For Reference

Not to be taken from this room

Encyclopedia of
African-American Writing:
Five Centuries of Contribution

Trials & Triumphs of Writers, Poets, Publications and Organizations

Encyclopedia of African-American Writing: Five Centuries of Contribution

Trials & Triumphs of Writers, Poets, Publications and Organizations

Shari Dorantes Hatch, Editor

Grey House Publishing

PUBLISHER: Leslie Mackenzie
EDITORIAL DIRECTOR: Laura Mars-Proietti
EDITORIAL ASSISTANT: Jael Bridgemahon
COMPOSITION: David Garoogian

EDITOR: Shari Dorantes Hatch
EDITORIAL CONSULTANT: Michael Strickland

MARKETING DIRECTOR: Jessica Moody

Grey House Publishing, Inc.
4919 Route 22
Amenia, NY 12501
518.789.8700
FAX 845.373.6390
www.greyhouse.com
e-mail: books @greyhouse.com

First edition published 2000
Second edition published 2009
Printed in the U.S.A.

Publisher's Cataloging-In-Publication Data
(Prepared by The Donohue Group, Inc.)

Encyclopedia of African-American writing : five centuries of contribution :
 trials & triumphs of writers, poets, publications and organizations / Shari Dorantes Hatch, editor. — 2nd ed.

 863 p. : ill. ; cm.
 Previous edition published as: African-American writers : a dictionary. Santa Barbara, Calif. : ABC-CLIO, 2000.
 Includes bibliographical references and index.
 ISBN: 978-1-59237-291-1

1. American literature--African American authors--Dictionaries. 2. African Americans--Intellectual life--Dictionaries. 3. African American authors--Biography--Dictionaries. 4. African Americans in literature--Dictionaries. I. Hatch, Shari Dorantes.

PS153.N5 A3444 2009
810.9/896073/03

Cover photography credits
Top row, from left: *Frederick Douglass* LoC; *Philippa Duke Schuyler* LoC/Carl Van Vechten; *Martin Luther King, Jr.* LoC; *Phillis Wheatley* LoC; *Jesse Jackson, Sr.* LoC; *Sojourner Truth* LoC; *Henry Van Dyke* LoC/Carl Van Vechten; *Ruby Dee* LoC/Carl Van Vechten

Bottom row, from left: *Shirley Graham Du Bois* LoC/Carl Van Vechten; *Booker T. Washington* LoC; *Barack Obama* White House Photo/ Pete Souza (http://creativecommons.org/licenses/by/3.0/us/); *Katherine Dunham* LoC; *Dorothy West*: AP/Wide World Photo/Alison Shaw

LoC – Library of Congress

To my husband, Bernie, who has supported and encouraged me for more than three decades; without you, this book would not have been possible, let alone pleasurable, to write. And to my daughter, Sarah, and her daughters, Savannah Grace and Elizabeth Rose. You four delight and inspire me.

Table of Contents

Foreword

From the first edition.

Many of my earliest memories center around my passionate love of reading. As a little girl, I was lucky enough to be able to walk to the little storefront branch library in my neighborhood. There, Mrs. Leux would greet me with a smile and a wink and would reach behind the counter to pull out a special book she had set aside just for me. I'd add to this special book a few other books I'd choose for myself, then I'd skip home, heavily laden with books but light of heart. Between visits, I'd spend many an hour pouring over my treasures.

Years later, in the mid-1950s, I started teaching schoolchildren, and among my favorite classroom activities was to read aloud to them and to find other ways to foster in them a love of reading. Two of my students flummoxed me, however. Everything I tried seemed destined to failure, so in the middle of the school year, I enrolled in a master's program in reading, to gain more insight into how to help them. What I learned in my studies helped my students-and helped me gain a deeper interest in finding out how to teach students to read. After a couple of years, I asked to teach first graders, so that I could be the first to teach young children how to read. This was a joyous task, watching my students' faces light up as they figured out the link between the printed symbols and meaningful words. Over time, my studies led me to become a reading specialist, a reading consultant, a professor of reading, and eventually the State of New Jersey Professor of Reading at Rutgers, my current position.

Throughout my own early experience with reading, I rarely came into contact with books involving children of color-certainly not during my experiences as a young reader-and even as a young schoolteacher, I rarely encountered such books. By the time my youngest son Michael was born, however, I was able to find numerous children's books to read to him that involved children and adults of color. In recent decades, young-and old-readers have available a wealth of literature centered in the life experience of African Americans and other persons of color. It give me great pleasure to see the long, long list of entries in *African-American Writers*, which my son Michael and his colleague Shari Hatch have edited. I sincerely hope that you will use this volume to enhance your enjoyment of the riches of African American literature.

—Dorothy Strickland

Preface

I thoroughly enjoyed creating this second edition of *African-American Writing: Five Centuries of Contribution*. When preparing the first edition, I discovered a tremendous wealth of noteworthy writers from whom to choose. At every turn, I came upon new riches, new discoveries, new treasures of literary achievement. Since the publication of the first edition, American writers of African descent have been writing and publishing abundantly, and this second edition reflects hundreds more entries. Making that final selection from more than 1,500 possible writers was a difficult task. The goal was to be as comprehensive as possible, yet provide a balanced historical survey.

This edition of *African-American Writing: Five Centuries of Contribution* is designed to highlight particular authors, publishers, and publications, and also act as a springboard for further investigation or as a source of ideas for creative writing. Open this volume at any page and you will find what inspired various African-American writers to create poems, plays, short stories, novels, essays, opinion pieces, scholarly analyses, and numerous other works.

This encyclopedia also explores the intriguing connections among authors. What are the common characteristics and distinctive aspects of the narratives of former slaves? Which African-American writers were helped by the 1930s-era Federal Writers' Project? Which were influenced by a distinctive region such as rural Mississippi or urban Detroit? Which writers were orphaned at a tender age? Which had to overcome tremendous economic and social hardships in order to put pen to paper? How did having light skin and European facial features—or dark skin and African facial features—affect these writers? Who mentored their contemporaries? Who put their careers on hold to raise children—their own or others? Which writers started writing to support their children? Who fled to Paris to escape racism in the United States? And who returned to their rural Southern roots after failing to make it in the urban North? While working on this volume, I discovered these and many other fascinating aspects of the lives of African-American authors. I hope that you will relish making your own discoveries as you read this work.

—Shari Dorantes Hatch

Acknowledgments

First and foremost, I thank my husband, Bernie. Second, I thank Laura Mars-Proietti, the Editorial Director at Grey House, editorial assistant Jael Powell, compositor David Garoogian, and proofreader, Nancy Furstinger.

Thanks also to Michael Strickland, who reviewed the composed pages. I also gratefully acknowledge Dorothy Strickland, as both she and Michael were instrumental in creating the first edition.

I particularly thank contributors Tonya Bolden, whose generous contributions greatly enriched the text; Lisa Bahlinger, who kindly filled in wherever there was a need; Michael Strickland, Diane Masiello, and Janet Hoover, who took on some of the heavyweights with grace and skill; Randall Lindsay, who conducted thorough and detailed research and offered intriguing analysis of his findings; and Brenda Pilson, who thoughtfully prepared her entry. Thanks also for the excellent research assistance conducted by numerous students of my daughter Sarah that kept the text lively and accessible.

I wish also to thank Cheryl Willis Hudson for working hard to ensure that the entries on her and her husband—and on their Just Us Books—are accurate. Thanks also to Dori Maynard and Jewell Parker Rhodes for their thoughtful responses to requests for information.

—Shari Dorantes Hatch

Introduction

This second edition of the *Encyclopedia of African-American Writing, Five Centuries of Contribution: Trials & Triumphs of Writers, Poets, Publications and Organizations* is the first published by Grey House Publishing. The first edition (*African-American Writers: A Dictionary*) was published by ABC-CLIO in 2000. This revised work is heavy with new material and features, and its new name better reflects its expanded content.

Section One: Profiles
This section, with 738 detailed profiles (210 more than the first edition) is so much more than just a collection of author biographies. In addition to biographies of individual writers, this section includes topics related to writing, such as newspapers, magazines, journals, slave narratives, publishers, awards, organizations, collaboratives, book clubs, self-publishing, and more. You'll read about the Civil Rights Movement, the Harlem Renaissance, and the Black Power Movement, and how African-American writers were influenced by the time they lived in.

Along with a new design, the A to Z profiles in this section begin with a bold face "genre line" that quickly identifies what the subject did (i.e. fiction, poems, slave narratives, short stories, sermons, etc.) and who the subject was (i.e. journalist, editor, publisher, mathematician, musician, columnist, etc.). These detailed profiles go on to tell the story not only of a writing life, but also of family, education and economic details, relationships with contemporaries, and how social issues played a part, ultimately influencing American culture today.

Each profile ends with a detailed list of references, as well as further reading, making it easy for the reader to continue their own research on individuals, groups, or historical events.

Section Two: Primary Documents
This brand new section includes nearly 100 pages of original documents. It takes the reader on a literary journey, from the 1635 contract used to bind African-American slaves to their masters, to the 2009 poem written by an African American for the inauguration ceremony of the first African-American U.S. President.

These 42 documents are categorized into nine sections, and have their own table of contents. Each section is supported by a brief introduction that sets the historical stage of the writing samples that follow. From letters and poems written by enslaved workers, to legal documents that freed the slaves and then restricted civil liberties, to well-known speeches by civil rights leaders, these Primary Documents provide a concise snapshot of five centuries of African-American writing. They combine with the individual profiles to bring alive the hundreds of African-American writers described throughout this edition.

Section Three: Appendices
This section is greatly expanded for this edition, with seven appendices - three more than the first edition:
* *Chronology of Writers* lists all individual writers by birth date;
* *Chronology of Firsts* summarizes significant "first" events by categories, such as book-publishing firsts, fiction firsts, and first to win the Nobel Prize for literature;
* *Timelines* are **NEW** and comprise seven historical linear timescales that pinpoint not only significant events in the writing lives of African Americans, but also relevant events, such as wars and terms of certain U.S. presidents;
* *Writers by Genre* categorizes all entries by one or more of 27 genres, from Anthologies to Criticism to Spoken Word;

- *Writers by Occupation* is **NEW** and categorizes all entries by one or more of 210 occupations, from Abolitionist to Judge to Language Consultant to Theologian;
- *References* is a **NEW** list which gives full citations for more than 300 references used throughout this edition;
- *Key to References* helps the reader identify references that are abbreviated at the end of the profiles because they are used repeatedly throughout.

This edition of the *Encyclopedia of African-American Writing, Five Centuries of Contribution* ends with a detailed index.

The *Encyclopedia of African-American Writing, Five Centuries of Contribution* is available in both print and ebook formats.

Praise for the first edition—

"Recommended for general and academic collections."

—CHOICE

"Finding information about African American writers has always entailed searching a variety of resources…the benefit of having information on so many authors in one place cannot be overstated. Recommended for high school, public, and academic libraries."

—Booklist

"No other single work seeks to include all past and present African American writers of significance in such an affordable format…The comprehensiveness of the work, its affordability, and the promise of future updates make this an appealing choice for all public and academic libraries."

—Library Journal

~A~

Abbott, Robert S. (Sengstacke)
11/24/1868–2/29/1940

Editorials; newspaper publisher and editor

On May 6, 1905, Abbott founded the *Chicago Defender*, a four-page weekly newspaper. The *Chicago Defender* was not Abbott's first contact with the newspaper business, however. While he was studying printing at the Hampton Institute in Virginia, he worked with his stepfather, John Sengstacke (whom his mother had married in 1874), to produce Sengstacke's the *Woodville Times* (in Georgia). Later, Abbott worked as a printer in Chicago to pay for his studies at Kent Law School (now Chicago-Kent College of Law). (The son of former slaves Thomas and Flora Abbott, he knew about and believed in the value of hard work.)

Although Abbott graduated from law school (1899) and started practicing law, within a few years he realized that his race would continually limit his ability to earn a living with the law, and his true calling was to serve African Americans by publishing his own newspaper. Reportedly, at first, he operated the paper out of his kitchen, with only about 20–25 cents in cash and about 25 dollars in borrowed resources to start his paper. He peddled it himself through African-American shops and churches, pubs and pool halls, as well as through door-to-door sales. During the paper's first several years of operation, Abbott's landlady, Henrietta Plumer Lee, almost single-handedly saved the paper from folding on several occasions. Among other things, Lee allowed Abbott to use the dining room of her apartment as the office for the paper; she took care of him during a bout of double pneumonia; and she accepted only nominal payments for the rent and food she provided him during those early years of the paper.

When Abbott started his paper, there were already three African-American newspapers in Chicago, and

Robert S. Abbott

none of them were faring too well financially. At that time, most newspaper publishers (e.g., Hearst and Pulitzer) used sensational stories, dramatic writing styles, and high-profile techniques to beef up their circulation. By 1910, Abbott's paper was doing likewise. That year, Abbott had hired J. Hockley Smiley, who encouraged Abbott to use banner headlines (often in red print); to include sections on theater, sports, and society; to highlight sensational news (e.g., editorials railing against prostitution in the African-American community)—and even to make up a few stories if the real news wasn't juicy enough. In addition, Smiley encouraged Abbott's natural inclinations to write aggressively outspoken editorials lambasting lynchings and other post-Reconstruction horrors, which helped boost the fledgling newspaper's circulation, particularly in the Southern states. Pullman porters also played an important role for the *Defender* at this time, both distributing the paper to railroad passengers and gathering news from various printed materials the passengers left behind. By the time Smiley died (in 1915), Abbott's *Defender* was an eight-page, eight-column, full-size paper, and throughout the 1920s, nearly one-quarter million readers were buying it each week.

Abbott's editorials also influenced his readers' opinions. For instance, he urged many Southern blacks to flee from the rural South to find work, better living conditions, and greater opportunities in the industrial North. The great migration to the North (with about 11/4 million African Americans fleeing North between World War I [the late 1910s] and the Great Depression [the early 1930s]) was at least partly attributable to Abbott's editorials. Another issue Abbott addressed was the segregation and unequal treatment of African-American soldiers during World War I. Despite some financial ups and downs, the paper flourished in the 1920s and even survived the Great Depression. Abbott had more difficulty, however, with the magazine he started a month before the 1929 stock-market crash. His *Abbott's Monthly* survived until 1933, but widespread unemployment among African Americans eventually led to the magazine's demise.

In the mid-1930s, Abbott brought his nephew, John H. Sengstacke, into the operation of the paper. After Abbott's death, Sengstacke took over the paper, and he adopted many of Abbott's editorial stances, opposing the segregation and mistreatment of African-American soldiers during World War II. (The U.S. military wasn't integrated until after World War II had ended.) When Sengstacke and other African-American newspaper publishers urged African Americans to reevaluate their military service in light of this mistreatment, the U.S. Justice Department threatened charges of sedition against them. Fortunately, Sengstacke was able to thwart those charges and to negotiate for African-American journalists to have greater access to federal government officials in exchange for tempering their remarks about the military.

Under Sengstacke's leadership, the paper attracted numerous outstanding authors, including poet and columnist (his "Simple Says" stories) **Langston Hughes**, poet Gwendolyn Brooks, and novelist Willard Motley. In 1956, Sengstacke successfully moved the *Defender* to daily publication and added other newspapers to create a chain of African-American papers. In its heyday, the *Defender* could reasonably have been called the most widely circulated and most influential African-American newspaper in the country, but by 1995, its circulation had dropped below 30,000, and its ability to shape opinion declined concomitantly.

Editor's note: There is some question about Abbott's birth and death dates. Abbott celebrated his birthday as November 24, 1870, but the parish register of the church where he was baptized lists his birth date as 11/28/1868. Also, at least one source gives his death date as 2/22, instead of 2/29.

REFERENCES: *EA-99. EB-99. PGAA.* Amana, Harry, in *GR-LRC,* and in *AMJ-00-60-1.* Folkerts, Jean Lange, in *ANJ-26-50-1* and in *GR-LRC.* Johns, Robert L., in *BH2C* and in *BB.* Toppin, Edgar Allan, in *WB-99.*

Abolition Literature *See* Antislavery Periodicals

Abu-Jamal, Mumia (né Wesley Cook)
4/24/1954–
Essays; talk-show host

Because of his political activism (in association with the Black Panther Party) and his outspoken views, Abu-Jamal was forced to resign from hosting his own radio talk show. Following an incident with Philadelphia police, and a highly questionable trial, he was convicted of first-degree murder and sentenced to death. In 2001, his death sentence was overturned, but this ruling could be overturned. In addition, he has three claims that might lead to a new trial or to a new evidentiary hearing. Abu-Jamal has written various articles for *Essence, Nation, Black Scholar,* and other periodicals; and he has published five books of essays: *Live from Death Row* (1995); *Death Blossoms: Reflections from a Prisoner of Conscience* (1996); *All Things Censored* (2000); *Faith of Our Fathers: An Examination of the Spiritual Life of African and African-American People* (2003); *We Want Freedom: A Life in the Black Panther Party* (2004). In 1994, National Public Radio (NPR) canceled a series of radio commentaries they had commissioned from Abu-Jamal, as a result of pressure from Senator Bob Dole and the Philadelphia police.

REFERENCES: *A.C-Wiki. CAO-02.* Jacobson, Robert R., in *BB.* Taylor, April, in *EA-99.*

Affrilachian Poets
1991–
Mutual-support organization for creative writers from the Appalachian region

In the fall of 1991, the Carnegie Center for Literacy and Learning in Lexington, Kentucky sponsored a celebration of "Southern Writing." Poet Frank X. Walker attended the event, having looked forward to hearing from Southern writers. Bobbie Ann Mason and two other European-American native Kentuckian writers were joined by one non-Kentuckian, South Carolinian Nicky Finney, the only African American on the panel. On reflecting on the experience, he investigated further, discovering that he could not find a single Kentucky publication that had cited the writings of a single one of the dozens of African-American Kentuckian writers he knew.

Clearly, the face of Kentucky writers—and of Appalachian writers—seemed to be all white. According to //en.wikipedia.org/wiki/Appalachia, Appalachia stretches from southern New York state to northern Alabama, including all of West Virginia and parts of Pennsylvania,

Ohio, Virginia, Tennessee, North Carolina, South Carolina, Georgia, Alabama, and Mississippi—not lily-white states. When Walker looked up the term "Appalachian," he found that the meaning was stated as "white residents of mountainous regions," yet African Americans had been among the earliest settlers to clear brush and haul household goods over the mountains into Appalachia. Outraged, Walker soon coined the term "Affrilachian."

By the spring of 1992, South Carolinian Finney had relocated to the University of Kentucky at Lexington, and she and Walker joined with Thomas Aaron, Gerald Coleman, Ricardo Nazario Colon, Miysan Crosswhite, Richard Donelan, Mitchell L. H. Douglass, Kelly Norman Ellis, Daudra Scisney-Givens, and Shanna Smith to form the Affrilachian Poets. Other members include Bernard Clay, Julian Long, Jude McPherson, Paul Taylor, Crystal Wilkinson, and Dan Woo. The Affrilachian Poets have also anointed several honorary members, such as Opal Palmer Adisa, **Henry Louis Gates, Jr.**, and **Nikki Giovanni**. Though most of the Affrilachian Poets come from cities in Appalachia, a few do not. Many also write in genres other than poetry, as well. For instance, one of the rare Affrilachian Poets raised on a rural Kentucky farm, Crystal Wilkinson has published two short-story collections (2000, 2002).

As a group, the poets are also becoming better known. Between the summer of 2008 and the summer of 2009, the Google entries for "Affrilachian poet" increased from 1,790 entries to 2,690.

REFERENCES: Burriss, Theresa L., in *GEAAL*. Finney, Nikky, "History of the Affrilachian Poets," in //www.mwg.org/education/archive/openstudio/walker/poets.html. //en.wikipedia.org/wiki/Appalachia. //findarticles.com/p/articles/mi_m0HST/is_2_3/ai_72275236.

African-American Book Publishing Authority, The *See* Journals and Magazines, Literary, *Black Issues Book Review*

African American Literature Book Club *See* BlackBoard African-American Bestsellers

African American Review (also *Negro American Literature Forum, Black American Literature Forum*)
1967–

This pioneering journal was one of the first to highlight African-American literary issues, and throughout its history, it has been on the cutting edge of African-American literary and cultural studies, being the first to focus on African-American writers, biography, film, critical theory, science fiction, and women's writing.

In 1967, John F. Bayliss, at Indiana State University, founded the *Negro American Literature Forum*. The journal originally focused on the teaching of literature, but as it evolved and came under the editorship of Hannah Hendrick and W. Tasker Witham from 1973 to 1976, it began to concentrate more and more on critical analysis of literary texts.

In 1976, current editor Joe Weixlmann reorganized and reformatted the journal and renamed it *Black American Literature Forum*, focusing on literary studies, poetry, and related cultural disciplines, including theater, art, and music. Under his leadership, it shifted its attention to include studies of theater, film, art, and music, as well as literature. In 1983 it received high praise from the Modern Language Association, an organization of literary scholars, and the association named it the official publication of the MLA Division on Black American Literature.

In the 1990s interest in cultural studies swept the academy, and the journal moved with the times and began to include more and more essays on nonliterary topics. It also shifted away from critical essays and gave more space to publishing high-quality fiction and poetry. In the spring of 1992, the shift in focus led to another new name for the journal: *African American Review*. It continues to provide brilliant and insightful commentary on issues of interest to African-American literature, media, and culture. The journal also continues to cover the cultural studies movement by publishing African-American autobiography, critical theory, women's writing, nonliterary essays, fiction, poetry, and other genres.

REFERENCES: Weixlmann, Joe, "*African American Review*," in *OCAAL. See also GEAAL.* //www.proquest.co.uk/assets/downloads/titlelists/serials/African-American-Press.pdf. —Diane Masiello and Lisa Bahlinger

African-American Vernacular English (AAVE; aka Black English; aka Negro dialect; aka Ebonics)
1619–present
Richly expressive variant of English, often used by poets and fiction writers, in addition to its spoken usage

For the first two and a half centuries after people of African descent arrived in what later became the United States of America, most African Americans lived in the South, where most of them were bound by legal slavery. By the late 1700s, it was illegal for enslaved people to be taught to read or write in most of the states where slavery remained legal. The penalties for violating these laws were harsh, so very few African Americans learned to read or write. During this time, for the vast majority of African Americans, their literary traditions were oral, not written. Their rich literature was passed along from person to person and generation to generation through the oral tradition.

Spirituals, folk songs, **folktales**, jokes, **proverbs**, and other literature emerging from the **oral tradition** among enslaved Southerners typically used African-American Vernacular English (AAVE), sometimes also called Black English, formerly called "Negro dialect." (Many people also use the term "Ebonics," but technically, "Ebonics" refers only to the phonic qualities of AAVE-"Ebony" "phonics.") Each of these terms is intended to convey the everyday speech of most African Americans during a given time in history. In part, AAVE emerged because most enslaved Southern African Americans lived in isolated housing or even isolated communities where their interactions with European Americans were limited and definitely not conversational. Though they needed to communicate clearly with European Americans so that they could understand and be understood by European Americans, they nonetheless had an opportunity to develop their own distinctive AAVE. This was particularly true of the enslaved fieldworkers, though less true of enslaved household workers and skilled laborers, who needed to speak Standard English (SE) fluently to perform their jobs well.

In addition, a few small communities of enslaved African Americans lived on plantations entirely isolated from European Americans, such as on the Sea Islands off the coast of Georgia and the Carolinas. The original enslaved residents had been kidnapped from various areas in Africa and arrived on the islands speaking different African languages. Over time, however, they developed their own creole language, which strongly preserved many Africanisms while creating their own discrete language forms, such as "Gullah" on the Sea Islands. Native monolingual speakers of creoles such as Gullah may find it difficult to understand speakers of SE, and vice versa, though many Gullah speakers also speak SE. For instance, though most of **James Edwin Campbell**'s poems in his poetry collections *Driftings and Gleanings* (1887) and *Echoes from the Cabin and Elsewhere* (1895) were written in Gullah or in AAVE, he also wrote poems in SE. More than half a century later, linguistics scholar **Lorenzo Dow Turner** wrote *Africanisms in Gullah Dialect* (1949), which revealed how much of African languages have been preserved in the speech of all Americans, especially African Americans, as well as in the distinctive Gullah creole language.

Unlike Gullah and other creoles, AAVE has been closely tied to SE; native speakers of AAVE and of SE have generally been able to understand one another. As soon as Southern slavery ended (1863-1865, depending on the location), African Americans were not only allowed to learn to read and write, but also actively encouraged to do so through Freedmen's Schools and other institutions. Ever since, African Americans have been taught to use SE in their writing, and many schools have tried to implement policies of encouraging students to speak SE during school hours. The use of AAVE versus SE in the classroom has been highly controversial, as in the 1996 decision of the Oakland, California, School Board resolution, "AAVE is neither slang nor incorrect language. Linguistically speaking, there is no such thing as incorrect language, because as long as someone is talking and is being understood by the person listening, communication occurs between speaker and listener-making language neither wrong nor right" (quoted from //en.wikipedia.org/wiki/African_American_Vernacular_English).

Of course, not all African Americans speak AAVE as a native language form, and not all speakers of AAVE are African Americans. Even among native speakers of AAVE, most African-American writers use SE in their formal writing (e.g., for publication or for business audiences), whether or not they do so in their informal writing (e.g., when texting, tweeting, e-mailing, or corresponding with family or friends). The tradition of African-American writers using SE goes back to the earliest days of African-American written literature.

Before the Civil War, most of the African-American writers who were establishing this written tradition lived in the North and were freeborn, legally emancipated, or self-liberated through their own escape from slavery. The chief publishing outlets available to these Northern African Americans during this time were **antislavery periodicals**, pamphlets, and books. These publications were mainly sponsored by and addressed to Northern abolitionists, most of whom were European Americans, chiefly because there were relatively few African Americans living in the North at that time. Of course, these abolitionists hoped that Southern slaveholders would read and be moved by this literature, as well, but with rare exceptions, these Southern slaveholders were also European Americans.

Northern African Americans who wrote for these publishing outlets tended to write in SE for several reasons. For one thing, many African Americans born and raised in the North spoke SE as their native tongue. For another, these writers needed to write in a manner that was directly comprehensible to their prospective European-American readers, as well as to literate fellow African Americans. Another motive to use SE was that they, their editors, and their publishers wished to ensure that their use of language did not impede the readers' ability to identify with the writers' ideas, thoughts, and feelings.

Editors and publishers wished to ensure that the readers felt strongly inclined to read their writings sympathetically. Had the authors used AAVE, their readers might have been tempted to disregard their words as the utterances of someone unlike them, perhaps even someone less deserving of liberty, humane treatment, and civil rights. For all of these reasons, before the Civil War, most African-American poets, essayists, autobiographers, and other writers of literature generally used SE in their written poetry and prose. Even **William Wells Brown**, in his novel *Clotel* (1853), used mostly SE, with AAVE only appearing occasionally for the utterances of some characters.

A major category of antebellum African-American literature was the **slave narrative**. As this dictionary's entry on slave narratives indicates, many slave narratives written before or during the Civil War were actually written by amanuenses, who listened to the dictation of the narrators and then wrote the narratives in SE. Even the slave narrators who wrote their own narrations were motivated to use SE for the reasons mentioned previously regarding all antebellum writers. As the entry on slave narratives suggests, the very last of the slave narrators were recorded by workers paid by the Works Progress Administrations' Federal Writers Project, and many of these amanuenses attempted to record the exact wording and speech sounds of the then-elderly narrators, with varying degrees of success.

Even after the Civil War and the all-too-brief period of Reconstruction, most writings by African Americans continued to be chiefly in SE, not in AAVE. In fact, European-American Southerners were more likely than African Americans to use a form of AAVE, typically through nostalgic stories of the good old days of plantation slavery. Typically, these narratives used highly stereotyped written representations of the phonics and syntax of AAVE, intended to portray the speakers as not only poorly educated but also unintelligent. The works of Thomas Nelson Page (1887, *In Ole Virginia*) and Thomas Dixon (1905, *The Clansman: An Historical Romance of the Ku Klux Klan*, later transformed into the racist movie *Birth of a Nation*) typify this tradition. One of the few exceptions to this glorified-plantation writing was **Joel Chandler Harris**, a white Southerner, who actually tried to use the authentic speech patterns of native AAVE speakers in his **folktales** (1880-1910). Rather than using the mocking, condescending interpretations of AAVE written by fellow European-American Southerners, Harris conducted extensive interviews, on which he based his narration by Uncle Remus, as well as his stories' dialogue.

Storyteller **Charles Chesnutt** offered his own twist on Harris's Uncle Remus stories and his own perspective on **trickster tales** (e.g., in *The Conjure Woman*, 1899) through a much more cunning Uncle Julius McAdoo, an AAVE speaker who cleverly outwitted the powerful European American, John. A few years earlier, novelist and poet **Frances Ellen Watkins Harper**, in her novel *Iola Leroy* (1892), had used AAVE for the speech of some of her characters and SE for the speech of other African-American characters, signaling differences in status and class through these linguistic differences. Two decades before publishing her novel, Harper had used AAVE in several poems in her collection *Sketches of Southern Life* (1872). The dialect poems in her collection were written through the voice of "Aunt Chloe," whom she alleged to have narrated the poems. Aunt Chloe's dialect poems addressed the difficulties of African Americans who had survived Southern slavery. In both of these books, Harper was able both to signal her own fluency in SE and to use AAVE to convey authentic speech.

Harper's dialect poems and Campbell's Gullah and AAVE dialect poems predated those of **Paul Laurence Dunbar**, who wrote numerous poems in SE, in addition to his dialect poems. Even so, Dunbar's dialect poems (written c. 1893-1906) have been much better known and more influential than either his own SE poems or the dialect poems of Harper or Campbell. Poet **Joseph Seamon Cotter, Sr.**, had become a literary and social friend of Dunbar's in 1894, and through Dunbar's influence, Cotter also experimented some with dialect poems. **James Weldon Johnson** used some dialect verse in his early writings, as well, but he also criticized some of the dialect poets who seemed tied to the European-American plantation tradition. **Raymond G. Dandridge** had been a bedridden teenager when Dunbar was the most celebrated African-American poet, and most of his poems emulated Dunbar's nostalgic and romantic dialect poems, even during the more poetically experimental, more politically attuned period of the **Harlem Renaissance**. Interestingly, Dunbar's wife, **Alice Ruth Dunbar Nelson**, took a different tack, writing to Dunbar, "I believe in everyone following his own bent. If it be so that one has a special aptitude for dialect work why it is only right that dialect work should be a specialty. But if one should be like me—absolutely devoid of the ability to manage dialect, I don't see the necessity of cramming and forcing oneself into that plane because one is a Negro or a Southerner." Similarly, poet **William Stanley Beaumont Braithwaite** praised Dunbar's dialect poetry for its lyricality and its sensitivity to the everyday speech of ordinary African Americans, but he carefully avoided using it in his own writing. Regarding scholarly appreciation of AAVE, in 1897, **William Sanders Scarborough** published a well-regarded paper on Negro dialect (AAVE) and folklore.

During the **Harlem Renaissance**, many authors began to use AAVE in their writing and to show fond appreciation for it. For instance, **Arna Bontemps** not only used his native Creole dialect in his personal correspondence to intimate friends such as **Langston Hughes**, but also studied dialects in order to use authentic AAVE in his writings so that he would neither sound stereotypical nor be incomprehensible to speakers of SE. Hughes, in turn, embraced the cadence of vernacular speech, both in his poetry and in his many other writings. **Zora Neale Hurston**, an anthropologist by training, seriously studied the vernacular speech of African Americans and incorporated AAVE into her writing, both fiction and nonfiction. **Georgia Douglas Johnson** was praised for her ability to use authentic folk speech in her writings, as was **Helene Johnson** (no relation to Georgia). African-American poet **Sterling Brown** lyrically celebrated AAVE in his own work, and Jamaican-American poet **Claude McKay** reveled in Jamaican speech patterns in his work. **Jean Toomer** also incorporated some AAVE in his major work, *Cane* (1923).

On the other hand, poet **Countee Cullen** wrote in the foreword to his anthology *Caroling Dusk* (1927), "If dialect is missed in this collection, it is enough to state that the day of dialect as far as Negro poets are concerned is in the decline. . . . In a day when artificiality is so vigorously condemned, the Negro poet would be foolish indeed to turn to dialect. The majority of present-day poems in dialect are the efforts of white poets" (quoted in //www.english.illinois.edu/maps/poets/a_f/cullen/dusk.htm).

During and following the **Black Arts Movement** of the 1960s and 1970s, many more authors began employing AAVE in their writings. For instance, in the 1970s, **Lucille Clifton** used AAVE in her picture books about Everett Anderson and her other books for children (1970-2001) whenever AAVE authentically suited the characters uttering the dialogue. Both **June Jordan**, with her *His Own Where* (1971), and **Alice Childress**, with her *A Hero Ain't Nothin' But a Sandwich* (1973), prompted controversy for their use of AAVE when writing for young adults (teens).

Just a few of the well-known African-American authors who have incorporated AAVE into at least some of their writings are **Toni Cade Bambara, Amiri Baraka, Gwendolyn Brooks, Frank London Brown, J. California Cooper, Ernest Gaines, Nikki Giovanni, Alex Haley, Paule Marshall, Patricia McKissack, Albert Murray, Ishmael Reed, Carolyn Rodgers, Sonia Sanchez, Ntozake Shange, Alice Walker, Margaret Walker, John Edgar Wideman, Brenda Wilkinson**, and **August Wilson**. Since the 1980s or so, many rappers and hip-hop poets have enthusiastically incorporated AAVE into their writings. In addition, **Michael Eric Dyson, Henry Louis Gates, Jr., Ivan van Sertima**, and others have critically analyzed topics related to AAVE.

European-American linguist William Labov was probably the first linguist to thoughtfully analyze the grammar of AAVE in his 1965 article and more thoroughly in his 1972 book (*see* "Further Readings"). In both his article and his book, he urged readers to recognize AAVE as a respected variety of English, with its own distinctive grammatical rules. The African-American scholar most renowned for her study of AAVE is **Geneva Smitherman**, who has written extensively on AAVE both in periodicals and in several books, including her seminal *Talkin and Testifyin: The Language of Black America* (1977/1996) (*see also* "Further Readings").

Though each speaker of AAVE is unique, and age, status, and contextual differences affect its use, some characteristics of AAVE have been detected across speakers and regions. Many of these characteristics reflect their African heritage, as well as their heritage in the American South. These features include distinctive phonology, or pronunciation; distinctive lexicon, or vocabulary; and distinctive syntax, especially regarding use of verb tenses and the *copula* (the "to be" verbs).

Linguists have noted that even across regions, AAVE typically has a distinctive phonology. This common phonology may have more to do with a shared past in the Southern United States and with racial segregation in the North than with common origins in Africa. For instance, both speakers of AAVE and European-American speakers of Southern variants of SE change the final sound of two-syllable words ending in "ng" (e.g., ending, morning, nothing) from the SE pronunciation of /ng/ to the AAVE (and Southern variant) sound of /n/. Similarly, some diphthongs (e.g., /oi/ or the "oi" sound in "boil") are reduced to monophthongs (e.g., pronounced as "ball" or even "bile"). Many other distinctive phonological features of AAVE are similar to those of Southern speakers of SE, although some differences exist. Often, distinctive phonological features depend on the location of a given sound within a word. For instance, /l/ and /r/ may be dropped when not followed by a particular vowel sound, but pronounced in other contexts. Articles and entire books have been written to describe the many other distinctive phonological features of AAVE.

Many of the distinctive lexical features of AAVE do reflect African origins. For instance, **Lorenzo Dow Turner** and other linguists have suggested that the *juke* joints where *jazz* was played, *banjos* were strummed, and listeners could *dig* it, may have originated from *dzug* (Wolof, meaning "misbehave"), *jaja* (Bantu), *mbanzo* (Kimdunu), and *dëgg* (Wolof). Not all of the origins suggested by Turner have been accepted by the gold-standard *Oxford English Dictionary* or by other linguists, but his findings are certainly suggestive if not definitive. AAVE has also made many linguistic contributions to SE, such as the distinctive contemporary meanings of "chill out," "funky," and "soul."

Probably the most frequently noted—and most controversial—features of AAVE relate to its syntax. Regarding AAVE syntax, the treatment of the *copula*, or the "to be" verb, is particularly distinctive. Fluent speakers of AAVE can distinguish between a habitual action and a nonhabitual action, without having to use adverbs such as "usually," "often," or "typically." For a nonhabitual action, the copula can be omitted, as in "She studying"—she is studying now but may or may not have studied much in the past. For a habitual action, however, the copula verb "be" is inserted, as in "She be studying"—she studies regularly. Fluent AAVE speakers also make numerous other distinctions in their use of the copula. (*See* "Further Readings" for resources offering more information.)

Use of negation is also distinctive in AAVE. For instance, like speakers of other variants of English, speakers of AAVE may use *ain't* to mean "am not," "isn't," "aren't," "haven't," and hasn't," but unlike them, speakers of AAVE may also use *ain't* to mean "don't," "doesn't," or "didn't." Also, whereas in SE, a double negative is a positive, in AAVE, a double negative—or even a triple or other multiple negative—remains a negative, with added negatives reinforcing the initial negative. Linguists have suggested that the origins of this pattern of negation may go back to the early days of the English colonies, when impoverished European indentured servants, who used this same pattern of negation, commonly shared living conditions and life experiences with early African servants and slaves.

The additional complexities and subtleties of AAVE syntax far exceed the scope of this dictionary. The interested reader may find much more comprehensive information by investigating the works suggested in the "Further Readings" section.

REFERENCES: **Harris, Trudier**, "speech and dialect," in *OCAAL*. Kelley, James B., "dialect poetry," in *GEAAL*. Osiapem, Iyabo F., "slang," and "vernacular," in *GEAAL*. //en.wikipedia.org/wiki/African_American_Vernacular_English. //en.wikipedia.org/wiki/Creole_language. //en.wikipedia.org/wiki/Ebonics. //en.wikipedia.org/wiki/Gullah_language. //www.english.illinois.edu/maps/poets/a_f/cullen/dusk.htm. *See also* **folktales**, **oral tradition** (including *griots, storytelling, not oratory and speeches*), and **slave narrative**, as well as the biographical entries for the many authors cited in bold type herein.

FURTHER READING: Delpit, Lisa, and Joanne Kilgour Dowdy. 2002. *The Skin That We Speak: Thoughts on Language and Culture in the Classroom*. New York: New Press. Dillard, John L. 1972. *Black English: Its History and Usage in the United States*. Random House. Labov, William. 1965. "Linguistic Research on the Non-standard English of Negro Children" (pp. 110-117). In A. Dore (Ed.), *Problems and Practices in the New York City Schools*. New York: New York Society for the Experimental Study of Education. _____. 1972. *Language in the Inner City: Studies in Black English Vernacular*. Philadelphia: University of Pennsylvania Press. Poplack, Shana. 2000. *The English History of African American English*. Oxford, England: Blackwell. _____, and Sali Tagliamonte. 2006. *African American English in the Diaspora*. Oxford, England: Blackwell. Rickford, John. 1999. *African American Vernacular English*. Oxford, England: Blackwell. _____, and Russell Rickford. 2000. *Spoken Soul: The Story of Black English*. New York: John Wiley & Sons. Smitherman, Geneva. 1977. *Talkin and Testifyin: The Language of Black America*. Boston: Houghton Mifflin. _____. 2000, *Black Talk: Words and Phrases from the Hood to the Amen Corner* (rev. ed.). Boston: Houghton Mifflin.

Ai (her self-chosen legal name, meaning "love" in Japanese) (née Florence Anthony; aka Florence Ai Ogawa)
10/21/1947–
Poems; educator

Ai's books of poetry and other creative writing include *Cruelty: Poems* (1973), *Killing Floor* (1979, Lamont Poetry Award winner), *Sin* (1985, American Book Award winner), *Fate: New Poems* (1991), *Greed* (1993), *Vice: New and Selected Poems* (1999, National Book Award winner), and *Dread: Poems* (2003). Her poems are dramatic monologues, narrated by a fictional or historical person. She reflected, "I always try to be true to the character. . . . Whatever character, I set up what I like to think are the keys to the character at the beginning of the poem, and then I proceed to go back over and enlarge throughout the poem" (quoted in *GEAAL*). Her work offers a distinctively egalitarian perspective on diverse people, at least in part because of her own multiethnic heritage (African American, Japanese American, Native American [Choctaw-Chickasaw, Southern Cheyenne, Comanche], and European American [Irish and Dutch]).

REFERENCES: *AAW:PV. Wiki*. Allen, Jessica, in *GEAAL*. Lee, A. Robert, in *OCAAL* and *COCAAL*. Willis, André, in *EA-99*. //english.okstate.edu/faculty/fac_pages/ai.htm. //www.english.uiuc.edu/maps/poets/a_f/ai/ai.htm. //www.nortonpoets.com/ai.htm. Amazon.com.

Alexander, Elizabeth
5/30/1962–

Poems, essays, literary reviews, verse play; educator, journal cofounder

On January 20, 2009, Elizabeth Alexander became best known as the fourth inaugural poet, heralding the first African-American president of the United States. Given her global audience, hers may have been the most widely heard poetry reading of all time. Alexander noted that she felt particularly honored to be chosen because **Barack Obama** "is aware of the kind of power language has, and aware of the kind of care with which we ought to try to speak to each other . . . as we move forward."

In thinking about this honor, she told Jeffrey Brown on PBS's *NewsHour* (January 13, 2009), "I think the fact that Barack Obama has decided that he wants to have a poem as part of the inaugural is tremendously significant, to say that here is a time when we can listen to language that shifts us a little bit, that allows us to pause for a moment and contemplate what's ahead of us, to think about how we can contribute to the challenges ahead of us, all of those things can be possible in the moment of pause and shift . . . that a poem makes possible." (*See also* inaugural poet **Maya Angelou**.)

In less exalted moments, Alexander writes essays, book reviews, short stories, and potent poems blending her own experiences and views with those of other African Americans, past (e.g., Emmett Till) and present (e.g., **Derek Walcott**). Her poems have been collected in *The Venus Hottentot* (1990), *Body of Life* (1996), *Antebellum Dream Book* (2001), *American Sublime* (2005), and *American Blue: Selected Poems* (2006), as well as being anthologized. Her essays have been published in an array of periodicals and have been collected in *The Black Interior* (2004) and in *Power and Possibility: Essays, Reviews, and Interviews (Poets on Poetry)* (2007). Alexander also coauthored the reverential *Workings of the Spirit: The Poetics of Afro-American Women's Writing* (1991, with Patricia Redmond and **Houston A. Baker, Jr.**). In 1996, her verse play, *Diva Studies,* was produced at Yale University. She also helped launch *Meridians* as a member of the feminist journal's founding editorial collective in 2002. A mother of two sons, she coauthored (with **Marilyn Nelson**) the history-inspired children's book, *Miss Crandall's School for Young Ladies and Little Misses of Color* (2007).

Among her numerous awards are three Pushcart Prizes for Poetry, a Pulitzer nomination, and a $50,000 Alphonse Fletcher Sr. Fellowship. Most recently, **Lucille Clifton**, Stephen Dunn, and Jane Hirshfield named her to receive the first $50,000 Jackson Prize for Poetry from Poets and Writers. Regarding her approach to poetry, she observed, "What poetry does is distill language with a kind of precision that reminds us what it means to take care with the word, that the word has tremendous power, that each word matters, and that . . . if we are mindful with our language to speak to each other across the many differences between us, that that is the way that I think we're more able to communicate precisely with one another" (on *NewsHour,* January 13, 2009).

In addition to her writing, Alexander has focused on fostering budding poets at University of Chicago, Smith College, Yale (chair of the African American Studies Department, starting July 2009), Harvard's Radcliffe Institute, **Cave Canem Poetry Workshop**, and elsewhere. In her teaching, she may draw on her 1992 doctoral dissertation, *Collage: An Approach to Reading African-American Women's Literature,* in which she observed that "a simulta-neous habitation of conflicting elements in the same space ... represents a particular strength and coherence of African-American women's cultural production." A line from her "Venus Hottentot" aptly conveys what a reader can expect from Alexander: "Elegant facts await me."

REFERENCES: *CAO-07. LFCC-07. VBAAP.* Pereira, Malin, in *AANB.* Pinto, Samantha, in *GEAAL.* Amazon.com. //bulletin.aarp.org/yourworld/politics/articles/the_intersection_of.html?CMP=KNC-360I-GOOGLE-BULL&HBX_OU=50&HBX_PK=elizabeth_alexander. //en.wikipedia.org/wiki/Elizabeth_Alexander_(poet). //www.blackculturalstudies.org/alexander/alexander_biblio.html. //www.elizabethalexander.net/home.html. //www.newsreel.org/guides/furious/alexande.htm. *NewsHour with Jim Lehrer,* January 13, 2009, last segment, at //www.pbs.org/newshour/bb/entertainment/jan-june09/inaug_poet_01-13.html. //www.poetryfoundation.org/archive/poet.html?id=84. //www.poets.org/poet.php/prmPID/245. //repository.upenn.edu/dissertations/AAI9308527/. //www.yale.edu/afamstudies/aboutfaculty.html.

Alexander's Magazine
1905–1909
Literary journal

Booker T. Washington could be supplicant to those who wielded power over him, such as European-American politicians, but he could be fiercely aggressive toward those who challenged his power, such as African-American journalists who criticized him. When **William Monroe Trotter** openly criticized Washington in the pages of the *Boston Guardian,* which Trotter cofounded with George Forbes in 1901, Washington became determined to drive them out of business. Washington then funded the founding of two Boston newspapers, the *Advocate* and the *Enterprise,* both of which promptly failed, and when a third, the *Boston Colored Citizen,* seemed about to die a similar death, Washington brought in Tuskegee graduate and Washington ally Charles Alexander to take over. Despite Alexander's efforts, he, too, failed to keep Trotter's competitor from collapsing within months.

Soon after, however, Alexander launched his monthly *Alexander's Magazine* (in 1905). Alexander offered more than just promotion of Tuskegee activities and philosophy. He included poems and essays, as well as occasional writings from viewpoints that diverged from his own. Both the photographs and the articles in the magazine touted the achievements of African Americans in the arts and the sciences, in business and in education. In step with the Tuskegee philosophy, the emphasis was on racial uplift and self-sufficiency in business. In addition, European-American writers were more likely to appear in its pages than in those of its contemporary, the *Colored American Magazine* (1900-1909).

Outside events soon affected the editor and the editorials of the magazine. On August 13, 1906 in Brownsville,

Texas, a European-American bartender was killed, and a European-American police officer was wounded. The white residents of Brownsville accused African-American soldiers from nearby Fort Brown of perpetrating the crimes, even though the all-white commanders at the fort confirmed that the soldiers were in their barracks at the fort during the time of the incident. President Teddy Roosevelt dishonorably discharged the accused soldiers, based on questionable evidence, without giving the soldiers a trial or any other opportunity to confront their accusers. When Booker T. Washington continued to support Roosevelt in order not to rock the boat, Alexander and many other Washington supporters started drifting apart from him and started leaning toward the Niagara Movement founded in 1905 by Washington's opponents, **W. E. B. Du Bois** and **William Monroe Trotter**.

In the fall of 1907, **Archibald Grimké** edited three issues of *Alexander's* (September-November), and he editorialized about Tuskegee's understated reaction to the Brownsville incident, while continuing to endorse the Tuskegee mission of educating African Americans. After the magazine editorship reverted back to Alexander's hands, Alexander reluctantly and weakly endorsed Roosevelt's chosen successor, William Howard Taft. After Taft's election, however, Alexander stopped publishing *Alexander's Magazine* and joined the Niagara Movement and then its successor, the NAACP.

REFERENCES: Alexander, Charles. 1969. *Alexander's Magazine: Volumes 4-5, 1907-1908*. New York: Negro Universities Press. Moses, Wilson Jeremiah. 1988. *The Golden Age of Black Nationalism, 1850-1925*. New York: Oxford University Press. Schneider, Mark. 1997. *Boston Confronts Jim Crow, 1890-1920*. Lebanon, NH: Northeastern University Press (University Press of New England, UPNE). Schneider, Mark R. 1995. "The 'Colored American' and 'Alexander's': Boston's Pro-Civil Rights Bookerites." in //www.questia.com/PM.qst?a=o&se=gglsc&d=5001657335. //en.wikipedia.org/wiki/Boston_Guardian. //en.wikipedia.org/wiki/Niagara_Movement. //www.liu.edu/cwis/cwp/library/historic.htm. //www.riverrunbookshop.com/cgi-bin/rrbooks/35696.html.

Allen, Richard
2/14/1760–3/26/1831
Sermons, devotional pieces, addresses, autobiography, hymnal; minister

Born into bondage, Allen's mind and spirit were freed before he was able to purchase his physical freedom. In 1777, he experienced both a spiritual awakening, converting to Methodism, and an intellectual awakening, teaching himself to read and write. In the early 1780s, Allen started serving as a lay preacher and was nominated for ministry of the newly denominated Methodist Episcopal (ME) Church.

Richard Allen, wood engraving, 19th century

By 1786, Allen had earned enough money to buy his freedom. Soon after, he met Absalom Jones and joined St. George's ME Church in Philadelphia. Although the church held segregated services and prayer meetings, the African-American congregants still supported the church with labor and donations. To provide aid to them, Allen and Jones organized the Free African Society in 1787. Allen's activism was guided by his religious conviction that Christianity and divine inspiration were intended to serve the needs of the oppressed, not the interests of the oppressors.

As the church authorities increasingly segregated blacks from whites, resentment built to the point where Allen and Jones led a walkout of the black congregants. Stories of the specific incident that triggered the walkout vary, but somehow, prayerful worship was interrupted by an affront to one or more black congregants. When they were asked to tolerate further segregation, enough was enough, and they left the sanctuary of St. George's to forge their own spiritual fellowship.

By 1794, the two leaders of the Free African Society formed two new churches: Most worshipers followed Jones, the elder spiritual leader, to form the first black Protestant Episcopal church. Those blacks who wished to remain Methodists followed Allen to form the Bethel Church. In 1799, Allen became the first black person officially ordained as a minister in the ME Church. Two years later, he compiled the first black hymnal—*Collection of Spiritual Songs and Hymns, Selected from Various Authors*—which included lyrics only, as the hymns were sung to the melodies of various traditional songs.

In 1816, Allen's Bethel Church hosted representatives from other Methodist congregations dissatisfied with how the ME Church was treating African Americans. Primed for action, they organized the African Methodist Episcopal (AME) Church, chose Allen as their first AME bishop, and named his Bethel Church the mother AME Church.

Allen also contributed to his community in various other ways: organizing schools for African-American children, preaching execution sermons for condemned African Americans, helping the **Freedom's Journal,** and denouncing slavery from any podium on which he could address a listening audience. Allen was also one of the first African Americans to author an autobiography (other than a **slave narrative**), titled *The Life, Experience and Gospel Labors of the Right Reverend Richard Allen* (published posthumously in 1833).

Allen was supported in his endeavors by his first wife, Flora, who helped him buy his church in 1794, as well as their home. After she died, he and his second wife, Sarah Bass, had six children (Richard Jr., James, John, Peter, Sara, and Ann). The Allens helped many of the fugitive slaves passing through Philadelphia's Underground Railroad, and after Richard died, Sarah continued doing so.

REFERENCES: *1TESK. AA:PoP. AWAW. B. BCE. BAL-1-P. BF:2000. CE. E-97. EB-98. G-95. SMKC. Wiki.* Nash, Gary B., in *USHC.* Saillant, John, in *OCAAL* and *COCAAL.* Watkins, Michael, in *BB.* Wilson, Ian W., in *GEAAL.*

Allen, Samuel W. (Washington) (aka Paul Vesey)
12/9/1917–

Poems, criticism, anthologies, translations; attorney, educator

Allen graduated magna cum laude from Fisk University in 1938. At Fisk, he had studied creative writing with **James Weldon Johnson**. After Fisk, he earned his J.D. from Harvard Law School. After a brief stint as a military officer, he spent the next two decades balancing a law career with his writing. For a time, he used his G.I. (veteran) benefits in Paris, where he learned French and studied at the world-renowned Sorbonne university. There, he met **Richard Wright**.

In 1949, Wright helped Allen get his verse published in *Présence Africaine*, a journal highlighting *negritude* poets (African Europeans and West Indians who wrote in French). When Wright left Paris for a while, he asked Allen to take over editing the journal's English materials.

While in this role, Allen unsuccessfully tried to interest American editors in the *negritude* poets' work, styles, and ideas.

During the 1950s and early 1960s, Allen focused on his law practice and worked in various governmental positions around the world. In Germany in 1956, he published his first volume of poetry (with all 20 poems in German and in English). When he returned to the United States, his poetry was virtually unknown until the 1960s, when **Arna Bontemps** (1963) and **Langston Hughes** (1964) first included his work in their anthologies.

In 1968, Allen stopped practicing law for profit, although he has still occasionally done *pro bono* (free of charge) work. Also, his second volume of poetry, *Ivory Tusk and Other Poems*, was published in the United States. To support his poetry habit, he also taught college from 1968 until 1981 (at the Tuskegee Institute, at Wesleyan University, and at Boston University). In addition, he volunteered to teach writers' workshops for prison inmates for two years.

In 1973, Allen compiled the anthology *Poems from Africa,* including several poems he translated. Two years later, his third original poetry collection was published: *Paul Vesey's Ledger,* which traces the long history of oppression against African Americans. Other Allen poems address key African-American heroes, martyrs, and resisters, such as **Nat Turner, Harriet Tubman, Martin Luther King, Jr.**, and **Malcolm X**. His collection *Every Round and Other Poems* (1987) includes most of his previously published poems, some reworkings of old ones, and some outstanding new poems. He has also published various essays on themes similar to those of his poetry. Throughout his writing, he interweaves African traditions and African-American culture.

Among the awards he has received are a National Endowment for the Arts Creative Writing Fellowship in Poetry and various residence grants. In 1981, Allen retired from teaching, but he continues to write, give poetry readings, and conduct workshops across this country and abroad. His works have been printed in more than 100 anthologies, as well as in countless periodicals (e.g., *Black World, Journal of Afro-American Studies, Massachusetts Review, Negro Digest*).

REFERENCES: *BAL-1-P. BWA. CAO-02. EBLG. TtW.* Brittin, Ruth L., in *AAP-55-85.* Brookhart, Mary Hughes, in *OCAAL* and *COCAAL.* Godfrey, Esther, in *GEAAL.* Manheim, James M., in *BB.*

American Negro Academy
1897–1924
Scholarly organization

On March 5, 1770, Crispus Attucks, a sailor of African-American and probably Native-American ancestry, was the first American killed in the Boston Massacre that initiated the American Revolution against British rule. Exactly 127 years later, a group of scholars commemorated the event by meeting in the U.S. federal district's Lincoln Memorial Church to formally inaugurate the all-male American Negro Academy. Two days earlier, one of its founding members, **Alexander Crummell**, had just celebrated his 78th birthday. The 18 founding members also included John Wesley Cromwell, **W. E. B. Du Bois, Francis J. Grimké,** and **William Sanders Scarborough**. Crummell was the Academy's first president. After Crummell's death (in 1908), Du Bois presided over the Academy, followed by Francis's brother **Archibald H. Grimke.**

After the inaugural meeting, the Academy members continued to meet annually, usually in December, as it was never intended as a writers' workshop or a social organization. The members meant for the Academy to serve as a think-tank or institute. As its constitution noted, it was intended "to raise the standard of intellectual endeavor among American Negroes," "to promote the publication of scholarly work," and "to gather into its archives . . . data and the work of Negro authors." Toward this aim, the Academy members paid an initial membership fee of $5 per member, with annual renewals of $2 per member. With its resources, the Academy funded half of the publication costs for each of the occasional papers, and the authors funded the other half.

Over the decades of its existence, the American Negro Academy produced 21 volumes of occasional papers, starting with **Kelly Miller**'s "A Review of Hoffman's Race Traits and Tendencies of the American Negro," as American Negro Academy Occasional Paper No. 1 (1897). Others followed, including **Archibald H. Grimke**'s "The Sex Question and Race Segregation," **William Pickens**'s "The Status of the Free Negro from 1860-1870," **Arthur Schomburg**'s "Economic Contribution by the Negro to America," and **Theophilus Gould Steward**'s "The Message of San Domingo of the African Race" and "How the Black San Domingo Legion Saved the Patriotic Army in the Siege of Savannah 1799." Washington-based attorney and historian John Wesley Cromwell edited the papers.

In addition to these occasional papers, the Academy published just one book-length monograph, Cromwell's *The Negro in American History* (1914). Unlike the authors' partial funding for the occasional papers, Cromwell funded his book's publication expenses entirely himself, intending for the book to be used as a textbook for secondary-school and college students. Other members of the Academy included poet **Paul Laurence Dunbar**, poet and editor **James Weldon Johnson**, scholar **Alain Locke**, educator **Booker T. Washington**, and the scholar known as "the father of Black History," **Carter G. Woodson**. The

Academy's pursuit of excellence in scholarship often led to elitism, and it constantly struggled to maintain its goal of including 50 members at any given time—a goal made more challenging because it failed to consider the female half of the African-American population. Perpetually underfunded, the Academy closed its virtual doors in 1924.

REFERENCES: Blaxton, Reginald, (Feb-March, 1997), The American Negro Academy: Black Excellence 100 Years Ago," *American Visions*, //findarticles.com/p/articles/mi_m1546/is_n1_v12/ai_19257620/. Jackson, Errin, "American Negro Academy," in //www.blackpast.org/?q=aah/american-negro-academy-1897-1924. Joyce, Donald F. 1991. *Black Book Publishers in the United States: A Historical Dictionary of the Presses, 1817-1990.* Westport, CT: Greenwood Publishing Group. //www.tbaal.org/history.html.

Amini [Swahili: "faithful"], Johari [Swahili: "jewel"] (née Jewel Christine McLawler; aka Johari Kunjufu)
1/13/1935–

Poems, essays, movie reviews, short stories, nonfiction—monographs on health; editor, publisher, educator, chiropractor

The widowed parent of a son and a daughter, she joined **Haki Madhubuti** and **Carolyn Rodgers** in 1967 to cofound **Third World Press**. In addition to editing for the Press, she participated in other Black Arts Movement institutions such as the Writers Workshop of the **Organization of Black American Culture (OBAC)**, its publication *NOMMO*, the Kuumba Theater, and the Gwendolyn Brooks Writers' Workshop. She also edited and wrote for *Black Books Bulletin*. Amini has authored numerous poetry collections, including *Images in Black* (1967), *Black Essence* (1968), *A Folk Fable* (1969), *Let's Go Somewhere* (1970), and *A Hip Tale in Earth Style* (1972). Her essays have been collected in *An African Frame of Reference* (1972), and many of her poems and short stories have been published in journals (e.g., *Black World*) and in anthologies (e.g., 1969-1983, by Arnold Adoff, **Amina and Amiri Baraka, Nikki Giovanni, Woodie King, Jr., Dudley Randall, Darwin Turner**). In addition, as a practicing chiropractor, she wrote *A Commonsense Approach to Eating* (1975). She now lives with her younger son Shikamana, by a second marriage.

REFERENCES: CAO-01. Brown, Fahamisha Patricia, in *AAP-55-85*. Reid, Margaret Ann, in *OCAAL* and *COCAAL*. //www.aaregistry.com/detail.php?id=2821.

Amsterdam News

12/4/1909–present

News reports of interest to African Americans, both locally and nationally

According to its website, "James H. Anderson . . . had $10 in his pocket, six sheets of paper, a lead pencil and a dressmaker's table" when he produced the first issue of the *Amsterdam News* on December 4, 1909. From his home at 132 W. 65th Street, near Amsterdam Avenue, he sold each copy for 2¢ apiece. Today, current subscribers pay $35/year for a weekly print subscription mailed to their homes or $10/month for desktop delivery to their computers. Interested readers can also pay $12 for home delivery of special print editions of Election Day and Inauguration Day newspapers.

The year after starting the *News*, Anderson moved the newspaper out of his home and into a Harlem office about 70 blocks north (and east) (135th St.). A few moves later, the paper reached its current location, at 2340 8th Avenue, in the 1940s. By that time, however, Anderson had sold his ownership in the paper (in 1926). Among the more interesting editors of the *News* are **Cyril Valentine Briggs** (editor, 1912-1919), who was fired for his radical editorials, and **Ted Poston** (staffer, 1929-1936; city editor, 1934-1936), who was fired for encouraging a history-making 6-week workers' strike in 1935. The strike made news as one of the first involving African-American employees of an African-American employer. (Financial problems interplayed with a second workers' strike nearly 50 years later, in 1983.)

When FDR swept in his New Deal, the *News* switched its affiliation from the Republicans to the Democrats. Around this time, from 1941 to 1943, the *News* changed its name to the *New York Amsterdam Star-News* and then back to the original name, *Amsterdam News*. Circulation also nearly tripled during this time, from less than 36,000 in 1940 to more than 110,000 in 1947, and for a time, the *News* was published semiweekly. As the Civil Rights era drew to a close, in 1964, the circulation dropped to about 75,000, and by 1993, it had dropped back to less than 33,000. Famous contributors to the *News* have included baseballer Jackie Robinson, poet and storyteller **Langston Hughes**, Congressman **Adam Clayton Powell, Jr.**, NAACP leader **Roy Wilkins**, scholar **W. E. B. Du Bois**, and competing newspaper founder **T. Thomas Fortune**.

At the time the *News* was founded, there were about 50 other African-American-owned and -operated newspapers in the nation. Like so many other African-American-owned businesses, especially newspaper businesses, chronic financial difficulties have plagued the *News*. Nonetheless, during nearly a century of its existence, the *Amsterdam News* has been one of just four African-American-owned and -operated newspapers that has continued to appeal both to local readers and to a national audience. Its age-mates include the **Baltimore Afro-American** (1892-), the **Chicago Defender** (1905-1956, *Chicago Daily Defender*, 1956-present), and the **Pittsburgh Courier** (1907-1965, *New Pittsburgh Courier*, 1965-present).

In 1971, a group of Harlem investors, including Wilbert A. ("Bill") Tatum, bought the paper for $2.3 million. In 1984, Tatum took the helm as publisher and editor, as well as principal stockholder. A quarter of a century after first investing in the paper (July 1996), Tatum bought out the last of the other investors, placing the paper in his family's hands. In 1997, Wilbert Tatum placed the jobs of editor-in-chief and publisher in the hands of his daughter, Elinor Ruth Tatum, while staying on as chair of the board.

REFERENCES: Bennett, Allison, in GEAAL. //en.wikipedia.org/wiki/ Amsterdam_news. s://secure.townnews.com/amsterdamnews.com/ subscriber_services/subscribe.php. //maps.google.com/maps?hl= en&num=100&q=amsterdam%20avenue&um=1&ie=UTF-8&sa= N&tab=wl. //www.aaregistry.com/african_american_history/467/ The_Amsterdam_News_founded. //www.amsterdamnews.com/. //www.amsterdamnews.com/our_newspaper/about_us/.

Anderson, Marian

2/27/1897–4/8/1993

Autobiography; opera singer

Anderson's autobiography *My Lord, What a Morning: An Autobiography* (1956/1984) focuses on her solo operatic singing career, during which she broke many racial barriers (and earned a 1939 **Spingarn medal**). Her later life included work as a diplomat and earning the highest civilian honor: the Presidential Medal of Freedom (1963). Her best known quote is, "As long as you keep a person down, some part of you has to be down there to hold him down, so it means you cannot soar as you otherwise might." Perhaps greater insight into her triumphs may be revealed by this one, however: "When you stop having dreams and ideals—well, you might as well stop altogether." **Note.** Though *AANB* and others give her birth date as February 17, Keiler, the biographer her nephew cited in her autobiography, gives it as February 27, as do other sources (e.g., Wikipedia, *Encyclopædia Britannica*, *Black Biography* at Answers.com). A few sources also give her birth year as 1902.

REFERENCES: A. B. BCE. CE. D. EB-BH-CD. FAD. ME. QB. S. USHC. W2B. Wiki. Fay, Robert, in EA-99. Green, Mildred Denby, in BWA:AHE. Handy, Antoinette, in AANB. Keiler, Allan. 2000. *Marian Anderson: A Singer's Journey.* New York: Scribner. Sanchez, Brenna, in BB. Sandage, Scott, in OCAAL and COCAAL. Turner, Patricia, in BH2C. //www.fembio.org/biographie.php/woman/ biography/marian-anderson/.

Interior Secretary Harold Ickes congratulates Marian Anderson (left) at her 1939 open-air concert held on the steps of the Lincoln Memorial, Washington, D.C.

Anderson, Regina M. (pen name: Ursala/Ursula Trelling; married surname, Andrews)
5/21/1901–2/5/1993
Plays; librarian, host

A gracious host, Anderson welcomed numerous notable **Harlem Renaissance** authors (e.g., **W. E. B. Du Bois, Countee Cullen, Langston Hughes, Jean Toomer**) at a seminal dinner she organized at Harlem's Civic Club in 1924. She and her two (female) roommates even opened their home as a salon for Renaissance writers, artists, and other intellectuals. By 1926, she had reached such "Talented Tenth" celebrity that *Crisis* literary editor **Jessie Fauset** was the maid of honor at her wedding to attorney William Trent Andrews, Jr. Three years later, when she challenged racial discrimination in her job as a librarian for the New York Public Library (NYPL), the NAACP—both representative W. E. B. Du Bois and acting secretary **Walter White**—championed her cause. On June 10, 1930, she was promoted, with a salary increase.

Andrews also hosted art exhibits, lectures, and plays at her branch library, where she helped found the Krigwa Players, later known as the Negro (aka Harlem) Experimental Theatre. In addition, Andrews both acted in and wrote (under her pseudonym Ursala or Ursula Trelling) her own plays, including *Climbing Jacob's Ladder* (1931, about a lynching, inspired by the writing of **Ida B. Wells-Barnett**), *Underground* (1932, about the Underground Railroad), *The Man Who Passed*, and *Matilda*. Even after retiring from the NYPL's Washington Heights branch, she remained active in literary life, coediting the historical work, *Chronology of African-Americans in New York, 1621-1966* (1971).

REFERENCES: *AA:PoP. EB-BH-CD. MWEL. OCWW. WDAA.* Jefferson, Annetta, in *BWA:AHE.* Ostrom, Hans, in *GEAAL. Wiki. MWEL.* Whitmire, Ethelene. "Breaking the Color Barrier: Regina Andrews and the New York Public Library." *Libraries and the Cultural Record.* 42.4 (Fall 2007): p. 409. *Literature Resources from Gale.* //mywebspace.wisc.edu/ewhitmire/web/reginaandrews.htm. //womenshistory.about.com/od/harlemrenaissance/p/regina_anderson.htm

Andrews, Raymond
6/6/1934–11/25/1991
Novels, essays, autobiography/memoir

A lifelong reader and writer, his first published work appeared in 1975: a *Sports Illustrated* piece on baseball. After that, his work appeared in numerous magazines (e.g., *Harper's*) and newspapers (e.g., *Atlanta Journal-Constitution*). His first novel, *Appalachee Road* (1978), was awarded the first **James Baldwin Prize** for literature, with Baldwin himself at the presentation ceremony. It and his next two novels, *Rosiebelle Lee Wildcat Tennessee* (1980) and *Baby Sweet's* (1983), formed a trilogy. Next, he wrote his first memoir, *The Last Radio Baby: A Memoir* (1991), and then his fourth novel, *Jessie and Jesus and Cousin Clare* (1991). His second memoir, *Once Upon a Time in Atlanta* (1997?), wasn't published until 1998, by Chattahoochee Review. Sadly, he had already taken his own life years earlier, before completing his fifth novel, *99 Years and a Dark Day*. Each of his books, including his memoirs, was illustrated by his brother, Benny Andrews. In 1987, the Brown Thrasher imprint of University of Georgia Press reprinted Andrews' books. Emory University has his collected letters and memorabilia.

REFERENCES: *CAO-00*. W. Beaty, Freda R., in *OCAAL* and *COCAAL*. Holloway, Anna R., in *GEAAL*. Taylor, Jeffrey, in *BB*.

Andrews, Regina M. *See* Anderson, Regina M.

Angelou, Maya (née Marguerite Annie Johnson)
4/4/1928–
Poems, autobiographies, plays, scripts; producer, actor, performer, singer, director, educator, journalist

The entire nation listened to Maya Angelou when she read her poem "On the Pulse of Morning" at Bill Clinton's 1993 inauguration as U.S. president. (*See also* inaugural poet **Elizabeth Alexander**.) The author of several volumes of poetry, Angelou is nonetheless best known for *I Know Why the Caged Bird Sings* (1970), the first of her many autobiographical novels, nominated for the National Book Award. Powerful and moving, this work chronicles Angelou's difficult childhood experiences.

Native to St. Louis, Missouri, Maya Angelou spent her infancy in California. The great-granddaughter of a woman born into slavery, Angelou had to endure her own heartbreaks and trials from an early age. When her parents divorced in the early 1930s, her father sent her and her brother to live with his mother, who ran her own small general store in Stamps, Arkansas. The experience of living in the pre-civil rights, segregated South made a deep impression on Angelou, and she has often written of the close-knit black community that somehow supported its members through the grueling hardships of the Depression and of segregation.

For a time, Angelou went to live with her mother's family in St. Louis, where she was raped at age eight and became mute for several years. When she returned to the South, Angelou took refuge in her grandmother's store and immersed herself in books, reading voraciously and building a foundation for her writing. As a teenager she moved back to California, finished high school, and gave birth to her only child, Guy Johnson.

Angelou's subsequent volumes of autobiography—*Gather Together in My Name* (1974), *Singin' and Swingin' and Getting Merry Like Christmas* (1976), *The Heart of a Woman* (1981), *All God's Children Need Traveling Shoes* (1986), and *Songs Flung Up to Heaven* (2002)—show her political, spiritual, and psychological development as she became increasingly known as a contemporary literary figure. The themes that emerge in the series are the struggle for civil rights in America and Africa, Angelou's involvement with the feminist movement, her ongoing relationship with her son, and her awareness of the difficulties of living in America's struggling classes.

I Know Why the Caged Bird Sings, generally considered the finest of the autobiographical works, shows great moral complexity and has generated universal appeal.

Editor's note: James Baldwin said, "I Know Why the Caged Bird Sings liberates the reader into life simply because Angelou confronts her own life with such a moving wonder, such a luminous dignity. I have no words for this achievement, but I know that not since the days of my childhood, when people in books were more real than the people one saw every day, have I found myself so moved."

Critic Lynn Z. Bloom believes the decreasing popularity of subsequent volumes result from Angelou appearing "less admirable" as time passed. In *Gather Together in My Name*, for instance, Angelou nearly falls into a life of prostitution and drug addiction, a situation for which readers may not have been able to muster understanding or empathy. Bloom goes on to say Angelou "jeopardizes the maturity, honesty, and intuitive good judgement toward which she had been moving in *Caged Bird*." Nonetheless, Angelou continued to receive praise from her critics for her strong sense of story and for her passionate desire to meet the challenges and injustices of her life with courage and an increasingly strong sense of self.

In *All God's Children Need Traveling Shoes*, Angelou looks to postcolonial Africa for ways black America can find intellectual, spiritual, and emotional sustenance in a poignant search for "home," both personally and metaphorically. For four years, Angelou lived and worked in Ghana as a freelance writer and editor. During this time, she explored the cultural similarities and differences between African and African-American society. She found much to admire about African culture yet affirmed that she is American and in some significant ways outside of traditional African culture. The critics praised this graceful exploration of African-American history and its important connections to Africa.

Critics have not given the same high praise and attention to Angelou's poetry that they've given to her prose. Nonetheless, her many volumes of poetry have helped Angelou to establish her reputation—including 1972 Pulitzer Prize nominee, *Just Give Me a Cool Drink of Water 'fore I Diiie* (1971), *Oh Pray My Wings Are Gonna Fit Me Well* (1975), *And Still I Rise* (1976), *Maya Angelou: Poems* (1981), *Shaker, Why Don't You Sing?* (1983), *Now Sheba Sings the Song* (1987, illustrated by **Tom Feelings**), *I Shall Not Be Moved* (1990), *The Collected Poems* (1993), *On the Pulse of Morning* (1993), *Life Doesn't Frighten Me* (1993), *Phenomenal Woman: Four Poems Celebrating Women* (1994), *Poems* (1994), *A Brave and Startling Truth* (1995), and *Amazing Peace* (2005). Most of Angelou's poetry consists of short lyrics with short lines, alliteration, and jazzy rhythms. Critics praise Angelou more for embracing the political in her poetry than for her mastery of the form. Angelou takes on social and political issues important to African Americans in her poems and challenges the sincerity of traditional American values.

REFERENCES: Angelou, Maya. 1994. *The Complete Poems of Maya Angelou.* New York: Random House. *Discovering Authors Modules,* at http://galenet.gale.com. Lionnet, Françoise, in *OCAAL* and *COCAAL.* Articles from resources in Gale's *Literature Resource Center* (Online): Baldwin, James (1970/1993), "Maya Angelou," originally in the *New York Times,* 3/20/1970, reprinted in *Children's Literature Review,* p. 44. Angelou, Maya, and Claudia Tate (1989/2001), from *Conversations with Maya Angelou* (Jeffrey M. Elliot, Ed.), Reprinted in *Poetry Criticism* (Ellen McGeagh, Ed.), Vol. 32, pp. 146-156. Angelou, Maya, and Lynn Neary, "At 80, Maya Angelou Reflects on a 'Glorious' Life," *Weekend Edition Sunday* (Apr. 6, 2008). —Lisa Bahlinger

Editor's note: While in Africa, Angelou worked as a journalist for Egyptian and Ghanaian newspapers and for a broadcaster and a journal in Ghana. Angelou's essays and other non-autobiographical nonfiction prose have been published in several collections: *Lessons in Living* (1993), *Even the Stars Look Lonesome* (1997), *Hallelujah! The Welcome Table: A Lifetime of Memories with Recipes* (2004), *Mother: A Cradle to Hold Me* (2006), and *Letters to My Daughter* (2008), written to all her nonbiological daughters, such as **Oprah Winfrey**, to whom she dedicated her memoir *Wouldn't Take Nothing for My Journey Now* (1993). Angelou's only biological child is her son, writer Guy Johnson. Angelou has been married numerous times, but she has remained faithful to her sole editor, Robert Loomis, at Random House, which has published all of her books. Two days after her 80th birthday,

Maya Angelou

Angelou told Lynn Neary, of National Public Radio, that "the last book in the autobiographical series is '*Songs Sung [Flung] Up to Heaven.*' Six books."

A dancer and actor on stage and on screen (TV and film), Angelou has written several plays produced in California, in New York, or on film, including *Cabaret for Freedom* (1960), *The Least of These* (1966), *Sophocles, Ajax* (1974), *And Still I Rise* (1976), *Poetic Justice* (1993), and *King* (1990, based on a book by **Lonne Elder III**). She also wrote numerous short and feature-length screenplays and teleplays (1968, 1972, 1974, 1975, 1976, 1979, 1982, 1993), as well as several plays (1966, 1967, 1983) not yet produced. A singer with a rich, sonorous voice, she has written musical scores and songs for some of her screenplays, as well as other songs. At least ten audio recordings offer listeners opportunities to hear her songs, poems, and prose. Her performances have garnered her a Tony nomination, an Emmy nomination, and three Grammy awards. Angelou's live performances have included song and dance, but she has been more often seen and heard as a speaker and as a lecturer to her students at the University of Ghana, the University of California at Los Angeles, and three other universities, until she settled at Wake Forest University in the early 1980s.

Angelou has also written numerous documentaries, documentary series, and dramatic series for television. Apparently wishing to provide something for the pleasure of every possible listener or reader, between 1986 and 2004, she wrote the text for at least nine children's picture books. In addition, she has contributed poetry and prose to numerous anthologies (e.g., *Ten Times Black: Stories from the Black Experience*, Julian Mayfield, Ed.) and periodicals (e.g., *Black Scholar, Ebony, Essence, Harper's, Mademoiselle, Ms. Magazine, Redbook*), and she has probably written more forewords and introductions than even she can count.

In an interview with Claudia Tate, Angelou indicated her own views of a writer's responsibilities to her readers: "I study my craft. I don't simply write what I feel, let it all hang out. That's baloney. That's no craft at all. Learning the craft, understanding what language can do, gaining control of the language, enables one to make people weep, make them laugh, even make them go to war. You can do this by learning how to harness the power of the word. So studying my craft is one of my responsibilities. The other is to be as good a human being as I possibly can be so that once I have achieved control of the language, I don't force my weaknesses on a public who might then pick them up and abuse themselves."

REFERENCES: *A. AANB. AAW:PV. AW:ACLB-96. B. BCE. CAO-08. CE. CLCS. D. LFCC-07. MAWW. MWEL. Q. W. W2B. Wiki.* Angelou, Maya, and Claudia Tate. 1989. *Conversations with Maya Angelou* (Ed. Jeffrey M. Elliot). University Press of Mississippi. pp. 146-156. Rpt. in McGeagh, Ellen (Ed.). (2001). *Poetry Criticism* (Vol. 32, pp. 146-156). Detroit: Gale Group. *Literature Resources from Gale.* "At 80, Maya Angelou Reflects on a 'Glorious' Life." *Weekend Edition Sunday* (Apr. 6, 2008). *Literature Resources from Gale.* Baldwin, James, in *WYA-1993.* Bloom, Lynn Z, in *AAW-55-85:DPW.* Graham, Joyce L., in *WYA-1997-3.* Hagen, Lyman B., in *T-CYAW.* Mueller, Michael E., and David Oblender, in *BB.* Renuard, Lindsey, *GEAAL.* Sylvester, William, in *CP-6.* Amazon.com.

Ansa, Tina McElroy
11/18/1949–

Novels, nonfiction—history, essays, articles; journalist, editor, educator, writers' retreat founder, publisher

A lifelong avid reader, Tina delightedly discovered a Floridian writer when she was a college student. "When I read **Zora Neale Hurston's** *Their Eyes Were Watching God* and *Mules and Men,* I thought to myself, 'You mean I can write about my people, the way we walk and talk, how we live and love and it can be literature?!'" (quoted in *BB*)

For Tina McElroy Ansa, Georgia is home. A native of Macon, Georgia, Tina was educated in Catholic school

there, then went on to earn a bachelor of arts degree at Spelman College in Atlanta (1971). After college, she became the first African-American woman to work on staff for the *Atlanta Constitution,* as a copyeditor, entertainment writer, features editor, and news reporter. After 8 years at the *Constitution,* she was hired by North Carolina's *Charlotte Observer* as a copy editor and editor (late 1970s-1981). Since 1982, she has worked as a freelance feature writer, news reporter, and columnist. She has also offered writing workshops in several Georgia colleges and universities, including Spelman College, Brunswick College, Coastal Georgia Community College, and Emory University. In the late 1980s, she wrote *Not Soon Forgotten: Cotton Planters and Plantations of the Golden Isles of Georgia, 1784-1812* (c. 1987) for the Coastal Georgia Historical Society.

Meanwhile, May 1, 1978, Tina McElroy married cinematographer Joneé Ansa, a fellow of the American Film Institute (AFI). The newlyweds honeymooned on St. Simons Island on the Georgia Sea Islands, world-renowned for having deeply rooted African-American cultural traditions, in part due to centuries of isolation from the mainland's mainstream ways. As she later recalled, "As our car neared the shores ... I heard a voice say clearly: This is where you belong" (from *Essence* article, quoted in *BB*). In 1984, Tina, Joneé, and their child, Afrika, moved to St. Simons Island. "Here in the Sea Islands, the cradle of African culture in this country, I have found the peace and acceptance of home" (in *BB*). In 1989, Ansa directed the Georgia Sea Island Festival, celebrating the islands' rich African-American cultural traditions. Fifteen years later, she and her husband founded Sea Island Writers Retreats, on Sapelo Island. Seminar leaders include best-selling writers, screenwriters, and professional editors, who guide both "emerging and established writers in honing their work and skills in fiction, nonfiction, memoir and editing" (//www.tinamcelroy ansa.com/bio.html). In the fall of 2004, she hosted three retreats. In 2006 and 2007, Ansa held retreats on the campus of Spelman College as "Sea Island Writers Retreats...On the Road."

More important, Ansa has set all her novels in the small fictional town of Mulberry in the middle of Georgia, much like her childhood home. As she has said, "I plan to remain in the little fictional middle Georgia town of Mulberry my entire writing career. It is here, in the heart of the South and the heart of Georgia, I explore the African-American family and the African-American community of this decade and earlier ones. It is an infinitely fascinating and rich subject" (quoted in *CAO-05*).

Ansa's characters inhabit not only a specific earthly geography but also a spiritual world, in which they may possess psychic powers, form relationships with deceased spirits, or receive guidance from their deceased ancestors.

Her fiction often evokes the spirit of a ghost story and sometimes employs its conventions. Though her characters enjoy middle-class comforts and seem untroubled by some of the harsh brutality of racism and sexism, they still experience psychic pain, personal loneliness, and yearnings for love. In part because of their ties to their ancestors, her characters come to appreciate African-American traditions while still enjoying success in the American mainstream.

The youngest of her parent's five children, Ansa titled her first novel *Baby of the Family* (1989), a coming-of-age novel suitable for young adults, as well as mature readers. Her protagonist, Lena McPherson, is born with a "caul" (part of the amniotic sac) over her eyes. The folks in Lena's community believe the caul to be a sign that Lena has special psychic powers for communing with the spirits of deceased people. Lena's mother doubts the existence of psychic powers, and she urges Lena to doubt her powers, too. As Lena reaches adolescence, her typical teen desire to be "normal" is compounded by her confusion about her psychic powers. "Ansa shows us that it's only through self-acceptance that we can uncover our distinctive 'powers' and effect positive change in our personal lives and the lives of others," said Shirley M. Jordan in *American Visions* (quoted in *BB*).

Other critics and reviewers welcomed *Baby*, too. In *The New York Times* (*NYT*) *Book Review*, Valerie Sayers said, "The novel offers dense rich scenes of black Southern life, scenes felt deeply by the characters who act them out, ... Tina McElroy Ansa tells a good quirky story, and she tells it with humor, grace and great respect for the power of the particular." *The NYT Book Review* named *Baby* a Notable Book of the Year (1989); the American Library Association named it a best book for young adults (1990); the Georgia Center for the Book named it one of the "Top 25 Books Every Georgian Should Read" (2001); and it was awarded the 1989 Georgia Authors Series Award. Regular readers gave Ansa the nod, too, putting *Baby* on the BlackBoard African-American Bestsellers list for Paperback Fiction. Tina and Joneé are adapting *Baby* to create a screenplay for a feature film starring Alfre Woodard, Loretta Devine, Vanessa Williams, and others. Tina will executive produce, and Joneé will direct and film the movie in Macon. Two decades after its release, *Baby* still ranks high in Amazon.com sales (#554,418; compare to #2,495,946 in Books for the 9-year-old edition of this dictionary).

In Ansa's second novel, *Ugly Ways* (1993), sisters Betty, Emily, and Annie Ruth Lovejoy are reunited to prepare for the funeral of their mother, Mudear. Their surname is ironic, as Mudear's emotional negligence and psychological abuse of them inhibited their ability to love joy. Countering the stereotype of African-American mothers, Mudear embodied the opposite of the strong,

warm, caring, selfless, nurturing mother. Ansa tells the story from the viewpoints of each of the three sisters, as well as of the deceased mother's spirit. Ansa observed, "In my novel *Ugly Ways*, I try to expand the canvas of American literature to include a mother, a black mother, who challenges the 'conventional wisdom,' the accepted line on what 'mother' is and means in African-American culture" (quoted in *CAO-05*). The NAACP nominated Ansa for its Image Award (1994), the BlackBoard African-American Bestsellers list named *Ugly Ways* among the Best Fiction (1994), the Georgia Center for the Book named the novel in its list of the "Top 25 Books Every Georgian Should Read" (2005), and the novel spent more than two years on the BlackBoard African-American Bestsellers list compiled by the *Quarterly Black Review of Books* and the *African American Literary Review.* Emmy, Globe, and Screen Actors Guild award-winning actress Alfre Woodard is working with Ansa to bring *Ugly Ways* to the screen.

In Ansa's third novel, *The Hand I Fan With* (1996), she returns to the story of Lena McPherson, now age 45 and a successful businesswoman. With her parents and her siblings deceased, no husband, and no children, Lena relies on her dear friend, "Sister," for companionship. When Sister plans to take a one-year sabbatical, the two women hold a mystical ritual to call forth the "perfect man" for her, in Sister's absence. The perfect man turns out to be a 100-year-old spirit, Herman, who is embodied for one year. In the *Washington Post Book World*, Natasha Tarpley called the novel "an absolutely delicious love story" (quoted in *CAO-05*). When *Hand* was awarded the Georgia Authors Series Award (1996), Ansa became the first author to win this award more than once.

You Know Better (2002), like *Ugly Ways*, tells a story from multiple viewpoints. In this case, Ansa tells the story of teenage LaShawndra, her mother Sandra, and her grandmother Lily. According to *Booklist* critic Lillian Lewis, as in her previous works, Ansa does "a superb job of weaving the supernatural and natural into an engrossing tale about women and relationships" (quoted in *CAO-05*). The American Library Association gave the novel its Best Fiction award.

Ansa's first four novels were published by mainstream publishers Harcourt (her first two), Doubleday (her third), and Morrow (her fourth). In March of 2007, Ansa launched her own publishing house, Down South Press. Her press's first title is her own sequel to *Ugly Ways*, *Taking after Mudear*, but she plans for her press to "publish established as well as emerging literary voices" (//www.tinamcelroyansa.com/bio.html). *Taking after Mudear* (2007) follows the Mudear sisters and their mother's spirit months after they have buried her body. The youngest sister, Annie Ruth, and the middle sister, Emily, have both moved in with Betty, the eldest sister, in their home town of Mulberry. When unmarried Annie Ruth gives birth to the first Lovejoy grandchild, Mudear's spirit returns to escalate sibling conflicts and to cause turmoil for the sisters.

In addition to her journalism and her novels, Ansa writes opinions, book reviews, articles, and other short pieces for periodicals such as the *Los Angeles Times*, (New York) *Newsday*, *Atlanta Constitution*, **Crisis**, *Ms.*, and *Essence*. Her short stories and other writings have also been anthologized, such as in Terry McMillan's *Breaking Ice* (1992), Rosemary Robotham's *Mending the World: Stories of Family by Contemporary Black Writers* (2003), and Atlanta's Task Force for the Homeless publication, *You Haven't to Deserve: A Gift to the Homeless: Fiction By 21 Writers (Signed By 8 Authors)* (1992). She has also regularly contributed "Postcards from Georgia" essays to *CBS Sunday Morning*, and she has presented lectures and readings at the Smithsonian Institution's African-American Center Author's Series, the **Richard Wright**/Zora Neale Hurston Foundation, the PEN/Faulkner Reading Series, the PEN American Center, the Folger Shakespeare Library, the **Schomburg** Center of the New York Public Library, the National Book Club Conference, and the Savannah College of Art and Design.

Ansa has served on the Advisory Council for the Georgia Center for the Book and on the host committee for the Flannery O'Connor Awards. For her literary contributions to Georgia, Ansa received the Stanley W. Lindberg Award (2005), and for her literary contributions overall, she was inducted into the International Literary Hall of Fame for Writers of African Descent at the **Gwendolyn Brooks** Center of Chicago State University (2002).

To promote literacy and to honor the contributions of women of color, Ansa founded the Good Lil' School Girl Foundation (2001) and established Good Lil' School Girl Book Clubs in schools at all levels across the country. In 2006, she joined Dazon Diallo of SisterLove to launch the South African African-American SisterLove Sisters Sharing (SAAASSS) book program. SAAASSS has collected and distributed more than 300 books, signed by African-American women authors, to book clubs and other women's organizations in South Africa. She also participates in many other charitable organizations and programs that benefit the homeless, including Habitat for Humanity, and she has helped to raise funds for Aid to Children of Imprisoned Mothers. She is also an *amateur*—French for "lover of"—naturalist, enjoying gardening and bird watching.

"To record, examine, and push the parameters of our lives is, I believe, the job and duty of literature" (quoted in *CAO-05*).

REFERENCES: *CAO-05*. *Wiki*. Brennan, Carol, in *BB*. Marsh-Lockett, Carol P., in *COCAAL* and *OCAAL*. Martin, Kameelah L., in *AANB*. Amazon.com. //en.wikipedia.org/wiki/Caul. //www.new georgiaencyclopedia.org/nge/Article.jsp?id=h-748. *News & Notes*, August 23, 2007, //www.npr.org/templates/story/story.php?storyId= 13895809.//www. tinamcelroyansa.com/bio.html.

FURTHER READING: *EAAWW. HAAL* Upchurch, Gail L., in *GEAAL*.

Anthologies of African-American Literature 1845–
Collections of the writings of numerous authors

Readers appreciate anthologies because they offer easy ways to discover new authors and new perspectives without investing a great deal of time or money in numerous volumes by numerous authors. Educators prize anthologies because they can readily introduce learners to a variety of authors in a particular genre (e.g., dramas or mysteries), from a particular time period (e.g., the Harlem Renaissance), from a particular cultural perspective (e.g., Latina women) or life experience (e.g., imprisoned writers), or about a particular topic (e.g., resistance to slavery). Editors enjoy compiling anthologies because they relish assembling a collection of writings that appeal to them or that well serve their particular purpose (e.g., introducing readers to Hispanic writers of African descent).

The first anthology of writings by Americans of African descent was *Les Cenelles* (1845), containing 85 poems written by 17 French-speaking freeborn New Orleans Creoles. The second, *Autographs for Freedom* (1853), edited by English abolitionist Julia Griffiths, included writings by European-American abolitionists, as well as African Americans. In addition to poetry by **William Wells Brown** and **George B. Vashon**, it included a nonfiction narrative "The Heroic Slave" by Griffiths's friend **Frederick Douglass** and prose by Vashon, **John Mercer Langston**, and John McCune Smith, among others.

The only collections of writings by African Americans for the next 70 or so years appeared in the pages of **antislavery periodicals**, African-American-owned and -operated **newspapers** (e.g., **Amsterdam News**, 1909-; **Baltimore Afro-American**, 1892-; **Chicago Defender**, 1905-; **Pittsburgh Courier**, 1907-) and journals (e.g., **The Woman's Era**, 1894-1897; **The Voice of the Negro**, 1904-1907; **The Messenger**, 1917-1928; **Negro World**, 1918-1933), as well as an occasional sprinkling in a few white-owned and -operated periodicals. A possible exception may be *The Work of the Afro-American Woman* (1894), by "Mrs. N. F. Mossell" (**Gertrude Bustill Mossell**). Not a true anthology, it did include a smattering of poems by other women poets, as well as a brief narrative history of African-American women's literature up to that time and some of her own poems.

After decades of neglect, in the 1920s, the first collections of writings by African Americans began to appear. The first ones were anthologies of poetry, verse, and songs, starting with **James Weldon Johnson**'s *Book of American Negro Poetry* (1922). (*See* **anthologies of African-American literature, specific genres, poetry, verse, and song** for further information on collections by Mossell, by Johnson, and by other poetry anthologists.)

The first multigenre anthologies also emerged in the 1920s. In the fall of 1924, the European-American editor of *Survey Graphic* (1921-1952), social-reform activist Paul Kellogg, asked scholar **Alain Locke** to guest-edit a special issue of the monthly journal Paul and his brother Arthur published. The following March (1925), Locke's special issue, "Harlem: Mecca of the New Negro" (Vol. 6, No. 6, aka "the Harlem Number"), sold out its first printing of 30,000, and the Kelloggs printed a second run of 12,000 copies. European-American patrons Amy and **Joel Spingarn**, Albert C. Barnes, and broadcasting award namesake George Foster Peabody each bought hundreds of 50¢ copies and distributed these copies to African-American organizations and educational institutions. As always, big sales numbers impress, so legendary publishers Albert & Charles Boni quickly asked Locke to expand the issue into a book-length publication. He did so, and they rushed it into print by the end of the year as *The New Negro* (1925). (For more on this publication, *see New Negro, The*.)

Three other publications deserve mention in this context, as well. The literary journal *Fire!!* (1926) was intended as a quarterly but ceased after one issue (*see also Fire!!*); contributions by numerous African-American writers appeared in the pages of its single issue. In addition, the National Urban League published what was essentially a special hardcover issue of its *Opportunity* magazine, *Ebony and Topaz: A Collectanea* (1927), edited by *Opportunity*'s editor, **Charles Spurgeon Johnson**. A more comprehensive anthology of contemporary (1920s-1933) African-American writers was *Negro: An Anthology* (1934), compiled by English heiress Nancy Cunard. Her 855-page volume included about 150 contributors from around the globe. (*See* **anthologies, writers from the New Negro era**, for more information on these and other anthologies of this era.)

Another editor of European descent was responsible for the first multigenre anthology to include not only contemporary African-American authors but also authors going back across one and a half centuries of African-American literature. The 535-page *Anthology of American Negro Literature* (1929/1969), edited by European-American V. F. (Victor Francis) Calverton (1900-1940), was published for the prestigious series, The Modern Library of the World's Best Books. Calverton, a devout Marxist, intended for the volume not only to

challenge white racist preconceptions, but also to highlight the role of economic forces in African-American literature and the arts. Some critics credit this volume with bringing to widespread national prominence writers such as **Countee Cullen, W. E. B. Du Bois, Langston Hughes, Claude McKay, Jean Toomer**, and others.

A more modest 388-page collection was *Readings from Negro Authors: For Schools and Colleges, with a Bibliography of Negro Literature* (1931), edited by Otelia Cromwell, **Lorenzo Dow Turner**, and Eva G. Dykes. In his pamphlet for the 135th Street Branch of the New York Public Library, Schomburg described the book as "a selection for classroom study or supplementary reading, with a bibliography." A decade later, a much more prestigious and comprehensive anthology appeared: *The Negro Caravan: Writings by American Negroes* (1941), edited by **Sterling A. Brown, Arthur Paul Davis**, and Ulysses Lee, containing more than 1,000 pages. According to *The Oxford Companion to African American Literature* (1997), "no single work has had greater influence in establishing the canon of African American literature. . . . It can still be read with profit decades after its compilation." *Caravan* included the entire sweep of African-American literature and included not only poetry, short fiction, and essays, but also autobiography, biography, folklore, speeches, pamphlets, and correspondence.

A few years later, The Modern Library of the World's Best Books series came out with a second collection, *Anthology of American Negro Literature* (1944), containing 481 pages, edited by Sylvestre C. Watkins. Other anthologies of this period included *American Literature by Negro Authors* (1950), edited by Herman Dreer; and *Black Voices* (1968), edited by European-American anthologist Abraham Chapman, who subsequently edited his 720-page *New Black Voices: an Anthology of Contemporary Afro-American Literature* (1972).

More than a quarter-century after the publication of *The Negro Caravan* (1941), mainstream publisher Free Press printed *Dark Symphony: Negro Literature in America* (1968; 2008, Paw Prints), edited by **James A. Emanuel** and Theodore L. Gross. The editors arranged the volume chronologically, including substantial introductions for each chronological period. Unfortunately, the 43 authors included only 6 females, even excluding **Phillis Wheatley** and **Zora Neale Hurston**. Nonetheless, the volume was praised as being well written, well organized, and selected according to "belles lettres" criteria, rather than "sociopolitical" ones.

On April 4, 1968, Dr. **Martin Luther King, Jr.**, was assassinated, and the resulting outrage among African Americans prompted many European Americans to awaken to the potential problems of continuing to ignore African Americans in academia, as well as in society at large. With pressure from African-American faculty and students, colleges began offering African-American studies courses and establishing departments of African-American studies. Publishers suddenly realized that they could make money by providing reading materials for these students. In 1970, Fawcett put out the 383-page *On Being Black; Writings by Afro-Americans from Frederick Douglass to the Present*, edited by Charles Twitchell Davis and Daniel Walden. That year, poet and literary critic **Darwin T. Turner** edited *Black American Literature: Essays, Poetry, Fiction, Drama* (1970), and a year later, literary critic, poet, scholar, and essayist **Houston A. Baker, Jr.**, edited *Black Literature in America* (1971). Baker's volume included some folklore but omitted works from the 1700s, included only six works from the 1800s, but covered 1900-1970 admirably.

Again, another standout appeared: Arthur P. Davis, who had coedited *The Negro Caravan* (1941), collaborated with **J. Saunders Redding** to edit *The Cavalcade: Negro American Writing from 1760 to the Present*. Their 905-page collection spanned nearly two centuries of African-American writing while trying to avoid "unneeded duplication" with other anthologies. Both Davis and Redding had integrationist leanings, so they tended to omit more militant, nationalist writings. When editing the subsequent *The New Cavalcade*, Redding was deceased, and Davis was joined by Joyce A. Joyce, who ensured inclusion of more militant authors in the second collection.

Another notable general anthology of this period was Richard Barksdale and Keneth Kinnamon's *Black Writers of America: A Comprehensive Anthology* (1972), published by mainstream publisher Macmillan, which sold more than 70,000 copies. Barksdale and Kinnamon said, "We have provided generous selections of autobiographies, essays, speeches, letters, political pamphlets, histories, journals, and folk literature as well as poems, plays, and stories. Our criteria for inclusion were both artistic and social; indeed, facile or rigid separation of the two seems to us misguided." They arranged the works from 85 writers into six parts, and they wrote generous part introductions and headnote introductions to the individual authors. The volume was also praised for its extensive bibliography.

Afro-American Writing: An Anthology of Prose and Poetry (1972; 2nd, enlarged ed., 1985), edited by Richard A. Long and **Eugenia W. Collier**, published by a university press, was smaller in scope than either *Cavalcade* or *Black Writers of America*, but it was praised for its judicious selections, other than the omission of Countee Cullen and **Richard Wright**, due to literary-property disputes. Also published were *Blackamerican Literature 1760-Present* (1971), edited by Ruth Miller, arranged in six chronological sections; and *I, Too, Sing America: Black Voices in American Literature* (1971), edited by Barbara Dodds

Standford, a small collection intended for high-school students.

The 1980s saw the flourishing of specialized anthologies. For more information on period-specific anthologies, *see* **anthologies, writers from the antebellum era**, and **anthologies, writers from the New Negro era**. For more information on anthologies written by and for homosexual and heterosexual women and men, *see* **anthologies, written by and for heterosexual or lesbian women**; and **anthologies, written by and for gay or heterosexual men**. *See also* **anthologies, written by and for juveniles**. For anthologies on specific genres of writing, *see* **anthologies, specific genres, poetry, verse, and song**; **anthologies, specific genres, drama and plays**; **anthologies, specific genres, fiction**; and **anthologies, specific genres, nonfiction**. *See also* **anthologies, regional**; **anthologies, from literary journals**; and **anthologies, special topics and audiences**.

The publication of the two-volume *The New Cavalcade* (1991-1992) revived interest in general anthologies. Some of the anthologies published during the 1990s include *African American Literature: An Anthology of Nonfiction, Fiction, Poetry, and Drama* (1993), edited by Demetrice A. Worley and Jesse Perry, Jr., with a foreword by **Nikki Giovanni**; *Crossing the Danger Water: Three Hundred Years of African-American Writing* (1993), edited by Deirdre Mullane, an 800-page volume including not only literary texts, but also historical documents, letters, songs, and autobiography, as well as fiction and poetry; *African-American Voices* (1995), edited by Michele Stepto, a 159-page collection of key authors such as Dove, Du Bois, Ellison, Morrison, and Richard Wright; *Cornerstones: An Anthology of African American Literature* (1996), edited by Melvin Donalson, a 1,001-page collection published by an imprint of St. Martin's Press; and *African-American Literature: A Brief Introduction and Anthology* (1997), edited by Al Young, a 500-page volume organized chronologically within each genre, featuring autobiography, fiction, poetry, and drama.

The end of the 1990s saw the publication of three superlative anthologies: First, **Henry Louis Gates, Jr.**, and **Nellie Y. McKay** coedited the highly esteemed 2,665-page *The Norton Anthology of African American Literature* (1997; also available with a CD), which incorporates many of the works of 120 writers, including a few complete long pieces. Starting with literary origins in the oral tradition, including folktales and spirituals, the volume continues through to 1996, with many writings by contemporary authors. Next, Patricia Liggins Hill and Bernard W. Bell coedited *Call and Response: The Riverside Anthology of the African American Literary Tradition* (1998; also includes a CD), a 2,039-page collection of about 550 selections, embracing both oral literature—from slave songs to rap pieces—and written literature. About half the size of the other two volumes, the 1,130-page *The Prentice Hall Anthology of African American Literature* (1999; with CD) edited by Rochelle Smith and Sharon L. Jones, offers paintings and photography, songs and speeches, as well as fiction, nonfiction, and poetry; the editors present the works chronologically and offer readers historical contexts for the literature.

The new millennium has continued to offer new anthologies, such as *The African-American Experience: Black History and Culture through Speeches, Letters, Editorials, Poems, Songs, and Stories* (2009, 720 pp.), edited by Kai Wright. Wright includes excerpts from more than 300 primary documents, organized chronologically. Other examples include *From Bondage to Liberation: Writings by and about Afro-Americans from 1700 to 1918* (2001, 487 pp.), edited by Faith Berry; *African American Literature Beyond Race: An Alternative Reader* (2006; 460 pp.), edited by Gene Andrew Jarrett; *Grace Abounding: The Core Knowledge Anthology of African-American Literature, Music, and Art* (2006, 2nd ed.; 910 pp.), edited by Robert D. Shepherd; and Prestwick House's truly concise *African American Literature: A Concise Anthology from Frederick Douglass to Toni Morrison* (2009; 232 pp.).

Anthologies of contemporary writers include *In the Tradition: An Anthology of Young Black Writers* (1993), edited by **Kevin Powell**, *Giant Steps: The New Generation of African American Writers* (2000), edited by **Kevin Young**, and a hip-hop urban novelist's collections *Nikki Turner Presents Street Chronicles: Tales from da Hood* (2006) and *Nikki Turner Presents Street Chronicles: Girls in the Game* (2007), among many others.

REFERENCES: Kinnamon, Keneth, in *OCAAL*. _____. (Spring 1997). "Anthologies of African-American Literature from 1845 to 1994." *Callaloo* (Vol. 20, No. 2), pp. 461-481. //en.wikipedia.org/wiki/Martin_Luther_King,_Jr. //en.wikipedia.org/wiki/Nellie_Y._McKay. //libpac.sdsu.edu/. //www.sandiego.gov/public-library/. //www.sdcl.org/. //www.worldcat.org/account/?page=searchItems. //worldcat.org/identities/. Amazon.com.

Anthologies of African-American Literature, from Literary Journals
1972–

Literature collections of the writings of numerous authors

In addition to providing all Americans with vibrant, stimulating literature, and offering African Americans culturally relevant literature, African-American literary journals have played a crucial role in nurturing the careers of African-American writers. It seems self-evident that anthologists would wish to draw on these rich resources to create compendiums of African-American literature. In addition, anthologies tied to particular literary journals not only pay homage to the specific journal, but

also indicate how a particular journal fits into the overall body of African-American literature. Further, such anthologies may offer distinctive insight into the surrounding historical context for these journals.

Perhaps the first literary journal to be so honored was *Umbra* (1963-1974), the literary journal that arose from the New York-based Society of Umbra (1962-1970s), more commonly called the **Umbra Workshop**. Workshop cofounder and journal editor (coeditor, 1963-1968; editor, 1968-1974) David Henderson edited three anthologies: *Umbra Anthology, 1967-1968* (1968), *Umbra Blackworks, 1970-1971* (1971), and *Umbra/Latin Soul 1974-1975* (1975), all published by the Society of Umbra.

While *Umbra* was being published from New York, in Chicago members of the **Organization of Black American Culture (OBAC)** Writers Workshop were publishing **NOMMO**, their own literary magazine. While the journal was still being published, William Henry Robinson (1922-) edited the 501-page *NOMMO: An Anthology of Modern Black African and Black American Literature* (1972). The same year, Paul Carter Harrison edited *Drama of Nommo: Black Theatre in the African Continuum* (1972). A decade and a half later, OBAC decided to celebrate its 20th anniversary by issuing *NOMMO: A Literary Legacy of Black Chicago 1967-1987: An OBAC Anthology* (1987), including some new unpublished material from OBAC Writers Workshop authors, as well as previously published works. Because poets dominate the OBAC Writer's Workshop, poetry dominates the celebratory anthology. It likewise dominates *NOMMO 2: Remembering Ourselves Whole* (1990), edited by the OBAC Writers Workshop, and published by its OBA House Press. OBA House Press also published *NOMMO 3: An OBAC Anthology of Contemporary Black Writing* (1992).

For more than a quarter of a century, the National Urban League published *Opportunity: A Journal of Negro Life* (1923-1949), much more a literary journal than a house organ, especially when edited by its founding editor, **Charles Spurgeon Johnson**. A few years after its inception, Johnson put together an anthology, *Ebony and Topaz: A Collectanea* (1927), published by the National Urban League as essentially a special hardcover issue of *Opportunity*. Half a century after *Opportunity* had ceased publication, Sondra Kathryn Wilson edited *The Opportunity Reader: Stories, Poetry, and Essays from the Urban League's* Opportunity *Magazine* (1999).

Sondra Kathryn Wilson also edited *The Crisis Reader: Stories, Poetry, and Essays from the N.A.A.C.P.'s* Crisis *Magazine* (1999), drawing on the long-lived **Crisis** magazine (1910-), originally titled *Crisis: A Record of the Darker Races*. Wilson's anthology has been lauded by Pulitzer Prize-winning author **David Levering Lewis** as an "excellent edition. It will be an indispensable source from the moment of issue."

Wilson followed that anthology with *The Messenger Reader: Stories, Poetry, and Essays from The Messenger Magazine* (2000). Unlike *Opportunity* and *Crisis*, **The Messenger** (1917-1928) was not directly affiliated with a civil-rights organization, but was instead tied to organized labor through its founding editors **A. Philip Randolph**, who helped found the highly influential Brotherhood of Sleeping Car Porters in 1925, and **Chandler Owen**, a labor organizer who remained on the masthead but ceased his direct involvement with *The Messenger* in 1924.

Much less well known, but still vitally important to African-American literature was *Freedomways* (1961-1986), cofounded by **Shirley Graham Du Bois**, wife of **W. E. B. Du Bois**, and Esther Cooper Jackson, among others. Jackson herself compiled a 416-page anthology, *Freedomways Reader: Prophets in Their Own Country* (2001). Over its quarter-century of existence, *Freedomways* had printed the writings of three Nobel laureates, leading intellectuals such as **James Baldwin** and W. E. B. Du Bois, emerging literati such as **Alice Walker** and **Alex Haley**, political activists such as **Angela Davis** and **Jesse Jackson**, and celebrities such as **Paul Robeson** and **Ruby Dee**, as well as known and unknown writers with intriguing ideas and literary talents.

Perhaps one of the best known African-American literary journals is *Callaloo*, which enjoys great prestige among scholars, as well as other literati. To celebrate its 25th anniversary, Charles Henry Rowell, *Callaloo's* founding editor, and poet **Carl Phillips** edited *Making Callaloo: 25 Years of Black Literature* (2002), highlighting some of the outstanding poetry, short fiction, and excerpts from longer works published in *Callaloo's* pages over the preceding quarter-century. Though the editors focus mostly on Americans of African descent, they also include some authors from the Caribbean and South America. (*See Callaloo* for more information on the journal and its contributors.)

REFERENCES: Kinnamon, Keneth, in *OCAAL*. ____. (Spring 1997). "Anthologies of African-American Literature from 1845 to 1994." *Callaloo* (Vol. 20, No. 2), pp. 461-481. //en.wikipedia.org/wiki/ Martin_Luther_King,_Jr. //en.wikipedia.org/wiki/Nellie_Y._McKay. //libpac.sdsu.edu/. //www.sandiego.gov/public-library/. //www.sdcl.org/. //www.worldcat.org/account/?page=searchItems. //worldcat.org/ identities/. Amazon.com.

Anthologies of African-American Literature, Regional African-American Literature
1936–

Literature collections of writings by authors in particular regions of the United States

Before the Civil War, African Americans in the North focused their literary efforts on opposing slavery, chiefly in **antislavery periodicals**. Following the Civil War, some clubs and other groups published literary journals or at least journals that included literature. (*See* **Ruffin, Josephine St. Pierre**, for information on *The Woman's Era*, 1894-1897.) While the Renaissance of the New Negro was still blossoming in Harlem, small groups of writers were gathering here and there across the country. Doubtless, some of them produced small collections of their work, published for themselves and possibly for others, which have remained obscure. (*See* **Quill Club** for information on Boston's *Saturday Evening Quill*, 1928-1930.)

In addition, some students of local literature gathered writings into modest regional anthologies. For instance, folklorist J. (John) Mason Brewer compiled and edited the 45-page anthology *Heralding Dawn: An Anthology of Verse*, still listed as having "limited availability," used, through //www.amazon.com. The poetry featured Texan poets, including Texas-born **Gwendolyn Bennett**, who left Texas early and made her home in Harlem, as well as Bernice Love Wiggins, who published her own volume of verse, *Tuneful Tales* (1925). Other Texas poets in the volume included Lauretta Holman Gooden, Maurine Lawrence Jeffrey, Lillian Tucker Lewis, and Birdelle Wycoff Ransom.

Most regions of the country have yielded at least one anthology of regional writings. For the Midwest, Conrad Balfour, Ta-coumba T. Aiken, and Seitu Jones coedited *The Butterfly Tree: An Anthology of Black Writing from the Upper Midwest* (1985, 190 pp.). For the West, Bruce A. Glasrud and Laurie Champion edited *African American West: A Century of Short Stories* (2000), featuring such prominent writers as **Charles Chesnutt** and **Walter Mosley**. (Glasrud also collaborated with Merline Pitre, James M. Smallwood, Angela Boswell, and Barry A. Crouch to write *Black Women in Texas History*, 2008, 248 pages.)

For the South, **John Oliver Killens** began and Jerry Washington Ward finished coediting *Black Southern Voices: An Anthology of Fiction, Poetry, Drama, Nonfiction, and Critical Essays* (1992, 608 pp.), including 56 authors, whom Killens introduced with the affirmation, "There is a black southern literary tradition, a voice that is special, profound, and distinct from any other in the country." More recently, William L. Andrews edited *The North Carolina Roots of African American Literature: An Anthology* (2006, 328 pp.), described as "thoughtful, comprehensive and very readable," making the case "that North Carolina produced a remarkable, indeed unmatched record of black authorship throughout the nineteenth century" (quoted in Amazon.com). A few examples include **Charles W. Chesnutt** (also claimed by the West), **Anna Julia Cooper**, David Bryant Fulton, **George Moses Horton**, **Harriet Jacobs**, **Moses Roper**, and **David Walker**. In addition, though they have not yet done so, it seems likely that the **Affrilachian Poets** will produce at least some modest anthology of their work in the future.

The Northeast offers a plethora of materials on the Harlem Renaissance (*see* **anthologies of African-American literature, writers from the New Negro era**). In addition, William H. Banks, Jr., edited *Beloved Harlem: A Literary Tribute to Black America's Most Famous Neighborhood: From the Classics to the Contemporary* (2005, 544 pp.). In addition to the authors of the **Harlem Renaissance** and the authors from the **Harlem Writers Guild** (1950-), founded by **John Oliver Killens, Rosa Guy,** Walter Christmas, and **John Henrik Clarke**, the volume embraces other writers, as well. The editors sort the 29 essays, excerpts, and short stories into periods, starting with Part 1 (1910s-1930s), including **W. E. B. Du Bois, Zora Neale Hurston, James Weldon Johnson,** and **Claude McKay**; Part 2 (1940s-1960s), including **Dorothy West, James Baldwin,** and **Langston Hughes**; Part 3 (1970-2000), including Grace F. Edwards, **Louise Meriwether, Toni Morrison, Walter Dean Myers,** and **John A. Williams**; and Part 4 (2000-), including novelist and playwright Brian Keith Jackson and journalist and fiction writer Rosemarie Robotham.

REFERENCES: Kinnamon, Keneth, in *OCAAL*. _____. (Spring 1997). "Anthologies of African-American Literature from 1845 to 1994." *Callaloo* (Vol. 20, No. 2), pp. 461-481. //en.wikipedia.org/wiki/Martin_Luther_King,_Jr. //en.wikipedia.org/wiki/Nellie_Y._McKay. //libpac.sdsu.edu/. //www.sandiego.gov/public-library/. //www.sdcl.org/. //www.worldcat.org/account/?page=searchItems. //worldcat.org/identities/. Amazon.com.

Anthologies of African-American Literature, Special Topics and Audiences
Literature collections including the writings of numerous authors for a particular audience or on a particular topic

The 1970s spawned an abundance of riches in African-American literature overall, and the **Black Arts Movement** in particular gave birth to numerous general anthologies. In addition, the 1970s brought to national attention the writings of prisoners.

Between early 1970 and late 1972, author, activist, fugitive, and defendant **Angela Yvonne Davis** popularized the cause of the accused murderers known as the Soledad brothers (named for Soledad Prison). By the middle of the decade, she had written two books about her experiences while a fugitive and while on trial, *If They Come in the Morning: Voices of Resistance* (1971) and best-selling *Angela Davis: An Autobiography* (1974). Two other bestsellers emerged about this time: fugitive Eldridge Cleaver's *Soul on Ice* (1968) and *Soledad Brother: The Prison Letters of George Jackson* (1970). Profiting from this heightened interest in the writings of prisoners were three anthologies: **Etheridge Knight**'s *Black Voices from Prison*

(1970), **Eugene Perkins**'s *Poetry of Prison: Poems by Black Prisoners* (1972), and Elena Lewis's *Who Took the Weight? Black Voices from Norfolk Prison* (1972).

An entirely different special topic documents a special event through anthology, such as *Million Man March/Day of Absence: A Commemorative Anthology: Speeches, Commentary, Photography, Poetry, Illustrations, Documents* (1995, 172 pp.), edited by **Haki R. Madhubuti** and **Maulana Karenga**, published by **Third World Press**. A more comprehensive documentation of the entire history of African-American political and social-reform writings is *Let Nobody Turn Us Around: Voices of Resistance, Reform, and Renewal: An African American Anthology* (2000, 598 pp.), edited by Manning Marable and Leith Mullings, arranged chronologically, from excerpts of the **slave narrative** of **Olaudah Equiano** to the contemporary remarks of **Cornel West** and others.

From the political to the personal, many anthologies address relationships and families, such as *Memory of Kin: Stories about Family by Black Writers* (1990), edited by Mary Helen Washington; *Adam of Ifé : Black Women in Praise of Black Men: Poems* (1992, **Lotus Press**, 235 pp.), edited by **Naomi Long Madgett**; *I Hear a Symphony: African Americans Celebrate Love* (1994, 334 pp.) edited by Paula L. Woods and Felix H. Liddell; and *Mending the World: Stories of Family by Contemporary Black Writers* (2008, 320 pp.), edited by Rosemarie Robotham, including both nonfiction and fiction, with a preface by **Maya Angelou** and a foreword by **Pearl Cleage**.

Given the all-embracing topic of folklore, Harold Courlander edited the 640-page *A Treasury of Afro-American Folklore: The Oral Literature, Traditions, Recollections, Legends, Tales, Songs, Religious Beliefs, Customs, Sayings and Humor of Peoples of African American Descent in the Americas* (1996/2002), which heavily emphasizes the **oral tradition** in African-American folklore. He draws on the oral literature not only from the United States, but also from the Caribbean and Latin America, where African captives also unwillingly settled centuries ago. Courlander even included dozens of musical scores and appendixes in his comprehensive volume.

When Courlander's anthology was being reprinted, Daryl Cumber Dance edited *From My People: 400 Years of African American Folklore (An Anthology)* (2002), a 736-page compendium of superstitions and folk beliefs, nursery rhymes and clapping games, speeches and sermons, stories and **folktales, spirituals** and work songs, **proverbs** and **trickster tales**, blues songs and rap lyrics, rumors and riddles, and recipes and photos of quilts and other folk arts. Like Courlander, Dance relies not only on written texts, but also on oral sources, to cover her vast territory. Of course she includes **Paul Dunbar, Langston Hughes,** and **Zora Neale Hurston**, but she also includes **W. C. Handy,** Jelly Roll Morton, and Bessie Smith, as well as **Frederick Douglass**, **Ralph Ellison**, and **Nikki Giovanni**, among others. Scholar **Arnold Rampersad** said of it, "This extraordinary book is a treasury that should prove of lasting value and appeal," and **Henry Louis Gates, Jr.** gushed, "What an astonishingly rich collection of African American folklore Dance has produced! A major contribution to African American scholarship" (quoted in //www.amazon.com).

Dance had previously applied her talents as an anthologist to *Honey, Hush! An Anthology of African-American Women's Humor* (1998, 720 pp.), finding the humor in the writings of African-American women from slave narrators to **Audre Lorde**. Her publisher, W. W. Norton, noted that "The eloquent wit and laughter of African American women are presented here in all their written and spoken manifestations: autobiographies, novels, essays, poems, speeches, comic routines, proverbial sayings, cartoons, mimeographed sheets, and folk tales. The chapters proceed thematically, covering the church, love, civil rights, motherly advice, and much more" (quoted in //www.amazon.com). Dance's volume embraces bawdy jokes and unkind humor, as well as tamer fare, but all readers will find something that prompts a chortle, a chuckle, or even a belly laugh. More recently, Paul Beatty edited *Hokum: An Anthology of African-American Humor* (2006, 468 pp.), which samples humorous poetry and prose, political speeches and songs, among other literary forms, by relative newcomers such as Darius James and **Harryette Mullen**, classics such as Langston Hughes and Zora Neale Hurston, serious writers such as **Toni Cade Bambara** and **W. E. B. Du Bois**, and celebrities, such as Mike Tyson and Al Sharpton.

The foregoing are just a tiny sample of the myriad anthologies addressing special topics. *See also* **anthologies of African-American literature, specific genres, nonfiction** for a sampling of topics addressed in nonfiction works. *See also* **anthologies of African-American literature, specific genres, fiction** for more information on fiction genres such as erotica, mystery and suspense, speculative fiction, and horror. Period-specific anthologies may also be found in the entries for **anthologies of African-American literature, writers from the antebellum era**, and **anthologies of African-American literature, writers from the New Negro era**. *See also* **anthologies of African-American literature, written by and for gay or heterosexual men**; **anthologies of African-American literature, written by and for heterosexual or lesbian women**; and **anthologies of African-American literature, written by and for juveniles**. In addition, special audiences, such as the **Cave Canem** fellows, produce their own annual anthologies (available at //www.cave canempoets.org/pages/store/Anthologies.htm).

REFERENCES: Kinnamon, Keneth, in *OCAAL*. ___. (Spring 1997). "Anthologies of African-American Literature from 1845 to 1994." *Callaloo* (Vol. 20, No. 2), pp. 461-481. //en.wikipedia.org/wiki/Martin_Luther_King,_Jr. //en.wikipedia.org/wiki/Nellie_Y._McKay. //libpac.sdsu.edu/. //www.sandiego.gov/public-library/. //www.sdcl.org/. //www.worldcat.org/account/?page=searchItems. //worldcat.org/identities/. Amazon.com.

Anthologies of African-American Literature, Specific Genres, Drama and Plays
1927–
Literature collections of the writings of numerous authors

As with other literary forms, many of the earliest collections of plays by African-American playwrights appeared in the pages of periodicals. The earliest known anthologies of plays appeared during the **Harlem Renaissance** when the "New Negro" was thriving: *Plays of Negro Life: A Source-book of Native American Drama* (1927), edited by literary scholar **Alain Locke** and T. Montgomery Gregory; *Plays and Pageants from the Life of the Negro* (1930; 1993, reissued, with an introduction by Christine R. Gray), edited by noted playwright **Willis Richardson**; and *Negro History in Thirteen Plays* (1935), edited by **Willis Richardson** and **May Miller**.

During World War II and its aftermath, and even the emerging civil-rights movement of the 1950s, playwrights had no anthologists collecting their works. At last, as the 1960s were giving way to the 1970s, play anthologies started appearing. *New Black Playwrights* (1968), edited by William Couch, included six plays by five playwrights, introducing rising stars **Adrienne Kennedy** and **Ed Bullins**. Ed Bullins himself edited two anthologies: *New Plays from the Black Theatre* (1969) and *The New Lafayette Theatre Presents* (1974). Anthologist and poet **Darwin T. Turner** edited *Black Drama in America: An Anthology* (1971; expanded and updated 2nd ed., 1994/2002, 736 pp.).

James V. Hatch and prolific playwright **Ted Shine** edited *Black Theater U.S.A.—Forty-Five Plays by Black Americans—1847-1974* (1974), which included 3 antebellum plays and 21 plays written before 1940, along with then-contemporary authors such as **Langston Hughes** and **Lorraine Hansberrry**. More than two decades later, they edited their revised, expanded, two-volume *Black Theatre USA: Revised and Expanded Edition, Vol. 1: Plays by African Americans; The Early Period 1847-1938* and *Vol. 2: Plays by African Americans, The Recent Period, 1935-Today* (1996). Hatch also published *Black Playwrights, 1823-1977; An Annotated Bibliography of Plays* (1977), and with Errol G. Hill, he wrote *A History of African American Theatre (Cambridge Studies in American Theatre and Drama)* (2006).

The other standout during this period was *Black Drama Anthology* (1972/1986), edited by playwright and anthologist **Woodie King, Jr.**, and his cofounder of the Concept East Theatre, **Ron Milner**. Their anthology features one early **Langston Hughes** play, but the other 22 plays are from the 1950s and beyond. King also founded the New Federal Theatre company (1970), based in New York City. King's other drama anthologies include *A Black Quartet: Four One-Act Plays* (1971), *New Plays for the Black Theatre* (1989), *The National Black Drama Anthology: Eleven Plays from America's Leading African-American Theaters* (1996/2000), and *Voices of Color: 50 Scenes and Monologues by African American Playwrights* (2000). In addition, King has published two retrospective views of his experiences in the theater: his essay collection, *Black Theater: Present Condition* (1981); and his notebook/memoir, *The Impact of Race: Theatre and Culture* (2003).

Numerous other drama anthologies continued to appear during the **Black Arts Movement** of the 1970s, and as with other genres, abundance led to specialization. Some anthologists have focused on plays written in earlier eras, such as *Roots of African American Drama: An Anthology of Early Plays, 1858-1938* (1990, 454 pp.), edited by Leo Hamalian, and *Classic Plays from the Negro Ensemble Company* (1995), edited by Paul Carter Harrison. *Wines in the Wilderness: Plays by African American Women from the Harlem Renaissance to the Present* (1990), edited by Elizabeth Brown-Guillory, both targets an earlier period and focuses on women playwrights. *Moon Marked & Touched by Sun: Plays by African-American Women* (1993, 448 pp.), edited by Sydné Mahone, features 11 women playwrights (e.g., **Thulani Davis, Anna Deavere Smith**) and includes biographical information on them, as well. *Plays of Black America* (1987), edited by Sylvia Kamerman, is intended for juvenile readers. *Crosswinds; An Anthology of Black Dramatists in the Diaspora* (1993), edited by William B. Branch, includes not only Americans, but also other playwrights of the African diaspora. *Colored Contradictions: An Anthology of Contemporary African-American Plays* (1996, 656 pp.), edited by Harry J. Elam, Jr., and Robert Alexander, includes 12 plays, all of which were written and produced in the 1990s by noteworthy playwrights such as Obie Award-winning **Suzan Lori-Parks**, Cheryl L. West, and Shay Youngblood. As this dictionary goes to press, other creative and resourceful anthologists are doubtless compiling and editing new and interesting collections of dramatic works.

REFERENCES: Kinnamon, Keneth, in *OCAAL*. ____. (Spring 1997). "Anthologies of African-American Literature from 1845 to 1994." *Callaloo* (Vol. 20, No. 2), pp. 461-481. //en.wikipedia.org/wiki/Martin_Luther_King,_Jr. //en.wikipedia.org/wiki/Nellie_Y._McKay. //libpac.sdsu.edu/. //www.sandiego.gov/public-library/. //www.sdcl.org/. //www.worldcat.org/account/?page=searchItems. //worldcat.org/identities/. Amazon.com.

Anthologies of African-American Literature, Specific Genres, Fiction
1950–
Literature collections of the writings of numerous authors

Many of the earliest collections of short fiction and fiction excerpts by African-American authors appeared in the pages of periodicals. The earliest known anthology of short fiction was *Best Short Stories by Afro-American Writers* (1950), edited by Nick Aaron Ford and H. L. Faggett, but two successors have been more highly praised than this groundbreaker. First, esteemed scholar **John Henrik Clarke** edited *American Negro Short Stories* (1966), which was later revised as *Black American Short Stories: 100 Years of the Best* (1993). Clarke also edited *Harlem* (1970), which included 20 stories by Harlem authors only. Second, superlative storyteller **Langston Hughes** edited *The Best Short Stories by Negro Writers* (1967); just a few he includes are **Charles Chesnutt, Alice Childress, Zora Neale Hurston, Ted Poston**, and **John A. Williams**. Two more anthologies came in the form of textbooks: *Black American Literature: Fiction* (1969), edited by **Darwin T. Turner**, which contains only 14 stories, but offers good pedagogical support; and *From the Roots: Short Stories by Black Americans* (1970), edited by Charles L. James, which contains 27 stories arranged in five chronological sections.

At this point, the **Black Arts Movement** kicked into high gear and yielded a high volume of volumes, most of which emphasized recent stories by contemporary authors. These included *Brothers and Sisters: Modern Stories by Black Americans* (1970), edited by Arnold Adoff (husband of storyteller **Virginia Hamilton**); *Black and White: Stories of American Life* (1971), edited by Donald B. Gibson and Carol Anselment; *Modern Black Stories* (1971), edited by Martin Mirer; *Tales and Stories for Black Folks* (1971), edited by **Toni Cade Bambara**; *What We Must See: Young Black Story Tellers* (1971), edited by Orde Coombs; *Black Short Story Anthology* (1972), edited by **Woodie King**; *We Be Word Sorcerers: 25 Stories by Black Americans* (1973), edited by **Sonia Sanchez**; and *Out of Our Lives: A Selection of Contemporary Black Fiction* (1975), edited by Quandra Prettyman Stadler.

Most of the aforementioned anthologies highlighted male writers, to the detriment of females. Meanwhile, Toni Cade (later **Toni Cade Bambara**) had edited her groundbreaking general anthology *The Black Woman: An Anthology* (1970), then Mary Helen Washington edited *Black-Eyed Susans: Classic Stories by and about Black Women* (1975), followed by *Midnight Birds: Stories by Contemporary Black Women Writers* (1980), combined and reissued as *Black-Eyed Susans and Midnight Birds: Stories by and about Black Women* (1989). (*See also* **anthologies of**

African-American literature, written by and for heterosexual or lesbian women, for more information on anthologies by and for women.)

A few of the general fiction anthologies have been written by celebrated and best-selling fiction writers, including **Terry McMillan's** *Breaking Ice: An Anthology of Contemporary African-American Fiction* (1990), **Gloria Naylor's** *Children of the Night: The Best Short Stories by Black Writers, 1967 to the Present* (1997), and **Marita Golden** and **E. Lynn Harris's** much-lauded *Gumbo: A Celebration of African American Writing* (2002), the sales of which benefit the **Hurston/Wright Foundation** Golden cofounded in 1990. **E. Lynn Harris** also edited *Best African American Fiction: 2009* (2009), which is the first volume in the series *Best African American Fiction,* for which **Gerald Early** is the series editor.

Another general anthology of short fiction, *Talk That Talk: An Anthology of African American Storytelling* (1989, 528 pp.), edited by Linda Goss (president of the Association of Black Storytellers) and fellow storyteller Marian E. Barnes, includes more than 100 entries, from Br'er Rabbit folktales to Leadbelly lyrics to Winnie Mandela's personal recollections, though the authors' tale-telling talents exceed their scholarly analysis of the material. Two other general anthologies are *Ancestral House: The Black Short Story in the Americas and Europe* (1995), edited by Charles Henry Rowell, founding editor of *Callaloo*; and *The Columbia Guide to Contemporary African American Fiction* (2005), edited by Darryl Dickson-Carr.

By far the greatest proliferation of fiction anthologies has been within specific subgenres, especially erotica, including *Erotique Noire: Black Erotica* (1992), edited by Miriam DeCosta-Willis; *Black Silk: A Collection of African-American Erotica* (2002), edited by Retha Powers; and Carol Taylor's series *Brown Sugar: A Collection of Erotic Black Fiction* (2001), *Brown Sugar 2: Great One Night Stands, Vol. 2* (2003), *Brown Sugar 3: When Opposites Attract, Vol. 3* (2003), and *Brown Sugar 4 Secret Desires: A Collection of Erotic Black Fiction* (2005). Other subgenres have their own anthologies as well, including *Dark Matter: A Century of Speculative Fiction from the African Diaspora* (2000) and *Dark Matter: Reading the Bones* (2008), both edited by Sheree R. Thomas. Brandon Massey, Zane, and **Tananarive Due** coedited *Dark Dreams: A Collection of Horror and Suspense by Black Writers* (2004, 336 pp.). Otto Penzler edited *Black Noir: Mystery, Crime, and Suspense Stories by African-American Writers* (2009). Mary Alicia Owen edited *Voodoo Tales: As Told Among the Negroes of the Southwest, Collected from Original Sources* (1969, 310 pp.). African-Canadian author Nalo Hopkinson edited *Mojo: Conjure Stories* (2003, 320 pp.), which contains 19 original stories, including se-

lections contributed by husband and wife **Tananarive Due** and **Steven Barnes**.

REFERENCES: Kinnamon, Keneth, in *OCAAL*. ____. (Spring 1997). "Anthologies of African-American Literature from 1845 to 1994." *Callaloo* (Vol. 20, No. 2), pp. 461-481. //en.wikipedia.org/wiki/Martin_Luther_King,_Jr. //en.wikipedia.org/wiki/Nellie_Y._McKay. //libpac.sdsu.edu/. //www.sandiego.gov/public-library/. //www.sdcl.org/. //www.worldcat.org/account/?page=searchItems. //worldcat.org/identities/. Amazon.com.

Anthologies of African-American Literature, Specific Genres, Nonfiction
1902–
Literature collections of the writings of numerous authors

Starting with the March 16, 1827, issue of *Freedom's Journal,* readers have been able to find collections of nonfiction writings by African Americans in newspapers and other periodicals. It was nearly a century before a true anthology of such writings appeared, however, with the publication of *Twentieth Century Negro Literature* (1902), edited by D. W. Culp, and including 100 nineteenth-century essays. A quarter-century later, a more scholarly collection could be found in *Negro Orators and Their Orations* (1925), edited by esteemed historian **Carter G. Woodson,** founder of the Association for the Study of African American Life and History, often called the "father of black history."

After another long lapse, things started revving up for nonfiction anthologies, starting with essays of resistance and protest in *The Angry Black* (1962), edited by **John A. Williams,** who followed up with his *Beyond the Angry Black* (1966/1969). After the assassination of Dr. **Martin Luther King, Jr.,** (4/4/1968) and its aftermath in American urban unrest, many European Americans awakened to the potential problems of continuing to ignore Americans of African descent. Colleges started offering African-American studies courses and establishing African-American studies departments. These new courses needed new reading materials, and publishers realized they could make money publishing for this new target market.

Among the many anthologies that appeared by 1972 were *Black on Black* (1968), edited by Arnold Adoff; *Rhetoric of Black Revolution* (1969), edited by Arthur L. Smith; *Black American Literature: Essays* (1969), edited by **Darwin T. Turner,** which includes works by 15 essayists—from **William Wells Brown** to **Eldridge Cleaver;** *Viewpoints from Black America* (1970), edited by Gladys J. Curry; *From a Black Perspective: Contemporary Black Essays* (1970), edited by Douglas A. Hughes; *The Black Aesthetic* (1971), edited by **Addison Gayle, Jr.,** including key contributors such as **Houston A. Baker, Jr.** and **Henry Louis Gates, Jr.** (*see also* **Black Aesthetic** and **Black**

Arts Movement); and *Bondage, Freedom, and Beyond: The Prose of Black Americans* (1971), edited by **Addison Gayle, Jr.**

Anthologies of speeches and essays also offer fundamental insight into the thinking of the most stimulating African Americans, starting with *Masterpieces of Negro Eloquence: The Best Speeches Delivered by the Negro from the Days of Slavery to the Present Time* (1914; multiple other editions published by 2007), edited by **Alice Moore Dunbar** (later **Alice Moore Dunbar-Nelson**). Later examples include *Historic Speeches of African Americans* (1993, 192 pp.), edited by Warren J. Halliburton; *The Voice of Black Rhetoric: Selections* (1971, 318 pp.), edited by Arthur L. Smith and Stephen Robb; and *The Voice of Black America: Major Speeches by Negroes in the United States, 1797-1971* (1972), edited by Philip S. Foner, who also edited *Lift Every Voice: African American Oratory, 1787-1900* (1998, with Robert J. Branham, 925 pp.). An outstanding example of such an anthology is *Speech and Power: The African-American Essay and Its Cultural Content, from Polemics to Pulpit* (1992, more than 900 pp.), edited by esteemed essayist **Gerald (Lyn) Early**, encompassing more than 100 essays by most of the major writers of the 20th century, among others. Early is also the series editor for *Best African American Essays*; Debra J. Dickerson is the guest editor for *Best African American Essays: 2009* (2009), which includes about 30 authors sorted into several general categories, entertainment, sports, the arts, sciences, technology, education, activism, and political thought; Amazon.com is already touting the next edition, *Best African American Essays 2010*, to be edited by Early. Although somewhat more specialized than the foregoing, **Benjamin Quarles**'s *Black Mosaic: Essays in Afro-American History and Historiography* (1988) deserves special mention.

An area of interest to readers of this volume is anthologies of literary criticism and history, including *Black Is the Color of the Cosmos: Essays on Afro-American Literature and Culture, 1942-1981* (1982/1989, 376 pp.), edited by Charles T. (Twitchell) Davis, published for **Howard University Press**'s series "Critical Studies on Black Life and Culture"; *Within the Circle: An Anthology of African American Literary Criticism from the Harlem Renaissance to the Present* (1994, 532 pp.), edited by Angelyn Mitchell, which includes **Barbara Smith**'s 1977 landmark essay, "Toward a Black Feminist Criticism"; and *Black Literature Criticisms: Excerpts from Criticism of the Most Significant Works of Black Authors Over the Past 200 Years* (1999, 489 pp.), edited by Jeffrey W. Hunter and Jerry (Gerald Eugene) Moore.

Because of the unique experiences of Americans of African descent, **slave narratives**, as well as other autobiographies and memoirs, have played a distinctive role in African-American literature. For information on anthologies on writers of the antebellum period, *see* **anthologies of African-American literature, writers from the antebellum era**. More contemporary autobiographies and memoirs abound, as well, such as **Henry Louis Gates, Jr.**'s *Bearing Witness* (1991), with the 20th-century writings of 28 authors. A different type of memoir may be found in Farah J. Griffin and Cheryl J. Fish's *A Stranger in the Village: Two Centuries of African-American Travel Writing* (1998, 366 pp.) and in Alasdair Pettinger's *Always Elsewhere: Travels of the Black Atlantic* (1998, 300 pp.).

Of course, African-American authors have written on a wide array of topics, and nonfiction anthologies can focus on nearly any topic. Just a few possibilities include protest literature, such as Roy L. Hill's *Rhetoric of Racial Revolt* (1964, 378 pp.); C. Peter Ripley's *Witness for Freedom: African American Voices on Race, Slavery, and Emancipation* (1993, 306 pp.); and Richard Newman, Patrick Rael, and Philip Lapsansky's *Pamphlets of Protest: An Anthology of Early African-American Protest Literature, 1790-1860* (2001, 326 pp.); and black-nationalist anthologies, such as Wilson Jeremiah Moses's *Classical Black Nationalism: From the American Revolution to Marcus Garvey* (1996, 257 pp.); Sterling Stuckey's *The Ideological Origins of Black Nationalism* (1972, 265 pp.); and William L. Van Deburg's *Modern Black Nationalism: From Marcus Garvey to Louis Farrakhan* (1997), 381 pp.).

Anthologies particular to the mid-twentieth-century Civil Rights Movement include Albert P. Blaustein and Robert L. Zangrando's *Civil Rights and the American Negro; A Documentary History* (1968, 671 pp.); Peter B. Levy's *Let Freedom Ring: A Documentary History of the Modern Civil Rights Movement* (1992, 275 pp.); Sondra Kathryn Wilson's *In Search of Democracy: The NAACP Writings of* **James Weldon Johnson**, **Walter White**, *and* **Roy Wilkins** *(1920-1977)* (1999, 524 pp.); Manning Marable and Leith Mullings's *Let Nobody Turn Us Around: Voices of Resistance, Reform, and Renewal: An African American Anthology* (1999, 643 pp.); and Jon Meacham's *Voices in Our Blood: America's Best on the Civil Rights Movement* (2001, 561 pp.).

History anthologies are also abundant. Regarding authors who wrote prior to the Civil War, *see* **anthologies of African-American literature, writers from the antebellum era**. Additional anthologies of nonfiction by and about African Americans could fill volumes. The aforementioned anthologies merely indicate a sample of the breadth and depth of anthologies now available and continuing to be released. If one considers also computer databases and Internet resources, the possibilities are truly limitless.

REFERENCES: Kinnamon, Keneth, in *OCAAL*. ___ . (Spring 1997). "Anthologies of African-American Literature from 1845 to 1994." *Callaloo* (Vol. 20, No. 2), pp. 461-481. //en.wikipedia.org/wiki/Martin_Luther_King,_Jr. //en.wikipedia.org/wiki/Nellie_Y._McKay.

//libpac.sdsu.edu/. //www.sandiego.gov/public-library/. //www.sdcl.org/. //www.worldcat.org/account/?page=searchItems. //worldcat.org/identities/. Amazon.com.

Anthologies of African-American Literature, Specific Genres, Poetry, Verse, and Song
1845–
Poetry collections written by numerous authors in a single volume

The first anthology of writings by Americans of African descent was a poetry collection, *Les Cenelles* (1845), comprising 85 poems written by 17 French-speaking free-born New Orleans Creoles. For decades, the only time African-American poets met in print were in the pages of antebellum **antislavery periodicals** (1827-1865) or later in African-American-owned and -operated **newspapers** (e.g., *Baltimore Afro-American*, 1892-; *Chicago Defender*, 1905-; *Pittsburgh Courier*, 1907-; *Amsterdam News*, 1909-).

As the nineteenth century drew to a close, "Mrs. N.F. Mossell" (**Gertrude Bustill Mossell**) published her *The Work of the Afro-American Woman* (1894/1908/1988), which included not only her own narrative history of African-American women's literature up to that time, but also 20 verses from fellow women poets, including **Phillis Wheatley, Frances Ellen Watkins Harper, Charlotte Forten Grimké, Cordelia Ray**, Josephine Heard, Alice Ruth Moore (later **Alice Dunbar Nelson**), Grace A. Mapps, and others, as well as some of her own poetry. (Text of the entire volume may be found online at the New York Public Library's Schomburg Center for Research in Black Culture, *African American Women Writers of the 19th Century*, //digilib.nypl.org/dynaweb/digs/wwm 9729/@Generic__BookView).

Though not truly an anthology, Mossell's work does represent an early collection of poetry written by women. In the second edition to Mossell's collection, she gives a nod to *The Woman's Era* (1894-1897), founded, edited, and published by **Josephine Ruffin**. Many nineteenth-century women poets were published in its pages. Similarly, both men and women poets found outlets for their poetry in early twentieth-century journals and magazines (e.g., *The Voice of the Negro*, 1904-1907; *The Messenger*, 1917-1928; *Negro World*, 1918-1933).

The first true postbellum anthologies of writings by African Americans were collections of poetry, verse, and songs. In 1922, **James Weldon Johnson** edited his *Book of American Negro Poetry* (1922); then he and his brother Rosamond coedited *The Book of American Negro Spirituals* (1925) and *The Second Book of Negro Spirituals* (1926). Rosamond Johnson alone edited *Shoutsongs* (1936) and his folksong anthology *Rolling Along in Song* (1937). In 1923, European-American anthologist Robert T. Kerlin published *Negro Poets and Their Poems* (1923), and the following year two other European Americans, Newman Ivey White and Walter Clinton Jackson (1892-1948), published *An Anthology of Verse by American Negroes* (1924/1968), including about 60 authors, followed by White's *American Negro Folk Songs* (1928).

In his foreword to *Caroling Dusk: An Anthology of Verse by Negro Poets* (1927), published by Harper, poet and editor **Countee Cullen** gave tribute to the foregoing volumes, "It is now five years since James Weldon Johnson edited with a brilliant essay on 'The Negro's Creative Genius' *The Book of American Negro Poetry*, four years since the publication of Robert T. Kerlin's *Negro Poets and Their Poems*, and three years since from the Trinity College Press in Durham, North Carolina, came *An Anthology of Verse by American Negroes*, edited by Newman Ivey White and Walter Clinton Jackson. . . . there would be scant reason for the assembling and publication of another such collection were it not for the new voices that within the past three to five years have sung so significantly as to make imperative an anthology recording some snatches of their songs. To those intelligently familiar with what is popularly termed the renaissance in art and literature by Negroes, it will not be taken as a sentimentally risky observation to contend that the recent yearly contests conducted by Negro magazines, such as *Opportunity* and *The Crisis*, as well as a growing tendency on the part of white editors to give impartial consideration to the work of Negro writers, have awakened to a happy articulation many young Negro poets who had thitherto lisped only in isolated places in solitary numbers. It is primarily to give them a concerted bearing that this collection has been published" (quoted in //www.english.illinois.edu/maps/poets/a_f/cullen/dusk.htm).

Cullen's volume included the work of 38 poets, the earliest being **Paul Laurence Dunbar**. As his foreword indicates, however, he mostly focused on his contemporaries, such as **Gwendolyn B. Bennett, Sterling A. Brown, Jessie Redmon Fauset, Georgia Douglas Johnson, James Weldon Johnson, Anne Spencer**, and the youngest poet in the collection, teenage poet Lula Lowe Weeden. Of course, he also included some of his own poems, as well as poetry from authors who wrote in multiple genres, such as **W. E. B. Du Bois, Arna Bontemps, Angelina Weld Grimké , Langston Hughes**, and **Alice Dunbar Nelson**. Each poet's entry included not only the selected poems, but also a biographical note written by the poet, or, in the case of Weeden, the note was written by her mother. In the case of deceased poets, Dunbar's note was written by his ex-wife, **Alice Dunbar Nelson**, and the note for **Joseph S. Cotter, Jr.**, was written by his father, **Joseph S. Cotter, Sr.** A further enhancement to this volume came from illustrations by renowned visual artist Aaron Douglas. Subsequent printings of his volume appeared in 1955, in 1993 (the first paperback edition), with the new subtitle *An Anthology of Verse by Black Poets,* and in 1998, with yet another subtitle, *An Anthology of Verse by Black Poets of the Twenties* (1998, 264 pp.).

More than two decades later, frequent collaborators and well-regarded poets Langston Hughes and Arna Bontemps edited *The Poetry of the Negro, 1746-1949: An Anthology* (1949), published by Doubleday. Some printings included the somewhat immodest subtitle *A Definitive Anthology.* Apparently, however, other potential anthologists confirmed it, and the next major poetry anthology did not appear for more than two decades—when Bontemps came out with their revised edition, *The Poetry of the Negro, 1746-1970: An Anthology: Revised Edition* (1970), published by Doubleday and by Viking. Interestingly, Bontemps edited *American Negro Poets* (1963) and Hughes compiled *New Negro Poets U.S.A.* (1964), both shorter collections offering some insight into what each poet brought to their joint efforts.

Because of the superabundance of African-American poets and poems, definitive anthologies have been few since then. Rather, anthologists seem to carve out a niche and compile collections aimed at special audiences and topics of interest. For instance, Joan R. Sherman edited *Collected Black Women's Poetry* (1988); **Naomi Long Madgett** edited *a Milestone Sampler: 15th Anniversary Anthology* (1988), celebrating the publications of **Lotus Press** (1972-); Joanne V. Gabbin edited *The Furious Flowering of African American Poetry* (1999), emerging from the 1994 Furious Flower Conference she organized; Fahamisha Patricia Brown edited *Performing the Word: African American Poetry as Vernacular Culture* (1999), rejoicing in the vernacular tradition; and Sascha Feinstein and **Yusef Komunyakaa** edited *The Jazz Poetry Anthology* (1991, 293 pp.), highlighting twentieth-century jazz poetry.

Other contemporary anthologies have zeroed in on specific time periods, such as *The New Black Poetry* (1969), edited by **Clarence Major** and including 76 poets, 63 of whom were not previously anthologized; *Dices or Black Bones: Black Voices of the Seventies* (1970), edited by Adam David Miller; *We Speak as Liberators: New Black Poets* (1970), edited by Orde Coombs; *Black Spirits: A Festival of New Black Poets in America* (1972), edited by **Woodie King, Jr.**; *African-American Poetry of the Nineteenth Century: An Anthology* (1992), edited by Joan Rita Sherman; *Every Shut Eye Ain't Asleep: An Anthology of Poetry by African Americans since 1945* (1994), edited by **Michael S. Harper**; *Voices in the Poetic Tradition (African-American Women Writers, 1910-1940)* (1996), introduced by Mary Anne Stewart Boelcskevy; *The Garden Thrives: Twentieth-century African-American Poetry* (1996, 470 pp.), edited and introduced by **Clarence Ma-**

jor; *I Am the Darker Brother: An Anthology of Modern Poems* (1997), edited by Arnold Adoff; *Catch the Fire!! A Cross-Generational Anthology of Contemporary African-American Poetry* (1998), edited by Derrick I. M. Gilbert (a.k.a. D-Knowledge) with special assistance from Tony Medina, presenting multiple generations of twentieth- and now twenty-first-century poets; *From Totems to Hip-Hop: A Multicultural Anthology of Poetry Across the Americas 1900-2002* (2002, 368 pp.), edited by **Ishmael Reed**; and *Beyond the Frontier: African-American Poetry for the 21st Century* (2002, 572 pp.), edited by **E. Ethelbert Miller**, published by Black Classic Press.

E. Ethelbert Miller had previously edited a less time-specific poetry anthology, *In Search of Color Everywhere: A Collection of African-American Poetry* (1994, 255 pp.), including both "contemporary and classic poems by African-American writers, celebrating freedom, love, family, and other universal aspects of life." Other such anthologies include Jerry W. Ward, Jr.'s *Trouble the Waters: 250 Years of African-American Poetry* (1997), Catherine Clinton's *I, Too, Sing America: Three Centuries of African American Poetry* (1998, 128 pp.), and **Michael S. Harper** and **Anthony Walton**'s *The Vintage Book of African American Poetry: 200 Years of Vision, Struggle, Power, Beauty, and Triumph from 50 Outstanding Poets* (2000, 403 pp.), as well as *African-American Poets: Phillis Wheatley through Melvin B. Tolson* (2003, 335 pp.), edited and introduced by Harold Bloom; and *Rainbow Darkness: An Anthology of African American Poetry* (2006, 226 pp.), edited by Keith Tuma, which emerged from Miami University's 2003 Marjorie Cook Conference on Diversity in African American Poetry.

While never claiming to produce a definitive poetry anthology, scholar **Arnold Rampersad**, along with his associate editor Hilary Herbold, makes an admirable attempt to represent the breadth and depth of African-American poetry in their *Oxford Anthology of African American Poetry* (2005, 464 pp.). *Publishers Weekly* said, "the diversity of the anthology's subject matter is trumped only by its poetic range. . . . The anthology, arranged by theme rather than author or time period, simultaneously grounds and sets the reader adrift in a terrain stretching from the American South to Africa, from the contemporary back to slavery." *Booklist* called it, "Thoughtfully organized, . . . Rampersad and Herbold's anthology creates a tide of powerful, melancholy, and ecstatic voices. There is much to admire about the artistry of the poems, and even more to discover about the African American experience." **Henry Louis Gates, Jr.** said, "This definitive volume captures, in verse, the history of African American life and culture. A landmark publication for African American literature and a major contribution to American poetry as a whole." Robert G. O'Meally said, "This is the volume awaited by scholars, teachers, poets and poet-in-training as well as everyday lovers of words set to the music of poetic pulses and colors. . . . this lovely book is a godsend. . . . Familiar poems look new in these new settings; poems we never saw before shimmer on these pages."

REFERENCES: Kinnamon, Keneth, in *OCAAL*. ____. (Spring 1997). "Anthologies of African-American Literature from 1845 to 1994." *Callaloo* (Vol. 20, No. 2), pp. 461-481. //en.wikipedia.org/wiki/ Martin_Luther_King,_Jr. //en.wikipedia.org/wiki/Nellie_Y._McKay. //libpac.sdsu.edu/. //www.sandiego.gov/public-library/. //www.sdcl.org/. //www.worldcat.org/account/?page=searchItems. //worldcat.org/ identities/. Amazon.com.

Anthologies of African-American Literature, Writers from 1619 through 1865, the Antebellum and Civil War Era
1619–1865
Literature collections of writings by authors who wrote during the time of legal slavery

Because the vast majority of African Americans were enslaved before the Civil War, an excellent way to gain insight into this era is to read *Slave Testimony: Two Centuries of Letters, Speeches, Interviews and Autobiographies* (1977), edited by scholar John W. Blassingame. In particular, **slave narratives** and other autobiographies and memoirs have played a distinctive role in African-American literature. Several editors have created their own distinctive narratives of the slaves' experiences by drawing on excerpts from slave narratives and placing those narratives within a larger historical context. These creatively excerpted anthologies include *To Be a Slave* (1968), edited by **Julius Lester**; *Black Slave Narratives* (1970), edited by John Bayliss; *Steal Away: Stories of the Runaway Slaves* (1971), edited by Abraham Chapman; and *Black Men in Chains: Narratives by Escaped Slaves* (1969), edited by Charles H. Nichols.

For more traditional anthologies, see *Great Slave Narratives* (1969), edited by scholar and creative writer **Arna Bontemps**; *Five Slave Narratives* (1969), edited by William Loren Katz, who also edited *Flight from the Devil: Six Slave Narratives* (1994); and *Puttin' On Ole Massa* (1969), edited by Gilbert Osofsky. **Henry Louis Gates, Jr.** has brought to light not only *The Classic Slave Narratives* (1987), but also many other early works by African Americans. *Six Women's Slave Narratives* (1988), edited by William L. Andrews, includes the narratives of Annie Louise Burton, Lucy Delaney, Kate Drumgoold, Old Elizabeth, **Mattie W. Jackson**, and **Mary Prince**.

Another type of narrative typically authored by women was the *spiritual narrative*, in which the author describes her prior wretched state, her spiritual awakening, and the blessings that have followed her awakening. Wil-

liam L. Andrews also edited *Sisters of the Spirit* (1986), which includes the narratives of **Jarena Lee**, Zilpha Elaw, and Julia A. J. Foote. Covering similar territory is *Spiritual Narratives* (1988), edited by Sue E. Houchins, which includes Virginia W. Broughton, Julia A. J. Foote, **Jarena Lee**, and **Maria W. Stewart**. A less specific set of narratives may be found in *Collected Black Women's Narratives* (1988), edited by Anthony G. Barthelemy, which includes writings from Louisa Picquet, **Nancy Prince**, **Susie King Taylor**, and Bethany Veney.

Two scholars of history and literature also compiled anthologies of the antebellum writings of African Americans: **Benjamin Brawley** edited *Early Negro American Writers* (1935), collecting 20 previously relatively obscure authors from the 1700s through 1865; and Dorothy Porter (later **Dorothy Burnett Porter Wesley**) edited *Early Negro Writing, 1760-1837* (1971; reprint Black Classic Press, 1995), drawn heavily from her master's thesis and including both literary works and historical documents. Vincent Carretta took a somewhat different tack, focusing on just the late 1700s, but encompassing authors from Britain, the West Indies, and Africa, as well as North America, in his *Unchained Voices: An Anthology of Black Authors in the English-Speaking World of the Eighteenth Century* (1996, 387 pp.; expanded ed., 2003, 416 pp.). Playwright, novelist, essayist, and autobiographer **John Edgar Wideman** edited *My Soul Has Grown Deep: Classics of Early African-American Literature* by (2001, 1,253 pp.), aptly named for its coverage of classic writings by a dozen early authors, such as **Richard Allen, Phillis Wheatley, Olaudah Equiano, Frederick Douglass, Ida B. Wells-Barnett, Paul Lawrence Dunbar**, and including his own brief biographical essays on each author, followed by one or more ample examples of each author's work.

Just a few of the many history anthologies covering this period are *American Negro Slavery: A Documentary History* (1976, 288 pp.), edited by Michael Mullin; *African Muslims in Antebellum America: A Sourcebook* (1984, 759 pp.), edited by Allan D. Austin; and *Stolen Childhood: Slave Youth in Nineteenth-Century America* (1997, 253 pp.) edited by Wilma King. Additional anthologies of just the slavery period of history would fill many pages.

REFERENCES: Kinnamon, Keneth, in *OCAAL*. ____. (Spring 1997). "Anthologies of African-American Literature from 1845 to 1994." *Callaloo* (Vol. 20, No. 2), pp. 461-481. //en.wikipedia.org/wiki/ Martin_Luther_King,_Jr. //en.wikipedia.org/wiki/Nellie_Y._McKay. //libpac.sdsu.edu/. //www.sandiego.gov/public-library/. //www.sdcl.org/. //www.worldcat.org/account/?page=searchItems. //worldcat.org/ identities/. Amazon.com.

Anthologies of African-American Literature, Writers from 1920 to the Early 1940s, during the New Negro Era
1920–1940s
Literature collections of the writings by authors who wrote during the time of the Harlem Renaissance and the New Negro era

During the heyday of the Harlem Renaissance, when **Alain Locke** and others were speaking of "The New Negro," interested readers—of whom there were many!—could always find collections of writings of African-American literature in the pages of three popular journals. The first into print was *Crisis: A Record of the Darker Races*, published by the National Association for the Advancement of Colored People (NAACP), starting in 1910. Fortunately, Sondra Kathryn Wilson edited the anthology *The Crisis Reader: Stories, Poetry, and Essays from the N.A.A.C.P.'s Crisis Magazine* (1999), so contemporary readers may find out directly what their forebears were reading. Though not quite as widely read, *The Messenger* (1917-1928), edited by labor organizers **A. Philip Randolph** and **Chandler Owen**, also included an array of fiction and nonfiction written by authors of the day. Luckily, Wilson edited an anthology for that periodical as well, *The Messenger Reader: Stories, Poetry, and Essays from The Messenger Magazine* (2000). She also edited *The Opportunity Reader: Stories, Poetry, and Essays from the Urban League's Opportunity Magazine* (1999), honoring the National Urban League publication, ***Opportunity: A Journal of Negro Life*** (1923-1949). In addition to Wilson's modern compilation from *Opportunity*, the journal's founding editor, **Charles Spurgeon Johnson**, also put together a contemporaneous anthology, *Ebony and Topaz: A Collectanea* (1927). (*See also* **anthologies of African-American literature, from literary journals**.)

In truth, the premier anthology of this era originated with a journal publication, as well. In the spring of 1925, the monthly social-reform magazine **Survey Graphic** (1921-1952) published a special issue, guest-edited by scholar **Alain Locke**, titled "Harlem: Mecca of the New Negro." Soon after, Locke expanded the issue to create his book-length anthology ***The New Negro*** (1925). (For more information, *see* the entries on each publication, as well as the general entry for **anthologies of African-American literature**.) Just one other literary journal deserves mention in this context: ***Fire!!*** (1926), in which contributions by numerous African-American writers appeared in the pages of its single issue.

The next significant anthology of New Negro writers was English heiress Nancy Cunard's ***Negro: An Anthology*** (1934). Her 855-page volume included about 150 contributors: European Americans, African Americans, and contributors from the West Indies, South America, Europe, and Africa. Contributions included poetry and prose, fiction and lots of nonfiction. Unable to find a daring publisher, Cunard paid for a private printing of just 1,000 copies. Despite its limited distribution, the volume deserves a special place in chronicles of African-American literature, both for its comprehensiveness and for its editor's distinctive multinational perspective.

Many other anthologies of writers from this era were published long afterward. During the prideful period of the **Black Arts Movement**, several anthologies appeared, including two edited by **Arthur P. (Paul) Davis**: *From the Dark Tower: Afro-American Writers from 1900 to 1960* (1974/1981, 306 pp.), referring to the celebrated "Dark Tower" literary salon of that era, and *The New Negro Renaissance: An Anthology* (1975, with Michael W. Peplow, 538 pp.). Another from that period was *Voices from the Harlem Renaissance* (1976), edited by Nathan Irvin Huggins, organized thematically. About two decades later, other anthologies of the New Negro era appeared, most notably *Classic Fiction of the Harlem Renaissance* (1994), edited by scholarly anthologist William L. Andrews; and *The Portable Harlem Renaissance Reader* (1994, 816 pp.), edited and introduced by Pulitzer-winning scholar **David Levering Lewis**.

Other anthologies include *Harlem Renaissance Re-Examined* (1997, 422 pp.), edited by Victor A. Kramer and Robert A. Russ, and *The Power of Pride: Stylemakers and Rulebreakers of the Harlem Renaissance* (1999, 272 pp.), edited by Carole Marks and Diana Edkins. To hear different voices, see *A Renaissance in Harlem: Lost Voices of an American Community* (1999, 302 pp.), edited by Lionel C. Bascom, compiled from manuscripts found in the Library of Congress's WPA Federal Writers' Project Collection, 1936-1940. To read more from women writers, see *Sleeper Wakes: Harlem Renaissance Stories by Women* (1993), edited by Marcy Knopf; *Harlem's Glory: Black Women Writing, 1900-1950* (1997), edited by Lorraine Elena Roses and Ruth Elizabeth Randolph; and *Shadowed Dreams: Women's Poetry of the Harlem Renaissance* (1989), edited by Maureen Honey.

Maureen Honey also coedited *Double-Take: A Revisionist Harlem Renaissance Anthology* (2001, with Venetria K. Patton, 619 pp.). The editors offer a balance of male and female authors (e.g., **Countee Cullen, Nella Larsen**) across a spectrum of genres (including even song lyrics), but do so with an emphasis on writings evidencing gay and lesbian themes, as well as class and gender issues. Another perspective may be found in *Gay Voices of the Harlem Renaissance* (2003), edited by A. B. Christa Schwarz (1972-).

REFERENCES: Kinnamon, Keneth, in *OCAAL*. ____. (Spring 1997). "Anthologies of African-American Literature from 1845 to 1994." *Callaloo* (Vol. 20, No. 2), pp. 461-481. //en.wikipedia.org/wiki/Martin_Luther_King,_Jr. //en.wikipedia.org/wiki/Nellie_Y._McKay.

//libpac.sdsu.edu/. //www.sandiego.gov/public-library/. //www.sdcl.org/. //www.worldcat.org/account/?page=searchItems. //worldcat.org/ identities/. Amazon.com.

Anthologies of African-American Literature, Written by and for Gay or Heterosexual Men
1925–

Literature collections of the writings of numerous authors

Some readers may wonder at the need for a separate entry for anthologies of writings by men. Most of the early anthologies comprised entirely the writings of men, and many of the anthologies through the early 1970s included very few women. For a listing of anthologies containing only or mostly males, merely scan the libraries and used bookstores for nearly anything printed prior to the mid-1970s; through the mid-1980s it was still not unusual to find an anthology claiming to be comprehensive while nonetheless largely excluding women writers from its pages.

From the 1970s through the mid-1990s, women began seeing collections of their own writings, to the exclusion of men. These anthologies were deemed necessary to compensate for the exclusion of women in nearly all previous collections. Further, comprehensive anthologies were no longer the sole province of male writers; any anthology claiming to be comprehensive necessarily included a representative sampling of women authors. By the mid-1990s, men began noticing that they could no longer find collections of exclusively male writers. Herb Boyd and Robert L. Allen decided that it was time for *Brotherman: The Odyssey of Black Men in America* (1995, 909 pp.), including more than 100 pieces, organized thematically. The wide array of writers include **Frederick Douglass** and **Cornel West**, **Malcolm X** and **Martin Luther King, Jr.**, **James Baldwin** and Wallace Terry (*Bloods*), **Paul Laurence Dunbar** and **Countee Cullen**; the book won both the American Library Association's Black Caucus Award and the Christopher Columbus Foundation's American Book Award. With a more narrow focus, Daniel J. Wideman and Rohan B. Preston edited *Soulfires: Young Black Men on Love and Violence* (1996, 398 pp.), introduced by **Henry Louis Gates, Jr.**

Another view from an all-male perspective may be found in *In the Life: A Black Gay Anthology* (1986, 255 pp.), edited by Joseph Beam, and *Brother to Brother: New Writings by Black Gay Men* (1991/2007, 274 pp.), edited by **Essex Hemphill**. Anthologies of a single genre by gay male authors include *Shade: An Anthology of Fiction by Gay Men of African Descent* (1996, 348 pp.), edited by Bruce Morrow and Charles Henry Rowell, introduced by one of the volume's 23 contributors, **Samuel Delany**, and *The Road Before Us: 100 Gay Black Poets* (1991, 191 pp.),

edited by Assoto Saint. For writers of the 1920s and 1930s, see *Gay Voices of the Harlem Renaissance* (2003), edited by A. B. Christa Schwarz. Gay literature including both female and male voices may be found in *Black Like Us: A Century of Lesbian, Gay, and Bisexual African American Fiction* (2002), edited by Devon W. Carbado and published by **Redbone Press**.

REFERENCES: Kinnamon, Keneth, in *OCAAL*. ____. (Spring 1997). "Anthologies of African-American Literature from 1845 to 1994." *Callaloo* (Vol. 20, No. 2), pp. 461-481. //en.wikipedia.org/wiki/ Martin_Luther_King,_Jr. //en.wikipedia.org/wiki/Nellie_Y._McKay. //libpac.sdsu.edu/. //www.sandiego.gov/public-library/. //www.sdcl.org/. //www.worldcat.org/account/?page=searchItems. //worldcat.org/ identities/. Amazon.com.

Anthologies of African-American Literature, Written by and for Heterosexual or Lesbian Women
1894–

Literature collections of the writings of numerous authors

At the close of the nineteenth century, "Mrs. N.F. Mossell" (**Gertrude Bustill Mossell**) published *The Work of the Afro-American Woman* (1894/1908/1988). In it, she included not only her own narrative history of African-American women's literature up to that time, but also 20 verses from fellow women poets, including **Phillis Wheatley**, **Frances Ellen Watkins Harper**, **Charlotte Forten Grimké**, **Cordelia Ray**, Josephine Heard, Alice Ruth Moore (later **Alice Dunbar Nelson**), Grace A. Mapps, and others, as well as some of her own poetry. (Text of the entire volume may be found online at the New York Public Library's Schomburg Center for Research in Black Culture, *African American Women Writers of the 19th Century*, //digilib.nypl.org/dynaweb/digs/wwm 9729/@Generic__BookView). Though not a true anthology, its inclusion of numerous other women poets earns it at least some recognition here. In Mossell's second edition, she gives a nod to *The Woman's Era* (1894-1897), founded, edited, and published by **Josephine Ruffin**. Many nineteenth-century women authors were published in its pages.

It was to be another 76 years before readers could enjoy the first true general anthology of African-American women's writings. At last, while women's studies courses were joining African-American studies courses and departments across the nation, Toni Cade (later **Toni Cade Bambara**) offered readers her groundbreaking *The Black Woman: An Anthology* (1970). A few years later, Mary Helen Washington edited *Black-Eyed Susans: Classic Stories by and about Black Women* (1975), followed by *Midnight Birds: Stories by Contemporary Black Women Writers* (1980), combined and reissued as *Black-Eyed Susans and*

Midnight Birds: Stories by and about Black Women (1989). Washington also published *Invented Lives: Narratives of Black Women, 1860-1960* (1987) and *Memory of Kin: Stories about Family by Black Writers* (1990).

Whereas Cade/Bambara and Washington focused on contemporary women authors, other anthologists brought to the fore writings by earlier women authors. Of course, most of the earliest writings by African-American women were **slave narratives**, such as those collected in *Six Women's Slave Narratives* (1988), edited by William L. Andrews, who includes the narratives of Annie Louise Burton, Lucy Delaney, Kate Drumgoold, Old Elizabeth, **Mattie W. Jackson**, and **Mary Prince**. *Collected Black Women's Narratives* (1988), edited by Anthony G. Barthelemy, including **Nancy Prince**, Louisa Picquet, Bethany Veney, and **Susie King Taylor**, is a volume in the multivolume *Schomburg Library of Nineteenth-century Black Women Writers* (1980s-1990s). Though the *Library* is a series, rather than an anthology, many references cite the entire collection as if it were one overarching work. Many works within the collection may be viewed, in their entirety, at //digital.nypl.org/schomburg/writers_aa19/toc.html.

Another type of narrative typically authored by women was the *spiritual narrative*, in which the author describes her prior wretched state, her spiritual awakening, and the blessings that have followed her awakening. William L. Andrews also edited *Sisters of the Spirit* (1986), which includes the narratives of **Jarena Lee**, Zilpha Elaw, and Julia A. J. Foote. Covering similar territory is *Spiritual Narratives* (1988), edited by Sue E. Houchins, which includes Virginia W. Broughton, Julia A. J. Foote, Jarena Lee, and **Maria W. Stewart**.

A broader collection with more varied genres may be found in *Afro-American Women Writers, 1746-1933: An Anthology and Critical Guide* (1988), edited by author and archivist **Ann Allen Shockley**, who covered 41 writers, for whom she included not only their writings but also some biographical information and critical notes. Other anthologies of early women writers include *With Pen and Voice: A Critical Anthology of Nineteenth-Century African-American Women* (1995, 169 pp.), edited by Shirley Wilson Logan; and *The Three Sarahs: Documents of Antebellum Black College Women* (1984, 335 pp.), edited by Ellen NicKenzie Lawson, with Marlene D. Merrill. Two anthologies of early twentieth-century women are *Short Fiction by Black Women, 1900-1920* (1991), edited by Elizabeth Ammons, including 46 short stories she gleaned from issues of **Colored American Magazine** and **Crisis**, and *Sleeper Wakes: Harlem Renaissance Stories by Women* (1993), edited by Marcy Knopf, including 27 stories by 14 writers. For a somewhat later period, see *Black Women's Blues: A Literary Anthology, 1934-1988* (1992), edited by Rita B. Dandridge.

For coverage of more expansive periods of time, anthologies include *Render Me My Song: African-American Women Writers from Slavery to the Present* (1990), edited by Sandi Russell; *Daughters of Africa* (1992), edited by Margaret Busby, with 84 U.S. writers and many more from elsewhere in the Americas, Africa, and Europe; and *Centers of the Self: Stories by Black American Women from the Nineteenth Century to the Present* (1994), edited and introduced by Judith A. Hamer and Martin J. Hamer, with 26 works. *The Prentice Hall Anthology of African American Women's Literature* (2005, 624 pp.), edited by Valerie Lee, offers a truly comprehensive multigenre anthology of more than 75 African-American women writers from three centuries, accompanied by some supporting pedagogy, including brief biographies, a map of the authors' birthplaces, a timeline, and some critical notes.

Many anthologists choose writings centered on particular topics, such as *Double Stitch : Black Women Write about Mothers and Daughters* (1991), edited by Patricia Bell-Scott, who also edited *Life Notes: Personal Writings by Contemporary Black Women* (1994); *Rise Up Singing: Black Women Writers on Motherhood* (2004), edited by Cecelie S. Berry; and *Wild Women Don't Wear No Blues: Black Women Writers on Love, Men, and Sex* (1993), edited by **Marita Golden**.

Though Cade/Bambara's *The Black Woman* is arguably feminist by its very existence, probably the first self-proclaimed feminist anthology is *Home Girls: A Black Feminist Anthology* (1983; 2nd ed., 2000, 364 pp.), edited by **Barbara Smith**, including the writings of 32 African-American feminists and lesbian activists from the United States and the Caribbean, with updated biographical information in the second edition. Though the second edition was published by Rutgers University Press, the original edition was published by **Kitchen Table: Women of Color Press**, which Smith cofounded and operated for many years. Kitchen Table: Women of Color Press also published an edition of *This Bridge Called My Back: Writings by Radical Women of Color* (1981, by Persephone Press; 1983, by Kitchen Table, 261 pp.; 2002, by 3rd Woman Press, 370 pp.), edited by Cherrie Moraga and Gloria Anzaldua, winning the Before Columbus Foundation's American Book Award (1986).

About a decade later, feminist scholar Beverly Guy-Sheftall edited *Words of Fire: An Anthology of African-American Feminist Thought* (1995, 577 pp.), including more than 60 authors, such as the antebellum orator **Sojourner Truth** and mid-1900s personal storytellers **Lorraine Hansberry** and **Shirley Chisholm**. With a narrower focus on just creative writing, Charlotte Watson Sherman edited *Sisterfire : Black Womanist Fiction and Poetry* (1994, 378 pp.). Taking a more culturally diverse approach, including even gay men, Gloria E. Anzaldua and Analouise Keating edited a more scholarly and theoretical follow-up to *This Bridge Called My Back*, titled *this bridge we call home: radical visions for transformation* (2002, 624 pp.); its 80 contributors' writings include not only short fiction, poems, and essays, but also letters, personal narratives, and theoretical pieces.

Numerous anthologies focus on particular genres, such as *Black Sister: Poetry by Black American Women, 1746-1980* (1981, 312 pp.), edited and introduced by Erlene Stetson, and *Shadowed Dreams: Women's Poetry of the Harlem Renaissance* (1989, 238 pp.; 2006, 297 pp.), edited by Maureen Honey, who also coedited *Double-Take: A Revisionist Harlem Renaissance Anthology* (2001, with Venetria K. Patton, 619 pp.). Dramatic works may be found in *Black Female Playwrights: An Anthology of Plays Before 1950* (1989), edited by Kathy A. Perkins. Short fiction may be found in *Revolutionary Tales: African American Women's Short Stories, from the First Story to the Present* (1995), edited by Bill Mullen, and *The Unforgetting Heart: An Anthology of Short Stories by African American Women, 1859-1993* (1995), edited by Asha Kanwar. Meri Nana-Ama Danquah edited *Shaking the Tree: A Collection of New Fiction and Memoir by Black Women* (2003), and **Joanne M. Braxton** edited *Black Women Writing Autobiography: A Tradition within a Tradition* (1989, 242 pp.). Robbie Jean Walker edited *The Rhetoric of Struggle: Public Address by African American Women* (1992, 445 pp.).

During the 1980s, numerous nonfiction anthologies by and about African-American women writers emerged, including Gloria T. Hull, Patricia Bell Scott, and **Barbara Smith**'s landmark *All the Women Are White, All the Blacks Are Men, But Some of Us Are Brave: Black Women's Studies* (1982); **Claudia Tate**'s insightful *Black Women Writers at Work* (1983); **Mari Evans**'s outstanding resource *Black Women Writers (1950-1980)* (1984); and **Barbara Christian**'s highly esteemed *Black Feminist Criticism: Perspectives on Black Women Writers* (1985). More recently, Yolanda Williams Page edited *Encyclopedia of African American Women Writers* (2007).

Nonfiction anthologies about African-American women have also abounded since the early 1990s, such as **Jessie Carney Smith**'s anthologies *Notable Black American Women* (1992) and *Powerful Black Women* (1996); as well as the comprehensive two-volume *Black Women in America: An Historical Encyclopedia* (1993), edited by **Darlene Clark Hine**, Elsa Barkley Brown, and Rosalyn Terborg-Penn. Two decades earlier, Gerda Lerner edited *Black Women in White America: A Documentary History* (1972, 630 pp.).

Many other comprehensive nonfiction anthologies have been published, and even more anthologies have focused on particular African-American women. Just a few of these include *Chained to the Rock of Adversity: To Be Free, Black and Female in the Old South* (1998, 96 pp.), edited by Virginia Meacham Gould; *Black Women in the Nursing Profession: A Documentary History* (1985, 165 pp.), edited by Darlene Clark Hine; *Black Women in Higher Education: An Anthology of Essays, Studies, and Documents* (1992, 341 pp.), edited by Elizabeth L. Ihle; and *Black Texas Women: A Sourcebook: Documents, Biographies, Timeline* (1996, 339 pp.), edited by Ruthe Winegarten, Janet G. Humphrey, and Frieda Werdens.

Lesbian authors have also created anthologies sharing their distinctive experiences and views, such as in the aforementioned *Home Girls: A Black Feminist Anthology* (1983), edited by **Barbara Smith**, published by Kitchen Table: Women of Color Press. More than a decade later, Catherine E. McKinley and L. Joyce DeLaney coedited *Afrekete: An Anthology of Black Lesbian Writing* (1995, 317 pp.). Soon after, **Redbone Press** published *Does Your Mama Know? An Anthology of Black Lesbian Coming Out Stories* (1998, 314 pp.), edited by Lisa C. Moore, including about 50 poems, essays, interviews, and personal narratives; followed by *Black Like Us: A Century of Lesbian, Gay, and Bisexual African American Fiction* (2002), edited by Devon W. Carbado.

REFERENCES: Kinnamon, Keneth, in *OCAAL*. ____. (Spring 1997). "Anthologies of African-American Literature from 1845 to 1994." *Callaloo* (Vol. 20, No. 2), pp. 461-481. //en.wikipedia.org/wiki/ Martin_Luther_King,_Jr. //en.wikipedia.org/wiki/Nellie_Y._McKay. //libpac.sdsu.edu/. //www.sandiego.gov/public-library/. //www.sdcl.org/. //www.worldcat.org/account/?page=searchItems. //worldcat.org/ identities/. Amazon.com.

Anthologies of African-American Literature, Written by and for Juveniles
1965–

Literature collections of the writings of numerous authors for, and sometimes by, children and youths

Probably the first anthology written just for young African-American readers was Arna Bontemp's Poetry Anthology for Youths: *Golden Slippers, An Anthology of Negro Poetry for Young Readers* (1941). Probably the first general anthology for African-American youth was *Negro Heritage Reader for Young People* (1965, 320 pp.), edited by Alfred E. Cain. Nearly two decades later, Dorothy S. Strickland edited *Listen Children: An Anthology of Black Literature* (1982/1986, 132 pp., illustrated by Leo and Diane Dillon), which included poetry and prose, a play and personal memoirs. Strickland also edited numerous language and literature textbooks for HBJ, a mainstream educational-textbook publisher, as well as *Families: Poems Celebrating the African American Experience* (1996, with Michael R. Strickland and John Ward).

Visual artist **Tom Feelings** both edited and illustrated *Soul Looks Back in Wonder* (1993), offering poetry by African-American authors such as **Maya Angelou, Langston**

Hughes, and **Askia Touré**. **Wade Hudson**, cofounder of **Just Us Books**, edited *Pass It On: African-American Poetry for Children* (1993, illustrated by Floyd Cooper), including poetry by **Lucille Clifton**, **Nikki Giovanni**, and **Eloise Greenfield**. Just Us Books published *In Praise of Our Fathers and Our Mothers: A Black Family Treasury by Outstanding Authors and Artists* (1997), edited by the copublishers Wade Hudson and **Cheryl Willis Hudson**. Davida Adedjouma edited *the Palm of My Heart: Poetry by African American Children* (1996, illustrated by Gregory Christie).

For the youngest of readers, Hyperion published *Jump at the Sun Treasury: An African American Picture Book Collection* (1993/2001, 205 pp.). For somewhat older youths, **Sam Cornish** and Lucian W. Dixon edited *Chicory: Young Voices from the Black Ghetto* (1969, 96 pp.). The aforementioned are just a small sampling of the literature anthologies available for young readers.

REFERENCES: Kinnamon, Keneth, in *OCAAL*. ____. (Spring 1997). "Anthologies of African-American Literature from 1845 to 1994." *Callaloo* (Vol. 20, No. 2), pp. 461-481. //en.wikipedia.org/wiki/ Martin_Luther_King,_Jr. //en.wikipedia.org/wiki/Nellie_Y._McKay. //libpac.sdsu.edu/. //www.sandiego.gov/public-library/. //www.sdcl.org/. //www.worldcat.org/account/?page=searchItems. //worldcat.org/ identities/. Amazon.com.

Anthony, Florence *See* Ai Ogawa, Florence

Antislavery Periodicals
1819–1829
Publication of antislavery fiction and nonfiction

(*See also* **antislavery periodicals, 1830-1839**; **antislavery periodicals, 1840-1849**; and **antislavery periodicals, 1850-1865**.) Slavery was, of course, opposed by enslaved persons from its inception, and many sympathetic freed and freeborn African Americans and European Americans sought ways to undermine it, if not openly to overturn it. The earliest existing public document opposing slavery was the 1688 "Petition Against Slavery" written by four members of the Religious Society of Friends, commonly known as Quakers, living in Germantown (now a section of Philadelphia), Pennsylvania. Though these Quakers forwarded their petition to larger meetings of Quakers, they were unsuccessful in getting others to take action in response to it.

About a century after the Germantown Quakers' petition, the war for American independence changed Northerners' sentiments toward slavery. In the North, state after state passed emancipation legislation—some much more slowly than others. Tennessee, however, was a slave state, where slavery was codified legally and deeply woven into the entire fabric of Tennessee society. Elihu Embree, a European-American Quaker Tennessean, had actually held slaves when, in 1812 (at age 29), he manumitted (freed) all the enslaved persons he "owned," at great financial cost to himself and his family. He also became an ardent abolitionist and an active member of the Manumission Society of Tennessee. In 1819, with the Society's approval and cooperation, Embree founded the *Manumission Intelligencer,* publishing its first issue that March, in Jonesborough. (Unfortunately, only 1–12 copies of Embree's weekly newspaper are known to be in existence today.) Until the following April, Embree published the *Intelligencer* each Tuesday, for the then-exorbitant annual subscription price of $3. Because he grew frustrated with the Society's insistence on approving each issue—and their irregular meetings to give approval—Embree disassociated his periodical from the Society, switched from a weekly to a monthly publication schedule, and changed its name to *The Emancipator.* Sadly, the premature death of Embree (at age 38) was also the demise of *The Emancipator* (October 31, 1820). In 1932, B. H. Murphy reprinted the entire 8-month, 112-page collection of *The Emancipator.* Though published in a slave state, *The Emancipator* had 2,000 paying subscribers, a large number for any Tennessee periodical published at that time.

In 1821, Benjamin Lundy, another European-American Quaker, founded the *Genius of Universal Emancipation* (1821-1839) in Ohio. After Embree's death, Quakers in Jonesborough, Tennessee urged Lundy to move the *Genius* to Jonesborough, which he did. Over the next 18 years, Lundy continued to edit and publish the *Genius,* even as he later relocated to Baltimore, Maryland; Washington, D.C.; and then Philadelphia, where Lundy's death proved the end of this second antislavery periodical.

Next-door to Tennessee, the Kentucky Abolition Society decided to publish a semimonthly antislavery periodical, to be edited by Reverend John Finley Crowe, in Shelbyville. From the start, the Society had trouble gathering enough subscriptions to pay for publication of the 16-page *Abolition Intelligencer and Missionary Magazine.* By the time the first issue appeared in May 1822, the Society had decided to publish *Abolition Intelligencer* monthly. Because of its advocacy of abolition, the Society was denounced, Reverend Crowe was threatened, and no more than 500 subscribers could be found for the magazine. After 12 issues, the *Abolition Intelligencer* was abandoned.

In 1827, Lundy made his own informal count of antislavery societies, finding just 24 societies with 1,500 members in the free states and four times that amount—106 societies with 5,125 members—in the slave states. These numbers seem astonishing at first glance. What Lundy did not point out, however, was that most of the self-proclaimed abolition societies in the slave states were actually proposing gradual emancipation, often even offering financial compensation to slaveholders for their financial losses through emancipation. Most Northern abolitionists called for immediate emancipation of all slaves based on its fundamental inhumanity and immorality.

In Philadelphia, mathematician Enoch Lewis, yet another European-American Quaker, was collecting antislavery essays, poems, legal summaries, African travel logs, statistical analyses, and other documents. In April of 1827, he had gathered enough antislavery material to publish his *African Observer: A Monthly Journal, . . . Illustrative of the General Character, and Moral and Political Effects of Negro Slavery* (1827-1828, Nos. 1-12). Google has scanned a facsimile of a 384-page book reprinting all 12 issues of the *African Observer.* Interested readers can simply choose "Books" from the "More" menu on the "Google.com" main page, then type in "African Observer" in the search box, then choose the full-view entry titled *The African Observer* by Enoch Lewis. The 12 issues start with the "Fourth Month" (April) of 1827 and end with "Third Month" (March) of 1828.

While Lewis was publishing *African Observer* in Philadelphia, and Lundy was still publishing his *Genius* in Baltimore, **Samuel E. Cornish** and **John B. Russwurm** started to publish their *Freedom's Journal* (3/16/1827-3/28/1829) in New York City. *Freedom's Journal* is significant to history not only as a vital antislavery periodical but also, even more important, as the first African-American weekly newspaper. Aware of previous and contemporaneous antislavery periodicals, published by European Americans, Cornish and Russwurm took pride in owning and operating their own publication, as evidenced in their paper's motto, "We Wish to Plead Our Own Cause." Interested readers can find links to rather difficult-to-read pdf files of the journal from //www.wisconsin history.org/libraryarchives/aanp/freedom/.

One more periodical deserves mention here, though it is not truly an abolitionist periodical. The American Colonization Society (ACS, founded in 1817) sought to send freed African Americans back to Africa and to establish a colony of American-Africans in Africa. In July of 1820, the ACS published a single issue of its planned monthly journal, *The African Intelligencer,* edited by European-American Jehudi Ashmun. Two years later, the ACS established its first group of emigrants in the colony, and two years after that, Ashmun became both the U.S. representative to the colony and the colony's governor (1824-1828). The colony later (1847) became the independent nation of Liberia; by 1867, 13,000 U.S. emigrants had arrived there.

In Britain, abolitionists were also fighting to end slavery in the British empire and published abolitionist periodicals there, as well. For instance, a Scottish abolitionist, Zachary Macaulay, published *The Anti-Slavery Reporter,* starting in 1825.

REFERENCES: Andrews, William L., and Mason I. Lowance, Jr., "Antislavery Movement," in *OCAAL*. Hinks, Peter P., John R. McKivigan, and R. Owen Williams (Eds.). 2007. *Encyclopedia of Antislavery and Abolition.* Westport, CT: Greenwood Publishing Group. "Jehudi Ashmun," in *B*, and in *Wiki*. //en.wikipedia.org/wiki/ Genius_of_Universal_Emancipation. //en.wikipedia.org/wiki/The_ 1688_Germantown_Quaker_Petition_Against_Slavery. //hcl.harvard. edu/libraries/widener/collections/newspapers/afam_alpha.cfm. //library.nyu.edu/research/news/historical/afr-am.html. //utc.iath. virginia.edu/abolitn/gallasrf.html. //web.library.emory.edu/subjects/ humanities/history/news/NewspAfam.html. //www.accessible.com/ accessible/about/aboutAA.jsp. //www.answers.com/topic/jehudi-ashmun. //www.blackvoicenews.com/content/view/37990/13/. //www.bpl.org/research/microtext/EthnicNewspapers.pdf. //www. gale.cengage.co.uk/controls/library.aspx?fileID=1284. //www.hup. harvard.edu/features/reference/danafr/samples.html. //www.jimcrow history.org/resources/lessonplans/hs_es_black_press.htm. //www.lib.fsu.edu/help/researchguides/index.php/African_American_ Newspapers. //www.loc.gov/exhibits/african/afam002.html. //www.loc. gov/exhibits/african/afam006.html. //www.pbs.org/wgbh/aia/rb_ index_hd.html. //www.spartacus.schoolnet.co.uk/USASnewspapers. htm. //www.wisconsinhistory.org/libraryarchives/aanp/. //www. wisconsinhistory.org/libraryarchives/aanp/freedom/. //www.wisconsin history.org/libraryarchives/aanp/freedom/docs/v1n01.pdf.

Antislavery Periodicals
1830–1839
Publication of antislavery fiction and nonfiction

(*See also* **antislavery periodicals, 1819-1829; antislavery periodicals, 1840-1849;** and **antislavery periodicals, 1850-1865.**) By the 1820s, Northern opposition to slavery had grown enough that abolitionist societies, usually including both African Americans and European Americans, emerged in every urban center, as well as in some smaller locales. These societies sponsored lectures and speeches preaching the antislavery message. In addition, some abolitionists printed broadsides (e.g., "Our Countrymen in Chains" poem by European-American Quaker John Greenleaf Whittier), pamphlets (e.g., **David Walker**'s *Appeal in Four Articles; Together With a Preamble, to the Coloured Citizens of the World, but in Particular, and Very Expressly, to Those of the United States of America,* 1829), and even books. Especially popular were **slave narratives**, documenting the horrors of slavery, but explanatory texts also directly explicated the moral evils of slavery and demanded—or pleaded for—its abolition. Not everyone could get to a lecture, however, and not everyone could afford a book, or even a pamphlet, but many people could afford a newspaper or other periodical. Soon, the antislavery periodical was one of the chief tools used by abolitionists to try to end slavery.

By the end of the 1820s, several antislavery periodicals had been published, most of them intermittent or short-lived (*see* **antislavery periodicals, 1819-1829**). Not short-lived, however, was the *Genius of Universal Emancipation,* published and edited by Benjamin Lundy, a European-American Quaker. In 1829, Lundy hired a young newspaper printer and editor to help him publish the *Genius* out of Baltimore, Maryland. The fiery young abolitionist, William Lloyd Garrison, soon grew impatient with Lundy's gradualist approach to emancipation. For Garrison, each additional hour of slavery's existence was an outrage. After Garrison was jailed for allegedly libeling a slave trader, he decided to leave Maryland and return to New England.

Back in Boston, Garrison started his unwaveringly weekly publication of *The Liberator* (January 1, 1831-December 29, 1865). In his first issue, he stated, "I am aware that many object to the severity of my language; but is there not cause for severity? I will be as harsh as truth, and as uncompromising as justice. On this subject, I do not wish to think, or to speak, or write, with moderation. . . . I am in earnest—I will not equivocate—I will not excuse—I will not retreat a single inch—AND I WILL BE HEARD" (quoted in //en.wikipedia.org/wiki/William_Lloyd_Garrison). His final issue stated, "The object for which the *Liberator* was commenced-the extermination of chattel slavery-having been gloriously consummated, it seems to me specially appropriate to let its existence cover the historic period of the great struggle; leaving what remains to be done to complete the work of emancipation to other instrumentalities, (of which I hope to avail myself,) under new auspices, with more abundant means, and with millions instead of hundreds for allies" (quoted in //en.wikipedia.org/wiki/William_Lloyd_Garrison). As this article shows, many other antislavery periodicals appeared in the 1800s, but Garrison's publication was probably the best known and the most widely read.

Though Garrison received many death threats, he survived to see universal U.S. emancipation arrive in 1865. The first martyr among the antislavery periodical publishers was Elijah Parish Lovejoy, who first denounced slavery in the pages of his *St. Louis Observer* (1834-1836), in the slave state of Missouri. In May of 1836, Lovejoy decried the lynching of Frank McIntosh, a free African American who had been accused of murder but was hanged before being tried. The day after Lovejoy's editorial, the mob that had killed McIntosh attacked and destroyed Lovejoy's printing press. Fearing for his family's safety, he moved them to the free state of Illinois, where he soon started publishing the *Alton Observer* (1836-1837). An Illinois mob stole Lovejoy's press two times, and each time, Lovejoy retrieved it. A mob then stole it a third time and tossed it in the river. The Ohio Anti-Slavery Society bought Lovejoy yet another printing press,

but in October of 1857, many leading citizens of Alton begged him to leave. He refused their pleas, and on November 7, 1837, a proslavery mob found where Lovejoy had hidden his press, and Lovejoy was murdered trying to protect it.

In New York, three abolitionist journals and one antislavery newspaper emerged in the mid-1930s. First, the American Anti-Slavery Society (AA-SS) published eight monthly issues of its *American Anti-Slavery Reporter* (1834, Nos. 1-8), which included brief **slave narratives** intended to prick the moral conscience of slaveholders and to bolster opposition to slavery, as well as essays and letters decrying slavery as anti-Christian and against God's commandments. Links to full text (html or pdf format) may be found at //www.archive.org/details/american antislav1.

The next year, the *Reporter* yielded to the AA-SS's *The Anti-Slavery Record* (1835-1837, Vol. 1-3, New York), published by R. G. Williams, which included poems, essays, brief slave narratives, and other documents. On the front of its 6-10 pages each month, it used an eye-grabbing woodblock print depicting one of the many cruelties of slavery described in the cover story. Many of these woodblocks may be seen at //utc.iath.virginia.edu/abolitn/gallasrf.html. Links to the text (html or pdf) may be found at //www.archive.org/details/antislaveryrecvol2no01amer. Fervently abolitionist essayists, pamphleteers, and lecturers **Sarah Grimké** and **Angelina Grimké Weld**, European-American Quaker-convert daughters of a slaveholder, gave testimony in the *Record*'s pages, as did some slaveholders and former slaveholders.

The Anti-Slavery Examiner (1836-1845, Nos. 1-14, New York), also published intermittently by the AA-SS, offered slave narratives, essays, and letters, as well as the text of speeches. A few of its pieces included "Bible against Slavery," "The Constitution, A Pro-Slavery Compact," and "American Slavery As It Is: Testimony of a Thousand Witnesses." Text of the *Examiner* may be found through Project Gutenberg at //www.gutenberg.org/dirs/1/1/2/7/11275/11275.txt.

On January 7, 1837, African-American journalist Phillip Bell started publishing *The Weekly Advocate,* a general-interest newspaper. As Bell was about to publish his ninth issue, on March 4, almost exactly eight years after **Samuel Cornish** had to give up on *Freedom's Journal* (later renamed *Rights of All*), Cornish and Charles Bennett Ray joined Bell to found a second African-American-owned and -operated weekly newspaper, newly named *The Colored American* (1836-1842, New York City) (*not* to be confused with the **Colored American Magazine**, 1900-1909, or with *The Colored American,* 1893-19??, a Washington, D.C., newspaper). The 4-6 pages of *The Colored American* specifically addressed the free African Americans living in the coastal states in the

North. Unlike other antislavery periodicals of its time, in addition to articles against slavery, it included articles intended to uplift its free African-American readers. Because its potential subscribers had little extra money, African-American churches, local abolition societies, and European-American abolitionists often funded purchases of the paper, which were then distributed to cash-strapped readers. The AA-SS also urged members to subscribe to it. From the start, Cornish was the editor, and Ray was identified as the "Publisher," and in 1839, Ray took over sole ownership of the newspaper. In 1842, Ray published his last issue on Christmas Day.

Two other periodicals started in the 1830s: **William Whipper** edited the *National Reformer* (1838-1839?), the journal of the American Moral Reform Society (AMRS), an integrated organization Whipper had cofounded. The *National Reformer* was distributed mostly along the eastern seaboard, but also elsewhere, so some have claimed that Whipper may have been the first African-American editor of a national magazine. In addition to opposing slavery, the *Reformer* emphasized racial uplift, racial integration, civil rights, women's equality, and nonviolent tactics for achieving abolition and other goals. The 16-page *Reformer* was published each month.

David Ruggles, the freeborn son of free African Americans, had regularly contributed to the *Emancipator* (1820) and to the *Liberator* (1/1/1831-12/29/1865), and he had opened the first known African-American bookshop (1834, New York City), where he had sold abolitionist pamphlets (some of which he authored) and other materials. He was probably also the first African American to publish his own pamphlets. Ruggles also founded the New York Committee for Vigilance, which worked with the Underground Railroad, interposing its members between slave catchers and fugitive slaves. In 1838, he started publishing the committee's *Mirror of Liberty* (1838-1840), perhaps the nation's first African-American magazine. Even after he ceased publishing *Mirror of Liberty,* Ruggles continued contributing to other antislavery periodicals.

REFERENCES: Andrews, William L., and Mason I. Lowance, Jr., "Antislavery Movement," in *OCAAL*. Hinks, Peter P., John R. McKivigan, and R. Owen Williams (Eds.). 2007. *Encyclopedia of Antislavery and Abolition*. Westport, CT: Greenwood Publishing Group. //chroniclingamerica.loc.gov/lccn/sn83027091/. //en.wikipedia.org/wiki/Anti-Slavery_Reporter. //en.wikipedia.org/wiki/Colored_American. //en.wikipedia.org/wiki/Elijah_Lovejoy. //en.wikipedia.org/wiki/Genius_of_Universal_Emancipation. //en.wikipedia.org/wiki/The_Colored_American. //en.wikipedia.org/wiki/The_Liberator. //en.wikipedia.org/wiki/William_Lloyd_Garrison. //hcl.harvard.edu/libraries/widener/collections/newspapers/afam_alpha.cfm. //library.nyu.edu/research/news/historical/afr-am.html. //onlinebooks.library.upenn.edu/webbin/serial?id=antislaveryexaminer. //utc.iath.virginia.edu/abolitn/gallasrf.html. //web.library.emory.edu/subjects/humanities/history/news/NewspAfam.html. //www.accessible.com/accessible/about/aboutAA.jsp. //www.archive.org/details/americanantislav1. //www.archive.org/details/antislaveryrecvol2no01amer. //www.archive.org/stream/americanantislav1/americanantislav1_djvu.txt. //www.blackvoicenews.com/content/view/37990/13/. //www.blackvoicenews.com/content/view/42452/3/. //www.blackvoicenews.com/content/view/42455/3/. //www.blackvoicenews.com/content/view/42458/3/. //www.bpl.org/research/microtext/EthnicNewspapers.pdf. //www.gale.cengage.co.uk/controls/library.aspx?fileID=1284. //www.jimcrowhistory.org/resources/lessonplans/hs_es_black_press.htm. //www.lib.fsu.edu/help/researchguides/index.php/African_American_Newspapers. //www.loc.gov/exhibits/african/afam002.html. //www.loc.gov/exhibits/african/afam006.html. //www.pbs.org/wgbh/aia/rb_index_hd.html. //www.spartacus.schoolnet.co.uk/USASnewspapers.htm. //www.wisconsinhistory.org/libraryarchives/aanp/. //www.wisconsinhistory.org/libraryarchives/aanp/freedom/.

Antislavery Periodicals
1840–1849
Publication of antislavery fiction and nonfiction

(*See also* **antislavery periodicals, 1819-1829; antislavery periodicals, 1830-1839;** and **antislavery periodicals, 1850-1865**.) While William Lloyd Garrison was continuing to publish the *Liberator,* most of the other antislavery periodicals of the 1830s had ceased to exist by 1840 or 1841. In 1840, the American Anti-Slavery Society (AA-SS) started a second long-lived weekly publication advocating abolition: the six-column *National Anti-Slavery Standard* (Vol. 1-30, 1840-1870), published in New York, as well as in Philadelphia some of the time. Though the *Standard* did include the Society's minutes, records, letters, and news, the chief content of the *Standard* was highly emotional appeals to the moral consciences of its readers, through **slave narratives** and other testimonies, as well as essays, speeches, debates, and other documents. The *Standard* was well known for its rhetorical flourishes to evoke strong antislavery sentiments in its readers.

Probably the *Standard's* most fiercely abolitionist and well-known editor was European-American **Lydia Maria Child**, a dear friend of **David Ruggles**. From 1841 to 1843, she and her husband, Boston abolitionist, attorney, and writer David Lee Child, edited the *Standard* each week. Lydia also edited the slave narrative of **Harriet Jacobs**, *Incidents in the Life of a Slave Girl* (1861), and she and David coauthored the highly influential *An Appeal in Favor of That Class of Americans Called Africans* (1833), probably the first published book denouncing slavery, segregation, and the mistreatment of African Americans. Her other antislavery writings include *Letters from New York* (1843), *The Duty of Disobedience to the Fugitive Slave Act* (1860), and *The Freedmen's Book* (1865). Meanwhile, the *Standard* continued to be published week in and week out, until 1870, when the 15th Amendment to the U.S. Constitution was ratified.

Also long-lived was the *National Era.* (Vol. 1-14, 1847-1860, Washington, D.C.), published and edited weekly by European-American Gamaliel Bailey. Bailey's associate editor was John Greenleaf Whittier, whose antislavery poems, editorials, and other prose often appeared in its pages. Though decidedly abolitionist, the *National Era* also published other material not directly related to abolition and opposition to slavery. The *Era* was also decidedly more moderate in its opposition to slavery than the *Standard* or the *Liberator.* Garrison accused it of being "tainted with the spirit of compromise." Its main claim to fame, however, is its serialization of **Harriet Beecher Stowe**'s hugely popular novel *Uncle Tom's Cabin,* from June 1851 through April 1852. By 1853, 25,000 subscribers were reading the four-page, seven-column *National Era.* During 1856, Bailey stepped up to daily publication of the *Era* to support the antislavery Republican candidate for U.S. president, returning to weekly publication after the Republican lost. Over time, Bailey also grew less moderate, and he used the details of the notorious *Dred Scott* case of 1857 to persuade others to endorse abolition. Bailey's 1859 death was the death of the *Era,* as well.

In 1846, George Washington Taylor, a Philadelphia Quaker and former student of Enoch Lewis (*see* **antislavery periodicals, 1819-1829**, *African Observer*), started publishing *The Non-Slaveholder.* Taylor's periodical (1st series, 1846-1850, Vol. 1-5; 2nd series, 1853-1854, Vol. 1-2) was distinctive because not only did he denounce the slaveholder, but he also particularly focused on awakening the consciences of all those who supported the slavery system but did not hold slaves. His paper's motto was "Whoso gives the motive, makes his brother's sin his own." Taylor used articles, dialogues, editorials, essays, letters, news bulletins, notices, poems, reports, and speeches, both original and reprinted, to exhort the non-slaveholder to stop buying or selling any goods produced by the labor of slaves, to stop shipping goods produced by slave labor, to stop manufacturing items with raw materials or other goods produced by slave labor, and of course to stop buying, selling, trading, or holding slaves. In *The Non-Slaveholder,* Taylor introduced documentary evidence of the slave trade in Brazil, Cuba, and the West Indies, as well as in the U.S. South, using material not only from U.S. sources, but also from the British and the Foreign Anti-Slavery Societies. Taylor also practiced what he preached, as owner of a Philadelphia store selling free-labor-only goods.

In upstate New York, Willis A. Hodges, a freeborn African American from Virginia, started publishing *The Ram's Horn* (1847-1848?), a weekly abolitionist newspaper. Both revolutionary warrior John Brown and adamant abolitionist **Frederick Douglass** contributed cash and articles to Hodges's paper. Brown's "Sambo's Mistakes" savaged free African Americans of the North for being too complacent about the enslavement of their Southern brethren. Though the *Ram's Horn* reached a peak circulation of 2,500, it lasted only a year, perhaps in part because another periodical, started the same year, superseded it.

Meanwhile, Harvard graduate **Martin R. (Robison) Delany** could not get his abolitionist writings published in local Pittsburgh newspapers, so in 1843, he founded and edited his own newspaper, the *Mystery* (1843-1847), credited as being unusually well written. When former fugitive slave and passionate abolitionist Frederick Douglass was ready to start publishing his own abolitionist periodical, in 1847, Delany decided he would be far more effective if he joined forces with Douglass, rather than continuing to publish his own newspaper.

The most important antislavery periodical to emerge during this decade was founded by former fugitive slave Frederick Douglass. On December 3, 1847, Douglass started publishing his weekly abolitionist newspaper, ***The North Star*** (1847-1851). Like most abolitionist newspapers, the *North Star* struggled financially, despite receiving some financial support from British abolitionists, who paid for his printing press. (*See North Star; see also* **antislavery periodicals, 1850-1865.**)

A regular contributor to Douglass's *North Star* was Douglass's fellow fugitive from slavery, **Samuel Ringgold Ward**. In describing Ward, Douglass said, "As an orator and thinker [he] was vastly superior to any of us," "the splendors of his intellect went directly to the glory of race" (quoted in //en.wikipedia.org/wiki/Samuel_Ringgold_Ward). In February 1849, while living and preaching in Cortland Village, New York, Ward founded the semimonthly *Impartial Citizen,* published both in Syracuse and in Boston, Massachusetts. Ward intended the *Impartial Citizen* to supplement Douglass's *North Star,* rather than to compete with it. The *Impartial Citizen* included the customary antislavery poems, editorials, letters to the editor, text from speeches, and organizational reports from antislavery societies. That June, he solicited 1,500 subscribers to pay $1 per year for the periodical to be published weekly, an amount that later proved inadequate. In 1850, the U.S. Fugitive Slave Act was passed, and in October of 1851, Ward found himself on the morally right but legally wrong side of the law trying to help a fellow fugitive escape. He quickly realized that he needed to move his family farther north, to Canada, leaving the *Impartial Citizen* behind.

REFERENCES: Andrews, William L., and Mason I. Lowance, Jr., "Antislavery Movement," in *OCAAL*. Hinks, Peter P., John R. McKivigan, and R. Owen Williams (Eds.). 2007. *Encyclopedia of Antislavery and Abolition.* Westport, CT: Greenwood Publishing Group. //docsouth.unc.edu/neh/holland/holland.html. //en.wikipedia.org/wiki/Emancipation_proclamation. //en.wikipedia.org/wiki/North_Star_(newspaper). //en.wikipedia.org/wiki/Samuel_Ringgold_Ward.

//hcl.harvard.edu/libraries/widener/collections/newspapers/afam_alpha
.cfm. //library.nyu.edu/research/news/historical/afr-am.html. //web.
library.emory.edu/subjects/humanities/history/news/NewspAfam.html.
//www.accessible.com/accessible/about/aboutAA.jsp. //www.blackvoice
news.com/content/view/37990/13/. //www.blackvoicenews.com/
content/view/42454/3/. //www.blackvoicenews.com/content/
view/42455/3/. //www.blackvoicenews.com/content/view/42456/3/.
//www.bpl.org/research/microtext/EthnicNewspapers.pdf. //www.gale.
cengage.co.uk/controls/library.aspx?fileID=1284. //www.jimcrow
history.org/resources/lessonplans/hs_es_black_press.htm. //www.lib.
fsu.edu/help/researchguides/index.php/African_American_Newspaper
s. //www.liu.edu/cwis/cwp/library/historic.htm. //www.loc. gov/exhibits
/african/afam002.html. //www.loc.gov/exhibits/african/ afam006.html.
//www.spartacus.schoolnet.co.uk/USASnews papers.htm.

Antislavery Periodicals
1850–1865
Publication of antislavery fiction and nonfiction

(*See also* **antislavery periodicals, 1819-1829**; **antislavery periodicals, 1830-1839**; and **antislavery periodicals, 1840-1849**.) By the 1850s, some European-American-owned and -operated mainstream papers were beginning to decry slavery and to advocate its abolition. While Horace Greeley edited the *New York Tribune* (1841-1872), it may well have been the nation's most influential newspaper, with a circulation nearing 300,000 on the eve of the Civil War. Greeley himself was often touted as the greatest editor of his day, so when he started editorializing against slavery by 1854, he wielded great power of the pen. Even Joseph Medill, managing editor of the *Chicago Tribune,* and known to have racist inclinations, began editorializing against slavery in the 1850s.

The most prominent dedicated abolitionist periodicals of this era were still William Lloyd Garrison's *The Liberator* (1831-1865), the American Anti-Slavery Society's *National Anti-Slavery Standard* (Vol. 1-30, 1840-1870), and **Frederick Douglass's** *The North Star* (1847-1851), which merged with Gerrit Smith's *Liberty Party Paper* and was renamed the *Frederick Douglass' Paper* (1851-1860?). In its new form, *Frederick Douglass' Paper* could boast of readers in England and the West Indies, as well as the United States, and the circulation of *Frederick Douglass' Paper* exceeded that of Garrison's *Liberator.* Like Garrison, Douglass also supported women's suffrage and women's civil rights. Sometime between 1858 and 1861, Douglass started publishing the *Douglass Monthly* and stopped publishing the weekly *Frederick Douglass' Paper,* probably with a period of overlap during which both periodicals were being published. From 1860 until 1863, Douglass continued to publish the *Douglass Monthly,* announcing Lincoln's January 1, 1863 Emancipation Proclamation in its pages. (*See North Star*; *see also* **antislavery periodicals,**

1840-1849, for more information on each of these periodicals.)

In addition to these national abolitionist periodicals, the *National Era* (Vol. 1-14, 1847-1860, Washington, D.C.), published and edited weekly by European-American Gamaliel Bailey, continued to publish antislavery poems, editorials, and other pieces, while also publishing material addressing other subjects. Numerous regional and even local antislavery periodicals also dotted the land, such as the *Anti-Slavery Bugle,* published by the Ohio Anti-Slavery Society's (later the Western Anti-Slavery Society), and even Providence Rhode Island's *The Instigator,* and New Orleans's *Liberalist.*

After the passage of the 1850 Fugitive Slave Law, increasing numbers of fugitives fled farther north to Canada, where they continued to publish antislavery periodicals. For instance, **Henry Bibb** and his wife fled to Canada in 1851, where he founded and edited *The Voice of the Fugitive,* probably the best-known African-Canadian abolitionist newspaper. He also persuaded freeborn **Mary Ann Shadd (later Cary)**, a regular contributor to Douglass's *North Star*, to move to Canada in 1850. In 1851, fugitive from slavery **Samuel Ringgold Ward** fled to Canada, as well. By 1853, Shadd and Bibb had a falling out, and in 1853, Shadd and Ward cofounded the weekly *Provincial Freeman,* in which the coeditors urged fellow African Americans to find refuge in Canada. As a native of the United States, Shadd was the first African-American woman to own and operate a periodical of any kind; though it was published in Canada, it was widely read South of the Canadian border.

Ward and slave narrator **James W. (William) C. (Charles) Pennington** were also named as coeditors of the weekly *Alienated American* (1853-), but Oberlin College graduate William Howard Day was actually the periodical's principal editor. The official newspaper of the Ohio Negro Convention Movement, it advocated integration, but not from a moderationist stance. Militant abolitionist John Brown was among the European Americans whose activities the newspaper endorsed. Day stopped publishing the *Alienated American* before leaving for England in 1856 and 1857, later settling in Canada before the Civil War.

Another short-lived periodical, *American Jubilee* (1854-1855, Nos. 1-12, New York), focused on political commentary and current events. Intermittently published, the *Anti-Slavery Tracts* (1855-1856, 1860-1862, New York) used essays, documentation, and other treatises to call for the abolition of slavery. William Goodell edited the *Radical Abolitionist* (1855-1858, Vol. 1-4, New York), which raised the legal and constitutional ramifications of slavery, based on the wording of the U.S. Constitution's preamble, "to establish justice, ensure domestic tranquility, provide for the common defense, promote the

general welfare and secure the blessings of liberty to ourselves and our posterity" (quoted in //www.liu.edu/
cwis/cwp/library/historic.htm). The year after the *Radical
Abolitionist* ceased publication, Goodell became editor
and publisher of another antislavery periodical (1859-
1866): *The Principia* (1859-1864), renamed the *Principia
and National Era* (1865), which was in turn renamed the
New York Principia (1866), then renamed the same year
the *National Principia* (1866). In all of its iterations, it was
sponsored by the Church Antislavery Society, which also
dedicated itself to moral uplift. To Goodell and his readers, slavery was simply sinful and therefore must be
abolished.

Many of the antislavery periodicals ceased publication after the start of the Civil War (*National Era*), the
publication of the Emancipation Proclamation (*Douglass
Monthly*), the end of the Civil War (*The Liberator*), or
soon afterward (*National Anti-Slavery Standard*). As freed
men and women began establishing new lives for themselves in the South and in the North, an abundance of
new African-American periodicals emerged, both to
serve the Freedmen (and women) as a group and to give
voice to free African-American communities arising
across the nation. (*See also* **newspapers**.)

REFERENCES: Andrews, William L., and Mason I. Lowance, Jr.,
"Antislavery Movement," in *OCAAL*. Hinks, Peter P., John R.
McKivigan, and R. Owen Williams (Eds.). 2007. *Encyclopedia of
Antislavery and Abolition*. Westport, CT: Greenwood Publishing Group.
Irvine Garland Penn 1891. *The Afro-American Press and its Editors*.
Wiley & Co., as accessed through Google Books. //docsouth.unc.edu/
neh/holland/holland.html. //en.wikipedia.org/wiki/Emancipation_
proclamation. //en.wikipedia.org/wiki/Horace_Greeley. //en.wikipedia.
org/wiki/Joseph_Medill. //en.wikipedia.org/wiki/North_Star_
(newspaper). //hcl.harvard.edu/libraries/widener/collections/
newspapers/afam_alpha.cfm. //library.nyu.edu/research/news/
historical/afr-am.html. //web.library.emory.edu/subjects/humanities/
history/news/NewspAfam.html. //www.accessible.com/accessible/
about/aboutAA.jsp. //www.blackvoicenews.com/content/view/
37990/13/. //www.blackvoicenews.com/content/view/42456/3/.
//www.bpl.org/research/microtext/EthnicNewspapers.pdf. //www.gale.
cengage.co.uk/controls/library.aspx?fileID=1284. //www.jimcrow
history.org/resources/lessonplans/hs_es_black_press.htm. //www.liu.
edu/cwis/cwp/library/historic.htm. //www.loc.gov/exhibits/african/
afam002.html. //www.loc.gov/exhibits/african/afam006.html.
//www.spartacus.schoolnet.co.uk/USASnewspapers.htm.

Asante, Molefi Kete (né Arthur Lee Smith, Jr.)
8/14/1942–
Scholarly writings; cofounding journal editor, educator

Arthur was the fourth child of Arthur and Lily Smith,
but he was their first son, and Arthur, Sr., gave him his
name. Thirty years later, while Arthur Smith, Jr., was visiting Ghana, King Opoku Ware II gave Arthur the last
name Asante, linking him to a Ghanaian tribe (once
commonly referred to as the Ashanti). Then, Asante

gave himself the first name Molefi, a Sotho name meaning "Keeper of the Traditions," and he chose as his middle
name Kete, meaning "One Who Loves Music and the
Dance." Asante's chosen first name aptly describes him,
as he is the founder of the Afrocentric school of thought
and a preeminent scholar of African-American history
and traditions. A prolific writer of scholarly works,
Asante has written at least 200 scholarly articles and has
authored or edited nearly 40 books, including
Afrocentricity: The Theory of Social Change (1980; 2nd
ed., 1983); *African Culture: The Rhythms of Unity* (1985,
edited with his wife, Kariamu Welsh Asante);
Afrocentricity (1988); *Kemet, Afrocentricity and Knowledge*
(1990); *Malcolm X as Cultural Hero and Other Afrocentric
Essays* (1993); *African American History: A Journey of Lib-
eration* (1995); *African Intellectual Heritage: A Book of
Sources* (1996, edited with Abu S. Barry); and *The
Afrocentric Idea* (rev. ed., 1998).

Asante perfected his scholarship while earning his
Ph.D. in Communication in 1968 at UCLA, where he
served as president of the Student Nonviolent Coordinating Committee. In addition to offering his books, he
has shared his knowledge with numerous students, first at
the State University of New York at Buffalo, then (since
1984) at Temple University in Philadelphia. At Temple,
Asante established the first Ph.D. program in African
American Studies; he also chaired the department of
Africology until 1997. For Asante, the key to Afrocentric
thought is an internal orientation, not merely an external
manifestation, such as adopting an African name. Instead, "the Afrocentric school of thought," says Asante,
"places Africans at the center of any analysis of ideas,
concepts, or people." That is, "Afrocentricity is an orientation to data, which says that African people are ancient, and should be seen as agents, as subjects, in history,
instead of as marginal players on the fringes of Europe."

In the mid-1990s, Asante was enstooled as a king
among the Akan of Ghana, partly in recognition for his
work on Afrocentricity and for increasing our knowledge
and awareness of the history and culture of Africa's
people.

REFERENCES: SMKC. Interview between Molefi Asante and Tonya
Bolden, Summer 1998. —Tonya Bolden

Editor's note: At the time of this publication, Asante had
authored or edited (or coauthored or coedited) more
than 60 books, including *The African-American Atlas:
Black History and Culture* (with Mark Mattson, 1998; revised from 1991 version), *100 Greatest African Americans:
A Biographical Encyclopedia* (2002), *Erasing Racism: The
Survival of the American Nation* (2003), and *Encyclopedia
of Black Studies* (Editor, 2003). His earliest books addressed the topics of rhetoric or mass, public, or
intercultural communication (e.g., *The Rhetoric of Black*

Revolution, 1969, written using his birth name). In addition to his scholarly writings, he has written a poetry book (1964, as Arthur L. Smith), an art and antiquities guide (1979, with his wife Kariamu Welsh), a novel (1984), popular books (e.g., two books of African names, 1991, 1999), a high school textbook (1993), an activity book (1997) and a "worktext" (2001), and teacher guides (1997, 2001). Asante also cofounded the bimonthly *Journal of Black Studies* in 1969 and has been its editor ever since. He has also served as an advisory-board member, advisory editor, associate editor, book reviewer, contributing editor, or editorial associate of several other journals. His writings have also appeared in newspapers (e.g., the *Los Angeles Times*) and magazines (e.g., *Utne Reader*), as well as dozens of scholarly journals (e.g., *Academe, Black Scholar, Communication Quarterly, Palestine Review*).

He and his second wife, Kariamu Welsh, have three children: Kasina Eka, Daahoud Ali, and Molefi Khumalo. "M. K." Asante has published his own nonfiction and poetry, and he wrote and produced the documentary films *500 Years Later* (2005), in which his father appeared, and *The Black Candle: A Kwanzaa Celebration* (2008), starring **Maya Angelou**.)

REFERENCES: *AANB. CAO-04. Wiki.* Bigelow, Barbara Carlisle, in *BB.* Amazon.com. "[Molefi Khumalo] "M. K. Asante," in //www.asante.info/, and in Amazon.com.

Ashe, Jr., Arthur Robert
7/10/1943–2/6/1993
Nonfiction-sports history, how-to books, autobiography/memoir; tennis player

Ashe's publications include his landmark *A Hard Road to Glory: A History of the Afro-American Athlete* (1988), in three volumes, covering 1619-1918, 1919-1945, and 1946-1988. After his death, the three volumes were reworked to create separate volumes on basketball (2000), baseball (1993), boxing (1993), and track and field (1993), also considered foundational, oft-cited texts. Ashe acknowledged the thorough, deep research evident in these books, telling the *Chicago Tribune*, "Once I made the decision to do it, I had to go at the book the way I've always done things-the way our teachers at Maggie Walker High School insisted upon-all out, with everything I've got."

He also wrote numerous how-to tennis books: *Getting Started in Tennis* (1977, with Louie Robinson, Jr., and with photographs by his wife **Jeanne Moutoussamy-Ashe**), *Mastering Your Tennis Strokes* (1978), *Arthur Ashe's Tennis Clinic* (1981), and *Arthur Ashe on Tennis: Strokes, Strategy, Traditions, Players, Psychology, and Wisdom* (with Alexander McNab, posthumous, 1995). His writings also appeared in newspapers (e.g., *New York Times, Washington Post*) and magazines (e.g., *People, Tennis Magazine*).

His achievements on the tennis court are too numerous to mention here, as is his list of "firsts"; to summarize, he was the first African American to achieve national (U.S.) and international ranking and to win numerous championships in tennis. Before he retired, his outstanding accomplishments on the tennis court merited numerous coauthored autobiographies and memoirs, including *Advantage Ashe* (with Clifford G. Gewecke, Jr., 1967), *Arthur Ashe: Portrait in Motion* (1975, with legendary sports commentator Frank Deford), *Off the Court* (with Neil Amdur, 1981), and *Days of Grace: A Memoir* (1993, with noted biographer **Arnold Rampersad**, finished just two days before Ashe died). His wife Jeanne's children's book *Daddy and Me: A Photo Essay of Arthur Ashe and His Daughter Camera* (1993) offers a more intimate view of him and their adopted daughter, Camera Elizabeth (born 12/21/1986).

A quadruple bypass surgery on his heart (1979) ended his tennis career, then a second bypass surgery (1983) included a blood transfusion that infected him with HIV, which took his life due to AIDS-related pneumonia. Though his biological heart failed him, his spiritual heart imbued him with both fierce determination to succeed and gracious forgiveness of circumstances and persons impeding his success. In addition to fighting his own civil-rights battles, he also championed the human and civil rights of others. For instance, in 1985, he was arrested protesting against South African apartheid, and in 1992, he was arrested for publicly objecting to the despicable treatment of Haitian refugees. He said it best himself, "From what we get, we can make a living; what we give, however, makes a life."

REFERENCES: *B. BCE. CAO-03. CE. EB-BH-CD. HD. QB. W2B. Wiki.* Jenkins, McKay, in *AANB.* Kram, Mark, and Ashyia N. Henderson, in *BB.* Robinson, Alonford James, Jr., in *EA-99.*

Atkins, Russell
2/25/1926–
Poems, drama; educator

A precocious artist, young Russell showed talent in visual arts from an early age, started studying piano at age 7 and was composing music soon after, wrote and staged short plays with puppets he had created himself, won several poetry contests by age 13, and published his first poem in his 1944 high school yearbook. After high school, he studied music, art, and theater in several Cleveland, Ohio schools of higher learning, then he served in the military in the late 1940s.

Atkins had a distinctive method for getting his early poems published: He wrote to some famous poets and art patrons and asked for their help. Sure enough, poet Edith Sitwell and literature champion **Carl Van Vechten** helped him get his poems published in journals such as *Experiment*, *View*, and *Beloit Poetry Journal*, and newspapers such as *The New York Times*. In 1950, Atkins cofounded (with Casper L. Jordan) *Free Lance*, probably the first African-American-owned literary magazine, which published avant-garde works by African-American and European-American writers until 1979. As an auspicious beginning, **Langston Hughes** wrote an introduction for the first issue, saying, "Skilled or unskilled, wise or foolish, nobody can write a poem without revealing something of himself. Here are people. Here are poems. Here is revolution" (quoted in *AAP-55-85*). Printed in England, the journal was soon distributed not only nationally, but also internationally. In fact, Atkins may be better known in Europe than in the United States.

The structure of Atkins's poetry reflected both of Atkins's other areas of knowledge: music and the visual arts. He particularly played with visual presentation of words on the page, to create what has been called "concrete poetry," "visual poetry," "pattern poetry," or "shape poetry." In a letter to writer, bookseller, and publisher Paul Breman, he said, "Many do not know that I was, possibly, the first to write [concrete poetry] over here in the U.S.A." (quoted in *AAP-55-85*). Casual readers may have been puzzled by his use of continuous words, embedded words, contracted words with numerous apostrophes, shifted parts of speech (e.g., by transforming adjectives into verbs), and other techniques, but intrigued readers enjoyed delving into his densely complex poetry. Just one example comes from his 1953 poem "Lisbon": multituDes per at En/trance of horror/o theR ush" (quoted in *BB*; multitudes desperate at entrance ...). He also enjoyed playing with onomatopoeia, such as in "Trainyard at Night," describing thunder, he wrote, "then huge bold blasts black / hiss, insists, upon hissing insists / on insisting on hissing hiss / hiss s ss sss ssss s" (quoted in *AAP-55-85*).

In describing his writing, Atkins said, "Originality is not necessarily what has never been done before. More often it is doing what has been done before differently" (quoted in *AAP-55-85*). Not only did he push the limits in his poetry style, but also in his poetic themes, probing such topics as sexual deviancy and drug addiction. After a decade of publishing poems in periodicals, in 1960, Atkins published *A Podium Presentation*, his first collection. Soon after, his other poetry collections appeared: *Phenomena* (1961), *Objects* (1963), *Objects 2* (1964), *Here in The* (1976), and *Whichever* (1978), many of them described as "pamphlets." His poems have also been widely anthologized (e.g., in Arnold Adoff's *Celebrations*, 1977).

In addition, Atkins collaborated with Hale Smith and with Langston Hughes to create *Elegy*, poetry set to music

(1968, published). Atkins wrote *The Nail, to Be Set to Music* (1970, published) as a poetic libretto to accompany an opera composed by Smith. He also wrote *By Yearning and by Beautiful*, poetry set to music by Smith (1986, performed at Lincoln Center for the Performing Arts). He has even written his own piano music to accompany his poetry *Objects* (1969, published).

Atkins's collection *Heretofore* (1968) includes not only poems but also a radio play, *Seventh Circle* (written in 1957). Meanwhile, Free Lance Press published *Two by Atkins: The Abortionist and The Corpse: Two Poetic Dramas to Be Set to Music* (1963; originally published separately in 1954), which he termed "poems in play forms." About 20 years ahead of his time, he presented these disturbing themes in a detached, abstract manner. Produced in the early 1960s, his play *The Exoneration* addressed police brutality using graphic language that would not have surprised viewers a decade later but that shocked his original viewers. Atkins also published a short-story collection, *Maleficium* (1971), which offered disconcerting portraits of violent or vicious characters. He also privately printed *Juxtapositions: A Manifesto* (1991). Amazon.com also lists these works by Russell Atkins: *Spyrytual* (1966, published by 7 Flowers Press), *From Gippsland to El Alamein* (1994, self-published), and *The war and I* (n.d., self-published), as well as *Experiment: A Quarterly of New Poetry* (1951, pamphlet).

He also published an essay on music theory, "A Psychovisual Perspective for 'Musical' Composition" in his 1955-1956 issue of *Free Lance*, urging fellow composers to compose for the brain of the listener, not for the listener's ear. Many of Atkins's other theoretical writings also appeared in *Free Lance* over the years. In his writings on education, he anticipated the **Black Arts Movement** of the 1960s by urging oppressed people to create their own forms of education, rather than trying to enter the educational institutions of the mainstream culture.

To supplement his income from his writing, from *Free Lance*, and from numerous grants and fellowships, he also taught writing, gave lectures, and served as writer in residence at various Ohio institutions. For his contributions, he was awarded an honorary doctorate from Cleveland State University (1976) and a Lifetime Literary Achievement award by the Poets' League of Cleveland (1997). Early in the new millennium, he reportedly is working on a new poetry collection, some operas, and a piano composition for *Spyrytuals*, and he continues to publish new poems in small presses.

REFERENCES: *AAP-55-85*. *CAO-01*. Burton, Jennifer, in *COCAAL*. Manheim, James M., in *BB*. Amazon.com. //heatstrings.blogspot.com/2007/07/russell-atkins.html.

FURTHER READING: Cuthbert, David, in *GEAAL*.

Attaway, William
11/19/1911–6/17/1986
Novels, play, short stories, scripts, songs, nonfiction—songbooks

After dropping out of college, Attaway spent two years living as a hobo during the Great Depression. After that, he spent some time working as a sailor, a salesperson, and a labor organizer before returning to the University of Illinois, where he earned his B.A. in 1936. Before graduating, he worked with the Federal Writers' Project, befriended fellow writer **Richard Wright**, and wrote *Carnival*, produced at his college in 1935.

In June 1936, he published his first short story in *Challenge*. About the time that John Steinbeck's 1937 *Of Mice and Men* was published, he wrote his first novel, *Let Me Breathe Thunder* (published 1939), about two white vagabonds who are joined by a good-natured homeless Mexican nine-year-old. While working on the novel, he sustained himself by toiling in an occupation more reliably lucrative than writing: acting. Whereas his first novel highlighted the Great Depression, the second focused on the Great Migration of African Americans from the rural South to the urban North. In *Blood on the Forge* (1941), three brothers fled from sharecropping on an impoverished Kentucky farm, seeking work as union busters in Pennsylvania steel mills, but finding death, blinding, and physical and mental crippling instead. Though critically acclaimed, the brothers' tragic story was overshadowed by Richard Wright's best-selling *Native Son*, published the previous year.

Discouraged that his books were widely praised but not big moneymakers, Attaway turned to song, arranging and composing songs for his friend Harry Belafonte and other performers. He also wrote *Calypso Song Book* (1957) and *Hear America Singing* (1967), a history of popular American songs. Belafonte also hosted Attaway's wedding ceremony December 28, 1962, to Frances Settele, with whom he later had a son, Bill, and a daughter, Noelle.

In 1966, he took his family for a weeklong vacation to Barbados—and stayed for 11 years before returning. In Barbados, he started writing scripts for radio, television, and film. For TV, he wrote scripts for *Wide Wide World*, *Colgate Hour*, and other programs. For film, he wrote an adaptation of Irving Wallace's best-selling novel *The Man*; the final filmed version was later rewritten by Rod Serling, who got the on-screen writing credits. His own scripts include *One Hundred Years of Laughter* (1967, TV show about African-American humor) and *The Atlanta Child Murders* (1985, about the tragic serial murder of numerous African-American boys).

REFERENCES: *AA. AANB. CAO-03. NYPL-AADR.* W. Accomando, Christina, in *OCAAL* and *COCAAL.* Garren, Samuel B., in *AAW-* 40-55. Prono, Luca, in *GEAAL.* Simms, L. Moody, Jr. "In the Shadow of Richard Wright: William Attaway." *Notes on Mississippi Writers 8.1* (Spring 1975), pp. 13-18. Rpt. in Narins, Brigham, and Debbie Stanley (Eds.), (1996). *Contemporary Literary Criticism* (Vol. 92, pp. 13-18). Detroit: Gale Research. From *Literature Resource Center.*

Aubert, Alvin (Bernard)
3/12/1930–
Poems, short stories, literary criticism, dramas

Aubert's poems are often anthologized and both his poems and his literary criticism have been published in periodicals. His poetry collections include *Against the Blues* (1972, by **Broadside Press**), *Feeling Through* (1975), *South Louisiana: New and Selected Poems* (1985), *If Winter Come: Collected Poems, 1967-1992* (1994), and *Harlem Wrestler: and Other Poems* (1995), as well as his chapbook, *A Noisesome Music* (1979). Praised for their word-craft, Aubert's poems are less emotion-imbued, less explicit, and less politically attuned than the poems produced by his **Black Arts Movement** peers of the 1960s and 1970s.

A college educator at several institutions starting in 1960, he settled in Detroit, Michigan, at Wayne State University in 1980. There, he initiated a course on African-American literature, which he continued to teach until he became professor emeritus in 1993. While still at the State University of New York (SUNY), in 1975, Aubert founded and started editing ***Obsidian****: Black Literature in Review*, a periodical that included poems, essays, short stories, and literary reviews, as well occasional dramatic pieces and bibliographies on specific authors or literary subjects. He took *Obsidian* with him to Wayne State, but he stopped publishing it in 1982. It has since been published by a series of editors at differing institutions and is now being published semiannually (Spring/Summer, Fall/Winter). His many awards and grants include being a 1968 Bread Loaf Writers Conference Scholar in poetry and receiving a 1959 Woodrow Wilson fellowship, two National Endowment for the Arts grants in poetry (1973, 1981), a 1979 Coordinating Council of Literary Magazines Editors fellowship, a 1988 *Callaloo* Award, and a 2004 Furious Flower Poetry Lifetime Achievement Award.

REFERENCES: *AAP-55-85. CAO-01.* Vander, R. Goldman, in *OCAAL* and *COCAAL.* Vander, R. Goldman, and Metzger, Sheri Elaine, in *BB.* Woodard, Loretta G., in *GEAAL.* //english.chass. ncsu.edu/obsidian/Obsidian%20History.html.

Autobiography/Memoir *See* **Slave Narratives**

~B~

Baisden, Michael
6/26/1963–

Novels, plays, anthologies; publisher, media host

Married (1993-1998), driving for the Chicago transit authority, and trying to start his own small business, Michael Baisden had been troubled by his friends' stories of heartache, guilt, and anguish arising when a love partner betrays the relationship by having a sexual relationship with someone outside the partnership. On his own initiative, Baisden interviewed countless men and women who had cheated on their partners by having sexual relationships with people other than their partners. He then compiled and analyzed the interviews, concluding that, "the cheating man depends on smooth talk, good looks, and the low morals of his victims to accomplish his goals. . . . What I am attempting to do, at the very least, is to expose the games that are quite seriously destroying our relationships with our women, and as a direct result, affecting our ability to maintain healthy relationships which could be beneficial to both ourselves and the children that are unsuspecting players in too many of those very games" (quoted in *BB*). Baisden was particularly tuned in to the effects on children, as he and his wife had a young daughter. He not only targeted the commitment-phobic men, but also the women who knowingly engage in sexual relationships with married or otherwise partnered men.

He tried to interest publishers in his resulting *Never Satisfied: How and Why Men Cheat*, to no avail. Undaunted, he sold his car, maxed out his credit cards, borrowed from friends and family, and founded his own Legacy Publishing, which published his book in 1995. He then promoted his book all over the place, in bookstores and book fairs, hair salons and barber shops, nightclubs and sorority conventions, and he managed to sell almost 50,000 copies within 8 months. Both *Essence* and *Emerge* listed his book as a bestseller. With his profits, he repaid his loans and took time out to write his first novel, *Men Cry in the Dark,* which his Legacy Publishing started selling in 1997. Using his tried-and-true strategies, he sold 30,000 copies within 6 months—in hardcover.

About the time he was working on his second novel, his own marriage dissolved. The following year, Legacy Publishing published *The Maintenance Man: It's Midnight, Do You Know Where Your Woman Is?* (1999). Publishing-industry rumors suggest that he turned down offers from mainstream publishers wanting to capitalize on his success. For his third novel, *God's Gift to Women: A Novel* (2002), Baisden allowed Touchstone to publish both a paperback and a hardcover edition, and Thorndike Press published a large-print edition (2003). Reviewers often call Baisden's novels part of the "Brotherman" genre of male-perspective books that counter the female-perspective books of the "Sistergirl" genre. Baisden adapted his novels *Men Cry in the Dark* and *The Maintenance Man* to stage, and they were produced in Texas in 2002 and 2003, respectively. *Maintenance Man* has also been optioned for film adaptation.

Meanwhile, Baisden's book-signing talks started drawing such large crowds that he started a series of "Love, Lust and Lies" seminars, addressing problems in contemporary relationships and suggesting how to form healthier love relationships. In 2001, he made numerous appearances on daytime talk shows and briefly had his own syndicated talk show, "Talk or Walk." In 2003, he developed his own nationally syndicated radio program, "Love, Lust and Lies," now simply the "Michael Baisden Show," broadcast in more than 35 cities, from Los Angeles to Miami to New York City to Cleveland, Ohio. He has broadened his audience to cable television, with African-American-owned TV One's *Baisden After Dark,* offering comedy, music, and talk on late Saturday nights, starting in 2007. He is also reputed to have a website offering online singles search services and advice for singles committed to remaining singles, at //happilysingle.com, but it was not reachable at the time of attempted access.

REFERENCES: CAO-04. *Wiki.* Brennan, Carol, in *BB.* //www.amazon.com/. //www.michaelbaisden.com/. //www.michaelbaisden.com/biography. //www.tvoneonline.com/shows/show.asp?sid=768&id=1722.

FURTHER READING: Williams, Dera R., in *GEAAL.*

Baker, Augusta (née Braxston; 2nd married surname: Alexander)
4/1/1911–2/23/1998

Nonfiction, story anthologies, bibliography, juvenile literature; spoken word—lectures, storytelling

Augusta Baker—granddaughter of a formerly enslaved "marvelous storyteller," only child of two college-educated teachers, mother of an only son, and children's librarian for the New York Public Library (NYPL)—literally wrote the book on storytelling, *Storytelling: Art and Technique* (1977, with Ellin Greene; 2nd ed. 1987; 3rd ed. 1996). A skilled storyteller herself, she taught storytelling at Columbia University for years, and in a 1995 interview, she discussed her storytelling workshops using the present tense—42 years after she was named the NYPL's head of Storytelling Services. In addition to her workshops, she also lectured often on oral narratives (*see* **oral tradition**) and **folktales**.

Frustrated with the paucity of high-quality African-American children's literature, she ardently advocated for developing and fostering such literature. Toward that end, she developed bibliographies of suitable African-American children's books, starting with an informally copied list in the 1930s, followed by two other annotated editions in 1946 and 1949. The 1949 edition was amplified and polished to create the widely distributed *Books about Negro Life* (1957, 1961, 1963; revised and expanded to *The Black Experience in Children's Books*, 1971). For the Children's Book Council, she wrote *Aids to Choosing Books for Children* (1967). Baker also offered readers carefully chosen tellable tales in her anthologies *The Talking Tree* (1955, 1960) and *The Golden Lynx and Other Tales* (1960), two highly regarded world folktale collections, as well as *The Young Years: Best Loved Stories and Poems for Little Children* (1960, 1963) and *Once Upon a Time* (1964).

At the Harlem branch of the NYPL (now named the **Countee Cullen** branch), Baker helped create the **James Weldon Johnson** Memorial Collection of books, a part of which is now included in the NYPL's Schomburg Center for Research in Black Culture. To further her literary outreach, she initiated a weekly radio series *The World of Children's Literature*. Later on, she consulted for the *Sesame Street* television show, sharing her vast knowledge of children's literature.

Among her numerous other awards from libraries, universities, and organizations, Baker received the American Library Association's first (1953) E. P. Dutton-John Macrae Distinguished Service Award. In 1961, she became the first African-American woman administrator in the NYPL when she was named coordinator of children's services for all 82 of the then-existing NYPL branches, a job she held until she retired in 1974. Another first: In 1980, she was named the first story-teller-in-residence at an American university, the University of South Carolina. Its Thomas Cooper Library now houses her papers and more than 1,600 children's books in its Augusta Baker Collection of African-American Children's Literature and Folklore.

Note: The spelling of her birth surname in a 1995 interview with *Horn Book* is Braxston, as it is in the re-

sources *Black Biography*, *BWA:AHE*, and GLRO's *Contemporary Authors Online*. The Braxton spelling appears in *AANB*, *Wikipedia*, and *Britannica*. Her son, James Henry Baker III, was named after her first husband, whom she divorced. She later married Gordon Alexander.

REFERENCES: *AANB*. *EBLG*. Edwards, Roanne, in *EA-99*. Jenkins, Betty L., in *BWA:AHE*. *Wiki*. Metzger, Sheri Elaine, and Ralph G. Zerbonia, in *BB*. *CAO-03*. Smith, Henrietta M., "An Interview with Augusta Baker." *The Horn Book Magazine*. 71.3 (May-June 1995) p. 292. From *Literature Resource Center*. //bccb.lis.uiuc.edu/1000gone. html. //www.britannica.com/EBchecked/topic/49465/Augusta-Braxton-Baker

Baker, Jr., Houston A. (Alfred)
3/22/1943–
Literary criticism, essays, poems; editor, educator

As a literary critic, Baker was instrumental in proposing a **"black aesthetic"** for interpreting and evaluating literature. To further this proposal, he has developed specific linguistic and sociohistorical strategies for studying the literature of persons from an oppressed culture living within a dominant culture. He has applied those strategies in several works of literary criticism, including *Long Black Song: Essays in Black American Literature and Culture* (1972), which analyzed African-American linguistic patterns and folklore in the works of **Frederick Douglass**, **W. E. B. Du Bois**, **Richard Wright**, and others; *A Many-Colored Coat of Dreams: The Poetry of Countee Cullen* (1974); *Singers of Daybreak: Studies in Black American Literature* (1974), essays on the works of **Paul Laurence Dunbar**, **Ralph Ellison**, **Jean Toomer**, and others; *The Journey Back: Issues in Black Literature and Criticism* (1980), examining both poetic and narrative language in African-American literature; *Blues, Ideology, and Afro-American Literature: A Vernacular Theory* (1984), probing the ways in which the blues have influenced and been influenced by African-American culture and how this idiom is expressed in literary phrasings and voice; *Modernism and the Harlem Renaissance* (1987), reflectively reassessing this period of intense African-American creativity; *Afro-American Poetics: Revisions of Harlem and the Black Aesthetic* (1988), in which he pays "special attention to the sociology, psychology, and entrancing sounding of race"; *Black Feminist Criticism and Critical Theory* (1988, with Joe Weixlmann); *Workings of the Spirit: The Poetics of Afro-American Women's Writing* (1991), assessing the literary contributions of such writers as **Zora Neale Hurston**, **Harriet Jacobs**, and **Toni Morrison**; *Black Studies, Rap, and the Academy* (1993), extending Baker's distinctive analysis to the rap form; *Critical Memory: Public Spheres, African American Writing, and*

Black Fathers and Sons in America (2001); *Turning South Again: Rethinking Modernism/Rethinking Booker T.* (2001); *I Don't Hate the South: Reflections on Faulkner, Family, and the South* (2007); and *Betrayal: How Black Intellectuals Have Abandoned the Ideals of the Civil Rights Era* (2008), arguing that many African-American leaders have failed to stay true to the progressive social ideals championed in the 1960s.

In addition, Baker has published collections of his own poems, such as *No Matter Where You Travel, You Still Be Black* (1979), *Spirit Run: Poems* (1982), *Blues Journey, Home* (1985), and *Passing Over* (2000), all published by **Lotus Press**. He has also edited various anthologies (e.g., his seminal *Black Literature in America*, 1971; *Renewal: A Volume of Black Poems*, edited by Baker and his wife, Charlotte Pierce-Baker, 1977; and *Three American Literatures: Essays in Chicano, Native American, and Asian-American Literature for Researchers of American Literature*, 1982) and other works. Contributor of more than 80 scholarly journal articles, essays, and reviews, he was named, in 2000, editor of *American Literature*, the oldest and probably most prestigious journal in the field.

The son of parents with master's degrees, Baker earned his B.A. (1965, magna cum laude) at Howard University and his M.A. (1966) and Ph.D. (1968) from the University of California at Los Angeles. In addition to writing, he taught in the English and the Afro-American Studies Departments of the University of Virginia, as well as Yale, Cornell, and Haverford College. Since 1974, he has taught at the University of Pennsylvania (UP), where he was given an endowed chair in 1982. Starting in 1986, Baker directed UP's Center for the Study of Black Literature and Culture. In 1999, he left UP to become the Susan Fox and George D. Beisher Professor of English and African and African American Studies. In addition to numerous other honors and awards, in 1992, Baker's peers honored him as the first African-American president of the exalted Modern Language Association (MLA). In 2003, the MLA awarded him the Hubbell Medal, the American Literature Section's award for lifetime achievement in American Literary Studies.

In the spring of 2006, Baker became embroiled in an incident in which white members of the Duke lacrosse team were accused of raping a black female entertainer. The charge was followed by hasty prosecution, many wild accusations, and lots of scurrilous blogging. In the fall of 2006, Baker left Duke to be welcomed as Distinguished University Professor and Professor of English at Vanderbilt University. In the spring of 2007, the North Carolina Attorney General dropped all charges, denouncing the local prosecutor and aiding in his disbarment. Many scholars have had similarly harsh responses either to Baker or to those who disparaged his handling of the situation.

REFERENCES: *EBLG. OC20LE. TtW. WDAA.* Awkward, Michael, in *A.CAAL* and *OCAAL.* Berube, Michael. "Hybridity in the Center: An Interview with Houston A. Baker, Jr." *African American Review.* 26.4 (Winter 1992) p. 547. From *Literature Resource Center.* Feldman, Keith, in *GEAAL. W. Wiki.* Jeffords, Susan, in *MAC-55-88.* //alsmla.org/HMBaker.htm. Patti, Nicholas S., in *BB. CAO-04. MWEL.* //encyclopedia.jrank.org/articles/pages/4108/Baker-Houston-A-Jr-1943.html. //sitemason.vanderbilt.edu/site/iGxZW8. //www.npr.org/templates/story/story.php?storyId=89434473, *News & Notes,* April 7, 2008. //www.phillwebb.net/regions/USA/Baker/Baker.htm. //www.us.oup.com/us/catalog/general/subject/LiteratureEnglish/AmericanLiterature/AfricanAmerican/~~/dmlldz11c2EmY2k9OTc4MDE5NTA4NDI5MA==. //www.vanderbilt.edu/news/releases/2006/5/25/five-prominent-african-american-literature-scholars-to-move-to-vanderbilt-hortense-spillers-houston-baker-among-new-hires. Amazon.com. *EB-BH-CD.*

Baldwin, James Arthur (né Jones)
8/2/1924–12/1/1987
Novels, plays, poems, short stories, essays, juvenile literature

When young Jimmy's mother, Emma Berdis Jones, married factory worker and itinerant evangelical preacher David Baldwin, Jimmy was just a toddler. David gave Jimmy his surname, but he never gave him his love, affection, or even his respect. Although Jimmy didn't know the underlying reason for his stepfather's scorn until years later, his stepfather always made it clear that he thought Jimmy was marked by the devil: a puny, ugly, and loathsome child. David also made sure Jimmy knew that he far preferred Jimmy's eight younger (step-)siblings over him; only later did he find out that his father treated him like a bastard because he considered him one.

In this harsh home environment, whenever Jimmy was free of household chores and child-care duties, he escaped into literature, borrowing heavily from the public libraries near him in Harlem. His love of learning and of reading were reinforced at school, where he found encouragement to write and to read further. At Frederick Douglass Junior High School, one of his teachers (and the advisor to the literary club he belonged to) was **Countee Cullen**. Cullen further stimulated Jimmy Baldwin's interest in literature and in writing. There, Jimmy edited the school's *Douglass Pilot* newspaper, to which he also contributed a short story, some sketches, and some editorials. At De Witt Clinton High School, he coedited the school's *Magpie* newspaper, to which he contributed short stories.

Between ages 14 and 17, Baldwin also embraced religion with great fervor, serving as a teen preacher at the Fireside Pentecostal Assembly, a storefront church in Harlem. Although his stepfather had showed him the harsh, punitive side of religion, Mother Horn, an evangelist leader of the assembly, showed him the warmth and affection of Christian love. During this time, Baldwin developed his rhetorical style and his flair for swaying human emotions with his words, and he gained a large following of devout listeners. He also read the Bible intensively and followed the church's admonitions to abstain entirely from worldly pleasures. By his late teens, however, the burgeoning hormones and life forces of the young man led him to abandon his mission and turn to literature as the source of his greatest passion.

After Baldwin graduated from high school (in 1942), he fled from his stepfather's home in Harlem and took various jobs, including a well-paid construction job in New Jersey, where he confronted a brand of racism he had not known previously in Harlem. In the summer of 1943, within 24 hours, his stepfather died in a mental hospital, and a huge riot erupted in Harlem. These events spurred him to leave his stable, but unpleasant job in New Jersey and move to Greenwich Village, determined to start his career in literature. Although he still had to earn a living in various war-related industries during the day, he worked on writing his first novel at night and on the weekends.

In the winter of 1944-1945, Baldwin met his mentor, **Richard Wright**, whom he had admired since high school. Wright soon recognized Baldwin's budding talent and recommended him for the Eugene F. Saxton Memorial Trust Award, Baldwin's first professional recognition of his talent. This award helped pave the way for his first published essay in the *Nation*, which was soon followed by essays, reviews, short stories, and other articles in the *Nation* and other publications.

Meanwhile, Baldwin continued to work on his first novel. The work was progressing *very* slowly, in part because Baldwin needed to work out his thoughts and feelings about his own sexual and racial identity. He even considered marrying a woman at this time, and the couple made wedding plans. In 1948, he nixed the engagement and firmly acknowledged his homosexuality; all of his subsequent intimate relationships were homosexual, although he occasionally chose bisexual partners. That year, he was also granted a Rosenwald Fellowship, with which he bought a one-way ticket to France, leaving the country of his birth November 11, planning never to return.

In France, although he still encountered race problems, he found much greater acceptance as an African-American homosexual writer than he had in America. There, his friends included fellow African-American expatriate **Richard Wright**, American writers Saul Bellow and Truman Capote, and French writers Jean-Paul Sartre and Simone de Beauvoir. By 1952, he had also formed a long-lasting intimate relationship with Swiss native Lucien Happersberger. By this time, however, the

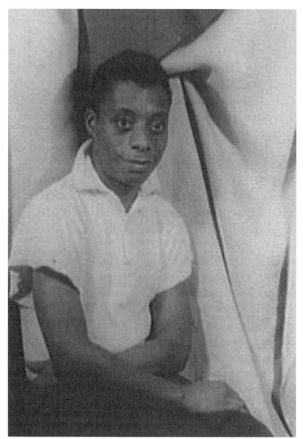

James Baldwin

friendship between Baldwin and Wright had ruptured, and the two never reconciled.

Until the late 1950s, Baldwin remained in Paris, but when the civil-rights movement heated up in the United States, Baldwin felt beckoned home, to participate actively in the struggle. He spent most of his time in the United States through most of the 1960s, dividing his time between the movement and his writing. (He even divided his interests geographically on occasion, living with the family of white writer William Styron in 1961 and with James Meredith and Medgar Evers in 1963.) Throughout this time, his writings eloquently elevated the discussion of civil and political rights, stirringly provoking his readers to reconsider their views on race in America. Following the murders of his friends Medgar Evers, **Martin Luther King, Jr.**, and **Malcolm X**, he fled to France again. During the remaining years of his life, he spent most of his time in France but often returned to the United States for extended periods. When here, Baldwin lectured and taught at various colleges across the United States (e.g., University of California at Berkeley, Ohio's Bowling Green State University, and the University of Massachusetts at Amherst).

Baldwin's writings included plays, novels, short stories, poems, and a children's book, as well as essays. In the middle of the twentieth century, Baldwin was one of the few African-American playwrights to have had more than one of his plays produced on Broadway. *Amen Corner*, his semiautobiographical work about a female evangelist, was first produced at Howard University (1954-1954) and later made it to the Broadway stage, where it was modestly successful. *Blues for Mr. Charlie*, inspired by the outrageous lynching of Emmett Till and other African Americans in the deep South, reached Broadway in 1964 and received mixed reviews. Baldwin's other plays included *Woman at the Well* (1972) and *One Day When I Was Lost* (1972).

Baldwin's poems were collected in *Jimmy's Blues: Selected Poems* (1983); his short stories were collected in *Going to Meet the Man* (1965); and his children's book was *Little Man, Little Man: A Story of Childhood* (1977, with Y. Cazac). Baldwin's best-known works, however, were his novels and his essay collections. The first of his novels, which was so long in the making, was *Go Tell It on the Mountain* (1953). Recall that he first started this novel in 1944, and he didn't finish it until 1952, while he was staying in Lucien's hometown in Switzerland. During this time, its title changed from "Crying Holy" to "In My Father's House" to its final version. Soon after Alfred Knopf published it (in 1953), it was widely acclaimed as brilliant, and many critics still consider it Baldwin's finest work.

The main action of the first section of the book is compressed into a single day, the fourteenth birthday of a preacher's stepson. Through this compression, readers clearly see how the cruel preacher abuses all his family members, particularly his teenage stepson. In the middle section of the book, which takes place during a midnight prayer meeting, Baldwin uses flashbacks to share with readers the background that led to this day, showing the personal history of the preacher and his wife. In the final section, the teenager experiences surrealistic visions, calling him to preach the gospel. Over time, the young man realizes that his conversion experience was not genuine, and he comes to believe that his hope for salvation is his emerging love for an older teenager, Brother Elisha.

Baldwin's next novel, *Giovanni's Room* (1956), frankly confronts issues of race and sexuality, so Knopf refused to publish it; the book was first published in Britain until an American publisher (Dial Press) was willing to publish it. The book is written from the viewpoint of a white American expatriate living in Paris, who is contemplating his engagement to a young woman and searching for his own sexual identity. While his girlfriend is away in Spain, he becomes embroiled in a homosexual love affair with a young Italian bartender (Giovanni). Because of his own homophobia, however, when his girlfriend joins him in Paris, he rejects Giovanni and makes plans to wed. When his girlfriend discovers him in a gay bar with a sailor, she

breaks off the engagement and flees home to America. Meanwhile, a desperate Giovanni has been fired by the bar owner, who then offers to hire him back in exchange for sexual relations. After the bar owner fails to follow through on his promise, Giovanni murders him and is later convicted and about to be executed for murdering the bar owner. The protagonist is left to contemplate his role in Giovanni's plight, as well as his own sexual identity.

Although Baldwin worried that he might be categorized as a homosexual African-American writer, he didn't shun issues of sexuality and race—or controversy—in his next novel, *Another Country* (1962). The book included a variety of white and black characters; settings in Greenwich Village (New York), Alabama, and Paris; and a loosely structured plot that wove back and forth across time. Nonetheless, the lyricality of his narrative made this book, too, a bestseller. Baldwin's subsequent novels, chiefly centered in New York, are less widely acclaimed and have been criticized for being somewhat repetitive and argumentative. These novels include *Tell Me How Long the Train's Been Gone* (1968), about two African-American brothers living in the ghetto, who face moral dilemmas during the civil-rights era; *If Beale Street Could Talk* (1974), written from the perspective of an unwed teenager who is pregnant with the baby of a young African American who has been unjustly imprisoned; and *Just Above My Head* (1979), about a homosexual gospel singer and his brother (published in France as the Prix Femina-nominated *Harlem Quartet*, 1987).

Baldwin's nonfiction includes several essay collections and a pair of conversations: *A Rap on Race* (1971) with European-American anthropologist Margaret Mead and *A Dialogue* (1973) with African-American poet **Nikki Giovanni**. His collections of essays, often written with the third-person plural voice, were probably the works that most firmly established him in the heart and soul of American literature—each one sold more than a million copies on publication. They certainly provoked thought and stirred controversy. Baldwin's critically acclaimed *Notes of a Native Son* (1955) and *Nobody Knows My Name: More Notes of a Native Son* (1961) gave a nod to his former mentor, **Richard Wright** (whose 1940 novel *Native Son* was probably his most celebrated work). Both works, and especially the second of these, eloquently indicted racism in America.

Baldwin's best-selling essay collection *The Fire Next Time* (1963) included essays on his experiences of abuse (by unscrupulous neighbors and by the police) as a teenager, his encounters with the Black Muslims, and his views on the civil-rights struggle. The title for his book came from the words of a spiritual Baldwin knew well, which alluded to impending catastrophe. In Baldwin's view, the racial tensions of the 1960s seemed destined to erupt in violence, and the riots that burst forth across the nation during the late 1960s seemed to confirm Baldwin's warnings. Baldwin himself, however, had concluded his book with hope for blacks and whites to work together to end racial hatred and avert this disaster.

Baldwin's subsequent writings included *Nothing Personal* (1964), with photographs by Richard Avedon, a high-school chum; *No Name in the Street* (1972), in which he wrote, "We are responsible for the world in which we find ourselves, if only because we are the only sentient force which can change it"; *The Devil Finds Work* (1976), addressing racial stereotypes and the history of African Americans in the movies; *Remember This House* (1980), his memoirs, mixed with biographical sketches of **Martin Luther King, Jr.**, Malcolm X, and Medgar Evers, assassinated leaders in the struggle for civil rights; *The Evidence of Things Not Seen* (1985), about the tragic serial murders of African-American boys in Atlanta, Georgia, in the late 1970s and early 1980s; and *The Price of a Ticket: Collected Non-Fiction 1948-1985* (1985), a collection of all previous essays, as well as some new ones.

Never one to shy away from lashing out at European Americans for their racist practices, Baldwin also never hesitated to express his views when they conflicted with the views being touted by African Americans of his day. Starting with his essay "Everybody's Protest Novel" (1949), Baldwin managed to irk many fellow African Americans for his distinctive views. Many of his essays provoked similar heated controversy among African-American political leaders.

When Baldwin died, he was still working on two never-completed projects: a play (*The Welcome Table*) and a biography of **Martin Luther King, Jr.** He died in France, shortly after the French government had named him a commander of the Legion of Honor, France's highest civilian award. At his memorial service, a who's who of African-American writers (e.g., **Maya Angelou**, **Amiri Baraka**, **Toni Morrison**, **Juan Williams**) sang his praises and credited him with having profoundly influenced their work. Among the many other writers whom he fostered are **Quincy Troupe, Suzan Lori-Parks, bell hooks**, and Nigerian author Chinua Achebe. In 2005, the U.S. Postal Service acknowledged his importance with a first-class postage stamp bearing his image on the front and a brief biography on the back of the peeling paper.

Just a few of the pearls he shared with all of us include "Children have never been very good at listening to their elders, but they have never failed to imitate them." (*OTD*, 6/26), and "You think your pain and your heartbreak are unprecedented in the history of the world, but then you read. It was books that taught me that the things that tormented me most were the very things that connected me with all the people who were alive, or who had ever been alive" (cited on p. 97 of *Pearls of Wisdom: A Harvest of Quotations from All Ages*). Perhaps the most telling quote of his is the goal he stated in 1955: "I want to be an honest man and a good writer." He succeeded at both.

REFERENCES: *1TESK. AA:PoP. AANB. AAW:AAPP. BAL-1-P. BWA. EBLG. EGW. OC2OLE. PGAA. RG20. WDAA.* Achebe, Chinua (1989), in *James Baldwin: The Legacy* (Ed. Quincy Troupe). NY: Simon & Schuster. Rpt. in Hunter, Jeffrey W. (Ed.). (2000). *Contemporary Literary Criticism* (Vol. 127. pp. 213-217). Detroit: Gale Group. From *Literature Resource Center.* Canfield, Rob, in *T-CAD-3rd.* Harris, Trudier, in *COCAAL* and *OCAAL.* Jones, Jacqueline C., in *ANSWWII-7th.* Kinnamon, Keneth, in *AW:ACLB-79.* McKay, Nellie Y., in *WB-99.* Miller, D. Quentin, in *B. BB. BCE. CAO-02. CE. CLCS. CPW. GEAAL. GLB. LFCC-07. QB. USHC. W. W2B. Wiki.* Pratt, Louis H., in "Author's Works. James Baldwin," *TUSAS-290.* Roberts, John W., in *AAFW-55-84.* Robinson, Lisa Clayton, in *EA-99.* Standley, Fred L., in *ANSWWII-1st* and in *T-CAD-1st.* Van Leer, David, in *AAW-1991.* //www.americanwriters.org/writers/baldwin.asp. //www.clpgh.org/books/booklists/africanamericanfiction.html. Abel, Joanne, Nancy Blood, and Phyllis Rogers, "African-American Fiction Writers," //0-web.ebscohost.com.dbpcosdcsgt.co.san-diego.ca.us/ novelist/detail?vid=76&hid=6&sid=02bf6a41-8618-414c-abf5-13f2 2fd219a5%40sessionmgr7&bdata=JnNpdGU9bm92ZWxpc3QtbGl2Z Q%3d%3d. *EB-BH-CD.* G-97.

Baltimore Afro-American
1892–

When it first appeared in 1892, the *Baltimore Afro-American* newspaper was published as a four-page sheet to advertise the church and community enterprises of Reverend William Alexander. John H. Murphy bought the paper for $200 from Alexander in 1910, and the paper merged with the *Ledger.* Murphy worked at the *Afro-American Ledger* (later, the *Afro-American*) after 1917, and the circulation grew from 8,500 to 79,952 in 1937. By then it was the largest-selling Black paper on the eastern seaboard. When Murphy died in 1922, his sons (*see* **Carl Murphy**) assumed leadership of the company and began to print editions in Washington, D. C., and Philadelphia in the 1930s. The *Baltimore Afro-American*, along with the *Houston Informer* and several others, has been published continuously for more than 100 years. It is the oldest family-owned Black newspaper in America. During its peak years between the two world wars, the newspaper printed 13 separate editions from New Jersey to South Carolina.

REFERENCES: *EAACH*, Vol. 1. Kellner, Bruce (Ed.). 1987. *The Harlem Renaissance: A Historical Dictionary for the Era.* New York: Methuen. Mack, Kibibi Voloria (Consulting Ed.). 1987. *The African American Encyclopedia Supplement* (Vol. 7). New York: Marshall Cavendish. Salzman, Jack, David Lionel Smith, and **Cornel West**. 1996. *Encyclopedia of African-American Culture and History* (Vol. 1). New York: Simon and Schuster. —Lisa Bahlinger

Bambara, Toni Cade (née Toni Cade)
3/25/1939–12/9/1995
Anthologies, short stories, novels, essays, scripts

After introducing Toni to the delights of the Apollo Theater, Toni's father left her and her brother Walter in her mother's capable hands. Helen Cade encouraged both her children to behave well, to think clearly, to read read read, to learn about African-American history, to tell stories, to write, and to take time "to wonder, to dawdle, to daydream" (p. 28, *BWWW*).

In 1959, when Toni graduated from Queens College (B.A. in theater arts and English literature), she published her first short story, "Sweet Town," and started winning awards for her fiction and her essays. From 1959 to 1965, she worked in various social-welfare positions, taking a little time off in 1961 to travel and study acting and mime in Italy and France.

After she earned her master's degree in African-American literature from City College of New York, CCNY (now CUNY) hired her to teach English and theater arts in the Search for Education, Elevation, Knowledge (SEEK) program there. From then on, she taught literature and theater arts at various colleges and universities—in addition to offering countless writers' workshops, readings, and lectures at prisons, museums, and so on. During the 1960s, Toni also started publishing short stories and essays in various magazines, newspapers, and journals (e.g., *New York Times, Ms., Essence*).

For Toni, 1970 was a highly productive—and reproductive—year. First, *Black Woman*, her stridently pro-civil rights, feminist anthology of poems, essays, and short stories, was published. *Black Woman* included consciousness-raising works by **Nikki Giovanni, Alice Walker, Audre Lorde**, and **Paule Marshall**, as well as pieces by some of her SEEK students. Ever since, many professors of literature, women's studies, and black studies have urged their students to read *Black Woman*. Although Toni's surname for *Black Woman* was Cade, she soon legally adopted the surname Bambara, taken from a signature on a sketchbook she found in her grandmother's trunk. In addition, Toni's only daughter, Karma, was born that year. Regarding how Bambara managed her personal life and her professional life, she said, "I have no shrewd advice to offer developing writers about this business of snatching time and space to work. . . . except to say that it will cost you something. Anything of value is going to cost you something" (p. 16, *BWWW*).

In 1971, Bambara produced *Tales and Stories for Black Folks*, which included stories by **Langston Hughes, Ernest Gaines**, and **Alice Walker**, as well as stories by her students. She compiled the volume chiefly to promote the study of cultural history, black folk traditions, and the richness of black English among African-American high school and college students. As with *Black Woman*, she succeeded in reaching a wide readership.

In 1972, Bambara published *Gorilla, My Love*, her first collection of her own short stories, earning rave reviews right away and the American Book Award in 1981. Of the 15 stories in the collection, 3 were original to this volume, and 12 had been written (and previously published) between 1950 and 1970. At that time, when stories included female characters, the females were usually helpless victims needing male rescuers—at best, females aided the male heroes. In contrast, most of Bambara's stories affectionately feature feisty teenage girls who tell their own stories, using their own African-American rhythms and styles of speech. These stories emphasize the strength and fortitude of memorable African Americans who learn about themselves, their families, and their communities. Bambara's stories also accent women's *interdependence* more than their independence, as her female characters support and nurture one another.

Bambara's trips to Cuba (1973) and to Vietnam (1975) broadened her view of interdependence and mutual support, fostering her increasing commitment to social activism and community organizing. The trips also deepened her ties between her writing and her sociopolitical beliefs and practices. "[In Cuba,] I learned what **Langston Hughes** and others . . . had been teaching for years—that writing is a legitimate way, an important way, to participate in the empowerment of the community that names me" (pp. 41-42, *BWW*). Her second collection of her own short stories, *The Sea Birds Are Still Alive* (1977), reflected both her cross-cultural experiences and her intense interest in community action. During the late 1970s, Bambara manifested the link between social organization and writing by cofounding the Southern Collective of African American Writers and participating in various other writers' guilds and organizations.

Bambara's first novel, *The Salt Eaters* (1980), is actually sort of a nonlinear patchwork of short stories about overlapping characters. The central character is Velma Henry, a burned-out community organizer, and the narrative thread tying the disparate pieces together is Velma's recovery from a suicide attempt. The community she had struggled to save, in turn, rallies to aid her recovery, offering her everything from traditional folk remedies through the spiritual guidance of the elders to modern medical miracles. Many critics disdained Bambara's forward and backward movement through time and space and her diverse array of characters and settings. On the other hand, many readers have praised her deft handling of dialogue and her richly idiomatic use of language. Among those who have prized her work is **Toni Morrison**, the Nobel-winning Random House editor who shepherded Bambara's novel through publication. Apparently, Morrison was not alone in her appraisal because the book won the 1981 American Book Award and the 1981 Langston Hughes Society Award, as well as additional awards.

Among Bambara's other novels are *If Blessing Comes* (1987), which addresses the tragic serial murders of Atlantan boys, and *Raymond's Run* (1990). Her final novel, published posthumously in 1997, was given the preliminary title of *Ground Cover*. In recognition of her overall contribution to literature, she received a 1981 National Endowment for the Arts Literature Grant.

In the 1980s, Bambara returned to her interest in the performing arts by spending time in film and video making, both as a writer and as a narrator. She wrote nine screenplays, including *Tar Baby,* based on the novel by her friend and editor Toni Morrison. She also worked on various television documentaries and participated in adapting several of her short stories to film.

Bambara's most memorable contributions have remained her short stories, including her many contributions to feminist anthologies. Her essays and short stories continue to be widely anthologized, both in the United States and in European and Asian publications. She clearly succeeded in achieving her primary goal: "I work to tell the truth about people's lives; I work to celebrate struggle, to applaud the tradition of struggle in our community, to bring to center stage all those characters, just ordinary folks on the block, who've been waiting in the wings, characters we thought we had to ignore" (p. 18, *BWWW*). Of her writing, she observed, "Writing was/is an act of discovery" (p. 19, *BWWW*); her readers might answer that to read her writing offers an opportunity for discovery, as well.

REFERENCES: *AANB. BASS. BI. BW:AA. BWW. BWWW. EBLG. MWEL. NAAAL. OC20LE. RT. TWT.* Byerman, Keith E., in *OCWW.* Cook, Michael, and Linda S. Watts, in *GEAAL.* Deck, Alice A., *AAW-55-85:DPW.* Doerksen, Teri Ann, in *ASSWSWWII-2nd.* Glickman, Simon, in *BB. CAO-03. CLCS. MWEL.* Stanford, Ann Folwell, in *OCAAL* and *COCAAL. B. W. //www.jimcrowhistory.org/scripts/jimcrow/women.cgi?state=New%20York. EB-98. G-97.*

Banks, Leslie Esdaile (aka L.A. Banks, Leslie)
12/11/1959–

Fiction, including romance, crime/suspense, vampire and other paranormal/fantasy, nonfiction—how to write romance

A mother of four with a masters in fine arts, Banks has developed a rich fantasy life. As "Leslie Esdaile," she has written than more a dozen romance novels, including *Sundance* (1996), *Slow Burn* (1997), *Love Notes* (2001), *Love Lessons* (2001), *Love Potions* (2002), *River of the Soul* (2001) and its sequel *Still Waters Run Deep* (2002), *Tomorrow's Promise* (2002), *Through the Storm* (2002), *Sister Got Game* (2004), *Keepin' It Real* (2005), *Take Me There* (2006), and *Better Than* (2008). Having shown herself as an expert, Esdaile also wrote *How to Write a Romance for the New Market* (1999).

As Leslie E. Banks, she wrote her "Soul Food" romance novels, *Soul Food: For Better, For Worse* (2002), *Soul Food: Through Thick and Thin* (2003), and *Soul Food: No Mountain High Enough* (2003).

As Leslie Esdaile Banks, she has written several crime/suspense novels, including *Betrayal of the Trust* (2004), *Blind Trust* (2005), *Shattered Trust* (2006), and *No Trust* (2007). She also wrote additional crime/suspense novels as "L. A. Banks," in the Scarface series, *Scarface, The Beginning, Volume 1* (2006) and *Scarface, Point of No Return, Volume 2* (2007).

L. A. Banks also authored dozens of paranormal/fantasy books. Her dozen-book Vampire Huntress Legend series featuring Damali Richards includes *Minion* (Book 1) (2003), *The Awakening* (Book 2) (2004), *The Hunted* (Book 3) (2004), *The Bitten* (Book 4) (2005), *The Forbidden* (Book 5) (2005), *The Damned* (Book 6) (2006), *The Forsaken* (Book 7) (2006), *The Wicked* (Book 8) (2007), *The Cursed* (Book 9) (2007), *The Darkness* (Book 10) (2008), *The Shadows* (Book 11) (2008), *The Thirteenth* (Book 12) (2009). Her Crimson Moon series started with *Bad Blood: A Crimson Moon Novel* (Book 1) (2008).

She has also written numerous romance, horror, and suspense short stories, which have been widely anthologized and published in periodicals.

REFERENCES: *CAO-05. Wiki. Amazon.com.*

FURTHER READING: LaFrance, Michell, in *GEAAL.*

Banneker, Benjamin
11/9/1731–10/9/1806

Almanacs, letters, essays, short narratives, poems; astronomer, mathematician, inventor, naturalist, amateur engineer

Although his maternal grandmother had taught him to read and write, Benjamin had no formal schooling until he was about 12 years old, when a Quaker opened a one-room school for boys of all races. Benjamin quickly mastered mathematics and various other subjects. During this time, Banneker adopted the plain clothing, the thinking, and many of the manners of Quakers.

While improving his mind, Banneker continued to help his family thrive, performing farm chores and making occasional trips to the coast to sell his family's tobacco crop. On one such trip, when he was about 22 years old, he met a man with a pocket watch. Banneker was so obviously captivated by it that the owner gave him the watch. Banneker spent quite a while taking apart and putting back together the watch. He then obtained a journal with a picture of a clock, a book on geometry, and Isaac Newton's *Principia*. Armed with these print materials, his own observations, a pocketknife, and some wood, he spent his free time for the next two years building his own clock, fashioning every single part from wood. By the time he was 24, he completed his clock—one of the first clocks ever built entirely in America, of American-made parts—and his clock continued to tick accurate time until it was destroyed, a few days after his death.

When Banneker was about 28 years old, he inherited his father's farm and tried to gain the hand (and the freedom) of his beloved Anola, a neighbor's slave. Through a series of misfortunes, he was prevented from doing so, nearly dying in the attempt, and a disheartened Anola drowned herself. Banneker never again found anyone whom he wished to marry.

In 1772, when Banneker was about 41 years old, another key Quaker entered his life: Andrew Ellicott and his sons moved into the area, and Ellicott and Banneker struck up a close friendship. During this time, Ellicott frequently loaned his astronomy books, telescope, and some other scientific instruments to Banneker, and when Ellicott died, he bequeathed these things to Banneker. As a farmer, Banneker had always been vitally interested in the night sky, but with Ellicott's books and telescope, Banneker the mathematician and farmer became a dedicated astronomer.

Once his interest in astronomy soared, he sold his farm to the Ellicotts, in exchange for a modest annuity and use of his cabin home and workshop. He then usually slept by day and watched the stars by night. When he accurately predicted a solar eclipse, his prestige as an astronomer was established. In 1792 (when he was 60), through contacts with abolitionist printers, he published the first of a series of almanacs, which prominently featured the *ephemerides* (astronomical tables) he had calculated. He also included weather forecasts for the year (vital for farmers), sunrise/sunset times, a Chesapeake Bay tide table, a list of holidays, lists of preventive medicines and of curative remedies, recipes, poems, essays, proverbs, and other practical information for farmers. Banneker didn't author all of the items in the almanac (other than the ephemerides), but he did write some of the verses and short narratives.

Banneker's almanacs were widely read throughout the middle states, even gaining him international recognition. Banneker took advantage of this popularity by including his opinions on slavery and racism, as well as his proposals for the betterment of society. For instance, his 1792 almanac included a proposal for establishing a national Department of Peace, instead of a Department of War. His proposal also included suggestions for establishing free schools for all children "in every city, village and township of the United States," and for abolishing capital punishment.

Banneker also wrote more narrowly focused tracts on various naturalistic subjects, such as a dissertation on bees and an insightful paper postulating the 17-year cycles of locust plagues. Other than his almanacs, however, perhaps the most well-known document written by Banneker was his letter to Thomas Jefferson, addressing Jefferson's appalling unwillingness to apply the sentiments of the Declaration of Independence to all people—or at least to all men. An excerpt highlights Banneker's message: "One universal Father hath given being to us all; and he hath not only made us all of one flesh, but he hath also, without partiality, afforded us all the same sensations and endowed us all with the same faculties; and that however variable we may be in society or religion, however diversified in situation or color, we are all in the same family and stand in the same relation to Him. . . . I freely and cheerfully acknowledge that I am of the African race and in that color which is natural to them of the deepest dye; . . . . Suffer me to recall to your mind that time in which the arms and tyranny of the British Crown were exerted with every powerful effort in order to reduce you to a state of servitude. This, Sir, was a time when you clearly saw into the injustice of a state of slavery and in which you had apprehensions of the horrors of its conditions."

Banneker accompanied the letter with a manuscript of his almanac, to show Jefferson that he had indeed authored it. Jefferson's response was rather obtuse, agreeing with Banneker that he had espoused the values of freedom and that Banneker clearly had great intellectual power, but still managing to weasel out of acknowledging his own blatant hypocrisy in continuing to endorse slavery despite his protestations regarding the equal rights of all "men."

In Banneker's modest cabin home and workshop, he entertained visiting scholars and other distinguished scientists and artists. On his death, just a few days before his seventy-fifth birthday, he was honored in the French Academy of Sciences and the English Parliament, but in this country, he was honored only privately, by those who knew him or knew of him. He left his scientific instruments, his books, and his correspondence with Jefferson to George Ellicott, the son of Andrew, who had so fortuitously helped him to lift his eyes heavenward. Unfortunately, two days after his funeral, his humble home burned to the ground, and his wooden clock, as well as most of his other writings, went up in smoke.

REFERENCES: *AA:PoP. AANB. BAL-1-P. BF:2000. BPSI. BWA. EBLG. SMKC.* Born, Brad S., in *COCAAL* and *OCAAL.* Engel, Bill, in *B. BCE. GEAAL. HD. W2B. Wiki.* Nash, Gary B., in *USHC. E-97. EB-98. G-95.*

Baraka, Amiri (né Everett LeRoy Jones; pseudonym: LeRoi Jones)
10/7/1934–
Poems, novels, plays, essays, anthologies, editorials

Amiri Baraka's activities and attitudes seem to be countercultural in any age, but they didn't start out that way. When writing in the late 1950s and early 1960s, Baraka used the name LeRoi Jones and was basically apolitical. Although Baraka wrote his poetry in the vernacular language of ordinary people, he did not use his art to further any political ideals or principles. The general political activism within the United States and a trip to Cuba changed the tone of Baraka's work in the 1960s and 1970s. Here Baraka integrated his art with his political views, helped initiate the **Black Arts Movement**, and founded the Black Arts Repertory Theatre-School. Since that time, Baraka has revised his politics, taught in universities, and continued to write and comment on society, culture, and poetry.

Born in Newark, New Jersey, Baraka apparently had an ordinary middle-class upbringing. His mother, Anna Lois Russ Jones, was a social worker, and his father, Coyt LeRoy Jones, was a postal worker. LeRoy was a good student in high school and attended first Rutgers and then Howard University, eventually flunking out of Howard. Jones then enlisted in the United States Air Force in 1954, where he served until receiving a dishonorable discharge, reportedly for submitting some of his poetry to what were considered communist publications.

After leaving the Air Force in 1957, Jones moved to Greenwich Village in New York City, where he began cultivating and using his writing talents more fully. He associated with and earned the respect of well-known artists in the area, including Allen Ginsburg. There, Jones met his first wife, Hettie Cohen, a white Jewish woman, and married her in 1958. Together, they edited *Yugen*, a literary journal that sought to publish works written by struggling authors.

Jones was invited to visit Cuba in 1960 because he was considered an important "Negro writer." This visit, along with the assassination of **Malcolm X**, the black-power movement, and the Civil Rights Act, altered Jones's view of poetry, politics, and the black community. Jones began to realize that his poetry and other writings could become vehicles for political views and could serve as catalysts for social and political change. Consequently, Jones started taking an active interest in promoting black nationalism in the African-American community.

Jones initiated the **Black Arts Movement**, encompassing the years 1965-1975. During this artistic and cultural movement, many African-American artists produced works calling for a rejection of white society and cultural norms and pride in African-American heritage

and culture. This new political attitude struck Jones on a personal level, as well. He divorced his first wife, moved to Harlem and later Newark, and committed himself to raising a new level of consciousness within the black community. This is also when Jones changed his name to Amiri Baraka and remarried, this time to a African-American woman, Sylvia Robinson (later known as Amina Baraka), with whom he eventually had five children.

Over time, Baraka decided that black nationalism was pandering to and imitating the white culture and power structure and therefore betraying black culture. Baraka's political awareness increased. He had so far discovered that neither apolitical stances nor black nationalism would bring about the society he envisioned. This observation pushed Baraka to make yet another ideological shift to a Marxist-Leninist position. This shift led Baraka to a vocal and public disagreement with controversial filmmaker **Spike Lee** about the making of **Malcolm X**, one of Lee's films.

To read Baraka's work in chronological order is to witness the personal and political evolution that he has experienced as a black man in the United States. Some scholars liken his personal political changes as a reflection of the changes taking place within the larger black community. Baraka's first collection of poetry is *Preface to a Twenty Volume Suicide Note* (1961). This early poetry evokes a sense of jazz with its off-beat rhythms and gives hints of Baraka's emerging political views.

Baraka's first drama, Obie Award-winning *The Dutchman* (1964), is an overtly political one-act play condemning racist oppression and startling audiences into consciousness. Baraka's semiautobiographical novel, *The System of Dante's Hell* (1965), further raises the issue of trying to reconcile the conflicts inherent in African Americans in white America. Robert J. Forman notes that "Western culture attracts [Baraka] intellectually, yet it morally damns him," that he remains "somewhere between black and white cultures, accepted by neither and estranged from both."

Other poetry by Baraka includes *The Dead Lecturer*, 1964; *Black Magic: Sabotage-Target Study-Black Art: Collected Poetry*, 1961-1967, 1969; *It's Nation Time*, 1970; *In Our Terribleness: Some Elements and Meaning Black Style*, 1970; *Spirit Reach*, 1972; *Hard Facts*, 1975; *Poetry for the Advanced* and *Selected Poetry of Amiri Baraka/LeRoi Jones*, both in 1979; *Reggae or Not!* 1981; *Transbluesency: The Selected Poems of Amiri Baraka/LeRoi Jones (1961-1995)*, 1995; and *Funk Lore: New Poems (1984-1995)*, 1996.

Other works by Baraka include dramas, *The Slave*, 1964; *Slave Ship: An Historical Pageant, The Baptism*, and *The Toilet*, all in 1967; and *Four Black Revolutionary Plays*, 1969. His other writings include *Home: Social Essays*, 1966; *Raise Race Rays Raze*, 1972; *Daggers and Javelins:*

Essays 1974-1979, 1984; *The Autobiography of LeRoi Jones/ Amiri Baraka*, 1984; and *The Music: Reflections on Jazz and Blues*, 1987.

Throughout his work, Baraka often seems like a man on a mission. He is a man who has something to say, a man who will have his say, and a man who will flatten, circumvent, or bypass any obstacles he finds—all the time creating a path for others to follow.

REFERENCES: *EBLG. NAAAL.* Ansen, D., & F. Chideya (1991), "The Battle for Malcolm X," *Newsweek, 118,* 9, pp. 52-55, *Magazine Academic Index Plus.* Brucker, Carl, "Dutchman," in *MAAL.* Draper, James P. (Ed.) (1992), "Amiri Baraka 1934-," in *BLC-1.* Forman, Robert J., "System of Dante's Hell," *Masterpieces of Azine Academic Index Plus.* Lacey, Henry C., "Baraka, Amiri," and "*Dutchman*," in *COCAAL* and *OCAAL.* Nazareth, Peter (1997), "World Literature in Review: English," *World Literature Today, 97,* 1, pp. 154-156. Popkin, Michael (Compiler and Ed.) (1978), "Baraka, Amiri," *Modern Black Writers,* New York: Ungar. Serafin, Steven R. (Compiler and Ed.) (1995), "Amiri Baraka," *Modern Black Writers: Supplement,* New York: Continuum. Zlogar, Laura Weiss, "Poetry of Amiri Baraka," in *MAAL.* —Janet Hoover, with Diane Masiello (on *The Dutchman*)

Editor's note: Baraka won an Obie Award for *The Dutchman* (1964), which portrays a shocking symbolic confrontation between blacks and whites. A political activist as well as a political writer, his militancy toward white society grew, as evidenced by the content of two subsequent plays, *The Slave* (1964) and *The Toilet* (1964).

After teaching at New York's New School for Research (1961-1964), San Francisco State College 1966-1967), Yale University (1977-1978), and George Washington University (1978-1979), in 1980, he moved to SUNY-Stony Brook, where he taught in its Department of African (now Africana) Studies (as a full professor since 1985) until his retirement in 1999.

He attended Rutgers on a scholarship, transferred to Howard for greater affirmation of his budding cultural awareness, and became disheartened with the lack of political and cultural awareness there in the early 1950s. While stationed in Puerto Rico as the base librarian, he started book-discussion groups, had his poems published in such magazines as *The New Yorker,* and stocked a wide array of books, including Marx's *Communist Manifesto.* His discharge reacted to all of these activities. After his discharge, he found a home with writers of the Beat Generation.

Among numerous other awards and honors, Baraka was named New Jersey's poet laureate, 2002. A controversy surrounding his poem asserting Jewish complicity in the 9/11 attacks led to the New Jersey legislature dissolving the post in 2003.

REFERENCES: *AANB AAW:PV.* Baraka, Amiri, and D. H. Mclhem. (1990). "Amiri Baraka: Revolutionary Traditions." *Heroism in the New Black Poetry: Introductions and Interviews.* University Press of Kentucky.

Rpt. in Hunter, Jeffrey W., and Deborah A. Schmitt (Eds.). (1999). *Contemporary Literary Criticism* (Vol. 115, pp. 215-263). Detroit: Gale Group. From *Literature Resource Center.* Baraka, Amiri, and David Ossman. (1963). "An Interview." *The Sullen Art: Interviews by David Ossman with Modern American Poets.* Corinth Books. Rpt. in *CLCS.* Detroit: Gale, pp. 77-81. From *Literature Resource Center.* Brown, Lloyd W., "Chapter 1: LeRoi Jones/Amiri Baraka," and "Author's Works," in *TUSAS-383.* Carrell, David, in *AA. ATG. B. BCE. CE. GEAAL. Q. W. WT. Wiki.* Fischer, William C., in *AW:ACLB-81.* Gaffney, Floyd, in *AAW-55-85:DPW.* Gardner, Stephen, in *APSWWII-1.* Goldsworthy, Joan, and Christine Miner Minderovic, in *BB. MWEL.* Harris, William J., in *AAW-1991.* Hurst, Catherine Daniels, in *T-CAD-1st.* Jurek, Thom, *All Music Guide,* in *A.* Lacey, Henry C., in *CAO-08. CLCS. COCAAL. LFCC-07.* Miller, James A. "Amiri Baraka. The Beats: Literary Bohemians in Postwar America." Ann Charters (Ed.). (1983). *Dictionary of Literary Biography, Vol. 16.* Detroit: Gale Research. From *Literature Resource Center.* Salaam, Kalamu ya. "Amiri Baraka Analyzes How He Writes." *African American Review. 37.2-3* (Summer-Fall 2003) p. 211. From *Literature Resource Center.* Wilson, Ted, "Ted Wilson Interviews Amiri Baraka." *Black Renaissance/Renaissance Noire. 7.3* (Fall 2007) p. 8. From *Literature Resource Center.* //www.poets.org/poet.php/prmPID/445, Amiri Baraka.

Barber, Jesse Max
7/5/1878–9/20/1949
Essays, articles; journal editor, journalist

A journalist, Barber was the sole managing editor of *Voice of the Negro,* a literary journal founded in Atlanta in January 1904. Initially, the journal included works by both accommodationists (e.g., **Booker T. Washington**) and radical activists (e.g., **W. E. B. Du Bois**), but with Barber's guidance, it soon had a reputation for progressive thinking, publishing works by **Charles Chesnutt, John Hope, Pauline Hopkins,** Kelly Miller, **William Pickens,** and **Mary Church Terrell**. In it, Barber also published works by poets such as **James D. Corrothers, Paul Laurence Dunbar,** and **Georgia Douglas Johnson**.

REFERENCES: *AANB. EA-99.*

Barnes, Steven Emory
3/1/1952–
Science fiction, screenplays, blog

When Barnes is not writing, he's teaching others how to write (e.g., at the University of California, Los Angeles, 1989-1994; at his own Life Writing Workshops, since 1990). Barnes told an interviewer, "When I was 16, I decided I wanted to be a writer and I've been one ever since" (quoted in *CAO-03*).

Barnes has written several science-fiction books on his own: *Streetlethal* (1982), *Gorgon Child* (1989), *Firedance* (1993), his series about do-gooder martial-arts expert Aubry Knight; his stand-alone sci-fi books *Ride the*

Angry Land (1980), *The Kundalini Equation* (1986), *Blood Brothers* (1996), *Iron Shadows* (1998), and *Charisma* (2002); and his series about the *Great Sky Woman* (2006), with its sequel *Shadow Valley* (2009). Perhaps most intriguing are his Bilalistan/Insh'Allah series books *Lion's Blood: A Novel of Slavery and Freedom in an Alternate America* (2002), which won the 2003 Endeavour Award, and *Zulu Heart* (2003). Set in 1800s America, African-American Muslims enslave European-American Christians. Critics praised this exploration comparing and contrasting Islamic and Christian values.

Barnes also wrote a novelization of *Star Trek: Deep Space Nine*, as *Far Beyond the Stars* (1998, with Ira S. Behr and Hans Beimler) and contributed to an anthology for the series, *The Lives of Dax* (1999). In addition, he wrote *The New York Times* best-seller-listed *The Cestus Deception: A Clone War Novel* (2004; available in audio and Kindle format), for the other dominant sci-fi dynasty in popular culture: Star Wars. His screenplays include *The Soulstar Commission* (1987) and numerous television scripts, including some for *The Twilight Zone* series (1985-1986). He even wrote a comic book miniseries, *Fusion* (1987, #1-#5, for Eclipse Comics); a Batman comic, *No Man's Land: Underground Railroad, Parts I and II* (1999, with Paul Ryan); and he was involved in developing the animated cartoon *The Secret of NIMH* (1982). According to Amazon.com, he also wrote *The Invisible Imam* (2007) as a paperback companion to the "Assassin's Creed" videogame. Asked why he writes science fiction, he answered, "Science fiction gives me the widest areas to play in" (quoted in *COCAAL*). Since 2004, Barnes has also written an almost-daily blog at //darkush.blogspot.com/.

Barnes is also a martial-arts expert: He has a Black Belt in Kenpo Karate and Kodokan Judo and a Brown Belt in Shorenji Jiu Jitsu, he has certification to teach several other martial arts, and he won second place in the National Korean Karate championships (1972). In addition to martial-arts themes in some of his novels (e.g., *The Kundalinin Equation, Firedance*), he also wrote the nonfiction work *Ki: How to Generate the Dragon Spirit* (1976). In his words, "My primary area of interest is human mental and physical development. To this end I research psychology, parapsychology, and kinesiology, practice and teach martial arts, and meditate and study comparative religious philosophy. My major viewpoint is that all human beings are perfect, but that we allow ourselves to dwell in our illusions of imperfection, creating fear, hate, and all negativity in human experience" (quoted in *CAO-05*). Barnes's outlook shaped his development of LifeWriting, inspired by Joseph Campbell's celebration of myths and of the "Hero's Journey to both life and writing" (quoted in *BB*). For more info on LifeWriting, see his website, //www.lifewrite.com; his workbook and tape set,

LifeWriting (1992); or his video recordings, *LifeWriting/TOTAL SUCCESS* (1993), *Lifewriting Writing System* (1999). His other videos include *Firedance Tai Chi* (1994), *The Art of Storytelling* (1999), and *Five Minute Miracle* (2005).

Barnes has also written several short stories, which have been anthologized and published in periodicals (e.g., *Analog*). With Hugo, Locus, Ditmar, and Nebula award-winning sci-fi novelist Larry Niven, he wrote "The Locusts," which was nominated for the prestigious Hugo award for science fiction. Barnes collaborated with Larry Niven, initially as Niven's apprentice, numerous other times. Together, they wrote *The Descent of Anansi* (1982), *Achilles' Choice* (1991), and *Saturn's Race* (2000). They have also written their Dream Park series of books, including *Dream Park* (1981), *The Barsoom Project* (1989), and *Dream Park: The Voodoo Game* (1991; published as *The California Voodoo Game*, 1992). Barnes and Niven joined with Niven's frequent cowriter Jerry Pournelle to begin their Heorot series, including *The Legacy of Heorot* (1987), *Beowulf's Children* (1995), and *The Dragons of Heorot* (1995). In a February 2005 blog, Barnes said, "Larry was my mentor...He (and uber-conservative Jerry Pournelle) taught me much of what I understand about SF extrapolation. . . . I . . . spent the next eight years writing rote adventure novels (more or less), hiding behind Larry's name" (quoted in *BB*). *The Legacy of Heorot* was a *New York Times* bestseller.

Another key collaborator for Barnes is his wife, **Tananarive Due**. When they married (8/1/2000), Barnes already had daughter from a previous marriage, Lauren Nicole (b. 3/16/1986; named to honor Barnes's collaborator Laurence "Larry" Niven). After Lauren graduated from high school, the couple adopted a son, Jason Kai. Better known is the couple's writing collaboration, especially on television and movie scripts. With actor Blair Underwood, Barnes and Due have cowritten the Tennyson Hardwick series of novels, including *Casanegra* (2007; also available as in audio format or Kindle format) and *In the Night of the Heat* (2009; also available in Kindle format). Barnes and Due also cowrote a tribute to deceased fellow sci-fi author Octavia Butler, published in *Black Issues Book Review* (2006).

REFERENCES: *CAO-03. Wiki.* Alic, Margaret, in *BB*. Sandra Y. Govan, in *COCAAL*. Amazon.com.

FURTHER READING: Cassidy, Thomas J., in *GEAAL*.

Barnett, Claude Albert
?/?/1889–8/2/1967
Founded the Associated Negro Press

An entrepreneur, Barnett noticed that newspapers catering to African Americans would benefit from having a source for news affecting African Americans. In 1919, he founded the **Associated Negro Press (ANP)**, modeled after the Associated Press news service. The ANP gathered, edited, and distributed articles to its member newspapers (about 200 of them by the start of World War II). After World War II, the press also included member newspapers in Africa, handling articles in French, as well as in English. During the 1960s, the number of African-American newspapers declined, and shortly after Barnett's death, the ANP ceased to exist. His widow of 33 years, actor and singer Etta Moten, continued the couple's cultural and civic activities, and Halle Berry presented an award to Etta at the Chicago International Film Festival to celebrate her 100th birthday in 2001.

REFERENCES: *AANB.* "African American Magazines and Newspapers," in *USHE.* //academic.lexisnexis.com/upa/upa-subject-area.aspx?pid=245&type=AS&parentid=212. //findingaids.library.northwestern.edu/fedora/get/inu:inu-ead-afri-0009/inu:EADbDef11/getDescriptiveSummary. //www.chicagohistory.org/static_media/pdf/historyfair/barnett_claude_a.pdf. //www.dlib.indiana.edu/reference/cshm/ohrc028.html. Hurst, Ryan, in //www.blackpast.org/?q=aah/barnett-claude-albert-1889-1967. *EA-99.*

Barnett, Marguerite Ross *See* Ross-Barnett, Marguerite

Barrax, Gerald W. (William)
6/21/1933–
Poems, literary criticism; educator

In 1969, Barrax moved to North Carolina and soon found his intellectual home among the faculty at North Carolina State University (NCSU), where he stayed until he retired in 1997. In 1985, when the literary journal **Obsidian** needed a home, Barrax brought it to NCSU and edited *Obsidian II: Black Literature in Review* there until 1996. (Since then, it has been renamed *Obsidian III: Literature in the African Diaspora* and the semiannual journal has passed through the hands of four other editors to reach its current editor, Sheila Smith McKoy.) Barrax also edited poetry for the prestigious **Callaloo** from 1984 to 1986.

In addition to nurturing young poets at NCSU, in workshops across the country, and through literary journals, Barrax writes his own poetry, published in numerous anthologies and journals. In 2008, Gale's *Literature Resource Center* included 135 "primary sources and literary works" by Barrax. His poetry has also been collected in *Another Kind of Rain* (1970), *An Audience of One: Poems* (1980), *The Deaths of Animals and Lesser Gods* (1984),

Epigraphs (1990), and Pulitzer- and National Book Award-nominated *Leaning against the Sun* (1992). He has since published his retrospective volume, *From a Person Sitting in Darkness: New and Selected Poems* (1998). Amazon.com also lists a self-published volume, *This Sky* (2003), currently out of print. Across the decades, his poetry shows mastery of both formal rhyme and meter and more informal forms and styles. He also can twist a form to satirize it, as in the opening lines of his 1970 "For a Black Poet" (anthologized in *Trouble the Water: 250 Years of African-American Poetry*):

BLAM! BLAM! BLAM! POW! BLAM! POW! RATTTTTTAT! BLACK IS BEAUTIFUL, WHITY! RAATTTTTTAT! POW! THERE GO A HONKIE! GIT'M, POEM! POW! BLAM! BANG!

In addition to his literary productivity, Barrax has produced five children: three sons from his first marriage and two daughters from his second. His own heritage includes Dutch and Native American, as well as African ancestry. Since retiring, he returned to Pennsylvania, where he was raised and educated.

REFERENCES: Hayden, Lucy K., in *AAP-55-85.* Kich, Martin, in *GEAAL.* Manheim, James M., in *BB. CAO-01.* Pettis, Joyce, in *APSWWII-3.* Scott, Daniel M. III, in *COCAAL* and *OCAAL.* //www.newsreel.org/guides/furious.htm.

Bass, Charlotta Amanda (née Spears)
2/14/1874–4/12/1969
Editorials, columns, autobiography/memoir; newspaper editor, publisher; political activist, U.S. vice-presidential candidate

For more than ten years, starting at age 20, Charlotta Spears had devoted herself to Rhode Island's *Providence Watchman*. Physically and mentally exhausted, Spears was told by her doctor to head West—and take some time out to rest, relax, and recuperate. She followed his suggestion to go West, but not his advice about resting. At first, she just sold subscriptions for the *Eagle*, the oldest **African-American newspaper** in the West (founded in 1879). Within a few years, however, its founding editor John Neimore asked her to take over as managing editor; her first issue was March 15, 1912. Soon after, Neimore died, and the following year, Spears bought the paper, which she renamed the *California Eagle*.

Charlotta Spears then took on another big commitment: She married Joseph Blackburn Bass, cofounder of the *Topeka Call* (later renamed *Topeka Plaindealer*), then of the *Montana Plaindealer*. She also promoted him from reporter to editor. The two of them boosted the paper's circulation to 60,000; by 1925, it was the largest West Coast African-American newspaper (20 pages a week), employing 12 workers. In the paper's pages, she championed workers' rights and fought against discrimination in the workplace, in housing, and in schooling. She also protested against D. W. Griffith's 1915 white-supremacist film *The Birth of a Nation;* deplored the U.S. Army's unfair court-martial, conviction, and punishment of the soldiers in the 24th Black Regiment in Houston, Texas, in 1917; and bitterly challenged the unjust legal prosecution—and persecution—of the innocent Scottsboro Boys in 1931. She even confronted the Ku Klux Klan and other racists, despite their bullying, threats of violence, and lawsuits against her. In fighting bigotry and injustice, she considered Mexicans, Jews, and other minorities her allies, who shared her aims.

After Joseph died (in 1934), Charlotta Bass kept up the struggle through her *California Eagle* until she sold it in 1951 (last issue published July 1964). Starting in the 1940s, however, she increasingly turned to politics as a medium for social change, including brief runs for Los Angeles city council and for the U.S. Congress. Having helped found California's Progressive Party, in 1952, the national Progressive Party chose her as their vice-presidential candidate. Because there was never a U.S. President Vincent Hallinan, you know that Bass and her running mate didn't win. Nonetheless, they stimulated public discussion of war (stop the Cold War and the Korean War) and peace (ban the bomb), as well as the need for addressing issues of social equity (for women, for all people of color, and for all impoverished people). After the election, she retired to write and self-published her *Forty Years: Memoirs from the Pages of a Newspaper* (1960, hardcover), still sometimes available from online booksellers.

Who was the winning vice-presidential candidate in the 1952 election? It was Richard Nixon, known for his virulent opposition to civil rights, civil liberties, and communism. In the 1950s, he backed Senator Joseph McCarthy's notorious witch hunt to punish and rebuke anyone who seemed remotely sympathetic with socialism, civil rights, or civil liberties. Because Bass was certainly sympathetic with all three, she suffered along with many others during McCarthy's Red Scare. Reportedly, the FBI surveillance of her that started in the 1940s continued even when she reached her 90s—a very dangerous woman indeed. McCarthy's backer is now better known for his deeds in the 1970s: As U.S. President, Nixon was forced to resign in disgrace for his lying and cheating. In the long run, Bass fared much better than her former rival, as we still remember her for her integrity and her willingness to fight for the welfare of others instead of seeking self-aggrandizement. As she said in her last issue as editor (4/26/1951), for "more than 40 years . . . I have tried to serve my people and my country, as a good neighbor, as an editor, and as a fighter for Negro liberation" (*Black Biography*).

Note. Though many sources list her birthdate as 2/14/1874, some give it as 1879, 1890, and even as October, 1880.

REFERENCES: *AANB. BAAW.* Bass, Charlotta Spears (1960), *Forty Years: Memoirs from the Pages of a Newspaper. Wiki.* Freer, Regina, and Marti Tippens, in //www.socallib.org/bass/story/index.html. Smith, Alonzo, in //www.blackpast.org/?q=aaw/bass-charlotta-1879-1969. Amazon.com. Stamatel, Janet P., in *BB* —Tonya Bolden

Bayley, Solomon
fl. c. 1800s
Slave narrative

Bayley was one of the first to write his own spiritual slave autobiography, *A Narrative of Some Remarkable Incidents in the Life of Solomon Bayley, Formerly a Slave in the State of Delaware, North America; Written by Himself, and Published for His Benefit* (2nd London ed., 1825), rather than dictating it to an *amanuensis* (someone who writes down what another person dictates aloud).

REFERENCES: *AANB. BAL-1-P.* Gautier, Amina. "Yolanda Pierce. Hell without Fires: Slavery, Christianity, and the Antebellum Spiritual Narrative." *African American Review. 41.4* (Winter 2007), p. 818. Shields, John C., "Literary History: Colonial and Early National Eras," in *COCAAL* and *OCAAL*, pp. 446-447. *Wiki. Literature Resources from Gale.* //www.webroots.org/library/usablack/norilsb0.html.

Beasley, Delilah
9/9/1872-8/18/1934
History; columnist

By age 12, Beasley started writing for the *Cleveland Gazette;* by age 15, she was a regular columnist for the Sunday edition of the *Cincinnati Enquirer.* Starting about 1910, she started writing a column for the Sunday *Oakland Tribune,* which she continued to write for another 20 years. One of her themes was her adamant opposition to racial discrimination and stereotyping, such as in the use of the words "darky" and "nigger" in mainstream American newspapers in her day. In addition, through her own archival research and collection of oral history, she gathered enough information on the history of African Americans in California to write *The Negro Trail-Blazers of California* (1919). Her self-published book was so highly respected by sociologists that it was nominated for inclusion in the *Guide to the Best Books.*

REFERENCES: *AANB. HR&B.* Crouchett, Lorraine J., in *BWA:AHE. Wiki.* Wilson, Francille Rusan. "Essay Review Ii: Black and White Women Historians Together?" *The Journal of African American History. 89.3* (Summer 2004) p266. From *Literature Resource Center. EA-99.*

Beckham, Barry
3/19/1944–
Novels, play, biography, nonfiction guide; educator, book publisher

Beckham's novels include *My Main Mother* (1969) and *Runner Mack* (1972, nominated for the National Book Award). Beckham also wrote a "novelized biography" of Harlem basketballer Earl Manigault, *Double Dunk* (1981; reissued by his Beckham House Publishing, 1993); a play, *Garvey Lives!* (1972, Brown University); and *Will You Be Mine?* (2006).

When he ran into difficulties finding someone to publish his *The Black Student's Guide to Colleges* (1982), he decided to start his own book publishing company, Beckham House Publishers, now part of the Beckham Publications Group. He eventually found another publisher for his first guide and for *The Black Student's Guide to Scholarships* (5th ed., 1999). Beckham House publishes his own *The College Selection Workbook* (2nd ed., 1987), some editions of his guides, and many works by other authors. A publishing innovator, Beckham may have been the first author to serialize via the Internet his entire novel, *You Have a Friend: The Rise and Fall and Rise of Chase Manhattan Bank*. In 1998, readers paid $9.95 total to receive e-mailed installments of the novel every three weeks. He continues to write, as well as publish, and all of his works remain in print.

REFERENCES: Bethel, Kari, in *BB. CAO-08.* Campenni, Frank, *CN-6.* Loeb, Jeff, in *COCAAL* and *OCAAL.* Ostrom, Hans, in *GEAAL.* Pinsker, Sanford. "A Conversation with Barry Beckham." *Studies in Black Literature 5.3* (1974), pp. 17-20. Rpt. in *Literature Resource Center.* Gale, Cengage Learning. From *Literature Resource Center.* Weixlmann, Joe, in *AAFW-55-84.* //www.beckhamhouse.com/barrybeckham.html. Amazon.com.

Bell, James Madison
4/3/1826–1902
Poems, spoken word—oratory; political and civic activist, orator, plasterer

Bell specialized in writing long (750-950 lines) verse orations on historical subjects, such as slavery, the Civil War, emancipation, and Reconstruction. His poetry books included *A Poem: Delivered August 1st, 1862 ... at the Grand Festival to Commemorate the Emancipation of the Slaves in the British West Indian Isles* (1862), *A Poem Entitled "The Day and the War"* (1864), *An Anniversary Poem Entitled "The Progress of Liberty"* (1866), and *A Poem Entitled "The Triumph of Liberty"* (1870), as well as his collection, *The Poetical Works of James Madison Bell* (1901). In his day, he was an esteemed advocate of emancipation and of civil rights.

REFERENCES: *AANB.* . Alic, Margaret, in *BB.* Lee, Truong, in *GEAAL.* Sherman, Joan R., in *COCAAL* and *OCAAL*

Bennett, Gwendolyn B.
7/8/1902–5/30/1981
Poems, criticism, essays, columns, short stories; graphic artist, editor, educator

Gwendolyn spent her preschool years on a reservation where her parents taught Paiute youngsters. In 1906, the family moved to Washington, D.C., to pursue new career options. Three years later, her parents divorced, and her mother was awarded custody. Her father then abducted her, moving frequently to avoid letting her mother find them. Not until Gwendolyn was a junior in high school did her father and she settle in Brooklyn, where she then won numerous school awards and contests.

As Bennett finished college, the **Harlem Renaissance** flowered, and Bennett's budding talent blossomed. She started contributing to literary journals, both creating covers and writing articles and poems for *Opportunity* and for *Crisis*. Many of her poems (e.g., her best-known poem, "To a Dark Girl") celebrate the natural grace, physical loveliness, and emotional qualities of African-American females. Her lyrical poems were distinctively refreshing during this time when many descendants of Mother Africa failed to appreciate their racial and cultural characteristics.

Between 1923 and 1928, Bennett wrote most of her stories, poems, and essays. During this highly productive period, she developed warm supportive relationships with her peers, especially **Langston Hughes** and **Countee Cullen**. To support her writing and her artwork, Bennett taught art and design at Howard University in Washington, D.C. She had no sooner begun teaching than she won a prestigious foreign-study award, which allowed her to study art in Paris from 1925 until 1926. While there, she kept corresponding with her peers in Harlem. They continually urged her to write for publication and told her of literary opportunities in the United States.

In 1926, Bennett returned to Harlem and joined Hughes and others to form the editorial board of *Fire!!*, a quarterly journal for work by young African-American artists. Sadly, soon after her return to the United States, much of her Parisian work caught fire—literally. From 1927 to 1928, she returned to teaching art at Howard but still kept in touch with her Harlem colleagues. She drew on these contacts for her "Ebony Flute" column (1926-1928) in *Opportunity,* which she described as "literary and social chit-chat": influential essays and news about African-American literary and artistic trends and activities. Her column is often cited as having documented, supported, and shaped the Harlem Renaissance.

In 1927, Bennett married a physician, and in May 1928, she left her teaching post to help her husband set up his private medical practice in Florida. Unable to tolerate the rigid segregation of the South, however, she eventually persuaded him to return to New York. Unfortunately, they arrived during the Great Depression, when support of the arts dried up, and the Harlem Renaissance shriveled up. Soon after, Bennett's husband died, and she had to turn from expressing her soul to feeding her body.

In 1937, she found a job suited to her artistic temperament at the Harlem Community Art Center, eventually becoming its director. She also found a man who appreciated her artistic talent, and in 1940, she married him, even though he was not black. At that time, interracial marriages were scorned—and worse—by many people of both races. She was also repudiated by Congress's House Un-American Activities Committee, which accused her of having communist sympathies. She was suspended from her job at the Center, then similar problems arose in her next two jobs. For a time, she worked anonymously for the Consumers Union, then she and her husband moved to Pennsylvania, where she spent the rest of her life collecting and selling antiques with her husband and then alone after his death in 1980.

REFERENCES: *BANP. EB-98. HR&B. MWEL. NAAAL. RLWWJ. RT. TtW.* Cassidy, Thomas J., in *GEAAL.* Daniel, Walter C., and Sandra Y. Govan, in *AAWHR-40.* Govan, Sandra Y., in *CAO-02. COCAAL* and *OCAAL. LFCC. MWEL. Wiki.* //catdir.loc.gov/catdir/toc/ecip064/2005035688.html. //www.poets.org/viewmedia.php/prmMID/19694.

Bennett, Hal
4/21/1930–
Novels, short fiction

Bennett sold his first short story at age 15, started writing features for the Newark *Herald News* at age 16, and edited a newsletter for soldiers when he was in the U.S. Air Force during the Korean War. His first published book was *The Mexico City Poems and House on Hay* (1961). Bennett's novels include *A Wilderness of Vines* (1966), *The Black Wine* (1968), *Lord of Dark Places* (1970), *Wait until Evening* (1974), and *Seventh Heaven* (1976); his short fiction has been collected in *Insanity Runs in Our Family* (1977). In 1973, Bennett won the prestigious PEN/Faulkner Award for literature.

REFERENCES: *AANB. CAO-04.* Bostian, Patricia Kennedy, in *GEAAL.* Le Rouge, Mary, in *BB.* Miller, James A., in *COCAAL* and *OCAAL.* Walcott, Ronald, in *AAFW-55-84.*

Bennett, Jr., Lerone
10/17/1928–
Nonfiction—history books, articles, biography; collaborative writer, journalist, editor

Bennett's best-selling *Before the Mayflower: A History of the Negro in America, 1619-1962* (1962) has sold more than 1 million copies and still counting. His other highly readable and well-researched books include *The Negro Mood, and Other Essays* (1964), *What Manner of Man: A Biography of Martin Luther King, Jr., 1929-1968* (4th rev. ed., 1976; originally 1964), *Confrontation: Black and White* (1965), *Black Power, U.S.A.: The Human Side of Reconstruction, 1867-1877* (1967), *Pioneers in Protest* (1968), *The Challenge of Blackness* (1972), *The Shaping of Black America: The Struggles and Triumphs of African-Americans, 1619 to the 1990s* (1975; 2nd ed., 1993), *Wade in the Water: Great Moments in Black History* (1979), *Listen to the Blood: Was Abraham Lincoln a White Supremacist? and Other Essays and Stories* (1994), and *Forced into Glory: Abraham Lincoln and the White Dream* (2000), his controversial book questioning Lincoln's role as the "Great Emancipator." Bennett also collaborated with founding publisher of **Jet** and **Ebony** magazines, **John H. Johnson**, to write Johnson's memoirs, *Succeeding against the Odds* (1989). The Johnson Publishing Company also published most of Bennett's books.

Writing about a dozen books is Bennett's sideline; his day job is journalism. He worked as a reporter and then city editor for **Atlanta Daily World** newspaper from 1949 to 1953. After a brief stay as associate editor at *Jet* magazine (1953-1954), he moved to *Ebony* magazine, eventually becoming its executive editor (since 1987). In his magazine work, he has also promoted the appreciation of African-American history (e.g., developing the four-volume compilation, *Ebony Pictorial History of Black America,* 1971), often contributing his own articles on the subject for the magazine. In addition, Bennett has had several of his poems and short stories published. When Bennett considered retiring in 2003, Johnson and his daughter **Linda Johnson Rice**, current CEO and president of Johnson Publications, persuaded him to stay. In 2002, the American Book Award honored Bennett for his lifetime achievement. In addition to numerous other honors, Bennett has been awarded more than ten honorary doctorates.

REFERENCES: *AANB. CAO-03. EBLG.* Robinson, Lisa Clayton, *EA-99.* Rosen, Isaac, *BB.* Stone, Les, in *BH2C. Wiki.* //library.msstate.edu/special_interest/Mississippi_African-American_Authors.asp.

Berry, Mary Frances
2/17/1938–

Nonfiction—history, contemporary issues; civil servant, educator

Among Berry's scholarly works of history are *Black Resistance/White Law: A History of Constitutional Racism* (1971; repr. 1995); *Military Necessity and Civil Rights Policy: Black Citizenship and the Constitution, 1861-1868* (1977); *Stability, Security, and Continuity: Mr. Justice Burton and Decision-Making in the Supreme Court, 1945-1958* (1978); *Long Memory: The Black Experience in America* (1982, with John W. Blassingame; pb 1986); *Why the ERA Failed: Politics, Women's Rights, and the Amending Process* (1986); *Black Self-determination: A Cultural History of African-American Resistance* (2nd ed., 1993, with V. P. Franklin); *The Politics of Parenthood: Child Care, Women's Rights, and the Myth of the Good Mother* (1993); her critically acclaimed *The Pig Farmer's Daughter and Other Tales of American Justice: Episodes of Racism and Sexism in the Courts from 1865 to the Present* (1999); *Overcoming the Past, Focusing on the Future: An Assessment of the U.S. Equal Employment Opportunity Commission's Enforcement Efforts, The Commission* (2000); *My Face Is Black Is True: Callie House and the Struggle for Ex-Slave Reparations* (2005); *And Justice For All: The United States Commission on Civil Rights and the Struggle for Freedom in America* (2009); as well as numerous articles in scholarly journals and popular periodicals.

In addition to the doctorate she earned from Howard University, she has been awarded more than 30 honorary doctorates, as well as many other awards for her scholarship and her service. Most prominently, she served on the U.S. Commission on Civil Rights (starting in 1980; chairing it since 1993), despite battles with Ronald Reagan and with George W. Bush—a battle she lost at the end of the latter's first term. She famously warned that the "watchdog of civil rights" should not become the "lapdog for the administration." She has also been a professor of history since 1966, at the University of Pennsylvania since 1987. Other positions include being Assistant Secretary for Education at the Department of Health, Education, and Welfare, 1977-1980, the first African-American woman to hold that position; chancellor at the University of Colorado, Boulder, 1976-1980, the first African-American woman to head a major research university; past president of the venerated Organization of American Historians, 1990-1991; controversial former national board chair of the Pacifica Radio Foundation, 1997-2001; and a nonviolent protester arrested and jailed several times for opposing apartheid in South Africa.

REFERENCES: *AANB.* Glenshaw, Peter, in *EA-99.* Harroun, Debra G., in *BB. CAO-01.* McNeil, Genna Rae, in *B. BH2C. BWA:AHE. Wiki.* //reference.findtarget.com/search/Pacifica%20Radio/.
//www.history.upenn.edu/faculty/berry.shtml. //www.maryfrancesberry.com/. Amazon.com, 8/1999, 3/2009.

Bibb, Henry (Walton)
5/10/1815–1854

Fugitive-slave narrative; newspaper editor, publisher

Since Bibb's mother was enslaved, he was born in slavery, despite his father reportedly being a white Kentucky state senator. Bibb is best known for his self-published *Narrative of the Life and Adventures of Henry Bibb Written by Himself* (1849, 1st ed.; also published as *Narrative of the Life and Adventures of Henry Bibb, An American Slave*). In his account, he describes escaping and being recaptured several times, including this account of his final escape: "The swift running steamer started that afternoon on her voyage, which soon wafted my body beyond the tyrannical limits of chattel slavery. When the boat struck the mouth of the river Ohio, and I had once more the pleasure of looking on that lovely stream, my heart leaped up for joy at the glorious prospect that I should again be free" (p. 114, *BAL-1-P*). In his day, he and his narrative were not nearly as well received as were **Frederick Douglass** and Douglass's narratives, but contemporary scholars have affirmed his narrative as one of the most reliable accounts of slavery in Kentucky and the South.

In 1842, Bibb made his final, successful escape to Detroit, leaving behind his first wife and their daughter. As a free man, he worked actively to defeat slavery, giving antislavery lectures and writing abolitionist articles. Following the 1850 passage of the Fugitive Slave Act, he and his second wife fled to Canada. There, in 1851, Bibb founded *The Voice of the Fugitive,* Canada's premier African-American abolitionist newspaper, which he edited. He also worked to aid the Underground Railroad and any other causes that would undermine or defeat slavery.

REFERENCES: *AANB. BAL-1-P. NYPL-AADR.* Gardner, Eric, in *GEAAL.* Lowance, Mason I., Jr., in *COCAAL* and *OCAAL. Wiki.* //www.gutenberg.org/etext/15398. *EA-99.*

FURTHER READING: *OCWW. BWA:AHE.*

Black Aesthetic
1960s–1970s

Supporters of the Black Arts Movement that lasted from the early1960s to the mid-1970s sought themes that arose from the context of African-American culture and were their own frame of reference. This became known as Black Aesthetic theory. It generated a remarkable amount of criticism and theory about African-American literature.

The spirit of the Black Arts Movement was captured in 1968 by Larry Neal and Amiri Baraka who edited *Black*

Fire: An Anthology of African American Writing. In examining how the political values of the Black Power Movement found expression in the aesthetic of African-American artists, Neal and Baraka postulated that there were two Americas, one black and one white. A central theme of Black Power was for African Americans to define the world in their own terms. The Black aesthetic held this concept from the vantage point of the artist. The artists' primary responsibility, according to Neal and Baraka, was to speak to the spiritual and cultural needs of Black people. "Therefore, the main thrust of this new breed of contemporary writers is to confront the contradictions arising out of the Black man's experience in the racist West ... Implicit in this reevaluation is the need to develop a Black Aesthetic ... the Western aesthetic has run its course: It is impossible to construct anything meaningful within its decaying structure. We advocate a cultural revolution in art and ideas."

Amiri Baraka amplifies the nature of the new aesthetic in his poem "Black Art" that ends with the lines:

We want a black poem. And a
Black World
Let the world be a Black Poem
And Let All Black people Speak This Poem
Silently
or LOUD

FURTHER READING: Clark, Norris B. "**Gwendolyn Brooks** and a Black Aesthetic." In Maria K. Mootry and Gary Smith (Eds.). 1987. *A Life Distilled: Gwendolyn Brooks, Her Poetry and Fiction* (pp. 81-99). University of Illinois Press. Rpt. in Daniel G. Marowski and Roger Matuz (Eds.). 1988. *Contemporary Literary Criticism* (Vol. 49). Detroit: Gale Research. From *Literature Resource Center.* Judy, Ronald A. T. "The New Black Aesthetic and W. E. B. Du Bois, or Hephaestus, Limping." *The Massachusetts Review 35.2* (Summer 1994), pp. 249-282. Rpt. in Deborah A. Stanley (Ed.). 1997. *Contemporary Literary Criticism* (Vol. 96). Detroit: Gale Research. From *Literature Resource Center.* Mackey, Nathaniel. "**Ishmael Reed** and the Black Aesthetic." *CLA Journal 21.3* (Mar. 1978): pp. 355-366. Rpt. in Michelle Lee (Ed.). 2006. *Poetry Criticism* (Vol. 68). Detroit: Gale. From *Literature Resource Center.* Martin, Reginald. "The FreeLance PallBearer Confronts the Terrible Threes: **Ishmael Reed** and the New Black Aesthetic Critics." *MELUS 14.2* (Summer 1987), pp. 35-49. Rpt. in Janet Witalec (Ed.). 2003. *Contemporary Literary Criticism* (Vol. 174). Detroit: Gale. From *Literature Resource Center.* Napier, Winston. "From the Shadows: Houston Baker's Move Toward a Postnationalist Appraisal of the Black Aesthetic." *New Literary History. 25.1* (Winter 1994) p. 159. From *Literature Resource Center.* Okafor-Newsum, Ikechukwu. "Afro-American Poetics: Revisions of Harlem and the Black Aesthetic." *Research in African Literatures. 28.2* (Summer 1997) p. 193. From *Literature Resource Center.* Shin, Andrew, and Barbara Judson. "Beneath the Black Aesthetic: James Baldwin's Primer of Black American Masculinity." *African American Review 32.2* (Summer 1998), pp. 247-261. Rpt. in Jeffrey W. Hunter (Ed.). 2000. *Contemporary Literary Criticism* (Vol. 127). Detroit: Gale Group. From *Literature Resource Center.* Thomas, Lorenzo. "The Need to Speak: Tom Dent and the Shaping of a Black Aesthetic. *African American Review. 40.2* (Summer 2006) p. 325. From *Literature Resource Center.*

Black American Literature Forum *See* African American Review

Black Arts Movement
1960s–1970s

The Black Arts Movement was the first major African-American artistic movement after the **Harlem Renaissance**. It lasted from the early 1960s through the mid-1970s, when the Civil Rights Movement was at its peak, as were new ways of thinking about African Americans. The Black Arts Movement was the literary, cultural, aesthetic, and spiritual wing of the **Black Power** struggle. Black Arts Movement participants sought to produce works of art that would be meaningful to the Black masses.

For the most part, African-American writers during this period were very supportive of separatist politics and Black nationalism. Many adherents viewed the artist as an activist responsible for the formation of racially separate publishing houses, theater troupes, and study groups. They acted in the spirit of **Malcolm X** more than in that of **Martin Luther King, Jr.** They believed that artists had a responsibility to be political activists.

The term "black arts" is of ancient origin, and had a negative meaning for centuries, similar to "black magic." It was first used in a positive sense by **Amiri Baraka** (formerly LeRoi Jones), a leader of the Black Arts Movement. Baraka and **Larry Neal** edited a collection of stories, plays, and essays by African-American writers that helped define the movement, *Black Fire: An Anthology of Afro American Writing (1968)*. In 1965, he founded the Black Arts Repertory Theatre in Harlem.

The proponents of this movement looked for inspiration in such sources as popular music, including John Coltrane's jazz and James Brown's rhythm and blues. The literature of the movement was confrontational in tone. In fact, some of the language used by these writers was intentionally vulgar and shocking to show the vitality of their position. Black Arts writing generally used **African-American vernacular English (AAVE)** and addressed such issues as racial tension, political awareness, and the relevance of African history and culture to Blacks in the United States. Baraka won an Obie Award for *Dutchman* (1964), a play portraying a shocking symbolic confrontation between Blacks and whites. A political activist as well as a political writer, Baraka's militancy toward white society grew, as evidenced by the content of two subsequent plays, *The Slave* (1964) and *The Toilet* (1964).

Rebelling against mainstream society by essentially being antiwhite, antimiddle class, and anti-American, participants in the movement were radically opposed to any concept of the artist that alienated him from his African-American community. These artists moved from the Harlem Renaissance view of art for art's sake to art for politics' sake. Other organizers of the movement include **Ishmael Reed**, who later dissented from some Black Arts doctrines and became inspired more by black magic and spiritual practices of the West Indies.

Another key figure was poet and essayist **Haki R. Madhubuti** (known as Don L. Lee until 1973). Madhubuti sold more than 100,000 of his books without a major distributor. Black contemporaries, lifestyles, music, and churches were the greatest influences on African-American poets of the times, according to Madhubuti. He became one of the movement's most popular writers with the publication of *Think Black* (1967) and *Black Pride* (1968). Madhubuti's collections of poetry such as *Don't Cry, Scream* (1969) used the rhythms of jazz music and the language of the streets to reach the masses of African Americans.

Leading theorists of the Black Arts Movement included **Houston A. Baker, Jr.**; **Henry Louis Gates, Jr.**; **Addison Gayle, Jr.**, editor of the anthology *The Black Aesthetic* (1971); and **Hoyt W. Fuller**, editor of the journal *Negro Digest* (which became *Black World* in 1970). African-American women also played an important role in the movement. **Sonia Sanchez** was a poet and playwright who brought the female voice, something often overlooked, into the nationalist movement. Her feminism and commitment to Black America came out in poetry collections such as *We a BaddDDD People* (1970). The book deals with the importance of positive role models for African Americans.

Among the numerous other writers associated with the Black Arts Movement were Obie Award-winning dramatist **Ed Bullins**; playwright Ben Caldwell; and poets **Margaret Taylor Burroughs**, **Jayne Cortez**, and **Eugene B. Redmond**. Other notable writers include **Toni Morrison**, **Ntozake Shange**, **Alice Walker**, and **June Jordan**. Characterized by an acute self-awareness, the movement produced such autobiographical works as *The Autobiography of Malcolm X* (1965) by **Alex Haley**, *Soul On Ice* (1968) by **Eldridge Cleaver**, and *Angela Davis: An Autobiography* (1974).

The Black Arts Movement served two functions that are significant to African Americans today. First, important African-American texts that had been ignored were discovered. Second, Black literature was defined in terms that differed from those used by white writers. Black Arts supporters sought themes that arose from the context of African-American culture and were their own frame of reference. This became known as **Black Aesthetic** theory. It generated a remarkable amount of criticism and theory about African-American literature. This era brought wide acclaim to many African-American writers

and fostered the growth of Black Studies courses and departments in higher education around the country. It also fostered the inclusion of African-American literature in the curriculum of elementary, middle, and high schools.
—Michael Strickland

FURTHER READING: Boyd, Melba Joyce. "'Prophets for a New Day': The Cultural Activism of Margaret Danner, Margaret Burroughs, Gwendolyn Brooks and Margaret Walker during the Black Arts Movement." *Revista Canaria de Estudios Ingleses* 37 (Nov. 1998), pp. 55-67. Rpt. in Janet Witalec (Ed.). 2003. *Twentieth-Century Literary Criticism* (Vol. 129). Detroit: Gale. From *Literature Resource Center*. Fenderson, Jonathan. "The Black Arts Movement: Literary Nationalism in the 1960s and 1970s." *The Journal of African American History.* 92.1 (Winter 2007) p. 139. From *Literature Resource Center.* Gladney, Marvin J. "The Black Arts Movement and Hip-hop." *African American Review.* 29.2 (Summer 1995) p. 291. From *Literature Resource Center.* Neal, Larry. "The Black Arts Movement." Visions of a Liberated Future. Ed. Michael Schwarz. New York: Thunder's Mouth, 1989. pp. 62-78. Roney, Patrick. "The Paradox of Experience: Black Art and Black Idiom in the Work of Amiri Baraka." *African American Review.* 37.2-3 (Summer-Fall 2003) p. 407. From *Literature Resource Center.* Salaam, Kalamu Ya. "A Primer of the Black Arts Movement: Excerpts from the Magic of Juju: an Appreciation of the Black Arts Movement." *Black Renaissance/Renaissance Noire* (Summer-Fall 2002) p. 40. From *Literature Resource Center.* Smethurst, James. "'Pat Your Foot and Turn the Corner': Amiri Baraka, the Black Arts Movement, and the Poetics of a Popular Avant-garde." *African American Review.* 37.2-3 (Summer-Fall 2003) p. 261. From *Literature Resource Center.* Smith, David Lionel. "The Black Arts Movement and Its Critics." American Literary History 3 (1991): pp. 93-110. Smitherman, Geneva. 1977. *Talkin and Testifyin: The Language of Black America.* Detroit: Wayne State UP, 1985. Thomas, Lorenzo. "'Classical Jazz' and the Black Arts Movement." *African American Review.* 29.2 (Summer 1995) p. 237. From *Literature Resource Center.* _____. "Dudley Randall, Broadside Press, and the Black Arts Movement in Detroit, 1960-1995." *African American Review.* 34.3 (Fall 2000) p. 541. From *Literature Resource Center.* _____. "Neon Griot: The Functional Role at Poetry Readings in the Black Arts Movement." Close Listening: Poetry and the Performed Word. Ed. Charles Bernstein. New York: Oxford UP, (1998) pp.300-23.

Black English *See* African-American Vernacular English (AAVE)

Black Fire: An Anthology of African-American Writing
1968

Literature collections of the writings of numerous authors

The goals of what the editors called the **Black Arts Movement** were first defined in *Black Fire: An Anthology of African American Writing* (1968), an important collection of writings in various genres by nearly 70 young African American writers from 1960s America.

Critics were neither unanimous nor generous with their praise of African-American poet **Amiri Baraka**, the former LeRoi Jones, and writer **Larry Neal**, the text's compilers. However, the critics recognized the aim of the editors to set the stage for a new **Black Aesthetic** unattached to European-American cultural standards.

Over time, the Black Arts Movement came to create a new mode of expression, define the role of Black artist in his community, and make art more meaningful by taking it to the black masses.

In the initial essay, James T. Stewart announces the paradigm of working exclusively from nonwhite literary models. Stewart compares wordsmiths to jazz musicians, championing the use of improvisation in all forms of aesthetic expression. Neal's closing statement offers the new African-American standards, as opposed to the abstract ideals that **W. E. B. Du Bois** characterizes as the double-consciousness of blacks in a white environment.

Neal embraces Black nationalist art to such an extent that the book sacrifices older works such as *Native Son* and *Invisible Man.* Instead he favors rewriting poetry to read like James Brown songs. Several of the poems included are devoted to musicians like Sun-Ra and Sonny Rollins.

Major and minor figures in the Black Arts Movement contributed stories. In one, an Uncle Tom is lectured by a burglar posing as God. Coeditor Amiri Baraka, then still using the name of LeRoi Jones, contributed "Madheart" to the collection. Other writers represented included **Stokely Carmichael (Kwame Toure)**, and **Charles Fuller.**

The work in *Black Fire,* as well as the criticism collected by **Addison Gayle, Jr.,** in *Black Expression* (1969) and in *The Black Aesthetic* (1971), codified Black Aesthetic theory. Supporters of Black Aesthetic theory sought forms and themes that arose from the context of African-American culture and were their own frame of reference. The Black Aesthetic theory generated a remarkable amount of theory and criticism about African-American literature.

The African-American canon, as defined by editors of earlier **anthologies** such as *The Negro Caravan* (1941), was literature that refuted white racist stereotypes and which embodied the "shared theme of struggle that is present in so much Negro expression." African-American writing was called on to reveal that racial classifications were irrelevant to European-American canon formation. *Black Fire* is at the opposite extreme in African-American canon formation. In *Loose Canons: Notes on the Culture Wars,* scholar **Henry Louis Gates, Jr.,** defined the canon put forth in *Black Fire* as "the blackest canon of all . . . defined by both formal innovations and by themes: formally, individual selections tend to aspire to the vernacular or to black music; or to performance; theoretically each selection reinforces the urge toward black liberation, toward 'freedom now,' with an up against the wall subtext." The hero in this volume, is the black vernacular (*see* **Afri-**

can-**American Vernacular English**). The desire of blacks to prove their common humanity with white people by demonstrating the depth of their intellect was completely absent.

REFERENCES: *AAP.* Neal, Larry, & Amiri Baraka. 1967. *Black Fire: An Anthology of African American Writing.* Time/Life Editors. 1994. *African Americans: Voices of Triumph, Creative Fire.* Alexandria, VA: Time Life Books. —Michael Strickland

Black Nationalism *See* Black Power *See also* Garvey, Marcus and Black Aesthetic

Black Opals
Late 1920s
Literary collective

Black Opals
1927–1928
Literary journal

By 1927, the literati in New York City boasted a plethora of journals publishing the writings of poets, storytellers, essayists, and others: The NAACP had long been publishing **The Crisis** (1910-), Randolph and Dodson were still publishing **The Messenger** (1917-1928), and, for several years, the National Urban League had been publishing **Opportunity: A Journal of Negro Life** (1923-1949). In addition, New York City's *The Crusader* (1918-1922), **The Brownies' Book** (1920-1921), and *Fire!!* (1926) had already come and gone, and *Fire!!'s* successor *Harlem* (1928) was being conceived. Other cities had also enjoyed their own publications, as well (e.g., Chicago's *The Half-Century Magazine,* 1916-1925; Boston's *Alexander's Magazine,* 1905-1909, and **Colored American Magazine,** 1900-1909; Atlanta's **Voice of the Negro,** 1904-1907; even Pittsburgh's *The Competitor: The National Magazine,* 1920-1921).

Meanwhile, Philadelphia, one of the earliest cities to host a large population of free African Americans, lacked a literary publication for its writers. At first an informal gathering of Philadelphia writers-the Black Opals-formed a literary collective, including Arthur Huff Fauset and Nellie Rathbone Bright, both of whom had been teachers who later became school principals, along with Bessie Calhoun Bird, Mae V. Cowdery, Ottie Beatrice Graham, Evelyn Crawford Reynolds, and Idabelle Yeiser. Bird's poem "Longings" included the line, "I want to look deep in a pool at night, and see the / stars / flash flame like fire in *black opals*" (quoted from *HR&B,* emphasis added), and when the literary collective was considering a name, they chose this metaphor.

The Black Opals, who met regularly each week, decided the participants needed a literary outlet for their work. In the Spring of 1927, the Black Opals published their debut issue of *Black Opals*, in a 5" × 8" format resembling a pamphlet. The subsequent issues were published on Christmas of 1927 and in June of 1928.

Fauset and Bright coedited the journal, and they include not only the poems, essays, drama criticism, and other writings by their members, but also the writings of non-Philadelphians, such as **Gwendolyn Bennett**, **Marita Occomy Bonner**, and Gertrude P. McBrown. Of course, Fauset also published some of the writings of his half-sister, **Jessie Redmon Fauset** and even her celebrated associates: poet, essayist, and storyteller **Langston Hughes** and scholar **Alain Locke**. By including both established writers and yet-undiscovered talented writers, the editors hoped to promote the careers of the newer authors, while providing outstanding literature for their readers. Bright's own contributions included not only literary criticism but also contributions highlighting early Philadelphia's rich African-American history and educational traditions. Both she and Fauset, as well as some of the other Black Opals, also published their work in other periodicals of the day.

Though many who knew of *Black Opals* praised it, the Philadelphia newspapers and other media ignored it entirely, as did most other African-American media outlets, and the *Black Opals* died of neglect.

REFERENCES: *HR&B*. "Arthur Huff Fauset," in *Wiki*. McHenry, Elizabeth. 2002. *Forgotten Readers: Recovering the Lost History of African American Literary Societies (a John Hope Franklin Center Book)*. Durham, NC: Duke University Press. //encyclopedia.jrank.org/articles/pages/4230/Fauset-Arthur-Huff-1899-1983.html#ixzz0MChBL2PK. //www.hsp.org/files/findingaid2057nelliebright.pdf. Amazon.com.

FURTHER READING: *See also* **Jessie Redmon Fauset**, **Harlem Renaissance, literary journals of the**, and **journals and magazines, literary**.

Black Power
1966–

Depending upon one's age and generation, the term "Black Power" brings different images to the minds of different Americans. Some people remember **Stokely Carmichael** telling a crowd at a Mississippi park in 1966 that the call for "freedom" and the chants of "We Shall Overcome" had not produced a better society for African Americans. He claimed that saying "Black Power!" would. On that summer day after Carmichael's call for "Black Power," Willie Ricks, an organizer of the Student Nonviolent Coordinating Committee (SNCC), rallied the crowd by repeating the question "What do you want?" The people repeated the answer: "Black Power!"

Others remember the 1968 Olympics when two African-American runners, Tommie Smith and John Carlos, stood on the medal platform with their raised black-gloved clenched fists over their tipped heads during the playing of the Star Spangled Banner. For their political action during what is supposed to be a nonpolitical event, the two men were sanctioned and removed from the Olympic Village.

Both incidents were viewed by some as militant and unnecessarily confrontational. **Martin Luther King, Jr.,** was quoted as saying that the phrase "Black Power" is "an unfortunate choice of words." Leadership within the National Association for the Advancement of Colored People (NAACP) also found this language less than helpful in furthering the cause of equality for African Americans. Although the 1966 call for "Black Power" came several years after the signing of the Civil Rights Amendment to the constitution, many Americans believed that change and improvement for African Americans was happening much too slowly.

This new call for "Black Power" signaled the beginning of several years of confrontation between two major factions within the African-American community. Each faction had the same basic goal in mind—equality for Blacks—but they had two very different ideas about how to achieve the goal and what needed to be done before equality could happen. Moderates believed that moderate methods must be used. Their voices for justice appealed to the conscience of America, noting that American society had made promises to all of its citizens—including Blacks. Martin Luther King, Jr.'s, "I Have a Dream" speech draws an analogy to America's giving African Americans a "blank check" where promises had been made, but they were not being kept. The more militant voices for social change were out of patience and generally believed that political power must be taken, and sometimes, taken by whatever means deemed necessary.

B.L. Martin notes the reaction within the African-American community to these new voices for equality and opportunity: "Young blacks—especially in the urban North—stopped using Negro, except in ridicule. Black was associated with youth, unity, militancy, and pride, while Negro increasingly connoted middle age, complacency, and the status quo." Interestingly, previous to the 1960s, "Black" was considered a derogatory term for many African Americans.

After the 1960s, "Black Power" became a term of empowerment and provided a cultural identity for African Americans, an identity that was not connected to white society. Additionally, other cultural changes occurred besides this change in vocabulary from Negro to Black. The "Afro" hairstyle became popular, and many whites copied this new style. The idea of observing Kwanzaa, a celebration of African-American heritage occurring in late December, began to take root. Many African Americans changed their given American names to names they believe better reflected their African roots.

In literature, the Black Power Movement (1965-1975/6) is often called the "Black Arts Movement," and the two movements are closely linked and intertwined. African-Americans writers such as **Amiri Baraka** (formerly LeRoi Jones), **Sonia Sanchez**, **Ishmael Reed**, and **Ed Bullins** were nurtured and cultivated within their own community, and this period brought numerous other African-American writers to the forefront of American society. Many of these writers saw and used the arts as a way to influence the prevailing political atmosphere. They no longer believed that art should be produced only "for art's sake." Instead they sought to create a new audience for their work by appealing directly to the general public instead of using the long-established and overwhelmingly white academic and publishing institutions. As a result, African Americans began new publishing and educational opportunities for Black writers and their audiences. Journals, magazines, anthologies, dramas, and collections of works produced by African Americans provided a means of communication with people who before this time did not have works specifically targeted for their needs.

This period also saw the rise of Black Studies departments within the university and college setting. William L. Van De burg notes in his book, *New Day in Babylon: The Black Power Movement and American Culture, 1965-1975*, success was not to be measured solely by the critical reception of a play, poem, or novel. The act of institution building in itself was deemed socially desirable and potentially empowering. It could facilitate the promotion of a broad cultural awareness that, in turn, would help individual Blacks discover important truths about themselves. No longer forced to view the world through a white interpretive lens, they could proceed to chart the future with confidence, knowing that they were supported by a strong, self-affirming, and distinctive culture.

Van De burg further notes that African-American artists developed particular themes in their works. These themes—"Defining 'Whitey'," "Identifying 'Toms'," "Understanding Black History," and "Achieving Liberation"—sought to influence prevailing attitudes in America. Through these themes, African-American artists sent messages that were usually angry, often filled with four-letter words, and sometimes fearful to white America. Yet, these artists succeeded in educating all Americans who were brave enough to listen to the oppressed in America and to question the social, economic, and cultural status quo. They also succeeded in offering a critically important idea to future African Americans, an idea that fundamentally said, "We are not powerless; we are

important; we can make a difference." Their messages helped African Americans gain a new identity as a distinct people with a valuable cultural heritage whose individual and corporate actions could influence the future of America as a country and African Americans as a people.

REFERENCES: Frayne, Trent. (1996). "Why Play National Anthems Anyway?" Maclean's. *109*(15), 60. *Magazine Academic Index Plus.* King, Martin Luther, Jr. 1993. "I Have a Dream." In *We Have a Dream: African-American Visions of Freedom.com. Diana Wells.* New York: Carroll & Graf. Martin, B.L. (1991). "From Negro to Black to African American: The Power of Names and Naming." *Political Science Quarterly,* 106(1), 83. **Neal, Larry.** "Black Arts Movement." In *NAAAL.* **Salaam, Kalamu ya.** "Black Arts Movement." In *OCAAL.* "Black Aesthetic (Arts) Movement." In *EBLG.* Van De burg, William L. 1992. *New Day in Babylon: The Black Power Movement and American Culture, 1965-1975.* Chicago: University of Chicago Press. —Janet Hoover

Black Scholar, The
1969–
Journal

Established in 1969 as the journal of the Black World Federation, the *Black Scholar* rose from the "**Black Power**" Movement and its emphasis on self-determination and social struggle. The *Black Scholar* was intended as a place where African-American ideologies could be discussed and critiqued. The journal published such writers as **Sonia Sanchez, Alice Walker, Maya Angelou, Gwendolyn Brooks, Gayl Jones, Clarence Major,** and John Stewart. The journal also published the work of Black intellectuals and activists and sought to be a bridge between Black academia and the Black community by promoting Black Studies programs and printing community-service listings of rallies, events, conferences, and the like.

REFERENCES: *EAACH,* Vol. 1. —Lisa Bahlinger

Black World See *Negro Digest*

BlackBoard African-American Bestsellers
1991–2001?
Recognize best-selling works by contemporary African-American authors

In the late 1980s, Faye Childs was looking for a publisher for her novel when a literary agent told her that African Americans do not buy books. Astounded, Childs decided to demonstrate the fallacy of that assertion. Over the next two years, Childs researched the book-buying habits of African Americans. She confirmed her preconception that African Americans do, indeed, buy and read books. In 1999, Childs reported that African Americans were spending $296 million on books each year. She was surprised, however, to find that many African-American book-buyers were not familiar with African-American writers whose names and book titles did not appear on the major bestseller lists (e.g., in *The New York Times*).

Childs decided to rectify this situation by creating her own research-based bestseller list of fiction and nonfiction titles written by or about African Americans. She surveyed 35 bookstores in 22 cities across the nation, to find out the retail book-buying preferences of African-American readers. Childs's first list included five nonfiction titles and five fiction titles and was first published in several newspapers in her home state of Ohio. A few months later, in the fall of 1991, the American Booksellers Association started printing her list in its newsletter, *Bookselling This Week*, distributed to nearly 9,000 booksellers. Childs's official BlackBoard African-American Bestsellers list comprised 10 nonfiction and 10 fiction titles. The following year, she was able to get *Essence*, a widely circulated magazine targeting African-American women, to pay her a fee to publish her list, and the BlackBoard African-American Bestsellers list's reputation soared. (In 2005, the Magazine Publishers of America reported that *Essence* had a paid readership of a little over 1 million; by comparison, **Ebony**'s was a little less than 11/2 million.)

Once the list started appearing in *Essence*, several things happened. Foremost, increasing numbers of readers came to rely on it to find appealing authors. According to Childs, *Essence* also started to have a more book-oriented editorial vision during the years it published her list. In addition, Childs has asserted, the sales of titles by many African-American authors skyrocketed, such as "**E. Lynn Harris**, **Terry McMillan**, Iyanla Vanzant, Eric Jerome Dickey. We've spurred sales growth in large numbers" (Childs, quoted in Patrick, 2001, *Publishers Weekly*). Reportedly, Terry McMillan confirmed that after the BlackBoard list named her *Disappearing Acts* the 1991 book of the year, "her publisher had to print 40,000 more copies" (Patrick, 2001, *Publishers Weekly*).

Over the next decade, Childs, the BlackBoard African-American Bestsellers list, *Essence* magazine, African-American authors, and readers enjoyed a mutually beneficial relationship. In the year 2000, however, Time Inc. bought a 49% share of the formerly African-American-owned and -operated *Essence*, and by March 2005, Time Inc. had bought the remaining 51% of *Essence*, removing it from African-American ownership and control. In December of 2000, *Essence* informed Childs that they would no longer be publishing her BlackBoard African-American Bestsellers list. Instead, *Essence* would be creating and publishing its own list. According to Childs, "Now *Essence* has stolen the list from me and taken it over without my permission or without compensating me" (quoted in //www.blackpress.org/editorial.htm). *Essence* started publishing its own list in its January 2001 issue. According to Patrik Henry Bass, *Essence's* books editor at the time, "It's an issue of branding. We wanted to have our name attached to the booksellers lists, and we wanted to have the booksellers list available on our website" (quoted in Dodson, 2001).

For a time, the American Booksellers Association's newsletter, *Bookselling This Week*, continued to print Childs's BlackBoard African-American Bestsellers list, although recent issues do not include the list. In 2001, Childs had announced plans to publish a *BlackBoard Biweekly* newsletter, which was to include not only the BlackBoard African-American Bestsellers list, but also book reviews, author-tour information, book-club columns, book and author feature articles, and a column by Childs. Noting that the list was based on 35 bookstores in 30 cities, Childs reported that she was negotiating with the American Booksellers Association (ABA) for its support of the biweekly publication. The plan was to distribute it free not only to the ABA's booksellers, but also to public libraries and others with an interest in its contents. She planned also to publish it on websites attracting African-American readers. According to //www.bookmarket.com/9.htm, the newsletter *BlackBoard Bi-Weekly* became a stand-alone publication in June 2001, naming Carr' Mel Ford White as its editor-in-chief; it operates out of Columbus, Ohio, where Childs founded the BlackBoard African-American Bestsellers list.

Childs also reported plans to work with the ABA's website BookSense.com, now //www.indiebound.org/, to enhance booksellers' awareness of titles for, about, and by African Americans. Meanwhile, BlackBoard African-American Bestsellers continued to announce Books of the Year in the categories of fiction, nonfiction, and children's books for a time. At the 2003 and 2004 Book Expo America, BlackBoard African-American Bestsellers announced those awards and an award for the BlackBoard Bookseller of the Year. In 2003, an honoree was also named for a new category, the African-American Publisher of the Year. The recipients were chosen based on the votes from booksellers across the nation.

At the 2006 Book Expo America's African American Pavilion, Faye Childs, "CEO, BlackBoard Multi Media Entertainment," received a Lifetime Achievement award. According to the blurb announcing her award, she is the publisher of the *BlackBoard National Provider (The BNP)*, described as "the first African American Globally Distributed Daily Newspaper." She also had plans to air a November 2006 television show, "the first BlackBoard WordStar Awards," in Los Angeles (quoted in //events.aalbc.com/the_bea_story_2006.htm).

Editor's note: Childs also returned to writing and finished coauthoring *Going Off!* with her sister, Noreen Palmer, described as "a psychotherapist, health professional, and founder of the BlackBoard Literacy Initiative."

Because a bestseller list can so powerfully affect book sales for the publisher, the author, and the bookseller, the motivation to manipulate a bestseller list can be quite high. The response of *The New York Times* is to closely guard and carefully scrutinize its list of reporting booksellers. *The New York Times Book Review* claims, "the rankings reflect sales at almost 4,000 bookstores, plus wholesalers serving 50,000 other retailers (gift shops, department stores, newsstands, supermarkets), statistically weighted to represent all such outlets nationwide" (quoted in Dodson, 2001). *Essence* takes the opposite tack, transparently listing its eight reporting stores (Ohio, Illinois, Michigan, Texas, Florida, California, Virginia, and Ontario, Canada) at the conclusion of its bestseller list of 20 books, comprising 10 hardcovers (5 fiction and 5 nonfiction) and 10 paperback books (5 fiction and 5 nonfiction). In 2001, *Essence's* Bass had noted that the selection of the bookstores was based on the stores' established marketing relationships with *Essence*.

Editor's note: According to Dodson, 2001, Essence compiled data from 20 African-American bookstores at that time, but the July 2009 online issue listed only 8 such stores.

Several other online bestseller lists are now also available. Black Expressions, a mail-order book retailer, lists bestsellers at //www.blackexpressions.com/ecom/pages/nm/browse/bestSellers.jsp. The Cush City website, //www.cushcity.com, has published a bestseller list since 2000, based on sales at both its website and its Houston retail outlet. The African American Literature Book Club, affiliated with Barnes & Noble, uses its online book sales (started in 1997) as a basis for its bestseller list at //books.aalbc.com/. At the website //mosaicbooks.com/whatshot.html, "bestsellers are based on Amazon.com click-throughs and sales that originate through links on Mosaicbooks.com." Of course, both //www.amazon.com and //www.barnesandnoble.com/ also offer not only global bestseller lists, but also tailored bestseller lists, based on the customer's purchases and preferences. Doubtless, additional retailers will continue to compile data on African-American book sales and to make their data available to prospective book buyers.

REFERENCES: Dodson, Angela, (3/2001), "Calculating African American Bestsellers," *Black Issues Book Review*, in //findarticles.com/p/articles/mi_m0HST/is_2_3/ai_72275266/. Patrick, Diane, (4/9/2001), "BlackBoard Chalks 10 Years: Faye Childs plans to expand her black bestseller list to a stand-alone publication," *Publishers Weekly*, in //www.publishersweekly.com/article/CA70921.html. Rhea, Shawn E., (2/1999), "Buy the Book - African American bookstores face challenges," *Black Enterprise*, in //findarticles.com/p/articles/mi_m1365/is_7_29/ai_54195610/. Schechner, Karen, (6/4/2003), "The BlackBoard Books of the Year Presented at BEA," in //news.bookweb.org/news/1492.html. //aalbc.com/reviews/so_you_wanna_write_a_best_seller.htm. //books.aalbc.com/. //en.wikipedia.org/wiki/American_Booksellers_Association. //en.wikipedia.org/wiki/Eric_Jerome_Dickey. //en.wikipedia.org/wiki/Essence_(magazine). //en.wikipedia.org/wiki/Virginia_DeBerry_%26_Donna_Grant. //events.aalbc.com/the_bea_story_2006.htm. //mosaicbooks.com/whatshot.html. //news.bookweb.org/news/1492.html. //news.bookweb.org/news/2635.html. //reviews.aalbc.com/so_you_wanna_write_a_best_seller.htm. //www.blacknews.com/pr/publisherpav101.html. //www.blackpress.org/editorial.htm. //www.bookmarket.com/9.htm. //www.bookmarket.com/qpublicity.htm. //www.cushcity.com. //www.DisilgoldSoul.com/default.asp?S=E3&Document=Disilgo - Published on: 6/22/2006 Last Visited: 2/9/2008. //www.essence.com/news_entertainment/entertainment/articles/july_bestsellers_books_list/. //www.francisray.com/presskit/Black%20writers%20carve%20out%20niche.htm. //www.hurston-wright.org/publishers.shtml. //www.qbr.com/. //www.thefreelibrary.com/Essence+of+the+deal:+what+does+Time+Inc.'s+takeover+mean+for+the...-a0129169844.

FURTHER READING: *See also* entries for Blackboard bestselling authors **Ansa, Tina McElroy**; **Harris, E. (Everette) Lynn**; **Hill, Donna**; **Hudson, Cheryl (Willis)**; and **Wesley, Valerie Wilson**. *See also* //aalbc.com/may2003.htm. //www.3blackchicks.com/3bcnews.html. //www.baip.org/news.asp. //www.bibookreview.com/. //www.hurston-wright.org/agents.shtml. //www.hurston-wright.org/resource_center.shtml. //www.unityfirst.com/trose.htm. //www.zoominfo.com/Search/PersonDetail.aspx?PersonID=79177599.

BLKARTSOUTH *See* **Free Southern Theater** *See also* **Nkombo**

Boasts, Toasts, Roasts, Signifying *See* **Oral Tradition**

Bogle, Donald
7/13/1944–
Film history

Young Donald's interest in films emerged early. By his own account (in *Blacks in American Films and Television: An Illustrated Encyclopedia*), "Black performers in movies and television cast a beguiling spell over me . . . . Even during those early years of my moviegoing and TV-watching experience, I think I was struggling to sort out incongruities of what I viewed, to clear up disparities. Always my curiosity and thirst for information led me to the library in search of some comment on a particular film, character, or personality. Usually, I returned home empty-handed, without any answers to some basic questions.

Comment: For instance, I wondered, as I watched on television a broadcast of the original 1934 version of *Imi-*

tation of Life, what effect this movie had had on the black community when first released. . . . Why, too, had Paul Robeson appeared in so many films made abroad? Had there really been a black director named **Oscar Micheaux**? . . ."

To our good fortune—and his—Bogle was able to make a living by informing himself—and us—about African Americans in American popular culture, with an emphasis on motion pictures and television. While satisfying his lifelong curiosity, he has become one of the nation's foremost authorities on this fascinating subject. Bogle shares what he has learned by:

- directly teaching (e.g., at Rutgers University, at the University of Pennsylvania, at New York University's Tisch School of the Arts)
- lecturing (at forums across the country)
- commenting on film for television (e.g., HBO's *Mo Funny: Black Comedy in America* and the American Movie Channel's documentary on African Americans in the movies, *Small Steps, Big Strides*)
- curating and cocurating several major film series in New York City (e.g., a retrospective on Sidney Poitier at the American Museum of the Moving Picture, and the Film Forum's *Black Women in the Movies: Actresses, Images, Films; Blacks in the Movies: Breakthroughs, Landmarks and Milestones;* and *Blaxploitation, Baby!*)
- writing countless articles and reviews for various periodicals (e.g., *Freedomways, Essence, Spin,* and *Film Comment*)
- writing books

For most of us, Bogle's books have been his most important contribution to what we know about African Americans involved in movies and television. Bogle's first book was the award-winning bestseller *Toms, Coons, Mulattoes, Mammies, & Bucks: An Interpretive History of Blacks in American Films* (1973; 3rd rev., updated ed., 1994). His next book, *Brown Sugar: Eighty Years of America's Black Female Superstars* (1980; rev. ed., 2007), was the basis for a documentary for the Public Broadcasting System, which he researched, adapted to film, and executive produced, and which the Association of American Women in Television and Radio named as one of the best documentaries of 1987. Bogle's *Blacks in American Films and Television: An Illustrated Encyclopedia* (1988) comprises hundreds of entries. His *Dorothy Dandridge* (1997) offers a rich, vivacious biography of the much-celebrated actress of the 1940s and 1950s, with whom Bogle had been enraptured as a young boy. In 1999, Halle Barre starred in the HBO film *Introducing Dorothy Dandridge* based on his book. Since then, Bogle wrote *Primetime Blues: African Americans on Network Television* (2001) and *Bright Boulevards, Bold Dreams: The Story of Black Holly-*

wood (2005), which garnered him a nomination for the 2006 Hurston-Wright Legacy Award.

If you're desperate to discover a few more words by Bogle, you may find them in his foreword for Spike Lee's *Mo' Better Blues*, his introduction to John Kisch and Edward Mapp's *A Separate Cinema: Fifty Years of Black-Cast Posters*, and a contemporary edition of **Ethel Waters's** 1951 autobiography *His Eye Is on the Sparrow*. Through all of these contributions, all those who share Bogle's curiosity about the history of African-American actors, producers, and directors can share in his abundant knowledge.

REFERENCES: *AANB. SMKC.* Brennan, Carol, in *BB. CAO-03.* Amazon.com. —Tonya Bolden

---

Bolden, Tonya
3/1/1959–

Biographies, juvenile books, criticism, articles, nonfiction—business, anthologies; columnist, journal editor

Bolden's literary reviews and other articles have appeared in *Black Enterprise, Essence, New York Times Book Review, Small Press,* and *Washington Post-Book World,* among other periodicals. From its inception in 1991 through its final issue in October 1996, she was the book-review columnist for *YSB* magazine. She was the editor of *Quarterly Black Review of Books* for its March 1994-June 1995 issues.

Bolden has authored, coauthored, or edited more than a dozen books. Her first published works included *The Family Heirloom Cookbook* (1990) and two "No Nonsense Success Guide" business titles: *Starting a Business from Your Home* (1993) and *Mail Order and Direct Response* (1994). She has since turned primarily to biographies, such as *The Book of African American Women: 150 Crusaders, Creators and Uplifters* (1997) and *Strong Men Keep Coming: The Book of African American Men* (1999). Most of her biographies are intended for young readers, such as *And Not Afraid to Dare: The Stories of Ten African American Women* (1998); *Tell All the Children Our Story: Memories and Mementos of Being Young and Black in America* (2001, told through the diaries and letters of young African Americans across time); *Portraits of African-American Heroes* (2003, illustrated by Ansel Pitcairn); an adaptation of Gail Buckley's *American Patriots: The Story of Blacks in the Military from the Revolution to Desert Storm* (2003); *Wake Up Our Souls: A Celebration of Black American Artists* (2004); *The Champ: The Story of Muhammad Ali* (2004, illustrated by R. Gregory Christie); *M.L.K.: The Journey of a King* (2006, photography edited by Bob Adelman); *Take-Off!: American All-Girl Bands during World War II* (2007; offered with a CD), *George Washington Carver* (2008, in Association with The Field Museum); *W. E. B Du Bois (Up Close)* (2008).

She also writes histories for young readers, such as *Rock of Ages: A Tribute to the Black Church* (2001, illustrated by R. Gregory Christie) and *Cause: Reconstruction America, 1863-1877* (2005). Her history-inspired fiction for young readers includes *Just Family* (1996, novel); *Through Loona's Door: A Tammy and Owen Adventure with Carter G. Woodson* (1997, illustrated by Luther Knox); *Doing It for Yourself: A Tammy and Owen Adventure With Madame C. J. Walker* (1999, now out of print); and *Maritcha: A Nineteenth-Century American Girl* (2005). She has also written study guides for the Carter G. Woodson Foundation Artists-in-the-Schools program.

Bolden also works well with others, having edited *Rites of Passage: Stories about Growing Up by Black Writers from Around the World* (1994); *33 Things Every Girl Should Know: Stories, Songs, Poems, and Smart Talk by 33 Extraordinary Women* (1998); *33 Things Every Girl Should Know about Women's History: From Suffragettes to Skirt Lengths to the E.R.A.* (2002). She has also collaborated with numerous celebrities, such as coauthoring a juvenile novel with playwright and radio personality Vy Higgensen, *Mama, I Want to Sing* (1992, based on Higgensen's musical); and motivational memoirs with talk-show host Mother Love, *Forgive or Forget: Never Underestimate the Power of Forgiveness* (1999) and *Half the Mother, Twice the Love: My Journey to Better Health with Diabetes* (2006); with "Santa Baby" chanteuse Eartha Kitt, *Rejuvenate!: It's Never Too Late*, (2001); with singer Chaka Khan, *Chaka!: Through the Fire* (2003); and with celebrity event planner Diann Valentine *Weddings Valentine Style: Rich Inspiration for Every Woman's Dream Day* (2006).

Many of Bolden's books have been honored: a Junior Library Guild selection, a Best Book for Young Adults by the American Library Association (ALA), a Coretta Scott King honor book (ALA), and more than one Book for the Teen Age (by the New York Public Library).

REFERENCES: Personal communication (1/5/99, 5/31/99); vitae/résumé (1999). Stiefer, Sandy J., in *BB. CAO-07*. //www.embracing thechild.org/africanamerican.htm. //www.tonyaboldenbooks.com/. Amazon.com.

Bonner, Marita (Odette) (married surname: Occomy; aka Joseph Maree Andrew)
6/16/1899 [or 1898]–12/6/1971
Essays, plays, short stories; educator

After earning her B.A. in English and comparative literature from Radcliffe College (1922), Bonner spent two years teaching at Bluefield Colored Institute in West Virginia; then she moved to Washington, D.C., where she taught until 1930. In 1930, she married accountant William Almy Occomy, with whom she moved to Chicago,

continued teaching, and raised three children (William Almy, Jr.; Warwick Gale Noel, and Marita Joyce).

Although Bonner never lived in Harlem, she was nurtured by fellow writers of the **Harlem Renaissance** period, especially those who congregated at the Washington, D.C., literary salon of **Georgia Douglas Johnson**, including such notables as **Countee Cullen, Jessie Fauset, Langston Hughes, Alain Locke, May Miller, Jean Toomer**, and **Willis Richardson**. In this stimulating and supportive environment, Bonner wrote two essays that aptly conveyed the spirit of the renaissance: In her autobiographical essay "On Being Young—A Woman—and Colored" (1925), she said, "You decide that something is wrong with a world that stifles and chokes; that cuts off and stunts; hedging in, pressing down on eyes, ears and throat. Somehow all wrong." Her militant essay "The Young Blood Hungers" (1928) warned of the dangers of continued racism.

In addition, Bonner wrote three plays: *The Pot Maker: A Play to Be Read* (1927), which indicts infidelity; *The Purple Flower* (1928), which provocatively suggests a revolt against racism; and *Exit, an Illusion: A One-Act Play* (1929), which probes multiracial ancestry. As the title of her first play suggests, she intended these plays to be read, and none were produced during her lifetime. In all of the plays, moral dilemmas challenge her characters.

In D.C. and then in Chicago, Bonner wrote numerous short stories, most of which were published in *Crisis* or in *Opportunity*, including "The Hands" (1925), "The Prison-Bound" (1926), "Drab Rambles" (1927), "Nothing New" (1928), "The Triple Triad on Black Notes" (1933), "Tin Can" (1934), "A Sealed Pod" (1936), "The Hongry Fire" (1939), "The Makin's" (1939), "The Whipping" (1939), and "Patch Quilt" (1940). "Tin Can" (the plot of which may have inspired **Richard Wright**'s *Native Son*) and several other stories won literary prizes and honors from *Crisis* and from *Opportunity*. Through her stories, Bonner addressed issues of poverty, interracial and intergenerational conflicts and connections, class and gender differences, harmful effects of the urban environment, and infidelity. A dark-skinned woman, she also addressed intraracial prejudice regarding skin color, and she considered the issue of beauty, which has resurfaced as an important contemporary issue. Her final short story, "One True Love" (1941), eloquently echoes the theme she described in her 1925 essay, on the double jeopardy of being African American and a woman. Following its publication, she turned her attention to her own family and her teaching career.

Many of Bonner's stories interconnected through her fictional "Frye Street," on which ethnically diverse characters interacted with one another. Years after Bonner's death, her daughter Joyce was instrumental in having *Frye Street and Environs: The Collected Works of Marita*

Bonner Occomy published (1987, edited by Joyce Flynn and Joyce Occomy Stricklin).

Her papers are housed at the Arthur and Elizabeth Schlesinger Library on History of Women in America, Radcliffe College of Harvard University.

REFERENCES: *AANB. HR&B. NYPL-AADR.* Brown-Guillory, Elizabeth, in *BWA:AHE.* Dillon, Kim Jenice, in *COCAAL* and *OCAAL. CAO-03.* Flynn, Joyce, in *AAWHR-40.* Meche, Jude R., in *T-CAD-2nd. EA-99.* Prono, Luca, in *GEAAL. Wiki.*

Bontemps, Arna Wendell
10/13/1902–6/4/1973
Poems, novels, short stories, children's literature, anthologies, nonfiction—history, biography; educator

Arna Wendell Bontemps

Arna Bontemps was born in Louisiana, the eldest of two children of Paul Bismark Bontemps (a Roman Catholic brick mason) and Maria Carolina Pembroke Bontemps (a Methodist former schoolteacher), both of Creole descent. Maria encouraged her son (and his younger sister, Ruby Sarah) to love reading books, but Paul had little interest in—and little use for—literature of any kind. Paul could see no reason why his son would need literature when laying bricks, as he intended for Arna to do.

Paul Bontemps was a stern, strong-willed man, and when two drunk white men threatened him just for being black in their presence, he decided to move his family away from the South. At age three, young Arna and his family settled into a big home in a mostly white neighborhood in Los Angeles, California. Pretty soon, Arna's maternal grandmother, his grandmother's brother Uncle Buddy, and other family members had moved to L.A., too. When Arna was just a dozen years old, his much-beloved mother died, and he moved in with his grandparents, developing a close relationship with his Uncle Buddy, a tall-tale-telling, hard-drinking charmer. Uncle Buddy encouraged Arna to write, and he told Arna delightful preacher-and-ghost stories and slave-and-master stories in his rich, native Creole dialect.

During their time in California, Paul Bontemps had converted to the Seventh-Day Adventist faith, and pretty soon, he decided he didn't want his son to come under Uncle Buddy's influence any more. Before Arna reached his fifteenth birthday, he was shipped off to a Seventh-Day Adventist boarding school, the San Fernando Academy. The school was mostly white, and before Arna left, Paul admonished him, "Now don't go up there acting colored." Instantly, Arna realized the appalling racial self-hatred embedded in that remark. When he later reflected on it, he challenged the very idea: "How dare anyone, parent, schoolteacher, or merely literary critic, tell me not to act *colored?*" Three school years later (in 1920, when he was 17), Arna graduated from the academy. From there, he went to the Seventh-Day Adventist's Pacific Union College, in Angwin, California, where he earned his B.A. in 1923.

After graduating from college, Bontemps got a job working nights in a Los Angeles post office while taking a series of postgraduate courses at UCLA. When he wasn't working or going to school, he was feverishly reading novels, biographies, dramas, poems, and anything else of interest from his local library. At work, he often discussed his readings with his coworker, **Wallace Thurman**. Soon, he was also writing poems of his own, sending them to various magazines, in hopes of having one of them published—to no avail. After noticing that **Jessie Redmon Fauset**, the editor of **Crisis** magazine, was interested in publishing the works of young African-American writers, Bontemps sent her "Hope," one of his poems rejected by other publishers.

Bontemps's hope was realized when his poem was printed in the August 1924, issue of the magazine. He quit his job at the post office and headed for Harlem, to catch the blossoming of the **Harlem Renaissance**. To support himself there, he got a job teaching at the Seventh-Day Adventist Harlem Academy, where he was eventually made principal. In addition, he sought to deepen his own knowledge, taking courses at Columbia

University, New York University, and the City College of New York.

On August 26, 1926, Bontemps married Alberta Johnson (a former student), who became his lifelong partner. In 1927, the couple had the first of their six children: Joan Marie Bontemps (Williams), followed by Paul Bismark Bontemps (II), Poppy Alberta Bontemps (Booker), Camille Ruby Bontemps (Graves), Constance Rebecca Bontemps (Thomas), and Arna Alexander Bontemps. This stable family man still managed to make time for his literary pursuits, however. As he said to a reporter for the *Nashville Tennessean* (February 18, 1951, quoted in *BH2C*), "I've done some of my best books at home with the children playing . . . all around me. I just pull up the card table, close the door (if that's possible) and go to work." It also helped that he started work at 5:00 a.m., and he could compose his works directly on the typewriter (working on a card table in the living room), often completing his works in just one or two drafts. Bontemps also constantly took notes. His eldest son (Paul) later recalled, "I thought this was the normal way that people lived, with a note pad beside the bed. In the morning there'd be scribbles all over it" (quoted in *BH2C*, p. 81).

Soon after Bontemps had moved to New York, he met **Countee Cullen**. Cullen told him of the frequent meetings of writers at the 135th Street Branch of the New York Public Library and invited him to a gathering of writers at the home (and literary salon) of **Regina Anderson** and Ethel Ray Nance. There, he met numerous fellow writers of the renaissance, such as his editor **Jessie Redmon Fauset** and the foster father of many literary careers, **Alain Locke**.

Probably the most important contact Bontemps made, however, was with the honoree of the gathering: **Langston Hughes**, who became his lifelong literary soul mate and dear friend. Even when they lived in separate cities, the twosome maintained frequent personal visits and exchanged about 2,500 letters until Hughes died (in 1967). According to Hughes biographer **Arnold Rampersad**, the two had "virtually a marriage of minds, that would last without the slightest friction" (quoted in *BH2C*, from Rampersad's *The Life of Langston Hughes*). Through their correspondence, they often proposed joint projects, shared project ideas and publishing tips, and encouraged one another in each of their solitary literary pursuits. In Bontemps's letters to Hughes, he frequently used the Creole dialect he had learned from his parents.

By mid-1931, Bontemps's first novel, *God Sends Sunday*, was published. Bontemps's literary pursuits had always been a source of friction between him and his Seventh-Day Adventist supervisors at the Harlem Academy. At the end of the school year in 1931, when the Adventists closed the academy in Harlem, they sent Bontemps to the Adventists' Oakwood Junior College in Huntsville, Alabama, far removed from the literary circles of Harlem. Some sources have claimed that Bontemps was sent away from New York against his will, but Bontemps's autobiographical sketch at Fisk University suggests that he was not unwilling to go. With the onset of the Great Depression, many artists and writers of the Harlem Renaissance were having to seek jobs elsewhere, so Bontemps was ready to leave Harlem when he did.

At Oakwood, Bontemps was both a librarian and an English instructor. Although he didn't enjoy Oakwood or Alabama, he was highly productive during his stay there, churning out quite a few publications. He also had a chance to visit Fisk University in Nashville, Tennessee, where he discovered a treasure trove of **slave narratives** that had been virtually ignored up until then. When his pal Langston Hughes visited him at Oakwood, the school's administrators admonished him against contact with Hughes. They further balked at his receiving so many books and spending so much time writing. Bontemps was a believer, but not a fundamentalist fanatic, and when the school administrators ordered him to stop writing novels, to stop teaching students about them, and to burn all of his books that were not of a religious nature, Bontemps decided he should resign, effective at the end of the school year in May of 1934. Bontemps moved his wife and children to Los Angeles, to live with his father and stepmother in their home. During the 1934-1935 school year, Bontemps studied dialects, analyzed children's books, and conducted other research in a local library; he also lectured to adults and held children's story hours there. The summer of 1935, while he and his family were cooped up in his father's house, Bontemps wrote *Black Thunder*, which was to become his most celebrated novel.

As soon as a publisher gave Bontemps an advance on royalties for the novel, he moved his family to Chicago. There, he found work as a principal and teacher at the Seventh Day Adventists' Shiloh Academy on the impoverished South Side of Chicago. He also found another blossoming bevy of talented African-American writers, such as **Margaret Walker** and fellow Seventh-Day Adventist **Richard Wright**. The critical acclaim of Bontemps's *Black Thunder* (1936) won him entry into this literary circle, and Wright and Bontemps developed a mutual respect for one another's work. Bontemps also found a new locale for his program of self-education (the Hall Branch of the Chicago Public Library), and he embarked on a program of formal education, as well. In 1936, he enrolled at the University of Chicago, taking postgraduate courses in library science and in English.

Bontemps soon won a Rosenwald Fund grant to write his third novel, *Sad-Faced Boy* (1937), and he used some of that money to travel to the Caribbean, to conduct research for his fourth novel, *Drums at Dusk* (1939). In 1938, Bontemps left the Shiloh Academy to take a position as editorial supervisor and technical assistant (in charge of African-American students) to the Illinois state director of the Federal Writers' Project (FWP) in the Works Progress Administration (WPA). Richard Wright, Jack Conroy, and other Chicago writers were also working for the WPA's FWP.

The same year that Bontemps started working for the FWP, **James Weldon Johnson** died, leaving vacant his position as professor of creative writing at Fisk University. Soon after, the head librarian position there also became available. The Fisk administrators offered Bontemps these posts, but Bontemps felt he lacked the formal training needed to fill these positions. By 1943, Bontemps had used two additional Rosenwald Fund fellowships to complete his master's degree in library science at the Graduate Library School, University of Chicago, writing his thesis on "the Negro in Illinois." The year he earned his degree, Bontemps felt ready to accept the position at Fisk.

As Fisk's head librarian, he established the James Weldon Johnson collection, as well as collections for the papers of his old Harlem Renaissance pals, Langston Hughes, **Countee Cullen**, and **Jean Toomer**. After retiring from Fisk in 1966, Bontemps returned to Chicago, where he was a professor of English at the University of Illinois, Chicago Circle, until 1969. In 1969, he moved on to Yale University, where he was instrumental in the African-American studies program and became curator of the James Weldon Johnson Memorial Collection in Yale's Beinecke Library. (Bontemps's own extensive correspondence with **Langston Hughes** is also housed there.) From 1970 until his death (1973), he returned to Fisk as writer-in-residence.

Bontemps wrote or edited more than 30 books, covering almost every literary genre: poems, plays, anthologies (of poems and of folklore), literary criticism, children's stories, novels, and nonfiction histories and biographies. Through all his works, he reflects the nobility of the African-American cultural heritage, while realistically depicting the struggles they have faced—and mixing in generous doses of humor. He also managed to use authentic dialect in his works, without sounding stereotypical or being incomprehensible to those who spoke other forms of American English.

Beginning with "Hope," Bontemps's earliest poems started appearing in **Crisis** (published by the NAACP) and **Opportunity** (published by the National Urban League) magazines from 1924 through 1931. In the mid-1920s, two of his poems ("Golgotha Is a Mountain" and "The Return") won *Opportunity* magazine's Alexander Pushkin prizes, and two ("A Black Man Talks of Reaping" and "Nocturne at Bethesda") won first honors from *Crisis*. Many of his poems were collected in his vol-

ume *Personals* (1936; 3rd ed., 1973). Although Bontemps's poems are entirely modern in their compactness, they clearly reflect his deep-seated Christian education and point of view. Critics often refer to his work as intellectually challenging, yet graceful, meditative, and serene.

During this early period, Bontemps also wrote short stories, including his *Opportunity* prize-winning "A Summer Tragedy" (1932), about the hardships of sharecropping in the South. This and a dozen or so more stories were collected decades later in his *The Old South: A Summer Tragedy and Other Stories of the Thirties* (1973).

Bontemps's very first novel (*Chariot in the Cloud*, written in 1929), set in Southern California, about the main character's psychological growth, was never published. The first of his novels to be published, *God Sends Sunday* (1931), was probably inspired by Bontemps's observations of his Uncle Buddy, as it depicts high living in St. Louis during the 1890s. In it, Little Augie, a fun-loving African-American jockey, manages horses better than he manages people. Bontemps and **Countee Cullen** later (in 1937) adapted the novel to the stage, and the retitled *St. Louis Woman* enjoyed success as a musical comedy on Broadway in 1946. In 1952, Metro-Goldwyn-Mayer bought the movie rights to the play. Despite its popularity and acclaim, many critics found fault with it; among others, **W. E. B. Du Bois** chided Bontemps for highlighting the less-than-morally-upright aspects of the African-American experience.

Two of Bontemps's novels focused on slave revolts. When Bontemps was younger, he had been taught a narrow view of slavery, typical of his day, and he had long wondered why none of the slaves had ever revolted. When he was older, and he heard of slave revolts in Haiti and in the antebellum South, he decided to ensure that other young African Americans wouldn't suffer in ignorance as he had. His novel *Black Thunder: Gabriel's Revolt, Virginia 1800* (1936) tells the story of Gabriel Prosser and the slave rebellion he attempted about two centuries ago. Bontemps revealed how bad weather and deceit foiled Prosser's efforts. Although the novel won no prizes, it was widely acclaimed; critic **Sterling A. Brown** praised it as "one of the six best African-American novels ever written." Bontemps's novel *Drums at Dusk* (1939) describes an eighteenth-century (1794) slave revolt on the island of Haiti.

Haiti was also the locale for the first book Bontemps wrote for children: *Popo and Fifina: Children of Haiti* (1932). He wrote this book (in collaboration with Langston Hughes), while he was teaching at Oakwood, when his own children were very young. The success of that book led him to continue, and he ended up writing a total of 16 books for children and youths, including such fiction works as *You Can't Pet a Possum* (1934), about an eight-year-old farm boy and his old yellow hound dog; *Sad-Faced Boy* (1937), about three country boys in Harlem; *We Have Tomorrow* (1945), about the extraordinary achievements of a dozen ordinary African-American youths; and *Lonesome Boy* (1955), about a trumpet-playing youth. With Jack Conroy (a thorough researcher, whom he knew from his early days in Chicago), he also wrote a few tall tales: *The Fast Sooner Hound* (1942); *Slappy Hooper, the Wonderful Sign Painter* (1946); and *Sam Patch, the High, Wide and Handsome Jumper* (1951). Bontemps also edited at least one poem anthology for youths: *Golden Slippers, An Anthology of Negro Poetry for Young Readers* (1941); one source suggests that his was the first such anthology for young people, and another source mentions that he edited another poetry volume for youths in 1968.

On his own, Bontemps also wrote quite a few nonfiction books intended for young readers, including his Jane Addams Children's Book Award-winning *The Story of the Negro* (1948), which traced African roots back to ancient Egyptian civilizations; *Chariot in the Sky: A Story of the Jubilee Singers* (1951), written while he was at Fisk University, enjoying their soulful songs; and biographies such as *Story of George Washington Carver* (1954); **Frederick Douglass**: *Slave, Fighter, Freeman* (1959, a brief biography); *Free at Last: The Life of Frederick Douglass* (1971, a full-length biography, written for youths and adults); and *Young Booker: The Story of* **Booker T. Washington***'s Early Days* (1972).

Bontemps also wrote a historical work for adults, *One Hundred Years of Negro Freedom* (1961), which follows from the period of Reconstruction immediately after the Civil War, highlighting the key roles played by **Frederick Douglass, W. E. B. Du Bois, Booker T. Washington**, and others. With Jack Conroy, Bontemps wrote *They Seek a City* (1945, revised as *Anyplace But Here*, 1966), which more narrowly focused on the great migration from the deep South to the North following Reconstruction. This work drew heavily on the research materials Bontemps and Conroy had gathered while working for the WPA's FWP in Chicago. While Bontemps was still in Alabama, he ghostwrote *Father of the Blues: An Autobiography of* **W. C. Handy** (1941), and he wrote *W.C. Handy's Compositions*.

Bontemps also enjoyed collecting and highlighting the outstanding works of fellow writers and edited numerous anthologies. With **Langston Hughes**, he edited the anthologies *The Poetry of the Negro 1746-1949* (1949), *The Book of Negro Folklore* (1958), *American Negro Poetry* (1963), and *I Too Sing America* (1964). After his coeditor died (in 1967), Bontemps continued to compile memorable anthologies: *Hold Fast to Dreams: Poems Old and New* (1969), including poems written by both African-American and European-American writers; *Great* **Slave** *Narra-*

tives (1969); and **Harlem Renaissance** *Remembered: Essays with a Memoir* (1972, reprinted 1984). Each of his anthologies has been touted as offering highly readable, yet thorough and scholarly explanations of literary and historical traditions linking the various works.

Along with the Rosenwald fellowships and the prizes he was awarded for individual works, Bontemps was awarded Guggenheim Fellowships (1949, 1954) for creative writing and honorary degrees from Morgan State University (1969) and Berea College (1973). In addition, his birthplace and early childhood home in Alexandria, Louisiana, is now the Arna Bontemps African American Museum and Cultural Center and was registered as the Arna Wendell Bontemps House on the National Register of Historic Places (9/13/1993). According to its website, //www.arnabontempsmuseum.com/, the museum was founded in 1988 and opened August 1992.

REFERENCES: *AA:PoP. AANB. AAW:AAPP. BAL-1-P. BWA. EA-99. EB-BH-CD. EBLG. G-97. NAAAL. OC2OLE. WDAA.* Alvarez, Joseph A. "The Lonesome Boy Theme as Emblem for Arna Bontemps's Children's Literature." *African American Review. 32.1* (Spring 1998) p. 23. From *Literature Resource Center*. Andrews, William L., in *WB-99*. Bader, Barbara, in *CBC*. Conroy, Jack. "Memories of Arna Bontemps, Friend and Collaborator." *American Libraries 5.11* (Dec. 1974): pp. 602-606. Rpt. in Literature Resource Center. Gale, Cengage Learning, pp. 602-606. From *Literature Resource Center*. Cosgrave, Mary Silva, in *T-CCW-4*. Duke-Sylvester, Jennifer, in //www.lib.utk.edu/refs/tnauthors/authors/bontemps-a.html. Fleming, Robert E., in //www.english.uiuc.edu/maps/poets/a_f/ bontemps/bontemps.htm. Gwin, Minrose C., in *AP1880-1945-2*. Harris, Melanie, in //www.csustan.edu/english/reuben/pal/chap9/ bontemps.html. Harris, Steven R., in *GEAAL*. Howard, Elizabeth F., in *WfC*. James, Charles L., in *COCAAL* and *OCAAL*. //www.english. uiuc.edu/maps/poets/a_f/bontemps/life.htm. Jones, Kirkland C., in *AAWHR-40*, and "Bontemps and the Old South." *African American Review. 27.2* (Summer 1993) p. 179. From *Literature Resource Center*. //www.arnabontempsmuseum.com/. //www.poets.org/poet.php/prm PID/128. Patti, Nicholas, in *BB. CAO-03. MWEL*. Smith, Jessie Carney, in *B. BCE. BH2C. CE. W. Wiki*.

Bourne, St. Clair (Cecil)
2/16/1943–12/15/2007
Documentary films; newspaper worker

Bourne's father, St. Clair Bourne, Sr., edited the *Amsterdam News* and reported for *People's Voice*. His childhood immersed in journalism probably helped the younger Bourne when the Peace Corps sent him to Lima, Peru, where he revived the nearly dead *El Comeno* newspaper there.

Bourne the younger's primary mission, however, was to make films, having producing and/or directed more than 40 films, many through Chamba, his own production company. Among other projects, Bourne's documentary films have included *Something to Build On* (1971), *Let the Church Say Amen!* (1973), *The Black and the Green*

(1982, commissioned by the British Broadcasting Corporation), *In Motion: **Amiri Baraka*** (1982), ***Langston Hughes**: Keeper of the Dream* (1987), *Making "Do the Right Thing"* (1989), *John Henrik Clarke: A Great and Mighty Walk* (1996), and participation in a Public Broadcasting System *American Masters* show, "**Paul Robeson**: Here I Stand." He has also directed other films, including a documentary executive produced and narrated by actor Wesley Snipes, *John Henrik Clarke: A Great and Mighty Walk* (1997).

REFERENCES: *EA-99. Wiki.* //www.imdb.com/name/nm0100093/bio. //www.nydailynews.com/entertainment/movies/2007/12/17/2007-12-17_filmmaker_st_clair_bourne_dies_at_64.html. //www.nytimes.com/2007/12/18/arts/18bourne.html.

Boyd, Melba (Joyce)
4/2/1950–
Poems, essays, biographies; educator

Boyd observed for *Contemporary Authors*, "I think like a poet. . . . inspired to write by whatever catches my eye or ear or heart." Her poems have been published in various periodicals (e.g., **Black Scholar** and **First World**) and anthologies and in her collections *Cat Eyes and Dead Wood* (1978), *The Inventory of Black Roses* (1989), *Letters to Che* (1996), and *The Province of Literary Cats* (2002), as well as two books published in both German and English: *thirteen frozen flamingoes* (1988) and *Song for Maya* (1989).

In addition, she has published two important nonfiction prose works, *Discarded Legacy: Politics and Poetics in the Life of **Frances E. W. Harper*** (1994) and *Wrestling with the Muse: **Dudley Randall** and the **Broadside Press*** (2003). Before writing the *Muse* book, she had written, directed, and produced the documentary film *The Black Unicorn: Dudley Randall and the Broadside Press* (1995). Even earlier, she was the assistant editor for the periodical *Broadside* (1972-1977, 1980-1982), and more recently, with M. L. Liebler, she edited the anthology *Abandon Automobile: Detroit City Poetry 2001* (2001). She has garnered at least a dozen awards and grants for her literary and cultural contributions and achievements. In addition, Boyd has taught high school, community college, and university students (since 1982; since 1996, as professor and head of the Africana Studies Department at Wayne State University). With her former husband, writer **Herb Boyd**, she has a son, John, and daughter, Maya.

REFERENCES: *CAO-07.* Bloom, Karen R., in *COCAAL* and *OCAAL.* Bostian, Patricia Kennedy, in *GEAAL.*

Bradley, Jr., David (Henry)
9/7/1950–
Novels, essays, book reviews, interviews; educator

A native of a rural coal-mining town, Bradley has spent most of his adult life in urban Philadelphia. After graduating summa cum laude from the University of Pennsylvania (1972), Bradley was awarded a Thouron Scholarship to attend the University of London (M.A., 1974). While there, he began work on his first novel, *South Street* (1975), about the observations and experiences of an African-American poet, an outsider who gets to know the habitues of Lightin' Ed's Bar and Grill, the Elysium Hotel, and the World of Life Church in an African-American neighborhood of Philadelphia. *South Street* was praised by critics for its characterizations. Bradley clearly relishes involving his readers in the lives of his characters: "When you sit down at your typewriter, you're having a good time. I can make you spend hours finding out about somebody that you would not invite to your dining table." (Blake and Millner, quoted in *NAAAL*, p. 2535).

By 1977, after teaching English elsewhere, Bradley joined the faculty at Temple University as a professor of English and creative writing, where he remained until 1996. Since then, he has returned to being a peripatetic professor, welcomed often at the University of Oregon. Meanwhile, Bradley wrote his critically acclaimed PEN/Faulkner Award-winning second novel, *The Chaneysville Incident* (1981, Book of the Month Club alternate selection). The novel centers on a fictional history professor and the revelations he discovers while trying to understand the suicide of his biological father. In truth, much of the information on which Bradley based his novel was uncovered by his mother, local historian Harriet M. Jackson Bradley, who wrote *The Kernel of Greatness: An Informal Bicentennial History of Bedford County* (for the 1969 bicentennial). Among the true incidents on which the story is based is one in which fugitive slaves in danger of re-enslavement chose instead to commit suicide.

In addition to his novels, Bradley has written numerous essays, interviews, and book reviews (e.g., in *New York Times Book Review* and *Washington Post Book World*); and his writings have been anthologized in works such as **Terry McMillan**'s *Breaking Ice* and Gates and McKay's *Norton Anthology of African-American Literature*. In 1998, he and Shelley Fisher Fishkin edited the three-volume *Encyclopedia of Civil Rights in America*, and in 2005, the duo edited the Modern Library volume *Paul Dunbar, Sport of the Gods: And Other Essential Writings*. Reportedly, he is currently working on an essay series, "The Bondage Hypothesis: Meditations on Race, History, and America"; a third novel, told as a series of stories; and a work tentatively titled "Orphan Pieces." Perhaps Bradley's own words (to *Contemporary Authors*) can help us understand why his writing receives such high praise: "I have faith in the ability of people to respond to a story that treats them with kindness, honesty, dignity, and understanding."

REFERENCES: *AA. AANB. AAW:PV. CAO-07. EA-99. MAAL. NAAAL.*. Ensslen, Klaus, in *COCAAL* and *OCAAL*. Hall, John Greer, in *GEAAL. W.* Metzger, Sheri Elaine, in *BB*. Pinsker, Sanford, in *CN-6*. Smith, Valerie, in *AAFW-55-84*. //www.litencyc.com/php/speople.php?rec=true&UID=535. //www.pabook.libraries.psu.edu/palitmap/bios/Bradley__David.html. //www.uoregon.edu/~crwrweb/faculty/davidbradley.htm.

FURTHER READING: *AWAW. BI. NYPL-AADR.. OCWW.*

Braithwaite, William Stanley Beaumont
12/6/1878–6/8/1962
Poems, criticism, anthologies, autobiography/memoir, biography; printer, editor, publisher, educator

William, the son of mixed-race parents, spent his first 12 years in a prosperous, well cultured home. That changed when his father died, and William had to stop his formal education to help support his family. Fortunately, in one of his jobs, he set type for some lyric poetry by the British Romantics—and fell madly in love with lyric poetry. Soon, he started writing poems himself, using traditional lyrical forms.

By 1903, his verse and his literary criticism were being published in various prestigious periodicals. His criticism spotlighted the poetry of both European Americans and African Americans. In 1904 and 1908, he published two collections of his own poems: *Lyrics of Life and Love* and *The House of Falling Leaves, with Other Poems*, respectively. In 1912, Braithwaite launched his *Poetry Journal*—which folded soon after. Undaunted, his next venture succeeded: His esteemed *Anthology of Magazine Verse and Yearbook of American Poetry* was published annually from 1913 until 1929. These anthologies included a wide assortment of poems highlighting themes of eternal truths and spiritual beauty. Notably absent were didactic, polemical, or narrowly political poems. He complemented the poems with his critical literary analyses and sensitive reviews.

Braithwaite preferred relatively traditional lyrical poetry and was initially wary of dialect poetry and other unconventional poetic forms. Perhaps because of his own abbreviated formal education, he worried that nontraditional forms would perpetuate stereotypes that African Americans were uneducated, uncultured, or unsophisticated in their grasp or expression of poetry. He also avoided segregating talented African-American poets from other fine literary artists in his anthologies and carefully included poets of other races.

William Stanley Braithwaite

Braithwaite was not entirely averse to novel poetic forms or themes, however, as he praised such dialect poets as **Paul Laurence Dunbar,** and he favorably reviewed many poems expressing the distinctive African-American experience. He introduced many African-American poets to a wider readership than they might otherwise have enjoyed. Similarly, he gradually introduced readers to various innovative poetic forms while maintaining his fondest love for lyrical poetry. For his contributions to African-American literature, in 1918, he won the NAACP's prestigious **Spingarn** Medal.

Braithwaite continued to contribute to American literature over the next three decades. For six years (1921-1927), he was editor of a publishing company he founded. His own published works included at least two novels and a short-story collection. During the Great Depression, however, he, his wife, and their seven children struggled financially. From 1935 to 1945, he taught creative literature in Atlanta and served on the editorial board of *Phylon*. In addition, he continued to write for periodicals and wrote his autobiography (1941), his last collection of his own poetry (1948), his biographical study of the Brontës (1950), and his last poetry anthology (1959).

REFERENCES: *AANB. BANP. BWA. EBLG. NAAAL. OC20LE. TtW.* Brawley, Benjamin, in *TNLAUS*. Brennan, Carol, in *BB. CAO-07. LFCC-07.* Clark, Patricia E., in *GEAAL*. Robinson, William H., in *AP1880-1945-3.* Schulze, Robin G., in *COCAAL* and *OCAAL*.

W. Wiki. Williams, Kenny J., in *AAWBHR.* //www.gutenberg.org/browse/authors/b#a865.

Brandon, Barbara (aka Barbara Brandon-Croft)
11/27/1958–
Comic strip, beauty and fashion articles

When Barbara was about 10 years old, her father, Brumsic Brandon, Jr., started publishing his comic strip, "Luther," in African-American newspapers across the country. His Luther was a city kid, like Barbara and her two older siblings. After Barbara Brandon studied illustration at Syracuse University, she created her "Where I'm Coming From" strip, featuring the perspectives and commentaries of a diverse set of nine young African-American women. At first, her strip was commissioned for *Elan,* an African-American women's lifestyle magazine, but before it was published, the magazine folded. Although *Essence* didn't want Brandon's strip, it did hire her to write beauty and fashion articles. In the late 1980s, the *Detroit Free Press* decided to seek some African-American-oriented comic strips and asked Barbara's dad (who had stopped drawing "Luther" in the mid-1980s) whether he happened to know of any talented cartoonists. Guess what he answered. In 1990, The United Press Syndicate decided to pick up Barbara Brandon's all-woman strip, making her the first African-American woman to have her cartoons syndicated nationally in mainstream, white-owned newspapers. Her first strip appeared nationwide September 1991. To pay her bills, she also does freelance fact-checking and other research for periodicals.

In 1993, fans of Cheryl, Nicole, Lekesia, Sonya, and Brandon's other five talking heads got a treat with the publication of the book *Where I'm Coming From,* with a foreword by **Ruby Dee** and **Ossie Davis**. Brandon introduced a little girl, Brianna, to the crew in the anthology *33 Things Every Girl Should Know* (Tonya Bolden, Ed.). Since marrying Monte Croft in 1997, with whom she has a son Chase (born October 1998), she uses the surname Brandon-Croft.

REFERENCES: *33T. AANB. BAAW.* Burgess, Marjorie, in *BB.* Thompson, Kathleen, in *BWA:AHE.* //aalbc.com/authors/barbara.htm. //lambiek.net/artists/b/brandon_barbara.htm. Amazon.com —Tonya Bolden

Brathwaite, Edward Kamau (né Lawson Edward Brathwaite)
05/11/1930–
Poems, literary and cultural criticism and history, plays; book publisher, journal founder, educator

Given the name Lawson Edward Brathwaite by his parents, Hilton and Beryl Gill Brathwaite, he was awarded the name Kamau by the grandmother of Kenyan author Ng g wa Thiong'o in Limuru, Kenya, while he was on a fellowship to study at the University of Nairobi in 1971. His works have been published under the names Edward Brathwaite, Edward Kamau Brathwaite, and Kamau Brathwaite.

After graduating from college at Cambridge University, Brathwaite spent several years (1955-1962) living in what is now Ghana. While in Ghana, Brathwaite wrote *Four Plays for Primary Schools* (1961, Ghana; 1965, England), his play *Odale's Choice* (produced in Ghana, 1962; published in London, 1967), and several other writings. He then returned to his native Barbados and married fellow Barbadian Doris Monica Welcome, a teacher and librarian (March of 1960), with whom he later had a son, Michael. He also obtained the first of several positions he was to have at the University of the West Indies (1962; in 1982, he became a full professor). Inspired by his environs, he cofounded the Caribbean Artists Movement (1966), which he continued to promote even while he returned to England to earn his doctorate of philosophy from the University of Sussex (1968).

Meanwhile, Oxford University Press was starting to publish the three poetry collections that would make up his celebrated *The Arrivants: A New World Trilogy* (1973), comprising *Rights of Passage* (originally 1967), *Masks* (originally 1968), and *Islands* (originally 1969). Since then, he wrote a second trilogy, comprising *Mother Poem* (1977), *Sun Poem* (1982), and *X/Self* (1987), later united as *Ancestors: A Reinvention of Mother Poem, Sun Poem, and X/Self* (2001). His other poetry collections include *Panda No. 349* (1969), *Day + Nights* (1975), *Other Exiles* (1975), *Black + Blues* (1976/1995), his much-honored *Word Making Man: A Poem for Nicolas Guillen* (1979), *Third World Poems* (1983), *Jah Music* (1986), *Sappho Sakyi's Meditations* (1989), *Shar* (1990), *Middle Passages* (1992/1993), *Barabajan Poems, 1492-1992* (1994), *Dream Stories* (1994) and *DS (2): Dreamstories* (2007), *Trench Town Rock* (1994), *Words Need Love Too* (2000), and *Born to Slow Horses* (2005), which won the esteemed 2006 International Griffin Poetry Prize.

Brathwaite's prose, especially literary and cultural criticism, include *Folk Culture of the Slaves in Jamaica* (1970; rev., 1981), *The Development of Creole Society in Jamaica, 1770-1820* (1971/2005), *Caribbean Man in Space and Time* (1974), *Contradictory Omens: Cultural Diversity and Integration in the Caribbean* (1974), *Wars of Respect: Nanny, Sam Sharpe and the Struggle for People's Liberation* (1977), *Soweto* (1979), *Barbados Poetry, 1661-1979: A Checklist: Books, Pamphlets, Broadsheets* (1979), *Jamaica Poetry: A Checklist: Books, Pamphlets, Broadsheets 1686-1978* (1979), *Afternoon of the Status Crow* (1982),

Gods of the Middle Passage (1982), *Kumina (Savacou Working Paper)* (1982), *National Language Poetry* (1982, as E. K. Brathwaite), *The Colonial Encounter: Language* (1984), *History of the Voice: The Development of Nation Language in Anglophone Caribbean Poetry* (1984), *Roots: Essay/ Literary Criticism* (1986/1993), *Visibility Trigger / Le détonateur de visibilité* (1986), *The Poet and His Place in Barbadian Culture* (1987), *Golokwati: A Tidaltectics History of Our Thymes* (2002/2009, 2 vols.), *MR (Magical Realism)* (2002), and *LX the Love Axe/l: Developing a Caribbean Aesthetic* (2009).

Brathwaite's edited works include *Iouanaloa: Recent Writing from St. Lucia* (1963), *Our Ancestral Heritage: A Bibliography of the Roots of Culture in the English-Speaking Caribbean* (1976), *Barbados Poetry, 1661-1979* (1979), *New Poets from Jamaica* (1979), and *Dream Rock* (1987). Brathwaite also founded the journal *Savacou* (starting in 1970 or 1971), to promote the Caribbean Artists Movement, and he has edited and contributed to the journal, as well. Savacou Publications (renamed Savacou North since the 1990s) has also published several of Brathwaite's poetry collections, his nonfiction prose, and his edited works.

Brathwaite carefully arranges and designs his poetry on the page, so that the visual effects enhance the poems' interpretation. Nonetheless, Brathwaite's highly rhythmic poems vivify when spoken aloud. Fortunately, Brathwaite has made audio recordings of his *Arrivants* trilogy: *Rights of Passage* (1969/1972), *Masks* (1972), and *Islands* (1973), and he has participated in producing several other recordings: *The Poet Speaks 10* (1968), *The Poetry of Edward Kamau Brathwaite* (1976), *Poemas* (1976), and two Library of Congress recordings, *Kamau Brathwaite Reading His Poems with Comment in the Recording Laboratory* (1970) and *Edward Kamau Brathwaite Reading His Poems* (1982). Brathwaite's live performances have been described as "electrifying" and "charismatic."

For more than a quarter century, he had enjoyed essential support from his wife, Doris. In May of 1986, Doris was given a death sentence when she was told cancer would kill her within a short time. During the next several months, he kept a diary of his powerless, helpless, hopeless observance of her dying. In his most personal, intimate work, *The Zea Mexican Diary, 7 Sept 1926-7 Sept 1986* (1993), he revealed himself, his wife, and his marriage to his readers through poignant poems, excerpts from his diary, letters, and other writings from this troubled time. He has since remarried, to Beverley Reid, a Jamaican (in the late 1990s).

In 1988, Hurricane Gilbert further assaulted Brathwaite, encasing in mud most of his extensive, priceless personal library of Caribbean literature and his personal papers. Devastated, Brathwaite was receptive to offers for change. Earlier, he had enjoyed visiting professorships at Harvard and Yale, and in 1991, he accepted an offer from New York University to become a professor of comparative literature there.

Among the honors he has received are Cuba's Casa de las Americas Prize for poetry (1976) and for literary criticism, the biennial Neustadt International Prize for Literature (2004), and the international Griffin Poetry Prize (2006). As a poet of West Indian origins, Brathwaite urges both himself and others "to restore our sense of an intimate, emotional connection with our past; to restore, in fact, our folk myths. But we also need to have a sense of connection and continuity—a sense of historicity—so that we may come to believe, in ourselves, in the credentials of our past" (from *Wars of Respect*, quoted in *T-CCBAW-2*). While he honors the country of his origins, to which he returns often, the country in which he has lived and worked for decades prizes his addition to our rich African-American heritage.

REFERENCES: *CAO-02. LF-07. MWEL. Wiki.* Breiner, Laurence A., in *T-CCBAW-2*. Brown, Lloyd W., in *CP-6*. Manheim, James M., in *BB*. //worldcat.org/identities/lccn-n50-43071. //www.poets.org/poet.php/prmPID/668. Amazon.com.

FURTHER READING: [Brathwaite, Kamau]. "Newstead to Neustadt: Kamau Brathwaite." [1994 Neustadt International Prize for Literature acceptance speech]. *World Literature Today*. 68.4 (Autumn 1994) p. 653. From *Literature Resource Center*. Brown, Lloyd Wellesley. 1978. "The Cyclical Vision of Edward Brathwaite." *West Indian Poetry*. Boston: G. K. Hall & Co. Rpt. in Janet Witalec (Ed.) (2004), *Poetry Criticism* (Vol. 56). Detroit: Gale. pp. 139-158. From *Literature Resource Center*. Irele, Abiola. "The Return of the Native: Edward Kamau Brathwaite's Masks." *World Literature Today*. 68.4 (Autumn 1994) p. 719. From *Literature Resource Center*. Kohli, Amor, in *BrWr*. Thiong'o, Ngugi wa. "Kamau Brathwaite: The Voice of African Presence." *World Literature Today* 68.4 (Autumn 1994), pp. 677-679. Rpt. in Literature Resource Center. Gale, Cengage Learning. From *Literature Resource Center*.

Brawley, Benjamin (Griffith)
4/22/1882–2/1/1939
Essays, textbooks, biographies, poems, short stories, literary criticism, literary history, social history, biography; educator

Among his works of scholarship are *A Short History of the American Negro* (1913; 4th rev. ed., 1939), *History of Morehouse College* (1917/1970), *The Negro in Literature and Art in the United States* (1918, with many subsequent editions), *A Social History of the American Negro* (1921/1971), *A Short History of the English Drama* (1921/1969), *New Survey of English Literature: A Textbook for Colleges* (1925/1930), *A History of the English Hymn* (1932), *Early Negro American Writers* (1935/1968), **Paul Laurence Dunbar**: *Poet of His People* (1936/1967), *The Negro Genius: A New Appraisal of the Achievement of the American Negro in Literature and the Fine Arts* (1937, short biographies), and *Negro Builders and Heroes* (1937/1965, biographies). He also wrote short stories, and his poems were posthumously collected in *The Seven Sleepers of Ephesys* (1971).

REFERENCES: *AANB. CAO-02. EBLG. Wiki.* Brennan, Carol, in *BB.* Williams, Jeffrey R., in *GEAAL,* Williams, Kenny Jackson, in *COCAAL* and *OCAAL.* //www.gutenberg.org/browse/authors/b#a4226.

Braxton, Joanne (aka Jodi) (Margaret)
5/25/1950–
Poems, criticism, interviews; educator

As a child, young Joanne had not only her parents and three brothers, but also her two grandmothers, who "taught me family history and genealogy, and told me stories they had heard about slavery; tales of horror and strength. This oral tradition constitutes the source of my artistic consciousness and my personal strength" (biographical note in *Sometimes I Think of Maryland*). Since the death of her beloved grandmothers and her brother, and the illness of her father, her writings have continued this oral tradition and reflect her close ties to family and the resulting risks of loss. Braxton's published work includes her poetry collection *Sometimes I Think of Maryland* (1977, as Jodi Braxton), with poems full of rich, sensual imagery; and her literary criticism *Black Women Writing Autobiography: A Tradition within a Tradition* (1989), based on her doctoral dissertation at Yale. She has also edited two works: *Wild Women in the Whirlwind: Afra-American Culture and the Contemporary Literary Renaissance* (1990, with Andree Nicola McLaughlin) and *The Collected Poetry of* **Paul Laurence Dunbar** (1993); and she contributes articles and poems to scholarly periodicals and anthologies (e.g., *My Magic Pours Secret Libations,* 1996, edited by Monifa A. Love; *The Private Self: Theory and Practice in Women's Autobiographical Writings,* 1988, edited by Shari Benstock). In addition, she has taught at Yale and at the University of Michigan, and at her intellectual home since 1980, the College of William Mary, where she has held an endowed chair since 1989.

REFERENCES: Clark, Keith, in *COCAAL* and *OCAAL. CAO-02.* Washington, Edward T., in *AAP-55-85.*

Briggs, Cyril Valentine
5/28/1888–10/18/1966
Editorials; founding journal editor

An outspoken radical militant in his day, Briggs advocated armed self-defense for African Americans. When he was evicted from his post with the *Amsterdam News* (in 1919) for an editorial attacking the League of Nations, he turned his attention to the journal he had founded the previous year, the *Crusader.* Initially, Briggs aligned himself with **Marcus Garvey** but then turned against virulent anticommunist Garvey when he aligned himself with the Communist Party USA. In 1929, he went to work for the communist-aligned *Harlem Liberator,* but in 1938, his championing of black nationalism led to his being ejected from the Communist Party.

REFERENCES: *AANB. EA-99. Wiki.*

Broadside Press
1965–

Almost by accident, **Dudley Randall** founded Broadside Press. Initially, he founded it just to publish a *broadside* (publication on a single [usually large] sheet of paper) of one of his poems, to preserve his copyright for it. Since that first publication, Randall's press has published the work of more than 200 other poets, as well as more than half a dozen of his own poetry collections. In particular, at the height of the **Black Arts Movement,** Broadside Press published the works of numerous important poets of that period (e.g., **Nikki Giovanni, Etheridge Knight,** Don Lee **[Haki Madhubuti], Audre Lorde, Sonia Sanchez**), including broadsides, chapbooks, full-length poetry collections, and even recordings of readings. He also published the works of poets from earlier literary periods, such as **Gwendolyn Brooks** and **Sterling Brown.** When Randall underwent a long-term illness, the press published very little. Briefly, the **Alexander Crummell** Center owned the press and published some works, then it, too, stopped publishing. In 1985, Don and Hilda Vest took over ownership of the press and restructured it as a nonprofit press, which has since started publishing new works and republishing backlist titles as "Broadside classics."

REFERENCES: **Madgett, Naomi Long,** in *OCAAL.*

FURTHER READING: Randall, Dudley. "Broadside Press: A Personal Chronicle." In Floyd B. Barbour (Ed.). 1970. *The Black Seventies* (pp.139-148). Boston: Porter Sargent Publisher. Rpt. in Jeffrey W. Hunter (Ed.). 2001. *Contemporary Literary Criticism* (Vol. 135). Detroit: Gale Group. From *Literature Resource Center.* Randall, Dudley, and Gwendolyn Fowlkes. "An Interview with Dudley Randall." *The Black Scholar* 6.9 (June 1975), pp. 87-90. Rpt. in Jeffrey W. Hunter (Ed.). 2001. *Contemporary Literary Criticism* (Vol. 135). Detroit: Gale Group. From *Literature Resource Center.*

Brooks, Gwendolyn (Elizabeth)
6/7/1917–12/3/2000
Poems, novel, autobiography/memoir; educator

Poet—this one word describes every cell of Gwendolyn Brooks's being. It was always poetry—from

Gwendolyn Brooks, Pulitzer Prize winner for poetry, 1950

her Chicago childhood to her 1950 Pulitzer Prize to her awakening social consciousness to her Illinois Poet Laureate status and through all the other honors and awards. It was always poetry—and few writers besides Brooks can speak volumes with so few words.

Born into a large and close-knit extended family, including memorable aunts and uncles whom Brooks later honored in her work, Brooks seems to always have been comfortable with herself. Her mother, Keziah Wims, met her father, David Anderson Brooks, in Topeka, Kansas in 1914. They soon married and relocated to Chicago. Keziah returned to family in Topeka to give birth to her first child, Gwendolyn. Keziah stayed in Topeka for several weeks before returning to her husband in Chicago with her infant daughter. Gwendolyn's only sibling, younger brother Raymond, was born 16 months later. Brooks's mother had been a schoolteacher in Topeka, and her father, son of a runaway slave, had attended Fisk University for one year in hopes of becoming a doctor. Economic survival became more important, however, so his desires for a medical career were dashed and he spent much of his life as a janitor. Despite financial constraints for the young family in Chicago, Brooks remembers a loving, family atmosphere throughout her childhood.

She had a more difficult time fitting in with her high-school classmates, however, attending three high schools: Hyde Park, which was mostly white; Wendell

Phillips, which was all black; and Englewood High School, the integrated school from which she eventually graduated in 1934. Two years later, she graduated from Wilson Junior College (1936). Even prior to her high school years, it became apparent to Brooks that she did not really fit in with her peers. She was a nonperson at Hyde Park and socially inept at Wendell Phillips. She kept her self-esteem, however, largely due to her strong family ties. Also, since she was seven years old, her mind had been someplace else. That place was poetry, which she had started writing at that young age. Her parents contributed to her love of language and story. As a former schoolteacher, Brooks's mother encouraged her daughter's interest, and her father often told stories and sang songs about his family's history with slavery. From her parents and her extended family, Brooks learned the honor and dignity found in living everyday life with love and integrity.

Her first published poem, "Eventide," appeared in *American Childhood Magazine* in 1930 when Brooks was 13. At 16, with her mother's help, Brooks met two prominent African-American writers, **James Weldon Johnson** and **Langston Hughes**. Although both writers read Brooks's work and told her that she had talent and should keep reading and writing poetry, only Hughes and Brooks developed a long and enduring friendship. She later wrote a poem tribute to him, "Langston Hughes," published in her *Bean Eaters* collection. She also remembered him fondly and with great respect in her autobiography, *Report from Part One.* In the meantime, she contributed regularly to the *Chicago Defender,* having 75 poems published there in two years.

Brooks was also looking outside herself, joining the Youth Council of the National Association for the Advancement of Colored People (NAACP) in 1938. There she met her future husband and fellow writer, Henry L. Blakey III, whom she married in 1939. Marriage took Brooks from the comfort of her parent's home and into a kitchenette apartment, the setting for her first volume of poetry, *A Street in Bronzeville,* published in 1945. She gave birth to their first child, Henry, Jr., in 1940, and to their daughter, Nora, in 1951. In between the births of her children, Brooks kept writing her poetry. She and her husband participated in a poetry workshop given by Inez Cunningham Stark, a reader for *Poetry* magazine. There, Stark and other workshop participants encouraged Brooks.

In 1943, Brooks received the Midwestern Writers' Conference Poetry Award. The Midwestern Writers' award proved to be the first of many for Brooks: In 1945, she was named as one of *Mademoiselle* magazine's "Ten Young Women of the Year"; in 1946, she won the American Academy of Letters Award; in 1947 and 1948, she won Guggenheim fellowships; and in 1949, she won the

Eunice Tietjens Memorial Award. Brooks published *Annie Allen* in 1949 and with it won the Pulitzer Prize for literature, becoming the first African American to do so.
The awards and honors continued for several years: being
invited to read at a Library of Congress poetry festival in
1962, at the request of then President Kennedy; named
Poet Laureate of Illinois in 1968 (lifelong post); nominated for the National Book Award in 1969; appointed
poetry consultant to the Library of Congress in 1985 (the
second African American and the first black woman in
that post, which was later retitled the nation's Poet Laureate); inducted into the National Women's Hall of Fame
in 1988; honored with a Lifetime Achievement Award in
1989 by the National Endowment for the Arts; named
the 1994 Jefferson Lecturer by the National Endowment
for the Humanities; presented with the National Book
Foundation's lifetime achievement medal in 1994;
awarded the National Medal of Arts in 1995 and the Order of Lincoln Medallion given by the Lincoln Academy
of Illinois in 1997; and received about 50 honorary
degrees.

Brooks also devoted herself to nurturing young writers of all races: She taught poetry at various colleges and
universities in the United States; sponsored writing contests for students; brought poetry to prisons, schools, and
rehab centers; funded and gave scholarships; and offered
awards of travel to Africa. She also wrote books to encourage budding authors, such as her *A Capsule Course in
Black Poetry Writing* (1975), *Young Poet's Primer* (1980),
and *Very Young Poets* (1983).

Above all, however, Brooks has been a prolific writer.
Her first published collection of poetry, *A Street in
Bronzeville* (1945), garnered immediate national acclaim.
The collection chronicles the life of poor urban Blacks in
a segregated setting reminiscent of Chicago's South
Side—essentially a series of portraits of people who fled
rural poverty and hopelessness only to find themselves
trapped in an urban ghetto. Realistic yet compassionate,
the poems unflinchingly examine the failed dreams and
small hopes of the maids, preachers, gamblers, prosti-
tutes, and others who live in "Bronzeville."

After Brooks received the Pulitzer for *Annie Allen*, her
major works included a novel, *Maude Martha*, 1953; and
more poetry collections, *Bronzeville Boys and Girls*, 1956;
The Bean Eaters, 1960; *Selected Poems*, 1963; *In the Mecca*,
1968; *Riot*, 1969; *Family Pictures*, 1970; *Aloneness*, 1971;
The Tiger Who Wore Gloves; or What You Are You Are,
1974; *Beckonings*, 1975; *A Primer for Blacks*, 1980; *To Dis-
embark*, 1981; *The Near Johannesburg Boy and Other
Poems*, 1986; *Blacks*, 1987; *Children Coming Home*, 1992;
and her posthumous collection, *In Montgomery*, 2001. (In
2005, **Elizabeth Alexander** edited *The Essential
Gwendolyn Brooks*.) Brooks also wrote her own story in

the autobiographies *A Report from Part One*, 1972; and
Report From Part Two, 1996.

Brooks's work always honored the everyday existence
of African Americans. She did, however, change her style
as the social situation in the United States changed. One
catalyst for this change was the Second Black Writers'
Conference, which she attended at Fisk University in
1967. There she met young black writers who were a part
of the **Black Arts Movement**, who wrote with overt anger and sometimes obscenities. This event gave Brooks
pause and her own sensibilities of her "blackness" came
into question. After this event, Brooks started selling her
work to smaller, African-American publishing houses.
Some have accused Brooks of becoming too much like
the newer poets—too polemic, leaving behind her subtle
and unique use of language and form as a way of seeing
the world. Others sense in Brooks's newer work a renewed vision of what it means to be African American in
the United States, a continuance of her abiding respect
and awe for the wonders of everyday existence and for her
unique way of finding universal truths within the specific
lives and events of ordinary people. In eulogizing Brooks
to *Essence* magazine, her long-time publisher and friend
Haki Madhubuti recalled, "She wore her love in her language." Her love has been returned, too, as shown in the
tribute book *To Gwen With Love* (1971) and the almost
worshipful celebrations of her 70th and 80th birthdays
(1987, 1997).

REFERENCES: *BLC-1* . *BW:SSCA*, pp. 64-65. *EBLG. NAAAL.* Lee,
A. Robert, "Poetry of Gwendolyn Brooks," in *MAAL.* McKay, Nellie.
1991. "Gwendolyn Brooks," *Modern American Women Writers*, New
York: Scribner's. McLendon, Jacquelyn, in *AAW.* Melhem, D. H.
1987. *Gwendolyn Brooks: Poetry & the Heroic Voice*, Lexington, KY:
University Press of Kentucky. Podolsky, Marjorie, "Maud Martha," in
MAAL. Williams, Kenny Jackson, "Brooks, Gwendolyn," and *Street in
Bronzeville*," in *OCAAL.* "Gwendolyn Brooks" in //www.black-
collegian.com, and in //www.greatwomen.org. "Brooks Brings
'Free-verse Kind of Time' to UIS," in //www.sj-r.com/news/97/11/13.
—Janet Hoover, with assistance from Lisa Bahlinger

REFERENCES: *AANB. AAW:PV. B. BCE. CAO-08. CE. CLCS.
LFCC-07. Q. W. W2B. Wiki.* Baker, Houston A., Jr. "The
Achievement of Gwendolyn Brooks." *CLA Journal* 16.1 (Sept. 1972):
Rpt. in Sharon R. Gunton and Laurie Lanzen Harris (Eds.). (1980).
Contemporary Literary Criticism (Vol. 15). Detroit: Gale Research.
From *Literature Resource Center.* Clark, Norris B. "Gwendolyn Brooks
and a Black Aesthetic." *A Life Distilled: Gwendolyn Brooks, Her Poetry
and Fiction* (Maria K. Mootry and Gary Smith, Eds.). University of
Illinois Press, 1987. Rpt. in Daniel G. Marowski and Roger Matuz
(Eds.). (1988). *Contemporary Literary Criticism* (Vol. 49, pp. 81-99).
Detroit: Gale Research. From *Literature Resource Center.* Doreski,
Carole K., in *AW:ACLB-91.* Griffin, Farah Jasmine, in *APSWWII-4.*
Hansell, William H. "The Uncommon Commonplace in the Early
Poems of Gwendolyn Brooks." *CLA Journal* 30.3 (Mar. 1987), pp.
261-277. Rpt. in Daniel G. Marowski and Roger Matuz (Eds.). (1988).
Contemporary Literary Criticism (Vol. 49). Detroit: Gale Research.
From *Literature Resource Center.* Israel, Charles, in *APSWWII-1.*
James, Charles L. in *CP-6.* Kent, George E., in *AAW-40-55.* Mckay,
Nellie, in *MAWW.* Mclendon, Jacquelyn, in *AAW-1991.* Miller, R.

Baxter, in *GEAAL*. Mueller, Michael E., and Jennifer M. York, in *BB*. Shaw, Harry B. 1980. "Gwendolyn Brooks." *Twayne's United States Authors Series 395*. Boston: Twayne Publishers. From *The Twayne Authors Series*. Shucard, Alan R., and Allison Hersh, in *RGAL-3*. Taylor, Henry. "Gwendolyn Brooks: An Essential Sanity." *Kenyon Review 13.4* (Fall 1991): pp. 115-131. Rpt. in Jeffrey W. Hunter (Ed.). (2000). *Contemporary Literary Criticism* (Vol. 125). Detroit: Gale Group. From *Literature Resource Center*.

Brown, Cecil
7/3/1943–
Novels, short stories, scripts, autobiography; educator

Brown's novels include *The Life and Loves of Mr. Jiveass Nigger* (1969) and *Days without Weather* (1982, winner of the Before Columbus Foundation American Book Award). His other major fiction work was the screenplay adaptation for *Which Way Is Up?*, the Richard Pryor movie that Brown cowrote with Carl Gottlieb (1977). His other works include his *Coming Up Down Home: A Memoir of a Southern Childhood* (1993), which French director Louis Malle had planned to make into a movie before Malle died in 1995. Brown's *Stagolee Shot Billy* (2003) offers a nonfiction probe of the legendary St. Louis shooting of Billy Lyons by Lee Shelton. Brown has also written articles and short stories, as well as scripts for screen and stage, some of which he has also produced and directed. He has also taught university students in France, California, and Illinois from 1967 until 2003.

REFERENCES: *AANB. CAO-03*. Alic, Margaret, in *BB*. Bright, Jean M., in *AAFW-55-84*. Carson, Warren J., in *COCAAL* and *OCAAL*. Han, John J., in *GEAAL*

Brown, "Charlotte Eugenia" (née Lottie Hawkins) Hawkins
6/11/1883–1/11/1961
Nonfiction—manners; fiction

History books point to Brown for her work as the almost-single-handed creator of a school, much like her contemporary, Mary McLeod Bethune. She raised funds and invested her bountiful energy and hard work in building the Palmer Memorial Institute in Sedalia, North Carolina. Her institute was considered one of the best African-American schools in the South in the middle of the twentieth century. During her day, however, across the nation, Mrs. Brown was known as the African-American Miss Manners because of her book *The Correct Thing to Do—to Say—to Wear* (1941).

Much of Brown's advice may seem quaint to us today (e.g., her "Earmarks of a Lady" chapter and her observation that "All food should be put into the mouth with the right hand"). Many of her suggestions seem very contem-

porary, however. For instance, she even recommends ways to save wear and tear on Mother Earth: "*Be saving.* Don't burn lights unnecessarily. Be sure that the hot water faucet is turned off. Don't leave the hose on too long in the back yard. Don't drive the automobile around the corner when you can walk. Don't turn the radio on in the morning and let it run all day. Don't leave the outside doors wide open when the furnace is going full blast." She also urges her readers to be thoughtful and considerate, such as by suggesting, "Don't save your table manners until company comes. You and your family are just as good and deserve just as much consideration as any of your friends or acquaintances." She even offers some good, sound, practical advice for young women: "[Do] not seek dark and secluded places in which to socialize."

Actually, Brown's book on the "social graces" was not her first venture into writing. She had published many articles and short stories. Her only short story published in book form, "*Mammy*": *An Appeal to the Heart of the South* (1919), was intended to shame former slaveholders who had allowed their former slaves to become totally destitute in old age.

REFERENCES: *AAWW. BAAW. EA-99*. Shockley, Ann Allen. *Afro-American Women Writers, 1746-1933: An Anthology and Critical Guide*: Boston: G.K. Hall, 1988; New York: Meridian/NAL, 1989. Thompson, Kathleen, in *BWA:AHE*. Vick, Marsha C., in *BH2C.*-
—Tonya Bolden

Brown, Claude
2/23/1937–2/2/2002
Autobiography/memoir, essays, articles, novel, spoken word—speeches; lecturer

Brown is mostly known for his best-selling autobiographical novel, *Manchild in the Promised Land* (1965), about his physically and psychologically brutal childhood and adolescence, including his own violent criminal activities in a youth gang. Selling more than 4 million copies, *Manchild* has been translated into more than a dozen languages and still appears on many high school and college curricula. The book led to a lucrative career as a popular lecturer. Brown also wrote *The Children of Ham* (1976), about the harsh realities and struggles of 13 African-American youths in a Harlem ghetto. Brown's countless essays and other articles appeared in such noteworthy periodicals as *Esquire, Saturday Evening Post, Life,* and the *New York Times Magazine*. At the time of his death, he was working on another novel, comparing his own troubled youth with the experiences of youths during the crack wars of the late 1980s and early 1990s.

Despite Brown's troubled youth, his adulthood offered fulfillment: He married in 1961, earned a bachelor's degree in 1965 (Howard University), and even took postgraduate law courses at Rutgers and Stanford until his lecturing career proved too profitable to neglect for his studies. The Browns later divorced, but they had a daughter (Denise) and a son (Nathaniel) together, and Brown was a grandfather at the time of his death. His obituary also noted he had a companion.

Brown recognized that mentoring and educational opportunities had made it possible for him to rehabilitate himself. His mentor Ernest Papanek, a psychologist at a special school for emotionally disturbed boys, had encouraged Brown to succeed and later helped launch Brown's writing career. After Brown's first literary and financial success, he involved himself in projects to help troubled youths transform their own lives and to offer educational opportunities to disadvantaged youths.

REFERENCES: *AA. AANB. CAO-07. EA-99. EBLG. G-97. W. Wiki.* Dudley, David L., in *COCAAL* and *OCAAL.* Manheim, James M., in *BB.* Nyangoni, Betty W., *GEAAL.* //findarticles.com/p/articles/mi_m0HST/is_3_4/ai_86041484. //www.pbs.org/newshour/essays/jan-june02/poverty_5-06.html. //www.racematters.org/manchildinthepromisedland.htm.

FURTHER READING: *AA:PoP. LLBL. MAAL.*

Brown, Elaine (Meryl)
3/2/1943–

Autobiography/memoir, songs; journalist, singer, lecturer, activist

A native of Philadelphia, Brown moved to California in the late 1960s and became deeply involved in the Black Power Movement. She worked for the *Harambee* newspaper of the Black Congress, and then joined the Black Panther Party (BPP) in 1968. She dedicated her first album, *Seize the Time* (1969), to the BPP. For both her first and her second album, *Until We're Free* (1973), she wrote and recorded each of the songs. Brown was already BPP Deputy Minister of Information when Party cofounder Huey Newton fled the country to avoid murder charges in 1974. Newton named her Minister of Defense, and in his absence, Brown shifted the BPP away from sexist chauvinism and toward political activism, such as voter registration drives, and community activism, such as free legal and medical clinics, free breakfasts, and educational programs. In 1977, when Newton returned after his acquittal, he and his followers pushed Brown out of the BPP, and she fled to France with her daughter, Ericka.

Nearly two decades later, she wrote a memoir of her childhood and of her experiences within the BPP, *A Taste of Power: A Black Woman's Story* (1992). Her book offers a refreshingly candid inside view of the BPP; it has been optioned for development by HBO. In 1996, Brown left France for Atlanta, Georgia, and again started championing the cause of the downtrodden and the oppressed. She devoted her next book, *The Condemnation of Little B* (2002), to prison reform, as viewed through the experiences of a 13-year-old accused of murder. She also edited an anthology of African-American prisoner autobiographies, *Messages from Behind the Wall* (2007). In Georgia, she again dallied with politics, offering to be the Green Party candidate for U.S. president for the 2008 election. At the end of 2007, however, she very publicly withdrew her candidacy and resigned from the Green Party, and soon after, she endorsed **Barack Obama**'s candidacy.

In addition to her extensive lecturing, Brown is writing *Melba and Al, A Story of Black Love in Jim Crow America* and coauthoring *For Reasons of Race and Belief, The Trials of Jamil Al-Amin (H. Rap Brown)* (with Karima Al-Amin).

REFERENCES: *AANB. CAO-06. EBLG. TAWH. Wiki.* Brown, Angela D., in *BWA:AHE.* Jennings, Regina, in *GEAAL.* Morin, Paula M., in *BB.* Amazon.com. //nh.barackobama.com/page/community/blog/elainebrown. //problemchylde.wordpress.com/2008/01/12/elaine-brown-withdraws-from-green-party-presidential-race-and-renounces-her-membership/. //www.elainebrown.org/. //www.thelecturebureau.com/speakers/elaine_brown.html.

Brown, Frank London
10/7/1927–3/12/1962

Novels, short stories & short story collection, journalism; jazz musician, union organizer, civil rights activist

A Chicagoan from age 12 to his all-too-soon death of leukemia at age 34, Brown fell in love with Chicago's jazz and gospel, blues and bebop. Morrie's Record shop offered him escape from his South Side slum home, and he enjoyed singing. After high school, he joined the army (1946-1948) and sang baritone in an army band. On leave, he married his high-school sweetheart, Evelyn Marie Jones, whom he also encouraged to continue her education. By the time of his death, they had three daughters, Debra, Cheryl, and Pamela, as well as a son who died soon after his birth. After the army, Brown used the G.I. Bill (college and housing grants awarded to honorably discharged veterans) to earn his baccalaureate at Roosevelt University (1951). Meanwhile, he worked as an organizer for Chicago's meat packers and other labor unions to support his growing family.

While in graduate school at the University of Chicago, Brown wrote articles and short stories for *Chicago Defender, Chicago Review, Chicago Sun-Times, Chicago Tribune, Ebony, Negro Digest,* and other periodicals. Brown also read his stories aloud at the Gate of Horn nightclub (1952-1953), accompanied by jazz, probably the first short-story writer to read aloud in public with musical accompaniment. After Brown's thoughtful interview of

Thelonious Monk ("More Man than Myth," *Down Beat*, 1958), Monk invited Brown to read some of his stories aloud at New York City's Five Spot, to Monk's musical accompaniment.

Brown also wrote journalistic pieces, such as his essay following his fearsome trip to Mississippi to report on the lynching of Emmett Till (1955). During the virulently antileftist McCarthy era, Brown challenged the status quo in his work, in his personal actions, in his writing, and in his family life. In 1954, Brown and his wife and children became the tenth black family to integrate the nearly all-white Trumbull Park, where they faced violent assaults, humiliating attacks, and virtual incarceration in their home until they left in 1957. His family had to travel in smelly, noisy police paddy wagons to get to and from home safely. Those experiences spawned his semiautobiographical novel, *Trumbull Park* (1959/2005), realistically depicting the experiences of an African-American family trying to escape an urban slum and integrate a Chicago housing development. His novel also celebrates the heroic role played by the wives of the integrating families. Critics praised Brown's storytelling skills, his sensitivity to vernacular speech, and his insights into human experience.

Brown also wrote a short play, *Short Ribs*, produced by the Penthouse Players in the late 1950s. He was firmly embedded in the Chicago literary scene, interviewing **Gwendolyn Brooks** and befriending **Willard Motley**. *Ebony* named him an associate editor in 1959, 14 years after he had walked into the *Ebony* office and audaciously asked for an editorial job while still in high school. Frank's wife, Evelyn, later recalled, "He was always in a hurry. He seemed aware that he didn't have enough time, so he never wasted it" (quoted in *AAW-40-55*).

In 1960, Brown completed his master's thesis, "The Myth Maker," and earned his master's degree. He was also accepted as a doctoral fellow into the University of Chicago's prestigious Committee on Social Thought and appointed to direct its Union Research Center. In *The Myth Maker*, racism psychologically traumatized the protagonist, Ernest Day, a drug-addicted bibliophile who lashed out by strangling an elderly black man who had innocently smiled at him. Most of the novel probes Day's mental anguish as his guilty conscience tortures him. Fortunately, Day comes into contact—socially and sexually—with Freda, who begins to humanize him just as he is apprehended by the police.

While still working on his doctorate, in 1961, Brown was diagnosed with leukemia. As his body failed him, his mind remained alert, and he continued to write. Sadly, his body died while Chicago's **Black Arts Movement** was still in the womb. After his death, his short stories were collected in *Short Stories of Frank London Brown* and published privately in 1965, and *The Myth Makers* was published in 1969. In a poetic tribute to Brown,

Gwendolyn Brooks said, "Armed arbiter, our scrupulous pioneer— / Out from the lushness of his legacy" (quoted in *AAW-40-55*).

REFERENCES: *CAO-03*. Brouwers, Bärbel R., in *AANB*. Hall, James C., in *COCAAL*. Hauke, Kathleen A., in *AAW-40-55*. Nelson, Emmanuel Sampath (Ed.). 1999. "Frank London Brown." *Contemporary African American Novelists: A Bio-Bibliographical Critical Sourcebook* (pp. 58-61). Santa Barbara: Greenwood Publishing Group. Amazon.com.

FURTHER READING: Williamson, Alicia D., in *GEAAL*.

Brown, Hallie Quinn
3/10/1845–9/16/1949
Biography, nonfiction—rhetoric, public speaking, spoken word—speeches

Brown's birth year is in question—listed as 1845 in *EA-99*; c. 1845 in *BWA:AHE*; c. 1847 in *OCAAL*; and 1850 in *EB-98*, *EB-BH-CD*, *EWHA*, and *WDAW*. Because it was common prior to the mid-twentieth century to alter women's birth years to make them appear younger, the earlier year seems the most probable one. Brown's parents, Frances Scroggins Brown and Thomas Arthur Brown, had both been slaves and had used their resources to aid fugitive slaves on the Underground Railroad. The Browns taught Hallie and her five siblings the value of working with others to effect social change. A lifelong social activist, Brown worked ardently for temperance and suffrage, participated in church organizations, lectured throughout America and abroad, and led women's clubs (e.g., president of the National Association of Colored Women, 1920-1924).

The Browns also taught their children the importance of education, moving their family from Canada to Wilberforce, Ohio, so that Hallie and her brother could attend Wilberforce University (B.A., 1873). Brown subsequently was awarded an honorary master's degree (1890, Chautauqua Lecture School) and an honorary doctorate (1936, Wilberforce University). After graduating, Brown dedicated herself to the education of others, teaching elementary school, working as a dean for Allen University in South Carolina, administering an adult night school, working as dean of women ("lady principal") at the Tuskegee Institute, and then professing elocution at Wilberforce University. Wilberforce honored her in 1948 with the dedication of its Hallie Q. Brown Library, which houses her unpublished papers. Her numerous published works include *Bits and Odds: A Choice Selection of Recitations* (1880); *First Lessons in Public Speaking* (1920); *The Beautiful: A Story of Slavery* (1924); *Tales My Father Told* (1925); *Our Women: Past, Present, and Future* (1925); *Homespun Heroines and Other Women of Distinction* (1926); and *Ten Pictures of Pioneers of Wilberforce* (1937). Scholars still use her *Homespun Heroines* as an important reference work, with its 60 illustrated biographies of important African-American women born between about 1750 and 1875.

REFERENCES: *AANB. EB-BH-CD. EWHA. HR&B. WDAW. Wiki.* Carter, Terry, in *GEAAL.* Fisher, Vivian Njeri, in *BWA:AHE.* Moody, Joycelyn K., in *COCAAL* and *OCAAL.* Robinson, Alonford James, Jr., in *EA-99.* //digital.nypl.org/schomburg/writers_aa19/bio2.html.

FURTHER READING: *PBW, p. xx.*

Brown, Linda Beatrice (aka Linda Brown Bragg)
3/14/1939–
Poems, novels; educator

Brown's poems have been published in various literary journals and anthologies and have been collected in her *A Love Song to Black Men* (1974). Her novels include *Rainbow Roun Mah Shoulder* (1984, as Linda Brown Bragg, reissued in 1989) and *Crossing over Jordan* (1994). Brown's writing has also appeared scholarly anthologies. In addition, she has raised a son (Christopher, born 1967) and a daughter (Willa, born 1969) from her first marriage, made numerous presentations, and taught countless college students (e.g., at the University of North Carolina at Greensboro, 1970-1986; Guilford College, 1986-1992). Since 1992, she has been the Willa B. Player Distinguished Professor of the Humanities at Bennett College for Women. The college also commissioned her to write *The Long Walk* (1998), about her aunt Willa B. Player, the first African-American female president of a U.S. four-year college. In an interview with *Contemporary Authors* (2007), she noted, "I see myself in solidarity with all those, of whatever ethnic origin, who have come before me and have resisted oppression. My writing provides a method of saying that I believe all humanity to be one."

REFERENCES: CAO-07. Brookhart, Mary, in *BWA:AHE.* Browne, Phiefer L., in *COCAAL* and *OCAAL.* Jones, Esther L., in *GEAAL.* //www.bennett.edu/sacs/docdirectory/focusedresponse/Faculty%20Development%20Report%2006222007.pdf. //www.unctv.org/bif/this season/descriptions.html.

Brown, Lloyd (né Lloyd Louis Dight)
4/3/1913–4/1/2003
Novel, short stories, essays; journalism, editor

Lloyd Dight was orphaned by his mother at age 4, when his father placed him and his three siblings in St. Paul's Crispus Attucks Home, an orphanage and old folks' home where some of the residents were former slaves. At age 16, Lloyd Dight changed his surname to Brown, honoring radical abolitionist John Brown. In 1929, Brown joined the Young Communist League, where he later met the love of his life, Lily Kashin (8/7/1913-6/5/1996), a Polish Jew. The couple married in

1937 and shared a life, joined by their two daughters, Linda and Bonnie. While supporting his family as a trade union organizer, he was imprisoned for several months for "conspiracy." In prison, he became friends with inmate Willie Jones, who was unjustly imprisoned for murder and sentenced to death. Despite the efforts of Brown efforts and others, Jones was wrongly executed November 24, 1941. Brown used his experiences in prison and in trying to help Jones as the basis for his novel *Iron City* (1951; reissued 1994), published by Masses and Mainstream. Brown urges the reader not only to sympathize with the plight of the wrongly imprisoned and executed protagonist, but also to understand that communism offers a more just alternative. *Iron City* has been translated into Chinese, German, Japanese, Polish, and other languages.

Meanwhile, starting in 1945, Brown worked as editor and then managing editor of *New Masses*, later retitled *Masses and Mainstream.* In its pages, he published the works of **James Baldwin**, **Ralph Ellison**, **Langston Hughes**, **Richard Wright**, and other literary noteworthies, as well as his own short stories, essays, reviews, editorials, and articles. Probably his most famous essay, "Which Way for the Negro Writer" (March, 1951), urged African-American writers to focus on their own distinctive cultural experiences in their own literature. In addition to his political and cultural writings in *Masses*, his work appeared in New York's *Amsterdam News, Nation, Negro Digest, The New York Times*, and other periodicals.

Brown's short stories included "Jericho, USA" (1946), "Battle in Canaan" (1947), and "God's Chosen People." He also worked on his second novel, *Year of Jubilee*, underscoring the relationship between communism and the struggle for civil rights. Although a chapter of his novel appeared in *Masses and Mainstream* (1953), titled "Cousin Oscar," the complete novel was never published, not even by the presses of *Masses and Mainstream.*

In 1951, Brown published his pamphlet *Lift Every Voice for* **Paul Robeson**, and in 1953 or so, Brown left *Masses* to begin a collaboration of more than 20 years with Robeson. For the Harlem newspaper *Freedom*, which Robeson edited (c. 1950-1955), Brown wrote columns and articles. Brown also collaborated with Robeson in writing other material for *Freedom* and in writing Robeson's autobiography *Here I Stand* (1958, on Valentine's Day; 1971/1988, reprinted with a preface by Brown). In the autobiography, Robeson discussed the McCarthy-era persecution of him and the anticommunist efforts to silence his outcries for equality for African Americans. In 1976, the year Robeson died, Brown published a pamphlet titled *Paul Robeson Rediscovered*, published by the American Institute for Marxist Studies. For the next two decades, Brown worked on his full-length biography *The Young Paul Robeson: On My Journey Now* (1997).

In an article titled "Robeson's *Here I Stand*: The Book They Could Not Ban" (published in *Paul Robeson: The Great Forerunner*, 1998; based on Brown's preface to the

1971 edition of *Here I Stand*), Brown recalled the attempted boycott of the autobiography, *"no white commercial newspaper or magazine in the entire country so much as mentioned Robeson's book. ...* [Outside the country, numerous reviewers praised the work, along with] the second area where the anti-Robeson ban was broken—in the black communities of America. The breakthrough began in Harlem where Othello Associates, an independent Negro publishing company, brought out Robeson's book. ... an important section of the Afro-American press moved with speed and energy to publicize and promote the sale of [the] book ... . The Baltimore *Afro-American* (with editions in several other cities) took the lead in the widespread defiance of the ban." He also recalled, "I am grateful I had the opportunity to serve as Robeson's collaborator in the writing of *Here I Stand,* and to be one of the 'Othello Associates' who published the book despite the ban."

In addition to the Robeson pamphlets, Brown wrote numerous other pamphlets, too, including *Young Workers in Action: Story of the South River Strike* (1932), *The Conspiracy Against Free Elections* (1941, unsigned), and *Stand Up for Freedom: The Negro People vs. the Smith Act* (1952). Though Brown left the Communist Party in 1953, for personal reasons, he remained a communist, lowercase "c." His writing continued to be published in communist journals, in periodicals intended for an African-American audience (e.g., *Freedomways*), and—rarely—in mainstream publications (e.g., *The New York Times*). Nonetheless, his leftist outlook barred him from widespread access to mainstream publications, so his writing is less well known than it would have been otherwise. In 1998, Brown received the Carey McWilliams Award for Outstanding Scholarly Work in Cultural Diversity.

Brown died two days shy of his 90th birthday; he was survived not only by his two daughters but also by his two grandchildren. His wife, also a community activist, had predeceased him, but the Lily Brown Playground (dedicated 11/16/2001) in New York's Fort Washington Park still honors her name. Herb Boyd noted that Brown's "closing remark [in his book on Robeson,] 'To fulfill his own potential, to serve his own people while advocating the oneness of mankind, he had to remain true to his principles regardless of the consequences' . . . could have been applied to Brown's remarkable life and commitment to peace and justice."

REFERENCES: CAO-04. Editors of *Freedomways*. 1998. *Paul Robeson: The Great Forerunner* (pp. 150-159). New York: International Publishers. Kornweibel, Karen Ruth, in COCAAL. Moody, Shirley C., in *AANB*. //lists.econ.utah.edu/pipermail/marxism-thaxis/2003-April/017865.html. //www.amazon.com. //www.highbeam.com/doc/1P1-79496060.html. //www.nycgovparks.org/parks/fortwashingtonpark/highlights/13151.

FURTHER READING: Asanti, Monifa Love, in *GEAAL*.

Brown, Sterling Allen
5/1/1901–1/13?/1989
Poems, folklore, criticism; educator

Born a slave, Sterling Nelson Brown had long been deeply embedded in the well-educated middle class of Washington, D.C., by the time he and his wife had their son, Sterling Allen Brown. Sterling Nelson Brown was a prominent, often-published professor of religion at Howard University, as well as a pastor; he counted **Frederick Douglass** and **Paul Laurence Dunbar** among his personal friends, and his wife had been the valedictorian of her graduating class at Fisk University. Young Sterling Allen Brown profited from this intellectually stimulating environment, attending public schools and graduating with honors (1918) from the prestigious Paul Laurence Dunbar High School, where he was taught by **Jessie Redmon Fauset** and **Angelina Weld Grimké**, among others.

His talents earned him a scholarship to Williams College in Williamstown, Massachusetts, where he was elected to the distinguished honor society Phi Beta Kappa and earned his baccalaureate with honors (1922). At Williams, he had been the only student awarded "Final Honors" in English, and he won the Graves Prize for his essay "The Comic Spirit in Shakespeare and Molière." After graduating, Brown went on to earn a master's degree in literature at Harvard University (1923). During his studies, he had been enthralled with the poetry of Carl Sandburg, Edwin Arlington Robinson, and Robert Frost, European-American poets who highlighted the voices and experiences of everyday folks in their own communities.

With his master's degree in hand, he took a series of teaching positions at various historically black colleges and universities in the South, including Virginia Seminary and College (1923-1926), Lincoln University in Jefferson City, Missouri (1926-1928), and Fisk University in Nashville, Tennessee (1928-1929). He later recalled that this period marked his most important education, as he embarked on a self-directed program of studying the speech patterns and the folklore and folk wisdom of the African Americans in the communities surrounding each of the colleges where he worked. He gathered sketches and anecdotes from the habitues of barbershops, and **folktales** and other stories from farmers way out in the country. He collected work songs, spirituals, ballads, and blues songs in the street, in the farmhouse, and in juke joints. All the while, he absorbed the dialect and manner of speaking of the folks around him.

In 1927, Brown wedded Daisy Turnbull, whom he had met in Virginia, and to whom he remained married more than 50 years (until her death in 1979). In 1929, Brown started another long-term relationship: He began teach-

ing English at the first university he had ever
known—Howard University, where he was to stay for another 40 years. In 1931 and 1932, Brown returned to Harvard to work on his doctorate, but even with this creden-
tial, most of his English Department colleagues at
Howard sneered at his appreciation for the folkways and
speech patterns common among the everyday African
Americans whom Brown had come to respect and admire. To this day, heated controversy continues to ignite
discussions among African-American scholars regarding
whether to celebrate or to scorn traditional African-American speech patterns and folk traditions within
the context of American literature, scholarship, and
education.

The English professors of Howard particularly disdained Brown's poetry, in which he occasionally dabbled
in such traditional poetry forms as sonnets, villanelles,
ballads, and children's songs, but more often used poetry
forms reminiscent of African-American work songs, spirituals, jazz riffs, blues rhythms and refrains, and other expressions rooted in the African-American folk and **oral
tradition**s. For Brown, the language he was celebrating
showed "tonic shrewdness, the ability to take it, and the
double-edged humor built up of irony and shrewd observation" (quoted in *OCAAL*). He observed, "I was first attracted by certain qualities that I thought the speech of
the people had, and I wanted to get for my own writing a
flavor, a color, a pungency of speech. Then later, I came to
something more important—I wanted to get an understanding of people, to acquire an accuracy in the portrayal of their lives" (quoted in *OCAAL*). Thus, his poetic themes addressed the everyday life experiences of
ordinary African Americans and often incorporated African-American folklore (e.g., tall tales and folk sermons).

Despite his poems' poor reception at Howard, they
were published in *Opportunity* and other literary publications and were widely anthologized (e.g., in **Countee
Cullen**'s *Caroling Dusk*, 1927; and in **James Weldon
Johnson**'s *The Book of American Negro Poetry*, 1931,
which Brown helped to revise). In 1932, Brown's first collection of verse, *Southern Road,* was published. The critics
and the general public praised it highly for its lyrical celebration of African-American speech patterns, of ordinary
African-American protagonists, and of traditional African-American songs and verses. Noted critic **Alain
Locke** extolled the virtues of Brown's freshly original
compositions as echoing the lyricality of authentic folk
ballads. Nonetheless, Brown's colleagues at Howard still
frowned on his poems for their obvious ties to and roots in
everyday African-American speech patterns, themes,
and musical traditions.

Sadly, during the Great Depression, publishers were
unwilling to take a chance on a poetry book that departed
too much from the literary traditions valued by the

Howard English professors, so Brown couldn't find any-
one to publish his second poetry collection, *No Hiding
Place.* Hence, Brown turned away from poetry. His next
collection didn't appear for another four decades: *The
Last Ride of Wild Bill and Eleven Narratives,* published in
1975—the same year that *Southern Roads* was reprinted.
The poems from *No Hiding Place* weren't published until
Michael S. Harper edited *The Collected Poems of Sterling
A. Brown* in 1980; the literary community responded to
those long-ago-rejected, long-neglected poems with the
Lenore Marshall Prize for the outstanding volume of poetry published in the United States in 1980. Among the
poems of Brown's that continue to be widely anthologized
are his "Strong Men," "Slim in Hell," and "Southern
Road."

Although he turned away from poetry, Brown did not
stop writing. Instead, he turned toward writing literary
criticism and historical analyses of African-American
culture. During the late 1930s, Brown served as the national editor of Negro Affairs for the Works Progress Administration's Federal Writers' Project (the WPA's FWP).
The job was a perfect match for Brown, as it provided federal government funding for Brown and other writers to
collect authentic American folklore. In connection with
that effort, Brown published two books in an Atheneum
series called the "Bronze Booklets" (originally published
in 1937, then reissued in the 1938 series): *The Negro in
American Fiction* and *Negro Poetry and Drama,* short surveys of the existing works in those fields.

In 1939, Brown worked on the staff of a Carnegie
Foundation-funded landmark study directed by Swedish
sociologist and economist Gunnar Myrdal. Whereas the
thrust of Myrdal's work was the detrimental effects of racism on African Americans, Brown focused on the ways in
which African Americans have risen to the challenge of
an often-hostile environment, using folk humor and
other defense strategies.

In 1941, Brown collaborated with Arthur Davis and
Ulysses Lee to edit the noted anthology *The Negro Caravan* (1941, repr. 1969), which offered a wide array of African-American literature, much of which the editors obtained from unpublished manuscripts. Their text was
groundbreaking at the time, a key reference text for decades after, and a valuable resource to this day.

From the 1940s on, Brown lectured at various colleges and universities (e.g., Atlanta University and New
York University), in addition to his post at Howard. After
three semesters of teaching at prestigious Vassar College,
in 1945, he was offered a full-time position there. He
turned it down, however, preferring to stay at Howard,
where he had his professional and familial home. Also, although he felt less than welcome by fellow English professors, he was greatly loved and admired by his students
there. Among those students were **Amiri Baraka,**

Stokely Carmichael, Ossie Davis, and Toni Morrison. Although he suffered from periodic bouts of deep depression (sometimes requiring hospitalization), he felt that his greatest legacy was the effect he had had on his students. In 1969, Brown retired from Howard, and through his many celebrated students, he enjoyed a revival of interest in his poetry.

In 1971, he was awarded an honorary doctorate from Howard, and before he died, he had been awarded additional honorary doctorates from Williams College, Vassar College, Harvard University, and Brown University. He had also been named poet laureate of the District of Columbia and elected to the Academy of American Poets. In 1979, Brown was invited to contribute a memoir of his experiences to the collection *Chant of Saints: A Gathering of Afro-American Literature, Art, and Scholarship.*

REFERENCES: *1TESK. AANB. AAW:AAPP. BAL-1-P. BWA. CAO-03. EBLG. EB-BH-CD. G-97. LFCC-07. MWEL. NAAAL. OC20LE. W. WDAA. Wiki.* Burnette, R. V., in *MAC-20-55.* Chester, Dennis, in *GEAAL.* Cohassey, John, in *BB.* Gabbin, Joanne V., in *AAWHR-40.* Henderson, Stephen E. in *AAW-1991.* Robinson, Lisa Clayton, in *EA-99.* Tidwell, John Edgar, in *COCAAL* and *OCAAL.* Wood, Don, in *AP1880-1945-2.* //muse.jhu.edu/login?uri=/journals/callaloo/v021/21.4omeally01.html.

Brown, William Wells
?/1814?–11/6/1884
Spoken word—speeches, autobiography/memoir/slave narrative, anthology, novels, plays, nonfiction—travel, essays, articles, history, biography; lecturer, physician

William failed in his first attempt to escape slavery, but his second attempt—aided by a Quaker couple, Mr. and Mrs. Wells Brown—succeeded. In appreciation of their help, he added their names to his own first name. From 1834 to 1843, he stewarded ships on the Great Lakes and was a conductor on the Underground Railroad. Meanwhile, he taught himself reading, writing, and other subjects, and he gained increasing confidence and skill as an abolitionist public speaker. In 1843, the Western New York Anti-Slavery Society (and other abolitionist societies) hired him to lecture around the country.

In 1847, his autobiography, *Narrative of William W. Brown, a Fugitive Slave, Written by Himself,* was published. In it, he modestly describes his experiences, revealing himself to have been a slave trickster, who used realistic—if less than exemplary—means of survival. Although his narrative frequently flouted nineteenth-century morality, the book underwent four American editions and five British editions before 1850.

In 1848, Brown published his poetry and song collection, *The Anti-Slavery Harp; a Collection of Songs for Anti-Slavery Meetings.* He spent 1849 through 1854 in Europe, delivering more than a thousand lectures to foster British support for abolition. His lectures led to his book *Three Years in Europe* (1852), credited as being the first published travel book by an African American. While in England, he also wrote and published *Clotel; Or, The President's Daughter: A Narrative of Slave Life in the United States,* believed to be the first novel published by an African American. As a contribution to African-American literature, its historical importance continues to outweigh its literary and aesthetic merit.

While Brown was abroad, several of his friends raised the funds to buy his emancipation, so he returned to the United States a fully free man. In 1856, he wrote the first dramatic work by an African American: *Experience; Or, How to Give a Northern Man a Backbone,* which has since been lost. That year, he also wrote his second play, *The Escape; Or, A Leap for Freedom,* about two slaves who secretly marry. This, his only published play, was the first play written by an African American to be published (in 1858).

He also wrote more than a dozen nonfiction books and pamphlets, including historical and biographical works such as *The Negro in the American Rebellion: His Heroism and Fidelity* (1867, the first military history of African Americans) and *My Southern Home; or, The South and Its People* (1880), his semiautobiographical final published book. Before the end of the Civil War, Brown had become a physician and continued his medical practice until he died about two decades later.

REFERENCES: *1TESK. AA:PoP. AANB. B. BAL-1-P. BCE. BF:2000. BWA. E-98. EB-98. EBLG. G-97. MWEL. NAAAL. W. Wiki.* Andrews, William L., in *COCAAL* and *OCAAL.* Candela, Gregory L., in *AAWBHR.* Dorsey, Peter A., in *AWS-2.* Katopes, Peter J., in *AWNYS.* Reed, Brian D., in *ATW.* Shearin, Gloria A., in *GEAAL.*

Brownie's Book, The
1920–1921

A magazine published especially for African-American children ages 6-16 years, the *Brownies' Book* was published by **W. E. B. Du Bois** and Augustus Granville Dill from January 1920 through December 1921. The magazine functioned as an independent counterpart to **Crisis,** the magazine of the National Association for the Advancement of Colored People (NAACP). The publication of the *Brownies' Book* is significant because it marks the beginning of African-American children's literature. With only one exception, Black artists made all of the drawings of Black children illustrating the magazine.

REFERENCES: Johnson-Feelings, Dianne, in *OCAAL.*

FURTHER READING: Martin, Michelle H. "Children's Literature of the Harlem Renaissance." *The Journal of African American History.* 91.3 (Summer 2006) p. 348. From *Literature Resource Center.* Smith, Henrietta M. "The Best of 'The Brownies' Book.'" (Children's

Review) (Brief Article). *The Horn Book Magazine. 72.3* (May-June 1996) p. 355. From *Literature Resource Center*. —Lisa Bahlinger

---

Bruce, Josephine Beall (née Willson)

10/29/1853–2/15/1923

Nonfiction: essays; educator, clubwoman

Blanche K. (Kelso) Bruce, husband

3/1/1841–3/17/1898

Spoken word—oratory; former slave, U.S. Senator, journalist

Henry Clay Bruce, brother-in-law

3/3/1836–9/1/1902

Autobiography/memoir, slave narrative; former slave, construction worker, civil servant

Roscoe Conkling Bruce, Sr., son

4/21/1879–8/16/1950

Letters, spoken word—lectures; journalist, editor, educator

Joseph Willson, father

2/22/1817–8/21/1895

Nonfiction—history; printer, dentist

When Josephine Beall Willson married Blanche Kelso Bruce, they formed a powerful alliance of two prominent families. Josephine's father, Joseph Willson, had already authored *Sketches of the Higher Classes among Colored Society in Philadelphia* (1841), about his own social circles, more than a decade before Josephine was born. In 1817, in Augusta, Georgia, Joseph was the freeborn son of Elizabeth Keating (later Willson), a freeborn woman of color, and John Willson, a Scots-Irish banker to whom she was not married. After John's death, John's estate provided a small inheritance for his "housekeeper," but the Black Codes so limited the activities of free people of color there that Elizabeth took Joseph and his four siblings to Philadelphia. There, she used the inheritance to buy a home for them in a largely white section of town. After Joseph graduated from the Pennsylvania Abolition Society's Clarkson School, he got a job as a printer for William Lloyd Garrison's *Liberator,* in Boston. After mastering the printing trade, he returned to Philadelphia and established his own printing shop. During this time, he wrote his *Sketches* under a pen name, but his authorship was an open secret.

Later on, he married a fellow Georgian, Elizabeth Hartnett, and the couple moved in with Willson's mother. After Elizabeth died in 1847, she left a tidy sum to be divided among her five children. With it, Joseph bought a home in an African-American part of town, where he raised his own children. Eventually, Joseph left the printing business to start a dentistry practice. In the mid-1950s, the

Willson family moved to Cleveland, Ohio, where the schools were desegregated and his dentistry practice could thrive—which it did. Josephine and her three sisters grew up in a household that valued education, and all four of the Willson girls went on to careers in education. Josephine became one of the first African-American teachers in Cleveland's integrated schools.

In June 1876, Josephine attended the Republican National Convention in Ohio, where she met Blanche Kelso Bruce. At that time, Bruce was already a U.S. Senator from Mississippi (3/4/1875-1881), about to become the first African American to serve a full six-year term in the U.S. Senate. Nonetheless, her family had some reservations about this informally educated former slave. Blanche was not a typical slave, however. He had been taught to read and write alongside his all-white half-brother, with the full knowledge of his father and "master."

Early during the Civil War, Blanche K. Bruce had escaped from the slave state of Missouri to the free state of Kansas. A year after the Emancipation Proclamation, in 1864, Bruce returned to Missouri, which now had to recognize his free status. There, he organized Missouri's first school for African-American children, in Hannibal, abolitionist Mark Twain's hometown. After the war, he returned to Mississippi and became a wealthy landowner. He also held some civil-service positions in his county before his election to the U.S. Senate. In addition, he edited Bolivar County's *Floreyville Star* newspaper. In the Senate, when the vice president was unavailable, Bruce presided over the Senate. According to the *New York Tribune,* "This is the first time a colored man ever sat in the seat of the Vice-President of the United States. Senator Bruce is universally respected by his fellow senators and is qualified both in manners and character to preside over the deliberations of the most august body of men in the land" (quoted in //library.msstate.edu/special_interest/Mississippi_African-American_Authors.asp). While in the Senate, Bruce also championed the causes of Native Americans and Chinese Americans, as well as African-American Union Army veterans.

On June 24, 1878, after two years of corresponding, Josephine and Blanche wedded in Cleveland and then honeymooned in Europe for four months. After Blanche's Senate term, he was named the first African-American Register of the U.S. Treasury by President James Garfield, becoming the first African American to sign his name on U.S. currency, making it legal tender. With an intervening post as the District of Columbia recorder of deeds (1891-1893), he served as Register until his death in 1898.

Blanche's older brother Henry Clay Bruce was also taught to read and write. When Blanche had moved to Missouri, Henry had moved to Kansas, where he earned enough as a bricklayer to buy a home for himself and his wife. After Blanche finished his Senate term, he helped Henry get a post office job in D.C., where he lived the rest of his life. Henry later wrote about his experiences in his slave narrative/autobiography, *The New Man: Twenty-nine Years As a Slave, Twenty-nine Years a Free Man; Recollections of H. C. Bruce* (1895; reprinted, 1969), "I had been taught the alphabet while in Missouri and could spell . . . words of two syllables, and [the planter's son] Willie took great pride in teaching me his lessons of each day from his books, as I had none and my mother had no money to buy any for me. This continued for about a year before the boy's aunt, Mrs. Prudence Perkinson, who had cared for Willie while we were in Missouri, found it out, and I assure you, dear reader, she raised a great row with our master about it. She insisted that it was a crime to teach a Negro to read, and that it would spoil him, but our owner seemed not to care anything about it and did nothing to stop it, for afterward I frequently had him correct my spelling. In after years I learned that he was glad that his Negroes could read, especially the Bible, but he was opposed to their being taught writing. . . . Willie Perkinson had become as one of us and regarded my mother as his mother. He played with the colored boys from the time he got home from school till bedtime, and again in the morning till time to go to school, and every Saturday and Sunday. Having learned to spell I kept it up, and took lessons from Willie as often as I could. My younger brother, B. K. Bruce (now Ex-Senator) had succeeded me as playmate and guardian of Willie, and being also anxious to learn, soon caught up with me, and by Willie's aid went ahead of me and has held his place during all the years since" (pp. 26-27 of narrative, available online at //docsouth.unc.edu/fpn/bruce/menu.html).

Meanwhile, Josephine and Blanche settled into a comfortable life in Washington, D.C., continuing to profit from the Bruce plantation in Mississippi during the protective, progressive era of Reconstruction. In 1879, Josephine gave birth to their son, Roscoe Conkling Bruce, named for Blanche's mentor in the Senate, Roscoe Conkling. In addition to her work as a mother and a prominent man's wife, she belonged to and presided over many charitable and cultural organizations and events. After Roscoe left for Phillips Exeter Academy boarding school in New Hampshire, she cofounded the Booklover's Club, started working with the Colored Women's League, and joined the National Association of Colored Women. Blanche died in 1898, and the following year, **Booker T. Washington** invited the former teacher to be "Lady Principal" at Tuskegee, essentially the dean of women there. She left Tuskegee in 1902 and turned to her real-estate holdings in Maryland; in Josephine, Mississippi (named for her), and in Washington, D.C., as well as her family's home in Indianapolis. She continued to be involved in club activities and to write essays for periodicals such as *Voice of the Negro*.

While Roscoe was at Phillips Exeter, he edited the school's *Exonian*, perhaps the oldest continuously operating high-school newspaper in the nation. After Exeter, he went on to Harvard, graduated magna cum laude (1902), and was elected to the Phi Beta Kappa honor society. About the time his mother left Tuskegee, Roscoe took a post as academic director and teacher there. For a glimpse into courtship of this era, see his 1903 letters to his fiancée, Clara Washington Bustill (*Letters from Black America*). In June of 1903, Reverend **Francis Grimké** married him to Clara, with whom he later had three children: Clara Josephine Bruce, Roscoe Conkling Bruce, Jr., and Burrill Kelso Bruce. In 1906, Roscoe left Tuskegee and took a series of public-school positions. In the early 1930s, he became editor in chief of the **Harriet Tubman** Publishing Company. His associate editors included **Georgia Douglas Johnson**, Kelly Miller (father of **May Miller**), **Arthur Schomburg**, **Mary Eliza Church Terrell**, his wife, and others. While there, he developed *Just Women*, intended as a supplementary reader for public-school 8th- and 9th-graders, honoring noteworthy African-American women such as those with whom he was deeply familiar.

REFERENCES: "Blanche Kelso Bruce," *B. BCE. W2B. Wiki.* Burke, Diane Mutti, in *AANB.* Collins, Grace E., and Jennifer M. York, in *BB.* Gardner, Eric, in *AANB.* //www.blackpast.org/?q=aah/ bruce-josephine-beall-willson-1853-1923. Harris, William C., in *AANB* and in *USHC.* //library.msstate.edu/special_interest/Mississippi_African-American_Authors.asp. "Henry Clay Bruce," Lohse, Bill, in //www.blackpast.org/?q=aaw/bruce-henry-clay-1836-1902. //docsouth.unc.edu/fpn/bruce/menu.html. //www.aaregistry.com/african_american_history/1843/He_told_his_story_well_Henry_Clay_Bruce. "Josephine Beall Willson Bruce," *NBAW.* "Roscoe Conkling Bruce, Sr.," Ingram, E. Renée, in *AANB.* Newkirk, Pamela. 2009. [1903 letters between Roscoe Conkling Bruce, Sr., and his fiancée Clara Bustill]. *Letters from Black America* (pp. 67-70). New York: Macmillan. //www.blackpast.org/? q=1905-roscoe-conkling-bruce-freedom-through-education. "Joseph Willson," Winch, Julie, in *AANB.* //www.encyclopedia.com/doc/1P3-109597847.html.

FURTHER READING: "Blanche Kelso Bruce," in Brawley, Benjamin G. 1937/1965. *Negro Builders and Heroes.* University of North Carolina Press. "Josephine Beall Willson Bruce," //www.brainyhistory.com/events/1923/february_15_1923_82970.html. //www.culturaltourismdc.org/info-url3948/info-url_show.htm?doc_id=204319&attrib_id=7974.

Bryan, Ashley F.

7/13/1923–

Folklore, children's literature, autobiography/memoir; illustrator, artist, educator

When Bryan was still in kindergarten, he created his first book—illustrating, binding, and distributing it himself. His first book was an alphabet book, and as he later recalled, "Number books, word books, sentence books followed" (p. 100, *CBC*). His large family (two parents, five siblings, three cousins being raised by his parents) gave his self-published books "rave reviews." "Encouraged, I published books as gifts to family and friends on all occasions. By the time I was in third or fourth grade, I had published hundreds of books." After earning degrees from Cooper Union Art School and Columbia University, Bryan has put together quite a few more books and taught painting and drawing at Dartmouth College, from which he is now retired.

Bryan's work clearly shows that "The illustrated book is my special love" (from Bryan's essay on the Children's Book Council website, //www.cbcbooks.org/cbcmagazine/meet/ashleybryan.html). As a child, Bryan had loved reading and yearned to see images of boys and girls who looked like him and his family, friends, and neighbors in books. Thanks to authors and illustrators such as Bryan, "Children can now see their images in illustrated books and in stories of their people. They make a direct connection to these pictures and stories."

Of the numerous children's picture books Bryan has illustrated and authored, he particularly revels in **folktales** and African-American spirituals. His first book of spirituals, which he considers "a gift from the musical genius of the Black people" (p. 100, *CBC*), was *Walk Together Children* (1974). *What a Morning: The Christmas Story in Black Spirituals* (1987/1996) celebrates the Christmas story through vivid paintings and five traditional spirituals. Bryan's *Climbing Jacob's Ladder: Heroes of the Bible in African American Spirituals* (1991) tells the stories of Noah, Abraham, Jacob, Moses, Joshua, David, Ezekiel, Daniel, and Jonah, through illustrations, along with the lyrics and musical notation of spirituals for each biblical hero. In addition, he published *All Night, All Day: A Child's First Book of African-American Spirituals* (1991), which illustrates and provides the lyrics and musical notation for 20 spirituals; *Spirituals* (2005); and *Let It Shine: Three Favorite Spirituals* (2007). Bryan observed, "With the birds trilling, my mother singing, and the general music-making that went on at home, it is only natural that I would one day do books of songs that had special meaning to me, the black American spirituals" (p. 16, quoted in *BBG*).

Other children's books by Bryan include assorted folktales, which he researches extensively, adapts to interest his readers, drafts as poems to be read aloud, and then illustrates vividly and appealingly. His first such book, *The Ox of the Wonderful Horns and Other African Folktales* (1971/1993), includes a few **trickster** folktales. His others include *The Adventures of Aku* (1976), a folktale explaining how the trickster Ananse was instrumental in why cats and dogs fight like—well, cats and dogs; *The Dancing Granny* (1977), about a grandmother who

deters the trickster Ananse from eating everything in her garden; his **Coretta Scott King** Award-winning *Beat the Story Drum, Pum-Pum* (1980; paperback 1987), with Nigerian folktales explaining how enmity emerged between other animals (e.g., bush cow vs. elephant; frog vs. snake); *Cat's Purr* (1985), about how the cat got its purr; *Turtle Knows Your Name* (1989), a West Indian folktale; *The Story of Lightning and Thunder* (1993, adapter/illustrator), Bryan's adaptation of a Nigerian folktale about the origins of rain, thunder, and lightning; and *Lion and the Ostrich Chicks: And Other African Folk Tales* (1996), Coretta Scott King Honor-winning book of four folktales, including the title tale about how a mongoose cleverly rescues six ostrich chicks from a lion. He also published *Ashley Bryan's African Tales, Uh-Huh* (1998), which includes 14 of the tales previously published in other volumes, and *Ashley Bryan Picture Book Autobiography* (2009).

In addition to his books of spirituals and of folktale adaptations, he has illustrated numerous poetry books for children, including *Greet the Dawn* (1978), with poems by **Paul Laurence Dunbar**; *Sing to the Sun: Poems and Pictures* (1992, author/illustrator), with about two-dozen of Bryan's own illustrated poems on the ups and downs of life, families, and nature ; *What a Wonderful World* (1995, song text by George David Weiss and Bob Thiele, popularized by Louis Armstrong); *The Sun Is So Quiet: Poems* by **Nikki Giovanni** (1996); *Ashley Bryan's ABC of African American Poetry* (1997), with 25 poems by noted African Americans, selected and illustrated by Bryan; *Carol of the Brown King: Nativity Poems* by **Langston Hughes** (1998); *The House with No Door: African Riddle-Poems* (1998, text by Brian Swann); *Jump Back Honey: Poems* by Dunbar (1999); *Salting the Ocean: 100 Poems by Young Poets* (2000, compiled by Naomi Shihab Nye); and *A Nest Full of Stars: Poems* (2004, by James Berry). Bryan also illustrated *Fablieux* (1964); *Christmas Gif': An Anthology of Christmas Poems, Songs, and Stories Written by and about African Americans* (1963/1993, compiled by **Charlemae Hill Rollins**); *Story of the Three Kingdoms* (1997, text by **Walter Dean Myers**); *Why Leopard Has Spots: Dan Stories from Liberia* (1999, tales adapted by Won-Ldy Paye and Margaret H. Lippert); *Aneesa Lee and the Weaver's Gift* (1999, by Nikki Grimes); *How God Fix Jonah* (rev. ed. 2000, text by **Lorenz Graham**, originally 1946); *My America* (2007, by Jan Spivey Gilchrist); and numerous other books. Always open to new discoveries, at nearly 80 years of age, Bryan explored a new artistic medium, cut-paper collage, to illustrate a Zambian folktale he adapted, *Beautiful Blackbird* (2003, Coretta Scott King Illustrator Award winner).

Bryan also practices reading poems aloud and lectures on African-American poetry; his voice may be heard on audiocassettes or CDs of *Ashley Bryan: Poems and Folk-*

tales (1994, audiocassettes; 2007, CD). Other Bryan books available for listening include *Lion and the Ostrich Chicks by Ashley Bryan* (1994, audiocassette) and *Ashley Bryan's Beautiful Blackbird and Other Folktales* (unabridged, 2004, CD). In addition, Bryan creates puppets from driftwood and other objects he finds on his daily walks at the beach, and he paints, creates stained-glass panels from glass he finds on the beach, exhibits his works in various one-man shows, and plays musical instruments.

REFERENCES: *1MPCA:BSB. BBG. CAO-08. EBLG.* . Brennan, Carol, in *BB.* Johnson, Virginia, in //www.kidspoint.org/columns2. asp?column_id=1553&column_type=author Lodge, Sally. "Talking with Ashley Bryan." *Publishers Weekly. 249.49* (Dec. 9, 2002) p.54. From *Literature Resource Center.* Ross, Ramon Royal, in *OCAAL.* S. H. H., in *CBC.* Thomas, Rhondda R., in *GEAAL.* Amazon.com. //0-web.ebscohost.com.dbpcosdcsgt.co.san-diego.ca.us/novelist/detail? vid=25&hid=7&sid=d408b38a-8f5e-4ec2-b75c-cf9c5b5097d7%40s essionmgr3&bdata=JnNpdGU9bm92ZWxpc3QtbGl2ZQ%3d%3d. //www.cbcbooks.org/cbcmagazine/meet/ashleybryan.html.

FURTHER READING: *WB-99.*

Bullins, Ed (né Edward Artie) (aka Kingsley B. Bass, Jr.)
7/2/1935–

Plays, novels, poems; journalist, theater director, editor, educator

Bertha Marie Queen and Edward Bullins probably wanted their son to steer clear of gangs and to stay in school, but in the tough Philadelphia neighborhood in which Ed grew up, it seemed a lot easier to join a gang than to join the chess club or the nerd squad at school. By the time Ed dropped out of school (at age 17), he had already been stabbed—and nearly died as a result—and he knew the ins and outs of marketing bootleg whiskey.

He escaped gang life by joining the U.S. Navy in 1952, and he spent the next three years going wherever the navy told him to go. When he was discharged, in 1955, he returned to Philadelphia for a while, but by 1958, he felt the need to escape the violence again, so he fled to Los Angeles—the big city farthest from Philadelphia, as far as he knew. There, he earned his high school diploma and attended classes at Los Angeles City College. In college, he started reading extensively and began writing short stories and poems; he even founded a campus literary magazine, the *Citadel.* After a while, he decided to move on, and after roaming the country for a while, in 1964, he settled in the San Francisco Bay Area. There, he enrolled in the creative writing program at San Francisco State College, and he started writing plays. (It wasn't until 1994 that Bullins earned his M.F.A. from San Francisco State University, after having earned his B.A. from Antioch University, in Yellow Springs, Ohio, in 1989.)

Because Bullins's plays drew on the violence of the street he experienced in his youth, he found it difficult to find a theater company to produce his plays. Rather than quit writing, he started looking for ways to produce his work himself. With several others (including playwright **Amiri Baraka**), he cofounded the Black Arts/West in the Fillmore District of San Francisco, a militant African-American cultural and political organization that produced plays in coffeehouses, bars, lofts, and almost anywhere else people could gather in small groups. In August of 1965, three of Bullins's one-act plays were produced: *How Do You Do?* (his first play); *Dialect Determinism, or The Rally*; and *Clara's Ole Man.*

From the Black Arts, Bullins (and Baraka) moved on to Black House, across the bay in Oakland. There, Bullins, Baraka, **Sonia Sanchez**, **Marvin X**, Black Panther Party (BPP) cofounders Huey Newton, Bobby Seale, and **Eldridge Cleaver**, and several other African-American theater artists and political activists joined forces to create Black House. For a short time, Bullins was the cultural director of Black House and the minister of culture for the BPP. After a while, however, the views of Bullins and the artistically oriented participants conflicted with those of the political activists. Although both groups valued theater as a means of expression and communication and shared similar political outlooks, they differed sharply as to the mission of theater: Should it be focused on art, from a given political perspective, or should it be focused on politics, with theater as one of the means for achieving political ends? In 1967, these divergent views led to a break, and Bullins accepted an invitation to move to Harlem, in New York City, the heart and soul of American theater.

The invitation had come from Robert Macbeth, a director who had read and liked Bullins's play *Goin' a Buffalo.* Macbeth and others were just establishing the New Lafayette Theatre in Harlem. By the time Bullins reached Harlem, he had also written *The Rally, How Do You Do, The Electronic Nigger,* and *In the Wine Time* (his first full-length play). At the Lafayette, Bullins started out as playwright-in-residence and eventually became the theater's associate director. After the Lafayette folded (in 1972), Bullins became playwright-in-residence at the American Place Theatre, also in New York City, in 1973. Meanwhile, Bullins also edited *Black Theatre* magazine (1969-1974). In 1974, Bullins became the producing director of Surviving Theatre, and during most of the 1970s, he was on the staff of the Public Theatre's New York Shakespeare Festival.

In 1978, Bullins's son, Edward Jr., died tragically; soon after, Bullins returned to California, where he founded the Bullins Memorial Theatre, and cofounded (later, with fellow playwright Jonal Woodward) the Bullins/Woodward Theater Workshop in San Francisco. Under Bullins's stewardship, in addition to offering theater workshops and playwriting seminars, the Theater Workshop also staged plays. During this time, Bullins also started teaching at various colleges and universities, including Amherst College, Columbia University, Dartmouth College, University of California at Berkeley (1988-1995), and Northeastern University in Boston (where he has taught theater since 1995).

Even Bullins's earliest plays, produced at the New Lafayette, earned critical praise (e.g., winning the Vernon Rice Drama Desk Award), although commercial success was slower in coming. Bullins was relentless in churning out dozens of plays throughout the 1960s and 1970s. By 1977, Bullins had written more than 50 plays, more than 40 of which have been produced professionally. Between 1968 and 1980, 25 of his plays were produced in New York theaters, and 3 of those won Obie Awards: *In New England Winter* (1969), *The Fabulous Miss Marie* (1971), and *The Taking of Miss Janie* (1975; also won the Drama Critics Circle Award as best American play of 1974-1975). Although Bullins slowed down considerably after 1980, in part because of feminist criticism of the frequent sexual violence in his work, he has still continued to write and produce plays, having written a total topping 100 plays by now.

With his great number also comes great range, from gritty realism to surrealistic fantasy; from a focus on the distinctive urban black experience to a focus on brutal interactions with white society; from tragedy to humor-inflected drama. Some of his dramas also play with "the fourth wall," inviting audience members to interact verbally with the characters onstage.

In the Wine Time (1968) was the first of a projected cycle (series) of 20 plays Bullins decided to write about African Americans in contemporary urban America, titled his "Twentieth-Century Cycle." Many of these plays feature two young African-American half-brothers: Cliff Dawson and Steve Benson, both of whom (like Bullins) had served in the navy. Family relationships, friendships, and violence figure prominently in many of these dramas. Among the plays in this cycle are *The Corner* (produced 1968), *In New England Winter* (1969), *The Duplex: A Love Fable in Four Movements* (produced 1970, published 1971), *The Fabulous Miss Marie* (1971), *Home Boy* (1976), and *Daddy* (1977), as well as *Boy x Man* (1995, 1996). Bullins's other plays (not included in his cycle of plays) include *The Gentleman Caller* (1969), *The Pig Pen* (1970), *Salaam, Huey Newton, Salaam* (1991), and *Eight-Minute Marathon* (1999). In addition, Bullins has written two children's plays (*I Am Lucy Terry*, 1976, and *The Mystery of Phillis Wheatley*, 1976); the books for two musicals (*Sepia Star* and *Storyville*, both 1977, and both in collaboration with European-American composer Mildred Kayden), and two antidrug plays (*A Teacup Full of Roses*, 1989, and *Dr. Geechee and the Blood Junkies*, 1991).

In addition, quite a few of his works have been collected in *New—Lost Plays by Ed Bullins* (1994).

Although Bullins is best known for his plays, he has also written poetry (e.g., *To Raise the Dead and Foretell the Future*, 1971), short stories (e.g., *The Hungered Ones, Early Writings*, 1971), and a novel (*The Reluctant Rapist*, 1973, about Steve Benson, from his cycle of plays). In addition, he has edited anthologies, including *Five Plays: New Plays from the Black Theatre* (1969, editor), *The New Lafayette Theatre Presents, The Theme Is Blackness* (1973), and *Four Dynamite Plays* (1971). Occasionally, he has used the pseudonym Kingsley B. Bass, Jr.

In addition to his three Obies, his two New York Drama Critics Circle Awards (1975, 1977), and his Vernon Rice Drama Desk Award, Bullins has been awarded four Rockefeller grants, two Guggenheim fellowships, an honorary doctorate from Columbia College in Chicago, two National Endowment for the Arts grants, Off- Broadway Awards for distinguished playwriting, and a Creative Artists Public Service Program award. In 1997, the National Black Theater Festival in Winston-Salem, North Carolina, named him a "Living Legend." Indeed.

REFERENCES: *AA. AA:PoP. AANB. AAW:PV. CAO-05. EB-BH-CD. EBLG. NAAAL. OC20LE. W. WB-99. WDAA. Wiki.* Diehl, Heath A., in *GEAAL.* Fay, Robert, in *EA-99.* Grant, Nathan L., in *COCAAL* and *OCAAL.* Manheim, James M., in *BB. MWEL.* Marranca, Bonnie, in *G-97.* Sanders, Leslie, in *AAW-55-85:DPW.* Scharine, Richard, in *T-CAD-1st.* Üsekes, ÇiÜdem, in *T-CAD-3rd.*

Bunche, Ralph (Johnson)
8/7/1904–12/9/1971
Nonfiction, memoir, spoken word—speeches; politics, diplomat

Bunche, a delegate and then an undersecretary to the United Nations, helped write the United Nations charter. Prior to that, he had collaborated with sociologist Gunnar Myrdal in producing *An American Dilemma: The Negro Problem and Modern Democracy*, considered a monumental landmark study of race relations in the United States. In addition to being the first African American to win the Nobel Peace Prize (in 1950), Bunche won the NAACP's **Spingarn** Medal (in 1950) and was awarded the presidential Medal of Freedom (in 1963), the highest honor given to civilians in the United States. Some of his insights and ideas may be seen in *Ralph J. Bunche: Selected Speeches and Writings* (1995).

REFERENCES: *AANB. B. BCE. CAO-03. CE. EB-BH-CD. EBLG. G-97. HD. PGAA. QB. Wiki.* Balfour, Lawrie, in *EA-99.* Fisher, R. A. "Review of Ralphe J. Bunche: Selected Speeches and Writings." *Choice* 34.3 (Nov. 1996): p. 527. Rpt. in *Literature Resource Center.* Gale, Cengage Learning, p. 527. Harris, Robert L., Jr., in *USHC.* Rosen, Isaac, in *BB.* Urquhart, Brian, in *MNAE.* Warren, Nagueyalti, in *BH2C.*

Ralph Bunche

gathered on trips to the Caribbean and to more than a dozen African nations). Nonetheless, the name accurately reflects its emphasis on African-American history, particularly focusing on the Midwest, especially Chicago.

Burroughs's contribution to literature has included children's books, short stories, and poems. Her most celebrated poem is the title poem of her first collection of verse, *What Shall I Tell My Children Who Are Black?* (1968). Her other works include *Jasper, the Drummin' Boy* (1947); *Did You Feed My Cow? Rhymes and Games from City Streets and Country Lanes* (1955); *Whip Me Whop Me Pudding and Other Stories of Riley Rabbit and His Fabulous Friends* (1966); her anthology *For Malcolm: Poems on the Life and the Death of **Malcolm X*** (1967, edited with **Dudley Randall**); and her second poetry collection, *Africa, My Africa* (1970). Her literary legacy may be best expressed in her own words, from her poem "What Shall I Tell My Children Who Are Black?": "I must find the truth of heritage for myself / And pass it on to them. . . . For it is the truth that will make us free!" In 2003, *Life with Margaret: The Autobiography of Dr Margaret Burroughs*, by Sterling Stuckey, was published.

REFERENCES: *AANB. BAAW. CAO-02. Wiki.* Bolden, B. J., in *GEAAL.* Dickerson, Mary Jane, in *AAP-55-85.* Harroun, Debra G., in *BB.* Long, Richard A., in *COCAAL.* Amazon.com. //www.thehistory makers.com/biography/biography.asp?bioindex=39. —Tonya Bolden

Burroughs, Margaret (née Taylor) (aka Margaret Taylor Goss, Margaret G. Taylor, Margaret G. Burroughs, Margaret Taylor-Burroughs)
11/1/1917–

Poems, short stories, children's books; artist, museum founder and curator

A graduate of the Art Institute of Chicago (BFA, 1944; MFA, 1948), Burroughs has created prints, paintings, and sculpture, specializing in portrayals of African-American heroes such as Crispus Attucks, **Harriet Tubman, Sojourner Truth**, and **Frederick Douglass**.

Her interest in history goes far beyond art, however. In 1961, she and her second husband, Charles Burroughs, opened part of their Chicago-area home as the Ebony Museum of Negro History. She raised funds for their museum and continued to expand it, renaming it the DuSable Museum of African-American History in 1968. (Its namesake, black fur trader Jean Baptiste Pointe DuSable, was among the first to settle the territory that formed the foundation for present-day Chicago.) As you might expect from an artist, the museum hosts a nice collection of African-American art (especially 1940s-1960s) and both fine and folk art from Africa (which Burroughs

Burroughs, Nannie Helen
5/2/1879–5/20/1961

Columns, play, nonfiction—organizational management

In addition to writing provocative columns for several African-American newspapers (e.g., the *Christian Banner*), Burroughs produced a wide variety of other publications. These include her guidebook *What to Do and How to Do It* (1907), her play *Slabtown District Convention: A Comedy in One Act* (1908), and several religious works, including *Grow: A Handy Guide for Progressive Church Women* and *Making Your Community Christian*. She also chaired a commission responsible for a major study, *Negro Housing: Report of the Committee on Negro Housing* (1932).

REFERENCES: *AANB.* Harley, Sharon, "Nannie Helen Burroughs: 'The Black Goddess of Liberty.' (Vindicating the Race: Contributions to African-American Intellectual History)." *The Journal of Negro History.* 81.1-4 (Annual 1996) p. 62. From *Literature Resource Center.* Higginbotham, Evelyn Brooks, in *BWA:AHE.* Jordan, Casper Le Roy, in *BH2C.* Robinson, Alonford James, Jr., in *EA-99.* //www.aaregistry. com/african_american_history/858/A_true_GirlFriend_Nannie_Burro ughs. //www.blackseek.com/bh/2001/47_NBurroughs.htm.

Butler, Octavia E. (Estelle)
6/22/1947–2/24/2006
Novels

Laurice Butler, a shoeshining man, died before he saw his daughter Octavia take her first steps. With the help of her own mother, Octavia M. Guy Butler gave little Octavia a strict Baptist upbringing. The three females lived in a racially integrated neighborhood in Pasadena, California, so Octavia grew up believing that African Americans, Asian Americans, Hispanic Americans, and European Americans could all share a culturally diverse community. Even the boarders her mother and grandmother hosted in their home reflected the cultural diversity of their community. Only when she accompanied her mother to work (as a maid in other people's homes) did Octavia realize the harsh realities of racial discrimination and segregation.

Tall for her age, Octavia was shy and withdrawn, preferring the company of books and her own thoughts to that of other children. Although she was dyslexic, she read avidly. She later recalled, "When I discovered that my first-grade teacher expected me to be content with Dick and Jane, I asked my mother if I could have a library card. From the day she took me to get one, I was a regular at the fairy tale shelves. I also explored, read anything else that looked interesting, got hooked on horse stories for a while, then discovered science fiction" (quoted in *BWA:AHE*). Among her favorites were Harlan Ellison, Isaac Asimov, Robert Heinlein, Ursula Le Guin (e.g., her *Dispossessed*), and Frank Herbert (especially the first book in his Dune series). She also read the numerous sci-fi magazines that were widely available during the era of the Cold War's race into space, and she enjoyed reading comic books (*Superman* and various superheroes in Marvel comics) and *Mad* magazine.

By age ten, Octavia had started writing her own stories, chiefly the same kinds of stories she was reading. When her reading shifted to science fiction, so did her writing. With the help and encouragement of her junior-high science teacher, Butler began submitting her stories to some sci-fi magazines, although they didn't end up in print.

After graduating from John Muir High School (1965) and from Pasadena City College (associate's degree, 1968), Butler started at California State University at Los Angeles (CSULA). She didn't stay long, though, because CSULA offered next to nothing in the way of creative-writing courses. In 1969 and 1970, she took some writing classes at UCLA and at the Writers' Guild of America West, through its "Open Door" program. At a Writers' Guild class, she met her mentor, Harlan Ellison. In addition to giving her encouragement and candid, constructive suggestions for improving her work, he urged her to attend the six-week Clarion Science Fiction Writers' Workshop, held in Clarion, Pennsylvania, in the summer of 1970. The workshop's instructors were well-known writers and editors of science fiction, who offered practical advice and realistic tips for writing in this genre. She often cited this training as being the most valuable she received for perfecting her writing craft.

At first, Butler patterned her own stories after the white-male-dominated, technologically oriented science-fiction stories that she was reading. After a while, however, it started to bother her that there were almost no people of color, no independent-minded leading women characters, and very few richly developed characters of any kind in the books she read. Soon, her own stories reflected the life experiences and the people whom she knew, and she offered fully developed characterizations in her work. Her novels and short stories are now widely acclaimed—both by science-fiction readers and by literary critics, and she became one of the few women to achieve success in this white-male-dominated genre.

"I began to write consciously, deliberately, about people who were afraid and who functioned in spite of their fear. People who failed sometimes and were not destroyed. . . . Every story I write adds to me a little, changes me a little, forces me to reexamine an attitude or belief, causes me to research and learn, helps me to understand people and grow. . . . Every story I create creates me. I write to create myself" (from the conclusion to her essay "Why I Write," quoted in *BWA:AHE*).

Her road to success was not without hardship, however, as she had to overcome not only publishers' resistance to sci-fi works centered on the experiences of African-American women, but also her family's pressures to get a job that would pay her a steady income, and her own feelings of discouragement during financially difficult times. Nonetheless, she persevered, and her perseverance paid off later on.

"Writing is difficult. You do it all alone without encouragement and without any certainty that you'll ever be published or paid or even that you'll be able to finish the particular work you've begun. It isn't easy to persist amid all that. ... I write about people who do extraordinary things. It just turned out that it was called science fiction." (Bloodchild, pages 143, 145)

By the mid-1990s, Butler had authored numerous novels and short stories and had won the two most prestigious awards given to works of science fiction: the Nebula and the Hugo. Her earliest works center around the ominous character Doro, a 4,000-year-old immortal Nubian who dominates his descendants through his supernatural psychic powers and his superhuman physical strength. Doro can invade other people's bodies whenever he wishes to, terrorizing his numerous descendants. Although he prefers the bodies of black males, he may choose to inhabit anyone, of any race or gender. He can even transcend time, inhabiting persons from various time periods. All Doro's descendants form a pattern of mentally linked individuals, so Butler calls this series her "patternist" novels. Other characters in these novels include several strong, self-confident females, such as

Doro's daughter Mary, a highly gifted telepath; Alanna, an African-Asian feral child who has to survive in a hostile environment of warring aliens; and Anyanwu, an African woman with great healing powers. Through her patternist novels, Butler addresses race, gender, and class differences, as well as ethical, social, and political issues. Butler's patternist novels include *Patternmaster* (1976), *Mind of My Mind* (1977), *Survivor* (1978), *Wild Seed* (1980), and *Clay's Ark* (1984). In 2007, four of the five novels (all but *Survivor*) were published in a single volume titled *Seed to Harvest*. Because these novels take place in the distant past, as well as in the future, they may be more accurately called "speculative fiction" than "science fiction."

While working on the patternist series, Butler wrote *Kindred* (1979), which she originally intended to be part of the series, but which turned out to be too closely tied to reality to fit into the series. In the novel, Dana Franklin, an African-American woman living in a 1970s Los Angeles suburb, is celebrating her 26th birthday with her European-American husband, when she is suddenly and unwillingly transported back in time. Much to her chagrin, she finds herself a slave on a Maryland plantation before the Civil War. It appears that she was summoned back by Rufus, an obnoxious, self-centered, hot-tempered white slave owner who is her grandmother Hagar's father. Apparently, he called her back because his life was in danger, and he needed her help to save him. Because he is Dana's biological ancestor, he has the power to force her to do so. As the novel unfolds, and Dana moves back and forth across space and time, she discovers the true physical and psychological brutality of slavery, even losing an arm in the process.

After the patternist series, Butler started a new set of novels, her Xenogenesis trilogy. Following a nuclear holocaust, the surviving humans are rescued by a species of extraterrestrials, who crossbreed with the humans. The alien species appreciates the intelligence of humans but dislikes the human tendency to form hierarchies, class divisions, stereotypes, and other categories that lead to conflict and prejudice. These novels are *Dawn: Xenogenesis* (1987), *Adulthood Rites: Xenogenesis* (1988), and *Imago: Xenogenesis* (1989); a collected edition was published as *Lilith's Brood* in 2000. After finishing this trilogy, Butler started a new trilogy, beginning with Nebula-nominated *The Parable of the Sower* (1993), about a 21st-century African-American teenage woman prophet in the midst of a spiritually decadent society where drug addiction has caused economic disintegration. The second in the trilogy, *The Parable of the Talents*, won the Nebula, but the third volume, tentatively titled *The Parable of the Trickster*, remained incomplete upon her death. Her last published novel, *Fledgling* (2005) uses a science-fiction context to explore a race of vampires involved in mutually beneficial relationships with humans.

In addition to her novels, Butler wrote numerous short stories, including her 1984 Hugo award-winning "Speech Sounds" (1983), about an anarchistic world in which communications deficits are the norm. Butler's "Blood-Child" (1984), about a society in which aliens exploit human males for purposes of reproduction, won a 1985 Hugo, a 1984 Nebula, and the Locus Award. Both short stories were printed in *Isaac Asimov's Science Fiction Magazine*. Butler collected and postscripted many of her shorter works in *Bloodchild: And Other Stories* (1995; expanded version, 2005). In all her works, she addressed themes of enslavement, race relations, and class and gender differences. Although she carefully researched the most recent scientific advances in the social, biological, and physical sciences, her fiction highlights human thoughts and feelings and human (or human-alien) interactions, rather than technological or scientific wizardry. When not fully engaged in her writing, she volunteered her time helping others learn how to read.

Butler was awarded a MacArthur Foundation Fellowship grant, often referred to as a "Genius" award, in 1995, and in 2000, she won a PEN American Center lifetime achievement award. In 2005, Butler was inducted into Chicago State University's International Black Writers Hall of Fame at the Gwendolyn Brooks Center. She was given one more major honor after her death: The Carl Brandon Society established the Octavia E. Butler Memorial Scholarship, to help writers of color attend the Clarion Science Fiction Writers' Workshop she considered invaluable to her own success, and where she had taught on five occasions, most recently in 2005.

REFERENCES: *AA:PoP. AANB. B. CAO-06. CLCS. EA-99. EB-BH-CD. EBLG. MWEL. NAAAL. OC20LE. W. W2B. WDAA. Wiki.* Benson, Linda G., in *T-CYAW.* Dunning, Stefanie K., in *AW:ACLB-03.* Ed. Daniel G. Marowski and Roger Matuz. Vol. 38. Detroit: Gale Research, 1986. pp. 37-49. From *Literature Resource Center.* Foster, Frances Smith, "*Kindred,*" in *COCAAL* and *OCAAL.* "Octavia Butler's Black Female Fiction." *Extrapolation* 23.1 (Spring 1982): pp. 37-49. Rpt. in *Contemporary Literary Criticism.* Francis, Diana Pharaoh, in *CPW.* Glickman, Simon, and Ralph G. Zerbonia, in *BB.* Govan, Sandra Y., in *OCWW.* Kendall, Lisa See. "Octavia E. Butler: In Her Science Fiction She Projects the Answers to Society's Ills." *Publishers Weekly.* 240.50 (Dec. 13, 1993) p. 50. From *Literature Resource Center.* McEntree, Grace, in *GEAAL.* Mickle, Mildred R., "Butler, Octavia E.," in *COCAAL* and *OCAAL.* O'Connor, Margaret Anne, in *AAFW-55-84.* Pfeiffer, John R., in *SFW:CSMA.* Salvaggio, Ruth. "Octavia Butler and the Black Science-Fiction Heroine." *Black American Literature* 18.2 (Summer 1984): pp. 78-81. Rpt. in *Contemporary Literary Criticism.* Ed. Jeffrey W. Hunter and Polly Vedder. Vol. 121. Detroit: Gale Group, 2000. pp. 78-81. From *Literature Resource Center.* Stevenson, Rosemary, in *BWA:AHE.* Sturgis, Susanna. "Octavia E. Butler: June 22, 1947-February 24, 2006." *The Women's Review of Books.* 23.3 (May-June 2006) p. 19. From *Literature Resource Center.* Govan, Sandra Y., in //www.femspec.org/editorial/Butler_Tribute.htm.

~C~

La medicina popular de Cuba: Medicos de antano, curanderos, santeros y paleros de hogano (1984, on traditional Cuban healing and medical and religious practices); *Supersticiones y buenos consejos* (1987, on superstitions and good advice); *Los animales en el folklore y la magia de Cuba* (1988, on animals in Cuban folklore and magic). From 1970 until 1991, Cabrera published at least three more short-story collections and nine more anthropological investigations.

REFERENCES: *CAO-03. MWEL. Wiki.* Edwards, Roanne, in *EA-99.* Hewitt , Julia Cuervo, in *MLAFW-2.* //ibisweb.miami.edu/search~ /a?a. //merrick.library.miami.edu/cubanHeritage/chc0339/. //www. habanaelegante.com/Summer99/Bustos.htm (in Spanish). Nelson, Renee, in //www.mnsu.edu/emuseum/information/biography/abcde/ cabrera_lydia.html.

Cabrera, Lydia
5/20/1900–9/19/1991
Short stories, nonfiction—cultural anthropology, ethnology, history

From an affluent Cuban family, Cabrera studied in France and lived mostly in Europe, especially after her parents died (her father in 1923, her mother in 1932). The eruption of the Spanish Civil War pushed her home to Cuba in 1936. There, she wrote two short-story collections offering insight into Afro-Cuban culture: *Cuentos Negros de Cuba* (1940, originally in French, 1936) and *Por Qué: Cuentos Negros de Cuba* (1948). Like most Cubans, her heritage included African roots. To enhance her readers' appreciation of the breadth and depth of Afro-Cuban culture, Cabrera did extensive anthropological research. Probably her most significant work was *El Monte: Notes on the Religion, the Magic, the Superstitions and the Folklore of Creole Negroes and the Cuban People* (1954, her study of Afro-Cuban folk culture). Most of her 100-plus published works were written and published only in Spanish, including *Refranes de Negros Viejos* (1955/1970, compiling Afro-Cuban proverbs); *Anagó: Vocabulario Lucumí* (1957, detailing the Yoruban vocabulary spoken in Cuba); *La Sociedad Secreta Abakuá* (1958, compiling an all-male secret society's legends and **folktales**). In 1959, another war—the Cuban Revolution—prompted Cabrera to flee her homeland for Florida, where she spent the rest of her life.

In Florida, Cabrera continued to publish her story collections, such as *Ayapa: Cuentos de Jicotea* (1971, Cuban turtle **trickster** tales, emerging from tales of an African tortoise trickster); and *Cuentos para adultos, ninos y retrasados mentales* (1983). She also continued her extensive Afro-Cuban ethnologies, such as *Otan Iyehiye: Las Piedras Preciosas* (1970, on the ritual meanings of precious stones); *Reglas de Congo* (1980, on Bantu rituals in Cuba);

Callaloo
1976–

First published in 1976 at Southern University in Baton Rouge, Louisiana, *Callaloo* is an African-American and African journal of arts and letters, established to ensure a creative outlet for the black Southern writing community that emerged in the late 1960s and early 1970s. (*See also* **Tom Dent**.) *Callaloo*'s editorial vision gradually expanded to include a wider range of writing, as well as visual art from Africa and the African diaspora, including original Afro-Brazilian poetry and West Indian and African literature. In 1977, the journal moved to the University of Kentucky with editor Charles H. Rowell, where it stayed nine years before moving to the University of Virginia in 1986 in a printing collaboration with Johns Hopkins University Press. *Callaloo* has dedicated whole issues to such authors as Chinua Achebe, Aime Cesaire, **Toni Morrison**, **Alice Walker**, and **Ernest Gaines**, as well as major younger writers such as **Yusef Komunyakaa**. The journal is contemporary with current trends in poetry, fiction, and drama.

REFERENCES: Keene, John R., in *OCAAL.* —Lisa Bahlinger

Campbell, (Elizabeth) Bebe (née Moore)
2/18/1950–11/27/2006
Articles, essays, short stories, autobiography/memoir, novels, radio plays, play, children's book, commentary; radio commentator

A public-school teacher for several years, Campbell started writing pieces for periodicals, eventually publishing about 100 articles and essays in newspapers (e.g., *Los Angeles Times, Washington Post*) and a diversity of magazines (e.g., *Ms., New York Times Magazine, Parents*). Next, she tackled her first book, *Successful Women, Angry Men: Backlash in the Two-Career Marriage* (1986), based on extensive interviews of women who juggled careers and families, as well as her own experience. She achieved her first critical and popular success with her memoir, *Sweet Summer: Growing Up with and without My Dad* (1989), about the summers she spent with her father and his family, as well as the school years at home with her mother and grandmother. Campbell told the *Philadelphia Inquirer*, "I think it's very important at this time for black people to see that there are fathers, despite divorce, that stuck around and were responsible."

Inspired by **James Baldwin, Toni Morrison, Alice Walker**, and other novelists, Campbell knew she wanted to write her own novels. After taking inspirational writing courses with **John Oliver Killens** and with **Toni Cade Bambara**, editor of the groundbreaking feminist anthology *Black Woman*, she decided to plunge in. Her first novel, *Your Blues Ain't Like Mine* (1992), centers on the struggle for civil rights, starting with the horrifyingly brutal race-motivated murder of Emmett Till in 1955 and spanning more than three decades. It was named a *New York Times* Notable Book of the Year and won the NAACP Image Award for Literature. All of Campbell's novels were critically acclaimed, and her next three novels were *New York Times* best-sellers. *Brothers and Sisters* (1994), set in the post-Rodney King-verdict riots in Los Angeles, focuses on the friendship of a black woman and a white woman. About the book, she told Knight-Ridder/Tribune News Service, "We've got to start getting past stereotypes, and anger, and fear, if we're going to have any semblance of racial harmony in this country. We have to make color our joy, not our burden." *Singing in the Comeback Choir* (1998) celebrates a grandmother who gives up her singing career to raise her granddaughter to adulthood, then tries to revive her singing career, eventually triumphing after overcoming challenging obstacles. Campbell's own family included her second husband, her daughter (Maia Campbell), and her stepson (Ellis Gordon, III). Her other novels included *What You Owe Me* (2001), about the relationship between two women: an African-American hotel maid and a Jewish Holocaust survivor, *Los Angeles Times* Best Book of the Year; and NAACP Image Award-winning *72 Hour Hold* (2005), about how an African-American family copes with a teenage daughter who has bipolar disease.

Campbell's first children's book, *Sometimes My Mommy Gets Angry* (2003; illustrated by E. B. Lewis), offers a child's eye view of her mentally ill mother. It won the Outstanding Literature Award by the National Alliance for the Mentally Ill. In her *Stompin' at the Savoy* (2006, illustrated by Richard Yarde), a young girl who feels anxious about her jazz recital is whisked away to the Savoy Ballroom during the Jazz Age, where she is immersed in its spirit and lets loose through jazz dancing. Campbell's *I Get So Hungry* (2008, illustrated by Amy

Bates) addresses childhood obesity in a warm and encouraging manner.

She also wrote a radio-play adaptation of her short story "Old Lady Shoes," an original radio play *Sugar on the Floor*, and her play *Even with Madness*, produced in New York in 2003. For the big screen, she sold the film rights to her novels *Sweet Summer* (1989, Motown Productions) and *Brothers and Sisters* (1995, Touchstone). Campbell also had even more listeners than readers, as her commentaries could often be heard on National Public Radio and other radio and television talk shows.

When asked how she would like to be remembered, Campbell told an interviewer, "That ... My work led to people talking with each other, and we began to dialogue about race. We began to focus on the love between us." She also said, "I like to be hopeful. I like to end where the characters still have work to do, but it's clear that if you do the work, your life is going to change for the better. ... when I'm writing, I'm thinking about me. I'm just trying to please, surprise, and delight me" (in *Callaloo*, Autumn 1999, quoted in GLRO *Literature Resource Center*). Let's end her story on a hopeful note, too: She helped us focus on our shared love, and though we may miss her living presence, Bebe Moore Campbell will continue to please, surprise, and delight many readers for the foreseeable future.

REFERENCES: *AANB. EBLG.* Campbell, Bebe Moore, and Jane Campbell. "An Interview with Bebe Moore Campbell." *Callaloo* 22.4 (Autumn 1999), pp. 954-972. Rpt. in *Contemporary Literary Criticism* (Vol. 246). Detroit: Gale. From *Literature Resource Center.* Campbell, Jane, in *ANSWWII-6th.* "Obituaries." *The Horn Book Magazine.* 83.2 (March-April 2007) p. 221. From *Literature Resource Center.* Johnson, Anne Janette, and David G. Oblender, in *BB. CAO-06. CLC-246.* Satz, Martha. "I Hope I Can Teach a Little Bit: An Interview with Bebe Moore Campbell." *Southwest Review.* 81.2 (Spring 1996) p. 195. From *Literature Resource Center.* See, Lisa. "PW Interviews: Bebe Moore Campbell." *Publisher's Weekly* 235.26 (June 30, 1989): pp. 82-83. Rpt. in *Literature Resource Center.* Gale, Cengage Learning. Amazon.com. Williams, Dera R., in *GEAAL. Wiki.*

Campbell, James Edwin
9/28/1867–1/26/1896
Poems, spoken word—speeches; journalist, educator

Campbell's dialect poems predated those of his contemporary, **Paul Laurence Dunbar**. Specifically, many of Campbell's poems were written in the Gullah language of the South Carolina sea islands. Nonetheless, like Dunbar, he also published many poems written in standard English, although his dialect poems are generally considered his better work. Campbell's poetry collections include *Driftings and Gleanings* (1887), the first collection of African-American dialect poems, and *Echoes from the Cabin and Elsewhere* (1895). His dialect poems may have heralded those of the **Harlem Renaissance** in their racial awareness, sense of satire, and skepticism of religion, while reflecting the lyricality of his own time in their phrasing, rhyme, and rhythm patterns.

In his brief lifetime, he supported himself by working as a teacher in African-American schools in Ohio (1884-1887) and West Virginia (1887-1891), and as a principal of a "colored institute" (1891-1894), now the West Virginia State University. In 1891, Campbell married schoolteacher Mary Champ. He also worked as a staff writer for the *Pioneer,* an African-American newspaper (1887-early 1890s), and for the Chicago *Times-Herald* (starting in 1894), and he contributed poems and articles to other periodicals, as well. In addition, Campbell was a gifted orator, whom historian **Carter G. Woodson** credited with inspiring Woodson to gain an education. Sadly, Campbell contracted pneumonia while visiting his parents for Christmas in Ohio, and it killed him early the following year, perhaps because he may already have had tuberculosis.

REFERENCES: *AANB. BV. EBLG. NYPL-AADR.* Kich, Martin, in *GEAAL.* Sherman, Joan R., in *COCAAL* and *OCAAL. Wiki. LF-07.* Thomas, Lorenzo, in *AAWBHR.*

Carmichael (chosen name: Kwame Touré), Stokely (Standiford Churchill)
6/29/1941–11/15/1998
Essays, spoken word—speeches; activist

Probably his best-known literary achievement is his having been credited with popularizing the term "black power." A graduate (with honors) from Howard University (1964), Carmichael is better known for his social activism as a Freedom Rider, a CORE (Congress of Racial Equality) activist, a SNCC (Student Nonviolent Coordinating Committee) voter registrar, and Black Panther Party (BPP) leader. In each of these pursuits, Carmichael demonstrated a mastery of rhetoric, delivering powerful speeches to large audiences. His speeches were provocative in challenging the white establishment, opposing nonviolence as a strategy for political change and integration as a political goal, fostering racial pride, and promoting political and economic independence and power. Many of these speeches were gathered in *Stokely Speaks* (1965), and he and political scientist Charles V. Hamilton coauthored *Black Power* (1967), published just before he left SNCC to join the BPP.

Two years later, he left the BPP to join a pan-African movement, and he himself moved to Guinea, West Africa, with his first wife, world-renowned South African singer Miriam Makeba (married 1968-1978). In 1971, he published *Stokely Speaks: Black Power Back to Pan-Africanism.* In 1978, he adopted the first name of Kwame Nkrumah and the last name of Sekou Toure (spelling it Ture), African leaders whom he admired. He later mar-

ried Guinean physician Marlyatou Barry, with whom he had a son, Boca Biro, and whom he later divorced (in 1992). Carmichael's ever-evolving message appealed to many black men and women, whom he inspired to political activism. Existing audio recordings of interviews of him can give an inkling of how powerfully articulate he was. Nevertheless, he offended many women listeners with his joking assertion that the position of women in SNCC is "prone." Before his death, Carmichael worked with Ekwueme Michael Thelwell to write his memoir, *Ready for Revolution: The Life and Struggles of Stokely Carmichael (Kwame Ture)* (2003, posthumous), which contains some inaccurate and controversial elements, many of which may have been introduced by Thelwell.

REFERENCES: *EBLG.* Balfour, Lawrie, in *EA-99.* Glickman, Simon, and David G. Oblender, in *BB. CAO-00. CE. LE. PD. Wiki.* Howe, Darcus. "In Memory of Stokely, My Friend, Who Said, Get Guns." *New Statesman* (1996). *127.4413* (Nov. 27, 1998) p. 14. From *Literature Resource Center.* Leak, Jeffrey B., in *OCAAL.* Nicholson, Dolores, in *B. BH2C.* Weisbrot, Robert. "Stokely Speaks." *The New York Times Book Review.* 108 (Nov. 23, 2003) *Book Review Desk,* p. 16. From *Literature Resource Center.* //en.wikiquote.org/wiki/Stokely_ Carmichael. *EB-BH-CD.*

Carroll, Vinnette (Justine)
3/11/1922–11/5/2002
Plays; director, actress, theater founder

In collaboration with composer and lyricist Micki Grant (née Minnie Perkins McCutcheon), Carroll wrote *Croesus and the Witch* (1971) and two Tony Award-nominated, award-winning musicals: *Don't Bother Me, I Can't Cope* (1971) and *Your Arms Too Short to Box with God* (1975; grossed more than $6 million after its 6-month tour ran almost 18 months). When she directed the Broadway production of *Your Arms,* she became the first African-American woman to direct a musical on Broadway, possibly even the first to direct a play of any kind there. Carroll also won awards for her acting (Obie, 1962) and her directing (e.g., Emmys, NAACP Image Award, Los Angeles Drama Critics Circle Award, Drama Desk Award), and she founded and artistically directed the Urban Arts Corps (1967; later renamed the Urban Arts Theatre). Even after she moved to Florida, she continued working, founding the Vinnette Carroll Repertory Company, in Fort Lauderdale, in 1984. Carroll also wrote many adaptations, such as *Trumpets of the Lord* (1963, adaptation of **James Weldon Johnson**'s poetry), *But Never Jam Today* (1969, adaptation of Alice in Wonderland), *All the King's Men* (1974, adaptation of Robert Penn Warren's novel), *When Hell Freezes Over I'll Skate* (1979, **Paul Laurence Dunbar**'s poetry), as well as original plays, such as *Step Lively Boy* (1973), *The Ups and Downs of Theophilus Maitland* (1974), *I'm Laughin' But I Ain't*

Tickled (1976), and *What You Gonna Name That Pretty Little Baby?* (1978).

REFERENCES: *EBLG. TAWH.* Dolen, Christine. "Vinnette Carroll: 1922-2002. (In Memoriam)." *American Theatre. 20.3* (Mar. 2003) p. 18. From *Literature Resource Center.* Manheim, James M., in *BB. CAO-05//www.jimcrowhistory.org/scripts/jimcrow/women.cgi?state=New%20York. //www.scils.rutgers.edu/~cybers/carroll.html.*

Cary, Mary Ann (née Shadd)
10/9/1823–6/5/1893
Pamphlets, news articles, spoken word—speeches; educator, publisher, newspaper cofounder

The eldest of 13 children of self-employed, free blacks Harriet and Abraham Shadd, Mary Ann Shadd learned responsibility and independence early on. She also learned a fierce dedication to abolition from her parents, who provided her with a Quaker education. Her father, a subscription agent for William Lloyd Garrison's *Liberator,* had been deeply involved in the Underground Railroad, and he fervently opposed the Back-to-Africa movement of the 1830s, believing that African Americans should work to abolish slavery and to establish racial justice here.

In the 1840s, Mary Ann Shadd applied her education to teaching African-American children, at first establishing her own school in Delaware and then accepting teaching jobs, first in New York and then in Pennsylvania. Through her teaching, she encouraged her pupils to foster independence and personal responsibility. In 1949, she wrote a pamphlet touting her belief in the importance of self-reliance, *Hints to the Colored People of North America,* and she wrote articles for **Frederick Douglass**'s *North Star.*

When the Fugitive Slave Act passed in 1850, Shadd was persuaded (by **Henry Bibb** and his wife) to join the exodus of African Americans seeking sanctuary in the abolitionist country of Canada West (as the province of Ontario was called at the time). When she (and her brother) reached the promised land in Canada West, she established a school, with financial support from the American Missionary Association and several African-American families. Soon, she decided to integrate the school, and she lectured and wrote, encouraging other African Americans to flee persecution in the United States, to find safety in Canada West.

Bibb, publisher of the *Voice of the Fugitive,* favored separatism and urged African Americans to return to the United States as soon as slavery was ended. He refused to publish Shadd's articles favoring integration and encouraging African Americans to consider Canada their permanent home. At the time, Bibb owned the only printing press in town. In 1852, Shadd decided to publish her own 44-page pamphlet, *Notes on Canada West,* which included statistical data and other facts documenting the bounty of that country, including information on farming, schooling, and churches. Her pamphlet is considered the first by an African-American woman to have used a factual database as the foundation for a persuasive message.

Bibb vehemently denounced Shadd's views in his *Voice,* so the funding for Shadd's school dried up, and in 1853, she had to close it. That year, with Samuel Ringgold Ward, Shadd founded, published, edited, and contributed to the weekly newspaper the *Provincial Freeman,* thereby becoming the first African-American woman to own and operate a periodical of any kind. In her paper, she scolded Bibb for promoting charity-supported self-segregated communities of fugitive slaves. Through her paper, she promoted abolition, integration, and most of all, her firm belief in the value of self-reliance.

In 1856, Shadd married Thomas F. Cary, with whom she had two children: their daughter Sarah and their son Linton. In 1858, while working hard for abolition, Mary Ann Shadd Cary attended an antislavery meeting at which John Brown described his bold plan. He and those he could convince to join him would raid the armory at Harpers Ferry, grabbing the weapons and distributing them to slaves. Brown knew in his heart that once the slaves had weapons, they would then rise up en masse, throwing off their bonds and freeing themselves, their loved ones, and all others in bondage. At that meeting, Brown met two of Cary's pals: Osborne P. Anderson, whom he conscripted to accompany him, and **Martin Delany**, later known as the father of black nationalism. In 1859, Brown and Anderson carried out their raid (for which Brown was executed), and Anderson ended up being the only African American to escape capture when their plan was thwarted. Thus, Anderson offered a distinctive eyewitness account of the historic event, detailed in *A Voice from Harpers Ferry,* which Mary Ann Shadd Cary edited and published in 1861.

The year of the Harpers Ferry raid, financial troubles caused Cary's paper to fold, and she returned to teaching. The following year, Cary's husband died and Cary continued teaching, supporting herself and her children. In 1863, however, in the middle of the Civil War, Cary moved her family back to the United States. There, with the encouragement of **Martin Delany**, she became a recruitment officer, encouraging African Americans in Indiana to fight for the Union Army. After the Civil War, she moved to Washington, D.C., where she became a school principal and wrote articles for **Frederick Douglass**'s *New National Era* and other periodicals. Meanwhile, she earned a law degree from Howard University in 1871, but Howard didn't grant her the degree for another decade, as the school officials feared negative publicity for giving a woman a degree. Needless to say, Cary became an ardent feminist and a suffragist. In fact, she was one of just a few woman who voted during Reconstruction.

REFERENCES: *AANB. ANAD. BAAW.* Blue, Rose, and Melodie Monahan, in *BB.* Born, Brad S., in *OCAAL.* Calloway-Thomas, Carolyn, in *BWA:AHE.* Gardner, Eric, in *GEAAL. Wiki.* Hudson, Peter, in *EA-99.* Yee, Shirley J. "Finding a place: Mary Ann Shadd Cary and the dilemmas of black migration to Canada, 1850-1870." *Frontiers. 18.3* (September-December 1997) p. 1. From *Literature Resource Center.* Shadd's papers have been collected at the Moorland-Spingarn Research Center at Howard University, as well as in the Public Archives of Canada in Ottawa, Ontario.

Cassells, Cyrus
05/16/1957–

Poems, literary criticism, film criticism, gay literature, Spanish-English translation; actor, educator

A graduate of Stanford University (1979), Cassells has been a creative writing fellow, a lecturer, and a poet-in-residence since 1982, and he currently teaches poetry as an associate professor at Texas State University in San Marcos. His poetry collections include *The Mud Actor* (1982), a National Poetry Series selection; *Soul Make a Path Through Shouting* (1994), nominated for the Pulitzer Prize, winner of the William Carlos Williams Award, and cited as one of the "Best Books of 1994" by *Publishers Weekly*; *Beautiful Signor* (1997), winner of the Lambda Literary Award; and *More Than Peace and Cypresses* (2004). His fifth collection, tentatively titled *Crossed-Out Swastika*, is intended for 2010 publication. He also contributes poetry to numerous periodicals (e.g., *Callaloo, Quilt, Sequoia*).

In addition, he has authored a short film (*Bayok*, 1980, about dancer Gregory Silva) and written film criticism (e.g., in *Bay Windows*, 1991). Cassells's other awards include a *Callaloo* creative writing award (1984), a Pushcart Prize (1995), the Peter I. B. Lavan Younger Poets Award, a Lannan Foundation Literary Award, and fellowships from the Rockefeller Foundation and the National Endowment for the Arts, along with numerous awards for individual poems, such as a prize from the Academy of American Poets for "The Women and Landscape with Traveler" (1979).

REFERENCES: CAO-06. *Wiki.* //www.cavecanempoets.org/pages/programs_faculty.php. //www.coppercanyonpress.org/catalog/dsp_author.cfm?Book_ID=1037. //www.loc.gov/bookfest/2006/authors/cassells.html. //www.poetryfoundation.org/archive/poet.html?id=98073. //www.poets.org/poet.php/prmPID/215. Amazon.com.

FURTHER READING: Lipkin, Elline, in *GEAAL.*

Cave Canem
1996–

Workshop, retreat, and mutual-support organization for African-American writers, especially poets

In 1996, poet-educators **Toi Derricotte** and **Cornelius Eady** were leading a weeklong summer workshop retreat for African-American poets when they realized that the need for their workshop retreat was perennial, and they vowed to conduct a similar workshop retreat each summer thereafter. To ensure the life of the workshop retreat, they decided to found a nonprofit organization to sponsor it. Derricotte, Eady, and Eady's wife, novelist Sarah Micklem, were discussing a name for their foundation when they recalled a trip to Pompeii, where they had observed the mosaic of a dog, with the inscription "CAVE CANEM" ("Beware of the Dog") at the entrance to the "House of the Tragic Poet." They quickly agreed that their protective safe haven for African-American poets would be well served by the title "Cave Canem."

The Cave Canem Foundation now has a full-time staff and an active board of directors, funded through grants from nonprofit foundations and governmental organizations, as well as from individual donations. Since its inception, the Cave Canem workshop retreat has greatly expanded its faculty. A variety of esteemed poets and other creative writers have led at least one workshop. The Cave Canem poets have included **Elizabeth Alexander**, **Cyrus Cassells**, Cheryl Clarke, **Lucille Clifton**, **Thomas Sayers Ellis**, **Michael S. Harper**, Terrance Hayes, **Angela Jackson**, **Yusef Komunyakaa**, Shara McCallum, **Colleen J. McElroy**, **Harryette Mullen**, **Marilyn Nelson**, G. E. Patterson, Willie Perdomo, **Carl Phillips**, Claudia Rankine, Ed Roberson, **Sonia Sanchez**, **Ntozake Shange**, Patricia Smith, **Al Young**, and **Kevin Young**.

The annual workshop retreat has made its home at the University of Pittsburgh at Greensburg since its early days. Any adult African-American poet may apply for admission to the summer workshop retreat. Though tuition for the intensive workshop retreat is free, participants are asked to pay a fee of $500 for room and board. Some limited financial aid is also available, on a first-come, first-served basis. A total of 54 fellows may attend the retreat, but because fellows are allowed to return, only about 18-22 new fellows are admitted each year. The workshop retreat is held Sunday evening through Saturday evening. Each fellow is required to present a new poem at 10:00 each morning of the workshop, and each morning, fellows may also choose a workshop to attend. In addition, fellows are randomly assigned to one of six workshops each afternoon. Each afternoon workshop contains 9 participants, led by a different faculty member, so that by the end of the six days of workshops, the 54 participants will have been taught by each of the six faculty members. Each evening, fellows may attend a reading presented by a faculty member or another fellow. Participants are thereafter known as Cave Canem fellows and encouraged to spread their newly gained knowledge and expertise to fellow poets wherever they may be.

In addition to the annual retreat, Cave Canem sponsors regional workshops, readings, and other events, as well as annual anthologies (available at //www.cavecanem poets.org/pages/store/Anthologies.htm). Former U.S. Poet Laureate **Rita Dove** chose **Natasha Trethewey's** first poetry collection, *Domestic Work* (2000), to become the first poetry collection to win the now-annual Cave Canem Poetry Prize for the best first collection of poems written by an African-American poet. Key events in poetry have been introduced at the Cave Canem workshop retreats. For instance, it was at a Cave Canem workshop that **Afaa M. Weaver** created his first "Bop" poetry, comprising three stanzas, each stanza of which is followed by a repeated line or refrain.

For more information about the organization, in the organizer's words, see //www.cavecanempoets.org/pages/about.php. Eady's account of the first decade of Cave Canem's existence may be found at //www.cavecanempoets.org/pages/pdfs/Cornelius-Poets_&_Writers_06.pdf. For links to 15 poems by Cave Canem poets, see //www.poets.org/notebookdetail.php/prmNotebookID/261218, which also includes links to biographies of two-dozen Cave Canem poets. For links to faculty and fellow Internet websites, see //www.cavecanempoets.org/pages/links.php.

REFERENCES: //www.bellaonline.com/articles/art54144.asp, re: Afaa M. Weaver. //www.cavecanempoets.org/pages/about.php. //www.cavecanempoets.org/pages/pdfs/Cornelius-Poets_&_Writers_06.pdf. //www.cavecanempoets.org/pages/pdfs/FAQs.pdf. //www.cavecanempoets.org/pages/programs.php. //www.poets.org/notebookdetail.php/prmNotebookID/261218.

FURTHER READING: *See also* **Toi Derricotte** and **Cornelius Eady**.

Cayton, Jr., Horace Roscoe
4/12/1903–1/22/1970
Nonfiction—sociology

Working with collaborators, Cayton coauthored two key sociological studies of African Americans: With George S. Mitchell, he wrote *Black Workers and the New Unions* (1939); and with **St. Clair Drake**, he wrote the award-winning sociological study of Chicago, *Black Metropolis* (1945). A columnist for the *Pittsburgh Courier*, Cayton was the son of publisher Horace Roscoe Cayton, Sr. and of writer, journalist, and college educator Susie Sumner Revels Cayton (daughter of Hiram Revels, first African-American U.S. senator); his brother was journalist and rights-activist Revels Hiram Cayton.

REFERENCES: *AANB. CAO-07. Wiki.* Robinson, Alonford James, Jr., in *EA-99* (see also the excerpt, "The Black Bugs," *EA-99*). Weitzman, Lisa S., in *BB*.

Channer, Colin
10/13/1963–
Novels, short stories; periodical editor, artistic director

Colin Channer's very first novel, *Waiting in Vain* (1998/2003), was both popularly acclaimed—a bestseller—and critically acclaimed, earning a Critic's Choice award from the *Washington Post* (1998). His subsequent novels have also sold well, including *Satisfy My Soul* (2002), *The Girl with the Golden Shoes* (2007), and *Lover's Rock* (2008). His novella *I'm Still Waiting* (2005), originally written as a screenplay, was chosen as one of four stories included in *Got to Be Real: Four Original Love Stories* (2000; also available unabridged on CD and audiocassette), also featuring **E. Lynn Harris**, Eric Jerome Dickey, and Marcus Major. Channer's interconnected collection of seven short stories, *Passing Through: Stories* (2004), was praised as "a remarkable literary achievement," and Channer was described as "a wonderfully funny, piercing, crafty and compassionate writer" (Dan Chaon, quoted in //www.amazon.com). In addition to his books, Channer has contributed numerous stories to anthologies (e.g., *Soulfires: Young Black Men on Love and Violence,* 1996) and to periodicals (e.g., *Billboard, Black Enterprise,* and *Ebony Man,* as well as *Essence,* for which he had been an assistant editor early in his career).

What's Channer's secret? As a husband (married to Bridgitte Fouche in 1993) and a father of two (Addis and Makonnen), Channer knows how to tell stories about love and personal relationships. As a youngster, Channer later recalled, he wrote "love letters to girls who didn't like me" (in *American Visions,* quoted in *BB*), then he wrote love letters and love poems for other boys at $1 per letter and $1.50 per poem. Love has inspired his writing ever since. He also sets his works in his native Jamaica, letting the warmth of the Caribbean heat up the passion in his stories. He differs from many other African-American male writers of love-relationship stories in another way, too; rather than aggrandizing the importance of males, he has said, "When I'm asked about the source of the tensions between Black women and men, I instantly know the answer: The problem with women is men. . . . If it appears that I'm being hard on men, it is because I think I must. My art, my existence as a novelist, is a public exploration of my inner life" (in *Essence,* quoted in *CAO-08*). He told an *American Visions* interviewer, "I think women should buy [*Waiting in Vain*] for their boyfriends" (quoted in *CAO-08*).

In 2001, Channer teamed up with Kwame Dawes to found the Caribbean's Calabash International Literary Festival Trust, a registered nonprofit entity of which he is the artistic director. The trust hosts annual literary festivals in Jamaica. In addition to attracting topnotch authors to the festivities, the festival spawned The Calabash

Chapbook Series of poetry books written by festival authors. Another outgrowth of the festival is *Iron Balloons: Hit Fiction from Jamaica's Calabash Writer's Workshop* (2006), which Channer edited. Channer also teams up with his New York-based reggae band named Pipecock Jaxxon, for whom he plays bass. Channer also has numerous other business ventures, including his own design and branding firm, Squad 1962.

In addition to all these activities, Channer is an assistant professor of English at City University of New York's Medgar Evers College, where he also coordinates the baccalaureate creative writing program. Perhaps the most valuable lesson Channer's students may learn from him is why he writes, "Like any writer, I write to preserve moments and ideas that I believe have lasting value. But on a fundamental level, I write because it brings me joy" (CAO-08).

REFERENCES: *CAO-08. Wiki.* Kiser, Helene Barker, in *BB. News & Notes,* 8/6/2007, in //www.npr.org/templates/story/story.php?storyId= 12533192. //www.cavecanempoets.org/pages/programs_faculty.php. //www.loc.gov/bookfest/2006/authors/cassells.html. //www.poets.org/ poet.php/prmPID/215 Amazon.com.

Chapman, Tracy
3/20/1964–
Songs; singer, performer

While being raised by her impoverished single mother, Chapman began singing, playing guitar, and writing her own songs by sixth grade. Since then, she gained popularity in the 1970s and 1980s by showing college students and others the power of simple melodies and lyrics written by the Grammy-winning singer. Her songs have included "Talkin' Bout a Revolution" and "Fast Car," and her albums have included *Tracy Chapman* (1988, reached Number 1 on *Billboard's* pop chart; more than 10 million sold), *Crossroads* (1989, 4 million sold), *Matters of the Heart* (1992), *New Beginning* (1995, more than 3 million sold), *Telling Stories* (2000), *Let It Rain* (2002), and *Where You Live* (2005, coproduced with Tchad Blake).

REFERENCES: *AANB. CAO-07. Wiki.* Tuttle, Kate, in *EA-99.* Weitzman, Lisa S., in *BB.*

Chase-Riboud, Barbara (née Dewayne)
6/26/1939–
Novels, poems, essays; sculptor, visual artist

Vivian (a medical assistant) and Charles (a building contractor) Chase encouraged their only child, Barbara, to develop her talents and interests in the arts, including classical piano, dancing (ballet), drawing, sculpting, and—of course—writing poetry. At age 8, she won her first prize for her artwork, and at age 15, she won a *Seventeen* magazine award and sold her prize-winning print to the Museum of Modern Art in New York. After high school, she went to the nearby Tyler Art School at Temple University (in Philadelphia, Pennsylvania), where she earned her B.F.A. (bachelor's in fine arts) in 1957. Awarded a John Hay Whitney Foundation Fellowship, she spent the following school year (1957-1958) studying art in Egypt and at the American Academy in Rome. Back in the states, she earned her M.F.A. (master's in fine arts) from Yale University (1960).

While exhibiting her work in Europe, the Middle East, Asia, Africa, and the United States over the next two decades, Barbara Chase met and married (12/25/1961) French photojournalist Marc Riboud. Although the couple had two children (David and Alexis), they managed to continue to travel extensively. The couple divorced in 1981, and she later married art expert and broker, archeologist, historian, and publisher Sergio Tosi. By the mid-1990s, she and Tosi had established homes in Paris and Rome.

Both her artwork (drawings and sculpture) and her writings (poems and novels) reflect the Asian, European, and African influences to which she has been exposed in her extensive travels. Through all her creative offerings, she expresses her hope for harmonious interactions among diverse races and cultures and between the sexes. Chase-Riboud's first poetry collection, *From Memphis and Peking* (1974), reflected on her travels through Africa (e.g., Memphis, Egypt) and China (Peking). In the People's Republic of China, Chase-Riboud was the first American woman to visit since the revolution of 1949. Her second poetry volume, *Portrait of a Nude Woman As Cleopatra* (1987), was inspired by a Rembrandt sketch with that title. In it, she tells Plutarch's story of Mark Antony and Cleopatra through an interwoven dialogue written in 57 sonnets. Her third poetry collection is *Egypt's Nights* (1994).

Chase-Riboud's best-known novel is *Sally Hemings* (1979), her neo-slave narrative of the long-term relationship between Thomas Jefferson and his slave mistress Sally Hemings (a quadroon who was Jefferson's wife's half sister). Chase-Riboud explored their relationship from various points of view and suggested its implications for gender relations, gender roles, race relations, and the role of each race in American society. As just one example, Chase-Riboud suggests that Jefferson's relationship with Hemings may have been at the root of his change in views about slavery. Although he had at first outspokenly opposed slavery, he eventually stopped opposing it, and Chase-Riboud suggests that perhaps part of his motivation was that Virginia law mandated that if she were emancipated, Hemings would have been required to leave Virginia, and he couldn't have beared to be parted from her.

When Chase-Riboud wrote the novel, based on the historical research of Fawn Brodie, this relationship was the subject of much controversy. Hemings's family members had long acknowledged the relationship, perhaps even before **William Wells Brown** wrote *Clotel* (1855), his novel about a relationship between Jefferson and one of his female slaves. Jefferson's white family members, however, had always repudiated the allegations of such a relationship. In the late 1990s, indisputable genetic evidence confirmed the relationship, forever putting the question to rest. Despite the controversy, *Sally Hemings* won the 1980 Janet Heidinger Kafka Prize for Excellence in Fiction by American Women, and the book has been translated into at least eight languages. Jacqueline Kennedy Onassis had been instrumental in encouraging Chase-Riboud to publish the novel and to have some of her works made into movies.

Chase-Riboud's next novel took place about the same time but was located in the Ottoman Empire of the late eighteenth century and early nineteenth century. In *Valide: A Novel of the Harem* (1986), Algerian pirates capture a Martinican woman and sell her to Sultan Abdulhamid I, who enslaves her in his harem. The women of the harem have little to do and lead self-indulgent lives, so they plot against one another to gain the favors of the sultan. Eventually, her son becomes the sultan, so she becomes *valide* (queen mother), the highest position for a woman in the Ottoman Empire.

Chase-Riboud's third and fourth novels also address slavery, but return to the United States as the location. Her *Echo of Lions* (1989) tells the fact-based story of Joseph Cinqué (Sengbe Pieh) and his fellow African slaves, who revolted against the crew of the slave ship *Amistad*. Since the publication of her book, the story has been made into a movie. In her book and in the movie, the slave ship lands off the coast of Long Island, and the Africans are jailed for slaughtering most members of the slave ship's crew. Former U.S. President John Quincy Adams successfully defends the prisoners in the U.S. Supreme Court, citing the illegality of the slave trade and the absolute right of anyone to commit homicide in self-defense.

Chase-Riboud's *The President's Daughter* (1994) takes the Hemings story forward from Sally to her daughter Harriet, carrying the narrative forward through the Civil War and its aftermath. More recently, Chase-Riboud wrote *Hottentot Venus* (2003), about the unfortunate South African woman who was vulgarly displayed in freak shows and circuses across 1700s Europe; the American Library Association offered it the 2004 Best Fiction Award. For her various artistic achievements, Chase-Riboud has earned a National Endowment for the Humanities fellowship (1973), first prize in the New York City Subway Competition for architecture (1973), the Academy of Italy gold medal for sculpture and drawing (1978), and an honorary doctorate from her alma mater, Temple University (1981).

REFERENCES: *AANB. EBLG.* Bolden, B. J., in *BWA:AHE.* Brennan, Carol, and Sara Pendergast, in *BB. CAO-04.* Mesa, Christina, in *GEAAL.* Richardson, Marilyn, in *AAFW-55-84.* //www.law.cornell.edu/background/amistad/bcr.html. Robinson, Lisa Clayton, in *EA-99.* Stanford, Ann Folwell, in *OCWW.* Tarver, Australia, in *AE. COCAAL* and *OCAAL. W. Wiki.*

Chesnutt, Charles Waddell
6/20/1858–11/15/1932
Short stories, novels, biography, journals, essays; educator, legal clerk, attorney

Charles was born with many choices not available to other African Americans of his era: Both he and his mulatto parents were free, and he was so light-skinned that he could have passed as white, although he chose not to do so. After the Civil War, Charles worked in his family's store while regularly attending school. By the time he was 14, however, Charles had to stop his formal education in order to help support the family, so he worked as a pupil-teacher at the school. At age 16, he started teaching full time, and in his late teens, he was appointed assistant principal at the school he had attended.

In 1878, Chesnutt married Susan Perry, also a teacher, and they started a family (Ethel, Helen, Edwin, and Dorothy) soon after. When he was in his 20s, he was a prominent principal with a wife and children, but he longed for a writing career. In 1879, he confided to his journal that he planned to move North to "get employment in some literary avocation, or something leading in that direction." Two years later, he confided to his journal, "Every time I read a good novel, I want to write one. It is the dream of my life—to be an author!"

In the early 1880s, Chesnutt tried to work as a journalist in Washington, D.C., returned to North Carolina, then tried working in New York City, and finally moved his wife and children to Cleveland, Ohio, where he worked as a legal clerk-stenographer. He soon set up his own profitable legal stenography business while studying to pass the bar. In 1887, he was admitted to the Ohio bar and added a law practice to his stenography firm. In addition, in his spare time in the evenings, he wrote short stories.

When his story "The Goophered Grapevine" became the first short story by a black writer to be published in the highly revered *Atlantic Monthly*, he was assured that his efforts were worthwhile. Like the traditional plantation stories by white authors, Chesnutt's story centered around an ex-slave African-American storyteller, Uncle

Julius McAdoo, who spun delightful antebellum recollections of Southern life. Unlike the white authors' narrators, however, Uncle McAdoo described a much less idyllic picture of the antebellum South and offered a much more realistic portrait of African-American folk culture. According to McAdoo, the slaves used trickery and deception to subvert their masters' dominance and brutality; they weren't cheerfully looking forward to complying with the kind requests of their masters.

The next year (1888), the *Atlantic Monthly* published Chesnutt's "Po' Sandy." Chesnutt continued to split his time between his literary pursuits and his legal career until the fall of 1899, when he closed his prosperous business to pursue writing as a full-time career. He felt certain that his book sales and his speaking engagements would suffice to support himself and his family, so he dedicated a few years to writing three novels. By the time he started writing his third novel, however, he realized that his particular books would not sell widely enough to sustain him and his family, so in 1902, he reopened his court-reporting business and his law practice.

Over his literary career, Chesnutt published more than 50 tales, short stories, and essays; his biography, *Frederick Douglass* (1899); and two short-story collections. His first short-story collection, *The Conjure Woman*, illuminates the relationships between white employers (or slave owners) and black servants (or slaves), as seen through the eyes of a black man who is a servant to a white man who has moved from the North to the South. It sold so well that his publisher (Houghton Mifflin) rushed the publication (the same year) of his second short-story collection, *The Wife of His Youth and Other Stories of the Color Line*. This second collection studies color prejudice among blacks, as well as between blacks and whites, by examining the racial identity of mixed-race Americans.

Chesnutt also wrote four novels. His first novel, *The House Behind the Cedars* (1900; originally called "Rena Walden"), dealt with interracial marriage and with a young girl's attempt to pass for white. Although it was generally well received, it didn't sell widely or well (although it did go to four printings rather quickly). His second novel, *The Marrow of Tradition* (1901), was based on a true incident and addressed the pervasive white-supremacist activities and violence of the post-Reconstruction South. Despite the book's nationwide reviews touting it as a timely but disturbing study, the book did not sell well. Chesnutt's next literary venture was a romance novel, for which he couldn't find a publisher. His 1905 novel *The Colonel's Dream* (published by Doubleday) explored the problems of freed slaves struggling against prejudice and exploitation in a Southern town. When this novel sold poorly, too, Chesnutt lost faith in his ability to become rich and famous through his literary career, and he turned away from novel-length fiction.

With two of his daughters in college and two younger children still at home, Chesnutt needed to realistically plan for the many demands on his financial resources. Perhaps he had also been unrealistic in his expectation that writing was likely to provide fame and fortune. He noted in his journal, "I want fame; I want money; . . . . literature pays—the successful." Chesnutt also loved writing for its own sake, however: "There is a fascination about this calling that draws a scribbler irresistibly toward his room. He knows the chance of success is hardly one out of a hundred; but he is foolish enough to believe, or sanguine enough to hope, that he will be the successful one."

Although his career in writing proved less successful than he had expected, he was pleasantly surprised by the financial rewards of his legal career. Thus, contrary to his expectations, his other pursuits proved more financially rewarding than did writing. He still continued to write and speak on social and political issues of interest to him, but he wrote only a handful of short stories and a novel (*The Quarry*, not published until 1999) during the final 25 years of his life.

Although his financial rewards for writing may have fallen short of his expectations, his literary achievements were nonetheless important. For one thing, he is now widely recognized as one of the first American writers to realistically portray the African-American experience. He is also generally considered the first major African-American novelist, though his short stories may have been a more valuable contribution to American literature than his novels. In any case, Chesnutt was the first African-American writer to have mainstream white-controlled presses publish his candid fiction about the racially oppressed lives of African Americans in the South.

Chesnutt used his fiction, rooted in African-American experience, to address social injustice, racial discrimination, and a wide array of other issues and problems in American life, particularly those among African Americans in the post-Civil War era. As he said, "The object of my writings would be not so much the elevation of the colored people as the elevation of the whites—for I consider [the unjust treatment of colored people] a barrier to the moral progress of the American people."

In 1928, the NAACP awarded Chesnutt its venerable Spingarn Medal for his "pioneer work as a literary artist depicting the life and struggles of Americans of Negro descent, and for his long and useful career as scholar, worker, and freeman of one of America's greatest cities." Despite poor health, he managed to publish his literary autobiographical essay, "Post-Bellum—Pre-Harlem" in 1931. After his death, his daughter Helen wrote his biography, *Charles W. Chesnutt: Pioneer of the Color Line*

(1952). Also posthumously published were an early un-published novel of his, *Mandy Oxendine*, in 1997; and his journals, his letters, and his essays and speeches, in 1993, 1997 and 2002, and 1999, respectively.

REFERENCES: *1TESK. AA:PoP. B. BAL-1-P. BASS. BCE. BDAA. BV. BWA. CAO-07. CE. E-98. EB-98. EBLG. G-95. LFCC-07. MAAL. MWEL. NAAAL. OC2OLE. SMKC. W. Wiki.* Andrews, William L., in *AAW-1991. AAWBHR. COCAAL* and *OCAAL.* Brodhead, Richard (Ed.). 1993. *The Journals of Charles W. Chesnutt.* Durham: Duke University Press. Crisler, Jesse S., Robert C. Leitz III, and Joseph R. McElrath, Jr. (Eds.). 2002. *An Exemplary Citizen: Letters of Charles W. Chesnutt, 1906-1932.* Stanford: Stanford University Press. Manheim, James M., in *BB.* McElrath, Joseph R., Jr., and Robert C. Leitz III (Eds.). 1997. *"'To Be an Author': Letters of Charles W. Chesnutt, 1889-1905.* Princeton: Princeton University Press. McElrath, Joseph R., Jr., Robert C. Leitz III, and Jesse S. Crisler (Eds.). 1999. *Essays and Speeches.* Stanford: Stanford University Press. Render, Sylvia Lyons, in *ASSW-1880-1910.* Richardson, Mark, *AAW-2004.* Scruggs, Charles W., in *ARN.*

Chicago Defender
5/5/1905–2/5/1956

Chicago Daily Defender
2/6/1956–present

News reports, features, and editorials of interest to African Americans, both locally and nationally

On its website, the *Chicago Defender* Online lists its "Homes" as "Landlady's Kitchen Table (1905-1920), 3435 South Indiana Avenue (1920-1960), 2400 South Michigan Avenue (1960-2006), 200 South Michigan Avenue (2006-2009), and 4445 South Martin Luther King Drive (2009-present day)." Proud of its humble roots, it nonetheless also claims, "By the start of World War I, the *Chicago Defender* was the nation's most influential Black weekly newspaper, with more than two thirds of its readership base located outside of Chicago" (//www.chicago defender.com/article-1369-about-us.html). Both statements appear to be accurate.

The *Defender's* founder, **Robert Sengstacke Abbott**, borrowed a chair, used his own card table, and invested 25¢ in a notebook and pencils to start the *Chicago Defender.* Though the *Defender* website highlights Abbott's initial investment of 25¢, Gerald Brennan's *International Directory of Company Histories*, Volume 66, 1995, points out that Abbott also obtained two $25 credit lines: one from the Western Newspaper Union and a second from the *Chicago Tribune*, the major European-American-owned newspaper. With his newly purchased notebook and pencils, he wrote up the local news he had gathered, adding cut-and-pasted news clippings from other newspapers. Once he had enough news material, he borrowed $13.75 from his credit line to print 300 copies of his four-page, six-column paper on May 5, 1905. On May

6, he started pounding the pavement, going door-to-door selling the first edition of the weekly *Chicago Defender*. He solicited readers in barber shops and clubs, pool halls and churches, wherever anyone might consider buying his newspaper. Before the week was out, Abbott had sold his copies and had gathered enough news to print the next edition.

At first, Abbott rented out a tiny office from which to publish his paper, but finances quickly dictated that he move out and cut his office-rental overhead to zero. Luckily, his landlady kindly offered him her kitchen table, and her kitchen hosted the *Defender* for its first 15 years. (Abbott later repaid her kindness by buying her a large house.) For the first few years, Abbott was errand boy and president, sales agent and editor, publisher and reporter of the *Defender*, which he sold to a local readership. He did have a little help from volunteer reporter-writers, such as attorney Louis B. Anderson and businessperson Julius Avendorph. When some European-American newsstand owners refused to sell his paper, Abbott solicited neighborhood youths to sell it for him, on street corners and for home or office delivery.

In 1909, Abbott's antivice campaign in his African-American neighborhood, nicknamed "Bronzeville," boosted local sales. Abbott also emulated the strategies of Hearst, Pulitzer, and other newspapers of his day, using dramatic writing styles and sensational stories to attract readers. The following year (1910), Abbott hired his first paid employee, J. Hockley Smiley, who suggested using banner headlines-often in red ink-graphic images, and satirical cartoons to further catch prospective readers' eyes. He also advised Abbott to delineate specific sections of the paper, such as editorial, theater, sports, and society sections. Further, Smiley envisioned a national readership for the *Defender* and encouraged Abbott to follow his natural inclination to write aggressively outspoken editorials lambasting lynchings and other post-Reconstruction horrors. All of these tactics further increased the fledgling newspaper's circulation, expanding it nationally, particularly in the Southern states.

Smiley also suggested a way to get around Abbott's distribution problem. No national distributors were willing to sell the *Defender* in the Southern states, particularly given Abbott's candid, blistering editorials against lynching, racism, and the Jim Crow practices of the South. Smiley advised Abbott to make use of the mostly African-American Pullman porters, who traveled the trains from town to town throughout the country. The railroad porters and waiters were given bundles of newspapers to take with them on their sojourns South, where they distributed the Chicago-based newspaper. The porters also gathered news from the Southern states for the *Chicago Defender*, so Abbott could more accurately report on current events relevant to his Southern readers. By the time Smiley died (in 1915), Abbott's *Defender* was an eight-page, eight-column, full-size paper, and by 1916, it was being distributed in 71 cities and towns across the nation.

Meanwhile, with his increased revenues, Abbott was able to hire more employees, including columnist and promoter extraordinaire Roscoe Conkling Murray Simmons. With Simmons, Abbott launched his "Great Northern Drive," promoting the Great Migration of African Americans from the rural Jim Crow South to the urban North, where they could escape the constant threat of lynchings and find jobs in the burgeoning industries of the North. Abbott not only encouraged readers with his editorials and articles, but also posted listings of jobs and housing, train schedules, and photos and descriptions of schools and parks, to appeal to Southern readers contemplating a move North. He published helpful "do's" and "don'ts" for newcomers. Between 1916 and 1918, the paying readership increased from 10,000 to 100,000. Abbott rewarded Simmons by making him the highest-paid African-American journalist.

When the United States became involved in "The War to End All Wars" (1917-1919, U.S. involvement), Simmons toured the South, stirring up patriotic sentiments to crowds of hundreds, often thousands of African Americans, as well as many European Americans. While attracting tens of thousands of loyal readers, Simmons was also recruiting distribution agents for the *Defender*. By the time World War I ended, the *Chicago Defender* had become the first African-American newspaper to have a truly national readership. In fact, the majority of the *Chicago Defender*'s nearly 230,000 paper purchasers lived in the Southern states. If one accepts the company's assertion that each paper sold was passed along to an additional four readers, the true readership may have exceeded 1 million. In addition to the *Defender*'s Pullman porter distribution system, entertainers such as **W. C. Handy** and athletes such as Negro League players were distributing the paper.

Editor's note: Unfortunately, in 1925, Simmons was implicated in a scheme to expropriate funds from the *Defender*. Though Abbott never brought formal charges against Simmons, Simmons did leave the *Defender*. Abbott later reemployed him for a few years until the Great Depression forced staff layoffs.

Meanwhile, during the Chicago Race Riot of 1919, lasting from July 27 until August 3, the *Defender*'s printer refused to work, fearing attacks by the rioting mobs. Abbott decided he never again wanted to be at the mercy of an outside printer, so in November, 1920, Abbott paid cash for his own high-speed rotary printing press and installed it at the *Defender*'s new headquarters at 3435 Indiana Avenue. By the early 1920s, the *Defender* had 68 employees, with branch offices in London and Paris as well as numerous U.S. cities.

Other factors also stimulated sales, such as the emergence of baseball's Negro National League (founded 2/13-14/1920; first game 5/2/1920) and Negro Southern League (founded 3/2/1920), and **Ida B. Wells-Barnett**'s reports on lynchings and riots. In 1921, the *Defender* introduced a children's section titled "Defender Junior." "Defender Junior" was edited by the fictional "Bud Billiken," who also presided over the "Bud Billiken Club," in which children could become members. The club later sponsored healthy activities for African-American children in Chicago, including an annual parade and picnic. The *Defender* also started publishing stories authored by youths. For instance, **Willard Motley**'s first published short story appeared in the pages of the *Defender* when Motley was just 13 years old. Soon after, Motley was writing the weekly "Bud Billiken" column (12/1922-7/1924).

During the 1930s, *Defender* journalists included sports editor (Frank) Fay Young, gossip columnist Dan Burley, and foreign editor Metz T. P. ("Doc") Lochard, who had earned a Ph.D., graduated from the Sorbonne, and taught at Howard University. During the 1930s and 1940s, the *Defender* staff included city editor Lucius Harper, war correspondent Enoch Waters, cartoonist Jay Jackson, children's editor Dave Kellum, theater and sports editor Alfred E. "Al" Monroe, and staffers Charles Davis, Richard Durham, Ben Burns, Vernon Jarrett, and Louis E. Martin. During the 1940s, Metz Lochard edited the paper, and the columnists included **Langston Hughes** (weekly, 1942-1962 or so), **Walter F. (Francis) White** (starting in 1919), **W. E. B. Du Bois**, and **Mary McLeod Bethune**. "Jackie" (née Zelda Jackson) Ormes got a job reporting for the *Chicago Defender*, where she launched her first comic strip, "Patty Jo 'n' Ginger" (1940s), and became the first African-American woman cartoonist to be nationally syndicated. **Ethel L. (Lois) Payne**, Washington, D.C., correspondent for the *Chicago Defender* during the 1950s, later sojourned to the deep South to cover critical civil-rights events, and to Vietnam, Nigeria, Zaire, China, Mexico, and elsewhere to cover current events.

Over the years, the *Defender* also published the works of such esteemed authors as **Gwendolyn Brooks**, who contributed at least 75 poems to the *Defender* (1930s); **John Henrik Clarke**, who contributed numerous articles on African-American history (starting in the 1960s); **Frank Rudolph Crosswaith**, a regular *Defender* columnist (c. 1930s); **Era Bell Thompson**, who wrote book reviews, feature articles, advertising copy, and news articles for the *Defender* (c. 1940s); and **James Baldwin** (1960s). In 1998, when **Coretta Scott King** was ready to warn readers that "homophobia is like racism and anti-Semitism and other forms of bigotry in that it seeks to dehumanize a large group of people, to deny their humanity, their dignity and personhood," she did so in the pages of the *Chicago Defender* (quoted in //en.wikiquote.org/wiki/ Coretta_Scott_King). She chose the *Defender* because when African-American soldiers were segregated and mistreated during World War II, the *Defender* defended them. In fact, the *Defender* almost certainly played a crucial role in persuading President Harry Truman to sign an Executive Order integrating the U. S. Armed Forces in 1948. When civil-rights activists were demonstrating, boycotting, holding sit-ins, protesting, being arrested and jailed, being attacked by dogs or by potent fire hoses, and otherwise struggling for their rights as citizens of this country, the *Defender* ensured that the nation saw their images in photos and heard their stories in its pages.

During the 1930s and 1940s, the *Defender* itself also underwent dramatic changes. In 1934, 65-year-old Abbott hired the son of his half-brother Alexander, John Herman Henry Sengstacke, III, as vice president and treasurer of the *Defender*. The following year, Abbott promoted Sengstacke to general manager of the Robert S. Abbott Publishing Company, grooming Sengstacke as his heir. The next year, in November, 1936, at Abbott's suggestion, Sengstacke founded Sengstacke Enterprises, which served as a holding company for the Abbott-Sengstacke family businesses, mainly newspapers. Sengstacke helped establish the *Michigan Chronicle*, which was later made the Sengstacke Enterprises's first subsidiary. Others followed, including even the *Chicago Defender* itself, formerly owned and run by the Robert Abbott Publishing Company. Sengstacke also took over some editorial duties, contributing numerous editorials to both the *Chronicle* and the *Defender*. In 1939, Abbott ceded control of the *Defender*, giving Sengstacke his controlling share of the Abbott Publishing Company. Abbott died on February 29, 1940.

Unfortunately, despite Abbott's clear wishes and his efforts to ensure a smooth transition, Abbott's death precipitated a decade-long legal battle over Abbott's estate. While fighting Abbott's widow Edna and her advocates on the *Defender's* board of directors, Sengstacke continued to manage and edit the *Defender* and to run the Robert S. Abbott Publishing Company and Sengstacke Enterprises. Astonishingly, he also made time to help create the Negro Newspaper Publishers Association (NNPA) in 1940 (renamed the National Newspaper Publishers Association in 1956), which promoted the interests of African-American journalists and newspaper publishers. The NNPA elected Sengstacke as its first president, and he later served several more terms.

At last, in 1951, Sengstacke gained sole control of both the *Defender* and the Robert S. Abbott Publishing Company and continued to preside over his own Sengstacke Enterprises. Other shareholders were Sengstacke's siblings-Fred, Florence, Ethel, and Whittier-and his son Robert. Meanwhile, Sengstacke had been continually expanding the assets of his publishing empire, creating the largest African-American-owned and -operated newspaper chain ever built. During the 1940s, Sengstacke had organized the *Columbus News, St. Louis News, Toledo Press,* and *Cincinnati News*. With his newfound authority, he founded the *Tri-State Defender,* a weekly newspaper serving Tennessee, Arkansas, and Mississippi in November 1951.

In 1952, Sengstacke bought the weekly **New York Age**, a decades-old newspaper originally edited and published by **T. Thomas Fortune**. During its illustrious career, the *New York Age* had included the writing of **Ida B. Wells-Barnett**, **James Weldon Johnson**, **Tom Dent**, and **Chuck Stone**. Sengstacke renamed it the *New York Age Defender* from 1953 until 1957, then restored its name as *New York Age* until it folded February 27, 1960.

In 1956, Sengstacke made an even bolder move: He changed the frequency of the paper's distribution, from a weekly to what can be called a daily. To reflect the new frequency, Sengstacke changed the name from the *Chicago Defender* to the *Chicago Daily Defender*. The new *Defender* includes four tabloid-style daily issues distributed Monday through Thursday, with an emphasis on local news, followed by a fifth weekend edition, with a national scope. Sengstacke continued as editor of both the four daily issues and the single weekend issue. By creating a daily, Sengstacke was then eligible to become the first African-American member of the American Society of Newspaper Editors. During the 1950s and 1960s, the *Defender's* staff of writers and editors included **Ethel Payne**, Vernon Jarrett, Lu Palmer, Doris Saunders, Charles Tisdale, Consuelo Young, cartoonist Chester Commodore, and fine arts editor Earl Calloway. By 1966, the *Defender* employed a total of 150 staffers. Circulation, however, started to decline in the 1950s and continued to decline thereafter. By 1977, the daily's circulation had declined to 34,000, and the weekend edition's circulation was just 38,000.

A decade after the *Defender* switched to daily circulation, when the *Pittsburgh Courier* was having financial trouble, Sengstacke acquired it, too. He then reorganized the paper as the *New Pittsburgh Courier,* folding it into his overarching Sengstacke Newspapers (now Real Times, LLC). About then, Sengstacke Enterprises also bought the *Florida (Miami) Courier*. With these acquisitions, Sengstacke's newspaper group became the largest and most influential African-American-owned and -operated newspaper chain in the nation, now also including the *(Detroit) Michigan Chronicle, Michigan Front Page,* and the *(Memphis) Tri-State Defender,* as well as the *Chicago Daily Defender*. While the overarching Sengstacke Enterprises has maintained control over the overall finances and operations of its newspapers and other subsidiaries, each newspaper has continued its own management responsible for day-to-day operations. Sengstacke continued to chair Sengstacke Enterprises and to maintain a major role in the company until his death May 28, 1997. At that point, his brother, Frederick Douglass Sengstacke, took over as publisher and chief operating officer of the *Chicago Defender*. John Sengstacke's trust dictated that the Northern Trust Company become the Trustee of his estate, and ownership of the *Defender* passed to his heirs. The trusteeship of the Trust changed hands, and each of the publications incurred significant debt. In January, 2003, all of the publications linked to the *Defender* were bought by Real Times, Inc., a corporation organized by John Sengstacke's nephew, Thomas Sengstacke Picou, and Sengstacke's son, Robert Abbott Sengstacke, as well as other investors.

Current print subscriptions to the *Defender* cost $20 for 6 months, $35 for 1 year, and $65 for 2 years; a digital subscription costs $10 per year. Sections in the online edition include Our City, Our Nation, Our World, Our Focus, Our Views, Our Health, Our Business, Our Entertainment, Our Culture, Our Faith, Our Sports, Our Events, Our Travel, Classifieds, Photos, and Archives.

REFERENCES: Brennan, Gerald. 1995. "Real Times, Inc." *International Directory of Company Histories* (Vol. 66), in //findarticles. com/p/articles/mi_gx5202/is_1995/ai_n19122501/, //findarticles.com/ p/articles/mi_gx5202/is_1995/ai_n19122501/pg_2/?tag=content;col1, //findarticles.com/p/articles/mi_gx5202/is_1995/ai_n19122501/pg_3/?t ag=content;col1. Jordan, William, "Simmons, Roscoe Conkling Murray," in *AANB*. Knight, Gladys L., in *GEAAL*. s://chicago defender.wehaa-server2.com/subscription_printNew.php. //en. wikipedia.org/wiki/Chicago_Defender. //en.wikipedia.org/wiki/ Chicago_riot_of_1919. //en.wikipedia.org/wiki/Negro_league_ baseball. //en.wikipedia.org/wiki/The_New_York_Globe. //mts.lib. uchicago.edu/collections/findingaids.html. //mts.lib.uchicago.edu/ collections/findingaids/abbottsengstacke.html. //www.chicagodefender. com/. //www.chicagodefender.com/article-1369-about-us.html. //www. chicagodefender.com/article-4679-ransom-notes-the-defender-is-hom e.html. //www.chicagodefender.com/article-5416-fred-sengstacke- dead-at-age-90.html. //www.chicagolife.net/content/other/The_ Defender_The_Beacon_to_the_North. //www.essortment.com/ all/robertsengstack_rhqz.htm. //www.inmotionaame.org/gallery/detail. cfm;jsessionid=f8301845191248876970983?migration=8&topic=5& id=465423&type=image&metadata=show&page=&bhcp=1. //www.state.il.us/HPA/Illinois%20History/Liesse405.pdf.

FURTHER READING: *See also* **Abbott, Robert Sengstacke**.

Child, Lydia Maria (née Francis)
2/11/1802–10/20/1880

Historical novels, volumes of advice for women, children's periodicals, abolitionist polemics

Although of European-American ancestry, after marrying Boston abolitionist, attorney, and writer David Lee Child (1794-1874) in 1828 and meeting **William Lloyd Garrison** in 1831, Child dedicated herself to fiercely opposing slavery, and most of her writings were in the service of abolition. She also edited the **slave narrative** of **Harriet Jacobs**, *Incidents in the Life of a Slave Girl* (1861). Her most noted work is her highly influential *An Appeal in Favor of That Class of Americans Called Africans* (1833, with her husband), which was probably the first published book denouncing slavery, segregation, and the mistreatment of African Americans. Her other antislavery writings include *Letters from New York* (1843), *The Duty of Disobedience to the Fugitive Slave Act* (1860), and *The Freedmen's Book* (1865). Child also edited the weekly periodical of the American Anti-Slavery Society, *National Anti-Slavery Standard* (1841-1843). Child and her husband were separated during the 1840s but reunited in 1850.

Child's other writings include the highly popular *The Frugal Housewife* (1829, a practical guide on domestic thrift; 33 editions were printed), *Ladies' Family Library* (1830s, a five-volume set of biographies), *The History of the Condition of Women, in Various Ages and Nations* (1835, a feminist account of history), several historical novels (e.g., *Hobomok*, 1824; *The Rebels, or Boston Before the Revolution*, 1825; *A Romance of the Republic*, 1867), several books on behalf of Native Americans (e.g., *An Appeal for the Indians*, 1868), and the lyric "Boy's Thanksgiving" (1844), which begins, "Over the river and through the woods, to grandmother's house we go." She also founded and edited the first American periodical for children, *Juvenile Miscellany* (1826-1834), from which she was ousted as editor because she had alienated her readers through the publication of her *Appeal*.

REFERENCES: *MWEL. WDAA. WDAW.* Mills, Bruce, in *EB-98. G-97. OCWW.* Woloch, Nancy, in *WB-99*

FURTHER READING: *TAWH*

Childress, Alice
10/12/1916 or 1920–8/14/1994

Plays, novels, children's literature, essays, columns; actress, lecturer, theater cofounder, director, consultant

After her parents divorced, they put Alice on a train headed for Harlem, where her grandmother Eliza welcomed her and raised her, and Alice started attending Public School 81. Eliza encouraged Alice's artistic and intellectual development, taking her to museums, art galleries, libraries, theaters, and concert halls. The two of them often sat at their window, watching people pass by, while Eliza asked Alice to imagine what the passersby were thinking.

Although Alice dropped out of high school, her grandmother had ensured that she would never lack an education: "Grandmother Eliza gently urged, 'Why not write that thought down on a piece of paper? It's worth keeping.' . . . Jottings became forms after I discovered the public library and attempted to read two books a day. Reading and evaluating form, I taught myself to know the difference of structure in plays, books, short stories, teleplays, motion picture scenarios, and so forth" (p. 114, *BWW*).

Childress married young, had her daughter Jean, and divorced soon after, so she had to work menial jobs (assistant machinist, domestic worker, salesperson, etc.) to support herself and her young daughter throughout the 1940s. These jobs helped her to keep in close touch with the working-class people she depicted in her plays and other fiction. Eventually, Jean fulfilled the dreams of the long line of Childress women, becoming the first college graduate in her mother's family.

In the early 1940s, Childress helped found the American Negro Theater (ANT), and she studied and worked with ANT, both on and off Broadway, until the early 1950s, participating in every aspect of producing plays. During that time, her long-standing friend Sidney Poitier raised the challenge that no one could write a strong play overnight. Childress took the challenge and in one night wrote her first play, *Florence*, a well-crafted one-act play centering on a black woman who comes to respect her daughter's pursuit of an acting career. What influences the mother? She happens to meet and converse with a white actress who presumes that she knows more about blacks than they know about themselves. As Childress observed, "Those who repress and exclude us also claim the right to instruct us on how best to react to repression. All too often we follow their advice" (p. 113, *BWW*). When ANT produced *Florence* in 1949, Childress directed it and starred in it.

Childress initially pursued a career in acting but, despite being nominated for a Tony award for her performance in the Broadway play *Anna Lucasta*, she found that racial prejudices limited her range of options. As she discovered, "I could more freely express myself as a writer" (p. 115, *BWW*). Thus, from the early 1950s until the late 1980s, Childress wrote a large number of plays, including several for juveniles, many for adults, and a few plays featuring music. Childress also set many of her plays within realistic African-American historical contexts, which she hoped might broaden the worldview of her viewers and readers, offering them new insights into how things came to be as they are.

Among literary critics, Childress was known for her skillful use of straightforward and direct language, her sensitively crafted characterizations, and her penetrating gaze into African-American lives. All of her plays involve realistic stories about everyday African Americans who courageously confront the debilitating effects of racism, sexism, and classism in America. Her heroes are not winners in the classical sense; instead, she writes "about those who come in second, or not at all—. . . the intricate and magnificent patterns of a loser's life. . . . My writing attempts to interpret the 'ordinary' because they are not ordinary. Each human is uniquely different. . . . I concentrate on portraying have-nots in a *have* society" (p. 112, *BWW*). Her protagonists, like Childress herself, inspire others as role models for not just surviving, but also maintaining their dignity in trying circumstances. They, too, collaborate with others and seek out familial and community support in surmounting the obstacles they face.

In addition to *Florence,* Childress wrote more than nine plays examining racial and social issues, including her Obie-winning *Trouble in Mind.* In this satiric indictment of racial stereotyping, staged as a play-within-a-play, the cast was presumably rehearsing a dramatic story about a lynching. How did she react when she discovered she was the first woman of any race to receive an Obie for her play? True to her convictions, she retorted that her honor merely highlighted the glaring absences of opportunities offered to other women of color.

Childress also wrote several plays that feature music (e.g., *Just a Little Simple,* based on **Langston Hughes**'s *Simple Speaks His Mind*) and plays for juveniles (historical *When the Rattlesnake Sounds* and parody *Let's Hear It for the Queen*). She also edited *Black Scenes* (1971), which excerpted various plays for children. Despite her prodigious output of plays, many readers know Childress better for her juvenile fiction than for her plays. Perhaps best known is her National Book Award-nominated *A Hero Ain't Nothin' but a Sandwich* (1973), a novel written for adolescents about a teenage drug addict who overcomes his addiction. Her book urges African Americans to take greater responsibility for nurturing their youths, especially males. The book was made into a film in 1978, for which Childress wrote the screenplay, but both the book and the film have been banned by many school systems. (Many of her plays have also been banned in many states.) Also considered controversial at the time was Childress's use of African-American vernacular, sometimes called Ebonics or "Black English," in her dialogue and narration.

Even more controversial was her 1989 young-adult novel, *Those Other People,* about a young high-school computer instructor who comes to terms with his own homosexuality while helping his students confront heterosexual abuse by a fellow teacher. Between that work and *Hero,* Childress wrote *Rainbow Jordan* (1981), revealing how a young African-American teen, neglected and abused by her biological parents, can find mothering from surrogates in her surrounding community; it, too, earned Childress critical praise (Coretta Scott King Honor, *New York Times* Outstanding Book of the Year, *School Library*

Journal Best Book). Throughout all her juvenile novels, young people realistically face many social ills with courage and integrity.

Childress's other long fiction includes *Like One of the Family: Conversations from a Domestic's Life* (1956 or 1953), which uses a series of witty and satirical monologues by Mildred, a domestic housemaid, who teaches her white employers to see their own inhumanity; and Pulitzer Prize-nominated *A Short Walk* (1979), which explores twentieth-century African-American history, from the **Harlem Renaissance** to the civil-rights movement of the 1960s, by chronicling the life experiences of a black woman. Childress's shorter fiction and dramas have been anthologized in **Langston Hughes**'s *The Best Short Stories by Negro Writers* and other works. Perhaps her variety of written expression can best be understood by noting her observation, "I try to bend my writing form to most truthfully express content" (*BWW,* p. 114). Among numerous honors and fellowships for her work, Childress was awarded a Jane Addams Children's Book Honor, a Lewis Carroll Shelf Award, a Rockefeller grant, and the prestigious MacDowell Colony writer-in-residence grant.

Little is known about Childress's private life as an adult. On July 17, 1957, she married Nathan Woodard, a professional musician and music instructor, with whom she was living in Long Island when she died of cancer in August of 1994. Tragically, her daughter had predeceased her on Mother's Day in 1990. When Childress died, she was working on her memoirs and on a sixth novel, never completed.

REFERENCES: *AA:PoP. AWA. BWW. CBC. E-95. EB-98. EBLG. MAAL. MWEL. OC20LE. RT.* Bader, Philip, in //0-web.ebscohost.com.dbpcosdcsgt.co.san-diego.ca.us/novelist/detail?vid=27&hid=7&sid=d408b38a-8f5e-4ec2-b75c-cf9c5b5097d7%40sessionmgr3&bdata=JnNpdGU9bm92ZWxpc3QtbGl2ZQ%3d%3d. Brown-Guillory, Elizabeth, in *COCAAL* and *OCAAL.* Cleary, Linda Miller, in *WYA-1997-3.* Hipple, Theodore W. 1997. *Writers for Young Adults* (Vol. 1, pp. 229–240). New York : Charles Scribner's Sons. Jennings, La Vinia Delois, in *AA. B. BCE. OCWW. W. Wiki. Wr.* Nilsen, Alleen Pace, in *T-CYAW.* Sussman, Alison Carb, in *BB. CAO-07. CLCS. MWEL.* Sweeney, Valerie Prince, in *RGAL-3.*

Chisholm, Shirley (Anita) (née St. Hill)
11/30/1924–1/1/2005
Autobiography/memoir, legislation; politician, activist, organizer, educator

In 1970, Chisholm wrote her first autobiography, *Unbought and Unbossed* (1970), including an account of how she became the first African-American woman elected to the U.S. Congress (in 1968, 12th Congressional District of Brooklyn, New York, a seat she held for several terms, leaving office in the early 1980s). In 1973, she had more to add about herself, so she wrote *The Good Fight,* describ-

Shirley Chisholm

ing her candidacy to become the Democratic nominee for president of the United States—the first woman and the first African American ever to do so. You don't recall hearing about the Chisholm-Nixon debates? There weren't any—the Democratic Convention didn't nominate her. As her book pointed out, though, she did manage to raise numerous issues of importance to African Americans and to women: child care (a former preschool teacher and child-care-center director herself), women's rights, employment opportunities and training, and civil rights, as well as the need for environmental protection and her opposition to the Vietnam War and to the seniority system in Congress.

After she left office, Chisholm cofounded the National Political Congress of Black Women to continue to raise important political and social-justice issues and to encourage more African-American women to pursue positions of leadership in society. In fact, Chisholm's 1972 presidential candidacy made lots of people think hard about who could—and should—hold high political offices. Partly as a result of her candidacy, many more women (and African Americans) entered politics and campaigned for various positions. Some might view the presidency of **Barack Obama** as part of Chisholm's legacy.

Though Chisholm never had children, she was married twice: first to Conrad Chisholm (1949-1977, divorced), then to Arthur Hardwick, Jr. (1977-1986, widowed). After leaving politics, Chisholm passed on her knowledge and experience at Mt. Holyoke College in Massachusetts (1983-1987). Unfortunately, in 1993, ill health prevented her from accepting President Clinton's offer for her to serve as U.S. Ambassador to Jamaica. After Chisholm's death, Shola Lynch documented her life in a film that aired at the Sundance Film Festival in 2004 and on public television in 2005; the film won a Peabody Award in 2006.

REFERENCES: *BAAW. B. BCE. CE. E-94. G-94. LE. PGAA. USGG. W2B. Wiki.* Mueller, Michael E., and Sara Pendergast, in *BB.* Gonsior, Marian, in *CAO-05.* —Tonya Bolden

Christian, Barbara (Theresa)
12/12/1943–6/25/2000
Scholarly, literary criticism; educator

A brilliant scholar, Barbara Christian entered Wisconsin's Marquette University at age 15 and graduated cum laude 4 years later (1963). While working on her doctorate in contemporary literature at Columbia University (Ph.D., 1970), she taught at the College of the Virgin Islands (1963), Hunter College (1963-1964), and the City College of the City University of New York (1965-1971). Married to poet and biographer David Henderson (later divorced), with her doctorate in hand and her daughter Najuma in her womb, in the Fall of 1971, Christian helped establish the Department of African-American Studies at the University of California at Berkeley (UCB). Later, she became the first African-American woman to gain tenure at UCB (in 1978), the first African-American woman promoted to full professor at UCB (in 1986), and the first African American to win UCB's Distinguished Teaching Award (in 1991), and she continued teaching at UCB the remainder of her life.

Christian not only wrote scholarly expositions of literary subjects, but also raised the rabble with her views as an African-American feminist. Her major works, landmarks in their day, include *Black Women Novelists: The Development of a Tradition, 1892-1976* (1980), which won the Before Columbus Foundation's American Book Award; *Black Feminist Criticism: Perspectives on Black Women Writers* (1985); and *From the Inside Out: Afro-American Women's Literary Tradition and the State* (1987). She also wrote a teaching guide for **Dorothy Sterling**'s *Black Foremothers, Three Lives* (1980; rev. ed. 1988), and she collaborated with Gloria Bowles, M.

Giulia Fabi, and Arlene Keizer to write *New Black Feminist Criticism, 1985-2000* (2007). She particular focused her literary analysis on **Alice Walker**, writing *Alice Walker's The Color Purple and Other Works: A Critical Commentary* (1987) and editing *Alice Walker, Everyday Use* (1994).

Christian also tirelessly edited or coedited numerous periodicals, including *Feminist Studies* (1984-1992), **Black American Literature Forum** (1985-1990), *Sage* (1987-1989), and *Contentions* (1990-2000). In addition, with Elizabeth Abel and Helene Moglen, she edited the provocative anthology *Female Subjects in Black and White: Race, Psychoanalysis, Feminism* (1997). She also wrote about 100 essays and reviews for journals such as *Black Scholar* and *Journal of Ethnic Studies,* and she contributed to anthologies such as *Black Women Writers, 1950-1980* (1984, edited by Mari Evans), *Reading Black, Reading Feminist* (1990, edited by **Henry Louis Gates, Jr.**), *The Norton Anthology of African American Literature* (1997, edited by Gates and by Nellie McKay), and others.

Among her many honors and awards are an Afro-American Society Hall of Fame award (1980), the Modern Language Association's MELUS award for contribution to ethnic studies and African-American scholarship (1994), a **Gwendolyn Brooks** Center award (1995), and a Citation for Distinguished Achievement from UCB (2000).

REFERENCES: *AAW:PV. CAO-01. MWEL. Wiki.* Jordan, June. "For Our Beloved Barbara Christian, June 19, 2000." **Callaloo**. *23.4* (Sept. 2000), p. 1172. Literature Resources from Gale. Morris, Paula J. K., in *BB.*

FURTHER READING: *EAAWW.* Black-Parker, Kimberly, in *GEAAL.*

Christian, Marcus Bruce
3/8/1900–11/21/1976
Poems, nonfiction—history, folklore; business owner, journalist, librarian, publisher, educator

Orphaned by his mother at age 3 and by his father at age 13, Marcus also tragically lost his fraternal twin sister at age 7. He and his remaining siblings were dispersed to relatives in the countryside near New Orleans, but while Marcus was still in his teens, he managed to get work to support his siblings and reunite his remaining family. An autodidact, Marcus also attended night school. His valedictory address to his night-school classmates was his first poem, "M-O-D-O-C-S of '22."

After unsuccessfully trying to self-publish his first poetry collection, *Ethiopia Triumphant and Other Poems,* through a printer, he bought his own printing press. After that, he published his own chapbooks. By 1932, Christian was also a poetry editor and special feature writer for *Louisiana Weekly* in New Orleans. In 1934, his poems started appearing in national publications such as the journals

Opportunity and *Phylon,* newspapers such as the *Pittsburgh Courier,* and even white-owned publications such as the *New York Herald Tribune.* He also started his second collection, *The Clothes Doctor and Other Poems,* inspired by his experiences running a dry-cleaning business.

Over his lifetime, Christian wrote about 2,000 poems. Nearly a quarter-century after his death, his collected poems were published in *I Am New Orleans and Other Poems* (1999, edited by Rudolph Lewis and Amin Sharif). Christian's original eight-page poem *I Am New Orleans: A Poem Published in Commemoration of the 250th Anniversary Celebration of the Founding of the Crescent City, 1718-1968* was published in 1968. His other poetry was also published in *From the Deep South* (1937), *High Ground: A Collection of Poems Published in Commemoration of the United States Supreme Court's Decision of May 17, 1954, and Its Final Decree of May ... Segregation in the Nation's Public Schools* (1958, 20 pp.), and *Song of the Black Valiants: Marching Tempo* (1960). Christian's *The Common Peoples' Manifesto of World War II* (1948) earned him an **Arthur Spingarn Crisis** book award (1948). His other writings include *In Memoriam: Franklin Delano Roosevelt* (1945), *Negro Soldiers in the Battle of New Orleans* (1965), and *Negro Ironworkers of Louisiana, 1718-1900* (1972). Christian's poetry was also anthologized in *Ebony Rhythm* (1948, edited by Beatrice M. Murphy), *American Negro Poetry* (1963, edited by **Arna Bontemps**), and *The Poetry of the Negro: 1746-1970* (1970), edited by **Langston Hughes** and Arna Bontemps, both of whom he had gotten to know in the early 1930s. Christian also contributed articles and poetry to *Crisis, Opportunity, The Louisiana Weekly, Negro Voices,* and other periodicals.

Starting in 1936, Christian working in a special "Negro unit" of the Federal Writers Project (FWP), part of the Works Progress Administration. His unit was located at Dillard University, and he continued in that role until the FWP closed in 1943. In 1943, a Rosenwald Fellowship enabled him to continue his research and writing of his still-unpublished manuscript, tentatively titled *The History of the Negro in Louisiana.* From 1944 until 1950, he worked as an assistant librarian at Dillard (1944-1950). Unfortunately, complaints about his lack of formal college education ended his employment there. After that, he founded the Bruce Printing and Publishing Co. in New Orleans, but he became financially destitute. In 1965, Hurricane Betsy devastated his home, and he was arrested for looting when he tried to save his papers wading through the filthy floodwaters. Ironically, this cruel blow reminded New Orleanians of Christian's importance to Louisiana culture, and he was awarded a bronze medal from the Sesquicentennial Commission of the Battle of New Orleans later that year. In 1969, he was invited to be a history instructor and poetry-writer-in-residence at Louisiana State University, where he was lecturing when

he collapsed a few days before his death in a charity hospital at age 76. The University of New Orleans houses hundreds of cubic feet of his personal and literary papers, bequeathed by his family.

REFERENCES: CAO-01. LF-07. *Wiki.* Mizell-Nelson, Michael, in *AANB.* //en.wikipedia.org/wiki/Works_Progress_Administration. Amazon.com.

FURTHER READING: Lewis, Rudolph, in *GEAAL.*

Clark, Kenneth B. (Bancroft)
7/24/1914–5/1/2005
Nonfiction—psychology; educator, psychologist, researcher, consultant

With his wife, **Mamie Phipps Clark,** Kenneth B. Clark wrote numerous influential studies on the influences of segregation on African-American youths, as well as on European Americans, which proved instrumental in the landmark *Brown v. Board of Education* Supreme Court decision of 1954. Born in the Panama Canal Zone, Clark and his sister had been brought to the United States by their mother, Miriam, a seamstress and labor activist. As a child, Clark had admired **Countee Cullen,** who had taught at his junior high school, and **Arthur Schomburg,** who curated the collection amassed at the Harlem branch of the New York Public Library. While Clark was still an undergraduate at Howard University, he met and married Mamie, his lifelong intellectual comrade, research collaborator, and domestic partner in rearing their two children (Kate and Hilton). (*See* the entry on **Mamie Clark,** for more on their collaborative efforts.)

From 1939 to 1941, Clark participated in research conducted by Swedish sociologist and economist Gunnar Myrdal, probing the problems of racial segregation and discrimination in the United States. During that time, Clark also earned his Ph.D. in psychology from Columbia University, the first African American to do so. In 1942, Clark was hired to teach at the City College of New York (CCNY), where he was made full professor in 1960, the first African American to earn that distinction there. (Clark retired from CCNY in 1975.)

In addition to numerous scholarly articles, Clark wrote *Prejudice and Your Child* (1953, 3rd ed., 1963), *Desegregation: An Appraisal of the Evidence* (1953), *The Negro Student at Integrated Colleges* (1963, with Lawrence Plotkin), *The Negro Protest* (1963, based on his televised interviews with **James Baldwin, Malcolm X,** and **Martin Luther King, Jr.**), *Social and Economic Implications of Integration in the Public Schools* (1965), *Dark Ghetto: Dilemmas of Social Power* (1965), *The Negro American* (1966, coedited with Talcott Parsons), *A Relevant War against Poverty: A Study of Community Action Programs and Observable Change* (1968, with Jeannette Hopkins), *Crisis in*

Urban Education (1971), *Pathos of Power* (1974), and *King, Malcolm, Baldwin* (1984). In 2004, Woody Klein edited the collection *Toward Humanity and Justice: The Writings of Kenneth B. Clark. Scholar of the 1954 Brown v. Board of Education Decision.*

Among the honors he received for his work on behalf of civil rights and for fostering the well-being of African-American youths were the 1961 NAACP Spingarn Medal and the Gold Medal Award from the American Psychological Association (APA), of which Clark had been elected its first African-American president (1970-1971). In the mid-1940s, he and Mamie founded the Northside Testing and Consulting Center; more than a decade later, he founded Harlem Youth Opportunities Unlimited (HARYOU), to help youths avoid delinquency, dropping out of school, and being unemployed; and in the 1970s, he and Mamie and their two children founded a consulting firm. Despite these impressive accomplishments and recognition, Clark lamented the lack of progress in educating America's youths, observing in a 1993 *Newsweek* interview, "Children must be helped to understand the genuine meaning of democracy from the earliest grades; . . . to understand that one cannot keep others down without staying down with them; and . . . to understand the importance of empathy and respect" (quoted on p. 134, *BH2C*).

REFERENCES: *B. CAO-05. CE. EBLG. G-97.* Balfour, Lawrie, in *EA-99.* Banks, Michelle, in *BH2C.* "Kenneth and Mamie Clark," in *Wiki.* Gutek, Gerald L., in *WB-99.* //c250.columbia.edu/c250_celebrates/remarkable_columbians/kenneth_mamie_clark.html. Martin, Jonathan, and Sara Pendergast, in *BB.*

Clark, Mamie (née Phipps)
10/18/1917–8/22/1983
Nonfiction-psychology; educator, psychologist, researcher

Mamie was one half of the legendary Clark-and-Clark team that provided research fundamental to the historic 1954 *Brown v. Board of Education* Supreme Court Decision. While still Mamie Phipps, she met **Kenneth B. Clark** at Howard University in the 1930s. The two married in 1938, the year she earned her bachelor's degree and he (with his master's degree in hand) was working as a psychology instructor at Howard. Later on, the couple moved to New York's Columbia University, where the two earned doctorates in psychology (his in 1940, hers in 1943), becoming the first African American (Kenneth) and the first African-American woman (and the second African American—Mamie) to do so. In fact, the Clarks were the first two African Americans to earn Ph.D.s of any kind at Columbia.

Given their primary status, were universities across the land rushing to make them inviting offers for the good life in the ivory tower? Well, if those towers were to preserve their ivory hue, apparently not. At last, Kenneth was hired as an assistant professor at Hampton Institute and at the College of the City of New York. Mamie wasn't. Apparently, her skin color was not the only physical barrier blocking her entry to academia. Still, she collaborated with Kenneth on his research, and in 1946 she and he founded the Northside Testing and Consulting Center, their Manhattan clinic for treating African-American children with special needs. Many of these children had been incorrectly identified as "retarded" by the public-school system or suffered from emotional disturbance, learning disabilities, or personality disorders for which they were not receiving treatment.

By the mid-1950s, the Clarks had written numerous articles about their observations of children, such as "Racial Identification and Preference in Negro Children" and "Emotional Factors in Racial Identification and Preference in Negro Children." Some attorneys at the NAACP noticed one of the Clarks' articles on the harmful effects of school segregation on African-American children. The NAACP chief counsel **Thurgood Marshall** asked the Clarks to conduct further research specifically to show those effects. They developed a study using white-skinned dolls and black-skinned dolls. When they asked children to identify the "bad dolls," both white children and black children overwhelmingly chose the black dolls. Next, when they asked the children to choose with which dolls they would want to play, most of the children—both white and black—chose the white dolls. Marshall asked Kenneth to give testimony on the Clarks' collaborative research in the Supreme Court. He did, and the justices decided to overturn the "separate but equal" doctrine—unanimously.

Meanwhile, back at the center, Mamie served as executive director for more than three decades. As the center's reputation grew, it started drawing clients from all races and was renamed the Northside Center for Child Development. By the time Mamie stepped down (in 1979), the center had helped more than 16,000 children and their families. In 1973, Mamie saw the need to provide schooling for emotionally disturbed and learning-disabled youngsters whom the public schools were not educating, so she founded the Northside Day School. In 1975, she and her husband and their two children, Kate Miriam Clark and Hilton Bancroft Clark (born while Mamie was earning her doctorate), founded a consulting firm to guide corporations in implementing affirmative programs for hiring African Americans and other nonwhites.

REFERENCES: *AANB. BAAW. Wiki.* Banks, Michelle, in *BH2C.* //c250.columbia.edu/c250_celebrates/remarkable_columbians/kenneth_mamie_clark.html. //faculty.frostburg.edu/mbradley/psyography/bioscopes_mamieclark.html. //www.columbia.edu/cu/lweb/digital/

collections/nny/clarkm/profile.html. //www.encyclopediaofarkansas.net/ encyclopedia/entry-detail.aspx?entryID=2938. //www.webster.edu/~woolflm/mamieclark.html.

FURTHER READING: *EA-99.*

Clark, Septima (née Poinsette)
5/3/1898–12/15/1987
Autobiographies; educator, activist

Clark participated in the writing of at least two books on her life story: Grace Jordan McFadden's *Oral Recollections of Septima P. Clark* (1980) and Clark's autobiography *Ready from Within: Septima Clark and the Civil Rights Movement* (1986, edited by Cynthia Stokes Brown), which won the National Book Award in 1987. Why would the life of a humble schoolteacher deserve so much discussion?

On April 19, 1956, after she had taught school for 40 years, Septima Clark was told that she had a choice: Give up her membership in the NAACP and her vocal protests for civil rights, or give up *not only* her teaching job, *but also* all of her retirement benefits. What would any sensible 58-year-old widow do in a situation like this? How on Earth could she give up her career, her livelihood, and her only means of supporting herself? If she could keep quiet and compliant for four more years, she could retire and do whatever she wanted to do. Well, the choice seemed obvious to anyone.

Well, it was obvious to her, too. She kept her NAACP membership, she kept up her protests—except that she did get a little louder—and she lost her job and was prevented from getting another one anywhere in South Carolina. Fortunately, when the Highlander Folk School in Chattanooga, Tennessee, found out about her situation, they invited her to be the school's director of education. Highlander already had a reputation for training community activists, and she had previously conducted a workshop for the school when she was hired. With Clark at the helm, the school had an excellent role model for how to live by your conscience when big issues are at stake. Among the people Clark inspired was a little-known bus-riding seamstress named Rosa Parks.

As an outgrowth of her work at Highlander, Clark founded various citizenship schools, designed to prepare African Americans to pass the citizenship tests required for them to become registered voters. A few of the people with whom she worked in the citizenship schools included Fannie Lou Hamer, John Lewis, and Andrew Young—all of whom went on to contribute significantly to the civil-rights struggle.

REFERENCES: *BAAW.* Brown, Cynthia Stokes, in *BH2C.* Fay, Robert, in *EA-99.* McFadden, Grace Jordan, in *BWA:AHE.* Clark's

papers have been collected at the College of Charleston, Robert Scott Small Library, in South Carolina. —Tonya Bolden

Clarke, John Henrik
1/1/1915–7/16/1998
History books, essays, anthologies, curriculum books, short stories, poems; editor, educator

As a young boy, Clarke so loved reading that in addition to the Holy Bible, he would read tin-can labels, signs, and any other words he could lay his eyes on. He borrowed books from the personal libraries of white folks whose children could but wouldn't read, and he forged white people's names on notes to be able to borrow books from Jim Crow-ruled public libraries.

This young word-hungry reader inspired many people to have faith in his promise, too: His mother, who saved 50 cents per week for his college education (but died when John was just 10 years old); his father and his uncles, who pooled their money to pull together the $3.75 they needed to buy his schoolbooks each semester; and his beloved teacher, Evelena Taylor, about whom he later recalled, she "took my face between her hands and looking me straight in the eyes said, 'I believe in you.'"

Taylor and the others had good reason to believe in John. He was quick to learn, as well as quick to raise questions about peculiarities he noticed. For instance, why was Jesus depicted in the Bible as being a blue-eyed blonde, yet the Bible described him as having dark eyes and dark hair, like the other people of that region?

When John sought a book on the contributions of Africans in ancient history, a kindly white lawyer whose books he borrowed told him that there was no such book, implying that there were no such contributions. John wondered why no such book existed—had Africans really made no contributions to world history at all—or had no one written about them—or had this attorney just been ignorant about the existing books and contributions?

By great good fortune, Clarke discovered the answer to that question while he was still in high school. While he was watching over the belongings of a guest speaker, he noticed a copy of *The New Negro*, an anthology compiled by **Alain Locke**. In it, he glimpsed an essay by **Arthur Schomburg**: "The Negro Digs Up His Past." Wow! Negroes had a past to dig up! As Clarke later remembered, he was thrilled to discover "I came from a people with a history older than the history of Europe. . . . [my people's] history was older than that of their oppressors."

Intrigued, Clarke pursued Schomburg in Schomburg's native habitat of the Harlem branch of the New York Public Library. Schomburg encouraged Clarke in his pursuits and told him that he would need to study not only African history, but also European and American history, to figure out how Africa contributed to European culture, why Europeans developed the slave trade, and how America figured into the picture. Clarke heeded Schomburg's advice—with vigor.

After a brief interruption while he served in the Air Force, he returned to his self-designed program of informal study, as well as formal studies at various universities (e.g., New York University, the New School of Social Research in New York, the University of Ibadan in Nigeria, and the University of Ghana). By the mid-1960s (and continuing through the mid-1980s), he taught his favorite subject around Harlem, in a variety of community centers, as well as at various colleges and universities (e.g., Columbia, Cornell). Even after he settled into being a professor of Black and Puerto Rican Studies at New York's Hunter College (1966-1988), he continued to lecture across the country and to develop curricula, study guides, and teaching materials for others to use.

In and among all his teaching and studying, Clarke managed to churn out quite a few short stories (including "The Boy Who Painted Christ Black," the most widely anthologized of his stories), as well as myriad articles on African-American history, contributing to **Robert Abbott**'s *Chicago Defender*, **W. E. B. Du Bois**'s *Phylon*, the European Négritude journal *Présence Africaine* (founded by Senegalese author Alioune Diop), and numerous other periodicals. He was also cofounder and associate editor of at least two journals: *Harlem Quarterly* (1949-1951) and *Freedomways* (starting in 1962). The nonfiction books he wrote include *Africans at the Crossroads: Notes for an African World Revolution* (1991), *Christopher Columbus and the African Holocaust* (1992), and *African People in World History* (1995); he even wrote a book of verse (*Rebellion in Rhyme*, 1948).

Then there are all the books he edited, including *Harlem U.S.A.: The Story of a City within a City* (1964); *American Negro Short Stories* (1966); **Malcolm X**: *The Man and His Times* (1969); *William Styron's* **Nat Turner**: *Ten Black Writers Respond* (1970); **Marcus Garvey** *and the Vision of Africa* (1973, with **Amy Jacques Garvey**); and *New Dimensions in African History: The London Lectures of Dr. Yosef ben-Jochanan and Dr. John Henrik Clarke* (1991).

Contemporary historians such as **John Hope Franklin** and Herb Boyd recognize Clarke's contributions, and his life has been documented in the film *John Henrik Clarke: A Great and Mighty Walk* (1997), directed by **St. Claire Bourne** and executive produced and narrated by actor Wesley Snipes. Fortunately, for those of us who follow in his absence, the proceeds from the film's premiere helped pay for cataloging and preserving the John Henrik Clarke Collection at the **Schomburg** Center for Research in Black Culture.

REFERENCES: *EBLG. SMKC.* Boyd, Herb. (1998). "The Griot of Our Time," *New York Amsterdam News*, July 23-29. Mix, Dusty. (1998). "Coming Home," *Ledger-Enquirer* (Columbus, GA), July 26. *EA-99.* —Tonya Bolden

Cleage, Pearl (Michelle) (1st married name: Lomax)
12/7/1948–
Plays, essays and articles, poems, novel, short stories, columns; magazine founding editor, theater artistic director, educator

A prolific playwright, Cleage has had many of her plays produced in New York, Washington, D.C., and her adulthood hometown of Atlanta, Georgia (e.g., *Hymn for the Rebels*, 1968; *Duet for Three Voices*, 1969; her audience-attendance-record-breaking *puppetplay*, 1983; her award-winning one-act *Hospice*, 1983; *Good News*, 1984; *Essentials*, 1985; *Banana Bread*, 1985; *Porch Songs*, 1985; *Chain*, 1992; *Late Bus to Mecca*, 1992; *Flyin' West*, 1994; *Bourbon at the Border*, 1997). In addition, many of her plays have been published, such as those in her *Flyin' West and Other Plays* (1999) and her plays *Blues for an Alabama Sky* (1999) and *A Song for Coretta* (2007). Many of Cleage's plays emphasize the strength of African-American women.

A strong woman herself, she has been named playwright-in-residence (1983) and artistic director (since 1987) of the Just Us Theater Company, as well as creative-writing instructor (1986-1991) and playwright-inresidence (1991) at Spellman College. Cleage also has a daughter, Diegnan Njeri, from her first marriage, and has been married to playwright and novelist Zaron "Zeke" W. Burnett, Jr. since 1994. She and Burnett have also cowritten performance pieces *Love and Trouble* (1987), *Live at Club Zebra!*, and *The Final Negro Rhythm and Blues Revue* (1988).

Cleage's creative writing has gone beyond drama to include her collection for young-adult readers, *The Brass Bed and Other Stories* (1991); her poetry collections *We Don't Need No Music* (1971), *Dear Dark Faces: Portraits of a People* (1980), and *We Speak Your Names: A Celebration* (2005, with her husband Burnett); and her chapbook *One for the Brothers* (1983). Also, in 1987, she founded the literary magazine *Catalyst*, which she has edited since.

Cleage also writes nonfiction. The daughter of a politically activist family, Cleage writes powerful, candid, thought-provoking columns, which have appeared regularly in the *Atlanta Gazette* (1976-) and the *Atlanta Journal-Constitution* (1977), and for about a decade (1988-1998) her "Stop Making Sense" column was published in the black-owned *Atlanta Tribune* newspaper. She has also contributed essays addressing issues of sex and race in America, as well as other articles, to numerous other periodicals, such as *Afro-American Review, Black Collegian, Essence, Journal of Black Poetry, Ms., New York Times Book Review, Promethean, Readers and Writers,* and *Southern Voices.* She also wrote two nonfiction books, *Mad at Miles: A Black Woman's Guide to Truth* (1991), and *Deals with the Devil and Other Reasons to Riot* (1993), which garnered both popular and critical acclaim.

Much of Cleage's fiction work is also inspired by historical events and settings. Since the mid-1990s, Cleage's fiction writing has primarily been novels, which sometimes carry characters from one novel into a subsequent one. Her first, *What Looks Like Crazy on an Ordinary Day: A Novel* (1997; audiocassette abridgement read by the author, 1998; large-print edition, 1999), earned much-coveted inclusion in Oprah's Book Club (*see* **Oprah Winfrey**) and rose to the top of the *New York Times* best-seller list. Her other novels have also won critical and popular acclaim: *Wish I Had a Red Dress* (2001; audiobook read by Cleage, 2001); *Some Things I Never Thought I'd Do* (2003; audiobook, 2003); *Babylon Sisters* (2005; audiobook read by Cleage, 2005); *Baby Brother Blues* (2006, which won the 2007 NAACP Image Award for Outstanding Literary Work in the area of fiction); and *Seen It All and Done the Rest: A Novel* (2008). At Amazon.com, customer reviewers have given her books at least four or five stars (out of five possible). Reviews in *Booklist, Chicago Sun-Times, Essence, Kirkus Reviews, New York Times, Publishers Weekly,* and *Washington Post* have praised her work, as have fellow writers **Tina McElroy Ansa, Bebe Moore Campbell, E. Lynn Harris**, Tayari Jones, Jill Nelson, Kevin Powell, and Jewell Parker Rhodes. For instance, **Nikki Giovanni** said, "Pearl Cleage is one of America's finest young writers. We fall in love with her characters—but maybe 'friends' is a better description—all over again. We laugh and cry [and do] all the things we do when you realize that these may be characters on a page or . . . they could be you."

REFERENCES: *AANB. BAWPP. EBLG.* Effinger, Marta J., in *T-CAD-2nd.* Kalfatovic, Mary, in *BB. CAO-08.* LaFrance, Michelle, in *GEAAL.* Marsh-Lockett, Carol P., in *COCAAL* and *OCAAL. W. Wiki.* Effinger, Marta J., in *T-CAD-2nd.* //www.scils.rutgers.edu/~cybers/cleage.html. //www.scils.rutgers.edu/~cybers/cleage2.html. Amazon.com, 7/1999, 1/31/2009.

Cleaver, (Leroy) Eldridge
8/31/1935–5/1/1998
Essays and letters, autobiography/memoirs; convict

After a troubled youth involving numerous incarcerations for drug deals and thefts, in 1954, Cleaver was imprisoned for two-and-a-half years for possessing marijuana. In prison (Soledad, Folsom, and San Quentin prisons in California), he completed high school and be-

Eldridge Cleaver

gan reading the works of Karl Marx and of **W. E. B. Du Bois**. After his release, he was again convicted and imprisoned in 1958, this time for rape and for assault with intent to commit murder. During this lengthier prison term, he joined the Black Muslims, enthusiastically following the teachings of **Malcolm X**. Following Malcolm's break with the Nation of Islam, Cleaver left, too, joining X's secular Organization of Afro-American Unity (OAAU).

Cleaver also started trying to have some of the essays he was writing published. When his essay "Notes of a Native Son," a homophobic assault on **James Baldwin**, was published in *Ramparts* magazine (a leftist publication), he gained the attention of various intellectuals, who helped him win parole in 1966. While writing and editing for *Ramparts,* he came to know Black Panther Party (BPP) cofounders Huey Newton and Bobby Seale. They named Cleaver the BPP's minister of information, and he was soon traveling nationwide promoting the message of the BPP. Within two years, he had published *Soul on Ice* (1968), a collection of his essays and letters reflecting on his criminal behavior, his experiences in prison, and the situation of African Americans within American culture, as well as gender relations and other topics. Just a couple months after *Soul on Ice* was published, Cleaver was arrested for assault and attempted murder following an armed confrontation between the police and BPP members. When it looked as though he would be returning to prison and asserted that he feared for his life, he jumped bail and fled the United States, spending the next several years in Cuba, in Algeria, and in France. Cleaver's new wife and fellow Panther Kathleen Neal joined him abroad, and the couple had two children (their son Maceo, born in Algiers; and their daughter Joju, born in North Korea).

At first, Cleaver continued to write leftist articles for such publications as *Black Panther*, *Ramparts*, and **Black Scholar**, and he wrote *Eldridge Cleaver: Post-Prison Writings and Speeches* and *Eldridge Cleaver's Black Papers* (both published in 1969). He also completed his autobiographical novella *Black Moochie* (1969), which he had begun while he was writing for *Ramparts*. Over time, however, he became disenchanted with leftist politics. By 1975, when he returned to the United States to face the charges against him, he had become a fundamentalist right-wing Christian. With his newfound religious and political beliefs, he was able to get the attempted-murder charges dropped in exchange for pleading guilty to the assault charges, for which he was given just five years probation and 1,000-2,000 hours of community service, with no prison time. (Ironically, many of his earlier speeches and writings were published a year later in the collection *The Black Panther Leaders Speak: Huey P. Newton, Bobby Seale, Eldridge Cleaver, and Company Speak Out through the Black Panther Party's Official Newspaper*.) Cleaver eventually embraced the Mormon faith and joined the Republican party, unsuccessfully running for the G.O.P.'s nomination for the U.S. Senate.

He wrote an account of his conversion experiences in *Soul on Fire* (1978). His religious beliefs did not suffice to keep him from turning to drugs, however, as he was arrested again in 1994 for intoxication and possession of cocaine. In addition to the aforementioned publications, Cleaver wrote poems, short stories, and pamphlets. Cleaver's lasting testament appears to be his early writings in *Soul on Ice*, however, as it is still prompting readers to praise or scorn (Amazon.com, 7/99).

REFERENCES: *EBLG. NAAAL.* Balfour, Lawrie, in *EA-99.* Berger, Roger A., in *COCAAL* and *OCAAL.* Kram, Mark, in *BB. CAO-03. CLCS.* Amazon.com, 7/1999. *EB-BH-CD.* Stone, Les, in *B. BH2C. CE. LE. QB. W. W2B. Wiki.* Weinstein, Henry, "Life on the Line: Conversation with Cleaver," 1969, quoted in *EA-99.*

Cliff, Michelle
11/2/1946–
Novels, poems, short stories, essays, autobiography/ memoir; editor, journalist, educator

Cliff's heritage blends African, Native American, and European ancestry, and her life experiences include her native Jamaica and the United States. Born in Jamaica, she lived in the United States (New York City) with her mother and sister from ages three until ten, becoming a naturalized American citizen, and she maintained her American citizenship after returning to Jamaica. On returning to Jamaica, light-skinned Michelle attended a private girls' school, where she saw firsthand the pernicious influence of a caste system based on color. Jamaica's colonial past had led to intraracial cruelty, oppression, and even violence; societal privileges were distributed according to color, and Michelle's darker-skinned compatriots suffered condemnation and alienation in their homeland.

Michelle also had a very personal experience of alienation and humiliation in Jamaica. While living with her aunt and attending private school, she continued to keep a diary of her most intimate thoughts and experiences. When her parents were visiting, they broke into Michelle's bedroom, broke the lock on her diary, and read it. Soon after, they read it aloud, in front of her, while she screamed, "Don't I have any rights?" Until then, she had always wanted to write, but that humiliation shut down her desire to write for many years.

After completing school, Cliff left Jamaica to study in London, then earned her B.A. in European history at Wagner College in Staten Island, New York (1969). The year she graduated, she started working as a researcher and then a production supervisor for New York publisher W. W. Norton. In the early 1970s, Cliff returned to London, where she earned her M.Phil. (master's in philosophy) from Warburg Institute (1974), writing her thesis on languages and comparative historical studies of the Italian Renaissance. Back in New York, she returned to publishing, working as a manuscript and production editor (specializing in history, politics, and women's studies) for the Norton Library Series. In the early 1980s (1981-1983), she and her life partner (since 1976), poet Adrienne Rich, coedited and published a lesbian feminist journal, *Sinister Wisdom*. Since then, Cliff has been a member of the editorial board of *Signs* (1980-1989) and a contributing editor of *American Voice* (since 1993).

While writing has been Cliff's main focus, she has also worked as a reporter and researcher and has lectured and taught extensively at various colleges and universities on both U.S. coasts, including Stanford University (Palo Alto, CA), the New School for Social Research (NY), Hampshire College and the University of Massachusetts at Amherst, Norwich University (Northfield, VT), the Martin Luther King, Jr., Public Library (Oakland, CA), the University of California at Santa Cruz, and Trinity College (Hartford, CT).

By the late 1970s, Cliff's essays, poems, and short stories were starting to appear in print. Her essay "Notes on Speechlessness" was published in the lesbian-feminist magazine *Conditions II* in 1977. Her essays often address themes of racial tension and of sexual identity. Two of her books include both essays and poems: *Claiming an Identity They Taught Me to Despise* (1980) and *The Land of Look Behind: Prose and Poetry* (1985). Many of her short works have been widely anthologized. In each of these works, she explores issues of colonialism, class struggle, sexual identity, racism, and feminist consciousness. Cliff also edited *The Winner Names the Age: A Collection of Writing by Lillian Smith* (1978). Her autobiographical prose and poetry collection, *If I Could Write This in Fire* (2008), has been praised by **Toni Morrison**, Tillie Olson, and others.

Cliff's *Bodies of Water* (1990) has been called a short-story collection, but it may also be viewed as a novel, as the characters appear across different stories, and their stories interweave, making use of folk myths and legends, as well as history. Prior to *Bodies of Water*, Cliff wrote two novels (*Abeng*, 1984; *No Telephone to Heaven*, 1988) featuring as their central character Clare Savage, a fair-skinned, middle-class Jamaican who must come to terms with her mixed cultural heritage and the privileges accorded to her because of her light complexion. (Sound familiar?) In *Abeng*, Clare and her dark-skinned friend Zoe confront a situation that highlights the difference in their status on the Caribbean island, and their friendship collapses under the weight of these disparities. By the end of the book, Clare is fleeing to the United States, leaving Zoe behind in Jamaica. *No Telephone to Heaven* continues Clare's story, weaving back and forth in time, as well as between the United States and Jamaica. Through both novels, Cliff explores the difficulties of affirming multiple aspects of a mixed cultural heritage. Cliff's third novel, *Free Enterprise: A Novel of Mary Ellen Pleasant* (1993), fictionalizes a real nineteenth-century abolitionist who aided fugitive slaves, interwoven with other historical and fictional figures.

Cliff has received critical praise for her more recent story collections *The Store of a Million Items: Stories* (1998), set in Jamaica and Manhattan, and her all-embracing collection *Everything Is Now: New and Collected Stories* (2009). In all her writings, Cliff blends broad aspects of history with highly personal autobiography, offering deeply personal insights within a richly detailed historical context. A fluent speaker of multiple languages, Cliff also intermingles the patois of the Caribbean with the speech patterns of standard American English. In appreciation of her work, Cliff has been awarded fellowships from the prestigious Macdowell Colony and the National Endowment for the Arts (NEA) (1982) and the Massachusetts Artists Foundation and the Yaddo Writers Colony (1984), as well as a Fulbright fellowship and a second NEA fellowship (1989).

REFERENCES: *EBLG. NAAAL. OC20LE.* Adisa, Opal Palmer. "Journey into Speech—A Writer between Two Worlds: An Interview with Michelle Cliff. *African American Review. 28.2* (Summer 1994) p. 273. From *Literature Resource Center.* Brice-Finch, Jacqueline, in *T-CCBAW-3.* Schwartz, Meryl F. "An Interview with Michelle Cliff." *Contemporary Literature. 34.4* (Winter 1993) p. 594. From *Literature Resource Center.* Fonteneau, Yvonne, in *BWA:AHE.* Pinto, Samantha, in *GEAAL.* Robinson, Lisa Clayton, in *EA-99.* Shea, Renee Hausmann. *Belles Lettres: A Review of Books by Women. 9.3* (Spring 1994) p. 32. From *Literature Resource Center.* Shepherd, Kenneth R. in *BB. CAO-07. GOE.* Wagner-Martin, Linda, in *OCWW. Wiki.* //www.english.emory.edu/Bahri/Cliff.html. //www.glbtq.com/literature/cliff_m.html. //www.glbtq.com/literature/cliff_m,2.html. Amazon.com.

Clifton, Lucille (née Thelma Lucille Sayles)
6/27/1936–
Poems, children's books, autobiography/memoir, novels, essays, short stories, screenplays; educator

You might say Lucille couldn't help becoming a poet and storyteller: Although neither of her parents had a formal education, Lucille grew up observing how to write poems and tell stories. Lucille's mother, a professional laundress and dedicated amateur poet, often read or recited poems to her children. Lucille's father, a steel worker by vocation and griot by avocation, frequently told his children stories about their African ancestors and their history in this country. In Clifton's own words: "I grew up a well-loved child in a loving family and so I have always known that being very poor . . . had nothing to do with lovingness or familyness or character or any of that" (p. 137, *BWW*).

When Lucille was just 16 years old, she won a full scholarship to study drama at Howard University (with fellow students **Amiri Baraka** and **Sterling Brown**). When she transferred to another college, she joined a drama group and met novelist **Ishmael Reed** and poet **Langston Hughes** (who later anthologized some of her poems). After a while, however, she became so absorbed in writing that she dropped out of college before earning a degree. Hardly a typical dropout, however, she eventually received four honorary doctorates in humane letters.

During the 1950s, in addition to writing, she worked for several years as a civil servant. In 1958, her mother died, Lucille married Fred Clifton, and she gave birth to their first child—quite a year! Over the next eight years or so, the couple had five more children. When the youngest of her children was a teenager (about a year before her husband Fred died, in 1984), she explained her priorities: "At home I am wife and mama mostly. My family has always come first with me" (p. 138, *BWW*).

Her children didn't prevent her from writing, however. In fact, she credits her four daughters and two sons with having inspired much of her work, and a large proportion of her literary output has been about children or addressed to them. Nonetheless, her children have often been less than encouraging about her poems and her books for young readers. When she was invited to share her children's books with classes all over the country, her own children begged her not to come to their classes—or if she *had* to come, they begged her, "You know how you walk? Don't walk that stupid walk. You know how you talk? Don't talk like that. Don't laugh your laugh. Don't wear your clothes" (p. 94, *LoL*). Although she may have felt a little hurt by their comments, her good humor got her past them, as shown in her poem "Admonitions": "Children / When they ask you / why your mama is so funny / say she is a poet / she don't have no sense" (p. 142, *BWW*).

In the 1970s, Clifton began various positions as a lecturer, a poet in residence, and a professor at several colleges and universities in Maryland and nearby Washington, D.C. After her children were grown and she was widowed, she accepted positions farther afield, such as at the University of California at Santa Cruz, North Carolina's Duke University, and the prestigious Cave Canem poetry workshops.

Clifton's poetry uses simple vocabulary and syntax to convey complex and subtle messages. As she has noted, "I am interested in being understood not admired" (p. 2219, *NAAL*). Clifton's voice is both realistic and optimistic, chiefly focused on everyday experiences and feelings. Her poetry illuminates the commonplace. For instance, she begins her poem "an homage to my hips," "these hips are big hips. / they need space to / move around in. / they don't fit into little / petty places. / these hips / are free hips."

Clifton has a hopeful, positive, life-affirming outlook, even when she writes about challenges and emotionally daunting experiences (as she often does). She describes difficult times without minimizing their fearsomeness or even their cruelty, yet she highlights the ways people face and get past the obstacles in their paths. Even when the ordinary people in her poems cannot entirely overcome the troubles they see, they do their best. As she has said, "Acting when you *are* afraid, *that's* where the honor is" (p. 95, *LoL*).

She particularly focuses on the responsibility and response-ability of humble heroes. She rails against injustice without fostering hatred, and she argues for taking personal responsibility, without preaching to her readers. By recognizing in herself and others both their vulnerability and their strength, Clifton encourages and empowers her readers as they confront their own problems. For instance, in concluding "Daddy," a poem she wrote to her

father after his death, she said, "When his leg died, he cut it off. / 'It's gone,' he said, 'it's gone / but I'm still here'" (p. 147, *BWW*). On the other hand, she noted in a 2000 interview, "I don't write because I have a mission to heal the world. My mission is to heal Lucille if I can, as much as I can. What I know is that I am not the only one who has felt the things I feel. And so, if what I write helps to heal others, that's excellent, but my main thing is for me not to fall into despair." Also, "For me, I think that writing is a way of continuing to hope. When things sometimes feel as if they're not going to get any better, writing offers a way of trying to connect with something beyond that obvious feeling" (Summer 2000, *Antioch Review,* quoted in GLRO *Literature Resource Center*).

Besides triumph over difficulties, Clifton's other dominant theme is continuity across generations. After her parents died, she carried on her father's griot tradition and wrote about her family in *Generations: A Memoir* (1976). Through all of her writing, she nudges her readers to acknowledge their indebtedness to generations past, as well as their obligation to generations to come. She asks readers to affirm the past—even when it is painful, such as in the experiences of slavery or of sexual molestation—to observe its effects in the present, and then to focus on moving forward into the future.

Clifton's poetry collections include *Good Times* (1969), named one of the year's ten best books by the *New York Times; Good News About the Earth: New Poems* (1972); *An Ordinary Woman* (1974); *Two-Headed Woman* (1980); *Good Woman: Poems and a Memoir: 1969-1980* (1987); *Next: New Poems* (1987); *A Meditation on Ten Oxherding Pictures* (1988); *Quilting: Poems 1987-1990* (1991); *The Book of Light* (1993); *The Terrible Stories* (1996); *Blessing The Boats: New and Selected Poems, 1988-2000* (2000), National Book Award winner; and *Mercy: Poems* (2004); and *Voices* (2008). In addition to her own collections, Clifton's poems are widely anthologized in other people's collections.

Many of her readers have never seen these works, however, knowing her solely through her children's books. These books focus on the everyday struggles of family life in the inner city. Perhaps her favorite central character is Everett Anderson, a six- or seven-year-old boy who lives with his single working mother in an inner-city neighborhood. Through him and other characters, Clifton shows that poverty and other material circumstances do not determine who you are or who you can become. These include *Some of the Days of Everett Anderson* (1970), *Everett Anderson's Christmas Coming* (1971), *Everett Anderson's Year* (1974), *Everett Anderson's Friend* (1976), *Everett Anderson's 1 2 3* (1977), *Everett Anderson's Nine Month Long* (1978), *Everett Anderson's Goodbye* (1983), and *One of the Problems of Everett Anderson* (2001).

Her stories encourage children to be proud of themselves and to act in ways that will make them proud of themselves. She's describes no goody-two-shoes children, however. She realistically addresses children's difficulties with moral and social dilemmas. Rather than demanding (or trying to show) perfection, she shows lovably flawed children trying to do the best they can with whatever they have. With a loving family (of whatever size) and through conscientious effort, each child can be an ordinary hero. To date, she has written more than 20 books of fiction and poetry for young readers, about half of which are about Everett Anderson and several of which spotlight history. Some of her other books for youngsters include *The Black BCs* (1970), *Good, Says Jerome* (1973), *Don't You Remember?* (1973), *My Brother Fine with Me* (1975), *Amifika* (1977), and *Three Wishes* (1992); for slightly older juveniles, she wrote *The Times They Used to Be* (1974) and *All Us Come Cross the Water* (1973); and for a little older still, she wrote *The Lucky Stone* (1979). She has also included nonblack protagonists in some of her children's books, such as *The Boy Who Didn't Believe in Spring* (1973), *My Friend Jacob* (1980), and *Sonora Beautiful* (1981). In addition to her children's books, her poetry, and her memoir, Clifton has written novels, essays, short stories, and screenplays.

Though Clifton generally shies away from celebrity, she has received many awards for her writing, including four National Endowment for the Arts fellowships (1969, 1970, 1972, 1973); four Pulitzer prize nominations (1980, 1987, 1988, 1991), the first author to receive more than one Pulitzer nomination for poetry books; a Coretta Scott King Award from the American Library Association (1984); a National Book Award (NBA; 2000) and an NBA nomination (1996); an Emmy Award; the Shelley Memorial Prize from the Poetry Society of America (1992); and the Poetry Foundation's $100,000 Ruth Lilly Poetry Prize for lifetime accomplishments (2007). She has also been named a fellow of the American Academy of Arts and Sciences (1999), a chancellor of the Academy of American Poets (1999-2005), and a Literary Lion by the New York Public Library (1989); and dozens of others. When she was first invited to become the Poet Laureate of Maryland (1974-1985), she asked **Gwendolyn Brooks** (Poet Laureate of Illinois) how the position would affect her life and how it would benefit her people. When Brooks told her that the honor was "what you make of it," Clifton decided to accept the award. She has since commented on celebrity, "I wish to celebrate and not be celebrated (though a little celebration is a lot of fun)" (p. 137, *BWW*).

When asked about her own life experiences, Clifton has responded, "I don't know if I think I've had a hard life, but I *have* had a challenging life. . . . but I was blessed with a sense of humor, . . . which has saved me on occasion. I can also see what I have gained from being challenged in my life" (pp. 81-82, *LoL*).

REFERENCES: *AANB. AAW:PV. AWAW. BWW. CBC. LoL. MAAL. MWEL. NAAAL.* Moody, Joycelyn K., in *COCAAL* and *OCAAL. PCPEL. Q:P. TTS. TtW. TWT. W. Wiki.* Baughman, Ronald, in *APSWWII-1* Bryan, T. J., in *BB. CAO-07. LFCC-07. MWEL.*. Glaser, Michael S. "I'd Like Not to Be a Stranger in the World: A Conversation/Interview with Lucille Clifton. *The Antioch Review.* 58.3 (Summer 2000) p. 310. From *Literature Resource Center.* Peppers, Wallace R., in *AAP-55-85.* //0-web.ebscohost.dbpcosdcsgt. co.san-diego.ca.us/novelist/detail?vid=44&hid=7&sid=d408b38a-8f 5e-4ec2-b75c-cf9c5b5097d7%40sessionmgr3&bdata=JnNpdGU9bm 92ZWxpc3QtbGl2ZQ%3d%3d. //www.cavecanempoets.org/pages/ programs_faculty.php. //www.poets.org/poet.php/prmPID/79, Lucille Clifton. Amazon.com.

Cobb, Jr., Charles E.
6/23/1943–
Poems, essays, autobiography/memoir; civil-rights activist

While still a teenager, Cobb left college to spend five years working as a field secretary with the Student Nonviolent Coordinating Committee (SNCC), struggling for civil rights. In 1967, he visited Vietnam, about a year before the peak of the United State's Vietnam War. His poetry collection *In the Furrows of the World* (1967), illustrated with photos he took himself, emerged from these experiences. Next, he worked for the Center for Black Education (1968-1969), visited Tanzania (1969), and then helped found Drum and Spear Press and served on its board of directors (1969-1974), while living in Tanzania for a time.

The insights he gained from his extended sojourn in Tanzania and other experiences inspired both his second poetry collection, *Everywhere Is Yours* (1971), and his nonfiction prose, *African Notebook: Views on Returning Home* (1971). For journals, magazines, and newspapers, he has also written various articles, many of which have been anthologized (e.g., "Whose Society Is This?" in *Thoughts of Young Radicals*, 1966, reflecting on why he joined SNCC). During the early 1970s, he worked as a Congressional staffer and a radio reporter. From 1976 to 1979, he reported on foreign affairs for National Public Radio (NPR); then from 1979 to 1985, he wrote and produced numerous documentaries, such as for Public Broadcasting Service's (PBS's) *Frontline*. From 1985 through 1996, he wrote on the staff of *National Geographic* (e.g., "Traveling the Blues Highway," 1999; articles on North Carolina's Outer Banks, Grenada, Zimbabwe). Since then, he has been senior diplomatic correspondent for AllAfrica.com, which has alliances with the British Broadcasting Corporation (BBC) and other European networks, as well as more than 100 African news organizations. With Robert P. Moses, his friend since they were both involved in SNCC, he wrote *Radical Equations: Civil Rights from Mississippi to the Algebra Project* (2001), tying the struggle for civil rights to the current need for struggle against poverty and impoverished education.

REFERENCES: *AANB.* Greene, Michael E., in *COCAAL* and *OCAAL.* CAO-05. Williams, Clara R., in *AAP-55-85.*

Cobb, Jewell (née Plummer)
1/17/1924–

Nonfiction—cell biology; scientist, educator, college administrator

Though her father and her grandfather were physicians, as a teenager, Jewell Plummer had planned to become a physical education teacher like her mother and her aunt. When her high school teacher gave her a chance to peek into cells through a microscope, though, she was hooked on cells. An honors student, she had to challenge racial discrimination to gain her college education, but she managed to earn a B.A. in biology and then an M.S. and a Ph.D. in cell physiology. Her 1950 dissertation was titled "Mechanisms of Pigment Formation." Since then, Cobb has published extensively on her scientific research, especially scholarly journal articles on cells with skin cancer, and how melanin, a skin pigment, can protect the skin from damaging ultraviolet radiation. She has also published some articles on social issues involving women and minorities. For instance, her article "Filters for Women in Science" (1979) describes how women are more commonly filtered out of scientific careers than are men. She also challenged sexism in her books *Breaking Down Barriers to Women Entering Science* (1979) and *Issues and Problems: A Debate* (1979).

After being named president of California State University, Fullerton (in 1981) and then trustee professor at California State University, Los Angeles (in 1990), Cobb has spent less time on research and writing. More recently, she has turned her attention to helping economically disadvantaged middle school and high school students have educational and career opportunities in science, math, and engineering, first as the principal investigator at Southern California Science and Engineering ACCESS Center and Network (1991-2001), and then as principal investigator for Science Technology Engineering Program (STEP) Up for Youth, the ASCEND project at California State University, Los Angeles (since 2001). She has worked hard to ensure that these students receive social support rather than discrimination in their endeavors. Cobb also has a son, Jonathan, born in 1957, with Roy Cobb, whom she married in 1954 and divorced in 1967. In addition to more than 20 honorary doctorates and many other awards, Cobb earned the Lifetime

Achievement Award from the National Academy of Science (1993).

REFERENCES: *AANB.* Irvin, Dona L., Jennifer M. York, and Ralph G. Zerbonia, in *BB.* Robinson, Lisa Clayton, in *EA-99.* Stille, Darlene R. (1995). *EWS.* Thompson, Kathleen, in *B. BWA:AHE.*

Cobb, William Montague
10/12/1904–11/20/1990

Nonfiction; editor, anatomist

In addition to writing more than 600 scholarly articles on physical anthropology and contributing to several standard reference works in medicine (e.g., *Gray's Anatomy*), Cobb wrote books on African-American medical care and on jobs in medicine, including *The First Negro Medical Society: A History of the Medico-Chirurgical Society of the District of Columbia* (1939). He also edited the *Journal of the National Medical Association* for 28 years.

REFERENCES: *AANB.* Fay, Robert, in *EA-99.*

Cole (1st married name; 2nd married name: Robinson), Johnnetta (née Betsch)
10/19/1936–

Scholarly, nonfiction—cultural anthropology, self-help; educator, college president

When Johnnetta enrolled at Fisk University at age 15 (through its early-admissions program), she knew right away that she had found her way into a magical, awesome environment. A bright girl, she was already well educated when she entered, but Fisk offered her a wealth of new opportunities for learning—as just one example, almost daily, she ran across the school librarian—scholar, novelist, storyteller, and poet **Arna Bontemps**.

Just before her junior year, Johnnetta then transferred to Oberlin, in the Midwest, where she met students and scholars from across the nation and around the world—and she discovered her passion for finding out about people from other places through the field of cultural anthropology. Anthropology revealed to her the link between African Americans and their West African ancestors, as evident in their cultural traditions. She pursued a bachelor's, then a master's, then even a doctorate in anthropology, so that she might teach to others, opening their eyes as hers had been opened. While earning her doctorate, Johnnetta Betsch married and became Johnnetta B. Cole.

Over the next two decades, Cole taught at several colleges, from Los Angeles to Washington State to Massachusetts to New York. In 1987, she was asked whether she would like to be considered as a candidate for the presidency of Spelman College. Shocked at first, she decided that she would. Soon after, she was appointed the first African-American woman to preside over that institution (following three European-American women and one African-American man). During her presidency, the daughter of **Camille and Bill Cosby** was attending Spelman, and they endorsed Cole's presidency to the tune of $20 million—a tremendous gift for a privately funded university.

In addition to numerous scholarly articles and a regular column in the popular magazine *McCall's*, Cole's publications include *Anthropology for the Eighties: Introductory Readings* (1982), *All American Women: Lines That Divide, Ties That Bind* (1986), *Anthropology for the Nineties: Introductory Readings* (1988), and *Conversations: Straight Talk with America's Sister President* (1993).

REFERENCES: *33T. BAAW. BWA:AHE. TAWH. WDAW*
—Tonya Bolden

Editor's note: Cole continued at Spelman until 1997, took a brief breather, and then presided over Bennett College in Greensboro, North Carolina, another historically black university for women. In addition to receiving at least 40 honorary degrees, Cole has been inducted into the Working Woman Hall of Fame and has received the Jessie Bernard Wise Woman Award and American Woman Award (both 1990). In addition to the aforementioned books, Cole has written *Traditional and Wage-Earning Labor among Tribal Liberians* (1975), *Race toward Equality* (1986), and *Dream the Boldest Dreams: And Other Lessons of Life* (1997). With Beverly Guy-Sheftall, she wrote *Gender Talk: Sexism, Power, and Politics in the African American Community* (2003; also subtitled *The Struggle for Women's Equality in African American Communities*). In addition, she has contributed to numerous periodicals and anthologies and serves on the editorial board of *Anthropology and Humanism Quarterly*, **Black Scholar**, *Emerge*, and *SAGE: A Scholarly Journal on Black Women*. She shares three sons (David, Aaron, and Ethan Che) with her first husband, economist Robert Cole (1960-1982), and two stepsons with her second husband, Arthur Robinson III (since 1988).

REFERENCES: *B. CAO-05. Wiki.* Goldsworthy, Joan, and Ralph G. Zerbonia, in *BB.* Rivo, Lisa E., in *AANB.* Amazon.com.

Coleman, Wanda (née Evans)
11/13/1946–

Drama, poems, short stories, columns, book reviews, novel; magazine editor, TV soap opera staff writer, radio cohost, educator, performance artist

Coleman had published several poems by age 15. Since then, she has garnered more than 4,500 rejection slips, but has managed also to publish numerous books of her poems and stories, including *Art in the Court of the Blue Fag* (1977), *Mad Dog Black Lady* (1979), and *Imagoes* (1983), all poetry collections; *Heavy Daughter Blues: Poems and Stories, 1968-1986* (1987/1991), *A War of Eyes and Other Stories* (1988), *The Dicksboro Hotel and Other Travels* (1989), *African Sleeping Sickness: Stories and Poems* (1990), her poetry collection *Hand Dance* (1993), *American Sonnets* (1994), her 1999 Lenore Marshall Poetry Prize-winning *Bathwater Wine* (1998), *Mambo Hips & Make Believe: A Novel* (1999), National Book Award-nominated *Mercurochrome: New Poems* (2001), *Ostinato Vamps: Poems* (2003), and *Jazz and Twelve O'Clock Tales: New Stories* (2008). She has also written nonfiction prose collections, *Native in a Strange Land: Trials and Tremors* (1996) and *The Riot Inside Me: More Trials and Tremors* (2004), which include essays, reports, interviews, and memoirs. Clearly, Coleman enjoys variety. She has also edited the writings of other writers. While writing more than 1,000 poems and giving more than 500 poetry readings, she has worked assorted day jobs, has raised three children—Anthony, Tunisia, and Ian Wayne—and has been married to her third husband, a poet, since 1981. Coleman has been awarded an Emmy for the best writing in a daytime drama, for *Days of Our Lives*, and has received writing grants from the National Endowment for the Arts and the Guggenheim Foundation.

REFERENCES: *AAW:PV. NAAAL. Wiki.* Magistrale, Tony, in *AW:ACLB-02.* Manheim, James M., in *BB. CAO-04. LFCC-07.* O'Mara, Kathleen K., in *ASSWSWWII-1.* Stanley, Sandra K., in *COCAAL* and *OCAAL.* //authors.aalbc.com/wandacoleman.htm. //www.poets.org/poet.php/prmPID/118.

Collier, Eugenia (Williams)
4/6/1928–

Stories, anthologies, literary criticism, play; educator

In Collier's best-known short story "Marigolds," the celebrated marigolds in eccentric Miss Lottie's garden offer a bright spot of color in her Depression-era neighborhood. Lizabeth, the 14-year-old narrator of the story, and her pack of pals amuse themselves by throwing rocks at Lottie's flowers. That evening, Lizabeth overhears her father crying as he tells her mother how deeply frustrated and angry he feels at not being able to find work to support their family. Shocked at hearing her father cry and at realizing that adults may sometimes feel vulnerable and afraid, she can't sleep, and she sneaks out of the house. She goes back to Miss Lottie's garden, where she furiously attacks the marigolds. As she finishes destroying the flowers and exhausts her rage, she looks up to see Miss Lottie, devastated and puzzled. In that instant, Lizabeth loses her childhood innocence and for the first time truly feels compassion for the pain of another human being. **Negro Digest** gave her the **Gwendolyn Brooks** Award for Fiction for "Marigolds" (1969). Her short stories have been collected in *Breeder and Other Stories* (1993). In addition, she adapted her short story "Ricky" to create the same-titled one-act play, produced by Kuumba Workshop at the Eugene Perkins Theatre in Chicago (1976).

Collier's other published works include *Steps Toward a Black Aesthetic: A Study of Black American Literary Criticism* (1976/1983), *The Four-Way Dilemma of Claude McKay (CAAS Occasional Paper)* (1971), and *Hurl (Broadside series)* (1974). Two sources (CAO-08 and //www.classzone.com/lol_demo/authors/09/9collier.htm) also list *Spread My Wings* (1992) as a book written by her (published by **Third World Press**), but the title is *not* listed in //www.amazon.com, in //worldcat.org, or in //www.thirdworldpressinc.com/search.php, so the title may refer to a short story or other writing included in an anthology or a periodical.

In addition, Collier has coedited several anthologies, including *Impressions in Asphalt: Images of Urban America* (1969, with Ruthe T. Sheffey), *A Bridge to Saying It Well* (1970, with Joel I. Glasser et al.), and the two-volume *Afro-American Writing: An Anthology of Prose and Poetry* (1972, with Richard A. Long; enlarged ed., 1985). Her short stories have appeared in *Brothers and Sisters* (1970, edited by Arnold Adoff), *Accent* (1972, edited by James B. Phillips, et al.), and *Oral and Written Composition: A Unit-Lesson Approach* (1972, edited by Albert Lavin, et al). Her nonfiction has appeared in anthologies such as **Langston Hughes**: *Black Genius* (1971, edited by Therman O'Daniel) and *Modern Black Poets: A Collection of Critical Essays* (1973, edited by Donald Gibson). She has also contributed stories, poems, essays, reviews, and articles to literary journals (e.g., *Phylon, College Language Association Journal*), popular magazines (e.g., **Black World**/*Negro Digest, TV Guide*), and newspapers (e.g., *The New York Times*).

For the small screen, she has participated in Morgan State University's televised lecture series *The Negro in History* and in a live videoconference discussing African-American literature and writers, *The Revival of Black Literature* (1996). She also taught literature and English to students at Morgan State College (now University, 1955-1966), Community College of Baltimore (1966-1974), University of Maryland (1974-1977), Howard University (1977-1987), Coppin State College (1987-1992), and came full circle to close her career at Morgan State University (1992-1996), where she retired from teaching. To earn a little extra cash, she was also a visiting professor for three summers in the early 1970s, and she offered numerous workshops. Decades earlier, she had graduated from Howard University magna cum laude (1948), had earned her master's degree from Columbia

University (1950), and earned her doctorate from the University of Maryland (1976). Even after her retirement, Collier continues to write stories and to visit classes to inspire creative writing.

REFERENCES: *CAO-01. Wiki.* //en.wikipedia.org/wiki/Marigolds_ (short_story). //worldcat.org/identities/lccn-n84-78276. //www.class zone.com/lol_demo/authors/09/9collier.htm. //www.newsreel.org/ guides/furious.htm. //www.thirdworldpressinc.com/search.php. //www.zimbio.com/Eugenia+Collier/articles/2/About+Eugenia+Colli er. //www.zimbio.com/Eugenia+Collier?overview=open. Amazon.com.

FURTHER READING: *EAAWW.* Carter, Linda M., in *GEAAL.*

Collins, Kathleen (née Conwell)
3/18/1942–9/?/1988
Plays, screenplays, novel; educator, filmmaker, director

Collins's screenplays have included *Losing Ground* (1982), *Madame Flor* (1987), and *Conversations with Julie* (1988) and have been aired on the Learning Channel and on the Public Broadcasting System. Her stage plays have included *In the Midnight Hour* (1981), *The Brothers* (1982), *The Reading* (1984), *Begin the Beguine* (1985), *Only the Sky Is Free* (1985), *While Older Men Speak* (1986), and *Looking for Jane* (198?). She finished writing her novel *Lollie: A Suburban Tale* the year she died.

REFERENCES: Carter, Steven R., in *COCAAL* and *OCAAL.* Keough, Leyla, in *EA-99.*

Colón, Jesús
1/20/1901–1974
Sketches, articles, columns

In 1923, Colón started writing for the Puerto Rican pro-labor paper *Justicia*, and soon after he was regularly writing columns for *Gráfico* and *The Daily Worker*. Many of his sketches and essays were collected in *Puerto Rican in New York and Other Sketches* (1961), awarded the American Book Award from the Before Columbus Foundation (1984, a decade after his death); and *The Way It Was and Other Writings: Historical Vignettes about the New York Puerto Rican Community* (1993, almost two decades after his death).

REFERENCES: *CAO-00. Wiki.* Vega-Merino, Alexandra, in *EA-99.*

Colored American Magazine, The
1900–1909
Literary journal

First published in 1900, the *Colored American Magazine* was the most widely distributed black journal before

1910. This monthly, edited for the first four years by **Pauline Hopkins**, featured articles of general interest to African Americans. The *Colored American Magazine* was important at the beginning of the century in encouraging and promoting the work of African-American writers. Hopkins's fiction and nonfiction also often appeared in the journal. Hopkins, who regarded herself as a race historian, pursued a politically risky agenda and sought to discredit **Booker T. Washington** as overly accommodating. She was fired in 1904 when Washington's ally, Fred Moore, purchased the magazine and moved its offices to New York. It ceased publication in 1909.

REFERENCES: Gruesser, John C., in *OCAAL*. —Lisa Bahlinger

Colter, Cyrus
1/8/1910–4/15/2002
Novels, short stories; attorney, civil servant

Cyrus Colter was an I.R.S. (Internal Revenue Service) tax collector (1940-1942), an attorney (1940-1942, 1946-1951), a U.S. Army captain (1942-1946), and Illinois's state Commerce Commissioner (1951-1973), before he published his first short story in 1960, at age 50. The story, "A Chance Meeting," was rejected by most of the popular magazines of that era and was finally published by *Threshold*, an Irish magazine. His next short story wasn't published until a year later, and between 1960 and 1976, Colter managed to have 24 of his short stories published in assorted literary journals and magazines.

The University of Iowa Press published his first collection, *The Beach Umbrella* (1970; 1996, TriQuarterly Books/Northwestern University Press), containing 14 stories. Soon after, his short story "The Beach Umbrella" won the 1971 Iowa School of Letters Award for Short Fiction, with Kurt Vonnegut among the jurors who chose it, as well as fiction awards from both the Chicago Friends of Literature and the Society of Midland Authors. Emboldened, Colter produced his first novel, *The Rivers of Eros* (1972, published by Swallow Press; 1991, University of Illinois Press). Next, he wrote his more experimental, disturbing, and provocative novel, *The Hippodrome* (1973/1994). The novel addresses fate and morality through the devoutly religious protagonist's guilt over murdering his wife and her lover, after which he evades the police by hiding in a brothel where he must perform sex acts to be viewed by others. The same year he published *Hippodrome*, Colter retired from civil service to become the Chester D. Tripp Professor of Humanities and Chair of the Department of African American Studies at Northwestern University in Evanston, Illinois

(1973-1978), the first African American in an endowed chair there.

After retiring from Northwestern, Colter traveled for a few months, then he culminated six years of work in publishing his third novel, *Night Studies* (1979, also by Swallow Press). This four-part narrative, which won the Friends of the Chicago Public Library's Carl Sandburg Literary Arts Award, probes the influences of African-American heritage on three contemporary African Americans: an African-American activist man, a wealthy African-American woman, and a young woman who has yet to recognize her African-American ancestry, due to her European-American appearance.

Nearly a decade later, at age 78, Colter published *A Chocolate Soldier* (1988), a complicated narrative that continues Colter's exploration of African-American history's effects on contemporary blacks. The story is unreliably narrated by an African-American theologian, in his relationship to and observation of the title's "Chocolate Soldier," as both men struggle with moral and psychological failings. In the same year *Chocolate Soldier* appeared, so did Colter's second short-story collection, *The Amoralists and Other Tales: Collected Stories* (1988). Colter's final novel, *City of Light* (1993), published when he was 83 years old, explores both the psychology of a man obsessed with his deceased mother and with his contentedly married mistress and the themes of class, race, and politics as the protagonist seeks to help Africans of the diaspora to settle in a new African homeland.

About his writing, Colter said, "What makes writing so intriguing for me is that it is a mission of self-discovery" (told to Susan Skramstad, quoted in *BB*). In his writings, his characters seem trapped in a deterministic world, striving to overcome feelings of isolation and meaninglessness. Colter's writings explored not only the distinctive struggles of racism but also the more universal challenges of being human. He told an interviewer, "When blacks solve their immediate problem, which is ridding the country of the denial of opportunity based on race ... then they will find themselves on the threshold of other monumental problems of the human condition" (told to John O'Brien, quoted in *BB*).

In addition to his books, Colter contributed short stories to periodicals (e.g., *Chicago Review, Northwest Review, Prairie Schooner*) and anthologies (e.g., *Soon One Morning: New Writing by American Negroes, 1940-1982* (1963). He also served on the editorial board of the *Chicago Reporter*. His works have been translated into at least four European languages and one Asian language. The University of Illinois awarded him an honorary doctorate (1977), and he was inducted into the Literary Hall of Fame for Writers of African Descent (1998).

REFERENCES: CAO-02. Houston, Helen R., in *AAFW-55-84*. Payne, James Robert, in *COCAAL*. Stamatel, Janet P., in *BB*. Amazon.com.

FURTHER READING: Raynor, Sharon D., in *GEAAL*.

Combahee River Collective (CRC)
1974–1980
Mutual-support organization for African-American feminist writers, especially including lesbian feminists

In 1973, when African-American lesbian feminist author **Barbara Smith** attended the first regional meeting of the National Black Feminist Organization (NBFO) in New York, she returned to Boston eager to start a chapter of NBFO there. While meeting with Demita Frazier, her twin sister Beverly Smith, and other prospective NBFO members, they realized that their own aims and visions for social change were more radical than those of the NBFO. Rather than found a Boston NBFO branch, they decided to form their own new, more militant organization, which would address the needs of African-American feminists, especially African-American lesbian feminists.

Barbara Smith then searched for a name to reflect their bolder mission. In a book on **Harriet Tubman**, she discovered that on June 1-2, 1863, Tubman had led a Union Army raid deep into the Port Royal region of South Carolina, along the Combahee River, where they freed more than 750 slaves. Smith suggested the name Combahee River Collective, telling the group that the Combahee River Raid had been the first military campaign in American history planned and led by a woman. The image of a woman leading others to freedom well suited their aims.

For the next few years, the members of the Combahee River Collective (CRC) met weekly at the Cambridge, Massachusetts Women's Center. The CRC took particular interest in the issue of violence against women, and several members helped found a shelter for battered women in an African-American community in Boston. When a dozen African-American women and one European-American were murdered in Boston in 1979, Barbara Smith wrote a pamphlet decrying the murders as racist and sexist crimes, signing it the "Combahee River Collective." Other CRC member activities included abortion-rights work, lesbian activism, and activities related to Third World Women's International Women's Day. Other activities considered by CRC members included workplace and labor organizing, rape-crisis work, and child-care concerns. The CRC also decided that in addition to consciousness-raising and activism, they would participate in a study group.

The best-known work of the CRC is its "Combahee River Collective Statement," drafted by Smith, Frazier, and Smith in April of 1977. In the CRC Statement, the authors asserted, "We are actively committed to struggling against racial, sexual, heterosexual and class oppression, and see as our particular task the development of integrated analysis and practice based upon the fact that the major systems of oppression are interlocking. The synthesis of these oppressions creates the conditions of our lives. As Black women we see Black feminism as the logical political movement to combat the manifold and simultaneous oppressions that all women of color face." They further asserted that "Black women are inherently valuable, that our liberation is a necessity . . . because of our need as human persons for autonomy." They pledged themselves to "working on those struggles in which race, sex, and class are simultaneous factors in oppression."

They acknowledged the little-known work of their historical foremothers, their own mothers, and their sisters, neglected by "outside reactionary forces and racism and elitism within the [feminist] movement." They further challenged European-American feminists to work harder to eliminate racism and to include all women in the battle against sexism, and they urged African-American leftists to oppose sexism and to include women in their battle against racism.

The CRC Statement also introduced the term "identity politics": "Focusing upon our own oppression is embodied in the concept of identity politics. We believe that the most profound and potentially most radical politics come directly out of our own identity, as opposed to working to end somebody else's oppression. . . . We believe that sexual politics under patriarchy is as pervasive in Black women's lives as are the politics of class and race. We also often find it difficult to separate race from class from sex oppression because in our lives they are most often experienced simultaneously" (quoted in //circuitous.org/scraps/combahee.html).

They also concluded that "the liberation of all oppressed peoples necessitates the destruction of the political-economic systems of capitalism and imperialism as well as patriarchy. We are socialists because we believe that work must be organized for the collective benefit of those who do the work and create the products, and not for the profit of the bosses. Material resources must be equally distributed among those who create these resources" (quoted in //circuitous.org/scraps/combahee.html). They further determined that a socialist revolution would not liberate African-American women if it were not also a feminist and antiracist revolution.

Following the drafting of the CRC Statement, in July of 1977, the CRC held a retreat for African-American women feminists in South Hadley, Massachusetts. In an interview with Duchess Harris, Barbara Smith later recalled, "Twenty Black feminists . . . were invited [and] were asked to bring copies of any written materials relevant to Black feminism—articles, pamphlets, papers, their own creative work—to share with the group. Frazier, Smith, and Smith, who organized the retreats, hoped that they would foster political stimulation and spiritual rejuvenation" (quoted in //en.wikipedia.org/wiki/Combahee_ River_Collective). That year, Barbara Smith also published her landmark *Toward a Black Feminist Criticism* (1977).

In November that year, the group held its second retreat in Franklin Township, New Jersey, followed by a third and fourth in March and July of 1978. At these retreats, participants were encouraged to publish their views on African-American feminism. Barbara Smith and Lorraine Bethel were coeditors of *Conditions* magazine, which was already planning an issue on Third World women, so Smith suggested that retreat participants write articles for this issue of *Conditions*. A fifth retreat, held the following July of 1979, suggested participants contribute articles on lesbian "herstory" to the journals *Heresies* and *Frontiers*. At the sixth retreat, participants discussed publications again, including a September 1979 *Essence* article by CRC member Chirlane McCray, "I am a Lesbian." A few months later, the seventh and final retreat was held in Washington, D.C., in February of 1980.

In addition to Smith, Smith, Frazier, and McCray, CRC members and retreat participants included Cassie Alfonso, Cheryl Clarke, **Gloria Akasha Hull**, **Audre Lorde**, Margo Okazawa Rey, and Sharon Page Ritchie, among others. Though the CRC disbanded in 1980, many of its participants went on to collaborate on other key African-American feminist projects, publications (e.g., **Barbara Smith**, **Gloria T. Hull**, and Patricia Bell Scott's *All the Women Are White, All the Blacks Are Men, But Some of Us Are Brave: Black Women's Studies*, 1981), and activities. Inspired and encouraged by **Audre Lorde**, **Barbara Smith** also went on to cofound **Kitchen Table: Women of Color Press**, which published many pamphlets and books by CRC members and other feminists of non-European-American heritage.

REFERENCES: Barnes, Sharon L., "feminism/black feminism," in *GEAAL*. Norman, Brian J., "Combahee River Collective," in *GEAAL*. //circuitous.org/scraps/combahee.html. //en.wikipedia.org/wiki/Barbara_Smith. //en.wikipedia.org/wiki/Beverly_Smith. //en.wikipedia.org/wiki/Black_feminism. //en.wikipedia.org/wiki/Combahee_River_Collective, //en.wikipedia.org/wiki/Combahee_River_Collective_Statement. //en.wikipedia.org/wiki/Raid_at_Combahee_Ferry. //www.lesbianpoetryarchive.org/book/export/html/27. //www.wifp.org/womenofcolorhistoric.html.

Cone, James H. (Hal or Hall)
8/5/1938–

Nonfiction—theology and other faith-inspired writings, autobiography/memoir; educator, pastor, activist

A cleric in the African Methodist Episcopal Church, Cone has taught religion and philosophy since 1964 at a few institutions, including the Union Theological Seminary, where he has taught since 1969, and as the Charles A. Briggs Distinguished Professor of Systematic Theology, since 1977. He has also been a visiting professor and a lecturer at more than 1,000 colleges, universities, churches, and other institutions. He created a new field of study with his *Black Theology and Black Power* (1969), integrating the emerging Black Power Movement and African-American religious traditions. In addition to critical and popular recognition in the United States, the book has been translated into German, French, Spanish, and Japanese.

Next, as Latin Americans were exploring Liberation Theology, Cone introduced *A Black Theology of Liberation* (1970; 2nd ed. 1986; 20th anniversary ed., 1990), also translated into *Teológia Negra: Teológia de la Liberación* (1974, by world-renowned educator Paulo Freire, with Eduardo I. Bodipo-Malumba and Hugo Assmann). Continuing his exploration of theology within a wider context, he wrote *The Spirituals and the Blues: An Interpretation* (1972/1991), *The God of the Oppressed* (1975; rev. ed. 1997), *The Social Context of Black Theology* (1977), *Black Theology Perspectives* (Documentation series—*Theology in the Americas*) (1978), *The Black Church and Marxism: What Do They Have to Say to Each Other* (1980), *The Theology of* **Martin Luther King, Jr.** (1985), *For My People: Black Theology and the Black Church* (The Bishop **Henry McNeal Turner** Studies in North American Black Religion, Vol. 1) (1984), *Black Spirituals: A Theological Interpretation* (1989), *Speaking the Truth: Ecumenism, Liberation, and Black Theology* (1986/1999), *Martin & Malcolm & America: A Dream or a Nightmare?* (1991; 2002 translation, **Malcolm X** et Martin Luther King: Même Cause, Même Combat, by Serge Molla), and *Risks of Faith: The Emergence of a Black Theology of Liberation, 1968-1998* (1999).

Cone also wrote his historical memoir, *My Soul Looks Back* (1982). Nearly as important as his writings is his two-volume anthology *Black Theology: A Documentary History, 1966-1979* (1979, with Gayraud S. Wilmore) and *Black Theology: A Documentary History. Vol. 2: 1980-1992* (1993, with Gayraud S. Wilmore). Cone also collaborated with John Ford Noonan and Denise Janha to produce *Teaching Minority Students* (New Directions for Teaching and Learning) (1983), and he worked with Joseph L. White to produce *Black Man Emerging: Facing the Past and Seizing a Future in America* (1998). Cone has also contributed articles to the *Encyclopædia Britannica*, to such popular publications as *Ladies' Home Journal* and *Ebony,* and to anthologies such as C. Eric Lincoln's *Is Anybody Listening to Black America?* (1968). In addition, he is a contributing editor to *Christianity & Crisis, Review of Religious Research,* and *Journal of the Interdenominational Theological Center.*

Cone's love life has been less than fortuitous. His first marriage ended in divorce (1958-1977) after he and his former wife had two sons, Michael and Charles; and his second wife (1979-1983) predeceased him.

REFERENCES: *B. CAO-07. Wiki.* Burgess, Marjorie, in *BB.* Mirra, Carl, in *AANB.* Rapoport, Nessa. "The Struggles of James H. Cone (Afro-American Theologian, and Author of 'Martin and Malcolm and America: a Dream or a Nightmare')." *Publishers Weekly 238.9* (Feb. 15, 1991) p. 30. From *Literature Resource Center.* //en.wikipedia.org/wiki/Black_liberation_theology. //en.wikipedia.org/wiki/Black_theology. Amazon.com.

FURTHER READING: Miller, Robert H., in *GEAAL.*

Cooper, Anna Julia (née Haywood)
8/10/1858–2/27/1964
Essays, spoken word—addresses; educator

After earning her bachelor's and master's degrees from Oberlin College, Cooper started teaching at Wilberforce University. She often went against the accepted wisdom of the day, insisting on the value of a liberal-arts education, contrary to **Booker T. Washington**'s emphasis on vocational training. In pursuit of her own liberal-arts education, she earned her Ph.D. at age 67, in the Sorbonne of Paris, writing her dissertation on "The Attitude of France toward Slavery during the Revolution." She was the fourth African-American woman to garner the doctorate. Throughout her life, Cooper gave addresses and contributed essays, which we have inherited in her *A Voice from the South by a Black Woman of the South* (1892), often cited as the first book-length work of African-American feminism. Among other feminist writings in her book are her "The Higher Education of Women" and "The Status of Woman in America."

REFERENCES: *AAWW. BAAW.* Guy-Sheftall, Beverly (Ed.). 1995. *Words of Fire: An Anthology of African-American Feminist Thought,* New York: New Press. —Tonya Bolden

Cooper, J. (Joan) California
c. mid-1900s–
Short stories, novels, plays; performance artist

A prolific writer, Cooper has written numerous plays (at least 17 by the mid-1990s, including *Everytime It Rains; System, Suckers, and Success; How Now; The Unintended; The Mother; Ahhh; Strangers;* and *Loners*), many of which have been produced on live stage, on radio, and on public television, and some of which have been anthologized. Despite her success as a playwright, Cooper may be better known for her short stories, having published several short-story collections (*A Piece of Mine,* 1984, published by **Alice Walker**'s publishing company and including a foreword by Walker; *Homemade Love,* 1986, winner of a 1989 American Book Award; *Some Soul to Keep,* 1987; *The Matter Is Life,* 1991; *Some Love, Some Pain, Sometime,* 1995; her highly praised *The Future Has a Past,* 2000; and *Wild Stars Seeking Midnight Suns: Stories,* 2006).

She has also written five novels: *Family* (1991), her Civil War-era novel about a slave and her family; *In Search of Satisfaction* (1994), about the black daughter and the mulatto daughter (and granddaughter) of a former slave from Reconstruction through the 1920s; *The Wake of the Wind* (1998), a family saga that begins in Africa in the 1760s when two friends are captured, enslaved, and brought to America, where their descendants' lives intersect in the troublesome and confusing period during and immediately following the Civil War; *Some People, Some Other Place* (2004), a five-generation story of an African-American family, as told by the unborn child of the protagonist; and *Life Is Short But Wide* (2009), about two families making their way in an Oklahoma town. Alice Walker praised Cooper's work as "a delight to read," and Nikki Giovanni named Cooper "my favorite storyteller." In addition to awards for her individual works, in 1988, Cooper was named a Literary Lion by the American Library Association and garnered the **James Baldwin** Writing Award.

In many of her works, Cooper shows the ways in which women offer one another support through times of abuse, neglect, economic difficulties, and other struggles. Despite the challenges they face, Cooper's characters show optimism, humor, and a strong spirit. They also tend to reinforce feminist family values and Cooper's firm belief that true happiness comes from within, often as a result of helping others. Some critics suggest that she tends toward preachiness, but others praise her clear moral stands. In her narratives, Cooper uses authentic vernacular dialogue and first-person accounts, offering one woman's insights into her own life crises or into the experiences of those whom she observes at close range. Readers frequently feel as though the narrator is speaking directly to them, using a folksy, chatty voice. Cooper's birthdate is nowhere to be found in available resources about her, and she closely guards her private life; it is known that from her first marriage, she has a daughter, Paris Williams, to whom she has dedicated her fiction.

REFERENCES: *EBLG. RP.* Golus, Carrie, in *BB. CAO-06.* Hickey, Kevin M., in *GEAAL.* King, Lovalerie, in *COCAAL* and *OCAAL.* Lawrence, Keith, *T-CAWW-2.* Yohe, Kristine A., in *OCWW. Wiki.* //www.mtsu.edu/~vvesper/afam.html. //www.nationalbookclub

conference.com/authors.aspx. //www.pageturner.net/gbc/previous.htm. Amazon.com, 7/1999, 2/2009.

Cornish, Sam (Samuel) (James)
12/22/1935–
Poems, essays, autobiography/memoir; bookseller, book publisher, self-publisher, editor, educator

After gaining a street education as a youth and serving in the U.S. Army Medical Corps (1958-1960), Sam Cornish needed to find ways to support his writing habit. He got jobs as a writing specialist at Baltimore's Enoch Pratt Free Library (1965-1966, 1968-1969); as a bookseller in the Fiction, Literature & Arts Bookstore in Brookline, Massachusetts (1966-1967); as an elementary-school editorial consultant for the Central Atlantic Regional Educational Laboratories (CAREL) (1967-1968); as a schoolteacher for Highland Park Free School in Roxbury, Massachusetts (1969-c. 1973); and as a staff adviser and children's writing consultant for the Education Development Center's Open Education Follow Through Project in Newton, Massachusetts (1973- 1978). Meanwhile, he managed to squeeze in some experience teaching at Baltimore's Edmondson High School and at Coppin State College. In 1968, Coppin State's Humanities Institute awarded him its Poetry Prize for his "influence on the Coppin poets," and the National Endowment for the Arts awarded him a grant. The spirited, peripatetic logophile also found time to be the literature director for the Massachusetts Council on the Arts and Humanities, and he coedited two literary magazines. For poetry aficionados, he and his wife, Jean Faxon, edited *Mimeo: Magazine of Poetry* (c. 1968-1969; Vol. 2 published in 1969). For children and young adults, he coedited *Chicory* (c. 1966-1969, with Lucian W. Dixon), while he worked for the Enoch Pratt Free Library. Cornish and Dixon also chose pieces from the magazine to create *Chicory: Young Voices from the Black Ghetto* (1969, edited with Lucian W. Dixon). The same year, he edited *The Living Underground: An Anthology of Contemporary American Poetry* (1969, edited with Hugh Fox).

In his moments of spare time, Cornish wrote his own poems. He was fortunate to find publishers for his first two poetry collections, *In This Corner: Sam Cornish and Verses* (1961/1964) and *People Beneath the Window* (1962/1987). While immersed in the literary underground at the Enoch Pratt Free Library, he decided to publish his own 16-page *Generations and Other Poems* (1964), edited and republished simply as *Generations* in 1966. He gained wider recognition when the anthologies *Black Fire* (1968, edited by LeRoi Jones [**Amiri Baraka**] and **Larry Neal**) and *New Black Poetry* (1969, edited by **Clarence Major**) included some of his poems. Numerous

other anthologers have continued to include his poems, as well.

Cornish found publishers for *Angles* (1965/1969), for *Winters* (1968, a limited-edition chapbook), and for *Short Beers* (1969), as well as for *A Reason for Intrusion: An Omnibus of Musings from the Files of Sam Cornish* (1969/1987). In 1971, Beacon Press published an enlarged edition of *Generations*. He also found another publisher for *Sometimes: Ten Poems* (1973), and **Third World Press** published *Streets* (1973).

Meanwhile, inspired by his experiences teaching poetry to children, he wrote *Your Hand in Mine* (1970), followed by two other poetry books for children: *Grandmother's Pictures* (1974) and *My Daddy's People Were Very Black* (1976, published by the Educational Development Center). Other Educational Development Center publications of his include *Cape Cod* (1974), *I Carry Words In* (1975), *Mary McLeod Bethune: 1875-1955* (1975), *Elizabeth Cotton* (1976), *William Grant Still* (1976), *Harriet* (1978), and *The First Black Man in Virginia* (1978). The Fiction, Literature & Arts Bookstore also published several Cornish books, including *My Father* (1979), *When My Grandmother Died* (1979), *The New Short Story: The Corner of the Landscape* (1981), and *The Harlem Renaissance: An Essay* (1981). Simon & Schuster published his juvenile book *Walking the Streets with Mississippi John Hurt* (1978), and Unicorn Press published his **Frederick Douglass** (1986). He also edited the anthology *Morgan School: Writing by Students* (1976).

In the late 1970s, Cornish started teaching in the Afro-American Studies Department of Emerson College in Boston, where he continued to teach until his retirement in 2004. While at Emerson, Cornish found publishers for *Sam's World: Poems* (1978), *Songs of Jubilee: New and Selected Poems, 1969-1983* (1986), *Folks Like Me* (1993), *Cross a Parted Sea: Poems* (1996), and *An Apron Full of Beans (Notable Voices)* (2008). Cornish has also written an autobiographical narrative blending poetry and prose, *1935: A Memoir* (1990), which is to be followed by its sequel, *1955*. He is said to be working on a critical study of **Langston Hughes**, as well.

Sam Cornish is credited with two other books in //www.amazon.com: *Forecast* (1968), published by Artists Against Racism & the War, and *The River* (1969), printed by William Ferguson for the Temple Bar Bookshop. He also regularly writes book reviews for popular periodicals such as *The Christian Science Monitor* and *Essence*, and he contributes poems and criticism to literary journals such as *Ann Arbor Review*, *Journal of Black Poetry*, and *Poetry Review*. In January of 2008, Cornish was appointed the first Poet Laureate of Boston.

REFERENCES: CAO-03. LF-07. Doreski, C. K., in COCAAL. Manheim, James M., in BB. Woodson, Jon, in AAP-55-85. Amazon.com.

FURTHER READING: Burris, Theresa L., in *GEAAL*.

Cornish, Samuel E.
?/1795–?/1858
Journalist, newspaper publisher; abolitionist, civil-rights activist, minister

In 1822, Samuel Cornish was ordained as an evangelist by the New York Presbytery and spent the next quarter of a century as a minister in various Presbyterian churches. In March of 1827, he and **John Brown Russwurm** made history when they printed the first edition of *Freedom's Journal*, the first African-American weekly newspaper, which the pair had cofounded. The paper's motto was "We Wish to Plead Our Own Cause"—the cause being abolition in the South and civil rights in the North. As part of pleading their own cause, the founders hired African Americans to print and run the paper. Cornish also strongly opposed the policies of the American Colonization Society, which urged freed (or fugitive) slaves to emigrate to Africa, to establish a colony of free African Americans in Liberia.

By the fall of 1827, Cornish felt that his duties as coeditor of the newspaper were taking him away from his ministry, so he resigned as coeditor, leaving the paper in Russwurm's hands. Much to Cornish's chagrin, Russwurm shifted the editorial policy of the paper away from fighting for abolition and civil justice in this country and toward emigration and resettlement (colonization) in Liberia. By the time of the paper's two-year anniversary, Russwurm had despaired of achieving any reforms in the United States and joined the American Colonization Society, embracing its aims. He turned the newspaper back to Cornish's control and moved to Liberia. Russwurm's editorial policies had damaged the paper's credibility as an advocate of abolition and social justice for African Americans in the United States, and even though Cornish renamed the paper the *Rights of All*, he was unable to revive it, and on October 29, 1829, he folded up shop.

In January 1837, Cornish started editing the *Weekly Advocate*, which changed its name to the *Colored American* (cf. **Colored American Magazine**) in March of that year. Cornish continued editing the periodical until April of the following year. In 1840, with Theodore S. Wright, he made clear his opposition to the American Colonization Society in *The Colonization Scheme Considered, in Its Rejection by the Coloured People—in Its Tendency to Uphold Caste—in Its Unfitness for Christianizing and Civilizing the Aborigines of Africa and for Putting a Stop to the African Slave Trade.*

Cornish's work as a journalist and a minister was not his only social and political involvement. He also worked with the American Anti-Slavery Society, the African Free Schools, and the American Missionary Society, working with others to oppose slavery, promote abolition, and evangelize his Christian beliefs. Perhaps he worked so hard to help others, in part, to divert himself from his personal troubles: his son William's emigration to Liberia, his wife Jane Livingston's death (1844), his daughter Sarah's death (1846), and his daughter Jane's mental collapse (1851). Only one of his four children outlived him, but his legacy as a crusader lives on.

REFERENCES: Button, Marilyn D., in *OCAAL*. Gardner, Eric, in *GEAAL*. Hodges, Graham Russell, in *AANB*.

Corrothers, James D. (David)
7/2/1869–2/12/1917
Poems, sketches, autobiography/memoir; journalist, minister

Though never as well known as **Charles W. Chesnutt**, **W. E. B. Du Bois**, and **Paul Laurence Dunbar**, Corrothers was widely published and popular in his day. In addition to having his poems and sketches published in various periodicals, his sketches were collected and published as *The Black Cat Club* (1902), and his autobiography, *In Spite of Handicap* (1916), was also published. Some sources suggest that he may also have published two other poetry volumes and perhaps even worked for a time as a columnist, but evidence for these has not yet surfaced. Raised chiefly by his deeply religious and fiercely honest Scotch-Irish and Cherokee paternal grandfather, he lived and was schooled among mostly whites, though his writing reflected his self-identification as an African American. When racism thwarted his intended career as a journalist, and he tired of menial jobs, he turned to ministry to support himself and his wife, Fanny Clemens, and two children. Sadly, she and his youngest son predeceased him in the late 1890s, and he sent his remaining son, Willard, to live with her family for a time. A second marriage ended in divorce, but in 1906, he married teacher Rosina Harvey, with whom he had a third son, Henry, and raised his eldest son, Willard.

REFERENCES: *NYPL-AADR*. Bruce, Dickson D., Jr., in *COCAAL* and *OCAAL*. Fischer, William C., in *AANB*. Williamson, Alicia D., in *GEAAL*. *LFCC-07*. Withem, Karen, in *CAO-03*. Yarborough, Richard, in *AAWBHR*.

Cortez, Jayne
5/10/1936–
Poems; performance artist, book and recordings publisher

Born on her father's army base at Fort Huachuca, Arizona, Jayne Cortez grew up in Watts, then an African-American ghetto of Los Angeles. Cortez grew up in a family of *bibliophiles* (book lovers), and from an early age, she was reading children's books and Bible stories. Soon, she was keeping notebooks full of new words she found in dictionaries, encyclopedias, and other reference books, and writing down the stories her family members enjoyed telling. Her literary interests expanded to include newspapers and the writings of African-American poets (e.g., **Langston Hughes** and **Sterling Brown**), as well.

Cortez also grew up listening to music, especially her family's huge collection of jazz and blues albums, as well as the songs her mother sang to her. By the time she reached her teens, she was taking piano lessons; she had learned to play the bass and the cello; and she was studying music harmony and theory. Often, while listening to local musicians at their jam sessions, she wrote and drew, inspired by the rhythms she was hearing. In 1951, she met avant-garde saxophonist Ornette Coleman; in 1954, she married him; in 1956, she and he had their son Denardo; and in 1960, the couple divorced. After her divorce, Cortez returned to writing poetry and started studying drama. Fifteen years later (1975), she married her second husband, artist Melvin Edwards, whose drawings are sometimes included in Cortez's books.

In the early 1960s, she worked with the Student Nonviolent Coordinating Committee (SNCC) to register African-American voters in Mississippi (the summers of 1963 and 1964). Back in Los Angeles, Cortez cofounded the Watts Repertory Theater and served as its artistic director, starting in 1964. By 1972, Cortez and her son had moved to New York, where she founded Bola Press. (*Bola* means "successful" in Yoruba.) Through Bola Press, she published not only her poetry collections, but also sound recordings of performances of her pieces, such as *Celebrations and Solitudes* (1975). From 1977 until 1983, she worked as writer-in-residence at Livingston College of Rutgers University in New Jersey. She has also lectured at Dartmouth College, Howard University, Queens College, and Wesleyan University, and she also travels extensively to perform her pieces and give readings across the country and around the world. She was named the M. Thelma McAndless Distinguished Professor in Humanities at Eastern Michigan University in 2003.

Cortez's poetic themes reflect her political concerns for justice and civil rights, and her opposition to racial prejudice and political oppression. Her poetic forms reflect her lifelong enchantment with music, particularly jazz and blues. In fact, music is often the theme of her poems (e.g., her often-quoted "How Long Has Trane Been Gone," an elegy to jazz saxophonist and composer John Coltrane). Although Cortez may be considered a performance poet—her works are most effective when heard as spoken aloud—her poems also visually dance across the page in printed form, and they have been widely anthologized and translated into multiple languages.

In Cortez's first collection of poetry, *Pisstained Stairs and the Monkey Man's Wares* (1969), she used her poetic artistry to celebrate the aesthetic expressions of African-American jazz musicians, thus firmly establishing herself as a poet of the **Black Arts Movement**. Renowned poet **Nikki Giovanni** noted, "We haven't had many jazz poets who got inside the music and the people who created it. We poet about them, but not of them. And this is Cortez's strength. . . . She's a genius." (p. 97, *Negro Digest*, Dec. 1969).

Cortez's second collection, *Festivals and Funerals* (1971), affirmed her appreciation of African-American culture, traditions, and language patterns. Starting with her third collection, *Scarifications* (1973), Cortez self-published most of her works through her Bola Press. As rap and hip-hop emerged at the end of the twentieth century, Cortez experimented and expressed her poetry with these forms, too. Her other collections include *Mouth on Paper* (1977), *Firespitter* (1982), *Coagulations: New and Selected Poems* (1984), *Poet Magnetic* (1991), *Somewhere in Advance of Nowhere* (1996), and *A Jazz Fan Looks Back* (2002).

In addition, Cortez has produced various recordings of her poetic readings accompanied by music. The music is performed by her jazz group, the Firespitters, which includes her son, Denardo Coleman, on the drums; on at least one of her albums (*Maintain Control*), her former husband Ornette Coleman played the sax. Her recordings include *Celebrations and Solitudes* (1975), *Unsubmissive Blues* (1980), *There It Is* (1982), *Maintain Control* (1986), *Everywhere Drums* (1990), *Mandela is Coming* (1991), *Taking the Blues Back Home: Poetry & Music* (1996), and *Borders of Disorderly Time* (2003). She and the Firespitters have also released a videotape of their performance. In addition to her published works (which have been translated into 28 languages), Cortez has performed her work in Africa, North and South America, and Europe, including her performance at the Berlin Jazz Festival and her "War against War" performance piece for UNESCO in Paris.

Cortez's achievements have earned her a Rockefeller Foundation grant (1970), two National Endowment for the Arts fellowships (1979-1980, 1986), a Before Columbus Foundation American Book Award for excellence in literature (1980), the New York Foundation for the Arts award for poetry (1987), and a Langston Hughes Medal from the City College of New York (2001).

REFERENCES: *AANB. EBLG. OC20LE. WDAA.* Black-Parker, Kimberly, in *GEAAL.* Melham, D. H. "A Melus Profile and Interview: Jayne Cortez." *MELUS. 21.1* (Spring 1996) p. 71. From *Literature Resource Center.* Minderovic, Christine Miner, in *BB. CAO-04. MWEL.* Wilkinson, Michelle J., in *COCAAL* and *OCAAL.* Woodson, Jon, in *A. AAP-55-85. EA-99. OCWW. Wiki.*

Cosby, Jr., Bill (William Henry)
7/12/1937–
Humor, spoken word—speeches; comedian, actor, TV host

As a high-school student, Bill was asked to join a class for gifted students, but family and work responsibilities led him to repeat the tenth grade and eventually to drop out of school. In 1956, Bill joined the U.S. Navy, where he earned his high-school equivalency and won awards for his athletic performance on the track. After his four-year stint in the Navy ended, he enrolled in Temple University, on an athletic scholarship, and majored in physical education.

While still in college, Cosby also worked as a bartender, continuing to develop the sense of humor that had helped him through difficult times in his early life. Occasionally, when the regular stand-up comedian didn't show, Cosby was asked to fill in. The money for that job was much better than what he earned as a bartender, so he started to seek other stand-up comedy jobs elsewhere. His exquisite timing, warm and friendly manner, and relaxed style of communicating made him appealing to audiences. By 1962, Cosby decided that he could earn pretty good money doing stand-up, so he left Temple in his sophomore year and worked in clubs in New York City, Chicago, and elsewhere. At first, he borrowed heavily from other successful comedians, but pretty soon, he was writing all his own material. In 1963, he recorded the first of about 30 comedy albums, which have cumulatively sold millions of copies.

After gaining national attention on Johnny Carson's *Tonight Show* and other venues, in 1965, Cosby landed a contract to star in *I Spy* (costarring Robert Culp), which aired until 1968. Through this role, Cosby became the first African American to star in a dramatic role on network television, and he earned a few Emmys in the process. *I Spy* was followed by other television series: several *Bill Cosby Specials* (1968-1971, 1975), his sitcom the *Bill Cosby Show* (1969-1971), regular appearances on the educational *Electric Company* (1971-1976), hosting his children's cartoon *Fat Albert and the Cosby Kids* (1972-1984; later called *The New Fat Albert Show*), his variety show *New Bill Cosby Show* (1972-1973), *Cos* (1976), his sitcom *The Cosby Show* (1984-1992), the game show *You Bet Your Life* (1992-1993), his detective show *The Cosby Mysteries* (1994), his People's Choice Award-winning sitcom *Cosby* (1996-2000), and the children's talk show *Kids Say the Darndest Things* (1997-2000). In addition, Cosby has appeared in numerous films and television commercials. For his television work, he has earned four Emmys, as well as a Lifetime Achievement Emmy (2003); two Golden Globe Awards; four People's Choice Awards, as well as an award for "Favorite All-Time Television Star" (1999); induction into the Academy of Television Arts and Sci-

ences Hall of Fame (1994); an NAACP Image Award (1976); Harvard's Hasty Pudding Theatricals "Man of the Year" award (1969); and numerous other awards.

Cosby's books include several books for adults: *Bill Cosby's Personal Guide to Power Tennis; or Don't Lower the Lob, Raise the Net* (1975/1986), his best-selling *Fatherhood* (1986, named the all-time best-selling nonfiction book by an African American [in *AABL*], selling more than 2 1/2 million hardcover copies), *Time Flies* (1987, about aging), *Love and Marriage* (1989), *Childhood* (1991, a memoir), *Kids Say the Darndest Things* (1998), *Congratulations! Now What?: A Book for Graduates* (1999), *Cosbyology: Essays and Observations from the Doctor of Comedy* (2001), *I Am What I Ate ... and I'm Frightened!!!* (2003), *Friends of a Feather* (2003, illustrated by Erika Cosby), and *Come On People: On the Path from Victims to Victors* (2007, with Alvin F. Poussaint, M.D.). Cosby also recorded numerous albums, audiocassettes, and audio CDs, including *Bill Cosby Is a Very Funny Fellow, Right!* (1963/1988), *I Started Out as a Child* (1964/1980), *Why Is There Air* (1965/1998), *Wonderfulness* (1966/1998), *200 mph* (1968/1980), *To Russell, My Brother, Whom I Slept with* (1968/1998), *The Wit and Wisdom of Fat Albert* (1973), *Bill Cosby at His Best* (1993), and *The Bill Cosby Collection* (2004). He has won eight Grammys for his albums.

While still a stand-up comedian, in 1963, Cosby met Camille Hanks (born in 1945), through mutual friends; despite the objections of her family, she left college and wedded Bill on January 25, 1964. Camille's parents foresaw that she would follow him as he rambled around the country doing stand-up routines in clubs, which Guy and Catherine Hanks considered less than a promising lifestyle for their daughter. Since then, the Cosbys had five children: Erika Ranee, Errin Chalene, Ensa Camille, Evin Harrah, and their third child and only son, Ennis William, who was tragically murdered January 16, 1997.

In response to this tragedy, Cosby created his charitable Hello Friend/Ennis William Cosby Foundation, for the early detection and treatment of dyslexia. Like two of his siblings, Ennis had struggled to overcome his own dyslexia. Before he died, he had been working on a Ph.D. in special education at Columbia University, was tutoring dyslexic youngsters, and planned to found his own school for children with learning difficulties. In an interview, Bill Cosby recalled that Ennis had wanted to write stories "about children with learning differences. Of course with his murder, this cut everything short. So I dedicated all of this to him" (*CBS Morning*, quoted in *Black Biography*). Since then, Cosby has published numerous "Little Bill Books for Beginning Readers" for elementary-school children (ages 7-10), including *The Best Way to Play* (1997), *The Meanest Thing to Say* (1997), *The Treasure Hunt* (1997), *Money Troubles* (1998), *One Dark and Scary Night* (1998), *Shipwreck Saturday* (1998), *Super-Fine Valentine*

(1998), *The Day I Was Rich* (1999), *Hooray for the Dandelion Warriors* (1999), *My Big Lie* (1999), and *The Day I Saw My Father Cry* (2000). As you might expect from the creator of Cliff Huxtable, these books humorously accept children's foibles while encouraging them to show pro-social behavior. As a further outreach, Cosby's program for preschoolers, *Little Bill*, debuted on Nickelodeon in 1999.

Within days of Ennis's murder, a young woman attempted to extort millions from Cosby, claiming that she was his daughter through an extramarital relationship. Though Cosby acknowledged an affair with the woman's mother, he denied paternity. The woman was tried and convicted of extortion. The conviction was later overturned but then was restored in 1999. While Cosby's myriad fans were struggling to reconcile this situation with Cosby's image as a loyal husband and devoted father, Cosby stirred further controversy. In 2004, on the fiftieth anniversary of the *Brown v. Board of Education* decision, Cosby made a provocative speech challenging African-American parents, especially fathers, to focus on educating their children and teaching their children strong moral values, instead of emphasizing sports, fashion, and acting tough. Michael Eric Dyson and numerous others have criticized his comments as a perceived unwarranted attack on economically disadvantaged African Americans, especially single parents. Still further travails arrived in 2006, when allegations of sexual assault surfaced against Cosby, but no complainants filed criminal charges, and the matter disappeared from the media.

In accord with his strong belief in the value of education, Cosby managed to return to college, earning his master's degree (1972) and his doctorate in education (1977) from the University of Massachusetts (UMass) at Amherst. Among the many honors he has received for his many achievements and contributions, he was awarded the NAACP's prestigious Spingarn Medal (1985); he has been named a Kennedy Center Honoree (1998); he has been given the Presidential Medal of Freedom (2002) and the Bob Hope Humanitarian Award (2003); and he has received honorary doctorates from Yale (2003), Carnegie Mellon (2007), and other universities, as well as an honorary degree from the Sisseton Wahpeton College on the Lake Traverse Reservation.

Bill's wife Camille had also dropped out of college to support her husband's career. She later earned her baccalaureate and master's degrees (1980, in education), and in 1989, she was awarded an honorary doctorate from Spelman College. In 1992, Camille earned her doctorate from UMass. Since Bill's early successes, she has been her husband's business manager, overseeing both his financial affairs (an estimated $300 million) and his philanthropic concerns. Together, the Cosbys have given millions to colleges (about $70 million by 1994, including $1.3 million to Fisk in 1986; $1.3 million to be shared among Central State at Wilberforce [Ohio], Howard University, Florida A&M State University, and Shaw University; $1.5 million to be shared between Meharry and Bethune-Cookman Colleges; and $20 million to Spelman; among others). Camille also co-owns her own documentary film production company. In addition, her own books include *Our Family Table: Recipes and Food Memories From African-American Life Models* (1993) and *Television's Imageable Influences: The Self-Perceptions of Young African-Americans* (1994). With her husband Bill and coauthor **David C. Driskell**, she wrote *The Other Side of Color: African American Art in the Collection of Camille O. and William H. Crosby, Jr.* (2001, with biographies written by Rene Hanks). She also coedited, with Howard Bingham, *A Wealth of Wisdom: Legendary African American Elders Speak* (2004).

REFERENCES: *AABL. EBLG. PGAA.* Bennett, Eric in *EA-99.* Brennan, Carol, "Camille Cosby," in *BB* and *CAO-07.* McCluskey, Malik. "An essay on the dispute between Bill Cosby & Michael Eric Dyson." *Black Renaissance/Renaissance Noire.* 6.3 (Spring-Summer 2006) p. 122. From *Literature Resource Center.* "William Henry Cosby," in *CAO-04.* //en.wikiquote.org/wiki/Bill_Cosby. *EB-BH-CD.* Smith, Jessie Carney, in *A. Act. B. BCE. BH2C. D. F. FAD. QB. W2B. Wiki.* Wankoff, Jordan, and David G. Oblender, "Bill Cosby," in *BB.*

Cose, Ellis (Jonathan)
2/20/1951–

Essays, novels, nonfiction—energy issues, equity issues, issues of race, gender, and class; journalist

When Ellis Cose was a senior in high school, his English teacher paved the way for him to be invited to join a writers group hosted by Illinois poet laureate **Gwendolyn Brooks**. Cose later recalled, "I joined for a while and in my typical rebelliousness didn't stay very long . . . . I'm 17 in with these guys in their 30s and 40s, a bunch of old farts" (quoted in Nixon, *Publishers Weekly,* 1992). Still a student, he wrote a novel, which was accepted by a publisher that went bankrupt before publishing it, and young Cose turned to writing nonfiction. At the University of Illinois at Chicago Circle, a scholarship student, Cose started writing commentaries for the student newspaper (1968). On the basis of these commentaries, he got a job writing columns and reporting for the *Chicago Sun-Times* (1970-1977), initially for the school edition and later for the regular edition, as well. Still a teenager, he became the youngest columnist in Chicago's newspaper history. After graduating (1972), Cose continued at the *Sun-Times,* becoming a national correspondent (e.g., covering Governor Jimmy Carter's unlikely 1976 campaign for the U.S. presidency) and an editor.

In 1977, Cose shifted gears to study for his master's degree (1978, George Washington University) and to become a senior research fellow and director of energy policy studies for the Joint Center for Political Studies in Washington, D.C. (1977-1979). For a time (1978-1979), he also served on the environmental advisory committee of the U.S. Department of Energy. Cose wrote his first book, *Energy and the Urban Crisis* (1978), published by the Center, while there. In it, he probed the effects of energy policy on the country's least advantaged citizens. The following year, the Iranian Revolution against a brutal dictator precipitated an energy crisis, during which President Jimmy Carter installed solar panels on the White House (which were later removed by President Ronald Reagan), and gas rationing and other energy-saving measures were considered. That year, he also edited *Energy and Equity: Some Social Concerns*, also published by the Center, and he returned to journalism, working as an editorial writer and columnist for the *Detroit Free Press* (1979-1981). He later left the *Free Press* to become a resident fellow at the National Academy of Sciences and the National Research Council (1981-1982).

Cose returned to journalism as a special reporter for *USA Today* (1982-1983), writing on labor policy and issues. He also wrote his second book on energy policy, *Decentralizing Energy Decisions: The Rebirth of Community Power* (1983). The academy then beckoned him again, luring him to the University of California at Berkeley, where he presided over and was chief executive officer of the Institute for Journalism Education (1983-1986). While at the Institute, Cose designed and directed a study, *The Quiet Crisis: Minority Journalists and Newsroom Opportunity*, published by the Institute. In 1987, he was offered a fellowship at Columbia University's prestigious Gannett Center for Media Studies. While there, he wrote a pamphlet titled *Minorities Research: Minority Journalists and Newsroom Opportunity* (1987).

In 1988, he returned to journalism, as a contributor and press critic for *Time* (1988-1990), and he researched and wrote *The Press: Inside America's Most Powerful Newspaper Empires—From the Newsrooms to the Boardrooms* (1989). He interviewed Katharine Graham of the *Washington Post*, Al Neuharth, the chief of Gannett (the chain that owns *U.S.A. Today*), and some other major figures in the newspaper business. Among other issues, his book addressed the changes emerging from the shift from family ownership to corporate ownership of newspapers, as well as the tensions arising between African-American reporters and their European-American editors. He then took on an editorial role himself, as an editorial page editor for *New York Daily News* (1991-1993). While there, he wrote *A Nation of Strangers: Prejudice, Politics, and the Populating of America* (1992), focusing on immigration issues and history, including interviews of native-born Americans and foreign residents of the United States; and his best-selling *The Rage of a Privileged Class: Why Do Prosperous Blacks Still Have the Blues?* (1993), lauded by **Arnold**

Rampersad in *The New York Times* book-review section. In 1993, Cose became a contributing editor for *Newsweek*, and in 1996, he started regularly contributing articles and essays to *USA Today*. He has also been interviewed on television in the United States, Britain, Canada, and Brazil.

Cose's subsequent books include *A Man's World: How Real Is Male Privilege—and How High Is Its Price?* (1995), which has been translated into Japanese and Korean; *Color-Blind: Seeing Beyond Race in a Race-Obsessed World* (1997); *The Envy of the World: On Being a Black Man in America* (2002), a bestseller; *Beyond Brown v. Board: The Final Battle for Excellence in American Education* (2004), published by the Rockefeller Foundation; and *A Bone to Pick: Of Forgiveness, Reconciliation, Reparation, and Revenge* (2004). Cose also edited the anthology *The Darden Dilemma: 12 Black Writers on Justice, Race, and Conflicting Loyalties* (1997). The next year, Cose published his first novel, *The Best Defense* (1998), a courtroom drama exploring issues of affirmative action, race, and gender.

In addition to garnering grants and fellowships from the Ford Foundation, the Andrew Mellon Foundation, the Rockefeller Foundation, and the Aspen Institute for Humanistic Studies, Cose has earned numerous honors, including the Newswriting award from the Illinois United Press International (1973), the Stick-o-Type Award from the Chicago Newspaper Guild (1975), the Lincoln University National Unity award for Best Political Reporting (1975, 1977), and the University of Missouri Honor Medal for Distinguished Service in Journalism (1997). He shared the National Association of Black Journalists Award with three colleagues for a *Newsweek* issue featuring "Black Like Who?" (1997), and in 2002, the New York Association of Black Journalists honored him with a Lifetime Achievement Award. Since then, he has won the National Association of Black Journalists' Best Magazine Feature Award (2003) and the New York Association of Black Journalists' award for best commentary and magazine feature (2003). In 2004, he became the first person to receive the now-annual Vision Award from the Maynard Institute for Journalism Education.

In 1992, lifelong bachelor Ellis Cose married Lee Llambelis.

REFERENCES: CAO-02. Fikes, Robert, Jr., in *AANB*. Martin, Jonathan, and Sara Pendergast, in *BB*. Nixon, Will. "Ellis Cose: Writing a History of Immigration, He Discovered a Deep Vein of Nativism in America's Past." *Publishers Weekly*. *239.15* (Mar. 23, 1992), p. 47. *Literature Resources from Gale*. //en.wikipedia.org/wiki/1979_energy_crisis. Amazon.com.

FURTHER READING: Huguely-Riggins, Piper G., in *GEAAL*.

Coston, Julia (née Ringwood)

fl. late 1800s

Magazines; publisher

In 1886, Julia Ringwood married minister and writer William Harry Coston and moved with him from Washington, D.C., to Cleveland, Ohio. In Ohio, in 1891, she started publishing the very first—ever—fashion magazine for African-American women, *Ringwood's Afro-American Journal of Fashion.* In 1893, she started up her second magazine, *Ringwood's Home Magazine,* another African-American women's first. Sadly, we know little else about Ringwood and nothing about either magazine after 1895.

REFERENCES: *BAAW.* —Tonya Bolden

Cotter, Jr., Joseph Seamon

1895–1919

Poems; journalist

The son of poet **Joseph Seamon Cotter, Sr.,** Cotter struck out on his own poetically. Although his father and their family friend **Paul Laurence Dunbar** wrote lyrical dialect poems, Cotter experimented with free verse, as well as traditional poetic forms (e.g., a 19-sonnet sequence "Out of the Shadows"). While still a college student, Cotter worked for the *Fisk Herald,* a monthly published by Fisk University's literary societies. In his second year at Fisk, he contracted tuberculosis, so he returned home, where he served as editor and writer for the Louisville *Leader* newspaper. Before tuberculosis took his life when he was just 23 years old, he wrote the poems in his collection *The Band of Gideon* (1918) and the poems later gathered in *Joseph Seamon Cotter, Jr.: Complete Poems* (1990, edited by James Robert Payne). In addition, his one-act play *On the Fields of France,* about the Great War being fought in Europe, was published in **Crisis** magazine.

REFERENCES: Gardner, Eric, in *GEAAL.* Payne, James Robert, in *AAWBHR. CAO-03. COCAAL,* and *OCAAL. LFCC-07.*

Cotter, Sr., Joseph Seamon

2/2/1861–3/14/1949

Poems, plays, short stories; educator

Fortunately, Joseph Cotter had learned to read at age 3 and lived with a mother who was a gifted poet, storyteller, and playwright, because by age 8, he had to leave school to earn money for his family. At age 22, he was able to return to school and quickly learned enough to begin teaching; his career as an educator (public-school teacher and administrator) lasted more than 50 years. Although Cotter is remembered best for his poetry, he also wrote several plays (e.g., his blank-verse four-act play *Caleb, the Degenerate,* 1901 or 1903), a short-story collection (*Negro Tales,* 1912), a pamphlet on his civic leadership, and a collection of miscellany (*Negroes and Others at Work and Play,* 1947). His eclectic poetry collections include *A Rhyming* (1895), *Links of Friendship* (1898), *A White Song and a Black One* (1909), *Collected Poems of Joseph S. Cotter, Sr.* (1938), and *Sequel to the "Pied Piper of Hamelin" and Other Poems* (1939). Among the poems that continue to receive scholarly attention are his "The Negro's Loyalty," on the loyalty of an African-American soldier during the Spanish American War, in the era of widespread lynchings in the American South; and his "Sequel to the 'Pied Piper of Hamelin,'" in response to Robert Browning's poem, "The Pied Piper." (**Note:** Robert Browning's mother was a dark-skinned Creole from St. Kitts in the Caribbean.) In 1894, Cotter and poet **Paul Laurence Dunbar** began a social and literary friendship, which prompted Cotter to experiment more with dialect poems. Tragically, Cotter's son, fellow poet **Joseph Seamon Cotter, Jr.,** predeceased him by 30 years.

REFERENCES: *AANB. EBLG.* Brooks, A. Russell, in *AAWBHR.* Gardner, Eric, in *GEAAL.* Metzger, Sheri Elaine, in *BB. CAO-03. LFCC-07.* Payne, James Robert, in *COCAAL* and *OCAAL.* Shockley, Ann Allen. "Joseph S. Cotter, Sr: Biographical Sketch of a Black Louisville Bard." *CLA Journal 18.3* (Mar. 1975): pp. 327-340. Rpt. in *Literature Resource Center.* Gale, Cengage Learning.

Craft, William

c. 1826–1900

Fugitive-slave narrative

After William Craft and his wife Ellen (1826-1891) daringly escaped from slavery, he chronicled their escape in *Running a Thousand Miles for Freedom* (1860).

REFERENCES: *AANB. NYPL-AADR.* Gardner, Eric, in *GEAAL.* Nelson, Dana D., in *B. COCAAL* and *OCAAL. W. Wiki.*

Crayton, Pearl

1930–

Poems, short stories; educator

Crayton's short stories and poems continue to be widely published in various journals and anthologies; for her work, she has been awarded the California Arts Council Poet in the Schools Fellowship (1987-1990), as well as several awards for her short stories. While continuing to write and to offer creative-writing workshops, she has raised five children as a single parent.

REFERENCES: *RP.* //www.word-hoard.com/AAA/crayton.html. Amazon.com.

Crews, Donald
8/30/1938–
Children's picture books

Crews and his wife, graphic artist Ann Jonas, had two daughters before he started his career illustrating and writing children's books. In addition to illustrating many children's picture books for other writers (e.g., *ABC Science Experiments*, 1970; *How Many Blue Birds Flew Away?: A Counting Book with a Difference*, 2005), Crews has written and vividly illustrated numerous books for young children, including *We Read: A to Z* (1967, an innovative alphabet book, named 1 of 50 "Books of the Year" by American Institute of Graphic Arts), *Ten Black Dots* (1970s; rev. ed., 1986), *Freight Train* (1978, Caldecott Honor, named "1 of the 100 books that shaped the twentieth century"), *Truck* (1980, Caldecott Honor), *Light* (1981), *Carousel* (1982/1987), *Harbor* (1982), *Parade* (1983), *School Bus* (1984), *Bicycle Race* (1985), *Flying* (1986/1989), *When the Box Is Full* (1993, offering Crews's take on the calendar), *Sail Away* (1995), *Night at the Fair* (1998), *Cloudy Day Sunny Day* (1999), *Chicken Coop* (2000), and his alternative view *Inside Freight Train* (2001). Many of Crews's books have since been published in board book format (e.g., *Truck*, *School Bus*), to make them more user-friendly for the youngest readers. His books also readily translate into other languages (e.g., *Ten Black Dots / Diez Puntos negros*, 1992; *Freight Train/Tren de carga*, 2003).

Most of Crews's books simply and boldly illustrate an aspect of the environment that appeals to young children. As he has observed, "Once I become fascinated with a subject, I'll do some freewheeling sketches. . . . thinking it through and exploring the visual possibilities. . . . I really believe in the idea of a *picture*-book. A picture-book is a book that really ought to tell the story with pictures" (*MAI-1*, pp. 24-25, emphasis in original). Crews also uses pictures and words to tell a narrative, as in his *Bigmama's* (1991/1998) and *Shortcut* (1992), which nostalgically take readers back to Crews's own visits to the home of his grandmother.

REFERENCES: *1MPPBAI. CAO-02. MAI-1. Wiki.* Bodmer, George, "Donald Crews: The Signs and Times of an American Childhood-Essay and Interview." *African American Review.* 32.1 (Spring 1998), pp. 107-117, //aar.slu.edu/in-intervws.html and From *Literature Resource Center.* Amazon.com, 1/2000, 2/2009.

Crisis, The
1910–
Official organizational publication and literary journal

The official magazine of the National Association for the Advancement of Colored People (NAACP), *Crisis* was founded in 1910 by **W. E. B. Du Bois**. Originally called *Crisis: A Record of the Darker Races*, the magazine is historically important as the register of African-American history, thought, and culture. Du Bois said the reason for publishing the *Crisis* was "to set forth those facts and arguments which show the danger of race prejudice, particularly as it is manifested today toward colored people. . . . The editors believe this is a critical time in the history of the advancement of men." After **Booker T. Washington**'s death in 1915, Du Bois assumed a role of national leadership through the *Crisis*. The monthly magazine published literature, editorials, reports from NAACP activities, feature articles, and so on. Du Bois served as editor for 24 years, retiring in 1934. Among its contributors, *Crisis* published work by George Bernard Shaw, Mahatma Gandhi, Sinclair Lewis, **Langston Hughes**, and others. Though the circulation dropped dramatically when Du Bois retired, by 1988, the circulation had risen again to 350,000 subscribers. The *Crisis* continues to publish contributors from all walks of life from clergy to lawyers, doctors, academics, and others.

REFERENCES: *AAW. EAACH* (Vol. 2). —Lisa Bahlinger

Crosswaith, Frank Rudolph
7/16/1892–6/17/1965
Nonfiction; journalist, labor leader, activist

A native of the West Indies, Crosswaith edited the *Negro Labor News* (1932-1934); wrote a column for the *Chicago Defender*; wrote articles and reviews for the *Messenger*; wrote *The Negro and Socialism*, one of the few pamphlets on socialism specifically for African-American readers; and coauthored two books on African-American labor: *True Freedom for Negro and White Workers* and *Discrimination Incorporated*.

REFERENCES: *AANB. Wiki.* Fay, Robert, in *EA-99.*

Crouch, Stanley
12/14/1945–
Essays, criticism, commentary

Touted by the renowned writer Tom Wolfe as "the jazz virtuoso of the American essay, the maestro of startlingly original variations and improvisations upon familiar themes," and by **Henry Louis Gates Jr.** as "a moment, or embodiment, of hard earned integrity and insight . . . among our generation of writers," Stanley Crouch is one of the most critically acclaimed jazz and cultural critics of our era. He is a contributing editor to the *New Republic*, a Sunday columnist for the New York *Daily News*, and a frequent guest on *The Charlie Rose Show*. He has written three extremely well-received books of essays. He was a jazz critic and staff writer for the *Village Voice* for a number of years and is also artistic consultant for jazz at Lincoln Center.

It is remarkable that he rose to such heights considering that his childhood was beset by extremely difficult circumstances. He was born in 1945 in Los Angeles to a father who was a heroin addict and a mother who worked long hours as a domestic. Despite her long working hours she nevertheless managed to find time to teach him to read before he entered school—and in a way may have set up a program of independent learning that he carried with him throughout his life. For although he attended Los Angeles Junior College and Southwest Junior College, he never received a degree—he is instead a self-educated man, but no less a writer for his lack of a diploma.

In the 1960s, Crouch was involved in the theater, working as an actor, director, and playwright. He also was a drummer in his own jazz band and even recorded an album. During that time he was interested in black nationalism, but upon reading the works of **Ralph Ellison** and **Albert Murray** began to distance himself from that movement.

Today he is called, by some, a "race traitor" because of his conservative views that include criticizing the civil-rights movement. His critical writing is said to be extremely harsh and biting—as almost all satire is—but with a wit that has led writer Saul Bellow to characterize him as "jazzy, breezy and playful," yet "willing to reject the taboos which restrict the free discussion of racial and other social questions." Despite his critics, he speaks his mind and denounces "all forms of cant, quackery and nonsense."

REFERENCES: Crouch, Stanley. 1998. *Always in Pursuit: Fresh American Perspectives, 1995-1997,* New York: Pantheon Books. Early, Gerald, in *COCAAL* and *OCAAL.* —Diane Masiello

Editor's note: Many of Crouch's *Village Voice* pieces were collected in his *Notes of a Hanging Judge: Essays and Reviews, 1979-1989* (1990). His views on race and other social issues may be found in his *The All-American Skin Game; or, The Decoy of Race: The Long and the Short of It, 1990-1994* (1995) and *Always in Pursuit* (1998). His other books include a poetry collection, *Ain't No Ambulances for No Nigguhs Tonight* (1972); *The Artificial White Man: Essays on Authenticity* (2004); and *Considering Genius: Writings on Jazz* (2006), as well as some coauthored works. Among the many recipients of his verbal attacks are **Amiri Baraka**, **Spike Lee**, and **Cornel West**. Crouch has also appeared unable to use his words for attacking on some occasions: He has punched two jazz critics and a letters editor with whom he disagreed; slapped and threatened a literary critic who unfavorably reviewed his first novel, *Don't the Moon Look Lonesome: A Novel in Blues and Swing* (2000); and used a choke hold on a fellow critic at the *Village Voice,* which led to the end of his tenure

there. Previously, Crouch's writings had earned him prestigious awards from the Whiting Foundation (1990) and the MacArthur Foundation (1991).

REFERENCES: *AANB.* Glickman, Simon in *BB. CAO-07.* Margolies, Edward. "Review - Stanley Crouch. The Artificial White Man: Essays on Authenticity." *African American Review. 40.3* (Fall 2006) p. 601. From *Literature Resource Center.* Amazon.com. Schmitt, Judith M., in *GEAAL. W. Wiki.*

Crummell, Alexander
3/3/1819–9/10/1898

Spoken word: sermons; nonfiction: religion, politics, culture; missionary, preacher

Crummell gained his early education in schools operated by African-American clerics and in integrated schools run by white abolitionists. (His schoolmates included **Henry Highland Garnet** and Ira Aldridge, later an internationally renowned actor.) When racist policies barred him from gaining the pastoral and theological education he sought, Crummell entered a program of self-study and of training in the Episcopal Seminary in Boston, and in 1844, he was ordained an Episcopal priest. When Crummell found it impossible to raise enough money to build a church in New York City for his impoverished parishioners, he went to England to raise funds. During the three years he traveled around Britain raising his church-building funds, he was also studying with a tutor, who prepared him to enter Queen's College in Cambridge. There, Crummell earned his baccalaureate (1853), but instead of returning to the United States, he moved to the newly independent (in 1847) African nation of Liberia, where he served as an Episcopalian missionary for the next 20 years. In Liberia, he faced many challenges, such as founding numerous churches and encouraging the moral uplift of his parishioners, but not the American ones of slavery, the Civil War, and the early Reconstruction era.

Although Crummell visited the United States several times to encourage African Americans to emigrate to Liberia and to raise funds for Liberian schools, churches, and other worthy causes, Crummell did not return to live in the United States until political upheaval in Liberia forced him to flee to America in 1872 or 1873. He then founded and pastored St. Luke's Episcopal Church in the nation's capital. In 1894, he retired from the ministry to teach theology at Howard University (1895-1897), after which he founded the American Negro Academy (1897), which included such celebrated scholars as **W. E. B. Du Bois** and **Paul Laurence Dunbar**. It was his hope that this premier scholarly society for African Americans would promote the publication of scholarly works on African-American history and culture.

Crummell's own publications included *The Relations and Duties of Free Colored Men in America to Africa* (1861) and *The Future of Africa* (1862), which encouraged Africans and African Americans to appreciate a shared resistance to the oppression they suffered; *The Greatness of Christ* (1882), a collection of sermons preaching the need for Christians to do good deeds, as well as to accept Christ as their Savior; and *Africa and America* (1891, collecting speeches and essays from the 1860s), on the relationship between the continent and the nation, particularly focusing on Africa's descendants in this country. Whatever he wrote or preached, he was always advocating on behalf of the civil rights and voting rights of Africans and of African Americans, although he often emphasized the need for developing moral character, more than for political action, as a means to that end. He often urged fellow African Americans to lift themselves up through education (especially vocational training)—thereby anticipating **Booker T. Washington**'s emphasis on vocational education—and he urged the well-educated African-American elite to lift up their race through service to others, thereby anticipating the views of Washington's intellectual adversary W. E. B. Du Bois.

REFERENCES: *AANB. AAW. BWA. EA-99. EB-BH-CD. W. Wiki.* Gay, Roxane, in *GEAAL*. West, Elizabeth J., in *COCAAL* and *OCAAL*.

Cruse, Harold Wright
3/8 or 3/18/1916–3/25/2005
Nonfiction essays and books

Cruse's thought-provoking books on politics include *The Crisis of the Negro Intellectual: A Historical Analysis of the Failure of Black Leadership* (1967); his collection of essays, *Rebellion or Revolution?* (1968); and *Plural but Equal* (1982). In 2002, William Jelani Cobb edited *The Essential Harold Cruse: A Reader*, highly praised by the *Library Journal*. Though he never graduated from college, Cruse's intellect was praised by many intellectuals, such as **Molefi Kete Asante**, who said Cruse had "arguably one of the sharpest minds of the twentieth century." On his death, Cruse was a professor emeritus from the University of Michigan, where he had founded the Center for Afro-American and African Studies. His birthdate is given as 3/18 in *GEAAL* and *EA-99*, but as 3/8 in *AANB*, *BB*, and *Wi*.

REFERENCES: *AANB*. Balfour, Lawrie, in *EA-99*. Briley, Ron, in *GEAAL*. *Wiki*. Henderson, Ashyia N., in *BB. CAO-05*.

Cullen, Countee (né Countée LeRoy Porter)
3/30/1903–1/9/1946
Poems, essays, plays, novel; educator

In 1918, Countée LeRoy Porter was adopted by Reverend Frederick Cullen and his wife Carolyn, leaders of one of the largest and most influential churches in Harlem (the exact date and circumstances of the adoption are unknown). There is scant information about Cullen's childhood, and Cullen was apparently unwilling to provide much information himself. His birthplace has been reported to be either Louisville, Baltimore, or New York City. Cullen is said to have claimed New York as his birthplace after he achieved celebrity for his work, but scholars believe that Louisville is correct, as Cullen himself wrote on official college documents; in addition, others who knew him well, such as his second wife, affirmed the Louisville origin.

Cullen was an excellent student, and he began writing poetry in elementary school. In high school, he achieved his first writing success by winning a citywide contest, and he was a published poet before he graduated. While still a college undergraduate, Cullen wrote most of the poems that were published in his first three books of poetry (*Color*, 1925; *Copper Sun*, 1927; *The Ballad of the Brown Girl*, 1927). He also won many poetry awards during this time. Cullen graduated with honors from New York University, where he earned a teaching degree, and he earned his master's degree from Harvard in 1927. After college, Cullen returned to school—as a teacher, inspiring countless students to become creative writers and thinkers (e.g., **James Baldwin** and **Kenneth Clark**).

Cullen is one of the earliest black writers (preceded by **Phillis Wheatley** and **Paul Laurence Dunbar**) to garner several important writing awards and widespread—though not unanimous—respect for his work. Cullen's poetry is most strongly characterized by bridges: His poetic aesthetic was founded on the belief that art could bridge the differences between white and black American cultures. Unlike some of his contemporaries writing during the **Harlem Renaissance**, he believed that black writers should attempt to work within English conventions rather than modeling their work on African arts. Eschewing experimentation with jazz, blues, or free-verse forms that characterize the work of many of his peers, he focused on writing in traditional lyric modes. He felt it was unnecessary to attempt to create distinctions between white and black poetry, believing, as he said in his foreword to *Caroling Dusk: An Anthology of Verse by Negro Poets* (1927), that "Negro poets, dependent as they are on the English language, may have more to gain from the rich background of English and American poetry than from any nebulous atavistic yearnings toward an African inheritance."

This aesthetic did not prevent Cullen from strongly indicting America's racism in his work. In poems such as "Heritage," "Atlantic City Waiter," "Incident," "Tableau," and "Ballad of a Brown Girl," Cullen expresses tremendous anger and frustration at the unfairness of racism.

Countee Cullen

Though racial in nature, these poems, like his others that focus on more traditional romantic themes of love and death, were geared at reaching Cullen's main aims—to show that blacks could write traditional poetry as well as anyone, to help bring more harmonious racial relations to America, and thus to achieve a complete sense of colorblind artistic freedom in the United States. In addition to the aforementioned volumes, Cullen published the collections *The Medea, and Some Poems* (1935), *The Lost Zoo (A Rhyme for the Young, But Not Too Young)* (1940), and *On These I Stand: An Anthology of the Best Poems of Countee Cullen* (1947, published after Cullen's death in 1946).

Ironically, because of his attempts to bridge African-American and European-American cultures and poetic expression, Cullen was criticized by many of his literary contemporaries, who asserted that the rigid structure of his traditional literary forms could not address the radical ideas that needed to be addressed. They also denounced him for being too quiet in his rejection of the white status quo, and although many of his poems clearly attack racism, Cullen himself has been quoted as saying that he did not strive to be a "Negro poet" but rather just a poet. Also, according to one scholar, Cullen completely abandoned racial themes after writing *The Black Christ and Other Poems* (1929). In addition to these apparent contrasts, Cullen felt conflicts about his sexual orienta-

tion and about his own spirituality. His spiritual conflict served as the basis for many of his works, including *The Black Christ*. In this and other works, he both rejects and accepts Christianity and the Christian God.

Although Cullen's poetic star waned later in his life, when the Great Depression drew attention and funding away from the work of the Harlem Renaissance, he stayed very active in teaching and turned his creative energy elsewhere. He wrote one novel, *One Way to Heaven* (1932), which deals with two different kinds of life in Harlem—that of the lower-middle-class church attendees that populated his father's church and that of the people of the intellectual circles in which he ran as a young man. Critics panned it as uneven and mediocre, so he abandoned novel writing to become quite an accomplished dramatist, working with **Arna Bontemps** to adapt Bontemps's novel into the play *St. Louis Woman*.

Cullen died before the play premiered on Broadway but left behind a luminous record of achievement. Though he is remembered most vividly for his early poetry, his less famous work as a teacher and an astute and fair literary critic was equally brilliant and more consistent. His resilience and determination to succeed despite setbacks in both poetic and novelistic endeavors makes him not only one of the great artists but also one of the great men of his time.

REFERENCES: *AAL. BW:SSCA. DANB.* Bloom, Harold.1994. "Countee Cullen, 1903-1946," *Black American Prose Writers of the Harlem Renaissance: Writers of English, Lives and Works,* New York: Chelsea. "Countee Cullen, 1903-1946," *BLC* (Vol. 1). Early, Gerald, in *OCAAL.* "Countee Cullen, 1903-1946," and "Harlem Renaissance, 1919-1949," in *NAAAL.* Lewis, David Levering.1994. *Harlem Renaissance Reader,* New York: Viking. Shackelford, D. Dean, "Poetry of Countee Cullen," in *MAAL.* —Diane Masiello and Janet Hoover

Cuney-Hare, Maud *See* Hare, Maud Cuney

Curtis, Christopher Paul
5/10/1953–

Juvenile novels; former auto plant worker

Each of Curtis's first two novels for young readers was honored twice by the prestigious American Library Association (ALA): *The Watsons go to Birmingham, 1963* (1995) won a Coretta Scott King Honor and the John Newbery Medal, and *Bud, Not Buddy* (1999) won both the Coretta Scott King Award and the Newbery Medal, the first book ever to receive both those awards. In Curtis's first book, ten-year-old Kenny Watson, a native of Flint, Michigan, must accompany his family to his grandparents' home in Birmingham, Alabama, where he views the civil-rights struggle up close. Kenny's story offers humor and compassion, as well as frank insights into the terrifying realities of Southern racism during that era. **Whoopi Goldberg** bought the story's film rights.

Curtis's second book, set during the Great Depression, tells the compelling story of a ten-year-old orphan who flees his foster home in Flint, hoping to find a father he has never known. His only clues come from some old flyers advertising a jazz band. In addition to the ALA awards, *Bud, Not Buddy* was named among the "Best Books" of the year by *Publishers Weekly, Horn Book,* and *New York Times Book Review,* among others. The Newbery Award selection-committee chair noted, "This heartfelt novel resonates with both zest and tenderness as it entertains questions about racism, belonging, love, and hope. Bud's fast-paced, first-person account moves with the rhythms of jazz and celebrates life, family and a child's indomitable spirit." For Curtis, however, "the highest accolade comes when a young reader tells me, 'I really liked your book.' . . . That is why I write" (//www.random house.com/teachersbdd.curt.html).

Curtis's other books include *Bucking the Sarge* (2004), about a 15-year-old boy's trials and tribulations with his morally questionable mother in contemporary Flint. His next two books were written as chapter books for young elementary-schoolers, *Mr. Chickee's Funny Money* (2005) and *Mr. Chickee's Messy Mission* (2005), part of his promised zany "Flint Future Detectives" series. In 2007, Curtis published *Elijah of Buxton,*, set in a town founded in 1849 by African-American fugitives who had freed themselves from slavery. Though 11-year-old Elijah was born free, he is immersed in a community of people who experienced slavery firsthand, and in 1860, he makes a heroic quest to help free others. This book, too, won prestigious awards—the 2008 Scott O'Dell award for historical fiction for young adults and the 2008 Coretta Scott King Author Award—and it was named *Booklist's* "Top of the List" winner for "Youth Fiction."

One reason Curtis's books are so compelling may be, as he noted in a *Booklist* interview (2/1/2008), "I like to write in first person; I feel as though that gives the story an intimacy and an immediacy that are difficult to reproduce in third person." As many critics have observed, Curtis also recognizes that "humor is the most marvelous of survival tools. It signals the beginning of healing. . . . I think my characters use humor to cope." Curtis's first two books have been adapted to the audiobook format, and his works have been translated into at least ten languages. When not writing for young readers, he contributes articles and reviews to periodicals such as the *Chicago Tribune, New York Times Book Review,* and *USA Weekend.* He also lectures widely, and he founded the Nobody but Curtis Foundation for raising literacy levels among youths in North America and Africa by providing scholarships, books, computers, and school supplies to juveniles.

Like the protagonists in his first three books, Curtis grew up in Flint, Michigan, where he worked for 13 years on an auto assembly line and attended the Flint branch of the University of Michigan. Curtis recalled, "I used to write during breaks because it took me away from being in the factory. . . . I was probably very young when I knew I wanted to write; but as a profession, that didn't come until [much, much later]. . . . The best advice I can give to any aspiring writer is to write. Write anytime you have the opportunity. . . . like any other skill, you have to work at it and you have to practice." Nowadays, Curtis does most of his writing in the library, having discovered it as a haven when he was still a young boy. His speech accepting his second Newbery Medal (2000) acknowledged, "I've been involved with librarians all of my life, and I, just like Bud, have always known where to go for a sympathetic ear or for information or for the key to the magical world of books. Libraries and librarians have always played such an important role in my life."

Christopher and his wife, registered nurse Kaysandra Sookram Curtis, live in Windsor (40 miles from Buxton), Ontario, Canada; they have two children, Steven Darrell and Cydney McKenzie. Christopher's family members have played key roles in his writing career. In his 2000 Newbery Medal acceptance speech, he thanked his wife, "In 1993 Kay took a tremendous leap of faith and said to me, 'Look, I know you hate your job, and I don't think you're doing everything you can with your life. I've read some of the things you've written and I bet you could be a writer. So why don't you take a year off work and see if you could write a book?'" During that year, he also completed the bachelor's degree (1996) he had been working on for years. In his speech, he also addressed his daughter, "Cydney, many people have told me that their favorite part of Bud is the song that you wrote." In an earlier interview, Christopher had noted appreciatively that for his first book, his son Steven typed Christopher's hand-written manuscript each evening, helpfully critiquing what worked and "what exactly doesn't work" (quoted in *Black Biography*).

REFERENCES: *CAITGM. CAO-08. Wiki.* Lamb, Wendy. *The Horn Book Magazine.* 76.4 (July 2000) p. 397. Lesinski, Jeanne M., in *BB.* "Coretta Scott King Author Award." *The Horn Book Magazine.* 84.2 (March-April 2008) p. 235. From *Literature Resource Center.* From *Literature Resource Center.* "Christopher Paul Curtis is Winner of the 2008 Scott O'Dell Award." *Booklist.* 104.12 (Feb. 15, 2008) p.75. From *Literature Resource Center.* Morgan, Peter E. "History for Our Children: An Interview with Christopher Paul Curtis, a Contemporary Voice in African American Young Adult Fiction." *MELUS.* 27.2 (Summer 2002) p. 197. From *Literature Resource Center.* "Newbery Medal Acceptance. Christopher Paul Curtis." *The Horn Book Magazine.* 76.4 (July 2000) p. 386. From *Literature Resource Center.* Rochman, Hazel. "The Booklist Interview: Christopher Paul Curtis." *Booklist.* 104.11 (Feb. 1, 2008) p. 54. From *Literature Resource Center.* "Scott O'Dell Award." *The Horn Book Magazine.* 84.2 (March-April 2008) p. 237. From *Literature Resource Center.*

//www.ala.org/newbery.html. //www.ala.org/news/newberycaldecott 2000.html. //www.hbook.com/magazine/articles/2000/jul00_lamb.asp. //www.library.uiuc.edu/blog/esslchildlit/archives/2008/02/african_amer ica.html. //www.randomhouse.com/features/christopherpaulcurtis/ activities.htm. //www.randomhouse.com/features/christopherpaul curtis/books.htm. //www.randomhouse.com/features/christopher paulcurtis/ christophercurtis.htm. //www.randomhouse.com/features/ christopherpaulcurtis/faq.htm. //www.randomhouse.com/teachersbdd. curt.html. Amazon.com, 1/2000, 2/2009. Gross, Terry, interview on National Public Radio, *Fresh Air,* 1/27/2000. *NPR-ME,* 2/6/2000.

~D~

Damas, Léon-Gontran
3/28/1912–1/22/1978
Poems, anthology, travel memoir

A native of French Guiana, Damas was comfortable in France, Africa, and the United States (spending the last years of his life here). Damas was one of three main poets to found and champion the *Négritude* movement, which celebrated the achievements of persons of African descent, particularly highlighting the work of French-speaking writers. (The other two were Aimé Césaire and Léopold Sédar Senghor.) His own writings include the travel books *Retour de Guyane* [Return from Guiana] (1938); the poetry collections *Pigments* (1937), *Graffiti* (1952), *Black-Label* (1956), and *Névralgies* (1966); and the anthology he edited *Poètes noirs d'expression française* [Black Poets in the French Language] (1948).

REFERENCES: *BB. CAO-02. CE. EA-99. FLC. NYPL-AADR. Wiki.* Cook, Mercer. "The Poetry of Leon Damas." *African Forum 2.4* (Spring 1967): pp. 129-132. Rpt. in *Twentieth-Century Literary Criticism* (Vol. 204). Detroit: Gale, p. 129-132. From *Literature Resource Center.* //en.wikipedia.org/wiki/L%C3%A9on_Damas.

Dandridge, Raymond G. (Garfield)
4/8/1882–2/24/1930
Poems, lyrics

Young Raymond had been an athletic runner and swimmer in high school, which he attended at night so he could work at various jobs by day. After high school, he expressed his artistic inclinations as a house painter and decorator, then in 1911, a fever and a mysterious illness sent him to bed for almost a year. Just as he thought he was recovering, his legs and his right arm became paralyzed in July of 1912. Some sources suggest that a stroke caused the paralysis, others that he had suffered from po-

lio. In any case, he never regained use of his right arm and his legs, so he taught himself how to write with his left hand.

Though bedridden, Dandridge was not isolated. In addition to his mother, who nursed him lovingly, and his sister and two brothers, Dandridge had visiting friends, and he read and corresponded widely. He also started writing poems. He had been a teenager while **Paul Laurence Dunbar** was the preeminent poet of the day, so most of his poems emulated Dunbar's dialect poems. For instance, these lines tell of his hopes of regaining his health, "Dar is somethin' I cain't tell, / Gibs me hopes ob gettin' well / Mebbe it's de home lak smell, / On de Hill," the "Hill" being "Price Hill," where he grew up (quoted in Gabbin, *AAWHR-40*).

One of Dandridge's friends gave him a telephone, which he used to earn money as an early telephone solicitor seeking orders for a coal company. When not working, he continued to write poems, which started appearing in various periodicals. He even served as the literary editor of the *Cincinnati Journal* for a while. Friends and patrons (e.g., the head of the coal company for which he worked) also helped him to get his three poetry collections published: *Penciled Poems* (1917), *The Poet and Other Poems* (1920), and *Zalka Peetruza and Other Poems* (1928).

During the heyday of the **Harlem Renaissance**, when other poets were experimenting with modern themes and forms, Dandridge continued to write much of his verse in the dialect poetry forms with the romantic and nostalgic themes he had read as a young man. Many critics of his day, such as **Sterling Brown**, questioned the value of his dialect poetry, but his poems nonetheless merited inclusion in several anthologies of that period, including posthumous publication in **James Weldon Johnson's** *The Book of American Negro Poetry* (rev. ed., 1931). In addition, Dandridge was cognizant of the Renaissance poets' subject matter and style. For instance, in his "Time to Die," he asked, "Black Brothers, think you life so sweet / That you would live at any price? / Does mere existence balance with / The weight of your great sacrifice?" (quoted in Gabbin, *AAWHR-40*). His body was bed bound, but his mind was free to roam.

REFERENCES: *CAO-02.* Gabbin, Joanne V., in *AAWHR-40.* Le Rouge, Mary, in *BB.* Amazon.com.

FURTHER READING: Tracy, Steven C., in *GEAAL.*

Danner, Margaret (Esse)
1/12/1915–1/1/1984
Poems

Caleb and Naomi Danner raised their daughter Margaret in Chicago, where she won her first poetry prize when she was still in the eighth grade. After graduating from Englewood High School, she went on to study poetry at Loyola College, Roosevelt University, and Northwestern University. We know little of Danner's private life: Danner married Cordell Strickland, and the pair had a daughter, whom they named Naomi, after Margaret's mother; Danner later married again, to Otto Cunningham, and she had at least one grandchild: her grandson, Sterling Washington, Jr., who inspired Danner to write what she called her "muffin poems."

During the 1940s, Danner was still writing poems, as she was awarded second prize in the Poetry Workshop of the Midwestern Writers Conference in 1945. From the 1950s through the 1970s, Danner's life as a writer became more public. From 1951 to 1957, she worked for *Poetry: The Magazine of Verse*, published in Chicago. She started out as an editorial assistant, and in 1956, she became the first African-American assistant editor there. At *Poetry*, she worked with Karl Shapiro and Paul Engle, who encouraged her as a poet; she later recalled her experiences there as being among the most rewarding she ever had. Her series "Far from Africa: Four Poems" was printed in a 1951 issue of the magazine, and it is still among her most widely anthologized poems. The series also won her the 1951 John Hay Whitney fellowship, which was to help pay for her to travel to Africa. It ended up being about a decade and a half before she finally made the trip.

By 1961, Danner had left Chicago and moved to Detroit, where she became the first poet-in-residence at Wayne State University. The following year, she convinced Dr. Boone, the minister of Detroit's King Solomon Church, that his parish needed a community arts center, and she persuaded him to let her convert an empty parish house into the Boone House for the Arts. Soon other notable African-American poets were also involved in Boone House, including **Dudley Randall**, **Robert Hayden**, and **Naomi Long Madgett**.

Both Boone House and Randall's **Broadside Press** helped make Detroit a major center of the **Black Arts Movement** and made Danner's poetry a prominent feature in that movement. In 1962, Broadside published Danner's *To Flower*. Four years later, Broadside published Danner and Randall's *Poem Counterpoem* (1966), which provided matched poems on facing pages, one written by each author; the poems treated a variety of subjects from each author's distinctive perspective and poetic viewpoint. That year, Danner finally made it to Africa, when she went to Dakar, Senegal, to present her work at the World Exposition of Negro Arts. She returned to the United States with a deepened commitment to highlighting African traditions among African Americans.

In 1968, Broadside Press published Danner's *Impressions of African Art Forms*. As the title suggests, many of her poems celebrated Africa's many gifts to African

Americans and encouraged African Americans to prize their African heritage. During the 1968-1969 academic year, Danner was poet-in-residence at Virginia Union University (in Richmond), and during the 1970s, she was poet-in-residence at LeMoyne-Owens College (in Memphis, Tennessee). During this period, Danner's poetry collections included *Iron Lace* (1968) and *The Down of a Thistle: Selected Poems, Prose Poems, and Songs* (1976). *The Down of a Thistle*, perhaps her most important collection, was dedicated to **Robert Hayden** and included poems illustrated with African images, as well as poems protesting against white racism and its effects on African Americans. Danner also participated in the 1973 **Phillis Wheatley** Poetry Festival, a gala event rejoicing in poetry written by African-American women.

REFERENCES: *AAW:AAPP. BAL-1-P. EBLG.* Aldridge, June M., in *AAP-55-85. OCWW.* Bethel, Kari, in *BB.* Carson, Sharon, in *COCAAL* and *OCAAL.* Thompson, Kathleen, in *BWA:AHE.* Woodard, Loretta G., in *GEAAL. CAO-01.*

Danticat, Edwidge
1/19/1969–
Short stories, novels, plays, autobiography/memoir, anthology, juvenile fiction; educator, documentary film producer

Though Edwidge's mother and then her father had moved to the United States when Edwidge was very young, she and her younger brother stayed in Haiti until she was 12 years old. After immigrating, she had to acquire English as a second language and to deal with a sharply contrasting culture, while going through pubescence and then adolescence.

Encouraged by her parents to become a nurse, she preferred to study literature. She earned her B.A. in French literature in 1990 at Barnard College, then went to Brown University on scholarship, to study writing. In 1992 and 1993, two of her plays were produced in Providence, Rhode Island. Her master's thesis at Brown evolved into her first book, the novel *Breath, Eyes, Memory* (1994). The Black Caucus of the American literary Association gave the *Breath* its fiction award, and GRANTA named her among the "Best Young American Novelists" (1996). Though Danticat's protagonist is a young Haitian woman who immigrated to New York City, Danticat says the experiences of sexual abuse described in the novel are fictional, not autobiographical. Mother-daughter relationships figure prominently in this novel and in many other Danticat works. Now, however, she views that relationship from two perspectives, as she has a daughter of her own (born c. 2005), named for her father, Mira.

In 1994, with her master's degree in hand and Haiti's troubles in the news, she decided to help John Demme produce his documentary film *Courage and Pain,* about the torture of Haitian citizens by their leaders, and she returned to Haiti for the first time since 1981. Her next book was her collection *Krik? Krak!* (1995), containing nine interwoven stories, also based on her experiences in Haiti. Critics loved it, honoring it with a National Book Award nomination. The same year, she was given a Woman of Achievement Award by Barnard College, and a prestigious Pushcart Prize for short story.

Danticat's second novel, *The Farming of Bones* (1998), offers a fictional first-person view of an actual 1937 incident, in which 12,000-15,000 Haitians were slaughtered in the Dominican Republic, in what may now be called "ethnic cleansing." Her third novel for adult readers, *The Dew Breaker* (2004), centers on a loving family man who tortures Haitian dissenters during Duvalier's regime.

Danticat has also written two novels for young adults (YA, librarians' term for teens). In *Behind the Mountains* (2002), a pubescent Haitian girl writes in her journal about her experiences at the time of the 2000 presidential elections in Haiti, then her experiences when she, her brother, and her mother join her father in Brooklyn. Danticat's historical YA novel, *Anacaona: Golden Flower, Haiti, 1490* (2005), revolves around the queen of Haiti at the time of Spanish conquest.

Danticat's memoir, *After the Dance: A Walk through Carnival in Jacmel, Haiti* (2002), describes her return to Haiti during its pre-Lenten Carnival. In it, she offers insights into her native land, as well as into herself. Her memoir *Brother, I'm Dying* (2007) focuses on the cherished uncle who helped raise her in Haiti and who escaped Haitian turbulence and violence only to die in the custody of U.S. Customs. It won the National Book Critics Circle Award in 2008. She also wrote two brief autobiographical essays, available online at the Gale Literature Resource Center, through most public libraries or to library card-holders: One appeared in the December 2004 issue of *The Writer,* and a second (nd, retrieved 1/2009), which includes poetry and prose, appeared in *Contemporary Authors.*

Many of Danticat's works have been published in other formats (sound recordings, large print) and have been translated into other languages. She also edited *The Beacon Best of 2000: Great Writing by Women and Men of All Colors and Cultures* (2000) and *The Butterfly's Way: Voices from the Haitian Dyaspora in the United States* (2001). In addition to her own writing, Danticat teaches others to do creative writing on the college level. In the epilogue of *Krik? Krak!* she wrote, "When you write, it is like braiding hair. Taking a handful of coarse unruly strands and attempting to bring them unity. Your fingers have still not perfected the task."

REFERENCES: *AANB. AAW:PV.* Brennan, Carol, in *BB. CAO. CAO-08. CLCS.* Cantave, Sophia, in *EA-99.* Charters, Mallay. "Edwidge Danticat: A Bitter Legacy Revisited." *Publishers Weekly.* 245.33 (Aug. 17, 1998) p. 42. From *Literature Resource Center.* Danticat, Edwidge, and Margaria Fichtner. "Author Edwidge Danticat Writes about Being Young, Black, Haitian, and Female." Knight-Ridder/Tribune News Service. Rpt. in *Contemporary Literary Criticism.* Ed. Jeffrey W. Hunter. Vol. 139. Detroit: Gale Group, 2001. From *Literature Resource Center.* Danticat, Edwidge, and Renee H. Shea. "The Dangerous Job of Edwidge Danticat: An Interview." *Callaloo* 19.2 (Jan. 17, 1996): pp. 382-389. Rpt. in Contemporary Literary Criticism. Ed. Jeffrey W. Hunter. Vol. 139. Detroit: Gale Group, 2001. pp. 382-389. From *Literature Resource Center.* Danticat, Edwidge, and Renée H. Shea. "An Interview." *Belles Letters: A Review of Books by Women 10.3* (Summer 1995): pp. 12-15. Rpt. in Contemporary Literary Criticism. Ed. Brigham Narins and Deborah A. Stanley. Vol. 94. Detroit: Gale Research, 1997. pp. 12-15. From *Literature Resource Center.* "Edwidge Danticat." *The Writer. 117.12* (Dec. 2004) p. 66. From *Literature Resource Center.* Vasconcelos, Elizabete, in *GEAAL. W. Wiki.* Vitone, Elaine. "PW Talks with Edwidge Danticat: Family Lines." *Publishers Weekly.* 254.30 (July 30, 2007) p. 66. From *Literature Resource Center.* SDPL catalog.

Dash, Julie
10/22/1952–
Screenplays, documentaries; filmmaker, director

Dash's documentaries include *Working Models of Success* (1973), *Four Women* (1978, focusing on experimental dance), *Illusions* (1983, about African-American women in the film industry), *Breaking the Silence: On Reproductive Rights* (1987), *Preventing Cancer* (1987), and a documentary on **Zora Neale Hurston**, as well as two music videos (1992, 1994). In addition to these works, the films she has written include *Diary of an African Nun* (1977, based on an **Alice Walker** short story) and *Daughters of the Dust* (the first full-length general-release film by an African-American woman). *Daughters of the Dust,* written primarily in Gullah patois, with occasional American English subtitles, premiered at the celebrated Sundance Film Festival in 1991 and aired nationally on Public Broadcasting System's *American Playhouse* series in 1992. Dash's own daughter, Nzinga, was conceived with cinematographer and critic Arthur Jafa, her former husband. Dash has directed numerous movies in the late 1990s and early 2000s (including *The Rosa Parks Story,* starring Angela Bassett), as well as several music videos. In addition to current movie projects, Dash is working on another novel. Dash's awards include grants from the Rockefeller Foundation, the National Endowment for the Arts, the Guggenheim foundation, United States Artists, and the Public Broadcasting Corporation; a Fulbright fellowship; and numerous film and cinema awards.

REFERENCES: *AANB. CAO-06. EA-99. F. Wiki.* Brennan, Sandra, *All Movie Guide,* in *Dir.* Goldstein, Nina, in *BB.* Goodall, N. H., in *BWA:AHE.* Ostrom, Hans, in *GEAAL.*

Dave, the Potter (aka David Drake)

c. 1800–after 1862, perhaps the mid-1870s
Poems; enslaved potter, typesetter

Enslaved all his life, Dave managed both to become literate and to develop skills as a potter and a typesetter. Having skills other than fieldwork was unusual, but knowing how to read and write was not just extraordinary. It could have been dangerous, as many whites both feared and loathed literate slaves. Dave's name may have appeared somewhere in inventories of enslaved persons, but his first known appearance on the legal record is June 13, 1818, when he was described as "a boy about 17 years old country born" who was "mortgaged to" Eldrid Simkins by Harvey Drake.

Despite legal sanctions barring the literacy of slaves, on many of the large, glazed stoneware pots Dave created, he inscribed poems, usually couplets in iambic tetrameter. Many poems suggested the uses of the vessel, such as "This noble jar will hold 20 / Fill it with silver then you'll have plenty / — April 8, 1858." Dave sometimes waxed philosophical, however, as in "I wonder where is all my relations / Friendship to all — and every nation / — Dave, Aug. 16, 1857." This tender poem was written after his beloved Louisa and their six children were all sold and separated from him, never to see each other again. (Both quotes may be found in //www.go-star.com/antiquing/stoneware0904.htm.) Nowadays, Dave's pots may be found in the Civil War collection at the Smithsonian Institution, and they may be bought at auctions for prices from $40,000 to six-figure numbers.

Dave's hometown of Edgefield, South Carolina, was the ancestral hometown of author Leonard Todd. Not only had Todd's ancestors owned a pottery business there, but also two of his ancestors had "owned" Dave the Potter. Repelled by his family's history and fascinated by Dave's pottery, Todd moved from Manhattan to Edgefield and began piecing together his family's letters, local records, and Dave's poems, to chronicle Dave's life story in *Carolina Clay: The Life and Legend of the Slave Potter Dave* (2008).

REFERENCES: *Wiki. All Things Considered,* 10/25/2008, //www.npr.org/templates/story/story.php?storyId=96140163. Kuebler-Wolf, Elizabeth, in *AANB.* //www.go-star.com/antiquing/stoneware0904.htm. Amazon.com.

FURTHER READING: "Drake, David," Ostrom, Hans, in *GEAAL.* Todd, Leonard. 2008. *Carolina Clay: The Life and Legend of the Slave Potter Dave.* New York: W. W. Norton.

Davis, Angela (Yvonne)

1/26/1944–
Essays, autobiography; educator, activist, spoken-word artist

During the 1970s, scholar and a militant political activist Angela Davis wrote a memoir (*If They Come in the Morning: Voices of Resistance,* 1971) and her best-selling autobiography (*Angela Davis: An Autobiography,* 1974) of her experiences. In the 1980s, she wrote several books on how women fit into our social, political, and economic structure, including *Women, Race, and Class* (1981) and *Women, Culture and Politics* (1989). Other books of hers include her *Blues Legacies and Black Feminism: Gertrude "Ma" Rainey, Bessie Smith, and Billie Holiday* (1998).

Despite her many contributions to scholarship, Davis may be best remembered for her Marxist rhetoric, her membership in the Communist Party and in the Black Panther Party, and her link to George Jackson, one of the Soledad Brothers who was charged with murdering guards at Soledad Prison. At Jackson's trial, there was an aborted attempt to help Jackson escape from a California courtroom, which ended up killing Jackson's brother, a trial judge, and two other people. Davis was accused of conspiring in the disastrous attempt, and she fled from prosecution. After being placed on the FBI's most-wanted list, within two months Davis had been arrested, denied bail, and imprisoned while she waited . . . and waited for a trial. At the end of the years-long process, an all-white jury acquitted her of all charges. Barred from teaching at any publicly funded institutions in California (by then-governor Ronald Reagan), she sought positions at various private institutions. In the early 1990s, Davis managed to regain a position teaching philosophy in the University of California at Santa Cruz.

REFERENCES: *BAAW.* Elliott, Joan C., in *OCAAL. EB-98. G-97.*

Editor's note: Davis won an American Book Award for her 1998 *Blues Legacies and Black Feminism.* As the twentieth century ended, Davis became a spoken-word artist, releasing the album *Prison Industrial Complex* (1999). Davis continues to write and to speak out against the death penalty and in favor of penal reform, as in *Policing the National Body: Sex, Race, and Criminalization* (2002); *Are Prisons Obsolete?* (2003); *Abolition Democracy: Beyond Empire, Prisons, and Torture* (2005); *Beyond the Frame: Women of Color and Visual Representations* (2005); and *Arbitrary Justice: The Power of the American Prosecutor* (2009); as well as articles in numerous periodicals. She also continues to be invited to lecture at various colleges and universities.

REFERENCES: *AANB.* Johnson, Anne Janette, in *BB. CAO-08.* Amazon.com. Steck, Stephen M., in *A. B. BCE. CE. D. GEAAL. LE. QB. W. Wiki.*

Davis, Arthur P. (Paul)
11/21/1904–4/21/1996
Anthology, literary criticism, columns, scholarly essays; educator

As a young man, Davis attended Columbia College (now University) in New York during the heyday of the **Harlem Renaissance**. While he felt alienated from his white peers at Columbia, he felt closely tied to the inspiring writers of the Renaissance nearby. He later wrote, "Believing strongly in the importance of the Negro's contribution to American literature, I have devoted practically all of my adult working years to teaching and writing in the field of Negro letters. It has been gratifying to note the subject's growth in popularity" (quoted in CAO-03). In fact, Davis is best known for his anthologies, though he wrote a newspaper column for nearly 20 years, contributed nearly 100 additional nonfiction pieces to periodicals, and wrote a major scholarly dissertation on English hymnist Isaac Watts.

After becoming the second African American to graduate Phi Beta Kappa from Columbia (1927), Davis started teaching English at North Carolina College (now North Carolina Central University) in Durham (1927-1928). He finished his master's degree at Columbia in 1929 and started teaching English at Virginia Union University in Richmond (1929-1944). While still at Virginia Union, he completed his doctorate at Columbia (1942), the first African American awarded a doctorate in English from Columbia, and self-published his doctoral dissertation, *Isaac Watts: His Life and Works* (1943). In 1944, Davis moved to Howard University in Washington, D.C., where he professed English until 1969, when he became professor emeritus.

Frustrated with the lack of adequate resources for teaching his students about African-American literature, he joined forces with **Sterling A. Brown** and Ulysses Lee to edit *The Negro Caravan: Writings by American Negroes* (1941; reprinted in 1970), containing more than 1,000 pages, and now considered a landmark in African-American literature. Meanwhile, Davis wrote abundantly: Between 1933 and 1950, he wrote a weekly newspaper column, "Cross Currents" (later titled "With a Grain of Salt"), for the *Norfolk Journal and Guide*. In addition, by 1979, he had written 27 book reviews for popular periodicals such as *Opportunity* and the *Washington Post*, as well as for scholarly journals such as the *CLA Journal* and the *Journal of Negro History*. He had also written 22 or more cultural commentaries and essays for popular periodicals such as *The Crisis*, **Negro Digest**, and *Southern Workman*. For the *Journal of Negro Education, Obsidian: Black Literature in Review, Phylon,* and other journals interested in pieces on African-American literature, Davis wrote 35 other scholarly articles and essays. His one and only pub-

lished fiction work is his short story, "How John Boscoe Outsung the Devil," published in several anthologies.

After he retired, he hosted a talk show, "Ebony Harvest," on Radio WAMU-FM (1972-1973). Davis also continued his interest in providing college students and others with adequate resources, editing *From the Dark Tower: Afro-American Writers 1900 to 1960* (1974/1981), which prominently featured the Harlem Renaissance writers. He also worked with Michael W. Peplow to edit *The New Negro Renaissance: An Anthology* (1975). A few years earlier, he and **J. Saunders Redding** had edited *Cavalcade: Negro American Writing from 1760 to the Present* (1971). Two decades later, while in his late 80s, Davis collaborated with Joyce Ann Joyce to create their two-volume *The New Cavalcade: African American Writing from 1760 to the Present* (1991, Vol. 1; 1992, Vol. 2), comprising more than "300 short stories, poems, and excerpts from essays, novels, plays, biographies and autobiographies. . . . [with] works by such classic authors as **Phillis Wheatley**, **Ralph Ellison**, and **James Baldwin** as well as selections from lesser-known and more contemporary writers" (from CAO-03).

During his long lifetime, Davis was honored numerous times, including with a Proudfit fellowship from Columbia University (1937), a National Hampton alumni award (1947), an award from Howard University's Institute for the Arts and Humanities (1973), an award from the College Language Association for distinguished contribution to literary scholarship (1975), a Distinguished Critic Award from the Middle Atlantic Writers Association (1982), an honorary doctorate in literature from Howard University (1984), and a Martin Luther King, Jr., Leadership Award from the Washington, D.C., Public Library (1992). Davis also shared his son, Arthur Paul Davis, Jr., with his wife, Clarice Winn, a librarian whom he married in 1928, but who predeceased him.

REFERENCES: CAO-03. DS:NLA. Morris, Paula J. K., in BB. Skinner, Beverly Lanier, in AANB.

FURTHER READING: HAAL. Carter, Linda M., in GEAAL. Emanuel, James A., and Theodore L. Gross. 1968. *Dark Symphony: Negro Literature in America* (2nd ed.). New York: Simon and Schuster.

Davis, Frank Marshall (one-time pen name Bob Greene)
12/31/1905–7/26/1987
Poems, memoir, editorials, criticism, columns; journalist

From 1930 until 1955, Davis, who never earned a college degree, worked as a feature writer, editorial writer, sports reporter, theater and music critic, correspondent, contributing editor, editor, managing editor, and executive editor for several African-American periodicals, including the Chicago-based *Evening Bulletin*, the *Whip*, and the *Star*; the Gary (Indiana) *American*, the *Negro Digest*, and various other periodicals. While managing editor at the Atlanta (Georgia) *World* (1931-1935), within two years, he transformed it from a semiweekly to the first successful African-American daily newspaper. In 1935, he was named managing editor and then executive director of the **Associated Negro Press**, where he stayed until 1947. He also wrote short fiction for some of these periodicals.

Other than journalism, Davis's chief literary love was poetry, which at first seemed to love him back. Davis's first poetry collection, *Black Man's Verse* (1935) was acclaimed by such notable critics as Stephen Vincent Benét, **Sterling Brown**, and **Alain Locke**, some of whom compared his poems to those of American folk poets Walt Whitman and Carl Sandburg. His next two poetry collections (*I Am the American Negro*, 1937, and *Through Sepia Eyes*, 1938) were less well received. Although his *47th Street: Poems* (1948) is considered by some to be his best effort, after his 1948 move to Hawaii, he seemed to fade into oblivion, operating a wholesale paper business and writing a weekly column, "Frank-ly speaking," for the Honolulu *Record*. Though literary critics may have ignored him there, the notorious House Un-American Activities Committee investigated him for comments made in the *Record* and other alleged ties to the U.S. Communist Party. Like his friend **Paul Robeson**, he was investigated not only for his socialistic sympathies with laborers, but also for his willingness to challenge racism's ugly manifestations such as segregation, lynching, and discrimination.

In 1968, he published *Sex Rebel: Black (Memoirs of a Gash Gourmet)*, under the pseudonym Bob Greene, and in 1970, he divorced his wife of 24 years, wealthy white socialite Helen Canfield, with whom he had four daughters and a son, and who was 19 years younger than he. In the late 1960s and early 1970s, poet and historian **Margaret Taylor Goss Burroughs**, literary critic Stephen Henderson, and publisher and poet **Dudley Randall** rediscovered his work, and soon Davis was giving readings and lectures at historically black colleges around the country. He also wrote many new poems, which were gathered in his *Jazz Interludes: Seven Musical Poems* (1977/1985). In 1978, he published his collection *Awakening, and Other Poems*. Even Davis's earlier poems were reprinted. After his death, Davis's *Livin' the Blues: Memoirs of a Black Journalist and Poet* was published in 1992, and *Writings of Frank Marshall Davis: A Voice of the Black Press* in 2007. During the 2008 political campaign, Davis's ties to communism and his scandalous *Sex Rebel* book were attacked by opponents of **Barack Obama**, because Obama had mentioned in *Dreams from My Father* that Davis was a friend of his mother's father when they both lived in Hawaii.

REFERENCES: *AANB. BV. EBLG. TtW.* Bostian, Patricia Kennedy, in *GEAAL.* Tidwell, John Edgar, in *AAWHR-40. CAO-07.* COCAAL and OCAAL. *G-97. Wiki.* //en.wikipedia.org/wiki/Frank_Marshall_Davis.

Davis, Ossie (né Raiford Chatman Davis)
12/18/1917–2/4/2005
Plays, scripts, novel, autobiography/memoir; actor, director

While Ossie was a wee little boy in Cogdell, Georgia, his father, Kince Charles Davis, was threatened by Ku Klux Klan (KKK) members. The Klan didn't go too far, however, because the white folks in the area needed his skills: He was a self-taught (though illiterate) railway-construction engineer who was willing to work for a black man's wages. Davis later commented that the KKK incident motivated him to become a writer in order to tell the world the truth about the African-American experience.

Because there were no schools in Cogdell, when Ossie was five years old, he had to move 23 miles away, to live with the father and stepmother of his mother (Laura Davis) in Waycross, where he could go to school. In high school, Ossie started writing plays, as well as acting in them. When he went on to Howard University (1935-1939), he studied under drama critic **Alain Locke**, who encouraged him to go to New York City to make his career in the theater. In New York, Davis joined the Rose McClendon Players of Harlem, making his stage debut with them in 1941. Meanwhile, Davis continued to write plays in his off hours.

World War II prompted Davis to take a temporary leave from the theater, while he served in the Medical Corps and in Special Services for the U.S. Army. Even in the military, he continued to write for the stage. He wrote and produced the musical variety show *Goldbrickers of 1944* while he was posted in Liberia. In 1945, following his discharge, he returned to New York right away. There, he was awarded the title role in *Jeb* (1946, written by Robert Ardrey), costarring with a talented young actress, **Ruby Dee**. Numerous other stage performances (e.g., *A Raisin in the Sun* (1959) followed—as did his (December 1948) marriage to Ruby Dee, with whom he shared the rest of his life.

Davis also performed on television, such as his 1969 Emmy-winning performance in *Teacher, Teacher,* for which he wrote the script; his regular role on *Evening Shade*, 1990-1994; his final role, in which he played a dying father struggling to accept his lesbian daughter's decision to have a child with her partner; and countless other appearances. He also acted in dozens of movies (e.g., the film version of *Raisin* and several Spike Lee features, such as *Do The Right Thing*, 1989) and directed them. Among the films he directed are these for which he also wrote the screenplays: *Cotton Comes to Harlem* (1970, written with Arnold Perl, based on a **Chester Himes** novel), *Black Girl* (1972, coscripted), and *Countdown at Kusini* (1976). Davis also coproduced *Countdown* with Dee; *Countdown* was the first American feature film that was filmed entirely in Africa, using all black professionals. Among the other television programs by Dee and Davis are "The Ruby Dee/Ossie Davis Story Hour" (1974) and the Public Broadcasting System arts education television series *With Ossie and Ruby* (1981).

Davis and Dee were also partners in civil-rights activism. In fact, during the 1950s, their activism cost them many opportunities to work, when they were blacklisted by the ruthless, right-wing anticommunists of the paranoid McCarthy era. During the 1960s, the red scare had subsided, and Davis and Dee's careers were resurrected. As they gained celebrity, they used their fame and popularity to promote civil-rights causes. Davis acted as master of ceremonies for the 1963 March on Washington and delivered memorable and moving eulogies for both **Martin Luther King, Jr.**, and **Malcolm X**. In 1972, Davis chaired the fund-raising drive to pay for **Angela Davis**'s defense against conspiracy charges of which she was later acquitted.

Davis's earliest plays include *The Mayor of Harlem* (1949), *Point Blank* (1949), *Clay's Rebellion* (1951), *What Can You Say, Mississippi?* (1955), and *Montgomery Footprints* (1956), about the civil-rights movement. Another of his early works was his one-act play *Alice in Wonder* (1952), which he then expanded into his full-length *The Big Deal* (1953). The story centers around the moral dilemma of an African-American television performer who is asked either to testify against his brother-in-law during a McCarthy-era witch hunt or to face being unable to find work in his field.

Davis's first commercially successful play was his satirical *Purlie Victorious* (1961), about an African-American preacher who seeks to build a racially integrated church in the South. When the play debuted on Broadway, Davis played the title role. He later adapted the play to make the feature film *Gone Are the Days* (1963). Davis even adapted the play into a musical version, *Purlie* (1970), in collaboration with Philip Rose, Peter Udell, and Gary Geld. In 1993, the play was published as *Purlie Victorious: A Commemorative*. Decades later, Davis adapted another work to the musical form: William Brashler's book *Bingo Long's Traveling All Stars and Motor Kings* (1985), about a baseball team during the days of the old Negro League.

Some of Davis's other plays honor the lives of important African Americans, such as *Curtain Call* (1963), about Shakespearean actor Ira Aldridge; and *Langston: A Play* (1982), about poet **Langston Hughes**. Davis's *Es-*

Ossie Davis as Gabriel in The Green Pastures

cape to Freedom: The Story of **Frederick Douglass**, *A Play for Young People* (1976; published by Viking Junior Books, 1978; republished in 1990 as *Escape to Freedom: A Play about Young Frederick Douglass*) won both the 1979 Jane Addams Children's Book Award from the Jane Addams Peace Association and the 1979 Coretta Scott King Book Award from American Library Association. Other plays by Davis include *Alexis Is Fallen* (1974) and *They Seek a City* (1974). In 1992, Davis wrote a novel intended for youths ages 10-14 years: *Just Like Martin*, set around the time of the 1963 March on Washington. The book centers on the relationship between an embittered father and his idealistic teenage son, who admires Martin Luther King's nonviolent means of effecting social change and achieving civil rights.

In 1998, Davis and Dee published their collaborative memoir *With Ossie and Ruby: In This Life Together*, in honor of their 50th wedding anniversary. The authors wrote the book in alternating chapters, starting with Dee in Chapter 1 and Davis's recollection of the KKK incident in Chapter 2. A *New York Times Book Review* critic observed that the book is "a conversation studded with anecdotes . . . inspiration, wisdom and gossip." In addition to their personal experiences, their family life with their children Nora, Guy, and Hasna, and their careers in entertainment, a central theme in their work is their participation in "The Struggle" for civil rights for all Americans.

Among Davis's numerous awards are the NAACP Hall of Fame Award for outstanding artistic achievement (1989) and two NAACP Image Awards (1989, 1996), induction into the Theater Hall of Fame (1994), the U.S. National Medal for the Arts (1995), the Presidential Medal for Lifetime Achievement in the Arts (1995), the Screen Actor's Guild Lifetime Achievement Award (2001), a joint Kennedy Center Honor for lifetime achievement with his wife Ruby Dee (2004), and a posthumous Grammy for his audiobook of *With Ossie and Ruby* (2007). At his funeral, attended by former U.S. President Bill Clinton, musician Wynton Marsalis, actors Alan Alda and Burt Reynolds, writer **Maya Angelou**, and filmmaker **Spike Lee**, Davis was eulogized by his friend of six decades, Harry Belafonte.

REFERENCES: *AA:PoP. AANB. EBLG.* Boxwell, David A., in *GEAAL.* Davis, Ossie, and Ruby Dee. 1998. *With Ossie and Ruby: In This Life Together,* New York: William Morrow. Jackson, Cassandra, in *Act. ATG. B. COCAAL* and *OCAAL. F. W. W2B. Wiki.* Edwards, Roanne, in *EA-99.* Ford, Sara J., in *T-CAD-3rd.* Greene, Michael E., in *AAW-55-85:DPW.* Mitchell, Louis D., in *CD-5.* Mulvaney, Jayne F., in *T-CAD-1st.* "Profile: Remembering Ossie Davis, who died at age 87." *All Things Considered.* (Feb. 4, 2005) From *Literature Resource Center.* Shuman, R. Baird, in //0-web.ebscohost.com.dbpcosdcsgt. co.san-diego.ca.us/novelist/detail?vid=54&hid=7&sid=d408b38a-8f 5e-4ec2-b75c-cf9c5b5097d7%40sessionmgr3&bdata=JnNpdGU9bm 92ZWxpc3QtbGl2ZQ%3d%3d. Amazon.com, barnesandnoble.com, 7/1999, 3/2009. *G-97.* Wankoff, Jordan, and Sara Pendergast, in *BB. CAO-07.*

Davis, Thulani (née Barbara Davis)
5/22/1948–
Poems, novels, articles, libretti, lyrics and liner notes, autobiography/memoir; educator, performance artist

After reporting for the *San Francisco Sun-Reporter* in the mid-1970s, Davis started regularly contributing essays, articles, interviews, and reviews to New York City's *Village Voice* (until 2004), as well as other periodicals. Davis's book-length published works include her poetry collections *All the Renegade Ghosts Rise* (1978) and *Playing the Changes* (1985); the text accompanying a photograph book, *Malcolm X: The Great Photographs* (1995, photos by Howard Chapnick); and her memoir, *My Confederate Kinfolk: A Twenty-First Century Freedwoman Confronts Her Roots* (2006). She also wrote two Book-of-the-Month Club-selected novels: *1959* (1992), about a pubescent girl's experiences in the civil-rights-era South; and 1997 American Book Award-winning *Maker of Saints* (1996), a contemporary murder mystery in Manhattan.

A performance artist herself, she has often collaborated with others to create numerous performance pieces. With **Ntozake Shange**, **Jessica Hagedorn**, and other spoken-word artists, she formed Third World Artists Collective in San Francisco in the mid-1970s. She, Shange, and Hagedorn also cowrote *Where the Mississippi Meets the Amazon* (1977) and *Shadow and Veil* (1982). She has written lyrics or libretti for several musical pieces in collaboration with her cousin, composer Anthony Davis (e.g., *See Tee's New Blues,* 1982; *Steppin' Other Shores,* 1987; *Amistad,* 1997); with composer Anne LeBaron (*The E & O Line,* 1989; *The Musical Railism,* 1998); and with composer Bernadette Speach (*Without Borders,* 1989; *Baobab Four,* 1994; *A Woman Unadorned,* 1994; *Reflections,* 2002). She has also collaborated with her husband, musician and Buddhist priest Joseph Jarman. On her own, she has written additional plays (e.g., *Paint,* 1982; *Ava & Cat in Mexico,* 1994; *Everybody's Ruby: Story of Murder in Florida,* 1999; *The Souls of Black Folk,* 2003), screenplay adaptations (*Paid in Full,* 2002; *Maker of Saints,* 2006, based on her own novel), libretti (e.g., *X: The Life and Times of* **Malcolm X,** 1986), documentaries (*Fanfare for the Warriors,* 1985; *Thulani Davis Asks, Why Howard Beach?,* 1987), a one-woman stage show (*Sweet Talk and Stray Desires,* 1979), and other performance pieces.

REFERENCES: *AANB. EBLG.* Black-Parker, Kimberly, in *CAO-07. GEAAL.*

de Burgos, Julia
2/17/1914–7/6/1953
Poems, mostly in Spanish; educator

De Burgos's fame is far greater in Puerto Rico than elsewhere in the United States, chiefly because she wrote primarily in Spanish, her first language. One of her translators, Jack Agüeros, is reputed to have called her "Puerto Rico's greatest poet," a *Booklist* reviewer called her "the most important Puerto Rican woman poet of the century," and a *Library Journal* reviewer called her "almost legendary" (quoted in *CAO-03*). Her Spanish-language collections include *Poemas Exactos a Mi Misma* [Exact Poems to Myself] (1937), *Poema en Veinte Surcos* [Poem in Twenty Furrows] (1938/1983), and *Canción De La Verdad Sencilla* [Song of the Simple Truth] (1939/1982).

Decades after de Burgos' death, Carmen D. Lucca translated some of her poems for a bilingual edition, *Roses in the Mirror* (1992); Rafael Ramos Albelo translated other poems to create *A Rose Made of Water* (1994); and Jack Agüeros translated all of her poems for a complete bilingual collection, *Song of the Simple Truth: The Complete Poems of Julia de Burgos* (1995). At last, with these translations, she received critical acclaim in the United States. Several Spanish-language editions were also published after her death, including *El Mar y Tu, y Otros Poemas* [The Sea and You, and Other Poems] (1954/1981), *Obra Poetica* [Works of Poetry] (1961/2005), *Poesías* [Poems] (1964), *Cuadernos de Poesia* [Poetry Notebooks] (1964), *Antología Poética* [Poetry Anthology] (1967; 1979, edited by Emilio M. Colon), *Julia de Burgos: Yo Misma Fui Mi Ruta* (1986, edited by Maria M. Sola), *Julia de Burgos* (1986/2004, selected poems and letters, edited by Manuel de la Puebla), *Julia de Burgos* (1990, selected poems), and *Julia de Burgos: Amor y Soledad* [Love and Solitude] (1994, selected poems, edited by Manuel de la Puebla).

The eldest child in a large family, de Burgos managed to earn a University of Puerto Rico teaching certificate after two years of study (1933). When further education was financially out of reach, she found work in child-care centers and in rural schools. An early feminist, she championed Puerto Rico nationalism and opposed dictators. Starting in the 1940s, she spent time in New York and in Cuba, finally settling in New York, where she died, unknown and uncelebrated.

REFERENCES: *CAO-03. Wiki.* Ocasio, Rafael, in *AANB.* Román-Odio, Clara, in *MSAP-2.* Amazon.com.

Deal, Borden (aka Loyse Deal, Lee Borden, Leigh Borden) (aka Her, Him, Us for his erotica)
10/12/1922–1/22/1985
Novels, short stories, nonfiction; journalist

The Great Depression took the Deal family's farm, and the Deals moved to a government-sponsored farming project where a community of family farmers barely eked out a living. When Borden's father died in a truck accident (1938), teenage Borden decided to make his own way in the world, finding assorted jobs as a sawdust hauler, Civilian Conservation Corps firefighter, antiaircraft fire-control instructor, telephone solicitor, labor auditor, migrant farm worker, and copywriter for radio stations in Mobile, Alabama. Cobbling together an assortment of paychecks, Deal managed to earn his B.A. from the University of Alabama at Tuscaloosa (1949).

Even before graduating, Deal won *Tomorrow* magazine's national contest for college writing (1948), and his short story "Exodus" was published in *Best American Short Stories of 1949.* Over the next few decades, he wrote more than 100 short stories, published in numerous periodicals—literary journals such as *Collier's, Saturday Evening Post,* and *Southwest Review,* as well as magazines such as *McCall's* and *Good Housekeeping.* They also appeared in many other anthologies, such as *Best American Short Stories of 1962, Ellery Queen's Double Dozen* (1964), *Witches Brew* (1975), *Alfred Hitchcock's Anthology* and *Al-*

fred Hitchcock's Tales to Send Chills Down Your Spine (both 1979), and even in high school and college textbooks. Many of his works appeared under pen names, such as Loyse Deal, Lee Borden, Leigh Borden, and even Her, Him, or Us for his erotica writings. He also published at least one essay, "The Function of the Artist: Creativity and the Collective Unconscious" (1966, *Southwest Review,* pp. 239-253).

Soon after graduating, Deal went to Mexico City College to do graduate work (1950), while supporting himself as a freelance journalist. He later worked as a correspondent for Association Films in New York City before he was able to support himself on his fiction writing (starting in 1954). He wrote nearly two dozen novels, and his stories and his books have been translated into at least 20 different languages. His first novel was *Walk through the Valley* (1956), which earned an honorable mention in the American Library Association's Liberty and Justice Awards contest. His best-known novel, *Dunbar's Cove* (1957), was chosen as a *Readers Digest Condensed Book* (1957); other novels of his were condensed for *Reader's Digest* in 1958, 1967, and 1983. Award-winning filmmaker Elia Kazan later said *Dunbar's Cove* strongly influenced his screenplay for *Wild River* (1960). In 1957, Deal also won a Guggenheim Fellowship for creative writing, and he produced his novels *Killer in the House* and *Search for Surrender* (both 1957). The following year, he published *Secret of Sylvia* (1958), and he closed out the 1950s with *The Insolent Breed* (1959), on which the Broadway musical *A Joyful Noise* (1966) was based. As in many of his other works, Deal set *The Insolent Breed* in farm country, showing both an appreciation for local culture and a disdain for judgmental, reactionary, parochial values.

In the 1960s, in addition to his short stories, Deal published several more novels: *Dragon's Wine* (1960), *Devil's Whispers* (1961), *The Spangled Road* (1962), and *A Long Way to Go* and *The Tobacco Men* (both 1965). Deal also started his first trilogy of novels probing the conflicts between traditional and contemporary value systems emerging in the "New South" of the 1960s and 1970s: *The Loser: A Novel* (1964), *The Advocate* (1968), and *The Winner* (1973). Deal's second trilogy, also begun in the 1960s, is set in a farming community in the Deep South, but during the Great Depression: *The Least One* (1967/1992), *The Other Room* (1974), and his overtly autobiographical *There Were Also Strangers* (1985).

In the 1970s, Deal wrote *Interstate* (1970), which pits developers against environmentalists who want to preserve a swamp that hosts a nearly extinct band of ivory-billed woodpeckers. He also wrote *Bluegrass* (1976; also titled *Legend of the Bluegrass,* 1977) and *Adventure* (1978). In addition to *A Joyful Noise,* other adaptations of his work have been produced for stage, film, radio, and television. According to //www.amazon.com, Deal's short story "Antaeus" has been published as a separate hard-cover work (1993), and his 27-page pamphlet *A Neo-So-cratic Dialogue on the Reluctant Empire* (1971) is also still available. Borden Deal's manuscripts and other papers are archived at Boston University.

A member of the Authors Guild and of P.E.N., Deal was also a fellow of the prestigious MacDowell Colony. Deal was married twice: first, briefly, to Lillian Slobtotosky (1950), with whom he had one child and then divorced soon after; and then to fellow novelist Bab Hodges (1952-1975), with whom he had three more children before they divorced.

REFERENCES: *Wiki.* Olson, Ted, in *AANB.* Waddell, James R., in *ANSWWII-2nd.* //en.wikipedia.org/wiki/A_Joyful_Noise. //en.wikipedia.org/wiki/Elia_Kazan. Amazon.com.

Dee, Ruby (née Ruby Ann Wallace)
10/27/1924–

Children's books, poems, stories, plays, memoirs; actor, activist

Her husband, **Ossie Davis**, introduced her *My One Good Nerve: Rhythms, Rhymes, Reasons* (1986) with this observation: "Here is a mind that diddles with nursery rhymes, that turns popular themes upside down in unex-pected stories and poems that are serious without half try-ing as they pay tribute, embrace or criticize. For example, the nursery rhymes—behind the chuckles—are com-ments about unemployment, loneliness, racism, housing, abortion, love and death. The stories are fantasies about overpopulation, growing old, looking for a hand-out from heaven, or eating pork. Some seem almost autobiographi-cal as she writes about childhood memories or an experi-ence in Hollywood. There is a real appreciation here of the people she salutes in poetry and prose." She and Da-vis published *With Ossie and Ruby: In This Life Together* in 1998, celebrating 50 years of marriage at the time.

You may know Dee better for her acting, which she started doing in the early 1940s, along with Sidney Poitier, Harry Belafonte, and the man whom she was to claim as her own, **Ossie Davis**. She has won an Obie and two Drama Desk Awards for her stage work and an Emmy for her television work (she has acted in more than 25 sil-ver-screen and made-for-TV movies since the 1950s, and she and Davis had their own PBS series, *With Ossie and Ruby* in 1981), and she has been nominated for an Emmy, an Oscar, and an Image Award. More importantly, she managed to create a fine acting career even though she consistently chose her conscience over opportunities to enhance her career by keeping quiet, by restraining her protests, by not supporting **Malcolm X**, the Black Pan-thers, or any other militants who asserted their rights and pursued freedom. Her activism included membership in

Ruby Dee

the Congress of Racial Equality (CORE), the Student Nonviolent Coordinating Committee (SNCC), the Na-tional Association for the Advancement of Colored Peo-ple (NAACP), and the Southern Christian Leadership Conference (SCLC), as well as friendship with both Dr. Martin Luther King, Jr., and Malcolm X.

For the world of literature, long before she published her *My One Good Nerve*, she started contributing poems to Harlem's *Amsterdam News* when she was still a teen-ager. Since then, she has edited poetry collections (e.g., *Glowchild and Other Poems*, 1972) and written children's books (e.g., *Two Ways to Count to Ten* and *Tower to Heaven*), stories, and plays, including the script for the musical *Take It from the Top*. In 1989, she received a Liter-ary Guild Award for her body of work.

REFERENCES: *BAAW.* Pagan, Margaret D., in *BWA:AHE. EA-99.* —Tonya Bolden

Editor's note: Dee also worked as a columnist for the *Amsterdam News* and as an associate editor for *Freedomways.* After the 1963 Birmingham church bomb-ing that killed four little girls, she founded Artists and Writers for Justice, which included **James Baldwin, John O. Killens,** and **Louis Lomax** and called for economic boycotts as a weapon for ending racial violence. With her husband, Dee was awarded the Presidential Medal for Lifetime Achievement in the Arts (1995), the Screen

Actors Guild Life Achievement Award (2001), the St. Louis International Film Festival Lifetime Achievement Award (1998), and a Kennedy Center Honor for lifetime achievement (2004), as well as two awards given after Davis died—a Lifetime Achievement Freedom Award from the National Civil Rights Museum in Memphis (2005) and a Grammy for Best Spoken Word Album (2007). She and Davis also had three children (Guy Davis, Nora Day, and Hasna Muhammad) and seven grandchildren by the time Davis died in 2005. Ruby's surname Dee was a remnant of her brief first marriage to blues singer Frankie Dee.

REFERENCES: "Dee, Ruby," and Gray, Pamela Lee, "Lomax, Louis Emanuel," in *AANB. Act. ATG. B. F. W2B. Wiki.* Harroun, Debra G., and Tom Pendergast, in *BB. CAO-07.*

Delaney, Sara ("Sadie") Marie (née Johnson) (1st married name: Peterson)
2/26/1889–5/4/1958
Nonfiction articles-library sciences, bibliography

Delaney's published works involve her articles on bibliotherapy (e.g., "Bibliotherapy in a Hospital," 1938, *Opportunity* magazine) and on the need for books about African Americans (e.g., "The Negro and His Books"), but perhaps her major contribution to literature was her initiation and promotion of books as a therapeutic means of recovery for African-American war veterans, in her role as chief librarian of the U.S. Veterans Administration Hospital in Tuskegee, Alabama (where she expanded the library's collection from 200 to 4,000 books, as well as other materials). Prior to her work at Tuskegee, Delaney had worked at the New York Public Library branch in the center of the **Harlem Renaissance**, where she learned firsthand about noteworthy African-American authors. (Sara's birth surname was Johnson, her first married surname was Peterson, and her second married surname was Delaney.)

RERERENCES: *BAAW.* —Tonya Bolden

Delany, Annie Elizabeth ("Bessie")
9/3/1891–9/25/1995
Memoir, inspirational advice; dentist

The third of ten children, Bessie Delany, like all her other siblings, worked her way through college. Initially, Bessie graduated from St. Augustine's College in Raleigh, North Carolina. With that start on her education, she taught school for a little more than two years, when a confrontation with an intoxicated white man just about got her lynched. Soon after, she and her sister left the Jim Crow South and moved to New York City, where she en-

rolled in dentistry courses at Columbia University in 1919. In 1923, she was awarded her doctorate of dental surgery and became the second African-American woman to become a licensed dentist in New York City. When she retired from her practice in 1950, she was still charging the same rates she had charged when she started her practice. After all, she said, she "was getting by OK. I was always proud of my work, and that was enough for me." After hours, political activists such as family friend **W. E. B. Du Bois**, sociologist **Edward Franklin Frazier**, and NAACP leader **Walter White** frequently met at Delany's dental office.

Bessie Delany's chief contribution to literature is the book she wrote with her sister **Sadie Delany**, *Having Our Say: The Delany Sisters' First 100 Years* (1993, with *New York Times* reporter Amy Hill Hearth). In their book, these two centenarians vividly and charmingly chronicled more than 100 years of their lives and of distinctive American experiences across the span of the twentieth century. Although they drop names (e.g., fellow Harlemite **Adam Clayton Powell** and various celebrities of the **Harlem Renaissance**), they do so with humor and grace. Camille Cosby (*see* **Bill Cosby**) purchased the film, stage, and television rights to their runaway best-seller, which became the basis for a Broadway play, which was subsequently made into a full-length TV movie. By popular demand, the two sisters then wrote *The Delany Sisters' Book of Everyday Knowledge* (1994, with Amy Hill Hearth), in which they offered uplifting inspiration and down-to-earth advice (e.g., they recommended reading the newspaper and watching Public Television's news-hour show each day, praying twice daily, doing yoga exercises, eating lots of vegetables and garlic every day, and taking cod-liver oil and vitamin supplements). Author **Samuel Delany** is Bessie and Sadie's nephew.

REFERENCES: *AANB.* Browne, Phiefer L., in *BH2C. CAO-03. EB-98. PBW. Wiki.* Amazon.com, 7/1999

Delany, Clarissa (née Scott)
?/1901–1927
Poems, essays

In association with the Urban League and the Women's City Club of New York, Delany published a study, "Delinquency and Neglect among Negro Children in New York City." Unfortunately, many of Delany's writings were unpublished and thereby lost to posterity when members of her immediate family died. Nonetheless, we do still have some of her works, which were published in anthologies and literary periodicals, including her essay "A Golden Afternoon in Germany" and poems "Interim," "The Mask," "Solace," and "Joy." Of these, the best known is her very long prize-winning poem "Solace," published in the Urban League's *Opportunity* magazine in 1925.

REFERENCES: *BAAW.* —Tonya Bolden

Delany, Martin R. (Robison)
5/6/1812–1/24/1885
Novel, nonfiction books and articles

One of the first African Americans to enter Harvard Medical School, Delany is better known for his writing, for which he is often called the "father of black nationalism."

In the mid-1840s (1843-1847), Delany launched *Mystery,* his weekly abolitionist, feminist, civil-rights newspaper. Even with his focus on abolition and civil rights, many of the articles he printed were later reprinted in white-owned newspapers because of the high quality of the writing and the journalism. In the late1840s (1847-1849), he stopped publishing his own paper and joined **Frederick Douglass** as coeditor of Douglass's *North Star,* another abolitionist weekly newspaper. At the end of the 1840s, he turned his attention to medical school and to his medical practice for a time, but by the early 1850s, he once again made time for his political views.

In 1852, Delany alienated—and infuriated—his fellow abolitionists with his *The Condition, Elevation, Emigration and Destiny of the Colored People of the United States, Politically Considered,* in which he appealed to African Americans to abandon hope of eliminating slavery and oppression in America and to emigrate to Africa instead. In 1856, he moved his family (which would eventually include seven children, all named after admirable Africans and African Americans) to Chatham, Ontario (the "Canada West" **Mary Ann Shadd** [Cary] described so invitingly and a hotbed of revolutionary abolitionism). There, in 1859, he published his highly popular insurrectionist, pan-African novel, *Blake, or The Huts of America,* considered to be the first black-nationalist novel. Sadly, in the copies still extant today, the last six chapters are missing.

Starting in the spring of '59, Delany practiced what he preached, sailing to Africa and exploring Liberia and the Niger Valley for three-quarters of a year. He published his account of that sojourn in his *Official Report of the Niger Valley Exploring Party* in 1861 (reprinted in 1969 by the University of Michigan Press). During the Civil War, Delany returned to the United States and served as surgeon for the 54th Massachusetts Volunteers. He also recruited numerous soldiers for the Union Army and became the first African American to receive a regular army commission (as a major, awarded by President Abraham Lincoln) for his efforts.

Delany's other writings include essays on international and national policy and politics, reflections on the Civil War, scholarly articles on botany, and *Principia of Ethnology: The Origins of Races and Color with an Archaeological Compendium of Ethiopian and Egyptian Civilizations* (1879), his study of African history from biblical times to his times, highlighting African achievements and contributions to ancient civilization. The first book *about* Delany, *Life and Public Services of Martin R. Delany* (1868), was authored by **Frances A. Rollin (Whipper)**.

REFERENCES: *PGAA. SMKC.* Austin, Allan D., in *OCAAL.* Davis, Matthew R., in *GEAAL. EB-98.* Sellman, James Clyde, in *EA-99.* —Tonya Bolden

Delany, Jr., Samuel ("Chip") R. (Ray) (occasional pen names: K. Leslie Steiner, S. L. Kermit)
4/1/1942–
Short stories, science-fiction novels, autobiography/ memoir, literary criticism; educator

Young Samuel was the namesake of his father, the prosperous owner of Levy and Delany, a Harlem funeral parlor, and he was the only child of Samuel Sr. and his wife, Margaret Carey Boyd Delany, a clerk on the staff of the New York Public Library. Other influences on young Samuel included his father's older sisters, **Sadie Delany**, a teacher, and **Bessie Delany**, a dentist. Samuel Sr. and Margaret provided their son with rich cultural experiences, including lessons in playing the violin and the guitar, in acting and ballet dancing. From 1947 through 1956, they sent him to the progressive Dalton elementary school, a private school where his chums were primarily upper-class liberal European Americans and Jewish Americans; even his summers were spent in racially integrated youth camps in upstate New York. Even given these advantages, Samuel Jr. suffered from dyslexia, which wasn't diagnosed at the time, so he always had to struggle with his schoolwork, despite being intellectually gifted and culturally privileged. Nonetheless, Samuel Jr. read widely, including the writings of numerous African-American authors, classical mythology, fantasy, and science fiction. He particularly enjoyed the stories of Ray Bradbury, Robert Heinlein, and Jules Verne, and later those of Arthur C. Clarke and others, as well.

In 1956, Delany enrolled in the prestigious public Bronx High School of Science. There, he excelled in math and science (especially physics), and he met Jewish poet and prodigy Marilyn Hacker. Delany was quite prodigious himself, singing folk songs, writing a violin concerto, keeping a journal, and writing science fiction. Before he reached his teens, he had written some sword-and-sorcery fantasies in his journals; in his teens, he wrote quite a few never-published novels (from 1954 to 1961). His adolescence was not problem free, however, as it included some unsettling sexual experimentation, a troublesome relationship with his father, and counseling sessions with a psychiatrist.

After graduating from high school, Delany attended the City College of New York (1960, 1962-1963). At age 19, Delany married Hacker, and she encouraged him to submit his manuscript to Ace Books, where she was working. While still 19, he published his novel *The Jewels of Aptor* (1962). Hacker went on to become a National Book Award-winning poet, and Delany and she coedited the first four issues of the speculative fiction quarterly *Quark* (1970-1971). (Eventually, after the couple had a daughter together, their relationship disintegrated; they separated in 1975 and divorced in 1980. Since then, Delany has openly identified himself as homosexual.)

During the 1970s, Delany lived in the Heavenly Breakfast commune in New York City and played in a rock band. In 1975, Delany was named Visiting Butler Chair Professor of English at the State University of New York at Buffalo. In 1977, he moved on to become senior fellow at the Center for Twentieth Century Studies at the University of Wisconsin, Milwaukee. Since 1988, he has been a professor of contemporary literature at the University of Massachusetts at Amherst.

Although Delany is best known for his novels, as well as his nonfiction, he has also written comic-book scripts, a film screenplay (the half-hour film *The Orchid*, which he also directed and edited), and short stories. His short stories include "Aye, and Gomorrah" (1967), which won a Nebula Award from the Science Fiction Writers of America; and "Time Considered as a Helix of Semi-Precious Stones" (1969), which won both a Nebula Award and a Hugo Award (at the World Science Fiction Convention at Heidelberg). His short stories have been collected in *Driftglass: Ten Tales of Speculative Fiction* (1971), *Distant Stars* (1981), *The Complete Nebula Award-Winning Fiction* (1983), *Driftglass/Starshards* (1993), *Atlantis: Three Tales* (1995), and *Aye, and Gomorrah: Stories* (2002).

Literary critics have divided Delany's novels into two periods: his early novels, which have been described as "space operas"; and his later novels, which are considered more complex and fully developed. His early novels used highly literary language, but though his tales were original, and his characters included females and blacks, the books still relied heavily on conventions typical of the sci-fi genre, such as exotic, futuristic settings with heavy emphasis on aliens, intergalactic conflicts, spaceships, and other technological gee-whiz gadgets. These novels include *The Jewels of Aptor* (1962), *The Ballad of Beta-2* (1964), and his *Fall of the Towers* trilogy: *Captives of the*

Flame (1963), *The Towers of Toron* (1964), and *City of a Thousand Suns* (1965). In 1965, he suffered a nervous breakdown, following which he tried to slow down the speed with which he whipped out his novels. In 1966, he published *Babel-17* (1966), which featured an artist as its protagonist and explored the ways in which language shapes human experience. *Babel-17* earned him the first of his five Nebula Awards and marked the beginning of his recognition as a major science-fiction writer. It was followed by his novella *Empire Star* (1966), Nebula Award-winning *The Einstein Intersection* (1967), and *Nova* (1968), sometimes considered the best of his space-opera novels.

His later novels can be read on multiple levels. In these works, he addresses issues of race and gender, freedom and slavery, and sexual desire and sexual identity. He once observed, "The constant and insistent experience I have had as a black man, a gay man, as a science fiction writer in racist, sexist, homophobic America, with its carefully maintained tradition of high art and low, colors and contours every sentence I write" (quoted in *OCAAL*). Delany also textures these later novels by using anthropology, linguistics, and philosophy to explore language and meanings, mythology and power. In addition, these novels reflect a greater mastery of his craft, with a sophisticated narrative structure and rich literary allusions. These novels include *The Tides of Lust* (1973, also published as *Equinox*), *Dhalgren* (1975), *Triton* (1976), *Stars in My Pocket Like Grains of Sand* (1984), *They Fly at Ciron* (1992), *The Mad Man* (1994), *Hogg: A Novel* (2004), *Phallos* (2004, a novella), *Dark Reflections* (2007), and what was said to be his forthcoming *Through the Valley of the Nest of Spiders* (2009).

Starting in the 1980s, Delany also returned to a genre he had enjoyed while still in his teens: sword-and-sorcery fantasies. Between 1979 and 1987, he wrote the four-volume *Return to Nevèrÿon* series: *Tales of Nevèrÿon* (1979, short stories), *Neveryóna: Or the Tale of Signs and Cities* (1983, novel), *Flight from Neveryóna* (1985, novella), and *The Bridge of Lost Desire* (1987, novella). The books are set in a prehistoric, precivilized, preindustrial empire.

Since the mid-1970s, Delany has also written numerous nonfiction works, including some books of literary criticism (sometimes using the pen names K. Leslie Steiner and S. L. Kermit for these works): *The Jewel-Hinged Jaw: Notes on the Language of Science Fiction* (1977), *The American Shore: Meditations on a Tale of Science Fiction* (1978), *Starboard Wine: More Notes on the Language of Science Fiction* (1984), *The Straits of Messina* (1989), *Silent Interviews: On Language, Race, Sex, Science Fiction and Some Comics* (1994), *Longer Views: Extended Essays* (1996), *Shorter Views: Queer Thoughts and Politics of the Paraliterary* (2000), and *About Writing: Seven Essays, Four Letters, and Five Interviews* (2005). He has also written the autobiographical books *Heavenly Breakfast* (1979), about his experiences in communal living during the late 1960s; *The Motion of Light in Water: Sex and Science Fiction Writing in the East Village* (1988/2004), about his experiences in the 1960s, when the counterculture of New York met the gay subculture; *Times Square Red, Times Square Blue* (1999), about interactions in New York City; *Bread & Wine: An Erotic Tale of New York; An Autobiographical Account* (1999), written in comic-book format; *1984: Selected Letters* (2000).

In addition to his Hugo and Nebula awards, Delany has been given the Pilgrim Award for excellence in science-fiction criticism from the Science Fiction Research Association (1985) and the Bill Whitehead Memorial Award for Lifetime Excellence in Gay and Lesbian Literature (1993).

REFERENCES: *AANB. AA:PoP. EBLG. NAAAL. OC20LE. WDAA.* Alterman, Peter S. in *T-CASFW.* Douglas, Barbour, in *SFW:CSMA.* Govan, Sandra Y. in *AAFW-55-84. COCAAL* and *OCAAL.* Shepherd, Reginald, in *BCE. GEAAL. W2B. Wiki.* Smethurst, James, in *EA-99.* Steiner, K. Leslie. "An Interview with Samuel R. Delany." *The Review of Contemporary Fiction.* 16.3 (Fall 1996) p. 97. From *Literature Resource Center.* Styrsky, Stefen. "Order Out of Chaos: Samuel R. Delany on Codes, Science Fiction and Philosophy." *Lambda Book Report.* 13.1-2 (August-September 2004) p. 6. From *Literature Resource Center.* //en.wikiquote.org/wiki/Samuel_R._Delany. Amazon.com. *EB-98. G-97.* SDPL catalog. Wainwright, Mary Katherine, in *BB. CAO-08. MWEL.*

Delany, Sarah "Sadie" (Louise)
9/19/1889–1/25/1999
Memoir, inspirational advice; educator, home economist

The second of ten children, Sarah ("Sadie") Delany and all her siblings earned their own way through a college education. For Sadie, that meant graduating from St. Augustine's College in Raleigh, North Carolina, after which she taught school for a while and then took on the job of county school superintendent, chauffeuring **Booker T. Washington** to show him the schools she supervised. When the brutality of Jim Crow laws confronted Sadie and her younger sister Bessie, the pair moved to New York, where Sadie graduated from the two-year program at the Pratt Institute, followed by a bachelor of science degree (1920) and then a master's degree (1925) from Columbia University. With her degrees in hand, while the Great Depression was making jobs scarce for everyone, she was appointed to teach at an all-white school. By evading a white-face-to-black-face interview with school personnel, she had become the first African-American woman home-economics ("domestic science") teacher in New York, where she taught from for 30 or so years. Both she and Bessie (one of the first Afri-

can-American women dentists) devoted their lives to their careers, rather than to marrying and to raising children.

When they were both centenarians, Sadie and her sister Bessie wrote *Having Our Say: The Delany Sisters' First 100 Years* (1993, with *New York Times* reporter Amy Hill Hearth), their spirited observations on 100 years of living well in the midst of turbulent times—from lynchings and the imposition of Jim Crow policies, through the **Harlem Renaissance**, the Great Depression, and the civil-rights movement, to the last decade of the twentieth century. This long-running best-selling book was the basis for a Broadway play and a full-length TV movie, and it inspired such reader demand that the sisters subsequently wrote *The Delany Sisters' Book of Everyday Knowledge* (1994, with Amy Hill Hearth). After Bessie's death in 1995, Sadie wrote *On My Own at 107: Reflections on Life without Bessie* (1997, with Amy Hill Hearth), in which she lovingly recalls her memories of her sister, while affirming life on her own. Author **Samuel Delany** is the son of Sadie and Bessie's youngest brother.

REFERENCES: *AANB.* Brown, Phiefer L., in *BH2C. CAO-01. PBW. W. Wiki.* Washington, Mary Helen. "Having Our Say: The Delany Sister's First 100 Years." *The Women's Review of Books.* 11.4 (Jan. 1994) p. 9. From *Literature Resource Center.* //www.hcoa.org/features/delaney.htm. Amazon.com, 7/1999.

Demby, William
12/25/1922–
Novels, screenplays; musician, journalist, ad writer, educator

William Demby and Gertrude Hendricks had first-hand experience with racial discrimination, having been barred from entering college (in Philadelphia) to study architecture and medicine, respectively. They also were aware of the race riots and the all-too-frequent lynchings of African Americans during the post-World War I era. After the couple married, William got a white-collar job in a munitions factory (and later in a natural-gas company), and they moved to Pittsburgh. There, William the younger arrived on Christmas day, and William's five sisters and one brother followed. The Dembys lived in a middle-class culturally diverse community, where families of first-generation immigrants (from Ireland, Poland, or Italy) mingled with African-American families. Much to the pleasure of the Dembys, members of this community understood that pride in being an American could coexist with pride in a cultural heritage from a distant land.

At Langley High School, young William became a jazz musician, a writer, and a socialist. He also observed how pride of ethnicity, religion, and political affiliation could lead to conflict. After William graduated (1941), his family moved to Clarksburg, West Virginia, a much more African-American community, which offered William a captivatingly new way of looking at the world. Demby started attending West Virginia State College, where he studied music, philosophy, and literature, taking writing classes from poet-novelist **Margaret Walker**. His love of playing jazz music also led him to the Cotton Club (in South Carolina), and soon he was skipping classes to play there (or to sleep in after playing the previous night). Eventually, he had missed so many classes that he wasn't making progress in school, and he decided to join the army to help the Allies in World War II.

He spent some of his military service in North Africa, but for most of his two-year tour, he was stationed in Italy. During that time, he wrote for the military newspaper *Stars and Stripes*. After his discharge from the service, he returned to college. This time, he enrolled in Fisk University, took his studies seriously, and delved into writing. While Demby was in his senior year at Fisk, poet **Robert Hayden** started teaching at Fisk and shepherding the militantly antifascist student newspaper, the *Fisk Herald*. Hayden also encouraged Demby to contribute to the paper, which Demby did. One of the stories Demby contributed to the *Herald*, "Saint Joey," was the basis for his first novel, *Beetlecreek* (1950, also released as *Act of Outrage*).

After he graduated (B.A., 1957) from Fisk, he returned to Rome. There, he supported himself by playing the alto saxophone in jazz groups and working for the Italian film and television industry (writing screenplays and adapting Italian screenplays for English-speaking audiences). In his free time, he studied literature at the University of Rome, published essays and other short pieces, painted, and traveled extensively. During this time, he also married Italian poet-writer Lucia Drudia, with whom he had a son, James, who composes music.

While in Italy, he wrote some nonfiction pieces and completed his novel *Beetlecreek*, set in an economically (and perhaps spiritually) depressed town in West Virginia. The novel centers around the rather desperate lives of three individuals: a reclusive elderly white man, a gang-affiliated black teenager, and an artist who gets involved with an unsavory woman. Mondavi, one of Italy's most prestigious publishers, produced this internationally acclaimed novel. In Demby's second novel, *The Catacombs* (1965), set in the area surrounding the Roman catacombs, Demby includes himself in the book as a fiction writer telling about a love affair between an African-American actress/dancer and an Italian count.

Around the time that *Catacombs* was published, Demby returned to the United States to live. For a while, he worked in public relations at a New York ad agency. Then in 1969, he started teaching at the College of Staten Island of the City College of New York (later the

William Demby

City University of New York, CUNY), from which he retired in 1987. In 1978, Demby published *Love Story Black* (1978), in which he again places himself in the novel, as Professor Edwards, the author of the novel. In the novel, Professor Edwards ends up in the fantasy life of an 80-year-old ex-vaudeville performer who is writing her memoirs. In 1979, Demby published *Blueboy*, which had limited publication.

In 2006, Demby earned the Anisfield-Wolf Book Awards' Lifetime Achievement Award. As he had noted earlier, "The black writer is . . . the only one who will be giving voice to the experience of black people." One of the early black novelists, Demby observed, "You are one of the very few among the family of your people who are putting things down in this form." He and others paved the way for the plethora of African-American novelists who write today.

In 2004, long after the death of his wife, Lucia, in 1995, William married Barbara Morris, a civil-rights activist and attorney whom he had known at Fisk. The couple moved to Florence, Italy, where they are involved in the music scene and Demby continues to write. Currently, he is working on a novel tentatively titled *King Comus*, about an army cook he knew when he was in the military.

REFERENCES: *BAL-1-P. BWA. EBLG.* Anderson, Joel, in *GEAAL*. Jacobson, Bob, in *BB. CAO-07*. O'Brien, John. "An interview with William Demby." *Studies in Black Literature 3.3* (Autumn 1972), pp. 1-6. Rpt. in Daniel G. Marowski and Roger Matuz (Eds.) (1982),

Contemporary Literary Criticism (Vol. 53). Detroit: Gale Research. From *Literature Resource Center.* Perry, Margaret, in *AAFW-55-84.* Smith, Virginia Whatley, in *COCAAL* and *OCAAL.* W. //en.wikipedia.org/wiki/1950_in_literature, 1950 in literature. //en.wikipedia.org/wiki/Anisfield-Wolf_Book_Awards. //en.wikipedia. org/wiki/List_of_African_American_writers. //en.wikipedia.org/wiki/ Mosaic_literary_magazine. Amazon.com. SDPL catalog.

Dent, (Thomas) Tom (Covington)
3/20/1932–6/6/1998
Poems, essays, oral histories, reviews, plays, autobiography/memoir; mentor, journal founder, collaborator, nurturer of culture

Tom's father had been the president of Dillard College, but Dent chose to attend Morehouse College, where he edited the college newspaper, *The Maroon Tiger,* in his senior year (1951-1952). During summer breaks, he reported for the *Houston Informer.* After graduating with a baccalaureate in political science, this native of New Orleans moved to New York City in 1959 and wrote for African-American weekly the **New York Age.** While in New York, at the inception of the **Black Arts Movement** in 1963 and 1964, Dent, **Calvin Hernton,** and David Henderson produced the poetry journal *Umbra,* as an outgrowth of the Umbra Workshop writing collective they had founded with **Ishmael Reed, Lorenzo Thomas, Askia M. (Muhammed) Touré,** and others.

In 1965, Dent returned to New Orleans where he wrote his best-known play, *Ritual Murder* (1967). While the associate director of the Free Southern Theater (FST), he wrote *The Free Southern Theater by the Free Southern Theater* (1969). Later, he helped launch the FST Writers' Workshop (also known as BLKARTSOUTH), through which he mentored **Kalamu ya Salaam** and other writers until 1973. In 1973, he founded Congo Square Writers Union, which fostered emerging writers, such as Quo Vadis Gex Breaux, with invited readings and lectures from visiting authors such as **Edward Kamau Brathwaite** and **Al Young.**

Dent also cofounded the literary journals *Nkombo* (in 1969, in association with BLKARTSOUTH) and *Callaloo* (starting in 1975) and helped fund the one-issue *The Black River Journal* (1977). His reviews and essays have appeared in numerous African-American periodicals, and his poetry was collected and published in *Magnolia Street* (1976) and *Blue Lights and River Songs* (1982). In addition, Dent was deeply involved in collecting oral histories about New Orleans jazz, about the civil-rights movement, and about the American South in the late twentieth century. In the early 1990s, he expressed this commitment as executive director of the New Orleans Jazz and Heritage Foundation. He left that position in or-

der to write his memoir, *Southern Journey: A Return to the Civil Rights Movement* (1997).

REFERENCES: *AANB.* Hall, John Greer, in *GEAAL.* Salaam, Kalamu ya. "Enriching the Paper Trail: An Interview with Tom Dent." *African American Review.* 27.2 (Summer 1993) p. 327. From *Literature Resource Center.* Thomas, Lorenzo, in *AAW-55-85:DPW.* Ward, Jerry W., Jr., in *CAO-05.* COCAAL and OCAAL. Gex Breaux, Quo Vadis. "Tom Dent's Role in the Organizational Mentoring of African American Southern Writers: A Memoir." *African American Review.* 40.2 (Summer 2006) p. 339. From *Literature Resource Center.* "In Memoriam: Thomas Covington Dent, 1932-1998." *The Mississippi Quarterly.* 52.2 (Spring 1999) p. 213. From *Literature Resource Center.*

Derricotte, Toi (née Toinette Marie Webster)
4/12/1941–
Autobiography/memoir, poems; educator

Starting at about age 10 and continuing through about age 35, Derricotte kept a secret journal documenting her personal experiences. This journal served as the basis for her *The Black Notebooks,* winner of the 1998 Anisfield-Wolf Book Award for Non-Fiction. Best known for her poetry, Derricotte's collections include *The Empress of the Death House* (1978); *Natural Birth* (1983, reprinted in 2000), about her experiences giving birth to her son Anthony 17 years earlier; *Captivity* (1989; reprinted in 1991 and 1993), exploring the lingering effects of slavery on modern-day African Americans; and *Tender* (1997), winner of the 1998 Paterson Poetry Prize. In 1998, she produced a sound recording, *The Poet and the Poem,* for the Library of Congress. For her work, Derricotte has won a Pushcart Prize and a prize nomination, the Distinguished Pioneering of the Arts Award from the United Black Artists, the Lucille Medmick Memorial Award of the Poetry Society of America, the Poetry Committee Book Award from the Folger Shakespeare Library, and other prizes; fellowships from the National Endowment for the Arts, the prestigious MacDowell Colony, the Guggenheim Foundation, the New Jersey State Council on the Arts, the Maryland State Arts Council, and other organizations; and she is a member of the Poetry Society of America and the Academy of American Poets. She has also taught and lectured at numerous colleges and universities, including the University of Pittsburgh (since 1991). In 1996, she and fellow poet **Cornelius Eady** cofounded **Cave Canem,** a prestigious poetry retreat and workshop for African-American poets.

REFERENCES: *AANB.* Allen, Jessica, in *GEAAL.* Richardson, James W., Jr., in *CAO-07.* COCAAL and OCAAL. *LFCC-07.* //www.cavecanempoets.org/pages/programs_faculty.php#toi. //www.newsreel.org/guides/furious.htm. //www.poets.org/poet.php/prmPID/107.

De Veaux (aka Deveaux), Alexis
9/24/1948–

Poems, short stories, children's story, biography, plays, novels, essays; illustrator, editor, lecturer, performance artist

Early in her career, De Veaux's jobs involved mostly visual arts and theater arts. She also worked for *Essence* magazine as poetry editor, feature writer, contributing editor, political commentator, and editor-at-large (1978-1991). For nearly three decades, however, when De Veaux is not writing and illustrating, she has been teaching college students, most recently at the State University of New York (SUNY) at Buffalo (since 1991; chair of the Department of Women's Studies since 2001). She has also lectured and performed across the United States and on five continents.

Internationally renowned, her writings have been published in several languages (e.g., Dutch, Japanese, Serbo-Croatian, and Spanish), and she has published in almost every genre. Across genres, De Veaux writes as an urban, African-American lesbian whose experiences are personal, yet relevant to other African-American women. De Veaux raises social and political issues of worldwide concern (e.g., racial, gender, and economic inequities) in both her fiction and her nonfiction, her poetry and her prose. While considering the big issues, she sensitively and caringly focuses on the distinctive experiences of an individual woman and her personal relationships (e.g., parent-child relationships or lesbian relationships). Also, she reflected, "The fact that I am a woman who loves women informs all of my work. . . . Part of what I try to do in my writing about women loving women is to counter traditional and stereotypic images of what that means. Even if that means being at odds with the African-American literary 'canon.' Even if that means being at odds with 'acceptable' or 'popular' notions of lesbian literature" (quoted in *Black Biography*, 2006, from *Gay and Lesbian Literature*, Vol. 2, 1998). In addition, as she noted herself (*BWWW*, p. 53), "Music is also a great influence on my work. Each piece has a different rhythm."

De Veaux's 1973 novel *Spirits in the Street* interweaves her own surrealistic drawings throughout her narrative about a young African American's experiences in Harlem during the turbulent 1970s. In 1973, De Veaux also wrote and illustrated an award-winning children's book, *Na-Ni*, set in Harlem, which compassionately tells the story of an impoverished child's longings in the face of urban crime and a callous social-welfare system. In 1981, De Veaux's fictionalized biography *Don't Explain: A Song of **Billie Holiday*** (1980) was named one of the American Library Association's Best Books for Young Adults; the book candidly puts the reader into the mindset of this talented and troubled singer. Both it and her children's book *An En-* *chanted Hair Tale* (1987) were named **Coretta Scott King** Honor books by the American Library Association. *An Enchanted Hair Tale* also garnered a Lorraine Hansberry Award for Excellence in African American Children's Literature, and it was featured on the PBS children's show *Reading Rainbow*.

In 1975, De Veaux published a prose poem, *Li Chen/Second Daughter First Son*. Next, De Veaux published her collection *Blue Heat: A Portfolio of Poems and Drawings* (1985). About a decade later, De Veaux started writing her biography of the pioneering African-American poet, librarian, and lesbian mother who boldly challenged stereotypes of all kinds, *Warrior Poet: A Biography of **Audre Lorde*** (2004); it took De Veaux about a decade to thoroughly research and to write the book. Meanwhile, De Veaux's poems, essays, and short stories have continued to appear in national journals, magazines, and anthologies.

De Veaux's play *A Little Play and Whip Cream* was produced in Harlem; her *Circles* was produced for KCET-TV; her *Tapestry* was produced in New York City on PBS; and her *A Season to Unravel* was produced by the Negro Ensemble Company in New York City. Her "choreo-poem," *No* (1981), offering a collection of poems, vignettes, and short stories highlighting the challenges confronting African-American lesbians who are politically active, was produced in New York City. Like her other performance pieces and plays, these explore family and intimate relationships. In addition to these works, De Veaux was involved in a video documentary, *Motherlands: From Manhattan to Managua to Africa, Hand to Hand*. In all her works, as she has noted, "I try to listen to language. I'm very interested in how words work. I try to write each piece in the language of the piece, so that I'm not using the same language from piece to piece."

In addition to her writing, De Veaux managed to cofound a theater company, a writing workshop, and an art gallery, which has exhibited some of her own paintings. She has also been given numerous awards, including two Coretta Scott King Awards, a National Endowment for the Arts fellowship, two Unity in Media Awards, a Fannie Lou Hamer Award for Excellence in the Arts, a PBS grant, and the Lorraine Hansberry Award for Excellence in African-American Children's Literature.

REFERENCES: *BFC. BWWW. EBLG.* Alic, Margaret, in *BB. CAO-07.* Hutchinson, Brandon L. A. in *GEAAL.* King, Lovalerie, in *COCAAL* and *OCAAL.* Moore, Lisa C. "Inside View: An Interview with Alexis De Veaux." *Lambda Book Report. 12.8* (March-April 2004) p. 9. From *Literature Resource Center.* Ramsey, Priscilla R., in *AAFW-55-84.* Amazon.com. SDPL catalog. Wilkerson, Margaret B., in *OCWW.*

Dialect *See* **African-American Vernacular English (AAVE; aka Black English; aka Ebonics; aka Black Dialect)**

"Diddley," "Bo" (né Otha Ellas Bates, adoptive name Ellas Bates McDaniel)
12/30/1928–6/2/2008
Songs; musician, performer

Initially a rhythm-and-blues guitarist, Diddley took to rock 'n' roll right away and soon had written and performed about a dozen hit songs, including "I'm a Man" and "Who Do You Love." In 1987, he was inducted into the Rock and Roll Hall of Fame, and he was later inducted into the Rockabilly Hall of Fame and then the Blues Hall of Fame. He was also given a star on the Hollywood Walk of Fame, a Grammy Lifetime Achievement Award (1998), and a Pioneer Lifetime Achievement Award from the Rhythm and Blues Foundation (1996). His daughter, Evelyn Kelly, posthumously accepted an honorary degree awarded to him by the University of Florida in August, 2008. He was also survived by his other 3 children, Ellas A. McDaniel, Tammi D. McDaniel, and Terri Lynn McDaniel; his 15 grandchildren, his 15 great-grandchildren, and his 3 great-great-grandchildren.

REFERENCES: A. *AANB.* D. *W2B.* "78-year-old Bo Diddley Suffered a Heart Attack on August 24 in Gainesville, Florida." *Sing Out!. 51.4* (Winter 2008) p. 10. From *Literature Resource Center.* Von Tersch, Gary. "Bo Diddley: 1928-2008." *Sing Out! 52.2* (Summer 2008) p. 168. From *Literature Resource Center.* EA-99.

Dodson, Owen (Vincent)
11/28/1914–6/21/1983
Plays, poems, novels

Young Owen was the ninth child in a Brooklyn family that was always short on cash but rich on intellectual stimulation. Owen's dad, a freelance journalist, directed the National Negro Press Association; through his contacts, he introduced Owen to noteworthy African Americans of that era, including the philosophical adversaries **Booker T. Washington** and **W. E. B. Du Bois**. After attending outstanding public schools, Owen went on to Bates College (in Lewiston, Maine, 1932-1936), where he earn his bachelor's degree, and then to Yale University School of Drama (in New Haven, CT, 1936-1939), where he earned his M.F.A. (master's in fine arts) in playwriting. His master's thesis was the manuscript of his play *Divine Comedy* (1938), which was produced at Yale, as was his play *The Garden of Time* (1939).

After Yale, Dodson served in the U.S. Navy and taught theater and literature at several colleges and universities, including the historically black Atlanta and Hampton universities. During this time, he also wrote and directed *New World A-Coming* (1944), about African-American contributions during World War II. In 1947, Dodson started teaching drama at Howard University and directing the Howard University Players. Through his work at Howard, he influenced an entire generation of African-American theater professionals.

In addition to teaching drama, Dodson wrote nearly 40 plays and operas, almost 30 of which have been produced, and 2 of those at the prestigious Kennedy Center. His thesis play, *Divine Comedy* (1938), was a verse drama about the lives of people who are drawn to a charismatic religious leader such as Father Divine. His *The Garden of Time* (1939) was also a verse drama, offering a new interpretation of the ancient Greek myth of Medea, a vengeful sorceress who kills her own children when their father betrays her. Dodson's other plays include *Bayou Legend* (1946) and *Media in Africa* (1964).

In addition to his dramas, Dodson also wrote poetry, some of which was collected in *Powerful Long Ladder* (1946). Dodson regarded as his finest work his *The Confession Stone* (1970), a series of verse monologues uttered by members of the Holy Family, about Jesus's life. Through simple language, Dodson communicates the speakers' humanity. In 1970, James Earl Jones used his rich, mellifluous voice to dramatically read and record Dodson's *The Dream Awake.* In 1978, Dodson's poetic captions accompanied funeral photos taken by celebrated photographer James Van Der Zee in *The Harlem Book of the Dead.* Although Dodson's final poetry collection, "Life on the Streets," was never published, it was performed on stage at the New York Public Theatre in May 1982. Probably his most critically praised poem is his "Yardbird's Skull," which pays homage to renowned jazz musician and composer Charlie "Yardbird" (or simply "Bird") Parker.

Dodson even tackled the novel form in his *Boy at the Window* (1951), published by the esteemed Farrar, Straus and Giroux. In this semiautobiographical novel, a nine-year-old boy in Brooklyn suffers the death of his much-beloved mother and must cope not only with his grief, but also with his guilt, for he believes that if he had undergone a religious conversion, her life might have been spared. The novel's somewhat surrealistic sequel, *Come Home Early, Child,* wasn't published until 1977.

Dodson has also won several major grants for his writing, including a General Education Board grant (1937), Rosenwald (1943) and Guggenheim (1953) fellowships, and a Rockefeller grant (1968). In 1964, President Lyndon Johnson invited Dodson to the White House to celebrate the 400th anniversary of fellow dramatist Shakespeare's birth. In recognition of his lifetime contributions to American drama, in 1974, the Black Repertory

Theater (Washington, D.C.) honored him with a pastiche of his writings, titled *Owen's Song*. While Dodson acknowledged that **Countee Cullen** and **Langston Hughes** influenced his writing, he is credited with influencing the writing of **Amiri Baraka** and others.

REFERENCES: *BAL-1-P. BWA. EBLG. G-97. MWEL. WDAA. Wiki* Claggett, Julie, in *GEAAL*. Hatch, James, in *COCAAL* and *OCAAL*.. Hatch, James V., in *AAW-40-55*.. Minderovic, Christine Miner, and Ralph Zerbonia, in *BB. CAO-07. LF-07. MWEL*.

Domino, Antoine "Fats" Dominique
2/26/1928–
Song lyrics

Domino's distinctive boogie-woogie piano work underscored his dynamic rhythm-and-blues and rock 'n' roll songs, including "Ain't It a Shame," "My Blue Heaven," and "Blueberry Hill." Although several popular white performers stole and marketed several of his songs, he managed to sell more than 65 million records in a dozen years (1950-1962), with at least 13 songs on the Top Ten charts. In 1986, he was inducted into the Rock and Roll Hall of Fame, and in 1987, he was given the Grammy Lifetime Achievement Award. In 1998, President Bill Clinton awarded him the National Medal of Arts. When Hurricane Katrina notoriously devastated Domino's home and its contents in New Orleans, President George Bush personally presented Domino with a replacement in 2006. In the immediate aftermath of Katrina, Domino and his ailing wife Rosemary had been rescued by Coast Guard helicopter, taken to a shelter, and then invited to sleep on the couch in the apartment of their granddaughter's football-player boyfriend. Despite by the devastation to his home and his lifestyle, Domino returned to the New Orleans stage in 2007, performing for a packed house. He and Rosemary have eight children—Antoinette, Antoine III, Andrea, Andre, Anatole, Anola, Adonica, and Antonio—in addition to their grandchildren.

REFERENCES: *AANB. W2B. Wiki*. Myers, Aaron, in *EA-99*.

Dorsey, Thomas (Andrew)
7/1/1899–1/23/1993
Songs—gospel and blues lyrics and tunes

From his earliest days, Dorsey was drawn to "the Lord's music," singing His praises in church, as well as to "the devil's music," getting low-down and funky in juke joints, honky-tonks, and houses of ill repute. The first blues composition he copyrighted (in 1920) was "If You Don't Believe I'm Leaving, You Can Count the Days I'm Gone." After a while, earning his living by playing the blues, he suffered a severe attack of the blues.

While his mother nursed him back to health, she also urged him back into the church, where he saw a new kind of music emerging, called "gospel music"; it melded traditional spirituals and shouts of praise with the contemporary jazzy, bluesy beats he had been enjoying outside the church. Soon, he had written his first sacred song, "If I Don't Get There"; along with his "Someday, Somewhere," it was printed in Willa A. Townsend's edited work, *Gospel Pearls* (1921), produced by the National Baptist Convention.

In the early 1920s (1921-1926), however, he strayed again from sacred music, composing and arranging jazzy, bluesy music for such notables as **Gertrude "Ma" Rainey**. For a time, it looked as though the "Father of Gospel Music" was going to be a son of the blues, instead. In the late 1920s (1926-1928), however, he suffered another severe depression, teetering on the deadly precipice of suicide on more than one occasion. Once again, he was brought back from the edge, and again, he turned to sacred songs in giving thanks for his recovery.

Making a living at gospel songs was tough going at first: Many church-goers rejected his jazzy rhythms as too secular, but folks outside the church rejected his sacred lyrics. On occasion, to put bread on his table, he still wrote decidedly "worldly" songs (e.g., "It's Tight Like That").

At last, in 1930, his "If You See My Savior, Tell Him That You Saw Me" hit big among Baptist church choirs, and Dorsey's career as a gospel songwriter was finally on its way. In 1931, Dorsey founded the first gospel-music publishing company, and he organized some church choirs to spread the gospel. A personal tragedy led to Dorsey's most beloved gift to gospel music: In 1932, his wife died in childbirth, and his newborn daughter died soon after. After three days of deep despair, Dorsey rose up with "Precious Lord, Take My Hand." Eventually, Dorsey was to compose more than 1,000 songs, about half of which were gospel songs, such as "The Lord Will Make a Way Somehow," "There'll Be Peace in the Valley for Me," "Walking Up the King's Highway," "If We Never Needed the Lord Before, We Sure Do Need Him Now," and "Search Me Lord."

REFERENCES: *EA-99. EAACH. PGAA. SMKC*.

Douglass, Frederick (né Frederick Auld)
2/?/1818–2/20/1895
Autobiography/memoir—slave narratives, editorials; journalist, orator

Frederick Douglass stands forth as a shining example of American achievement and ingenuity. Although he was born a slave in Maryland in 1818, in 1895 he died a free man who not only had bought his own freedom with

Frederick Douglass

ings he witnessed during his youth were another major force behind his dissatisfaction as a slave, although he never received such abuse himself. During his childhood he suffered less from violence than from deprivation—in his biography he claims that as a young boy he was not so much beaten as deprived of food, clothing and human contact, his mother having died when he was very young.

He was given his first tool to use in fighting his way out of slavery in 1826, when he was sent to work for his master's son-in-law's brother, Hugh Auld. There, Auld's new bride, Sophia, who had just moved to Maryland from the North, took it as her Christian duty to help Douglass learn to read. When Hugh Auld returned home one day to find her giving Frederick reading lessons, he forcefully forbade his wife to continue, telling her that teaching slaves was both illegal and unsafe. He told her that teaching a slave to read would give him ideas, and that since a slave should think of nothing but his master's wishes, teaching him to read would only make him unhappy and unmanageable, and thus less valuable. While Auld's words effectively put an end to Mrs. Auld's lessons, they inspired Douglass to teach himself how to read and write. Auld's words showed Douglass the power that could be gained from the ability to read ideas and write them down, and he became wholeheartedly determined to acquire that power.

Douglass's determination to break free of slavery increased when, in 1833, he was returned to the Maryland farm on which he was born because of a quarrel between Hugh Auld and his brother. By this time, Douglass had become increasingly resentful of his masters, and his owner decided to send him to work at the farm of Edward Covey, a local slave-breaker. While Douglass was working on the farm, Covey used brutal whippings, unrelenting work, and terrible humiliations to break Douglass's spirit so that he would become an obedient worker. This physical and mental brutality actually had an opposite effect on the 16-year-old Douglass—instead of submitting and becoming more obedient, he fought back, intimidating Covey to such a great extent that the slave breaker refrained from ever touching Douglass again.

Frederick tried to escape from slavery for the first time in 1836, but failed. His master sent him to Baltimore to work in the shipping yards. This setting provided him with a perfect opportunity to escape, and escape he did. In 1838, with the help of some of the money he earned from working in the yards, as well as the assistance of a woman, Anna Murray, who would become his wife, he posed as a free black merchant sailor and boarded a train bound for New York. Although he arrived in New York the next day, his freedom was by no means secure, as the Fugitive Slave Act of 1793 imposed stiff penalties on those who aided in the escape of a slave or abetted an escaped slave. Despite the fact that the Northern states had

the money he earned from his publications and public speaking tours but also had risen to the highest position an African American could hold in the United States government. He became one of the most influential African Americans of the nineteenth century, and throughout his lifetime earned the respect not only of his friends and supporters but also of the entire nation and the U. S. government. By the time of his death he had in many ways become an example both to newly freed black Americans and to white Americans—he showed black Americans that their color need not stand in the way of their achieving great things, and he made whites more aware of their obligation to allow black Americans access to the same opportunities that they were making available to their own children.

Frederick Douglass received no such opportunities—he was, in the purest sense, a self-made man, having received little help from anyone in securing his freedom or making his way in life. He was born of a slave, Harriet Baily, and an unknown white man; his name was originally Frederick Auld, as he bore the last name of the man who owned him. He spent a large portion of his life trying to find information about his birth, but to little avail (although recent historical scholarship has placed it as around 1818). In his biography he records that his resentment at not knowing his birthday was one of the earliest forces behind his desire to break out of slavery. The beat-

passed personal freedom laws to protect escaped slaves, many men and women were returned to slavery in the South after their escape.

Nevertheless, Douglass remained free for the rest of his life. Although he did not know it right away, he had effectively escaped from slavery on September 3, 1838. Within a month, Anna Murray joined him and they married. They moved to a thriving African-American community in New Bedford, Massachusetts, and he changed his name from Auld to Douglass to protect himself. Within three years, he had joined the abolitionist movement led by William Lloyd Garrison, beginning his career as a full-time lecturer in 1841 during an antislavery meeting in Nantucket. He became an eloquent and powerful speaker, and in many ways was known more in his time as an orator than as the brilliant writer for which we know him today.

He began his career as a writer in 1845 when he published his life story: *Narrative of the Life of Frederick Douglass, an American Slave, Written by Himself.* Although he was not the first slave to publish his story, his book was the most successful of all **slave narratives** of the time, selling more than 30 million copies in five years. The success could be attributable to any number of things—his clear, direct, first-person narrative style that made the story both powerful and accessible; the belief that his story well represented the experience of slavery; the highly compelling portrait he painted of African-American selfhood; or the fact that the book was *"Written by Himself"* and thus disrupted many expectations and conventions, as many previous slave narratives were transcribed by amanuenses who recorded the narrators' oral tales. This desire to overturn conventions was in many ways deliberate—Douglass specifically designed this biography and his future writings to create an image of himself that is nothing less than heroic, so as to break social stereotypes in the minds of both whites and blacks.

Yet before those stereotypes could be overturned, Douglass knew he needed to first help to topple the institution of slavery. However, he was still very much afraid he would be captured and returned to his master, more so now that he was receiving a large amount of attention because of the popularity of his book. So, after the book was published he went on a two year speaking tour of Great Britain and Ireland. He returned to the United States in 1847 and, with the money he had earned from his book and his lecture tour, he bought his freedom. Then he began his own newspaper, the *North Star*, both to show that a newspaper run by a black man could succeed and to give himself a forum to freely express himself without needing the approval of other abolitionists. He not only edited and managed the paper, but also wrote most of the articles and editorials. It was in this paper that he first published his novella, "The Heroic Slave."

In the early 1850s, Douglass fought with his close associate William Garrison, leader of the Garrisonian abolitionists. After they split, Douglass did a great deal of reflection and soul-searching and came to the realization that, although progress was still possible, the abolitionists had not yet helped him to fully reach his goals as a free man. Instead he felt he needed to turn to the Northern black community in order to feel a truly liberated sense of self. This period of reflection and realization culminated in Douglass's 1855 publication of his second autobiography, *My Bondage and My Freedom*. In this book, Douglass reevaluates his life after 15 years of being free, reflecting on his goals as a reformer and setting out his realizations about the Garrisonian abolitionists.

Soon after the publication of his second autobiography, in 1859, he had to flee to Canada because he was publicly linked to John Brown, the man who had initiated the raid on Harpers Ferry. While he was in Canada, Abraham Lincoln was elected president, and after the Civil War broke out, Douglass began lobbying Lincoln to allow black men join in the fighting. In 1863, African-American men began to be recruited into the Union Army, and Frederick Douglass delivered inspirational speeches to get men to join in the fight against slavery.

After the war ended, Douglass turned his efforts toward getting President Andrew Johnson to pass a national voting rights act that would make it possible for black men to vote in all states. As a result of his political involvement and his loyalty to the Republican Party, he was appointed to the position of federal marshal and recorder of deeds for Washington, D.C.; assistant secretary of the Santo Domingo Commission; U.S. minister to Haiti; and president of the Freedman's Bureau Bank. These were, at the time, the highest offices that any African American had ever won.

As a result of these appointments and the income from his books and lectures, he earned enough money to live in comfort for the last 20 years of his life. He published his last memoir, *Life and Times of Frederick Douglass*, in 1881 and published an expanded version in 1892. Although the book did not reach the critical or economic success that his earlier autobiographies received, it enunciates the ending of a life of great achievement—what he called a "life of victory, if not complete, at least assured." It also serves as a conclusion of a life that served as an inspiration for African-American writers such as **Booker T. Washington** and **W. E. B. Du Bois**, who were greatly influenced by Douglass in writing their own biographies. Douglass's life serves as a model for heroism, self-advancement, self-liberation, and self-reliance to this day.

REFERENCES: *NAAAL*. Andrews, William L., in *OCAAL*.
—Diane Masiello

Editor's note: Anna Murray Douglass and Frederick had three sons—Charles Remond; Frederick, Jr.; and Lewis Henry—and two daughters—Rosetta and Annie. Anna also provided a home life that facilitated Frederick's career successes. Frederick recognized the value of women's contributions and advocated for women's suffrage and other civil rights, and the couple's four granddaughters were active suffragists and feminists during the twentieth century. Douglass nonetheless had a traditional marriage and held that the rights of women would have to be subordinate to the rights of African Americans. He further confounded his biographers with his second marriage (following Anna's death) to his former secretary, Helen Pitts, a white woman. (*See* Martin, Waldo E., Jr., "Douglass, Frederick," *BWA:AHE.*)

Douglass Monthly See *North Star*

Douglass (married name), Sarah (née Mapps)
9/9/1806–9/8/1882
Articles, essays

A lifelong Quaker, Douglass was a regular contributor to William Lloyd Garrison's abolitionist *Liberator* newspaper. Through her antislavery efforts, she became close pals with fellow abolitionists, including both the **Forten** sisters (prominent African Americans) and the **Grimké** sisters (prominent European-American Quakers). Her correspondence with the Grimké sisters remains a testament of insightful abolitionist sentiments. A well educated teacher herself, she was instrumental in promoting education among African-American youths.

REFERENCES: *AANB. TAWH.* Lerner, Gerda, in *BWA:AHE.* "Selected Websites on Sarah Mapps Douglass's Life and Works." *Gale Online Encyclopedia.* Detroit: Gale. From *Literature Resource Center.* Robinson, Lisa Clayton, in *EA-99.*

Dove, Rita (Frances)
8/28/1952–
Poems, a novel, short stories, essays, verse drama; educator

Rita's parents, Ray and Elvira Dove, prized education, but they recognized that the material rewards of education may not be immediately forthcoming, particularly to African Americans: Even though Ray was at the top of his class when he earned his master's degree, he had to work as an elevator operator at Goodyear for several years before he became one of the first African-American chemists in the U.S. tire and rubber industry. Elvira and Ray raised their four children to be proud of their racial heritage, to be wary of the evils of racism, and to watch for changing times, when their abilities and knowledge would be recognized.

As Dove noted in *The Poet's World*, "Education was the key: That much we knew, and so I was a good student. . . . I adored learning new things and looked forward to what intellectual adventures each school day would bring; some of the luckiest magic was to open a book and to come away the wiser after having been lost in the pages" (p. 75, 1995, Library of Congress). "I read everything I could get my hands on . . . . Our parents allowed me and my siblings to read whatever we wanted to read. Some of my most wonderful memories are of wandering along the bookshelves in our house thinking, 'What book am I going to read this time'" (pp. 118-119, *LoL*).

Rita also showed an early interest in writing plays, stories, and poetry (inspired by Robert Frost and other poets). When one of her high-school teachers took her to a local writers conference, her desire for a career in writing blossomed. In an interview for the *Chicago Tribune*, Dove noted, "When I told my parents that I wanted to be a poet, they looked at me and said 'OK.' They didn't know what to make of it, but they had faith in me."

After high school, Dove graduated summa cum laude from Ohio's Miami University (1973), accepted a Fulbright/Hays fellowship to study modern European literature at the University of Tübingen in Germany (1974-1975), and completed her master of fine arts at the University of Iowa (M.F.A., 1977). Her master's thesis later served as the basis for her first book-length poetry collection. While she was in Iowa, she met and married (in 1979) German novelist Fred Viebahn, with whom she had a daughter, Aviva (b. 1983). This international family loves to travel, and Dove roams extensively in Europe, northern Africa, and Israel. She considers travel "a good way to gain different perspectives and to avoid becoming complacent" (quoted from *Contemporary Authors*, p. 115).

As a writer, Dove came of age a decade after the **Black Arts Movement** had peaked, and her poetry differs markedly from poems produced during that era. Unlike the loose, improvisational, jazz style of that era, her poetry style shows tremendous discipline and technically precise lyricality. Similarly, she rejected the narrow focus of that movement, in favor of a more inclusive, encompassing worldview and a broader perspective on human experience. Her lovingly crafted work offers deep insights into universal themes through precise depictions of specific individuals at particular moments.

This is not to say that Dove shies away from complex racial issues. Rather, such issues don't form the central focus of her work. Her works often highlight the experiences of African-American individuals, both past and present, but she sets them within a larger context of history, culture, and world literature. As she noted in a 1991 interview (in *Callaloo*), "I would find it a breach of my integrity as a writer to create a character for didactic or propaganda purposes." She tries "very hard to create characters who are seen as individuals—not only as Blacks or as women, or whatever, but as a Black woman with her own particular problems, or one White bum struggling in a specific predicament."

Following is a brief chronology of her literary output: From 1977 through 1988, she produced four chapbooks (*Ten Poems*, 1977; *The Only Dark Spot in the Sky*, 1980; *Mandolin*, 1982; *The Other Side of the House*, 1988). *The Yellow House on the Corner*, her first book-length poetry collection, was published in 1980. In 1983, she published *Museum*, her first of several poetry collections, which was favorably received. Her collection of short stories, *Fifth Sunday*, was published in 1985. In 1986, her Pulitzer Prize-winning *Thomas and Beulah* was published, a volume of narrative verse tracing the life experiences of her maternal grandfather and grandmother. A collection of previously published poems with some unpublished poems appeared in *Grace Notes: Poems* (1989). In 1992, she published her novel *Through the Ivory Gate*, which tells the life story of a talented young African-American woman, interweaving present experiences and flashbacks to past incidents. Her poem *Lady Freedom among Us* was read when the statue *Freedom* was returned to the U.S. Capitol in 1993. That same year, she published *Selected Poems*, containing her previously published volumes *The Yellow House on the Corner*, *Museum*, and *Thomas and Beulah*. Her verse drama, *The Darker Face of the Earth: A Verse Play in Fourteen Scenes*, was published in 1994 (rev. ed., 2000) and then produced at the Kennedy Center (1997) and the Royal National Theatre in London (1999). In 1995, she published *Mother Love*, her sixth book of poetry, written chiefly in sonnet form and focusing on the mother-daughter relationship; and *The Poet's World*, a collection of her essay-lectures presented to the Library of Congress during her tenure as Poet Laureate. She published another chapbook, *Evening Primrose*, in 1998, and the next year, she published her poetry collection, *On the Bus with Rosa Parks: Poems* (1999), inspired by an actual bus trip on which she and her daughter shared a bus with the segregation-defying Parks. Five years later, she published her collection *American Smooth* (2004). Her collection *Sonata Mulattica: Poems by Rita Dove* was due for release in April, 2009. She collaborated with composer John Williams on *Seven for Luck* and on *Song for the Twentieth Century*; the latter was included in Steven Spielberg's 1999 documentary *The Unfinished Journey*. She has also written lyrics for at least seven other composers. Sound recordings have been made of some of her lectures, interviews, and poetry readings, as well as panels and other collaborative works. She edited *The Best

American Poetry 2000*, and her work is often published in periodicals and anthologies.

Her academic career may be chronicled as follows: Starting in 1981, she began as an assistant professor at Arizona State University (ASU) at Tempe. From there, she spent a year as writer-in-residence at the Tuskegee Institute before returning to ASU and staying there until 1989. In 1989, she joined the faculty at the University of Virginia, the Center for Advanced Studies, and in 1993 was promoted to the endowed Commonwealth Professor of English, University of Virginia, where she still teaches creative writing. Meanwhile, she has served on the literary advisory panel for the National Endowment for the Arts (NEA), has been named chair of the poetry grants panel for the NEA, and served on the board of directors of the Associate Writing Programs (serving as its president, 1986-1987). In 1987, she became linked to two key institutions of African-American culture: as the associate editor of **Callaloo**, a journal of criticism and the arts known for publishing contemporary poetry; and as commissioner of the **Schomburg Center for Research in Black Culture**.

In 1993, President Bill Clinton named her to two terms as the United States Library of Congress Poet Laureate Consultant in Poetry—the first black person, the first woman, and the youngest person to hold that post. Dove was delighted to have the opportunity to inspire young African Americans and young girls to fulfill their dreams, but her very public role impeded her time spent in private contemplation needed for her writing. When the position concluded, she needed to regain her sense of privacy, so she had a one-room writing cabin built in the backyard of her home, overlooking a pond. When she visits it each evening, she works at the stand-up desk her father built for her. In 1998, her writing sanctuary proved providential when her house's attic and second story was incinerated by lightning, and then the whole house was flooded to contain the fire. Though her family had to move to temporary housing, she could continue to retreat to her writing cabin until permanent housing was complete.

In addition to being 1993-1995 U.S. Poet Laureate, Dove has received numerous other honors: Starting in 1970, she was awarded a Presidential scholarship and was invited to the White House. She since has been awarded a National Achievement Scholarship, a Fulbright/Hays scholarship, literary grants from the NEA, numerous fellowships (including John Simon Guggenheims and Andrew W. Mellons), a Pulitzer Prize in poetry (the second African American to receive that honor, following **Gwendolyn Brooks**), a National Book Critics Circle Award nomination, more than 20 honorary doctorates, a Bellagio residency from the Rockefeller Foundation, citations as a Literary Lion of the New York Public Library, appointment to numerous prestigious panels (e.g., the National Book Award poetry panel), an invitation to read at the White House and to speak at the 200th anniversary celebration of the U.S. Capitol, and many, many more honors. She has also judged or juried on numerous prize committees, such as for the Walt Whitman Award, the Academy of American Poets, the Pulitzer Prize in Poetry, the National Book Award in poetry, the Anisfield-Wolf Book Award, the Amy Lowell Fellowship, and the Shelley Memorial Award. Her memberships include PEN; Poetry Society of America; Poets and Writers; Associated Writing Programs (president, 1986-87); American Society of Composers, Authors, and Publishers; American Philosophical Society, Phi Beta Kappa (senator, 1994-2000); and Phi Kappa Phi.

REFERENCES: *1TESK. AA:PoP. AANB. AAP. AAW:PV. BF:2000. EBLG. LoL. MAAL. MWEL. NAAAL. OC20LE. PBW. RT. TtW.* Cavalieri, Grace. "Rita Dove: An Interview." *The American Poetry Review.* 24.2 (March-April 1995) p. 11. From *Literature Resource Center.* Dove, Rita, and Steven Ratiner. "In an Interview." *The Christian Science Monitor.* pp. 16-17. Rpt. in Contemporary Literary Criticism. Ed. James P. Draper and Jeffery Chapman. Vol. 81. Detroit: Gale Research, 1994. pp. 16-17. From *Literature Resource Center.* Jones, Kirkland C., in *APSWWII-3.* Kitchen, Judith, and Stan Sanvel Rubin. "A Conversation with Rita Dove." *Black American Literature Forum* 20.3 (Fall 1986): pp. 227-240. Rpt. in *CLCS.* Detroit: Gale, pp. 227-240. From *Literature Resource Center.* Li, Wenxin, in *GEAAL.* Pereira, Malin. "An Interview with Rita Dove." *Contemporary Literature.* 40.2 (Summer 1999) p. 183. From *Literature Resource Center.* Sale, Maggie, in *COCAAL.* Shaughnessy, Brenda. "Rita Dove: Taking the Heat." *Publishers Weekly.* 246.15 (Apr. 12, 1999) p. 48. From *Literature Resource Center.* Stanford, Ann Folwell, in *OCWW.* Sussman, Alison Carb, in *BB. CAO-04. CLCS. LFCC-07. MWEL.* Wheeler, Lesley, in *AW:ACLB-96.* //www.poets.org/poet.php/prmPID/ 185. Amazon.com. *E-98. EB-98. G-95.* SDPL catalog. Williams, Kenny Jackson, in *B. BCE. CE. COCAAL* and *OCAAL. W. W2B. Wiki.*

Drake, St. Clair
1/2/1911–6/14/1990
Nonfiction—anthropology, sociology; educator, civil servant, researcher, social worker

After graduating from college, Drake headed South, working with the Religious Society of Friends (Quakers), teaching high school in Virginia, and helping to conduct research at Dillard University in New Orleans. In 1936, he moved to Chicago, where he teamed up with University of Chicago professor **Horace Cayton**, doing research for the Works Progress Administration there. Their research led to Cayton and Drake's classic, the Anisfeld-Wolf Award-winning sociological study of Chicago's South Side (known as "Bronzeville"), *Black Metropolis* (1945). In 1942, he married fellow sociologist Elizabeth Johns, with whom he had two children, Sandra and Kail.

Drake returned briefly to Dillard, then in 1946, he completed his Ph.D. at the University of Chicago and started professing sociology and anthropology at Roosevelt University in Chicago. Other than a three-year professorship in Ghana, and a couple other visiting professorships, he stayed there until 1969. While there, he wrote *Race Relations in a Time of Rapid Social Change* (1966) and *Our Urban Poor: Promises to Keep and Miles to Go* (1967). In 1969, he was invited to move to Stanford, where he founded and shaped one of the preeminent African and Afro-American Studies Departments in the United States. While there, he wrote *The Redemption of Africa and Black Religion* (1970) and his two-volume work, *Black Folk Here and There: An Essay in History and Anthropology* (1987-1990). Throughout his career, he also wrote various pamphlets, lectures, and books for governmental and nongovernmental organizations; edited numerous journals and books, and contributed to various periodicals and anthologies.

REFERENCES: *AANB. CAO-03. Wiki.* Balfour, Lawrie, in *EA-99.*

Draper, Sharon M. (Mills)
4/11/1952–
Juvenile, children's, and young-adult literature, nonfiction, humor, poems, short stories, essays; educator

A Cincinnati public-school teacher for nearly 30 years (1970-1997), Sharon Draper was named U.S. Teacher of the Year in 1997, in addition to winning more than a dozen other education awards. Six years earlier, Draper's short story, "One Small Torch," had won first prize in an *Ebony* Literary Contest (1991). Since then, she has contributed numerous poems and short stories to various literary magazines, as well as some essays.

In 1994, she started her *Ziggy and the Black Dinosaurs* series for children ages 8-12 years, featuring Ziggy, Jerome, Rashawn, and Rico, four African-American boys who form the "Black Dinosaurs." In these adventure tales, the boys revel in exploring history and science, as well as friendship. Just Us Books, owned and operated by **Cheryl Hudson Willis** and her husband **Wade Hudson**, published three of Draper's Ziggy books: *Ziggy and the Black Dinosaurs* (1994/2006), *Ziggy and the Black Dinosaurs: Lost in the Tunnel of Time* (1996/2006), and *Ziggy and the Black Dinosaurs: Shadows of Caesar's Creek* (1997/2006). Aladdin and other publishers have produced other Ziggy and the Black Dinosaurs books, including *The Backyard Animal Show, The Buried Bones Mystery,* and *The Space Mission Adventure* (all 2006), and *Stars and Sparks on Stage* (2007), which introduces a strong girl to the all-boy quartet.

For young adults (YA), the audience with which the former junior-high and high-school teacher is most familiar, Draper has written her "Hazelwood Trilogy" of novels.

Her first novel, *Tears of a Tiger* (1994/2003; also in kindle and audio format), won the American Library Association (ALA) and **Coretta Scott King John Steptoe** Genesis Award for an outstanding new book; was named as an ALA Best Book for Young Adults, was recognized as a Best Book by the Children's Book Council (CBC) and Bank Street College, was chosen as a Book for the Teen Age by the New York Public Library (NYPL), was named a Notable Trade Book in the Field of Social Studies by the National Council for Social Studies, was named the Best of the Best by Voice of Youth Advocates (VOYA), and was named one of the top 100 YA books by the ALA. The second in the trilogy, *Forged by Fire* (1997; also in audio format), won the Coretta Scott King Award (1997), the ALA Best Book Award, the Parent's Choice Award, and many of the other honors bestowed on *Tears*. The third of the three books, *Darkness before Dawn* (2001; also in audio format), was named a Top Ten Quick Pick by the ALA and both given a Children's Choice Award and a Young Adult Choice Award from the International Reading Association (IRA).

Draper's second trilogy of young-adult novels features Jericho Prescott, a junior at **Frederick Douglass** High School, who longs to belong and must make crucial decisions about the kind of person he wants to be while trying to get what he wants. The first in the trilogy, *The Battle of Jericho* (2003; also in audio format), was named a Coretta Scott King Honor Book by the ALA, a Book for the Teen Age by the NYPL, and a Young Adult Choice Book by the IRA. The second, *November Blues* (2007; also in audio format), features November, a female student, as well as Jericho, and it, too, was named a Coretta Scott King Honor Book by the ALA. Draper completed the Jericho trilogy with *Just Another Hero* (2009), featuring Arielle Gresham, who struggles with problems at home and at school.

Draper's contemporary take on Shakespeare, *Romiette and Julio* (1999/2001), was named a Best Book by the ALA, chosen as Notable Book for a Global Society by the IRA, and a Book for the Teen Age by the NYPL (all 2000). *Double Dutch* (2002; also in audio format) was named a Notable Social Studies Trade Book for Young People by the Children's Book Council, designated one of the Top Ten Sports Books for young adults by the ALA (both 2003), and chosen as the Best of the Best (2004). *Copper Sun* (2006; also in audio format) won the Coretta Scott King Author Award from the ALA, was nominated for an NAACP Image Award for Literature, and was named one of the Top Ten Historical Fiction Books for Youth by *Booklist* (all in 2007). Draper's other novels for young adults include *Blackout* (2003) and *Fire from the Rock* (2007).

Draper has also written two books in her "Sassy" series for elementary-schoolers: *Little Sister Is Not My Name*

(2009) and *The Birthday Storm* (2009). For students, Draper created *Jazzimagination: A Journal To Read And Write* (1999/2002), as well as a volume titled *Sprint Reading* (Scholastic, Level 600) (2003). She also edited two poetry collections, *Let the Circle Be Unbroken: Collected Poetry for Children and Young Adults* (1997) and *Buttered Bones—Adult Poetry* (available through her website, //sharondraper.com/books.asp).

For fellow teachers, Draper has written two motivational humor books: *Teaching from the Heart: Reflections, Encouragement, and Inspiration* (1999) and *Not Quite Burned Out but Crispy around the Edges: Inspiration, Laughter, and Encouragement for Teachers* (2001). Draper has also collaborated on two other volumes: *We Beat the Street: How a Friendship Pact Led to Success* (2005, with Sampson Davis, George Jenkins, and Rameck Hunt; available in hardcover or kindle editions), and *Tramp Art: An Itinerant's Folk Art* (1975, with by Helaine W. Fendelman, George Jenkins, and Rameck Hunt).

In addition to her numerous awards for individual books, as well as her education awards, Draper has been awarded two honorary doctorates.

REFERENCES: CAO-08. Donaldson, Catherine V., in *BB*. //wiki. answers.com/Q/What_is_sharon_mills_draper's_birthday. //www.ala. org/ala/emiert/corettascottkingbookaward/cskpastwinners/alphabetical list/cskalphabetical.cfm#au. //sharondraper.com/bio.asp. //sharon draper.com/bookdetail.asp?id=14. //sharondraper.com/bookdetail. asp?id=16. //sharondraper.com/bookdetail.asp?id=25. //sharondraper. com/books.asp. Amazon.com.

Driskell, David Clyde
6/7/1931–
Nonfiction—art; painter, art curator, educator

Driskell has been quoted as saying, "I make art to free myself, to give a new dimension to life, and hopefully to other people's lives" (quoted in *Black Biography*). He certainly is freewheeling, as he has lectured, curated exhibits, and exhibited his own work at New York City's Whitney Museum of Art and Metropolitan Museum of Art; Washington D.C.'s Corcoran Gallery of Art, Smithsonian Institute, and White House; and in numerous other locations in North America, Europe, and Africa. Nonetheless, after a few visiting professorships and a decade-long professorship at Fisk University (1966-1976), Driskell made his intellectual home as a professor of art at the University of Maryland from 1977 to 1998, when he was named an emeritus professor there. Driskell's primary visual artistic medium is paintings, but he also carves trees and stones. Driskell is not only productive but also reproductive; he and his wife Thelma DeLoatch have two children: Daviryne Mari and Daphne Joyce.

Some of Driskell's books have been written and published as companions to art exhibitions he has curated, such as *Two Centuries of Black American Art* (1976), *Hidden Heritage: Afro-American Art, 1800-1950* (1985), *Contemporary Visual Expressions: The Art of Sam Gilliam, Martha Jackson-Jarvis, Keith Morrison, William T. Williams* (1987), *Introspectives: Contemporary Art by Americans and Brazilians of African Descent* (1989, with Henry J. Drewal), and *Narratives of African American Art and Identity: The David C. Driskell Collection* (1998, toured until 2001). He also collaborated with the Cosbys, who own some of Driskell's artwork, to write *The Other Side of Color: African American Art in the Collection of Camille O. and William H. Cosby, Jr.* His other books include *Harlem Renaissance: Art of Black America* (1994, coauthored with David Levering Lewis and Deborah Willis Ryan) and *African American Visual Aesthetics: A Postmodernist View* (1995, editor). He also often contributes articles to assorted periodicals, and he participated in the 1990 British television film *Hidden Heritage: The Roots of Black American Painting*, which emerged from a similarly named exhibit he curated. The Rockefeller Foundation, the Harmon Foundation, and numerous other U.S. and European institutions have given Driskell fellowships, grants, scholarships, honorary doctorates, and awards. At the close of his second term, President Bill Clinton awarded Driskell the National Humanities Medal (2000).

REFERENCES: *AANB. Wiki.* Sussman, Alison Carb, in *BB. CAO-01. EA-99.* //www.embracingthechild.org/africanamerican.htm. SDPL catalog.

Du Bois, Shirley (Lola) (née Graham)
11/11/1896?–3/27/1977
Biographies, plays, libretti, novel

By the time she reached her mid-20s, Shirley was the widow of Shadrack McCanns, with two young boys to support. With help from her parents, she managed to complete her training as a musician and to earn her bachelor's (1934, in music) and her master's (1935, music history and fine arts) degrees.

In the 1930s and 1940s, Shirley Graham wrote several plays. First was her one-act play *Tom-Tom*, which she developed into the opera *Tom-Tom: An Epic of Music and the Negro* (1932), the first major opera written and produced by a woman, featuring an all-black cast. She also wrote several other plays while a Julius Rosenwald Fellow at the Yale University School of Drama (following a brief stint with the WPA's Federal Theater Project), including *Deep Rivers* (1939, a musical), *It's Morning* (1940, a one-act tragedy set in the brutal times of slavery), *I Gotta Home* (1940, a one-act drama), *Track Thirteen* (1940, a radio script), *Elijah's Raven* (1941, a three-act comedy), and

Shirley Graham Du Bois

Dust to Earth (1941, a three-act tragedy). In recognition of her work, she was given a National Institute of Arts and Letters Award in 1950.

Starting in the 1940s, Graham also began writing biographies of important African Americans and Africans, such as *Dr. George Washington Carver, Scientist* (1944); *Paul Robeson: Citizen of the World* (1946); *There Was Once a Slave: The Heroic Story of Frederick Douglass* (1947); *Your Most Humble Servant* (1949, about Benjamin Banneker); *The Story of Phillis Wheatley* (1949); *The Story of Pocahontas* (1953); *Jean Baptiste Pointe du Sable: Founder of Chicago* (1953); *Booker T. Washington: Educator of Hand, Head, and Heart* (1955); *His Day Is Marching On* (1971, a memoir of W. E. B. Du Bois); *Gamal Abdel Nasser, Son of the Nile* (1972); *Julius K. Nyerere: Teacher of Africa* (1975); and *A Pictorial History of W. E. B. Du Bois* (1976). She also wrote a novel, *Zulu Heart* (1974), giving her distinctive view of whites in South Africa.

While she was gaining awareness of important contributors to African-American history, she was also becoming increasingly politically active, as evident in her articles for progressive periodicals such as *The Masses* and *The Harlem Quarterly* during the late 1940s and the 1950s. During this time, she had grown closer to W. E. B. Du Bois, whom she had known since she was a teenager (and he was nearing 50) and with whom she had corresponded since 1936. In 1951, a year after the death of Nina Du Bois, W. E. B.'s wife of 55 years, Graham married him. For the next dozen years, Shirley Du Bois virtually stopped her own writing and dedicated herself to helping him with his, aiding him to write what would have been his magnum opus, the *Encyclopedia Africana*.

Throughout the 1950s and into the 1960s, however, the red scare (anticommunist frenzy) inflamed the U.S. government's zeal for persecuting civil-rights activists and anyone else they suspected of communist sympathies. In 1961, Shirley and her husband emigrated to Ghana. They still kept in touch with the politics of the United States, however. In the early 1960s, she, W. E. B., and **Paul Robeson** cofounded the cultural and literary journal, *Freedomways*, which called itself "a journal of the Freedom Movement." The U.S. government continually barred the Du Boises from returning to this country (other than for visits in 1971 and 1975), and she (like her husband) died in exile.

REFERENCES: *BAAW.* Brown-Guillory, Elizabeth, in *BWA:AHE.* Edwards, Roanne, in *EA-99.* Nishikawa, Kinohi, in *GEAAL.* Warren, Nagueyalti, in *OCAAL.* —Tonya Bolden

W.E.B. Du Bois

Du Bois, W. E. B. (William Edward Burghardt)
2/23/1868–8/27/1963
Essays, novels, biography, autobiography/memoir, nonfiction—political and social issues, history

Any serious student of African-American culture, history, and intellectual life finds much to glean from the life and work of William Edward Burghardt Du Bois. Du Bois's influence remains strong today both in the memory of **Martin Luther King, Jr.**, and the works of author and scholar **Cornel West**. A superbly well-educated man and a prolific writer, Du Bois played an integral role in the African-American community's call for racial equality and social justice. Du Bois believed that the African-American community needed to be intellectually astute and politically active, the latter position sometimes bringing Du Bois into conflict with other black and white leaders of the time, including **Booker T. Washington**.

Du Bois was born in Great Barrington, Massachusetts, into a family of free blacks who had no roots with slavery, but instead had roots in the American Revolution. Du Bois lived with his mother, Mary Slyvina Burghardt Du Bois, for much of his childhood, as his father, Alfred Du Bois, left his wife and son soon after the boy's birth. Du Bois grew into a fine student, graduating first in his 1884 high school class. Others recognized his intelligence and encouraged his intellectual talents. Du Bois enjoyed life in Massachusetts, remembering no discrimination, even though the town was by and large populated by whites. Du Bois and his mother attended the First Congregational Church as the only black members. His mother died soon after Du Bois graduated from high school, and at that time, he apparently had no plans or

money for college, although he was industrious, always attending the annual town meetings and writing for the *New York Globe*. Eventually, the members of Du Bois and his mother's church provided the money for his fees to attend Fisk University in Nashville, Tennessee, in 1885.

After graduating from Fisk in 1888, Du Bois received a scholarship to Harvard University, earning a second bachelor's degree in 1890 and a master's degree in 1891. Du Bois continued with his studies, spending two years at the University of Berlin and gaining his Ph.D. from Harvard in 1896. Du Bois holds the distinction of being the first African American to receive such a degree from Harvard. Additionally, Du Bois's doctoral dissertation, *The Suppression of the African Slave-Trade to the United States of America, 1638-1870*, was published in 1896 as volume 1 of Harvard's multivolume *Historical Series*.

Du Bois found a teaching post in Ohio at Wilberforce University, and while he was there, he met his future wife, Nina Gomer, marrying her in 1896. That same year, Du Bois was hired by the University of Pennsylvania to teach and conduct a sociological study of blacks. His work culminated in the publishing of *The Philadelphia Negro* in 1899, the first work of its kind. Du Bois's innovative and serious academic work earned him another job offer. This one came from Atlanta University and included leading the sociology department. Du Bois continued to study

African-American life and to teach in Georgia until 1910. While at Atlanta, Du Bois continued to produce groundbreaking sociological work about the lives of African Americans.

In Atlanta, Du Bois also wrote his most famous and enduring work, *The Souls of Black Folk*. This book landed Du Bois right in the middle of the fight for equality. It also landed him in the middle of a long controversy with the most prominent black leader at the time, Booker T. Washington. During his early years, Du Bois had had no firsthand experience with the racial inequities so prevalent in many areas of the United States, yet when he attended Fisk, Du Bois saw a new side to the world—and he did not like what he saw. Washington, too, did not like the situation in the United States. What separated the two intellectual giants was not the goal of equality but the method by which to achieve it.

Du Bois believed that Washington, who was closely allied with the more practical Tuskegee Institute in Alabama, promoted methods for achieving equality that were submissive, focusing around the common economic self-interests of blacks and whites instead of demanding equality based on rational and philosophical grounds. Du Bois argued that African Americans needed to be highly educated and then serve as ladders to help others achieve similar status. Thus, *The Souls of Black Folk* directly challenged Washington, and Du Bois gained both popularity and notoriety.

Washington's political stance also continued to gain popularity with blacks and whites alike. Du Bois responded by founding the Niagara Movement in 1905. Although the organization folded in 1910, some consider it to be the first African-American protest movement of the twentieth century. Du Bois went on to become the only African American founding officer of the National Association for the Advancement of Colored People (NAACP) in 1910.

While with the NAACP, Du Bois started the organization's journal **Crisis**, which Du Bois also edited and wrote for. Although Du Bois published new black writers, such as **Countee Cullen** and **Langston Hughes**, he became frustrated by what he considered their lack of commitment to political action. After 24 years, Du Bois resigned from the NAACP because of a conflict with its executive board. Du Bois returned to Atlanta University in 1934, heading the sociology department there until his forced retirement when he was 76 years old. Du Bois then returned to the NAACP in 1944, engaged in more conflict with the leadership over his renewed interest in and promotion of communism, and he was fired in 1948.

In 1950, Du Bois ran for the Senate as a Labor Party candidate, and he lost. Du Bois later led the Peace Information Center and entered into more controversy. He was indicted by a grand jury in 1951, which accused him

of being a foreign agent, and he had to forfeit his U.S. passport in the process. Although a judge threw the case out of court, it took some time for Du Bois to regain his passport. When he did, however, he traveled to Europe, including the Soviet Union.

Editor's note: About this time, Du Bois's wife Nina died, and about a year later, he married **Shirley Graham**, nearly 30 years his junior.

Du Bois saw an international community in the world's future and continued to be frustrated by the tiny steps of progress toward racial equality within the United States. Years earlier, Du Bois had accurately identified two conflicts in America that continue to this day: (1) "Double consciousness" questions whether African Americans can be true to both their cultural heritage and their national identity, and (2) as Du Bois noted, "The color line" will be the problem of the twentieth century.

Du Bois's frustration grew until he eventually left America in 1961, moving to Ghana. He became a naturalized citizen of Ghana and died there in 1963. Ironically, Du Bois died on the exact date when **Martin Luther King, Jr.**'s famous March on Washington took place. To some, it seemed as if the baton had been passed. Others mourned the loss of one of the African-American community's greatest intellectuals. All, however, agree that Du Bois's legacy, work, and influence will not soon be forgotten.

In addition to the works previously mentioned, Du Bois published the following: *John Brown*, 1909 (a biography); *The Quest of the Silver Fleece*, 1911 (a novel); *The Negro*, 1915 (pan-African history); *Darkwater: Voices from within the Veil*, 1920 (a collection of prose and verse); *The Gift of Black Folk: Negroes in the Making of America*, 1924; *Dark Princess*, 1928 (a novel); *Black Reconstruction in America*, 1935 (a massive treatise); *Dusk of Dawn: An Essay toward an Autobiography of a Race Concept*, 1940 (an autobiography); *In Battle for Peace: The Story of My Eighty-Third Birthday*, 1952 (a memoir); a novel trilogy, *The Black Flame* (comprising *The Ordeal of Mansart*, 1957; *Mansart Builds a School*, 1959; and *Worlds of Color*, 1961); and *The Autobiography of W. E. B. Du Bois: A Soliloquy on Viewing My Life from the Last Decade of Its First Century*, 1968, published posthumously.

REFERENCES: *EBLG*. Blight, David W. (1990), "Up From 'Twoness': Frederick Douglass and the Meaning of W. E. B. Du Bois's Concept of Double Consciousness," *Canadian Review of American Studies*, 21(3) Online, EBSCO Host. Coates, Rodney D., "Autobiography of W. E. B. Du Bois: A Soliloquy on Viewing My Life from the Last Decade of Its First Century," in *MAAL*. Cunningham, George P., "W. E. B. Du Bois," in *AAW*. Franklin, Robert Michael (1990), "W. E. B. Du Bois and the Strenuous Person," *Liberating Visions: Human Fulfillment and Social Justice in African-American Thought*, Minneapolis: Fortress. "From 1909 to the Great Depression: A Partial Chronicle" (1994), *Crisis*, 101(1) Online, EBSCO Host. **Rampersad, Arnold**, in *BLC* (Vol. 1).

OCAAL. Richardson, Ben, & William Fahey (Eds.) (1976), *Great Black Americans* (2nd rev. ed.; formerly titled *Great American Negroes*), New York: Thomas Crowell. Townsend, Kim (1996), "'Manhood' at Harvard: W. E. B. Du Bois," *Raritan*, 15(4), Online, EBSCO Host. —Janet Hoover

Editor's note: Du Bois's work was made much easier by Nina Gomer, his wife of 55 years, and by his second wife, **Shirley Graham Du Bois**, who followed him to Ghana, to spend his last years with him there. Graham also helped him with his massive work, *Encyclopedia Africana*, which was incomplete at the time of his death.

Due, Tananarive
1966–
Horror, science fiction, supernatural fiction, autobiography/memoir, fictional biography; journalist

Tananarive Due yearned to be a writer from an early age. She told an interviewer, "I've wanted to write since I was four years old, ... It seems to me that I came into this world wanting to tell stories and write" (quoted in CAO-03). As a sixth grader, she wrote "My Own Roots," inspired by **Alex Haley**'s *Roots* television miniseries. Even in college, she won awards for her essays and plays and her oratory. She earned her baccalaureate in journalism and a master's degree in literature from the University of Leeds (United Kingdom), specializing in Nigerian literature. Afterward, she supported herself with her journalism as an intern for the *Miami Herald* (while still in high school), *The New York Times*, and the *Wall Street Journal*, and then as a columnist and feature writer for the *Miami Herald* (1988-1996). Meanwhile, she built her stash of fiction writings—and her pile of rejection slips.

Due's first published novel, *The Between* (1995), was nominated for the Bram Stoker Award for Outstanding Achievement in a First Novel from the Horror Writers Association. Better known, however, is her trilogy of gothic supernatural horror novels. *My Soul to Keep* (1997) and *The Living Blood* (2001), both named as *Publishers Weekly* Best Books, was followed by *Blood Colony: A Novel* (2008). *My Soul to Keep* was also nominated for a Bram Stoker Best Novel award, and Blair Underwood is planning to produce and star in a film version of *My Soul. The Living Blood* also won an American Book Award from the Before Columbus Foundation. Underwood said of *Blood Colony*, "Her storytelling is at once intimate and wholly epic. Her characters, though otherworldly and supernatural, are profoundly relatable and eerily familiar" (quoted in //www.amazon.com).

Due's other supernaturally themed novels include *The Good House* (2003) and *Joplin's Ghost* (2005). Underwood and actor Forest Whitaker are interested in developing *The Good House* for the big screen. Asked why she chooses supernatural themes, Due told an interviewer, "By looking at the world through a supernatural prism I can step back from my own real-life fears of loss and death, and make them feel a little bit safer when I write stories with characters who are facing things that I'll never have to face" (quoted in Dziemianowicz, 2001).

She has also participated in a collaborative satirical mystery novel *Naked Came the Manatee* (1996), contributed a horror novella to *The Ancestors* (2008, with Brandon Massey and **L.A. Banks**), and contributed stories to anthologies (e.g., *Mojo: Conjure Stories*, 2003). In addition, using notes given to her by the estate of Alex Haley, she wrote the fictionalized biography *The Black Rose: The Magnificent Story of Madam C. J. Walker, America's First Black Female Millionaire* (2000), nominated for an NAACP Image Award.

In 1997, Due met sci-fi novelist **Steven Emory Barnes** at a panel discussion of science fiction, fantasy, and horror, and they married three years later. When they married, Barnes already had daughter from a previous marriage, Lauren Nicole, and the couple later adopted a son, Jason Kai. Though she usually writes horror and he typically writes science fiction, they have collaborated on writing speculative fiction and fantasy for television and movie scripts. Also, with actor Blair Underwood, Due and Barnes have cowritten the Tennyson Hardwick series of novels, including *Casanegra* (2007; also available in audio format or kindle format) and *In the Night of the Heat* (2009; also available in kindle format). Barnes and Due also cowrote a tribute to deceased fellow sci-fi author **Octavia Butler**, published in *Black Issues Book Review* (2006).

Due has also collaborated with her mother to write *Freedom in the Family: A Mother-Daughter Memoir of the Fight for Civil Rights* (2003, with Patricia Stephens Due). She later recalled, "My family is very close as a rule, but the time I spent with my mother on this book was particularly precious. . . . For the first time in my life, I KNOW the chronology of my mother's life story. I saw glimpses of her as a young person, I better understood the emotional scars she wears, and I better understood the dynamic of my parents' relationship, which began as a civil rights partnership and has remained one all these years later. There is no price for such a gift. . . . I'm grateful to have written it, I'm grateful my mother has been such a diligent historian over the years, and I'm grateful that she has unburdened these episodes from her heart" (in Glave, 2004). Her mother also affects her other writing. She observed, "All of the strong women in my novels are different versions of my mother. I thought of her a great deal while I was writing *The Black Rose*, for example" (in Glave, 2004).

A deliciously fun collaboration has been to perform on the keyboard and as a vocalist and dancer for

"Rockbottom Remainders," the celebrated rock band formed by writers Stephen King, Dave Barry, and Amy Tan, which often performs to great delight at book expos, fairs, and conferences. Overall, however, Due says, "I'm happiest when I can write a story the way I did when I was a kid: finding the place the story naturally begins and having great fun in the telling. . . . What continues to surprise me is that writing doesn't get easier—in fact, if anything, sometimes I think it gets more difficult with each book. . . . I'm always trying to stretch myself" (quoted in CAO-03).

REFERENCES: CAO-03. Wiki. Dziemianowicz, Stefan. "PW Talks to Tananarive Due." Publishers Weekly. 248.12 (Mar. 19, 2001), p. 81. Literature Resources from Gale. Glave, Dianne. "'My Characters Are Teaching Me to Be Strong': An Interview with Tananarive Due." African American Review. 38.4 (Winter 2004), p. 695. Literature Resources from Gale. Kalfatovic, Mary, in BB. //darkush.blogspot.com/. //en.wikipedia.org/wiki/Larry_Niven. //www.amazon.com. //www.blogger.com/profile/13630529492355131777.

FURTHER READING: Gay, Roxane, in GEAAL.

Dumas, Henry L.
7/20/1934–5/23/1968
Poems, short stories

Born in Sweet Home, Arkansas, Dumas spent the early years of his childhood in the South before his family moved to Harlem, when he was 10 years old. Dumas's short fiction reflects his deep understanding of the African-American experience both in the rural South and in the urban North. After graduating from high school, Dumas enrolled in the City College of New York, but he soon left to join the U.S. Air Force (1953-1957). While in the Air Force, he married Loretta Ponton (September 24, 1955), and he contributed poems and short stories to Air Force periodicals, winning creative writing awards for his efforts. After his military service, he enrolled at Rutgers University, but family responsibilities for his sons David (born in 1958) and Michael (born in 1962) led him to quit school and focus on earning a steady income.

In 1967, Dumas was invited to teach, counsel students, direct language workshops, and direct the "Experiment in Higher Education" at Southern Illinois University. There, he met **Eugene Redmond**, a fellow teacher and poet who was to become his friend and literary conservator. In the late spring of 1968, when his literary career seemed so promising and his young family so needed his promise, Dumas's life was tragically ended in a violent clash with a New York City transit officer on a subway platform, who mistakenly shot him. Much of Dumas's work centered on the theme of the metaphorical clash between African- and European-American cultures. Other important influences on his writings were religion,

supernatural phenomena, folk traditions (e.g., African-American music and lore), and the struggle for civil rights. After his death, Redmond edited several collections of Dumas's works, including his short-story collections Ark of Bones and Other Stories (1974, edited by Hale Chatfield and Eugene Redmond), Rope of Wind and Other Stories (1979), and Good-bye Sweetwater: New & Selected Stories (1988), which included stories from his previous collections, as well as excerpts from his unfinished novel Jonoah and the Green Stone (published in 1976); and his poetry collections Poetry for My People (1970; republished as Play Ebony, Play Ivory, in 1974) and Knees of a Natural Man: Selected Poetry of Henry Dumas (1989).

REFERENCES: AANB. EBLG. WDAA. Alic, Margaret, in BB. CAO-03. MWEL. Brown, Deborah, in GEAAL. Harris, Trudier, in COCAAL and OCAAL. Wiki. Mitchell, Carolyn A., in AAP-55-85. //www.nathanielturner.com/playebonydumasbio.htm. EB-BH-CD. G-97.

Dunbar, Paul Laurence
6/27/1872–2/9/1906
Poems, short stories, novels, essays, musical, operetta

Although slavery had ended years before Paul was born, both of Paul's parents had known well the oppressive burden of slavery. Paul's father, Joshua Dunbar, had escaped slavery to join a black regiment during the Civil War, and after the war, he had worked as a plasterer. Paul's mother, Matilda Glass, had worked as a launderer after gaining her freedom. Both Joshua and Matilda enjoyed telling their young son stories of their experiences on the plantations of the South. Sadly, however, while Paul was still young, his parents divorced, and his father died soon afterward.

The only African American in his Dayton, Ohio, Central High School class, young Paul already showed literary talent: He was named class poet, president of the literary society, and editor-in-chief of the school newspaper. Although he couldn't afford to continue his education after high school, within two years after graduating he had some of his poems published in the Dayton Herald. Soon after, Wilbur Wright (of first-flight fame) financed Dunbar's founding of the Dayton Tattler, which Dunbar also edited. When the Tattler folded, Dunbar sought jobs with local newspapers, but not one was willing to hire an African American, regardless of his talent. With that avenue closed to him, he got work as a hotel elevator operator, which allowed him time for writing.

In 1892, one of Dunbar's former teachers asked him to address the Western Association of Writers in Dayton. At that meeting, Dunbar was introduced to James Newton Matthews, who was to become another of his champions. For starters, Matthews wrote to an Illinois newspaper singing Dunbar's praises, and Matthews's letter was widely reprinted in other newspapers across the land. One of the people who read of Dunbar was poet James Whitcomb Riley. Intrigued, Riley read numerous poems by Dunbar, and he, too, started singing the young poet's praises.

With the financial help of Wilbur Wright, Dunbar self-published his first collection of poems, *Oak and Ivy* (1893). Many of these poems were written in standard English (e.g., "Ode to Ethiopia," a poem celebrating the achievements of African Americans; "Sympathy," a somber verse about the dismal plight of African Americans). In addition, many of the poems in this volume were written in plantation dialect, which reflected the Southern slaves' speech patterns he had learned at his parents' knees. The poems in *Oak and Ivy* were well received, and attorney Charles A. Thatcher offered to help pay for Dunbar to attend college. Appreciative of the offer, Dunbar nonetheless decided to turn him down to pursue writing ever more diligently. Apparently, Dunbar's refusal was gracious, as Thatcher continued to promote Dunbar's work in Ohio, helping him find opportunities to read his poems at various gatherings, such as at meetings in libraries. At this point, however, Dunbar's writings did not free him (or his mother) from having to earn money by other means.

While doing odd jobs at the 1893 World's Columbian Exposition in Chicago, Dunbar met **Frederick Douglass**, who was working as the commissioner in charge of the Haitian exhibit there. Douglass immediately recognized Dunbar's talent and inscribed one of his books to Dunbar, "From Frederick Douglass to his dear young poet friend Paul Dunbar, one of the sweetest songsters his race has produced and a man of whom I hope great things" (Bryan, 1978, p. 7). Douglass also paid Dunbar five dollars a week (out of his own funds) to work as his clerical assistant during the fair. At the exhibition's Colored Americans Day, Douglass invited Dunbar to sit on the platform with him and other celebrities and to read his own poetry.

Another of Dunbar's supporters was psychiatrist Henry A. Tobey, who helped him distribute *Oak and Ivy* and sent him money from time to time. Tobey and Thatcher then collaborated in helping Dunbar to publish his next book, *Majors and Minors*, published in 1895. The "Majors" were complex poems written in standard English, and the "Minors" were his dialect poems. The standard-English poems absorbed most of his attention during these early years, and they reflected his voracious appetite for reading the English romantic poets (e.g., John Keats, William Wordsworth, Samuel Taylor Coleridge) and for contemporary European-American poets (e.g., Riley, John Greenleaf Whittier, Henry Wadsworth Longfellow). Perhaps surprisingly, Dunbar's dialect poems were actually more popular among his readers, most

Paul Laurence Dunbar U.S. commemorative postage stamp, 1975

of whom were European Americans. It was chiefly these dialect poems that earned him national fame. They also earned him the friendship and affection of fellow writer Alice Ruth Moore, with whom he began a lengthy correspondence.

Thatcher and Tobey also introduced Dunbar to a literary agent, who secured many more opportunities for Dunbar to give readings and even gained Dunbar a literary contract. With this contract, Dunbar published *Lyrics of a Lowly Life* (1896). Most of the poems in this collection had previously appeared in his *Oak and Ivy* and his *Majors and Minors* collections.

On Dunbar's 24th birthday, he received an unexpected gift: The prestigious journal *Harper's Weekly* published an essay by novelist and celebrated literary critic William Dean Howells, praising Dunbar's *Lyrics of a Lowly Life*. At that time, Dunbar was still working as an elevator operator in a hotel in Dayton, Ohio. After that time, Dunbar was widely recognized as the first important African-American poet, and according to Smythe (1976, p. 48), he had a greater impact than any other African-American writer of his time. More than two decades later, **James Weldon Johnson** called him the first true African-American master of writing and recognized him as the first to earn and keep high honors for what he wrote (Johnson, 1922, p. 34). Perhaps the best evidence of his acclaim, however, is that after the publication of his book, he was able to eke out a (humble) living based solely on his writing—a feat that remains difficult to this day.

To begin with, Dunbar started a six-month tour of England, giving readings of his poetry. While there, he found a British publisher for his *Lyrics of a Lowly Life,* and he earned the friendship of musician Samuel Taylor Coleridge, with whom he wrote an operetta, *Dream Lovers.*

In 1897, Dunbar returned to the United States, but not to the Midwest. Instead, he gained work as a clerk for the Library of Congress in Washington, D.C. With this stable income in hand, he and Moore wedded (in secret, over the objections of her family and friends) (*see* **Alice Ruth Moore Dunbar-Nelson**). The continual exposure to dust from the library shelves caused Dunbar respiratory difficulties, and his health began to suffer. Nonetheless, he continued to write, and in 1898, Dunbar published *Folks from Dixie,* his first short-story collection, and *The Uncalled,* his first novel. That year, he left the Library of Congress and toured the country, giving readings. Although his health continued to decline, he still published *Lyrics of the Fireside* in 1899.

In the spring of 1899, he was diagnosed with tuberculosis and fled to the mountains to rest and recuperate. In the early 1900s, Dunbar published his collection of tales, *The Strength of Gideon and Other Stories* (1900), and three more novels. After the publication of his fourth novel, *The Sport of the Gods* (1902), his respiratory problems (including a bout of pneumonia) worsened, and Dunbar exacerbated his health problems by abusing alcohol. That year, he and Alice separated. The following year, Dunbar suffered a nervous breakdown, followed by yet another attack of pneumonia.

Despite being so ill he could barely walk, Dunbar managed to continue writing, publishing *Lyrics of Love and Laughter* (1903), *When Malindy Sings* (1903), *Li'l Gal* (1904), *Howdy, Honey, Howdy* (1905), and *Lyrics of Sunshine and Shadow* (1905), one after another. Ultimately, however, tuberculosis was the death of him, at just 33 years of age.

Although Dunbar wrote several outstanding novels, short stories, essays, and many poems in standard English, his literary reputation has always chiefly rested on his "dialect poems," written to reflect the speech patterns of African-American folks living on antebellum plantations. During his lifetime, this poetry was praised widely among both European Americans and African Americans. Following World War II, however, critics lamented his use of dialect and whined about his stereotypes of plantation life, often depicting African Americans as being servile. During the early 1960s, critics viewed Dunbar as a victim of circumstance, who muted his protest against injustice and tempered his praise of African Americans to please his European-American patrons, publishers, and readers.

Starting in the late 1960s, however, Dunbar's work was once again viewed in a new light. The 1972 Centenary Celebration on Paul Laurence Dunbar at the University of California, Irvine, reflected a new appreciation of this preeminent poet, given the postslavery Reconstruction era in which he emerged, and his own struggle to survive as a writer. Dunbar was recognized for awakening American readers to dialect poetry and to the valuable contributions of Africa and of that continent's descendants in America. Dunbar's "Little Brown Baby" and other lyrical poems have uplifted countless young African Americans (e.g., *see* **Patricia McKissack**), and have been hailed as inspirational by numerous subsequent African-American poets, such as **Nikki Giovanni**, who named him a "natural resource" of his people (Giovanni, 1988, p. 122).

Evidence of Dunbar's continuing importance may be seen in the fact that following the 1913 publication of his *Complete Poems of Paul Laurence Dunbar,* this volume has remained in print, year after year, continually rediscovered by new generations of Americans who appreciate the skill with which he expressed the yearnings and the fears, the humor and the turmoil of African Americans at the turn of the twentieth century.

REFERENCES: **Bontemps, Arna** (1976), "The Black Contribution to American Letters," in Mabel M. Smythe (Ed.), *The Black American Reference Book,* Englewood Cliffs, NJ: Prentice-Hall. **Bryan, Ashley** (1978), *I Greet the Dawn: Poems by Paul Laurence Dunbar,* New York: Atheneum. **Giovanni, Nikki** (1988), in *Contemporary Authors* (Vol. 124), Detroit: Gale Research. **Johnson, James Weldon** (1922), *Book of American Negro Poetry,* Orlando: Harcourt, Brace and World. Smythe, Mabel M. (Ed.) (1976), *The Black American Reference Book,* Englewood Cliffs, NJ: Prentice-Hall. —Michael Strickland

Dunbar Nelson, Alice Ruth (née Alice Ruth Moore)
7/19/1875–9/18/1935
Novel, poems, essays, short stories, literary criticism, edited volumes, diary; journalist, newspaper copublisher, public speaker, educator

Alice excelled in school, both as a student (through the master's degree) and as a teacher at the elementary, secondary, and college levels. *Violets, and Other Tales,* Alice's first book, was published privately in 1895. This collection of sketches, reviews, stories, poems, and essays expresses her characteristic fascination with language and with various literary forms. It also introduced her recurring themes: class differences, ambivalent attitudes toward women's roles, and romance. Her writing notably neglects issues of racial identity, perhaps reflecting her conflicts regarding how her own Creole cultural and racial heritage and her fair skin affected her self-concept and her sociopolitical outlook.

The year her first book was published, **Paul Laurence Dunbar** was attracted to one of her poems and began corresponding with her. Alice analyzed the contrast between her writing and his in a letter she wrote to him: "You ask my opinion about the Negro dialect in literature? Well, frankly, I believe in everyone following his own bent. If it be so that one has a special aptitude for dialect work why it is only right that dialect work should be a specialty. But if one should be like me—absolutely devoid of the ability to manage dialect, I don't see the necessity of cramming and forcing oneself into that plane because one is a Negro or a Southerner."

In 1898, she married Dunbar in secret, over the objections of her family and friends. In 1899, her 14-tale collection, *The Goodness of St. Rocque, and Other Stories*, was published as a companion to Dunbar's *Poems of Cabin and Field*. Some critics consider these stories to be her finest work, establishing her reputation for skillful depiction of Creole culture. In 1902, Paul Dunbar's extensive travel, poor health, and alcohol abuse led Alice to separate from him, but they never divorced and stayed friends until his death in 1906. Some biographers have also suggested that another factor in their relationship was that Dunbar's heterosexual affairs distressed Alice; Alice in turn may have had homosexual affairs that upset Dunbar; their arguments occasionally may have led Dunbar to alcohol-inflamed outbursts of violence.

On separating, Alice moved to Wilmington, Delaware, where she taught English for 18 years. During this time, she married again—and again: In 1910, she married again but soon divorced; then in 1916, she married journalist and poet Robert J. Nelson, with whom she spent the rest of her life. Alice and Robert owned and operated the *Wilmington Advocate*, a civil-rights newspaper, which included her "As in a Looking Glass" and "A Women's Point of View" (later "Une Femme Dit") columns. Her columns also appeared in the *Pittsburgh Courier* and the *Washington Eagle*, and she contributed to numerous other periodicals, such as *Crisis, Opportunity*, and *A.M.E. Church Review*. In addition, her interest in public speaking and oratory led to two edited volumes: *Masterpieces of Negro Eloquence* (1914) and *The Dunbar Speaker and Entertainer* (1920; republished as *The Dunbar Speaker and Entertainer: Containing the Best Prose and Poetic Selections*, 1996).

Alice also continued to write poetry, such as her "I Sit and Sew" (1918), which decried the government's unwillingness to take make use of women's contributions during World War I. She was also socially active in other ways, such as helping to found the White Rose Mission (later White Rose House for Girls) in New York City and the Industrial School for Colored Girls in Marshalltown, Delaware; field-organizing for women's suffrage, volunteering for the Circle of Negro War Relief, fostering black women's volunteerism in the South, striving to end lynching, and working for numerous social and political causes.

During the 1920s and early 1930s, Dunbar Nelson was primarily known for her poems, which were precisely crafted, incisive, romantic, and traditional in form. These works appeared in *Crisis* and *Opportunity* magazines and were often anthologized. In addition, her literary reviews influenced fellow poets, such as **Langston Hughes**. Dunbar Nelson continued to write steadily throughout the **Harlem Renaissance** period, but much of her work was not published until after her death, as *Give Us Each Day: The Diary of Alice Dunbar-Nelson* (1984) and *The Works of Alice Dunbar-Nelson* (1988), both edited by Gloria T. Hull.

REFERENCES: *1TESK. BANP. EBLG. HR&B. NAAAL. OC20LE. RLWWJ. RT.* McKoy, Sheila Smith, in *OCWW.* Nixon, Timothy K., in *GEAAL.* Titus, Mary, in *COCAAL* and *OCAAL. EB-98.*

Dunham, Katherine
6/22/1909–5/21/2006
Nonfiction—anthropology, autobiography/memoir; dancer/choreographer, educator, library assistant

Although Dunham is most widely known for her dancing, her direction of her dance troupe, and her choreography, she is well regarded in scholarly circles for her anthropological study of dance. Dunham's love of dance had begun before she graduated from high school, and she took dance lessons while attending Joliet Junior College. Her brother, Albert, persuaded her to transfer to the University of Chicago, where she supported herself by giving dance lessons, as well as assisting in the library. In Chicago, she studied various kinds of dance and formed an African-American dance troupe, Ballets Negre. During this time, she met **Langston Hughes** and other luminaries of the **Harlem Renaissance**. She also met and married fellow dancer Jordis McCoo, who worked nights at the post office, while she attended school by day.

At the university, her ethnology professor Robert Redfield inspired her interest in anthropology by emphasizing the role of dance in the social and ceremonial life of a culture. Perhaps also, she was already primed to be interested in cultural diversity, as her own ancestry included West African, Malagasyan, Madagascan, French Canadian, and Native American heritage. With encouragement from psychologist Erich Fromm and sociologist **Charles (Spurgeon) Johnson**, she was soon awarded a Julius Rosenwald Foundation fellowship to do fieldwork in the West Indies (Haiti—observing the Vaudun cere-

Katherine Dunham

monies, Jamaica—the Accompong, and Martinique and Trinidad). As her research continued, she also received funding from Guggenheim and Rockefeller Foundation fellowships, and she founded a dance school and a medical clinic in Haiti.

Eventually, this research led to her receiving bachelor's and master's degrees in anthropology from the University of Chicago, and a doctorate from Northwestern University, based on her doctoral thesis on the dances of Haiti. With her impressive credentials and distinctive knowledge, she gave lectures on her investigations at Yale, the Royal Anthropological Society of London, and other institutions throughout the Americas and Europe.

Dunham has also demonstrated a lifelong commitment to civil rights, justice, and freedom from oppression. As just one example, despite pressure from the U.S. State Department, she and her troupe toured internationally performing her dance *Southland,* which dramatized a lynching, following the outrageous lynching of young Emmett Till. In 1992 (in her 80s), she also went on a 47-day fast to publicize the despicable U.S. policies toward Haitian refugees in the United States. Humorist **Dick Gregory**, dancer and actor Debbie Allen, minister and activist Louis Farrakhan, and other celebrities visited her home to show respect for her and her cause.

While working for the Federal Theatre Project in the 1940s, Dunham met Anglo-Canadian set and costume designer and artist John Thomas Pratt. Soon, he was collaborating with her and helping her manage her career. After divorcing her first husband, on July 10, 1939, she married 24-year-old Pratt, to whom she remained married until his death in 1986. In 1952, Pratt and Dunham adopted a daughter, a mixed-heritage French Martinican four- or five-year-old, Marie Christine Columbier, who is now a designer herself, living in Rome.

About the time of her marriage, The Dunham Dance Company formed in 1939, the first all-African-American modern-dance company. The troupe toured internationally throughout the 1940s and into the 1950s. About 1944 or 1945, Dunham opened the Katherine Dunham School of Arts and Theatre in New York. There, in addition to studying dance and theater arts, students learned about literature and world cultures until the school closed in 1955. Her students had included actors Marlon Brando and James Dean, dancer Eartha Kitt, and choreographer Arthur Mitchell.

Meanwhile, Dunham continued to choreograph ballets, stage shows, and films (e.g., *Stormy Weather*), and in 1963, she was invited to choreograph Verdi's *Aida* for the Metropolitan Opera, becoming their first African-American choreographer. After her 1965 performance at Harlem's Apollo Theatre, Dunham spent two years involved in dance in Senegal (1965-1967), as President Lyndon Johnson's cultural adviser there. On returning to the United States, she moved to East St. Louis and opened the Performing Arts Training Center (since named the Katherine Dunham Centers for the Arts and Humanities) of Southern Illinois University, where she again encouraged cross-cultural understandings through dance, literature, and other arts. In association with the center are a children's workshop and the Katherine Dunham Museum. Even from a wheelchair and despite having diabetes, Dunham continued her work. Dunham won numerous honorary degrees and other awards from American institutions (e.g., the Albert Schweitzer Music Award, 1973; the Kennedy Center Award for Lifetime Achievement in the Arts, 1983; the Distinguished Service Award of the Anthropological Association, 1986; induction into the Hall of Fame of National Museum of Dance, 1987; National Medal of Arts, 1989) and from the Haitian government (Haitian Legion of Honor and Merit Chevalier, 1950; Commander, 1958; Grand Officer, 1968).

In addition to writing numerous scholarly journal articles and popular magazine essays, Dunham contributed short stories to various popular magazines, sometimes using the nom de plume Kaye Dunn. Dunham's book-length publications include her Jamaican observations, *Journey to Accompong* (1946, 1971 reprint titled *Katherine Dunham's Journey to Accompong*); her first memoir, *A Touch of Innocence: Memoirs of Childhood* (1959/1994); her Haitian memoir written while she was living in Senegal, *Island Possessed* (1969/1994); her fiction set in Senegal, *Kasamance, a Fantasy* (1969); and her authoritative work based on her 1947 doctoral thesis, *Dances of Haiti* (1983). At her death, she was said to be working on an additional memoir.

REFERENCES: *EBLG. HR&B. PGAA. WDAW.* Aschenbrenner, Joyce, in *BWA:AHE.* Jackson, Gregory, in *COCAAL* and *OCAAL.* Martin, Jonathan, in Amazon.com, 7/1999. *BB. CAO-06. EB-BH-CD.* Moss, Shondrika L., in *GEAAL.* Odom, Selma Landen in *WB-99.* Tobias, Tobi, in *G-95.* Wood, Phyllis, in *BH2C.* Dunham's papers, films, and artifacts are archived at the Missouri Historical Society in St. Louis. *A. B. BCE. CE. D. DD. Wiki.*

Dyson, Michael Eric

10/23/1958–

Literary and cultural criticism, biographies; cleric, educator, journalist

In 2008, *Ebony* included Michael Eric Dyson as 1 of 10 educators in its list of the "150 Most Influential Black Americans." *Ebony* also included **Maya Angelou**; **Lerone Bennett, Jr.**; **John Hope Franklin**; **Henry Louis Gates, Jr.**; **Neil DeGrasse Tyson**; and **Cornel West** in its list of the most influential educators. Though now known as an educator, he started his professional life as a licensed Baptist minister (1979) and an ordained minister (1981). Anyone who has heard Dyson speak would not be surprised at these origins, given his commanding presence, his resonant voice, his rhetorical flourishes, and his biblically poetic cadences. A frequent talk-show guest on radio (e.g., National Public Radio) and television (e.g., HBO), he has also appeared in at least two films, *Tupac: The Hip Hop Genius* (2004) and *Waist Deep* (2006), as well as some TV episodes and shows. For a little over a year (1/2006-2/2007), Dyson hosted an eponymous syndicated weekday talk radio show.

After earning his baccalaureate magna cum laude (1985), Dyson was called from the pulpit to the lectern. After a brief position as assistant director of a poverty project at the Hartford Seminary (1988-1989), he started teaching at the Chicago Theological Seminary (1989-1992), during which time he earned his M.A. (1991) at Princeton, where he later earned his Ph.D. (1993). Next, Dr. Dyson moved on to Brown University (c. 1993-1995), University of North Carolina at Chapel Hill (c. 1995-1997), Columbia University in New York City (1997-1999), DePaul University in Chicago (1999-2002), University of Pennsylvania in Philadelphia (2002-2007), and Georgetown University in Washington, D.C. (since 2007), the oldest Roman Catholic Jesuit university in the nation.

Though he may broadly be called a cultural critic, the range of his interests may be seen in his varied book titles, chiefly essay collections. These titles include *Reflecting Black: African-American Cultural Criticism* (1993), *Between God and Gangsta Rap: Bearing Witness to Black Culture* (1995), *Making Malcolm: The Myth and Meaning of* **Malcolm X** (1995), *Race Rules: Navigating the Color Line* (1996), *Open Mike: Reflections on Philosophy, Race, Sex, Culture, and Religion* (2002), *Why I Love Black Women* (2003), *The Michael Eric Dyson Reader* (2004), *Pride: The Seven Deadly Sins* (2006; also, *Soberbia/ Pride: Los Siete Pecados Capitales/ The Seven Capital Sins*), *Is* **Bill Cosby** *Right?: Or Has the Black Middle Class Lost Its Mind?* (2006), *Come Hell or High Water: Hurricane Katrina and the Color of Disaster* (2006), *Debating Race: With Michael Eric Dyson* (2007), *Know What I Mean?: Reflections on Hip Hop* (2007), *Can You Hear Me Now?: The Inspiration, Wisdom, and Insight of Michael Eric Dyson* (2009), *April 4, 1968:* **Martin Luther King, Jr.***'s Death and How it Changed America* (2009), *Full of the Hope That the Present Has Brought Us: Obama and America (The W. E. B. Du Bois Lectures)* (2009), and *Untitle on the Church* (2009).

In addition to these diverse books of cultural criticism, Dyson has written several biographical works, including *I May Not Get There with You: The True Martin Luther King, Jr.* (2000, a biography), *Holler If You Hear Me: Searching for* **Tupac Shakur** (2001), and *Mercy, Mercy Me: The Art, Loves, and Demons of Marvin Gaye* (2004). Many of Dyson's books, particularly his essay collections, have been published in audio and in kindle formats, as well as print. In addition to his own books, he has collaborated with others, contributed to anthologies, written forewords and other material for other authors, and contributed countless articles, commentaries, and columns to periodicals such as the *Black Issues Book Review, Chicago Tribune, Nation, The New York Times, Rolling Stone,* and *Vibe.*

Among his many awards and honors are the National Magazine Award from the National Association of Black Journalism (1992) and an Image Award for Outstanding Literary Work of Nonfiction from the National Association for the Advancement of Colored People (2006). Dyson has been married three times. After divorcing his first two wives, he has been married to author, marketer, and P.R. specialist Marcia Louise since 1992. He has dedicated at least one of his books to his two children, Michael Eric Dyson, II, who was born while the senior Dyson was still a teenager, and Maisha.

REFERENCES: *CAO-07. Wiki.* Kram, Mark, and Ralph G. Zerbonia, in *BB.* //www.amazon.com. //www.ebonyjet.com/ebony/articles/index.aspx. //www.michaelericdyson.com/.

FURTHER READING: Nishikawa, Kinohi, in *GEAAL.*

~E~

Eady, Cornelius
1954–
Poems; educator

Many of Eady's urban bluesy poems have been collected in his volumes *Kartunes* (1980); *Victims of the Latest Dance Craze* (1985/1997), winner of the Academy of American Poets' 1985 Lamont Poetry Prize; *BOOM BOOM BOOM: A Chapbook* (1988); *The Gathering of My Name* (1991), nominee for the 1992 Pulitzer Prize in Poetry; *You Don't Miss Your Water* (1995), reflecting on the death of his father; *The Autobiography of a Jukebox* (1997); and *Brutal Imagination* (2001), finalist for the National Book Award in Poetry; and *Hardheaded Weather* (2008). Eady's other awards include fellowships from the Rockefeller Foundation, the Guggenheim Foundation, and the National Endowment for the Arts, as well as a Lila Wallace-Reader's Digest Award. His poems also appear in *Blackbird*, *Ploughshares*, and other literary journals. Just four lines from his "Radio" shows how readily Eady can squeeze a lot of delight into a small package: "There is the school boy / Whose one possession / Is an electric box / That scrambles the neighborhood." In 1996, he and **Toi Derricotte** cofounded **Cave Canem**, a workshop retreat for poets. Eady also has taught at numerous colleges and universities, most recently as director of the Creative Writing program at the University of Notre Dame, where his wife, novelist Sarah Micklem, also teaches. He and she had been friends since high school when they married.

REFERENCES: *VBAAP*. Powers, Stephen Roger, in *GEAAL*. "Cornelius Eady," in *Wiki*. "Sarah Micklem " in *Wiki. CAO-02*. //www.cavecancmpocts.org/pagcs/programs_faculty.php#toi. //www.firethorn.info/ftautobio.htm. Amazon.com.

Early, Gerald (Lyn)
04/21/1952–
Cultural criticism, essays, autobiography/memoir, scholarly anthologies; educator, editor

After Early graduated cum laude from the University of Pennsylvania (1974), he married Ida Haynes (later a college administrator) in 1977, then he finished his M.A. (1980) at Cornell University in Ithaca, New York. By the time he earned his Ph.D. from Cornell (1982), Gerald and Ida already had two daughters, Linnet Kristen Haynes Early and Rosalind Lenora Haynes Early. Unlike many scholars who roam from campus to campus moving up the academic ladder, Early has managed to keep one academic home, at Washington University in St. Louis. There, he has moved from being an instructor (1982) to an assistant professor (1982-1988), an associate professor (1988), and a professor (since 1988). In 1996, he was honored to be named the Merle Kling Professor of Modern Letters, which he continues to be. He did have an interim visit as a writer in residence at Randolph Macon College for Women in Lynchburg, Virginia (1990), however. His nonacademic jobs include advising Warner Brothers Communications on the script for the television series *The Mississippi* (1983), consulting for Ken Burns's documentaries *Baseball* (1994) and *Jazz* (2001), and commentating for *Fresh Air* on National Public Radio (NPR).

A prolific author, Early's essays, literary reviews, and poetry have been featured in countless periodicals and anthologies. Early has also published his own essay collections, starting with *Tuxedo Junction: Essays on American Culture* (1989), covering a broad range of cultural topics, from boxing to literature, Miss America to jazz musicians, with currents of racial politics flowing throughout. His next collection jabs directly at boxing, but he sets it in a broader context of sports and culture. *The Culture of Bruising: Essays on Prizefighting, Literature, and Modern American Culture* (1994) won the National Book Critics Circle Award. Though it might seem that his other book of that year, *One Nation Under a Groove: Motown & American Culture* (1994), contrasted the visceral and tangible with an appreciation of the aesthetic and ethereal, the two books are not unrelated. Berry Gordy had been a boxer before starting Motown Records, and in both books Early aptly uses the particular of his given topic, boxing and Motown, to explore broader issues of interracial relations, popular culture, and American politics.

On a much more personal, intimate note, Early also published his memoir, *Daughters: On Family and Fatherhood* (1994). As always, however, he offered a cultural and sociological context even for his personal life experiences. After producing three big works in a single year, Early waited nearly a decade for his next big collection, *This Is Where I Came In: Black America in the 1960s* (Abra-

ham Lincoln Lecture) (2003), which comprises a series of lectures he gave on three key cultural icons: boxer Muhammad Ali, entertainer Sammy Davis Jr., and NAACP leader Cecil B. Moore. In the interim, between prose collections, Early published his poetry collection, *How the War in the Streets Is Won: Poems on the Quest of Love and Faith* (1995). He also wrote Grammy-nominated album-liner notes for *Yes I Can! The Sammy Davis Jr. Story* (2000) and for *Rhapsodies in Black: Music and Words From the Harlem Renaissance* (2001).

If Early had never written any essays, his career as an editor would still make him an important literary figure. His two-volume collection, *Speech and Power: The African-American Essay in Its Cultural Content from Polemics to Pulpit* (1992, Vol. 1; 1993, Vol. 2), comprised more than 100 essays altogether. Early's other edited works include *My Soul's High Song: The Collected Writings of **Countee Cullen*** (1991), *Lure and Loathing: Essays on Race, Identity and the Ambivalence of Assimilation* (1993), *Ain't But a Place: An Anthology of African American Writings About St. Louis* (1998), *Body Language: Writers on Sport* (1998), *I'm a Little Special: The Muhammad Ali Reader* (1998; with Muhammad Ali), *Miles Davis and American Culture* (2001), and *The Sammy Davis, Jr. Reader* (2001). In addition to the aforementioned editing of *Best African American Essays* in 2009 and 2010, Early is also slated to edit *Best African American Fiction* (2009, with **E. Lynn Harris**; 2010, alone).

In addition to National Book Critics Circle Award and the National Magazine Award, Early has won numerous other fellowships (1977, 1978-1980, 1980, 1981, 1981, 1984, 1985-1987) and grants (1983), as well as awards (1978, 1979, 1981, 1988), most notably the Whiting Writer's Award of $25,000 from the Whiting Foundation (1988). In addition, on September 5, 2007, an appreciative Washington University unveiled a portrait of Early, which now presides over the Journals Reading Room in the school's Olin Library.

REFERENCES: *QB. W. Wiki.* Chura, Patrick, in *AANB.* Daily, Eileen, and Lorna Mabunda, in *BB.* Martin, Daniel J., in *COCAAL.* //en.wikipedia.org/wiki/Ken_Burns. //news-info.wustl.edu/sb/page/normal/134.html. Amazon.com.

FURTHER READING: Rutledge, Rebecka Rychelle, in *GEAAL.*

Ebonics *See* African-American Vernacular English (AAVE)

Ebony
1945–

Popular magazine, including both features and news articles

(*See also* **Johnson Publishing Company** (1942-.) In 1942, **John H. Johnson** published his first issue of his first periodical, a *Reader's Digest*-sized 68-page magazine he called **Negro Digest**. Like *Reader's Digest*, *Negro Digest* included entirely reprinted articles from other sources, both African-American-owned and -operated periodicals and European-American-owned and -operated ones. Within three years, *Negro Digest*, which later included some original articles, was a reliable moneymaker for Johnson, and he was ready to try something new.

On November 1, 1945, Johnson launched a second periodical. This time, Johnson's models were the highly popular *Life* and *Look* magazines, both large-size, photo-studded magazines showing current events and feature articles. Eunice, Johnson's business-savvy wife, suggested calling the new magazine *Ebony*. *Ebony*'s large, photo-rich pages highlighted African Americans and an African-American perspective on the news. Johnson's primary aim was to shine a positive light on African-American achievements and successes. The existing European-American magazines celebrated European Americans' weddings, births, graduations, and festivals; they featured the small and large achievements of famous and not-so-famous European Americans; and they reveled in the lifestyles of rich and famous European Americans. Johnson planned for *Ebony* to do so for African Americans.

In the inaugural issue, Johnson described his positive outlook, "We're rather jolly folks, . . . Sure, you can get all hot and bothered about the race question (and don't think we don't) but not enough is said about all the swell things we Negroes do and accomplish" (quoted in Berry, //www.lib.niu.edu/2007/iht07140113.html). As this introduction indicates, Johnson used an informal chatty style to invite readers into his magazine. Readers could almost feel his arm around their shoulder, as he told them what he had found about their neighbors and their distant cousins across the nation.

Johnson expected the new magazine to sell well, so he printed 25,000 copies. *Ebony*'s first printing sold out within hours, and a second printing of another 25,000 copies sold out, as well. At its birth, *Ebony* had vastly superseded its parent, *Negro Digest*. Like *Life*, *Ebony* continued as a weekly publication until the 1970s, when it went to monthly distribution.

Johnson was delighted that *Ebony* was selling well, but he still had a big problem. In order to boost readership, he was selling the magazine for just 25¢ each-less than it cost to produce it. Johnson was losing money on each magazine he printed. While *Negro Digest* was being outsold by *Ebony*, *Negro Digest*'s modest production costs made it much more profitable than *Ebony*. Johnson used the profits from the parent magazine to help support its offspring until *Ebony* was mature enough to support itself.

In truth, few periodical publishers can pay for all publication costs solely with subscriptions and single-issue sales. Like television broadcasters, Internet webcasters, and other media producers, the periodical publishers' lifeblood is advertising revenue. Therefore, while Johnson was keeping two weekly magazines in print, he was also trying to drum up advertising business for his newborn magazine. Though a skilled salesperson, Johnson was having trouble luring advertisers to buy into Ebony's pages.

His solution? He launched yet another business: Beauty Star, a mail-order business selling hair-care products, wigs, and vitamins. Of course, he advertised the Beauty Star products in his magazines, which in turn shared the profits from his Beauty Star sales. In May of 1946, Ebony also started printing ads for Murray's Hair Pomade and for Johnson's old employer, Supreme Life Insurance. At last, in 1947, Johnson persuaded Eugene F. McDonald, head of radio- and electrical-appliance-manufacturer Zenith, to advertise in Ebony. With McDonald's influence, Johnson was then able to sell ad space to Armour Foods, Elgin Watch, Quaker Oats, and Swift Packing (Chicago meat packers), followed by Beech-Nut canned foods, Colgate personal-hygiene products, Old Gold tobacco products, Pepsi-Cola, Seagrams alcoholic products, and numerous other advertisers.

A key to the success of these advertisers has always been to tailor the ads to the readers, featuring African-American models wearing the watch, eating the oatmeal, or drinking the soda pop. Johnson Publishing Company (JPC) blazed the trail in this regard. As **Langston Hughes** recalled on Ebony's 20th anniversary, "to see ourselves presented so handsomely in commercial advertising (which now has spread to other national publications) is a great achievement on the positive side due, I believe, largely to EBONY" (from November 1965, Ebony, quoted in //findarticles.com/p/articles/mi_m1077/is_1_56/ai_66455747/).

Once Ebony was making a profit, Johnson invested some of his profits in the magazine by hiring talented African Americans to work for him. For instance, he hired **Era Bell Thompson** as associate editor (1948-1951), then comanaging editor with Herbert Nipson (1951-1964), and then international editor (1964-1986). He also hired Moneta Sleet, Jr., the first African-American photojournalist to win a Pulitzer Prize and the first journalist from a black-owned publication to win the Pulitzer. Sleet won his Pulitzer for his photos following the 1968 assassination of **Martin Luther King, Jr.** Johnson also paid for professional historians to offer expert advice on documenting African-American history for Ebony's readers.

Since its earliest issues, photographers have vied to see their work appear on the cover of Ebony. Covers usually portray photos of successful African-American entertainers (e.g., Dorothy Dandridge, Lena Horne, Tina Turner; Redd Foxx, Eddie Murphy, **Richard Pryor**), politicians (e.g., Douglas Wilder, Andrew Young, Nelson Mandela), and other notables (e.g., Colin Powell, Shaquille O'Neal, Tiger Woods). The photographs almost always show beaming faces, often with the celebrity's smiling loved ones close at hand. The August 2008 issue, identifying "25 Coolest Brothers of All Time," featured eight separate covers, and collectors no doubt purchased all eight, featuring **Barack Obama**, Muhammad Ali, Marvin Gaye, Samuel L. Jackson, Jay-Z, Prince, Denzel Washington, and Billy Dee Williams.

Critics have charged that Ebony's persistent focus on the positive aspects of the lives of successful African Americans has come at the cost of failing to reveal the persistent problems of poverty, racial discrimination, and oppression suffered by African Americans. Since the 1960s, many advocates of **Black Power** and of the **Black Aesthetic** have denounced Ebony as emphasizing the rich and famous, accepted into the European-American mainstream, while ignoring Afrocentric topics and values.

In 1965, Langston Hughes offered a contrarian view: "An especially happy event . . . was the birth of EBONY in the autumn of 1945-a new young and handsome journalistic child of which to be proud. I liked EBONY from its very beginning, . . . From the start EBONY has had consistently eye-catching and interesting covers . . . . I remember well . . . the massed faces, Negro and white, . . . the crowd surging forward in the great March on Washington of 1963 . . . . One picture is sometimes worth a million words, and much easier to take in quickly. The files of EBONY . . . could well serve as an overall history of the American Negro . . . . While the main emphasis has been on the presentation of the positive side of Negro achievement, EBONY has not hesitated to face the grim realities of such ugly episodes in American life as the Emmett Till lynching or the Birmingham brutalities and to present them in all their horror. The careless charge some critics have made that EBONY presents only successful Negroes, colorful sports and entertainment personalities and pretty fashion models is not true. Even if it were true, there has been such a need in Negro lives to see themselves pictured beautifully, to view on the printed page something other than slums, and to learn that at least some Black men and women can be successful in this highly competitive world, that a magazine presenting nothing but the positive side would still be of value, even if the balance were a bit overboard. I do not feel that EBONY has gone overboard" (from November 1965, Ebony, quoted in //findarticles.com/p/articles/mi_m1077/is_1_56/ai_66455747/).

Fortunately for all people interested in deciding the value of *Ebony*'s content for themselves, Google has scanned in the issues from November 1959 through November 2008. The interested reader can simply choose "Google Books" from the "More" menu on the "Google.com" main page, then type in "Ebony Magazine" in the search box. As an example, the November 1959 issue (Vol. 15, NO. 1, 184 pp., available for 35¢) highlights "Opera Singers," "Harry Truman and the Negro: Was He Our Greatest Civil Rights President?" by **Carl T. Rowan**, and "Six Ways to Stop Negro Crime" on its cover. The "Contents" page lists two articles in the "Race" section, including the Rowan article; three in the "Education" section; three in the "Children" section; four in the "Entertainment" section, including one titled "Ballet Star: Arthur Mitchell is top soloist with New York Co."; two in the "Occupations" section; two in the "Medicine" section, including one titled "Have Wheel Chair—Will Travel: Polio victim propels self hundreds of miles"; two in the "Organizations" section; two in the "Personalities" section, including "Civil War Reporter: Thomas Chester wrote about Negro troops in battle" and "Jim Brown, Gentleman Juggernaut by Francis Mitchell: Modest Cleveland back is maturing into football's top pro"; and two in the "Foreign" section. The three "Departments" listed include "Photo-Editorials: Six Ways to Stop Negro Crime"; "Date with a Dish: Meat Tenderizer"; and "Fashion Fair: The Magic of a 'Paris Original'."

The Magazine Publishers of America (MPA) reported *Ebony*'s circulation as 1,372,297 in 2008, with 2008 subscription revenues of $25,995,264, single-copy revenues of $9,548,062, for a total of $35,543,326 for the year. The figures for its little sister *Jet* were $29,659,969 for subscriptions, $4,576,586 for single issues, and $35,236,555 total. Comparable figures for *Ebony*'s chief competitor, *Essence*, were $16,230,698 for subscriptions, $12,022,979 for single issues, and $28,253,677 total. On the other hand, all three of these were overshadowed by *O, the Oprah Magazine*, which had revenues of $47,595,030 for subscriptions, $36,719,757 for single issues, and $84,314,787 total. *People* magazine had $250,161,652 in subscription revenues, $308,930,282 in single-issue revenues, and $559,091,933 total revenues. To earn those revenues, in 2009, new subscribers paid $15.97 for a 1-year, 12-issue print subscription to *Ebony*, or $3.99 per single issue ($47.88/year).

The *Ebony* brand has become so highly regarded and well known that many other products and product lines have used the *Ebony* label to assure potential purchasers of the products' appeal and quality. For instance, *Ebony* was linked to several other magazines: *Ebony, Jr.!* (1973-1985), *Ebony Man (EM)* (1985-1998), *E Style* (1993-1996), and *Ebony South Africa* (1995-2000). Books, too, used this label, such as *The Ebony Cookbook: A Date with a Dish - A Cookbook of American Negro Recipes* by Freda De Knight (1962), Margaret Peters's *The Ebony Book of Black Achievement* (1970), and JPC's four-volume *Ebony Pictorial History of Black America* (1971).

Even entirely new business ventures were introduced with the *Ebony* brand, such as the Ebony Fashion Fair. In 2005, Rice announced that *Ebony* would be seeking to license the *Ebony* brand to a wide variety of products, from games and toys to financial products. For the $773 billion African-American consumer market, *Ebony* is a recognized, well-respected brand, and if Rice carefully chooses the licensed products to fit with the lifestyle *Ebony* conveys, she may even enhance the *Ebony* brand-as well as JPC's profits.

In reflecting on the mission of *Ebony*, John H. Johnson recalled, "We wanted to give blacks a new sense of somebodiness, a new sense of self-respect . . . . We believed then—and we believe now—that blacks needed positive images to fulfill their potentialities" (quoted in Lamb, 2005).

REFERENCES: Berry, William E., "The Johnson Publishing Company: Historical Research and Narrative," in //www.lib. niu.edu/2007/iht07140113.html. Cabell, A. K. "brandchannel," (7/21/2005), "Branding," in //www.businessweek.com/innovate/ content/jul2005/di20050721_807102.htm. "From *Negro Digest* to *Ebony, Jet* and *EM* - Special Issue: 50 Years of JPC - Redefining the Black Image." *Ebony*, in //findarticles.com/p/articles/mi_m1077/is_ n1_v48/ai_12811539/. Hughes, Langston, ("55 EBONY's Nativity - Magazine's History," reprinted from November 1965, *Ebony*), *Ebony*, (November, 2000), in //findarticles.com/p/articles/mi_m1077/is_ 1_56/ai_66455747/. Huguley-Riggins, Piper G., "*Ebony*," in GEAAL. Lamb, Yvonne Shinhoster, (8/9/2005) "Publisher Helped Chronicle Black Life with *Ebony* and *Jet*," p. A01, in //www.washingtonpost.com/ wp-dyn/content/article/2005/08/08/AR2005080801607.html. "Top Negro Publisher: John H. Johnson of Chicago," (March, 1952), *Kiplinger's Personal Finance* (Vol. 6, No. 3), p. 37. //books.google.com/ books?id=r9QDAAAAMBAJ. //en.wikipedia.org/wiki/Ebony_ (magazine). //www.ebonyjet.com/. //en.wikipedia.org/wiki/John_H._ Johnson. //www.flickr.com/photos/vieilles_annonces/collections/ 72157602208090748/. //www.fundinguniverse.com/company- histories/Johnson-Publishing-Company-Inc-Company-History.html. //www.magazine.org/consumer_marketing/circ_trends/16117.aspx. //www.magazine.org/CONSUMER_MARKETING/CIRC_TRENDS/ ABC2008TOTALrank.aspx. //www.magazine.org/consumer_ marketing/circ_trends/index.aspx, [link from] for 2008 Circulation Revenue for All ABC Magazines.

FURTHER READING: *See* the main entry and the many references cited in the entry for **Johnson Publishing Company.** *See also* the main entry and the many references cited in the entry for **Johnson, John H.**

Edelman, Marian Wright
6/6/1939–

Inspirational/motivational books of child advocacy, autobiography/memoir; attorney, founding president of the Children's Defense Fund

The parents of Marian, her sister, and her three brothers prized education and cherished children. Although they lacked many financial resources, every one of the Wright children went to college, and the Wrights raised 12 foster children in addition to their own. Marian's daddy, a Baptist minister (Marian's "the aunt, granddaughter, daughter, and sister of Baptist ministers"), built a playground and snack bar behind his church to ensure that the black children of the neighborhood, barred from white play areas in Jim Crow South Carolina, would have somewhere to enjoy themselves, to belong, and to feel safe. In 1954, when Marian was 14 years old, the U.S. Supreme Court case *Brown v. Board of Education* was a major topic of conversation in her household. Sadly, her father died the week before the decision was handed down, so he never knew how that case would affect future generations of African-American children. By the time Marian's father died, she had already learned to rely on her religion to guide her to serve those in need.

Early on, Marian Wright was active in the civil-rights movement. For instance, she was among the 14 students arrested at an Atlanta sit-in. After she earned her baccalaureate from Spelman College (1960), while a student at Yale University Law School, she spent the summer working on the voter-registration campaign in Mississippi. In 1963, after she graduated from Yale Law, she became a staff attorney for the NAACP Legal Defense and Education Fund, which helped release jailed students for their civil-rights activities. She put her beliefs to the test when assaulted by Southern sheriffs' fire hoses and attack dogs, as well as being incarcerated in Southern jails. During that time, she became the first African-American woman to pass the Mississippi bar (at age 26). She also joined the board of the Child Development Group of Mississippi, a major Head Start program.

During the Mississippi Freedom Summer of 1964 and her battles for Head Start in 1965, Wright observed the tremendous hunger, homelessness, and illiteracy of children (and their families), and she determined that local, specific actions seemed ineffectual in addressing those needs. As a result, she conceived of a broader, more encompassing organization that could address these needs on a national level. In 1968, she was awarded a Ford Foundation Grant, which she used to start the Washington Research Project, to investigate national policies and investment strategies that might address the needs she saw. Following a brief stint (1971-1973) as director of the Harvard University Center for Law and Education, she re-

turned to Washington and built on the foundation she had erected for the Washington Research Project to found the highly esteemed Children's Defense Fund (CDF), a non-profit organization lobbying on behalf of children's issues. She has since presided over the CDF, tackling such issues as child care, children's health, and youth employment. One of the most widely recognized CDF programs is its nationwide multimedia and community-based campaign to prevent or reduce teen pregnancy.

Meanwhile, Marian's personal life also came to center around children. In 1967, in Mississippi, she met fellow attorney Peter Edelman, the grandson of Russian Jews, who shared her dedication to civil rights. In 1968, they married, and fairly soon after, they had three sons (Josh, Jonah, then Ezra). As she said in her 1992 book, *The Measure of Our Success: A Letter to My Children and Yours*, she has been fortunate to have a job that allowed her to ensure that her children "came first in any crunch." Not only was she *able* to put her own children ahead of her work for the nation's children, however, but she also *chose* to do so, such as ensuring that when one of her children was sick, either she or her husband stayed home with them. She also attended most school parent meetings and baked her share of cookies and brownies—and then she went to work the next morning, to fight for the well-being and education of other people's children. Now that her three sons are adults, her four grandchildren continue to spur her to action on behalf of the nation's children.

Senator Edward Kennedy described her effectiveness, "She has real power in congress, and uses it brilliantly." Among her myriad awards is a 1985 MacArthur fellowship (nicknamed a "genius grant"), a 2000 Robert F. Kennedy Lifetime Achievement Award, a 2000 Presidential Medal of Freedom, and a 2006 NAACP Image Award. Among her many appointments to prestigious and influential bodies are appointments to the Council on Foreign Relations and to the board of trustees of Spelman College. She was soon the first African American and the second woman to chair the college's board of trustees.

In addition to countless legal documents and other advocacy writings, she has written several books: Her 1987 book *Families in Peril: An Agenda for Social Change (The W. E. B. Du Bois Lectures)* shows how poverty is the most pressing national problem and urges readers to ensure support for poor mothers and children of all races. Her 1992 *The Measure of Our Success: A Letter to My Children and Yours* warmly describes her own interracial family life and spells out her beliefs regarding how we as a society can best promote the well-being of our children and youths. Her 1995 *Guide My Feet: Prayers and Meditations on Loving and Working for Children* offers prayers by the author and by others, intended to cry out for help to protect and care for our children. Her impassioned 1996 speech at a Stand for Children gathering was adapted to picture-book format with quilts by Adrienne Yorinks to create *Stand For Children* (1998). Her 1999 memoir *Lanterns: A Memoir of Mentors* highlights those who have inspired her and illuminated her path. After the Bush Administration twisted the meaning of her campaign to "Leave No Child Behind," she published *Hold My Hand: Prayers for Building a Movement to Leave No Child Behind* (2001) and *I'm Your Child, God: Prayers for Children and Teenagers* (2002). She also edited a multicultural collection of poems, stories, and art for children, *I Can Make a Difference: A Treasury to Inspire Our Children* (2005, illustrated by Barry Moser). Most recently, she wrote *Sea Is So Wide and My Boat Is So Small, The: Charting a Course for the Next Generation* (2008), formatted as a series of open letters to all of us who should be working to improve the lives of our nation's children.

REFERENCES: *1TESK. AA:PoP. AAB. AANB. BF:2000. EBLG. H.* Edelman, Marian. 1992. *The Measure of Our Success: A Letter to My Children and Yours* Boston: Beacon Press. *B. LE. QB. Wiki.* Lee, Cathleen Collins; Isaac Rosen; and Jennifer M. York, in *BB. CAO-07.* //womenshistory.about.com/od/aframerwriters/tp/african_american_women_writers.htm. Amazon.com, 8/1999, 2/2009. SDPL catalog. *G-95.*

Edmonds, Kenneth (Brian) "Babyface"
4/10/1959–

Songs; singer, musician, record and film producer

Among award-winning songwriter Edmonds's many hits are "Tender Lover," "Unbreak My Heart," "Take a Bow," and "Change the World," and Grammy winners "I'll Make Love to You" and "When Can I See You," recorded by such singers as Whitney Houston, Madonna, and Eric Clapton. In addition to at least 10 Grammy awards, he was awarded the 1992 NAACP Lifetime Achievement Award.

REFERENCES: Crockett, Kenneth, in *A. BH2C. D. Wiki.* Glickman, Simon, Jim Henry, and Jennifer M. York, in *BB.*

Elder, III, Lonne
12/26/1931–6/11/1996

Plays, screenplays; theater founder, director

Elder's stage plays include his highly celebrated *Ceremonies in Dark Old Men* (1969), as well as *Charades on East Fourth Street* (1967) and his first—still unproduced—play, *A Hysterical Tale in a Rabbit Race* (1961). His screenplays include episodes of *N.Y.P.D.* (for ABC television, 1967-1969) and of *McCloud* (for NBC TV, 1970-1971) and the movies *Sounder* (1972, based on the novel by William Armstrong), *Day of Absence* (1975, adapted from **Douglas Turner Ward**'s stage play),

Melinda (c. 1972), *The Terrible Veil* (1963), and *A Woman Called Moses* (1978). He also wrote the screenplay adaptation of **Richard Pryor**'s story *Bustin' Loose* (1981). Elder's first mentor, who inspired him to write, was poet **Robert Hayden**; his second was the Harlem Writer's Guild cofounder and patron saint **John O. Killens**. His roommate, **Douglas Turner Ward**, was also instrumental in guiding Elder's writing toward the theater.

REFERENCES: Cherry, Wilsonia E. D., in *AAW-55-85:DPW.* Frye, Karla Y. E., in *COCAAL and OCAAL.* Hart, William Bryan, in *T-CAD-1st.* Manheim, James M., in *BB. CAO-03.* McCarty, Joan F., in *AA. F. GEAAL. W. Wiki. Wr.* Millichap, Joseph, in *AS-2.* "An Interview with Lonne Elder III." *The Black American Writer, Volume II: Poetry and Drama.* Ed. C. W. E. Bigsby. Everett/Edwards, 1969. Rpt. in Lawrence J. Trudeau (Ed.), *Drama Criticism* (Vol. 8). Detroit: Gale Research, 1998. pp. 219-226. From *Literature Resource Center.*

Ellison, Ralph (Waldo)
3/1/1914–4/16/1994

Novels, essays, short stories, literary criticism, spoken word—speeches, lectures; educator

A descendant of slaves, Ralph Waldo Ellison was named after nineteenth-century European-American philosopher and writer Ralph Waldo Emerson. Lewis Alfred Ellison, a construction worker and small-time entrepreneur, gave his son that name in the hope that young Ralph would someday become a writer. Lewis was an avid reader and was exposing his son to books by the time Ralph started learning to walk. Lewis and Ida Millsap Ellison had moved to Oklahoma City, Oklahoma, from the deep South in the hope that this western frontier state was a land of greater opportunities for African Americans to prosper. Even after Lewis died, when Ralph was just three years old, the Ellisons held fast to their belief in limitless possibilities.

Ida worked as a domestic servant, a custodian, and occasionally even a cook, to earn enough to support Ralph and his brother Herbert. She also moved herself and her sons into the parsonage of a local church, and she continued to organize for the Socialist Party, enlisting African Americans. Ida often brought discarded popular magazines, books, and records home from the white householders for whom she worked. Ralph, an avid reader like his father, later recalled, "These magazines and recordings . . . spoke to me of a life that was broader and more interesting and although it was not really a part of my own life, I never thought they were not for me because I happened to be a Negro. They were things which spoke of a world which I could some day make my own" (quoted in *NAAAL*). Ida always affirmed Ralph's youthful beliefs about his possibilities for fulfillment. Even his wider community seemed to affirm these possibilities, as everywhere he saw African Americans courageously rising to challenges they faced.

In 1920, young Ralph started attending the segregated public schools in town. By the time he finished high school, in 1931, he had studied music theory and classical music and had started playing the trumpet and several other brass instruments. At that time, Oklahoma City was a haven for jazz and other music, so the blacks-only schools emphasized music education. In addition, Ralph made every effort to find places where he could listen to jazz music—which wasn't hard in Oklahoma City. To ensure that this talented young African American would not try to attend one of the whites-only colleges in Oklahoma, the state gave Ellison a scholarship to attend the Tuskegee Institute (in Alabama). The scholarship wasn't enough to pay for his living expenses in Alabama, however, so it was two years before Ellison had saved enough money to attend Tuskegee. In 1933, he hitched a ride (like a hobo) on a freight train headed to Alabama and entered Tuskegee to study music composition.

In his second year at Tuskegee, a sophomore English class opened Ellison's eyes and ears to the world of modern literature, such as T. S. Eliot's poem *The Waste Land*, with its jazzlike rhythms. Increasingly, he found himself spending more and more time in the library, delving into literature and history, while continuing his music major. For him, European-American poets such as T. S. Eliot and Ezra Pound wrote poems more closely linked to jazz than did the African-American poets of that time. Through their works, he started realizing that his interests in literature and in music could be merged, and a career in writing gained appeal for him. During this time, he met literary critic **Alain Locke**, who also encouraged him to think about writing as a career. Ellison developed an intense interest in sculpture, too.

Over time, the relatively anti-intellectual college life at Tuskegee, centered around campus politics and athletics, appealed to him less and less. The school's accommodationist philosophy also grated on Ellison, who had grown up believing in limitless possibilities, not quiet acceptance of whatever constraints were imposed on him by white society. Each summer, Ellison had to work to earn money for living expenses the following year. After his junior year (summer of 1936), he decided to find work in New York City, where he thought he might also pursue his interest in sculpture. In New York, he contacted Alain Locke again; Locke introduced him to **Langston Hughes** and **Arna Bontemps**. Enraptured by the pro-intellectual literary haven of New York City, Ellison never returned to Tuskegee. The following year, Ellison's mother died, and Ellison spent half the year with his brother, grieving, hunting, and reading. When he returned, Ellison knew that New York City was his home, and his career aim was to become a writer.

Ralph Ellison

In 1937 (the year Ellison's mother died), **Richard Wright** moved from Chicago to New York, and Hughes and Bontemps introduced Wright to Ellison. Wright proved to be a tremendous mentor to Ellison, encouraging Ellison to read widely, including European (e.g., James Joyce, Joseph Conrad, Fyodor Dostoyevsky) and European-American (e.g., Henry James, Ernest Hemingway) novelists. He also urged Ellison to work on perfecting his writing craft. Wright even allowed Ellison to see a master artisan at work, while Wright was writing his most widely acclaimed novel, *Native Son*. Ellison shared many of Wright's political views, too, although he never joined the Communist Party, and he was much more optimistic about the possibilities for change than Wright was, as Ellison had adopted his parents' deep-seated optimism. Nonetheless, Wright was pretty much the literary center of Ellison's universe at that time.

Wright also urged Ellison to contribute writings to the *New Challenge*, a Marxist literary magazine that Wright had started editing in Harlem. The first issue of *New Challenge* included Ellison's review of *These Low Grounds*, by Waters Turpin. A subsequent issue included Ellison's short story "Hymie Bull": Ellison could officially call himself a writer. The late 1930s were nothing like the 1920s (the era of the **Harlem Renaissance**), however, so writing for a living was pretty tough. Most writers had to earn a living doing menial jobs that left them a little time for writing after work. Fortunately, one of the New Deal programs was the Federal Writers' Project (FWP), which employed quite a few writers to conduct research and write reports on their findings. Through Wright, Ellison managed to get an FWP job in 1938, earning $103 each month to gather and record folklore and oral histories through extensive interviews with Harlem residents. In 1940 and 1941, Ellison wrote a couple of essays on the value of African-American folklore in African-American fiction, and he continued to contribute short stories, essays, and articles to *New Challenge, New Masses,* and other periodicals.

Ellison's earliest short stories (e.g., "Slick Gonna Learn," 1939; "The Birthmark," 1940) closely paralleled Wright's literary style and political outlook; far from being flattered, Wright rebuked Ellison for his derivative work, and their close relationship grew distant. Soon, Ellison started finding his own voice, style, and aesthetic and political outlook, and his writing became distinctively his own. In 1942, Ellison started editing *The Negro Quarterly,* and by 1944, he had written almost five dozen published articles (including a *New York Post* article on the 1943 Harlem riot), more than half a dozen stories, and various sketches and book reviews. No longer working for the FWP, he also started working on a novel, which was to be his masterpiece.

In 1943, Ellison joined the U.S. Merchant Marine, serving as a cook while continuing to write. After the war ended and he left the service, he planned to start writing a novel about a Tuskegee Airman captured by the Nazis during World War II, based on his 1944 short story "Flying Home." Instead, he found himself developing a novel based on a few words he had scribbled on a sheet of paper: "I am an invisible man." Fortunately, a publisher encouraged him to write it, and a Rosenwald Fellowship provided him enough money to do so. About seven years later, he completed his best-selling *Invisible Man* (1952).

The complex novel is seen through the eyes of an unnamed idealistic and naïve young black male who seeks his identity and his place in the world. On graduating from high school, the young man goes off to a well-respected college, where he hopes to find his way but instead finds himself invisible in a college much like Tuskegee, where neither the accommodationist founder nor the white patrons can see African Americans as an integral part of American society, instead seeing them only in terms of preconceived roles. After failing to find what he seeks in the South, the young man moves to Harlem, where he is again invisible as an individual and is instead urged to define himself in terms of various political stances (e.g., black nationalism, communism). Throughout the novel, the young man yearns for respect and equality and only at the end of the book does he realize that he has wrongly sought to define himself through others—others to whom he is invisible as an individual. Instead, he must define himself through a solitary quest for self-awareness and self-knowledge, drawing on his own

intellect and cultural heritage. Only then is he ready to enter a society full of possibilities for him, ready to forge his own identity and to create his own place (as a writer) in the world.

Although some African-American activists and scholars criticized the work for Ellison's response to militant African-American political activists, most literary critics of all races lauded the work. Among the many awards Ellison received for the book was a 1953 National Book Award for fiction, making him the first African American to win it. At the awards ceremony, Ellison credited the richness of African-American speech as central to his writing.

Ironically, one of several colleges and universities to award Ellison an honorary degree was his alma mater, which he had left without graduating and which he had not too subtly indicted in his novel; in 1963, the Tuskegee Institute awarded him an honorary Ph.D. in Humane Letters. In 1974, Harvard University awarded him an honorary doctorate, as well. In 1967, the Oklahoma State Legislature recognized him for his "outstanding contribution to the creative arts." In 1969, President Richard M. Nixon awarded Ellison the Medal of Freedom, the highest civilian honor. Perhaps the most remarkable honor, however, was awarded in 1965, when a poll of 200 book critics, editors, and authors named *Invisible Man* "the most distinguished American novel written since [the end of World War II]." The poll, published in *Book Week,* was taken more than a decade after the book was published and was based on the assessment of critics who had read countless books each year, including books by J. D. Salinger, Mary McCarthy, Norman Mailer, Joseph Heller, Jack Kerouac, Truman Capote, and Eudora Welty.

In the mid-1950s, Ellison went to Europe, lecturing in Germany and Austria; in 1955, he was awarded the Prix de Rome by the American Academy of Arts and Letters; the prize money paid for him to live in Italy for a while. When he returned to the United States, numerous colleges and universities invited him to lecture, teach, and work as writer-in-residence. Between 1958 and 1964, he taught at Bard College (in New York) and the University of Chicago; he was a writer-in-residence at Rutgers University (in New Jersey); he was a visiting fellow at Yale University; and he lectured at such prominent colleges and universities as Antioch, Bennington, Columbia, Fisk, Oberlin, Princeton, and UCLA. In 1970, he was named the Albert Schweitzer Professor of Humanities at New York University, from which he retired after 1979.

In addition to the novel on which his literary reputation rests, Ellison wrote short stories and essays, which have been widely anthologized. A couple years after his death, many of Ellison's short stories were collected in *Flying Home: And Other Stories* (1996). Of the 13 short stories in the collection, 6 were found after his death and had never been published before. All the stories were written between 1937 (his return to New York) and 1954 (before he left for Europe), including "Flying Home"; "Hymie's Bull," his first published short story; 4 humorous stories about Buster and Riley, adventurous preteens; and "A Party Down at the Square," a white Northern boy's observation of a lynching in the South.

When Ellison died, two volumes of Ellison's essays had been published: *Shadow and Act* (1964) and *Going to the Territory* (1986). Ellison dedicated *Shadow and Act* to Monteza Sprague, the English teacher at Tuskegee who had opened his eyes to the world of modern literature. Both collections include autobiographical observations of his own emergence as a writer, literary reviews and criticism, and essays, speeches, and interviews on the African-American experience (jazz and blues music, art and culture, and social issues). *Shadow and Act* included sections on literature and folklore ("The Seer and the Seen"), music ("Sound and the Mainstream") and African Americans in a social, cultural, and societal context ("The Shadow and the Act"). *Going to the Territory* also included excerpts from his second novel, still incomplete at the time of his death. *The Collected Essays of Ralph Ellison* (1995, edited by John F. Callahan) includes all the works from both collections, along with nearly two dozen previously uncollected or newly discovered works. His other major nonfiction work, also published posthumously, is *Conversations with Ralph Ellison* (1995, edited by Amritjit Singh and Maryemma Graham).

Ellison started his long-awaited second novel in the mid-1950s. He claimed that a fire at his summer home in Plainsfield, Massachusetts, had made ashes of more than a year's work, but **Arnold Rampersad** later disputed that claim. For the next three decades or more, Ellison had to try to recreate what he had written and then further develop the manuscript. At the time of his death, at least eight excerpts had been published (in his essay collection, in literary journals, and in readings during Ellison's appearances on television or on college campuses), but the work was still considered incomplete.

Ellison's literary executor, John F. Callahan, pulled together numerous sections of his work (about one third of the 2,000-page manuscript Ellison had written) to create the novel *Juneteenth*, published in 1999. Many critics have hailed its arrival as a major achievement, while others have decried both the completed work and even the effort to complete a work that Ellison himself was unable to finish during his lifetime. In *Juneteenth*, U.S. Senator Adam Sunraider, a white-complected racist, suffers a fatal gunshot wound while delivering a speech to fellow senators. To the great surprise of all who thought they knew him, on his deathbed, Sunraider asks to see Reverend Alonzo ("Daddy") Hickman, a black revivalist preacher. Apparently, the two have a long history to-

gether, and their lives are intertwined in ways never revealed before. Publication of Ellison's entire 2,000-page manuscript is still being planned.

Although Ellison made himself highly accessible to college students, he enjoyed his privacy. He and his wife, Fanny McConnell (whom he had married in 1946), lived in a flat in Manhattan, where he enjoyed listening to music, playing the jazz trumpet, making furniture, and experimenting with photography. He recognized his own way of contributing, however, when he observed, "[Writing] offers me the possibility of contributing not only to the growth of the literature but to the shaping of the culture as I should like it to be." Ellison also observed, "What moves a writer to eloquence is less meaningful than what he makes of it" (from "The World and the Jug," quoted in *NAAAL*). Other insights into Ellison may be found in *Ralph Ellison: An Interview with the Author of Invisible Man* (sound recording) (1974); *Is the Novel Dead?: Ellison, [William] Styron and [James] Baldwin on Contemporary Fiction* (sound recording) (1974); *Conversations with Ralph Ellison* (1995, edited by Maryemma Graham and Amritjit Singh); *Trading Twelves: The Selected Letters of Ralph Ellison and Albert Murray* (2000, edited by Albert Murray and John F. Callahan); and a *Paris Review* interview reprinted in *Contemporary Literary Criticism* (1999, edited by Jeffrey W. Hunter and Deborah A. Schmitt, Vol. 114).

REFERENCES: *1TESK. AA:PoP. AAW:AAPP. BAL-1-P. BF:2000. BWA. EBLG. EB-BH-CD. EGW. NAAAL. OC20LE. RG20. WDAA.* Busby, Mark, in *ANSWWII-6th.* Callahan, John F. "Frequencies of Memory: A Eulogy for Ralph Waldo Ellison (March 1, 1914 - April 16, 1994) (Obituary)." *Callaloo.* 18.2 (Spring 1995) p. 298. From *Literature Resource Center.* Cannon, Steve. "Reminiscin' in C: Remembering Ralph Waldo Ellison." *Callaloo.* 18.2 (Spring 1995) p. 288. From *Literature Resource Center.* Deutsch, Leonard J. in *AAW-40-55,* and in *ANSWWII-1st.* Early, Gerald, "Decoding Ralph Ellison," in *EA-99.* Ellison, Ralph, Vilma Howard, and Alfred Chester. "An Interview." *Paris Review.* pp. 53-55. Rpt. in Jeffrey W. Hunter and Deborah A. Schmitt (Eds.) (1999), *Contemporary Literary Criticism* (Vol. 114, pp. 53-55). Detroit: Gale Group. From *Literature Resource Center.* **Gayle, Addison,** in *G-97.* Kinnamon, Keneth. "Ellison in Urbana: Memories and an Interview." *Callaloo.* 18.2 (Spring 1995) p. 273. From *Literature Resource Center.* McKay, Nellie Y., in *WB-99.* McPherson, James Alan. "Listening to the Lower Frequencies: Ralph Ellison (1914-1994)." *World Literature Today.* 68.3 (Summer 1994) p. 444. From *Literature Resource Center.* Miller, D. Quentin, in *GEAAL.* O'Meally, Robert, in *AAW-1991. AW:ACLB-81.* Reckley, Ralph, Sr., in *B. BB. BCE. CAO-02. CE. CLCS. COCAAL* and *OCAAL. MWEL. QB. USHC. W. W2B. Wiki.* Robinson, Lisa Clayton, "Ellison, Ralph Waldo," in *EA-99.* Rosenmeier, Rosamond. "Chapter 1: Coming from the Territory: Geography, Biography, and Fate." *Ralph Ellison.* Mark Busby. *Twayne's United States Authors Series 582.* Boston: Twayne Publishers, 1991. From *The Twayne Authors Series.* Stern, Richard G. *Callaloo.* 18.2 (Spring 1995) p. 284. From *Literature Resource Center.* Amazon.com and barnesandnoble.com, 8/1999, Amazon.com, 2/2009.

Emanuel, Sr., James A. (Andrew)
6/15/1921–
Poems, literary criticism and biography, essays, anthology; educator

Editor's note: *AANB* lists Emanuel's birth month as January, rather than June, as it is listed in multiple other sources.

In 1950, Emanuel graduated summa cum laude from Howard University. He then worked as a civilian chief for the military while earning his M.A. from Northwestern University (1953). After that, he taught at the Harlem YWCA Business School (1954-1956), and he and his wife, Mattie, had a son, whom they named James Andrew, Jr. (Tragically, James the younger died in 1983.) James Sr. left the "Y" to teach at the City College of New York (CCNY) (1957-1962) while earning his Ph.D. from Columbia University (1962). While still an undergraduate, Emanuel's poems were published in *Ebony Rhythm* (in 1948) and in college publications. Within a decade, Emanuel was seeing his poems published in popular periodicals such as **Negro Digest** and *The New York Times*, as well as in nationally known literary periodicals such as *Freedomways* and *Midwest Quarterly*. By 1961, Emanuel was reading his poems in public, and he has since estimated that he has given a few hundred poetry readings to date (//www.james-a-emanuel.com/).

While Emanuel was still writing his doctoral dissertation on poet and creative writer **Langston Hughes**, he had an opportunity to form a friendship with Hughes, starting in 1959. Hughes also mentored Emanuel as a poet, both encouraging him and critiquing some of his poetry. Even after completing his dissertation, Emanuel continued to broaden his knowledge of Hughes, eventually publishing the comprehensive biography *Langston Hughes* (1967) for Twayne's United States Authors Series (number 123), still considered a fundamental resource in the study of Hughes.

Hughes's profound appreciation of African-American literature and of American writers of African descent influenced Emanuel to seek out the works of neglected African-American writers. He wrote of his emerging awareness in "The Invisible Men of American Literature," published in *Books Abroad, 37* (Autumn 1963, pp. 391-394). Emanuel continued his discoveries of unappreciated, undiscovered African-American authors, culminating with his landmark anthology *Dark Symphony: Negro Literature in America* (1968), which he coedited with Theodore L. Gross. Not only did they unearth buried treasures, but they also placed these writings in historical context, so that their anthology continues to be an invaluable resource to students of literature.

At CCNY, after Emanuel earned his doctorate, he was promoted to assistant professor (1962-1970), associate professor (1970-1972), and then professor of English (1973-1984). While still an assistant professor, he was awarded a Fulbright Professorship in American Literature, to teach at France's University of Grenoble (1968-1969). When Emanuel got home, he agreed to serve as the general editor for **Broadside Press**'s Broadside Critics Series (1969-1975), overseeing the publication of five volumes on African-American poets. In 1971, France's University of Toulouse invited him to become a visiting professor of American Literature (1971-1973). In 1975, Emanuel was awarded a second Fulbright, this time, to teach at Poland's University of Warsaw (1975-1976). In 1979, the University of Toulouse invited Emanuel to return (1979-1981). While teaching students to appreciate literature, Emanuel also collaborated with two other writers to create *How I Write/2* (1972); MacKinlay Kantor told readers how to write fiction, Lawrence Osgood described how to write a play, and Emanuel suggested how to write poetry by critically analyzing his own poems and those of other African-American poets.

Between his first tour at the University of Toulouse and his Fulbright in Warsaw, James's marriage to Mattie dissolved, and James Sr.'s relationship to James Jr. became estranged. His poem, "A Clown at Ten," was written during happier times, "We should have known / His pull-ups on the closet pole, / His swimming in the kitchen zone, / His pugilistic body roll / On the church pew / And museum queue / Were ways to storm the pass / For the smallest in his class" (quoted in *BB*).

Throughout this period, Emanuel wrote poems. His early poems tended toward traditional themes such as love or reminiscences of childhood, expressed through relatively formal verse. Over time, Emanuel's themes increasingly reflected those of the **Black Arts Movement**, expressed more often through free verse. His years abroad also influenced his poetry and continue to do so. In 1992, Emanuel toyed with haiku and developed what he calls "jazz haiku" or "jazz-and-blues haiku," adapting the traditional Japanese form to jazzier, more African-American rhythms, more playful language, including rhymes, and a wider array of subjects and themes. The first three lines of his "Jazzanatomy" catch the feel of this form: "EVERYTHING is jazz: / snails, jails, rails, tails, males, females, / snow-white cotton bales" (quoted in //www.poemhunter.com/poem/jazzanatomy/). In performance, these poems are read to musical accompaniment. Listeners can hear Emanuel reading 42 of his poems, accompanied by saxophonist Noah Howard, on *Middle Passage* (2001), an audio CD.

Readers can observe these thematic and form changes through his collections, starting with his early collections, published by Broadside Press: *The Treehouse and Other Poems* (1968), *At Bay* (1969), and *Panther Man* (1970); Emanuel also recorded his reading of the first and the third collections on Broadside Voices (1968 and 1970, respectively). **Lotus Press** published another five of Emanuel's collections: *Black Man Abroad: The Toulouse Poems* (1978), *A Chisel in the Dark: Poems, Selected and New* (1980), *The Broken Bowl: New and Uncollected Poems* (1983, including poems written 1946-1982), *Deadly James and Other Poems* (1987), and *Whole Grain: Collected Poems, 1958-1989* (1990). Lotus Press also published *The Force and the Reckoning* (2001), sort of an autobiographical retrospective of his poems, grouped by decade, along with memoirs, travel notes, handwritten drafts of poems, and other documents revealing insights into Emanuel's poetic process and development. Reportedly, Emanuel has also written two unpublished autobiographies: "From the Bad Lands to the Capital (1943-1944)" and "Snowflakes and Steel: My Life as a Poet, 1971-1980."

The same year that Lotus published *The Broken Bowl*, Jean McConochie edited an anthology of his poems, along with pedagogical materials, to be used by foreign students learning English as a second language. Since 1988, four of Emanuel's collections have been published abroad: *The Quagmire Effect* (1988, Paris), *De la Rage au Coeur* (1992, bilingual with French translations by Jean Migrenne, published in Thaon, France), *Blues in Black and White* (1992, with Belgian visual artist Godelieve Simons, privately printed in Brussels), and *Reaching for Mumia: 16 Haiku* (1995, Paris). Emanuel and Simons have also collaborated on numerous exhibits (1991-2000) across Europe, the United States, and Brazil. In 1999, Broadside Press published Emanuel's multilingual anthology of jazz haiku, *Jazz: From the Haiku King*, with original jazz haiku in English, as well as jazz haiku written in French, German, Italian, Spanish, and Russian with English translations; several translators aided him in this work (G. L. Simons, Jean Migrenne, Andrey C. Masevich, et al.). Emanuel currently resides in Paris.

Emanuel has estimated that he has published more than 345 poems, about 32 literary essays, and has had his work published in more than 145 anthologies, as well as in countless journals (e.g., *American Speech*, *Negro Digest/Black World*, *Phylon*) (//www.james-a-emanuel.com/). In addition to his Fulbrights, among Emanuel's other honors are John Hay Whitney fellowships (1952, 1953), a Saxton memorial fellowship (1964), and a Black American Literature Forum Special Distinction award (1978).

REFERENCES: *CAO-07*. Alic, Margaret, in *BB*. Hinton, KaaVonia, in *AANB*. Watson, Douglas, in *AAP-55-85*. //en.wikipedia.org/wiki/Grenoble. //en.wikipedia.org/wiki/Toulouse_Sciences_University. //en.wikipedia.org/wiki/University_of_Warsaw. //www.cranberrybooks.com/si/12768.html. //www.james-a-emanuel.com/. //www.poemhunter.com/poem/jazzanatomy/. Amazon.com.

FURTHER READING: Burton, Brian, in *GEAAL*.

Equiano, Olaudah (Gustavus Vassa)
c.1745–3/31/1797
Slave narrative, spoken word—lectures; sailor, hairdresser, abolitionist lecturer

Born into the Ibo tribe in the village of Essaka (or Benin) in the kingdom of Benin (what is now southeastern Nigeria), west Africa, Olaudah was captured by black slave raiders at age 11 (or 12), then he and his sister were kidnapped. Shortly after their abduction, he and his sister were separated, and he spent months in the service of a black chieftain, whose treatment of him was mild, compared to the brutality of the British slave traders to whom he was sold soon after. The slave traders then took him to Barbados in the West Indies, but he was not sold there, so he was taken to the mainland English colony of Virginia, where he was purchased by a plantation owner.

Fortunately for Olaudah, he was soon sold to a British Royal Navy officer (a captain or a lieutenant), who renamed him Gustavus Vassa, after the 16th-century Swedish king and freedom fighter. Olaudah worked for the navy officer either as a personal servant or as a ship steward, and he traveled widely with the officer to many countries and colonies on the North Atlantic and the Mediterranean. Several friendly white sailors helped him learn to speak, read, and write English, and they introduced him to Christianity.

By the early 1760s, Equiano had spent about 10 years on several vessels, engaged mostly in commerce but sometimes in naval warfare. In 1762, he was sold to a West Indian trader, who soon sold him to Robert King, a Philadelphia Quaker and merchant. King taught him about seagoing commercial enterprises and allowed him enough free time to work at other enterprises to earn enough money to purchase his freedom. Finally, on July 10, 1766, he had put aside enough money not only to purchase his freedom but also to start his own business career, working on commercial vessels and occasional scientific expeditions to Central America and to the Arctic regions.

In 1767, he moved to England to start an entirely new career, working as a hairdresser for affluent Londoners (at a time when wigs for men and women were quite popular). He also learned how to play the French horn, expanded his knowledge of math, and experienced a long, intense spiritual conversion, at least in part a result of his much earlier introduction to Christianity. He joined the Methodists, known for their opposition to slavery.

In 1773, he returned to the sea to join a scientific expedition to the Arctic and the North Pole. This trip started his return to working on ships, traveling to Europe, the middle East, the Caribbean, and North, Central, and South America. During his seafaring experience, he handled a variety of tasks and situations: taking charge of a ship during a storm, serving as parson when needed,

Olaudah Equiano

Gustavus Vassa, the African (1789: England; 1791: United States), in order to document and collect evidence on the sufferings of slaves. His narrative is credited with being the prototype starting the **slave-narrative** genre, as well as the spiritual autobiography genre among African-American writers. Although some critics trace his distinctive autobiographical form highlighting spiritual conversion to Saint Augustine's *Confessions* (c. 400), his addition of the element of social protest makes the form of his book distinctive. Specifically, he paralleled the three-part structure of a life of sin, a conversion experience, and an emergence into a spiritually awakened life with a life in slavery, a struggle for freedom, and then a freedom from the physical bonds of slavery. Stylistically, Equiano's narrative interweaves a direct, straightforward, graphic style (especially in describing his personal experiences and adventures) and an elaborate, elevated style (especially in relation to his spiritual awakening).

Although Equiano wasn't the first African-born former slave to *tell* his life experiences of enslavement and emancipation, he was the first to write his life story himself, without help or direction from white ghostwriters, amanuenses, or editors. Perhaps for this reason, his slave narrative much more compellingly indicts slavery as the brutal institution it was, emphasizing the atrocities of slavery and adamantly urging its total and immediate abolition. His autobiography is so compelling a narrative, so insightful a spiritual awakening, and so forceful an indictment of slavery that John Wesley, the founder of Methodism, the religion to which Equiano had converted, had the book read to him on his deathbed.

His book also included an idealized, sentimental, affectionate description of his early life in Benin. He describes his fellow Africans as having simple manners, highly just moral values, and a profoundly harmonious society. In contrast, he describes the terror he felt on seeing the mean-faced white men with long hair and red faces, who packed him and fellow slaves as human cargo to be crammed into the dark foul-smelling bowels of slave ships. His account was the first to show the extreme brutality (suffocating stench, filth, disease, sexual abuse, near starvation, and physical tortures) of the journey of the Middle Passage, from Africa to the Americas.

Another highlight of his book was his revelation of the effects of slavery on the master, as well as on the slave. He also mixed personal remembrances with his wide range of reading in the areas of history, geography, religion, politics, and commerce. His account powerfully describes his dichotomous feelings of terror and awe during his first contacts with Europeans and European Americans. He concludes his account with two goals: to lobby for the abolition of the slave trade and to become a Christian missionary to Africa. After his book was published in 1789, he traveled extensively throughout England and

governing a vessel when the captain died and then conducting it safely into port, and even overseeing slaves on occasion. Whenever he visited England, however, he further pursued his education, and eventually, in 1777, he decided to settle in England.

In the 1780s, the British Parliament debated whether to end the slave trade. Equiano became an active abolitionist, lecturing against slavery and petitioning the British Parliament, calling for abolition. Among other things, he railed against the cruel practices of British slave owners in Jamaica. In 1787, he was appointed commissary of provisions and stores aboard the *Vernon*, which was carrying 500 to 600 male and female impoverished freed slaves to Freetown, Sierra Leone, on the west coast of Africa, to establish a colonial settlement there. Some disputes with the venture management led to his returning to England, rather than settling back in his native land.

Back in England, British abolitionists paid for Equiano to publish his thick two-volume autobiography, *The Interesting Narrative of the Life of Olaudah Equiano, or*

Ireland promoting it—and abolition. In 1792, he married an English woman, Susanna Cullen, in England, and the couple had two daughters. His book was so popular that by 1794, there had been eight editions printed in England and one in the United States. The book was also translated into Dutch (1790), German (1792), and Russian (1794). By the middle of the nineteenth century, about 20 or more editions had been produced in America and Europe, and it has been printed in several new editions since the 1960s. In addition, many writers have used his book to create biographies of Equiano (e.g., Vincent Carretta's *Equiano, the African: Biography of a Self-Made Man*, 2005), and radio dramas, stage and television dramas, films, and children's books have dramatized his life.

In his autobiography and his later *Miscellaneous Verses*, he idealized his African past, taking pride in his race, yet he condemned those Africans who trafficked in slavery. While being transported to the slave ship on the coast, he further observed how European intrusion into African societies had a corrupting influence on them, such as by introducing the weaponry of war and by fostering hostilities and greed to elicit the Africans' aid in the Europeans' barbarous venture. He further showed appreciation of his own master's kindness and of the English abolitionists and others who befriended him.

REFERENCES: *1TESK. AA:PoP. AANB. BAL-1-P. BWA. CSN. EBLG. MAAL. NAAL.* Costanzo, Angelo. 1987. "The Spiritual Autobiography and Slave Narrative of Olaudah Equiano." *Surprizing Narrative: Olaudah Equiano and the Beginnings of Black Autobiography.* Greenwood Press. Rpt. in James E. Person, Jr. (Ed.) (1991), *Literature Criticism from 1400 to 1800* (Vol. 16, pp. 41-90). Detroit: Gale Research. From *Literature Resource Center.* COCAAL and OCAAL. Hickey, Kevin M., in *B. GEAAL. MWEL. W. Wiki.* O'Neale, Sondra, in *AWER.* Potkay, Adam. "Olaudah Equiano and the Art of Spiritual Autobiography." *Eighteenth-Century Studies* 27.4 (Summer 1994), pp. 677-692. Rpt. in Thomas J. Schoenberg and Lawrence J. Trudeau (Eds.), *Literature Criticism from 1400 to 1800* (Vol. 143). Detroit: Gale. From *Literature Resource Center.* Samuels, Wilfred D., in *AAWBHR. EB-98.* "A Review of *The Interesting Narrative of the Life of Olaudah Equiano, or Gustavas Vassa, the African.*" *The Monthly Review* 80 (1789), pp. 551-552. Rpt. in *Literature Resource Center.* Gale, Cengage Learning. //www.csustan.edu/english/reuben/pal/chap2/equiano.html. //www.wwnorton.com/college/english/naal7/contents/A/authors/equiano.asp.

Essence *See* BlackBoard African-American Bestsellers *See also* Ebony

Evans, Mari
7/16/1923–
Poems, children's books, anthologies, essays, plays, short stories, reviews, lectures; educator

A native of Toledo, Ohio, Evans credits her father with encouraging her literary development. As she said in "My Father's Passage," her autobiographical essay in the volume she edited, *Black Women Writers* (1984, p. 165), "No single living entity really influenced my life as did my father." For instance, he had saved her first printed story, written when she was in the fourth grade, and printed in the school newspaper. As she recalled, her father had "carefully noted on it the date, our home address, and his own proud comment" on her achievement.

Evans attended Toledo public schools and the University of Toledo, where she studied fashion design—a career she never pursued after college. As she noted, "I moved from university journalism to a by-lined column in a Black-owned weekly and, in time, worked variously as an industrial editor, as a research associate with responsibility for preparing curriculum materials, and as director of publications for the corporate management of a Job Corps installation." Her "industrial editor" job involved being an assistant editor at a local chain-manufacturing plant, where precise language and discipline in writing were essential. Although her supervisor was wary of having a young black woman working for him, he knew how to write well, and his model and his demands for her work encouraged her to revise endlessly. Eventually, she was able to turn out prose as precise as he demanded, and he allowed her some creative freedom.

By the end of her three years working with him, she fully understood "that writing is a craft, a profession one learns by doing. One must be able to produce on demand, and that requires great personal discipline. . . . I cannot imagine a writer who is not continually reaching, who contains no discontent that what he or she is producing is not more than it is. . . . discipline is the foundation of the profession" (p. 167). "I have always written, it seems. I have not, however, always been organized in my approach. Now, I find I am much more productive when I set aside a specific time and uncompromisingly accept that as commitment."

Beginning in 1969, Evans began teaching at a series of American universities and began lecturing widely and frequently as a much-sought-after speaker (e.g., at the biennial National Black Writers Festival, held at Medgar Evers College). These appointments included the following: 1969-1970—instructor of African-American literature and writer-in-residence at Indiana University at Purdue; 1968-1973—producer, writer, and director, *The Black Experience,* a WTTV, Channel 4, Indianapolis TV show; 1969-1970—consultant, Discovery Grant Program, National Endowment for the Arts; 1970-1973 —consultant in ethnic studies, Bobbs-Merrill Co.; 1970-1978—assistant professor and writer-in-residence at Indiana University, Bloomington; 1972-1973—visiting assistant professor, Northwestern University, Evanston, Illinois; 1975—fellowship residency at the MacDowell Colony, Peterboro, New Hampshire; 1975-1980—member, board of management, Fall Creek Parkway YMCA; 1976-1977—Chair of Literary Advisory Panel, Indiana Arts Commission; 1978-1979—member, Indiana Corrections Code Commission; 1978-1980—visiting assistant professor at Purdue University, West Lafayette, Indiana; 1980—visiting assistant professor at Washington University, St. Louis; 1981-1984—visiting assistant professor and distinguished writer, Africana Studies and Research Center, at Cornell University; other appointments as visiting professor at SUNY Albany (1985-1986) and at Spelman College (1989-1990).

Evans's literary career has primarily involved poetry and plays, but she has also published many short stories, essays, book reviews, children's books, articles, and works of literary criticism and biography. Many of her writings have been translated into Swedish, French, Dutch, Russian, German, and Italian, and her work has been published in countless textbooks, anthologies, and periodicals. Her poetry has also been choreographed and used on record albums, filmstrips, calendars, radio, television specials, and two Off-Broadway productions. She has even attempted to write a novel.

Starting in 1963, her poetry was published in **Phylon, Negro Digest**, and *Dialog*. Thereafter, her work has been published in **Black World**, *Okike*, **Callaloo**, *Essence, Ebony, Black Collegian*, and myriad other journals and magazines. By the time she published her first poetry collection, *Where Is All the Music?* (1968), addressing various aspects of intimate love affairs, she was already able to craft tight verse.

Her second poetry collection, *I Am a Black Woman* (1970), begins with the theme of romantic love but expands into a more complex volume, embracing historical and political themes. She progresses from the intimate relations between two African Americans to the entire African-American community, then she further extends her embrace to encompass others who have been impoverished and oppressed, whether here in America or elsewhere in the world. In it is her oft-anthologized poem "Who Can Be Born Black": "Who / can be born black / and not / sing / the wonder of it / the joy / the / challenge / / Who / can be born / black / and not exult!" Next, she wrote *Whisper* (1979), then her next collection, *Nightstar: Poems from 1973-1978* (1981), patterned as an ever-widening progression from the personal and individual to the political and global. In *Nightstar*, she used more innovative rhetorical devices and more complex poetry techniques than in her earlier work. In this work, in her *A Dark and Splendid Mass* (1991 or 1992), and in her *Continuum: New and Selected Poems* (2007), she deftly shows the uncommon courage of ordinary black folks, using authentic African-American voices.

Her plays, featuring vividly realistic characters and richly textured details, highlight the valor and strength of African Americans who face many small and large challenges. Evans's *Rivers of My Song* (first performed, 1977) incorporates poetry and prose, music and dance in a distinctively African-American drama. Her *Portrait of a Man* (1979) intersperses episodes showing the struggles of a young and an old African-American man, whom the viewers soon realize are one and the same. Her other plays include *Boochie* (1979) and *Eyes* (1979), her screenplay for a musical adapted from **Zora Neale Hurston**'s *Their Eyes Were Watching God*.

Although widely known for her poems and plays, many readers know Evans best for her children's books, which include *I Look at Me!* (1974), *JD* (1973), *Rap Stories* (1974), *Singing Black: Alternative Nursery Rhymes for Children* (1976/1998), *Jim Flying High* (1979), and *The Day They Made Biriyani* (1982). More recently, she wrote *Dear Corinne, Tell Somebody! Love, Annie: A Book about Secrets* (1999), a juvenile epistolary novel addressing the issue of child abuse; and *I'm Late: The Story of Leneese and Moonlight and Alisha Who Didn't Have Anyone of Her Own* (2006), addressing many issues surrounding teen pregnancy. Her books highlight a nurturant, positive perspective of the African-American community and foster a positive self-concept among African-American youths. Although she sometimes introduces unfamiliar words for young readers, she does so in a self-explanatory context. Divorced, Evans also has two sons of her own.

The other literary work for which Evans is well known is her landmark critical analysis *Black Women Writers (1950-1980): A Critical Evaluation* (1984, editor). The volume covers 15 poets, novelists, and playwrights, including for each author an autobiographical commentary on her own literary development, two critical essays (offering differing perspectives), and a brief biographical summary and list of key publications. This book celebrates the diversity of African-American women writers, offering a broad spectrum of critical approaches to their writings. More than two decades later, she published *Clarity as Concept: A Poet's Perspective* (2005), a collection of critical essays and commentary.

Among the numerous awards she has been given are a John Hay Whitney fellowship (1965); a Woodrow Wilson grant (1968); the Most Distinguished Book of Poetry by an Indiana Writer (for her *I Am a Black Woman*) (1970); the Indiana University Writers' Conference Black Academy of Arts and Letters First Poetry Award (1975); MacDowell Fellow, MacDowell Colony, Peterboro, New Hampshire (1975); Outstanding Woman of the Year, Alpha Kappa Alpha Sorority graduate chapter, Indiana University, Bloomington (1976); Builder's Award, Third World Press, Chicago (1977); Indiana Committee for the Humanities grant for *Eyes* (1977); Commins Engine Company Foundation grant (stage project) (1977); Black Liberation Award, Kuumba Theatre Workshop Tenth

Anniversary, Chicago (1978); an honorary doctorate of humane letters degree from Marian College (1979); Copeland Fellow, Amherst College, Amherst, Massachusetts (1980); Black Arts Celebration Poetry Award, Chicago (1981); and a National Endowment for the Arts Creative Writing Award (1981-1982).

Evans's body of work celebrates African-American culture and shows a strong sense of social responsibility. She passionately combats oppression on both personal and institutional levels and illuminates the heroic struggles of ordinary African Americans. The simplicity of her lyrical verse eloquently expresses her straightforward themes; her plays have been produced repeatedly over the years; her children's books are praised for their constructive values and positive view of the African-American community; and her essays logically and coherently reveal her deeply held political beliefs. Evans's beliefs have also led her to political action and community activism, championing such causes as prison reform and opposing various forms of oppression, such as capital punishment.

REFERENCES: AA:PoP. BAL-1-P. BV. BWA. BWW. EBLG. MWEL. NAAAL. TtW. TWT. Bostian, Patricia Kennedy, in GEAAL. Dorsey, David F., Jr., in COCAAL and OCAAL. Golus, Carrie, in BB. CAO-01. MWEL. Peppers, Wallace R., in AAP-55-85. EB-98. Wagner-Martin, Linda, in OCWW. Wiki.

Everett, II, Percival (Leonard)
12/22/1956–

Novels, short story collections, children's book; educator

Before he dedicated himself to the world of academe, Everett found work as a ranch hand and as a jazz musician, experiences that later helped him create richly detailed settings for his novels. After earning his baccalaureate from Florida's University of Miami (1977) and his master's from Rhode Island's Brown University (1982), Everett taught high school for a while before starting at the academy.

In 1983, Everett published his first novel, Suder (1983), about a major-league baseball player who hits a slump and decides that a road trip will fix what ails him, described as a "mad work of comic genius" by Carolyn See in the Los Angeles Times (quoted in CAO-08). His next novel, Walk Me to the Distance (1985), centers on a Vietnam War veteran who seeks the isolation of a Wyoming ranch house and finds some solace, followed by tragedy. The novel's plot was later altered to create an ABC TV movie titled Follow Your Heart. The year he published Walk Me, he got work in the academy, first as an associate professor of English and director of a graduate creative-writing program at the University of Kentucky in Lexington (1985-1989), then as professor of English at the University of Notre Dame in Indiana (1989-1992),

professor and chair of the creative writing program at University of California at Riverside (1992-1999), and finally professor of creative writing, American studies, and critical theory at University of Southern California in Los Angeles (since 1999).

He has since written more than a dozen novels, including Cutting Lisa (Voices of the South) (1986/2000), the "cutting" referring to a cesarean section, and Zulus (1989), a New American Writing Award-winning futuristic, postapocalyptic fantasy about a woman who evades forced sterilization then becomes pregnant after a forcible rape. Next, Everett reinterprets Euripides's classic Greek play Medea in his novel, For Her Dark Skin (1989). In 1994, he published two novels, The Body of Martin Aguilera (1994) and God's Country (1994), a western novel about an African-American tracker hired by a European-American racist to find his wife, who was kidnapped by bandits who appear to have been Native Americans. Two years later, two more novels were published: Watershed (1996), with a western setting, and Frenzy (1996), set in Greek mythology, featuring the demigod Dionysus and his hapless human assistant, time travel, mind-reading, and other fantastic elements. Next came Glyph: A Novel (1999), narrated by a four-year-old genius, recalling his experiences as a brilliant baby, when he was kidnapped multiple times; Grand Canyon, Inc. (2001), his first novella; and then Erasure (2002), featuring Thelonius "Monk" Ellison, an intellectual who decides to broaden his readership by writing "ghetto prose" and ends up creating a pseudonym-authored bestseller nominated for a prominent book award. In a delightful twist of fate, Erasure won the prestigious 2002 Hurston/Wright Legacy Award for Fiction; also, a German translation, Ausradiert, appeared in 2008.

In 2004, Everett teamed with fellow USC professor James Kincaid to create an epistolary novel, A History of the African-American People (Proposed) by Strom Thurmond, As Told to Percival Everett and James Kincaid (2004). That same year, Everett published American Desert: A Novel (2004), about a suicidal college professor who is tragically killed in a car crash on the way to his suicide—and then comes back to life for a literally soul-searching adventure. In Everett's 2006 PEN USA Literary Award for Fiction winner, Wounded: A Novel (2005), Everett returns to a western setting, with an African-American horse trainer and rancher who has managed to avoid ruffling feathers in his Wyoming ranching community until homophobia and anti-Native American racism confront him, forcing him to respond. In The Water Cure (2007), the narrator, Ishmael Kidder, is confessing to torturing the person whom he believes raped and killed the narrator's 11-year-old daughter. As a Washington Post reviewer observed, "This is a book that not only makes you feel, but think" (quoted in //www.amazon.com). The title character in *I Am Not Sidney Poitier: A Novel* (2009) may seem to have sprung from the old Abbott and Costello "Who's On First?" comedy sketch, in which the protagonist's first name is "Not," and his next two names point to the actor whom he uncannily resembles.

While cranking out novels one after another, Everett has managed to continue to publish short stories in periodicals (e.g., *Aspen Journal of the Arts, Black American Literature Forum,* **Callaloo**), and in anthologies (e.g., *Pushcart Prize Anthology* and *Best American Short Stories*). He has also published his own collections, including *The Weather and Women Treat Me Fair: Stories* (1989); *Big Picture: Stories* (1996), which won a PEN/Oakland Josephine Miles Award for Excellence in Literature; and *Damned If I Do: Stories* (2004). On a playful note, Everett published a children's book, too. In *The One That Got Away* (1992), cowhands try to corral fugitive "1" numerals. In addition to prose, Everett has also published poetry, including his two collections: *re:f (gesture)* (2006), which prominently displays a painting by Everett's own hand on the cover, and *Abstraktion und Einfühlung* [Abstraction and Empathy] (2008), for Chris Abani's Black Goat poetry series. Everett was also invited to write the foreword to *Making Callaloo: Twenty-five Years of Black Literature, 1976-2000* (2002). His other honors include a D. H. Lawrence fellowship (1984), a Lila Wallace-Reader's Digest fellowship, a Hillsdale Award for Fiction from the Fellowship of Southern Writers (1999), and the esteemed Academy Award for Literature from the American Academy of Arts and Letters (2003).

Long a bachelor, Everett married novelist **Danzy Senna**.

REFERENCES: CAO-08. *Wiki.* Burrell-Stinson, Denise, in *AANB.* //dictionary.paralink.com/. //search.barnesandnoble.com/Wounded/ Percival-Everett/e/9781555974275/?itm=4. //thefsw.org/page/awards/. //translation.babylon.com/German. //www.artsandletters.org/awards2_ search.php. //www.hurston-wright.org/legacy_winners2002.shtml. //www.worldcat.org/oclc/310129621&referer=brief_results. Amazon.com.

FURTHER READING: Feerst, Alex, in *GEAAL*.

Evers-Williams, Myrlie (Louise) (née Beasley)
3/17/1933–
Memoirs; organization leader

The widow of civil-rights activist Medgar Evers, she cowrote *For Us, the Living* (1967, with William Peters), a candid account of her life with Evers and their three children. Through her persistent efforts, the killer of Evers was caught, prosecuted, convicted, and imprisoned on February 5, 1994—about 30 years after Evers was assassinated. Since then, Evers-Williams has written a second memoir (which she has called "an instructional autobiography"), *Watch Me Fly: What I Learned on the Way to Becoming the Woman I Was Meant to Be* (1999, with Melinda Blau), which documents her childhood and youth, her up-and-down relationship with Evers, her valiant struggle to raise her children as a single mother following his assassination, her experiences as she welcomed her second husband into her life and her heart—and then shared his final fight against terminal cancer, her rise to chairing the NAACP, and her triumphs in business. Evers-Williams also participated in two other book projects: She wrote the introduction to Steven Kasher's *The Civil Rights Movement: A Photographic History, 1954-68* (1996), and she participated in writing *No Mountain High Enough: Secrets of Successful African American Women* (1997). She also collaborated with scholar Manning Marable to put together *The Autobiography of Medgar Evers: A Hero's Life and Legacy Revealed Through His Writings, Letters, and Speeches* (2006).

REFERENCES: *AANB. EA-99. EB-BH-CD. G-99. WB-99.* Assensoh, A. B., in *BH2C.* Bailey, Ronald, in *BWA:AHE.* Fowler, Gregory W., "Medgar Evers," in *B. GEAAL. Wiki.* Goldsworthy, Joan, in *BB.* Two reviews of her own autobiography and five reviews of her editing of Medgar Evers's autobiography in Gale's *Literature Resource Center* online. Amazon.com. SDPL catalog.

Fabio, Sarah (née Webster)
1/20/1928–11/7/1979
Poems, anthology; educator, spoken word artist

Sarah Webster studied poetry under **Arna Bontemps** at Fisk University, from which she graduated at age 18, then she paused for almost two decades to marry Cyril Fabio and raise their three sons and two daughters. After earning her master's degree in language arts, creative writing, she helped establish a Black Studies department at the University of California at Berkeley in the late 1960s. After divorcing her husband in 1972, she went to Oberlin College in Ohio, then to the University of Wisconsin in 1974, and then to Pinole, California, where she lived with her eldest daughter, Cheryl, for two years before her death of colon cancer. Her writings mirror the **Black Aesthetic** of the **Black Arts Movement**, during which she published the books *Saga of a Black Man* (1968); *A Mirror, a Soul* (1969); *Dark Debut: Three Black Women Coming* (1966); *Return of* **Margaret Walker** (1966); *Double Dozens: An Anthology of Poets from* **Sterling Brown** *to Kali* (1966, editor); *No Crystal Stair: A Socio-Drama of the History of Black Women in the U.S.A.* (1967); *Black Talk: Shield and Sword* (1973); and her seven-volume poetry collection *Rainbow Signs* (1973). In addition, she recorded three spoken-word albums: *Boss Soul* and *Soul Ain't, Soul Is* (1972, both for the Folkways label) and *Jujus: Alchemy of the Blues* (1975).

REFERENCES: *AANB.* Manheim, James M., in *BB.* Ratcliff, Anthony J., in *GEAAL.* Warren, Nagueyalti, in *COCAAL* and *OCAAL. CAO-03.*

Fauset (married name: Harris), Jessie Redmon
4/27/1882–4/30/1961
Novels; literary editor, educator

Jessie was born in Camden County, NJ, the youngest of seven children born to Annie Seamon Fauset and Reverend Redmon Fauset, an Episcopal minister. Both of her parents were well educated and literary but not as well off financially as they were intellectually. Sadly, Jessie's mother died when Jessie was a small child, leaving her father as sole provider and role model for her and her siblings. As if there weren't enough children to care for, Reverend Fauset then married a widow with three children, and the couple went on to have three children of their own. Far from living a life of privilege, her younger half-brother, Arthur Huff Fauset (b. 1899), described their family as "dreadfully poor." (As an adult, Arthur wrote short stories, biographies, and nonfiction books, essays, and articles, e.g., for **Crisis** and ***Opportunity***, and he was a public-school teacher, a school principal, a noted anthropologist, and a businessperson. He earned a Ph.D. from the University of Pennsylvania.)

By the time Jessie started high school, her family was living in Philadelphia. Jessie responded to her family's emphasis on the importance of education, excelling in her studies at a public high school (the High School for Girls) known for its high academic achievers. When she graduated, in 1900, based on her outstanding scholarship, she applied to Bryn Mawr College. That school managed to avoid permitting a black girl to enter by obtaining a scholarship for her to attend Cornell University. In 1905, she earned her B.A. from Cornell University (when she was about 23 years old). She was the first black woman to be elected to the Phi Beta Kappa honor society at Cornell, and she was probably the first—or at least one of the first—black woman to be given a Phi Beta Kappa membership key in the United States. Even after she began her career, she continued her education, earning her master's degree at the University of Pennsylvania in 1919 and spending six months studying at the world-renowned Sorbonne university in Paris during 1925 and 1926.

Upon graduating from Cornell, she spent the next 13 years (1905-1918) teaching high school. Initially, she sought a teaching position in Philadelphia but was barred from doing so because of her race. Hence, she moved to Baltimore to teach at the Douglass High School for a year. The next year, she started teaching French and Latin at Dunbar High School, an all-black high school in Washington, D. C., where she continued to teach until she decided to return to college to complete her master's degree.

Starting when she was in her 30s, Fauset had begun to write articles for the NAACP's **Crisis** magazine, then edited by **W. E. B. Du Bois**. After a bit, she became one of the magazine's four staff editors. After Fauset finished her master's degree, when she was in her late 30s, Du Bois convinced her to move to New York and become *Crisis's* literary editor at a crucial epoch in African-American literary history: the first blossoming of the **Harlem Renais-**

Jessie Redmon Fauset

sance (1919-1926). This accident of timing put her in a position to shape the literature emerging in this exciting, dynamic period. Specifically, she chose the literary selections for each magazine and was thereby able to mentor many young writers (e.g., **Countee Cullen, Nella Larsen, Claude McKay, Jean Toomer**). In fact, **Langston Hughes** said she was one of "the three people who mid-wifed the so-called New Negro literature into being" during the Harlem Renaissance. With her knack for discovering talented writers and her willingness to work long and hard, she managed to bring to full bloom the literary careers of many a budding writer. She often encouraged them through letters and through invitations to her home. There, her guests would read poetry aloud, discuss literature, and converse in French. Meanwhile, she continued her own writing projects, such as essays and fiction works.

When Du Bois began his short-lived (1920-1921) monthly periodical for African-American children, **The Brownies' Book**, he asked Fauset to edit the periodical and to do much of the writing for it. The periodical featured historical biographies of notable African Americans, such as Denmark Vesey and **Sojourner Truth**, as well as articles on current events and Africa, as well as games, riddles, and music.

In 1926, Fauset quit her position as literary editor for *Crisis,* hoping to turn her attention to her own writing as a full-time occupation. (There may also have been some tension in her relationship with Du Bois, and a decline in the magazine's circulation may have been a contributing factor in her decision.) During this time, she traveled and lectured, wrote poetry, and explored her new role as a wife: At age 47 (in 1927), she married insurance broker Herbert E. Harris. Unfortunately, however, she was unable to earn a living from her writing, so from 1927 until 1944, Fauset (Harris) returned to teaching (starting at DeWitt Clinton High School in New York). She wrote only three more novels after she left *Crisis.*

As a teacher, Fauset decried the lack of nonwhites in classroom curricula, textbooks, and other reading materials. She denounced the absence of positive role models and urged the creation of biographical materials on important African Americans. She intended to write some herself, but her teaching duties took up her time, and she never got around to writing the biographies she wished to see. A few years after she retired from teaching high school, she worked briefly (September 1949-January 1950) as a visiting professor at the Hampton Institute. When she retired, she was still living with her husband in Montclair, New Jersey, until he made her a widow in 1958. After he died, she left New Jersey and returned to Philadelphia, to live with her stepbrother, Earl Huff, with whom she lived until her death, in 1961, of heart disease.

Between the 1910s and the early 1930s, Fauset wrote numerous essays, poems, and short stories, which were published in various periodicals of the day, as well as in anthologies, such as those by Countee Cullen and **Alain Locke**. Between 1924 and 1933, Fauset produced four novels, each of which reflected her belief in the importance of self-acceptance as a key to personal success. Most of her characters are light-skinned, well-educated, middle-class African Americans. For them, self-hatred posed a greater challenge than did racial prejudice and discrimination, which have more profoundly oppressed darker-skinned, less-educated, working-class African Americans. By focusing on mulattos and African Americans who can pass for white, Fauset explored issues of identity and race, class, and gender differences.

Fauset's 1924 novel *There Is Confusion* centers on an African-American family confronting racial discrimination. *Plum Bun: A Novel without a Moral* (1928 or 1929) is about Angela Murray, a light-skinned young black artist who constantly seeks to "pass" as white among New York white artists. Only when she eventually stops posing and embraces her African-American heritage and accepts her ties to the African-American world does she succeed in finding happiness. Fauset's 1931 novel *The Chinaberry Tree: A Novel of American Life* deals with interracial marital relationships and is not considered her finest effort.

Her best-known novel is *Comedy: American Style* (1933), in which the black female protagonist, Carey, longs to be white and hates being black, but her son and her husband take pride in their African-American cultural heritage.

REFERENCES: *AA:PoP. AWA. BANP. BF:2000. BFC. EBLG. MAAL. NAAAL. OC20LE. RLWWJ. RT.* Le, Truong, in *GEAAL.* Mcdowell, Deborah E., in *MAWW.* McLendon, Jacquelyn Y., in *COCAAL* and *OCAAL.* Sylvander, Carolyn Wedin, in *AAWHR-40.* Wagner, Wendy, in *B. BCE. OCWW. W. Wiki.* Wainwright, Mary Katherine, in *BB. CAO-00. LFCC-07.* //catdir.loc.gov/catdir/toc/ecip064/ 2005035688.html. //womenshistory.about.com/od/aframerwriters/ tp/african_american_women_writers.htm. //www.poets.org/ viewmedia.php/prmMID/19694. *EB-98.*

Fax, Elton C. (Clay)
10/9/1909–3/13/1993
Juvenile and children's literature, travel, biography; illustrator, cartoonist

Before he was 20 years old, Elton Fax married Grace Elizabeth Turner (1929), with whom he had three children: Betty Louise (Mrs. James Evans), Virginia Mae (deceased), and Leon. He attended the historically black Methodist-affiliated Claflin College (now University) for a while but then got his B.F.A. in painting from Syracuse University (1931). At first, Fax found work teaching art and art history at Claflin (1935-1936). He then found work teaching life drawing at the Harlem Art Center, under the auspices of the Works Progress Administration (WPA) (1936-1940). In 1940, he made the bold move to go freelance, producing *Susabelle,* a weekly cartoon strip highlighting African-American history and issues, published in the numerous African-American-owned newspapers of the day. He also illustrated 30 or more books, mostly for children (e.g., books by Verna Aardema), by 1972. He supplemented those jobs by occasionally illustrating some of the many of the pulp magazines popular in the 1940s and 1950s.

In the mid-1950s, Fax and his family moved to Mexico (1953-1956). With Mexico as their home base, they also traveled to several other Latin American countries. Everywhere they went, Fax sketched scenes that sympathetically documented the living conditions of the everyday people. In 1955, he received a special U.S. Department of State grant for international cultural exchange to South America and the Caribbean. As he later reported in "It's Been a Beautiful but Rugged Journey" (*Black American Literature Forum,* 1986; per *BB*) United States embassy officials often questioned him as to whether he had seen any communist activity in his travels.

Fax soon became a worldwide lecturer, developing his distinctive "chalk talks" during which he spontaneously illustrated his oratory for adults and for children. In 1957-1958, he returned to the States to teach watercolor painting and art history at the City College (now of the City University) of New York. After that, he was offered a series of artist-in-residence and consultant posts at numerous institutions (e.g., Purdue University, Princeton University, Fisk University, Western Michigan University, University of Hartford, Texas Southern University). Meanwhile, he continued to establish himself as a man of the world. In 1959, he was a delegate to Second International Congress of Society of African Culture in Rome, Italy, hosted by the American Society of African Culture (AMSAC). Afterward, he toured Africa (e.g., Nigeria and elsewhere in West Africa), creating the verbal and graphic sketches published a year later in his first book, *West African Vignettes* (1960; expanded edition, 1963). His other travels included going to East Africa (e.g., Sudan, Ethiopia) as a State Department lecturer (1963), visiting the U.S.S.R. (Union of Soviet Socialist Republics) as a guest of the Soviet Writers Union (1971, 1973), and participating in the Union of Bulgarian Writers Conference in Sofia, Bulgaria, alongside Gore Vidal, John Cheever, and William Saroyan (1977).

During the 1970s, Fax was invited to exhibit his paintings in such prestigious locales as the Smithsonian Institution's National Gallery of Art and the Corcoran Gallery of Art, in Washington, D.C., the Kerlan Collection at the University of Minnesota, and the National Museum in Tashkent, Uzbekistan. He also published a number of other books highlighting African-American history, including *Contemporary Black Leaders* (1970) and *Seventeen Black Artists* (1971), which won the **Coretta Scott King** Award (for authors) from the American Library Association (1972). Fax's *Garvey: The Story of a Pioneer Black Nationalist* (1972), with its foreword by esteemed historian **John Henrik Clarke**, was perhaps the most critically acclaimed of his books. In *Garvey,* Fax provided not only a detailed narrative of Garvey's life, but also the historical events in which Garvey's life unfolded.

Fax's next book was a travelogue, *Through Black Eyes: Journeys of a Black Artist in East Africa and Russia* (1974), which he both wrote and illustrated himself. The areas of Russia (still the U.S.S.R. at the time) he highlighted were in central Asia, rather than the more European areas with which most people are more familiar. As always, both his drawings and his text revealed extraordinary sensitivity to the ordinary people he observed. He then wrote *Black Artists of the New Generation* (1977), this time with a foreword by world-renowned visual artist **Romare Bearden**.

In the 1980s, Fax continued to travel, and his next three books also emerged from his travel, and he provided both the text and the illustrations for all three. *Hashar* [Working Together] (1980, published in Moscow), arose from his continued travels in the central Asian states of what is now Russia. *Elyuchin* [For the People] (1983) and *Soviet People as I Knew Them* (1988) followed. He also wrote and illustrated *Black and Beautiful,* which was privately printed. At nearly 80 years of age, he illustrated one last project: *Take a Walk in Their Shoes* (1989), written by Glennette Tilley Turner.

Fax's numerous honors included a gold medal from the Women's Civic League Contest (1932), a prestigious MacDowell Colony fellowship (1968), an Arena Players award (1972), a Rockefeller Foundation fellowship (1976), and a Chancellor's Medal from Syracuse University (1990). His painting, "Machinists Board U.S.S. Hunley, Charleston, SC, March 1969" was awarded a Louis E. Seley NACAL gold medal (1972).

REFERENCES: *CAO-03.* Martin, Frank, in *AANB.* Routledge, Chris, in *BB.* //library.syr.edu/digital/guides/f/fax_e.htm. //www.bucknell.edu/x36626.xml.

Feelings, Tom
5/19/1933–8/25/2003
Children's picture books, book illustrations; graphic artist

Since childhood, Tom had immersed himself in art, studying graphic arts in vocational school, specializing in cartooning and illustration at the School of Visual Arts, and even serving the U.S. Air Force as a graphic artist. While he was still an art student, his comic strip "Tommy Traveler in the World of Negro History" started being regularly published in the *New York Age.* More than 30 years later, his "Tommy Traveler" materials led to his book, *Tommy Traveler in the World of Black History,* 1991, featuring **Frederick Douglass** and other notables.

From the mid-1960s through the early 1970s, Feelings lived abroad, doing illustrating for the Ghanaian government's printing house and for *African Review,* and directing a children's book project while teaching art in Guyana. During the 1970s, he and his first wife, writer Muriel (Grey) Feelings, collaborated on three award-winning children's books, inspired by their experiences in Africa: *Zamani Goes to Market* (1970), *Moja Means One: Swahili Counting Book* (1971), and *Jambo Means Hello: Swahili Alphabet Book* (1974). During this time, he also wrote his autobiographical *Black Pilgrimage* (1972).

Editor's note: The couple also had two sons, Zamani and Kamili, before divorcing in 1974.

In addition, Feelings illustrated books for such distinguished authors as **Julius Lester** (*To Be a Slave,* 1968; *Black Folktales,* 1969), **Eloise Greenfield** (*Daydreamers,* 1981), and **Maya Angelou** (*Now Sheba Sings the Song,* 1987). Other books he illustrated include celebrations of African lore and crafts, *Tales of Temba: Traditional African Stories* (1969, with text by Kathleen Arnot) and *African Crafts* (1970, with text by Jane Kerina). In his *Soul Looks Back in Wonder* (1993), he offered lively paintings of children engaged in various activities—from dreaming to daring—as his vision of poems written by noteworthy authors such as **Lucille Clifton** and **Mari Evans.**

His most masterful piece, however, is almost surely *The Middle Passage: White Ships/Black Cargo* (1995). Comprising more than 60 magnificent black-and-white paintings of the nightmare that was the slave trade, his pièce de résistance took him about two decades—and a great deal of emotional, physical, and intellectual energy—to create.

REFERENCES: *SMKC.* C. H. S., in *CBC.*
—Tonya Bolden

Editor's note: The American Library Association (ALA) gave its Coretta Scott King Award for illustrating to *Something on My Mind* (1979, text by **Nikki Grimes**) and to *Soul Looks Back in Wonder* (1994, editor, illustrator). His *Black Pilgrimage,* based on a conversation with an 8-year-old girl, was named a Coretta Scott King Honor book (1973), and his *Jambo Means Hello* was nominated for a National Book Award. His other awards included an ALA notable book citation, a Horn Book honor listing, and a Boston Globe-Horn Book Award.

Feelings's last book, *I Saw Your Face* (2004), was published posthumously. Before his death, Feelings had showed poet Kwame Dawes his collection of drawings of young African and African-American faces, gathered across a lifetime. The drawings inspired Dawes to write the accompanying verses, and the twosome collaborated to complete the manuscript. After his death, **Marvin X** wrote a tribute poem to Feelings, and **Amiri Baraka, Askia Touré, Quincy Troupe,** and many other literary celebrities celebrated his life's work.

REFERENCES: *Wiki.* Steele, Vincent. "Tom Feelings: A Black Arts Movement." *African American Review. 32.1* (Spring 1998) p. 119. From *Literature Resource Center.* Wolf, Gillian, and Sara Pendergast, in *BB. CAO-04.* "Obituaries." *The Horn Book Magazine. 79.6* (November-December 2003) p. 788. From *Literature Resource Center.* //ncanewyork.com/feelings/tom_feelings_tribute.htm. //www.june teenth.com/Tom_Feelings.htm. //www.nathanielturner.com/tom feelings.htm. Amazon.com.

Ferguson, Lloyd Noel
2/9/1918–
Nonfiction—chemistry textbooks; educator, chemist

After graduating from high school, Lloyd Ferguson earned enough money to enter the University of California at Berkeley, from which he earned a B.S. with honors (1940) and a Ph.D. (1943), both in chemistry. After earning his doctorate, Lloyd was offered a job teaching in the chemistry department of North Carolina Agricultural and Technical College in Greensboro (1944-1945). Next, he moved to Howard University (1945-1965), where he later chaired the chemistry department (1958-1965). While at Howard, he wrote numerous scholarly and pedagogical articles, and he published three chemistry textbooks, *Electron Structures of Organic Molecules* (1952), *Textbook of Organic Chemistry* (1958), and *The Modern Structural Theory of Organic Chemistry* (1963). When not teaching or writing textbooks, Ferguson studied the chemistry involved in taste and odor sensation. Ferguson was also awarded a Guggenheim fellowship to work in Copenhagen, Denmark (1953), and a National Science Foundation fellowship to work in Zurich, Switzerland (1961-1962).

In 1965, Ferguson moved again, to teach at California State University in Los Angeles. While there, he wrote three more chemistry textbooks, *Organic Chemistry: A Science and an Art* (1972), *Highlights of Alicyclic Chemistry* (1973, two volumes), and *Organic Molecular Structure: A Gateway to Advanced Organic Chemistry* (1975). His other appointments included the U.S. national committee to the International Union of Pure and Applied Chemistry (IUPAC) (1973-1976), the National Sea Grant Review Panel (1978-1981), and the National Institute of Environmental Health Sciences (1979-1983). He is also a member of the American Chemical Society (ACS), the American Association for the Advancement of Science, and the Royal Chemical Society. Ferguson was awarded numerous teaching awards (1974, 1976, 1978, 1979, 1981), and was appointed chair of American Chemical Society's Division of Chemical Education (1980). He also became increasingly involved in finding ways to recruit nonwhite students into science fields, helping to establish a program to aid economically disadvantaged youths and a national organization of African-American scientists. Ferguson retired from CSULA as professor emeritus in 1986.

REFERENCES: Fikes, Robert, Jr., in *AANB*. Kessler, James H., J. S. Kidd, Renee A. Kidd, and Katherine A. Morin. 1996. *Distinguished African American Scientists of the 20th Century* (Distinguished African Americans Series) (pp. 95-99). Phoenix, AZ: Oryx Press. //jchemed. chem.wisc.edu/JCEWWW/Features/eChemists/Bios/Ferguson.html. //www.bookrags.com/biography/lloyd-n-ferguson-woc/. Amazon.com.

Fields, Julia
1/21/1938–
Poems, fiction, plays, children's books; educator

As a young girl growing up on an Alabaman farm, Fields reveled in biblical verses and works by British poets such as Robert Burns, Lewis Carroll, William Shakespeare, and William Wordsworth. When she was just 16 years old, her poem "Horizons" was published in *Scholastic* magazine.

After earning her bachelor's degree at Knoxville (Tennessee) College and studying (later earning her master's degree) at Breadloaf College in Middlebury, Vermont, Fields taught for a while in Alabama, then went to the University of Edinburgh to study in Robert Burns's homeland. In Britain, she met **Langston Hughes** and South African writer Richard Rive. On returning to the United States, **Georgia Douglas Johnson** and **Robert Hayden** offered her inspiration, and for two years, she spent countless hours in the Library of Congress.

In 1966, one of Fields's plays, *All Day Tomorrow*, was produced at Knoxville College. Two years later, Fields published her first book of poetry, aptly titled *Poems* (1968); wrote her eulogy of the fallen leaders Medgar Evers, **Malcolm X**, and **Martin Luther King, Jr.** titled "Poem"; and had her short story "Not Your Singing, Dancing Spade" anthologized in LeRoi Jones (later **Amiri Baraka**) and **Larry Neal's** landmark *Black Fire* (see the **Black Arts Movement**). Fields's book-length works include *East of Moonlight* (1973); *A Summoning, A Shining* (1976); her critically acclaimed poetry collection *Slow Coins* (1981); and her verse picture book for children *The Green Lion of Zion Street* (1988). Other poems and short stories have been anthologized and have been published in periodicals such as *Callaloo, Black World*, and *Negro Digest*, which awarded her the 1972 Conrad Kent Rivers Memorial Fund Award. The two daughters Fields and her husband raised are adults now.

REFERENCES: *BAL-1-P.* Burger, Mary Williams, in *AAP-55-85*. Hauke, Kathleen A., in *COCAAL* and *OCAAL*. Manheim, James M., in *BB. CAO-08*. Wald, Gayle, in *OCWW.* Amazon.com, 7/1999.

Fire!!
1926

Published in 1926, this avant-garde journal was intended to be a quarterly dedicated to the second generation of the **Harlem Renaissance**. Unfortunately, only one issue was published by editor **Wallace Thurman**, who was chosen for the position by **Langston Hughes**. Hughes had wanted the journal to be by and for black artists, a break from the social commentary of the day's established journals. Several associate editors included **Zora Neale Hurston** and poet **Gwendolyn Bennett**. The journal failed due to a lack of financing, poor distribution, and bad luck—most copies of *Fire!!* burned in an actual apartment fire. Two years later, Thurman tried again with *Harlem: A Forum for Negro Life*, but it also failed after its premier issue.

REFERENCES: *AAW.* White, Craig Howard, in *OCAAL*.
—Lisa Bahlinger

Editor's note: The editorial board appealed to readers for funding, "We would appreciate having fifty people subscribe ten dollars each, and fifty more subscribe five dollars each," but not enough readers responded, despite dazzling writings by **Arna Bontemps, Countee Cullen, Zora Neale Hurston,** and **Langston Hughes,** bolstered by Richard Bruce's handsome typographic design and drawings, and African wood-block prints.

REFERENCES: Schwarz, A. B. Christa, in *GEAAL.* //www.liu.edu/cwis/cwp/library/historic.htm.

First World *See* Negro Digest

Fishburne, III, Laurence
7/30/1961–
Play; actor, director, producer

A prominent film and television actor, Fishburne wrote, directed, and starred in *Riff Raff,* a one-act play. In 2000, he produced, directed, and wrote the screenplay for *Once in the Life,* his adaptation of *Riff Raff.* Fishburne is better recognized for his film roles such as *Boyz N the Hood, What's Love Got to Do With It, The Matrix* and its sequels, and his television role on the series *CSI* (starting in 2008).

REFERENCES: *AANB. Act. F. QB. W2B. Wiki.* Glickman, Simon, and Rebecca Parks, in *BB. EA-99.* //www.laurence-fishburne.com/. Amazon.com.

Fisher (married name), Abby
c. 1832–?
Cookbook

Fisher's *What Mrs. Fisher Knows about Old Southern Cooking* (1881, containing 160 recipes) is probably the first published cookbook authored by an African-American woman. Because Fisher could neither read nor write, she dictated her 160 recipes, based on 35-plus years of experience in cooking. Apparently, her evident expertise was much admired and desired.

REFERENCES: *BAAW.* Fisher, Abby (1881/1995), *What Mrs. Fisher Knows About Old Southern Cooking, Soups, Pickles, Preserves, Etc.* (reprint, with historical notes by Karen Hess), Applewood Books. —Tonya Bolden

---

Fisher, Rudolph (John Chauncey) ("Bud")
5/9/1897–12/26/1934
Novels, short stories; physician

Rudolph Fisher

Born in Washington, D.C., but raised in Providence, Rhode Island, Fisher was an outstanding scholar at Brown University (B.S., 1919; M.S., 1920) in Providence, and he earned high honors from Howard University Medical School (M.D., 1924) in D.C. After graduating, Fisher spent a year interning at the Freedman's Hospital, then he garnered a fellowship for postgraduate study in the medical school at Columbia University (ending in 1927). After completing his studies, Fisher opened his medical practice in New York.

While still attending Brown, Fisher had met **Paul Robeson,** whose singing he would accompany on the piano. During the early 1920s, the pair toured the eastern seaboard, earning money to pay for their college tuition. After earning his M.D., Fisher also managed to meet (1924) and then marry (1925) Jane Ryder, and the couple soon completed their family with the birth of their son Hugh (1926). Quite a busy fellow, Fisher also managed to write and have published some of his short stories (e.g., "The City of Refuge," 1919, in *Atlantic Monthly,* the first Harlem Renaissance author to be published there; "High Yaller," 1926, Amy Spingarn Prize for fiction) during this time.

While practicing medicine as a roentgenologist (X-ray specialist) during the **Harlem Renaissance**, Fisher wrote two novels—*The Walls of Jericho* (1928) and *The Conjure-Man Dies: A Mystery Tale of Dark Harlem* (1932)—now considered classic texts of the 1920s era among African-American New Yorkers. Fisher's first novel satirizes class and race distinctions through his portraits of black and white New Yorkers of each class. His second novel is widely recognized as the first African-American detective novel and might also be considered an early psychological thriller. Its central character is Dr. John Archer, a Harvard-educated psychiatrist from Africa, who uses his knowledge of deviant psychology (especially paranoia) to catch a killer, with help from detective Perry Dart. Fisher also adapted his second novel to write the play *Conjur' Man Dies*, which was first produced more than a year after his death, on March 11, 1936, in Harlem.

Although almost all of his short stories (e.g., "Common Meter," "The Conjure Man Dies," "Miss Cynthie") were published individually during his all-too-brief lifetime, it wasn't until more than half a century after his death that his stories were collected and published in *The City of Refuge* (1987). Sadly, Fisher died at age 34, due to complications of a digestive-tract disorder. News of his death shared the newsstand with his novelette (or long short story) "John Archer's Nose," his sequel to *The Conjure-Man*, published in the sole issue of *Metropolitan*, January 1935. He had planned at least two more novels featuring Archer and Dart.

REFERENCES: *AANB. EBLG.* Cohassey, John, in *BB. CAO-03.* Henry, Oliver Louis. "Rudolph Fisher: An Evaluation." *Crisis 78.5* (July 1971), pp. 149-154. Rpt. in Lawrence J. Trudeau (Ed.) (1997), *Short Story Criticism* (Vol. 25). Detroit: Gale Research. From *Literature Resource Center.* McCluskey, John, Jr., in COCAAL and OCAAL. Perry, Margaret (1987). "A Fisher of Black Life: Short Stories." *The Harlem Renaissance Re-Examined.* AMS Press. Rpt. in Lawrence J. Trudeau (Ed.) (1997), *Short Story Criticism* (Vol. 25, pp. 253-262). Detroit: Gale Research. From *Literature Resource Center.* Potter, Vilma Raskin, in *ASSW-1910-1945-2.* Schwarz, A. B. Christa, in *AA. BCE. GEAAL. W. Wiki.* Tignor, Eleanor Q., in *AAWHR-40,* and "The Short Fiction of Rudolph Fisher." *Langston Hughes Review 1.1* (Spring 1982), pp. 18-24. Rpt. in Lawrence J. Trudeau (Ed.) (1997), *Short Story Criticism* (Vol. 25). Detroit: Gale Research. From *Literature Resource Center. G-97.*

Folklore *See* Folktales; Oral Traditions; Proverbs; and Trickster Tales

Folktales
Time immemorial-

In the past, many white scholars contended that African Americans had a poor and shallow literary tradition imitative of white culture. These scholars studied only British and Anglo-American influences on African-American tradition, pointedly ignoring the influence of Africa and the Caribbean. To the contrary, the African-American folk tradition is actually rich and diverse, drawing on oral and written traditions from the West Indies, West Africa, and Europe, as well as white America. The distinctive qualities of the African-American folk tradition are well illustrated in folktales, where many cultural strands are interwoven.

In fact, folktales are part of a long, continuing **oral tradition** of creating and passing on the stories, customs, and traditions of a culture. When slaves were brought to America from Africa, they carried a literary tradition with them—an oral one that had been passed down in towns and villages through many generations. Because African-American folktales come from the common people's storytelling tradition brought over by slaves, many elements of folktales—the characters, motifs, styles of telling, story types—strongly resemble the stories told in sub-Saharan and western Africa. As time passed, however, and African-Americans came in contact with the folktales of other cultures—the Native Americans, as well as the European Americans-they assimilated elements of other cultures into their own stories. African-American folktales thus contain an amalgam of many different cultural ideas and views.

A major distinction between African-American folktales and their African counterparts is the institution of slavery. The slaveholders' attempt to obliterate the African identities of the slaves (their language, cultural traditions, and ways of seeing and ordering the world around them) was effected by forbidding slaves to learn how to read or write. The only way slaves could preserve their stories and cultural views was by word of mouth. In doing so, African Americans passed on their stories as a form of underground rebellion against their masters. Thus as **Nikki Giovanni**, a scholar of African-American folktales, says, African-American folktales were "built and focused on a quest for freedom and equality."

Also, in many ways, African-American folktales resemble the folktales of many other cultures—they mirror people's hopes and fears, explain relationships, interpret the nature of the world, ask and answer questions of existence and origin, and clarify people's doubts about life. They order the world and create both a foundation on which to construct reality and a filter through which to process daily events. They convey people's culture, religion, and social customs, and they impart history, explain the unexplainable, express values, identify acceptable and unacceptable behavior, identify fears and dreads, and communicate aspirations and goals. They are stories to live by but are also lived through—they not only teach but also provide their listeners with hope.

African-American folktales fall into seven categories: tales of origins (how things became as they are); stories dealing with trickery and trouble (with people getting into each other's business, with varying consequences); tales of noble black figures triumphing over natural and supernatural evils; funny stories that gladden the heart; mothers' narratives for teaching about expectations of marriage, family, and parenthood; ghost stories; and master-slave stories in which the clever slave outwits the foolish master (most of the time).

Many African-American folktales are *animal tales* —tales in which the main characters are animals with human characteristics. Animal tales can be seen to contain, in varying forms, all seven categories attributed to African-American folktales. Many of these stories deal with origins—"How the Snake Got His Rattles," "The Story of the Skunk and Why He Has Such a Bad Smell," "Why Hens Are Afraid of Owls." Origin stories across all cultures emerge because most people have lacked the scientific knowledge to explain why things are as they are, such as why animals behave and look as they do. The need for these stories in African-American culture was exaggerated because of the slave trade, which thrust slaves into a land with creatures and plants they had never seen before.

Nonetheless, most animal tales deal less with origins and more with teaching morality, for as time passed, African Americans had less need to make the unfamiliar landscape explainable and instead needed tales to provide entertainment and instruction. One of the most famous characters in the moral animal tales is Brer Rabbit—a wise and shrewd **trickster** who regularly outwits and gains victory over a physically stronger adversary. In some stories, the function of Brer Rabbit is that of teacher—in outwitting his adversary, he implicitly teaches the right way to treat others and the punishment that may befall any creature who fails to do so. In many stories, however, Brer Rabbit can be seen as a powerless slave who outwits a powerful master, making such stories into tales of rebellion, where a clever slave uses trickery to undermine the system of slavery by which the slave had seemed insurmountably trapped. Such tales can also be cautionary tales to warn potential tricksters to be wary of overestimating their own trickery.

Another genre of tale that serves to caution and even scare children into proper behavior are the supernatural stories—tales of monsters (the bogeyman being the most famous), witches, devils, and evil spirits who plague wayward children who are too curious, wander too far from home, disobey their parents and other elders, lie, talk back, get too lazy to do their chores, or try to be something they are not. These tales are based largely on re-membered stories of supernatural beings from African homelands but are set in the lands of rural America—the woods, swamps, mountains, rivers, and, of course, cemeteries.

Some of the stories are set in times before the advent of humans, and some even take place as recently as postslavery eras, but most are set either during the time of slavery or in ancient times. The ancient legends focus mostly on teaching proper ways of behaving and show brave black figures triumphing over supernatural tests and temptations. The tales set in times of slavery derive mostly from actual historical events in which African Americans took part. In these tales, the supernatural activity does not turn against wayward children but instead punishes a cruel, evil, greedy, or abusive master. Such stories serve not only as warnings but also as a release—a fantasy in which cruel people get the punishment they deserve but do not seem to receive in real life.

Release, relief from frustration, and diverting entertainment are among the most common features of all African-American folktales. The tales that serve this purpose most clearly are the humorous tales, designed purely to make folks laugh. Such tales are set in every time period, from preslavery days to the present and have existed since slaves first arrived here. **Langston Hughes** said that slaves would joke about their food, their masters, their bodies, their preachers, and even the devil, all because "they were laughing to keep from crying." Unlike all other genres of folktales—the animal tales, the ghost stories, the fables—humorous folktales are not really meant to teach anything. They focus less on moralizing and more on entertaining, while giving listeners a way to celebrate cultural traditions and make political statements.

Jokes are one form of humorous tales enjoyed widely by both urban and rural African Americans. In the African-American tradition, jokes often have taken the form of verbal jesting and games that tested people's verbal skill. These verbal contests had firm rules; the loser was the person who allowed his or her emotion to interfere, allowing an impersonal insult to become personalized. Another form of verbal play in the African-American tradition is jive. *Jive* is a playful way to communicate that excludes most whites. Some of the words African Americans have brought into the English language are "jazz," "boogie," "gumbo," and "okra," as well as the expressions, "uh-huh," and "unh-uh" for yes and no.

Within the past few decades, jokes and humorous tales can be found in the performances of black comedians such as Dave Chappelle, **Bill Cosby**, Redd Foxx, **Whoopi Goldberg**, Eddie Murphy, Richard Pryor, and Chris Rock. These comedians carry on the tradition of the humorous folktale by taking pieces of everyday life and, through exaggeration, showing the subtle psychological relationships that go on between people in any slice of life. In many ways, they also serve to heal their listeners, helping them laugh at their hardships.

In addition to the work of contemporary African-American comedians, African-American folktales have inspired many contemporary African-American writers, such as **Arna Bontemps, Sterling Brown, Paul Laurence Dunbar, Ralph Ellison, Virginia Hamilton, Langston Hughes, Zora Neale Hurston, James Weldon Johnson, Julius Lester, Paule Marshall, Toni Morrison** (whose *Song of Solomon* was inspired by tales of flight such as "All God's Chillen Had Wings"), **Jean Toomer, Alice Walker**, and **Richard Wright**. In fact, not only did Hughes, Hurston, and Lester gather inspiration from folktales, but they also compiled collections of them that are still available today—Zora Neale Hurston's *Mules and Men* represents one of the earliest efforts to accurately record the **oral tradition** of African-American communities, and Langston Hughes and Arna Bontemps's *The Book of Negro Folklore* holds a wonderful collection of stories, as do Lester's *Black Folktales* (1969), *The Knee-High Man and Other Tales* (1972), and his numerous Brer Rabbit books.

The readers of African-American folktales, however, must realize that the written versions differ in many ways from the tales as told orally. The written versions do show that such folktales are often told in a combination of languages, with African words translated into English either directly or told as asides, and text notes may inform readers that tales are often told with rhythmic chants and wails, as well as with various instruments, but such notes cannot immerse readers in the experience of listening to oral storytelling.

When the tales are told aloud, the storyteller may incorporate music, costume, voices, chanting, screaming, and rhythmic language, as well as emotion, humor, and wisdom in order to hold the attention of the listeners. In oral tellings, the listeners are just as important as the teller, for the audience in many ways directs how the story will go by asking questions, making comments, and responding in other ways. When a storyteller has a specific audience, he or she may also make topical references to people in the audience, drawing parallels between the tale being told and things that have occurred in the community. Many of these elements are lost when the tales are written down. In the hands of the best storytellers (whether oral or written), however, African-American folktales still maintain their main characteristic—as tales that are not so much heard as experienced.

In addition to being interwoven as a subtext for storytelling, music is often a vehicle for storytelling, particularly as it emerged on plantations before emancipation. In work songs, hollers, story songs, and spirituals, slaves were able to hold onto their hopes and to affirm their faith in God and in their own self-worth. By acknowledg-

ing their sorrows, despair, and feelings of worthlessness through shared song, slaves were able to transcend these feelings, to comfort themselves and others. These songs later paved the way for blues, jazz, gospel, rap, and hip-hop.

The folktale tradition continues to develop today in so many ways, through the written works of contemporary authors, through contemporary music, and through preaching. There is a need for more serious scholarship of the African-American folk tradition, to preserve and pass on the beautiful art of this tradition for future generations.

REFERENCES: *AAL. NAAAL.* Abrahms, Roger D. 1985. *Afro-American Folktales: Stories from Black Traditions in the New World*, New York: Pantheon Books. Bristow, Margaret Bernice Smith, "Hamilton, Virginia," in *OCAAL.* Coffin, Tristram Potter, "Folktales," in *E-98.* Goss, Linda, & Marian E. Barnes 1989. *Talk That Talk: An Anthology of African American Storytelling*, New York: Simon and Schuster. Harris, Trudier, "Folk literature," in *OCAAL.* **Hughes, Langston,** and **Arna Bontemps** 1958. *The Book of Negro Folklore*, New York: Dodd, Mead and Company. **Hurston, Zora Neale** c. 1935/1978. *Mules and Men*, Bloomington: Indiana University Press. Olson, Ted, "Folklore," in *OCAAL.* —Diane Masiello and Lisa Bahlinger

Ford, Nick Aaron
8/4/1904–7/17/1982

Literary criticism, poems, anthology, short stories, autobiography/memoir; educator

After earning his baccalaureate at Benedict College in Columbia, South Carolina (1926), Nick Ford worked as a principal at Schofield Normal School in Aiken, between Columbia and Augusta (1926-1928). He then taught English at Florida Normal and Industrial Institute (now Florida Memorial College) in Miami (1929-1936), while earning his M.A. at the University of Iowa (1934), where he later earned his Ph.D. (1945). After Florida, he moved to San Antonio, Texas, where he was the dean of faculty at St. Philips Junior College (1936). From there, he moved to nearby Langston, Oklahoma, where he was an associate professor of English at Colored Agricultural and Normal University (now Langston University) (1937-1944). In 1945, with his doctorate in hand, he moved to Baltimore, Maryland, where he became professor of English and department chair (1945-1973), then Alain Locke Professor of Black Studies (1973-1974) at Morgan State College. His next move was to nearby Coppin State College, as professor and coordinator of the Union for Experimenting Colleges and Universities, Baltimore Urban Regional Learning Center, Union Graduate School (1974-1976), and then professor and director of the Center for Minority Students (1976-1979). Meanwhile, he consulted for the U.S. Office of Education (1964-1966).

His teaching career also fostered Ford's writing. He wrote both literary criticism and pedagogical materials on English usage and literature. Regarding the former, he published *The Contemporary Negro Novel: A Study in Race Relations* (1936; reprinted in 1968 and still available) and *American Culture in Literature* (1967, now out of print, with limited availability), as well as numerous articles of literary criticism published in journals such as *Black World, College English*, **Langston Hughes** *Review*, and *Phylon*. Regarding the latter, he wrote *Remedial English: Presenting the Minimum Essentials of Grammar and Composition for Students with Different Backgrounds in the Knowledge and Use of Correct English* (1955; now out of print, with limited availability) and *Basic Skills for Better Writing: A Guide and Practice Book for Those Who Intend to Master the Essentials of Good English* (with **Waters E. Turpin**, 1959; 2nd ed., "Form B," 1962, also out of print, limited availability). He and Turpin also coedited *Extending Horizons: Selected Readings for Cultural Enrichment* (1969). Previously, he had edited *Language in Uniform: A Reader on Propaganda* (1967, still available), and he subsequently edited a textbook, *Black Insights: Significant Literature by Black Americans—1760 to the Present* (1971, still available).

With H. L. Faggett, Ford coedited *Best Short Stories by Afro-American Writers* (1950, still available; later published as *Baltimore Afro-American: Best Short Stories by Afro-American Writers, 1925-1950*, 1977). He also contributed short stories to his anthology, and his stories continue to appear in anthologies published in the new millennium (e.g., *The African American Studies Reader*, 2001). He also published a collection of his poetry, *Songs From the Dark: Original Poems* (1940, now out of print, with limited availability). His other two major publications, however, reflected his primary identity as a teacher: In *Black Studies: Threat or Challenge?* (1973), he crucially advocates the establishment of the discipline of African-American studies. In *Seeking a Newer World: Memoirs of a Black American Teacher* (1982, still available), he reflects on his life in the classroom, published in the year of his death. His awards indicate not only his dedication, but also his talent as a teacher: grants from United States Office of Education (1964) and the National Endowment for the Humanities (1970-1972); awards from the Maryland Council of Teachers of English (1971), the African Association of Black Studies (1974), Benedict College (1975), and the National Association for Equal Opportunity in Higher Education (1981). In addition, he was named the Outstanding Educator of America (1971), and he earned the Paul L. Dunbar Memorial Award (1978) and the Distinguished Literary Critics Award from the Middle Atlantic Writers Association (1982).

REFERENCES: CAO-03. Alic, Margaret, in *BB*.

FURTHER READING: *HAAL*. Carter, Linda M., in *GEAAL*.

Forrest, Leon
1/8/1937–11/6/1997
Novels, essays, short stories, libretti; journalist, educator

While working on his first novel, Forrest supported himself as a journalist, initially for community newspapers and then for *Muhammad Speaks*, the Nation of Islam newspaper, named associate editor in 1969 and then managing editor in 1972. In 1973, he left journalism for teaching at Northwestern University (Evanston, IL), where he was associate professor (1973-1984), then full professor (1985-1997); he chaired the Department of African-American Studies from 1985 to 1994.

Meanwhile, Saul Bellow and **Ralph Ellison** persuaded Random House acquisitions editor **Toni Morrison** to take on Forrest's first novel, *There Is a Tree More Ancient than Eden* (1973). As he did in his other novels, he used stream-of-consciousness writing to tell his story of the descendants of a former slave-owning family. Critics both lauded and deplored it. Readers gave wider praise and more popular approval to Forrest's second novel, *The Bloodworth Orphans* (1977), another complexly plotted story about the family's descendants, focusing on the family's numerous mixed-race orphans. His next novel, *Two Wings to Veil My Face* (1984), continued the story of the protagonist from his first novel. His critically acclaimed fourth novel, *Divine Days* (1992), was named a Book of the Year by the *New York Times* (1993) and the *Chicago Sun-Times* (1992), was called the "*War and Peace* of the African American novel" by **Henry Louis Gates**, and was sometimes compared to James Joyce's *Ulysses*. His final novel, *Meteor in the Madhouse* (2001), was published after his death.

Forrest also wrote essays (*The Furious Voice for Freedom*, 1992; *Relocations of the Spirit*, 1994), short stories (published in *Callaloo* and elsewhere, 1977-1984), a play (*Theater of the Soul*, 1967), and libretti (*Re-Creation*, 1978; *Soldier Boy, Soldier*, 1982). In an interview in *Callaloo* following the publication of *Divine Days*, Forrest observed, "The writer is taking a tremendous gamble in whatever he or she is working on. That it will all come out. And if you're ambitious enough you're rolling dice with some pretty rugged people who are no longer around, but their books are there to outwit." In a 1999 interview with *African-American Review*, Forrest noted, "A writer is working alone with his materials, hopefully finding things that will engage an audience, of course, but more than that."

REFERENCES: *AANB*. *WDAA*. Byerman, Keith. "Angularity: An Interview with Leon Forrest." *African American Review*. 33.3 (Fall 1999) p. 439. From *Literature Resource Center*. Grimes, Johanna L., in *AAFW-55-84*. McQuade, Molly. "The Yeast of Chaos: An Interview with Leon Forrest." *Chicago Review*. 41.2-3 (Spring-Summer 1995), p. 43. From *Literature Resource Center*. Miller, James A., in *COCAAL* and *OCAAL*. Reid, Calvin. "Leon Forrest's Chicago." *Publishers*

Weekly. 244.48 (Nov. 24, 1997) p. 17. From *Literature Resource Center.* Routledge, Chris, in *BB. CAO-07. MWEL.* Warren, Kenneth W. "The Mythic City: An Interview with Leon Forrest." *Callaloo.* 16.2 (Spring 1993) p. 392. From *Literature Resource Center.* Williams, Seretha D., in *GEAAL. Wiki.* //www.mtsu.edu/~vvesper/afam.html.

Forten, Charlotte Vandine *See* Fortens, Grimkés, and Purvises

Forten, James *See* Fortens, Grimkés, and Purvises

Forten (Purvis), Sarah (Louisa) *See* Fortens, Grimkés, and Purvises

Fortens, Grimkés, and Purvises

James Forten, Sr.
9/2/1766–3/4/1842

Sarah (Louisa), Forten (Purvis)
1814–1883
Essays, poems

Charlotte L. ("Lottie") Forten (Grimké)
8/17/1837?–7/23/1914
Diaries, poems, essays; educator, abolitionist

Robert Purvis, Sr.
8/4/1810–1898
Essays, pamphlets, letters, petitions, spoken word—speeches, eulogies

Sarah (Moore) Grimké
11/26/1792–12/23/1873
Essays, pamphlets, lectures

Angelina (Emily) Grimké (Weld)
2/20/1805–10/26/1879
Essays, pamphlets, lectures

Archibald Henry Grimké
8/17/1849–2/25/1930
Essays, biographies, scholarly works; political and social activist

Francis J. (James) Grimké
1850–1937
Sermons; minister

Angelina Grimké (Weld)
2/27/1880-6/10/1958
Poems, plays, essays, short fiction; educator

The Fortens, the Grimkés, and the Purvises were highly literary families who played vital roles in political and social activism, as well as literature, throughout the 1800s and the early 1900s. The patriarch of the Forten family was **James Forten, Sr.** (9/2/1766-3/4/1842), born the son of free African-American parents in Philadelphia. As a boy, he had studied in a school run by a Quaker abolitionist, Anthony Benezet, but James had quit at age 15 to serve the navy in the American Revolution. When the British captured his vessel, they imprisoned him for months. After the war, he was apprenticed to a sailmaker, and by 1798, he had purchased the sailmaking business. After inventing—and patenting—a special sail-positioning device, his company prospered, and by 1832, he was a wealthy employer of 40 European- and African-American workers.

James Forten used much of his fortune to promote causes of abolition, women's suffrage, civil rights, and temperance. His home gave birth to the American Anti-Slavery Society (in 1833). He also often hosted abolitionists such as William Lloyd Garrison, whose *The Liberator* he helped to fund; and the poet John Greenleaf Whittier, who dedicated a poem "To the Daughters of James Forten." Probably the most noteworthy of the social- and political-activist pamphlets he wrote was his pamphlet of protest against a Pennsylvania bill barring free African Americans from immigrating into the state. In addition, Forten and his second wife, CHARLOTTE VANDINE FORTEN (1784-1884), raised five strongly abolitionist children, including their daughters Margaretta, Harriet, and Sarah, and their sons James Jr. and Robert Bridges, as well as their granddaughter Charlotte Forten Grimké. Charlotte Forten and her daughters were charter members of the Philadelphia Female Anti-Slavery Society.

MARGARETTA FORTEN (1808-1875) taught for years in a private school her father and **Sarah Mapps Douglass** had opened for African-American children in Philadelphia, leaving it only to start her own grammar school. When **Sarah (Louisa) Forten (Purvis)** (1814-1883) was only 19 or 20, using the pen name Ada (for her protest poems) or Magawisca (for her fiery essays), Sarah began contributing to antislavery periodicals such as *The Liberator.* Composer Frank Johnson even set to music her poem "The Grave of the Slave," which became kind of an abolitionist anthem. She found it bitterly ironic that her father and many others had fought so fervently for the nation's liberty, only to have slavery embraced by the new nation, as the following excerpt shows (*PBW,* p. 254):

Where—where is the nation so erring as we,
Who claim the proud name of the

'HOME OF THE FREE'? . . .

Speak not of 'my country,' unless she shall be,
In truth, the bright home of the 'brave and the free.'
Till the dark stain of slavery is washed from her hand,
A tribute of homage she cannot command.

Early in 1838, Sarah married Joseph Purvis, the younger brother of her sister Harriet's husband Robert. After her marriage, bearing and rearing eight children (alone after Joseph widowed her) took most of her time. Nonetheless, she still managed to write some antislavery verses and prose. Sarah's sister HARRIET FORTEN (PURVIS) (1810-1875) had been highly active in numerous abolitionist organizations and conventions before marrying Robert Purvis. Afterward, she and he offered their home as a way station (complete with a specially designed room with a hidden trap door) of the Underground Railroad and a hostel for fellow abolitionists.

Robert Purvis, Sr. (8/4/1810–1898) (essays, pamphlets, letters, petitions, spoken word—speeches, eulogies) was the son of a wealthy white English immigrant and his freeborn mulatto mistress. Well educated, he was among the first African Americans to attend Amherst College. After his father's death, Robert and his brother Joseph, both residents of Philadelphia by this time, each inherited a fortune. Soon after, when Robert was about 20 years old, he met fervent abolitionists William Lloyd Garrison and Benjamin Lundy, who encouraged him to embrace antislavery causes. In addition to his work for the Underground Railroad, he supported the "Free Produce Movement," buying, eating, and serving only food that had been planted and harvested by free laborers, not slaves. He joined fellow abolitionist James Forten in opposing Pennsylvania's fugitive-slave legislation. He wrote pamphlets trying to prevent the disenfranchisement of African-American men of Pennsylvania. **William Still** recalled that "he gave with all his heart his money, his time, his talents" to the antislavery cause. Purvis also advocated on behalf of women's rights, civil liberties and rights, temperance, prison reform, and the education of all African Americans. For instance, when his local township tried to bar African-American children from attending public schools, Purvis threatened to withhold his considerable school taxes unless they reintegrated the schools.

Two contemporaries of the Fortens and the Purvises were two European-American sisters, the daughters of South Carolinian slave owners: **Sarah (Moore) Grimké** (11/26/1792-12/23/1873) and **Angelina (Emily) Grimké (Weld)** (2/20/1805-10/26/1879) (essays, pamphlets, lectures). Although raised with riches, they were denied formal education because of their gender. Nonetheless, the two girls would sneak into their father's ample library. Sarah furtively studied law, although she was prevented from practicing because of her gender. The two sisters rebelled against these constraints, and when Sarah (and later Angelina) converted to the Religious Society of Friends (Quakerism), the sisters embraced abolition, as they had long been aware of the injustices of slavery. In 1821, Sarah moved to Philadelphia, and her sister Angelina joined her in 1829. In the 1830s, the sisters started touring New England, lecturing against slavery, the first white women to speak to "promiscuous audiences" (containing both men and women). (**Maria W. Stewart** had been the first woman of any color to do so.) As former slave owners, they provided candid insights into the abuses of slavery.

In addition to their lectures, the sisters wrote abolitionist essays and pamphlets. Angelina's best-known work was her *An Appeal to the Christian Women of the South*, urging Southern women to rise up and oppose slavery. Sarah's best-known work is her *An Epistle to the Clergy of the Southern States*, pleading for Southern ministers and other clerics to fight against slavery and to encourage their parishioners to abolish it. Copies of these works were burned in the South, and the sisters were threatened with imprisonment if they ever returned to South Carolina. In contrast, Sarah Forten (Purvis) began corresponding with Angelina and welcomed the sisters' writings with her own "Lines Suggested on Reading *An Appeal to the Christian Women of the South* by A. E. Grimke," praising Grimké and urging other white feminists and Southern women to join her in opposing slavery.

Soon afterward, the sisters persuaded their mother to deed over the family slaves as their part of the family estate after their father's death. She did so, and the sisters immediately freed the slaves. The sisters are less well known for Sarah's 1838 *Letters on the Equality of the Sexes, and the Condition of Woman* and Angelina's 1837 *Letters to Catherine Beecher in Reply to an Essay on Slavery and Abolitionism Addressed to A. E. Grimké*, among the first American writings calling for women's rights. Although Sarah opposed marriage, turning down two proposals, her sister Angelina relented, marrying adamant abolitionist Theodore Weld in 1838. The marriage signaled the end of the sisters' careers as lecturers, and they turned their attention toward helping Weld run liberal schools in New Jersey. Nonetheless, Sarah continued to write on abolition and women's rights. After the Civil War, at ages 78 (Sarah) and 65 (Angelina), the sisters led a suffrage demonstration, casting symbolic votes in a separate ballot box, despite being hindered by a severe snowstorm.

Before the Grimké sisters were able to free their family's slaves, their brother Henry and his slave Nancy Weston had parented **Archibald Henry Grimké** (8/17/1849-2/25/1930) (essays, biographies, scholarly works; political and social activist) and **Francis J. (James) Grimké** (1850-1937) (sermons; minister). The

Grimké sisters sponsored Archibald's education at Lincoln University in Pennsylvania and then at Harvard Law School, where he earned his degree in 1874. Five years later, he married Sarah Stanley, a white Bostonian writer whose father opposed the marriage. Soon after, the couple had a daughter, **Angelina Weld Grimké**, but Sarah Stanley soon abandoned her husband and daughter, never to see her daughter again.

In addition to his law practice, Archibald was editor of the Boston *Hub* newspaper, an executive officer of the NAACP, a consul to the Dominican Republic, president of the American Negro Academy (which his brother Francis founded), and recipient of the NAACP's prestigious **Spingarn** Medal. An active abolitionist, Archibald wrote major biographies of William Lloyd Garrison (1891) and Charles Sumner (1892). He continued to publish extensively throughout his life, including some writings seeking to heal the divisions in African-American leadership erupting as a result of **Booker T. Washington**'s accommodationist policies.

Like his older brother, **Francis J. (James) Grimké** was educated at Pennsylvania's Lincoln University; then his aunts paid for him to attend Princeton Theological Seminary, from which he graduated in 1878. After graduating, Francis married into the Forten family, wedding James Forten's granddaughter (and the niece of Sarah Forten Purvis and of Robert Purvis) **Charlotte Forten (Grimké)**. A noted theologian and outspoken integrationist, he served as a Presbyterian minister in Washington, D.C. Renowned historian **Carter G. Woodson** (editor) collected Francis's writings into *The Works of Francis James Grimké* (4 vols., 1942).

When **Charlotte ("Lottie") L. Forten (Grimké)** (8/17/1837?-7/23/1914) (diaries, poems, essays; educator, abolitionist) was a child, her mother died, so she was raised in various Forten (and Purvis) households, immersed in political activism. Although Philadelphia schools were segregated, she was well educated, learning from private tutors until she was old enough to go to integrated schools in Massachusetts, attending grammar school and then studying to become a teacher. While in New England, she began the first of her five journals, recording her impressions of political activists, abolitionists, and intellectuals (e.g., **Frederick Douglass**, John Greenleaf Whittier, William Lloyd Garrison, **William Wells Brown**, **Lydia Maria Child**, Ralph Waldo Emerson, and Wendell Phillips), as well as political events and her own experiences. For instance, she wrote of being barred from Philadelphia ice cream parlors and from Boston museums. Although her white classmates treated her kindly enough while in the school setting, they ostracized her when they met outside of school, in public settings. She also wrote essays and poems, and her *Parting Hymn* was chosen as the class song from among about 40 entries.

After she graduated, though she was ill with tuberculosis, she became the first African American to teach white students in Massachusetts. Once she had recovered somewhat, at the encouragement of family friend William Lloyd Garrison, she journeyed to South Carolina, to participate in South Carolina's Port Royal Experiment. There, on the Sea Islands, she was to teach former slaves, freed by the advancing Union Army. She shared virtually no life experiences with her illiterate, ill-fed, ill-clad, ill-housed, and impoverished students. Because of the isolation of the islands, their cultural experiences much more closely resembled that of their African homeland than that of this well-educated Northerner. She didn't even share a language with them, as most of them spoke a distinctive dialect developed in isolation from both Africa and the American mainland. Young Charlotte faced a formidable challenge, which she recorded in her journal. After nearly two years on those islands, she experienced many setbacks but ultimately succeeded. She even had some fun occasionally, such as when she met **Harriet Tubman** and listened to her recount her tales of life along the Underground Railroad. In addition to her journal records, she wrote many firsthand accounts of her work for several Northern periodicals. Her two-part essay, "Life in the Sea Islands," appeared in the prestigious *Atlantic Monthly*.

On her return to Philadelphia, Charlotte served as a nurse for "contraband" slaves and Union soldiers (including the all-black 54th Regiment, defeated so resoundingly at Fort Wagner). She also wrote and published more poems and essays (often using a pseudonym) and translated a novel, but she took a 20-year hiatus from her journal. While in her forties, she married Reverend Francis J. Grimké and devoted herself to being a minister's wife and hosting the African-American intellectual elite of Washington, D.C. Sadly, their only child, Theodora Cornelia, died six months after her birth. Afterward, Charlotte focused her motherly love on being the cherished aunt of Angelina Weld Grimké. She returned to her journals again from 1885 to 1892 but was silent again until her death. Her insightful, politically revealing journals (*The Journal of Charlotte L. Forten: A Free Negro in the Slave Era*) were published in 1953, nearly 40 years after her death.

Charlotte Forten Grimké unifies the politically active literary families of the Grimkés, the Fortens, and the Purvises. Her grandfather was James Forten; her aunts were his famous daughters Sarah, Margaretta, and Harriet, who was married to Robert Purvis. Her husband, Francis Grimké, and his brother, Archibald Grimké, were the nephews of abolitionists Sarah Moore Grimké and Angelina Grimké Weld. Her brother-in-law Archibald was the father of her niece, the talented Angelina Weld Grimké. Got it?

Archibald pampered his motherless daughter, but he demanded a great deal in return. Born in Boston, **Angelina Weld Grimké** (2/27/1880-6/10/1958) (poems, plays, essays, short fiction; educator) was educated at the finest liberal, integrated schools in New England, as well as the Carleton Academy in Minnesota. In 1902, she graduated from what was later to be a part of Wellesley College. After graduating, she taught English during the school year in Washington, D.C., while taking summer classes at Harvard University for several years. She continued teaching school until 1926, when poor health led her to retire. After her father died, a few years later, she moved to Brooklyn, where she lived until her own death.

Angelina showed early promise as a writer, first publishing a poem in 1891, in her community's *Gazette.* Her essays and her prose were highly polished and expressed her familial inclination for political activism. Her plays and short stories similarly expressed her social and political awareness, particularly of racism. Unfortunately, she was writing at a time when African Americans—and especially African-American women—were not often published, although her works did occasional appear in magazines such as *Crisis* and *Opportunity.* The **Harlem Renaissance** was blooming just as her poor health was inhibiting her literary output. Thus, although she longed for a full-time literary career, ultimately, she was unable to support herself on her writing, and many of her works have yet to be published. Nonetheless, because of her lyrical skills and her distinctive African-American woman's perspective, many of her verses are often anthologized (e.g., in **Alain Locke**'s 1925 *The New Negro* and **Countee Cullen**'s 1927 *Caroling Dusk*).

Grimké's earliest verses follow conventional lyrical forms and themes (e.g., love, longing, and loss, such as her elegy "To **Clarissa Scott Delany**"; motherhood; nature; philosophy; poetic tributes), but in the early 1900s, she started experimenting a little with both the form (e.g., brief, with vivid images) and the content (politics, race) of her poems, anticipating the trends of the **Harlem Renaissance**. Though best known for her poetry, Grimké also wrote a play, *Rachel* (first produced in 1916 and published in 1920), and some short stories. *Rachel,* which addressed lynching and the effect of racism on a middle-class African-American family, gained attention as the first successful full-length drama written by an African-American woman and performed by African-American actors, for a European-American audience. The NAACP even sponsored several productions of the play, as a means of dispelling some of the racist myths perpetuated by D. W. Griffith's racist *The Birth of a Nation* (1915). Grimké's second drama, *Mara* (unpublished), also explored the effects of racism, as did her short story "The Closing Door" (published in 1919). In this story, after a lynching, a hysterical mother murders her own newborn son. Although Weld was not well known for her short stories, this story was well received. Some of her stories and poems have been collected in *Selected Works of Angelina Weld Grimke* (1991).

Within the past decade or more, feminist and lesbian scholars have noted that Grimké's writings, especially her love poems and her journals, almost certainly indicate her sexual attraction to women and possibly also to men. Grimké also would have felt pressured to conceal any homosexual identity in an era when she already faced huge challenges as an African-American woman, let alone a woman whose love interests and expressions stirred deep-seated and sometimes violent animosities. It has even been suggested that the paucity of written work and her social withdrawal from fellow writers in her later years may have been due to a perceived need to suppress her sexual identity.

REFERENCES: *1TESK. AA:PoP. ANAD. BAAW. BF:2000. BFC. BWA. EBLG. MWEL. NAAAL. RT. TtW.* Beemyn, Brett, "Grimké, Archibald Henry," and "Grimké, Francis James," in *GEAAL.* Bruce, Dickson D., Jr., "Grimké, Archibald," and "Grimké, Francis J.," in *OCAAL.* "Grimké, Angelina Weld," in *OCWW.* Campbell, Jane, "Grimké, Sarah Moore, and Angelina Grimké Weld," in *OCWW.* Carruth, Mary C., "Grimké, Angelina Weld," in *COCAAL* and *OCAAL.* Carson, Warren J., "Angelina Weld Grimke," in *GEAAL.* Clem, Bill, "Grimké, Charlotte Forten," in *GEAAL.* Cobb-Moore, Geneva, "Forten, Charlotte," in *OCAAL.* Davis, Hugh. "Forten, James a Gentleman of Color: the Life and Times of James Forten." *Biography.* 26.2 (Spring 2003) p. 358. From *Literature Resource Center.* "Forten, James," in *AANB.* Hubbard, Dolan, "Grimké, Charlotte Forten," in *OCWW.* Johnson, Sherita L., "Grimké, Sarah Moore," and "Grimké (Weld), Angelina Emily," in *GEAAL.* Angelina Weld Grimke, in *W* and *Wiki.* "Angelina Weld Grimke," in *CAO-02; LFCC-07; MWEL;* Greene, Michael, *AAWBHR;* Miller, Jeanne-Marie A., *AP1880-1945-3;* and Neumann, Caryn E., *GLB.* "Charlotte L(ottie) Forten Grimke," in *CAO-03;* Braxton, Joanne M., "Charlotte Forten Grimke and the Search for Public Voice." Shari Benstock (Ed.) (1988), *The Private Self: Theory and Practice of Women's Autobiographical Writings.* The University of North Carolina Press. Rpt. in *Literature Resource Center.* Gale, Cengage Learning, pp. 254-271; Harris, Trudier, in *AAWBHR;* Rodier, Katharine, in *AWPW:1820-1870.* "Angelina Weld Grimke," in //catdir.loc.gov/catdir/toc/ecip064/2005035688.html and //www.glbtq.com/literature/grimke_aw.html. *E-98. EB-98. G-96.*

Fortune, Amos
1710?–11/17/1801
Enthusiastic appreciation

After purchasing his freedom from slavery—at age 60—Fortune was able to earn a good living by working as a tanner. His important contribution to literature was to help to found the public library in Jaffrey, New Hampshire (1/28/1796), and using his skills to bind the library's books.

REFERENCES: *AANB. Wiki.* Liander, Margit, in *EA-99.*

Fortune, T. (Timothy) Thomas
10/3/1856–6/2/1928
Articles, editorials, poems, spoken word—speeches; journalist, editor, newspaper founder and publisher

Born a slave and a son of slaves, Fortune had Irish and Native-American ancestors, as well as African ones. He observed the Civil War as a young child and attended a Freedmen's Bureau school for a while after the Civil War. His father was a prominent Republican politician during Reconstruction; this status enabled Thomas to hold various patronage positions when he was a teenager. His relationship with the Republican Party grew strained, however, when Fortune decried the party's 1877 Compromise, which ended Reconstruction and left the constitutional protections and civil rights of southern blacks in the hands southern whites.

Earlier, in 1876-1877, Fortune had started his studies at Howard University, but he left after a couple of semesters to start a career in journalism. Within a short time, he had become a compositor for an African-American newspaper in Washington, D.C., and had married Carrie Smiley of Jacksonville, Florida. The couple later had Jessie, Stewart (who died in infancy), and Fred, before they separated in 1906. In 1878, the young couple moved to New York City, and he worked as a printer for the white-owned and -operated *New York Sun* and wrote articles for various white and black publications. The *Sun* editor appreciated Fortune's writing skills and promoted him to the paper's editorial staff.

By 1882, Fortune was editor and publisher of a daily African-American newspaper called the *New York Globe.* A militant defender of African-Americans' civil rights, he urged African Americans to question their loyalty to Abraham Lincoln's party, which didn't seem to be serving their interests. When Fortune came close to endorsing Grover Cleveland, conflicts with the management led to the death of the paper in 1884. In 1885, he published a pamphlet, *The Negro in Politics,* admonishing readers to support "Race first, then party!" Despite lack of advertising and other financial support from the Republican party, Fortune soon founded the *New York Freeman,* which was essentially the old *Globe,* with a new name and a new owner. This paper, renamed the *New York Age* in 1887, became the leading African-American newspaper at that time. From 1887 until 1907 (with some interruptions), he was also the paper's editor.

Though he wrote more than 300 articles during his career as a journalist, his editorials made him famous to civil libertarians and notorious to racists. In them, Fortune spoke out stridently against racial discrimination and segregation, and he championed African-Americans' civil rights in both the North and the South. Fortune also coined the term "Afro-American" and used it instead of the term "Negro" in his New York newspapers. To get a feel for his editorials, a contemporary of his once said, "He never writes unless he makes someone wince." In his words, "Let us agitate! *Agitate! AGITATE!* until the protest shall awake the nation from its indifference." Among his causes was the segregation of children into separate schools for black and white schoolchildren—a cause the nation failed to address until Supreme Court's *Brown* decision in 1954. Of course, the white press labeled him a firebrand.

In 1884, Fortune published *Black and White: Land, Labor, and Politics in the South,* in which he decried the exploitation of black labor by both agriculture and industry in the post-Reconstruction South, and he advocated for blacks to ally with white laborers to promote labor unionism. In 1890, he conceived of and established the Afro-American League, to promote African-American autonomy and to develop African-American political thinking. Essentially, this organization was the ideological forebear of the Niagara Movement, which was the basis for the NAACP. Unfortunately, the league became inactive after a few years. About this time, he also offered fiery journalist **Ida B. Wells** a job at the *Age,* to continue her antilynching campaign after her printing presses were destroyed and her newspaper offices were burned down.

Though Fortune's paper reached a weekly circulation of about 6,000 at a time when the *New York Times's* daily circulation was less than 9,000, he was always struggling to meet his financial obligations. In 1895, his *New York Age* and he were in deep financial difficulties, and he solicited and received both personal loans and subsidies to the *Age* from **Booker T. Washington,** whose accommodationist views were opposed by militant civil-rights advocates such as **W. E. B. Du Bois.** As a result of Fortune's link to Washington, his influence declined. Many prominent militants felt that Fortune had compromised his principles by lending Washington moral support in exchange for Washington's financial support. Fortune may also have ghostwritten many of Washington's speeches, his *A Negro for a New Century* (1899) and *The Negro in Business* (1907), and even parts of Washington's autobiography, *The Story of My Life and Work* (1900). In 1900, Fortune helped Washington organize the National Negro Business League.

Meanwhile, Fortune published two of his own very different books: *The Kind of Education the Afro-American Most Needs* (1898) and *Dreams of Life: Miscellaneous Poems* (1905). Many of his poems had already been published, and he was often invited to speak at public ceremonies and other occasions. Not too long after, however, Fortune's relationship with Washington became strained—both personally and politically—and in 1906, Fortune denounced Washington's support for President Theodore Roosevelt's actions following the Brownsville affair, in which an entire regiment of black troops was wrongly dishonorably discharged for inciting a riot. (The troops were exonerated in 1972.) In 1907, his relationship with Washington had deteriorated to the extent that Washington and his allies forced Fortune to sell them the *Age*. That same year, shortly before he was forced to sell the *Age*, he had suffered a mental breakdown, induced by marital discord and alcoholism. For the next decade or so, Fortune was virtually destitute—and definitely depressed—barely supporting himself by editing several short-lived newspapers and writing columns for the *Age* every once in a while. In 1915, he published *The New York Negro in Journalism*, but it offered him little financial aid. Starting in 1919, he rebounded and started writing editorials for the *Norfolk Journal and Globe*, which he continued to write the rest of his life.

Starting in 1923, Fortune also tied himself to another prominent African-American leader who promoted African-American business interests: **Marcus Garvey**. This association, too, involved mixed sentiments and yielded mixed results for Fortune. Prior to 1923, Fortune had absolutely rejected the notion of allegedly repatriating African Americans to Africa. From 1923 until his death, however, he worked as chief editorial writer of Garvey's *Negro World*. He never fully endorsed Garvey's views or joined Garvey's Universal Negro Improvement Association, but he still appreciated Garvey's ability to garner support from the masses through his dramatic message. Fortune also shared Garvey's aversion to Du Bois and the rest of the NAACP leadership, and when Garvey was charged with stock fraud, Fortune defended him against the charges. This action tarnished his reputation as a staunch defender of rights against wrong-doers.

REFERENCES: *AA:PoP. AANB*. Beasley, Maurine H., in *ANJ-1873-1900. EB-98. G-95.* //www.lib.uchicago.edu/efts/AAP/ AAP.bib.html Blight, David W., in *USHC*. Fitzgerald, Michael W., in COCAAL and OCAAL. Podesta, James J., in *BB. CAO-07.* Sloat, Mary J. in *B. GEAAL. Wiki.*

Foster, Frances Smith
2/8/1944–
Literary criticism and biography, anthology; educator

Almost anyone who has read widely in the field of African-American literature has read something edited or written by Frances Smith Foster. Perhaps the most prominent of her works in this area are *The Norton Anthology of African American Literature* (1997, edited with **Henry Louis Gates, Jr.**, Nellie McKay, et al.) and *Oxford Companion to African American Literature* (1997, edited with William L. Andrews and **Trudier Harris**). Both of these works were published after Foster had arrived at Emory University, where she was a professor of English and of

Women's Studies (1994-1996) and was then named the Charles Howard Candler Professor of English and Women's Studies (since 1996).

Before arriving at Emory, Foster had earned her B.S. in education (1964, Miami University) and her M.A. (1971, University of Southern California) and her Ph.D. in British and American literature (1976, University of California, San Diego [UCSD]). Once she had earned her master's degree, she started professing literature at San Diego State University (1971-1988). After that, she moved across town to profess literature at UCSD (1988-1994). At Emory, her specialties have broadened to include African-American family life before the twentieth century, as well as African-American literature, especially the literature of slavery. Foster's first key publication was *Witnessing Slavery: The Development of Antebellum* **Slave Narratives** (1979/1994), which sparked national scholarly interest in this field, and which remains a key resource in the field. While still at UCSD, she authored another landmark work, *Written by Herself: Literary Production by African American Women, 1746-1892* (1993).

Since then, Foster has continued to publish numerous essays in anthologies and in scholarly journals (e.g., *African American Review, Black Academy Review, CLA Journal, English Language Notes, Journal of Black Studies, Legacy*), as well as reviews (e.g., in *African American Review, American Literature, Black American Literature Forum, Fiction International, The Journal of American History, MELUS, The New York Times Book Review*). Her other edited works include *A Brighter Coming Day: A Frances Ellen Watkins Harper Reader* (1990); *Minnie's Sacrifice, Sowing, and Reaping, Trial and Triumph: Three Rediscovered Novels by Frances Ellen Watkins Harper* (1994/2007); *Behind the Scenes by Elizabeth Keckley* (1998); *Norton Critical Edition of Incidents in the Life of a Slave Girl* (2001, with Nellie Y. McKay; the slave narrative of **Harriet Jacobs**); *The Family in Africa and the African Diaspora: A Multidisciplinary Approach [La Familia en Africa y La Diaspora Africana: Estudio Multidisciplinar]* (2004, with Olga Barrios); *Till Death or Distance Do Us Part: Love and Marriage in Early African America* (2007); and *Still Brave: Legendary Black Women on Race and Gender* (2009, with Beverly Guy-Sheftall); as well as two volumes in the *Schomburg Library of Nineteenth-Century Black Women Writers* series (Octavia V. Rogers Albert and **Frances E. W. Harper**).

REFERENCES: *AAW:PV. CAO-02.* //cslr.law.emory.edu/index.php? id=1913. //www.law.emory.edu/index.php?id=1666&tx_cslrpubs_ pi1[cslrpubsauthor]=69&tx_cslrpubs_pi1[cslrpubscat]=18&cHash= 5158132117. //www.law.emory.edu/index.php?id=1913. //www. womensstudies.emory.edu/facstaff/faculty_foster.shtml. Amazon.com.

FURTHER READING: Liggins, Saundra K., in *GEAAL.*

Franklin, J. E. (Jennie Elizabeth)
8/10/1937–
Plays, autobiographies/memoirs; educator, activist

A schoolteacher and civil-rights activist, Franklin has worked at numerous youth and educational organizations, schools, colleges, and universities, including work as a resident playwright at Brown University (1982-1989) and as a teacher for the Harlem School of the Arts since the 1990s. She is also the founding artistic director of Blackgirl Ensemble Theatre since the 1990s. Initially, Franklin started writing plays as a means to interest her students in reading. Her plays include *A First Step to Freedom* (1964), *Prodigal Daughter* (c. 1965), *The In-Crowd* (1965), *Mau Mau Room*, *Two Flowers*, her highly acclaimed *Black Girl* (1971), and her musical *The Prodigal Sister* (1976). She adapted her *Black Girl* to a screenplay, which **Ossie Davis** directed for film. In addition, she has written a nonfiction book on her experiences as a playwright, *Black Girl, from Genesis to Revelations* (1977), as well as numerous unpublished plays and other writings. She and her now-deceased husband, Lawrence Siegel, had one child, Malika N'zinga. Among her honors and awards are a New York Drama Desk Most Promising Playwright Award (1971) and fellowships from the National Endowment for the Arts (1979) and the Rockefeller Foundation (1980).

REFERENCES: Houston, Helen R., in *COCAAL* and *OCAAL*. McCarty, Joan F., in *GEAAL*. Shostak, E. in *BB*. *CAO-01*.

Franklin, John Hope
1/2/1915–3/25/2009
Nonfiction—history, biography, essays; educator

Though the son of a lawyer in the all-black town of Rentiesville, Oklahoma (then "Indian Territory"), young John had no running water, indoor plumbing, or electricity in his childhood home. Despite a financially impoverished youth, Franklin was well schooled by his parents and grew up to be one of the leading scholars of U.S. history, particularly illuminating the American Civil War era and the American civil-rights movement. He earned his A.B. from Fisk University, in Nashville, Tennessee, in 1935; his A.M. from Harvard University in 1936; and his Ph.D. in history from Harvard in 1941. He went on to teach at Howard University, Washington, D.C. (1947-1956); at Brooklyn College (1956-1964), where he became the first African American to chair a department at a white-dominated college; at the University of Chicago (1964-1982), where he also chaired the history department for a few years; and at Duke University (1982-1985, now emeritus), where he was the James B. Duke Professor of History and a professor of legal history

at the university's law school, where he continued to teach some classes until 1992. In 2000, Duke opened the John Hope Franklin Center for Interdisciplinary and International Studies, named in his honor. During Franklin's academic career, he also taught at Fisk and at North Carolina Central University.

Alongside Franklin for 59 years (starting June 11, 1940) was his wife, librarian Aurelia Whittington, whom he met in college, and with whom he had a son, John Whittington Franklin (born August 24, 1952). In 1997, the younger John noted that Aurelia had served as the elder John's research assistant, editor, and proofreader, and "They are partners in the complete sense of the term" ("Remarks," 9/20/1997). That year, the elder John and his son coedited *My Life and an Era: The Autobiography of Buck Colbert Franklin*, about his father Buck.

Franklin may be best known to history for helping to shape the legal brief for the landmark *Brown v. Board of Education of Topeka* Supreme Court decision (1954). When he heard that the *Brown v. Board* decision was unanimous, he later recalled, "I let out some kind of shriek, and it was dancing in the streets after that" (*All Things Considered*, October 30, 2005). Franklin made history himself by presiding over several historical organizations, including the American Studies Association (1967), the Southern Historical Association (1970), the Organization of American Historians (OAH, 1975), and the American Historical Association (1979), the first African American to do so. He also presided over the United Chapters of Phi Beta Kappa (1973-1976).

In 2006, Franklin was named the third person to receive the John W. Kluge Prize for lifetime achievement in the study of humanity, a $1 million prize he shared with historian Yu Ying-shih. Franklin also received about 150 honorary doctorates, numerous fellowships from the Guggenheim and other foundations and institutions, and many other major honors, awards (e.g., OAH Award for Outstanding Achievement, 1995; American Book Award, 1997), and medals (e.g., Encyclopedia Britannica Gold medal for dissemination of knowledge, 1990; the Charles Frankel Prize for contributions to the humanities, 1993; NAACP **Spingarn** Medal, 1995), most significantly the Presidential Medal of Freedom (1995), the highest honor a civilian can be given by a grateful nation. The taint of racism attached even to this honor, however. Following a dinner honoring him for the Presidential Medal, he was at the elite Cosmos Club, where he was a member, when a white woman mistook him for a coat-check clerk, rather than the honoree. In 1997, President Clinton appointed Franklin to chair the advisory for the Initiative on Race and Reconciliation. In 2008, Franklin endorsed Barack Obama's presidency, and he lived long enough to see Obama inaugurated and taking the reins of government in 2009. (To see a video of Franklin commenting on Obama's nomination, see //www.npr.org/blogs/newsandviews/2008/06/john_hope_franklin_calls_obama.html.)

Franklin's most acclaimed text is his *From Slavery to Freedom: A History of African Americans* (1947, original; 2000: 8th revised edition, coauthored with Alfred A. Moss, Jr., extending the coverage through the 1990s; 2008, paperback with study guide). Including German, Japanese, Chinese, French, and Portuguese translations, as well as all editions, more than 3 million copies of the book have been sold. Probably the preeminent textbook on African-American history, it traces the story of African Americans from the beginnings of civilization through the early 1990s. In it, he elaborates the history, cultures, and peoples of Africa and ties them to the experiences of African Americans and other people of African descent in Latin America, the West Indies, and Canada. He also insightfully analyzes the ways in which African Americans have influenced and been influenced by American history and culture. The book also offers an extensive bibliography, an appendix of numerous important documents, and illustrative graphics such as maps and photographs.

Franklin's other publications include *The Free Negro in North Carolina, 1790-1860* (1943/1995); *The Militant South, 1800-1861* (1956/2002); *Reconstruction: After the Civil War* (1961/1995); *The Emancipation Proclamation* (1963/1995); *Racial Equality in America* (1976/1993); *The Color Line: Legacy for the Twenty-first Century* (1993); *Black Intellectuals: Race and Responsibility in American Life* (1996, with William M. Banks); *Runaway Slaves: Rebels on the Plantation* (1999, with Loren Schweninger); and *In Search of the Promised Land: A Slave Family in the Old South* (2005, with Loren Schweninger). In addition, he wrote or cowrote numerous other books, and he edited or coedited about a dozen others, such as *The Civil War Diary of James T. Ayers* (1947), *Color and Race* (1968), *Illustrated History of Black Americans* (1970), and *Black Leaders of the Twentieth Century* (1982, with August Meier). He also published *Race and History: Selected Essays, 1938-1988* (1989). Among scholars, Franklin may be best known for his *George Washington Williams: A Biography* (1985/1998), which culminates 40 years of Franklin's scholarly research into the life and the achievements of a pioneering nineteenth-century African-American historian. He also served on the editorial board of the *Journal of Negro History*, which dedicated its entire Winter-Spring 2000 issue to him and his texts.

In addition to numerous biographies of Franklin, his life is highlighted in a VHS tape and a DVD titled *First Person Singular: John Hope Franklin* (1999, 2007). In 2005, he managed to recruit a legendary historian and biographer to tell the story of his life: himself, in his *Mirror to America: The Autobiography of John Hope Franklin*. The

book was also adapted to audio format and abridged to make six CDs. Following its release, in a 2005 interview with Debbie Elliott, of National Public Radio, Franklin recalled an incident when he and his mother were thrown off of a train for defying the Jim Crow laws requiring them to sit in segregated seating. Only 6 years old at the time, he was crying, when his mother said, "Don't you fret about that. . . . You must spend your energy and time to prove to that man and to every other white person that you are as good as they are. And if you do that, you won't be crying. You'll be defying." Indeed, he did.

REFERENCES: *AANB. EBLG. SMKC.* Elliott, Debbie, "Remembrances: Civil Rights Activist, Historian Franklin Dies At 94," *Morning Edition*, 3/26/2009, //www.npr.org/templates/story/story.php?storyId=102371121, and in *All Things Considered*, National Public Radio, 3/25/2009, //www.npr.org/templates/story/story.php?storyId=102371121, and in *All Things Considered*, 10/30/2005, //www.npr.org/templates/story/story.php?storyId=4982081, with links to Franklin discussing Tulsa Race Riots of 1921, Reparations for Slavery, Lynching of a Classmate at Fisk, and FDR's Visit to Fisk University. Mathai, Varghese in *B. BCE. CE. GEAAL. Wiki.* Moses, Olufunke, in *EB-98. G-95.* //www.indyweek.com/gyrobase/Content?oid=oid%3A88747. Moss-Coane, Marty, in *Radio Times*, 3/27/2009 (re-airing) and 2/9/2006, interview with John Hope Franklin, searchable from //www.whyy.org/91FM/RadioTimesSearch.html. Podesta, James J. in *BB. CAO-07. The Journal of Negro History.* 85.1-2 (Winter-Spring 2000) [whole issue]. From *Literature Resource Center.* "Biography of John Hope Franklin," in //library.duke.edu/special collections/franklin/bio.html.

Frazier, E. (Edward) Franklin
9/24/1894–5/17/1962
Nonfiction—sociology; educator

Frazier's influential, yet controversial sociological works include his dissertation, *The Negro Family in Chicago* (1931), *The Free Negro Family* (1932), Anisfield-Wolf Award-winning *The Negro Family in the United States* (1939), *Negro Youth at the Crossways: Their Personality and Development in the Middle States* (1940), *The Negro Family in Bahia, Brazil* (1942), the textbook *The Negro in the United States* (1949/1957), *Black Bourgeoisie* (1957/1997; originally *Bourgeoisie Noire*, 1955), *Race and Culture Contacts in the Modern World* (1957, rev. 1965), *The Negro Church in America* (1963), and *On Race Relations: Selected Writings* (1968). Frazier never hesitated to challenge white Americans to think about race and to prod black Americans to think about socioeconomic class. Though he and his wife Marie Brown were married from 1922 until his death 40 years later, he often had prickly relationships, feuds, and fall-outs with colleagues and mentors, such as **Charles Spurgeon Johnson** and **W. E. B. Du Bois**. In 1995, Howard University established the E. Franklin Frazier Center for Social Work Research in its School of Social Work.

REFERENCES: *AANB.* Balfour, Lawrie, in *EA-99.* Cohassey, John, in *BB. CAO-03.* Sloat, Mary J., in *B. BCE. GEAAL. Wiki.*

Frederick Douglass' Paper *See* North Star

Free Southern Theater (FST)
1963–1979
Theater organization

By the middle of 1963, civil-rights activists and workers from the North were congregating in Mississippi, gearing up for Freedom Summer of 1964. Freedom Summer launched a monumental voter-registration drive in Mississippi, as well as other states in the Deep South. Among these Northerners were African-American activists Doris Derby, John O'Neal, and Gil (Gilbert) Moses. In association with Freedom Summer's sponsoring organizations-the Congress of Racial Equality (CORE) and the Student Nonviolent Coordinating Committee (SNCC)-these three dramatist-activists founded the Free Southern Theater (FST) at Tougaloo College, near Jackson, Mississippi.

From their home base at Tougaloo, the intentionally integrated theater group toured throughout the Deep South, seeking out nearly inaccessible rural African-American audiences and staging productions anywhere they could. The founders viewed theater as a means not only of promoting a political message through artistic means, but also of reaching out to people in distant, rural locales who had never seen theater productions. After two years of touring, Derby left the troupe in 1965, and O'Neal and Moses, FST's director and its artistic director, respectively, moved FST from Tougaloo to New Orleans.

Part of FST's mission had been to reach out to the communities in which they were located, but their integrated troupe was unwelcomed by the New Orleans Creole community. Within the company, disputes arose regarding whether FST should remain integrated or should become an all-African-American troupe. Eventually, segregation won out, and FST reconstituted itself as an all-black company, relocating from the Creole part of town to the African-American Ninth Ward. As many in the company had hoped, the racial segregation of the group and the move to a racially segregated community led to better integration of FST into the community. From its new home, FST not only offered adventurous theater productions to the community, but also extensive training to aspiring actors, directors, and playwrights, many of whom went on to stage productions on Broadway and film and TV productions in Hollywood.

According to **Kalamu ya Salaam,** "around 1967, FST lost all funding and suspended the touring ensemble of professional actors." During this time, O'Neal and Moses returned to New York City, although O'Neal later returned to New Orleans to rejoin FST. In 1970, FST obtained enough funding to resume touring, and FST continued to tour across the South, though not as intensively as in its early days.

Meanwhile, after FST settled into New Orleans, poet, playwright, and activist **Thomas Covington Dent** became deeply involved in FST and was soon its associate director (1966-1970). In 1968, **Kalamu ya Salaam** joined FST (1968-1971) as a playwright, director, and actor. A little before then, Dent had established an FST Writers' Workshop, through which he and Salaam then launched the literary journal *Nkombo* (1968-1974), which Dent and Salaam coedited. By the end of 1969, Dent and Salaam stopped publishing the journal for about 15 months, and Dent published *The Free Southern Theater by the Free Southern Theater* (1969). About 1969 or 1970, the FST's Writers' Workshop was renamed BLKARTSOUTH, which continued to publish *Nkombo.* In 1973, Dent left BLKARTSOUTH to found the Congo Square Writers Union, separate from FST.

Soon after FST ceased operating in 1979, former founder John O'Neal created Junebug Productions, Inc. in 1980, through which he toured the nation as a solo performer. More recently, O'Neal has announced plans to establish "a formal training program and cultural laboratory" he plans to call the Free Southern Theater Institute (FSTI) (quoted in //www.junebugproductions.org/#/ free-southern-theater-institut/4528633641).

REFERENCES: Fisler, Ben, in *GEAAL. The Free Southern Theater by the Free Southern Theater* (1969), in //www.amazon.com. Jacobson, Robert R., "Gilbert Moses," in *BB.* //biography.jrank.org/pages/2514/ Dent-Thomas-Covington.html. //en.wikipedia.org/wiki/Doris_Derby. //en.wikipedia.org/wiki/Gilbert_Moses. //en.wikipedia.org/wiki/ Kalamu_ya_Salaam. //www.answers.com/topic/gilbert-moses-2. //www.jstor.org/pss/2904579. //www.junebugproductions.org/#/ free-southern-theater-institut/4528633641. //www.nathaniel turner.com/legacyfreesouttheater.htm. //www.nathanielturner.com/ tomdentspeaks.htm.

FURTHER READING: *See also* entries for **Nkombo,** as well as for **Thomas Covington Dent** and **Kalamu ya Salaam.**

Freedom's Journal
3/16/1827–1829

Founded in 1827 in New York City, *Freedom's Journal* was the first black weekly newspaper, established by **Samuel E. Cornish,** a minister, and **John B. Russwurm,** to respond to racist commentary in local white papers in New York, with its motto, "We Wish to Plead Our Own Cause." *Freedom's Journal* used current events, anecdotes, and editorials to convey a message of moral reform and other issues of interest to northern free blacks, such as prejudice, slavery, and the threat by the American Colonization Society to expatriate free blacks to Africa. The newspaper was widely supported by blacks outside of New York City. Russwurm was gradually convinced of the benefits of colonization, damaging the paper's credibility. *Freedom's Journal* ceased publication in 1829, and Russwurm departed for the American Colonization Society's settlement in Liberia. Cornish was unable to revive the newspaper under a new name, the *Rights*.

REFERENCES: *EAACH* (Vol. 2). Wagner, Wendy, in *OCAAL*.

Freedomways: A Quarterly Review of the Negro Freedom Movement
1961–1986
Literary and cultural journal

Decades before there was a Student Nonviolent Coordinating Committee, militant student activists formed the Southern Negro Youth Congress (SNYC), formed in 1937 and continuing for more than a decade. When SNYC folded in 1949, a group of these young activists, including Esther Cooper Jackson, her husband James Jackson, Edward Strong, and Louis Burnham, moved to New York City. There, in 1950, they joined celebrity singer and civil-rights activist **Paul Robeson** to found the monthly newspaper *Freedom,* of which Burnham was the managing editor. Key figures of the day, such as **John Oliver Killens**, contributed to *Freedom.*

Unfortunately, the 1950s were soon dominated by virulently anticommunist McCarthyism, and Robeson became deeply embroiled in battles with the federal government regarding his outspoken political views and his Communist Party affiliations. Others in the group were also harassed, and many of them feared being charged and imprisoned under the Smith Act, which targeted outspoken leftists. The FBI went so far as to have one of Esther and James Jackson's children expelled from her publicly funded preschool. James Jackson went "underground" for several years. Soon after he reemerged in 1956, he was convicted of "conspiracy" under the Smith Act. Jackson then became one of the defendants in the landmark 1957 Supreme Court case *Yates v. United States,* in which the Court decided that it was unconstitutional to prosecute people for their beliefs under the Smith Act-even if those beliefs seem abstractly to support violent overthrow of the government.

Though *Freedom* had struggled on for a few years, it ended in 1955. Almost immediately, Burnham and Strong developed a prospectus for creating an African-American militantly progressive civil-rights journal

to replace it. Burnham was also inspired by the burgeoning liberation and nation-building movements taking place in Africa and elsewhere, and he envisioned the new journal as global in perspective. He also viewed it as a link between his younger generation such as his fellow SNYC activists and the older generation of activists-such as **Shirley Graham Du Bois**, her husband **W. E. B. Du Bois**, **Paul Robeson**, Chicagoan African-American history museum founder **Margaret Burroughs**, writers **Alice Childress** and **John Oliver Killens**, and even playwright **Lorraine Hansberry**. The new journal would offer not only political, social, and economic commentary, but also literature and art, drawing on the resources of the older generation, such as Elizabeth Catlett (Mora), Jacob Lawrence, and Samella Lewis, as well as younger visual artists, such as **Tom Feelings**.

Burnham and Strong circulated the prospectus among the activists who had cofounded *Freedom,* but it initially failed to interest the disheartened and fearful activists. Burnham continued to press them, however, with the aid of the budding civil-rights movement toward the end of the 1950s. Once the Jacksons' legal troubles were behind them, Burnham enlisted Esther Cooper Jackson to his cause in 1959, and she became instrumental in raising funds and gathering an editorial board. The core group of activists also expanded to include historian and storyteller **John Henrik Clarke**, Louis's wife and fellow activist Dorothy Burnham, and pan-Africanist writer W. (William) Alphaeus Hunton, Jr. Even after Burnham died in 1960, his cohorts continued to work on fulfilling his dream, joining forces with Shirley Graham Du Bois, and with encouragement from her husband W. E. B. Du Bois and from Robeson.

In April 1961, this small collective published its first issue of *Freedomways,* with a print run of 2,000 copies, 600 of which were sent to new subscribers. Initially, *Freedomways* was edited by Shirley Graham Du Bois, who later called it "a magazine ... that would encompass the Negro freedom movement" (quoted in *BB*). Before the year was out, however, Ghanaian President Kwame Nkrumah invited her and her husband to move to Ghana for W. E. B. Du Bois to undertake Du Bois's long-dreamed-of *Encyclopedia Africana*. When W. E. B. gladly accepted the invitation, Shirley resigned as *Freedomways'* editor and moved to Accra, Ghana, in 1961. Esther Cooper Jackson took over as editor of *Freedomways* for the next quarter of a century, with the help of associate editors, such as **John Henrik Clarke, Ruby Dee**, and Jack O'Dell. At Jackson's insistence, the editorial board and the management and operation of the journal was entirely African American. Nonetheless, the journal did print articles by some sympathetic Hispanic Americans and European Americans, such as Jewish scholar of African-American history and communist Herbert Aptheker.

In essence, the pages of *Freedomways* documents the sweep of the civil-rights movement, as seen through the eyes of those engaged in the struggle-from memoirs of African-American activists who organized in the Jim Crow South during the 1930s to the most current reports from Freedom Riders during the 1960s. Its pages included early essays arguing against the Vietnam War and South African apartheid, as well as fiction, poetry, and other creative works. The older generation of writers was well represented, such as by **Gwendolyn Brooks, Sterling Brown, James A. (Andrew) Emanuel (Sr.), John O. Killens, Claude McKay, Beah Richards, Joel Augustus Rogers,** and **Margaret Walker,** as was the then-younger generation, such as **Donald Bogle, Lloyd Brown, Tom Dent, Mari Evans, Nikki Giovanni, Rosa Guy,** David Henderson, **Calvin Hernton, Woodie King, Audre Lorde, Haki Madhubuti, Paule Marshall, Loften Mitchell, Aishah Rahman, Askia Touré, Alice Walker,** and **Sarah E. (Elizabeth) Wright.** *Freedomways* also built close working relationships with **Umbra Workshop, OBAC Writers Workshop,** OBAC Visual Arts Workshop, and other writers and artists collectives. Many of the Black nationalists criticized *Freedomways'* socialist foundation, but they nonetheless accepted invitations to contribute to it. *Freedomways* also included scholarly contributors, such as book columnist Ernest Kaiser, a research librarian at New York City's Schomburg Library, now the Schomburg Center for Research in Black Culture.

In addition to publishing the journal, *Freedomways* sponsored numerous events, including book parties, readings, art shows, benefit concerts, holiday celebrations, and tributes to important political and cultural figures, such as Gwendolyn Brooks, **Paul Robeson,** and W. E. B. Du Bois. These benefits often attracted leading lights of the African-American community, such as jazz musicians John Coltrane and Dizzy Gillespie, folk singer Len Chandler, opera singer Leontyne Price, and comedians **Dick Gregory** and Godfrey Cambridge. Actors Ruby Dee and her husband **Ossie Davis** often emceed or otherwise participated in these events, as well as contributing to the journal.

Freedomways came to an end in 1986, and a decade and a half later, Esther Cooper Jackson edited the anthology *Freedomways Reader: Prophets in Their Own Country* (2001). Among the many other authors not previously mentioned, included in Jackson's anthology, are African Americans **James Baldwin, Angela Y. Davis, Alex Haley, Jesse Jackson,** and **Thurgood Marshall**; writers from elsewhere in Africa and the African diaspora Jomo Kenyatta (Kenyan), Kwame Nkrumah (Ghana), Julius Nyerere (Tanganyika), and C. L. R. James (Trinidad); Nobel laureates **Martin Luther King, Jr.** (1964), **Pablo Neruda** (1971, Chilean), and **Derek Walcott** (1992); and ordinary African Americans, such as prisoners, a memoir-writing coal miner, labor organizers, and feminists.

REFERENCES: Bonds, Jean Carey, (2006), "Roots of the Fight for Rights: Esther Jackson and *Freedomways* Magazine," in //www.blackagendareport.com/?q=content/freedomways-magazine-and-roots-fight-rights. Cosby, Camille, Rene Poussaint, and Howard Bingham. 2007. *A Wealth of Wisdom: Legendary African American Elders Speak.* New York: Simon and Schuster. Golus, Carrie, "Shirley Graham DuBois," in *BB,* //www.answers.com/topic/shirley-graham-dubois. Jackson, Esther Cooper (Ed.). 2001. *Freedomways Reader: Prophets in Their Own Country.* New York: Basic Books. Robeson, Paul, and Philip Sheldon Foner. 2002. *Paul Robeson Speaks: Writings, Speeches, Interviews, 1918-1974.* New York: Citadel Press. Rocksborough-Smith, Ian, (2003), "Bearing the Seeds of Struggle: *Freedomways* Magazine, Black Leftists, and Continuities in the Freedom Movement," in //ir.lib.sfu.ca/retrieve/2139/etd1772.pdf. //bayarearobeson.org/Chronology_6.htm. //bayarearobeson.org/Chronology_8.htm. //en.wikipedia.org/wiki/List_of_people_from_Harlem,_New_York. //en.wikipedia.org/wiki/Paul_Robeson. //en.wikipedia.org/wiki/Smith_Act. //en.wikipedia.org/wiki/W._E._B._Du_Bois. //proquest.com/en-US/catalogs/collections/detail/African-American-Press.shtml. //www.amazon.com. //www.answers.com/topic/herbert-aptheker. //www.betweenthecovers.com/btc/item/1872/. //www.blackcommentator.com/147/147_odell_operation_dixie.html. //www.filmreference.com/film/85/Ruby-Dee.html. //www.geocities.com/SouthBeach/Breakers/5116/farewell.html. //www.library.cornell.edu/africana/clarke/jourmag1.html. //www.library.cornell.edu/africana/clarke/jourmag2.html. //www.marxists.org/history/usa/parties/cpusa/encyclopedia-american-left.htm. //www.noeasyvictories.org/interviews/int04_mitchell.php. //www.nyu.edu/public.affairs/releases/detail/1205.

FURTHER READING: *See also* all the authors shown in bold typeface, for further information.

French, William P. (Plummer)
2/19/1943–1/14/1997
Bibliographical pamphlets, anthology

While working in a bookstore specializing in African Americana, catering to noteworthy collectors **Arthur Schomburg** and **Arthur Spingarn,** French became an expert on African-American books and bibliography. Based on his expertise, he compiled two biographical pamphlets on African-American poets and coedited a bibliographical book, *Afro-American Poetry and Drama, 1760-1975,* which includes thousands of works. In recognition of his work, Harvard University's Afro-American Studies department commemorates him with a book-collecting prize.

REFERENCES:
//www.lib.virginia.edu/digital/collections/text/ch_afam_poetry.html. Newman, Richard, in *EA-99.*

Fuller, Jr., Charles H. (Henry)
3/5/1939–

Plays and screenplays, short stories, essays, poems; educator, director

This son of Lillian Anderson Fuller and Charles H. Fuller, a prosperous printer, developed an early love of reading and writing, at least partly because of his father's occupation. For one thing, his father sometimes asked him to proofread some of his printing projects. In addition, his parents exposed young Charles to a constant stream of different personalities and life experiences, as they opened their home to foster children. At age 23, Charles started his own family with Miriam Nesbitt (married 8/4/1962), with whom he has two sons, Charles Henry III and David.

While still a high school student, Charles was stage-struck when he saw a Yiddish-theater play: He didn't understand a word being spoken but "it was live theater, and I felt myself responding to it." His college education began at Villanova University (1956-1958); was briefly interrupted by some time in the U.S. Army, when he was stationed in Japan and in South Korea (1959-1962); and finished up at La Salle College while he worked at various jobs (1965-1967).

From 1967 until 1971, Fuller cofounded and served as director of the Afro-American Arts Theatre in Philadelphia. He also wrote and directed "Black Experience" on WIP radio station in Philadelphia. Meanwhile, he was developing his play-writing skills, evolving from writing dialogue-filled short stories to writing skits to writing one-act plays and finally into creating full-length dramas. In 1968, while he was working as a housing inspector in Philadelphia, Princeton University's McCarter Theatre offered to produce his *The Village: A Party*, his drama about intermarriage and racial tensions. He now refers to it as "one of the world's worst interracial plays," but he nonetheless profited from this experience, as he met members of the Negro Ensemble Company (NEC) while that play was being produced. In 1974, his *In the Deepest Part of Sleep* was produced by NEC, and throughout the 1970s, he wrote plays for New York's Henry Street Settlement theater.

In 1975 or 1976 , Fuller wrote his hit play *The Brownsville Raid* for NEC's tenth anniversary. The play is based on the historic Brownsville, Texas, incident of 1906, in which an entire regiment of African-American U.S. Army troops was dishonorably discharged, on President Theodore Roosevelt's orders, after being falsely accused of inciting a riot that led to fatalities. (The soldiers were exonerated in 1972.) Although Fuller describes himself as a playwright who happens to be black, rather than a black playwright, he addresses issues of race realis-

tically and sensitively, never hesitating to approach society's cruelty in a humanistic yet forceful light.

Fuller's next major play was *Zooman and the Sign* (produced in 1980, published in 1982), an Obie Award-winning melodrama in which a father searches for the murderer of his daughter in Philadelphia. His best-known work, however, was *A Soldier's Play* (produced in 1981, published in 1982), for which he won the 1982 Pulitzer Prize for Drama (only the second African-American playwright to win this award), as well as the new York Drama Critics Circle Award, the Outer Critics Circle Award, and the Theatre Club Award. In it, African-American army Captain Richard Davenport investigates the murder of African-American army Sergeant Vernon C. Waters at an army base in Fort Neal, a backwater of New Orleans, Louisiana, in 1944, during World War II. Fuller crafted the play as a series of interviews by Davenport, in which each enlisted man's story is revealed; each character's story at least partly overlaps with the story of other characters. Fuller adapted his play to a screenplay, retitled *A Soldier's Story*, which Columbia Pictures produced in 1984. The resulting movie was nominated for an Academy Award for Fuller's screen adaptation. **Amiri Baraka** and others have criticized Fuller for abetting white racists by showing a black man responsible for the murder, but Fuller has defended his work, "I'm trying to capture my experience. I'm translating the kind of contact that I've made with people, most of them black. But how I would write anything that is presumptuous enough to masquerade as being something that speaks for black people is beyond me. I'm just not that sort of person" (interview with Esther Harriott, 1988).

Fuller's early produced plays include *The Rise*, 1968; *An Untitled Play*, 1970; *In My Many Names and Days*, 1972; *The Candidate*, 1974; *First Love*, 1974; *The Lay Out Letter*, 1975; and *Sparrow in Flight*, 1978. He also wrote the play series *The Sunflowers*, 1969, comprising *Ain't Nobody Sarah, But Me*; *Cain*; *Indian Giver*; *J. J.'s Game*; *The Layout*; and *The Sunflower Majorette*. The scripts he has written, which have been produced, include *Mitchell*, 1968; *The Wall* (segment titled "The Badge"), 1998; *Love Songs*, 1999; TV scripts *Roots, Resistance, and Renaissance* (12-part series), 1967; *Mitchell*, 1968; *Black America*, 1970-1971; and a radio script, *The Black Experience*, 1970-1971. He also wrote original screenplays and screen adaptations of the works of others, such as **Ernest Gaines**'s *The Sky Is Gray* (1980) and his *Gathering of Old Men* (1987).

In addition to two Obies, a Pulitzer, and an Edgar Allan Poe award from the Mystery Writers of America, Fuller has been awarded a fellowships from the Guggenheim Foundation, Rockefeller Foundation, National Endowment for the Arts, and CAPS, as well as numerous other awards. Since 1988, Fuller has also been professor of Afro-American Studies at Temple University. His plays since then have included *Eliot's Crossing* (1988) and *We* (1989-1990), a series of plays including *[I] Sally, [II] Prince, [III] Jonquil,* and *[IV] Burner's Frolic,* all produced by the NEC. Asked what else he writes, he noted, "I write short stories and essays." He also pointed out, however, that "part of the problem with the novel is that it takes a long time to be read by lots of people. The one advantage of working in the theater is that I know I'm going to get an instant response. On the other hand, if someone writes poetry or fiction, he can count on more people reading him than a playwright can count on people seeing him. And if a play isn't produced, nobody at all is going to know what you've written. ... People are not reading a whole lot of black material. But if there's a play that you can come to, sit for two hours, and be moved in some way, and get up and tell your friends, that's a lot easier than spending a week with a book. And then a writer isn't quite sure, after you've read it, what you've got out of it. I'm fairly certain when an audience walks out whether they like or dislike what I've done" (interview with Esther Harriott, 1988). In a 1999 interview (with playwright N. Graham Nesmith), he remarked, "I have been writing for a long time, more than 30 years, and it is the most enjoyable thing in my life."

REFERENCES: *1TESK. AA:PoP. AANB. EBLG. MWEL. MAAL.* Githii, Ethel W., in *AAW-55-85:DPW.* Harriott, Esther. "In an Interview." Esther Harriott (Ed.) (1988), *American Voices: Five Contemporary Playwrights in Essays and Interviews.* McFarland & Company, Inc., Publishers. Rpt. in *CLCS* (pp. 112-125). Detroit: Gale. From *Literature Resource Center.* Knight, Gladys L., in *GEAAL.* Macon, Wanda, in *AA. COCAAL* and *OCAAL.* W. Nesmith, N. Graham. "Charles Fuller STEADFAST." *American Theatre.* 16.8 (Oct. 1999), p. 99. From *Literature Resource Center.* Sussman, Alison Carb, in *BB. CAO-05. CLCS. MWEL.* Üsekes, Çiôdem, in *EB-98. T-CAD-4th.*

Fuller, Hoyt
9/10/1923–5/11/1981
Criticism, editorials; journalist, educator

Starting in 1949, Fuller reported for newspapers in Detroit and Chicago, then he worked for a Dutch newspaper as a correspondent in Africa. This experience led to Fuller's only book, his collection of essays, *Journey to Africa* (1971). From 1960 to 1961, he helped edit *Collier's Encyclopedia* in New York, then he moved to Chicago and became a major force in the **Black Arts Movement**. Chiefly, he became executive editor of ***Negro Digest***, later renamed *Black World*. Fuller also helped found the African-American writers' collective Organization of Black American Culture (OBAC), which nurtured the careers of **Haki Madhubuti** (Don L. Lee), **Carolyn Rodgers**, **Nikki Giovanni**, **Angela Jackson**, and others. He also taught college students at a few universities from 1969 through 1974. After *Black World* folded in 1976, Fuller moved from Chicago to Atlanta. There, he collaborated in forming the First World Foundation, where he helped launch ***First World***, a magazine of opinion, scholarship, and literature. He edited *First World* for the remainder of his life. Unfortunately, his premature death prevented him from finishing a novel and book-length nonfiction on the Black Arts Movement.

REFERENCES: *AAW:AAPP.* Barnett, Rachael, in *GEAAL.* Brennan, Carol, in *BB. CAO-07.* Long, Richard A., in *COCAAL* and *OCAAL.* Amazon.com. SDPL catalog.

Gaines, Ernest J. (James)
1/15/1933–
Novels, short stories, essays; educator

Young Ernest, son of Manuel and Adrienne Gaines, was born on River Lake Plantation in Point Coupée Parish County, Louisiana, where his father worked and where later, he, too worked cutting sugarcane and digging potatoes for about half-a-dollar a day during his childhood. His aunt Augusteen Jefferson, who literally had no useful legs to stand on but had an iron will and tremendous courage and determination, raised him until he turned 15 years old. Because the parish had no high school for African-American youths, Ernest was sent to live with his mother and stepfather in Vallejo, California, to attend high school and then junior college there. A huge advantage of his move to California from Louisiana: He was not barred from entering the local public library, so the world of literature opened to him. Decades later, when his Louisiana town built a new library branch, he was the first person invited to give a reading there. In a 2007 interview with Wiley Cash, he recalled that his reading "was the first gathering in a library of blacks and whites in this city."

Homesick for Louisiana, Gaines tried to find books about the African-American, Anglo-American, Creole (Spanish- or French-African-American), and Cajun (French-Canadian-American) people whom he had known growing up—to no avail. Failing that, he read American (e.g., Ernest Hemingway and William Faulkner), Russian (e.g., Leo Tolstoy, Ivan Turgenev, and Nikolai Gogol), French, and Anglo-Irish authors who talked about rural ways of life across the country and around the world. Though these writers spoke of rural and peasant experiences similar to his own, they lacked the flavor of the down-home front-porch stories he had heard while growing up. As he later recalled in an inter-view with Ruth Laney, "I wanted to read about the South, and I wanted to read about the rural South. But at that time you had very few people writing anything that was in any way complimentary about blacks or the rural South. So I decided to write a novel myself." Even now, though Gaines spent most of his adolescence and half of his adulthood in the San Francisco Bay area, his writings continue to be immersed in Louisiana's cultural gumbo.

In 1953, after a couple years of junior college, Gaines was drafted into the army, where he served for two years. After his discharge, he went to San Francisco State College (now University), where he earned a bachelor's degree in English in 1957. During the mid to late 1950s, San Francisco was a haven for writers of the Beat generation, and Gaines responded to this stimulating environment enthusiastically. As he reported to Wiley Cash (in 2007), "Once I discovered a library and started writing in San Francisco I couldn't think of anything else in the world I wanted to do." While still in college, in 1956, he started having his short stories published—at first in the *Transfer*, a tiny campus periodical. A white literary agent, Dorothea Oppenheimer, saw one of his first stories and decided he had promise. With her support, in 1958, he was awarded a Wallace Stegner Creative Writing Fellowship to study creative (fiction) writing at Stanford University's graduate school.

Eventually, Oppenheimer also helped Gaines get a contract with Dial Press to publish his first novel, *Catherine Carmier* (1964/1993), a third-person narrative about a star-crossed couple (an African-American man and a Creole woman whose father opposes their relationship). Ever since, he has spent part of his time writing and part of his time teaching or working as writer-in-residence at various colleges, including Denison and Stanford universities. Since 1983, he was named professor of English (now emeritus) at the University of Southwestern Louisiana, Lafayette, where he spends part of each year; the rest of his time is spent in San Francisco, writing.

Through the process of "knowing the place, knowing the people," Gaines vividly describes the rural Louisiana settings of his stories, using authentic speech in dialogues and in first-person narratives. Even those for whom this setting and these people might seem foreign if they were to visit, through Gaines's narratives, they feel intimately engaged with his characters and become familiar with their settings and experiences. Through Gaines's compassion for his people, readers, too, care deeply about his stories' characters. Also, even in the most desperate of circumstances, Gaines satisfyingly incorporates humor as it would naturally emerge in the real lives of courageous people. His characters face racism, other forms of oppression, and personal tragedies and difficulties with dignity and determination—and with the love and support of their family and their community.

Gaines's second novel, *Barren Summer*, was completed in 1963 but has never been published. His second published novel, *Of Love and Dust* (1967/1994), tells a story of forbidden (i.e., interracial) love. This novel characteristically uses Gaines's first-person narration, such that the reader observes the events in the life—and death—of Marcus Payne, as seen through the eyes of Jim Kelly. This novel gained Gaines some critical notice, but the novel that roused the literary world to notice Gaines was his next novel, *The Autobiography of Miss Jane Pittman* (1971/2009). In it, the centenarian Miss Pittman tells her own story, describing more than 100 years of her personal experiences, while revealing an intimate account of slavery, Reconstruction, Jim Crow policies and practices, and the civil-rights movement. The best-selling novel was even made into an Emmy Award-winning (nine Emmys!) made-for-TV movie (1974), as well as an unabridged audio format (cassette, 1984; CD, 2006). Almost certainly his most memorable character, Pittman honors the qualities Gaines treasured in his beloved aunt: resourcefulness, integrity, stamina, determination, and loving compassion.

His next book, *In My Father's House* (1978/2008), returned to third-person narration and was set chiefly in a town, instead of in the countryside. This novel wasn't as widely acclaimed or as popular as the novel before it or the novel that followed it, *A Gathering of Old Men* (1983/2000). In the opening of the *Gathering*, a white Cajun farmer is murdered, and the white folks in town decide that a black man must pay—with his life. The reader hears the story through the first-person narratives of more than a dozen older African-American men, who act together to defend the black man targeted by the white folks. They do so by having each old man admit his guilt and accept responsibility for the murder. Although the actual events of the story are compressed into a single day, heightening their drama, each storyteller helps the reader see that these events are embedded within the context of a long history of racial injustice. This novel, too, was made into a movie (1987). Both *Miss Pittman* and *Gathering* were awarded gold medals by the Commonwealth Club of Northern California.

Gaines's subsequent novel, *A Lesson Before Dying* (1993/2001), was also made into a television (HBO) movie (1999), as well as an audio CD (2005). Readers view the novel through the eyes of Grant Wiggins, a teacher who was raised by his elderly aunt. As the story opens, a young African-American man is wrongly convicted of participating in a robbery that leads to murder. In a futile attempt to spare the young man's life, the youth's (European-American) lawyer says that the barely literate young man shouldn't be executed because to do so would be the equivalent of executing a hog, as the youth's mental level is no different than that of a hog. As

the youth awaits execution, his elderly godmother asks Wiggins's aunt to get Wiggins to help the youth realize his own worth and to see that he has human dignity much greater than that of a hog. Wiggins is unenthusiastic about this task, to say the least, and the young man has no great interest in Wiggins, either. In deference to his aunt, however, Wiggins grudgingly complies, and the young man agrees to do so, out of respect for his godmother's wishes. Over time, Wiggins succeeds in helping the young man to read and to write in a journal, recording his increasingly philosophical thoughts and feelings. By the time the youth is executed, he has come to acknowledge his worth and his journal reflects his tremendous dignity. The critically acclaimed novel won Gaines a National Book Critics Circle Award in 1994 and was chosen for both the Book-of-the-Month Club (1993) and Oprah's Book Club (1997).

In a 1987 interview with Marcia Gaudet and Carl Wooton, Gaines observed, "I would think that a writer never stops working as long as he is conscious; as long as he is awake, he is thinking about his work. And then he sits down four or five hours, six hours, whatever he does a day and does his work there. Work means having your antennae out, too, that you're tuned in." In addition to his novels, Gaines has published many short stories, some of which have been collected in *Bloodline* (1968/1997), comprising five different first-person narratives, one of which—"The Sky Is Gray"—was made into a TV movie (1980). Two more collections are *A Long Day in November* (1971) and *Mozart and Leadbelly: Stories and Essays* (2005), a collection of short stories and autobiographical essays offering insight into his writing. Gaines has also been very generous in offering interviews to interested listeners; many are available in print, and at least two are also available in audio format. Gaines's voice may also be heard reading *A Gathering of Old Men* (1986). His current project, *The Man Who Whipped Children*, has been churning in his mind for more than a dozen years, off and on, but book tours, personal travel, and home projects seem to be interrupting its progress.

In addition to the previously named awards and several honorary degrees, Gaines has garnered a Guggenheim (1971), a National Endowment for the Arts (1967), a Rockefeller (1970), a Wallace Stegner (1957), and a MacArthur Foundation fellowship (often called a "genius grant," 1993) in appreciation for his many literary contributions. He was also awarded the Joseph Henry Jackson Literary Award (1959), the National Governors' Arts Award (2000), and the National Humanities Medal (2000); inducted into the American Academy of Arts and Letters (2000) and the French Order of Arts and Letters (Commander, 1996; Chevalier, or knight, 2000); and nominated for the Nobel Prize in Literature (2004). In 2007, the Baton Rouge Area Foundation established Ernest J. Gaines Award for Literary Excellence, which Gaines wholeheartedly appreciates, "From experience I know what it means to young writers to receive recognition and monetary awards when struggling in the early years. We hope that this important award will encourage and help young writers to continue their struggles and aspirations to write." In 1993, when he married his first and only wife, assistant district attorney Dianne Saulney, he observed, "What frightens me is that so many things are falling into place."

REFERENCES: *AA:PoP. AAL. AAW:PV. BWA. EBLG. NAAAL. OC20LE. WDAA.* Byerman, Keith E., in *AAFW-55-84. ANSWWII-4th.* Campbell, P., in *T-CR&HW.* Cash, Wiley. "'What Men Dream about Doing': A Conversation with Ernest J. Gaines." *The Mississippi Quarterly.* 60.2 (Spring 2007) p. 289. From *Literature Resource Center.* Davis, Thadious M., in *AAW-1991.* Gaudet, Marcia, Ernest J. Gaines, and Carl Wooton. "An Interview with Ernest J. Gaines." *New Orleans Review* 14.4 (Winter 1987), pp. 62-70. Rpt. in David M. Galens (Ed.) (2003), *Novels for Students* (Vol. 16). Detroit: Gale. From *Literature Resource Center.* Harroun, Debra G. in *BB. CAO-04. CLCS. MWEL.* Laney, Ruth. "A Conversation with Ernest Gaines." *The Southern Review* 10.1 (Jan. 1974), pp. 1-14. Rpt. in Jennifer Baise (Ed.) (2000), *Children's Literature Review* (Vol. 62). Detroit: Gale Group. From *Literature Resource Center.* Lang, John, in *COCAAL* and *OCAAL.* Lepschy, Wolfgang. "A MELUS Interview: Ernest J. Gaines." *MELUS.* 24.1 (Spring 1999) p. 197. From *Literature Resource Center.* Robinson, Lisa Clayton, in *EA-99.* Summer, Bob. "Ernest Gaines: The Novelist Describes His Arduous Efforts to Educate Himself as a Writer." *Publishers Weekly.* 240.21 (May 24, 1993) p. 62. From *Literature Resource Center.* //blog.nola.com/new south/2008/01/pulitzernominated_olympia_vern.html. *EB-BH-CD. G-97.* Yon, Veronica Adams, in *GEAAL. W. Wiki.*

Garland (married name), Hazel B. (née Hazel Barbara Maxine Hill)
1/28/1913–4/5/1988
Journalist, editor

The eldest of the 16 children in her family, and a bright student who loved learning and excelled in school, Garland was urged by her father to drop out of high school. Why? To make it easier for her younger brother to finish school. As she later recalled (quoted on p. 97, *PBW*), "My father was a dear soul. I loved him dearly. But his idea was, 'Why waste your money on sending a girl to college? She's going to get married. Save your money for the boys.' I used to go to the library where I would read and read. . . . I lived in libraries. I read everything." On January 26, 1935, she did exactly as her father predicted: She married (wedding business owner and photographer Percy A. Garland), and a little over nine months later, she had her only child (her daughter Phyllis) and settled down to homemaking.

With encouragement from her mother-in-law, Janey Garland, Hazel started getting involved in various civic organizations, including the local YWCA. When a *Pitts-burgh Courier* reporter got lost on the way to a club function, Garland- the club's reporter and a member of the publicity committee-wrote up the event herself. Editors at the *Courier* were impressed with her writing skills and her journalistic intuition, so they invited her to work for them as a "stringer"—a freelance reporter who got paid ($2) for each item she wrote but received no salary otherwise. She was to cover local events in various nearby communities. Pretty soon, Garland was turning in so many items that the editors encouraged her to combine her items into a column, titled "Tri-City News," starting in 1943. When the *Courier* offered training for the stringers, Garland made good use of the opportunity, and pretty soon she was filling in for staff reporters whenever they went on vacation. In 1946, she was invited to join the staff full time, and her column's title was changed to "Things to Talk About." Garland's highly popular column was published in various editions of the *Pittsburgh Courier* until her death in 1988.

In 1952, Garland won a prestigious regional journalism competition, beating out many white journalists and at least one Pulitzer Prize winner. The same year, when the *Courier* decided to start a new magazine section, the paper named Garland to be its associate editor. In 1955, Garland started writing another column, her weekly "Video Vignettes," which she also continued writing until the year she died. In it, she praised TV networks, producers, and executives that provided positive images of African Americans, put African Americans in front of the camera, and addressed issues of concern to African Americans—and she scorned them when they canceled those programs, dismissed those performers, or showed negative images of African Americans. To drive home her point, she often sent copies of her column to the TV executives and station managers she was honoring or scolding. She was the first African-American journalist to start a column critiquing television, and when she died, hers was one of the longest-running newspaper columns about television ever published.

When the magazine section was phased out, Garland became the woman's editor and then in 1960, her job expanded to include being the entertainment editor, as well. When the newspaper started having grave financial woes in the mid-1960s, and staffers' checks started to bounce, Garland's commitment never flagged. As she later recalled, "I loved the *Courier.* It was everything to me. I had spent the greater part of my life there, so I wanted to work even if I didn't get paid. I thought maybe we could keep on and hold it together." In 1966, *Chicago Defender* publisher John Sengstacke (**Robert Sengstacke Abbott**'s nephew) bought the *Courier,* adding it to his chain of African-American newspapers and renaming it the *New Pittsburgh Courier.*

Sengstacke, a savvy publisher, promoted Garland to city editor, considered a management-level position at a newspaper. In that position, Garland influenced the newspaper's policies and staff assignments. In 1972, Sengstacke further promoted her to editor-in-chief, making her the first woman to head a nationally circulated African-American newspaper chain. According to the Negro Press Association, she was also the first African-American woman to edit any nationally circulated periodical. In that role, Garland reorganized the paper into different sections, developed new "beats" for the paper, and emphasized various features. In 1974, the National Newspaper Publishers Association named her "Editor of the Year." That same year, poor health forced Garland to step down as editor-in-chief, but she continued on as assistant to the publisher, so she still had a hand in editorial operations and decision making, and she continued writing her columns and occasional feature articles. In 1977, Garland retired from her full-time position at the paper, but she still continuing working for the paper as an editorial coordinator and consultant. In addition to working one day a week, doing editing and layouts, she kept writing her columns and her occasional feature articles, which she continued to do until three weeks before her death. In both 1978 and 1979, she was honored as a juror of journalism's most prestigious prize: the Pulitzer. She also won a National Sojourner Truth Award, a News Hen of the Year award from the Women's Press Club of Pittsburgh, and a National Headliner Award from Women in Communications. In thinking about success, Garland commented, "We must not let anything turn us aside. And to be truly successful, we must always reach back and try to lift someone else as we climb" (quoted on p. 100, *TAWH*). She continues to lift others, through the Garland-Goode Scholarship for journalism students, founded by Pittsburgh's *Renaissance Too* magazine, and named to honor her and Malvin "Mal" Goode, a former *Courier* journalist and national news broadcaster.

REFERENCES: *PBW.* Almeida, Eugenie P., in *AANB.* Garland, Phyl, in *CAO-1998.* //query.nytimes.com/gst/fullpage.html? res=940DE7DF153CF932A25757C0A96E948260.

FURTHER READING: *TAWH.*

Garnet, Henry Highland (né ?Trusty)
12/23/1815–2/13/1882
Spoken word—sermons and lectures, nonfiction—abolitionist writings; cleric

Enslaved by the Trusty family, in 1824, Henry's father George, a descendant of a Mandingo chieftain, absconded his family from Maryland's eastern shore to New Hope, Pennsylvania, and then to New York City. George gave each member of his family not only their freedom but also a new first name and family surname, Garnet. Thereafter, Henry grew up not knowing the constraints of slave life, though he was never far removed from racial hatred and discrimination. When he was just 14, he went to sea as a cabin boy, but on his return to his home port, he found that his sister had been caught by slave hunters and the rest of his family had been forced into hiding to avoid capture. From then on, he carried a large knife, although his friends did manage to persuade him to hide in Long Island, rather than openly trying to defend himself from the slave hunters.

In New York, Henry attended the African Free School with his neighbor and friend **Alexander Crummell**, his cousin **Samuel Ringgold Ward**, future Shakespearean actor Ira Aldridge, future physician James McCune Smith, and future college professor **Charles Reason**. He went on to the Canal Street High School and then, along with Crummell and Aldridge, enrolled in the newly founded Noyes Academy in Canaan, New Hampshire, which had been all white prior to their enrollment. As if that weren't enough to rile the locals, the brazen young Garnet and Crummell spoke boldly against slavery in a local church. An outraged mob of white neighbors of the school used a fleet of oxen to drag the school's main building into a nearby swamp. Undaunted, Garnet and Crummell continued their schooling at Oneida Theological Institute, from which Garnet graduated in 1840. That year, he ended a long battle with an unhealed sports injury by having his leg amputated at the hip; he used crutches the rest of his life.

In 1841, Garnet married Julia Ward Williams, a schoolteacher who had been a student at both daring Prudence Crandall's interracial school in Canterbury, Connecticut, and the Noyes Academy. The couple later had three biological children (James Crummell, 1844-1851; Mary Highland, born c. 1845; and a second son, b. 1850) and one adopted daughter, Stella, who had been a fugitive slave. Julia died in 1870, two of her children having predeceased her. Less than a decade later, Henry married Susan Smith Thompkins, a widow whose two children predeceased her. Susan had been appointed the first African-American principal in the New York Public School System in 1863, after she had been teaching school for about a decade. Garnet widowed her in 1882, and in 1892, when **Ida B. Wells**'s presses were destroyed, Susan was instrumental in raising funds to replace them.

Garnet, following his graduation, gained his own pastorship at a Presbyterian church. It was soon a center of abolitionist activity, as well as the location for a grammar school. He was ordained an elder in 1841, licensed to preach in 1842, and ordained a minister in 1843. He gained national notoriety when he addressed the National Convention of Colored Citizens (also called the "National Negro Convention") in Buffalo, NY, proclaiming his 1843 "Call to Rebellion," urging listeners to take whatever steps they needed to in order to resist and oppose slavery. He admonished them, "THEREFORE IT IS YOUR SOLEMN AND IMPERATIVE DUTY TO USE EVERY MEANS, BOTH MORAL, INTELLECTUAL, AND PHYSICAL THAT PROMISES SUCCESS. . . . Brethren arise, arise! Strike for your lives and liberties. . . . Let your motto be resistance! *resistance!* RESISTANCE! . . . What kind of resistance you had better make, you must decide by the circumstances that surround you, and according to the suggestion of expediency."

In addition to his speeches from the pulpit, he lectured widely and wrote and edited numerous pieces for newspapers, such as the *National Watchman* and *The Clarion*. In 1848, Garnet published *The Past and Present Condition, and the Destiny, of the Colored Race*, which detailed his views on abolition and his opposition to emigration to Africa. At that time, he noted that many racist whites supported emigration, and he observed that the reasons for their support was that abolition was more likely to occur if freed African Americans remained in America to advocate and work for abolition. He also believed that if African Americans emigrated, they would be abandoning their legitimate claim to the fruits of their labor in America. He later (by the late 1850s) changed his mind and advocated emigration to Africa and the Caribbean.

In 1849, he published **David Walker**'s *Appeal in Four Articles; Together with a Preamble, to the Coloured Citizens of the World, but in Particular, and Very Expressly, to Those of the United States of America*, with which he included his 1843 speech. The compounded effect of Walker's appeal and his own was to inspire countless slaves to revolt by whatever means they had available, including the murder of their masters if necessary. These two abolitionists' ideas also influenced sympathetic whites, such as William Lloyd Garrison (editor of *The Liberator*) and John Brown, who helped Garnet financially in this publication, and who was later to become rather famous himself, at the little town of Harpers Ferry.

From 1850 to 1855, Garnet left the United States to lecture against slavery in Great Britain and Germany, as well as to do missionary work in Jamaica. Meanwhile, in the United States, abolitionist sentiments were gaining ground, and Garnet's ideas about slave resistance and violence—and his opposition to emigration—were becoming increasingly acceptable to militant abolitionists. Even **Frederick Douglass**, who had denounced Garnet's violence in 1843, agreed that nonviolent moral suasion was unlikely to succeed in abolishing slavery and that violent means may be necessary to achieve abolition.

When Garnet returned to the United States in 1855, he became the pastor of Shiloh Presbyterian Church in New York City. During the Civil War, he offered aid to persons who were displaced and distressed because of the Civil War. In 1864, while he was pastor of the 15th Street Presbyterian Church in Washington, D.C., he urged President Lincoln to enlist African-American troops, and he helped recruit African Americans for the Union Army.

Another of Garnet's speeches also made history: On February 12, 1865, he became the first African-American minister to deliver a sermon in the U.S. Congress. In it, he admonished the representatives to "emancipate, enfranchise, educate, and give the blessings of the gospel to every American citizen." After the Civil War, Garnet supported government workers in developing programs to benefit former slaves. He also outspokenly advocated on behalf of civil rights, such as by urging land reform to get rid of the land monopolies held by white Southerners. In addition, his reach extended beyond the American continent, as he championed Cuban independence, maintained an interest in the West Indies, and promoted strong ties to Africa. Although Garnet married (two times, actually—first to Julia and second to women's rights activist Sarah Thompson), his primary devotion was to abolition, and his second was to his church and followers, leaving little for his personal life.

During his later years, he became increasingly disillusioned about the possibilities for African Americans in the United States and became interested in emigrating to Africa. In 1881, an appointment as Minister to Liberia (established as a free state of Africa during the era of American slavery) offered him a way out. Exactly 17 years after his groundbreaking speech to the Congress, less than two months after his arrival in Liberia, he died there. He was buried on African soil, as was his wish, in a Liberian cemetery overlooking the Atlantic Ocean.

REFERENCES: *1TESK. AA:PoP. AANB. BAL-1-P. BF:2000. BWA. NAAAL. SMKC. VBA.* Eiselein, Gregory, in *B. BCE. CE. COCAAL* and *OCAAL. EB-98. G-95. W. Wiki.* Gardner, Eric, in *GEAAL.*

Garvey, Amy Euphemia (née Jacques)
12/31/1896–7/25/1973
History, editorials; journalist, editor

A native of Jamaica, Amy Euphemia Jacques's main claim to fame is her link to fellow Jamaican and black nationalist leader **Marcus Garvey**, whom she wedded July 27, 1922, and with whom she had two sons (Marcus Jr., born in 1930, and Julius Winston, born in 1933), raising them alone after Marcus widowed her in 1940. Before marrying Garvey, Amy Jacques had migrated to the United States in 1917, had joined UNIA in 1918, and had worked as Garvey's private secretary and office manager, replacing Marcus's first wife in those roles by 1922. Eventually, she became the associate editor of UNIA's *Negro World* newspaper, editing the women's page and writing her own column, "Our Women and What They Think." When they married, Marcus was already under indictment for mail fraud, and when he was convicted and jailed, she ardently campaigned for his release, through her editorials in *Negro World* and by giving speeches throughout the United States. She also compiled and edited Marcus Garvey's writings in the *Philosophy and Opinions of Marcus Garvey, or Africa for the Africans* (vol. 1, 1923; vol. 2, 1925; vol. 3, published posthumously in 1977, with E. U. Essien-Udom) and two volumes of Marcus's poems in *The Tragedy of White Injustice* and *Selections from the Poetic Meditations of Marcus Garvey* (both published privately by her in 1927).

Though she and Marcus were estranged by the time of his death, she continued to share his aims, writing letters to pan-Africanists and articles about pan-Africanism the remainder of her life, including numerous articles for *The African: Journal of African Affairs*. She also wrote her own account of Garveyism in *Garvey and Garveyism* (1963) and *Black Power in America: The Power of the Human Spirit* (1968, a booklet).

REFERENCES: *AANB*. Taylor, Ula, in *BWA:AHE*. *CAO-1998*. *Wiki*. Amy Garvey's papers are collected in the Marcus Garvey Memorial Collection at Fisk. //www.pbs.org/wgbh/amex/garvey/peopleevents/p_jacques.html.

FURTHER READING: *BH2C*.

Garvey, Jr., Marcus (Moziah)
8/17/1887–6/10/1940
Essays, poems, speeches; newspaper and magazine founder and editor, entrepreneur, convict

During his lifetime and continuing to this day, Marcus Garvey has been a controversial character. There is even disagreement as to whether Garvey's middle name may have been Moziah (per *EB-98* and *EBLG*), Mosiah (per *EA-99* and *BH2C*), or even Mozian Mannasseth (per *BF:2000*). The son of a bold, brilliant, and book-loving stonemason, Garvey was born and raised in Jamaica. In Garvey's *The Philosophy and Opinions of Garvey* (quoted in *BH2C*, p. 253), he said of his mother that she was "a sober and conscientious Christian, too soft and good for the time in which she lived."

After a superb elementary education, Garvey was apprenticed as a printer for his godfather during his early teens. At age 16, he had learned the trade well enough to go to Kingston and get work as the youngest foreman printer in Jamaica. While in Kingston, he printed his periodical, *Garvey's Watchman*, and his political club's newsletter, *Our Own*. In his early 20s, Garvey left Jamaica,

traveling through Central and South America and Europe, everywhere observing the exploitation of African-descended workers and the appalling living conditions of African descendants on the American and European continents. After a while, he settled down in London for a couple years, where he worked for the *Africa Times and Orient Review*, the leading pan-African journal of that time, and attended law lectures at the University of London. Increasingly, Garvey became outraged at the suffering of African people everywhere, including the people in African nations subject to European imperial rule, as well as African descendants whom the diaspora had scattered across the globe.

Before leaving London, Garvey read **Booker T. Washington**'s *Up from Slavery*, after which he was inspired to become "a race leader," destined to lead Africans everywhere to join him in uplifting his race. Within days of returning to Jamaica in 1914, he founded the pan-African organization Universal Negro Improvement and Conservation Association and African Communities League, usually called UNIA (for Universal Negro Improvement Association). UNIA's aim was to unite "all the Negro peoples of the world into one great body to establish a country and Government absolutely their own" (quoted in *BWA*, p. 566). Garvey began corresponding with Washington and embarked on a program to affirm a bond (which he called "confraternity") among Africans everywhere, aid the needy, establish education facilities like Washington's Tuskegee Institute, and improve the status of women.

Early in 1916, Garvey made a fund-raising tour to the United States, where he was able to stir a much greater following than he had in Jamaica. During this time, many African Americans were migrating from the rural South to the urban North, only to find segregated housing, job discrimination, and other forms of racism, so Garvey's message of racial pride and economic independence was welcome indeed. By 1918, Garvey moved the UNIA headquarters to Liberty Hall in Harlem, and he established UNIA branches in numerous other large African-American ghettos of the urban North. He also founded his weekly newspaper, **Negro World**, through which he communicated to followers across the nation and around the world, and through which he gave voice to many writers of the **Harlem Renaissance**. By 1919, Garvey had attracted at least a million followers (estimates range from 1 million to 11 million; the exact number of UNIA members was never certain) in North America, the West Indies, Central and South America, West Africa, and England.

At his side starting in 1914 was Amy Ashwood (1897-1969), who met him in Jamaica and helped him in founding UNIA, becoming its first general secretary, as well as a management-board member. After moving to the United States to join Garvey, she helped launch the *Negro World* newspaper. Against her family's wishes, she married Garvey on December 25, 1919, attended by her friend and maid of honor, Amy Jacques, who became their roommate, along with Amy Ashwood's brother and another man. In part because she refused to comply with Garvey's insistence that she stay at home, out of the public eye, their marriage quickly grew troubled. Early in 1920, Garvey announced their separation and tried to get their marriage annulled. Two years later, Garvey sued her in a bitterly battled divorce. About a month later, Garvey remarried, choosing a second Amy: Amy Jacques, another feminist who played key roles in UNIA and *Negro World*.

Through his speeches (delivered weekly in UNIA headquarters at Liberty Hall) and his newspaper articles, poems, and essays, he told of the "new Negro," one who was no longer servile, but rather proud of a triumphant African heritage. Garvey regaled his followers with accounts of the great achievements of African culture and of the historic contributions of African Americans. He promised, "I shall teach the black man to see beauty in himself" (quoted in *BWA*, p. 565)—and he did so. While working toward the establishment of an independent nation in Africa, Garvey urged his followers to develop an independent, self-sustained African-American economy within European-American capitalist societies. Toward these ends, he formed the Black Star Line Steamship Corporation and the Negro Factories Corporation, which employed more than 1,000 African Americans to produce dolls, tailor clothes, and run a printing press, a hotel, and various restaurants, grocery stories, and laundries.

Among Garvey's many ardent supporters were **T. Thomas Fortune**, editor of *Negro World*, and his second wife, **Amy Jacques Garvey**, associate editor of the newspaper. Not everyone in the black community supported Garvey, however. Labor leader **A. Philip Randolph** and NAACP leader **W. E. B. Du Bois** opposed Garvey's championing of segregation (which linked him to the Ku Klux Klan) and of racial purity (a troublesome goal for almost all Americans). Others criticized Garvey's haphazard, slapdash business practices, and still others found his flamboyant manner to be pompous and arrogant. In 1922, his inattention to minding his own businesses led to his being indicted for mail fraud (in connection with sales of Black Star Line stock). The next year, he (with some other UNIA members) was convicted and sentenced to five years in prison—by a judge who was an NAACP member. While he awaited imprisonment, his *Aims and Objects of Movement for Solution of Negro Problem Outlined* was published by UNIA (1924). In 1925, he started serving his sentence in a federal penitentiary in Atlanta. While he was in prison, Garvey's (second) wife Amy campaigned for his release and compiled and edited his writ-

Marcus Garvey, Jr.

ings in the *Philosophy and Opinions of Marcus Garvey, or Africa for the Africans* (vol. 1, 1923; vol. 2, 1925; vol. 3, published posthumously in 1977, with E. U. Essien-Udom). She also compiled and published two volumes of his work in *The Tragedy of White Injustice* and *Selections from the Poetic Meditations of Marcus Garvey* (both published in 1927). After Garvey had served two years in prison, his sentence was commuted by President Calvin Coolidge, and he was deported as an undesirable alien.

On returning to Jamaica in 1927, he established another newspaper, the *New Jamaican*, and a monthly magazine, *The Black Man*. Amy joined him and gave birth to his sons Marcus Jr. (in 1930) and Julius (in 1933) there. Garvey also tried to participate in the political process in Jamaica, but he ran into legal difficulties, and in 1934, he left Jamaica for England. While living in a cottage in London, he still published *The Black Man* for a few years, although he ended up dying in relative obscurity. Since his death, however, he has been much honored (with numerous roads, schools, and other buildings named after him; his likeness produced on statues, coins, and postage stamps; and his story told through songs and poetry). Ironically, despite his wide travels and his lifelong aim to establish a settlement in Africa, Garvey ended up never stepping foot on African soil.

In 1937, Garvey gave his top UNIA organizers his *Message to the People: The Course of African Philosophy*, which was published for wider circulation in 1986 (as the seventh title in "The New Marcus Garvey Library" series). Although Garvey failed in his avowed goal for UNIA and in his business dealings, he achieved great success in stirring millions of African Americans to take pride in their African heritage (e.g., motivating the Jamaican Rastafarian movement), in prompting subsequent movements to establish economic independence for African Americans (e.g., the Nation of Islam), and in inspiring many African-American writers to create poetry and prose, fiction and nonfiction reflecting a proud people with a grand heritage. The red, green, and black colors that now symbolize liberation for African peoples were originally the colors of the UNIA flag. Even today, Garvey's words continue to arouse and embolden his readers: "The time has come for the Negro to forget and cast behind him his hero worship and adoration of other races, and to start out immediately to create and emulate heroes of his own. We must canonize our own saints, create our own martyrs, and elevate to positions of fame and honor black men and women who have made their distinct contributions to our racial history. . . . We must inspire a literature and promulgate a doctrine of our own without any apologies to the powers that be" (from his "African Fundamentalism," quoted in *BH2C*, p. 257). In the 1930s, he had aptly prophesied, "I am only the forerunner of an awakened Africa that shall never go back to sleep" (quoted in *BWA*, p. 567). As he predicted in prison in 1925, "Look for me in the whirlwind or the storm, look for me all around you" (quoted in *Wikipedia*).

REFERENCES: *AANB. AAW:AAPP. BAL-1-P. BF:2000. BWA. EBLG. PGAA.* Cohassey, John, in *BB.* Engel, Bill, in *GEAAL.* King, Martha, in *EA-99.* Martin, Tony, in *BH2C.* Stein, Judith, in *CAO-03. USHC.* Waskey. Andrew J., in *ARRW-2. EB-BH-CD.* Williams, Patricia Robinson, in *B. BCE. CE. COCAAL* and *OCAAL. HD. QB. W2B. Wiki.* Resources about Amy Ashwood Garvey: //www.aaregistry.com/african_american_history/1954/Amy_Garvey_and_frontline_activist. //www.allmusic.com/cg/amg.dll?p=amg&sql=11:0zfpxqr0ld6e~T1. //www.answers.com/topic/amy-ashwood-garvey, Wikipedia: Amy Ashwood Garvey. //www.pbs.org/wgbh/amex/garvey/peopleevents/p_ashwood.html.

Gates, Jr., Henry Louis "Skip"
9/16/1950–

Scholarly literary criticism, cultural criticism, nonfiction—history, biography, autobiography/memoir; educator

Currently Harvard University's Alphonse Fletcher Professor and the Director of Harvard's W. E. B. Du Bois Institute for African and African American Research, as well as the former Chair of Harvard's Afro-American Studies Department, Gates is one of America's leading literary and cultural critics. In *Figures in Black: Words, Signs, and the Racial Self* (1987), a seminal work of literary criticism, he tells how being the first black student in

English at Cambridge, or at least the first in anyone's recollection, was all-important to him. "I had allowed myself to be on fantasies of meeting a certain challenge for 'the race,' in literature just as **W. E. B. Du Bois** had done in sociology at Heidelburg, or as **Alain Locke** had done in philosophy at Oxford," Gates (1987, p. xvi) said.

Since his days in graduate school, Gates has drawn on the extraordinarily rich body of contemporary literary theory, using it to analyze the writings of a wide range of African-American and African authors published in English between the eighteenth century and the present.

Gates grew up in Piedmont, West Virginia, a backwoods town of about 2,000 people. He spent a year at a junior college before applying to Yale. After graduating summa cum laude, he received a fellowship to Cambridge. Gates physically limped through both universities. At age 14, he had suffered a hairline fracture while playing touch football at a Methodist summer camp. His joint calcified and began to fuse over the next 15 years. Despite aspirin, ibuprofen, heating pads, and massages, Gates couldn't escape the tremendous pain. "My leg grew shorter, as the muscle atrophied and the ball of the ball and socket joint migrated into my pelvis" (Gates, 1992a, p. 633). When Gates turned 40, doctors finally agreed to replace Gates's hip, and after surgery, he ceremonially trashed his corrective shoe and began wearing matching normal pairs for the first time. He describes this experience in his essay "A Giant Step" (1992a).

While his legs were weak at Cambridge, Gates's intellectual ambition was strong: "It is somewhat embarrassing to admit this today, but I felt as if I were embarked upon a mission for all black people, especially for that group of scholars whom our people have traditionally called 'race men' or 'race women,' the intellectuals who collect, preserve, and analyze the most sublime artifacts of the black imagination" (Gates, 1987, p. xvii).

It was at Cambridge that Gates met Nigerian writer Wole Soyinka, who encouraged him to study African-American literature. Soyinka had been recently released from two-year confinement in a Nigerian prison. He was on campus to deliver a lecture series on African literature. In *Loose Canons: Notes on the Culture Wars* (1992), Gates tells the story of how African writing was not seen as a legitimate area of literary study when Soyinka had come to the university in 1973. He had been pursuing a two-year lectureship in English, but Soyinka was forced to accept an appointment in social anthropology instead. Gates contended that moving the African material to this area blatantly devalued the African work from the perspective of literary theory.

Shortly after he heard Soyinka's story, Gates asked the tutor in English at Clare College, Cambridge, why Soyinka had been treated this way. Gates told the tutor, as politely as he could, that he would very much like to write a doctoral thesis in "black literature." The tutor replied with great consternation, "Tell me sir, . . . what is black literature?" Gates said that when he responded to the tutor "with a veritable bibliography of texts written by authors who were black, [the tutor's] evident irritation informed me that I had taken as serious information what he had intended as a rhetorical question" (Gates, 1992b, p. 88).

Editor's note: Since that time, Gates has written reviews of Soyinka's work and has edited a few volumes about the Nobel-winning playwright's work, including *Wole Soyinka: A Bibliography of Primary and Secondary Sources* (1986, with James Gibbs and Ketu H. Katrak), *Wole Soyinka: Critical Perspectives Past and Present* (1997), and *The Essential Soyinka: A Reader* (1998); and he edited and introduced *In the House of Oshugbo: A Collection of Essays on Wole Soyinka* (1988, 2003).

Gates overcame this sort of suspicion, hostility, and skepticism, however, to pursue black literature at Cambridge. He eventually encountered professors there who, while professing their ignorance of the topic, worked with him on his thesis in African-American literature. Gates had to intellectually begin anew, abandoning his undergraduate training in history.

In 1977, he developed a close relationship with a professor named John Holloway. Holloway allowed Gates to experiment by letting contemporary literary theories inform his close readings of black texts. The theories came from French, Russian, Anglo-American, British, and other perspectives. Most of his later work was shaped by those experimental exercises with Holloway.

After completing his Ph.D. in English, Gates returned to Yale, this time as a professor. He has also taught English, comparative literature, and African Studies at Cornell, and he held an appointment at Duke before joining the faculty at Harvard.

Gates has a reputation as a literary archeologist. While looking at books in a Manhattan bookstore, he came across a copy of *Our Nig*. The autobiographical text was written in 1859 by **Harriet E. Wilson**, a free black woman. After investigating, Gates showed that this was the first novel published by a black person in the United States. Gates wrote the first extensive critical commentary of *Our Nig* in *Figures in Black*, along with a biography of Wilson. It was only the second time Wilson's work had been written about.

Editor's note: In 1983, Gates edited and introduced *Harriet E. Wilson, Our Nig; or, Sketches From the Life of a Free Black*. Some scholars have raised questions about Wilson's authorship and her primacy, but Gates's claims remain widely accepted in the literary community.

Gates has written extensively on the African-American vernacular. His writings also tackle topics ranging from the contentious issue of multiculturalism to the idea of race as a meaningful category in the study of literature and the shaping of critical theory. Gates won the American Book Award for *The Signifying Monkey: A Theory of Afro-American Literary Criticism* (1988, Anisfield-Wolf Book Award winner). Other publications include *Bearing Witness* (1991) and *Colored People* (1994). In 1996, he published *The Future of the Race* with **Cornel West**, who is a close colleague and professor of Afro-American studies and the philosophy of religion at Harvard. That year, Gates also wrote *Africa: The Art of a Continent.*

Editor's note: Some of the other works Gates has authored include *Colored People: A Memoir* (1994); *Speaking of Race, Speaking of Sex: Hate Speech, Civil Rights, and Civil Liberties* (1995); *Thirteen Ways of Looking at a Black Man* (1997), profiles of diverse African-American men drawn chiefly from his previously published *New Yorker* essays; *Back to Africa* (2002); *The Trials of Phillis Wheatley: America's First Black Poet and Her Encounters with the Founding Fathers* (2003); *America behind the Color Line: Dialogues with African Americans* (2004); *Finding Oprah's Roots: Finding Your Own* (2007); and *In Search of Our Roots: How 19 Extraordinary African Americans Reclaimed Their Past* (2009).

In 1981, Gates was identified by the MacArthur Foundation as one of the exceptionally talented individuals to receive a research award. He has received many other awards, including the Zora Neale Hurston Society Award for Cultural Scholarship and a Ford Foundation National Fellowship. Gates has also been awarded grants from the National Endowment for the Humanities.

Editor's note: In addition to these, Gates has been awarded more than four dozen honorary degrees and other awards, including the National Humanities Medal (1998), election to the American Academy of Arts and Letters (1999), and chair of the Pulitzer Prize Board (2005). He also serves on prominent boards such as the New York Public Library, the Council on Foreign Relations, the Aspen Institute, the Brookings Institution, the Studio Museum of Harlem, and the NAACP Legal Defense Fund. After tracing his own roots back to John Redman, a free black soldier in the Revolutionary War, he was inducted into the Sons of the American Revolution in 2006.

Gates has written numerous articles and edited a number of books. He is known as an expert on African-American-Jewish relations. Gates is the general editor of the 30-volume *Schomburg Library of Nineteenth Century Black Women Writers* (1991/ 2002). Gates is also general editor of the *Norton Anthology of African American Literature* (1997, with Nellie Y. McKay). In the text, he attempts to define the canon of African-American literature for instructors and students at any institution. Gates said that he was especially driven to complete the book so that no one could ever again use the excuse of unavailability of texts in order not to teach about writings by African Americans. The book brings together the crucially central authors who are essential for understanding the shape and shaping of the tradition. "A well marked anthology functions in the academy to define and create a tradition, as well as to define and preserve it," Gates said. "A Norton anthology opens up literary traditions as simply as opening the cover of a carefully edited and ample book" (Gates, 1992b, pp. 31-32).

REFERENCES: Gates, Henry, Louis, Jr. 1987. *Figures in Black: Words, Signs and the Racial Self* (pp. xvi, xvii). New York: Oxford University Press. ____. 1992a. "A Giant Step," in William L. Andrews et al. (Eds.), *African American Literature*. Austin, TX: Holt, Rinehart and Winston. ____. 1992b. *Loose Canons: Notes on the Culture Wars* (pp. 31-32, 88). New York: Oxford University Press. —Michael Strickland

Editor's note: Perhaps most notably, Gates and his Harvard colleague, Evelyn Brooks Higginbotham, coedited the massive eight-volume *African American National Biography* (AANB), including about 4,000 entries, published early in 2008, after many years of effort. In addition, some of the other works of general African-American literary criticism, biography, and history Gates has edited include *Black Literature and Literary Theory* (1984); *The Slave's Narrative: Texts and Contexts* (1985, with Charles T. Davis); *"Race," Writing, and Difference* (1986); *The Classic Slave Narratives* (1987); *Reading Black, Reading Feminist: A Literary Critical Anthology* (1990); *Three Classic African-American Novels* (1990); *Bearing Witness: Selections from 150 Years of African-American Autobiography* (1991); *Black Biography, 1790-1950: A Cumulative Index* (1991, with Randall K. Burkett and Nancy Hall Burkett); *The Amistad Chronology of African-American History from 1445-1990* (1993); *Dictionary of Global Culture* (1995, with (Kwame) Anthony Appiah); *Identities* (1996); *Pioneers of the Black Atlantic: Five Slave Narratives from the Enlightenment, 1772-1815* (1998, coedited); *The Civitas Anthology of African American Slave Narratives* (1999, with William L. Andrews); *Black Imagination and the Middle Passage* (1999, with Carl Pederson); *Africana: The Encyclopedia of the African and African-American Experience* (1999/2003, with Anthony Appiah); *Wonders of the African World* (1999); *Slave Narratives* (2000); *The African American Century: How Black Americans Have Shaped Our Century* (2000, with Cornel West); *Unchained Memories: Readings from the Slave Narratives* (2002); *African American Lives* (2004, with Evelyn Brooks Higginbotham); *Africana: Civil Rights: An A-to-Z Reference of the Movement That Changed America* (2004, with Anthony Appiah); and *Lincoln on Race and Slavery* (2009, with Donald Yacovone).

His edited works of particular authors include *Black Is the Color of the Cosmos: Charles T. Davis's Essays on Black Literature and Culture, 1942-1981* (1982); *W. E. B. DuBois, The Souls of Black Folk* (1989); four works by **Zora Neale Hurston**: *Their Eyes Were Watching God, Jonah's Gourd Vine, Tell My Horse,* and *Mules and Men* (all in 1990); *Langston Hughes and Zora Neale Hurston, Mule Bone: A Comedy of Negro Life* (1991, with George H. Bass); *Frederick Douglass: Autobiographies* (1994); *The Complete Stories of Zora Neale Hurston* (1995); and based on his most recent discovery, *The Bondwoman's Narrative* by Hannah Crafts (2002, 1st ed.) and *Searching for Hannah Crafts: Essays in the Bondwoman's Narrative* (2004, with Hollis Robbins). He and Anthony Appiah have also coedited a series, subtitled, *Critical Perspectives Past and Present,* with each book profiling the following authors: *Gloria Naylor, Alice Walker, Langston Hughes, Richard Wright, Toni Morrison,* and *Zora Neale Hurston* (all in 1993); *Ann Petry, Chinua Achebe, Harriet A. Jacobs, Ralph Ellison, Wole Soyinka,* and *Frederick Douglass* (all in 1997). He and Hollis Robbins coedited *The Annotated Uncle Tom's Cabin* (2007).

Gates has also turned to film and television to broaden the audience for African-American literature and culture. Projects in which he has been involved include *The Image of the Black in the Western Imagination* (1982), *From Great Zimbabwe to Kilimatinde* (1996), *The Two Nations of Black America* (1998), *Leaving Eldridge Cleaver* (1999), *Wonders of the African World* (1999, six-part series), *America Beyond the Color Line* (2004, four-part series), *African American Lives* (2006), *African American Lives 2* (2008), and *Looking for Lincoln* (2009). He has even appeared on such popular TV programs as *Jeopardy* (February 25, 2009).

He also collaborated with Anthony Appiah to create a CD-ROM of *Microsoft Encarta Africana Comprehensive Encyclopedia of Black History and Culture* (1999, 1st ed.).

REFERENCES: *AANB. AAW:PV.* Feldman, Keith, in *BCE. CE. GEAAL. W. Wiki.* Nagel, Rob, and Christine Miner Minderovic, in *BB.* Warren, Kenneth W., in *CAO-07. COCAAL.* Olney, James, in *MAC-55-88.* "The Booklist Interview: Henry Louis Gates Jr." *Booklist. 93.12* (Feb. 15, 1997) p. 972. From *Literature Resource Center.* Amazon.com. SDPL catalog.

Gayle, Jr., Addison
6/2/1932–10/3/1991
Literary criticism, essays, biographies, autobiography/memoir, poems, short stories; educator

Gayle's dedication to his literary endeavors started early, as he completed a 300-page novel by the time he finished high school and wrote numerous short stories and poems before a single work of his was published. In 1965, he married lecturer Rosalie Norwood, and the next year, he started lecturing at the City University of New York (CUNY). About that time, his works started to appear in **Hoyt Fuller**'s *Black World*. Inspired by his students, he published anthologies of literary criticism he had edited, *Black Expression: Essays by and about Black Americans in the Creative Arts* (1969); *Bondage, Freedom and Beyond: The Prose of Black America* (1970); and *The Black Aesthetic* (1971). In his introduction to *The Black Aesthetic,* he wrote, "The question for the black critic today is not how beautiful is a melody, a poem, or a novel, but how much more beautiful has the poem, the melody, play, or novel made the life of a single black man." He also authored his essay collection, *The Black Situation* (1970); his literary history, *The Way of a New World: The Black Novel in America* (1975); his three literary biographies, *Oak and Ivy: A Biography of* **Paul Laurence Dunbar** (1971), **Claude McKay**: *The Black Poet at War* (1972), and **Richard Wright**: *Ordeal of a Native Son* (1980); and his autobiography, *Wayward Child: A Personal Odyssey* (1977). Although he was occasionally a visiting lecturer or professor at other colleges and universities, CUNY offered him an intellectual home as professor and then distinguished professor until his death.

REFERENCES: *AANB. AAW:AAPP.* Donaldson, Bobby, in *COCAAL* and *OCAAL.* Morris, Paula J. K., in *BB. CAO-03.* Wallace, Earnest M., in *GEAAL. W.*

Gerima, Haile
3/4/1946–
Plays, screenplays, scripts; filmmaker, bookseller

His films include *Harvest: 3,000 Years* (1974, filmed in his native Ethiopia), *Bush Mama* (1976), the documentary *Wilmington 10-USA 10,000* (1977), *Ashes and Embers* (1982), and the documentary *After Winter:* **Sterling Brown** (1985). In his *Sankofa* (1994), a modern-day African-American model goes to notorious Elmina Castle for a photo shoot, when she's abruptly taken back in time and across the sea to a Southern plantation, where she's a house slave; when she's returned again to the present, she has gained a greater awareness of her African roots. Instead of moving to Hollywood, he has stayed near Howard University, in Washington, D.C., where he has been a professor since 1975. With the proceeds from *Sankofa,* Gerima opened Sankofa Video and Bookstore, which also housed his film-production company, Negodgwad Productions, and Mypheduh Films. Gerima's African-American wife, Shirikiana Aina, is his partner not only in marriage and in raising their five children, but also in his business ventures. After *Sankofa,* he made the documentary *Adwa: An African Victory* (1999), about a

key battle in the Ethiopians' defeat of Italian colonialism. Next, he produced *Teza* (2008), about the emotional turmoil of an Ethiopian expatriate who returns home, to find violence and despair in his homeland. It was given a Special Jury Prize at the 65th Venice Film Festival. Among his other awards and honors are two **Oscar Micheaux** Awards, two awards from the Black Filmmakers Hall of Fame, Best Cinematography Award from the Pan African Film and Television Festival, First Prize in the African Film Festival.

REFERENCES: *Wiki.* Heath, Elizabeth, in *EA-99.* Kande, Sylvie. "Look Homeward, Angel: Maroons and Mulattos in Haile Gerima's 'Sankofa.'" *Research in African Literatures. 29.2* (Summer 1998) p. 128. From *Literature Resource Center.* LaBalle, Candace, in *BB.*

Gibson, P. J. (Patricia Joann)
1952–
Plays, as well as short stories, poems; theater director, educator

By the end of the twentieth century, Gibson had written at least 26 plays, many of which have been produced in countries around the globe. Some of these include *Shameful in Your Eyes* (1971), *The Black Woman* (1971, as a one-act play; 1972, as a three-act play), companion one-act plays *Void Passage* and *Konvergence* (1973), *The Ninth Story Window* (1974), her children's play *Spida Bug* (1975), *The Zappers and the Shopping Bag Lady* (1979), *The Androgyny* (1979), her musical *Ain't Love Grand?* (1980), *Miss Ann Don't Cry No More* (1980), *Brown Silk and Magenta Sunsets* (1981), *My Mark, My Name* (1981), *Angel* (1981), *The Unveiling of Abigail* (1982), *Clean Sheets Can't Soil* (1983), *Long Time Since Yesterday* (1985/1992), and *Deep Roots* (1998), as well as her play triology, *Private Hells, Sketches in Reality* (1981), which included *You Must Die Before My Eyes as I Have Before Yours,* "*But I Feed the Pigeons*" / "*Well, I Watch the Sun,*" and *Can You Tell Me Who They Is?* Her collection *Destiny's Daughters: 9 Voices of P.J. Gibson* (2002) has been critically acclaimed and praised by such notables as **Woodie King** and **Gloria Naylor**. Her unproduced plays include *Strippa, Swing/Slide, Majorna and the Man Thief, A Man, Masculine and Glass Fist, Marie,* and *In Search of Me* (also titled *Trial*). Other literary forms she has tried include poems, short stories, and a novel. After assorted teaching and playwright-in-residence experiences, including Rutgers University, the University of California at Berkeley, and a lengthy stay at the College of New Rochelle, she arrived at her current home as Professor of English at John Hay College of Criminal Justice at the City University of New York (CUNY). Her honors and awards include a Schubert fellowship with which she earned her M.F.A. at Brandeis University, a grant from the National

Endowment for the Arts, and two Audelco Awards for playwrighting.

REFERENCES: Brown, E. Barnsley, in *OCAAL*. Kich, Martin, in *CAO-02*. *GEAAL*. //www.jjay.cuny.edu/academics/513.php. //web.jjay.cuny.edu/~english/gibson.htm. //www.post-gazette.com/magazine/19990525gibson3.asp. //www.scils.rutgers.edu/~cybers/gibson.html. //www.scils.rutgers.edu/~cybers/gibson2.html.

Giddings, Paula (Jane)
11/16/1947–
Nonfiction—history; educator, journalist, editor

Early in her career, Giddings worked as a book editor for Random House (1969-1972) and for Howard University Press (1972-1975). Since then, she served as the Paris bureau chief for Encore America and Worldwide News (1975-1979), edited the *Afro-American Review*, and she helped found and continues to edit the peer-reviewed literary journal *Meridians: Feminism, Race, Transnationalism*. After numerous itinerant professorships and fellowships, including time at Princeton and a few years at Duke University, she settled in at Smith College as Professor of Afro-American Studies in 2001.

Her work has been published in newspapers such as the *Washington Post*, *The New York Times*, and the *Philadelphia Inquirer*, in popular periodicals such as *Essence* and the *Nation* (founded by abolitionists in 1865), and in scholarly periodicals such as *Sage: A Scholarly Journal on Black Women*. She even wrote a play, *The Reunion*, which had a public reading in 1991. Her work has also been anthologized, and she has written some important books. Her first, *When and Where I Enter: The Impact of Black Women on Race and Sex in America* (1984; 2nd ed., 1996), offers a history of African-American women, using primary documents (letters, speeches, diaries) written by such celebrated women as **Ida B. Wells**, **Zora Neale Hurston**, and **Shirley Chisholm**. Nobel laureate **Toni Morrison** and others lauded the work, it was translated into several languages, and the Book-of-the-Month Club chose it as an alternate selection. In her preface to the book, she noted, "For a black woman to write about black women is at once personal and an objective undertaking." Her next book also highlighted the little-known history of African-American women, *In Search of Sisterhood: Delta Sigma Theta and the Challenge of the Black Sorority Movement* (1988/1994), about this prestigious organization of college-educated women. The topic of her next book was better known, *Ida: A Sword among Lions: Ida B. Wells and the Campaign against Lynching* (2008), called "Best Book of the Year" by the *Washington Post* and the *Chicago Tribune*, finalist for the National Book Critics Circle Award, winner of the *Los Angeles Times* Book Prize. In addition, she edited *Regarding* **Malcolm X**: *A Reader*

(1995, with **Cornel West**) and *Burning All Illusions: Writing from the Nation on Race 1866-2002* (2002).

REFERENCES: *AANB*. *EBLG*. *Wiki*. "At the Gates of the 20th Century" panel, "*Los Angeles Times* Festival of Books," 4/25/2009, on *BookTV*, aired 8/22/2009. McDermott, Jim, in *BB*. *CAO-07*. Amazon.com, barnesandnoble.com, 8/1999. Amazon.com, 3/2009. SDPL catalog.

FURTHER READING: *TAWH*.

Giovanni, Nikki (née Yolande Cornelia Giovanni, Jr.)
6/7/1943–
Poems, essays, children's poetry books

"If I could come back as anything, I'd be a bird first, but definitely the command key is my second choice."
— Nikki Giovanni

A small woman with towering talent, Nikki Giovanni is one of America's most respected poets. She has won numerous awards and is internationally renowned for her powerful poetry and prose. The author is also famous for recorded albums of her poetry, essays, and her many acclaimed books of poetry for children.

She is one among many notable African-American artists and writers who emerged from the 1960s **Black Arts Movement**, a loose coalition of African-American intellectuals who wrote politically and artistically about black rights and equality. Like much of the literature of the 1960s and 1970s, Giovanni's poetry was colorful and combative. Her early poems dealt with the black social revolution, whereas her later works are more personal, focusing on the themes of childhood, family, and love. During the civil-rights movement, her popularity soared and she became known as a poet of the people.

Born in Knoxville, Tennessee, Yolande Cornelia Giovanni, Jr., was the second child of Jones Gus, a probation officer, and Yolande Cornelia Giovanni, a social worker. In August of 1943, the family moved to the Lincoln Heights neighborhood of Cincinnati, Ohio, a place Giovanni still calls home. There, she remained in close contact with her maternal grandmother, Emma Louvenia (Luvenia Terrell) Watson, and spent summers and holidays with her in Knoxville.

Giovanni grew up in a happy, close-knit family. She was especially close to her older sister, Gary, who studied music and inherited her strong sense of racial pride from her grandmother, who instilled in her an intense admiration for and love of her race. Watson spoke her mind and was extremely intolerant of the way blacks were treated by whites. Once, her husband, John Brown, had to smuggle her and the rest of the family out of Albany, Georgia, because Emma's outspokenness had given them cause to worry that her life was in danger. The family finally settled in Knoxville, the first town they found to be large enough for them (Pellow, 1992).

At age 17, Giovanni enrolled in the all-black Fisk University in Nashville, Tennessee. There, eventually, her strong will and independent nature caused her to abide by her own rules, and she became involved in a conflict with the school's dean of women and was asked to leave (Giovanni, 1994, p. 179). Determined to receive her degree, in 1964, she returned to Fisk and became a dedicated student. She also joined the Writer's Workshop and restored Fisk's chapter of the Student Nonviolent Coordinating Committee (SNCC). As a teenager, Giovanni had been conservative in her outlook. In college, however, a roommate named Bertha succeeded in persuading Giovanni to adopt revolutionary ideals (Giovanni, 1994, p. 150).

In 1967, Giovanni graduated from Fisk with honors and a degree in history. Two years later, she gave birth to a son, Thomas Watson Giovanni. She later told *Harper's Bazaar*, "I can't imagine living without Tommy, but I can live without the revolution."

At age 25, Giovanni published her first volume of poetry, *Black Feeling, Black Talk* (1968/1969), which was later followed by *Black Judgement* (1968/1970) and *Re: Creation* (1970). These early poetry collections were extremely popular among black audiences. They also established her as a prominent new voice in black poetry and led to numerous poetry readings and speaking engagements.

Editor's note: Her other early poem collections include *Poem of Angela Yvonne Davis* (1970), *My House* (1972), *The Women and the Men* (1975), *Cotton Candy On A Rainy Day* (1978), and *Those Who Ride The Night Winds* (1983).

In 1971, Giovanni began experimenting with sound recording, which led to *Truth Is On Its Way*, her best-selling spoken-word album of that time. The album features Giovanni reading her poetry accompanied by gospel music. She remarked to *Ebony* magazine that she chose this genre because she wanted to make something her grandmother would listen to. With the success of *Truth*, Giovanni went on to make subsequent recordings, as well as audio- and videotapes in which she discussed poetry and African-American issues with famous writers such as the legendary **James Baldwin**.

Giovanni is beloved for her poetry for children and has published several volumes of children's poetry: *Spin a Soft Black Song* (1971, rev. ed. 1985), *Ego-Tripping and Other Poems for Young People* (1973), and *Vacation Time: Poems for Children* (1979/1980). In fact, the places where she grew up often provide her with subject matter for much of her poetry for children. She has a sweet, mesmerizing ability to relate to children. When Nikki Giovanni

Nikki Giovanni with her son Thomas at the P.U.S.H. Soul Picnic in New York City, March 26, 1972

speaks to kids, she hits that perfect pitch between irreverence and sincerity, humor and sensitivity, toughness and approachability (Pilson, 1997).

Her essays are popular, as well. In 1988, she published *Sacred Cows . . . And Other Edibles*, a book of essays. *Racism 101*, her provocative collection of essays about race relations was published in 1994, winning the Ohioana Library Award.

Editor's note: Her other essay collections include *Gemini: An Extended Autobiographical Statement on My First Twenty-Five Years of Being A Black Poet* (1971, nominated for the National Book Award) and *The Prosaic Soul of Nikki Giovanni* (2003). She also published two conversations, *A Dialogue: James Baldwin and Nikki Giovanni* (1973) and *A Poetic Equation: Conversations Between Nikki Giovanni and Margaret Walker* (1974).

She published a collection of her works in *The Selected Poems of Nikki Giovanni* (1996, nominated for the NAACP Image Award). Her next book, *Love Poems* (1997), a tender collection of emotionally candid poems, features 20 new poems, including "All Eyez On You" written for the late rapper, **Tupac Shakur**.

Editor's note: *Love Poems* won the 1998 NAACP Image Award. Her other poetry collections include *Blues: For All the Changes* (1999; 2000 NAACP Image Award winner), *Quilting the Black-Eyed Pea: Poems and Not Quite*

Poems (2002, NAACP Image Award winner, American Library Association's Black Caucus Award for nonfiction), *The Collected Poetry of Nikki Giovanni* (2003), *Acolytes* (2007), *The Collected Poetry of Nikki Giovanni: 1968-1998* (2007; American Book Award winner, 2008), and *Bicycles: Love Poems* (2009). She has also edited three anthologies, *Night Comes Softly: Anthology of Black Female Voices* (1970), *Appalachian Elders: A Warm Hearth Sampler* (1991), and *Shimmy Shimmy Shimmy Like My Sister Kate: Looking at the Harlem Renaissance Through Poems* (1996).

Giovanni has been honored as Woman of the Year by such magazines as *Ebony, Essence, Mademoiselle,* and *Ladies' Home Journal* and has received numerous other prestigious awards. She writes frequently for national magazines and scholarly journals and makes many stage and TV appearances. She is also an inspirational lecturer. She lives in Roanoke (Christiansburg), Virginia, and is a distinguished professor of English at Virginia Polytechnic Institute and State University in Blacksburg, Virginia (starting in 1987). Today, her work remains an international treasure.

Editor's note: Giovanni had warned college officials of her grave concerns about the compositions and behavior of her creative-writing student Cho Sueng-Hui, who later massacred 32 students at Virginia Tech in April of 2007. At the school's memorial service, her chant poem inspired listeners both there and around the world, through the international news media. The following fall semester of 2007, she served as distinguished visiting professor at her alma mater, Fisk University, before returning to Virginia Tech.

Among the myriad honors and awards she has received are a Literary Achievement Award from McDonald's, to be presented in Giovanni's name in perpetuity (starting in 1988); a Nikki Giovanni Annual Artistic Award to be presented by Delta Sigma Theta Sorority (starting in 1992); a Langston Hughes Medal for outstanding poetry from the City College of New York (1996); induction into the National Literary Hall of Fame for Writers of African Descent, at the Gwendolyn Brooks Center of Chicago State University (1998); an invitation to serve on the 2000 Poetry Panel of the National Book Awards; the first Rosa Parks Woman of Courage Award (2002); citation as one of "The Legends" by *O, the Oprah Magazine* (2004-2005); and honorary degrees from more than 20 colleges and universities.

REFERENCES: Giovanni, Nikki (1994), in *Contemporary Authors New Revision Series* (Volume 41, pp. 150, 179), Detroit: Gale Research. Pellow, Arlene Clift (1992), in Jessie Smith (Ed.), *Notable Black American Women* (p. 404), Detroit: Gale Research. Pilson, Brenda (1997), "The Reason She Applauds Reading," *Creative Classroom,* May/June, p. 31. —Brenda Pilson

Editor's note: Giovanni's sound recording of *One Ounce of Truth—The Nikki Giovanni Songs, Truth Is On Its Way* (1971) was named Best Spoken Word by the National Association of Radio and Television Announcers; her other sound recordings include *Like a Ripple on a Pond* (1973), *The Way I Feel* (1975), *Legacies—The Poetry of Nikki Giovanni—Read by Nikki Giovanni* (1976), *The Reason I Like Chocolate (and Other Children's Poems)* (1976), *Cotton Candy On A Rainy Day* (1978), *Nikki Giovanni and the New York Community Choir* (1993), *In Philadelphia* (1997), *Stealing Home: For Jack Robinson* (1997), and *The Nikki Giovanni Poetry Collection* (2002, nominated for a Best Spoken Word Grammy, 2004). She has also appeared in films and multimedia presentations, as well as on countless radio (e.g., *News & Notes,* 2005) and television (e.g., *Bill Moyers Journal,* 2009) shows.

Giovanni's other books of children's poetry include *Knoxville, Tennessee* (1994), *The Sun Is So Quiet* (1996; Ashley Bryan, illustrator; Parents' Choice Award), *The Girls in the Circle (Just for You!)* (2004; Cathy Ann Johnson, illustrator), *The Genie in The Jar* (1996; Chris Raschka, illustrator), and *Hip Hop Speaks to Children (with CD): A Celebration of Poetry with a Beat* (2008). She has edited two children's anthologies, *Grand Mothers: A Multicultural Anthology of Poems, Reminiscences, and Short Stories About the Keepers of Our Traditions* (1994) and *Grand Fathers: Reminiscences, Poems, Recipes, and Photos of the Keepers of Our Traditions* (1999). Her other children's books include her best-selling *Rosa* (2005; Bryan Collier, illustrator; awarded a Caldecott Honor, the Coretta Scott King Illustrator Award, and *Child Magazine's* Best Children's Book of the Year), *On My Journey Now: Looking at African-American History Through the Spirituals* (2007), *The Grasshopper's Song: An Aesop's Fable Revisited* (2008; Chris Raschka, illustrator), and *Lincoln and Douglass: An American Friendship* (2008; Bryan Collier, illustrator).

REFERENCES: AANB. Batman, Alex, in *APSWWII-1.* Collier, Andrea King. "A Poetic Force: Nikki Giovanni: This Powerful Poet Doesn't Shy Away from Tough Topics, and Audiences of All Ages and Colors Love Her for It." *The Writer.* 118.10 (Oct. 2005) p. 22. From *Literature Resource Center.* Fowler, Virginia C., in COCAAL. Giovanni, Nikki, and Arlene Elder. "A MELUS Interview: Nikki Giovanni." *MELUS* 9.3 (Winter 1982), pp. 61-75. Rpt. in Jeffrey W. Hunter and Timothy J. White (Eds.), *Contemporary Literary Criticism.* Giovanni, Nikki, with Claudia Tate. "An Interview in *Black Women Writers at Work.*" *Continuum.* pp. 60-78. Rpt. in Carol T. Gaffke (Ed.) (1997), *Poetry Criticism* (Vol. 19). Detroit: Gale Research. From *Literature Resource Center.* Harris, Steven R., in *A. D. GEAAL. QB. W. W2B. Wiki.* Mitchell, Mozella G., in *AAP-55-85.* Reid, Calvin. "Nikki Giovanni: Three Decades on the Edge." *Publishers Weekly.* 246.26 (June 28, 1999), p. 46. From *Literature Resource Center.* Rosenmeier, Rosamond. "Chapter 1: An Introduction to the Life of Nikki Giovanni," "Appendix: A Conversation with Nikki Giovanni," and "Author's Works," in Virginia C. Fowler.1992. *Twayne's United States Authors Series 613.* New York: Twayne Publishers. From *The Twayne Authors Series.* Amazon.com. SDPL catalog. //www.authorsontheweb.

com/features/0302-bhm/bhm-authors.asp. //www.pbs.org/moyers/ journal/02132009/profile2.html, February 13, 2009 interview on *Bill Moyers Journal* (transcript and brief biography available). Wainwright, Mary Katherine, and Ralph G. Zerbonia, in *BB. CLCS. CAO-08. LFCC-07. MWEL.*

Giscombe, C. (Cecil) S.
11/30/1950–
Poems, essays, autobiography/memoir, travel writing

Formerly a professor at Illinois State University, at Cornell University, and other universities, Giscombe now teaches at the University of California at Berkeley. A long-distance cyclist, Giscombe has deepened his love of the outdoors since moving to northern California, showing almost a missionary zeal to encourage his students outdoors, too, "So often in the woods I'm the only black person I see, unless my sister is there with me, or my daughter," Madeline Wright (with his wife, teacher and zoo curator Katharine E. Wright).

His poems, which use distinctively staccato spacing, occasional deviant spellings, and punchy punctuation, have been published in *Callaloo* and other notable periodicals, as well as collected in the volumes *Postcards* (1977), *At Large* (1989), *Here* (1994), *Inland* (2001), and *Prairie Style* (2008). Perhaps his best-known works are his collections about his possible Jamaican-Canadian ancestor John Robert Giscome: *Giscome Road, Second Section* (1994, winner of the Carl Sandburg Award), *Two Selections from Giscome Road* (1995), *Giscome Road* (1998), and *The Northernmost Road* (1997). He also edited the journal *Epoch* during the 1980s, and he edited the anthology *Mixed Blood* (2008).

He wrote his travel memoir, *Into and Out of Dislocation* (2000), as a series of linked essays. His work for children, "Archie Underground," remains unpublished, and his **Cave Canem** biography noted that his current work in progress "is a prose book about trains and train metaphors, *Railroad Sense.*" Among his numerous awards are a Fulbright Research award and a National Endowment for the Arts fellowship. In addition, his "All (Facts, Stories, Chance)" was chosen for *The Best American Poetry 1996* (Adrienne Rich, Ed.).

REFERENCES: *CAO-07. VBAAP.* //andrewkenower.typepad.com/ a_voice_box/ 2007/12/cs-giscombe—s.html. //canadianstudies. uoregon.edu/pdf/giscombe.pdf //ls.berkeley.edu/?q=node/770. //muse.jhu.edu/journals/callaloo/v024/24.3giscombe.html. //www.cave canempoets.org/pages/programs_faculty.php. //www.epoetry.org/issues/ issue1/alltext/cngis.htm. //www.goodreads.com/author/show/ 306787.C_S_Giscombe. Amazon.com. SDPL catalog.

Gladwell, Malcolm
9/3/1963–
Nonfiction books; journalist

The United Kingdom can claim Malcolm Gladwell as a native-born Brit, Canada can claim him because he was raised and educated in Ontario and his father professes civil engineering at the prestigious University of Waterloo, Jamaica can claim him as the motherland of his mother, and the United States has happily claimed him as a resident for more than two decades. After Gladwell earned his baccalaureate in history from the University of Toronto (1984), he found his way to a career in journalism at the *American Spectator* (a conservative monthly magazine), then to the world-renowned *Washington Post* (starting in 1987), at first as a business and then a science reporter and eventually as chief of its New York bureau. Once in New York, he started writing freelance articles for the *New Yorker* (starting in 1992). In 1996, Gladwell officially left the *Post* to write on the staff of the *New Yorker*. In early 2006, he also launched his blog site, //www.gladwell.com, where readers can find not only his blog, but also an archive of his *New Yorker* articles and information on some of his books.

Gladwell's typical approach to a subject is to zero in on one or more particular examples of individuals, then to zoom out and observe how the particular relates to the universal—or at least to his much broader big-picture idea or theme. This approach has not only served him well in his articles, but also in his three *The New York Times* (NYT) bestsellers: *The Tipping Point: How Little Things Can Make a Big Difference* (2002), which was on the *NYT* bestseller list for more than half a year; *Blink: The Power of Thinking without Thinking* (2004), which stayed on the *NYT* list for more than a year; and *Outliers: The Story of Success* (2008), which was still at number TWO on the *NYT* list for Hardcover Fiction on Thursday, June 4, 2009, more than six months after its release.

REFERENCES: *CAO-06. Wiki.* Curry, Jennifer, in *AANB.* Interview, *Charlie Rose*, December 20, 2008. //gladwell.typepad.com/ gladwellcom/. //www.biblio.com/author_biographies/2893843/ Malcolm_Gladwell.html. //www.gladwell.com/bio.html. //www.gladwell.com/blink/index.html. //www.gladwell.com/outliers/ index.html. //www.gladwell.com/tippingpoint/index.html. Amazon.com.

Goines, Donald (occasional pseudonym: "Al C. Clark")
12/15/1937–10/21/1974
Novels; convicted criminal

Goines wrote authoritatively about the life of crime and drug use in the streets of Detroit. A high-school dropout, he had lied about his age to join the U.S. Air

Force. While serving in Japan during the Korean War, Goines became addicted to heroin, and he remained addicted for the rest of his short life (except while he was in prison). Arrested 15 times, Goines was in prison six-and-a-half years, serving seven different prison sentences for crimes he committed to support his addiction. While in prison, Goines started writing fiction. At first, he tried his hand at westerns and other novels, but he soon found these genres unsuitable. After reading **Ice-berg Slim**'s *Trick Baby,* however, he turned to writing his novels about criminals and drug users in the ghettos of Detroit.

The first novel he wrote, *Whoreson: The Story of a Ghetto Pimp* (1972) was his most autobiographical work and the only one he wrote in the first person. Although *Whoreson* was the first novel he wrote, the first of his novels to be published was *Dopefiend: The Story of a Black Junkie* (1971), about the power of a drug dealer to rule the life of a drug user. In his next novel, *Black Gangster* (1972), he showed how American society makes it difficult for African-American males to succeed in legitimate business endeavors and revealed the temptations to turn to illegal ones instead. His next books were *Black Girl Lost* (originally published in 1973, reprinted in 1995), his only book written from a woman's point of view; *Street Players* (1973/1996); and *White Man's Justice, Black Man's Grief* (1973/1988), about the injustices of the bail-bond system in a racist society.

When he wrote a series of books centered on his revolutionary leader Kenyatta, who fought both black criminals and white police officers, Goines's publisher (Holloway House) asked him to use a pseudonym, which he did, choosing his friend's name, Al C. Clark. These books included *Crime Partners* (1974/1995), *Cry Revenge* (1974/1996), *Death List* (1974/1996), *Kenyatta's Escape* (1974/1992), and *Kenyatta's Last Hit* (published posthumously in 1975, reprinted in 1998). Under his own name, he also wrote *Daddy Cool* 1974/1996), *Eldorado Red* (1974/1992), *Never Die Alone* (1974/1995), *Swamp Man* (1974/1995), and his last novel, *Inner City Hoodlum* (posthumously published 1975, reprinted in 1992). Goines's life was cut short when he and his live-in lover, Shirley Sailor, were both shot and killed at home, leaving their two daughters and his seven other children orphans. Unlike the murders in his novels, the murderer(s) and the motives remain a mystery. His books have never gone out of print, and in fact, all of his works were reprinted as mass-market paperbacks in the 1990s, more than two decades after his death. Goines's publisher once claimed that he was the best-selling African-American author, and the fact that his books are still being reprinted for a mass market speaks volumes about his continuing popularity. In addition, rappers such as Ludacris and **Tupac Shakur** have paid him tribute.

REFERENCES: *EBLG.* Goode, Greg, in *AAFW-55-84. SJGCMW.* //archive.salon.com/march97/noir2970307.html. Loomis, Craig, in *GEAAL.* Manheim, James M., in *BB. CAO-04.* Matthews, Valerie N., in *COCAAL* and *OCAAL. Wiki.* Amazon.com, 7/1999.

Goldberg, Whoopi (née Caryn Johnson)
11/13/1949 or 1950 or 1955–
Spoken word—humor, comic sketches, autobiography/memoir, children's books; actor

Young Caryn was bright but dyslexic, so she had difficulties in school, but she excelled as a performer. A native of New York City, she had been a child actor (1958-1960) and had acted on Broadway in various plays. In 1974, she moved to California, where she was a founding member of the San Diego Repertory Theatre and joined Spontaneous Combustion, an improvisational comedy troupe.

Acting jobs for an African-American woman were difficult to find, however, and she increasingly worked on developing her own repertoire as an improvisational comedian. Over time, she developed a series of distinct characters, through whom she offered her distinctively refreshing insights into contemporary life. In 1983-1984, she had developed her character monologues into a one-woman show, titled *The Spook Show,* and she took it on tour throughout the United States and Europe. Celebrated producer-director Mike Nichols saw her show in New York and got it moved to Broadway, where she expanded it and renamed it *Whoopi Goldberg* (1984-1985), where it won the Drama Desk Award for Best Solo Performance and a Theatre World Award, as well as a Grammy for the recording of it. Between the time Nichols saw her show and the time it opened on Broadway, Goldberg won a Bay Area Theatre Award for her show *Moms,* her one-woman play (cowritten with Ellen Sebastian) about deceased comedian Moms Mabley.

In 1985, Stephen Spielberg saw her show and invited her to star in *The Color Purple,* based on **Alice Walker**'s novel. For her work, Goldberg garnered a best-actress Academy Award nomination, a Golden Globe award, and an NAACP Image Award. Through the rest of the 1980s and the 1990s, Goldberg performed and starred in dozens of films, some light (e.g., *Jumpin' Jack Flash,* 1986; two *Sister Act* movies, 1992, 1993), some serious (e.g., as a housekeeper struggling to get by in the segregated South of the 1950s, *The Long Walk Home,* 1990; as **Myrlie Evers** in *Ghosts of Mississippi,* 1996). For a more thorough listing of her 100-plus film projects, see //www.answers.com/topic/whoopi-goldberg, "Filmography" and "Black Biography," as well as //en.wikipedia.org/wiki/Whoopi_Goldberg.

In addition to her big-screen work, she has also performed on the small-screen, starring in a short-lived television program based on the film *Bagdad Cafe*, playing a recurring role as a humanoid bartender on *Star Trek: The Next Generation*, as the middle square on *Hollywood Squares*, in her sitcom *Whoopi* (2003), in her *Littleburg* preschool specials for Nickelodeon (2004), and now as moderator and cohost of daytime television's *The View* since 2007. Before she started at the *View*, she had hosted her own national radio show, *Wake Up with Whoopi*, starting in 2006.

Although her successful acting career has now overshadowed her career as a comedian, Goldberg won the Mark Twain Prize for American Humor in 2001 and a Grammy for best comedy album in 1985. She has had three HBO specials and continues to perform for charitable events, such as *Comedy Relief* (which she, Billy Crystal, and Robin Williams cofounded). She was also the first African American to host the Academy Awards (1994; also 1996, 1999, 2002), as well as the first female to host the show without a cohost. In addition to her 1985 Academy Award nomination, she has won an Academy Award (the "Oscar," 1990, for best-supporting actress, the second African-American woman to receive it), an Emmy (daytime Emmy, 2002; Emmy nominations, 1986, 1991, 1996; daytime Emmy nomination, 1999), Golden Globes (Best Actress, 1986; Best Supporting Actress, 1991; nominations, 1986, 1993, 1996), a Gracie Allen Award (2003), a Hans Christian Andersen Award (1987), a Muse Award (2003), five Nickelodeon Kids' Choice Awards as Favorite Movie Actress (1988-1997), seven NAACP Image Awards (1988-2004), six People's Choice Awards, and a Tony Award (2002); only a dozen other people have won an Emmy, a Grammy, an Oscar, and a Tony, not to mention her other acting awards and numerous humanitarian awards. In 2001, she was given a star on the Hollywood Walk of Fame.

Until now, her charming, vibrant live performances have upstaged her books, including her memoir *Book* (1997), some coauthored recipe books (*A Taste of Africa: With Over One Hundred Traditional African Recipes Adapted for the Modern Cook*, 1994; *Alaska Roadhouse Recipes: Memorable Recipes from Roadhouses, Lodges, Bed and Breakfasts, Cafes, Restaurants and Campgrounds along the Highways and Byways*, 1999), and her preface to *Breaking the Walls of Silence: AIDS and Women in a New York State Maximum-Security Prison* (1998). A mother and a grandmother at an early age, she has also written some children's books. Her first, *Alice*, was an urban take on *Alice in Wonderland*, 1992. Her next three are the first of four anticipated children's books, *Whoopi's Big Book of Manners* (2006; Olo, illustrator), *Sugar Plum Ballerinas #1: Plum Fantastic* (2008, with Deborah Underwood; Maryn Roos, illustrator), and *Sugar Plum Ballerinas #2: Toeshoe Trouble* (2009; Maryn Roos, illustrator). From her first (brief) marriage, Goldberg has a daughter,

Alexandrea Martin, and three grandchildren, including an adult granddaughter, Amarah Skye, who shares her grandmother's November 13 birthdate.

REFERENCES: *AANB*. Bennett, Eric, in *EA-99*. Cain, Joy Duckett, in *GEAAL*. Nagel, Rob, and Christine Miner Minderovic, in *BB*. *CAO-08*. *G-97*. Simmons, Simmona E., in *BH2C*. Thompson, Kathleen, in *A*. *Act*. *B*. *BWA:AHE*. *D*. *F*. *QB*. *W2B*. *Wiki*. //www.acme webpages.com/whoopi/bio.htm. //www.amfar.org/spotlight/article. aspx?id=4420. //www.kennedy-center.org/calendar/index.cfm?fuse action=showIndividual&entitY_id=3951&source_type=A. //www. pbs.org/weta/onstage/twain2001/bios/whoopi.html. //www.scils.rutgers. edu/~cybers/goldberg2.html.

Golden, Marita
4/28/1950–
Autobiography/memoir, novels, anthologies, poems; educator

At age 29, Golden started writing her first memoir, *Migrations of the Heart: A Personal Journey* (1983; subtitled *An Autobiography*, paperback, 2005). When asked, she told *Washington Post* reporter Jacqueline Trescott, "What I wanted to do was write a book that would take my life and shape it into an artifact that could inform and possibly inspire" (quoted in *CAO-07, Contemporary Authors Online*). A little more than a decade later, she published *Saving Our Sons: Raising Black Children in a Turbulent World* (1994), based on her journal of her experiences raising her son, Michael Kayode. A few years later, she wrote *A Miracle Every Day: Triumph and Transformation in the Lives of Single Mothers* (1999). Her next memoir was *Don't Play in the Sun: One Woman's Journey Through the Color Complex* (2004).

Meanwhile, she started publishing her novels: *A Woman's Place* (1986), *Long Distance Life* (1989), *And Do Remember Me* (1992), *The Edge of Heaven* (1997), and *After: A Novel* (2005), which won the Award for Fiction from the American Library Association's Black Caucus (2007). She has also edited the anthologies *Wild Women Don't Wear No Blues: Black Women Writers on Love, Men, and Sex* (1993) and *It's All Love: Black Writers on Soul Mates, Family and Friends* (2009), and she coedited *Skin Deep: Black Women and White Women Write about Race* (1995, with Susan Richards Shreve) and *Gumbo: A Celebration of African-American Writing* (2002, with **E. Lynn Harris**). She also contributes poetry and other writings to periodicals and to anthologies.

In 1990, she funded and launched the **Zora Neale Hurston/Richard Wright** Foundation, over which she now presides and serves as CEO. In addition to honoring other writers, she has received many honors herself. Probably the most prestigious award she has received was being inducted into the International Literary Hall of Fame of Writers of African Descent by the Gwendolyn Brooks Center at Chicago

State University. She has also taught at universities from Lagos, Nigeria, to Roxbury, Massachusetts.

REFERENCES: Brennan, Carol, in *BB. CAO-07.* Browne, Phiefer L., in *COCAAL* and *OCAAL.* Lindsay, Elizabeth Blakesley, in *GEAAL.* //en.wikipedia.org/wiki/Marita_Golden. Amazon.com. "African-Americans in the Publishing Industry," Book TV, C-SPAN2, 9/25/1999.

Gomez, Jewelle
9/11/1948–
Poems, novels, short stories, essays; editor, educator, executive

Raised from ages 2 to 22 years by her African-American and Native-American great-grandmother, Gracias Archelina Sportsman Morandus, Jewelle has always appreciated the "intellectual curiosity and graciousness that no amount of education could have created. [My great-grandmother] formed the basis of much of my intellectual yearnings. I wanted a book that would celebrate the life of people like her and that would still be read by people like her" (quoted in GLRO—*Contemporary Authors Online,* 2002). She even used the name Grace Publications to self-publish her first two volumes of poetry, *The Lipstick Papers* (1980) and *Flamingoes and Bears* (1987). In addition, the works of **Ntozake Shange**, **Audre Lorde**, **Lorraine Hansberry**, and other African-American women and men inspired Gomez to write about her own experiences and about those of other African-American women, especially but not exclusively women who share her lesbian identity. Her more recent work has also explored her Ioway and Wampanoag Native American heritage.

Gomez's next poetry collection was *Oral Tradition: Selected Poems Old and New* (1995), published by Firebrand Books. Firebrand also published her collection *Forty-three Septembers: Essays* (1993), as well as her novel *The Gilda Stories: A Novel* (1991, winner of two Lambda literary awards—for fiction and for science fiction), about a conscientious feminist lesbian African-American vampire; and her story collection *Don't Explain: Short Fiction* (1998), which includes another Gilda story. In addition, Urban Bush Women Company commissioned her to adapt her Gilda stories, resulting in the stage play *Bones and Ash: A Gilda Story,* which toured the United States in 1996. In 2001, Quality Paperback Book published the novel and the play, *Bones and Ash: A Gilda Story.* Gomez is currently writing another novel, "a comedy ... about a group of black student activists from the '60s at their 30th anniversary reunion, and it is about how they maintain a level of activism when they are middle aged and middle class" (quoted in GLRO, *It's in Her Blood,* 2004).

Gomez also coedited the anthologies *Swords of the Rainbow* (1996, with Eric Garber) and *Best Lesbian Erotica 1997* (with Tristan Taormino), and she participated in creating *Over the Rainbow: Lesbian and Gay Politics in America Since Stonewall* (1995, with David Deitcher and others). Her own works have been widely anthologized and published in various periodicals, too. She has also worked as a poetry editor for *Essence* magazine, an instructor at Hunter college, and executive director of The Poetry Center and American Poetry Archives at San Francisco State University. She has been the director of the Cultural Equity Grants Program of the San Francisco Arts Commission since 2001. In 2008, she and her long-time partner Diane Sabin were involved in California's all-too-brief experiment with gay marriage, which ended—for now—with the passage of "Proposition Hate [8]." She once noted, "What do I hope to achieve by writing? Changing the world!" (quoted in GLRO, 2002). Good idea!

REFERENCES: *AAW:PV.* Maguire, Katia. "It's in Her Blood: Jewelle Gomez Talks about Activism, Feminist Playwriting, and a Kinder, Gentler Vampirism." *Iris: A Journal About Women. .49* (Fall-Winter 2004) p. 18. From *Literature Resource Center.* //en.wikipedia.org/wiki/ Jewelle_gomez. Mitchell, Keith B., in *GEAAL.* Sanchez, Brenna, in *BB. CAO-02.* Ricketts, Wendell, in //www.glbtq.com/literature/ gomez_j.html. **Shockley, Ann Allen,** in *COCAAL* and *OCAAL. Wiki.* Amazon.com.

Gordone, Charles (né Charles Edward Fleming)
10/12/1925–11/16/1995
Plays, screenplays; educator, actor, director

A native of the Midwest, Gordone has a mixed racial heritage, including French-, Irish-, African-American, and Native-American ancestry. He felt accepted by neither the whites who dominated his hometown nor the blacks whom he knew there. Still, he was an outstanding student and athlete and started at UCLA before leaving school to serve in the air force. After the military, he studied music at L.A. City College, then earned a B.A. in drama from the state college in Los Angeles (1952). With his diploma in hand, he moved to New York City, where he waited on customers in a Greenwich Village bar, while trying to make his way in the theater. For a time, he even managed his own theater, the Vantage, in Queens.

Meanwhile, Gordone was also writing plays. His *No Place to Be Somebody* (1969) was set in a bar similar to the Greenwich Village bar he had tended. That Broadway production of the play earned him a 1970 Pulitzer Prize for drama, making him the first African American to win this prize; it also garnered him a Drama Desk Award, New York and Los Angeles Critics Circle awards, and a Vernon Rice Award. Gordone's other dramas include

Chumpanzee (1970), *Gordone Is a Mutha* (1970), *Willy Bignigga* (1970), *Baba Chops* (1975), *The Last Chord* (1976), *Anabiosis* (1979), and two incomplete works: "Roan Brown and Cherry" and "Ghost Riders." He adapted *A Little More Light Around the Place* (from a Sidney Easton novel, 1964), *Mamzel Jolie* (from Strindberg's *Miss Julie*, 1982), and *The W.A.S.P.* (from the Julius Horwitz novel). His screenplays include *Heart and Soul* (1986) and *Under the Boardwalk* (1989; play, 1979).

His dramas also earned him awards from the American Academy of Arts and Letters, the National Institute of Arts and Letters, and the NAACP, as well as a fellowship from the National Endowment for the Arts and a D. H. Lawrence fellowship. In addition to his drama prizes, he received a Best Actor Obie for his 1953 performance in *Of Mice and Men*. His death widowed Susan Kouyomjian (married 1987; met in 1981), but he had previously been married to Juanita Barton (in 1947; divorced), had a long relationship with Jeanne Warner (1959-1973), and had four children and nine grandchildren. As a child, Gordone had been captivated by cowboys and westerns, and in the mid-1980s, he and his wife Susan ventured west. Cowboy poetry and the West captivated him, and they settled down. In 1987, Texas A&M University named him a distinguished lecturer, and he taught English and theater there until he died.

REFERENCES: *AANB*. Decker, Ed, in *BB*. *CAO*. *CAO-04*. *CLCS*. Fisler, Ben, in *GEAAL*. Gordone. Charles. "I Am a Black Playwright, But." *The New York Times*, p. D1. Rpt. in Lawrence J. Trudeau (Ed.) (1998), *Drama Criticism* (Vol. 8). Detroit: Gale Research. From *Literature Resource Center*. Leonard, Charles, in *AA*. *COCAAL* and *OCAAL*. *W. Wiki*. Pogrebin, Robin. "Charles Gordone Is Dead at 70; Won a Pulitzer for His First Play." *The New York Times*, p. 51. Rpt. in *CLCS*. Detroit: Gale, p. 51. From *Literature Resource Center*. Ross, Jean W., in *T-CAD-1st*. Smith, Susan Harris, in *EB-98*. "An Interview with Charles Gordone." In Philip C. Kolin and Colby H. Kullman (Eds.) (1996), *Speaking on Stage: Interviews with Contemporary American Playwrights*. University of Alabama Press. Rpt. in Lawrence J. Trudeau (Ed.) (1998), *Drama Criticism* (Vol. 8, pp. 167-175). Detroit: Gale Research. From *Literature Resource Center*. //en.wikipedia.org/wiki/Charles_Gordone.

Graham, Lorenz (Bell)
1/27/1902–9/11/1989
Children's and juvenile literature, novels, short stories, folklore, comic-book adaptations; educator, missionary, social worker

A former missionary, Graham showed missionary zeal in creating juvenile literature portraying authentic African-American children, youths, and adults in positive ways. Long before his first children's book was published, however, he and his wife, Ruth Morris (married, 1929), had five children of their own: Lorenz Jr., Jean, Joyce, Ruth, and Charles. It took Graham 15 years to find a publisher for his first story collection, *How God Fix Jonah* (1946), which included 21 biblical stories, related in West African speech patterns. A family friend, **W. E. B. Du Bois**, wrote the book's introduction. Five years later, Du Bois married Graham's older sister, **Shirley Graham Du Bois**, who had taught Lorenz to read before he entered school.

While teaching in Liberia, Graham had encouraged his students to become health-care workers. Two decades later, in Virginia, he sought treatment for malaria, and he was treated by Dr. Momolu Tugbah, one of his former students. Graham borrowed Momolu's name to create two books of coming-of-age stories: *Tales of Momolu* (1946) and *I, Momolu* (1966). To put food on his table, he wrote story adaptations of *The Story of Jesus* (1955) and *The Ten Commandments* (1956), Shakespeare's *Macbeth* (1955), Clark's *The Ox-Bow Incident* (1955), and Wells's *The Time Machine* (1955) for Classics Illustrated comic books. He also wrote dozens of short stories that were anthologized in textbooks by Houghton Mifflin (*Directions 1, 2, 3*, and *4*, 1972) and by the Los Angeles Public Schools (*Happenings* and *Voices of Youth*, 1965).

Meanwhile, Graham continued writing novels for juveniles ("young adults"). In his popular four-volume *South Town* series (*South Town*, 1958/2003; *North Town*, 1965/2003; *Whose Town?* 1969/2003; *Return to South Town*, 1976/2003), a young man strives to become a physician, while struggling against racist oppression and despite sometimes encountering violence. At first, he had trouble finding a publisher again, though the books earned him the Charles W. Follet Award and the Child Study of America Award in 1959, the Book World First Place Award in 1969, and the *Boston Globe-Horn Book* and Children's Book Showcase awards in 1976. Some of his earlier stories were later illustrated and published separately, such as *Every Man Heart Lay Down* (1970; Colleen Browning, illustrator), *A Road Down in the Sea* (1970; Gregorio Prestopino, illustrator), *David He No Fear* (1971; Ann Grifalconi, illustrator), *God Wash the World and Start Again* (1971; Clare Romano Ross, illustrator), and *Hongry Catch the Foolish Boy* (1973; James Brown, illustrator), all originally in *How God Fix Jonah*; and *Song of the Boat* (1975; **Leo and Diane Dillon**, illustrators), originally in *Tales of Momolu*. In 1972, he published a quartet of novelettes for teens: *Carolina Cracker*, *Detention Center*, *Stolen Car*, and *Runaway*. He also published two biographies, *John Brown's Raid: A Picture History of the Attack on Harpers Ferry* (1971) and *John Brown: A Cry for Freedom* (1980).

REFERENCES: *A*. *CAO-03*. *CBC*. *Q*. Alic, Margaret, in *BB*. Kich, Martin in *GEAAL*. Williams, Kim D. Hester, in *COCAAL* and *OCAAL*. Williams, Ora, in *AAW-40-55*. //www.ala.org/ala/emiert/corettascottkingbookaward/cskpastwinners/alphabeticallist/cskalphabetical.cfm#au.

Graham, Shirley (Lola) *See* Du Bois, Shirley Graham

Granville, Evelyn (née Boyd)
5/1/1924–
Nonfiction—math; educator

In addition to her dissertation and her other scholarly publications, Granville coauthored *Theory and Application of Mathematics for Teachers* (1975, with Jason Frand), a textbook widely used in colleges. She is one of the first three African-American woman to receive a doctorate in mathematics in the United States. She taught at the California State University at Los Angeles from 1967 until she retired in 1984, then she moved to Tyler, Texas, where she later became a mathematics professor at the University of Texas, once again focusing on mathematics education. In 1989, Smith College awarded Granville an honorary doctorate in mathematics, the first African-American woman to receive such an honor. In 1999, she became one of three African-American women honored by the National Academy of Science.

REFERENCES: *AANB. BAAW.* Kenschaft, Patricia Clark, in *B. BB. BWA:AHE. CAO-07. Wiki.* //en.wikipedia.org/wiki/Evelyn_Boyd_Granville. —Tonya Bolden

Greaves, "Bill" (né William Garfield Greaves)
10/8/1926–
Film scripts; dancer, actor, editor, film director and producer

According to *BB*, Greaves has "produced more than 200 documentary films" about key African-Americans personages. The *AANB* says, "Since 1968 the prolific Greaves has written, produced, edited, and directed more than 175 films, ranging from historical documentaries to avant-garde and commercial feature films." One of his four feature films was Richard Pryor's *Bustin' Loose* (1980), of which he was executive producer. Asked why he has focused on documentaries, Greaves has said he does so "because of their role in consciousness-raising and as an advocacy instrument, . . . They also tend to have a longer shelf life" (quoted in *BB*).

Before 1968, Greaves was a dancer (1940s), an actor on stage and screen (1943-1949), and a member of the then-new Actors Studio (1948)-founded by Lee Strasberg, with classmates Marlon Brando, Anthony Quinn, and others. Years later, Greaves occasionally offered classes at the Actors Studio (1969-1982). Despite his acting talents, he became frustrated by the lack of suitable roles for African Americans, so he studied film under Louis DeRochemont at the Film Institute of the

City College of New York (c. 1950-1952). Unable to get his start as a U.S. filmmaker, Greaves moved to Canada, where he was involved in writing, editing, directing, or assistant directing more than 80 films for Canada's National Film Board (1952-1960). Next, he worked as a public information officer for the United Nations' International Civil Aviation Organization in Montreal (1960-1962). In 1963, he returned to the United States, where he made three films for UN-TV (United Nations television). He then founded his own William Greaves Productions (in 1964) and created additional films.

From 1968 through 1970, he wrote, hosted, and produced *Black Journal*, an Emmy Award-winning series offering cultural and political commentary, as well as news relevant to the African-American community. Greaves's *Symbiopsychotaxiplasm: Take One* (1967) may have been too far ahead of its time, with its sophisticated cinema verité, innovative camera techniques, and ironically humorous improvisational narration. Seen by very few, it was nonetheless critically acclaimed and eventually was aired occasionally at film festivals (starting in the 1990s) and on U.S. cable channels (starting in 2002). Actor Steve Buscemi helped to promote *Take One,* and he appeared in Greaves's sequel, *Symbiopsychotaxiplasm: Take Two* (2005).

Among Greaves's 80-plus national and international awards are the aforementioned Emmy, four Emmy nominations, a 2004 Career Achievement Award from the International Documentary Association, and one of the first Dusa Awards from the Actors Studio (1980).

REFERENCES: *CAO-06. Wiki.* Natambu, Kofi, in *AANB.* Sanchez, Brenna, in *BB.*

Green, J. (Jacob) D.
?/1813–?
Autobiography/memoir, slave narrative

Green's 43-page fugitive-slave narrative is *Narrative of the Life of J. D. Green, a Runaway Slave from Kentucky, Containing an Account of His Three Escapes in 1839, 1846, 1848* (1864), which candidly describes his three attempts at escape, the last of which proved successful, due to his clever trickery. At the time, 8,000 copies were printed. In his narrative, he revealed not only that he had outwitted slaveholders, but on more than one occasion, he also used deception to avoid his own punishment, resulting in the punishment of innocent fellow slaves. Yolanda Pierce noted that his revelations of disreputable behavior differ sharply from the typical slave narrative, "Green is everything that the slave narrator is not supposed to be: dishonest, dishonorable, prideful, and selfish. . . . We want to like him, but we cannot. We want to trust him, but we do not. We want to pity him, but we will not. In this subversive slave narrative, the reader is put into the position of having to work, having to think."

REFERENCES: *AANB*. *NYPL-AADR*. Andrews, William L., in *COCAAL* and *OCAAL*. Pierce, Yolanda. "The Narrative of the Life of J. D. Green, a Runaway Slave: Some New Thoughts on an Old Form." *ANQ*. 14.4 (Fall 2001) p. 15. From *Literature Resource Center*. //docsouth.unc.edu/neh/greenjd/menu.html. //infomotions.com/ etexts/gutenberg/dirs/1/5/1/2/15128/15128.htm.

Greenfield, Eloise
5/17/1929–
Poems, children's books, juvenile biography, autobiographies/memoirs

This versatile writer has produced several famous, critically acclaimed, award-winning books for children and has compiled an extensive, honored list of picture books, biographies, essays, collections of poetry, and novels to her name.

Among the prestigious awards she has earned is the Carter G. Woodson Award for her biography, *Rosa Parks* (1973). *Paul Robeson* (1975) won the Jane Addams Children's Book Award. Three of her picture books received major citations: *She Come Bringing Me That Little Baby Girl* (1974) won the Irma Simonton Black Award, *Africa Dream* (1977) won the **Coretta Scott King** Award, and *Me and Neesie* was an American Library Association Notable Book.

Greenfield is a master poet. Her verse collections include *Honey I Love* (1978), *Under the Sunday Tree* (1988), and *Nathaniel Talking* (1988). The poems in *Nathaniel Talking* celebrate the life of an African-American boy who shows the deep, gentle, and joyful feelings to which all children relate. Greenfield's recording of *Honey I Love* has been widely praised by critics. Her first attempt at poetry, the book was twice named a Notable Book by the American Library Association and is the most popular of all Greenfield's books.

Greenfield was born in Parmele, North Carolina, at the beginning of the Great Depression. When she was four months old, her family moved to Washington, D.C. Her father had gone ahead a month earlier, looking for work. Once he found a job, he sent for Greenfield, her mother, and her brother, and she has lived there ever since.

Greenfield believes that during her early years, when she loved the words that she read, writing was being stored (Greenfield, 1983, p. 137). She dreaded writing but loved the sounds and rhythms of words while reading. Greenfield even liked strange things about language, such as homonyms and silent letters. The future author also grew fond of books and movies. It was by channeling her love of words to love for the craft of writing that

Greenfield went on to become one of the most renowned modern children's authors.

The path to this high level of artistry was not easy, but the strife is what inspired Greenfield the most. Washington, D.C., was segregated when Greenfield grew up, and she faced racist treatment on a regular basis. While her parents explained that the rude people were ignorant, the experience of oppression for being African American engendered in the author a serious commitment to uplift her community. Greenfield (1980, p. 143) later described how she educated herself in her poor surroundings:

Until I was 14, there was no library within close walking distance of our house, so every few weeks my father would take us in the car to the nearest one to get a supply of books. Finally, though, a branch of the public library was opened in the basement of a nearby apartment building. For the next few years, I practically lived there, and I worked there part-time during the two years that I was in college.

Later on, on her way to becoming an outstanding prose artist and poet, she attended Miner Teacher's College.

Part of Greenfield's overall inspiration came from music, which is still very important in her life. Greenfield took piano lessons and sang in her school's glee club. Early on, her only goal was to be the teacher in charge of plays and singing. Greenfield abandoned that limited career track as she grew into adulthood. In her early twenties, she began a search for satisfying work, which she later found in writing. The craft combined her enjoyment of sounds and rhythms with her interest in story and words. In a May 23, 1975 speech to the International Reading Association, she talked of this connection:

If you love home and you love music and you love words, the miracle is that the poet chose those words and put them together in that order, and it is something to shout about. I [feel] like the Southern Black preachers who, in reciting from the Scriptures, would suddenly be surprised by an old, familiar phrase and would repeat it over to savor and to celebrate this miracle of words.

Greenfield's bountiful spirit led her to make the change to a writing life in the 1960s, when she was married and raising two children while holding a full-time civil-service job. Her husband, Robert, was a Procurement Specialist for the U.S. Department of the Navy. Attention to him and to their children, Monica and Steve, was her priority. Nonetheless, Greenfield's second passion continued to emerge. She believed that there were far too few books that told the truth about African Americans.

Bored with her job as a clerk typist for the government, Greenfield decided to write three stories. If none of them sold, she would give up writing and try something else. She received three rejection slips and thought she had no writing talent. During this time, Greenfield wrote in solitude, nervously avoiding discussion of her work with other writers. Eventually, she began to believe that talent must have direction. Greenfield poured herself into books about the craft, sought the ideas of other writers, and realized that she needed a knowledge of techniques in order to utilize talent. Over the next several years, she read and spoke with many people about writing.

Greenfield's first publication was a poem that appeared on the editorial page of the *Hartford Times*. She then began to publish stories in the **Negro Digest**. Greenfield wrote one or two stories a year until she began writing for children. As an influential writer, she has also contributed to *Ebony Jr.!*, *Ms.*, *The Horn Book Magazine*, and the *Interracial Books for Children Bulletin*.

In 1990, Greenfield received the Recognition of Merit Award presented by the George G. Stone Center for Children's Books in Claremont, California. Many other organizations have officially praised her, including the Council on Interracial Books for Children, the District of Columbia Association of School Librarians, and Celebrations in Learning.

Greenfield's work is shared and loved in schools and homes across the country. Greenfield has often found time to work with other writers. She headed the Adult Fiction and Children's Literature divisions of the D.C. Black Writer's Workshop. The group, which no longer exists, encouraged the writing and publishing of African-American literature. She does most of her workshops in the D.C. area, but travels also, sometimes giving free workshops on the writing of African-American literature for children.

Greenfield is now a member of the African American Writers Guild. She was awarded grants from the D.C. Commission on the Arts and Humanities, with whom she has taught creative writing to elementary and junior high students. Greenfield believes that the value of a book comes from its application. In keeping with this philosophy, she has taped her works for the blind and visits schools regularly. Greenfield told the *Washington Post* (Trescott, 1976) that "seeing the reaction to the words and the realism and respect that you have touched makes you feel like continuing."

REFERENCES: Greenfield, Eloise (1983), in Sally Holtze (Ed.), *Fifth Book of Junior Authors and Illustrators* (p. 137), New York: W.H. Wilson. _____. (1980), in *Something about the Author* (Vol. 19, p. 143), Detroit: Gale Research. _____. (1975, May 23), "Something to Shout About," speech given at the International Reading Association—Children's Book Council Preconvention Institute: Books Open Minds, in New York, NY. Trescott, Jacqueline (1976), "Children's Books and Heroes," *Washington Post*, Friday, October 29. —Michael Strickland

Editor's note: Many of Greenfield's books have been printed as board books (all of which were illustrated by Jan Spivey Gilchrist, and most of which were also printed in paperback format): *Big Friend, Little Friend* (1991), *I Make Music* (1991), *My Daddy and I* (1991), *My Doll, Keshia* (1991), *Aaron and Gayla's Alphabet Book* (1992), *Aaron and Gayla's Counting Book* (1992), *Sweet Baby Coming* (1994), *Kia Tanisha* (1996/1997), and *Kia Tanisha Drives Her Car* (1996/1997). Greenfield's other prose picture books for young children include *Bubbles* (1972, illustrated by Eric Marlow; retitled *Good News*, 1977, illustrated by Pat Cummings), *She Come Bringing Me That Little Baby Girl* (1974, illustrated by **John Steptoe**), *Me and Neesie* (1975, illustrated by Moneta Barnett; 2005, illustrated by Jan Spivey Gilchrist), *First Pink Light* (1976, illustrated by Moneta Barnett; 1991, illustrated by Jan Spivey Gilchrist), *Africa Dream* (1977/1992, illustrated by Carole Byard), *I Can Do It by Myself* (1978, written with her mother, Lessie Jones Little; illustrated by Carole Byard), *Darlene* (1980, illustrated by George Cephas Ford), *Grandmama's Joy* (1980, illustrated by Carole Byard), *Grandpa's Face* (1988, illustrated by Floyd Cooper; 1993, *La Cara de Abuelito*), *Lisa's Daddy and Daughter Day* (1991, illustrated by Jan Spivey Gilchrist), *William and the Good Old Days* (1993, illustrated by Jan Spivey Gilchrist), *On My Horse* (1995, illustrations by Jan Spivey Gilchrist), and *Easter Parade* (1997/2001, illustrated by Jan Spivey Gilchrist).

Greenfield's illustrated poetry books for children include *Honey, I Love and Other Love Poems* (1978, illustrated by **Leo and Diane Dillon**), *Daydreamers* (1981, illustrated by **Tom Feelings**), *Nathaniel Talking* (1988, illustrated by Jan Spivey Gilchrist), *Under the Sunday Tree* (1988, illustrated by Amos Ferguson), *Night on Neighborhood Street* (1991, illustrated by Jan Spivey Gilchrist), *Angels: An African-American Treasury* (1998, illustrated by Jan Spivey Gilchrist), *Water, Water* (1999, illustrated by Jan Spivey Gilchrist), *I Can Draw a Weeposaur and Other Dinosaurs* (2001, illustrated by Jan Spivey Gilchrist), *Honey, I Love* (2003, 25th anniversary edition, illustrated by Jan Spivey Gilchrist), *In the Land of Words: New and Selected Poems* (2004, illustrated by Jan Spivey Gilchrist), *The Friendly Four* (2006, illustrated by Jan Spivey Gilchrist), *When the Horses Ride By: Children in the Times of War* (2006, illustrated by Jan Spivey Gilchrist), and *Brothers & Sisters: Family Poems* (2008/2009). Greenfield also introduced *Children of Long Ago: Poems*, written by her mother, Lessie Jones Little (2000, illustrated by Jan Spivey Gilchrist).

Greenfield has also written nonfiction biographies and memoirs for children, including *Rosa Parks* (1973, illustrated by Eric Marlow; 1995, reillustrated by Gil Ashby), *Paul Robeson* (1975, illustrated by George Ford), *Mary McLeod Bethune* (1977, illustrated by **Jerry Pinkney**),

Childtimes: A Three-Generation Memoir (1979, with Greenfield's mother, Lessie Jones Little; additional material by Patricia Ridley Jones; illustrated by **Jerry Pinkney** and with family photographs), *Alesia* (1981, written with Alesia Revis; illustrated by George Ford, with photographs by Sandra Turner Bond), *For the Love of the Game: Michael Jordan and Me* (1997, illustrated by Jan Spivey Gilchrist), and *How They Got Over: African Americans and the Call of the Sea* (2003, illustrated by Jan Spivey Gilchrist). Last, but not least, she has written longer fiction for children in middle-school grades, including *Sister* (1974, about a 13-year-old girl), *Talk about a Family* (1978/1993, illustrated by James Calvin, about a sixth-grade girl), and *Koya DeLaney and the Good Girl Blues* (1992, about an 11-year-old girl). Recordings have been made of *Honey, I Love* and *Lisa's Daddy and Daughter Day. Daydreamers* was dramatized for the PBS television series *Reading Rainbow.*

REFERENCES: Haywood, Chanta M., in *COCAAL.* Hinton-Johnson, KaaVonia, in *CA/I. GEAAL.* Johnson, Anne Janette, in *BB. CAO-04.* Amazon.com. SDPL catalog.

Greenlee, Sam
7/13/1930–
Poems, novels, essays, screenplays; educator

Most readers know Sam Greenlee for his novel *The Spook Who Sat by the Door* (1969, Meritorious Service Award). It was adapted to make a same-titled movie (1973) and was named a London *Sunday Times* Book of the Year. Greenlee's other published novels include *Baghdad Blues: A Novel* (1976; 1991, with a new subtitle, *The Revolution That Brought Saddam Hussien to Power*), inspired by his travels through Iraq in the 1950s, and *Djakarta Blues* (2002). His poetry collections include *Blues for an African Princess* (1960/1971), *Ammunition: Poetry and Other Raps* (1975), and *"Be-bop Man/Be-bop Woman," 1968-1993: Poetry and Other Raps* (1995). His stories and other works have also been anthologized (e.g., in *Black Short Story Anthology,* 1972, edited by **Woodie King**). In 1990, he was named Illinois's Poet Laureate.

REFERENCES: *AANB.* Hunt, Imelda, in *GEAAL.* Macon, Wanda, in *COCAAL* and *OCAAL.* Routledge, Chris, in *BB. CAO-01.* //en.wikipedia.org/wiki/Sam_Greenlee. //www.coe.ohio-state.edu/beverlygordon/834/miller.html. Amazon.com.

Gregory, "Dick" (Richard Claxton)
10/12/1932–
Spoken word—comedy sketches, autobiography/memoir, political writings; performer, civil-rights activist, health advocate

Dick Gregory

After his father left his mother alone to raise Dick and his five siblings (three brothers and two sisters), Momma used the "relief" money from the "welfare" agencies—and a healthy dose of hope and humor—to raise all six children as ably and skillfully as she could. Dick described how she managed in his autobiographical book *Nigger* (p. 25): "Like a lot of Negro kids, we never would have made it without our Momma. When there was no fatback to go with the beans, no socks to go with the shoes, no hope to go with tomorrow, she'd say, 'We ain't poor, we're just broke.' Poor is a state of mind you never grow out of, but being broke is just a temporary condition. . . . She taught us that man has two ways out in life—laughing or crying. There's more hope in laughing."

Although his mother made sure he stayed in school, Dick had to begin working as a shoeshine boy and at sundry other jobs to help his mother support his siblings. Despite his impoverished circumstances, however, Dick "never learned hate at home, or shame." As he said, "I had to go to school for that" (*Nigger*, p. 29). In high school, Dick became involved in a variety of sports and social causes. His skill as a middle-distance runner earned him an athletic scholarship in 1951 to go to Southern Illinois University. While there, he was welcome to participate in all athletic endeavors, and he was named the university's outstanding student athlete in 1953. On the other hand, he was prohibited from eating a celebratory meal with his white teammates in a local restaurant, and he was banned from sitting in the orchestra section (instead of the balcony) at the local movie house with his date.

In 1954, Gregory was drafted into the U.S. Army, where he spent two years. His natural sense of humor caught the attention of his colonel, who called Gregory into his office and said, "Gregory, . . . you are either a great comedian or a goddamned malingerer. There is an open talent show at the service club tonight. You will go down there, and you will win it. Otherwise, I will court-martial you. Now get the hell out of here" (*Nigger*, p. 90). Gregory won that show and the two shows after that, and then he was transferred to Special Services and thereafter hosted and performed comedy routines in military shows. By the time he got out of the military in the spring of 1956, he was an experienced stand-up comic. Although he briefly returned to his alma mater, he soon started his professional career in the private sector. By 1958, Gregory was serving as a master of ceremonies at various Chicago nightclubs.

Around April of 1958, Dick met Lillian Smith, a secretary at the University of Chicago, after one of his nightclub acts. He saw her a few times, then that summer, when he was in the hospital for six weeks for jaundice, she visited him. Over the next several months, they developed an on-again, off-again relationship. On Thursday, January 29, 1959, "I went to see Lillian Smith. . . . She had quit her job at the University and she was leaving town. I had to ask her twice before she told me why. 'I'm pregnant, Greg. I'm going to have a baby.'" Recalling his own fatherless childhood, he quickly decided what to do. "I asked Lil to marry me. She refused. She said she didn't want to do anything to stand in my way. This time I didn't ask her, I told her . . . , and on Monday, February 2, 1959, I was a married man" (*Nigger*, pp. 115-116). By1964, Dick and Lil had four children: Michele, Lynne, and the twin babies Pamela and Paula. Sadly, however, their infant son, Richard, Jr., had died suddenly in 1962. In 1981, when the Gregorys had ten children, including Stephanie (aka Xenobia), Gregory, Christian, Ayanna, Missy, Youhance, he announced his plans to be celibate as part of his self-purification program. In a 1997 speech honoring Dr. **Martin Luther King, Jr.**, Dick acknowledged Lillian's crucial support in fostering his success in all his endeavors.

On January 13, 1961, Gregory got his big career break: What was meant to be a one-nighter at the Chicago Playboy Club ended up being a six-week gig, which netted him a prized appearance on the highly acclaimed *The Jack Paar Show*, as well as a profile in *Time* magazine. From that point on, he was invited to appear on television, in nightclubs, on college campuses, and wherever his brand of comedy could be showcased. He avoided slapstick, stereotypical jokes, and personal jibes, and instead, his satirical sketches and routines bitingly attacked poverty, segregation, and racial discrimination.

Following is an outline of his sketch, as he described it in *Nigger*, pp. 132-133: First, he started out with a self-mocking comment, such as "Just my luck, bought a nice white suit with two pair of pants today. . . . burnt a hole in the jacket." Next, he poked fun at the contemporary racial situation: "They asked me to buy a lifetime membership in the NAACP, but I told them I'd pay a week at a time. Hell of a thing to buy a lifetime membership, wake up one morning and find the country's been integrated." Then he'd get the members of the mostly white audience to laugh at themselves: "Wouldn't it be a hell of a thing if all this was burnt cork and you people were being tolerant for nothing?" After that, he could talk about virtually anything he wanted to—as long as he didn't stray into talking about sex, which would put him back into being stereotyped as a black comedian.

Once Gregory had achieved national prominence (e.g., being listed in the 1963 edition of *Who's Who in America*), he used his fame to benefit civil-rights causes. During the 1960s, he participated in numerous demonstrations, was arrested for civil disobedience several times, and was even jailed for his activities. Dr. Martin Luther King, Jr., never hesitated to call on Gregory to focus attention on civil-rights activities, and Gregory was a close associate of Medgar Evers. Ironically, Evers was the person who told Richard that Richard, Jr., had died, and soon after Gregory had buried his son, he got the call telling him that Medgar Evers had been murdered.

Starting in the 1960s, Gregory recorded numerous albums: *In Living Black and White* (1961), *East & West* (1961), *Dick Gregory Talks Turkey* (1962), *The Two Sides of Dick Gregory* (1963), *Dick Gregory Running for President* (1964), *So You See . . . We All Have Problems* (c. 1960s), *Dick Gregory On* (1969), *The Light Side: The Dark Side* (1969), *Dick Gregory's Frankenstein* (1970), *Live at the Village Gate* (1970), *At Kent State* (1971), *Caught in the Act* (1974), and *The Best of Dick Gregory* (1997). He also wrote several books, reflecting both his comedic outlook and his political views. For instance, he published *From the Back of the Bus* (1962); *Nigger: An Autobiography by Dick Gregory* (1964/1990, with Robert Lipsyte); *What's Happening* (1965); *Write Me In* (1968); *The Shadow That Scares Me* (1968); *No More Lies: The Myth and the Reality of American History* (1971/1972, written under full birth name); *Dick Gregory's Political Primer* (1972); *Dick Gregory's Natural Diet for Folks Who Eat: Cookin' with Mother Nature* (1973); *Dick Gregory's Bible Tales, with Commentary* (1974/1978); his autobiography *Up From Nigger* (1976, with James R. McGraw); *Code Name "Zorro": The Murder of Dr. Martin Luther King, Jr.* (1977, with Mark Lane); *Murder in Memphis: The FBI and the Assassination of Martin Luther King* (1993, with Mark Lane); and *Callus on My Soul: A Memoir* (2000, with Shelia P. Moses).

Gregory's focus has gradually shifted away from comedy and toward politics. In 1966, he ran for mayor of Chicago, and in 1968, he ran for president of the United States on the Peace and Freedom Party ticket. During the 1970s, he broadened the range of issues he opposed to include war and other forms of violence, capital punishment, drug abuse, and poor health care. Gregory also began fasting to call attention to the problems of world hunger, and he started to promote vegetarianism as a statement of nonviolence. During the 1980s, he returned to distance running, and he taught himself to become an expert on nutrition. After he developed his own nutritional product, the "Bahamian Diet," he founded Dick Gregory Health Enterprises, Inc., both as a successful entrepreneurial enterprise and as a vehicle for promoting better health and longer life expectancy of African Americans.

Problems with his business partners, however, led to financial difficulties, and Gregory briefly returned to the comedy circuit in the mid-1990s, when he starred in his critically acclaimed off-Broadway *Dick Gregory Live!* (1996). About this time, he also engaged in political activism at a local level, promoting a crime-fighting campaign in the neighborhoods of St. Louis. He continues to keep his eye on national and international issues, however, using nonviolent tools such as fasting and protesting to gain attention for the causes he champions. In 2002, he struggled to prevent the FBI from naming its headquarters for J. Edgar Hoover, the notoriously racist opponent of civil rights and civil liberties. In 2004, he was arrested for his protest at the Sudanese Embassy, opposing that government's genocide of its citizens. From 2000 to 2005, he battled against lymphoma and won, crediting his use of diet and alternative healing methods for his victory. In 2006, he eulogized James Brown. Eight years earlier, at the 1998 celebration of Dr. Martin Luther King, Jr.'s birth, Gregory addressed an audience including President Bill Clinton, who was later quoted as saying, "I love Dick Gregory, he is one of the funniest people on the planet" (quoted on Gregory's website).

REFERENCES: *AANB. EBLG.* Ankeny, Jason, *All Music Guide,* in A. Goldsworthy, Joan, and Tom Pendergast, in *BB. CAO-01. EB-98. G-95. WB-98.* Gregory, Richard. 1965. *Nigger: An Autobiography of Dick Gregory,* New York: Pocket Books (Hardcover: 1964, New York: E. P. Dutton). Simonson, J'Lyn, in *B. D. GEAAL. QB. Wiki.* //en.wikiquote.org/wiki/Dick_Gregory. //www.dickgregory.com/. //www.dickgregory.com/about_dick_gregory.html.

Griggs, Sutton E. (Elbert)
6/19/1872–1/3/1933
Novels, nonfiction—politics, essays, biography, spoken word—sermons and speeches; publisher, minister, social worker, educator

Through his Orion Publishing Company, Griggs published his own 5 novels (*Imperium in Imperio,* 1899, his best-selling and most widely praised book, reprinted in 1969; *Overshadowed,* 1901; *Unfettered,* 1902; *The Hindered Hand; or, the Reign of the Repressionist,* 1905; *Pointing the Way,* 1908) and a few of his other books (*The One Great Question ...,* 1907; *Pointing the Way,* 1908; *Needs of the South,* 1909; *The Race Question in A New Light,* 1909, then enlarged as *Wisdom's Call,* 1911). In the 1910s, he turned to social work, founding the National Public Welfare League, which published many of his works of nonfiction (*The Story of My Struggles,* 1914; *How to Rise,* 1915; *Life's Demands; or, According to the Law,* 1916; *The Reconstruction of a Race,* 1917; *Light on Racial Issues,* 1921; *Guide to Racial Greatness; or, The Science of Collective Efficiency,* 1923; *The Negro's Next Step,* 1923; *Kingdom Builders' Manual: Companion Book to Guide to Racial Greatness,* 1924; *Paths of Progress; or, Cooperation Between the Races,* 1925; *The Winning Policy,* 1927). Another of his books was *Triumph of the Simple Virtues, or the Life Story of John L. Webb* (1926?).

The son of a former slave, Griggs used themes of militant black separatism and racial pride in his work decades before the Black Power movement, and even before **Marcus Garvey**'s black-pride, back-to-Africa militancy. Although Griggs's novels and other works are little known now, as some of his contemporaries showed more enduring literary skills, his books sold well in his day, in part because his ability to promote their sale directly as their publisher. He may also be considered the first African American to write a political novel. The Wall Street Crash of 1929 bankrupted his Tabernacle Baptist Church, where he had been pastor for 19 years and had provided the only swimming pool and gymnasium open to African Americans in Memphis.

REFERENCES: *AANB. NYPL-AADR.* Elder, Arlene A., in *COCAAL* and *OCAAL.* Fleming, Robert E. "Sutton E. Griggs: Militant Black Novelist." *PHYLON: The Atlanta University Review of Race and Culture* 34.1 (Mar. 1973), pp. 73-77. Rpt. in Jennifer Gariepy (Ed.) (1998), *Twentieth-Century Literary Criticism* (Vol. 77). Detroit: Gale Research. From *Literature Resource Center.* Moses, Wilson J. "Literary Garveyism: The Novels of Reverend Sutton E. Griggs." *PHYLON: The Atlanta University Review of Race and Culture* 40.3 (Fall 1979), pp. 203-216. Jennifer Gariepy (Ed.) (1998), *Twentieth-Century Literary Criticism* (Vol. 77). Detroit: Gale Research. From *Literature Resource Center.* Mulcahy, Judith, in *CAO-00. GEAAL. QB. W. Wiki.* Thompson, Betty E. Taylor, in *AAWBHR.*

Grimké, Angelina Weld *See* **Fortens, Grimkés, and Purvises**

Grimké, Angelina (Emily) (married name: Weld) *See* **Fortens, Grimkés, and Purvises**

Grimké, Archibald Henry *See* **Fortens, Grimkés, and Purvises**

Grimké, Charlotte L. Forten *See* **Fortens, Grimkés, and Purvises**

Grimké, Francis J. (James) *See* **Fortens, Grimkés, and Purvises**

Grimké, Sarah (Moore) *See* **Fortens, Grimkés, and Purvises**

Grooms, Anthony ("Tony")
1/15/1955–
Poems, short stories, novel; educator

After earning his baccalaureate in theater and speech from the College of William and Mary (1978) and his masters of fine arts in English from George Mason University (1984), Grooms moved to Georgia to teach English, first at Macon Junior College (1984-1986), then at Clark Atlanta University in Atlanta (1986-1988), then at the University of Georgia in Athens 1988-1994, and at Morehouse College in Atlanta (1994). Meanwhile, each summer, he taught at Oglethorpe University (1991-1994) and at the Summer Writing Institute of Emory University (1991-1995), and he edited *Our Era* (1990-1991). At last, in 1994, Grooms settled at Kennesaw State University near Atlanta, starting as an assistant professor of creative writing and now working as a full professor of creative writing. The year he moved to Kennesaw, he also served as fiction editor for the *Atlanta Review* (1994).

While teaching creative writing, Grooms has modeled his creative writing talents as a playwright, a poet, a storyteller, and a novelist. His plays include *Accidents* and *Dr. Madlove* (both 1975), both produced at William and Mary Premier Theatre. His poems and short stories have been published in numerous magazines (e.g., *Atlanta Magazine*), journals (e.g., *African-American Review,*

Callaloo), and anthologies (e.g., *Crossing the Color Line: Recent Readings in Black and White,* 2000). In addition, his poems have been published in his chapbook *Ice Poems* (1988), and his short stories have been collected in *Trouble No More* (1995; 2nd ed., 2006), which won a prestigious Lillian Smith Award (1996). His historical novel *Bombingham* (2001) was nominated for the prestigious Hurston-Wright Foundation Legacy award (2002). Grooms has also contributed essays, book reviews, and other nonfiction to both periodicals (e.g., *Chattahoochee Review, Humanities in the South, Our Era*) and anthologies (e.g., *Eudora Welty: Writers' Reflections upon First Reading Welty,* 1999). He also continues to write and is now working on another novel and a book of narrative poems. In addition to the aforementioned awards, Grooms has been honored with a fellowship from the National Endowment for the Arts (1991), a David R. Sokolov Scholarship in Fiction from the Breadloaf Writers' Conference (1991), a Lamar lectureship at Wesleyan College (1997), and many other grants.

REFERENCES: CAO-06. Leak, Jeffrey B., in *AANB.* //www.georgia encyclopedia.org/nge/Multimedia.jsp?id=m-499. //www.highlands. edu/webzine/backbytes/features30/grooms.htm. //www.hurston-wright. org/legacy_winners2002.shtml. //www.kennesaw.edu/english/ faculty.htm. //www.kennesaw.edu/ksupress/troublenomore.shtml. Amazon.com.

FURTHER READING: Metress, Christopher, in *GEAAL.* //www.randomhouse.com/catalog/display.pperl?isbn=9780345452931.

Guinier, (Carol) Lani
4/19/1950–
Nonfiction—social, political, and legal issues; educator

The daughter of a Jamaican-American father and a Jewish mother, this provocative and distinguished civil-rights attorney has published several books offering her insights: *The Tyranny of the Majority: Fundamental Fairness in Representative Democracy* (1970/1994), comprising the controversial essays of legal opinions that cost her President Bill Clinton's nomination to assistant attorney general; *Becoming Gentlemen: Women, Law School, and Institutional Change* (1997, with Michelle Fine, and Jane Balin), which discusses her take on how law-school education is a male-gendered experience; *Lift Every Voice: Turning a Civil Rights Setback into a New Vision of Social Justice* (1998), which offers a clear explanation of Guinier's views that cost her the nomination; *Who's Qualified?* (2001, with Susan Sturm), which offers an alternative to affirmative action to ensure that the most meritorious candidates have educational and job opportunities; *The Miner's Canary: Enlisting Race, Resisting Power, Transforming Democracy* (2002, with Gerald Torres), which blends personal anecdotes (including her biracial son Niklas's experiences) and hard facts to show why "color-blind" approaches fail to provide equal opportunities. Guinier is the first African-American woman to be appointed to a tenured professorship at Harvard Law School (since 1998) and continues to write scholarly and popular articles; she also cofounded (in 1996) the non-profit organization Commonplace, dedicated to stimulating enlightened discussion of racial issues between the media and academia.

REFERENCES: *AANB. Wiki.* Le Blanc, Ondine E., and Christine Miner Minderovic, in *BB. CAO-07. EA-99.* //minerscanary.org/pubs/pubs_by_lani.shtml. //www.kepplerspeakers.com/speakers/speakers.asp?Lani+Guinier. Amazon.com, 7/1999, 3/2009.

Guy, Rosa (née Cuthbert)
9/1/1925– or 1928–
Novels—adult and juvenile; organizer

Soon after Rosa was born, her parents, Audrey and Henry Cuthbert, emigrated to the United States, leaving Rosa and her sister behind in Trinidad. Seven years later, the two girls emigrated to Harlem, New York City, to join their parents. Their family reunion was short-lived, however, as in 1933, their mother became ill, and the two girls were sent to live with a Garveyite cousin in Brooklyn. The next year, their mother died, their father remarried, and the girls returned to Harlem, to live with their father and his new wife. Even this period of a blended family life was not to last long, as their father died in 1937, abandoning his two orphaned daughters to life in an orphanage. When Rosa was only 14 years old, she left school to work in a brassiere factory in the garment district.

When Rosa was only 16—and still working in the factory, she met and married Warner Guy in 1941. The next year, Rosa gave birth to her only child, Warner, her husband's namesake. While she attended to Warner the younger (and continued to work in the factory), her husband was serving the military in World War II. Rosa continued to work in the factory but sought creative ways to express herself. Young and energetic—and in need of creative and intellectual outlets—Rosa started attending classes at New York University (NYU). At about the same time, one of her coworkers introduced her to the relatively newly formed American Negro Theater (ANT). Rosa did not perform in any of the ANT productions (despite her youthful energy, the need to work and to care for her child did impose *some* limits), but she did study acting with ANT. Her association with ANT and with NYU led her to start writing plays and short stories.

When the war ended and the soldiers returned home, Rosa, her husband, and her son moved to Connecticut. Sadly, Rosa was not able to forge a lasting family life in Connecticut to replace the family she missed as a child. In

just five short years, her marriage disintegrated, and she and her son returned to New York, where she returned to work in a clothing factory. Unfortunately, by that time, her ANT family had also disappeared, but another organization, the Committee for the Negro in the Arts, had appeared in its place. The goal of the committee was to rid the arts of racial stereotypes. It was through Rosa's interactions with this group that she wrote and performed in her first play, *Venetian Blinds* (1954), a one-act play successfully produced Off-Broadway by ANT at the Tropical Theater.

Through the committee, Guy also met various other writers, including **John O. Killens**, who was to play an important role in her life. In 1951, she and Killens founded a workshop for African-American writers, which soon became known as the Harlem Writers Guild. Among the many notable participants were **Maya Angelou, Audre Lorde, Paule Marshall,** and **Douglas Turner Ward**. In fact, some have estimated that at least half of all the noted African-American writers between 1951 and 1970 were linked to the guild's workshop. Both Killens and the guild offered Guy (the guild's president from 1967 to 1978) the nurture and encouragement she needed to pursue her writing craft while overcoming her lack of education and continuing to handle her responsibilities as a single parent and a factory worker.

Although Guy may lack formal education, she clearly loves exploring language, and her mastery of it reflects both her natural talent and her lifelong self-education. In addition to speaking English, Guy speaks French and Creole, and she enjoys researching African languages as a relaxing pastime. Guy has further expanded her grasp of language, as well as culture and folkways, through her travels to Africa and to two Caribbean countries with deep roots in Africa: Haiti and her native Trinidad.

Guy's writing also reflects her personal history as a cultural outsider, a family outsider, and an urban dweller struggling to survive and to come into her own identity. Most of her books are centered around African-American or West-Indian-American youths who are facing great adversity in the inner city. After writing and publishing a couple of short stories, Guy tackled the novel form. *Bird at My Window* (1966/2001), her tragic first novel, written for adults and dedicated to **Malcolm X**, despairingly showed how her protagonist, Wade Williams, was eventually crushed by oppressive poverty and racism in a Harlem ghetto. Although Guy wrote other novels for adults—*A Measure of Time* (1983); *My Love, My Love: Or the Peasant Girl* (1985/2002, an adaptation of Hans Christian Andersen's "The Little Mermaid," set in the Caribbean); and *The Sun, the Sea, a Touch of the Wind* (1995)—her literary focus shifted chiefly to young adults.

Like many other Americans, Guy was shaken by the assassinations of Malcolm X and of **Martin Luther King,**

Jr., and she decided to investigate how African-American youths (ages 13-23 years) viewed their world during the turbulent 1960s. She ventured into the American South and interviewed numerous youths, then returned North to edit her volume *Children of Longing* (1970), a collection of essays, synthesizing the firsthand accounts of young people's experiences, aspirations, and fears.

After finishing her essay collection, Guy traveled in the Caribbean and lived for a time in Haiti and in Trinidad, and several of her subsequent novels reflected the cultural experiences on these islands. Her trilogy *The Friends* (1973/1995, *The New York Times* Outstanding Book of the Year), *Ruby* (1976/2005), and *Edith Jackson* (1978/1993) describes the psychological development of three young girls within the context of race, gender, class, and cultural discrimination. As the trilogy opens, two sisters (Ruby and her younger sister, Phyllisia) emigrate from the West Indies to join their parents in Harlem. In Harlem, their mother is dying, so the two girls feel ill at ease at home, and they feel like outsiders at school. (Wonder what inspired that perspective?) Edith Jackson, an outcast orphan herself, offers Phyllisia her friendship, but Phyllisia's father discourages that relationship. In the second novel, after Phyllisia and Ruby's mother dies, their domineering father raises them, and each of the girls finds her own path to escape from their situation. The third novel centers on young Edith, who vainly strives to keep her three younger sisters with her. Each of the novels was named the Best Book of the Year by the American Library Association at the time of publication.

Guy followed this dramatic trilogy with a trilogy of detective stories, centered on Imamu Jones, a 16-year-old Brooklyn probationer who is trying to do well: *The Disappearance* (1979/1991; *The New York Times* Outstanding Book of the Year), *New Guys around the Block* (1983/2005; Parents' Choice Award for Literature), and *And I Heard a Bird Sing* (1987). Guy also produced a variety of other books for young readers: *Mother Crocodile* (1981/1995), a Coretta Scott King Award-winning picture-book adaptation of an African fable, and *Billy the Great* (1991, illustrated by C. Binch), about the friendship of two young boys. Her other novels for youths include *Mirror of Her Own* (1981), about a younger sister emerging from behind the shadow of her older sister; *Paris, Pee Wee, and Big Dog* (1984), about three 10-year-olds enjoying a Saturday in New York city; *The Ups and Downs of Carl David III* (1989), about a preteen boy sent South to stay with his grandmother; and *The Music of Summer* (1992), which explores issues of class and of color differences among African Americans. She also wrote *Caribbean Carnival: Songs of the West Indies* (1992), a collection of songs for children.

REFERENCES: *AA:PoP. CBC. EBLG. MAAL. MWEL. OC20LE.* Bader, Philip, in *EB-98.* //0-web.ebscohost.com.dbpcosdcsgt.co.san-diego.ca.us/novelist/detail?vid=67&hid=7&sid=d408b38a-8f5e-4ec 2-b75c-cf9c5b5097d7%40sessionmgr3&bdata=JnNpdGU9bm92ZWx pc3QtbGl2ZQ%3d%3d. Guy, Rosa. *Speaking for Ourselves: Autobiographical Sketches by Notable Authors of Books for Young Adults.* Ed. Donald R. Gallo. Urbana, Ill.: National Council of Teachers of English, 1990. Rpt. in *Children's Literature Review.* Ed. Tom Burns. Vol. 137. Detroit: Gale, pp. 85-86. From *Literature Resource Center.* Hinton-Johnson, KaaVonia, in *GEAAL.* Lawrence, Leota S., in *AAFW-55-84.* Sussman, Alison Carb, in *BB. CAO-05. MWEL.* Warren, Nagueyalti, in *COCAAL* and *OCAAL. Wiki.*

Haley, Alex (Alexander Murray Palmer)
8/11/1921–2/10/1992
Autobiographical/biographical novels; reporter

Simon Henry Haley and Bertha George Palmer were both students in Ithaca, New York, where they met, married, and had young Alex. The young family soon moved to Henning, Tennessee, where Alex and his two brothers spent most of their childhoods. Although both of his parents were educators (his father a professor of agriculture and his mother a grade-school teacher), Alex was less captivated by his schooling than he was by the stories of his ancestors, as told by his mother's mother, her sisters, and the other members of his large extended family. At age 15, Alex graduated from high school, and he started attending college in Mississippi; then he transferred to a teachers college in North Carolina. After a couple of years there, in 1939, Alex enlisted in the U.S. Coast Guard.

While in the Coast Guard, Haley started writing articles and short stories. After several years of writing and submitting his works for publication, he eventually started having some of his short stories printed in magazines such as *Coronet, Reader's Digest, Atlantic,* and *Harper's.* By 1952, the Coast Guard recognized his writing talents, and he was given a new title as chief journalist, handling public relations for the Coast Guard. After putting in his 20 years of service, Haley retired from the Coast Guard in 1959.

After retiring, Haley moved to New York City to pursue a writing career, with his Coast Guard pension as a financial safety net. As a freelance writer, he started out with assignments for *Reader's Digest,* then he went on to initiate a series of interviews (e.g., with Miles Davis, **Martin Luther King, Jr.**, Cassius Clay [later Muhammad Ali], and **Malcolm X**) for *Playboy* magazine. His interview with Malcolm X proved crucial to Haley's career, as

the two eventually established a collaboration that led to the writing of Malcolm's autobiography.

Although the famous Muslim leader was initially reticent to reveal much to Haley, over time, Haley earned his trust, and through intensive interviews, he elicited from Malcolm the frank and engaging story of his life. Haley chronicled Malcolm's terrifying early childhood experiences as the son of a militant **Garvey**ite preacher, his youth as an unrepentant criminal, his prison conversion to Islam as expressed by the Black Muslims, his increasing prominence as a spokesperson for the Black Muslims, and his eventual spiritual awakening to traditional Islam during his pilgrimage to Mecca. Tragically, Malcolm X (renamed El Hajj Malik El-Shabazz following his sojourn to Mecca) was assassinated (by Black Muslims) before the book went into print, so he never saw how profoundly his autobiography influenced Americans of both black and white races. Nor did he know that his critically acclaimed book sold more than 6 million copies; was required reading in many college classes in literature, African-American studies, and contemporary history; was translated into at least eight languages; and was made into a popular movie (in 1992).

The success of Haley and Malcolm X's collaboration firmly established Haley's writing career, and he continued to publish short articles, including a *Saturday Evening Post* exposé of Elijah Muhammad and the Nation of Islam. When Haley considered what major project to tackle next, he soon recalled the stories of his ancestors, which his mother's mother family members recounted to him during his childhood. With the success of *The Autobiography* and his military pension, Haley could afford to spend the time—and pay for research assistance—to probe his family's history and genealogy.

Haley ended up spending the next 12 years of his life probing his family's past. His investigations took him to many libraries (e.g., the Library of Congress and the Daughters of the American Revolution Library) and archives, as well as to several countries in Africa and elsewhere. He even followed the approximate route that a slave ship might have taken from Africa to America, across the Atlantic Ocean. Haley was soon giving lectures about his research in the United States and Great Britain, and he was publishing numerous magazine articles on his findings. He was even awarded several honorary doctorate degrees, recognizing his scholarship in African-American history and genealogy.

As might be imagined, there were many times when the research bogged down, when it was difficult to know how to proceed, or when Haley might have felt a little discouraged. On the other hand, he was encouraged when he found many of the people identified in his grandmother's stories listed in United States census records in our National Archives. He was able to trace much of his family's history in this way. How was he to trace his family back to Africa, however? Africa was a huge continent, and there was no continental archive listing all Africans who left for America.

Haley thought perhaps that the few words and expressions that were carried through the generations might be one way of finding out the *part* of Africa from which his ancestor originated. With a little diligence, he found someone who had studied African languages extensively. When he told this scholar the terms he had learned from his grandmother, the scholar identified the terms as being Mandinka, a language spoken in modern-day Gambia and Senegal.

With that bitty clue in hand, Haley went to Gambia and searched for their equivalent of national archives: a *griot,* a storyteller whose job it is to memorize and recall the history of the persons in each village. After interviewing various village griots, he found one in the village of Juffure, whose narrative matched what he knew of his own ancestor. The griot told of a youth named Kunta Kinte, whose capture and kidnapping matched the story relayed to Haley by his grandmother. The griot provided Haley with rich information on Kunta's biography in Africa, which complemented what Haley had heard and had been able to find out about Kunta after he left Africa. The story of Kunta Kinte formed the major part of Haley's historical novel *Roots:* We last read of Kunta Kinte, as his daughter Kizzy is torn away from his arms, on page 453 of 729 pages. The remaining pages tell the story of Kizzy and her descendants, as well as about 20 pages documenting Haley's own investigation into his family's history.

Initially, Haley's story was excerpted in *Reader's Digest* in 1974, so when it was finally published in the fall of 1976, the critics had already heralded its arrival, and *Roots: The Saga of an American Family* (1976) succeeded phenomenally well, winning special citations from the Pulitzer Prize and National Book Award committees and the NAACP's **Spingarn** Medal in 1977, being translated into 26 languages, and selling millions of copies. When the book was adapted to be a TV miniseries (in 1977), about 130 million Americans watched at least one of the several episodes of the series, making it one of the most popular TV shows in American history. In recognition of *Roots,* the U.S. Senate passed a resolution honoring Haley, and a *Scholastic Magazine* survey of 4,000 college and university deans and department heads found that Haley was named "America's foremost achiever in the literature category." Perhaps the greatest honor awarded to Haley was that his work prompted tremendous popular interest in Africa and in African-American genealogy and history among everyday Americans. Haley also reinforced the literary tradition of having his characters speak in the vernacular of the larger African-American community.

Not everyone praised Haley, however. At least two published authors (**Margaret Walker**, author of *Jubilee;* and Harold Courlander, author of *The African*) accused Haley of plagiarism. Haley eventually gave Courlander a large settlement, saying that his researchers had provided him with any of the questionable passages, without citing Courlander as the source. Other critics have found serious flaws in his genealogical research, pointing to many discrepancies in his data and problems in his research methods. Others have pointed out that the *griot* Haley encountered may have known what Haley wanted to hear and therefore may have fabricated some of the story told to Haley. Further, the final book contains no bibliographical citations and did not show the rigorous type of research that would be expected for a scholarly work. Regardless of how we view the legitimacy and importance of these criticisms, Haley's story will continue to be a significant contribution to African-American literature, and its role in stimulating a national discussion of African-American history cannot be questioned.

Following *Roots,* Haley chiefly focused on various TV productions (e.g., *Roots: The Next Generation* [1979], a sequel to the original *Roots* miniseries; *Roots: The Gift,* a story about a Christmas Eve slave escape involving two of the principal characters from *Roots*). When he died, Haley left several unfinished manuscripts; one of them, *Alex Haley's Queen* (1993), about the ancestors of his paternal grandparents, was subsequently finished and then published by David Stevens. A TV miniseries about the story in the book was shown at about the time the book was published.

In addition to his manuscripts, Haley left his family behind. While in the Coast Guard, Haley had married Nannie Branch in 1941, and the pair had two children. He subsequently divorced her and then married Juliette Collins in 1964, with whom he had one daughter. After they divorced, Haley eventually remarried for a third time, although he had no additional children. After Haley died of cardiac arrest, he was buried on the grounds of the Alex Haley Museum in Henning, Tennessee.

REFERENCES: *1TESK. AANB. BF:2000. DA* (for *Roots* and for *Malcolm X*). *EBLG. MAAL. OC20LE.* Berger, Roger A., in *COCAAL* and *OCAAL.* Haley, Alex, and Jeffrey Elliot. "In an Interview." *Negro History Bulletin 41.1* (January-February 1978), pp. 782-785. Rpt. in *CLCS.* Detroit: Gale. From *Literature Resource Center.* Harris, Steven R., in *B. BCE. GEAAL. QB. SD. W. W2B. Wiki.* Johnson, Anne Janette, in *BB. CAO-03. CLCS. MWEL.* Kern-Foxworth. Marilyn, in *AAW-55-85:DPW.* O'Brien, Maureen. "Alex Haley's Hometown Burial." *Publishers Weekly. 239.12* (Mar. 2, 1992) p. 20. From *Literature Resource Center.* E-97. EB-98. G-95.

Hamilton, Virginia
3/12/1936–2/19/2002
Children's picture books and novels

Virginia Hamilton, a prolific children's author, was honored with every prestigious award for writers of children's books. She is best known for her novel M.C. *Higgins, the Great* (1971), the first book to win both the National Book Award and the John Newbery Award. The Newbery is given annually for the most distinguished contribution to literature for children published in the United States. Hamilton raised the standards for children's literature. Her graphic descriptions of emotional and physical landscapes give the reader a view of the real world and the fanciful world with equal and exceptional clarity.

Hamilton attended to the heritage, culture, and pride of African-American history, writing or editing stories for more than 30 children's books, including contemporary novels about teenagers and biographies of such historical figures as **Paul Robeson** and **W. E. B. Du Bois**. She produced collections of African-American folklore and slavery-era "liberation" stories of people, including **Harriet Tubman**, **Sojourner Truth**, and **Frederick Douglass**, as well as lesser known contemporaries such as Henry Box Brown.

Hamilton grew up on a small farm near the college town of Yellow Springs, Ohio, in the 1940s. The town is an old station on the Underground Railroad where her maternal grandfather, Levi Perry, had settled after escaping from slavery in Virginia, by crossing the Ohio River to freedom. Born into a big farm family, she was the daughter of Kenneth James and Etta Belle (Perry) Hamilton. With two older brothers and two older sisters, she was also surrounded by a large extended family of cousins, uncles, and aunts, and by the sights, sounds, and smells of rural America. These experiences later played a large role in the children's stories Hamilton spun as an adult.

Nonetheless, the fact that her own parents were storytellers was probably the biggest influence on the author, whom *Entertainment Weekly* called "a majestic presence in children's literature." In her acceptance speech for the 1988 Boston Globe/Horn Book Award for nonfiction, Hamilton said, "The past moves me and with me, although I remove myself from it. Its light often shines on this night traveler: and when it does, I scribble it down. Whatever pleasure is in it I need pass on. That's happiness. That is who I am."

Young Virginia, named for her grandfather's home state, listened at her mother's and father's knee: "My mother said that her father sat his ten children down every year and said, 'I'm going to tell you how I escaped from slavery, so slavery will never happen to you.'"

Hamilton received a full scholarship to Antioch College and after three years transferred to Ohio State University. She went on to the New School for Social Research in New York City where she continued her study of writing. In New York, she fell in love with a young poet, Arnold Adoff, whom she married in March 1960. The couple's honeymoon in Africa was another influence on her work. They began a life together in the big city and settled there for 15 years. They wrote as much as possible, making a living however they could. During those early years, Hamilton relates, she worked at such varied jobs as cost accountant for an engineering firm, nightclub singer, and museum receptionist. Virginia and Arnold had two children: a daughter, Leigh Hamilton, and a son, Jaime Levi, now an author in his own right. In 1967, Virginia published her first book, *Zeely*, and shortly thereafter, she and her family moved back to Yellow Springs.

Zeely (1967) was praised for its promotion of racial understanding. The novel tells the story of 11-year-old Elizabeth (Geeder) Perry, who sees a portrait of a beautiful Watusi queen. She fantasizes that her 6 1/2-foot-tall neighbor, Zeely Tayber, is also a Watusi queen, only to find out that she actually is. Geeder watches the beautiful Zeely walk at night, and she frightens her brother with stories about night travelers. Zeely helps Geeder understand the difference between fantasy and reality, and she leads Geeder to an even greater understanding of herself and the beauty of being who you are.

"*Zeely* was one of the very first books where black characters are simply being people and living; it's not a problem book about integration," Hamilton said. As a result, *Zeely* attracted considerable attention. Written during the era of racial strife across the country, mixed with a rising credo of "black is beautiful," the time was right for the novel.

Family, an important theme in most of Hamilton's books, is the emphasis of M.C. *Higgins the Great*. The novel is set in southern Ohio, where 13-year-old Cornelius Higgins and his close-knit family live on old family property just beneath a slag heap (created by strip miners). The slow moving heap threatens to engulf their home, and M.C. dreams of moving his family to safety. He surveys the world from a 40-foot steel pool, his place of refuge. From there, M.C. sees a "dude" he imagines will make his mother a singing star and enable them to move. Another outsider, Luthreta, who is hiking through this section of Appalachia, awakens M.C. to the reality that he is never going to solve his problems by daydreaming about them. This moves M.C. to finally take a small but symbolic action.

In 1968, Hamilton published *The House of Dies Drear*, a mystery centering on the Underground Railroad, which won the Edgar Allan Poe Award for best juvenile mystery of the year. Rich with the historical research that would characterize many of her subsequent works, the story of this house, which held an incredible secret, reflected the stories of liberation Hamilton grew up with in Yellow Springs, located just 60 miles north of the Ohio River—the legendary boundary between "slave" states and free. The isolated individual is the focus of *The Planet of Junior Brown* (1971), in which lonely people find support in each other, a story of urban life in New York.

Hamilton mixed realism, history, and folklore. *Justice and Her Brothers* (1978), *Dustland* (1980), and *The Gathering* (1981) are the fantasy novels comprising the "justice" trilogy. They deal with time travel, clairvoyance, and global disaster. *The Time Ago Tales of Jadhu* (1969) mimics traditional folktales while containing elements of fantasy. Other Hamilton books include *Bells of Christmas* (1990), *The Dark Way: Stories from the Spirit World* (1993), and *Plain City* (1993), a book in which Hamilton takes up the issues of homelessness and racial prejudice.

Jaguarundi (1995) is a picture book for young children. The animal tale offered an environmental slant on Hamilton's liberation theme. *Her Stories, African American Folktales, Fairy Tales, and True Tales* (1995) won the **Coretta Scott King** Award. She published *When Birds Could Talk and Bats Could Sing* in 1996.

Hamilton also edited numerous publications of the United States Committee for Refugees and wrote reviews of books related to the history of the American South. She was awarded a MacArthur Foundation grant in 1995.

Hamilton was the first African-American writer to receive the John Newbery Award. She also earned the American Book Award, the Coretta Scott King Award, the Boston Globe-Horn Book Award, the National Book Award, and the most prestigious of all, the Hans Christian Andersen Medal. In 1995 she was awarded the Laura Ingalls Wilder Medal. Her books are frequently placed on the American Library Association's list of Notable Books and Best Books for Young Adults.

Hamilton was instrumental in wiping out the glaring lack of children's literature about the ethnic experience that existed until recent years. One way she helped do this was by loaning her name for the past decade to an annual conference on multicultural children's literature, allowing writers to follow her lead.

REFERENCES: Cullinan, Bernice E., & Lee Galda. 1994. *Literature and the Child*. Orlando, FL: Harcourt Brace. Hamilton, Virginia (1996), "Home Page Away from Home," //www.cris.com/~Bonfire2/index.shtml. *Entertainment Weekly*, 2/5/1993. _____. 1974. *M.C. Higgins, the Great*. New York: Macmillan. _____. 1967. *Zeely*. New York: Macmillan. Huck, Charlotte S., Susan Helper, Janet Hickman, & Barbara Z. Kiefer. 1997. *Children's Literature in the Elementary School*., Dubuque, IA: Brown and Benchmark Publishers.

Editor's note: Hamilton's most recent books include *A Ring of Tricksters: Animal Tales from America, the West Indies, and Africa* (1997); *Second Cousins* (1998); *Bluish: A Novel* (1999), *The Girl Who Spun Gold* (2000, illustrated by **Leo and Diane Dillon**); *Wee Winnie Witch's Skinny: An Original Scare Tale for Halloween* (2001, illustrated by Barry Moser); *Time Pieces: The Book of Times* (2002); *Bruh Rabbit and the Tar Baby Girl* (2003); *Wee Winnie Witch's Skinny: An Original African American Scare Tale* (2004); a picture-book adaptation of *The People Could Fly Picture Book and CD* (2007, illustrated by Leo and Diane Dillon).

REFERENCES: *AANB*. Apseloff, Marilyn F. in *AWC-1960-86*. Ball, Jane, in *AAFW-55-84*. Bristow, Margaret Bernice Smith, in *COCAAL* and *OCAAL*. *Wiki*. Green, Heidi Hauser, in *GEAAL*. Hearne, Betsy, in *FTC*. Oleck, Joan, in *BB*. *CAO-04*. "Obituaries." *Publishers Weekly*. 249.9 (Mar. 4, 2002) p. 38. From *Literature Resource Center*. "Obituaries. (The Hunt Breakfast)." *The Horn Book Magazine*. 78.3 (May-June 2002) p. 366. From *Literature Resource Center*. //0-web.ebscohost.com.dbpcosdcsgt.co.san-diego.ca.us/novelist/detail?vid=79&hid=7&sid=d408b38a-8f5e-4ec2-b75c-cf9c5b5097d7%40sessionmgr3&bdata=JnNpdGU9bm92ZWxpc3QtGl2ZQ%3d%3d. //www.ala.org/ala/emiert/corettascottkingbookaward/cskpastwinners/alphabeticallist/cskalphabetical.cfm#au. //www.embracingthechild.org/africanamerican.htm. //www.hickorygov.com/library/bibs/aaf.htm. //www.library.uiuc.edu/blog/esslchildlit/archives/2008/02/african_america.html. //www.virginiahamilton.com/home.htm. //www.virginiahamilton.com/pages/about.htm. Amazon.com.

Hammon, Briton
fl. 1700s
Autobiography/memoir—slave narrative

All we know of Briton Hammon is contained in his 14-page memoir, *A Narrative of the Uncommon Sufferings, and Surprising Deliverance of Briton Hammon, A Negro Man—Servant to General Winslow* (printed in Boston in 1760). From it, we learn that he lived as a slave, obtained permission to leave his master's service to go to sea, and sailed to Jamaica on Christmas Day, 1747. On his return to the mainland, his ship—heavily laden with wood—got caught on a reef off the coast of Florida. The captain refused to dump any of the cargo, choosing instead to send some of his crew ashore in a small boat. When a landing party approached the shore, natives from the mainland chased them back to the ship and killed the captain and all his fellow crew members. Hammon managed to escape being killed, only to be held captive by them. Although he describes them as "barbarous and inhuman Savages" and "Devils," his description of their treatment of him is rather mild, noting that they fed him what they ate and "us'd me pretty well." After a time, some Spaniards helped him to escape to Havana, where the "Indians" pursued him. The Cuban governor refused to turn him over to them. Following a series of misadventures (including several years of wrongful detainment), Hammon managed to make his way to England. Next, he got work on a vessel headed back to Boston, only to find that his old master was a passenger, too. Hammon expressed his gratitude that "Providence" delivered him back into the hands of his master. Although this narrative is often cited as the first African-American **slave narrative**, many have questioned whether Hammon himself authored it.

REFERENCES: *AANB. BAL-1-P.* Murray, Keat E., in *GEAAL.* Williams, Roland L., Jr., in *COCAAL* and *OCAAL. W. Wiki.*

Hammon, Jupiter
10/17/1711–c. 1806
Poems, essays

A slave all his life, Hammon was well educated, and his intellect was given free expression within the circumstances to which he had adapted. A modest man who had become a deeply religious and devout Christian, Hammon wrote profoundly religious poems and essays. For a slave to be well educated and to write poetry was quite unusual, but Hammon went on to do something even more unusual: He had his writings published. The first literary work written by an African American and published in the United States was Hammon's 88-line "An Evening Thought. Salvation by Christ with Penitential Cries: Composed by Jupiter Hammon, a Negro belonging to Mr. Lloyd of Queen's Village, on Long Island, the 25th of December, 1760." The poem was published as a *broadside* (a work printed on single large sheet of paper) in 1761. Although he probably wrote many poems in the interim, the next published poem of Hammon's that survives to this day was written for the other famous African-American poet of his day: "An Address to Miss Phillis Wheatly [sic], Ethiopian Poetess, in Boston, who came from Africa at eight years of age, and soon became acquainted with the gospel of Jesus Christ" (1778). As is so often the case with trailblazers, he is better known for being first than for being foremost. His poems are simple and straightforward, focused on a single theme; subsequent literary critics have compared his verse rather unfavorably with that of his contemporary, **Phillis Wheatley**, as well with those who followed him.

Actually, **Lucy Terry Prince**'s poetry predates the work of both Hammon and Wheatley, and she is therefore the first African American to have written poems that survive to this day, but her poetry was published after that of both Hammon and Wheatley. Thus, Hammon was the first African American to have his writings published here, and Wheatley was the first African-American woman to have her works published. Two other poems of Hammon's are still extant: his "A Poem for Children with Thoughts on Death" (1782) and his verse "A Dialogue Entitled the Kind Master and Dutiful Servant" (1786). From the title of the 1786 poem, you may correctly infer that he recommended that slave owners be

kind to their slaves, but he also urged slaves to be patient in waiting for the bonds of slavery to be lifted. After all, he believed, they would be free forever in the world hereafter. He expressed these views in his *Address to the Negroes of the State of New York*, presented at the September 24, 1786, meeting of the African Society in New York City (published in 1787 and again in 1806). He did lament, however, that the patriotic African Americans who had fought in the Revolutionary War were not freed following the war, and he wished that slave owners would free their young slaves. Hammon's prose works include *A Winter Piece: Being a Serious Exhortation, with a Call to the Unconverted* (c. 1782), *A Short Contemplation on the Death of Jesus*, and *An Evening's Improvement, Showing, the Necessity of Beholding the Lamb of God* (c. 1783). In addition, *An Essay on the Ten Virgins* was advertised in a December, 1779, issue of the Connecticut *Courant* but has still not been found in printed form.

REFERENCES: *AANB. AAW:AAPP. BAL-1-P. BWA. EBLG. G-97.* Kaplan, Sidney. *The Black Presence in the Era of the American Revolution, 1770-1800.* New York Graphic Society Ltd, 1973. Rpt. in *Poetry Criticism.* Ed. Margaret Haerens and Christine Slovey. Vol. 16. Detroit: Gale Research, 1997. pp. 171-180. From *Literature Resource Center.* Munro, Karen, in *GEAAL.* O'Neale, Sondra, in *COCAAL* and *OCAAL. W. Wiki.* O'Neale, Sondra A., in *AAWBHR. ACW.* Palmer, R. Roderick. "Jupiter Hammon's Poetic Exhortations." *CLA Journal 18.1* (Sept. 1974), pp. 22-28. Rpt. in Margaret Haerens and Christine Slovey (Eds.) (1997), *Poetry Criticism* (Vol. 16). Detroit: Gale Research. From *Literature Resource Center.* Robinson, Lisa Clayton, in *EA-99.* Wegelin, Oscar. "Biographical Sketch." In Stanley Austin Ransom, Jr. (Ed.) (1970), *America's First Negro Poet: The Complete Works of Jupiter Hammon of Long Island.* Kennikat Press. Rpt. in Margaret Haerens and Christine Slovey (Eds.) (1997), *Poetry Criticism* (Vol. 16). Detroit: Gale Research. From *Literature Resource Center.* //www.csustan.edu/english/reuben/pal/chap2/hammon.html. //www.lib.uchicago.edu/efts/AAP/AAP.bib.html.

Handy, W. C. (William Christopher)
11/16/1873–3/28/1958
Blues composer, musician

A masterfully musical horn man, Handy realized that he would do better to publish his own music than to accept short money from someone else to publish it. Hence, in 1908, he and lyricist Harry H. Pace cofounded the song-publishing outfit Pace and Handy Music Company. Their company published countless blues and ragtime songs, including many he wrote himself (e.g., "Memphis Blues," reportedly the first blues song to be published as sheet music; as well as "Aunt Hagar's Children's Blues," "Joe Turner's Blues," "Beale Street Blues," and "St. Louis Blues"). He was able to claim the title "Father of the Blues" not only for the blues he wrote and played, but also for his writings, including *Blues: An Anthology* (1926),

W. C. Handy

Book of Negro Spirituals (1938), and *Father of the Blues* (1941, his autobiography).

REFERENCES: *DANB. EA-99. EAACH. SMKC.* —Tonya Bolden

Hansberry, Lorraine Vivian
5/19/1930–1/12/1965
Plays, essays, newspaper articles, poems; journalist

Lorraine Hansberry's writing was profoundly influenced by her family elders. Her uncle William Leo Hansberry was a scholar of African history at Howard University, so Lorraine learned from an early age to link the experiences and challenges of African Americans with those of Africans struggling for liberation in their native land. Lorraine's mother, Nannie Perry Hansberry, was a schoolteacher, an influential politician, and a prominent society matron (entertaining in their home such cultural luminaries as poet **Langston Hughes**, scholar **W. E. B. Du Bois**, actor **Paul Robeson**, musician Duke Ellington, and novelist **Walter White**). The educational and cultural opportunities Lorraine's mother provided enriched the texture of Lorraine's writing.

When Lorraine was a young girl, her father, Carl Augustus Hansberry, Sr., was a realtor who specialized in sub-

dividing large houses vacated by whites and selling the subdivided kitchenette units to African Americans migrating from the South. He was also a civil-rights activist, and these two roles combined to have a tremendous impact on Lorraine's childhood experiences. When Lorraine was just eight years old, the NAACP sponsored her father to challenge Chicago's discriminatory housing *covenants*—written agreements that prohibited African Americans and other people of color from moving into segregated European-American neighborhoods. With that support, Carl moved his wife and children into Hyde Park, a wealthy whites-only Chicago neighborhood. Needless to say, the Hansberrys weren't greeted with a welcome wagon at their front door. Instead, threats and curses were hurled at the family members, and bricks were tossed at—and into—their home, one brick (thrown through the front window) just barely missing young Lorraine. The NAACP even had to provide armed guards to protect the family for a time. Not long after, an Illinois court evicted the Hansberrys from the home they had purchased, enforcing the city's covenants. This eviction started a two-year-long judicial crusade, which ended up in the U.S. Supreme Court. At last, the most exalted court in the land upheld the Hansberrys' right to live in whatever neighborhood they chose, and it overturned Chicago's segregationist covenants as being unconstitutional.

Unfortunately, the precedent of the *Hansberry v. Lee* decision was not widely applied until further court cases broadened its applications. The whole experience so deeply discouraged Carl Hansberry that he was preparing to move away from an America he deemed hopelessly racist, to go to Mexico, when he died suddenly at age 51. The experience also profoundly affected Lorraine, who never forgot the daily hostility she felt as she walked to and from the local school. Once the Hansberrys returned to a working-class community, Lorraine and her two older brothers and older sister attended public schools. Although the Hansberry children continued to enjoy cultural and financial privileges unknown to their working-class schoolmates, their parents taught them to take pride in their race and to admire the courage shown by their working-class peers. The Hansberry children were also encouraged to show civic responsibility, challenging discriminatory practices wherever they met them—such as at local stores and restaurants.

After high school, Lorraine decided not to follow the family tradition of attending a black college, and she enrolled at the University of Wisconsin at Madison, a predominantly white university, to study journalism, as well as theater and the visual arts. At Madison, she integrated an all-white women's dormitory and was soon active in leftist politics, becoming the president of the Madison campus chapter of the Young Progressive Association. She also saw a production of Sean O'Casey's *Juno and the*

Paycock, about Irish peasants whose struggles, hopes, and dreams were dramatically portrayed; his play inspired Hansberry to consider how to dramatically depict the strivings, hopes, and dreams of working-class African Americans. Meanwhile, she noticed she was more interested in stage design than in other subjects, so she decided to pursue painting more rigorously, studying art at Chicago's Art Institute and in a school in Guadalajara, Mexico. After exploring her talents at art, however, she decided that she wasn't talented enough to make it her chief occupation, so she quit studying art and moved to New York.

In New York, Hansberry found odd jobs to support herself, while she perfected her skill as a writer. She frequently published articles, essays, reviews, and poetry in progressive periodicals such as **Paul Robeson**'s *Freedom*. *Freedom* soon hired Hansberry as a reporter and then as associate editor. When Robeson was unable to attend an international peace conference in Uruguay (because the U.S. State Department had revoked his passport), Hansberry went in his place. During this time, her civil-rights activism intensified, and she read ever more widely the works of African Americans (e.g., W. E. B. Du Bois, Frederick Douglass, and Langston Hughes). She also studied whatever she could find about African-American history, politics, and culture, and she increasingly spoke out at public rallies and meetings, attacking U.S. policies she deemed racist or imperialist.

While participating in a civil-rights demonstration at New York University (NYU), Hansberry met Robert Barron Nemiroff, the son of Russian Jewish immigrants, who had just earned his master's degree at NYU. The two courted briefly, then married on June 20, 1953, and moved to Greenwich Village. While Nemiroff pursued a career as a songwriter and music publisher, Hansberry left *Freedom* to write more creatively, such as sketches about the people and lifestyles she observed in Greenwich Village. Nemiroff also encouraged Hansberry to pursue her goal of writing a play. When one of Nemiroff's ballads became an instant hit, he offered financial support, as well as emotional and intellectual support, to Hansberry. Freed from having to earn a living, Hansberry devoted herself fully to writing her first play: *A Raisin in the Sun*. (In the early 1960s, after Hansberry had recognized and acknowledged her own lesbianism, she and Nemiroff divorced, but the two remained close friends.)

By 1957, Hansberry completed her play. Her title comes from Langston Hughes's *Harlem:* "What happens to a dream deferred? / Does it dry up / Like a raisin in the sun . . . ?" Fortunately, after she read her play to a friend of hers, her friend agreed to produce it. The play was a smash hit in its trial runs in New Haven, Philadelphia, and Chicago, and the rave reviews helped her garner enough financial support to produce the play on Broad-

Lorraine Hansberry

way, starring Sidney Poitier, **Ruby Dee**, and other outstanding actors.

What was the underlying story of this smash hit? The play was set in Chicago in the 1940s and showcases a working-class black family contemplating a move from a Chicago ghetto to a white-dominated Chicago suburb. The play opens as the recently widowed Lena Younger realizes that the payment from her deceased husband's insurance policy is enough to fulfill her husband's lifelong wish to buy a home in an upscale neighborhood. Lena's son, Walter, has other plans for the money. He sees it as his once-in-a-lifetime chance to take advantage of a business opportunity. The play revolves around these hopes and dreams of the principle characters, as well as the feelings and longings of Walter's sister, Beneatha, his wife, Ruth, and his son, Travis.

In addition to Hansberry's expert crafting of the drama, the play arrived at a propitious time in American history: closing out a decade in which African Americans were celebrating the *Brown v. the Topeka Kansas Board of Education* decision and the successful Montgomery bus boycott, and heralding the decade of civil-rights activism among both whites and blacks, including student sit-ins, Freedom Riders, and Freedom Summer. For all these reasons, *Raisin* instantly achieved critical, popular, and financial success. The play's 538 performances across 19 months made *Raisin* the longest-running play by an African American on Broadway. At age 29, Hansberry became the youngest person, the first African American, and the fifth woman to win the New York Drama Critics Circle Award for the Best Play of 1959, surpassing plays by Tennessee Williams and Eugene O'Neill. The play was later (1961) made into a movie starring Poitier (which won a special award at the Cannes film festival) and into a Tony Award-winning musical (in 1973).

Following Hansberry's success with *Raisin*, NBC commissioned Hansberry to write a drama commemorating the one-hundredth anniversary of the Civil War. The network executives judged her resulting drama, *The Drinking Gourd*, "superb," but because of her frank treatment of slavery, the executives decided not to produce it. Another of Hansberry's works, *What Use Are Flowers?* (written in 1962, published in 1972), about the aftermath of nuclear war, was also never produced.

The next play of Hansberry's to be produced was *The Sign in Sidney Brustein's Window* (1964). She set the play in Greenwich Village, the racially (and religiously) mixed community in which she lived. The title character is a Jewish liberal intellectual who continually fluctuates between his political conviction and commitment to action and his sense of disillusionment and existentialist apathy. This play opened in mid-October 1964, earning mixed reviews, and it closed on January 12, 1965—the same day that Hansberry died of cancer.

When Hansberry died at age 34, she left several unfinished plays, including *The Arrival of Mr. Todog*, a satire of Samuel Beckett's *Waiting for Godot;* a play about the eighteenth-century feminist Mary Wollstonecraft; and *Les Blancs*. Hansberry left her works in good hands, designating her ex-husband, Robert Nemiroff, the literary executor of her estate. Nemiroff took his role very seriously and spent the rest of his life devoted to completing, publishing, and producing her works. Among other works, he gathered her essays and articles against racism, homophobia, war, and oppression into the books *To Be Young, Gifted and Black* and *The Movement: Documentary of a Struggle for Equality*. Hansberry's legacy lives on through the work of others, as well. **Woodie King, Jr.**, discovered that two thirds of the contemporary playwrights he questioned acknowledged that Hansberry had either aided them directly or influenced them in their work.

REFERENCES: *1TESK. AA:PoP. AANB. BF:2000. EBLG. MAAL. NAAAL. OC20LE. RLWWJ.* Adams, Michael, in *T-CAD-1st.* Bigsby, C. W. E. *Confrontation and Commitment: A Study of Contemporary American Drama, 1959-66.* University of Missouri Press, 1968. Rpt. in Roger Matuz and Cathy Falk (Eds.) (1991), *Contemporary Literary Criticism* (Vol. 62). Detroit: Gale Research. pp. 156-173. From *Literature Resource Center.* Carter, Steven R., in *AAW-55-85:DPW,* and in *AW:ACLB-96.* Cheney, Anne. "Preface." "Chapter 1: White Fur and Football in the Depression." "Chapter 2: Nobody Is Crying: It's Just Quiet." "Chapter 3: The Talented Tenth and Long-headed Jazzers." "Chapter 5: Trying Not to Care: The Sign in Sidney Brustein's Window." "Chapter 7: The Human Race Concerns Me: To Be Young, Gifted and Black." "Chronology." "Author's Works." "Bibliography." *Twayne's United States Authors Series 430.* Boston: Twayne, 1984. From *The Twayne Authors Series.* Clark, Keith, in *OCWW.* Fisler, Ben, in *GEAAL.* Patti, Nicholas S., in *BB. CAO-03. CLCS. MWEL.* Miller, Jordan Y., in *BAW:P&D,* and in *RGAL-3.* Skolnik, Leslie-Anne, in *FW.* Wilkerson, Margaret B., in *AAW-1991. B. BCE. CE. COCAAL* and *OCAAL. E-97. EB-98. G-95. W. WB-98. Wiki.*

Hansberry, William Leo
2/25/1894–11/3/1965
Scholarly; educator

Editor's note: In *AANB,* Hansberry's death date is listed as October 17, which differs from other resources.

Long before European-American or even African-American scholars and intellectuals showed much interest in Africa, past or present, Hansberry was fascinated by his ancient homeland in Africa. At a time when precious few African Americans had more than a high-school education—and many had less—William Leo Hansberry earned a baccalaureate (1921) and a master's degree (1932) from Harvard University, which did not offer a doctorate in African studies. Despite the lack of American colleges offering postgraduate African studies, Hansberry continued his education, attending the Oriental Institute at the University of Chicago (1936), Oxford University (1937-1938) in England (funded by a Rockefeller Foundation grant), and Cairo University (1953) in Egypt. He shared what he was learning about Africa by teaching at Howard University in Washington, D.C., from 1922 until 1959.

After he retired, he traveled extensively throughout the continent to which he had devoted his study for nearly four decades. As modern African nations started emerging from colonial rule during the 1950s, Africans started to notice Hansberry's research. He won several Awards of Honor from the African Student Association of the U.S. and Africa (1951, 1959, 1963), a Fulbright scholarship to conduct field research in northeastern Africa (1953), a Bronze Citation for his "Forty Years of Service in the Cause of African Freedom" from the United Friends of Africa (1961), the First African Research Award from the Haile Selassie I Prize Trust (1964), and an honorary doctorate from the University of Nigeria. In addition, the University of Nigeria established the Hansberry College [or Institute] of African Studies in his name (1963). He delivered *Africana at Nsukka: Inaugural Address Delivered at the Hansberry College of African Studies, Nsukka, Eastern Nigeria, September 22, 1963* at the formal opening of the school and served as a distinguished visiting professor that year.

Eventually, Hansberry's American colleagues started to notice his work and to honor him with awards such as an Achievement Award from Omega Psi Phi Fraternity (1961), an honorary doctorate from Morgan State College, and a posthumous dedication naming a Howard University lecture hall in his honor (1972). Not until about a decade after his death, however, was his extensive research published in a two-volume compendium, *Pillars in Ethiopian History: The William Leo Hansberry African History Notebook, Volume I* (1974) and *Africa and Africans as Seen by Classical Writers: The William Leo Hansberry History Notebook, Volume II* (1977), both edited by Joseph E. Harris and both published by Howard University Press, at Hansberry's scholarly home.

Hansberry and his wife, Myrtle Kelso (married 1937), had two daughters—Gail Adelle and Myrtle Kay—but he may be better known for his ties to his niece, playwright **Lorraine Hansberry**.

REFERENCES: *CAO-03*. *Wiki*. Harris, Joseph E., in *AANB*. Wolf, Gillian, in *BB*. //library.msstate.edu/special_interest/Mississippi_African-American_Authors.asp.

Hansen, Joyce (Viola)
10/18/1942–
Novels for adults and juveniles; educator

While teaching middle-school students identified as learning disabled, Hansen was reminded of the importance of interesting, motivating reading materials for students who found reading to be burdensomely difficult. Dissatisfied with the relative lack of stimulating stories about nonwhite youths from low-income areas, she decided to write her own. Her contemporary novels—known for their realistic experiences and settings, their authentic dialogue, and believable characters—include her trilogy: *The Gift-Giver* (1980/2005); *Yellow Bird and Me* (1986/2005), cited as a Parents Choice book; and *One True Friend* (2001; edited by James Cross Giblin as an epistolary novel); as well as *Home Boy* (1982/2005). Her historical novels include her trilogy: *Which Way Freedom?* (1986/1992), a Coretta Scott King Honor Book; *Out from This Place* (1988/1992); and *The Heart Calls Home* (1999/2001). Two other historical novels are inspired by real characters: *The Captive* (1994/1995), which won the African Studies Association's Children's Book Award and was named a Coretta Scott King Honor Book; and *I Thought My Soul Would Rise and Fly: The Diary of Patsy, a Freed Girl* (1997), given a Coretta Scott King Award from the American Library Association. All of Hansen's books reflect her careful observation of the people from her own childhood and of her students, as she draws not only from their experiences but also their authentic voices.

Hansen has also published nonfiction history books, *Between Two Fires: Black Soldiers in the Civil War* (1993); *African Americans. Breaking Ground, Breaking Silence: The Story of New York's African Burial Ground* (1997, with Gary McGowan), a Coretta Scott King Honor Book; *"Bury Me Not in a Land of Slaves": African-Americans in the Time of Reconstruction* (2000); and *Freedom Roads: Searching for the Underground Railway* (2003, with Gary McGowan; illustrated by James Ransome). Her nonfiction biographies include *Women of Hope: African Americans Who Made a Difference* (1998/2007) and *African Princess: The Amazing Lives of Africa's Royal Women* (2004, illustrated by Laurie McGaw; for grades 4-8). Though she retired from teaching in 1995, she clearly has not retired from writing.

REFERENCES: Cain, Joy Duckett, in *GEAAL*. Foster, Frances Smith, in *CA/I*. *CAO-05*. *COCAAL* and *OCAAL*. Sandmann, Alexa L., in //0-web.ebscohost.dbpcosdcsgt.co.san-diego.ca.us/novelist/detail?vid=93&hid=7&sid=d408b38a-8f5e-4ec2-b75c-cf9c5b5097d7%40sessionmgr3&bdata=JnNpdGU9bm92ZWxpc3QtbGl2ZQ%3d%3d. //www.ala.org/ala/emiert/corettascottkingbookaward/cskpastwinners/alphabeticallist/cskalphabetical.cfm#au. //www.embracingthechild.org/africanamerican.htm. //www.joycehansen.com/bio.htm. Amazon.com.

Hare (aka Cuney-Hare), Maud (née Cuney)
2/16/1874–2/13/1936
Plays, nonfiction—music, history, folklore, biographies

Coming from a musical family and following her own talent, Maud Cuney studied at the New England Conservatory of Music. After school, one of her first jobs was to direct music at the Deaf, Dumb, and Blind Institute in Austin. When she was in her early 30s, she married William P. Hare and returned to New England.

Over the next three decades, Hare contributed greatly to music history and criticism, as well as to literature, writing a regular column for **Crisis**, into which she poured the wealth of folk songs and dances she had collected in Mexico and the Caribbean, tracing the African origins of many works. In her masterwork, *Negro Musicians and Their Music* (1936, just one month before her death), she provides priceless information on African-American performers, shows how many African-American musical expressions have African origins, and even offers an appendix of African musical instruments. Her medley of other offerings illustrate the breadth and range of this talented woman, including her biography of her father, *Norris Wright Cuney: Tribune of the Black People* (1913); her anthology of poems, *The Message of the Trees: An Anthology of Leaves and Branches* (1918); her musicological text, *Creole Songs* (1921); and her play, *Antar of Araby* (1929).

REFERENCES: *BAAW*. Koolish, Lynda, in *OCAAL*. Roses, Lorraine Elena, in *BWA:AHE*. —Tonya Bolden

Hare, Nathan
4/9/1934–

Nonfiction—sociology, psychology; educator, clinical psychologist, scholarly-journal founder

Before founding **Black Scholar**, *Journal of Black Studies and Research* (in 1969), Hare started the African-American studies department at San Francisco State University (in 1968), becoming perhaps the first to coordinate a black-studies department. In addition, Hare has published several books, including three edited books: *Contemporary Black Thought: The Best from The Black Scholar* (1973, coedited with Robert Chrisman), *Pan-Africanism* (1974, coedited with Robert Chrisman), and *Crisis in Black Sexual Politics* (1989, coedited with his wife, writer Julia Reed Hare). He also wrote *The Black Anglo-Saxons* (1965). In 1979, Nathan and his wife, Julia, founded the Black Think Tank (BTT), through which they have published the subsequent books they coauthored, including *The Endangered Black Family: Coping with the Unisexualization and Coming Extinction of the Black Race* (1984), *Bringing the Black Boy to Manhood: The Passage* (1985), *The Miseducation of the Black Child: The Hare Plan to Overhaul the Public Schools and Educate Every Black Man, Woman, and Child* (1991), and *The Black Agenda* (2002). With Mabel B. Little, he and Julia helped write *Fire on Mount Zion: My Life and History As a Black Woman in America* (1992), also a BTT publication. On her own, Julia wrote *How to Find and Keep a BMW: Black Man Working* (1995), also through BTT. Nathan also writes essays and other articles for periodicals such as *Black Collegian*, *Ebony*, and *Massachusetts Review* and for anthologies.

REFERENCES: *EBLG*. Alic, Margaret, in *BB*. CAO-08. Amazon.com.

Harlem Renaissance
1919–1940

Within the African-American community, a cultural movement called the Harlem Renaissance emerged in America during the 1920s. The renaissance called for greater awareness, increased artistic activity, and overt political comment by African Americans about the racial disparity and the insulting caricatures of blacks. Black artists consequently saw an opportunity and responsibility to influence prevailing views about themselves and their community through art. During the renaissance, many African-American artists moved to urban areas, including Harlem, New York and Chicago, and they produced an unprecedented amount of creative, culturally affirming works. These works are of varying genres, but all attempted to use art to highlight oppression and preju-

dice while promoting African Americans and their culture in a logical, artistic fashion.

The Harlem Renaissance, generally considered the first significant movement of black writers and artists in the United States, emerged during the Great Migration from the rural South to the urban North, following the end of World War I, and these two events contributed to its emergence. Between 1820 and 1920, a series of agricultural crises, coupled with a labor shortage in the Northern industrial centers, led approximately 2 million African Americans to move from the rural South to the urban North, in search of jobs and a better life. Their participation in the urban industrial work force resulted in greater racial cohesiveness and economic independence. This met with resistance from some conservative whites, provoking a revival of the Ku Klux Klan and an outbreak of racial violence.

This period of social conflict and upheaval inspired black intellectuals to reexamine their role in American society and their unique cultural heritage. Lured by the promise of employment, African Americans migrated to cities such as Chicago, Cleveland, Detroit, Philadelphia, and—especially—New York City. African Americans had fought in World War I to make the world safe for democracy but returned home to be confronted with racism, unemployment, and poverty. However, their racial identity had been solidified by their experiences in Europe, which had made African Americans more aware of this country's prejudices. "The war to end all wars" had made them now more eager than ever to change their condition. After World War I, African Americans began to fully recognize that racism and poverty could not take away their culture, which they prized increasingly.

First called New Negro Movement, the Harlem Renaissance was a dramatic upsurge of creativity in African-American literature, music, and visual art. The celebration of African-American culture came at a time in America's history when the restraints of the Victorian era were giving way to the boldness of the Roaring Twenties. The word *renaissance* means rebirth, but the Harlem Renaissance was more of a birth, unprecedented in its variety and scope, than a rebirth. Its participants celebrated the uniqueness of African-American poetry, fiction, drama, essays, music, dance, painting, and sculpture. Such flowerings of unusually fertile cultural activity are often referred to as times of renaissance.

During this period, the first influential African-American literary journals were established, and African-American authors and artists received their first serious critical appraisal and widespread recognition. New and established African-American writers published more fiction and poetry than ever before.

Many young African-American writers came into prominence during the Harlem Renaissance. With both black and white readers eager to experience a slice of African-American life, the literature of the time provided that experience. The most popular and prolific poet of the 1920s was **Langston Hughes**, whose work delves into the lives of the black working class. **Arna Bontemps**'s poems "The Return" and "Golgotha Is a Mountain" won awards given by *Opportunity* magazine. Another major figure of the period, **Countee Cullen**, wrote poems exploring the problem of racism and the meaning of Africa for African Americans. Among fiction writers, **Claude McKay** stands out as author of *Home to Harlem* (1928), the first commercially successful novel by a black writer. Other notable novels of the era include **Nella Larsen**'s *Passing* (1929), which focuses on sophisticated middle-class black women who are unable to escape the restrictions of racism, and **Jean Toomer**'s innovative novel *Cane* (1923), which demonstrates a strong identification with poor blacks. Many other authors, including poet **James Weldon Johnson**, folklorist **Zora Neale Hurston**, novelist **Rudolph Fisher**, **Georgia Douglas Johnson**, poet and critic **Sterling Brown**, and **Jessie Fauset** received recognition for their poetic short stories, dramas, and novels. Essayist **Eric Walrond**, novelist **Walter White**, and poet William Waring Cuney are just some of the other writers associated with the Harlem Renaissance.

To carve a niche for themselves in the literary scene, young, educated African Americans traveled to New York City, in particular to Harlem, which was the cultural and artistic center of African Americans. Something approaching cultural revolution took place. Although there were a few centers that approached Harlem's significance, their significance was to accentuate that the Harlem Renaissance constituted a racial awakening on a national and perhaps even a world scale. This national scope of the phenomenon has led some to dispute the very existence of the Harlem Renaissance, with some downplaying its identification with one district in New York City. Nonetheless, the term *Harlem Renaissance* has remained popular.

Much of the extraordinary creativity took place in Harlem, the gathering place for what black leader, sociologist, and historian **W. E. B. Du Bois** had labeled the Talented Tenth. Du Bois envisioned that this ten percent of African-American intellectuals and artists would lead African Americans in the United States. In Harlem, these intellectuals and artists debated about the future of African Americans. The impulse of artists was to create boldly expressive, high-quality art as a response to their social conditions. Younger, radical African Americans believed that a "realistic" view of African-American life had to be presented because it was art. Some conservative African-American critics believed that the literature should "uplift" the race by showing African Americans only in a positive light. A common goal and theme was an affirmation of African-American dignity and humanity in the face of poverty and racism.

However, most publishers and readers in the United States were still white, and a controversy developed over the degree to which the perceived expectations of the white establishment should be met. Many African-American writers felt that whites, interested only in stereotypical portrayals of blacks as primitive, were unduly fascinated by the more sensational aspects of Harlem and African-American sexuality. While this primitivism was rejected by some African-American authors as a destructive stereotype, it was actually fostered by others, who considered it a continuation of African custom and a defiance of white Puritanism. Among the poets who embraced primitivism was Bontemps.

The Harlem Renaissance was formally recognized as a movement in 1925 with the publication of **Alain Locke**'s anthology *The New Negro: An Interpretation*, in which he described the "New Negroes" of the 1920s. According to scholar **Arnold Rampersad**, *The New Negro* is the Harlem Renaissance's "definitive text, its Bible. Most of the participants in the movement probably held the book in similar regard." *The New Negro* "represents the triumph of the compiler's vision of a community and a nation changing before its eyes," Rampersad contends. It offered a definition of the cultural movement.

The Harlem Renaissance artists took on the self-appointed challenge to communicate the ills of racism through art rather than argument. They sought to chisel out a unique, African-centered culture for blacks and to simultaneously improve relations with whites. Johnson, with his influential anthology of verse, *Book of American Negro Poetry* (1922), set the manipulation of language and other patterns of signification as the heart of the African-American poetic enterprise. Thus, literature of the era was marked by a shift away from moralizing and political ideals, which had been characteristic of much post-Reconstruction writing.

At the same time, growing interest among white Americans in jazz and blues music and the discovery of some African sculpture by modernist artists broadened the audience for African-American writing. Some black critics, including Du Bois and **Benjamin Brawley**, welcomed the increase in white patronage and stressed the value of literature in fostering racial equality. Others, including Alain Locke and **Charles W. Chesnutt**, decried such overt use of literature for propaganda purposes. While few black critics asserted the complete independence of art from social concerns, most believed that literature could best promote racial equality by showing that black writers could produce works rivaling or surpassing those of their white counterparts.

During the Harlem Renaissance, New York City provided a wide variety of publishing opportunities. Major publishing companies began soliciting and publishing literary works by black writers. Several agencies had magazines that published work by young black writers and sponsored writing contests. Two such periodicals were *Crisis*, published by the National Association for the Advancement of Colored People (NAACP) and edited by Du Bois, and *Opportunity*, published by the Urban league and edited by **Charles S. Johnson**. Independent magazines, such as *The Messenger*—a militant socialist journal edited by **A. Philip Randolph** and **Chandler Owen**—published up and coming African-American writers. Some writers, such as **Wallace Thurman**, Langston Hughes, Zora Neale Hurston, Aaron Douglas, John P. Davis, **Bruce Nugent**, and **Gwendolyn Bennett**, even tried to start their own literary journal—*Fire!!*—which lasted only one issue.

Du Bois, continuing work he had started at the beginning of the century, produced books and essays on the position of African Americans in this country and on the steps African Americans needed to take to achieve equality. The appearance of African-American journals such as Du Bois's *Crisis* and Johnson's *Opportunity* made it much easier for black writers to publish in a style that suited their tastes.

The Harlem Renaissance writers reflected both the "uplifting" theme of the conservative African-American critics and the "realistic" artist movement of the younger, more radical African-American critics. Both sides succeeded in showing African Americans and the world that their culture was a worthy literary topic, that it was beautiful—a theme that would reemerge during the black-power movement of the mid-1960s and early 1970s.

REFERENCES: EBLG. **Baker, Houston A. Jr.** 1987. *Modernism and the Harlem Renaissance*. Chicago: University of Chicago Press. Bassett, John E. 1992. *Harlem in Review: Critical Reactions to Black American Writers, 1917-1939*. Selinsgrove: Susquehanna University Press. Bloom, Harold. 1994. *Black American Prose Writers of the Harlem Renaissance: Writers of English, Lives and Works*. New York: Chelsea. "Harlem Renaissance, 1919-1949," in *NAAAL*. Lewis, David Levering. 1981. *When Harlem Was in Vogue*. New York: Knopf. Britannica Online—Biographies, Audio/Video, *Bibliography: Harlem Renaissance*, //blackhistory.eb.com/micro/259/32.html. Encarta Schoolhouse (1997), "The Harlem Renaissance," //www.encarta.com/schoolhouse/Harlem/harlem.asp. —Janet Hoover and Michael Strickland

Harlem Renaissance, literary and scholarly journals of the "New Negro" era
c. 1919–1939

Publication venues for prominent African Americans during this time period

From about 1915 to 1930 or so, about 1.3 million African Americans participated in the Great Migration from the rural South to the urban North. These migrants sought to escape from the violent and legally codified racism of the Jim Crow South to find jobs and educational opportunities for themselves and their children in the urban North, where racism persisted, but less savagely so than in the South. Though African Americans congregated in Chicago, Cleveland, Detroit, Philadelphia, and other urban areas, they particularly sought homes in the Harlem community of New York City. Hence, a shorthand term for this period is the "Harlem Renaissance," though it might just as well have been less glamorously called the "Big Northern City Renaissance." During this literary flowering, numerous literary journals appeared-many just as briefly as a summer blossom, a few continuing as perennials.

A few journals heralded the new era of rebirth: *Colored American Magazine* (1900-1909), originated by **Pauline Hopkins** in Boston, then bought out by an ally of **Booker T. Washington** and moved to New York City; *Voice of the Negro* (1904-1907), founded by John Wesley Edward Bowen and **Jesse Max Barber**, in Atlanta, Georgia, then moved in 1906 to Chicago, where Barber struggled on for another year; and *Alexander's Magazine*, founded in Boston by Charles Alexander, an ally of Booker T. Washington. Also of note was *Negro Music Journal: A Monthly Devoted to the Educational Interest of the Negro in Music* (1902-1903, Vol. 1-2), founded in Washington, D.C.

As 1919 approached, other journals came into existence, most notably **The Crisis** (1910-; originally subtitled *A Record of the Darker Races*), founded by **W. E. B. Du Bois** as the official magazine of the National Association for the Advancement of Colored People (NAACP); and **The Messenger** (1917-1928), founded by **A. Philip Randolph** and **Chandler Owen**. (*See* the main entries for these two journals for more information.) In 1918, **Cyril Valentine Briggs** (editor of the **Amsterdam News**, 1912-1919) founded *The Crusader* (1918-1922), subtitled *Journal of the Hamitic League of the World and the African Blood Brotherhood*, an African-American nationalist organization that aimed "To inspire the Negro with new hopes; to make him openly proud of his race and of its great contributions to the religious development and civilization of mankind and to place in the hands of every race man and woman and child the facts which support the League's claim that the Negro Race is the greatest race the world has ever known" (quoted in //en.wikipedia.org/wiki/Hamitic_League_of_the_World). In addition, *The Half-Century Magazine* (1916-1925, Vol. 1-18) was founded in Chicago; and *Stylus* (1916-1929) started its intermittent publication at Washington, D.C.'s, Howard University, where it was reputed to be the first African-American literary journal to be published by a historically black college or university. *Stylus* published noteworthy literary figures such as Chesnutt, Du Bois, Dunbar-Nelson, and Hurston. More clearly academic, *The Journal of Negro History* (1916-2002; 2002-present as *The Journal of African American History*) was founded by historian **Carter G. Woodson**, as a quarterly journal of the Association for the Study of Afro-American Life and History (now the Association for the Study of African American Life and History).

At last, the 1920s dawned, and with it the era of renaissance. The most noteworthy new literary journals included *Brownies' Book* (January 1920-December 1921), intended for African-American children ages 6-16 years, published by W. E. B. Du Bois and Augustus Granville Dill. Du Bois invited **Jessie Redmon Fauset** to edit the periodical, and she not only edited it but also wrote many of the pieces for it. Fauset featured historical biographies of notable African Americans, such as Denmark Vesey and **Sojourner Truth**, as well as articles on current events and Africa, plus games, riddles, and music. For the National Urban League, **Charles Spurgeon Johnson** founded *Opportunity: A Journal of Negro Life* (1923-1949), which published fiction, poetry, and book reviews, as well as nonfiction articles addressing the issues of concern to the National Urban League. *Fire!! Devoted to Younger Negro Artists* (1926) also ignited during this era. The brainchild of **Langston Hughes**, it was edited by **Wallace Thurman**, with associate editors **Zora Neale Hurston** and **Gwendolyn Bennett**. Lack of financing turned it to ashes after one issue. Two years later, Thurman tried again, launching *Harlem: A Forum for Negro Life* (1928), also with the editorial help of Hurston, Hughes, and Bennett, but again inadequate financing killed it after its first issue.

In June of 1923, the official entity of the **Howard University Press** launched *The Howard Review* (1923-1925), which scholar **Rayford W. Logan** called "among the best of its kind" and said, Howard's "College of Liberal Arts at no subsequent time has published as scholarly a belle-lettristic periodical as *The Howard Review*" (quoted in Logan, 2004). Howard's Dudley Woodard served as editor-in-chief, with **Alain Locke, Ernest Everett Just**, St. Elmo Brady, and Dwight O. W. Holmes his associate editors. Pieces covered every aspect of academia, from esoteric science articles to highly literary works. Howard's other publications of that time included the newsletter-style *Howard University Record* (starting in 1907) and the student journal *The Hill Top* (starting January 22, 1924).

Other journals of this era include *The Competitor: The National Magazine* (1920-1921, Vol. 1-3), founded in Pittsburgh, with the aim of highlighting African-American achievements in all fields of endeavor, featuring essays and articles, as well as short stories and poems. *The Negro Churchman* (1923-1931), an official organ of the African Orthodox Church, was edited by Garveyite George Alexander McGuire. It was also during this time that the European-American-owned and -operated *Survey Graphic* (1921-1952) published its famed "Harlem: Mecca of the New Negro" issue in the spring of 1925, guest-edited by scholar Alain Locke.

Even as the economic crisis of the 1930s and world events started crashing in on the New Negro renaissance, new journals continued to emerge. By far the most noteworthy literary journal was *Challenge* (1934-1937), founded by **Dorothy West**, whose editorial vision was highly aesthetic and apolitical. She had founded the magazine with $40 of her own money, and despite struggling to finance it, she managed to publish five or six issues between 1934 and 1937. Though she was able to include esteemed authors such as **Arna Bontemps, Countee Cullen**, Zora Neale Hurston, Langston Hughes, **Helene Johnson, Claude McKay**, and **Pauli Murray**, she was often given less than their finest work.

Pressured to present a broader editorial vision and to include more of the younger, less well-established writers, in 1937, West renamed the journal *New Challenge* (1937) with **Richard Wright** as her associate editor and a broad editorial board including **Sterling A. Brown, Owen Dodson, Margaret A. Walker**, and others. These new voices gave the *New Challenge* a more leftist, political leaning, which did not suit West, so she let the journal's continuing financial problems shut it down after a single issue. That one issue, however, introduced **Ralph Ellison**, and it included Wright's landmark essay, "Blueprint for Negro Writing."

Several journals had more clear political purposes, such as *The Black Man: A Monthly Magazine of Negro Thought and Opinion* (1933-1939), the organ of **Marcus Garvey**'s UNIA organization; and *Race: Devoted to Political and Economic Equality* (1935-1936), which published only two issues but included book reviews and poems, as well as articles by **Ralph Bunche, E. Franklin Frazier**, Langston Hughes, and Alain Locke, among others. *The Brown American* (1936-1945) included articles by NAACP leaders W. E. B. Du Bois, **Roy Wilkins**, and **James Weldon Johnson**, as well as by educator Mary McLeod Bethune and singer Marian Anderson.

The 1930s also saw the emergence of professional journals, such as the *National Negro Health News* (January 1933-June 1950), published in collaboration with the United States Public Health Service, to provide communities and social-service organizations with health-related information, as well as to highlight the work of African-American physicians and other health-care workers. Numerous journals of education appeared, such as *The Negro Needs Education* (1935-1936); *Quarterly Review of*

Higher Education among Negroes (1933-1960), which published conference papers, essays, symposia reports, and other articles pertaining to African-American college educators and education; and *Education: A Journal of Reputation (Negro Needs Society)* (1935-1936), which included not only articles and essays for educators, but also poems, short stories, editorials, and local notices touting the importance of education.

Howard University's *The Journal of Negro Education* (*JNE*, 1932-present, now subtitled *A Howard University Quarterly Review of Issues Incident to the Education of Black People*) deserves special mention. For its first 31 years, the journal was edited by Charles H. Thompson, whose 100-plus articles and editorials denounced Jim Crow educational policies and other racist practices that harmed African-American students. From its start, the journal was intended both to publish data and analyses of what was known regarding the education of African Americans and to stimulate further research to gain deeper understanding of both the existing education of African Americans and the desired best educational practices for educating African Americans. For instance, the *JNE* published "Some Psychogenic Hazards of Segregated Education of Negroes" by Howard Hale Long and "Emotional Factors in Racial Identification and Preference in Negro Children" by **Kenneth B. Clark** and **Mamie P. Clark**, reporting their classic investigation revealing African-American children's preference for white dolls versus black dolls. This research was later critical to the U.S. Supreme Court's unanimous 1954 decision on *Brown v. Board of Education*, overturning legal racial segregation in public schools. In addition to Long and the Clarks, other esteemed contributors have included **Ralph J. Bunche**, W. E. B. Du Bois, **E. Franklin Frazier**, Dorothy Height, **Charles Spurgeon Johnson**, Alain L. Locke, **Thurgood Marshall, Benjamin E. Mays, Dorothy Burnett Porter (Wesley)**. The journal's editors make it clear that the *JNE* is "edited and published under the sponsorship of the School of Education at Howard . . . [but] the Journal is not now and has never been merely a local organ of Howard University" (quoted in //www.journalnegroed.org/generalinfo.html).

FURTHER READING: Huggins, Nathan Irvin (Ed.). 1995. *Voices from the Harlem Renaissance*. New York: Oxford University Press. Logan, Rayford W. 2005. *Howard University: The First Hundred Years 1867-1967*. New York: New York University Press. Wintz, Cary D., and Paul Finkelman (Eds.). 2004. *Encyclopedia of the Harlem Renaissance*. London: Taylor & Francis. //africanamericanlit.suite101.com/article.cfm/dorothy_west. //biography.jrank.org/pages/2886/West-Dorothy.html. //en.wikipedia.org/wiki/Dorothy_West. //en.wikipedia.org/wiki/Great_Migration_(African_American). //en.wikipedia.org/wiki/Hamitic_League_of_the_World. //en.wikipedia.org/wiki/Journal_of_African_American_History. //en.wikipedia.org/wiki/The_Journal_of_Negro_History. //mts.lib.uchicago.edu/collections/findingaids.html. //www.answers.com/topic/new-challenge. //www.asalh.org/.

//www.jaah.org/index.html. //www.journalnegroed.org/general info.html. //www.liu.edu/cwis/cwp/library/historic.htm. //www.notable biographies.com/supp/Supplement-Sp-Z/West-Dorothy.html.

FURTHER READING: *See* **journals and magazines, literary**, and the entries for specific journals mentioned herein, for more information. *See also* the entries and references for the authors named herein.

Harlem Writers Guild
1950–
Mutual-support group for African-American writers

In 1950, the blossom of the **Harlem Renaissance** had long since withered, and the **Black Arts Movement** was decades away. More immediately, **Richard Wright**, the rare African-American author to have two books published in the 1940s (1940, 1945), had fled to Paris, and **Ralph Ellison** was still writing his *Invisible Man* (1952). These were tough times for African-American writers. It seemed almost outrageously bold to proclaim oneself an African-American writer at that time, given the overwhelming odds against getting published at all, let alone eking out a living from the sale of published work.

Many African-American and other writers sought succor from writer groups forming in Greenwich Village, guided and mostly populated by European-American writers. Those writer groups that welcomed African-American writers were often led by leftists who had predetermined political agendas to which they expected their African-American colleagues to adhere. Still, these European-American writers could offer technical assistance, literary critiques, and writing tips. They could also affirm the worth of their African-American colleagues' serious efforts to write. They could not, however, provide nourishment and empathy, and they could not affirm the cultural experiences of their African-American colleagues.

To meet these needs, Walter Christmas, **John Henrik Clarke, Rosa Guy**, and **John Oliver Killens** banded together to form what has become the oldest continuously operating organization of African-American writers in the United States. In a small storefront office one story above the corner of 125th Street and Lenox Avenue (now called **Malcolm X** Boulevard), these hearty souls founded what they called the "Harlem Writers Club." From the small storefront office, the club moved to libraries, empty offices, meeting halls, and a rotating array of members' apartments, picking up new members along the way as the itinerant club moved from place to place. At last, in the 1980s, the Harlem Writers Guild (HWG) officially designated its permanent home as the Schomburg Center for Research in Black Culture, part of the New York Public Library, located at 515 Malcolm X Boulevard, with its entrance at 103 West 135th Street, about 10 blocks from its original meeting place. According to a 1999 article (by Nikki Terry), the Guild meets there on the first Tuesday and the third Wednesday of each month.

According to **John Henrik Clarke**, the first fiction piece published by a Harlem Writers Guild member was his own "The Boy Who Painted Christ Black" (1948). Probably the first book published by a Harlem Writers Guild member was John Oliver Killens's *Youngblood* (1954). Other early members of the Harlem Writers Guild included **Maya Angelou, Alice Childress, Ossie Davis, Ruby Dee, Lon Elder III, Lorraine Hansberry, Audrey Lorde, Paule Marshall, Julian Mayfield, Louise Meriwether, Loften Mitchell**, Henry Moon, Willard Moore, **Douglas Turner Ward**, and **Sarah Elizabeth Wright**, still an active member of the Guild.

By the mid-1980s, John Oliver Killens estimated that Guild members had produced more than a few-hundred original works of poetry and prose, fiction and nonfiction, stage plays and screenplays. Members have also edited or contributed to luminous periodicals such as *Black Scholar, Crisis*, and *Freedomways*. Even as most of the founders went on to other ventures, other writers found a haven at the guild, such as William H. Banks, Jr., **Joyce Hansen, Terry McMillan, Walter Mosley, Valerie Wilson Wesley**, and **Brenda Wilkinson**. Current members include **Walter Dean Myers**, Betty Anne Jackson, Gammy L. Singer, and Sandra L. West.

The Guild's executive secretary is Grace F. Edwards, whose novel *In the Shadow of the Peacock* was reprinted by the newly founded Harlem Writers Guild Press. In addition, in the summer of 2006, the HWG Press published works by these current members: Judy C. Andrews, Eugene Landon Hobgood, and K. C. Washington. The HWG Press was developed through a partnership with digital publisher iUniverse.com, announced in 2000.

The Guild also participates in educational programs, both formal, such as a creative writing workshop for the writing program of the New School University, and informal, such as community workshops in public libraries throughout New York City and Brooklyn. Many members also participate in the annual Harlem Book Fair each summer. HWG members also started a television (WNYE, channel 25) and radio (WNYE, 91.5) program called *In Our Own Words* in 1990. Members Grace Edwards and Terry McMillan have appeared on the program, as have guests **Edwidge Danticat, Nikki Giovanni, Dick Gregory, Ishmael Reed, Ntozake Shange**, and many others.

REFERENCES: Banks, William H., Jr. (Ed.). 2005. *Beloved Harlem: A Literary Tribute to Black America's Most Famous Neighborhood: From the Classics to the Contemporary*. New York: Harlem Moon (Doubleday). Terry, Nikki, (Summer 1999), "Profile: The Harlem Writers Guild," *Mosaic*, p. 93, in //mosaicmagazine.org/pdf/mosaic%20summer% 201999.pdf. //biography.jrank.org/pages/2862/Killens-John-O.html. //crimesistahs.blogspot.com/2006_02_01_archive.html. //en.wikipedia. org/wiki/African_American_art. //en.wikipedia.org/wiki/Schomburg_ Center_for_Research_in_Black_Culture. //theharlemwritersguild.org/ history.htm. //theharlemwritersguild.org/hwg_press.htm. //theharlem writersguild.org/members.htm. //www.islandmix.com/backchat/f17/dr-john-henrik-clakrke-harlem-writers-guild-38695/. //www.nathaniel turner.com/johnoliverkillens.htm. //www.npl.org/Pages/Programs Exhibits/PressReleases/PR_BHM08_010208.html. //www.thefree library.com/Harlem+Writers+Guild+&+iUniverse.com+Partner+t o+Create+New+Publishing...-a059652285.

FURTHER READING: *See also* cross-references to authors shown in bold type.

Harper, Frances Ellen Watkins (née Frances Ellen Watkins; occasional pseudonym: "Effie Afton")
9/24/1825–2/20/1911

Poems, novels, short stories, columns, spoken word—speeches; journalist, columnist, orator, social reformer/activist, literary journal coeditor

Young Frances was born free, the only child of free parents, in the slave state of Maryland. Sadly, her mother and father died before she was old enough to have any memories of them. Luckily, she was raised by her uncle William Watkins and his wife and their children. The William Watkins Academy for Negro Youth had an excellent reputation for rigorous instruction in vocational subjects (such as seamstress training), academic subjects (such as languages and oratory), and moral leadership (such as abolition, radical politics, and biblical studies). Unfortunately, as was common at that time, financial pressures forced Frances to stop her formal education at age 13 and to start working as a housekeeper. Fortunately, her employers owned a bookstore, so in her spare time, she was able to read widely to advance her own self-education.

While still a teenager, Frances began writing poetry, and when she was about 20, her early poems were gathered into the collection *Forest Leaves*, published in about 1845. (The collection has since gone out of print, and no known copies remain.) When Frances Watkins was about 25 years old, she put into practice her self-teaching and her talent for public speaking, becoming the first female instructor (teaching "domestic science") at the Union Seminary (later a part of Wilberforce University) in Columbus, Ohio. In 1853, Maryland passed a law prohibiting any free blacks from entering or returning to that state. Thereafter, if Watkins had been caught in her home state of Maryland, she risked being either imprisoned or enslaved. That law inflamed Watkins's abolitionist passions. Hence, after a couple of years teaching in Ohio and in Pennsylvania, she was easily persuaded by **William Grant Still** to join the Underground Railroad and to begin speaking out on abolition.

Watkins started lecturing for the Maine Anti-Slavery Society, delivering her fiery oratory throughout the northeastern United States and in Canada. Despite the difficulties of transportation during that era, she carried out a grueling schedule of lectures, often lecturing in a new city every other day, commonly giving more than one lecture in each city. She spiced her speeches with her own original poems, which she managed to jot down while on the road. Although most of her poems addressed the issue of slavery, she also focused on feminist issues and topics such as religion, racial pride, and African-American history. While frantically scurrying from city to city, she virtually created the genre of protest poetry. This energetic, enthusiastic orator published her poems, essays, anecdotal sketches, and letters in various periodicals.

In 1854, her volume *Poems on Miscellaneous Subjects*, including both poems and essays, was published in both Boston and Philadelphia. It sold briskly, easily establishing her reputation as the most popular African-American poet of the era, and going through 20 more editions over the next 20 years. Following is an excerpt from just one of the poems in that volume, from her well-regarded "Bury Me in a Free Land" (quoted in *BWA*, p. 225):

Make me a grave where'er you will,
In a lowly plain, or a lofty hill;
Make it among earth's humblest graves,
But not in a land where men are slaves.
. . . [three stanzas] . . .
I'd shudder and start if I heard the bay
Of bloodhounds seizing their human prey,
And I heard the captive plead in vain
As they bound afresh his galling chain.
. . . [two stanzas] . . .
I ask no monument, proud and high,
To arrest the gaze of the passers-by;
All that my yearning spirit craves,
Is bury me not in a land of slaves."

Also in that volume was her poignant poem "The Slave Mother":

Heard you that shriek? It rose
So wildly in the air,
It seemed as if a burdened heart
was breaking in despair.
. . . [two stanzas] . . .
He is not hers, although she bore
For him a mother's pains;
He is not hers, although her blood
Is coursing through his veins!
He is not hers, for cruel hands
May rudely tear apart
The only wreath of household love
That binds her breaking heart.
. . . [four stanzas] . . .

This poem of devastating separation at the slave-auction block is among the most frequently anthologized of Harper's poems.

With **Frederick Douglass** and several other notables, she coedited and contributed to the *Anglo-African Magazine,* probably the earliest African-American literary journal. In that journal, in 1859, she published "The Two Offers," generally believed to be the first short story by an African American to appear in print. Although not her best literary effort, the work was revolutionary in its message that conscientious, smart women may choose options for their lives other than marriage.

In November 1860, Watkins chose to marry Fenton Harper, a widower with three children, and she used the proceeds from her book sales to buy a farm for her new family. Meanwhile, Frances continued to write. Considered one of the most popular African-American poets and most prolific women writers of the nineteenth century, her stories, poems, letters, and essays continued to appear in various abolitionist and African-American periodicals. Nonetheless, she, Fenton, and the children settled into domestic life, and after a time, Frances gave birth to their new daughter, Mary. Less than four years later, Fenton died, and after creditors claimed the farm and most of their other belongings, Frances was left penniless with four children to support.

Frances Harper hit the lecture circuit again, with full vigor (and her infant daughter Mary). She spent the next five years traveling throughout the post-Civil War South, lecturing to whites and blacks—separately and in integrated forums—in every southern state but Texas and Arkansas. She prodded whites to fully integrate Negroes into the mainstream of American life, and she urged former slaves to build up their race by enhancing their own lives, such as by mastering reading, writing, political participation, and home management. While in the South, she also wrote for Northern newspapers, exhorting their readers to lend their financial, moral, and physical support for Reconstruction.

Soon after she returned to the lecture circuit, she joined the newly founded American Equal Rights Association. (Fellow members included abolitionists and suffragists **Frederick Douglass**, Harriet Forten Purvis and **Robert Purvis**, **Sojourner Truth**, Susan B. Anthony, Lucretia Mott, and Elizabeth Cady Stanton.) Much to her dismay, these passionate idealists ended up dividing over whether the Fifteenth Amendment to the U.S. Constitution should extend the right to vote to blacks *and* to women, to black men (but not to women), or to white women (but not to blacks). She rejected both the racism underlying the focus on women and the sexism underlying the focus on blacks. Unless the franchise was extended to both blacks and women, Harper would not have the right to vote. Nonetheless, most agreed that the amendment stood little chance of passing at all if the white men in the U.S. Congress and in state legislatures were asked to extend the voting privilege so broadly.

Harper tried to negotiate some agreement between the factions, often reminding them that "We are all bound up together in one great bundle of humanity." Despite her tremendous oratory gifts and persuasive charms, Harper was unable to unify the conflicting parties and ended up having to divide her attentions between increasingly separate interest groups. She spoke out fervently in opposition to lynching and in support of educational and economic opportunities for blacks; she lectured widely for the American Women's Suffrage Association; and she railed against alcohol for the Women's Christian Temperance Union. As in her youth, whenever she spoke, she lectured without notes, but she often pulled poems, short stories, or anecdotal sketches from her writings, to make particular points or to highlight her commentary.

In addition to her lectures, her essays, her letters, and her poems, Harper managed to write four novels. In all genres, Harper attended to the aesthetics of her writing, manipulating form and technique to suit her purpose. Her purpose was vital, too, however, as all her writing was intended to uplift her people. In the late 1860s, she published her blank-verse allegory, *Moses: A Story of the Nile*, narratively addressing the hopes and strivings of African Americans in the era of Reconstruction. At about the same time, she used the Moses allegory in her serialized novella, *Minnie's Sacrifice*, which encouraged African Americans to dedicate themselves to high ideals for elevating the race. She also dedicated her late-1860s novel, *Sowing and Reaping: A Temperance Story*, serialized in the *Christian Recorder*, to the temperance movement.

In the 1870s, she published her collection simply entitled *Poems*, followed soon after by her collection *Sketches of Southern Life* (1872). In her *Sketches*, she addressed the difficulties of Southern blacks through a series of dialect poems allegedly narrated by "Aunt Chloe." Aunt Chloe valiantly survived slavery and models the best in what African-American women could achieve in a postslavery era. Aunt Chloe summons the courage she needed to survive slavery to take on a monumental task at age 60: learning to read. In other verses, Aunt Chloe poetically gives an oral history of her life under slavery, and she describes her current political and community activism (e.g., helping to build churches and schools and encouraging the menfolk to vote conscientiously). Like other African-American women of her era, Aunt Chloe may never have considered herself a feminist, but she exemplifies feminist thought and womanly strength in all she does and says.

Shortly after her *Sketches* was produced, Harper started writing a newspaper column in which she created the characters of Jenny, a recent college graduate and aspiring poet, and her Aunt Jane, a socially conscientious woman who encourages Jenny's aspirations while reminding her to shape them to societal improvement. Through their "conversations" and activities, Harper discussed issues of aesthetics, politics, social reform, economics, and morality. Following her example, **Langston Hughes** used his character Simple as a vehicle for exploring twentieth-century social issues. Several other journalists have similarly followed suit.

In the late 1880s, Harper published *Trial and Triumph*, her temperance novel that refuted the myths of the happy slave, the chivalrous plantation owner, and the treacherous black freedman being propounded by white Southern plantation-school literature. In 1892, she published her novel *Iola Leroy: Or, Shadows Uplifted* (1892), considered the first book to depict the experiences of African Americans during Reconstruction, as told by an African American. *Iola Leroy* tells the melodramatic story of an octoroon who initially passes for white, then is discovered to be black and is sold into slavery. During the Civil War, she becomes a nurse. When a white doctor proposes marriage to her, contingent on her willingness to again pass for white, she refuses him. She later meets and marries an African-American doctor who shares her devotion to social reform and racial uplift. Although Harper's mulatta suffers, she is not a typical tragic mulatta: She is not martyred for her race, but she dedicates herself to working to uplift her race. Further, Harper's fiction does not equate lightness of skin with nobility or accomplishment. Though she was a product of her time, Harper's feminism, positive values, and racial pride heralded sentiments that were not to be more fully appreciated for nearly a century.

In addition to her fiction, between 1890 and 1901, Harper published several poetry collections, including *The Sparrow's Fall and Other Poems, Atlanta Offering: Poems, Martyr of Alabama and Other Poems, Poems*, and *Idylls of the Bible* (1901). More recently, Harper's poems have been anthologized in *Complete Poems of Frances E. W. Harper* (1988) and *A Brighter Coming Day: A Frances Ellen Watkins Harper Reader* (1990).

When Harper was in her midseventies, her health began to fail, and she had to slow down and eventually stop lecturing. Her daughter Mary, a social worker, continued to lecture until Mary died in 1909. Two years later, the heart that had so vigorously sustained the life—and the liveliness—of Frances Ellen Watkins Harper gave out. Though she did not survive, her literary descendants live on. Her protest poetry can be seen in the writings of **Nikki Giovanni, Sonia Sanchez**, and **Audre Lorde**; her early feminist themes can be found today in the works of **Alice Walker** and **Gloria Naylor**. Her biblical and literary allusions and her love of lyrics are today expressed in the work of **Margaret Walker** and **Rita Dove**. Her journalistic legacy has lived on through the work of **Ida B. Wells** and of contemporary African-American reporters, correspondents, and newspaper publishers.

REFERENCES: *1TESK. AANB. AA:PoP. BAL-1-P. BF:2000. BWA. EBLG. MAAL. MWEL. NAAAL. PBW. RT. TtW.* Campbell, Jane, in *OCWW.* Diana, Vanessa Holford, in *GEAAL.* Foster, Frances Smith, in *B. COCAAL* and *OCAAL. W. Wiki.* Gautier, Amina. "African American women's writings in the Woman's Building Library." *Libraries & Culture.* 41.1 (Winter 2006): p. 55. *Literature Resources from Gale.* //digital.nypl.org/schomburg/writers_aa19/bio2.html. *EB-98. WB-98.* Rubiner, Joanna, in *BB.*

Harper, Michael S. (Steven)
3/18/1938–
Poems; educator

Born in Brooklyn, Michael Harper grew up in a mostly white area in western Los Angeles. His parents, Walter Warren Harper (a postal supervisor) and Katherine Johnson Harper (a medical stenographer), provided their son with middle-class comforts (e.g., an extensive record collection and lots of books)—and expectations. When Michael was in junior high school, his asthma prevented him from participating much in gym class, so his gym teacher flunked him. That failing grade kept him from being on the school's honor roll, and Michael lost his enthusiasm for studying. At Dorsey High School, a school counselor started to put Michael in classes on the vocational-education track. Walter Warren Harper would have none of that, and he soon made it clear that his son was destined for a career in medicine, not for a career in industrial arts. Michael's own interests, however, inclined more toward writing poems than toward probing human physiology.

In 1955, Harper enrolled at Los Angeles City College and then transferred to Los Angeles State College. At first, Michael compliantly took premed courses—until his zoology professor advised him that no African American would be able to get into medical school. In the face of this racist advice, he turned to literature, studying the letters of poet John Keats, the philosophical writings of **W. E. B. Du Bois**, and **Ralph Ellison**'s *Invisible Man*— and earning a bachelor's degree from L.A. State (1961). Meanwhile, he also worked in the post office, where many of his coworkers were well-educated African-American men much like his father. They told him how racial prejudice had blocked their progress and encouraged him to continue his education further.

Harper went on to attend the prestigious Iowa Writers' Workshop in the winter of 1961. While there, he was obliged to live in segregated housing, apart from fellow students, and he was the only African American in his poetry and fiction classes. Despite these affronts, Harper began writing poetry in earnest there. After leaving Iowa, he taught for a year at Pasadena City College (1962), then he returned to Iowa to earn his master's degree in English (1963). From there, he taught at Contra Costa College (1964-1968) and at California State College (now University, 1968-1969). Since the early 1970s, Harper has been on the faculty of the renowned Ivy League college Brown University, where he has taught literature and creative writing and is the "longest serving professor of English" there. His former students include novelist, playwright, and poet **Gayl Jones**.

Harper is best known for his poetry, which draws heavily on his lifelong love of African-American music, especially jazz rhythms and blues lyricality. By his own account, Harper has said, "I'm trying to write a poem for the ear as well as the eye" (quoted in *NAAAL*). His poems are intended to be read aloud, so that the listener can hear his off-beat rhythms and cadences, his bluesy refrains and repetitions, and his off-balance improvisations. Although his messages often allude to philosophical abstractions, he uses concrete imagery to make them accessible to his readers' senses. While Harper readily confronts racism in his writings, he offers messages of hope through human creativity and encourages Americans to embrace multiple cultures, rather than focus on either/or dualisms. In an 1990 interview, he said, "For me literature is a study in comparative humanity" (quoted in *GEAAL*, originally from *Callaloo*). Harper often celebrates and honors African Americans in his poems, especially highlighting the lives of musicians, such as John Coltrane, who is also his close friend.

When Harper was first launching his teaching career, he was already publishing his poems in various literary journals. His first poetry collection, *Dear John, Dear Coltrane* (1970) was nominated for the 1971 National Book Award, and thus Harper's very first book established his national reputation as a writer. Since then, numerous other poetry collections have followed, including *History Is Your Own Heartbeat: Poems* (1971), which earned him the Poetry Award of the Black Academy of Arts and Letters; *Photographs: Negatives: History as Apple Tree* (1972), published as a limited edition; *Song: I Want a Witness* (1972), which responds to religion, history, and other literary works; *Debridement* (1973), which is dedicated to his children (Roland Warren, Patrice Cuchulain, and Rachel Maria, as well as his two deceased sons Reuben Masai and Michael Steven); *Nightmare Begins Responsibility* (1975), which considers personal experiences in a literary and historical context; *Images of Kin: New and Selected Poems* (1977), which earned the Melville-Cane Award and was nominated for the 1978 National Book Award; *Rhode Island: Eight Poems* (1981); *Healing Song for the Inner Ear: Poems* (1984), which reflects on the thinking of **Frederick Douglass**, **Booker T. Washington**, and **W. E. B. Du Bois**; *Songlines: Mosaics* (1991), another lim ited-edition publication; *Honorable Amendments: Poems* (1995); *Songlines in Michaeltree: New and Collected Poems* (2000/2002); *Selected Poems* (2002); and *Debridement/ Song: I Want a Witness* (2002).

His other works include his recording, *Hear Where Coltrane Is* (1971), and edited collections of works by other poets, *The Collected Poems of* **Sterling A. Brown** (1980) and a limited edition of **Robert Hayden**'s *American Journal*. Harper has also edited some anthologies: *Heartblow: Black Veils* (1975) and the contemporary literary classic *Chant of Saints: A Gathering of Afro-American Literature, Art, and Scholarship* (1979, with Robert B. Stepto). With his former student Anthony Walton, he coedited *Every Eye Ain't Asleep: An Anthology of Poetry by Afro-Americans Since 1945* (1994) and *The Vintage Book of African-American Poetry* (2000).

In recognition of his literary contributions, he has received the National Institute of Arts and Letters Creative Writing Award (1972), a Guggenheim Fellowship (1976), a National Endowment for the Arts grant (1977), and an American specialist grant (1977), which he used to travel to Ghana, South Africa, Zaire, Senegal, Gambia, Botswana, Zambia, and Tanzania. He has also served as a judge of poetry for the National Book Awards in 1978, 1993, and 2001, as well as for the Pulitzer Prize in poetry, 1993. Harper was named the first Poet Laureate of Rhode Island (1988-1993), and he has worked on the faculty of **Cave Canem**. Perhaps he summarized his writing best, "My hope is that the best of what I have to say is offered in that moment, where the weight of what I know and what I need to discover, including the mysteries around aesthetic process, will be useful to readers. What I strive for is a unique blend of eloquence and original phrasing as practiced by the best musicians, and equivalence of interior speech and historical wakefulness as a person alive in a dynamic reality. I surprise myself often by what I write" (2000, interview with Michael Antonucci).

REFERENCES: *AANB. AAW:AAPP. AAW:PV. EBLG. LoL. MWEL. NAAAL. OC20LE. WDAA.* Allen, Jessica, in *GEAAL.* Antonucci, Michael. "The Map and the Territory: An Interview with Michael S. Harper." *African American Review.* 34.3 (Fall 2000) p. 501. From *Literature Resource Center.* Clark, Norris B., in *AAP-55-85.* Leonard, Keith D., in *COCAAL* and *OCAAL. QB. W. Wiki.* Manheim, James M., in *BB. CAO. CAO-04. LFCC-07. MWEL.* Robinson, Lisa Clayton, in *EA-99.*

Harrington, Oliver ("Ollie") Wendell
2/14/1912–11/7/1995
Cartoons and comic strips

By the time Harrington was 20 or so, his comic strips were being published in such African-American newspapers as the *Pittsburth Courier, [Harlem's] Amsterdam News,* and *Baltimore Afro-American.* His most famous cartoon character, "Bootsie," soon took on a life of its own, and he ended up publishing a collection of Bootsie comic strips in *Bootsie and Others* (1958). Harrington also worked as a war correspondent, journalist, and illustrator of books (e.g., classic novels).

REFERENCES: *AANB.* Von Blum, Paul, in *GEAAL. Wiki.* Jacobson, Robert R., in *BB.* Fabre, Michel. "Dark Laughter: The Satiric Art of Oliver W. Harrington." *African American Review.* 30.2 (Summer 1996) p. 305. From *Literature Resource Center. EA-99.*

Harris, E. (Everette) Lynn
6/20/1955–7/23/2009
Gay literature, novels, autobiography/memoir; lecturer, salesperson, self-publisher

Editor's note: *AANB* and *BB* list Harris's birth year as 1957, but numerous other sources list it as 1955.

Best-selling novelist E. Lynn Harris graduated with honors from the University of Arkansas at Fayetteville (1977) and then went to work in corporate sales for IBM, AT&T, and Hewlett- Packard (1977-1990). After 13 years of this work, he was driving a fancy car and earning nearly six figures a year, but he was miserable, so he quit his job. While watching an episode of *The* **Oprah Winfrey Show,** on which gay men talked about living "in the closet," he was inspired to write his first novel, *Invisible Life.* Once it was written, he couldn't find any publisher interested in publishing it. Undefeated, he paid tens of thousands of dollars to have 5,000 copies printed (1991) and literally sold it out of the trunk of his car. Putting his sales skills to work, Harris found buyers in African-American-owned bookstores and book clubs and he left copies in beauty salons to generate word-of-mouth sales. Word-of-mouth eventually led to an article in the *Atlanta Constitution,* which then led to a mainstream publisher's notice.

Doubleday's Anchor Books saw the book's potential for sales and republished it as a trade paperback (1994); it was soon first on the Blackboard African-American Booksellers' list of books. Doubleday took a chance and published his second novel, *Just As I Am* (1994), in hardcover, and they were repaid many times over when Harris became the first male writer to have his hardcover book listed first by Blackboard, which also named the book "Novel of the Year." *Invisible Life* and *Just As I Am* form the first two novels in a trilogy of books about handsome, wealthy attorney Raymond Tyler. Tyler has been living out loud as a heterosexual man with a long-term girlfriend, but he has also been attracted to men, has had intimate and sexual relationships with men, has frequented gay bars, and has otherwise sought out the gay community—but always in secret. Like Harris's other novels, it made it to the premier *The New York Times* bestseller list, as well as lists published by *Wall Street Journal, Publishers Weekly, USA Today, Entertainment Weekly, Washington Post,* and *Los Angeles Times.*

Harris's third and fourth novels focus on groups of people. *And This Too Shall Pass* (1996) focuses on a group of young African-American professionals, both gay and straight, male and female. *If This World Were Mine* (1997) centers on a group of almost-40 upwardly mobile diarists who meet regularly to offer support both for their journal writing and for their personal lives. *If This World Were Mine* won the James Baldwin Award for Literary Excellence (1997).

Editor's note: No other James Baldwin Award for Literary Excellence recipients appeared in the first 100 responses to a Google search for the award.

Both it and his next novel, *Abide with Me* (1998), were nominated for NAACP Image Awards. *Abide with Me* completed Harris's trilogy about Raymond Tyler. Like Harris's second novel, his sixth and seventh novels, *Any Way the Wind Blows* and *A Love Of My Own,* both won Blackboard's "Novel of the Year" award.

Like his earlier novels, Harris's twenty-first century novels have reached *The New York Times* and other bestseller lists, including *Not A Day Goes By* (2000), *Any Way The Wind Blows* (2001), *A Love of My Own* (2002), *I Say A Little Prayer* (2006), *Just Too Good To Be True* (2008), and *Basketball Jones* (2009). Even his memoir, *What Becomes of the Brokenhearted* (2003), became *The New York Times* bestseller, in addition to winning the Lambda Literary Bridgebuilder Award (2004). Some estimate that more than 4 million of Harris's books are in print. Harris's memoir and many of his novels are also available in audio format (download, CD, and/or cassette); some are available in Amazon.com's Kindle format; *Just As I Am* is available in Spanish as *Tal Como Soy* (2005); and *Not A Day Goes By* was adapted as a musical for the stage (2004). Harris also wrote a screenplay entitled *Sparkle.* His *Mama Dearest* (due for release in the fall of 2009) is predicted to sell well, too. Harris has also lavished praise and appreciation on his own mother and bought her a house with his literary windfall.

Harris also participated in several collaborative projects. With Eric Jerome Dickey, Marcus Major, and **Colin Channer**, he published *Got to be Real: Four Original Love Stories* (2000), also available unabridged on audiocassette. With **Marita Golden**, he edited the much-praised *Gumbo: A Celebration of African American Writers* (2002). Alone, he edited *Freedom in the Village: Twenty-five Years of Black, Gay Men's Writing* (2004), nominated for a Lambda Literary Award (2005). He also collaborated with **Gerald Early** to edit the first of many expected annual editions of *Best African American Fiction: 2009* (2009). Harris's writ-

ings also appeared in anthologies by other editors (e.g., *Brotherman: The Odyssey of Black Men in America* and *Go The Way Your Blood Beats*), as well as in periodicals (e.g., *Atlanta Journal Constitution, Essence, Sports Illustrated, The New York Times Book Review,* and *Washington Post Sunday Magazine*).

Harris was a visiting professor of English and a writer-in-residence at his alma mater, the University of Arkansas at Fayetteville, and he was a lecturer at dozens of other colleges and universities (e.g., Princeton, Harvard, Morehouse). He appeared in two Broadway plays, and he guest-hosted episodes of Public Television's *In the Life* (2000, 2003). He was named to many popular lists, including *Ebony's* "Most Intriguing Blacks," *Out Magazine's* "Out 100," *New York Magazine's* "Gay Power 101," *Savoy's* "100 Leaders and Heroes in Black America," and *SBC Magazine's* "Brother of the Year" in literature. In addition, Arkansas honored its celebrated resident with induction into the Arkansas Black Hall of Fame (2000), and the University of Arkansas honored its alumnus with a Citation of Distinguished Alumni for outstanding professional achievement (1999) and the Silas Hunt Award for Outstanding Achievement. His other honors include the Sprague Todes Literary Award and the Harvey Milk Honorary Diploma. He also served on the Hurston/Wright Foundation's Board of Directors, and he founded the E. Lynn Harris Better Days Foundation, offering aid to aspiring writers and other artists.

While visiting Los Angeles to attend a business meeting, Harris spent the night in a hotel. He was found unconscious and was later pronounced dead at a local hospital. A subsequent autopsy determined that the cause of death was heart disease. Harris had celebrated his 54th birthday just a little more than a month earlier.

REFERENCES: *CAO-08. Wiki.* Clay, Stanley Bennett, in *AANB.* Labbe, Theola S. "E. Lynn Harris Black, Male, Out and On Top." *Publishers Weekly* 248.31 (July 30, 2001), p. 53. *Literature Resources from Gale.* Millard, Elizabeth. "Writing to Find Some Kind of Peace of Mind: PW Talks with E. Lynn Harris. (Nonfiction)." *Publishers Weekly.* 250.24 (June 16, 2003), p. 62. *Literature Resources from Gale.* Quart, Alissa. "E. Lynn Harris: Tales of the Good Life." *Publishers Weekly.* 246.16 (April 19, 1999), p. 44. *Literature Resources from Gale.* Stratton, Stephen, and Christine Miner Minderovic, in *BB.* Weaver, Kimberly, in *COCAAL.* //www.aalbc.com/authors/e.htm. //www.elynnharris.com/e_lynn_harris.htm. //www.legacy.com/obituaries/latimes/obituary.aspx?n=e-lynn-harris&pid=130259932. //news.bookweb.org/news/1492.html. Amazon.com.

FURTHER READING: Bell, Chris, in *GEAAL.* "Calculating African American Bestsellers," in //findarticles.com/p/articles/mi_m0HST/is_2_3/ai_72275266/.

Harris, Joel Chandler
12/9/1848–7/3/1908
Humorous trickster tales, short stories, novels, folklore

Joel Chandler Harris

A journalist of European-American ancestry, Harris took a profound interest in the trickster tales told by African Americans in the rural South (*see also* **oral tradition**). Based on his extensive study of this oral literature, Harris's "Negro Folklore: The Story of Mr. Rabbit and Mr. Fox, as Told by Uncle Remus" first appeared in the *Atlanta Constitution* on July 20, 1879. The story was enthusiastically well received, and he continued to publish more stories. The following year, Harris collected various Brer Rabbit stories in *Uncle Remus, His Songs and Sayings* (1880). This collection was followed by seven more, including his *Nights with Uncle Remus* (1883) and *Uncle Remus and His Friends* (1892), as well as his posthumously published *Uncle Remus and the Little Boy* (1910).

In these stories, Harris was conscientious in retaining the authentic dialect of the many African-American storytellers whom he interviewed, and he remained true to the folktales they told, yet he set these stories within a context reflecting his European-American Southern background: He has the storyteller, Uncle Remus, tell these stories to the blue-eyed, blond son of his former master (and current employer), rather than telling them to his family and friends, which would have been much more believable. Further, as a white Southerner, Harris found it difficult to avoid perpetuating stereotypes of African Americans, such as portraying Uncle Remus as a jo-

vial old man, content with his lot in life. Nonetheless, Harris's efforts to preserve this important aspect of African-American oral literature deserves credit, and because of his efforts, many others were inspired to pay attention to this important body of literature. In addition to the Uncle Remus stories, Harris published other short-story collections, such as *Mingo and Other Sketches in Black and White* (1884), *Free Joe and Other Georgian Sketches* (1887), *On the Wing of Occasions* (1900). He also wrote novels, including *Sister Jane, Her Friends and Acquaintances* (1896) and *Gabriel Tolliver* (1902). His other children's books included *Little Mr. Thimblefinger and His Queer Country* (1894), *The Story of Aaron* (1896), and *Aaron in the Wildwoods* (1897). Harris also published *On the Plantation* (1892), his autobiography, and in 1907, he and his son Julian cofounded *Uncle Remus's Magazine*, which he edited until his death.

REFERENCES: *WDAA*. Gribben, Alan, in *WB-99*. Paulsen, Frank M., in *G-97*. P. R., in *CBC*. *EB-98*.

Harris, Trudier (aka Trudier Harris-Lopez)
2/27/1948–

Scholarly, literary biography and criticism, anthologies, autobiography/memoir, newspaper column; educator

Harris's mother named her "tru-DI-er," but she renamed herself "TRU-di-er," as she explains in *Summer Snow: Reflections from a Black Daughter of the South* (2003). In her memoir, as in her other writings, Trudier embraces her Southernness, starting with her upbringing in deeply racist Tuscaloosa, Alabama, where she also earned her baccalaureate at Stillman College (1969). She left the South briefly to earn her M.A. (1972) and her Ph.D. (1973) at Ohio State University, but then she quickly returned South to accept her first job as assistant professor of English at College of William and Mary in Williamsburg, Virginia (1973-1979). From there, she moved to the University of North Carolina (UNC) at Chapel Hill, where she has made her academic home since 1979, except for a brief (3 years) stay as the Augustus Baldwin Longstreet Professor of American Literature at Emory University in Georgia. In 1996, she was enticed home to UNC as the J. Carlyle Sitterson Professor of English, where she remains, other than during visiting professorships and occasional lectures and conferences sending her to Canada, France, Germany, Italy, Jamaica, Poland, Spain, and the United Kingdom.

Like Frances Smith Foster, Trudier Harris may be better known to many students of African-American literature as an editor than as an author. Probably her best-known edited work is *The Oxford Companion to African American Literature* (1997), which she coedited with William L. Andrews and **Frances Smith Foster**. She and

they also coedited *The Concise Oxford Companion to African American Literature* (2001). In the 1980s, she and Thadious M. Davis coedited numerous volumes for the *Dictionary of Literary Biography*: Volume 33, *Afro-American Fiction Writers After 1955,* (1984); Volume 38, *Afro-American Writers After 1955: Dramatists and Prose Writers* (1985); Volume 50, *Afro-American Writers Before the Harlem Renaissance* (1986); and Volume 51, *Afro-American Writers From the Harlem Renaissance to 1940* (1987). She also served as sole editor of two more volumes of the *Dictionary of Literary Biography*: Volume 41, *Afro-American Poets Since 1955* (1985), and Volume 76, *Afro-American Writers, 1940-1955* (1988). Not surprisingly, she also served on the *Dictionary of Literary Biography's* editorial and advisory board, just as she has served on the boards of numerous other scholarly journals and series, including **Black American Literature Forum**, **Callaloo**, *Journal of American Folklore, South Atlantic Review,* and others.

In addition to these works, Harris has coedited *The Oxford Companion to Women's Writing in the United States* (1995, as the fourth of seven editors with Cathy N. Davidson, Linda Wagner-Martin, Elizabeth Ammons, et al.), *The Literature of the American South: A Norton Anthology* (1997, as the third editor with William L. Andrews, Minrose C. Gwin, and Fred Hobson), and *Call and Response: The Riverside Anthology of the African American Literary Tradition* (1997, as the third editor with Patricia Liggins Hill, Bernard W. Bell, and William J. Harris). As a soloist, she has edited the *Selected Works of Ida B. Wells-Barnett* (1991), for the Schomburg Library of Nineteenth-Century Black Women Writers, *New Essays on [James Baldwin's] "Go Tell it on the Mountain"* (1996), and *Reading Contemporary African American Drama: Fragments of History, Fragments of Self* (2007; Jennifer Larson is listed as her assistant editor). In 2007, she also edited *Failed, Forgotten, Forsaken: Christianity in Contemporary African American Literature* for UNC's Program in the Humanities and Human Values. Also, as a longtime member of the Wintergreen Women Writers' Collective, she participated in the collective's *Shaping Memories: Reflections of African American Women Writers* (2009, edited by Joanne V. Gabbin).

Harris has also authored numerous works plumbing the depth and breadth of African-American literature, starting with her dissertation, *The Tie That Binds: The Function of Folklore in the Fiction of* **Charles Waddell Chesnutt**, **Jean Toomer**, *and* **Ralph Ellison** (1973), followed by *From Mammies to Militants: Domestics in Black American Literature* (1982), *Exorcising Blackness: Historical and Literary Lynching and Burning Rituals* (1984), and *Black Women in the Fiction of James Baldwin* (1985), which garnered her the College Language Association Creative

Scholarship Award. In the 1990s, she wrote *Fiction and Folklore: The Novels of* **Toni Morrison** (1991) and *The Power of the Porch: The Storyteller's Craft in* **Zora Neale Hurston**, **Gloria Naylor**, *and* **Randall Kenan** (1996). In 2001, she published *Saints, Sinners, Saviors: Strong Black Women in African American Literature* as Trudier Harris; in 2002, she published *South of Tradition: Essays on African American Literature* under the surname Harris-Lopez; and in 2009, she published *The Scary Mason-Dixon Line: African American Writers and the South (Southern Literary Studies)* under her original surname.

In addition to her numerous books, Harris has written a newspaper column for the *Chapel Hill News* since her return to UNC. She has also authored countless articles for such periodicals as *African American Review, Black American Literature Forum, Callaloo, CLA Journal, MELUS, Modern Fiction Studies, Southern Cultures, Southern Humanities Review,* and many others. Her essays and articles also have appeared in numerous books since the 1980s, covering specific authors (e.g., James Baldwin, Toni Morrison), comparative studies of authors, and topical analyses of literature. Awards for her scholarship include a National Endowment for the Humanities grant (1977-1978, 1988-1989), a Bunting Institute grant (1981-1982), a Ford Foundation/National Research Council grant (1982-1983), a Center for Advanced Study in the Behavioral Sciences grant (1989-1990), a University of North Carolina grant (1990), a Rockefeller fellowship to Bellagio, Italy (1994), a National Humanities Center fellowship (1996-1997), and a John Hurt Fisher Award for outstanding contributions to English scholarship from the South Atlantic Association of Departments of English (2005). She has also received a teaching award from the South Atlantic Modern Language Association (1987), a Roscoe B. Tanner Teaching Award (1988), and the UNC System Board of Governors' Award for Excellence in Teaching (2005). In addition, her alma mater, Ohio State University, presented her with its first annual Award of Distinction for the College of Humanities (1994). In 2008, she was invited to serve as the judge for the Penelope Niven Creative Nonfiction Award, presented by the Salem College Center for Women Writers.

REFERENCES: *CAO-05.* Gale Group's online "Literature Resource Center." Knoenagel, Axel. "Trudier Harris-Lopez: South of Tradition: Essays on African American Literature." *International Fiction Review.* 32.1-2 (Jan. 2005), p. 122. *Literature Resources from Gale.* Pereira, Malin, in *AANB.* San Diego State University library catalog, at //libpac.sdsu.edu/. //aalbc.com/reviews/summersnow.htm. //english.unc.edu/faculty/harrist.html. //www.salem.edu/index.php? option=com_content&task=view&id=460&Itemid=559. //www.worldcat.org. Amazon.com.

FURTHER READING: Steward, Douglas, in *GEAAL.*

Haskins, James ("Jim") S.
9/19/1941–7/6/2005
Biography, children's literature, juvenile nonfiction, criticism, autobiographies/memoirs; educator

Barred from using the public library in the Jim Crow South in which he grew up, Haskins spent his free hours lazily poring over the encyclopedias his mother, Julia, had purchased for him, one volume at a time. Julia later persuaded her white employer to check out library books for James each week. These childhood explorations fostered in him a love of learning and of reading about what's true. Years later, with his college degrees in hand, Haskins sold ads for the *New York Daily News* and sold stocks on Wall Street. After a while, though, he decided to earn a living with his love of learning, becoming a teacher in 1966. A lifelong diarist, Haskins wrote his first book based on his experiences as a special-education teacher in a public school, *Diary of a Harlem Schoolteacher* (1969). While teaching, he saw the need for outstanding nonfiction books for children and youths. In his lifetime, Haskins wrote and published about 150 nonfiction books for children and adults, making him one of the most prolific authors in the country. While being so prolific, Haskins also managed to teach English to college students starting in 1970, working as a full-time professor at the University of Florida since 1977.

In 1970, Haskins published his first nonfiction book for youths, *Resistance: Profiles in Nonviolence*. Thereafter, one estimate stated that he had "written, cowritten, or edited more than 160 books" (*GEAAL*). Haskins wrote on a wide assortment of topics, such as the Underground Railroad, gambling, careers, the Special Olympics, handicaps, civil rights, history of U.S. street gangs, child abuse, blacks in colonial America and in the Civil War, Exodusters, the Vietnam War, India, ghost stories, jokes, labor history, the consumer movement, boat people of Cuba and of Vietnam, the Statue of Liberty, werewolves, Methodism, world religions, and teen alcoholism, as well as dictionaries of African languages and of African cultures. One of his most cherished topics, however, was music, as can be seen in his biographies of legendary singers Nat King Cole, Scatman Crothers, Lena Horne, Michael Jackson, Diana Ross, his award-winning books *The Story of Stevie Wonder* (1976, **Coretta Scott King** Award), *Scott Joplin: The Man Who Made Ragtime* (1978, with Kathleen Benson, ASCAP [American Society of Composers, Authors, and Publishers] Deems Taylor Award for music writing), *Black Music in America: A History through Its People* (1987, the National Council for Social Studies' **Carter G. Woodson** Book Award), and *Black Dance in America* (1990). With musician Lionel Hampton, he wrote *Hamp: An Autobiography* (1989; rev. 1993). His new-millennium music-inspired books include *One Nation Under a Groove: Rap Music and Its Roots* (2000) and *One Love, One Heart: A History of Reggae* (2001).

Haskins also wrote numerous other biographies, including biography collections (e.g., the Black Stars series, 2000-2005) on African-American entrepreneurs, explorers, inventors, military heroes, political and governmental leaders, and athletes. In addition, he has written individual biographies on civil-rights activists **Martin Luther King, Jr.,** Rosa Parks, and **Bayard Rustin**; as well as biographies of other leading African Americans such as astronaut Guion Bluford, **Ralph Bunche, Shirley Chisholm, Bill Cosby, Katherine Dunham, Langston Hughes, Jesse Jackson, Barbara Jordan, Spike Lee, Thurgood Marshall, Toni Morrison,** politician **Adam Clayton Powell, Jr.** former head of the Joint Chiefs of Staff Colin Powell, the Scottsboro Boys, **Carter G. Woodson, Malcolm X,** photographer James Van Der Zee, politician Andrew Young, several sports stars and musicians, and many more. He has also written biographies of other prominent people in the world, such as Corazón Aquino, Shirley Temple Black, Christopher Columbus, Indira and Rajiv Gandhi, Winnie Mandela, and Pele. He also wrote a series of counting books on Africa, the Arab lands, Brazil, Canada, China, France, Germany, Greece, India, Ireland, Israel, Italy, Japan, Korea, Mexico, and Russia; four of these won the Alabama Library Association Award for best writing for children (1988).

Haskins's books for adults include *The Psychology of Black Language* (1973, with Hugh Butts), *Black Manifesto for Education* (1973, editor), *Snow Sculpture and Ice Carving* (1974), *Voodoo and Hoodoo: Their Tradition and Craft as Revealed by Actual Practitioners* (1978), and several biographies (e.g., of Scott Joplin, Mabel Mercer, and Richard Pryor). In addition, Haskins wrote numerous critical essays and reviews of literature for scholarly journals and other periodicals. The *Washington Post* awarded him its Children's Book Guild Award for his body of nonfiction works (1994). The American Library Association (ALA) named his *The Sixties Reader* (1988) a Best Book for Young Adults, and it awarded its Coretta Scott King Honor to six of his books. His books have also been commended by the Child Study Association, and he received awards from the World Book Year Book, the National Council of Christians and Jews, the English-Speaking Union Books-Across-the-Sea, Parents Choice, the National Endowment for the Humanities, the Joseph P. Kennedy Foundation, and others too numerous to note here. His adult book *The Cotton Club* (1977; rev. 1994) was honored as only Hollywood can do it: It was adapted to create Francis Ford Coppola's movie by that name. In an essay for the *Something about the Author Autobiography Series* (quoted in *Contemporary Authors Online,* 2007), he noted, "It has always seemed to me that truth is not just 'stranger than fiction,' but also more interesting." Indeed.

REFERENCES: *EBLG*. Courtot, Marilyn, in //www.childrenslit.com/childrenslit/mai_haskins_jim.html. Fikes, Robert, Jr., in *COCAAL* and *OCAAL*. Henderson, Ashyia, Sheri Elaine Metzger, and Tom Pendergast, in *BB. CAO-07*. Kich, Martin, in *GEAAL*. L.F.A., in *CBC. CA/I. Wiki.* "Obituaries." *The Horn Book Magazine.* 81.6 (November–December 2005) p. 757. From *Literature Resource Center.* Moore, Kay, in //0-web.ebscohost.com.dbpcosdcsgt.co.san-diego.ca.us/novelist/detail?vid=102&hid=7&sid=d408b38a-8f5e-4ec2-b75c-cf9c5b5097d7%40sessionmgr3&bdata=JnNpdGU9bm92ZWxpc3QtbGl2ZQ%3d%3d. Reid, Suzanne Elizabeth, in *WYA-2000.* //www.ala.org/ala/emiert/corettascottkingbookaward/cskpastwinners/alphabeticallist/cskalphabetical.cfm#au. //www.embracingthechild.org/africanamerican.htm, African-American/Black History and Heritage. Amazon.com.

Hawkins Brown, "Charlotte Eugenia" (née Lottie) *See* Brown, "Charlotte Eugenia" (née Lottie Hawkins)

Hayden, Robert (né Asa Bundy Sheffey)
8/4/1913–2/25/1980
Poems

Although Robert Hayden described himself as "a poet who teaches to earn a living so that he can write a poem or two now and then," history will record him as being much more than that. Although he did teach English at various universities for more than 30 years, he was an artist of the highest caliber whose remarkable poetic ability led him to be named Consultant in Poetry to the Library of Congress. This honor is equivalent to the distinction of poet laureate in England, and in both nations, the poets named to these positions are seen as the representative poets of the nation. Hayden was the first black poet to achieve this distinction in the United States.

Asa Bundy Sheffey was born as to his parents, Ruth and Asa Sheffey, but after his parents' marriage fell apart and his mother left to get her life together, his foster parents, Sue Ellen and William Hayden, raised him. Although his mother did come by periodically to visit, he considered the Haydens his parents and took their name as his own. Nearsighted from an early age, he was a reclusive child who preferred indoor pastimes such as reading and writing to outdoor sports. In 1932, at 18 years of age, he published his first poem and began attending Detroit City College, where he majored in foreign languages.

After graduating in 1936, he joined the Federal Writers' Project, where he did research on black history—specifically the Underground Railroad and the antislavery movement—and black folk culture. He left the Federal Writers' Project in 1938 and married Erma Morris in 1940—the same year he published his first volume of poetry, *Heart-Shape in the Dust.* He then enrolled in the University of Michigan, where he pursued a mas-

ter's degree and studied under a world-famous modern poet, W. H. Auden. He received his master's degree in 1944 and began teaching at Fisk University in Tennessee, where he stayed for 22 years. In 1968, he gained a position at the University of Michigan at Ann Arbor, where he worked until his death in 1980.

During his lifetime, he produced eight volumes of poetry, and although he is best known for the poems that focus on African-American historical figures, he cannot be classified as a historical poet. Indeed, as a poet, his expansive array of work, written in a wide variety of forms, deals with a great diversity of topics and themes, so he defies classification. Some critics have described his work as "kaleidoscopic" because the patterns in his work are always shifting, never focusing on the same themes, ideas, images, or styles twice. In each successive poem or collection of poems, Hayden finds ways to integrate new material, ask new questions, and add new perspectives. It is hard to find one thematic or stylistic preoccupation in even a majority of his works. This is very rare, as most poets, either because of the lives they have led or because of their general interests, tend to return to the same topics, themes, or ideas over and over again.

Part of the reason that Hayden avoids such repetition has to do with his philosophy about poetry. He believed that for a poet to focus on his own personal or racial identity in his work would limit the poetry, and that poetry should never be constrained by such concerns. While he acknowledged that poetry, because it comes from the mind of a living, breathing person, is unavoidably rooted in personal concerns, he also believed that the poet is responsible for moving the ideas of the poems from dealing with the personal to communicating something universal. Thus, while one of his poems, "Monet's Waterlilies," begins with his feelings about the Vietnam War and the fact that he by chance catches a glance of Monet's famous painting, it continues to make a statement about the way to escape history through contemplating art.

This theory of poetry occasionally earned him censure from some critics of his time. This criticism largely arose because, as William Meredith wrote in his foreword to Hayden's *Collected Prose*, "Hayden declared himself ... an American rather than a black poet, when for a time there was posited an unreconcilable difference between the two roles." At the time, critics were advancing the notion that black poetry could only be understood in terms of black themes, black feelings about life, black speech, and black music. Hayden, in his belief that poetry should transcend the personal (which included not just personal experiences but also racial identity), vehemently disagreed with such ideas. He felt such notions put boundaries around the artist, confining the poet's reality to a very narrow space. He wanted to be an American writer and would not settle for anything narrower.

He also disagreed with many powerful critics as to how African-American art should be judged. At the time, it was said that black poetry should be judged by separate ethnic criteria. He believed that, although his poems originated in the real facts of his "blackness," his race was really only "a point of departure into that magic realm where all artists of unmistakabl[e] . . . merit" become so all-inclusive as to affect the whole world. He said that he wanted his poetry to be "human rather than racial," to "speak . . . to other human beings and . . . not [be] limited by time and place and not limited by the ethnic."

Hayden's decision to prevent his work from being classified along racial lines was probably inspired by his adherence to the Baha'i faith. This Eastern religion shaped many of his ideas about identity, poetry, the personal and the universal. Baha'is believe in a coming world civilization and believe that all people and all religions are united by an essential oneness. The assertion of this spiritual unity led him to believe that humankind would overcome divisiveness, and he certainly didn't want his poetry adding to that separation by being classified as "black poetry" or being judged by different standards than other poetry of the English literary tradition.

Despite his desire to transcend classification, Hayden is nevertheless best known for his poetry that deals with African-American history and experiences. After reading "John Brown's Body," a poem written by white poet Stephen Vincent Benét, he was struck by Benét's admission that he could not adequately "sing" the "black-skinned epic" because he had "too white a heart," but that he hoped "some day, a poet will rise to sing you/And sing you with . . . truth and mellowness." These words inspired Hayden to write a "black epic," and throughout the 1940s he published poems that adhere to his desire to sing African-American history.

"The Middle Passage" is known as one of Hayden's best poems and can be seen in and of itself as a black epic. In this poem, Hayden uses a lot of the research that he had done while working for the Federal Writers' Project after college. The poem deals with the stories of the African slave trade, specifically the story of the Amistad mutiny and the legal battle that followed it. It is told through a montage of elements ranging from straight narration, to tales told by a variety of voices and characters, to log entries from the ships, to hymns sung by the slaves in the belly of the ship, to testimony of the mutineers of the Amistad. Even within the poem, Hayden refuses to be pinned down to one style, but rather uses the entire gamut of forms at his disposal.

Although "The Middle Passage" is his best-known work, he also wrote poems about **Harriet Tubman** and the Underground Railroad, **Nat Turner**, **Frederick Douglass** (all of which use research he unearthed during his time at the Federal Writers' Project), and **Malcolm X**.

All of these topics would lead one to think that Hayden did become what he never wished to be—a racial poet. However, even within these poems, Hayden slips away from such classification largely because the historical poems do not really focus on the past but always end with something—words, or actions—that point toward the future. In closing this way, Hayden meant to show that the hero is not gone but is still a force to contend with, that the heroes of the past are still acting on us today, whether in the facts of our day-to-day life or in our imagination.

In many ways, the historical figure becomes a symbol—something that serves a dual purpose by having its own characteristics but also standing for something else. For instance, "The Middle Passage" deals with the character Cinquez, who has a physical presence in the history of the Amistad but who also stands for a kind of spiritual emancipation that overcomes physical bondage. The poem then becomes a work that is not only about the African-American slave experience but also speaks to anyone who has been enslaved or anyone who has found spiritual freedom. It fails to fall into the category of "historical poetry" or "racial poetry" but instead moves to a more universal arena—one that deals with the struggle between humans' spiritual and imaginative nature and the realities of life on earth.

For this, in essence, was Robert Hayden's project—to write works of art that are meant to delight the senses and allow the spiritual side of humans to flourish. While he acknowledges that people are tied to the real world and have their possibilities limited by the tragedies of everyday life and the evils of the world, he nevertheless will not give up on the idea that people can overcome those limits. This transcendence can be achieved not by escaping the horrors but by rising above them in such a way that the tragedies and evils are changed into something beautiful, good, and sacred.

REFERENCES: AAW. BW:SSCA. EA-99. OCAAL.

Haynes, Elizabeth (née Ross)
7/30/1883–10/26/1953
Nonfiction—sociology, biographies

Haynes's publications included sociological essays on African-American women workers and two biographies, including *The Black Boy of Atlanta* (1952, about college president and banker Richard Robert Wright, Sr.) and *Unsung Heroes* (1921, about 17 people of African descent, three of whom were women and three of whom weren't Americans, published by **Du Bois** and Dill Publishers).

REFERENCES: AANB. Dagbovie, Pero Gaglo. "Black Women Historians from the Late 19th Century to the Dawning of the Civil

Rights Movement." *The Journal of African American History.* 89.3 (Summer 2004) p. 241. From *Literature Resource Center.* Robinson, Lisa Clayton, in *EA-99.* Wilson, Francille Rusan, in *BWA:AHE.* //www.aaregistry.com/african_american_history/1932/Elizabeth_R_Ha ynes_a_gallant_administrator. //www.blackpast.org/?q=aah/haynes-elizabeth-ross-1883-1953.

Haynes, Lemuel
7/18/1753–9/28/1833
Nonfiction—theology, spoken word—sermons

The primary publication of cleric and theologian Haynes was *Universal Salvation, a Very Ancient Doctrine,* published in about 70 editions. Although he was no abolitionist activist, he preached against slavery and the slave trade, and he wrote a manuscript, "Liberty Further Extended," urging that the freedoms and principles underlying the American Revolution be extended to liberate slaves. Other publications include a short story, "Mystery Developed" (1820), about the false murder conviction of two brothers, and a sermon, "The Prisoner Released" (1820), a moral admonition against convictions based on circumstantial evidence. He also composed a poem included in his funeral sermon for poet **Lucy Terry**. In 1975, his last home, located in South Granville, New York, was named a National Historic Landmark.

REFERENCES: *AANB.* Carter, Linda M., in *GEAAL.* Saillant, John, in *COCAAL* and *OCAAL. EA-99. Wiki.*

Heard, Nathan C. (Cliff)
11/7/1936–3/16/2004
Novels, spoken word—speeches; performer, educator, newsletter editor

While Heard was in prison for armed robbery, a fellow inmate introduced him to **Langston Hughes, Amiri Baraka, James Baldwin,** and other writers, and in addition to reading about 2,000 books, he started writing himself. In an interview with Eric Beaumont, he modestly observed, "The only thing that I believe was behind the creative instinct back then was that there were no televisions or radios or furloughs to distract you. Had they had television in the cells when I was in prison, I probably never would have been a writer." Initially, he wrote about music and about African history. By 1963, he had written the initial draft of his violent urban street-life novel, the best-selling *Howard Street* (1968/1992), which was published a month before he was released from prison. His other novels include *To Reach a Dream* (1972, which he had drafted before he wrote *Howard Street*), *A Cold Fire Burning* (1974/1995), *When Shadows Fall* (1977), and *House of Slammers* (1983, which Heard considered his best effort). He often left his completed manuscripts for long periods before submitting

them, noting, "No manuscript is good enough until you've finished it and can go back ten years later and it still excites you." While trying to support his three children—Melvin, Cliff, and Natalie—he worked as a musician, educator, speechwriter, newsletter editor, TV host, and actor, and he wrote numerous articles, such as for *The New York Times.* His almost complete manuscript, *Summer's Fool,* remains unpublished.

REFERENCES: *AANB.* Banks, Marva O., in *COCAAL* and *OCAAL.* Beaumont, Eric. "The Nathan Heard Interviews." *African American Review.* 28.3 (Fall 1994) p. 395. From *Literature Resource Center.* Kich, Martin, in *GEAAL. Wiki.* Manheim, James M., in *BB. CAO-04.* Yarborough, Richard, in *AAFW-55-84.* Amazon.com.

Hemphill, Essex
4/16/1957–11/4/1995
Poems, essays; editor, self-publisher, performance artist, gay-rights activist

In *Ceremonies: Prose and Poetry* (1992/2000), Hemphill recalled, "My sexual curiosity would have blossomed in any context, but in Southeast Washington, where I grew up, I had to carefully allow my petals to unfold. If I had revealed them too soon they would have been snatched away, brutalized, and scattered down alleys. I was already alert enough to know what happened to the flamboyant boys at the school who were called 'sissies' and 'faggots.' I could not have endured then the violence and indignities they often suffered" (quoted in *CAO-03*). Hemphill found little succor from the publishing world, either. Before *Ceremonies* was published, he used his own savings to self-publish his only two poetry collections, the two chapbooks *Earth Life: Poems* (1985) and *Conditions: Poems* (1986). A posthumous collection, *Standing in the Gap* (1999), is now out of print and does not appear in the WorldCat titles for Hemphill.

Hemphill also edited the anthology *Brother to Brother: New Writing by Black Gay Men* (1991), and his work has appeared in numerous anthologies (e.g., *In the Life: A Black Gay Anthology,* 1986; *Boys Like Us: Gay Writers Tell Their Coming Out Stories,* 1996). His poems and other writings have also been published in *Black Scholar, Callaloo, Essence, Gay Community News, Obsidian, Painted Bride Quarterly,* and other periodicals. In addition, Hemphill appeared in and/or contributed to several documentaries, including *Tongues Untied* (1990/2007), *Looking for Langston* (1992/2007), and *Black Is ... Black Ain't* (1994/1995). Several sources also list him as narrator of *Out of the Shadows,* an AIDS-related documentary, pointing out that complications of AIDS ended his life.

REFERENCES: *AAW:PV. CAO-03. Wiki.* Dickel, Simon, in *AANB.* Sussman, Alison Carb, in *BB.* //www.worldcat.org. Amazon.com.

FURTHER READING: Clem, Bill, in *GEAAL.*

Henson, Matthew Alexander
8/8/1866–3/9/1955
Adventure memoir

Matthew A. Henson

A key member of Robert Peary's 1909 expedition to the North Pole, Henson wrote *A Black Explorer at the North Pole* (1912), describing his role as navigator and as translator for the four native Inuits (also called "Eskimos") who accompanied him and Peary.

REFERENCES: *EA-99. EB-BH-CD.*

Heralding Dawn See **Anthologies**

Hercules, Frank
2/12/1911–5/6/1996
Novels, nonfiction—history

Editor's note: Hercules's year of birth is given as 1917 in *CAO-03*, but as 1911 in other resources.

Frank's father Felix Hercules was banished from their home in the British colony of Trinidad. Allegedly, Felix had incited disorder when he had offered verbal support for African-English workers during World War I. While Felix was living in the United States, Frank was being well educated in Trinidad. As a young teen, Frank was sent to England, to study for the bar at University Tutorial College in Reading (1934-1935), then at the prestigious

Honorable Society of the Middle Temple of Inns of Court (1935-1939), established in the 1200s. On returning to Trinidad, Frank married musician and music scholar Olive Walke, who later became pregnant with his son. Before their son was born, however, Frank left her to move to the United States, and they later divorced.

In the United States, Hercules eventually settled in Harlem, where he launched his own clothing line. When that business failed, he went to work for an insurance company. He married a second time, in 1946, to Dellora Howard, a schoolteacher who later became one of the first African-American school administrators in New York City. Hercules may also have had a second son (according to *CAO-03*), presumably with Dellora. In 1950, he returned to studying at the Honorable Society of the Middle Temple of Inns of Court, but he returned to the United States and to the insurance business in 1951. In the late 1950s, with Dellora's encouragement, 40-something-year-old Frank decided to try his hand at writing.

Hercules used Trinidad as the setting for his first novel, *Where the Hummingbird Flies* (1961), which was translated into German as well. While telling a story, he also satirized the colony's intraracial caste system in which skin color and hair texture affected social standing. *Newsweek* named *Hummingbird* one of the five best first novels of the year, and Vermont's prestigious Bread Loaf Writers' Conference awarded Hercules the Fletcher Pratt Memorial Fellowship in Prose. Hercules set his second novel, *I Want a Black Doll* (1967), in the United States. This tragic story about an interracial marriage was darker than his first novel and fared better in Europe than in the States, published in translation in Czechoslovakia, (West) Germany, the Netherlands, Sweden, and Switzerland. In his third novel, *On Leaving Paradise* (1980), Hercules returned to Trinidad and to more light-hearted storytelling. At his death, he had nearly completed a fourth novel, tentatively titled *Sunrise at Midnight*, and he had begun work on a fifth novel, tentatively titled *The Portuguese Earrings*, involving the slave trade.

Hercules's other major work was his nonfiction volume *American Society and Black Revolution* (1972/1980). In it, he attacked racism as being central to the American social and political system, yet he optimistically looked forward to change. The NAACP purchased copies of the book for inclusion in the libraries and classrooms of American historically black colleges and universities. Nearly two decades before he published his first book, Hercules had been publishing numerous essays in periodicals (e.g., *Harper's Bazaar* [German edition], *International Herald Tribune* [Paris], *National Geographic, New York Herald Tribune Sunday Magazine, Opportunity,* and *Reader's Digest*) and in books (e.g., *Voices for Life: Reflections on the Human Condition,* 1974). His article "To Live in Harlem" appeared in the January 1977, issue of *Na-*

tional Geographic, was reprinted in *Reader's Digest*, and was even read into the Congressional Record by Senator Jacob Javits of New York.

Hercules was awarded a Rockefeller fellowship from the Institute for Humanistic Studies (1977), and he was invited to be a writer-in-residence at Xavier University in New Orleans and a visiting scholar at Loyola University there. The National Endowment for the Humanities also invited him to become a member of its final award review panel. Lamentably, Hercules may have been better known in Europe than in his adopted homeland, and much better known here than in his native homeland, where his works were nearly unknown.

REFERENCES: *CAO-03*. Manheim, James M., in *BB*. Marsh, Carol P., in *AAFW-55-84*. //en.wikipedia.org/wiki/Middle_Temple. //en.wikipedia.org/wiki/Trinidad. //www.utcollege.org.uk/.

FURTHER READING: Carson, Warren J., in *GEAAL*.

Hernton, Calvin C. (Coolidge)
4/28/1932–10/1/2001

Nonfiction, novels, poems, essays; educator, social worker, journalist

After earning a B.A. in social science (Talladega College, 1954) and an M.A. in sociology (Fisk, 1956), Hernton taught history and sociology at four different colleges across the south from Florida to Louisiana (1957-1960). Hernton then briefly left teaching to get hands-on experience as a social-welfare counselor in New York City (1960-1961), and he cofounded *Umbra*, a New York-based literary magazine, in 1963. Next, Hernton wrote his first major literary work, his thought-provoking treatise *Sex and Racism in America* (1965; with new introduction, 1988; 1992), in which he reflected on case studies and his own understanding to propose how racism and sex are interrelated in American society. In his view, the puritanical beliefs of white men prevented them from viewing white women as sexual beings, so they pursued black women as objects of sexual desire; in turn, white men's guilt over their lust for black women led them to fear that black men felt lust for white women. Thus, according to Hernton, "all race relations tend to be, however subtly, *sexual* relations" (quoted in *OCAAL*, p. 353). This thesis permeates much of Hernton's other writings. Starting in 1965, Hernton studied with radical therapist R. D. Laing as a research fellow at the London Institute of Phenomenological Studies (*phenomenology* is an aspect of philosophy concerning human consciousness and self-awareness). After returning to the United States in 1969, he became a writer-in-residence at Oberlin College in Ohio, where he served as a tenured professor from 1973 until 1999.

While in London, Hernton wrote his essay collection *White Papers for White Americans* (1966), reviewing the events of the civil-rights movement up to that time. While at Oberlin, he wrote his analysis *Coming Together: Black Power, White Hatred, and Sexual Hang-ups* (1971), his novel *Scarecrow* (1974), his nonfiction *The Cannabis Experience: The Study of the Effects of Marijuana and Hashish* (1974, with Joseph Berke), his poetry collections *Medicine Man: Collected Poems* (1976) and *The Red Crab Gang and Black River Poems* (1999), and his nonfiction "womanist" volume *Sexual Mountains and Black Women Writers: Adventures in Sex, Literature, and Real Life* (1987). Hernton also wrote three plays, *Glad to Be Dead* (1958), *Flame* (1958), and *The Place* (1972), and in the 1980s, he wrote television scripts for *A Man Called Hawk*, starring his former Oberlin student Avery Brooks. His most recent work was to edit *The Collected Stories of Chester Himes* (2000). He and his first wife, Mildred, had a child, Antone, before she died; he predeceased his second wife, Mary O'Callaghan, whom he had married in 1998.

REFERENCES: *EBLG. TtW.* Boelcskevy, Mary Anne Stewart, in *COCAAL* and *OCAAL*. Magistrale, Anthony S., in *AAW-55-85: DPW.* Manheim, James M., in *BB. CAO-02.* Ramey, Lauri, in *GEAAL. Wiki.* //reportingcivilrights.loa.org/authors/bio.jsp?authorId =117. Amazon.com, 7/1999, 3/2009.

Herron, Carolivia
7/22/1947–

Novels, short fiction, juvenile literature; educator, business owner

Herron edited the *Selected Works of **Angelina Weld Grimké*** (1991), a book in the **Schomburg** Library series on nineteenth-century African-American women writers. Perhaps today, however, more readers know her children's books, *Nappy Hair* (1997), *Little Georgia and the Apples: Aunt Georgia's First Catalpa Tale* (2006), and *Always an Olivia* (2007, about her African-Jewish family ancestors). She also wrote a print novel, *Thereafter Johnnie* (1991/2001), which addresses the theme of incest through her lyrical prose; an online "academic novel," *Asenath and Our Song of Songs*; and some short stories. According to her website, in the new millennium, Herron shifted her career focus from teaching at Harvard University, Mt. Holyoke College, and California State University at Chico, to working on numerous multimedia online educational products and specialty courses through her Epicenter Literary Software company. Among her specialties is African-American Judaica, and she edits *Bridges*, a Jewish feminist journal. Her children's works in progress include *High Seas* (about her Jewish ancestor in a Geechee community on a Georgia Sea Island) and *The*

Journey of Phillis Wheatley. In 2005, she was reported to be working on a memoir titled *Peacesong.*

REFERENCES: An, Jee Hyun, in *GEAAL.* Coleman, Alisha R., in *CAO-02.* COCAAL and OCAAL. *Wiki.* //www.carolivia.org/. //www.carolivia.org/asenath.html. //www.carolivia.org/cohbio.html. //www.carolivia.org/cohhome.html. //www.carolivia.org/teach.html. //www.carolivia.org/tj.html. Amazon.com. SDPL catalog.

Heyward, (Edwin) DuBose
8/31/1885–6/16/1940
Novels, poems, plays, other fiction

European-American writer DuBose Heyward often collaborated with his wife, Dorothy (née) Kuhns Heyward (1890-1961), who had studied at Harvard University, married Heyward in 1923, had a play of her own produced on Broadway (1924), and collaborated with other writers, as well as with her husband. Dubose Heyward's most famous work is his best-selling novel *Porgy* (1925), which he and his wife Dorothy dramatized in the Pulitzer Prize-winning play *Porgy* (produced in 1927, published in 1928). George Gershwin, in turn, spent a summer with Heyward, adapting Heyward's play to create Gershwin's popular opera *Porgy and Bess* (1935), for which Heyward and Ira Gershwin wrote the libretto (lyrics). A quarter of a century later, the opera was made into a movie, *Porgy* (1959).

Although Heyward was European American—his family directly descended from a signer of the Declaration of Independence, Thomas Heyward—his work sensitively yet unsentimentally portrayed the experiences of African Americans living in Charleston and on the sea islands of South Carolina. Because Heyward's family was impoverished, although Heyward had been crippled by polio as an infant and suffered poor health all his life, he had to leave school at age 14, in order to earn money for his widowed mother and family. His jobs included working as a retail clerk in a hardware store, working on the docks, working as a checker in a cotton warehouse, and working for an insurance company until grave health problems forced him to stop. In many of these jobs, Heyward worked alongside African Americans as an equal coworker.

Heyward's other works include the novels *Angel(s)* (1926); *The Half-Pint Flask*(s); *Mamba's Daughters: A Novel of Charleston* (1929; reprinted 1995), about the efforts of three generations of an African-American family to improve their economic situation, which he and his wife, Dorothy, adapted into a play (1939); *Peter Ashley* (1932), a Civil War chronicle; *Lost Morning* (1936); and *Star-Spangled Virgin* (1939), about the economic struggles of African Americans in the Virgin Islands. In addition to the plays he and his wife adapted from his novels,

Heyward wrote the play *Brass Ankle* (1931), about a mixed-race romance. Heyward's poetry collections include *Carolina Chansons: Legends of the Low Country* (1922, with Hervey Allen), *Skylines and Horizons* (1924), and *Jasbo Brown and Selected Poems* (1931). Heyward also wrote an outstanding children's book, *Country Bunny and the Little Gold Shoes* (1939; reprinted in 1949 and 1974 and available on audiocassette in 1999). His book was far ahead of its time, showing that a clever, kind, wise, poor, hard-working, brown mother of 21 (rabbits) can do whatever she sets out to do, even when big, brawny, rich, white males try to thwart her efforts. Heyward also cowrote a nonfiction work, *Fort Sumter* (1938, with H. R. Sass).

REFERENCES: *OC20LE. RG20. WDAA.* French, Warren, in *G-97.* Hitchcock, Bert, in *WB-99.* Osborne, Elizabeth A., in *EB-98.* "Heyward, [Edwin] DuBose (1885-1940) and Dorothy [Hartzell Kuhns] Heyward (1890-1961)," in *GEAAL.* San Diego Summer Pops program, 8/28/1998.

Higginbotham, Jr., A. (Aloysius) Leon
2/25/1928–12/14/1998
Nonfiction—law and civil rights; jurist, civil rights leader

Evelyn (Titania) Higginbotham (née Brooks)
6/4/1945–
Scholarly, biography; educator

In 1948, Leon Higginbotham married Jeanne L. Foster, with whom he later had Stephen, Karen, and Kenneth. He earned his B.A. (1949) from Antioch College a year later, and his LL.B. (1952) from Yale University four years later, then he was hired as an assistant district attorney for Philadelphia County (1953-1954). He then went into private practice (1954-1962) and left that to serve on a series of federal and state commissions (1962-1964). In 1964, he was appointed judge of the U.S. District Court for the East District (1964-1977), and in 1977, he was appointed judge of the U.S. Court of Appeals Third Circuit (1977-1993), the chief judge by the time he retired. After retiring, he became a professor at Harvard University's John F. Kennedy School of Government (1993-1998) while also doing some private-practice work. Meanwhile, in 1994, he served as an international mediator for the first South African election in which black South Africans were allowed to vote.

Throughout this time, Leon Higginbotham published hundreds of articles for law reviews and other publications. Probably his best-known article was a 1992 article for *University of Pennsylvania Law Review,* "An Open Letter to Clarence Thomas from a Federal Judicial Colleague," in which he said, among other things, "I could not find one shred of evidence suggesting an insightful understanding on your part of how the evolutionary movement of the Constitution and the work of civil rights organizations have benefited you" (quoted in *LE*). The article was reprinted in the *Philadelphia Inquirer* and was reported in the *Chicago Tribune, Los Angeles Times, The New York Times,* and *Wall Street Journal.* He also wrote three books: American Book Award-nominated *In the Matter of Color: Race and the American Legal Process: The Colonial Period* (1978), *Race, Values, and the American Legal Process* (1987), and *Shades of Freedom: Racial Politics and Presumptions of the American Legal Process* (1996), described as a sequel to *Matter of Color.* Many of his lectures and speeches have also been published, and his essays and other writings have been published in anthologies by other authors. In addition to his dozens of honorary degrees, Higginbotham was honored with many awards, including the first Spirit of Raoul Wallenberg Humanitarian Award (1994); a Presidential Medal of Freedom (1995), the country's highest civilian honor; and the prestigious **Spingarn** Medal of the NAACP (1996).

In his personal life, after 40 years of marriage, Leon divorced Jeanne, and he married Harvard law professor Evelyn Brooks. It was the second marriage for both of them, and Leon adopted Evelyn's daughter Nia. Evelyn was born the year Leon entered Antioch, but the two shared common values and common ideals. In contrast to Leon's very modest beginnings as the son of a domestic servant, Evelyn was the daughter of well-educated teachers and public-school administrators who were fascinated by history. Evelyn's paternal grandfather, Reverend Walter Henderson Brooks, wrote poetry, and he had published an article in one of the earliest volumes of the *Journal of Negro History.* Both sets of inlaws had valued education, however, as Leon had recalled that his mother " knew that education was the sole passport to a better life" (quoted in *LE*).

By the time Evelyn Brooks married Leon Higginbotham, she had earned a B.A. (1969), an M.A. (1974), and a Ph.D. (1984) in U.S. history. Before earning her M.A., Brooks had taught high-school history and social studies, as her parents had done. Afterward, she spent a year as a manuscript research associate at the prestigious Moorland-Spingarn Research Center of Howard University in Washington, D.C. She then began a series of college teaching jobs (1979-1992) at Simmons College, Harvard's Divinity School, Dartmouth College, University of Maryland at College Park, University of Pennsylvania in Philadelphia, and Princeton. In 1993, Evelyn Brooks Higginbotham began a joint appointment as Professor of Afro-American Studies in Harvard's College of Arts & Sciences and of African American Religious History in Harvard's Divinity School (1993-1998). Starting in 1998, she began focusing on being a Professor of History and Afro-American Studies at the College of Arts & Sciences. In addition to these appointments, she

has been the principal investigator and general manager of the *Harvard Guide to African-American History* (1993-2001), published in 2001 (with Darlene Clark Hine and Leon Litwack), and the principal investigator and project coordinator of the Black Religion Evaluation of the Lilly Endowment (1994-present).

Meanwhile, Evelyn Brooks Higginbotham wrote her comprehensive *Righteous Discontent: The Women's Movement in the Black Baptist Church, 1880-1920* (1993), honored with the Joan Kelly Memorial Prize in Women's History from the American Historical Association (1994), the Award for Excellence from the American Academy of Religion (1993), the Letitia Woods Brown Memorial Award from the Association of Black Women Historians (1993), and a book prize from the Association for Research on Non-Profit and Voluntary Organizations (ARNOVA; 1994). She has also collaborated with **Henry Louis Gates, Jr.** to coedit some fundamental references that will benefit scholars for decades to come. Chief among these is their eight-volume *The African American National Biography* (2008), but they have also collaborated on *African American Lives* (2004) and on *Harlem Renaissance Lives* (2009). She also collaborated with Barbara Laslett, Ruth-Ellen B. Joeres, Mary Jo Maynes, and Jeanne Barker-Nunn to coedit *History and Theory: Feminist Research, Debates, Contestations* (1997). In addition, Higginbotham has contributed numerous articles to journals (e.g., *Gender and History, Signs*) and to anthologies (e.g., *The Dictionary of American Negro Biography,* 1982, as Evelyn Brooks; *Black Women in America: An Historical Encyclopedia,* 1993; *The House that Race Built: Black Americans,* 1997; *African American Women and the Vote, 1837-1965,* 1997). She has also delivered many conference papers (e.g., for the Library of Congress's American Odyssey exhibition, for the American Historical Association, for the Organization of American Historians).

Evelyn Brooks Higginbotham's fellowships include a National Humanities Center fellowship (1993-1994), a Lilly Faculty Fellowship (1988-1989), a Ford Foundation fellowship from the National Research Council (1987-1988), a National Endowment for the Humanities summer fellowship at Princeton University (1986), and a J. Franklin Jameson fellowship from the American Historical Association and the Library of Congress (1985-1986). She was also named a Distinguished Rochester Scholar by the University of Rochester (1994) and won an article prize from the Berkshire Conference of Women Historians (1993). In addition, Higginbotham has served on numerous boards and committees of historical organizations, conferences, and associations. She also helped form the Association of Black Women Historians (1977).

REFERENCES: "A. Leon Higginbotham, Jr." *CAO-05. LE. Wiki.* Jackson, Kenneth T., Karen Markoe, and Arnie Markoe (Eds.). 1998. *The Scribner Encyclopedia of American Lives* (Vol. 5, pp. 261-262). New York: Simon and Schuster, in //books.google.com/books?id=7QsOn9_NviAC. Lach, Edward L., Jr., in *AANB*. Niven, Steven J., in *AANB*. Strumolo, Amy Loerch, and David G. Oblender, in *BB*. //blog.oup.com/2009/01/a-leon-higginbotham-jr/. "Evelyn Brooks Higginbotham." "Models and Mentors." *The Women's Review of Books.* 15.5 (Feb. 1998) p. 24. From *Literature Resource Center.* //aaas.fas.harvard.edu/faculty/evelyn_brooks_higginbotham/index.html. //www.fas.harvard.edu/~amciv/faculty/higginbotham.shtml. Amazon.com.

Hill, Anita Faye
7/30/1956–

Autobiography/memoir, scholarly; educator, civil servant

As an attorney who had worked for Clarence Thomas, Hill came forward during the hearings for Thomas's nomination to the U.S. Supreme Court, asserting that he had sexually harassed her during her employ. She has since written *Speaking Truth to Power* (1997) about her experiences in regard to the Thomas matter. She also writes scholarly articles on legal issues, and she wrote a biographical article about a legal legend, "The Scholarly Legacy of A. Leon Higginbotham: Voice, Storytelling and Narrative."

REFERENCES: B. *CAO-06. LE. SEW. Wiki.* Goldsworthy, Joan, in *BB*. Keough, Leyla, in *EA-99*. //www.heller.brandeis.edu/faculty/guide.php?emplid=e69d2f368b67d9 63832f9d1d8a5b8a07c6e976d5.

Hill, Donna
8/6/1955–

Columns, fiction, especially romance; public relations

Though Donna Hill had always aspired to write, especially romantic fiction, she never expected that she would be able to do so successfully. While working as an office manager in an architectural firm (1985-1988), she studied business management at Pace University (1986-1988). She worked as an executive (1988-1944) until she settled in as public relations associate for New York's Queens Borough Public Library System (1995-present). Throughout this time, Hill was married with children, eventually having three—Nichole, Dawne, and Matthew—whom she has raised alone since divorcing.

In 1987, she finally started putting her writing skills to work, and she published "A Long Walk," her first short story in *Black Romance* magazine (1987). Soon, she was writing advice columns for *Black Romance*, then for *Jive* magazine as well (1987-1988), while continuing to have her short stories published in both magazines. With encouragement from her editor, she started writing her first

novel (manuscript completed in 1989). After a couple of rejections, she found a publisher for *Rooms of the Heart* (1990/1998). Her second romance novel, *Indiscretions* (1991/2007), interwove a murder mystery into the tale; it was soon the first African-American romance novel to appear on a bestseller list, when it showed up on *Emerge* magazine's listing. Her subsequent romance novels included *Temptation* (1994/2008), *Scandalous* (1995) and its sequel *A Scandalous Affair* (2000), *Deception* (1996), *Intimate Betrayal* (1997), *Chances Are* (1998), *Charade* (1998), *A Private Affair* (1998/2009), *Quiet Storm* (1998/2007), *Interlude* (1999/2006), and *Pieces of a Dream* (1999/2009), winner of an Award of Excellence from *Romance in Color* (1999).

In the new millennium, Hill decided to try a new genre. Instead of writing another romance novel, she tried her hand at a mainstream fiction novel, *If I Could* (2000/2003). Though bookstores resisted placing a Donna Hill book in their mainstream fiction section, *If I Could* could indeed, making the BlackBoard African-American Bestsellers list in *Essence* magazine. Having shown that she could do it, Hill wrote two more romance novels, *Soul to Soul* (2000/2006) and *Through the Fire* (2001). Mainstream publisher St. Martin's Press published her next two mainstream novels, *Rhythms* (2001) and *An Ordinary Woman* (2002). St. Martin's Griffin published her next romance novel, the wildly popular *Divas Inc.* (2004), and Kensington/Dafina Books published her romance *Say Yes* (2004; mass-market paperback [mmpb], Arabesque, 2007). St. Martin's Press then published *In My Bedroom* (2004), tackling the difficult topic of incest, and it published *Getting Hers* (2005) and its sequel *Wicked Ways* (2007), as well as *Guilty Pleasures* (2006).

Hill's other romance novels, mostly published by BET/Arabesque or by Kimani Press, include *Dare to Dream* (2004), *Courageous Hearts* (2005), *Long Distance Lover* (2006), *Love Becomes Her* (2006), *Saving All My Lovin'* (2005), *After Dark* (2007), *If I Were Your Woman* (2007), *Moments Like This* (2007), *On the Line* (2008), and her three novels about the covert female operatives of the Tender Loving Care sales force: *Sex and Lies* (early 2008), *Seduction and Lies* (late 2008), and *Temptation and Lies* (2009). Another romance novel is due after this dictionary goes to press: *Prize of a Lifetime* (2009, mmpb).

Three of Hill's books have been adapted for the small screen: *A Private Affair* and *Intimate Betrayal*, both novels, and her novella *Masquerade*; all were shown on BET. She also cowrote a screenplay, *Fire* (2000). In addition to her solo works, Hill edited *Midnight Clear: A Holiday Anthology* (2000), a short-story collection, and she has contributed to many other anthologies (e.g., *Winter Nights*, 1998; *Della's House of Style*, 2000; *Welcome to Leo's*, 2000; *Living Large*, 2003; *A Whole Lotta Love*, 2004; *Let's Get It On*, 2004; *Big Girls Don't Cry*, 2005). She has also collabo-

rated with other writers to create a novella, *Rockin'
around That Christmas Tree* (2003, with Francis Ray); a
trilogy of novellas, *Sister, Sister* (2001, with Carmen
Green and *Janice Sims*); an anthology of mystery stories,
Where There's A Will (2004); and many other projects too
numerous to mention here. As this dictionary goes to
press, Hill is doubtless busily creating additional novels,
novellas, and stories for inclusion in anthologies and
periodicals.

Among Hill's many honors are a Career Achievement
Award from *Romantic Times* (1998), a Gold Pen Award
for Best Romantic Anthology (2000), a Trailblazer Award
(2002), and a Favorite Romance Author Award from Sister Circle.

REFERENCES: *CAO-07.* Saunders, Shellie M., in *BB.* Amazon.com.

FURTHER READING: Williams, Dera R., in *GEAAL.*
//www.publishersweekly.com/article/CA70921.html.

Chester Himes

Himes, Chester (Bomar)
7/29/1909–11/12/1984
Novels, autobiographies/memoirs

To get a feel for how Himes viewed his life, we might
glimpse at these titles: *The Quality of Hurt: The Autobiography of Chester Himes* (1972) and *My Life of Absurdity:
The Autobiography of Chester Himes* (1976). Following a
troubled childhood, he spent his young adulthood in
prison (sentenced to 20-25 years, starting at age 19). In
prison, he started writing, and after a while, his stories
started being published in the *Baltimore Afro-American*,
Abbott's Monthly, and other African-American periodicals of the 1930s. In 1934, he sold "Crazy in the Stir" to
Esquire magazine, his first professional story to appear in a
mainstream white-owned periodical. Two years later, he
was paroled.

Nearly a decade later, he started publishing his largely
autobiographical novels *If He Hollers Let Him Go* (1945),
Lonely Crusade (1947), *Cast the First Stone* (1952), *The
Third Generation* (1954), and *The Primitive* (1955). Of
these, his first two are often cited as his best, and all are
sometimes cited as "protest novels." By the mid-1950s,
Himes started pumping out his crime-thriller novels featuring Coffin Ed Johnson and Grave Digger Jones,
cop-detectives in Harlem. These novels include *For Love
of Imabelle* (1957, a.k.a. *A Rage in Harlem*, 1965), *The
Crazy Kill* (1959), *All Shot Up* (1960), *Cotton Comes to
Harlem* (1965), *The Heat's On* (1966), and *Blind Man with
a Pistol* (1969). If you think you recognize the name of one
of them, it's probably because it was adapted to a 1970
film, directed by **Ossie Davis**: *Cotton Comes to Harlem*.
(His *The Heat's On* was also adapted to film as *Come
Back, Charleston Blue*, but this 1972 pic didn't do well at

the box office.) Whereas his first two novels are deemed
his greatest literary achievements, his last eight were definitely his greatest popular and financial successes.

In addition to his early novels and his detective novels, Himes wrote the novels *A Case of Rape* (1963) and *Be
Calm* (1961); a satire on sexual attraction between whites
and blacks, *Pinktoes* (1961); and his collection *Black on
Black: Baby Sister and Selected Writings* (1973). Also, after
his death, his short stories were gathered into *The Collected Stories of Chester Himes* (1990).

REFERENCES: *EAACH. EBLG. SMKC.* Sanders, Mark A., in
OCAAL. —Tonya Bolden

Hine, Darlene Clark
2/7/1947–
Nonfiction—history

Hine has interviewed history watchers and storytellers, dug around in archives and libraries, plumbed the
depths of basements, and climbed the heights of attics to
gather information on her primary passion: African-American history, particularly the special contributions of African-American women. As a result of her long
hours of research, she has written and edited numerous
works. The books she has authored include *When the
Truth Is Told: A History of Black Women's Culture and Community in Indiana, 1875-1950* (1981); *Black Women in
White: Racial Conflict and Cooperation in the Nursing Pro-*

fession, 1890-1950 (1989); *Black Victory: The Rise and Fall of the White Primary in Texas* (1979); *Hine Sight: Black Women and the Reconstruction of American History* (1994), and *A Shining Thread of Hope: The History of Black Women in America* (1998, with Kathleen Thompson). Her edited works include *The State of Afro-American History: Past, Present, and Future* (1986); the 16-volume collection *Black Women in United States History: From Colonial Times to the Present* (1990); the 2-volume *Black Women in America: An Historical Encyclopedia* (1993, with Elsa Barkley Brown and Rosalyn Terborg-Penn, comprising 641 biographical essays and 163 essays on various topics relevant to African-American women's history); and *"We Specialize in the Wholly Impossible": A Reader in Black Women's History* (1995, with Wilma King and Linda Reed). In addition, her contributions to periodicals are too numerous to count.

REFERENCES: *BAAW.* —Tonya Bolden

Editor's note: Other key publications edited by Hine include her 16-volume *Milestones in African American History* (1993, with Clayborne Carson), for middle- and high-school students; *The Harvard Guide to African American History* (2001, with Evelyn Brooks Higginbotham, Leon F. Litwack, and Randall K. Burkett); *The African-American Odyssey* (1999-2009, multiple versions and editions, with William C. Hine and Stanley C. Harrold); *African Americans: A Concise History* (starting by 2003, multiple volumes and editions, also with William C. Hine and Stanley C. Harrold); and *Beyond Bondage: Free Women of Color in the Americas* (2004, with David Barry Gaspar). She has also written, edited, and coedited numerous other works.

REFERENCES: Golus, Carrie, in *BB. CAO-03.* Amazon.com.

Hoagland, III, Everett H.
12/18/1942–
Poems, columns; educator

Hoagland's poetry collections include *Ten Poems: A Collection* (1968), *Black Velvet* (1970), *Scrimshaw* (1976), *This City and Other Poems* (1997), and *Here: New and Selected Poems* (2002). His best-known collection, *Black Velvet,* opens with the affirming lines, "our art is beyond reproach but never beyond reach / its in the streets not the colleges what we can't / learn we don't teach and what we don't learn ain't / worth it we got what it takes." His poems are frequently anthologized, and he has received fellowships from Brown University (1971-1973), Massachusetts Arts and Humanities Foundation (1975), and the National Endowment for the Humanities (1984). Hoagland also wrote a weekly column for the *New Bedford Standard-Times* (1979-1982).

REFERENCES: CAO-01. Halil, Karen Isabelle, in *COCAAL* and *OCAAL.* Routledge, Chris, in *BB.* Scott, Linda E., in *AAP-55-85.* Torian, Stacy, in *GEAAL.* //www.newsreel.org/guides/furious.htm.

Billie Holiday

Holiday, Billie (née Eleanora Fagan)
4/17/1915–7/17/1959
Songs, autobiography/memoir; singer

With journalist William Duffy, jazz singer "Lady Day" wrote her somewhat self-mythologizing autobiography *Lady Sings the Blues* (1956). The book, which she had wanted to title *Bitter Crop* (from the last line of her signature song, "Strange Fruit"), emphasizes her personal tragedies—often inaccurately—and gives short shrift to her musical talents and career. For instance, both the book and the 1972 movie made from the book neglect her talent as a songwriter (e.g., "God Bless the Child" and "Don't Explain").

REFERENCES: *AANB.* Cook, Susan, in *BWA:AHE.* Griffin, Farah Jasmine, in *COCAAL* and *OCAAL.* Sellman, James Clyde, in *EA-99.* Vasconcelos, Elizabete, in *EB-BH-CD. GEAAL.*

Holly, James Theodore
10/30/1829–3/13/1911
Autobiography/memoir, sermons; journalist, cleric, emigrationist, colonizationist, missionary

Born free during a time of slavery, James Holly favored abolition, but he also angered many fellow abolitionists through his support of the African colonization movement in the years leading up to the Civil War. As a first step, James Holly was drawn to Canada, where so many fugitives from slavery were finding refuge. In 1851, he and his wife, Charlotte Ann Gordon, with whom he eventually had five children, moved to Windsor, across the Canadian border from Detroit, Michigan. There, he coedited **Henry Bibb**'s *Voice of the Fugitive* newspaper. While advocating emigration in the *Voice*, he left Roman Catholicism and became a deacon (1855) and then an ordained priest (1856) of the Protestant Episcopal Church.

After three years in Canada, Holly returned to the United States, all the while plotting to create an African-American colony in Haiti. Among the many letters he wrote, conferences he attended, visits he made, and lectures he gave was *Vindication of the Capacity of the Negro Race for Self Government and Civilized Progress* (1857), which championed emigration to Haiti as a means of establishing a self-governing colony of African Americans. At last, in 1861, Holly's numerous strategies for obtaining financial, clerical, and Haitian governmental support for the colony led to success. He and about 100 other émigrés left for Haiti, where their high hopes were soon dashed by illnesses, deaths, and desertions. Holly's own wife and mother, and two of his five children were among the 43 who perished that first year. Holly and just a few of his followers remained after 1862, and Holly had to return to the United States to drum up church financial support for his mission. Holly later remarried, and he and his second wife, Sarah Henley, helped populate their little mission with nine children. In 1874, he was ordained a bishop in New York City and was named Bishop of the Anglican Orthodox Episcopal Church of Haiti; in 1897, he was named bishop of the Dominican Republic, as well. In 1897, Holly wrote *Facts about the Church's Mission in Haiti: A Concise Statement*, including a brief autobiography and a history of his small mission in Haiti. Overall, Holly returned to the United States seven times in the years from 1861 until his death in 1911.

REFERENCES: Dean, David M., in *AANB*. "Episcopal Church," in //www.answers.com/topic/episcopal-church. //anglicanhistory.org/usa/jtholly/facts1897.html. //satucket.com/lectionary/James_Holly.htm. //specbuffalo.bfn.org/bishop_holley.htm. //www.blackpast.org/?q=aah/theodore-james-holly-1829-1911. //www.haititimeline.com/n422/james-theodore-holly-elected-bishop.html.

FURTHER READING:
//connection.ebscohost.com:80/content/article/1022127243.html. //www.io.com/~kellywp/LesserFF/Mar/Holly.html.

Holman, M. (Moses) Carl
6/27/1919–8/9/1988
Poems, plays; editor, educator, activist

Carl Holman got off to an auspicious start. While still in his teens, he won a $350 prize in a radio-play contest. He later wrote other plays, including *The Baptizin'* (1971), which won first prize in the National Community Theatre Festival. He graduated magna cum laude from Missouri's Lincoln University (1942) then earned two master's degrees, one from the University of Chicago (1944) and one from Yale University (1954). By 1948, he had found his true calling, teaching English and the humanities at Clark College (now Clark Atlanta University) (1948-1962). In the late 1950s and early 1960s, Holman was in the right place at the right time. When students were rising up to advocate civil rights, Holman unofficially advised them on effective strategies and helped them negotiate for desegregation and for equal employment opportunities.

In 1960, when Clark College launched the weekly *Atlanta Inquirer* (1960-present) to report on civil-rights issues there and in the wider South, Holman took on the job as its editor. Under his leadership, the *Inquirer* came to be valued for its hard-hitting news analysis and indepth reporting. About that time, his personal life also blossomed, as he met and married the love of his life, Mariella, with whom he had two sons, Kwasi and Kwame, and a daughter, Kinshasha. In 1962, President Kennedy appointed Holman to work for the U.S. Commission on Civil Rights, in Washington, D.C., and in 1966, he was named deputy staff director of the commission. A year later, widespread urban riots prompted him to leave that post to join the National Urban Coalition, as vice president of programs (1967), then as president (1971). Before he was 50, *Ebony* listed Holman as one of the 100 most influential African Americans (1968).

Meanwhile, Holman filled his off hours with award-winning poetry, which has been often anthologized (e.g., in **Arna Bontemps's** *American Negro Poetry*, 1963), **Arnold Adoff's** *The Poetry of Black America: Anthology of the 20th Century*, 1973; as well as *The North America Book of Verse*, 1939; and *Soon One Morning: New Writing by American Negroes, 1940-1982*, 1963). In addition to earning the John B. Fiske Poetry Prize and the Blevins Davis Playwriting Prize, Holman received a Rosenwald fellowship and a John Hay Whitney fellowship.

REFERENCES: *Wiki*. Burke, Chesya, in *AANB*. Table 7.1, "African American Mississippi Writers, Historians, and Journalists," and Table 7.2, "Black Writers in Mississippi, 1940-2000," in *AT*. //library.msstate.edu/special_interest/Mississippi_African-American_Authors.asp. Amazon.com.

FURTHER READING: Adoff, Arnold (Ed.). 1973. *The Poetry of Black America: Anthology of the 20th Century.* New York: Harper & Row. From *LitFinder.* Bontemps, Arna (Ed.). 1963. *American Negro Poetry.* New York: Hill & Wang. From *LitFinder.*

hooks, bell (née Gloria Jean Watkins)
9/25/1952?–

Feminist and social-criticism essays, nonfiction books, autobiography/memoir, juvenile literature; scholar, educator

Rosa Bell and Veodis Watkins raised young Gloria, her brother, and her five sisters in a segregated, working-class Southern neighborhood. At home, her parents taught her the same patriarchal, patriotic values her teachers and textbooks were teaching her in all-black public-school classrooms. At home and at school, she learned that African-American girls were of little worth. How did she respond to such belittlement? She enlarged her mind by escaping into a world of literature, particularly the verses of Walt Whitman and the romantic poets. Secretly, she scribbled her own poems, too.

When Gloria stepped onto the Stanford campus, she entered an unsegregated environment. For the first time, she was interacting continuously with whites. At about this time, the campus women's movement was starting to raise people's consciousness of sexism, and Gloria started to question the patriarchal values she had known all her life. She soon started to question many other values she had been taught. As she extended her questioning further, she noticed a distinct absence of African-American women and other women of color in the women's movement. Women's studies was usually white-women's studies. (Similarly, black studies was usually black-male studies.) In her academic studies, her white (mostly male) professors engaged in covert racism, ignoring their nonwhite students, perhaps without even realizing they were doing so. After earning her B.A. (1973) in English literature from Stanford, she went on to earn her M.A. (1976) from the University of Wisconsin and her Ph.D. (1983) from UC Santa Cruz.

At age 19, while still earning her undergraduate degree, Watkins began her first book project, a full-length book, *Ain't I a Woman: Black Women and Feminism.* This book harshly criticized the feminist movement for its unwillingness to explore issues of race and class, as well as issues of sexism as they apply uniquely to women of color. She provided a feminist analysis of the history of African-American women from the days of slavery through the 1970s. Her analysis asserted that nineteenth-century African-American women had developed greater feminist consciousness than contemporary African-American women seem to evidence. Both men and women involved in the struggle for black liberation ignored the distinctive plight of African-American women.

When she was ready to publish her first book, Gloria Jean Watkins changed her name to bell hooks. She took the name from her maternal great-grandmother, an outspoken woman whom hooks describes as "a sharp-tongued woman, a woman who spoke her mind, a woman who was not afraid to talk back." In addition to her admiration for her grandmother, she chose the name to pay homage to matriarchal legacies. If outspoken clarity is the criterion, bell hooks has indeed honored her namesake. She spells her name in lowercase letters as a way to emphasize that her work's substance has more importance than her celebrity.

Needless to say, the blunt and irreverent bell hooks had trouble finding a publisher for her book, as even the feminist presses and independent black publishers were less than enthusiastic about it. At last, when speaking at a feminist bookstore, she was put in touch with South End Press, which published *Ain't I a Woman* (in 1981) and her subsequent books through the mid-1990s. Academics didn't welcome her book with open arms, but many others responded favorably to it. A reviewer in *Publishers Weekly* called the book one of the "twenty most influential women's books of the last twenty years."

While she was still earning her doctorate, she lectured in English and ethnic studies at the University of Southern California. Once she had her doctorate, she became an assistant professor at Yale, teaching African and African-American studies and English literature there. In 1988, she became an associate professor of American literature and women's studies at Oberlin College (the first college to admit women, as well as men, and an early interracial institution). She left Oberlin to become a distinguished professor of English at the City University of New York, from 1994 until 2001. A popular lecturer, her courses in African-American women's fiction and the politics of sexuality were always filled to capacity.

Her subsequent books have further elaborated her analysis of feminism. For instance, in *Feminist Theory from Margin to Center* (1984), she posited that mainstream feminism has put middle-class white women at the center of the movement and has marginalized working-class women and women of color. In her *Talking Back: Thinking Feminist, Thinking Black* (1989/1999), she prodded women of color to start speaking out to advocate liberation of the oppressed. In it, she wrote, "Moving from silence into speech is for the oppressed, the colonized, the exploited, and those who stand and struggle side by side, a gesture of defiance that heals, that makes new life and new growth possible. It is that act of speech, of 'talking back,' that is no mere gesture of empty words."

In *Yearning: Race, Gender and Cultural Politics* (1990/1999), hooks questioned sexism, classism, and racism in the arts (especially cinema), winning the Before Columbus Foundation's American Book Award. She and **Cornel West** co-authored a dialogue, *Breaking Bread: Insurgent Black Intellectual Life* (1991/1999), which probes the challenge of African-American intellectuals who emerge from working-class backgrounds. Her *Black Looks: Race and Representation* (1992) questions the manipulation of dominant cultural images of African-American women and the ways in which those images reinforce inequality. *Sisters of the Yam* (1993/2005) shares its name with a support group for black women, which hooks established in the 1980s. In her *Outlaw Culture, Resisting Representation* (1994), hooks critiques various facets of American culture. Her *Teaching to Transgress: Education as the Practice of Freedom* (1994) prods young men and women of color to participate fully and actively in their own education. She also wrote *Art on My Mind* (1995), some essays on modern art; *Killing Rage: Ending Racism* (1995); *Reel to Real: Race, Sex, and Class at the Movies* (1996/2008); *All About Love: New Visions* (2000); *Feminism is for Everybody: Passionate Politics* (2000); *Where We Stand: Class Matters* (2000); *Salvation: Black People and Love* (2001); *Rock My Soul: Black People and Self-Esteem* (2003); *Teaching Community: A Pedagogy of Hope* (2003); *We Real Cool: Black Men and Masculinity* (2003); *The Will to Change: Men, Masculinity, and Love* (2004); and *Homegrown: Engaged Cultural Criticism* (2006, with Amalia Mesa-Bains. Her poems have been collected in *And There We Wept* (1978), a chapbook, and *When Angels Speak of Love* (2007). Her memoirs include *Bone Black: Memories of Girlhood* (1996), and *Wounds of Passion: A Writing Life* (1997/1999), as well as *Remembered Rapture: The Writer at Work* (1999), collected memoir essays.

In her more recent books, hooks noted in a *Publishers Weekly* interview with Robert Fleming, "I moved toward a more accessible language that addressed a wider audience. When I get letters from readers who say my books opened up debate and introspection among them and their loved ones, I feel affirmed." For her ever-widening audience, she also edited *Gumbo Ya Ya: Anthology of Contemporary African-American Women Artists* (1995). In addition, she has written several books for young children, most of them illustrated by Chris Raschka, including *Happy to be Nappy* (1999; board book, 2001), *Be Boy Buzz* (2002/2004), *Skin Again* (2004), and *Grump Groan Growl* (2008). Her second children's book, *Homemade Love* (2001), illustrated by Shane W. Evans, was named the prestigious Bank Street College's Children's Book of the Year in 2002. Her other awards include 2001 nominations for an NAACP Image Award and for a Hurston/Wright Legacy Award.

REFERENCES: *1TESK. AANB. EBLG. PBW.* Chay, Deborah G., in *COCAAL* and *OCAAL.* Davis, Amanda, in *B. GEAAL. W. W2B. Wiki.* Evans, Melissa L., in *FW.* Fleming, Robert. "Feminist Revolutionary Comes down to Earth. (PW Talks with bell hooks)." *Publishers Weekly.* 249.47 (Nov. 25, 2002) p. 54. From *Literature Resource Center.* Henderson, Carol E., in *T-CACT.* Le Blanc, Ondine E., in *BB. CAO-06. CLCS.* Reid, Calvin. "Books - and More Books - from bell hooks." *Publishers Weekly.* 242.13 (Mar. 27, 1995) p. 24. From *Literature Resource Center.* //en.wikiquote.org/wiki/Bell_hooks. //www.harpercollins.com/authors/19422/bell_hooks/index.aspx?author ID=19422. *EB-98. G-95.*

Hopkins, Pauline (Elizabeth) (occasional pen name: Sarah Allen)
?/1859–8/13/1930
Novels, short stories, plays, essays, commentaries, nonfiction—biography; journalist, editor, publisher

While still a teenager, Hopkins won an essay contest, for which **William Wells Brown** awarded her the ten-dollar prize. After finishing public school, Hopkins toured the country, singing with her mother and stepfather in their group Hopkins' Colored Troubadours for a dozen years. While touring, she wrote and performed her first two plays: *Slaves' Escape; or, The Underground Railroad* (also called *Peculiar Sam;* written 1879, produced 1880), a musical lauding **Harriet Tubman**, **Frederick Douglass**, and other slaves who escaped to freedom, and *One Scene from the Drama of Early Days*, about the biblical character Daniel. Eventually, she grew tired of having no steady income and no home, so she left the family business to get a civil-service job as a stenographer for the Massachusetts Decennial Census in the Bureau of Statistics during the 1890s.

In 1900, she started her professional association with the newly founded Colored Cooperative Publishing Company in Boston, becoming a shareholder and a member of the company's board of directors. That year, the company started publishing *Colored American Magazine*. In the first issue were Hopkins's first published short story, "The Mystery within Us," and an announcement that Hopkins was to be the first editor of the magazine's women's department. In October, the company published Hopkins's first novel, *Contending Forces: A Romance Illustrative of Negro Life North and South* (1900), about a multigenerational mixed-race family. The novel followed the family members from their enslavement in Bermuda in 1790, through slavery in North Carolina and the brutality of the post-Civil War era, to their experiences in Boston late in the nineteenth century. In it, Hopkins highlights strong women characters, who show the role of mothers as keepers and conveyors of culture, and the value of education and employment for women.

While working as an editor, Hopkins also contributed numerous short stories, essays, editorials, social and political commentaries, and biographical sketches of famous African-American men (e.g., **William Wells Brown,**

Frederick Douglass) and women (e.g., **Sojourner Truth**, Harriet Tubman), as well as serialized versions of her novels. The only literary form this great-grandniece of poet **James Monroe Whitfield** did not contribute was poetry. Whatever form she used, all of her works reflected her aims of racial pride, social justice, racial and gender equality, and protest against Jim Crow racist policies and practices. Worried that her own name was appearing too often in the magazine, she sometimes used her mother's maiden name, Sarah A. Allen, as a pseudonym for her works. Her serialized novels included her traditional romances *Hagar's Daughter: A Story of Southern Caste Prejudice* (1901-1902, using her pseudonym), about an upper-class woman who discovers she has African ancestry, and *Winona: A Tale of Negro Life in the South and Southwest* (1902), about a mulatta's struggle to resist and escape slavery; and her fantasy *Of One Blood; or, the Hidden Self* (1902-1903), which highlights the splendorous achievements of ancient African civilizations. In her short stories, she dabbled in westerns, detective stories, and other popular genres of her day.

Through all her fiction—even her traditional romance novels—Hopkins explored racial and social themes, including such issues as miscegenation and racial intermarriage, racial politics, pseudoscientific theories about race, segregation, and racial inequities. In 1903, Hopkins was named the magazine's literary editor, and many of her male colleagues resented having a woman in such an important role on the magazine. In that role, she exerted powerful influence on the magazine's editorial policies, helping to ensure that racial uplift and protest against racism were reflected in the magazine's articles, editorials, and fiction items. Male literary critics of her day and subsequent male historians may have underestimated her influence in this regard.

Hopkins's outspoken views eventually reached the eyes and ears of **Booker T. Washington**, who was outraged by her opposition to his accommodationist, segregationist policies and beliefs. In 1904, Washington's supporters bought the *Colored American Magazine,* and a month after they bought it, the magazine announced that "ill health" had forced Hopkins to resign. Poor, sickly Hopkins was actually in such vibrantly good health that she soon started publishing articles in the *Voice of the Negro* (edited by Max Barber and **T. Thomas Fortune**), including her series of articles "The Dark Races of the Twentieth Century," which predicted that the two major crises of that century would be the "Negro Problem" and the conflict between laborers and capitalists. Income from her articles in *Voice of the Negro* wasn't enough to support her and her aging mother, however. In 1905, she founded her own publishing company, P.E. Hopkins and Co., which published her *A Primer of Facts Pertaining to the Early Greatness of the African Race,* making use of her ex-

tensive knowledge of ancient African civilizations. A decade later, she tried to found another journal, which she hoped would become the equivalent of the *Colored American Magazine* she had known and loved (1915-1916, with Walter Wallace). Sadly, only two issues of her *New Era* were published before financial difficulties forced her to stop. Her last publication was her novella *Topsy Templeton,* published serially in *New Era* in 1916. That year, she returned to working as a stenographer, employed by the Massachusetts Institute of Technology. This incendiary writer was killed by a fire in her home in Cambridge, Massachusetts; any remaining unpublished manuscripts that she may have written went up in smoke with her.

Hopkins was not as well known as many of her male contemporaries, and it was not until 1972 that **Ann Shockley** rediscovered her works, and by the 1980s, her works started being recognized more widely. Since then, some of her works have been republished in paperbacks, and biographers frequently identify her as a pioneer in African-American literature.

REFERENCES: *AANB. EBLG. MWEL. NAAAL. OC20LE. WDAA.* Beebe, Ann, in *GEAAL.* Campbell, Jane, in *AAWBHR. BWA:AHE. EB-BH-CD. OCWW.* Robinson, Lisa Clayton, in *EA-99.* Tate, Claudia, in *COCAAL* and *OCAAL.* Hopkins's papers are archived at Fisk University Library. *BCE. W. Wiki. CAO-03. MWEL.* //digital.library.upenn.edu/women/_generate/AFRICAN%20AMERICAN.html - texts of three of her works. //www.coe.ohio-state.edu/beverly gordon/834/miller.html.

Horton, George Moses
?/1797?–1883?
Poems

When George was a young boy, music prompted him to sing out his own poems, and as soon as he could, he struggled to learned to read a few words, in the hope that someday, he might write down his own verses. Some of his first verses were inspired by Scripture and by Methodist hymns. Particularly appealing were verses on freedom, which he had never known but had always longed for.

When Horton was leaving his teen years behind, and he was hawking his master's produce at the University of North Carolina (UNC) in Chapel Hill, he started reciting some of the verses he had composed, within earshot of some of the students there. Pretty soon, he was being commissioned to make up verses for the students. He wrote some of these on the 8-mile walk to and from the university each Sunday—or while taking care of his farm chores during the week, or perhaps just before his weary mind slipped into unconsciousness in his bed each night. He might charge a quarter—or even two or three—for writing a special love poem or a poem centered around the letters of a sweetheart's name. In any case, he always received a cash payment, upon delivery, when he recited the poem to the patron. After a while, people started calling him the "Colored Bard of North Carolina," perhaps mocking at first, but then with reverence. His patrons also became his coaches, providing him with classical poetry from Byron to Shakespeare, with stops for Homer and Milton along the way.

When he was making up verses on his own self-chosen themes, frequent subjects were freedom—and his longings to enjoy it—and slavery—and the depredations of that institution. Soon, the wife of one of the UNC professors, writer Caroline Hentz, started rallying support for gaining him his liberty. She sent some of his poems to the *Lancaster* (Massachusetts) *Gazette,* which published two of them, and in the summer and fall issues, *Freedom's Journal* was urging every African American in New York to donate a penny toward his manumission. In 1829, Horton's *The Hope of Liberty, Containing a Number of Poetical Pieces,* was published, becoming the third book of poetry by an African American published in the United States (*see* **Phillis Wheatley** for the first) and the first book of any kind authored by an African American, which was published in the South. In 1830, able to see a bright new life for himself, he married; later on, the couple had two children: their daughter, Rhoda, and their son, Free. At about this time, he also mastered reading and writing, so from the early 1830s forward, he could read poetry and write down his own verses.

Although his hope of liberty was not extinguished, he was unable to raise enough money to buy it despite the efforts of his supporters. After a few years, his owner recognized that Horton was far better suited to poetry than to farming, thereafter allowing Horton to buy his own time for a quarter a day. When he couldn't earn the money by selling poems, he did odd jobs at UNC. Still, despite all his efforts, he couldn't buy more than a day of freedom at a time. Discouraged with waiting for his freedom, in the mid-1830s, Horton decided that liquor was quicker in easing his troubled mind.

At last, toward the end of the 1830s, his *Hope of Liberty* was printed twice more, retitled *Poems by a Slave* in 1837, and as an addition to the reprint of *Memoir and Poems of Phillis Wheatley* in 1838. In 1843, after Horton's lifelong owner died, and the owner's son was Horton's new owner, the son started charging Horton two quarters a day for his freedom. At that rate, freedom for more than a day or two seemed a long way off.

He decided to step up his efforts. In addition to taking on as many wage-earning jobs as he could, he sold subscriptions to his second book of poetry, for which he charged 50 cents a subscription. Once he had gathered enough money, he published his *Poetical Works of George M. Horton, The Colored Bard of North Carolina, To Which Is Prefixed the Life of the Author, Written by Himself* (1845). He firmly believed that if he could sell just 100 copies of his book, with a final (nonsubscription) price of $2, he would be able to buy his freedom. Just as he was reaching his goal, in 1852, his new owner told him that the full sale price for his body and soul was now $250. So near, but yet so far. Throughout his struggle for freedom, Horton also summoned the financial aid of prominent white abolitionists, such as *Liberator* publisher William Lloyd Garrison and Horace Greeley. By all accounts, neither obliged him. Why not? Because the person who was to have posted these summons, new UNC president (and future North Carolina governor) David Swain failed to send them.

After decades of dedicated labor to free himself, in April 1865, Horton and his fellow slaves were liberated by Captain Will Banks and the entire Union Army's 9th Michigan Cavalry. Horton's poor new master didn't get a dime for his "property." Over the next several months, Horton wrote poem after poem about being enslaved, being at war, leading the Yankees, leading the Rebels, and even about writing poetry. By September of that year, Banks compiled Horton's new poems—and a few of his previously published ones—into a new volume, *Naked Genius.*

The following year, Horton moved to Philadelphia, parting company with Banks and leaving behind his wife and children. Sadly, the "Colored Bard of North Carolina" never received in freedom anything close to the "celebrity" he had while in bondage.

REFERENCES: *SMKC.* Sherman, Joan R. (Ed.) 1989. *Invisible Poets: Afro-Americans of the Nineteenth Century* (2nd ed.). Urbana and Chicago: University of Illinois Press. _____. 1997. *The Black Bard of North Carolina: George Moses Horton and His Poetry.* Chapel Hill: University of North Carolina Press. —Tonya Bolden

Houston, Charles (Hamilton)
9/3/1895–4/22/1950
Nonfiction—legal matters, legal briefs, columns; editor, attorney, educator

Although we know of no books he authored, Charles Houston's writings made history. Yes, he was the first African-American member of the editorial board of the *Harvard Law Review,* and yes, he wrote a seminal report on constitutional law, funded by a Rockefeller grant, "The Negro and His Contact with the Administration of the Law" (1928). He also headed Howard University's law school, turning it upside down to make it the finest he could make it, and by 1932, it was fully accredited and approved by the American Bar Association and the Association of American Law Schools.

On leave from Howard, as the full-time special counsel to the NAACP, he wrote columns for various periodicals, such as the *Baltimore Afro-American.* Those columns were important for rallying support for the battle he was starting to wage. His historic writings, however, were his legal briefs for the NAACP's series of Supreme Court cases, designed to force the nation to obey its own laws, especially the equal protection clause of our Constitution's Fourteenth Amendment. His writing also influenced two life-or-death decisions (in 1935 and 1938) in the cases of two African-American men; for each, his death sentence was reversed when Houston showed the Court that their trials had been unfair because African Americans had been specifically barred from serving on their juries.

By the time Houston turned over his NAACP job to his protégé (and former student) **Thurgood Marshall**, he had guided Marshall well in how to write a persuasive brief. Houston went on to serve as counsel to various union and governmental organizations, and he continued to advise his colleagues at the NAACP. One of his last services for the NAACP was to file a brief for a case involving segregated schools in Washington, D.C. That case was later subsumed, along with several others, into the case now known as *Brown v. Board of Education* (1954), which Thurgood Marshall fought and won. As Marshall readily acknowledged, Houston had taught him well.

REFERENCES: *BH2C. EAACH. SMKC.* McNeil, Genna Rae. 1983. *Groundwork: Charles Hamilton Houston and the Struggle for Civil Rights.* Philadelphia: University of Pennsylvania Press. Tushnet, Mark V. 1987. *The NAACP's Legal Strategy against Segregated Education, 1925-1950.* Chapel Hill: University of North Carolina Press. —Tonya Bolden

Houston, Drusilla (née Dunjee)
6/20/1876–2/8/1941
Nonfiction—history, cultural anthropology, paleontology, archeology; educator, journalist, self-publisher

As a child, Drusilla had loved roaming through history in her father's massive library. As a young woman, she wrote history-related columns while working with her brother, Roscoe Dunjee, founding editor of the *Black Dispatch*, a weekly newspaper. Later still, she applied her historical research and expertise to writing a masterwork of African history. As celebrated bibliophile **Arthur Schomburg** said of her self-published *The Wonderful Ethiopians of the Ancient Cushite Empire* (1926/1985), "I can assure everyone that the author must have used considerable oil in her lamp represented by her extensive research, the indefatigable labor that resulted in the astonishing compilation before me." At a time when few others were studying Africans and African Americans, Houston embarked on a planned massive three-volume survey of ancient sub-Saharan African history, highlighting its gifts to Western civilization. Sadly, she was able to publish only this first of the three before her death, and the manuscripts for the other two have been lost.

REFERENCES: *BAAW.* Coates, W. Paul, in *BWA:AHE.* —Tonya Bolden

Howard University Press
1972–
Scholarly publisher of literature by, for, and about African Americans

Howard University, established in 1867, did not officially establish the current Howard University Press until 1972. By then, various Howard professors and scholars had been stamping the Howard University Press imprint on monographs and other scholarly works for nearly a century (since 1882, at the latest). These early "Howard University Press" publications were written by Howard scholars but then edited, produced, marketed, and distributed by persons or entities outside of Howard itself.

On February 7, 1919, Howard University's board of trustees resolved to make the Howard University Press an official entity of the university. Although several monographs appeared under this imprimatur, the press did not truly exist as a distinct publishing entity at the university. In addition to the monographs, for a brief time, starting in June of 1923, Howard University Press (HUP) published *The Howard Review* (1923-1925), which covered every aspect of academia, from esoteric science articles to highly literary works. The *Review's* editor-in-chief was Dudley Woodard, with **Alain Locke**, **Ernest Everett Just**, St. Elmo Brady, and Dwight O. W. Holmes his associate editors. Among the contributors were Locke, Just, and sociologist **E. Franklin Frazier**. (For more information, *see* **Harlem Renaissance, literary and scholarly journals of the "New Negro" era.**)

In 1926, the HUP bought printing machinery, type, and supplies for the press, but in 1933, during the Great Depression, the university sold the equipment, the press closed, and Howard University scholars were forced to contract with outside entities for any publication work they sought. In 1959, the trustees reestablished HUP, but in name only. All publication work continued to be done off-site by outside contractors. In 1971, the university hired Charles F. Harris to establish and then manage a fully functioning scholarly press for the university. The following year, new bylaws were written, and the renewed HUP was established. Even after the HUP's official launch on April 8, 1974, Harris continued on as the HUP's first director and the chief executive officer of its publishing operations (1971-1986). Within 4 years after its launch, the HUP had published 37 new titles. During Harris's reign, the press followed the rigorous process of becoming a member of the Association of American University Presses in 1979. In the early 1980s, the HUP established its Library of Contemporary Literature, which included works by **Barry Beckham** (1983), **John Oliver Killens** (1983), **William Melvin Kelley** (1984), and Junius Edwards (1985). By the time Harris left in the mid-1980s, several of HUP's titles had not only won honors and awards but also been listed as bestsellers.

Before Harris left, in 1980, HUP inaugurated the HUP Book Publishing Institute, as part of its mission as a university press. The Book Publishing Institute offers an intensive 5-week summer institute offering coursework in all aspects of book production, including editing, marketing, and design, through hands-on workshops, as well as classroom sessions and site tours. In addition to university sponsorship, the Book Publishing Institute enjoys some scholarship and other funding from book-publishing industry sources.

As the first scholarly press owned and operated by a historically black college or university, HUP is "dedicated to publishing noteworthy new scholarship that addresses the contributions, conditions, and concerns of African Americans, other people of African descent, and people of color around the globe" (quoted from //www.hupress.howard.edu/). Since the 1990s, the university has reduced its financial support of its HUP, in part because many other mainstream publishers offer outlets for African-American scholars' publications. Though HUP now publishes only a few titles per year, given its backlist, it still offers a large list of books. In 2009, the Howard University Press (HUP) website listed 121 titles and 123 discrete authors (e.g., **Arthur P. Davis**, **Nikki Giovanni**, **Chester Himes**, **Woodie King**, Alain Locke, **Larry Neal**, **Darwin T. Turner**, **Margaret Walker**) in its current repertoire. Starting in 2004, the HUP website announced plans to publish digital reprints of 92 titles as "Classic Editions" to fall within the categories of 14 "libraries," including African American Literature & Criticism, African American Political Studies & Economics, African Diasporic Literature & Criticism, African Diasporic Studies, African Political Science & Economics, Biography, Black Professional Achievement, Caribbean Studies, Drama & Drama Criticism, Education, Literary Anthology, National Archives Research Studies, Psychology, and Slavery Studies. In addition to publishing books, HUP publishes three scholarly journals under its auspices: the *Journal of Negro Education*, the *Journal of Religious Thought*, and the *Howard Journal of Communication*.

REFERENCES: Byrne, Dara N., "Howard University Press," in *GEAAL*. Jones-Wilson, Faustine Childress (Ed.). 1996. *Encyclopedia of African-American Education*. Westport, CT: Greenwood Publishing Group. Logan Rayford W. 2005. *Howard University: The First Hundred Years 1867-1967*. New York: NYU Press. //en.wikipedia.org/wiki/Howard_University. //en.wikipedia.org/wiki/List_of_Howard_University_people. //www.hupress.howard.edu/. //www.hupress.howard.edu/Authors.htm. //www.hupress.howard.edu/huclassics/classiclibrary.htm. //www.hupress.howard.edu/Titles.htm.

FURTHER READING: *See also* **Harlem Renaissance, literary and scholarly journals of the "New Negro" era**. *See also* entries for each of the authors mentioned herein.

Hudson, Cheryl (Willis)
4/7/1948–
Juvenile and children's literature, nonfiction and fiction; book publisher

Wade Hudson
10/23/1946–
Juvenile and children's literature, plays, nonfiction; book publisher

In 1971, while Cheryl Willis was working as an art editor for Houghton Mifflin, she met writer, playwright, and public-relations specialist Wade Hudson. They married the following summer. In 1976, their daughter Katura was born, and they went looking for African-American art and other materials to decorate Katura's nursery. They found none. Undefeated, Cheryl created her own decorations: alphabet letters that looked like African-American children.

Over the years, they had their son, Stephan (b. 1982), and they continued to elaborate on the elements from Katura's nursery decor. Eventually, Cheryl created a complete alphabet, then she and Wade tweaked the concept and coined the term AFRO-BETS® Kids. The kids who formed the letters were modeled on Katura ("Tura") and Stephan ("Stef") and four other characters—Langston, Robo, Glo, and Nandi. Cheryl wrote and illustrated a 24-page concept book, *AFRO-BETS® ABC Book* (e.g., "A" was for Africa, alligator, and apple). With their innovative manuscript in hand, they went looking for interested children's book publishers. They found none. Undaunted, in 1987, the Hudsons took a leap of faith and became business partners. They gathered $7,000 of their savings and had 5,000 copies of their *AFRO-BETS® ABC Book* printed. They sold out their print run within three months and had more printed.

In 1988, they published *AFRO-BETS® 123 Book*. Now with two books in print, **Just Us Books** was officially launched as a publishing company, starting out in their own home. The company has prospered and now operates in an office building near their home, with more than just the Hudsons on staff. (*See* the separate entry on **Just Us Books** for more information on their publishing company.)

Cheryl has continued to author and edit many more appealing books for youngsters. For Just Us Books, she coauthored *Bright Eyes, Brown Skin* (1990) with Bernette G. Ford; George Ford's illustrations won the Publishers Marketing Association's Ben Franklin Award (1991). Alone, Cheryl wrote *Glo Goes Shopping* (1999); she adapted *Many Colors of Mother Goose* (1997); and she created *Come by Here, Lord: Everyday Prayers for Children* (2001), named 2003 "Children's Book of the Year" by BlackBoard African-American Bestsellers. In 2002, she collaborated with her daughter Katura (as coauthor) and her son Stephan (as illustrator) to create *Langston's Legacy: 101 Ways to Celebrate the Life and Work of **Langston Hughes*** (2002), offering biographical information and activities.

In addition, for Scholastic, Cheryl has written four board books for babies, all illustrated by George Ford: *Good Morning, Baby* (1992; rev., 1997) and *Good Night, Baby* (1992; rev., 1997), *Let's Count, Baby* (1995; rev., 1997), and *Animal Sounds for Baby* (1995), as well as an activity book, *The Kwanzaa Sticker Activity Book* (1994), and a picture book, *What Do You Know? Snow!* (2004). For Candlewick Press, Cheryl wrote *Hands Can* (2003) and *Construction Zone* (2006). The Hudsons collaborated with Kensington Publishing to create a new imprint, Marimba Books, for which Cheryl has written *Clothes I Love To Wear (I Love To...)* and *From Where I Stand* (both 2008), with two more in the works: *Sights I Love to See* and *Sounds I Love to Hear*. Cheryl's other books include *The Harlem Renaissance: Profiles in Creativity* (2002) and *My Friend Maya Loves to Dance* (2009). Cheryl has also contributed poems and illustrations to *Ebony Jr!* and to *Wee Wisdom*.

In addition, the Hudsons have compiled two collections for Scholastic: Cheryl edited *Hold Christmas in Your Heart: African-American Songs, Poems, and Stories for the Holidays* (1995), and she and Wade edited *How Sweet the Sound: African-American Songs for Children* (1995). She and Wade also edited two collections for Just Us Books, *Kids Book of Wisdom: Quotes from the African-American Tradition* (1996) and *In Praise of Our Fathers and Our Mothers: A Black Family Treasury by Outstanding Authors and Artists* (1997), designated a Cooperative Children's Book Center Choice.

Wade, too, has authored or coauthored, edited or coedited numerous other books. Under the Marimba imprint, Wade published *Places I Love to Go* and *It's Church Going Time* (both 2008). For their AFRO-BETS® "best-selling children's book series," Wade has written *Afro-Bets Alphabet Rap Song* (1990) and *Afro-Bets Kids: I'm Gonna Be!* (1992). Wade also collaborated with **Valerie Wilson Wesley** to write the wildly popular *Afro-Bets Book of Black Heroes from A to Z: An Introduction to Important Black Achievers* (1988). Wade also collaborated with Debbi Chocolate to write the first book in the series *NEATE: To the Rescue* (1992) and he authored *NEATE: Anthony's Big Surprise* (1998).

For Just Us Books, Wade also authored *Jamal's Busy Day* (1991), which won awards and honors from the *Boston Globe*, the National Council of Social Studies, and the former Multicultural Publisher's Exchange (all 1992); and *Scientists, Healers, and Inventors: An Introduction for Young Readers* (2002). Wade also edited and introduced

Poetry from the Masters: The Pioneers (2003, illustrated by his son Stephan). For Scholastic, Wade has authored *I Love My Family* (1993) and *The Two Tyrones* (2004, illustrated by Mark Page), as well as his trilogy *Five Brave Explorers* (1995), *Five Notable Inventors* (1995), and *Five Bold Freedom Fighters* (2001). He also edited two collections for Scholastic, *Pass It On: African-American Poetry for Children* (1993) and *Powerful Words: More than 200 Years of Extraordinary Writing by African Americans* (2004, illustrated by Sean Qualls). For other publishers, he has written *Beebe's Lonely Saturday* (1974); *God Smiles When* (2002) and *God Gave Me* (2003); and *The Underground Railroad* (2005). He also authored several stage plays: *Freedom Star* (published by Macmillan), "Sam Carter Belongs Here," "The Return," "A House Divided ...," "Black Love Story," and "Dead End."

For both his publishing and his writing, Wade has earned a Stephen Crane Literary Award (2001) and induction into the Writers of African Descent Literary Hall of Fame (2003). In addition, Wade and Cheryl have both been honored with the **Ida B. Wells** Institutional Leadership Award from the National Black Writers Conference and with the **Phillis Wheatley** Award from the Harlem Book Fair (both 2008).

For Just Us Books, their daughter Katura has authored or coauthored two books, and son Stephan has illustrated two publications and is currently illustrating two more. Wade and Cheryl are currently looking forward to the publication of a cherished project: *African American Heritage Bible for Children* (due in October 2009) and *African American Heritage Bible for Teens* (due in February 2010), to be published by Zondervan).

REFERENCES: "Cheryl Willis Hudson," *CA/I*. Personal communication, 5/17/2009. //news.bookweb.org/news/1492.html. //www.fleamarketcollectibles.com/tau907.html. //www.unitycsl. org/history.htm. San Diego Public Library catalog, s://sddp.sirsi.net/uhtbin/cgisirsi/x/x/0/5?library=ALL&user_id=catalog&searchdata1 =hudson%2C+cheryl&srchfield1=AU%5EAUTHOR%5EAUTHO RS%5EAuthor+Processing%5Eauthor&submit=Find+It+%21. "Cheryl Willis Hudson and Wade Hudson," Lesinski, Jeanne, "Wade and Cheryl Willis Hudson," in *BB*. //booksofsoul.com/2008/07/wade-and-cheryl-hudson-to-be-honored-at-harlem-book-fair-with-wheatley-book-award/. //en.wikipedia.org/wiki/Bakke_case. //www.justusbooks.com/modules/content/index.php?id=2. //www.justusbooks.com/modules/content/index.php?id=3. //www.justusbooks.com/modules/content/index.php?id=87. //www.justusbooks.com/modules/content/index.php?id=225C. //www.justusbooks.com/modules/content/index.php?id=226. //www.justusbooks.com/modules/content/index.php?id=236. //www.justusbooks.com/modules/extgallery/public-photo.php? photoId=64. http://www.justusbooks.com/search.php?query=&mid= 15&action=showallbyuser&andor=AND&uid=2&start=100. //www.marimbabooks.com/. Personal communication, 6/24/2009. "Wade Hudson," *CAO-06. CA/I. News & Notes*, 8/23/2007, in //www.npr.org/templates/story/story.php?storyId=13895809. Personal communication, 6/24/2009. Amazon.com.

Hughes, (James Mercer) Langston
2/1/1902–5/22/1967
Poems and news columns, as well as short stories, novel, plays, screenplay, autobiographies, children's books, anthologies

James Langston Hughes was born in Joplin, Missouri, and grew up in Lawrence, Kansas, with his maternal grandmother, Mary Langston. Hughes moved to Lawrence with his mother, Carrie Langston Hughes, when his father and mother separated. His father, James Nathaniel Hughes, moved to Mexico to practice law in a place where he would not be discriminated against because of racism, leaving his family behind. Hughes was often lonely as a boy, left with his grandmother while his mother was frequently away looking for work and pursuing a dream of being an actress. Growing up with his grandmother was difficult. They were poor, and Hughes's grandmother did not want him to play with children who lived nearby.

She did read to him, though, sometimes from the Bible, and she often told Langston stories, many of them true stories about the brave history of Langston's family. She told him about her first husband, Lewis Sheridan Leary, who had ridden with John Brown and was killed at Harpers Ferry in the struggle to end slavery. Langston's grandfather, her second husband, was also a militant abolitionist. John Mercer Langston, a brother of Langston Hughes's grandfather, was one of the best-known black Americans in the nineteenth century. She also told him about two uncles who were heroes, "buffalo soldiers," the Native Americans called them, because of their curly hair. The Native Americans considered the buffalo soldiers to be the bravest of the brave. Langston's grandmother herself helped with the Underground Railroad, and she told him stories about helping slaves escape to the safety of the North. Langston's grandmother may have been poor, but she knew and claimed a rich and proud history for her grandson. She knew how to feed his imagination and his dreams with real-life heroes.

As Langston's grandmother grew older, she withdrew into herself, becoming silent for long periods of time. In his loneliness, Langston Hughes discovered new possibilities for his life in books: "Then it was that books began to happen to me, and I began to believe in nothing but books and the wonderful world in books—where if people suffered, they suffered in beautiful language."

By the time Hughes enrolled at Columbia University in New York he had already published his first poem, "The Negro Speaks of Rivers," in *Crisis* magazine, edited by **W. E. B. Du Bois**. He had also realized that he wanted to write, and to write specifically about being an African American in America. Hughes left Columbia in 1922 and spent the next three years working menial jobs, as well as

Langston Hughes

traveling abroad. Hughes moved frequently, working on a freighter on the west coast of Africa, living for a time in Paris, and as a busboy in Washington, D.C. By 1924, when he returned to the United States, he was known in African-American circles as a gifted young poet.

Though Hughes wrote in many genres, he is best known for his poetry. In his early work, he embraced jazz and blues rhythms and the cadence of vernacular speech. Hughes's poetry was often written in free verse or loosely rhymed verse, reflecting the poet's admiration for Walt Whitman and Carl Sandburg. Hughes had an ear tuned to the music of black speech, however, and came to see black American culture as his primary influence and black Americans as his most important audience.

Hughes's first two books, *The Weary Blues* (1926) and *Fine Clothes to the Jew* (1927), established Hughes as a major poet of the **Harlem Renaissance**. With the fame came a great deal of criticism in the middle-class black press for dwelling on lower-class black culture, and taking as his subject matter sexuality, poverty, loss, sorrows, and violence. In 1926, Hughes published an essay titled "The Negro Artist and the Racial Mountain" in the *Nation,* which became a manifesto for the young artists and writers who were determined to claim the freedom to write about racial issues from a perspective of racial pride.

In a search for more stability in his life, Hughes enrolled at Lincoln University, a historically black college in Pennsylvania, graduating in 1929. Two years earlier, in 1927, Hughes had met Mrs. Charlotte Mason, or "Godmother," an older white woman who became his patron until 1930. During the period of her patronage and under her intense encouragement and meticulous editing, Hughes wrote his first novel, *Not without Laughter* (1930). When she suddenly withdrew her friendship for reasons still not known today, Hughes was devastated and became ill. He fled to Cuba and Haiti with 400 dollars from the Harmon Prize for Literature, and he spent several weeks on Haiti's northern coast, evidently reviewing his life choices and direction for the future.

When he returned, his politics had become leftist, so he spent the following year in the Soviet Union (1932-1933), during which he wrote his most radical verse. His poetry was no longer lyrical and blues based; the poem "Goodbye Christ," published without his knowledge in Germany, attacked American imperialism and Christianity in favor of communist/Marxist values. He would later repudiate this work. He spent the following year (1934) in Carmel, California, under the patronage of Noel Sullivan, a liberal patron of the arts. Despite the friendship of his white patron, Hughes wrote *The Ways of White Folks*, Hughes's satiric, bleak, and cynical collection of short stories about race relations in America. While the collection was unprecedented in its harshness and bitter portrayal of whites in their confused and insincere dealings with blacks, it established Hughes as a fiction writer, which helped him to live solely by his writing.

When Hughes's father died in 1934, Hughes went to Mexico, spending several months there, translating the work of several short pieces by young Mexicans for possible publication in the States. American editors had no interest in this material, however, and Hughes returned in 1935 almost broke, to live with his mother in Oberlin, Ohio, where her parents had lived during their youth before the Civil War.

Hughes then wrote *Mulatto*, a dramatized account of American race relations in the segregated South, with its disastrous denial of the humanity of blacks and their essential role in the country. Despite harsh reviews, *Mulatto* remained on Broadway longer than any play by a black playwright until *A Raisin in the Sun* many, many years later. After *Mulatto* opened on Broadway in 1935, Hughes wrote other plays: *Little Ham* (1936), *Troubled Island* (1936), *Joy to My Soul*, *Front Porch*, *Soul Gone Home*, and *Don't You Want to be Free?* In 1938, Hughes published his only collection of socialist poetry, *A New Song*, with an introduction by Mike Gold, a radical writer. Most of Hughes's plays made virtually no money, so throughout the 1930s, he lived near poverty.

In 1939, he worked as a writer in Hollywood on *Way Down South*, a movie written for the popular young singer Bobby Breen. Unfortunately and to Hughes's dismay, the movie, set on a plantation in the days of slavery, was de-

nounced in liberal circles when it opened. In 1940, a major luncheon in Pasadena, California, to present Hughes's new autobiography, *The Big Sea*, was canceled due to picketing by an evangelical group that accused Hughes of communism and atheism. The basis for their outrage was Hughes's poem "Goodbye Christ" from 1932. Hughes then repudiated the poem as a youthful error, ending his reputation as a socialist.

During World War II, Hughes completed his withdrawal from leftist politics. *Shakespeare in Harlem* (1942) took him back to the blues. In *Jim Crow's Last Stand* (1943), he attacked racial segregation. In what may have been his finest literary achievement during the war, however, he began writing a weekly column in the *Chicago Defender* in 1942, which continued for 20 years. The column introduced Jesse B. Semple, or Simple, a character from Harlem who commented on racism, race, and other matters. Simple was Hughes's most beloved character and became the subject of five collections edited by Hughes, beginning with *Simple Speaks His Mind* (1950). Two postwar books of poetry, *Fields of Wonder* (1947) and *One-Way Ticket* (1949), were not well received, but *Montage of a Dream Deferred* (1951) was an important work, blending poetry with the new bebop jazz in a discordant reflection of the despair of many urban blacks living in the North.

In 1953, Hughes was subpoenaed by Senator Joseph McCarthy to testify in Washington, D.C., about his politics. Humiliated and frustrated, Hughes cooperated with McCarthy, though he had no respect for McCarthy or his aims. Hughes testified he had never been a party member but admitted "Goodbye Christ" had been ill advised. Some leftists criticized Hughes for cooperating with McCarthy, but overall, Hughes's career was not hurt by this episode, unlike that of **Paul Robeson** and W. E. B. Du Bois. Soon McCarthy himself was discredited. Hughes then wrote *I Wonder as I Wander* (1956), an account of his year in the Soviet Union and an admired second volume to his autobiography.

In the 1950s, Hughes was finally able to break the seemingly endless poverty he had lived in all his life. Becoming prosperous, he bought a home in Harlem. Hughes looked to the stage again, first with a show based on the Simple books, *Simply Heavenly* (1957), which met with some popularity. His next show, *Tambourines to Glory* (1963), was a gospel musical, but it failed badly. Some critics accused Hughes of caricaturing black Americans. Hughes went on to write other gospel-based stage shows, including *Black Nativity* (1961) and *Jericho-Jim Crow* (1964).

Versatile and prolific, Hughes also wrote a dozen children's books throughout his career, beginning with *Popo and Fifina* (1932, written with **Arna Bontemps**), which drew on Hughes's visit to Haiti in 1931. Many of his children's books sought to introduce children to various aspects of black culture or black Americans, such as *The First Book of Jazz* (1957), one of a series of "first" books, and *Famous American Negroes* (1954).

Hughes also edited and anthologized the work of others in books such as *The Poetry of the Negro 1746-1949*, which included work of Caribbean writers; *New Negro Poets USA* (1964); and *The Best Short Stories by Negro Writers* (1967), which included the first published story of **Alice Walker**.

Hughes was distinctively able to write for the needs of his black audience, as he held to a vision of a more inclusive America. Hughes's work celebrates and lifts up the lives and dreams of average black Americans, who in turn, praised and celebrated him. His poetry, with its jazz rhythms and blues influence, is some of the best and most influential of any written this century by any black poet. "The Negro Speaks of Rivers," "Mother to Son," and "Harlem" are anthems of black America.

Langston Hughes died in a New York hospital, still hard at work on various projects until just before his death. *The Panther and the Lash* (1967), a collection of poetry published posthumously, focuses on the civil-rights and black-power movements.

Hughes's work was rooted in racial pride and freedom. He based his often-controversial politics on the belief that art should be accessible to the largest number of people possible. Langston Hughes was one of our most creative and prolific African-American poets.

REFERENCES: *AAW.* **Haskins, James S.** 1976/ *Always Movin' On: The Life of Langston Hughes.* New York: Watts. **Rampersad, Arnold** in *COCAAL* and *OCAAL. EA-99.* 1986. *The Life of Langston Hughes, 1902-1941: Vol. 1. I, Too, Sing America.* New York: Oxford University Press.. —Lisa Bahlinger

Hull, Akasha (née Gloria Theresa Thompson)
12/6/1944–

Scholarly, poems, literary criticism; educator

The first time Gloria Theresa Thompson changed her name, she was merging her identity with that of her husband, Prentice R. Hull (in 1966). That year, she graduated from Southern University, summa cum laude. She and Prentice had a son, Adrian Prentice Hull, but she and Prentice later divorced (1983). Nearly a decade later, she legally changed name again, this time to distinguish her own separate identity as Akasha Gloria Hull (1992), a proud African-American lesbian feminist.

By that time, her name had already appeared in print numerous times. She had written and published her doctoral dissertation (1972) on women in Lord Byron's Romantic poetry; her literary analysis *Color, Sex and Poetry:*

Three Women Writers of the Harlem Renaissance (1987), critiquing **Alice Dunbar-Nelson, Georgia Douglas Johnson,** and **Angelina Weld Grimké**; and her poetry collection, *Healing Heart, Poems 1973-1988* (1989), published by Kitchen Table: Women of Color Press. She had also coedited the landmark *All the Women Are White, All the Blacks Are Men, but Some of Us Are Brave: Black Women's Studies* (1982, with Patricia Bell Scott and **Barbara Smith**), winner of the National Institute of Women of Color Award (1982). In addition, she had edited and introduced *Give Us Each Day: The Diary of Alice Dunbar-Nelson* (1984), her three-volume *The Works of Alice Dunbar-Nelson* (1988), and Dunbar-Nelson's *The Dunbar Speaker and Entertainer: The Poet and His Song (African-American Women Writers, 1910-1940)*. She also recorded a videotape titled *A Day with Alice Dunbar-Nelson* (1976), made by the University of Delaware. In addition, she has written countless articles for scholarly literary and cultural journals.

In the new millennium, Akasha Gloria Hull published *Soul Talk: The New Spirituality of African-American Women* (2001) under her new name. For a decade or so, she had been asking interesting women the question, "How do you see yourself as a spiritual being and how does that spirituality manifest in your life and work?" Her book includes responses from the late **Toni Cade Bambara, Sonia Sanchez,** and **Alice Walker**.

Meanwhile, Hull rose through the academic ranks at the University of Delaware in Newark (1971-1988), reaching full professor in 1986. While there, she worked as advisory editor on the highly esteemed *Black American Literature Forum* (subsequently the **African American Review**) (1978-1986). During her last year at Delaware, she served as a visiting scholar at Stanford University. The following year, she started as professor of women's studies and literature (1988-2000), serving as department chair for a time (1989-1991) and retiring as professor emerita in 2000. She is said to be working on two novels, and one of her short stories has already been published in an anthology, *Age Ain't Nothing but a Number: Black Women Explore Midlife* (2003). Her awards and honors include a stipend from the National Endowment for the Humanities (1979), a Rockefeller Foundation fellowship (1979-1980), a Ford Foundation fellowship (1987-1988), a Mellon Foundation fellowship and Fulbright scholarship to the University of West Indies in Jamaica (1984-1986), and a grant from the American Association of University Women (1991).

REFERENCES: *CAO-08.* Brennan, Carol, in *BB.* Johnson, Sharon D., in *AANB.* Amazon.com.

FURTHER READING: Black-Parker, Kimberly, in *GEAAL.*

Hunter, Alberta
4/1/1895–10/17/1984
Songs; singer, nurse

Chiefly known as a blues singer, Hunter wrote many of her own songs, such as "Downhearted Blues" (1922), recorded by fellow blues singer Bessie Smith. From 1955 until 1977, Hunter retired from singing and songwriting to work as a nurse, but when she returned to singing, at age 82, she once again returned to the fore in her profession.

REFERENCES: *WDAW.* Meadows, Eddie S., in *BWA:AHE. EA-99. EB-BH-CD.*

Hunter (second married name: Lattany), Kristin (née Eggleston)
9/12/1931–

Novels, children's/juvenile novels, short stories, plays, screenplays; journalist, columnist, advertising copywriter, educator

School principal George Lorenzo Eggleston and his wife Mabel planned that their only child would become a schoolteacher. A former teacher herself, Mabel had been forced to retire from teaching when she became a mother, as her school district barred mothers from teaching. Kristin's family home held a wealth of books, and her parents encouraged her to read, but she was rarely allowed to speak in this "children-were-seen-and-not-heard household." She later recalled, "I escaped into books very early. When I picture myself as a child, I see myself somewhere reading, usually hiding and reading" (*BWWW,* p. 85). She also learned early that if she wished to express herself, she would have to do so through writing. In retrospect, Hunter noted, "I always knew I wanted to be a writer."

When Kristin was 14 years old, her aunt helped her get work writing a youth column for the *Pittsburgh Courier.* After a bit, she started writing feature articles for the paper. During her 6-year association with that paper, she also had some of her poems and "a short story or two" published, and she graduated from the University of Pennsylvania (in 1951). On graduation, she briefly tried to fulfill her parents' wishes for her to teach in public school. After teaching third grade for less than a year, however, she realized that she needed to follow her own goals, not her parents' dreams for her. In 1952, Kristin moved away from her parents' home, married journalist Joseph Hunter, and resigned her teaching job to begin her writing career, starting as an advertising copywriter.

Although Kristin and Joseph divorced a decade later, most of her writings were published under her first married name. She later regretted this decision, observing, "Sometimes I wish I had come to terms with this early enough to revert to my maiden name when I was di-

vorced in 1962, rather than continuing to use Hunter, ... But at the time I did not like my maiden name, Eggleston, because I thought it sounded awkward, ugly, and . . . because . . . I did not like my father. I thought of 'Hunter' not as my ex-husband's name but as my own. And by the time of my second marriage, to John Lattany in June 1968, I had established a solid professional identity . . . as Kristin Hunter" (quoted in *Children's Author/Illustrator* at Answers.com). Not until 1995 did she start using the surname Lattany for her writings.

At first, Hunter pursued other kinds of writing only after her copywriting job. In 1955, she won a national Fund for the Republic Award competition for a television script, having submitted her script *Minority of One.* Her script involved black-white school integration, but by the time the teleplay aired, the CBS network had transformed the script into a story about a French-speaking immigrant starting out in an all-Anglo school.

Hunter continued to write fiction at night and on weekends while working as a copywriter, an information officer, and then a freelance writer (e.g., with articles in *Philadelphia Magazine* and other publications) by day. In 1964, Hunter had another breakthrough when her social-criticism novel *God Bless the Child* was published. The central character, Rosie Fleming, tragically believes that because her poverty has oppressed her, the secret to happiness must be to achieve high financial status and success at all costs. She ends up sacrificing her relationships with loved ones and even her own health in the effort. The next year, Hunter's play *The Double Edge* was produced. In 1966, her novel *The Landlord* was published. In it, a young wealthy white landlord buys a black-ghetto apartment building and starts to try to shape the lives of his tenants. Over time, however, his tenants have far more influence on him than he has on them. The novel was made into a 1970 movie, which portrayed a far harsher view of the landlord and the tenants than Hunter had described.

In the late 1960s, Hunter turned to writing novels for young adults. Many readers now know her primarily as an author of these works. Her first young-adult novel was *The Soul Brothers and Sister Lou* (1968/2005), centered around Louetta Hawkins. "Lou" forms a singing group whose rise in popularity carries them up and out of their urban ghetto. In this work, Hunter uses the authentic speech of African-American urban youths, a relatively novel approach at the time. The Council on Interracial Books recognized this book with its 1968 Children's Prize, and the book sold more than 1 million copies. Hunter's other novels and novellas for young readers include *Boss Cat* (1971), *The Pool Table War* (1972), *Uncle Dan and the Raccoon* (1972), and her sequel *Lou in the Limelight* (1981). She also wrote a short-story collection for young adults, *Guests in the Promised Land* (1973), which earned her a National Book Award nomination and the 1973 Chicago Tribune Book World Prize for juvenile literature. Her works have been widely translated.

When her husband, John's, children were youngsters around the house, Kristin had to create a room of her own in which to work. Since 1984, Kristin and John have lived in the same house in which Kristin was raised, and their home still often overflows with grandchildren, nephews, nieces, and other family and friends. Although Kristin's own experiences have been centered in the middle class, she writes both realistically and optimistically, with sensitivity, warmth, and humor, about the black urban ghetto.

She also continues to writes novels for adults, including *The Survivors* (1975), about a friendship between a lonely middle-aged dressmaker and a neglected, homeless 13-year-old boy. Hunter's novel *The Lakestown Rebellion* (1978, reprinted 2003) tells how a small community of blacks cleverly sabotages a powerful corporation's attempt to bulldoze through their town to build a highway. Along the lines of the **trickster** tradition in African-American and world literature, the protagonist Bella Lake leads the residents of the town to innovatively create comical disruptions that foil the plans of the out-of-towners. Hunter reported that her account is fictional, but she based it on an actual rebellion.

Nearly two decades after *Lakestown*, Lattany published *Kinfolks* (1996), about lifelong friends and former activists whose children are about to wed. Lattany also "enjoyed the high point of my career in 1996, when I was given the Lifetime Achievement Award by Larry Robin's Moonstone Foundation, which celebrated black writing annually for seventeen years." She has since published *Do unto Others* (2000), about the cultural ties and clashes that emerge when a middle-class African-American entrepreneur and wife temporarily offers her home to a homeless African woman; and *Breaking Away* (2003), "which fictionalizes an racist incident that occurred at the University of Pennsylvania while [Lattany] was teaching there" (from *Something about the Author*, quoted in *Children's Authors/Illustrators*).

In 1972, after establishing her writing career, Kristin returned to the University of Pennsylvania campus to teach, offering instruction in creative writing and African-American literature until she retired in 1995. She has enjoyed "working with young people, finding out what's on their minds, seeing them develop. It's a source of energy even though it drains the writing energy" (*BWWW*, p. 86). Although teaching also provided needed income, she found that it inhibited her writing, particularly if she taught more than two courses per semester. In an interview, she observed, "I don't think I'll ever run out of ideas. I may run out of energy. Stories are waiting to be written. It's whatever grabs my imagination. It finds form, as a novel, as a short story. What is most ur-

gent I do first. I have a dozen more stories I haven't done yet. You see this box of future projects; it's full" (*BWWW*, p. 84). "My main problem these days is a tendency to have far more ambition than energy. Writing projects abound. Right now (summer 2004), along with revising my play, I am working on a short story collection and a revision of my husband's book of village memories, which we wrote together. . . . It's been a rich, fulfilling life—and it isn't over" (from *Something about the Author*, quoted in *Children's Authors/Illustrators*).

REFERENCES: *BI. BWWW. EBLG. MAAL. MWEL*. Collier, Eugenia W., in *OCWW*. Fowler, Anne Marie, "Lattany, Kristin Hunter," in *GEAAL*. O'Neale, Sondra, in *AAFW-55-84*. *G-95*. Tate, Claudia, in *CA/I. CAO-02. COCAAL* and *OCAAL. MWEL. Wiki*.

Hunter, Latoya
6/13/1978–
Memoir

Hunter's *The Diary of Latoya Hunter: My First Year in Junior High School* was published when she was just 12 years old. Since then, she has continued to write and aspires to be a journalist.

REFERENCES: *33T.* Amazon.com, 3/2009. —Tonya Bolden

Hunter-Gault, Charlayne
2/27/1942–
Autobiography/memoir, articles; print and broadcast journalist

At age 12, Charlayne already knew she wanted to be a journalist like her comic-strip heroine Brenda Starr. In high school, she was editor of her school newspaper, but her guidance counselor tried to dissuade Charlayne from journalism because of her double jeopardy: being both female and black. Undaunted, Charlayne decided to attend a college with an outstanding journalism program; the one she chose (with a little nudging from the NAACP) was the all-white University of Georgia. That started her two-year legal battle to become the first African-American woman to attend the University of Georgia since its start 176 years earlier. While her NAACP lawyers were working her case through the legal system to the Supreme Court, Charlayne started studying journalism at Wayne State University in Detroit. At last, in January of 1961, the court ordered that Charlayne Hunter and Hamilton Holmes be admitted as the first two African Americans to desegregate the University of Georgia. That's when the real battle began, with white racists violently protesting her presence. She later observed, "There was conflict and there was pain. . . . But I emerged as a whole person and the university came out the better for it" (quoted in *TAWH*, p. 189). In belated appreciation, the university renamed the building where they registered the Hunter-Holmes Academic Building in 2001. A short time before she graduated (B.A. in journalism, 1963), she married fellow (white) student Walter Stovall, and a few years later, the couple had a daughter, Susan. Although the marriage didn't last, the two have stayed friends.

After graduating, Hunter-Stovall started out as a secretary for *New Yorker* magazine, began contributing items for the magazine's "Talk of the Town" column. Soon, she was promoted to a writing position on the staff, becoming the first African-American reporter for the *New Yorker*. In 1967, she studied social science through a Russell Sage Fellowship and started working for *Trans-Action* magazine. The magazine sent her to cover the Poor People's Campaign in Washington, D.C., and soon she was anchoring and reporting the local evening news for WRC-TV there. In 1968, she joined the staff at *The New York Times*, following Nancy Hicks Maynard to be the second African-American woman *Times* reporter. There, she founded and managed the paper's Harlem bureau. Hunter-Gault has since observed, "I have never apologized for doing black stories, being interested in black stories, and insisting that every institution that I work for report black stories" (quoted in *RWTC*, p. 43). While working for the *Times,* she took time out to codirect the Michele Clark Fellowship program for minority students at Columbia University's school of journalism. In 1971, Hunter married a second time, to African-American banker Ronald Gault, with whom she has a son, Chuma.

In 1978, she joined the *MacNeil/Lehrer Report,* and in 1983, she became the program's national correspondent when it expanded to the one-hour *MacNeil/Lehrer NewsHour.* In 1997, Hunter-Gault left the *NewsHour* to take a job as South Africa bureau chief for National Public Radio, during the critical times of that nation's history. In 1999, CNN hired her as its African correspondent, too. Among Hunter-Gault's awards are the prestigious George Foster Peabody Award for Excellence in Broadcast Journalism (1986, 1999), the Journalist of the Year Award from the National Association of Black Journalists (1986), the National Urban Coalition Award for Distinguished Urban Reporting, *The New York Times* Publisher's Award, the American Women in Radio and Television Award, two national news (outstanding coverage of a single breaking story and outstanding background/analysis of a single current story) and documentary Emmy Awards, a Lifetime Achievement Award from the Annenberg School of Communication at the University of Southern California (2000), and more than two dozen honorary degrees. In addition to writing numerous articles for national publications (e.g., *Essence, Life, Saturday Review*), Hunter-Gault wrote her autobiography of her early life, *In My Place* (1992), and she has coauthored

and contributed to other volumes. Her most recent book returns to reporting *New News Out of Africa: Uncovering Africa's Renaissance* (2006/2007), based on lectures she presented at Harvard University in 2003. In it, she attempts to contradict the prejudices about Africa as a continent of "death, disaster, disease, and despair," to offer her analysis presenting a more hopeful perspective.

REFERENCES: *AANB. EBLG. EWJ. RWTC.* Decker, Ed, and Jennifer M. York, in *BB. CAO-08.* Amazon.com, 7/1999, 3/2009. Garza, Hedda, in *G-97.* Robinson, Lisa Clayton, in *EA-99.* Smith, Jessie Carney, in *BWA:AHE. Wiki.*

Hurston, Zora Neale
1/7/1891–1/28/1960
Essays, short stories, novels, nonfiction—anthropology, folklore; journalist, librarian, teacher

Zora Neale Hurston is probably best known as the author of *Their Eyes Were Watching God* (1937) and as one of the most prolific participants in the **Harlem Renaissance**. She has influenced such writers as **Ralph Ellison, Toni Morrison, Gayl Jones,** and **Toni Cade Bambara**. The author of four novels and a number of short stories, essays, and other nonfiction works, Hurston is also acknowledged as the first African American to collect and publish African-American folklore.

Hurston was raised in the first incorporated African-American town—Eatonville, Florida. Eatonville had a mayor, a charter, a marshal, and a council. She described it as the first attempt at self-government on the part of African Americans. A rich source of African-American cultural tradition, the locale inspired most of her fiction.

Hurston's mother, Lucy Potts Hurston, a former schoolteacher, died when Zora was about nine years old. Her father, John Hurston, was a carpenter, a Baptist preacher, and three-term mayor of Eatonville. Hurston, the fifth of John and Lucy's eight children, had a rocky relationship with her family. Her father had remarried shortly after Lucy's death, and Hurston's dislike of her stepmother caused her relationship with her father to deteriorate.

Hurston was taken out of school at age 13, and she left home to take a job as a wardrobe girl in a repertory company touring the South. Eighteen months later, she left the troupe in Baltimore, Maryland, and an employer later arranged for her to complete her primary education. She completed her high-school requirements at Morgan Academy in Baltimore. She went on to Howard Prep School and Howard University and earned an associate's degree. She completed her undergraduate education at Barnard College and Columbia University, becoming a soror of Zeta Phi Beta. In college, she studied under es-

Zora Neale Hurston

teemed anthropologist Franz Boas, an experience that influenced her work.

While in New York, Hurston become a part of the **Harlem Renaissance** literati, making regular company of artists such as **Langston Hughes**, **Wallace Thurman**, and **Jessie Fauset**, and calling the black literati the "niggerati." She became well-known not only for her writing but for her outspokenness, her distinct way of dress, and her refusal to be ashamed of her culture.

Ironically, several members of the "niggerati" harshly criticized Hurston for her rugged individualism. Like many other black artists of the period, Zora received funds from white patrons and philanthropical organizations to do her work. She was very adept in her quest for funds. To some of her contemporaries, however, this was just another reason to criticize her, even though many of them relied on the same patrons and organizations for their livelihood.

From 1927 to 1931, Hurston collected African-American folklore in Alabama and Florida, working on a private grant. She also traveled to the Caribbean and Latin America for her folklore writings. Her most active years were the 1930s and early 1940s. During that time, she was awarded a Guggenheim fellowship, joined the

Federal Writers' Project in Florida, published four novels and an autobiography, and worked as a story consultant for Paramount Pictures.

Hurston drew on the folklore material for her plays, musicals, short stories, and novels. In *Zora Neale Hurston: A Literary Biography*, Robert Hemenway quotes Hurston's definition of folklore: "Folklore, Hurston said, is the art people create before they find out there is such a thing as art; it comes from a folk's 'first wondering contact with natural law'—that is, laws of human nature as well as laws of natural process, the truths of a group's experience as well as the principles of physics."

Hurston's search for the "inner heart of truth," which she believed could be found in folklore, took her on many perilous adventures. Her study of African-American folklore took her into the secret world of hoodoo (voodoo), and because she believed in personally participating in her research, she learned how to conjure. Albert Price III, a man to whom Hurston was married for a short time, claimed that she had supernatural powers and could "fix him." The belief in voodoo features in Hurston's fictive Eatonville, which is often controlled by seemingly supernatural forces.

Fearing for her life, Hurston fled Haiti shortly after writing *Their Eyes Were Watching God*, which is an intense blend of black folklore and Western literary tradition. Her intensive study of voodoo, which she believed to be rooted in African mysticism, came to an abrupt end. Hemenway states, "She had gone deeply enough into the Caribbean night."

Hurston embraced hoodoo for artistic inspiration because it freed her of the institutional restraints that restricted the freedom of a black woman in white patriarchy. *Their Eyes Were Watching God*, considered Hurston's best work by many critics, tells the story of a woman's quest for fulfillment and liberation. In the novel, when Tea Cake, Janie's third husband, becomes ill after being bitten by a rabid dog, he fears that he has been conjured. He is suspicious that Janie wants to be free of him so that she can marry a lighter-skinned man. In an attempt to quell his fear, Janie says, "Maybe it wuz uh witch ridin' yuh, honey. Ah'll see can't Ah find some mustard seed whilst Ah's out."

Her novel *Jonah's Guard Vine* (1934) combines her knowledge of folklore with biblical themes. *Mules and Men* (1935) incorporates **folktale** elements drawn from her hometown culture. In *Moses, Man of the Mountain* (1937), an allegorical novel of American slavery, Hurston made use of her studies in voodoo in New Orleans. Her autobiography *Dust Tracks on a Road* was published in 1942. Hurston's individualism was mixed with a strong sense of optimism. In her *Dust Tracks on a Road*, she recalled her mother urging her eight children to aim high: "Jump at de sun. . . . We might not land on the sun, but at least we would get off the ground." She shocked many, while delighting others, by living her life as she pleased.

In an essay called "How It Feels to Be Colored Me," Hurston said,

I am not tragically colored. There is no great sorrow dammed up in me or lurking behind my eyes. I do not mind at all. I do not belong to the sobbing school of Negrohood who hold that nature somehow has given them a lowdown dirty deal and whose feelings are all hurt about. . . . No, I do not weep at the world—I am too busy sharpening my oyster knife.

Hurston was raised to be a Christian but became a pagan. Educated to be a scholar, Hurston believed in the integrity of the genius of black vernacular. Hurston was an African-American woman who achieved fame in a white man's world. Hurston was an artist, an urban New Yorker, and a rural Floridian. In "How It Feels to Be Colored Me," Hurston describes herself as "a brown bag of miscellany propped against a wall."

During the mid-1940s, Zora began to publish less and less. It was not that she did not produce work, but her work was rejected with increasing frequency, and she had to find other ways to make a living. During the remaining years of her life, she worked variously as a newspaper reporter, librarian, and substitute teacher. For a while in 1950, she worked as a maid in Rivo Island, Florida. During that period, she published an article in the *Saturday Evening Post*. She moved to Belle Glade, Florida, late that year, and she continued to write and publish, including another article in the *Saturday Evening Post*.

However, her finances and health faltered. Like many other artists who were before their time, Zora lived her last few years in relative obscurity. In 1959 she suffered a stroke and had to enter the St. Lucie County Welfare home. She died there penniless and was buried in an unmarked grave in a segregated cemetery in Fort Pierce, Florida.

In 1973, writer **Alice Walker** discovered her grave and put a gravemarker on the site. Walker published the essay "In Search of Zora Neale Hurston" in *Ms.* magazine in March 1975 and resurrected the literary world's interest in Zora. Since 1989, there has been an annual festival in her honor in Eatonville.

REFERENCES: *EBLG.* Hemenway, Robert E. 1977. *Zora Neale Hurston: A Literary Biography.* Chicago: University of Chicago Illinois Press. Hooks, Rita (1996), "Conjured into Being, Their Eyes Were Watching God," //splavc.spjc.cc.fl.us/hooks/Zora.html. Hurston, Zora Neale. 1979. "How It Feels to Be Colored Me," in **Alice Walker** (Ed.), *I Love Myself When I Am Laughing . . . And Then Again When I Am Looking Mean and Impressive.* Old Westbury, New York: Feminist Press. _____. 1937. *Their Eyes Were Watching God.* New York: Harper and Row. —Michael Strickland

Hutson, Jean (née Blackwell)
9/7/1914–2/3/1998
Nonfiction—bibliography, short stories; librarian

A frequent contributor to bibliographic works, particularly on African-American writers and writings, Hutson also wrote short stories and the introductions to numerous books. Nonetheless, Hutson is chiefly known for her work as a librarian, starting in 1936 at the New York Public Library (NYPL). While still a relatively new NYPL librarian, Jean Blackwell was invited to the NYPL's Division of Negro Literature, History, and Prints, principally comprising the books and other materials donated by bibliophile **Arthur A. Schomburg**, who considered the division his domain. She later recalled, "he arranged the books according to their color and size. So working late one night, I decided to arrange them according to the Dewey Decimal System. When he discovered what I had done the next day, he was so angry that he fired me. I was immediately banished from the Library" (quoted in *AANB*).

Schomburg died in 1938, but Blackwell was still banished from his collection. In 1939, she left the NYPL to become a junior high school librarian in Baltimore, and the same year, she married lyricist **Andy Razaf**. In 1942, she returned to the NYPL, but she continued to work at other locations and branches of the NYPL, always looking for ways to serve her patrons. For instance, she helped expand the Spanish-language materials available to the Spanish-speaking residents of her library's community. Finally, in 1948, she was appointed the fourth curator of the **Arthur A. Schomburg** Collection within the Harlem branch of the library. By then, she had divorced Razaf (in 1947), and in 1950, she married library security guard John Hutson. The couple adopted a daughter, Jean, Jr., in 1952. Sadly, John died in 1957, and Jean Jr. also predeceased her mother, in 1992.

By 1972, Hutson had so expanded the collection that she was appointed chief of the collection, now known as the Schomburg Center for Research in Black Culture. When Hutson took over the collection, it comprised Schomburg's 15,000-book library and was located in a small, decaying Carnegie library building. For the next eight years, she raised funds and elevated public awareness of the collection, now considered the preeminent research center of its kind, comprising more than 5 million separately catalogued items, housed in a spacious new facility. She also supervised the development of the *Dictionary Catalog of the Schomburg Collection of Negro Literature and History* (1962), a massive undertaking. Her bibliographical writings are also included in *Nine Decades of Scholarship: A Bibliography of the Writings, 1892-1983, of the Staff of the Schomburg Center for Research in Black Culture*.

REFERENCES: *AANB. BAAW.* Gunn, Arthur, in *BWA:AHE.* Newman, Richard, in *EA-99.* Wolf, Gillian, in *BB.* —Tonya Bolden

~I~

Ice-T (né Tracey [or Tracy] Lauren Morrow [or Marrow])
2/16/1958–
Rap lyrics, opinion; performer, actor

While still a young teenager, Tracy was orphaned and sent away from Newark, New Jersey, to live with his father's sister in Los Angeles. In high school, he started getting involved with petty crimes, local gangsters, and rap music. As his pals started heading to prison, they and his girlfriend, Darlene Ortiz (pictured on his first two albums), urged him to focus on the rap and steer away from crime. Soon considered one of the most prolific and outspoken rap artists, Ice-T named himself in deference to **Iceberg Slim**, whom Ice-T knew personally. Known for his "bad-boy" image and his provocative "gangsta rap" lyrics, which tout violence and misogyny, Ice-T has also spoken out against gang violence, drug abuse, and censorship. Many cite his *Rhyme Pays* (1987) as the first successful West Coast hip-hop album, and even his harshest social critics praise his clever rhymes. Nonetheless, Ice-T's 1991 album *O.G.—Original Gangster* was slapped with a sticker warning, "Parental guidance is suggested," perhaps the first album to receive such a warning. He retorted, "In my book, parental guidance is always suggested. If you need a sticker to tell you that you need to guide your child, you're a dumb f*****' parent anyhow." Soon after, on his *Body Count* album, his song "Cop Killer" inflamed national outrage by self-proclaimed music critics and rap fans such as then-President George Bush the elder and his V.P. Dan Quayle. In addition to Ice-T's numerous rap lyrics (e.g., "The Coldest Rap," "Colors," "Cop Killer"), his literary contributions include his book *The Ice Opinion: Who Gives a F***?* (1994, with Heidi Siegmund).

While rhyme was still paying, Ice-T began his acting career, appearing in dozens of films, starting in 1984. In 1995, he had a recurring role as a drug dealer on *New York Undercover,* cocreated by *Law & Order* creator Dick Wolf. In 1997, Ice-T proposed his ex-convict crime-fighters drama, *Players,* to Wolf, and Wolf gave it a try. Though the show didn't have a long run, it helped in the transition from "Cop Killer" to cop, and Ice-T landed his regular role as Detective Fin Tutuola on *Law & Order: Special Victims Unit,* starting in 2000. After parting company with Ortiz, Ice-T married swimsuit model Nicole "Coco" Austin. In October 2006, his first rap album in the new millennium, *Gangsta Rap,* featured his gorgeous wife provocatively posed over him. The same month, VH1 started airing Ice-T's Rap School, in which he trained eight teens to become a hip-hop group, culminating with a public performance opening for Public Enemy in mid-November. In 2008, he came out with *Black Ice—Urban Legends.* Still sometimes a "bad boy," Ice-T included his teenage son trash-talking in his 2008 video response to a fellow rapper.

REFERENCES: *AANB. D. F. Wiki.* Buchanan, Jason, *All Movie Guide,* in *Act.* Erlewine, Stephen Thomas, *All Music Guide,* in A. Glickman, Simon, and Leslie Rochelle, *BB. EA-99.* Amazon.com.

Iceberg Slim (né Robert Lee Maupin; aka Robert Beck)
8/4/1918–4/30/1992
Autobiography/memoir, novels, essays, short stories, spoken word—poems; criminal, salesperson

After earning a scholarship to the Tuskegee Institute at age 15 and spending 2 years studying there, Robert was kicked out for selling bootleg whiskey to fellow students. Renamed as Iceberg Slim, he ended up spending the next 25 years of his life either imprisoned or involved in street crime, as noted in his autobiography *Pimp: The Story of My Life* (1967). After that, he married, fathered four children, and spent several years writing his novels *Trick Baby: The Story of a White Negro* (1967), *Mama Black Widow: A Story of the South's Black Underworld* (1969), *Death Wish: A Story of The Mafia* (1976), and *The Long White Con: The Biggest Score in His Life!* (1977), a sequel to *Trick Baby.* He also wrote *Doom Fox* in 1978, but it was not published until 1998. His short stories were published in *Airtight Willie and Me: The Story of Six Incredible Players* (1979). *Mama Black Widow* was his most critically acclaimed work but not his most popular. Nonetheless, there have been discussions of making *Mama Black Widow* and *Pimp* into movies. In 1973, *Trick Baby* was adapted to make a blaxploitation movie released by Universal Studios. Slim also made a spoken-word album of his poems, titled *Reflections* (1976/1994). His poems inspired many followers, including **Ice-T**; while still in high school, Ice-T often recited Slim's poems. *The Naked Soul* *of Iceberg Slim* (1971) included many of his essays and word sketches. In 1982, he married Diane Millman, a fan with whom he had been corresponding for two years. By the time he died at age 73, he had sold more than 6 million copies of his books, including Dutch, French, German, Greek, Italian, Spanish, and Swedish translations. Initially, he sold many of his books through nontraditional channels, especially black-owned businesses such as beauty and barber shops and liquor stores. His largest audience continues to be his prison readership.

REFERENCES: *AANB.* Kergan, Wade, *All Music Guide,* in *A.* Leverette, Marc, in *GEAAL.* Oliver, Terri Hume, in *COCAAL* and *OCAAL.* Rubiner, Joanna, in *BB. D. Wiki.* "Robert Lee Maupin," in *CAO-08.*

~J~

Shango Diaspora: An African-American Myth of Woman-hood and Love (1980), *When the Wind Blows* (1984), and *Comfort Stew* (1997). She also wrote *Cowboy Amok* (1992) and the novels *Treemont Stone* (1984) and *Where I Must Go: A Novel* (2009).

REFERENCES: *AANB. BAWPP. CAO-03. CAO-09.* Clark, Cameron Christine, in *GEAAL.* Conyers, James L., in *Afrocentric Traditions, 2005* By Transaction Publishers, 2005. Patterson, Tracy J., in *COCAAL* and in *OCAAL.* Smith, D. L., in *AAP-55-85.* Amazon.com. //library.ms state.edu/special_interest/Mississippi_African-American_Authors.asp.

Jackson, Angela
July, 25, 1951–
Poems, plays, other fiction; educator, workshop leader

As a young girl, Angela relished bringing home armfuls of books from the Hiram Kelly Branch library and occasional hand-me-down books from the daughter of her mother's employer. She later recalled, "It is because of Alcott's Jo that I at an early age, before ten, began to dream myself as writer" (in *CAO-09*). In college, "poems called me to create myself in the hot and glorious moment. . . . I dared myself to make a life for myself as a writer, a life of dignity, passion, joy, and enduring achievement" (in *CAO-09*). Jackson's poetry emerged during the **Black Arts Movement**, and her poetry continues to reflect her roots in this movement. Jackson's writing career was nurtured by poet **Mari Evans** at Northwestern University and by the Chicago-based Organization of Black American Culture (OBAC) founded by **Haki Madhubuti, Carolyn Rodgers, Johari Amini**, and **Hoyt Fuller**, whom she succeeded as OBAC's coordinator until 1990. She has also nurtured aspiring writers at Columbia College (in Chicago), Framingham State College (in Massachusetts), and Howard University (Washington, D. C.).

Jackson has been awarded the Pushcart Prize, the Carl Sandburg Award, the *Chicago Sun Times*/Friends of Literature Book of the Year Award, an American Book Award, a Shelley Memorial Award from the Poetry Society of America, and numerous other prizes and fellowships for her poetry, which includes her collections *Voodoo/Love Magic* (1974), *The Greenville Club* (1977, a chapbook), *Solo in the Boxcar Third Floor E* (1985), *The Man With the White Liver: Poems* (1987), *Dark Legs and Silk Kisses: The Beatitudes of the Spinners* (1993), and *And All These Roads be Luminous: Poems Selected and New* (1998). Jackson has also written numerous short stories and several poetic dramas, including *Witness!* (1978),

Jackson, Elaine
1943–
Plays; actor, educator

Jackson's plays include *Toe Jam* (1971) and *Paper Dolls* (1979), about African-American actors, *Cockfight* (1976), about a problematic marriage; and *Birth Rites* (1987), about a mother-daughter relationship. She is also working on a musical version of *Birth Rites* (with composer-lyricist <u>Martin Weich</u>) and a new play, *Puberty Rites*. For her playwriting, she has earned awards from the National Endowment for the Arts and from the Rockefeller Foundation. She has also taught since the late 1970s, including experiences as playwright-in-residence at Lake Forest College and at Wayne State University.

REFERENCES: Manora, Yolanda M., in *OCAAL.* Ostrom, Hans, in *GEAAL.*

Jackson, George Lester
9/23/1941–8/21/1971
Memoir, letters

The Soledad Prison writings of Jackson, compiled in his *Soledad Brother: The Prison Letters of George Jackson* (1970/1994), had tremendous impact at the time of their publication, sparking heated controversy and much admiration among revolutionary thinkers of the early 1970s. He wrote his second book, *Blood in My Eye* (1972/1996), while in San Quentin, completing it just days before his death at the hands of prison guards, just as his posthumously published book had predicted. Guards and prison officials alleged that he was killed while attempting an armed escape, but prisoners and others disputed that allegation.

REFERENCES: *AANB. CAO-03. EA-99. Wiki.* Briley, Ron, in *GEAAL.* Jacobson, Robert R., in *BB.* Amazon.com.

Jackson, Jesse
1/1/1908–4/14/1983
Juvenile fiction and biography; journalist, educator, reader

This Jesse Jackson never ran for U.S. President and never preached in a pulpit, but he has influenced many youths nonetheless. Following three years at Ohio State University's School of Journalism (1927-1929), Jackson left school and started working on the *Ohio State Press.* After that, he worked in a variety of jobs, including that of juvenile probation officer (1936). While working with African-American adolescents, he saw a need for young-adult novels relevant to their experiences. He later recalled, some of these "boys had dropped out of school because they were ashamed to tell their teachers they could not read. Their ages ran from fourteen to sixteen when this occurred. How to write something nonreaders would want to read became an obsession of mine and still is" (quoted in *CAO-03*).

In Jackson's first novel, *Call Me Charley* (1945/1968), the title character, Charles Moss, strives for acceptance and respect—a difficult task for a black youth living in an all-white neighborhood and attending an all-white public school. Jackson's book was among the first young-adult books to address racial prejudice as a central theme. At the time, this book blazed a trail that many others were to follow. (The *Brown v. Board of Education* decision was not handed down until 1954, the Little Rock Nine didn't integrate Central High School until 1957, and James Meredith didn't integrate the University of Mississippi until 1962.) In light of contemporary experiences and understandings, however, many critics question the tremendous forbearance Charley shows in responding to the racial insults to which he is subjected.

Jackson's subsequent books for young adults include two sequels to his first novel (*Anchor Man,* 1947/1968; and *Charley Starts from Scratch,* 1958); *Room for Randy* (1957); and *Tessie* (1968) and *Tessie Keeps Her Cool* (1970), about a young African-American girl in Harlem who earns a scholarship to attend an all-white private school. Jackson also wrote nonfiction for young adults, including two biographies of Stonewall Jackson, *The Sickest Don't Always Die the Quickest* (1971) and *The Fourteenth Cadillac* (1991), as well as his two **Carter G. Woodson** Award-winning books, *Black in America: Fight for Freedom* (1971) and *Make a Joyful Noise unto the Lord! The Life of **Mahalia Jackson**,* Queen of the Gospel Singers (1974). He had also written an earlier biography of Mahalia, *I Sing Because I'm Happy* (1972). In 1974, he started working as a lecturer, instructor, and writer-in-residence at Appalachian State University, where he continued to work until his death.

REFERENCES: *BAWPP. CAO-03. EBLG.* Lowe, Barbara, in *COCAAL* and in *OCAAL.*

Jackson, Sr., Jesse (Louis) (né Jesse Louis Burns-Robinson)
10/8/1941–
Nonfiction—civil rights, spoken word—sermons, speeches; preacher, politician, activist

What makes Jesse Jackson such an effective political and religious leader? His ability to craft words and to deliver them with gusto. From his earliest days as a student sitting-in in Greensboro, North Carolina, through his U.S. presidential campaigns in 1984 and 1988, he has given eloquent voice to the pleas and the demands of those who suffer oppression, poverty, and injustice. He has cried out for us in our despair at losing **Martin Luther King, Jr.**, whose blood stained his shirt; he has exclaimed jubilantly for us at the March on Washington; and he has triumphantly urged us to proclaim, "I am somebody," always including those whom many others disparage, ignore, and neglect.

Always one to lead with words, but never one to stop with them, he has organized boycotts, led corporations to do good, stirred support for African-American entrepreneurship, spearheaded enrichment programs for youths, and negotiated peaceful international win-win settlements when it seemed everyone was about to lose. Through his Operation PUSH (People United to Save Humanity) and his Rainbow Coalition, he has accomplished a great deal. Just what does he want to be the outcome of his words and his actions? No one says it better than he does. In his address at the 1984 Democratic National Convention, he said, "We are not a perfect people. Yet we are called to a perfect mission: to feed the hungry, to clothe the naked, to house the homeless, to teach the illiterate, to provide jobs for the jobless, and to choose the human race over the nuclear race."

In addition to giving speeches and writing forewords and introductions to numerous books, Jackson authored *Time to Speak: The Autobiography of Reverend Jesse Jackson* (1988). He also coauthored *Keep Hope Alive: Jesse Jackson's 1988 Presidential Campaign: A Collection of Major Speeches, Issue Papers, Photographs, and Campaign Analysis* (1989, with Frank Clemente, Frank E. Watkins), *Legal Lynching: Racism, Injustice, and the Death Penalty* (1996, with Jesse Jackson, Jr., and Bruce Shapiro), and other books. Reflecting his new-millennium shift in focus from politics in Washington D. C. to in finances on Wall Street, he and his son Jesse Jackson, Jr., cowrote *It's About the Money! The Fourth Movement of the Freedom Symphony: How to Build Wealth, Get Access to Capital, and Achieve Your Financial Dreams* (Times Business, 2000).

Jesse Jackson, Sr.

The younger Jackson also wrote *A More Perfect Union: Advancing New American Rights* (2001, with Frank E. Watkins).

Occasionally, Jackson's words have gotten him into trouble, as when he disparaged Jews in New York City and he verbally emasculated presidential candidate Barack Obama. His actions, too, have sometimes brought shame to himself and suffering to his family, including his wife Jacqueline Brown Jackson and their five children- Santita (b. 1963), Jesse Jr. (1965), Jonathan Luther (1966), Yusef DuBois (1970), and Jacqueline Lavinia (1975)- when he fathered a daughter, Ashley Laverne (b. 1999), with his staffer Karin Stanford. Jesse's own birth father, Noah Robinson, never married Jesse's mother, Helen Burns. Jesse's stepfather, Charles Jackson, adopted Jesse, gave Jesse his surname, and raised Jesse to be proud to be somebody.

REFERENCES: *AANB. B. CAO-05. EAACH. HD. LE. PB. QB. SMKC. W2B. Wiki.* Knight, Gladys L., in *GEAAL.* Ryan, Bryan, and Jennifer M. York in *BB.* Williams, Nicole L. Bailey, in *BH2C.*

Jackson, Joseph Harrison
9/11/1900–8/18/1990
Opinion

Jackson is perhaps best known for being an African-American Baptist minister opposed to civil disobedience and the civil-rights movement, favoring instead economic independence and self-development, as expressed in his book *Unholy Shadows and Freedom's Holy Light* (1967). The head of the National Baptist Convention (1953-1982), he also wrote numerous other works, including *Stars in the Night* (1950), *The Eternal Flame* (1956), *The Story of a Preaching Mission in Russia* (1956), *Many But One: The Ecumenics of Charity* (1964), *The Ecumenic of Charity* (1964), *Nairobi, a Joke, A Junket, or a Journey? Reflections upon the Fifth Assembly of the World Council of Churches* (1976), and *A Story of Christian Activism: The History of the National Baptist Convention, U.S.A., Incorporated* (1980).

REFERENCES: *AANB. Wiki.* Newman, Richard, in *EA-99.* //library. msstate.edu/special_interest/Mississippi_African-American_Authors.asp

Jackson, Mae
1/3/1946–
Poems; activist, educator, social worker

Jackson's poems, reflective of the **Black Arts Movement**, have frequently been published in literary journals and anthologies. Her poetry has also been collected in her *Can I Poet with You?* (1969/1972). She also wrote several children's plays highlighting African-American biography, history, and culture; as well as short stories and an audio documentary on prison reform for Pacifica Radio. She also contributes poetry and prose, fiction and nonfiction to various periodicals. Among her many community-service activities, she directs the Children Without Walls arts program for children of imprisoned mothers.

REFERENCES: *BAWPP. CAO-01.* LaFrance, Michelle, in *GEAAL.* Lindberg, Kathryne V., in *OCAAL.*

Jackson, Mahalia
10/26/1911–1/27/1972
Autobiography

Jackson, a world-renowned gospel singer, wrote her autobiography, *Movin' On Up* (1966), with the help of writer Evan Wylie. Perhaps her most memorable performance was at the 1963 rally in Washington, D.C., at which **Martin Luther King, Jr.,** gave his unforgettable "I Have a Dream" speech. Two decades after her death, Oxford University Press published an account of her life, *Got to Tell It: Mahalia Jackson, Queen of Gospel.*

REFERENCES: *EA-99. EB-CD-98. SEW. WDAW.* Jackson, Joyce Marie, in *BWA:AHE.*

Mahalia Jackson

Jackson, Mattie J.
c. 1846–?
Autobiography/memoir, slave narrative

With her *amanuensis* (a person who writes down dictation), Dr. L. S. Thompson (the second wife of Mattie's mother's second husband), Jackson authored her book, *The Story of Mattie J. Jackson: Her Parentage, Experience of Eighteen Years in Slavery, Incidents During the War, Her Escape from Slavery: A True Story* (1866), describing her family's valiant struggle for freedom from slavery. She authored the book at age 20, to pay for obtaining a formal education—with which she might write her own words in her own hand.

REFERENCES: Moody, Jocelyn K., in *OCAAL*. //docsouth.unc.edu/neh/jacksonm/menu.html.

FURTHER READING: Jones, Regina V., in *GEAAL*.

Jackson, Rebecca (née Cox)
?/1795–1871
Spiritual autobiography/memoir, nonfiction—religion

A freeborn child of a free family, Jackson found her spiritual home in the African Methodist Episcopal (AME) church and married. In 1830, she experienced a religious conversion experience and felt called to become an evangelist, leaving her husband and her childhood home to travel and preach. She was excommunicated from the AME church for heresy (women preachers were considered heretics), and she soon embraced the Shaker faith and was embraced by them in turn, becoming an eldress in that church. Between 1830 and 1864, Jackson wrote a spiritual autobiography describing her experiences with prophetic visions, religious revelations, and spiritual healings. In 1981, Jean McMahon Humez compiled and edited Jackson's spiritual writings into the volume *Gifts of Power: The Writings of Rebecca Jackson, Black Visionary, Shaker Eldress*.

REFERENCES: Humez, Jean McMahon, in *BWA:AHE*. Moody, Jocelyn K., in *OCAAL*. *Wiki*. //www.pbs.org/wgbh/aia/part3/3p247.html.

FURTHER READING: *AANB*. *Wiki*. Gardner, Eric, in *GEAAL*.

Jacobs, Harriet Ann (pen name: "Linda Brent")
c. 1813–3/7/1897
Slave narrative

Whatever we know of Harriet Jacobs, we have learned from Harriet herself. Born into slavery in Edenton, North Carolina, she was allowed to live with her family until she was six years old. Her family included her mother (Delilah), her father (Elijah or Daniel, a skilled carpenter, who was the son of a white farmer and who was enslaved by a doctor), and her brother William ("Willie" or John), who was two years younger than she. Sadly, her mother died when Harriet was just six years old, and Harriet was sent to live with Margaret Horniblow, who had "owned" her mother. For the next six years, her new "mistress" was kindly toward young Harriet, teaching her to sew, to read, and to spell, and letting her run outside to gather berries or flowers from time to time.

When Harriet was 12, however, Margaret Horniblow died, and instead of freeing Harriet, Margaret bequeathed her "property" to her sister's daughter, Mary Matilda Norcom, a 5-year-old white girl. At first, Harriet seemed to be treated fairly well in the Norcom household, but as she ascended into puberty, she became the victim of Dr. James Norcom's sexual harassment. By the time she was 15 years old, she was subject to unrelenting sexual aggression. In an attempt to gain an ally against this aggression, when Harriet was just 16 years old, she initiated an intimate relationship with a young white neighbor, attorney Samuel Tredwell Sawyer.

By the time she reached her early 20s, Jacobs had moved into the home of her grandmother, baker Molly Horniblow, who had been freed in 1828, when Hannah Pritchard purchased Molly's freedom. Jacobs had fled there to try to escape the Norcoms—both the doctor and his wife, who was furious with jealous rage toward Jacobs. There, Jacobs had borne two children with Sawyer: her son Joseph (born c. 1829) and her daughter Louisa Matilda (c. 1833-1913). Outraged that Jacobs had these children by another man, James Norcom sent Jacobs away from Edenton, to his son's plantation out in the country, where the working conditions were harsh. When Jacobs heard that Norcom planned to sell her children to a plantation owner, she made plans to escape, hoping that either her own father (who had, by then, purchased his freedom) or her children's father would be able to purchase and then free her children once Norcom believed that Jacobs was gone altogether.

In June of 1835, Jacobs escaped from Norcom's grasp, hiding in sympathetic white and black neighbors' houses and in a nearby snake-riddled swamp until her grandmother and her uncle had built a tiny (3' high × 9' × 7') hiding place for her above her grandmother's porch. Jacobs later reflected that her strong, dignified, compassionate "good old grandmother" was a "special treasure," about whom she had "tender memories" (quoted in *CSN* and in *BWA:AHE*). Later in 1835, Sawyer was allowed to buy their children, as well as Jacobs's brother—but he didn't free them, although he let them live with Jacobs's grandmother. For nearly seven years, Jacobs was confined to her grandmother's crawlspace, writing letters that she would have other people mail to Norcom from Boston or New York.

In 1842, abolitionists helped her escape to the North, where she soon was reunited with her children. In 1849, she moved to Rochester, New York, where she joined her brother, an abolition activist and associate of **Frederick Douglass**. There, she told her story to her friend Amy Post, a feminist Quaker, who urged Jacobs to write it down, as Post believed the story would incite the sympathies of Northern women, thereby aiding the abolitionist cause.

In 1850, the year the Fugitive Slave Law was passed, Norcom died, but his daughter Mary continued to try to capture Jacobs. For quite a while, Jacobs did domestic work for writer Nathaniel Parker Willis and Cornelia Grinnell Willis. Mary Norcom sent agents to New York to try to kidnap Jacobs from their home. In 1852, Ms. Willis began arranging for Jacobs's freedom to be purchased, which it was in 1853. Although Jacobs was relieved to be free from fear of recapture, she bitterly resented having her wrongful enslavement sanctioned through the exchange of money.

Meanwhile, Jacobs was mulling over Post's suggestion, and she practiced her writing skills by contributing letters to the *New York Tribune*. From 1853 to 1861, Jacobs corresponded with Amy Post about her narrative, starting with her initial conception of the book and concluding with its publication. At first, she hoped that **Har-**

riet Beecher Stowe would serve as her *amanuensis,* so that Stowe would record her story as she dictated it to her. Instead, Stowe had offered to incorporate some of Jacobs's experiences into her fictional sequel to *Uncle Tom's Cabin* (1851), *The Key to Uncle Tom's Cabin* (1853).

Somewhat reluctantly, but with determination, Jacobs decided to write her own life story—with continuing encouragement from Post. For the next several years, she worked on the manuscript whenever she had completed her child-care and other domestic duties for the day. When at last she had completed her manuscript, she had great difficulty finding a publisher, perhaps largely because of her candor in revealing the sexual abuse she had suffered. She even sought letters of introduction from Boston abolitionists and took the letters to England, in the unrewarded hope of getting British abolitionists to publish the work. At last, in 1860, African-American author **William C. Nell** introduced her to European-American author **Lydia Maria Child**. Child agreed to edit the work (which Child described as "making minor grammatical alterations"), to add an introduction to the work, and to act as Jacobs's literary agent in getting the work published.

At last, in the spring of 1861, *Incidents in the Life of a Slave Girl: Written by Herself* was published. Jacobs was the first published author to reveal the truth of how African-American slaves had been sexually exploited, as well as physically abused. She also frankly described the racial prejudice she encountered in the North, the horrors of the Fugitive Slave Law, and the support she received from other women.

Only Child's name appeared on the title page (listed as the book's editor), and Jacobs used a pseudonym both for herself ("Linda Brent") and for the people in her book (e.g., Norcom became "Dr. Flint"). Among other concerns, Jacobs feared that her candor about her sexual exploitation might make life very difficult for her—a single mother—and for her children. Unfortunately, although the book was well received in the abolitionist press, her book's publication preceded the outbreak of the Civil War by just a month or so, and potential readers—North and South—were otherwise distracted.

During the war, with the support of Quakers and other abolitionists, Jacobs and her daughter worked behind the Union Army lines to offer emergency relief. They also helped establish the Jacobs Free School (owned and operated by African Americans), to teach freed slaves in Union-occupied Alexandria, Virginia. After the war, mother and daughter did similar work in Savannah, Georgia. Jacobs continually supplied the Northern press with reports on their activities. In 1868, the mother-daughter team went to England, to raise funds to build an old-age home and orphanage in Savannah. On their return, however, white rage erupted in the post-Civil War South, and Jacobs and her daughter fled North again, moving to Cambridge, Massachusetts. There, Jacobs managed a boarding house for students and faculty members of Harvard University.

From 1877 to 1897, Harriet and Louisa lived in Washington, D.C., where Harriet continued her work on behalf of freed slaves, and Louisa taught at Howard University and other schools. A few years before she died, Harriet sold the house and lot that her grandmother had owned, and where she had found refuge so many decades before.

When Jacobs's book was first published, abolitionists believed it was an authentic narrative, written by an African-American woman. As time went by, however, scholars questioned both its authenticity and its authorship. In 1981, however, literary historian Jean Fagan Yellin did a thorough examination of the evidence, including correspondence documenting Jacobs's work on the manuscript. In 1987, Yellin published an annotated edition of Jacobs's book, thereby establishing the widespread acceptance of Jacobs's authorship and of the work's authenticity. Some skeptics remain (e.g., John Blassingame), who question the plausibility of some of the events and who find many of her descriptions melodramatic. Despite the skeptics, however, Jacobs's autobiography has become an important part of the canon of American literature, telling a crucial aspect of American history.

REFERENCES: *1TESK. CSN. NAAAL.* Robinson, Lisa Clayton, in *EA-99.* Woodard, Helena, in *OCWW.* Yellin, Jean Fagan, in *BWA:AHE,* and in *COCAAL* and *OCAAL. G-97.*

FURTHER READING: *AANB. B. EAAWW. W. Wiki.* Harriet A(nn) Jacobs. Gale Online Encyclopedia. Detroit: Gale. From *Literature Resource Center.* McCaskill, Barbara, in *GEAAL.* Riemer, James D. *AWPW:1820-1870.* //digital.library.upenn.edu/women/_generate/AFRICAN%20AMERICAN.html

---

Jakes, T. D. (Thomas Dexter)
6/9/1957–

Faith-inspired literature, spoken word—sermons, novels; cleric

While still in his teens, Jakes attended Center Business College (1972) and then West Virginia State College (1976). He later received a B.A. (1990), an M.A. (also 1990), and a Doctorate of Ministry (1995) from Friends University in Kansas, a private college that does not indicate any accreditation at its website, //www.friends.edu/. While earning his degrees, Jakes worked for business and industry (1976-1982) to support himself and his wife, Serita (married in 1980), with whom he has five children: Jamar, Jermaine, Cora, Sarah, and Thomas Jakes, Jr.

Meanwhile, in 1979, Jakes was called to the ministry. At first, he ministered part-time out of a storefront he called the Greater Emanuel Temple of Faith in West Virginia. He grew his small, interracial congregation from just 10 members in 1980 to a congregation large enough to support him as a full-time pastor. Part of his attraction was his ability to attract an integrated congregation of members crossing racial lines that had previously divided his community.

Jakes also moved from his small storefront to a larger church in another West Virginia town (1990) and then to a still-larger church in yet another West Virginia town (1993). In 1996, he and his family along with about 50 other families in his congregation left Virginia to found a church near Dallas, Texas. There, they founded The Potter's House, a nondenominational, multiracial Christian church. Within two years, 14,000 congregants were attending various services in his megachurch's 5,000-seat auditorium. Since then, his congregation has grown to exceed 30,000 members.

While enlarging the flock in his church, Jakes was also extending his ministry beyond the church. He started his "The Master's Plan" radio program, on which he was both the producer and the host (1982-1985); his "Bible Conference" ministry (1983-); and his *Get Ready with T.D. Jakes* TV show, which he hosts, aired on both Trinity Broadcasting Network (TBN) and Black Entertainment Television (BET) (1993-). Soon after, Jakes founded T.D. Jakes Ministries, a nonprofit conference and television ministry (1994-). His televangelist *The Potter's House* church services and sermons can now be seen both on TBN and on The Word Network (TWN). For a time, Jakes also wrote a column for *Ministries Today* (1996-1997). Before the end of the millennium, Jakes also extended his ministry directly into prisons by creating the Prison Satellite Network (1999), enabling prisoners to view live conferences, church services, and bible study while incarcerated.

In the early 1990s, Jakes added another dimension to his ministry with his book *Woman, Thou Art Loosed! Healing the Wounds of the Past* (1993/1996). It was soon the second-best-selling Christian book (in 1995) and the third-best-selling religious book (1996), selling more than 800,000 copies by 1996. In 1997, the book was adapted into a musical recording, *Woman, Thou Art Loosed: The Songs of Healing and Deliverance,* nominated for a Grammy and honored with the Gospel Music Association's prized Dove Seal (both 1997). It was also adapted to the stage (produced in 1999), to television (2001), and to an independent film featuring Jakes and produced by T.D. Jakes Enterprises (2004). Jakes also wrote another play, *Behind Closed Doors* (1999/2000).

By 2008, *Woman, Thou Art Loosed!* was available in hardcover, paperback, Kindle (electronic format), and audio formats. Jakes has also produced both audio and videotapes of *Woman, Thou Art Loosed: The Songs of Healing and Deliverance*, as well as a *Live at the Superdome* album. These have been followed by *Sacred Love Songs* albums (1999), named the top Gospel Album of the year by *Billboard* magazine (1999); and *Storm Is Over* (2001), which he produced on his label, Dexterity Sounds, in collaboration with EMI Gospel. *The Storm Is Over* was not only nominated for Dove and Grammy awards, but also honored with NAACP Image and Stellar Gospel awards for Best Gospel Album in the Contemporary genre. His other albums include *God's Leading Ladies* and his *Follow the Star* album of Christmas songs.

The success of *Thou Art Loosed* led to a three-day national conference ministry attended by more than 18,000 women. Though his "Thou Art Loosed" conference for women is probably the most popular of his conferences, Jakes also sponsors numerous other conferences and various other seminars, such as the "Manpower" series for men, the "When Shepherds Bleed" events for pastors and their spouses (starting in 1995), and an annual "MegaFest" reminiscent of an old-fashioned revival, attracting more than 100,000 worshipers.

Jakes has explored the novel form with his *Cover Girls: A Novel* (2003/2008), *Woman, Thou Art Loosed!: A Novel* (2004), and *Not Easily Broken: A Novel* (2006). He has achieved his greatest print success, however, by writing inspirational, spiritual, self-help books. Including his *Women, Thou Art Loose!*, he has sold millions of copies of his books, thereby becoming one of the best-selling African-American authors in history. Before the year 2000, he had written *Water in the Wilderness* and *Why? Because You Are Anointed* (both 1994/2008); a workbook *Can You Stand to Be Blessed?* (1995), *Help Me, I've Fallen and I Can't Get Up!* (1995), *The Harvest* (1995/2008), *Loose That Man and Let Him Go!* (1995) and a related workbook, *Naked and Not Ashamed: We've Been Afraid to Reveal What God Longs to Heal* (1995), and *When Shepherds Bleed: A Study Guide for Wounded Pastors* (1995, with Stanley Miller); *Help! I'm Raising My Children Alone* (1996/2006), *Daddy Loves His Girls* (2006), and *T.D. Jakes Speaks to Women! Deliverance for the Past, Healing for the Present* (1996); *Anointing Fall on Me: Accessing the Power of the Holy Spirit* (1997/2008), *A Fresh Glimpse of the Dove* (1997), *I Choose to Forgive* (1997), *Lay Aside the Weight: Taking Control of It Before It Takes Control of You!* (1997), *So You Call Yourself a Man? A Devotional for Ordinary Men with Extraordinary Potential* (1997), and *Woman, Thou Art Loosed! Devotional* (1997/2007); *The Lady, Her Lover, and Her Lord* (1998); *Maximize the Moment: God's Action Plan for Your Life* (1999), *Intimacy with God: The Spiritual Worship of the Believer* (1999), and *His Lady: Sacred Promises for God's Woman* (1999). He also edited *Holy Bible:*

Woman, Thou Art Loosed! Edition: New King James Version (1998).

Nor did Jakes slow down in the new millennium, producing *Celebrating Marriage: The Spiritual Wedding of the Believer* (2000), *Experiencing Jesus: God's Spiritual Workmanship in the Believer* (2000), *The Great Investment: Faith, Family, and Finance* (2000), *Life Overflowing: The Spiritual Walk of the Believer* (2000), and *Loved by God: The Spiritual Wealth of the Believer* (2000); *Woman Thou Art Loosed Cookbook* (2001); *God's Leading Lady: Out of the Shadows and into the Light* (2002); *Follow the Star: Christmas Stories That Changed My Life* (2003/2007), *God's Leading Ladies: Conference Workbook: Taking Your Place on Life's Center Stage* (2003), *Overcoming the Enemy: The Spiritual Warfare of the Believer* (2003), and *Transforming Your Relationships: An Action Plan for Love That Lasts* (2003); *He-motions: Even Strong Men Struggle* (2004/2007); *Promises from God for Single Women* (2005), and *The Ten Commandments of Working in a Hostile Environment* (2005/2009); *Mama Made the Difference* (2006; winner of a Quill Award in the Religion/Spirituality category), *Not Easily Broken* (2006; also being made into a movie), *Promises from God for Parents* (2006), and *The Potter's House Presents Your Harvest without Limits* (2006); *Hope for Every Moment: 365 Days to Healing, Blessings, and Freedom* (2007), *Reposition Yourself: Living Life without Limits* (2007, also available in Spanish; a workbook is also available), *T.D. Jakes Speaks to Men: Three Bestselling Books in One Volume!* (2007), and *Woman, Thou Art Loosed! Workbook* (2007); *Before You Do: Making Great Decisions That You Won't Regret* (2008), *Hope for Every Moment: 365 Inspirational Thoughts for Every Day of the Year* (2008), *Insights to Help You Survive the Peaks and Valleys: Can You Stand to Be Blessed?* (2008; also available as a "Personal Study Guide"), *It's Time to Reveal What God Longs to Heal: Naked and Not Ashamed* (2008), *Life Overflowing, 6-in-1: 6 Pillars for Abundant Living* (2008), *Release Your Anointing 40-Day Devotional Journal: Tapping the Power of the Holy Spirit in You* (2008), and *Reposition Yourself Reflections: Living a Life without Limits* (2008); and *40 Days of Power* (2009), *Healing, Blessings, and Freedom* (2009), *Highly Favored: A Christmas Story* (2009), *Making Great Decisions Reflections: For a Life without Limits* (2009; available in Spanish), *Power for Living* (2009), and *Strength for Every Moment* (2009); and *Positioning Yourself to Prosper* (n.d.). Many of these books are available in audio and Kindle formats, as well. T. D. Jakes has also collaborated with his wife, Serita Ann Jakes, to write *T. D. and Serita Ann Jakes Speak to Women, 3-in-1* (2006). He and his sister, Jacqueline Jakes, also collaborated on two books, *Sister Wit: Devotions for Women* (2004) and *God's Trophy Women: You Are Blessed and Highly Favored* (2006).

Jakes was named one of the "Ten Most Influential Christian Leaders of 1997" by *Home Life* magazine

(1998). In 2001, a *Time* magazine cover and CNN both named Jakes "America's Best Preacher," and in 2009, on the morning of the inauguration, President-elect Barack Obama attended a private church service where Jakes was invited to preach.

REFERENCES: *CAO-08. D. W2B. Wiki.* Bush, John, *All Music Guide,* in A. Gruen, Dietrich, and Ralph G. Zerbonia, in *BB.* Jenkins, Maureen. "T. D. Jakes." *Publishers Weekly.* 245.21 (May 25, 1998), p. S14. *Literature Resources from Gale.* "PW Talks with T.D. Jakes. (PW Forecasts)." *Publishers Weekly.* 249.18 (May 6, 2002), p. 54. *Literature Resources from Gale.* //en.wikipedia.org/wiki/Islam_in_Nigeria. //en.wikipedia.org/wiki/Nigeria. //en.wikipedia.org/wiki/Religion_in_Nigeria. //www.friends.edu/. //www.newsday.com/news/nationworld/nation/sns-ap-rel-inauguration-religion. Amazon.com.

Jeffers, Lance (né Lance Flippin)
11/28/1919–7/19/1985
Poems, novels

After graduating from high school in 1938, Jeffers attended a series of colleges then joined the army in 1942. After his discharge from the army (1946), he graduated with honors and earned his master's degree from Columbia University. Starting in 1951, he began teaching at various colleges and universities (from California to North Carolina). In 1974, he finally joined the faculty at North Carolina State University in Raleigh, where he continued to teach until he died.

Jeffers's first poetry collection, *My Blackness Is the Beauty of This Land* (1970), highlights the courage and endurance of African Americans who face racial oppression; and his second collection, *When I Know the Power of My Black Hand* (1974), expands this theme to embrace the oppression of other American minorities, such as Native Americans, and other oppressed people around the globe, such as the Jews of the Buchenwald concentration camp (during World War II) and the people of Vietnam (during the Vietnam War). His subsequent collections include *O Africa, Where I Baked My Bread* (1977) and *Grandsire* (1979). In his poetry, Jeffers employed *anaphora* (repetition of the initial words and phrases in sequential poetic lines), *alliteration* (repeated initial sounds in the words of a poetic line or stanza), *litany* (repeated phrasings reminiscent of chanting), and *metaphor* (figurative speech), which reflect the African-American **oral tradition**. Jeffers also often coined compound words such as "bluecool" and "corpse-head." Although Jeffers's work is not as widely read as that of many of his contemporaries more strongly identified with the **Black Arts Movement**, his work has appeared in numerous literary journals and has been widely anthologized (e.g., in the definitive **Black Aesthetic** volume *Black Fire* by LeRoi Jones [later **Amiri Baraka**] and **Larry Neal**), and his last three collections are still in print.

Jeffers dedicated three volumes of his poetry to his second wife, Trellie James (whom he married in 1959). With Trellie, he had three daughters; with his first wife, social worker Camille Jones, he had a son.

In addition to his poetry, Jeffers wrote the novel *Witherspoon* (1983), about a minister who tries to spare the life of a convict facing execution.

REFERENCES: *EBLG. TtW.* Harris, Trudier, in *COCAAL* and in *OCAAL.* Amazon.com, 7/1999.

FURTHER READING: *AANB. CAO-02.* Brown, Deborah, in *GEAAL.* Dorsey, David F. Jr., in *AAP-55-85.*

Jenkins, Beverly (née Hunter)
2/15/1951–
Novels; librarian

While enrolled at Michigan State University (MSU), Beverly Hunter majored in English literature. Though she ended her enrollment, she continued on as a librarian in the school's graduate library (1974-1980). While at MSU, she wrote poetry, gave poetry readings, helped start a theater company, and met her future husband, with whom she later had two children. The couple returned to the Detroit area, where she worked for a while as a librarian.

Jenkins wrote her first romance novel in the early 1980s. Over the next decade or so, she wrote and rewrote *Night Song* (1994). Unlike most romance novelists, Jenkins set her book in the 1880s, where African Americans had settled in and created their own Midwestern town, following the Civil War. Jenkins took a long time because she did extensive research to ensure that the novel was historically accurate. Once she finished the writing, it took her four years to find a publisher. At last, she hired an agent, who hooked her up with Avon Books. *Night Song* became an alternate book of the month for both the Doubleday Book Club and the Literary Guild, and it was a bestseller at Waldenbooks that year.

That book's success allowed her to quit her librarian job and start writing romantic stories full-time, and the next year she published *Vivid* (1995), which won a four-star review in the *Detroit Free Press* and sold very well. Ever since, Jenkins has written about one romance each year. Many of her books set her African-American characters in the pre- and post-Civil War years. Her third novel, *Indigo* (1996), takes place during the days of the Underground Railroad, and her fourth romance novel, *Topaz* (1997), uses a western setting. *Topaz* was followed by Civil War-era *Through the Storm* (1998), western-set *The Taming of Jessi Rose* (1999), and *Always and Forever* (2000), a sequel to *Topaz*. That same year, she published *Before the Dawn* (2000).

Two years later, Jenkins tried her hand at a young-adult novel, *Belle and the Beau* (2002), also involving the Underground Railroad. That year, she also published *A Chance at Love* (2002), and she collaborated with Geri Guillaume, Francis Ray, and Monica Jackson to write *Gettin' Merry: A Holiday Anthology* (2002). The next year, she wrote a second young-adult novel, *Josephine and the Soldier* (2003).

In the following years, she started publishing some romantic-suspense novels: *The Edge of Dawn* (2004), *The Edge of Midnight* (2004), *Black Lace* (2005), *Sexy/Dangerous* (2006), and *Deadly Sexy* (2007). During those years she also wrote historical-romance novels: *Something Like Love* (2005), *Winds of the Storm* (2006), and *Wild Sweet Love* (2007), followed by *Jewel* (2008), *Belle* (2009), and *Josephine* (2009). Her *Bring on the Blessings* (2009) has a contemporary setting, but with a twist: She sets her modern-day protagonist in a town settled by freed slaves following the Civil War, and her protagonist seeks to preserve the town's heritage. When this dictionary went to press, Jenkins's novel *Captured* was available for late-2009 preorder. According to an Amazon.com blurb, "Beverly Jenkins has received numerous awards, including three Waldenbooks Best Sellers Awards, two Career Achievement Awards from Romantic Times magazine, and a Golden Pen Award from the Black Writer's Guild. In 1999, Ms. Jenkins was voted one of the Top Fifty Favorite African-American writers of the 20th Century by AABLC, the nation's largest on-line African-American book club."

REFERENCES: *CAO-08*. Decker, Ed, in *BB*. Amazon.com.

FURTHER READING: Dandridge, Rita B., in *GEAAL*.

Jet *See* **Johnson Publishing Company**

Joans, Ted
7/4/1928–4/25/2003
Poems, stories; musician, painter, performer

A jazz musician since age 13, and a surrealist painter who earned his bachelor of fine arts (1951, Indiana University), Joans moved to Greenwich Village in New York during the heyday of the Beat Generation. There, his jazz, his artwork, and his poems were appreciated, and he published *Beat Poems* (1957). In 1959, he published his collection *Funky Jazz Poems*, followed by *The Truth* (1960) and *The Hipsters* (1961). Soon, however, he became disillusioned with how the Beat Generation was being commercialized, and in 1961, he published *All of Ted Joans and No More: Poems and Collages*, bidding adieu to the Beat phase of his career to travel through Europe and Africa.

While abroad, he published his *Black Pow-wow: Jazz Poems* (1969/1973), which revealed his link to the American **Black Arts Movement**. On returning to America, he published *Afrodisia: New Poems* (1970/1976), which he had written abroad; *A Black Manifesto in Jazz Poetry and Prose* (1971/1979); a German-English volume *The Aardvark-Watcher: Der Erdferkelforscher* (1980); *Sure, Really I Is* (1982); *Razzle Dazzle* (1984); *Teducation: Selected Poems, 1949-1999* (1999); and *Our Thang* (2001). Joans married and fathered three sons and one daughter. At the time of his death, he had an autobiography, a novel, and another poetry collection in progress.

REFERENCES: *AANB. CAO-04. EBLG. TtW. Wiki*. Kohli, Amor, in *GEAAL*. Lindberg, Kathryne V., in *COCAAL* and *OCAAL*. Amazon.com, 7/1999. Miller, James A. "The Beats: Literary Bohemians in Postwar America." Ann Charters (Ed.), *Dictionary of Literary Biography* (Vol. 16). Detroit: Gale Research, 1983. From *Literature Resource Center*. Woodson, Jon, in *AAP-55-85*.

Joe, Yolanda (aka Garland, Ardella)
3/13/1962?–
Mystery novels, juvenile fiction, novels; television and radio newswriter and producer

While attending Yale University, Yolanda Joe spent a summer in England at Oxford University. After earning her B.A. in English from Yale and her master's degree from Columbia University's School of Journalism (in the 1980s), Yolanda Joe went to work as a news producer and a news writer for news radio stations in Chicago (1987-1997), and she still does freelance work for Chicago's WGN-TV.

Meanwhile, Joe was working on her first novel, *Falling Leaves of Ivy* (1992), about an interracial friendship among four Yale students who become involved in a crime and a cover-up that plague them in the years that follow. Her next novel, *He Say, She Say* (1997), tells a romantic-comedy narrative from each of the four main characters' viewpoints—females Sandy and Bebe, Sandy's male love interest T.J., and his father Speed. After her second book hit the bookstores, Joe quit her full-time news job and turned to writing full-time. Since then, she has published *Bebe's by Golly Wow* (1998), which also tells the story from four viewpoints: Bebe and Sandy from her second novel, as well as Isaac, a new romantic interest for Bebe, and Isaac's teenage daughter Dash. Praised for the authenticity of each character's voice, the book was chosen for the Literary Guild book club. Joe's next novels included *This Just In...* (2000), featuring five women battling both racism and sexism in a news room; *The Hatwearer's Lesson* (2003), exploring a relationship between a granddaughter and the grandmother who raised her; and *My Fine Lady* (2004; also available unabridged in audio format), about an aspiring singer who must find her own way despite all the "help" she receives from the men in her life.

Joe has also written mystery novels using the pen name "Ardella Garland": *Details at Ten* (2000) and *Hit Time: A Mystery* (2002; also available unabridged in audio format), both featuring African-American Chicago TV journalist Georgia Barnett. On her second mystery novel, she also listed her own name, as well as her pen name. She penned her third Georgia Barnett novel, *Video Cowboys: A Georgia Barnett Mystery* (2006), under her own name.

REFERENCES: *CAO-05*. Decker, Ed, in *BB*. //www.simonsays.com/content/destination.cfm?tab=73&pid=597068. Amazon.com.

FURTHER READING: LaFrance, Michelle, in *GEAAL*.

Johnson, Amelia E. (Etta) (née Hall)
?/1858–?/1922

Novels, as well as poems, short stories, articles

Johnson is best known for her three faith-inspired novels (*Clarence and Corinne, or God's Way*, 1890; *The Hazeley Family*, 1894; *Martina Meriden, or What Is My Motive?* 1901), published by the white-dominated American Baptist Publication Society. Nonetheless, she called for the African-American community to create black-owned and -operated publishers, and she started her own eight-page monthly magazine, *Joy* (1887), and a monthly magazine for children, *Ivy* (1888), but no issues have survived of either one. Documents from that era confirm that she also published poems, short stories, and articles in various periodicals, such as *New York Age*, and she edited the children's section of a Louisville, Kentucky, Baptist periodical.

REFERENCES: *AANB. BAWPP. NYPL-AADR. W.* Bolden, Tonya, in //digital.nypl.org/schomburg/writers_aa19/bio2.html. Draggoo, Kimberly P., in *GEAAL*. Fabi, M. Giulia, in *COCAAL* and *OCAAL*. Wagner, Wendy, with the assistance of Heidi L. M. Jacobs and Jennifer Putzi, in *AWPW:1820-1870*.

Johnson, Angela
6/18/1961–

Juvenile literature for both children and young adults, poems, novels; educator

Before turning her attention to writing, Angela Johnson attended Kent State University and worked with young children for the Volunteers in Service to America (VISTA) (1981-1982). Ever since 1989, she has made her way by writing books for youths of all ages. Her first book was a picture book, *Tell Me a Story, Mama* (1989, illustrated by David Soman), in which a little girl's plea for a familiar bedtime story turns into the girl's recital of most of the tale. In *Do Like Kyla* (1990), illustrated by James Ransome), a younger sister tells of how she "does like" her older sister Kyla during the day, but then at bedtime, "Kyla does like me." In *When I Am Old with You* (1990, illustrated by David Soman), a grandson tells his grandfather what they will do when the grandson catches up in age and is "old with you"; it was named an American Library Association (ALA) **Coretta Scott King** Honor Book. In *One of Three* (1991, illustrated by David Soman), Johnson returns to the theme of older siblings, narrated by the youngest of three sisters.

Johnson's other picture books also focus on loving yet realistic relationships among family and friends, written from the perspective of a young child and often narrated by a child storyteller. These include *The Leaving Morning* (1992, illustrated by David Soman), *The Girl Who Wore Snakes* (1993, illustrated by James Ransome), *Julius* (1993, illustrated by Dav Pilkey), *Shoes like Miss Alice's* (1995, illustrated by Ken Page), *The Aunt in Our House* (1996, illustrated by David Soman), *The Rolling Store* (1997, illustrated by Peter Catalanotto), *Daddy Calls Me Man* (1997, illustrated by Rhonda Mitchell), *The Wedding* (1999, illustrated by David Soman), *Those Building Men* (1999, illustrated by Mike Benny), *Down the Winding Road* (2000, illustrated by Shane W. Evans), and *Violet's Music* (2004, illustrated by Laura Huliska-Beith) and *Lily Brown's Paintings* (2007, illustrated by E. B. Lewis)-both about little girls who delight in expressing themselves creatively. A few of Johnson's picture books weave historical events or settings into the story, such as *I Dream of Trains* (2003, illustrated by Loren Long), *Just like Josh Gibson* (2003, illustrated by Beth Peck), *A Sweet Smell of Roses* (2005, illustrated by Eric Velasquez), and *Wind Flyers* (2007, illustrated by Loren Long). She also collaborated with illustrator Rhonda Mitchell to create four board books: *Joshua by the Sea* and *Joshua's Night Whispers* (both 1994), *Mama Bird, Baby Birds* (1994), and *Rain Feet* (1994/2001).

In addition to her picture books, Johnson has written short stories and novels for older children and young adults (teens). Her novels include Coretta Scott King Award winner *Toning the Sweep* (1993/2000) and *Humming Whispers* (1995). In 1998, Johnson published *Songs of Faith* (1998) and *Heaven* (1998). *Heaven* is also the protagonist in her later novel *The First Part Last* (2003). Both *Heaven* and *First Part Last* won ALA Coretta Scott King Awards (1998 and 2004, respectively), and *First Part Last* won the ALA's Michael J. Printz Award, as well. Johnson's third book in the trilogy, *Sweet, Hereafter* (2010), was available for preorder in 2009. Johnson wrote a humorous pair of novels, too: *When Mules Flew on Magnolia Street* (2001, illustrated by John Ward) and *Maniac Monkeys on Magnolia Street*

(2005). Johnson addresses more serious issues in *Running Back to Ludie* (2002), *Looking for Red* (2002), *A Cool Moonlight* (2003), and *Bird* (2004).

In addition to her novels and her picture books, Johnson wrote a Coretta Scott King Honor Book collection of poetry for middle-schoolers, *The Other Side: Shorter Poems* (1998); and a collection of 12 stories for young adults, *Gone from Home: Short Takes* (2001). Her writings have also been anthologized. For her outstanding contributions to juvenile literature, Johnson has earned not only numerous Coretta Scott King Awards and Honors, but also an Ezra Jack Keats New Writer Award from the U.S. Board on Books for Young People (1991) and a revered "Genius" grant from the MacArthur Foundation (2003).

REFERENCES: *CA/I. CAO-08.* Chris Routledge, in *BB.* //www.scare crowpress.com/Catalog/SingleBook.shtml?command=Search&db= ^ DB/CATALOG.db&eqSKUdata=0810850923. Amazon.com.

FURTHER READING: Green, Heidi Hauser, in *GEAAL.* Hinton, KaaVonia. (2006). *Angela Johnson: Poetic Prose (Scarecrow Studies in Young Adult Literature).* Lanham, MD: Scarecrow Press.

Johnson, Charles (Richard)
4/23/1948–

Novels, short stories, essays, editorial cartoons, screenplays, literary criticism; educator

Starting when Johnson was just 17 years old, he was drawing editorial cartoons for various newspapers (e.g., the *Chicago Tribune*, **Black World**). With more than 1,000 of his drawings already published in newspapers, he published two collections of his cartoons (*Black Humor*, 1970; *Half-Past Nation Time*, 1972). While he was still a college student, he had his own how-to-draw show on PBS, *Charley's Pad* (1971, comprising 52 segments), too. During this time, he also wrote several "apprentice" novels, sailing along on the inspiration of writers he deeply admired—**James Baldwin**, Albert Camus, **Ralph Ellison**, Hermann Hesse, Nathaniel Hawthorne, Thomas Mann, Herman Melville, Jean-Paul Sartre, **Jean Toomer**, **John A. Williams**, and **Richard Wright**, among others.

While Johnson was a doctoral student in phenomenology (an aspect of philosophy) and literary aesthetics, he published his surrealistic first novel, *Faith and the Good Thing* (1974/2001), which built on literary traditions from African-American folklore (*see also* **folktales**) and on his predilection for philosophical inquiry. Johnson constructed his next novel, *Oxherding Tale* (1982/2005), on the basis of African-American **slave** narratives (especially **Frederick Douglass**'s first autobiography), which continued to reflect his philosophical explorations. Meanwhile, he started teaching English at the University of Washington in Seattle (since 1976), and he wrote some

biographical screenplays for PBS (*Charlie Smith and the Fritter Tree*, 1978, about an African-American cowboy; and *Booker*, 1984, about **Booker T. Washington**).

Johnson's next major publication, his *The Sorcerer's Apprentice: Tales and Conjurations* (1986/1994), made even more obvious his enthusiasm for experimenting with various literary forms. The eight stories in this collection addressed Johnson's philosophical questions through different literary genres, including sci-fi ("Popper's Disease") and horror ("Exchange Value"). The prestigious literary guild PEN nominated Johnson's collection for a PEN/Faulkner Award, in recognition of his achievement.

Next, Johnson addressed literature directly, through his nonfiction book of literary criticism, *Being and Race: Black Writing Since 1970* (1988/1990). The next genre he took on was the sea adventure, through his novel *Middle Passage* (1990/1998). Johnson had conducted extensive research (e.g., reading ship logs, dictionaries of nautical terms and of Cockney slang, and "every sea story that I could get my hands on") before writing the book. He was rewarded for his effort with the 1990 National Book Award for Fiction (only the second African American to receive the award; **Ralph Ellison** being the first, in 1953). In 1990, he also tackled another literary form, with his play *All This and Moonlight*, and in 1993, he completed a screenplay for a film version of *Middle Passage*.

In Johnson's next novel, *Dreamer* (1998), he integrated his love of philosophy, his interest in biography, and his fascination with the novel form. The dreamer of whom he speaks is, of course, **Martin Luther King, Jr.** Perhaps more than a fictionalized biography, it is a fictional exploration of King's Christian philosophy. Johnson explores how King lives and breathes his philosophy of nonviolence as an outgrowth of unconditional love, founded on his soul-deep Christian beliefs. The same year Johnson's *Dreamer* appeared in print, Johnson himself was given an award that will allow him to pursue his own dreams—the John D. and Catherine T. MacArthur Foundation's $300,000 so-called "Genius Award." Doubtless, he will be finding still newer ways to use his genius to explore the objects of his passion: literature and philosophy.

REFERENCES: *SMKC.* Nash, William R., in *COCAAL* and *OCAAL.* *G-96.* —Tonya Bolden

Editor's note: Numerous biographers have written about Johnson, and he has also participated in some auto/biographies of him, including *I Call Myself an Artist: Writings By and About Charles Johnson* (1999, edited by Charles Richard Johnson and Rudolph P. Byrd) and *Passing the Three Gates: Interviews with Charles Johnson* (2004, edited by Jim McWilliams). Some of his lectures have been collected in *In Search of a Voice (The National Book Week Lectures)* (1991), and he published another play, *Olly Olly*

Oxen Free: A Farce in Three Acts (1988). He also worked with Patricia Smith and the research team of WGBH television to produce the companion volume for the TV series *Africans in America: America's Journey through Slavery* (1998). Johnson also continues to write short stories, collected in *Dr. King's Refrigerator: And Other Bedtime Stories* (2005) and *Soulcatcher: And Other Stories* (2008). In his essay collection, *Turning the Wheel: Essays on Buddhism and Writing* (2003), he explores how Buddhism has been deeply tied to his creativity and to his intellectual pursuits. In addition to awards for his individual works, he received the American Academy of Arts and Letters Award in Literature in 2002.

REFERENCES: *AAW:PV.* Nishikawa, Kinohi, in *GEAAL.* Amazon.com.

FURTHER READING: *BB. CAO-01. CAO-07. W. Wiki.* Amazon.com, March 23, 2009. //www.npr.org/templates/story/ story.php?storyId=1035635, *All Things Considered*, March 25, 1998. Graham, Maryemma, in *AAFW-55-84.* Hawkins, Shayla. *The Writer. 121.2* (Feb. 2008) p. 58. From *Literature Resource Center.* Nash, William R., in *AW:ACLB-01.* Whalen-Bridge, John, in *ANSWWII-7th.* A Conversation with Charles Johnson. Rob Trucks. TriQuarterly. 107-108 (Winter-Summer 2000) p. 537. From *Literature Resource Center.* A Conversation with Charles Johnson. Charles Johnson and William R. Nash. New England Review 19.2 (Spring 1998): pp. 49-61. Rpt. in Contemporary Literary Criticism. Ed. Janet Witalec. Vol. 163. Detroit: Gale, 2003. pp. 49-61. From *Literature Resource Center.* A conversation with Charles Johnson and Maxine Hong Kingston. John Whalen-Bridge. MELUS. 31.2 (Summer 2006) p. 69. From *Literature Resource Center.* A Conversation with Charles Johnson. Charles Johnson and Rob Trucks. TriQuarterly 107-108 (Winter-Summer 2000): pp. 537-560. Rpt. in Contemporary Literary Criticism. Ed. Janet Witalec. Vol. 163. Detroit: Gale, 2003. pp. 537-560. From *Literature Resource Center.* An Interview with Charles Johnson. Charles Johnson and Michael Boccia. African American Review 30.4 (Winter 1996): pp. 611-618. Rpt. in Contemporary Literary Criticism. Ed. Janet Witalec. Vol. 163. Detroit: Gale, 2003. pp. 611-618. From *Literature Resource Center.* An interview with Charles Johnson. Michael Boccia. African American Review. 30.4 (Winter 1996) p. 611. From *Literature Resource Center.* From narrow complaint to broad celebration: a conversation with Charles Johnson. Nibir K. Ghosh. MELUS. 29.3-4 (Fall-Winter 2004) p. 359. From *Literature Resource Center.* with Farai Chideya, //www.npr.org/templates/story/story.php? storyId=4569040, *News & Notes*, March 31, 2005. with Susan Stamberg, //www.npr.org/templates/story/story.php?storyId=877654, *Morning Edition*, December 16, 2002.

Johnson, Charles (Spurgeon)
7/24/1893–10/27/1956
Nonfiction—sociology, anthology; founding journal editor

Charles S. Johnson had been educated alongside the son of his parents' master. He then went on to earn a divinity degree at the Richmond Institute, later named the Virginia Union University (VUU). On receiving his degree, Reverend Johnson and his wife, Winifred Branch Johnson, established a pastorate in Bristol, Virginia, in

Charles Spurgeon Johnson

1890. As Charles the younger and his four younger siblings were growing up, Reverend Johnson's congregation built him a fine big church. When it came time for Charles the younger to go to college, he was sent to Wayland Baptist Academy (affiliated with VUU). Within three years, he had earned his degree, with distinction (B.A., 1916). At Wayland, he started to believe that racism often interrelates with economic hardship and social deprivation. To investigate this notion further, he went on to the University of Chicago, to do postgraduate work with the esteemed trail-blazing urban sociologist Robert Ezra Park.

While Johnson was studying with Park, Park was president of the Chicago Urban League and helped Johnson get a position directing research and records for the league, so that Johnson could study the Great Migration (of African Americans from the rural South to the urban North). In response to a race riot (July 1919), Chicagoans established the Chicago Commission on Race Relations to investigate the origins of the riot, and Johnson was asked to direct the commission (1919-1921). The commissioners gathered sociological data based on surveys of blacks and whites in the area. The commission's report, chiefly Johnson's effort, comprehensively analyzed the underlying causes of the riot, particularly focusing on flaws in the social infrastructure, such as in employment, housing, education, and social services. The report further warned that if these conditions did not change, further riots were entirely possible. The final report was published in 1922 as *The Negro in Chicago: A Study in Race Relations and a Race Riot*.

In 1921, the National Urban League appointed Johnson to direct research for the league in New York City. In that role, he founded *Opportunity: A Journal of Negro Life*, in 1923. He served as the league's magazine editor and director of research until 1928. Johnson's timing was flawless, as he was editing *Opportunity* when it was one of the two most important literary magazines publishing work by African-American writers and artists at the height of the **Harlem Renaissance**. (The other was the NAACP's journal, *Crisis*.)

In 1928, Johnson left the Urban League to accept a position as professor of sociology at Fisk University in Nashville, Tennessee, where he chaired the Department of Social Sciences until he was named president of Fisk in 1946, the first African American to take the helm of that historically black university (established in 1867). Johnson also continued to probe the ways in which economic and social conditions influence race relations in this country. As an expert in that field, he was consulted by Presidents Franklin D. Roosevelt, Herbert Hoover, and Dwight D. Eisenhower. Johnson also served in the League of Nations (1930), worked with the U.S. Department of Agriculture (1936-1937), and helped Japanese educators reorganize the Japanese educational system following World War II.

Among his many publications are his books *The Negro in American Civilization* (1930), *Economic Status of the Negro* (1933), and *Shadow of the Plantation* (1934; reprinted 1996), about the near-serfdom of tenant cotton farmers in Macon County, Alabama. The book interwove sociological data with commentaries from oral interviews with the tenant farmers. That work was followed by *The Collapse of Cotton Tenancy* (1935, with Will Alexander and Edward Embree, director of the Julius Rosenwald Fund), *The Negro College Graduate* (1936), and *Growing Up in the Black Belt* (1941), which argued that race relations in the United States was not truly a caste system, as social protest and progressive governmental action would erode the castelike boundaries between the races. Johnson's *Patterns of Negro Segregation* (1943) continues to be a sociological reference work on the insidious ways that segregation harms Americans. He also wrote *Educational and Cultural Crisis* (1951) and *Bitter Canaan* (published posthumously in 1987), a sociological history of Liberia. Johnson's son Robert continued his father's interest in sociology, and Johnson and his wife, drama and music teacher Marie Antoinette Burgess Johnson, had three other children: Charles II, Patricia, and Jeh.

REFERENCES: *AA:PoP. BF:2000. MWEL.* Robbins, Richard, in *BH2C. EA-99. EB-BH-CD. G-97.* Toppin, Edgar Allan, in *WB-99.*

FURTHER READING: *AANB. B. CAO-03. Wiki.* Cohassey, John, in *BB.* Dunne, Matthew William. Next steps: Charles S. Johnson and southern liberalism." *The Journal of Negro History.* 83.1 (Winter 1998) p. 1. From *Literature Resource Center.* Gasman, Marybeth, in *GEAAL.* Hauke, Kathleen A., in *AAWHR-40.* Stroman, Carolyn A., *AMJ-00-60-1.*

Johnson, Fenton
5/7/1888–9/17/1958
Poems, short stories, essays, plays; journalist, educator, self-publisher

Elijah H. Johnson (a railroad porter) and his wife Jesse (Taylor) Johnson were among the wealthiest African-American families in Chicago, and their son Fenton started writing fiction when he was just nine years old. His first published poem appeared in a Chicago-area newspaper in 1900. On graduating from Chicago public schools, he had intended to become a cleric, but after enrolling in the University of Chicago (in 1910), he realized that his interests had changed. He studied at Northwestern University for a while then moved to New York (around 1913), to study at the highly acclaimed Columbia University School of Journalism. He also wrote for the *New York News* and for the Eastern Press association. After college, he taught at a private African-American Baptist-owned college in Louisville, Kentucky, but a year later, he decided to turn his attention to magazine editing and publishing. During this decade, he also married Cecilia Rhone.

In 1916, Johnson moved back to Chicago, where he founded *Champion Magazine* and *Favorite Magazine*, but by the end of the decade, financial difficulties and other problems drove the magazines out of business. He also wrote and self-published several collections of his own works. His *A Little Dreaming* (1913; reprinted 1969) includes both poems written in standard English and poems written in language expressing traditional African-American speech patterns; all of the poems were conventional in form, including his lyrical 300-line blank verse poem "The Vision of Lazarus."

Between this collection and the next, Johnson's poetry changed dramatically. He left behind conventional forms and embraced irregular rhythms and unrhymed lines, keeping his poems closer to actual speech and to realistic urban situations, rather than the more romantic expressions of his earlier works. These poems also echo a much more profound sense of despair than he expressed in his earlier poems. He also used more deviant spellings and nonstandard syntax in these works. Johnson also started incorporating more elements of African-American musical forms such as spirituals (reminiscent of the rural South) and blues (representing the urban North). His last two volumes were *Visions of the Dusk* (1915; reprinted 1971) and *Songs of the Soil* (1916; reprinted 1969). After Johnson's death, about 40 of his poems were collected and published posthumously by the Works Progress Administration's "Negro in Illinois" program. Johnson also published a collection of his short stories, *Tales of Darkest America* (1920), and his essays, *For the Highest Good* (1920).

In addition, Johnson wrote plays. By the time he was 19 years old, some of his plays had been produced at the old Pekin Theatre, in Chicago. In 1925, his *The Cabaret Girl* was performed at the Shadow Theatre there. None of the scripts for his plays has survived.

Perhaps Johnson was just a little too far ahead of his time, for by the middle of the next decade, a renaissance was blooming in Chicago just as much as in Harlem. What was poor timing for Johnson, however, proved invaluable for literary historians, as his work bridges the gap between the turn-of-the-century writings of African Americans and those of the renaissance. Quite a few of Johnson's poems are repeatedly anthologized, representing that narrow window between the two highly productive periods in African-American literature. Among his poems that are most widely anthologized are "The Scarlet Woman" (1922), "The Minister," and "Tired" (1919). By the end of the renaissance period, Johnson's only contact with the artistic community was his continuing correspondence with **Arna Bontemps**.

REFERENCES: *AAW: AAPP. BAL-1-P. BAWPP. BWA. EBLG. NAAAL.* Bruce, Mary Hanford, in *GEAAL.* Engelhardt, Elizabeth Sanders Delwiche, in *COCAAL* and *OCAAL. G-97.* Johnson's unpublished poems and papers are collected at Fisk University.

FURTHER READING: *CAO-03. CAO-06. LFCC-07. Wiki.* Johnson, Fenton. "The Story of Myself. Tales of Darkest America." *The Favorite Magazine,* 1920. Rpt. in *Literature Resource Center.* Gale, Cengage Learning, pp. 5-8. From *Literature Resource Center.* Lumpkin, Shirley, in *AP1880-1945-1.* Worthington-Smith, Hammett, in *AAWHR-40.*

Johnson, Georgia (Blanche) Douglas (née Camp)

9/10/1877–5/14/1966

Poems, short stories, plays, spoken word—lectures; music composer, educator, civil servant, self-publisher

There are questions about the year in which Georgia Camp was born—given variously as 1877, 1880, and 1886, with more than one source citing each year. During her era, it was common practice for women to have their birth years accelerated somewhat by the women themselves and by their parents, so it seems safe to conjecture that the earliest of these dates is probably the most accurate. Georgia's heritage well reflects America's diversity, as her father, George Camp, had African-American and

English ancestry, and her mother, Laura (Jackson) Camp, had African-American and Native-American ancestry.

When Georgia was attending public schools in Atlanta, Georgia, she was often her teachers' favorite, although she was quite shy and reserved. Georgia chose her friends carefully, often preferring her own company. She also considered music to be a great companion and taught herself to play the violin. After high school, she studied music extensively at Atlanta University's Normal School, where she met her future husband, Henry Lincoln Johnson (the son of former slaves, born in 1870). The university had been a haven for her, and she was sorry to leave it when she graduated in 1896. She went on to study musical composition at Howard University, in Washington, D.C., and then she traveled even farther from her home in Georgia to study at the Oberlin Conservatory of Music and the Cleveland College of Music, both in Ohio. When she finished her studies, she returned to Georgia, where she taught and worked as an assistant principal in the public schools. By the time she married "Link" Johnson (September 28, 1903), she had shifted her main interest from composing music to composing lyric poetry.

For a few years, Georgia and Link remained in Atlanta, where Link was a prominent attorney and an up-and-coming Republican politician. By the end of the decade, Link's interest in politics attracted him to Washington, D.C. There, Georgia settled into her roles as a wife and the mother of two sons (Henry Lincoln, Jr., and Peter Douglas), and Link was soon embedded in Republican politics, appointed as Recorder of Deeds by President Taft (in 1912). Link definitely had traditional expectations that Georgia would assume full responsibility for the home and primary responsibility for bringing up their two sons. In Link's view, if she wanted to write, it would have to be *after* she had taken care of these duties. Georgia, however, far preferred reading and writing to cooking and cleaning, which sometimes caused friction in their relationship. Nonetheless, Link financially supported all of Georgia's creative pursuits, even if he did not endorse them altogether.

During this period, Georgia wrote numerous poems and short stories. When **Kelly Miller**, a dean at Howard University, read her work, he encouraged her to continue writing. She occasionally submitted some of her writings to newspapers and magazines, but it wasn't until 1916 that her poems were first published in the NAACP's journal, **Crisis**. Her love of music is evident in the lyricism of all her poems, which tend to center on emotional, often romantic, themes. Any of her poems that address sociopolitical issues do so through personal, emotional experiences. For instance, in her poems "Black Woman," "The Mother," and "Shall I Say, 'My Son, You're Branded,'" she explores the feelings of enslaved women who face the abomination of bearing a child who will be enslaved for a lifetime.

Two years after her first poem was published, her poems were collected in *The Heart of a Woman and Other Poems* (1918). Celebrated poet and poetry critic **William Stanley Braithwaite**, whom Georgia greatly admired, praised the volume for offering unique insights into the experiences of African-American women. Other critics and intellectuals acknowledged her gift for language and her lyricality, but they lambasted her for failing to focus on racism, racial issues, and race-centered experiences.

Johnson's next collection, *Bronze: A Book of Verse* (1922), focused chiefly on racial themes (including racism, racial prejudice, integration, interracial romance, and children of mixed racial heritage), while continuing to address gender issues and motherhood—issues closely tied to her own experiences. **W. E. B. Du Bois**, **Jessie Fauset**, and other critics and commentators of the day lauded this work. Johnson, however, felt that these were not her best works, as she preferred to write on more intimate, romantic, sentimental human themes, as she confided in a letter to **Arna Bontemps**.

Eighteen days before Georgia and Link would have celebrated their twenty-second wedding anniversary, Link died, leaving Georgia to find a way to support herself and her two teenage sons and to pay for their college educations. By hook and by crook, she managed to send her son Peter Douglas through Williston Seminary, Dartmouth College, and Howard University's medical school, and she sent Henry Lincoln, Jr., to Asburnham Academy, Bowdoin College, and Howard University's law school. At first, she shifted from job to job (e.g., substitute teacher, civil-service file clerk), always having to work very long hours for very little pay. Fortunately, Link's political contacts led to her gaining an honorary post in President Coolidge's administration, as Commissioner of Conciliation in the Department of Labor. In that job, she investigated the living and working conditions of laborers in various places across the land.

Despite her long work hours, she managed to continue writing, and she traveled across the land, giving lectures and readings of her writings; in her travels, she also met with other writers (e.g., Carl Sandburg in Chicago, **Charles Waddell Chesnutt** in Cleveland). Meanwhile, the **Harlem Renaissance** was in full swing, and Johnson made her home at 1461 S Street NW, the Washington, D.C., outpost of the renaissance, hosting a literary salon in her home. In addition to offering writers' workshops there, she hosted the "Saturday Nighters' Club," a weekly open house for writers, such as **Countee Cullen**, W. E. B. Du Bois, **Alice Dunbar-Nelson**, **Jessie Fauset**, **Angelina Weld Grimké**, **Langston Hughes**, **Zora Neale Hurston**, **Alain Locke**, **Anne Spencer**, and **Jean Toomer**. In addition, artists, politicians, and other intellectuals often attended. Douglas kept up correspondences with prisoners, and when they were released from prison, they, too, were invited to attend the weekly gatherings. She called her house "Half-Way Home," allegedly for two reasons: She saw her home as a common ground for anyone who was willing to meet halfway, and she offered her home to visiting writers (e.g., Hurston, Hughes), paroled prisoners, and anyone else who was willing to fight halfway to make it.

Johnson's unflagging encouragement of writers (young and old, female and male), parolees, and others in need made her one of the most beloved and cherished of renaissance poets. During this time, she produced the collection often cited as her finest work: *An Autumn Love Cycle* (1928). In this volume, she returned to focusing on women's experiences, especially regarding romantic love, but she also took steps in a new direction, exploring free verse, rather than the more traditional forms she had used in her earlier volumes. The collection made Johnson the first African-American woman since **Frances Ellen Watkins Harper** to gain national attention for her poetry. It included Johnson's oft-anthologized "I Want to Die While You Love Me," which playwright and poet **Owen Dodson** read at her funeral.

Johnson had dedicated her *Autumn Love Cycle* collection to Zona Gale, a European-American writer who had prompted Johnson to give playwriting a try. From the mid-1920s to about 1940, Johnson did just that, completing 28 plays—most of which, sadly, are no longer available. Regarding the plays that remain, critics have praised Johnson's ability to express the drama through authentic folk speech, rather than stereotypical dialect. Her plays, unlike her poems, focus on race issues such as the harmful impact of racism, the need for harmony between the races, interracial relationships, and the distinctive experiences of African Americans. Apparently, at least some of her plays were produced during the 1920s, and several more won literary prizes.

Johnson's *Plumes: Folk Tragedy, A Play in One Act* (1927), about modern medicine versus folk customs, won first prize in a contest for best new play of the year, held by the Urban League's *Opportunity* magazine; the play was also anthologized by Alain Locke in 1927 and published as a single work in 1928. Her controversial play *Blue Blood* (1926) also won honorable mention in an *Opportunity* contest. *Blue Blood*, in which an African-American woman is raped by European-American men, was performed in New York City (by the Krigwa Players) in the fall of 1926 and was published in 1927. Even more controversial was Johnson's *A Sunday Morning in the South* (1928; written in 1925), in which an innocent black teenager is lynched, in the throes of Southern white hysteria. The play also showed how the Ku Klux Klan and the police conspired to create—and to cover up—the atrocity. The play was included in a 1974 anthology. After 1928, Johnson continued to write poems and plays, but she found it harder and harder to get her work published as the Great Depression descended on the country. Still, Johnson was able to publish a series of newspaper columns: *Homely Philosophy*, which was syndicated in 20 newspapers across the country (1926-1932); *Wise Sayings; Beauty Hints;* and an interracial news column for the *New York Amsterdam News*.

In 1934, Douglas lost her job in the Department of Labor, and from then on, she struggled to find clerical jobs and whatever other jobs she could find, and for three decades, she applied to numerous fellowships to get funding for her writing. None of these efforts was rewarded, and she continued to struggle to produce poems, short stories, and plays in spite of her financial difficulties. Fortunately, her son, attorney Henry Lincoln, Jr., and his wife moved in with her, so they helped her financially; she also continued to show generosity toward any writers, artists, or other needy souls to whom she could offer shelter, despite her limited financial resources. From 1930 to 1965, she founded and managed an international correspondence club, and for some time, she sponsored a lonely hearts club.

During this period, Johnson wrote several historical plays, including *Frederick Douglass* (1935), **William and Ellen Craft** (1935), and *Frederick Douglass Leaves for Freedom* (1940). She also wrote two more lynching-related plays, in association with the Federal Theater Project: *Blue-Eyed Black Boy* (1935) and *Safe* (1936). The plays were never chosen for production by the project—in all likelihood because of their controversial subject matter. In the late 1940s, Johnson also collaborated in a musical work with composer Lillian Evanti, the only specifically musical composition resulting from her early musical training.

In the early 1960s, Johnson compiled a "Catalogue of Writings," listing her 200-plus poems, 28 plays, and 31 short stories. Many of her short stories were probably never published, and only 3 of them have been found: "Free," "Gesture," and "Tramp"; the last 2 were published in **Dorothy West**'s journal *Challenge* in 1936 and 1937, under the pseudonym "Paul Tremaine." Like her poems, her short stories focus on intimate human relationships, rather than race relations. The catalogue also mentions an unpublished biography she wrote about her late husband, *The Black Cabinet;* a novel, *White Men's Children;* and a book-length manuscript about the literary salon she hosted during the 1920s and 1930s. Her final work, *Share My World* (1962), was a small poetry collection she published privately. To the end, however, she was known for wearing a tablet around her neck, so she could quickly and easily jot down any idea that came to mind.

In addition to the awards she received for her individual works, and the awards she received from various organizations for her work, in 1965, she received an honorary doctorate from her alma mater, Atlanta University. Sadly, soon after she died, workers cleaned out her house, discarding her numerous unpublished manuscripts and other documents, depriving the literary world of ever knowing what else she may have had to contribute.

REFERENCES: *1TESK. AAL. AA:PoP. EBLG. NAAAL. OC20LE. RLWWJ.* Collier, Eugenia W., in *OCWW.* Donlon, Jocelyn Hazelwood, in *BWA:AHE.* Honey, Maureen, in *COCAAL* and in *OCAAL.* Robinson, Lisa Clayton, in *EA-99.*

FURTHER READING: *AANB. BAWPP. CAO-02. HR&B. LFCC-07 Wiki.* Diehl, Heath A., in *GEAAL.* Effinger, Marta J., in *T-CAD-3rd.* Fletcher, Winona, in *AAWHR-40.* Stamatel, Janet P., in *BB.* //www.poets.org/viewmedia.php/prmMID/19694

Johnson, Helene (née Helen)
7/7/1906–1995
Poems

After finishing high schools and briefly attending Boston University, 18-year-old Helene Johnson and her cousin **Dorothy West** left Massachusetts to embrace the literary reawakening of the **Harlem Renaissance** in New York. There, she attended classes in journalism at Columbia University, although she never earned a degree. From 1925 to 1927, the founding editor of the National Urban League's *Opportunity* magazine, **Charles Spurgeon Johnson** (no relation), published many of Helene Johnson's poems.

About Helene's prize-winning work, Charles said, "Helene Johnson has a lyric penetration which belies her years, and a rich and impetuous power" (quoted in *OCWW,* p. 448). More recently, **Rita Dove** said, "Helene Johnson proved herself a lyricist of utmost delicacy yet steely precision; restraint attends her every meditation on love, race and loss." Her use of vernacular language and themes of racial pride led others to sang her praises, as well, including poet **Countee Cullen**, novelist and *Fire!!* editor **Wallace Thurman**, and novelist and critic **Carl Van Vechten**. From 1928 to 1934, Johnson published only about a dozen poems, and after she married William Hubbell (from whom she later separated) and had her daughter, Abigail, she stopped writing poems altogether and didn't start writing them again until the 1960s. Her poems have never been collected in a single volume, although they have appeared in numerous periodicals and anthologies.

REFERENCES: *AANB. BAWPP. HR&B.* Boxwell, David A., in *GEAAL.* Dove, Rita, in //www.washingtonpost.com/wp-srv/style/books/feed/a39265-2000feb26.htm. Ferguson, Sally Ann H., in *COCAAL* and *OCAAL.* Keough, Leyla, in *EA-99.* Patterson, Raymond R., in *OCWW.* //catdir.loc.gov/catdir/toc/ecip064/2005035688.html. //www.aaregistry.com/african_american_history/992/Helen_Johnson_wrote_words_with_a_melody.

FURTHER READING: *CAO-01. LFCC-07.* Patterson, Raymond R., in *AAWHR-40.* Wheeler, Lesley. "This Waiting for Love: Helene

Johnson, Poet of the Harlem Renaissance." *African American Review.*
36.2 (Summer 2002) p. 340. From *Literature Resource Center.*

Johnson, James Weldon
6/17/1871–6/26/1938
Lyrics, poems, novels, criticism, autobiography/memoir, editorials, anthologies; educator, journalist, publisher, attorney, diplomat, organization leader

As the celebrated lyricist of what is now called the Black National Anthem, "Lift Every Voice and Sing," James Weldon Johnson's talent and influence seem unending. He is perhaps most well known for his Broadway productions and the compositions written with his brother, John Rosamond Johnson, and their partner, Bob Cole.

That is, however, only one of James Johnson's accomplishments. He also served as a United States diplomat to Venezuela and Nicaragua, started a newspaper, was the first African American since the end of Reconstruction to be admitted to the bar in Florida, and served as an officer in the National Association for the Advancement of Colored People (NAACP), as well as being a poet, novelist, editor, principal, and English professor. Johnson played a vital role in the **Harlem Renaissance**, and his untiring enthusiasm, activism, and talent took him to various areas of interest and places where he never failed to distinguish himself.

Johnson was born in Jacksonville, Florida, as was his younger brother, Rosamond. Their parents, James and Helen Louise Dillet Johnson, had moved to Florida from the Bahamas after a hurricane destroyed their sponge fishing and hauling businesses in 1866. Initially, Helen taught James at home. He then attended and graduated from the Stanton School at age 16 and went on to Atlanta University, writing poetry and graduating in 1894. Johnson then returned to Florida and served as principal of the Stanton School.

During this time, Johnson started writing poetry and also published the *Daily American*, a newspaper where Johnson did most of the work. The content of the newspaper focused on issues important to the African-American community, including racial injustice. Unfortunately, the paper had financial difficulties and lasted only a year. Continuing as principal of the Stanton School, Johnson then studied law, passed the Florida bar, and built up a successful law practice in Jacksonville. Practicing law did not satisfy Johnson, however, and when his brother Rosamond returned to Jacksonville after completing studies at the New England Conservatory of Music (1897), the two collaborated to produce music and lyrics, with James's poems serving as lyrics to Rosamond's music. One of the brothers' most famous compositions, "Lift Ev-

James Weldon Johnson

ery Voice and Sing," was written in 1900 for the students at the Stanton School to sing during a celebration of Abraham Lincoln's birthday. Apparently the Johnson brothers did not intend a broader audience for their song. Yet after the song was published, it took root with students all over the South, finally culminating in the NAACP adopting it as the "Negro National Anthem" around 1920. The brothers had a successful partnership and split their time between New York and Jacksonville for several years before both moved permanently to New York City.

The brothers met Bob Cole in New York, and the three of them wrote more than 200 songs, often for Broadway productions. One production, *The Shoo-Fly Regiment*, was a musical-comedy staged in 1906 with an all-black cast. Johnson also met his future wife, Grace Nail, while in New York. As Bob and Rosamond started to travel with a successful vaudeville act, Johnson stopped songwriting to accept two successive government posts, first as consul to Venezuela (1906) and then as consul to Nicaragua (1909).

While a diplomat, Johnson wrote the novel *The Autobiography of an Ex-Coloured Man* (1912). When the book was published, the reading audience perceived it as the true story of a African-American male who is light-skinned and consequently can choose between moving within the white world or the black world. Ultimately, out of fear, the main character chooses to turn away from his African heritage and pass as white. Johnson originally had the novel published anonymously, though in 1927 he admitted that he had written the book and that it was a work of fiction. The book was subsequently republished with Johnson's name on it. Carolyn Dirkson notes that *Autobiography* was the first of its kind, in that it chronicles the black perspective of white society, the tension within the black community about fair-skinned and dark-skinned blacks, and provides insights into the black community. This was a groundbreaking work at the time and opened the door for future African-American writers to pursue similar interests.

Johnson switched careers again in 1913, taking a job as editorial writer for the *New York Age* newspaper. (His editorials have since been collected into a book, published in 1995 by Oxford University Press and edited by Sondra Kathryn Wilson.) Johnson also moved into the larger public sphere by taking a post with the NAACP in 1920.

During the next several years, Johnson produced numerous written works, including authoring *Fifty Years and Other Poems* (1917), and editing *The Book of American Negro Poetry* (1922), *The Book of American Nero Spirituals* (1925), and *The Second Book of American Negro Spirituals* (1926). In 1927, one of Johnson's most famous works, *God's Trombones: Seven Negro Sermons in Verse*, was published. Additionally, Johnson chronicled the achievements of African Americans on the New York artistic scene in *Black Manhattan* (1930).

Johnson's autobiography, *Along This Way*, was published in 1933 while Johnson was teaching at Fisk University, a post he accepted in 1931. In part, Johnson was motivated to write his autobiography to settle any confusion that had occurred as a result of *Autobiography* being published. *Negro Americans, What Now?*, Johnson's last major literary contribution to the world, was published in 1934. Johnson was killed in a car accident in 1938 and is buried in Brooklyn, New York.

By examining Johnson's work and life, it seems clear that Johnson worked hard to preserve African-American culture and heritage, highlight the positive influence of blacks on America in general, and encourage young black writers to pursue their talents and choices of vocations. All of these things he did with grace and diplomacy in an attempt to bridge the differences between blacks and whites in the early twentieth century and to produce a more humane society for all.

REFERENCES: *BLC-2. EBLG. NAAAL.* Beavers, Herman, "Johnson, James Weldon," in *OCAAL.* Dirkson, Carolyn, "The Autobiography of an Ex-Coloured Man," in *MAAL.* Fleming, Robert E. (1997), "Reviews," *African American Review, 31*(2), pp. 351-352, *Magazine Academic Index Plus.* Morgan, Thomas L. (1997), "Bob Cole, J. Rosamond Johnson, and James Weldon Johnson," //www.redlt.com/jass/c&j.html. —Janet Hoover

Johnson, John H. (Harold) (né Johnnie Johnson)
1/19/1918–8/8/2005
Autobiography/memoir, nonfiction; editor, magazine and book publisher

Born and raised in desperate poverty in Arkansas, Johnson amassed a vast fortune by publishing materials of interest to African-American readers. After his family moved to Chicago, Johnson started high school, edited the *Phillipsite* (his school's newspaper), and was the class president of his junior and his senior classes. A frequent visitor to the public library, Johnson read whatever he could find on African-American history and literature, including the works of **W. E. B. Du Bois, Booker T. Washington,** and **Langston Hughes.** After high school, Johnson got a job working for Supreme Life Insurance, intending to work his way through the University of Chicago. In 1939, Johnson was promoted to editor of the company's monthly newsletter, the *Guardian,* and he quit college.

After several years of editing the Supreme publication, Johnson decided that the news he was gathering for Supreme's top executives might interest other African Americans, so he used his mother's furniture as collateral to borrow $500 with which to start his own magazine. With that capital, he sent out mailings to Supreme's client list and sold 3,000 advance subscriptions to his proposed magazine (for $2 apiece). At last, in 1942, he began publishing his 68-page **Negro Digest**, patterned after the highly popular *Reader's Digest,* and reprinting articles from both white and black periodicals. After distributing copies to his subscribers, he had to sell 2,000 more copies to be able to pay his bills and print the next issue. Through his hard work and industry in finding outlets for his magazine, he made money on his first issue—so there could be a second issue.

Starting in 1943, Johnson also included original articles and essays in the digest. By late 1943, Johnson had made enough money to be able to buy his first building: a three-story apartment building with an apartment for his mother and stepfather, as well as for himself and his wife, Eunice Walker. He and Eunice shared an adopted son, John Jr., who died in 1981; and a daughter, Linda Johnson Rice, who became broadcaster and Johnson Publishing Company president and chief operating officer, starting in 1989, and was named the chief executive officer in 2002.

Until 1944, Johnson's only employee was a full-time secretary (although he fudged the masthead with names of some of his relatives), but after that, he hired his mother (whom he employed until her death in 1977) and other staffers. With *Negro Digest* running smoothly, in 1945, Johnson started publishing *Ebony* magazine, a photo-rich periodical showing African Americans in news articles about current events and in feature articles. (It was similar in format to *Life* magazine, a popular magazine of that time.) Its first printing of 25,000 copies sold out within hours, and the second printing of 25,000 sold out, too. In no time at all, *Ebony* had outsold *Negro Digest* to become the most widely circulated African-American magazine. Among the talented African Americans he hired were **Era Bell Thompson** and Moneta Sleet, Jr. (the first African-American photojournalist to win a Pulitzer Prize and the first journalist from a black publication to win the Pulitzer, for his photos following the 1968 assassination of **Martin Luther King, Jr.**). That year, Negro Digest Publishing Company also published its first—and its last—book, *The Best of Negro Humor*, which Johnson edited himself.

In 1949, Johnson renamed his company the eponymous Johnson Publishing Company. In 1951, Johnson suspended publication of *Negro Digest* (*see* **Negro Digest** for more on the ups, downs, and various rebirths of this periodical), which had a circulation of about 60,000. That same year, he launched *Jet*, a small-format (51/4" × 4") news magazine that predated *USA Today* in offering bite-sized news features and articles on politics, sports, and entertainment. Almost immediately, its circulation passed 300,000, and in the new millennium, *Jet* has claimed nearly 1 million readers. *Ebony* has claimed more than 10 million readers, including more than 1 million subscribers. Other Johnson magazine ventures have included *Tan Confessions* (a true-confessions magazine), *Proper Romance, Beauty Salon, Ebony Man*, and *Ebony South Africa*, as well as *Ebony, Jr.!* a monthly magazine for African-American children. In 1996, Johnson wrote *Every Wall a Ladder* (1996, with Quinn Currie), described as a children's book of less than 200 pages.

In 1962, in addition to its periodicals, Johnson Publishing Company started publishing books, such as **Lerone Bennett**'s *Before the Mayflower: A History of the Negro in America, 1619-1962* (1962). The book division now also publishes books for children, as well as for adults. Johnson's enterprises also expanded to include many other business ventures (e.g., radio stations, clothing, cosmetics, wigs, vitamins). His numerous awards include receiving the Presidential Medal of Freedom (1996), the NAACP's prestigious **Spingarn** Medal (1966), and various honorary degrees; being named one of the U.S. Junior Chamber of Commerce's top ten young men (1951); and being inducted into the Black Press Hall of Fame (1987) and the Chicago Journalism Hall of Fame (1990).

In 1993, Johnson wrote his autobiography, *Succeeding against the Odds*, which esteemed Chicago journalist Clarence Page called "a fascinating read for anyone who wants to do what the title suggests." In his book, Johnson said, "If you can somehow think and dream of success in small steps, every time you make a step, every time you accomplish a small goal, it gives you confidence to go on from there" (quoted in *BusB*). John H. Johnson had surely become a very confident man.

REFERENCES: *AANB. B. BCE. CAO-05. CE. PGAA. Wiki.* Goldsworthy, Joan, and Tom Pendergast, in *BB*. McQueen, Lee, in *BusB*. Patton, June O. "Remembering John H. Johnson, 1918-2005." *The Journal of African American History.* 90.4 (Fall 2005) p. 456. From *Literature Resource Center*. Roberson, Patt Foster, in *AMJ-00-60-2*. Smith, Jessie Carney, in *BH2C. EA-99. EB-BH-CD. G-97*. Toppin, Edgar Allan, in *WB-99*.

Johnson, Kathryn Magnolia
12/15/1878–5/?/1955
Autobiography/memoir; educator, subscription salesperson, bookseller

A well-educated schoolteacher, in 1910, Johnson started selling subscriptions to the NAACP journal **W. E. B. Du Bois** had started, **Crisis**, promoting NAACP membership in the process. Although she had done quite well for the NAACP, after she started outspokenly denouncing their inclusion of whites in leadership positions, she was asked to take her services elsewhere—which she did, for the YWCA.

During World War I, the YMCA asked her, Addie Waites Hunton, and another woman to go to France to watch over the rights and the well-being of segregated African-American soldiers fighting for their own country in that country. When Johnson and Hunton returned, they published an account of their travels and their experiences, *Two Colored Women with the American Expeditionary Forces* (1922). That done, she returned to the road, selling the "Two-Foot Shelf of Negro Literature," the 15 books then published by the Association for the Study of Negro Life and History and its Associated Publishers. One of the best-selling authors on the shelf was the "Father of Black History," **Carter G. Woodson**, who had founded both the association and its publishing affiliate. By mid-1928, Johnson had traveled more than 9,000 miles and had sold more than 15,000 books.

REFERENCES: *BAAW. TAWH.* Arnold, Thea, in *BWA:AHE*.
—Tonya Bolden

Johnson Publishing Company
1942–
Publishing empire

In 1939, 21-year-old **John H. (Harold) Johnson** (né Johnnie Johnson) had edited his school's newspaper and was already the editor of the *Guardian*, the newsletter of the Supreme Life Insurance. After a couple of years of gathering articles for the *Guardian*, Johnson realized that these articles might also appeal to a wider African-American readership. In the early 1940s, he used his mother's furniture as collateral to borrow $500 with which to start his own magazine. He used that loan money to send out mailings to Supreme's client list. As a result, he sold 3,000 advance subscriptions to his proposed magazine, for the pricey cost of $2 each. With the net of $5,500 (3,000 × $2 = $6,000 $500 loan = $5,500), he paid for a *Reader's Digest*-sized 68-page magazine he called **Negro Digest**. Like *Reader's Digest*, *Negro Digest* included entirely reprinted articles from other sources, both African-American-owned and -operated periodicals and European-American-owned and -operated periodicals.

Johnson's Negro Digest Publishing Company printed 5,000 copies of the new monthly magazine. After distributing the 3,000 copies to his subscribers, he needed to sell the other 2,000 at 25¢ apiece, in order to fund his next issue. An excellent salesperson, he managed to do so. One of his sales techniques was to get 30 of his associates to go to newsstands all around town, asking for *Negro Digest*. This tactic and others worked, and *Negro Digest* was a going concern. In 1943, Johnson started introducing some original articles and essays, along with the reprinted materials. That year, his only employee was a full-time secretary. The additional names on the masthead were his relatives, whose names he used to make the *Digest* seem more stable.

In 1944, Johnson also hired his mother, who remained on the employee roster until she died in 1977, and a few other staffers. The following year, Johnson launched a second periodical, along the lines of *Life* and *Look* magazines, popular magazines of that era. Johnson's wife Eunice suggested calling the new magazine **Ebony**. Like *Life*, *Ebony* was a large-size, photo-rich magazine of current events and feature articles. Unlike *Life*, *Ebony* highlighted African Americans and an African-American perspective on the news. Johnson expected the new magazine to sell well, so he printed 25,000 copies. On November 1, 1945, *Ebony*'s first printing sold out within hours, and a second printing of another 25,000 copies sold out, as well. At its birth, *Ebony* had vastly superseded its parent, *Negro Digest*. *Ebony* remained a weekly publication until the 1970s, when it went to monthly distribution.

Johnson had one tiny problem with *Ebony*, though. It cost a lot more to produce it than it cost to produce *Negro Digest*. In fact, it cost more to produce it than Johnson was charging for each issue. To boost readership, he was keeping the price of each issue low, just 25¢ each (increased to just 35¢ by 1959). The only way to fix the problem was to obtain advertisers, the lifeblood of almost all periodical publications. Ever the entrepreneur, Johnson started another new business, Beauty Star, which in turn advertised in the pages of *Ebony*. Sales of Beauty Star

hair-care products, wigs, and vitamins financially supported the costly production of *Ebony*, and *Ebony*, in turn, boosted the sales of Beauty Star. Several months after launching *Ebony*, in May of 1946, two other advertisers started appearing in *Ebony*. The following year, after extensive smooth-talking by Johnson, Zenith started advertising in *Ebony*. Soon after that, a few more advertisers bought space in *Ebony*, and pretty soon, big-name brands such as Quaker Oats, Colgate, and Pepsi-Cola were appearing alongside numerous other advertisers in *Ebony*. Company legend has it that Johnson sent a sales representative to Detroit every week for nearly a decade until he finally got the Chrysler Corporation to advertise its cars in *Ebony* in 1954. By the time *Ebony* reached its 40th anniversary in 1985, *Ebony* had been instrumental in making Johnson 1 of the 400 richest individuals in the United States.

Negro Digest Publishing Company published one book, *The Best of Negro Humor*, edited by Johnson, then it quietly bowed out and was renamed the Johnson Publishing Company (JPC) in 1949. Two years later, Johnson halted publication of *Negro Digest* and launched another, *Jet*, Johnson's second inexpensive digest on the African-American experience. Johnson packaged *Jet*, "The Weekly Negro News Magazine," in a small-format (51/4" × 4"), offering bite-sized news features and articles on politics, sports, and entertainment. Almost immediately, its circulation passed 300,000. Countless African Americans first learned of the savage murder of young Emmett Till in the pages of *Jet*. There, they also learned about the burgeoning Civil Rights Movement, including events such as the Montgomery Bus Boycott, and key leaders, such as **Martin Luther King, Jr.**

Until December 27, 1999, *Jet* had been printed entirely or almost entirely in black and white, when it went to color printing. In 2009, *Jet*'s senior editor, Terry Glover, changed *Jet*'s format so that it continues to be published weekly, but with the end-of-the-month issue a double issue. The Magazine Publishers of America (MPA) identified *Jet* as 1 of the top 100 magazines of its 1,000-plus titles in 2005, with a total paid circulation of 956,909, up from 927,402 in 2004. *Jet* wasn't among MPA's top 100 in 2006, 2007, or 2008, but *Jet* did report 2008 subscription revenues of $29,659,969, single-issue revenues of $4,576,586, for a total of $35,236,555 for the year. New 2009 subscribers pay $30.97 for a 1-year, 52-issue print subscription to *Jet*, or $1.99 per issue ($103.48/year). (See the entry for **Ebony** for further information on that magazine's circulation, revenues, and prices.).

Not all of JPC's magazine ventures were enduring and prosperous, however. The year between starting *Ebony* and starting *Jet*, JPC jumped into the burgeoning romance-magazine market with *Tan Confessions* (1950-1971), a true-confessions romance magazine that also included home-making and child-care articles and columns, as well as features on the love affairs of celebrities. *Tan* was replaced by *Black Stars* (1971-1981), an entertainment-celebrity fan magazine, until JPC ended its affairs. Among JPC's other short-lived ventures were *Copper Romance* (1953-1954); *Hue* (November 1953-October 1959), a pocket-size features magazine; *Beauty Salon* (1960s), a trade magazine for beauticians; *Ebony Man (EM)* (1985-1998); *Ebony South Africa* (1995-2000), which was impeded by linguistic barriers, leading to low circulation numbers; and *E Style* (1993-1997), a joint catalog venture with Spiegel. JPC also published *Ebony, Jr.!* (1973-1985) for African-American children, with 10 issues per year (including June/July and August/September).

In 1961, JPC revived *Negro Digest*, with the talented **Hoyt Fuller** as its managing editor. Fuller, who also later edited the more literary **NOMMO** (1969-1976), soon became the most influential African-American journal editor of the 1960s and early 1970s. Through Fuller, *Negro Digest* continued to offer reprints of news and feature articles, but with a greater emphasis on African-American literature, history, and culture. As the **Black Power** movement and the **Black Aesthetic** emerged, Fuller reflected these societal changes in the magazine, also changing its name to *Black World* in 1970. In 1976, against the wishes of Fuller, JPC stopped publishing *Black World*, at least in part due to its drastically declining circulation and its reduced revenues to JPC. (*See Negro Digest* for a fuller explanation of *Black World's* demise.)

Meanwhile, Johnson the entrepreneur was finding new business ventures. The Civil-Rights Movement of the 1950s and 1960s was prompting a dawning awareness of African-American history, and as Johnson later recalled, he "detected a growing interest in black history and authorized a path-finding Black history series. The response was so enthusiastic that we published a book, **Lerone Bennett**'s *Before the Mayflower* [1962], which became one of the most widely read Black history books ever. This marked the beginning of the [JPC] Book Division" (quoted from p. 289 of Johnson and Bennett's *Succeeding against the Odds*). Bennett had briefly been an associate editor at *Jet* magazine (1953-1954) before moving to *Ebony* magazine (1954-), eventually becoming its executive editor (1987-?). (On April 15, 2008, *Ebony* mentioned Bennett as its executive editor emeritus; see //www.ebonyjet.com/ebony/articles/index.aspx?Page=6.) Bennett also developed JPC's four-volume *Ebony Pictorial History of Black America* (1971). When Johnson wanted to write his memoirs, he asked Bennett to collaborate with him on *Succeeding against the Odds* (1989). The Johnson Publishing Company also published most of Bennett's many other books,

even Bennett's highly controversial *Forced into Glory: Abraham Lincoln and the White Dream* (2000).

In 1962, Johnson's new Book Division also published *The Ebony Cookbook: A Date with a Dish—A Cookbook of American Negro Recipes* by Freda De Knight (1962). De Knight's "Date with a Dish" columns had been a featured "Department" of *Ebony* for many years, and she had previously published *A Date with a Dish* in 1948 with Hermitage Press. By far, JPC's greatest book-publishing interest, however, was children's books and other educational materials. Johnson sought to use his publishing empire to remedy the appalling lack of books about and for African-American children. Just a few of JPC's books include Margaret Peters's *The Ebony Book of Black Achievement* (1970), with biographies of key historical African Americans, Helen H. King's *The Soul of Christmas* (1972), a picture book showing urban African Americans celebrating Christmas, Lucille Giles's *Color Me Brown* (1972), a picture book for young children, and D. W. Robinson's *The Legend of Africania* (1974), a picture-book allegory depicting Africa's struggle against colonialism. JPC also created some video products for the educational market.

Over the years, in addition to its magazine and book publishing divisions, JPC has undertaken numerous other ventures, often with Johnson's wife, Eunice, playing a key role. For instance, in 1973, JPC's highly lucrative Fashion Fair Cosmetics line was started because of one of Eunice's observations. While Eunice was watching models preparing for JPC's Ebony Fashion Fair (traveling charity fashion shows), she noticed the models had a lot of trouble mixing just the right color of cosmetics to suit their skin color. After trying to persuade existing cosmetics manufacturers to create a line for African-American women, she and John hired a private lab to create the cosmetics for them, and Fashion Fair Cosmetics was born. Their cosmetics line was later subsumed under JPC's Supreme Beauty Products, which also embraced several other product lines, including Linda Fashions, a mail-order clothing business, as well as the old Beauty Star line. Other company ventures have included three radio stations (WJPC, WLOU, WLNR), a travel service (Ebony-Jet Tours, of course), and ownership stock in Supreme Life Insurance (until 1991). In the company's early days, Johnson had also started the *Negro Digest* Book Club, through which it sold books from other publishers. In 2005, JPC announced plans to license the *Ebony* brand to a wide variety of products, from games and toys to financial products.

In 1972, Johnson was named publisher of the year by the major magazine publishers in the United States; he built an $8-million 11-story steel, concrete, and marble building for JPC's downtown Chicago headquarters; and he had an estimated net worth of at least $50-60 million. In 1988, Johnson was inducted into the Publishing Hall of Fame, along with highly esteemed book editor Maxwell Perkins, Simon & Schuster founders Richard Leo Simon and Max Lincoln Schuster, and William Randolph Hearst.

When Johnson's daughter Linda was just 15 years old, she started working summers at JPC. After earning her M.B.A., she took her place in the company, later becoming its president and chief operating officer in 1989 and then its chief executive officer in 2002, while her father stayed on as publisher and board chair. Soon after his death, in 2005, she recalled, "He was in his office and alert and active until the end, . . . He was the greatest salesman and CEO I have ever known, but he was also a father, friend and mentor with a great sense of humor who never stopped climbing mountains and dreaming dreams" (quoted in Lamb, 2005).

REFERENCES: Berry, William E., "The Johnson Publishing Company: Historical Research and Narrative," in //www.lib.niu.edu/2007/iht07140113.html. Cabell, A. K., "Branding" (July 21, 2005), in //www.businessweek.com/innovate/content/jul2005/di20050721_807102.htm. "From *Negro Digest* to *Ebony, Jet and EM* - Special Issue: 50 Years of JPC—Redefining the Black Image." *Ebony*, in //findarticles.com/p/articles/mi_m1077/is_n1_v48/ai_12811539/. Hamilton, Kendra, "Writers' Retreat: Despite the Proliferation of Black Authors and Titles in Today's Marketplace, Many Look to Literary Journals to Carry on the Torch for the Written Word - Cover Story." *Black Issues in Higher Education*, in //findarticles.com/p/articles/mi_m0DXK/is_19_20/ai_111112027/, //findarticles.com/p/articles/mi_m0DXK/is_19_20/ai_111112027/pg_2/?tag=content;col1. Henderson, Laretta. 2008. *Ebony Jr!: The Rise, Fall, and Return of a Black Children's Magazine*. New York: Rowman & Littlefield. "Honoring the 50th Anniversary of *Jet* Magazine - (House of Representatives - November 15, 2001)," p. H8229, in //thomas.loc.gov/cgi-bin/query/z?r107:H15NO1-0068. Hughes, Langston, ("55 EBONY's Nativity - Magazine's History," reprinted from November 1965, *Ebony*), *Ebony*, (November, 2000), in //findarticles.com/p/articles/mi_m1077/is_1_56/ai_66455747/. *Kiplinger's Personal Finance* (March 1952; Vol. 6, No. 3). Lamb, Yvonne Shinhoster, "Publisher Helped Chronicle Black Life with *Ebony* and *Jet*," *Washington Post*, Tuesday, August 9, 2005, p. A01, in //www.washingtonpost.com/wp-dyn/content/article/2005/08/08/AR2005080801607.html. Magazine Publishers of America, "2008 Average Total Paid & Verified Circulation for Top 100 ABC Magazines," in //www.magazine.org/CONSUMER_MARKETING/CIRC_TRENDS/ABC2008TOTALrank.aspx. Magazine Publishers of America, "2008 Circulation Revenue for All ABC Magazines," [link from] //www.magazine.org/consumer_marketing/circ_trends/index.aspx. Magazine Publishers of America, "Average Circulation for Top 100 ABC Magazines, 2005," in //www.magazine.org/consumer_marketing/circ_trends/16117.aspx. Munro, Karen, "magazines, literary," in GEAAL. Patton, June O. "Remembering John H. Johnson, 1918-2005." *The Journal of African American History*. 90.4 (Fall 2005) p456. From *Literature Resource Center*. Ricigliano, Lori, "Negro Digest," in GEAAL. "The New Black Power & The Power 150" (4/15/2008), //www.ebonyjet.com/ebony/articles/index.aspx?Page=6. Sale, Maggie, "First World," in OCAAL. s//www.neodata.com/jpc/ebny/. s://www.neodata.com/jpc/jett/. //en.wikipedia.org/wiki/Ebony_(magazine). //en.wikipedia.org/wiki/Jet_(magazine). //www.ebonyjet.com/. //www.flickr.com/photos/vieilles_annonces/collections/7215760220809048/.

FURTHER READING: *See also* **Johnson, John H.** entry in this dictionary, as well as Huguley-Riggins, Piper G., "Johnson Publishing Company," in GEAAL. McQueen, Lee, in BusB. Smith, Jessie Carney, in BH2C. Toppin, Edgar Allan, in WB-99.

Johnson, William
?/1809–1851
Diaries, slave narrative

Johnson's 13-volume set of diaries cover his life experiences as a freed slave in Mississippi. His diaries began October 12, 1835, initially as a record of his income and outgo; they expanded in scope to consider social, economic, and political events; and they continued until his death 16 years later. Considered the longest and most detailed narrative of the antebellum South written by an African American, Johnson's diaries offer deep and broad insights into that period. (*See also* **slave narratives**.)

REFERENCES: Andrews, William L., in OCAAL.

Jones, Edward P.
10/5/1950–
Novels, short stories; columnist, educator

Edward Jones did not lead a life of privilege in his youth and young adulthood, though a scholarship enabled him to earn his B.A. from Holy Cross College (1972). While he was unemployed and living in a homeless shelter, he wrote and published his first story in *Essence* magazine (1975). Encouraged, Jones wrote additional stories, putting together a short-story collection. Meanwhile, he worked in a series of jobs while earning his M.F.A. from the University of Virginia (1981) and continuing to write. At last, in 1992, he published *Lost in the City*. Much lauded, the book was nominated for a National Book Award from the National Book Foundation and won an Ernest Hemingway Foundation/PEN Award (both 1992).

For more than a decade, Jones worked as a columnist and proofreader for the newsletter *Tax Notes* (1990-2002). When he was laid off work, he spent several months writing *The Known World* (2003/2006). The book centers on an African-American man and his wife, who "own" enslaved fellow African Americans, a little-known, rare phenomenon of Southern history. When the husband dies, his widow inherits her husband's slaves and must figure out her own response to the situation. Critics showered the book with praise, and *The Known World* won Jones a second National Book Award nomination (2003), a Pulitzer Prize for Fiction (2004), a National Book Critics Circle Award (2004), an International

IMPAC Dublin Literary Award (2005), and the lucrative Lannan Literary Award (2003).

Since the publication of his first novel, Jones has been a guest instructor at several universities (2000s). He has also continued writing short stories, including "A Rich Man," which won the 2005 O. Henry Prize. He later published his collection *All Aunt Hagar's Children: Stories* (2006). Jones also edited *New Stories from the South: The Year's Best, 2007*. In addition to his many other awards, Jones received a grant from the National Endowment for the Arts and the prestigious MacArthur "Genius" Fellowship (2004).

REFERENCES: CAO-06. CLCS-08. *Wiki. Hollins Critic. 44.3* (June 2007) p. 8. From *Literature Resource Center*. Jackson, Lawrence P. "An Interview with Edward P. Jones." *African American Review. 34.1* (Spring 2000) p. 95. From *Literature Resource Center*. Lesinski, Jeanne M., in *BB*. //en.wikipedia.org/wiki/Lannan_Literary_Award. //en.wikipedia.org/wiki/Macarthur_fellowship. //en.wikipedia.org/wiki/Pulitzer_Prize_for_Fiction. Amazon.com.

FURTHER READING: Ostrom, Hans, in *GEAAL*.

Jones, Gayl (Amanda)
11/23/1949–
Novels, short stories, poems, plays, criticism; educator

Young Gayl grew up in a storytelling family: Her grandmother wrote plays for her church, and her mother constantly made up stories to entertain the children and other family members. As Gayl recalls, "I began to write when I was seven, because I saw my mother writing, and because she would read stories to my brother and me, stories that she had written" (*BWW*, p. 234).

Although Gayl received little encouragement for her storytelling and her writing in school, she continued to write. Finally, while earning her bachelor's degree in English from Connecticut College, she was awarded several prizes for her poems. After graduation, she sought her graduate degrees in creative writing (M.A., 1973; D.A., 1975) at Brown University. As she later noted (*BWW*, p. 234), "The individuals who have influenced my work are my mother, Lucille Jones; [and] my creative writing teachers, **Michael Harper** and **William Meredith**," with whom she studied at Brown.

As soon as Jones earned her D.A., she moved to the University of Michigan, where she taught creative writing and African-American literature as an associate professor of English (1975-1983). Her academic interests have included African-American folklore, narrative strategies, fictional forms, and **oral tradition**. Although Jones enjoyed teaching and found that "teaching other writers can make you think more about certain themes, literary techniques, and strategies, which I think can be helpful"

(*BWW*, p. 235), she also found that full-time teaching detracted from her writing.

The year Jones earned her D.A. and started teaching, she also published both her play *Chile Woman* and her first novel, *Corregidora* (1975/1987). *Corregidora* tells the story of a blues singer whose foremothers' abuse under slavery mirrors the contemporary abuse she receives from her husband. Jones credits her editor, **Toni Morrison**, with helping to shape the work. In her next novel, *Eva's Man* (1976/1987), the protagonist Eva tells how she ends up being imprisoned in an institution for the criminally insane. In it, Eva reports having poisoned her abusive lover. Through the story, Jones experiments with the definitions of sanity and psychosis, reality and fantasy. Jones further explores psychological distortions in her short-story collection *White Rat: Short Stories* (1977/2005).

While teaching at the University of Michigan, Jones met Bob Higgins, who was arrested in 1983 for using a shotgun to threaten a gay-rights demonstrator. The couple married and fled to Europe for a few years. Higgins, who was convicted in absentia, took Jones's surname as his own. On their return to this country, they stayed with her ailing mother, remaining reclusive and out of the limelight. In 1997, Gayl's mother died, and Gayl published *The Healing*, in which the narrator offers a stream-of-consciousness recollection of her experiences; her novel was the first work of fiction ever published by 150-year-old Beacon Press. When *The Healing* started receiving critical acclaim (including a National Book Award nomination), the police discovered Bob's true surname and location, and they issued an arrest warrant for him. When the police arrived at the Jones household, Gayl tried to prevent their entry, and Bob slit his own throat, dying instantly. Gayl was forcibly removed and held in a Kentucky mental hospital for a couple weeks, after which she resumed her reclusive lifestyle. Nonetheless, she resurfaced to create her novel *Mosquito* (1999), narrated by "an African American truck driver with a mind as flighty as the insect she's named for" (from a review in Amazon.com), and fictionally addressing the issue of illegal immigration from Mexico.

Although best known for her novels, Jones has also written in other genres. In the early 1980s, Jones started publishing poetry collections with Lotus Press. Her collection *Song for Anninho* (1981/2000) had started out as a novel she titled *Palmares*, which explored man-woman relationships, set in seventeenth-century Brazil; *Anninho* particularly focused on an early Brazilian slave revolt. Her other poetry collections include *The Hermit-Woman* (1983) and *Xarque and Other Poems* (1985). In addition to essays, Jones's nonfiction prose includes her highly praised critical exploration of the African-American oral tradition, *Liberating Voices: Oral Tradition in African American Literature* (1991). "I am very much interested in form and structure. I am as interested in *how* things are said as I am in what is said" (*BWW*, p. 235). For her poems and her fiction, she has been recognized with many grants and other awards, including a National Endowment for the Arts grant in writing (1976-1977) and the *Mademoiselle* Award for Fiction (1975).

REFERENCES: *AA:PoP. BAWPP. BI. BWW. BWWW. CAO-03. CLCS. EBLG. MAAL. OC20LE. RT. W. Wiki.* Brewer, Kathryn A., in *ANSWWII-7th.* Byerman, Keith E. in *AAFW-55-84. OCWW.* Davison, Carol Margaret, in *GEAAL.* Gottfried, Amy S., in *COCAAL* and in *OCAAL.* Manheim, James M. in *BB.* Smith, Cynthia J., in *AAW-1991.*

Jones, Sarah
11/29/1974–
Poems, spoken word—poetry, plays; performer, poetry slam artist, actor

Because Sarah Jones's father was a medical doctor in the military, she and her family moved often. To adapt, she quickly picked up the local speech patterns and gestures. Further enriching her verbal and gestural vocabulary, she attended New York City's United Nations International School during her late teens. After high school, Jones garnered a Mellon Minority Fellowship to attend Bryn Mawr University, but after a while, she left Bryn Mawr and moved to Brooklyn. There, she read her poems aloud, seeking out spoken-word competitions. In doing so, she also developed distinct narrative voices for many of her pieces. She also crossed the Brooklyn Bridge to New York City's Nuyorican Poets Cafe, where she started competing in poetry slams. In 1997, she won the citywide Grand Slam Championship with her winning poem, "Your Revolution."

"Your Revolution" used the rhythms and stylings of hip-hop but defied and denounced much of hip-hop's emphasis on money, sex, and violence. When an independent radio station in Portland, Oregon broadcast her poem, The Federal Communications Commission (FCC) fined the station. The fine provoked public controversy, earning Jones a lot of attention. The FCC ended up reversing its decision and rescinding the fine in early 2003, and stations were again free to air her work. Meanwhile, Jones published a poetry collection, *Your Revolution: Poems* (2000).

Jones also started developing her characterizations more fully to create monologues for a series of critically acclaimed one-woman shows. She presented her first one-woman show, *Surface Transit*, at the Nuyorican Poets Cafe in 1998, then at the New York Hip Hop Theater Festival in 2000. *Surface Transit* was nominated for the Drama Desk Award and won HBO's Best One Person Show award. Next, human rights organization Equality

Now commissioned her to create and perform *Women Can't Wait*, dramatically demonstrating why discriminatory laws in various countries violate women's human rights. Jones first performed it at the International Conference on Women's Rights in 2000. Her third one-woman show, *Waking the American Dream*, was also a commissioned piece intended to address human-rights issues. *Waking the Dream* served as a springboard for Jones's fourth, better-known show.

Jones's fourth show, *Bridge & Tunnel* (2004), won an Obie and ran for six months to sold-out audiences. After further development at Berkeley Repertory Theatre, it reached Broadway in early 2006. On Broadway, the show garnered Jones a special Tony Award. The W. K. Kellogg Foundation commissioned Jones's fifth one-woman show, *A Right to Care* (2005). Her mission was to create a show that would raise the audience's awareness of disparities in the provision of health to people of differing races and ethnic backgrounds.

Audiences have seen and heard Jones's live performances in Europe, Asia, and Africa. She has performed for United Nations delegates, for U.S. congressional representatives, and for the small screen, such as on HBO's *Def Poetry Jam* and on Bravo's *The Sarah Jones Show* special (2005). She also offers workshops and lectures across Europe and the United States. In addition to her Obie and her Tony, Jones has been honored with a Van Lier Literary Fellowship (1998), a Helen Hayes Award, two Drama Desk nominations, grants from the Lincoln Center Theater and the Ford Foundation, as well as a Best One Person Show award at the HBO Aspen Comedy Arts Festival. Jones has also been featured in *Mother Jones, Nation, Vanity Fair,* and *Vibe* and has appeared on the covers of *Ms. Magazine* and the *Utne Reader.*

REFERENCES: *Wiki.* Minderovic, Christine Miner, in *BB.* "20 Questions." *American Theatre.* 23.1 (Jan. 2006), p. 144. *Literature Resources from Gale.* //www.playbill.com/news/article/86210-Small_Tragedy_Mark_Russell_and_George_C._Wolfe_Among_2004_Off-Broadway_Obie_Awards_Winners. Amazon.com.

FURTHER READING: McCarty, Joan F., in *GEAAL.*

Jones, Tayari
11/30/1970–
Novels; educator

Tayari Jones's literary imagination was captured when African-American children her own age were disappearing and then being found, murdered, in her home town of Atlanta (1979-1981). When Tayari was 10 years old, the murderer was caught, and the killings ended. After high school, Jones earned her B.A. (1991), magna cum laude, from local Spelman College, where she studied with poet and playwright **Pearl Cleage**. Cleage helped her get her first story published in *Catalyst* magazine. Jones then earned her M.A. (1994) from the University of Iowa, where she worked as a graduate-student instructor (1992-1994). After grad school, she coordinated and taught in a developmental reading program on the faculty of Prairie View A&M University in Texas (1994-1997). She left Texas to return home to Atlanta for a while, where she studied with **Kevin Young** and Judith Ortiz Cofer at the University of Georgia.

After leaving Atlanta, Jones started writing her first novel and she moved to Arizona State University, where she studied with novelists Ron Carlson and **Jewell Parker Rhodes**, earning an M.F.A. (2000) and earning a little cash as a graduate-student instructor (1999-2000). She stayed on in Tempe, working as a public arts assistant in the city's Cultural Services Department (2001). She left Arizona for Johnson City to become the Geier Writer in Residence at East Tennessee State University (2003-2004). She left Tennessee to become an assistant professor at the University of Illinois in Urbana-Champaign (2004-200?). At some point, she also taught creative writing at George Washington University in D.C., and by 2008 she had become an assistant professor in the M.F.A. program at Rutgers-Newark University in New Jersey.

Meanwhile, she finished her first novel, *Leaving Atlanta* (2002), told mostly from the viewpoints of two girls and a boy living in Atlanta during the time of the Atlanta Child Murders. The disappearances and murders affect each of the three children differently, as they struggle with their own issues. Jones's book won the Hurston/Wright Legacy Award for Debut Fiction, and it was named "Novel of the Year" by *Atlanta Magazine*, "Best Southern Novel of the Year" by Creative Loafing Atlanta, and one of the best of 2002 by both the *Atlanta Journal-Constitution* and the *Washington Post*. Jones's second novel, *The Untelling* (2005), also set in Atlanta, tells the story of a woman still recovering from a childhood trauma, which she keeps secret. *The Untelling* was awarded the Lillian C. Smith Award for New Voices (2005) by the Southern Regional council and the University of Georgia Libraries. Jones has also contributed numerous short stories to periodicals (e.g., *Langston Hughes Review* and *Sou'wester*) and to several anthologies (e.g., *Gumbo*, 2002; *New Stories from the South: The Year's Best 2004*, 2004). Her creative nonfiction and literary criticism have appeared in periodicals and in anthologies. In addition, many readers will enjoy reading her blogs, past and present, through links at //www.tayarijones.com/blog/.

Her numerous awards include a **Zora Neale Hurston/Richard Wright** Foundation Award (2000), a MacDowell Colony fellowship (2002), a Bread Loaf Writers Conference fellowship (2004), a Yaddo fellow-

ship, and a Collins fellowship from the United States Artists Foundation (2008).

REFERENCES: *CAO-06. Wiki.* //en.wikipedia.org/wiki/Atlanta_Child_Murders. //english-newark.rutgers.edu/03_faculty_12_tayari_jones.html. //www.georgiaencyclopedia.org/nge/Article.jsp?id=h-3501. //www.hurston-wright.org/hw_legacy.shtml. //www.tayarijones.com/about/. //www.tayarijones.com/blog/. //www.tayarijones.com/blog/archives/2005/02/where_do_i_writ.html. //www.tayarijones.com/blog/archives/2008/11/prebliss_links.html. //www.tayarijones.com/blog/archives/2008/11/37_years_ago_to.html. //www.tayarijones.com/blog/archives/2008/12/post_birthday_l.html. //www.tayarijones.com/blog/archives/the_writing_life/index.html.

Jones-Meadows, Karen
1953–
Stage plays, screenplays; dramaturge

Starting in 1985, Jones-Meadows managed to have *Henrietta,* the second play she ever wrote, produced Off-Broadway, by the Negro Ensemble Company. **Woodie King, Jr.,** included *Henrietta* in landmark *The National Black Drama Anthology* (1995). Since then, she has written *Tapman* (1988), *Major Changes* (1989), *Crystals* (1994), *Mystery Cycle Plays* (1989), *In the Name of the Woman* (1993), and *Harriet's Return!* (1994), which probes the mental life of Harriet Tubman, as well as her experiences on the Underground Railroad. She has also written two stage plays for young adults—*Private Conversations* (1991-1992) and *Everybody's Secret* (1994), as well as several television and film scripts.

REFERENCES: Brown, E. Barnsley, in *OCAAL*. Kich, Martin, in *GEAAL*.

Jordan, Barbara (Charline)
2/21/1936–1/17/1996
Autobiography/memoir, spoken word—oratory; attorney, politician, scholar, educator

Best known as a politician, Jordan became the first African-American state senator in Texas since 1883, the first woman state senator ever (1966-1972), and the first African-American congresswoman from the South (1972-1978). Despite her status as a ground-breaker, Jordan announced, "I am neither a black politician nor a female politician, just a politician" (quoted in *EA-99*). In 1974, she was a member of the House Judiciary Committee during the Nixon impeachment hearings, and her eloquent and explicit observations were among the most memorable and stirring during that historic time. For instance, she noted, "My faith in the Constitution is whole. It is complete. It is total. I am not going to sit here and be an idle spectator in the diminution, the subversion, and the destruction of the Constitution" (quoted in *BH2C*, p.

Barbara Jordan gives the keynote address to the Democratic National Convention, July 12, 1976

398). In 1976 (and again in 1992), she delivered the keynote address to the Democratic National Convention, the first woman and the first African American ever to do so. Again, she inspired her listeners with her observation, "That this [keynote address] is possible is one additional bit of evidence that the American Dream need not forever be deferred" (quoted in *TAWH*, p. 87).

In 1978, Jordan left Congress and taught social sciences (specializing in political ethics and public policy) at the University of Texas at Austin. A decade later, she was diagnosed with multiple sclerosis (a neuromuscular disorder). Her published works include her autobiography, *Barbara Jordan: A Self-Portrait* (1979, with Shelby Hearon); *Local Government Election Systems* (1984, with Terrell Blodgett); and a collection of her speeches, *Selected Speeches* (1999, edited by Sandra Parham). Among Jordan's numerous awards are the Eleanor Roosevelt Humanities Award (1984), the NAACP's **Spingarn** Medal (1992), the Presidential Medal of Freedom (1995), and more than 20 honorary doctorates from prominent American universities.

REFERENCES: *EBLG*. Duckworth, James, in *BH2C*. Edwards, Roanne, in *EA-99*. Hamilton, Charles V., in *WB-99*. Amazon.com, 7/1999. Pitre, Merline, in *BWA:AHE*. *EB-BH-CD*. *G-97*.

Jordan, June (aka her former married name, Meyer)
7/9/1936–6/14/2002

Poems, essays, columns, young-adult and juvenile novels, short stories, anthologies, plays, libretti; journalist, educator, political activist

Granville and Mildred Jordan had emigrated from a life of desperate poverty in Jamaica to the Bedford-Stuyvesant neighborhood of Brooklyn before their daughter June was born. June's mother, a nurse, had longed to be an artist but had to abandon her dreams to address more practical concerns. As an adult, Jordan reflected back on the situation of her mother in her essays "Notes of a Barnard Dropout" and "Many Rivers to Cross" (1985) and in poems such as "Getting Down to Get Over" (1977). In these works, she placed her mother's situation and eventual suicide (in 1966) in the historical context of other black women whose longings and aspirations have been unfulfilled and whose voices and creative works have been ignored. June's relationship with her father, a postal clerk, was complicated: He beat her savagely—to the point of scarring her physically, as well as emotionally. Yet he also shared with June his love of literature, especially the verses of the Bible, Shakespeare, Poe, and **Paul Laurence Dunbar**.

At age seven, June started writing her own poems. Over the years, her changing interests in poets (the major Romantic poets, African-American male poets, women poets, etc.) influenced shifts in her own poetry. Both her parents worked hard to ensure that young June would have what they considered an outstanding education. In most of the schools she attended, she was among a small minority of blacks—in Midwood High School, a long commute from Bedford-Stuyvesant, she was a minority of 1 black among 3,000 students. She felt unwelcome, to say the least. The situation wasn't much different in Northfield School for Girls (in Massachusetts) or in Barnard College (in New York City).

In each of these exclusive schools, Jordan was faced with a white-male-oriented curriculum, which in no way related to her, her family, her friends, her community, or her cultural background. Although she had once been turned on to literature through the works of white males, as a youth, she resisted the exclusive focus on a heritage and life experiences she did not share. On her own, she sought out African-American writers such as **Margaret Walker**, **Robert Hayden**, and **Langston Hughes**.

While Jordan was still an undergraduate at Barnard College, she married Michael Meyer, a white liberal graduate student at Columbia. They wedded in 1955, when interracial marriage was still illegal in 43 states—and was reviled in all 50. When Meyer went on to the University of Chicago, June followed him to that university, taking a year off from Barnard. The following year, she returned to Barnard for a year, but she dropped out the following year, and the next year (1958) she and Michael had a son, Christopher David Meyer.

After leaving college, Jordan tried out several different jobs, including assistant movie producer. She also worked closely with innovative architect Buckminster Fuller, developing a plan for renovating Harlem, for which she was awarded a 1970 Prix de Rome in environmental design. She also took her young son with her and rode to Baltimore, Maryland, with the Freedom Riders, despite her husband's fear that she and her son would be in danger doing so. As she became increasingly involved in the civil-rights movement in New York, and he became increasingly involved in his work in Chicago, the couple drew apart, and in 1966 (the same year her mother committed suicide), the two divorced, though June kept the surname Meyer until 1969. June did freelance journalistic writing to support herself and her son, but she still wrote poems every day.

Supporting a son on freelance writing proved difficult, and starting in 1967, Jordan began teaching English, literature, African-American literature, and writing at several colleges in Connecticut (e.g., Yale) and in New York (e.g., City College of New York, Sarah Lawrence College, State University of new York at Stony Brook). She also accepted positions as poet- and playwright-in-residence, children's workshop leader, and lecturer at various schools and institutions. In 1989, she was named Professor of African American Studies and Women's Studies at UC Berkeley. At the same time, she started writing political columns for *The Progressive* magazine. In a *Los Angeles Times* tribute, Lynell George observed that Jordan "spent her life stitching together the personal and political so the seams didn't show" (quoted in CAO-06).

In the academic community, Jordan attempted to rectify the educational flaws she observed in her own schooling. Hence, she fervently advocated for including African-American and third-world studies within the university curricula. She also championed the use of Black English (or Ebonics) as an acceptable, lovely, and efficacious form of English language expression. She further argued that the resistance to Black English centers more on the power dynamics in the mainstream culture than on any qualities intrinsic to either Black English or Standard American English: "Language is political. . . . the powerful don't play; they mean to keep that power, and those who are the powerless (you and me) better shape up—mimic/ape/suck—in the very image of the powerful, or the powerful will destroy you—you and our children" (*QB*).

Jordan applied her own use of language to a variety of genres, including more than two-dozen books: poetry collections, children's fiction and nonfiction books, plays,

and essay collections, as well as countless short stories and columns. She also edited several anthologies (e.g., *Soulscript: A Collection of Classic African American Poetry*, 1970/2004, chosen a Best Young Adult Book by the American Library Association [ALA]). Jordan's free-verse poems have been widely published and anthologized. In *Who Look at Me* (given the ALA's Notable Book Award in 1969), she interwove her dialect poem into a series of paintings depicting the history of blacks in America. *Some Changes*, her first poetry collection, followed in 1971, including highly personal poems, as well as poems that addressed political, social, and racial issues, and even poems responding to aesthetic questions.

Her subsequent poetry publications include *Poem: On Moral Leadership as a Political Dilemma (Watergate, 1973)* (1973), *New Days: Poems of Exile and Return* (1974), *Okay Now* (1977), *Things That I Do in the Dark: Selected Poetry, 1954-1977* (1977), *Passion: New Poems, 1977-1980* (1980), *Living Room: New Poems, 1980-1984* (1985/1993), *High Tide—Marea Alta* (1987), *Lyrical Campaigns: Selected Poems* (1989), *Naming Our Destiny: New and Selected Poems* (1989), *Haruko/Love Poems* (1993), and *Kissing God Goodbye: Poems 1991-1997* (1997). After Jordan's death, Jan Heller Levi edited the collection *Directed by Desire: The Collected Poems of June Jordan* (2005). These collections reflect Jordan's expanding sense of inclusiveness, as she first embraced African Americans, then other U.S. ethnic groups, women around the globe, and all people who are struggling everywhere. While wrapping her poetic attention around humanity throughout the world, she still moved in close to give readers an intimate view of universal experiences.

In addition to her poetry, Jordan wrote several plays (*In the Spirit of Sojourner Truth*, 1979; *For the Arrow That Flies by Day*, 1981), musicals (*Freedom Now Suite*, 1984; *The Break*, 1984; *The Music of Poetry and the Poetry of Music*, 1984; *Bang Bang Uber Alles*, 1985 or 1986, picketed by the Ku Klux Klan), and libretti (lyrics) (e.g., *I Was Looking at the Ceiling and Then I Saw the Sky*, 1995). She is probably better known, however, for her juvenile fiction. Her novel *His Own Where* (1971) was written entirely in Black English, about a mid-teens protagonist who undertakes an urban-renewal project to renovate his neighborhood; it was named among the "Most Outstanding Books" by *The New York Times*, "Best Books for Young Adults," by the ALA, and "Books for the Teen Age" by the New York Public Library, as well as a National Book Award finalist. Her historical novel *Dry Victories* (1972) and her biography *Fannie Lou Hamer* (1972) explore African-American history from the Reconstruction era through the civil-rights movement. Jordan also recorded the narratives of children directly in the reader she edited with Terri Bush, *The Voice of the Children: Writings by Black and Puerto Rican Young People* (1970/1974). To round out this genre, she wrote two picture books for children: *New Room, New Life* (1974/1975, illustrated by Ray Cruz), about adjusting to a new sibling, and *Kimako's Story* (1981, illustrated by Kay Burford), about moving to New York City, "inspired by the young daughter of [her] friend, fellow writer **Alice Walker**" (quoted in *CAO-06*).

Jordan's nonfiction writings include the essay collections *Civil Wars: Selected Essays: 1963-1980* (1981/1995), *On Call: Political Essays, 1981-1985* (1985), *Moving Towards Home: Political Essays* (1989), *Technical Difficulties: African-American Notes on the State of the Union* (1992), *Affirmative Acts: Political Essays* (1998), and *Some of Us Did Not Die: New and Selected Essays* (2002, released about a month after her death). As with her poetry, Jordan frequently addressed international issues and themes in her work. Jordan didn't hesitate to address tough questions to her own situation, either. For instance, she observed how her own experiences and worldview as a black vacationer in the Caribbean differed from those of the black women and men who made her bed and served her drinks. In a *Publishers Weekly* interview, she noted, "I write for as many different people as I can, acknowledging that in any problem situation you have at least two viewpoints to be reached. . . . I'm also interested in telling the truth as I know it" (quoted in *Black Biography*). In 2000, she published her childhood memoir, *Soldier: A Poet's Childhood.*

Throughout her career, Jordan received numerous awards for her activism and for her writing, including a 1969 Rockefeller grant in creative writing, a 1979-1980 Yaddo fellowship, a 1982 National Endowment for the Arts fellowship, a 1984 National Association of Black Journalists Award, a 1987 MacDowell Colony fellowship, a 1991 PEN West Freedom to Write Award, a 2001 Writers for Writers Award from Barnes and Nobel, and a Lifetime Achievement Award from the 2002 National Black Writers Conference. Fellow writer Jewelle Gomez observed, "The passionate flame of justice burned deep inside and was always shining through in her essays, poems and activism. . . . probably the most published Black author in the United States" (in *CLCS-08, v3*). Nobel literary laureate and former editor **Toni Morrison** treasured her long-standing friend's work, "In political journalism that cuts like razors, in essays that blast the darkness of confusion with relentless light; in poetry that looks as closely into lilac buds as into death's mouth . . . she has comforted, explained, described, wrestled with, taught and made us laugh out loud before we wept . . . I am talking about a span of forty years of tireless activism coupled with and fueled by flawless art" (quoted in a review of the 2004 reissue of *Soulscript*).

Much of Jordan's later work centered on her UC Berkeley forum for aspiring poets, the Poetry for the People program, through which she sought to develop the poetic talents of students and community members. In 1991, she published *Poetry for the People in a Time of War,* and in 1995, she published a guidebook on her program, *June Jordan's Poetry for the People: A Revolutionary Blueprint.* The blueprint suggests not only how to teach poetry in a community setting but also how to ensure that poetry reaches diverse communities, including people who are children, women, gay or lesbian, or deaf, or who have ancestors of various ethnicities. About her own sexuality, she wrote, "Bisexuality means I am free and I am as likely to want to love a woman as I am likely to want to love a man, and what about that? Isn't that what freedom implies?" (quote found at //sunsite3.berkeley.edu/gaybears/jordan/). About her life, she wrote, "Freedom requires our steady and passionate devotion" (quoted in *G&LL-98-2*). Even after Jordan's death, Poetry for the People Press published *Poetry Should Run for Office (June Jordan's Poetry for the People, an Anthology of Student Poets)* (2004) and *Poetry for the People Fall 2005 Anthology: And Our Eyes Were Watching* (2005). She lives on.

REFERENCES: *AA:PoP. AANB. AAW:PV. B. BAWPP. CAO-06. CBAPD. CLCS-08,* version 1. *CLCS-08,* version 2. *EBLG. LDW. MAAL. MWEL. NAAAL. OC2OLE. QB. TtW. TWT. W. Wiki.* Ards, Angela. "Tribute: The Faithful, Fighting, Writing Life of Poet-Activist June Jordan 1936-2002." *Contemporary Literary Criticism Select.* Detroit: Gale. From *Literature Resource Center.* Gomez, Jewelle, in *CLCS-08,* version 3. Johnson, Ronna C., in *COCAAL* and in *OCAAL.* Lewis, Leon, in *T-CYAW.* Norman, Brian J., in *GEAAL.* Sussman, Alison Carb, and Pat Donaldson, in *BB.* Swartz, Patti Capel, in *G&LL-98-2.* Towns, Saundra, in *CP-6.* Zevenbergen, Susan J., in *EB-98. G-95. OCWW.* Amazon.com, March 27, 2009. -

FURTHER READING: Bashir, Samiya A. "June Jordan's True Grit." *CLCS.* Erickson, Peter B., in *AAW-55-85:DPW.* "The Love Poetry of June Jordan." *CLCS.* Freccero, Carla, in *AAW.* MacPhail, Scott. "June Jordan and the New Black Intellectuals." *CLCS.*

Josey, E. J. (Elonnie Junius)
1/20/1924–

Nonfiction—library sciences, bibliography; librarian, civil libertarian, educator

A rabble-rousing librarian, Josey effectively desegregated the American Library Association (ALA) in the four Southern states that still officially sanctioned segregation (1950s and 1960s), founded and led the Black Caucus of the ALA (1970), presided over the ALA (1984-1985), and garnered the ALA's highly prized Joseph W. Lippincott Award (1980), its Equality Award (1991), and Honorary Membership (2002). The National Association for the Advancement of Colored People gave Josey its President's Award (1986), five colleges awarded him honorary doctorates (1973, 1987, 1989, 1995, 2001), and the United States Information Agency invited him to lecture in Ethiopia, Zimbabwe, and Zambia, under its auspices (1987). In addition, he inspired aspiring librarians at several colleges and universities until he retired from the University of Pittsburgh School of Library and Information Science in 1995.

In addition to writing more than 400 (mostly scholarly) articles, he wrote *Opportunities for Minorities in Librarianship* (1977, with Kenneth E. Peeples, Jr.). Josey also edited (or coedited) nearly a dozen volumes, including *The Black Librarian in America* (1970) and *The Black Librarian in America Revisited* (1994), as well as *What Black Librarians Are Saying* (1972); *New Dimensions for Academic Library Service* (1975); *The Information Society: Issues and Answers* (1978); *Libraries in the Political Process* (1980); and *Libraries, Coalitions, and the Public Good* (1987). Josey's coedited books include *A Century of Service: Librarianship in the United States and Canada* (1976, with Eleanor B. Herling and Sidney L. Jackson), *Handbook of Black Librarianship* (1978, with **Ann Allen Shockley**; 2nd ed., 2000, with Marva DeLoach), *Ethnic Collections in Libraries* (1983, with Marva L. DeLoach), and *Politics and the Support of Libraries* (1990, with Kenneth D. Shearer). He also edited the library trade journal, *The Bookmark* (1976-1986; coedited for 5 more years).

REFERENCES: *AANB. CAO-01. EBLG. Wiki.* Patti, Nicholas, in *BB.* Amazon.com

Journalism *See* National Association of Black Journalists and names of specific newspapers

Journals and Magazines, Literary
Literary journals and magazines

The first African-American to edit a national magazine was **William Whipper**, who founded and edited the *National Reformer* (c. 1830), the Journal of the American Moral Reform Society. Probably the earliest African-American literary journal was the *Anglo-African Magazine,* coedited by **Frederick Douglass, Frances Ellen Watkins Harper**, and others (1859). The key literary journals and magazines included as main entries in this dictionary are *African American Review* (aka *Negro American Literature Forum, Black American Literature Forum*) (1967-); *Alexander's Magazine* (1905-1909); *Black Opals* (1927-1928); *The Black Scholar* (1969-); for *Black World, see* **Negro Digest**; *The Brownies' Book* (1920-1921); *Callaloo* (1976-); *The Colored American Magazine* (1900-1909); *The Crisis* (1910-); *Ebony* (1945-); *Fire!!* (1926); for *First World, see* **Negro Digest**; for *Douglass' Monthly* (1860-1863), *see* **North Star**; *Freedomways: A Quarterly Review of the Negro Free-*

dom Movement (1961-1986); *The Messenger* (1917-1928); *Negro Digest* (1942-1951, 1961-1970), renamed *Black World* (1970-1976) and then *First World* (1977-1983); *Negro World* (1918-1933); *Nkombo* (aka *Echoes from the Gumbo*) (1968-1974); **NOMMO** (1969-1976); *Obsidian: Black Literature in Review* (1975-1982), *Obsidian II: Black Literature in Review* (1986-1998), *Obsidian III: Literature in the African Diaspora* (1999-2006), and *Obsidian: Literature in the African Diaspora* (2006-?); *Opportunity: A Journal of Negro Life* (1923-1949); *Phylon* (1940-); *Quill Club's Saturday Evening Quill* (1928-1930); *Sage: A Scholarly Journal on Black Women* (1984-1995); *Survey Graphic* (1921-1952); *Umbra* (1963-1974); and *The Voice of the Negro* (1904-1907).

Additional information on literary journals may be found in these entries on anthologies: **anthologies of African-American literature** (1845-); **anthologies of African-American literature, from literary journals** (1972-); and **anthologies of African-American literature, writers from 1920 to the early 1940s, during the New Negro era.** The entries on antislavery periodicals also contain information on periodicals containing literature by African Americans; these entries include **antislavery periodicals, 1819-1829; antislavery periodicals, 1830-1839; antislavery periodicals, 1840-1849;** and **antislavery periodicals, 1850-1865.** Another entry may be of interest: **Harlem Renaissance, literary and scholarly journals of the "New Negro" era.** (c. 1919-1939). In addition, the entry on the **Johnson Publishing Company** includes information on several of its magazines.

Just, Ernest Everett
8/14/1883–10/27/1941
Nonfiction—biology; cellular zoologist, educator

Just sped through the Kimball Academy (prep school, four-year course completed in three years, graduated with honors, 1903) and Dartmouth College (B.S. in biology, with minors in Greek and in history, magna cum laude, 1907) and started teaching English and rhetoric at Howard University. Fortunately for science, in 1909, Howard needed an instructor of biology, zoology, and physiology for its newly expanded science curricula, and it pressed Just into service. In 1912, Just married fellow Howard instructor Ethel Highwarden, and later on, the couple had three children.

While developing the science program from fall through spring, Just spent his summers at the world-renowned Marine Biological Laboratory (MBL) in Woods Hole, Massachusetts. Frank R. Lillie, the director of the MBL also headed the zoology department at the University of Chicago, and he took an interest in the bright and hard-working Just. With Lillie's encouragement, Just earned his Ph.D. in 1916 from the University of Chicago, while maintaining his teaching duties at Howard and continuing to work at MBL each summer. Before Just even received his doctorate, he had started publishing scientific articles on his research (e.g., "The Relation of the First Cleavage Plane to the Entrance Point of the Sperm," 1912, a well-regarded study). In 1915, the NAACP recognized his contributions and his potential by awarding him the first NAACP **Spingarn** Medal. They knew what they were doing when they awarded it, as Just published about 60 research papers in various scientific journals during his 30-plus-year career at Howard. Most of these focused on the life of normal and abnormal cells, which Just believed held the promise of giving insight into how various diseases (such as cancer) came into being—and could possibly be eradicated.

Because Just's true passion was his research, he viewed his teaching duties as a distraction. He loved to get research grants that would take him to Europe and other places, so that he could be free of his teaching duties and could focus solely on his research. (Needless to say, his wife and children weren't thrilled to have him be away so much; the couple eventually divorced.) In 1939, he published *The Biology of the Cell Surface*, which revolutionized biologists' view of cells by showing that the life of the cell depended just as much on the activities in the ectoplasm (the outer part of the cell) as on the functions of the cell nucleus (the figurative heart and brain of the cell).

The year after his revolutionary book appeared in print, Just was studying at a biological research arm of the prestigious Sorbonne university in France. By that time, he had remarried—a graduate student whom he had met previously in Germany. His health was failing, but he never flagged in his dedication to his work. In June, the Germans invaded France and interred Just in a prison camp until his new wife's father intervened and had him released. Just quickly escaped to the United States. By the end of the following year, Just was dead, having succumbed to a disease caused by abnormal cell growth: cancer. Given his dedication to his work, he probably died, saying to himself, "If only I could have unlocked a few more secrets of the cell. . . ."

REFERENCES: *EAACH. SMKC.* Manning, Kenneth R. 1983. *Black Apollo of Science: The Life of Ernest Everett Just.* New York: Oxford University Press. Tuttle, Kate, in *EA-99.* —Tonya Bolden

Just Us Books
1988–
Publisher of books for juveniles, from preschool through high school

Cheryl and **Wade Hudson** had their first child, their daughter Katura, in 1976. Eager to share their Afri-

can-American heritage with their newborn, Cheryl and Wade looked for African-American art, posters, books, and learning materials suitable for Katura's nursery. Katura had arrived during the culmination of the **Black Aesthetic** movement, so the Hudsons were heartily disappointed at the lack of suitable materials. Undeterred, Cheryl, a visual artist and graphic designer, created her own decorations: several alphabet letters that looked like African-American children. Between then and the birth of their second child, Stephan, in 1982, Cheryl further elaborated her concept to create a complete alphabet. Children of the Hudsons' friends were welcomed into their community with the Hudsons' gift of customized nameplates, created by Cheryl.

With the encouragement of all who saw Cheryl's work, the Hudsons tweaked the concept and coined the term AFRO-BETS® Kids. Katura and Stephan became the initial inspirations for the AFRO-BETS® Kids Tura and Stef. Four other characters-Langston, Robo, Glo, and Nandi-were added to complete the gang. Using these six characters, Cheryl created a 24-page concept book, *AFRO-BETS® ABC Book* (e.g., A was for Africa, alligator, and apple), featuring the AFRO-BETS® Kids. Once the Hudsons were satisfied with the book, Cheryl was determined to see her book in print because she "strongly believes that African-American children have a right to see themselves portrayed positively and accurately in the literature of this society" (quoted in *CA/I*). Wade pitched the book and its underlying concept to a number of commercial children's book publishers, facing rejection after rejection. One editor stated simply, "There's no market for Black children's books."

Wade and Cheryl had confidence in the value of their book, however, and in 1987, they pulled $7,000 out of savings and found a typesetter and printer to help them self-publish 5,000 copies of *AFRO-BETS® ABC Book*. By appealing directly to African-American bookstores, as well as parents and teachers, they sold all 5,000 copies of the title in less than three months and had more printed. Cheryl recalled the most inspirational responses: "We received letters written in crayon from 3- and 4-year old children who couldn't wait to show us that they could write the alphabet, or share drawings they did of their favorite AFRO-BETS® . . . character" (from //www.justus books.com/modules/content/index.php?id=2). Within a decade, 220,000 copies of *AFRO-BETS ABC Book* had been sold.

While the Hudsons were getting their first book published, Cheryl had already started on a second, *AFRO-BETS® 123 Book*. This time, charming-and-flexible!- African-American children form the numerals, accompanied by the correct number of vividly illustrated items and a chubby preschooler's hand (or two) holding up the correct number of digits. With the 1988 publication of their second book, the Hudsons founded Just Us Books as a publishing company, starting out in their own home. While Cheryl supervises the editorial aspects of the company- coordinating the writers and illustrators and editing the books in development- Wade oversees the business aspects, such as marketing, dealing with suppliers, and handling distribution. They now operate in a nearby office building, with a staff larger than just the two original Hudsons.

Just Us Books now publishes not only many of Cheryl's books, Wade's books, and their cowritten books, but also the books of many other authors. In mid-2009, their website listed about 15 illustrators (including Stephan, as well as R. Gregory Christie and Morrie Turner) and about 30 authors (including Katura, Cheryl, and Wade, as well as **Mari Evans**, Nikki Grimes, **Rosa Guy**, **James Haskins**, Angela Medearis, **Eleanora E. Tate**, **Omar Tyree**, **Valerie Wilson-Wesley**, and **Camille Yarbrough**). No matter who does the writing or the illustrating, however, all Just Us Books are written for young readers, ages preschool through "young adult" (teens).

The Hudsons carefully choose the six to eight titles they will publish each year. Within 8 years of their launch, more than 3 million of their books were in print, and their company grossed about $1 million. What is their secret to such success? Cheryl has said, "What distinguishes us from the [major publishers] . . . is that our products are designed to truly reflect black culture. Our children see black characters that are substantial and unique. They see themselves and their surroundings on the pages of our books" (quoted in CA/I).

Wade and Cheryl have also been innovative in developing new book series. Their first series, the AFRO-BETS(r) books, was named the "best-selling children's book series" by **BlackBoard African-American Bestsellers** (1995). One book in the series, *AFRO-BETS(r) Book of Black Heroes: Volume II. Great Women in the Struggle* (1991), written **Valerie Wilson Wesley**, Toyomi Igus, and others, garnered a Book Award of Excellence from the now-defunct Multicultural Publishers Exchange, and aired on PBS's popular *Reading Rainbow* television show. Wade and Cheryl also helped **Sharon Draper** develop and publish her first *Black Dinosaur* (1995) book, now a series published by Aladdin and other publishers. Wade collaborated with Debbi Chocolate to develop *NEATE to the Rescue* (1992), about five junior-high-school friends, Naimah, Elizabeth, Anthony, Tayesha, and Eddie. The first *NEATE* has been followed by four other *NEATE* books, authored by Chocolate, by Wade, and by two other authors. Cheryl and Wade also worked with Dwayne J. Ferguson to develop his *Kid Caramel* series (illustrated by Don Tate), including four books so far. Other award-winning books they have published include Nikki Grimes's *From a Child's Heart* (1994), illustrated by Brenda Joysmith, who won the Publishers Marketing Association's Ben Franklin Award for illustration; and N. Joy's *The Secret Olivia Told Me* (2007), illustrated

by Nancy Devard, which was named a **Coretta Scott King** Honor Book for Illustration.

Wade, as marketer-in-chief, directly markets their company's books to a few hundred African-American-owned bookstores throughout the nation. He has also directly established contacts with the corporate offices of larger bookstore chains and even large retail outlets such as Toys 'R Us. He has even ventured some of Just Us Books's precious financial resources on large ads in targeted publications, such as *Publishers Weekly, School Library Journal*, and even *The New York Times Book Review*. He attends book fairs, conferences, and expos, often with Cheryl, to promote their books and their publishing company. He and Cheryl also attend book signings, offer workshops, consult with publishers and writers, and meet with educators.

Within a decade of its founding, Just Us Books had been named a "Small Business Pioneer of the Year" by *Income Opportunities* magazine (1997) and had garnered the New Jersey Small Business Success Award (1998). Within two decades, the African American Pavilion named Just Us Books the "**Haki Madhubuti** Publisher of the Year" (2006) at BookExpo America (BEA), and the National Black Writers Conference honored Wade and Cheryl Hudson with the **Ida B. Wells** Institutional Builders Award for their contributions to literature (2008).

Wade and Cheryl have also taken the initiative to strike out in new directions. In 2004, Just Us Books established its first imprint, Sankofa Books (2004), to return out-of-print books to the marketplace, so that interested readers could gain access to now-classic books by esteemed authors Rosa Guy, James Haskins, Camille Yarbrough, and others. Four years later, the Hudsons collaborated with Kensington Publishing Company to create a new imprint, Marimba Books (2008), "a cultural melody of diversity and creativity," with the motto, "Educate. Entertain. Empower." The motto well suits Just Us Books, too.

REFERENCES: Lesinski, Jeanne, "Wade and Cheryl Willis Hudson," in *BB*. //www.fleamarketcollectibles.com/tau907.html. //www.justusbooks.com/modules/content/index.php?id=2. //www.justusbooks.com/modules/content/index.php?id=3. //www.justusbooks.com/modules/content/index.php?id=87. //www.justusbooks.com/modules/content/index.php?id=225C. //www.justusbooks.com/modules/content/index.php?id=226. //www.justusbooks.com/modules/content/index.php?id=236. //www.justusbooks.com/modules/extgallery/public-photo.php?photoId =64. //www.marimbabooks.com/. "Cheryl Willis Hudson," in *CA/I*. Personal communication, 5/17/2009, 8/3/2009. //news.bookweb.org/ news/1492.html. //www.unitycsl.com/history.htm. San Diego Public Library catalog, s://sddp.sirsi.net/uhtbin/cgisirsi/x/x/0/5?library= ALL&user_id=catalog&searchdata1=hudson%2C+cheryl&srchfield 1=AU%5EAUTHOR%5EAUTHORS%5EAuthor+Processing%5Ea uthor&submit=Find+It+%21. "Wade Hudson," CAO-06. *CA/I*. *News & Notes*, 8/23/2007, in //www.npr.org/templates/story/ story.php?storyId=13895809. Amazon.com.

FURTHER READING: *See also* main entries for **Hudson, Cheryl (Willis)** and **Hudson, Wade**.

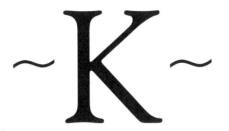

~K~

Karenga, Maulana Ron (né Ronald McKinley Everett)
7/14/1941–
Scholarly, nonfiction—philosophy; political and cultural activist

More than anything else, Maulana Ron Karenga is best known for his 1966 invention of Kwanzaa-an annual seven-day celebration of Pan-Africanism extending from December 26 to January 1, observed chiefly in the United States. As Karenga has pointed out, Kwanzaa is an outgrowth of the "Black Liberation Movement," specifically of the black nationalist Organization Us, which Karenga founded. Not a religious holiday or a birthday commemoration, *Kwanzaa*, or "first fruits" (Swahili), is intended as a family and community festival of values. Karenga explicates the holiday in his books *Kwanzaa: Origin, Concept and Practice* (1978) and *The African American Holiday of Kwanzaa; A Celebration of Family, Community and Culture* (1988; later abbreviated as *Kwanzaa; A Celebration of Family, Community and Culture*, 1996/2007). About the time Karenga invented Kwanzaa, he changed his name from his birth name to *Maulana*, Swahili for "master teacher" or "lord," *Karenga*, meaning "nationalist." An interim name of his was Ron Ndabezitha Everett-Karenga, *Ndabezitha* meaning "your majesty."

In addition to Karenga's Kwanzaa books, he has written *The Quotable Karenga* (1967, with Clyde Halisi & James Mtume, Eds.); *Beyond Connections: Liberation in Love and Struggle* (1978), *Essays on Struggle: Position and Analysis* (1978); *Selections from the Husia: Sacred Wisdom of Ancient Egypt* (1984/1989); *Kemet and the African Worldview: Research, Rescue and Restoration* (1986, with Jacob H. Carruthers); *The Book of Coming Forth by Day: The Ethics of the Declarations of Innocence* (1988); *The Million Man March Day of Absence: Mission Statement* (1995) and *Million Man March/Day of Absence: A Commemora-*

tive Anthology, Speeches, Commentary, Photography, Poetry, Illustrations & Documents (1996, with **Haki R. Madhubuti**); *Reconstructing Kemetic Culture* (1996); *Odu Ifa: The Ethical Teachings* (1999); *Maat, The Moral Ideal in Ancient Egypt (African Studies: History, Politics, Economics and Culture)* (2003); and *Kawaida Theory: An African Communitarian Philosophy* (2003)

Now an elder statesman of African-American studies in academia, Karenga was at one time convicted (1971) and imprisoned (until 1975) for brutally assaulting, falsely imprisoning, and torturing two young women from his Organization Us (United Slaves). After his release, he reorganized US and earned his first of two doctorates (from United States International University and from University of Southern California). Karenga also chaired the Black Studies Department at California State University, Long Beach (1989-2002). He has since written *Introduction to Black Studies* (2002) and *Handbook of Black Studies* (2005, with **Molefi Kete Asante**). In addition to his books, Karenga is widely published in scholarly articles and anthologies. He has also received numerous awards for his contributions to African-American studies, and his colleague Molefi Kete Asante listed him as 1 of the "100 Greatest African Americans."

REFERENCES: *AANB*. //www.officialkwanzaawebsite.org/index.shtml. //www.officialkwanzaawebsite.org/origins1.shtml. Amazon.com.

FURTHER READING: *PGAA*. Yarbough, Stephanie M., in *GEAAL*.

Kaufman, (Robert) "Bob" (Garnell)
4/18/1925–1/12/1986
Poems; journal editor

The son of a German Jewish father and a Roman Catholic mother from Martinique, a native of New Orleans, and a former Merchant Marine, Kaufman made his home in San Francisco. In 1959, Kaufman cofounded and edited *Beatitude*, a San Francisco literary magazine, in which he popularized—and perhaps even coined—the term *Beat* to characterize the offbeat poets who gathered in coffeehouses in North Beach (San Francisco) and Greenwich Village (New York City) during the late 1950s and the 1960s. In tune with other Beat poets, his poems reflect a jazz-riffs feel, and he embraced both the oral tradition of improvisational spoken-word poetry and Buddhism.

Unfortunately, Kaufman's tendency not to write down his words, his Buddhist vow of silence from Kennedy's assassination in 1963 until the end of the Vietnam War in 1973, and his tendency toward hermitage after that kept much of his work in obscurity. Nonetheless, some of his poems were published broadsides; for instance, "Abomunist Manifesto" (1959) was published by

City Lights, the press and bookstore that published Ferlinghetti, Ginsberg, and many other Beat poets. Also, his poems have been widely anthologized and have been collected in *Solitudes Crowded with Loneliness* (1965), which was translated into Arabic, Danish, French, German, Italian, Polish, Russian, and Spanish; *Golden Sardine* (1966), which his friend Mary Beach collected from his manuscript paper scraps; *The Ancient Rain: Poems, 1956-1978* (1981); and *Cranial Guitar: Selected Poems by Bob Kaufman* (1996, published posthumously). Between silences, he once told an interviewer, "I want to be anonymous . . . my ambition is to be completely forgotten" (CAO-04). Though he almost gained his wish, readers in France and Britain, as well as the United States, continue to sing his praises.

REFERENCES: *AANB. BAWPP. CAO-04. MWEL. VBAAP. Wiki.* Lindberg, Kathryne V., in COCAAL and in OCAAL. Matta, Allia A., in GEAAL. Amazon.com, 3/2000.

FURTHER READING: Winans, A. D., in *TB:LBPA.* Woodson, John, in *AAP-55-85.*

Keckley, Elizabeth (née Hobbs)
c. 1824–5/26/1907
Memoir

Predating many contemporary Washington scandals by more than a century, Elizabeth Hobbs Keckley published her tell-all memoir of her experiences with folks in the White House. Keckley's memoir wasn't her first show of industry and initiative. Born and raised a slave in St. Louis, Missouri, Elizabeth had become quite handy with a needle. When the "owner" of Elizabeth and her elderly mother threatened to hire out Elizabeth's frail mother, Elizabeth offered to hire out her own services as a seamstress. Within three years, she had not only provided an income for 17 people, but also bought freedom for herself and her son (the product of a rape by a white man). For $1,200, including her own savings and some money she borrowed from her clients, she was free to leave St. Louis and set up shop in Baltimore, Maryland.

In Baltimore, Elizabeth met and married the disreputable James Keckley. In less than a year, she left the swindler behind and moved to Washington, D.C., where she set up yet another seamstress shop, employing up to 20 women at times. In no time at all, many of the best-dressed and most esteemed women of Washington were seeking her services. The wives of Stephen Douglas (Lincoln's proslavery rival for the presidency) and of Jefferson Davis (soon to be president of the Confederacy) were among her patrons. When the First-Lady-to-be spilled coffee on her inaugural gown, Mrs. McClean (General Sumner's daughter) recommended that Mary Todd Lincoln seek the help of Elizabeth Keckley. After

rescuing the future First Lady, Keckley was soon the only fashion designer to work for Mrs. Lincoln.

Just as nowadays, many barbers, hairdressers, and "personal trainers" become the confidantes of their clients, in those times, dressmakers heard all the juicy details of the lives of their patrons. Even after Abraham Lincoln died, Keckley continued her close relationship with Mrs. Lincoln. At first, she even followed Lincoln to Chicago, but when it seemed apparent that her business would do better back in the nation's capital, Keckley returned to D.C. When Lincoln decided to auction off her White House wardrobe, she asked Keckley to help her in this mission. Sadly, the auction netted Lincoln more ridicule than cash.

In some ways, the same could be said for Keckley when, in 1868, she published her memoirs, *Behind the Scenes: Or, Thirty Years a Slave and Four Years in the White House.* In it, she included quite a few letters Mary Todd Lincoln had written to her, as well as many recollections from confidences Lincoln had shared with her in person. Although Keckley protested that she had written her book to stir up public sympathy for Mrs. Lincoln, Mary was outraged, perceiving that her privacy and her friendship had been betrayed. Robert Todd Lincoln, the only surviving (and oldest) son of the Lincolns, tried to have booksellers remove the book from their shelves. When that effort failed, he rather fruitlessly tried to remove them by buying up as many copies as he was able to.

Needless to say, Keckley's business suffered, too. For the 1892-1893 school year, she taught domestic arts at Wilberforce University in Ohio. The following year, she retired to D.C., where her failing health eventually overshadowed her other troubles.

REFERENCES: *BAAW.* Keckley, Elizabeth Hobbs. 1868. *Behind the Scenes: Or, Thirty Years a Slave and Four Years in the White House.* —Tonya Bolden

FURTHER READING: *AANB. BAWPP. BWA:AHE. CAO-07. EA-99. EAAWW. TAWH. Wiki. W.* McCaskill, Barbara, in *AWPW:1820-1870.* Saulsbury, Rebecca R., in *GEAAL.* Warner, Anne Bradford, in COCAAL. and in OCAAL. //digital.library.upenn.edu/women/_generate/AFRICAN%20AMERICAN.html. //digital.nypl.org/schomburg/writers_aa19/bio2.html

Keene, Jr., John R.
6/18/1965–
Poems, novels, short stories; librarian, educator, editor

A Harvard graduate (1987), Keene earned a masters of fine arts degree from New York University, then returned to Cambridge, Massachusetts as a librarian and then an assistant director for the Laboratory for Manufacturing and Productivity Collegium at the Massachusetts Institute of Technology, Cambridge (1991-1993).

He left Cambridge for the University of Virginia in Charlottesville, where he taught English and became involved in the Global Studies for Teachers Program (1993-1995). While there, he also served as the managing editor of *Callaloo*. He left Virginia to spend a year in New York City, teaching creative writing at the East Side Community High School (1995-1996). He has since become an associate professor of English and African American Studies at Northwestern University in Evanston, Illinois.

Keene's first novel, *Annotations* (1995), was lauded as 1 of the "top 25 fiction books of 1995" by *Publishers Weekly* and was given the Critics Choice Award from the *San Francisco Review of Books* and *Today's First Edition* (1995). While he was germinating his second book, he contributed poems and stories to numerous periodicals (e.g., *African American Review, Ploughshares*) and anthologies (e.g., *Brother to Brother: New Writings by Black Gay Men*, 1991; *Ancestral House*, 1995).

Keene's second book, *Seismosis* (2006, with visual artist Christopher Stackhouse), presents a collection of his poems. Even before it appeared, Keene had won the prestigious Whiting Writers' Award for fiction/poetry (2005). His other honors include a Fiction fellowship from the Artists Foundation of Massachusetts and Massachusetts Cultural Council (1990) and fellowships from the New Jersey State Council of the Arts, *The New York Times* Foundation, the Yaddo colony, and the Bread Loaf Writer's Conference. A graduate fellow of the **Cave Canem** poet retreats, he also participated for many years in the now-defunct Dark Room Collective of writers. Keene is currently working on a new poetry collection, a short-story collection, and a second novel.

REFERENCES: *CAO-05. Wiki.* //en.wikipedia.org/wiki/Whiting_Prize. //en.wikipedia.org/wiki/Yaddo. //www.whitingfoundation.org/whiting_2005_bios.html.

FURTHER READING: Kich, Martin, in *GEAAL*.

Kelley (aka Kelley-Hawkins), Emma Dunham
11/11/1863–10/22/1938
Novels

Since at least 1972, scholars and others formerly have believed her to be of African-American descent, but Katherine Flynn, an independent researcher, and Holly Jackson, a doctoral student at Brandeis University (Massachusetts) have since shown that Kelley was of European-American ancestry. Future editions of the *African American National Biography* and of the *Schomburg Library of 19th-Century Black Women Writers* will not include her.

REFERENCES: Chideya, Farai, and Holly Jackson, in *News & Notes*, March 21, 2005, //www.npr.org/templates/story/story.php?storyId=4543971, link to audio file available. Jackson, Holly, "Mistaken Identity: What If a Novelist Celebrated as a Pioneer of African-American Women's Literature Turned out Not to Be Black at All?" February 20, 2005, in //www.boston.com/news/globe/ideas/articles/2005/02/20/mistaken_identity/. McDaniel, Caleb, "The Latest on Emma Dunham Kelley Hawkins," //hnn.us/blogs/entries/26410.html. (Plastic), John, in //www.plastic.com/article.html;sid=05/03/02/10155368;cmt=11.

Kelley, William Melvin
11/1/1937–
Novels, short stories, essays; editor, educator

Young William Kelley grew up in an Italian-American Bronx neighborhood in New York. As a young man, he went to a private prep school, Fieldston School, in New York, then he went on to attend Harvard University. At Harvard, his instructors included Archibald MacLeish and novelist John Hawkes. While still an undergraduate, Kelley was awarded the Dana Reed Prize for his writing (1960). After college, Kelley garnered grants from the New York Writers Conference, the Bread Loaf Writers Conference, the John Hay Whitney Foundation, and the Rosenthal Foundation of the National Institute of Arts and Letters, which he used to write his first novel, *A Different Drummer* (1962/1989). He has also taught or worked as writer-in-residence at New School for Social Research, State University of New York at Geneseo, and Sarah Lawrence College.

A Different Drummer, often named his best novel, centers around an intriguing what-if: What would happen if all the black residents of a Southern state left the state in a mass exodus? What would happen to the blacks (especially those of the Caliban family) who left and to the whites (especially those of the Willson family) who were left behind?

Kelley's next novel, *A Drop of Patience* (1965/1996) tracks the life story of Ludlow Washington, a blind saxophone-playing jazz musician, starting in his childhood and progressing through his adulthood. In the story, Ludlow ends up in a misguided sexual relationship with a white woman, who becomes pregnant by him and then abandons him, thereby driving him to madness. *A Drop of Patience* is loosely connected to *A Different Drummer* in that Ludlow's daughter Bethra ends up marrying a member of the Caliban family.

Kelley dedicates his next novel, *dem* (1967/2000), to "the Black people in (not of) America" (quoted in *BWA*). The novel is narrated by Mitchell Pierce. In the novel, Pierce's wife, Tam, gives birth to fraternal twins: one white and one black. This rather surrealistic novel satirizes white family life in relation to African Americans.

Kelley's *Dunfords Travels Everywheres* (1970) has been compared to James Joyce's *Finnegans Wake* because of its dream sequences, fantasy, and playful linguistic experimentation. In the novel, Kelley compares and contrasts

William Melvin Kelley

the two main characters—Chig Dunford, a middle-class writer, and Carlyle Bedlow, a working-class hustler.

Kelley's short-story collection, *Dancers on the Shore* (1964/1984, dedicated to his mother's mother, Jessie Garcia), also includes many stories involving the Dunfords and the Bedlows. Of the 16 stories in the collection, 6 focus on the Dunfords (e.g., "A Visit to Grandmother," "Saint Paul and the Monkeys," "Christmas with the Great Man") and 4 focus on the Bedlows. Kelley also forms links between the stories and his other novels. For instance, one of the characters in his first story, "The Only Man on Liberty Street," is the illegitimate daughter of a white (former slave-owning) member of the Willson family. In the last story, "Cry for Me," Wallace Bedlow (a refugee from the mythical Southern state, who knows the Calibans) flees to New York, where he gets to know his nephew Carlyle, who was an important character in *dem* and in *Dunfords Travels Everywheres*.

In addition, Kelley has written numerous essays about the African-American experience, which have appeared in various national periodicals throughout the 1960s (e.g., *The New York Times Magazine, Esquire, Mademoiselle,* and *Negro Digest*). He also edited Norman Bel Geddes's autobiography, *Miracle in the Evening* (1960).

In addition to his writing, Kelley has taught at the New School for Social Research in New York and both taught and worked as writer-in-residence at the State University of New York at Geneseo. He has also taught literature and writing at the University of Paris, Nanterre, and has lived in France, Italy, and Jamaica. In 2008, he was awarded the prestigious Anisfield-Wolf Book Award in 2008 for Lifetime Achievement. He has also been given New York Writers' Conference and Bread Loaf Writers' Conference fellowships, as well as awards from the John Hay Whitney Foundation and the Rosenthal Foundation.

REFERENCES: *AAL. AANB. BAL-1-P. BAWPP. BWA. G-97.* Fleming, Robert E., in *COCAAL* and in *OCAAL*. Skerrett, Joseph T., Jr., in *GEAAL*. //aalbc.com/authors/williamkelley.htm. //worldcat.org/identities/lccn-n50-48130. //www.Amazon.com. //www.answers.com/topic/william-melvin-kelley. Wardi, Anissa J., in //www.questiaschool.com/read/101383396?title=William%20Melvin%20Kelley.

Kenan, Randall
3/12/1963–
Novels, short stories, essays, biography, autobiography/memoir; editor, educator

Before finishing his B.A. in English and creative writing from the University of North Carolina (UNC) (1985), Kenan spent a summer in England at Oxford University. After graduation, an instructor recommended him to Random House editor **Toni Morrison**, who helped him find a job working for the publisher in New York City. Within a year, he had worked his way from receptionist to an assistant editor at Random House's prestigious Knopf imprint, where he remained while he worked on his first novel.

In 1989, Kenan left his publishing job and became a published author of *A Visitation of Spirits* (1989/1996), which explores both first- and third-person narratives and experiments with time, as well as the boundary between fantasy and reality. After leaving publishing, Kenan started teaching writing at Sarah Lawrence College (1989), Vassar College (1989), and Columbia University (1990–?). Five years later, he was named the first William Blackburn Visiting Professor of Creative Writing at Duke University (1994), and the following year, he was named the Edouard Morot-Sir Visiting Professor at UNC (1995); other positions included the John and Reneé Grisham Writer-in-Residence at the University of Mississippi and professor of creative writing at the University of Memphis. He has since returned to North Carolina as an associate professor of English at UNC at Chapel Hill, and he is on the creative nonfiction and fiction faculty at Pine Manor College.

Kenan's second book, *Let the Dead Bury the Dead and Other Stories* (1992), offers a collection of novellas and other short fiction, in which spirits and superstition again play a part. *Let the Dead* was nominated for a Los Angeles Times Book Award for Fiction and a National Book Critics Circle Award (1993), it was named a "Notable Book" of 1992 by *The New York Times,* and it won a Lambda Award for best gay men's fiction. Kenan's third book, *James Baldwin* (1994, with Amy Sickels), is part of a series written for teen readers. Soon after, he wrote the text for a photography book, *A Time Not Here: The Mississippi Delta* (1996, photos by Norman Mauskoff).

Kenan's fourth book, *Walking on Water: Black American Lives at the Turn of the 21st Century* (1999), was nominated for the Southern Book Award. The writing involved a multiyear, 75,000-mile road trip during which Kenan interviewed about 200 African Americans in the United States and Canada. His interviewees included both literati and dozens of ordinary people from all walks of life. Kenan's fifth book *The Fire This Time* (2007), inspired by Baldwin's *The Fire Next Time* (1963), has been described as "alternating memoir and commentary." In it, Kenan offers both historical perspective and his analysis of current issues.

When not working on his books, Kenan is writing short stories, reviews, interviews, and articles published in various periodicals and anthologies. He is working on a new novel, tentatively titled *The Fire and the Baptism,* and a play, tentatively titled *The Meek Shall Inherit the Earth.* In addition to his book awards, Kenan has received a Guggenheim fellowship, a lucrative Whiting Writers Award (1994), the Sherwood Anderson Foundation Writers Award (1995), the Rome Prize in Literature from the American Academy (1997), and the John Dos Passos Award (2002).

REFERENCES: *AANB. AAW:PV. CAO-05. W. Wiki.* "Becoming a Writer," *News & Notes,* August 27, 2007, at //www.npr.org. Byerman, Keith E., in *21-CAN.* Yohe, Kristine A., in *COCAAL.* //en.wikipedia.org/wiki/John_Dos_Passos_Prize. //en.wikipedia.org/wiki/Sherwood_Anderson_Foundation. //en.wikipedia.org/wiki/Whiting_Prize. //www.pmc.edu/mfa-faculty-staff. Amazon.com.

FURTHER READING: Nixon, Timothy K., in *GEAAL.*

Kennedy (married name), Adrienne (née Adrienne Lita Hawkins) (occasional pseudonym Adrienne Cornell)
9/13/1931–

Plays, spoken word—lectures; educator

Adrienne's parents were Cornell Wallace Hawkins, executive secretary of the YMCA, and Etra Haugebook Hawkins, a teacher. Their first child (and their only daughter), she was quite gifted, learning to read when she

was just three years old. After Adrienne turned four, her family moved from Pittsburgh, Pennsylvania, to an integrated, middle-class neighborhood in Cleveland, Ohio. In Cleveland, she attended public schools, where her own racial heritage was part of the multiethnic blend of the community. Her strict parents always stressed the importance of both education and religion. While still a youth, Adrienne saw Tennessee Williams's play *The Glass Menagerie,* which dramatically portrays the emotional dynamics in a troubled family. As she later recalled, seeing that play was "when the idea of being a writer and seeing my own family onstage caught fire in my mind" (quoted in *COCAAL* and in *OCAAL.,* from her memoir). As time went on, she recalled, "I often saw our family [as] if they were in a play" (quoted from *NAAAL*). Kennedy compensated for a certain rigidness in her childhood by developing a dramatic inner life.

In 1949, Adrienne entered Ohio State University to study writing. There, she faced tremendous racial hostility, which she had never before encountered in the multiethnic community of her childhood. Nonetheless, many good things came out of that experience, not the least of which were a B.A. in education (1953) and meeting the man she married two weeks after graduating: Joseph C. Kennedy. Within six months, she was pregnant, and Joseph was on his way to Korea, courtesy of the U.S. Army. While Joseph was in Korea, Adrienne moved back in with her parents, and she started writing her earliest plays.

When Joseph returned, Adrienne and he—and their infant son Joseph C., Jr.—moved to New York so that Joseph Sr. could further his education at Columbia's Teachers College. Soon, Adrienne, too, returned to school at Columbia, where she studied drama and creative writing. She also continued to write, including her autobiographical play *Pale Blue Flowers* (1955) and some unpublished autobiographical fiction. In 1958, she started studying at the American Theatre Wing of the New School for Social Research in New York.

In 1960, Adrienne accompanied her Josephs (Sr. and Jr.) to Ghana, where Joseph Sr. was to do research. On board the ship to Ghana, Adrienne wrote her short story "Because of the King of France," which was published in 1963 under the pseudonym of Adrienne Cornell, in *Black Orpheus: A Journal of African and Afro-American Literature.* During this trip, she also gained a sense of connection to African culture and came in contact with the writings of Chinua Achebe and Wole Soyinka.

This trip also inspired her to start writing her play *Funnyhouse of a Negro* (which was produced in 1964). In addition to being productive, Adrienne was reproductive, and when her pregnancy with her second child proved difficult, she and Joseph Jr. went to Rome, where she could have easy access to physicians and other conveniences while she awaited the birth of Adam Patrice (named after Patrice Lumumba, an African leader who had been assassinated, whom Adrienne also included as a character in *Funnyhouse*) and Joseph Sr. completed his research.

When she returned to New York, Adrienne submitted *Funnyhouse* to Edward Albee's play-writing workshop at Circle-in-the-Square Theatre. The Theatre produced this surrealistic play featuring many outstanding actors of the day as historic characters in nightmarish dreamscapes. Albee liked the play well enough to option it for an Off-Broadway production at the East End Theatre, where it ran for 46 performances and won a *Village Voice* Obie Award for distinguished play of 1964 and a Stanley Drama Award. Her very first play made her an instant hit as a playwright.

Kennedy favored her next play, *The Owl Answers* (1965), a one-act play in which she uses composite characters to portray multiple aspects (and selves) of an African-American woman's search for identity in a white man's world. Kennedy went on to write several more one-act plays by the end of the 1960s: *A Beast Story* (1966); *A Rat's Mass* (written in 1963, named one of the best plays of the season when it was produced in 1966), in which humans are transformed into rats; *A Lesson in a Dead Language* (1968), which surrealistically depicts pubescent sexual maturation as a rite of passage in a classroom setting; *Boats* (1969); and *Sun: A Poem for Malcolm X Inspired by His Murder* (commissioned in 1968, produced in 1969 and 1970, published in 1971 and 1972), in which a male voice dominated the drama. *The Owl Answers* and *A Beast Story* were produced together at the New York Shakespeare Festival (by Joseph Papp) as *Cities in Bezique* (1969), again using surrealistic, nonlinear dreamscapes and composite characters to highlight the inhumanity of humans, in relation to beasts.

To create her surrealistic effects, she often uses nontraditional music, masks, religious symbols (both pagan and Christian), rich imagery, and other theatrical devices. She also has some characters played by more than one actor; she has some characters transform into other characters; and she includes composite characters. Many of her composite characters include members of her immediate family, as well as other people from her childhood, along with historical figures. Her use of nonlinear narratives, unconventional plots, and dreamlike sequences further the surrealism of her work. She also adds to her works' complexity by infusing the plays with poetic, figurative language, which can convey multiple levels of meaning.

Adrienne and Joseph divorced in 1966, and Adrienne took her sons to England for three years. In 1967, Kennedy worked with John Lennon and Victor Spinetti, to dramatically adapt Lennon's writings to make Kennedy's first full-length play, *The Lennon Play: In His Own Write*

(first produced in 1967; published in 1968 and 1973). With her son Adam, she later reflected on this experience in the book *Mom How Did You Meet the Beatles? A True Story of London in the 1960's, Adam P. Kennedy Talks to Adrienne Kennedy* (2008, published by Kennedy Publishing, owned by Adam and Renee Kennedy). Adrienne's subsequent plays include *Evening with Dead Essex* (1973), about a Vietnam War incident involving a sniper; *A Movie Star Has to Star in Black and White* (1976), her best-known full-length play, which probes dysfunctional family relationships through the lens of movie-stars' fantasy lives; *Orestes and Electra* (1980), a commissioned adaptation of the Greek tragedies; *A Lancashire Child* (1980), her first play for children, a commissioned musical based on the memoirs of Charlie Chaplin; *Diary of Lights* (1987), a music-inspired play about an idealistic young African-American couple living in New York City's Upper West Side; and *Motherhood 2000* (1994), a brief single-scene play. *Sleep Deprivation Chamber* (1991, with Adam Kennedy), dramatizing a true incident involving the beating of her son Adam by outlaw police officers, featured Adrienne and Adam's alter egos Suzanne and Teddy Alexander.

In 1992, Kennedy came out with *The Alexander Plays*, a set of four one-act plays about a character named Suzanne Alexander: *She Talks to Beethoven* (first produced in 1989); *The Ohio State Murders*, in which the protagonist acts out some of the wrenching experiences Kennedy had during her undergraduate studies at Ohio State; *The Film Club: A Monologue*; and *The Dramatic Circle*, in which the action of *The Film Club* is dramatized. Each of the four plays comprises a story that is resolved in one act, and they were published individually in *Plays in One Act* (1991). In 1993, Kennedy came out with a fifth Suzanne Alexander story: *Letters to My Students on My 61st Birthday by Suzanne Alexander*. Kennedy actually introduced Suzanne Alexander to readers in her mystery novella (with two solved puzzles), which incorporated journal entries from her experiences in London (between 1966 and 1969), *Deadly Triplets: A Theatre Mystery and Journal* (1990).

Kennedy has written more than one play for children (e.g., *Black Children's Day*, 1980; *Lancashire Child*, 1980). She also wrote *Adrienne Kennedy in One Act* (1988) and her memoir, *People Who Led to My Plays* (1987). *People* lists both fictional characters and actual persons who influenced her in her early years, thus extending the surrealistic quality of her plays into her memoir; it was adapted to a play format as *June and Jean in Concert* (1995). In addition, many of Kennedy's plays have been anthologized in various collections, including the *Norton Anthology of Literature,* one of only five playwrights included therein. Some of her essays have also been published. In thinking about how she writes, Kennedy has said, "I think about things for many years and keep loads of notebooks, with images, dreams, ideas I've jotted down" (quoted in *NAAAL*). Much of her work may be found in *The Adrienne Kennedy Reader* (2001). Her works have been broadcast in Great Britain and in Denmark and have been translated into Danish, French, German, and Portuguese.

When the Kennedys returned from England, Adrienne started teaching and lecturing at Yale University, where she was a fellow at the Yale School of Drama and a visiting professor (1972-1974), a visiting professor at Princeton University (1977), at Brown University (1979-1980), at the University of California (U.C.) at Davis, at U.C. Berkeley (1986), and at Harvard University (1990-1991). She was also invited to serve as playwright-in-residence for the 1995-1996 season with the Signature Theater Company in New York, where previous honorees include Pulitzer Prize-winning playwrights Horton Foote and Edward Albee.

In addition to many commissions to write plays, Kennedy has received numerous grants, including a Guggenheim Memorial Fellowship (1968), several Rockefeller grants (1967-1969, 1973-1974, 1976), a National Endowment for the Arts grant (1973), a CBS Fellowship at the School of Drama (1973), a Creative Artists Public Service Grant (1974), a Yale Fellowship (1974-1975), and a New England Theatre Conference Grant. She also received two Obie Awards (1964, 1996), an American Book Award (1990), a Lila Wallace-Reader's Digest Fund's Writers Award (1994), an honorary doctorate from her first alma mater (2003), a Lifetime Achievement Award from the Anisfield-Wolf Book Awards (2003, only the eighth person ever to receive it), and a Lifetime Achievement Award from the Obie Awards (2008).

REFERENCES: *AA. AANB. BAWPP. CAO-01. EBLG. NAAAL. OC20LE.* W. Carter, Steven R., in *OCWW.* Dunbar, Eve, in *GEAAL.* French, Ellen Dennis, in *BB.* King, Lovalerie, in *COCAAL* and in *OCAAL.* Robinson, Lisa Clayton, in *EA-99.* Turner, Beth, in *T-CAD-5th.* Wilkerson, Margaret B., in *AAW-55-85:DPW.* //worldcat.org/identities/lccn-n86-109553. //worldcat.org/identities/viaf-DNB%7C119083264. //www.adriennekennedy.com/. //www.Amazon.com. //www.kennedypublishing.biz/.

Killens, John Oliver
1/14/1916–10/27/1987
Novels, essays

Young John was exposed early to a love of literature. Every week, his father read aloud **Langston Hughes**'s newspaper column, and his mother presided over the Macon, Georgia, Dunbar Literary Club. Going even farther back in the family, John's great-grandmother used to

John Oliver Killens

tell him stories about living under the burden of slavery and about her first taste of freedom.

Though Killens longed to be a writer, a career as a lawyer seemed a lot more practical. He pursued the law, but when World War II broke out, he took time out for a tour of duty in the South Pacific. On returning home, he took to labor relations, union work, and political activity. By the late 1940s, Killens was living in New York and taking classes at Columbia University and New York University, studying how to write well. Pretty soon, he was coming into contact with **W. E. B. Du Bois**, **Langston Hughes**, and **Paul Robeson**, and he started thinking that a writing career might be possible for him. Soon, he was writing for Du Bois and Robeson's *Freedomways* magazine and Robeson's newspaper, *Freedom*.

Realizing the value of writers supporting one another, Killens joined up with **John Henrik Clarke**, Walter Christmas, and **Rosa Guy** to form the writing workshop later known as the Harlem Writers Guild. During the 1950s and beyond, some of the writers whose careers were bolstered by the Guild included **Maya Angelou, Alice Childress, Ossie Davis, Joyce Hansen, Paule Marshall, Walter Mosley**, and **Brenda Wilkinson**, to name just a few.

Killens was also the first to show that the Guild could produce publishable outcomes. In 1954, he published his first novel, *Youngblood*, revealing the agony of staying down home in Georgia, suffering under Jim Crow, while many blacks were fleeing North. His subsequent novels included *And Then We Heard the Thunder* (1962, a Pulitzer Prize nominee, about racism in the U.S. Armed Forces during World War II), *'Sippi* (1967, about the one-man-one-vote struggle in the South), *Slaves* (1969), and *The Cotillion; Or, One Good Bull Is Half the Herd* (1971, a Pulitzer Prize-nominated satire on social-class climbing and assimilation within the African-American community). In the 1970s, Killens wrote inspiring biographies for young readers: *Great Gittin' Up Morning: A Biography of Denmark Vesey* (1972) and *A Man Ain't Nothin' but a Man: The Adventures of John Henry* (1975). He also wrote a novel about Russian novelist Alexandr Pushkin, *The Great Black Russian: A Novel on the Life and Times of Alexander Pushkin* (1989), which wasn't published until after Killens's death. Killens even tackled nonfiction in his essay collection, *Black Man's Burden* (1965), and he wrote numerous plays and screenplays, including adaptations of his novels *Slaves* and *The Cotillion*, as well as *Winter Soldier* and *Odds Against Tomorrow*.

REFERENCES: *BAAW. EA-99. EAACH. EBLG. SMKC.* —Tonya Bolden

FURTHER READING: *AA. AANB. BAWPP. CAO-07. F. W. Wiki.* Brennan, Carol, in *BB* and in *All Movie Guide,* W.R. Carter, Linda M., in *GEAAL.* Macon, Wanda, in *COCAAL* and in *OCAAL.* Wiggins, William H., Jr., in *AAFW-55-84.* //aalbc.com/authors/killens.htm. //theharlemwritersguild.org/history.htm. //www.nathanielturner.com/johnoliverkillens.htm.

Kincaid, Jamaica (née Elaine Potter Richardson)
5/25/1949–
Novels, essays, short stories, anthology; journalist

Born and raised in the West Indies British colony of Antigua, young Elaine—a prolific reader—was taught that all the greatest literature had been written in Britain, prior to 1900. Although she had won scholarships to colonial schools in Antigua, at age 16 or 17, Elaine fled to New York City, to be an au pair, earning her room and board by doing domestic work for a white family, the father of which happened to write for the *New Yorker* magazine. While with them, she completed her high-school equivalency, grew to love the big city, and studied photography.

Elaine won a full scholarship to New Hampshire's Franconia College but left after two years, drawn irresistibly back to Manhattan, where she found secretarial work. She soon started doing freelance writing for various magazines. As a freelancer, she gained some recognition for an interview of Gloria Steinem, whom she wrote about for *Ingenue* magazine. After a time, she was invited to write a "Talk of the Town" piece for *New Yorker* maga-

zine, and in 1976, she was hired for a *New Yorker* staff position. The "Talk" pieces she wrote between 1974 and 1983 have been collected in *Talk Stories* (2000).

While at the *New Yorker*, she changed her name to Jamaica Kincaid, in recognition of her Caribbean island heritage. The magazine's legendary editor, William Shawn, also became her literary mentor, and then her father-in-law when she married his son Allen, a composer and college professor, in 1979. The couple has a daughter, Annie (b. 1985), and a son, Harold (b. 1989). Decades later, Allen and Jamaica divorced; since then, Jamaica has remarried and has another daughter, Camryn.

Much of Kincaid's work is autobiographical fiction, often centered around a feminist exploration of her intensely emotional relationship with her mother. She explores this relationship within the context of her childhood experiences in the West Indies and her adolescent and young-adult experiences as a U.S. immigrant. In addition to editing *Best American Essays 1995*, Kincaid has written some novels and many columns, essays, short sketches, and short stories. In 1983, several of her short stories (seven of which originally appeared in the *New Yorker*) were collected and published in the volume *At the Bottom of the River*. Most of these stories center on her experiences growing up in Antigua, and the collection was recognized with the Morton Dauwen Zabel Award. Though these stories are works of prose, she uses repeated phrases and other lyrical elements reminiscent of poetic styling.

In 1985, Kincaid published her novel *Annie John*, a series of eight interconnected chapters, originally published as discrete short stories in the *New Yorker*. The stories describe a young girl coming of age on a Caribbean island, striving for independence and individuality despite her overbearing, possessive mother. Although the girl deeply loves her mother, she desperately longs to establish her own identity, free of her mother's domination. *Library Journal* recognized the book as one of the best books of the year, and the book was a finalist for the Ritz Paris Hemingway Award. The following year, the Whitney Museum of American Art published Kincaid's *Annie, Gwen, Lilly, Pam and Tulip* (an oversized limited-edition art book, with drawings by artist Eric Fischl). Kincaid's text was essentially a conversation among the title characters. (A regular trade edition of the book was published in 1989.)

Kincaid's second novel was *Lucy* (1990), about a Caribbean Island girl who moves to the United States as an au pair for a white family (sound familiar?). As in *Annie John*, the turbulence of the mother-daughter relationship looms large in this work. Although physically separated from her mother and from her island home, she still feels tied to them and feels psychologically unconnected to her new environment and to the people in it. *Annie John* is a more continuous narrative than *Lucy*, which was more a series of interconnected but discrete short stories.

Critics often comment on Kincaid's blurring of the lines between fiction and nonfiction, autobiography and novel, but Kincaid has said, "I am so happy to write that I don't care what you call it" (quoted in *AW:ACLB-01*). Her next two novel/memoirs were *Autobiography of My Mother* (1995) and *My Brother* (1997), about her brother, who died of AIDS in Antigua; the former won the National Book Award, and the latter was nominated for that award. Her next novel/memoir, *Mr. Potter: A Novel* (2002), was inspired by her biological father, an uneducated taxi driver who fathered and discarded numerous children with less care and concern than a short-order cook might feel toward a stack of pancakes. One of the daughters of *Mr. Potter* narrates the story of this emotionally detached illiterate chauffeur. Kincaid herself considers David Drew, who married her mother shortly after Elaine's birth, to be her true father.

In addition, Kincaid wrote a nonfiction polemical essay about Antigua, *A Small Place* (1988). She wrote it after having returned to visit Antigua after a 20-year absence. In it, she describes the social and economic consequences arising as Antigua creeps forward out of its British colonial domination. Her furious indictment of colonization and imperialism evoked harsh criticism in the United States and England but were better received in Europe. Her other essay books include *Poetics of Place* (1998) and *My Garden* (1999/2001). She also edited *My Favorite Plant: Writers and Gardeners on the Plants They Love* (1998). More recently, she wrote a travel memoir, *Among Flowers: A Walk in the Himalaya* (*National Geographic Directions*, 2007).

REFERENCES: *AANB. AAW:PV. B. BW. CAO-04. CE. CLCS-08. EBLG. G-95. LDW. NAAAL. OC20LE. TWT. W. Wiki.* Johnson, Anne Janette, in *BB.* Kincaid, Jamaica, and Ivan Kreilkamp. "An interview with Jamaica Kincaid." *Publishers Weekly*, pp. 54-56. Rpt. in Jeffrey W. Hunter (Ed.), *Contemporary Literary Criticism* (Vol. 137). Detroit: Gale Group, 2001. From *Literature Resource Center*. Kuilan, Susie Scifres, in *GEAAL*. Margulis, Jennifer, in *COCAAL* and in *OCAAL*. Seaman, Donna, in *AW:ACLB-01*. Yohe, Kristine A., in *OCWW*. //www.Amazon.com.

FURTHER READING: Andrade, Susan Z., in *T-CCBAW-3*. Covi, Giovanna. (1990). "Jamaica Kincaid and the Resistance to Canons." In Carole Boyce Davies and Elaine Savory Fido (Eds.), *Out of the Kumbla: Caribbean Women and Literature* (pp. 345-354). Africa World Press. Rpt. in Jeffrey W. Hunter (Ed.), *Contemporary Literary Criticism* (Vol. 137). Detroit: Gale Group, 2001. From *Literature Resource Center*. Grewal, Gurleen, in *FW*. Kreilkamp, Ivan. "Jamaica Kincaid: Daring to Discomfort." *Publishers Weekly. 243.1* (Jan. 1, 1996) p. 54. From *Literature Resource Center*. McDowell, Margaret B., in *CN-6*. Morgan, Karen Ferris, in *T-CYAW*. Simmons, Diane, in *ANSWWII-6th*. _____."The Rhythm of Reality in the Works of Jamaica Kincaid." *World Literature Today* 68.3 (Summer 1994) pp. 466-472. Rpt. in Elizabeth Bellalouna, Michael L. LaBlanc, and Ira Mark Milne (Eds.), *Literature of Developing Nations for Students: Presenting Analysis, Context, and Criticism on Literature of Developing Nations* (Vol. 1).

Detroit: Gale Group, 2000. From *Literature Resource Center*. //aalbc.com/authors/jamacia.htm.

King, "B. B." (Riley B.)
9/16/1925–
Songs, autobiographies/memoirs; guitarist, singer, performer, business owner

Originally nicknamed "The Blues Boy from Beale Street," King was soon "Blues Boy" and then simply "B. B." His style of blues playing is reminiscent of the *call-and-response* of the African-American **oral tradition**, in which he sings a line of his lyric, then responds with a guitar riff. In his blues lyrics, King highlights the pleasure and pain of true love (e.g., in "The Thrill Is Gone" 1970), rather than glorifying sexual promiscuity or violence. His most recent "Farewell Tour" was in 2006, but he has already had more than one, despite his age and his two-decade-long battle with diabetes. In 2008, he performed in two blues festivals, the Kennedy Center Honors Award show for Morgan Freeman (an honor King received in 1995), and several other venues. One estimate suggests that in 52 years, he has given more than 15,000 performances.

The fifteen-Grammy winner received a Grammy Lifetime Achievement Award in 1987, and he has been inducted into the Blues Hall of Fame (1980), the Rock and Roll Hall of Fame (1987), and the Hollywood Bowl Hall of Fame (2008). A museum dedicated to him opened in Indianola, Mississippi, in 2008. In addition to receiving an honorary doctorate from Yale and at least three other universities, he has been awarded the National Medal of Arts (1990), the National Heritage Fellowship from the National Endowment for the Arts (1991), and the Presidential Medal of Freedom (2006). A licensed pilot, he neither drinks nor smokes nor eats meat, though he does gamble. Over his long lifetime, he has had two wives (Martha Denton, 1946-1952; Sue Hall, 1958-1966) and has fathered numerous children by different women. In addition to his CDs, he can be heard (and seen) on more than a dozen videos of his performances. In 1996, he authored his autobiography, *Blues All Around Me: The Autobiography of B.B. King* (with David Ritz).

Regarding the Blues, King has been quoted (in Ferris, 2006) as saying, "I think this is how the blues actually started. . . . A lot of the chanting and singing was to warn other people in the field that the boss was coming or something else was happening. The earliest sound of the blues that I can remember was in the fields, where people would be picking or chopping cotton. Usually, one guy would be plowing by himself, or take his hoe and chop way out in front of everybody else. You would hear this guy sing most of the time—just a thing that would kind of begin, no special lyrics, just what he felt at the time. . . . I think young people like blues. One reason is they like to associate blues with truth. A lot of the lines we use are like warnings to people about certain habits that one maybe wouldn't like. . . . Young people are for . . . honesty, and they're for living. And I think that's one of the reasons why they can relate to blues and to many other branches of music. I like to think that rock and roll and soul music are sons of the blues."

REFERENCES: *AANB. EB-BH-CD.* Bennett, Eric, in *EA-99.* Ferris, William R. "'Everything Leads Me Back to the Feeling of the Blues,' B.B. King, 1974." *Southern Cultures. 12.4* (Winter 2006) p. 5. From *Literature Resources from Gale.* Johns, Robert L., in *BH2C.* //en.wikipedia.org/wiki/B_B_King.

King, Coretta (née Scott)
4/27/1927–1/30/2006
Memoir, columns

Following the assassination of her world-renowned husband, Coretta wrote a memoir of her experiences as the wife of **Martin Luther King, Jr.**, *My Life with Martin Luther King, Jr.* (1969). She also edited *Martin Luther King, Jr., The Words of Martin Luther King, Jr.* (1983) and helped produced *The Martin Luther King, Jr. Companion: Quotations From the Speeches, Essays, and Books of Martin Luther King, Jr.* (1999). She also wrote a nationally syndicated newspaper column (starting in the 1980s) and numerous articles in various periodicals. Additionally, in 1969, an award was established in her honor- the Coretta Scott King Book Award- to recognize the contributions to children's literature provided by African-American authors and illustrators. Since that time, numerous honorees have been recognized. King broadened her scope to include women's rights and the rights of gays, lesbians, and transsexuals in her vision of civil rights; like her husband, she also fought to end war, capital punishment, and poverty. In 1998, she warned, "Homophobia is like racism and anti-Semitism and other forms of bigotry in that it seeks to dehumanize a large group of people, to deny their humanity, their dignity and personhood" (*Chicago Defender*, quoted in //en.wikiquote.org/wiki/Coretta_Scott_King).

Coretta raised the couple's four children, Yolanda Denise (1955-2007), Martin Luther III (1957-), Dexter Scott (1961-), and Bernice Albertine (1963-). She and her husband leave two other lasting legacies: (1) the celebration of Martin's birthday as a national holiday, which she championed, and (2) the Martin Luther King, Jr., Memorial Center for Nonviolent Social Change (conceived in 1968, opened in 1981), which not only offers training for civil-rights advocates, but also houses more than 1 million documents related to the civil-rights movement. She was the Center's first president and CEO until she

Coretta Scott King

handed it over to their son Dexter, who had persuaded her to adopt a vegan diet as an extension of nonviolence. Her funeral was attended by then-future U.S. President Barack Obama, as well as the current and former living presidents at that time, other than the ailing Gerald Ford. Jimmy Carter and Joseph Lowery (who gave a benediction at Obama's inauguration) offered provocative eulogies that garnered standing ovations. Following her funeral, her body lay in state at the Georgia State Capitol, the first woman and the first African American to be so honored. In 1987, the *Boston Globe* had quoted her saying, "I've never seen myself as a person who would fit into the traditional female role. My parents instilled in me the idea that I had the intellectual capacity and physical strength to be the best, to achieve excellence in my life. I never felt limitations" (quoted by Vicki Crawford in *The Journal of African American History*, 2007).

REFERENCES: *AANB. B. CAO-06. CE. EB-BH-CD. QB. SEW. W2B. Wiki.* Carson, Clayborne, & Angela D. Brown, in *BWA:AHE.* Chappell. David. "RIP: Coretta Scott King." *Books & Culture. 12.3* (May-June 2006) p. 5. From *Literature Resource Center.* Crawford, Vicki. "Coretta Scott King and the Struggle for Civil and Human Rights: An Enduring Legacy." *The Journal of African American History. 92.1* (Winter 2007) p. 106. From *Literature Resource Center.* Edwards, Roanne, in *EA-99.* Marren, Susan M., in *BB.* //en.wikiquote.org/wiki/Coretta_Scott_King.

King, Jr., Martin Luther
1/15/1929–4/4/1968
Nonfiction—theology, civil rights

Martin Luther King, Jr., is the best-known leader of the civil-rights movement, which took place in the 1950s and 1960s. Indeed, he was so deeply involved in the movement and so instrumental in its successes that it is often hard to distinguish the story of the civil-rights movement from the story of Martin Luther King's life, and vice versa. In many ways, his upbringing and schooling taught him the philosophy that would make the movement a success, so the conflation of the man and the movement is not altogether unfounded.

Martin Luther King, Jr., was born in Atlanta, Georgia in 1929, the son of Martin Luther, a Baptist minister and Alberta Christine Williams, a teacher. Martin Luther King, Sr., had inherited his ministry at the Ebenezer Baptist Church in Atlanta from his wife's father, Adam Daniel Williams. King's childhood was spent listening to his father's and his grandfather's thunderous, wall-shaking sermons. From them, he learned the ideals of Christian love that would later permeate his writings and speeches, as well as the African-American Baptist oratory techniques that would make him into one of the best public speakers in the country.

While Martin Luther King, Sr., hoped that his son would follow in his footsteps and become a copastor of the congregation of Ebenezer Church, as a young man, Martin Luther King, Jr., did not want to become a pastor like his father and his grandfather. Despite the fact that he went to better schools than many African-American children in Atlanta, he had witnessed the evils of segregation firsthand growing up in the South and did not think that becoming a minister would allow him to combat the social evils he saw around him. He entered Morehouse College in 1944, determined to become a doctor or a lawyer, but, under the tutelage of his religion professor and the president of the college, he learned of the influence that ministers had on society, both socially and intellectually throughout history.

Thus, in 1948, King began studies at the Crozer Theological Seminary, where he was first introduced to the philosophy of passive resistance—nonviolent, direct confrontation. This philosophy was first espoused by Mahatma Gandhi, who led a nonviolent revolution against colonial British rule in India in the 1950s. Through using this method of protest, the people of India had won their independence from British rule without spilling any blood. King was so moved by this ideology that he embraced nonviolent resistance as the best, most moral, and most practical way to achieve social reform in the United States. However, he was still not ready to implement these ideas on a social scale, so after finishing his studies at the seminary, he began doing Ph.D. work in theology at Boston University. It was during his time in Boston that he married Coretta Scott, who would remain his partner throughout his life.

After he completed his Ph.D. coursework, he decided not to join his father in the Ebenezer Baptist Church in

Martin Luther King, Jr.

Atlanta but instead took a pastorship in Montgomery, Alabama, knowing that Montgomery was one of the areas in the United States where segregation was most heartily enforced and where he might do the most good combating it. He rose to the head of the Civil Rights Movement rather quickly, brought into the spotlight by his role in the Montgomery bus boycott of 1955. This boycott was initially organized by a number of black activist groups who came together to protest the arrest of Rosa Parks, an African-American woman who had been arrested for refusing to give up her seat on a city bus to a white passenger (as the segregation laws required her to do). These groups all joined together to create the Montgomery Improvement Association (MIA), a group that was supposed to work with city and bus line officers to establish better treatment of blacks in Montgomery. They elected King as the MIA's first president.

It was during his time as president of the MIA that King delivered his first civil rights address at Holt Street Baptist Church. The speech urged the boycotters to continue their fight for equal rights, which they did for 382 days. During this time King helped to organize various means of alternate transportation for the boycotters and kept the pressure high on the city and bus line officials. As a result, he was arrested, received hate mail and verbal insults, and even had his house bombed. Nevertheless, he managed to maintain his adherence to the philosophy of nonviolence, and as a result of his teachings and beliefs, the protesters won their battle when the Supreme Court declared Montgomery's bus segregation laws to be unconstitutional in 1956.

King's work, however, had only just begun, and in 1957, he gathered with other black leaders to form the Southern Christian Leadership Conference (SCLC), which was created to spread the movement out from Montgomery and through the South as a whole. The movement's first goal was to increase black voter registration in the South, which had been held back by various discriminatory laws that allowed for literacy tests and poll taxes that prevented many African Americans from access to the voting booths. Their ultimate goal, of course, was the complete elimination of segregation.

To achieve this end, King began an extensive tour of the country, giving speeches and sermons attacking segregation, meeting with various public officials, and writing a book, *Stride Toward Freedom: The Montgomery Story*, which chronicled the experience of the bus boycott in Montgomery and explained King's politics of nonviolence. He also took a trip to Ghana, a country in sub-Saharan Africa, where he spoke at a ceremony celebrating its independence. The cornerstone of his travels, however, was a trip to India, where he and his wife met with various people who had known Gandhi and visited the major sites where the Indian leader waged his nonviolent struggle against the British. Upon returning, King was infused with a greater commitment to nonviolence, not only as a philosophy and a way of achieving social change but also as a way of life. He resigned from his position at Dexter Church and joined his father as copastor of Ebenezer Church so he would have more time to devote to his work for civil rights.

His work reached a crucial stage when he decided to focus on fighting segregation in Alabama's capital, Birmingham, which King believed was the most segregated city in America. In Birmingham, every place from restaurants to stores was segregated, and African Americans did not have equal opportunities in gaining employment. Local leaders invited King and the SCLC to their city to help them remedy these conditions. They decided to march in protest, and in preparation for the march, King and the SCLC trained the protesters in nonviolent techniques, exposing them to the kinds of abuse they would receive as they marched and teaching them how to take the physical and verbal abuse and not hit or talk back.

Volunteers took part in a series of marches that turned out to be some of the most gruesome events in American history. The Birmingham police met the first set of absolutely peaceful demonstrators with attack dogs and clubs. One thousand protesters were arrested and a

court order was issued forbidding any more protests. King defied the court order and was arrested and placed in solitary confinement. While in jail, King wrote his famous essay "Letter from a Birmingham Jail," in response to the criticism that he was hearing from local white opponents to his work. This letter became one of the classic protest pieces not only of the civil-rights movement but also of literary history, and it became a definitive work in laying out the principles of nonviolent protest.

King was released from jail on appeal after being convicted of contempt and soon rejoined the protesters. As the enthusiasm of the adult marchers began to falter under the constant opposition of the police and the repeated refusals of the Birmingham business owners to end their segregationist practices, King decided to use children in the demonstrations. This decision proved to be a crucial one, as it created one of the most lasting pictures of the evils of segregation ever recorded. The peaceful children were met with the same clubs and dogs that the police had turned on the adults; the police also employed tear gas and high-pressure fire hoses to turn back the protesters. The millions of viewers who saw this on television and the even greater numbers of people who saw pictures of this published in their newspapers were outraged by the brutality being turned against innocent children, and a national and international cry went up to bring an end to segregation.

President Kennedy, responding to this public outcry, quickly dispatched a representative from the U.S. Justice Department to negotiate between the protesters and the Birmingham business owners. Fearing the negative publicity, the Birmingham officials agreed to meet King's major demands, resulting in the desegregation of drinking fountains, restrooms, lunch counters, and fitting rooms. They also agreed to more equal hiring practices, which allowed African Americans to gain employment in positions that had always been closed to them. While the nation, the Kennedy Administration, and the protesters celebrated this victory, white supremacists displayed their anger at the agreement by bombing King's hotel and the home of King's brother. These actions inspired rioting, and the Kennedy Administration ordered federal troops into Birmingham to stop the violence so that the agreement would have time to take effect.

Editor's note: King's sermon collection, *Strength to Love* (1963), was also published during this time.

After this victory, King became involved in a massive march on Washington, which he had planned with leaders of other civil-rights groups, with the goal of raising national consciousness of the civil-rights movement and to urge Congress to pass a civil rights bill that was coming up for a vote. In front of 250,000 people, King delivered his famous "I Have a Dream" speech in front of the Lincoln

Memorial. This speech, which was largely improvised, has been called "the most eloquent of his career." He mesmerized the crowd with his deep, resounding voice, his rhythmic repetition of the phrase "I Have a Dream," and the picture he painted of a "promised land" where there was racial equality and equal justice for all. He pointed out that although the nation was celebrating the centennial anniversary of Lincoln's Emancipation Proclamation, the children of the freed slaves did not feel emancipated at all, but rather were still fighting for equal rights. Early in 1964, King stood by as President Lyndon Johnson signed the Civil Rights Act of 1964, which declared that the federal government was firmly dedicated to ending segregation and discrimination in all public places.

The "I Have a Dream" speech and the signing of the Civil Rights Act marked King's elevation to a position of national and international prominence. This status was confirmed as he became the first black American to be named as *Time* magazine's "Man of the Year" in 1964. In November of the same year, he was awarded the Nobel Peace Prize, becoming the youngest person to ever win the award.

He continued his efforts on behalf of the civil-rights movement, focusing on a campaign for voter's rights in Selma, Alabama. Again, he and his protesters were met with violent opposition—the multitude of schoolchildren who had cut school to join King's protest were arrested for juvenile delinquency; adults were arrested for picketing the county courthouse; nonviolent demonstrators who were marching from Selma to Montgomery to present their demands for voting rights to the governor were beaten by state troopers. In frustration, King asked for help from ministers throughout the nation and was gratified when they joined him in the march, only to feel great sorrow when he learned that two of the white ministers who had joined him were beaten so severely by white supremacists that one of them died.

The death of the minister, however, did gain President Johnson's attention and within days he appeared on television urging that Congress pass a voting rights bill, which became the Voting Rights Act that was signed into law in 1965. King had finally gained one of his main objectives as a civil-rights leader, as the act made literacy tests illegal, gave the U.S. Attorney General power to oversee federal elections in seven southern states, and asked the Attorney General to challenge the legality of poll taxes in local and state elections.

Editor's note: The "literacy tests" were actually spurious, in that the testers would ask prospective African-American voters incredibly arcane questions about obscure passages of the law and would judge their answers harshly to prevent them from being able to vote, whereas they'd give European-American voters ridiculously easy questions and would judge their answers generously, so they could vote.

However, not all of King's protests were successful. In 1966, he and the SCLC launched a campaign in Chicago, which was designed to expand the civil-rights movement into the North and to raise awareness of racial discrimination as manifested in urban areas and in the issues of housing, schools, and employment. The protests broke into violent rioting just two days after they began. This was followed by rioting in Boston, Detroit, Milwaukee, and other Northern cities throughout the United States.

These events marked the beginning of discord in the civil-rights movement, as more radical black leaders such as **Malcolm X** and the black-power movement refused to accept King's nonviolent ethos, believing that violence could and should be used when necessary. In his book *Where Do We Go From Here: Chaos or Community,* King fought the ideology of the black-power group. He reasserted his unequivocal belief in the philosophy of peaceful protest and pointed out that by resorting to violence, the black community would become self-destructive, pessimistic, and separatist. He also expressed the concern that in resorting to violence, the movement would lose the support of whites by creating fear instead of understanding. However, more and more, he witnessed the nonviolent ideals among his earlier protesters breaking down.

He soon turned his attentions to human-rights issues as he began to speak against the Vietnam War and on behalf of the poor in urban and rural areas. Many civil-rights leaders begged him not to take on the Vietnam War, fearing that in speaking out against it, he would lose the support for the movement from those who believed in the war. However, he felt that his Nobel Peace Prize had given him a commission to work for peace in all areas of the world, even if that meant speaking out against the actions of his nation.

While still speaking out against the Vietnam War, King also turned his attentions back to the nation and in 1967 initiated the Poor People's Campaign, designed to recruit the poor of all races and backgrounds, train them in nonviolent techniques, and lead them in a protest designed to fight for greater economic rights. They were supposed to march on Washington, D.C., to begin a series of marches, sit-ins, rallies, and boycotts designed to disrupt the government so that they would pass antipoverty legislation. This movement was never fully realized, however, because on April 4th, 1968, while staying at a hotel in Memphis to plan a demonstration, he was assassinated on the hotel balcony.

News of his death was met with a myriad of reactions—in 150 cities, furious blacks rioted; world leaders praised him as a great man and a martyr; close friends and family determined to establish a permanent memorial on his behalf and succeeded in establishing his birthday as a national holiday—the only national holiday commemorating the birthday of a person from the 20th century. This holiday, as well as his published and collected speeches, essays and books and the profound changes he had effected in American society during his 12 years of working toward civil rights assured that his memory would live on.

REFERENCES: *BW:SSCA.* Bigelow, Barbara Carlisle.1992. *Contemporary Black Biography: Profiles from the International Black Community* (Vol. 2). Detroit: Gale Research. Miller, Keith D., and Emily M. Lewis, in *COCAAL* and in *OCAAL.* —Diane Masiello

FURTHER READING: *AANB. AB. B. BAWPP. BCE. CAO-01. CE. CLCS. D. HD. LE. PB. USHC. W. W2B. Wiki.* Ankeny, Jason, *All Music Guide,* in A. Carlin, David R., Jr. A Man to Remember: Martin Luther King, Jr., Moral Hero. *Commonweal. 121.1* (Jan. 14, 1994) p. 10. From *Literature Resource Center.* Han, John J., in *GEAAL.* Ryan, Bryan, in *BB.* "Martin Luther King, Sr." *CAO-02.*

King, Jr., Woodie
7/27/1937–

Essays, short stories, anthologies, plays, scripts, drama criticism, autobiography/memoir; director, producer, actor, educator

No matter what, King would be important to African-American theater for founding the Concept East Theatre (1960, with **Ron Milner**; manager and director until 1963), housed in a 100-seat Detroit bar; and the New Federal Theatre (1970) company, based in New York City. Perhaps more important, he made major contributions to the **Black Arts Movement** as an anthologist, producer, and director, as well as a shepherd to the careers of more than a few aspiring writers (e.g., **Ntozake Shange, Ron Milner, Elaine Jackson, J. E. Franklin, Ed Bullins, Amiri Baraka**). He has also taught at numerous universities (e.g., Yale, Penn State, Hunter College). He and his wife (since 1959), casting agent Willie Mae Washington, jointly produced three children: Michelle, W. (Woodie) Geoffrey, and Michael.

King adapted **Langston Hughes**'s poetry and short stories to the stage in *The Weary Blues* and *Simple's Blues,* respectively, and he adapted **Julian Mayfield**'s novel to the big screen in *The Long Night* (1970). He also wrote and directed a documentary film (*The Black Theatre Movement: "A Raisin in the Sun" to the Present,* 1979), and he has written original movie scripts (*The Torture of Mothers,* 1980; *Death of a Prophet,* 1982) and television scripts (e.g., for *Sanford and Son*). His approach to writing and directing dramas: "We give the audience a lot of fun—and let the message sneak up on them" (quoted in *CAO-01*).

King has contributed many short stories and drama-criticism pieces to numerous periodicals, and

some of his own short stories have appeared in the anthologies of others (e.g., Langston Hughes), but he is better known for editing outstanding anthologies of other writers' works, including *A Black Quartet: Four One-Act Plays* (1971), *Black Drama Anthology* (1972/1986, with Ron Milner), *Black Poets and Prophets: The Theory, Practice, and Esthetics of the Pan-Africanist Revolution* (1972, with Earl Anthony), *Black Short Story Anthology* (1972), *Black Spirits: A Festival of New Black Poets in America* (1972), *The Forerunners: Black Poets in America* (1975, with Addison Gale and Dudley Randall), *New Plays for the Black Theatre* (1989), *The National Black Drama Anthology: Eleven Plays from America's Leading African-American Theaters* (1996), and *Voices of Color: 50 Scenes and Monologues by African American Playwrights* (2000). King has published two retrospective views of his experiences in the theater: his essay collection, *Black Theater: Present Condition* (1981) and his notebook/memoir, *The Impact of Race: Theatre and Culture* (2003). In 1997, he was given an Obie Award for Sustained Achievement, and in 2003, he was given a Paul Robeson Award.

REFERENCES: *BAWPP. CAO-01. Wiki.* Carter, Steven R., in *COCAAL* and in *OCAAL.* Jacobson, Robert R., in *BB.* Salaam, Kalamu Ya. "Black Theatre—The Way it Is: An Interview with Woodie King, Jr." *African American Review.* 31.4 (Winter 1997) p. 647. From *Literature Resource Center.* and //aar.slu.edu/in-intervws.html. Vallillo, Stephen M., in *AAW-55-85:DPW.* Warnes, Andrew. "The Impact of Race: Theatre and Culture." *African American Review.* 38.3 (Fall 2004) p. 544. From *Literature Resource Center.* Wattley, Ann S., in *GEAAL.*

Kitchen Table: Women of Color Press
1981–1992

Publisher of books by, about, and for African-American feminists and other feminists of non-European-American descent, particularly including lesbians

The Kitchen Table: Women of Color Press can directly trace its roots to the National Black Feminist Organization (NBFO), which led twins Beverly and **Barbara Smith** and their associate Demita Frazier to cofound the **Combahee River Collective (CRC)**. Barbara Smith later recalled an early or mid-October 1980 phone conversation with poet **Audre Lorde**, CRC member and Barbara's friend, in which Lorde said, "We really need to do something about publishing" (quoted in //en.wikipedia.org/wiki/Kitchen_Table:_Women_of_Color_Press).

By Halloween weekend, Barbara Smith had called together a group of feminists of color, who met with her in Boston. This meeting led to the cofounding of Kitchen Table: Women of Color Press, which claims to be the first publisher owned and operated by American women of color and dedicated to publishing their literary and critical works. The cofounders have since been identified as

Rosie Alvarez, Helena Byard, Leota Lone Dog, Alma Gomez, Hattie Gossett, **Audre Lorde**, Cherrie Moraga, Ana Oliveira, Smith, and Susan Yung.

When Smith left the University of Massachusetts at Boston, she took the Press with her to New York. (On most of the Press's publications, it lists its location as Latham, New York, near Albany.) Among the first three publications of Kitchen Table: Women of Color Press were three groundbreaking anthologies still considered to be landmarks: Alma Gómez and Cherríe Moraga's *Cuentos: Stories by Latinas* (1983); Cherríe Moraga and Gloria Anzaldúa's *This Bridge Called My Back: Writings by Radical Women of Color* (1984, 2nd ed.; originally published by Persephone Press in 1981); and Barbara Smith's *Home Girls: A Black Feminist Anthology* (1983; reprinted by Rutgers University Press, 2000).

In addition to these books, in 1986, Kitchen Table: Women of Color Press published its Freedom Organizing Pamphlet Series, including Combahee River Collective's *The Combahee River Collective Statement: Black Feminist Organizing in the Seventies and Eighties* (No. 1), Audre Lorde and Merle Woo's *Apartheid U.S.A. / Freedom Organizing in the Eighties* (No. 2), Audre Lorde's *I Am Your Sister: Black Women Organizing Across Sexualities* (No. 3), Barbara Omolade's *It's a Family Affair: The Real Lives of Black Single Mothers* (No. 4), **Angela Y. Davis**'s *Violence Against Women and the Ongoing Challenge to Racism* (No. 5), and Merle Woo's *Our Common Enemy, Our Common Cause: Freedom Organizing in the Eighties*.

Other press publications include Cheryl Clarke's *Narratives: Poems in the Tradition of Black Women* (1983); Mila D. Aguilar's *A Comrade Is as Precious as a Rice Seedling* (1987); Mitsuye Yamada's *Desert Run: Poems and Stories* and *Seventeen Syllables and Other Stories* (both 1988), and *Camp Notes and Other Poems* (1992); **Gloria T. Hull**'s *Healing Heart: Poems, 1973-1988* (1989); and Audre Lorde's *Need: A Chorale for Black Woman Voices* (1990).

Audre Lorde died in 1992, and the Press became inactive soon after. Barbara Smith turned her attention to politics and other concerns, later becoming a member of the city council of Albany, New York.

REFERENCES: Rigney, Melisssa A., "Kitchen Table: Women of Color Press," in GEAAL. //en.wikipedia.org/wiki/Barbara_Smith. //en.wikipedia.org/wiki/Beverly_Smith. //en.wikipedia.org/wiki/Home_Girls. //en.wikipedia.org/wiki/Kitchen_Table:_Women_of_Color_Press. //en.wikipedia.org/wiki/Lorraine_Bethel. //en.wikipedia.org/wiki/This_Bridge_Called_My_Back. //maps.google.com/maps?hl=en&tab=wl&q=latham%2C%20ny. //www.lesbianpoetryarchive.org/book/export/html/27. //www.wellesley.edu/womensreview/archive/2003/01/highlt.html. //www.wifp.org/womenofcolorhistoric.html.

FURTHER READING: *See also* **Combahee River Collective (CRC)** and **anthologies of African-American literature, written by and for heterosexual or lesbian women**.

Knight, Etheridge
4/19/1931–3/10/1991
Poems, anthology; magazine editor, educator

One of seven children in an impoverished family, Etheridge dropped out of school at age 14 and hung out with older men and other adolescent males in pool halls, bars, and juke joints. Although he learned few or no marketable vocational skills in that environment, he did learn the distinctly African-American craft of *toasting*: long, humorous, rhyming oratory, requiring great verbal competence and skill—as well as a little audience participation. As a youth, his oratorical skills may have earned him the respect of his peers in the juke joints, but they didn't win him any honest means of earning a living. In 1947, when Etheridge was 16 years old, he pursued one of the only legitimate means of livelihood available to him in the segregated South: the deadly career of soldier—and he joined the U.S. Army.

In the juke joints, Knight had learned to use alcohol and other drugs, and his service career didn't teach him to stop that use. At first, he was a medical technician in the Korean War and learned about the appropriate uses for pharmaceuticals. After he suffered a shrapnel wound, however, he was given narcotics to treat the pain of his wound, and he eventually became addicted to narcotics.

When he was discharged from the service, he rambled from city to city frequently, often staying in Indianapolis, Indiana, but never for long at a time. His drug addiction, his lack of education, and his restlessness made steady work virtually impossible for him, and in 1960, he was arrested for robbery and sentenced to prison. While in prison, Knight started educating himself, reading the poetry of **Langston Hughes**, **Gwendolyn Brooks**, and Don L. Lee (**Haki Madhubuti**), as well as the traditional poetry of the Anglo-American tradition and the poetry of Greece, China, ancient Rome, and Japan—especially haiku.

Knight also started to draw on the verbal skills he had developed in his youth. Soon, he was writing poems, and such noteworthy poets as Gwendolyn Brooks, **Dudley Randall**, and **Sonia Sanchez** recognized his talent. Their receptivity to his work may have been aided by the times in which he was imprisoned. The 1960s was a time of tremendous political foment for prison reform, for civil rights, and for black power. For instance, the flickering flames of **Martin Luther King, Jr.,** and **Malcolm X** came to full brightness—and were extinguished. By the time Knight's sentence was up for parole review, Gwendolyn Brooks had visited him in prison and Dudley Randall's **Broadside Press** was in the process of publishing his *Poems from Prison*.

In 1968, Knight was released from prison, although he was not freed from his habitual use of alcohol and other drugs. (In fact, for the rest of his life, he intermittently incarcerated himself in Veterans' Administration hospitals to undergo treatment attempting to free himself from drugs.) Soon after his release, the high school dropout Etheridge Knight was invited to hold academic positions at a few different universities, and he met and married Sonia Sanchez. Despite his newfound success, Knight was unable to control his drug addiction, and the marriage to Sanchez disintegrated as a result.

About a year after divorcing Sanchez, Knight married Mary Ann McAnally, with whom he had two children. The peripatetic Knight continued moving from city to city (in Minnesota, Missouri, Connecticut, Pennsylvania, Tennessee, and his most-frequent home state, Indiana). A frequent contributor to magazines, he also served as magazine editor (of *Motive* and of *New Letters*) on occasion. During the 1970s, he also got to know and mutually respect several contemporary white male poets, such as Robert Bly, Galway Kinnell, and James Wright, and he was frequently invited to give poetry recitations (not readings, as he could movingly recite long works without glancing at the text). By 1978, Knight's marriage to McAnally had dissolved, and in December of that year, Knight married Charlene Blackburn, with whom he had a son.

As a leading voice of the **Black Arts Movement** of the 1960s and 1970s, Knight rejected the traditional techniques and themes of lyrical verse. In terms of techniques, he used free verse, highly graphic street language, jazzy and bluesy rhythms, and unconventional punctuation in his works. Although he often wrote of love (sexual, as well as familial or companionate), his poetic themes frequently centered on the experiences of a black man in a racist society, oppressed by racial segregation but uplifted by a rich African-American cultural heritage. He often talked of imprisonment, particularly focusing on incarceration, but also in terms of the constraints of slavery, poverty, and racism. Using the prison as a metaphor, he even acknowledged his own self-imposed imprisonment due to his addiction to drugs. Other common themes in his work included sex, families, violence, and African-American identity.

His writings on imprisonment influenced not only the literary world of the Black Arts Movement, but also the very down-to-earth world of the inmates of the Attica Penitentiary. Many have said that his writings helped shape the thoughts and actions of the prisoners who staged a revolt in Attica in the 1970s. His great prestige rarely earned him financial rewards, however, and he and his family usually lived in—or very near—poverty. He was, nonetheless, well received among white and black audiences. In 1972, he was given a National Endowment for the Arts grant, and in 1974, he was awarded Guggenheim Fellowship. Although he spoke in a distinc-

tively African-American voice, he clearly acknowledged that much of what he said applied to the experiences and emotions of both blacks and whites.

Knight's first volume of verse, *Poems from Prison* (1968), clearly emerges from his experiences as a toastmaster and is probably his best-known work. His *Belly Song and Other Poems* (1973) diverges from the prison theme and includes many poems on love and ancestry. In his title poem "Belly Song," he speaks of how love's pain and passion is centered in the belly. Often considered his finest work, this collection earned him nominations for both the Pulitzer Prize and the National Book Award. In his 1980 collection, *Born of a Woman: New and Selected Poems*, he acknowledges the role women have played in his life, turning him toward life-affirming expressions and away from life-threatening outlets. Perhaps his most outstanding poem in the collection is "The Stretching of the Belly," in which he observes that his wife's scars (stretch marks) appear as evidence of the growing life within her, whereas the scars on black men's bodies show evidence of violence, such as war (and slavery). In 1986, he published *The Essential Etheridge Knight* (1986), which features many of the poems from each of his previous poetry collections, embracing topics from freedom to family.

In addition to his poetry, Knight published the anthology *Black Voices from Prison* (1970), which includes not only his own poems about his prison experiences, but also the poetic and prose writings of many other male prisoners. Ironically, given all of Knight's addictions, the addiction that killed him was cigarettes: He died at age 59 from lung cancer.

REFERENCES: *BWA. EB-98. EBLG. G-95. MAAL. MWEL. NAAAL. TtW.* Premo, Cassie, in *COCAAL* and in *OCAAL.*

FURTHER READING: *AANB. BAWPP. CBAPD. CAO-00. LFCC-07. W. Wiki.* Lumpkin, Shirley, in *AAP-55-85.* Steck, Stephen M., in *GEAAL.* Sussman, Alison Carb, in *BB.* Tracy, Steven C. "An Interview with Etheridge Knight." *MELUS* 12.2 (Summer 1985): pp. 7-23. Rpt. in Literature Resource Center. Detroit: Gale. From *Literature Resource Center.* //library.msstate.edu/special_interest/ Mississippi_African-American_Authors.asp. //www.english.uiuc.edu/ maps/poets/g_l/ knight/life.htm. //www.poets.org/poet.php?prmPID/158.

Komunyakaa, Yusef (né James Willie Brown, Jr.)
4/29/1947–
Poems; educator

When Komunyakaa won the Pulitzer Prize for Poetry in 1994, he grabbed the attention of the literary world, but his love of words had started decades earlier. When Komunyakaa was a child, his mother fostered his love of reading, buying a set of encyclopedia for him at a grocery store in Bogalusa, Louisiana. His grandmother later remembered, "He was always reading something or writing something" (quoted in *Black Biography*). As a young teenager, he read all the sonorous verses of the Bible—twice. At age 16, he discovered **James Baldwin**'s essay collection *Nobody Knows My Name*, which inspired him to try his own hand at writing. His first verses were modeled on the British poets he had heard in school. At some point, James Willie realized that his name did not adequately reflect his cultural heritage. He recollected family lore that his great grandparents had been forced to give up their surname Komunyakaa when they arrived here from Trinidad, so James Willie Brown, Jr., renamed himself Yusef Komunyakaa.

After high school, Komunyakaa moved to Phoenix, started working on an assembly line, and joined the U.S. Army. In early 1969, his daughter, Kimberly Ann, was born, and within a month, he was shipped to Vietnam, taking along two books of poetry. There, he reported from the battlefield, was awarded a Bronze Star, and edited *The Southern Cross*, a military newspaper. He later recalled, "Vietnam helped me to look at the horror and terror in the hearts of people and realize how we can't aim guns and set booby traps for people we have never spoken a word to. That kind of impersonal violence mystifies me" (quoted in *Black Biography*).

Disillusioned, Komunyakaa returned home and completed a baccalaureate (University of Colorado, 1975) and two master's degrees (Colorado State University, 1979; University of California at Irvine, 1980). Meanwhile, he footed the bill to self-publish his first two poetry collections, *Dedications and Other Darkhorses* (1977) and *Lost in the Bonewheel Factory* (1979/2006). University presses and other small presses published his other early poetry collections, including *Copacetic* (1984), *I Apologize for the Eyes in My Head* (1986), *Toys in a Field* (1986), *Dien Cai Dau* (1988), *February in Sydney* (1989), *Magic City* (1992), *Neon Vernacular* (1994, the Pulitzer winner), *Thieves of Paradise* (1998, nominated for the National Book Award), *Scandalize My Name: Selected Poems* (2002), and *Pleasure Dome: New and Collected Poems, 1975-1999* (2001). The prestigious Farrar, Straus, & Giroux has published many of his subsequent collections, such as *Talking Dirty to the Gods* (2000), *Taboo: The Wishbone Trilogy, Part I* (2004), and *Warhorses: Poems* (2008).

Komunyakaa also works well with others. Radiclani Clytus edited an eclectic collection of Komunyakaa's work in *Blue Notes: Essays, Interviews, and Commentaries (Poets on Poetry)* (2000). Komunyakaa collaborated with Chad Gracia to dramatically adapt the ancient Sumerian epic, *Gilgamesh: A Verse Play* (published in 2006; performed in 2008). He also collaborated with photographer Tyagan Miller to create the large-format *Covenant: Scenes from an African American Church* (2007). In addition, Komunyakaa edited an issue of *Ploughshares: Poems and Stories* (Spring 1997), *Jazz Poetry Anthology* (1991, with Sascha Feinstein), *Second Set (The Jazz Poetry Anthology,*

Vol 2) (1996, with Sascha Feinstein), and *The Best American Poetry 2003* (series editor David Lehman).

In addition to his Pulitzer, he has won two fellowships from the National Endowment for the Arts (1981, 1987), the second annual $50,000 Kingsley Tufts Poetry Award (1994), and other poetry awards. He was also elected a Chancellor of the Academy of American Poets (1999). Komunyakaa has supported his poetry habit through teaching, first in the New Orleans public schools (1984-1985) and at the University of New Orleans (1984-1985), then at Indiana University in Bloomington (1985-1996), despite absences to teach at the University of California at Berkeley (1992) and at Washington University in St. Louis (1996). In 1997, he started teaching creative writing at Princeton University, which he left to become Professor and Distinguished Senior Poet at New York University.

Though Komunyakaa's poetry has been considered brilliantly radiant, his love life has been darkly tragic: He married Australian fiction writer Mandy Jane Sayer (1985-1995), whom he later divorced. He was later involved with poet Reetika Vazirani, with whom he had a son, Jahan Vazirani Komunyakaa (2001), but she apparently killed herself and their son in 2003.

REFERENCES: *AANB. AAW:PV. CAO-07. CLCS. LFCC-07. W. Wiki.* Ashford, Tomeiko, in //www.ibiblio.org/ipa/poems/komunyakaa/ biography.php. Claggett, Julie, in *GEAAL.* Harris, Trudier, in *COCAAL* and in *OCAAL.* Jones, Kirkland C., in *APSWWII-3.* Komunyakaa, Yusef, and Muna Asali (2000). "An Interview with Yusef Komunyakaa." Radiclani Clytus (Ed.), *Blue Notes: Essays, Interviews, and Commentaries.* Ann Arbor: University of Michigan Press, Rpt. in Jeffrey W. Hunter (Ed.), *Contemporary Literary Criticism* (Vol. 207). Detroit: Gale, 2005, pp. 76-84. From *Literature Resource Center.* Rourke, Elizabeth, in *BB.* Sutphen, Joyce, in *AW:ACLB-03.* //www.Amazon.com. //www.cavecanempoets.org/pages/ programs_faculty.php. //www.poets.org/poet.php/prmPID/22.

Kweli, Talib (né Talib Kweli Greene)
10/3/1975–

Poems, spoken word—rap, hip-hop; performer, social activist, bookstore co-owner

Kweli's parents, an English professor and a sociology professor, named their son *Talib*, Arabic for "seeker" or "student," *Kweli*, Swahili for "truth or knowledge," Greene. While still in high school, Kweli met Dante Smith, better known now as actor and rapper Mos Def, who encouraged Kweli's rapping. While still in his teens, Kweli met Tony Cottrell, better known as DJ [disc jockey] Hi-Tek. Later, DJ Hi-Tek invited Kweli to emcee some tracks on Hi-Tek's 1997 album *Doom* with Hi-Tek's rap group Mood. Soon afterward, Kweli and Hi-Tek formed the duo Reflection Eternal and recorded *Fortified Live* (1997). The following year, the duo became a trio when they invited Mos Def to join them, renaming themselves Black Star, and putting out an album labeled simply *Black Star* (1998). Their highly acclaimed album offered an alternative to gangsta rap or hip-hop versions of popular songs. They even captured some mainstream attention for their emphasis on rhythms, rhymes, and real life. The highly popular Dave Chappelle's Show invited the whole group and individual members of the group onto his show numerous times, and Chappelle and Kweli have since become friends.

The following year (1999), Kweli and Mos Def bought Nkiru, the oldest African-American-owned bookstore in Brooklyn, but Mos Def soon struck out on his own as an artist, releasing his debut solo album, *Black on Both Sides* (1999), and then moving away from rapping and toward acting. Kweli and Hi-Tek revived their Reflection Eternal duo and released a second album, *Reflection Eternal* (2000), which went gold, but it earned the duo more critical acclaim than money. Next, Kweli made his own solo album, *Quality* (2002), which also included some tracks with up-and-coming artists such as Kanye West. This album, too, earned more respect and admiration than money, but it, too, sold enough to go gold.

Two years later, Kweli released his second solo album, *The Beautiful Struggle* (2004), which included lyrics featuring his trademark social-political commentary. Soon after, Kweli created his own record label, Blacksmith Records (distributed by Warner Bros. Records). His label released his third solo album, *Right About Now: The Official Sucka Free Mix CD* (2005), then he collaborated with producer Madlib to create a digital-only album, *Liberation* (2006). Next, Blacksmith released Kweli's *Ear Drum* (2007) album, available in tangible, as well as digital format.

Through collaborations with Chappelle, Mos Def, West, and others, and appearances on television (e.g., on MTV's *Wild 'N Out* and *MADE*), Kweli has promoted his own work. He is currently working on an album titled *Prisoner of Consciousness*, giving a nod both to his labeling as a "conscious rapper" and to Nigerian reggae artist Majek Fashek's album *Prisoner of Conscience*. In addition, he and his old partner DJ Hi-Tek have announced plans to record a follow-up to their *Reflection Eternal* album, and he is collaborating with R&B singer Res and musician Graph Nobel as the group Idle Warship to make an album titled *Party Robot*.

Kweli's more personal collaborations include having a son and a daughter with Brooklyn-based novelist Darcel Turner, and marrying DJ Eque in 2009.

REFERENCES: *D. Wiki.* Birchmeier, Jason, *All Music Guide,* in A. "Getting 'The Message' from Hip-Hop Lyrics (15:00-16:00 PM)." *Talk of the Nation* (Jan. 23, 2008). From *Literature Resource Center.* "20 Questions." *American Theatre. 23.1* (Jan. 2006), p. 144. Literature Resources from Gale. Osborne, Gwendolyn E. "Nkiru Preserving a Legacy—African American Bookstore." *Black Issues Book Review* (Jan. 2001), in //findarticles.com/p/articles/mi_m0HST/is_1_3/ai_71317314/. Wallace, Earnest M., in *GEAAL.* //en.wikipedia.org/wiki/RIAA_ certification. //en.wikiquote.org/wiki/Talib_Kweli. //talibkweli.com/. //talibkweli.com/bio. //talibkweliblog.com/.

FURTHER READING: //www.myspace.com/talibkweli. //www.youtube.com/talibkweli.

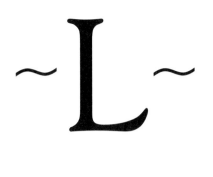

~L~

Ladner, Joyce A.
10/12/1943–

Nonfiction—sociology, autobiography/memoir, anthologies; educator, administrator

Most notable among Ladner's many important works on teen pregnancy, cultural diversity, the value of higher education, urban issues, public policy, human sexuality, and child welfare is her pioneering sociological study of African-American teenage girls, *Tomorrow's Tomorrow: The Black Woman* (1995, rev. ed.). In it, she reveals that these soon-to-be-women feel positive about themselves and about their futures. Ladner also authored *Mixed Families: Adopting across Racial Boundaries* (1977), based on interviews of 136 transracial adoptive families; *The Ties That Bind: Timeless Values for African-American Families* (1999), in which she also recalled her civil-rights activism with the Student Nonviolent Coordinating Committee (SNCC); and *The New Urban Leaders* (2001); and she coauthored *Lives of Promise, Lives of Pain: Young Mothers After New Chance* (1994, with Janet Quint and Judith Musick). In addition, Ladner edited the anthologies *The Death of White Sociology* (1998), *Adolescence and Poverty: Challenge for the 1990s* (1991, with Peter Edelman, husband of **Marian Wright Edelman**), and *Launching our Black Children for Success: A Guide for Parents of Kids from Three to Eighteen* (2003, with Theresa Foy DiGeronimo), which offers guidance based on a sound understanding of child development.

After teaching at Southern Illinois University (1968-1969), Wesleyan University (1969-1970), University of Dar es Salaam, Tanzania (1970-1971), Hunter College of the City University of New York (1976-1981), and Howard University (1981-1998), Ladner was Howard's vice president of academic affairs (1990-1994) and then was the first woman president of Howard University (1994-1995). She was also a senior fellow at the Brookings Institution until chronic fibromyalgia forced her into retirement in 2003. Among Ladner's numerous awards are doctorates of humane letters from Howard University and from Tougaloo College (from which she earned her B.A. in sociology, 1964), and the Distinguished Alumni award from Washington University (from which she earned her M.A. in 1966 and her Ph.D. in 1968). In addition to writing numerous scholarly articles, she has been a guest editor for the *Western Sociological Review* and has participated in peer review for several publishers, including Cambridge University Press, Greenwood Press, Simon & Schuster, and University of California Press. She has also been invited as a social commentator on the CBS *Evening News*, NBC *Evening News*, CBS *Sunday Morning*, ABC's *Nightline*, and PBS's *Newshour*. She has served on numerous boards of directors and as a fellow of numerous prestigious institutions. Even in retirement, Ladner continues to write a blog, "The Ladner Report," at //theladnerreportblog.blogspot.com/, and she does abstract painting.

REFERENCES: *33T. AANB. CAO-08. Wiki.* Bankole, Katherine Olumkemi, and Jennifer M. York, in *BB.* //library.msstate.edu/special_interest/Mississippi_African-American_Authors.asp. //theladnerreportblog.blogspot.com/. //www.olemiss.edu/mwp/dir/ladner_joyce/index.html, Joyce A. Ladner. //www.thehistorymakers.com/biography/biography.asp?bioindex=445&category=educationMakers. Personal communication, 6/14/1999.

Lane (married name), Pinkie (née Gordon)
1/13/1923–

Poems; educator

Louisiana's first African-American poet laureate, Lane has written several noteworthy poetry collections, including *Wind Thoughts* (1972), her first collection; *The Mystic Female* (1978), nominated for the Pulitzer Prize; *I Never Scream: New and Selected Poems* (1985), published by Lotus Press; and *Girl at the Window* (1991) and *Elegy for Etheridge* (2000), both published by Louisiana State University Press. In addition, she edited *Discourses on Poetry* (1972) and the third volume of *Poems by Blacks* (1973), both of which were published by South & West, which also published her first two poetry collections. Lane's poetry has also been published in numerous anthologies and literary journals. In 2005, she recalled that poet **Gwendolyn Brooks** had nominated Lane for a Nobel Prize for Literature. Though Lane taught English and world literature at Southern University (in Baton Rouge, Louisiana; first home of *Callaloo* literary journal) from 1959 until 1986, she was invited to archive her papers at Louisiana State University, and she accepted the invitation; some of her writings are also kept in the James Weldon Johnson Memorial Collection at Yale University.

In 1948, Pinkie Gordon married Ulysses Lane, both schoolteachers at the time, and the twosome later had a son, Gordon. After Lane's husband died (1970), she alone raised her son (b. 1963), who has since given her two much-loved granddaughters, Jessica Ulelia and Simone Rose (after "Pinkie").

REFERENCES: *BAWPP. CAO-01.* Craig, Marilyn B., *AAP-55-85.* Lowe, John, in *COCAAL* and *OCAAL.* _____. "'Pulling in the natural environment': An Interview with Pinkie Gordon Lane." *African American Review.* 39.1-2 (Spring-Summer 2005), p. 17. From *Literature Resource Center.* Martin, Shelley, in *GEAAL.* //www.newsreel.org/guides/furious.htm.

Langston, John Mercer
12/14/1829–11/15/1897
Autobiography/memoir, spoken word—lectures, oratory; attorney, abolitionist, politician, civil servant, educator, administrator

The son of Ralph Quarles, a European-American planter, and Lucy Langston, the African-American and Native-American slave of the planter, Virginia law dictated that John Mercer Langston was born a slave. On his death, Ralph manumitted his children with Lucy and provided for their education in his will. John was just five years old when he and his brothers were orphaned and freed, then forced to leave Virginia because the state law dictated that freed slaves must leave the state or risk re-enslavement. All of the Langston brothers moved to Oberlin, Ohio, where they were farmed out to family friends. In Ohio, a free state, the Langstons were educated. At age 14, John entered Oberlin College and earned a bachelor's degree and a master's degree a few years later (1849). He had wanted to study law, but no law schools would admit him because of his race. As an alternative, he returned to Oberlin and studied theology, earning another degree (1853). Meanwhile, he found an attorney, Philemon Bliss of Elyria, Ohio, who was willing to train and tutor him in the practice of the law. A year later, John became the first African American admitted to the Ohio bar, and he married Caroline M. Wall.

Langston was also a champion of civil rights and civil liberties. An active abolitionist, he organized antislavery societies and helped runaway slaves. In 1855, the small town of Brownhelm elected him to the office of town clerk, thereby probably making him the first African American to hold an elective office in America. During the Civil War, Langston recruited regiments of United States Colored Troops, as the chief recruiter of the 5th Ohio and a major recruiter for the legendary 54th and 55th Massachusetts regiments. He was also being considered for an officer's commission when the war ended. After the war, he continued to fight for civil rights,

cofounding the African-American voting-rights organization-the National Equal Rights League-over which he presided for a time.

Langston was also named an educational inspector general for the Freedmen's Bureau, trying to ensure educational opportunities for former slaves throughout the South, as well as helping to organize the National Negro Labor Union. Back home in Oberlin, he became president of the Oberlin Board of Education (1867-1868) and worked hard for the education of African Americans in Ohio, organizing schools and recruiting teachers.

In 1869, Langston left Ohio for Washington, D.C., to become a professor and dean of the Howard Law School (1869-1872), then acting president of the law college (1872). Under his administration the Howard Law School admitted and graduated the first African-American woman lawyer in the United States, Charlotte E. Ray. About that time, President Ulysses S. Grant named him to the Washington, D.C., Board of Health, over which he was elected secretary in 1875. The next president, Rutherford B. Hayes, named him U.S. Minister to Haiti and chargé d'affaires to San Domingo (1877-1885). He had left diplomacy to resume his law practice, when he was appointed the first president of Virginia Normal and Collegiate Institute (now Virginia State University) in Petersburg (1885-1888). He left that post when he was elected to the U.S. House of Representatives from his native state of Virginia. The highly contested election finally seated him in 1890, 6 months before the term ended. He lost his reelection bid but remains the first African American elected to Congress from Virginia, and he remained the only one for a century.

In his later years, Langston published a collection of his speeches, *Freedom and Citizenship* (1882), which reveals his powerful oratory in the best of African-American **oral tradition**. He also wrote his autobiography, *From the Virginia Plantation to the National Capitol* (1894), oddly doing so in the third person. In Ohio, the John Mercer Langston Bar Association in Columbus and the Langston Middle School in Oberlin are both named for him. In Virginia, the former John Mercer Langston High School in Danville was named for him. A branch of the Langstons moved to Oklahoma, where Langston University is named in his honor. Perhaps most importantly, however, his great-nephew was named **James Mercer Langston Hughes**.

REFERENCES: *AANB. B. Wiki.* Eiselein, Gregory, in *COCAAL.* //womenslegalhistory.stanford.edu/papers/RayC-Osborne01.pdf.

FURTHER READING: Gardner, Eric, in *GEAAL.*

Larsen, Nella (née Nellie Walker)
4/13/1891–3/30/1964
Novels, short stories; library worker, nurse

Nellie Walker's African-West Indian father died when she was just two years old. Soon after, her Danish-American mother remarried and had another child. Dark-skinned Nella felt like an outsider in her all-white, Danish-American family. Raised outside the African-American community, Nella also felt alienated from African Americans. Rather than being biracial, she felt nonracial—neither white nor black.

An accomplished nursing supervisor, Nella married Elmer Imes, an African-American research physicist. The couple made a home in the intellectual world of Harlem, becoming friends with Nina and **W. E. B. Du Bois**, siblings Arthur and **Jessie Fauset**, and other literary luminaries of Harlem. In 1921, Nella quit nursing to work for the New York Public Library, and she began writing (publishing her first two stories in 1926). As the **Harlem Renaissance** blossomed, so did her writing. Eventually, she left the library, finishing her novels *Quicksand* (1928) and *Passing* (1929) in rapid succession.

Quicksand's protagonist Helga—an urban, middle-class, well-educated mulatto—struggles with her racial identity. When her all-white family rejects her for her dark skin, she goes South to teach in an all-black school. There, too, she feels alien. After seeking an identity and a sense of belonging in various locales, she marries a Southern preacher and submerges her identity in mothering their four children. Just when she seems ready to leave them, to forge her own identity, she discovers she is pregnant with a fifth child. The novel ends without revealing how she responds to this circumstance. Like other critics, W. E. B. Du Bois praised *Quicksand* as "the best fiction that Negro America has produced since the heyday of **[Charles] Chesnutt**."

Du Bois also praised her *Passing,* calling it "one of the finest novels of the year." *Passing's* protagonist Clare easily "passes" in white society, not even telling her white husband of her black ancestry. By chance, she runs into an old acquaintance, Irene, a middle-class African American who knows Clare's heritage. Irene has her own problems, however, as she fears that her husband will be attracted to her light-skinned friend. Neither woman is entirely satisfied with who she is.

Larsen's novels immediately earned her prominence as a visionary novelist, illuminating the inner psyche of a bicultural, urban woman of her time. Just as her literary star was ascending, however, she was dragged into a nasty scandal (falsely accusing her of plagiarism), followed by a humiliatingly sensationalized divorce. Afterward, Nella left for Europe on a Guggenheim fellowship (the first African-American woman to win one).

Nella Larsen

In Europe, she started two new novels, but her publisher rejected both of them—and a third novel, too. Larsen then withdrew entirely from the Harlem literary scene, eventually returning to nursing. After her death, her two published novels and her short stories have been republished several times.

REFERENCES: *1TESK. AA:PoP. BAAW. BF:2000. EB-98. EBLG. MAAL. NAAAL. OC20LE. RLWWJ. RT.* Davis, Thadious M., in *COCAAL* and in *OCAAL*. Larson, Charles R., in *OCWW.*

FURTHER READING: *B. CAO-02. MWEL. W. Wiki.* Davis, Thadious M., in *AAWHR-40.* Gloster, Hugh M. 1948. "Fiction of the Negro Renascence: Nella Larsen." *Negro Voices in American Fiction.* Chapel Hill: University of North Carolina Press. Rpt. in *Twentieth-Century Literary Criticism* (Vol. 200, pp. 141-146). Detroit: Gale. From *Literature Resource Center.* Hayes, Melissa Hamilton, in *GEAAL.* McKoy, Sheila Smith, in *RGAL-3.* McLendon, Jacquelyn Y., in *AAW-1991. FW.* Smith, Whitney Womack, in *AW:ACLB-09.* Wainwright, Mary Katherine, in *BB.*

Latifah, Queen (née Dana Elaine Owens)
3/18/1970–

Rap lyrics, autobiography/memoir; performer, actor, business owner

Rita Owens was 18 years old and already the mother of Lance Owens, Jr., when she gave birth to Dana. When Dana was about 8 years old, her parents' troubled marriage fell apart (although she and her brother, who since died in 1992, continued to keep in touch with her father); she was given the name Latifah (meaning "delicate" and "sensitive" in Arabic) by a Muslim cousin; she was identified as intellectually gifted; and she started attending Saint Anne's parochial school. Rita Owens rose to the challenges posed by these changes, working one full-time job and one part-time job to pay for Latifah's schooling. While raising her children and working two jobs, Rita also managed to complete a two-year community-college program. When Latifah was 10 years old, Rita started working as an art teacher at Irvington High School—which Latifah later attended.

During high school, Latifah started singing with a rap group, Ladies Fresh, and through contacts with a local D.J., she made a demo, which ended up in the hands of Tommy Boy Music. In 1988, Tommy Boy released Latifah's first single, "Wrath of My Madness" and "Princess of the Posse," and her second single, "Dance for Me" and "Inside Out." The following year was even more eventful: She made her first video ("Dance for Me"), her first European tour, her first appearance at the Apollo, and her first rap album, *All Hail the Queen*. Her subsequent albums include *Latifah's Had It Up 2 Here, How Do I Love Thee*, and *Nature of a Sista'* (all in 1991); *Black Reign* (1993); *Order in the Court2* (1998); and her compilation *She's a Queen: A Collection of Hits* (2002). In 1993, Latifah was producing her own records and was soon signing other rap artists to produce their records. In 1994, she and Salt-N-Pepa were the only two rappers to receive a Grammy. Latifah's raps address womanist issues, as well as issues of poverty, homelessness, and segregation; a victim of carjacking herself, she doesn't glorify criminal violence. More recently, Latifah has produced *The Dana Owens Album* (2004, nominated for a Best Jazz Vocal Album Grammy) and *Trav'lin' Light* (2007, nominated for a Best Traditional Pop Vocal Album Grammy), which showcase her singing skills instead of her rap lyrics.

Latifah has also branched into acting. Her television roles include those on *The Fresh Prince of Bel-Air* (1991), *Living Single* (1993), and *Spin City* (2001), as well as the TV movie *Life Support* (2007), which won Screen Actors Guild, Golden Globe, and NAACP Image Awards, as well as an Emmy nomination. She also hosted her own talk show from 1999 through 2001. Her numerous film roles started with *Jungle Fever* (1991) and include her Os-car-nominated role in *Chicago* (2002), her starring role in *Last Holiday* (2006), her much-acclaimed role in *Hairspray* (2007), and her role as Nina Brewster in *Mad Money* (2008); she has other films currently in production. Latifah also lent her voice to the animated feature-length movie *Ice Age: The Meltdown* (2006). For her many roles, she has been nominated for an Academy Award (Oscar), two Golden Globe Awards, a Black Movie Award, and an Emmy Award—not bad for a second career. She also earned an NAACP Image Award in 2004, for her role in *Bringing Down the House*, the first film produced by her company Flavor Unit Entertainment. In addition to her music and her movies, Latifah has published her memoir, *Ladies First: Revelations from a Strong Woman* (1999); authored a story for a screenplay, *The Cookout* (2004, with Shakim Compere); and written a children's book, *Queen of the Scene* (2006, illustrated by Frank Morrison).

REFERENCES: *AANB. CAO-08. D. F. W2B. Wiki.* Buchanan, Jason, *All Movie Guide*, in *Act*. Ferran, Christine, and Robert L. Johns, in *BB*. Huey, Steve, *All Music Guide*, in *A*. Johns, Robert L., in *PBW*. //aalbc.com/authors/queen_latifah.htm. //www.Amazon.com, 7/1999.

FURTHER READING: *TAWH*.

Latimer, Catherine A. (née Allen)
c.1895–9/1948

Bibliography

Soon after the New York Public Library (NYPL) hired Latimer—the first African-American professional librarian hired by the NYPL—she began enthusiastically studying the story of African Americans. At the NYPL Harlem branch library (where she worked 1920-1946), she started collecting clippings on African-American history while carrying out her duties. By the time the library became the home of the **Schomburg** Collection (in 1926, later named the Schomburg Center for Research in Black Culture), she was the reference librarian in charge of African-American literature and history. In "Where Can I Get Material on the Negro?" an article Latimer wrote for **Crisis** magazine (June, 1934), she described the collection as comprising about 7,000 books, 500 prints and portrait engravings, and 800 "manuscripts, letters, poems, plays, and sermons of writers and prominent citizens." Latimer wrote numerous other articles on bibliography for various publications, and she wrote *The Negro: A Selected Bibliography* (1943). Latimer also guided her protégé Ernest D. Kaiser in continuing to expand and index the clipping collection. He did so, continuing the clippings file until 1985, when the index was first marketed as the *Ernest D. Kaiser Index to Black Resources*.

REFERENCES: *BAAW*. Gubert, Betty K., in *BWA:AHE*.

Latimer, Lewis Howard
9/4/1848–12/11/1928
Nonfiction—electricity textbook; inventor

A newspaper peddler in his youth, Latimer made numerous inventions in various fields (e.g., an improvement for bathroom facilities on a train), but his specialty was electric lighting. Latimer's textbook *Incandescent Electric Lighting* (1896) was a key reference for understanding Edison's developments in the field.

REFERENCES: Bennett, Eric, in *EA-99*.

FURTHER READING: *AANB. B. BAWPP. Wiki.* Hayden, Robert C. "Black Inventors in the Age of Segregation: Granville T. Woods, Lewis H. Latimer, and Shelby J. Davidson." *The Journal of African American History.* 89.3 (Summer 2004) p. 271. From *Literature Resource Center.* Martin, Jonathan, in *BB*.

LaValle, Victor
2/3/1972–
Novel, short stories; educator

After earning his B.A. from Cornell University and his M.F.A. from Columbia University, LaValle has been a teacher at the Bank Street School (with Writers in the Schools) and at the Bronx Council for the Arts, an assistant professor at Columbia University in New York, and the distinguished visiting writer at Mills College in California. Before publishing his first book, LaValle was named a fellow at the Fine Arts Work Center in Provincetown, Massachusetts (1998). A year later, he published his collection *Slapboxing with Jesus: Stories* (1999), which earned him a PEN/Open Book Award and the Key to Jamaica, in Southeastern Queens, New York. The book's 11 interlinking stories are all set in New York during the time of LaValle's childhood and youth, and the characters are mostly African-American and Hispanic-American males. The following year, LaValle was an invited fellow at the Bread Loaf Writer's Conference in Middlebury Vermont (2000).

Two years later, LaValle published *The Ecstatic: A Novel* (2002), for which he earned nominations for a Hurston-Wright Legacy Award and a PEN/Faulkner Award (both 2003). In it, LaValle's protagonist, morbidly obese Anthony James, introduced in his previous book, may be showing the beginning signs of schizophrenia. For his literary achievements, he won the lucrative Whiting Writers' Award for fiction (2004). Two years later, he was awarded the United States Artists Ford Fellowship (2006). Three years later, his second novel, *Big Machine: A Novel* (2009), was available for preorder when this dictionary went to press. In addition to his books, LaValle has written essays and book reviews for periodicals (*GQ, Essence Magazine, The Fader, The Washington Post,* et al.), and his short fiction has appeared in anthologies (e.g., *Gumbo*).

REFERENCES: *CAO-05. Wiki.* [author interview in] Jacobe, Monica F., in *GEAAL*. //en.wikipedia.org/wiki/Whiting_Prize. //www.authorsontheweb.com/features/0302-bhm/bhm-authors.asp. //www.hobartpulp.com/website/october/NarrativeVoice.pdf. //www.worldcat.org/search?q=lavalle%2C+victor&qt=results_page. Amazon.com.

Lawrence-Lightfoot, Sara
8/22/1944–
Nonfiction

The daughter of sociology professor Charles Radford Lawrence and child psychiatrist Margaret Morgan Lawrence, Sara earned her B.A. (1962-1966) from Pennsylvania's Swarthmore College, studied child development and early childhood education at New York's prestigious Bank Street College of Education (1966-1967), and earned her Ed.D. (1968-1972) in the sociology of education from Massachusetts's Harvard University. Meanwhile, she conducted research on the battered-child syndrome at Harlem Hospital, studied cognitive development from birth to age 2 years at the Albert Einstein School of Medicine, and researched and evaluated social studies curriculum for the Educational Development Center in Cambridge, Massachusetts. Lawrence-Lightfoot, the divorced mother of Tolani and Martin, has spent her adult life concerned about the well-being and education of all children.

She has since taught at the Harvard Graduate School of Education (starting in 1972), only the second African-American woman to become a permanent Harvard faculty member. She rose through the academic ranks from assistant professor (1972-1976) to faculty fellow at Radcliffe (1976-1978) to associate professor (1976-1980) to professor (1980-1998). In 1998, she became the Emily Hargroves Fisher Professor of Education, and upon her retirement, she will become the first African-American woman in Harvard's history to have an endowed professorship named in her honor. Her alma mater, Swarthmore, already created an endowed professorship named in her honor. She also enjoyed a fellowship (1983-1984) at the Center for Advanced Study in the Behavioral Sciences in Stanford, California.

In addition to numerous scholarly articles, Lawrence-Lightfoot has written numerous book-length works. Before she earned her doctorate, as Sara Lawrence, she wrote *A Critical Review of Ability Grouping* (1969). As Sara Lawrence-Lightfoot, she wrote her doctoral dissertation, *An Ethnographic Study of the Status Structure of the Classroom* (1972). Since then, she has written *Worlds Apart: Relationships between Families and Schools* (1978), *Beyond Bias: Perspectives on Classrooms* (1979, with Jean V. Carew), *The Good High School: Portraits of Character and Culture* (1983), her biography of her mother in *Balm in Gilead: Journey of a Healer*

(1988/1995), *I've Known Rivers: Lives of Loss and Liberation* (1995), *The Art and Science of Portraiture* (1997, with Jessica Hoffmann Davis), *Respect: An Exploration* (1999), *The Essential Conversation: What Parents and Teachers Can Learn from Each Other* (2003), and *The Third Chapter: Passion, Risk, and Adventure in the 25 Years after 50* (2009).

In addition to her writing, her teaching, and her research, Lawrence-Lightfoot has served on numerous professional committees and national boards. Lawrence-Lightfoot's awards include numerous book awards, a prestigious MacArthur Foundation fellowship (1984-1989), a Candace Award from the National Coalition of 100 Black Women (1990), a Radcliffe College Graduate Society Medal (1991), Harvard's George Ledlie Prize (1993), a Meridian Award from the Indianapolis Children's Museum (1995), a Spencer Senior Scholar Award (1995), a Crossing the River Jordan Award from the Public Education Network (2003), a Ferguson Award for Service to Children and Families from National Louis University (2004), and a Margaret Mead Award from the American Academy of Political and Social Science (2008). In addition, she has received more than two dozen honorary doctorates from numerous U.S. and Canadian colleges. She was also featured in the Bill Moyers *World of Ideas* specials (1989) and the PBS documentary *African American Lives* (2006).

REFERENCES: *CAO-05. Wiki.* Newman, Richard. "Sara Lawrence-Lightfoot: 'To Chart Different Journeys'" (*PW* Interview). *Publishers Weekly 241.36* (Sept. 5, 1994) p. 80. From *Literature Resource Center.* Sehgal, Parul. "PW Talks with Sarah Lawrence-Lightfoot: The Golden Age." *Publishers Weekly. 255.48* (Dec. 1, 2008) p. 38. From *Literature Resource Center.* Sussman, Alison Carb, in *BB.* //gseweb.harvard.edu/faculty_research/profiles/awards.shtml?vperson_id=440#awards. //gseweb.harvard.edu/faculty_research/profiles/profile.shtml?vperson_id=440. //gseweb.harvard.edu/faculty_research/profiles/publications.shtml?vperson_id=440#publications. //www.gse.harvard.edu/faculty_research/profiles/cv/sara_lawrence-lightfoot.pdf. //www.pbs.org/moyers/journal/05082009/transcript3.html. Amazon.com.

Lee, Andrea
1953–
Autobiography/memoir, novel, short stories; journalist

A former staff writer for the *New Yorker*, Lee has written for numerous periodicals (e.g., *The New York Times Magazine, The New York Times Book Review, Time, Vogue*), and her work has appeared in several anthologies. Lee's own books include her National Book Award-nominated travel memoir *Russian Journal* (1981/2006), based on her 1978-1979 experiences in Russia; her semiautobiographical novel *Sarah Phillips* (1984/1993), containing several stories originally appearing in the *New Yorker; Interesting Women: Stories* (2002), about her experiences as an expatriate in Europe; and *Lost Hearts in It-* aly: *A Novel* (2006), about an affluent African-American wife and mother who has an adulterous relationship with a wealthy Italian scoundrel. Though critically acclaimed, she hasn't garnered the popular sales her critics say she deserves. One reason may be that she writes about her own authentic experiences as an African-American woman who was raised in an upper-class family and who continues to enjoy a more cosmopolitan lifestyle than most Americans of any racial heritage. She, her husband, and her two children live in Torino, Italy.

REFERENCES: *CAO-03. Wiki.* Gallego, Mar, in *AANB.* LaFrance, Michelle, in *GEAAL.* Smith, Valerie, in *COCAAL* and in *OCAAL.*

Lee, Barbara
7/16/1946–
Autobiography/memoir, legislation, spoken word—oratory; congresswoman, peace and justice activist

A graduate of Mills College (1973), Lee earned an M.A. in social work from the University of California at Berkeley (1975), then joined the staff of California's Ninth District U.S. congressional Representative Ron Dellums (1975), eventually becoming his chief of staff. With his encouragement, she ran for election to the California state assembly, which she won (1990-1996). In 1996, she ran for and won election to the California state senate (1996-1998). When Dellums retired from the U.S. Congress, he endorsed her as his replacement, and she won the election. While in Congress, she was the sole member to vote against the bombing of Yugoslavia in 1999, then she won her 2000 bid for reelection by a margin of 85% to 9%. Lee went on to be the sole member of Congress—in either chamber—to vote against authorizing President George Bush's use of military force following the September 11, 2001 attacks. Ranked the sixth-most-liberal member of the House by the *National Journal*, she was rated at 97% by a progressive organization and 4% by a conservative one.

While in Congress, Lee has authored bills such as the **"Shirley A. Chisholm** United States-Caribbean Educational Exchange Act, H.R. 176," intended to enhance foreign relations by improving educational opportunities in Caribbean nations; and the "Benign Brain Tumor Cancer Registries Amendment Act," intended to enhance data collection on benign brain tumors. In addition, she has authored her autobiography, *Renegade for Peace and Justice: Congresswoman Barbara Lee Speaks for Me* (2008). Lee also offers eloquent oratory when championing the rights of the oppressed and when advocating peace.

REFERENCES: *Wiki.* Manheim, James M., in *BB.* //barbaraleespeaksforme.org/. //barbaraleespeaksforme.org/meet-barbara/. //barbaraleespeaksforme.org/meet-barbara/accomplishments.html. //barbaralee

Lee, Jarena
2/11/1783–c.1850
Autobiography/memoir, spoken word—sermons; itinerant preacher

A freeborn woman, Jarena Lee felt called to the Christian faith at about age 21 (c. 1804) and felt called to preach about 7 years later (c. 1811). When she asked **Richard Allen**, cofounder of the African Methodist Episcopal Church and her pastor at Philadelphia's Mother Bethel Church, he reminded her of the church's ban on women preachers. She soon married Joseph Lee, with whom she had two children, and she set aside her call to preach. When Joseph Lee died (1818), Jarena Lee again pressed Allen for permission to preach. At this point, Allen was the church's bishop, and he permitted Lee to hold prayer meetings in her home for a while. Soon after, the minister who was scheduled to preach was not available, and Lee was allowed to preach at the last minute. Allen heard her sermon, recognized her call for the ministry, and allowed her to be ordained as a preacher, thereby becoming the first African-American woman whom an established church officially recognized as a preacher.

From then on, Lee preached all around the North, traveling as far west as Ohio. Decades later, she wrote an account of her early experiences and her life as an itinerant preacher, *The Life and Religious Experiences of Jarena Lee, a Coloured Lady, Giving an Account of Her Call to Preach the Gospel* (1836), which she later expanded for an updated edition (*The Religious Experience and Journal of Mrs. Jarena Lee*, 1849). That account was reprinted in *Sisters of the Spirit: Three Black Women's Autobiographies of the Nineteenth Century* (1986, William L. Andrews, Ed.). With her initial autobiographical account, Lee became the first African-American woman to publish a book-length account of her own life. The book comprises four sections: her early life, her call to preach, her marriage, and "The Subject of My Call to Preach Renewed."

REFERENCES: *AANB. W.* Bolden, **Tonya**, in //digital.nypl.org/schomburg/writers_aa19/bio2.html. LaPrade, Candis, in *COCAAL.*

FURTHER READING: *EAAWW.* Ralston, Pamela, in *GEAAL.*

Lee, Spike (né Shelton Jackson Lee)
3/20/1957–
Scripts, screenplays, autobiography/memoir; director, producer, business owner, business executive

After Lee graduated from his father and grandfather's alma mater, Morehouse College in Atlanta (1979), he interned at Columbia Pictures for the summer, then started at New York University's Institute of Film and Television, at which he earned his M.A. (1982). The film he made for his master's degree was *Joe's Bed-Stuy Barbershop: We Cut Heads,* which was awarded the Student Academy Award for best director by the Academy of Motion Picture Arts and Sciences (i.e., a student Oscar). After a false start with a film about a bicycle messenger, Lee's next film was *She's Gotta Have It* (1986), which he produced in just 12 days, for $175,000—not much money for a movie. The film grossed more than $7 million and won several awards, most notably the Prix de Jeunesse for the best new film by a newcomer at the Cannes Film Festival.

Columbia Pictures produced his next film, *School Daze* (1988), about his undergraduate experiences and exposing the caste system among lighter- versus darker-skinned blacks. Grossing $15 million, *School Daze* paved the way for Lee's critically acclaimed blockbuster, *Do the Right Thing* (1989), produced by Universal Studios for $6.5 million. Set in the Bedford-Stuyvesant borough of Brooklyn, it highlighted the tensions between Italian Americans (e.g., actor Danny Aiello) and African Americans (featuring actors **Ossie Davis** and **Ruby Dee**) struggling to make a living. Among its many awards and nominations was an Oscar nomination for best original screenplay; the film grossed $28 million. This film, like many others of his, sparked great controversy. Lee views his writing this way, "All I want to do is tell a story. When writing a script I'm not saying, 'Uh-Oh, I'd better leave that out because I might get into trouble.' I don't operate like that" (quoted in *BH2C*, p. 442).

Lee's subsequent films have included *Mo' Better Blues* (1990), about a musician involved with two women; *Jungle Fever* (1991), about an interracial sexual relationship; **Malcolm X** (1992), a three-hours-plus film about the black-nationalist leader; *Crooklyn* (1994), about growing up in Brooklyn; *Clockers* (1995), about a murder investigation involving the relationship between two brothers, one of whom was a low-level worker in the illegal drug trade; *Get on the Bus* (1996), about a journey to the Million Man March; *He Got Game* (1998), about a convict's relationship with his son, a promising basketball player; *Summer of Sam* (1999), about the terror (white) New Yorkers felt when a (white) serial killer was stalking the city; *Bamboozled* (2000), a satire of the television industry; *She Hate Me* (2004), a humorous rant; *Inside Man* (2006), a high-gloss heist thriller; and *Miracle at St. Anna* (2008, adapted from a James McBride novel), an atypical murder mystery in which viewers know right away who committed the 1983 crime but must probe much more deeply to discover the killer's motivation, which dates back to World War II, in German-occupied Tuscany. Lee has not only directed, but also acted (usually in minor roles) in his films, along with such noteworthy actors as

Ossie Davis, Ruby Dee, **Laurence Fishburne**, and Denzel Washington. In addition to his film-production company, Forty Acres and a Mule, which produces not only Lee's films, but also those by other filmmakers, Lee has numerous other business and advertising ventures.

Other than *Summer of Sam*, Lee's films have been rooted in the African-American community. As he noted in a 1991 interview, "I try to show African-American culture on screen. Every group, every culture and ethnic group needs to see itself on screen. What black filmmakers can do is show our culture on screen the same way Fellini's done for Italians and Kurosawa's done for the Japanese. . . . I don't think my films are going to get rid of racism or prejudice. I think the best thing my films can do is provoke discussion" (quoted in "He's Gotta Have It," 1991/1998). Others have pointed out that his films have universal appeal precisely because he so deeply probes the psyches of particular individuals.

Lee also produced the documentary *Four Young Girls* (1997), about the four Sunday-school girls whose lives were blown to smithereens in their Birmingham church in 1963; the film garnered an Oscar nomination for best documentary (1999). In 2002, he created and produced the laudatory documentary *Jim Brown: All American* (2002), about the legendary football player. His *When the Levees Broke: A Requiem in Four Acts* (2006) documents the devastation wrought by governmental neglect of vital infrastructure, nature's Hurricane Katrina, and further governmental negligence and ineptitude. The HBO documentary won two Emmys in 2007: Exceptional Merit in Nonfiction Filmmaking and Outstanding Directing for Nonfiction Programming. Lee has written the scripts for most of his films; the exceptions are *Crooklyn*, written with his sister Joie and his brother Cinqué; *Clockers*, written with Richard Price, adapting Price's novel; *Get on the Bus*, written by Reggie Rock Bythewood; *Girl 6*, written by **Suzan-Lori Parks**; and *25th Hour* (2002), written by David Benioft, based on his novel. His *Malcolm X* was also written with Arnold Perl, based both on work by James Baldwin and Alex Haley's *Autobiography of Malcolm X*. (Joie, née Joy Lee, has also written numerous television scripts, such as for Nickelodeon and for the British Broadcasting Company.)

Lee has written several companion books for his films: *Spike Lee's Gotta Have It: Guerrilla Filmmaking* (1987, with photographs by his brother David), *Uplift the Race: The Construction of School Daze* (1988, with Lisa Jones), *Do the Right Thing: The New Spike Lee Joint* (1989, with Lisa Jones), *Mo' Better Blues* (1990, with Lisa Jones), *Five for Five: The Films of Spike Lee* (1991), *By Any Means Necessary: The Trials and Tribulations of Making Malcolm X* (1992, with Ralph Wiley), *The X Factor* (1992). He also wrote *Best Seat in the House: A Basketball Memoir* (1997, with Ralph Wiley), about his fanatical love of the New

York Knicks basketball team. He has since written a broader memoir, *Spike Lee: That's My Story and I'm Sticking to It* (2005). Interviews of him were collected in *Spike Lee: Interviews* (2002, edited by Cynthia Fuchs).

In 1993, Lee married attorney and children's television producer Tonya Linnette Lewis, with whom he has a daughter (Satchel Lewis Lee, born in 1994) and a son (Jackson Lee, born in 1997). With Tonya, Spike wrote two lively picture books for young children: *Please, Baby, Please* (2002) and *Please, Puppy, Please* (2005). With Crystal McCrary Anthony, Tonya wrote the novel *Gotham Diaries* (2004), set in New York City.

REFERENCES: *AANB. B. BCE. CAO-08. CE. CLCS. EBLG. G-97. PGAA. QB. W2B. Wiki.* Ankeny, Jason, *All Movie Guide,* in *Dir.* Armstrong, Stephen. "Rebel without a Pause: Once Hollywood's Enfant Terrible, Spike Lee Is Now Directing Blockbusters and TV Shows. But, He Tells Stephen Armstrong, He Is Still Fighting for Black Cinema." *New Statesman* (1996). 136.4860 (Sept. 3, 2007) p. 32. From *Literature Resource Center.* Ashwill, Gary, in *COCAAL* and *OCAAL.* Crowdus, Gary, and Dan Georgakas. "Thinking about the Power of Images: An Interview with Spike Lee. *Cineaste.* 26.2 (Spring 2001) p. 4. From *Literature Resource Center.* Crowdus, Gary, Spike Lee, and Dan Georgakas. "Our Film Is Only a Starting Point: An Interview with Spike Lee." *Cineaste* 19.4 (1993) pp. 20-24. Rpt. in Deborah A. Schmitt (Ed.) (1998), *Contemporary Literary Criticism* (Vol. 105). Detroit: Gale Research. From *Literature Resource Center.* Goldstein, Nina, and Rebecca Parks, in *BB.* Knight, Gladys L., in *GEAAL.* Lee, Spike, and Janice Mosier Richolson. "He's Gotta Have It: An Interview with Spike Lee." *Cineaste* 18.4 (1991): pp. 12-15. Rpt. in Deborah A. Schmitt (Ed.) (1998), *Contemporary Literary Criticism* (Vol. 105). Detroit: Gale Research. From *Literature Resource Center.* Massood, Paula J. "The Quintessential New Yorker and Global Citizen: An Interview with Spike Lee." *Cineaste.* 28.3 (Summer 2003) p. 4. From *Literature Resource Center.* Sklar, Robert, in *WB-99.* Tuttle, Kate, in *EA-99.* Wise, Flossie E., in *BH2C.* //www.memorabl equotations.com/African-American.htmm. *See also* "Tonya Lewis Lee," *CAO-05.* //www.book-remarks.com/Reading_List.htm. //www.childrenslit.com/childrenslit/th_af_cskawards.html. //www.library.ci.corpus-christi.tx.us/readingroomafrauthos.htm. *See also* "Joie Susannah Lee," *CAO-07.*

Legends and Myths *See* Folktales *See also* Oral Tradition; Trickster Tales

---

Lester, Julius
1/27/1939–

Novels, juvenile fiction, short stories, opinion and commentary, nonfiction [folk songs, history], folktales, poems, autobiography, black history; educator, journalist, musician

The son of a Methodist minister, Woodie Daniel Lester, and his wife, Julia B. Smith Lester, Julius Lester converted to Judaism in 1982 (at age 43). Born in St. Louis, Missouri, he grew up in the Midwest (Kansas City, Kansas) and in the segregated South (Nashville, Tennessee). In addition to a semester at San Diego State College, he earned his B.A. from Fisk University (1960). After graduating, Lester worked as an organizer for the Student Nonviolent Coordinating Committee (SNCC), primarily in Mississippi, but he also traveled to Cuba (with **Stokely Carmichael**), North Vietnam, and Korea. Lester also pursued a career as a folksinger and musician, and he has recorded two albums of original songs. He wrote a newspaper column, he hosted both television and radio programs, and he has written more than 200 essays and reviews published in periodicals such as *Boston Globe, Los Angeles Times Book Review, New Republic, The New York Times Book Review,* and *Village Voice.*

In 1971, Lester earned his M.A. from the University of Massachusetts, Amherst, which then hired him as a professor (until he retired in 2003); he has also been writer-in-residence at Vanderbilt University (Nashville, TN, 1985) and has lectured or presented papers at more than 100 colleges and universities. Lester has written quite a few pieces for adults, including his double-novella *Two Love Stories* (1972) and his novels *Do Lord Remember Me* (1985/2004), inspired by the life of his minister father, and *And All Our Wounds Forgiven* (1994), centered in the civil-rights movement. He has edited the collection *The Seventh Son: The Thought & Writings of* **W. E. B. Du Bois** (1971), and he has coauthored some folksong books, *We Shall Overcome! Songs of the Southern Freedom Movement* (1963, with Guy Carawan, Candie Carawan, Ethel Raim, and Joseph Byrd) and *The 12-String Guitar as Played by Leadbelly: An Instructional Manual* (1965, with folksinger Pete Seeger). He has also authored several books of political writings, including *The Angry Children of* **Malcolm X** (1966) and *Look Out, Whitey! Black Power's Gon' Get Your Mama!* (1968), his essay collection *Revolutionary Notes* (1969), and his collection of essays on race, religion, and education, *Falling Pieces of the Broken Sky* (1990), and *Search for the New Land: History as Subjective Experience* (1969).

Despite these impressive credits, Lester is probably best known for the works he has written for young adults and for children, primarily works intended to instill pride in African-American history and cultural heritage. He has said, "Writing for children is a curious thing because you're writing for people who don't buy books. So what I have consistently done is write for both audiences, children and adults. I put things in my books for the enjoyment of the teacher, parent, or librarian who is reading to the child, and I also try to spark the child to ask, "oh, gee, what does this mean?"" ("The *Booklist* Interview," 1995). His first black-history book for juveniles, *To Be a Slave* (1968/2005), earned a 1969 Newbery Honor from the American Library Association, a Lewis Carroll Shelf Award (1970), and sold about half a million copies. It comprised six short stories that incorporated oral histo-

Julius Lester

ries from former slaves, collected by the Federal Writers' Project. Through their stories (and his text), Lester tells the history of slavery from revolutionary times to the end of the Civil War, from the Middle Passage journey (sailing from Africa to America) through enslavement on Southern plantations and slave revolts to Civil War and emancipation.

Lester's *The Long Journey Home: Stories from Black History* (1972) also won a Lewis Carroll Shelf Award and was nominated for a 1973 National Book Award. *Journey* presented six more stories, also interweaving slave narratives, about the post-Civil War Reconstruction era. These stories included accounts of a roaming blues singer ("Satan on My Track") who observes the plight of sharecroppers and of a formerly enslaved cowboy who ponders what he is doing as he rounds up (entraps) a herd of wild (free) mustangs. Lester's more recent nonfiction for young folks has included *Black Cowboy, Wild Horses: A True Story* (1998, illustrated by Jerry Pinkney), *From Slave Ship to Freedom Road* (1998, illustrated by Rod Brown), *The Blues Singers: Ten Who Rocked the World* (2001, illustrated by Lisa Cohen), and *Let's Talk about Race* (2004, illustrated by Karen Barbour).

Lester has also been captivated by traditional African-American **folktales**, so he has written numerous books based on this lore. Some of these tales originated on African soil, some emerged from the unique African-American experience, and all have been passed down through the generations via the **oral tradition**. In many of the folk stories in *Black Folktales* (1969/1994, illustrated by **Tom Feelings**) and in *The Knee-High Man and Other Tales* (1972), clever beasts and crafty people outwit those who would dominate them through force of greater size and might. In such stories as "People Who Could Fly" and "Stagolee," those who are oppressed escape from and resist their oppressors. *Knee-High* also won Lester a third Lewis Carroll Shelf Award. Several other books mingle Lester's appreciation of folktales and his warmly open feelings of religious faith, such as *What a Truly Cool World* (1997, illustrated by Joe Cepeda), *When the Beginning Began: Stories about God, the Creatures, and Us* (1999, illustrated by Emily Lisker), and *Why Heaven Is Far Away* (2002, illustrated by Joe Cepeda). For older readers, he wrote *The Autobiography of God: A Novel* (2004).

Perhaps the best-known folktales in America are the adventures of a wily rabbit and the mighty but foolish animals that he outwits. Lester has written numerous books about their adventures: *The Tales of Uncle Remus: The Adventures of Brer Rabbit* (1987); *More Tales of Uncle Remus: Further Adventures of Brer Rabbit, His Friends, Enemies, and Others* (1988); *Further Tales of Uncle Remus: The Misadventures of Brer Rabbit, Brer Fox, Brer Wolf, the Doodang, and Other Creatures* (1990); and *The Last Tales of Uncle Remus: As Told by Julius Lester* (1994), and collected as *Uncle Remus: The Complete Tales* (1999, illustrated by Jerry Pinkney). These books earned him two Parents' Choice Awards and a Reading Magic Award. In all these adventures, Lester celebrates African-American storytelling with vivid language, delectable humor, and delightful triumphs by the cunning rabbit. Lester has also written *How Many Spots Does a Leopard Have? and Other Tales* (1989), a collection of a dozen folktales from the African and the Jewish traditions; *The Man Who Knew Too Much: A Moral Tale from the Baile of Zambia* (1994); and *John Henry* (1994), the traditional American story of a hard-working man fighting for his survival against modern technology. *John Henry* garnered a *Boston Globe-Horn Book* Award, a Caldecott Honor, and an American Library Association Notable Book, which was also given to his *Sam and the Tigers: A New Telling of Little Black Sambo* (1996, illustrated by Jerry Pinkney).

As he noted, "We all live in and move back and forth between many worlds. . . . We all live in multiple cultures, and move back and forth between them and put on and take off identities and parts of identities as we go, and we do it pretty effortlessly" ("The *Booklist* Interview," 1995). Lester's other juvenile fiction draws on a wealth of world literature and lore as seen from his own distinctive perspective, as in *Othello: A Retelling* (1995), in which Desdemona and Iago are black; *Shining* (1997/2003, illustrated by John Clapp), in which an apparently mute

young girl teaches the value of listening; *Albidaro and the Mischievous Dream* (2000, illustrated by Jerry Pinkney), in which teddy bears invite children to do whatever they want, then the children encourage animals to do likewise, and bedlam ensues; *Pharaoh's Daughter: A Novel of Ancient Egypt* (2000/2009), Lester's view of the Moses story; *Ackamarackus: Julius Lester's Sumptuously Silly Fantastically Funny Fables* (2001, illustrated by Emilie Chollat), original stories imagined by Lester; and *The Old African* (2005, illustrated by Jerry Pinkney), a slave legend retold through magical realism.

Lester's 2006 Coretta Scott King Award winning *Day of Tears: A Novel in Dialogue* (2005) was inspired by an 1859 auction of 400 slaves, the largest in U.S. history. For older readers, his young-adult fiction includes the deeply psychological murder mystery *When Dad Killed Mom* (2001), as told by the orphaned sister and brother; a magical-realism novel inspired by Nat Turner's rebellion, *Time's Memory* (2006); the Greek-myth-based *Cupid: A Tale of Love and Desire* (2007); and *Guardian* (2008), about false accusations, moral courage, and a lynching in a Southern town. Lester has also written a collection of stories about romances among enslaved African Americans, *This Strange New Feeling* (1982; reissued as *This Strange New Feeling: Three Love Stories from Black History*, 2007). He has written a collection of poems, *Who I Am: Photopoems* (1974), illustrated with his photographs; his photographs have also appeared in numerous exhibits, including one at the Smithsonian Institution. He has also written three books recollecting his own life story—*All Is Well: An Autobiography* (1976), *Lovesong: Becoming a Jew* (1988), and *On Writing for Children and Other People* (2004). When asked why he writes, he said, "I write because there is something I want to know and the only way I can find out is to write about it" (from //members.authorsguild.net/juliuslester/events.htm).

Lester has been married three times (1962-1970, 1979-1993, 1995-present) and has five children: Jody Simone and Malcolm Coltrane (first marriage); Elena Milad (stepdaughter) and David Julius (second marriage); and Lian Amaris Brennan (stepdaughter, third marriage). He and his wife and two cats live in a small town in western Massachusetts. "Deep down we all want to see ourselves in the other person. Storytelling gets us past all the personal crap that we do to each other and gives us something to focus on, and for those moments, when we are involved in the story, we do have a sense of community and belonging to each other" ("The *Booklist* Interview," 1995).

REFERENCES: *AAL. AANB. BAWPP. CAO-08. EBLG. WB-99. Wiki.* Bloom, Karen R., in *COCAAL* and in *OCAAL*. Davis, Mary Virginia, Salem Press for EBSCO Publishing, July 2003, //0-web.ebscohost.com.dbpcosdcsgt.co.san-diego.ca.us/novelist/detail?vid=113&hid=7&sid=d408b38a-8f5e-4ec2-b75c-cf9c5b5097d7%40sessionmgr3

&bdata=JnNpdGU9bm92ZWxxpc3QtGl2ZQ%3d%3d. Del Negro, Janice. "The Booklist Interview: Julius Lester." *Booklist.* 91.12 (Feb. 15, 1995) p. 1090. From *Literature Resource Center.* Johnson, Anne Janette, in *BB.* Johnson, Virginia, CRRL Staff, in //www.kidspoint.org/columns2.asp?column_id=665&column_type=author. Lodge, Sally. "Working at His Creative Peak." *Publishers Weekly.* 248.7 (Feb. 12, 2001) p. 180. From *Literature Resource Center.* McDaniels, Pellom, III, in *GEAAL.* P. D. S., in *CBC.* //members.authorsguild.net/juliuslester/bio.htm, Biography. //members.authorsguild.net/juliuslester/events.htm, FAQ. //members.authorsguild.net/juliuslester/index.htm. //www.Amazon.com. //www.library.uiuc.edu/blog/esslchildlit/archives/2008/02/african_america.html. //www.umass.edu/judaic/faculty/juliuslester.html.

Lewis, David Levering
5/25/1936–
Scholarly history, biography, literary criticism, anthologies; educator

David Levering Lewis graduated Phi Beta Kappa from Tennessee's Fisk University (1956), earned his M.A. in U.S. history from Columbia University (1958), and earned his Ph.D. in modern European and French history from the London School of Economics and Political Science (1962). Meanwhile, he also served in the U.S. Army's Medical Corps (1961-1963). With his degrees in hand, he went on to teach modern French history at the University of Ghana at Accra (1963-1964), at Howard University in Washington, D.C. (1964-1965), at the University of Notre Dame in Indiana (1965-1966), at Morgan State College in Baltimore, Maryland (1966-1970), and at Federal City College in Washington, D.C. (1970-1974). In 1974, he broadened his field of scholarship and became a professor of history at the University of the District of Columbia (1974-1980) and then the University of California at San Diego (1981-1985) before settling down at Rutgers University in New Brunswick, New Jersey, as the **Martin Luther King, Jr.** Professor of History (1985-1994) and then as the Martin Luther King, Jr. University Professor of History since 1994. In 1995, he started his association with New York University, starting as a visiting professor (1995-1996, fall of 2000) and then as the Julius Silver University Professor and professor of history (since 2003).

Lewis's books include *King: A Critical Biography* (1970/1978), *Prisoners of Honor: The Dreyfus Affair* (1973/1995), *District of Columbia: A Bicentennial History* (1976), *When Harlem Was in Vogue: The Politics of the Arts in the Twenties and Thirties* (1981/1997), and *The Race to Fashoda: European Colonialism and African Resistance in the Scramble for Africa* (1988). In 1994, he wrote his first award-winning biography, **W. E. B. Du Bois**: *Biography of a Race, 1868-1919* (1994), for which he won the Pulitzer Prize in Biography, the Anisfield-Wolf Book Award, the Francis Parkman Prize in History from the Society of American Historians, the Bancroft Prize in American History and Diplomacy, the Ralph Waldo Emerson Award from Phi Beta Kappa, the English Speaking Union Book Award, and the Book Award of the Black Caucus of the American Library Association, as well as nomination for the National Book Award for nonfiction, a 1995 Outstanding Book Award from the National Conference of Black Political Scientists, and a 1997 J. E. K. Aggrey Medal from the Phelps Stokes Fund.

While working on the second volume of his Du Bois biography, he was awarded the prestigious John D. & Catherine T. MacArthur Foundation Fellowship (1999-2004). In the new millennium, his *W. E. B. Du Bois: The Fight for Equality and the American Century, 1919-1963* (2000) was published, winning Lewis a second Pulitzer Prize for Biography (2001), the first author ever to win two Pulitzers for two consecutive volumes. He also garnered a second Anisfield-Wolf Book Award (2001) and a Horace Mann Bond Book Award from Harvard University (2000). The following year, he was named a fellow of the American Philosophical Society and of the American Academy of Arts & Sciences (2002), as well as president of the Society of American Historians (2002-2003). In 2004, he was given the inaugural **John Hope Franklin** Award; during Franklin's lifetime, Lewis also listed Franklin as a reference in his curriculum vita. In the fall of 2008, Lewis published *God's Crucible: Islam and the Making of Europe, 570-1215,* certainly a timely topic.

In addition to his solo book-length projects, Lewis has contributed articles and chapters to the *Encyclopedia Britannica* and more than a dozen other books, as well as numerous forewords and introductions to books. Lewis also edited two readers, *The Portable Harlem Renaissance Reader* (1994) and *W. E. B. Du Bois: A Reader* (1995). He has also contributed dozens of articles and reviews to *American Historical Review, Nation, The New York Times, New Yorker,* and numerous other periodicals. He has presented dozens of invited papers at historical associations, colleges and universities, and other events.

In addition to the aforementioned awards, fellowships, and honors, Lewis has been honored with a dozen other grants and fellowships and numerous honorary doctorates (1995-2005). He has also served on numerous editorial boards and panels. Lewis speaks and writes French, reads Italian and Spanish, can read a little Russian, and modestly claims to have studied Arabic "with poor results." Lewis has four children and is married to Ruth Ann Stewart, also a professor.

REFERENCES: *AA. AANB. CAO-04. W. Wiki.* Johnson, Anne Janette, in *BB.* //en.wikipedia.org/wiki/Francis_Parkman_Prize. //history.fas.nyu.edu/object/davidleveringlewis. Amazon.com.

Lewis, Samella Sanders
2/27/1924–
Art history, documentary films; artist, curator, educator, arts journal founder

In addition to being an artist (specializing in paintings and serigraphs), an educator, a museum founder, and an art-gallery curator, Lewis has written books on art, founded an art journal, and created documentary films on art. Her art books include *Black Artists on Art* (1969, with Elizabeth Waddy, 2 vols.; revised 1976), on contemporary African-American artists; *Art: African American* (1978; revised 1990), on art history; and *The Art of Elizabeth Catlett* (1984/2001), which appraises the work of this highly acclaimed and innovative artist.

Editor's note: Her other writings include *The Art of African Peoples* (1973), *African American Art for Young People* (1991), *African American Art and Artists* (1990; revised, 2003), and *Caribbean Visions: Contemporary Painting and Sculpture* (1995).

Lewis has been making films on African-American artists, past and present, since the late 1960s. Her films include both short features on individual artists (e.g., *To Follow a Star: The Sculpture of Richmond Barthé* and *Feathers of Wood: The Art of Charles Hutchinson*) and full-length works embracing the work of multiple artists (e.g., *The Black Artists*). In addition, Lewis has extended her celebration of African-American artists through the journal she founded in 1976, *Black Art Quarterly* (since renamed *The International Review of African American Art*). Among the aspects of art she has featured have been artists from particular times (the 20th century, the 1930s and 1940s), specific places (e.g., Trinidad and Tobago, the American North and West), special genres (e.g., contemporary folk art), women artists, and even art collectors (e.g., collections at African-American institutions).

Editor's note: Volume 21, Number 1, the 30th anniversary issue of *The International Review of African American Art*, now published by Hampton University Museum, honored Lewis as the founder of the journal, then titled *Black Art: An International Quarterly*, and her art collections, which she started gathering in 1942.

REFERENCES: *BAAW.* —Tonya Bolden

FURTHER READING: *AANB. CAO-03. Wiki.* Manheim, James M., in *BB.* Olin, Ferris Aurora. "Collecting and the Cultural Politics of Race and Community Survival: Samella Sanders Lewis. *The Journal of the History of Art.* 4 (Annual 2003) p. 201. From *Literature Resource Center.*

Literary Journals of the Harlem Renaissance (1919-1940) *See* Harlem Renaissance, Literary Journals of the

Locke, Alain (LeRoy)
9/13/1886–6/9/1954
Essays, anthology, nonfiction—philosophy, art, music, biography; educator

The Lockes were well established in Philadelphia's intellectual elite, starting with Ishmael Locke (1820-1852) and his wife, both educators; their son Pliny Locke (1850-1892) and his wife Mary Hawkins Locke (1853-1922), also both educators; and their grandson (Pliny and Mary's only child), Alain, also an educator, as well as a writer. Therefore, even though Pliny died when Alain was just six years old, Mary was able to continue ensuring that her son had an excellent education. At first, Mary hoped that Alain would have a career in medicine, but a childhood bout of rheumatic fever permanently injured Alain's heart, so that career path was blocked. Mary quickly shifted gears and ensured that her son had a broad artistic education, studying piano, violin, and literature. By the time Alain graduated from Central High School (second in his class), he was an accomplished musician, as well as a gifted student.

After high school, Alain attended the preparatory school where his father had taught, the Philadelphia School of Pedagogy (1902-1904), finishing first in his class. The following fall, Locke enrolled at Harvard University, where he was named to the prestigious honor society Phi Beta Kappa and earned a B.A. in philosophy (and English), magna cum laude (1907). On graduating, he became the first African American to be awarded a Rhodes Scholarship, which enables a scholar to study at Oxford University in England. (Considered by many to be the highest honorary academic scholarship in the world, no other African Americans were awarded this scholarship during Locke's lifetime.) Despite the scholarship and his outstanding record as a student, several Oxford colleges denied him admittance because of his race. At last, Hertford College at Oxford admitted him, and Locke spent the next three years there, studying philosophy, Greek, Latin, and literature. In 1910, Locke was awarded Oxford's B. Litt. degree. Next, Locke went to Germany, where he studied at the University of Berlin (1910-1911), then he studied under Henri Bergson in Paris at the College de France (1911). After that, Locke left Europe to travel through territory that was entirely foreign to him: the American South, where he searched for jobs at various Southern universities and closely observed the distinctive brand of discrimination and racial prejudice practiced there.

At last, in 1912, Howard University (in Washington, D.C.) appointed Locke as "Assistant Professor of the Teaching of English and Instructor in Philosophy and Education." In 1915, Locke proposed establishing a course on race relations at Howard, but the school's trustees (all white at that time) rejected the idea. Locke then collaborated with Howard's Social Science Club and its NAACP chapter to develop a lecture series on that subject. During the 1916-1917 school year, Locke took a sabbatical to complete his doctorate at Harvard University. In 1918, Harvard awarded him his Ph.D., making Locke the first African American to receive this degree there. That year, Locke was named the chair of the philosophy department at Howard. During his tenure at Howard, Locke also enjoyed occasional stints as a visiting professor elsewhere (e.g., at his alma mater Harvard, in Haiti, at Fisk University, at the University of Wisconsin, at New York's New School for Social Research, at the City College of New York, and at the Salzburg [Austria] Seminar in American Studies), and in 1924, he conducted archeological studies in the Sudan and in Egypt.

In the late 1920s, Locke had a conflict with Howard's president, which led to Locke's dismissal from Howard, to which he didn't return until 1928. During this period of time—the very peak of the **Harlem Renaissance**—Locke moved to Harlem. There, Locke was tireless in helping artists, musicians, dramatists, and writers to promote their careers. Among other things, Locke helped writers get their work published; acted as liaison between such writers as **Langston Hughes**, **Zora Neale Hurston**, and **Claude McKay** and wealthy white patrons (e.g., Mrs. Charlotte Osgood Mason) who could support their literary pursuits; paved the way for writers to wend their way through American cultural institutions; and encouraged writers and other artists to seek inspiration from African culture and artistic expression.

In 1928, Locke returned to Howard, where he remained until his retirement just before he died. The year he retired, Howard University awarded Locke an honorary doctorate of humane letters. Ironically, in 1954, a year after Locke's retirement, Howard honored Locke in a more important way: It established an African Studies Program, which Locke had been advocating for many years. He had also encouraged the expansion of Howard University's art collection, urged the establishment of an African-American theater at Howard, and celebrated African-American music as America's most authentic folk music.

In *Callaloo* (February-October, 1981), "Alain Locke: A Comprehensive Bibliography of His Published Writings" listed more than 300 articles, books, and other writings published by Locke between 1904 and 1953 (per *OCAAL*). The topics he addressed include African studies, anthropology, art, culture, education, literature, music, philosophy, political science, race relations, and sociology, among others. A recurrent theme throughout many of his writings was the importance of Africa's influence on American culture, chiefly through African-

Alain Locke

American culture, but also through having permeated all of the American cultural experience.

Other than his doctoral dissertation ("The Problem of Classification in Theory of Value"), Locke's first book-length work was *Race Contacts and Inter-Racial Relations* (1916). Starting in 1923, Locke began contributing essays to the National Urban League's literary journal *Opportunity* (established by **Charles Spurgeon Johnson**). In addition, starting in 1929, Locke wrote an annual critical review of African and African-American literature published in the preceding year. In 1942 or 1943, *Opportunity*'s editorship changed hands, and Locke stopped publishing his annual reviews, but in 1946, he started publishing them again in the social-science and literary journal *Phylon* (founded by **W. E. B. Du Bois** in 1940).

Another of the major ways in which Locke contributed to American literature started in March 1925, when he was invited to edit a special issue of the sociology magazine *Survey Graphic*, titled "Harlem, Mecca of the New Negro." Locke wrote the lead essay and organized the issue into sections: "The Greatest Negro Community in the World," "The Negro Expresses Himself," and "Black and White—Studies in Race Contacts." The issue was such a hit that he expanded it into his anthology *The New Negro: An Interpretation* (1925; reprinted 1968). Both the special issue and the anthology included fiction, poetry, drama, music criticism, and essay contributions from such African-American writers as **Countee Cullen,** W. E. B. Du Bois, **Rudolph Fisher,** Langston Hughes, **Charles S. Johnson, James Weldon Johnson, Anne Spencer, Jean Toomer,** and **Walter White,** as well as various white writers. Writers whose contributions were added in the anthology include **William Stanley Braithwaite, Jessie Redmon Fauset, E. Franklin Frazier, Angelina Weld Grimké,** Zora Neale Hurston, Claude McKay, **Kelly Miller,** and J. (Joel) A. (Augustus) Rogers. In addition to the writings, the special issue and the anthology also included lush African artworks and vivid depictions of the African-American experience, by such artists as Miguel Covarrubias, Aaron Douglass, Winold Reiss (a Bavarian artist), and Walter Von Ruckteschell. Many literary critics and scholars have credited the anthology as being the definitive text of the Harlem Renaissance.

In 1934, Locke launched another initiative intended to promote African-American culture, founding the Associates in Negro Folk Education (ANFE). Through the ANFE, Locke edited nine volumes in the "Bronze Booklets" series on African-American scholarship and culture, especially art and music. ANFE also published works of criticism by **Sterling A. Brown** and other African-American critics. Locke's volumes included *Negro Art: Past and Present* (1936), *The Negro and His Music* (1936), and *The Negro in Art: A Pictorial Record of the Negro Artists and the Negro Theme in Art* (1940; reprinted 1971), probably Locke's most celebrated work since his 1925 *The New Negro.*

As a champion of African-American culture, he wrote *Four Negro Poets* (1927), celebrating the writings of Countee Cullen, Langston Hughes, Claude McKay, and Jean Toomer; and edited *Plays of Negro Life* (1927, edited with T. Montgomery Gregory), the first collection of African-American dramatic works. Other works in this vein include *A Decade of Negro Self-expression* (1928), *Frederick Douglass, a Biography of Anti-Slavery* (1935), and *The Negro in America* (1953). His greatest achievement, however, was to be his final volume, *The Negro in American Culture,* which he worked on for years. In 1954, however, when he realized that his lifelong heart problems would prevent him from completing his work himself, he asked the daughter of **Ernest Everett Just,** his colleague at Howard, Margaret Just Butcher, to complete it for him. In 1956, she published the work, based on his guidelines, notes, and other materials, but the consensus of critical opinion suggests that the work reflects the style and vision of Butcher more than that of Locke.

All aspects of African-American culture were at the forefront of Locke's interests, and he wrote numerous essays on his philosophy of "cultural pluralism." Locke opposed segregation and favored integration, emphasizing the need for all Americans to respect and appreciate the value of America's rich cultural diversity, within a democratic context. He opposed the notion of the "melting pot" and favored instead what contemporary educators metaphorically call a "stew" or a "salad." Toward this end, from 1940 until his death, he regularly contributed essays about African-American culture for the *Encyclopædia Britannica's* Book of the Year. In addition, he studied and wrote about race relations, coediting an anthology on global race relations, *When Peoples Meet: A Study in Race and Culture Contacts* (1942, edited with Bernhard J. Stern), which included analytical pieces by prominent anthropologists such as Ruth Benedict and Margaret Mead.

Locke never married and always presented himself as the definition of elegance, culture, and refinement. Although he had several serious conflicts with many writers (often over his rather intrusive and fussy intervention when he edited their works), he was instrumental in promoting the careers of many, and he never hesitated to encourage his students and aspiring writers in their literary pursuits. In addition, his own numerous writings show penetrating insight into African-American culture and helped readers appreciate its distinctive contribution to American (and world) culture.

REFERENCES: *1TESK. AA:PoP. AANB. AAW:AAPP. B. BAL-1-P. BAWPP. BF:2000. BWA. CAO-03. EB-BH-CD. EBLG. G-97. MWEL. NAAAL. OC20LE. PGAA. W. WDAA. Wiki.* Born, Brad S., in *WB-99.* Buck, Christopher, in *AW:ACLB-04.* Fitchue, M. Anthony. "Alain Locke: Faith and Philosophy." *The Journal of African American History.* 92.1 (Winter 2007) p. 131. From *Literature Resource Center.* Long, Richard A., in *COCAAL* and *OCAAL.* Mason, Ernest D., in *AAWHR-40.* Ostrom, Hans, in *GEAAL.* Podesta, James J., in *BB.* Rainey, Cortez, in *BH2C.* Robinson, Lisa Clayton, in *EA-99.* //aalbc.com/authors/Alainlocke.htm.

Logan, Rayford W. (Whittington)
1/7/1897–11/4/1982

Nonfiction—African-American history and biography; educator, organization leader, civil servant on Franklin Roosevelt's "Black Cabinet"

After earning his baccalaureate from Williams College in Williamstown, Massachusetts (1917), Logan enlisted as an officer in the U.S. Army during "The Great War" to end all wars. Even in his segregated unit, he faced such intense racism that he asked for and received a discharge in 1919, staying in Europe for the next five years. Decades later, when the conditions left by the first world war led to the second one, he was already serving on President Franklin Delano Roosevelt's "Black Cabinet" and helped draft the president's executive order barring the military from excluding blacks during World War II. Meanwhile, he had earned two master's degrees (1929 from Williams; 1932 from Harvard University) and a Ph.D. (1936, from Harvard), and he had started professing at Virginia Union University (1925-1930), Atlanta University (1933-1938), and Howard University (1938-1974; emeritus 1974-1982). In addition, Logan was assistant director (1932-1933) and director (1950-1951) of the Association for the Study of Negro Life and History, which he helped **Carter G. Woodson** to found.

A whirlwind of activity, Logan also managed to write *Education in Haiti* (1930); *The Diplomatic Relations of the United States with Haiti, 1776-1891* (1941/1969); *The Operation of the Mandate System in Africa, 1919-1927: With an Introduction on the Problem of the Mandates in the Post-War World* (1942); *The Negro and the Post-War World: A Primer* (1945); *The Senate and the Versailles Mandate System* (1945/1975); *The African Mandates in World Politics* (1949); *The Negro in American Life and Thought: The Nadir, 1877-1901* (1954, later published as *The Betrayal of the Negro from Rutherford B. Hayes to Woodrow Wilson,* 1965); *The American Negro: Old World Background and New World Experience* (1967, with Irving S. Cohen); and *Four Took Freedom: The Lives of Harriet Tubman, Frederick Douglass, Robert Smalls, and Blanche K. Bruce* (1967, with Philip Sterling, illustrated by Charles White). He also wrote *The Negro in the United States: A Brief History* (1957), later published as *Volume 1: A History to 1945: From Slavery to Second-Class Citizenship,* 1970) and *The Negro in the United States, Volume 2: The Ordeal of Democracy* (1971, with Michael R. Winston). His obituary anticipated the posthumous publication of his final book, *The International Struggle for Human Rights.*

In addition, Logan helped **W. E. B. Du Bois** with his *Encyclopedia of the Negro,* and he edited the *Journal of Negro History.* He also edited *The Attitude of the Southern White Press toward Negro Suffrage, 1932-1940* (1940); *What the Negro Wants* (1944); *Memoirs of a Monticello Slave, as Dictated to Charles Campbell in the 1840's by Isaac, One of Thomas Jefferson's Slaves* (1951); *The New Negro Thirty Years Afterward: Papers Contributed to the Sixteenth Annual Spring Conference of the Division of Social Science* (1955); and *W. E. B. Du Bois: A Profile* (1971); and he coedited the *Dictionary of American Negro Biography* (1982, with Michael R. Winston), with about 700 entries, which **Henry Louis Gates, Jr.**, coeditor of the esteemed *African American National Biography,* called "the standard of excellence . . . for any future black biographical dictionary." For his numerous contributions, he was awarded the NAACP's prestigious **Spingarn** medal (1980). Logan's wife, musician and choir director Ruth Robinson, predeceased him in 1966, less than two months before their thirty-ninth anniversary.

REFERENCES: *AANB. CAO-07. Wiki.* Robinson, Alonford James, Jr., in *EA-99.* Shepherd, Kenneth R., in *BB.* Stuckey, Sterling. "Rayford W. Logan and the Dilemma of the African-American Intellectual." *African American Review.* 30.1 (Spring 1996) p. 125. From *Literature Resource Center.*

Lomax, Louis E. (Emanuel)
8/16/1922–7/30/1970
Nonfiction, commentary; journalist

In his young adulthood, Lomax earned a Ph.D. from Yale University (1947) and parole from Joliet Prison (1954; imprisoned starting in 1949, for selling a rented car). He had briefly professed philosophy at Georgia State University before his incarceration, but after his release, he turned to work as a print news reporter (e.g., initially for Associated Negro Press papers such as *Baltimore American* and *Chicago American*; later for mainstream magazines such as *Harper's, Life, Look, The Nation,* and the *Saturday Evening Post*). In 1959, he joined Mike Wallace's news staff, where he became the first African American to appear on television as a news reporter. His opportunity was created when **Malcolm X** refused to be interviewed unless his interviewer was African American. Hence, instead of Wallace, Lomax interviewed fellow ex-convict Malcolm X for Wallace's documentary *The Hate That Hate Produced,* on the Nation of Islam. Lomax continued to work in broadcasting as a news commentator, analyst, and narrator, and he hosted a semiweekly television show (1964-1968). He also wrote several important books on domestic and global social and political issues: *The Reluctant African* (1960), which earned him the prestigious Anisfield-Wolf Award; *The Negro Revolt* (1962), which sold well and was required reading in many college courses; *When the Word Is Given: A Report on Elijah Muhammad, Malcolm X, and the Black Muslim World* (1963); *Thailand: The War That Is, the War That Will Be* (1966), which included a rare interview of Ho Chi Minh; and *To Kill a Black Man: The Shocking Parallel in the Lives of Malcolm X and* **Martin Luther King, Jr.** (1968). For a snippet of his writing, see "The Negro Revolt against 'The Negro Leaders'" (*Harper's,* June 1, 1960, available at //reportingcivilrights.loa.org/authors/selections.jsp?authorId=45). In the 1950s, the FBI intensively investigated him—and many others who outspokenly opposed racism—in pursuit of possible ties to the Communist Party. His love life was troubled, but there, too, he persisted, marrying his fourth wife in 1968.

REFERENCES: *CAO-03. EBLG.* Gray, Pamela Lee, in *AANB.* //reportingcivilrights.loa.org/authors/selections.jsp?authorId=45. //www.gibbsmagazine.com/Louis%20E%20Lomax.htm. //www.nathanielturner.com/louislomaxbioandnotes.htm.

Lorde, Audre (née Audrey Geraldine Lorde) (aka Gamba Adisa)
2/18/1934–11/17/1992
Poems, essays, autobiography/memoir; librarian, educator

Linda Gertrude Belmar, a native of Grenada, and Frederic Byron Lorde, an African American, had moved

Audre Lorde

to Harlem from Grenada, with plans of returning to Grenada—until the Great Depression dashed their plans of gaining enough money to return. In Harlem, the couple had three daughters, the youngest of which was Audrey. Little Audrey was so nearsighted that she was identified as legally blind, and she didn't learn to speak until she was four or five years old—the same age at which her mother taught her to read and write. From the very start, Audrey started shaping the words she encountered. When she learned to write her own name, she disliked having the tail of the "y" of "Audrey" hanging below the line, so she soon omitted it altogether.

As Lorde herself later noted, "I was very inarticulate as a youngster. I couldn't speak. I didn't speak until I was five, in fact, not really until I started reading and writing poetry. I used to speak in poetry. I would read poems, and I would memorize them. People would say, 'Well, what do you think, Audre? What happened to you yesterday?' And I would recite a poem and somewhere in that poem there would be a line or a feeling I was sharing. In other words, I literally communicated through poetry. And when I couldn't find the poems to express the things I was feeling, that's when I started writing poetry. That was when I was 12 or 13" (p. 106, *BWWW*).

Lorde also observed, "Words had an energy and power and I came to respect that power early. Pronouns, nouns, and verbs were citizens of different countries, who really got together to make a new world" (quoted in *OCWW*,

from Karla M. Hammond, *Denver Quarterly*, Spring 1981). When Audre was 15, her first published poem appeared in print. Her school newspaper had refused to print the poem, as it discussed Audre's first love affair with a boy, but *Seventeen* magazine was happy to print it.

Audre's retreat into literature and poetry helped her escape her parents' strict upbringing and the dictatorial educational environment of the Catholic schools (St. Mark's and then St. Catherine's) she attended while growing up. In addition to its stern manner, the schools' racism created an unwelcoming environment for this shy, sensitive girl. Only through words was she able to protect herself. When Audre hit her teen years, she started embracing her status as an outsider and rebelled against the harshness of her environment. At last, when Audre was in high school, she was enrolled in Hunter College High School, where she became the school arts magazine's literary editor and found a sisterhood of rebellious poets. One of her fellow sister-outsiders was poet Diane Di Prima, with whom she maintained a close friendship after high school.

After high school, Lorde continued her studies part-time at Hunter College, while earning a living in various low-paying jobs, such as factory worker, medical clerk, x-ray technician, ghostwriter, social worker, and arts and crafts supervisor. While working in a factory, Lorde had her first lesbian affair. In 1954, she went Mexico, where she spent a year studying at the National University of Mexico. There, she began speaking in full sentences and came into her own, identifying herself as a poet and as a lesbian, enjoying an affair with a woman she knew there. When she returned to New York, Lorde entered Greenwich Village's mostly white "gay-girl" culture there.

Back in New York, Lorde also decided that she wanted to study librarianship in order to better understand how to organize and analyze information. In March 1955, she got a job at the New York Public Library Children's Services while studying library sciences at Hunter. She also continued to write poetry and started being interested in the Harlem Writers Guild. At the guild, **Langston Hughes** encouraged her writing, but many other guild members were homophobic, and Lorde soon felt alienated from the guild. In 1959, Lorde earned her B.A. in English literature and philosophy from Hunter College.

After graduation, Lorde started working as a librarian at Mount Vernon Public Library and earned her master's degree from Columbia University's School of Library Science (M.L.S., 1961). For the next seven years, Lorde worked as a librarian for various libraries, including a job as the head librarian at the Town School Library in New York (1966-1968). Meanwhile, on March 31, 1962, Lorde married Edward Ashley Rollins, with whom she had two children, Elizabeth (1963) and Jonathan (11/2 years younger than Elizabeth). Although the marriage ended in divorce (in 1970), Lorde's role as a mother became central to much of her writing thereafter.

In 1968, Lorde's poetry was recognized with a grant from the National Endowment for the Arts, and her first book, *The First Cities* (1968) was published. In the spring of that year, she enjoyed a six-week position as poet-in-residence at historically black Tougaloo College in Mississippi. Lorde's experience at Tougaloo changed her life. During those six short weeks, she discovered that she loved teaching far more than being a librarian; she realized that her poetry was appreciated by a wide community of African Americans; she met Frances Clayton, who was to become her long-term partner in life; and she wrote most of the poems for her second poetry collection, *Cables to Rage* (1970). Lorde later recalled, "[Tougaloo] was pivotal for me. Pivotal. In 1968 my first book had just been published; it was my first trip into the Deep South; it was the first time I had been away from the children; the first time I worked with young black students in a workshop situation. I came to realize that this was my work. That teaching and writing were inextricably combined, and it was there that I knew what I wanted to do for the rest of my life. . . . I realized that writing was central to my life" (p. 110, *BWWW*; see also p. 262, *BWW*).

When Lorde returned to New York, she started offering poetry courses at the City College of New York (1968-1969), and from then on, she taught English, creative writing, and literature at various colleges and universities, including Lehman College (1969-1970), John Jay College of Justice (1970-1980), and Hunter College (starting in 1980). In addition, during the 1970s, Lorde traveled extensively, touring Africa, the Caribbean, and Europe (including Russia).

Starting in September 1978, Lorde was diagnosed with breast cancer, launching her 14-year war against cancer. She triumphed in her first battle, although she didn't emerge unscathed: She underwent a *radical mastectomy* (surgically removing her breasts, lymph nodes, and some muscle tissue) and decided against wearing *prostheses* (artificial breasts), rebelling against male-centered notions of how females should look. Six years later (February, 1984), she was diagnosed with liver cancer, and more than eight years later (November 1992), the liver cancer killed her. Before it did, however, she returned to her mother's birthplace in the Caribbean, and the Quaker poet was given an African name: Gambia Adisa, which means "Warrior: She Who Makes Her Meaning Clear."

In 1962, Langston Hughes included Lorde's poetry in his anthology *New Negro Poets, USA*, and after that, her poems were published in numerous African-American literary magazines and anthologies. It was not until the early 1970s, however, that Lorde gave a public reading of one of her lesbian love poems, thus "outing" herself as a lesbian. (The same poem was later published in *Ms.* magazine.) In 1974, Lorde, **Alice Walker**, and Adrienne Rich were nominated for the National Book Award. When Rich won the award, she announced that she would accept it as a coequal with her two fellow nominees, saying, "We symbolically join here in refusing the terms of patriarchal competition and in declaring that we will share this prize among us, to be used as best we can for women." Seven years later, Rich further championed Lorde's poetry when Rich published an interview with Lorde (in *Signs: Journal of Women in Culture and Society*, 1981).

Lorde was herself a champion of rights and respect for African Americans, for women, and for homosexuals. Through her poems, essays, and autobiographies, she opposed homophobia, sexism, and racism forthrightly and vociferously. Although she outspokenly denounced oppression and injustice, she wrote often of love (especially motherly love and romantic/lesbian love), not of hatred. She embraced diversity and urged her readers to work together to use difference as a creative, productive force to heal the wounds caused by conflict and strife, and to promote positive change.

Stylistically, Lorde wrote free-verse poems rich with figurative imagery. She presented global, political questions and comments through highly personal, specific experiences. Lorde's old pal from high school, Diane Di Prima, edited Lorde's first collection, *The First Cities* (1968), and helped her get the collection published by Poet's Press. Many of Lorde's contemporaries criticized Lorde for writing such personal, introspective poems during a time when most African-American poets were focusing on militantly confrontational political poems. Not everyone shared this view, however. **Dudley Randall**, founder of **Broadside Press**, observed that Lorde "does not wave a black flag, but her blackness is there, implicit in the bone."

Randall's press distributed Lorde's next collection, *Cables to Rage* (1970), which explored her feelings about her marriage, her husband's betrayal, her experiences raising her children, and her embracing of her identity as a lesbian. Nonetheless, the tone of this volume was less introspective and more centered on social injustices than was her first volume. That trend continued with Broadside's publication of Lorde's National Book Award-nominated *From a Land Where Other People Live* (1973). Two more volumes followed: her most politically oriented volume, *New York Head Shop and Museum* (1974), and her chapbook, *Between Ourselves* (1976).

In 1976, major mainstream publisher W. W. Norton published Lorde's *Coal* (1976), thereby introducing Lorde to a much wider audience and offering her a chance for greater critical notice. Many of the poems in

Coal had been published in her previous collections, but the volume also introduced many previously unpublished poems. Probably Lorde's most highly acclaimed collection, however, was *The Black Unicorn* (1978, also published by Norton), in which she highlighted themes of African ancestry, the diaspora of Africans across other continents, mythology, motherhood, lesbian relationships, and other close ties among women. Both collections included laudatory blurbs by Adrienne Rich on the book jackets.

Lorde's next collection, *Chosen Poems, Old and New* (1982), included poems from each of the preceding volumes, as well as new poems. This volume was followed by *Our Dead Behind Us* (1986), *Undersong: Chosen Poems Old and New* (1992), and *The Marvelous Arithmetics of Distance, Poems 1987-1992* (1993). In addition, Lorde edited two anthologies: *Lesbian Poetry: An Anthology* (1982) and *Woman Poet—The East* (1984). Lorde's prose was collected in several collections, including *Sister Outsider: Essays and Speeches* (1984, Crossing Press), which has since been used extensively in women's studies courses. In addition, many of Lorde's essays have been published in numerous anthologies and periodicals.

Lorde's other major contribution to literature is her distinctive approach to autobiography, much of which centers on her war against cancer, starting with *The Cancer Journals* (1980), documenting her personal battle against breast cancer, a pioneering exploration of one woman's battle against this epidemic disease. As a teacher, Lorde had decided to use her own battle against breast cancer as an opportunity to educate women about this disease. As she herself noted, "I couldn't believe that what I was fighting I would fight alone and only for myself. I couldn't believe that there wasn't something there that somebody could use at some other point because I know that I could have used some other woman's words, whatever she had to say. Just to know that someone had been there before me would have been very important, but there was nothing. Writing *The Cancer Journals* gave me the strength and power to examine that experience, to put down into words what I was feeling. It was my belief that if this work were useful to just one woman, it was worth doing" (p. 116, *BWWW*).

She described her further struggles in her autobiographical collection of journal entries and essays *A Burst of Light* (1988), which won an American Book Award in 1989. In it, she describes her decision to abstain from further invasive medical treatments and to explore alternative treatment modalities. Between her first and her second nonfiction autobiographies, she introduced her experimental "biomythography," which combines autobiography with myth, poetry, and prose fiction forms, in her book *Zami: A New Spelling of My Name* (1982). *Zami* peers into Lorde's childhood and early adulthood (through 1959), exploring in depth the complexities of the mother-daughter relationship, the difficulties of growing up homosexual in a homophobic society, and the delight in discovering the power of language. Touted for its rich imagery and allegory, the book is considered a landmark in African-American women's autobiography.

Among the many awards Lorde received were a National Endowment for the Arts residency grant (1968), a Creative Artists Public Service award grant (1972, 1980), a Broadside Press Poet's Award (1975), appointment to the Hunter College Hall of Fame (1980), a Cultural Council Foundation grant for poetry, and two Lambda Literary Awards for Lesbian Poetry. In addition, in 1991, New York's Governor Mario Cuomo named Lorde the Poet Laureate of New York state.

REFERENCES: *AA:PoP. AAW:AAPP. BAWPP. BWW. BWWW. CAO-01. CBAPD. EAAWW. EB-BH-CD. EBLG. LFCC-07. MWEL. NAAAL. OC20LE. RLWWJ. RWTC. WDAA. WDAW.* Balfour, Lawrie, in *EA-99.* Davis, Amanda, in *GEAAL.* Homans, Margaret, in *AAW-1991* and in *BWA:AHE.* Johnson, Anne Janette, in *BB.* Kimmich, Allison, in *FW.* Kohl, Judith C., in *GLB.* Kulii, Beverly Threatt, in *COCAAL* and *OCAAL.* Levy, Sholomo B., in *AANB.* Lorde, Aúdre, and Charles H. Rowell. "Above the Wind: An Interview with Audre Lorde." *Callaloo 23.1* (Winter 2000): pp. 52-63. Rpt. in Thomas J. Schoenberg and Lawrence J. Trudeau (Eds.) (2006) *Twentieth-Century Literary Criticism* (Vol. 173). Detroit: Gale. From *Literature Resource Center.* McClaurin-Allen, Irma, in *AAP-55-85.* Ridinger, Robert B. Marks, in *GLL* and in *RGAL-3.* Trapasso, Ann, in *OCWW.*

FURTHER READING: *B. BCE. EAAWW. QB. W. Wiki.* //aalbc.com/authors/audre.htm.

Lotus Press
1972–1992, 1998–

Michigan State University Press's Lotus Press Series
1993–1997
Publisher of poetry by, for, and about African Americans

In 1972, although **Naomi Long Madgett** had already published three previous poetry collections, she was having trouble finding someone to publish her fourth poetry collection, *Pink Ladies in the Afternoon: New Poems 1965-1971* (1972). Unlike many of the militant, strident poems of the **Black Arts Movement** being published at that time, Madgett's poems were, as she later recalled, "quiet and subtle and she was unable to find a publisher who would accept it." Undeterred, with the help of three Detroit-based friends, she founded a publishing company in order to publish this collection. When considering a name for her new venture, she recalled seeing "the Egyptian lotus and saw the best of black poetry as a part of Africa transplanted to American soil." Having chosen a name, she also settled on a motto, "Flower of a New Nile" (quoted from //www.lotuspress.org/).

As Madgett notes on her website, she did not originally intend to publish poems by other authors. As a long-time educator, however, she had always been committed to ensuring "fairer representation of literature by African Americans in high school and college textbooks." She soon decided to showcase the breadth and variety of contemporary African-American poets by creating a series of 20 broadsides, or "poster-poems," which she titled *Deep Rivers, A Portfolio: 20 Contemporary Black American Poets* (1972). She intended the poster-poems to be used in classrooms, displayed on bulletin boards. For each set of 20 poster-poems, she also wrote a teacher guide, suggesting discussion questions, classroom activities, and other strategies for integrating poetry into English courses. The prestigious National Council of Teachers of English bought several hundred sets for distribution to American secondary-school teachers. According to Julius Thompson (Table 4.5, Table 4.6, pp. 156-157), Madgett sold each set for $7.00, and the 20 broadsides included poems by **Gerald Barrax**, Madgett's daughter Jill Witherspoon Boyer, **Michael S. Harper, Robert Hayden, June Jordan, Bob Kaufman, Etheridge Knight, Pinkie Gordon Lane, Audre Lorde, Dudley Randall, Eugene B. Redmond, Margaret Walker**, and **Paulette Childress White**.

In 1974, Madgett's cofounders turned the press over to her as sole proprietor. The following year, Madgett published Paulette Childress White's *Love Poem to a Black Junkie*, **May Miller**'s *Dust of Uncertain Journey*, and a chapbook of poems by one of her students, Pamela Cobb (now Baraka Sele) (all 1975). A novice in book production, she used as models existing poetry books, to figure out layout and the correct placement of title page, copyright, and so on for each book. Madgett published all three books by typing them on a proportional-font typewriter, printing them on a duplicator with interchangeable tubes of color, collating and stapling the books by hand, and then trimming them with a heavy-duty paper cutter. In 1976, she was helped by another small publisher to develop what appeared to be perfect binding for her books, and her publication of Herbert Woodward Martin's *The Persistence of the Flesh* (1976) was bound using her new technique. The following year, Lotus Press published its first professionally bound book, **Lance Jeffers**'s *O Africa, Where I Baked My Bread* (1977), and the year after that, the Press published its first typeset book, **Toi Derricotte**'s *The Empress of the Death House* (1978). That year, Lotus Press also published Madgett's fifth poetry collection, *Exits and Entrances* (1978). By 1979, Lotus Press had published 17 books, in addition to the series of 20 broadsides. That year, the Press received a generous do-

nation, making it possible to acquire a computer system and a laser printer.

Throughout the life of Lotus Press, Madgett sought to keep the purchase price of each book very low to make the books more accessible to potential readers. For instance, for the 58 books published by Lotus Press between 1980 and 1993, 36 of the titles cost just $3-$6, 15 cost $7-$9, 2 cost $10, and 5 cost $11-$25 (according to Thompson, 2005). During this time, a typical poetry book published by the Press was 40-90 pages. In 1980, Madgett, along with her third husband, elementary school principal Leonard Patton Andrews (who died in 1996), and her daughter, poet Jill Witherspoon Boyer, incorporated Lotus Press as a nonprofit corporation. The following year, Lotus Press achieved tax-exempt status as a federal 501(c)(3) organization, so that donations to the Press would be tax-exempt, and the press could apply for grants. Even after this time, however, the Press continued to need financial infusions from Madgett. All along, Lotus Press has been a labor of love, in which Madgett not only has not taken a salary or charged the Press for her expenses, but also has funded each of the Press's new ventures out of her own pocket.

After Madgett's 1984 retirement from teaching, she delved into developing her small, independent press. By the early 1990s, the press had published 75 titles, many of which are still in print. The press has been instrumental in keeping African-American poetry in print and was the first to publish the writings of such notables as **Houston Baker, Gayl Jones**, and many of the aforementioned authors. In fact, Lotus Press has been distinctive in offering the poetry of multiple generations of African-American poets, including established poets such as **James Emanuel**. After 1992, Madgett and her Lotus Press were unable to continue financing new titles, however, so the separate entity of Lotus Press was suspended that year.

In 1993, however, Madgett was able to arrange a deal with Michigan State University (MSU) Press to have them finance two new titles each year, with Madgett as the senior editor of MSU Press's Lotus Poetry Series. That year, Lotus Press established its annual Naomi Long Madgett Poetry Award, the winner of which was to have a volume published by MSU Press the following year. The first two titles published under this agreement were Madgett's anthology *Remembrance of Spring: Collected Poems* (1993) and the first winner of the annual poetry award, Adam David Miller's *Forever Afternoon* (1993). MSU Press also agreed to handle the distribution of Lotus Press's backlist. In recognition of Madgett's work as publisher and editor, the Before Columbus Foundation honored her with its American Book Award in 1993.

The arrangement with MSU Press continued through 1997, publishing the first five of the recipients of the annual Naomi Long Madgett Poetry Award. After that,

Madgett resumed responsibility for publishing the winners of the annual poetry award (through 2009, *Chronicles of the Pig and Other Delusions* by Edward Bruce Bynum). She also continues to try to handle distribution of the Press's list. Her website lists 16 current authors and 31 backlist authors (many with multiple titles). Regrettably, however, many Lotus Press books are now out of print, as Madgett cannot afford to publish additional copies after selling the last copy of an earlier print run. Her website notes that "Among the poets whose books are now out of print are Louie Crew, **Tom Dent**, Toi Derricotte, Kamaldeen Ibraheem, Gayl Jones (3 books), Dolores Kendrick, Pinkie Gordon Lane, **Haki R. Madhubuti**, Herbert Woodward Martin (2 books), **E. Ethelbert Miller**, Dudley Randall, Isetta Crawford Rawls, Sarah Carolyn Reese, Satiafa (Vivian V. Gordon), and Helen Earle Simcox, editor. . . . she plans to continue [publishing and distributing books] as long as she is able, but she is very much concerned about the future of Lotus Press, Inc. when she is no longer able to function. Except for entries in the annual Naomi Long Madgett Poetry Award, Lotus Press is not considering any unsolicited manuscripts." As of the printing of this dictionary, the next deadline for submission of entries was identified as March 31, 1910. Perhaps a reader of this dictionary will take up the torch Madgett is ready to pass.

REFERENCES: Black-Parker, Kimberly, "Madgett, Naomi Long"in *GEAAL*. Byrne, Dara N., "Lotus Press," in *GEAAL*. Thompson, Julius E. 2005. *Dudley Randall, Broadside Press, and the Black Arts Movement in Detroit, 1960-1995*. Jefferson, NC: McFarland. //newsreel.org/guides/furious/madgett.htm. //www.lotuspress.org/.

FURTHER READING: *See also* **anthologies of African-American literature, special topics and audiences; anthologies of African-American literature, specific genres, poetry, verse, and song;** and **Madgett, Naomi Long.**

Love, Nat (aka "Deadwood Dick")
6/??/1854–1921
Slave narrative, autobiography/memoir

Nat Love was born into plantation slavery, but he spent most of his adult life constantly in motion—as a cowboy in the western United States (1869-1889) and then as a Pullman porter (1890-1921). Though he lacked formal education, he did learn to read and write, and when the Civil War freed him, he worked for a while on the farm his father had rented, even after his father's death. On February 10, 1869, young Nat Love left the farm and started walking west. A couple of decades later, Love leaped from horseback to Pullman train.

In his fifties, Love wrote his self-celebratory autobiography, *The Life and Adventures of Nat Love: Better Known in the Cattle Country as "Deadwood Dick"* (1907), includ-

Nat Love "Deadwood Dick"

ing photographs of himself wearing a cowboy getup. Though the book may be viewed as a slave narrative—which it is—it also has some elements of the western tall tale, of a captivity narrative, and of the rags-to-riches story. Sadly, his narrative also offers insight into the deeply held prejudices of many Americans in the West at that time, such as his references to Native Americans as "red devils" and "painted savages" and to Mexicans as "greasers," though he acknowledges that his "first love" was a Mexican woman. For whatever reason, Love never mentions an instance in which he experienced racial prejudice against himself, though it would be astounding if such incidents never occurred. His account also fails to mention ever seeking the company of other African-American westerners, although he later married an African-American woman (in 1889), whom he describes as his "second love." He does, however, do a lot of name-dropping of prominent Americans he met while working as a Pullman porter, including George M. Pullman himself.

REFERENCES: *AANB. B. Wiki.* Costanzo, Angelo. "The Life and Adventures of Nat Love." *MELUS.* 22.3 (Fall 1997), p. 218. Literature Resources from Gale. Smith, Caroline B. D., in *BB.*

FURTHER READING: Gordon, Stephanie, in *GEAAL.*

Love, Rose Leary
12/30/1898–6/2/1969
Juvenile literature, autobiography/memoir, poems; educator

Rose Leary, of African, Irish, French, Scotch, and Native-American ancestry, was the cousin of **Langston Hughes**. She also earned a B.A. from Johnson C. Smith College in Charlotte, North Carolina, then did postgraduate work at the Hampton Institute in Hampton, Virginia, and at Columbia University in New York. Rose passed on her knowledge and education to youngsters in the Charlotte-Mecklenburg public elementary schools (1925-1964), having a special fondness for first-graders. Pretty soon, she also had a special fondness for George Leary Love (1937-1995), the son she had with her husband, George W. Love, who worked at the Tuskegee Institute. Rose also took breaks from Charlotte-Mecklenburg to teach in Greensboro, North Carolina, where her brother John was a principal, and in Jakarta, Indonesia (1957-1958), when her husband was a technical advisor there.

Rose Leary Love is best known to history as a writer, having written her children's story, *Nebraska and His Granny* (1936), and her brief textbook, *A Collection of Folklore for Children in Elementary School and at Home* (1964). After retiring, Love wrote her memoir, *Plum Thickets and Field Daisies* (preface dated 1965; published 1996; electronic version copyright 1998), the manuscript of which was donated to the Public Library of Charlotte and Mecklenburg County. It is available in its entirety at //www.cmstory.org/exhibit/plum/chapters.htm and through links at //www.cmstory.org/african/default.asp. Love also wrote a three-part children's serial, "George Washington Carver: A Boy Who Wished to Know Why," published in *Negro History Bulletin* in early 1967. Many of her poems were individually published in various periodicals. Love also wrote an unpublished collection of songs and an unpublished collection of poems. Most of her papers are archived at the University of North Carolina in Charlotte.

FURTHER READING: *AANB. BAWPP. HR&B.* //dlib.uncc.edu/ special_collections/manuscripts/html/339.php. //dlib.uncc.edu/ special_collections/manuscripts/subject_list.php?ms_subjectno=1. //www.cmstory.org/african/default.asp. //www.cmstory.org/exhibit/ plum/chapters.htm. //www.cmstory.org/exhibit/plum/preface.htm. //www.marshall.edu/melus/archives/mla2001_text.html.

John Roy Lynch

Lynch, John R. (Roy)
9/10/1847–11/2/1939
Nonfiction—history, autobiography/memoir, spoken word—speeches; former enslaved plantation worker, photographer, justice of the peace, politician, civil servant, soldier, attorney, business person

Born into slavery, John Roy Lynch was freed by the Union Army in 1863. After the Civil War, Lynch mastered photography and earned a living as a photographer. With nearly no formal education, he taught himself to read and write. Nonetheless Lynch became a Justice of the Peace, the first African-American Speaker of the House in Mississippi, then one of the first African-American members of the U.S House of Representatives (at age 26). Each of his three Congressional elections was contested, then he lost his fourth bid to Congress by 600 votes. During the 1870s, several of his speeches were published, including *Civil Rights: Speech of Hon. John R. Lynch, of Mississippi, in the House of Representatives, February 3, 1875* (1875); *Southern Question, Reply to Mr. Lamar:*

Speech of Hon. John R. Lynch of Mississippi, in the House of Representatives, August 12, 1876 (1876); *Speech of Hon. John R. Lynch, of Mississippi, in the House of Representatives, March 1, 1877* (1877); and *Speech of John R. Lynch* (1882). Though none are still in print, all are available at least to a limited degree. He also wrote the book *The Late Election in Mississippi* (1877).

In 1884, Lynch married Ella Sommerville, with whom he had a daughter before their subsequent divorce. After that, he returned to Mississippi to pursue farming while continuing to be active in the Republican Party. In 1889, he started civil-service work (1889-1893) and studied law, being admitted to the Mississippi bar in 1896. He practiced law for a couple of years before returning to civil service during the Spanish-American War in 1898. During his civil service, he wrote *Colored Americans: John R. Lynch's Appeal to Them* (c. 1900).

In 1901, Lynch joined the U.S. Army, from which he retired in 1911. That year, he married Cora Williams, and the couple moved to Chicago, where he practiced law and earned money from real estate. While in Chicago, he wrote *The Facts of Reconstruction* (1913/1970), which has been available free online since 2005 through the Gutenberg Project, at //www.gutenberg.org/etext/16158. He also wrote *Some Historical Errors of James Ford Rhodes* (1922), and he wrote at least one article for the *Pittsburgh Courier* (1930). After Lynch's death, the esteemed historian **John Hope Franklin** edited *Reminiscences of an Active Life: The Autobiography of John Roy Lynch* (1970/2008). Lynch was buried in the Arlington National Cemetery with military honors.

REFERENCES: *AANB. Wiki.* Table 7.1, "African American Mississippi Writers, Historians, and Journalists," and Chapter 7, "Selected Bibliography," in *AT.* //bioguide.congress.gov/scripts/biodisplay.pl?index=L000533. //library.msstate.edu/special_interest/Mississippi_African-American_Authors.asp. //www.aaregistry.com/african_american_history/349/John_R_Lynch_congressman_from_the_Magnolia_State. //www.gutenberg.org/etext/16158. //www.gutenberg.org/files/16158/16158-h/16158-h.htm. Amazon.com.

FURTHER READING: Foner, Eric (Ed.). 1996. "Lynch, John Roy," in *Freedom's Lawmakers: A Directory of Black Officeholders During Reconstruction* (rev. ed.). Baton Rouge: Louisiana State University Press. Franklin, John Hope. 1982. "Lynch, John Roy," in Rayford W. Logan and Michael R. Winston (Eds.), *Dictionary of American Negro Biography* (1982 pp. 407-409). New York: W. W. Norton.

~M~

Mackey, Nathaniel
10/25/1947–
Poems, essays, criticism, novels, anthology; journal editor, educator

A graduate of Princeton (B.A., with high honors) and Stanford (Ph.D., 1975, English and American literature), Mackey has taught at the University of California at Santa Cruz since 1979. His poems have been collected in *Four for Trane* (1978, chapbook), *Septet for the End of Time* (1983, chapbook), *Eroding Witness: Poems* (1985, a National Poetry Series selection), *Outlantish* (1992), *School of Udhra* (1993/2001), *Song of the Andoumboulou, 18-20* (1994), *Whatsaid Serif* (1998), and his National Book Award-winning *Splay Anthem* (2006). A biographer said that all his cross-culturally rich writings were deeply and idiosyncratically erudite, yet "his poetry remains true to an ideal of spontaneous, joyous musicality ultimately derived from improvisational jazz" (Scroggins, 1996). He can also be heard on his recording, *Strick: Song of the Andoumboulou 16-25* (1995), and on his weekly KUSP radio program "Tanganyika Strut," which offers a heterogeneous cross-cultural blend of music with Mackey's expert commentary.

Mackey's essays have been collected in *Discrepant Engagement: Dissonance, Cross-Culturality, and Experimental Writing* (1993/2009), a critical reflection on cross-cultural and experimental aspects of U.S. poetry; and *Paracritical Hinge: Essays, Talks, Notes, Interviews* (2005), a diverse array of literary insights, biography, and history, as well as Mackey's ongoing theme linking music and creative writing. In 1974, Mackey coedited the first issue of the literary journal *Hambone*, which ceased publication until 1982; since he resurrected it, he has been its sole editor. Regarding its creation, he said, "My idea was to simply put my sense of a community of writers and artists on a kind of map, in one place. . . . [W]hat little magazines . . .

do best . . . [is to] put a particular editor's sense of 'what's up' out there, and you find out who out there is interested in that" (from his 1995 Funkhouser interview). He also guest-edited an issue of *Callaloo: A Journal of African-American and African Arts and Letters* (Winter 1995); in turn, *Callaloo* dedicated its Spring 2000 issue to essays on Mackey and his writings. Mackey also coedited the anthologies *Moment's Notice: Jazz in Poetry and Prose* (1993, with Art Lange) and *American Poetry: The Twentieth Century* (2000, two volumes, with Carolyn Kizer, John Hollander, Robert Hass, and Marjorie Perloff). Further, he participated in *Conversations with Nathaniel Mackey* (1993/1999, edited by Kamau Brathwaite and Chris Funkhouser).

Having conquered poetry and nonfiction prose, Mackey tackled a series of epistolary novels, in which letters written by jazz musician "N" carry the action. The series, entitled *From A Broken Bottle Traces of Perfume Still Emanate*, includes the volumes *Bedouin Hornbook* (1986/2000), *Djbot Baghostus's Run* (1993/2000), *Atet, A.D.* (2001), and *Bass Cathedral* (2008). A reviewer in *Publishers Weekly* described his novels as poetic and avant-garde, but also "dense and challenging." The letters from "N" actually originated in poems in Mackey's *Eroding Witness* collection. His poetry, short fiction, fiction excerpts, and literary criticism have been published in a variety of periodicals (e.g., *MELUS: The Journal of the Society for the Study of the Multi-Ethnic Literature of the United States, San Francisco Review of Books, World Literature Today*). Throughout his writings, he marries music and literature. Almost two decades ago, he married Pascale Gaitet, with whom he shares a stepson, Joe, and a biological daughter, Naima.

REFERENCES: *AANB. AAW:PV. BAWPP. CAO-06. LFCC-07. VBAAP. Wiki.* Funkhouser, Christopher. "An Interview with Nathaniel Mackey." *Callaloo*. 18.2 (Spring 1995) p. 321. From *Literature Resource Center.* Habell-Pallán, Michelle, in COCAAL and in OCAAL. Mackey, Nathaniel, and Edward Foster. "An Interview with Nathaniel Mackey." *Talisman: A Journal of Contemporary Poetry and Poetics*.9 (Fall 1992): pp. 48-61. Rpt. in David M. Galens (Ed.) (2003), *Poetry Criticism* (Vol. 49). Detroit: Gale. From *Literature Resource Center.* Maynard, James, in GEAAL. O'Leary, Peter. "An Interview with Nathaniel Mackey. *Chicago Review. 43.1* (Winter 1997), p. 30. From *Literature Resource Center.* Scroggins, Mark, in *AAP-WWII-1996-5th.* Amazon.com

Madgett (2nd married name), Naomi Long (née Naomi Cornelia Long)
7/5/1923–
Poems, anthologies, autobiography/memoir, nonfiction

Naomi Long was encouraged to love learning and reading at an early age, and she had a promising start as a poet, with her *Songs to a Phantom Nightingale* (1941) published in her maiden name, just a few days after she graduated from high school. After high school, she attended her mother's alma mater, Virginia State College, at which she earned her B.A. (1945). Later, she noted that she felt very isolated from other African-American poets during this time, and many of the poems she wrote during this period were not published until later, in *Phantom Nightingale: Juvenilia, Poems 1934-1943)* (1981).

Although she started graduate school at New York University, she withdrew after just one semester, when she married Juan F. Witherspoon. The pair then moved to Detroit, where she worked as a reporter and copyreader for the African-American weekly the *Michigan Chronicle* until her daughter Jill was born (in 1947). During this time, a few of her poems were published appearing under her married name, Naomi Long Witherspoon. Between 1948 and 1949, she and Witherspoon divorced, and she started working for one of the Bell telephone companies, which she continued until 1954. She then married William H. Madgett, whose surname she has used for her writing ever since.

In 1955, she started teaching in Detroit-area public schools and attended Wayne State University. In 1956, she earned her master's degree in English education and published her second poetry collection, *One and the Many* (1956). Throughout her teaching career, she tried to encourage high-schoolers and junior-high-schoolers to develop an appreciation of African-American literature. (Among her students was **Pearl Cleage**, who later acknowledged the importance of Madgett's encouragement.) In 1965, she introduced both a course in creative writing and the first African-American literature course ever taught in the Detroit public schools.

Meanwhile, Madgett took additional postgraduate courses (1961-1962, University of Detroit). During the 1965-1966 school year, Madgett received the first grant of a $10,000 fellowship from the Mott Foundation to pursue her research interests at the Oakland University in Rochester, Michigan. She used this time to write her third poetry collection, *Star by Star: Poems* (1965), and an African-American literature textbook for high-school students, *Success in Language and Literature/B* (1967, with Ethel Tincher and Henry B. Maloney). In 1968, Madgett was offered a position teaching creative writing and African-American literature in the English language and literature department at Eastern Michigan University in Ypsilanti. She continued to teach there until her retirement in 1984. As a complement to the textbook she wrote for her high-school students, she wrote a college-level textbook, *A Student's Guide to Creative Writing* (1980). That same year, she was awarded a Ph.D. in literature and creative writing from the International Institute for Advanced Studies.

Early in the 1970s, three of Madgett's friends founded **Lotus Press**, and they asked to publish her fourth poetry collection, *Pink Ladies in the Afternoon: New Poems 1965-1971* (1972). In 1974, Madgett arranged to take over the press, handling its existing books and using its name. Four years later, Madgett's Lotus Press published her fifth poetry collection, *Exits and Entrances* (1978). Two years after that, she and her daughter, Jill Witherspoon Boyer, and her third husband, elementary school principal Leonard Patton Andrews (died in 1996), incorporated Lotus Press as a nonprofit, tax-exempt corporation. After Madgett's 1984 retirement, she delved into developing this small, independent press. By the early 1990s, the press had published 75 titles, most of which are still in print. The press has been instrumental in keeping African-American poetry in print and was the first to publish the writings of such notables as **Houston Baker**, **Toi Derricotte**, **Lance Jeffers**, **Gayl Jones**, **Pinkie Gordon Lane**, and **Paulette Childress White**. In recognition of her work as publisher and editor, the Before Columbus Foundation honored her with its American Book Award in 1993; before and since, she has earned countless other awards, including her designation as Detroit's poet laureate in 2001.

Madgett wrote two poetry collections honoring her Aunt Octavia Long: *Octavia and Other Poems* (1988, published by **Third World Press**), which included poems about other family members, and *Octavia: Guthrie and Beyond* (2002, Lotus Press), which focuses on the Octavia poems but adds family photographs and history. Madgett's other poetry collections include *Remembrances of Spring: Collected Early Poems* (1993) and *Connected Islands: New and Selected Poems* (2004), both published by Lotus Press. She has also written some "poster-poems," such as *Hymns Are My Prayers* (1997, Lotus Press), comprising seven hymn-inspired poems. Madgett has also edited several anthologies, including *Deep Rivers, a Portfolio: Twenty Contemporary Black American Poets, with Teachers' Guide* (1974/1978); *A Milestone Sampler: Fifteenth Anniversary Anthology* (1988); and *Adam of Ife: Black Women in Praise of Black Men, Poems* (1992); and her own poems have been anthologized in nearly 200 volumes and have been translated into several languages. Whether writing in free verse, prose poems, or her own distinctively rhyming, metered poetry, Madgett pierces to the core of her subject, simply and eloquently voicing its essence. In 2006, Lotus Press published her comprehensive chronological autobiography *Pilgrim Journey*.

REFERENCES: *BAWPP. BV. CAO-02. EBLG. LFCC-07. TtW. W. Wiki.* Black-Parker, Kimberly, in *GEAAL.* Deck, Alice A., in *BWA:AHE.* Madgett, Naomi Long. 2006. *Pilgrim Journey.* Detroit: Lotus Press. Sedlack, Robert P., in *AAW-40-55. OCWW.* Wedge, George F., in *COCAAL.* Amazon.com. Madgett's early papers are archived in the Special Collections of Fisk University Library, and her more recent works, as well as copies of her earlier ones, are archived at the University of Michigan Special Collections Library.

Madhubuti, Haki (né Don L. [Luther] Lee)
2/23/1942–
Poems; publisher

In Little Rock, Arkansas, Don Lee was born to Jimmy L. and Maxine Graves Lee. The following year, the small family moved to Detroit, Michigan, where Jimmy abandoned the family just before the birth of Lee's sister, during the last half of 1943. Maxine had to support herself and her young children through her earnings as a janitor in the three-story apartment building where they lived. Unbeknownst to Don and his sister, the young and beautiful Maxine also had to perform sexual favors for the landlord—an African-American preacher and undertaker— in exchange for rent. Maxine's mopping, sweeping, hauling of trash, and other janitorial duties put food on the table and clothes on their backs.

In addition to providing a home for her children, Maxine encouraged them to read. Although "poetry in my home was almost as strange as money" (Madhubuti, 1988, p. 295), reading was not at all foreign in the Lee home. When Don was just 13 years old, Maxine urged him to go to the Detroit public library and check out a book titled *Black Boy* by **Richard Wright**. Initially, he avoided doing so. As he later recalled, "I refused to go because I didn't want to go anywhere and ask for anything black. The self hatred that occupied my mind, body and soul simply prohibited me from going to a white library in 1955 to request from a white librarian a book by a black author, especially with 'Black' in the title" (Madhubuti, 1994, p. 9). (As Madhubuti has observed since, the American educational system subtly reinforces white supremacy and black self-loathing.) Despite his aversion, Don eventually responded to her repeated requests and read Wright's autobiographical novel. That book changed his life forever, as he felt that his life was very similar to that of Wright. He further realized that by reading Wright, he was beginning to see African Americans in a new light, and he began reading works by other African-American authors.

By the time Don read *Black Boy*, Maxine had changed jobs and was serving drinks in Sonny Wilson's, one of the top bars in Detroit. Sadly, Maxine was also heavily imbibing alcohol, as well. By the time Don was 15, Maxine had also become addicted to other drugs. At about that time, Don's sister (barely 14 years old) revealed that she was pregnant, and soon after, Don picked a fight with the 21-year-old gang leader who had impregnated her. Needless to say, Don was ill prepared for the beating he took, and when he told his mother what had happened, she gave him another licking for having been beaten. Maxine's addiction to alcohol and other drugs continued to deepen, and she turned to prostitution to support her

habits. Fifteen-year-old Don ended up spending many a night searching cheap motels looking for Maxine.

Pretty soon, Don's younger sister was pregnant again, and soon after, Maxine took a fatal overdose of drugs. (His younger sister was unwed with six children by the time she was 30 years old.) At age 16, Don Lee was on his own and moved to Chicago, where he stayed with an aunt. There, he sold magazines, worked two newspaper routes, and cleaned a local bar. After a while, he rented a room at the Southside YMCA and finished his high school education at Dunbar High School. Not long after that, he moved to St. Louis, Missouri, where he joined the U.S. Army.

When Don Lee got off the bus at boot camp, he was 1 of 3 African Americans in a group of 200 recruits. In his hand was a copy of *Here I Stand*, by **Paul Robeson**. The white drill sergeant grabbed the book from his hand, made a racist remark, tore pages from the book, and handed a page to each recruit, ordering them to use the pages for toilet paper. This did not bode well for Lee's military career. It did, however, teach Lee an important lesson about the power of ideas to incite humans to action. Lee became ever more devoted to reading books by and about African Americans. Throughout the remainder of his two-year military career, Lee read just about a book a day.

By the time he left the service, in August 1963, he was determined to use words to serve the interests and wellbeing of African Americans. Four years later, Lee and two fellow poets (**Carolyn M. Rodgers** and **Johari Amini**) bought a mimeograph machine and cofounded **Third World Press** (TWP). By the late 1990s, black-owned TWP was one of the largest African-American publishers in the United States and abroad.

Another of Lee's goals was to uplift and educate fellow African Americans, so in 1969, he started the Institute of Positive Education/New Concept Development Center. He also cofounded the Organization of Black American Culture (OBAC) Writer's Workshop. By 1970, Lee had published his collections *Don't Cry, Scream* (1969) and *We Walk the Way of the New World* (1970). He was also a star performer of the **Black Arts Movement**, giving about three readings a week throughout the country. Since then, he has been invited to speak throughout the world, including Algiers, Tanzania, Senegal, Nigeria, India, and Brazil. In 1973, Don Lee rejected his birth name (his "slave name") and named himself Haki Madhubuti, which means "strong" and "precise" in Swahili.

Madhubuti writes his poems to be spoken aloud, using a distinctively African-American voice, and inviting his listeners to participate with him during his readings. He credits African-American music, lifestyles, churches, and people as the inspiration for his poetry, which expresses both the beauty and the joy of the African-American experience and his outrage at the oppression African Americans endure. As critic Liz Gant said, his "lines rumble like a street gang on the page" (Madhubuti, 1988, p. 295). **Gwendolyn Brooks**, with whom he shared a special mentoring relationship, said of his poetry, "The last thing these people crave is elegance. It is very hard to enchant, with elegant song, the ears of a fellow whose stomach is growling" (Madhubuti, 1969, p. 9).

In addition to his poetry, Madhubuti has been a poet in residence at Cornell University, the University of Illinois (Chicago), Howard University, and Central State University. He taught English at Chicago State University and directed the university's Gwendolyn Brooks Center. Madhubuti is also one of the best-selling authors of poetry and nonfiction in the world, with more than 3 million copies of his books in print—one of the few writers of the **Black Arts Movement** who is still widely read today. In addition to his books, his poetry is published in newspapers and in such journals as *Journal of Black Poetry*, **Negro Digest**, Black Dialogue, Soulbrook, Freedomways, Umbra, Liberator, and many others. In addition to these publications, Madhubuti also has appeared on several radio and television programs. According to scholar Steven Henderson, Madhubuti is more widely imitated than any other African-American poet except **Amiri Baraka**.

Madhubuti also has been much honored for his work as a writer, publisher, educator, and social activist. His numerous awards include the American Book Award, the Black Caucus Award of the National Council of Teachers of English, honors from the African American Cultural Center of Los Angeles Foundation, a leadership award from the National Council of Black Studies, a community service award from the African American Heritage Studies Association, and the Paul Robeson Award of the African American Arts Alliance. He was also named 1991 Author of the Year in the state of Illinois. Madhubuti is also a founding board member of the National Association of Black Book Publishers and is editor of the *Black Books Bulletin.*

In addition to his books and other publications, Madhubuti's legacy will be his advocacy of a distinctively African-American literature, which celebrates the life experiences and views of African Americans and his belief that African-American literature should positively enhance the living conditions of African Americans. Another of Madhubuti's successes was also self-taught, as he never observed it in his own childhood: He has had a stable marriage and has been an involved father to his children.

REFERENCES: Madhubuti, Haki R. 1994. *Claiming Earth: Race Rage, Rape and Redemption, Blacks Seeking a Culture of Enlightened Empowerment.* Chicago: Third World Press. _____. (1988), in *Contemporary Authors* (New Revision Series, Vol. 24), Detroit: Gale Research. _____. 1969/ *Don't Cry, Scream/* Chicago: Third World Press. —Michael Strickland

Editor's note: The author's poetry collections as Don L. Lee included several published by Broadside Press: *Think Black* (1967; enlarged edition, 1969/1983); *Black Pride* (1967), *Don't Cry, Scream* (1969), *We Walk the Way of the New World* (1970), and *Directionscore: Selected and New Poems* (1971); Broadside also published Lee's essay collections, *Dynamite Voices I: Black Poets of the 1960s* (1971) and *From Plan to Planet-Life Studies: The Need for Afrikan Minds and Institutions* (1973; reprinted in 1992 by Third World Press). Lee cofounded Third World Press in 1967 with Carolyn Rodgers, Roschell Rick, and his first wife, Johari Amini, with whom he had his son Don. TWP published Lee's nonfiction, *For Black People (and Negroes Too)* (1968), and Johnson Publishing published his anthology, *To Gwen with Love* (1971, edited with P. L. Brown and F. Ward). Lee also wrote *Back Again, Home: Confessions of an Ex-executive* and *One Sided Shootout* (both in 1968).

In 1973, Lee renamed himself Haki Madhubuti, and Broadside Press published his poetry collection *Book of Life.* Broadside later published *A Capsule Course in Black Poetry Writing* (1983), which he produced with Gwendolyn Brooks, Keorapetse Kgositsile, and Dudley Randall. Lotus Press published his poetry collection *Killing Memory* in 1987. Third World Press (TWP), over which he has presided as publisher and editor, has printed his other writing, including his poetry collections *Ground-Work: New and Selected Poems, Don L. Lee/Haki R. Madhubuti from 1966-1996* (1996), *Heartlove: Wedding and Love Poems* (1998), *Run Toward Fear: New Poems and a Poet's Handbook* (2004), and *Liberation Narratives: Collected Poems 1966-2007* (2009); his poetry and essay collection *Earthquakes and Sunrise Missions: Poetry and Essays of Black Renewal, 1973-1983* (1984); and his essay collections *Enemies: The Clash of Races* (1978), *Black Men: Obsolete, Single, Dangerous? Afrikan American Families in Transition: Essays in Discovery, Solution, and Hope* (1990), *Tough Notes: A Healing Call for Creating Exceptional Black Men: Affirmations, Meditations, Readings, and Strategies* (2002), and *Freedom to Self-Destruct: Much Easier to Believe Than Think, New and Collected Essays* (due out in 2009).

His other nonfiction prose published by TWP include *Kwanzaa: A Progressive and Uplifting African American Holiday* (1987), and *Claiming Earth: Race, Rage, Rape, Redemption: Blacks Seeking a Culture of Enlightened Empowerment* (1994), as well as his memoir *YellowBlack: The First Twenty-One Years of a Poet's Life* (2005). TWP also published *African-Centered Education: Its Value, Importance, and Necessity in the Development of Black Children* (1991), which he wrote with his wife, Safisha L. Madhubuti (married since 1974), with whom he has three children, Laini Nzinga, Bomani Garvey, and Akili Malcolm. She also teaches in the School of Education at Northwestern University, and the two of them cofounded the Institute of Positive Education. The Institute published some pamphlets and other nonfiction, including *The Need for an Afrikan Education* (1972) and *Black People and the Coming Depression* (1975, with Jawanza Kunjufu); and it republished his *From Plan to Planet-Life Studies: The Need for Afrikan Minds and Institutions* (1992; originally Broadside Press, 1973). TWP published his pamphlet *Developmental Manual for Young Black Males* (1996) and his *Malcolm X: Visionary: El Haj Malik, El Shabazz, and the 21st Century* (1993).

Madhubuti has also edited numerous TWP anthologies, including *Say That the River Turns: The Impact of Gwendolyn Brooks* (1987), including both poetry and prose; *Confusion by Any Other Name: Essays Exploring the Negative Impact of the Blackman's Guide to Understanding the Blackwoman* (1990); *Children of Africa* (1993); *Why L.A. Happened: Implications of the '92 Los Angeles Rebellion* (1993); *Million Man March/Day of Absence: A Commemorative Anthology: Speeches, Commentary, Photography, Poetry, Illustrations, Documents* (1996, with Maulana Karenga); and *Black Culture Centers: Politics of Survival and Identity* (2005, with Fred Hord). Madhubuti also edited two other TWP anthologies in conjunction with Chicago's Gallery 37 Project, an educational program in the visual and literary arts for youths ages 14 to 21 years: *Releasing the Spirit* (1998, with Gwendolyn Mitchell) and *Describe the Moment: A Collection of Literary Works from Gallery 37* (2000/2008). TWP also published two of Madhubuti's spoken-word audio recordings: *Medasi* (1990) and *Rise Vision Comin* (2003).

REFERENCES: *AAW:PV. BAWPP. CAO-05. CBAPD. MWEL. Wiki.* Hurst, Catherine Daniels, in *AAP-55-85.* Jennings, Regina, in *GEAAL.* Joyce, Joyce A., in *COCAAL.* McAninch, Jerry B., in *APSWWII-1.* Wainwright, Mary Katherine, in *BB.* Amazon.com, April 5, 2009. //www.poets.org/poet.php/prmPID/484/.

Magazines and Journals *See* Journals and Magazines, Literary

---

Major, Clarence
12/31/1936–

Novels, poems, short stories, nonfiction books and essays, anthologies, autobiography/memoir, columns; educator, editor, publisher

Clarence Major's roots extend from the South (both urban Atlanta, where he was born, and the rural South, where he visited his grandparents each summer) to the North (Chicago, where he moved at age 10 with his mother, after his parents divorced). As a youngster, in Chicago, Clarence was captivated by an exhibit of modern art, highlighting Van Gogh and other European artists; these paintings stirred him deeply—particularly the Impressionists—and fostered his lifelong fascination with the visual arts. Books also fascinated him, and he read avidly in his youth.

When Clarence was 17 years old, he thought he would pursue painting and studied at the Chicago Art Institute. From there, he went on to study at the New School for Social Research (in New York), the State University of New York, and the Union for Experimental Colleges and Universities. During this educational journey, Major also decided to earn his daily bread through literature and to pursue painting as an avocation. He also expresses his artistry through photographs, which have been showcased in exhibits and in publications. He often manages to combine visual and literary arts, however, as he did in his books *Reflex and Bone Structure* (1975/1996) and *Emergency Exit* (1979), which integrate his paintings and photography into the body of the text. Major is also a teacher, starting with young adolescents and then continuing to teach young adults at various colleges and universities, most recently as professor of literature and creative writing in the English Department at the University of California, Davis (since 1989).

Major has written hundreds of pieces published in periodicals such as *Kenyon Review, The New York Times Book Review, The Nation, Poetry,* and the *Washington Post* and in numerous anthologies. In addition, Major has edited an issue of the *Journal of Black Poetry* and has been a member of the Fiction Collective (comprising mostly white authors), which published *Jerry Bumpus, Things in Place* (1975), a collection of short stories Major edited. Major's own published works also include short stories, poetry, novels, a dictionary of slang (three editions), and other nonfiction. In nearly all of these works, Majors shows his artistic predilection for experimentation and exploration. In his fiction, he bends, twists, and chops plot structure; toys with the narrative voice; and plays with characters, manipulating identity. Through these devices, he communicates his postmodernist view regarding the difficulty of forming a coherent identity and of finding a clear meaning within our incoherent contemporary society. He has described his own writing process in this way: "I often think that the best writing is done after you've forgotten what you wanted to say, but end up putting something down anyway just as though it were the actual evidence of your original intention" (quoted on p. 48, *TWL*).

In *Fun and Games: Short Fictions* (1988/1996), Major collected several of his short experimental fiction works, earning a *Los Angeles Times* Book Critics Award nomination. His nonfiction books include *The Dark and Feeling: Black American Writers and Their Work* (1974), a collection of essays and interviews, and the *Dictionary of*

Afro-American Slang (1970; in England, *Black Slang: A Dictionary of Afro-American Talk*, 1971), which was revised, expanded, and updated as *Juba to Jive: A Dictionary of African-American Slang* (1994). In the new millennium, Major published *Afterthought: Essays and Criticism* (2000), *Trips: A Memoir* (2001), and *Necessary Distance* (2001), which includes book reviews and critical pieces, as well as more autobiographical essays. Probably his most widely acclaimed nonfiction work is his essay "A Black Criterion," in which he urged African-American poets and other artists to use authentically African-American criteria for writing and judging their own works, rather than using European or European-American standards for their work. Major also encourages all artists to preserve the integrity of their artistic vision and to focus on the quality of their work, rather than on any particular ideological standards—black or white—for their work.

Major applied the standards he proposed in selecting the materials for his anthologies: *Writers Workshop Anthology, Harlem Education Program* (1967); *Man Is Like a Child: An Anthology of Creative Writing by Students* (1968); *The New Black Poetry* (1969/1970), an eclectic anthology highlighting the work of young poets from across the nation; *Calling the Wind: Twentieth-Century African-American Short Stories* (1993), a collection of both short stories and essays; and *The Garden Thrives: 20th-Century African-American Poetry* (1996). He edited and performed other duties for several periodicals: as associate editor, *American Book Review* (1978-), *Bopp* (1977-1978), *Caw* (1967-1970), *Gumbo* (1978), and *Journal of Black Poetry* (1967-1970); columnist, *American Poetry Review* (1973-1976); editor, *American Book Review* (1977-1978); editor and publisher, Coercion Press (1958-1966), which published *Coercion Review* (1958-1961); editorial board member, *Umojo: A Scholarly Journal of Black Studies* (1979); fiction editor, *High Plains Literary Review* (1986-); and staff writer, *Proof* (1960-1961).

Major's original poetry volumes include *The Fires That Burn the Heaven* (1954), published when he was just 18 years old; his mimeographed Coercion Press volumes *Love Poems of a Black Man* (1965) and *Human Juices* (1966); *Swallow the Lake* (1970); *Private Line* (1971); *Symptoms and Madness* (1971); *The Cotton Club: New Poems* (1972); *The Syncopated Cakewalk* (1974); *The Other Side of the Wall* (1982); *Inside Diameter: The France Poems* (1985); *Surfaces and Masks* (1988), a book-length poem about links between Europeans and Americans, as viewed through a journey to Venice; *Some Observations of a Stranger at Zuni in the Latter Part of the Century* (1989), from a sojourn inspired by the true story of an African who explored the American Southwest as a servant of sixteenth-century Spanish adventurers; *Parking Lots: A Poem* (1992); his retrospective *Configurations: New & Selected Poems, 1958-1998* (1998), nominated for the Na-

tional Book Award; and *Waiting for Sweet Betty* (2002), praised as "his most subtle and beautiful book yet, highlighting his impressive range of styles and his precision of expression" (in *Publishers Weekly*).

Major's *All-Night Visitors* (1969), a well-written, often-erotic interracial story was censored and expurgated when originally published; an unexpurgated edition was published in 2000. Major's other novels include *No* (1973), which has been described as a "literary detective story"; *Reflex and Bone Structure* (1975), a murder mystery; *Emergency Exit* (1979), incorporating black-and-white reproductions of Major's paintings, and in which Major surrealistically explores the relationships between the narrator, the reader, and the story; *My Amputations: A Novel* (1986/2008), inspired by Cubist paintings; *Such Was the Season: A Novel* (1987/2003), Major's relatively conventional, realistic narrative, a memoir about African-American middle-class Atlantans; *Painted Turtle: Woman with Guitar, a Novel* (1988), about a Native-American (Zuni) woman who questions—and seeks—her own cultural identity; and *Dirty Bird Blues: A Novel* (1996), about a blues musician to whom the line "If it wasn't for bad luck, I wouldn't have no luck at all" truly applies. Major's experimental novels have been called "metafictional," in that they go beyond fiction to include narratives in which the author/narrator reflects on his own narrative stance. Major's highly praised *One Flesh* (2003) strays from his metafictional style into a conventional linear narrative about an interracial love story, written from a third-person viewpoint. In an interview, he observed, "Exploring different personae in my earlier novels was something that grew out of my sense of personal fragmentation. Those feelings have changed somewhat as I've gotten older and had the opportunity to resolve some of those conflicts about myself and recognize integration rather than separation. When you're young, you haven't had the experiences that allow perspective on who you are or how to know what 'you' consist of" (in Kutnik and McCaffery, 1994). Major also wrote a television script, *Africa Speaks to New York* (1970).

Although distinctively African American in his voice, his work clearly shows the influence of European and European-American writers and artists. He has been honored with a Fulbright fellowship, a National Council on the Arts fellowship, two Pushcart Prizes (1976, 1989), and numerous other awards and prizes, in addition to his National Book Award in Poetry nomination. He also served on a jury for the National Book Award for fiction (1994).

REFERENCES: AANB. AAW:PV. BAL-1-P. BAWPP. BB. CAO-01. CBAPD. EBLG. G-97. LFCC-07. NAAAL. OC20LE. TWL. W. Wiki. Byerman, Keith E., in COCAAL and in OCAAL. Cassidy, Thomas J., in GEAAL. Cruz, Victor Hernández, Walt Shepperd, and Clarence Major. (1972). "An Interview with Clarence Major and Victor Hernandez Cruz." Abraham Chapman (Ed.), *New Black Voices: An*

Anthology of Contemporary Afro-American Literature. New York: New American Library. Rpt. in Elisabeth Gellert (Ed.) (2002), *Poetry Criticism* (Vol. 37, pp. 545-552). Detroit: Gale Group. From *Literature Resource Center.* Klinkowitz, Jerome in *CN-6.* Kutnik, Jerzy, and Larry McCaffery. "I Follow My Eyes": An Interview with Clarence Major. African American Review. 28.1 (Spring 1994) p. 121. From *Literature Resource Center.* Reilly, John M., in *CP-6.* Weixlmann, Joe, in *AAFW-55-84.* //www.nathanielturner.com/clarencemajor.htm. //www.poetryfoundation.org/archive/poet.html?id=4320. //www.poets.org/poet.php/prmPID/488. Amazon.com.

Malveaux, Julianne (Marie)
9/22/1953–

Essays, articles, nonfiction—economics; economist, scholar, educator, entrepreneur, executive, administrator

Malveaux's first published work was poetry (while she was still in her teens) and a literary review. Her primary genre, however, has been nonfiction prose—specifically, nationally syndicated columns, as well as essays and articles on scholarly and popular topics, for which her Ph.D. in economics from M.I.T. (Massachusetts Institute of Technology) prepared her well. She has collected her popular newspaper columns into *Sex, Lies, and Stereotypes: Perspectives of a Mad Economist* (1994) and *Wall Street and the Side Street: A Mad Economist Takes a Stroll* (1999), which offered prescient commentary on the 2008 economic disaster. Her writings have inspired rabble-rousing scholar **Cornel West** to say, "Julianne Malveaux is the most provocative, progressive and iconoclastic public intellectual in the country." She has also edited volumes on how economic issues affect black women, *Slipping through the Cracks: The Status of Black Women* (1986, with Margaret Simms), *Voices of Vision: African American Women on the Issues* (1996), and *State of Black America 2008: The Black Woman's Voice* for the National Urban League (2008, with Stephanie J. Jones). In addition, she has written pamphlets on economics (e.g., *The Status of Women of Color in the Economy: the Legacy of Being Other,* 1984; *The Economic Predicament of Low-income Elderly Women,* 1992). She has also cowritten *Black Women in the Labor Force* (1980, with Phyllis A. Wallace and Linda Datcher) and *Unfinished Business: The 10 Most Important Issues Women Face Today* (2003, with Deborah Perry), originally titled *Unfinished Business: A Democrat and a Republican Take on the 10 Most Important Issues Women Face Today* (2002). Malveaux furthered her iconoclast credentials by coediting *Paradox of Loyalty: An African American Response to the War on Terrorism* (2002), with Reginna A. Green.

Green is a research associate at Malveaux's multimedia production company Last Word Productions, which produces public-affairs radio and television programs for a national audience. A frequent television guest, Malveaux has also hosted her own radio show. Malveaux has also worked as a junior staff economist for the White House Council of Economic Advisers (1977-1978), a research fellow for the Rockefeller Foundation (1978-1980), an assistant professor at the New School for Research (1980-1981) and San Francisco State University (1981-1985), a research associate for the University of California, Berkeley (starting in 1985), and a diversity-in-residence scholar at Bennett College for Women (2006-2007) in Greensboro, North Carolina, where she replaced Johnnetta Betsch Cole as the school's fifteenth president (starting June, 2007). Malveaux also serves her community as a member or officer of numerous boards, foundations, and other organizations.

REFERENCES: *AANB. CAO-06. Wiki.* Sanchez, Brenna, in *BB.* Smith, Jessie Carney, in *PBW.* //library.agnesscott.edu/about/events/Julianne_Malveaux_Bibliography.htm. //www.bennett.edu/administration/pdf/BiographicalSummaryofthePresident.pdf. //www.diverseeducation.com/artman/publish/article_7158.shtml. //www.juliannemalveaux.com/aboutjulianne.html. Amazon.com.

Marrant, John
6/15//1755–4/15/1791

Captivity narrative, spiritual autobiography; missionary

Marrant's first known published work, *A Narrative of the Lord's Wonderful Dealings with John Marrant, a Black* (1785, London), describes him experiencing a religious conversion and then being captured by Native Americans (Cherokees). His conversion occurred when he overheard an English evangelist. Following that experience, he sought spiritual guidance while hiking through the forest. Cherokees saw him, captured him, and initially appeared to threaten him. After a time, however, he won their favor through his appreciation of their culture, adopting their dress and their manners. He rather unsuccessfully attempted to convert them, and they released him, after which he followed a devoutly religious lifestyle. During the Revolutionary War, he was captured again—this time by British sailors, who forced him into service for six years. Upon his release, Marrant studied for the ministry and devoted himself to missionary work in Canada, which he described in his *Journal* (1790).

REFERENCES: Costanzo, Angelo, in *COCAAL* and in *OCAAL.*

FURTHER READING: *AANB. BAWPP. W. Wiki.* Barthelemy, Anthony G. "Black Atlantic Writers of the 18th Century: Living the New Exodus in England and the Americas." *African American Review.* 31.3 (Fall 1997) p. 525. From *Literature Resource Center.* Brooks, Joanna. "Genius in Bondage: Literature of the Early Black Atlantic." *Early American Literature.* 37.2 (Spring 2002) p. 354. From *Literature Resource Center.* Carretta, Vincent. "'Face Zion Forward': First Writers of the Black Atlantic, 1785-1798." *Early American Literature.* 39.1 (Winter 2004) p. 175. From *Literature Resource Center.* Chiles, Katy L., in *GEAAL.* Cullick, Jonathan S. "Unchained Voices: An Anthology of Black Authors in the English Speaking World of the Eighteenth Century." *ANQ.* 12.2 (Spring 1999) p. 50. From *Literature Resource*

Center. May, Cedrick. "John Marrant and the Narrative Construction of an Early Black Methodist Evangelical." *African American Review.* 38.4 (Winter 2004) p. 553. From *Literature Resource Center.* Walker, James W. St G. "Marrant, John, Freeborn Black American," in //www.biographi.ca/009004-119.01-e.php?&id_nbr=2048.

Marshall (married name), Paule (née Burke)
4/9/1929–

Novels, novellas, short stories, essays; journalist, educator, library assistant

Ada and Samuel Burke left their humble home in Barbados at just the right time to reach Brooklyn, New York, during the Great Depression. There, in a "Bajun" (Barbadian) section of the Bedford-Stuyvesant borough, young Paule learned early to savor the sounds, smells, and tastes of her Barbadian mother's kitchen; the rhythms, rhymes, and reasons of African-American culture in her neighborhood; and the European-American culture described in her school.

At home, Paule learned from the "kitchen poets": the womenfolks gathered around her mother's kitchen table, speaking their folk poetry in the rhythmic lyricism of their West Indian homeland. At school, young Paule devoured grandiose novels written by white English men in the nineteenth and twentieth century (e.g., Charles Dickens and William Makepeace Thackeray). After high school, Burke attended New York's Hunter College for a time, but an illness soon forced her to drop out. When she returned to college, Paule majored in English at Brooklyn College, was invited to join Phi Beta Kappa (a prestigious honor society), and graduated cum laude (in 1953).

After graduation, Burke worked briefly at the New York Public Library then joined the staff of *Our World* magazine—initially as a research assistant and then as a full-time writer. *Our World* sent Burke to the Caribbean and to Brazil, to observe the life experiences of Africa's descendants elsewhere in the Americas. On her own, Burke continued her literary education. In college, she had read only two African-American writers: **Paul Laurence Dunbar** and **Richard Wright**. In the late 1950s and early 1960s, she read the writings of other African-American men, citing **Ralph Ellison**'s 1964 *Shadow and Act* as her "literary bible" and identifying **James Baldwin**'s essays as powerful influences on her writing and her thinking.

During this time, Burke also started writing her novel *Brown Girl, Brownstones.* She had no reason to believe her book would ever be published, as she had never seen any published novels by African-American women. Before the 1960s, if a book written by African-American women was somehow published, it was usually ignored and quickly went out of print. Not until Burke finished her own novel did she discover **Zora Neale Hurston**'s *Their*

Paule Marshall

Eyes Were Watching God (1937), **Dorothy West**'s *The Living Is Easy* (1948), and especially **Gwendolyn Brooks**'s *Maud Martha* (1953), which Burke later called "the finest portrayal of an African American woman in the novel to date." Despite the apparent lack of published African-American women novelists, Burke persisted in writing, figuring that she would at least develop her writing skills and deepen her insights into the human experience.

As Paule Burke extended her literary world, she also expanded her personal world. In 1957, she married Kenneth Marshall, and in 1958, she gave birth to Evan-Keith, her only child. Like other men of the 1950s, Kenneth expected his wife to stay home, contentedly caring for him and for their child. Although he was pleased—and proud—that his wife was intelligent and a gifted writer, he could see no reason why she would take time and energy away from the family in order to write. To make matters more difficult, Paule decided that she needed a private place in which to write, so she found someone to supervise her son and started writing in a friend's apartment. Over Kenneth's objections, Paule spent the next two years writing *Brown Girl, Brownstones.*

Marshall set her autobiographical novel in a Barbadian community in Brooklyn during and following the Great Depression. Marshall's exquisitely crafted dialogue keenly reveals the coming-of-age experiences of Selina Boyce, the adolescent daughter of Barbadian immigrants. Her pubescent awakening and identity development are complicated by issues of acculturation in a society that devalues her parents' native culture, by the conflicting values and marital difficulties of her parents, and by her own strength and independence within a society that prizes female submissiveness and dependence. Marshall's work was not a superficial survey of these issues, however. Rather, she explored these issues on an intimate level, psychologically probing the emerging sexuality of a young girl, the complexities of forging a mature mother-daughter relationship, and the struggle for personal identity within a family context.

The 1959 publication of Marshall's book presciently heralded the writings of subsequent novelists. In her work, she urged women to recognize their intrinsic power and strength, but her feminist view of gender issues didn't gain prominence for about a decade. She encouraged African Americans to proudly affirm their African heritage, but her distinctively African-American view of race and class issues didn't become popular until a decade later. Marshall also recognized the value of African-American linguistic forms long before intellectuals started discussing Ebonics and Black English. Although Marshall's talent was critically acclaimed and earned her many awards, she suffered the fate of many other artists who are too far ahead of their time: Her novel was virtually ignored when it first was published, although a Feminist Press reprint of it in the early 1980s was popularly acclaimed and at last enjoyed some commercial success.

Next, Marshall turned her attention to *Soul Clap Hands, and Sing*, a Rosenthal Award-winning set of four novellas published in 1961 (reprinted in 1988). The novellas, titled to match their settings—*Barbados, Brooklyn, British Guiana*, and *Brazil*—tell the stories of four elderly men who reflect back on their lives and must come to terms with how poorly their materialistic values served them in the end. For a while, Marshall then turned her attention to short stories. Her 1962 story "Reena" highlighted the experiences of a college-educated activist African-American woman—again, Marshall was ahead of her time, and the work was neglected then but widely anthologized a decade or two later. In the early 1980s, the Feminist Press reprinted it, along with several of Marshall's other stories in *Reena and Other Stories* (reprinted in 1993, with the novella *Merle*).

After a time, Marshall turned her hand again to novel writing, and her home life finally fell apart. She and Kenneth divorced while she was writing her second novel, *The Chosen Place, The Timeless People*. This novel takes place on a fictional Caribbean island, where Marshall examines issues of colonialism, neocolonialism, cultural oppression, and economic imperialism. In the novel, West Indian villagers, the descendants of slaves, are confronted by the well-meaning but patronizing staff of an American aid project. Cultural conflicts lead to a revolt, in which the villagers rebel against their would-be benefactors.

After her second novel was published (1969/1984), Marshall remarried and started to teach creative writing at Yale, Columbia, and various other universities. She also started spending some of her time living in Haiti. Given her many commitments, Marshall did not complete and publish her third novel, *Praisesong for the Widow*, until 1983. This Before Columbus American Book Award-winning novel centers around Avatara ("Avey") Johnson, a middle-aged, middle-class, well-acculturated African-American suburban New York widow. Avey takes a physical, cultural, and spiritual journey to a Caribbean island, where she reclaims her African heritage. Marshall followed *Praisesong* with her 1983 *Merle and Other Novellas*, another step in her literary and spiritual development.

In Marshall's novel *Daughters* (1991/2004), Ursa, a young African-American New Yorker, confronts a moral dilemma complicated by her relationship with her parents and her mixed cultural heritage. Ursa's mother is African American, and her father is an African-West Indian politician. When her domineering father's reelection campaign gets into trouble, he asks Ursa to help him. She agrees to help but then realizes that the help he needs is not the help he has requested. In order to truly help him, she must resist his powerful influence over her and persuade him to redeem himself, restoring his intrinsic decency and refuting the corrupt political system in which he has become embroiled.

Marshall's *The Fisher King: A Novel* (2000) was "highly recommended" by *Library Journal*, and *Publisher's Weekly* said, "Marshall's triumphant new novel reminds us why she is one of our premier African-American voices. . . . Marshall writes with verve, clarity and humor, capturing the cadences of black speech while deftly portraying the complexity of family relationships and the social issues that beset black Americans" (in //www.Amazon.com). In it, Marshall's protagonist, an eight-year-old boy who grew up in Paris, uncovers the history of two African-American branches of his family. As the youngster opens old wounds, he helps to heal them.

In addition to Marshall's fiction work, she has written numerous essays and articles. Notably, her "From the Poets in the Kitchen" (*The New York Times Book Review*, 1983) acknowledges how profoundly her work was influenced by the **oral tradition** of the women folk poets who gathered in her mother's kitchen years before. Marshall's work is also widely anthologized (e.g., in collections by **Langston Hughes** and **Toni Cade Bambara**) and admiringly reviewed. **Alice Walker** has been quoted as observing that Paule Marshall is "unequaled in intelligence, vision, [and] craft by anyone of her generation, to put her contributions to our literature modestly." In addition to recognition by her peers, Marshall has been given many awards for her writings, as well as several acknowledging her overall stature as a writer: a prestigious MacArthur fellowship for lifetime achievement (in 1992), a Guggenheim fellowship, a National Endowment for the Arts fellowship, and awards from the Ford Foundation, the National Institute of Arts and Letters, and the Yaddo Corporation.

In 2009, Marshall published *Triangular Road: A Memoir,* in which she recalls her life through her personal geography: her youth in Brooklyn, her 1965 U.S. State Department-sponsored whirlwind trip to Europe with legendary Langston Hughes, her government-sponsored trip to Nigeria, and her trip to her parents' birthplace in Barbados, as well as her other experiences, such as her civil rights activism and her work with both noteworthy and notorious editors. *Publishers Weekly* called it an "elegant, passionate, elliptical memoir of self-exploration and revelation"; *Booklist* said, "Acclaimed novelist Marshall . . . poignantly chronicles her travels"; and //www.Amazon.com said, "In this unflinchingly honest memoir, Paule Marshall offers an indelible portrait of a young black woman coming of age as a novelist in a literary world dominated by white men." Marshall's fans will doubtless feel grateful that she applied her superlative storytelling skills to reveal her own narrative.

REFERENCES: *AANB. AAW:PV. AWAW. B. BAWPP. BCE. BASS. BFC. BI. BV. BW:AA. BWA. BWW. CAO-04. CLC-253. EB-98. EBLG. G-95. MAAL. MWEL. NAAAL. OC20LE. VBA. VOO. W. Wiki.* Barnett, Rachael, in *GEAAL.* Christian, Barbara T., in *AAW-1991.* and in *AAFW-55-84.* Davies, Carole Boyce, *T-CCBAW-3.* Gold, Sarah F. "PW Talks with Paule Marshall: To Barbados and Beyond." *Publishers Weekly.* 256.4 (Jan. 26, 2009) p. 106. From *Literature Resource Center.* Mitchell, Keith Bernard, in *COCAAL* and *OCAAL.* Pettis, Joyce, in *ANSWWII-6th* and in *OCWW.* Pettis, Joyce. "A MELUS Interview: Paule Marshall." *MELUS. 17.4* (Winter 1991) pp. 117-129. From *Literature Resource Center.* Pettis, Joyce Owens. 1995. *Toward Wholeness in Paule Marshall's Fiction.* University of Virginia Press. Available at //books.google.com/books?id= KiJWVD33Ov0C&dq=%22joyce+pettis%22&source=gbs_summary _s&cad=0. Reilly, John M., in *CN-6.* Wainwright, Mary Katherine, in *BB.* Watson, Dana Cairns, in *AW:ACLB-02.* Zlogar, Laura Weiss, in *RGAL-3.* Amazon.com.

Marshall, Thurgood
7/2/1908–1/24/1993
U.S. Supreme Court opinions, legal briefs; attorney, U.S. Supreme Court Justice

Young Thurgood graduated from his all-black high school at age 16. In 1930, he graduated with highest honors from Pennsylvania's Lincoln University and married Vivien "Buster" Burey. In 1933, Marshall graduated first

Thurgood Marshall

in his class from Howard University Law School, Washington, D.C.

After a few years in private practice, Marshall started working as an NAACP attorney. A few years later, he became the NAACP chief counsel, helping to develop and implement a plan for using the federal courts to achieve racial equality. He implemented the plan by winning 29 of the 32 cases he argued before the U.S. Supreme Court.

When presenting cases to the Supreme Court, opposing attorneys state why they believe that the justices should decide a case in a particular way. The justices also question the attorneys, probing their reasoning and any constitutional ramifications of the case. The Supreme Court then evaluates how to interpret the relevant laws in light of the U.S. Constitution. For instance, when Marshall won the 1944 *Smith v. Allwright* decision, the justices declared that a Texas law excluding black voters from primary elections was unconstitutional. Other Supreme Court cases that Marshall argued and won during the 1940s and 1950s helped to integrate neighborhoods, public parks, swimming pools, athletic facilities, local bus systems, and university law schools, professional training, and graduate instruction.

Marshall's most celebrated victory was the 1954 *Brown v. Board of Education of Topeka* case. As a result, the United States Supreme Court unanimously ruled that the existing racial segregation in American public schools violated the Constitution of the United States. This decision completely changed the history of segregation in the United States. Marshall's persuasive argument cited the Fourteenth Amendment, which includes an "equal-protection clause" requiring that all citizens be treated alike, regardless of race, color, or creed. This groundbreaking decision provided the historical basis for many of the changes brought about by the civil-rights movement of the 1950s and 1960s. For his outstanding achievements, the NAACP awarded Marshall its prestigious **Spingarn** Medal.

Sadly, in 1955, Marshall's wife "Buster" died. Later, Marshall married Cecilia, with whom he had two sons. In September, 1961, Marshall was nominated to the U.S. Court of Appeals, where he wrote nearly 100 judicial opinions, none of which was overturned by the Supreme Court. Many of his opinions defended civil liberties, such as academic freedom and the right to a fair trial, as well as civil rights. In 1965, Marshall was named U.S. Solicitor General, arguing on behalf of the federal government before the Supreme Court. Two years later, Marshall became the first African American to serve on the Supreme Court, where he wrote countless judicial opinions affecting the lives of all Americans.

REFERENCES: *1TESK. AA:PoP. BaD. BF:2000. E-97. EB-98. G-95. MW-10. WB-98.*

FURTHER READING: *AANB. B. BCE. CE. HD. LE. QB. USGG. W2B. Wiki.* Bloch, Susan Low, in *USSC.* Kennedy, Randall, in *USHC.* Kram, Mark, and Sara Pendergast, in *BB.* Lasch-Quinn, Elisabeth. "Thurgood Marshall: American Revolutionary." *The Wilson Quarterly. 23.1* (Winter 1999) p. 105. From *Literature Resource Center.* National Public Radio, *All Things Considered,* July 2, 2008. Portwood, Shirley J. "Thurgood Marshall: Warrior at the Bar, Rebel on the Bench." *The Mississippi Quarterly. 47.2* (Spring 1994) p. 346. From *Literature Resource Center.*

Matheus, John F. (Frederick)
9/10/1887–2/19/1983
Short stories, plays, book reviews

Among Matheus's 20-plus short stories are "Fog" (*Opportunity*, 1925), "Clay" (*Opportunity*, 1926), and "Sallicoco" (*Opportunity*, 1937); many of his stories were privately published in a collection edited by Leonard A. Slade, Jr. (1974). His six plays, most of which highlight the oppression of African Americans, include *Black Damp,* '*Cruiter* (winner of the 1926 *Opportunity* prize), *Guitar, Ouanga!, Tambour,* and *Ti Yette.* Many of Matheus's plays and short stories have been widely anthologized in important works of his era (e.g., in *Ebony and Topaz, The Negro Caravan, The New Negro, Plays of Negro Life*). Earlier, while he was teaching modern lan-

guages (1910-1922), he also published numerous articles and book reviews in scholarly journals related to his work.

REFERENCES: Dandridge, Rita B., in *COCAAL* and in *OCAAL.*

FURTHER READING: *AANB. BAWPP. CAO-02.* Carson, Warren J., in *GEAAL.* Perry, Margaret, in *AAWHR-40.*

Mathis (married name), Sharon (née Bell)
2/26/1937–
Children's and juvenile books, juvenile biography, columns, poems; educator, librarian

A voracious reader as a child, Mathis recalled, "When I was little I . . . fashioned letters of the alphabet into what I thought were real words. It was fun! It was the beginning of my own desire to write. Then I learned to read! Books were a zillion different kinds of candy and I wished to discover all the flavors" (quoted by Heidi Grosch, Children's Literature Network). Mathis has devoted her adulthood to helping young people develop a similar love of reading. Not only did she do so with her own children, Sherie, Stacy, and Stephanie, but also with other people's children, working as a librarian, a teacher, and a writer in residence. Mathis's books include her juvenile storybooks *Brooklyn Story* (1970); *Sidewalk Story* (1971/1986), chosen by **Tom Feelings** and **John Oliver Killens** for the Council on Interracial Books for Children Award; The *Hundred Penny Box* (1975/2009), winner of a Newbery Honor and a *Boston Globe-Horn Book* Honor; and *Cartwheels* (1977), about three young gymnasts who compete for a prize and triumph over moral challenges. Her juvenile biography *Ray Charles* (1973/2001) won the American Library Association's **Coretta Scott King** Award.

For young adults, she wrote *Teacup Full of Roses* (1972), named a Coretta Scott King Honor book; and *Listen for the Fig Tree* (1973), an American Library Association Notable Book about an intrepid young girl who is blinded at age 10, loses her father at age 15, but has loving support from neighbors and friends. More recently, Mathis's *Red Dog Blue Fly* (1991) offers poems about a football team, and her *Running Girl: The Diary of Ebonee Rose* (1997) uses diary entries to tell the protagonist's story, as well as that of other women athletes of African-American descent. In addition to her books and her published short stories, starting in 1972, Mathis began writing a monthly column "Ebony Juniors Speak!" (in *Ebony Jr.!*) and a biweekly column "Society and Youth" (in *Liteside: D.C. Buyers Guide*). In addition to her individual book awards and honors, she was granted prestigious fellowships for Vermont's Bread Loaf Writers' Conference (1970) and New Hampshire's MacDowell Colony (1978), the oldest artist colony in the nation. About her work, literary biographer Frances Smith Foster said,

"Sharon Bell Mathis writes honestly and respectfully about black people coming to terms with themselves and with those whom they love."

REFERENCES: *BAWPP. CAO-01.* Davis, Mary Virginia, Salem Press for EBSCO Publishing, July 2003, in //0-web.ebscohost.com.dbpcos dcsgt.co.san-diego.ca.us/novelist/detail?vid=26&hid=8&sid=02bf6a 41-8618-414c-abf5-13f22fd219a5%40sessionmgr7&bdata=JnNpdGU 9bm92ZWxpc3QtbGl2ZQ%3d%3d. Foster, Frances Smith, in *AAFW-55-84.* Grosch, Heidi, in //www.childrensliteraturenetwork.org/birth bios/brthpage/02feb/2-26mathis.html. Hinton-Johnson, KaaVonia, in *GEAAL.* Liggins, Saundra, in *COCAAL* and in *OCAAL.*

Matthews (married name), Victoria (née Earle)
5/27/1861–3/10/1907
Novella, edited work, children's stories, articles, essays, spoken word—oratory; activist, organizer, librarian, orator, journalist

Born a slave, Victoria had to spend many of her early years supporting her family through domestic service while trying to educate herself on her own. In 1879, she married William Matthews and soon after started having her essays and short stories appear in various periodicals (e.g., *New York Weekly* and *Waverly*). She also corresponded for the *Boston Advocate* and the *New York Globe* and worked on the staff of **T. Thomas Fortune**'s *New York Age*. While at the *Age*, she compiled and edited the collection *Black Belt Diamonds: Speeches, Addresses and Talks of* **Booker T. Washington** (1898). She also wrote a novella (*Aunt Lindy*, 1893, penned by "Victoria Earle") and quite a few children's stories.

In the late 1890s and early 1900s, after her son died (at age 16), she devoted her attention more fully to social and political activism, helping to organize a women's group and to establish a travelers' aid society for young women from the South. She also raised funds for **Ida B. Wells-Barnett**, after Wells's newspaper offices had been destroyed by Southerners who wished to stop her from publishing her antilynching articles. Shortly afterward, Wells-Barnett joined Matthews at the *New York Age*.

Matthews also founded a nonsectarian Christian home for homeless African-American women and children. There, she set up a library of books by and about African Americans, which she used for her own research in preparing lectures and addresses on African-American history. Perhaps her most famous address, given in 1895 to the first national conference of African-American women, was "The Value of Race Literature," in which she urged the conferees to recognize and preserve the works of African Americans. Two years later, she addressed the Society of Christian Endeavor with her speech, "The Awakening of the Afro-American Woman." Surely, she had contributed to that awakening.

REFERENCES: *BAAW. EA-99.* Cash, Floris Barnett, in *BWA:AHE.*
—Tonya Bolden

FURTHER READING: *AANB. EAAWW. Wiki.* Garfield, Deborah, in *COCAAL.* Gentry, April, in *GEAAL.* Logan, Shirley Wilson, with the assistance of Heidi L. M. Jacobs editorial assistant, and Jennifer Putzi editorial assistant. (2000). *American Women Prose Writers, 1870-1920.* In Sharon M. Harris, Heidi L. M. Jacobs, and Jennifer Putzi (Eds.), *Dictionary of Literary Biography* (Vol. 221). Detroit: Gale Group, From *Literature Resource Center.*

Mayfield, Curtis
6/3/1942–12/26/1999
Songs

Among Mayfield's numerous hit songs are "For Your Precious Love" (1958), "People Get Ready" (1965), "We're a Winner," and the songs for movies such as *Superfly* (1972) and *Let's Do It Again* (1975). In 1990, Mayfield was injured when a lighting rig fell on him, causing him to be paralyzed from the neck down. Since then, in 1994, he was recognized with a Grammy Legend Award.

REFERENCES: *EA-99.*

FURTHER READING: *AANB. All Movie Guide,* in *Act. BCE. D. F. W2B. Wiki.* Bianco, David, and Catherine V. Donaldson, in *BB.* Unterberger, Richie, *All Music Guide,* in *A.*

Mayfield, Julian (Hudson)
6/6/1928–10/20/1984
Novels, plays, scripts, critical essays

After marrying a Mexican physician, Ana Livia Cordero, Mayfield moved to Mexico (in 1954), where he cofounded Mexico's first English-language radio station, for which he also served as newscaster. In addition, he began editing and writing theater reviews for Puerto Rico's *World Journal.* During that time, he also started writing fiction and wrote the novels *The Hit* (1957, based on a one-act play, *417,* which he had written previously), *The Long Night* (1958), and *Grand Parade* (1961). From 1961 to 1966, Mayfield lived in Ghana, where he was the founding editor of *African Review,* while advising Ghana's President Kwame Nkrumah. From 1971 to 1973, he lived in Guyana and advised Guyana's Prime Minister Burnham Forbes. Meanwhile, he edited the short-story collection *Ten Times Black* (1972). Since then (and from 1966 to 1971), he lived in the United States, writing dozens of critical essays and articles for various periodicals.

REFERENCES: Rodney, Ruby V., in *COCAAL* and *OCAAL.*

FURTHER READING: *BAWPP. CAO-02.* Kich, Martin, in *GEAAL.* Taylor, Estelle W., in *AAFW-55-84.*

Julian Mayfield

Maynard, Nancy Hicks (né Nancy Alene Hall)
11/1/1946–9/21/2008
Journalism; reporter, newspaper publisher, educator

Robert (Clyve) Maynard, husband
6/17/1937–8/17/1993
Journalism; reporter, editor, ombudsman, newspaper publisher, educator

Dori J. Maynard, daughter
5/4/1958–
Journalism; reporter, educator, organization leader

Nancy Hall had started at the *New York Post* while still studying journalism at Long Island University (graduating in 1966). In 1968, however, the *Post* refused to let her go to Memphis to report on a garbage-workers' strike, where **Martin Luther King** was later assassinated. Soon after, she left the *Post,* and she became the first African-American woman to work as a full-time regular news reporter for *The New York Times* (1969). During this time, she also married Daniel Hicks, with whom she had a son, David, before Daniel died in 1974. A single parent, reporter Nancy Hicks continued to write articles regarding

science, education, and health, as well as newsworthy race-related stories.

Meanwhile, Robert Maynard was gaining experience as a journalist. He dropped out of high school to report for African-American weekly newspapers such as the *New York Age-Defender.* When still in his teens (1956), he moved to Greenwich Village and freelanced articles for newspapers such as the *Baltimore Afro-American.* By 1960, he already had a wife and a young daughter when he caught a lucky break. As a stringer for the *York [Pennsylvania] Gazette and Daily,* he finagled an interview with Cuban president Fidel Castro. In 1961, the *Gazette* offered Robert steady work as a reporter.

In 1965, Robert won a Nieman Foundation fellowship to attend Harvard University (1965-1966). During his fellowship, brash Robert Maynard had doggedly questioned guest lecturer Ben Bradlee, the new editor-in-chief of the *Washington Post.* When Maynard went to Bradlee's office and asked for work, Bradlee surprised him by responding enthusiastically. Maynard was required to eturn to the *Gazette* for a short time, but exactly one year after he met with Bradlee, Bradlee hired him as the first African-American national news correspondent (1967-1972). Maynard arrived at the *Post* in time to report on Nixon's Watergate scandal and his subsequent resignation from the presidency, as well as other key stories of the day. For a time, he was also the first African-American White House correspondent.

Maynard, who was also single parenting his teenage daughter Dori, remained mindful of the need to mentor other reporters, as well. He codirected the Summer Program for Minority Group Members at Columbia University Graduate School of Journalism (1972, 1973). When Columbia suspended the program in 1974, he, Nancy Hicks, and several other journalists created the summer program anew at the University of California at Berkeley. He also tirelessly sought new minority recruits for the Nieman Foundation's Harvard fellowships. The *Post* named him an associate editor and the *Post's* ombudsman (1972-1974), then it invited him to write editorials (1974-1977).

At a convention of African-American journalists, Nancy Hicks renewed her acquaintance with Robert Maynard. Both single parents, they shared a commitment to journalism and to ensuring that their children would grow up in a world where a diverse array of people would be reporting and managing the news. In 1975, they married. For a while after their marriage, Nancy continued at the *Times* in its Washington bureau, while Robert stayed on at the *Post.* In the summers, they operated their summer program at the University of California's Berkeley campus (UCB).

In 1977, the Maynards left their secure jobs in Washington, D.C., moved across the country to California, and dedicated themselves to a new nonprofit endeavor to diversify the staffing of newsrooms and news offices by training prospective journalists. They joined fellow journalists to found the nonprofit Institute for Journalism Education (IJE) in Berkeley, over which Nancy presided as its first president. This multicultural group was determined to help "the nation's news media reflect America's diversity in staffing, content and business operations" (quoted from //www.mije.org/founders) and has since educated hundreds of students of color to become journalists. Two years later, Nancy and Robert expanded their family with the birth of their son Alex (1979).

Initially, the IJE focused on training reporters for the news desk, but as other institutions developed programs for reporters, the IJE shifted its emphasis to training professionals to work at the editor's desk and in the news manager's office. While Nancy presided over the IJE, Robert chaired it until 1979 and then continued on its faculty until his death in 1993.

Robert also wrote a semiweekly syndicated column (1979-1993) and regularly contributed to numerous television news shows. Robert also made time to consult for the Gannett Company (publishers of USA Today and dozens of other newspapers), as its affirmative-action advisor. In 1979, after Gannett bought the financially ailing Oakland Tribune, it hired Robert as editor-in-chief, making him the first African-American editor-in-chief of a major metropolitan (circulation over 100,000) daily newspaper. In 1983, Gannett sold the Tribune to the Maynards making them the first African Americans to own a major metropolitan daily newspaper. Unfortunately, at the time of Nancy's death, several sources acknowledged that no other African Americans had done so yet.

The Maynards decided just to focus on Oakland and Berkeley, and within two years, the Tribune's circulation had increased to more than 150,000. Its advertising rose, too. The Maynards recruited journalists from across the country, some of whom even accepted pay cuts to work for the Tribune. The paper earned high praise from colleagues, and it won about 150 awards for its reporting, including the Pulitzer, remarkable for the daily newspaper of the eighth-largest city in the state. At one time or another, Robert also served on the boards of directors of numerous organizations, including several Pulitzer Prize committees, the American Society of Newspaper Editors, and the Associated Press.

Robert and Nancy also continued to write articles and criticism for various periodicals, and Nancy wrote a column for the Tribune. Robert also garnered eight honorary doctorates, a 1989 John Peter Zenger Award for Freedom of the Press, a George Chaplin Scholar honor, and the 1991 Elijah Parish Lovejoy national award from Maine's Colby College. Unfortunately, however, honors, prizes, awards, and prestige could not pay the rent. The Maynards

managed to keep the Tribune afloat during a century when more than 1,000 daily newspapers folded, but in 1992, when Robert was diagnosed with prostate cancer, the couple decided to sell their cherished newspaper to William Dean Singleton's Alameda Newspaper Group.

The following year, Robert died, yet he, too, lives on. In honor of Robert's memory, his colleagues at the Institute for Journalism Education renamed it the Robert C. Maynard Institute for Journalism Education (MIJE) in 1993. Since then, the Institute has ensured that editors and publishers can never legitimately complain that they cannot find qualified journalists of color when making hiring or promotion decisions. Two years after his death, Robert's daughter Dori edited his nationally syndicated columns to create the book Letters to My Children (1995),and she continues to honor his work through her own work at the MIJE.

After the sale of the Tribune and Robert's death, Nancy graduated from Stanford Law School and formed Maynard Partners Inc., a media consulting company over which she presided. She also continued to champion diversity in the newsroom and to write, chairing the Freedom Forum Media Studies Center at Columbia University serving on the MIJE board. In 1995, her Nancy Hicks Maynard Press published Joan Kenley's book, Woman's Right to Know—Health and Hormones After 35 (1995). Three years later, the National Association of Black Journalists honored her with a Lifetime Achievement Award (1998). Two years after that, Nancy authored Mega Media: How Market Forces Are Transforming News (2000). Upon her death, Nancy was still revising and polishing her autobiography, tentatively titled Covenant. Several of her friends and colleagues have discussed collaborating to complete it and have it published.

Both Nancy and Robert had high hopes for the future of journalism. Their daughter, Dori J. Maynard has presided over the MIJE since 2001. Prior to taking that post, she had earned her B.A. in American history from Middlebury College in Vermont, and she had followed her father in becoming a Nieman fellowship scholar at Harvard University (1993), the first father-daughter duo to receive this honor. Her journalistic experience has reached beyond the academy, too. She has reported on each coast and in the Midwest, having reported for the Bakersfield Californian, Quincy Massachusetts's Patriot Ledger, and the Detroit Free Press.

As the MIJE's president and chief executive officer, Dori faces a daunting challenge. Though the proportion of journalists of color in daily newsrooms increased from less than 1% to more than 10% during her father's lifetime, it remains at about 13% now, though about 33% of the whole population are people of color—a disparity of 20%. In addition to her work for the MIJE and her work as shepherd of her parents' papers and champion of their work, Dori blogs (available at //www.mije.org/dorimaynard, 2007-2008; and at //www.pbs.org/idealab/dori_j_maynard/, 2007-present). Dori Maynard has also been honored as a prestigious "Fellow of Society" from the Society of Professional Journalists (2001), winner of the 2007 Knight News Challenge, and winner of the 2008 Asian American Journalists Association's Leadership in Diversity Award. She was also voted one of the "10 Most Influential African Americans in the Bay Area" (2004).

REFERENCES: Najjar, Orayb, "ASNE Efforts Increase Minorities in Newsrooms," *Newspaper Research Journal,* Fall 1995, p. 4 of 12, //findarticles.com/p/articles/mi_qa3677/is_199510/ai_n8718252/pg_4/. //en.wikipedia.org/wiki/Oakland,_California. //en.wikipedia.org/wiki/Robert_C._Maynard_Institute_for_Journalism_Education. //www.mije.org/founders. Personal communication, Dori J. Maynard, June 12-15, 2009. "Nancy Hicks Maynard," *Wiki.* Burt, Elizabeth V. 2000. *Women's Press Organizations, 1881-1999.* Westport, CT: Greenwood Press. Christian, Margena A., "Nancy Hicks Maynard, 61, *Oakland Tribune* Publisher," *Jet,* October 13, 2008, in //findarticles.com/p/articles/mi_m1355/is_14_114/ai_n30938424/. "Death of Nancy Hicks Maynard a Terrible Loss," *Oakland Tribune,* September 22, 2008, in //findarticles.com/p/articles/mi_qn4176/is_20080922/ai_n28114597/?tag=rel.res4. "Diversity Advocate Nancy Hicks Maynard Dies at 61," //www.usatoday.com/life/television/news/2008-09-22-maynard-obit_N.htm. Drummond, Tammerlin, "Legacy of Nancy Hicks Maynard Lives on in Journalists of Color," *Oakland Tribune,* Sep 23, 2008, in //findarticles.com/p/articles/mi_qn4176/is_20080923/ai_n28114809/?tag=rel.res3. Hevesi, Dennis, "Nancy Hicks Maynard Dies at 61; A Groundbreaking Black Journalist," in //www.nytimes.com/2008/09/23/business/media/23maynard.html?_r=1&oref=slogin. Holley, Joe, in //www.washingtonpost.com/wp-dyn/content/article/2008/09/21/AR2008092102296.html. Maher, Sean, "Nancy Maynard, Trailblazer and Former *Oakland Tribune* Co-owner, Dies," *Oakland Tribune,* September 21, 2008, in //findarticles.com/p/articles/mi_qn4176/is_20080921/ai_n28114517/?tag=rel.res4. May, Meredith, "Journalist Nancy Hicks Maynard Dies," September 22, 2008, in //www.sfgate.com/cgi-bin/article.cgi?f=/c/a/2008/09/22/BA0T132AII.DTL. *News Watch* Interviews Nancy Maynard, Center for Integration and Improvement of Journalism, in //www.ciij.org/newswatch?id=105. *Newshour with Jim Lehrer,* September 22, 2008. Stepp, Carl Sessions, "A Nonhysterical View of Where News Is Heading," *American Journalism Review,* September 2000, in //www.ajr.org/Article.asp?id=2957, for *American Journalism Review.* //belvadavis.com//?p=399. //en.wikipedia.org/wiki/Kerner_Commission. //news.newamericamedia.org/news/view_article.html?article_id=52d26c57029e749acea009ade44faf27. //worldcat.org/identities/lccn-n00-20611. //www.aaja.org/features/articles/2008_09_22_01/, Asian American Journalists Association. //www.maynardije.org/programs/history/collection/nancy_maynard/. //www.mije.org/nancy-maynard. //www.mije.org/richardprince/nancy-hicks-maynard-dies-61. //www.mije.org/richardprince/nancy-maynard. //www.nyslittree.org/index.cfm/fuseaction/DB.PersonDetail/PersonPK/1363.cfm. //www.nytimes.com/2008/09/23/business/media/23maynard.html?_r=1&oref=slogin. //www.usatoday.com/life/television/news/2008-09-22-maynard-obit_N.htm. "Robert Clyve Maynard," *B. CAO-07. QB.* Bonner, Alice, in *AANB.* Favre, Gregory E., "Maynard: 'Give All Front Door Access to the Truth,'" in //poynter.org/column.asp?id=58&aid=147392. Kram, Mark, in *BB.* //en.wikipedia.org/wiki/Elijah_Lovejoy. //en.wikipedia.org/wiki/Nieman_fellowship. //en.wikipedia.org/wiki/The_NewsHour_with_Jim_Lehrer. //en.wikipedia.org/wiki/Watts_riots_of_1965. //www.amazon.com. //www.gannett.com/about/company_profile.htm. //www.mije.org/history project/caldwell_journals/chapter18. //www.mije.org/robertmaynard.

//www.nieman.harvard.edu/NiemanFoundation/NiemanFellowships/Eligibility.aspx. Amazon.com. "Dori J. Maynard," *Wiki.* //en.wikipedia.org/wiki/Nieman_fellowship. //www.aaja.org/features/articles/2008_09_22_01/2008_09_22_02/. //www.mije.org/blindsided. //www.mije.org/blog/diversity-isnt-only-front-burner-its-not-even-kitchen. //www.mije.org/dorimaynard. //www.mije.org/frontdooraccess. //www.mije.org/richardprince/outing_rappers_given_names. //www.mije.org/staff. //www.mije.org/staffpicks/aaja_awards. //www.nieman.harvard.edu/NiemanFoundation/NiemanFellowships/Eligibility.aspx. //www.pbs.org/idealab/dori_j_maynard/.

Mays, Benjamin Elijah
8/1/1894–3/28/1984
Autobiography/memoir, faith-inspired nonfiction, essays, spoken word—sermons; educator, administrator

Benjamin Elijah Mays was the youngest of eight children in the first generation of his family born free of enslavement in South Carolina, yet he was able to graduate with honors from Bates College in Lewiston, Maine (1920), then earn his M.A. (1925) and then his Ph.D. (1935) from the University of Chicago. While earning his postgraduate degrees, Mays had taught mathematics at Morehouse College in Atlanta, Georgia (1921-1924), while becoming an ordained Baptist minister (1922) and pastor of Shiloh Baptist Church (1922-1924), then an English instructor at South Carolina State College in Orangeburg (1925-1926), executive secretary of the Tampa Urban League in Florida (1926-1928), national student secretary of the YMCA (Young Men's Christian Associations) in New York City (1928-1930), and director of a national study of African-American churches (1930-1932). Mays then collaborated with Joseph William Nicholson to write a report of the study, *The Negro's Church* (1933/1969). While completing his doctorate, he became dean of the School of Religion at Howard University in Washington, D.C. (1934-1940). After earning his doctorate, Mays wrote *The Negro's God as Reflected in His Literature* (1938/1969).

In 1940, Mays was named president of Morehouse College (1940-1967) and then president emeritus (1967-1984). While presiding over Morehouse, he compiled *A Gospel for the Social Awakening: Selections from the Writings of Walter Rauschenbusch* (1950), and he wrote *Seeking to Be Christian in Race Relations* (1957). After his retirement, he wrote a collection of his sermons, *Disturbed about Man* (1969); two autobiographies, *Born to Rebel: An Autobiography* (1971) and *Lord, the People Have Driven Me On* (1981); and *Quotable Quotes of Benjamin E. Mays* (1983). A weekly columnist in the *Pittsburgh Courier* (starting in 1946), Mays was a contributing editor to the *Journal of Negro Education,* and he contributed many articles to other periodicals and to anthologies.

His awards could fill pages of this volume, but a few deserve mention here, such as the Man of the Year Award from the Society for the Advancement of Management (1968), the Religious Leaders Award from the National Conference of Christians and Jews (1970), the **Russwurm** Award from the National Newspaper Publishers (1970), the Roy Wilkins Award from the NAACP (1977), the Distinguished American Educator Award from the U.S. Office of Education (1978), the Hale Woodruff Award from the United Negro College Fund (1978), the Top Hat Award from the *Chicago Defender* (1978), and the **Spingarn** Medal from the NAACP (1982). He was also named to the South Carolina Hall of Fame (1984) and received more than 45 honorary degrees, from Dartmouth, Brandeis, and Harvard to Kalamazoo, the University of Southern California, and the University of Ife in Nigeria.

Mays also consulted for the U.S. Office of Education (1969) and the Ford Foundation (1970), and he presided over the United Negro College Fund (1958-1961). He also played key roles for the World Council of Churches (1948-1953), the U.S. Committee for the United Nations (1959), the Peace Corps (1961), the U.S. National Commission for UNESCO (1962), the Atlanta Board of Education (1969-1981), the Danforth Foundation, and the National Fund for Medical Education. A member of Phi Beta Kappa and Delta Sigma Rho, he spoke at more than 200 educational institutions. He was married and widowed twice, to Ellen Harvin and then to Sadie Grey.

REFERENCES: *AANB. B. BAWPP. CAO-02. EE. Wiki.* Smith, Caroline B. D., in *BB.* //www.bates.edu/about-bates.xml.

FURTHER READING: Cassidy, Thomas J., in *GEAAL.*

McDonald, Janet A.
8/10//1953–4/11/2007
Young-adult novels, essays, autobiography/memoir, journalism, attorney

Few would have expected that a woman who grew up in a public-housing project in Brooklyn would have a B.A. from Vassar College, an M.A. from Columbia University, and a J.D. from New York University Law School. Janet McDonald did so, however, and she lived to tell the tale in her memoir, *Project Girl: An Inspiring Story of a Black Woman's Coming-of-Age* (1999), which was named a Best Book by the *Los Angeles Times.*

McDonald's subsequent works have been novels written for young adults (teens), including *Spellbound* (2001), named a Best Young Adult Novel by the American Library Association (ALA); *Chill Wind* (2002), given a **Coretta Scott King/John Steptoe** New Talent Award from the ALA (2003); *Twists and Turns* (2003), a Quick

Pick for Young Adults selection from the ALA (2003); *Brother Hood* (2004), called "hard-hitting yet thoughtful" by a *Horn Book* reviewer; *Harlem Hustle* (2006), called "a gripping tale of the hood" by *Kirkus Reviews*; and *Off-color* (2007), about which a starred *Booklist* reviewer said, "McDonald dramatizes the big issues from the inside, showing the hard times and the joy in fast-talking dialogue that is honest, insulting, angry, and very funny" (quoted in //www.amazon.com). McDonald's short story, "Zebra Girl," was anthologized in *Skin Deep* (2004), and she contributed to numerous periodicals (e.g., *Literary Review, O Magazine, Village Voice*). She was said to be working on additional adult and young-adult novels when she died prematurely of cancer in Paris, France.

REFERENCES: *CA/I. CAO-07. Wiki.* Engberg, Gillian. "The *Booklist* Interview: Janet McDonald (Spotlight on Black History)." *Booklist* 98.12 (Feb. 15, 2002), p. 1026. Literature Resources from Gale. _____. "Sad News." *Booklist* 103.18 (May 15, 2007), p. 42. Literature Resources from Gale. Kennedy, Thomas E. "Up from Brooklyn: An Interview with Janet McDonald." *The Literary Review 44.4* (Summer 2001), p. 704. Literature Resources from Gale. "Obituaries." *The Horn Book Magazine 83.4* (July-August 2007), p. 430. Literature Resources from Gale. Powers, Retha, in "Janet McDonald 1953-2007: Make Some Noise for the Project Girl," *Black Issues Book Review*, May-June, 2007, //findarticles.com/p/articles/mi_m0HST/is_/ai_n19395093. Rellihan, Heather (2002), "Janet McDonald (1953-)," in Emmanuel Sampath Nelson (Ed.), *African American Autobiographers: A Sourcebook* (pp. 270-273), Westport, CT: Greenwood Publishing Group. Whelan, Debra Lau, "Young Adult Author Janet McDonald Dies at 53," *School Library Journal*, 4/16/2007, in //www.school libraryjournal.com/article/CA6434296.html. Williams, Jennifer, "Twists and Turns: An Interview with Janet McDonald," in //www.hip mama.com/node/197. //biography.jrank.org/pages/127/McDonald-Janet-1953-Sidelights.html. //biography.jrank.org/pages/128/McDonald-Janet-1953.html. //us.macmillan.com/author/janet mcdonald. //www.childrenslit.com/childrenslit/mai_mcdonald_janet.html. //www.schoollibraryjournal.com/blog/620000062/post/1610008561.html.

FURTHER READING: Sloan, Karen, in *GEAAL.*

McElroy (married name), Colleen (née Johnson)
10/30/1935–
Poems, short stories, plays, screenplays, nonfiction, travel autobiography/memoirs, novel; speech clinician, educator, visual artist

McElroy's poetry books include *The Mules Done Long Since Gone* (1973), *Music from Home: Selected Poems* (1976), *Winters without Snow* (1980), *Looking for a Country under Its Original Name* (1985), *Queen of the Ebony Islands* (1984, winner of the American Book Award), *Bone Flames: Poems* (1987), *Lie and Say You Love Me* (1988), *Blue Flames* (1989), *What Madness Brought Me Here: New and Selected Poems, 1968-1988* (1990), *Travelling Music* (1998), and *Sleeping with the Moon* (2007). Her short-story collections include *Jesus and Fat Tuesday and Other Short Stories* (1988) and *Driving under the Cardboard Pines: And Other Stories* (1991), and her individual short stories are widely anthologized. McElroy has also written a choreopoem, *The Wild Gardens of the Loup Garou*, and a play about **Harriet Tubman**, *Follow the Drinking Gourd*, both with **Ishmael Reed**, as well as some filmscripts and dozens of TV screenplays. She is still working on a novel (once tentatively titled *Study War No More*).

McElroy's first work of nonfiction, *Speech and Language Development of the Preschool Child: A Survey* (1972), grew out of her experience as a speech clinician. Her experiences as a sojourner led to her nonfiction travel memoirs, *A Long Way from St. Louie: Travel Memoirs* (1997) and *Over the Lip of the World: Among the Storytellers of Madagascar* (1999). She also worked as editor-in-chief of the *Seattle Review* (1992-2006) and later edited the collection *Page to Page: Retrospectives of Writers from the Seattle Review* (2006). Aside from her honors for particular books, she has been awarded two National Endowment for the Arts Creative Writing fellowships, two Fulbright fellowships, a Rockefeller fellowship, and a Breadloaf Conference scholarship. In addition to her prodigious writing output, she has been a speech pathologist, a TV-program moderator, an exhibited visual artist, a professor at University of Washington at Seattle (now emeritus), and a mother to her children, Kevin and Vanessa.

REFERENCES: *AANB. AAW:PV. BAWPP. CAO-07. LFCC-07.* Gailey, Jeannine Hall, in //www.seattlewomanmagazine.com/articles/sept06-1.htm. Margulis, Jennifer, in *COCAAL* and *OCAAL*. Skeeter, Sharyn, in //africanamericanlit.suite101.com/article.cfm/colleen_mcelroy__part_2. Williamson, Alicia D., in *GEAAL*. //www.cavecanempoets.org/pages/programs_faculty.php. Amazon.com. SDPL catalog.

McFadden, Bernice L. (aka Geneva Holliday)
9/26/1965–
Novels, short stories

Bernice McFadden, who has earned praise for her writing from Nobel Literature laureate **Toni Morrison** and from best-selling author **Terry McMillan**, did not take the typical path to a writing career. First, she attended the Laboratory Institute of Merchandising (1983) in New York City and worked in the retail garment industry for a while. Then she took time out to have her daughter, R'yane Azsa, and earned a Travel and Tourism Certificate from Marymount College in Tarrytown, New York. She then worked for a while for the travel and tourism industry (1988-1990, 1991-1999). In 1990, however, she was laid off from a resort-reservation company and it was another 12 months before she found her next travel in-

dustry job. During that year, McFadden took care of her daughter and wrote, wrote, wrote.

In the new millennium, McFadden found a publisher for her first completed novel, *Sugar* (2000). It was awarded a Black Caucus Fiction Honor from the American Library Association (ALA) and a Best New Author of the Year Award from the Go On Girl Book Club. With this encouragement, she published her second novel, *The Warmest December* (2001), which won Golden Pen Awards for Best Mainstream Fiction and for Best New Author, earned a nomination for the **Zora Neale Hurston/Richard Wright** Legacy Award for fiction (2002), and prompted Toni Morrison to write, "Riveting. . . . I am as impressed by its structural strength as by the searing and expertly imagined scenes" (quoted in *BB*). McFadden next tackled *Sugar*'s sequel, *This Bitter Earth* (2002). Like her first two novels, it was a bestseller. The next year, she published *Loving Donovan: A Novel in Three Stories* (2003), followed by *Camilla's Roses* (2004). She then took a little detour before publishing *Nowhere Is a Place* (2006).

In 2005, McFadden decided to dabble in erotic melodrama and used the nom de plume Geneva Holliday for a series of books in this genre: *Groove* (2005) and its sequel *Fever* (2006), then *Heat* (2007), *Seduction* (2008), and *Lover Man* (2009). In addition, her Holliday story "One Night Stand" was anthologized in *Black Silk: A Collection of African-American Erotica* (2002).

REFERENCES: *CAO-07.* Burns, Ann. "In the Spotlight: Bernice McFadden." *Library Journal 130.18* (Nov. 1, 2005), p. 93. Literature Resources from Gale. LaBalle, Candace, in *BB*. Peterson, V. R. "The Name Game: Don't Confuse the Author of *Fever* with the Author of *Nowhere Is a Place*." *Publishers Weekly 253.10* (Mar. 6, 2006), p. 44. Literature Resources from Gale. //www.campusexplorer.com/colleges/FE387F69/New-York/Tarrytown/Marymount-College-of-Fordham-University/. //www.hurston-wright.org/legacy_nominees2002.shtml. //www.limcollege.edu/. Amazon.com.

FURTHER READING: LaFrance, Michelle, in *GEAAL*. //www.clpgh.org/books/booklists/africanamericanfiction.html. //www.randomhouse.com/broadway/blackink/authors.html.

McGhee, "Brownie" (Walter Brown)
11/30/1915–2/16/1996
Blues songs

Widely known for his collaboration with blues harmonica player Sonny Terry, McGhee wrote numerous blues songs, many of which have been performed with and by other folk singers, both white (Woody Guthrie, Pete Seeger, etc.) and black (e.g., his and Terry's former roommate, Huddie Ledbetter, a.k.a. Leadbelly).

REFERENCES: *EB-BH-CD.* "Obituary. McGhee, Walter Brown," 1997 Book of the Year, *Encyclopedia Britannica*.

FURTHER READING: *AANB. D. F. Wiki.* Brennan, Sandra, *All Movie Guide,* in *Act.* Dahl, Bill, *All Music Guide,* in *A.*

McGirt, James E. (Ephraim)
9/??/1874–6/13/1930
Poems, short stories, songs; magazine editor and publisher

Raised on a family farm in Greensboro, North Carolina, James McGirt went on to earn a B.A. from nearby Bennett College (1895). After college, McGirt established businesses as a launderer and a drayman. Despite his difficult manual labor, McGirt managed to write and have published his first collection, *Avenging the Maine, A Drunken A.B., and Other Poems* (1899; rev. enlarged ed., 1900; 2nd rev. ed., 1901). In the preface, he apologized for the small number and the weakness of the poems, noting that long days of manual labor prevented him from writing more and writing better. Next, he published his collection of lyrics, *Some Simple Songs and a Few More Ambitious Attempts* (1901).

McGirt subsequently moved to Philadelphia. There, he founded his own publishing company, which published both books and his own *McGirt's Magazine* (1903-1910), starting with the September 1903 issue. McGirt not only published but also edited his illustrated monthly magazine. *McGirt's* published or reprinted poems by **Paul Laurence Dunbar** and **Frances Ellen Watkins Harper**, fiction by John Edward Bruce, essays by **Kelly Miller**, articles by **Anna Julia Cooper** and **W. E. B. Du Bois**, and writings by other literary luminaries of the day. In addition, of course, it included McGirt's poems, short stories, a long fictional piece titled "Black Hand," and articles. Article topics included African-American arts and sciences, general culture, and politics. McGirt's political views led to his founding the Constitutional Brotherhood of America, an organization dedicated to promoting voting rights for African Americans and ensuring that chosen candidates would truly serve the African-American community. He even called his magazine the organization's "official organ," and in *McGirt's,* he admonished readers that the key to opportunities and uplift for African Americans was their use of the vote.

McGirt's third collection was *For Your Sweet Sake: Poems* (1906; enlarged ed., 1909). The next year, the McGirt company published his short-story collection, *The Triumphs of Ephraim* (1907/1972). A few of his poems have since been reprinted in *African-American Poetry of the Nineteenth Century* (1992). Unfortunately, declining sales forced McGirt to slow his output from a monthly to a quarterly publication in 1909. The following year, McGirt gave up his admirable pursuit, closed up his publishing house, and returned to Greensboro. There, he went into business with his sister Mary Magdalene, running Star Hair Grower Manufacturing Company, which manufactured and distributed cosmetics (beginning 1910). He also made money buying and selling real estate, and he continued to write songs.

REFERENCES: *AANB. BAWPP. CAO-00.* Andrews, William L., in *COCAAL.* Daniel, Walter C., in *AAWBHR.* //en.wikipedia.org/wiki/Bennett_College. //www.bookrags.com/biography/james-ephraim-mcgirt-dlb/.

McGruder, Aaron (Vincent)
5/29/1974–
Comic strips; graphic artist

Editor's note: McGruder's birth month is listed as March in *BB,* but as May in *W2B, Wiki,* //www.imdb.com/name/nm1412298/bio, and other resources.

While still an African-American studies student at the University of Maryland (now UMUC, University of Maryland University College), Aaron McGruder started drawing his comic strip. The year he graduated (1997), the student newspaper published *Boondocks.* After McGruder graduated, fellow student, DJ, and writer Rhome Anderson helped him get his strip onto the Internet, where it attracted enough attention to have *The Source,* a hip-hop print magazine, publish it. As the strip gained popularity—or perhaps notoriety—it was syndicated for national distribution. On April 19, 1999, *Boondocks* first appeared in about 160 newspapers across the United States and in 200 papers by the end of the year. In the strip, preteen African-American brothers Huey and Riley Freeman both live with their grandfather out in "the boondocks," predominantly European-American suburbs. After the second President Bush was elected, Huey and his younger brother Riley, as well as their biracial pal Jazmine DuBois, were grabbing headlines, too. During most of the Bush presidency, the wise-cracking brothers asked provocative questions and raised controversial issues, prompting many newspapers to move the strip to the editorial page. Even so, the strip was carried in more than 300 U.S. papers in 2004.

Meanwhile, McGruder also published collections of his *Boondocks* strips, including *The Boondocks: Because I Know You Don't Read the Newspapers* (2000), *Fresh for '01—You Suckas!: A Boondocks Collection* (2001), *A Right to Be Hostile: The Boondocks Treasury* (2003), and *Public Enemy Number 2: An All-New Boondocks Collection* (2005). He also collaborated with Reginald Hudlin of Black Entertainment Network (BET) to create their graphic novel, *Birth of a Nation: A Comic Novel* (2004, illustrated by cartoonist Kyle Baker).

In 2005, McGruder started toying with an animated version of his cartoon, and the following year he put his daily strip on hiatus and focused solely on his animated cartoon on the Cartoon Network. Reportedly, he offered BET a chance to adapt the strip to animated format, but BET turned him down. Since then, BET sued Cartoon Network to prevent it from airing two episodes that lampooned BET, though the two episodes are included in a DVD of the series. While a second season of the series is being delayed, McGruder is experimenting with yet another medium. His "The Official Unofficial YouTube Channel of Aaron McGruder," the "Boondocks Bootleg Comedy Channel," features "The Super Rumble Mix Show" and numerous other videos, touted as "Brand new comedy from 'The Boondocks' creator, Aaron McGruder's Partner Rumble studio!," available for subscription.

McGruder has since written *All the Rage: The Boondocks Past and Present* (2007), which includes three parts: (1) a collection of strips from 2003 to 2005; (2) interviews of McGruder for newspapers, magazines, and television, in which he directly opines; and (3) reprints of the comic strips that various newspaper editors withheld from print. In 2002, McGruder won the NAACP Chairman's Award for his comic strip, and in 2009, he was nominated for an NAACP Image Award for his animated series. He has also appeared on television at the Image Awards (2002) and on four episodes of *Real Time with Bill Maher* (2003-2004), and his voice can be heard as the young Granddad in some episodes of the *Boondocks* cartoon.

REFERENCES: *AANB. CAO-06. W2B. Wiki.* Henderson, Ashyia, Melissa Walsh Doig, Jennifer M. York, and Tom Pendergast, in *BB.* Mcgrath, Ben. "The Radical." *The New Yorker* 80.9 (Apr. 19, 2004), p. 153. Literature Resources from Gale. //www.diamondbackonline.com/. //www.imdb.com/name/nm1412298/awards. //www.imdb.com/name/ nm1412298/bio. //www.imdb.com/name/nm1412298/filmoseries. //www.imdb.com/name/nm1412298/maindetails. //www.imdb.com/ name/nm1412298/news?year=2008#ni0617941. //www.youtube. com/boondocksbootleg. Amazon.com.

McKay, Claude (né Festus Claudius McKay)
9/15/1889 [or 1890]–5/22/1948
Poems, novels

Although many critics have disagreed as to the merit of Claude McKay's literary works, his historical importance in the field of African-American literature in the twentieth century is indisputable. He was a key figure in, if not the first major poet of, the **Harlem Renaissance**, and many of his works paved the way for the 1920s literary movement, as well as defining the trends that would characterize it. His political activism, as well as his literary achievements, garnered both praise and condemnation, making him one of the more controversial figures of the time.

Born in Sunny Ville, Jamaica, McKay was raised by his father and mother, who were relatively prosperous members of the peasant class. He was educated as a subject of the British colonial empire, learning British poetry and conventional verse forms such as the sonnet. However, he received an alternative education from his father, whose own father was brought over from West Africa as a slave. McKay's father attempted to teach him the customs and traditions of the Ashanti, his native people, and repeatedly told him the story of how his father was enslaved. This story instilled in McKay a certain distrust of whites.

This distrust only deepened when, in 1911, he moved away from rural Sunny Ville to the Jamaican capital of Kingston. There, at 19, he became a constable but left in less than a year because he felt as if he was oppressing his people by enforcing laws that were unjustly slanted against the black residents of the city. It was in Kingston that he first encountered racism and bigotry. The town of Sunny Ville was populated mostly by blacks, so while growing up, he had encountered relatively little racism there. However, Kingston's predominantly white and mulatto population held dark-skinned blacks in contempt and often exploited them, allowing them access to only the most menial of jobs—and this troubled McKay to no end.

The contrast between life in Sunny Ville and life in Kingston struck a deep chord in McKay, and in 1912 he published his first two books of poetry, *Songs of Jamaica* and *Constab Ballads*. These books were published by Walter Jekyll, a British man who came to Jamaica to study folklore. He had, earlier in McKay's career, encouraged McKay to stop writing conventional poetry and instead to write poetry rooted in Jamaican folk culture and using the Jamaican dialect. Jekyll's influence can be seen in these books, which, though published separately, when read together clearly illustrate the differences McKay found in both lifestyle and sentiment when he compared the lives of rural citizens and city dwellers in Jamaica.

Songs of Jamaica focuses largely on presenting the peasant life as idyllic—tied to nature and the land, free from bigotry and oppression, and ultimately peaceful. *Constab Ballads*, based on McKay's experiences as a constable, centers on life in the city, which is shown to be dark, bleak, and full of bigotry, exploitation, and contempt for blacks. These works were well received by the public, and McKay became the first black writer to receive the Medal from the Jamaican Institute of Arts and Sciences. The frankness, realism, and honesty of these works differed from the work that African Americans were producing in the United States, which focused less on issues of racism and equality and more on conventional poetic topics such as death, life, love, and beauty.

The award he received from the Jamaican Institute came with a stipend, and in 1912, McKay used this money to transport himself to the United States, where he began to pursue a degree in agriculture at Alabama's Tuskegee Institute. In two months, he transferred to Kansas Sate College but by 1914 had decided to abandon his course of study and return to work as a writer. He worked at various jobs to finance his move to Harlem in New York City, where he continued to work at menial jobs to support himself. The racism he encountered on the trip and in the city made him more determined to pursue his career as a poet.

After arriving in New York, he made contacts with various publishers, sending his works not only to black magazines but also to white publications, particularly leftist political magazines. Once a part of these literary circles, McKay became involved with various radical liberals such as Max Eastman, who was a major leader of leftists in the literary field. In addition to having his poetry and essays published in these magazines, McKay worked on the editorial staff of Eastman's magazine *The Liberator* and wrote various reviews.

It was in *The Liberator* that McKay first published what may be his most famous poem, "If We Must Die." This poem was inspired by the "Red Summer" of 1919 when racial violence directed against blacks broke out throughout the United States but particularly in Chicago. It asserts and defends the rights of blacks to fight back against such abuse and is a rallying cry to battle, saying that blacks will not "die like hogs" but will instead "face the murderous, cowardly pack/Pressed to the wall, dying, but fighting back!" The poem brought him instant fame when it was published and endured as a poem that Jean Wagner notes "voices the will of oppressed people of every age who, whatever their race and wherever their region, are fighting with their backs against the wall to win their freedom." It became so famous that it was still remembered in the late 1930s when Winston Churchill used it in a speech against the Nazis, and it became an unofficial battle cry of the Allied Forces in World War II.

McKay was not affected by the fame the poem brought to him but instead traveled to England where he became even more politically active. He began writing for a British socialist named Sylvia Pankhurst, who published a communist magazine called *Worker's Dreadnaught*. In these writings, he urges the communist leadership in Europe and America to accept blacks as equals and to oppose European imperialism in other countries. He claims that only after the leadership does this will the black workers in Europe and America join the movement, and he points out that without them, the communist revolution will never succeed.

McKay continued to write poetry during his time in England, and in 1920, he published his third book of poetry, *Spring in New Hampshire*. The book was deeply respected by both **Countee Cullen** and **Langston Hughes** and was praised by I. A. Richards, an extremely well respected literary critic of the time, as "the best work that the present generation is producing" in England. While it included poems that dealt with both island life and race relations in the United States, McKay made a conscious effort to avoid publishing very many poems focusing on racial themes in that book. As a result, a year later, after returning to New York, he published *Harlem Shadows*, which contained many works from his previous books and magazine publications. The masterful treatment of racial issues in this book assured his position as the leading member of the Harlem Renaissance. Before, poems about matters of race were only occasionally used as subjects for poetry. This pioneering book proved to the other writers of the Harlem literary circle that a black writer's insights on racial issues could succeed as the focus of an entire collection of literary works.

By this time, McKay had become dissatisfied with the efforts he saw being made toward confronting racism in the United States and abroad, so he used his fame to redouble efforts toward that end. He traveled to the Soviet Union and attended the Fourth Congress of the Third Communist International as a special delegate-observer. The Moscow crowds loved him so much that the Soviet leaders sent him on a six-month tour of the Soviet Union, during which he lectured on art and politics. He also wrote for Soviet journals and magazines, analyzing the history of African Americans in the United States from a Marxist perspective. These works were published under the title *Negroes in America* in 1923.

McKay soon got tired of acting as a politician rather than as a poet and also got tired of being seen as a novelty, so he left the Soviet Union to embark on what he did not know would be 10 years of travel throughout Western Europe and North Africa. His health began to fail him but he still continued to write, producing his first novel, *Home to Harlem*, during the time he spent in Paris. Published in 1928, it became the first best-seller written by a black author. The book focuses on a black soldier who leaves the army to return to Harlem and who falls in love and finds happiness with a former prostitute. The characters the soldier encounters along the way and upon his arrival in Harlem are not necessarily positive—they are rough, hard, and not fully respectable figures who often cross lines of morality and legality in their daily lives.

This work differed from much of the writing produced by African-American writers of the time. Many black authors had decided to assert only the positive aspects of blacks in both the cities and the countryside. McKay's decision to realistically portray the negative elements of black society, which he had encountered during his travels as a young man, earned him scathing criticism from various figures. **W. E. B. Du Bois** claimed that the book was disgusting; other critics stated that it was written to appeal to whites' stereotypes of blacks for commercial success. Others, however, defended the book as celebrating lives of the most marginal black figures of the ghettos and showing their strength and staying power.

Undeterred by critics, McKay continued his efforts at realism in his later books, *Banjo* and *Banana Bottom*, published in 1929 and 1933, respectively. *Banana Bottom* is considered to be his best work by far. Set in Jamaica, it initially appealed to audiences because of its realistic depictions of the lush tropical landscape. Today, however, it is praised for its affirmation of black culture. In the book, the heroine, Bita—a peasant girl who is adopted by white missionaries after being raped—discovers the dangers that Western imperialists pose to African Americans and learns that her healing can only commence when she escapes from her white guardians and returns to her native people. This book asserts McKay's belief that African Americans needed to derive their basic values from their racial heritage, cultural traditions, and experiences, rather than Western traditions that actually put black life and culture into danger. He felt that the only way African Americans had resisted the deadly effects of slavery, racism, and segregation was by rooting themselves in such tradition. He also believed that the only way they would acquire equal rights would be to unite and build their own labor, business, and social institutions within their own communities so that they could integrate into American life as a whole.

Claude McKay's ideas and politics did not always make him popular, but they did make him a pioneer in the African-American community. His novels inspired the founders of the *Négritude* movements in West India and French West Africa. He helped initiate the New Negro movement. He is an important touchstone for those who defend the idea of black cultural autonomy and became an important reference for black nationalism during the civil-rights era. He reached new heights in racial poetic achievement, refusing to hide his impatience with racism behind traditional poetic forms despite the fact that other writers felt he should do just that. When he died of heart failure, after years of illness, he left behind a life that was devoted to art and social protest—and whether or not critics consider him to be a figure of great literary merit, he is most certainly a figure of great historical importance: He is the man who began an era of Renaissance in Harlem.

REFERENCES: *AAW. BW:SSCA. NAAAL.* Hathaway, Heather, in *COCAAL* and *OCAAL.*

FURTHER READING: *AANB. B. BAWPP. BCE. CAO-03. CE. LFCC-07. MWEL. W. Wiki.* Ali, Schavi Mali, *AAWHR-40.* Cagan, Penni, in *AP1880-1945-1.* Callahan, John F. "Claude McKay: A Black Poet's Struggle for Identity." *Contemporary Literature.* 34.4 (Winter

1993) p. 767. From *Literature Resource Center.* Chauhan, P. S. "Rereading Claude McKay." *CLA Journal 34.1* (Sept. 1990) pp. 68-80. Rpt. in Mary K. Ruby (Ed.), *Poetry for Students* (Vol. 4). Detroit: Gale, 1999. From *Literature Resource Center.* Cohassey, John, in *BB.* Cooper, Wayne F., in *AAW-1991.* Giles, James R. Claude McKay, Chapter 1: The Renaissance, Jamaica, the Party, and the Church. Chapter 2: The Poetry: Form versus Content. Chapter 3: The Novels: Instinct versus Intellect. Chapter 4: Gingertown: Studies of Self-hatred. Chapter 5: The Nonfiction: Harlem and the World. Chapter 6: A Long Way From Home. James R. Giles. Chronology. Author's Works. Bibliography. *Twayne's United States Authors Series 271.* Boston: Twayne Publishers, 1976. From *The Twayne Authors Series.* Grant, William E., in *AWP-1920-1939.* Holcomb, Gary E. "Complete Poems." *African American Review.* 40.2 (Summer 2006) p. 383. From *Literature Resource Center.* McLeod, Alan L., in *T-CCBAW-1.* Munro, Karen, in *GEAAL.* Singh, Amritjit, in *RGAL-3.* Soitos, Stephen, in *AW:ACLB-02.* Swartz, Patti Capel, in *G&LL-98-2.* //www.poets.org/poet.php/prmPID/25.

McKay, Nellie Yvonne (née Reynolds)
5/12/1930–1/22/2006
Literary criticism and biography, scholarly, anthologies; educator

Editor's note: McKay's birth year is given as 1947 in *GEAAL,* as a range between 1931 and 1947 in *Wiki,* and about 1930-1932 in her *The New York Times* obituary.

The daughter of Jamaican immigrants, Nellie McKay was already a divorced, single mother when she entered college in her 30s. She earned a B.A. in English from Queens College (1969), and an M.A. (1971) and a Ph.D. (1977) in English and American literature from Harvard. After earning her master's degree and before completing her doctorate, McKay started teaching in Boston (1973-1978) as an assistant professor of English and American literature at Simmons College and as a visiting professor of Afro-American literature at Massachusetts Institute of Technology.

In 1978, McKay moved to the University of Wisconsin at Madison, where she taught multicultural women's literature, African-American literature, and African-American women's literature. In 1984, she was tenured, and by the time of her death, she was the Evjue-Bascom Professor of American and African-American Literature there. In addition, she helped to establish the university's **Lorraine Hansberry** Visiting Professorship in the Dramatic Arts, and she has been said to have played a big part in **Henry Louis Gates**'s appointment to his post in Harvard's Afro-American Studies Department (in 1991).

For her students, as much as for her colleagues, McKay contributed more than 60 nonfiction pieces of literary scholarship on various topics, such as African-American women literary biography, African-American literature, and social and political issues of interest to her and to the wider community. She was also advisory editor and then associate editor for the *African American Review*. McKay's articles have also appeared in numerous literary biographical dictionaries, including two volumes in the *Dictionary of Literary Biography* (1985, 1987) and two volumes in the *Scribner Writers Series* (both 1991). McKay also authored three books: *Black Women in the Academy* (1982), *20th Century Third World Women Writers, Black American and African: Selected Bibliography* (1983), and **Jean Toomer**, *the Artist: A Portrait in Tragedy* (1977; rev. *Jean Toomer, Artist: A Study of His Literary Life and Work, 1894-1936*, 1984; reprinted 1987). She also coauthored *Black Studies in the United States: Three Essays* (1990, with Robert L Harris and **Darlene Clark Hine**).

Perhaps even more important, McKay edited numerous crucial references in African-American literature, the most well-known and widely read of which is the *Norton Anthology of African-American Literature* (1996; 2nd ed., 2005), which she coedited with **Henry Louis Gates, Jr.** McKay also edited numerous other volumes, including *Critical Essays on* **Toni Morrison** (1988; rev. ed., 1998), *Race-ing Justice, En-Gendering Power: Essays on Anita Hill, Clarence Thomas, and the Construction of Social Reality* (1992, with Toni Morrison and Michael Thelwell), *The Sleeper Wakes: Harlem Renaissance Stories by Women* (1993, with Marcy Knopf), *Approaches to Teaching the Novels of Toni Morrison* (1997, with Kathryn Earle), and *Toni Morrison's Beloved: A Casebook* (1999, with William L. Andrews). She also edited and/or introduced **Ann Petry**'s *The Narrows: A Novel* (1988/1999); **Ellen Tarry**'s *Third Door: The Autobiography of an American Negro Woman* (1992); **Mary Church Terrell**'s *Colored Woman in a White World* (African-American Women Writers, 1910-1940) (1996); and **Harriet A. Jacobs**'s *Incidents in the Life of a Slave Girl: Contexts, Criticisms* (Norton Critical Editions) (2000, with **Frances Smith Foster**; originally, 1861).

She had hoped to finish a revised edition of the landmark African-American feminist anthology *All the Women Are White, All the Blacks are Men, But Some of Us Brave: Black Women's Studies* (1982, originally edited by **Gloria T. Hull**, Patricia Bell Scott, and **Barbara Smith**), but she literally died trying. In addition to her fellowships, awards, and other honors, she was memorialized in "Nellie McKay—A Memorial," in *African American Review*, in which more than a dozen prominent scholars and public figures offered her tribute. McKay also had two children, one grandchild, and one great-grandchild.

REFERENCES: *AANB, Wiki.* Moody, Joycelyn. "Nellie McKay—A Memorial." *African American Review 40.1* (Spring 2006), p. 5. Literature Resources from Gale. //worldcat.org/identities/lccn-n83-176065. //www.nytimes.com/2006/01/28/national/28mckay.html?ex=1162180800&en=12fedf03e8fa476c&ei=5070. //www.simmons.edu/. Amazon.com.

FURTHER READING: Morton, Clay, in *GEAAL*.

McKissack (married name), Patricia L'Ann (née Carwell)
8/9/1944–
Juvenile books

Each day after school, Pat and her siblings stayed with her mother's parents: Her "Mama Frances" told them family stories, and her "Daddy James" spun **trickster tales** featuring his grandchildren. In addition, her father's mother, "Mama Sarah told creepy, scary stories at twilight."

In an autobiographical sketch, McKissack recalled, "Somewhere around age seven I discovered reading. And so began my lifelong love affair with the printed word. To me, reading is like breathing; both are essential to life" (from //www.randomhouse.com/author/results.pperl?author id=20049&view=full_sptlght). Pat grew up loving the public library, a refuge from Jim Crow segregation. An avid reader, Pat particularly enjoyed "world myths, legends, and fairytales." She also made up her own stories: "I was forever scribbling a poem, a play, or a story" (*CYI*, p. 13).

At Tennessee State, Pat rediscovered her childhood acquaintance Fredrick McKissack. In 1964, Pat got her B.A. in English and education—and married Fredrick. The couple has since coauthored many books, managed a business partnership, and raised Fredrick Jr., Robert, and John.

When her sons were young, Patricia spent a lot of time with them in the library. At this time, her lifelong journal writing was her main literary output. In 1969, Pat started teaching eighth graders and noticed the need for biographies of noteworthy African Americans. She particularly wanted a juvenile biography of **Paul Laurence Dunbar**. When she could find none, she spent the summer of 1971 gathering information and writing one. That fall, she invited her students to respond honestly to her manuscript: They said it was boring. Several revisions later, they responded more enthusiastically. As she later said, "My students taught me [to] keep the material interesting, fast-moving, and up-beat."

In 1975, Pat earned her master's degree in early childhood literature and media programming. The next year, she started teaching a college course on "Writing for Children" (1976-1982) and working as a children's book editor (1976-1981). Later on, with Fred's encouragement, she quit these jobs and started writing full time. Soon after, the couple founded All-Writing Services, conducting educational workshops, book talks, and lectures, and consulting about multicultural children's literature. The McKissacks often cowrite books: Fred does most of the research, and Pat does most of the writing. Their sons and other family members often help, too. Pat and Fredrick Jr. (a journalist) also cowrote an award-winning children's book, and Robert wrote a children's book, too.

Alone, Pat has written nearly 60 books; alone or with Fredrick, she has written at least a dozen dozens (144) of books; with other authors (e.g., political consultant and Southern storyteller James Carville), she has cowritten an additional seven books. Just a listing of her bibliography would cover numerous pages. Among her almost countless works, Pat has written numerous children's picture books echoing Daddy James's rural Southern dialect; her picture books include *Mirandy and Brother Wind* (1989), named an American Library Association (ALA) Notable Book, a Caldecott Honor Book, a Notable Children's Trade Book in the Field of Social Studies, and a **Coretta Scott King** Illustrator Award Winner; *Nettie Jo's Friends* (1989), a Parents' Choice Award winner; and *A Million Fish...More or Less* (1992/1996), named a Junior Library Guild Selection. Alone or with Fred, Pat has also written dozens of books on assorted topics, including African-American folktales, such as her Newbery Honor and Coretta Scott King Author Award-winning *The Dark-Thirty: Southern Tales of the Supernatural*); biographies, such as her Coretta Scott King Honor Award and *Boston Globe-Horn Book* Award-winning *Sojourner Truth: Ain't I a Woman?* (1999, with her husband Fred); diverse cultures, such as *The Aztec* (1985) and *The Apache* (1985); and history, such as her Coretta Scott King Author Award-winning books *A Long Hard Journey: The Story of the Pullman Porter* (1990, with Fred; also won the Jane Addams Children's Book Award) and *Christmas in the Big House, Christmas in the Quarters* (1995, with Fred), and her Coretta Scott King Author Honor-winning books *Black Diamond: Story of the Negro Baseball League* (1995, with her son Fredrick Jr.), *Rebels Against Slavery: American Slave Revolts* (1997, with her husband Fred), *Black Hands, White Sails: The Story of African-American Whalers* (2000, with Fred), and *Days of Jubilee: The End of Slavery in the United States* (2003, with Fred; illustrated by Leo and Dianne Dillon).

Pat has also written several religion-related books, including her NAACP Image Award-winning *Let My People Go: Bible Stories of Faith, Hope, and Love, as Told by Price Jefferies, a Free Man of Color, to His Daughter, Charlotte, in Charleston, South Carolina, 1806-1816* (1998, with Fred), and her two books awarded the C.S. Lewis Silver Medal from the Christian Educators Association, *Abram, Abram, Where Are We Going?* (1984, with Fred) and *It's the Truth, Christopher* (1984, illustrated by Bartholomew). The *Christopher* book is part of a series, including three other books by the McKissacks. Other series in which she has participated include the Big Bug Books (which she and Fred coedit the series and write many of its books), Corner-

stones of Freedom, Dear America (historical fictional diaries), Early Readers, Great African Americans, Little Beastie Good Behavior Builders, People of Distinction (biographies), Reading Well (which she and Fred coedit the series and write many of its books), Rookie Readers (including several of her *Messy Bessey* books), Royal Diaries (historical fictional diaries), Scraps of Time (historical fiction), Start Off Stories (updated classic folktales, many translated into Spanish), Stepping Stone Chapter Books, Taking a Stand, and World of Stamps (telling history through stamps). In addition to her 140-plus books, Pat has written radio and television scripts and collaborated on an award-winning movie script. Also, "I enjoy teaching other people to write too. What better way to combine all my training as teacher and writer? For the past ten years I've been teaching a course in writing for children at the University of Missouri at St. Louis" (from //www.random house.com/author/results.pperl?authorid=20049&view= full_sptlght).

In addition to Pat's numerous awards for individual books, including the American Library Association's Notable Books, Caldecott, Newbery, and Coretta Scott King honors; the National Association for the Advancement of Colored People's Image Award, and the Women's International League for Peace and Freedom's Jane Addams Children's Book Award, Patricia has won the third annual **Virginia Hamilton** Literary Award (2001), and the McKissacks have been awarded honorary doctorate degrees (1994).

REFERENCES: *AANB. CA/I. CAO-06. CBC. CYI. EBLG. Wiki.* Frederick, Heather Vogel, "PW Talks with Patricia McKissack." *Publishers Weekly.* 248.32 (Aug. 6, 2001) p. 90. From *Literature Resource Center.* Heath, Lisa, 5/23/01, //voices.cla.umn.edu/vg/ Bios/entries/mckissack_patricia.html. Hinton-Johnson, KaaVonia, in *GEAAL.* MacCann, Donnarae, in *COCAAL* and *OCAAL.* McKissack, Patricia C. (1992). "That's Why I Write." Gary D. Schmidt and Donald R. Hettinga (Eds.), *Sitting at the Feet of the Past: Retelling the North American Folk Tale for Children.* Westport, CT: Greenwood Press. Rpt. in Tom Burns (Ed.) (2008), *Children's Literature Review* (Vol. 129, pp. 64-68). Detroit: Gale. From *Literature Resource Center.* Smith, Jessie Carney, and Phyllis Wood, in *PBW.* //www.ala.org/ala/emiert/corettascottkingbookaward/cskpastwinners/al phabeticallist/cskalphabetical.cfm#au. //www.eduplace.com/kids/ hmr/mtai/mckissack.html. //www.library.uiuc.edu/blog/esslchildlit/ archives/2008/02/african_america.html. //www.randomhouse.com/ author/results.pperl?authorid=20049&view=full_sptlght. //www.ucalgary.ca/~dkbrown/k6/mckissack.html. Amazon.com.

McMillan, Terry
10/18/1951–
Novels, anthologies

Port Huron, Michigan, is just 60 or so miles northeast of Detroit. In that economically depressed community, Madeline Washington Tillman and Edward Lewis

McMillan struggled to raise their five children—Madeline working as a domestic servant and a factory worker, and Edward working intermittently as a sanitation worker and a factory worker. When Terry, their oldest child, had just entered her teen years, Madeline decided she had had enough of Edward's alcoholism and abuse, and she divorced him, taking charge of raising her five children alone. Edward died three years later. Terry later recalled that her mother's example taught her and her siblings "how to be strong and resilient. She taught us about taking risks" (quoted in *BWA:AHE*).

The only contacts that Terry had with books during her childhood were with the Bible and her required textbooks for school. Her parents never read to her or her siblings. When she was 16, however, Terry got a job (paying $1.25/hour) shelving books for the local public library, to help support her family. As she wrote in her introduction to her anthology *Breaking Ice* (1990), "As a child, . . . I did not read for pleasure, and it wasn't until I was sixteen . . . that I got lost in a book. It was a biography of Louisa May Alcott. I was excited because I had not really read about poor white folks before; . . . . I related to Louisa because she had to help support her family at a young age, which was what I was doing at the library" (p. xv).

Up to that time, she had never read—or even heard of—any African-American writers. "Then one day I went to put a book away, and saw **James Baldwin**'s face staring up at me. 'Who in the world is this?' I wondered. . . . not only had there not been any African-American authors included in any of [my] textbooks, but I'd never been given a clue that if we did have anything important to say that somebody would actually publish it. Needless to say, I was not just naïve, but had not yet acquired an ounce of black pride. I never once questioned why there were no representative works by us in any of those textbooks. After all, I had never heard of any African-American writers, and no one I knew hardly read *any* books."

Later on, however, "I read **Alex Haley**'s biography of [**Malcolm X**] and it literally changed my life. First and foremost, I realized that there was no reason to be ashamed of being black, that it was ridiculous. That we had a history, and much to be proud of. I began to notice how we had actually been treated as less than human; began to see our strength as a people . . . . I started *thinking*. Thinking about things I'd never thought about before, and the thinking turned into questions. But I had more questions than answers. . . . So I went to college" (pp. xv-xvi).

After finishing high school in Port Huron, she enrolled in Afro-American Literature at Los Angeles City College. Again, as McMillan herself observed, "I remember the textbook was called *Dark Symphony: Negro Literature in America* because I still have it. I couldn't believe the rush I felt over and over once I discovered **Countee Cullen, Langston Hughes, Ann Petry, Zora Neale Hurston, Ralph Ellison, Jean Toomer, Richard Wright**, and rediscovered and read James Baldwin, to name just a few. I'm surprised I didn't need glasses by the end of the semester. My world opened up. . . . Not only had we lived diverse, interesting, provocative, and relentless lives, but during, through, and as a result of all these painful experiences, some folks had taken the time to write it down" (p. xvi, *BI*).

During this time, McMillan also had a love affair that broke her heart. As she recalled, "I was so devastated and felt so helpless that my reaction manifested itself in a poem. I did not sit down and say, 'I'm going to write a poem about this.' It was more like magic. I didn't even know I was writing a poem until I had written it. Afterward, I felt lighter, as if something had happened to lessen the pain. And when I read this 'thing,' I was shocked because I didn't know where the words came from" (pp. xvi-xvii). "I read that poem over and over in disbelief because *I* had written it. One day, a colleague saw it lying on the kitchen table and read it. . . . he liked it, then went on to tell me that he . . . . wanted to publish it. Publish it? He was serious and it found its way onto a typeset page" (p. xvii). "Seeing my name in print excited me. And from that point on, [almost everything inspired me to write poems.] . . . Years passed. . . . Those poems started turning into sentences. . . . Writing became an outlet for my dissatisfactions, distaste, and my way of trying to make sense of what I saw happening around me" (p. xvii).

By the time McMillan transferred to the University of California at Berkeley (1973), writing had become easy for her, and she majored in journalism. In 1976, with encouragement from her teacher, mentor, and friend **Ishmael Reed**, she published her first short story in a campus literary magazine. "The End" was her beginning, and by the time she graduated (B.S., 1979), she had realized that writing news stories was not the kind of writing she enjoyed. She had already submitted a collection of her short stories to major mainstream publisher Houghton Mifflin. The editors there rejected her stories, but they told her they liked her writing well enough that if she submitted a novel, they might be interested in seeing it.

With Berkeley behind her, McMillan left California to go to New York City. There, she entered Columbia University, to study screenwriting. She didn't complete the master's program there, however, because she had already realized that this type of writing was not her main interest. She left Columbia, got a job doing word processing, became involved with Leonard Welch, and continued to write fiction. When Welch lost his job, he started selling cocaine, and he and she got involved in using cocaine and alcohol. On April 24, 1984, McMillan and Welch had a son, Solomon Welch; within a year, McMillan left Welch, overcame her addiction, and started raising Solomon on her own. She has stayed away from alcohol and other drugs ever since.

Meanwhile, in 1982, McMillan spent time at the Yaddo artists colony (in Saratoga Springs, NY), and she enrolled in a writing workshop at the Harlem Writers Guild. Fellow writers there had encouraged her to turn her short story "Mama" into a full-length novel. In 1983, while at the prestigious MacDowell Colony (in Peterborough, NH), she started writing the first draft of *Mama*. Once she completed it, she sent it to Houghton Mifflin, and they accepted it. Even before the book's 1987 publication, however, McMillan decided that she would do whatever she could to promote it. Through her contacts with other writers, she knew that publishers make very little effort to promote the work of most authors, particularly first-time novelists. Hence, she wrote (thanks to her word-processing skills) and sent out (thanks to her friendly contacts with the guys in her firm's mail room) more than 3,000 letters to bookstores, college campuses, and African-American organizations.

As she later recalled, "I did it all summer long: my friends were hanging out at the beach, and I was licking envelopes" (p. 140, *WYL2*). In her letters, she encouraged recipients to promote her book and offered to give talks or readings. She launched her own publicity tour, going wherever she was invited to speak. *Mama* had sold out its first printing before it was published, and it was in its third printing by the time it was two months old. Even her editors at Houghton Mifflin acknowledged, "Terry, we don't think this would happened if you had not done all this" (*BI*). A paperback edition was published by Washington Square Press in 1991, and a pocket paperback (Pocket Books) appeared in 1994.

In *Mama*, the 27-year-old protagonist Mildred Peacock struggles to raise her five children in Port Haven, Michigan, an economically depressed town with few job opportunities for African Americans. After getting herself and her children away from her alcoholic, abusive husband, she works whatever jobs she can find, draws on her inner strength, and somehow manages to create a decent—though very difficult—life for herself and her children. (Wonder where she got that story idea?) Mildred is definitely no saint, but she teaches her children how to rely on themselves and their family to get through the hard times. In *The New York Times Book Review*, critic Valerie Wayers called *Mama* "original in concept and style, a runaway narrative pulling a crowded cast of funny, earthy characters" (quoted in *PBW*), and the book won an American Book Award in 1988.

The year *Mama* was published, McMillan was invited to be a Visiting Writer at the University of Wyoming, Laramie (1987-1988), and the following year (1988), she was named an associate professor in creative writing at the University of Arizona, Tucson. That year, she was also awarded a literary fellowship by the National Endowment for the Arts. The next year, she published her second novel, *Disappearing Acts* (1989), which sold even more copies than her first novel. Houghton Mifflin didn't receive the benefit of those sales, however, as the publisher and McMillan had parted company because of disputes regarding how McMillan was approaching the work. While Houghton Mifflin was still dickering about making an offer, Viking Penguin bought the manuscript within a couple days of hearing about it. Washington Square Press sold more than 100,000 copies in paperback (1990), and Pocket Books sold additional copies (1993). In 2000, HBO released a film version of it.

Disappearing Acts comprises alternating first-person narrations by Zora Banks, a college-educated aspiring songwriter, and by Franklin Swift, a poorly educated and often unemployed laborer. Although their relationship is troubled and unhappy, the story isn't, as McMillan's humor and compassion sizzle throughout the book. Leonard Welch apparently thought their story too closely resembled his experiences with McMillan, and in 1990, he sued her for defamation of his character. Eventually, McMillan prevailed in their legal battles, winning both the case and a later appeal, just as she had emerged triumphant (i.e., drug free and with her beloved son) from the earlier battles of their previous relationship. Meanwhile, MGM purchased the movie rights to the book, optioned by Tri-Star, and McMillan was commissioned to write the screenplay herself, which she did while on sabbatical from the University of Arizona.

While McMillan was still teaching in Arizona, she made it her mission to find an anthology of American literature reflecting the cultural diversity of American culture. She looked through all her own books and all the books in the library, but she found none. She then decided just to augment a European-American-centered anthology with an African-American-centered one. Every anthology in her own library—and in her college's—included works from the 1960s or before. She called friends and colleagues around the country, asking them for recommendations of anthologies of contemporary African-American fiction. No one knew of anything worthwhile.

Once McMillan was satisfied that nothing existed to meet her specifications, she decided she'd have to create her own anthology—and thus was born the manuscript for *Breaking Ice: An Anthology of Contemporary African-American Fiction* (1990). All 57 of the works are by post-1960s authors, which she categorized as "seasoned, emerging, and unpublished." The works represent diverse topics, perspectives, and orientations, few of which focus on race as a central theme. McMillan chose these pieces from nearly 300 submissions she received, and she ended up choosing quite a few excerpts from novels, as she wasn't satisfied with the selection of superb short stories available. In thinking about this dearth of fine short stories, she observed that publishers frequently encourage talented writers to abandon short stories in favor of novels, which they believe will sell better and will be more deserving of critical attention. As if the 300 submissions weren't enough fiction reading to satisfy anyone, McMillan also served as a judge for the National Book Award for fiction the year that *Breaking Ice* was published.

While still retaining her tenured position in Arizona, McMillan and her son moved from Tucson to Danville, California, in the San Francisco Bay area. She was still working on completing her third novel, *Waiting to Exhale* (1992), while the movers were loading—and then unloading—her desk. Viking, McMillan's publisher, set a $700,000 bidding minimum each for the movie rights and for the paperback rights. Not to worry: The paperback rights were sold to Pocket Books (paperback, 1993) for $2.64 million. Viking then paid for a 20-city, 6-week, nearly 30-bookstore tour—quite a change from McMillan's industrious self-promotion of her first novel.

Viking's investment paid off big-time, too: *Waiting to Exhale* had sold more than 700,000 hardcover copies by the end of 1992. In its first week of publication, it went on *The New York Times Bestseller* list, where it stayed for months. That same year, award-winning novelist **Alice Walker**'s *Possessing the Secret of Joy* and Nobel laureate **Toni Morrison**'s *Jazz* had been released, but McMillan's *Waiting* outsold both books by 3 to 1 (eventually selling more than 3 million copies). The 1995 film made from the book was also a smash hit. McMillan hadn't exactly predicted this great success herself, however. She later recalled, "After about 90 pages [of writing the *Waiting* manuscript], I'm saying to myself, 'Are they going to think this is as good as *Disappearing Acts*? Are they going to be disappointed?' Eventually, I just had to say, 'I cannot think about my audience; I can't guess what people are going to like'" (p. 142, *WYL2*). Regarding the book's tremendous success, she noted, "It's like having a baby and praying that people think it's cute" (*OCAAL*).

Waiting to Exhale is about four smart, funny, sexy African-American professional women and the ups and downs of their relationships with men (lovers, husbands, ex-lovers, friends, sons), with one another, and with their careers. As with all McMillan's previous novels, her writing style is warm and conversational. Although some critics have scorned her work for treating African-American men too negatively, critic **Charles R. Johnson** called it "a tough love letter to black males everywhere." Other critics have whined that *Waiting* and McMillan's other novels use too much profanity and vulgarity, but McMillan has rebutted, "basically, the language that I use is accurate. . . . That's the way we talk. And I want to know why I've

never read a review where they complain about the language that male writers use!" (p. 142, *WYL2*).

Between the 1992 publication of the *Waiting* book and the 1995 release of the *Waiting* movie were 1993 and 1994, two very tough years for McMillan. Her mother had been living with her, both in Arizona and in California, and in early September, Terry bought her mother a house and a new car, to offer her 59-year-old mama a little comfort and security after a challenging life of self-sacrifice. Then she left for a European tour to promote *Waiting*, while her mother stayed in her home with Solomon. On September 30, Madeline suffered a fatal asthma attack. While Terry was still reeling with grief, her dearest friend, novelist and columnist Doris Jean Austin, was diagnosed with inoperable liver cancer. Austin died before the anniversary of Madeline's death.

With 1993 and 1994 behind her, McMillan needed to celebrate life. In 1995, she took a vacation to Jamaica, where she met a charming man who was about half her age, Jonathan Plummer. The twosome had a deliciously romantic affair, and she wrote her fourth novel, *How Stella Got Her Groove Back*, within a few weeks. After completing her manuscript, she invited Plummer to come to the States and live with her and her 11-year-old son, who was skeptical about the relationship at first. The tremendous success of *Waiting* helped McMillan gain a $6 million publishing deal for *Stella* (1996), and Terry, Solomon, and Jonathan had a home custom built for them in Danville. After she sold her film rights for *Stella*, the couple married, and for a time lived happily after, just as anyone who saw the 1998 film would imagine.

In the novel, the 42-year-old protagonist Stella has been highly successful in her corporate career, as well as in raising her child single-handedly, but she still feels dissatisfied, discontent. Her fun-spirited—and outrageously outspoken—friend gets her to take a vacation in Jamaica. There, Stella meets a handsome 20-year-old Jamaican cook, who seduces her, falls in love with her, and charms her into loving him in turn. Complicating the situation are the young man's parents—who at first seem horrified at their son's relationship—and Stella's two sisters, Vanessa (a single parent) and Angela (married and pregnant). Vanessa is highly impulsive herself, so she encourages Stella to go for it, but Angela is unable to appreciate anything outside the traditional family she prizes. By the end of the story, the couple defies expectations and social conventions; readers and viewers imagine that they will live happily ever after. Unfortunately, the real-life couple did *not* live happily ever after. In March 2005, McMillan filed for a divorce, and Plummer received an undisclosed settlement amount. Almost exactly two years later, McMillan sued Plummer and his attorney for $40 million, citing that they intentionally embarrassed and humiliated her, including Miller's assertion that he is gay.

"McMillan's allegations also include 'emotional distress, invasion of privacy and placing her in a "false light" to harm her professionally and personally.' McMillan also claims Plummer violated a restraining order by calling her to speak with her son" (from //rodonline.typepad.com/rodonline/2007/03/terry_mcmillan_.html). From what she has said in interviews, she believed that he had never truly loved her and that he sought only U.S. citizenship and financial gain from their relationship. Since then, Plummer has offered his own fictional take on their relationship, *Balancing Act* (2007, with Karen Hunter). McMillan's resilience helped her through, though. In a July 11, 2005 interview with *People* magazine, she said, "I never thought my happiness was contingent on having a man. A man should enrich it. But when that ceases to be the case, he's gotta go" (quoted in *Black Biography*).

While her marriage was still a romance story, McMillan completed her fifth novel, *A Day Late and a Dollar Short* (2001), which she had actually started in the mid-1980s. The novel offers the perspectives of six family members—two parents, three daughters, and one son—after the children are grown. In addition to their struggles within the family, each person has her or his own individual struggles, such as alcohol and other drug abuse, child molestation, and marital infidelity. McMillan explores the narrative form by allowing each person to tell her or his own story, managing to keep each person's voice and perspective distinct, without confusing the reader. McMillan also introduces tragedy to achieve her happy, hopeful ending. The mother of the family dies in a sudden asthma attack, but she leaves letters for each of her loved ones, urging them to spend one final Thanksgiving meal together. At the meal, each one reads aloud Mama's letter, and by the end of the meal, they pledge to meet again the next year.

In McMillan's *The Interruption of Everything* (2005), 44-year-old wife and mother Marilyn Grimes feels she's underappreciated, and she relishes her monthly "Private Pity Parties" with her two best girlfriends. At last, with her three children out of the nest, Marilyn can finally start thinking about what she wants for her own life, without first considering the needs of her children, her mid-life-crisis husband, her live-in mother-in-law, and her own needy mother and sister. She soon considers some radical changes: dumping her current boring and now-boorish husband for a dalliance with her former husband, and ditching her part-time craft-store job for her long-longed-for career as an artist. But then a possible pregnancy seems to be the interruption of everything. *Interruption* has been adapted to audiocassette format, narrated by Emmy-winning actor Lynn Whitfield; most of McMillan's other novels have been adapted to the audiocassette format, too: *Waiting to Exhale* (1992, abridged), *Disappearing Acts* (1993, abridged), *How Stella Got Her Groove Back* (1996, unabridged, narrated by actor Lynne Thigpen), and *A Day Late and a Dollar Short* (2001).

In all her works to date, McMillan speaks to the heart of her readers, tying the experiences of her characters to their own. Through candor and humor, she depicts spirited, independent African-American women who care deeply about their relationships with loved ones and who seek to form meaningful relationships with men, without losing their own identities or their independence. Because her writing is so forthright, she appeals to a far wider audience than just African-American readers or film viewers. McMillan also hopes her own example will encourage other African Americans to become writers.

In a 2001 interview (*Writer*, August, quoted in *CAO-05*), McMillan said, "I write because the world is an imperfect place, and we behave in an imperfect manner. I want to understand why it's so hard to be good, honest, loving, caring, thoughtful, and generous. Writing is about the only way (besides praying) that allows me to be compassionate toward folks who, in real life, I'm probably not that sympathetic toward. I want to understand myself and others better, so what better way than to pretend to be them."

McMillan has also offered advice to writers, "It took [a long time] to realize that writing was not something you aspired to, it was something you did because you had to" (p. xviii, *BI*). "Persist. Acknowledge your bewilderment. Remember. Writing is personal. Try to write the kind of stories you'd like to read. Do not write to impress. Do not write to prove to a reader how much you know, but instead write in order *to know*. At the same time, you want to snatch readers' attention, pull them away from what they're doing and keep them right next to your characters. You want them to feel what your characters feel, experience it with them so the readers are just as concerned about their outcome as the character is. Perhaps, if you do your job well and you're lucky, readers may recognize something until it clicks" (p. xxiii, *BI*). "I don't force things on my characters; I wait and watch them grow" (p. 144, *WYL2*).

McMillan's most recent book emerged from advice she offered at her son's high-school commencement ceremony. *It's OK If You're Clueless: And 23 More Tips for the College Bound* (2006) started out as a pamphlet for Solomon's fellow grads. As with all of her writings, her frankness, wit, and charm let her wisdom slide down effortlessly, so popular demand by other students—and their parents—led her to have Viking publish her 64-page book. Apparently, her advice was particularly sound, too: Her son Solomon graduated from Stanford University, where she was once a visiting lecturer.

Although Solomon's graduation may be the honor about which she feels proudest, her readers also offer her kudos and popular acclaim, making her books bestsellers. In addition, the literary world has honored McMillan with an American Book Award (1987), a National Endowment for the Arts fellowship (1988), an invitation to serve on the 1990 National Book Award for fiction panel, two NAACP Image Awards (1992, for *Waiting,* and 1996, for *Stella*), an *Essence* Award for Excellence in Literature (2002), the Walter Mosley Author of Distinction Award (2005, National Book Club Conference), and an *Essence* Lifetime Achievement Award (2008). Not too shabby for a woman who didn't enjoy books until she reached her teens.

REFERENCES: *AA:PoP. AANB. B. BI. CAO-05. CLCS. EB-BH-CD. EBLG. MWEL. NAAAL. QB. W. WDAA. Wiki.* Bolden, B. J., in *RGAL-3.* Bronson, Tammy J., in *CPW.* Champion, Laurie, in *21-CAN.* Darnell, Debra G., and Sara Pendergast, in *BB.* Esselman, Mary D., in *T-CYAW.* Hall, John Greer, in *GEAAL.* Heininge, Kathy, in *AW:ACLB-02.* Mason, Wanda, in *COCAAL* and *OCAAL.* McMillan, Terry, and Evette Porter. "My Novel, Myself." *Village Voice.* Rpt. in Jeffrey W. Hunter and Deborah A. Schmitt (Eds.) (1999), *Contemporary Literary Criticism* (Vol. 112). Detroit: Gale Group. *Literature Resource Center.* Robinson, Lisa Clayton, in *EA-99.* Shaw, Brenda Robinson, in *PBW.* Smith, Wendy, "An Interview with Terry McMillan." *Publishers Weekly* 239.22 (May 11, 1992): pp. 50-51. Rpt. in *Contemporary Literary Criticism Select.* Detroit: Gale. From *Literature Resource Center.* _____. "Terry McMillan: The Novelist Explores African American Life From the Point of View of a New Generation." *Publishers Weekly.* pp. 50-51. Rpt. in Literature Resource Center. Detroit: Gale, p50-51. From *Literature Resource Center. WYL2.* Thompson, Kathleen, in *BWA:AHE.* Wolcott, James, *The New Yorker* 72.10 (Apr. 29, 1996): p. 102. Rpt. in Jeffrey W. Hunter and Deborah A. Schmitt (Eds.) (1999), *Contemporary Literary Criticism* (Vol. 112). Detroit: Gale Group. *Literature Resource Center.* Woodard, Helena, in *OCWW.* //aalbc.com/authors/terry.htm, Terry McMillan. //books.simonandschuster.com/Balancing-Act/Karen-Hunter/9781416537403. //findarticles.com/p/articles/mi_m1355/is_7_108/ai_n15691161/. //search.barnesandnoble.com/Terry-McMillan/Terry-McMillan/e/9780671993092. //us.penguingroup.com/static/pages/authors/popular/terry mcmillan.html. //www.gbmnews.com/articles/2802/1/Terry-McMillan-Gets-Achievement-Award/Page1.html. //www.imdb.com/name/nm0573334/bio, Biography for Terry McMillan. //www.nationalbook clubconference.com/authors.aspx. Amazon.com.

McPherson, James Alan
9/16/1943–

Short stories, essays, autobiography/memoir; educator

Little James's father, also named James, shared his love of comic books with his two sons. The three McPherson males would leave Mable (Smalls) McPherson behind and go to a comic book wholesale house in Savannah, where they'd luxuriate in bins of remaindered comic books. The white man who ran the operation was a pal of big James, and he'd let the boys take home as many leftover comic books as their arms could hold.

While James was growing up, segregation was the rule in schools, libraries, and other public places, so when young James was a little older, he found his way to the Colored Branch of the Carnegie Public Library, within a block of their home. As he later recalled, "I liked going there to read all day. At first the words, without pictures, were a mystery. But then, suddenly, they all began to march across the page. They gave up their secret meanings, spoke of other worlds, made me know that pain was a part of other people's lives. After a while, I could read faster and faster and faster and faster. After a while, I no longer believed in the world in which I lived. I loved the Colored Branch of the Carnegie Public Library" (*TWL*).

After finishing public school, McPherson worked as a Pullman waiter aboard the Great Northern Railroad while attending college at Morgan State University (in Baltimore, 1963-1964) and then at Morris Brown College (in Atlanta; B.A., 1965). After graduating, Harvard University Law School recruited him, and in 1968, he earned his L.L.B. there. After Harvard, he went to the University of Iowa Writers' Workshop, where he earned a master's degree (M.F.A., 1969). After all that schooling, McPherson was ready to go out into the world and—teach English at several universities, including the University of Iowa Law School; University of California, Santa Cruz; Morgan State University; and the University of Virginia, Charlottesville. In 1981, he became an English professor at the University of Iowa Writers' Workshop. Other than a few visiting professorships (e.g., Harvard and Stanford), he has been there ever since. From 2005 to 2007, he even served as acting director of the Iowa Workshop.

Meanwhile, in the late 1960s, McPherson entered his short story "Gold Coast" in a fiction contest sponsored by the editors of *Atlantic Monthly* magazine. "Gold Coast" won first prize, and McPherson gained a prestigious start to his literary career. By the end of the decade, *Atlantic* had awarded McPherson a writer's grant and had invited him to become a contributing editor for the magazine. More of his short stories started being published in other periodicals, as well. Rarely does a writer earn a distinguished literary reputation based on short stories, but McPherson has done so, based chiefly on two collections of his stories: *Hue and Cry: Short Stories* (1969/2001) and *Elbow Room* (1977/1996).

The stories in *Hue and Cry* were written while McPherson was still a student, yet they were praised by such literary luminaries as **Ralph Ellison** for his mastery of the writing craft. Although race is not central to his stories, his stories nonetheless indict social injustice and discrimination based on race, class, and sex. His stories "On Trains" and "A Solo Song: For Doc" offer readers a glimpse into the lives of the legendary Pullman porters with whom McPherson had worked; his stories "Hue and Cry" and "Cabbages and Kings" tell of the travails of interracial relationships; "Gold Coast" explores race, class, and age differences between two men; and "An Act of Prostitution" reveals some of the injustices of legal justice. In these stories, McPherson withholds judgment, permitting his readers to form their own opinions about the characters and their situations. In recognition of his work, McPherson was awarded a National Institute of Arts and Letters grant (1970), a Rockefeller grant (1970), and a Guggenheim fellowship (1972-1973).

McPherson's next collection, *Elbow Room* (1977), was also lauded by Ralph Ellison and was awarded a Pulitzer Prize for Fiction (1978), making McPherson the first African American to receive this honor. The stories in this book range from reminiscence ("Why I Like Country Music," in which a New Yorker recalls a partner at a country dance during his Southern boyhood) to tall tale ("The Story of a Dead Man," about a mythical African-American folk figure) to travel ("I Am an American," about a young African-American couple in London). As with *Hue and Cry,* most of his characters are still confronting social constraints and limitations, but they seem better equipped to face their challenges. All of his stories are realistic and centered around his richly detailed characters. Both his stories and his essays have been widely published in periodicals (e.g., *The New York Times magazine, Esquire*) and in anthologies (e.g., *Best American Short Stories, Best American Essays,* 1990, 1993, 1994, 1995). He also edited two issues of the literary journal *Ploughshares* (1985, 1990), and two anthologies (*Railroad: Trains and Train People in American Culture,* 1976, with Miller Williams; and *Fathering Daughters; Reflections by Men,* 1998, with DeWitt Henry). After unsuccessful child-custody battles over his daughter, Rachel (born in 1979), McPherson chose to focus on fathering, rather on writing, during the 1980s and 1990s. As his coeditor DeWitt Henry noted, "Once his daughter was in college, McPherson felt 'free to get back to my work'" (quoted in *Ploughshares,* Fall 2008).

Since publishing *Elbow Room,* McPherson has written mostly essays, including both personal ones and political ones addressing his vision of a cultural synthesis among America's diverse people. His more personal pieces appeared in *Crabcakes: A Memoir* (1998), covering almost two decades of his experiences. Despite many trials and tribulations, McPherson observed, "If nothing in the future of the present seems permanent . . . one can always focus on . . . the future enjoyment of a Maryland crabcake. Such exercises of the imagination keep hope alive" (quoted by *Kirkus Reviews,* in //www.Amazon.com). Richard Burns "highly recommended" it, noting, "This dramatic memoir reaches for the essence of life in search of an epiphany" (*Library Journal,* quoted in //www.Amazon.com). Others called this work "lilting," "inspirational," "beautiful," "thoughtful," "incomparable," and "dazzling" (from *The New York Times Book Re-*

view, Philadelphia Inquirer, Ploughshares, People, Bloomsbury Review, and *Cleveland Plain Dealer,* respectively, quoted in //www.Amazon.com).

Next, McPherson published many of his more political and cultural essays in *A Region Not Home: Reflections from Exile* (2000/2009). Though less personal than his memoir, this book, too, uses his own experiences to illuminate more universal themes, such as his part-time parenting of his cherished daughter Rachel. *Kirkus Reviews* called it "a rich feast for the hungry mind" (quoted in //www.Amazon.com). The publisher called it "a meditation on what it means to be human—an enlightening and soulful work reaching to the core of suffering and joy" (quoted in //www.Amazon.com).

In 1981, McPherson was one of three African-American writers to be awarded a five-year "genius" grant by the MacArthur Foundation, for his exceptional writing talent. He has also served as a trustee for *Ploughshares* (1989-2005) and a panelist for the Whiting Foundation (starting in 1985), and he has been inducted into the American Academy of Arts and Sciences (1995). In addition, he earned a Pushcart Prize (1995) and a Lannan Foundation fellowship (2003). McPherson has admirably taken his own advice to African-American writers, when he suggested, "employing our own sense of reality and our own conception of what human life should be to explore, and perhaps help define, the cultural realities of contemporary American life" (from *Atlantic Monthly,* 1970; quoted in *CAO-08*).

Asked why he became a writer, he said, "I suppose because I seemed to do it well, and there was joy in that. . . . And being able to use my imagination. . . . I suppose to find a way of expressing that, I chose writing. The freedom of it is also something that attracted me. Not that being tied to your typewriter or pen and paper day after day is especially a free occupation, but there is a lot of freedom, room to move and grow, inherent in the . . . writing . . . lifestyle. . . . But it's also a way of dealing with things. . . . A lot of mean things have happened to me, and the only way I can deal with them, or beat them, is to take it inside myself, turn it over and look at it and try to humanize the experience, try to understand why it happened" (interview with Bob Shacochis, 1983; reprinted 2007).

REFERENCES: *AA:PoP. BAWPP. CAO-08. E-98. EB-BH-CD. MWEL. NAAAL. OC20LE. TWL. W. WDAA. Wiki.* "About James Alan McPherson, a Profile." *Ploughshares.* 34.2-3 (Fall 2008) p. 187. From *Literature Resource Center.* Beavers, Herman, in *ASSWSWWII-4th.* Knutson, Lin, in *GEAAL.* McPherson, James Alan, and Bob Shacochis. "Interview with James Alan McPherson." *Iowa Journal of Literary Studies 4.1* (Winter 1983): pp. 6-33. Rpt. in Short Story Criticism. Ed. Jelena O. Krstovic. Vol. 95. Detroit: Gale, 2007. pp. 6-33. From *Literature Resource Center.* Perry, Patsy B., in *AAW-55-85:DPW. RGAL-3.* Schafer, William J., in *CN-6.* Wallace, Jon, in *COCAAL* and *OCAAL.* Amazon.com. *News & Notes,* National

Public Radio, "Becoming a Writer," August 27, 2007, link to audio at //www.npr.org.

Mebane, Mary E. (Elizabeth)
6/26/1933–3/5/1992
Autobiography/memoirs, literary criticism, juvenile literature, play; educator

The daughter of a farmer and a tobacco-factory worker, Mary Mebane graduated summa cum laude from North Carolina College at Durham (now North Carolina Central University) (1955). She then spent another five years teaching music and English in North Carolina public schools (Martin County, 1955-1956; Pinehurst, 1957; and Durham City, 1957-1960). After that, she returned to her alma mater to teach English (1960-1965), first as an instructor and then as an assistant professor. Meanwhile, she earned her M.A. (1961) from the University of North Carolina (UNC), and she published her first volume of literary criticism, *Existential Themes in Ellison's Invisible Man* and **Wright's** *The Outsider* (1961/1962).

She left the assistant professorship in 1965, and she received fellowships from the Southern Fellowship Fund in 1965 and 1966. The following year, she became an associate professor of English at South Carolina State College in Orangeburg (1967-1974) while completing her Ph.D. (1973) from UNC. Her doctoral dissertation, *The Family in the Works of Charles W. Chesnutt and Selected Works of Richard Wright* (1973) was published and is still available in numerous libraries. She also contributed to at least two anthologies during that time, *A Galaxy of Black Writing* (1970) and *The Eloquence of Protest: Voices of the Seventies* (1972). While working toward her doctorate, she received a Woodrow Wilson Career Teaching fellowship (1968) and a third Southern Fellowship Fund grant (1971) for working on her dissertation.

From Orangeburg, she moved to Columbia as associate professor of English at the University of South Carolina (1974-1977). While there, she wrote a two-act play, *Take a Sad Song* (produced in 1975). Unable to rise through the academic ranks as quickly as she wished, she left academia for a few years, during which time she contributed to *Southern Panorama* (1979). She then accepted a position as a lecturer in composition at the University of Wisconsin—Madison (1980-1983). During that time, she wrote two autobiographies, *Mary: An Autobiography* (1981), about her impoverished Depression-era youth; and *Mary, Wayfarer* (1983), which highlights her experiences as a young teacher viewing the harmful effects of legal segregation in the U.S. South.

Throughout the 1970s and 1980s, Mebane contributed to *The New York Times*, often using the pseudonym "Liza" for her op-ed pieces. Her work was recognized with a Distinguished Alumnus Award in Literature from UNC at Chapel Hill (1982), a Milwaukee Artists Foundation grant (1983), and a creative writing fellowship grant from the National Endowment for the Arts (1983). Little is known about her life after she left Madison, except that she died alone and impoverished in a Milwaukee nursing home.

REFERENCES: *BAWPP. CAO-02.* Bobo, Kristina D., in *AANB.* //worldcat.org/identities/lccn-n80-82804. Amazon.com.

Meriwether (1st married name; 2nd married name: Howe), Louise (née Jenkins)
5/8/1923–
Novels, short stories, biographies, articles

When Julia and Marion Lloyd Jenkins left South Carolina, they surely didn't expect to arrive in the North on the precipice of an economic depression. By the time Louise came along (their only daughter and their third child), they were living in Haverstraw, New York, where Julia was busy caring for a houseful of children while Marion worked as a bricklayer. When the Great Depression hit, there were five Jenkins children, and Marion had lost his job. To make ends meet, Marion worked as a "numbers runner" (small-time helper in an illegal gambling operation) and Julia collected welfare checks. In those days, the Jenkins family was not alone in their poverty—or in their various ways of trying to get by.

After Louise finished P.S. (public school) 81 and then graduated from Central Commercial High School (in downtown Manhattan), she went on to study English at New York University, where she earned her B.A. By the 1960s, Louise had married Angelo Meriwether and had moved with him to Los Angeles, where she worked as a freelance reporter for the *Los Angeles Sentinel* (1961-1964). Her book reviews, biographical sketches of local African-American heroes and of Arctic explorer **Matthew Henson**, and other writings started appearing in the *Los Angeles Times* and in the *Sentinel*. During the mid-1960s, Louise had become a dedicated social activist, fighting for better working conditions for African-American laborers; working with the Congress of Racial Equality (CORE) for civil rights; and collaborating with the Deacons, a self-defense coalition that maintained an all-day, all-night patrol to protect the African-American community from Ku Klux Klan attacks.

In 1965, she earned an M.A. in journalism from the University of California at Los Angeles, and she got a job as the first African-American story analyst for Universal Studios (1965-1967). In 1967, William Styron's white-male account of *The Confessions of Nat Turner* sparked fury among many African Americans, including Meriwether, who helped prevent the prize-winning book from being made into a movie. In the late 1960s, she joined the Watts Writers' Workshop and started writing short stories (e.g., "Daddy Was a Number Runner," 1967; "A Happening in Barbadoes," 1968; and "The Thick End Is for Whipping," *Negro Digest*, 1969).

While protesting Styron's work, Meriwether had temporarily set aside work on her novel, *Daddy Was a Number Runner* (1970/2002), which she had started writing as a short story in the mid-1960s. Her five years of labor paid off, however, in terms of critical acclaim, including high praise from such noted authors as **James Baldwin**, and the monetary rewards of writing, including a grant from the National Endowment for the Arts (1973) and a grant from the Creative Arts Service Program, an auxiliary of the New York State Council on the Arts (1973). The semiautobiographical novel views the Great Depression through the eyes of 12-year-old Francie Coffin. Despite the youth of the narrator, the story is no fairy tale. Pubescent Francie watches her father abandon his family to run off with a young woman, her mother beg welfare workers to help her feed her family, and her brother become a pimp. Award-winning novelist **Paule Marshall** said of *Daddy*, "In her perceptive and moving first novel about the social death of one Harlem family, Meriwether reaches deeply into the lives of her characters to say something about the way black people relate to each other" (quoted in *CAO-01*). In 1988, a Dutch publisher reprinted the work as *Francie's Harlem*.

After finishing *Daddy*, Meriwether wrote three biographies of notable African Americans, intended for young-adult (teenage) readers: *The Freedom Ship of Robert Smalls* (1971), about a former slave who became a national politician; *The Heart Man: Dr. Daniel Hale Williams* (1972), about the first doctor to perform open-heart surgery; and *Don't Ride the Bus on Monday: The Rosa Parks Story* (1973), about the Alabama seamstress and civil-rights activist who initiated a major protest action for social change. Meriwether later noted, "I have been deeply concerned for many years by the way African Americans fell through the cracks of history, and I reacted by attempting to set the record straight" (*BWA:AHE*, quoting a 1981 letter from Meriwether to article author Rita Dandridge). Thus, her writing may be viewed as an extension of her devotion to social activism.

By the late 1970s, Meriwether had left California, returning to the East Coast, where she served on the faculty of Sarah Lawrence College in Bronxville, New York (with a little time out for teaching creative writing at the University of Houston, Texas). In 1994, Meriwether's second novel for young adults, *Fragments of the Ark*, was published. This Civil War-era historical novel fictionally recreates the story of Robert Smalls, in the character of Peter Mango, a fugitive slave from Charleston, North Carolina, who runs away to aid the Union army and gain his free-

dom. A 1980s grant from the Mellon Foundation helped fund her research for the novel, so that she could make several trips to the Sea Islands, off the coast of Charleston, in North Carolina. She has also taught writing at Frederick Douglass Creative Arts Center, at Sarah Lawrence College, and at the University of Houston Creative Writing Program.

In the new millennium, Meriwether wrote a novel for adults, *Shadow Dancing* (2000), about a well-respected writer who has more difficulty managing her love life and her emotions than she has had in handling her professional life and her career. Meriwether's own life has paralleled her protagonist's; despite her success as a writer, she was twice divorced: from her first husband, Angelo Meriwether, and from her second husband, Earl Howe. Meriwether's long-time friend **Maya Angelou** described *Shadow Dancing* as "lusty and gutsy and sexy and true. Louise Meriwether has written a woman's book which will knock men's socks off. We will all enjoy Shadow Dancing."

REFERENCES: *AANB. BAWPP. CAO-01. EBLG.* Brown-Guillory, Elizabeth, in *OCWW.* Dandridge, Rita, in *AAFW-55-84. BWA:AHE. COCAAL*, and *OCAAL*. Holt, Amanda, in *GEAAL.* //www.writers center.org/brownmeriwether.html. Amazon.com.

Merrick, Lyda (née Moore)
11/19/1890–2/14/1987
Periodical for the blind

While raising her two daughters, Merrick worked in the library her father had founded for his community. (Her father, a physician, had also cofounded a hospital and a life-insurance company.) While working with members of the library's club, Library Corner for the Blind, she discovered the need for a periodical that would appeal to blind African-American readers. In June 1951, Merrick established the journal *Negro Braille Magazine*, serving as its editor until 1969. Even after she had stepped down as editor, she continued to be involved with the journal for another 10 years. As the journal gradually addressed a wider audience and no longer focused exclusively on blind African-American readers, it was renamed *Merrick-Washington Magazine for the Blind* (in 1981).

REFERENCES: *BAAW.* —Tonya Bolden

Messenger, The
1917–1928
News reports, features, and editorials of interest to African Americans, both locally and nationally

In 1917, **A. Philip Randolph** and **Chandler Owen**, both members of the Socialist Party of America, were asked to edit *Hotel Messenger,* a labor-union journal of the Headwaiters and Sidewaiters of Greater New York. When differences between the editors and the labor union emerged, Randolph and Owen decided to start their own pro-labor monthly magazine. The first issue of *The Messenger: The Only Radical Negro Magazine in America* appeared that November (1917).

Randolph and Owen had to work hard to attract readers because other African-American periodicals were already in print, such as the NAACP's *The Crisis* magazine (1910-) and **William Monroe Trotter** and George Forbes's *Boston Guardian* newspaper (1901-1950s). Still more appeared in print soon after the arrival of *The Messenger,* such as **Cyril Valentine Briggs**'s *The Crusader: Journal of the Hamitic League of the World and the African Blood Brotherhood* (1918-1922) and **Marcus Garvey**'s *Negro World* (1918-1933), as well as the National Urban League's *Opportunity: A Journal of Negro Life* (1923-1949). All but the *Guardian* were also being published in New York City. As socialists, Owen and Randolph also distinguished *The Messenger* as the "first publication to recognize the Negro problem as fundamentally a labor problem" (quoted in *COCAAL*). In it, they urged African Americans to join forces with other laborers, along class lines and across racial lines.

The same year Randolph and Owen launched *The Messenger,* the United States got involved in World War I (1917-1919, U.S. involvement). The editors clearly stated, "Patriotism has no appeal to us; justice has. Party has no weight with us; principle has. Loyalty is meaningless; it depends on what one is loyal to" (quoted in //en.wikipedia.org/wiki/The_Messenger_Magazine). In their editorials, Randolph and Owen not only opposed World War I but also urged African Americans to resist the government's draft into segregated armed forces designed to preserve a racially discriminatory society.

As always, during wartime, the federal government clamped down on free speech, and on August 4, 1918, Randolph and Owen were arrested and held for federal investigation. The investigation led to their being indicted for violating the Espionage Act. After just two days, the two were brought to trial, where the charges were surprisingly dismissed. As Randolph later recalled, "The judge said, why, we were nothing but boys. He couldn't believe we were old enough, or, being black, smart enough, to write that red-hot stuff in the *Messenger.* There was no doubt, he said, that the white Socialists were using us, that they had written the stuff for us" (quoted in Anderson, 1986).

More problematic in the end was the U.S. Postmaster General's revocation of *The Messenger's* second-class postage-rate privilege, which was not reinstated until 1921. Even in 1919, the U.S. Justice Department still said *The Messenger* was "the most able and the most dangerous of all Negro publications" (//nnpa.org/news/media/pdfs/769.pdf). Fellow Harlemites nicknamed the duo "Lenin" (Owen) and "Trotsky" (Randolph). To see for oneself the contents of the November 1917 issue of *The Messenger,* see //www.nlc.edu/archives/2.8a.html, which shows Randolph as the paper's president and Owen as its secretary-treasurer. In it, pages 6-10 include 14 "Editorials," pages 11-21 include 9 items on "Economics and Politics," pages 22-26 include 3 items on "Education and Literature," pages 27-28 include 4 poems by Walter Everett Hawkins in the "Poets' Corner," pages 29-30 include 6 items on "Theatre-Drama-Music," page 31 includes "Messages from the *Messenger,*" and page 32 includes 8 items of "Who's Who." A smattering of extracts may be found at //www.spartacus.schoolnet.co.uk/USAC messenger.htm. A lengthier excerpt, "If We Must Die," may be found in the //www.amazon.com entry for Wilson's *The Messenger Reader.*

Soon after Randolph and Owen returned to New York in mid-August of 1918, Owen was drafted. Both Randolph and Owen were conscientious objectors (C.O.s) to the war, but neither of them had declared their C.O. status by formally applying to the draft board. Luckily for Randolph, he was classified 4-A as the sole support of his wife and children. In fact, he and his wife, fellow Socialist Lucille E. Green, a widowed former schoolteacher and Howard University graduate, never had any children. The premise of the classification was also ironic because Lucille's beauty shop kept the Randolphs financially afloat, while A. Philip focused on his less-than-profitable ventures, such as *The Messenger.*

After Owen finished his military service, he moved to Chicago, leaving Randolph to run *The Messenger,* though Owen's name and title continued to appear on the paper's masthead. In 1923, Randolph hired former socialist and increasingly conservative **George Samuel Schuyler** as staff writer, then assistant editor, and then managing editor of *The Messenger.* Under Schuyler's stewardship, *The Messenger* greatly diminished its editorializing and broadened its inclusion of literary works, such as poetry by **Arna Bontemps, Countee Cullen, Alice Dunbar-Nelson, Georgia Douglas Johnson,** and **Claude McKay,** as well as **Langston Hughes,** who also contributed his first short stories to *The Messenger.* A short story by **Dorothy West** and "The Eatonville Anthology" by **Zora Neale Hurston** were also printed there. **Edward Christopher Williams**'s epistolary novel *The Letters of Davy Carr: A True Story of Colored Vanity Fair* (reprinted in 2004 as *When Washington Was in Vogue*) was serialized in *The Messenger* from January 1925 through June 1926. Before *The Messenger* ceased publication in 1928, its numerous contributors had also included sociologist **E. Franklin Frazier,** *Negro World* editor Hubert Henry Harrison, journalist and critic Theophilus Lewis, entertainer and activist **Paul Robeson**, journalist **Joel Augustus Rogers**, novelist and creative writer **Wallace Thurman** (who briefly took over as managing editor from Schuyler in 1926), journalist and storyteller **Eric Walrond**, and journalist and NAACP leader **Roy Wilkins**.

As radical politics was drained out of *The Messenger*, the masthead's motto changed from "The Only Radical Negro Magazine in America" to "A Journal of Scientific Radicalism" to "The World's Greatest Negro Monthly" to "New Opinion of the New Negro." Sadly, though *The Messenger* had at one time exploded into print, it truly went out not with a bang, but a whimper.

REFERENCES: Anderson, Jervis. 1986. *A. Philip Randolph: A Biographical Portrait.* Los Angeles: University of California Press. Jimoh, A. Yemisi, "*The Messenger*," in *GEAAL*. White, Craig Howard, "*The Messenger*," in *COCAAL*. Wilson, Sondra Kathryn. 2000. *The Messenger Reader: Stories, Poetry, and Essays from The Messenger Magazine.* New York: Modern Library. //en.wikipedia.org/wiki/A._Philip_Randolph. //en.wikipedia.org/wiki/Boston_Guardian. //en.wikipedia.org/wiki/Chandler_Owen. //en.wikipedia.org/wiki/The_Messenger_Magazine. //nnpa.org/news/media/pdfs/769.pdf. //www.blackpast.org/?q=aah/owen-chandler-1889-1967. //www.liu.edu/cwis/cwp/library/historic.htm. //www.nlc.edu/archives/2.6a.html. //www.nlc.edu/archives/2.8a.html. //www.spartacus.schoolnet.co.uk/USACowen.htm. //www.spartacus.schoolnet.co.uk/USACmessenger.htm.

FURTHER READING: *See also* **Alexander's Magazine**, **Chandler Owen**, **A. Philip Randolph**, and **George Samuel Schuyler**.

Micheaux, Oscar
1/2/1884–3/25/1951
Screenplays, novels; self-publisher

Of the 50 or more films Micheaux made, only about a dozen are still available for viewing today. Before he started writing screenplays, though, he wrote a string of novels, starting with his highly autobiographical *The Conquest: The Story of a Negro Pioneer* (1913). Who would publish the first novel of an African-American Midwestern homesteading farmer named "Oscar Devereaux," who is romantically involved with a white woman? Western Book Supply Company—owned and operated by Micheaux. Surprisingly, the stockholders and even the first purchasers of his books were mostly European-American Midwestern farmers. His next two novels were just as obviously autobiographical: *The Forged Note: A Romance of the Darker Races* (1915) and *The Homesteader* (1917).

When the owners of Lincoln Film Motion Picture Company, one of the first African-American movie companies ever, offered to turn *The Homesteader* into a film, Micheaux agreed to letting them do so—as long as they let him direct the film. They refused, so Micheaux—ever the intrepid entrepreneur—started the Micheaux Book

and Film Company. Without any prior experience as a film producer, director, publicity agent, and so on, Micheaux managed to complete his film by 1919 and personally sold the film, traveling from movie house to movie house and town to town.

Pretty soon, Micheaux's productions included *Within Our Gates* (1919) and *The Brute* (starring the prizefighter Sam Langford), *Son of Satan*, *The Millionaire*, and *Wages of Sin* (all produced in the 1920s). Micheaux could sell you two nickels for a quarter, and his ability to sell his films-in the North and the South—was legendary. For that reason, African-American actors jumped at the chance to launch their careers through his films. The acting titan **Paul Robeson** made his moving-picture debut in Micheaux's *Body and Soul* (1924).

It must be acknowledged that Micheaux's films may have starred some acting geniuses, but Micheaux himself was no writing genius. His hastily produced films were melodramatic, technically flawed, and far from exalting African-American virtues. In fact, many intellectuals carped that skin hue correlated very strongly with virtue—and definitely not the blacker the berry, the sweeter the juice. Nonetheless, at least he gave work to African-American actors and film workers, and he gave African-American theater audiences something to see on a Saturday afternoon, without having all white faces on the screen. Given what was available at the time—and the prevailing sentiments of his era—he contributed a great deal. The mere fact that his film company survived the Great Depression says something about the man. His films from this era include *The Exile* (the first all-black-cast talkie, 1931), *Harlem after Midnight* (1934), *Underworld* (1937), *Lying Lips* (1939, coproduced by black star aviator Hubert Julian), and *The Notorious Elinor Lee* (1940).

In the 1940s, Micheaux returned to novel writing; what he lacked in creativity, he definitely compensated for with stamina and selling skill. His 1940s-era books include *The Wind from Nowhere* (1941, another autobiographical novel, reworking the material in his first novel and his first film), *The Case of Mrs. Wingate* (1944, a detective novel), *The Story of Dorothy Stanfield* (1946, about an insurance con), and *The Masquerade* (1947, which owes much to **Charles Chesnutt**'s *The House Behind the Cedars*). There was one last film made from Micheaux's work: In 1948, *The Betrayal* (adapted from *The Wind from Nowhere*), essentially the story from his first novel and his first film, was a fitting last work. The final tributes to Micheaux came in 1974, when the Oscar Micheaux Award was created by the Black Filmmaker's Hall of Fame, and in 1987, when the Oscar Micheaux star was placed on Hollywood's Walk of Fame.

REFERENCES: *EAACH. SMKC.* —Tonya Bolden

FURTHER READING: *AANB. BAWPP. CAO-07. F. Wiki.* Brennan, Sandra, *All Movie Guide,* in *Dir.* Cole, Kevin L., in *GEAAL.* Fontenot, Chester J. "Black Novelist and Film Maker." Virginia Faulkner (Ed.) 1982. *Vision and Refuge: Essays on the Literature of the Great Plains.* University of Nebraska Press. Grupenhoff, Richard. "The Rediscovery of Oscar Micheaux, Black Film Pioneer." *Journal of Film and Video 40.1* (Winter 1988) pp. 40-48. Hebert, Janis. "Oscar Micheaux: A Black Pioneer." *South Dakota Review 11.4* (Winter 1973) pp. 62-69. Johnson, Anne Janette, in *BB.* Lopate, Phillip. "Micheaux, Oscar: Oscar Micheaux, the Great and Only: The Life of America's First Black Filmmaker." *Biography. 30.4* (Fall 2007) p. 700. From *Literature Resource Center.* Sampson, Henry T. 1977. "The Micheaux Film Corporation; Oscar Micheaux." *Blacks in Black and White: A Source Book on Black Films.* The Scarecrow Press. Soitos, Stephen F., in *COCAAL.* Woodland, J. Randal, in *AAWBHR.*

Miller, E. (Eugene) Ethelbert

11/20/1950–

Poems, essays, literary criticism, autobiography/ memoirs; editor, educator

Miller's poetry has been collected in *Andromeda* (1974), *The Land of Smiles and the Land of No Smiles* (1974), *The Migrant Worker* (1978), *Season of Hunger/Cry of Rain: Poems 1975-1980* (1982), *Where Are the Love Poems for Dictators?* (1986/2001), *First Light: New and Selected Poems* (1993), *How We Sleep on the Nights We Don't Make Love* (1996/2004), *Whispers, Secrets, and Promises* (1998), *Buddha Weeping in Winter* (2001), and *On Saturdays, I Santana With You* (2009), as well as his chapbook, *The Fire This Time: 1992 and Beyond Los Angeles* (1993). Premier poet **Gwendolyn Brooks** said Miller is "one of the most significant and influential poets of our time" (quoted in *CAO-03*).

Of his own writing, Miller has said, "I've always written short poems. I try and practice what I define as an economy of words. Say more with less. I hope people take time to read my short poems more than once. I think the white space on the page around the words provides the opportunity for the reader to enter a stage or level of contemplation. Take the words in. Breathe. This is how the words are able to touch the heart as well as mind. . . . The creative writing process . . . is fraught with difficulties and challenges. It's a very rigorous undertaking: to master a form is a challenge" (quoted in "I Can Make Music," 2006).

In addition to his poetry, Miller has written two memoirs, *Fathering Words: The Making of an African American Writer* (2000) and *The Fifth Inning* (2009). As a "literary activist," Miller archives rare African-American literature and history, which he has collected as director of the African American Studies Resource Center at Howard University (since 1974). Miller also champions up-and-coming African-American writers and is considered "a core faculty member" at Bennington College's Writing Seminars. For many years, he guided aspiring writers through a series of readings and professional workshops via the Ascension Poetry Series he founded (in 1974) and directed (until 2000). He has also served as senior editor of **African American Review** and of *Washington Review,* an editorial advisor for *Black Issues Book Review,* and a contributor to **Callaloo.** Miller suggests, "I hope the term 'literary activist' is one that other writers will feel comfortable placing before or after their names. . . . I think being a literary activist and being interested in documenting literary history is another reason for doing anthologies" (quoted in "I Can Make Music," 2006). Miller's anthologies include *Synergy: An Anthology of Washington D. C. Black Poetry* (1975, with Ahmos Zu-Bolton II), *Women Surviving Massacres and Men* (1977), his highly acclaimed *In Search of Color Everywhere: A Collection of African American Poetry* (1994, a Book-of-the-Month Club selection), and *Beyond the Frontier: African American Poetry for the 21st Century* (2002).

Miller's scholarship and dedication have been recognized with honors such as the Columbia Merit Award (1993), the PEN Oakland Josephine Miles Award (1994), the O. B. Hardison, Jr. Prize (1995), an honorary doctorate from Emory and Henry College (1996), the Stephen Henderson Poetry Award (1997), an invitation to the National Book Festival by Laura Bush (2001, 2003), and a Fulbright fellowship (2004). **Charles Richard Johnson** said, "No one, to my knowledge, has done and is doing more, day in, day out, to promote contemporary black writing, and especially poetry, than Miller" (quoted in "I Can Make Music," 2006).

It might seem surprising that he would have the time or the energy to do so, but Miller has also fathered two children, Jasmine-Simone and Nyere-Gibran, whom he shares with his wife, Denise L. King. Although he spent his own boyhood in a decidedly nonintellectual family, he grew up savoring words. In his memoir *Fathering Words* (quoted in "I Can Make Music," 2006) he recalled, "One night a poem comes to me. Words. Revelations. In the beginning I was a small boy standing on a corner in the Bronx waiting for my father. . . . Suddenly words are escorting me across the street. I reach the other side, proud of what I've done. I can write. My prayers are songs. I can make music. I can give color to the world. This is my life. This is my gift." Truly.

REFERENCES: *CAO-03. MAAL. Wiki.* Ghosh, Nibir K. "'I Can Make Music. I Can Give Color to the World': Interview with E. Ethelbert Miller." *MELUS. 31.2* (Summer 2006) p. 119. From *Literature Resource Center.* Hall, John Greer, in *GEAAL.* Haywood, Elanna N., in *COCAAL* and *OCAAL.* Ramsey, Priscilla R., *AAP-55-85.* //www.newsreel.org/guides/furious.htm. //www.poets.org/poet.php/prmPID/485. Amazon.com.

Miller, Kelly
7/23/1863–12/29/1939
Nonfiction—sociology, poems; educator

Despite an impoverished upbringing, Kelly Miller won a scholarship to attend Howard University, graduating in 1886. Afterward, he was tutored in advanced mathematics (1886-1887), then he became the first African American admitted to Johns Hopkins University, where he studied physics, astronomy, and mathematics (1887-1889), but he ran out of funds before completing a degree there. In 1890, he joined the faculty of Howard University, where he was to continue another 44 years. After a few years at Howard (in 1894), Miller married Annie May Butler, and they later had five children, including poet and playwright **May Miller**.

At first, Miller was a professor of mathematics (1890-1895). As the nineteenth century drew to a close, however, Miller persuaded Howard to add sociology to its curricula. Initially, Miller taught both math and sociology (1895-1907) while he earned his A.M. (1901) and his L.L.D (1903). Eventually, Miller focused solely on the study of sociology, becoming the new department's chair (1915-1925).

A prolific writer, Miller wrote countless articles and essays. His pamphlet *The Disgrace of Democracy: An Open Letter to President Woodrow Wilson* (1917/1976) was banned on military posts, but more than 250,000 copies were sold. In addition to his numerous individually published essays, Miller published several collections of his essays, including *A Review of Hoffman's Race Traits and Tendencies of the American Negro* (1897/1969); *As to The Leopard's Spots: An Open Letter to Thomas Dixon, Jr.* (1905/1972); *From Servitude to Service: Being the Old South Lectures on the History and Work of Southern Institutions for the Education of the Negro* (1905); *An Appeal to Reason: An Open Letter to John Temple Graves* (1906); *Race Adjustment: Essays on the Negro in America* (1908/1970); *Progress and Achievements of the Colored People* (1913/1917); *Out of the House of Bondage* (1914/1971); his concisely titled *Kelly Miller's History of the World War for Human Rights; Being an Intensely Human and Brilliant Account of the World War and Why and for What Purpose America and the Allies Are Fighting and the Important Part Taken by the Negro, Including the Horrors and Wonders of Modern Warfare, the New and Strange Devices, Etc.* (1919/1977; available through Project Gutenberg at //www.gutenberg.org/etext/19179); *An Appeal to Conscience; America's Code of Caste, A Disgrace to Democracy* (1918/1969); and *The Everlasting Stain* (1924). In addition, a collection of his essays was published posthumously as *Radicals and Conservatives, and Other Essays on the Negro in America* (1968).

In addition to this voluminous output, Miller wrote a regular newspaper column, and he was a contributing ed-itor to **W. E. B. Du Bois**'s *Crisis* magazine. A listing of his papers, archived at Emory University, includes 49 journal articles, as well as more than half a dozen boxfuls of newspaper articles and other short works he wrote between 1894 and 1939. He was even a published poet.

In 1907, Miller was asked to serve as dean of the College of Arts and Sciences (1907-1919). In 1919, a new Howard president demoted Miller to dean of a short-lived new junior college (1919-1925). After that, Miller's power and influence on and off campus declined in the years leading up to and following his 1934 retirement.

REFERENCES: *BAWPP. Wiki.* Dunbar, Paul Laurence. (1993). *The Collected Poetry of Paul Laurence Dunbar* (p. 337). University Press of Virginia. From *LitFinder*. Rodgers, Lawrence R., in COCAAL. Winston, Michael R., in AANB. //en.wikipedia.org/wiki/Kelly_Miller_High_School. //findarticles.com/p/articles/mi_qa3812/is_199907/ai_n8868901/. //marbl.library.emory.edu/findingaids/content.php?el=c01&id=millerkelly1050_series4. //marbl.library.emory.edu/findingaids/content.php?el=c02&id=millerkelly1050_subseries2.1. //webapps.jhu.edu/jhuniverse/information_about_hopkins/about_jhu/a_brief_history_of_jhu/index.cfm. //worldcat.org/identities/lccn-n50-33697. //www.blackpast.org/?q=aah/american-negro-academy-1897-1924. //www.gutenberg.org/etext/19179.

Miller (married name: Sullivan), May
1/26/1899–2/8/1995
Plays, poems; educator

Kelly Miller was a prominent sociology professor and dean at Howard University (in Washington, D.C.), as well as a published poet, but to May and her four siblings, he was best known as their dad and the husband of her mother, Annie May (Butler) Miller. At their home, **W. E. B. Du Bois** and **Booker T. Washington** were frequent guests. At M Street School (later Paul Dunbar High School), her instructors included playwrights **Angelina [Weld] Grimké** and Mary Burrill. Burrill encouraged May to write her first play, *Pandora's Box*, published in 1914.

In 1916, May graduated from Dunbar and entered her father's university, where she once again studied drama, acting, directing, and producing plays. She collaborated with Howard professor **Alain Locke** and others to found an African-American drama movement on campus. She also earned a best-play award for her one-act *Within the Shadows*, thereby becoming the first student from Howard University to receive this award. Four years after she entered, she graduated at the academic head of her class at Howard (B.A., 1920).

After graduation, Miller taught drama, speech, and dance at the Frederick Douglass High School in Baltimore. While school was out during the summer, she studied playwriting at Columbia University, and she continued to write her own plays. Miller's timing could not have been better. While the **Harlem Renaissance** was blooming in New York, poet and playwright **Georgia Douglas Johnson** was hosting her weekly literary salon in Washington, D.C., offering a major gathering place for writers to share their works and to give one another support and encouragement. Each weekend, Miller commuted to 1461 S Street NW, Johnson's home, where she joined such celebrated writers as **Langston Hughes, Zora Neale Hurston, Willis Richardson,** and **Carter G. Woodson** in the warm, nurturing ambience of Johnson's salon. Soon, Miller was probably the most widely published and produced woman playwright of that highly productive era.

Miller's plays included *The Bog Guide* (1925), her humorous but provocative *Riding the Goat* (1925), her prize-winning *The Cuss'd Thing* (1926), and *Moving Caravans* (1930s?). Several of her plays focused clearly on addressing racial issues, such as *Scratches* (1929), highlighting the biases within the African-American community (e.g., color distinctions and class differences); *Stragglers in the Dust* (1930), about African Americans in the military; and her anti-lynching play *Nails and Thorns* (1933). Less successful were her plays *Christophe's Daughters* (1935), set in Haiti, and *Samory* (1935), set in the African Sudan. She also wrote many historical plays, four of which (including plays on **Harriet Tubman** and **Sojourner Truth**) were anthologized in *Negro History in Thirteen Plays* (1935), which she and playwright Willis Richardson edited. The last play she wrote, *Freedom's Children on the March* (1943), was also a historical play. Like other African-American women writers of her era, Miller focused on social and political issues in her works. Unlike most others, however, her work strayed from the home and family; in addition, she was innovative in including both African-American and European-American characters in many of her works, so that she could more fully explore issues of race from multiple perspectives.

May had married John Sullivan, a high school principal, in 1940. In 1943, she retired from teaching in the Baltimore public school system, and the couple moved to Washington, D.C. In addition to teaching public-school students, Miller taught college students as a visiting lecturer and poet at Monmouth College; the University of Wisconsin, Milwaukee; and the Philips Exeter Academy.

Miller did not retire from writing, however. To the contrary, she turned her attention from plays to poetry, and she was at least as prolific in her new genre as she had been in her old one. Her poetry was well received, too, earning praise from poets **Gwendolyn Brooks** and **Robert Hayden**. Although her poems were rather conventional in form and language, they inspired readers to question social conventions. Just as she had posed ethical and spiritual questions in her plays, her poems raised issues of humanistic values. Soon, her poems were widely published in such periodicals as **Phylon**, *Antioch Review,*

Crisis, Nation, The New York Times, and *Poetry.* Miller's poetry collections include *Into the Clearing* (1959); *Poems* (1962); *Lyrics of Three Women: Katie Lyle, Maude Rubin, and May Miller* (1964); *Not That Far* (1973); *The Clearing and Beyond* (1974); *Dust of Uncertain Journey* (1975); *The Ransomed Wait* (1983); and *Collected Poems* (1989). She also wrote a collection of poems for children, *Halfway to the Sun* (1981).

REFERENCES: *EB-BH-CD. WDAA.* Koolish, Lynda, in *COCAAL* and *OCAAL.* Perkins, Kathy A., in *BWA:AHE.*

FURTHER READING: *AANB. BAWPP. CAO-01. HR&B. MWEL. Wiki.* Stoelting, Winifred L., *AAP-55-85.* Woodard, Loretta G., in *GEAAL.*

Millican (2nd married name), Arthenia (Bernetta) J. (née Jackson) Bates (1st married name)
6/1/1920–

Poems, short fiction, novel, articles, essays, biography; educator

A poet at age 10 and a published poet at age 16, Arthenia was raised in a home that valued literature and intellectual pursuits. A 1941 magna cum laude graduate of Morris College, Arthenia Jackson was married to Noah Bates from 1950 until 1956 (ending in divorce) and to Wilbert Millican, with whom she has a stepson Wilbert, from 1969 until 1982 (when he died). Both men were of working-class backgrounds, with working-class jobs, and Arthenia's mother never forgave her for choosing them. Some of Arthenia's works were published under her former married name and then changed to her latter in subsequent printings. Her first published work was her highly acclaimed first short-story collection *Seeds Beneath the Snow* (1969; with the subtitle *Vignettes from the South,* 1975). Next, she tackled the novel with *The Deity Nodded* (1973), inspired by her sister's conversion from Baptism to Islam and her own conversion from Baptism to Catholicism. She also published a second short-story collection, *Such Things from the Valley* (1977, as Arthenia J. Bates Millican), as well as her doctoral dissertation on **James Weldon Johnson** (1972, for Louisiana State University).

For nearly two decades, Millican's chief publications were scholarly and critical articles, short stories, and poems published in numerous periodicals (e.g., *African American Review, Negro Digest, Obsidian: Black Literature in Review,* **Callaloo**) and anthologies (e.g., *The Heath Anthology of American Literature,* 1990; *National Poetry Anthology,* 1958, 1962, 1963, and 1973; *Rhetoric and Readings for Writing,* 1975, 1977, 1979, and 1981). In 1993, she published the biography *Hand on the Throttle: Touchstones in the Life of Lionel Lee, Sr., Volume 1: Holding On.* //www.Amazon.com also lists several other works as being currently out of print by unnamed publishers: her 16-page *A Note from Cell Thirty-three* (1985), her 79-page, 13-story *Bottoms and Hills: Virginia Tales* (1985), and her *A Journey to Somewhere: A Novella* (1985), as well as what may be brief individual poems or short stories, *Blame it on Adical* (1985, 13 pages), *Laugh If You Will* (1985), *Wake Me Mama* (1985, 12 pages), *Folk and Fetters* (1986), and *Heartbeat* (1986). As Millican was approaching her tenth decade of life, she was working on a sequel to her novel *Deity Nodded* and on a series of short stories about mother-daughter relationships among Southern women, across the previous century. In addition, Millican taught English and creative writing to high school students and to college students (at Southern University in Baton Rouge, 1956-1980, with a brief hiatus at Norfolk State University, 1974-1976).

REFERENCES: *BAWPP. CAO-01.* Dandridge, Rita B., in *GEAAL.* Gill, Glenda E., in *COCAAL* and *OCAAL.* Smith, Virginia Whatley, *AAW-55-85:DPW.* Amazon.com.

Milner, Ronald
5/29/1938–7/9/2004
Plays, screenplays, anthology, criticism, novel, short stories; educator, theater founder and director

Although Milner's first published book was a novel (*The Life of the Brothers Brown*, 1965), he is chiefly known for his plays, which include *Who's Got His Own* (1967), *The Warning: A Theme for Linda* (1969), *The Monster* (1968), *(M)Ego and the Green Ball of Freedom* (1968), *What the Wine-Sellers Buy* (1973/1974), *These Three* (1974), *Season's Reasons* (1976), *Work* (1978), *Jazz Set* (1980), *Crack Steppin'* (1981), *Roads of the Mountaintops* (1986), *Checkmates* (1987), *Don't Get God Started* (1988), *Defending the Light* (2000), and *Urban Transition: Loose Blossoms* (2002).

He has also published several short stories and articles of literary criticism, and he has been writing film and television scripts, while continuing to teach creative writing, particularly playwriting.

Perhaps his most notable achievements have been with **Woodie King**, with whom he coedited *Black Drama Anthology* (1971) and cofounded the Concept-East Theatre company (1962). King later recalled, "Ron Milner and I worked together for more than 40 years. We laughed a lot at our observations and jokes, experienced and explored aspects of black literature and its creators.... Milner loved literature in which the writer told a story.... On March 21, at the Charles Wright Museum of African American Culture in Detroit, 400 friends—actors, singers, poets, producers and politicians from across America—came together to roast and toast Ron Milner.... After everyone had toasted him, Milner had the last word.... He ... said

that he was overcome with all the love in the room; he just wanted to thank everyone and wanted them all to meet his [four] children and [his] grandchildren" (from "Ron Milner: 1938-2004").

REFERENCES: *BAWPP. CAO-07. Wiki.* Aguilar, Marian, in *EA-99.* Anderson, Gary, *CD-5.* Cunningham, Beunyce Rayford, in *AAW-55-85:DPW.* Hall, John Greer, in *GEAAL.* King, Woodie, Jr. "Ron Milner: 1938-2004." *American Theatre. 21.8* (Oct. 2004) p. 22. From *Literature Resource Center.* Metzger, Sheri Elaine, in *BB.* Williams, Derek A., in *COCAAL* and *OCAAL.*

Mitchell, Loften
4/15/1919–5/14/2001
Plays, novels, nonfiction—drama history, anthology; educator

After completing his A.B. (Talladega College in Alabama, 1943) and a tour in the navy (1944-1945), Mitchell went to Columbia University, where he studied playwriting with John Glassner (M.A., 1951). Mitchell's first three plays—*Shattered Dreams* (1938), *The Bancroft Dynasty* (1948), and *The Cellars* (1952)—received little notice, but his *A Land Beyond the River* (1957) was both popularly and critically acclaimed. It probably helped that the play appeared just three years after the landmark *Brown v. Board of Education* decision and dramatized a court case ending school segregation.

His many other plays include *The Photographer* (1962), *Ballad of [or for] Bimshire* (1963), *Ballad for [or of] The Winter Soldiers* (1964), *Star of the Morning* (1965), *Tell Pharaoh* (1967), *The Phonograph* (1969), *Sojourn to the South of the Wall* (1973, a one-act play; expanded to the full-length *The Walls Came Tumbling Down*, 1976), and *Bubbling Brown Sugar* (1975, with Rosetta LeNoire), a popular musical that won a 1976 Tony Award nomination and was named the Best Musical of the Year in 1977 in London. In addition, paperbacks have been published about his musical *Bubbling Brown Sugar: A Musical Revue* (1985) and his plays *A Land Beyond the River at the Greenwich Mews* (1957) and *Tell Pharaoh* (1987). He also wrote several radio plays, and he wrote four screenplays between 1954 and 1972. Having observed theater history for decades, Mitchell published two histories of drama: his essay collection *Black Drama: The Story of the American Negro in the Theatre* (1967) and his oral-history anthology *Voices of the Black Theatre* (1975). He contributed articles and other pieces to numerous periodicals (e.g., **Amsterdam News**, **The Crisis**, Freedomways, **Negro Digest**, and *The New York Times*). *GEAAL* notes that he edited the NAACP's *Freedom Journal* and that he wrote an essay collection, *Harlem, My Harlem*, but the book is not listed in //www.Amazon.com or in other references. He also tackled the novel form in his *The Stubborn Old Lady*

Who Resisted Change (1973). From 1971 through 1985, Mitchell taught drama at the State University of New York at Binghamton. Mitchell had two sons, Thomas and Melvin, with his first wife, Helen March (married 1948-1956); he married Gloria Anderson in 1991.

REFERENCES: *BAWPP.* Aguiar, Marian, in *EA-99.* Anderson, Addell Austin, and Jennifer M. York, in *BB.* Jahannes, Ja A., *AAW-55-85: DPW.* LaFrance, Michelle, in *GEAAL.* Mueller, Michael E., in *CAO-02.* Walker, Robbie Jean, in *COCAAL* and *OCAAL.* Amazon.com.

Monroe, Mary (née Nicholson)
12/12/1949 or1951–
Novels, short stories

Editor's note: Monroe's birth year is given as 1949 in *EAAWW* and as 1951 in *CAO-08* and *GEAAL.*

The daughter of sharecroppers, Mary fell in love with reading and writing early, even penning a lengthy biography of her mother's employer before Mary reached her teens. While still in her teens, she earned her first money as a writer for a story published in *Reader's Digest.* She also wrote true-confession stories for *Bronze Thrills.* The first high-school graduate in her family, Monroe has since earned two prestigious awards for her writing.

In 1985, Monroe published *The Upper Room* (1985/2001). As a single mother, supporting her daughters Michelle and Jacquelyn, Monroe has washed cars, picked apples and beans, cleaned houses, done doggie day care, and worked as a secretary. Unsurprisingly, it took another 15 years before she completed the manuscript and found a publisher for her second novel, *God Don't Like Ugly* (2000), which won the PEN/Oakland Josephine Miles National Literary Award. The following year, Kensington Books (also the Dafina Books imprint) signed a contract with her for six more books (2001). Monroe's next book, *Gonna Lay Down My Burdens* (2002), won the Best New Southern Fiction Award from the Memphis Black Authors Group. Since then, Monroe has produced at least a book a year, starting with her sequel *God Still Don't Like Ugly* (2003), followed by *Red Light Wives* (2004), *In Sheep's Clothing* (2005), *God Don't Play* (2006), *Deliver Me from Evil* (2007), *She Had It Coming* (2008), and *The Company We Keep* (2009). Her *God Ain't Blind* was due for late summer 2009 publication when this dictionary went to press. Monroe also wrote a novelette, *Nightmare in Paradise,* and she collaborated with Victor McGlothin on the volume *Borrow Trouble* (2006), which includes a novella she wrote.

REFERENCES: *CAO-08.* Manheim, James M., in *BB.* //www.kensingtonbooks.com/catalog.cfm?dest=dir&linkid =1808&linkon=subsection. Amazon.com.

FURTHER READING: *EAAWW.* Olson, Debbie Clare, in *GEAAL.*

Mary Monroe

Moody, Anne (née Essie Mae)
9/15/1940–
Short stories, autobiography/memoir, essays; activist, organizer

Mississippi sharecroppers Fred and Elmire Moody had nine children, the oldest of whom was Anne (Essie Mae at birth). Eventually, Fred got tired of the harsh fieldwork and the impoverished living conditions, and he left Elmire to raise the children as best she could. Although the segregated schools of rural Mississippi could not be said to have offered an outstanding education, Anne drew every bit of learning she could from the limited opportunities available. A couple weeks before Anne turned 15 years old, the week before high school started, 14-year-old Chicagoan Emmett Till was lynched and murdered in Mississippi for being black in the wrong place. In addition to the 100,000 people who went to Mississippi to pay him a final tribute, the nation—and the world—was outraged by this egregious wrong. While Anne was in high school, an all-male, all-white jury acquitted the men who had been positively identified as involved in the lynching. These events stirred Anne's emotions; they probably would have affected her anyway, but Emmett's physical proximity and his age deepened and intensified their impact. Nonetheless, Anne continued her academic achievements and added to them athletic success as a basketball player.

After high school, Anne went on to spend two years at Natchez Junior College on a basketball scholarship. From there, she transferred to Tougaloo College, in Jackson, Mississippi, on a full academic scholarship. Meanwhile, however, Anne was becoming deeply committed to and involved in the civil-rights movement, raising funds and organizing people and activities for the Congress of Racial Equality (CORE) in the state noted for its most violent opposition to civil rights: Mississippi. When sit-in demonstrations were held to integrate a Woolworth's lunch counter in Jackson, Mississippi, Anne sat in. She also became involved in other civil-rights organizations, including the National Association for the Advancement of Colored People (NAACP) and the Student Nonviolent Coordinating Committee (SNCC). After graduating (B.S.) from Tougaloo in 1964, she continued her civil-rights activities, working for Cornell University as a civil-rights project coordinator. Eventually, however, she grew disenchanted with the movement, feeling that it had become too narrowly focused on black nationalism and too factional, hoping instead that African Americans would see themselves as part of a global struggle for civil rights and freedom from oppression.

Moody has written numerous short stories and essays, which have appeared in national magazines such as *Ms.* and *Mademoiselle*; in 1970, *Mademoiselle* awarded her its silver medal for her article "New Hopes for the Seventies." A few of her short stories have also appeared in her collection *Mr. Death* (1975). Her best-known literary work, however, is her autobiography, *Coming of Age in Mississippi* (1968/2004), which was favorably reviewed by critics and was lauded with the Best Book of the Year Award from the National Library Association (1969) and the Brotherhood award from the National Council of Christians and Jews. The book traces her childhood of desperate poverty, segregation, and discrimination in rural Mississippi, and her efforts to win civil rights for the African Americans of Mississippi—and the nation. Through her very personal one-woman account, she revealed the troubles and travails of many people, both in Mississippi and anywhere people face cruel poverty and oppressive racism. Moody also has a daughter, Sascha, and is divorced.

REFERENCES: *AANB. CAO-01. EBLG. OC20LE. SMKC. W. Wiki.* Beavers, Gina, in *BWA:AHE.* Bohde, Cheryl D., in *GEAAL.* Conyers, James L. 2005. *Afrocentric Traditions.* Transaction Publishers, available at //books.google.com/books?id=ibsI6DK7jdgC&pg=PA128&lpg= PA128&dq=%22effie+t.+battle%22&source=web&ots=21l8N5joe R&sig=nWlt1pZF15b40WUVgVqqMkWIxMM&hl=en&sa=X&oi =book_result&resnum=21&ct=result. Eckard, Paula Gallant, in *COCAAL* and *OCAAL.* Fay, Robert, in *EA-99.* //library.msstate.edu/ special_interest/Mississippi_African-American_Authors.asp. Amazon.com.

Moore, Alice Ruth *See* Dunbar-Nelson, Alice Ruth Moore

Moore, Opal
1953–
Poems, short stories, essays, literary criticism of children's literature; educator

In 1970, Moore started writing journal entries and poems in an effort to cope with the racism she was encountering in art school. In 1975 she wrote *Why Johnny Can't Learn,* seeking changes in how we educate our youths. Her poems have been collected in *Lot's Daughters* (2004, published by **Third World Press**). //www.Amazon.com already lists her forthcoming (2010) publication, *Gwendolyn Brooks: Her Life and Letters* (*Women Writers of Color*), and she is said to be working on a short-story collection. In collaboration with painter, performance artist, and Spelman College Art educator Arturo Lindsay, Moore is creating *Children of Middle Passage,* a poetry collection to accompany visual artworks, inspired by her visit to West Africa's secularly sacred sites of enslavement. Moore has also published numerous short stories, poems, and critical essays focusing on children's literature. Among the writers who have shaped Moore's work have been her teachers **Paule Marshall** and **James Alan McPherson,** her first idol **Gwendolyn Brooks,** and **Toni Morrison.** She teaches in Spelman College's English Department, which she previously chaired.

REFERENCES: Dance, Daryl Cumber, in *COCAAL* and *OCAAL.* Randall, Kelli, in *GEAAL.* //cavecanempoets.org/pages/poems/ ourtown.html. //libpac.sdsu.edu/. //www.newsreel.org/guides/furious/ omoore.htm. Amazon.com.

Morrison, Toni (née Chloe Anthony Wofford)
2/18/1931–
Novels, literary criticism, juvenile literature, lyrics, libretti, anthologies; editor, educator

In 1993, Toni Morrison became the first black woman to receive the Nobel Prize for Literature. Her works are noted for their powerful storytelling, provocative themes, and poetic language. Morrison's novels explore racial and gender conflicts and the various ways that people express their identities. She writes about familiar subjects and themes, but her approaches to them distinctly differ from any other American author. For example, in her novel *The Bluest Eye* (1970), Morrison uses the unique style of fairy tale motifs. In *Song of Solomon* (1977), she uses Greek tragic motifs; and in *Tar Baby* (1981/2004), she uses garden metaphors and Christian symbolism. Her troubled characters seek to find themselves and their cul-

Toni Morrison

tural riches in a society that impedes and warps such crucial growth.

Chloe Anthony Wofford was born in Lorain, Ohio. Her parents had moved to Ohio from the South to escape racism and to find better opportunities. Chloe was the second of four children of George Wofford, a shipyard welder, and Ramah Willis Wofford. While the children were growing up, George worked three jobs at the same time for almost 17 years. He took a great deal of pride in the quality of his work, so that each time he welded a perfect seam, he'd also weld his name onto the side of the ship. He also made sure to be well-dressed, even during the Depression. Chloe's mother was a church-going woman who sang in the choir.

At home, Chloe heard many songs and tales of Southern African-American folklore. The Woffords were proud of their heritage. Lorain was a small industrial town populated with immigrant Europeans, Mexicans, and Southern blacks who lived side by side. Chloe attended an integrated school. She was the only African-American student in her first-grade class and the only child who could already read. She was friends with many of her white schoolmates and did not face racism until she started dating.

Chloe hoped to one day become a dancer like her favorite ballerina, Maria Tallchief. She also loved to read. Her early favorites were the Russian writers Tolstoy and Dostoyevsky, French author Gustave Flaubert, and English novelist Jane Austen. She graduated with honors from Lorain High School in 1949.

The sense of community that Wofford acquired from her youth in Lorain is very important to her life. Under-

lying themes of family and community are present throughout all of her later work. Wofford's father, a dignified man, impressed a positive self-image on his daughter. Biographers Clenora Hudson and Wilfred Samuels suggest that although her father died before she began her third novel, she continues to hold up her accomplishments for his approval. The resonance of such authority resides in all of Morrison's books.

The Bluest Eye is set in Lorain. Its explicit portrayal of an interwoven African-American community can be seen as a partially autobiographical picture of her childhood home. The sense of community expands and diversifies with her later novels, but the essence of that community remains. There, the lives and business of its inhabitants are only, as Morrison writes, "Quiet as it's kept" (Morrison, 1970). Even in her novel *Jazz* (1992), in which she depicts the complex social structure of New York City in the 1920s, Morrison suggests that the same principles of community that existed in the small town of Lorain, Ohio, can be found in the great metropolis.

After high school, Wofford attended Howard University, where she majored in English with a minor in classics. It was there that she changed her name to Toni because many people couldn't pronounce Chloe correctly. Toni Wofford joined a repertory company, the Howard University Players, with whom she made several tours of the South. She experienced firsthand the life of the African Americans there, the life her parents had escaped by moving North.

Wofford graduated from Howard in 1953 with a B.A. in English. She then attended Cornell University and earned a master's degree in 1955. After graduating, Wofford was offered a job at Texas Southern University in Houston, where she taught introductory English. Negro History Week was a regular event at Texas Southern. There, Wofford was introduced to the idea of black culture as a discipline, rather than just personal family reminiscences.

In 1957, Wofford returned to Howard University as a member of the faculty. The civil-rights movement was gaining momentum, and she met several people who were later active in the struggle. She met the young poet **Amiri Baraka** (at that time called LeRoi Jones) and Andrew Young, who later became a mayor of Atlanta. Her students included **Stokely Carmichael** and **Claude Brown**.

At Howard, Wofford met and fell in love with a young Jamaican architect, Harold Morrison. They married in 1958, and their first son, Harold Ford, was born in 1961. She continued teaching after her marriage, while helping take care of the family. Her married life was unhappy, however, so she joined a small writer's group as temporary escape, filling her need for companionship with other lovers of literature. Members of the writer's circle were required to bring a story or poem for discussion each week.

One day, having nothing to bring, Morrison quickly wrote a story, loosely based on a girl she knew in childhood, who had prayed to God for blue eyes. The group received the story well, and feeling satisfied, Morrison put it away.

Meanwhile, Morrison's marriage continued to deteriorate. While pregnant with their second child, she left her husband and her job at the university. Toni divorced Harold and returned to her parents' house in Lorain with her two sons.

In the fall of 1964, Morrison began work with a textbook subsidiary of Random House in Syracuse as an associate editor. She hoped to be transferred to New York City. She found writing exciting and challenging, doing her own work while the children were asleep. With the exception of parenting, Morrison found everything else boring in comparison to writing. She went back to the story she had composed for the writer's group and decided to make it into a novel. She utilized her childhood memories, expanding the facts with her imagination. This made the characters develop a life of their own.

In 1967, she was transferred to New York and became a senior editor at Random House. While editing books by prominent black Americans such as Muhammad Ali, Andrew Young, and **Angela Davis**, she was busy sending her own novel to various publishers. The *Bluest Eye* was eventually published in 1970, to much critical acclaim, although it was not commercially successful.

From 1971 to 1972, Morrison was the associate professor of English at the State University of New York at Purchase while she continued working at Random House. In addition, she soon started writing her second novel, *Sula* (1973/2004). *Sula* examines (among other issues) the dynamics of friendship between two adult black women and the expectations for conformity within the community. *Sula* became an alternate selection by the Book-of-the-Month Club, excerpts were published in *Redbook* magazine, and it was nominated for the 1975 National Book Award in fiction.

From 1976 to 1977, Morrison was a visiting lecturer at Yale University. She was also writing her third novel. This time, she focused on strong black male characters, with insight gained from watching her sons. *Song of Solomon* (1977) brought Morrison national attention, winning the National Book Critic's Circle Award and the American Academy and Institute of Arts and Letters Award. In 1980, Morrison was appointed by President Jimmy Carter to the National Council on the Arts. The next year, she published her fourth novel, *Tar Baby* (1981). For the first time, she described the interaction between black and white characters, exploring conflicts of race, class, and gender.

Morrison continued to forge her place in American literary history. Her picture appeared on the cover of the March 30, 1981 issue of *Newsweek* magazine. In 1983, she left her position at Random House, having worked there for almost 20 years. In 1984, she was named the Albert Schweitzer Professor of the Humanities at the State University of New York in Albany. While living in Albany, she started writing her first play, *Dreaming Emmett*. It was based on the true story of Emmett Till, a black teenager killed by racist whites in 1955 after being accused of making a snide remark to a white woman. The play premiered January 4, 1986 at the Marketplace Theater in Albany.

Morrison's next novel, *Beloved* (1987), was influenced by a published story about a slave, Margaret Garner, who in 1851 escaped with her children to Ohio from her master in Kentucky. When she was about to be recaptured, she tried to kill her children, rather than return them to a life of slavery. Only her infant daughter died, and Margaret was imprisoned for her deed. She refused to show remorse, saying she was unwilling to have her children suffer slavery as she had. *Beloved* became a bestseller, winning a 1988 Pulitzer Prize for fiction.

In 1987, Morrison was named the Robert F. Goheen Professor in the Council of Humanities at Princeton University. She became the first black woman writer to hold a named chair at an Ivy League university. She taught creative writing and also took part in the African-American studies, American studies, and women's studies programs. In 1993, Toni Morrison received the Nobel Prize in Literature. She was the eighth woman and the first African American to do so. A work of criticism, *Playing in the Dark, Whiteness and the Literary Imagination*, was published in 1992.

REFERENCES: Bauer, Eric Jerome (1997), "Biographical Information on Toni Morrison," //www.viconet.com/~ejb/bio.htm. _____. (1997), "Toni Morrison: Women of Hope, African Americans Who Made a Difference," //www.mvhs.srvusd.k12.ca.us/~jaymeyer/toni.html. Century, Douglas. 1994. *Toni Morrison*. New York: Chelsea House Publishers. Lifetime Online (1997), "Connections: Toni Morrison," //www.lifetimetv.com/Connections/toni.htm. Morrison, Toni.1970. *The Bluest Eye*. New York: Knopf. Samuels, Wilfred D., and Clenora Hudson-Weems. 1990. *Twayne's United States Authors Series: Toni Morrison*. Boston: Twayne.

Editor's note: After writing *The Bluest Eye* (1970/1993), National Book Award-winning *Sula* (1973/2004), best-selling *Tar Baby* (1981/2004), Pulitzer Prize and American Book Award-winning and National Book Award and National Book Critics Circle Award nominated *Song of Solomon* (1977/2004), Morrison has written several other novels: *Jazz* (1992/2004), *Paradise* (1998), *Love: A Novel* (2003), and *Mercy* (2008). Several of her novels have been adapted to other media: *Beloved* was adapted to a 1998 movie, Oprah's Harpo Productions bought the rights to adapt *Paradise* to a TV miniseries, and *Beloved, The Bluest Eye, Jazz, Paradise, Tar Baby*, and *Song of Solomon* have been adapted to audio format. In addition to writing *Playing in the Dark, Whiteness and the*

Literary Imagination (1992), Morrison's nonfiction includes her essay collection, *What Moves at the Margin: Selected Nonfiction* (2008), as well as her lectures upon accepting the Nobel Prize for Literature (published in 1994) and the National Book Foundation Medal for Distinguished Contribution to American Letters (published in 1996).

Morrison's other prizes and awards include the New York State Governor's Art Award (1986), Elizabeth Cady Stanton Award from the National Organization of Women (1988), Pearl Buck Award (1994), Rhegium Julii Prize (1994), Condorcet Medal (1994, Paris, France), Commander of the Order of Arts and Letters (1994, Paris, France), and the National Humanities Medal (2001). She was also named a National Endowment for the Humanities Jefferson Lecturer (1996) and one of *Time* magazine's 25 Most Influential Americans (1996). Paris's Louvre Museum invited her to be the second foreigner to guest-curate a series of events on the arts, titled "The Foreigner's Home" (2006). She has also received more than 15 honorary doctorates (e.g., Oxford University, 2005), and Barnard College awarded her its Medal of Distinction (1979). The Toni Morrison Society was founded in 1993 (with biennial conferences) as one of the American Literature Association's Coalition of Author Societies.

Morrison has also written fiction for children, including her Coretta Scott King Book Award-winning historical fiction for children 9-12 years old, *Remember: The Journey to School Integration* (2004). With her ex-husband Harold Morrison, Morrison has two sons, Harold and Slade. With painter and musician Slade, she has written numerous books suitable for children 4-8 years old, perhaps inspired by his daughter Kali. These include *The Big Box* (1999/2002), *The Book of Mean People* (2002), and their Who's Got Game series: *The Ant or the Grasshopper?* (2003), *The Lion or the Mouse?* (2003), *Poppy or the Snake?* (2004), and *The Mirror or the Glass?* (2007). Expected soon is their *Peeny Butter Fudge*.

Morrison also wrote the lyrics for *Honey and Rue* (1992), *Four Songs for Soprano, Cello, and Piano* (1995), *Sweet Talk: Four Songs* (1996), and *Spirits in the Well: For Voice and Piano* (1998), and the libretto for *Margaret Garner: Opera in Two Acts* (performed in 2005). She has edited several works, including *The Black Book* (1974), *Race-ing Justice, En-Gendering Power: Essays on Anita Hill, Clarence Thomas, and the Construction of Social Reality* (1992), *To Die for the People: The Writings of Huey P. Newton* (1995), Toni Cade Bambara, *Deep Sightings and Rescue Missions: Fiction, Essays, and Conversations* (1996), *Birth of a Nation'Hood: Gaze, Script, and Spectacle in the O. J. Simpson Case* (1997, with Claudia Brodsky Lacour), and

the forthcoming publication, *Burn This Book: PEN Writers Speak Out on the Power of the Word* (2009).

REFERENCES: *AANB. AAW:PV. B. BAWPP. BCE. CAO-06. CE. CLCS-08. LFCC-07. QB. S. W. W2B. Wiki.* Heinze, Denise, and Sandra Adell. *Nobel Prize Laureates in Literature, Part 3. Dictionary of Literary Biography* (Vol. 331). Detroit: Gale, 2007. From *Literature Resource Center.* Marren, Susan, in *BB.* Miller, D. Quentin, in *GEAAL.* Mobley, Marilyn Sanders, in *COCAAL.* //www.africanvoices.com/e-events.htm. //www.lorain.lib.oh.us/author_biography.aspx?PID=71&ID=17. //www.ncteamericancollection.org/litmap/morrison_toni_oh.htm. Amazon.com.

FURTHER READING: *EAAWW. MWEL.* Blake, Susan L., in *AAFW-55-84.* Blue, Bennis, in *CPW.* Carabi, Angels, *Belles Lettres: A Review of Books by Women.* 9.3 (Spring 1994) p. 38 and 10.2 (Spring 1995) p. 40. From *Literature Resource Center.* Denard, Carolyn C., in *MAWW.* Evans, Elizabeth, Toni Morrison, Wilfred D. Samuels (1990). *Twayne's United States Authors Series 559.* Boston: Twayne Publishers. From *The Twayne Authors Series.* Heinze, Denise, and Catherine E. Lewis, in *ANSWWII-3rd.* Joyner, Nancy Carol, *ANSWWII-2nd.* Lubiano, Wahneema, in *AAW-1991.* Ott, Bill, *Booklist.* 90.12 (Feb. 15, 1994) p. 1136. From *Literature Resource Center.* Smith, Valerie, in *AW:ACLB-91.* //www.africanvoices.com/e-events.htm.

Mosley, Walter (Ellis)
1/12/1952–

Novels (especially mysteries), nonfiction essays and books, opinion/commentary, anthologies, coloring book, short stories; educator

Walter Mosley's parents, Leroy (an African-American school custodian) and Ella (a Jewish-American schoolteacher and school administrator), raised him in South Central Los Angeles, where he attended public schools. Leroy plays a central role in many of Walter's novels, in that Walter's Easy Rawlins character bears a striking resemblance to Leroy: Both of them grew up in a ghetto in Houston, Texas; both were involved in combat during World War II; and both knew how to tell a captivating story. In appreciation for his father's literary gifts—his love of language, storytelling skills, and specific tales of Leroy's experiences—Walter dedicated three of his novels to him.

After high school, Mosley went on to college, eventually earning a political-science degree from Vermont's Johnson State College in 1977. After college, he flitted through a few different jobs, working as a potter and a caterer before settling into work as a computer programmer. After a while, he enrolled in a creative-writing program at the City College of New York, where he pursued an interest in poetry and then in fiction. By the end of the 1980s, Mosley had quit his job writing computer programs and had written his first novel.

His first novel, *Devil in a Blue Dress* (published in 1990), is set in the Watts section of Los Angeles in 1948 and is narrated by Mosley's Easy (Ezekiel) Rawlins character. In this novel, World War II veteran Easy loses his aircraft-industry job. He has an upcoming mortgage payment and other bills to pay, so he somewhat reluctantly takes a job as a private detective, searching for Daphne Monet, a missing white woman known to hang out in jazz clubs in black parts of town. The case ends up embroiling Easy in an organized-crime ring, and issues of race relations and sexual mores during that era further complicate the situation. The novel earned Mosley the John Creasey Award for the year's best first crime novel, the Private Eye Writers of America's Shamus Award, a nomination for the Mystery Writers of America's Edgar Award, and that most lucrative award of all: a 1995 film starring Denzel Washington.

Mosley's next Easy Rawlins novel was set in 1953: *A Red Death* (1991). In it, Easy is working as a janitor but secretly buys some apartments, thereby getting into some trouble with the I.R.S. To wiggle out of this problem (and avoid prosecution), he's asked to do a dirty job for the F.B.I.: He is supposed to spy on a labor-union organizer. This McCarthy-era dirty deed leads Easy into an investigation for murder.

The next Easy Rawlins sequel, *White Butterfly* (1992), takes place in 1956. Easy has married, and he and his wife have a new baby girl. Three young African-American women are viciously slaughtered, but the police show only lackluster interest in solving the crimes. However, when the serial killer murders Cyndi Starr, a white college coed and stripper known as the "White Butterfly," the police decide they need outside help to solve the crime, so they call on Easy to help them find the murderer.

The events in Mosley's fourth Easy Rawlins novel, *Black Betty* (1994), occur in 1961. By this time, Rawlins has separated from his wife and child, and he has two children living with him. His adopted Mexican son Jesus was made mute by traumatic early experiences as a child prostitute, and his adopted daughter Feather was orphaned when her white grandfather killed her mother after finding out that Feather's father was black. A wealthy Beverly Hills family hires Easy for another missing-persons case. It turns out that the missing housekeeper is Elizabeth Eady, with whom Easy was infatuated when he was a young boy.

Mosley's model for Easy, his father Leroy, died of cancer in 1993, but Mosley continued to write more Rawlins novels: a sequel, *A Little Yellow Dog* (1996); a prequel, *Gone Fishin'* (1997); and *Bad Boy Brawley Brown* (2002), which was nominated for the Hammett Prize by the North American Branch of the International Association of Crime Writers (2003). Next were *Six Easy Pieces: Easy Rawlins Stories* (2003), a series of interlocking short stories that form a novella; *Little Scarlet* (2004/2008); *Cinnamon Kiss* (2005); and *Blonde Faith* (2007), after which Mosley said, "I'm not thinking about writing any more Easy Rawlins

books at this time. . . . this one is very likely the last Easy, and . . . I really feel that this is the best Easy Rawlins novel. It's not that it's my favorite book, but I think it's my best novel. And I've never said that before" ("PW Talks with Walter Mosley: The End of Easy?" 2007). The NAACP agreed, honoring *Blonde Faith* with its Image Award for Outstanding Literary Work—Fiction (2008).

Easy's character appeals to readers because this working-class hero is imperfect, flawed. He has financial woes, trouble with his personal relationships, and anger-control issues. Although he's streetwise and crafty, he often makes mistakes in his sleuthing. He tries to stick to his principles, but practical concerns sometimes make him stray a little from time to time. Mosley's character never whines, but he does candidly tell of his interactions with racist police officers and other situations of racial discrimination and prejudice. Also, Easy sometimes gets help from his sidekick and best friend, Raymond "Mouse" Alexander, who often explodes into violence with little provocation. Overall, Mosley's characters have added to the American literary canon some distinctive twentieth-century African-American perspectives, experiences, and language.

Another series of Mosley novels centers around his character "Socrates," a streetwise philosopher of sorts. Like the Easy Rawlins stories, the Socrates stories take place in the Watts section of Los Angeles, but unlike Rawlins, Socrates lives in contemporary times. The stories begin after Socrates has been released from a 27-year prison term for rape and murder and is struggling with trying to redeem himself while facing challenges of poverty and racism. In *Always Outnumbered, Always Outgunned: The Socrates Fortlow Stories* (1998), a series of interwoven short stories introduce him through his interactions, such as with an injured two-legged dog he names "Killer," a troubled youth, and a cancer patient. *Always* garnered one of two Anisfield-Wolf Book Awards for 1998, in recognition that it made "important contributions to our understanding of racism and our appreciation of the rich diversity of human culture." A Socrates short story had already won an O'Henry Award in 1996. *Walkin' the Dog* (1999) also tells Socrates's story through interconnected short stories, in which he continues to confront moral questions while coping with problems such as eviction from his home and abusive police. In *The Right Mistake: The Further Philosophical Investigations of Socrates Fortlow* (2008), a 60-year-old Socrates is troubled by the street violence, poverty, and racism he sees and responds to it by forming the weekly Thinkers' Meetings, comprising a racially and religiously diverse assortment of people, including businesspeople, attorneys, gangsters, killers, a gambler, undercover cops, preachers and others, hoping they can effect changes in their community.

Mosley's "Fearless Jones" series centers on two characters, the World War II veteran Fearless Jones and his pal, used-book-store owner Paris Minton. Paris, who narrates the tales, is book-smart, whereas Fearless is street-smart; Paris fears violence and trouble, whereas Fearless seems to seek the most fearsome and threatening of situations, perhaps because he handles them so well. These books, too, are set in Los Angeles, starting in the 1950s, with *Fearless Jones* (2001), in which Paris tries to help a damsel in distress and ends up being beat up, shot at, robbed of his car and his money by the damsel, and having his much-cherished bookstore burned down. Paris posts bail for Fearless, who in turn helps Paris. In *Fear Itself* (2003) and in *Fear of the Dark* (2006), the twosome search for missing persons and find trouble. Mosley's Fearless borders on superheroism, and Mosley has called the series "comic noire," because no matter how violent and impossibly difficult the situation, Mosley will offer the reader a chance to chuckle. Where Socrates is sincere and serious, Fearless is almost comically heroic. Whereas Socrates feels wary of his own strength, Fearless relishes it.

Each of Mosley's series characters has earned a big- or small-screen adaptation: Easy was honored with the film *Devil in a Blue Dress* (1995); Fearless Jones appeared in Episode 15, "Fearless," of the *Fallen Angels* TV series; and Socrates appeared in the HBO movie starring Laurence Fishburne, *Always Outnumbered* (1998).

In 2009, Mosley introduced a new series in *The Long Fall, the First Leonid McGill Mystery* (2009), set in a new location: Mosley's own new home of New York City. In a //www.Amazon.com exclusive, Mosley said, "My new detective series about the bad-guy-turned-good, Leonid McGill, has been a long time coming. . . . Leonid McGill . . . lives in the modern world. Rather than being a victim, he has spent his entire life as a victimizer. . . . Leonid McGill has not been a good man. . . . But Leonid has gotten as good as he's given. . . . He's gone from orphanage to foster home to the streets—fighting hard and never taking a backward step. . . . one day when he wakes up to realize that he has been on the wrong path for all of his fifty-odd years, Leonid . . . decides to change direction against all the wrong that he's done. Leonid is a man looking for redemption among the people he's wronged in the city that he has betrayed." Further complicating his story, "Leonid is married with three children (though only one of them is his by blood). He and his wife have a relationship of sorts but there is little love in that bond. One gets the feeling that the only reason he hasn't left this loveless union is that he just doesn't know how to back down in a fight."

In 1995, Mosley published a different kind of novel, *RL's Dream* (1995), set in late-1980s New York, written while Mosley's father was dying of cancer in 1993. In it, musician Atwater "Soupspoon" Wise, dying of cancer, is evicted from his apartment when his young white neighbor Kiki Waters mercifully offers him sanctuary in her apartment. The two are sharing less-than-nostalgic memories of their past in the South, when Soupspoon reminisces about legendary blues musician Robert (Leroy) Johnson. The Black Caucus of the American Library Association gave *RL's Dream* its Literary Award in 1996.

Nearly a decade later, Mosley wrote the psychological suspense novel *The Man in My Basement* (2004), about an odd pairing and an odd situation: European-American Anniston Bennet arrives at the door of African-American Charles Blakely, recently fired for stealing from the bank where he worked. Anniston makes a proposal to Blakely, a total stranger: He offers to give him $50,000 if Blakely will let Bennet live in his basement for the next two months. Blakely accepts, and the story ensues.

Next, Mosley wrote a novella, "Archibald Lawless, Anarchist at Large: Walking the Line" (2005) for Ed McBain's third volume in his *Transgressions* series. (Presumably, with McBain's death, the series ended at Volume 4.) About the novella, reviewers have noted, "Felix Orlean is a New York City journalism student who needs a job to cover his rent. An ad in the paper leads him to Archibald Lawless, and a descent into a shadow world where no one and nothing is as it first seems." *Booklist* said, "Walter Mosley profiles an irresistible, offbeat hero through a journalism student who answers a want ad for a 'scribe.'" *Mystery Scene* observed, "Mosley introduces . . . one of the most bizarre and off-beat detectives in fictional history." *Entertainment Weekly* hoped, "Mosley debuts a promisingly eccentric new hero," and *Kirkus Reviews* opined, "such great prose."

Mosley's short stories have been published in periodicals (e.g., **Callaloo**, *The New Yorker, Gentleman's Quarterly, Savoy*) and anthologies (e.g., *Spooks, Spies, and Private Eyes: Black Mystery, Crime, and Suspense Fiction*, Paula L. Woods, Ed., 1995; *Shades of Black*, Eleanor Taylor Bland, Ed., 2004). He also coedited the anthology *The Best American Short Stories 2003*, with Katrina Kenison. Mosley has written two books available chiefly in Kindle (electronic reader) format: *Whispers in the Dark* (2000), originally available in hardcover, but now available only in Kindle format, and *The Greatest* (2008) available only for the Kindle. In *Whispers*, when the sister of ex-convict Chill Bent dies, Chill must take care of her son Ptolemy, "Popo," an astonishing genius whom predators want to exploit. In Mosley's futuristic sci-fi thriller *The Greatest*, genetically engineered Fera Jones is a boxer who can "float like a butterfly" and sting "like a B-1 Bomber." With the help of her gene-drug-addicted father and trainer and her streetwise boyfriend, she must face a death match with an undefeated heavyweight champion.

Mosley's other science fiction includes the novel *Blue Light* (1998), set in 1965, when bizarre blue light rays strike some San Francisco residents, giving them super-powers; the collection *Futureland: Nine Stories of an Imminent World* (2001); and the novel *The Wave* (2006). Many of Mosley's other novels venture into other genres, as well. In his fantasy novel, *The Tempest Tales* (2008), Tempest Landry is shot, killed, and sent to heaven, where he's stopped at the gate. Throughout his life, Tempest has done wrong in order to do good, such as using stolen money to buy groceries for his sick aunt and perjuring himself to send a murderous rapist to jail for a crime the murderer didn't commit. Tempest defends himself to St. Peter, who returns Tempest to Earth, along with a heavenly auditor, while the dispute is being resolved. Mosley's *Fortunate Son: A Novel* (2006) has been called a "fairy tale or parable about race, fate, luck, love, and redemption" (from *Bookmarks*, quoted in //www.Amazon.com). In it, the son of a white father and the son of a black mother form a familial bond in childhood but then are separated by cruel circumstances. Though they end up experiencing very different fates, their strong bond remains.

Mosley has also written two erotic novels, *Killing Johnny Fry: A Sexistential Novel* (2006) and *Diablerie: A Novel* (2008); and a graphic novel, *Maximum Fantastic Four* (2005, with Stan Lee and Jack Kirby). He even wrote a speculative-fiction novel for young adults. In Mosley's *47* (2005), the title character and narrator meets an extraterrestrial who appears to be a fugitive slave and who asks 47 to help him free his fellow slaves; *47* was the first book to receive the Carl Brandon Society Parallax Award, "given to works of speculative fiction created by a person of color."

Leaving no genre untried, Mosley even wrote and self-published *Alien Script: Coloring Book* (1998). Mosley has also written numerous short and long nonfiction works. His essays have been published in numerous periodicals (e.g., *Los Angeles Times Book Review, The New York Times Magazine, The Nation, Whole Earth*) and anthologies (e.g., *Critical Fictions: The Politics of Imaginative Writing*, Philomena Mariani, Ed., 1991; *Defining Ourselves: Black Writers in the 90s*, Elizabeth Nunez and Brenda M. Greene, Eds., 1999). His book *Workin' on the Chain Gang: Shaking off the Dead Hand of History* (1999, available also in audio format) gives a social analysis of how capitalism affects everyday people, and it describes how methods of resistance used by African Americans may be used more broadly, to beneficial effect. In *What Next: A Memoir toward World Peace* (2003), Mosley urges African Americans to lead the way to achieving world peace and harmony, and he suggests how to do so. *Life out of Context: Which Includes a Proposal for the Non-Violent Takeover of the House of Representatives* (2006) offers Mosley's guide for broadening Americans' worldview and for challenging the existing political parties to more effectively respond to the current world situation. In addition, he introduced

and coedited (1999, with Manthia Diawara, Clyde Taylor, and Regina Austin Norton) *Black Genius: African-American Solutions to African-American Problems*, essays by intellectuals proposing solutions to various problems.

Nearly a decade ago, Mosley wrote *The New York Times* article, "For Authors, Fragile Ideas Need Loving Every Day" (7/3/2000), which offered clear, straightforward advice to aspiring writers. He followed up with his book for aspiring novelists, *This Year You Write Your Novel* (2007). In a National Public Radio *Talk of the Nation* (4/17/2007) interview about the book, he said, "If you aren't writing every day, you're going to lose the thread of your novel and it's never going to work. . . . no less than an hour and a half. I don't expect anybody to write more than three hours. I just expect that every day, seven days a week, 365 days a year. . . . the first draft, . . . it's going to be flawed. . . . it's not going to be good enough . . . to be published . . . . You have to work at it. You have to work and rework and rework. Rewriting is when the novel really begins, after you've gotten that first draft down."

The smart reader will heed his advice, if his awards are any indication of its efficacy. In addition to the aforementioned awards for individual books, Mosley has been awarded a Lifetime Achievement Award at the 21st Annual Celebration of Black Writing (2005, Art Sanctuary of Philadelphia), a TransAfrica International Literary Prize, a Grammy Award for best album liner notes on *Richard Pryor And It's Deep, Too! The Complete Warner Bros. Recordings (1968-92)* (2002), a Risktaker Award from the Sundance Institute (2005) "for both his creative and activist efforts," and an honorary doctorate from City College of the City University of New York in 2005. His work has been translated into 21 languages, and in 1992, then-President Bill Clinton's said "Walter Mosley" was his favorite writer.

Mosley tries to support African-American enterprises, such as by publishing a few of his books through the small independent Black Classic Press. He also joined forces with City College of the City University of New York to develop "a new publishing degree program aimed at young urban residents . . . the only such program in the country" (quoted from his website, //www.hachettebook group.com/features/waltermosley/).

REFERENCES: *AANB. AA:PoP. AAW:PV. CAO-08. CE. CLCS-08. EB-98. EBLG. MAAL. MWEL. NAAAL. OC20LE. W. Wiki.* Berg, Rebecca, in *AW:ACLB-02.* Cobbs, John L., in *AMDW.* Decker, Ed, and David G. Oblender, in *BB.* Foster, Frances Smith, in *COCAAL* and *OCAAL.* Hahn, Robert C. "PW Talks with Walter Mosley: The End of Easy?: On October 10, Little, Brown published Blonde Faith, Walter Mosley's 10th and Possibly Final Novel to Feature Los Angeles Investigator Easy Rawlins." *Publishers Weekly.* 254.52 (Dec. 31, 2007) p. 25. From *Literature Resource Center.* Lindsay, Elizabeth Blakesley, in *GEAAL.* Lock, Helen. "Invisible Detection: The Case of Walter Mosley." *MELUS.* 26.1 (Spring 2001) p. 77. From *Literature Resource Center.* Mosley, Walter, and Robert C. Hahn. "PW Talks with Walter

Mosley." *Publishers Weekly* 248.22 (May 28, 2001): p. 54. Rpt. in Contemporary Literary Criticism. Ed. Tom Burns and Jeffrey W. Hunter. Vol. 184. Detroit: Gale, 2004. p. 54. From *Literature Resource Center.* Rogers, Michael. *Library Journal.* 129.10 (June 1, 2004) p. 107. From *Literature Resource Center. Talk of the Nation.* "Stop Reading and Starting Writing" (Apr. 17, 2007). From *Literature Resource Center.* //en.wikipedia.org/wiki/Always_Outnumbered. //en.wikipedia.org/wiki/Anisfield-Wolf_Book_Awards. //en.wikipedia.org/wiki/List_of_Fallen_Angels_episodes. //www.answers.com/topic/walter-mosley. //www.bellaonline.com/articles/art54701.asp. //www.carlbrandon.org/awards.html. //www.coe.ohio-state.edu/beverlygordon/834/miller.html. //www.hachettebookgroup.com/features/waltermosley/. //www.imdb.com/title/tt0146425/. //www.naacpimageawards.net/40/winners.php. //www.nationalbookclubconference.com/authors.aspx. //www.nytimes.com/library/books/070300mosley-writing.html. //www.pen.org/author.php?prmAID/244/prmID/1832. //www.philsp.com/homeville/msf/d109.htm. //www.waltermosley.com. Amazon.com.

FURTHER READING: MWEL. Coale, Samuel, in *CPW.* Frumkes, Lewis Burke. "A Conversation with Walter Mosley." *The Writer.* 112.12 (Dec. 1999) p. 20. From *Literature Resource Center.* McCullough, Bob. "An Interview with Mosley. *Publishers Weekly* 241.21 (May 23, 1994): pp. 67-68. "Walter Mosley: The Crime Novelist Explores Black Life in Postwar America through His Reluctant PI." *Publishers Weekly.* 241.21 (May 23, 1994) p. 67. From *Literature Resource Center.* Wallmann, Jeffrey M., in *SJGCMW.* //aalbc.com/january2003.htm. //www.thepickledpig.com/cgi-bin/apf4/amazon_products_feed.cgi?Operation=ItemLookup&ItemId=B00139YYRM.

Moss (married name), Thylias (née Thylias Rebecca Brasier)
2/27/1954–

Poems, plays, autobiography/memoir, children's picture book; educator

Moss's writing reflects the diversity of her African-American, Native- American, and European-American heritage. Though her parents were not well-educated professionals, young Thylias was their only child, and she took to literature right away, publishing her first short story at age 6 and her first poem at age 7, in her local church bulletin. After she married John Lewis Moss (in 1973), with whom she raised their two sons, Dennis and Anstead, Moss started having her writings published in nationally distributed periodicals. Since then, Moss's poems have been collected in *Hosiery Seams on a Bowlegged Woman* (1983), *Pyramid of Bone* (1988, nominated for the National Book Critics Circle Award), critically acclaimed *At Redbones* (1990), *Rainbow Remnants in Rock Bottom Ghetto Sky* (1991, winner of the National Poetry series Open competition and the Ohioana Book Award), *Small Congregations: New and Selected Poems* (1993/1994), *Last Chance for the Tarzan Holler: Poems* (1998/1999, nominated for the National Book Critics Circle Award), *Slave Moth: A Narrative in Verse* (2003, named a "best book" by *Village Voice*), and *Tokyo Butter: A Search for Forms of*

Deirdre (2006). In addition, her work was included in *The Best of the Best American Poetry: 1988-1997* (1998, Harold Bloom, Ed.). Her canny ability to vividly express profound feelings can be seen in a stanza from "Lessons from a Mirror": "I am the empty space where the tooth was, that my tongue / rushes to fill because I can't stand vacancies."

Moss has also written plays, including *The Dolls in the Basement* (1984) and *Talking to Myself* (1984), as well as a sound recording, *Larry Levis and Thylias Moss Reading Their Poems* (1991). Moss's other works include her children's picture book *I Want To Be* (1993, an exuberant, imaginative response to the question adults perennially ask young children) and her haunting yet hopeful memoir *Tale of a Sky-Blue Dress* (1998). Adventurous not only with her writing but also with technology, Moss has created what she calls "poams," "Products Of Acts of Making," multimedia works combining visual and auditory expressions, available as podcasts, on YouTube, and through other media outlets. As she says on //www.youtube.com/forkergirl, she's interested in "Experiments in interacting visual systems and sound systems on multiple scales in multiple formats simultaneously—to see what happens and to leap from those outcomes into what can happen. I'm hoping for compelling shifting, temporary modes of meanings and sensory invigoration in any of the forms of realities to which a tine of Limited Fork Theory can connect (in some way on some scale for some duration of some form of time). Writing with a Limited Fork need not produce recognizable text at all —but it can. . . . each tine can bifurcate; in fact, each tine-set can take on as many bifurcations as the entire limited fork, and although these tine-set systems of bifurcations and the limited fork itself may be equally infinite, they are not necessarily the same size." Very daring.

For her literary contributions, Moss has received a Pushcart Prize (1990), a Dewar's Profiles Performance Artist Award in Poetry (1991), a Whiting Writer's Award (1991), and a Witter Bynner Prize from the American Academy and Institute of Arts and Letters (1991); she has won grants and fellowships from the Kenan Charitable Trust (1984-1987), the Artists' Foundation of Massachusetts (1987), the National Endowment for the Arts (1989), the Guggenheim Foundation (1995), and the MacArthur Foundation (1996). In addition to her writing, she teaches English at the University of Michigan (since 1993). She also taught at the prestigious Phillips Academy (Andover, MA, 1984-1992) and has been the Fannie Hurst Poet at Brandeis University (1982), as well as a visiting professor at the University of New Hampshire (1991-1992).

REFERENCES: AANB. CAO-07. CBAPD. VBAAP. Wiki. Bates, Gerri, in APSWWII-3. Vertreace-Doody, Martha Modena, in GEAAL. //www.youtube.com/forkergirl. Amazon.com, 3/2000.

Mossell, Gertrude Bustill
7/3/1855–1/21/1948
Poems, essays, juvenile literature

The most memorable work by Mossell is her book *The Work of the Afro-American Woman* (published under her married name, Mrs. N. F. Mossell, 1894; reprinted 1988, with an introduction by **Joanne Braxton**). In it, she offers 17 poems and 8 essays celebrating the achievements of African-American women in almost every field of endeavor. She also wrote *Little Danisie's One Day at Sabbath School* (1902, a book for children) and myriad articles for both white and black periodicals. Mossell shared her beliefs in the value of her race and her sex with her family. Her great-aunt was abolitionist and educator Grace Bustill Douglass (whose daughter was **Sarah Mapps Douglass**), and her nephew was **Paul (Bustill) Robeson**.

REFERENCES: *BAAW.* Ashe, Bertram D., in *COCAAL* and *OCAAL*.

FURTHER READING: *AANB. EAAWW.* Donaldson, Patricia A., in *BB.* Ostrom, Hans, in *GEAAL.* //digital.library.upenn.edu/women/_generate/AFRICAN%20AMERICAN.html. //digital.nypl.org/schomburg/writers_aa19/bio2.html.

Motley, Willard
7/14/1909–3/4/1965
Novels, diaries, essays

When Willard was only 13 years old, the *Chicago Defender* (*see* **Robert Abbott**) published his first short story, after which he wrote a weekly column for the *Defender* under the pseudonym "Bud Billiken" from December 1922 through July 1924. (A few sources have incorrectly said he was born in 1912, which would have made his first publication at age 10.) Though a good student, active on his high school newspaper and yearbook, Motley was prevented from going to college by the Great Depression. Instead, Motley plunged into writing full time, with help from the Federal Writers' Project (in 1940) and a couple of fellowships. He also cofounded a literary journal during this time. Motley's novels include his best-seller *Knock on Any Door* (1947), *Let No Man Write My Epitaph* (1958), *We Fished All Night* (1951), and *Let Noon Be Fair* (1966). His first two novels were made into movies. Although his novels addressed issues of social class and poverty, they were not strongly identified with his race at a time when race consciousness was emerging, so his reputation and popularity declined. He died in relative poverty and near obscurity in Mexico, where this lifelong bachelor had adopted a son. Since his death, however, his diaries have been published (*The Diaries of Willard Motley,* 1979, Jerome Klinkowitz, ed.).

REFERENCES: *AANB. BAWPP. CAO-02.* Fikes, Robert, Jr., in *COCAAL* and *OCAAL.* Fleming. Robert E., in *AAW-40-55 ANSWWII-* 3rd. Lewin, James A., in *AW:ACLB-08.* Prono, Luca, in *GEAAL.*

Moutoussamy-Ashe, Jeanne
7/9/1951–
Nonfiction—photograph books

Among Moutoussamy-Ashe's photo essays are her *Daufauskie Island: A Photographic Essay* (1982), about the cultural heritage evident in the Gullah-speaking residents of a South Carolina sea island, and *Viewfinders: Black Women Photographers* (1986, including photographers as early as the 1860s). She also produced *Daddy and Me: A Photo Story of Arthur Ashe and His Daughter, Camera* (1993), showcasing Moutoussamy-Ashe's photos of everyday experiences of her husband with their daughter; Camera wrote the text. In addition, Moutoussamy-Ashe provided the photographs for her husband's book *Getting Started in Tennis* (1977). Since Ashe died of AIDS-related complications (in 1993), Moutoussamy-Ashe has continued her photojournalism work for such periodicals as *Life, Smithsonian, Sports Illustrated, Ebony, Essence,* and *Black Enterprise.*

REFERENCES: *33T. AANB.* Alexander, Adele Logan, in *BWA:AHE.* Johnson, Anne Janette, in *BB.* McDaniel, Karen Cotton, in *PBW.*

FURTHER READING: "Arthur (Robert) Ashe, (Jr.)," in *CAO-03.*

Mowry, Jess
3/27/1960–
Juvenile literature, young-adult fiction, novels, short stories

When little Jess was just a few months old, his European-American mother abandoned him and his African-American father, Jessup Willys Mowry. When Jess was just a little boy, Jessup and he moved from rural Mississippi to urban Oakland, California, where Jessup supported Jess working as a mechanic and a crane operator.

An eighth-grade dropout, Jess Mowry hated school but loved reading. After leaving school, he helped his father, also an avid reader, collect scrap metal. For a while, Jess succumbed to his gang-riddled neighborhood's criminal lifestyle and made cash acting as a bodyguard for a drug dealer. At age 16, however, he started a long-term relationship with Markita Brown, with whom he eventually had four children. She urged him to leave the gang life, and reading showed him "there was another world out there some place" (quoted in *BB*). He was also concerned for the welfare of his own children if he continued in the gang lifestyle, so at age 17, he abandoned drugs and gang life.

For decades, Mowry made money for his growing family doing odd jobs such as garbage hauling and yardwork, always just eking out a living, sometimes living in an abandoned bus, but never seeking public assistance. Pretty soon, the Mowry's home—however modest—attracted children from all over their neighborhood, children who needed a refuge from street violence or from an abusive home life. To entertain them, Mowry would tell them stories.

Soon, Mowry started writing down his stories, with a pencil in longhand at first. After he sold his first short story (1988), he paid $10 for an electric typewriter that he used to write other stories. Since 1988, Mowry has been contributing his work to numerous periodicals (e.g., *Alchemy, Santa Clara Review, Sequoia*), including the prestigious literary journal **Obsidian** and the popular magazine *Writer's Digest*. In 1990, Mowry's stories were collected in *Rats in the Trees* (1990), which won the PEN Oakland-Josephine Miles Award for excellence in literature (1991). His second story collection, *Crusader Rabbit and Other Stories*, was due to be published in August of 2009, as this dictionary went to press.

With this encouragement from the literary community, Mowry tackled the novel form, writing a series of best-selling young-adult (teen) novels set in the urban ghetto context in which he had lived since a small child. His first young-adult novel was *Children of the Night* (1991), followed by *Way Past Cool* (1992) and *Six Out Seven* (1993), both on the *Quarterly Black Review of Books* bestseller list, and both published by the esteemed Farrar, Straus, & Giroux. Mowry turned down a $250,000 offer from the Walt Disney Studio to write a screenplay based on *Way Past Cool*. He did accept their $75,000 offer to option the novel for the screen but was later relieved to hear they planned not to make the movie.

Mowry's subsequent novels include *Ghost Train* (1996), *Babylon Boyz* (1999, illustrated by Leonid Gore), *Bones Become Flowers* (2001), *Phat Acceptance* (2007), *Skeleton Key* (2007), *Tyger Tales* (2007), and *Voodu Dawgz* (2007). *Knight's Crossing*, available for preorder, was due to be published in August of 2009, as this dictionary went to press. Mowry has donated some of his book earnings to charitable causes, and he had planned to keep his family in his childhood neighborhood despite his more stable finances. Unfortunately, disputes with his neighbors led them to leave. He, Markita, their own children, and a few extra children needful of a home moved to a modest house in another area in Oakland. He still writes in an abandoned bus.

REFERENCES: CAO-02. Anne Janette Johnson, in *BB*.

FURTHER READING: Kich, Martin, in *GEAAL*.

Mullen, Harryette (Romell)
7/1/1953–
Poems, literary criticism; educator

The daughter of a teacher and a social worker, Harryette Mullen has spent nearly her entire adult life in academia. She earned her B.A. from the University of Texas in Austin (1971-1975), then her M.A. (1987) and Ph.D. (1990) from the University of California—Santa Cruz (UCSC). She also taught for a while at Austin Community College (1975-1977) and then did temporary office work in Austin (1977-1979). Meanwhile, she worked for the Artists-in-Schools program sponsored by the Texas Commission on the Arts (1978-1981). While doing her postgraduate work at UCSC, she worked as a teaching assistant (1985-1989) and then as a visiting lecturer and dissertation fellow (1988-1989). In 1989, she moved across the country to become an assistant professor of African-American and other ethnic literature at Cornell University in Ithaca, New York (1989-1995). In 1995, she returned to California as an associate professor (1995-2003) and then a full professor (since 2003) of African-American literature and creative writing at the University of California in Los Angeles (UCLA).

While still an artist in schools, Mullen wrote her first poetry collection, *Tree Tall Women* (1981), which had broad appeal. Her graduate work and her teaching duties slowed her down for a while, then a decade later, she published *Trimmings* (1991). She took an even more playful approach with her next collection, *S*PeRM**K*T* (1992)—which, of course, refers to *supermarket*. Both books include chiefly short, fragmented prose poems. Departing from these freer verses, Mullen explored more formal quatrains—from a feminist angle—in her next collection, *Muse & Drudge* (1995), referring to the dichotomous roles of females throughout the history of art. The collection also probed issues of race and continued Mullen's facility for surprising her readers with her rhymes—or their absence. In 2002, Mullen released *Blues Baby: Early Poems* (2002) in the Bucknell Series in Contemporary Poetry, as well as her more adventurous word-play prose-poem collection, *Sleeping with the Dictionary* (2002), nominated for the National Book Award for poetry, the National Book Critics Circle Award for poetry, and the *Los Angeles Times* Book Prize for poetry (all 2002). In it, she revivifies tired metaphors, toys with Shakespearean sonnets, and creates "alphabetical language salads" (quoted in *CAO-05*). She followed it with *Dim Lady* (2003) and her retrospective *Recyclopedia: Trimmings, S*PeRM**K*T, and Muse and Drudge* (2006). Her poetry has also appeared in periodicals (e.g., *Antioch Review*, **Callaloo**, *Hambone*) and in anthologies (e.g., *Trouble the Water: 250 Years of African-American Poetry*, 1997).

In addition to her poetry, Mullen has written literary criticism, contributing essays and reviews to periodicals (e.g., *American Book Review, MELUS, Meridians*). Some of these articles have been anthologized (e.g., in *African American Literary Theory: A Reader*, 2000, and in *The Black Studies Reader*, 2004). Her own books of literary criticism and commentary include *Gender and the Subjugated Body: Readings of Race, Subjectivity, and Difference in the Construction of Slave Narratives* (1990/1994) and *Freeing the Soul: Race, Subjectivity, and Difference in Slave Narratives* (1997).

Mullen also writes short stories, which have been published in periodicals, in anthologies, and even in textbooks. Her honors include faculty fellowships (1991-1992, 1994-1995), a Gertude Stein Award for Innovative American Poetry (1994-1995), a Katherine Newman First Prize Award (1996), and a Guggenheim fellowship (2005). She is also a graduate fellow of the Cave Canem poetry workshop retreats.

REFERENCES: *AAW:PV. CAO-05. Wiki.* Hostetler, Ann, in *AANB.* Minderovic, Christine Miner, in *BB.* Williams, Emily Allen. "Harryette Mullen, 'The Queen of Hip Hyperbole': An Interview." *African American Review 34.4* (Winter 2000), p. 701. Literature Resources from Gale. //worldcat.org/identities/lccn-n85-818788, Mullen, Harryette Romell. //www.cavecanempoets.org/pages/programs_faculty.php. //www.poets.org/poet.php/prmPID/237. Amazon.com.

FURTHER READING: *EAAWW.* Pinto, Samantha, in *GEAAL.*

Murphy, Beatrice M.
6/25/1908–5/12/1992
Poems, columns, reviews, anthologies, nonfiction; columnist, editor, archivist

Before she started losing her sight, Murphy's poetry was collected in *Love Is a Terrible Thing* (1945), and she edited the poetry anthologies *Negro Voices: An Anthology of Contemporary Voices* (1938/1971) and *Ebony Rhythm: An Anthology of Contemporary Negro Verse* (1948/1968). Her anthologies included works by luminaries such as **Langston Hughes**, who shed light on novices, including even promising high-school and college students. Her own poems also were published in other editors' anthologies (e.g., *Contemporary American Women Poets: 1937, Crown Anthology of Verse, Golden Slippers,* and *Poetry of the Negro*), and her poems and critical reviews appeared in various periodicals (e.g., *Crisis, The New York Times, Tan Confessions*). She also guided aspiring writers in her *Catching the Editor's Eye* (1949). An early victim of McCarthy-style anticommunism in the 1950s, she was fired from her job with the Veterans Administration but was later reinstated, with back pay. Meanwhile, she worked as a columnist (e.g., for the Associated Negro Press, *Washington Tribune*) and a book-review editor (e.g., for the *Afro-American*).

Even after she started losing her sight in 1967, she continued to write, collaborating with Nancy L. Arnez to produce her poetry collections *The Rocks Cry Out* (1969) and *Home Is Where the Heart Is,* and alone she wrote *Get with It Lord: New & Selected Poems* (1977). Although Murphy was eventually declared legally blind, she still managed to edit *New Negro Voices: An Anthology by Young Negro Poets* (1970), which brought to prominence the work of young and previously unknown poets. Even so, perhaps her most significant contribution to literature was to found and direct the Negro Bibliographic and Research Center in the 1960s, later named the Minority Research Center, which published the *Bibliographic Survey: The Negro in Print* she edited (1965-1972). The center also contributed 3,000 books to the Martin Luther King Library in 1968. In 1977, she founded the Beatrice M. Murphy Foundation, which donated nearly 2,000 books to the King Library that year. As the foundation's executive director until her death, she ensured that the foundation fostered the development of African-American literature, in addition to collecting, preserving, and distributing literature by and about African Americans.

REFERENCES: *CAO-03. HR&B.* Adams, Katherine H., in *AAW-40-55.* Andrews, Larry R., in *COCAAL* and *OCAAL.*

Murphy, Carl
1/17/1889–2/26/1967
Newspaper publisher

Carl's father, John Henry Murphy, had founded the weekly *Baltimore Afro-American* before Carl was old enough to remember a time when it didn't exist. After Carl had graduated from Howard and Harvard universities, in 1918, John Henry's health began to fail, so Carl Murphy took the reins as editor of his father's paper. When John Henry died four years later, Carl became the paper's publisher, overseeing a circulation of about 14,000. Carl's vision extended beyond Baltimore, and he expanded the paper's reach to Washington, D.C.; Richmond, Virginia; Philadelphia, Pennsylvania; and Newark, New Jersey. He also expanded the paper's coverage to include national and international events, as well as local news. Under his stewardship, the paper had a circulation of more than 200,000, with semiweekly editions. The paper, still in publication, is the second oldest continuously published African-American newspaper (founded in 1892). For his (and his paper's) contributions to numerous civil-rights endeavors (e.g., providing funding for court cases opposing Jim Crow laws), Murphy was awarded the NAACP's prestigious **Spingarn** Medal in 1955.

REFERENCES: *SMKC.* —Tonya Bolden
FURTHER READING: *AANB. Wiki.*

Murray, Albert L.
5/12/1916–
Essays, novels, criticism, nonfiction, biography, poems, spoken word—lectures; military career, educator

Mattie (James) Murray, a homemaker, and her husband, a manual laborer (named either Hugh or Albert Lee), adopted little Albert and raised him in Magazine Point, a little town outside of Mobile, Alabama. Early on, Albert developed a passionate interest in literature and music. With the guidance of Mobile County Training School principal Benjamin Francis Baker, Albert excelled academically and became a talented athlete.

In 1935, he won a scholarship to the Tuskegee Institute, where he delved deeply into studying literature, reading both the assigned texts and numerous other works, including those by scholars championing modern literature. He was there at the same time as **Ralph Ellison**, but at that time, Ellison was a music major, so the two did not become close friends until later on. Nonetheless, Murray shared Ellison's interest in America's cultural complexity, especially the influence of African Americans, and Murray highlighted Ellison's literary influence in a series of lectures he gave in the 1970s. Decades later, John Callahan edited *Trading Twelves: The Selected Letters of Ralph Ellison and Albert Murray* (2000), documenting the gradual building of their deep friendship. The letters cover the years 1949 through 1960, when Ellison and Murray turned to long-distance phone calls instead of letters to maintain their ties. Their gain in ease of communication is our loss.

After Murray earned his bachelor's degree at Tuskegee (1939), he went on to graduate study at the University of Michigan. He returned to Tuskegee for a while, to teach English and theater there, then in 1943, he enlisted in the U.S. Air Force, where he stayed for the next two decades. While in the service, he earned a master's degree at New York University (1948). In 1962, Murray retired from the Air Force as a major. Since then, he has lived on the East Coast (mostly in New York City) and has been a visiting professor, writer in residence, and special lecturer in various schools, including Barnard (New York City [NYC]), Colgate University (Hamilton, NY), Columbia University School of Journalism (NYC), Emory University (Atlanta), the University of Massachusetts at Boston, and Washington and Lee (Lexington, VA).

Through his essays, literary criticism, memoirs, and even his fiction, Murray has made clear his belief in the powerful influence of African Americans on American culture. He particularly values the blues idiom and touts its importance to American culture, not just in music, but also in literature and other aspects of artistic expression. He expresses similar sentiments for jazz, as well.

Murray's first published volume was his collection of essays and reviews, *The Omni-Americans* (1970), in which he criticized what he called "social science fiction," which emphasizes the subordination of African Americans in American culture. Instead, Murray contends that African Americans have always played a vital role in the cultural development of this country, and he supports this contention with examples from history, music, and literature. As he observed, "The background experience of U.S. Negroes includes all of the negative things that go with racism and segregation; but it also includes all of the challenging things that make for ambition, integrity, and transcendent achievement" (quoted in *AAW:AAPP*). In Murray's view, African Americans, far from being marginalized victims of the dominant culture, are the quintessential Americans, *Omni*-Americans who embrace the riches of America's diverse cultural heritages.

After showing the national—and perhaps global—impact of African Americans, Murray took his readers on a very personal journey into his own experiences in his memoir *South to a Very Old Place* (1971/1991). In the narrative, Murray takes his readers along a geographical journey from New York to Alabama and a chronological journey from the present to the days of his boyhood. Along the way, Murray visits with and interviews a wide array of Southerners, white and black, humble and high ranking. His work is an intriguing blend of the **oral tradition** and the new journalism, chronicling the changes from the rule of Jim Crow through the heyday of the civil-rights movement, to the end of the 1960s.

Murray's next major publication was a collection from the Paul Anthony Brick lectures he gave at the University of Missouri, *The Hero and the Blues* (1973/1996). The theme of these lectures centers on the importance of the blues (and jazz) idiom to contemporary literature, illustrated by the works of Ralph Ellison and **Richard Wright**, as well as those of James Joyce, Ernest Hemingway, and Thomas Mann. In it, Murray also offers this sound advice to aspiring artists of all kinds: "Such is the nature of art that the only thing the creative person is justified in straining for is his personal point of view, and paradoxically this probably has much to do not with straining but with learning to relax so as to discover how one actually feels about things" (quoted in *AAW:AAPP*).

Stomping the Blues (1976/1989) continued Murray's emphasis on the blues (and jazz) idiom, highlighting its value as a life-affirming, constructive response to deprivation and misery. Touted as one of the best—if not the best—books on the aesthetics of jazz, it won the ASCAP Deems Taylor Award for music criticism in 1977.

Murray's next major project was to cowrite jazz pianist, bandleader, and composer Count Basie's autobiography *Good Morning Blues* (1985/2002). Through this work, he was able to personalize the aesthetic theory he had described in previous works. In Murray's most recent essay collection, *The Blue Devils of Nada* (1996), he describes the process of writing Basie's autobiography, and he analyzes the artistry of Romare Bearden, Duke Ellington, and Ernest Hemingway, showing—once again—the influence of the blues idiom. In Murray's view, the best way to triumph over "the blue devils of nada" (the meaninglessness and randomness of the forces of decay) is through embracing the blues.

In addition to his nonfiction, Murray has written a few novels tracing the life of a charming, clever fellow named "Scooter," whose life experiences resemble Murray's own. Murray started working on his first novel after retiring from the military, and he continued to work on it intermittently for the next three decades. At last, in 1974, *Train Whistle Guitar* appeared in print (reprinted in 1998), winning for Murray the Lillian Smith Award for Southern Fiction. The novel starts in the 1920s, during Scooter's boyhood in Alabama. There, Scooter learns not just from his school textbooks, but also from the adults in his community and his home. The next part of Scooter's story appears in *The Spyglass Tree* (1991), in which he goes to college (a very Tuskegee-like institution) and his worldview grows ever wider. In *Seven League Boots* (1996), Scooter, renamed Schoolboy, has graduated from college and gets a job playing bass with a Duke Ellington-like band.

Murray's most recent—though perhaps not final—volume, *The Magic Keys: A Novel* (2005), picks up Schoolboy's story in 1940s Greenwich Village. There, Schoolboy meets up with such thinly disguised notables as novelist Taft Edison (Ralph Ellison) and artist Roland Beasley (Romare Bearden). Schoolboy relishes exploring the streets, libraries, galleries, jazz clubs, and other venues in Manhattan. When not prowling Manhattan, he is home with his new bride, Eunice, or attending graduate school at New York University. As the novel concludes, Schoolboy is invited to collaborate in writing the autobiography of Daddy Royal (Count Basie) and to teach in Alabama. As you'd expect, in all these works, Murray pays careful attention to rhythm in his storytelling, and his stories have a jazzy, bluesy feel to them.

Reviewers have commented on the musicality of Murray's poetry, collected in *Conjugations and Reiterations* (2001). For instance, *Publishers Weekly* sang out, "Whether in the slow blues refrains or in a later poem that mixes academy-speak with black vernacular, his prosody always seamlessly supports his content, his eye and ear jointly keeping time" (quoted in //www.Amazon.com). In *Antioch Review,* Ned Balbo said, "Murray's

poems engage in serious play both challenging and rewarding, accessible on the surface but, like the best musicianship, yielding new pleasures with each listening" (quoted in CAO-07).

Murray's other nonfiction works include *Reflections on Logic, Politics, and Reality: A Challenge to the Sacred Consensus of Contemporary American Thinking* (1989) and *From the Briarpatch File: On Context, Procedure, and American Identity* (2001), his collection of lectures, essays, book reviews, and interviews. In addition, *Conversations with Albert Murray* (1997, edited by Roberta S. Maguire) "brings together previously published interviews with the author and critical articles on his works with an introduction, a chronology, and a recent, previously unpublished interview by the editor" (Carson, *African American Review*, 2000). For his body of work, Murray has been given the Ivan Sandrof Lifetime Achievement Award from the National Book Critics Circle (1996), the Alabama Writer's Forum Harper Lee award for Literary Excellence (1998), and the Distinguished Artist Award from the Alabama State Council on the Arts (2003), as well as honorary doctorates from Colgate University (1975) and Spring Hill College (1996). Another of Murray's legacies promotes another of his loves: the program Jazz at Lincoln Center, which he and musician/composer Wynton Marsalis cofounded.

REFERENCES: AANB. AAW:AAPP. AAW:PV. BAWPP. CAO-07. EB-BH-CD. EBLG. MWEL. NAAAL. W. WDAA. Wiki. Borshuk, Michael, in GEAAL. Brown, Eva Stahl, in EA-99. Carson, Warren J. "Conversations with Albert Murray." *African American Review*. 34.3 (Fall 2000) p. 547. From *Literature Resource Center*. Manheim, James M., in BB. Schultz, Elizabeth, in AAW-55-85:DPW. Shank, Barry, in COCAAL and OCAAL. Amazon.com.

Murray, Daniel Alexander Payne
3/3/1852–3/31/1925

Nonfiction—history and biography, bibliography; librarian

In 1871, young Daniel Murray was hired as personal assistant to the Librarian of Congress, becoming the second African-American to hold a professional position at the Library of Congress. Few people were professionally trained librarians at the time; no U.S. school for librarians existed until 1884. Like most of his colleagues, Murray learned librarianship on the job. A decade after starting, Murray was appointed an assistant librarian (in 1881), a title beyond which he never moved over the next forty-plus years. Meanwhile, in 1879, Murray married Anna Evans, an Oberlin College-educated teacher, with whom he later had seven children.

In 1899, Murray was asked to organize an exhibit on "Negro Authors" for the 1900 Paris Exposition. The Library also published Murray's bibliographical pamphlet cataloging the collection of books and pamphlets he organized for the exhibit. Photos of the exhibit and of the pamphlet he created for the exhibit can be seen at //lcweb2.loc.gov/ammem/aap/aapexhp.html. The exhibit and its catalog soon formed the core of the Library of Congress's "Colored Author Collection," to which Murray continually added, growing to 1,100 titles within a year.

Murray also formed his own personal library of 1,448 books and pamphlets by African Americans, bequeathed to the Library of Congress upon his death. Pamphlets offered an inexpensive and highly popular means for African Americans to assert their political views when they were often denied other avenues of expression. The pamphlets cover a variety of genres, such as political speeches, poetry collections, **slave narratives**, sermons, legal documents, biographies, and libretti; and they address such topics as African colonization by freed slaves, lynching and other hate crimes, segregation, voting rights, racial pride, and racial uplift. Both accommodationists and militant rebels expressed their views in these pamphlets, though Southern writers were more common than Northern ones. Since Murray's death, the Library of Congress has created the "Daniel A. P. Murray Pamphlet Collection, 1818-1917" including more than 350 pamphlets now available online at //memory.loc.gov/ammem/aap/aaphome.html. More information on this collection may be found at the library's website, //lcweb2.loc.gov/ammem/aap/aapcoll.html.

Murray not only collected writings, but also produced his own. His first bibliography, *Preliminary List of Books and Pamphlets by Negro Authors* (1900), tied to the Paris exhibition, was followed by others. Eventually, his bibliography expanded to 2,000 titles by African-American authors. In selecting which authors were or were not African Americans, he used the "one-drop rule," commonly used to discriminate against African Americans in the segregated South, by which any person with even a drop of African ancestry would be deemed an African American.

Murray also wrote essays and articles (1899-1925), which frequently appeared in African-American journals, particularly the *Voice of the Negro* (e.g., his article "The Industrial Problem of the United States and the Negro's Relation to It," 1904) and the *Colored American Magazine* (e.g., his article "Color Problems in the United States," 1904). In addition to his bibliographies and articles, he assigned himself the job as editor-in-chief of his extensive, six-volume *Murray's Historical and Biographical Encyclopedia of the Colored Race throughout the World*. Sadly, he never completed or published it, despite his perseverance and dedication. Microfilm reels of his manuscript include about 500 biographical essays, as well as tens of thousands of handwritten cards on a variety of topics. In addition to his own writings, he obtained contributions from many other authors, such as John Edward Bruce, **William Sanders Scarborough**, and **Arthur Schomburg**. Murray was prevented from achieving his goal due to the need to obtain sufficient subscriptions to publish the work, as no publisher was willing to take the financial risk to publish it without advance subscriptions.

While happy to tout the strengths, talents, and accomplishments of his race, Murray never wrote his own autobiography, so few of his literary and bibliophilic descendants have recognized his importance. In his day, he was nonetheless widely recognized for his expertise.

REFERENCES: *Wiki*. Simoneau, Elizabeth, in *AANB*. Walker, Billie E. "Daniel Alexander Payne Murray (1852-1925), Forgotten Librarian, Bibliographer, and Historian." *Libraries & Culture 40.1* (Winter 2005), p. 25. Literature Resources from Gale. //en.wikipedia.org/wiki/Benjamin_W._Arnett. //en.wikipedia.org/wiki/Melvil_Dewey. //lcweb2.loc.gov/ammem/aap/aapbib.html. //lcweb2.loc.gov/ammem/aap/aapexhp.html. //lcweb2.loc.gov/ammem/aap/aaphome.html. //lcweb2.loc.gov/ammem/aap/timeline.html. //memory.loc.gov/ammem/aap/aapcoll.html. //memory.loc.gov/ammem/aap/murray.html.

Murray, (Anna) "Pauli" (Pauline)
11/20/1910–7/1/1985
Biography, autobiographies/memoirs, poems, nonfiction—law; attorney, civil-service commissioner, social activist, cleric

Before she died, Agnes Georgianna Fitzgerald Murray gave birth to six children, the fourth of whom was Pauli. Both Agnes and her husband, William Henry Murray, were of racially mixed ancestry and middle-class status. Sadly, however, Agnes died in March of 1914, before little Pauli was four years old. William was overwhelmed with grief and with the care for his many children, so Pauline Fitzgerald Dame, Agnes's oldest sister, adopted her namesake and moved her from Baltimore to her home in Durham, North Carolina, near the Fitzgeralds, Agnes and Pauline's parents. In 1917, William was committed to a mental institution, and in 1923, he died there.

Pauline was a schoolteacher, and she taught little Pauli to read and write when Pauli was quite young. Pauli attended Durham's segregated public schools, graduating from Hillside High School in 1926. After that, she moved to New York City, where she hoped to enter Hunter College, but before she could do that, she had to attend Richmond Hill High School for one year because of rigorous college entrance requirements. At Hunter, she majored in English and minored in history, and she immersed herself in the world of literature. She had entered Hunter just as the Great Depression was forcing an end to the **Harlem Renaissance**. Nonetheless, while there, she met **Sterling A. Brown, Countee Cullen, Robert Hayden, Langston Hughes,** and **Dorothy West,** and she was stirred profoundly by Stephen Vincent Benét's poetry, especially his "John Brown's Body." Although a brief marriage temporarily interrupted her studies, she graduated from Hunter in 1933, among the 4 African-American students in the class of 247 women. Later on, Hughes and Benét were important mentors for Murray, encouraging her and helping her get her works published.

After college, Murray worked for a while as a schoolteacher. After unsuccessfully trying to be the first African American to enroll at the University of North Carolina at Chapel Hill (which later awarded her an honorary degree and honored her with a scholarship in her name), she was accepted to the Howard University Law School in Washington, D.C. There, she was the top student in her class and the only female when she earned her LL.B. in 1944. As if this weren't enough, she also actively participated in nonviolent civil-rights demonstrations, such as by taking Freedom Rides and leading student sit-ins at Washington-area restaurants. The next obstacle she faced was while trying to enter Harvard Law School, where her race posed no problem; rather, she was denied entry to the all-male graduate law program at Harvard University because she was a woman. Once again, Murray found another way, completing an L.L.M degree at Boalt Hall of Law at the University of California at Berkeley in 1945.

In the mid-1940s, Pauli Murray was clearly an up-and-comer, named 1 of the 12 outstanding women in Negro life (1945) by the National Council of Negro Women, and Woman of the Year by *Mademoiselle* magazine (1947). After serving as the first woman Deputy Attorney of California (1946), she went into private law practice, which included being a member of the California, New York, and Supreme Court bars, serving on a presidential (Kennedy) commission (1962-1963), and championing the victims' rights in numerous sex-discrimination cases. In 1966, she, Betty Friedan, and others helped found the National Organization for Women (NOW). The previous year, she had become the first African American (man or woman) to be awarded Yale University Law School's Doctor of Juridical Science degree (1965), with her dissertation "Roots of the Racial Crisis: Prologue to Policy." Starting in 1968, she taught law and constitutional history at Brandeis University, as well as at Yale and in Ghana.

During this time, she wrote and published several books on law and jurisprudence. These included *Human Rights U.S.A., 1948-1966* (1967) and *States' Law on Race and Color* (1951; supplement, 1955; reprinted, 1997), which **Thurgood Marshall** touted as the best available reference book for lawyers who advocated civil rights and fought segregation in the courts. She also coauthored *The Constitution and Government of Ghana* (1961, with Leslie Rubin), held to be the first textbook on law there. Murray received numerous honorary degrees in recognition of

her scholarship and her legal work on behalf of civil rights.

After a lifetime of achievement, when many others would have happily retired and savored their successes, in 1972, Murray "heard (and heeded) the call" to the ministry. Four years later, she had earned her master's in divinity degree from General Theological Seminary, and in January, 1977, she was consecrated as a minister, the first African-American female priest to be ordained in the 200-year-old Episcopal Church.

Murray's law books were not the only—or even the first—publications she wrote. Her interest in writing had started in early adolescence, and in the early 1950s, she had been a resident at the prestigious MacDowell Colony for writers, with **James Baldwin**. In 1956, after years of research, she published *Proud Shoes: The Story of an American Family* (1956; revised 1978), a memoir of the interracial Fitzgerald family. Through her family's personal history, Murray offers readers greater insight into the wider historical context of racism, interracial relationships, and sexism. Three decades later, Murray finished her own autobiography, *Song in a Weary Throat: An American Pilgrimage* (1987), which chronicles her commitment to political and social activism and her spiritual quest leading to her ordination. The book, not published until after her death, was honored with the Robert F. Kennedy Book Award and the Christopher Award, and it was reprinted in 1989 as *Pauli Murray: The Autobiography of a Black Activist, Feminist, Lawyer, Priest, and Poet*. As with her family memoir, her personal memoir illuminates the broader historical context in which she lived, and to which she contributed greatly.

Starting in the 1930s, while Murray was first opening herself to the world of literature, she began writing poems, and she continued to publish her poems in periodicals and anthologies over the next four decades. In 1970, her poems were collected in *Dark Testament and Other Poems*. As with her other works, these poems include insights into both her personal experiences and her political and social concerns. Because the poems were written in such a historically and politically dynamic time, they aptly reflect the historical changes that occurred during their writing.

REFERENCES: *AANB. B. BAWPP. CAO-00. EA-99. EBLG. G-97. HR&B. OC20LE. Wiki.* Hughes, Sheila Hassell, in *COCAAL* and *OCAAL*. Jacobs, Sylvia M., in *BWA:AHE.* Murray, Stephen Butler, in *GEAAL.* Sanchez, Brenna, in *BB.*

Myers, Walter Dean (né Walter Milton Myers)
8/12/1937–

Juvenile/young-adult novels, nonfiction, picture books, poems, novels; book acquisition editor

When young Walter was just 3 years old, Herbert and Florence Dean adopted him and moved him from Martinsburg, West Virginia, to New York City's Harlem neighborhood. As he later wrote, "I loved Harlem. I lived in an exciting corner of the renowned Black capital and in an exciting era. The people I met there, the things I did, have left a permanent impression on me" (quoted from *Something about the Author Autobiography Series*, CAO-08). For Myers, Harlem was an engaging community, rich with opportunities for playing games with his pals on the street, for daydreaming about being a cowboy or a famous athlete, for listening to his grandfather's biblical stories or his stepfather's scary stories, and for delving into the world of books. As a young boy, he especially enjoyed *The Three Musketeers* and *Little Men*, but as a teenager, he started longing for books that more realistically related to his own experiences. Unfortunately, on those all-too-rare occasions when he could find *anything* written about African Americans, they were depicted as criminals or as victims, and in any case people who didn't make positive contributions to the world. Two glorious exceptions to this rule occurred when Myers discovered two writers whose works he admired: **Frank Yerby** and **Langston Hughes**.

Later, as Myers recalled, "After leaving school and a stint in the army, I bounced around in a series of jobs, none very satisfying, until I finally reached a point where I was writing full time. I was writing fiction primarily, putting my world on paper, exploring the real and imagined lives that comprise my existence. I had found that my real life, the life in which I found my truest self, was the life of the mind. And this life is the one I would use to write my books" (Myers, "Voices of the Creators," in *CBC*). When he was first learning his craft, he joined **John Killens**'s writers' workshop, where he got to know fellow writers such as **Askia Touré**. Today, Myers remains a member of the Harlem Writers guild and of the authors' association PEN. In 1970, he became an acquisitions editor for the publisher Bobbs-Merrill. In this role, he was able to help **Nikki Giovanni**, **Ann Shockley**, and other writers get their work published—and he figured out quite a lot about writing and publishing in the process.

Since then, Myers has written and published nearly 100 fiction and nonfiction books, and his writing has been widely published in numerous periodicals and anthologies. Many of his books have been named with honors, such as a Golden Kite Honor Book, a Jane Addams Honor Book, and an Orbis Pictus Honor Book. Some honors have been bestowed on more than one of his books, such as *Boston Globe/Horn Book* Honor Books, Best Books for Young Adults by the American Library Association (ALA), ALA's Notable Children's Books, ALA's Newbery Honor Books, two National Book Award nominations, and ALA's **Coretta Scott King** Honor

Books. His books have also earned multiple Coretta Scott King Author Awards, numerous Parents' Choice Awards from the Parents' Choice Foundation (PCF), a Lee Bennett Hopkins Poetry Award from the International Reading Association, and the ALA's first Michael L. Printz Award. For his body of work, he has been awarded the Margaret A. Edwards Award from the ALA and its *School Library Journal* (1994) and the May Hill Arbuthnot Honor Lecture Award of the ALA (2009), and he has been nominated for *World Literature Today*'s NSK Neustadt Prize for Children's Literature (2006).

One of the earliest and most important honors Myers received, however, was the appreciation of his son Christopher, to whom he told his stories, and who offered him excellent critical feedback regarding how to tell a captivating story. "My son . . . finds it amusing to walk into a room to discover me in conversation with imaginary companions, or to see in my face the reflection of some inner dialogue, some adventure of the mind" ("Voices of the Creators," *CBC*). Myers has two other children, Karen and Michael Dean, by his first marriage to Joyce, during the late 1950s. In 1973, Myers married Constance "Connie" Brendel, with whom he shares his second son, Christopher. Christopher has also delved into his father's fanciful world. Not only has Christopher creatively illustrated several of his father's books, including *Shadow of the Red Moon* (1995) and *Monster* (1999), but he has also created the rhythmic rap and the illustrations for his own Coretta Scott King Honor picture book *Black Cat* (1999).

In Myers's young-adult novel *Monster* (1999/2008), 16-year-old Steve is on trial for participating in a crime that led to a murder. An amateur filmmaker, Steve decides to write a movie script of the trial, and he records in a journal his most private thoughts about how his past experiences and choices led to his present situation. Myers thus tells the story by interweaving scenes from the movie script with passages from the journal. In January, 2000, the American Library Association awarded Myers the first Michael L. Printz Award for Excellence in Young Adult Literature, as well as a Coretta Scott King Honor and a National Book Award nomination for the book. The Printz selection committee chair noted, "The detached style of the screen play, juxtaposed with the anguished journal entries, reveals the struggle within Steve's conscience. . . . [Myers's] distinctive format creates narrative and moral suspense that will leave readers with questions that have no real answers" (//www.ala.org/news/printzaward.html). In this book and others, Myers, "[creates] windows to my world that all may peer into. I share the images, the feelings and thoughts, and, I hope, the delight" ("Voices of the Creator," *CBC*).

Monster exemplifies the works for which Myers is best known: his young-adult novels, most of which revolve around young folks growing up in Harlem. Although he never glosses over issues such as gang violence, street crime, drug use and abuse, economic and racial oppression, and sexuality, his novels are neither heavy nor disheartening. Humor and optimism prevail among his quirky but very likeable characters. Although most of his characters are males, and he focuses mostly on male-male relationships, the female protagonists in his works are depicted as realistic and nonstereotypical. Both Coretta Scott King Author Award-winning *Motown and Didi: A Love Story* (1984) and Parents' Choice Award-winning *Crystal* (1987) include female protagonists; in the former, family troubles pose obstacles to a young woman's success, and in the latter, a highly successful young woman feels unsatisfied with her fame and fortune. In ALA Notable Book *Me, the Mop, and the Moondance Kid* (1988) and in *Mop, Moondance, and the Nagasaki Knights* (1992), Mop is a white girl who pals around with two adopted brothers and their softball team.

A selection of Myers's many young-adult novels include *Fast Sam, Cool Clyde, and Stuff* (1975), named a Notable Book by the ALA and given a Woodward Park School Annual Book Award; *Mojo and the Russians* (1977); *It Ain't All for Nothin'* (1978), which addresses problems of the elderly and of family members involved in criminal activities, named a Best Book for Young Adults by the ALA; *The Young Landlords* (1979), a Coretta Scott King Award winner, named a Best Book for Young Adults by the ALA; *Hoops* (1981), an ALA Best Book for Young Adults and runner-up for the Edgar Allan Poe Award; *Won't Know Till I Get There* (1982), about peer loyalties, friendships, and youth crime, given a Parents' Choice Award from the PCF; and *The Outside Shot* (1984), about the racial prejudice at a Midwestern college confronting an athletic scholarship student from Harlem, garnering a Parents' Choice Award from the PCF.

Probably one of Myers's best-known novels is *Scorpions* (1988/2008), an ALA Notable Book and Newbery Honor Book about a seventh-grader who longs to feel he's important and that he belongs, so he ends up in a world of trouble by agreeing to hold onto a gun for an older teen who belongs to a gang; *Scorpions* has been adapted to video (1990), Spanish (1992), and audio (1998) formats. Inspired by the death of his own brother on his first day as a soldier in Vietnam, Myers's *Fallen Angels* (1988) follows a Harlem youth to Vietnam. There, he must literally battle to survive, as well as to keep from losing his heart and his soul; *Fallen Angels* was named a Best Book for Young Adults by the ALA, and it won a Coretta Scott King Author Award, a Parents Choice Award from the PCF, a New Jersey Institute of Technology Authors Award, and a Children's Book Award from the South Carolina Association of School Librarians.

Another theme in many Myers books is the father-son relationship, such as the troubled one he explores in

Somewhere in the Darkness (1992). In *Somewhere*, Lonnie's father gets out of prison and decides to get close to his son by having Lonnie go with him to his native Arkansas. Myers ("Voices of the Creators," *CBC*) later reflected, "A book like *Somewhere in the Darkness* deals more with imagined feelings and encounters that might have been. Although I did meet my real father, I had never had an intimate moment with him, had never seen him in that wholeness of being with which we get to know people." *Somewhere* was designated a *Boston Globe/Horn Book* Award Honor Book, a Coretta Scott King Honor Book, and a Newbery Medal Honor Book. Myers's other contemporary, urban juvenile or young-adult fiction includes *Darnell Rock Reporting* (1994), also adapted to video format (1996); *Slam!* (1996/2008), Coretta Scott King Author Award winner, also adapted to audio format (2000); *The Beast* (2003); *The Dream Bearer* (2003/2008), a dark urban fantasy; *Shooter* (2004), about the antecedents and the consequences of a school shooting, also adapted to audio format; *Autobiography of My Dead Brother* (2005), National Book Award nominee about a friendship tested by drugs, gangs, and violence, also adapted to audio format (2006); *Game* (2008), also adapted to large-print format; *Sunrise over Fallujah* (2008), an epistolary novel focusing on the nephew of the protagonist from *Fallen Angels*, set during the Iraq War, also adapted to audio format; and *Dope Sick* (2009), also a dark urban fantasy. In *Handbook for Boys* (2002), Myers seemed to invent his own genre, which critics have called "advocacy fiction," in which his story more pointedly guides the reader onto the right path than he does in his other fiction works.

Myers has also addressed another major category of juvenile and young-adult fiction for young adults: historical fiction. Three of these books were written as journals: *The Journal of Scott Pendleton Collins: A World War II Soldier* (1999), *The Journal of Joshua Loper: A Black Cowboy* (1999), and *The Journal of Biddy Owens, the Negro Leagues* (2001). His other historical fiction includes *The Glory Field* (1994/2008), *Patrol: An American Soldier in Vietnam* (2002), and *Riot* (2009). Myers also offers a wide variety of other fiction for young readers. Just a sampling: Parents' Choice Award-winning *The Mouse Rap* (1990), droll word-play tale; Parents' Choice Award-winning *The Righteous Revenge of Artemis Bonner* (1992), a humorous, fanciful Wild West tale; *Sniffy Blue, Ace Crime Detective: The Case of the Missing Ruby and Other Stories* (1996); and *A Time to Love: Stories from the Old Testament* (2003). Myers has written young-adult adventure tales set in foreign lands, such as *The Nicholas Factor* (1983) and *The Hidden Shrine* (1985), set in Peru and Hong Kong, respectively. *The Hidden Shrine* is part of Myers's Arrow Series, which also includes *Adventure in Granada* (1985), *Duel in the Desert* (1986), and *Ambush in the Amazon* (1986). Myers also created and edits the Eighteen Pine Street series, which won the Jeremiah Ludington Award from the Educational Paperback Association; for the series, he also sometimes writes young-adult novels under the pen name Stacie Johnson, including *Sort of Sisters* (1993), *The Party* (1993), and *The Prince* (1993). To date, Myers has also written nearly two dozen other juvenile or young-adult fiction works, including *The Legend of Tarik* (1981), named a Best Book for Young Adults by the ALA and a Notable Children's Trade Book in the Field of Social Studies by the National Council for Social Studies/Children's Book Council, and *Tales of a Dead King* (1983), given a New Jersey Institute of Technology Authors Award.

In the children's picture-book format, Myers's first was *Where Does the Day Go?* (1969), the only of his books published under his birth name of Walter Milton Myers; thereafter, he honored his foster parents by taking their surname as his middle name, "Dean." *Where* won a picture-book competition sponsored by the Council on Interracial Books for Children and was published by *Parent's Magazine* Press. As he later recalled, he entered the contest "more because I wanted to write *anything* than because I wanted to write a picture book" (quoted in CBC). Since then, he has conquered that format, as well. *The Dancers* (1972) was named Book of the Year by the Child Study Association of America. Myers's other picture books include *The Golden Serpent* (1980), an Indian (Asian) fairy-tale picture book; *The Black Pearl and the Ghost; or, One Mystery after Another* (1980) and *Mr. Monkey and the Gotcha Bird: An Original Tale* (1984), picture-book ghost stories and legends he heard when he was young; and *The Blues of Flats Brown* (2000), about a hit-record-making fugitive puppy and the "owner" who tries to capture him; as well as *The Dragon Takes a Wife* (1972), *Fly, Jimmy, Fly!* (1974), *The Story of the Three Kingdoms* (1995), *How Mr. Monkey Saw the Whole World* (1996), and Myers's young-adult picture book, *Amiri & Odette: A Love Story* (2009), called a hip-hop version of Swan Lake, illustrated by Javaka Steptoe, son of esteemed illustrator **John Steptoe**.

Christopher Myers has also illustrated several of his father's picture books, including *Looking Like Me* (2009). In a 2007 interview (in *World Literature Today*), Walter Dean Myers noted, "When I work with my son, Chris, we feed off each other. I'll present a text and then Chris will respond to that text with his art. He doesn't just want to illustrate my words but to contribute his own vision to the overall piece. When I see what he's done, the nuances he brings to the work, I'll often change the text to add accents to his images. Sometimes, as we discuss ideas that we might like to work on in the future (a constant conversation) I will try to build a vocabulary around his visual concepts or try to change the rhythm of my text to contrast with his style."

Walter Dean and Christopher Myers have also collaborated on three poetic art books: *Harlem: A Poem* (1997; available in audio format), named a *Boston Globe/Horn Book* Honor Book and given the prestigious Caldecott Honor for illustration; *Blues Journey* (2003); and *Jazz* (2006). Without Chris, Walter has created two other poetically and visually artistic books, *Brown Angels: An Album of Pictures and Verse* (1993), in which he interweaves his own poems with turn-of-the-twentieth-century photos of African-American children; and *The Great Migration* (1994), in which Myers intersperses his own poems with the artwork of noted artist Jacob Lawrence. Other poetry-laced books by Myers include *Remember Us Well: An Album of Pictures and Verse* (1993), *Glorious Angels: A Celebration of Children* (1995), *Angel to Angel: A Mother's Gift of Love* (1998), and *Here in Harlem : Poems in Many Voices* (2004), which won the Lee Bennett Hopkins Poetry Award from the International Reading Association.

Myers has also written numerous nonfiction works for juveniles and young adults. Though he mostly focuses on history and biography, he also wrote two other nonfiction books—*The World of Work: A Guide to Choosing a Career* (1975) and *Social Welfare* (1976). His history *Now Is Your Time! The African-American Struggle for Freedom* (1991/2009) won the **Coretta Scott King** Author Award and was named a Golden Kite Honor Book, a Jane Addams Honor Book, and an Orbis Pictus Honor Book. *A Place Called Heartbreak: A Story of Vietnam* (1992) peers into the true experiences of an African-American Air Force Pilot who was imprisoned in North Vietnam for almost 8 years. Myers's other historical nonfiction includes *One More River to Cross: An African American Photograph Album* (1995), *Turning Points: When Everything Changes* (1996), *Amistad: A Long Road to Freedom* (1998/2001), *Antarctica : Journeys to the South Pole* (2004), *USS Constellation: Pride of the American Navy* (2004), *The Harlem Hellfighters : When Pride Met Courage* (2006), and *New York Draft Riot* (2009). He has also written nonfiction picture books: *Young Martin's Promise* (1992) and *We Are America: Tribute from the Heart* (2008), illustrated by Christopher Myers.

Myers's nonfiction biography **Malcolm X**: *By Any Means Necessary* (1993) incorporates photographs, newspaper clippings, interviews, and magazine snippets. His own description of how he approached the writing of this book offers an insight into how a master artisan executes his craft: "To write *Malcolm X: By Any Means Necessary*, a biography of the fiery black leader, I played his taped voice constantly, surrounded myself with pictures of him as a boy and as a young man, walked down the same Harlem streets that he walked down, and tried to put myself in his classroom when a teacher said that it wasn't practical for him to be an attorney because of his race. In seeing what Malcolm saw, in allowing his voice to fill my imagination, by touching upon those instances of racism that touched my life and mirrored his, I recreated Malcolm as surely as I have created fictional characters. As I wrote, I felt him looking over my shoulder, and so I could write with a sureness of voice, with an authority that went beyond the factual material" (Myers, "Voices of the Creators," in CBC). Myers is clearly a highly innovative, creative, and careful writer.

In 2005, Myers wrote his autobiographical *Bad Boy: A Memoir*, which was also adapted to large print and audio formats. His other nonfiction biographies include *Toussaint L'Ouverture: The Fight for Haiti's Freedom* (1996), *At Her Majesty's Request: An African Princess in Victorian England* (1999), a second biography of *Malcolm X: A Fire Burning Brightly* (2000), *The Greatest: Muhammad Ali* (2001), *I've Seen the Promised Land: The Life of Dr. Martin Luther King, Jr.* (2004), and *Ida B. Wells: Let the Truth Be Told* (2008). This list will undoubtedly be incomplete by the time this volume is published, as Myers is constantly at work, creating fiction and nonfiction to inspire and to entertain us all.

REFERENCES: *BAWPP. CA/I. CAO-07. CAO-08. EBLG. WB-99. Wiki. WYA-1997-2.* Bishop, Rudine Sims, in *WYA-1997-3.* Forman, Jack, in *T-CYAW.* Foster, Frances Smith, in *COCAAL* and *OCAAL.* "Interview with Walter Dean Myers." *Journal of Adolescent & Adult Literacy. 50.8* (May 2007) p. 688. From *Literature Resource Center.* Ishola, Olubunmi, "An Interview with Walter Dean Myers." *World Literature Today. 81.3* (May-June 2007) p. 63. From *Literature Resource Center.* Johnson, Anne Janette, in *BB.* Kuilan, Susie Scifres, in *GEAAL.* M. F. S., in *CBC.* Myers, Walter Dean, "Voices of the Creators," in *CBC.* Reynolds, Tom (2005). "A Place within Myself: Walter Dean Myers and the Fiction of Harlem Youth." NoveList Bibliographic Article, NoveList/EBSCO Publishing, //web.ebscohost.com.sdplproxy.sandiego.gov/novelist/detail?vid=3&hid=112&sid=53e96d33-78bf-47ec-b344-06f159a40337%40sessionmgr104&bdata=JnNpdGU9bm92ZWxpc3QtbGl2ZQ%3d%3d. Rochman, Hazel. "The Booklist Interview." *Booklist. 96.12* (Feb. 15, 2000) p. 1101. From *Literature Resource Center.* Smith, Amanda. "Walter Dean Myers: This Award-winning Author for Young People Tells It Like It Is." *Publishers Weekly. 239.32-33* (July 20, 1992) p. 217. From *Literature Resource Center.* Subryan, Carmen, in *AAFW-55-84.* //www.ala.org/ala/emiert/corettascottkingbookaward/cskpastwinners/alphabeticallist/cskalphabetical.cfm#au. //www.ala.org/news/kingawards2000.html. //www.ala.org/news/printzaward.html. //www.ala.org/yalsa/index.html. //www.ala/org/yalsa/printz/2000winnerpr.html. //www.library.uiuc.edu/blog/esslchildlit/archives/2008/02/african_america.html. //www.nationalbookclubconference.com/authors.aspx. //www.walterdeanmyers.net/biblio.html. //www.walterdeanmyers.net/bio.html. //www.walterdeanmyers.net/reviews.html. Amazon.com. SDPL catalog.

Myths *See* **Folktales**

~N~

National Association of Black Journalists
1975–present
Mutual-support organization for African-American journalists

On December 12, 1975, at the Sheraton Park Hotel in Washington, D.C. (now the Marriott Wardman Park Hotel), a group of 44 men and women came together to form the National Association of Black Journalists (NABJ). They included 15 broadcast journalists (radio, e.g., National Public Radio, and television, e.g., stations in Boston, New York, and Washington, D.C.) and 29 print journalists (newspapers, e.g., *Christian Science Monitor*, *The New York Times*, *Washington Post*; and magazines, e.g., **Ebony**, *U.S. News & World Report*). The NABJ welcomes "journalists, journalism professors, and students interested in pursuing a career in journalism, who are full members, associate members or student members of the organization" (quoted in //www.nabj.org/members/documents/story/183p-222c.php).

The first president of the NABJ was **Chuck Stone** (1975-1977), and the most recent past president is Barbara Ciara (2007-2009). An eighteenth president will be elected as this dictionary goes to press in August of 2009. Today, NABJ has 4,100 members and is the largest of the four associations that compose UNITY: Journalists of Color, Inc. Among the NABJ's 10 task forces are the Digital Journalism Task Force, which "keeps NABJ members on the cutting edge as they navigate rapidly evolving newsrooms" and the Lesbian, Gay, Bisexual, and Transgender Task Force, formed "so they may support and strengthen one another [and] to assist the NABJ in carrying out its mission of inclusion and excellence" (quoted in //www.nabj.org/about/taskforces/index.php).

The preamble of the NABJ constitution (dated 8/7/2005) reads, "We, the members of the National Association of Black Journalists, believing that Black journal-ists nationwide should bind themselves together in an effort to increase Black employment in the media, to increase the number of Blacks in management positions, to encourage and educate young Blacks interested in pursuing a journalism career, and to monitor and sensitize all media to racism, do enact and establish this Constitution for the governance of our members" (quoted in //www.nabj.org/members/documents/story/183p-222c.php).

According to its constitution, "The purpose of the NABJ shall be to bring about a union of Black journalists dedicated to truth and excellence in the news, and full equality in the industry in order: (a) To expand and balance the media's coverage of the Black community and Black experience. (b) To encourage students to identify careers in journalism. (c) To actively seek out and identify job opportunities for Black journalists, and to serve as a clearinghouse for such opportunities. (d) To assist Black journalists in upgrading their skills for upward mobility toward managerial and supervisory positions. (e) To strengthen the ties between Blacks who work in majority-owned media and Blacks who work in the Black-owned media. (f) To sensitize the majority-owned media to racism. (g) To award scholarships and internships to Black students. (h) To be an exemplary group of professionals that honors excellence and outstanding achievement among Black journalists. (i) To encourage journalism schools to appoint Black professors. (j) To work with high schools to identify potential Black journalists" (quoted in //www.nabj.org/members/documents/story/183p-222c.php).

In its mission to help aspiring journalists, the NABJ awards more than $100,000 in scholarships annually to African-American college journalism students, sponsors brief journalism courses at historically black colleges and universities, and offers paid internships to about 15 students each year. Each summer, the NABJ also holds a national convention, where hundreds of job recruiters may meet with current and aspiring journalists seeking employment opportunities in journalism. Speakers at the NABJ convention have included Liberian President Ellen Johnson Sirleaf, Senegalese President Abdoulaye Wade, and Bill Clinton, the first sitting U.S. president to address the convention, as well as two U.S. senators who now hold executive positions: President **Barack H. Obama** and Secretary of State Hillary Rodham Clinton.

At the organization's 30th anniversary, members selected "30 Moments in Journalism (1975-2005), Crucial milestones, achievements and events in which black journalists affected the profession" (quoted in //www.nabj.org/30/moments/thirty/index.php). The number-one milestone was when "**Robert C. Maynard** becomes editor of *The Oakland Tribune* in 1979, and in 1983 becomes editor and president in the newspaper industry's first management-leveraged buyout. By doing so, he becomes the first African American to own a major metropolitan newspaper." Other key moments in journalism included when **Charlayne Hunter-Gault** joined PBS's half-hour *MacNeil/Lehrer Report* (1978) and later became the national correspondent for the one-hour *MacNeil/Lehrer NewsHour* (1983); **Max Robinson** became a coanchor of ABC's *World News Tonight* (1978); Robert Johnson launched Black Entertainment Television, the first African-American-owned national cable-TV network (1980); Ed Bradley joined CBS News's *60 Minutes* (1981); Bernard Shaw moderated the 1988 U.S. presidential debate; Pearl Stewart became the first African-American woman to edit a U.S. daily metropolitan newspaper, at *The Oakland Tribune* (1992); Isabel Wilkerson became the first African-American journalist to win a Pulitzer Prize for individual reporting and the first African-American woman to win a journalism Pulitzer (1994); Jack White became the first African-American journalist with a regular column ("Dividing Line") in a major weekly newsmagazine, *Time* (1/16/1995); Mark Whitaker was named *Newsweek's* editor, the first African-American journalist to become editor of a major weekly newsmagazine (1998); *The New York Times* reporters Dana Canedy, Steven A. Holmes, and Ginger Thompson, along with then-deputy-managing-editor Gerald Boyd, won a Pulitzer Prize for their series, "How Race is Lived in America" (2000); and Sheila Cherry was inaugurated the first African-American president of the National Press Club (2004).

The first seven inductees into the NABJ Hall of Fame, established in 1990, are *Washington Post* reporter, editor, and columnist Dorothy Butler Gilliam; the first African-American network news correspondent, hired by ABC News in 1962, Malvin (Mal) Goode; NABJ cofounder and the first female reporter at Cox Radio and Television News, and later their first female White House correspondent, Mal Johnson; photojournalist and filmmaker **Gordon Parks**; award-winning *New York Post* reporter **Ted Poston**; veteran network anchor and correspondent at NBC News, CNN, and PBS, Norma Quarles; and esteemed columnist **Carl T. Rowan**. In 2004, the NABJ Board of Directors also voted to induct 10 legendary journalists: **Robert Sengstacke Abbott**, founder (1905) of the *Chicago Defender*; **Samuel E. Cornish** and **John B. Russwurm**, copublishers (1827-1829) of *Freedom's Journal*, the first African-American-owned and -operated newspaper; **Frederick Douglass**, abolitionist and former slave who published the *North Star* and other periodicals (1847-1863); **W. E. B. Du Bois**, founding editor (1910) of the NAACP magazine, *The Crisis*; **T. Thomas Fortune**, editor and publisher of numerous New York-based newspapers (late 1870s-late 1910s); **Marcus Garvey**, publisher of *Negro World* (1918-1933); **Ethel Payne**, Washington, D.C., correspondent for the *Chicago Defender*; John Herman Henry Sengstacke, III, publisher of the **Chicago Defender** and the *New Pittsburgh Courier* (reorganized from the *Pittsburgh Courier* in 1965), and founder of the *Michigan Chronicle*; and **Ida B. Wells-Barnett**, newspaper editor, antilynching crusader, and reporter (1889-1931). In 1979, the NABJ named Acel Moore and Les Payne its first two Journalists of the Year, and since then, the NABJ has named 28 more Journalists of the Year, the 2009 honoree being Michele Norris, cohost of National Public Radio's "All Things Considered." (No honorees were named in 1980 or 1991.)

REFERENCES: //dailysally.blogspot.com/2007/11/mal-johnson-boss-and-friend.html. //en.wikipedia.org/wiki/National_Association_of_Black_Journalists. //feministlawprofs.law.sc.edu/?p=2513. //members.nabj.org/halloffame.html. //www.nabj.org/30/founders/index.php. //www.nabj.org/30/index.php. //www.nabj.org/30/moments/index.php. //www.nabj.org/30/moments/othermoments/index.php. //www.nabj.org/30/moments/thirty/index.php. //www.nabj.org/about/taskforces/index.php. //www.nabj.org/awards/hall/inductees2004/index.php. //www.nabj.org/awards/honors/past_winners/index.php. //www.nabj.org/conventions/2009/about.html. //www.nabj.org/conventions/2009/index_redirect.html. //www.nabj.org/index2.php. //www.nabj.org/members/documents/story/183p-222c.php. //www.pabj.org/30thpioneers.htm.

FURTHER READING: *See also* the periodicals and journalists cross-referenced here with bold type.

Naylor, Gloria
1/25/1950–
Novels, screenplays, fictionalized memoir

Best known for her first novel, *The Women of Brewster Place* (1982), which received the American Book Award for best first novel in 1983, Gloria Naylor has become a prominent voice in modern African-American fiction. Her works, which also include *Linden Hills* (1985), *Mama Day* (1988), and *Bailey's Café* (1992), all focus sharply on, as Donna Perry has put it, women's friendships and interrelationships, "love, tragedy, self-sacrifice and the enduring strength of women."

The Women of Brewster Place is composed of the interrelated tales of seven African-American women living on a dead-end street in a Northern ghetto. Besieged and betrayed by men—one character has been stripped of her home and money; one completely deprived of the ability to form her own identity because of her reliance on men; one forced into an abortion that makes her neglect her living child, who then dies of electrocution; and one gang-raped by a group of men who are threatened by her lesbian relationship and feel the need to teach her a lesson—these women, who range in age from their twenties to their fifties, rely on each other for the support they need to get through their devastating experiences.

The novel has been criticized by various critics for creating extremely negative and violent portraits of black men. Naylor claims that her focus, however, comes less out of any dislike she holds for black males and more out of her desire to concentrate intently on black females. She believes that any good story needs to have some type of conflict and turns to male characters as a great many of her conflict-bearers. Her desire to hone in on portraits and issues of women comes out of her belief that society has been taught to value men's stories over those of women. She wants her readers to question their own resistance to reading stories solely about women so as to fight this subconscious discrimination.

Her intention to move her readers to a greater awareness of women's issues stems largely from the fact that she had little to no exposure to African-American literature during her younger years. Although she was born in New York City, she was nevertheless born before the height of the civil-rights movement and the end of legally sanctioned segregation in the South. Thus, Naylor grew up in a society that had not yet acknowledged the place of African-American writers in the English curriculum. Growing up in New York City as a shy, introverted child who wrote poetry and short science-fiction stories, and who kept a vast array of journals, she thought that her penchant for writing was freakish because she honestly believed that black women did not write books. Her high-school education did little to disabuse her of this notion, as it focused on the English and white American male writers but never exposed her to the vast array of African-American literature that was beginning to gain critical attention during those years.

It took a while for her to gain exposure to that literature because after high school she became a Jehovah's Witness missionary for seven years. Her decision to join the fundamentalist group came as a result of her disillusionment with the current system of government. Influenced largely by the presence of the Vietnam War throughout her years in high school and the assassination of **Martin Luther King, Jr.**, in her senior year, she came to believe things could only get better if the current system of government was overthrown by a theocracy. After seven years, she left the missionary life because despite her belief and hard work, things had not gotten any better. She decided to try to make a difference by operating from within the system rather than hoping that the system would just somehow go away.

She began to study nursing at Medgar Evers College but found herself less interested in nursing and much more interested in English literature, so she decided to pursue her B.A. in English at Brooklyn College. It was while at Brooklyn College that she took a class with poet Joan Larkin, which exposed her to books by **Toni Morrison**, **Alice Walker**, and **Paule Marshall**. These books inspired her to study African-American literature and also to begin writing the short stories that would become *The Women of Brewster Place*. She has claimed, in an interview with Donna Perry, that "*Brewster Place* really got written as a result of my discovering these writers." She continues on to point out that her focus on women in her novels came out of her realization that "women were despised to the point that [students] weren't even taught that they did such wonderful things for the country and the arts," and that her "presence as a black woman and [her] perspective as a woman in general had been underrepresented in American literature."

Spurred on by these beliefs, she decided to pursue a master's degree in African-American studies at Yale. *Linden Hills*, her second book, was her master's thesis. Unlike *Brewster Place*, which she describes as "a gush of raw emotion," *Linden Hills* is structured like, and loosely based on, Dante's *Inferno*, with hell being a black middle-class neighborhood. It is a scathing judgment against a black middle-class life, which strives more toward assimilation into white culture than attempting to rise up in society by maintaining black identity.

The figures in this book, particularly the men, are again extremely negative characters. The main character, Luther Nedeed, is a Satanic figure, a descendent of several generations of Nedeeds, all of whom presided over the community and its descent into hollowness by encouraging its members to turn away from their past and who they are. The wives of the Nedeed men have all been "despised" figures stripped of their identity, and the wife of the latest Nedeed, Willa, is left the task of reclaiming their identities by finding the ways that the women of the household had left their mark—in Bible scribblings, photos, and recipes. In reviews of this book, Naylor has been harshly criticized for creating such negative images of blacks, particularly by those critics who believe that there are enough images of destructive blacks in literature and that black writers should portray positive images.

This criticism has led her to enunciate some of her ideas about the separation of her personal self from her writerly self, as well as leading her to explain the role she believes she plays in the writing of her novels. Naylor feels that her books are "something separate and apart from the way I live my life and try to help my community." Her books seem to have a life of their own and develop organically, almost out of her control. She sees herself as a filter for stories that come to her, stories that begin as images in her mind, which do not go away and which develop as she writes to try to figure out what the images mean. Sometimes she is sad at what she finds, as the writing leads her to write the deaths of characters that she hopes will live, or the suffering of characters she hopes will find peace. She allows these developments to just happen rather than altering them to make herself or anyone else happy because she feels she is entrusted with the story and must tell it as it comes. She makes conscious decisions not to censor her characters because she does not believe her art should serve a particular political end—she saves that for her private life. Yet just because she does not skew her art to conform to political ideas does not mean that her work does not have a particular ideology. She feels that every writer has an ideology and that she may be more political than other writers because she feels that her "existence [as an African-American woman] in this country was an act of politics."

Although still ideological, her later novels, *Mama Day* and *Bailey's Café*, seem much more subdued than her earlier ones, with many more positive male characters and strong female ones. These works focus much more on the supernatural but hearken back to her earlier works, if only because all of her novels are linked by carrying over characters from one novel to another. Yet they are also linked by her inimitable writerly style, which is characterized by naturalism and a poetic prose that has the spiritual rhythms of gospel riffs. They are also connected by her move toward constant experimentation, which leads her to draw on both European and American traditions. For instance, *Mama Day* has been seen as being loosely based on both Shakespeare's *The Tempest* and Toni Morrison's *The Song of Solomon*, and *Bailey's Café* has been seen both as a continuation of the experimental narrative work of William Faulkner and as bearing a strong resemblance to Morrison's *Jazz*. She continues to write, working to produce screenplays of her books, as well as working on writing plays. She says that she hopes to continue writing, to have something to say in the twenty-first century, whether in the medium of the novel, the screenplay, the dramatic play, or in producing movies of her earlier works.

REFERENCES: *AAW. BW:SSCA.* Gates, Henry Louis Jr., & K. A. Appiah. 1993. *Gloria Naylor: Critical Perspectives Past and Present.* New York: Amistad Press. Perry, Donna.1993. *Backtalk: Women Writers Speak Out* (pp. 216-244). New Brunswick, NJ: Rutgers University Press. Yohe, Kristine A., in *OCAAL.* —Diane Masiello

Editor's note: In the twenty-first century, Naylor wrote a fictionalized memoir, *1996* (2004/2007), describing her own experiences of governmental harassment, within the wider context of governmental antagonism toward artists and activists, particularly those of color. A few of Naylor's other writings include her American Book Award-winning novel *The Men of Brewster Place* (1998), a children's play titled *Candy*, an inprogress sequel to *Mama Day*, and numerous articles and essays for various periodicals (e.g., *Callaloo, Essence, Yale Review*). Her work has also appeared in anthologies (e.g., *The Writing Life: Writers on How They Think and Work: A Collection from the Washington Post Book World* [2003]). She also edited the short-story anthology *Children of the Night: The Best Short*

Stories by Black Women Writers, 1967 to the Present (1995). Naylor refers to her first four novels as a quartet, many of which have been adapted to other formats, such as her audio recording, *Gloria Naylor Reads "The Women of Brewster Place" and "Mama Day"* (1988), a stage adaptation of *Bailey's Cafe*, a miniseries adaptation of *Women of Brewster Place* (1989, produced by **Oprah Winfrey** and Carole Isenberg), which was also made into a weekly television series (1990, produced by Oprah Winfrey and others).

In addition to her American Book Awards, Naylor garnered a Lillian Smith Book Award from the Southern Regional Council (1989) for *Mama Day*, and she has earned a National Endowment for the Arts fellowship (1985) and a Guggenheim fellowship (1988). In a 2002 interview with Angels Carabi, Naylor observed, "I talk to myself and to my characters—and I let them speak to me. I feel that they have chosen me, for whatever reason, to convey their stories to the world. I try really hard to listen internally. I often do things with my own life to make myself a more fitting vessel to communicate their stories. I always worry if I am saying the right thing, because I have the words and they have the story, which I am recording. The best writing comes out when you just are quiet and you let happen what must happen."

REFERENCES: *AANB. AAW:PV. B. CAO-04. CLC-261. MWEL. W. Wiki.* Barnett, Rachael, in *GEAAL.* Decker, Ed, and Jennifer M. York, in *BB.* Denison, D.C. "Interview with Gloria Naylor." *The Writer.* 107.12 (Dec. 1994) p. 21. From *Literature Resource Center.* Fowler, Virginia C. (Ed.). "Author's Works." *Gloria Naylor: In Search of Sanctuary.* Twayne's United States Authors Series 660. New York: Twayne Publishers, 1996. From *The Twayne Authors Series.* Haralson, Eric L., in *AAW-1991.* Lewis, Vashti Crutcher, ANSWWII-5th. Naylor, Gloria, and Tomeiko R. Ashford. "Gloria Naylor on Black Spirituality: An Interview." *MELUS* 30.4 (Winter 2005): pp. 73-87. From *Literature Resource Center.* Naylor, Gloria, and Angels Carabi. "Interview with Gloria Naylor." *Belles Lettres* 7.3 (Spring 1992): p. 36. Rpt. in Contemporary Literary Criticism. Ed. Janet Witalec. Vol. 156. Detroit: Gale, 2002. p. 36. From *Literature Resource Center.* Rosenmeier, Rosamond. "Appendix: A Conversation with Gloria Naylor." "Chapter 1: Writing as Witnessing: An Introduction to the Life of Gloria Naylor." Virginia C. Fowler (Ed.), *Gloria Naylor: In Search of Sanctuary.* Twayne's United States Authors Series 660. New York: Twayne Publishers, 1996. From *The Twayne Authors Series.* Yohe, Kristine A., in *COCAAL.* //www.amazon.com.

FURTHER READING: *EAAWW.*

Neal, "Larry" (Lawrence Paul)
9/5/1937–1/6/1981
Poems, essays, plays, criticism, folklore, anthology; theater founder, editor

Neal wrote two plays (*The Glorious Monster in the Bell of the Horn*, 1976, and *In an Upstate Motel: A Morality Play*, 1980), numerous literary reviews (published in various periodicals), and many poems (collected in the books *Black Boogaloo: Notes on Black Liberation*, 1969, and *Hoodoo Hollerin' Bebop Ghosts*, 1971/1974). In addition, some of his writings have been published in the posthumous collection *Visions of a Liberated Future: Black Arts Movement Writings* (1989). His importance to the **Black Arts Movement**, however, may be more closely related to his work in cofounding a repertory theater (with **Amiri Baraka**), founding and editing several literary journals of that movement (e.g., *Journal of Black Poetry, Cricket, Liberator Magazine*), and coediting the anthology *Black Fire: An Anthology of Afro-American Writing* (1968, also with Baraka). His essays in *Black Fire* are considered some of the clearest statements of the **Black Aesthetic**.

REFERENCES: Engelhardt, Elizabeth Sanders Delwiche, in *COCAAL* and *OCAAL*. Hudson, Peter, in *EA-99*.

FURTHER READING: *AANB. BAWPP. CAO-03. HAAL. Wiki.* Funkhouser, Christopher. "LeRoi Jones, Larry Neal, and The Cricket: Jazz and Poets' Black Fire." *African American Review*. 37.2-3 (Summer-Fall 2003) p. 237. From *Literature Resource Center*. Harris, Norman, in *AAW-55-85:DPW.* Knight, Gladys L., in *GEAAL*. LaBalle, Candace, in *BB*.

Neely, Barbara
1941–
Short stories, novels; community activist, radio producer, organization leader

The protagonist of Neely's novels-queen-sized, middle-aged, dark-skinned Blanche White-earns her living as a domestic, but those around her know her true calling: amateur detective, in the true sense of love of the craft. Whenever someone dies under suspicious circumstances, Blanche applies her perceptive powers to reveal the murder and identify the murderer. *Blanche on the Lam* (1992) won an Agatha Award, an Anthony Award, a Macavity Award, and a Go On, Girl! Award from the Black Women's Reading Club, for best first mystery novel. Neely's other novels, *Blanch among the Talented Tenth* (1994), *Blanche Cleans Up* (1998), and *Blanche Passes Go* (2000), have also been well received. For instance, a 1998 *Publishers Weekly* reviewer said Blanche's "streetwise attitude and lusty approach to life . . . add sparks to an already sizzling mystery." In addition, Naylor thoroughly enjoys writing in the short-story form, and her stories are widely published in periodicals (e.g., *Essence, Obsidian II*) and anthologies (e.g., **Terry McMillan**'s *Breaking Ice*). In all her stories—long and short—Neely considers issues of race, gender, homophobia, and class, reflecting her life's work as a feminist social activist.

REFERENCES: *AANB. AAW:PV. CAO-03.* W. Govan, Sandra Y., in *COCAAL* and *OCAAL*. McEntree, Grace, in *GEAAL*. //www.amazon.com.

FURTHER READING: *EAAWW.*

Negro American Literature Forum *See Black American Literature Forum*

Negro: An Anthology
1934

An editor of European descent, English heiress Nancy Cunard, put together a significant anthology of African-American literature, *Negro: An Anthology* (1934). Her original work weighed 8 pounds, encompassed 855 oversize pages, and included about 150 contributors of poetry and prose, fiction and nonfiction, both European American (e.g., V. F. Calverton, Theodore Dreiser, William Carlos Williams) and African American, as well as contributors from the West Indies, South America, Europe, and Africa. Just a few of the many African-American writers she included were **Countee Cullen**, **W. E. B. Du Bois**, **Langston Hughes**, **Zora Neale Hurston**, **Alain Locke**, **Arthur Schomburg**, **George Schuyler**, and **Walter White**. She even featured more than 20 pages on the notorious trial of the Scottsboro Boys. No publisher would take the chance on producing it, so Cunard paid for its publication out of her own ample pocket, printing just 1,000 copies. Despite its limited distribution-and the scandalous lifestyle of its editor-the volume deserves a special place in the annals of African-American literature, both for its comprehensiveness and for its editor's distinctive multinational perspective.

More recently, Greenwood Press reprinted the full 855-page volume in 1969; Ungar Publishing published a greatly abridged (464-page) edition of the volume in 1970; Quartet Publishing published an abridged version in 1981; and Continuum International Publishing Group reprinted the abridged version in 1996.

REFERENCES: "Nancy Cunard," in *CAO-04*. Cunard, Nancy, and Hugh D. Ford (Eds.). 1981/1996. *Negro: An Anthology - Abridged*. London: Quartet Books, available at Google Books. Hopkins, Chris. 2001. "Nancy Cunard." In William B. Thesing (Ed.), *Late Nineteenth- and Early Twentieth-Century British Women Poets. Dictionary of Literary Biography* (Vol. 240). Detroit: Gale Group. Kaplan, Carla, (7/28/2007), "When 'High Society' Had a Conscience: The Life of Nancy Cunard," *The Nation*, in //www.alternet.org/story/58178/?page=entire. Kinnamon, Keneth, in *OCAAL*. _____, (Spring 1997), "Anthologies of African-American Literature from 1845 to 1994," *Callaloo* (Vol. 20, No. 2), pp. 461-481. "Nancy Cunard: An Inventory of Her Collection at the Harry Ransom Humanities Research Center," in //research.hrc.utexas.edu:8080/hrcxtf/view?docId=ead/00031.xml. Scott, Bonnie Kime. (July, 1997). *Women's Review of Books*, in //findarticles.com/p/articles/mi_hb4397/is_199707/ai_n15307047/. Wintz, Cary D., and Paul Finkelman (Eds.). 2004. *Encyclopedia of the Harlem Renaissance*. London. Taylor & Francis. //en.wikipedia.org/wiki/Nancy_Cunard. amazon.com. //www.bolerium.com/cgi-bin/

bol48/117879.html. //www.bookride.com/2008/03/henry-crowder-nancy-cunard-henry-music.html. //www.negrophilia.com.jm/?q=nancy-cunard-and-hurricane-katrina.

Negro Caravan See **Anthologies, Negro Caravan**

Negro Digest (1942-1951, 1961-1970); renamed *Black World* (1970-1976), and later *First World* (1977-1983)

(*See also* **Johnson Publishing Company**.) In 1942, publisher **John H. Johnson**, who later published *Ebony, Tan,* and *Jet* magazines, created *Negro Digest,* originally a monthly, published between 1942 and 1951. Its style imitated *Reader's Digest,* and it contained articles of general interest to African-American life, with an emphasis on racial progress and occasional reprints from mainstream white publications. *Negro Digest* ceased publication in 1951 then reappeared 10 years later with the same basic mission, but a greater emphasis on African-American literature, history, and culture.

Hoyt Fuller, the digest's managing editor, became the most influential editor among African-American journal editors at that time. When Fuller's ideology became more focused on **Black Power** and the **Black Aesthetic,** the change was reflected in the magazine, with an increasing emphasis on what Fuller perceived as the responsibility of African-American writers to be politically and publicly committed to African-American causes. By 1970, the name of the magazine changed to *Black World* to more accurately reflect the new direction. During its heyday, *Black World* was an excellent source of literature, as well as of political commentary, ranging from left (e.g., the NAACP's **Walter White** and future U.S. Congress member **Charles Rangel**) to right (e.g., **George Schuyler**). Unfortunately, its final issue appeared in 1976.

Editor's note: The immediate successor to *Negro Digest* was Johnson Publishing Company's pocket-sized, highly popular *Jet* magazine. *See* the main entry for the Johnson Publishing Company for more on this publication and how it emerged from and compares with *Negro Digest.*

Numerous reasons have been given for the demise of *Black World.* For one thing, *Black World's* circulation dropped drastically from 100,000 to 15,000. Publisher, author, and protégé of Fuller, **Haki Madhubuti,** has suggested that Fuller's occasional pro-Palestinian articles and columns so enraged Jewish advertisers that they threatened to pull their ads from *Ebony* and *Jet* if Johnson continued to publish it. Scholar and political scientist Jerry Watt has questioned that assertion, noting that Johnson could simply have fired Fuller and continued publishing *Black*

World under new leadership, especially since *Black World* included very few columns and articles on the Middle East. Watt believed that Johnson simply wanted to make more money than *Black World* was providing him. According to author and educator **Lorenzo Thomas,** *Black World* "didn't carry any advertising," usually the financial foundation of any periodical. Another source suggested that Johnson was looking for a way to fund his new commercial venture-Ebony Fashion Fair, traveling fashion shows-and *Black World* was a vulnerable target.

In any case, Fuller facilitated the publication's subsequent reappearance as *First World,* a relatively more polished journal. When *First World* emerged a year later (1977), it was under the auspices of the First World Foundation of Atlanta, Georgia, which Fuller had cofounded, not the Johnson Publishing Company. Fuller also shared the editorial helm with Carole A. Parks. Under their stewardship, *First World* published poetry, short fiction, scholarly articles, and journalistic pieces addressing a broad range of issues, including apartheid, environmental issues, and desegregation. Its esteemed contributors included scholar **John Henrik Clarke,** historian Sterling Stuckey, novelist **Chester Himes,** and multigenre creative writers **Mari Evans** and **June Jordan.** *First World* continued for another two years after Fuller's death (1981) and then ceased to exist (1983).

REFERENCES: "From *Negro Digest* to *Ebony, Jet* and *EM* - Special Issue: 50 Years of JPC - Redefining the Black Image." *Ebony,* in //findarticles.com/p/articles/mi_m1077/is_n1_v48/ai_12811539/. Hamilton, Kendra, "Writers' Retreat: Despite the Proliferation of Black Authors and Titles in Today's Marketplace, Many Look to Literary Journals to Carry on the Torch for the Written Word - Cover Story." *Black Issues in Higher Education,* in //findarticles.com/p/articles/mi_m0DXK/is_19_20/ai_111112027/, //findarticles.com/p/articles/mi_m0DXK/is_19_20/ai_111112027/pg_2/?tag=content;col1. Henderson, Laretta. 2008. *Ebony Jr!: The Rise, Fall, and Return of a Black Children's Magazine.* New York: Rowman & Littlefield. Munro, Karen, "magazines, literary," in GEAAL. Ricigliano, Lori, "Negro Digest," in GEAAL. Sale, Maggie, "First World," in OCAAL.
—Lisa Bahlinger

Negro World
1918–1933

The literary journal of **Marcus Garvey's** Universal Negro Improvement Association (UNIA), *Negro World* was published from 1918 to 1933. This journal may have been the most widely read black periodical of its time. Marcus Garvey was a journalist and activist, and *Negro World* promoted art and writing that supported racial equality and freedom, especially among new and emerging writers. If Garvey had not been arrested and deported, *Negro World* would probably have rivaled the currently better known and more politically moderate journals: **Crisis, Opportunity,** and the *Messenger.*

REFERENCES: Sale, Maggie, in *COCAAL* and *OCAAL*. —Lisa Bahlinger

Nell, William C. (Cooper)
12/20/1816–5/25/1874
Nonfiction—history; journalist, orator

As a young man, Nell apprenticed himself as a printer for William Lloyd Garrison's *Liberator* newspaper. A little later, he switched to working with **Frederick Douglass**, publishing his *North Star*, also an abolitionist newspaper. Meanwhile, Nell was doing research, making notes, interviewing those with first- or second-hand information, checking cemeteries for facts and figures, gathering honorable-discharge papers and war memorabilia (e.g., flags or banners), and investigating whatever he could find out about African-American soldiers who had fought in the American Revolutionary War and the War of 1812. In 1851, he published his 23-page pamphlet, *Services of Colored Americans in the Wars of 1776 and 1812*, which he revised and published again in 1852. By 1855, he had expanded his pamphlet to a full-length book—nearly 400 pages—published as *The Colored Patriots of the American Revolution, with Sketches of Several Distinguished Colored Persons: To Which Is Added a Brief Survey of the Condition and Prospects of Colored Americans*. In addition to this historic—and historical—writing, Nell continued as an abolitionist orator and journalist, and he is reputed to have helped **Harriet Ann Jacobs** publish her autobiography.

REFERENCES: *SMKC*. Eiselein, Gregory, in *COCAAL* and *OCAAL*. **Quarles, Benjamin** (1988), in *BM:EAAHH*. —Tonya Bolden
FURTHER READING: *AANB*. *Wiki*. Gardner, Eric, in *GEAAL*.

Nelson, Alice Ruth Moore Dunbar *See* Dunbar Nelson, Alice Ruth Moore

Nelson, Jill
6/14/1952–
Autobiography/memoirs, novels, anthology, columns, essays, documentary, screenplays; journalist

Jill Nelson earned her B.A. (1977) from City College of the City University of New York (CUNY) and her M.S. (1980) from the Columbia School of Journalism, where she also did further graduate study (1983-1984). During her graduate studies, Nelson also lectured as an adjunct for her alma mater (1982) and for CUNY's Hunter College (1983). Meanwhile, starting in 1978, Nelson worked freelance for numerous periodicals (1978-1986), including newspapers such as New York City's *Village Voice* and magazines such as *Essence*. One of her key themes was to write to right wrongs for the needy, the underserved, the

neglected, and the oppressed. Over time, her reportorial assignments grew more important and more prestigious. She wrote *Mandela* (1985), a documentary screenplay for PBS-TV, and *Essence* sent her to South Africa on assignment (1986). Five years later, Nelson wrote a third documentary screenplay, *Michael's Journal* (1991), for the U.S. Department of Education.

That same year, the *Washington Post* launched its *Washington Post Magazine* and invited Nelson to join the writing staff for its new weekly (1986-1990). By that time, Nelson was the divorced mother of her daughter, Misu, and the twosome went to the District of Columbia, where they experienced extreme culture shock. Although the *Post* had hired **Robert Maynard** (1967-1977) and a few other African-American staffers, when Nelson arrived, the *Post* was still a white, male, corporate environment in a Southern city.

From the start, Nelson's editors questioned her reportorial judgment. After two years at the *Magazine*, she switched to the *Post*'s city desk. Despite further difficulties there, Nelson was honored as the Washington D.C. Journalist of the Year. She also wrote a second PBS-TV, documentary screenplay, *Two Dollars and a Dream* (1989), which she narrated as well. In 1990, she couldn't take the cultural conflict anymore, and she left the *Post*, to return to New York and to freelancing. Since then, Nelson has freelanced for numerous other newspapers, many magazines and journals, and MSNBC.com. She has been a columnist for *USA Today*, a contributing editor to *USA Weekend*, and a contributing columnist to NiaOnline.com, and she now contributes monthly to *USA Today*'s Op-Ed page.

When not writing for others, Nelson wrote her memoir about her *Post* experience. *Volunteer Slavery: My Authentic Negro Experience* (1993) earned Nelson critical praise and the American Book Award. Nicole Quinn later adapted Nelson's memoir as the TV screenplay *Volunteer Slavery*, broadcast by Showtime (1996-1997). Next, Nelson collected her essays in *Straight, No Chaser: How I Became A Grown-Up Black Woman* (1997). She also edited *Police Brutality: An Anthology* (2000).

Nelson took a break from nonfiction to write her first novel, *Sexual Healing: A Novel* (2003), and its sequel, *Let's Get It On: A Novel* (2009). Between her two novels, Nelson wrote *Finding Martha's Vineyard: African Americans at Home on an Island* (2005), which combines historical fiction with historical fact, as well as with memoirs of her own experiences in the Vineyard, where she now lives some of the year. A Harlem community activist the rest of the year, Jill Nelson is now listed as a Professor of Journalism in the College of Liberal Arts and Science at the City College of New York (//www.ccny.cuny.edu/advisement/undergradadvisors.htm). She has also spoken to students across the country (e.g., Harvard University,

New Orleans's Tulane University, University of Illinois at Urbana-Champaign), and she enjoys both motherhood and grandmotherhood.

REFERENCES: *CAO-05. Wiki.* Johnson, Anne Janette, and Sara Pendergast, in *BB.* //findarticles.com/p/articles/mi_m1365/is_n4_v24/ai_14651235. //findarticles.com/p/articles/mi_m1546/is_n4_v8/ai_13284567/. //jillnelson.com/biography.html. //www.ccny.cuny.edu/advisement/undergradadvisors.htm. //www.tanglewoodfilms.com/profile-march.htm. Amazon.com.

FURTHER READING: Feerst, Alex, in *GEAAL.*

Nelson, Marilyn *See* Waniek, Marilyn (née Nelson)

New York Age
1880–1960
News reports, features, and editorials of interest to African Americans, both locally and nationally

T. Thomas Fortune both published and edited this weekly African-American-owned and -operated newspaper, originally named the *New York Globe* (1880-11/8/1884). After Fortune stirred up political controversy in its pages, the *Globe* died, and soon after, the *New York Freeman* (11/22/1884-10/8/1887) emerged, also edited and published by Fortune. Later renamed the *New York Age* (10/15/1887-2/27/1960), Fortune continued to edit the newspaper until 1907. Under his leadership, at a time when the readership of *The New York Times* was 9,000, the readership of the *New York Age* reached 6,000 despite-or perhaps because of-his fiery antilynching and antiracism rhetoric. Nonetheless, financial difficulties plagued the *Age*, and in 1895, he had to seek financial aid from **Booker T. Washington**, who then dictated the paper's editorial policies to be much less militant and much more accommodationist than it had been previously. Fortune stuck it out for another dozen years but finally ceded the editorship in 1907. While Fortune was still at the helm, the *Age*'s staff included such impressive journalists as **Gertrude Bustill (Mossell)**, who edited the "Women's Department" for both the *Freeman* and the *Age*; **Victoria Earle Matthews**; and **Ida B. Wells-Barnett**, who also bought a partial interest in the *Age.* **Amelia E. (Etta) Johnson** also contributed poems, short stories, and articles to the *Age.*

Even after Fortune left the *Age*, the paper continued to find outstanding writers, such as **James Weldon Johnson**, who worked as an editorial writer for the *Age* (1914-1916). In 1952, John Herman Henry Sengstacke, publisher of the **Chicago Defender**, bought out the weekly *New York Age*, renaming it the *New York Age Defender* from 1953 until 1957. During the 1950s, the *Age* contin-

ued to employ such noteworthy journalists as **Robert Maynard**, then a teenage reporter (c. 1955), and experienced journalist **Chuck Stone**, as an editorial consultant (1957-1958) and then an editor (1958-1960). During its illustrious career, the *New York Age* was the first to regularly publish **Tom Feelings'** comic strip "Tommy Traveler in the World of Negro History" (1950s), and **(Thomas) Tom (Covington) Dent** reported for the *Age* (1959-1960). In 1957, Sengstacke restored the name as *New York Age* until it folded on February 27, 1960.

REFERENCES: Salaam, Kalamu ya. "Enriching the paper trail: an interview with Tom Dent." African American Review. 27.2 (Summer 1993): p. 327. Literature Resource Center. //biography.jrank.org/pages/2514/Dent-Thomas-Covington.html. //en.wikipedia.org/wiki/James_Weldon_Johnson. //en.wikipedia.org/wiki/The_New_York_Globe. //mts.lib.uchicago.edu/collections/findingaids/abbottsengstacke.html.

FURTHER READING: *See also* **Chicago Defender, (Thomas) Tom (Covington) Dent, Tom Feelings, T. Thomas Fortune, Amelia E. (Etta) Johnson, James Weldon Johnson, Victoria Earle Matthews, Robert Maynard, Gertrude Bustill Mossell , Chuck Stone**, and **Ida B. Wells-Barnett**.

Newsome, (Mary) Effie (née Lee)
?/?/1885–1979
Poems, juvenile literature; columnist

Newsome's primary contribution to literature was her work as **Crisis** magazine's editor of a literary column for children (1925-1929), filling the column with delicious verses and short stories (e.g., fables and parables). Some of her poems for children also appear in her anthology *Gladiola Garden* (1940), and her poems for adults have been anthologized by **Langston Hughes** and **Arna Bontemps**.

REFERENCES: MacCann, Donnarae, in *COCAAL* and *OCAAL.*

FURTHER READING: *AANB. BAWPP. CAO-05. HR&B.* Honey, Maureen (Ed.), "Table of Contents for *Shadowed Dreams: Women's Poetry of the Harlem Renaissance,*" at //catdir.loc.gov/catdir/toc/ecip064/2005035688.html. Musser, Judith, in *GEAAL.* Zeigler, Mary B., in *AAW-40-55.*

Newspapers
1827–present
News reports, features, and editorials of interest to African Americans, both locally and nationally

The key newspapers included as main entries in this dictionary are, in chronological order by date of founding, **Freedom's Journal** (3/16/1827-1829); **North Star**, subsequently renamed **Frederick Douglass' Paper** (12/3/1847-1863); **New York Age** (1880-1960, originally *New York Globe*); **Baltimore Afro-American** (1892-);

Chicago Defender (5/5/1905-2/5/1956), and *Chicago Daily Defender* (2/6/1956-present); *Pittsburgh Courier* (1907-1965) and *New Pittsburgh Courier* (1965-present); and the (New York) *Amsterdam News* (12/4/1909-present). Additional information about antebellum newspapers may be found in **antislavery periodicals, 1819-1829**; **antislavery periodicals, 1830-1839**; **antislavery periodicals, 1840-1849**; and **antislavery periodicals, 1850-1865**. Information on newspapers in relation to **Booker T. Washington** and his rivals may be found in *Alexander's Magazine* (1905-1909). The entry on the **National Association of Black Journalists** (1975-present) includes not only information on its organization and its members, but also on the history of journalism. Within each of these entries, there are also names of editors and publishers in boldface type, referring the interested reader to biographies of journalists herein.

Nkombo (aka *Echoes from the Gumbo*)
1968–1974
Literary magazine

In 1963, African-American civil-rights activists Doris Derby, John O'Neal, and Gil (Gilbert) Moses founded the **Free Southern Theater (FST)** at Tougaloo College, near Jackson, Mississippi. The FST's integrated theater troupe toured throughout the most rural areas of Mississippi and the Deep South. In 1965, Derby left the troupe, and O'Neal and Moses, FST's director and its artistic director, respectively, moved FST from Tougaloo to New Orleans. Soon after moving to New Orleans, FST became an all-African-American company. According to **Kalamu ya Salaam**, "around 1967, FST lost all funding and suspended the touring ensemble of professional actors." O'Neal and Moses returned to New York, and FST did not gain a new funding source until 1970, when it could resume touring.

Meanwhile, in 1965, **Thomas Covington Dent** had returned to New Orleans from New York City. There, Dent had cofounded the New York City-based **Umbra Workshop** and coedited its poetry journal *Umbra*. He was soon the associate director of the FST, and-drawing on his Umbra experience-started a writers' workshop through FST. Around 1968 or so, the FST Writers' Workshop had become BLKARTSOUTH. In December of 1968, Dent launched BLKARTSOUTH's literary journal *Echoes from the Gumbo*, with the help of Vallery Ferdinand III (**Kalamu ya Salaam** after 1969), an FST playwright, actor, and director. Accustomed to innovation on the stage, the coeditors designed their journal as if it were a recipe book. Ferdinand/Salaam's introduction was titled, "Food for Thought," and the table of contents was identified as the "Recipe." The journal's four sections

were titled, "Meat and Seafoods," "Seasonings," "Spices," and "Miscellaneous Ingredients." The ingredients included **Black Arts Movement** poetry, drama selections, short narrative fiction, and essays. The chefs included not only their own writings and writings by Movement celebrities such as **James Baldwin** and LeRoi Jones (soon renamed **Amiri Baraka**), but also the works of many local poets of Creole and African descent. In addition to the spicy New Orleans flavor, the journal offered a rich broth of Black Arts Movement political commentary on civil rights and the struggle against economic and other forms of oppression.

With the second issue, the editors renamed the journal *Nkombo*, said to be "named for the food the maroons created out of necessity to survive in the wilderness," though an online dictionary (//www.websters-online-dictionary.org/translation/Tsonga/nkombo) lists *nkombo* as a Kenyan Chuka word for "bond servant" or "slave." Perhaps both meanings are correct. In any case, Dent and Ferdinand/Salaam devoted the second issue to poetry. They published two more issues by 1969, when they took a 15-month break from publishing the journal. During that hiatus, Dent wrote *The Free Southern Theater by the Free Southern Theater* (1969). When Dent and Salaam returned to editing *Nkombo*, partially funded by a grant from the Coordinating Council of Literary Magazines, they sought writers from all of the Deep South, not just New Orleans. The seventh and eighth issues, published in June 1971 and August 1972, respectively, included authors from Georgia, Texas, Mississippi, and Florida, as well as Louisiana.

In 1973, Dent left BLKARTSOUTH to found the Congo Square Writers Union, which mentored emerging writers, such as Quo Vadis Gex Breaux, and offered invited readings and lectures from visiting authors, such as **Edward Kamau Brathwaite** and **Al Young**. In 1974, the ninth and final issue of *Nkombo* was published. In 1975, *Nkombo: A Quarterly Journal of Neo-Afrikan/American Culture* appeared, but without the panache or the critical acclaim of its predecessor and namesake. A search of //www.worldcat.org listed seven U.S. libraries (including the New York Public Library and the Tulane University Library) holding *Nkombo* but none holding its successor. The following year, Dent later helped Charles Henry Rowell found the esteemed literary journal *Callaloo* (1976-), based in nearby Baton Rouge.

REFERENCES: Gabbin, Joanne V., "Overview," *Furious Flower: African American Poetry*, kin //newsreel.org/guides/furious/introduc.htm. Salaam, Kalamu ya (Summer 1993), "Enriching the Paper Trail: An Interview with Tom Dent." *African American Review*, 27.2, p. 327. Literature Resource Center. Strathearn, Judith, in *GEAAL*. //biography.jrank.org/pages/2514/Dent-Thomas-Covington.html. //en.wikipedia.org/wiki/Doris_Derby. //en.wikipedia.org/wiki/Gilbert_Moses. //en.wikipedia.org/wiki/Kalamu_ya_Salaam. //www.bluegecko.org/kenya/tribes/chuka/history.htm. //www.doollee.

com/PlaywrightsS/salaam-kalamu-ya.html. //www.gnocdc.org/orleans/ 2/61/snapshot.html. //www.nathanielturner.com/tomdentspeaks.htm. //www.worldcat.org/oclc/3383991&referer=brief_results.

FURTHER READING: *See also* entries for **Free Southern Theater (FST)**, **Thomas Covington Dent**, **Kalamu ya Salaam**, and *Umbra*.

NOMMO
1969–1976
Literary journal

In 1967, several Chicago-based writers formed the Writers' Workshop of the **Organization of Black American Culture (OBAC)**. The original founders of the Writers' Workshop included Don L. Lee (later known as **Haki Madhubuti**), **Carolyn Rodgers**, **Johari Amini**, and **Hoyt Fuller**, the editor of *Negro Digest* (1961-1970), subsequently renamed *Black World* (1970-1976). Though the membership has changed dramatically during the multiple decades of OBAC, it still offers workshops and other mutual support to African-American writers. Some members credit OBAC as being the oldest continuously operating African-American writers' workshop, but that designation probably goes to the **Harlem Writers Guild**.

Two years after helping to found OBAC's Writers' Workshop, Fuller helped found OBAC's first literary magazine, NOMMO (1969-1976), using a grant from the Illinois Arts Council. He also edited it for many years. According to playwright Sandra Jackson-Opoku, who presided over the Writers' Workshop in 1987, NOMMO was named for the Bantu word meaning the magical power of the word to effect material change. (*Nommo* is also the name of an unrelated quarterly student journal founded in late 1968, at the University of California, Los Angeles, and reportedly, other *Nommo* journals have been published out of Oberlin, OH; Athens, GA; Nashville, TN; Saginaw, MI; Heidelberg, Germany; and Paris, France.) Volume 1, Number 1 of NOMMO appeared as the Winter 1969 issue. Originally intended as a quarterly, NOMMO was published rather irregularly from the outset.

Though NOMMO's chief contributors were poets, many of them felt strongly about the issues of the day and expressed themselves both in poetry and in prose. In the spirit of the times, they celebrated an Afrocentric **Black Aesthetic**, and they aimed to empower their African-American readers through literature that affirmed their culture and championed their political and economic well-being. In addition to Amini, Fuller, Madhubuti, and Rodgers, contributors included poet and playwright Nora Brooks Blakely-daughter of Pulitzer Prize-winning poet **Gwendolyn Brooks**, and poet **Sterling Plumpp**, as well as less-well-known authors Jamila-Ra, Jeff Donaldson, Randson Boykin, and Walter Bradford. NOMMO was later followed by the OBAC *Newslettah*, and *Cumbaya*, which briefly replaced NOMMO in the 1980s.

In addition to the journal, OBAC's publishing arm, OBA House, published three NOMMO anthologies, the first of which was under Fuller's leadership. Three years after the founding of NOMMO, William Henry Robinson edited NOMMO: *An Anthology of Modern Black African and Black American Literature* (1972, 501 pp.), the first of three NOMMO anthologies. That same year, Paul Carter Harrison edited *Drama of NOMMO: Black Theatre in the African Continuum* (1972, 245 pp.). A decade and a half later, OBAC celebrated its 20th anniversary with NOMMO: *A Literary Legacy of Black Chicago 1967-1987: An OBAC Anthology* (1987), edited by Carole Parks, who included a lengthy commemoration of founding editor **Hoyt Fuller**. It was soon followed by NOMMO 2: *Remembering Ourselves Whole* (1990) and NOMMO 3: *An OBAC Anthology of Contemporary Black Writing* (1992), both published by OBAC's OBA House Press and edited by the OBAC Writers' Workshop.

REFERENCES: Cyganowski, Carol Klimick, "NOMMO" and "Organization of Black American Culture," in GEAAL. Thompson, Julius E. 2005. *Dudley Randall, Broadside Press, and the Black Arts Movement in Detroit, 1960-1995.* Jefferson, NC: McFarland.

FURTHER READING: *See also* entries for **Black Aesthetic**, **Black Arts Movement**, **Hoyt Fuller**, **Angela Jackson**, **Haki Madhubuti**, *Negro Digest*, **NOMMO**, and **Carolyn Rodgers**.

North Star, Frederick Douglass' Paper, and *Douglass Monthly*
1847–1863
Publication of antislavery fiction and nonfiction

(*See also* **antislavery periodicals, 1840-1849**, and **antislavery periodicals, 1850-1865**). After spending two decades enslaved in Maryland, **Frederick Douglass** managed to escape North to freedom in 1838, with the help of freeborn Anna Murray, whom he soon wedded. With the encouragement of William Lloyd Garrison, he started lecturing for the abolitionist movement in 1841. In 1845, he wrote his first autobiography, *Narrative of the Life of Frederick Douglass, an American Slave, Written by Himself,* the best-selling **slave narrative** of the time. That August, Douglass left for Britain, where he spent two years giving lectures decrying the horrors of slavery. During that time, some British abolitionists purchased his freedom, so he could return to the United States a free man, not a fugitive.

While in Britain, Douglass contemplated, as he recalled in his 1892 version of his autobiography, "At that time there was not a single newspaper in the country, regularly published by the colored people, though many attempts had been made to establish such, and had from one cause or another failed. These views I laid before my friends. The result was that nearly two thousand five hundred dollars were speedily raised toward my establishing such a paper as I had indicated" (quoted in //doc south.unc.edu/neh/dougl92/dougl92.html). Bolstered by the encouragement he received from British abolitionists, Douglass returned to the United States in March 1847, determined to start his own antislavery periodical.

Rather than return to New Bedford, Massachusetts, where he would have been directly competing with Garrison's *Liberator,* Douglass decided to declare his independence, moving his family to Rochester, New York. Both Garrison, who had been Douglass's mentor and ally, and the other leaders of the American Anti-Slavery Society felt hurt that Douglass did not return to their loving embrace, which Douglass sometimes viewed more as a stranglehold. In 1892, Douglass recalled, "From motives of peace, instead of issuing my paper in Boston, among New England friends, I went to Rochester, N. Y., among strangers, where the local circulation of my paper—'THE NORTH STAR'—would not interfere with that of the *Liberator* or the *Anti-Slavery Standard,* for I was then a faithful disciple of Wm. Lloyd Garrison, and fully committed to his doctrine touching the pro-slavery character of the Constitution of the United States" (quoted in //docsouth. unc.edu/neh/dougl92/dougl92.html).

Over the next several months, Douglass prepared to launch his periodical. Among others, **Martin Robison Delany**, publisher and editor of the *Mystery,* pledged his support for Douglass's paper. At last, on December 3, 1847, Douglass published the first issue of his weekly abolitionist newspaper, *The North Star* (1847-1851). According to Douglass's 1892 autobiography, "The North Star was a large sheet, published weekly, at a cost of $80 per week, and an average circulation of 3,000 subscribers" (quoted in //docsouth.unc.edu/neh/dougl92/dougl92. html). From the beginning, Douglass wrote not only the editorials, but also most of the paper's articles.

To see Douglass's opening editorial of *The North Star,* see //docsouth.unc.edu/neh/douglass/support15.html. It begins, "We are now about to assume the management of the editorial department of a newspaper, devoted to the cause of Liberty, Humanity and Progress. The position is one which, with the purest motives, we have long desired to occupy. It has long been our anxious wish to see, in this slave-holding, slave-trading, and Negro-hating land, a printing-press and paper, permanently established, under the complete control and direction of the immediate victims of slavery and oppression. . . . It is scarcely necessary for us to say that our desire to occupy our present position at the head of an Antislavery Journal, has resulted from no unworthy distrust or ungrateful want of appreciation of the zeal, integrity, or ability of the noble band of white laborers, in this department of our cause; but, from a sin-

cere and settled conviction that such a Journal, if conducted with only moderate skill and ability, would do a most important and indispensable work, which it would be wholly impossible for our white friends to do for us. It is neither a reflection on the fidelity, nor a disparagement of the ability of our friends and fellow-laborers, to assert . . . that the man who has suffered the wrong is the man to demand redress,—that the man STRUCK is the man to CRY OUT—and that he who has endured the cruel pangs of Slavery is the man to advocate Liberty." Right away, Douglass made clear the authority with which he wrote.

Even before publishing his first issue, Douglass had written a pamphlet introducing it, in which he explicated the editorial stance he was taking: "The object of The North Star will be to attack slavery in all its forms and aspects; advocate UNIVERSAL EMANCIPATION; exact the standard of public morality; promote the moral and intellectual improvement of the COLORED PEOPLE; and to hasten the day of FREEDOM to our three million enslaved fellow countrymen" (quoted in //www.loc.gov/exhibits/african/afam006.html). Douglass also quietly participated in the Underground Railroad, hiding fugitives both in his home and in his newspaper offices. For instance, starting in 1849, escaped former slave **Harriet Jacobs** and her brother hid out in a Rochester antislavery reading room and bookstore above Douglass's newspaper offices for about a year and a half. About a decade later, Jacobs published her historic slave narrative, *Incidents in the Life of a Slave Girl* (1860). Like Garrison, Douglass also supported women's suffrage and women's civil rights.

Like most abolitionist newspapers, the *North Star* struggled financially, despite receiving some financial support from British abolitionists. As he recalled in 1892, "There were many times when, in my experience as editor and publisher, I was very hard pressed for money, but by one means or another I succeeded so well as to keep my pecuniary engagements, and to keep my antislavery banner steadily flying during all the conflict from the autumn of 1847 till the union of the States was assured and emancipation was a fact accomplished. I had friends abroad as well as at home who helped me liberally" (quoted in //docsouth.unc.edu/neh/dougl92/dougl92.html).

European-American abolitionist Gerrit Smith merged his *Liberty Party Paper* with Douglass's *North Star,* which changed its name to *Frederick Douglass' Paper,* starting with the December 1850 issue (according to an 1895 biography of him by Frederic May Holland; dates of April 17, 1851 and June, 1851 are given elsewhere). Douglass later explained the name change, "During the first three or four years my paper was published under the name of the North Star. It was subsequently changed to Frederick Douglass's Paper, in order to distinguish it from the many papers with 'Stars' in their titles" (quoted in

//docsouth.unc.edu/neh/dougl92/dougl92.html). *Frederick Douglass' Paper* could boast of readers in England and the West Indies, as well as the United States, and its circulation exceeded that of Garrison's *Liberator*. Douglass continued to be the paper's major contributor, even contributing a novella, "The Heroic Slave" (1852). According to Holland, "In 1852 it contained more news, more poetry, more humor, more about politics, and more about Woman's Rights and other new reforms than had been found in the 'North Star.' Mr. **[Samuel Ringgold] Ward** was prominent among the colored contributors, and among the white ones were J. G. Birney and Gerrit Smith" (//docsouth.unc.edu/neh/holland/holland.html).

During this time, Douglass also wrote to Gerrit Smith, "The North Star sustains itself, and partly sustains my large family. It has reached a living point. Hitherto, the struggle of its life has been to live. Now it more than lives" (quoted in //www.history.rochester.edu/class/DOUGLASS/part3.html). British abolitionist Julia Griffiths had been instrumental in this financial turn of events, just as she had played a key role in helping him finance the initial launch of the *North Star*.

According to Holland, "in 1858 . . a little magazine, called 'Douglass's Monthly,' and designed especially for circulation in England, made its first appearance. The first number was that for June; the price was five shillings a year; . . . . The weekly paper, it may here be added, was merged in the 'Monthly' in August, 1860." Other sources confirm that sometime between 1858 and 1861, Douglass started publishing the *Douglass Monthly* for U.S. readers, and by 1861, the *Monthly* had replaced the weekly *Frederick Douglass' Paper*, probably with a period of overlap during which both periodicals were being published.

The years 1859 and 1860 were turbulent in other ways, as well. On October 16-18, 1859, virulently abolitionist John Brown failed in his attempt to launch a widespread slave revolt, starting at the Harpers Ferry arsenal. Douglass knew that his association with Brown could prove dangerous to himself, both legally and physically, so he fled to Canada and then to England for a time. While Douglass was in England, his youngest daughter, Annie, died in Rochester in March of 1860. The following month, he returned to Canada and then slipped across the border home to Rochester. On November 6, 1860, Lincoln was elected as the 16th president of the United States, and on December 20, 1860, South Carolina became the first of seven Southern states to secede from the Union.

Douglass continued to publish the *Douglass Monthly* until 1863, announcing Lincoln's January 1, 1863 Emancipation Proclamation in its pages.

REFERENCES: Andrews, William L., "Douglass, Frederick" in *OCAAL*. Hinks, Peter P., John R. McKivigan, and R. Owen Williams (Eds.). 2007. *Encyclopedia of Antislavery and Abolition*. Westport, CT: Greenwood Publishing Group. Martin, Waldo E., Jr., "Douglass, Frederick," *BWA:AHE*. //docsouth.unc.edu/fpn/jacobs/bio.html. //docsouth.unc.edu/neh/dougl92/dougl92.html. //docsouth.unc.edu/neh/douglass/bio.html. //docsouth.unc.edu/neh/douglass/support15.html. //docsouth.unc.edu/neh/holland/holland.html. //en.wikipedia.org/wiki/Abraham_Lincoln. //en.wikipedia.org/wiki/Emancipation_proclamation. //en.wikipedia.org/wiki/Frederick_Douglass. //en.wikipedia.org/wiki/John_Brown %27s_Raid. //en.wikipedia.org/wiki/Military_history_of_African_Americans_in_the_American_Civil_War). //en.wikipedia.org/wiki/North_Star_(newspaper). //rmc.library.cornell.edu/abolitionism/resistance/Monthly.htm. //www.accessible.com/accessible/about/aboutAA.jsp. //www.blackvoicenews.com/content/view/42450/3/. //www.history.rochester.edu/class/DOUGLASS/part3.html. //www.library.rochester.edu/index.cfm?PAGE=2884. //www.liu.edu/cwis/cwp/library/historic.htm. //www.loc.gov/exhibits/african/afam006.html. //www.winningthevote.org/FDouglass.html.

Northup, Solomon
7/?/1808–1863 or after

Autobiography/memoir, slave narrative; manual and semiskilled laborer—both free and enslaved, abolitionist lecturer

Solomon Northup's 1853 *Twelve Years a Slave: Narrative of Solomon Northup* may be unique among slave narratives: Solomon Northup was born free but was kidnapped, smuggled deep into the deepest South, and enslaved there for a dozen years. Eventually, Northup managed to get a letter to his wife, Anne, who found help to free Solomon and return him to New York.

After returning, Northup participated in writing his narrative, the first book-length narrative to document such a horrific tale of kidnapping and enslavement. Though Northup was literate, the actual writing was done by an amanuensis, so the writing style was not Northup's, but the experiences and the details of events were authentically Northup's. Northup also went on the abolitionist lecture circuit across the northeastern United States. Little is known of him, however, after a lecture he gave in Boston in 1863.

REFERENCES: *Wiki*. Born, Brad S., in *COCAAL*. Smith, David Lionel, in *AANB*. //www.accd.edu/sac/english/bailey/aframlit.htm.

FURTHER READING: Blaque, Ellesia Ann, in *GEAAL*.

Nugent, Richard (Bruce) (a.k.a. Richard Bruce, Bruce Nugent)
7/2/1906–5/27/1987

Poems, short stories, plays; journalist, visual artist, journal cofounder

Nugent securely ensconced himself in the center of the flame of the **Harlem Renaissance** when he cofounded the short-lived literary journal *Fire!!* with **Wallace Thurman** (the journal's editor), **Langston**

Hughes (the driving force behind it), **Zora Neale Hurston**, and Aaron Douglas. The solitary issue of *Fire!!* included two of Nugent's brush-and-ink drawings and his "Smoke, Lilies and Jade," which was probably the first published short story written by an African American, explicitly depicting a homosexual encounter. (Nugent had been openly gay since his late teens, but he often used pseudonyms to protect his mother from being denigrated or embarrassed because of his homosexuality.) Although some certainly shunned him for his gay identity, he had numerous gay or bisexual contemporaries with whom to associate, including E. M. Forster, Langston Hughes, **Alain Locke**, and **Carl Van Vechten**.

After *Fire!!* flickered out, Nugent coedited (with Thurman) and boldly illustrated *Harlem* (1928). Both his artwork and his poems were published in ***Opportunity*** and ***Crisis*** magazines, as well as *Ebony* and other periodicals, and many were anthologized (e.g., his first poem, "Shadows," which was anthologized by **Countee Cullen** in 1927), although they haven't been collected into a single volume. His short story "Sahdji," which includes themes of homosexuality and biblical imagery, served as the starting point for his one-act musical *Sahdji: An African Ballet* (with music by William Grant Still). The play was later anthologized in Alain Locke's *Plays of Negro Life : A Source-book of Native American Drama* (1927) and was produced in 1932. In addition to his writing and his artwork, Nugent acted.

REFERENCES: *BAWPP. CAO-01. EA-99. EB-BH-CD. WDAA. Wiki.* Garber, Eric, in *AAWHR-40.* Grant, Nathan L., in *COCAAL* and *OCAAL.* Morris, Paula J. K., in *BB.* Schwarz, A. B. Christa, in *GEAAL.*

OBAC, Organization of Black American Culture
1967–
Mutual-support organization for African-American writers

At the height of the **Black Arts Movement**, some writers and other artists formed the Organization of Black American Culture in 1967. The organization's first home was in Chicago's South Side Community Art Center and **Margaret Burroughs**'s DuSable Museum, but it later found a home in the Abraham Lincoln Center. In addition to its Writers' Workshop, the organization comprised a community workshop, a drama workshop, and a visual-arts workshop.

Of all the workshops, the Writers' Workshop is the only one that has continued since its origins. The founders of the Writers' Workshop included Don L. Lee (later known as **Haki Madhubuti**), **Carolyn Rodgers**, **Johari Amini**, and **Hoyt Fuller**, the editor of *Negro Digest*. Later, established Chicago poet **Gwendolyn Brooks** lent her prestige to the Workshop, and New York-based **Amiri Baraka** visited Chicago as an advisor to the Workshop. Though the membership has changed dramatically over time, the Writers' Workshop is one of the two oldest continuously operating African-American writers' workshops (*see* **Harlem Writers Guild**).

The organization's more familiar name, OBAC, pronounced "oh-BAH-see," was intended to be reminiscent of the Yoruba word for leader, *oba*, according to Writers' Workshop participant Jeff Donaldson. OBAC aimed to promote an Afrocentric perspective and the **Black Aesthetic**. To do so, it not only nurtured the workshop's writers, but also immersed the writers within the context of the larger community, so that participants offered community workshops, participated in a public-library reading program, and organized a speakers' bureau.

While Hoyt Fuller was editing the Chicago-based *Negro Digest* (1961-1969), subsequently renamed **Black World** (1970-1976), he also helped found OBAC's first literary magazine, **NOMMO** (1969-1976), which he also edited. *NOMMO* was later followed by OBAC's *Newslettah,* and *Cumbaya*. In addition, OBAC's publishing arm, OBA House, published three *NOMMO* anthologies, the first of which was under Fuller's leadership. Fuller was also OBAC's workshop coordinator. When *Black World* folded in Chicago, only to be reborn in Atlanta as *First World* (1977-1983), Fuller followed it to Atlanta. Creative writer and educator **Angela Jackson**, then about 25 years old, took over as OBAC coordinator, a post she continued to hold until 1990.

Within four years of its inception, only two of the original members remained active, but those who drifted away were replaced by newer members, who reinvigorated the organization.

REFERENCES: Cyganowski, Carol Klimick, "NOMMO" and "Organization of Black American Culture," in *GEAAL*. Thompson, Julius E. 2005. *Dudley Randall, Broadside Press, and the Black Arts Movement in Detroit, 1960-1995*. Jefferson, NC: McFarland.

FURTHER READING: *See also* entries for **Johari Amini**, **Black Aesthetic**, **Black Arts Movement**, **Hoyt Fuller**, **Angela Jackson**, **Haki Madhubuti**, *Negro Digest*, **NOMMO**, and **Carolyn Rodgers**.

Obama, II, Barack (Hussein)
8/4/1961–
Autobiography/memoirs, spoken word—oratory, political position papers; journal editor, politician, executive

Barack Obama is the son of a biracial marriage: his father an African from Kenya, his mother a European American from Kansas. Raised by his maternal grandparents, as well as his mother, Barack attended Occidental College (1979-1981), graduated from Columbia University (1983), and earned his J.D., magna cum laude, from Harvard Law School (1991). Meanwhile, Barack Obama met Michelle LaVaughn Robinson while he was working as a summer associate at a Chicago law firm (1989), where she was his adviser. Despite initial resistance, she eventually accepted his requests for dates, and they were married in 1992. Six years later, Malia was born (1998), followed by Sasha (2001).

Before Barack met Michelle, he had worked as a writer and financial analyst (1984-1985), then as a community organizer (1985-1988). While at Harvard, he had become the first African-American president of the *Harvard Law Review* (1990). After earning his J.D., he chaired a Chicago voter-registration drive (1992) and taught constitutional law at the University of Chicago Law School (1993-2004). Starting in 1993, he also worked as a Chicago attorney, specializing in civil-rights matters. He left the law for politics, as an Illinois state senator (1997-2004), a U.S. senator (2005-2008), and then the first African-American U.S. president (starting in 2009).

One of the key factors that elevated Obama so quickly is his powerful gift for oratory. In 2004, he delivered the keynote address to the Democratic National Convention (DNC), wowing both conveners in Boston and television viewers across the nation and around the world. Obama has similarly inspired listeners to his subsequent speeches, from the Senate Chamber to the White House Rose Garden.

Though known worldwide for his oratory, Obama has actually earned more money from his writing than from his speaking. His bestselling first book, *Dreams from My Father: A Story of Race and Inheritance* (1995; rev. ed., 2004), candidly but inspiringly told his life story. Reviewers such as **Toni Morrison** have praised it; the abridged audiobook he narrated won the 2006 Grammy Award for Best Spoken Word Album; and the book has been translated into at least seven Asian, European, and Middle Eastern languages.

Obama's bestselling *The Audacity of Hope: Thoughts on Reclaiming the American Dream* (2006) may emphasize inspiration more than candor, as it highlights many of the themes from his 2004 keynote speech. The book hit number one on both *The New York Times* and the Amazon.com bestseller lists. Again, the abridged audiobook narrated by Obama won a Grammy Award for Best Spoken Word Album (2008). Obama's subsequent books include *Change We Can Believe In: Barack Obama's Plan to Renew America's Promise* (2008); *The Essential Barack Obama: The Grammy Award-Winning Recordings* (abridged audio CD, 2008); *The Inaugural Address, 2009: Together with Abraham Lincoln's First and Second Inaugural Addresses and The Gettysburg Address and Ralph Waldo Emerson's Self-Reliance* (2009); and *President Barack Obama's Inaugural Address and Other Speeches and Debates* (2009).

Most other awards and honors pale in comparison to Obama's earning election as the leader of the world's leading nation. A couple of earlier honors deserve mention, however: The National Newspaper Publishers Association gave him the Newsmaker of the Year Award (2004) and the National Association for the Advancement of Colored People gave him the Chairman's Award (2005).

REFERENCES: *AN. BCE. CAO-08. CE. W2B. Wiki.* Kennedy, Randall, in *AANB.* Manheim, James M., in *BB.* Southern, Nathan, *All Movie Guide,* in *Act.* Amazon.com. //en.wikipedia.org/wiki/ Dreams_from_My_Father. //en.wikipedia.org/wiki/The_Audacity_ of_Hope. //web.archive.org/web/20010509024017/, //www.law. uchicago.edu/faculty/obama/cv.html. //www.theonion.com/content/ news_briefs/black_man_given_nations.

Obsidian: Black Literature in Review
1975–1982

Obsidian II: Black Literature in Review
1986–1998

Obsidian III: Literature in the African Diaspora
1999–2006

Obsidian: Literature in the African Diaspora
2006–?
Literary journal

After teaching at several educational institutions, creative writer **Alvin (Bernard) Aubert** stayed for a while at the State University of New York (SUNY), where he founded and started editing the literary journal *Obsidian: Black Literature in Review.* In it, Aubert published poems, essays, short stories, literary criticism, and book reviews, as well as occasional dramatic pieces and bibliographies on specific authors or literary subjects. In 1980, Aubert moved to Wayne State University and took *Obsidian* with him. By 1982, he had developed other interests and stopped publishing it.

While **Gerald Barrax** was editing **Callaloo** (1984-1986), he brought *Obsidian* to his academic home at North Carolina State University (NCSU) in 1985. There, he relaunched the journal as *Obsidian II: Black Literature in Review,* and he continued to edit the journal until 1996. When Barrax sought some relief, **Afaa Weaver** took up the reins in 1997, and under his stewardship, the journal was transformed from *Obsidian II: Black Literature in Review* to *Obsidian III: Literature in the African Diaspora.* In the new millennium, Doris Laryea, Joyce Pettis, and Thomas Lisk were starting to take turns editing *Obsidian III.*

Sheila Smith McKoy is identified as the current editor of *Obsidian: Literature in the African Diaspora,* published semiannually (Spring/Summer, Fall/Winter), with poetry editors Duriel E. Harris and Lenard D. Moore, fiction editors **Opal Moore** and Rochelle Spencer, criticism editor Kwame Dawes, and book review editor John Charles. McKoy has dedicated some issues to particular writers, such as **Pearl Cleage**, or to particular topics, such as the 50th anniversary of Ghanaian independence. The writing guidelines for the journal states that "*Obsidian: Literature in the African Diaspora,* [is] a nonprofit organization hosted by North Carolina State University, ... We publish contemporary poetry, fiction, drama, and nonfiction prose from within, about, and contextualizing the African Diaspora." Unfortunately, a library and Internet search for 2007, 2008, or 2009 issues of *Obsidian,* articles in *Obsidian,* or contributors to *Obsidian* has proven fruitless; perhaps the journal is experiencing another lull before its next burst of creative activity.

REFERENCES: //english.chass.ncsu.edu/obsidian/Obsidian%20 History.html. //english.chass.ncsu.edu/obsidian/Staff_Editors.html. //english.chass.ncsu.edu/obsidian/writing_guidelines.html. //find articles.com/p/articles/mi_m0DXK/is_19_20/ai_111112027/pg_6/. //www.columbia.edu/cu/lweb/indiv/africa/African_Diaspora_African_ Literatures.html. //www.h-net.org/announce/show.cgi?ID=150850. //www.worldcat.org/search?q=obsidian&qt=search_items&search= Search. personal communication sent to "Editor or editors of Obsidian," <obsidian@social.chass.ncsu.edu>.

FURTHER READING: *See also* entries for **Alvin (Bernard) Aubert**, **Gerald Barrax**, and **Afaa Weaver**.

Oliver, Diane (Alene)
7/28/1943–5/21/1966
Short stories; journalist

While at the University of North Carolina at Greensboro, Oliver was managing editor of her campus newspaper, started writing short stories, studied poetry under Randall Jarrell, and served as guest editor of the June 1964 issue of *Mademoiselle* magazine. Just days before she graduated from college, she was killed in an auto/motorcycle accident, thus cutting short her promising literary career. Several of her short stories were published, but we can only imagine what works she might have produced had she lingered a little longer.

REFERENCES: Smith, Virginia Whatley, in *COCAAL* and *OCAAL.*

FURTHER READING: *BAWPP. EAAWW.* //academic.regis.edu/ jstclair/EN%20311Q/civil_rights.htm.

Opportunity: A Journal of Negro Life
1923–1949
Official organizational publication and literary journal

Opportunity, the official publication of the National Urban League, was originally intended as a scientific journal with a sociological point of view of African-American life. During the 1920s, however, the magazine was instrumental in encouraging young writers and artists of the **Harlem Renaissance**, including **Langston Hughes**, **Countee Cullen**, **James Weldon Johnson**, **Claude McKay**, **Gwendolyn Bennett**, and **Sterling Brown**. The 1930s brought some dissension on the editorial board as to the vision of the journal, and the Great Depression brought financial difficulties. In the 1940s, despite a lack of funds, the journal was an important voice for wartime discussions of racial equality. *Opportunity* journal was an early champion of integration.

REFERENCES: *EAACH* (Vol. 4).

Oprah's Book Club (1996-) *See* **Winfrey, Oprah**

Oral Tradition (including Griots, Storytelling, not Oratory and Speeches)

The *oral tradition* is the custom of preserving and transmitting a culture's body of beliefs, knowledge, and literature, through word of mouth, from person to person, across generations. Since the first human grunted, wailed, or chortled to a fellow human, the oral tradition was the primary means of communicating and preserving the shared knowledge of a culture. Such knowledge, known as folklore, included ancestry, lineage, and history, as well as myths, legends, religious beliefs, and the oral equivalent of how-to books. Other aspects of folklore may be aided by the oral tradition but rely more on shared observance than on speaking and listening; these aspects include festivals, ritual celebrations (e.g., harvest, planting), rites (e.g., birth, coming-of-age, marriage, death), dances, music and rhythms, costumes, games, foods, arts and crafts, and other customs.

When specialized knowledge must be preserved orally across generations, particular individuals often assume responsibility for memorizing and transmitting that information. For instance, tribal *shamans* take charge of the extensive spiritual, religious, and healing beliefs and practices of a culture. In addition to knowing how to use folk medicines, shamans must know words of healing and power: charms, remedies, superstitions, omens, divination rituals, spells, religious beliefs, and perhaps communications with deceased ancestors, spirit guides, or deities. Village *griots* memorize the lineage and folk history of families within their communities; traveling *troubadours* learn and perform the folk songs of a given region; chiefs and other leaders master the laws, codes, and mores of the groups they lead; elders transmit **folktales** from one generation to the next; and eyewitnesses to important events tell family and friends about what they saw.

By definition, the knowledge preserved through the oral tradition must be memorized. Hence, oral folklore usually has distinctive features that aid memorization. For instance, folk songs usually include repetitive refrains and predictable rhythms and rhymes; they may use the same familiar tunes with various lyrics. Folk stories usually include a predictable set of phrases (e.g., "Once upon a time") and actions (e.g., the antagonist challenges the protagonist, then the protagonist defeats the challenger). These stories follow predictable plot lines, with recurring themes. Folk stories also evoke vivid imagery and intense emotions, which help the storyteller (and the listeners) envision the characters and events. The stories center on plot, as the setting is either ambiguous (e.g., "Long ago and far away") or unvarying. These stories usually rely on a set of somewhat stereotyped characters with relatively predictable behavior. Whatever the form of folk information, however, it must be exciting—or at least attention getting—or listeners will not learn and retain the folk-lore. The information must be as simple and concise as possible. As **Zora Neale Hurston** said, "Folklore is the boiled-down juice, or pot-likker, of human living."

Within the oral tradition, oral literature serves important functions: communal sharing of an experience, entertainment and diversion, shared understandings of communal history and religious beliefs, moral and social education, and safe opportunities to flout social conventions and cultural taboos. Oral literature takes a wide variety of forms: very brief forms (e.g., **proverbs**, riddles, and jokes), poems (e.g., rhymes, verse narratives), chants and songs (e.g., lullabies, ballads, work songs), realistic short stories and anecdotes, and various folktales.

There are many variations within each type of folktale, and the various forms of folktales often overlap. In *myths*, deities and demigods use superhuman powers to create the universe and all the habitants of it. In *folk epics*, *legends*, and *tall tales*, a hero (e.g., John Henry, Odysseus, Robin Hood) who lacks superhuman powers still manages to accomplish seemingly impossible feats. *Fairy tales* and *märchen* are unbelievable fantasies involving magical assistance, such as from fairy godmothers, golden-egg-laying geese, or Jack's amazing beans. The most common *animal tales* are **trickster tales** and fables. *Fables* are brief moralistic or cautionary stories in which animal characters speak and act like humans. *Formula tales* follow a predictable pattern. These include *cumulative tales*, in which the storyteller continually adds new elements to a base statement or phrase (e.g., "The House That Jack Built"); *endless stories*, in which the story action is repeated—endlessly; *catch stories*, in which the story seems to be proceeding down one predictable path, when suddenly the story ends in a surprising—and usually humorous—way; and *dilemma tales*, in which the storyteller sets up a tricky situation or problem and invites the listeners to supply the ending or solution.

Africa has a particularly rich oral literature, at least in part because there was no written language in most of sub-Saharan Africa until the nineteenth century. Exceptions include Ge'ez (Ethiopia), Arabic (Saharan Africa), Swahili (East African coast), and Arabic-influenced Hausa writing (parts of Nigeria, Niger, and Chad). Christian missionaries spread the written word in the rest of Africa during the nineteenth century, chiefly using the Latin alphabet and European languages (e.g., English, French). For the most part, distinctive written literature didn't emerge in sub-Saharan Africa until after World War II. Even now, African illiteracy rates are still extremely high, so the power of the oral tradition remains great.

Many African peoples use *praise names* (elaborate descriptions of revered personages), myths, trickster tales, legends, songs, proverbs, and riddles. Other oral literature includes dance-stories, chants, magical spells, incantations, and divinations. Throughout Africa, oral literature is closely linked to music and rhythm (e.g., the "talking drum"). Storytelling and singing also often involve a call-and-response form, in which the narrator frequently elicits the participation of the listeners in a back-and-forth interaction.

Starting in the 1500s and continuing into the 1800s, west Africans were captured, enslaved, and brought to the Americas. The captives were forced to leave behind their belongings, their names, and even their identities. Their only remaining possession was their folklore. As **Ralph Ellison** observed, they had *rites*, not *rights*. Over time, the African Americans adapted their traditional lore to suit their new environment and their new life circumstances. Myths about how the giraffe got its long neck disappeared, and tales about tricksters undermining cruel oppressors gained popularity. In America, various African cultures blended and interacted with Native-American and European-American cultures. As Christianity spread among the slaves, they adapted biblical stories to their circumstances, particularly finding solace in the stories of Moses leading his people—Jews enslaved in Egypt—to the promised land in Israel.

African story types, plots, characters, themes, and storytelling styles mutated and changed, and new stories and story forms emerged. Whatever their modifications and variants, however, these stories retained a distinctively African-American flavor. For one thing, these stories have a definite oral character, with distinctive story sounds, vocal inflections, pauses, whispers, and roars. They highlight rhythm and often feature ear-pleasing music and rhyme. Vivid metaphors and similes help listeners picture the stories being told. Many stories also retain the call-and-response interaction of narrator and listeners. Through frequent call-and-response interactions of storytellers and listeners, improvisation has emerged, and spontaneous verbal cleverness has been prized.

Through their oral literature, slaves were able to preserve their own cultures and beliefs, affirm their own perceptions and experiences, and create their own identities and self-definitions, separate from their oppressors. African-American literature has included proverbs, trickster tales, jokes, folk epics, folk sermons and testimonials, ghost stories, story-songs such as blues ballads, and legends, myths, and tall tales of heroes (e.g., John Henry) and scoundrels (e.g., Stagolee), some realistic (e.g., Harriet Tubman) and some mythical (e.g., High John the Conqueror).

A distinctively African-American oral form is the toast, traditionally a male form of literature. *Toasts* are highly stylized dramatic narratives comprising a long series of rhyming couplets, with a definite rhythm and meter—usually four stressed syllables per line in each couplet. Toasters gain prestige by being entertaining and establishing dominance in verbal skill. They use active verbs and vivid imagery to regale their listeners with stories of bad characters (e.g., Stagolee and the Signifying Monkey) who exhibit tremendous sexual prowess, great physical strength, brutal aggression, and sneaky treachery, using any means to get whatever they want.

Related to toasts are *boasts,* in which the narrator brags of his own sexual prowess, physical strength, aggressive ability and readiness, and other masculine characteristics, offering autobiographical evidence of these traits. When competing narrators add insulting put-downs and challenges to their boasts, they are *sounding.* Typical put-downs may be mild challenges (e.g., "Let the door hit you where the good Lord split you"), direct insults (e.g., "You so stupid you don't believe fat meat is greasy"), or metaphorical threats (e.g., "Your ass is grass, and I'm the lawnmower").

To escalate the competition, however, speakers *play the dozens,* derogating one another's family members. As **Maya Angelou** said in her *All God's Children Need Traveling Shoes* (1986), "Blacks concede that hurrawing, jibing, jiving, signifying, disrespecting, cursing, even outright insults might be acceptable under particular conditions, but aspersions cast against one's family call for immediate attack." For instance, a player might say, "Yo' mama so short she can sit on a sheet of paper and swing her legs." More aggressive insults refer to sexual acts. Typically, adolescent males boast, sound, and play the dozens, but girls, women, and adult men may also do so.

Men and women, boys and girls may engage in signifying. *Signifying* communicates indirectly, usually signaling insults and criticism without explicitly stating them. Signifying exalts verbal power over economic and physical power. Humor is important in signifying, as signifiers communicate not only the insult, but also a sense of shared understanding among a community of listeners. Variations of signifying include *loud-talking* (in which the speaker talks so loudly to a primary listener that others can overhear, thereby embarrassing the primary listener), *jiving* (playful conversations using distinctively African-American vernacular foreign to European Americans), *rapping* (lively, highly stylized conversation, usually intended to persuade listeners), and *marking* (mocking someone's words or mannerisms).

Related to signifying is *masking,* in which a speaker hides his or her true intentions, attitudes, feelings, thoughts, beliefs, and abilities from listeners. Masking provides an excellent complement to signifying, in that the speaker can mask the truth from one listener (such as a slave owner or other person in authority), while signifying to other listeners who overhear the communication (e.g., fellow slaves or other African Americans). Masking and signifying have been vital means of hiding and re-

vealing messages in oppressive circumstances. Literary examples of masking include Ralph Ellison's grandfather character in *Invisible Man* (1952), who advises his grandson to "overcome 'em with yeses"; **Paul Laurence Dunbar**'s poem "We Wear the Mask," in which the masker "grins, lies, hides our cheeks, and shades our eyes"; and **Charles Waddell Chesnutt**'s passing and conjuring stories, **Langston Hughes**'s *Not Without Laughter,* and **Richard Wright**'s *Uncle Tom's Children.*

Because African-American slaves were barred from learning to read and write, they continued to prize the oral tradition despite being immersed in a culture that prized written language. They preserved their histories and their literature through word of mouth. Distinctively African-American music and oral literature emerged. By the dawn of the twentieth century, a distinctive African-American written literature also emerged. Paul Laurence Dunbar's poems (e.g., *Oak and Ivy,* 1893) and Charles Waddell Chesnutt's short stories (e.g., *The Conjure Woman,* 1899) were steeped in African-American folklore. Decades later, Zora Neale Hurston (*Mules and Men,* 1935) studied and described African-American folklore of the South. Hurston illustrated what she had learned in her novel *Their Eyes Were Watching God* (1937), which she filled with proverbs, signifying, playing the dozens, trickster tales, folk wisdom and wit, and folksy patterns and styles of speech (e.g., mock call-and-response among multiple narrators). (Her 1934 *Jonah's Gourd Vine* similarly highlights African-American folklore.) Other writers of the **Harlem Renaissance** shared her appreciation of African-American oral literature as fundamental elements in their own works (e.g., Langston Hughes, *The Weary Blues,* 1926; **James Weldon Johnson**, *God's Trombones,* 1927; **Jean Toomer**, *Cane,* 1923; Richard Wright, *Native Son,* 1940).

Subsequently, many other writers have drawn on the wealth of African-American oral tradition in their written literature: **James Baldwin** (*Go Tell It On the Mountain,* 1952), **Toni Cade Bambara** (*The Salt Eaters,* 1980), Ralph Ellison (*Invisible Man,* 1952), **Ernest Gaines** (*The Autobiography of Miss Jane Pittman,* 1971), **Paule Marshall** (*Praisesong for the Widow,* 1983), **Toni Morrison** (*Song of Solomon,* 1977; *Tar Baby,* 1981; *Jazz,* 1992), **Gloria Naylor** (*Mama Day,* 1988), **Ntozake Shange** (*sassafras, cypress & indigo,* 1982), **Alice Walker** (*The Temple of My Familiar,* 1989; *Possessing the Secret of Joy,* 1992), **Sherley Anne Williams** (*Dessa Rose,* 1986), and others. Children's works also frequently reflect the oral foundation of written literature, such as Verna Aardema's (1975) *Why Mosquitoes Buzz in People's Ears;* Phillis Gershator's (1994) *The Iroko-Man: A Yoruba Folktale;* and **Virginia Hamilton**'s (1985) *The People Could Fly: American Black Folktales.*

Increasingly, written records accompany—or even replace—the oral tradition as a means of communicating and preserving important information. Nonetheless, in the workplace, within the family, and in neighborhoods, gossip, stories, sayings, anecdotes, and lore continue to be *told*: "Did I tell you what Johnnetta did?" "You'll never guess what happened to me today!" Some things simply don't translate easily from spoken to written language. For instance, how can an author write down distinctive sounds such as the "tst, tst, tst" of the tongue tip swiftly sucked away from the back of the teeth? Would a standup comic's joke be funny without the comic's vocal expression and facial gestures? Would playgoers pay so much to see a play if reading the script had the same emotional impact? Increasingly, new communications technologies are being added to written ones, but it's probably not time yet to predict the end of the oral tradition. In fact, with *YouTube*, podcasts, web-cams, and other video and audio formats available through the Internet, the oral tradition may overtake written culture in some ways and among some people.

REFERENCES: *AP. AP&W. EBLG. MSD-CD (AHD-3). NAAAL.* "Aesop," "Fables," and "Folklore," in *WB-98.* "African arts" and "Folk arts," in *EB-98.* "African literature," "African religion," and "Folklore," in *G-96.* "African literature" and "Tutuola, Amos," in *MSE-CD.* "African literature," in *WCE-CD.* "Folk literature" and "Folklore," in *MWEL.* "Folklore," in *BRE.* "Folklore," in *OCWW.* "Folklore," "Folktale," "Oral transmission," in *AHL.* "Folklore," "Mythology," and "Native American religions," in *E-98.* "Humor," in *OCAAL.* Lowe, John, and Theodore O. Mason, Jr., "Signifying," in *OCAAL.* Olson, Ted, "Folklore," in *OCAAL.* Peters, Pearlie, "Masking," in *OCAAL.*

Organizations, Clubs, and Collectives
Antebellum–present

The key organizations, clubs, and collectives included as main entries in this dictionary are, in approximate order of their founding, the Woman's Era Club (1893-1903?, described in the entry on **Josephine Ruffin**), **American Negro Academy** (1897-1924), **Quill Club** (1925-1930?), **Black Opals** (late 1920s), **Harlem Writers Guild** (1950-), Umbra Workshop (1962-1963, listed under its literary journal, *Umbra*), **Free Southern Theater (FST)** (1963-1979), **OBAC, Organization of Black American Culture** (1967-), **Combahee River Collective (CRC)** (1974-1980), **National Association of Black Journalists (NABJ)** (1975-present), **Affrilachian Poets** (1991-), and **Cave Canem** (1996-). In addition, information on **Oprah's Book Club** may be found in the entry on **Oprah Winfrey.** Many other organizations would be worthy of separate entries (e.g., the Dark Room Collective, the Furious Flower Conferences, Krigwa, the Langston Hughes Society, the Last Poets, the Louder Arts poets, the Nuyorican Poets Cafe), but regret- tably, time and space constraints do not permit their inclusion in this edition.

Ormes, "Jackie" (née Zelda Jackson)
8/1/1917–12/26/1985
Comic strip; visual artist, journalist

On May 1, 1937, "Torchy Brown in Dixie to Harlem" first appeared as a comic strip in the *Pittsburgh Courier.* Although this was the first comic strip to feature an African-American female, it was not the first work of Jackie Ormes to appear in that newspaper. Ormes had started on the paper's staff about a year earlier, contributing feature articles and pieces of art. Unlike her creator, Torchy was born and raised on a farm in Dixie and migrated to New York to make it big in show business. In later strips, however, Torchy decided to become a newspaper reporter, rather emulating her creator. In any case, Torchy may have been naïve, but she sure wasn't helpless or stupid. With wit and plucky independence, she made her way in the world (despite frequent encounters with male chauvinism and white racism).

While in Pittsburgh, Ormes had started art school, and when she and her husband Earl made a new home in Chicago in the early 1940s, she continued her schooling at the Art Institute of Chicago and got a job reporting for the *Chicago Defender.* Pretty soon, she had developed a new strip for her new locale: "Patty Jo 'n' Ginger," about a pair of sisters, featuring their experiences with educational segregation and inequality, with sexism and gender issues, and with political issues of the day (e.g., the unprovoked murder of Emmett Till). The sisters were soon being published in African-American newspapers across the land, making Ormes the first African-American woman cartoonist to be nationally syndicated. (*See* **Barbara Brandon** for the first African-American woman to have her cartoon nationally syndicated in mainstream white-owned papers.) After a while, the popularity of Ormes's strip was so great that she even made a few bucks on some dolls based on the two sisters. In the late 1960s, rheumatoid arthritis forced Ormes to stop drawing her popular strip, but she still remained active in Chicago community activities.

REFERENCES: *BAAW.* Brown, Elsa Barkley, in *BWA:AHE.*
—Tonya Bolden

Editor's note: *AANB* gives her birthdate as 8/1/1911, citing the Social Security Death Index, but the year of her birth has been noted elsewhere as 1910, 1917, and 1918, as well. Her death date has been listed as December 26, 1985 and as January 2, 1986.

REFERENCES: *AANB. CAO-1998. Wiki.*

Osbey, Brenda Marie
12/12/1957–
Poems; librarian, educator

Osbey's poetry and essays have appeared in numerous periodicals (e.g., *Callaloo, Obsidian*), and her poetry has been collected in *Ceremony for Minneconjoux* (1983, 86 pages), *In These Houses* (1988, 63 pages), and *Desperate Circumstance, Dangerous Woman: A Narrative Poem* (1991, 96 pages), and her American Book Award-winning *All Saints: New and Selected Poems* (1997, 128 pages), about her native New Orleans. Her other awards include the Loring-Williams Prize from the Academy of American Poets (1980); the Associated Writing Program award (1984); fellowships from the National Endowment for the Arts (1990), the MacDowell Colony (1984), and the Millay Colony (1986); and inresidence opportunities at Marion County, Kentucky (1986-1987) and Southern University (1999-2001). Even her prose is poetic, as in this casual observation about a bookshop: "There is a smell that permeates antiquarian book shops that is unmistakable. It is the smell not only of parchment and leather, of ink and goldleaf and mildew sometimes. No. It is the smell also of the passage of time. Antiquarian book dealers are, in fact, dealers in time." This observation and others can be found in "Writing Home" (2008), her autobiographical essay offering personal insights through her narrative about her family origins, her life experiences, and her literary mentors.

REFERENCES: *AANB. CAO-02. LFCC-07.* Brice-Finch, Jacqueline, in *APSWWII-3.* Lowe, John. "An Interview with Brenda Marie Osbey. *The Southern Review.* 30.4 (Autumn 1994) p. 812. From *Literature Resource Center.* COCAAL and OCAAL. Osbey, Brenda Marie. "Writing Home." *The Southern Literary Journal.* 40.2 (Spring 2008) p. 19. From *Literature Resource Center.* //www.amazon.com.

FURTHER READING: *EAAWW.*

Owen, Chandler
4/5/1889–1967?
Nonfiction—political issues; journalist

Owen coedited (with **A. Philip Randolph**) *The Messenger,* a socialist pro-union magazine, after which he worked as managing editor of *The Chicago Bee,* a less radical African-American newspaper. He also wrote a pamphlet encouraging African Americans to fight in World War II (*Negroes and the War*), distributed in the millions by Democrat Franklin D. Roosevelt's U.S. Department of War, and Owen wrote numerous speeches for Republican Party politicians (including presidential candidates such as Dwight Eisenhower).

REFERENCES: *AAL. EA-99.*

FURTHER READING: *AANB. Wiki.* Adams, Luther, in //www.blackpast.org/, //www.blackpast.org/?q=aah/owen-chandler-1889-1967.

~P~

Packer, ZZ (Zuwena)
1/12/1973–
Short stories; educator

ZZ Packer earned a B.A. from Yale University (1994), an M.A. from Johns Hopkins University (1995), an M.F.A. from the Iowa Writers' Workshop of the University of Iowa (1999), and was named a Wallace Stegner Fellow in Fiction at Stanford University (1999). She is also listed as a Truman Capote fellow and a Jones Lecturer at Stanford (*CAO-07*). During the 2007-2008 school year, she was Writer-in-Residence at Tulane University's English Department Creative Writing Program (Fall 2007) and the Lurie Distinguished Visiting Professor of Creative Writing at San Jose State University (Spring 2008). She has also served on the faculty of the California College of the Arts, as a Senior Visiting Professor of Creative Writing.

Meanwhile, Packer attracted grants for her writing, including the Rona Jaffe Writers Foundation Grant (1997), the highly lucrative Whiting Writers' Award for fiction from the Ms. Giles Whiting Foundation (1999), and the Bellingham Review Award for her short story "Brownies" (1999). She started the new millennium highly productively: Her short story "Drinking Coffee Elsewhere" appeared as Debut Fiction in the *New Yorker* (2000), and several other stories were published in *Seventeen, Harper's,* and *Ploughshares,* as well as in the anthology *The Best American Short Stories* (2000). Emboldened, Packer collected "Brownies" and seven other stories in *Drinking Coffee Elsewhere* (2003), earning praise from critics in *The New York Times, Harper's,* and numerous other periodicals. Pulitzer- and National Book Award-winning novelist John Updike personally chose it for his Today Book Club on NBC's *Today Show* (June 2003); it was named The New York Times Notable Book and nominated for the PEN/Faulkner Award for Fiction

(2004). Soon after, Packer won an esteemed Guggenheim Fellowship in fiction (2005). She has since been invited to edit 20 stories in the anthology *New Stories from the South: The Year's Best* (2008). Her major current project is a novel, said to be about the African-American "Buffalo Soldiers" who served in the post-Civil War U.S. Army.

REFERENCES: *CAO-07. Wiki.* "Letters: ZZ Packer Travels in Time." *Talk of the Nation* (Mar. 18, 2008), *Literature Resources from Gale.* //en.wikipedia.org/wiki/Whiting_Writers_Award. //news.stanford. edu/news/2008/september24/books-092408.html. //www.answers.com/ topic/brownies-story. //www.answers.com/topic/brownies-story-1. //www.answers.com/topic/brownies-story-2. //www.answers.com/topic/ brownies-story-3. //www.answers.com/topic/brownies-story-4. //www. answers.com/topic/brownies-story-5. //www.answers.com/topic/ brownies-story-6. //www.answers.com/topic/brownies-story-7. //www. answers.com/topic/brownies-story-8. //www.barnesandnoble.com/ writers/writer.asp?cid=1069496&userid=18KS2DILFG&qu=1. //www.barnesandnoble.com/writers/writerdetails.asp?cid=1069496#in terview. //www.clpgh.org/books/booklists/africanamericanfiction.html. //www.stanfordalumni.org/news/magazine/2004/mayjun/red/awards.ht ml. Amazon.com.

FURTHER READING: Foster, Guy Mark, in *GEAAL.*

Page, Clarence
6/2/1947–
Columns, essays, articles; journalist

While still a teenager, before starting college, Page did freelance writing and photography for the *Middletown Journal* and the *Cincinnati Enquirer.* While earning his B.S. in journalism (1969) at Ohio University, he reported on civil-rights and antiwar issues for the university's student newspaper, and just before his senior year he interned for the *Dayton Journal-Herald.*

After graduation, Page got a job as reporter and then assistant city editor for the *Chicago Tribune* (1969-1980). During that time, Page took a nonoptional two-year break to serve in the military (1970-1971). After returning to the *Tribune,* he collaborated on a Pulitzer Prize-winning *Tribune* task force writing a series on voter fraud (1972); he earned the Edward Scott Beck Award for his coverage of South African politics (1976); and he won an Illinois United Press International award for a series of investigative reports (1980). While at the paper, he married his *Tribune* colleague Lenita McClain.

In 1980, Page left print journalism for broadcast journalism at Chicago's WBBM-TV (1980-1984), and soon after, Page and McClain amicably divorced. Meanwhile, he freelanced for several print outlets. In 1984, McClain committed suicide, entrusting Page with her writings. Her death left the *Chicago Tribune* short-handed, and he was lured back there as a member of the editorial board and a semiweekly columnist. Two years later, he edited and introduced Lenita McClain's collected writings in *A Foot in Each World: Essays and Articles* (1986), published by Northwestern University Press. The following year, Page won the American Civil Liberties Union's James P. McGuire Award for his columns on constitutional rights (1987); his column was nationally syndicated; and he married Lisa Johnson.

Two years later, about the end of April, Page was told he had become the first African-American columnist to win the Pulitzer Prize for Commentary (1989). Two months later, he and Lisa celebrated the birth of their only son, Grady Johnson Page. Two years later, Page moved his family to Washington, D.C., where he works out of the *Tribune's* D.C. bureau (since 1991). Meanwhile, he has continued doing freelance writing for numerous periodicals. In broadcast media, Page often appears on TV news shows, such as on ABC's *Nightline*, PBS's *The McLaughlin Group*, NBC's *The Chris Matthews Show*, and Black Entertainment Television's weekly *Lead Story*. He also offers occasional commentary on National Public Radio's *Sunday Morning Edition* and on PBS's *NewsHour*. He also hosted the PBS documentary *Closing the Achievement Gap* (2004) and other PBS documentaries.

For anyone lacking a television, a radio, or a newspaper in which Page's column appears, his writing may also be found in *Showing My Color: Impolite Essays on Race and Identity* (1996). Page also produced another collection of McClain's work, *What Killed Lenita McClain?: Essays on Living in Both Black and White Worlds*. In addition to his journalism awards, Page has received honorary doctorates from numerous Midwestern colleges and universities.

REFERENCES: *AANB. CAO-07. Wiki*. Glickman, Simon, in *BB*. Amazon.com. //www.chicagotribune.com/news/columnists/chi-clarencepage,0,3614106,bio.columnist. //www.pulitzer.org/awards/1989. Amazon.com.

Painter, Nell (née Irvin)

8/2/1942–

Scholarly, biography, nonfiction—history; educator

While working toward her B.A. in anthropology, cum laude, from the University of California at Berkeley (1964), Nell Irvin took a year to study French medieval history at France's University of Bordeaux (1962-1963). In 1965, she married Colin Painter and became Nell Irvin Painter, even after the couple divorced. Ms. Painter then studied at the University of Ghana's Institute of African Studies (1965-1966) and was a lecturer in French at the Institute of Languages (1964-1965). She earned her M.A. in African History at the University of California at Los Angeles (1967). Within two years, she went back to school again, this time as a Teaching Fellow in Afro-American studies (1969-1970) and in history (1972-1974) at Harvard University, while she earned her Ph.D. in American history.

With her doctorate in hand, Painter became an assistant professor (1974-1977) of history at the University of Pennsylvania, then a resident associate of Afro-American studies at the W. E. B. Du Bois Institute at Harvard University (1977-1978). She then spent two years as an associate professor (1978-1980) before becoming a full professor of history at the University of North Carolina (UNC) at Chapel Hill (1980-1988). While still at UNC, she took time out to be the Russell Sage Visiting Professor of History at Hunter College of the City University of New York (CUNY) (1985-1986). Painter's next move was to Princeton University, where she became a professor of history (1988-1991), then the Edwards Professor of American History (1991-2000), and then professor emeritus (since 2000). She also served as the acting director (1990-1991) and later the director (1997-2000) of the program in African American Studies.

Meanwhile, she married Glenn R. Shafer (in 1989), but her writings have continued to appear under her earlier married surname. Her first book, *Exodusters: Black Migration to Kansas after Reconstruction* (1976; 2nd ed., 1986/1992), was named a Notable Book of the Year by *The New York Times Book Review* and a History Book Club selection. Her second, *The Narrative of Hosea Hudson: His Life as a Negro Communist in the South* (1979/1993) was also named a Notable Book of the Year by *The New York Times Book Review*. Her other books include *The Progressive Era* (1984) and *Standing at Armageddon: The United States, 1877-1919* (1987; reissued as *Standing at Armageddon: A Grassroots History of the Progressive Era*, 2008), which was also named a Notable Book of the Year by *The New York Times Book Review* and won the Letitia Brown Book Prize of the Association of Black Women Historians.

Painter's essay "Soul Murder and Slavery: Toward a Fully Loaded Cost Accounting" (1995) won the Brown Article Prize of the Association of Black Women Historians, and her next book, **Sojourner Truth**: *A Life, A Symbol* (1996/2008), was selected by both the Book of the Month Club and the History Book Club, and it won the Nonfiction category of the Black Caucus of the American Library Association. Next, Painter collected many of her essays in *Southern History Across the Color Line* (2002), including her "Soul Murder" piece and her introduction to her *Hosea Hudson* book. Painter's *Creating Black Americans: African American History and Its Meanings, 1619 to the Present* (2005), which was given the Gustavus Myers Center Outstanding Book Award, offers not only text, but also artwork by African-American artists.

Painter's *The History of White People* was due out in March of 2010 as this dictionary went to press, and a second book, *Personal Beauty: Biology or Culture?*, is said to be forthcoming. In addition, Painter edited the *Narrative of Sojourner Truth: A Bondswoman of Olden Time, with a His-*

tory of Her Labors and Correspondence Drawn from Her Book of Life (1998) and **Harriet Jacobs**'s *Incidents in the Life of a Slave Girl* (2000), both for Penguin Classics. She is also a member of several editorial boards and contributes to both periodicals and anthologies.

Her awards and honors are too numerous to mention here (see her c.v. at //www.nellpainter.com/cv.html), but a few may deserve mention here, such as fellowships from the Ford Foundation (1971-1972), the Radcliffe Institute (1976-1977), the John Simon Guggenheim Foundation (1982-1983), the National Endowment for the Humanities (1992-1993), and an honorary doctorate from Yale University.

REFERENCES: *AANB. CAO-06. Wiki.* Kalfatovic, Mary, in *BB.* //worldcat.org/identities/lccn-n79-27041. //www.nellpainter.com/ cv.html. //www.nellpainter.com/publications/books_authored.html. //www.nellpainter.com/publications/books_edited.html. //www.pbs.org/ moyers/journal/02292008/profile2.html. Amazon.com.

Park, Robert E. (Ezra)
2/14/1864–2/7/1944
Nonfiction—urban sociology, textbooks; journalist

After graduating from the University of Michigan (1887), Park went to work as a newspaper reporter in Detroit, New York City, and some other big cities, spending the next 11 years closely scrutinizing how people behave in urban environments. With philosopher and educator John Dewey and others, he later founded the short-lived newspaper *Thought News*, dedicated to providing indepth coverage and analysis of serious contemporary social issues. In the late 1890s, Park took graduate coursework from Dewey (at the University of Michigan), from psychologist and philosopher William James (at Harvard University, from which he earned a master's degree in 1899), and from sociologist Georg Simmel (in Heidelberg, Germany, where he earned a Ph.D.). With his doctorate in hand, Park returned to the United States and taught at Harvard (1904-1905), at the University of Chicago (1914-1933), and at Fisk University in Nashville (1936-1943). In the interim between teaching at Harvard and at the University of Chicago, he became secretary of the Congo Reform Association and wrote two articles about Belgian colonial oppression of the Congolese. Through that association, he got to know **Booker T. Washington**. When he turned his attention to Americans of African descent, he became Washington's secretary and is believed to have ghostwritten most of Washington's *The Man Farthest Down* (1912).

At the University of Chicago, Park led the prestigious Chicago school of sociology, where he shaped the field and guided the research in that discipline. In that role, he and Ernest E. Burgess wrote their landmark textbook, *In-troduction to the Science of Sociology* (1921), which was later updated and revised. He also guided the thinking of many of his students, such as **Charles Spurgeon Johnson**. With his background in psychology and philosophy, he fostered a multidisciplinary approach to sociology and popularized (and perhaps even coined) the terms *human ecology*, referring to both the physical and the moral and social environment in which humans live; and *collective behavior*, referring to the actions of people in groups, which often differ from their behavior as individuals. Park also wrote numerous journal and magazine articles and essays, many of which were collected and published posthumously in three volumes: *Race and Culture, Human Communities,* and *Society* (1950-1955, edited by Everett C. Hughes et al.). Park's other books include *The Principles of Human Behavior* (1915) and *The Immigrant Press and Its Control* (1922).

REFERENCES: *EB-98. G-97.* Marx, Gary T., in *WB-99.*

FURTHER READING: *B. BCE. Wiki.* Coser, Lewis A. (1977). "Robert Ezra Park, 1864-1944." *Masters of Sociological Thought: Ideas in Historical and Social Context.* Harcourt Brace Jovanovich, Publishers. Rpt. in Jennifer Gariepy (Ed.), (1998), *Twentieth-Century Literary Criticism* (Vol. 73, pp. 257-383). Detroit: Gale Research. From *Literature Resource Center.* Elsner, Henry, Jr. (1972). "Introduction." In Henry Elsner, Jr. (Ed.), *Robert E. Park: The Crowd and The Public and Other Essays.* The University of Chicago Press. Rpt. in Jennifer Gariepy (Ed.), (1998), *Twentieth-Century Literary Criticism* (Vol. 73, pp. vii-xxv). Detroit: Gale Research. From *Literature Resource Center.* Goist, Park Dixon. (1977). "A Sociologist and The City: The Experience of Robert Park." *From Main Street to State Street: Town, City, and Community in America.* Kennikat Press Corp. Rpt. in Jennifer Gariepy (Ed.), (1998), *Twentieth-Century Literary Criticism* (Vol. 73, pp. 110-120). Detroit: Gale Research. From *Literature Resource Center.* Turner, Ralph H. (1967). "Introduction." In Ralph H. Turner (Ed.), *Robert E. Park: On Social Control and Collective Behavior.* The University of Chicago Press. Rpt. in Jennifer Gariepy (Ed.), (1998), *Twentieth-Century Literary Criticism* (Vol. 73, pp. ix-xlvi). Detroit: Gale Research. From *Literature Resource Center.* Velazquez, Sheila, in *CAO-03.*

Parker, Pat (née Patricia Cooks)
1/20/1944–6/4/1989
Poems, performance poetry, lesbian and gay literature; publisher, health-care center director

While still in her teens, Pat Cooks left her parents' home in Texas and moved to California, where she attended Los Angeles City College and worked odd jobs. She then moved north to the Bay Area and attended San Francisco State College (now University) for a while. Between 1962 and 1966, she married playwright **Ed Bullins**, wrote poems, gave her first poetry reading, divorced Bullins, married writer Robert Parker, and continued to work on her poetry. She also worked in a series of service jobs and writing-related jobs.

As the 1960s drew to a close, Parker started regularly reading her poetry to women's gatherings at counterculture bookstores, coffeehouses, and feminist consciousness-raising events. By the end of the 1960s, Pat divorced Robert Parker, had her first intimate relationship with a woman, and realized that she was a lesbian—not necessarily in that order. In 1969, Parker worked with a lesbian feminist collective, helping to found an all-female publishing company, the Women's Press Collective (WPC), in Oakland. The WPC published Parker's first two collections, *Child of Myself* (1972) and *Pit Stop* (1974). Two years later, Olivia Records released the audio recording *Where Would I Be Without You: The Poetry of Pat Parker and Judy Grahn* (1976), also a WPC poet.

In 1978, Parker was named director of the Oakland Feminist Women's Health Center (1978-1989), a post she held until breast cancer prevented her from doing so. That same year, vandals destroyed the WPC's equipment, effectively putting it out of business. Fortunately, the commercial feminist publisher Diana Press published Parker's *Womanslaughter* (1978). *Womanslaughter* was Parker's outraged response to the murder of her older sister by her sister's husband, for which he was sentenced to one year in a work-release program. Diana Press also published Parker's comprehensive *Movement in Black: The Collected Poetry of Pat Parker, 1961-1978* (1978; expanded ed., Firebrand Books, 1999). Firebrand Books published her final collection, *Jonestown and Other Madness* (1985). Meanwhile, Parker contributed to numerous periodicals and anthologies.

In recognition of her contributions, the National Women's Studies Association (NWSA) offers a Pat Parker Memorial Poetry Award, and two decades after Parker's death, Berkeley was still hosting an annual memorial tribute to Parker (early 2009). In New York, The Pat Parker/Vito Russo Center Library honors the names of Parker and fellow writer, Vito Russo.

REFERENCES: *AAW:PV. CAO-00. Wiki.* Beaulieu, Elizabeth Ann (Ed.). 2006. *Writing African American Women: K-Z* (pp. 692-693). Westport, CT: Greenwood Publishing Group. Castro, Ginette, and Elizabeth Loverde-Bagwell (Eds.). 1990. *American Feminism: A Contemporary History* (p. 251). New York: NYU Press. Escamilla, Brian, in *BB.* //en.wikipedia.org/wiki/Firebrand_Books. //en.wikipedia.org/wiki/Judy_Grahn. //voices.cla.umn.edu/vg/Bios/entries/parker_pat.html. //www.berkeleydaily.org/issue/2009-01-29/article/32121?headline=Poetry-Events-Honor-Pat-Parker-Feature-Adnan-and-Fraser. //www.lesbianpoetryarchive.org/book/export/html/27. //www.ncrw.org/digest/umaryland.htm. Amazon.com.

FURTHER READING: *EAAWW.* Beemyn, Brett, in *GEAAL.*

Parks, Sr., Gordon
11/30/1912–3/7/2006
Novels, autobiographies, screenplays, documentary scripts, nonfiction books-photography; photographer, filmmaker, visual artist, composer

For most people, Parks's accomplishments as a photographer would be sufficient to merit claiming a lifetime of satisfying achievement. The same could be said about his writing, his filmmaking, his painting, and even his composing. Parks's writings include his books on photography (*Flash Photography*, 1947; *Camera Portraits: Techniques and Principles of Documentary Portraiture*, 1948); his best-selling autobiographical novel (*The Learning Tree*, 1963/1987); his collection of essays and photographs (*Born Black*, 1970); six collections of poetry and photographs (*Gordon Parks: A Poet and His Camera*, 1968; *Gordon Parks: Whispers of Intimate Things*, 1971; *In Love*, 1971; *Moments without Proper Names*, 1975; *A Star for Noon—An Homage to Women in Images Poetry and Music*, 2000; and *Eyes With Winged Thoughts: Poems and Photographs*, 2005); his collection of his photographs, his poems, and his paintings (*Glimpses Toward Infinity*, 1996); his second (nonautobiographical) novel (*Shannon*, 1981); a biography of J. M. W. Turner (*The Sun Stalker*, 2003); and five autobiographies (*A Choice of Weapons*, 1966/1986; *To Smile in Autumn: A Memoir*, 1979; *Voices in the Mirror: An Autobiography*, 1990/2005; *Half Past Autumn: A Retrospective*, 1998; and *A Hungry Heart*, 2005/2007). Parks even provided illustrations for a children's book written by Ann Parr, *Gordon Parks: No Excuses* (2006).

In addition to the photographs featured in his books, his photographs have appeared in nearly every prestigious magazine, including fashion magazines such as *Vogue* and *Glamour,* as well as the ultimate lifestyles magazine *Life.* His musical compositions include a libretto and music for a five-act ballet titled *Martin,* which aired on national TV on King's birthday, as well as several pieces performed by symphony orchestras around the country and many musical scores for his films. Some of his films have been documentaries: *Diary of a Harlem Family* and *Mean Streets,* both made in the 1960s; and biographies **Leadbelly** (1976, on the folk-music legend), *Flavio* (1978, on impoverished Brazilian boy Flavio da Silvia), *The Odyssey of Solomon Northrup* (1984, about a freeborn man who was kidnapped in 1841 and enslaved for 12 years), and of course, *Gordon Parks: Moments without Proper Names* (1988). Parks's first nondocumentary film was *The Learning Tree* (1968, Warner Brothers), adapted from his autobiographical novel of the same name. This film made him the first African American to produce, direct, and script a major Hollywood movie, and in 1989 the National Film Registry of the Library of Congress named it among the 25 most significant films in America. Parks also knew how to make commercially successful films: *Shaft* (1971, featuring Richard Roundtree), *Shaft's Big Score* (1972), and *The Super Cops* (1974).

On December 7, 1934, Gordon Parks, Jr., entered the lives of Parks and his wife, Sally Alvis. Junior worked as a camera operator on several of Senior's films, and as an adult, Junior started making his own films, virtually creating the blaxploitation genre with his film *Superfly* (1972), which grossed more than $24.8 million at the box office. After producing three more feature films in this country, Junior moved to Kenya, where he tragically died in a plane crash April 3, 1979.

After the Senior Parks's death (3/7/2006), Michelle Norris of National Public Radio recalled an earlier interview in which Parks had said, "I think curiosity is what has helped me and I just think that 90 percent of us don't pursue the things that we could possibly do well in. Some people say, oh, I wanna write a novel. I say, well, why don't you sit down and write it? You know. That's the way my first novel popped up."

REFERENCES: *AANB. AE. B. BAWPP. BCE. CAO-06. CE. F. MWEL. SMKC. Wiki.* Aguiar, Marian, "Parks, Sr., Gordon" and "Parks, Jr., Gordon," in *EA-99.* Ball, Jane, *AAFW-55-84.* Bianco, David, and Pat Donaldson, in *BB.* Erickson, Hal, *All Movie Guide, Dir.* "Gordon Parks, Photographer, Filmmaker, Dies at 93." (Mar. 7, 2006). *All Things Considered.* From *Literature Resource Center.* Houston, Helen R., in *BH2C.* McDaniels, Pellom, III, in *GEAAL.* "Pioneering Photographer Gordon Parks Dies at 93." (Mar. 8, 2006). *Talk of the Nation.* From *Literature Resource Center.* Schultz, Elizabeth, in *COCAAL, OCAAL,* and *PE.* Watkins, Mel. "Renaissance Photographer." *The New York Times Book Review* (p. 7). Rpt. in *Literature Resource Center.* Detroit: Gale. Amazon.com.
—Tonya Bolden

Parks, Suzan-Lori
5/10/1963–
Plays; educator

The distinctive spelling of her first name arose from a typo. As she later explained, "When I was doing one of my first plays in the East Village, we had fliers printed up and they spelled my name wrong. I was devastated. But the director said, 'Just keep it, honey, and it will be fine.' And it was" (quoted in *Wiki*). "'Who am I?' [is] the question at the very center of every one of my plays. Who am I? I'm not just Suzan-Lori Parks, ... It's all those who came before me'" (quoted in "The Possession of Suzan-Lori Parks," 2000).

Parks's plays include *The Sinner's Place* (1984), *Fishes* (1987), *Betting on the Dust Commander* (1987/1990), Obie Award for Best New American Play-winning *Imperceptible Mutabilities in the Third Kingdom* (1989), *The Death of the Last Black Man in the Whole Entire World*

(1990/1992), *Greeks (or The Slugs)* (1990, a short work from *Imperceptible*), *Devotees in the Garden of Love* (1991/1992), *The America Play* (1992/1994), Obie Award for Playwriting-winning *Venus* (1996/2001), *In the Blood* (1999/2001), *F****** A* (2000/2003), Pulitzer Prize for Drama-winning *Topdog/Underdog* (2001), and *Ray Charles Live!* (2001). Probably her most ambitious task was her series *365 Days/365 Plays* (2006-2007), the result of her self-appointed task of writing one play each day from November 13, 2002 through November 12, 2003. With her producing partner Bonnie Metzgar, she coordinated productions that launched November 13, 2006, and eventually included more than 700 theatres across the United States and Canada. Parks has also written three radio plays: *Pickling* (1990), *Third Kingdom* (1990), and *Locomotive* (1991). Many of her plays have been published, such as *The America Play and Other Works* (1994, which also includes *The Death of the Last Black Man in the Whole Entire World*), *Venus* (1998), *Imperceptible Mutabilities in the Third Kingdom* (2000), *Red Letter Plays* (2000, including *In the Blood* and *F****** A*), *Topdog/Underdog* (2004), and *365 Days/365 Plays* (2006).

In addition to the Pulitzer Prize and the two Obies, Parks's playwriting has earned her two NEA fellowships (1990, 1991), a New York Foundation for the Arts grant (1990), a Rockefeller Foundation grant (1990), a Whiting Writers' Award (1992), a grant from the W. Alton Jones Grant Kennedy Center Fund for New American Plays (1994), a Lila-Wallace/Reader's Digest Award (1995), a Guggenheim fellowship (2000), a PEN-Laura Pels Award for Excellence in Playwriting (2000), the prestigious John D. and Catherine T. MacArthur Foundation "genius grant" (2001), and the Eugene McDermott Award in the Arts from the Council for the Arts (2006). Further, her *In the Blood* was nominated for a Pulitzer Prize for Drama, and her *Topdog/Underdog* was nominated for Drama Desk Award for Outstanding New Play and a Tony Award for Best Play.

In addition, Parks has written several screenplays. Her *Girl 6* (1996) became a **Spike Lee** movie. She has also written screenplays for Jodie Foster and Danny Glover, as well as *Anemone Me* (1990), for Apparatus Productions. For **Oprah Winfrey**'s Harpo Productions, Parks has written the film screenplay for *The Great Debaters* (2007, with Robert Eisele), as well as ABC television screenplay adaptations of **Zora Neale Hurston**'s *Their Eyes Were Watching God* (2005, with Misan Gagay and Bobby Smith, for ABC) and of **Toni Morrison**'s *Paradise*. At the end of 2003, Parks discontinued her work for Disney Theatricals on her libretto for *Hoopz*, a musical about the Harlem Globetrotters.

Parks tackled a new form when she wrote *Getting Mother's Body: A Novel* (2003). As one might expect for an award-winning playwright, critics lavish praise on her dialogue and her narrative, but they also praise her ability to weave a diverse assortment of characters into a novel with "easy grace and infectious rhythms." To support her literary and theatrical artistry, Parks has also resided and taught at several colleges and universities (e.g., Yale School of Drama), most recently as director of the writing for performance program at the California Institute of the Arts (since 2000). In a 2004 essay, Parks wrote, "I don't know if writers have things to say as much as writers, at least in my case, are possessed by things. Writing it down is the only way to get it out of your system. It's like having the flu, and to get rid of the flu you have to write it down. That's why I write" (January, *The Writer*). Her advice to aspiring writers: "First, keep at it. . . . You're a writer if you put the time in, and if you have the desire. . . . believe that if you have the desire to write, that's what you should be doing . . . . If you really love it, chances are you'll get better at it."

REFERENCES: *AANB. CAO-05. NYPL-AADR. Wiki.* Garrett, Shawn-Marie. "The Possession of Suzan-Lori Parks." *American Theatre* 17.8 (Oct. 2000): pp. 22-26. Rpt. in Timothy J. Sisler (Ed.), (2004), *Drama Criticism* (Vol. 23). Detroit: Gale. From *Literature Resource Center.* Kanter, Jodi, in *T-CAD-5th*. Langer, Adam. "The New Multitasker: Suzan-Lori Parks (Ten to Watch in 2003)." *Book* (January-February 2003), p. 44. From *Literature Resource Center.* Minderovic, Christine Miner, in *BB.* Parks, Suzan-Lori. *The Writer.* 117.1 (Jan. 2004) p. 66. From *Literature Resource Center.* Pearce, Michele. "Alien Nation: An Interview with the Playwright." *American Theatre.* 11.3 (Mar. 1994) p. 26. From *Literature Resource Center.* Smith, Wendy. "Words as Crossroads: Suzan-Lori Parks (Interview)." *Publishers Weekly.* 250.19 (May 12, 2003) p. 37. From *Literature Resource Center.* Walat, Kathryn. "These Are the Days: Suzan-Lori Parks's Year of Writing Dangerously Yields 365 Plays." *American Theatre.* 23.9 (Nov. 2006) p. 26. From *Literature Resource Center.* Wilmer, S.E. "Restaging the Nation: The Work of Suzan-Lori Parks." *Modern Drama.* 43.3 (Fall 2000) p. 442. From *Literature Resource Center.* Young, Harvey, in *GEAAL.* //www.nytimes.com/2000/12/29/movies/on-stage-and-off-half-court-press-for-hoopz.html?sec=&spon=&pagewanted=1. //www.playbill.com/news/article/83566.html. Amazon.com.

FURTHER READING: *EAAWW.*

Parsons (common-law husband's surname), Lucy Gonzalez
3/?/1853–3/7/1942
News articles, editorials, spoken word—oratory

Parsons's heritage included African, Mexican, and Native-American (Creek) ancestry, and she felt a deep sympathy for all peoples who suffered oppression of any kind, particularly economic oppression. Her 1871 interracial marriage to Albert Parsons forced her to flee from Texas to Chicago. In 1886, her labor-activist husband was arrested, tried, and eventually executed (1887) for his alleged conspiracy to incite the Haymarket Riot. Parsons continued to write articles against lynchings and other racist violence several years before **Ida B. Wells-Barnett** did so. In addition to writing articles for several leftist periodicals, she edited and published *Freedom: A Revolutionary and Anarchist-Communist Monthly* (1892). In 1905, she helped found the Industrial Workers of the World (IWW) and started editing the *Liberator,* which championed the IWW in Chicago. Even in her 80s, Parsons continued to advocate for the downtrodden, inspiring noted Chicago writer Studs Terkel to take up their cause.

REFERENCES: *AANB. B. EA-99. Wiki.* Kelley, Robin D. G., in *BWA:AHE.* Moore, Melissa, in *ARRW-2.* //womenshistory.about.com/od/aframerwriters/tp/african_american_women_writers.htm.

Patterson, Lillie
5/3/1917–3/11/1999
Biographies, juvenile fiction and nonfiction; media librarian, teacher

Patterson published more than two-dozen books, most of them for juveniles (chiefly readers in grades 4-6). Her biographies include *Francis Scott Key: Poet and Patriot* (1963), *Sun Queen: A Novel About Nefertiti* (1967), *Sequoyah: The Cherokee Who Captured Words* (1975), *David, the Story of a King* (1985), and biographies of celebrated African Americans, such as **Booker T. Washington** (1962), **Frederick Douglass**: *Freedom Fighter* (1965/1981), *Sure Hands, Strong Heart: The Life of Daniel Hale Williams* (1981), **Oprah Winfrey**: *Talk Show Host and Actress* (1990, with C. H. Wright), and **A. Philip Randolph**: *Messenger for the Masses* (1996). Patterson's **Martin Luther King, Jr.**: *Man of Peace* (1969) won the **Coretta Scott King** Author Award, and three of her books earned the Coretta Scott King Author Honor: *Coretta Scott King* (1977), **Benjamin Banneker**: *Genius of Early America* (1978), and *Martin Luther King, Jr. and the Freedom Movement* (1989/1993; originally *Martin Luther King, Jr. & the Montgomery Bus Boycott,* 1988). Before Patterson's death, she was said to be working on a biography of **James Weldon Johnson**. Her other nonfiction includes *The Book Of Three Festivals* (1961), *Meet Miss Liberty* (1962), *Halloween* (1963), *Birthdays* (1965), *Easter* (1966), *Lumberjacks of the North Woods* (1967), *Christmas Feasts and Festivals* (1968), *Christmas in America* (1969), and *Christmas in Britain and Scandinavia* (1970). Her fiction includes *The Grouchy Santa* (1979), *Haunted Houses on Halloween* (1979), *The Jack-O'Lantern Trick* (1979), *Janey, the Halloween Spy* (1979), and *Christmas Trick or Treat* (1979). She also edited *Poetry for Spring* (1973).

REFERENCES: *CAO-00.* Smith, Karen Patricia, in *COCAAL* and *OCAAL.* //www.ala.org/ala/emiert/corettascottkingbookaward/cskpastwinners/alphabeticallist/cskalphabetical.cfm#au. Amazon.com.

Patterson, Orlando
6/5/1940–
Novels, scholarly works, nonfiction—history

A native of Jamaica, educated at Kingston University and at the London School of Economics, in 1971, Patterson was awarded an honorary degree from Harvard University, where he also teaches. Patterson's first novel was *The Children of Sisyphus* (1964/1986), "now required reading in Jamaica" (Amazon.com review, May 5, 1998) and named the best novel in English at the Dakar Festival of Negro Arts (1965). His next two novels were *An Absence of Ruins* (1967) and *Die the Long Day* (1972). His scholarly works include *The Sociology of Slavery: An Analysis of the Origins, Development, and Structure of Negro Slave Society in Jamaica, 1655-1838* (1967), *Ethnic Chauvinism: The Reactionary Impulse* (1977), *Slavery and Social Death: A Comparative Study* (1982/1985), *Freedom* (Vol. 1: *Freedom in the Making of Western Culture*, 1991, National Book Award; Vol. 2: *Freedom in the Modern World*, 1993/2008), *The Ordeal of Integration: Progress and Resentment in America's "Racial" Crisis* (1997), *Rituals of Blood: Consequences of Slavery in Two American Centuries* (1998), and *Chronology of World Slavery* (1999, with Junius Rodriguez). His awards include Commonwealth scholarships (1962-1965), National Endowment for the Humanities grants (1973, 1978, 1981, 1983), a Guggenheim fellowship (1978-1979), the American Political Science Association's Ralph Bunche Award for best scholarly work on pluralism (1983, cowinner for *Slavery and Social Death*), and the American Sociological Association's Distinguished Contributor to Scholarship Award (formerly the Sorokin Prize) (1983).

REFERENCES: *AANB. BAWPP. CAO-05. OC20LE. Wiki.* Patterson, Orlando. *Commentary.* 105.3 (Mar. 1998) p. 43. From *Literature Resource Center.* Rosen, Isaac, in *BB.* Amazon.com, 7/1999, 4//2009.

Patterson, Raymond R.
12/14/1929–4/5/2001
Poems, column; educator

To earn a living, Patterson taught English both to junior-high-school students (1959-1968) and to college students (at the City University of New York, 1968-1992). To satisfy his passion, Patterson wrote poems, many of which were published in periodicals and anthologies. His poems were collected in *Dangerous River* (1954/1990), *Get Caught: A Photographic Essay* (1964, with Lawrence Sykes), *Twenty-six Ways of Looking at a Blackman and Other Poems* (1969), *The Elemental Blues: Poems 1981-1982* (1983/1994), and *Elemental Bliss* (1989). Stanza "XXIII" of the title poem in *Twenty-six Ways* highlights his gift: "By moonlight / We tossed our

pebbles into the lake / And marveled / At the beauty of concentric sorrows. / You thought it was like the troubled heart / Of a blackman, / Because of the dancing light." He also wrote a weekly syndicated column on African-American history, "From Our Past" (1960-1962). James Madison University awarded him its Furious Flower Lifetime Achievement Award in Literature; he earned two grants from the National Endowment for the Arts (1969-1970); and he was the third vice president of the poetry Society of America.

REFERENCES: *BAWPP. CAO-02. LFCC-07. VBAAP.* Bostian, Patricia Kennedy, in *GEAAL.* Amazon.com.

Patterson, William
8/27/1891–3/5/1980
Nonfiction—political issues, autobiography; labor leader, attorney, political activist

Patterson wrote articles and edited such communist newspapers as the *Daily Record* and the *Daily Worker.* In 1951, he and **Paul Robeson** petitioned the United Nations, accusing the United States of genocide, and the same year, he edited the book *We Charge Genocide: The Crime of Government Against the Negro People.* Two decades later, he published his autobiography, *The Man Who Cried Genocide* (1971).

REFERENCES: Schmidt, Jalane, in *EA-99.*
FURTHER READING: *AANB. CAO-03. Wiki.*

Payne, Daniel A. (Alexander)
2/24/1811–11/2/1893
Poems, nonfiction—history; educator

A lifelong learner who pursued a self-directed program of study, Payne opened his first school in 1829 in South Carolina, when he was just a teenager himself, teaching youths during the day and adults during the evenings. He continued teaching until the mid-1830s, when the state legislature passed a law prohibiting anyone from teaching slaves to read or write. With his school outlawed, in effect, Payne moved to Gettysburg, Pennsylvania, where he studied at the Lutheran Seminary. By 1837, however, his failing eyesight forced him to leave school. Despite the abbreviation of his education, he was licensed to preach, and in 1839, a synod of the Lutheran Church ordained him as its first African-American minister. Unable to serve a Lutheran parish, Payne briefly ministered to a Presbyterian Church in New York, then he returned to Pennsylvania and opened a church in Philadelphia in 1840. When he was still unable to find a Lutheran parish to shepherd, he became a minister (and later a bishop) of the African Methodist Episcopal (AME) Church in 1841, although he did not readily warm to the less intellectual and more emotional style of most AME services. For years, Payne traveled from place to place, establishing churches and schools. During those years, Payne published his poetry collection, *The Pleasures and Other Miscellaneous Poems* (1850), most of which focused on the need for "moral purity" and "holy virtue." Among his most affecting poems were tributes to his wife and daughter, both of whom had died in the late 1840s, and a poem celebrating emancipation in the West Indies in 1838.

In 1863, Payne had raised enough money to purchase Wilberforce University, in Xenia Ohio, from the Methodist Episcopal Church, and to establish it as an AME institution. That done, Wilberforce became the first U.S. college governed by African Americans, and Payne became the first African American to preside over the college. Raising funds and attracting faculty and students dominated his early years there. By 1876, the school was established academically and financially, and he resigned as president but stayed on as chancellor.

In his later years, Payne wrote *Treatise on Domestic Education* (1885), on his experiences as an educator, and his massive *History of the African Methodist Episcopal Church* (1891, two vols.), which he had started more than four decades earlier. Even his autobiography, *Recollections of Seventy Years* (1888), was largely theological and historical, including detailed descriptions of the AME Church, the abolition movement among African Americans, and the civil and social activism of African Americans during the Reconstruction era (to 1888). Also, about eight decades after his death, his sermons and other addresses were gathered in *Sermons and Addresses, 1853-1891* (1972).

REFERENCES: *EA-99.* Carson, Sharon, in *COCAAL* and *OCAAL.*

FURTHER READING: *AANB. BAWPP. Wiki.* Walker, Billie E. "Daniel Alexander Payne Murray (1852-1925), Forgotten Librarian, Bibliographer, and Historian." *Libraries & Culture.* 40.1 (Winter 2005). From *Literature Resource Center.* //www.lib.uchicago.edu/efts/AAP/AAP.bib.html. //www.lib.virginia.edu/digital/collections/text/ch_afam_poetry.html.

Payne, Ethel L. (Lois)
8/14/1911–5/28/1991
Nonfiction, column; journalist

As the Washington, D.C., correspondent for the *Chicago Defender* during the 1950s, Payne covered many historic events from our nation's capital. She considered herself an "advocacy journalist," rather than an objective reporter, never hesitating to press the high and the mighty for social and political progress. She also so-

journed to the deep South whenever she needed to cover critical civil-rights events, such as the Montgomery bus boycott; the desegregation of Central High School in Little Rock, Arkansas; and demonstrations in Birmingham, Alabama, in 1963. Although her advocacy had prompted President Dwight Eisenhower to avoid her questions in Washington press conferences, they led President Lyndon Johnson to invite her to attend his signing of the 1964 Civil Rights Act and the 1965 Voting Rights Act. In the late 1960s and the 1970s, Payne reported on her travels to Vietnam; Nigeria, Zaire, and many other African nations; the People's Republic of China; and Mexico. In addition to her work for the *Defender*, she was a commentator for a thrice-a-week network news broadcast (1972-1982) and wrote a nationally syndicated column.

REFERENCES: Streitmatter, Rodger, in *BWA:AHE.*

FURTHER READING: *AANB. Wiki.* Saunders, Shellie M., in *BB.* //members.nabj.org/pr060502.html.

Paynter, John H.
?/1862–1947
Memoirs, fiction; civil servant

Paynter's memoirs serve as bookends to his life experiences and his change in perspective: In his first memoir, *Joining the Navy, or Abroad with Uncle Sam* (1895), he seldom says much about the racial discrimination he experienced in the navy, but in his final memoir, *Horse and Buggy Days with Uncle Sam* (1943), he angrily deplores the racial persecution he endured during his nearly 40 years in the Treasury Department. Paynter also wrote a travel book, *Fifty Years After* (1940, about his travels abroad and his experiences in Washington, D.C.), and a historical novel, *Fugitives of the Pearl* (1930/1970).

REFERENCES: *BAWPP.* Carson, Sharon, in *COCAAL* and *OCAAL.*

Pennington, James W. (William) C. (Charles) (né Jim Pembroke)
?/1807–1870
Essays, slave narrative, spoken word—oratory, sermons, lectures; cleric, abolitionist, social activist, educator

In 1828, Pennington fled from slavery in Maryland and found his way to the home of a Pennsylvania Quaker, who taught him to read and write. Soon after, he moved to Long Island, New York, where he blacksmithed by day and attended school at night. In 1834, Pennington moved still farther north, to New Haven, Connecticut, where he audited classes at Yale and pastored a local Congregational church. For a time, he contributed articles to the *Colored American,* and when it folded, he founded and edited his own *Clarksonian* newspaper for a short time. Wherever he was, Patterson constantly sought ways to help fellow African Americans, through aid societies and through teaching and preaching. In fact, it was Pennington who performed the wedding ceremony for Anna Murray and **Frederick Douglass** on September 15, 1838, a dozen days after Douglass had escaped from slavery. Pennington also helped fellow abolitionists to free the mutineers of the *Amistad* slave ship.

Pennington published his slave narrative, *The Fugitive Blacksmith, or Events in the History of James W. C. Pennington* (1849), just before passage of the 1850 Fugitive Slave Act, which made it easy to recapture and return runaways from anywhere in the nation. Fortunately, several of Pennington's associates banded together to formally purchase his freedom from the estate of his former "owner" for $150. The narrative was serialized in the *Afro-American* in 1859. Although Pennington's best-known literary work is his slave narrative, that was not his first published book. His first book, *A Text Book of the Origin and History . . . of Coloured People* (1841), was intended to be used as a guide for teachers, to help them to enlighten, inform, and uplift their students with knowledge of their distinctive history. In addition, several of his sermons, abolitionist lectures, and other addresses were published as pamphlets.

REFERENCES: *AANB*. *Wiki*. Gardner, Eric, in *GEAAL*. Wilson, Charles E., Jr., in *COCAAL* and *OCAAL*. //academic.sun.ac.za/forlang/bergman/real/amistad/history/msp/bio_penn.htm. //www.gutenberg.org/browse/authors/p#a5872. //www.spartacus.schoolnet.co.uk/USASpennington.htm.

Perkins, Eugene (aka Useni Eugene Perkins)
9/13/1932–

Poems, plays, nonfiction essays and books, anthologies, musical; social worker

At age 10, on seeing **Paul Robeson** portray the title character in Shakespeare's *Othello*, Perkins decided he wanted to become a writer, and at age 11, he published his first poem (in the *Chicago Tribune*). During high school, he edited his school's newspaper, in which he published his own poems, essays, and short plays. Even after earning his master's degree and starting his career as a social worker, he continued to write poems and other works. His poetry collections include *An Apology to My African Brother: And Other Poems* (1965), *Black Is Beautiful* (1968), *West Wall* (1969), *Silhouette: Poems* (1970), *When You Grow Up: Poems for Children* (1982/1989), *Midnight Blues in the Afternoon and Other Poems* (1984), *Hey Black Child: and Other Children's Poems* (2003), and *Memories & Images: Selected Poems* (2003).

Perkins has also edited the poetry anthologies *Black Expressions: An Anthology of New Black Poets* (1967), *Dark*

Meditations: A Collection of Poems (1971), and *Poetry of Prison: Poems by Black Prisoners* (1972). Perkins's *Poetry from the Masters: The Black Arts Movement* blends poetry and biography, offering an anthology of representative poetry, as well as biographies of the key poets of that era. His other nonfiction addresses his lifelong concern with urban underprivileged youths, including *Home Is a Dirty Street: The Social Oppression of Black Children* (1975/1991), *Harvesting New Generations: The Positive Development of Black Youth* (1987; 2nd ed., 2005), *Explosion of Chicago's Black Street Gangs: 1900 to Present* (1987), and *Afrocentric Self-Discovery Workbook for Black Youth* (1991), a brief workbook written for young adults ages 12-15 years. Perkins is also the editor and publisher of Free Black Press, which published many of his poetry books. For a time, Perkins also published and edited *Black Child Journal* (ca. 1980-1996) and edited *Successful Black Parenting Magazine* (ca. 1995-1997). He has practiced parenting himself, as well: He and his wife, Janis, (married, 1969) raised their three children, Julia, Russell, and Jamila Saran.

Perkins has also used fiction to engage youths, having written *Black Fairy and Other Plays for Children* (1993/2008). Overall, he has written 6 musicals (e.g., *The Black Fairy*, 1974/1976), and 19 other stage plays, including *Turn a Black Cheek* (1965), *The Legacy of Leadbelly* (1966), *Assassination of a Dream* (1967), *Thunder Is Not Yet Rain* (1968), *Nothing but a Nigger* (1969), *Black Is So Beautiful* (1970), *Cry of the Ghetto* (1970), *Fred Hampton* (1970/1975), *The Image Makers* (1973), *It Can Never Be in Vain* (1973), *Brothers* (1974), *God Is Black, but He's Dead* (1974), *Our Street* (1974), *Professor J. B.* (1973), *Cinque* (1975), *Quinn Chapel* (1975), and *Pride of Race* (1984), as well as *Maternity Ward*. Perkins's *Ghetto Fairy* (later *The Black Fairy*) won the 1972 Special Award from the Council on Interracial Books for Children. For his body of work, he was inducted into the Literary Hall of Fame for Writers of African Descent in Chicago (1999), and February 25, 1999, was proclaimed Useni Eugene Perkins Day in Chicago.

REFERENCES: *BAWPP*. *CAO-02*. Greene, Michael, in *AAP-55-85*. Kich, Martin, in *GEAAL*. Toombs, Charles P., in *COCAAL* and *OCAAL*. //www.aafp.org/fpr/sept96/blkparnt.html. //www.doollee.com/PlaywrightsP/PerkinsEugene.htm. //www.etacreativearts.org/classes/instructor_bios.html. //www.highbeam.com/doc/1P2-10615802.html. //www.thehistorymakers.com/biography/biography.asp?bioindex=423. //www.writeanalysis.com/press.asp. Amazon.com.

Peterson, Louis (Stamford)
6/17/1922–4/27/1998

Television and film scripts, plays; stage actor, educator

Peterson's highly celebrated *Take a Giant Step* (1953) was performed 76 times at Broadway's Lyceum Theater, starring Louis Gossett, Jr., before it closed; starting in 1956, it had an additional 264 Off Broadway performances. Peterson's other plays include *Entertain a Ghost* (1962), *Crazy Horse* (1979), and *Another Show* (1983). At the time of his death, Peterson was cowriting a musical, *Numbers*, with Ken Lauber. In addition, he wrote screen adaptations of his *Take a Giant Step* (1958, with Julius Epstein) and of *The Tempest* (1957, with Alberto Lattuada). He also wrote television screenplays during the 1950s and early 1960s for such then-popular dramas as *Wagon Train* and *Dr. Kildare*. After devoting decades to the theater, Peterson turned to professing theater arts at the State University of New York at Stony Brook, from which he retired in the 1990s.

REFERENCES: *BAWPP. CAO-03.* W. Carter, Steven R., in *AAW-40-55.* Smith, Virginia Whatley, in *COCAAL* and *OCAAL*.

Ann Petry

Petry, Ann (née Lane)
10/12/1908–4/28/1997

Novels, short stories, children's nonfiction and fiction books, essays; reporter, columnist

Ann's childhood home rested atop her father's drugstore in Old Saybrook, Connecticut, an almost-all-white New England town. Ann longed to be a writer, but instead, she dutifully earned her pharmacology degree in 1931 and spent several years working in her family's drugstore, writing unpublished short stories in her spare time. Her life changed, however, when she met and married George Petry, who whisked her away to Harlem in 1938.

In Harlem, Ann focused on writing. She started out reporting for the *Amsterdam News*, then switched to the *People's Voice*. There, she also edited the women's page and then wrote a weekly column, "The Lighter Side," about the goings-on of Harlem's upper middle class.

Meanwhile, Petry studied creative writing at Columbia University and started submitting her stories to magazines. Though she frequently faced rejection, with persistence, some of her stories were eventually published in **Phylon** and **Crisis**. One of her *Crisis* stories earned her a chance to compete for a Houghton Mifflin Literary Fellowship Award. The first five chapters of her first novel, *The Street*, won her the $2,400 fellowship in 1945.

When Houghton Mifflin published *The Street*, the critically acclaimed 1946 novel quickly made Petry the first African-American woman to write a book selling more than a million copies. Petry's vividly crafted main character, Lutie Johnson, a working-class African-American mother of an eight-year-old son, dreams of escaping Harlem's violence, street crime, economic exploitation, and psychological despair. Tragically, poverty, sexism, and racism prevent her escape. Although Lutie's story ended tragically, it transformed Petry's career felicitously. Reissued at least twice, the novel has sold close to 2 million copies to date and is still considered Petry's best-known novel and an American literary classic.

Petry's second novel, *The Country Place* (1947), turns away from urban, mostly black Harlem and returns to white-dominated small-town New England. Petry's novella *Darkness and Confusion* was also published that year, and the following year, the Petrys returned to Old Saybrook, where they raised their only daughter. For the next several years, Petry wrote short stories, as well as her third novel, *The Narrows* (published in 1953).

Petry also wrote children's books, including *The Drugstore Cat* (1949); **Harriet Tubman**, *Conductor on the Underground Railroad* (1955); *Tituba of Salem Village* (1964); and *Legends of the Saints* (1970); as well as her short-story collection *Miss Muriel and Other Stories* (1971). Her novels and juvenile works have been widely translated, and her poems, short stories, and essays have been widely anthologized. Petry's short stories and essays have appeared in national magazines such as *The New Yorker*, *Redbook*, and the *Horn Book*.

Petry's work and talent have been recognized in various ways, including honorariums, lectureships, and honorary doctorates at several universities, as well as placement in various *Who's Who* guides since the 1970s.

REFERENCES: *1TESK. AANB. AA:PoP. BASS. BAWPP. BFC. BV. BWA. CAO-03. EB-98. EBLG. HR&B. LDW. MAAL. MWEL. NAAAL. OC20LE. RT. W. Wiki.* Alexander, Sandra Carlton, in *AAW-40-55.* Brennan, Carol, in *BB.* Ervin, Hazel Arnett, in *COCAAL* and *OCAAL.* Hoeness-Krupshaw, Susanna, in *GEAAL.* Holladay, Hilary. (1996). "Author's Works. Ann Petry." *Twayne's United States Authors Series 667.* New York: Twayne Publishers. From *The Twayne Authors Series. OCWW.* Miller, Leah, in "A Unit of African American Mystery Writers and Their Works," //www.coe. ohio-state.edu/beverlygordon/834/miller.html. Mobley, Marilyn Sanders, in *AAW-1991.* Rosenmeier, Rosamond. (1996). "Chapter 1: Ann Petry, Neighborhood Novelist." In Hilary Holladay (Ed.), *Twayne's United States Authors Series 667.* New York: Twayne Publishers. From *The Twayne Authors Series.*

FURTHER READING: *EAAWW.*

Pharr, Robert Deane
7/5/1916–4/1/1992
Novels, short stories

Robert Deane Pharr attended St. Paul's Normal and Industrial School (now St. Paul's College) in Lawrenceville, Virginia (1933) and then Lincoln University in Pennsylvania (1934) before earning his B.A. at Virginia Union University (1939), where he was the feature editor of the school's newspaper. Pharr went on to do postgraduate studies at Fisk University, and he wrote a play that won a nationwide contest. His hopes for the future looked bright, but tuberculosis and alcoholism impeded his progress.

By the late 1940s, the chief work he could find was as a waiter at posh resort hotels and private clubs. Meanwhile, he returned to writing in his off hours. By the mid 1960s, he had finished his first novel and was in search of a publisher. Luckily, someone at Columbia University's faculty club, where he was working, helped him make connections with a publisher. In 1969, Doubleday published Pharr's *The Book of Numbers* (1969; London, 1970; reprinted by University Press of Virginia, 2001). The protagonist of *The Book of Numbers*, David Greene, is a smart African-American man living in the black section of a small Southern city; Greene makes his living in the "numbers" game, operating a small lottery business. Critics praised the work for its believable story with authentic dialogue. The publisher printed more than 10,000 hardcover copies of the book, and Avon eventually printed 300,000 copies. In 1973, Avco Embassy released a film adaptation of the book.

Doubleday soon published Pharr's second book, *S.R.O.* (1971; reprinted by Norton, 1998). Pharr set the book in a Harlem S.R.O., where impoverished men and women find refuge from homelessness. Critics and book buyers liked this book less, but three more of Pharr's novels found their way into print: *The Welfare Bitch* (1973), *The Soul Murder Case: A Confession of the Victim* (1975),

and *Giveadamn Brown* (1978/1997). In addition, a short story of Pharr's, "The Numbers Writer," has been reprinted, both in a periodical and republished in at least one anthology. Pharr also received grants from the Rockefeller Foundation, the New York State Council on the Arts, and other funders of the arts.

REFERENCES: *BAWPP. CAO-03.* Scott, Daniel M., III, in *COCAAL.* Yarborough, Richard, in *AAFW-55-84.* //worldcat.org/identities/lccn-n50-47687. Amazon.com.

FURTHER READING: Yost, David, in *GEAAL.*

Phillips, Carl
7/23/1959–
Poems; educator

Phillips has always had a distinctive perspective as an outsider: The son of a biracial couple, Phillips spent his early years moving annually with his family, wherever his father, an Air Force medic, was asked to go. He also realized early that he has a special gift for connecting with others. As an adolescent living in Zweibrücken, Germany, he realized he could easily acquire new languages. Back in the States, he became proficient in Latin and Greek, and he majored in these classical languages at Harvard. While there, he also worked on *The Harvard Advocate* literary magazine, he started writing poetry, and then he graduated magna cum laude (1981). He continued to write poetry while teaching high-school Latin and earning two master's degrees (in classical studies and in creative writing). In 1993, Phillips started professing English and African and Afro-American Studies at Washington University (St. Louis, Missouri), where he has also directed the Creative Writing Program (1996-1998, 2000-2002). He also feels at home in his Provincetown, Massachusetts, writing studio.

Phillips's celebrity springs from his finely crafted free-verse poems. About his preference for tercets, he has said, "Tercets are the shortest odd-numbered stanzas and make for unevenness. If you refuse to close any stanzas, that forces the eye down the page. And when that's combined with an unusual syntax, there's a kind of seduction where meaning can't be reached without propelling yourself forward over several stanzas. Bits of the final meaning are given, but because most of the sentences are inflected, there's a sense that satisfaction can't be reached, that meaning isn't clear until the very end. And it seems to work, since the things I write about don't seem to be realistically resolvable" (quoted in "*PW* Talks to Carl Phillips").

Phillips's critically acclaimed poetry collections include *In the Blood* (1992), winner of the 1992 Samuel French Morse Poetry Prize; *Cortége: Poems* (1995), nominated for a National Book Critics Circle Award and for the Lambda Literary Award for Gay Poetry; *From the De-*

votions: Poems (1997/2002), nominated for the National Book Award for poetry; *Pastoral: Poems* (2000), winner of the 2001 Lambda Literary Award for Gay Poetry; *The Tether: Poems* (2001), winner of the Kingsley Tufts Poetry Award; *Rock Harbor: Poems* (2002); *The Rest of Love: Poems* (2004), also nominated for the National Book Award for poetry and awarded the Theodore Roethke Memorial Foundation prize and the Thom Gunn Award for Gay Male Poetry; *Riding Westward: Poems* (2006); *Quiver of Arrows: Selected Poems, 1986-2006* (2007); and *Speak Low: Poems* (2009). After his second National Book Award nomination, Phillips humbly noted, "At some level, it means that my work is not only being read, but is also being deemed worthy of particular attention. But I also know that there are many deserving, excellent poets at work, and that not everyone has the good fortune to have their work recognized. The nomination reminds me . . . to be grateful. I'm grateful each time I can write a poem" (quoted by S. K. McGinn, 10/27/2004).

While still the U.S. Poet Laureate, Robert Pinsky chose Phillips for a Witter Bynner Foundation fellowship from the Library of Congress (1997-1998), calling Phillips "a tremendously gifted poet" who has the "unmistakable voice and subject, rhythm and cadence of an original writer" (quoted in //news-info.wustl.edu/sb/page/normal/143.html). Phillips has earned numerous other awards, too: at least one Pushcart Prize, a Guggenheim Foundation grant (1998), an Award for Literature from the American Academy of Arts and Letters (2001), induction into the American Academy of Arts and Sciences (2004), and a James Merrill fellowship from the Academy of American Poets (2006), which named him its Chancellor.

Phillips's poems have been published in at least eight of the annual series *The Best American Poetry* (e.g., 1994, 1995, 1996, 2000, 2001, 2002) and other anthologies, and his translations, essays, and poems have appeared in various periodicals, such as the prestigious *Atlantic Monthly, Kenyon Review, The New Yorker, Paris Review,* and *Yale Review.* He also published a translation of Sophocles's *Philoctetes* (2003) and an essay collection, *Coin of the Realm: Essays on the Art and Life of Poetry* (2004).

REFERENCES: *AANB. CAO-08. LFCC-07. VBAAP. Wiki.* Helfrich, Karen. "Symbolic Changes: Interview with Carl Phillips." *Lambda Book Report.* 6.9 (Apr. 1998) p. 15. From *Literature Resource Center.* Hennessy, Christopher. "About Carl Phillips." *Ploughshares.* 29.1 (Spring 2003) p. 199. From *Literature Resource Center.* Lewin, Jennifer. "PW Talks to Carl Phillips." *Publishers Weekly.* 246.49 (Dec. 6, 1999) p. 71. From *Literature Resource Center.* McGinn, Susan Killenberg. (10/27/2004). "Poet Carl Phillips Is Finalist for National Book Award," in //news-info.wustl.edu/news/page/normal/4156.html. Shepherd, Reginald, in *GEAAL.* //news-info.wustl.edu/sb/page/normal/143.html. //www.amazon.com, 3/2000, 4/2009. //www.cavecanempoets.org/pages/programs_faculty.php. //www.poets.org/poet.php/prmPID/247.

FURTHER READING: "Carl Phillips, Coin of the Realm." *Ploughshares.* 30.2-3 (Fall 2004) p. 215. From *Literature Resource Center.* "Carl Phillips, Quiver of Arrows." *Ploughshares.* 33.2-3 (Fall 2007) p. 219. From *Literature Resource Center.* Dabydeen, Cyril. "Carl Phillips. The Rest of Love." *World Literature Today.* 80.3 (May-June 2006) p. 73. From *Literature Resource Center.* Hammer, Langdon. "The Leaves Rush, Greening, Back: Carl Phillips." *American Scholar.* 75.4 (Autumn 2006) p. 58. From *Literature Resource Center.*

Phylon
1940–

This scholarly review was founded in 1940 by **W. E. B. Du Bois**, who served as its editor until 1944. *Phylon*, which primarily focuses on the social sciences, was founded on the principle that the idea of "race" is a social, cultural, and historical construct and not based on biological or psychological differences among people. *Phylon* broadened its readership by the inclusion of poetry, fiction, and book reviews, and it still continues to make an important contribution to African-American cultural studies.

REFERENCES: *COCAAL* and *OCAAL.* —Lisa Bahlinger

William Pickens

Pickens, William
1/15/1881–4/6/1954
Essays, articles, autobiographies, fiction

In addition to writing numerous provocative and outspoken articles for *Voice of the Negro* (starting in 1904), Pickens wrote two autobiographies (*Heir of Slaves,* 1911; greatly expanded to create the much more strident

Bursting Bonds, 1923), a collection of essays (*The New Negro: His Political, Civil and Mental Status,* 1916), and a somewhat preachy fiction work (*The Vengeance of Gods and Three Other Stories of the Real American Color Line,* 1922).

REFERENCES: *BAWPP.* Andrews, William L., in *COCAAL* and *OCAAL.*

FURTHER READING: *AANB.* //www.routledge-ny.com/ref/harlem/thematic.html.

Pickett, Wilson
3/18/1941–1/19/2006
Songs; musician

Starting at age 15, Pickett wrote some of the songs his band made popular, such as "I Found a Love" (1962), "Mustang Sally," and "It's Too Late." In 1991, he was elected to the Rock and Roll Hall of Fame.

REFERENCES: Tuttle, Kate, in *EA-99.*

FURTHER READING: *AANB. D. Wiki.* Unterberger, Richie, *All Music Guide, Art.*

Pietri, Pedro Juan
3/21/1943–3/3/2004
Poems, plays; educator, performer

A United States resident since 1947, Afro-Puerto Rican poet and playwright Pietri started writing poetry in high school. After high school, he worked some odd jobs before being drafted into the Army and sent to fight the Vietnam War. After returning, he wrote his celebrated *Puerto Rican Obituary* (1971; *Obituario Puertorriqueño,* 2000), a response to his experiences during the Vietnam War. Since then, he published several more poetry collections, including *Traffic Violation* (1973/1984), *The Blue and the Gray* (1975), *Invisible Poetry* (1979), *Out of Order* (1980; *Fuori servizio,* 2001), and *Uptown Train* (1980).

Pietri's poems have been widely anthologized, including his all-punctuation-marks poem in *Nuyorican Poetry: An Anthology of Puerto Rican Words and Feelings,* edited by Miguel Algarín and Miguel Piñero. Pietri, Algarín, and Piñero were also instrumental in founding the U.S. Afro-Puerto Rican poetry movement known as *Nuyorican poetry,* affirming both African and Hispanic heritage within a U.S. context—often with verse rich with puns in both English and Spanish. To foster this movement, they cofounded the Nuyorican Poets Café with Sandra María Esteves, **Ntozake Shange,** and 15 other Nuyorican poets; additional Nuyorican poets include Felipe Luciano and Victor Hernández Cruz. Still operating as a nonprofit organization dedicated to creating "a multi-cultural venue that both nurtures artists and

exhibits a variety of artistic works," the Café's "programming [now] includes poetry and prose readings, theatrical and musical performances, and visual art exhibits" (from //www.nuyorican.org/history.php); it offers highly popular weekly poetry slams, weekly Latin Jazz Jam sessions, Obie and Audelco Award-winning theater, screenplay readings, Hip Hop events, and monthly performances by the Nuyorican Rule comedy troupe. In the oral tradition of the Café, Pietri recorded his poetry on two Folkways albums, *Loose Joints* (1979) and *One Is a Crowd* (after 1979).

Pietri wrote plays, too, including *The Livingroom* (1975/19778), *Lewlulu* (1976), *What Goes Up Must Come Down* (1976), *Dead Heroes Have No Feelings* (1978), *Appearing in Person Tonight—Your Mother* (1978), *Jesus Is Leaving* (1978), *The Masses Are Asses* (1983/2007; *Las Masas Son Crasas,* 1997), *Mondo Mambo/A Mambo Rap Sodi* (1990), and *Illusions of a Revolving Door: Plays / Ilusiones de una Puerta Giratoria: Teatro* (1993, with Alfredo Matilla Rivas), as well as *No More Bingo at the Wake, Eat Rocks!,* and his unproduced *I Dare You to Resist Me.* Pietri also wrote *An Alternate* (1980), *Missing Out of Action* (1992), *Get the F*** out of Vieques* (2001), and his narrative *Lost in the Museum of Natural History/Perdido en el Museo de Historia Natural* (1980). Pietri also taught creative writing to college students, offered poetry workshops to children, and with his wife, Phyllis Nancy Wallach, (married 1978), he raised his children, Diana, Evava, and Speedo. His free-spirited writings, readings, and other performances celebrated intellectual freedom, iconoclasm, and nonconformity.

REFERENCES: *CAO-04. EA-99. Wiki.* //www.nuyorican.org/history.php. Amazon.com.

Pittsburgh Courier
1907–1965

New Pittsburgh Courier
1965–present
Newspaper

Edwin Harleston, an aspiring poet and a security guard at the H. J. Heinz food-packing plant, founded the local *Pittsburgh Courier* in his hometown in 1907. During the *Courier's* first year, Harleston printed just 10 copies of each of several editions of his paper; Harleston's poems filled most of each edition. It continued as a local outlet for a handful of African-American residents of Pittsburgh for another two years. In 1909, Harleston decided he wanted wider distribution for the paper, and he sought help from **Robert Lee Vann,** a young African-American attorney, to offer legal counsel and to help him get financial backing.

The following year, Vann had become the newspaper's editor, publisher, treasurer, and legal counsel (1910). Vann quickly transformed the *Courier* into a national newspaper addressing a broad spectrum of issues and current events appealing to African Americans across the country, far beyond Pittsburgh. During his lifetime (1879-1940), the *Courier* had reached a circulation approaching 1/4 million, employed more than 400 workers in 14 U.S. cities, and published 14 editions of the paper, becoming one of the most influential African-American newspapers of the day. The best and the brightest of African-American journalists and other writers contributed to the *Courier* at one time or another, and many of them regularly did so (e.g., **Marcus Garvey**'s column in the 1930s; **W. E. B. Du Bois**'s weekly column, 1936-1938; **Zora Neale Hurston**'s reports in 1952; Elijah Muhammad's columns, 1956-1963).

While Vann was at the helm, he used his editorials to advocate improvements in housing, health, and education for African Americans, both in Pittsburgh and across the country. He also sought to empower African Americans, socially, economically, and politically. He encouraged his readers to join organizations such as the National Urban League and the National Association for the Advancement of Colored People (NAACP), and he urged them to align with FDR's Democratic Party, offering a New Deal to all Americans. He also ranted against racist images of African Americans in the media, such as in the daily radio serial *Amos 'n' Andy*. Vann even paid correspondents to report on events in the wider world beyond U.S. borders. Before the U.S. involvement in World War II, *Courier* correspondent **Joel Augustus Rogers** reported on the invasion of Italian fascists into Ethiopia (1935-1936), thereby becoming the first African-American war correspondent and the only African-American foreign war correspondent during World War II.

After Vann's death in the fall of 1940, Vann's hand-picked successor, Ira Lewis, took the helm. Lewis had started as a sports writer in 1914 and had become the *Courier*'s managing editor by the time Vann died. Lewis even further expanded the *Courier*'s circulation, especially in response to his "Double V" campaign, in which "Victory" in war would be matched by "Victory" at home: That is, African-American soldiers who risked and sometimes forfeited their lives for their country should receive full rights of citizenship on their return home. Following the 1948 death of Lewis, the *Courier*'s circulation started declining, and it continued to decline throughout the 1950s and the early 1960s. The *Courier* nonetheless continued to make news. While other newspapers published the story of a sit-in on the inside pages, the *Courier* gave the story front-page prominence, with a photo, implying that this strategy was becoming a widespread phenomenon—and it soon was.

Meanwhile, just a few years before Vann took over the *Courier*, **Robert S. (Sengstacke) Abbott** had founded the ***Chicago Defender*** (on May 6, 1905), a four-page weekly newspaper. Within a decade, Abbott's *Defender* was an eight-page, eight-column, full-size paper, and throughout the 1920s, nearly 1/4 million readers were buying it each week. In the mid-1930s, Abbott brought his nephew, John H. (Herman Henry) Sengstacke, into the operation of the paper, and when Abbott died in 1940, Sengstacke took over the paper. Sengstacke started publishing the *Defender* daily in 1956 and renamed it the *Chicago Daily Defender*.

In 1965, John Sengstacke bought the *Courier*, folding it into his overarching Sengstacke Newspapers (now Real Times, LLC). The newspaper group Sengstacke founded has become the largest and most influential African-American-owned and -operated newspaper chain in the nation, including the *Michigan Chronicle*, *Michigan Front Page*, and the (Memphis) *Tri-State Defender*, as well as the *Chicago Daily Defender*, and the newspaper Sengstacke renamed *New Pittsburgh Courier*.

The current editor is Rod Doss, and the *Courier* offers both home-delivered print ($35/52 issues) and desktop-delivered digital ($10/52 issues) editions. The online edition may be viewed at //www.newpittsburghcourier online.com/, including This Week's Issue and these sections: Metro, National, Forum/Opinion, Business, Sports, In The Spirit, Lifestyle, Entertainment, Youth Connection, Health, Classifieds. In addition, it offers these links: Site Search, Tools, Advertise, Real Time Media, and Special Sections.

REFERENCES: *Wiki*. Jaap, James A., in *GEAAL*. Yu, Karlson, in //www.blackpast.org/?q=aah/vann-robert-lee-1879-1940. //lbis. kenyon.edu/research/guides/aaperiodicals. //www.newpittsburgh courieronline.com/. //www.newpittsburghcourieronline.com/ articlelive/pages/About-Us.html. //www.pbs.org/blackpress/ news_bios/courier.html.

Plato, Ann
fl. 1800s
Essays, biographies, poems

The only published book of Plato's work that has survived to this day is her *Essays: Including Biographies and Miscellaneous Pieces of Prose and Poetry* (1841/1988), which includes 4 biographies (of deceased personal acquaintances), 16 brief essays, and 20 poems. The very brief introduction written by her preacher, **James W. C. Pennington**, mentions that she is young but does not tell how young. Little else is known about her, as she reveals little about herself in her work, said to be the second book by an African-American woman, published in this country.

REFERENCES: Williams, Kenny Jackson, in *COCAAL* and *OCAAL*.

FURTHER READING: *AANB. EAAWW. W. Wiki.* Knight, Gladys L., in *GEAAL.* Smith, Katharine Capshaw, in *AWPW:1820-1870.* //digital.nypl.org/schomburg/writers_aa19/bio2.html.

Plumpp, Sterling
1/30/1940–
Poems, criticism; educator, editor

Born and raised a sharecropper in Clinton, Mississippi, young Sterling was traumatized by the murder of Emmett Till for having supposedly flirted with a white woman. Soon after, he underwent a deep religious conversion to Catholicism and sought means of escaping Mississippi and the deep South altogether. While attending St. Benedict's College in Kansas on an academic scholarship, he read **James Baldwin** and ancient Greek literature and decided to become a writer, leaving college after two years. He then moved to Chicago, finished college there, and continued to write. His poetry books include *Portable Soul* (1969), *Half Black, Half Blacker* (1970), *Muslim Men* (1972), his narrative poem *Steps to Break the Circle* (1974), his autobiographical narrative *Clinton* (1976), his award-winning collection of his major poems *The Mojo Hands Call/I Must Go* (1982/1988), *Blues: The Story Always Untold* (1989), *Johannesburg and Other Poems* (1993, following a trip to South Africa), *Hornman* (1995), *Ornate with Smoke* (1998), *Blues Narratives* (1999), and *Velvet BeBop Kente Cloth* (2003), as well as his poetic broadside *Blues for My Friend's Longings* (1993).

Plumpp also wrote two biographies for children ages 4-8 years, *Paul Robeson* (1999) and *Harriet Tubman* (2005); *Black Rituals* (1972/1987), prose about how particular behavior reinforces the oppression of African Americans; and he edited a poetry anthology, *Somehow We Survive: An Anthology of South African Writing* (1982). His own poems have been anthologized and have been published in periodicals (e.g., *Black Scholar, Black World,* **Callaloo,** *Journal of Black Poetry, Obsidian*). Since 1971, he has taught at the University of Illinois at Chicago Circle, as an instructor (1971-1984) and then as associate professor (since 1984). Since 1970, he has been the editor of **Haki Madhubuti**'s Third World Press, which has published many of Plumpp's works. He is also the editor of Madhubuti's Institute for Positive Education and the poetry editor for *Black American Literature Forum* (since 1982), and he served as the managing editor of *Black Books Bulletin* (1971-1973). His works in progress are reported to include works on **Henry Dumas, Ernest Gaines,** and black critics; a novel about a blues singer, and his collection *Superbad and the Hip Jesus.* He and his wife, Falvia Delgrazia Jackson, also raised their daughter, Harriet Nzinga.

REFERENCES: *AANB. BAWPP.* Antonucci, Michael A., in *GEAAL.* "Velvet BeBop Kente Cloth." *African American Review.* 39.1-2 (Spring-Summer 2005) p. 257. From *Literature Resource Center.* Basel, Marilyn K., in *CAO-01.* Collins, Michael, in *COCAAL* and *OCAAL.* Conyers, James L., (2005), *Afrocentric Traditions,* available at //books.google.com/books?id=ibsI6DK7jdgC&pg=PA128&lpg=PA128&dq=%22effie+t.+battle%22&source=web&ots=2ll8N5joeR&sig=n Wlt1pZF15b40WUVgVqqMkWIxMM&hl=en&sa=X&oi=book_re sult&resnum=21&ct=result. Cunningham, James, in *AAP-55-85.* //library.msstate.edu/special_interest/Mississippi_African-American_ Authors.asp. Amazon.com.

Polite, Carlene (née Hatcher)
8/28/1932–
Novels, essays; activist, performer, educator

Polite has published two novels, which have been labeled by some as "experimental" and by others as "innovative": *The Flagellants* (1966 in French, 1967/1988 in English) and *Sister X and the Victims of Foul Play* (1975); both are still in print. In addition, her 1968 article in *Mademoiselle* magazine offered four distinctive views of black power, presented through four distinctive voices. Hatcher is perhaps better known, however, as a dancer and a civil-rights activist, as well as a professor at the State University of New York at Buffalo (as faculty since 1971; as professor since the mid-1990s).

REFERENCES: *AANB. BAWPP. CAO-01.* Donald, Kalenda C. Eaton, in *GEAAL.* Dubey, Madhu, in *BWA:AHE.* Johnson, Ronna C., in *COCAAL* and *OCAAL.* Worthington-Smith, Hammett, in *AAFW-55-84.* //www.amazon.com, April 17, 2009.

Porter, James Amos
12/22/1905–2/28/1970
Art history; visual artist

An artist (chiefly a portrait painter) himself, Porter wrote an outstanding text on art history, *Modern Negro Art* (1943), which is still studied. He also wrote a biography of an African-American artist of the Civil War era, *Robert S. Duncanson, Midwestern Romantic-Realist* (1951). In 1965, the National Gallery of Art chose Porter and 24 other honorees as the best art teachers in the nation, to be presented with an award by First Lady Lady Bird Johnson. Porter's wife, **Dorothy Burnett Porter** (later Wesley), was the curator of the Moorland-**Spingarn** Research Center at Howard University.

REFERENCES: *AANB. CAO-03. EA-99. Wiki.* Jacobson, Robert R., in *BB.* //artnoir.com, 1999.

Porter Wesley, Dorothy Louise (née Burnett)
5/25/1905–12/17/1995
Bibliographies, anthologies; librarian and curator

The eldest of the Burnetts' four children, Dorothy Louise—like her siblings—was expected to get a college education. She surely did so. She graduated from a teacher's college, then earned her A.B. from Howard University (1928), and then she earned another bachelor's degree and a master's degree at Columbia University's School of Library Science—and then she was awarded a few honorary doctorates for good measure.

A year after Dorothy graduated from Howard, she married **James Porter**—art historian, painter, Howard grad, and Howard faculty member—with whom she had a daughter, Constance Burnett Porter (later Uzelac), on August 22, 1939. Starting even before she graduated, however, Dorothy had been working in the university's library, cataloging materials. In 1930, newlywed Mrs. Porter and her boss realized that a wealth of African-American literature was in danger of being lost to history unless special care was taken to preserve it. They agreed that Porter was just the person to take charge of that task. Porter spent the next 40-plus years doing just that.

First, she cataloged about 3,000 items donated to Howard by Jesse Moorland, Lewis Tappan, and a few others. Next, she set about collecting additional materials by asking everyone she could find (including bibliophile and enthusiastic book collector **Arthur Spingarn**) to donate them. She also searched through discard heaps, book sales, and even the estates of deceased African Americans. By the time Porter retired in 1973, the Moorland-Spingarn Collection comprised 180,000 items, including documents, microfilms, books, and periodicals. After she retired, Howard expanded the collection to embrace other parts of the library, founding the Moorland-Spingarn Research Center and naming Porter its curator emerita. In that role, Porter continued to consult and do research for the center until about a month before she died. Three years before she retired, Porter was widowed, and in 1979, she married noted Howard historian **Charles Wesley**.

Throughout her career, Porter (Wesley) had published hundreds of articles, including biographies, bibliographies, and histories of books and libraries. Probably her best-known book is her *Early Negro Writing, 1760-1837* (1971; reprint Baltimore: Black Classic Press, 1995), based on her master's thesis. She also wrote several bibliographies: *A Selected List of Books by and about Negroes* (1936); *North American Negro Poets: A Bibliographical Checklist of Their Writings 1760-1944* (1945), with annotations on poetry anthologies, as well as pamphlets and books by individual poets; *Catalogue of the African Collection at Howard University* (1958); *The Negro in American Cities: A Selected and Annotated Bibliography* (1967); *A Working Bibliography on the Negro in the United States* (1969); *Negro Protest Pamphlets: A Compendium* (1969, editor); *The Negro in the United States: A Selected Bibliography* (1970/1978); *Howard University: A Selected List of References* (1965); *Documentation on the Afro-American: Familiar and Less-Familiar Sources* (1969); and *Afro-Braziliana: A Working Bibliography* (1978).

Porter Wesley was given numerous awards for her outstanding achievements, including the Charles Frankel Award, given to her in 1994 by President and Mrs. Clinton, in a White House ceremony.

REFERENCES: *EA-99.* Barnes, Bart, "Obituaries, Librarian Dorothy Wesley Dies: Black History Curator at Howard," *Washington Post* (December 19, 1995), p. E05. Bhan, Esme, "Legacy of a Job Well Done," *Washington Post* (December 31, 1995), p. C08. Ferguson, Sally Ann H., in *COCAAL* and *OCAAL.* Gunn, Arthur C., in *BWA:AHE.* Weeks, Linton, "The Undimmed Light of Black History Dorothy Porter, Collecting Forgotten Memories," *Washington Post* (November 15, 1995), p. C01. //www.artnoir.com, 1999.

FURTHER READING: *AANB. HR&B. Wiki.* Escamilla, Brian, in *BB.* Nyangoni, Betty W., in *GEAAL.* //digital.library.upenn.edu/women/_generate/AFRICAN%20AMERICAN.html.

Poston, Ted (né Theodore Roosevelt Augustus Major Poston)
7/4/1906–1/11/1974
Autobiography/memoir, essays, short stories; journalist

While still attending Crispus Attucks High School, young Ted Poston worked as a copy clerk (starting in 1922) for his family's weekly *Hopkinsville Contender* newspaper in Kentucky until it was run out of town. After high school, Poston earned his bachelor's degree (1928) from Tennessee Agricultural and Industrial College (now Tennessee State University). Next, Poston moved to New York City, where he finagled a job writing materials for Governor Al Smith's run for the presidency. After Smith lost the election, Poston served food on a railroad while he wrote freelance, including a weekly column for the **Pittsburgh Courier** (1928-1929).

In 1929, Poston got a job at the **Amsterdam News**, which sent him to cover the trials of the Scottsboro boys (1931) and other major stories. In 1932, Poston traveled to Moscow, to work as an extra for the film *Black and White*, which was never produced. In 1934, Poston was promoted to city editor at the *News*, but when he helped lead a workers' strike to unionize the *News*, the owners fired him (1936). For a while, Poston worked as a writer for the federal W.P.A., Works Progress Administration.

Eager to work again as a journalist, Poston managed to wow the editors at the then-all-white *New York Post* by lucking onto a front-page story the day they interviewed him. That started Poston's 34-year career at the *Post*

(1937-1972), thereby becoming one of the first African-American staffers on a daily New York newspaper. At first, the *Post* assigned Poston to cover New York City Hall, but he was later sent to cover juicier—and riskier—stories, such as the 1955 Montgomery bus boycotts in Alabama. While there, he called his boss nightly just to reassure his boss he was still alive. Among his numerous awards was the American Newspaper Guild's Heywood Broun Award (1949).

Poston also enjoyed expressing himself through fiction, writing at least 20 short stories that appeared in numerous periodicals, anthologies, and even textbooks between 1927 and 1967. Most were set in his hometown of Hopkinsville. Poston was also married and divorced twice, but the woman most devoted to his legacy may be Kathleen A. Hauke, who edited a 144-page collection of his fiction, *The Dark Side of Hopkinsville: Stories by Ted Poston* (1991), wrote a 326-page biography of Poston, *Ted Poston: Pioneer American Journalist* (1998), and edited a 256-page collection of his articles, *A First Draft of History* (2000).

REFERENCES: *BAWPP. CAO-07.* Boyd, Melanie, in *COCAAL.* Hauke, Kathleen A., "Theodore Roosevelt Augustus Major Poston," in *AAWHR-40.* Niven, Steven J., in *AANB.* //en.wikipedia.org/wiki/Alfred_smith. //en.wikipedia.org/wiki/Heywood_Broun_Award. //en.wikipedia.org/wiki/Huey_Long. //en.wikipedia.org/wiki/Scottsboro_boys. //en.wikipedia.org/wiki/The_Newspaper_Guild. //www.newsguild.org/index.php?ID=906. //www.newsguild.org/index.php?ID=910. //www.pbs.org/blackpress/modern_journalist/dreyfuss.html. Amazon.com.

Poussaint, Alvin Francis
5/15/1934–

Nonfiction—education, psychology, psychiatry; educator, psychiatrist, consultant

In addition to serving as educational consultant to long-time friend **Bill Cosby**'s TV shows, Poussaint is a professor of psychiatry and associate dean of Harvard's Medical School. He has written dozens of scholarly and popular articles on how racism affects the psychological development of African-American children and about the development and experiences of children of interracial marriages. His writings have been published in *Grolier Encyclopedia Yearbook* and numerous anthologies, as well as in scholarly journals (e.g., *Black Scholar, International Journal of Psychiatry*) and popular periodicals (e.g., *Boston Globe, The New York Times, Psychology Today, Redbook*). His books include *Why Blacks Kill Blacks* (1972), *Black Children: Coping in a Racist Society* (1987), *Raising Black Children: Two Leading Psychiatrists Confront the Educational, Social, and Emotional Problems Facing Black Children* (1992, with James Comer, originally *Black Child Care: How to Bring Up a Healthy Black Child in*

America—A Guide to Emotional and Psychological Development, 1975), *Single Parenthood: Implications for American Society* (1997), *Lay My Burden Down: Unraveling Suicide and the Mental Health Crisis among African-Americans* (2000, with Amy Alexander), and *Come On People: On the Path from Victims to Victors* (2007, with Bill Cosby). Poussaint also wrote the foreword for Cosby's *Fatherhood* (1986), and he fathered his own black child, his son, Alan. His niece, Renee Poussaint, coedited *A Wealth of Wisdom: Legendary African American Elders Speak* (with Howard Bingham and Camille Cosby).

REFERENCES: *AANB. B. CAO-08. Wiki.* Armstrong, Robin, in *BB.* Goodson, Martia Graham, in *BH2C.* Myers, Aaron, in *EA-99.* Amazon.com.

Powell, Jr., Adam Clayton
11/29/1908–4/4/1972

News articles and columns; newspaper publisher, politician, cleric

In the mid-1930s, Powell wrote many political pieces for the *New York Post*, followed by a popular column (aptly titled "Soap Box") for the *Amsterdam News* of Harlem. From 1942 to 1946, he published the *People's Voice*, which he founded. More often, however, his words could be heard from the pulpit (after taking over the ministry of a Baptist church from his father, **Adam Clayton Powell, Sr.**, in 1937) and in the chambers of the U.S. Congress (representing his New York City district from 1945 to 1970). Legendary for his civil-rights activism, he was also notorious for his financial indiscretions.

REFERENCES: *EA-99. EB-BH-CD. PGAA.* Stone, Les, in *BH2C.*

FURTHER READING: *AANB. BCE. CAO-07. LE. QB. USGG. Wiki.* Glickman, Simon, in *BB.* Hargrove, Claude, in *ARRW-2.*

Powell, Sr., Adam Clayton
5/5/1865–6/12/1953

Sermons, books; cleric

Perhaps best known as the Baptist minister who fathered **Adam Clayton Powell, Jr.**, Powell Sr. wrote three books and countless sermons.

REFERENCES: Balfour, Lawrie, in *EA-99.*

FURTHER READING: *AANB. BAWPP. Wiki.*

Powell, Kevin
4/24/1966–

Poems, essays, hip-hop history; journalist, educator, performer

Kevin Powell earned his bachelor's degree at Rutgers University, the State University of New Jersey (1984-1988), then he freelanced nonfiction articles and wrote poetry while teaching English at New York University in New York City (1990-1992). In 1992, he became a writer, a host, and the oldest cast member of the first season of MTV's *Real World* series. After leaving *Real World*, Powell got a job as a senior staff writer (1993-1996) for the then-brand-new *Vibe* magazine. Among other projects, he interviewed and profiled **Tupac Shakur** and Colin Powell. Meanwhile, Kevin Powell has continued to write freelance for various periodicals (e.g., *Esquire, Essence, Newsweek, Rolling Stone*).

While still on the *Vibe* payroll, Powell published his first poetry collection, *Recognize: Poems* (1995). Afterward, he published four essay collections: *Keepin' It Real: Post-MTV Reflections on Race, Sex, and Politics* (1997), *Essence* best-selling *Who's Gonna Take the Weight?: Manhood, Race, and Power in America* (2002), *Someday We'll All Be Free* (2006), and *Open Letters to America: Essays by Kevin Powell* (2009). A year before publishing his latest essay collection, he published another poetry collection, *No Sleep Till Brooklyn: New and Selected Poems* (2008). According to *Wiki*, Powell has two more books in progress: a memoir of his childhood, *homeboy alone* (due out in 2010), and *The Kevin Powell Anthology* (due out in 2011). In addition, he has written a screenplay and an MTV documentary.

Powell has also edited several anthologies, including *In the Tradition: An Anthology of Young Black Writers* (1993), *Step into a World: A Global Anthology of the New Black Literature* (2000), *Who Shot Ya?: Three Decades of Hiphop Photography* (2002), and *The Black Male Handbook: A Blueprint for Life* (2008). Despite receiving unwanted attention for having been involved in domestic abuse, Powell prefers the public eye to the life of the solitary writer. He has lectured in nearly all 50 states, in a variety of settings. He also guest-curated the Brooklyn Museum's "Hip-Hop Nation: Roots, Rhymes, and Rage" exhibit (2001). In addition, he has hosted programs for HBO and BET (Black Entertainment Television) and has often appeared as a guest on VH1, MTV, BET, and other media outlets. He has also run two unsuccessful bids for the U.S. Congress (2006 and 2008) and has hinted that he may seek a seat again in 2010. He received fellowships from the Joint Center for Political and Economic Studies and from the Phelps Stokes Fund.

REFERENCES: *CAO-05. Wiki.* Sanchez, Brenna, in *BB*. //en.wiki pedia.org/wiki/Black_Entertainment_Television. //en.wikipedia. org/wiki/Vibe_(magazine). //www.vibe.com/news/magazine_features/ 2005/02/vibe_magazine_love_hurts_raps_black_eye/. //www.vibe.com/ news/news_headlines/2007/11/other_side_of_hiphop_documentary/. //www.vibe.com/news/news_headlines/2009/03/106_and_park_dedicat ing_show_to_teen_abuse/. //www.vibe.com/tags/Kevin-Powell. Amazon.com.

FURTHER READING: treco, eboni, in *GEAAL*.

Prince, Mary
c. 1788–after 1833
Slave narrative

Mary Prince's *The History of Mary Prince, A West Indian Slave, Related by Herself*, published in London in 1831, was the first published slave narrative written by a woman of African descent living in the Americas. (**Harriet Jacobs** wrote the first American-published slave narrative [in 1861], authored by an African-American woman.) Slave narratives written by African-American men had been published previously (e.g., **Olaudah Equiano**'s [1789, England; 1791, United States], Charles Ball's [1836], and **Moses Roper**'s [1838, U.S.; 1837, England), and some of these accounts described some of the sexual abuse and violently cruel treatment of women. Nonetheless, Prince's vivid description of her slave experiences awakened many Americans to the brutality of slavery that women were forced to endure in the Americas (she was enslaved in Bermuda, Antigua, and other islands in the West Indies).

Previously, many whites had unquestioningly asserted that slaves really didn't mind being enslaved and didn't really seek to escape bondage. This assertion was rather unconvincing after Prince's highly popular and controversial book came to light, including this observation: "They [whites] put a cloak about the truth. It is not so. All slaves want to be free. . . . I have been a slave myself—and I know what slaves feel—I can tell by myself what other slaves feel, and by what they have told me. The man that says slaves be quite happy in slavery—that they don't want to be free—that man is either ignorant or a lying person" (quoted in *CSN*, p. xvi). She gave first-person testimony to the emotionally scarring sexual exploitation and physically scarring savage beatings she suffered, as well as her long hours of labor in harsh chemicals that deformed her feet.

While traveling with her barbarous "owners," the Woods, in England, Prince escaped from them and fled to the Moravian Church in London, seeking sanctuary. There, the British Anti-Slavery Society offered her legal and financial aid. Through the society, British abolitionist poet Susan Strickland recorded Prince's firsthand telling of her experiences, and society secretary Thomas Pringle edited the work (with Prince's approval of the final wording), added some supporting documentation, and published it as an abolitionist tract. Pringle also hired Prince as his paid employee and offered to purchase her freedom from the Woods. They refused, insisting that she return with them to Bermuda. Prince refused to return with them (realizing that she would never again see her husband, a free black man whom she had married in 1826), remaining in England to fight in the courts, in the press, and in the British parliament. Ultimately, in 1833, she won her battle through parliament, when it abolished slavery in Britain and its colonies (including those in the West Indies). Almost nothing is known about Prince after she gained her freedom. Perhaps she managed to return to her husband on a slavery-free Caribbean island; perhaps she started a new life in England; perhaps . . . . During the twentieth century, Prince's work was rediscovered and republished (1987, in *CSN*).

REFERENCES: *AANB. CSN. W. Wiki.* Keough, Leyla, in *EA-99.* Paquet, Sandra Pouchet, in *COCAAL* and *OCAAL.*

FURTHER READING: *EAAWW.* Jackson, Gale P. "Mary Prince" (a poem about her). *Bridge Suite.* Storm Imprints, 1998. p. 35. From *LitFinder.* Whitlock, Gillian. "Merry Christmas, Mary Prince." *Biography.* 26.3 (Summer 2003): p. 440. Literature Resources from Gale. //digital.nypl.org/schomburg/writers_aa19/bio2.html.

Prince (married name), Nancy (née Gardner)
9/15/1799–1856 or after?
Autobiography, travel chronicles

Nancy Prince's major literary contribution is her *Narrative of the Life and Travels of Mrs. Nancy Prince, Written by Herself* (1850), in which she describes some family history, her own experiences and living conditions as a free black in New England before the Civil War, as well as her travels through Europe and the Caribbean. In describing her family history, she shows her outrage that Africans were abducted from their homeland, subjected to bondage and inhumane cruelty in a foreign land, and then forced to live in abject poverty if they managed to gain their freedom. Her account also imparts the pride she feels for her racial heritage and her forebears, including her mother's father, an African brought to this country as a slave, who fought at Bunker Hill during the Revolutionary War; her mother's mother, a Native American, who had been captured and enslaved by the British; and her African-born stepfather, who literally leaped to freedom when he jumped off a slave ship. Nancy's mother was widowed twice: first, by Nancy's father, when Nancy was just three years old, and then by Nancy's stepfather. After he died, Nancy's mother was overwrought, and Nancy had to take charge of parenting her six siblings, including her oldest sister, whom she and a cane-wielding friend abducted from a brothel and returned home.

In 1824, Nancy married Nero Prince (a former sailor and a servant to a Russian princess). With him, she traveled through Europe to Russia, where she spent nearly a decade working as a seamstress, directing an orphanage,

and doing various other jobs—as well as learning several languages and observing world events from this distinctive vantage point. In 1833, the Princes returned to the United States, and Nancy was widowed soon after. Before long, Nancy Prince was working for the American Anti-Slavery Society in Boston, where she established an orphanage for "colored children." A deeply religious woman, in 1840-1841 and 1842, Prince made two evangelistic trips to Jamaica, hoping to ignite Christian zeal in the newly freed former slaves she met there. Back in Boston in 1843, she wrote her autobiography in the hope that she might gain enough from its sale to support herself. Her preface to the 1856 third edition of her book notes that she is gravely ill, and nothing more has been uncovered about her life or her death.

REFERENCES: *EA-99.* Henderson, Australia Tarver, in *BWA:AHE.* Winter, Kari J., in *COCAAL* and *OCAAL.*

FURTHER READING: *AANB. W.* Zabel, Darcy A., in *AWPW:1820-1870.* //digital.nypl.org/schomburg/writers_aa19/bio2.html. //voices.cla.umn.edu/vg/Bios/entries/prince_nancy_gardner.html. //www.blackpast.org/?q=aah/prince-nancy-gardner-1799-c-1856. //www.bookrags.com/biography/nancy-gardner-prince-dlb/.

Prison Writings and Writers *See* Anthologies of African-American Literature, Special Topics and Audiences

Proverbs

A *proverb* is a short, highly meaningful folk saying, originating in and preserved by word of mouth, which memorably expresses a widely recognized truism about human experience and the ways of the world. Proverbs generally have no known author, or at least they are customarily quoted without identifying an author. In contrast, *aphorisms* are widely quoted pithy sayings for which the author is known. Thus, some expressions may originate as quotations, gain such popularity that they become aphorisms, then lose their association with their distinctive authors to become proverbs. For instance, even within the past few decades, many people don't recall that it was **Eldridge Cleaver** who said, "You're either part of the solution or part of the problem." By the middle of the next century, this may slip from being an aphorism to being a proverb.

Proverbs are a form of *folklore*, a particular culture's large body of commonly recognized knowledge, which people transmit across generations through the **oral tradition**. Often, proverbs are *maxims*, basic propositions or widely accepted rules about how the world works, how to behave, or how to handle various situations (e.g., "Never say never"). Maxims give advice or make observations about common situations (e.g., "Feed a cold, starve a fever"), practical matters of everyday living (e.g., "Don't put all your eggs in one basket"), moral conduct (e.g., "Waste not, want not"), or the ways of the world (e.g., "Nature abhors a vacuum"). Some proverbs are *admonitions,* giving warnings (e.g., "Don't throw the baby out with the bathwater"). Some proverbs are epigrams, although the authors of epigrams are often identifiable. *Epigrams* are concise, ingeniously clever or satirical poems (e.g., Ogden Nash's "'Neath tile or thatch / That man is rich / Who has a scratch / For every itch.") or witty prose statements (e.g., Oscar Wilde's "Experience is the name everyone gives to his mistakes.").

In addition to losing their connection to a known author, proverbs change in other ways as they pass from generation to generation. For one thing, as a spoken language changes, some of the words, idioms, or word meanings within proverbs drop out from common use in the language. For instance, in the proverb "tide and time wait for no man," the word *tide* means "season," but that meaning of the word is archaic now. In addition, the original meanings of the proverbs themselves sometimes get lost along the way. For example, in the proverb "The exception *proves* the rule," the original meaning of "proves" is "tests." Nowadays, however, we commonly infer that "proves" means "shows a known truth," which is almost the opposite of the original meaning.

Because human experience is so complex and often paradoxical, many proverbs have conflicting counterparts. For instance, "Nobody tells all he knows" (Senegal) seems to contradict "Wisdom is not like money to be tied up and hidden" (Akan); "Too many cooks spoil the broth" goes against "Many hands make light work"; "Birds of a feather flock together" contrasts with "Opposites attract"; and "Look before you leap" challenges "He who hesitates is lost."

Given the problems associated with proverbs—changes in meanings, archaic terms and idioms, contradictions—why do we so often use them and cherish them across countless generations? Because these little truisms offer sound advice, comfort in times of trouble, and brief summaries of shared knowledge. What helps us to remember these folk sayings? In addition to their brevity, proverbs often use several memorable features:

- metaphors with vivid imagery ("If you bring your firebrand into your hut then do not complain of the smoke," West Africa)
- repetition ("An eye for an eye, a tooth for a tooth," Jewish)
- rhyme ("If I'm lying, I'm flying," African American)
- alliteration and consonance (e.g., "Strategy is better than strength," Hausa)

- parallelism ("Pretty is as pretty does," African American) or comparison ("The blacker the berry, the sweeter the juice," African American)
- antithesis ("Do as I say, not as I do," British) or contrast ("A healthy ear can stand hearing sick words," Senegal)
- irony ("Before healing others, heal thyself," Nigeria)

Proverbs, as expressions of common human experiences, may be found across cultures and across time. Because they often express universal truths, differing cultures frequently express the same ideas through distinctive proverbs. For instance, the Nigerian proverb "Some birds avoid the water, ducks seek it" conveys the same sentiment as the Roman proverb "One man's meat is another man's poison." The African-American proverb "What goes around comes around" expresses the same idea as the Jewish proverb "You reap what you sow."

Unfortunately, the only way of being sure when a particular proverb came into use is to search for written records showing where and when the proverb emerged. For instance, written records show ancient Egyptian collections of proverbs dating from 2500 b.c., and one of the earliest sources of proverbs in the Western tradition is the book of Proverbs in the Old Testament (400s-300s b.c.). Because most of sub-Saharan Africa had no written language before the nineteenth century, there is no way to be sure of when or where most African proverbs emerged.

Nonetheless, proverbs play a vital role in African culture and in the African oral tradition. In fact, Africans highly revere the ability to cite proverbs in conversations, arguments, and speeches. Elders and other leaders generally have a great command of pithy proverbs, by which they guide people's behavior. One illustration of proverbs' importance can be seen in various proverbs *about proverbs,* such as "Proverbs are the palm oil with which words are eaten" (Ibo); "One who applies proverbs gets what he wants" (the Shona of Zimbabwe); and "A wise man who knows proverbs reconciles difficulties" (the Yoruba of Nigeria).

In addition to African proverbs, other sources of African-American proverbs are the Old and New Testaments of the Bible and various British authors (e.g., George Herbert: "He that makes his bed ill, lies there" paved the way for "If you make your bed hard, you're gonna have to lie in it"). Many other African-American proverbs have originated in songs, such as spirituals (e.g., "If you cain't bear no crosses, / You cain't wear no crown"), blues songs (e.g., "You never miss your water 'til the well runs dry"), civil-rights songs (e.g., "Keep your eyes on the prize"), and soul songs (e.g., "Different strokes for different folks"). Several Americanisms have also become common African-American folk sayings, such as "If you can't stand the heat, get out of the kitchen" and "You can lead a horse to water, but you can't make him drink."

In addition, the struggles for abolition and for civil rights have led to folk sayings, such as "We ain't what we wanna be; we ain't what we gonna be; but thank God we ain't what we was" and "In the South they don't care how close you get, as long as you don't get too high. In the North they don't care how high you get, as long as you don't get too close." In addition, several contemporary aphorisms are headed toward becoming proverbs: **Frederick Douglass**'s "If there is no struggle, there is no progress"; **Fannie Lou Hamer**'s "I'm sick and tired of being sick and tired"; **Jesse Jackson**'s "We must turn to each other and not on each other" and "Your children need your presence more than your presents"; and **Martin Luther King, Jr.**'s "Injustice anywhere is a threat to justice everywhere."

REFERENCES: *AHL. AP&W. BRE. E-98-CD. G-96-CD. MSD-CD. MSE-CD. MWEL. WB-98-CD.* Beilenson, John, & Heidi Jackson.1992. *Voices of Struggle, Voices of Pride.* White Plains, NY: Peter Pauper Press. Bell, Janet Cheatham.1986/1995. *Famous Black Quotations.* New York: Warner Books, Time Warner. Diggs, Anita Doreen.1995. *Talking Drums: An African-American Quote Collection.* New York: St. Martin's Griffin. Hudson, Cheryl & Wade. 1996. *Kids' Book of Wisdom: Quotes from the African-American Tradition.* East Orange, NJ: Just Us Books. Leslau, Charlotte & Wolf . 1962, 1985. *African Proverbs.* White Plains, NY: Peter Pauper Press. Scheffler, Axel.1997. *Let Sleeping Dogs Lie and Other Proverbs from Around the World.* Hauppage, NY: Barron's Educational Series. Simpson, John.1982. *The Concise Oxford Dictionary of Proverbs,* New York: Oxford University Press.

Pryor, Richard
12/1/1940–12/10/2005
Spoken word—performance comedy, humor, autobiography/memoir; actor, performer

Almost anyone who went to a movie theater or watched television during the 1970s and 1980s has seen Richard Pryor act in at least 1 of the 40-plus films or the countless TV shows in which he performed, or has seen him cohost 2 Academy Awards shows. He also was nominated for both an Emmy Award and a National Association for the Advancement of Colored People (NAACP) Image Award for his guest appearance on the TV series *Chicago Hope* (1996). Some readers may even be old enough and fortunate enough to have seen his nightclub stand-up performances in the 1960s.

By the end of the 1960s, Pryor started recording some of his performances on comedy albums, such as *Richard Pryor* (1968 or 1969), *Craps (After Hours)* (1971/1993), *Pryor Goes Foxx Hunting* (1973), and his Grammy Award-winning *That Nigger's Crazy* (1974), which went gold and then platinum. During the 1970s, he also wrote for television's *Flip Wilson Show* series (1970) and for Lily

Tomlin's TV special *Lily* (1973), for which he won an Emmy Award (1973). He also collaborated with funnyman Mel Brooks to write the screenplay for the hit film *Blazing Saddles* (1974), for which he won both a Writers Guild Award and an American Academy of Humor Award (both 1974).

Through the rest of the 1970s, he released many more comedy albums, including *Down-N-Dirty* (1975), Grammy-winning *Is It Something I Said?* (1975/1991), *Richard Pryor Meets Richard & Willie & the S.L.A.* (1976), Grammy-winning *Bicentennial Nigger* (1976), *L.A. Jail* (1976), *Are You Serious???* (1977), *Richard Pryor's Greatest Hits* (1977), *Richard Pryor Live* (1977), *Who Me? I'm Not Him* (1977/1994), *Black Ben the Blacksmith* (1978), *The Wizard of Comedy* (1978/1995), *Outrageous* (1979), *Wanted: Live in Concert* (1979, two-album set), *Insane* (1980), *Holy Smoke!* (1980), *Richard Pryor's Greatest Hits* (1980), Grammy-winning *Rev. Du-Rite* (1981), Grammy-winning *Live on Sunset Strip* (1982), *Supernigger* (1983), and *Here and Now* (1983). All told, he won five Grammys for his spoken-word comedy albums. He also released a picture disc, *Richard Pryor Live!* (1982). In addition, he wrote and starred in a TV special, *The Richard Pryor Special?* (1977) then a short-lived TV series, *The Richard Pryor Show* (1977), a variety show that lasted just 5 weeks, due to constant battles with the network.

Pryor also earned writing credits, either solo or shared, for numerous films and TV shows, including *Silver Streak* (1976) and *Blue Collar* (1978). In 1978, Pryor suffered a serious heart attack; had a tumultuous divorce; and stored up material for writing his next film, *Richard Pryor: Live in Concert* (1979). Next, Pryor wrote and acted in *Stir Crazy* (1980), and he wrote and starred in *Bustin' Loose* (1981). While filming *Bustin' Loose*, on June 9, 1980, Pryor was severely burned. Accounts differ as to the cause, but all accounts reference his abuse of alcohol or other drugs. It took Pryor 6 weeks to recover from his immediate injuries and much longer to recover fully. The film and album he produced afterward, *Richard Pryor Live on Sunset Strip* (1982), have been touted as his best work of all. After that, he wrote and starred in the films *Richard Pryor-Here and Now* (1983, which he also directed), *Richard Pryor: Live and Smokin'* (1985), and his autobiographical *Jo Jo Dancer, Your Life Is Calling* (1986).

Pryor continued to act in films, but by the end of the 1980s, multiple sclerosis ended his public career. He then collaborated with Todd Gold to write his memoir, *Pryor Convictions: And Other Life Sentences* (1995). In the new millennium, Rhino Records released a series of boxed sets of his previous recordings, to both critical and popular acclaim. In addition to his aforementioned awards, Pryor received the NAACP Hall of Fame Award (1996), the first annual Mark Twain Prize for American Humor from the John F. Kennedy Center for the Performing Arts

(1998), an MTV Lifetime Achievement Award (2000), and was voted number 1 on Comedy Central's list of the 100 Greatest Stand-ups of All Time (2004).

REFERENCES: *B. CAO-06. CE. D. F. W2B. Wiki.* Ankeny, Jason, *All Music Guide,* in *A.* Erickson, Hal, *All Movie Guide,* in *Act.* Phelps, Shirelle, Anne Janette Johnson, David G. Oblender, and Tom Pendergast, *BB.* Smydra, David F., Jr., in *AANB.* //en.wikipedia.org/wiki/Bustin%27_Loose.

Publishers
1942–

The key publishers included as main entries in this dictionary are, in approximate order of their founding, **Johnson Publishing Company** (1942-), **Broadside Press** (1965-), **Third World Press (TWP)** (1967-), **Howard University Press** (1972-), **Lotus Press** (1972-1992, 1998-), **Kitchen Table: Women of Color Press** (1981-1992), **Just Us Books** (1988-), and **Redbone Press** (1995-). In addition, numerous African Americans have published **newspapers**, as well as **journals and magazines** (*see* those entries for cross-references and other information).

In addition, religious publishers, such as A.M.E. Book Concern, of Philadelphia, originally started publishing church newsletters and other publications in 1817. The AME's *Christian Recorder* was first published in 1854. The AME Sunday School Union and Publishing House was founded in 1882 and started printing Sunday-school materials in 1886. The AME Zion Book Concern was founded in 1841, to publish its church-related materials.

Many of these religious publishers also published periodicals, in which they published the literary works of their members, and some also occasionally published suitable books by their members.

Perhaps most important, however, is African-American authors' long tradition of self-publishing their own works, such as **Pauline Elizabeth Hopkins**'s 1905 P. E. Hopkins & Co.; the Hudsons' first 1987 self-published book prior to founding Just Us Books; and **E. Lynn Harris**'s legendary 1991 self-published best-seller. Just among the "B" entries in this volume, these self-published authors appeared: **Gerald W. (William) Barrax, Charlotta Amanda Spears Bass, Delilah Beasley, Henry Bibb,** and **Ashley F. Bryan.** When African-American writers are faced with rejection by European-American-owned and -operated publishers, they try to make a way out of no way.

REFERENCES: Barksdale, Richard, and Keneth Kinnamon (Eds.). 1972. *Black Writers of America: A Comprehensive Anthology.* New York: Macmillan. Joyce, Donald F. 1991. *Black Book Publishers in the United States: A Historical Dictionary of the Presses, 1817-1990.* Westport, CT: Greenwood Publishing Group. //www.hup.harvard.edu/features/reference/danafr/samples.html.

Purvis, Robert *See* Fortens, Grimkés, and Purvises

Purvis, Sarah (Louisa) Forten *See* Fortens, Grimkés, and Purvises

Lift Every Voice: The Lives of Booker T. Washington, W. E. B. Du Bois, Mary Church Terrell, and James Weldon Johnson (1965), and he edited the volumes Blacks on John Brown and Narrative of the Life of Frederick Douglass: American Slave, Written by Himself (1960/1997). He was married twice and had two daughters: Roberta by his first wife, Vera Bullock (died in 1951), and Pamela by his second wife, Ruth Brett (married in 1952).

REFERENCES: AANB. CAO-03. EBLG. G-97. Wiki. Fay, Robert, in EA-99. McConnell, Roland C. "In Memoriam." The Journal of Negro History. 86.2 (Spring 2001) p. 200. From Literature Resource Center. Toppin, Edgar Allan, in WB-99. Wolf, Gillian, in BB. //www.amazon.com, 7/1999.

Quarles, Benjamin
1/23/1904–11/16/1996
Histories, essays, textbooks; educator

The son of a subway porter, Benjamin Quarles dedicated his adult life to learning and teaching others about African-American history, particularly the people and events emerging before the start of the twentieth century. Toward this end, Quarles earned a B.A. (1931) from Shaw University and both an M.A. (1933) and a Ph.D. (1940) from the University of Wisconsin. After earning his degrees, he taught briefly at Shaw, then was dean at Dillard University (New Orleans) and then history department chair at Morgan State University (Baltimore).

Starting with his first published journal article ("The Breach between Douglass and Garrison," 1938, *Journal of Negro History*) and his first book (**Frederick Douglass**, 1948), Quarles probed race relations throughout American history, and he told true, well-researched stories that inspired an appreciation of African-American contributions to American life and history. Quarles went on to publish numerous other scholarly articles, contribute to the journal *Phylon*, and serve as an associate editor of the *Journal of Negro History*.

Among Quarles's scholarly books are his *The Negro in the Civil War* (1953, reprint 1989), *The Negro in the American Revolution* (1961, reprint 1996), *Lincoln and the Negro* (1962, reprint 1991), *Black Abolitionists* (1969, reprint 1991), *Allies for Freedom: Blacks and John Brown* (1974), and *Black Mosaic: Essays in Afro-American History and Historiography* (1988). Quarles also wrote two textbooks to inform a wider readership of what he and other scholars had learned: *The Negro in the Making of America* (1964; 3rd ed., 1996) and *The Negro American: A Documentary History* (1967; later rev. ed. retitled *The Black American: A Documentary History*, 1970, with Leslie H. Fishel). He collaborated with Dorothy Sterling to write

Quill Club
1925–1930?

Saturday Evening Quill
1928–1930
Literary organization and literary journal

While the **Harlem Renaissance** was in full flower in New York City, African-American intellectuals in Boston were seeking ways to nurture one another's literary interests and expressions, as well. In July of 1925, a group of published authors, aspiring authors, and apreciators of literature gathered to form the Quill Club, also known as the Boston Quill Club and even the Saturday Quill Club. True to their times, though nearly all the members were women, the president of the club was journalist Eugene F. Gordon, husband of member Edythe Mae Gordon. Among the club's 23 or more members, ranging in age from about 21 through 60-plus, were Marion G. Conover, Waring Cuney, Alice Chapman Furlong, the club's treasurer and *Boston Post* staffer Florence M. Harmon, Alvira Hazzard, Gertrude P. McBrown, club secretary Grace Vera Postles, **Florida Ruffin Ridley** (daughter of *The Woman's Era* editor **Josephine St. Pierre Ruffin**), Gertrude Schalk, and Roscoe Wright. Also early members were **Helene Johnson (Hubbell)** and **Dorothy West**, cousins who both moved to New York City in 1926.

In 1928, the Quill Club started publishing a literary journal containing the writings of club members, titled *Saturday Evening Quill*. The *Quill*, edited by Eugene Gordon, included all genres, including poetry, short fiction, and essays, as well as illustrations. Though the journal steered clear of political comment, **W. E. B. Du Bois** said it was "by far the most interesting and the best" of the small local literary journals. The club published just 250 copies of each annual edition, so that each member could distribute copies to family and friends, but it was never intended for national distribution. Nonetheless, the editors were continually asked to send copies to would-be readers who had caught glimpses of it or had heard of it. Finally, in 1930, the club published its first issue for sale, and it turned out to be the club's last issue.

REFERENCES: McHenry, Elizabeth. 2002. *Forgotten Readers: Recovering the Lost History of African-American Literary Societies.* Durham, NC: Duke University Press. Roses, Lorraine Elena. 1990. *Harlem Renaissance and Beyond: Literary Biographies of 100 Black Women Writers 1900-1945.* Boston, MA: G.K. Hall. (*See* biographical entries for each of the aforementioned club members.) Wintz, Cary D., and Paul Finkelman 2004, *Encyclopedia of the Harlem Renaissance.* London: Taylor & Francis.

~R~

Rahman, Aishah (née Virginia Hughes)
1936–
Plays, short stories, anthologies, memoir

Rahman's surrealistic, avant-garde plays include her *Lady Day: A Musical Tragedy* (1972), about the life and times of **Billie Holiday**, and her AUDELCO Award-nominated *Transcendental Blues* (1976). Her *Unfinished Women Cry in No Man's Land While a Bird Dies in a Gilded Cage* (1977), inspired by her own experiences as a high-school senior, takes place in a home for unwed mothers on the day jazz saxophonist Charlie Parker dies. Rahman based *The Tale of Madame Zora* (1986) on the life of **Zora Neale Hurston**.

Rahman won the Doris Abramson Playwriting Award for *The Mojo and the Sayso* (1987/2007), "inspired by a true 1973 incident. 'A 10-year old boy, . . ., was walking with his father one morning in Queens, N.Y., and two [plain-clothes] policemen stopped them,' explained Rahman. 'Not realizing who the men were, the boy and his father ran.' The son was shot in the back by the police and killed, and 'the father had to live with that,' Rahman said. Pregnant at the time with her daughter Yoruba, Rahman was deeply affected by the case" (Berson, *Seattle Times*). The boy's family later won a cash settlement for his wrongful death, but a crooked minister swindled them out of their money.

Next, Rahman wrote the libretto for *The Opera of Marie Laveau* (1989, later renamed *Anybody Seen Marie Laveau?*). Her other plays include *Only in America* (1993), *Public Spaces* (1997, published, not produced), *Chiaroscuro a Light (And Dark) Comedy* (1999), and *Mingus Takes (3)* (2003). Some of her plays have been published in *Plays by Aishah Rahman* (1997). In 2001, she published two works in new formats: Her short-story collection, *"If Only We Knew,"* was inspired by Amadou Diallo's death resulting from a brutal police attack; her

recollections of her childhood in a cruelly abusive foster family appear in *Chewed Water: A Memoir* (2001). She also continues to work on her novel, *Internal Exiles*; a documentary film, *Yeabo*; and a drama, *Pffssst*.

Emerging from her work as a professor at Brown University (Providence, RI; since 1992; as full professor since 1997), she has also edited at least two annual anthologies: *NUMUSE: An anthology of plays from Brown University's New Plays Festival* (1994) and *NuMuse: New Plays from Brown University* (1995, 2nd issue). Before Brown, she taught at Nassau Community College (New York) and Columbia University School of the Arts. In addition to the Abramson award and the Audelco nomination, Rahman has received fellowships from the Rockefeller Foundation (1988) and the New York Foundation for the Arts (1988) and from the prestigious artist colonies MacDowell (1992) and Yaddo (1992). She has also been invited to help adjudicate MacArthur Fellowship playwright grants (2005), Schomburg Library Scholars-in-Residencies (2005), Howard playwriting fellowships (2000), and other awards.

REFERENCES: *BAWPP.* Berson, Misha (9/6/2007), "The Raw Issues in 'Mojo' Still Cry Out for Discussion," *The Seattle Times*, in //seattletimes.nwsource.com/html/thearts/2003870559_sayso06.html. Diehl, Heath A., in *GEAAL.* Margulis, Jennifer, in *COCAAL* and *OCAAL.* Metzger, Sheri Elaine, in *BB.* //research.brown.edu/pdf/10199.pdf. Amazon.com.

FURTHER READING: *EAAWW.*

Rainey, Gertrude (née Pridgett) "Ma"
4/26/1886–12/22/1939
Songs; performer, theater manager, business owner

Among the 93 or so songs she performed and recorded, Rainey wrote more than a third of them. For her singing and songwriting, she was inducted into the Blues Foundation Hall of Fame (1983) and the Rock 'n' Roll Hall of Fame (1990). She also inspired playwright **August Wilson** to write his *Ma Rainey's Black Bottom* (1984) and poet **Sterling Brown** to write "Ma Rainey."

REFERENCES: *A. AANB. B. BCE. D. EA-99. EB-BH-CD. SEW. Wiki.* Griffin, Farah Jasmine, in *COCAAL* and *OCAAL.* Lieb, Sandra, in *BWA:AHE.* Minderovic, Christine Miner, in *BB.*

Rampersad, Arnold
11/13/1941–
Literary and cultural criticism, biography

Most readers know Rampersad for his comprehensive accounts of the lives of other literary figures: *The Art and Imagination of W. E. B. Du Bois* (1976), *The Life of* **Langston Hughes** (Volume 1: *1902-1941: I, Too, Sing*

America, 1986; Volume 2: *1941-1967: I Dream a World*, 1988), and ***Ralph Ellison*** (2007). These thoroughly researched works are considered preeminent authorities on these outstanding African Americans; the first volume on Hughes was a National Book Critics Circle Award nominee, an Anisfield-Wolf Book Award winner, and a Clarence L. Holte Literary Prize winner for works on African-American heritage; the second volume was a Pulitzer finalist and an American Book Award winner. Rampersad also authored *Melville's Israel Potter: A Pilgrimage and Progress* (1969), coauthored **Arthur Ashe's** autobiography *Days of Grace* (1993), and authored *Jackie Robinson: A Biography* (1997; available in unabridged audio format).

Among the many volumes he has edited are *Slavery and the Literary Imagination* (1989, with Deborah E. McDowell), the prestigious two-volume Library of America edition of **Richard Wright**, *Works* (1991), *Race and American Culture* (1993, series coedited with Shelley Fisher Fishkin), *Collected Poems of Langston Hughes* (1995), *Richard Wright: A Collection of Critical Essays* (1995), *Collected Works of Langston Hughes* (3 volumes, including *The Poems: 1921-1940*, and *The Poems: 1951-1967*, 2001), and *Poetry for Young People: Langston Hughes* (with David Roessel; a **Coretta Scott King** Illustrator Honor book) (2006).

For his scholarship, Rampersad has been recognized with a MacArthur Fellowship (1991-1996), and he has been elected to the American Academy of Arts and Sciences and the American Philosophical Society. Rampersad has spent most of his scholarly career at Stanford University (1974-1983, 1998-present), with intervening stays at Rutgers, Columbia, and Princeton universities. From January 2004 through August 2006, he also served as Stanford's Senior Associate Dean for the Humanities.

REFERENCES: *AANB. CAO-01. EBLG. W. Wiki.* Mandell, Gail Porter, in *ALB-2.* Mason, Theodore O., Jr., in *COCAAL* and *OCAAL.* Wanyama, Mzenga Aggrey, in *GEAAL.* Amazon.com.

Randall, Alice (née Mari-Alice Randall) (aka Alice Randall Ewing)
5/4/1959–
Songs, novels, screenplays, essays; cultural organization activist

Mari-Alice Randall earned her B.A. in English and American literature from Harvard University (1977-1981), then she started writing songs at the Wolf Trap Performing Arts Center in Vienna, Virginia, just outside of Washington, D.C. Soon after, Randall moved to Nashville, Tennessee to write country-music songs (starting in 1983). Among Randall's 30-plus recorded song credits

are three top-40 hits, two of which are also top-10 hits, and one of which hit number-one on Billboard's Country Music charts, probably making her the first African-American woman to have written a number-one song on the Country Music charts. Also that year, CBS aired a TV screenplay titled *XXX's and OOO's* (1994), the same title as her number-one hit song, which Randall cowrote with John Wilder. Randall has also been involved in three screenplay adaptations.

More noteworthy than these achievements, however, Randall wrote *The Wind Done Gone* (2001), a novelistic parody of Margaret Mitchell's *Gone with the Wind* (1936). In it, she tells the familiar story from the viewpoint of the enslaved daughter of "Mammy." About a month before the book was due to be published, Mitchell's estate claimed that Randall's work infringed on Mitchell's copyright and filed an injunction to bar its release. Eventually, the courts overruled the injunction, and the book was released with great fanfare and publicity. Soon after the book was released, it was a *The New York Times* bestseller and remained so for many weeks.

Randall's next critically acclaimed novel, *Pushkin and the Queen of Spades* (2004), also satirical, is set in contemporary times. Her third novel, *Rebel Yell: A Novel* (2009), due for fall 2009 release, promises to provoke both interest and discussion, as well. In addition to her songs and her novels, Randall has written short pieces for several periodicals. She is also a Writer-in-Residence at Vanderbilt University in Nashville.

Among her many awards are membership in the ASCAP Number One Club (1994), the Al Neuharth Free Spirit Award (2001), a Literature Award of Excellence from the Memphis Black Writers Conference (2002), and a nomination for the NAACP Image Award (2002).

REFERENCES: *CAO-07. Wiki.* Morris, Paula J. K., in *BB.* "Parody," Mathai, Varghese, in *GEAAL.* //en.wikipedia.org/wiki/Steve_Earle. //en.wikipedia.org/wiki/XXX%27s_and_OOO%27s_(An_American_Girl).

FURTHER READING: *EAAWW.*

Randall, Dudley (Felker)
1/14/1914–8/5/2000
Poems; publisher, editor, librarian, educator

The son of a teacher (Ada Viola Bradley Randall) and a preacher (Arthur George Clyde Randall), Randall was just 13 years old when a poem of his was published in the *Detroit Free Press*, and thus began his literary career. Like many other African Americans of his era, his early work was influenced mostly by his reading of English poets. Only later was he awakened to the works of African-American writers such as **Countee Cullen** and **Jean Toomer**. Randall was highly influential in changing that situation, so that subsequent generations of budding African-American writers were reading and learning about African-American poets early on.

After high school, Randall worked in a foundry for the Ford Motor Company, and served in the Army during World War II before returning to his education when he was in his early 30s. While earning his bachelor's in English (1949, Wayne [State] University) and his master's in library science (1951, University of Michigan), Randall worked in the post office. Later, after working as a reference librarian at Morgan State and Lincoln (Missouri) universities for a few years, he returned to Detroit, to take a job with the Wayne County Federated Library System. In 1969, he briefly tried teaching poetry at the University of Michigan before becoming a librarian and poet-in-residence at the University of Detroit, from which he retired in the mid-1970s.

In 1965, Randall published a *broadside* (a publication printed on a single sheet of paper) of his poem "Ballad of Birmingham," about the 1963 racism-motivated bombing of a Birmingham church, in which four little girls were attending Sunday school. With that initial publication, he founded **Broadside Press**. In his memoir, *Broadside Memories: Poets I Have Known* (1975), Randall recalled, "Broadside Press began without capital, from the 12 dollars I took out of my paycheck to pay for the first Broadside, and has grown by hunches, intuitions, trial and error" (quoted in *Black Biography*). On a more humorous note, Randall said he had founded Broadside Press, "Because I was ignorant. . . . If I had known all the toil and problems that running a business entails, perhaps I wouldn't have started a business. But folksinger Jerry Moore wanted to set my 'Ballad of Birmingham' to music, and in order to get it copyrighted I published it as a broadside. That's how Broadside Press began. Now we have eighty-nine broadsides, forty books, and eight anthologies. We have also published posters, tapes, books of criticism, and the autobiography of **Gwendolyn Brooks**" (from *The Black Scholar*, 1975, quoted in *CLC-01*).

The first poetry collection the press published was *Poem Counterpoem* (1966), which included 10 poems by Randall and 10 poems by **Margaret Esse Danner**, with each poet addressing the same theme in poems printed on facing pages. One of his most intriguing poems in this collection was "Booker T. and W. E. B.," which concisely articulates the philosophical differences that separated **Booker T. Washington** and **W. E. B. Du Bois**. In the following years, the press published several of Randall's poetry collections, including *Cities Burning* (1968), in response to a riot in Detroit; *Love You* (1970), with 14 love poems; *More to Remember: Poems of Four Decades* (1971), with 50 poems on diverse subjects; and *After the Killing* (1973), addressing issues of racial pride and black nationalism. Another independent publisher, **Lotus Press**, pub-

lished Randall's *A Litany of Friends: New and Selected Poems* (1981), four dozen new poems and two dozen old poems on a variety of topics. Across his body of work, Randall explored various poetry structures (haiku, triolet, sonnet, dramatic monologue, etc.), poetry techniques (slant rhyme, blues stylings, typographical arrangements on the page, etc.), and even poetry styles (e.g., trying on the styles of fellow poets).

In addition to poetry, Randall edited or wrote several other works, including two anthologies, *For Malcolm: Poems on the Life and Death of Malcolm X* (1967), which Randall edited with **Margaret Burroughs**; and *Black Poetry: A Supplement to Anthologies Which Exclude Black Poets* (1969); as well as *A Capsule Course in Black Poetry Writing* (1975, with **Gwendolyn Brooks**, Keorapetse Kgositsile, and Haki R. Madhubuti). Broadside Press did far more than publish and promote the works of Dudley Randall, however. Broadside also played a crucial role in the development of the **Black Arts Movement** of the late 1960s and early 1970s, publishing broadsides, chapbooks, and literary criticism by such poets and critics as Gwendolyn Brooks, **Lucille Clifton**, **Nikki Giovanni**, **Etheridge Knight**, **Audre Lorde**, **Haki Madhubuti** (Don L. Lee), **Carolyn Rodgers**, **Sterling Plumpp**, and **Sonia Sanchez**. Through the press's affordable paperbacks, writers were able to reach an audience eagerly waiting to read their works. By the time Randall sold the press in 1977, it had published more than 90 broadsides and 55 books; even afterward, he continued on the staff as a consultant for another decade. When asked what he was trying to accomplish through the press (*Black Books Bulletin*, 1972), Randall answered, "I'm trying to encourage poetry, because I like poetry. I'm trying to give people joy, because poetry gives joy. I'm helping to create black literature, and pride in black literature, therefore, pride in ourselves. I'm helping to create black consciousness, and values for black people to live by." Randall published two other works, as well: *Black Poets* (1971; reissued in 1985), an anthology he edited; and *Homage to* **Hoyt Fuller** (1984).

In 1980, Randall founded Broadside Poets Theater and Broadside Poetry Workshop. His honors include numerous Detroit and Michigan arts awards, a celebration honoring him at the Twenty-Fifth Anniversary of Broadside Press (1990), and an endowed scholarship in his name in the Department of Africana Studies at Wayne State University, donated by the Chrysler Corporation Fund (1997). In addition to his many literary children, Randall has a daughter, Phyllis Ada, with his first wife; he shared most of his life with his third wife, Vivian Spencer (married in 1957). When asked about the traits of young writers who offer great promise (*Black Books Bulletin*, 1972), Randall responded, "Traits that indicate promise are: strong motivation, love of words (since they are the poet's medium), seriousness, dedication to craftsmanship, willingness to study, learn, grow and change, health, stamina, and staying power"—all traits that he showed in abundance himself.

REFERENCES: *AANB. BAWPP. CAO-01. CLCS. EA-99. EBLG. TtW. Wiki.* Bianco, David, and Sara Pendergast, in *BB.* Cassidy, Thomas J., in *GEAAL.* Madgett, Naomi Long, in *COCAAL* and *OCAAL.* Melhem, D. H. (1990). "Dudley Randall: The Poet as Humanist." *Heroism in the New Black Poetry: Introductions and Interviews.* Lexington: University Press of Kentucky. Rpt. in *Poetry Criticism* (Vol. 86, pp. 41-83). Detroit: Gale. From *Literature Resource Center.* Miller, R. Baxter, *AAP55-85.* Randall, Dudley. "Interviews: Dudley Randall." *Black Books Bulletin 1.2* (Winter 1972): pp. 23-26. Rpt. in Jeffrey W. Hunter (Ed.), (2001), *Contemporary Literary Criticism* (Vol. 135). Detroit: Gale Group. From *Literature Resource Center.* Randall, Dudley, and Lena Ampadu. "The Message Is in the Melody: An Interview with Dudley Randall." *Callaloo 22.2* (Spring 1999): pp. 438-445. Rpt. in *Poetry Criticism* (Vol. 86). Detroit: Gale. From *Literature Resource Center.* Randall, Dudley, and Gwendolyn Fowlkes. "An Interview with Dudley Randall." *The Black Scholar 6.9* (June 1975): pp. 87-90. Rpt. in Jeffrey W. Hunter (Ed.), (2001), *Contemporary Literary Criticism* (Vol. 135). Detroit: Gale Group. From *Literature Resource Center.* Thompson, Julius E. (1999). "Dudley Randall, Black Life and Culture in Detroit, 1900-1959." *Dudley Randall, Broadside Press, and the Black Arts Movement in Detroit, 1960-1995.* Jefferson, NC: McFarland. Rpt. in *Poetry Criticism* (Vol. 86, pp. 5-19). Detroit: Gale. From *Literature Resource Center.* Amazon.com, 7/1999, 4/2009.

Randolph, A. (Asa) Philip
4/15/1889–5/16/1979
Essays, articles, commentaries; labor leader, political activist

By the time Randolph was in his 20s, he was well versed in progressive politics and a self-proclaimed socialist. In 1914, he married Lucille Green, whose unflagging support for Randolph and his beliefs was more than emotional and moral: Her highly successful beauty-parlor business provided the sole means by which the Randolphs stayed financially afloat.

In 1917, he cofounded the outspokenly radical monthly magazine the *Messenger* (with **Chandler Owen**, who left the *Messenger* in 1923). The *Messenger* unflinchingly denounced leaders in the African-American community (e.g., **Booker T. Washington**, for his accommodationism; **Marcus Garvey** for his separatism; and **W. E. B. Du Bois**, for his failure to recognize the importance of class struggle). Randolph also attacked job and housing discrimination, railed against lynching, condemned African-American participation in World War I, and generally provoked the U.S. Justice Department to call him "the most dangerous Negro in America" in 1919, holding the *Messenger* to be "the most able and the most dangerous of all Negro publications." Despite the best ef-

A. Philip Randolph

forts of the government, however, Randolph continued delivering his message month after month, year after year.

Randolph also took up the cause of the Pullman porters who worked for the railroads, leading them to found the Brotherhood of Sleeping Car Porters in 1925. Through the 1930s, 1940s, 1950s, and 1960s, A. Philip Randolph was always in the lead, championing the rights of hard-working folks to earn a decent wage, without suffering discrimination, and with full civil rights.

REFERENCES: *EAACH. SMKC.* Anderson, Jervis (1986, reprint). *A. Philip Randolph: A Biographical Portrait* (originally published 1973). Berkeley: University of California Press. Johns, Robert L., in *BH2C.* Pfeffer, Paula F. (1996, reprint). *A. Philip Randolph: A Pioneer of the Civil Rights Movement* (originally published 1990). Baton Rouge: Louisiana State University Press. —Tonya Bolden

FURTHER READING: *AANB. B. BCE. CAO-03. CE. LE. USMHC. Wiki.* Amana, Harry, in *AMJ-00-60-1.* Briley, Ron, in *GEAAL.* Isaac Rosen, in *BB.* Stein, Judith in *USHC.*

Raspberry, William (James)
10/12/1935–
Editorials

Raspberry wrote three politically conservative "Potomac Watch" opinion columns each week for the *Washington Post* from 1966 until his retirement in 2005; two of those columns were nationally syndicated each week. In 1991, 50 of his columns were collected in the book *Looking Backward at Us*. His honors include a 1982 Pulitzer Prize nomination, a 1994 Pulitzer Prize for Commentary (*see also* **Clarence Page**), honorary degrees from at least four universities, and being named the Capital Press Club's "Journalist of the Year" in 1965, for his coverage of the Los Angeles Watts riot.

REFERENCES: *AANB. CAO-07. EBLG. Wiki.* Conyers, James L. (2005). Afrocentric Traditions. Transaction Publishers. ISBN 1412804787, 9781412804783. 198 pages, in //books.google.com/books?id=ibsI6DK7jdgC&pg=PA128&lpg=PA128&dq=%22effie+t.+battle%22&source=web&ots=2118N5joeR&sig=nWlt1pZF15b40WUVgVqqMkWIxMM&hl=en&sa=X&oi=book_result&resnum=21&ct=result. Freiman, Fran Locher, in *BB*. //library.msstate.edu/special_interest/Mississippi_African-American_Authors.asp. //www.pulitzer.org/awards/1994. //www.pulitzer.org/finalists/1982. Amazon.com.

Ray, Henrietta Cordelia
c. 1849-1916
Poems; educator

In her collections *Sonnets* (1893) and *Poems* (1910), Ray's lyrical sonnets, ballads, and quatrains explore traditional poetic themes (nature, platonic love, religious ideals) and pay homage to members of her family, as well as to other heroic figures of her era (e.g., **Frederick Douglass**, **Paul Laurence Dunbar**, Harriet Beecher Stowe). Her poetry also reflects her superb formal education, including her master's degree in pedagogy from the University of the City of New York (1891), and her mastery of the Greek, Latin, French, and German languages. In fact, before Ray started earning money for her poetry, she taught at the Colored Grammar School Number One. Many of her poems were published in the *A.M.E. Review* before they were gathered into her collections.

Ray's poem "Verses to My Heart's-Sister" (published in her *Poems*) reveals her passionately profound affection and loyalty toward her older sister, Florence, who was her lifelong companion. She and Florence also wrote *Sketches of the Life of Rev. Charles E. Ray* (1887), a brief biography of their father, an abolitionist and editor of a periodical. Another of Ray's poems, "Commemoration Ode" or "Lincoln/Written for the Occasion of the Unveiling of the Freedman's Monument in Memory of Abraham Lincoln/April 14, 1876" was read at the unveiling in Washington, D.C. (printed in her *Sonnets*).

REFERENCES: Sanders, Kimberly Wallace, in *COCAAL* and *OCAAL*.

FURTHER READING: *AANB. BAWPP. CAO-02.* Gautier, Amina. "African American women's writings in the Woman's Building Library." *Libraries & Culture.* 41.1 (Winter 2006): p. 55. *Literature Resources from Gale.* Mollis, Kara L., in *GEAAL*.

//digital.nypl.org/schomburg/writers_aa19/bio2.html. //encyclopedia.jrank.org/articles/pages/ 4435/Ray-Charles-B-1807-1886.html. //oldpoetry.com/oauthor/show/Henrietta_Cordelia__Ray. //www.aaregistry.com/detail.php?id=2772. //www.bookrags.com/biography/henrietta-cordelia-ray-dlb/. //www.jimcrowhistory.org/scripts/jimcrow/women.cgi?state=New%20York. //www.questia.com/PM.qst?a=o&d=28142910. //www.uiowapress.org/books/pre-2002/grashewie.htm. Amazon.com.

Razaf, Andy
12/15/1895–2/3/1973
Song lyrics

The second lyricist to have a long-standing collaboration with noted composer Eubie Blake, Razaf wrote the lyrics for *Blackbirds of 1930,* including "Memories of You," a popular song of the day. He also collaborated with Thomas ("Fats") Waller, producing such hit songs as "Honeysuckle Rose," "Ain't Misbehavin'," and "The Joint Is Jumpin'." With other collaborators, he wrote the lyrics to "Stompin' at the Savoy" (1936), "In the Mood" (1939), "Gee Baby, Ain't I Good to You?," and many, many more popular songs. Among his four wives was the Schomburg Collection curator and librarian **Jean Blackwell (later Hutson)**.

REFERENCES: "Eubie Blake," in *EB-98*. Fay, Robert, "Andy Razaf," in *EA-99*.

FURTHER READING: A. *AANB. CAO-98. Wiki.* Manheim, James M., in *BB*. Singer, Barry, in *ASL-00-60*.

Reagon, Bernice (née Johnson)
10/4/1942–
Music history, songs; educator

Reagon has always interwoven her dedication to family, music, civil rights, and education. In the early 1960s, while she was studying music at Spelman College, she joined SNCC's Freedom Singers and married fellow Freedom Singer Cordell Reagon. (SNCC is the Student Nonviolent Coordinating Committee.) In 1964, her daughter, Toshi, was born, and she became pregnant with her son, Kwan. Before Kwan was born, she and Cordell separated and eventually divorced. In 1966 and 1967, Reagon released her first and second solo song albums, while raising her children and conducting her own research on traditional African-American songs and stories. Her research eventually led to her earning a Ph.D. from Howard University (in the 1970s) in American history, with a concentration in African-American history, cultural and oral history methodologies.

In 1973, she founded the group Sweet Honey in the Rock, the dynamic all-woman a cappella ensemble, with whom she has produced various albums and numerous concerts. The group's repertoire includes songs from musical styles as varied as gospel, blues, reggae, folk songs, rap, and West African chants. Their songs speak of the cultural riches of African-American heritage and of the struggles of Africa's descendants in America, past and present. These powerful women sing out against racism, sexism, and oppression of all kinds. The group has won numerous Grammies and other awards and has a wealth of recordings, including such items as a CD accompanying a life- and love-affirming children's book (Ysaye M. Barnwell, 1998, *No Mirrors in My Nana's House*). Reagon's work with her group also led her to write *We Who Believe in Freedom: Sweet Honey In The Rock . . . Still on the Journey* (1993).

Reagon has also worked for the Smithsonian Institution in various capacities (as cultural historian of the African Diaspora Project in the Division of Performing Arts Festival of American Folklore, 1974-1976; for the National Museum of American History as cultural historian of the Program in Black Culture, 1976-1988; and as curator of the Division of Community Life, 1988-1993). During her tenure there, she wrote various articles, including "African Diaspora Women: The Making of Cultural Workers," "The Albany Georgia Movement," "Women as Culture Carriers in the Civil Rights Movement," and "The Power of Communal Song." She has also spearheaded several projects: *Voices of the Civil Rights Movement: Black American Freedom Songs 1960-66*, a three-record collection, and *Voices of the Civil Rights Movement, 1960-1965*, a remastered two-CD collection with booklet anthology. She also edited *"We'll Understand It Better By and By": Pioneering African-American Gospel Composers* (1992). That served as the start of her Smithsonian Institution/National Public Radio series *Wade in the Water: African-American Sacred Music Traditions*, for which she was conceptual producer and host narrator. The Peabody Award-winning 26-hour-long radio programs started airing in January 1994. Other prize-winning projects with which she has been associated are the TV documentary series *Eyes on the Prize*, for which she was music consultant, performer, and music producer; and the PBS *American Experience* series film on the Underground Railroad, "Roots of Resistance," for which she was music consultant, composer, and music producer.

Meanwhile, Reagon raised her children, and her daughter Toshi has become an accomplished musician, composer, band leader, and recording producer in her own right, as well as an outspoken champion of gay rights and other civil rights. Reagon has also managed to hold visiting fellow posts and to lecture at various colleges around the country, and in 1993, the College of Arts and Sciences at American University appointed her its Distinguished Professor of History. She was also granted a 1989 John D. and Catherine T. MacArthur Foundation award (often called a "Genius Award"), a Trumpet of Conscience Award from the **Martin Luther King, Jr.**, Center for Nonviolent Social Change, and a National Endowment for the Humanities 1995 Charles Frankel Prize for outstanding contribution to public understanding of the humanities.

REFERENCES: *BAAW. WDAW.* Reagon, Bernice Johnson, and Toshi Reagon, "Remember . . . Believe . . . Act," in *33T.* —Tonya Bolden

Editor's note: Other writings by Reagon include *The African Diaspora: World Family of Black Culture* (1980), *Black American Culture and Scholarship, Contemporary Issues* (1986), *Compositions One: The Original Compositions of Bernice Johnson Reagon* (1986), *If You Don't Go, Don't Hinder Me: The African American Sacred Song Tradition* (2001), and contributions to numerous anthologies. She also edited *We Who Believe in Freedom: Sweet Honey in the Rock ... Still on the Journey* (1993) and *We'll Understand It Better By and By: Pioneering African American Gospel Composers* (1992). She was also music consultant and composer for the prestigious PBS series *Eyes on the Prize* (1987), *Roots of Resistance* (1990), and *Freedom Never Dies: The Legacy of Harry T. Moore* (2001). In 1995, President Clinton presented her with a Charles Frankel Prize, and in 2003, the Heinz Family Foundation honored her with the Ninth Heinz Award in the Arts and Humanities.

REFERENCES: *A. AANB. CAO-07. D. QB. Wiki.* Le Blanc, Ondine, in *BB.*

Reason, Charles L.
7/21/1818–8/16/1893
Essays, poems; educator, activist

A friend of abolitionists and social activists Charles Ray (father of **Henrietta Cordelia Ray**), **Frederick Douglass**, and **Robert Purvis** (husband of **Charlotte Forten [Grimké]**), Reason devoted his life to issues of social justice, civil rights, and suffrage. A college graduate, he also firmly believed in the value of education, working as a teacher and a principal in various schools and colleges in New York City and in Philadelphia, Pennsylvania. His essays and poems, which have been anthologized but not yet published as a collection, were also focused on the issues of importance to him and reflected his broad and deep knowledge of many subjects. His poems include his 86-line ode "The Spirit Voice" (1841) and his 48-stanza poem "Freedom" (1846) both eloquently express his fervor for freedom for African Americans.

REFERENCES: *AANB. Wiki.* Sherman, Joan R., in COCAAL and OCAAL. //www.lib.uchicago.edu/efts/AAP/AAP.bib.html.

FURTHER READING: Reason, Charles L. "Freedom." *LitFinder Classic Collection.* Detroit: Gale. From *LitFinder.* _____. (1992). "O Freedom! Freedom! O! How Oft, from Freedom," and "The Spirit

Voice; Or, Liberty Call to the Disenfranchised." In Joan R. Sherman (Ed.), *African-American Poetry of the Nineteenth Century.* University of Illinois Press. From *LitFinder.*

Redbone Press
1995–
Publisher

Lisa C. Moore already had publishing experience as an editorial assistant for *HealthQuest* magazine and copy editor for the *Atlanta Journal-Constitution* when she decided to publish her anthology *Does Your Mama Know? An Anthology of Black Lesbian Coming Out Stories* (1995). To pay the 49 contributors to the collection, Moore worked three part-time jobs. Once she had assembled her anthology, she realized the only way to maintain her collection as she had edited it was to self-publish it. She raised some more money, and in 1995 she paid for a print run of 3,000 copies, to start. To sell the book, she contacted African-American bookstores, gay and lesbian bookstores, African-American lesbian organizations, and anyone else whom she thought might be interested. Through her endeavors, she sold out her first print run within 6 months. In 1997, *Does Your Mama Know?* was awarded two Lambda Literary Awards: the Lesbian Studies award and the Small Press award.

The Lambda awards paved the way for Moore to find a distributor for her book, and more than 8,000 copies are currently in print. Lisa C. Moore officially became the chief editor at Redbone Press, and she published Redbone's second title, Sharon Bridgforth's short-story collection, *The Bull-Jean Stories* (1998), with more than 4,000 copies in print. Bridgforth's book won Redbone its third Lambda Literary Award, as a Small Press winner, and her book was a finalist in the Lesbian Fiction category. It was also a finalist for the American Library Association's Gay/Lesbian Book Award.

According to its website, "Redbone Press publishes work celebrating the cultures of black lesbians and gay men, and work that further promotes understanding between black gays and lesbians and the black mainstream." Redbone Press has also published "three more books [in] September 2004: *love conjure/blues,* a novel by Sharon Bridgforth; *last rights* and *nothin' ugly fly,* both books of poetry by Marvin K. White. In the summer of 2005, Redbone published *Where the Apple Falls,* poetry by Samiya Bashir. Published in 2006 are *Spirited: Affirming the Soul and Black Gay/Lesbian Identity, Blood Beats: Vol. 1,* and *Erzulie's Skirt.* Published in 2007 are *Voices Rising: Celebrating 20 Years of Black Lesbian, Gay, Bisexual and Transgender Writing; Carry the Word: A Bibliography of Black LGBTQ Books;* and *Brother to Brother: New Writings by Black Gay Men.* Published in 2008 are *Blood Beats: Vol.*

2 and *In the Life: A Black Gay Anthology.* Most titles since 2004 have been Lambda Literary Award finalists; additionally, *Blood Beats: Vol. 1* won a 2007 PEN/Beyond Margins Award" (quoted in //www.redbonepress.com/about/).

REFERENCES: Gay, Roxane, in *GEAAL.* [blogs from November 2005 through July 2009; a list of authors, and a list of books], //www.redbonepress.com/. //www.lambdaliterary.org/awards/previous_winners/paw_1996_1999.html. //www.lambdaliterary.org/awards/previous_winners/paw_2004_2006.html. //www.redbonepress.com/about/.

Redding, (James) "Jay" Saunders
10/13/1906–3/2/1988
History, social and literary criticism, novel; educator

In high school, one of Redding's teachers was **Alice Moore Dunbar-Nelson.** After high school, Redding spent most of his life in academia: earning his bachelor's (Ph.B., 1928) and master's (M.A., 1932) from Brown University, and teaching English at several colleges and universities (Morehouse College, 1928-1931; Louisville Municipal College 1934-1936; Southern University in Baton Rouge, Louisiana, 1936-1938, where he chaired the English department; Hampton Institute, 1943-1966; visiting professor at Brown University, becoming the first African American to be on the faculty at an Ivy League school; George Washington University, 1968-1970; and Cornell University, 1975-1988).

An ardent integrationist, Redding lost his job at Morehouse for denouncing the views of **Booker T. Washington,** favoring those of **W. E. B. Du Bois** instead. In the 1960s, his views cost him the favor of **Amiri Baraka** and other black nationalists who called for cultural separatism. Through his teaching and his writing, Redding challenged his peers, his students, and his readers to rethink their existing views of literature and history. In his first book, *To Make a Poet Black* (1939), he critically surveyed and analyzed African-American literature, suggesting the development of a **Black Aesthetic** and showing how individual poets (e.g., **Paul Laurence Dunbar)** and novelists (e.g., **Zora Neale Hurston)** participated in that development. Impressed with his scholarship in this work, the Rockefeller Foundation awarded him a fellowship to study African Americans in the South. This study yielded his *No Day of Triumph* (1942), which includes a chapter on his own family. That book further enhanced his scholarly reputation, as did his subsequent works, including *They Came in Chains: Americans from Africa* (1950), *The Lonesome Road: The Story of the Negro's Part in America* (1958), and *The Negro* (1967). These works combine biographical vignettes with information from primary sources to tell the story of race relations in America and to chronicle African-American history. With Arthur P. Davis, Redding edited the landmark anthology *The Cavalcade: African-American Writing from 1760 to the Present* (1971; revised as *The New Cavalcade*, 1991). Redding also wrote some popular works, writing articles for *Atlantic Monthly, Saturday Review,* and other national magazines.

A Guggenheim fellowship made it possible for him to take time out to write his only novel, *Stranger and Alone* (1950; reprinted 1989), about the son of a black mother and a white father, set in the segregated South in the 1920s and 1930s. In addition to Rockefeller and Guggenheim fellowships, Redding was awarded a Ford Foundation fellowship and numerous honorary degrees.

REFERENCES: *EA-99. EBLG.* Ashwill, Gary, in *COCAAL* and *OCAAL.* Amazon.com, 7/1999.

FURTHER READING: *AANB. BAWPP. CAO-00.* Chapman, Ryan, in *GEAAL.* Golus, Carrie, in *BB.* Savery, Pancho, in *MAC-20-55.* Thompson, Thelma Barnaby, in *AAW-40-55.*

Redding, Otis
9/9/1941–12/10/1967
Songs; performer

Redding's love of playing and singing music began at an early age, and when he had to drop out of school, to take menial jobs to help support his family, he still managed to squeeze in time for his music. In the mid-1950s, he played the drums for gospel performers on a local radio station, and by the late 1950s, he was singing in local amateur contests. In 1961, he made his first record, on a small local label in Georgia. In 1963, Redding's original rhythm-and-blues (R&B) ballad "These Arms of Mine" earned him a recording contract with Stax Records in Memphis. His sonorous, gravelly voice and original songs were soon strongly identified with the Memphis Soul sound. Among Redding's hits in 1965 and 1966 were "Mr. Pitiful," "I've Been Loving You Too Long," and "Try a Little Tenderness." In 1967, Aretha Franklin popularized his song "Respect," and other singers (e.g., the Rolling Stones) started showing interest in his songs. When Redding appeared at the 1967 Monterey Pop Festival, his career seemed destined for meteoric heights. By the end of that year, a plane crash ended his life, but ironically, it didn't end his fame. Redding's first number-one pop single was his song "Sittin' on the Dock of the Bay," recorded three days before he died, and released in 1968.

REFERENCES: *EA-99. G-97.*

FURTHER READING: *A. AANB. D. W2B. Wiki.* Cohassey, John, in *BB. See also* "Interview: Steve Cropper, Producer and Guitarist, Discusses Otis Redding." (Oct. 7, 2000). *Weekend Edition Saturday.* From *Literature Resource Center.*

Redmond, Eugene
12/1/1937–
Poems, plays, criticism, spoken word—poetry; journalist, publisher, literary executor, educator, actor, performer

"Motherless and fatherless at age eight" years, Redmond was raised by his "grandmother and a group of neighborhood fathers" in his East St. Louis community (quoted in *CAO-01*). Starting in high school, Redmond was involved with journalism, working on his high school newspaper and later his college newspaper and yearbook, then working as associate editor of the *East St. Louis Beacon.* While still a student, he cofounded the East St. Louis *Monitor,* working for that paper in various editorial capacities.

In college, he shifted his focus to literary writing, and his poems started appearing in periodicals (e.g., *Black Scholar, Journal of Black Poetry*) and anthologies (*The New Black Poetry,* 1969; *The Poetry of Black America,* 1972). He published several collections of poetry, too, including *A Tale of Two Toms, or Tom-Tom (Uncle Toms of East St. Louis and St. Louis)* (1968), *A Tale of Time & Toilet Tissue* (1969), *Sentry of the Four Golden Pillars* (1970), *River of Bones and Flesh and Blood: Poems* (1971), *Songs from an Afro/Phone* (1972), *Consider Loneliness as These Things* (1973), *In a Time of Rain & Desire: New Love Poems* (1973/1986), and American Book Award-winning *Eye in the Ceiling: Selected Poems* (1991). His spoken-word album *Bloodlinks and Sacred Places* (1973, Black River Writers Press) uses musical accompaniment to his poetry reading. He and several fellow poets also invented the *kwansaba,* a seven-line poem of seven words per line, with only one to seven letters in each common word—exceptions include proper nouns and foreign terms. A former consultant to master performer and choreographer **Katherine Dunham,** Redmond is said to be working on a poetic biography of Dunham.

Redmond also wrote *Drumvoices: The Mission of Afro-American Poetry: A Critical History* (1976), covering the period from 1946 through 1976; *Drumvoices* was adapted to a play format (produced in 1976). Redmond wrote several other plays, as well, many of which have been produced, including *The Ode to Taylor Jones* (1968), *9 Poets with the Blues* (1971), *The Face of the Deep* (1971), *River of Bones* (1971), *The Night John Henry Was Born* (1972), *Will I Still Be Here Tomorrow?* (1972), *Kwaanza: A Ritual in 7 Movements* (1973), *Music and I Have Come Home at Last* (1974), and *There's a Wiretap in My Soup* (1974). Redmond's teleplays include *Cry-Cry, Wind, through the Throats of Horns and Drums: A Jazz Ballet* (1977), *If You Love Me Why Don't You Know It: A Blues Ballet* (1977), and *Shadows before the Mirror,* and he has adapted other writers' work for television.

A man of many talents, Redmond is also an accomplished photographer, whose work has been exhibited across the United States and in Africa, as well as published in *Eighty Moods of Maya & Other Photo-Poetic Moments*. Redmond also edited *Griefs of Joy: Anthology of Contemporary Afro-American Poetry for Students* (1977/1986) and *A Confluence of Colors: The First Anthology of Wisconsin Minority Poets* (1984, with Angela Lobo-Cobb and Credo James Enriquez). In addition to his writing, Redmond has taught at various universities in Nigeria, Canada, and the United States (e.g., Southern Illinois University, 1967-1969 and since 1990, now emeritus; Oberlin College, 1969-1970; California State University, Sacramento, 1970-1985; East St. Louis School District, 1985-1989; Wayne State University, 1989-1990). Even in retirement, he continues to be an invited lecturer in Africa and the United States.

A poet and playwright of the **Black Arts Movement**, Redmond helped shape the movement through the company he cofounded (with **Henry Dumas** and Sherman Fowler), Black River Writers Press (aka Black River Writers Publishing Company), which published most of Redmond's collections. After Dumas's life was tragically cut short, Redmond was instrumental in preserving and promoting Dumas's remaining literary works. Redmond coedited Dumas's *Ark of Bones and Other Stories* (1970, with Hale Chatfield) and *Poetry for My People* (1970, with Hale Chatfield), and he edited Dumas's *Play Ebony, Play Ivory* (1974), *Jonoah and the Green Stone* (1976), *Rope of Wind, and Other Stories* (1979), *Goodbye, Sweetwater* (1988), *Knees of a Natural Man: The Selected Poetry of Henry Dumas* (1989), and *Echo Tree: The Collected Short Fiction of Henry Dumas* (2003). In the 1990s, Redmond also founded and edits (or coedits) the semiannual journal *Drum Voices Revue: A Confluence of Literary, Cultural and Vision Arts* (e.g., Fall/Winter 1991/1992, Fall/Winter 1992/1993, Fall/Winter/Spring 1997/1998, Fall/Winter 1998/1999, Summer/Fall 2000; the 2005 and 2006 editions feature Nigerian poets). He became the first poet laureate named by a municipality when East St. Louis named him its poet laureate (1976); he has also been honored with a Pushcart Prize, a Pyramid Award for lifetime literary contributions to Pan-Africanism from the Pan-African Movement USA (1993), a fellowship from the National Endowment for the Arts, induction into the International Hall of Fame for Writers of African Descent, and an honorary doctorate of humane letters from Southern Illinois University at Edwardsville.

REFERENCES: *BAWPP. CAO-01.* Burton, Jennifer, in *COCAAL* and *OCAAL.* Pettis, Joyce, in *AAP-55-85.* Torian, Stacy, in *GEAAL.* Weitzman, Lisa S., in *BB.* //www.nathanielturner.com/ eugenebredmondtable.htm. //www.newsreel.org/guides/furious.htm. Amazon.com.

Reed, Ishmael
2/22/1938–
Novels, essays, poems, songs, plays; editor, publisher, musician

Perhaps the most widely reviewed African-American literary figure since **Ralph Ellison**, Ishmael Reed has created a distinct niche in American letters. His experimental works often parody both the white and the black establishment. In addition to being a novelist, poet, teacher, and essayist, he is a songwriter, television producer, publisher, magazine editor, playwright, and founder of the Before Columbus Foundation and There City Cinema, both of which are located in northern California.

Reed and **Amiri Baraka** are probably the most controversial African-American literary figures. An innovative poet, he uses phonetic spellings and word play blended with what he calls neo-Hoodooism, offering an alternative cultural tradition for African Americans. Despite criticism from other African-American writers and from feminists, he remains committed to his satiric commentaries.

Two of Reed's books have been nominated for National Book Awards, and he has received numerous honors, fellowships, and prizes, including the Lewis H. Michaux Literary Prize, awarded to him in 1978 by the Studio Museum in Harlem. He has taught at Harvard, Yale, and Dartmouth, and for more than 20 years, he has been a lecturer at the University of California at Berkeley.

Reed was born in Chattanooga, Tennessee. In 1942 he moved to Buffalo, New York, growing up in the city's working-class neighborhoods. He attended Buffalo public schools and the State University of New York at Buffalo. He married Priscilla Rose in 1960, but they divorced a few years later, after which Reed settled in New York City. There, he helped found an underground newspaper, *East Village Other*, and participated in several cultural organizations, experiences that helped shape his artistic development.

By the late 1960s he had published and won critical acclaim for his first novel, *The Free Lance Pallbearers* (1967), a parody of the African-American confessional narrative. His second novel is a parody, as well: *Yellow Black Radio Broke Down* (1969) targets Western pulp fiction and what Reed sees as the repressiveness of American society. In the work, Reed also introduces his theory called neo-Hoodooism, a blend of Italian voodoo, West African religious practices, and nonlinear time.

By the late 1960s, Reed had begun teaching at the University of California at Berkeley, and in 1970, he married Carla Blank. In the ensuing decade he helped establish the Before Columbus Foundation and cofounded both Yardbird Publishing and Reed, Cannon & Johnson Communications. During this time, he also published his first major work of poetry, *Conjure: Selected Poems 1963-1970* (1972), which garnered him a Pulitzer Prize nomination. He also produced the mystery parodies *Mumbo Jumbo* (1972), set during the **Harlem Renaissance**, and *The Last Days of Louisiana Red* (1974), featuring voodoo trickster detective PaPa LaBas.

Mumbo Jumbo was the work that first achieved wide celebrity for the author, and it is considered by several scholars to be his best, along with *Flight to Canada* (1976), in which Reed parodies the **slave narrative** form. *Mumbo Jumbo* is a mythic/magic epic centered in such places as New Orleans and Harlem during the Jazz Age and the Harlem Renaissance of the 1920s. The story depicts the struggle among Jes Grew, purveyors of the black cultural impulse, and supporters of the Western monotheistic tradition, whom Reed calls the Atonists. Reed incorporates illustrations, footnotes, and bibliographies in parody of the documentary conventions of black realism.

Throughout the 1980s, Reed won critical respect more for his poetry and his essays than for his novels. His 1980s poetry was collected in *New and Collected Poems* (c. 1988), which blends black dialect with mythic elements. His essays were collected in *God Made Alaska for the Indians* (1982) and *Writin' Is Fightin': Thirty Seven Years of Boxing on Paper* (1988). Among his novels are *The Terrible Twos* (1982), a satire of the Reagan years; its 1989 sequel, *The Terrible Threes*; and *Reckless Eyeballing* (1986), an attack on literary politics.

Under the pseudonym of Emmett Coleman, Reed edited *The Rise, Fall, and ...? of Adam Clayton Powell*. In 1993 he published both a novel, *Japanese by Spring*, a parody of academia, and a nonfiction collection, *Airing Dirty Laundry*, a compilation of writings addressing such subjects as the news media and black anti-Semitism.

Reed's literary style is best known for its use of parody and satire in attempts to create new myths and to challenge the formal conventions of literary tradition. Reed's works have been criticized as incoherent, muddled, and abstruse. Other critics have praised him as multicultural, revolutionary, vivid, and profoundly aware of mythic archetypes. He wrote his fiction in a tone that was irreverent and harsh. He mixed standard English with a vernacular from the street, television, and popular music.

Reed constructs a resistance to the dominant Western conceptions of literature in his mixing of multimedia into the text. Reed's novel *Mumbo Jumbo* establishes him as a multimedia enthusiast much in the same vein as Kathy Acker, a notoriously controversial author who clearly rejects the constraints of pure text. On one page of *Mumbo Jumbo* is a picture of a Black Panther demonstration, obviously relevant to the plot of African-American resistance to Anglo traditions, but extremely anachronistic in a book about the 1920-1930s. Reed makes deliberate use of this apparent absurdity. In *Japanese by Spring*,

Reed mixes literary forms constantly, shuffling back and forth from fiction to nonfiction to narrative to essay to description to commentary, and so on.

Placing himself as a character in *Japanese by Spring*, Reed wrote,

"Historically, when whites moved among yellows, blacks and reds, death always resulted. . . . Reed believed that racism was learned. That racism was the result of white leaders of western nations placing little value on nonwhite life, or indeed, projecting violent impulses upon those who lived under constant fear of white terror."

Reed's books possess a common theme of resistance to cultural and racial oppression. It is tied in with the repulsion of dominant ideologies and formats. This repulsion and resistance is manifested in the multimedia formats.

Two albums of Reed's songs, *Conjure I: Music for the Texts of Ishmael Reed* and *Conjure II: Cab Calloway Stands in for the Moon* have been released by Pangaea Records. Reed lives in Oakland, California.

REFERENCES: *EBLG*. Dougherty, Brian Fox (1995), "Metalanguages and Contemporary Authors, Page: Ishmael Reed, *Mumbo Jumbo*," http://www.uiowa.edu/~english/litcult20/bdougherty/reed.html. Medgar Evers College (1995), Website produced by Arts Wire, a program of the New York Foundation for the Arts; Panel entitled "Politically Correct in a Politically Incorrect World" at the Fourth National Black Writers Conference, http://www.tmn.com/CGI/Artswire/black/reed.htm. Reed, Ishmael. 1996. *Japanese by Spring*. New York: Penguin. _____. 1972. *Mumbo Jumbo*. Garden City, NY: Doubleday. University of Delaware Library (1996), "Treasures of the University of Delaware Library," //www.lib.udel.edu/ud/spec/exhibits/treasures/american/reed.html.

Editor's note: Reed has been married twice. With his first wife, Priscilla Rose Thompson, he has a son, Timothy, and a daughter, Brett; with his second wife, Carla Blank, he has a daughter, Tennessee María. He and Carla also cowrote a mystery play, *The Lost State of Franklin* (1976, Reed, Blank, and Suzushi Hanayagi), which was awarded New York City's Poetry in Public Places Award. Reed also wrote the plays *Hell Hath No Fury . . .* (1980), *Hubba City* (1988), *Savage Wilds* (1988), *Savage Wilds II* (1990), and *The Preacher and the Rapper* (1994). Many of his plays have been collected in *Ishmael Reed: The Plays* (2009).

Reed and Carla also collaborated to edit *Pow-Wow: Charting the Fault Lines in the American Experience—Short Fiction from Then to Now* (2009). Other works Reed has edited include *The Rise, Fall, and ...? of Adam Clayton Powell* (1967, pen name Emmett Coleman); *19 Necromancers From Now: An Anthology of Original American Writings for the 1970s* (1970), awarded a Certificate of Merit from the California Association of English Teachers; the five-volume *Yardbird Reader* (1972-1976); *Yardbird Lives!* (1978, with Al Young), *Calafia, the Califor-*

nia Poetry (1979); *The Before Columbus Foundation Poetry Anthology* (1991, with Kathryn Trueblood and Shawn Wong); *Multi-America: Essays on Cultural Wars and Cultural Peace* (1997); and *From Totems to Hip-Hop: A Multicultural Anthology of Poetry Across the Americas 1900-2002* (2002). He and Al Young also created the video script for *Personal Problems* (1980), and they coedited *Quilt 1, 2, 3, 4, and 5* (1981-1987).

Reed has garnered a Pushcart Prize for one of his essays, and he has collected many of his essays in *Shrovetide in Old New Orleans* (1978), *God Made Alaska for the Indians: Selected Essays* (1982), *Writin' Is Fightin': Thirty-Seven Years of Boxing on Paper* (1988), *Airing Dirty Laundry* (1993), *Another Day at the Front: Dispatches from the Race War* (2003), *Blues City: A Walk in Oakland (Crown Journeys)* (2003), and *Mixing It Up: Taking On the Media Bullies and Other Reflections* (2008). His poetry has been collected in *Catechism of D Neoamerican Hoodoo Church* (1970), *Chattanooga: Poems* (1973), *A Secretary to the Spirits* (1978), and *New and Collected Poems 1964-2006* (1988/2006), as well as his Pulitzer Prize-nominated and National Book Award-nominated *Conjure; Selected Poems, 1963-1970* (1972). Reed has also recorded his spoken words in *Ishmael Reed Reading His Poetry* (1976), *Ishmael Reed and Michael Harper Reading in the UCSD New Poetry Series* (1977), "Sky Diving" (1978), *The Poet and the Poem: Ishmael Reed and Garrett Hongo Reading Their Poems in the Mumfoud Room* (1996, Library of Congress). He has also done vocals with Kip Hanrahan, Taj Mahal, and other Latin and jazz musicians; these collaborations led to *Conjures 1, 2, and 3*. In 2007, he released *For All We Know: Ishmael Reed Quintet Featuring David Murray*, on which he plays jazz piano. Though he retired from teaching at UC Berkeley after 35 years, he has definitely not retired altogether.

Reed has also written several novels, including *The Freelance Pallbearers* (1967/1999), *Yellow Back Radio Broke-Down* (1969/2000), National Book Award-nominated *Mumbo Jumbo* (1972/1996), and *The Last Days of Louisiana Red* (1974/2000), which won awards from the Richard and Hinda Rosenthal Foundation Award and the National Institute of Arts and Letters. While writing *Mumbo Jumbo*, he wrote *Cab Calloway Stands in for the Moon*, which became a contribution in *19 Necromancers* and then was published separately as a book (1986). In 1988, an audio version was recorded on CD (compact disc). Reed's other novels include *Flight to Canada* (1976/1998), *The Terrible Twos* (1982/1999), *Reckless Eyeballing* (1986), *The Terrible Threes* (1989/1999), and *Japanese by Spring* (1993).

In addition to his honors and awards for individual works, Reed has earned John Simon Guggenheim Memorial Foundation award for fiction, 1974; a Guggenheim

fellowship, 1975; an American Academy Award, 1975; a National Institute of Arts and Letters honor, 1975; a Lewis Michaux Award, 1978; an American Civil Liberties Union Award and publishing fellowship, 1978; a Wisconsin Arts Board fellowship, 1982; an associate fellowship of Calhoun College, Yale University, 1982; an associate fellowship, Harvard Signet Society, 1987 on; a Langston Hughes Medal for Lifetime Achievement, 1994; an honorary doctorate from the State University of New York at Buffalo, 1995; a MacArthur Foundation fellowship, 1998; three New York State publishing grants for merit; three National Endowment for the Arts publishing grants for merit; and a California Arts Council grant.

REFERENCES: *AANB. AAW:PV. B. BAWPP. CAO-04. CBAPD. CLCS. D. W. Wiki.* Bokinsky, Caroline G., in *APSWWII-1.* Cowley, Julian, in *ANSWWII-6th.* Duff, Gerald, in *ANSWWII-1st.* Fox, Robert Elliot, in *COCAAL.* Friedman, Robert S., in *APSWWII-5.* Gates, Henry Louis, in *AAFW-55-84.* Gates, Henry Louis, Jr. *AAW-1991.* Guzzio, Tracie Church, in *AW:ACLB-02.* Li, Wenxin, in *GEAAL.* Nastos, Michael G., *All Music Guide*, in *A.* Wankoff, Jordan, in *BB.* Zamir, Shamoon. "An Interview with Ishmael Reed." **Callaloo**. *17.4* (Fall 1994) p. 1130. From *Literature Resource Center.* Amazon.com.

Remond, Sarah (née Parker)
6/6/1826–12/13/1894
Nonfiction—abolitionist lectures

Starting in July 1842, Sarah Parker Remond joined her brother Charles Lenox Remond in delivering more than 50 abolitionist lectures across this country and in England. A letter of hers was published in London's *Daily News* (1865), and a lecture was published in London's *The Freedman* (1867). In 1866, she moved to Europe, studied medicine in Florence, and received her diploma for professional medical practice in 1868, and she practiced medicine there for more than two decades. In 1877, she married Italian Lorenzo Pintor and remained in Italy thereafter.

REFERENCES: *EA-99.* **Wesley, Dorothy Porter,** in *BWA:AHE.*

FURTHER READING: *AANB. Wiki.* Smith, Laura, in *GEAAL. See also* Winch, Julie. "'Doers of the Word': African-American Women Speakers and Writers in the North (1830-1880)." *The Women's Review of Books.* 13.9 (June 1996) p. 20. From *Literature Resource Center.*

Rhodes, Jewell Parker
2/12/1954–
Autobiography/memoir, novels—historical fiction, plays, lyrics; educator

Jewell Parker Rhodes earned her B.A., her M.A., and her Ph.D. at Carnegie Mellon University in Pittsburgh, Pennsylvania. She then worked as an assistant professor of English at Central Missouri State University in

Warrensburg, and then settled down at Arizona State University in Tempe. There, she has risen through the professorial ranks to hold the Piper Endowed Chair. She is also both Artistic Director for Piper Global Engagement and the founding artistic director of the Virginia G. Piper Center for Creative Writing. As an educator, she has won numerous awards.

Rhodes's first book was *Voodoo Dreams: A Novel of Marie Laveau* (1993), set in the 1800s. Critics praised it; Barnes & Noble chose the book for its "Discover Great New Writers" series (1993); and the audio version garnered an Audio Distinction/ Earphones Award (2002). Rhodes's next two novels were *Magic City* (1997), named a "Favorite Book of the Year" by the *Chicago Tribune*, and *Douglass' Women* (2002), awarded the PEN Oakland Josephine Miles Award for Outstanding Writing, the 2003 American Book Award, the Award for Literary Excellence in Fiction from the Black Caucus of the American Library Association, and numerous other awards. Rhodes also wrote two how-to books for aspiring writers. In *Free Within Ourselves: Fiction Lessons for Black Authors* (1999), she uses writings from 67 fiction writers to illustrate how best to perfect the craft of writing fiction. In *The African American Guide to Writing and Publishing Nonfiction* (2002), she offers a similar guide to writing autobiography, memoir, and other personal narratives, using the work of 30 other authors.

At last, Rhodes wrote a sequel to her first novel, *Voodoo Season: A Marie Laveau Mystery* (2005), centered on the present-day great-great granddaughter of Marie Laveau. The book earned Rhodes a nomination for the African American Literary Awards in the Mystery Category. Rhodes's third novel in the Laveau trilogy, *Yellow Moon: A Novel* (2008), follows Laveau's great-great granddaughter into the twenty-first century. While germinating the third Marie Laveau story, Rhodes wrote two tributes to her grandmother: *Porch Stories: A Grandmother's Guide to Happiness* (2006), given two Arizona Book Awards (both 2007), and *Down South: A Granddaughter's Memories* (2007), a digital-downloadable essay describing the values she gained from her grandmother. Rhodes also has two more books in progress: her sixth novel, *Hurricane Levee Blues*, and her first novel for young adults, *Ninth Ward*, both expected out some time in 2010.

In addition to her novels, Rhodes has written a dramatic adaptation of *Voodoo Dreams* (2001), which was named the "Most Innovative" Theater Piece of the Arizona Professional Theater Season (2000-2001). She also wrote both the story and some of the lyrics for *Water Rhythms*, and she is currently developing a dramatic adaptation of *Douglass' Women*. In addition, Rhodes has contributed to numerous periodicals and several anthologies. Along with the aforementioned awards and honors, Rhodes has been awarded a prestigious Yaddo Creative Writing Fellowship and a National Endowment for the Arts Award in Fiction.

REFERENCES: *CAO-06. Wiki.* Ramsey, Allen, and Barbara C. Rhodes. "An Interview with Jewell Parker Rhodes." *African American Review.* 29.4 (Winter 1995), p. 593. *Literature Resources from Gale.* //en.wikipedia.org/wiki/American_Book_Award. //jewellparkerrhodes. blogspot.com/. //www.hurston-wright.org/legacy_nominees2003.shtml. //www.jewellparkerrhodes.com/bio.html. //www.pulitzer.org/bycat/ Fiction. Personal communication, 5/18/2009. Amazon.com.

FURTHER READING: *EAAWW.* Boxwell, David A., in *GEAAL.*

Richards, Beah (aka Beulah Richardson)
7/12/1926–9/14/2000
Plays, poems, children's literature; actor

Known as an actor on stage (e.g., her Tony-nominated performance in *The Amen Corner*, 1965), in film (e.g., her Oscar-nominated performances in *Guess Who's Coming for Dinner*, 1967, and in *Beloved*, 1998), and on television (e.g., her Emmy-winning performances in *Frank's Place*, 1988, and in *The Practice*, 2000), Beah Richards also won an All-American Press Association Award (1968) and was inducted into the Black Filmmakers Hall of Fame (1974).

More important to literature, Richards also wrote plays and poetry. Her plays include *All's Well That Ends* (n.d.), her three-act play *One Is A Crowd* (1951, 1970), her one-act dramatic monologue *A Black Woman Speaks* (1950), and her one-woman show *An Evening with Beah Richards* (1979). *A Black Woman Speaks* was also published in **Freedomways** (1964), written by "Beulah Richardson"; reprinted with a collection of her poetry, in her volume *A Black Woman Speaks and Other Poems* (1974); and anthologized (1986). After Richards's death, LisaGay Hamilton highlighted one of Richards's poems to create the children's picture book *Keep Climbing, Girls* (2006).

REFERENCES: *BAWPP. CAO-01. QB. Wiki.* LeVasseur, Andrea, *All Movie Guide,* in *Act.* Naden, Corinne J., in *BB.* //library.msstate.edu/ special_interest/Mississippi_African-American_Authors.asp. Amazon.com.

Richardson, Willis
11/5/1889–11/7/1977
Plays, anthologies; theater director

Richardson is best known as the first African American to have a nonmusical play produced on Broadway (his *The Chip Woman's Fortune*, 1923). Prior to that landmark event, however, he wrote several one-act plays, which were published in **The Brownie's Book**. Also a director, Richardson wrote many other plays for adults, including *The Deacon's Awakening* (1920, published in **Cri-**

sis); *Mortgaged* (1924); *Broken Banjo, A Folk Tragedy* (1925, which won *Crisis*'s first drama contest, established by **W. E. B. Du Bois**); and *The Bootblack Lover* (1926, also a *Crisis* drama-contest winner). Richardson also published three important anthologies of African-American dramas: *Plays and Pageants from the Life of the Negro* (1930), *Negro History in Thirteen Plays* (1935, coedited with **May Miller**, including 5 of his own plays), and *The King's Dilemma and Other Plays for Children* (1956, including 6 of his own plays). In addition to his 30-plus published plays, Richardson wrote numerous other unpublished plays, which may be found in collections at the **Schomburg** Center and at the Howard University library. A playwright of the **Harlem Renaissance**, Richardson anticipated the **Black Arts Movement**, lobbying for the development of an African-American theater, which would promote plays written and performed by and about African Americans.

REFERENCES: *NYPL-AADR.* Houston, Helen A., in *COCAAL* and *OCAAL.*

FURTHER READING: *AANB. BAWPP. CAO-02. W. Wiki.* Nesmith, N. Graham. "Forgotten Pioneer of African-American Drama." *African American Review.* 35.2 (Summer 2001) p. 331. From *Literature Resource Center.* Ostrom, Hans, in *GEAAL.* Perry, Patsy B., in *AAWHR-40.*

Ridley, Florida Ruffin *See* **Ruffin, Josephine, George Lewis Ruffin, & Florida Ruffin Ridley**

Ridley, John
10/??/1965–

Screenplays [TV/film], commentary, humor routines, detective novels

After earning a baccalaureate from New York University in East Asian languages and culture, John Ridley tried doing standup comedy in New York nightclubs. He made it to the late-night talk shows but soon decided that he preferred writing to performing, so he moved to Los Angeles (1990). There, he started out writing scripts for TV sitcoms, including *Martin*, then *The Fresh Prince of Bel-Air* and *The John Larroquette Show.* Ridley's other TV work includes scripts for the critically acclaimed series *Third Watch* (1999-2001), *Static Shock* (2000), *Platinum* (2003, which he also directed), *Justice League* (2004), and *Barbershop: The Series* (2005, which he also directed).

While writing scripts, Ridley tried writing novels, too. His first novel, *Stray Dogs* (1997), didn't immediately sell as well as he had hoped, so he adapted it to create a screenplay, which was made into the feature film *U Turn* (1997), directed by Oliver Stone. Ridley's other screenplays include *Cold Around the Heart* (1997), *Positively*

Fifth Street (2007), and *Let Me Take You Down* (2007), all three of which he also directed, as well as *The Night Watchman* (2008). George Lucas is currently developing Ridley's *Red Tails*, about the Tuskegee Airmen. Meanwhile, Ridley became the only nonsoap-opera writer to choose "financial core status" with the Writers Guild of America and continued to work during the writers' strike of 2007-2008.

Ridley also developed some materials for Urban Entertainment. First, he developed an animated series for UrbanEntertainment.com, released on the Internet, then he adapted it to a movie format, writing the screenplay for the animated film *Undercover Brother* (2002), which was nominated for Best Screenplay from Black Reel Theatrical (2003). For Urban Entertainment, Ridley also wrote *Those Who Walk in Darkness* (2003), released the same year as Ridley's novel of the same name. In addition, Ridley wrote the story "Spoils of War," which led to the film *Three Kings* (1999); it garnered him a shared Writers Guild of America nomination for Best Screenplay Written Directly for the Screen (1999, with screenwriter David O. Russell). Ridley also wrote a stage play, *Ten Thousand Years* (2005), about World War II kamikaze pilots.

After *Stray Dogs*, Ridley penned several more novels, including *Love Is a Racket* (1998), *Everybody Smokes in Hell* (1999), *A Conversation with the Mann* (2002), and *The Drift* (2002). He also wrote *Those Who Walk in Darkness* (2003) and its sequel, *What Fire Cannot Burn* (2006). Ridley also collaborated with artist Ben Oliver to create the graphic novel *The Authority: Human on the Inside* (2004) for DC Comics. His second graphic novel, *The American Way*, was a collaboration with artist Georges Jeanty (2006).

In addition, Ridley writes short pieces for assorted periodicals; he occasionally commentates for National Public Radio; and he serves as a regular panelist on MSNBC's daily *Morning Joe.* In the past, he was an occasional guest on PBS's *California Connected* (2002-2007) and on MSNBC's *Scarborough Country* (2003-2007). He occasionally comments on public radio's *Weekend America* segment, "Good News, Bad News, No News." He also briefly hosted *Movie Club with John Ridley* (2004) on American Movie Classics (AMC) television, and he cohosted an episode of *Ebert & Roeper* (2006).

REFERENCES: *CAO-03. F. Wiki.* Bozzola, Lucia, *All Movie Guide,* in *Wr.* Feerst, Alex, in *GEAAL.* //en.wikipedia.org/wiki/Those_Who_Walk_In_Darkness. //en.wikipedia.org/wiki/Undercover_Brother. //www.imdb.com/name/nm0725983/. //www.imdb.com/name/nm0725983/awards. //www.imdb.com/name/nm0725983/bio.

Riggs, Marlon Troy
2/3/1957–4/5/1994

Film screenplays; filmmaker, educator, journalist, gay and civil-rights activist

Riggs independently wrote, directed, and produced numerous antihomophobic and antiracist films, including his 1988 Emmy-winning *Ethnic Notions* (produced in 1986). His other films include *Tongues Untied* (1989), made famous by the attacks from fundamentalists Senator Jesse Helms and political columnist and perennial presidential candidate Patrick Buchanan; *Anthem* (1990); *Color Adjustment* (1991), Peabody Award-winning documentary; and his final film *Black Is . . . Black Ain't* (1995), completed by his collaborators after his death. He also wrote and directed *Open Window: Innovations* (1988); wrote, directed, and edited *Visions Toward Tomorrow: Ida Louise Jackson* (1989); and directed and produced *Warring Ideals: A Portrait of Henry O. Tanner* (1989), *Affirmations* (1990), and *Non Je Regrette Rien/No Regret* (1991). Riggs was awarded grants from the National Endowment for the Arts and was posthumously inducted into the National Lesbian and Gay Journalists Association Hall of Fame (2006).

REFERENCES: *AANB. Wiki.* Balfour, Lawrie, in *EA-99.* Le Blanc, Ondine E., and Sara Pendergast, in *BB.*

FURTHER READING: Riggs, Marlon. "Black Is ... Black Ain't." *Cineaste. 22.4* (Fall 1996), p. 55. From *Literature Resource Center.* Wood, Irene. "Black Is ... Black Ain't." *Booklist. 92.12* (Feb. 15, 1996) p. 1031. From *Literature Resource Center.*

Ringgold (2nd married name), Faith (née Faith Willi Jones)
10/8/1930–

Children's books, memoirs; visual artist, educator

Faith Ringgold was born in Harlem Hospital in New York City and has lived in or near Harlem ever since. In recent years, she has been living in Englewood, New Jersey, but she still keeps her art studio in Harlem; she also spends almost half the year in La Jolla, California, where she taught and is now professor emeritus at the University of California at San Diego. Because young Faith had asthma (which makes breathing difficult), she was frequently kept home from school. At home, in addition to doing her schoolwork, she was allowed to draw with crayons and to create clothes and other items from the fabric, thread, and needles her mother gave her. (Faith's mother earned a living by designing fashions and making dresses.) Her family also included her brother Andrew (the oldest) and her older sister Barbara. During her early years, Faith's father, a sanitation-department truck driver, also lived with them.

When Faith was still in high school, she came to realize that she wanted to be an artist, and in 1948, she enrolled in the City College of New York, to study art. During that time, women weren't allowed to enroll in the liberal-arts program, so she had to attend the School of Education. While still attending college, she married Robert Earl Wallace, with whom she had two daughters: Barbara and Michelle; her marriage (and later divorce) slowed her down a little in completing her degree, but she nonetheless earned her B.A. in art (her major) and education (her minor) in 1955. Four years later, she had earned an M.F.A. (master's in fine arts, 1959) there, as well. By 1960, she started teaching art in the public schools while continuing to paint. Soon after, she married Burdette Ringgold, with whom she raised her daughters; their daughters have since enriched the family with three granddaughters: Martha, Teddy, and Faith.

Within a few years after graduating, Faith had started painting professionally. Through the 1960s and 1970s, Ringgold expanded her art to include sculpture and performance art, and the subject of her art has often centered on the experiences of African-American women (and men and children). To gain a deeper understanding of African-American culture and history, Ringgold began reading extensively, such as the works of **James Baldwin** and **Amiri Baraka**, and studying African art traditions, having learned about European art traditions almost exclusively during her schooling. Both her paintings and her sculpture often depict her family members and important African Americans such as **Martin Luther King, Jr.**

Ringgold's sculptures draw on a lifetime of experience in creating artwork with fabric, as she creates soft sculptures with fabric that she stuffs and paints. As she said on page 14 of her pictorial autobiography, *Talking with Faith Ringgold* (1996/1998; with Linda Freeman and Nancy Roucher), "My soft sculptures began as dolls, then masks, then hanging figures, then free-standing sculptures." Interestingly, one of the next steps in Ringgold's artistic evolution arose out of a practical concern. As she said on pages 16-17 of *Talking...*, "When I was starting out, there were hardly any galleries that showed the work of black women or women in general. . . . I had an opportunity to show my work provided I could ship it easily. Framed paintings have to be packed in crates, which are heavy and expensive to ship. In Amsterdam, Holland, I saw several examples of Tibetan *tankas*, which are paintings that are framed in cloth. I thought this was an excellent alternative to framing paintings in wood, because the painting could be rolled up and placed in a trunk and shipped rather inexpensively. So when I got home I shared the idea with my mother and she started making cloth frames. And it worked. I got a lot of exhibitions and lectures for which I was paid. Then I decided to write stories and put them on my paintings."

This development led to Ringgold's creation of her "story quilts": huge fabric quilts onto which she paints important scenes from African-American culture and history, and onto which she writes out a story about the scene and the characters depicted there. As Ringgold observed, the process of making quilts reflects not only her own childhood experiences but also the experiences of African-American women through the centuries. In her own family, Ringgold's great-great grandmother had made quilts for the plantation owners who enslaved her, and she had taught the skill to Ringgold's mother's grandmother, and so on down the generations. Further, Africans have a long-standing tradition of making useful objects beautiful, and much of African art reflects this tradition.

In 1980, Faith Ringgold and her mother, Willi Posey, worked together to create Ringgold's first vividly painted quilt, *Echoes of Harlem*. Within three or four years, she started including in her quilts fabric swatches onto which she wrote story text, beginning with *Who's Afraid of Aunt Jemima?* and continuing for at least 75 more story quilts. Subsequent quilts include *Sonny's Quilt* (1986; showing Sonny Rollins playing the jazz saxophone on the Brooklyn Bridge) and *Tar Beach* (1988; showing a scene from Ringgold's childhood).

Tar Beach led to yet another progression in Ringgold's evolution as an artist: She adapted the story quilt into a children's book (1991/1996), which was named a Caldecott Honor Book (1992), *The New York Times* Best Illustrated Book, and an American Library Association Notable Book; it was also featured as a Reading Rainbow selection and given a **Coretta Scott King** Award for illustration, a Parents Choice Gold Award, and numerous other honors. On page 7 in *Talking...*, Ringgold noted, "If you look closely at *Tar Beach*, you may learn more about me. It's really about going up to the roof, which has a tar floor, in the summertime when I was a child. My father would take the mattress up and my mother would place a sheet on it and some pillows and we kids would lie on the mattress. It was very hot and we could have food up there—watermelon and fried chicken and all kinds of goodies. The adults would play cards and the children would lie there and listen to them talking and it was cool. I wrote about this little girl [eight-year-old Cassie Louise Lightfoot] in the picture who is dreaming that she owns all the skyscraper buildings that she can see from the roof and the George Washington Bridge. She imagines that she can fly and that she can make life better for her family." Since its publication in hardcover in 1991, it has been published in library binding (1992), as a puzzle and paperback (1992), as a (13") doll and paperback (1992), as a paperback (1995), and as a "Turtleback" (1996). It has also inspired Ringgold's two board books, *Cassie's Colorful Day: A Tar Beach Board Book* (1999) and *Counting to Tar Beach: A Tar Beach Board Book* (1999).

Since the publication of *Tar Beach*, Ringgold has published several other books for children, including *Aunt Harriet's Underground Railroad in the Sky* (1992/1995), winner of the 1993 Jane Addams Children's Book Award, in which Cassie and her brother journey across time and space to find out about how African Americans escaped from slavery through the Underground Railroad; *Dinner at Aunt Connie's House* (1993/1996), which introduces a dozen famous African-American women who have made substantial contributions to American history (and is adapted from her 1986 story quilt, *The Dinner Quilt*); *My Dream of Martin Luther King* (1995/1998), a whimsical yet powerful biography of the great man; *Bonjour, Lonnie* (1996), which explores African-American history and mixed cultural ancestry with Lonnie, an orphan, who travels back in time to World War I Paris, where he meets his African-American grandfather and French grandmother, and then forward to World War II, where he meets his father and his Jewish mother, who ensured his safekeeping before she was discovered by Nazis; *The Invisible Princess* (1998/2001), a rather frightening fairytale in which a charming princess saves her parents and others from slavery through her own courage; *If a Bus Could Talk: The Story of Rosa Parks* (1999/2003); *My Grandmother's Story Quilt* (1999); and *Cassie's Word Quilt* (2002/2004). Many of these books have been praised in such noteworthy review publications as *Horn Book*, *School Library Journal*, *Publishers Weekly*, *Booklist*, and *Kirkus Reviews*, among others.

In 2004, Ringgold lent her name to *What Will You Do for Peace? Impact of 9/11 on New York City Youth*, illustrated and written by young people representing New York City's diverse peoples and calling for peace and understanding across cultures and life experiences. She has also illustrated the writings of other writers in *Bronzeville Boys and Girls* (2006, text by **Gwendolyn Brooks**), *The Three Witches* (2006, text by **Zora Neale Hurston** and **Joyce Carol Thomas**), and *O Holy Night: Christmas with the Boys Choir of Harlem* (2004, with text in the public domain). Her artwork has also been published on bookplates (1992), on stationery (1995), in an address book (2002), and in calendars (2003, 2004, 2005).

In addition to these works, Ringgold has written and illustrated exhibit catalogs, such as *Faith Ringgold: Twenty Years of Painting, Sculpture, and Performance, 1963-1983* (1984), *Faith Ringgold: Painting, Sculpture, Performance* (1985, Art Museum, College of Wooster), *Faith Ringgold: Change: Painted Story Quilts* (Bernice Steinbaum Gallery, January 13 through February 7, 1987), *Faith Ringgold: Changes 2: Painted Story Quilts* (Bernice Steinbaum Gallery, November 5-December 3, 1988), *Faith Ringgold: A Twenty-Five-Year Survey* (1990, Fine Arts Museum of

Long Island), *Faith Ringgold* (The Saint Louis Art Museum, March 22-May 8, 1994), *Dancing at the Louvre: Faith Ringgold's French Collection and Other Story Quilts* (1998), *Faith Ringgold: A View From the Studio* (2005, with Curlee Raven Holton). Her artwork has also been showcased in *7 Passages To A Flight* (1995) and in *Faith Ringgold: The David C. Driskell Series of African American Art, Vol. 3* (2004, with Lisa E. Farrington).

More than a decade ago, Ringgold told her life story in *We Flew over the Bridge: The Memoirs of Faith Ringgold* (1995), glowingly reviewed in the American Library Association's *Booklist*; and in her autobiography for young readers, *Talking with Faith Ringgold* (1996; with Linda Freeman and Nancy Roucher), mentioned previously. Her daughter Michelle Wallace edited *Faith Ringgold: Twenty Years of Painting, Sculpture and Performance (1963-1983)* (1984). Wallace's other works include *Black Macho and the Myth of the Superwoman* (1979), *Invisibility Blues: From Pop to Theory* (1991), *Dark Designs and Visual Culture* (2004), and numerous essays, short stories, poetry, and articles published in various periodicals and anthologies.

In addition, a few videos have been produced by or about Ringgold: *Faith Ringgold: The Last Story Quilt* and *Faith Ringgold Paints Crown Heights* (both produced by Linda Freeman), *Crown Heights Children's History Story Quilt* (1994), and *Tar Beach*, with Faith Ringgold (produced by Rosemary Keller). In addition to the awards she has received for her literary works, Ringgold has received quite a few awards honoring her artistic achievements, including at least five honorary doctorates, a grant from the National Endowment for the Arts (for her sculpture), a Creative Artistic Public Service Award Grant, a Banks Street School of Education award, an NAACP Image Award, and a Guggenheim fellowship. Perhaps the greatest honor of all, an elementary and middle school in Hayward, California, was named in her honor in 2007. New Yorkers are also planning the development of The Faith Ringgold Museum of Art and Storytelling in Harlem.

REFERENCES: *33T. AA:PoP. AANB. AAW:PV. AE. B. BCE. CAO-07. EA-99. EB-BH-CD. SEW. WDAW. Wiki.* Anderson, Joyce Owens. "We Flew Over the Bridge: The Memoirs of Faith Ringgold." *The Journal of African American History.* 91.3 (Summer 2006) p. 364. From *Literature Resource Center.* Cousins, Emily, in *BWA:AHE.* Goldstein, Nina, in *BB.* Johnson, Virginia, CRRL Staff, "Faith Ringgold: Stories in Stitches" in //www.kidspoint.org/columns2. asp?column_id=1239&column_type=author. "Michele Faith Wallace." *CAO-06.* Ringgold, Faith, Linda Freeman, & Nancy Roucher (1996), *Talking with Faith Ringgold,* New York: Crown Publishers. Simon, Stephanie (2/18/2008), in "Faith Ringgold Museum Secures Location In West Harlem," //www.ny1.com/ny1/content/index.jsp?stid=120&aid=78591. treco, eboni, in *GEAAL.* Amazon.com, 8/1999, 4/2009. //artnoir.com, 7/1999. //faithringgold.blogspot.com/. //www.faithringgold.com/ringgold/bio.htm. //www.faithringgold.com/ringgold/book12.htm. //www.faithringgold.com/ringgold/books.htm. //www.faithringgold. com/ringgold/chron_rev.pdf. //www.faithringgold.com/ringgold/default.htm. //www.faithringgold.com/ringgold/faq.htm. //www.library.uiuc.edu/blog/esslchildlit/archives/2008/02/african_america. html. //www.nwhp.org/whm/honorees.php. //www.nwhp.org/whm/ringold_bio.php. Amazon.com.

Rivers, Conrad Kent
10/15/1933–3/24/1968
Poems, as well as short stories and a play

While still a college student, Rivers had his first poetry collection, *Perchance to Dream, Othello* (1959), published. His subsequent collections include *These Black Bodies and This Sunburnt Face* (1962), *Dusk at Selma* (1965), *The Still Voice of Harlem* (1968, which appeared a few weeks after his death), and *The Wright Poems* (1972, a posthumous collection in homage to **Richard Wright**, edited by Paul Breman); Rivers's poems have also been published widely in journals and anthologies. Rivers's play and his short stories remain unpublished.

REFERENCES: Foster, Frances Smith, in *COCAAL* and *OCAAL.*

FURTHER READING: *BAWPP. CAO-03.* Coleman, Edwin L., II, in *AAP-55-85.* Vertreace-Doody, Martha Modena, in *GEAAL.*

Robeson (married name), Eslanda ("Essie") Cardozo (née Goode)
12/12?/ or 12/15?/1896–12/13/1965
Biography, memoir

Although Robeson is best known for managing the career of her famous husband, **Paul Robeson**, she was quite a shining intellect in her own right. After marrying him in 1921, she earned a B.S. in chemistry (1923, Columbia University) and a Ph.D. in anthropology (Harvard Seminary). Both she and he well deserved their reputations as fervent leftist social activists and outspoken advocates of social justice. The couple had a son, Paul Jr., in 1927, and although they separated for a time (following an adulterous affair of Paul's), they later reunited, staying together until her death separated them. She wrote a biography of him, *Paul Robeson, Negro* (1930), relatively early in his career.

Starting in the 1930s, Eslanda Robeson worked ardently to champion the cause of colonized people in Africa and other places in the world. In 1936, she and her young son traveled to Africa, and she later published her diary of the experience in *African Journey* (1945). Over the next three decades, the Robesons—as a couple and as individuals—traveled all over the globe, going wherever they thought their voices would help the causes they believed in: supporting anti-Fascist forces in Franco's Spain, attending pan-African conferences in Ghana, and living in the Soviet Union for a time. Because of their outspoken dissent, they were caught up in the anticommunist fervor of the 1940s and 1950s, and when Eslanda refused to cooperate with the witch hunts being staged by Senator Joseph McCarthy and by the House Un-American Activities Committee, Paul was prevented from getting work in this country.

REFERENCES: *AANB. B. CAO-03. HR&B. Wiki.* Myers, Aaron, in *EA-99.* Ransby, Barbara, in *BWA:AHE.* Wolf, Gillian, in *BB.*

Robeson, Paul
4/9/1898–1/23/1976
Autobiography, columns; founder of periodical, singer, performer

The story of Paul Robeson has been called an "American Tragedy," and this appellation does not seem to be an exaggeration at all. Paul Robeson was a man who rose to great heights because of his brilliance and talent—but that meteoric rise made his eventual fall all the more tragic. During the course of his life, Robeson was a scholar, an all-American football player, a lawyer, a singer, an actor, and an author. He did all of these with tremendous grace and skill but it was his acting that earned him international fame. He was cut down at the height of his career because he chose to defend the principles of communism (which he thought would eventually bring racial equality to the world) during the beginning of the Cold War. It was a fall from which he never recovered.

Paul Robeson was born in Princeton, New Jersey in 1898 to William Drew and Maria Louisa Robeson. His father was a runaway slave who became a cleric and raised Paul alone after Paul's mother died when Paul was only six years old. Despite this early loss, Robeson grew up to be immensely successful—he was admitted to Rutger's College (now a university) on a full scholarship, elected to the Phi Beta Kappa honor society in his junior year, and graduated as valedictorian of his college class. On top of his academic honors, he also excelled in athletics. He chose academics over sports in the end, earning a law degree from Columbia Law School in 1923.

During his first job at a law firm, however, he realized that the legal profession in 1923 would never allow a Black American to reach his fullest potential. After facing a great deal of discrimination from employees who refused to work under an African American, he concluded that, as Martin Duberman states in his biography of Robeson, law was a profession "where the highest prizes from the start were denied to me." He decided to leave the law firm less than a year after starting work there.

While in law school, he had acted in a few small theater productions; after deciding to leave law, he returned

Paul Robeson

to the theater. In 1924 he joined an acting group called the Provincetown Players, which was associated with and put on plays written by famous playwright Eugene O'Neill. Robeson starred in two O'Neill plays—*The Emperor Jones* and *All God's Chillun Got Wings* (a controversial play about interracial marriage)—and a star was born. He achieved tremendous critical acclaim and before long became an internationally celebrated figure in both dramatic and musical theater. Unlike many of his fellow contemporary African-American singers and actors, whose opportunities on stage were usually limited to playing comic characters or characters with racist stereotypes, Robeson became a prominent actor who performed in serious roles.

While touring in Europe, he was introduced to leftist views, and their emphasis on justice and racial and economic equality immediately appealed to him. Over the following years, he became increasingly outspoken about his views. His political opinions made him one of many prominent Americans dragged into the McCarthy hearings, a witch hunt in which Americans who were suspected of having any communist leanings were browbeaten with questions as United States senators tried to insinuate that they posed a threat to the national security of the United States. Finding that Robeson was even then unwilling to renounce his beliefs in the rectitude of communism, a senator asked him why he didn't stay in the Soviet Union. He paid dearly for his response, which was, "Because my father was a slave, and my people died to build this country, and I am going to stay right here and have a part of it just like you. And no fascist-minded people will drive me from it. Is that clear?"

So clear was his statement that it, in essence, heralded the end of his career. His popularity fell drastically. A riot erupted outside of a building in Peekskill, New York where he was to hold a concert when people who opposed his political views began to harass and assault his audience. Thereafter, he was never able to put on the concerts and found few opportunities to perform. His income plummeted as he became blacklisted by concert managers, falling from $104,000 in 1947 to $2,000 afterward. In 1950, the United States revoked his passport, which cut off Robeson's access to Europe and his audiences there because he would not sign an anticommunist oath of loyalty. When he published his autobiography, *Here I Stand* (1958), *The New York Times* and prominent literary journals not only refused to review it, but even refused to put its title on their lists of new books.

Robeson, who was described in the journal *American Heritage* in 1943 as a man "being hailed as America's leading Negro," had been transformed into, as Sterling Stuckey pointed out in *The New York Times Book Review*, a man whose name had become "a great whisper and a greater silence in black America." Although his passport was restored in 1958 after a Supreme Court ruling on a similar case agreed with Robeson's complaint that Americans cannot be prohibited from traveling because of their political views, the ruling came too late. Robeson made one more trip to the Soviet Union, but he soon fell ill. As his health failed, he remained in the United States, cut off from audiences and friends, and he refused even to attend tributes organized in his honor. He died in 1976 after suffering a stroke.

While some condemn Robeson's adherence to communism despite knowing that doing so would bring about his own downfall, others praise him, saying that his story is, as Jim Miller said in a *Newsweek* article, "a pathetic tale of talent sacrificed, loyalty misplaced and idealism betrayed." **Coretta Scott King**, wife of **Martin Luther King, Jr.**, told the people who gathered at a gala celebration of Robeson's seventy-fifth birthday (which he refused to attend) that Robeson "had been buried alive . . . [because he had] tapped the same wells of latent militancy" among African Americans that her husband had.

Whatever one chooses to believe, it is irrefutable that Paul Robeson must be seen as one of the great, if tragic, figures in African-American history—he was a man who achieved much, rose to great heights, and fell to greater depths, but all the while kept the goal of the advance-

ment of African Americans and the fight against racism uppermost in his heart. —Diane Masiello

REFERENCES: *BW:SSCA. EB-BH-CD. EBLG.* Bigelow, Barbara Carlisle (1992), *Contemporary Black Biography: Profiles from the International Black Community* (Vol. 2), Detroit: Gale Research. Mason, Theodore O., Jr., in *COCAAL* and *OCAAL*.

FURTHER READING: *AANB. All Movie Guide, in Act. ATG. B. BCE. CE. D. F. FAD. MD. ME. Wiki.* Cummings, Robert, *All Music Guide*, in A. Foner, Eric, in *USHC*. Howard, H. Wendell. "Paul Robeson Remembered." *The Midwest Quarterly*. 38.1 (Autumn 1996) p. 102. From *Literature Resource Center*. Kozikowski, Thomas, in *CAO-05*. Lankford, Ronnie D., Jr., *All Music Guide*, in A. Nagel, Rob, in *BB*. Nasaw, David. "His Father's Voice: Paul Robeson Jr. on the Life of Paul Robeson Sr." *The New York Times Book Review*. 106.14 (Apr. 8, 2001) Book Review Desk: p. 18. From *Literature Resource Center*. "Paul Robeson, Jr." *CAO-02*. Wadman, Mark, in *GEAAL*. *See also* **Brown, Lloyd; Davis, Frank Marshall; Du Bois, Shirley Graham; Fisher, Rudolph; Freedomways; Mossell, Gertrude Bustill; Greenfield, Eloise; Hansberry, Lorraine Vivian.**

Robinson, Max (né Maxie)
5/1/1939–12/20/1988
Broadcast journalist

Randall Robinson, brother
7/6/1941–

Nonfiction—social/political commentary/analysis, novel, biography, memoir; organization founder and leader

Max and Randall Robinson are the sons of Maxie Cleveland Robinson, a high-school history teacher and athletics coach, and Doris Jones Robinson, a former teacher and homemaker, who also had two daughters, Jewell and Jeanie.

Max attended Oberlin College (1957-1958) and Indiana University (1959-1960), then auditioned for a job reading the news at then-all-white WTOV-TV in Virginia. He got the job—but only on the condition that he had would read the news out of sight. One night, he managed a way to have viewers see his nonwhite face reading the news. The next day, the station manager fired him. After a stint in the Air Force, he got another chance to work in broadcast journalism. WTOP-TV in Washington, D.C., hired him as a reporter-cameraman trainee and then a full-time reporter, earning $25 less each week than his white colleagues, and doing traffic reports and other uneventful news (1965).

When WRC-TV offered him a job as a correspondent (1965-1969), he grabbed it. Despite the racist job climate there, he won six journalism awards, including an award from the National Education Association (1966), a Journalist of the Year award from Capitol Press Club (1967), and two Regional Emmy awards from the National Academy of Television Arts and Sciences. For a while, he also worked as associate professor of communicative arts at

Federal City College (1968-1972). Despite his awards, WRC refused to fulfill Robinson's ambition for an anchor position. His old employer, WTOP-TV, offered him an anchor job, at first as coanchor of the midday newscast (starting in 1969), where he was the first African-American TV news anchor in Washington, D.C. Two years later, he was coanchoring the 6 pm and 11 pm newscasts there (until 1978), another first.

ABC decided to try having a trio of anchors for its *ABC World News Tonight* broadcast: Frank Reynolds reported from Washington, D.C.; Peter Jennings reported from London, England; and ABC needed a third anchor, reporting from Chicago. ABC hired Max Robinson to become the first African-American anchor on a nationally broadcast TV news program, coanchoring out of Chicago (1978-1983). Sadly, Robinson knew how to excel at his job, but not how to win friends and influence people. When his coanchor Reynolds died in 1983, Robinson very prominently avoided the very public event.

Outraged, ABC demoted him to weekend anchor and gave Jennings the solo weekday anchor job. Soon after, Robinson left ABC to become WMAQ-TV's first African-American anchor in Chicago (1983-1985). Meanwhile, his long battle with alcohol continued, and he moved in and out of alcoholism-treatment centers. He seemed ready for full recovery when he was diagnosed with AIDS-related pneumonia. Reverend **Jesse Jackson** delivered the eulogy at Max Robinson's funeral. His awards included a National Media Award from the Capitol Press Club (1979), several honorary doctorates, a national Emmy Award (1981) for his 1980 election coverage, an Excellence in Journalism award from the College of William and Mary (1981), a Drum Major for Justice Award from the **Martin Luther King, Jr.**, Memorial (1981), and recognition awards from the **National Association of Black Journalists** (NABJ) and other organizations (1981).

Max's brother, Randall Robinson, earned his bachelor's degree (1967) from Virginia Union University and his law degree (1970) from Harvard University Law School, and then he passed the Massachusetts bar exam. In the summer after graduating (1970), Randall Robinson went to Tanzania, where he became disturbed that the United States was hindering African nations' progress, rather than helping them. He then returned to Massachusetts, where he worked for the Boston Legal Assistance Project (BLAP) (1971) and then directed the development division of the Roxbury Multi-Service Center (1972-1975). In his next two jobs, he aided U.S. congressional representatives William Clay (1975) and then Charles C. Diggs, Jr. (starting in 1976). He then worked as a staff attorney for the Lawyer's Committee for Civil Rights (1976-1977) while conceiving his next post.

In 1977, Randall Robinson founded and became the executive director and president of TransAfrica, Inc. (1977-1995), and then of the nonprofit organization, TransAfrica Forum (1995-2001), which has lobbied for and advocated on behalf of the human rights of people of African descent in Africa, in the Caribbean, and elsewhere in the diaspora. At first, he hired exactly one assistant for his staff. Since then, TransAfrica has grown tremendously, as has its advocacy. As a champion of the rights of people of the African diaspora, Robinson has often appeared on TV programs on ABC, CBS, NBC, PBS, CNN, and C-Span. In 2001, Robinson resigned his post, packed up his family, and moved to St. Kitts, his second wife's native island.

Decades earlier, Robinson had written a novel, *The Emancipation of Wakefield Clay: A Novel* (1978). He has since written his memoir, *Defending the Spirit: A Black Life in America* (1998) and several other nonfiction books. *The Debt: What America Owes to Blacks* (2000) discusses the need for reparations to the descendants of African-American slaves. *The Reckoning: What Blacks Owe to Each Other* (2002) outlines what African Americans of privilege owe to their less fortunate peers. *Quitting America: The Departure of a Black Man from His Native Land* (2004) explains why Robinson left his own country. *An Unbroken Agony: Haiti, from Revolution to the Kidnapping of a President* (2007) champions the case of Haiti's ousted president Jean-Bertrand Aristide, who had been the nation's first democratically elected president and its ardent advocate for that nation's poorest residents.

For his humanitarian work, Robinson has earned a Ford Foundation fellowship (1970), several humanitarian awards, and nearly 20 honorary doctorates.

REFERENCES: "Max Robinson," B. *CAO, 1986/2009. CAO-00. Wiki.* Kuskowski, Joe, in *BB.* "Randall Robinson," B. *CAO-07. Wiki.* Rosen, Isaac, Barbara Carlisle Bigelow, and Tom Pendergast, in *BB.* Veney, Cassandra, in *AANB.* //en.wikipedia.org/wiki/TransAfrica_Forum. Amazon.com.

Rock, Chris (né Christopher Julius Rock III)
2/7/1965–

Spoken word—humor, screenplays, scripts, autobiography/memoir; actor, performer

Editor's note: Rock's birth year is given as 1965 in *Wiki* and in *AANB*, but 1966 in *Act, BB*, and *CAO-06*. According to *Wiki*, "Reliable sources differ on his year of birth. In his book, *Rock This!*, Rock gives his birth date as February 7, 1966. But Rock stated he was 42 years old on his February 28, 2007 appearance on *The Oprah Winfrey Show*."

Chris Rock honed his comedic talents as a standup comic at New York City's Catch a Rising Star, starting in 1985. Meanwhile, Rock started getting acting parts on TV episodes, such as *Miami Vice* (1985) and *The Fresh Prince of Bel-Air* (1995), and making appearances on late-night shows, such as *Saturday Night Live* (1996) and *Chappelle's Show* (2003). He also started getting voice parts, such as on the live-action movie *Doctor Dolittle* (1998), the animated TV show *King of the Hill* (1998), and the animated movie *Madagascar* (2005), which won him the Kids' Choice Award for Best Voice in an Animated Movie (2006). Rock also started showing up in films, such as *Beverly Hills Cop II* (1987) and *Lethal Weapon 4* (1998).

Rock was also writing and performing for numerous spoken-word comedy albums, including *Born Suspect* (1992), *Roll with the New* (1997), *Bigger & Blacker* (1999), and *Never Scared* (2004). His second and third albums won Grammys (1998, 2000) for Best Spoken Comedy Album, and his fourth album, released on DVD (2004) as well as CD (2005), won a Grammy for Best Comedy Album (2006). Rock has also cowritten several screenplays with other writers, including *Comedy's Dirtiest Dozen* (1988), *CB4* (1993), *Down to Earth* (2001), *Head of State* (2003), and *I Think I Love My Wife* (2007).

Rock was soon hired as a cast member of *Saturday Night Live* (1990-1993), for which he was also a writer, and of *In Living Color* (1993-1994). In addition, he wrote and performed in two episodes of *Politically Incorrect* for Comedy Central (1996), and he wrote and performed in an NBC special, *Saturday Night Live: The Best of Chris Rock* (1999). He also wrote and/or performed in other specials for HBO, NBC, and PBS, and he participated in numerous awards ceremonies for MTV (1993, 1997, 1998, 1999, 2000) and for NBC (1994), as well as Billboard Music Awards (1996), Cable ACE Awards (1997), Emmy Awards (1997, 1998), Grammy Awards (1998), and Essence Awards (1998).

HBO invited Rock to write and perform in three specials: *Chris Rock—Big Ass Jokes* (1994), *Chris Rock: Bring the Pain* (1996), and *Chris Rock: Bigger & Blacker* (1999). *Bring the Pain* won Rock two Emmys (1997) and *Bigger & Blacker* earned Rock an American Comedy Award (2000). HBO also hired him to write, host, and executive produce *The Chris Rock Show* (1997-2000), which earned him two Cable ACE awards (1997) and another Emmy (1999). A DVD boxed set of the show's first two seasons was released in 2006.

Rock also managed to write his humor-filled memoir, *Rock This!* (1997). Fewer Americans have read about his childhood, however, than have seen his semiautobiographical TV sitcom, *Everybody Hates Chris* (9/2005-5/2009), created, developed, and executive produced by Rock and Ali LeRoi, and narrated in voice-over by Rock. Its four seasons included 88 episodes. Set in the 1980s, it featured a young Chris, living in the mostly African-American Bedford-Stuyvesant neighborhood, but busing to a mostly European-American neighborhood school. The show earned widespread praise and was nominated for two Emmys, one Golden Globe, and more than two dozen other awards, as well as winning a Young Artist Award for Best Comedy Family Television Series and an Image Award for Outstanding Writing in a Comedy Series (2008). It also won the adult Chris a Nickelodeon Kids' Choice Wannabe Award (2006).

REFERENCES: *CAO-06. D. F. W2B. Wiki.* Brennan, Sandra, *All Movie Guide*, in *Act.* Erlewine, Stephen Thomas, *All Music Guide*, in *A.* Peters, Ann M., and David G. Oblender, in *BB.* Redmond, Shana L., in *AANB.* //en.wikipedia.org/wiki/Catch_a_Rising_Star. //en.wikipedia.org/wiki/CB4. //en.wikipedia.org/wiki/Comedy %27s_Dirtiest_Dozen. //en.wikipedia.org/wiki/Down_to_Earth_ (2001_film). //en.wikipedia.org/wiki/Everybody_Hates_Chris. //en.wikipedia.org/wiki/Head_of_State_(film). //en.wikipedia.org/ wiki/I_Think_I_Love_My_Wife. //en.wikipedia.org/wiki/ Kids%27_Choice_Award. //en.wikipedia.org/wiki/Never_Scared. //en.wikipedia.org/wiki/Pootie_tang. //en.wikipedia.org/wiki/TCA_ Award. //en.wikipedia.org/wiki/The_Chris_Rock_Show. //en.wikipedia.org/wiki/WGA_Award. //www.imdb.com/Sections/ Awards/Cable_Ace_Awards/awards_summary.

Rodgers, Carolyn (Marie)
12/14/1945–
Poems, literary criticism and theory, novel, short fiction; self-publisher, lecturer, social worker, educator

At age nine, Carolyn started writing a journal. By the time she reached adolescence, she was reciting poems and had started writing her own poems. In college, she met **Gwendolyn Brooks**. With Brooks's encouragement, Rodgers submitted some of her poems to **Hoyt Fuller**, editor of **Negro Digest**.

After several of her poems had been published, Rodgers self-published her first volume of verses, *Paper Soul*, in 1968. The volume was reviewed favorably, and she was soon active in the **Black Arts Movement**. During the late 1960s and early 1970s, Rodgers traveled widely, giving readings and lectures. Often, she gained appointments as lecturer or writer-in-residence at various colleges across the country. Wherever she went, she read of cultural revolution and African-American traditions, advocating a black aesthetic through street dialect and free verse, while voicing feminist objections to "The Movement."

During this time, Rodgers cofounded the **Third World Press** in Chicago, which published several of her poetry collections, such as *Paper Soul* (1968), *Songs of a Black Bird* (1969), and *2 Love Raps* (1969). **Dudley Randall**'s Broadside Press also published her *Now Ain't That Love* (1970), *For H. W. Fuller* (1970), *For Flip Wilson*

(1971), and *Long Rap/Commonly Known as a Poetic Essay* (1971). Her written poems used unconventional capitalization, punctuation, spacings, and spellings, thereby reinforcing her distinctive free-verse, nonmetrical, nonrhyming style. Her themes often focused on racial issues, as well as relationships between men and women or between mothers and daughters.

In the mid-1970s, Rodgers's poetic themes shifted away from militant nationalist politics and toward more personal and introspective themes, such as loneliness and love, and even some religious themes. Her *how i got ovah: New and Selected Poems* was published by mainstream publisher Anchor/Doubleday in 1975 and was nominated for the National Book Award in 1976. In 1978, Anchor/Doubleday published her *The Heart as Ever Green: Poems*. In both collections, Rodgers viewed politics from a feminist perspective and revealed the spiritual and personal guidance she receives from her church and from her mother. Her subsequent poetry volumes include *Translation* (1980), *Eden and Other Poems* (1983), *Finite Forms: Poems* (1985), *Morning Glory: Poems* (1989), *We're Only Human* (1994), *The Girl with Blue Hair* (1996), *A Train Called Judah* (1996), and *Salt* (1998), which were published by Eden Press, as was her novel, *A Little Lower Than Angels* (1984). Many of Rodgers's poems have been published in periodicals such as *Ebony* and *Essence,* and in more than a dozen anthologies. She also edited the anthologies *For Love of Our Brothers* (1970) and *Roots* (1973).

In addition to her poetry, Rodgers often publishes short fiction and literary criticism, noting that literature "speaks not only to the political sensibility but to the heart, the mind, the spirit, and the soul of every man, woman, and child." Rodgers has received numerous awards, such as a National Endowment for the Arts award and P.E.N. Awards. Even after receiving such praise and recognition, however, she "continued writing and publishing and practically starving to death" (*MAAL*, p. 435). Apparently, in this country, poetry writing is not lucrative for an African-American woman—even a highly talented one.

REFERENCES: *BAWPP. BWW. CAO-07. CBAPD. EBLG. MAAL. NAAAL.* Davis, Jean, in *AAP-55-85.* Holm, Janis Butler, in *GEAAL.* Vick, Marsha C., in *COCAAL* and *OCAAL.* Woodson, Jon, in *OCWW.* Amazon.com.

FURTHER READING: *EAAWW.*

Rogers, Joel Augustus
9/6/1880?–3/26/1966
Novels, nonfiction—history; Pullman porter, self-publisher, journalist

In 1906, Rogers emigrated from Jamaica to the United States. Luckily for him, he managed to get a job as a Pullman porter (1909-1919), giving him a chance to travel, visit libraries in cities all across the country, and observe and meet a wide array of people. A year before Rogers became a naturalized citizen (1918), he self-published his first book, *From "Superman" to Man* (1917), presented as a novel in which an African-American train porter is arguing with a racist Southern European-American politician. When the politician asserts the intrinsic inferiority of Africa's descendants, the porter documents the myriad achievements of Africans and the people of the African diaspora. To create his counterattacks, Rogers drew on both classical and contemporary sources, using information from an array of fields, including biology and anthropology, as well as history. Rogers also used his novel to show the paltry scientific basis for the very concept of race, given the widespread intermarrying and intermingling of peoples from all continents of the world.

Joel Augustus Rogers was probably one of the best-educated men of his era. He receiving minimal education in his homeland, only briefly attended the Chicago Art Institute, and was barred from enrolling in the University of Chicago because he lacked a high-school diploma. Nonetheless, using his own funds, Rogers taught himself in the great libraries, museums, art galleries, and archives of Europe and Africa, as well as the United States. To further his studies, he managed to teach himself four languages: French, German, Portuguese, and Spanish. Perhaps because he was never trained in a single academic discipline, he freely ranged across disciplines, including history and archaeology, art and science, anthropology and sociology. France's Paris Society of Anthropology, the oldest anthropological society in the world, elected him to become a member (1930), and he won memberships in numerous other American and French scholarly societies.

In addition to being self-taught, he was also a self-financed self-publisher of most of his many books. After writing his novel, he wrote four nonfiction works: *As Nature Leads: An Informal Discussion of the Reason Why Negro and Caucasian Are Mixing in Spite of Opposition* (1919), *The Approaching Storm and How It May Be Averted: An Open Letter to Congress and the 48 Legislatures of the United States of America* (1920), *The Maroons of the West Indies and South America* (1921), and *The Ku Klux Klan Spirit: A Brief Outline of the History of the Ku Klux Klan Past and Present* (1923, published by Messenger). He then published two more novels, *Blood Money* (1923) and *The Golden Door* (1927).

During this time, he left his porter job and found work as a freelance journalist. He had already been working for the *Chicago Enterprise* during the 1910s. After moving from Chicago to Harlem, he became a correspondent

(1921-1966) and a columnist (1934-1966) for the **Pittsburgh Courier**, and he freelanced for the *New York Amsterdam News* (1920s) and for other periodicals, such as **Crisis**, **Freedomways**, *Journal of Negro History*, **The Messenger**, and **Negro World**. In the 1930s, Rogers went to Africa as a foreign correspondent, covering the 1930 coronation of Emperor Haile Selassie I of Ethiopia. A few years later, he returned to Ethiopia, when the Italian fascists invaded that country, among the first battles of World War II (1935-1936). His coverage of the conflict may have made Rogers the first African-American war correspondent and the only African-American foreign war correspondent during World War II. Between his first and his second trip to Ethiopia, Rogers wrote four thoroughly researched books: *World's Greatest Men of African Descent* (1931, self-published), *100 Amazing Facts about the Negro, with Complete Proof: A Short Cut to the World History of the Negro* (1934; rev., enlarged ed., 1957; 24th rev. ed., 1963), *Real Facts about Ethiopia* (c. 1935, self-published), and *World's Greatest Men and Women of African Descent* (1935, self-published). In addition, he contributed to the federal Works Progress Administration's *Negroes of New York* (1936-1941).

In the 1940s, Rogers continued to earn money as a freelance journalist. He also produced two major works: His three-volume *Sex and Race: Negro-Caucasian Mixing in All Ages and All Lands* (1940-1944, self-published) and his two-volume *World's Great Men of Color* (1946-1947, self-published), later edited and introduced by noted scholar and historian **John Henrik Clarke** and published by mainstream Macmillan after Rogers's death (1972). In the 1950s, Rogers wrote *Nature Knows No Color Line: Research into the Negro Ancestry in the White Race*, which argues that color prejudice and racial preferences appear whenever differences excuse domination, subjugation, and war. He also wrote and self-published *Africa's Gift to America: The Afro-American in the Making and Saving of the United States* (1959; 1961, published with a new supplement, *Africa and Its Potentialities*, by Sportshelf). The following year, Lincoln Park Studios published Rogers's *Facts about the Negro* (1960). Two of Rogers's last two publications were another novel, *She Walks in Beauty* (1963, published by Western), and a pamphlet, *Five Negro Presidents* (1965, published by Helga M. Rogers).

More than two decades after Rogers's death, Kinya Kiorgozi edited the *Selected Writings of Joel Augustus Rogers* (1989, published by Pyramid). For all of his works, Rogers not only conducted meticulous research and analysis, but also provided detailed references for his works, that others might follow him. Days before Rogers suffered his fatal stroke, he was in Washington, D.C., studying at the Smithsonian Institutions, with plans to visit the Library of Congress. His unfinished projects were *Color Mania*, addressing U.S. whites regarding their apparent color phobia, and a study of the early contacts between Africans and the Olmecs of Mexico (cf. **Ivan Van Sertima**).

REFERENCES: *BAWPP. CAO-03. Wiki.* Asukile, Thabiti, in *AANB.* Joyce, Donald Franklin. *Black Book Publishers in the United States: A Historical Dictionary of the Presses, 1817-1990.* 1991. Westport, CT: Greenwood Press. Manheim, James M., in *BB.* Rashidi, Runoko, in //aalbc.com/authors/jarogers.htm, and in //www.africawithin.com/bios/joel_rogers.htm. "Joel Rogers, 85, Author Of Afro-American Books," *The New York Times* (3/27/1966). p. 86. (from ProQuest, document ID: 356764092, //proquest.umi.com/pqdweb?did=356764092&sid=2&Fmt=1&clientId=9477&RQT=309&VName=HNP. //en.wikipedia.org/wiki/Haile_Selassie. //isbndb.com/d/publisher/helga_m_rogers.html. Amazon.com.

Rollin Whipper (married name), Frances A.
See **Whipper, Frances A. Rollin**

Rollins, Charlemae (née Hill)
6/20/1897–2/3/1979

Biography, bibliographies, anthologies, children's books; librarian

We rarely think of children's librarians as crusaders, but Charlemae Hill Rollins indeed crusaded on behalf of promoting worthwhile books for children. She strived to make available to children books that clearly portrayed the valuable contributions African Americans have made to American history and contemporary experience. The only thing worse than the total absence of African Americans from most of American literature was the distorted caricatures and stereotypes she saw in many books written for children and adolescents. To champion her cause, she lectured widely; taught workshops on storytelling; wrote numerous articles for professional journals; wrote bibliographies, anthologies, and biographies; and led by example in her own work as a librarian and storyteller.

After graduating from Western University in 1915, Charlemae Hill went on to study library sciences at Columbia University and the University of Chicago. In 1918, she married Joseph Walker Rollins, with whom she had a son, Joseph, Jr. At home with her son, she gained lots of practice in reading and telling stories, perfecting the most artful ways of charming and delighting a child through words. In 1926, Rollins started working for the Chicago Public Library (CPL), which was to be her professional home for the next 36 years. In 1932, the CPL opened its George C. Hall Branch and appointed her its children's librarian. From 1949 until 1960, she also found another avenue for her crusade: teaching students about outstanding African-American literature at Roosevelt University.

When Rollins wasn't captivating children with her storytelling skills or lecturing to adults, she was writing.

Her first book, *We Build Together: A Reader's Guide to Negro Life and Literature for Elementary and High School Use* (1941), listed nonfiction and fiction books suitable for children, which portrayed African Americans through authentic characters, realistic events, and interesting narratives. This bibliography was published by the National Council of Teachers of English and was revised in 1948 and again in 1967. In 1963, she offered a selection of works in *Christmas Gif': An Anthology of Christmas Poems, Songs, and Stories, Written by and about Negroes* (1963; reprinted 1993).

Rollins also wrote quite a few children's books of her own, including *Magic World of Books* (1952), and she edited *Call of Adventure* (1962). Most of her books were biography collections, such as *They Showed the Way: Forty American Negro Leaders* (1964), *Famous American Negro Poets for Children* (1965), *Great Negro Poets for Children* (1965), and *Famous American Negro Entertainers of Stage, Screen, and TV* (1965). In addition, as an outgrowth of her personal friendship with poet **Langston Hughes**, she wrote *Black Troubadour: Langston Hughes* (1970), which won a **Coretta Scott King** Award (1971). Rollins was also given numerous other awards by the American Library Association and by various book associations and women's groups, and she was awarded an honorary doctorate from Columbia College in Chicago. Perhaps most impressively, she inspired fellow Chicagoan **Gwendolyn Brooks** to write a poem in her honor.

REFERENCES: *AANB. B. BAWPP. CAO-03. EBLG. Wiki.* Jenkins, Betty L., in *BWA:AHE*. Lesinski, Jeanne M., in *BB*. //library.msstate.edu/special_interest/Mississippi_African-American_Authors.asp.

Roper, Moses
c. 1816–4/15/1891
Slave narrative

Roper's *A Narrative of the Adventures and Escape of Moses Roper, from American Slavery* (1837, London; 1838, America; later editions, 1838-1840, London and Philadelphia; 10th ed., 1856) was one of the first such narratives by an African American to appear in print. Roper's chronicle vividly documents the brutal treatment of slaves across the American Southeast before he escaped North to New England and then to England in 1835 (where slavery had been abolished in 1833), with the aid of American abolitionists. (See the editorial note for slave narratives for more on other narrators.)

REFERENCES: *AANB. BAWPP. Wiki.* Wilson, Charles E., Jr., in *COCAAL* and *OCAAL*.

FURTHER READING: Hovis, George. "Four Slave Narratives from the Old North State." *The Mississippi Quarterly.* 58 (Winter 2004) p. 397. From *Literature Resource Center.* Puffer, Raymond. "Andrews,

William L., ed. *North Carolina Slave Narratives.*" *Kliatt. 40.1* (Jan. 2006) p. 27. From *Literature Resource Center.*

Ross-Barnett, Marguerite
5/21/1942–2/26/1992
Nonfiction—political science, Indian- and African-American studies, scholarly writings and edited works; educator, administrator

In addition to writing 40 to 50 articles, University of Houston president (1990-1992) Ross-Barnett wrote *The Politics of Cultural Nationalism in South India* (1976) and *Images of Blacks in Popular Culture: 1865-1955* (1985), and she coedited *Public Policy for the Black Community: Strategies and Perspectives* (1976, with James Hefner). She also edited Volumes 7, 8, and 9 of *Readings on Equal Education,* including *Educational Policy in an Era of Conservative Reform* (Vol. 9, 1986, coedited with Charles Harrington and Philip White). Before becoming the first African-American woman to preside over a major American university, Ross-Barnett taught at Princeton University (1970-1976), Howard University (1976-1980), and Columbia University (1980-1983), where she was also director of the Institute for Urban and Minority Education; after that, she was a professor and vice-chancellor at the City University of New York (1983-1986), then a professor of political science and chancellor of the University of Missouri—St. Louis (1986-1990). Meanwhile, in 1962, she had a daughter, Amy Douglass Barnett, from her first marriage, which ended in divorce; she married Walter Eugene King in 1980.

REFERENCES: *AANB. B. Wiki.* Aguilar, Marian, in *EA-99.* Brennan, Carol, in *BB.* Williams-Andoh, Ife, in *BWA:AHE.*

FURTHER READING: Sargent, Lyman Tower. "Editorial." *Utopian Studies.* 15.1 (Winter 2004) pvi. From *Literature Resource Center.*

Rowan, Carl T. (Thomas)
8/11/1925–9/23/2000
Biographies, history, political commentary; journalist

Although young Carl was born in Ravenscroft, Tennessee, his family had moved to McMinnville, Tennessee, a small lumber mill town, when he was still an infant. During Carl's childhood, the entire country was suffering an economic depression, and the Rowan family suffered particularly greatly. Thomas David Rowan, Carl's father, stacked lumber for 25¢ an hour, and his mother, Johnnie Rowan, earned a little by doing laundry for other folks. Johnnie also taught young Carl how to find various wild plants to add to the family meals. Nonetheless, Carl, his brother, Charles, and his sister, Ella, never had electricity in their home, they marked the time by the trains that rattled past their house, and they lived in terror of the rats that infested their home and stalked them in their nightmares.

From an early age, Carl started working at various menial jobs to help out his family, but he managed always to have hope of using education to lift himself out of his desperate poverty. Fortunately, while he was still at McMinnville's segregated Bernard High School, Miss Bessie Taylor Gwynn encouraged his belief in himself and in the value of education. As he later wrote in his autobiography *Breaking Barriers*, Miss Bessie used to say, "If you don't read, you can't write, and if you can't write, you stop dreaming." She inspired him to want to pursue journalism, and she helped him more directly by smuggling books to him from the whites-only library in town. He later said, "The library is the temple of learning, and learning has liberated more people than all the wars in history" (*QB*).

After Carl graduated as valedictorian of his high school class, he left McMinnville with 77¢ in his pocket, wearing his best clothes, carrying a cardboard box of his other belongings, and hoping to go to college. His grandparents lived in Nashville, and he planned to stay with them while studying journalism at Fisk University. Originally, he had hoped to get a football scholarship, as he had played football in high school. When Fisk turned him down, he went to work mopping floors and delivering food in a local hospital where his grandfather worked, earning $30 per month. By the fall (1942), he had saved up enough money to enroll in Tennessee A&I (agricultural and industrial) College (now Tennessee State University).

In 1943, while Rowan was still in college, a professor recommended him for taking a written examination to enter the U.S. Navy's V-12 officer-training program. Rowan passed the test and became one of the first 15 African Americans to train to become a commissioned officer in the U.S. Navy. At first, he trained at Washburn University in Topeka, Kansas, then later he attended Oberlin (Ohio) College and then the Naval Reserve Midshipmen School in Fort Schuyler, in the Bronx, New York. After his training, he was commissioned as an officer and assigned to sea duty, serving as a deputy commander of communications aboard the USS *Chemung* during World War II. In the Navy, even white Southerners had to listen to him and follow his orders in regard to communications.

After being discharged, Rowan returned to McMinnville. While riding the train home, he read numerous African-American newspapers of that era—the *Pittsburgh Courier*, the *Baltimore Afro-American*, the *Chicago Defender*, and so on—and became even more determined to pursue a career in journalism. After a very brief stay in McMinnville, Rowan headed back to Oberlin to complete his college degree in journalism. While finishing his bachelor's degree (B.A., 1947), he worked as a freelance writer for the *Baltimore Afro-American*. During graduate school at the University of Minnesota (M.A., journalism, 1948), he continued working for the *Afro-American* as a Northern correspondent, and he started working for the *Minneapolis Spokesman* and the *St. Paul Recorder*.

Once Rowan had his M.A. in hand, the formerly all-white *Minneapolis Tribune* hired him as a copywriter, and two years later, he was made a general-assignment reporter, thereby becoming one of the first few African-American reporters to be employed by a major urban daily newspaper. In 1951, Rowan wrote a series of 18 articles titled "How Far from Slavery?" while he took a 6,000-mile sojourn through 13 Southern states. Actually, the idea for the articles emerged much earlier, from a discussion with a white Texan when he was still in the Navy. This seamen had encouraged Rowan to write about "all the little things it means being a Negro in the South, or anyplace where being a Negro makes a difference." Rowan's articles opened the eyes of Northern readers about the realities of the Jim Crow South, describing his own experiences and those of others in Southern hotels, restaurants, buses, trains, and other public places. The series earned Rowan a 1952 Sidney Hillman Award for the best newspaper reporting in the nation and a check for $500 (the equivalent of six of Rowan's weekly paychecks at the time). The articles also became the basis of Rowan's first book, *South of Freedom* (1952).

For another of Rowan's series, "Jim Crow's Last Stand," Rowan returned to the South again, this time to document the various court cases leading to the historic 1954 *Brown v. Board of Education of Topeka* Supreme Court decision. This series gained Rowan a 1954 Sigma Delta Chi Journalism Award from the Society of Professional Journalists, for the best general reporting of 1953, and it played a role in his being named among the 10 most outstanding men of 1953 by the U.S. Junior Chamber of Commerce. Another of his series, "Dixie Divided," probed the South's efforts to resist the Supreme Court's desegregation orders following the *Brown* decision. During the 1955 Montgomery bus boycott led by **Martin Luther King, Jr.**, Rowan was the only African-American reporter covering the story for a national newspaper.

Rowan was also asked to cover international affairs, such as the United Nations, the Suez Canal crisis (in Egypt, when England, France, and Israel tried to seize the canal) and the Hungarian uprising (in which the Soviet Union brutally suppressed a Hungarian attempt to break free from the Soviet bloc). In 1954, the U.S. State Department invited Rowan to travel to India and to Southeast Asia, to lecture on the importance of the free press. While in India, he also wrote a series of articles for the *Tribune*, and in Southeast Asia, he wrote about the political tensions of that region, as well as about the 1955

Bandung Conference, attended by representatives from 23 less-developed nations. In recognition of his journalistic skills, Rowan won two more Sigma Delta Chi awards (for foreign correspondence) and was invited to become the first African-American member of the Gridiron Club, an organization of Washington, D.C., journalists (founded in 1885).

In 1961, Rowan left the *Minneapolis Tribune* and accepted appointments in the Kennedy and then the Johnson administrations. From 1961 to 1963, he served as Kennedy's deputy assistant secretary of state for public affairs, handling press relations for the State Department. In that role, he made top-secret negotiations with the Soviet Union to free U.S. pilot Francis Gary Powers, whose U2 spy plane had been shot down over the USSR. He also became not only the first African American to serve on the National Security Council (NSC) but also the first ever to attend an NSC meeting. Rowan also toured Southeast Asia, India, and Europe with then-Vice President Lyndon Johnson. In 1963, Rowan was appointed the ambassador to Finland, thereby becoming the youngest ambassador and only the fifth African American ever to serve as an envoy.

In 1964, President Johnson asked Rowan to leave his ambassadorship to become the director of the United States Information Agency (USIA). The USIA operates an assortment of educational and cultural programs abroad, including the worldwide radio broadcasts of the "Voice of America." Again, Rowan broke ground as the first African American to lead this important post and was then the highest-ranking African American ever to serve in the State Department and the highest-ranking African American in the federal government at that time.

In 1965, Rowan left his USIA position to return to journalism. From 1965 to 1978, he wrote a column for the *Chicago Daily News*. In 1978, he started writing a column for the *Chicago Sun-Times* and he since wrote a nationally syndicated column for the *Chicago Tribune*. In addition to his columns, Rowan made regular appearances as a broadcaster on radio (his five-day-a-week *The Rowan Report*) and television (frequently appearing on *Meet the Press, Inside Washington,* and other programs).

Rowan also wrote several books, including the previously mentioned *South of Freedom* (1952; reprinted in 1997). Rowan's other books include *The Pitiful and the Proud* (1956), about his experiences in Asia; *Go South to Sorrow* (1957), a provocative book about the need for immediate action in civil rights; *Wait Till Next Year: The Life Story of Jackie Robinson* (1960); *Just Between Us Blacks* (1974); his nationally best-selling *Breaking Barriers: A Memoir* (1991); *Dream Makers, Dream Breakers: The World of Justice Thurgood Marshall* (1993/1994), about the memorable Supreme Court justice and their 40-year

friendship; and *The Coming Race War in America: A Wake-Up Call* (1996), about the country's highly charged racial relations following the O.J. Simpson case, exacerbated by increasing disparities between rich and poor, the rising number of right-wing militias and other hate groups, the growing opposition to affirmative action and to welfare support of the underclass, and burgeoning prison populations.

In addition to his written work, Rowan hosted two documentaries, *Searching for Justice: Three American Stories* (1987) and *Thurgood Marshall: The Man* (1987). Rowan also established "Project Excellence," a million-dollar scholarship fund for Washington, D.C., high school students who wish to become journalists. Rowan and his wife, Vivien Louise Murphy, raised three children: Barbara, Carl Jr., and Geoffrey. In addition to his numerous awards for his reporting, in 1997, Rowan won the Spingarn Medal for his outstanding achievements and contributions.

REFERENCES: *AA:PoP. AAB. AANB. B. BF:2000. CAO-01. EBLG. G-99. QB. Wiki.* Aguiar, Marian, in *EA-99.* Emery, Michael, in *WB-99.* "Analysis: Newspaper Columnist Carl Rowan Dies at Age 75." (Sept. 23, 2000). *Weekend All Things Considered.* From *Literature Resource Center.* Mueller, Michael E., & Michelle Banks, in *BH2C.* Mueller, Michael E., and Ashyia N. Henderson, in *BB.* Oder, Norman. "Carl T. Rowan: In His New Book, the Veteran Columnist Recalls the Man He Calls Justice 'Thurgood' (PW Interviews)." *Publishers Weekly.* 240.3 (Jan. 18, 1993) p. 444. From *Literature Resource Center.* Amazon.com, 8/1999, 4/2009.

Ruffin, Josephine St. Pierre
8/31/1842–3/13/1924

Columnist, journalist, journal publisher, editor, activist, organization leader

George Lewis Ruffin, husband
12/16/1834–11/19/1886

Literary criticism, opinion pieces; attorney, judge, politician, activist

Florida Ruffin Ridley, daughter
1/29/1861–3/?/1943

Essays, history, short stories; educator, journalist, organization activist

The Woman's Era, the journal Josephine created with the help of her daughter
3/1894–1/1897

Club news, opinion, advocacy, poetry, short fiction, essays, literary criticism, editorials, motivational pieces; first monthly periodical published by African-American women

When Josephine St. Pierre was just 16 years old, she married George Lewis Ruffin, the son of one of Boston's wealthiest African-American families. Immediately after their marriage, they moved to England, but soon after the Civil War started, they returned to Boston, where George attended Harvard Law School and Josephine became involved in charity work. Ruffin also joined Lucy Stone and Julia Ward Howe in founding Boston's American Woman Suffrage Association in 1869. She later joined Stone and Howe's New England Woman's Club.

In 1869, George became one of Harvard Law School's first African-American graduates, and soon after he entered politics, becoming Boston's first African-American city councilman and then a Massachusetts state legislator. In 1883, George was appointed the first African-American judge in New England. As a prominent judge, his literary criticism and other writings commanded the respect of his readers. By the time George was named a judge (1883), the Ruffins had five children, including their only daughter, Florida Yates Ruffin. Sadly, Judge Ruffin did not live to see Florida's 1888 marriage to folklorist Ulysses A. Ridley, also from one of Boston's most socially prominent and wealthy families.

In the early 1890s, Josephine started writing a column for the weekly *Boston Courant*, owned and operated by African Americans. For a time, she was the *Courant's* editor-in-chief, and she joined the New England Women's Press Association. In 1893, she held the first meeting of the Woman's Era Club in Boston, one of the first U.S. clubs for African-American women. She opened her first meeting to both black women and white women, in line with her aims for racial uplift, but also for women's rights, especially women's suffrage, and integration. For the next decade, Ruffin presided over the club, ably assisted by her daughter, Florida, and by her friend, Maria Louise Baldwin. Two years after starting her Woman's Era Club in Boston, Ruffin organized the First National Conference of Colored Women (1895), to which she invited woman's club members from across the land. This conference led to the founding of the National Federation of Afro-American Women (NFA-AW), from which the National Association of Colored Women (NACW) emerged in 1896.

To publicize and promote the Woman's Era Club's activities, Ruffin soon founded, edited, and published *The Woman's Era*, which she distributed nationally. The *Era*, the first monthly periodical published by African-American women, first appeared in March 1894. It showcased literature by African-American women, including poetry, short stories, essays, and other literary works, as well as reviews of literature, drama, and music by African Americans. It also included articles of national interest, and Ruffin frequently editorialized on key issues of the day. Club activities throughout the NFA-AW and then the NACW were publicized in each issue, and Ruffin included the opinions of other women, as well as her own. Ruffin always struggled to finance the magazine, however,

and in November, the magazine started including advertisements. Despite these efforts, it eventually became impossible to continue, and its final issue appeared in January 1897.

Ruffin's daughter, Florida Ruffin Ridley, also helped with her mother's club work, helped edit the *Era*, and occasionally editorialized. In addition, she wrote essays, short fiction, poetry, and articles, both for the *Era* and for other periodicals. Ridley was also a member of Boston's Saturday Evening Quill Club of African-American intellectuals. Like her mother, Ridley was a suffragist, deeply involved in community service, and dedicated to racial uplift. The Ridleys also had a son and a daughter, Josephine's grandchildren. Before marrying, Florida had been the second African-American teacher in Boston's public schools. After marrying, she and her husband, Ulysses, founded Boston's Society for the Collection of Negro Folklore.

REFERENCES: "Florida Ruffin Ridley," *HG:BWW. HR&B.* "George Lewis Ruffin," *Wiki.* "Josephine St. Pierre Ruffin," *Wiki.* Bair, Barbara, in *AANB.* Gatewood, Willard B. 2000. *Aristocrats of Color: The Black Elite, 1880-1920.* Fayetteville: University of Arkansas Press. in //books.google.com/books?id=CyQEzCEV9XkC&pg=PA211&lpg=PA211&dq=Ulysses+Ridley+-scott&source=bl&ots=6tBSpCb0hG&sig=kdiLXMkDcnGJZJ9UfmPsHxFbOdk&hl=en&ei=zbZGSqyLF46OMbSnsLAC&sa=X&oi=book_result&ct=result&resnum=8. Hall, Nora, in *AMJ-1850-1900-1.* Larson, Jennifer, in *AANB.* Moses, Wilson Jeremiah. 1988. *The Golden Age of Black Nationalism, 1850-1925* (2nd ed., pp. 105-110). New York: Oxford University Press. //books.google.com/books?id=xnZQhKB5_f8C&pg=PA105&lpg=PA105&dq=the+women's+era&source=bl&ots=HS5Vdlrp Yi&sig=7aFinEuT_OwBsL58vpTmakS9ifY&hl=en&ei=tbhGSq_FA oyCNPy79KIB&sa=X&oi=book_result&ct=result&resnum=25. Schuppert, Roger A., in *AANB.* //en.wikipedia.org/wiki/National_ Association_of_Colored_Women. //www.howard.edu/library/Social_ Work_Library/guides/african_american_social_workers.htm#Ridley,% 20Florida%20Ruffin. //www.town.brookline.ma.us/planning/PDFs/ Update/UpdateJanFeb2007.pdf.

Ruggles, David
3/15/1810–12/26/1849

Abolitionist pamphlets, lectures; publisher, journalist, bookseller

David Ruggles wasn't shy about his beliefs. Although he was born free, of free parents, in a free state (Connecticut), he had passionate feelings against slavery. When he was just 20 years old, he wrote a letter to the French Marquis de Lafayette, asking him to help abolish slavery. As Ruggles said, "The pleas of crying soft and sparing never answered the purpose of a reform, and never will." A self-educated man, he worked in a temperance (anti-alcohol) grocery, a bookstore, a reading room, and a printing business.

Ruggles was a regular contributor to the *Emancipator* and the *Liberator*, and in 1833, Ruggles was working as an agent lecturing for the *Emancipator*, drumming up business for the abolitionist newspaper and stirring his listeners to oppose slavery. The next year (1834), in New York City, he opened the first known African-American bookshop. There he sold abolitionist pamphlets (some of which he authored) and other materials. He was probably also the first African American to publish his own pamphlets, including his anticolonization *Extinguisher, Extinguished . . . or David M. D. 'Used Up'* (1834), his abolitionist *The Abrogation of the Seventh Commandment by the American Churches* (1835), and his anticolonization *An Antidote for a Poisonous Combination* (1838).

Ruggles also founded the New York Committee for Vigilance, putting his beliefs into action. The committee worked with the Underground Railroad, interposing its members between slave catchers and fugitive slaves. In this way, Ruggles risked his own life and well-being to protect more than a thousand fugitive slaves, including **Frederick Douglass**. He suffered attacks on his person and arson at his business. In 1838, he started publishing the committee's *Mirror of Liberty*, perhaps the nation's first African-American magazine. Ruggles also published a *New York Slaveholders Directory* (1839), unmasking whites who were thought to have captured and enslaved free men and women. A dispute with *Colored American* editor **Samuel Cornish** divided the local abolitionist community, leaving a nearly blind Ruggles financially devastated. Fortunately, his friend, fellow abolitionist **Lydia Maria Child**, suggested that he join her in Northampton, Massachusetts, which he did.

In Massachusetts, Ruggles continued his abolitionist activities, and he resisted segregation in the North. In an 1841 incident that foretold Rosa Parks's later actions, Ruggles refused to leave his seat to allow segregation on a Bedford, Massachusetts, railroad car. (*See also* **Ida B. Wells-Barnett**). Nonetheless, the *Mirror* stopped publication in 1841, and the Vigilance Society folded in 1842. In 1844, Ruggles tried to start a second magazine, *Genius of Freedom*, but with little success. By then, Ruggles had started a hydropathy ("water cure") business, which proved quite successful.

REFERENCES: *AANB. Wiki.* Aguiar, Marian, in *EA-99.* Carruth, Mary C., in *COCAAL* and *OCAAL.*

Rush, Gertrude E. (née Durden)
8/5/1880–9/5/1962
Songs, plays; attorney

Rush's plays include *Satan's Revenge* (a staging of Milton's *Paradise Lost*), *Sermon on the Mount* (1907), *Uncrowned Heroines* (1912), and *Black Girls Burden* (1913). Her songs include "Jesus Loves the Little Children." One source (*BWA:AHE*) said she died in 1918, but she actu-

ally started her career as an attorney in that year, becoming the first African-American woman to be admitted to the Iowa bar. When she and four other African-American attorneys were barred from joining the American Bar Association, they formed the National Bar Association. In 2003, the Iowa Chapter of the National Bar Association established the annual Gertrude Rush Award for Distinguished Service, in her honor.

REFERENCES: Duthie, Peg, in *AANB.* Warwick, Judy, in *BWA:AHE.* //en.*Wiki.* .org/wiki/Gertrude_Rush. //www.aaregistry.com/detail.php?id=2497.

FURTHER READING: //goliath.ecnext.com/coms2/gi_0199-3923577/. //www.answers.com/topic/sharon-sayles-belton. //www.iowawomenattorneys.org/awards.htm. //www.law.uiowa.edu/documents/rush_award.pdf.

Russwurm, John (né Brown)
10/1/1799–6/9/1851
Journalist, editor

John Brown's mother was a Jamaican slave, impregnated by a white American merchant. On the insistence of his father's wife (and John's stepmother), Mr. Russwurm acknowledged his paternity and gave his son his surname. In 1807, Russwurm sent his son to Quebec for his early schooling. When John was a teenager, his father brought him home to Portland, Maine, and young John Russwurm attended the Hebron Academy, starting in 1812. After completing his studies at the academy in Hebron, Russwurm went to Bowdoin College, from which he graduated in 1826, one of the first African Americans to earn a bachelor's degree from an American college. An early advocate of emigration, in the speech he gave on graduation, he urged African Americans to leave America and resettle in Haiti.

The following year, Russwurm moved to New York City, and on March 16, 1827, he and **Samuel E. Cornish** (an African-American Presbyterian minister) published the first issue of **Freedom's Journal**, the first African-American weekly published in this country. "In presenting our first number to our Patrons, . . . we believe, that a paper devoted to the dissemination of useful knowledge among our brethren, and to their moral and religious improvement, must meet with the cordial approbation of every friend to humanity" (*Freedom's Journal,* 3/16/1827, quoted in "The History of *Freedom's Journal,* 2003). Cofounders Russwurm and Cornish coedited the paper and employed itinerant African-American abolitionists to print and operate the paper, thereby affirming the paper's motto, "We Wish to Plead Our Own Cause." Their cause, of course, was the abolition of slavery in the South and of inequality in the North. One of the most powerful arguments for this cause was **David Walker**'s

Appeal, which was first printed in the pages of this paper in December of 1828. While Cornish was involved in editing the paper, the official editorial policy of the paper was to oppose the emigration of African Americans, holding that African Americans had built this nation and had every right to enjoy the full benefits of their labor within it. In September of 1827, however, Cornish resigned from his editorial duties, in order to give more of his time to his ministry. Russwurm was less firmly committed to opposing emigration.

About the time of the paper's two-year anniversary, Russwurm had despaired of achieving any reforms in the United States and joined the American Colonization Society, embracing its aims of having all African Americans free to leave the country and resettle in Africa. He turned the newspaper back to Cornish and moved to Liberia, which had been established as an independent nation in 1822, offering a homeland in which freed African-American slaves could resettle. There, he joined the American Colonization Society's settlement and accepted a job as the Superintendent of Education. Russwurm also edited the *Liberia Herald* and continued to advocate the emigration of African Americans to Liberia. In 1833, he married Sarah McGill, the daughter of Monrovia's lieutenant-governor, with whom he later had a daughter and three sons. With these excellent family ties and his own fine talents, Russwurm was elected the first African-descended governor of his "Maryland" section of Liberia, starting in 1836, and in that position, he continued striving to improve Liberia's economic conditions and diplomatic status the rest of his life.

Meanwhile, back in the States, Cornish tried to revive the paper as the *Rights of All,* but after a year, Cornish found it impossible to keep the paper financially afloat and folded its operation. The end of the paper was not, however, the end of Russwurm's legacy. The Black Press celebrated its 180th anniversary in 2007, and each year, the National Newspaper Publisher's Association, an African-American newspaper syndicate (with a cumulative circulation of 10 million) honors recipients with the John Russwurm Trophy and Merit Award.

REFERENCES: *AANB. B. EA-99. G-97. PGAA. SMKC. Wiki.* Andrews, William L., in *COCAAL* and *OCAAL.* Bacon, Jacqueline. "The History of Freedom's Journal: A Study in Empowerment and Community. *The Journal of African American History.* 88.1 (Winter 2003) p. 1. From *Literature Resource Center.* Bardolph, Richard, in *WB-99.*

FURTHER READING: Kent, Holly M. "Freedom's Journal: The First African-American Newspaper." *Journal of the Early Republic.* 27.4 (Winter 2007) p. 737. From *Literature Resource Center.*

Bayard Rustin (left) helping to organize the 1963 March on Washington for Jobs and Freedom

Rustin, Bayard
3/17/1910–8/24/1987
Nonfiction essays and books

Raised among Quakers, Rustin learned early the importance of nonviolent struggle for civil rights, and he perfected his political strategies as a protégé of **A. Philip Randolph.** Having spent more than two years in prison as a conscientious objector to World War II, he never hesitated to risk arrest or take other bold nonviolent actions if they would help achieve the civil-rights movement's aims. In addition to his numerous essays, many of which were collected in *Down the Line: The Collected Writings of Bayard Rustin* (1971), Rustin published *Which Way Out? A Way Out of the Exploding Ghetto* (1967) and *Strategies for Freedom: The Changing Patterns of Black Protest* (1976). He also ghostwrote many of the civil-rights writings and speeches by and about **Martin Luther King, Jr.,** and he kept a journal of his thoughts and experiences.

REFERENCES: *AANB. B. BCE. CE. EA-99. EB-BH-CD. EB-98. EBLG. E-98. G-95. USMHC. Wiki.* Martin, Jonathan, in *BB.* Szymczak, Jerome, in *BH2C.* Wiloch, Thomas, in *CAO-03.*

Rux, Carl Hancock (né Carl Stephen Hancock)
3/24/1968–1974?–
Poems, plays, novel, essays; performance artist

Editor's note: Rux's birth year is given as 1974 in *Wiki*, retrieved 6/28/2009, but was 1971 in *Wiki*, retrieved 10/29/2008, as well as 1970 in *CAO-07*, and c. 1968 in *GEAAL*. Raised by the foster-care system of New York City, with more than one surname, Rux's vital records may be difficult to track down.

While Carl Hancock was an infant, he and his two brothers ended up in separate foster-care residences after their mother was institutionalized for schizophrenia. Members of his mother's family offered him sporadic and negligent care, changing his surname to Rux. Rux attended Columbia University, but his true alma mater is the Nuyorican Poets Café in New York City's East Village (1990s), where he started developing his poetry and spoken-word performances. Soon, he was including jazz, hip-hop, and rhythm-and-blues musical elements into his performances.

His evolution as a spoken-word performer may be tracked through his albums and other sound recordings, starting with his 1996 CD *Cornbread, Cognac, Collard Green Revolution* (1996), which was never distributed. Most biographers consider his second album, *Rux Revue* (1999), his debut album because it was the first to gain adequate distribution. In *The New York Times's* Year in Music, *Rux Revue* was voted one of the top ten alternative music CDs. It was followed by *Apothecary Rx* (2004) and *Good Bread Alley* (2006). He has also collaborated with others on several other CDs.

Rux is always seeking new experiences. He has traveled throughout West Africa, where he lived in Ghana for a while. He has also collaborated with dance performers and earned a Bessie Award for directing the dance musical *Stained* (1994). He has also tried acting, taking the title role in the folk opera production of *The Temptation of St. Anthony* (2003, Germany).

Rux has also offered numerous spoken-word performances at New York City's world-renowned Joseph Papp Public Theater and many other venues. In addition, Rux has written numerous plays, including *Song of Sad Young Men* (1990), *Chapter and Verse* (1991), *Geneva Cottrell,*

Waiting for the Dog to Die (1991), *Singing in the Womb of Angels* (1992), and *Smoke, Lilies, and Jade* (1999); he also wrote the libretti for two operas, *The Blackamoor Angel* and *Makandal*. His Obie Award-winning *Talk* (2002) was also published as a paperback in 2005. Between 1990 and 2002, Rux wrote an additional 15 theater and/or dance productions. Rux also cowrote and narrated the radio documentary *Walt Whitman; Songs of Myself*, awarded the 2006 New York Press Club Journalism Award for Entertainment News.

Rux also writes poetry, which has been appearing in anthologies and periodicals since 1994, and which was collected in his early chapbook, *Elmina Blues* (1992). Rux's poetry and prose collection *Pagan Operetta* (1998; 2nd ed., 2000) was featured in a *Village Voice* cover story and earned the *Village Voice* Literary Prize. His other major publication is his novel *Asphalt* (2004), following which he was featured on the cover of *The New York Times* magazine.

Rux has enjoyed six theater residencies, seven artist residencies at educational institutions, and he has been the head of the Writing for Performance M.F.A. program at the California Institute of the Arts. He has frequently appeared as a radio essayist and guest host on XM radio's *The Bob Edwards Show* and WNYC's *Soundcheck*. Voices of America TV documentary about him, *Carl Hancock Rux, Coming of Age* (produced by Larry Clamage and Richard Maniscalo), received the CINE Golden Eagle Award.

Rux received a Fresh Poet Award from the Nuyorican Poets Café (1994) and a lucrative CalArts/Alpert Award in the Arts (2003). To see his many other honors and awards, as well as a complete listing of his publications, performances, and discography, visit //www.carlhancockrux.com/index.php?section=15.

REFERENCES: *CAO-07*. *Wiki*. Ankeny, Jason, *All Music Guide*, in *A*, and in //www.allmusic.com/cg/amg.dll. Chaplin, Julia, "Carl Hancock Rux - interview with writer-performer from Harlem - Interview," in //findarticles.com/p/articles/mi_m1285/is_2_29/ai_53747381/?tag=content;col1. //en.wikipedia.org/wiki/Alpert_Awards_in_the_Arts. //en.wikipedia.org/wiki/Bessie_Award. //www.carlhancockrux.com/index.php?section=8. //www.carlhancockrux.com/index.php?section=15. //www.discogs.com/artist/Carl+Hancock+Rux. //www.npr.org/templates/story/story.php?storyId=1975321. Amazon.com.

FURTHER READING: Clark, Patricia E., in *GEAAL*.

Sage: A Scholarly Journal on Black Women
1984–1995

Literary journal

By 1983, **Toni Cade (Bambara)** had published *Black Woman* (1970), Mary Helen Washington had published *Black-Eyed Susans: Classic Stories by and about Black Women* (1975), and both women's studies programs and African-American studies programs had emerged on campuses across the nation (throughout the 1970s and early 1980s). In 1982, Gloria T. Hull, Patricia Bell Scott, and **Barbara Smith** published their landmark *All the Women Are White, All the Blacks Are Men, But Some of Us Are Brave: Black Women's Studies*. Despite all these groundbreaking events, there were still no scholarly journals dedicated to the writings of African-American women by April of 1983. That month, Atlanta's Spelman College professors Beverly Guy-Sheftall and Patricia Bell-Scott decided to remedy the situation. They founded Sage Women's Educational Press (SWEP), along with editorial staffers Ruby Sales, Janet Sims-Wood, and Jacqueline Jones Royster. With a lot of hard work and industry, this small team published their first issue of *Sage: A Scholarly Journal on Black Women* in May of 1984.

They intentionally adopted an interdisciplinary, global, cross-cultural perspective, with three key objectives: (1) It would publish articles written by feminist African-American scholars, such as mathematicians Sylvia Trimble Bozeman and **Evelyn (née) Boyd Granville**. (2) It would publish scholarly articles about African-American women, such as its special issue, "Artists and Artisans" (Spring 1987, Vol. 4, No. 1), which included artist profiles and essays on African-American quilt-makers; and its issue "Black Women in Science and Technology" (Fall 1989, Vol. 6, No. 3), which included articles on engineers, mathematicians, biologists, and choosing a career in the sciences. (3) It would offer a print forum for discussion of issues important to African-American women, such as articles about mother-daughter relationships and female-male relationships among African Americans, topics ignored in other scholarly journals.

The editors of *Sage* also broadened their scope to include photo essays, excerpts from women's diaries, and bibliographies, as well as the typical book reviews and scholarly articles found in other scholarly journals. Among its myriad notable contributors were **Pearl Michelle Cleage, Alexis De Veaux**, Mae G. Henderson, **bell hooks, Claudia Tate**, and Gloria Wade-Gayles. Also in its pages were book reviews and literary criticism regarding African-American women writers of the past, such as **Frances Ellen Watkins Harper, Zora Neale Hurston, Nella Larsen**, and **Phillis Wheatley**, and of recent times, such as **Octavia Butler, Paule Marshall, Toni Morrison, Gloria Naylor, Alice Walker**, and **Sherley Anne Williams**.

Sage's last issue appeared in Summer, 1995. Meanwhile, Beverly Guy-Sheftall had helped establish the Women's Research and Resource Center at Spelman College (1980s) and had edited *Words of Fire: An Anthology of African-American Feminist Thought* (1995), and Patricia Bell-Scott had edited both *Double Stitch : Black Women Write about Mothers and Daughters* (1991) and *Life Notes: Personal Writings by Contemporary Black Women* (1994).

REFERENCES: Beaulieu, Elizabeth Ann. 2006. *Writing African American Women: K-Z*. Westport, CT: Greenwood Publishing Group. Black-Parker, Kimberly, in *GEAAL*. Johnson, Anne Janette, "Beverly Guy-Sheftall," in *BB*. //www.loc.gov/rr/scitech/tracer-bullets/africanwomenb.html. //www.si.edu/encyclopedia_SI/nmah/afamwom.htm.

Salaam, Kalamu ya (né Vallery Ferdinand III)
3/24/1947–

Plays, poems, essays, literary and cultural criticism, short stories; educator, performer

After writing the poetry collection *The Blues Merchant* (1969), Vallery Ferdinand III renamed himself Kalamu ya Salaam, Swahili for "Pen of Peace." Salaam's other poetry collections include *Pamoja Tutashinda: Together We Will Win* (1974), *Iron Flowers: A Poetic Report on a Visit to Haiti* (1979), and *A Nation of Poets: Poems* (1989; available with CD, 1992). He also wrote two collections that include both poems and essays: *Hofu Ni Kwenu: My Fear Is for You* (1973), his best-known volume *Revolutionary Love: Poems & Essays* (1978; illustrated by Douglas Redd, with photos by Kwadwo Oluwale Akpan), and *Raise Beauty: Essay and Poetry* (1989, self-published). Salaam's nonfiction includes his essay collection *What Is Life? Reclaiming the Black Blues Self* (1994); *The Magic of Juju: An Appreciation of the Black Arts Movement* (1998), his recollections of this crucial time in literary history; and *Our Women Keep Our Skies from Falling: Six Essays in Support of the Struggle to Smash Sexism, Develop Women* (1980). Salaam also wrote numerous nonfiction pamphlets, including *Tearing the Roof off the Sucker: The Fall of South Afrika* (1977), *Nuclear Power and the Black Liberation Struggle* (1978), *South African Showdown: Divestment Now* (1978), *The Political Act of Writing* (1983, self-published), *Our Music Is No Accident* (1987), and *He's the Prettiest: A Tribute to Big Chief Allison "Tootie" Montana's 50 Years of Mardi Gras Indian Suiting, July 12-August 31, 1997* (1997).

Salaam has also created fiction. An actor and director with the Free Southern Theater (1968-1971), later named BLKARTSOUTH, Salaam has also written plays. During the **Black Arts Movement**, he wrote *The Picket* (1968), *Mama* (1969), *Happy Birthday Jesus* (1969), *Black Liberation Army* (1969), *Homecoming* (1970), *Black Love Song* (1971), and *The Quest* (1972). Since then, he has written the plays *Somewhere in the World* (1982) and *Malcolm, My Son* (1993, published in *African American Review*), among others. Salaam's *Ibura* (1976, illustrated by Arthrello Beck, Jr.) includes poems and short stories. With three other authors, he wrote the short-story collection *Anansi: Fiction of the African Diaspora* (1999, with Sheree Renée Thomas, Angeli R. Rasbury, and Martin Simmons). With his wife, Tayari kwa Salaam, he has five children (including a daughter named Asante), and he coauthored a book for young readers, *Who Will Speak for Us? New Afrikan Folktales* (1978); he also authored *Herufi: An Alphabet Reader* (1978).

In addition, many of Salaam's stories, essays, plays, poems, and reviews of music, books, and plays have been published in various scholarly and literary journals (e.g., *Journal of Black Poetry*) and anthologies (e.g., **Sonia Sanchez**'s *We Be Word Sorcerers: 25 Short Stories by Black Americans*, 1973). He also edited the anthologies *Word Up: Black Poetry of the 80s from the Deep South* (1990), *Fertile Ground—Memories & Visions* (1996, with Kysha N. Brown), *360°: A Revolution of Black Poets* (1998; 2001 edition with Kwame Alexander), and *From A Bend in the River: 100 New Orleans Poets* (1998). Salaam also cofounded Ahidiana (1973-1984), a Pan-African organization, which published many of his poetry and essay collections and other works, and he founded the publishing company Runagate Press, now Runagate Multimedia, which published his anthologies *Fertile Ground* and *360*. BLKARTSOUTH chose him to coedit its quarterly journal *Nkombo*; and he cofounded (1970) and edited *Black Collegian Magazine*. He is also the poetry editor of *QBR Black Book Review*, and he has edited *Black River Journal* (1988) and some issues of *African American Review* (1993, with Jerry W. Ward, Jr.; 1995). Salaam founded the weekly workshop NOMMO Literary Society, he has mod-

erated the listserv e-Drum for African-American writers, he has led the performance poetry ensemble WordBand, he hosted a radio show, and he and his son, Mtume, comoderated "The Breath of Life—A Conversation about Black Music." He also produced the spoken-word album *My Story, My Song* (1997), and he has written dozens of liner notes for both music and poetry albums.

A lifelong resident and native of New Orleans, Salaam has been involved in numerous post-Hurricane Katrina activities, such as an oral history project, "Listen to the People," available online. Among his awards are two Deems Taylor Awards from the American Society of Composers, Authors, and Publishers (ASCAP) (1981, 1989), for his writings about music.

REFERENCES: *AAW:PV. BAWPP. CAO-01. Wiki.* Hall, John Greer, in *GEAAL.* Miller, E. Ethelbert, "Interview with Kalamu ya Salaam," //www.fpif.org/fpiftxt/4232. Millican, Arthenia J. Bates, *AAW-55-85:DPW.* Toombs, Charles P., in COCAAL and OCAAL. Ward, Jerry W., Jr. "Kalamu ya Salaam: A Primary Bibliography. *The Mississippi Quarterly.* 51.1 (Winter 1997) p. 105. From *Literature Resource Center.* Amazon.com. *See also* Gale Literature Resource Center online, for many of Salaam's poems, plays, and interviews of fellow writers.

Sanchez, Sonia (Benita) (née Wilsonia Driver) 9/9/1934–
Poems; educator

Sonia Sanchez's work has an impact on readers like that of few other writers. A prolific writer, Sanchez sometimes functions as a prophet when she calls for justice and equality for all peoples of the world. At other times, she writes passionately of love and intimate relationships. Her honesty can be loving and sensual, angry and biting, or hopeful and humorous. Sanchez grew up listening to jazz and blues music, and consequently, much of her work is imbued with a distinctive lyrical quality. Ultimately, her powerful language and her universal messages make her one of the most significant African-American writers to emerge from the **Black Arts Movement**.

Wilsonia Driver was born in Birmingham, Alabama, one of the two daughters of Lena and Wilson L. Driver. When Sonia was one year old, her mother died, and she and her older sister, Patricia, lived with extended family until Sonia was nine years old. For many years of her childhood and youth, Sonia stuttered. When Sonia was nine, her musician father took her and Patricia to live with him in Harlem, New York, leaving Sonia's half-brother in the South. Her half-brother later moved to New York, where he died from AIDS in 1981. Sanchez's *Does Your House Have Lions?* reflects on this family tragedy.

Sanchez graduated from Hunter College in New York in 1955, with a B.A. in political science. She spent the next year at New York University, studying poetry with Louise Bogan, who encouraged Sanchez to publish her work.

Twice divorced, Sanchez has one daughter (1957) and twin sons (1968). One of her marriages was to fellow writer and political activist **Etheridge Knight**.

Sanchez began her academic career in 1965 at the Downtown Community School in San Francisco. She then taught at San Francisco State College (1967-1969), where she helped establish the first Black Studies program in the United States. During these years, Sanchez became politically active in the Congress of Racial Equality (CORE) and the Nation of Islam (1972-1975). After several posts at various colleges and universities, Sanchez settled in Philadelphia at Temple University in 1977. She remains on the faculty there, teaching and maintaining a schedule of national and international readings of her work. Her travels include trips to China, Africa, and the Caribbean.

Sanchez has published more than 10 books of poetry: *home coming* (1969); *We are a Baddddd People* (1970); *Love Poems* (1973); *Blues Book for Blue Black Magical Women* (1974); *Selected Poems, 1974* (1975); *homegirls & handgrenades* (1984); *I've Been a Woman: New and Selected Poems* (1985); *Generations: Poetry, 1969-1985* (1986); *Under a Soprano Sky* (1987); *Wounded in the House of a Friend* (1995); *Does Your House Have Lions?* (1997); and *Like the Singing Coming off the Drums: Love Poems* (1998). She has also published six plays and three children's books: *It's a New Day: Poems for Young Brothas and Sistuhs* (1971); *The Adventures of Flathead, Smallhead, and Squarehead* (1973); and *A Sound Investment: Short Stories for Young Readers* (1980). Sanchez also edited two books, and her work has been anthologized in numerous books and published in many journals and magazines. She has also garnered several important academic distinctions and literary awards, notably the 1985 American Book Award for *homegirls & handgrenades*.

During the early years of her writing career, Sanchez played a prominent role in the Black Arts Movement, and her poetry reflects the political turmoil present in the United States at that time. In the 1960s, African Americans sought to publish and promote their own creative work for a general audience. Alternative publishing houses and periodicals were established, and they served as arenas for a wellspring of innovative works. This aggressive business and political venture was later named the Black Arts movement. This movement included other celebrated African-American writers, such as **Mari Evans** and **Nikki Giovanni**. These and other writers realistically focused on the minority-black experience in a majority-white America prior to civil rights and affirmative action.

Sanchez's work has evolved as she has grown as an artist. Her first published book of poetry, *home coming*, is hard-hitting and controversial, with its cries for social justice and black pride and its condemnation of the established white power structure. Poems such as "the final solution," and "definition for blk/children" use a form and vocabulary so distinctive and powerful that Sanchez's words crush the printed page. Here Sanchez is her most angry and militant, cursing and rejecting white culture and encouraging blacks to embrace their own blackness as a positive image. She has said of that time and her work that "you have to really understand the time and what the politics were about."

In contrast, Sanchez's more recent work, *Like the Singing Coming off the Drums: Love Poems*, follows a more traditional form, vocabulary, and subject matter. In this book, Sanchez uses the haiku extensively and writes with sensuality, wisdom, and humor. One selection, simply titled "Haiku," says, "is there a fo rent /sign on my butt? / you got no / territorial rights here." In another, Sanchez writes, "i am who i am. / nothing hidden just black silk / above two knees."

Throughout all of her work, Sanchez has continued to lobby for a more humane society for all peoples of the world. In a "Poem for July 4, 1994," Sanchez says, "All of us must finally bury / the elitism of race . . . sexual . . . economic . . . [and] religious superiority." A speech she gave to Temple University's 1998 graduation class reads not like a speech but like poetry, and it, too, calls for a just world. Sanchez writes, "How can I bind you together . . . Away from Racism. Sexism. Homophobia. Exploitation. Militarism. Extreme materialism. Towards Unity. . . . Inaugurate a new way of breathing for the world, . . . and it will get better."

These short excerpts give only a small taste of the feast of words that Sanchez spreads before her readers. Sanchez has shown that a poet can be an activist, a loving sister, and a creative commentator on the American political scene. Whether structured or unstructured, loud or serene, Sanchez's work always retains its impact.

REFERENCES: *BWW.* "Selected Bibliographies," in *NAAAL.* "Sonia Sanchez," in *NAAAL.* Madhubuti, Haki, "Sonia Sanchez: The Bringer of Memories," in *BWW.* Melhelm, D. H. 1990. "Sonia Sanchez: The Will and the Spirit," *Heroism in the New Black Poetry: Introductions & Interviews.* Lexington, KY: University Press of Kentucky. **Salaam, Kalamu ya,** "Black Arts Movement," in *OCAAL.* Sitter, Deborah Ayer, "Sonia Sanchez," in *OCAAL.* Williams, David, "The Poetry of Sonia Sanchez," in *BWW.* http://english.cla.umn.edu/LKD/VFG/Authors/SoniaSanchez. —Janet Hoover

Editor's note: Since the 1960s, Sanchez has written several plays (e.g., *The Bronx Is Next*, 1970; *Sister Son/Ji*, 1970; *Dirty Hearts*, 1973; *Malcolm Man Don't Live Here No Mo'*, 1972/1979, intended for children; *Uh, Huh: But How Do It Free Us?* 1975; *I'm Black When I'm Singing, I'm

Blue When I Ain't, 1982; and *Black Cats Back and Uneasy Landings*, 1995), at least five of which have been produced. Whereas plays require collaboration, poems do not. Nonetheless, Sanchez's poetry also reflects her collaborative spirit. When Sanchez and fellow poets **Haki R. Madhubuti** (Don L. Lee), Nikki Giovanni, and **Etheridge Knight** published their early works with **Broadside Press**, they helped supported the press financially by returning their royalties to the press. About that period, she has written, "A lot of the Black poetry that we wrote during the sixties was playing the dozens on a very interesting level and also playing with words on a very interesting level" (quoted by Salaam, *AAP-55-85*).

Sanchez has a daughter, Anita (b. 5/24/1957), from her first marriage, and with Knight, her second husband, she gave birth to twin sons, Morani and Mungu (b. 1/26/1968). While her sons were young, she wrote three books for children: a poetry collection (1971), a moral fable about a pilgrimage to Mecca (1973), and a collection of short stories (1979). During her association with the Nation of Islam (1972-1975), Sanchez wrote a column for its publication *Muhammad Speaks,* and she wrote *Ima Talken Bout the Nation of Islam* (1971). Her speeches have been published in *Crisis in Culture—Two Speeches* (1983) and in *Shake Down Memory: A Collection of Political Essays and Speeches* (1991/1994). One source estimated that she had lectured at more than 500 U.S. campuses by 2003, in addition to her long career at Temple University (1977-1999) and other academic institutions.

Since her retirement from Temple, Sanchez has continued to write poetry, collected in *Shake Loose My Skin: New and Selected Poems* (1999), celebrating Black English in haiku, among other poems; and *Ash* (2001). Sanchez's *Morning Haiku* is due out in early 2010. Her previous poetry collections include *Autumn Blues: New Poems* (1994) and *Continuous Fire: A Collection of Poetry* (1994). Sanchez also edited two anthologies: *360 Degrees of Blackness Coming at You: An Anthology of the Sonia Sanchez Writers Workshop* at **Countee Cullen** *Library in Harlem* (1971), and *We Be Word Sorcerers, 25 Stories by Black Americans* (1973); and she both compiled and introduced *Allison Funk, Living at the Epicenter: The 1995 Morse Poetry Prize* (1995). In addition, she has produced several spoken-word recordings of her work: *Sonia Sanchez* (1968), *Homecoming* (1969), *We a BaddDDD People* (1969/1979), *A Sun Lady for All Seasons Reads Her Poetry* (1971), *Sonia Sanchez and Robert Bly* (1971), *Sonia Sanchez: Selected Poems, 1974* (1975), *IDKT: Capturing Facts about the Heritage of Black Americans* (1982), *Every Tone a Testimony* (2001), and *Full Moon of Sonia* (2004).

Sanchez has received numerous grants, honors, and awards for her work. Her *Homegirls and Handgrenades*

(1984/2007) earned the American Book Award, and her *Does Your House Have Lions?* was nominated for both the NAACP Image and the National Book Critics Circle Award. For her literary contributions, she has earned a PEN Writing Award (1969), a National Institute of Arts and Letters grant (1970), a grant from the American Academy of Arts and Letters (1972), a National Education Association Award (1977-1978), a National Endowment for the Arts fellowship (1984), a Pew Fellowship in the Arts (1992-1993), a PEN fellowship in the arts (1993-1994), the Robert Frost Award from the Poetry Society of America (2001), the John Oliver Killens Lifetime Literary Award (2008), and honorary doctorates from Wilberforce University (1973) and Baruch College (1993). For her overall contributions, she has been named Honorary Citizen of Atlanta (1982), and she has earned a Tribute to Black Women Award from the Black Students of Smith College (1982), a Lucretia Mott Award (1984), a Pennsylvania Governor's Award for Excellence in the Humanities (1989), a Welcome Award from Museum of Afro-American History (1990), an Oni Award from the International Black Women's Congress (1992), a Women Pioneers Hall of Fame Citation from the Young Women's Christian Association (1992), a Roots Award from the Pan-African Studies Community Program (1993), and a Legacy Award from Jomandi Productions (1995). She has also been awarded the Community Service Award from the National Black Caucus of State Legislators and the Peace and Freedom Award from the Women's International League for Peace and Freedom (WILPF).

Sanchez offers sage advice to aspiring writers: "Read and read and read and read everything you can get your hands on. One of the things Louise Bogan told me was, 'Whatever you write, read aloud. Your ear will be the best friend you will ever have.' And join a workshop at some point when you really feel you want to work more and/or apprentice yourself to a poet or writer and study with her or him" (quoted in Sanchez & Melhem, 1985). When Melhem asked Sanchez whether she revised, she answered, "Oh, sure, sure. I write in notebooks, so I have all my poems that, as it moved towards a second, third, fourth, fifth revision, et cetera." Next, Melhem asked, "Do you wait for inspiration or do you write regularly?," she chuckled, "I write regularly. If I waited for inspiration, I'd be finished." Sanchez's visceral delight in her craft of writing permeates her work. According to *Black Biography,* she told Susan Kelly of the *African American Review,* "It is that love of language that has propelled me, that love of language that came from listening to my grandmother . . . . It is that love of language that, when you have written a poem that you know works, then you stand up and you dance around, or you open your door and go out on the porch and let out a loud laugh."

REFERENCES: *AANB. AAW:PV. B. BAWPP. CAO-03. CBAPD. CLCS-08* (2 articles). *LFCC-07. MWEL. W. Wiki.* Kelly, Susan. "Discipline and Craft: An Interview with Sonia Sanchez." *African American Review.* 34.4 (Winter 2000) p. 679. From *Literature Resource Center.* Salaam, Kalamu ya, *AAP-55-85.* Sanchez, Sonia, and Herbert Leibowitz. "Exploding Myths: An Interview with Sonia Sanchez." *Parnassus 12-13.2-1* (1985): pp. 357-368. Rpt. in Jeffrey W. Hunter and Timothy J. White (Eds.) (1999), *Contemporary Literary Criticism* (Vol. 116). Detroit: Gale Group. From *Literature Resource Center.* Sanchez, Sonia, and D. H. Melhem. "Sonia Sanchez: Will and Spirit." *MELUS 12.3* (Fall 1985): pp. 73-98. Rpt. in Jeffrey W. Hunter and Timothy J. White (Eds.) (1999), *Contemporary Literary Criticism* (Vol. 116). Detroit: Gale Group. pp. 73-98. From *Literature Resource Center.* Sanchez, Sonia, and David Reich. "'As Poets, As Activists': An Interview with Sonia Sanchez." *World 13.3* (1999, pp. 12-18). Rpt. in Jeffrey W. Hunter (Ed.) (2006), *Contemporary Literary Criticism* (Vol. 215). Detroit: Gale. From *Literature Resource Center.* Sanchez, Sonia, and Danielle Alyce Rome. "An Interview with Sonia Sanchez." In Farhat Iftekharuddin, Maurice Lee, and Mary Rohrberger (Ed.) 1997. *Speaking of the Short Story: Interviews with Contemporary Writers.* Jackson: University Press of Mississippi. Rpt. in Contemporary Literary Criticism. Ed. Jeffrey W. Hunter. Vol. 215. Detroit: Gale, 2006. pp. 229-236. From *Literature Resource Center.* Sitter, Deborah Ayer, in *COCAAL.* Sussman, Alison Carb, and Sara Pendergast, in *BB.* Upchurch, Gail L., in *GEAAL.* Wood, Jacqueline. "'This thing called playwrighting': An Interview with Sonia Sanchez on the Art of Her Drama." *African American Review. 39.1-2* (Spring-Summer 2005) p. 119. From *Literature Resource Center.* //www.cavecanempoets.org/pages/programs_faculty.php. //www.poets.org/poet.php/prmPID/276. Amazon.com.

FURTHER READING: *EAAWW.*

Sanders, Dori
6/8/1930? or 1934? or 1935?–
Juvenile novels, nonfiction—cookbook, autobiography/memoir

Editor's note: Sanders is not forthcoming about her birth year, and it is given as 1930 in *GEAAL*, 1934 in *COCAAL*, c. 1935 in *BB*, and either 1934 or 1935 in *CAO-03*.

Dori and her seven older siblings and two younger siblings were raised on their family's farm, but only Dori and her brother Orestus stayed on the farm, where they sold their produce at the roadside Sanders's Peach Shed. During the winter, she sometimes worked at a banquet hall. In 1982 or so, while on a break, Dori's banquet-hall manager read what she wrote and encouraged her to write more. She did just that. Inspired by her observations of two funeral processions, she created a novel imagining the relationship that might arise between a 10-year-old African-American girl and her European-American stepmother, if the father and husband who united them died within hours of the marriage. In *Clover* (1990), the two very different people, who scarcely know each other, must work through their grief and share a life. *Clover* spent 10 weeks on the *Washington Post* fiction bestseller list, was cited as a Best Book for Young Adults by the American Library Association, and won the prestigious Lillian Smith Award from the Southern Regional Council and the University of Georgia Libraries (both 1990). Disney also bought the option to make it into a motion picture.

Sanders's second novel, *Her Own Place* (1993), is a family love story, in which a World War II-era abandoned wife and mother struggles to raise her family on a farm and how her family returns her love as she grows older. In her third book, *Dori Sanders' Country Cooking: Recipes and Stories from the Family Farmstand* (1995), Sanders tells stories about farm life and offers family recipes. It was nearly a decade before Sanders's next book, the 31-page memoir *Promise Land: A Farmer Remembers* (2004), was published.

REFERENCES: Johnson, Anne Janette, in *BB*. Knight, Gladys L., in *GEAAL*. Vick, Marsha C., in *COCAAL.* //en.wikipedia.org/wiki/Lillian_Smith_Book_Award. Amazon.com.

FURTHER READING: *EAAWW.*

Sapphire (née Ramona Lofton)
8/4/1950–
Poems, novel, prose, lesbian short fiction; performance artist

While a premed student at San Francisco City College in the 1970s, Ramona Lofton renamed herself Sapphire, rejecting the name given to her by her father, who had repeatedly raped her before she was old enough to see over the dashboard of her father's car, and her mother, who had abandoned her. Veering away from premed, Sapphire studied dance at a small private California college and started giving poetry and dance performances. In 1977, Sapphire moved to Brooklyn, New York, where her first published work appeared in *Azalea: A Magazine by and for Third World Lesbians* (1977). She also returned to college, graduating with honors from the City College of New York (CCNY) (1983). Meanwhile, she earned a living in a wide array of menial jobs and service jobs. She also taught remedial reading in Harlem and the Bronx, earning the City of New York's Outstanding Achievement in Teaching Award. Sapphire also earned her M.F.A. in modern dance from Brooklyn College (c. 1993), and she has taught literature, fiction, and poetry workshops at numerous institutions of higher learning.

Starting in 1986, she returned her attention to writing, gathering her poems into *Meditations on the Rainbow: Poetry* (1987). She also published several short pieces in lesbian literary journals and started publicly reading her poems again. In 1989, Sapphire's poem "Wild Thing" was published in *The Portable Lower East Side Queer City,* a journal that had received some funding from the National Endowment for the Arts (NEA). A right-wing minister contacted then-Senator Jesse Helms, leading to a huge uproar about NEA funding, and drawing unwanted attention to Sapphire. The following year, Sapphire staged her 50-minute choreopoem (choreographed poem) "Are You Ready to Rock?" (1990). Sapphire published a collection of prose and poems, *American Dreams* (1994), which included graphic stories and poems inspired by Sapphire's experiences and observations. Critics and fellow writers admired her talent but found her subjects and her tone challenging. That year, Sapphire was also awarded the Year of the Poet III Award from *Downtown* magazine and a MacArthur Foundation Scholarship for poetry (both 1994).

Sapphire's next major work was her novel *Push* (1996), narrated by the protagonist, Precious Jones. Precious is an overweight, illiterate Harlem teenager who is raped and impregnated twice by her father and is also physically, verbally, and sexually abused by her mother. Though challenging, the book gained a wide readership and earned both the First Novelist Award from the Black Caucus of the American Library Association and the Stephen Crane Award for First Fiction from the Book-of-the- Month Club (both 1997).

Sapphire's next book, like her first book, combines poetry and prose, *Black Wings & Blind Angels: Poems* (1999). Her work has also been published in periodicals and in anthologies (e.g., *Women on Women: An Anthology of American Lesbian Short Fiction*, 1990).

Editor's note: According to CAO-08, Sapphire also has two children of her own, but *AANB* says only that she helped raise her two younger siblings before leaving Los Angeles for San Francisco.

REFERENCES: *AAW:PV. CAO-08. TWL. Wiki.* Brennan, Carol, in *BB.* Dismukes, Ondra Krouse, in *AANB.* Howard, W. Scott, in *GEAAL.* Amazon.com.

Satuday Evening Quill See **Quill Club**

Scarborough, William Sanders
2/16/1852–9/9/1926
Scholarly works, textbook, translation, opinion—advocacy; educator, scholar, administrator

William's father was believed to be the great-grandson of an African chief, and his mother was of Spanish, Native-American, and African-American ancestry; his father was freed by the time William was born, and his mother was a slave in name only, as her "owners" allowed her to live with her husband and children. Because the

children of slave mothers were legally considered slaves, William was born into slavery and was not freed until the Civil War. Nonetheless, despite the strictures against slaves learning to read and write, both of William's parents were literate, and William, too, learned to read and write while still considered a slave.

After emancipation, William was able to gain a formal education, eventually attending Atlanta University and graduating from Oberlin College (in Ohio) in 1875. After brief attempts to teach school in the South, where angry whites fought the reforms of Reconstruction, Scarborough returned North to Ohio, earning an M.A. at Oberlin and then becoming a professor of Latin and Greek at Wilberforce University (also in Ohio). In 1881, Scarborough married Sarah Bierce, a white woman on the Wilberforce faculty, 1877-1914. From 1892 to 1897, he had a hiatus from Wilberforce, as the demand for instruction in the classic languages was slight. During this hiatus, he taught at Payne Seminary in South Carolina. When he returned to Wilberforce, he was made vice president, then in 1908, he was named president of the university.

While maintaining his administrative duties, Scarborough continued to write scholarly works on language (specifically, linguistics and philology), as well as translations (e.g., of Greek playwright Aristophanes's *The Birds,* 1886). In addition to Greek and Latin, Scarborough knew Sanskrit and Hebrew, as well as Slavonic languages. In recognition of his scholarship on language, he was elected to the American Philological Association (the third African American to be so honored). His most acclaimed work was his *First Lessons in Greek* (1881), which was used on campuses across the United States; in 1897, he published a highly esteemed paper on black folklore and dialect. In addition, he advocated for civil rights and wrote articles and other works championing that cause. His *The Educated Negro and His Mission* (1903) was well-regarded enough to be reprinted and published again in 1969.

REFERENCES: *AANB. BDAA. Wiki.* Hairston, Eric Ashley, in *GEAAL.*

Schomburg, Arthur A. (né Arturo Alfonso Schomburg) (occasional pseudonym: Guarionex)
1/24/1874–6/10/1938
Bibliography, essays, articles, nonfiction—history; bibliophile, curator

Arturo's mother, West Indian laundress Maria Josepha (Mary Joseph), was not married to his father, German-born merchant Carlos Federico Schomburg, when she gave birth to Arturo. Although Arturo adopted

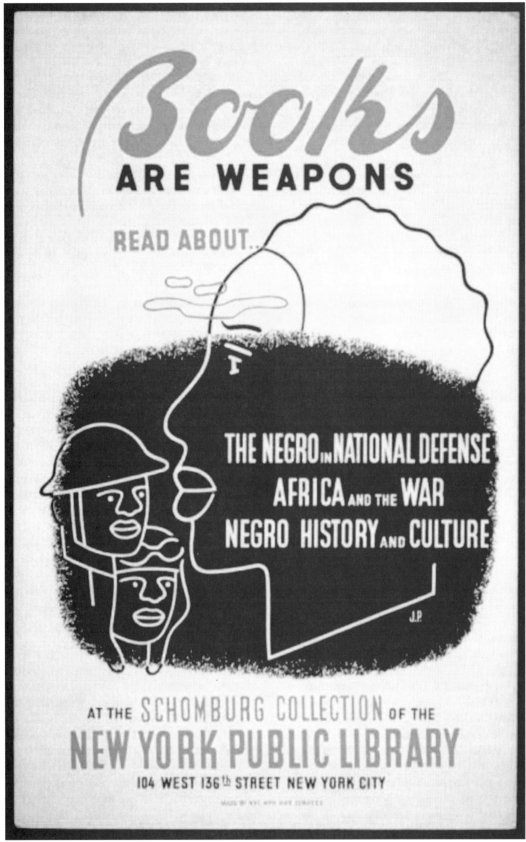

Work Projects Administration (WPA) poster of the Schomburg Collection at the New York Public Library

his father's surname, it appears that his father failed to support or even to acknowledge his son. Born in St. Thomas, in the U.S. Virgin Islands, young Arturo was raised by his mother's family in Puerto Rico. Later in life, Arthur Schomburg provided very little information about his childhood experiences, and biographers have not been able to dig up much more information. Apparently, he had an older sister, Dolores María (called "Lola"), and his mother's parents were born free in St. Croix.

Accounts of his schooling vary, including suggestions that he attended school in San Juan, Puerto Rico, at a Jesuit school, the Instituto de Párvulos, or at the Institute of Popular Teaching (or of Instruction); that he attended school in the Virgin Islands; or that he was entirely self-educated, never having attended school. At one point, Schomburg reported that he attended St. Thomas College in the Virgin Islands, but no documentation supports that claim. Accounts also vary as to whether his mother lived with him and her parents in Puerto Rico, or she remained in the Virgin Islands, sending him to Puerto Rico alone to live with her parents.

At some time during his adolescence, someone (reportedly a teacher of his) told young Arturo that Africans in the Americas had no history. In Puerto Rico and in other Latin American countries, many persons of Spanish heritage have celebrated the splendid achievements of their Spanish ancestors, neglecting to appreciate the heritage of the pre-Columbian native civilizations in the Americas and discounting altogether the fact that Africans ruled Spain for many centuries until very shortly before Ferdinand and Isabella sent Columbus across the Atlantic. Apparently, this person's offhand remark moved Schomburg to prove otherwise. Essentially, Schomburg dedicated the rest of his life to demonstrating the long, rich history of Africans, both in Africa and in the Americas, and to showing the countless profoundly important contributions of persons of African descent around the world.

Whatever his educational background, there can be no doubt that Schomburg was a well-educated man, who continually sought to enrich his knowledge of his own cultural heritage and that of other persons of African descent in the Americas. While still in Puerto Rico, he joined a literary club, frequently participating in intellectual discussions, and he read widely, in both Spanish and English. He particularly loved studying the history of the Caribbean and elsewhere in the Americas. Eventually, he realized that he would have greater opportunities for educating himself if he moved to the United States. Some reports suggest that he worked as a printer (typesetter) to earn money to move, and in 1891, at age 17, Arturo Schomburg left Puerto Rico.

On April 17, 1891, Arthur Schomburg arrived in New York City, where he settled in the Puerto Rican and Cuban section of the east side of Manhattan. He had brought with him some letters of introduction confirming his experience as a typographer, and he got work right away as a printer, as well as doing various service jobs (bellhop, porter, elevator operator, etc.). In addition, he attended night school at Manhattan's Central High School. Meanwhile, he continued to use his excellent memory to plumb the depths of history about Africans around the world, especially in the Americas. He also became active in political organizations involved with the Cuban and Puerto Rican independence movements.

By the time he had been in New York City a decade, he had gained work as a researcher clerking in a law office. For a time, he also studied law and had aspirations of becoming an attorney. When the state of New York barred him from taking the New York State Regents examination to qualify for a "law certificate," however, he abandoned that goal and left the law firm in 1906. That year, he began working for the Bankers Trust Company (BTC), in the Latin American section of their mailroom. After a while, he was promoted to supervisor of the department, and he remained in that position until he retired in 1929, with a medical disability. On his modest salary from the BTC, he managed to support himself and his very large family, as well as his chief true love: books and other materials about the history of Africa's descendants.

Actually, Schomburg had already been married twice by the time he started working at BTC. Schomburg had married Elizabeth ("Bessie") Hatcher June 30, 1895, and she and he had three sons: Maximo Gomez, Arthur Alfonso Jr., and Kingsley Guarionex. Bessie died in 1900, and two years later (March 17, 1902), Schomburg married Elizabeth Morrow Taylor, with whom he had two more sons: Reginald Stanfield and Nathaniel José. She, too, died young, and both sets of children were sent to live with their respective maternal relatives out of state. Undaunted, Schomburg married a third Elizabeth—Elizabeth Green—with whom he had three more children: Fernando, Dolores Marie (his only daughter, named after his older sister), and Plácido Carlos.

In addition, he was an active member of the Prince Hall Masons, serving as the grand secretary of the Grand Lodge of New York from 1918 to 1926. Despite these diversions, Schomburg's primary energies and efforts were always focused on his main love—African-American culture and history. In 1911, Schomburg joined John Edward Bruce's Men's Sunday Club, dedicated to discussing race-related issues and books. The club had an extensive library of materials on African-American history, and club members had been raising funds to buy additional materials for it. Bruce's club served as a springboard for the Negro Society for Historical Research, which Schomburg and Bruce cofounded that year. The society (of which Schomburg was secretary-treasurer and librarian for many years) was dedicated to publishing articles on African-American history, based on research conducted by society members. Participation in these groups encouraged Schomburg to be more rigorous and systematic in his own collection of books and other artifacts.

In 1914, Schomburg was invited to join the American Negro Academy (ANA), which **Alexander Crummell** had founded in 1879. Fellow members included **W. E. B. Du Bois**, **Alain Locke**, Kelly Miller, **Carter G. Woodson**, and numerous other scholars. This association helped him further refine his bibliophilic research skills and encouraged his abiding dedication to research in African-American culture and history. In 1922, he was elected the ANA's fifth (and last) president, although he was chiefly an absentee executive for the Washington, D.C.-based academy. In 1929, when the academy ceased operation, Schomburg had already become rather disillusioned with it. Schomburg also had rocky relationships with many other organizations (including the NAACP, the National Urban League, the Negro Writers' Guild, and about 25 or more others). He often resigned from these organizations over a disagreement, particularly if he felt that his opinion was unappreciated or he felt slighted or overlooked. Perhaps because of his lack of formal educational credentials, we may speculate that he was overly sensitive to criticism or neglect from African-American intellectuals, but we can only guess as to the reason.

Over time, Schomburg amassed a wealth of literary works and visual artworks by persons of African descent. By the time he had been in New York for a couple of decades, he had accumulated a broad, well-organized, prodigious collection. He had also become well known for his sophisticated ability to recognize choice items and to find rare or missing materials. In 1926, the New York Public Library (NYPL) opened its Division of Negro Literature, History, and Prints at its 135th Street (off of Lenox Avenue in Harlem) branch, based largely on Schomburg's private collection. That year, the Carnegie Corporation had paid Schomburg $10,000 for his collection, which it donated to the NYPL. At the time of the purchase, Schomburg's collection included more than 10,000 items (about 5,000 books, 3,000 manuscripts, numerous pamphlets and prints, 2,000 etchings and drawings, and countless other artifacts). Sadly, the original inventory of his contribution has been lost, so these numbers are just estimates.

What did Schomburg do with all that money? (To give you an idea of what he could have done, at that time, a Sears, Roebuck and Co. catalogue sold kits for building your own five-room home for about $2,000.) He crossed the country and the globe, contacting booksellers in Europe, Latin America, and elsewhere, to gather still more materials, which he continued to contribute to the NYPL. Fortunately, during the era of the **Harlem Renais-**

sance, many writers and scholars came to recognize Schomburg for his dedication to African-American scholarship and research, as well as for his collection. He was frequently invited to lecture across the country, and he inspired **James Weldon Johnson**, **Kenneth Clark**, **Claude McKay** (probably his closest friend), **Walter White**, and others in their literary and scholarly pursuits. Schomburg also admired **Marcus Garvey** and valued Garvey's goals of fostering African-American pride, independence, and self-sufficiency. Schomburg's collection itself also offered a tremendous resource to writers and other artists of the Harlem Renaissance and of every era since.

Another of Schomburg's close associates was historian **Charles Spurgeon Johnson**. Through his contact with Johnson, in 1929 or 1930, Schomburg was invited to establish and curate a collection of resources on African-American history and culture for the library of Fisk University (in Nashville, Tennessee). There, he not only established a highly respected collection but also mapped out a plan for the library to continue to add to its collection through future acquisitions.

In 1932, Schomburg received another job offer, which he found irresistible: An additional Carnegie Corporation grant funded the NYPL's appointment of Schomburg as the curator of his own collection at the Harlem branch. There, he remained for the next several years until his death (in 1938). During his final years, in addition to his own travels and contacts, Schomburg asked other scholars and writers (e.g., **Langston Hughes**) to help him find further materials for the collection. Frequently, if he was unable to get the library to purchase materials he deemed important, he purchased them out of his own funds. He also managed to persuade composers, visual artists, scholars, writers, and others to contribute their manuscripts and other materials to the collection. At some point, the collection was renamed the Schomburg Collection of Negro Literature and History (in 1934 or 1940) and still later was renamed the Schomburg Center for Research in Black Culture (in 1973).

Many researchers acknowledge the Center as the world's largest and most important repository of materials on African and African-American history and culture, now including more than 5 million items. The five divisions of the center are the art and artifacts division; the general research and reference division; the manuscripts, archives, and rare books division; the moving image and recorded sound division; and the photographs and prints division. The Center also offers online resources at //www.nypl.org/research/sc/digital.html, such as "African American Women Writers of the 19th Century," "Images of African Americans from the 19th Century," "Manuscripts, Archives, and Rare Books Division Finding Aids," "Studies Dedicated to Fernando Ortiz

(1880-1969): A Bibliography of Afro-Cuban Culture," "The State of Black Studies: Methodology, Pedagogy and Research," "Harlem 1900-1940: An African-American Community," and "The African Presence in the Americas, 1492-1992."

Schomburg's own publications included a bibliography (A *Bibliographical Checklist of American Negro Poetry*, 1916), an exhibition catalogue, and various articles published in the *A.M.E. Review*, **Crisis**, the *Messenger*, **Negro Digest**, **Negro World**, *New Century*, **Opportunity**, and *Survey Graphic*. Among his best-known articles are "Economic Contribution by the Negro to America" (1916), published by the ANA; and "The Negro Digs Up His Past" (1925), published in *Survey Graphic* and reprinted in Alain Locke's anthology *The New Negro*. Given that English was his second language and that he lacked much formal education, his writing served him well. Nonetheless, he profited from having skilled editors such as W. E. B. Du Bois, Charles Spurgeon Johnson, and Alain Locke edit his work for readability. With their help, he was able to show his great analytical skills, his keen insight into African-American culture and history, and his tremendous scholarship in the field.

REFERENCES: *AA:PoP. EA-99. NAAL.* Barnes, Deborah H., in *OCAAL.* Fay, Robert, "Schomburg Library," in *EA-99.* **Smith, Jessie Carney**, in *BH2C.*

FURTHER READING: *AANB. GEAAL. Wiki. See also* Holton, Adalaine. "Decolonizing History: Arthur Schomburg's Afrodiasporic Archive." *The Journal of African American History.* 92.2 (Spring 2007) p. 218. From *Literature Resource Center.*

Schuyler, George Samuel
2/25/1895–8/31/1977
Satire, novels, political commentary, autobiography

Although Schuyler was a socialist associated with **A. Philip Randolph** as a young adult, he is better known for his anticommunist, conservative political views in his later years. For about a decade, starting in 1923, his writing centered on articles and columns (e.g., "Shafts and Darts: A Page of Calumny and Satire") appearing in several newspapers. For Randolph's the *Messenger* (1923-1928), he started out as a staff writer, then became an assistant editor and then managing editor. Starting in 1924, he was also the New York correspondent for the *Pittsburgh Courier*, which he continued to be until the mid-1960s. Nine of his essays were published in H. L. Mencken's *American Mercury* (1927-1933), and many other articles and columns of his were published in other white-owned publications, such as *Nation, Plain Talk*, and *Common Ground*. Schuyler also wrote nonfiction books, including *Racial Intermarriage in the United States* (presaged by his own marriage to a white woman, Josephine

George Samuel Schuyler

Cogdell, in 1928), *Slaves Today: A Story of Liberia* (1931, an account of the slavelike working conditions of laborers in Liberia), and *Black and Conservative: The Autobiography of George S. Schuyler* (1966).

In the 1930s, Schuyler turned his attention to fiction. Schuyler's best-known novel is his satire *Black No More, Being an Account of the Strange and Wonderful Workings of Science in the Land of the Free* (1931), which satirically addresses the issue of race in America. In addition, between 1933 and 1939, he wrote 54 short stories and 20 serialized novels or novellas, which were published under pen names. In the 1990s, four of these serialized novels were printed in two volumes: *Black Empire* (1991) and *Ethiopian Stories* (1995). Perhaps Schuyler's most distinguished production, however, was his daughter—musician, composer, and writer **Philippa Duke Schuyler** (b. 1931)— the fruit of his marriage to Cogdell.

REFERENCES: *BAAW. EBLG.* Davidson, Adenike Marie, in *COCAAL* and *OCAAL.* Fay, Robert, in *EA-99.*

FURTHER READING: *BAWPP. CAO-07. W. Wiki.* Brennan, Carol, in *BB.* Fleener, Nickieann, in *ANJ-26-50-1.* Jones, Norma R., in *AAWHR-40.* Walker, Yvonne, in *GEAAL.*

Philippa Duke Schuyler

Schuyler, Philippa Duke
8/2/1931–5/9/1967

Autobiography/memoir, nonfiction—politics, religious biographies, dream interpretation, war observations; journalist

Schuyler's parents certainly knew how to provoke controversy. Josephine "Jody" Cogdell, a wealthy European-American journalist from Texas, firmly believed that the ultimate solution to America's race problems was interracial marriage. What's more, she believed that the offspring of such marriages would be extraordinary, as a result of "hybrid vigor." When she met **George Schuyler**, the novelist and journalist who wrote the highly provocative *Black No More,* she found a soulmate to share her theory and her life. To their delight, their daughter, Philippa (named after both Philip of Macedon and Revolutionary War hero Philip Schuyler), turned out to be exceptional in many ways.

Of course, Philippa's parents provided her with private tutoring and almost every other cultural and educational advantage they could offer, and she flourished in this environment: reading at age 2 1/2 years, playing the piano at age 3, and composing at age 4. By the time she was 13 years old, Philippa had already composed more than 100 pieces, including *Manhattan Nocturne,* which won the Grinnell Foundation's young composers contest for both originality and skill (including parts for 100 instruments), and which has since been performed by the New York Philharmonic and several other major symphony orchestras in this country. At age 15, she herself debuted for the New York Philharmonic in Lewisohn Stadium, to an audience of about 12,000 listeners.

Despite her early promise, however, her career as a concert pianist didn't take her to the stratosphere, so she shifted from music to writing. As her parents' daughter, she felt right at home lecturing on "The Red Menace in Africa" for the John Birch Society and other right-wing organizations. Her book *Who Killed the Congo?* (1962) elaborated on that theme. Her other published books include an autobiography, *Adventures in Black and White* (1960); *Jungle Saints: Africa's Heroic Catholic Missionaries* (1963); a book on dream interpretation, *Kingdom of Dreams* (1966, coauthored with her mother, Josephine Schuyler); and her eyewitness view of the Vietnam War, *Good Men Die* (1969, published posthumously).

Schuyler wrote her final published book while covering the war as a journalist. She had been working as a journalist for various American and European publica-

tions, often corresponding in French and German, as well as English. While in Vietnam, she was helping to rescue children from a battle site in Hue to a school in Da Nang when the helicopter in which she was riding crashed.

Schuyler also left behind some unpublished fiction, which she hadn't completed: *Sophie Daw,* a novel about the oppression of women, and *Dau Tranh,* about a tragic American mulatto. Ironic.

REFERENCES: *BAAW. EA-99.* Richardson, Deborra A., in *BWA:AHE.* Talalay, Kathryn 1995. *Composition in Black and White: The Life of Philippa Schuyler.* New York: Oxford University Press. —Tonya Bolden

FURTHER READING: *AANB. CAO-03. Wiki.* Manheim, James M., in *BB. See also* Richardson, Marilyn. "Composition in Black and White: The Life of Philippa Schuyler." *The Women's Review of Books.* 13.7 (Apr. 1996) p. 9. From *Literature Resource Center.*

Scott, Jr., Nathan A. (Alexander)
4/24/1925–12/20/2006

Literary criticism, nonfiction—theology, philosophy and literature, scholarly anthologies; journal editor

Scott attended Michigan's Wayne State University (1940-1941) before earning his B.A. from University of Michigan (1944); he then earned his M.Div. from New York City's Union Theological Seminary (1946) and his Ph.D. from Columbia University (1949). While still in college, Scott was the dean of chapel (1946-1947), and he started teaching at Howard University in Washington, D.C. (1948-1950). After earning his doctorate, he stayed on at Howard until 1955. He then moved to the University of Chicago Divinity School (1955-1977), where he rose through the academic ranks to become the Shailer Mathews Professor of Theology and Literature (1972-1977). He had also held several visiting or adjunct posts and was also a fellow of the school of letters at Indiana University (1965-1972). Meanwhile, he was ordained as a priest in the Episcopal Church (1960) and became a canon theologian at the Cathedral of St. James in Chicago (1966-1976).

He left Chicago for the University of Virginia in Charlottesville to become a professor of English and the William R. Kenan, Jr., Professor of Religious Studies (1976-1990), from which he retired in 1990. Among many of his fellowships and memberships, he was a fellow of both the Society for Religion in Higher Education and the American Academy of Arts and Sciences, and he was a member of both the Modern Language Association of America and the American Academy of Religion.

Scott's prodigious literary output reflects his deep insights into the intersection of literature and theology. In the 1950s, he wrote *Rehearsals of Discomposure: Alienation and Reconciliation in Modern Literature* (1952), *Modern Literature and the Religious Frontier* (1958), and a lecture published by National Council of the Protestant Episcopal Church, *The Broken Center: A Definition of the Crisis of Values in Modern Literature* (1959). In the 1960s, he wrote books about existentialist *Albert Camus* (1962, 2nd. rev. ed., 1969), dramatist and poet *Samuel Beckett* (1965, 2nd. rev. ed., 1969), and Nobel Prize-winning novelist and journalist *Ernest Hemingway: A Critical Essay* (1966); a pamphlet about theologian *Reinhold Niebuhr* (1963); and the books *The Broken Center: Studies in the Theological Horizon of Modern Literature* (1966), *Craters of the Spirit: Studies in the Modern Novel* (1968), *Negative Capability: Studies in the New Literature and the Religious Situation* (1969), and *The Unquiet Vision: Mirrors of Man in Existentialism* (1969). In the 1970s, he wrote literary criticism on *Nathanael West* (1971), *Three American Moralists: Mailer, Bellow, Trilling* (1973), and *The Poetry of Civic Virtue: Eliot, Malraux, Auden* (1976); and the books *The Wild Prayer of Longing: Poetry and the Sacred* (1971), *The Legacy of Reinhold Niebuhr* (1975), and *Mirrors of Man in Existentialism* (1978). The other two books he authored were *The Poetics of Belief: Studies in Coleridge, Arnold, Pater, Santayana, Stevens, and Heidegger* (1985) and *Visions of*

Presence in Modern American Poetry (1993). Most were published by scholarly presses such as Johns Hopkins University Press and Yale University Press, and many of these works are still available through Amazon.com.

Astonishingly, Scott also made time to edit numerous collections, including *The Tragic Vision and the Christian Faith* (1957), *The New Orpheus: Essays toward a Christian Poetic* (1964), *The Climate of Faith in Modern Literature* (1964), *Forms of Extremity in the Modern Novel* (1965), *Four Ways of Modern Poetry* (1965), *Man in the Modern Theatre* (1965), *Adversity and Grace: Studies in Recent American Literature* (1968), and *Reading George Steiner* (1994, coedited with Ronald A. Sharp). Also, according to the biographical introduction to the piece he contributed to *The New Cavalcade: African American Writing from 1760 to the Present* (1992), Scott "contributed articles to fifty books edited by others, and published essays or articles in more than one-hundred journals in literature, philosophy, and theology" (Redding et al., 1992). In addition to his literary contributions to periodicals, Scott also served as advisory editor for **Callaloo**, a coeditor of *Christian Scholar* and of *Journal of Religion*, and a member of the advisory board for *Religion and Literature* (formerly *Notre Dame English Journal*). He also was awarded at least 15 honorary doctorates.

REFERENCES: *BAWPP. CAO-0-7.* Redding, J. Saunders, Arthur P. Davis, and Joyce Ann Joyce (Eds.). 1992. *The New Cavalcade: African American Writing from 1760 to the Present* (pp. 96ff). Washington, D.C.: Howard University Press. Schlueter, Paul. "A Tribute to Nathan A. Scott, Jr." *Christianity and Literature.* 56.3 (Spring 2007) p. 458. Literature Resources from Gale. Amazon.com, June 29, 2009.

Scott-Heron, Gil
4/1/1949–

Poems, novels, song lyrics, spoken word—poetry; musician, performer

While attending DeWitt Clinton High School in the Bronx, Gil Scott-Heron was granted a full scholarship to attend the private Fieldston School of Ethical Culture. After high school, Scott-Heron decided to attend the historically black Lincoln University, in Pennsylvania, from which **Langston Hughes** had graduated in 1929. While there, he earned the school's Langston Hughes Creative Writing Award (1968) and met his long-time collaborator Brian Jackson. After a year or so, he left Lincoln and never earned a baccalaureate degree.

After leaving Lincoln, Scott-Heron returned to New York City, where he wrote two novels, *The Vulture* (1970/1996) and *The Nigger Factory* (1972/1996), as well as a poetry and photography collection, *Small Talk at 125th and Lenox: A Collection of Black Poems* (1970). Having put his words on paper, he began recording his words on albums, starting with a spoken-word recording of his poetry collection, accompanied by percussions and vocals, *Small Talk at 125th & Lenox* (1970), followed by *Pieces of a Man* (1971), *Free Will* (1972), and *The Revolution Will Not Be Televised* (1972).

While continuing to work on his creative productions, Scott-Heron earned an M.A. in creative writing from Baltimore's Johns Hopkins University (1972) then taught creative writing at Federal City College in Washington, D.C. (1972-1976). After a few years, he left teaching to focus on his music. While still in D.C., he produced his highly acclaimed album *Winter in America* (1974), followed by *Midnight Band: The First Minute of a New Day* (1975), *From South Africa to South Carolina* (1975), his live album *It's Your World* (1976), *Bridges* (1977), and *Secrets* (1978). His last album of the 1970s was *The Mind of Gil Scott-Heron* (1979), a return to spoken-word poetry.

Scott-Heron started off the 1980s with *1980, Real Eyes*, and *Gil Scott-Heron and Brian Jackson* (all 1980), *Reflections* (1981), *Moving Target* (1982), *The Best of Gil Scott-Heron* (1984), and *The Revolution Will Not Be Televised* (1988). He also contributed to several albums. In addition, **Third World Press** published his poetry collection *So Far, So Good* (1988/1990). Also, in 1982, filmmaker Robert Mugge made a 79-minute documentary film about Scott-Heron. In the 1990s, Scott-Heron released *Tales of Gil Scott-Heron and His Amnesia Express* and *Glory: The Gil Scott-Heron Collection* (both 1990), *Minister of Information* and *Spirits* (both 1994), *The Gil Scott-Heron Collection Sampler: 1974-1975* and *Ghetto Style* (both 1998), and *Evolution and Flashback: The Very Best of Gil Scott-Heron* (1999).

In the new millennium, Scott-Heron was arrested and convicted for possessing cocaine and was in and out of jail, prison, and drug-rehabilitation facilities between 2001 and 2007. Meanwhile, he returned to print with *Now and Then: The Poems of Gil Scott-Heron* (2001). He also created his own record label, Rumal-Gia, as an imprint of TVT Records. His label released *Gil Scott-Heron & Brian Jackson—Messages* (2005). Scott-Heron was also featured on the album *Malik & the OG's—Rhythms of the Diaspora* (2009) and on the documentary film *Word Up—From Ghetto to Mecca*. In his live comeback performance in 2007, he announced plans to release a new album and to complete work on his book *The Last Holiday*. A subsequent drug arrest has impeded his progress, but he has still managed a few live appearances while resolving his legal difficulties.

REFERENCES: *CAO-02. D. Wiki.* Bush, John, *All Music Guide*, in *A.* Hinton, KaaVonia, in *AANB.* Woodson, Jon, in *AAP-55-85.* //cn.wikipedia.org/wiki/Fore-Word_Press. //en.wikipedia.org/wiki/Robert_Mugge. //worldcat.org/identities/lccn-n50-3969. //www.robert

mugge.com/films.htm. //www.worldcat.org/search?q=scott-heron%2C+gil&fq=&dblist=638&start=21&qt=next_page. Amazon.com.

FURTHER READING: Blaque, Ellesia Ann, in *GEAAL.*

Séjour, Victor (né Juan Victor Séjour Marcon-Ferrand)
6/2/1817–9/21?/1874
Plays, poems, novel

Though New Orleans can claim Séjour as its native son, most Americans know little or nothing of his work, as most of it was written in French. As the son of a free mulatto from the West Indies and a free octoroon from New Orleans, Séjour was born a free Creole of color. After finishing school at New Orleans's Sainte-Barbe Academy, his family realized that adequate educational and career opportunities would be denied him if he remained in the United States.

Séjour soon left for Paris (1836), where he became associated with the noted African-French novelist, playwright, and correspondent Alexandre Dumas, père. In 1837, Séjour's writing first appeared in print in *La Revue des Colonies*, a journal edited by African-French abolitionist Cyrille Bisette. In Séjour's short story "Lemulâtre" ("The Mulatto"), one of the earliest works of African-American fiction to openly address slavery, an enslaved man murders his "master," whom he then discovers was also his father. Séjour's subsequent writings never addressed racism directly. Séjour's heroic ode *Le Retour de Napoléon* (1841) brought him literary recognition both in France and in the United States, where Armand Lanusse included it in his *Les Cenelles* (1845), the first anthology of poetry written by African-American authors. From 1844 until 1869, Séjour enjoyed great prominence and fame in the Parisian theater, where more than 20 of his plays were produced. In addition, 20 of his plays were also published, and some were also produced in other venues around the world. Among his plays were numerous verse dramas. After 1870, his career declined, but he still wrote the novel *Le Compte de Haag* (1872, "The Count of Haag"), which was published serially.

REFERENCES: *AAWBHR. W. Wiki.* Barnard, Philip, in *COCAAL.* Kadish, Doris Y. "Sejour, Victor. The Jew of Seville." *Nineteenth-Century French Studies. 33.1-2* (Fall-Winter 2004), p. 190. Literature Resources from Gale. Pederson, Nadine D., in *AANB.* Perkins, A. E. "Victor Séjour and His Times." *The Negro History Bulletin. 5.7* (1942, April), pp. 163-166. Literature Resources from Gale. Perret, J. John. "Victor Séjour, Black French Playwright from Louisiana." *The French Review. 57.2* (1983, Dec.), pp. 187-193. Literature Resources from Gale. Roussève, Charles Barthelemy. (1937). "Negro Literature in Ante Bellum Louisiana: Victor Séjour." *The Negro in Louisiana: Aspects of His History and His Literature* (pp. 82-90). New Orleans: Xavier University Press. Literature Resources from Gale. //www.bookrags.com/biography/victor-sejour-dlb/.

FURTHER READING: *HAAL*. Coates, Jennifer R., in *GEAAL*.

Senna, Carl
4/13/1944–
Nonfiction, essays, literary criticism, biography, columns; book acquisition editor, journalist, educator

Danzy (Maria) Senna, daughter
9/13/1970–
Novels, essays, autobiography/memoir; journalist, publisher

After Carl Senna attended Boston University (1962-1967), while he was just starting to attend Columbia University (1968-1970), he married Irish-American Protestant writer Fanny Quincy Howe. She and Carl also produced three children: Ann Lucien Quincy, Danzy Maria, and Maceo Carl.

As a newlywed, soon to be a father, Carl worked as an editor for Boston's Beacon Press (1968-1969), a lecturer in English at the Medford campus of Tufts University (1968-1969), and a creative-writing instructor at Boston's Northeastern University (1969). While working as a lecturer in English at the University of Massachusetts in Boston (1969-1973), he gave up on finishing his degree at Columbia. In 1974, Carl and Fanny, parents of three young children, divorced. During the 1970s and 1980s, the children lived with Howe, but Senna still participated in their lives.

Carl wrote a pamphlet, *Beyond the Basics: Text and Content* (1975), and edited two books, *Parachute Shop Blues and Other Writings of New Orleans* (1972) and *Fallacy of IQ* (1973). He also authored the first of several Cliff's Notes he wrote, *"Black Boy" Notes* (1971). Carl copublished a book as the "Senna" of "Senna & Shih, Inc." (1976-1977). He also worked as a teaching assistant at Harvard University (1978-1979). Meanwhile, he contributed to numerous periodicals (e.g., *Commonweal*, *The New York Times Book Review*, *Ploughshares*). In the 1980s, he was a lecturer at Northeastern University (1983-1985) and at Roger Williams College (later University) in Bristol, Rhode Island (1985). He also authored two more Cliff's Notes, *"One Hundred Years of Solitude" Notes* and *"Alice in Wonderland" Notes* (both 1984), as well as an essay collection, *Pumping 800 and Other Essays* (1986). In the 1990s, Senna wrote a biography, *Colin Powell: A Man of War and Peace* (1992) and a young-adult nonfiction work, *The Black Press and the Struggle for Civil Rights* (1993). Senna also wrote a fourth Cliff's Notes, *Cliffs Notes on Shakespeare's Sonnets* (2000). In addition, he worked as a columnist for the *Providence (Rhode Island) Journal* for a while.

Danzy Senna gives her own account of her childhood family life in her memoir *Where Did You Sleep Last Night?: A Personal History* (2009), published by the prestigious Farrar, Straus and Giroux. The book seems have to cracked open fault lines in the family, exacerbated by Danzy's fair skin and nearly straight hair and her older sister Lucien's somewhat darker skin and curlier hair. Before publication of the memoir prompted a rupture in their relationship, Danzy and Carl had collaborated on researching a key aspect of Danzy's memoir. Both of them wanted to find out more about Carl's mother, Anna Maria "Ria" Franklin Senna, who was rumored to have had an affair with Reverend Francis E. Ryan, an Irish-American Josephite priest. Through Danzy and Carl's investigation, they discovered that Carl and his brother Adrian had a biological sister, Carla Latty, who was adopted, while Carl and Adrian remained in an Alabama orphanage. DNA evidence has linked both Adrian and Carla to Ryan.

Prior to writing the memoir, Danzy Senna earned a B.A., with honors, from Stanford University (1992) and then an M.F.A. from the University of California at Irvine (1996). Between those two academic achievements, she worked as a researcher and reporter for *Newsweek* (1992-1994) in New York City. After earning her master's degree, she became a contributing editor for *American Benefactor* (back in New York City, 1996-1997). Danzy Senna has also taught writing and literature at the College of the Holy Cross, a Roman Catholic liberal arts college in Worcester, Massachusetts.

While working on her first novel, Senna was awarded a prestigious fellowship to the MacDowell Colony in Peterborough, New Hampshire (1997). Her novel, *Caucasia* (1998, published as *From Caucasia with Love*, 2000), is set in the 1970s and 1980s. The protagonist and narrator, Birdie, looks more like her white mother, and her sister, Cole, looks more like her black father. Danzy Senna's fictional story departs from Danzy Senna's life story, but it still touches on themes of racial identity in biracial families. *Caucasia* was honored with both the Book-of-the-Month's Stephen Crane Award for First Fiction and the American Library Association's Alex Award (1999).

Danzy Senna won the prestigious and lucrative Whiting Writers' Award for fiction (2002) before publishing her second novel, *Symptomatic* (2003), in which racial identity also plays a role, as a biracial narrator finds herself involved in an increasingly creepy situation. While working on her book-length fiction, Senna has also contributed essays to books edited by others. Since publishing *Symptomatic*, Senna was named a fellow of the New York Public Library's Cullman Center for Scholars and Writers (2004). She and her husband, novelist and educator **Percival Everett**, have a son.

REFERENCES: "Fanny Howe," in //www.poets.org/poet.php/
prmPID/881. Sege, Irene. (6/9/2009). "Fractured Family Tree: To
Danzy Senna, Her Memoir Is Personal History. To Her Father, It's
Character Assassination." *Boston Globe*, in //www.boston.com/ae/
books/articles/2009/06/09/to_danzy_senna_her_memoir_is_personal_
history_to_her_father_its_character_assassination_boston_globe/.
"Carl Senna," *BAWPP. CAO-08.* https://isbndb.com/d/publisher/
senna_and_shih.html. //en.wikipedia.org/wiki/Roger_Williams_
University. //www.betterworld.com/T-i-t-l-e-id-0894600001.aspx.
//www.worldcat.org/search?q=carl+senna&qt=search_items.
Amazon.com. "Danzy Senna," *CAO-04. CLCS. Wiki.* Curry, Ginette,
in *AANB.* LaFrance, Michelle, in *GEAAL.* //en.wikipedia.org/wiki/
Alex_Award. //en.wikipedia.org/wiki/College_of_the_Holy_Cross.
//en.wikipedia.org/wiki/MacDowell_Colony. //en.wikipedia.org/
wiki/Whiting_Writers%27_Award. //www.flickr.com/photos/8541955
@N07/1323070115. //www.goodreads.com/author/show/19027.
Danzy_Senna. //www.worldcat.org/isbn/3404145690. Amazon.com.

Shadd Cary (married name), Mary Ann *See* Cary, Mary Ann Shadd

Shakur, Assata Olugbala (née JoAnne Deborah Byron; married name: Chesimard)
7/16/1947–
Autobiography

In her book, *Assata: An Autobiography* (1987/2001), she candidly (and often with good humor) describes her formative years, as well as her experiences as an activist in the Black Panther Party (early and mid 1970s), as a questionably convicted accomplice to the murder of a white state trooper (1977), as a prisoner, and as an escaped prisoner residing with political asylum in Cuba (since 1979).

REFERENCES: *BAAW.* —Tonya Bolden

Editor's note: In 1985, Assata's daughter, Kakuya, joined Assata in Cuban exile. In 1993, Assata Shakur collaborated with Dhoruba bin Wahad and politically active convict Mumia Abu-Jamal to produce *Still Strong, Still Black*; many of Shakur's less formal writings can be found on the Internet. In the mid-1990s, the notorious murder of her stepnephew, rapper **Tupac Shakur**, revived Assata's visibility.

REFERENCES: *AANB. CAO-07.* "Assata Shakur" and "Assata aka Joanne Chesimard," in *Wiki.* Sipal, Iva, in *BB.* Amazon.com.

Shakur, Tupac (2Pac)
6/16/1971–9/13/1996
Rap songs

One of Shakur's first rap hits was "Brenda's Got a Baby," which depicted the hardships faced by single African-American mothers, much like his own mother, Black Panther Party activist Afeni Shakur. Sadly, the drugs and violence Shakur described in his songs (e.g., "If I Die 2Nite" and "Death around the Corner") also mimicked his own life experiences: He was shot multiple times, jailed and imprisoned, and eventually died as a result of a shooting. His career had been promising before his demise, as his records had sold millions of copies, and he was nominated for two Grammy Awards.

REFERENCES: Robinson, Alonford James, Jr., in *EA-99.*

FURTHER READING: *A. Act. CAO-03. D. F. W2B. Wiki.* Gilley, D. Shane, in *GEAAL.* Glickman, Simon, in *BB.* //www.afropoets.net/tupacshakur.html. Amazon.com.

Shange, Ntozake (née Paulette Williams)
10/18/1948–
Plays, poems, novels, essays, children's fiction and nonfiction picture books, nonfiction— cookbook, food history; entertainer, director, educator

The Williams family—Eloise (a psychiatric social worker), Paul T. (a surgeon), and their four children—regularly enjoyed a broad array of cultural experiences, including jazz, blues, soul, Latin, and classical music; selected readings from William Shakespeare, **Paul Laurence Dunbar**, and **Langston Hughes**; attendance at ballets and concerts; and Sunday afternoon family variety shows, with Paul T. playing the congas and the children dancing or playing an assortment of instruments. These family events were often highlighted with visits from such outstanding entertainers as Josephine Baker, Chuck Berry, Dizzy Gillespie, and Charlie Parker. On at least one occasion, **W. E. B. Du Bois** illumined Paulette's family's home, and guests from "virtually all of the colonized French-, Spanish-, and English-speaking countries" were welcome in the Williams home. Paulette and her younger siblings felt very much connected to Africa's descendants around the world, as well as to a breadth of Third World cultures.

After Paulette's birth, the Williamses spent eight years in Trenton, New Jersey, then five years in St. Louis, Missouri, before returning again to Trenton. During their years in St. Louis, Paulette was among the first African-American children to integrate the public-school system, and she experienced firsthand the poignant cruelty of racism. While her parents took pride in their courageous, independent young racial pioneers, Paulette was developing a belly-deep rage toward racism. Although Paulette had been writing stories since her early years, when she heard in school that Negroes don't write, she stopped writing.

When the family returned to Trenton, Paulette started reading all the literature she could put her hands on: Carson McCullers, Simone de Beauvoir, Fyodor

Dostoyevsky, and Herman Melville. In high school, she even started writing again. After some of her poetry was published in her high-school magazine, she felt encouraged to write more. In her English class, she wrote essays about African Americans. After writing numerous essays, however, she was told that she should start writing about other topics, and she again stopped writing until after she finished high school.

After high school, Paulette entered Barnard College (in 1966) and soon married a law student. After she and her husband went through an agonizing separation, Paulette underwent a series of suicide attempts. Compounding her emotional distress was her intensifying awareness that the society in which she lived—unlike her supportive family—devalued intelligent African-American women. Despite this emotional turmoil, she managed to graduate cum laude with a B.A. in American Studies in 1970.

After Barnard, Paulette moved to Los Angeles, where she lived communally with several other performance artists and writers. During this time (in 1971), she adopted her name Ntozake Shange. *Ntozake* is a Zulu name for "she who comes with her own things," and *Shange* means "she who walks like a lion." By the time she earned her master's degree (in 1973), she signed all of her work with her self-chosen name.

With her master's degree in hand, Shange moved to the San Francisco Bay area, where she taught at various colleges until 1975. During this period, she also made numerous public appearances as a performance artist, dancing and reciting her own original poetry. Even after her literary career took off, Shange has continued to teach (e.g., at Yale, Howard, University of Houston, and Maryland Institute's College of Art).

Through Shange's numerous performances, she developed a distinctive form, which she calls a "choreopoem"—verse narratives, which are presented on stage, accompanied by music and dance. Her first finished choreopoem was *for colored girls who have considered suicide / when the rainbow is enuf* (published in 1976). In this choreopoem, seven African-American women act, sing, dance, and recite 20 poems. Their characters are identified as the Lady in Brown, the Lady in Yellow, in Red, Green, Purple, Blue, and Orange. Each woman takes a turn reciting her story as a poetic monologue. Each story highlights an aspect of African-American women's experiences across the life span (e.g., a childhood crush, a first sexual experience, an abusive relationship with a violent Vietnam veteran).

While many critics praised the play for its freshness and wit and for highlighting the experiences of courageous, outspoken women who triumph over despair, some critics condemned it for its lack of winsome men and its superficial characterizations. Apparently, the praises out-

weighed the detractions, as her choreopoem was performed on Broadway (only the second play by an African-American woman to reach Broadway) for two years in the mid-1970s, winning an Obie Award, as well as Emmy, Tony (for best play), and Grammy Award nominations. The play also earned Outer Critics Circle, Audelco, Off-Broadway, Village Voice, and *Mademoiselle* awards and was chosen for international performances. Shange's peers recognize her achievement, too. For instance, **Nikki Giovanni** (*BWWW*, p. 67) said of her, "I loved *For Colored Girls*. First of all Ntozake is an extremely bright, sensitive, *good poet*. She writes exceptionally well. . . . *For Colored Girls* is . . . one of my favorite poems."

Additional plays by Shange include *Where the Mississippi Meets the Amazon* (1977, coauthored with Jessica Hegedorn and Thulani Nkabinda); her 1981 Obie Award-winning *Mother Courage and Her Children* (1980), a Civil War-era adaptation of Bertolt Brecht's play *Mother Courage*; her 1981 *Los Angeles Times Book Review* Award-winning *Three Pieces: Spell #7: A Photograph: Lover in Motion: Boogie Woogie; Three for a Full Moon* (1982) and *Bocas* (1982); her choreopoem *From Okra to Greens! A Different Kinda Love Story: A Play! With Music and Dance* (1985); *Three Views of Mt. Fuji* (1987); *Betsey Brown* (1989), based on her 1985 novel; *Daddy Says* (1989), a somewhat conventional one-act play; *The Love Space Demands: A Continuing Saga* (1991), a choreopoem performance piece; *Fire's Daughters* (1993); and *Lavender Lizards and Lilac Landmines: Layla's Dream* (2003).

In addition to her plays, Shange has written several novels. As with her plays, Shange has developed her novels in her own distinctive way. Often, she has taken work from one medium (e.g., a play) and adapted it to another medium (e.g., a novel), or she has taken a smaller work (e.g., a novella) and amplified it to create a much broader work (e.g., a novel). For instance, she transformed her dance-drama *Sassafras*, presented in 1976, into a novella, *Sassafras: A Novella*, published in 1977; then she developed that work further and expanded it to create her novel *Sassafras, Cypress & Indigo: A Novel*, published in 1982. Her novel tells the story of three sisters: Sassafras, a weaver, Cypress, a dancer, and Indigo, a midwife. Each sister is struggling with her own identity and her need for creative freedom and purpose. Also, in Shange's initial novella, she minimally punctuated the book, "because I didn't want the reader to be able to put the book down" (*BWWW*, p. 156); the novel, however, follows standardized punctuation conventions. Additional novels by Shange include *Betsey Brown* (1985), a semiautobiographical novel set in the late 1950s, when the author and the civil-rights movement were coming of age; and *Liliane: Resurrection of the Daughter* (1994), about the psychological development of a wealthy African-American woman living in the South.

In addition, Shange has written several free-verse poetry collections, which also flout conventional language forms: *Nappy Edges* (1978), exulting in outspoken independent women's voices; *Some Men* (1981), presented as a pamphlet that looks like a dance card; *A Daughter's Geography* (1983); *From Okra to Greens: Poems* (1984); *Melissa and Smith: A Story* (1985); *Ridin' the Moon in Texas: Word Paintings* (1987), which highlights the African-American **oral tradition** through nonconformist syntax, capitalization, spelling, and idiomatic vocabulary and language structure; *I Live in Music* (1994); and *The Sweet Breath of Life: A Poetic Narrative of the African-American Family* (2004), a photo and poetry collage of African-American children, women, and men.

Regarding her distinctive spellings, Shange has said, "The spellings result from the way I talk or the way the character talks or the way I heard something said. Basically, the spellings reflect language as I hear it" (*BWWW,* p. 163). Bridging the gap between prose and poetry is Shange's collection *Natural Disasters and Other Festive Occasions* (1977). Her nonfiction writings have been gathered in *See No Evil: Prefaces, Essays and Accounts 1976-1983* (published in 1984). More recently, Shange wrote *If I Can Cook You Know God Can* (1998), in which she collects essays discussing the foodways of people of African descent around the world, as well as representative recipes, from the traditional and familiar to the exotic. Amazon.com also listed *How I Come by This Cryin' Song,* authored by Shange and Ifa Bayeza, as forthcoming in June 2009; its contents and genre remain a mystery until then.

Venturing into new territory herself, Shange wrote a juvenile picture book, *Whitewash* (1997), about a young African-American girl and her brother, who suffer an attack by white gang members on their way home from school, and who recover with the help of her grandmother and her classmates. Her next two picture books were inspired by reminiscences of her childhood and youth: *Float Like a Butterfly: Muhammad Ali, the Man Who Could Float Like a Butterfly and Sting Like a Bee* (2002) offers a picture-book biography of Ali, who visited Shange's home when she was a teen; her sparely written poetic picture book *Ellington Was Not a Street* (2004, illustrated by Kadir Nelson) pays tribute to the musicians, artists, and writers who graced her childhood home. In *Coretta Scott* (2009, illustrated by Kadir Nelson), Shange used her simple, unpunctuated, uncapitalized poetry to evoke the early life of the woman who married **Martin Luther King, Jr.** By the end of 2009, Shange's picture book *We Troubled the Waters* is due in readers' hands. For preteen and young-teen readers, Shange's *Daddy Says* (2003) revolves around 12- and 14-year-old sisters orphaned by their rodeo-champion mother, as their cowboy-rancher father starts forming a relationship with a new girlfriend. Previously, Shange had written a play titled *Daddy Says* and a video screenplay titled *Whitewash,* produced in 1989 and 1994, respectively.

Among the many honors and awards Shange has earned are an NDEA fellowship (1973), a Frank Silvera Writers' Workshop Award (1978), a Columbia University Medal of Excellence (1981), a Guggenheim fellowship (1981), Barnard College's Nori Eboraci Award (1988), naming as the World Heavyweight Champion at the Taos Poetry Circus (1991, 1992, 1993, 1994), the Arts and Cultural Achievement Award from the National Coalition of 100 Black Women (1992, PA chapter), the Lila Wallace-Reader's Digest Fund annual writer's award (1992-1995), Paul Robeson Achievement Award (1992), the Claim Your Life Award from WDAS-AM/FM (1993), the Living Legend Award of the National Black Theatre Festival (1993), the Pew fellowship in fiction (1993-1994), the Black Theatre Network Winona Fletcher award (1994), the City of Philadelphia Literature Prize (1994), the Lincoln University President's Award (1994), the Monarch Merit Award from the National Council for Culture and Art, a Pushcart Prize, and appointment to the New York State Council of the Arts. Perhaps more astonishingly, Shange has managed to achieve such success while raising her daughter, Savannah (b. 1981), as a single working mother.

REFERENCES: *1TESK. AA:PoP. AANB. AAW:PV. B. BWWW. CA/I. CAI-07. CBAPD. CLCS-08-a. CLCS-08-b. EBLG. MAAL. MWEL. NAAAL. OC20LE. W. Wiki.* Brown, Elizabeth, in *AAW-55-85:DPW.* Fisler, Ben, in *GEAAL.* Lester, Neal, in *OCWW.* Lester, Neal A., in *RGAL-3.* O'Connor, Jacqueline, in *T-CAD-3rd.* Power, Will. "Catching up with Ntozake Shange Her Innovations in Stage Verse and Movement Have Inspired a New Generation." *American Theatre.* 24.4 (Apr. 2007) p. 30. From *Literature Resource Center.* Richards, Sandra L., in *AAW. CD-5.* Shange, Ntozake, and Henry Blackwell. "Interview." *Black American Literature Forum* 13.4 (Winter 1979): pp. 134-138. Rpt. in *Contemporary Literary Criticism Select.* Detroit: Gale. From *Literature Resource Center.* Shange, Ntozake, and Brenda Lyons. "Interview with Ntozake Shange." *Massachusetts Review* 28.4 (Winter 1987): pp. 687-696. Rpt. in Jeffrey W. Hunter (Ed.) (2000), *Contemporary Literary Criticism* (Vol. 126). Detroit: Gale Group. From *Literature Resource Center.* Taylor-Thompson, Betty, in *COCAAL* and *OCAAL.* Vandergrift, Kay E., in *T-CYAW.* Wainwright, Mary Katherine in *BB.* Walton, Priscilla L., in *CP-6.* Wilson, J. J., in *FW.* //worldcat.org/identities/lccn-n94-60380. //www.cavecanempoets.org/pages/programs_faculty.php. //www.poets.org/poet.php/prmPID/147. Amazon.com.

FURTHER READING: *EAAWW.*

Shepherd, Reginald
4/10/1963–9/10/2008
Poems, anthologies, essays, memoir—blog; educator

As a gay black man, Shepherd observed, "I have been oppressed by many things in my life, but not by literature, which for me has always represented potential and not closure" (in *CAO-08*). Shepherd's poems have been collected in six volumes in the Pitt Poetry series: *Some Are Drowning* (1994), *Angel, Interrupted* (1996), *Wrong* (1999), Lenore Marshall Poetry Prize-nominated *Otherhood: Poems* (2003), *Itinerary: Poems* (2006), and *Fata Morgana: Poems* (2007), which won a Silver Medal for poetry from the Florida Book Awards. More than 400 of his poems have also been published in his chapbooks *This History of His Body* (1998) and *New and Selected Poems* (n.d.), and in various literary journals (e.g., *Kenyon Review, Nation, Paris Review, Poetry*); they have also appeared in four editions of *The Best American Poetry*. Shepherd's award-winning poetry explores such diverse themes as interracial homosexual relationships, ancient Greek mythology (e.g., three poems on Narcissus), contemporary music, and historical and current social dilemmas. Shepherd also edited *The Iowa Anthology of New American Poetries* (2004) and *Lyric Postmodernisms: An Anthology of Contemporary Innovative Poetries* (2008).

The recipient of two M.F.A. degrees (Brown University, 1991; University of Iowa, 1993), Shepherd taught at Northern Illinois University, Cornell University, and Antioch University, among others. He also wrote a regular blog, where he discussed his approaches to literature, especially poetry. Shepherd's nonfiction is collected in *Orpheus in the Bronx: Essays on Identity, Politics, and the Freedom of Poetry* (2007), which was nominated for the National Book Critics Circle award in January 2009. Shepherd's other awards include two Pushcart Prizes, a grant from the National Endowment for the Arts, and a Guggenheim fellowship (2008). An online literary publication established The 2009 International Reginald Shepherd Memorial Poetry Prize in his honor. In addition, Robert Philen, Shepherd's beloved and his literary executor, is preparing both a poetry collection and an essay collection of Shepherd's works, to be published posthumously. Readers may gain some insight into Shepherd's intriguing views from his observation, "Every writer is as much the tool of language as its wielder" (in *CAO-08*).

REFERENCES: *CAO-08. VBAAP.* Adolf, Antony, in *GEAAL.* //reginaldshepherd.blogspot.com/. //reginaldshepherd.blogspot. com/2008/ 09/reginald-shepherd-1963-2008.html. //www.amazon. com, 3/2000, 4/2009. //www.knockoutlit.org/rsprize.htm. //www. poets.org/poet.php/prmPID/1053. //www.thevalve.org/go/valve/ article/ reginald_shepherd_1963_2008/.

Shine, Ted (Theodis)
4/26/1931–
Plays, television scripts, anthology

Editor's note: Shine's birth year is given as 1931 in *CAO-01, COCAAL, GEAAL,* but as 1936 in *BAWPP.*

While Ted Shine was still studying at Howard University in Washington, D.C., he wrote the play *Cold Day in August* (1950), which was produced at Howard. Shine's next two plays were *Sho Is Hot in the Cotton Patch* (1951; published in *Encore,* 1967; produced as *Miss Weaver,* 1968) and his one-act *Dry August* (1952). Each of his first three plays addressed serious matters through humor. His attempt at tragedy, "My Mother Came Crying Most Pitifully," proved unsuccessful.

After earning his B.A. (1953), Shine gained a Rockefeller scholarship to study at Karamu House in Cleveland (1953-1955), and he wrote a musical, "Entourage Royale," which was never produced. While serving in the military (1955-1957), his musical *Good News* (1956) entertained troops in Germany. After his military service, Shine obtained a scholarship to enroll in a play-writing program at the Iowa State University of Science and Technology (now the University of Iowa). His thesis project, *Epitaph for a Bluebird* (1958), was produced at the university, earning him an M.A. (1958), but his "A Rat's Revolt" has never been produced.

After Iowa, Shine moved to New Orleans briefly to teach drama and English at Dillard University (1960-1961), then he returned to Howard University as an assistant professor of drama (1961-1967). While there, he wrote his three-act *Morning, Noon and Night* (1964), which won Howard University's Brooks-Hines Award for Playwriting and which was published in *The Black Teacher and the Dramatic Arts* (1970). The play introduced a strong, influential, powerful female character type, who was to reappear in many of Shine's other plays. By the end of his stay at Howard, Shine had written and seen produced three full-length plays, a musical, and several one-act plays.

In 1967, Shine moved to Prairie View, Texas to become a professor and head of the drama department at Prairie View A & M University (1967-). Six years later, he earned his Ph.D. (1973) from the University of California at Santa Barbara (UCSB). While at UCSB, he served as the UCSB Players' playwright. Shine's next full-length play, *Comeback after the Fire* (1969), was a sequel to *Morning, Noon and Night.* In a departure from his stage work, over the next few years (1969-1973), Shine wrote 60 or more half-hour scripts for the *Our Street* TV series produced by the Maryland Center for Public Broadcasting and aired by 22 public-television stations. Meanwhile, Shine continued to teach, to work toward his doctorate, and to write some stage plays. During this time, he also wrote a musical, "Jeanne West" (completed in 1968, not produced), as well as 11 one-act or other short plays, including *Shoes* (1969), *Idabel's Fortune* (1969), *Flora's Kisses* (1969), *Hamburgers at Hamburger Heaven Are Impersonal* (1969), and *Contribution* (1969), each of which have been produced multiple times.

After the *Our Street* series ended, Shine wrote another full-length play, *The Night of Baker's End* (1974), followed by his one-act *Herbert III* (1975), which was also published in *Black Theatre, U.S.A.: Forty-five Plays by Black Americans, 1847-1974* (1974), for which the editor James V. Hatch gives Shine credit as a consultant. The book has been updated to create *Black Theatre USA Vol. 1 (rev., expanded ed.): Plays by African Americans, The Early Period 1847 to 1938* and *Black Theatre, USA, Vol. 2: Plays by African Americans: The Recent Period, 1935-Today* (both 1996). Shine's other produced plays include *Baby Cakes* (1981), *The Woman Who Was Tampered with in Youth* (1983), *Good Old Soul* (1984), *Going Berserk* (1984), *Ancestors* (1986), and *Deep Ellum Blues* (1986). He also wrote at least eight more unpublished, unproduced plays. His play *The Earthworms* was published (1958) but never produced, and his short story "Bury Miss Emma in a White Satin Coffin and Cover Her with Pure White Sand" was also published (1969).

In addition to his writing, Shine's expertise was highlighted when the John F. Kennedy Center for the Performing Arts' board of trustees chair asked him to serve on the Task Force on Playwrights and Black Producing Theatres in Washington, D.C. (1977). Shine also served as a judge for the **Lorraine Hansberry** Playwriting Award presented by the American Theatre Association as part of the American College Theatre Festival (1980-1981). He is a board member of the Texas Non-Profit Theatres, Inc., as well.

REFERENCES: *BAWPP. CAO-01.* Carter, Steven R., in *COCAAL.* Fletcher, Winona L., in *AAW-55-85:DPW.* McCarty, Joan F., in *GEAAL.* Amazon.com.

Shockley, Ann (née Ann Allen)
6/21/1927–

Criticism, novels, short stories, bibliographies, biographies, essays, compilations; journalist, columnist, librarian, educator, archivist, newsletter editor

Henry and Bessie Lucas Allen, both social workers, raised Ann, their only daughter, to savor reading and writing. In junior high school, Ann edited her school newspaper, and she was soon writing short articles for the local *Louisville [Kentucky] Defender.*

While working toward her B.A. at Fisk University, Ann wrote essays and short stories for the *Fisk Herald.* She earned her B.A. in 1948, and in 1949 she married William Shockley, with whom she had a son and a daughter, William Leslie and Tamara Ann; the Shockleys subsequently divorced. Between 1949 and 1959, Ann wrote weekly newspaper columns focusing on African-American political, cultural, social, community, family, and women's issues. Shockley also worked as a public-school

teacher and then a librarian. By 1959, she had earned an M.S. in library science, and for years, she curated various African-American collections at nearby colleges. At last, by 1969, she had earned her way home to Fisk, where she has since been recognized as one of the leading university archivists of African-American women's writing.

Shockley's first book-length projects were outstanding reference works, used by fellow librarians and other archivists: Her *History of Public Library Services to Negroes in the South, 1900-1955* (unpublished) thoroughly describes the inadequacies of segregated public-library services in the Jim Crow South; and her *Living Black American Authors: A Biographical Directory* (1973, with Sue P. Chandler) encompasses numerous African-American writers. Shockley's *A Handbook for the Administration of Special Black Collections* (1970) and her *A Handbook for Black Librarianship* (1977, with **E. J. Josey**) specifically tell how to gather and protect materials on African-American history; the second handbook was nominated for the 1978 Ralph R. Shaw Award for Outstanding Contributions to Library Literature. Shockley's widely appealing *Afro-American Women Writers (1746-1933): An Anthology and Critical Guide* (1988) places more than 40 writers in their historical, cultural, and literary context. In addition, Shockley has written *Joseph S. Cotter, Sr: Biographical Sketch of a Black Louisville Bard* (1975), as well as numerous articles. She has also edited volumes about issues of interest to professionals (e.g., oral history, literacy, racism in children's literature); for a time, she edited the American Library Association Black Caucus's newsletter (1972-1974).

Shockley's fiction includes *Loving Her* (1974/1997), considered the first novel written by an African-American woman to focus on an interracial lesbian love affair. Her second novel, *Say Jesus and Come to Me* (1982/1987), addresses the issue of homophobia in the African-American church. In her long-awaited third novel, *Celebrating Hotchclaw* (2005), faculty scandals disrupt the one-hundredth anniversary celebration of a historically black college. Shockley's other fiction book, a collection of short stories, *The Black and White of It* (1980/1987), centers on lesbian love and issues of race. For instance, her "A Meeting of the Sapphic Daughters" reveals racism in the women's movement. In this collection and elsewhere, Shockley's short stories address a wide range of issues (homophobia in the African-American community, de facto public-school segregation, interracial dating, etc.). Her short stories and her essays have also been widely anthologized and published in numerous periodicals (e.g., *Essence, Phylon , Umbra*).

Despite the triple jeopardy she has faced— being black, female, and homosexual in a racist, sexist, and homophobic society—Shockley has been honored for her work, including a 1962 National Short Story Award from the American Association of University Women, a 1982 **Martin Luther King** Award for literature, a 1988 Susan Koppelman Award, and a 1990 OUTlook Award for her pioneering contribution to lesbian and gay writing.

REFERENCES: *AANB. BAWPP. CAO-07. EBLG.* Dandridge, Rita B., in *COCAAL* and *OCAAL.* Harris, Steven R., in *GEAAL.* Houston, Helen, R., in *AAFW-55-84.* Schulz, Elizabeth, in *OCWW.* Amazon.com.

FURTHER READING: *EAAWW.*

Simmons, Herbert Alfred
3/29/1930–
Novels, play, poems; journalist

Simmons has written some poetry, the award-winning play *The Stranger* (1956), and the novels *Corner Boy* (1957/1996), which earned him a Houghton Mifflin literary fellowship, and *Man Walking on Eggshells* (1962/1997), both of which have an improvisational, jazzlike quality. For a time, he also edited the now-dead literary journal *Spliv.* He is said to be working on *Some Jazz Called Life; and Freedom Bound.*

REFERENCES: *BAWPP. CAO-01.* Henderson, Australia, in *AAFW-55-84.* Margulis, Jennifer, in *COCAAL* and *OCAAL.* Nishikawa, Kinohi, in *GEAAL.* Amazon.com.

Noble Sissle

Simmons, William J.
6/26/1849–10/30/1890
Biographies; magazine editor, educator, administrator

Despite being born into slavery and spending his childhood as a fugitive from slavery, Simmons ended up gaining a good education and became an educator himself. In 1880, he was appointed the president of the Normal and Theological Institution, run by Baptists, which later became the State University of Kentucky at Louisville under his leadership. In 1881, he earned his M.A. from Howard University, and the following year (1882), he was named editor of the *American Baptist* magazine. Five years later, Simmons published his landmark biographical dictionary of important African-American men: *Men of Mark: Eminent, Progressive, and Rising* (1887; reprinted 1968; now out of print, but available online at //docsouth.unc.edu/neh/simmons/menu.html). When Simmons died, at age 41, he left behind his wife, Josephine Silence Simmons, and their seven children.

REFERENCES: *AANB. BDAA. Wiki.* //docsouth.unc.edu/neh/simmons/menu.html. //www.blackrefer.com/literature11.html.

Sissle, Noble
7/10/1889–12/17/1975
Songs, musical

Sissle was the primary lyricist to collaborate with noted pianist and composer Eubie Blake, such as in their ground-breaking 1921 show, *Shuffle Along,* one of the first musicals to be written, directed, and produced by African Americans, as well as performed by blacks. Their "I'm Just Wild about Harry" was popular for years.

REFERENCES: *A. AANB. BAWPP. CAO-1998. EA-99. Wiki.* Manheim, James M., in *BB.* //en.wikisource.org/wiki/Special:Search/Noble_Sissle.

Slave Narratives

Slave narratives are the recordings and recollections of slaves and former slaves. Slave narratives give voice to history, enabling us to trace more than 300 years of history in which millions of people were brought to the United States, literally in chains. The narratives provide distinctive insight into the everyday experiences of slaves and former slaves, from the earliest days of 15th- and 16th-century slave trading in Africa through the postemancipation period. Without such narratives, these experiences are otherwise invisible to most readers of traditional history books. Across the history of slavery, slave narratives help us to piece together a genuine understanding of the life, experiences, and humanity of those who have been enslaved in our country. As Frazier (1970) said, "Much of the writing and teaching of American history, when it has considered the black man at all, has considered him as a slave up to 1863 and as a problem after that." Slave narratives may shed light on the value of the men and women whom this country enslaved and whose unpaid arduous labor helped create a nation of great wealth.

The narratives also offer distinctive insight into particular aspects of U.S. history. For instance, many of these narratives show how Southern plantations underwent historical changes. In the early years, most of these plantations were relatively small, independent farms with a few slaves, located mainly in the coastal colonies of Virginia and the Carolinas. Over time, however, the plantations grew to large, complex slave-holding plantations, which spread east from the coastal colonies through the southern colonies and states to Texas.

Types of Narratives

Slave narratives may be sorted into three types, based on the origin of the account: (1) authentic narratives, written directly by slaves, in their own words, during or soon after their enslavement; (2) narratives recorded by *amanuenses* (people who wrote down what others dictated) during or soon after the narrator's enslavement, which were often heavily edited by the amanuenses; or (3) narratives recorded after slavery had officially ended (in 1863), based on interviews between former slaves and government workers. Clearly, the credibility and reliability of the account varies across these three basic forms. Therefore, readers need to know which type of account they are reading in order to know how readily to believe the account.

Often, scholars disagree about how to categorize particular narratives, with some giving evidence that an account was authentic, while others firmly believe that the same account was recorded and edited by an amanuensis. The age, gender, and literacy of the slave or former slave and of the possible amanuensis are closely analyzed in trying to assess the true origin of accounts in question. For instance, if an account seems to be written by a well-educated 50-year-old man, but its author is identified as a poorly educated 20-year-old woman, questions will emerge.

Authentic Narratives

Authentic, unedited narratives, written directly by the slaves themselves were more likely to emerge during the early slavery period, when slaves were still being captured and brought to this country. Because some of the enslaved were already literate when they were captured, they were able to record their narratives in their native languages. If they then mastered English or another European language, they could easily write their narratives themselves. On the other hand, if they didn't arrive in this country knowing how to read and write, they were unlikely to learn that skill here.

A rare example of a slave narrative, written during the time of his enslavement, was that of Omar ibn Sied (born in 1770). Ibn Sied, a literate Muslim abducted from what is now Senegal, wrote his life story on the walls of his cell in North Carolina. After learning English, he then transcribed his autobiography into English. More commonly, these narratives were by former slaves, such as Ukawsaw Gronniosaw and **Olaudah Equiano** (also called "Gustavus Vassa"), both of whom gained their freedom in the United States. Gronniosaw wrote his narratives in the United States, and Equiano wrote his in England. According to Frazier (1970), both men's writings were "highly emotional and introspective autobiographies," which gave lie to the slave owners' pretense at justifying slavery on the basis of the intellectual inferiority of the slaves.

Equiano's narrative is one of the most widely referenced narratives describing enslavement in West Africa. Equiano was born into the family of an Ibo tribal elder in 1745 in what is now Nigeria (the Benin Empire at that time). Kidnapped at age 11, Equiano described the white men on the slave ship as having "horrible looks, red faces and long hair," and the journey through the *Middle Passage* (the trip from Africa to America) as "a scene of horror almost inconceivable." He recorded that, on landing in Barbados, he and others feared that the whites were cannibalistic, remembering that "there was much dread and trembling among us, and nothing but bitter cries." (Blassingame, 1979). The narratives written during the early period of slavery help to dispel the myth that all slaves were nonliterate.

Once the majority of slaves were born in this country (rather than being kidnapped and shipped here), it became less and less likely that a narrative would be authored by a slave during her or his time of captivity. Customarily, slave owners tried to ensure that their slaves were *prevented* from learning to read and write. In fact, toward the end of the slavery period, slave owners imposed harsh penalties on any slave who could read or write and on anyone who was caught teaching a slave to read or write. This made it highly unlikely for a narrative to be written by a slave during his or her time of enslavement.

Therefore, during this later period, authentic slave narratives were chiefly written by former slaves who had escaped, had bought their freedom, or had been proclaimed emancipated (after 1863).

The degree to which former slaves were able to master reading and writing varied widely. Most of these former slaves had only rudimentary writing skills, and their narratives reflected the speech patterns they had acquired during their time of enslavement, rather than the patterns of educated Northerners. Some former slaves, however, had illicitly learned to read and write before their escape, and some escaped at a young enough age to master the new skill. For instance, **Frederick Douglass**, born in slavery about 1817, was taught the rudiments of English from his second owner, and young white boys had helped him learn to read. His later mastery of reading and writing are without question. To summarize, the authors of authentic narratives included fully literate people during or soon after their enslavement, former slaves who had rudimentary literacy skills, or former slaves who were educated after their emancipation, who recollected their earlier experiences of enslavement. In all cases, these narratives were written in the authentic words of the slave or former slave. In reflecting on the slave writings of the 19th century, Andrews (1999) noted that "the slave wrote not only to demonstrate humane letters, but also to demonstrate his or her own membership in the human community."

Narratives through Amanuenses

As you may have guessed, there are very few authentic slave narratives, based on firsthand experiences of the author, after the early period of American slavery. After 1800, the most prevalent slave narratives were the second type of slave narrative: the account of an amanuensis, who purportedly recorded the words dictated by the narrator. In these accounts, only through the record of the amanuensis does the reader discover the horrors of the Middle Passage, life and work on the plantations, and the period following emancipation.

The amanuensis could have been a fellow slave, a freed slave, a white plantation worker or owner, or a white abolitionist. The amanuensis may have been writing a letter, a report to a Freedmen's Bureau, or an antislavery tract. Whatever the source, their writings remain few when compared to the large number of slaves, but as Gutman (1976) says, "These few letters are quite unusual historical documents . . . the letters' importance does not rest upon whether they were a common form of expression. They were not. What is important is their relationship to the beliefs and behaviors of other slaves who left no such historical record."

Although many amanuenses took pains to record the narratives as faithfully as possible, many others heavily edited the narratives. The prevalence of editing and other distortions is in little doubt. Andrews (1999) observed that "the great nineteenth-century slave narratives typically carry a black message in a white envelope." Editing ranged from modest changes in wording or emphasis to entirely ghostwritten text, as well as recollections edited much later, far from the narrator. Abolitionists played an important role in these writings. They often imposed their own biases on the narratives, whether or not they acknowledged doing so. Nonetheless, there is reason to believe that many amanuenses recorded the actual words of the former slaves with great care.

One such narrator who relied on the help of an amanuensis was **Venture Smith**. Smith dictated his *A Narrative of the Life and Adventures of Venture Smith* (1789) to an amanuensis, probably Elisha Niles, a schoolmaster in Connecticut. The narrative described Smith's life in Guinea after he had been given his freedom by his third owner (Frazier, 1970). In it, Smith remembered his father, a wealthy prince, as "a man of remarkable strength and resolution, affable, kind and gentle, ruling with equity and moderation" (Blassingame, 1979). It seems likely that the recollections are genuine, but the wording may be influenced by the amanuensis.

Even when narratives were from the author's own pen, white abolitionists or others often added prefatory or appended writings, intended to legitimize the works. This was true even for Frederick Douglass's narrative (1845/1963). Wendell Phillips, in a letter included as part of the introduction of Douglass's moving narrative wrote, "I am glad the time has come when the 'lions write history.' We have been left long enough to gather the character of slavery from the involuntary evidence of the masters."

Postemancipation Interviews

The third type of slave narratives appeared after the proclamation of emancipation in 1863. These were gained through interviews of former slaves, conducted by volunteer or paid employees of the federal government. These were funded by two different federal programs, implemented decades apart. Immediately following the Civil War (starting in the late 1860s), many states' Freedmen's Bureaus conducted interviews of former slaves. Decades later, during the 1930s, interviews were conducted as part of the Federal Writers' Project (FWP), for the Works Progress Administration (WPA; part of President Franklin D. Roosevelt's New Deal).

Narratives submitted to the Freedmen's Bureaus highlighted the variety of work relationships that emerged through slavery. In states from Alabama to Texas, owners of many large plantations had impersonal relations with their slaves, with a white overseer supervising huge gangs of field workers. On plantations in the eastern states, from the Carolinas to Georgia, owners had more personal relationships with the slaves who worked for them, identifying them by face and knowing them by name. The narratives gathered during this early postslavery period also served as records of slave families, documenting that some family members resided together while others were separated from the main family, often because of having been sold (Tyler & Murphy, 1974).

Regarding the second main federal program for recording slave narratives, John Cade, a Southern professor, was one of the first to conceive of interviewing former slaves in the 1930s. His initial work was published in 1935. Lawrence Reddick is credited with suggesting to New Deal leaders what came to be known as the Federal Writers' Project.

The accuracy and authenticity of the interviews gathered through this program have been questioned. For one thing, it had been almost 70 years since emancipation, so the informants (former slaves or children of slaves) had had a *long* time to forget their experiences and the stories they had heard about slavery. Also, most of them were very old, so age may also have impaired their memories. In addition, most of the WPA workers were white and lacked knowledge of the history of slavery, and very few had any training in techniques for conducting oral-history interviews. What's more, the interviewers rarely used recording devices for conducting the interviews, so whatever they didn't write down at the time or recall later on was left out. This project depended heavily on the memories of the interviewers, as well as of the interviewees. Finally, the interviews were edited by government workers in Washington, D.C., or some other locale.

Even with these limitations, however, these narratives contain many truths. Much of the information and many of the events revealed in the FWP interviews were corroborated by earlier interviews and other evidence (Elkins, 1963). In addition, these narratives aptly chronicled daily experiences. For instance, former slaves such as Hannah Davidson described her hard daily life in her interviews with an FWP worker. She recalled working six days a week from dawn to midnight, with Sunday being used for home chores: "Work, work, work, . . . I been so exhausted working, I was like an inchworm crawling along a roof. I worked till I thought another lick would kill me" (Jones, 1985).

Distinctive Perspective

In combination, the various types of narratives are important in countering the perspectives of white owners and historians who had depicted the slave as being well cared for, well fed, and rarely mistreated, or slave life as being more bearable in one part of the South than another (Tyler & Murphy, 1974). In fact, these diverse narratives chronicle the full range of interactions with own-

ers and other whites. The records range from brutal treatment for minor infractions to slaves' recollections of getting sick when working in the hot sun and having their owners insist they sit in the shade until they had recovered (Genovese, 1974). These narratives provide a voice to the story, correcting distortions in much of recorded history and documenting the participation of slaves and former slaves in the human community, as evidenced by Frederick Douglass in the closing paragraph of his narrative:

Sincerely and earnestly hoping that this little book may do something toward throwing light on the American slave system, and hastening the glad day of deliverance to the millions of my brethren in bonds—faithfully relying upon the power of truth, love, and justice, for success in my humble efforts—and solemnly pledging my self anew to the sacred cause,—I subscribe myself,

FREDERICK DOUGLASS, Lynn, Mass., April 28, 1845.

REFERENCES: Andrews, William L., & Henry Louis Gates, Jr. 1999. *The Civitas Anthology of African American Slave Narratives.* Washington, DC: Civitas/Counterpoint. Bennett, Jr., Lerone. 1964. *Before the Mayflower: A History of the Negro in America 1619.* New York: Penguin Books. Berlin, Ira. 1974. *Slaves without Masters: The Free Negro in the Antebellum South.* New York: Vintage Books. Blassingame, John W. 1979. *The Slave Community: Plantation Life in the Antebellum South.* New York: Oxford University Press. Douglass, Frederick. 1963. *Narrative of the Life of Frederick Douglass: An American Slave* (originally published 1845). Garden City, NY: Dolphin Books of Doubleday. Elkins, Stanley M. 1963. *Slavery: A Problem in American Institutional and Intellectual Life.* New York: Universal Library. Franklin, John Hope, & Alfred A. Moss, Jr. 1988. *From Slavery to Freedom.* New York: McGraw-Hill. Frazier, Thomas R. (Ed.) 1970. *Afro-American History: Primary Sources.* New York: Harcourt Brace and World. Genovese, Eugene D. 1974. *Roll Jordan Roll: The World the Slaves Made.* New York: Vintage Books. Gutman, Herbert G. 1976. *The Black Family in Slavery and Freedom, 1750-1925.* New York: Pantheon Books. Herskovits, Melville J. 1958. *The Myth of the Negro Past.* Boston: Beacon Press. Jones, Jacqueline. 1985. *Labor of Love, Labor of Sorrow: Black Women, Work, and the Family, from Slavery to the Present.* New York: Vintage Press. Lerner, Gerda (Ed.). 1972. *Black Women in White America: A Documentary History.* New York: Vintage Books. Myrdal, Gunnar. 1972. *An American Dilemma: The Negro Problem and Modern Democracy* (Vol. 2). New York: Pantheon Books. Shields, John, "Literary History: Colonial and Early National Eras," and "Smith, Venture," in OCAAL. Tyler, Ronnie C., & Lawrence R. Murphy (Eds.). 1974. *The Slave Narratives of Texas.* Austin: Encino Press. Weinstein, Allen, & Frank Otto Gatell (Eds.). 1968. *American Negro Slavery: A Modern Reader.* New York: Oxford University Press. - Randall Lindsey

Editor's note. Some of the better-known slave narratives include *The Interesting Narrative of the Life of Olaudah Equiano, or Gustavus Vassa, the African* (1789: England; 1791: United States); *The History of **Mary Prince**, A West Indian Slave, Related by Herself* (1831, published in London); *Slavery in the United States: A Narrative of the Life and Adventures of Charles Ball, a Black Man* (1836, written with abolitionist Isaac Fisher; reprinted 1970); *A Narra-*

tive of the Adventures and Escape of **Moses Roper**, from American Slavery (1837, London; 1838, America); Narrative of the Life of Frederick Douglass, an American Slave, Written by Himself (1845); and **Harriet Jacobs**'s Incidents in the Life of a Slave Girl (1861), regarding her escape in 1835, edited and promoted by **Lydia Maria Child**, the first slave narrative written by a woman, published in America. Perhaps the earliest narrative written by a slave—but hardly a characteristic slave narrative—was A Narrative of the Uncommon Sufferings, and Surprising Deliverance of **Briton Hammon**, A Negro Man—Servant to General Winslow (1760, published in Boston), a 14-page memoir of his experiences as a sailor and as a captive of Floridian Cherokees and of a press-gang in Cuba, and his joy and gratitude that "Providence" returned him to his master.

REFERENCES: AA:AJS, pp. 270-273, notes pp. 461-462. Andrews, William L., "Slave Narrative," in OCAAL.

Slim, Iceberg See Iceberg Slim

Smith, Amanda (née Berry)
1/23/1837–2/24/1915
Autobiography; periodical publisher

To raise funds for an orphanage and industrial school she wanted to establish for African-American children, Smith wrote a monthly newspaper, the Helper, and she wrote her autobiography, An Autobiography: The Story of the Lord's Dealings with Mrs. Amanda Smith, the Colored Evangelist (1893), describing her own spiritual quest, her pursuit of an education, and her struggles with sexism in the African Methodist Episcopal Church, which led to her becoming an independent evangelist.

REFERENCES: Wiki. Carruth, Mary C., in COCAAL and OCAAL. Israel, Adrienne, in BWA:AHE.

FURTHER READING: AANB. Bolden, Tonya, //digital.nypl.org/schomburg/writers_aa19/bio2.html. Dodson, Jualynne E. "Amanda Berry Smith: From Washerwoman to Evangelist." The Journal of Religion. 81.1 (Jan. 2001) p. 131. From Literature Resource Center. Mathai, Varghese, in GEAAL. Patton, Venetria K., with the assistance of Heidi L. M. Jacobs editorial assistant, and Jennifer Putzi editorial assistant, in AWPW:1870-1920. Smith, Amanda, An Autobiography: The Story of the Lord's Dealings with Mrs. Amanda Smith, the Colored Evangelist, a Machine-readable Transcription, in //digilib.nypl.org/dynaweb/digs/wwm97264/@Generic__BookView. See also EAAWW.

Smith, Anna Deveare
9/18/1950–
Plays, documentaries; performer, director, educator

After her experiences as an actor, director, and drama teacher, Smith initiated a series of one-woman shows, starting with On the Road: A Search for American Character (1983). Each of her performances comprises multiple characters with differing voices and identities. Her Fires in the Mirror (1992; published, 1993/1998), comprising 26 characters, based on a series of riots that erupted in Crown Heights following a tragic accident, won her an Obie Award, a Drama Desk Award, a Pulitzer Prize nomination, a Kesselring Prize (for $10,000), and other awards. She was then commissioned to write Twilight: Los Angeles 1992 (1993; published, 1994/2003), about the riots that erupted following the acquittal of the police officers who had severely beaten motorist Rodney King. After a Los Angeles run, Twilight opened on Broadway in New York, the first play by an African-American woman to do so since 1983, and it won two Tony nominations, an Obie, a Drama Desk, and an Outer Circle Critics Special Achievement Award. Because the play was based on the actual testimony of participants and observers, Smith was denied a Pulitzer nomination for Twilight. In 1996, Smith was given a MacArthur Foundation award, which enabled her to take time to create House Arrest: First Edition (1997) and House Arrest: A Search for the American Character in and Around the White House, Past and Present (1998; published, 2004). Her Piano (2000; published, 1989; published with House Arrest, 2004), set in prerevolutionary Cuba, includes an upstairs/downstairs array of characters. In 2003, she was invited to perform The Best of Anna Deveare Smith at Carnegie Hall. In 2008, she debuted her play Let Me Down Easy, which explores the meaning of grace, and her one-woman show The Arizona Project, which explores "women's relationships to justice and the law" (quoted in Wiki). Smith's other plays include A Birthday Card and Aunt Julia's Shoes (1983), Aye, Aye, Aye, I'm Integrated (1984), Building Bridges Not Walls (1985), On the Road: ACT (1986), Chlorophyll Post-Modernism and the Mother Goddess: A Convers/Ation (1988), Voices of Bay Area Women (1988), Gender Bending: On the Road (1989), From the Outside Looking In (1990), On Black Identity and Black Theatre (1990), Fragments (1991), Identities Mirrors and Distortions I, II, III, and IV (1991), Other Identities (1992), and Rounding It Out (2000).

Smith has documented her creative process for playwriting in her critically acclaimed Talk to Me: Travels in Media and Politics (2000) and her Letters to a Young Artist: Straight-up Advice on Making a Life in the Arts—For Actors, Performers, Writers, and Artists of Every Kind (2006). In an interview, Smith reported, "When I sit and I interview somebody, I'm not just looking for any old thing they say. I'm looking for that thing they say which is that poem that they're speaking. . . . My intention is not to turn art into activism, but to walk that line, . . . , which is dangerous" (quoted in Rubino, 2008). Smith also teaches theater and literary arts at Tisch School of the Arts and "listening skills" at the School of Law at New York University (since 2000); previously, she taught at Carnegie-Mellon University (1978-1979), University of Southern California (1980s), National Theater Institute (1980s), Yale University (1982), New York University (1983-1984), American Conservatory Theater (1986), Radcliffe's Bunting Institute (1991), and Stanford University (1990-2000). Even those unable to see her plays or attend her courses may have seen her perform in TV shows such as *West Wing* and in movies such as *Dave*. In addition to being given 20 or so honorary degrees, numerous awards for her plays, and the MacArthur fellowship, she has earned a 2006 Fletcher Foundation Fellowship and a 2008 Matrix Award from the New York Women in Communications.

REFERENCES: *AANB. ATG. CAO-04. CLC-241. EA-99. W. Wiki.* Abbott, Charlotte. "PW Talks with Anna Deveare Smith." *Publishers Weekly.* 247.38 (Sept. 18, 2000) p. 94. From *Literature Resource Center.* Glickman, Simon, and Sara Pendergast, in *BB.* Rubino, Cecilia, in *T-CAD-5th.* Smith, Anna Deavere, and Carl Weber. (1995). "Brecht's 'Street Scene'-On Broadway, of All Places? A Conversation with Anna Deavere Smith." *Brecht Then and Now: The Brecht Yearbook 20*, pp. 51-64. Rpt. in Jeffrey W. Hunter (Ed.) (2007), *Contemporary Literary Criticism* (Vol. 241). Detroit: Gale. From *Literature Resource Center.* Young, Harvey, in *GEAAL.* //www.annadeaveresmithworks. org/. Amazon.com. National Public Radio, *Day to Day,* September 29, 2008.

FURTHER READING: Bernstein, Robin. "Rodney King, Shifting Modes of Vision, and Anna Deavere Smith's Twilight: Los Angeles, 1992." *Journal of Dramatic Theory and Criticism* 14.2 (Spring 2000): pp. 121-134. Rpt. in Jeffrey W. Hunter (Ed.) (2007), *Contemporary Literary Criticism* (Vol. 241). Detroit: Gale. From *Literature Resource Center.* Feffer, Steve. "Extending the Breaks: Fires in the Mirror in the Context of Hip-Hop Structure, Style, and Culture." *Comparative Drama* 37.3/4 (Fall 2003): pp. 397-415. Rpt. in Jeffrey W. Hunter (Ed.) (2007), *Contemporary Literary Criticism* (Vol. 241). Detroit: Gale. From *Literature Resource Center.* Modleski, Tania. "Doing Justice to the Subjects: Mimetic Art in a Multicultural Society: The Work of Anna Deavere Smith." In Elizabeth Abel, Helene Moglen, and Barbara Christian (Eds.). 1997. *Female Subjects in Black and White: Race, Psychoanalysis, Feminism.* Berkeley: University of California Press. Rpt. in Jeffrey W. Hunter (Ed.) (2007), *Contemporary Literary Criticism* (Vol. 241). Detroit: Gale. From *Literature Resource Center.* Reinelt, Janelle. "Performing Race: Anna Deavere Smith's Fires in the Mirror." *Modern Drama* 39.4 (Winter 1996): pp. 609-617. Rpt. in Jeffrey W. Hunter (Ed.) (2007), *Contemporary Literary Criticism* (Vol. 241). Detroit: Gale. From *Literature Resource Center.* Schechner, Richard. "Anna Deavere Smith: Acting as Incorporation." *Drama Review* 37.4 (Winter 1993): pp. 63-64. Rpt. in Jeffrey W. Hunter (Ed.) (2007), *Contemporary Literary Criticism* (Vol. 241). Detroit: Gale. From *Literature Resource Center.* Smith, Anna Deavere, and Carol Martin. "Anna Deavere Smith: The Word Becomes You." *Drama Review* 37.4 (Winter 1993): pp. 45-62. Rpt. in Jeffrey W. Hunter (Ed.) (2007), *Contemporary Literary Criticism* (Vol. 241). Detroit: Gale. From *Literature Resource Center.* Thompson, Debby. "'Is Race a Trope?': Anna Deavere Smith and the Question of Racial Performativity." *African American Review* 37.1 (Spring 2003): pp. 127-138. Rpt. in Jeffrey W. Hunter (Ed.) (2007), *Contemporary*

Literary Criticism (Vol. 241). Detroit: Gale. From *Literature Resource Center.* Trudell, Scott. "Critical Essay on 'Fires in the Mirror.'" Anne Marie Hacht (Ed.). 2006. *Drama for Students* (Vol. 22). Detroit: Gale. From *Literature Resource Center.* Weatherston, Rosemary, "'The True Words of Real People': Documenting the Myth of the Real in Anna Deavere Smith's Twilight: Los Angeles, 1992." *ARIEL. 39.1-2* (January-April 2008) p. 189. From *Literature Resource Center.*

Smith, Barbara
11/16/1946–
Nonfiction criticism, anthologies; educator, publisher

Little has been written about Barbara Smith, but she has written a great deal to deepen our understanding of other important African-American women writers. While teaching at the University of Massachusetts, she was drawn to the burgeoning feminist movement. In 1974, she cofounded the Cohambee River Collective, a Boston-based community of African-American socialist feminists, and in 1977, she wrote *Toward a Black Feminist Criticism*. A few years later, Gloria T. Hull, Patricia Bell Scott, and she published their groundbreaking anthology *All the Women Are White, All the Blacks Are Men, But Some of Us Are Brave: Black Women's Studies* (1981; paperback, 1986). Smith herself is brave indeed: To the double jeopardy of being African American and female, Smith adds her identification as an openly gay woman—triple jeopardy! Undaunted by these challenges, in 1981, Smith cofounded (with Myrna Bain, Cherríe Moraga, and Mariana Romo-Carmona) Kitchen Table: Women of Color Press, the first American publisher dedicated to publishing the writings of women of color (including Third World women). The press has chiefly published poetry, fiction, and literary and social criticism (e.g., Cherríe Moraga and Gloria Anzaldúa's landmark *This Bridge Called My Back: Writings by Radical Women of Color,* 1981). Until 1995, Smith directed, edited, and published for the press, while trying to eke out a living with speaker fees, fellowships, and teaching positions.

Smith continues to write and edit other publications, including her essay collection *The Truth That Never Hurts: Writings on Race, Gender, and Freedom* (1998, published by Rutgers University Press), her opinion piece *Yours in Struggle: Three Feminist Perspectives on Anti-Semitism and Racism* (1991, with Elly Bulkin and Minne Bruce Pratt), and her anthology *Neither Separate nor Equal: Women, Race, and Class in the South* (1999, in the Women in the Political Economy series published by Temple University Press). Smith's other anthologies include *Conditions: Five, the Black Women's Issue* (1979, with Gloria T. Hull), a special issue of *Conditions* magazine, and *Home Girls: A Black Feminist Anthology* (1983), including essays and stories from 34 African-American lesbians. Smith's twin sister, Beverly, is also a lesbian feminist activist, and the two have occasionally written together.

Of her work, Smith has said, "I think whenever the invisible is made visible, to me that's a political act. As a lesbian, of course coming out is the logical outcome of that mentality, in a lesbian context, but there are other kinds of identities in American society that are completely, completely suppressed. So I think documentation is really important. I think there's some of us who do the kind of work that we do as writers because we have that kind of vision" (quoted in Heath, 1998).

REFERENCES: *AA:PoP. AANB. CAO-02. TWT. W. Wiki.* Bell, Chris, in *GEAAL.* Heath, Terrance. "Making History: An Interview with Barbara Smith." *Lambda Book Report.* 6.11 (June 1998) p. 1. From *Literature Resource Center.* LaBalle, Candace, in *BB.* www.amazon.com, 7/1999, 4/2009.

Smith, Effie Waller
1/6/1879–1/2/1960
Poems, short stories

Smith's published poetry collections include *Songs of the Months* (1904), *Rhymes from the Cumberland* (1909), and *Rosemary and Pansies* (1909), but she also wrote many more poems and several short stories, continuing to write poems until she died. Her works may be found in *The Collected Works of Effie Walker* (1991, with an introduction by David Deskins).

REFERENCES: *LFCC-07. Wiki.* Barnes, Paula C., in *COCAAL* and *OCAAL.*

FURTHER READING: Bolden, Tonya, in //digital.nypl.org/schom burg/writers_aa19/bio2.html. Williams, Sarah Lynsey, in *GEAAL. See also* George, Hermon, Jr. "The Schomburg Library of Nineteenth-Century Black Women Writers." *Nineteenth-Century Prose.* 20.1 (Spring 1993) p100. From *Literature Resource Center.*

Smith, Jessie (née Carney)
9/24/1930–

Nonfiction—African-American history and biographies, bibliography, anthologies; librarian, educator

Readers need to have an outstanding scholar of African-American history and biography write a definitive essay on the life experiences and contributions of Jessie Carney Smith. Ironically, one of the persons best known for writing such biographies about talented, interesting African-American women is Smith herself. We do know that Smith has a twin sister, Jodie, and she married Frederick Smith in 1950, with whom she had a son in the early 1950s before they divorced in 1963. The daughter of college-educated parents, she earned four degrees from four universities: North Carolina A&T State University (B.S., home economics), Michigan State University (M.A.,

child development), Peabody College of Vanderbilt University (M.A., library sciences), and the University of Illinois (Ph.D., 1964, library science). Thereafter, she began her tenure as a librarian and professor of library science at Fisk University in Nashville, Tennessee, later taking the reins from **Arna Bontemps** as Fisk's head librarian. She has since been named the **William and Camille Cosby** Professor at Fisk, and she has guest-lectured at numerous other U.S. academic institutions (e.g., Cornell University, Howard University, Bennett College) and at international venues, where her literacy in French and German may be highlighted. She has also spoken on TV and radio talk shows, such as National Public Radio's *Talk of the Nation* (2003).

In addition to numerous reports on library science, Smith has written several books intended to facilitate the work of fellow librarians, including her first book, *Bibliography for Black Studies Programs* (1969), as well as *A Handbook for the Study of Black Bibliography* (1971), *Minorities in the United States: Guide to Resources* (1973), *The Literature of Minority Cultures: A Guide for Students* (1976), and *Black Academic Libraries and Research Collections: An Historical Survey* (1977). Smith has also edited many books on African-American genealogy, history, and biography, including *Ethnic Genealogy: A Research Guide* (1983); *Images of Blacks in American Culture: A Reference Guide to Information Sources* (1988); *Notable Black American Women* (1991); *Epic Lives: 100 Black Women Who Made a Difference* (1993); *Black Firsts: 2,000 Years of Extraordinary Achievement* (1994, with Robert Johns and Casper L. Jordan); *Historical Statistics of Black America: Agriculture to Labor and Employment* (1994, with Carrell Peterson Horton); *Statistical Record of Black America* (1990, with Carrell P. Horton; 4th ed., 1996, with Carrell P. Horton); *Notable Black American Women, Book II* (1996); *Powerful Black Women* (1996); *Black Heroes of the 20th Century* (1998/2001); *Notable Black American Men* (1998); *Notable Black American Scientists* (1998); *The African American Almanac* (1999, with Joseph M. Palmisano); *Reference Library of Black America* (5 volumes, 2001, with Joseph M. Palmisano); *Black Firsts: 4,000 Ground-Breaking and Pioneering Historical Events* (2002); *Notable Black American Women, Book III* (2003, with Shirelle Phelps); *Encyclopedia of African American Business* (vol. 1 & vol. 2, 2006); and *Freedom Facts and Firsts: 400 Years of the African American Civil Rights Experience* (2009, with Linda T. Wynn). Jay P. Pederson and she also edited a work for middle-school-aged students, drawing on her *Black Firsts*, titled *African American Breakthroughs: 500 Years of Black Firsts* (1994). Many of her books have been cited by *Library Journal* or by the American Library Association as crucial reference works.

Smith has noted, " Writing is a rewarding part of my life, and it provides a balance between professional responsibilities and personal gratification so necessary in the complexities of contemporary society." More important, "I learned from my mother [who was 98 years old in 2002] and my maternal grandparents that one must share resources with others, that helpfulness is a gift to be passed along" (quoted in *CAO-01*). For her own helpfulness, Smith has been honored with the 1982 **Martin Luther King, Jr.** Black Author's Award, named the 1985 Academic/Research Librarian of the Year by the Association of College and Research Library, given the United Negro College Fund's 1986 Distinguished Scholars Award, the 1992 Women's National Book Association Award, the National Coalition of 100 Black Women's Candace Award for excellence in education, and *Sage* magazine's Anna J. Cooper Award (for *Epic Lives*).

REFERENCES: *B. CAO-01. EBLG.* Shellie M. Saunders, in *BB.* Amazon.com, 7/1999, 4/2009.

FURTHER READING: *BH2C. BWA:AHE.*

Smith, Lillian Eugenia
12/12/1897–1966
Novels, essays; journal editor, publisher

A lifelong resident of the American South, this European-American woman's most important literary contributions were her books confronting issues of race in the middle of the twentieth century. Although Smith had attended Piedmont College and a college in Maryland, she had to leave school early to take over managing her parents' summer camp when their health failed. In 1936, Smith started her own magazine, eventually titled *The North Georgia Review,* the first journal published by a white Southerner, which regularly printed literary and scholarly writings by blacks.

As if that wasn't stirring up enough trouble, Smith's very first novel, *Strange Fruit* (1944), told the story of how an interracial love relationship within a racist environment could lead to murder and a public lynching. Not only was the book banned in the South, but it was also banned in the North (Massachusetts), supposedly for "obscenity," and even the U.S. Post Office barred it from being sent through the U.S. mail until First Lady Eleanor Roosevelt intervened on behalf of Smith—and the U.S. Constitution. Much to the chagrin of the racists who opposed her, these actions stirred up tremendous publicity for her book, which ended up selling quite well. The novel was later (1945) made into a play, produced by José Ferrer.

Her subsequent works include *Killers of the Dream* (1949), which openly and unhesitatingly attacked segregation; *One Hour* (1959), a novel covertly assailing McCarthyism; and several other books, none of which engendered as much public attention as did *Strange Fruit.* She still, however, managed to irk white Southern racists,

Lillian Eugenia Smith

and mysteriously ignited arson fires destroyed her manuscripts and other materials twice in 1955 and once in 1958. Among the documents that went up in flames were about 9,000 letters she had written during the 1940s and 1950s, which the U.S. Library of Congress had requested for the nation's archives. Smith was also active in the nonviolent struggle for civil rights during the 1950s and 1960s. She was in the process of writing her autobiography when cancer took her life.

REFERENCES: *BC. RLWWJ.* National Public Radio, *Writer's Almanac,* 12/12/1998.

FURTHER READING: *B. BWA:AHE. CAO-07. CE. OCWW. QB. W. Wiki.* //www.answers.com/topic/quote-4?author=Smith,%20Lillian &s2=Lillian%20Smith. *See also* Belton, Don. "Lillian Smith: Walking a Trembling Earth." *Hollins Critic.* 20.3 (June 1983) p. 1. From *Literature Resource Center.* Johnson, Cheryl L. "The Language of Sexuality and Silence in Lillian Smith's *Strange Fruit.*" *Signs.* 27.1 (Autumn 2001) p. 1. From *Literature Resource Center.*

Smith, Venture
c. 1729–9/19/1805
Slave narrative

A native of Guinea, West Africa, Venture was captured, enslaved, and shipped to a colonial port in Rhode Island when he was about 8 years old. By his own account, he spent the next 28 years of his life seeking his own freedom, and then spent the rest of his life earning enough money to purchase the freedom of his wife, Meg, his daughter ,Hannah, his sons, Solomon and Cuff, and three enslaved men of African descent. In 1798, he dictated his life story to an *amanuensis* (someone who writes down the words spoken by another), probably Elisha Niles, a white schoolmaster in Connecticut, who clearly never believed Smith to be his intellectual equal—or perhaps his equal in other terms, as well. His autobiographical story, *A Narrative of the Life and Adventures of Venture Smith, A Native of Africa: But Resident above Sixty Years in the United States of America, Related by Himself* (1789), describes the three phases of Smith's life in three discrete chapters: his youth in Africa, his decades-long struggle to free himself, and his dedicated efforts to free his family and acquaintances. Despite having a less than sympathetic amanuensis, Smith's narrative makes clear that he resents the treatment he received as a black man of African descent, even after his liberation from bondage.

REFERENCES: *NYPL-AADR.* Shields, John C., in *COCAAL* and *OCAAL.*

FURTHER READING: *AANB. Wiki.* Shearin, Gloria A., in *GEAAL.* See also Brooks, Joanna. "*Genius in Bondage: Literature of the Early Black Atlantic.*" *Early American Literature.* 37.2 (Spring 2002) p. 354. From *Literature Resource Center.* Markley, Robert. "*Unchained Voices: An Anthology of Black Authors in the English-Speaking World of the Eighteenth Century.*" *Studies in English Literature, 1500-1900.* 37.3 (Summer 1997) p. 637. From *Literature Resource Center.*

Smith, William Gardner
2/6/1927–11/6/1974
Novels

Smith's novels include *Last of the Conquerors* (1948), *Anger at Innocence* (1950), *South Street* (1954), *The Stone Face* (1963), and *Return to Black America* (1960).

REFERENCES: Dawson, Emma Waters, in *COCAAL* and *OCAAL.* Fay, Robert, in *EA-99.*

FURTHER READING: *AANB. BAWPP. CAO-03.* W. Feerst, Alex, in *GEAAL.* Jackson, Jacquelyn, in *AAW-40-55.* Amazon.com.

Smitherman, Geneva (aka Geneva Smitherman-Donaldson)
12/10/1940–

Scholarly, nonfiction—linguistics, literary criticism; educator, language-policy expert, language consultant

Smitherman earned her B.A. (1960) and her M.A. (1962) from Detroit's Wayne State University, then she earned her Ph.D. from the University of Michigan (1969). While doing her postgraduate work, Smitherman taught English and Latin at public junior and senior high schools in Detroit, Michigan (1960-1965) and taught English at Eastern Michigan University in Ypsilanti (1965-1966) and at her alma mater, Wayne State University (1966-1989?). There, her posts have included being the director at the University Center for Black Studies (1977-1980) and the senior research associate and acting director of the school's Linguistics Program (1982-1983).

Smitherman also took interim hosts as a lecturer in Harvard University's newly established Afro-American Studies Department (1971-1973), and she has been a visiting or adjunct professor or lecturer at several other colleges and universities. She was also named to serve on then-new Students' Right to Their Own Language Committee, for the Conference on College Composition and Communication (CCCC) (1971), an intermural organization; years later she chaired the CCCC's Language Policy Committee (1987) and still later received the CCCC's Exemplar Award (1999). She has also participated in numerous Detroit organizations for the arts and culture.

In 1989, Smitherman moved to Michigan State University, where she is the University Distinguished Professor of English and Director of the African American Language and Literacy Program. In addition, she cofounded the doctoral program in African American and African studies and served on its executive committee (through 2007). The divorced mother of a son, Robert Anthony, she also directs My Brother's Keeper, a middle-school male-mentoring program at Detroit public schools' **Malcolm X** Academy. With Clifford Watson, she cowrote *Educating African American Males: Detroit's Malcolm X Academy Solution* (1996, published by **Third World Press**).

Smitherman has also made time to write columns (e.g., "Soul 'n' Style," for *English Journal,* given the Award for Excellence in Journalism from the Educational Press Association, 1974), articles for periodicals (e.g., *Black Scholar, Essence, Harvard Educational Review*), and contributions to anthologies (e.g., *Black Culture: Reading and Writing Black,* 1972; *The State of the Language,* 1980). An article she wrote about playwright **Ed Bullins** (1984, *Black World*) won the **Richard Wright**-Woodie King Award for drama criticism. She was also a member of the editorial board of the short-lived *Journal of Afro-American Issues* (1975-1977).

Smitherman's first book-length project was her dissertation, *A Comparison of the Oral and Written Styles of a Group of Inner-City Black Students* (1969), and a few years later she published a brief work, *Black Language and Culture: Sounds of Soul* (1975). Most sources, however, cite as her first book *Talkin and Testifyin: The Language of Black America* (1977/1996), which pleased both academicians and a wider readership. Through *Talkin,* Smitherman argued that African-American Vernacular English (AAVE) has a distinctive lexicon and syntax that differ from other variants of English, and she ties many distinctive aspects of AAVE to its African origins. She further suggests how to apply this understanding of AAVE to educational policy.

Smitherman's subsequent authored works include her best-selling *Black Talk: Words and Phrases from the Hood to Amen Corner* (1994/2000) and *Talkin that Talk: Language, Culture, and Education in African America* (1999), which won the David H. Russell Research Award from the National Council of Teachers of English (NCTE) (2001). In these two books, she further develops the ideas presented in *Talkin and Testifyin* and addresses the history of Ebonics, closely tied to AAVE, and the ways in which school and educational policies about Ebonics affect the educational experiences of young people. Her next book, *Words from the Mother: Language and African Americans* (2006), has been called awesome in "its depth, comprehensiveness, and relevance" (quoted in Amazon.com).

In addition to her authored works, Smitherman has edited several works, including *Black English and the Education of Black Children and Youth: Proceedings of the National Invitational Symposium on the King Decision* (1981); *African American Women Speak out on Anita Hill-Clarence Thomas* (1995); *Black Linguistics: Language, Society and Politics in Africa and the Americas* (2003, with Sinfree Makoni, Arnetha F. Ball, Arthur K. Spears); and *Language Diversity in the Classroom: From Intention to Practice (Studies in Writing and Rhetoric)* (2003, with Victor Villanueva). She has also been involved in the recordings *The Legitimacy of the Black Idiom* (1972), *The Voice of Black America* (1974), and *Geneva Smitherman Talks about the Legitimacy of Black English* (1977).

Smitherman has also directed workshops on the education of African-American students, judged writing contests, served as an expert witness on language and education, and appeared on radio and television programs. For these and other deeds, Smitherman has received numerous grants. In addition to the aforementioned awards, Smitherman has received NCTE's James R. Squire Award, honoring a scholar has provided a "transforming influence and has made a lasting intellectual contribution" (quoted in *AANB*).

REFERENCES: *BAWPP. CAO-02*. Davis, Ella, in *GEAAL*. Dumas, Bethany K., in *AANB*. //worldcat.org/identities/lccn-n87-909683. //www.worldcat.org/search?q=no:000816014. //www.worldcat.org/search?q=no:005629354. //www.worldcat.org/search?q=no:007740138. //www.worldcat.org/search?q=no:017353926. //www.worldcat.org/search?q=no:051203753. //www.worldcat.org/search?q=no:059721342. //www.worldcat.org/search?q=no:082421736. Amazon.com.

Society of Umbra *See* Umbra Workshop

Southerland, Ellease (aka Ebele Oseye)
6/18/1943–

Poems, essays, short stories, novels, travel memoir; educator, publisher

Southerland's poems have been published in various periodicals, earning her *Black World's* **Gwendolyn Brooks** Poetry Award (1972); they have also been collected in *The Magic Sun Spins* (1975). Her fiction includes numerous published short stories and her novella *White Shadows* (1964), which won the John Golden Award for Fiction from the Queens College of the City University of New York. Southerland's first novel, *Let the Lion Eat Straw* (1979/2004), fictionally celebrates her mother's daunting and difficult life. Ellease, named for her mother, was her mother's third of 15 children and her eldest daughter, and the two women had been close friends when the elder Ellease died of cancer at age 45 (1965). A 1980 **Coretta Scott King** Author Honor book, *Lion* was named one of 1979's "Best Books for Young Adults" by the American Library Association and the alternate selection of the Book-of-the-Month Club; it was included in the New York Public Library's Black Heritage Series (1987); and it was lavishly praised by almost 100 reviewers, who often cite its lyricality and its concision. The book has since been adapted to audio format (unabridged audiocassettes, 2004; unabridged CD, 2004).

In 1996, Southerland changed her name to Ebele ("mercy"; Nigerian Igbo) Oseye ("happy one"; Beninese or Nigerian). She published her second novel, *A Feast of Fools: A Novel* (1998), under both her birth name and her self-chosen name; the novel continues her family's story from her first novel, as they migrate from the South to the North. Through her own Eneke Publications, Southerland has produced *Opening Line: The Creative Writer: From Blank Page to Finished Story* (2000, as Ellease Southerland), a pamphlet; and *This Year in Nigeria: Memoir* (2001, as Ebele Oseye), reminiscing about her travels in Africa across many years. These and other works reflect her fondness for Africa, especially Nigeria and Egypt. She is also said to be working on a third novel, a second poetry collection, a short-story collection, and a nonfiction book on communication. Her essays and reviews have been published in both literary journals (e.g., *Présence Africaine*) and popular magazines (e.g., *Black World*). From 1966 until 1972, Southerland worked as a social worker to help support her mother's large family; from 1972 until 1976, she taught at Columbia University. Since 1975, she has taught Creative Writing and the Literature of the African Peoples at Pace University (New York City).

REFERENCES: *AANB. BAWPP.* Brookhart, Mary Hughes, "Ellease Southerland" in *AAFW-55-84*. Dandridge, Rita B., in *COCAAL* and *OCAAL*. "Ebele Oseye," in *CAO-08*. Falvey, Kate, in *EAAWW.* Mitchell, Caroline, in *BWA:AHE.* Ramey, Lauri, in *GEAAL*. //www.goodreads.com/book/show/1525583.Opening_line_The_creativ e_writer_from_blank_page_to_finished_story. //www.goodreads. com/book/show/2308698.This_year_in_Nigeria_A_memoir. Amazon.com.

Southern, Eileen Stanza (née Jackon)
2/19/1920–10/13/2002
Nonfiction—music criticism, historiography, biography, bibliography; concert pianist, educator, journal publisher, editor

After her doctoral dissertation on Renaissance music (1961, New York University), Southern's first publication was *The Buxheim Organ Book* (1963). Most of Southern's publications, however, focus on the music history and biography, such as *The Music of Black Americans: A History* (1971; 3rd ed., 1997; Spanish ed., *Historia De La Musica Negra Norteamericana*, 2001), honored by ASCAP, the American Society of Composers, Authors, and Publishers; *Source Readings in Black American Music* (editor, 1971/1983); *Biographical Dictionary of Afro-American and African Musicians* (1982); *Afro-American Traditions in Song, Sermon, Tale and Dance, 1630-1920: An Annotated Bibliography of Literature, Collections, and Artworks* (1990, with Josephine Wright); *African American Theater* (editor, 1994); and *Images: Iconography of Music in African-American Culture (1770s-1920s)* (2000, with Josephine Wright). She also contributed to the highly esteemed *The New Grove Dictionary of Music* (1980) and *The New Grove Dictionary of American Music* (1986), to encyclopedias and other reference works, and to numerous scholarly journals. For a time, she also edited the journal *Nineteenth-Century African-American Musical Theater*.

Southern had been a concert pianist since age 20, and she taught music in both public school and university settings, starting in 1941. Since 1987, she was professor emerita of music and Afro-American studies at Harvard University; she had started teaching there in 1976, the first African-American woman to be tenured in Harvard's College of Arts and Sciences. With her husband, Joseph, she founded and edited the journal *Black Perspectives in Music* (1973-1991), the first journal dedicated to African-American music, and they raised their children, April and Edward. In addition to Southern's many other awards, the Society of American Music honored her with a Lifetime Achievement Award (2000), noting that "she helped transform the field of musicology into a more inclusive discipline . . . and championed the intellectual viability and legitimacy of research in all areas of African

American music"; and the National Endowment for the Humanities awarded her the National Humanities Medal (2001) for being a "musicologist who helped transform the study and understanding of American music."

REFERENCES: *AANB. BAAW. CAO-03. Wiki.* Shostak, E. M., in *BB.* RW, in //www.neh.gov/news/humanities/2002-05/medalists.html. Amazon.com. //www.neh.gov/whoweare/nationalmedals.html. Amazon.com.

Spence, Eulalie
6/11/1894–3/7/1981
Plays; educator, actor

Spence's 13 known plays include *Being Forty* (1920), *Brothers and Sisters of the Church Council* (1920), *Fool's Errand* (1927), *Her* (1927), *Hot Stuff* (c. 1927), *Episode* (1928), *La Divina Pastora* (1929), *Undertow* (1929), and *The Whipping* (1932). In addition, she wrote *Foreign Mail* (1926), which won second place in a **Crisis** magazine drama contest, as well as *The Hunch* (1926) and *The Starter* (1926), the second- and third-place winners of **Opportunity** magazine's 1927 competition. At least 8 of Spence's plays were published, 7 of them were produced, and 1 of them was sold to Paramount Pictures, though it was never produced.

REFERENCES: *Wiki.* Perkins, Kathy A., in *BWA:AHE.*

FURTHER READING: *BAWPP. HR&B.* Dandridge, Rita B. "Black Female Playwrights: An Anthology of Plays before 1950." *MELUS. 19.1* (Spring 1994) p. 141. From *Literature Resource Center.* Macki, Adrienne C. "'Talking B(l)ack': Construction of Gender and Race in the Plays of Eulalie Spence." *Theatre History Studies. 27* (Annual 2007) p.86. From *Literature Resource Center.* Parascandola, Louis J., in *GEAAL.*

Spencer (married name), "Anne" (née Annie Bethel Bannister)
2/6/1882–7/12/1975
Poems; librarian

Annie's future did not look bright when she was born on a Virginia plantation to parents whose marriage was turbulent from the outset—her mother, Sarah Louise Scales, the mulatta daughter of a former slaveholder; and her father, Joel Cephus Bannister, a man of African, Native-American, and European-American descent. When Annie Bethel Bannister was just 5 years old, she and Sarah left Joel in Virginia and moved to Bramwell, a mining town in West Virginia. There, Annie roomed with the Dixies, a foster family, while Sarah supported herself and her daughter by working as an itinerant cook. Although Annie loved to read and voraciously plowed through dime-store novels, newspapers, and whatever else was available, she didn't received any formal education until she was 11 years old.

When Annie was 11, Joel threatened to take her with him unless Sarah enrolled Annie in school. As soon as she could, Sarah enrolled Annie at the Virginia Seminary in Lynchburg, under the name Annie Bethel Scales (Sarah's maiden name). Annie was the youngest student ever to attend the seminary, and she graduated as valedictorian when she was just 17 years old. She also started writing poetry, including her sonnet "The Skeptic" (1896). The road to the valedictory address was not untroubled, however. Although Annie excelled in all her humanities courses, she had difficulty with her science courses. In order to do well in these courses, she sought the help of a tutor, Edward Spencer.

Immediately after her 1899 graduation, Annie returned to Bramwell, where she taught school. Two years later, however, Annie returned to Lynchburg, where she married Edward on May 15, 1901, and the two of them subsequently raised three children: their daughters, Bethel Calloway (Stevenson) and Alroy Sarah (Rivers), and their son, Chauncey Edward (who later became a pioneer aviator). Annie was not devoted to homemaking and childrearing, however. Her primary interests were poetry and lovingly tending to their backyard garden. She was so attentive to her garden that Edward built her a cottage (named "Edenkraal") looking onto it. Fortunately, Edward was able to pay for housekeepers and caregivers for the children, liberating Annie to work in her garden and to write poetry. These two passions often intersected, too, as Annie often used the garden as imagery for her poetic themes.

During these early decades of the twentieth century, Spencer also became increasingly interested in political activism. She stirred up a protest against the employment of all-white faculty at the segregated black-students-only high school in Lynchburg, and her actions led to the hiring of African-American teachers there. She boycotted Lynchburg's segregated public transportation and defiantly rode on the all-white trolley, refusing to leave when asked. She offered refuge to Ota Benfa, an African pygmy who had been exhibited in zoos, allegedly to show the presumed intrinsic inferiority of Africans, but instead showing the intrinsic inferiority of people who would treat fellow humans so inhumanely. In 1918, she worked with NAACP secretary **James Weldon Johnson** to establish an NAACP chapter in Lynchburg. In 1923, she was instrumental in starting the only library in Lynchburg that was open to African Americans, and she served as its librarian until 1945. Spencer also did just plain outrageous things for her day, such as wearing pants in public, having interracial friendships, and writing stinging editorials denouncing any claims about the superiority of whites over blacks.

Spencer's contact with Johnson led to far more than her political activism, however. For one thing, Johnson and Spencer formed a friendship that lasted the rest of his life. For another, while Johnson was visiting her home as they were working together to found the Lynchburg NAACP chapter, he happened to see some of her poetry. He liked what he read and urged her to publish some of her poems, using the name "Anne Spencer," rather than the informal-sounding "Annie." With his help, 38-year-old Anne Spencer published her first poem, "Before the Feast of Shushan" (February 1920) in the NAACP journal **Crisis**. Johnson also published 5 of her poems in his anthology *The Book of American Negro Poetry* (1922), and 10 of her poems were published in **Countee Cullen**'s anthology, *Caroling Dusk* (1927).

Although Spencer treasured Johnson's friendship and his advice, she didn't always follow it. For instance, he introduced her to H. L. Mencken, the well-regarded editor of the popular *American Mercury* magazine, advising her that Mencken had frequently launched the careers of African-American writers. When Mencken criticized Spencer's work, however, she refused to accept his suggestions, not because he was not African American, but because he was not a poet and therefore had no right to comment on her poetry. After Mencken helped her publish "Before the Feast of Shushan," she refused any further collaboration with him.

Spencer showed similar resistance to the editorial process with other editors, feeling that they misunderstood her meanings and intentions and that they tried to censor her either for being too assertive about the need for racial and sexual equality or for being too subtle in asserting those needs. These quarrels ended up limiting the degree to which her works were published. For instance, no collection of her poetry was ever published during her lifetime, and of her thousands of writings (including a novel, as well as poems and cantos), only 50 remain, with fewer than 30 of those having ended up in print during her lifetime. Despite these difficulties, however, Spencer's work was favorably reviewed and highly esteemed during her day, and at least one of her poems appeared in virtually every poetry anthology that appeared between the start of the 1920s and the end of the 1940s, including those by Johnson, by Cullen, by **Alain Locke**, by **Sterling Brown**, and by **Langston Hughes** and **Arna Bontemps**.

Perhaps part of Spencer's appeal was her contradictions: While she embraced spiritual appreciation of the beauty of nature (e.g., in her poems "At the Carnival," 1922; "Lines to a Nasturtium," 1926; "Substitution," 1927; and "Requiem," 1931) and often used biblical and mythological imagery and allusions, she bluntly rejected religious dogma and prudery. For instance, her "Black Man O'Mine" revels in the erotic pleasures of lovemaking between an African-American man and woman. While her poems could never be categorized as "protest poems," she nonetheless addressed issues of racial oppression of blacks by whites (e.g., in "White Things," 1923) and feminist issues (e.g., in "The Wife-Woman," 1922; "Lady, Lady," 1925; and "Letter to My Sister," 1927). Her poetry reflected the more traditional themes of the earlier Romantic poets (e.g., nature's beauty, friendship, love), yet she wholeheartedly plunged into modern poetic forms, such as slant rhymes, haunting rhythms, and obscure symbolism. She has even been called the most modern, original, and unconventional poet of her time. Unsurprisingly, the adjective most often used to describe her poetry is "ironic."

Although Lynchburg, Virginia, certainly was a far cry from Harlem, her home was nonetheless a welcome hostel for numerous literary notables associated with the **Harlem Renaissance**, such as **Maya Angelou**, **Gwendolyn Brooks**, Sterling Brown, **W. E. B. Du Bois**, Langston Hughes, **Georgia Douglas Johnson**, **Claude McKay**, and **Paul Robeson**, as well as George Washington Carver and others. To be sure, one of the reasons for her gracious hospitality and for their appreciative welcoming of it was because Jim Crow laws prohibited African Americans from staying in most hotels anywhere in the South. During those troublesome times, most African Americans expected to open their homes to visiting African Americans who were traveling through the South. Nonetheless, Spencer's home and its splendid garden at 1313 Pierce Street offered cordial, hospitable lodgings to her visitors. In addition to enjoying Spencer's agreeable accommodations, these visitors also exchanged ideas and literary critiques with their hostess.

In 1938, Spencer's mentor, James Weldon Johnson, died unexpectedly, and her tribute to him, "For Jim, Easter Eve," was the last of her poems to be published during her lifetime. After his death, she retreated from literary circles. After her husband died in 1964, she retreated further into being a recluse, even allowing her garden to go to seed, but she never stopped writing. She wrote various historical pieces, and she began revising her poems by making notes on whatever slips of paper were handy. Unfortunately, when she died, her friends couldn't figure out what she intended with these scraps and tossed them out. On the other hand, most of the completed poems that were found were gathered into *Time's Unfading Garden: Anne Spencer's Life and Poetry* (1977, edited by J. Lee Greene). In addition, Spencer's garden and the cottage, Edenkraal, have been restored and placed on the National Register of Historic Places.

REFERENCES: *BANP. NAAAL.* Aguiar, Marian, in *EA-99.* Barnes, Paula C., in *BWA:AHE.* Clark, Keith, in *OCWW.* McCaskill, Barbara, in *COCAAL* and *OCAAL.*

FURTHER READING: *AANB. BAWPP. HR&B. LFCC-07. Wiki.* Chester, Dennis, in *GEAAL.* Dean, Sharon G., in *AP1880-1945-3.* Greene, J. Lee, in *AAWHR-40.* Johnston, Sara Andrews, in *AWW-1900-45.* Leverich, Jean M., in *CAO-07.* Manheim, James M., in *BB.*

Spillers, Hortense J.
c. 1944–
Literary criticism, essays; educator

Precious little has been written about Hortense Spillers, except to observe what she has written about other African-American women writers (e.g., **Gwendolyn Brooks, Jessie Redmon Fauset, Amelia E. Johnson, Paule Marshall**). An astute, outspoken literary critic and essayist, she is invariably mentioned whenever writers speak of African-American literary critics. Often invited to write the introductions to books identified with the **Schomburg** Library, Spillers also edited the Library's *Clarence and Corinne; or God's Way* (originally 1890, by Mrs. A. E. Johnson; 1988, edited by Spillers). Her other edited works include *Conjuring: Black Women, Fiction, and Literary Tradition* (1985, with Marjorie Pryse) and a special issue of *Boundary 2* titled *The Sixties and the World Event* (2009, with Christopher Connery). Her own writings include *Comparative American Identities: Race, Sex and Nationality in the Modern Text* (1991); *Black, White, and in Color: Essays on American Literature and Culture* (2003); and *The Idea of Black Culture* (2007, in the Blackwell Manifestos series). After teaching at Cornell University, Spillers moved into the Gertrude Conaway Vanderbilt Chair in Vanderbilt University's English Department. Spillers has diverse scholarly interests, including literature, African-American culture, feminism, and psychoanalysis, about which she writes articles (e.g., in *African American Review*). In addition to her own awards and honors, she was invited to choose the 2007 winner of the Andrew J. Kappel Prize in literary criticism.

REFERENCES: Nishikawa, Kinohi, in *GEAAL.* "Twentieth-Century Literature's Andrew J. Kappel Prize in Literary Criticism, 2007." *Twentieth Century Literature.* 53.2 (Summer 2007) p. vi. From *Literature Resource Center.* //aalbc.com/authors/hortensespillers.htm. //www.amazon.com, 7/1999, 4/2009. //www.blackculturalstudies.org/spillers/spillers_index.html. //www.vanderbilt.edu/english/hortense_spillers.

FURTHER READING: *BWA:AHE. OCAAL. OCWW.*

Spingarn, Arthur B. (Barnett)
1878–1971
Bibliophile

Joel Elias Spingarn

Joel Elias Spingarn
1875–1939
Nonfiction, literary criticism; publisher

Though both Spingarn brothers have European-American heritage, they were heavily involved in the activities of the National Association for the Advancement of Colored People (NAACP): Arthur, an attorney, chaired the NAACP's legal committee for many years and served as the organization's president (1940-1965); Joel chaired the NAACP board in 1914, and at that time, he established the organization's prestigious Spingarn medal, awarded to outstanding African Americans who have made significant contributions to their community in various fields of endeavor. Joel also encouraged many writers of the **Harlem Renaissance** and wrote such works of literary criticism as *A History of Literary Criticism in the Renaissance* (1899) and *The New Criticism* (1911). Those volumes serve as bookends to his career teaching literature at Columbia University (1899-1911). Another of Joel Spingarn's books was *Creative Criticism and Other Essays on the Unity of Genius and Taste* (reprinted 1979). Joel also worked closely with **Walter White**, whom he had met when White had consulted with him about White's first novel (in 1922), when Joel

was an editor at Harcourt and Brace. White and Joel Spingarn were instrumental in shaping the NAACP's financial and administrative policies during the 1930s.

In 1946, Arthur Spingarn, a noted collector of literature by (and about) people of African descent (especially rare editions of Cuban, Haitian, and Brazilian authors), made available his 5,000-plus books to Howard University. Howard's president at the time, Mordecai Wyatt Johnson, observed that it was "the most comprehensive and interesting group of books by Negroes ever collected in the world." Even after Howard acquired his collection, Arthur Spingarn continued to send to Howard a copy of every book he could find, written by an author of African descent, including books on various academic topics, written in African and European languages. In recognition of his contribution, Howard named their world-renowned research center the Moorland-Spingarn Research Center in 1973.

REFERENCES: Hornsby, Alton, "Spingarn, Joel Elias," in *WB-99.* Myers, Aaron, "Moorland-Spingarn Research Collection," in *EA-99.* Sekora, John, "Libraries and Research Centers," in *OCAAL.* Moorland-Spingarn Research Center online card catalog, 5/1999. //www.amazon.com, 8/1999. //www.founders.howard.edu/moorland-spingarn/HIST.HTM.

FURTHER READING: *CE.* "Arthur B. Spingarn," and "Joel Elias Spingarn" in *Wiki.*

Spirituals

African-American spirituals are overtly religious songs that are believed to have been sung since the days when African-Americans were brought to the New World as slaves. While the word "spiritual" originally referred only to songs sung at religious congregations, as time progressed, they were greatly influenced by African-American slave songs, and as such, the songs of slavery are included in the category of spirituals. Like **folktales**, spirituals were probably created to help slaves adjust to the conditions they found upon arriving in the New World from Africa, and also to help them come together as a single people despite the fact that they came from different areas of the African continent and thus had different traditions. Also, like folktales, when African Americans tried to get out from under the yoke of slavery, spirituals became instruments of underground rebellion.

The earliest spirituals remain mostly unknown to us because, also like folktales, these songs are part of the African-American **oral tradition**, arising from the interactions of people and thus composed by a group. No one composer, lyricist, or musician can be associated with any one song, nor do we have dates of composition because nothing was written down until 1801 when **Richard Allen** gathered some of them into a book. By then, however, many spirituals had been lost because they had fallen out of use or had been modified through the generations. Thus, even Allen's versions of the songs cannot be said to be authoritative, and when looking through the recorded texts and music of the spirituals, a researcher will find that the same song may be sung to a variety of tunes; additionally, a researcher might discover that the same phrases will appear in the lyrics of different songs.

Spirituals probably emerged out of the contact between the traditions of the African slaves and the Protestant Christianity of the South, intent on spreading its religion to all races. Although African-American spirituals may have picked up the details of the Bible stories, evangelical sermons, and hymns from the Protestants, they are distinct from white religious songs because of the African influences that the slaves incorporated into their spirituals. Protestant hymns were very European, traditional, and stately, stiffly sung. In contrast, African-American spirituals have long, repetitive choruses, employ *call-and-response* patterns of West and Central Africa (in which the lead singer sings a line and the rest of the congregation sing the same line or a responding line back), include percussion and syncopation (if not performed with instruments, singers would use their hands and feet to keep the beat), and encourage the congregation and singers to incorporate rhythmic body movements.

African-American spirituals differ from white spirituals not only in their melodic or performative elements, but also in the layers of meanings beneath the words of the songs. Because they were slaves, when African Americans were singing to God, they were singing not only of a spiritual redemption but also of a physical redemption. Slaves sang spirituals not only in congregations or at church time but also while they were working in the fields, while they were resting after a long day, and even during children's playtimes. In many ways, these songs were a way of mentally shielding themselves from the abuses of the slaveholders, the restrictions of slavery and its cruelties. In imagining a kind God as father and heaven as a loving home where they would arrive after their work on Earth was through, the songs may have made the day easier to get through.

In many ways the songs were also more than shields—they were songs of protest, and in some cases a call to arms. Spirituals were often linked with slave uprisings, and in those instances, the songs brought together both religious and secular meanings. While songs such as "Swing Low, Sweet Chariot" and "Go Down Moses" call for a spiritual liberation that is overtly religious, they also hint at an actual yearning for freedom that slaves were denied and yet were striving toward. When viewed in light of the fact that these were songs sung by slaves, the fact that many of the spirituals seem to speak to three basic themes—the desire for justice, the desire for freedom, and the ways to survive unbearable hardship—becomes significant.

When the spirituals recalled and referred to the biblical tales of Daniel who was freed from the lion's den by a redeeming savior God, Jonah who was swallowed by a whale and also rescued by God, and the Israelites who were guided by Moses and aided by God in their escape from slavery in Egypt, African Americans were transforming songs about the past into songs about the present, as well. So threatening were these double meanings that slaveholders forbade slaves to sing some songs, such as "Go Down Moses" (which powerfully expresses the desire for human liberation in referring to the freeing of the Israelites) as they worked the plantations.

Although critics have disputed whether the slaves were really using the double meanings as they sang, conflating the yearning for spiritual release and actual release from bondage, testimonies of former slaves such as **Frederick Douglass** confirm that the spirituals were loaded with symbolic language. The song, "Swing Low, Sweet Chariot," which refers to a chariot that will sweep down and "carry me home," seems to refer to a chariot coming from heaven to take people back there. In actuality, it often signified the Underground Railroad or some means of escape and was sometimes sung to signal such liberating opportunities. Other words with double meanings in the songs include Egypt or Babylon, which meant the oppressive South; the river Jordan, which represented any body of water that could be crossed to reach the North and thus freedom; and home, Canaan or the Promised Land which could mean anywhere slaves could be free, be it the North, Africa, free states, or even Canada.

Because they are based on experiences unique to slaves in the Americas, in many ways, African-American spirituals have been seen as the first indigenous music of the United States. In their mixture of sorrow and joy, spirituals paved the way for other genres of music such as blues and jazz. **Ralph Ellison** said that the blues "is an impulse to keep the painful details and episodes of a brutal experience alive in one's aching consciousness, to finger its jagged edge, and to transcend it . . . by squeezing from it near-tragic, near-comic lyricism." In many ways, spirituals are full of the sorrows of slaves and gave the oppressed people a way to finger the jagged edges of their sorrow while still affirming notions of what Richard Newman calls "divine redemption and human triumph."

Yet the influence of the spirituals is seen not only in modern music, but also in the works of both African-American and European-American writers for more than a century. Some writers incorporated spirituals into their works to structure their stories. Others, such as **Zora Neale Hurston**, drew on the biblical parallels between African-American slaves and Moses's Israelites to develop her works. **James Baldwin**'s *Go Tell It On the Mountain* is informed by spirituals, and **Richard Wright** and Ralph Ellison both pay tribute to the formative effect spirituals had on their writing in various works, with Wright using a spiritual as an epigraph in one of his novels and Ellison's *Invisible Man* using spirituals as influences on the novel's characters, plot, and language. **Toni Morrison**'s *Song of Solomon* uses the spiritual's call-and-response patterns to advance the plot. Poets such as **James Weldon Johnson**, **Paul Laurence Dunbar**, and **Langston Hughes**, playwrights such as Eugene O'Neill, and novelists such as William Faulkner all incorporated spirituals into their work, using them as inspiration and models as they wrote.

The heart-piercing lyrics of the spirituals still hold as strong an impression for writers, readers, musicians, and listeners today as they did when they were first created. **Cornel West** sees in them a "depth of inarticulate anguish," and "a level of questioning about the nature of suffering previously unknown" that is made only more poignant by the fact that in these same songs, strength is found not by exacting murderous revenge but "in an all-embracing love and mercy." Thus, it is no wonder that one in particular, "Free at Last," became the cornerstone of **Martin Luther King, Jr.**'s "I Have a Dream" speech. Starting as songs that helped an uprooted people adjust to their new surroundings, continuing as songs of solace and eventually of rebellion against unjust oppressors, and finding their place in rallying cries for equality in the civil rights movement, spirituals truly seem to have the lasting power found only in great works of art.

REFERENCES: *NAAAL.* Connor, Kimberly Rae, in *COCAAL* and *OCAAL.* Newman, Richard. 1998. *Go Down, Moses: Celebrating the African-American Spiritual.* New York: Clarkson Potter. West, Cornel. 1998. Foreword, in *Go Down, Moses: Celebrating the African-American Spiritual.* New York: Clarkson Potter. —Diane Masiello

Spivey, Victoria Regina
10/15/1906–10/3/1976
Songs

Hired as a songwriter for the St. Louis Publishing Company, Spivey both wrote and recorded songs (e.g., "TB Blues") during the late 1920s. During the 1960s, she wrote and recorded songs (e.g., "Murder in the First Degree") for her own Queen Vee (later named Spivey) Records and for the Bluesville and the Folkways labels.

REFERENCES: *EA-99.* Flandreau, Suzanne, in *BWA:AHF.*

FURTHER READING: *A. AANB. D. Wiki.*

Steele, Claude M. (Mason)
1/1/1946–
Scholarly; social psychologist, journal editor, educator

Shelby Steele, twin brother
1/1/1946–
Scholarly; educator

Ruth Hootman, a European-American social worker, met Shelby Steele, an African-American self-educated truck driver, while both were working in the civil-rights movement. The two wedded and had identical twin sons, Claude and Shelby Jr. As their sons grew, the Steeles continued to be active in nonviolent protests in support of the civil-rights movement. The two sons viewed these experiences very differently. Claude was impressed by the effectiveness of their parents' nonviolent tactics, such as their use of a boycott to shut down the nearby segregated school. Shelby observed that their efforts were often futile or pointless, such as by trying to desegregate a lunch counter where the Steeles had never intended to eat. The two Steele sons continued to differ further as they grew older.

Claude left the Steele household to attend Hiram College in Ohio, then transferred to nearby Ohio State University, where he specialized in social psychology, earning an M.A. (1969) and then a Ph.D. (1971). After a brief assistant professorship in psychology at the University of Utah in Salt Lake City (1971-1973), Claude joined the faculty of the University of Washington in Seattle (1973-1987). While there, he specialized in studying alcohol abuse, winning several grants from the National Institute of Alcohol Abuse and Alcoholism.

Claude's next move was to the University of Michigan in Ann Arbor, as a professor of psychology (1987-1991), where he also became a research scientist at the school's Institute for Social Research (1989-1991). At Ann Arbor, he was invited to join a committee studying how to recruit and retain students. African-American students with high SAT (Scholastic Aptitude Test) scores were nonetheless dropping out of college at an alarming rate, and the African-American students who continued in school were earning grades slightly lower than those of their European-American counterparts.

Steele decided to study the origins of this phenomenon. Neither systematic racism among the faculty nor class differences in the students' backgrounds could explain the differences. Through further investigations, Claude developed his theory of "stereotype threat," in which the students' anxiety about fulfilling racial stereotypes of intellectual inferiority harmed the students' performance. Claude not only theorized about the problem, but also helped work toward its solution. With others at the university, he developed the 21st Century Program, which succeeded in significantly decreasing the grade gap between the African-American and the European-American students. By the time the 21st Century Program was fully implemented, however, Claude had moved on to Stanford University in California (1991-).

Before leaving the University of Michigan, Claude was an associate editor of the *Personality and Social Psychology Bulletin* (1984-1987) and a consulting editor to the *Personality and Social Psychology Bulletin* (1977-1983), to the *Journal of Social Issues* (1983-1990), and to the *Journal of Experimental Social Psychology, Journal of Personality and Social Psychology, Motivation and Emotion, Basic and Applied Social Psychology, Attitudes and Social Cognition,* and *Psychological Review* (all 1990-). He had also been publishing his research findings in various scholarly journals.

In 1992, however, Claude wrote "Race and the Schooling of Black Americans" for the *Atlantic Monthly,* a well-regarded popular magazine, explaining his findings on "stereotype vulnerability." Claude Steele's further investigations have confirmed his concept of stereotype vulnerability, as reported in many scholarly social-psychology journals. He also explained his further findings in "Thin Ice: 'Stereotype Threat' and Black College Students" for *The Atlantic Monthly* (1999) and in "Colorblindness as a Barrier to Inclusion: Assimilation and Nonimmigrant Minorities," which he cowrote with his wife, Dorothy M. Steele, and with Hazel Rose Markus for *Daedalus.* His findings have also been published in anthologies and in textbooks. In addition to these articles, Claude Steele cowrote *Young, Gifted, and Black: Promoting High Achievement among African American Students* (2003, with Theresa Perry and Asa Hilliard III), offering each author's view of how to foster school success among African-American students. Steele's *Whistling Vivaldi: And Other Clues to How Stereotypes Affect Us (Issues of Our Time Series)* is also forthcoming.

In 2001, Claude Steele was named director of Stanford's Center for Advanced Study in the Behavioral Sciences (2001-2009). Years earlier, he had been awarded a fellowship to study at the Center (1994-1995), as well as several other fellowships. Among his other honors, he has been awarded the Gordon Allport Intergroup Relations Prize in social psychology (1997), the Donald Campbell Award from the Society for Personality and Social Psychology (2001), and the Kurt Lewin Memorial Award from the Society for the Psychological Study of Social Issues (2002), as well as the Senior Award for Distinguished Contributions to Psychology in the Public Interest and the Distinguished Scientific Contribution Award from the American Psychological Association (2002) and the William James Fellow Award for Distinguished Scientific Career Contribution from the American Psychological Society (2000). In addition to memberships in numer-

ous professional and scholarly organizations , he has served on the board of directors of the American Psychological Society (1991-1996) and has presided over the Western Psychological Association (1996-1997) and the Society for Personality and Social Psychology (2002-2003). In addition, he has been elected to the American Academy of Arts and Sciences (1996), the National Academy of Education (1997), and the National Academy of Sciences (2003). He also has several honorary doctorates and has offered expert testimony on affirmative action before the U.S. Supreme Court (2003). In 2009, Steele left Stanford to become Provost of Columbia University in New York City.

Though Claude and Shelby Steele now agree not to publicly discuss each other's work, at one time, Shelby could have been considered one of the harshest critics of Claude's analysis of his research. Shelby Steele enrolled in Coe College in Cedar Rapids, Iowa. After graduating, by day, Shelby taught high-school students in an East St. Louis, Illinois ghetto, and by night, he earned his master's degree from Southern Illinois University (1971). To earn his Ph.D. in English (1974), he moved to Salt Lake City's University of Utah (UU). After he earned his doctorate, UU offered him a job with tenure, but he and his wife already had their first of two children and did not want to raise their family in the climate of racial hostility they found in Salt Lake City.

Instead, Shelby and his family moved to California, where he became a professor of English literature at San Jose State University. At first, he followed the traditional path of the English literature professor, writing literary criticism, such as articles on the works of **Richard Wright** and **Ralph Ellison,** for publication in scholarly literature journals. In time, however, he began expressing his views on race, for publication in popular periodicals such as his columns in the *Wall Street Journal.* Unlike his brother Claude, Shelby relies on his own personal experiences and observations to formulate his views, rather than looking to research findings for his assertions. Their choice of audience also differs: Whereas Claude writes chiefly for scholarly journals, Shelby chiefly writes for popular audiences, such as his best-selling collection of essays *Content of Our Character: A New Vision of Race in America* (1990), for which he won the National Book Critics Circle Award for nonfiction (1990). Steele also created and narrated the PBS *Frontline* special *Seven Days in Bensonhurst* (1990), which won an Emmy Award and a Writer's Guild Award for television documentary writing, as well as a San Francisco Film Festival Award for television documentary writing (all 1991).

To Shelby, the civil-rights movement had achieved its aims decades earlier, and now individual African Americans must take charge of personally overcoming any racial vulnerability they may experience if they wish to succeed. Shelby therefore attacks affirmative-action programs as stigmatizing and as further victimizing African Americans by singling them out for special treatment, rather than encouraging them to buck up and create their own opportunities for advancement. Though Shelby enjoys a warm welcome from conservatives, chiefly European Americans, but also some African Americans, he has received chilly reception from liberal academics, especially African-American academics.

After teaching at San Jose State University for two decades, Shelby Steele left it to become a research fellow at the Hoover Institution at Stanford University (1994-). A few years later, Shelby Steele published *A Dream Deferred: The Second Betrayal of Black Freedom in America* (1998), which expands on many of his views presented in *Content*. In *White Guilt: How Blacks and Whites Together Destroyed the Promise of the Civil Rights Era* (2006), Steele goes on to suggest how liberals have used affirmative action to keep African Americans from taking responsibility for their own lives, becoming self-sufficient, and creating their own success. Steele further elaborated on his views in *A Bound Man: Why We Are Excited About Obama and Why He Can't Win* (2007).

Shelby Steele earned the San Jose State University President's Award, the National Humanities Medal (2004), and the Bradley Prize from the Lynde and Harry Bradley Foundation (2006). He has also been invited to share his views on race on numerous television shows, including *Good Morning America*, *60 Minutes*, *Nightline*, and *This Morning*.

REFERENCES: "Claude Steele," *Wiki*. Lesinski, Jeanne M., in *BB*. Pendergrass, Sabrina, in *AANB*. //en.wikipedia.org/wiki/Daedalus_ (journal). //psychology.stanford.edu/~steele/. //psychology.stanford. edu/~steele/vita.html. Amazon.com. "Shelby Steele," *CAO-07*. *Wiki*. Chura, Patrick, in *AANB*, Strumolo, Amy Loerch, in *BB*. Amazon.com.

Steptoe, John (Lewis)
9/14/1950–8/28/1989
Children's picture books; visual artist

From an early age, John loved art, often preferring to draw and paint at home, rather than play outside. In his teens, John attended the New York High School of Art and Design, then during a summer art program in Vermont, he wrote and illustrated his first book, *Stevie*.

What motivated a 19-year-old to write *Stevie*? For one thing, he wanted to see more children's books featuring African-American children. In *Stevie*, Steptoe's characters use authentic urban African-American speech patterns. The main character's sentiments also ring true, as an older child candidly expresses his jealousy and resentment toward—and then reconciliation with and accep-

tance of—his younger brother Stevie. *Stevie* earned Steptoe numerous awards and national recognition.

After engendering his own readership—his children Bweela and Javaka—Steptoe wrote *My Special Best Words* (1974) and *Daddy Is a Monster . . . Sometimes* (1980), exploring the complexities of father-child relationships. Steptoe's *Marcia* (1976), a young-adult novel, underscores the need for responsibility with sexual activity. This novel seems particularly poignant, given that Steptoe died young due to AIDS.

In the 1980s, Steptoe focused on folktales. In 1981, he illustrated **Rosa Guy**'s *Mother Crocodile*, an adaptation of an African fable (first recorded by Birago Diop). He also wrote and illustrated the Caldecott Honor Book *The Story of Jumping Mouse: A Native American Legend* (1984). When he created his masterpiece, *Mufaro's Beautiful Daughters: An African Tale* (1987), Steptoe spent about two and a half years researching, writing, and illustrating it. He studied African zoology, anthropology, and archeology, unearthing the architectural and technological sophistication of ancient residents of what is now Zimbabwe. The story, similar to the European Cinderella tale, explores universal feelings of sibling rivalry. Steptoe's lush illustrations dazzle the eyes with vivid landscapes and beautiful Africans. Steptoe's major effort paid off, as the book earned 1988 Caldecott Honors and a 1987 *Boston Globe-Horn Book* Honor Award for Illustration.

Steptoe's other books include *Uptown* (1970), *Train Ride* (1971), *Birthday* (1972), *Jeffrey Bear Cleans Up His Act* (1983), and *Baby Says* (1988). In addition, he illustrated several picture books written by **Arnold Adoff** (two books), **Lucille Clifton**, and **Eloise Greenfield**. When accepting the 1982 **Coretta Scott King** Award for illustrating *Mother Crocodile*, Steptoe commented, "I'm gratified sometimes by the positive social effect my work may have had. But an effect comes after the aesthetic statement." In reviewing the body of his work, he clearly achieved both positive social effect and glorious aesthetics.

Javaka Steptoe has become an illustrator and artist, as well. His first book, *In Daddy's Arms I Am Tall: African Americans Celebrating Fathers*, offers a collection of poems Javaka edited and illustrated, including one of Javaka's own poems. It won the Coretta Scott King Illustrator Award and at least half a dozen other key awards. When asked about following in his father's footsteps, he answered, "I might do the same things that he does, but I can't do them the way he did them, so I do things the way that I do them. I don't have a problem being identified with them, but ultimately I will make my own footsteps" (quoted in *CA/I*). With *The Jones Family Express* (2003), Javaka took yet another of his own steps by writing and illustrating his own book about a young boy named "Steven."

REFERENCES: *CBC. EBLG. IPOF.* Brown, Jennifer M., Nathalie Op De Beeck, Cindi Di Marzo, Heather Vogel Frederick, Emily Jenkins, and Shannon Maughan, et al. "Flying Starts: Six Children's Authors and Artists Discuss Their Fall '97 Debuts." *Publishers Weekly.* 244.52 (Dec. 22, 1997; p. 28). *Literature Resources from Gale.* "Javaka Steptoe," *CA/I.* Lowe, Barbara, in COCAAL and OCAAL.

FURTHER READING: *BAWPP. CAO-03. Wiki.* Ostrom, Hans, in *GEAAL.*

Sterling (married surname), Dorothy (née Dannenberg)
11/23/1913–12/1/2008
Juvenile nonfiction and fiction books, anthologies, autobiography; journalist

A Jewish-European-American mother of a daughter, Anne, and a son, Peter, Sterling wrote many biographical narratives for juveniles, such as *Freedom Train: The Story of Harriet Tubman* (1954/1987); *Captain of the Planter: The Story of Robert Smalls* (1958/1978); *Lucretia Mott: Gentle Warrior* (1964/1999); *Lift Every Voice: The Lives of Booker T. Washington, W.E.B. Du Bois, Mary Church Terrell and James Weldon Johnson* (1965, with Benjamin Quarles); *The Making of an Afro-American: Martin Robison Delany, 1812-1885* (1971/1996); *Black Foremothers: Three Lives* (1979/ 2nd ed., 2004), about Ellen Craft (wife of William Craft), Ida B. Wells, and Mary Church Terrell; and *Ahead of Her Time: Abby Kelley and the Politics of Antislavery* (1991/1994). Sterling's historical accounts include *Forever Free: The Story of the Emancipation Proclamation* (1963), *Tear Down the Walls! A Story of the American Civil Rights Movement* (1968), and *It Started in Montgomery: A Picture History of the Civil Rights Movement* (1972). Among those who sing her praises are Houston A. Baker, Jr., Toni Morrison, and Nikki Giovanni, who said, "She tells our story with such compassion and understanding that it is difficult to believe she is non-Black" (quoted in CAO-08).

Sterling also edited *Speak out in Thunder Tones: Letters and Other Writings by Black Northerners, 1787-1865* (1973/1998), *We Are Your Sisters: Black Women in the Nineteenth Century* (1984/1997; adapted to a play produced in 1998), and *Turning the World Upside Down: Proceedings of the Anti-Slavery Convention of American Women Held in the City of New York, May 9-12, 1837* (1987/1993), as well as *The Trouble They Seen: Black People Tell the Story of Reconstruction* (1976; reprinted with the subtitle *Story of Reconstruction in the Words of African Americans*, 1994), which garnered the Carter G. Woodson Book Award from the National Council for the Social Studies. For adults, Sterling wrote *Tender Warriors* (1958), resulting from her interviews of African-American children entering schools that were newly desegregated. She also wrote nature-study nonfiction for juveniles, including *Insects and the Homes They Build* (1954), *Creatures of the Night* (1960), and *Caterpillars* (1961); two other nonfiction books for children; seven books of juvenile fiction, including *Sophie and Her Puppies* (1951), *The Cub Scout Mystery* (1952), and *The Brownie Scout Mystery* (1955); and a book of young-adult fiction, *Mary Jane* (1959/1972), about a 12-year-old African-American girl who faces many challenges when integrating a large Southern junior-high school. In all, Sterling wrote more than 30 books. In her early years, she had worked for *Life* magazine (1941-1949); in her later years, she wrote *Close to My Heart: An Autobiography* (2005).

REFERENCES: *CAO-08. Wiki.* B. B., in *CBC.* Amazon.com.

Steward, Theophilus Gould
4/17/1843–1/11/1924
Novel, nonfiction—theology, history; theologian, cleric, military chaplain

Steward's history books include *The Haitian Revolution* (1914) and *The Colored Regulars* (c. 1899); his theology books include *Genesis Reread* (1885) and *The End of the World* (1888); and his novel was titled *Charleston Love Story* (1899).

REFERENCES: Myers, Aaron, in *EA-99.*

FURTHER READING: *AANB. Wiki.* Andrews, William L., in COCAAL. Bailey, Julius H., in *GEAAL. See also* Perry, Kennetta Hammond. "Elevating the Race: Theophilus G. Steward, Black Theology, and the Making of an African American Civil Society, 1865-1924." *The Journal of African American History.* 90.3 (Summer 2005) p. 326. From *Literature Resource Center.*

Stewart, Maria W. (née Maria Miller)
?/1803–12/17/1879
Essays, pamphlets, poems, spoken word—speeches; domestic servant, activist

Born free, but orphaned at age five, Maria was indentured to a European-American cleric's family to earn her bed and board as a domestic servant. Released at age 15, she sought literacy and religious education while supporting herself through domestic service.

In 1826, she married James Stewart, a prosperous shipping agent. Sadly, after only three childless years of marriage, James died, and his estate's executors cheated Maria of her inheritance. Penniless, she returned to domestic service. Shaken, Maria awakened to her belief that opposition to slavery and oppression of African Americans was God's will. In 1830, she began writing religious tracts, inspiring fellow African Americans to share her revelation.

In 1831, Stewart wrote *Religion and the Pure Principles of Morality, the Sure Foundation on Which We Must Build,* using both the Bible and the U.S. Constitution as authorities for asserting a universal right to freedom, equality, and justice. Stewart urged African Americans to organize resistance to slavery in the South and to oppose racist discrimination and restrictions in the North: "Sue for your rights and privileges. . . . You can but die if you make the attempt; and we shall certainly die if you do not."

William Lloyd Garrison, publisher of the *Liberator,* printed her manuscript as a pamphlet; thereafter, he published the texts of all her essays, speeches, and other writings. Stewart's second public speech made history: In 1832, she became the first American-born woman documented to have given a public lecture to a "promiscuous audience" (both men *and* women) on political topics. A year later, at her fourth public lecture, Stewart announced her retreat from public speaking, noting that both blacks and whites, women and men had reproached her for speaking to promiscuous public audiences. Not one to leave whimpering, however, she cited numerous powerful women of the Old Testament and in world history, asking, "What if such women . . . should rise among our sable race?"

Stewart's published works include her pamphlet *Meditations from the Pen of Mrs. Maria Stewart* (which she enlarged and published herself half a century later) and her 1835 *Productions of Mrs. Maria W. Stewart,* a collection of her speeches, some biographical facts, and several poems and essays on topics from abolition, human rights, and women's rights to economic equality, education, and moral uplift. Whenever she spoke or wrote, Stewart exhorted well-off white women to sympathize with the plight of their darker-skinned brothers and sisters, and she encouraged all women and African-American men to gain education, citing it as a source of uplift. Further, she urged all women to participate fully and equally in the political and social life of their communities.

After retreating from lecturing, Stewart taught school, worked for abolition, and promoted literacy. A little over a century after Stewart's death, Marilyn Richardson edited the 1987 collection *Maria W. Stewart, America's First Black Woman Political Writer: Essays and Speeches.*

REFERENCES: *1TESK. BAAW. NAAAL. PBW.* Richardson, Marilyn, in *COCAAL* and *OCAAL.*

FURTHER READING: *AANB. B. W. Wiki.* Bolden, Tonya, in //digital.nypl.org/schomburg/writers_aa19/bio2.html. Dasher-Alston, Robin M., in *AWPW:1820-1870.* Golus, Carrie, in *BB.* Saulsbury, Rebecca R., in *GEAAL. See also EAAWW. See also* reviews of *Black Women's Intellectual Traditions: Speaking Their Minds;* of *"Doers of the Word": African-American Women Speakers and Writers in the North, 1830-1880;* of *Memorial Narratives of African Women in Antebellum New England;* and of *Sentimental Confessions: Spiritual Narratives of Nineteenth-Century Women.*

Still, William
1821–7/14/1902
Nonfiction—history, biography; abolitionist, Underground railroad conductor and station master

From an early age, William Still knew that there were certain things he was never to mention: his parents' true names (Levin and Sidney Steele, not Levin and Charity Still), his mother's escape from slavery with his two older sisters, and his two older brothers-left behind in bondage so that the rest of the family might have a chance for escape. Sidney had at first tried to escape with all her children, but the slavehunters found her and returned her to her owner—and cruel punishment for her attempt. On a small farm in New Jersey, the fugitive Still family grew quite large, and William, the youngest, never revealed his secret. For more than 40 years, he knew that slavehunters might come to steal him, his siblings, and his mother back to slavery, so it was easy to keep quiet.

In the mid-1840s, William moved to Philadelphia and did odd jobs to earn his keep, while learning to read and write. In 1847, the Pennsylvania Anti-Slavery Society hired him to do odd jobs for them, and gradually, his responsibilities expanded. He raised funds and disbursed them to conductors on the Underground Railroad, trained and coordinated the activities of the slavehunter lookouts, established safe houses, and found ways to provide forged free papers, food, clothing, medical care, jobs, money, and friends to fugitive slaves. He also provided contacts and resources for fugitives to escape farther north, to the safety of Canada. He and his wife, Letitia George Still, also opened their homes to fugitives. In various ways, Still managed to help about 800 people find their way to freedom.

Still also started keeping a journal. At first, he just kept track of his expenses. Then something happened to motivate him to keep more explicit records. In 1850, a former slave named Peter, somewhere in his 40s, had reached Still's office, searching for some way to find his family. His grandmother had told him and his brother that their family was somewhere "up the Delaware River," just before the boys were sold down the river to Alabama. Peter also knew that his mother was named Sidney, and his father was Levin. After 40 years, Peter was reunited with a baby brother he never knew he had and with his mother, his older sisters, and his numerous younger siblings. Sadly, Levin had died several years earlier, so he was never able to celebrate that reunion. William then worked with Peter for three years to have his wife and two children rescued from bondage and reunited with him, when at last they succeeded.

With this remarkable motivation, Still expanded his journal to include the names, aliases, and owners' names of everyone he served for the Anti-Slavery Society. He

William Still

also recorded whatever details he could discover about their relatives, either still enslaved or in freedom. In 1872, long after Emancipation and the close of the Civil War, Still published the first edition of his book, including all the information he had been able to gather over the years: *The Underground Rail Road: a Record of Facts, Authentic Narratives, Letters, &c., Narrating the Hardships Hair-Breadth Escapes and Death Struggles of the Slaves in Their Efforts For Freedom, as Related by Themselves and Others, or Witnessed by the Author; Together with Sketches of Some of the Largest Stockholders, and Most Liberal Aiders and Advisers on the Road.*

After his years of service to the cause of abolition, following Emancipation, Still continued to serve, donating time and money to those in need. He also worked with various social and civic organizations, encouraging other people to donate whatever resources they had to their community, helping to found an old folks home, an orphanage, and a YMCA. In 1888, Still and his son-in-law Matthew Anderson started the Berean Building and Loan Association, which enabled many Philadelphia families to buy property, including their own homes. Anderson was the second husband of Still's daughter, Caroline Virginia Still Wiley Anderson, one of the first African-American women to graduate from a medical school (in 1878) and to practice medicine.

REFERENCES: *DANB. EAACH. SMKC.* —Tonya Bolden

FURTHER READING: *AANB. B. BAWPP. Wiki.* Gardner, Eric, in *GEAAL.* Kenneth W. Goings, in *COCAAL.*

Stone, Chuck (né Charles Sumner Stone, Jr.)
7/21/1924–
Nonfiction books, articles, novel; Tuskegee airman, journalist, columnist, newspaper editor, educator, etc.

Soon after Charles Sumner Stone enrolled in Springfield College (1942-1943), his Uncle Sam invited him to join the U.S. Army Air Forces (1943-1945), where he served among the Tuskegee airmen. After his military service, Stone earned his A.B. in political science and economics from Wesleyan University (1948). Next, he earned his M.A. in sociology from the University of Chicago (1950). Even after that, he continued to further his education, attending the University of Connecticut Law School (1954-1955) and the Eastern Baptist Theological Seminary (1989-1991).

Though best known as a journalist, Stone has worked in international relations, public service, politics, and education, as well as journalism. Early in his career, he worked for nongovernmental organizations (NGOs) in the Middle East and India (1952-1957). After returning, he found work as an editorial consultant (1957-1958) and then an editor (1958-1960) for the *New York Age* newspaper. When Chuck Stone left the *Age*, he remained in New York City as the associate director of the American Committee on Africa (1960).

Next, Stone moved his family to D.C., where he became editor and the White House correspondent for the *Washington Afro-American* (1960-1963). After a few years there, the peripatetic Stone moved his family again, this time to Chicago, where he became editor-in-chief (1963-1964) of the *Chicago Daily Defender* (the **Chicago Defender** until 1956). Forced to leave the *Defender* for his fiery rhetoric, he became a lecturer in journalism at Columbia College (1963-1964) and then a speechwriter and special assistant to U.S. Congressman **Adam Clayton Powell, Jr.** (1965-1967) of Harlem. During the years 1967-1970, Stone was an editorial research specialist for U.S. Congressman Robert N. C. Nix of Pennsylvania (1968), a visiting professor at Trinity College in Connecticut (1969), a politician-in-residence at Morgan State College (1969), and a commentator on NBC's *Today* TV show (1969-1970). He spent most of his time writing books, however. He wrote two nonfiction books, *Tell It Like It Is, a Provocative, Timely and Biting Report on the American Racial Scene* (1968) and *Black Political Power in America* (1968; rev. ed., 1970), and one novel, *King Strut* (1970).

In 1970, Stone moved again, to Princeton, New Jersey to become director of minority affairs and educational opportunities for the Educational Testing Service (ETS) (1970-1972). In 1972, Stone resigned, outraged at ETS's insensitivity to issues of racial bias in testing. More than a decade later, Stone was motivated to cofound FairTest, the National Center for Fair and Open Testing (1986, Cambridge, MA). After leaving ETS, Stone settled into his second long-term commitment—his first being to his wife Louise—at the *Philadelphia Daily News* as a syndicated columnist (1972-1991) and a senior editor (1979-1991). While working at the *News,* he also lectured in sociology at Philadelphia's Antioch-Putney Graduate School of Education (1973), hosted PBS-TV's *Black Perspective on the News* (later *Another Voice*) (1979-1980), hosted a radio talk show for WWDB (1983-1985), and professed English and journalism at the University of Delaware (1984-1991). Meanwhile, he took the time to cofound the National Association of Black Journalists (NABJ), over which he presided for the organization's first two terms (1975-1977). Stone was also a fellow at Harvard University's John F. Kennedy School of Government (1982).

In 1991, Stone left Philadelphia to become the Walter Spearman Professor at the School of Journalism and Mass Communication at the University of North Carolina (UNC) at Chapel Hill (1991-2005). Before retiring, Stone wrote a children's picture book, *Squizzy the Black Squirrel: A Fabulous Fable of Friendship* (2003). Amazon.com lists four other works, one or more of which may be book-length writings. Stone's writings have also appeared in numerous periodicals, and he is a contributing editor to *The Black Scholar.* His essays have also appeared in numerous anthologies. According to *AANB,* Stone wrote more than 4,000 columns, articles, and essays for newspapers, magazines, and scholarly journals.

Stone's journalism awards stretch across more than four decades, including being named "Journalist of the Year" by the Capitol Press Club of Washington, D.C. (1961), a Lifetime Achievement Award from the NABJ (1992), and induction into the NABJ Hall of Fame (2004). In addition, he has received several awards for his teaching and five honorary doctorates, and he was named an honorary federal warden by the U.S. Bureau of Prisons (1983).

REFERENCES: *BAWPP. CAO-07. Wiki.* Hunt, Karen Jean, in *AANB.* Jackson, Dennis, in *BB.* //en.wikipedia.org/wiki/Bobbs-Merrill. //en.wikipedia.org/wiki/Chicago_Defender. //en.wikipedia.org/wiki/ Columbia_College_Chicago. //en.wikipedia.org/wiki/Educational_ testing_service. //en.wikipedia.org/wiki/FairTest. //en.wikipedia.org/ wiki/National_Association_of_Black_Journalists. //en.wikipedia.org/ wiki/Robert_N.C._Nix,_Sr. //en.wikipedia.org/wiki/United_States_ Army_Air_Forces. //www.fairtest.org/. //www.highereducation.org/ crosstalk/ct0306/news0306-fairtest.shtml. //www.nabj.org/30/ moments/thirty/index.php. //www.nabj.org/awards/hall/inductees 2004/index.php. //www.nabj.org/awards/honors/past_winners/ index.php. //www.nabj.org/front/nabj/story/9220p-12723c.php. //www.nabj.org/front/story/870p-1389c.php. //www.nabj.org/ newsroom/news_releases/2004/v-print/story/512p-23c.php. //www.nabj.org/newsroom/news_releases/2007/v-print/story/52974p-8 1655c.php. //www.nabj.org/newsroom/publications/committed/story/ 418p-572ac.php. //www.nabj.org/newsroom/publications/committed/ story/418p-582c.php. //www.tbaal.org/history.html. //www.unc.edu/ news/archives/oct06/vetsday102506.htm. Amazon.com.

Stowe, Harriet Beecher
6/14/1811–7/1/1896
Novels, biographical sketches, essays, short stories, poems

Lithograph poster c.1899 for Al W. Martin's production of Uncle Tom's Cabin *by Harriet Beecher Stowe*

Stowe's novel *Uncle Tom's Cabin* (1852) was turned down by several publishers, and the publisher that finally accepted the work offered either to provide a 10% royalty or to share both the costs of the printing and the profits from the book's sales. European-American abolitionist Stowe unwisely chose the former option. The book sold 3,000 copies the first day out its initial printing of 5,000 copies in 2 days and half a million copies within 5 years. Later, on meeting her, Civil War President Abraham Lincoln said, "So you're the little woman who wrote the book that made this great war." She had based her novel on several slave narratives, such as those of **Frederick Douglass** and Josiah Henson (6/15/1789-5/5/1883). Henson subsequently claimed the title "Uncle Tom" and wrote two more narratives after Stowe's book was published. Many other African-American authors (e.g., **Martin R. Delany, Frances Ellen Watkins Harper**, and **Paul Laurence Dunbar**) have written works directly or indirectly referring to Stowe and her antislavery novel.

REFERENCES: *SEW.* Wagner, Wendy, in *COCAAL* and *OCAAL.*

FURTHER READING: B. BCE. CAO-03. CE. LFCC-07. MWEL. QB. Spot. USHC. W. W2B. Wiki. Adams, John R. (1989). "Chapter 1: Early Years." "Chapter 9: Afterword." "Author's Works." *Harriet Beecher Stowe.* In *Twayne's United States Authors Series 42.* Boston: Twayne Publishers. From *The Twayne Authors Series.* Bussey, Susan Hays, in *GEAAL.* Gatta, John, in *AWPW:1820-1870.* Hovet, Theodore R., and William E. Grant, in *ASSW-to1880.* Johnson, Paul David, in *AW:ACLB-79-V2-S1.* Lenz, Millicent, in *AWCto1900.* Ryan, Barbara, in *ARNE-4.* Stern, Madeleine B., in *ARN,* in *ARNE-1,* and in *RGAL-3.* Wright, Sarah Bird, in *ATW-1850-1915.*

Sundiata, Sekou (né Robert Franklin Feaster)
8/22/1945–7/18/2007
Poems, spoken word—poetry; performer

Born in Harlem, but with roots in South Carolina and in Florida, Sundiata grew up relishing the call-and-response patterns of African-American church services. Sundiata preferred to view himself as an oral poet, who recorded and performed his highly rhythmic, alliterative, sonorous poems. He usually gave his performances with jazz, blues, or other musical accompaniment, sometimes with video projections, too, thereby blurring the lines separating music, poetry, and theater. Nonetheless, Sundiata wrote down many of his poems, such as in his collection *Free* (1977). He also edited an anthology with Keith Gilyard and **Toi Derricotte**, *Spirit and Flame: An Anthology of Contemporary African American Poetry* (1997). In addition, Sundiata wrote a script based on his performance piece, *The Circle Unbroken Is a Hard Bop,* while a fellow at the Sundance Film Institute; the play garnered three Audelcos and a Bessie Award. He wrote his musical *The Mystery of Love* (1994) with songwriting help from Doug Booth, who also collaborated with him on his album *The Blue Oneness of Dreams* (1997), nominated for a Grammy. His other albums included *Are & Be, The Sounds of the Memory of Many Living People,* and *Longstoryshort* (2000).

In addition to his writing and his performing, Sundiata taught and worked as writer-in-residence (the first there) at the New School for Social Research in New York City. In 2001, he accompanied his former student Ani DiFranco on her "Rhythm and News" tour. His own performance pieces include *Udu,* about modern Mauritanian slavery; *Blessing the Boats,* his multimedia and multigenre tribute to the friend whose donated kidney saved his life; and *The 51st (dream) state,* a multicultural-jazz, multimedia, spoken-word piece responding to the 9/11/2001 events. He also appeared on HBO's *Def Po-*

etry series and on PBS's *The Language of Life* series. A taste of his lyricism may be found in "Shout Out": "Here's to what you forgot and who you forgot. / Here's to the unforgettable. / To the was you been to the is you am / To what's deep in deep to what's down in down / To the lost, and the blind, and the almost found" (quoted in Abrash, 2007). Abrash, a fan and colleague of his, noted that he ended his e-mails to her with the closing, "All of a sudden ... Sekou." This abrupt ending surely describes how his wife, Maurine Knighton, his daughter, Myisha Gomez, his stepdaughter, Aida Riddle, and his grandson, Amman, felt on his leaving them.

REFERENCES: *D. LoL. Wiki.* Abrash, Victoria. "Sekou Sundiata: 1948-2007." *American Theatre. 24.10* (Dec. 2007) p. 22. From *Literature Resource Center.* Bush, John, *All Music Guide,* in A. Gener, Randy. "New York City and Stanford, Calif.: Poems in the Key of Empire." *American Theatre. 23.4* (Apr. 2006) p. 23. From *Literature Resource Center.* Troupe, Quincy. "Remembering Andrew Hill and Sekou Sundiata." *Black Renaissance/Renaissance Noire. 7.3* (Fall 2007) p. 6. From *Literature Resource Center.* //www.poets.org/viewmedia.php/prmMID/580.

Survey Graphic
1921–1952
European-American-owned and -operated literary journal

Paul Kellogg, a European-American social-reform activist and social-work advocate, had been editing *Charities and the Commons* since 1907, under the auspices of a charitable organization. In 1912, Paul and his brother Arthur formed a separate entity, Survey Associates, with which they officially took over publishing the journal, as editor and business manager, respectively. They also changed the journal's name to *The Survey.* Anyone interested could become a member of Survey Associates by paying an annual membership fee of $10/year (or more was welcome), entitling them to a subscription to *The Survey* as well as the right to vote for members of *The Survey's* board of directors, among whom was social-reform activist Jane Addams.

In line with the emerging field of sociology, *The Survey* took a scientific approach to social reform, presenting statistical data on issues such as worker safety and prevention of occupational hazards, fair treatment of laborers, elimination of exploitative child labor, and employee hours and wages. It also addressed the Kelloggs' social issues, such as housing, prison reform, women's suffrage, discrimination against immigrants, and racial discrimination. Unfortunately, the highly data-driven materials were both challenging to read and unappealing to readers so that *The Survey* was inaccessible to the very people whom they wished to reach.

In 1921, the Kelloggs created a supplement to *The Survey, Survey Graphic,* which used photos and drawings as well as charts and graphs to present their information in a much more readable, accessible format than its companion *The Survey* (now known as *Survey Midmonthly*). Soon, the brothers published the two journals as separate entities, with *Survey Graphic* sent to readers on the first of each month and *Survey Midmonthly* two weeks later. Readers could choose to subscribe to just one or to both publications. Before the Great Depression, *Survey Graphic* sent out journals to about 25,000 paid subscribers, and during the Great Depression and the New Deal years, it boasted a few more subscribers.

Often, the Kelloggs devoted entire issues of the journal to key topics of the day. In the fall of 1924, Paul Kellogg asked scholar **Alain Locke** to guest-edit a special issue of *Survey Graphic* (Vol. 6, No. 6), to broaden the awareness of the journal's mostly European-American readership. The following March (1925), Locke's special issue, titled "Harlem: Mecca of the New Negro" (aka "the Harlem Number"), included not only nonfiction articles and essays, but also short fiction and poetry. Among the many noteworthy contributors were **Countee Cullen, W. E. B. Du Bois, Rudolph Fisher, Angelina Grimke, Langston Hughes**, Eunice Roberta Hunton (Carter), **Charles Spurgeon Johnson, James Weldon Johnson, Claude McKay, Kelly Miller, Joel Augustus Rogers, Arthur Schomburg, Anne Spencer, Jean Toomer**, and **Walter F. White**. See //etext.virginia.edu/harlem/ for a complete electronic edition of the entire journal, right down to images of the classified advertisements. In addition, a 1981 reprint version has been published by Black Classic Press.

The Harlem Number sold out its first printing of 30,000, and the Kelloggs printed a second run of 12,000 copies. European-American patrons Amy and **Joel Spingarn**, Albert C. Barnes, and broadcasting award namesake George Foster Peabody each bought hundreds of 50¢ copies and distributed these copies to African-American organizations and educational institutions. This special issue of *Survey Graphic* directly led to Locke's subsequent publication of his anthology, **The New Negro** (1925).

Years later, *Survey Graphic* published two other special issues devoted to topics of special interest to African Americans: *Color: The Unfinished Business of Democracy* (1942) and *Segregation: Color Patterns from the Past-Our Struggle to Wipe It Out* (1947). In 1948, financial problems dictated that *Survey Graphic* merge with *Survey Midmonthly*. Four years later, both Survey Associates and its journal went out of business (1952).

REFERENCES: Finnegan, Cara, "Social Welfare and Visual Politics: The Story of *Survey Graphic*," in //newdeal.feri.org/search_details. cfm?link=http://newdeal.feri.org/sg/essay02.htm, //newdeal.feri.org/ search_details.cfm?link=http://newdeal.feri.org/sg/essay03.htm, and //newdeal.feri.org/search_details.cfm?link=http://newdeal.feri.org/sg/e ssay04.htm. "Introduction," in //newdeal.feri.org/search_details.cfm? link=http://newdeal.feri.org/sg/index.htm. Kirschenbaum, Matthew G., and Catherine Tousignant, "Harlem: Mecca of the New Negro: A Hypermedia Edition of the March 1925 Survey Graphic Harlem Number." in //etext.virginia.edu/harlem/. //etext.virginia.edu/harlem/. //etext.virginia.edu/harlem/contents.html. Mellon, Michelle, in GEAAL. //en.wikipedia.org/wiki/Survey_Graphic. *See also* **anthologies of African-American literature, writers from 1920 to the early 1940s, during the New Negro era; Harlem Renaissance, literary and scholarly journals of the "New Negro" era; Locke, Alain**; and *New Negro, The*.

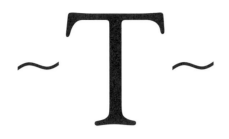

Tanner, Benjamin Tucker

12/25/1835–1/14/1923

Nonfiction—theology and ethnology, editorials, poems; cleric, theologian, editor, publisher

In addition to writing poems and journal articles, Tanner wrote several scholarly and theological books, including *Paul versus Pius Ninth* (1865), *An Apology for African Methodism* (1867), *The Negro's Origin, or Is He Cursed of God?* (1869), *The Outline of Our History and Government for African Methodist Churchmen* (1884), *Theological Lectures* (1894), *The Color Solomon: What?* (1896), *The Negro in Holy Writ* (1898), and *A Hint to Ministers, Especially Those of the African Methodist Episcopal Church* (1900). Tanner also edited publications of the African Methodist Episcopal (A.M.E.) Church and founded and edited the quarterly *A.M.E. Church Review*, the first African-American scholarly journal. With his wife, Sarah Miller, he had seven children, including painter Henry Ossawa Tanner; his daughter Mary's daughter was economist, attorney, and civil-rights activist Sadie Tanner (née) Mossell Alexander.

REFERENCES: *AANB. EA-99.* Connor, Kimberly Rae, in *COCAAL* and *OCAAL.*

FURTHER READING: Bailey, Julius H., in *GEAAL.*

Tarry, Ellen

9/26/1906–9/23/2008

Editorials and columns, children's fiction books, biographies, autobiography; journalist, educator, social worker

Tarry's writing career started with editorials and an African-American heritage column ("Negroes of Note") for the *Birmingham Truth* (1927–1929). After she moved to New York City, she was welcomed into a circle of jour-nalists and creative writers such as **Countee Cullen, Langston Hughes, James Weldon Johnson,** and **Claude McKay.** There, she continued to write, as in her outspo-ken essay, "Native Daughter: An Indictment of White America by a Colored Woman," discussing how U.S. racists shoved **Richard Wright** into the arms of godless communists (1940, republished in Lorraine Roses's *Harlem's Glory: Black Women Writing, 1900–1950,* 1996). At Harlem's Friendship House, Tarry started a story hour for children, and she soon began writing children's literature. She subsequently wrote *Janie Bell* (1940, illustrated by Myrtle Sheldon), *Herekiah Horton* (1942/1962, illustrated by Oliver Harrington), *My Dog Rinty* (1946/1964, with Marie Hall Ets; photographs by Alexander and Alexandra Alland), and *The Runaway Elephant* (1950, illustrated by Oliver Harrington), which depicted nonstereotyped African Americans and interracial friendships among children.

An adult convert to Catholicism, she also wrote biographies of notable fellow Catholics, including *Katherine Drexel: Friend of the Neglected* (1958), retitled *Saint Katherine Drexel: Friend of the Oppressed* (2000); *Martin de Porres, Saint of the New World* (1963), about a seventeenth-century South American; and *The Other Toussaint: A Modern Biography of Pierre Toussaint, A Post-Revolutionary Black* (1970/1981) and *Pierre Toussaint: Apostle of Old New York* (1998), about a pious enslaved Haitian brought to New York just after the Revolutionary War ended, who bought not only his own freedom but also that of others. In addition, she wrote a biography of *Young Jim: The Early Years of James Weldon Johnson* (1967) and her own autobiography, *The Third Door: The Autobiography of an American Negro Woman* (1955/1971; new edition, 1992, introduced by Nellie McKay). During her brief marriage, she had a daughter, Elizabeth Tarry Patton.

REFERENCES: *AANB. BAWPP. CAO-01. HR&B. Wiki.* Osborne, Elizabeth A., in *GEAAL.* Roberts, Janet M., in *OCAAL.* Amazon.com.

FURTHER READING: *EAAWW.*

Tate, Claudia

12/14/1946–7/29/2002

Literary criticism, biography, literary psychoanalysis; educator

A high-school honor student, Claudia Tate went on to major in English and American Literature, earning her A.B. at the University of Michigan (1968) and then her M.A. (1971) and her Ph.D. (1977) from Harvard University. After earning her doctorate, Tate became an associate professor of English at historically black Howard University in Washington, D.C. (1977–1989), then a professor of English at nearby George Washington University (1989–1997), and then at Princeton University in New Jersey (1997–2002). In addition, she was awarded at least four fellowships, and she was a Distinguished Visiting Scholar at the University of Delaware (1986) and at Rutgers University (1987).

Even before she completed her doctorate, Tate was writing freelance, and during her career, she wrote both reviews of specific books and broader essays of literary criticism on particular writers. Her book reviews and literary criticism, articles and essays were published in scholarly journals, in newspapers, in popular magazines, and in book-review resources. She also served on the advisory editorial boards of *African American Review, American Literature, American Quarterly,* and *SIGNS: Journal of Women in Culture and Society.* She was also a member of the American Studies Association, the College Language Association, and the Modern Language Association of America, and she chaired the board of directors of the Association for the Psychoanalysis of Culture and Society.

Tate first came to national prominence with her *Black Women Writers at Work* (*BWWW,* 1983), the research for which was partly funded by a grant from the National Endowment for the Humanities (1979). For *BWWW,* Tate interviewed 14 prominent African-American writers, edited the interviews, and introduced each author. In Tate's next book, *Domestic Allegories of Political Desire: The Black Heroine's Text at the Turn of the Century* (1992), she turned her critical eye to the literature of African-American authors whose writings were disregarded, ignored, or denigrated for their emphasis on marriage, family, and domesticity.

In addition to her authored books, Tate edited five books offering readers insight into the literature of five African-American authors: *The Works of **Katherine Davis Chapman Tillman*** (1991), ***Richard Wright**: Critical Perspectives Past and Present* (1993), *Conversations with **Toni Morrison*** (1994), **W. E. B. Du Bois**'s *Dark Princess: A Romance* (1995), and *Selected Works of Georgia Douglas Johnson Camp* (1997). Her final book was *Psychoanalysis and Black Novels: Desire and the Protocols of Race* (1998), in which she critically examined five novels written by African-American authors during the 1940s and 1950s that feature protagonists who are not African American. At the time of her death, she was said to be working on a short-story collection, two longer works of fiction, critical essays on **Ralph Ellison** and **Gwendolyn Brooks**, a major work on African-American women as portrayed in film, and a history of the African-American literary canon.

REFERENCES: *CAO-03. Wiki.* //en.wikipedia.org/wiki/American_ Quarterly. //en.wikipedia.org/wiki/Signs_(journal). Painter, Nell Irvin, "Claudia Tate: In Memoriam—Obituary." *African American Review.* 36.4 (Winter, 2002), p. 705. Literature Resources from Gale; also in //findarticles.com/p/articles/mi_m2838/is_4_36/ai_97515905. ____. "Introduction: Claudia Tate and the Protocols of Black Literature and Scholarship." *The Journal of African American History.* 88.1 (Winter 2003), p. 60. Literature Resources from Gale. Amazon.com.

FURTHER READING: *EAAWW.*

Tate, Eleanora E.
4/16/1948–
Juvenile literature, poems, short fiction, anthologies; journalist, storyteller, educator

Tate's books for juveniles include *Just an Overnight Guest* (1980/1997), adapted to television and aired on Public Broadcasting System's *Wonderworks* series; and its sequel, *Front Porch Stories at the One-Room School* (1992), designated Pick of the Lists by the American Booksellers Association (ABA). She also wrote three juvenile novels set in Gumbo Grove: *The Secret of Gumbo Grove* (1987), honored as Parents' Choice Award winner and California Young Reader Medal nominee, also available in audio format; and *Thank You, Dr. **Martin Luther King, Jr.**!* (1990), named a Notable Children's Trade Book in the Field of Social Studies by the National Council for the Social Studies (NCSS) and the Children's Book Council (CBC), chosen as Children's Book of the Year by the Child Study Children's Book Committee, and available in audio format; and *Blessing in Disguise* (1995), also designated Pick of the Lists by the ABA. In keeping with her appreciation of folktales, she wrote *Retold African Myths* (1993) and *Don't Split the Pole: Tales of Down-home Folk Wisdom* (1997).

Tate's historical fiction for juveniles includes an American Girl History Mystery, *The Minstrel's Melody* (2001), set in early 1900s Missouri, and designated a Notable Children's Trade Book in the Field of Social Studies; and *Celeste's Harlem Renaissance* (2007/2009), given the American Association of University Women North Carolina Book Award for Juvenile Literature, and the International Reading Association Teachers' Choice Award. Her nonfiction for young readers includes *African American Musicians* (2000) and *To Be Free* (2003). In addition, her stories, poems, and essays have appeared in numerous anthologies (e.g., **Rosa Guy**'s *Children of Longing,* 1970; **Jim Haskins**'s *Black Stars of the Harlem Renaissance,* 2002) and periodicals (e.g., *African American Review, American Girl, Obsidian III, Washington Post*). Above and beyond the aforementioned honors, she garnered a Bread Loaf Writers Conference fellowship (1981); received a **Zora Neale Hurston** Award from the National Association of Black Storytellers (1999, shared with **John Hope Franklin**); and earned numerous other honors. She also edited *Wanjiru: A Collection of Blackwomanworth* (1976, privately printed). With her husband Zack E.

Hamlett III, she edited the poetry anthology *Eclipsed* (1975, privately printed), and they have a daughter, Gretchen. Tate has been quoted as saying, "Children's childhoods can be happy if they can learn that they can do anything they set their minds to, if they try" (quoted in CAO-08).

REFERENCES: *BAWPP. CAO-08.* Hinton-Johnson, KaaVonia, in *GEAAL.* Johnson-Feelings, Dianne, in *COCAAL* and *OCAAL.* Amazon.com.

FURTHER READING: Knuth, Carole Brown. "African-American Children and the Case for Community: Eleanora Tate's South Carolina Trilogy." *African American Review.* 32.1 (Spring 1998) p. 85. From *Literature Resource Center.* Tate, Eleanora E. "Tracing the Trilogy." *African American Review.* 32.1 (Spring 1998) p.77. From *Literature Resource Center.*

Taylor, Mildred (Delois)
9/13/1943–
Juvenile novels; educator, editor

When Mildred was just a few months old, her father had to flee from their home in Jackson, Mississippi, to avoid a violent confrontation with a white man. A few months later, his family joined him in Toledo, Ohio. Although her father left the South, he never left behind the rhythms and idioms of rural African-American Southern speech, the lifestyles and folkways of African-American Southern culture, and the Southern storytelling craft. Young Mildred sat at his knee and listened—and learned.

An excellent student (and editor of her high-school newspaper), Mildred questioned the history taught in her textbooks, noting the distinct absence of African Americans. Perhaps, someday, she could write books that more accurately reflected American history. After earning a bachelor's in education (1965) at the University of Toledo, she joined the Peace Corps, spending two years in Ethiopia teaching English and history. After her return, she earned her master's degree and spent several years teaching, but she eventually realized that if she was to write, she would have to get a less demanding job. In 1971, she resigned, moved to Los Angeles, and did proofreading and editing while spending her free time writing. In 1972, she married Errol Zeal-Daly, with whom she has a child, P. Lauren, but whom she divorced in 1975.

After a few unsuccessful publishing attempts, Taylor reworked a story for a writing contest sponsored by the Council on Interracial Books for Children. That story became Taylor's novella, *Song of the Trees*, published in 1975. This book introduces readers to the Logan family, who lived through slavery, Reconstruction, and the Jim Crow South. Her book's simple story, vividly appealing characters, and poetically authentic speech were critically acclaimed (cited as *The New York Times* Outstand-

ing Book of the Year and a Jane Addams Honor book). Taylor's protagonist, Cassie Logan, is less like Mildred (a quiet, bookish girl) and more like Mildred's sister and her aunt—spirited adventurers.

Taylor's second book about the Logans was *Roll of Thunder, Hear My Cry* (1976), often cited as a contemporary classic of children's literature, having won a Newbery Medal (the second book by an African American to do so), as well as a Notable Book Citation from the American Library Association 1976, National Book Award nomination, an Honor Book citation from *Boston Globe/Horn Book*, a Jane Addams Honor citation, and a Buxtehuder Bulle Award (in 1985). The book was also adapted to create a three-part television miniseries broadcasted on ABC (1978). The next of the Logan family stories was *Let the Circle Be Unbroken* (1981), nominated for an American Book Award, given a **Coretta Scott King** Author Award, and cited as Outstanding Book of the Year by *The New York Times* and as a Jane Addams Honor book. Other books in the Logan saga include *The Friendship* (1987), given a *Boston Globe/Horn Book* Fiction Award and a Coretta Scott King Author Award; *Mississippi Bridge* (1990), told from the viewpoint of one of the white characters in the Logan story; *The Road to Memphis* (1990), which takes the Logan children to the brink of adulthood, and which won the Coretta Scott King Author Award; *The Well: David's Story* (1995), which goes back in time to the childhood of Cassie's father, David, and which won a Jason Award; and *The Land* (2001), the Scott O'Dell Historical Fiction and Coretta Scott King Author Award–winning book that goes even farther back in time to the Reconstruction era, telling the story of Cassie's great-grandfather, whose father was a European-American planter, and whose a mother was a former slave of Native-American and African-American descent. Taylor is writing an additional Logan family book, tentatively titled *Logan*. In an interview with Hazel Rochman (2001), she said, "The last book will take the Logan children, all grown up, through the end of World War II, the years following, and then the beginning of the civil rights movement. For the first time, I'll have to weave a part of my own life into the story."

Taylor also wrote her semiautobiographical *The Gold Cadillac* (1987), primarily set in 1950s Toledo, cited as a Notable Book by *The New York Times*. In these works, Taylor presents a view of American history that complements the flawed, incomplete versions of history she was taught as a young girl. In 1988, the Children's Interracial Book Council honored Taylor "for a body of work that has examined significant social issues and presented them in outstanding books for young readers." In 1997, she won the ALAN Award for her significant contribution to young adult literature from the National Council of Teachers of English. In the new millennium, Mississippi's

Governor Haley Barbour declared April 2 "Mildred D. Taylor Day." In 2003, Taylor became the first recipient of the biennial NSK Neustadt Prize for Children's Literature, "intended to enhance the quality of children's literature by promoting writing that contributes to the quality of their lives" (quoted from //www.ou.edu/worldlit/ NSK/NSK.htm). "NSK" stands for Nancy, Susan, and Kathy, the children of Walter and Dolores Neustadt, who sponsor the $25,000 prize, in concert with the journal *World Literature Today*.

In all of her books, Taylor offers first-person narratives frankly addressing issues of racist segregation, race-based beatings and lynchings, and racial injustice. Despite the wishes of some critics, Taylor's dialogue accurately reflects the raw racism evidenced during those times, including the all-too-meaningful uses of the word "nigger." In response to critics who question her candor in books for young readers, she has answered, "Just as I have had to be honest with myself in the telling of all my stories, I realized that I also must be true to the feelings of the people about whom I write, and I must be true to the stories told. . . . When there was humor, my family passed it on. When there was tragedy, they passed it on. When the words hurt, they passed them on. My stories will not be 'politically correct,' so there are those who will be offended by them, but as we all know, racism is offensive. It is not polite, and it is full of pain" (from her 2003 NSK Neustadt Prize acceptance speech; see Taylor, 2004). Far from being grim stories, however, the Logan family rises to confront these issues with dignity, strength, perseverance, determination, and hope. Also, any stories containing spunky Cassie's humor and warmth will leave readers feeling good.

REFERENCES: *AANB. B. CAO-05. CBC. E-95. MAAL. Wiki. WYA-2000*, pp. 273–282, Vol. 3. Bader, Philip, "Mildred D. Taylor," Salem Press for EBSCO Publishing, July 2003, in //0-web.ebscohost. com.dbpcosdcsgt.co.san-diego.ca.us/novelist/detail?vid=47&hid=8& sid=02bf6a41-8618-414c-abf5-13f22fd219a5%40sessionmgr7&bdata =JnNpdGU%2bm92ZWxpc3QtbGl2ZZQ%3d%3d. Con Davis-Undiano, Robert. "Mildred D. Taylor and the Art of Making a Difference." *World Literature Today* 78.2 (May-August 2004) p. 11. From *Literature Resource Center*. Conyers, James L. 2005. *Afrocentric Traditions*. Transaction Publishers, in //books.google.com/books?id=ibsI6DK7jdg C&pg=PA128&lpg=PA128&dq=%22effie+t.+battle%22&source =web&ots=21l8N5joeR&sig=nWlt1pZF15b40WUVgVqqMkWIxM M&hl=en&sa=X&oi=book_result&resnum=21&ct=result. Harde, Roxanne, in *GEAAL*. Harper, Mary Turner, in *OCWW*. Johnson, Dianne. "A Tribute to Mildred D. Taylor." *World Literature Today*. 78.2 (May-August 2004) p. 4. From *Literature Resource Center*. "Mildred D. Taylor." *World Literature Today*. 78.2 (May-August 2004) p. 3. From *Literature Resource Center*. Johnson, Virginia, "Mildred Taylor's Stories from the Heart," //www.kidspoint.org/columns2.asp?column_id=436 &column_type=author. Kirk, Susanne Porter, in *WYA-1997-3*. Lesinski, Jeanne M., in *BB*. Rochman, Hazel. "The Booklist Interview: Mildred Taylor." *Booklist*. 98.2 (Sept. 15, 2001) p. 221. From *Literature Resource Center*. Taylor, Mildred D. "My Life as a Writer." *World Literature Today*. 78.2 (May-August 2004) p. 7. From *Literature*

Resource Center. Warren, Nagueyalti, in *COCAAL* and *OCAAL*. Wright, David A., in *AWC-1960–86*. //falcon.jmu.edu/~ramseyil/ taylor.htm. //library.msstate.edu/special_interest/Mississippi_African-American_Authors.asp. //us.penguingroup.com/nf/Author/Author Page/0,,0_1000031974,00.html. //www.ala.org/ala/emiert/corettascott kingbookaward/cskpastwinners/alphabeticallist/cskalphabetical.cfm#a u. //www.hickorygov.com/library/bibs/aaf.htm, African American Children's Fiction. //www.library.uiuc.edu/blog/esslchildlit/archives/ 2008/02/african_america.html. //www.ou.edu/worldlit/NSK/Neustadt Family.htm. //www.ou.edu/worldlit/NSK/NSK.htm Amazon.com.

FURTHER READING: *EAAWW*. Bosmajian, Hamida. "Mildred Taylor's Story of Cassie Logan: A Search for Law and Justice in a Racist Society." *Children's Literature: Annual of the Modern Language Association* 24 (1996): pp. 141–160. Rpt. in Scot Peacock (Ed.) (2004), *Children's Literature Review* (Vol. 90). Detroit: Gale. From *Literature Resource Center*. Brown, Jennifer M. "Stories Behind the Book." *Publishers Weekly*. 248.43 (Oct. 22, 2001) p. 24. From *Literature Resource Center*. Taylor, Mildred. "The Friendship." *Horn Book Magazine* 65.2 (Mar. 1989): pp. 179–182. Rpt. in Scot Peacock (Ed.) (2004), *Children's Literature Review* (Vol. 90). Detroit: Gale. From *Literature Resource Center*.

Taylor, Susan L.
1/23/1946–

Memoirs, editorials, columns; former actor and cosmetologist, editor, executive

In 1970, Taylor was the newly divorced mother of Shana-Nequai with a part-time job at *Essence* magazine. By 1980, she was *Essence*'s editor-in-chief. In less than a decade after she took the helm, *Essence* was being circulated to 800,000 purchasers and perhaps 4 million readers in all. In addition to writing her regular "In the Spirit" column, she has published several collections of her columns, including *Lessons in Living* (1995) and *All About Love: Favorite Selections from* In the Spirit *on Living Fearlessly* (2008). She has said of herself, "I come by my strong opinions naturally: In that respect I am my mother's child. . . . It is not for nothing that black women have acquired a reputation for speaking out. Historically, our words have been our only weapons, and our voices often our only defense" (quoted in *BB*). Her nationally best-selling memoir *In the Spirit: The Inspirational Writings of Susan L. Taylor* (1993), tells Taylor's personal story of faith, determination, and perseverance. She also cowrote a set of biographies, *Essence: 50 of the Most Inspiring African-Americans* (2006, with Patricia M. Hinds). With her husband, Khephra Burns, she wove together a series of inspirational writings from diverse spiritual traditions, *Confirmation: The Spiritual Wisdom That Has Shaped Our Lives* (1996).

REFERENCES: *AANB. PGAA*. Patti, Nicholas, in *BB*. Amazon.com.

Taylor, Susie (née Baker King)
8/6/1848–1912
Autobiography/memoir; nurse, educator, domestic servant

Taylor's *A Black Woman's Civil War Memoirs: Reminiscences of My Life in Camp with the 33rd United States Colored Troops, Late 1st S. C. Volunteers* (1902, republished 1988, ed. Patricia W. Romero and Willie Lee Rose) describes her experiences teaching illiterate freed slaves on Union Army–controlled St. Catherine Island, off the South Carolina coast, then (after marrying Sergeant Edward King) as a laundress and a nurse (working with Clara Barton) for the Union Army. Her book is the only known personal account of the Civil War (and Reconstruction) written by an African-American woman. A few months before the birth of their first child, Edward died in 1866. In 1879, she married former Union soldier Russell Taylor. In the 1890s, after caring for her dying son, she wrote her *Reminiscences.*

REFERENCES: *B. EA-99. SEW. Wiki.* Moody, Joycelyn, in *COCAAL* and *OCAAL.* Romero, Patricia W., in *BWA:AHE.* Wolf, Gillian, in *BB.* //www.georgiaencyclopedia.org/nge/Article.jsp?id=h-1097.

FURTHER READING: Bolden, Tonya, in //digital.nypl.org/schomburg/writers_aa19/bio2.html. Dagbovie, Pero Gaglo. "Black Women Historians from the Late 19th Century to the Dawning of the Civil Rights Movement." *The Journal of African American History.* 89.3 (Summer 2004) p. 241. From *Literature Resource Center.* Moody, Joycelyn K., with the assistance of Heidi L. M. Jacobs editorial assistant, and Jennifer Putzi editorial assistant, in *AWPW:1870–1920.* Tanter, Marcy L., in *GEAAL.* //digital.library.upenn.edu/women/_generate/AFRICAN%20AMERICAN.html. *See also EAAWW.*

Terrell, Mary Eliza (née Church)
9/23/1863–7/24/1954
Autobiography, articles, lectures; journalist, lecturer

Mary's father, a former slave, was perhaps the first African-American millionaire in the South, so the Churches ensured that their daughter received an outstanding education by sending her to Northern schools. In 1884, she earned her baccalaureate at Oberlin College, one of the first three African-American women to do so. Despite Oberlin's liberal reputation, Church still felt the sting of racism. For instance, when Matthew Arnold observed her reciting verses in Greek, he showed surprise that she could do so: He had heard that African tongues were incapable of uttering Greek words.

After Mary graduated, despite her father's objections, she taught at Ohio's Wilberforce University and then in a segregated Washington, D.C., high school for African Americans. After a year of teaching, however, she agreed to a two-year tour of Europe, where she mastered French, Italian, and German. On returning to America, she became one of the first African-American women to receive a graduate degree, earning her master's degree (1888) from Oberlin. Three years later, she married Robert Terrell, a lawyer who later became the first African-American municipal-court judge in the District of Columbia. The Terrells had four children, only one of whom survived to adulthood—their daughter Phyllis, named after **Phillis Wheatley**.

In 1890, Terrell embarked on a 30-year public-speaking career. In her lectures and her writings, she advocated for women's rights, women's suffrage, African-American voting rights, civil rights, racial and civil justice, world peace, educational reform, and even kindergartens and child-care centers for the children of African-American working mothers. She also opposed lynching, racial segregation, racial discrimination in employment and schooling, unfair prosecution, and injustice and oppression in any form.

Although Terrell wrote numerous articles, her major literary contribution was her autobiography, *A Colored Woman in a White World* (1940), which reflected on racial and social justice, African-American history and life experiences, and notable persons in whom she was interested (e.g., **Frederick Douglass**, Phillis Wheatley, and **George Washington Carver**). A lifelong learner, Terrell received doctor of letters degrees from Oberlin, Wilberforce, and Howard Universities during the 1940s. A well-respected scholar, she fought for three years to force the American Association of University Women (AAUW) to accept her and other nonwhite women as members; she was admitted in 1949, when she was in her mid-eighties.

Terrell also participated actively in various political, social, and cultural organizations, and she was the first African-American woman appointed to a school board. Terrell also reached out globally, representing numerous American delegations at conventions in Germany, Switzerland, and England (addressing those gatherings in fluent German, French, and English). At ages 89 and 90, Terrell leaned on her cane as she led sit-ins, pickets, and boycotts to desegregate lunch counters and restaurants in our nation's capital. After a year of such actions, several department stores relented and desegregated their lunchrooms, but it took her lawsuit, culminating in a 1953 U.S. Supreme Court case, to desegregate the remaining eateries.

REFERENCES: *1TESK. BAAW. BF:2000. EB-98. G-95. PGAA.* Eckard, Paula Gallant, in *OCAAL.*

FURTHER READING: *AANB. B. HR&B,* pp. 310–313. *LE. W. Wiki.* Johnson, Anne Janette, in *BB.* Nyangomi, Betty W., in *GEAAL.*

Terry (married name: Prince), Lucy
c. 1730–8/?/1821
Poems, stories; enslaved worker, homemaker

Although she was born free in West Africa, Lucy was just an infant when she was captured—too young to remember a time before her enslavement. She spent her first few years in Rhode Island, then at age 5, she was sold away to Massachusetts. In 1746, when she was about 16 years old, she wrote "Bars Fight," the first poem known to have been penned by a female African American. ("Bars Fight" wasn't actually published until 1855, so the first published poetry by an African American was by **Jupiter Hammon**, and the first published poetry by an African-American woman was by **Phillis Wheatley**.) You might be thinking that Terry was writing about a tavern brawl, but actually, the "Bars" to which she was referring was a patch of open meadow land by that name, and the "Fight" she was describing was an engagement resulting when some Native Americans (encouraged by French colonists) ambushed some English colonists.

With such an auspicious start in her midteens, Terry became renowned for her storytelling over the years. Fortunately for her, her life also provided quite a story to tell. In 1756, Justice of the Peace Ephraim Williams (later the founder of Williams College in Williamstown, Massachusetts) married her to Abijah Prince, from Curaçao, who was almost 25 years older than she. By the time they wedded, Prince was able to buy Lucy out of bondage and owned quite a bit of land. Their union proved fruitful—yielding six children, including one who later served in the Revolutionary War. Feisty to the end, even after her beloved Prince died, Lucy was always ready to take up a challenge and to fight for what she believed was right.

REFERENCES: *BAAW.* —Tonya Bolden

FURTHER READING: *AANB. BAWPP. MWEL. W. Wiki.* Andrews, William L., in *COCAAL.* Beebe, Ann, in *GEAAL. See also EAAWW.* Kubitschek, Missy Dehn. "Written by Herself: Literary Production by African American Women, 1746-1892." *The Mississippi Quarterly.* 50.1 (Winter 1996) p. 175. From *Literature Resource Center.*

Third World Press (TWP)
1967–

Established in 1967, TWP is one of the oldest existing African-American publishing houses in the United States. It publishes fiction, history, essays, poetry, drama, and both young adult and children's literature. TWP's purpose statement is to "publish literature that contributes to the positive development of people of African descent." During the 1990s, TWP found a profitable niche for itself by publishing black authors who found it difficult to gain acceptance and publication by white publishers, due to the controversial nature of their books. By publishing for this niche market, TWP has become financially stable and has remained black-owned.

REFERENCES: *EAACH* (Vol. 5). —Lisa Bahlinger

Thomas, Joyce Carol
5/25/1938–
Poems, novels, plays, juvenile literature, anthologies; educator

While raising her first three children and working as a telephone operator, Joyce Carol Thomas took college courses at night, earning her B.A. in Spanish (1966, San Jose State University, minoring in French) and her master's degree in education (1967, Stanford University). Then she really got busy. She has taught Spanish and French languages in California public schools and taught creative writing, African-American studies, and literature at several colleges in California (San Jose State University; Contra Costa College, in San Pablo; St. Mary's College, in Moraga; the University of Santa Cruz) and across the nation (Purdue University and University of Tennessee at Knoxville). She has lectured, offered seminars, and presented workshops on creative writing in the United States, Nigeria, and Haiti; and she has been a commissioner at Berkeley Civic Arts and a visiting scholar at Stanford's Center for Research on Women.

And then, of course, she writes. For starters, she has contributed works to numerous periodicals, such as the **Black Scholar** and *Calafia,* and she edited *Ambrosia,* an African-American feminist magazine published on the West Coast. Her lyrical poems have also been collected in *Bittersweet* (1973), *Crystal Breezes: Poems* (1974), *Blessing: Poems* (1975), and *Inside the Rainbow: Poems* (1982, including both new and earlier poems). In addition, *A Mother's Heart, a Daughter's Love: Poems for Us to Share* (2001) offers 25 poems pairing a mother and a daughter's harmonizing voices.

Thomas has also written five plays, all of which have been produced in northern California: *A Song in the Sky* (1976), *Look! What a Wonder!* (1976), *Magnolia* (1977), *Gospel Roots* (1981), and *I Have Heard of a Land* (1989). She developed her sixth play, *When the Nightingale Sings* (1991), into a novel. In fact, many readers know Taylor solely as a novelist. Her first novel, *Marked by Fire* (1982; reprinted 1999) won the National Book Award and the Before Columbus Foundation American Book Award, and was cited as a best book by the American Library Association (ALA) and an outstanding book by *The New York Times* (NYT). *Bright Shadow* (1983), her sequel to *Fire,* was named a **Coretta Scott King** Honor Book. Taylor's subsequent novels include *The Golden Pasture* (1986), an American Booksellers "Pick of the Lists"; *Water Girl* (1986), *Journey* (1988), and *When the Nightingale Sings* (1992). Her next novel, *House of Light* (2001), which has been adapted to audio format, continues the story of *Fire* and *Shadow,* as does *Healer* (2007). Usually classified as novels for young adults, her books also address themes and issues of interest to more mature adults.

She also often creates her happy endings via mystical means.

Thomas has also edited anthologies for young folks. Her multicultural anthology *A Gathering of Flowers: Stories about Being Young in America* (1992) won a Chancellor's Award for Research and Creativity from the University of Tennessee and was named a Selected Title for Children and Young Adults by the National Conference of Christians and Jews. Reflecting back on an earlier time, Thomas edited *Linda Brown, You Are Not Alone; the Brown V. Board of Education Decision* (2003, illustrated by Curtis James), including the recollections of 10 contemporary writers who were young at the time of this landmark decision. For parents and their infants, she edited *Hush Songs: African-American Lullabies* (2000, illustrated by Brenda Joysmith), which offers not only traditional lullabies but also contemporary ones, including three original lullabies by Thomas.

Thomas has also written numerous other books for younger readers. For older infants and toddlers, she has written three board books: *You Are My Perfect Baby* (1999, illustrated by Nneka Bennett), *Angel's Lullaby* (2001, illustrated by Pamela Johnson), and *Joy!* (2001, illustrated by Pamela Johnson). Preschoolers and other very young readers enjoy her lovingly written verse picture books, such as *Brown Honey in Broomwheat Tea* (1993/1996, illustrated by Floyd Cooper), named a Coretta Scott King Honor Book, a New York Public Library (NYPL) top 100 Children's Book, and a Notable Children's Book by the National Council of Teachers of English (NCTE). Her other verse picture books include *Gingerbread Days: Poems* (1997, illustrated by Floyd Cooper), which earned a *People* magazine Celebrated Storyteller Award, and *Cherish Me* (1998, illustrated by Nneka Bennett). For elementary-school students, she wrote *Crowning Glory: Poems* (1999), a collection celebrating African-American hair; *The Blacker the Berry: Poems* (2008, illustrated by Floyd Cooper), rejoicing in all shades of black; and *Shouting!* (2007, illustrated by Annie Lee), exuberantly reveling in worship and faith; as well as her narrative poem *I Have Heard of a Land* (1999, illustrated by Floyd Cooper), about African-American pioneers, chosen for an International Reading Association (IRA) Teacher's Choice Award and named an ALA Notable Children's Book, a Notable Children's Trade Book in Social Studies, and a Coretta Scott King Illustrator Honor Book.

Throughout her works, Taylor shows her appreciation of African-American culture, and many of her books have adapted traditional folktales, building on research and story gathering done by anthropologist and storyteller **Zora Neale Hurston**. For elementary-school readers, she has adapted many of these tales to create the books *Bottle Up and Go: The Illustrated Zora Neale Hurston* (1996, illustrated by Bob Callahan), *The Bowlegged Rooster: And Other Tales That Signify* (2000, illustrated by Holly Berry), *The Skull Talks Back: And Other Haunting Tales* (2004, illustrated by Leonard Jenkins), *What's the Hurry, Fox?: And Other Animal Stories* (2004, illustrated by Bryan Collier), *The Six Fools* (2006, illustrated by Ann Tanksley), and *The Three Witches* (2006, illustrated by **Faith Ringgold**). Thomas also offered her own spin on a European fairy tale with *The Gospel Cinderella* (2004, illustrated by David Diaz).

All of Taylor's writings highlight the importance of children and their families within a community context. She knows whereof she speaks; by the time she published her first novel, she was the single mother of four: Monica (now Pecot), Gregory Withers, and Michael Withers, and Roy T. Thomas, III.

REFERENCES: *CAO-05. Wiki. WYA-2000*, pp. 293–301, Vol. 3. Bader, Philip, "Joyce Carol Thomas," July 2003, Salem Press for EBSCO Publishing, //0-web.ebscohost.dbpcosdcsgt.co.san-diego.ca.us/novelist/detail?vid=61&hid=8&sid=02bf6a41-8618-414c-abf5-13f22fd219a5%40sessionmgr7&bdata=JnNpdGU9bm92ZWxpc3Qtb Gl2ZQ%3d%3d. Cook, Leslie S. in *WYA-1997-3*. Duke-Sylvester, Jennifer, in //www.lib.utk.edu/refs/tnauthors/authors/thomas-j.html. Harper, Mary Turner, in *OCWW*. Henderson, Darwin L., and Anthony L. Manna. "Evoking the 'Holy and the Horrible': Conversations with Joyce Carol Thomas." *African American Review*. 32.1 (Spring 1998) p. 139. From *Literature Resource Center*. Hinton-Johnson, KaaVonia, in *GEAAL*. McKinney, Caroline S., in *T-CYAW*. Toombs, Charles P., in *AAFW-55–84*, in *COCAAL* and *OCAAL*. //www.amazon.com, 7/1999, 4/2009. //www.childrenslitera turenetwork.org/aifolder/aipages/ai_t/thomjc.html.

FURTHER READING: *EAAWW*.

Thomas, Lorenzo
8/31/1944–7/4/2005

Poems, criticism, anthologies, translation, essays; librarian, editor, correspondent, educator

Lorenzo Thomas was born in Panama, but he and his parents immigrated into the United States a few years later (1948). Because Lorenzo was not a native English speaker, he decided to read and write English as much as possible. In 1962, when Lorenzo Thomas was still in his teens, he enrolled in Queens College, now part of the City University of New York, and he found his way to the **Umbra Workshop**, where he met with fellow writers each week. These writers went on to write dozens of published volumes of prose and poetry, as well as numerous produced plays. The Umbra Workshop also contributed to the **Black Arts Movement** of the 1960s. After the workshop fell apart, Thomas continued at Queens College, earning his B.A. (1967), then going on to do graduate study at New York City's Pratt Institute, where he was also an assistant reference librarian (1967–1968).

In 1968, at the height of the Vietnam War, Thomas served in the U.S. Naval Reserve (1968–1972) and did a tour in Vietnam (1971). After returning from his service, he worked for a while as a librarian at Pace College in New York City (1972), then he moved to Houston's Texas Southern University, where he was a writer-in-residence (1973). While there, he helped edit the school's literary journal *Roots*. After completing his residency, he stayed on in Houston, conducting creative-writing workshops at the then-new community-based Black Arts Center (1974–1976). Eventually, the brief writing residency became a lifetime residency in Houston. He became a professor of English, teaching creative writing and American literature at the University of Houston (1984–2005), and one of the first African Americans to work in the Poetry-in-the-Schools program in Texas, as well as Arkansas, Florida, Georgia, New York, and Oklahoma. Thomas's *Blues Music in Arkansas* (1982, cowritten with Louis Guida and Cheryl Cohen) grew out of his experiences with the schools programs.

Thomas also maintained a national presence, as a correspondent for Chicago's bimonthly *Living Blues* (1976–2005) and as a freelance writer of poems published widely in national journals. His published poetry included broadsides and pamphlet poems, such as *A Visible Island* (1967), *Fit Music: California Songs, 1970* (1972), his book-length poem *Dracula* (1973), *Framing the Sunrise* (1975), *Sound Science* (1978; later the title poem of his 1992 collection), *Hiccups* (1975), and *Hoo-doo 6 1/2* (1978, with Adesanya Alakoye and **Ahmos Zu-Bolton**). In 1979, Thomas published his first poetry collection, *Chances Are Few* (1979; expanded 2nd ed., 2003), closely followed by *The Bathers* (1981), which included some of his earlier individually published poems, as well as his earlier unpublished poetry. A year after *Chances Are Few* was reissued, Thomas published his chapbook *Time Step: 5 Poems, 4 Seasons* (2004) and his long-awaited collection *Dancing on Main Street: Poems* (2004), expressing his poetic take on his lifetime of experiences.

In addition to his individual publications, his work has appeared in numerous anthologies (e.g., *FURIOUS FLOWER: African American Poetry, 1960-1995. A "Facilitator Guide" to the Video Series*, 1994). Thomas also edited two poetry anthologies, *Ankh: Getting It Together* (1974) and *I Luv It!: A Selection of Poems by Children in Grade 4-6* (1977). In addition, Thomas was an advisory editor of the literary journal *Nimrod* and a contributing editor of *Black Focus*, and he contributed to several periodicals.

Along with his poetry, Thomas published literary and music criticism for both scholarly and popular audiences. His prose works include an anthology he edited, *Sing the Sun Up: Creative Writing Ideas from African American Literature* (1998). Two years later, he published *Extraordinary Measures: Afrocentric Modernism and Twentieth-Century*

American Poetry (2000). After his death, Aldon Lynn Nielsen edited a final essay collection that Thomas had been compiling, *Don't Deny My Name: Words and Music and the Black Intellectual Tradition* (2008). Thomas is also credited with helping to translate poetry in *Tho Tu Viet-Nam*. He also cowrote several books, including *DiverseWorks Artspace: 1983–93* (1993, with Elizabeth McBride), *There Are Witnesses* (1996, written in German, with Thomas et al.), and *If the Stones Could Speak* (1998, with Ann Trask, Glen K. Merrill, Paul Kittelson). He also participated in some video productions, including *The Strange Demise of Jim Crow* (1997, 1998), *Color: A Sampling of Contemporary African American Writers* (1994), and *New Forms, New Functions: An Expert Roundtable Discussion of Prominent American Poets Asking, Do Historical Contexts Influence a Poet's Immediate Needs of Expression?* (1988).

For his work, Thomas was awarded the Dwight Durling Prize in poetry (1963), two Poets Foundation awards (1966, 1974), a Committee on Poetry grant (1973), a Lucille Medwick Award (1974), a National Endowment for the Arts Creative Writing Fellowship (1983), and a Houston Festival Foundation Arts Award (1984).

REFERENCES: *BAWPP. CAO-06. Wiki.* Dent, Tom, in *AAP-55–85.* Harter, Christopher, in *AANB.* Poulos, Jennifer H., in *COCAAL.* //en.wikipedia.org/wiki/Living_Blues. //www.worldcat.org/ identities/lccn-n79-85301. //www.aaregistry.com/sources.php. //www.newsreel.org/guides/furious.htm. //www.worldcat.org/ search?q=no:173303903. Amazon.com.

FURTHER READING: Lipkin, Elline, in *GEAAL.*

Thomas, Piri (né Juan Pedro Tomás)
9/30/1928–

Autobiographies, plays, young-adult book, short stories, spoken word—lectures, documentary film; prison counselor and rehabilitation worker, educator

Thomas's autobiographies include *Down These Mean Streets* (1967), a critically acclaimed best-seller; *Saviour, Saviour, Hold My Hand* (1972); and *Seven Long Times* (1974), all of which reflect his Afro–Puerto Rican roots and the Nuyorican Movement. Although he started writing his first autobiography in 1952, while in prison for attempted armed robbery (1950–1956), he has since done volunteer work in prisons and in drug-rehabilitation programs, and he has offered lectures and workshops across the world. "I do that part as my dues, because I promised when I was in prison that whenever I got out alive I'd do my very best to help out" (in McGill, 2000).

About his first book, Thomas later recalled, "when I was writing the book I did not realize that I was going back in time to see the sees and do the dos and hear the hears and feel the feelings over and over again seven times stronger" (in Greenberg, 2001). "I was bursting with all of that rage that was in me. The only way to get at it was to put it onto a paper" (in McGill, 2000). What may have been his salvation, however, was that "There was a childlike quality that I always fought to keep within me: that was my sense of amazement and wonderment and joy" (in McGill, 2000). Though he considers himself a loner, Thomas also gives credit to writer and workshop leader **John Killens** for encouraging his early writing.

Thomas also wrote a play, *Las calles de oro* (1970, [The Golden Streets]); a collection of short stories for young adults, *Stories of El Barrio* (1978); and a film documentary, *Petey and Johnny* (1964, on youth gangs). Thomas's wife translated *Down These Mean Streets* into Spanish. Thomas also wrote and narrated a film about himself, *The World of Piri Thomas* (1968), directed by **Gordon Parks**. Thomas is working on a sequel titled "A Matter of Dignity," and a film version, as well as an educational film tentatively titled "Dialogue with Society."

REFERENCES: *AANB. CAO-01. EA-99. W. Wiki.* Dudley, David L., in *COCAAL* and *OCAAL.* Greenberg, Dorothee von Huene. "Piri Thomas: An Interview." *MELUS. 26.3* (Fall 2001) p. 77. From *Literature Resource Center.* McGill, Lisa D. "A Conversation with Piri Thomas." *Bilingual Review. 25.2* (May-August 2000) p. 179. From *Literature Resource Center.* Steck, Stephen M., in *GEAAL.* Amazon.com.

Thompson, Era Bell
8/10/1905–12/29/1986
Autobiography, criticism, nonfiction articles; journalist, editor

Thompson wrote book reviews, feature articles, advertising copy, and news articles for various periodicals, including the *Bugle* (a weekly) and the *Chicago Defender.* She also edited **Negro Digest** (1947; later called *Black World*) and *Ebony,* as associate editor (1947–1951), co–managing editor (1951–1964), and then international editor (1964–1986). During this time, she still contributed essays to other journals, such as *Phylon.* She also wrote her autobiography, *American Daughter* (1946, funded by a fellowship from the Newberry Library), and a thoughtful pondering of her connection to Africa, *Africa, Land of My Fathers* (1954). She also edited *White on Black* (1963, with Herbert Nipson White), a collection of articles by European Americans, about African Americans.

REFERENCES: *AANB. CAO-03. HR&B. W. Wiki.* Cole, Kevin L., in *GEAAL.* Roberts, Janet M., in *COCAAL* and *OCAAL.* Thompson, Kathleen, in *BWA:AHE.*

FURTHER READING: *EAAWW.*

Thurman, Howard
11/18/1900–4/10/1981
Autobiography, nonfiction—religion; cleric, theologian, educator

The author of 20 books (e.g., his autobiography *With Head and Heart: The Autobiography of Howard Thurman,* 1980) and many journal articles, Thurman also lectured widely on the importance of Christian cooperation among the races and on the value of passive resistance, as demonstrated by Mohandas Gandhi (whom he met personally on a trip to India). His nonfiction includes *Deep River: An Interpretation of Negro Spirituals* (1945, rev. ed. 1955), *The Negro Spiritual Speaks of Life and Death* (1947), *Meditations for Apostles of Sensitiveness* (1948), *Jesus and the Disinherited* (1949/1981), *Meditations of the Heart* (1953/1972), *The Creative Encounter* (1953/1972), *Footprints of a Dream: The Story of the Church for the Fellowship of All Peoples* (1959), *Mysticism and the Experience of Love* (1961), *The Inward Journey* (1961/1973), *Disciplines of the Spirit* (1963), *The Luminous Darkness* (1965), *The Centering Moment* (1969/1984), and *The Search for Common Ground: An Inquiry Into the Basis of Man's Experience of Community* (1971/1986). Many of his writings have also been collected in *For the Inward Journey: The Writings of Howard Thurman* (1984, selected by his daughter, Anne Spencer Thurman).

REFERENCES: *AANB. BAWPP. CAO-02. EA-99. EBLG. Wiki.* Connor, Tim, in *BB.*

FURTHER READING: Strong, Robert, in *GEAAL. See also* Allen, Mathews F. "Howard Thurman: Paradoxical Pavior." *The Journal of Negro History. 77.2* (Spring 1992) p. 84. From *Literature Resource Center.* Hardy, Clarence E. III. "Imagine a World: Howard Thurman, Spiritual Perception, and American Calvinism." *The Journal of Religion. 81.1* (Jan. 2001) p. 78. From *Literature Resource Center.*

Thurman, Wallace (Henry)
8/16/1902–12/22/1934
Novels, poems, play, articles, editorials, literary criticism; journal editor, publisher, screenwriter

Wallace was born and raised in Utah, continuing to live there after graduating from high school. After his first two years of studying medicine at the University of Utah, however, he suffered a nervous breakdown and withdrew from school. After he recovered, he transferred to the University of Southern California (USC), while he worked nights in a Los Angeles post office. At work, he often discussed literature and other topics with his coworker, **Arna Bontemps.** He also wrote his column "Inklings" for a local African-American newspaper. As time went by, his interest in medicine diminished, and his interest in literature increased, fueled by news of the flourishing **Harlem Renaissance.** In 1925, while working at the post office by night and studying at USC by day, Thurman founded *Outlet*, a literary magazine he had hoped would germinate a West Coast renaissance similar to that taking place in Harlem. Unfortunately, not. After just six months of operation, Thurman was forced to recognize that his best-laid plans weren't working, so in September of 1925, he packed his bags and left USC and L.A. for Harlem, as did his pal and coworker Bontemps.

Regarding his early years in Harlem, Thurman remarked, "Three years in Harlem have seen me become a New Negro (for no reason at all and without my consent), a poet (having had 2 poems published by generous editors), an editor (with a penchant for financially unsound publications), an exotic (see articles on Negro life and literature in *The Bookman, New Republic, Independent, World Tomorrow*, etc.), an actor (I was a denizen of Cat Fish Row in *Porgy*), a husband (having been married all of six months), a novelist (viz: *The Blacker the Berry*, Macaulay's, Feb. 1, 1929: $2.50), a playwright (being coauthor of *Black Belt*). Now—what more could one do?" Quite a bit, apparently.

The first of Thurman's "financially unsound publications" had been *Outlet*, but it was not to be his last. The most famous of these ventures was the literary journal *Fire!! A Quarterly Devoted to the Younger Negro Artists*. In the summer of 1926, **Langston Hughes** asked Thurman to cofound and edit a quarterly literary journal dedicated to publishing the works of the up-and-coming young writers of the Harlem Renaissance. Joining them in this venture were **Gwendolyn Bennett**, John P. Davis, Aaron Douglas, **Zora Neale Hurston**, and **Richard Bruce Nugent**, all of whom agreed that Thurman should edit the quarterly. This group of impoverished writers pooled all their resources—and came up with next to nothing—to finance the start of the journal. Thurman had to borrow a thousand dollars to get out the first issue, which included not only works by the coventurers, but also works by Arna Bontemps and others. With Thurman's guidance, the journal was an outstanding achievement, highlighting the avant-garde brilliance of these young, aspiring luminaries.

Without enough money to promote the journal and to ensure enough sales to pay back the loan, the journal was in trouble. When an actual fire erupted in a basement storing numerous issues of *Fire!!*, Thurman's (and his cofounders') hopes for continuing its publication went up in smoke. Thurman was left still owing $1,000 to creditors, which took him four years to pay off. Since then, copies of the journal have become priceless rarities, which collectors treasure. In 1985, the demand for these 60-year-old works was great enough that a paperback copy of the journal was reprinted and made available as a book, still in print.

Less well known—and less avant-garde—was Thurman's third attempt to launch a journal. In November of 1928, he published the first issue of *Harlem, a Forum of Negro Life*, which included contributions from Hughes and other young writers, as well as from **Alain Locke**, **George Schuyler**, and **Walter White**. Despite the contributions of these established writers and scholars, this journal, too, failed after just one issue—again chiefly because it was underfinanced.

To finance his own livelihood, Thurman had sought work as an employee for various other publications. When he first arrived in New York, he started working as an editorial assistant and then a reporter for *Looking Glass* (a small magazine); next, he got work as the managing editor at the left-wing African-American periodical the *Messenger*, to which he contributed essays, reviews, and a short story ("Grist in the Mill") for about six months. Before the end of 1926, he took over as circulation manager for *The World Tomorrow*, a magazine intended for religious white readers, operated by whites. He also wrote numerous articles for other periodicals, including four essays that earned him particular praise: "Negro Artists and the Negro" (*The New Republic*, August 1927), "Nephews of Uncle Remus" (*The Independent*, September 1927), "Harlem Facets" (*The World Tomorrow*, November 1927), and "Negro Poets and Their Poetry" (*The Bookman*, July 1928). He also wrote a pamphlet, *Negro Life in New York's Harlem: A Lively Picture of a Popular and Interesting Section* (1927). In his writings, he criticized **W. E. B. Du Bois**, Alain Locke, and other intellectuals of the day for tempering what they said in order to gain the approval of whites.

While Thurman was trying to recover from the financial disaster of *Fire!!* and perhaps germinating the idea for *Harlem*, he was hired at Macaulay's Publishing Company, a book-publishing house. There, he was the only African-American reader (low-level editor) and one of the first blacks to be hired as an editor by a major publishing house owned and operated by whites.

While continuing to earn a living at Macaulay's, Thurman also started writing novels and plays. He wrote his first play, *Harlem: A Melodrama of Negro Life in Harlem*, in collaboration with playwright William Jourdan Rapp, a European-American editor of *True Story* magazine, with whom he also produced the play. Originally titled *Black Mecca* and then *Black Belt*, the play grew out of "Cordelia the Crude, a Harlem Sketch," a short story he had contributed to *Fire!!* In the play, the Williams family of South Carolina struggles to make it in their new home in the heart of the Harlem ghetto. The play—which includes a provocatively erotic dance, a violent shootout, and various other sensational elements—earned mixed reviews but was a popular success, running for 93 performances after its opening at the Apollo Theater in February 1929. Despite its popularity, however, Thurman's ability to attract financial difficulties continued, and even though this play was his greatest financial success, it left him further in debt. His other three-act play, *Jeremiah, the Magnificent* (also written with Rapp), was never produced. He also started writing *Black Cinderella*, addressing color prejudice within the black community, but he never completed it. By the early 1930s, a California filmmaker had recruited Thurman to move back to California and write screenplays, reportedly paying him an exorbitantly high salary for doing so. After writing just two scripts, however, Thurman returned to New York in 1934.

The same year that *Harlem* was being produced on Broadway and driving Thurman into deeper debt, his first novel, *The Blacker the Berry: A Novel of Negro Life*, also appeared in print. Ever the iconoclast, Thurman addressed in this novel themes that continue to spark controversy in this new millennium: abortion, homosexuality, ethnic conflict (between African Americans and Caribbean Americans), and intraracial prejudice (between light-skinned and dark-skinned blacks). An ebony-skinned man himself, Thurman was especially sensitive to intraracial color prejudice. Thurman's protagonist, Emma Lou Morgan, is similarly dark-skinned, and she suffers both self-criticism and criticism from her middle-class black family members and "friends" for her dark skin. Hoping to escape at least the persecution by others, she flees from her home in Boise, Idaho (suspiciously close to Salt Lake City, Utah), and runs first to Los Angeles and then to the Black Mecca of Harlem. Nowhere does she find a safe haven from this prejudice, however, and she must decide whether to continue her self-loathing for her skin coloring or to reject European-American-based standards of physical beauty. This 1929 book was reprinted in hardcover in 1972 and in paperback in 2008, with large numbers of copies in each printing.

Thurman's next novel, *Infants of the Spring* (1932), bitingly satirizes the Harlem Renaissance and its participants. A critic said of the work, "every serious student of the Harlem Renaissance must come to grips with this fictional critique by one of its most talented participants" (quoted in *BWA*). Thurman centers the action in "Niggerati Manor," a mansion in Harlem where various writers and other artists congregate. In addition to thinly disguised cameo appearances by Cullen, Hughes, Hurston, and Locke, Thurman includes an ensemble of characters meant to depict composite stereotypes of renaissance writers. Thurman takes sharp aim at the "New Negro" and other aspects of the renaissance, but he reserves his harshest critiques for Raymond Taylor, a self-aggrandizing young writer who most closely resembles Thurman himself. Thurman mocks Taylor's pretense and his presumed dedication to high art, and he ridicules Taylor's alcoholic proclivities and his cynical attitude.

Through his novel, Thurman challenges readers to contemplate individual aspirations within the context of collective interests, the pursuit of art within a politically charged environment, and the conflicts between the goals of integration and of forging an independent cultural identity. This 1932 novel has been reprinted in paperback in 1992 and in two 1999 paperback editions, and as the first volume (1997) in the prestigious Modern Library's series about the Harlem Renaissance.

Thurman wrote his third and final novel, *The Interne* (1932), with Abraham Furman, a white writer. Their novel exposed the unethical behavior and social injustices perpetrated at City Hospital on Welfare Island (now Roosevelt Island). The novel does not really touch on racial issues but instead focuses on medical abuses of disadvantaged persons. Two years after the novel was published, Thurman was taken to that very hospital, after he collapsed at a reunion party celebrating his return to New York. A few months later, he died in the charity ward of Bellevue Hospital, due to tuberculosis exacerbated by chronic alcoholism.

His friends and acquaintances recalled that he aspired to be not just a good ("journalistic") writer, but a great writer (like Thomas Mann, Herman Melville, Marcel Proust, or Leo Tolstoy). He was a voracious reader and might have achieved greatness had he not been one of his own worst enemies. In fact, his frequent self-deprecation occasionally lapsed into threats of suicide, particularly when he had been drinking. His sexual (and bisexual) appetites and his thirst for alcohol also frequently diverted him from his literary pursuits. His perpetual financial difficulties also often led him to write (or ghostwrite) trashy stories for *True Story* magazine or other publications of questionable literary merit. Amritjit Singh and Daniel M. Scott III have put together *The Collected Writings of Wallace Thurman: A Harlem Renaissance Reader* (2003), published by Rutgers University Press.

REFERENCES: *AANB. BAWPP. BWA. CAO-03. EA-99. EB-BH-CD. EBLG. MWEL. NAAAL. W. WDAA. Wiki.* Cohassey, John, in *BB.* Ferguson, Sally Ann H., in *COCAAL* and *OCAAL.* Kich, Martin, in *GEAAL.* Klotman, Phyllis R., in *AAWHR–40.* Robinson, J. E., in *G&LL-98-2.* //www.amazon.com, 8/1999, 4/2009.

FURTHER READING: *BWA:AHE. HAAL. MAAL. NYPL-AADR.* Ghosh, Nibir K. "*The Collected Writings of Wallace Thurman: A Harlem Renaissance Reader.*" *MELUS* 30.1 (Spring 2005) p. 250. From *Literature Resource Center.* Harris, Reginald. "*The Collected Writings of Wallace Thurman: A Harlem Renaissance Reader.*" *Lambda Book Report* 12.7 (Feb. 2004) p. 6. From *Literature Resource Center.* Washington-Favors, Sarah M. "*The Harlem Renaissance, 1920–1940, Vol. 3*, Black Writers Interpret the Harlem Renaissance." *African American Review.* 33.4 (Winter 1999) p. 697. From *Literature Resource Center.*

Tillman, Katherine Davis (née Chapman)
2/19/1870–?
Poems, novels, plays, biographical essays

Chapman's two novellas (*Beryl Weston's Ambition: The Story of an Afro-American Girl's Life*, 1893; *Clancy Street*, 1898–1899) were serialized in the *A.M.E. Church Review*, which also published many of her poems and biographical essays (e.g., of Aleksandr Pushkin, Alexandre Dumas, and many famous African-American women). Her other works include a collection of verse (*Recitations*, 1902) and three dramas (*Aunt Betsy's Thanksgiving*, n.d.; *Thirty Years of Freedom*, 1902; *Fifty Years of Freedom, or From Cabin to Congress*, 1910), all of which were published by A.M.E. Book Concern. Her works have since been gathered in *The Works of Katherine Davis Chapman Tillman* (1991, introduced by Claudia Tate).

REFERENCES: *AANB. BAWPP.* Tate, Claudia, in *COCAAL* and *OCAAL.*

FURTHER READING: *EAAWW.* Holliday, Deloice, in *GEAAL. See also* George, Hermon, Jr. "The Schomburg Library of Nineteenth-Century Black Women Writers." *Nineteenth-Century Prose. 20.1* (Spring 1993) p. 100. From *Literature Resource Center.*

Tolson, Melvin (Beaunorus) ("Cap")
2/6/1898?–8/29/1966
Poems, plays, newspaper columns, novels; journalist, educator

When Reverend Tolson, an itinerant minister, moved from church to church through various Midwestern towns, his four children moved from school to school. Tolson had only an eighth-grade education, but he had a great thirst for knowledge, having taught himself more than one classical language. Although he was skeptical about the need for a college education, he taught his children the value of learning.

The Tolsons also encouraged their children to appreciate music, visual arts, and literature, as well as a broad range of cultural riches. Initially, Melvin seemed destined to become a painter, but when an unconventional artist invited Melvin to accompany him to Paris, Melvin's mother squelched that ambition. Fortunately for lovers of literature, Melvin merely turned his creative pursuits to poetry, and in 1912, his "The Wreck of the *Titanic*" was published in the Oskaloosa, Iowa, newspaper. In high school, he gave outstanding dramatic recitations of **Paul Laurence Dunbar** poems and other dramatic performances. In his last year of high school, he was elected senior class poet, and he had two of his poems and two of his short stories published in the school yearbook.

After high school, while earning his B.A. (with honors, 1923), Tolson met Ruth Southall, whom he married January 29, 1922. Shortly after they wedded, Ruth gave birth to the first of their four children. After graduating, Tolson started teaching English and speech at Wiley College in Marshall, Texas, where he remained until 1947. In addition to his academic duties, he was deeply involved in extracurricular organizations, organizing and cofounding various student clubs and coaching an athletic team.

During the 1931–1932 school year, Tolson took a sabbatical to pursue his master's degree in comparative literature from Columbia University in New York City. Tolson and his family lived in Harlem during the last days of the **Harlem Renaissance**, and he wrote his thesis about "The Harlem Group of Negro Writers." While at Columbia, he also started writing *Harlem Gallery*, his much-celebrated poetry collection (not published until 1965). In 1940, Tolson earned his master's degree from Columbia.

In 1947, Tolson left Wiley and moved to Langston, Oklahoma to become a professor of creative literature and the director of the Dust Bowl Theatre at Langston University. In addition to his professional, literary, and artistic pursuits, Tolson served as the mayor of Langston for four terms. In the mid-1960s, Tolson was invited to become the Avalon Professor of the Humanities at Tuskegee Institute, as well as a writer in residence. According to former students at each of the institutions at which he taught, Tolson was an outstanding, enthusiastic teacher, deeply interested in the intellectual development of his students. He also encouraged his students to follow his lead in developing and using a broad, deep vocabulary, in the pursuit of clarity.

Throughout Tolson's career, he wrote numerous novels and plays, as well as stage adaptations of other authors' novels. Although these works went unpublished, his poems appeared regularly in various literary journals. In addition, Tolson wrote a weekly column, "Caviar and Cabbage," for the *Washington Tribune* (1937–1944). An idealistic Marxist, he addressed a wide range of social, political, and even religious topics in his columns, attacking racism and class-based oppression, and promoting cultural pride and civil rights. These columns were published posthumously in 1982, in *Caviar and Cabbage: Selected Columns by Melvin B. Tolson*, edited by Robert M. Farnsworth.

The writings for which Tolson is best known, however, are his poems. "Dark Symphony," probably his best-known work, contrasts the historical contributions of African Americans with those of European Americans, addresses issues of class and race oppression, then reaches a finale optimistically predicting great progress for African Americans through their unity with other oppressed peoples around the world. Tolson arranged the poem in six "movements," comparable to the musical movements of a symphony. Listen to the lyricality of the middle verse of his "Andante Sostenuto" movement: "They tell us to forget / Democracy is spurned. / They tell us to forget /

The Bill of Rights is burned. / Three hundred years we slaved, / We slave and suffer yet: / Though flesh and bone rebel, / They tell us to forget!" "Dark Symphony" won the National Poetry Contest of the 1939 American Negro Exposition in Chicago, then in 1941, *Atlantic Monthly* published it. Fortunately, his editor at *Atlantic Monthly* moved to a book publisher. She so liked Tolson's poem that she asked him to produce his first published collection, *Rendezvous with America* (1944). Popularly and critically acclaimed, the book went through three editions.

In 1947, Liberia's president appointed Tolson to be the Liberian poet laureate. Tolson's only previous connection to Liberia was that a former student of his had once introduced him to the daughter of a Liberian consul. As poet laureate, he was commissioned to write a poem commemorating Liberia's first 100 years for the 1956 Liberian Centennial and International Exposition. Tolson completed his *The Libretto for the Republic of Liberia* in 1953. Tolson's complex, modernistic *Libretto* comprises eight sections, each one named for a sequentially ascending note on the diatonic musical scale, each section prefaced with the question, "Liberia?" Making extensive use of literary, classical, mythical, and cultural allusions, Tolson's *Libretto* attacks colonial exploitation, embraces universal brotherhood, celebrates African history and achievements in science and the humanities, and looks forward to an African continent of free and independent nations. While many critics praised the work's complex splendorous language and subject matter, many others considered it to be modernism run amok—too unlyrical, too scholarly, and too allusive.

Tolson's next published collection of poems—*Harlem Gallery: Book I, The Curator*—was actually the collection he first started in the early 1930s, finally published in 1965. He originally planned this project to comprise five books, but only one was published during his lifetime. Each of the five books were to represent a distinct phase in the history of the African *diaspora* (the scattering of Africans throughout the world). The name "Gallery" suggests Tolson's strong orientation in the visual arts, and the poems in this first book are written from the point of view of the curator of a gallery illustrating the African-American experience.

Tolson's *Gallery* included a richly diverse wealth of scenes and of portraits. In the *Gallery*, Tolson retained some of the modernism and metaphorical language of the *Libretto*, but he blended it with African-American oral storytelling and blues traditions, yielding lyrical vignettes, conversations, and folk philosophy. This blending makes the poetry compelling, but also makes it difficult to classify. A devout nonconformist, he probably relished his resistance to categorization. Further enriching this blend, Tolson combined playfully humorous insights and investi-

gations with serious study of the role of the artist in African-American culture.

Tolson died soon after the publication of his *Gallery*, and that might have been the end of his publications. Fortunately, Robert Farnsworth (who later published Tolson's posthumous essay collection) amplified the original *Gallery* with various free-verse monologues by a culturally diverse cross-section of Tolson's characters to create *A Gallery of Harlem Portraits* (1979). This collection reflects Tolson's love of lyrics, his passion for plays, and his fondness for blues. As with his previous gallery, this gallery portrays a community of individuals who together illustrate the strengths of the culturally diverse Harlem community. Throughout this work, Tolson manages to highlight class and race oppression while maintaining an optimistic outlook for the future.

Tolson himself is also difficult to define. He came into his poetic voice after the Harlem Renaissance had waned and before the **Black Aesthetic** emerged. While embracing African-American folk traditions, he explored European-American modernism. While addressing issues of past and present class and racial oppression, he optimistically predicted a future in which such oppression would be thrown over by a culturally and nationally diverse union of oppressed peoples. An inveterate iconoclast, he never hesitated to express ideas starkly clashing with those of his contemporaries. Yet he was no sourpuss, winning the abiding affection of his students and of the citizens whom he served as mayor. This irreverent scholar received an honorary doctorate from Lincoln University in 1965, as well as numerous other awards, fellowships, and grants. He was also well respected by fellow poets, such as Robert Frost, Theodore Roethke, John Ciardi, and William Carlos William.

REFERENCES: *AA:PoP. BAL-1-P. BWA. EB-98. EBLG. G-95. MAAL. NAAAL.* Beaulieu, Elizabeth Ann, in *COCAAL* and *OCAAL.*

FURTHER READING: *AANB. BAWPP. CAO-07. CLCS. MWEL. W. Wiki.* Farnsworth, Robert M., in *AAW-40–55* and in *AP1880–1945-2.* Gibson, Donald B., in *RGAL.* Harris, Steven R., in *GEAAL.* Metzger, Sheri Elaine, in *BB.* Mvuyekure, Pierre-Damien, in *AAA-1745–1945.* Williams, Wilburn, in *AAW-1991.*

Toomer, Jean (né Nathan Pinchback Toomer)
12/26/1894–3/30/1967
Poems, essays, plays, novels

Jean Toomer's life was consumed by a search for spiritual wholeness. The search both preoccupied him throughout his life and has been blamed for ruining his promise as a brilliant writer. During his lifetime, Toomer produced only one great work—the novel *Cane*—but it was so brilliantly and artistically composed that it won Toomer great praise and renown as one of the most famous writers of the **Harlem Renaissance**. The fact that his first work exhibited such promise, however, led many to judge him to be, as Cynthia Kerman and Richard Eldridge say in their biography *The Lives of Jean Toomer*, "a comet that had one burst of glory before burning up." Yet Toomer did not die, or stop living after the publication of *Cane*, but led an extremely active life in pursuit of religion and spiritual identity.

Nathan Pinchback Toomer was born to his parents Nina Pinchback and Nathan Toomer. His father was a farmer and his mother the daughter of P. B. S. Pinchback, a prominent politician in Louisiana during the period of Reconstruction. Toomer's father and his maternal grandfather both claimed to have "black blood," but had very fair-skinned appearances, which Toomer inherited. After his mother and father divorced two years after he was born, Toomer's mother took him to live with her parents who, because of their wealth and fair skin lived in a prominent white upper-middle-class neighborhood. A few years later, his mother married and moved to upstate New York with her (white) husband and her son.

Because the neighborhoods he lived in for the first 14 years of his life were predominantly white and upper class, and because his skin was so fair, Toomer did not come into contact with real racial issues until his mother died in 1910. At that time, he moved from New York back to Washington, D.C., to live once again with his mother's parents. His grandparents' economic situation had taken a turn for the worse, however, and they had been forced to move out of their mansion in the upper-class white section of town and into a middle-class interracial community. Although, for the most part, he quickly adapted to his new environment and was almost invigorated by the change, it was at this point that he came into contact with issues of race and began to formulate his theories on the meaning of racial identity in a person's relationship with the world.

The fact that Toomer once described himself having a mixture of "Scotch, Welsh, German, English, French, Dutch, Spanish and some dark blood" might indicate his ideas about the importance he gave to racial identity. In essence, he tried to avoid labels and hated the idea of being classified; he once said, "I am of no particular race. I am of the human race, a man at large in the human world, preparing a new race." When pressed, he would reject the idea that he had to define himself as either black or white and insisted that he was a member of the "American" race—which he felt all Americans should claim to be.

However, as seems to be the case for many writers who eschew racial labels, Toomer is best known for the work that deals most clearly with racial themes—*Cane*. Toomer decided to become a writer in 1919 after spending five years meandering through four different colleges and receiving no degrees. He found college disappointing

because it failed to offer him "a sort of whole into which everything fits . . . a body of ideas which holds a consistent view of life." He thus turned to writing in an attempt to find that whole and moved to Greenwich Village in New York City, where he met a number of prominent writers and critics, including Waldo Frank, a writer who would later help him publish his novel. It was in New York that he changed his name from Nathan to Jean because he felt that the main character of Romain Rolland's *Jean Christophe* best embodied whom he would like to be as a writer.

Despite the time spent in New York, *Cane* was actually inspired by a trip he took to Sparta, Georgia. He traveled there to take a position as an acting principal at the Sparta Agricultural and Industrial Institute. While there, he was struck by the landscape of Georgia and by its rich history of slavery and segregation. He was also amazed to hear folk songs and spirituals being sung by the residents of the area, and hearing that music made him realize that in that place, black folk culture had remained untouched by white cultural influences. In a sense, the segregation of the South had served to preserve an African-American folk culture that Toomer never knew existed. He noticed, however, that the culture was being lost, as many young black people in the area moved away from the Southern rural areas and into the large industrialized Northern cities where they were forgetting their rich cultural history and instead taking up the values of white society. On the way home from his two-month stay, he began penning the poem "Georgia Dusk" and many of the vignettes that would compose the first section of *Cane*.

The novel is divided into three sections. The first depicts the black experience in the rural South and tells, in vignettes interspersed with verse, the experiences of five Southern women. All the women are presented as beautiful, strong, and vulnerable, and they represent different parts of the black community throughout history. The second section depicts the life of African Americans in the North and comprises vignettes interspersed with verse. This section attempts to illustrate the way that the natural tendencies of human nature are destroyed by the sterile, harsh, and mechanical elements of the modern city. It also focuses on the detrimental effects segregated society has on the human spirit and the way it prevents African Americans from achieving wholeness of mind or body, and warns black Americans of the danger they face if they lose sight of the values of black folk life when they appropriate the sterile values of white society.

The third part of the novel attempts a kind of synthesis of Northern and Southern black experience and offers a resolution of the two; it is a drama called "Kabnis," which enacts the story of an urban black writer who travels to the rural South. This section is written entirely in prose. The black writer in the story is having difficulty with his African-American identity, and that prevents him from succeeding as a writer. With some fear, he undertakes a spiritual quest for identity, and on the way, he ends up dealing with issues of racial inequality. The end of the novel is mostly optimistic, as the writer spends a night in a basement with a number of Southern blacks, all of whom talk about the damage that they have experienced because of racial conflict. He emerges from the basement determined to write of the struggles of blacks throughout history and thus finds a place for himself in African-American history.

Whether he intended it to be or not, the third section of *Cane* is highly autobiographical—for after his trip to the South, Toomer did write of the struggles of blacks in the North and the South and does make a place for himself in history with that one novel. After its publication, however, Toomer dropped out of literary circles and rejected all his friends. He had become a writer because he felt that his writings could help to stem the rapid flow of technology that was causing people to become increasingly isolated and materialistic; after publishing *Cane*, he came to believe that the literary arts were proving to be completely ineffective at helping resolve many of the world's problems. He also became very angry at the fact that in writing *Cane*, he began to be classified as a black writer and that it made people expect that he would continue to write about issues of race. He stated that "*Cane* was a song of end," that had helped him come to terms with his racial identity but which was really only a part of his search for a unifying principle in himself.

His quest for wholeness continued after he abandoned his literary community when, in 1924, he became involved with Georgei I. Gurdjieff, a spiritual philosopher who propounded theories of human development. Toomer hoped this spiritual program would help him to attain a higher consciousness that would help him to locate where his self existed in relationship to the universal whole. During this time, he continued to write and tried to publish his writings, but no publishers were interested in his rather abstract, spiritual work.

In the mid-1930s, Toomer formally disassociated himself with Gurdjieff, although the ideas of his teachings would appear in Toomer's writing for many more years. During that time he was married, twice—his first wife, Marjery Latimer, died in childbirth in 1931, and three years later, he married Marjorie Content. Continuing in his quest for spiritual wholeness, he and Marjorie became interested in the Society of Friends (known as the Quakers) in 1934 and became members in 1940.

His second and last literary milestone was achieved in 1936 when *New Caravan* agreed to publish his poem, "Blue Meridian." Although at the time it was published it received little attention, some contemporary critics have claimed that it is artistically equal to *Cane*. In this poem,

Toomer writes about the fusion of black-, white-, and red-skinned people into a new creation, the blue man. This poem is extremely idealistic and still contains a great deal of Gurdjieff's philosophy, but it also makes some important social statements in an extremely artistic way. The blue man represents a person who has shed all classifications—being of no sex, class, or color. This blue man lives in a new America, which has indeed become a melting pot. Everyone exists in harmony and oneness.

In many ways, "Blue Meridian" is yet another part of Toomer's quest to reconcile disparate parts—of the self, the nation, and the world. As in *Cane*, Toomer draws the readers' attention to the possibility of transformation and synthesis, for this is what Toomer had been searching for, unsuccessfully, throughout his life. His expectations for literature, religion, and the world were always unfulfilled, but in many ways, that kept him always reaching—an activity that kept him active as a thinking, living person, but which stood in the way of fulfilling his promise as a brilliant writer. Gorham Munson, a friend of Toomer's for 45 years, wrote a review of Toomer's life after hearing of his death in 1967: "We must realize that there are many casualties on the road to self-development." The fact that Toomer was one of them makes him, if nothing else, abundantly human.

REFERENCES: *AAW. BW:SSCA. NAAAL.* Byrd, Rudolph P., in *COCAAL* and *OCAAL.* Kerman, Cynthia Earl, & Richard Eldridge. 1987. *The Lives of Jean Toomer: A Hunger for Wholeness.* Baton Rouge: Louisiana State University Press. —Diane Masiello

FURTHER READING: *AANB. B. BAWPP. BCE. CAO-03. CE. LFCC-07. MWEL. QB. W. Wiki.* Bremen, Brian A., in *AW:ACLB-02-S3.* Deakin, Motley, in *AP1880–1945-1.* Guzzio, Tracie Church, in *AW:ACLB-02.* Le Blanc, Ondine E., in *BB.* McKay, Nellie, in *AAW-1991,* and in *AAWHR-40.* Reilly, John M., in *RGAL-3.* Wilson, Ian W., in *GEAAL.* //www.poets.org/poet.php/prmPID/71.

Torrence, Jackie
2/12/1944–11/30/2004
Stories, folklore; librarian, storyteller

A small portion of Torrence's rich treasure may be found in her collection of folklore and stories, *The Importance of Pot Liquor* (1994). Although her specialty was ghost stories (reputedly able to tell 300 or so), Torrence could vividly recount a wealth of African and African-American stories, as well as stories from other lands and other times.

REFERENCES: *BAAW.* —Tonya Bolden

Editor's note: Ironically, while still a schoolgirl, Jackie had been taunted by her peers for having a speech impediment. After corrective dental work, however, she worked hard to overcome her difficulties and superlatively overcompensated. While raising her daughter, Lori, as a single mother, Torrence was working as a reference librarian when the children's librarian was unavailable to lead a story time. Torrence filled in, thus beginning her career as "The Story Lady." Audio editions of her storytelling have been distributed as *The Story Lady* (1982), *Mountain Magic Jack Tales* (Vol. 1 and 2, 1984), *Brer Rabbit Stories* (1985), *Country Characters* (1986), *Tales for Scary Times* (1987), *Classic Children's Tales* (1993), *Jump Tales* (1993), *Traditions: A Potpourri of Tales* (1994), *The Accidental Angel* (n.d., audio download), and *My Grandmother's Treasure* (n.d., audio download). She also passed on her storytelling techniques in *Jackie Tales: The Magic of Creating Stories and the Art of Telling Them* (2001).

REFERENCES: B. "Obituaries." *The Horn Book Magazine*. 81.2 (March-April 2005) p. 237. From *Literature Resource Center*. Amazon.com.

Touré, Askia Muhammad Abu Bakr el
(né Rolland Snellings)
10/13/1938–
Poems; educator, lecturer

After writing his illustrated biography, *Samory Touré* (1963, illustrated by **Tom Feelings** and designed by Matthew Meade), as Rolland Snellings, this poet converted to Islam and changed his name to Askia Muhammad Abu Bakr el Touré. Under his new name, his subsequent publications include *Juju: Magic Songs for the Black Nation* (1970, with Ben Caldwell, published by **Third World Press**), his poetry and prose collection; *Songhai!* (1973), his collection of poems and sketches; *From the Pyramid to the Projects: Poems of Genocide and Resistance* (1989), which won the American Book Award for Literature; *Dawnsong: The Epic Memory of Askia Touré* (2000), which won the Stephen Henderson Poetry award from the African-American Literature and Culture Society; and *African Affirmations: Songs for Patriots* (2007). He was also honored with the Gwendolyn Brooks Lifetime Achievement Award (1996). Touré has also cofounded (with **Larry Neal**) *Afro World* newspaper (1965); written on the staff for *Liberator Magazine* (1965–1966), *Soulbook* (1960s–1970s), and *Umbra* (1962–1963); regularly contributed to and served as associate editor of *Black Dialogue* (1965–1970s), which then became the *Journal of Black Poetry* (now *Kitabu Cha Juai*), for which he has been editor-at-large ever since. In 2003, Touré was working on adapting his play *Double Dutch: A Gather of Women* into a screenplay, and his epic poem "From the Pyramid to the Projects" into a libretto.

REFERENCES: CAO-01. Bethel, Kari, in *BB*. Gabbin, Joanne V., in *AAP-55–85*. Kich, Martin, in *GEAAL*. Richardson, James W., Jr., in *COCAAL* and *OCAAL*. Amazon.com.

Trethewey, Natasha
4/26/1966–
Poems; educator

When European-Canadian poet and graduate student Eric Trethewey wanted to wed African-American social worker Gwendolyn Ann Turnbough, the couple had to leave the South for Ohio as their interracial marriage violated the laws of 16 Southern states in the 1960s. Such laws were not ruled unconstitutional until 1967. After the Tretheweys married, Gwendolyn and baby Natasha returned to Gwendolyn's mother's home in Gulfport, Mississippi. Eric moved to New Orleans to earn his Ph.D. at Tulane, returning to Gulfport each weekend to be with his family. When Natasha was about a year old, the Tretheweys moved to Canada for a year.

For various reasons, the Tretheweys' union dissolved by the time Natasha entered elementary school, and she moved to Decatur, Georgia with her mother. She also spent time with her father in New Orleans and with her grandmother in Gulfport. Eric later moved to Virginia to teach at Hollins University, where he remarried. Gwendolyn later remarried, too, but in 1985, when Natasha was still a teenager, Gwendolyn was murdered by her estranged second ex-husband.

Heartbroken and orphaned, Natasha continued to earn her B.A. in English from the University of Georgia in Athens (1989). She then moved to her father's school, Hollins University, where she earned her M.A. in English and creative writing (1991). Her next stop was the University of Massachusetts at Amherst (1995), where she earned her M.F.A. in poetry, as well as the Distinguished Young Alumna Award. While in Massachusetts, she participated in the **Dark Room Collective** (1988–1998) of African-American poets, who offered each other mutual support.

After earning her second master's degree, Trethewey returned South to become an assistant professor of English at Alabama's Auburn University and at the University of North Carolina at Chapel Hill, and then an associate professor at Atlanta's Emory University (since 2002), where she now sits in the **Phillis Wheatley** Distinguished Chair in Poetry. Meanwhile, she had an interim post at Duke University (2005–2006). While teaching aspiring writers, Trethewey continues to write her own poetry, which has appeared in numerous periodicals as well as in volumes of *The Best American Poetry* (2000, 2003). Based on the publication of her individual poems, the National Endowment for the Arts awarded her a Literature Fellowship (1999).

Trethewey has explored an array of formal poetic forms in her work, such as the ghazal, the pantoum, the villannelle, and the sonnet, as well as the blues poem, tied to African origins. Starting in the new millennium,

Trethewey has published three award-winning poetry collections. Her first, *Domestic Work* (2000), was chosen by former U.S. Poet Laureate **Rita Dove** to become the first poetry collection to win the now-annual **Cave Canem** Poetry Prize for the best first collection of poems written by an African-American poet. It also won both the Mississippi Institute of Arts and Letters Book Prize and the Lillian Smith Award for Poetry (both 2001).

While working on her second book, *Bellocq's Ophelia* (2002), Trethewey was awarded a National Endowment for the Arts grant (2002), and after its publication, she received a Guggenheim Fellowship (2003). The collection also earned her another Mississippi Institute of Arts and Letters Book Prize (2003) and nomination for two prestigious awards from the Academy of American Poets: the James Laughlin Award and the Lenore Marshall Poetry Prize. It was also named a Notable Book by the American Library Association (2003).

For Trethewey's third poetry collection, *Native Guard* (2006), she was writing a series of poems about Louisiana's Native Guard, African-American Union soldiers. While working on it, she was also writing some elegies for her mother. As she continued to work on each series of poems, she noticed some interrelationships, and she decided to include both series in her collection. *Native Guard* earned Trethewey the Pulitzer Prize for Poetry, a second Lillian Smith Award for Poetry, and a third Mississippi Institute of Arts and Letters Book Prize (all 2007).

In addition to the many aforementioned awards and honors, Trethewey has received three prestigious fellowships (for the Radcliffe Institute at Harvard, 2000; a Guggenheim fellowship, 2003; and a Bellagio-residency fellowship, 2004). Following the award of her Pulitzer, Trethewey was also awarded the Mississippi Governor's Award for Excellence in the Arts for Poetry and was named the Georgia Woman of the Year (both 2008). Reportedly, Trethewey is currently working on a memoir.

REFERENCES: CAO-07. W2B. Wiki. Hostetler, Ann, in *AANB*, McHaney, Pearl Amelia. "An Interview with Natasha Trethewey." Five Points: A *Journal of Literature and Art*. 11.3 (Sept. 2007), p. 96. Literature Resources from Gale. Rowell, Charles Henry, and Carl Phillips (Eds.). 2002. *Making **Callaloo**: 25 Years of Black Literature*. New York: St. Martin's Griffin. //en.wikipedia.org/w/index.php?title=Special%3ASearch&search=dark+room+collective. //en.wikipedia.org/wiki/Ghazal. //en.wikipedia.org/wiki/Hollins_University. //en.wikipedia.org/wiki/List_of_winners_of_the_Lenore_Marshall_Poetry_Prize. //en.wikipedia.org/wiki/Pantoum. //en.wikipedia.org/wiki/Sonnet. //en.wikipedia.org/wiki/University_of_Georgia. //en.wikipedia.org/wiki/Villanelle. //www.newsreel.org/guides/furious/darkcoll.htm. //www.poets.org/poet.php?prmPID/442. //www.poets.org/viewmedia.php?prmMID/5652. //www.oah.org/pubs/magazine/family/cruz-berson.html. Amazon.com.

FURTHER READING: Lipkin, Elline, in *GEAAL*.

Trickster Tales
Time immemorial–

(e.g., *Anansi, Brer Rabbit*). A *trickster tale* is a folktale in which the action of the story centers on a trickster character, and the fictional events in the story are intended to represent events in the real world. In most trickster tales, animal characters represent humans, speaking and behaving like humans, but occasionally, tricksters are actually humans—or even superhumans with some godlike characteristics. In all cases, *trickster* characters are wily, charming, and mischievous, and they almost invariably come into conflict with characters who are physically larger and more powerful than they, so they must use their craftiness to trick these more powerful adversaries. Some tricksters may have supernatural powers, but most do not. The fundamental nature of the trickster may also vary cross-culturally. For instance, one culture's trickster may play a benevolent, creative role, whereas another culture's may play an evil, destructive role. The trickster may be a childlike, impulsive prankster; a wise, wily charmer; or a seemingly innocent fool whose actions seem coincidentally to outwit a powerful enemy.

Usually, the trickster encounters a difficult situation posed by an antagonist, to which the trickster responds with some clever trickery. In some variants, however, the trickster is simply mischievous, thereby creating her or his own problem. In most trickster tales, the prankster manages to get out of the difficulty through chicanery, but sometimes, the scamp is too clever for her or his own good and ends up being undone by the knavery. The undoing often results because the trickster has shown some human fallibility, such as pride or greed.

Another variant is the *escape story*, in which the trickster appears to be caught in a situation from which escape seems impossible. Occasionally, a powerful adversary presents the trickster with an impossible task, and the trickster must counter it by imposing an impossible condition on the adversary. In one tale, for instance, a wicked Dahomean king demanded that his subjects build him a castle, starting the building from the *top* and building *downward*. He warned them that their failure to do so would mean death for all. The terrified Dahomeans saw no way to avoid a seemingly certain death. A wise old trickster came up with a solution: He told the king that his people were ready begin construction, and he asked the king to honor them by laying the foundation stone, as was customary.

What purposes do trickster tales serve? For one thing, whatever the outcome, the story usually teaches the reader a lesson (e.g., "Even if you're weaker than your adversary, you can succeed," or "Don't be greedy"). Often, trickster tales are told by folks without much power (physical, financial, political, etc.), and the trickster serves as a cultural hero, triumphing over more powerful foes. Such tales also allow the storytellers to poke fun at their more powerful nemeses, at human foibles shown by the story characters, or even at themselves (e.g., when the trickster is undone by greed or gluttony). Because trickster tales are allegorical, storytellers can parody more powerful members of a culture, signifying the failings of these adversaries without explicitly stating those faults—and risking the opponents' wrath. Around the world and across time, almost every culture offers amusing trickster tales, so that storytellers and listeners can project their hopes and fears onto these charming rascals. In addition, in some cultures, tricksters have supernatural powers and serve important roles in sacred rituals.

In Africa, tricksters may take on human forms, animal forms (e.g., hare, monkey, Ijapa the tortoise, or Anansi the spider), or divine forms (e.g., the trickster god Eshu). Both Anansi and Eshu may take on mythological characteristics. For instance, Eshu carries messages between gods and humans and influences luck. Tricksters often change as they travel from place to place, adapting to new environments and situations. For instance, in America, Eshu was transformed into the signifying monkey.

When differing cultures interact, interesting combinations sometimes emerge. For instance, when African slaves were brought to the American continent, African trickster tales and the hare trickster tales of Southeastern American Indians may have given birth to the Brer Rabbit tales of the American South. Certainly, the need for trickster tales was magnified by the slaves' almost total powerlessness. The trickster could become an icon of survival and resistance in a savagely oppressive environment, where outright rebellion almost surely meant death.

As African slaves adapted to the American continent, they modified their tales to suit their new environs. They dropped animals native to Africa and incorporated animals of the American South. As Christianity became more widespread among African Americans, tricksters lost their mythical powers. Increasingly, tricksters used sly cunning rather than supernatural powers to succeed. Perhaps because of the slaves' grim circumstances, their trickster tales highlighted humorous characterizations, plots, and even wordings. Further, these slaves, forbidden from gaining any formal education or even learning to read in a land where education connotes success, tell of tricksters who have masterful verbal skills and cunning wit.

Prevented from open revolt, the African-American trickster uses artful subversion to undo the oppressor. Within the context of slavery, increasingly prominent characteristics of African-American tricksters are *masking*, in which tricksters conceal their true feelings, thoughts, intentions, and actions; and *signifying*, in which tricksters covertly communicate with their sympathizers without revealing their true meanings to their oppressors. When

overt resistance was foolhardy, subversive tactics became ever more appealing. In most of these tales, the trickster uses wile and guile to trick the oppressor in some way.

Some stories, however, serve as cautionary tales, showing how the trickster's greed, gluttony, pride, or selfishness ends up harming the trickster at least as much as the object of the trickery. Perhaps the best-known example is the traditional story of "Brer Rabbit and the Tar Baby": Brer Fox (a trickster in his own right) sets up a tar baby alongside the path he knows that Brer Rabbit takes. Brer Rabbit greets the tar baby, but the tar baby says nothing in response. Brer Rabbit, affronted that the tar baby doesn't politely greet him, chides the tar baby for such rudeness. When it continues to ignore him, Brer Rabbit swats it. When this effort not only fails but also gets Brer Rabbit's arm stuck in the tar baby, Brer Rabbit strikes the tar baby with his other fist, then kicks it with both legs, and finally thumps it with his tail. Once Brer Rabbit is thoroughly stuck, Brer Fox and his associates Brer Wolf and Brer Bear gleefully rejoice in having caught the prideful rabbit. Don't worry too much, though; Brer Rabbit finds a way to be released before much harm comes to him. In this case, Brer Rabbit uses reverse psychology on his animal foes, begging them to *please* burn him, hang him, drown him, boil him, or inflict any other kind of torture they wish, as long as they *please* don't throw him in the briar patch—his native home.

Many traditional African-American trickster tales were popularized by a white Southerner, **Joel Chandler Harris**. Harris had actually done extensive research into African-American folklore when he wrote his Brer Rabbit tales. Harris may have been drawn to the Brer Rabbit stories because he, too, identified with the underdog. Small, painfully shy, and raised by an unwed mother, he often used humor and practical jokes to win acceptance by others.

Harris's stories were pretty true to the original versions, and he tried his best to preserve the authentic dialect of the numerous storytellers whom he interviewed. What makes the tales inauthentic, however, is that he couches the stories within a peculiar framework: He has the storyteller, Uncle Remus, tell these stories to the blue-eyed, blond son of his master. In truth, slaves almost always told such stories *within* the slave community; they rarely tempted fate by telling these thinly disguised subversive tales to slave owners. In addition, Harris couldn't help but perpetuate stereotypes of African Americans, intrinsic to his worldview as a white Southerner. Thus, he portrayed Uncle Remus as a jovial old man, delighted to have enjoyed the blessings of slavery. More contemporary writers, such as **Zora Neale Hurston** and **Julius Lester**, give more authentic versions of these tales—without the ludicrous Uncle Remus character.

After the Civil War, the trickster tale was modified to more specifically describe the situation of the slave. The small trickster animals were replaced by the servant John, and the oppressive larger animals were replaced by the master himself, usually called "Ol' Massa." In one particularly appealing John-and-Ol'-Massa tale, John manages to earn his freedom, and as he is walking down the road away from the plantation, the master, the mistress, and their children keep calling after him how much they love him and how well they will treat him in the future if he chooses to stay with them. John keeps walking down that road. The reader is left to imagine the puzzled expressions on the former slave owners' faces. In other stories, John tricks the master by staging a contest in which John has rigged the outcome. For instance, John may use trickery to appear to have some special talent (such as fortune telling) and taunts the master to do what John has done. The master, not to be outdone by a mere slave, attempts to show similar talent but fails. By this means, John may win his freedom, earn money toward gaining his freedom, or at least get out of a particularly onerous task or punishment of some sort.

At the turn of the century, **Charles Waddell Chesnutt** took a different tack with his *The Conjure Woman* (1899), featuring former slave Uncle Julius McAdoo, who entertains white Northerners with stories that covertly reveal the tragedy of slavery. In Uncle McAdoo's stories, the trickster usually manages to turn the tables on the oppressor. During this era of Ku Klux Klan terrorism, lynchings, and Jim Crow laws, a new set of tales also emerged, which still might loosely be called "trickster tales." These tales center on self-identified "Bad Niggers" such as High John the Conqueror and Stagolee. Such protagonists are aggressive, cruel, and even bloodthirsty, lacking social conscience or moral constraints. Though not truly heroes, their bold fierceness held strong appeal to African Americans being brutalized around the turn of the twentieth century. Even legendary heroes such as John Hardy and Railroad Bill may be construed along these lines. Another kind of trickster tale was the popular genre of stories about light-skinned African Americans who passed for white. A distinctive nonfiction version of this type of story was blue-eyed **Walter White**'s "I Investigate Lynchings" (1929), describing how he interviewed lynchers for the NAACP during the 1920s.

More contemporary trickster tales include **Toni Morrison**'s *Tar Baby* (1981); **Ishmael Reed**'s *The Last Days of Louisiana Red* (1974); **Ralph Ellison**'s *Invisible Man* (1952), featuring con artist, gambler, and petty criminal Bliss Proteus Rinehart; and **Kristin Hunter**'s *The Laketown Rebellion* (1978), in which Bella Lake unites her community to slyly thwart the wishes of a huge corporation. A contemporary poem referring to tricksters is **Col-**leen McElroy's "The Griots Who Know Brer Fox" (1979). Contemporary children's books featuring African or African-American trickster tales include Gerald McDermott's *Anansi the Spider* (1972) and his West African *Zomo the Rabbit* (1992); **Ashley F. Bryan**'s *The Adventures of Aku* (1976) and *The Dancing Granny* (1977), featuring "Ananse"; **Louise Bennett**'s books about "Brer Anancy"; Eric Kimmel's *Anansi and the Talking Melon* (1994); and **Julius Lester**'s *The Last Tales of Uncle Remus: As Told by Julius Lester* (1994).

REFERENCES: *CBC. E-98. EB-98. EBLG. G-96. MSE-98. MSI-98. MWEL. NAAAL. WB-98.* Harris, Trudier, "Passing," in *OCWW.* Newson, Adele S., "African-American Oral Tradition," in *OCWW.* Smith, Jeanne R., "Trickster," in *OCAAL.*

Trotter, Geraldine ("Deenie") (née Pindell)
10/3/1872–10/8/1918
Editorials; publisher, activist

Geraldine's childhood friend (and boyfriend, for a time) was **W. E. B. Du Bois**, who described her as both "fine" (because of her intellect, her cultured refinement, and her strength of purpose) and "fragile" (because of her precarious health). In 1899, after marrying her beloved Monroe (**William Monroe Trotter**), she started to settle into a life of relative comfort and ease in the upper-class Dorchester neighborhood of Boston.

A couple of years later, Monroe cofounded his *Guardian,* in which he lambasted **Booker T. Washington** and other accommodationist African Americans, just as he opposed injustice, discrimination, and segregation wherever he saw it. In 1903, Monroe infuriated Washington when his cohorts interrupted Washington's address at a local meeting. Washington ensured that Monroe was arrested and jailed. For a month, Deenie worked for his release and helped keep the *Guardian* running in his absence.

Washington continued to retaliate against the *Guardian* and its founders with the power and fierceness he was so capable of mustering. Pretty soon, Monroe's cofounder bailed out on him, leaving Deenie to fill in on a permanent basis. She was soon associate editor, business manager, bookkeeper, circulation manager, society-column editor, and in charge of whatever other tasks were needed. Despite their joint efforts, Washington's all-out effort to crush them (through smear campaigns, dirty tricks, subterfuge, and full financing of rival papers) led to financial disaster, and Monroe had to sell his formerly prosperous real-estate business—and even their lovely home. When Monroe was out of town, spreading his message or rallying support, Deenie was left to run the *Guardian* on her own.

Deenie had her own activist pursuits, as well. Raised in a family of activists, she wrote and gained signatures for petitions, organized committees, chaired societies, and raised funds for whatever causes she believed in—such as a shelter for women and children and the Boston Literary Society. She championed the cause of unjustly imprisoned African Americans, and she fought against lynching. Despite her fragile health and weak physical stamina, she believed that "those of us who have had the advantages of education, who have seen life in its broadest light, [should] be willing to sacrifice . . . to do for our own down-trodden people all in our power . . . to make their cause our cause, their suffering, our suffering" (from a 1905 speech on the 100th anniversary of abolitionist William Lloyd Garrison's birth).

REFERENCES: *BAAW.* —Tonya Bolden

FURTHER READING: *AANB.* //www.answers.com/topic/monroe-trotter. //www.answers.com/topic/william-monroe-trotter.

Trotter, James Monroe
2/7/1842–2/26/1892
Nonfiction—musicology, biography; soldier, civil servant

Young James learned early about the complexities of race relations in a slavery-based society: His European-American father "owned" his African-American mother, as well as James and his two siblings. In 1854, when James's father decided to marry, he sent his children and their mother to Cincinnati, Ohio, where slavery was outlawed. There, James had to work (e.g., as a hotel bellboy, a riverboat cabin boy), but he still managed to educate himself.

During the Civil War, Trotter's passion for equality and for civil rights became evident; among other things, he led black soldiers in the fight to be paid equal pay for equal rank and work—comparable to white soldiers—and after the soldiers refused to accept inferior pay for more than a year, the federal government relented and gave them commensurate pay. After the war, he turned to civil-service employment and continued to champion civil rights and equality.

In 1868, Trotter married Virginia Isaacs, with whom he had three children, including his son **William Monroe Trotter.** James Trotter's main claim to fame, however, was his book *Music and Some Highly Musical People* (1878), in which he asserted that slave **spirituals** are "our only distinctively *American* music" (emphasis in original). Although he touted the musical achievements of African Americans, he nonetheless was a man of his times, expressing the biases and worldview of those around him, which praised Eurocentric "classical" music traditions

above Afrocentric and other non-European musical forms and traditions.

REFERENCES: *BDAA. SMKC.*
FURTHER READING: *AANB. Wiki.*

Trotter, (William) Monroe
4/7/1872–4/7/1934
Editorials; business owner, newspaper founder and publisher

The son of a Civil War veteran, successful real-estate broker, and author (about African-American achievements in music), young William attended mostly white schools, graduated magna cum laude from Harvard in 1895, and earned a master's degree a year later. In these early years, he had frequent near-misses with **W. E. B. Du Bois**, a year or two ahead of him at Harvard, and a boy-friend of William's wife-to-be, **Geraldine Louise Pindell (Trotter)**.

Monroe (the name most folks called him) and "Deenie" wedded in 1899 and settled into a comfy lifestyle among the Boston bourgeoisie. With his ample inheritance and his own prospering real-estate business, they both could see much more comfort ahead. Naturally, the couple became involved in cultural and intellectual pursuits. He soon participated in founding the Boston Literary and Historical Association, which attracted the attention of some African Americans with decidedly noncomfy views of things. In fact, his cohorts at the association tended toward rabble rousing. A frequent subject of conversation was their disapproval of the accommodationist policies and practices of **Booker T. Washington**, whom they considered a traitor to their race.

Over the course of a couple of years, Trotter had worked up quite a feverish opposition to Washington, and in 1901, he and George Forbes founded the Boston *Guardian*, in large part to speak out against accommodationism and its traitorous champion from the Tuskegee Institute, whose *Up from Slavery* came out in March of the same year. At first, Trotter intended the *Guardian* to be a sidelight to his real-estate business, but he made the mistake of giving the paper this motto—"For every right, with all thy might!"—and then trying to live up to it.

Late in July 1903, Trotter and the troops he had rallied attended a speech by Washington. Some of them (not Trotter in particular) loudly voiced their opposition to Washington's policies and practices. In the fracas that followed, Washington managed to have Trotter arrested and jailed for a month, and Washington—with many powerful friends and allies—launched an all-out campaign to destroy Trotter and his *Guardian*. Washington was able to finance rival papers, dig up—or make up—smears on Trotter and his wife, and pull any number of filthy tricks to demolish Trotter. In not too long, Forbes saw the futility of trying to oppose Washington, and he left Trotter in the lurch.

Trotter's frail wife Geraldine filled in, working as business manager, associate editor, and whatever else was needed. So much for a comfy lifestyle. For a time, while waging war against lynching, Jim Crow, and foot-dragging-take-it-slow Washingtonites, Trotter joined forces with his former classmate and former rival W. E. B. Du Bois, and they were united in founding the Niagara Movement, progenitor of the NAACP, which emerged in 1909. Even Du Bois wasn't militant enough for Trotter, however, so Trotter split from W. E. B. to found the Negro Equal Rights League (NERL), with African Americans squarely (and solitarily) in positions of leadership. Through the nineteen-teens, Trotter continued to lead the way, opposing segregation in the federal government, protesting against D. W. Griffith's racist *Birth of a Nation*, and practicing in-your-face activism at every turn.

In the fall of 1918, Trotter lost his closest ally, his best friend, his beloved wife Deenie. Almost everything was slower and harder going after that. Still, he never faltered or wavered from his course. Over the next 16 years, Trotter continued to fight racism, segregation, discrimination, and injustice wherever he saw it. He spent every last penny of his—of which there had once been quite a few—fighting "For every right." When at last, his might gave out, and he couldn't see how to continue the fight, he took his own life. Had he only known that he had made an important difference and that we would remember his efforts. His contemporary, W. E. B. Du Bois, later said of him that he "was a man of heroic proportions, and probably the most selfless of Negro leaders during all our American history"; one of his many successors, **Lerone Bennett Jr.**, later wrote, "Trotter laid the first stone of the modern protest movement"; and Boston schools and libraries now honor Trotter by bearing his name.

REFERENCES: *BAAW. SMKC.* Fox, Stephen R. 1970/1971. *The Guardian of Boston: William Monroe Trotter.* New York: Scribner.
—Tonya Bolden

FURTHER READING: *AANB. B. Wiki.* Cohassey, John, in *BB.*

Troupe, Jr., Quincy (Thomas)
7/23/1943–

Poems, anthology, biography, spoken word—poetry; journals editor

Although Troupe loved reading from an early age, and his mother encouraged him to read widely, the kids in his neighborhood frowned on his love of books, and he never really thought he'd grow up to be a writer. For a time, Troupe attended Grambling College (now Grambling State University) in Louisiana, then he joined the military. Years later, while traveling the world with the U.S. Army basketball team, he started writing. In Europe, he was encouraged to write poetry by Jean-Paul Sartre and came under the influence of many other poets (e.g., **Sterling Brown**, Aimé Césaire, Pablo Neruda, **Jean Toomer**). When he moved to Los Angeles, he studied journalism, joined the Watts Writers' movement, and edited *Watts Poets: A Book of New Poetry and Essays* (1968).

As Troupe started advancing his writing career, he also began lecturing and teaching creative writing at various colleges and universities, including Columbia University, the University of California at Berkeley, the University of Ghana, Lagos University (in Nigeria), the City University of New York, and a few others. By the mid-1990s, Troupe was a professor of creative writing and American and Caribbean literature at the University of California at San Diego. In 2002, Troupe was named California's first Poet Laureate, but shortly after he took office, a background check showed that he hadn't been truthful about having earned a degree from Grambling. He chose to resign the laureate post and to retire from UCSD. When asked about these events, Troupe responded, "I don't feel bad about talking about it, because I felt liberated by saying, finally, that I didn't have a college degree. It has cleansed the rest of my life in many ways, and that's good for my mental health. . . . I regret what happened, but I don't regret it in the way a lot of people have discussed it, because of morality. I did become a full professor and when the students evaluated us, I was always in the top one percent of all professors on every campus where I taught. I didn't cheat any student out of anything. I was a great professor. . . . I haven't looked back because life goes on. But . . . it was an honor and privilege to be named the first official Poet Laureate of the state of California" (quoted in Castro, 2005). Troupe has since moved to New York City, where he continues to write and performs both spoken-word poems and jazz music.

When asked why he writes poetry, Troupe responded, "I write poetry because I *need* to write poetry. I need the music of language and the instant communication that I feel I get in writing poetry" (quoted in p. 413, *LoL*). That need is clear when viewing the abundance of poems he has produced. Troupe has had many of his poems published in such diverse periodicals as *Black Scholar*, *Black World*, *Callaloo*, *Umbra*, and *Village Voice*. He is also tireless in editing numerous literary journals. He was the founding editor of *Confrontation: A Journal of Third World Literature* (1970), *American Rag* (1978), and *Code* magazine (2000); he has been associate editor of *Shrewd* magazine (starting in 1968), guest editor of *Mundus Artium*

(1973), contributing editor of *Conjunctions* magazine, and senior editor of *River Styx* magazine (starting in 1983). He also edits the *Black Renaissance Noire* for New York University (since 2004). In addition to editing journals, he edited a second anthology, *Giant Talk: An Anthology of Third World Writings* (1975, with Rainer Schulte), and the much-lauded *James Baldwin: The Legacy* (1989).

Troupe's poems have been widely anthologized, as well. In addition, his poems have been gathered in his collections *Embryo Poems, 1967–1971* (1972); *Snake-Back Solos: Selected Poems, 1969–1977* (1979), which won an American Book Award; *Skulls along the River* (1984); *Weather Reports: New and Selected Poems* (1978/1996); *Avalanche: Poems* (1996); *Choruses: Poems* (1999); *Transcircularities: New and Selected Poems* (2002); and *The Architecture of Language* (2006). Troupe's poems reflect his love for improvisational jazz and often have a jazzy, spontaneous, go-with-the-flow feel to them. He observed, "I think every language has a musical core.... the sounds of the American language come from *all* our different ethnic communities, and these sounds are beautiful to me. As a poet, I try to get the music that's underneath all that.... I grew up listening to blues and to the old African American people talking.... and I especially loved to listen to jazz musicians talk. So all that musical language that I grew up listening to is what I try to make *my* language" (quoted in p. 413, *LoL*). In describing his own poetry (and that of other African Americans), Troupe sees the link between the rhythms and refrains of his poems and those of blues music, noting, "We tend to speak in circles—we come back and say things over and over again, just for emphasis—and there you have the whole repetition of lines coming back like refrains." He also feels that the improvisational aspects of jazz permeate and guide his own work: "Jazz provides the model for taking a text and improvising on it in a performance. That's why performance is part of the whole concept of poetry for me" (quoted in p. 417, *LoL*).

When giving spoken-word performances, Troupe often reads his poems with a musical accompanist (e.g., George Lewis, Donal Fox). "In order to get into people's blood and into people's consciousness and into people's lives, poetry has to sing" (quoted in p. 417, *LoL*). His recordings include two Library of Congress recordings—*The Architecture of Language* (1968) and *Michael S. Harper and Quincy Troupe Reading Their Poems* (1994, with **Michael S. Harper**, Library of Congress)—as well as *Shaman Man* (1990), *George Lewis Changing with the Times* (1993), *Root Doctor* (1995), and *Quincy Troupe with Pianist Donal Fox* (1996).

Troupe also worked closely with jazz musician Miles Davis to produce their *Miles: The Autobiography* (1989, with Miles Davis), for which he won a second American Book Award. He also wrote and coproduced the *Miles Davis Radio Project* (1991–1992, PBS), for which he won a Peabody Award and the Ohio State Award. The book has been translated into Spanish (*Miles y Yo*, 2001), and **Spike Lee** is said to be producing a film based on the book. Troupe even wrote a memoir about their relationship in *Miles and Me* (2000). Troupe's other biographical tributes include *Take It to the Hoop, Magic Johnson* (2000, illustrated by Lisa Cohen) and *Little Stevie Wonder* (2004, illustrated by Shane Evans), both written as poetic picture books for young readers.

Troupe was twice crowned the "World Heavyweight Poetry Champion" at the Taos Poetry Circus. "You have to make what you're coming from *live*. You have to find your central metaphor and your central meaning, and you have to make your language *live* — going back to the whole idea of language as being alive—so that when you read your poems you can become something else, a force" (quoted in p. 423, *LoL*). "Great art ... reveals our humanity and puts us in touch with it. That's what *all* great art is supposed to do" (quoted in p. 428, *LoL*). At present, Troupe is continuing to perform, he is collaborating to write an autobiography of a self-made millionaire, and he is writing several other books—a collection of essays and articles titled *Crossfertilizations*; a novel, tentatively titled *The Footmans*; and what he calls his "auto-memoir, *The Accordion Years*." His other writings include *Soundings* (1988), a film script on Thelonious Monk, and a screenplay (with musician Hugh Masekala).

REFERENCES: A. AANB. AAW:PV. BAWPP. CAO-07. LoL. NAAAL. TtW. Wiki. Castro, Jan Garden. "Quincy Troupe: An Interview by Jan Garden Castro." *The American Poetry Review*. 34.2 (March-April 2005) p. 49. From *Literature Resource Center*. Coleman, Horace, in AAP-55–85. Dillon, Kim Jenice, in COCAAL and OCAAL. Kester, Alicia, in GEAAL. Turner, Douglas. "Miles and Me: an Interview with Quincy Troupe." *African American Review*. 36.3 (Fall 2002) p. 429. From *Literature Resource Center*. //www.amazon.com, 7/1999, 4/2009. //www.poetryfoundation.org/ archive/poet.html?id=82127. //www.poets.org/poet.php/prmPID/489

Truth, Sojourner (legal name: Isabella Van Wagenen; slave name: Isabella Baumfree) c.1797 or 1799–11/26/1883
Spoken word—speeches, sermons, slave narrative; enslaved domestic servant, itinerant preacher, abolitionist orator, military recruiter and nurse

Born into slavery in Hurley, Ulster County, New York, Isabella Baumfree (or Bomefree) was the second-youngest child of James and Elizabeth Baumfree's 10 or 12 children. The Baumfrees' primary language was Dutch, the language spoken by the family that "owned" them. While still a child, Isabella was sold again and again, ending up with John Dumont from 1810 until 1827, when the state of New York's Gradual Emancipation Act freed her.

When Isabella was about 14 years old, another of Dumont's slaves, Thomas, married her, and the twosome had five children: Diana, Sophia, Elizabeth, Peter, and perhaps Hannah (there is some question about her; maybe she died in infancy). Even before Isabella's own emancipation, however, she boldly resisted the constraints of slavery. A year before New York's emancipation law was enacted, she chose to leave the Dumonts and went to work for Isaac Van Wagenen's family. Further, when Dumont illegally sold her son Peter into perpetual slavery in Alabama (just as New York state law was about to abolish slavery in New York), she solicited the aid of Ulster County Quakers and went to court to sue for his return—and won the suit!

About that time, she also underwent a religious conversion and pursued various unorthodox Christian faiths, while supporting herself through domestic work. In 1843, she felt called to ramble around the country, preaching the gospel as she understood it, and on June 1 of that year, she renamed herself "Sojourner Truth," thereby acknowledging her calling as an itinerant preacher. By the end of that year, Truth moved to a utopian community in Massachusetts, where she became a feminist abolitionist (and where she met fellow abolitionists **Frederick Douglass**, **David Ruggles**, and William Lloyd Garrison). To add to her meager income, to pay off her mortgage on a house she bought in Florence, Massachusetts, Truth dictated a slave narrative to Olive Gilbert, her neighbor in Massachusetts. Like most slaves, Truth had never learned to read or write. By her own admission, "I cannot read a book, but I can read the people." The Boston printer of Garrison's *Liberator* newspaper printed it as *The Narrative of Sojourner Truth: A Bondswoman of Olden Time* (1850; six or seven more editions by 1884), and Truth sold copies for 25¢ apiece to listeners at her sermons and speeches.

A powerful, insightful, and witty orator, Truth gave perhaps one of the most famous speeches in American history to the Ohio Women's Rights Convention in 1851: "And A'n't I a Woman?" (quoted either as "Ain't" or as "Ar'n't"). In that speech, she cited numerous ways in which she (and, by implication, other African-American and working-class women) had worked hard and had suffered much, thereby showing that many women are neither fragile nor protected from hardship. In her speeches, she tended to take poetic license by exaggerating her authentic experiences in slavery, to dramatic effect, such as stating that she had 13 children, rather than 5, and that she lived 40 years a slave, rather than about 30. This speech (printed on June 21, 1851, in the *Anti-Slavery Bugle*) and a contact with **Harriet Beecher Stowe** (author of the 1852 book *Uncle Tom's Cabin*) helped publicize Truth and her book, thereby increasing her readership and her live audiences. In 1858, when a rude male listener challenged her femininity, asserting that no one as

Sojourner Truth

strong and smart and outspoken as she could be a woman, she bared her breast, scorning his ridicule.

In 1856, Truth moved to Battle Creek, Michigan, and a neighbor there, Frances Titus, reprinted Truth's *Narrative* (1875, 1878), along with some additional material from Truth's "Book of Life" (a scrapbook with letters, clippings, and kudos from friends) and some articles by Stowe ("Sojourner Truth, The Libyan Sibyl," *Atlantic Monthly*, April 1863) and by another abolitionist feminist. In 1884, Titus came out with a final (posthumous) edition, which included eulogies for and obituaries about Truth.

During the Civil War, Truth helped supply food and clothing to African-American Union soldiers, and she fervently encouraged other African Americans to join that army. On October 29, 1864, President Abraham Lincoln received her at the White House. During the post-Civil War period, Truth worked tirelessly to aid former slaves and war refugees in gaining employment and job skills.

REFERENCES: *1TESK. ANAD. BAAW. EB-BH-CD. EWHA. H. HWA. NAAAL. PGAA. SEW. WDAW. WW:CCC.* "Ain't I a Woman," in *EA-99*. Lewis, Ronald L., in *G-99*. Painter, Nell Irvin, in *BWA:AHE* and in *COCAAL* and *OCAAL*. Ross, Cheri Louise, in *OCWW*. Scruggs, Otey M., in *WB-99*. Sellman, James Clyde, in *EA-99*.

FURTHER READING: *AANB. B. BCE. CE. HD. LE. QB. W. W2B. Wiki.* Davison, Carol Margaret, in *GEAAL.* Blight, David W. in *USHC. Gale Online Encyclopedia.* Detroit: Gale. From *Literature Resource Center.* //digital.library.upenn.edu/women/_generate/ AFRICAN%20AMERICAN.html. //www.americanwriters.org/writers/ truth.asp. //www.jimcrowhistory.org/scripts/jimcrow/women.cgi?state= New%20York. //www.lib.virginia.edu/small/exhibits/rec_acq/history/ truth.html.

Harriet Tubman

Tubman, Harriet (née Araminta Ross; renamed Harriet by her mother)
c. 1820–3/10/1913
Spoken word—speeches, songs; enslaved worker, abolitionist, Underground Railroad conductor, military scout, spy, nurse, social worker

Born a slave, she escaped to freedom in 1849—but not with the help of her husband, John Tubman. A free man himself, he not only refused to leave Maryland with her, but also threatened to reveal her plans for running away. After her successful escape, she did not seek safety and security for herself. Instead, for a decade or more, she led about 300 people out of bondage—including her parents and several other relatives of hers. In her 20 or so trips, she never lost a single Underground Railroad passenger, although she sometimes had to use some powerful motivation to get tired, worn-out, and just-plain-scared passengers to continue—sometimes even prodding with the point of a gun. By the time Civil War was declared, slavehunters and slaveholders had posted a $40,000 price tag on her head.

Although she never learned to read or write, she certainly knew how to turn a phrase to move people to action. Her speeches rallied support for abolition and motivated listeners to contribute time and money, and she even inspired some to put their own lives on the line just as she did, conducting and safe-housing fugitives on the Underground. "Wade in the Water" (her song for signaling escape) and several other **Negro spirituals** are attributed to her.

During the Civil War, she worked for the Union Army, spying, scouting, nursing, and even cooking as close to the action as she heard the call. She even led a Union raid, which freed 750 enslaved African Americans, and she served at the Battle of Fort Wagner, at which the 54th Massachusetts Colored Regiment fought so valiantly. Tubman's recollections of this battle and many others inspired many a writer who followed (e.g., **John Oliver Killens**'s *And Then We Heard the Thunder,* 1962). After the war, in about 1868, Tubman married a Union Army veteran, Nelson Davis, who was about 20 years younger than she. About three decades later, in 1896, Tubman bought 25 acres of land adjacent to her house (a former way station on the Underground Railroad). There, she built The Harriet Tubman House for Aged and Indigent Colored People. She herself moved into that home in about 1911. On her death, she was given a burial with full military honors, in recognition of her service to the Union Army. Both her funeral and her headstone were paid for by the National Association of Colored Women.

REFERENCES: *ANAD. BAAW.* —Tonya Bolden

FURTHER READING: *AANB. B. BCE. CE. HD. W. W2B. Wiki.* Barnes, Deborah H., in *COCAAL.* Mallory, Devona, in *GEAAL.* Patterson, Tiffany R. L., in *USHC.* Wainwright, Mary Katherine, in *BB.*

Turner, Darwin T. (Theodore Troy)
5/7/1931–2/11/1991
Poems, criticism; educator

In addition to his poetry collection, *Katharsis* (1964), Turner contributed poetry to dozens of anthologies and numerous literary journals. Turner's literary criticism also appeared in various journals and encyclopedia (e.g.,

Encyclopædia Britannica, Encyclopedia International, Dictionary of American Biography, Contemporary Dramatists, and *Encyclopedia of World Literature in the Twentieth Century*), as well as in his books *Nathaniel Hawthorne's "The Scarlet Letter"* (1967) and *In a Minor Chord: Three Afro-American Writers and Their Search for Identity* (1971), and *The Teaching of Literature by Afro-American Writers: Theory and Practice* (1972, cowritten for the National Council of Teachers of English).

Turner edited several anthologies, including *Images of the Negro in America* (1965, with Jean Bright), *Afro-American Writers* (1970), *Black American Literature: Essays, Poetry, Fiction, Drama* (1970; 1969, as 3 separate volumes, for essays, poetry, and fiction), *Black Drama in America: An Anthology* (1971; 2nd ed., 1994), *Voices from the Black Experience: African and Afro-American Literature* (1972), *Responding: Five* (1973), *The Wayward and the Seeking: A Collection of Writings by Jean Toomer* (1980), and *The Art of the Slave Narrative: Original Essays in Criticism and Theory* (1982, with John Sekora). He and his wife, M. Jean Lewis Turner, had a daughter, Pamela, and two sons, Darwin and Rachon. His university named a theatre and a scholars program in his honor.

REFERENCES: *AANB. BAWPP. CAO-00. EBLG.* Carter, Linda M., in *GEAAL.* //www.news-releases.uiowa.edu/2006/ january/011206the-meeting.html. //www.nytimes.com/1991/02/21/obituaries/ darwin-turner-59-a-professor-of-english.html. //www.uc.edu/sas/ documents/eps/ TurnerApplication2008-2009.pdf. //www.uiowa.edu/ ~theatre/programs/dtat.html.

Turner, Henry McNeal
2/1/1834–5/8/1915

Spoken word—sermons, nonfiction—theology, hymnal; cleric, book publisher, church—periodicals founder, publisher, editor

Despite South Carolina laws prohibiting the education of African Americans, Henry McNeal Turner was surreptitiously taught to read and write as a youngster. In 1851, he started traveling through the South as an itinerant preacher, and in 1856, the Methodist Episcopal Church licensed him as a preacher and evangelist (1856–1857). In 1858, Turner discovered the African Methodist Episcopal Church (AME), which served African-American churchgoers, and he became a lifelong AME member. For two years, he studied AME theology (1858–1860), after which he was made a deacon (1860), then an elder (1862). Finally he was named the pastor of Washington, D.C.'s, largest AME church, the Union Bethel Church (1862–1865). There, he preached fiery sermons that warmed the hearts of his parishioners but inflamed the anger of European Americans who heard of him.

During the Civil War, Turner urged African-American men to fight for the Union Army, and President Abraham Lincoln named Turner the first African-American chaplain in the Union Army (1863). After the war ended, President Andrew Johnson appointed Turner to work as an agent of the Freedman's Bureau in Georgia, but he soon left that post to return to his church duties, organizing AME churches and missions in Georgia (1865–1867). He then worked as a delegate to Georgia's constitutional convention (1867) and was elected to the Georgia legislature, but the legislature refused to seat Turner and his fellow African-American legislators. Instead, Turner accepted appointments as postmaster in Macon, and then a customs inspector in Savannah, Georgia. In 1870, he was named pastor of a church in Savannah (1870–1876).

In 1876, Turner was asked to be the business manager of the AME Book Concern in Philadelphia (1876–1880), during one of its periods of greatest profitability. In 1880, he was elected an AME Church bishop, and a decade later, he was named to preside over the AME Church's newly established Morris Brown College in Atlanta (1890–1902). While there, he made four trips to Africa (1891–1898) and organized a national convention of African Americans in Cincinnati, Ohio (1893).

In addition to his provocative sermons, Turner wrote extensively for AME Church periodicals and for newspapers and other periodicals for the general public. Two favorite topics of his articles and editorials were bold attacks on racism wherever he found it and schemes for urging African Americans emigrate to their African motherland. Years after he left management of the AME Book Concern, he was involved in publishing Nashville's *Southern Christian Recorder* (1888–?), and he founded two church periodicals out of Atlanta: *Voice of Missions* (1892–1900) and *Voice of the People* (1901–1904), which he also edited and published. His other publications include an AME catechism, an AME hymnal, *The Genius and Theory of Methodist Polity* (1885), and *The Barbarous Decision of the Supreme Court...* (1883, revised as *The Black Man's Doom*, 1896).

In Oakville, Ontario, a small group of former fugitive slaves built their own church out of bricks and named it Turner Chapel, one of many churches in the African-Canadian community named in his honor.

REFERENCES: *B. Wiki.* Angell, Stephen W., in *AANB.* Joyce, Donald F. 1991. *Black Book Publishers in the United States: A Historical Dictionary of the Presses, 1817-1990.* Westport, CT: Greenwood Publishing Group. In //books.google.com/books?id=zzNHVYJR_AAC &pg=PA14&lpg=PA14&dq=ame+book+concern&source=bl&ots =AVpv1ymRXE&sig=yqW46MCV-qpZPHvtwFxVb9-P6zY&hl=en &ei=nyZQSt2eL5SsswOsxfyqDQ&sa=X&oi=book_result&ct=resu lt&resnum=5. Martin, Jonathan, in *BB.*

FURTHER READING: Bailey, Julius H., in GEAAL. Mixon, Gregory. "Henry McNeal Turner versus the Tuskegee Machine: Black Leadership in the Nineteenth Century." *The Journal of Negro History.* 79.4 (Fall 1994), p. 363. From *Literature Resource Center.* Wolfe, Margaret Ripley. "Bishop Henry McNeal Turner and African-American Religion in the South." *The Mississippi Quarterly.* 47.1 (Winter 1993), p. 186. From *Literature Resource Center.*

Turner, Lorenzo Dow
8/21/1890–1969
Nonfiction—linguistics; educator, scholar

Turner's *Africanisms in Gullah Dialect* (1949) was instrumental in revealing how much of African languages have been preserved in the speech of African Americans. For example, there's *danshiki* (Yoruba), from which we have the *dashiki; dzug* (meaning "misbehave" in Wolof), which led to our *juke* joints; *mbanzo* (Kimdunu), our *banjo*; and *jaja* and *nyambi* (Bantu) gave us our *jazz* and *yam*. Turner also turned out numerous articles and essays on linguistics, as well as his doctoral dissertation (*Anti-Slavery Sentiment in American Literature Prior to 1865*), and he wrote two more books, based on his proverb- and folktale-gathering sojourn to West Africa: *An Anthology of Krio Folklore and Literature and Interlinear Translations in English* (1963) and *Krio Texts: With Grammatical Notes and Translations in English* (1965).

REFERENCES: *SMKC.* —Tonya Bolden

FURTHER READING: *AANB. Wiki.*

Turner, Nat
10/2/1800–11/11/1831
Memoir; enslaved worker, rebel leader

We know him chiefly through his *"Confessions."* Although Turner had learned to read and write at an early age—unusual for a boy raised in slavery—he wasn't offered a means for writing his story in his own hand. Instead, he dictated it to his white confessor, Thomas Ruffin Gray, Turner's court-appointed attorney and unsympathetic scribe. Gray, who offered no defense of Turner in court, doubtless interpreted Turner's offerings through his own way of seeing things. For three days, Gray recorded Turner's story. In Gray's eyes, Turner was a mad fanatic whose religious fervor led him to insane acts of savage violence.

In Turner's eyes, God had specially chosen him to be His instrument of vengeance and of violent insurrection against white oppressors who were holding fellow blacks in bondage. Born a slave himself, Turner was a deeply religious child and youth. He believed that God had revealed to him his mission through divine visions: The first, in 1825, showed him "white spirits and black spirits engaged in battle, and the sun darkened—the thunder rolled in the heavens, and blood flowed in streams." His second vision, May 12, 1828, gave him his messianic assignment to lead his slave rebellion: "I heard a loud noise in the heavens, and the Spirit instantly appeared to me and said . . . Christ had laid down the yoke he had borne for the sins of men, and that I should take it on and fight . . . . And by the signs in the heavens that it would make known to me when I should commence the great work, and until the first sign appeared I should conceal it from the knowledge of men."

When, in February of 1831, Turner saw a solar eclipse, he believed it to be the sign he awaited, and he started making his bold plan and sharing it with others. Though he had planned the strike for freedom to start on Independence Day, he ended up postponing his uprising until August 21. On that day, he and his followers (said to number 70 or 80 at the peak of the revolt) started on a 40-hour rampage, killing 57 white men, women (starting with the widow of his former owner), and children. Turner had expected not to have to murder every last white person. He had envisioned that once the whites were terrified into seeing the error of their cruel enslavement of blacks, the whites would surrender, and the bloodshed could stop.

This part of Turner's vision was definitely not to come to pass. A white militia had been called to arms, which killed many of the rebels outright, caught and hanged others of them, and scattered the rest, and Turner went into hiding. On the eve of Hallow's Eve, Turner was captured and jailed. After his trial during the first few days of November, he was hanged on November 11. So furious were his executioners that his skin and his bones were stripped from his flesh. Following the rebellion, blacks—enslaved or not—were targets for every malicious white brute in the South, and any Southern whites who may have been sympathetic to abolition were either turned around or silenced. The crime of teaching an African American to read drew much harsher penalties, African-American preachers had to go underground and avoid public notice, and the Bible was barred from being held by black hands. White Southerners intuitively knew that reading and writing could promote a little too much *free* thinking, and those passages about Moses in Egypt were downright dangerous.

REFERENCES: *DNPUS. EAACH. SMKC.* —Tonya Bolden

FURTHER READING: *AANB. BCE. CE. HD. USMD. W. W2B. Wiki.* Andrews, William L. in COCAAL. Watts, Linda S., in GEAAL. //etext.virginia.edu/subjects/African-American.html.

Turpin, Waters (Edward)
4/9/1910–11/19/1968
Novels, plays, drama criticism, nonfiction textbook; social worker, educator, newsletter editor

Turpin's plays include two he produced and directed: *And Let the Day Perish* (1950) and *St. Michael's Dawn* (1956, about **Frederick Douglass**). He also wrote the libretto for *Li'l Joe* (1957). His other writings include three novels that were published (*These Low Grounds*, 1937; *O Canaan!* 1939; *The Rootless*, 1957), and some other novels and numerous short stories and poems that were not published. With Nick Aaron Ford, he wrote a textbook (*Basic Skills for Better Writing*, 1959) and edited a reader (*Extending Horizons: Selected Readings for Cultural Enrichment*, 1969). Turpin also was the editor-in-chief of Morgan State College's *Morgan Newsletter.*

REFERENCES: *BAWPP.* W. Carter, Linda M., in *GEAAL.* Hollis, Burney, in *AAWHR–40.* Reid, Margaret Ann, in *COCAAL* and *OCAAL.* Thomas, Elizabeth, in *CAO-02.*

Tyree, Omar (Rashad) (né Antwynne McLaurin; aka "Urban Griot")
4/15/1969–
Novels, juvenile literature, nonfiction business book, screenplay; journalist, self-publisher, speaker

An outstanding high-school student, Tyree was admitted to the University of Pittsburgh (UP) as 1 of 30 students in a challenge grant scholarship program for minority students (fall 1987). In the spring of 1988, Tyree won a tuition scholarship to study pharmacy sciences for his academic excellence in math and science. The following fall (1988), Tyree enrolled in a selective creative-writing course. Later on, his personal journal, "The Diary of a Freshman," was published in one of the school's minority counseling news pamphlets.

Following some incidents of racism on campus, Tyree transferred to historically black Howard University (in 1989), where he changed his major from pharmacy studies to journalism. In his senior year there, Tyree's column "Food for Thought" was featured in Howard's award-winning newspaper, *The Hilltop*, making him the first student whose column was featured in its pages. In 1991, Tyree graduated cum laude (with honors) in print journalism.

After graduating, Tyree was hired as a reporter, assistant editor, and advertising salesperson for D.C.'s *Washington Capital Spotlight*, a weekly newspaper (1991). He was later hired as chief reporter for *News Dimensions*, another D.C. weekly. Meanwhile, he supplemented his income freelancing for *Washington View* magazine. In 1992, he realized that his calling was to write fiction, but he knew that a first-time novelist would have trouble finding a publisher. Undaunted, he used money borrowed from

friends and family along with the knowledge he had gained about typesetting and printing while working in print journalism, moved to Delaware, and founded his own publishing company, MARS Productions.

Tyree's first novel, *Colored, On White Campus: The Education of a Racial World* (1992), was loosely autobiographical, based on his experiences at UP. Though it did not make *The New York Times*—or any other—bestseller list, it did sell well enough for him to publish his second novel, *Flyy Girl* (1993), a coming-of-age book with a female African-American protagonist, Tracy Ellison Grant. Because of Tyree's aggressive marketing campaign, *Flyy Girl* was reviewed by critics and sold much better than his first novel. Tyree then repackaged *Colored* and published it again as *Battlezone: The Struggle to Survive the American Institution* (1994). That year, Tyree's MARS Productions also published his *Capital City: The Chronicles of a DC Underworld* (1994), set in the late 1980s and early 1990s, featuring the struggles of urban African-American males. According to Tyree, these books established him as the author of a new genre of books, "urban classics."

Meanwhile, Tyree was lecturing to high schools, colleges, and organizations; speaking at community events; and writing articles to promote his books. For instance, his article "Meet the New Invisible Man: The Young Black Male Nobody Knows" was published in the Sunday "Outlook" section of the *Washington Post* (July 18, 1993, p. C5), making himself one of the youngest African-American journalists with an article published in the *Post*'s commentary page. The article was also reprinted both nationally and internationally, leading to an interview on a BBC television show in England (1993). A couple of years later, he was interviewed on a Black Entertainment Television (BET) by Julian Bond on the *America's Black Forum* show, titled "For Black Men Only" (1995). Tyree sold 25,000 copies of his self-published books.

In 1995, mainstream publisher Simon & Schuster offered Tyree a two-book contract. The first of the two books was a hardcover republication of *Flyy Girl*, which ended up selling about 200,000 copies. The second book was Tyree's new novel, *A Do Right Man* (1997), in which the title character, Bobby Dallas, is succeeding in his career as a radio talk-show host but is struggling with his love life. The book sold well enough for Simon & Schuster to agree to publish more of Tyree's novels, eventually publishing 11 more. Tyree's next novel, *Single Mom* (1998), became a national bestseller. The book's protagonist, self-made businesswoman Denise Stewart, is raising three sons by three different fathers, each of whom has his own ideas regarding his involvement in his son's life. Tyree's next novel was *Sweet St. Louis: An Urban Love Story* (1999), about a player who is tempted into doing all his playing at home, with one woman.

Tyree's next book, his sequel *For the Love of Money* (2000), picks up the story with Tracy at age 28, an up-and-coming film actress, screenwriter, and author (of the book *Flyy Girl*). The sequel earned Tyree an NAACP Image Award for Outstanding Literature in Fiction (2001), and it was the first of Tyree's books to make it to *The New York Times* bestseller list. Tyree followed it with *Just Say No!* (2001), and then he made his first entry into the new urban-horror literary genre, *Leslie* (2002), in which voodoo mixes with murder. Tyree's *Diary of a Groupie* (2003) mixes sex and suspense with challenges to morality.

Meanwhile, Tyree was writing a series of novels using the pen name "The Urban Griot." Tyree's Urban Griot novels include *The Underground* (2001), *One Crazy-A** Night* (2003), *College Boy* (2003), and *Cold Blooded: A Hardcore Novel* (2004). Tyree also collaborated with Donna Hill, Monica Jackson, Kevin S. Brockenbrough, Linda Addison, and Angela C. Allen to create the vampire-fiction anthology *Dark Thirst* (2004, Pocket; 2006, Simon & Schuster).

Tyree's third Tracy Ellison Grant novel, *Boss Lady* (2005), is narrated by Tracy's 16-year-old mentee and cousin, Vanessa Tracy Smith, who is eager for the glamour and fame she sees her cousin enjoying. Tyree followed it with *What They Want* (2006), *The Last Street Novel* (2007), and *Pecking Order* (2008). Tyree has said that *Pecking Order* will be his "final adult fiction novel," noting that his 15 books had "sold more than 1.5 million copies worldwide" (quoted in //thedailyvoice.com/voice/2008/06/street-lit-000748.php). By the time he published *The Last Street Novel,* Tyree had been awarded the **Phillis Wheatley** Literary Award for Body of Work in Urban Fiction (2006).

Tyree's next entrepreneurial enterprise was to found a record company, Hot Lava Entertainment, and to found a magazine publisher, *Flyy Girl* Incorporated (2005). He also continues to write. He wrote a collection of short stories, *12 Brown Boys* (2008), for youngsters ages 9–12 years. He also ventured into nonfiction with *The Equation: Applying the 4 Indisputable Components of Business Success* (2008, published by Wiley). Tyree has also been anthologized. Several of his books have been adapted to audio format (unabridged and abridged), and he recorded *Rising Up!* under his pen name The Urban Griot (2003). He has written a screenplay about the music industry, "Move the Crowd," and he is seeking to have both it and an adaptation of *Flyy Girl* made into movies. He also has an Internet presence at the websites //www.omartyree.com and //www.theurbangriot.com.

REFERENCES: *CAO-08. Wiki.* Decker, Ed, in *BB.* Henderson, Carol E., in *21-CAN.* Tyree, Omar, "An Urban 'Street Lit' Retirement," in //thedailyvoice.com/voice/2008/06/street-lit-000748.php. //www.allied-media.com/Publications/african_american_newspapers.htm. //www.omartyree.com. //www.theurbangriot.com. Amazon.com.

FURTHER READING: Schmitt, Judith M., in *GEAAL.*

Tyson, Neil deGrasse
10/5/1958–
Autobiography/memoir, nonfiction—science; educator, educational television host

Neil deGrasse Tyson has been looking up at the stars since he was in elementary school. In his teens, Tyson was spending as much time as possible at the nearby Hayden Planetarium, where he attended astronomy courses and sky shows, and he queried the staff. At age 15 years, he had gained enough knowledge that he was already giving talks to his local New York City astronomy community. While attending the Bronx High School of Science (1973–1976), he was made editor-in-chief of the school's *Physical Science Journal.* After high school, Tyson majored in physics at Harvard University, where he earned his B.A. (1980), then he earned his M.A. at the University of Texas at Austin (UT—A) (1983). After a few years of postgraduate work at UT—A, Tyson transferred to New York City's Columbia University (in 1988), where he earned his Ph.D. in astrophysics (1991).

With his Ph.D. in hand, Tyson moved southwest to Princeton University's Department of Astrophysics, as a postdoctoral research associate (1991–1994), and then a visiting research scientist and lecturer (1994–2003). While continuing to teach sometimes at Princeton, Tyson moved home to the American Museum of Natural History (AMNH) Department of Astrophysics on Manhattan's Upper West Side in New York City, where he is now the first Frederick P. Rose Director of the Hayden Planetarium (since 1996), as well as a research associate at the AMNH (since 2003). In addition to his scientific and administrative duties, Tyson makes sure to take time to stimulate and foster the curiosity of budding young scientists much like himself as a child, such as through the AMNH Department of Education's "Science in the City" program.

Tyson has also worked to promote scientific thinking and appreciation of the scientific method. He regularly attends and addresses scientific colloquia, and he is frequently interviewed on television as a science expert (e.g., on ABC *World News Tonight,* CBS *Evening News, Charlie Rose*). Tyson has also found ways to demonstrate his sense of humor, within a scientific context, having appeared numerous times on Comedy Central programs (e.g., *The Colbert Report, The Daily Show with Jon Stewart*), at least twice on *Late Night with Conan O'Brien,* and at least once on the National Public Radio (NPR) quiz show, *Wait Wait ... Don't Tell Me!*

Tyson has also been involved in television science-education series. For the History Channel, Tyson has been a key expert interviewed on numerous episodes of its science program, *The Universe*. Tyson has also been involved in the Public Broadcasting System (PBS) television series NOVA. In 2000, he hosted the *One Universe* NOVA special, and with Charles Tsun-Chu Liu and Robert Irion, he coauthored the show's companion volume, *One Universe: At Home in the Cosmos* (2000), which won the Science Writing Award from the American Institute of Physics (2001). In 2004, he hosted the four-part *Origins* miniseries, and with Donald Goldsmith, he cowrote the companion volume *Origins: Fourteen Billion Years Of Cosmic Evolution* (2004). Since 2006, he has hosted NOVA's summer series *NOVA scienceNOW* (2006–2009).

In print, Tyson has been a science consultant for both a newspaper and a textbook publisher. He has also authored numerous research papers (1980s–1990s). In 1983, while still working toward his doctorate, he also started writing for a wider audience with a regular question-and-answer column for *Star Date* magazine. Tyson later collected the columns into his book *Merlin's Tour of the Universe* (1989). Both the columns and the book are supposedly authored by Merlin, a scholar visiting Earth from his native planet, Omniscia. About 8 years later, the book was published as *Merlin's Tour of the Universe: A Skywatcher's Guide to Everything from Mars and Quasars to Comets, Planets, Blue Moons, and Werewolves* (1997). Tyson also reworked this material to create a more cohesive look at the *Universe Down to Earth* (1994).

While continuing to write his *Star Date* column, in 1995, Tyson started also writing his "Universe" column for *Natural History* magazine. The married father of two children, Tyson has also contributed his writing to *Highlights for Children*. Tyson's subsequent books have included *Just Visiting This Planet: Merlin Answers More Questions about Everything under the Sun, Moon, and Stars* (1998), *Cosmic Horizons: Astronomy at the Cutting Edge* (2000, published by AMNH), *City of Stars: A New Yorker's Guide to the Cosmos* (2002, published by AMNH), his memoir *The Sky Is Not the Limit: Adventures of an Urban Astrophysicist* (2000; 2nd ed., 2004), *Death by Black Hole: And Other Cosmic Quandaries* (2007), and *The Pluto Files: The Rise and Fall of America's Favorite Planet* (2009). In addition to these works, he has participated in producing *My Favorite Universe* (2003), his 12-part lecture series, available in several formats. He also coedited *Cosmic Horizons: Astronomy at the Cutting Edge* (2001, with Steven Soter).

Tyson's memberships include the American Physical Society, Astronomical Society of the Pacific, International Planetarium Society, and a fellowship in the New York Academy of Sciences. He presides over the Planetary Society, where he was formerly vice president and then chaired the board of directors, he served on the board of the American Astronomical Society, and he serves on the board of directors of the Astronauts Memorial Foundation. Former President George W. Bush named Tyson to serve on two aerospace-related commissions (2001, 2004), and Tyson was later awarded NASA's Distinguished Public Service Medal. Tyson also won the Columbia University Medal of Excellence (2001) and the Klopsteg Memorial Award (2007), and he received at least eight honorary doctorates. The International Astronomical Union named asteroid 13123 "Tyson" in his honor, *Craines* magazine named him 1 of the 40 most influential and up-and-coming New York City residents (1996), *People Magazine* voted him the "Sexiest Astrophysicist Alive" (2000), and *Time* magazine named him 1 of 100 Most Influential People of 2007.

REFERENCES: *CAO-07. Wiki.* Decker, Ed, in *BB.* Kolker, Amy Sparks, in *AANB.* //en.wikipedia.org/wiki/NASA_Distinguished_Service_Medal. //www.colbertnation.com/the-colbert-report-videos/232270/june-29-2009/neil-degrasse-tyson. //www.haydenplanetarium.org/tyson/category/media/colbertreport. //www.thedailyshow.com/video/index.jhtml?videoId=81508&title=neil-degrasse-tyson-pt.-1. //www.tv.com/the-daily-show/neil-degrasse-tyson/episode/1122134/summary.html. Amazon.com.

~U~

Umbra
1962–1974

Society of Umbra (aka the Umbra Workshop)
1962–1963

Literary journal and mutual-support group for African-American poets

In 1962, New York City poets **Thomas (Covington) Dent**, 19-year-old David Henderson, and **Calvin C. (Coolidge) Hernton** noticed that European-American poets had benefited from forming artist collectives, but these collectives had neglected African-American poets. They decided to remedy the situation by forming their own collective of largely yet-unpublished poets, who originally met in Dent's Lower East Side apartment. The weekly workshops included Lloyd Addison, Steve Cannon, Ann Guilfoyle, Albert Hayes, Joe Johnson, Charles and **William Patterson**, Oliver Pitcher, Norman Pritchard, Lennox Raphael, **Ishmael Reed**, Rolland Snellings (later **Askia Muhammad Touré**), college student **Lorenzo Thomas**, James Thompson, Brenda Walcott, and others. Men did all of the reading, and Walcott later recalled that the women poets "were there to serve or observe. It was a very macho group" (quoted in *GEAAL*). The Society of Umbra (better known as the Umbra Workshop) also included European-American poets Art Berger and Nora Hicks. The name "Umbra" was taken from a line in one of Addison's poems.

The year after the workshops started, Umbra members decided to publish their own literary journal, and *Umbra* emerged into the light in March of 1963, printed on an offset press on heavily textured paper, with a cover designed by then-unknown artist **Tom Feelings**. That first issue featured poems by **Julian Bond, Lerone Bennett, Julia Fields**, David Henderson, **Raymond Patterson, Alice Walker**, and others; subsequent issues featured **Nikki Giovanni** and **Quincy Troupe**, among others. Dent, Henderson, and Hernton coedited the journal until 1968, when Henderson took over as sole editor. Initially, the journal had no particular political outlook, other than opposing racism, so the criterion for publication was literary excellence. As is so common among the best-intentioned groups, many factors tended to pull it apart. In the case of the Umbra Workshop, these factors included outside pressures and demands on members' time and energy, petty jealousies, and political differences between the three editors and the more activist Pattersons and Rolland Snellings, who soon converted to Islam and changed his name to Askia Muhammad Abu Bakr el Touré.

In November of 1963, President John Fitzgerald Kennedy (JFK) was assassinated, and the three editors refused to publish a poem critical of JFK in the second issue of *Umbra*, published in December of 1963. As a result, the group largely disbanded. After Henderson took over as sole editor, he also published three anthology issues: *Umbra Anthology, 1967-1968* (1968), *Umbra Blackworks, 1970-1971* (1971), and *Umbra/Latin Soul 1974-1975* (1975). By 1975, *Umbra* and the Umbra Workshop had receded into the shadows. Lorenzo Thomas created the archival "Umbra Poets Workshop collection, 1976-1986," which included Michael Oren's oral-history interviews with 13 of the poets, Thomas's interview of **Amiri Baraka**, and Thomas's manuscript, "Annotated Bibliography of the Umbra Workshop 1962-1982."

REFERENCES: Alic, Margaret, "David Henderson," in *BB*. Cole, Terry Joseph, "David Henderson," in *AAP-55-85*. "David Henderson," in *CAO-06*. Dent, Tom, "Lorenzo Thomas," in *AAP-55-85*. Rodriguez, Raquel, in *GEAAL*. //en.wikipedia.org/wiki/Lennox_Raphael. //www.worldcat.org/identities/lccn-n81-23042. //www.worldcat.org/search?q=au%3ASociety+of+Umbra.&qt=hot_author. //www.worldcat.org/search?q=no:173303903. //www.newsreel.org/guides/furious.htm.

Uncle Tom *See* Henson, Josiah *See also* Stowe, Harriet Beecher

~V~

Van Dyke, Henry
10/3/1928–
Novels; journalist, book acquisitions editor

Van Dyke's novels include *Ladies of the Rachmaninoff Eyes* (1965), *Blood of Strawberries* (1968, dedicated to **Carl Van Vechten**), *Dead Piano* (1971/1997), and *Lunacy and Caprice* (1987). In addition, he has contributed numerous short pieces to various literary journals. Van Dyke started his first novel while working as a journalist, completing it while on the editorial staff of Basic Books.

REFERENCES: *BAWPP. CAO-04.* McGehee, Edward G., in *AAFW-55-84.* Senter, Caroline, in *COCAAL* and *OCAAL.* Amazon.com.

Van Peebles, Melvin (né Melvin Peebles)
8/21/1932–
Novels, screenplays, plays, rap lyrics, musical play, television scripts, autobiography/memoir, nonfiction—economics and finance, graphic novel; filmmaker, director, composer, actor

After graduating from Ohio Wesleyan's literature department, Van Peebles served for 31/2 years in the U.S. Air Force, then found that civilian airlines weren't as willing as the government to employ an African American. After meeting and marrying his wife, Maria, in California, the couple moved to Mexico, where he worked for a time as a portrait artist and where their son Mario was born. When they returned to California, Van Peebles worked as a cable-car operator and wrote a pictorial book about San Francisco cable cars, targeted to tourists: *The Big Heart* (1957). He then made a few shoestring-budget films, which Hollywood rejected.

At this point, Van Peebles decided to earn a Ph.D. in astronomy in Amsterdam, so he and his family (now also including his daughter Megan) left for Europe. While in

Henry Van Dyke

Amsterdam, he was urged to go to France, told that the French film industry offered great opportunities. In France, those opportunities were rather ephemeral at first, so Van Peebles wrote crime reports; he edited the French equivalent of *Mad* magazine; and he wrote five novels in French (e.g., *Un Ours pour le F.B.I.,* 1964 [A Bear for the F.B.I., 1968]; and *Un American en enfer,* 1965 [The True American, 1976]; *La Fete a Harlem,* 1967; *La Permission,* 1967). With those works under his belt, he was then able to make his first feature film, the critically acclaimed *La Permission* (c. 1968, [The Story of the Three-Day Pass]).

Back in the United States, Van Peebles recorded his *Br'er Soul* (1968) album of jazz-accompanied raps. He then filmed his *Sweet Sweetback's Baadasssss Song* (1971), for which he wrote the script and the music, as well as directing, producing, and starring in the film, which eventually earned $10 million, making it one of the biggest-earning independent films of that time. Recommended viewing by the Black Panther Party for its authenticity and its political viewpoint, its amazing success didn't lead to further financing for his films. After telling readers how he made it in *The Making of Sweet*

Sweetback's Baadasssss Song (1972), Van Peebles turned to writing plays, creating *Ain't Supposed to Die a Natural Death* (1971), for which he wrote the words, the music, the lyrics, and directed the play, which he produced on Broadway; he also adapted the play to a novel of the same name (1973). He wrote two more Broadway shows: *Don't Play Us Cheap* (1972), adapted from his novel *Don't Play Us Cheap: A Harlem Party,* and adapted for film in 1973; and *Waltz of the Stork* (1982), in which both he and his son Mario acted. He also toured the nation with his one-man show *Out There by Your Lonesome* (1973). In the late 1970s, he wrote two screenplays produced as films by the NBC network (*Just an Old Sweet Song,* 1976; *Sophisticated Gents,* 1979).

Astonishingly, this Black Panther Party-approved entrepreneur became the only African-American trader on the American Stock Exchange in 1985, and he ended up writing two books about his experiences there: *Bold Money: A New Way to Play the Options Market* (1986) and *Bold Money: How to Get Rich in the Options Market* (1987). In the 1990s, Van Peebles wrote another novel and returned to film work, acting in *Posse* (1993), a film written by his son Mario. Melvin and Mario then collaborated on the film *Panther* (1995), based on Melvin's 1995 same-named novel, with Melvin writing the script and producing the film and Mario directing it (once again directing his father, who acted in the film). Melvin has since retitled the novel *Panther: The Novel That Inspired the Movie* (2000). As might be expected, the father-son duo have cowritten a book about their collaboration: *No Identity Crisis: A Father and Son's Own Story of Working Together* (1990). Mario Van Peebles also produced the film *BAADASSSSS!* about the making of his father's film (2004). Mario and Melvin also appeared as father and son on an episode of the soap opera *all My Children* (2008).

A fitting medium for describing Melvin is a documentary entitled *How to Eat Your Watermelon in White Company (and Enjoy It)* (2005). His most recent film is *Confessionsofa Ex-Doofus-ItchyFooted Mutha* (2008), for which Van Peebles is coming out with a graphic novel version in 2009. Returning to his musical roots, Van Peebles is working on a two-disc album with Madlib, to be released on Stones Throw Records. In addition to *Br'er Soul,* his previous recordings include *As Serious As A Heart-Attack* (1974), *What the....You Mean I Can't Sing?!* (1974), and *Ghetto Gothic* (1995), as well as sound tracks for music he composed for films or plays, such as *Watermelon Man* (1970), which he did not write but which he directed and for which he composed the music; *Sweet Sweetback's Baadasssss Song* (1971); *Ain't Supposed To Die A Natural Death* (1970); and *Don't Play Us Cheap* (1973). What is the secret to his continuing health and productivity? In a 2005 interview, he noted that he considers neck bones to be "health food," he's "into Uncle Ben's

and fat," and he reported running seven miles that morning, preparing for the annual Boston Marathon (quoted by Williams). The reader should decide whether any of these practices contributes to Van Peebles's stamina and his prolific productivity.

REFERENCES: *AANB. B. BAWPP. CAO-08. D. F. W. Wiki.* Briley, Ron, in *GEAAL.* Erickson, Hal, *All Movie Guide,* in *Wr.* Kellman, Andy, *All Music Guide,* in *A.* Robinson, Alonford James, Jr., in *EA-99.* Taft, Claire A., in *BH2C.* Wankoff, Jordan, in *BB.* Williams, Kam, in //reviews.aalbc.com/melvin_van_peebles.htm. Amazon.com.

van Sertima, Ivan (Gladstone)
1/26/1935–5/25/2009
Poems, novel, essays, scholarly writings, nonfiction—history, linguistics, anthropology, and biography

Born in British Guiana (now Guyana), van Sertima finished his primary and secondary education in his homeland. He then worked for a few years as a Press and Broadcasting Officer and writer for the Government Information Services in Georgetown, British Guiana (1956-1959). In 1959, he moved to London, England, where he freelanced in broadcasting and writing. Among other things, he made weekly broadcasts about literature for BBC, to both Africa and the Caribbean. Meanwhile, he earned his B.A. in African languages and literature, with honors, from the London School of Oriental and African Studies (1969). He also managed to learn to speak both Swahili and Hungarian fluently. After college, he got a job broadcasting for the Central Office of Information in London (1969-1970).

While still in British Guiana, van Sertima published his poetry collection *River and the Wall* (1958), which was sold in Britain, as well. While earning his baccalaureate in London, van Sertima conducted linguistic fieldwork in Tanzania (1967), which led to his publication of his *Swahili Dictionary of Legal Terms* (1968). He also published *Caribbean Writers: Critical Essays* (1968/1971), a collection of his critical essays on novels written by Caribbean authors. He even wrote a novel called *Blackhouse,* which was filmed under the title of *The Black Prince.*

In 1970, he took a trip to the United States—and stayed here ever since. Van Sertima settled in New Brunswick, New Jersey as both a student working toward his M.A. in anthropology (1977) and an instructor in the newly formed African Studies department (1970-1972). He later became an assistant professor (1972-1979), and then an associate professor of African studies in the Department of Africana Studies until his retirement (1979-2006). While completing his master's degree, van Sertima was also completing his masterwork, *They Came before Columbus: The African Presence in Ancient America* (1977/2003). The bestseller went on to enjoy dozens of printings. In *They Came*, van Sertima offers an abundant array of evidence (e.g., from anthropology, archeology, architecture, botany, linguistics, metallurgy, navigation, and oceanography) that Africans had reached Latin America centuries before Columbus's arrival.

Many mainstream scholars of anthropology have since attacked his evidence, questioning individual points and charging van Sertima with extracting selected bits of information from their explanatory contexts. Other historians have countered that all published histories involve the historian's selection and analysis of information. Even his detractors do not question his ability to write captivatingly. The Book-of-the-Month Club chose it as a featured selection, and in 1981 it won van Sertima the Clarence L. Holte Prize. Perhaps an even greater tribute, however, is that educators started using van Sertima's book in their college-level African studies courses, and eventually his work was represented in some Afrocentric curriculum in urban primary and secondary schools. He was also invited to present his evidence to the U.S. Congressional Subcommittee on Census and Population on July 7, 1987 and to the Smithsonian Institution in 1991.

In 1979, van Sertima founded the *Journal of African Civilizations*, which his widow, Jacqueline, said she will continue to publish. Van Sertima contributed to and edited numerous volumes as issues of the *Journal* and as anthologies published by Transaction Press. Some volumes appeared first in the *Journal* and then were published by the Press, and vice versa. These edited volumes included *African Presence in Early Europe* (1981/1986), *The African Presence in the Art of the Americas* (1981), *Blacks in Science: Ancient and Modern* (1983/1990), *Egypt Revisited* (1983, 160 pp.; 1983, 454 pp.; rev. ed., 1991; 1999), *Black Women in Antiquity* (1984/1988), *Nile Valley Civilizations: Proceedings of the Nile Valley Conference, Atlanta, September 26-30, 1984* (1985; as *Nile Valley Civilizations*, 1989), *African Presence in Early Asia* (with Runoko Rashidi, 1985; rev. ed., 1988), *Great African Thinkers, Volume I: Cheikh Anta Diop* (1986, with Larry Obadele Williams), *African Presence in Early America* (1987/1995), *Great Black Leaders: Ancient and Modern* (1988), *The Golden Age of the Moor* (1991/1993), *Egypt: Child of Africa*, (1994/1995), and *Early America Revisited* (1998).

In addition, van Sertima authored several major literary reviews published in Europe and Asia, as well as the United States (e.g., *Inter-American Review*), and he published essays on the Gullah language spoken on the Sea Islands off the Georgia Coast. He also contributed articles to books. On his death, his widow, Jacqueline, said she planned to publish a book of his poetry. More than a decade before **Toni Morrison** was awarded the Nobel Prize in Literature (1993), the Swedish Academy invited van Sertima to serve as a nominator for the Nobel Literature

Prize committee (1976-1980). The international agency UNESCO also invited van Sertima to join its International Commission for Rewriting the Scientific and Cultural History of Mankind. Two years before he retired from Rutgers, The Rutgers African-American Alumni Alliance inducted van Sertima into the Alumni Hall of Fame (2004).

REFERENCES: CAO-01. *Wiki.* Manheim, James M., in *BB.* //en.wikipedia.org/wiki/Guyana. //en.wikipedia.org/wiki/Transaction_Publishers. //voices.washingtonpost.com/postmortem/2009/06/controversial_afrocentric_scho.html. //www.blackvoices.com/boards/welcome/welcome/bv-welcome-forum/orisons-ivan-van-sertima-died/30182/1?utc=true. //www.nj.com/news/ledger/jersey/index.ssf?/base/news-14/1244174855241290.xml&coll=1. //www.nytimes.com/1981/03/08/books/van-sertima-wins-prize-for-book-on-africa-van-sertima-wins-7500-book-prize.html?scp=3&sq=Ivan%20van%20Sertima&st=cse. //www.rutgersblackalumni.org/HallofFame/hof2004/inductees2004/vansertima.htm. //www.theblacklibrary.com/standard.htm. //www.transactionpub.com/cgi-bin/transaction publishers.storefront/4a51f83f000908dcea6fc0a80aa50674/Cartridge/ss1257027b/AdvSearch/Run/MASK989?searchTerm=6&attr=6&tempSearchString=ivan+van+sertima&nr=ivan+van+sertima&SearchMaskLogic=2&attr_1011=&attr_1070=&attr_1073=&attr_1087=&attr_1094=&attr_1100=ivan+van+sertima&attr_1101=ivan+van+sertima&attr_1010=ivan+van+sertima&attr_1103=ivan+van+sertima&name=ivan+van+sertima. Amazon.com.

FURTHER READING: Internet links from //aliciabanks.blogspot.com/.

Van Vechten, Carl
6/17/1880–12/21/1964
Novels, music and literary criticism, fashion commentary, nonfiction books, anthology; photographer, journalist

Of European-American ancestry, Van Vechten spent much of his life championing the literature and culture of African Americans. Among other things, he collected African-American literary works and founded the **James Weldon Johnson** Memorial Collection of Negro Arts and Letters (housed at Yale University), the Carl Van Vechten Collection at the New York City Public Library, and the George Gershwin Memorial Collection of Music and Musical Literature (music books) at Fisk University (in Nashville, Tennessee). He also hosted a literary salon during the **Harlem Renaissance** and advanced the writings of **Langston Hughes**, **Helene Johnson**, James Weldon Johnson, **Nella Larsen**, and other writers of that era. It could easily be said that he was the most prominent European American associated with the Renaissance in New York. His most acclaimed novel was written about these experiences and was intended to showcase the riches of African-American culture, but his choice of title, *Nigger Heaven* (1926), divided the African-American literary community. Langston Hughes provided songs for the book, and many other gay and bisexual participants in

During the Harlem Renaissance, a view of the Renaissance Casino in Harlem, New York, 1927

the Renaissance appreciated the work, but many others were outraged by the title—and by Van Vechten. **Jessie Carney Smith** took a neutral view of him in her brief biographical essay on **Arna Bontemps** (in *BH2C*), referring to Van Vechten as "the benefactor of the period and unofficial record-keeper of the 'New Negro' movement."

After Van Vechten graduated from the University of Chicago in 1903, he started working as a reporter, joining *The New York Times* in 1906 as an assistant music critic. In that role, he encouraged New Yorkers to enjoy jazz and ragtime music, introducing those forms to a wider audience. In 1907, Van Vechten went to Europe as the *Times's* Paris correspondent. There, he met Mabel Dodge (Luhan), and she introduced him to a host of literary figures, including Gertrude Stein, who later named him as her literary executor. His popularly acclaimed novel *Peter Whiffle: His Life and Works* (1922) describes the experiences of a young man in Paris during that era.

While still in Europe, Van Vechten also married (1907) and divorced (1912) Anna Elizabeth Snyder. Snyder was awarded alimony, but by mutual consent, he never paid it. In 1914, stateside, Van Vechten married again (to Fania Marinoff), prompting his first wife to decide that alimony would be nice indeed, and she pressed for back payments. Van Vechten refused to pay (at least in part because he simply didn't have the money), so he

ended up spending four months in jail—with a piano in his cell and a plethora of visitors passing through. Money problems continued to plague him through most of the 1920s, until his older brother died, leaving him $1 million in 1928—when being a millionaire was rare wealth indeed.

By 1928, Van Vechten had published five more novels (*The Blind Bow-Boy*, 1923, reprinted 1977; *The Tattooed Countess: A Romantic Novel with a Happy Ending*, 1924, reprinted 1987; *Firecrackers*, 1925; *Nigger Heaven*, 1926; and *Spider Boy: A Scenario for a Moving Picture*, 1928), and he had written several nonfiction works (*Music after the Great War*, 1915; *Music and Bad Manners*, 1916; *Interpreters and Interpretations*, 1917, 1920, a collection of music reviews; *The Merry-Go-Round*, 1918; *The Music of Spain*, 1918; *In the Garret*, 1920; *The Tiger in the House*, 1920, reprinted 1996; *Red*, 1925; and *Excavations: A Book of Advocacies*, 1926). He had also edited an anthology of cat stories, *Lords of the Housetops* (1921); and *My Musical Life* (1924, with composer Nikolay Andreyevich Rimsky-Korsakov). After receiving his inheritance, he produced two more novels (*Feathers*, 1930. and *Parties: Scenes from Contemporary New York Life*, 1930, reprinted 1993), a set of autobiographical essays (*Sacred and Profane Memories*, 1932), and *Fragments* (1955). He also edited Gertrude Stein's *Selected Writings of Gertrude Stein* (1946; reprinted 1990) and *Last Operas and Plays* (1949).

Although he clearly had published works after 1932, some sources suggest that after publishing *Sacred and Profane Memories*, he vowed never to write again. He did turn his attention to photography and soon established his reputation as a preeminent portrait photographer of his time. Many of his photographs are considered crucial to the documentary collections at the New York Museum of Modern Art and other institutions. His photographs may be seen in *Dance Photography of Carl Van Vechten* (1981), *Passionate Observer: Photographs by Carl Van Vechten* (1993), and *Generations in Black and White: From the James Weldon Johnson Memorial Collection* (1997). Two other books are listed as being authored by him in Amazon.com: *Ex-Libris* (1981) and *"Keep A-Inchin' Along"* (1979), with publication dates following his death.

REFERENCES: *EB-98. G-97. OC20LE. RG20. WDAA.* French, Warren, in *G-97.*

FURTHER READING: *B. CAO-06. CE. MWEL. W. Wiki.* Gunther, Carol, in *AWP-1920-1939.* Kellner, Bruce, in *AAWHR-40, AW:ACLB-81-2,* and in *RGAL-3.* Lueders, Edward, in *AN-1910-45.* Owens, David M., in *GEAAL.*

Vann, Robert Lee
8/27/1879–10/24/1940
Newspaper editor, publisher, journalist, attorney

Although Vann was a criminal-defense attorney and participated in politics (as a Republican, then a Democrat, then a Republican again), he probably had the greatest influence on U.S. history through his work as editor of the *Pittsburgh Courier* (1910-1940), a preeminent black-owned and -operated newspaper with national readership. Educated at the Waters Training School (valedictorian, 1901, a Baptist college in Winton, North Carolina), the Wayland Academy (1901-1903, Richmond, Virginia), Western University of Pennsylvania (starting in 1903, in Pittsburgh), and Wesleyan's law school, Vann was admitted to the Pennsylvania bar at the end of 1909 (cf. **George Vashon**, 1840). Within a few months, he was an attorney for the *Pittsburgh Courier*, and within another few months, he was the newspaper's editor and publisher, a position he continued to hold until his death. Through Vann's editorial policies, the *Courier* became known nationwide for its passionate stands against segregation and other forms of racial discrimination. Vann also challenged other newspapers of both the black press and the white press to address these issues. In fact, many credit the *Courier* with prompting coverage of these issues in the mainstream white-owned press. The *Courier* was also instrumental in motivating the Great Migration of blacks from the rural South to the urban North.

Vann was not without contradictions, however. For instance, although he opposed segregation in public institutions, he supported the efforts of **Booker T. Washington** and of **Marcus Garvey** to develop separate black businesses and vocations rather than attempting to integrate white businesses and professions. Vann also endorsed Garvey's plans for establishing a colony for African Americans in Africa, yet he urged African Americans to fight for Uncle Sam in World War I and World War II. He outspokenly opposed some union activity (e.g., strikes to have the workday limited to *just* 12 hours/day), yet he supported **A. Philip Randolph**'s attempt to unionize the Pullman porters—and then within a few years, he urged Randolph to resign from the leadership of that union because of Randolph's socialist views. Although many blacks and whites strongly disagreed with many of Vann's views, they always appreciated that his words could stimulate discussion and could prompt people to think deeply about the issues of his day.

During Vann's tenure, the *Courier*'s circulation varied from a low of 8,000 to a peak of 250,000, depending on the economic circumstances, his editorial policies, and the newsworthiness of events. (It reached its all-time peak of 357,212 in 1947.) At the time of his death, the *Courier* was the most widely circulated black newspaper in the nation.

REFERENCES: *BDAA. AANB.* Dematteis, Philip B., in *ANJ-26-50-1.* Parker, Roy, Jr. (1998), in //www.ncnewspapersineducation.org/ About_Newspapers/NC_Newspaper_History/RoyParker%2024.pdf. Yu, Karlson, in //www.blackpast.org/?q=aah/vann-robert-lee-1879-1940. //www.aaregistry.com/detail.php?id=329. //www.explorepahistory.com/hmarker.php?markerId=1060. //www.pbs.org/blackpress/news_bios/courier.html. //www.pbs.org/ blackpress/news_bios/vann.html. //www.routledge-ny.com/ref/ harlem/thematic.html.

Vashon, George B. (Boyer)
7/25/1824?–10/5/1878
Poems, essays; attorney, educator, administrator

In 1838, 14-year-old George was secretary of the first Junior Anti-Slavery Society in America, and in 1844, he made history as the first African American to graduate from Oberlin College. He then studied to become an attorney in Pittsburgh, Pennsylvania, but his race barred him from admission to the state bar. After a 30-month sojourn to Haiti, he returned to the States and was admitted to the New York bar in 1848, the first African American to do so in that state. He returned to Haiti and taught at College Faustin in Port-Au-Prince for a couple years, then he returned to New York, where he practiced law (1850-1854) and then taught college in McGrawville, New York for three years. In 1856, Vashon published his *Autographs of Freedom* collection, which included his epic narrative about Haitian revolutionary hero "Vincent Oge," believed to be the first published narrative poem by an African American. In 1857, he married Susan Paul Smith, with whom he had seven children, and for the next decade, he worked as a teacher and a school principal in Pittsburgh schools. After that, he held various governmental positions in Washington, D.C. Meanwhile, many of Vashon's essays, poems, and letters were published in numerous periodicals.

REFERENCES: *BAWPP. W.* Sherman, Joan R., in *COCAAL* and *OCAAL.*

FURTHER READING: *AANB.* Gardner, Eric, in *GEAAL.* Thornell, Paul N. D. "The Absent Ones and the Providers: A Biography of the Vashons." *The Journal of Negro History.* 83.4 (Fall 1998) p. 284. From *Literature Resource Center.*

Vernon, Olympia
5/22/1973–
Novels

After graduating from Southeastern Louisiana University, Olympia Vernon was given the Top Alumnus of the Year Award (1999). While still in graduate school, her writing was nominated for the Robert O. Butler Award in Fiction (2000). She went on to earn her M.F.A. from Louisiana State University (2002), which honored her with the M.F.A. Thesis Award for *Eden. Eden: A Novel* (2003, Grove Press) offers a surrealistic, richly sensual, but grim account of Maddy Dangerfield, a 14-year-old who is sent each weekend to nurse her mother's dying sister, with whom Maddy's reprobate father had one of his countless extramarital sexual relationships.

Eden went on to be nominated for the Pulitzer Prize for Fiction (2004), to win the Richard and Hinda Rosenthal Foundation Award from the American Academy of Arts and Letters (2004), and to be chosen as a Best Book of 2003 for Southern reading by the *Atlanta Journal-Constitution.* By the time Vernon received those honors, she had already been twice awarded the Matt Clark Memorial Scholarship, had won a Words and Music Scholarship at Louisiana State University, and had won the Director's Award for Outstanding Personal Achievement in literature and language, from Louisiana State University.

Meanwhile, Vernon published her second novel, *Logic* (2004), an experimental, surrealistic, almost hallucinogenic view of a pregnant teen who has been repeatedly raped by her father. Vernon's third novel, *A Killing in This Town: A Novel* (2006), was inspired by the brutal 1998 murder of James Byrd, set in the context of more than a century of Southern lynchings of African Americans.

REFERENCES: *CAO-05. Wiki.* //en.wikipedia.org/wiki/American_ Academy_ of_Arts_and_Letters. //en.wikipedia.org/wiki/Kip_Holden. //www.groveatlantic.com/. //www.groveatlantic.com/grove/bin/wc.dll? groveproc~genauth~1694. Amazon.com.

FURTHER READING: Ostrom, Hans, in *GEAAL.*

Voice of the Negro, The
1904–1907
Literary journal

In the early 1900s, Austin N. Jenkins, the European-American vice president of Atlanta-based publisher J. L. Nichols, decided to start up a new publication to reach African-American readers. He hired two African Americans to head the publication: John Wesley Edward Bowen as the journal's founding editor, hired in October 1903, and **Jesse Max Barber** as the journal's managing editor, hired that November. Astonishingly the two managed to publish the first monthly issue of the *Voice of the Negro* in January 1904, the first magazine published in the South that was edited by African Americans.

Bowen's associate editor, Emmett Jay Scott, was **Booker T. Washington**'s private secretary. Whereas Bowen and Scott tended to agree with Booker T. Washington's more accommodationist outlook, Barber tended to take a more radical view, holding that African Americans should demand civil rights, rather than accommodating to a European-American timetable for benevolently granting civil rights when it suited. The first issue of the *Voice* included pieces by both Washington and Barber. Washington had little tolerance for anyone who disagreed with him, so he helped fund a competing journal, hoping to diminish-or eliminate-Barber's readership (*cf.* ***Alexander's Magazine****; see also* **William Monroe Trotter**). As soon as J. L. Nichols got wind of Washington's rival journal, the publisher cut its ties with Washington, accepted Scott's resignation, and gave Barber a free hand to openly oppose Washington's accommodationism.

In September, 1905, the *Voice* endorsed the Niagara Movement, spearheaded by Washington's chief opponent **W. E. B. Du Bois**, who was also a *Voice* contributor. Contributors also included noted scholars **John Hope, Kelly Miller,** and **William Sanders Scarborough**; journalists **T. Thomas Fortune, Archibald Grimké, Pauline Hopkins, William Pickens,** and **Mary Church Terrell**; poets **William Stanley Beaumont Braithwaite, James D. (David) Corrothers, Paul Laurence Dunbar,** and **Georgia Douglas Johnson**; scientist **George Washington Carver**; writers **Benjamin Brawley,** John Edward Bruce, and Fannie Barrier Williams; and others. In addition to politics and social issues, the *Voice's* topics included art, education, history, religion, and science. Among other features, the *Voice* included pieces on the history and development of several historically black colleges and universities, including industrial schools such as Hampton and Tuskegee, as well as academic institutions such as Fisk University (Nashville, TN), Rust College (Holly Springs, MS), and Talladega College (AL). In 1906, the number of subscribers had reached a peak of 12,000-15,000.

Meanwhile, Booker T. Washington continued to fund opponents to Barber's *Voice,* and the *Voice's* white owners offered to sell the journal in June of 1906. About three months later (September 22-26, 1906), a race riot erupted in Atlanta, with whites attacking blacks. Bowen, who was also president of the Gammon Theological Seminary, offered refuge to blacks trying to escape attack. Three days after the riot started, Bowen himself was beaten and arrested by white police officers. Barber feared a similar fate, especially after Atlantans discovered it was he who had written an anonymous letter (9/23/1906) to *New York World* denying the charges that black Atlantans had initiated the riots. He moved the journal to Chicago, Illinois, where he struggled on, without Bowen or J. L. Nichols, for another year. The *Voice* was silenced in Chicago in October of 1907, when Barber sold it to **T. Thomas Fortune,** who soon had problems of his own.

REFERENCES: Luker, Ralph E., "John Wesley Edward Bowen," and "Jesse Max Barber," *AANB.* Pound, DaNean, in *GEAAL.*

//en.wikipedia.org/wiki/Historically_black_colleges_and_universities. //en.wikipedia.org/wiki/List_of_historically_black_colleges_of_the_United_States. //www.answers.com/topic/voice-of-the-negro-the. //www.liu.edu/cwis/cwp/library/historic.htm.

Vroman, Mary Elizabeth
c. 1923?–4/29/1967
Short stories, novels, movie script, nonfiction

Vroman is most noted for her short story "See How They Run" (1951), about an African-American teacher's enthusiastic efforts to educate impoverished rural African-American third graders; her story was later adapted to become the film *Bright Road* (starring Harry Belafonte and Dorothy Dandridge), for which she wrote the screenplay (1953). On writing the script, she became the first African-American woman to join the Screen Writers Guild. Vroman also wrote a novel for adults (*Esther,* 1963), a nonfiction book (*Shaped to Its Purpose,* 1965, about the history of Delta Sigma Theta sorority), and a novel for juveniles (*Harlem Summer,* 1967).

REFERENCES: *AAL. CAO-02.* Blicksilver, Edith, in *AAFW-55-84,* in *COCAAL* and *OCAAL,.* Jordan, Shirley, in *BWA:AHE.*

FURTHER READING: *AANB. BAWPP.* Kich, Martin, in *GEAAL. See also EAAWW.*

Walcott, Derek (Alton)
1/23/1930–

Poems, plays, essays, criticism, nonfiction; educator, self-publisher, journalist

Editor's note: The birthdate of Derek Walcott is given as January 23 in *B, BB, BCE, CAO-07, LF-07, MWEL, T-CCBAW-1, Wiki,* and Baugh (2007), but as June 23 in *AANB.*

A year after future Nobel laureate Derek Walcott was born in Castries, St. Lucia, West Indies, he and his twin brother and their older sister were orphaned by his father, and single-handedly raised by his mother, Alix, a teacher, headmistress, and seamstress. While still a teenager, Derek saw a poem of his published in the local newspaper. After graduating from the local high school, where he later taught (1947-1950), he self-published two poetry collections: *25 Poems* (1948) and *Epitaph for the Young: XII Cantos* (1949). He also wrote half a dozen plays, all of which were produced in the West Indies (1950-1951).

He then left for Kingston, Jamaica to earn his B.A. at the University College of the West Indies (1953), where he published his third collection, *Poems.* Between 1954 and 1957, he taught at several secondary schools, then he found work writing features on literature and theater for the Jamaican weekly *Public Opinion* (1956-1957). During this time, he also did a lot of West Indies island hopping. Meanwhile, he wrote and directed a radio broadcast, *Harry Dernier: A Play for Radio Production* (1952), as well as numerous stage plays—*The Wine of the Country* (1953, 1956), *The Charlatan* (starting in 1954), and *Ti-Jean and His Brothers: A Play in One Act* (starting in 1957). He also wrote four other plays that he did not direct: *The Sea at Dauphin: A Play in One Act* (starting in 1953), *Crossroads* (1954), *Ione: A Play with Music* (1957), and *Drums and Colours: An Epic Drama* (1958; 1961, published).

Drums and Colours won Walcott a Rockefeller Fellowship to study drama in New York, but he left in the middle of the following year, returning to the Caribbean. In Trinidad, he became the founding director of Little Carib Theatre Workshop and Basement Theatre (later named the Trinidad Theatre Workshop) (1959-1976). He also wrote features (1960-1962) and drama criticism (1963-1968) for the *Trinidad Guardian,* as well as many more poetry collections: *In a Green Night: Poems* (1962), *Selected Poems* (1964), *The Castaway and Other Poems* (1965), *The Gulf and Other Poems* (1969), *Sea Grapes* (1976), *The Star-Apple Kingdom* (1979), and *The Fortunate Traveller* (1981).

Meanwhile, Walcott wrote and directed numerous plays, including *Batai* (1965), *Dream on Monkey Mountain* (1967), *Franklin: A Tale of the Islands* (1969), *In a Fine Castle* (1970), *O Babylon!* (1976; 1978, published in *The Joker of Seville and O Babylon!: Two Plays*), *Remembrance* (1977), and *Marie Laveau* (1979; excerpts published). He also wrote *Malcauchon; or, The Six in the Rain* (1959), *Jourmard; or, A Comedy till the Last Minute* (1959), *The Isle Is Full of Noises* (1970), *The Joker of Seville* (1974), and *Pantomime* (1978). He also wrote the television play *The Snow Queen* (1977). In addition, Farrar, Straus published two collections of his plays, *Dream on Monkey Mountain and Other Plays* (1970) and *Remembrance & Pantomime: Two Plays* (1980).

In the late 1970s, Walcott moved to the U.S. Virgin Islands, where he taught at the College of the Virgin Islands. The Guggenheim Foundation awarded Walcott a fellowship (1977-1978), and he briefly taught at Yale's School of Drama, Columbia, and New York Universities, then received a fellowship for the New York Institute for the Humanities. In 1981, he was awarded a John D. and Catherine MacArthur Foundation Fellowship. Soon after, he started teaching creative writing and English at Boston University (starting in early 1982). He has also been a visiting professor at Columbia University (1981) and Harvard University (1982, 1987) and a lecturer at Rutgers University and Yale University.

Since moving to the United States, Walcott has also written additional poetry collections, including *The Caribbean Poetry of Derek Walcott and the Art of Romare Beardon* (1983), *Midsummer* (1984), *The Arkansas Testament* (1987), *Omeros* (1990), *Poems, 1965-1980* (1992), *The Bounty* (1997), *Tiepolo's Hound* (2000), and *The Prodigal* (2004). He has also published several retrospective collections, including *Another Life* (1973; 2nd ed., 1982; *Another Life: Fully Annotated,* 2004), *Selected Verse* (1976; rev. ed., 1993), *Collected Poems, 1948-1984* (1986), *Derek Walcott: Selected Poems* (1993), and *Selected Poems* (2007). In addition, Walcott has contributed poems to numerous periodicals (e.g., *London Magazine*).

Walcott has also continued to write plays. His produced plays include *Beef, No Chicken* (1981), *A Branch of the Blue Nile* (1983), *To Die for Grenada* (1986), *Ghost Dance* (1989), *Steel* (1991; 2005, rev.), *Walker* (1993; 2001, rev.), and *The Capeman: A Musical* (1997; published, 1998). Many of his plays have also been published in *Three Plays: The Last Carnival; Beef, No Chicken; and A Branch of the Blue Nile* (1986), *The Odyssey: A Stage Version* (1993, adapted from Homer), *The Haitian Trilogy* (2002), and *Walker and Ghost Dance* (2002).

Walcott's other books include *The Poet in the Theatre* (1990), *The Antilles: Fragments of Epic Memory: The Nobel Lecture* (1993), *Conversations with Derek Walcott* (1996, edited by William Baer), *Homage to Robert Frost* (1996, with Joseph Brodsky and Seamus Heaney), and his essay collection, *What the Twilight Says* (1998). He also contributed to at least a dozen anthologies between 1966 and 1985 (e.g., *Oxford Book of Contemporary Verse, 1945-1980*, 1980). His nonfiction prose has also appeared in numerous periodicals (e.g., *New Republic, The New York Times Magazine*).

In 1992, Derek Walcott was awarded the Nobel Prize in Literature, the first U.S. resident of African descent to receive this honor. In addition, he has received numerous awards for his poetry, such as the *American Poetry Review* Award (1979), the *Los Angeles Times Prize* in poetry (1986), and the Queen Elizabeth II Gold Medal for Poetry (1988). His plays have earned him prizes as well, including the Heinemann Award of the Royal Society of Literature (1966) and an Obie Award (1971). Walcott's other honors and awards include numerous grants and fellowships. In addition, Walcott was named a fellow of the Royal Society of Literature (1966), an Officer of the Order of British Empire (O.B.E., 1972), and an honorary member of the American Academy and Institute of Arts and Letters (1979). In 1973, the University of the West Indies honored him with a doctorate, making him the first of its graduates to be so honored.

REFERENCES: *AAW:PV. B. BCE. CAO-07. CE. CLCS-08. LF-07. MWEL. QB. Wiki.* Baugh, Edward. "Derek Walcott." *Nobel Prize Laureates in Literature, Part 4. Dictionary of Literary Biography* (Vol. 332). Detroit: Gale, 2007. *Literature Resources from Gale.* Cabrera, Enriqueta. "Derek Walcott: The Voice of the Caribbean: Saint Lucia's Favorite Son Discusses the Emerging Identity in Literature and Prose Unique to the Islands." *Americas (English Edition)*. 59.3 (May-June 2007), p. 38. *Literature Resources from Gale.* Castro, Jan Garden. "Derek Walcott." *Black Renaissance/Renaissance Noire.* 6.2 (Spring 2005), p. 76. *Literature Resources from Gale.* "Derek Walcott: A Life in Poetry." *Weekend All Things Considered.* (Mar. 18, 2007). *Literature Resources from Gale.* Gaspar, David Barry, in *AANB.* Hamner, Robert D., in *T-CCBAW-1.* _____. (1993). *Derek Walcott. Twayne's World Authors Series 600.* New York: Twayne. *Literature Resources from Gale.* Hartigan, Patti. "The passions of Derek Walcott." *American Theatre.* 10.5-6 (May-June 1993), p. 14. Literature Resources from Gale. Johnson, Anne Janette, in *BB.* //nobelprize.org/nobel_prizes/literature/laureates/. Amazon.com.

Walker, A'Lelia (née Lelia McWilliams)
6/6/1885–8/16/1931
Host of literary salon

Though her own writings were pretty much limited to business correspondence and business documents related to the business empire of her mother, Madame C. J. Walker, A'Lelia did quite a bit to promote African-American literature during the full blossom of the **Harlem Renaissance**. Although she was never at all as charitable as her mother, she made her houses the home of writers and other artists. Her townhouse, in particular, became the Dark Tower Tea Club (after **Countee Cullen**'s "Dark Tower" column in *Crisis* magazine), her formal and stylish literary salon. Among those whom she hosted were **Langston Hughes, Zora Neale Hurston, James Weldon Johnson, Richard Bruce Nugent**, and **Jean Toomer**, as well as **Carl Van Vechten** (among the many whites at Walker's gatherings).

REFERENCES: *BAAW.*

FURTHER READING: *AANB. MWEL. Wiki.* Brennan, Carol, in *BB.* //www.glbtq.com/sfeatures/afamlitlesbian.html.

Walker, Alice
2/9/1944–

Poems, essays, short stories, novels, anthology, memoirs, juvenile literature, nonfiction books; social worker, civil-rights and peace activist, educator, publisher

Alice Walker writes directly, and openly about people who live the kinds of lives she has always known, and sometimes lived. Walker was born in rural Eatonton, Georgia, the eighth and last child of sharecroppers Willie Lee and Minnie Lou Grant Walker. She went on to become one of the best known and most respected writers in the United States. She was raised in a shack minutes from Flannery O'Connor's house, "Andalusia." Perhaps because of this proximity, O'Connor's writing has also influenced Walker's own work. At an early age, Walker was encouraged by her mother to read, study diligently, and appreciate doing so.

Alice suffered a traumatic injury at age 8 years, when a brother accidentally blinded her right eye with an air rifle. From a self-confident, "womanish" little girlhood, she sank into a period of adolescent depression and uncertainty. She secluded herself from the other children, and as she explains, "I no longer felt like the little girl I was. I felt old, and because I felt I was unpleasant to look at, filled with shame. I retreated into solitude, and read stories and began to write poems" (quoted in Christian, p. 56).

Nonetheless, the accident made Walker begin taking note of other people and their feelings. She arose from the despair to become a leader and valedictorian of her high-school class. That achievement, coupled with a "re-habilitation scholarship" for disabled students, made it possible for her to go to Spelman, a college for black women in Atlanta, Georgia. Her involvement in various civil-rights demonstrations led to her dismissal. She then won another scholarship at the progressive Sarah Lawrence College. In 1964, she traveled to Uganda, Africa, where she studied as an exchange student. Upon her return in 1965, she received her bachelor of arts degree. One of Walker's teachers at Sarah Lawrence was Muriel Rukeyser, who saw Walker's poems and helped to publish her first poetry collection. Years later, in a commencement speech at Sarah Lawrence, Walker spoke out against the absence of African-American culture and history from that institution's curriculum.

After college, Walker was awarded a writing fellowship and planned to spend it in Senegal, West Africa. However, after working as a case worker in the New York City welfare department, her plans changed. She decided to volunteer her time working at the voter-registration drive in Mississippi in the summer of 1966. Walker later stated that her decision had been based on the realization that she could never live happily in Africa or anywhere else until she could live freely in Mississippi.

From the mid-1960s to the mid-1970s, she lived and worked in Tougaloo, Mississippi, and remained active in the civil-rights movement. There she met and married a civil-rights lawyer, Mel Leventhal. They had a daughter, Rebecca, in 1969. In her novel *Meridian* (1976), Walker used her own and others' experiences of this time as material for her searing examination of politics and black-white relations.

Later, Walker came to greatly admire **Zora Neale Hurston**, whose works she discovered and read. She also found Hurston's weed-covered gravesite and provided a marker for it, and she helped bring Hurston back to literary eminence. In 1979, Walker edited an anthology of Hurston's writing, *I Love Myself When I'm Laughing.*

In her first novel, *The Third Life of Grange Copeland* (1970), Walker told of how three generations of one family were affected by their move from the South to the North. She focused on a matrix that includes sexual and racial realities within black communities. For exposing this, she has been criticized by some African-American male critics and theorists. The book also highlights the unavoidable connections between family and society. For exploring this, she has been awarded numerous prizes while winning the hearts and minds of countless black and white readers.

Walker's writing career began to take off when she started teaching. She taught at Jackson State, then Tougaloo, and finally at Wellesley College. Walker was also a fellow at the Radcliffe Institute from 1971 to 1973.

In her last year there, she published her first collection of stories, *In Love and Trouble* (1973).

Perhaps Walker's most famous work is *The Color Purple* (1982), for which she won the American Book Award and the Pulitzer Prize. She was the first African-American woman to win the Pulitzer for a novel. The *Color Purple* captured the attention of mainstream America through the film adaptation by Steven Spielberg. In that novel of incest, lesbian love, and sibling devotion, Walker also introduces blues music as a unifying thread in the lives of many of the characters. *The Color Purple* also gained fierce criticism when Spielberg turned it into a movie. In her collection of essays, *The Same River Twice: Honoring the Difficult* (1996) Walker grapples with some of the issues raised in the making of the film.

Walker refuses to ignore the tangle of personal and political themes in her novels, which also include *Temple of My Familiar* (1989) and *Possessing the Secret of Joy* (1992). She has also written a collection of short stories titled *You Can't Keep a Good Woman Down* (1979), as well as numerous volumes of poetry and many books of essays.

Though she has attained fame and recognition in many countries, Walker has not lost her sense of rootedness in the South or her sense of indebtedness to her mother for showing her what the life of an artist entailed. Writing of this central experience in her famous essay, "In Search of Our Mothers' Gardens," she talks about watching her mother at the end of a day of back-breaking physical labor on someone else's farm return home, only to walk the long distance to their well to get water for her garden, planted each year at their doorstep. Walker observed her mother design that garden, putting tall plants at the back and planting so as to have something in bloom from early spring until the end of summer. As an adult, Walker names her mother an artist full of dedication, with a keen sense of design and balance and a tough conviction that life without beauty is unbearable.

Among Walker's numerous awards and honors are the **Lillian Smith** Award from the National Endowment for the Arts, the Rosenthal Award from the National Institute of Arts and Letters, the Townsend Prize, the Lyndhurst Prize, the Front Page Award for Best Magazine Criticism from the Newswoman's Club of New York, and a nomination for the National Book Award, as well as a Radcliffe Institute fellowship, a Merrill fellowship, and a Guggenheim fellowship.

Walker is still an involved activist. She has spoken for the women's movement, the antiapartheid movement, and the antinuclear movement, and she has cried out against female genital mutilation. Walker started her own publishing company, Wild Trees Press, in 1984.

REFERENCES: 2CAAWA, pp. 291-293. BW:SSCA, pp. 571-573. OCAAL, pp. 163-164. Christian, Barbara T. 1994. *Everyday Use.* New Brunswick, NJ: Rutgers University Press. Jokinen, Anniina (1996),

"Anniina's Alice Walker Page,"
//www.alchemyweb.com/~alchemy/alicew/. McNaron, Toni (1996),
"Voices From the Gaps: Women Writers of Color," University of
Minnesota, Department of English and Program in American Studies.
//english.cla.umn.edu/lkd/vfg/Authors/AliceWalker. //www.simonsays.
com/279104371934306/0671521101/kidzone/teach/colorpurple/alicew
alker.html. Simon and Schuster (1997), *Teacher's Guide to the Color
Purple*, New York: Simon and Schuster. Walker, Alice. 1982. *The Color
Purple*. Orlando: Harcourt Brace. Zinn, Howard (1996), "Lit Chat
with Alice Walker," in *Salon: An Interactive Magazine of Books and
Ideas*. //www.salon1999.com/09/departments/litchat1.html.
—Michael Strickland and Lisa Bahlinger

Editor's note: Walker's first published book was her poetry collection, *Once: Poems* (1968/1976), followed by a four-page collection, *Five Poems* (1972), published by **Broadside Press**. Her other poetry collections include *Revolutionary Petunias and Other Poems* (1973), *Goodnight, Willie Lee, I'll See You in the Morning* (1979/1984), *Horses Make a Landscape Look More Beautiful* (1984), *Her Blue Body Everything We Know: Earthling Poems, 1965-1990* (1991; 2005, titled *Collected Poems: Her Blue Body Everything We Know—Earthling Poems 1965-1990*), *Absolute Trust in the Goodness of the Earth: New Poems* (2003), and *A Poem Traveled Down My Arm: Poems And Drawings* (2003).

Walker also wrote a juvenile biography, **Langston Hughes**: *American Poet* (children's biography) (1973; 2001/2005, illustrated by Catherine Deeter). Hughes had been the first to publish her short story "To Hell with Dying," in his 1967 anthology. Walker later used that story to create her second book for children, *To Hell with Dying* (1988, illustrated by Catherine Deeter), on how human memory can transcend physical mortality. Her next three children's books were *Finding the Green Stone* (1991, illustrated by Catherine Deeter), a fantasy, and two verse books for children, *There Is a Flower at the Tip of My Nose Smelling Me* (2006, illustrated by Stefano Vitale), a series of whimsical short verses celebrating sensory delights in the surrounding world, and *Why War Is Never a Good Idea* (2007 illustrated by Stefano Vitale), imploring readers to choose peace.

Walker has written at least seven novels: *The Third Life of Grange Copeland* (1970/2003), *Meridian* (1976/2003), *The Color Purple* (1982/2006), *The Temple of My Familiar* (1989), *Possessing the Secret of Joy* (1992/2008), *By the Light of My Father's Smile: A Novel* (1998), and *Now Is the Time to Open Your Heart: A Novel* (2004; available in hc, pbk, Kindle, audio download). Her third, fourth, fifth, and sixth novels were best-sellers. She has also written at least three short-story collections, including *In Love and Trouble: Stories of Black Women* (1973/2003), *You Can't Keep a Good Woman Down: Stories* (1981/2003), and *The Complete Stories* (1994/2005). Her collection *The Way Forward Is with a Broken Heart* (2000) offers both autobiographical and fictional narratives. Her publisher has also created boxed sets of her poetry (1985) and of her fiction (1985).

Walker's nonfiction collections often include essays, personal memoirs, journal entries, short fiction, or poems, and even materials from other sources (e.g., periodical clippings, photos). These collections include *In Search of Our Mothers' Gardens: Womanist Prose* (1983/2003), which won the Lillian Smith Book Award (1984); *Living by the Word: Selected Writings, 1973-1987* (1988), containing travel notes, speeches, and personal memoirs, as well as essays; *The Same River Twice: Honoring the Difficult; A Meditation of Life, Spirit, Art, and the Making of the Film "The Color Purple," Ten Years Later* (1996), a scrapbook collage of memoirs and artifacts; *Sent By Earth: A Message from the Grandmother Spirit after the Attacks on the World Trade Center* (2001), essays and poems inspired by Walker's response to this crisis; and *We Are the Ones We Have Been Waiting For: Inner Light in a Time of Darkness* (2006), offering poetry and prose, writings and speeches guiding readers to create the world they wish to inhabit. In her earlier essay collection *Anything We Love Can Be Saved: A Writer's Activism* (1997), she noted, "My heart is by now in its rightful place, in proximity to my hands, which are made to reach out, as I write, to all those around me" (quoted by Margaret Nolan, *School Library Journal*, in //www.amazon.com).

Walker has also written nonfiction monographs. *Warrior Marks: Female Genital Mutilation and the Sexual Blinding of Women* (1993, with Pratibha Parmar) affirms her abhorrence of this still-extant practice. In *Alice Walker Banned* (1996), she responds to having two of her short stories removed from a statewide examination by the California Board of Education; the stories were "Roselily" (1973), banned for being "anti-religious," and "Am I Blue?" (1986), banned for being "anti-meat-eating." She also wrote lengthy text introducing *Dreads: Sacred Rites of the Natural Hair Revolution* (1999, with Francesco Mastalia and Alfonse Pagano), a large-format coffee-table book celebrating this splendid hair style; and she edited *I Love Myself When I'm Laughing ... and Then Again When I Am Looking Mean and Impressive: A Zora Neale Hurston Reader* (1979/1993).

In addition to her print works and Spielberg's film adaptation of *The Color Purple*, Walker has been involved in two projects published in audio format: *Pema Chodron and Alice Walker in Conversation* (1999, cassette, CD, and download, as well as video) and *Gardening the Soul* (2000, with Michael Toms, cassette). Her writings have been translated into 25 or more languages. Her personal and literary papers are being catalogued and archived at Emory University (starting in 2007). Her fellowships and scholarships include a Bread Loaf Writer's Conference scholarship (1966), a Merrill writing fellowship (1967), a McDowell Colony fellowship (1967, 1977-1978), a grant from the National Endowment for the Arts (1969, 1977), a Radcliffe Institute fellowship (1971-1973), and a Guggenheim fellowship (1977-1978). She has been awarded honorary doctorates from the Russell Sage College (1972) and the University of Massachusetts (1983), and she has been inducted into both the Georgia Writers Hall of Fame (2001) and the California Hall of Fame (2006). Her short story "Kindred" (1985, *Esquire*) won the O. Henry Award (1986). Her books have been awarded a Pulitzer Prize for Fiction, a National Book Critics Circle Award nomination, and an American Book Award (all for *The Color Purple*), two Lillian Smith Awards (*Revolutionary Petunias* and *In Search of Our Mothers' Gardens*), a Richard and Hinda Rosenthal Foundation Award from the American Academy and Institute of Arts and Letters (*In Love and Trouble*), a National Book Award nomination (*Revolutionary Petunias*), and an American Library Association citation for "Best Books for Young Adults" (*In Search of Our Mothers' Gardens*). Her other awards include a Langston Hughes Award from New York City College (1989), a Nora Astorga Leadership award (1989), a Fred Cody award for lifetime achievement from the Bay Area Book Reviewers Association (1990), a Freedom to Write award from PEN West (1990), a California Governor's Arts Award (1994), a Humanist of the Year award from the American Humanist Association (1997), and a Literary Ambassador Award from the University of Oklahoma Center for Poets and Writers (1998).

REFERENCES: *AANB. AAW:PV. B. BAWPP. BCE. CAO-00. CAO-07. CE. CLCS-08. GOE. LFCC-07. MWEL. QB. W. W2B. Wiki.* "Author's Works." Donna Haisty Winchell. (1992). *Alice Walker: Twayne's United States Authors* (Series 598). New York: Twayne Publishers. From *The Twayne Authors Series*. Christian, Barbara T., *AAFW-55-84*. Davis, Thadious M., in *ANSWWII-2nd*. Gray, Janet, in *AW:ACLB-91*. Howard-Hill, T. H., in *T-CBBCB-1*. King, Debra Walker, in COCAAL. Mueller, Michael E., and Ralph G. Zerbonia, in *BB*. Rosenmeier, Rosamond. (1992). "Chapter 1: Survival, Literal and Literary." Donna Haisty Winchell. *Alice Walker: Twayne's United States Authors* (Series 598). New York: Twayne Publishers. From *The Twayne Authors Series*. Tate, Claudia, in *MAWW*. Upchurch, Gail L., in *GEAAL*. Walker, Alice, and John O'Brien. "Alice Walker: An Interview." Henry Louis Gates, Jr. and K. A. Appiah (Eds.) (1993), *Alice Walker: Critical Perspectives, Past and Present*. Rpt. in Ellen McGeagh and Linda Pavlovski (Eds.) (2000), *Poetry Criticism* (Vol. 30, pp. 326-346). Detroit: Gale Group. From *Literature Resource Center*. Winchell, Donna Haisty, in *ANSWWII-3rd*. //en.wikiquote.org/wiki/Alice_Walker, Alice Walker. //www.georgiaencyclopedia.org/nge/Article.jsp?id=h-998. Amazon.com. *See also* **Walker, Rebecca.**

Walker, David
9/28/1785–6/28/1830
Pamphlets; abolitionist, self-publisher

His pamphlet, *David Walker's Appeal in Four Articles; Together With a Preamble, to the Coloured Citizens of the World, but in Particular, and Very Expressly, to Those of the United States of America,* was certainly not the first abolitionist writing he did, but it was very likely the cause of his own end. This outcome was no surprise to Walker himself: "I will stand my ground. *Somebody must die in this cause.* I may be doomed to the stake and the fire, or to the scaffold tree, but it is not in me to falter if I can promote the work of emancipation." His wife (Eliza) and his friends beseeched him to escape to Canada, on hearing that there was a reward being offered for his capture: $1,000 if caught dead, and $10,000 if captured alive.

What had he said that so enraged the white folks? He vociferously recited the atrocities of slavery, and he denounced all those who participated in perpetuating it—predicting that slave traders, slaveholders, and any others who dealt in the ownership of humans would suffer the wrath of God and the torment of hell. He also sought a more earthly retribution for these vile traders and owners of human beings, urging slaves to revolt and escape their enslavement.

Walker spared no one from his appeal, as he scathingly rebuked any blacks who were complicit in the bondage of their fellows, and he offered cold comfort to free blacks who didn't work hard to free their black sisters and brothers. He himself had been born the son of a free woman, yet he never hesitated to give every fiber of his being to the cause of abolition. He had little tolerance, too, for those of the American Colonization Society, whom he believed were falling prey to the wishes of slaveholders who wanted all free blacks out of earshot of their slaves, lest these free souls give their slaves any undesirable ideas. He even aroused the anger of fellow abolitionists who opposed violent insurrection as a means to that end. Walker was also a firm believer in the subversive power of education, holding that "for coloured people to acquire learning [in] this country, makes tyrants quake and tremble on their sandy foundations." Apparently, many white Southerners agreed, for they tightened restrictions against letting slaves learn to read and write after Walker's pamphlet was published.

A self-educated man, Walker self-published his *Appeal* (although an earlier, briefer version had appeared in *Freedom's Journal*, to which he was a frequent contributor). Among those who welcomed his *Appeal* with open arms was **Maria Stewart**, who may have had a hand in promoting its distribution in the South. Despite the banning of its circulation by several state legislatures (including Georgia's) and other energetic attempts to block its distribution, it slipped subversively into circulation. By early 1830, Walker had managed to release his third (revised) edition of his *Appeal*. By the end of that year, Walker was found dead, probably murdered by poisoning. His pregnant wife, Eliza, was left to raise their son, Edward Garrison Walker, alone.

For a time, it seemed that his *Appeal* might go out of print, but in 1848, **Henry Highland Garnet** reprinted it, along with his own provocative *Address to the Slaves of the United States*. Like all the great ideas of great people, they could slay the person, but not the idea.

REFERENCES: *EB-98. SMKC.* Eiselein, Gregory, in COCAAL and OCAAL.

FURTHER READING: *AANB. B. BAWPP. BCE. W. Wiki.* Blight, David W., in *USHC.* Davis, Matthew R., in *GEAAL.* //docsouth.unc.edu/nc/walker/menu.html.

Walker (married name: Alexander), Margaret (Abigail)

7/7/1915–12/1/1998

Poems, novel, essays, biography, criticism, memoir; educator

Margaret's parents, Methodist Episcopal minister Sigismund Walker and music teacher (and church musician) Marion Dozier, expected a great deal from their children. They instilled not only a love of church and of music, but also a love of scholarship and of literature. Young Margaret grew up listening to biblical verse, her father's sermons, her mother's readings of classical verse, and countless anecdotes, vignettes, and discussions. By the time Margaret was 11 years old, she was reading not only William Shakespeare and John Greenleaf Whittier but also **Countee Cullen** and **Langston Hughes**. As a youth, she met **James Weldon Johnson, W. E. B. Du Bois**, and other African-American celebrities. In many ways, Margaret's parents provided enriched cultural experiences that helped to shield their children from the personal sting of Southern racism, although they made their children well aware of racism's effects on other African Americans.

As a minister's daughter, Margaret was raised across various states in the Jim Crow South, attending numerous denominational schools in Alabama, Mississippi, and Louisiana. She earned her high-school diploma from New Orleans's Gilbert Academy when she was just 14 years old. Despite her obvious talent and inclination, however, few of her teachers ever encouraged her to write. Later, in her "For My People," she wrote this about school: "For the cramped bewildered years we went to school to learn to know the reasons why and the answers to and the people who and the places where and the days when, in memory of the bitter hours when we discovered we were black and poor and small and different and nobody wondered and nobody understood."

After high school, Margaret attended New Orleans University (later Dillard University), where her parents both taught (Walker was a third-generation college graduate). While there, in 1931, she met Langston Hughes, who read some of Margaret's poems and—at last—encouraged her to become a writer. Hughes also encouraged her to complete her education outside of the South—which she did, transferring to Northwestern University, from which she earned a B.A. in English in 1935, just before she turned 20 years old. While at Northwestern, she published her first poem ("Daydreaming") in **Crisis** magazine in 1934. She also started working for the Works Progress Administration (WPA) as a social worker for troubled youths. She later wrote an unpublished novel, *Goose Island,* about this experience.

After graduating, she started working for the WPA's Federal Writers' Project. During this time, through **Margaret Burroughs**, Walker also became friends with **Gwendolyn Brooks**. While mastering the writing craft, she profited from friendships with novelists (e.g., **Frank Yerby**), poets (e.g., **Arna Bontemps**), and playwrights (e.g., **Theodore Ward**). Perhaps most importantly, she got to know **Richard Wright**, with whom she shared her political outlook, enjoyed a close friendship, and collaborated on literary works until he ended their friendship abruptly in 1939. That same year, Walker stopped working for the WPA and returned to graduate school to earn her M.A. in creative writing (1940) at the University of Iowa.

Walker's master's thesis was essentially her first volume of poems, *For My People* (1942), only the second volume of poetry published by an African-American woman for more than two decades. In the 1941-1942 school year, she started teaching at Livingstone College in South Carolina. That summer, she won the Yale University Younger Poet's Award for her *For My People,* thereby becoming the first African-American woman to win a prestigious national literary competition. In 1990, she recalled that she wrote most of the title poem (first published in 1937) within 15 minutes, after having been asked, "What would you want for your people?"

Walker's poem resonates with the rhythm, alliteration, and consonance; biblical phrasings; emotive tone; and cultural cadences of the sermons Walker had heard throughout her youth. Her poem exults in the endurance and the triumphs of African Americans, mourns her people's suffering and losses, proudly points to their struggles, and demands freedom and fairness for her people ("Let another world be born. . . . let a people loving freedom come to growth. . . . Let a race of men now rise and take control!"). Other poems in her *For My People* collection echo these themes, as well as her interpretations of characters from African-American folktales, Southern settings, and African-American history.

In 1943, Margaret Walker married Firnist Alexander, and the following year, she gave birth to the first of their four children, after which her writing slowed considerably, and her teaching stopped altogether for a while (although she did continue to lecture occasionally). Her mentor Langston Hughes warned her, "All these babies you're having, every baby you have could have been a book." Years later, she observed, "I have four children, nine grandchildren, and eleven books."

In 1949, she returned to teaching, to support her children (all of whom were less than six years old, including a nine-week-old) and her husband, who was "sick and disabled from the war." This started her 30-year tenure at Jackson State College in Mississippi. To boost her bread winning, Walker-Alexander spent several summers and a full academic year earning her Ph.D. in creative writing from the University of Iowa in 1965. She used her Civil War novel (started many years earlier) as the basis for her doctoral dissertation (published as *Jubilee* in 1966). In 1968, she founded the Institute for the Study of the History, Life and Culture of Black People at Jackson State, serving as its director until she retired 11 years later. The center has since been renamed in her honor.

Walker's subsequent poetry collections include *Ballad of the Free* (1966); *Prophets for a New Day* (1970), hailing abolitionist and civil-rights leaders and comparing them with biblical prophets; and *October Journey* (1973), honoring Walker's personal heroes, such as **Harriet Tubman**, **Gwendolyn Brooks**, and her father. In 1989, she published *This Is My Century: New and Collected Poems*, which includes her poems from her earlier volumes *Prophets for a New Day* and *October Journey*. Her works have been widely anthologized, such as by **Robert Hayden**, by Bontemps, and by Hughes and Bontemps.

Walker started writing her novel *Jubilee* in 1934, and she continued to work on it through her 1965 doctoral-dissertation version until her final version was published in 1966. She centered the well-researched novel on the true life experiences of her maternal great-grandmother, Margaret Duggans (named "Vyry Brown" in the novel), from slavery, through the Civil War, to the end of Reconstruction. Walker observed that the long process of writing this novel was enriched by her own life experiences. Although Walker herself never knew the nightmares of slavery, Civil War, and Reconstruction terrorism, she nevertheless vividly recounted the stories she heard from her maternal grandmother (Elvira Ware Dozier), describing Walker's great-grandmother's firsthand accounts. In *Conversations with Margaret Walker* (p. 133), Walker discussed having sued **Alex Haley**, author of best-selling *Roots*, for copyright infringement in 1977. She accused him of using 6 of her characters, 15 of her

scenes, more than 150 of her verbatim expressions, and parts of 400 pages from *Jubilee* in his best-seller. The case was dismissed in 1988.

Walker's other prose includes *How I Wrote* Jubilee (1972), in which she tells just how she researched and wrote her novel; and *A Poetic Equation: Conversations between* **Nikki Giovanni** *and Margaret Walker* (2nd ed., 1983). Perhaps her most important prose work, however, is her biography of her former friend Richard Wright, entitled *Richard Wright, Daemonic Genius: A Portrait of the Man, A Critical Look at His Work* (1988). In reflecting on her biography, Walker noted, "Wright was just like somebody in my family" (*BWWW*, pp. 194-195). "I felt Wright wanted me to write his biography because nobody is going to be more sympathetic and understanding than I."

In addition to these books, she recorded three spoken-word albums of her poetry on the Folkways label for the Smithsonian Institution, and she contributed to two other Folkways albums. Walker also wrote countless essays and scholarly articles on African-American literature and culture. Before she died, Walker was working on a sequel to *Jubilee*, focusing on the life experiences of Vyry's son and daughter-in-law; an autobiography; and her novel *Mother Broyer*, based on a folk story. As she noted, "I've got to write for the rest of my life, no matter how short or long it is. I've got to write. . . . Writing is the first thing on my list, and I can't live long enough to write all the books I have in me" (*BWWW*, p. 200). Sadly, she was right.

Walker's honors and awards include a 1944 Rosenwald Fellowship for Creative Writing, a 1954 Ford Fellowship at Yale University, a 1966 Houghton Mifflin literature fellowship, and a 1979 Ford grant for completing her biography. Also, the mayor of her home town, Birmingham, Alabama, proclaimed June 17, 1976, Margaret Walker Alexander Day.

REFERENCES: *AA:PoP. BAAW. BAL-1-P. BWA. BWW. BWWW. EB-98. EBLG. G-95. MWEL. NAAL. NPR-ME-12/1/98. OC20LE.* Ashford, Tomeiko, in //www.ibiblio.org/ipa/walker.php & //www.ibiblio.org/ipa/poems/walker/biography.php. Campbell, Jane, in *OCWW.* Graham, Maryemma. "The Fusion of Ideas: An Interview with Margaret Walker Alexander." *African American Review* 27.2 (Summer 1993), p. 279. From *Literature Resource Center.* Odom, Maida, in //writing.upenn.edu/~afilreis/50s/walker-margaret.html. Walker, Margaret, and Maryemma Graham. (2002). *Conversations with Margaret Walker.* Jackson: Univ. Press of Mississippi, available via //books.google.com/books. Ward, Jerry W., Jr., in *COCAAL* and *OCAAL.* //www.folkways.si.edu/searchresults.aspx?sPhrase=Margaret%20Walker&sType='phrase'/.

FURTHER READING: *AANB. AT. B. BAWPP. CAO-05. HR&B, pp. 332-336. LFCC-07. MWEL. W. Wiki.* Alexander, Margaret Walker, and Kay Bonetti (1992). "An Interview with Margaret Walker Alexander." *The Missouri Review* 15.1, pp. 112-131. Rpt. in Janet Witalec (Ed.) (2003), *Twentieth-Century Literary Criticism* (Vol. 129). Detroit: Gale. From *Literature Resource Center.* Campbell, Jane, in *AAW*, and in *ANSWWII-4th.* Grierson, Patricia. "An Interview with

Dr. Margaret Walker Alexander on Tennessee Williams. *The Mississippi Quarterly* 48.4 (Fall 1995) p. 587. From *Literature Resource Center.* Hall, John Greer, in *GEAAL.* Kalfatovic, Mary, in *BB.* Pettis, Joyce, in *AAW-40-55.* Walker, Margaret, and Lucy M. Freibert (1987). "Southern Song: An Interview with Margaret Walker." *Frontiers: A Journal of Women's Studies* 9.3, pp. 50-56. Rpt. in Janet Witalec (Ed.) (2003), *Twentieth-Century Literary Criticism* (Vol. 129). Detroit: Gale. From *Literature Resource Center.* //library.msstate.edu/special_interest/ Mississippi_African-American_Authors.asp. *See also EAAWW.*

Walker, Rebecca (né Rebecca Leventhal)
11/17/1969–
Essays, autobiographies/memoirs, anthologies, nonfiction; feminist, activist

Editor's note: Rebecca Walker's birthdate is identified as 11/17 in *Wiki* and in the biography of her mother, **Alice Malsenior Walker**, in *AANB*, but as 11/11 in *CAO-07* and in *BB.*

Following the divorce of Rebecca's parents, African-American author Alice Malsenior Walker and European-Jewish-American attorney Mel Leventhal, she alternated two-year periods with each of her parents. At age 18, Rebecca Leventhal changed her surname to her mother's maiden name, Walker. While earning her B.A. from Yale University (1992), Rebecca Walker was already a contributing editor to *Ms.* magazine (1989-). After graduating cum laude, she cofounded her nonprofit Third Wave Direct Action Corporation (1992) and then edited the anthology *To Be Real: Telling the Truth and Changing the Face of Feminism* (1995). Meanwhile, she continued to contribute nonfiction pieces to numerous periodicals (e.g., *Black Scholar, Essence, Harper's, Vibe*) and to anthologies (e.g., *Listen Up: Voices from the Next Feminist Generation,* 1995). For a while, she also co-owned a cyber café. Eventually, however, she moved back to the West Coast, settling in Berkeley, California.

After a brief attempt at novel writing, Walker realized that writing nonfiction was her calling. In 2001, she wrote her best-selling memoir *Black, White, and Jewish* (2001). In it, Rebecca Walker offers her take on being the daughter of a famous parent who is deeply involved in activities outside the house, often to the detriment of the loved ones left at home. Rebecca's memoir led to turbulence in her relationship with her mother, and that schism only deepened over the following years. Rebecca followed her memoir by editing another anthology, *What Makes a Man: 22 Writers Imagine the Future* (2004).

As Rebecca Walker had recorded in her journal, she had long felt ambivalent about becoming a mother. This journal eventually became her second book, *Baby Love: Choosing Motherhood After a Lifetime of Ambivalence* (2007). For a time, she and her long-time partner considered asking a male friend to be the biological father of their child. Her mother's opposition to Rebecca's decision to have a child led to further ruptures in their relationship. By the time Rebecca's son was born, the two Walkers were still not communicating. During Rebecca's distressing separation from her mother, she formed a new tie, to Glen, the biological father of her son, Tenzin. She, Glen, and Tenzin now share a home. For Rebecca, becoming a mother is a new opportunity to become the parent she had longed to have for herself.

While raising her son and writing for *Ms.* and other periodicals, Rebecca Walker also edited another anthology, *One Big Happy Family: 18 Writers Talk About Polyamory, Open Adoption, Mixed Marriage, Househusbandry, Single Motherhood, and Other Realities of Truly Modern Love* (2009). Her anthology of 18 essays presents family members from a wide array of family compositions, across race, class, sexual preference, and gender boundaries. She is said to be working on a third memoir, about her travels in Africa.

For her excellence in African-American scholarship, Rebecca Walker won the Pickens Prize from Yale University (1992). For her feminist activism, she has won several other awards. *Time* magazine named her 1 of the 50 most influential leaders of her generation and a future leader (1994), and the League of Women Voters gave her its Women Who Could Be President Award. In addition to her own writing, Walker consults on nonfiction manuscripts and teaches writing workshops. She also gives speeches and has been featured on television (e.g., CNN and MTV), in print (e.g., in the *Chicago Times, Esquire, The New York Times, Shambhala Sun*).

REFERENCES: *CAO-07. Wiki.* Brennan, Carol, in *BB.* Driscoll, Margarette, "The Day Feminist Icon Alice Walker Resigned as My Mother: *The Color Purple* Brought Alice Walker Global Fame, but Her Strident Views Led to an Irreconcilable Rift, Her Daughter Tells Margarette Driscoll," in //entertainment.timesonline.co.uk/tol/arts_ and_entertainment/books/article3866798.ece. Fleming, Robert. "PW Talks with Rebecca Walker." *Publishers Weekly. 247.45* (Nov. 6, 2000), p. 78. *Literature Resources from Gale.* Lauret, Maria, "Walker, Alice Malsenior," in *AANB.* //www.oah.org/pubs/magazine/family/cruzberson.html. Amazon.com.

FURTHER READING: Feerst, Alex, in *GEAAL.*

Walker, Wyatt Tee
8/16/1929–
Nonfiction—musicology, theology

A minister instrumental in shaping the strategies of the Southern Christian Leadership Conference (SCLC), Walker wrote *"Somebody's Calling My Name": Black Sacred Music and Social Change* (1979). His other books, most of which were published through **Martin Luther King** Fellows Press, include *The Soul of Black Worship: A Trilogy—Preaching, Praying, Singing* (1984), *Road to Da-*

mascus: A Journey of Faith (1985), *Common Thieves: A Tithing Manual for Christians and Others* (1986), *Spirits that Dwell in Deep Woods: The Prayer and Praise Hymns of the Black Religious Experience* (1987-1991, 3 vols., with musical notations and arrangements by C. Eugene Cooper), *Gospel in the Land of the Rising Sun* (1991), *The Harvard Paper: The African-American Church and Economic Development* (1994), *A Prophet from Harlem Speaks: Sermons & Essays* (1997), *Race, Justice & Culture: Pre-Millennium Essays* (1998), *Millennium End Papers: The Walker File '98-'99* (2000), and *My Stroke of Grace: A Testament of Faith Renewal* (2002). In addition to honorary doctorates from Virginia Union University and Princeton University, Walker has been inducted into the International Civil Rights Walk of Fame.

REFERENCES: *AANB. CAO-02. Wiki.* Fay, Robert, in *EA-99.* //mlk-kpp01.stanford.edu/index.php/kingpapers/article/walker_wyatt_tee_1929/. Amazon.com.

Walrond, Eric (Derwent)
12/18/1898–8/8/1966
Short stories, novels; journalist, editor, publisher

A native of British Guiana (now Guyana), Walrond was educated at a boys' school in Barbados and in public schools in Panama. From 1916 to 1918, he reported for the Panama *Star-Herald,* while working as a government clerk. In 1918, Walrond left Panama and came to the United States, where he lived for a decade before emigrating to Europe. During that decade, he continued his education at the College of the City of New York and at Columbia University, and he played an important role in the **Harlem Renaissance.**

When Walrond first arrived in New York, he felt assaulted by racism and was soon drawn both to **Marcus Garvey**'s Universal Negro Improvement Association (UNIA) and to the Urban League, the director of which, **Charles Spurgeon Johnson,** soon became Walrond's mentor. Soon, Walrond was contributing articles on Harlem and the Great Migration (from the rural South to the urban North) to newspapers, and in 1921, he started editing the *Brooklyn and Long Island Informer,* an African-American weekly, which he also co-owned. In 1923, he wrote "The New Negro Faces America," in which he analyzed and critiqued the philosophies of Marcus Garvey, **Booker T. Washington,** and **W. E. B. Du Bois.** That same year, he left the *Informer* to accept a job as associate editor of the UNIA organ, *Negro World,* which he continued until 1925, when he and Garvey had a falling-out, and Walrond took over as business manager of the Urban League's *Opportunity* magazine.

In the early and mid-1920s, Walrond started contributing short stories to various periodicals (e.g., the *New Republic, Opportunity, Smart Set*), and in 1926, he published his collection of eight short stories, *Tropic Death* (1926), which addressed themes of race relations in America, migration, and the diaspora of Africa's descendants. In 1928, Walrond was awarded a Guggenheim fellowship and was named a Zona Gale scholar at the University of Wisconsin before moving to Europe. While in Europe, he and Garvey (then an exile) patched things up, and Walrond did some writing for Garvey. During the 1930s, Walrond's writing slowed to a trickle, and by 1940, he stopped writing entirely.

REFERENCES: *EA-99. EBLG. WDAA.* Barceló, Margarita, in *COCAAL* and *OCAAL.*

FURTHER READING: *AANB. BAWPP. CAO-02. MWEL. W. Wiki.* Berry, Jay R., in *AAWHR-40.* Christensen, Peter Glenn, in *GEAAL.*

Walter, Mildred Pitts
9/9/1922–
Children's picture books, novels, juvenile nonfiction

Walter's fiction for children and youths includes her *Lillie of Watts: A Birthday Discovery* (1969) and its sequel *Lillie of Watts Takes a Giant Step* (1971), *The Liquid Trap* (1975), her pair of novels on school integration (*The Girl on the Outside,* 1982; *Because We Are,* 1983, Parents' Choice award winner), *My Mama Needs Me* (1983), *Have a Happy . . .* (1984, about a family's celebration of Kwanzaa during a difficult time; retitled *Kwanzaa: A Family Affair,* 1995), *Trouble's Child* (1985), *Justin and the Best Biscuits in the World* (1986, **Coretta Scott King** Award winner about an Exoduster family who settled in Missouri), *Mariah Loves Rock* (1988), *Mariah Keeps Cool* (1990), and *Two and Too Much* (1990). Her affection for 11-year-old boys may be seen in *Suitcase* (1999, illustrations by T. Flavin), about a very tall 11-year-old who's drawn more to drawing than to basketball, much to his father's dismay; and in *Ray and the Best Family Reunion Ever* (2002), where a young boy learns about his Louisiana Creole ancestry and his own family's troubles.

Her nonfiction book *The Mississippi Challenge* (1992, winner of Coretta Scott King Award and Carter G. Woodson Book Award: Secondary) describes the historic struggle for the right to vote in Mississippi up through the mid-1960s. She explored slavery in two juvenile historical-fiction books. *Second Daughter: The Story of a Slave Girl* (1996) views slavery as Aissa, the fictitious teenage younger sister of Elizabeth Freeman, "Mum Bett," who successfully sued her "owner" for her freedom in Massachusetts; it was named a Jane Addams Honor Book and was honored by the Virginia Library Association. *Alec's Primer* (2004/2008) novelizes the true story of Alec Turner (1845-1923), who illicitly learned to read a primer as a young boy on a Virginia plantation, escaped slavery by becoming a Union soldier during the Civil War, and managed to buy farmland in Vermont (published by the Vermont Folklife Center, winner of a Carter G. Woodson award).

Walter's picture books include *Ty's One Man Band* (1980) and her original folktale *Brother to the Wind* (1985, Parents' Choice award winner), *Little Sister, Big Trouble* (1990, illustrated by Pat Cummings), *Tiger Ride* (1993, illustrations by C. Hanna), and *Darkness* (1995, illustrations by M. Jameson), about the delights found in darkness.

REFERENCES: Harris, Violet J., in *COCAAL* and *OCAAL*. Hinton-Johnson, KaaVonia, in *GEAAL*. Kozikowski, Thomas, in *CAO-02*. M. F. S., in *CBC*. Wilson, Sharon K. (July 2003), Salem Press for EBSCO Publishing, //0-web.ebscohost.com.dbpcosdcsgt.co.san-diego.ca.us/novelist/detail?vid=65&hid=16&sid=02bf6a41-8618-414c-abf5-13f22fd219a5%40sessionmgr7&bdata=JnNpdGU9bm92ZWxpc3QtbGl2ZQ%3d%3d. //www.ala.org/ala/emiert/corettascott kingbookaward/cskpastwinners/alphabeticallist/cskalphabetical.cfm#au. Amazon.com.

Walton, Anthony
1960–
Poems, articles, essays, anthologies, memoir, nonfiction—biography/history

Walton earned his B.A. from the University of Notre Dame and his M.F.A. from Brown University and now teaches at Bowdoin College in Maine. Many of his poems were collected in *Cricket Weather* (1995). He has also published his family memoir, *Mississippi: An American Journey* (1996), and numerous articles and essays (e.g., in *Harper's*, *Atlantic Monthly*, *The New Yorker*, **Callaloo**, *Kenyon Review*). With his mentor and friend **Michael S. Harper**, he coedited *Every Eye Ain't Asleep: An Anthology of Poetry by African Americans Since 1945* (1994) and *The Vintage Book of African American Poetry: 200 Years of Vision, Struggle, Power, Beauty, and Triumph from 50 Outstanding Poets* (2000). He also collaborated with Kareem Abdul-Jabbar to write *Brothers in Arms: The Epic Story of the 761st Tank Battalion, WWII's Forgotten Heroes* (2004).

REFERENCES: *AT. VBAAP. Wiki.* Olson, Debbie Clare, in *GEAAL*. //www.amazon.com, 3/2000, 5/2009.

Waniek (1st married name; 2nd married name: Wilkenfield), Marilyn (née Nelson) (aka Marilyn Nelson)
4/26/1946–
Poems, criticism, biography, translations; educator

Even before she had her own children, Marilyn was writing of family life and love. In 1970, she married Erdmann F. Waniek, a German in this country on a grad-

uate student visa. After two years, due to visa difficulties, they moved to Denmark for a year before returning to the States. Their troubled marriage, about which she wrote in *Partial Truth* (1992), ended in 1979. Later that year, she married Roger R. Wilkenfeld, with whom she had two children, Jacob (b. 1980) and Dora (b. 1986), before they divorced in 1998. Meanwhile, Marilyn had still used Marilyn Nelson Waniek as her pen name until the late summer of 1995, when she officially returned to using her maiden name, Marilyn Nelson; some of her titles list both names.

As Waniek, her poetry collections include *For the Body* (1978), using free verse to reveal childhood experiences; *The Cat Walked through the Casserole and Other Poems for Children* (1984, with Pamela Espeland), humorously exploring family life and the foibles of family pets; *Mama Promises* (1985), using ballad stanzas to unveil the conflicts of trying to write while trying to mother a young child; *The Homeplace* (1990), using multiple poetic forms (e.g., sonnet, villanelle, ballad, dramatic dialogue) and photos to tell family stories; *Partial Truth* (1992, originally published under the pen name Lynn Nelson), probing marital turmoil in a chapbook of 14 Pushcart Prize-winning sonnets; and *Magnificat: Poems* (1994), meditating on Christian spiritual themes. *Homeplace*, nominated for a National Book Award (1991), received an Anisfield-Wolf Award (1992). After her first collection, the poet has often turned to more formal poetry, using rhyme, rhythm, and meter to enrich readers' enjoyment of her poems.

Waniek also translated Danish author Pil Dahlerup's *Literary Sex Roles* (1975) and Danish poet Halfdan Rasmussen's *Hundreds of Hens and Other Poems for Children* (1982, with Pamela Espeland), humorous rhyming-couplets poetry. As Marilyn Nelson, she translated Rasmussen's *Ladder* (2004/2006, illustrated by Pierre Pratt), a whimsical verse narrative for children about a wandering ladder that enables others to reach skyward; and *Selected Verse of Halfdan Rasmussen* (2004). She also translated the poems of her friend, Danish poet Inge Pedersen, in *The Thirteenth Month* (2005), which won the American Scandinavian Foundation (ASF) Translation prize. In addition to translating these contemporary works, Nelson was invited to translate Euripides's ancient Greek classic play, "Hecuba" (originally 424 b.c.e.), about the enslaved widow of a king, for the Penn Greek Drama series' *Euripides 1* (1997). As she later recalled, "I spent the entire semester weeping, reading of Hecuba's descent from the throne of Troy into slavery, and of African American women in the throes of slavery.... The first production of the play, performed in 1998 by the African Continuum Theatre Company of Washington, D.C., was directed by my sister, Jennifer Nelson" (quoted in *CAO-09*). Soon after, the United States Military Academy at West Point commissioned Nelson to edit *Rumors of Troy: Poems Inspired by "The Iliad"* (2001), offering modern poems about the events in Homer's war epic, for use in the school's freshman English course. She has also written articles of literary criticism and review, and both her criticism and her poems have been published in numerous periodicals (e.g., *MELUS, Obsidian II*) and anthologies (e.g., *The New Bread Loaf Anthology of Contemporary American Poetry*, 1999).

Nelson's friend Pamela Espeland compiled *The Fields of Praise: New and Selected Poems* (1997), winner of the Poets' Prize (1999), and nominated for a National Book Award (1997), the Lenore Marshall Poetry Prize, and the L.L. Winship/PEN New England Award. In 2001, Nelson published two chapbooks: *She-Devil Circus*, using seven sonnets to challenge the meaning of love; and *Triolets for Triolet*, using triolets to journey through the Mauritian village of Triolet. More notably, she also published her verse biography, *Carver: A Life in Poems* (2001), comprising dozens of free-verse poems for young adults. Her book was nominated for the National Book Award and was named a Newbery Honor Book, a **Coretta Scott King** Honor Book, and one of the Best Books for Young Adults by the American Library Association (2002). It also won the Flora Stieglitz Straus Award for Nonfiction and the *Boston Globe-Horn Book (BG-HB)* Award. In her *BG-HB* acceptance speech, she said, "I did not intend this to be a book for children. I wrote the poems as I always do, striving for clarity and truthfulness, and imagining an audience of grown-ups" (2002).

Her next verse biography, *Fortune's Bones: The Manumission Requiem* (2004), also appeals to young adults, as well as older ones. Commissioned by the Mattatuck Museum in Waterbury, Connecticut, her text provides a libretto for music played by the Waterbury Symphony. Given a Coretta Scott King Honor and the 2005 Lion and the Unicorn Award for Excellence in North American Poetry, Nelson said, "What was a dirge for the dead becomes a celebration of life" (quoted by Bridgford in *AW:ACLB-09*).

Andrea Pinkney, senior editor and publisher of children's books at Houghton Mifflin, commissioned Nelson to write *A Wreath for Emmett Till* (2005), to enlighten contemporary young adults about this darkly tragic lynching of a teenage boy in 1955. Nelson calls the work "a heroic crown of sonnets," having chosen sonnets because they so aptly signify poems of love. She recalled, "I wrote this poem with my heart in my mouth and tears in my eyes, breathless with anticipation and surprise" (quoted by Bridgford in *AW:ACLB-09*). Among its laurels are a Coretta Scott King Honor (2006), a *BG-HB* Honor (2005), a Michael L. Printz Honor for Excellence in Young Adult Writing (2006), and a Lee Bennett Hopkins Poetry Award Honor (2006).

Nelson employed an array of poetic forms (e.g., sestinas, sonnets, free verse) for her next verse biography, *The Freedom Business: Connecticut Landscapes through the Eyes of **Venture Smith**: Poems* (2006, illustrated by Deborah Muirhead). Smith, a former slave, told his own story in his 1798 narrative, and Nelson's work pairs side-by-side excerpts from his narrative with her poetic responses. She also paired her writing with inauguration poet **Elizabeth Alexander** in *Miss Crandall's School for Young Ladies and Little Misses of Color: Poems* (2007, illustrated by Floyd Cooper). Written for young adults, the paired sonnets of Alexander and Nelson address shared themes, highlighting Alexander's more conversational style and Nelson's more formal sonnets.

For adults, Nelson has written *The Cachoeira Tales, and Other Poems* (2005), described as an homage to Chaucer, as "a group of African American 'pilgrims' who tell stories as they travel on their pilgrimage" (quoted in CAO-09). It won the L. E. Phillabaum Award and was nominated for the *Los Angeles Times* Book Award. At present, Nelson has several children's picture books at different stages of production: *Snook Alone* (in press), about "a little dog marooned on an uninhabited island" (CAO-09); *The Baobab Room*, soon to be published, in collaboration with her dear friend Abba Jacob; another collaborative picture book being written with Abba Jacob, about the plight of the Kalahari Bush people of Botswana; and *Ostrich and Lark*, which uses Bush people artists' illustrations. For young adults, Nelson collaborated with Tonya Hegamin on *Pemba: A Ghost Story* (in press), in which Nelson's 10 sonnets are accompanied by Hegamin's prose.

Nelson's manuscripts and other documents related to her writing are being archived in the Kerlan Collection at the University of Minnesota and in the archives of the University of Connecticut. Nelson taught English for more than three decades, starting in 1970 in Oregon, Denmark, and Minnesota, before settling at the University of Connecticut at Storrs in 1978, where she taught until 2002. After retiring, she went to the University of Delaware until 2004, then she returned to claim her emerita status in Connecticut. She was also a visiting professor in Hamburg, Germany (1977), and in several colleges across the United States, including West Point's U.S. Military Academy (2000).

In the summer of 2002, Nelson "joined the Cave Canem family by leading a week-long workshop. . . . Like every Cave Canem student and faculty member, I was . . . touched to my very core. This was the first time I had ever been in a community of African American artists. . . . I told the directors that I was going to try to buy a house which could be a retreat for Cave Canem graduates; a place where they could replicate, on a much smaller scale, that intense, trust-based workshop community. In my mind, I was already calling the place 'Soul Mountain.' . . . I became obsessed with real estate, looking for the right house in which to plant Soul Mountain. . . . I found the house in Connecticut: nine bedrooms, three living rooms, three kitchens, and a large deck, on six acres of lawn, meadow, and woods, with a large pond. . . . I bought the house in 2003. . . . I . . . moved to Soul Mountain in the summer of 2004. Tonya Hegamin, a young woman I had met at a Cave Canem workshop, joined me soon afterward, to be the first program director of Soul Mountain. . . . We invited our first guests, two Cave Canem poets. And Soul Mountain was off and running."

In addition to her numerous book honors, Nelson has been awarded a Kent fellowship (1976), two National Endowment for the Arts creative-writing fellowships (1981, 1990), a Connecticut Arts Award (1990), and a J. S. Guggenheim Memorial Foundation Fellowship (2001), as well as a Fulbright teaching fellowship (1995), a Contemplative Practices fellowship from the American Council of Learned Societies (2000), and three honorary doctorates. The State of Connecticut's Connecticut Commission on the Arts named her the state's Poet Laureate for 2001 through 2006. In 2006, Nelson was honored for her Lifetime Achievement in Service to the Literary Community, from the Connecticut Book Awards. In her speech accepting that honor, she said, "My achievements are really blessings for being in the right place at the right time" (CAO-08). Elsewhere, she was quoted as saying, "The greatest masters of our tradition sought not to see their own eyes, but to see through them" (quoted by Kim Bridgford, in AW:ACLB-09). More than a decade earlier, she had written, "I hope my poems are windows. So many people have been windows for me" (quoted in the 1995 section of her autobiographical essay, CAO-09).

REFERENCES: CA/I. CAO-08. CAO-09. Blackwell, Jacqueline A., in GEAAL. Boelcskevy, Mary Anne Stewart, in COCAAL and OCAAL. Bridgford, Kim, in AW:ACLB-09. Goldsmith, Shari. "Obituaries." Library Journal 126.20 (Dec. 2001) p. 42. From Literature Resource Center. Griffith, Paul A., in NFP. Jones, Kirkland C., APSWWII-3. Nelson, Marilyn, in //www.hbook.com/magazine/articles/2002/jan02_nelson.asp. //classics.mit.edu/Euripides/ hecuba.html. //en.wikipedia. org/wiki/Poets%27_Prize. //www.afro poets.net/marilynnelson.html. //www.blueflowerarts.com/ mnelson.html. //www.britannica.com/ EBchecked/topic/259223/ Hecuba. //www.cavecanempoets.org/pages/ programs_faculty.php. //www.embracingthechild.org/african american.htm. //www.hbook. com/bghb/past/past.asp. //www.soul mountainretreat.org/marilyn_ nelson.html. Amazon.com.

FURTHER READING: EAAWW.

Ward, Douglas Turner
5/5/1930–
Plays; journalist, actor

A native of Louisiana, Ward graduated from public school at age 15, then left for Xenia, Ohio, to attend Wilberforce University. From there, he transferred to the University of Michigan, where he played junior-varsity football. In 1948, his knee was injured, and at the end of the school year, he moved to New York, where he started writing articles and satirical sketches for the *Daily Worker*, a leftist newspaper. Soon, he was arrested, convicted, and shipped to Louisiana for draft evasion; he stayed there for two years until the U.S. Supreme Court reversed his conviction.

He returned to New York, eager to start a career in theater, writing plays. To better learn the craft, he studied acting and performed in several plays. He debuted Off-Broadway in 1957, on Broadway in 1959 (**Lorraine Hansberry**'s *A Raisin in the Sun*), and won an Obie for acting in 1966 and a Tony nomination for acting in 1974. Soon, he was also writing his own one-act satirical plays *Day of Absence* (1965) and *Happy Ending* (1966), while continuing to act. *Day of Absence*, probably his best-known play, showed how much European Americans rely on African Americans and how much power African Americans can exert when united in their aims. *Happy Ending* shows the flip side, in which African Americans depend on European Americans, as well: A nephew and his two aunts, domestic servants, fear they may lose their jobs—until the happy ending. In the play, all the African Americans in a small Southern town go on strike, bringing the town to its knees. His first two plays ran as *Two Plays* for 504 Off-Broadway performances, among the longest-running Off-Broadway plays, winning Ward a Vernon Rice/Drama Desk Award for playwriting. He also wrote his full-length *The Reckoning: A Surreal Southern Fable* (1969), *Brotherhood* (1970), and *The Redeemer* (1979). His first three plays were reprinted in the 1990s.

In 1966, Ward wrote *The New York Times* article "American Theatre: For Whites Only?" in which he assaulted the racist practices of the New York theater establishment and proposed the need for a permanent African-American theater, to showcase the talents of African-American playwrights, actors, technicians, and managers. In 1967, Ward, Robert Hooks, and Gerald Crone cofounded the prestigious Negro Ensemble Company (NEC) of New York City, using a $434,000 grant from the Ford Foundation, and naming Ward its artistic director. NEC produced the plays of **Lonne Elder III** (*Ceremonies in Dark Old Men*), **Charles Fuller** (Pulitzer Prize-winning *A Soldier's Play*), **Wole Soyinka** (*Kongi's Harvest*), Joseph Walker (Tony-winning *The River Niger*), and **Richard Wright** and Louis Sapin (*Daddy Goodness*), and many actors got their start through NEC. During the 1980s, the right-wing policies of the executive branch meant that funding of arts programs was cut dramatically, in favor of bigger weapons programs. As a result, NEC struggled to stay afloat, and in 1991 and 1992, NEC produced no plays. In 1993, NEC opened for business again, with Ward at the helm as company president.

Ward and his wife, Diana Hoyt Powell (an editor, married in 1966), have two children.

REFERENCES: *AT. BAL-1-P. BAWPP. G-97. W. WB-99.* Gaffney, Floyd, in *COCAAL* and *OCAAL.* Prescott, Jani, in *CAO-01.* Shepherd, Kenneth R., in *BB.* Stewart, Gail, in *T-CAD-1st.* Vallillo, Stephen M., *AAW-55-85:DPW.* Wattley, Anne S., in *GEAAL.* Amazon.com.

Ward, Samuel (Ringgold)
10/17/1817–1866?
Essays, autobiography/slave narrative; enslaved worker, abolitionist

Born a slave, three-year-old Samuel escaped to freedom with his parents. In New York, he was deeply involved in the abolitionist movement and contributed to **Frederick Douglass**'s *North Star.* After passage of the fugitive-slave law, he had to flee farther north to Canada, where he wrote his 1855 *Autobiography of a Fugitive Slave.*

REFERENCES: *AANB. AAW:AAPP. Wiki.*

Ward, Theodore
9/15/1902–5/8/1983
Plays

Ward wrote 30 plays, including his most critically acclaimed works *Big White Fog* (1938) and *Our Lan'* (1941), which were produced on Broadway, as well as *Sick and Tiahd* (c. 1936-1937), *Deliver the Goods* (1942), *John Brown* (1950), *Candle in the Wind* (1967), and *The Daubers* (1973). *Big White Fog* was performed again in London in 2007 (May 11-July 30).

REFERENCES: *NYPL-AADR.* Barthelemy, Anthony Gerard, in *COCAAL* and *OCAAL.*

FURTHER READING: *AANB. BAWPP. CAO-02. W. Wiki.* Brown, Fahamisha Patricia, in *AAW-40-55.* Osborne, Elizabeth A., in *GEAAL.* Shandell, Jonathan, in *T-CAD-5th.* //wanhonlinedn.net/1173.html?*session*id*key*=*session*id*val*.

Washington, Booker T. (né Booker Taliaferro)
4/5/1856–11/14/1915
Essays, autobiography/slave narrative, spoken word—speeches

Even as a young boy, Washington sensed that education was the key to success. As he put it himself, "I had the feeling that to get into a schoolhouse and study in this way would be about the same as getting into paradise." As soon as he gained his freedom, he started his own self-ed-

Poster for the Federal Theatre Project presentation of Big White Fog *by Theodore Ward*

ucation, using an old copy of Noah Webster's *Elementary Spelling-Book* as his first text. In 1872, he heard about the Hampton Normal and Agricultural Institute, some 500 miles away, and he stuffed everything he owned (which wasn't much) in a satchel, stuffed all his money (less than two dollars) in his pocket, and journeyed to "Virginny." Once there, he cleaned his way into the classroom, janitored his way through school, and graduated with honors three years later. At that school, he learned not only the knowledge he had sought, but also a fundamental belief in self-reliance and industry as the sole route to success for African Americans. At Hampton, he also came to believe that civil-rights activism was frivolous foolishness that would stand in the way of economic progress.

After a brief detour studying the law and then theology, Washington returned to Hampton to teach and, soon after, brought with him his longtime beloved Fannie Norton Smith. In 1881, Washington was recommended for the opportunity to start a new school in Tuskegee, Alabama. He was to use the $2,000/year he received from the state of Alabama to convert "a broken down shanty

Booker T. Washington

and an old hen house" into the Tuskegee Normal and Industrial Institute. Tuskegee was to offer vocational training to artisans and tradespersons, as well as schoolteachers. A hard worker himself, Washington instilled in his teachers and his students the importance of working hard.

In 1882, Washington married Fannie, and the couple had a daughter, Portia, in 1883. In 1885, Fannie died, and just a year later, widower Washington married Tuskegee teacher and Lady Principal Olivia America Davidson. Nine months and 18 days after their wedding, Olivia gave birth to Booker, Jr. (5/29/1887), and a little over a year-and-a-half later, Ernest Davidson was born (2/6/1889). Tragically, within a few months, Olivia, too, was dead (5/9/1889). Grief-stricken and broke (due to the expenses of trying to save Olivia's life), Washington tried to raise his sons and daughter alone. In 1892, however, he gave marriage another chance, choosing again Tuskegee's Lady Principal (since 1890), Margaret Murray James.

Despite his personal and family tragedies, he managed to build his institute for African-American education in the hostile territory of the post-Reconstruction South. In this hostile environment, Washington developed his philosophy of accommodation. He opposed the Northward emigration of Southern blacks and quietly complied with segregation. A hard worker but never a rabble rouser, he noted that "the wisest among my race understand that the agitation of questions of social equality is the extremest folly." Needless to say, many Northern blacks denounced him as a race traitor, but most Southern whites praised Washington as a leader of great insight, and many white Northerners liked what he had to say, too. More than one publisher encouraged him to write his life story. With the collaboration of African-American journalist Edgar Webber, Washington wrote *The Story of My Life and Work* (1900), which was published by a small press. Despite the protests of black (and white) civil-rights activists, Washington's *Story* sold well.

Washington realized that if he wrote an even better book, he could raise even more funds for his institute. Hence, he joined forces with Max Bennett Thrasher, a European-American journalist, and the two produced *Up from Slavery*, published by Doubleday, Page and Company. With Doubleday's backing, the book was published serially in *Outlook* magazine (November 3, 1900-February 23, 1901) before it was published as a book. When the book was released, it was an immediate best-seller. Not only did the book bring in bucks directly, but it also prompted many rich white folks to open up their pocketbooks and to start writing checks to the Institute. Among the new benefactors was millionaire Andrew Carnegie (the industrialist), whose gifts included a Carnegie Library and $600,000 in U.S. Steel bonds. Over the years, Washington would commission or produce many more books promoting his philosophy, his school, and himself.

As closely as the wealthy whites (North and South) drew him to their hearts, well-educated blacks drew away from him. The more praise whites heaped upon him, the more scorn blacks piled on. He soon had virulently outspoken opponents among civil-rights activists such as **William Monroe Trotter** and **W. E. B. Du Bois**. Much to their chagrin, their cries of opposition in no way deterred Washington's supporters. In fact, Washington was ever more the darling of high society and of folks with power. He dined at the White House, was consulted by Presidents Theodore Roosevelt and William Howard Taft, and was respected as *the* African-American expert on race matters. If Washington smiled upon you, you were likely to receive healthy endowments and generous philanthropy for your cause. His good deeds to his supporters were numerous. He definitely had enough power to make it very rewarding to have him as a friend. If Washington didn't smile on you, however, you were in for some *real* trouble. He *definitely* could make it painful to be his enemy, and he was not at all opposed to dirty tricks and manipulations to punish those whom he perceived as opposing him.

Washington was not completely averse to some quiet actions on behalf of civil rights, however. In the background, he managed to subvert a few Jim Crow laws. He also had some mixed messages about the value of education. For instance, he espoused the value of vocational training and denigrated scholarly pursuits as irrelevant, scorning the well-educated intellectuals who were criticizing him. On the other hand, he saw to it that his own children received a college education.

When Washington died, 34 years after he had opened the school (which started out with 1 teacher, 2 ramshackle buildings, and 50 students), the Tuskegee Institute had a faculty of nearly 200 instructors, more than 100 well-equipped buildings, and an endowment of about $2 million.

REFERENCES: *SMKC.* Harlan, Louis R. 1972. *Booker T. Washington: The Making of a Black Leader, 1856-1901.* New York: Oxford University Press. _____. 1983), *Booker T. Washington: The Wizard of Tuskegee, 1901-1915.* New York: Oxford University Press.

FURTHER READING: *AANB. B. BAWPP. BCE. CAO-03. CE. HD. QB. W. W2B. Wiki.* Beavers, Herman, in *COCAAL.* Blight, David W., in *USHC.* Engel, Bill, in *GEAAL.* Jones, David M., in *ARRW-2.* Martin, Jonathan, in *BB.* Mixon, Gregory, in *EE.* //www.american writers.org/writers/washington.asp.

Waters, Ethel
10/31/1896–9/1/1977
Autobiographies; performer

Songbird Ethel Waters wrote two autobiographies: *His Eye Is on the Sparrow* (1951, with Charles Samuels) and *To Me It's Wonderful* (1972).

REFERENCES: *EB-BH-CD.* Griffin, Farah Jasmine, in *COCAAL* and *OCAAL.* Morse, Evan, in *BWA:AHE.*

FURTHER READING: *AANB. AT. B. BCE. CAO-02. D. F. Wiki.* Armstrong, Robin, in *BB.* Erickson, Hal, *All Movie Guide,* in *Act.* Pinto, Samantha, in *GEAAL.* Yanow, Scott, *All Music Guide,* in *A.*

Weatherly, Tom
11/3/1942–
Poems; theater producer, press agent

Emerging in the **Black Arts Movement**, Weatherly's poetry volumes are *Maumau Cantos* (1970), *Thumbprint* (1971), and his chapbook *Climate* (1972), and his individual poems have been anthologized. He also coedited *Natural Process: An Anthology of New Black Poetry* (1972).

REFERENCES: *BAWPP. CAO-01.* Kich, Martin, in *GEAAL.* Roberts, Evelyn Hoard, in *AAP-55-85.* Toombs, Charles P., in *COCAAL* and *OCAAL.* Amazon.com.

Weaver, Afaa M. (Michael) (né Michael S. Weaver)
11/26/1951–
Poems, plays, anthology; factory worker, journal editor, publisher, educator

At age 16, Michael S. Weaver graduated from high school as a National Merit Scholarship Finalist and entered the University of Maryland in College Park. While in college, he wrote extensively. By the end of two years of college, however, Weaver had impregnated his muse and married her in 1970. Needing to support his new family, he left the university and got a job at Bethlehem Steel. Other than a semester at historically black Morgan State University in 1975, Michael did not return to college for more than 15 years. Michael S. Weaver, Jr., was born with Down's syndrome. As a result, little Michael suffered from complications that killed him before he reached school age. Little Michael's death sent big Michael into an emotional tailspin, and he and his wife divorced in 1976. Two marriages and two divorces later, he had three ex-wives and a second son, Kala Oboi. Weaver also gained insight into the roots of his own pain, as he had been the victim of incest during his childhood.

Meanwhile, Michael Weaver, Sr., continued to write short nonfiction and fiction, as well as poetry. He also founded 7th Son Press, cofounded (with Melvin E. Brown) the literary magazine *Blind Alleys,* and found support and aid from fellow poets, who helped him find freelance work with the *Baltimore Sun.* Weaver also coedited *Gathering Voices: An Anthology of Baltimore Poets* (1985, with David Beaudouin and James Taylor), and he published his first poetry collection, *Water Song* (1985). That same year, Weaver received a grant from the National Endowment for the Arts, and Rhode Island's Brown University offered him a full university fellowship to its graduate writing program. While earning his M.A. in creative writing from Brown (1987), he simultaneously enrolled in Regents College in Albany, New York, where he earned his B.A. in English-language literature (1986).

After completing his master's degree, Weaver got a series of teaching jobs (1987-1990), then took a tenure track position at Rutgers University in New Jersey (1990-1998). During this time, Weaver published five more poetry collections: *some days it's a slow walk to evening* (1989), *My Father's Geography* (1992), *Stations in a Dream* (1993), and *Timber and Prayer* (1995). He also wrote three plays: *Rosa* (1987, his master's thesis project; 1993, produced), *The Last Congregation* (semifinalist at the University of Colorado's theater competition), and *Elvira and the Lost Prince* (1993, produced in Chicago, where it received the Playwrights Discovery/Development Award).

In 1995, Weaver was told that he would die within five years unless he received a heart transplant. Instead, Weaver drastically changed his diet and his lifestyle. Decades earlier, Weaver had started studying Chinese culture and the Daoist (aka Taoist) faith, and he now delved into Asian healing practices. Meanwhile, he was named a Dodge Poet by the Geraldine R. Dodge Foundation and a member of the Literature Panel for the Pennsylvania Arts Council (1993-?), which also awarded him a fellowship (1994). In the spring of 1997, he was named the first African-American to become a poet in residence at Bucknell University's Stadler Poetry Center in Pennsylvania.

In 1997, Michael S. Weaver, Senior, also came to terms with the death of Michael S. Weaver, Junior. To honor his son with a distinctive name, Weaver decided to adopt a new first name for himself. On reading a list of Ibo names, he chose the name "Afaa," which he later discovered means "oracle" or "prophet." In 1998, the former Michael S. Weaver, Senior, legally changed his name to Afaa M. (Michael) Weaver. His subsequent books use either his new name or both his old and his new names.

Afaa M. Weaver moved to Boston, Massachusetts in 1998 to accept an endowed chair as the Alumnae Professor of English at Simmons College. There, he also cofounded and directs the **Zora Neale Hurston** Literary Center (1998-). In 2001, he was awarded a Fulbright fellowship to teach at Taiwan's National University, during which time he traveled extensively in China. He soon started formally studying the Chinese language (2002), studying at Taiwan's Taipei Language Institute (2004-2005), and probably becoming the first African-American poet who can speak, write, and read Chinese.

While at Simmons, Weaver has published several additional poetry collections, including *Talisman* (1998), *Multitudes: Poems Selected & New* (2000), *Sandy Point* (2000), *The Ten Lights of God* (2000), and *The Plum Flower Dance/Poems 1985 to 2005* (2007), which included his Pushcart Prize-winning (2008) poem "American Income." He also edited the literary journal *Obsidian III: Literature in the African Diaspora* (1997-2002), and he edited the anthology *These Hands I Know: African-American Writers on Family* (2002). His own poetry and short fiction have also appeared in other anthologies, as well as in journals (e.g., *American Poetry Review*, **Callaloo**).

In addition to the aforementioned grants, awards, and other honors, Weaver has been named a Pew Fellow in Poetry and the first Elder of **Cave Canem**. He also won Paris's Sidney Becht Prize (1996), a Penn Fellowship in the Arts (1998), and a gold friendship medal from the Chinese Writers' Association in Beijing (2005). He is a member of American P.E.N., Poetry Society of American Dramatists Guild, Academy of American Poets, National Writers Union, and PEN New England, in addition to being a Cave Canem fellow.

REFERENCES: *AAW:PV. CAO-06*. Alger, Derek, //www.pif magazine.com/SID/882/. Aucoin, Don, "A Poet Forged in Heartbreak: One-time Factory Worker Afaa Michael Weaver Broke through a Dam from His Past—and the Words Flowed Forth," in //www.boston.com/ae/books/articles/2007/12/11/a_poet_forged_in_heartbreak/. Brownlow, Ron, "Afaa Weaver: Once upon a Trauma. Noted US Poet and Literature Professor Afaa Weaver Has Found a Kindred Spirit in the People of Taiwan," in //www.taipeitimes.com/News/feat/archives/2007/07/08/2003368561. Danois, Ericka Blount, "Tao and Then: East Baltimore and Eastern Philosophy Transformed Afaa Michael Weaver into the Poet He Is," in //www.baltimoremag.com/article.asp?t=1&m=1&c=30&s=481&ai=70772. Minderovic, Christine Miner, in *BB*. Wilson, Sonya L., "Afaa Michael Weaver—Artist and Survivor," in //www.bellaonline.com/articles/art54144.asp. //en.wikipedia.org/wiki/Brown_University. //en.wikipedia.org/wiki/Bucknell_University. //en.wikipedia.org/wiki/Daoism. //en.wikipedia.org/wiki/Excelsior_College. //en.wikipedia.org/wiki/Morgan_State_University. //en.wikipedia.org/wiki/National_Merit_Scholarship_Program. //www.afaamweaver.com/. //www.pen.org/MemberProfile.php/prmProfileID/19293. //www.poets.org/poet.php/prmPID/170. Amazon.com.

FURTHER READING: Ostrom, Hans, in *GEAAL*.

Weaver, Robert C. (Clifton)
12/29/1907–7/17/1997
Nonfiction—economics, sociology

Weaver's explorations in the fields of sociology and economics include nearly 200 articles and 4 books: *Negro Labor: A National Problem* (1946), *The Negro Ghetto* (1948), *The Urban Complex* (1964), and *Dilemmas of Urban America* (1965). These works (and his involvement in several governmental positions) contributed to his becoming the first African American appointed to the U.S. Cabinet, as the Secretary of Housing and Urban Development (1966-1968).

REFERENCES: *EB-BH-CD*. Fay, Robert, in *EA-99*. Thieme, Darius L., in *BH2C*.

FURTHER READING: *AANB. B. CAO-03. CE. PB. Wiki*. Armstrong, Robin, and Sara Pendergast, in *BB*.

Webb, Frank J. (Johnson)
1828–1894
Novel; abolitionist

All that remains of the literary work of Frank J. Webb are one novel, *The Garies and Their Friends* (1857); two novelettes, "Two Wolves and A Lamb" and "Marvin Hayle," published in *New Era: A Colored American National Journal*, in the January-February and the

Robert C. Weaver, chief of the Negro Employment and Training Branch (NETB), Washington, D.C.

March-April, 1870 issues, respectively; and a handful of poems and several articles, also published in *New Era*. He is nonetheless important to African-American literature. *The Garies* was just the second of four published antebellum novels written by African-American writers. In addition, *The Garies* was the first such novel to touch on topics such as free-born Northern African Americans, "passing" as white, interracial marriage, intraracial color biases, Northern racism, class differences within the African-American community, and African-American entrepreneurship. These issues emerge through the interactions among the novel's three families: the interracial Garies, the dark-skinned Ellises, and the white Stevenses.

Regarding Webb himself, little is known. After the 1857 publication of his novel, British friends found him a post in the Kingston, Jamaica post office (1858). His first wife died in Kingston in 1859. Frank stayed in Jamaica, marrying a Jamaican woman with whom he soon had four children (1865-1869). In 1870, Frank returned to the United States, alone. In Washington, D.C., he clerked for the Freedmen's Bureau and attended Howard University's law school. He continued to write, and he claimed

to have completed a second novel, "Paul Sumner," which never reached print; the manuscript has never been found.

When Webb's Freedmen's Bureau job ended, and he was not able to earn a living from his writing, he moved to Galveston, Texas, where he found another post office job and edited the short-lived *Galveston Republican* newspaper. In 1873, Webb sent for his Jamaican family to join him, had two more children, and in 1881, Webb became principal of the Barnes Institute. Webb's novel was largely neglected during his day and remained so until the 1960s, when scholars such as **Arthur P. Davis** brought him to long-overdue prominence.

REFERENCES: *BAWPP. W.* Bogardus, R. F. "Frank J. Webb's The Garies and Their Friends: An Early Black Novelist's Venture Into Realism." *Studies in Black Literature.* 5.2 (1974, Summer), pp. 15-20. Reprinted in Russel Whitaker (Ed.), 2005, *Nineteenth-Century Literature Criticism*, Vol. 143). Detroit: *Literature Resources from Gale.* Candela, Gregory L., in *AAWBHR.* Gardner, Eric, in *AANB*, and " 'A Gentleman of Superior Cultivation and Refinement': Recovering the Biography of Frank J. Webb." *African American Review.* 35.2 (Summer 2001), p. 297. *Literature Resources from Gale.* Lapsansky, Phillip S. 1991. "Afro-Americana: Frank J. Webb and His Friends." *The Annual Report of the Library Company of Philadelphia for the Year 1990.*

Philadelphia: Library Company of Philadelphia. Reprinted in Russel Whitaker (Ed.), 2005, *Nineteenth-Century Literature Criticism*, Vol. 143). Detroit: *Literature Resources from Gale*. Rodgers, Lawrence R., in COCAAL.

FURTHER READING: "Frank J. Webb," Davis, Arthur P. (1969). "The Garies and Their Friends: A Neglected Pioneer Novel," *CLA Journal, 13* (No. 1), pp. 27-34. "Mary Webb," Gardner, Eric, in GEAAL. Reuben, Paul P. "Chapter 3: Frank J. Webb." *PAL: Perspectives in American Literature-A Research and Reference Guide.* //www.csustan.edu/english/reuben/pal/chap3/webb.html. Saulsbury, Rebecca R., in GEAAL.

Wells-Barnett (née Wells), Ida B. (Bell) (aka "Iola")
7/16/1862–3/25/1931
Essays, pamphlets, diaries, editorials, autobiography, travel journal; journalist, newspaper co-owner; lecturer

Ida B. Wells-Barnett

This daughter of slaves was freed by the Civil War, but she was not to live a carefree life. In 1878, her youngest brother and her parents died of yellow fever, leaving teenage Ida to care for her six remaining younger siblings. Fortunately, she had received a good grammar-school education at Rust College, where her father was a trustee after the Freedman's Aid Association set up the school in her home town in Mississippi. With that education, she got a teaching job and supported her siblings on her $25/month salary. After five years of struggling to support them, she decided to move to Memphis (in 1883) to get a better-paying teaching job and to attend Fisk University during summer breaks.

While at Fisk, Wells started writing for the student newspaper, and she soon started editing two church-related newspapers. In her subsequent reflections on this experience, Wells commented, "I wrote in a plain, common-sense way on the things which concerned our people." Wells soon started writing for numerous African-American newspapers on various topics, especially on issues relating to race and gender. Wells also kept a diary of her experiences and of her observations of racism in the Jim Crow South, which she used later for writing her autobiography.

Among her many topics was an experience that heralded Rosa Parks's stand against segregated bus transportation in 1955. In 1884, Wells had paid for a first-class ladies coach ticket on a train, but she was physically removed from that car and dragged to the smoking car, where all "colored" people were ordered to ride. She sued the Chesapeake, Ohio, and Southwestern Railroad and won a $500 settlement in a Tennessee circuit court. Unfortunately, she later lost when the railroad appealed to the Tennessee Supreme Court, which overturned the lower-court decision.

Another of her favorite topics was the inferiority of segregated schools for African-American children. As a teacher and a former student of segregated schools, she knew her subject firsthand. Although she wrote all her newspaper articles under the pseudonym "Iola," the Memphis school board eventually realized she had authored these critical articles, and in 1891, the board refused to renew her teaching contract. Fortunately, two years earlier (1889), Wells had used her savings to buy a one-third interest in the Memphis *Free Speech and Headlight*. Now, with more time on her hands—and a greater need to earn money from her writing—Wells turned her attention to journalism full time.

Did losing her teaching job make Ida's articles milder? Not at all. Then on March 9, 1892, three co-owners of a profitable grocery business were lynched, one of whom (Thomas Moss) was a close friend of hers. Did that violence quiet her voice? Definitely not. Instead, she wrote scathing editorials denouncing lynching as a brutal means of squelching economic competition from African Americans—not, as was often claimed, an overly enthusiastic defense of white women's virtue against black men's sexual aggression: "Nobody in this section of the country believes the old thread-bare lie that Negro men assault white women." She urged the African Americans of Memphis to flee from lynching and Jim Crow racism, to go West, to find genuine economic and social opportunity.

After publishing these editorial attacks on lynching, Wells took a trip up North to visit **Frances E. W. Harper** and to rally Northern support for her antilynching efforts. While there, an enraged mob of Memphis whites destroyed her newspaper's offices and loudly warned Wells never to return to Memphis—under penalty of death. That threat got her attention, and she stayed clear of Memphis, but she didn't stop speaking out against lynching and other aspects of racism.

Sarah Garnet (wife of **Henry Highland Garnet**) and other prominent African-American women helped raise funds for Wells to replace her ruined press equipment and offices. Once she realized she couldn't return to Memphis, Wells moved to New York and bought a partial interest in **T. Thomas Fortune**'s *New York Age,* and she was soon writing and editing for that paper. After conducting extensive research on incidents of lynching, she published her 1892 pamphlet, *Southern Horrors: Lynch Law in All Its Phases.* Her pamphlet cited numerous incidents, giving all the specifics of each case, and clearly documenting her assertion that lynching relates far more closely to economic competition by African Americans than to any alleged instances of rape.

Occasionally, Wells attacked problems of Northern racism. For instance, when African Americans were not included in the planning—and barely included in the exhibition—of the 1893 Chicago World's Fair, Wells asked **Frederick Douglass**, Chicago attorney and newspaper publisher Ferdinand Lee Barnett, and other prominent African Americans to join her in publishing 20,000 copies of her pamphlet *The Reason Why the Colored American Is Not in the World's Columbian Exposition.* Douglass wrote the foreword, and Barnett contributed an essay to the publication. During 1893 and 1894, Wells continued to denounce lynching and traveled throughout the North and in England to muster support for her antilynching campaign. Her travel journal was later published in her autobiography.

In 1895, she published *A Red Record: Tabulated Statistics and Alleged Causes of Lynching in the United States, 1892 – 1893 – 1894.* This publication provided extensive statistics and analyses of lynchings, which backed up her premise: Two out of three victims of lynching were never even accused of rape, and those who were accused of rape may have engaged in consensual relations with white women who later were forced to cry rape. In any case, most of the lynch victims had been economically competitive, educationally advanced, or politically assertive in relation to local whites. Among the statistics she cited were these: "During these years more than ten thousand Negroes have been killed in cold blood, without the formality of judicial trial and legal execution. . . . the same record shows that during all these years, and for all these murders only three white men have been tried, convicted, and executed." Wells also pointed out how the

transition from slavery to Reconstruction meant that whites no longer had an economic interest in the bodies of blacks, which had previously constrained whites from murdering or maiming blacks, so brutality against African Americans actually *increased* following emancipation.

On June 27, 1895, Wells married Barnett, the Chicagoan with whom she had collaborated previously. Barnett was a widower with two sons, and Wells later gave birth to four additional children: Charles Aked, Herman Kohlsaat, Ida B. Wells, Jr., and Alfreda (who later edited her mother's autobiography, shortly after her mother's death). The Wells-Barnett merger also yielded journalistic fruit, as Wells purchased her husband's *Chicago Conservator.* Although her duties as the wife of an assistant state attorney (Illinois's first African American to have that job) and mother of six did slow down Wells's activism and her journalistic output, they certainly didn't stop her. She often took her babies with her to speaking engagements, expecting that local sponsors (usually, women's clubs) would provide suitable child-care arrangements.

Her postmarriage writings included her 1900 pamphlet on lynching, *Mob Rule in New Orleans,* and the essays "Lynching and the Excuse for It" (1901) and "Our Country's Lynching Record" (1913). She also wrote "**Booker T. Washington** and His Critics" (1904), one of the first articles questioning Washington's willingness to abandon the pursuit of civil rights in order to seek economic advancement—a surefire prescription for continuation of lynching, as far as Wells could see. In 1917, the *Chicago Tribune* published her letter warning that racial violence might erupt the following summer. The next summer, she wrote a series of articles on the race riot that did indeed erupt. In 1922, she wrote and raised money to publish and distribute 1,000 copies of her pamphlet *The Arkansas Race Riot,* probing the unjust murder indictment of a dozen African-American farmers.

Wells continued to write diaries during many periods of her life, and between 1928 and 1934, she wrote her autobiography. Just as she was about to complete it, mid-sentence, uremic poisoning overtook her, and she died. Her daughter Alfreda M. Duster completed the work and oversaw its publication as *Crusade for Justice: The Autobiography of Ida B. Wells* (1970).

Wells also joined with others in support of racial and gender equality. In addition to joining many organizations, she founded or cofounded the Ida B. Wells Club of Chicago (1893); the National Association of Colored Women (1896); the Niagara Movement (1905) and its successor, the NAACP (1910); the Negro Fellowship League (1910); and the Alpha Suffrage Club of Chicago (1913), the first African-American women's suffrage organization. In 1930, she rejected her Republican Party affiliation and ran as an independent candidate for the Illinois senate, but she lost her bid. Sixty years later, however, she won a place on a

U.S. postage stamp, the first African-American woman journalist to be so honored.

REFERENCES: *1TESK. AA:PoP. ANAD. BAAW. BaD. BF:2000. EB-98. EBLG. G-95. H. NAAAL. PGAA. RLWWJ. WW:CCCC.* DeCosta-Willis, Miriam, in *OCAAL.* Harris, Trudier, in *OCWW.*

FURTHER READING: *AANB. AT. B. BCE. CE. HR&B*, pp. 339-342. *LE. QB. W. Wiki.* Athey, Stephanie, et al., in *AWPW: 1870-1920.* Hall, Nora, *ANJ-1873-1900.* Hine, Darlene Clark, in *USHC.* "Iola," *CAO-00.* Podesta, James J., in *BB.* Willis, Sharese Terrell, in *GEAAL.* //digital.library.upenn.edu/women/_generate/AFRICAN %20AMERICAN.html. *See also* "Wells-Barnett, Ida B.," *EAAWW.*

Welsing, Frances (née Cress)
3/18/1935–
Commentary

A Washington, D.C., psychiatrist since the early 1960s, Frances Cress Welsing gained media attention for her 1970 essay, "The Cress Theory of Color Confrontation and Racism (White Supremacy)." In it, she hypothesized that the lack of melanin that leads to white skin "is a genetic inadequacy or a relative deficiency or disease based upon the inability to produce the skin pigments of melanin which are responsible for all skin color." She further noted that "the majority of the world's people are not so afflicted, suggesting that the state of color is the norm for human beings and absence is abnormal." As a result of the "numerical inadequacy" and "color inferiority" of melanin-deprived white people, whites respond by defensively asserting white supremacy. She further elaborated her theory in *The Isis Papers: The Keys to the Colors* (1991, published by **Third World Press**), which remained on the then-new **BlackBoard African-American Bestsellers** list long after its publication.

REFERENCES: *CAO-02. Wiki.* Sussman, Alison Carb, in *BB.* Amazon.com.

Wesley, Charles Harris
12/2/1891-8/16/1987
Nonfiction—African-American history, biography; cleric, educator, administrator

This A.M.E. minister and president of Wilberforce University wrote numerous articles on African-American history. He also wrote or edited 13 general history books, including *Negro Labor in the United States, 1850-1925* (1927), *Collapse of the Confederacy* (1937), *The Negro in the Americas* (1940), *Negro Makers of History* (1958, 5th ed., with Carter G. Woodson), *Neglected History: Essays in Negro History* (1965), *International Library of Negro Life and History* (1967, 10 vols.), *Negro Americans in the Civil War: From Slavery to Citizenship* (1967), *Negro Citizenship in the United States: The Fourteenth Amendment and the*

Negro-American, Its Concepts and Developments, 1868-1968 (1968); as well as 6 histories of organizations, such as *The History of the National Association of Colored Women's Clubs: A Legacy of Service* (1984). He also wrote four biographies, including *Richard Allen, Apostle of Freedom* (1935), *Women Builders* (1970, with Sadie Iola Daniel and Thelma D. Perry), *Henry Arthur Callis, Life and Legacy* (1977), and *Prince Hall: A Life and Legacy* (1977). In 1979, he wedded writer, historian, and archivist **Dorothy Burnett Porter**. Among his honors are a Guggenheim Fellowship (1930-1931), a Phi Beta Kappa Key (1953), and an Amistad Award (1972).

REFERENCES: *EA-99. Wiki.* //wapedia.mobi/en/Charles_H._Wesley. //wapedia.mobi/en/Charles_H._Wesley?t=1.#2. //www.worldcat.org/identities/lccn-n50-3883.

FURTHER READING: *AANB. CAO-02.* Aptheker, Herbert. "Charles H. Wesley: Some Memories." *The Journal of Negro History.* 83.2 (Spring 1998) p. 153. From *Literature Resource Center.* Harris, Janette Hoston. "In Memoriam: Charles Harris Wesley," "Selected Words of Wisdom of Charles Harris Wesley," and "Woodson and Wesley: a Partnership in Building the Association for the Study of Afro-American Life and History." *The Journal of Negro History.* 83.2 (Spring 1998) pp. 109, 150, 155. From *Literature Resource Center.* Wilson, Francille Rusan "Racial Consciousness and Black Scholarship: Charles H. Wesley and the Consciousness of 'Negro Labor in the United States.' (Vindicating the Race: Contributions to African-American Intellectual History)." *The Journal of Negro History.* 81.1-4 (Annual 1996) p. 72. From *Literature Resource Center.*

Wesley, Dorothy Burnett Porter *See* **Porter, Dorothy Burnett**

Wesley, Valerie Wilson
11/22/1947–
Mysteries and other novels, nonfiction, juvenile literature; editor

Richard (Errol) Wesley, husband
7/11/1945–
Plays; educator

After Valerie Wilson earned her B.A. from Howard University (1970), she worked as an assistant editor for *Scholastic News* (1970-1972). She also met and then married (May 22, 1972) playwright Richard Wesley, with whom she had two daughters, Thembi and Nandi. While raising her girls, she studied at the Bank Street College of Education, earning her M.A. in Early Childhood Education. While working on her master's thesis, she renewed her love of writing. She started attending workshops at the Harlem Writers' Guild and writing poems, short stories, and short nonfiction. Her byline started appearing in educational periodicals (e.g., *Creative Classroom*) and in mainstream ones (e.g., *The New York Times*). Wesley then earned a second M.A. from the Columbia Graduate School of Journalism.

In 1988, Valerie Wilson Wesley collaborated with **Wade Hudson** to write a children's book, *Afro-Bets Book of Black Heroes from A to Z: An Introduction to Important Black Achievers for Young Readers* (1988). She also started her long association with *Essence* magazine, as a travel columns editor (1988), a senior editor for travel (1989), a senior features editor (1990), and the executive editor (1992-1994). Meanwhile, she was continuing to write freelance. In 1994, she demoted herself to contributing editor so she could focus on her freelance work, including not only articles for periodicals but also books.

Wesley's second book was a young-adult novel, *Where Do I Go from Here?* (1993), cited as a Best Book for Reluctant Readers by the American Library Association (ALA). She also premiered her well-known series of Tamara Hayle mystery novels, written for adult readers. Her first, *When Death Comes Stealing, a Tamara Hayle Mystery* (1994), was nominated for a Shamus Award for Best First P.I. Novel (1995). More than half a dozen other Tamara Hayle mysteries have followed, including *Devil's Gonna Get Him* (1995), *Where Evil Sleeps, a Tamara Hayle Mystery* (1996), *No Hiding Place, a Tamara Hayle Mystery* (1997), *Easier to Kill, a Tamara Hayle Mystery* (1998), *The Devil Riding* (2000), *Dying in the Dark: a Tamara Hayle Mystery* (2004), and *Of Blood and Sorrow: A Tamara Hayle Mystery* (2008). She has also written at least three more novels for adults: *Ain't Nobody's Business If I Do* (1999), given an Award for Excellence in Adult Fiction by the ALA's Black Caucus (2000); *Always True to You in My Fashion* (2002); and *Playing My Mother's Blues* (2005).

Wesley has also continued to write for juvenile readers. Her *Freedom's Gifts: A Juneteenth Story* (1997) introduces young readers to the battle to end slavery and the struggle to achieve broader civil rights. Wesley also started her "Willimena Rules" series of picture books for young children, all of which have been illustrated by Maryn Roos. The numbered books in her series include *Willimena Rules!: How to Lose Your Class Pet* (2003), *How to Fish for Trouble* (2004), *How to Lose Your Cookie Money* (2004; published previously as *Willimena and the Cookie Money*, 2001), *How to (Almost) Ruin Your School Play* (2005), *23 Ways to Mess Up Valentine's Day* (2005), and *How to Face Up to the Class Bully* (2007). Earlier Willimena books include *Willimena and Mrs. Sweetly's Guinea Pig* (2002) and *Tales of Willimena* (2003).

Valerie's husband, Richard Wesley, earned his B.F.A. from Howard University (1967), where his first play, *Put My Dignity on 307*, was produced (1967). After graduating, he authored two unproduced plays, "Springtime High" (1968) and "Another Way" (1969). Soon after, he started working with Harlem's New Lafayette Theatre

(1969-1973), where he wrote numerous plays. Many of these plays were produced elsewhere, such as *The Streetcorner* (1970), *Headline News* (1970), *Knock Knock, Who Dat* (1970), *The Black Terror* (1971), *Gettin' It Together* (1971), and *Strike Heaven on the Face* (1973). *The Black Terror* won the Drama Desk Award for Outstanding Playwrighting (1972). In addition, two of these plays were also published in anthologies. During this time, he was also the managing editor of *Black Theatre Magazine* (1969-1973), and he contributed to periodicals. Wesley also was awarded a Rockefeller grant in 1973.

In 1974, four of Wesley's plays were produced: *Goin' thru Changes* (1974), *The Sirens* (1974), *The Past Is the Past* (1974), and *The Mighty Gents* (1974). Wesley was awarded NAACP Image Awards for each of these plays, and he was honored with an AUDELCO Award. *The Sirens* (1975) and *The Mighty Gents* (1979) were both published by the Dramatists Play Service, as was *The Past Is the Past and Gettin' It Together: Two Plays* (1975). In addition, *The Past Is the Past* (1975) was published in *The Best Short Plays of 1975*. During this time, Wesley also wrote two screenplays, *Uptown Saturday Night* (1974) and its sequel, *Let's Do it Again* (1974), both of which were box-office hits. In 1979, Wesley's musical, *On the Road to Babylon*, was both produced (1979) and published.

Wesley started off the 1980s as a guest lecturer in creative writing at Manhattan Community College (1980-1981, 1982-1983). After that, Wesley wrote two more stage plays, *The Dream Team* (1984) and *The Talented Tenth* (1989). He has since written plays for both large and small screens. In the mid-1980s, he adapted *Fast Forward* (1985 for Columbia Pictures) and *Native Son* (1986, for Cinecom). He also adapted **Virginia Hamilton**'s 1968 novel *The House of Dies Drear* for the Public Broadcasting Service (1984).

Since 1990, Wesley has written four teleplays, *Murder without Motive* (for NBC, 1991), *Mandela and De Klerk* (for Showtime, 1997), *Bojangles* (for Showtime, 2000), and *Deacons for Defense* (for Showtime, 2003). He has also written episodes for two TV series: *Fallen Angels* (for Showtime) and *100 Centre Street* (for A&E). A member of the Writers Guild of America East, Wesley is also the associate chair of the Goldberg Department of Dramatic Writing in the Tisch School of the Arts at New York University.

REFERENCES: "Valerie Wilson Wesley," *CAO-05. CA/1. Wiki.* Drew, Bernard Alger. 2007. *100 Most Popular African American Authors: Biographical Sketches and Bibliographies.* Santa Barbara, CA: Libraries Unlimited. Wolf, Gillian, in *BB.* //cityonthemove.us/html/east_orange_public_library.html. //en.wikipedia.org/wiki/American_Civil_War. //en.wikipedia.org/wiki/Emancipation_proclamation. //en.wikipedia.org/wiki/Shamus_Award. //www.goongirl.org/. //www.goongirl.org/Read/TheGoOnGirlLibraryList.pdf. //www.tamarahayle.com. //www.thrillingdetective.com/trivia/triv72.html. Amazon.com.

FURTHER READING: Moss, Shondrika L., in *GEAAL*.

REFERENCES: "Richard (Errol) Wesley," *BAWPP. Wiki*. Carter, Steven R., in *AAW-55-85:DPW.* Malinowski, Sharon, in *CAO-07.* //en.wikipedia.org/wiki/The_House_of_Dies_Drear. //theater2. nytimes.com/mem/theater/treview.html?res=950DE3D9123CF933A2 5752C1A96F948260. //www.imdb.com/name/nm0921759/bio. //www.imdb.com/title/tt0264696/. //www.manhattanville.edu/. Amazon.com.

West, Cornel (Ronald)
6/2/1953–

Nonfiction—sociology, anthologies, scholarly works; educator

Teacher? Philosopher? Writer? Theologian? Sociologist? Which of these disciplines best describes Cornel West and his large body of work? None of them—and all of them. Some say that West is the first leading African-American intellectual to rise to prominence since **W. E. B. Du Bois** in the late nineteenth and early twentieth centuries. Others say that West says a lot without saying anything. West's admirers like his prophetic speech and his intellectual ability to cross and integrate disciplines, while his detractors say that West never fully completes his ideas and thoughts and has no plan to implement change. Regardless of one's opinion of West's writings, politics, or philosophies, it is apparent that West defies being placed into a simple category. He and his work are far too complex for that.

West was born in Tulsa, Oklahoma. His mother was a schoolteacher and then a principal, and his father worked for the United States Air Force, as a civilian. West has one brother, Clifton. After several moves, the family resided in Sacramento, California, in a middle-class African-American neighborhood. After high school, West graduated with a degree in Near Eastern languages and literature from Harvard University and later earned both his master's and his doctorate (in philosophy) degrees from Princeton University. West then went to Union Theological Seminary.

In 1988, West led Princeton's Afro-American Studies program. In 1994, he went to Harvard University with dual teaching appointments (in the School of Divinity and in the Faculty of Arts and Sciences). West and his Harvard colleague **William Julius Wilson** simultaneously became full professors in 1995, the first African Americans to achieve the highest academic post possible at Harvard. Unlike associate professors, full professors can teach across academic disciplines, meaning that as a theologian, West can teach courses that encompass theological concerns within the law or history department, for example. This seems to be the perfect position for someone like West, who has a vision of the various academic disciplines akin to a spider's web, intricately linked and interdependent.

For West, scholarship is not done only in the ivory towers of colleges and universities. He believes that intellectuals must come down from those towers and help meet the needs of the society in which they live; their knowledge must be applicable on the streets. West adheres to what he calls a "prophetic pragmatism." *Pragmatism* emphasizes the idea that "knowledge [is] derived from experience and experimentation"; it desires to "solve practical problems," and thus the philosophy's "truth is tested by its utility and consequences."

Additionally, West believes that there is a *prophetic* component to his philosophy. He sees a connection between prophecy and pragmatism. While West does not seem to believe that he is speaking directly and literally for God, he does believe in the Christian idea of speaking the "truth in love," although he also says that prophetic insight is available "through a number of different traditions." For West, prophetic pragmatism means telling the truth about the human condition, the human struggle, and the chances for improvement. For West, practical problems in society are economic disparity, racism, cross-cultural relations, families and children, and homophobia.

West's lectures, speeches, interviews, essays, and books hold true to these beliefs. *Prophesy Deliverance!: An Afro-American Revolutionary Christianity* (1982/2002), West's first book, mixes several of his beliefs and ideas. These include Christian theology, the African-American experience, philosophy, and political ideologies. West's paternal grandfather was a Baptist preacher in Tulsa for 40 years and apparently influenced West profoundly, as West dedicated this book to his grandfather. West notes in that dedication that his grandfather is one "who through it all kept the faith." That, too, seems to be what West is trying to do. Ultimately, West sees Christianity as a liberating force for people to "have the opportunity to fulfill [their] potentialities," and West is not talking about eternal life; he is talking about the here and now. To many, this is a radical view of Christianity; to West, it is absolutely accurate and essential for the transformation of society, a transformation for which West hopes.

In the preface of *Prophesy Deliverance!* West describes himself and states his intellectual presuppositions. West says that he is "committed to the prophetic Christian gospel," has an "affinity to a philosophical version of American pragmatism," and has an "abiding allegiance to progressive Marxist social analysis and political praxis." Additionally, West notes that he does not understand philosophy to be merely an intellectual exercise full of empty jargon and rhetoric, but a discipline that affects and is affected by its cultural context, a context that is full of various problems and choices. West's other works follow this same pattern, mixing various intellectual ideas with various practical, real-life problems.

His body of work includes the following titles: *Theology in the Americas: Detroit II Conference Papers* (1982, edited with Caridad Guidote and Margaret Coakley), *Post-Analytic Philosophy* (1985, edited with John Rajchman), *Prophetic Fragments: Illuminations of the Crisis in American Religion and Culture* (1988; 1993, with Richard Abanes), *The American Evasion of Philosophy: A Genealogy of Pragmatism* (1989), *Out There: Marginalization and Contemporary Cultures* (1990, edited with Russell Ferguson, Martha Gever, and Trinh T. Minh-ha), *The Ethical Dimensions of Marxist Thought* (1991), *Breaking Bread: Insurgent Black Intellectual Life* (1991, with **bell hooks**), *Beyond Eurocentrism and Multiculturalism: Volume 1. Prophetic Thought in Postmodern Times* (1993) and *Volume 2. Prophetic Reflections: Notes on Race and Power in America* (1993), *Race Matters* (1993; 2001, with new preface), *Keeping Faith: Philosophy and Race in America* (1993/2008), *Jews and Blacks: Let the Healing Begin* (1995, with Michael Lerner), *The Future of the Race* (1996, with **Henry Louis Gates, Jr.**), and *The War Against Parents: What We Can Do for America's Beleaguered Moms and Dads* (1998), coauthor.

His best-selling *Race Matters* earned West the most celebrity, leading him to accept numerous speaking engagements across the United States. *Race Matters* also is the most accessible of his books to the general public, leading some to call him a "public intellectual." West says that current race problems within the United States are "an everyday matter of life and death." He further says that the current political atmosphere does not work, that neither liberals nor conservatives can effectively address or solve the problems of race. West also has strong beliefs on other current social issues, but none are a simple affirmation or condemnation of one perspective over another. West calls for individual responsibility and a political system structured for fairness and opportunity.

In *The War Against Parents*, West and coauthor Sylvia Ann Hewlett call for both political and cultural changes, saying that parents are drowning in economic, social, and family demands, but that children must have this nurturing from their parents because the values taught serve as "the glue that holds society together." In a 1993 interview with *Black Collegian,* West seems to agree that both the Christian Bible and the Islamic Qur'an say that homosexuality is unacceptable behavior, yet West calls for a "different kind of dialogue" where a "fundamental concern is to keep track of the humanity of folk."

Concerning relationships among Jews, non-Jewish whites, and non-Jewish blacks, West says that Jews do not fully understand the African-American identification with the plight of Palestinians living in Israel, nor do African Americans fully understand the importance of the state of Israel for Jews. West further states that African Americans should choose to put neither whites nor Jews "on a pedestal or in the gutter," that "the very ethical character of the black freedom struggle largely depends on the open condemnation by its spokespersons of any racist attitude or action." Like a prophet, West is calling for change; like a pragmatist, West is calling for this change to be exhibited on the street corners in America. West maintains an "audacious hope," saying that it is essential for any transformation to a more humane and equal American society, claiming that "Either we learn a new language of empathy and compassion or the fire this time will consume us all."

REFERENCES: Bolden, Tonya (1993), "Recovering Hope," *Black Enterprise, 23*(12), Online, EBSCO Host. Bowman, Jim (1994), "A Conference on Racism," *Commonweal, 121*(4), Online, EBSCO Host. Cose, Ellis (1993), "A Prophet with Attitude," *Newsweek, 121*(23), Online, EBSCO Host. Donovan, Rickard (1991), "Cornel West's New Pragmatism," *Cross Currents, 41*(1) Online, EBSCO Host. Edwards, Audrey (1995/1996), "Cornel West: In Praise of the Combative Spirit," *Heart & Soul, Dec95/Jan 96* (12), Online, EBSCO Host. Engelhardt, Elizabeth Sanders Delwiche, "West, Cornel," in *COCAAL and OCAAL.* Gooding-Williams, R. (1991), "Evading Narrative Myth, Evading Prophetic Pragmatism: Cornel West's *The American Evasion of Philosophy,*" *Massachusetts Review, 32*(4) Online, EBSCO Host. "Healing the Rift between Blacks and Jews," (1995), *Christian Century, 112*(29), Online, EBSCO Host. Iannone, Carol (1993), "Middle Man," *National Review, 65*(14), Online, EBSCO Host. Kazi, Kuumba Ferrouil (1993), "Cornel West: Talking about Race Matters," *Black Collegian, 24*(1), Online, EBSCO Host. Lewis, Judith A. (1995), "The Impact of Racism on American Family Life," *Family Journal, 3*(2), Online, EBSCO Host. McKim, Donald K. (1996), "Pragmatism," *Westminster Dictionary of Theological Terms,* Louisville, KY: Westminster John Knox Press. Pinsker, Sanford (1994), "What's Love, and Candor, Got to Do with it?" *Virginia Quarterly Review, 70*(1), Online, EBSCO Host. Sanoff, Alvin P. (1993), "A Theology for the Streets," *US News & World Report, 113*(25), Online EBSCO Host. Smith, Sande (Ed.) (1994), "West, Cornel," *Who's Who in African-American History,* New York: Smithmark. Van Leeuwen, Mary Stewart (1998), "Parenting and Politics: Giving New Shape to 'Family Values,'" *Christian Century, 115*(21), Online, EBSCO Host. West, Cornel (1982), *Prophesy Deliverance!: An Afro-American Revolutionary Christianity,* Philadelphia: Westminster Press. "West, Wilson Named 'University Professor' at Harvard" (1998), *Black Issues in Higher Education, 15*(8), Online, EBSCO Host. White, Jack E. (1993), "Philosopher with a Mission," *Time, 141*(23), Online EBSCO Host. —Janet Hoover

Editor's note: West also wrote *Jews and Blacks: A Dialogue on Race, Religion, and Culture in America* (1996, with Michael Lerner), *The Future of American Progressivism : An Initiative for Political and Economic Reform* (1998, with Roberto Mangabeira Unger), *Restoring Hope: Conversations on the Future of Black America* (1998, edited by Kelvin Shawn Sealey), and *The Cornel West Reader* (1999), about which a Publishers Weekly reviewer said, "This collection amply attests that West's reputation as a brilliant, humane voice in American intellectual discourse is richly deserved" (CAO-07).

In the new millennium, West's writings include *The African-American Century: How Black Americans Have Shaped Our Century* (2000, with **Henry Louis Gates, Jr.**), *Cornel West: A Critical Reader* (2001, edited by George Yancy), *Democracy Matters: Winning the Fight Against Imperialism* (2004, also available in audio format), *Commentary on The Matrix, Matrix Reloaded and Matrix Revolutions* (2004, with Ken Wilber), *Heart of American Darkness: The Underside of the City on the Hill* (2005), *Hope on a Tightrope: Words and Wisdom* (2008), and his forthcoming *Brother West: Living and Loving Out Loud, A Memoir* (2009, with David Ritz).

West has also edited or coedited many additional volumes, including *White Screens, Black Images: Hollywood from the Dark Side* (1994, with Colin MacCabe and James Snead), *Encyclopedia of African-American Culture and History* (1996, with Jack Salzman and David Lionel Smith), *Struggles in the Promised Land: Toward a History of Black-Jewish Relations in the United States* (1997, with Jack Salzman), *The Courage to Hope: From Black Suffering to Human Redemption: Essays in Honor of James Melvin Washington* (1999, with Quinton Hosford Dixie), *The Other Malcolm, "Shorty" Jarvis: His Memoir* (2001, writings by Malcolm Jarvis and Paul D. Nichols; edited by West), *Taking Parenting Public: The Case for a New Social Movement* (2002, with Sylvia Ann Hewlett and Nancy Rankin), *African-American Religious Thought: An Anthology* (2003, with Eddie S. Glaude, Jr.), and *Racist Traces and Other Writings: European Pedigrees/African Contagions* (2003, with Kara Keeling, Colin MacCabe, and James A. Snead). Among the many periodicals to which he contributes are *Nation, The New York Times, The New York Times Book Review, The Progressive,* and *Tikkun.*

In addition to having been named the Du Bois fellow at Harvard University, the iconoclastic West has garnered more than 20 honorary degrees, an American Book Award from the Before Columbus Foundation (1993), a Critics Choice Award from the American Educational Studies Association (1993), a listing as *The New York Times* Notable Book of the Year (1992), a Literary Lion Award from New York Public Library (1993), an Outstanding Book Award from the Gustavus Myers Center for the Study of Human Rights in North America, a listing as a *Publishers Weekly* Best Book of the Year (1993), and a James Madison Medal from Princeton University (1996).

West's spoken-word albums include *Race Matters* (1994), an audio version of his same-titled book, *Sketches of My Culture* (2001), and *Never Forget: A Journey of Revelations* (2006/7?). His *Sketches* album triggered a nasty public dispute with Harvard's then-president Larry Summers (now an Obama economic advisor). As a result, West left Harvard to return to Princeton (2002), which gladly welcomed its alma filium (soul son).

In his political outlook, though West identifies with economic and political aspects of Marxist socialism, he disagrees with Marx's opposition to religion. He has said, "I was attracted by the black Baptist theology and the idea of Jesus as a figure who expressed love and caring. . . . The leftist tradition in the modern West has been deeply secular. . . . But we have to recognize other historical traditions, as well. We've got a black tradition [that includes many] deeply religious folks" (*The Progressive,* 1/1997). For West, the multiracial Democratic Socialists of America, which named him its honorary chair, best reflects his political views.

West strongly opposed President Bush's response to the 9/11 attacks on the World Trade Center, particularly the Iraq War, as well as many other policies of the Bush Administration. In 2000, West had endorsed Bill Bradley's Democratic candidacy and then Ralph Nader's Green Party candidacy; in 2004, he endorsed Al Sharpton; and in 2008, he encouraged voters to elect Barack Obama. In addition to supporting many human-rights causes, West supports the People for the Ethical Treatment of Animals. Known for his natty attire and his full-bodied Afro hairstyle, West often responds to contemporary issues on such TV shows as *Real Time with Bill Maher, Tavis Smiley,* and *BookTV.*

In an interview, West aptly described his own outlook: "People ...are still out there, fighting against the darkness and thunder. For me, that's a form of bearing witness, and, of course, intellectuals try to reflect critically on the witness that they bear. There are always hundreds and hundreds, thousands and thousands, millions and millions of folk around the world who are cutting against the grain. That's the kind of movement and motion that we hope, somewhere down the line, will lead to the higher-level organizing and mobilizing necessary to transform these societies that are shot through with so many institutional forms of evil. . . . I have a deep, existential confidence in the rightness of radical democracy. I will try to actualize it to the best of my ability. But there's no rational certainty, there's no historical inevitability to the causes that we promote" (*The Progressive,* 1/1997). In an earlier interview, he suggested, "Subversive joy is the ability to transform tears into laughter, a laughter that allows one to acknowledge just how difficult the journey is, but to also acknowledge one's own sense of humanity and folly and humor in the midst of this very serious struggle. So it's a joy that allows one both a space, a distance from the absurd, but also empowers one to engage back in the struggle when the time is necessary" (West & Moyers, 1991).

REFERENCES: *AANB. B. CAO-07. CLCS-08. D. W. Wiki.* "Cornel West," *The Progressive* 61.1 (Jan. 1997), pp. 26-29. Rpt. in *Contemporary Literary Criticism Select.* Detroit: Gale. From *Literature Resource Center.* Cordor, Cyril, *All Music Guide,* in A. Engelhardt, Elizabeth Sanders Delwiche, in *COCAAL.* Kunnie, J. E., *T-CACT.* Nishikawa, Kinohi, in *GEAAL.* Patti, Nicholas S., and Christine Miner Minderovic, in *BB.* West, Cornel, and Bill Moyers. "Subversive Anger, Subversive Joy-An Interview." *Cross Currents: Religion and Intellectual Life* 41.4 (Winter 1991): pp. 538-546. Rpt. in Jeffrey W. Hunter (Ed.) (2001), *Contemporary Literary Criticism* (Vol. 134). Detroit: Gale Group. From *Literature Resource Center.* //www.bookfinder.com/author/cornel-west/. Amazon.com.

West, Dorothy
6/2/1907–8/16/1998
Novels, short stories, essays, columns; publisher, editor of a literary journal

Dorothy's blue-eyed middle-aged father, Isaac West, had been born into slavery. After gaining his freedom, he built a profitable wholesale fruit business in Boston. When Dorothy's young mother, South Carolinian Rachel West, married Isaac, she began using her husband's wealth to support her large Southern family. Decades later, Dorothy wrote *The Living Is Easy,* about a woman much like her mother.

Dorothy was provided with an excellent education, starting with tutoring at age 2, continuing through her 1923 graduation from the prestigious Girls' Latin High School, and ending with her studies at Boston University and the Columbia University School of Journalism. Clearly precocious, West started writing short stories when she was 7 years old. At age 15, her short story "Promise and Fulfillment" was published in the *Boston Post,* and thereafter she contributed regularly to the *Post,* also winning several literary prizes for her stories. As she once wrote, "I have no ability nor desire to be other than a writer, though the fact is I whistle beautifully."

In 1926, West and her cousin, poet **Helene Johnson,** attended the annual *Opportunity* magazine awards dinner, held in New York City. There, West's "The Typewriter" tied with **Zora Neale Hurston**'s "Spunk" for second place. With that recognition and encouragement, West stayed in New York. That year, West started publishing her stories regularly in various literary journals. Most of these stories featured urban African Americans who felt constrained by their environment, as well as by racism and sexism.

In the early 1930s, West spent a year in the Soviet Union with about 20 other African-American intellectuals and artists. When she returned to New York, she founded *Challenge* magazine, to promote the high-quality works of many **Harlem Renaissance** writers. Unfortunately, the Great Depression—and her own financial difficulties—forced her to stop publishing it. Many critics also charged

Dorothy West, 87, at her home in Oak Bluffs, Martha's Vineyard, MA on January 20, 1995

that *Challenge* published only highly aesthetic, nonpolitical works by established writers, ignoring the works of many talented but unknown or highly political writers.

Although she was considered the youngest—and longest surviving—member of the Harlem Renaissance, most of her stories were published after the renaissance had peaked. In 1937, West scrounged together a little more money and launched *New Challenge,* with **Richard Wright** as associate editor, broadening the range of contributors. The sole issue of *New Challenge* included Wright's "Blueprint for Negro Writing" and the first piece to be published by then-unknown **Ralph Ellison.** Unhappily, editorial disagreements and financial problems sabotaged this journal, too.

To survive the Depression, West worked as a welfare investigator and then worked for the Federal Writers' Project until it ended in the mid-1940s. After that, West moved back to Massachusetts, settling permanently in Martha's Vineyard. There, she wrote *The Living Is Easy* (1948), an autobiographical novel satirizing the snobbery, shallowness, racism, sexism, and elitism of middle-class African-American New Englanders. Favorably reviewed when it was first published, the novel was even more widely acclaimed when reprinted in 1982, and it's now viewed as central in African-American women's literature.

West continued to write short stories until 1960, publishing more than two-dozen stories. In 1995, her stories were collected in *The Richer, the Poorer, Sketches and Reminiscences.* That same year, her second novel, *The Wedding,* was published. Set in Martha's Vineyard, the novel's dominant themes center around social class, financial status, and skin-color variations among African Americans. In 1998, **Oprah Winfrey** produced a TV-film adaptation of West's second novel. In addition, West contributed weekly columns, essays, and other pieces to her local *Vineyard Gazette.*

REFERENCES: *About Books* TV show, 12/7/1997, 8/28/1998. *EBLG. NAAAL. NPR-ME-98. OC20LE. PBW.* Ferguson, Sally Ann H., in *OCWW.* Griffin, Farah Jasmine, in *COCAAL* and *OCAAL.*

FURTHER READING: *AANB. BAWPP. CAO-05. HR&B,* pp. 343-345. *W. Wiki.* Durham, Joyce. "Dorothy West and the Importance of Black 'Little' Magazines of the 1930s: Challenge and New Challenge." *Langston Hughes Review* 16.1 & 2 (Fall-Spring 1999), pp. 19-31. Rpt. in Thomas J. Schoenberg and Lawrence J. Trudeau (Eds.), *Twentieth-Century Literary Criticism* (Vol. 194). Detroit: Gale, 2008. pp. 19-31. From *Literature Resource Center.* Ferguson, Sally Ann H., in *AAW-40-55.* Harris, Jennifer, in *GEAAL.* Rampson, Nancy, and Sara Pendergast, in *BB.* Steinberg, Sybil. "Dorothy West: Her Own Renaissance." *Publishers Weekly.* 242.27 (July 3, 1995) p. 34. From *Literature Resource Center.* Whitney Womack Smith. American Writers: A Collection of Literary Biographies. New York: Charles Scribner's Sons, 2009. From *Scribner Writers Series. See also EAAWW.*

Wheatley (married surname: Peters), Phillis
?/?/1753?–12/5/1784
Poems; enslaved domestic servant

One of the earliest known African-American writers and the first to publish a book of poetry, former slave Phillis Wheatley has nevertheless been both revered and ignored by the African-American community.

Wheatley was "purchased" by John and Susanna Wheatley in 1761 Boston, and, as was the custom, she was promptly given her master's surname. Although Wheatley is believed to have been born in West Africa, nothing is known about her life previous to her coming to the United States. Her birthdate is also unknown, though John Wheatley estimated her age to have been seven or eight in 1761.

Susanna Wheatley is said to have taken pity on the frail black girl and begged her husband to purchase the child. John obliged his wife, and Phillis became Susanna's personal maid, an assignment that gave Phillis only light household responsibilities. This situation proved beneficial for Phillis, whom the Wheatleys recognized as being particularly bright. She was subsequently tutored by the Wheatleys' daughter and perhaps others, and Phillis attained a level of education that most *white* females did

Phillis Wheatley

not enjoy at that time. Wheatley's education was rooted in literary classics, including the Bible and the writings of Alexander Pope and John Milton. Wheatley and her poetry thus compose what was considered to be an odd combination—a black female slave with much education and low social status who wrote critically acclaimed poetry.

This combination of factors was so unusual that when Wheatley's book, *Poems on Various Subjects, Religious and Moral by Phillis Wheatley, Negro Servant to Mr. John Wheatley, of Boston, in New England,* was released in London in 1773, it included statements that testified to the authenticity of Wheatley and her 38 poems. One such statement, written by John Wheatley, retold the author's personal story, and another included the signatures of 18 well-respected Boston men, such as the governor of Massachusetts and soon-to-be-notorious-rebel John Hancock.

Wheatley sailed to England in the spring of 1773 to participate in the publication of her book. While in London, Wheatley toured the city as a free human being, giving readings of her poetry and meeting Benjamin Franklin and other noted personalities. Unfortunately, she had to return to Boston prematurely in the fall of 1773 when Susanna Wheatley became seriously ill. Susanna's death in March 1774 deeply affected Phillis, as she truly cared for her mistress. Around the time of her return to Boston, John Wheatley granted Phillis her freedom, although she stayed with the Wheatley family until John's death in March 1778.

Phillis married John Peters, a free black man, in April 1778. They had three children, two of whom preceded their mother in death. Peters often changed occupations, and the family struggled to survive financially. Eventually, John Peters was sentenced to a Massachusetts debtors' prison, and Phillis worked in a boardinghouse, trying to support herself and her last surviving child. Phillis died, though still a young woman, on December 5, 1784. Her third child died soon after, and they are buried together at an unknown location.

Though *Poems on Various Subjects* gained Wheatley much recognition and respect, it was not her first or last important work. She was previously published in New England area newspapers, and she continued to write for several more years after the publication of her book. Her works include elegies written upon the deaths of either well-known citizens or her own children. She also wrote a letter and poem to George Washington in 1776, which so impressed him that Wheatley gained an audience with him during the Revolutionary War.

Some scholars have criticized Wheatley for placating white society and neglecting to include antislavery messages in her poetry. The first line of her poem, "On Being Brought from Africa to America" can be read to exhibit a certain emotional distance from Africa, which she calls "my Pagan land." The last two lines of the poem, however, call for equality and justice. Here Wheatley writes, "Remember, Christians, Negroes, black as Cain, / May be refined, and join the angelic train." These two lines serve as a reminder to Christians—a religion Phillis knew well, as she had been baptized in 1771—that the Christian God accepts everyone, regardless of race or ethnicity, with the same love and grace.

Wheatley has also been accused of being too imitative of Milton and Pope. While it is true that Wheatley's poetry leans on the styles of Milton, Pope, and the neoclassic period of literature, readers must remember that Wheatley's education included these writings, and it follows that they would influence her work.

In recent years, therefore, Wheatley's work has enjoyed a revival. She is being reread with more consideration given to her high command of both the English language and the art of poetry. Many scholars believe that her vulnerable social status led her to realize that she could not disrupt the status quo with too much vigor, but that she did indeed find a way to send antislavery messages.

As a Christian and an ardent supporter of the Revolutionary War, Wheatley initially decried slavery by promoting principles attested to by Christianity and the framers of the new republic. Her 1773 poem to the Earl of Dartmouth compares the oppression of the colonies by England with the oppression of the slaves by whites. Wheatley writes, "can I then but pray / Others may never feel tyrannic sway?" A letter written to Samson Occom in 1774 shows sarcasm for those who "Cry for Liberty" when their "Words and Actions are so diametrically opposite" where slaves are concerned. In her later years, her protest became even more candid. By 1778, in Wheatley's poem, "On the Death of General Wooster," she writes that Africa's people are a "blameless race," and that whites "disgrace [blacks] / And hold [blacks] in bondage."

Wheatley was indeed a remarkable woman and writer, one who lived in two worlds—the slave and the free. Yet while still a young woman, she managed to work within a political system and produce poetic works that reflect both an unusually high level of education and a growing social conscience.

REFERENCES: *AAWW. BLC-3. NAAAL.* Abarry, Abu (1990), "The African-American Legacy in American Literature," *Journal of Black Studies,* 20, 379-399, *Infotrac: Magazine Index Plus.* Flanzbaum, Hilene (1993), "Unprecedented Liberties: Rereading Phillis Wheatley," *MELUS,* 18, 71-82, *Infotrac: Magazine Index Plus.* Hayden, Lucy K., "The Poetry of Phillis Wheatley," in *MAAL.* Shields, John C., in *COCAAL* and *OCAAL.* —Janet Hoover

FURTHER READING: *AANB. B. BAWPP. BCE. CE. LFCC-07. MWEL. W. W2B. Wiki.* Bolden, Tonya, in //digital.nypl.org/schomburg/ writers_aa19/bio2.html. Griswold, Rufus Wilmot, "Mrs. Phillis Wheatley Peters," *FPA.* Mallory, Devona, in *GEAAL.* O'Neale, Sondra A., "Phillis Wheatley (Peters)," in *ACW.* Perry, Margaret, in *RGAL-3.* "Phillis Wheatley's 'Poems on Various Subjects'." *The Monthly Review* 49 (Dec. 1773), pp. 457-459. Rpt. in James E. Person, Jr. (Ed.) (1986), *Literature Criticism from 1400 to 1800* (Vol. 3). Detroit: Gale Research. From *Literature Resource Center.* Shields, John C., in *COCAAL,* and "Phillis Wheatley (Peters)," in *AAW-1991.* Washington, George. "An Excerpt from a Letter to Phillis Wheatley on February 28, 1776." In Jared Sparks (Ed.) (1858), *The Writings of George Washington.* Little, Brown, and Company. Rpt. in James E. Person, Jr. (Ed.) (1986), *Literature Criticism from 1400 to 1800* (Vol. 3). Detroit: Gale Research. From *Literature Resource Center.* Williams, Kenny J., "Phillis Wheatley (Peters)," in *AAWBHR.* //digital.library. upenn.edu/women/_generate/AFRICAN%20AMERICAN.html. //www.poets.org/poet.php/prmPID/431. //www.wwnorton.com/college/ english/naal7/contents/A/authors/wheatley.asp. *See also EAAWW.*

Whipper, Frances A. (née Rollin)
11/19/1845–10/17/1901
Biography, diaries

Young Frances Rollin certainly went out of her way to repay a favor. In 1865, **Martin R. Delany**, in his work for the Freedmen's Bureau in South Carolina, helped her press—and win—a lawsuit against a South Carolina steamer captain who had refused to let her travel in first class, despite her possession of a first-class ticket. During the course of that case, Rollin and Delany struck up a friendship, and Delany mentioned his interest in having a biography written about himself. Rollin was quite a skilled writer, and the pair soon agreed that he would pay her to write it.

Around the end of 1867, Rollin had finished gathering materials for her endeavor, and she was ready to start writing the book. She trudged off to Boston, bringing along her prodigious notes, as well as Delany's own writings. Unfortunately, Delany ran out of funds for the project before he finished paying Rollin to complete it. At that point, Rollin was committed, and even though her own father was undergoing financial difficulties, too, she managed to continue writing in the time she had left after doing clerical work and sewing to keep herself afloat financially. She also got a little financial help from some distinguished African-American Bostonians.

In 1868, *The Life and Services of Martin R. Delany*, by Frank A. Rollin, was published. "Frank" was Rollin's nickname, and the reason she used it instead of "Francis" has been the source of much speculation. In any event, the book sold modestly well, and when the first print run ran out, the book was reissued again in 1883.

If that book had been Rollin's sole contribution to literature, it would merit her inclusion in this volume. It wasn't all she wrote, however. Perhaps an even greater treasure was her diary. The oldest surviving diary by a southern African-American woman, it reveals her thoughts, her experiences, and her opinions.

Rollin also offers glimmers about noteworthy African Americans of her day, such as **William C. Nell**, Richard Greener (the first African American to graduate from Harvard College), **William Wells Brown**, **Elizabeth Hobbs Keckley**, and **Charlotte Forten**. Rollin also makes comments about various Europeans and European Americans of her day—**Lydia Maria Childs**, Frances A. Kemble, Charles Dickens, Ralph Waldo Emerson, and William Lloyd Garrison, among others.

On July 28, 1868, with her book published, Rollin returned to her home in South Carolina. There, she went to work for William J. Whipper, an attorney who was a partner in what was probably the first all African-American law firm in the country. Soon after she started there, she married William and became Mrs. Whipper. Although their marriage ended in 1881, their union produced five children, three of whom survived to adulthood: Leigh (who became a noted actor of the 1940s and 1950s), Winifred (who became a schoolteacher), and Ionia (who became an obstetrician and founded the Whipper Home for Unwed Mothers).

Another of Frances A. Rollin Whipper's descendants, her great-granddaughter Ione, inherited her ancestor's interest in writing. Carol Ione's 1991/2001 book *Pride of Family: Four Generations of American Women of Color* includes a recollection of her delight in discovering her great-grandmother's diary.

REFERENCES: *BAAW.* —Tonya Bolden

FURTHER READING: Lewis, Carole Ione, in //www.blackpast.org/ ?q=aah/whipper-ionia-rollin-1872-1953. Wartts, Adrienne, in //www.blackpast.org/?q=aah/whipper-leigh-1876-1975. //www.slavery inamerica.org/scripts/ sia/glossary.cgi?term=w&letter=yes.

Whipper, William
2/22/1804–3/9/1876
Spoken word: oratory, essays, epistles, legal documents; editor, journalist, library cofounder, public speaker, Underground Railroad station master

Whipper's mother was an African-American servant in the household of his father, a European-American lumber merchant in Little Britain township, Pennsylvania. At his father's request, the same tutor who educated Williams's half-siblings also educated him. By the time Whipper was in his 20s, in literary circles he had become well known as a lecturer on moral reform, giving addresses at conventions, small meetings, and other gatherings. In 1828, Whipper published his landmark "Address on Non-Resistance to Offensive Aggression," which suggested moral suasion through nonviolence as a route to political change, more than a century ahead of the 1960s civil-rights movement's nonviolent strategies of social protest. (The address was widely read when it appeared in the *Colored American* in 1837.)

Editor's note: An entirely different journal, ***Colored American Magazine***, was published from 1900 to 1909.

By 1830, he had moved to Philadelphia, where he managed a grocery store that promoted temperance and advertised that its goods were made and sold using only free (i.e., not enslaved) labor; he also operated a business for cleaning clothes using a special steam-scouring process. In 1832, he joined **James Forten** and Forten's son-in-law **Robert Purvis** in sponsoring a petition opposing the enforcement of the Fugitive Slave Act in Pennsylvania. In 1833, this upright grocer joined eight other Philadelphians in cofounding the Philadelphia Library of Colored Persons. In 1835, he moved to Columbia, Pennsylvania, where he formed a business partnership that made him one of the richest African Americans of his day. He used his wealth to promote the causes in which he believed, which were chiefly moral reform and abolition.

In addition to contributing numerous essays and letters to abolitionist papers such as the *Liberator*, the *North Star*, and the *National Antislavery Standard*, he edited the *National Reformer*, the journal of the American Moral Reform Society (AMRS), which he had helped found. Some sources say that he was therefore the first African American to edit a national magazine. Whipper also drafted the organizational documents and constitutions for the AMRS (which folded in 1841) and for the National Negro Convention, which he attended through the 1830s,

1840s, and 1850s. In Columbia, Whipper also offered his home as a safe house for the Underground Railroad and spent nearly $1,000 each year, helping runaway slaves. In 1853, Whipper bought property in Canada and considered emigration, but after the Civil War, he returned to live in Philadelphia.

REFERENCES: *1TESK*. Andrews, William L., in *COCAAL* and *OCAAL*. Myers, Aaron, in *EA-99*.

FURTHER READING: *AANB*. *Wiki*. Gardner, Eric, in *GEAAL*.

White, Paulette (née Childress)
12/1/1948–
Short stories, poems

An artist's wife and the mother of five boys (Pierre, Oronde, Kojo, Kala, and Paul), White has had two major works published: her poetry collection *Love Poems to a Black Junkie* (1975) and her narrative poem *The Watermelon Dress: Portrait of a Woman* (1984). In addition, both her poems and her short stories have appeared in several periodicals (e.g., **Callaloo**, *Essence*) and anthologies (e.g., *Black-Eyed Susans/Midnight Birds*, 1990; **Tonya Bolden**'s *Rites of Passage*, 1994). When asked why she writes, White has said, "I write . . . because I want to make sense of my experience of life" (quoted in *CAO-02*).

REFERENCES: *AAL. CAO-02*. **Madgett, Naomi Long**, in *COCAAL* and *OCAAL*. Woodard, Loretta G., in *GEAAL*. Amazon.com.

FURTHER READING: *EAAWW*.

White, Walter F. (Francis)
7/1/1893–3/21/1955
Autobiography, historical fiction, novels, essays, nonfiction; columnist, activist

George White had finished high school and his freshman year of college (at Atlanta University) when his parents died, forcing him to end his formal education. George got a job as a mail carrier and saved up his money to buy a lot. Soon, he built a five-room house on the lot and married Madeline Harrison, a teacher. Eventually, George built an eight-room house on the lot, moved the smaller house to the back of the lot, and earned extra income by renting out the little house.

George's racial heritage was one-fourth black and three-fourths white; Madeline's was one-sixteenth black, one-sixteenth Native American, and seven-eighths white. George and Madeline had seven children: two boys (the eldest—George, Jr.-and Walter—the middle child) and five girls (Alice, Olive, Ruby, Helen, and Madeline). George looked so white that when he was injured and struck unconscious in a car accident in 1931, he was at first taken to the white part of the hospital; only when his brown-skinned son-in-law asked about him did the staff realize that George was black and took him to the black part of the hospital, where he died a little over two weeks later.

George and Madeline's son Walter was a blond-haired, light-skinned, blue-eyed boy, and in his racially mixed neighborhood—or anywhere, he could easily have "passed" as white. He chose not to, however— except when it was advantageous to the civil-rights cause for him to do so. Why was Walter so committed to his African-American heritage and to civil rights? Long before racism took the life of his father, he had another experience with his father that wakened him to the injustice of racial prejudice. In September 1906, Atlanta erupted in race riots. A marauding band of whites threatened to invade and burn down the White home when they noticed guns protruding from the house and changed their plans. Walter decided then and there to do whatever he could to oppose racism and to embrace his own African-American identity.

By the time of this incident, White had also developed a ravenous appetite for literature, having read his family's copies of books by Shakespeare, Dickens, Thackeray, and Trollope, as well as countless books he borrowed from his church's library. Public libraries were not available to young black boys in Atlanta and other places in the South; although White may have been able to check out books, unnoticed as being black, he chose not to do so.

Walter attended high school at Atlanta University, as there were no public high schools for blacks at the time. After graduating from high school, White went on to college at Atlanta University, working as a hotel bellhop. In 1915, the summer before he graduated from college, White started selling life insurance for Harry Pace's insurance company. (Pace later used his profits from his insurance business to establish a music-publishing company.) A city boy, White learned a lot about country living conditions as he roamed the rural South, selling insurance.

In 1916, after White had graduated from Atlanta University, the Atlanta public school board moved to cut out education for black students beyond the sixth grade, so that they'd have more money to pay for superb education for Atlanta's white students. Previously, they had successfully cut out eighth-grade education for blacks for the same reason, so they didn't anticipate any problems with cutting out the seventh grade. For White and his boss, Harry Pace, however, that action was all they needed to motivate them to form an NAACP branch, involving the Atlanta African-American community. With Pace as the chapter president and White as the secretary, the NAACP and the local community forced the school board to back down on its plans, and in 1920, Atlanta established its very first high school for African-American students.

By 1917, the NAACP national field secretary, **James Weldon Johnson**, noticed how fervently and effectively the newfound Atlanta chapter was fighting for civil rights. He was particularly impressed with the chapter secretary, and in 1918, Johnson helped White get a position in New York as assistant secretary for the national organization. White served as the NAACP's assistant secretary until 1929 and then as the executive secretary from 1931 until his death in 1955.

On the last day in January of 1918, White started doing clerical and office duties in the New York office, but within two weeks, he and Johnson had decided that he would best serve in a very different role. On February 12, Johnson and White read about an atrocious lynching in Estill Springs, Tennessee. White proposed that he go to Estill Springs and investigate the lynching, using his European-American appearance to pose as a white journalist uncovering exactly what happened. Johnson agreed, and this turned out to be the first of many times White put his life at risk to investigate lynchings and other manifestations of racial hatred, such as segregation, restrictions on voting, and job and housing discrimination. On numerous occasions, White narrowly escaped being lynched, shot, and otherwise attacked during his investigations.

White sent his reports of 41 lynchings and 8 race riots not only to the NAACP, but also to various periodicals, so that blacks and whites across the country would read about what was going on throughout the nation, particularly in the South. These reports were instrumental in getting the U.S. Congress to pass an antilynching law, as well as laws opposing discrimination, segregation, and voting restrictions. Also, during White's tenure at the NAACP, the organization grew in size and status, becoming the preeminent civil-rights organization in the land. Among White's numerous achievements at the helm of the NAACP, he established the organization's Legal Defense and Education Fund, which made possible the 1954 *Brown v. Board of Education* Supreme Court decision. In 1937, White was awarded the NAACP's **Spingarn** Medal for his work in advancing the civil rights of African Americans.

In addition to his civil-rights work, White was well respected as a writer of much more than reports and articles on his NAACP-related activities. In fact, White wrote a great deal, including six books, two of which were novels. White's articles were printed in numerous major national magazines such as *Saturday Evening Post* and *Reader's Digest*, as well as in anthologies of his era. For instance, when **Alain Locke** was putting together his historic anthology *The New Negro* (1925) (see **Anthologies of African-American Literature, Writers from 1920 to the**

Early 1940s and **Survey Graphic**), Locke invited White to contribute an essay to it. Two noteworthy essays by White are "Negro Literature" (printed in John A. Macy's *American Writers on American Literature*, 1931) and "Why I Remain a Negro" (*The Saturday Review of Literature*, October 11, 1947). White also wrote a regular column for the *Chicago Defender* and a syndicated column for the *New York Herald-Tribune*, and he even worked for a while as a correspondent for the *New York Post* (1943-1945), reporting on the conditions of African-American troops serving in World War II. His 1945 nonfiction book, *A Rising Wind*, was based on his reports for the *Post* during that war. White also wrote a couple of small booklets, labeled as "Little Blue Books," for a well-known series: *The American Negro and His Problems* (1927) and *The Negro's Contribution to American Culture* (1928).

In 1922, in the presence of the famous editor and writer H. L. Mencken, White disparaged a white author who had written a novel about blacks. Mencken challenged White to write something better and more relevant. White had long been praised for his ability to tell a good—though true—story, so White took up Mencken's challenge. In the summer of 1922, White and his family vacationed in the Massachusetts cottage of Mary White Ovington, and after 12 days of intensive work, White had completed his first draft of his first novel. Within four years of Mencken's challenge, White had produced two novels: *The Fire in the Flint* (1924) and *Flight* (1926). Both books address the ways in which well-educated African Americans respond to racial injustice.

In *Fire in the Flint* (1924), Kenneth Harper, an African-American native of a small town in Georgia, has just returned home after having completed his training (in Northern schools) to become a physician. Back home, he works hard to help improve the health and the economic conditions of the blacks in his home town, but in doing so, he butts heads with the local whites. As White reported all too often in his real-life experiences, this conflict led to Harper's lynching death at the hands of the local whites. The novel was printed in hardcover by prestigious major publisher Knopf in 1924 and has since been reprinted (1996, paperback, Brown Thrasher Books). A modest best-seller in America (particularly good for a first novel), the book did well in several European editions.

Flight (1926/1998) centers on Mimi Daquin, a light-skinned Creole woman from New Orleans, who "passes" for white for a while. When Mimi finds herself unexpectedly pregnant—and unmarried—she flees North, first to Philadelphia, and then to Harlem. Eventually, Mimi embraces her African heritage and abandons her attempts to "pass." As you might expect, this novel sparked a lot of controversy in 1926.

In 1926, White was awarded a Guggenheim fellowship for his literary accomplishments. He used his fellowship money to move with his family to southern France for about a year (mid-1927-1928), where he intended to write his third novel. Despite his best intentions, he ended up writing *Rope and Faggot: A Biography of Judge Lynch* (1929; hardcover reprint 1978), a sharp attack of lynching. In it, White analyzed the ways in which politics, economics, sexuality, religion, and social policies and conditions influenced lynching. White also wrote about 45,000 words of an expected 70,000-word novel, telling the story of three generations of his family, but he ran out of steam—and money—before he ever finished it.

After returning to the States and taking on the executive secretary job at the NAACP, White found little time to write any book-length projects. As mentioned previously, however, he did pull together his writings on the experiences of African-American soldiers during World War II and produced the book *A Rising Wind: A Report on the Negro Soldier in the European Theater of War* (1945/1978). Just before he died, he completed another nonfiction work analyzing racial relations in America, *How Far the Promised Land?* (1955), published after his death. White also produced his critically acclaimed autobiography, *A Man Called White: The Autobiography of Walter White* (1948/1995), documenting his own experiences, particularly those related to the NAACP, as an illustration of race relations in America during the first half of the twentieth century.

In addition to his civil-rights work and his own writing, White encouraged the careers of other writers. For one thing, White introduced numerous other African-American writers of the **Harlem Renaissance** to **Carl Van Vechten**, a European American and an ardent patron of African-American literature. Van Vechten valued White's friendship, his writing, and his opinion of other people's writing. White also used other NAACP contacts to help young writers and other artists (e.g., **Countee Cullen, Claude McKay**, and even **Paul Robeson**) in their careers, and he helped start the Negro Fellowship Fund to support young writers directly.

White also enjoyed close relationships with friends (e.g., James Weldon Johnson) and family. On February 15, 1922, White married Leah Gladys Powell, a fellow NAACP staffer. Before they divorced in 1948, the couple had two children: Jane (b.1923) and Walter Carl Darrow (b. 1927). In 1949, he married Poppy Cannon, a white woman, prompting a huge controversy among NAACP board members. He was allowed to stay in his position, but his influence had diminished greatly. His obituary reported that he was survived by his two children and his widow; Cannon wrote a biography of him in 1956, *A Gentle Knight: My Husband, Walter White*. In 2002, **Molefi**

Kete Asante named White to be among the "100 Greatest African Americans."

REFERENCES: *AA:PoP. AANB. BWA. EA-99. EB-BH-CD. EBLG. PGAA. Wiki.* "African Americans Challenge the President," "NAACP's Legal Strategy in the 1930s," and "Walter Francis White (1893-1955)," in *1TESK*. Cady, Edwin H., in *WB-99*. Johns, Robert L., in *BH2C*. Wald, Gayle, in *COCAAL* and *OCAAL*. Zangrando, Robert L., in *G-99*. Amazon.com, 8/1999.

FURTHER READING: *B. BAWPP. CAO-03. CE. W.* Connor, Tim, in *BB*. Daniel, Walter C., in *AAWHR-40*. Goodman, Carol, in *GEAAL*.

Whitfield, James Monroe
4/10/1822–4/23/1871
Poems, essays

Whitfield's poems were published in his collection *America and Other Poems* (1853) and his 400-line epic *Poem* (1867). Many more of his poems, as well as his letters and essays, were published in the *North Star* and other periodicals.

REFERENCES: *AANB. NYPL-AADR.* Sherman, Joan R., in *COCAAL* and *OCAAL*.

FURTHER READING: *BAWPP. LFCC-07. W.* Gardner, Eric, in *GEAAL*. Laryea, Doris Lucas, in *AAWHR-40*. *See also HAAL*.

Whitman, Albery Allson
5/30/1851–6/29/1901
Poems

Among Whitman's five poetry books are his *Leelah Misled* (1873), 118-stanza poem; *Not a Man, and Yet a Man* (1877), 197-page narrative poem; *The Rape of Florida* (1884, reprinted as *Twasinta's Seminoles*, 1885), comprising 251 Spenserian stanzas; *The World's Fair Poem* (1893), comprising two poems; and *An Idyl of the South: An Epic Poem in Two Parts* (1901), another narrative poem, often cited as his finest work.

REFERENCES: *AANB. NYPL-AADR.* Sherman, Joan R., in *COCAAL* and *OCAAL*.

FURTHER READING: *BAWPP. CAO-03. W.* Bostian, Patricia Kennedy, in *GEAAL*. Jackson, Blyden, in *AAWBHR*. *See also HAAL*.

Wideman, John Edgar
6/14/1941–
Plays, novels, short stories, autobiography/memoir; educator

As a novelist, John Edgar Wideman has been compared to William Faulkner. Such praise is not uncommon for this author, a two-time recipient of the PEN/Faulkner award, the only major award in the United States to be judged, administered, and largely funded by writers. He is best known for his writings about his childhood neighborhood Homewood, an African-American community on the eastern side of Pittsburgh. Wideman's characters, like Faulkner's, are often haunted by their pasts, and both authors have an ear for voices. Enthusiastic reviews have established Wideman as a major talent. He is one of America's premier writers of fiction.

John was the oldest of five children of Edgar and Betty French Wideman. They moved to Homewood shortly before Wideman's first birthday, and there he spent the first 10 years of his life. Sybela Owens, his great-great-great grandmother, had escaped slavery with the help of her "owner's" son (who later became her husband), and settled in Homewood. Much of Wideman's extended family still lived there when John was a boy. John's father worked as a paperhanger, a waiter, and a garbage collector. Even though the family was poor, they followed what Wideman called "the traditional middle class pattern," moving to the predominantly white, upper-middle-class neighborhood of Shadyside in 1951.

In Shadyside, Wideman associated with his white friends in the classroom and gym and his black friends outside of school. He was senior class president, valedictorian, and a basketball star. Recruited to the University of Pennsylvania for its basketball team, Wideman's grades earned him a Benjamin Franklin scholarship.

In college, Wideman began to deal with the issues of race that he had compartmentalized in high school. He later described what he has called his collegiate theatrical performance in the autobiographical novel, *Brothers and Keepers* (1984): "Just two choices as far as I could tell: either/or. Rich or poor. White or black. Win or lose . . . . To succeed in the man's world you must become like the man and he sure didn't claim no bunch of nigger relatives in Pittsburgh." Wideman first majored in psychology, but he switched to English after he discovered that he'd be spending time with lab rats, as opposed to the mysteries of the human psyche.

Wideman played basketball well enough to be named to the Philadelphia Basketball Hall of Fame. When his lifelong dream to play in the National Basketball Association waned, however, he concentrated on a different achievement. In 1963, he became the second African American to earn a Rhodes Scholarship (*see* **Alain Locke**). Wideman began to concentrate on his writing. His first novel, *A Glance Away* (1967), was published shortly after he received his degree from Oxford. Wideman had written it while a Kent Fellow at the University of Iowa's Writer's Workshop. The story of a day in the life of a drug addict, *A Glance Away* reflects the harsh realities Wideman saw and experienced during his youth in Homewood. Although he later resided in other locales, including Wyoming, his novels continued to depict black urban experiences. His critically acclaimed "Homewood Trilogy" comprises the short-story collection *Damballah* (1981) and two novels, *Hiding Place* (1981) and *Sent for You Yesterday* (1983), which traces the lives of two Homewood families between the 1920s and the 1970s. Switching back and forth across the eras, Wideman celebrates the power of humanity to transcend adversity and restore bonds between people.

Literary devices that Wideman uses include stream of consciousness, first-person and third-person narrators, flashback, fast-forward, journals, identity exchange, interior monologue, epiphanies, dreams (historical and personal), letters, and puns. Wideman is much more than a storyteller, however. His characters represent aspects of the African-American mind, the elements that have been at the center of the recent African-American experience. His complex psychological approach uses language that ranges from ghetto slang and Ebonics to a style reminiscent of James Joyce, T. S. Eliot, and William Faulkner, often at the flip of a page.

After *A Glance Away*, Wideman chose to support himself through teaching while he continued to write, holding a faculty position at the University of Pennsylvania from 1967 to 1973. He published his second novel, *Hurry Home*, in 1970. Wideman directly faced the crisis of the African-American intellectual in his third novel, the *Lynchers* (1973). In it, Littleman is a crippled genius whose idea it is to lynch a white police officer as a way to save the spirit of the black community, and he is willing to sacrifice a few "insignificant" African-American lives to that "higher" purpose. He comes into conflict with Orin Wilkerson, the schoolteacher who finally destroys the bizarre, inhuman plot. Critic Philip Keith said "The issue is also faced implicitly in the relation between *The Lynchers* and the other major works in the tradition of black novels, particularly Wright's *Native Son*, the novel that led black writers away from the minstrel novels into serious naturalistic fiction that spoke of and to the condition of the black masses."

In 1973, Wideman began teaching at the University of Wyoming at Laramie, where he studied the history and linguistics of African-American writers and searched for a new language to express the people, places, and experiences that he found important. Another event happened while Wideman was in Wyoming that also greatly influenced his work. His younger brother Robby was arrested, tried for murder, and sentenced to life in prison without parole.

Wideman ventured into nonfiction for the first time with *Brothers and Keepers* (1984). In it, he continued to draw inspiration from the same source, Homewood. In *Brothers and Keepers*, Wideman comes to terms with Robby's fate. Robby, younger by 10 years, was influenced by the street, its drugs, and its crime. The book is

Wideman's attempt to understand what happened. The author writes, "Even as I manufactured fiction from the events of my brother's life, from the history of the family that nurtured us both, I knew something different remained to be extricated." The book depicts the inexorably widening chasm that divides middle-class African Americans from underclass ones.

Wideman often uses storytelling to deal with painful realities. *Reuben* (1987) harshly indicts the judicial system through its portrayal of a lawyer to poor African Americans in Homewood. In *Philadelphia Fire* (1990), Wideman brings together two stories, combining fact and fiction. In the first, he describes the events in which Philadelphia police, under the direction of Mayor Wilson Goode, bombed the headquarters of the MOVE organization, which had received city eviction notices. The bombing killed six adults and five children and left 262 people homeless. The other story is the tale of Wideman's youngest son, who, in real life, like Robby, is serving a life sentence for murder. These prose pages convey enormous pain and the author's feelings of confusion as a father.

In 1992, Wideman gathered two previous collections of short stories into *All Stories Are True*, and in 1995, Wideman published *Fatheralong: A Meditation on Fathers and Sons, Race and Society*. Wideman's *The Cattle Killing* (1996) is a passionate and revealing novel about ancestors, family, and subjugation to the shackles of racial ideology. With fiercely poetic prose, the novel spans two centuries and three continents in haunting, powerful, and mythic fashion. In plague-infested eighteenth-century Philadelphia, a young itinerant black preacher searches for a mysterious, endangered African woman. Most blacks living there were free, but the freedom was precarious due to poverty and prejudice. The preacher's struggle to find her and to save them both plummets him into the nightmare of a society violently dividing itself into white over black. White demagogues blame the blacks for the killing fever. They irrationally accuse the blacks of being carriers of the pestilence, who are somehow immune to it. The blacks are nearly wiped out, however, and nonetheless make great efforts to attend to the dying. Wideman utilizes the core image of a cattle killing, the Xhosa people's ritual destruction of their herd in a futile attempt to resist European domination. Out from this metaphor the narrator spirals a search for meaning and love in the America, Europe, and South Africa of yesterday and today. Wideman grapples with the nature of truth. He has spent his career challenging, testing, and pushing the boundaries of writing.

In 1992, he was elected to the American Academy of Arts and Sciences, and in 1993, the MacArthur Foundation awarded Wideman a $350,000 "genius" grant. He also won the American Book Award. Wideman has spoken extensively throughout Europe and the Near East.

He teaches in the English department in the University of Massachusetts at Amherst.

REFERENCES: *NAAAL*. Houghton Mifflin Company Web Page (1996), Fiction and Poetry Aisle: *The Cattle Killing*, by John Edgar Wideman. //www.hminet.com/hmco/trade/fictionpoetry/catalog/Title0-395-78590-1.html. Keith, Philip (1974, Winter), Philadelphia Story, *Shenandoah: The Washington and Lee University Review*, pp. 99-102. Nasso, Christine (Ed.) (1980), *Contemporary Authors*, Detroit: Gale Research. Strahinich, John (1995), "Oh Brother," *Globe Magazine*, 12(3). Wideman, John Edgar. 1996. *The Cattle Killing*. Boston: Houghton Mifflin. —Michael Strickland

Editor's note: In addition to the aforementioned works, Wideman wrote *Two Cities: A Novel* (1998; 1999 subtitle, *A Love Story*), which interweaves the stories of a widow, a mysterious man who seeks to draw her out of her bereavement, and her tenant who recalls five decades of African-American history in Philadelphia and Pittsburgh. In *Hoop Roots—Basketball, Race, and Love* (2001), another of his thematic memoirs, Wideman rediscovers basketball as a means of recovering from the breakup of his three-decade marriage to attorney Judith Ann Goldman (1965-2000), with whom he has three children: Daniel, Jacob, and Jamila. Jamila plays professional basketball in the Women's National Basketball Association and the Israeli League. Wideman has since married journalist Catherine Nedonchelle (2004), with whom he has a third son, Romeo Alexander.

An entirely different tone emerges in Wideman's lyrical travel memoir about *The Island Martinique* (2003) for the National Geographic Society. Perhaps Wideman's most difficult-to-categorize work is *Fanon* (2008, also in Kindle & audio download format), which includes a nonfiction narrative about African-French Martinique-born psychiatrist, philosopher, and revolutionary Frantz Fanon; a horror fantasy about a novelist who is writing a screenplay about Fanon; and a narrative written by the novelist's twin brother, a character named John Edgar Wideman, whose life experiences are remarkably similar to those of the author. Wideman has also written two more short-story collections: *Fever: Twelve Stories* (1989) and *God's Gym: Stories* (2006). His edited works include *The Best American Short Stories* (1996), *My Soul Has Grown Deep: Classics of Early African-American Literature* (2001), and *20: Best of the Drue Heinz Literature Prize* (2001). At least two of Wideman's books have been translated: *Brothers and Keepers: A Memoir* (1984/2005) into Spanish (*Hermanos y guardianes*, 1986) and *The Cattle Killing* (1996) into French (*Le Massacre du Bétail*, 1998). He also participated in making an audio titled *John Edgar Wideman, Interview* (1987) and a video titled *John Edgar Wideman* (1993). In addition to his other awards, Wideman was nominated for a National Book Award for *Fatheralong* and a National Book Critics Circle Award for *Brothers and Keepers*, and he has received numerous other awards and honors. He was also the first African-American author to receive two Pen/Faulkner Awards (1984 for *Brothers and Keepers*, 1991 for *Philadelphia Fire*).

REFERENCES: *AANB. AAW:PV. BAWPP. BCE. CAO-05. CLCS-08. GOE. LFCC-07. MWEL. QB. W. Wiki.* Allen, Jeffery Renard. "Talking and Walking the Line: An Interview with John Edgar Wideman." *Black Renaissance/Renaissance Noire.* 6.2 (Spring 2005) p. 92. From *Literature Resource Center. Book* (Sept. 2001), p. 12. From *Literature Resource Center.* Bunyan, Scott, in *GEAAL.* Byerman, Keith E., in *ANSWWII- 3rd.* Coleman, Jame W., *AAW.* Ferreira, Patricia, in *AW:ACLB-02.* Johnson, Anne Janette, in *BB.* Samuels, Wilfred D., in *AAFW-55-84,* and in *COCAAL.* Wideman, John Edgar, and Jessica L. Lustig. "Home: An Interview with John Edgar Wideman." *African American Review* 26.3 (Fall 1992), pp. 453-457. Rpt. in Jeffrey W. Hunter (Ed.) (2000), *Contemporary Literary Criticism* (Vol. 122, pp. 453-457). Detroit: Gale Group. From *Literature Resource Center.* //en.wikipedia.org/wiki/Frantz_Fanon. Amazon.com.

Wilkins, Roger Wood
3/25/1932–
Biography/history, autobiography/memoir, anthology; journalist, scholar, educator

Roy (Ottaway) Wilkins, uncle
8/30/1901–9/8/1981
Autobiography/memoir, spoken word—speeches; journalist, journal editor, organization leader, activist

The son of Earl Williams Wilkins, business manager of the African-American weekly *Kansas City Call,* and Helen Natalie Wilkins, a national board member of the Young Women's Christian Association, Roger Wood Wilkins will probably always be best known for one thing: He was one of the journalists to expose the Watergate scandal that brought down the presidency of Richard Nixon. After earning his A.B. (1953) and then his LL.B. (1956) from the University of Michigan, Wilkins started out as a welfare worker in Cleveland, Ohio (1957) until he was admitted to the Bar of the State of New York (1958). He then worked as an attorney in private practice (1958-1962), a special assistant administrator for the Agency for International Development (1962-1964), a director of community relations for the U.S. Department of Commerce (1964-1966), and an assistant attorney general for the U.S. Department of Justice (1966-1969), all in Washington, D.C. He then left to work for the Ford Foundation in New York City (1969-1972).

In 1972, Wilkins returned to Washington, D.C., to join the editorial page staff of the *Washington Post* (1972-1974). He arrived just before the *Post* started probing the notorious Watergate scandal, and Wilkins was one of four *Post* journalists awarded the 1973 Pulitzer Prize for Public Service Journalism, "for its investigation of the Watergate case." In 1974, Wilkins returned to New York City to join the editorial board of *The New York*

Times (1974-1977) and then to become an urban affairs columnist for the *Times* (1977-1979). He was also named to the Pulitzer Prize board (1979-, chair, 1987-1988) and to the PEN/Faulkner Foundation board. He left the *Times* to work both as an associate editor for the now-extinct *Washington Star* (1980-1981) and a radio news commentator for CBS-Radio, for its New York City "Spectrum" program (1980-1983). He also often appears on television (e.g., PBS's *Newshour,* ABC's *Nightline*). Meanwhile, he continued to offer dozens of print columns and commentaries on segregation, race relations, affirmative action, feminism, nuclear weapons, presidential administrations, and myriad other topics for a variety of magazines (e.g., *Esquire, New Yorker*) and newspapers (e.g., *Los Angeles Times*).

In 1982, Wilkins wrote *A Man's Life: An Autobiography* (1982), and he became a senior fellow of the Washington, D.C., think tank the Institute for Policy Studies (1982-). In 1985, Wilkins turned his attention to directly educating young minds, becoming a Regents Lecturer for the University of California (1985) and an Otis Lecturer for Wheaton College (1985), then a Commonwealth Professor of George Mason University in Fairfax, Virginia (1985-1986). The following year, he became a professor of history and American culture there (1987-) and is currently the Clarence J. Robinson Professor of History and American Culture.

In the late 1980s, Wilkins was honored with the Roger Baldwin Civil Liberties Award (1987), and he developed, wrote, and narrated two PBS *Frontline* programs: *Keeping the Faith* (1987) and *Throwaway People* (1989). He also edited *Quiet Riots: Race and Poverty in the United States* (1988, with Fred R. Harris). More than a decade later, he authored *Jefferson's Pillow: The Founding Fathers and the Dilemma of Black Patriotism* (2001). The journal of the National Association for the Advancement of Colored People (NAACP), *Crisis,* names Wilkins as the chair of the *Crisis* board of directors and the journal's "Publisher." He is said to be working on "a book assessing the strengths and weaknesses of Great Society programs, based primarily on the experiences and insights of poor, black, inner-city residents who were the objects of those programs" (quoted in *CAO-03*).

In addition to his other honors, Wilkins has been awarded several honorary doctorates, is a member of numerous organizations, and serves or has served on numerous boards, including the NAACP Legal Defense Fund and WETA television. He has been a member of board of trustees of the African-American Institute and the Fund for Investigative Journalism, and he has served on the editorial board of *The Nation* (since 1979).

Roger's uncle, Roy Wilkins, earned his A.B. (1923) from the University of Minnesota. While there, he was the secretary of the local chapter of the National Association for the Advancement of Colored People (NAACP),; he won an oratorical contest for his powerful speech denouncing lynching; he was the first African-American reporter for the university's student newspaper; and he edited the *St. Paul Appeal*, an African-American-owned and -operated weekly newspaper. After college, Roy Wilkins moved to Kansas City, Missouri, where he started out as a reporter for the boldly antiracist African-American weekly newspaper the *Kansas City Call*. In its pages, he denounced segregation and urged African Americans to register to vote. Roy was soon the *Call*'s managing editor (1923-1931), and Roger's father Earl was the *Call*'s business manager. Meanwhile, Roy settled down to married life with social worker Aminda Badeau (1929).

Wilkins's militant editorials attracted the attention of **Walter White**, the NAACP executive secretary, who persuaded Wilkins to join him in the NAACP's New York City office as assistant executive secretary (1931-1949). In that role, Wilkins continued to do investigative reporting, including his first report to the NAACP, "Mississippi Slave Labor," which was used to prompt the U.S. Congress to legislate better wages and working conditions for workers on federal levee projects. During the following decades, Wilkins was involved in providing financial and other support for the NAACP's Legal Defense Fund and its attorneys. This legal strategy was designed to use the U.S. courts as means of overturning bogus "separate-but-equal" access to facilities and institutions, achieving desegregation, and ensuring equal opportunity for all Americans, especially the right to vote. These efforts continued making progress throughout the 1930s and 1940s. Occasionally, Wilkins backed up the legal strategy with a strategy of leading peaceful public demonstrations to call national attention to the plight of African Americans, especially in the South, where lynchings were still commonplace. These actions also included civil disobedience, sometimes leading to the arrest of participants, including Wilkins on a few occasions.

In 1934, the editor of NAACP's *Crisis* magazine, **W. E. B. Du Bois**, resigned, and Roy Wilkins took over the job, editing the *Crisis* for a decade and a half (1934-1949). As editor, Wilkins had yet another means of crusading against all forms of segregation. His editorials particularly championed voting rights. During Wilkins's editorship, the *Crisis's* readership increased, and its formerly increasing debts were eliminated.

In 1949, Wilkins resigned as editor and became the NAACP's acting executive secretary (1949-1950), while Walter White took a leave of absence. During that time, Wilkins collaborated with **A. Philip Randolph** and Arnold Aronson to found the Leadership Conference on Civil Rights (LCCR). Throughout the 1950s, the LCCR coalition was instrumental in promoting both legislative campaigns and other strategies on behalf of civil rights.

When White returned to leadership in 1950, Wilkins became the NAACP's administrator of internal affairs (1950-1955), continuing his coalition building and his legal strategy, culminating in the victorious *Brown v. Board of Education* (1954) Supreme Court decision. The unanimous decision determined that segregation in public schools violated the equal protections provided in the U.S. Constitution. After the *Brown* decision, the NAACP started winning more of its battles in the Jim Crow South, as it continued to fight against segregation and for equal opportunities for all Americans.

After Walter White died (3/21/1955), Roy Wilkins was unanimously elected the next executive secretary (later renamed executive director) by the NAACP's Board of Directors, and he continued to head the NAACP until 1977. At its height, in the early 1960s, the NAACP could boast having half a million members. In addition to legal strategies, public demonstrations, collaboration with Presidents John F. Kennedy and Lyndon B. Johnson to pass civil-rights legislation, and other strategies, such as supporting black-owned banks over white-owned ones, Wilkins authored a weekly column in New York City's *Amsterdam News* (until 1970). He later wrote a column syndicated by the Register and Tribune Syndicate (1969-1980).

By the early 1970s, Wilkins's approach was no longer popular among civil-rights activists, and many activists disdained his tactics. Wilkins's differences with the up-and-coming more militant advocates for the rights of African Americans eventually led to his reluctant resignation in 1977, and Benjamin Hooks was named his successor. After his retirement, Roy Wilkins's wife, Aminda Wilkins, and her collaborator, Helen Solomon, compiled *Talking It Over with Roy Wilkins: Selected Speeches and Writings* (1977), and Roy collaborated with Tom Matthews to write his *Standing Fast: The Autobiography of Roy Wilkins* (1982). Decades earlier, he had contributed to **Rayford W. Logan**'s *What the Negro Wants* (1944), and he published the collection *The Roy Wilkins Column: Selections from Mr. Wilkins' Nationally Syndicated Columns Published During 1972 and 1973* (1973). Individual congressional testimony, interviews, speeches, and addresses by Wilkins have also been published separately or in anthologies.

Wilkins received the Congressional Gold Medal (5/17/1984), the University of Minnesota's Outstanding Achievement Award (1960), the NAACP's Spingarn Medal (1964), Freedom House's Freedom Award (1967), the Theodore Roosevelt Distinguished Service Medal (1968), the Zale Award (1973), and the Joseph Prize for Human Rights. He was made an honorary fellow of Hebrew University (1972), and he received dozens of honorary degrees from colleges and universities. Perhaps most impressive of all, the University of Minnesota's

Humphrey Institute of Public Affairs established the Roy Wilkins Centre for Human Relations and Human Justice (1992).

REFERENCES: "Roger Wood Wilkins," CAO-03. Wiki. Fikes, Robert, Jr., in AANB. Taylor, B. Kimberly, in BB. //en.wikipedia.org/wiki/ Watergate_scandal. //www.ips-dc.org/about/history. //www.pulitzer.org/ awards/1973. //www.thecrisismagazine.com/boardofdirs.htm. //www.thecrisismagazine.com/bodbios.htm#wilkins. Amazon.com.

FURTHER READING: Wilson, Ian W., in GEAAL.

REFERENCES: "Roy Wilkins," B. BCE. CAO-02. CE. LE. Wiki. Kram, Mark, in BB. Thurber, Timothy N., in AANB. //en.wikipedia. org/wiki/Category:Presidential_Medal_of_Freedom_recipients. //en.wikipedia.org/wiki/Civil_Rights_Act_of_1960. //en.wikipedia.org/ wiki/Civil_Rights_Act_of_1964. //en.wikipedia.org/wiki/Civil_ Rights_Act_of_1965. //en.wikipedia.org/wiki/List_of_Congressional_ Gold_Medal_recipients. //en.wikipedia.org/wiki/List_of_Presidential_ Medal_of_Freedom_recipients. //en.wikipedia.org/wiki/March_ Against_Fear. //en.wikipedia.org/wiki/Presidential_Medal_of_ Freedom. //en.wikipedia.org/wiki/Voting_rights_act. //www.jfklibrary. org/Historical+Resources/Archives/Reference+Desk/Presidential+M edal+of+Freedom.htm. //www.mnhs.org/library/tips/history_topics/ 129wilkins.htm. //www.thecrisismagazine.com/bodbios.htm#wilkins. Amazon.com.

FURTHER READING: Ostrom, Hans, in GEAAL.

Wilkinson, Brenda (Scott)
1/1/1946–
Poems, short stories, nonfiction, juvenile novels, biographies; homemaker

As a child, Brenda Wilkinson grew up with many younger siblings, and as an adult, she raised her own children, Kim and Lori. She knows how to appeal to middle-school and juvenile readers in her historical novels (e.g., her Ludell trilogy), in her contemporary novel about resisting peer pressure (*Definitely Cool*, 1993), and in her nonfiction (e.g., *Jesse Jackson: Still Fighting for the Dream*, 1990). Her Ludell trilogy includes *Ludell* (1975), nominated for the National Book Award; *Ludell and Willie* (1976), named the best book of the year for children by *The New York Times* and for young adults by the American Library Association (both in 1977); and *Ludell's New York Time* (1980). Ludell is a high-spirited teenage girl, showing all the conflicting emotions and behavior characteristic of her age and stage in life (childish/mature, insensitive/thoughtful, etc.). In *Not Separate, Not Equal* (1987), African-American teens cope with 1960s integration, as well as all the other difficulties of adolescence. For some readers, Wilkinson's use of irregular spellings to convey the distinctive dialect sounds of her speakers may be troublesome; for other readers, these spellings enhance their enjoyment of her stories. For nearly all readers, however, her characters are irresistible.

Wilkinson has also written some nonfiction books for juveniles, such as *Civil Rights Movement: An Illustrated*

History (1996) and her biography of Jesse Jackson. She has written three biographies for the "Black Stars" series edited by **Jim Haskins**, including *African American Women Writers* (1999), *Black Stars of Colonial Times and the Revolutionary War: African Americans Who Lived Their Dreams* (2002, with Jim Haskins and Clinton Cox), and *Black Stars of the Harlem Renaissance* (2002, Jim Haskins, **Eleanora E. Tate**, and Clinton Cox). Amazon.com also lists two out-of-print publications: *Under the Baobab Tree: Children of Africa* (2000), published by the missionary arm of the United Methodist Church, and a pamphlet, *What About Women?: Employer's Guide to Efficiency and Equal Opportunities* (1989). Wilkinson also has written *Angels in Art* (1994) and has contributed both poems and short stories to various periodicals.

REFERENCES: BAWPP. CAO-08. Bennett, Susan G., in WYA-1997-3, pp. 381-390. Harris, Violet J., in COCAAL and OCAAL. Amazon.com.

FURTHER READING: EAAWW.

Williams, Chancellor
12/22/1898–12/7/1992
Novels, nonfiction; educator, scholar

Editor's note: Williams's birthdate is given as 1898 in *CAO-01* and *Wiki*, but as 1902 in *BAWPP* and 1905 in *AAW-40-55* and in //www.bookrags.com/Chancellor_Williams.

As soon as he could afford it, in 1925, Chancellor Williams enrolled in Howard University's school of education and graduated in 1930. After graduating, he obtained a Rosenwald fellowship (1931-1932), then he returned to Howard to study for his M.A. in history (1935). In 1935, Williams became the administrative principal at the Cheltenham School for Boys in Maryland (1935-1937), while starting his postgraduate work as a nonresident student of the University of Chicago and the University of Iowa (1935-1941). In 1939, he left Maryland to teach in the Washington, D.C., public schools (1939-1941). In 1941, Williams left teaching to work in several civil-service posts (1941-1946).

Meanwhile, he wrote his first novel, *The Raven: A Novel of Edgar Allan Poe* (1943/1975), and his first nonfiction book, *And If I Were White* (1946). In 1946, Williams left his government post to become a social sciences instructor at Howard University (1946-1952), while completing work for his Ph.D. in history and sociology from American University (1949). He also wrote his second novel, *Have You Been to the River?* (1952).

In 1953, Williams became a visiting resident scholar at Oxford University and the University of London (1953-1954). In 1956, he traveled to Africa, conducting field research in African history at Ghana's University College. In the following decade, he returned to Africa again and again, gathering information on African achievements and precolonial civilizations. Eventually, he visited more than 25 African nations and studied more than 100 African language groupings (by 1964).

In 1961, Williams returned to Howard as professor of African studies in the history department. He also published three books interpreting his findings from his studies in Africa, *The Rebirth of African Civilization* (1961; rev. ed. 1993), *Problems in African History* (1964), and his magnum opus, *The Destruction of Black Civilization: Great Issues of a Race from 4500 B.C. to 2000 A.D.* (1971; rev., expanded ed., 1987). *Destruction* earned him the Book Award from the short-lived **Black Academy of Letters and Arts** (1971), prompting him to expand and revise it. The second edition received much wider critical attention. For it, Williams became the first person ever to receive the Clarence L. Holte International Biennial Prize from the 21st Century Foundation (1979). In 1979, Williams published his third novel, *The Second Agreement with Hell* (1979). During his long writing career, Williams also contributed to anthologies and to periodicals.

REFERENCES: *BAWPP. CAO-01. Wiki.* Jennings, La Vinia Delois, in *AAW-40-55.* //en.wikipedia.org/wiki/British_museum. //en.wikipedia.org/wiki/Cooperative_movement. //en.wikipedia.org/wiki/John_Ruskin_College. //en.wikipedia.org/wiki/Office_of_Price_Administration. //en.wikipedia.org/wiki/Rhodes_House. //www.bookrags.com/Chancellor_Williams. //www.cwo.com/~lucumi/williams-ref.html. Amazon.com.

Williams, Edward Christopher (aka Bertuccio Dantino)
2/11/1871–12/24/1929

Novel, plays, nonfiction—book, essays and articles, poems, short stories; librarian, library educator, journal editor

Edward Christopher Williams earned a B.A. as valedictorian of the Adelbert College of Western Reserve University (WRU; later Case Western University) (1892). He then enrolled in the New York State Library School, where he became the first African American to graduate from a library school. As the first African American to work as a professionally trained librarian, he worked for his alma mater as an assistant librarian (1892-1894), librarian (1894-1898), and university librarian (1898-1899). He then took a sabbatical to earn a master's degree in librarianship at the New York State Library School and returned to his librarian post at WRU (1900-1909).

During that time, Williams published *A Sketch of the History and Present Condition of the Library of Adelbert College* (1901). He also married **Charles Waddell**

Chesnutt's daughter Ethel (in 1902), with whom he had one child, Charles Edward Williams. Williams had been teaching courses in bibliography when he joined the faculty of WRU's newly established Library School (1904). There, he taught bibliography and reference, while continuing as a librarian (until 1909). He also cofounded the Ohio Library Association and was elected to serve as vice-president of New York State's Library School Association (1904). In 1909, Williams left the library and Ohio to become a high school principal in Washington, D.C. (1909-1916).

Next, he switched to Howard University, where he became head librarian (1916-1921), professor of bibliography, and director of library-training classes. In addition, Williams taught courses in foreign languages and literature for a while, as he could speak, read, and write fluently in French, German, Italian, and Spanish. In 1921, he was named head of Howard's Romance languages department (1921-1929). He nonetheless continued in the library, working summers at the New York Public Library (1921-1929). He also continued his involvement in the American Library Association (ALA). In addition, Williams was the associate faculty editor of the *Howard University Record;* he hosted a book club that met at D.C.'s Carnegie library; and he helped found a D.C. literary society that fostered the talents of **Georgia Douglas Johnson** and others.

In 1929, Williams was awarded a Julius Rosenwald fellowship (1929-1930) to pursue a doctorate in librarianship at New York's Columbia University, where he would surely have become the first African American to earn a Ph.D. in library sciences, but his sudden death prevented his completion of his coursework. Meanwhile, Williams had been writing both fiction and nonfiction. He wrote three plays, *The Exile* (1924), *The Chasm* (1926), and *The Sheriff's Children* (n.d.), all of which were produced at Howard and were published in the *Messenger* magazine (1925-1927). Williams also published numerous essays, short stories, and poems that appeared in print, often under the pen name Bertuccio Dantino, or even published anonymously.

Williams's best-known work, however, was his epistolary novel—probably the first epistolary novel authored by an African American. *Letters of Davy Carr, A True Story of Colored Vanity Affair,* first published serially, and anonymously, in the pages of the *Messenger* (1925-1926), immersed readers in the lives of African Americans living in D.C. during the 1920s. It has since been published as *When Washington Was in Vogue: A Love Story* (2004), with Williams's name revealed. For lovers of libraries, however, Williams was not only an outstanding professional librarian but also a champion of making public libraries available to African Americans, of providing adequate funding to both build and maintain library buildings and library staffs, and of ensuring that African-American librarians had opportunities to gain the education and knowledge they needed to become leaders in their field.

REFERENCES: *CAO-05. Wiki.* McKible, Adam, in *AANB.* "The Messenger Magazine," in *Wiki.*

FURTHER READING: McKible, Adam, in *GEAAL.*

Williams, George Washington
10/16/1849–8/2/1891
Nonfiction—history, political commentary; soldier, theologian, cleric, attorney, lecturer

Williams, generally recognized as the first major African-American historian, wrote *History of the Negro Race in America from 1619 to 1880* (1883), considered the first fully encompassing history of African Americans up to that time. Williams started his historical writing with his 80-page *History of the Twelfth Street Baptist Church* (1875), of which he was pastor for a few months. A Union Army Civil War veteran, Williams also wrote the *History of the Negro Troops in the War of Rebellion* (1887). His other works include *1862—Emancipation. The Negro as a Political Problem* (1884), *Memorial Day. The Ethics of War* (1884), *An Open Letter to Leopold* (1890), and *Report upon the Congo State and Country to the President of the Republic of the U.S.* (1886). In addition, he was an ordained minister (1874) and a practicing attorney admitted to the Ohio bar (1881) and to the Massachusetts bar (1883). In his spare time, he founded two newspapers: *The Commoner* (Washington) and *The Southern Review* (Cincinnati). In his role as a historian, he said, "I have striven to record the truth, the whole truth, and nothing but the truth.... My whole aim has been to write a thoroughly trustworthy history, and what I have written, if it have no other merit, is reliable" (quoted in *BAWPP*).

REFERENCES: *AANB. BAWPP. EA-99. NYPL-AADR. USMD. Wiki.* Hall, Stephen Gilroy, in *COCAAL* and *OCAAL.* McDermott, Jim, in *BB.*

FURTHER READING: Feerst, Alex, in *GEAAL.* //www.findagrave.com/cgi-bin/fg.cgi?page=gr&GRid=12551659. *See also* **John Hope Franklin**'s *George Washington Williams* (1985).

Williams, John A. (Alfred)
12/5/1925–
Novels, biography, essays, travel account, poems, play, libretto; educator

A native of Mississippi, Williams grew up in Syracuse, New York. After a stint in the navy during World War II, Williams graduated from high school, went on to Syracuse University (B.A., English and journalism, 1950), and started graduate school. Lack of finances forced Williams to leave school and earn money in various jobs: foundry worker, grocery clerk, social worker, insurance-company employee, television publicity coordinator, and publicity director for a vanity press. Meanwhile, Williams was contributing articles to such periodicals as *Ebony, Newsweek,* and *Jet.* Early in his career, *Holiday* magazine commissioned Williams to write a series of articles about his experiences and the people he met while traveling across the country in 1963, which he later printed in his book *This Is My Country Too* (1965). By the early 1970s, Williams was able to leave menial jobs behind and started teaching at various colleges in the Virgin Islands, New York, and California, and from 1973 to 1977, he was named a distinguished professor of English at the City University of New York; during most of his career, he was the **Paul Robeson** Distinguished Professor of English at Rutgers University at Newark, New Jersey, from which he retired in 1994.

By the late 1950s, Williams had started writing novels, and in 1960, he published his first novel, *The Angry Ones* (reprint 1996), followed by *One for New York* (1960/1975), *Night Song* (1961), and *Sissie* (1963/1993; London *Journey Out Of Anger,* 1965). In all of these works, Williams's African-American protagonists successfully triumph over the racist oppression they confront in this country. *Night Song* was later adapted to film as *Sweet Love, Bitter* (1967), but years earlier, in 1962, the American Academy of Arts and Letters sent Williams a letter, informing him that he would be awarded the *Prix de Rome* for *Night Song.* He was also asked to be interviewed, as a mere formality before being awarded the prize. Apparently, the interview didn't go well, as the academy then withdrew the prize. In Williams's eyes, their actions were an outrageous act of racism. Williams reported this experience in his essay "We Regret to Inform You That" (reprinted in his essay collection *Flashbacks,* 1973), and he then fictionalized this incident in his celebrated novel *The Man Who Cried I Am* (1967). This incident occurred around the time that the civil-rights movement seemed to be losing ground—two great African-American leaders had been assassinated (**Malcolm X** in 1965, **Martin Luther King, Jr.**, in 1968), black-nationalist fervor was peaking, and the **Black Arts Movement** was in full swing.

The next few novels Williams wrote were far more pessimistic about race relations in Williams's native land, including *Sons of Darkness, Sons of Light* (1969); *Novel of Some Probability* (1969); and *Captain Blackman* (1972). By the middle of the 1970s, both the mood of the country and Williams's next few novels seemed milder and more hopeful, including his *Mothersill and the Foxes* (1975); *The Junior Bachelor Society* (1976), which was made into a television miniseries, *Sophisticated Gents* (1981); *Click Song* (1982), which won the Before Columbus Foundation's American Book Award (1983); *The Berhama Ac-*

count (1985); *Jacob's Ladder* (1987); and *Clifford's Blues* (1999).

In addition to his articles and his travel account (*This Is My Country Too*, 1965), Williams has written numerous other nonfiction works, including *Africa: Her History, Lands, and People, Told with Pictures* (1962) and two essay collections (*Flashbacks: A Twenty-Year Diary of Article Writing*, 1973, and *Flashbacks 2: A Diary of Article Writing*, 1991).His biographies include *The Most Native of Sons: A Biography of* **Richard Wright** (1970) and *If I Stop I'll Die: The Comedy and Tragedy of Richard Pryor* (1991, with his son, Dennis A. Williams). In *The King God Didn't Save: Reflections on the Life and Death of Martin Luther King, Jr.* (1970), Williams indicts King's nonviolent methods of social and political change. Williams's numerous anthologies include *Beyond the Angry Black* (1966), and *Amistad 1* (1970) and *Amistad 2* (1971), both edited with Charles F. Harris. With Gilbert H. Muller, he created *Bridges: Literature across Cultures* (1993), *Ways in: Approaches to Reading and Writing about Literature* (1994), and *The McGraw-Hill Introduction to Literature* (1995).

In 1998, Williams published *Safari West*, a collection of his poetry, written from the mid-1950s through 1997; this collection won the Before Columbus Foundation's 1998 American Book Award. Amazon.com lists a 1953 collection titled simply *Poems*. Not one to leave any literary avenue untraveled, Williams wrote at least two plays (1981, 1991), two TV scripts (1965, 1966), and the libretto for the opera *Vanqui* (1999). He has also been published widely in anthologies (e.g., *Censored Books*, 1993; *Brotherman*, 1995; *Norton Anthology of African-American Literature*, 1997) and in periodicals (e.g., *Jet, Los Angeles Times, Nation*). Williams was inducted into the National Literary Hall of Fame (1998) and the Black Literary Hall of Fame (1999), and Rutgers honored him with the John A. Williams Lecture Series (1999). His collected manuscripts are archived in New York (at Syracuse University and at University of Rochester). Williams is married and has three sons (Gregory, a drug-company executive; Dennis, a writer, former *Newsweek* journalist, and college administrator; and Adam, a musician).

REFERENCES: *1TESK. AANB. AAW:PV. BAWPP. CAO-03. EBLG. G-97. NAAAL. OC20LE. W. Wiki.* de Jongh, James L., in *AAFW-55-84.* Dickinson, Gloria H., *RGAL-3.* Ferguson, Brenda R., *CN-6.* Helterman, Jeffrey, *ANSWWII-1st.* Manheim, James M., in *BB.* Mazique, Marc, in *EA-99.* Nash, William R., in *COCAAL* and *OCAAL.* Ostrom, Hans, in *GEAAL.* Pfeiffer, John, in *SJGSFW.* www.amazon.com, 7/1999, 5/2009. His papers are collected at the John A. Williams Archive, founded at the University of Rochester in New York in 1987.

Williams, Myrlie Evers *See* Evers, Myrlie

Williams, Patricia J. (Joyce)
8/28/1951–

Cultural criticism, scholarly, columns, autobiography/ memoir; attorney, educator

Patricia Williams's first four decades were spent being a student, learning the law, practicing the law, and teaching the law. She earned her B.A. from Wellesley College (1972) and then her J.D. from Harvard University Law School (1975). She then became a deputy city attorney (1975-1978), a staff attorney (1978-1980), and an associate professor of law, first at Golden Gate University in San Francisco (1980-1984) and then at the City University of New York in Queens (1984-1988). Next, she held interim posts at Stanford University in California (1988-1989) and at Duke University in North Carolina (1990). After Duke, Williams moved to Madison to become a professor of law at the University of Wisconsin, which honored her with the Romnes Endowment for Excellence in Scholarship. After another interim post at Harvard University (1992), she settled into being a professor of law in New York City at the Columbia Law School (1992-), where she was later named the James L. Dohr Professor of Law. In 1993, the National Women's Political Caucus honored Williams with its Exceptional Merit Media Award.

Just before settling in at Columbia, Williams published her first book, *The Alchemy of Race and Rights: Diary of a Law Professor* (1991), which earned the Bruce K. Gould Book Award (1992). Between 1992 and 1995, she also contributed to another seven books. She then authored a second book, *The Rooster's Egg: On the Persistence of Prejudice* (1995), and a third book, *Seeing a Color-Blind Future: The Paradox of Race* (1998; 1997, England), based on several of her academic lectures.

In 1998, she started writing "Diary of a Mad Law Professor" columns for *The Nation* (1998-). She also continues to contribute pieces to newspapers (e.g., *Washington Post*), journals (e.g., *Harvard Law Review*), and magazines (e.g., *New Yorker*). In June of 2000, the MacArthur Foundation awarded Williams its prestigious five-year fellowship (2000-2005). During her fellowship, Williams wrote *Open House: Of Family, Friends, Food, Piano Lessons and the Search for a Room of My Own* (2004), which includes essays discussing more personal issues, such as her single parenthood of her adopted son, Peter, her interracial friendships, and her experiences as a female attorney.

REFERENCES: *CAO-07. Wiki.* Oleck, Joan, and Sara Pendergast, in *BB.* //www.amazon.com. //www.thenation.com/directory/bios/bio. mhtml?id=408.

FURTHER READING: Nishikawa, Kinohi, in *GEAAL.*

Williams, Jr., Peter
?/1780–10/10/1840
Spoken word—hymns, sermons; newspaper founder

In 1827, Williams helped found *Freedom's Journal*, an ardently abolitionist newspaper. Williams, the first African-American Episcopalian priest, was active in the American Anti-Slavery Society until rumors that he had celebrated an interracial marriage abruptly ended his leadership role, although he continued his church service. Williams also wrote hymns, as well as sermons.

REFERENCES: *AANB. EA-99.*

Williams, Robert Franklin
2/26/1925–10/15/1996
Autobiography, nonfiction—politics

Williams's grandfather had edited the *People's Voice*, a civil-rights-crusading newspaper, and Williams grew up listening to stories of how his grandfather had challenged white supremacy during the virulently racist Reconstruction era. In the 1960s, Williams initially affiliated with the NAACP, but when he decided against nonviolent tactics and organized a militia to fight off Ku Klux Klan terrorism, Williams was ousted from the NAACP. Williams became more certain that armed struggle was the best route to civil rights for African Americans. During this time, because of legal trouble, Williams had exiled himself to Cuba and then to North Vietnam and to China. In Cuba, he published his own newsletter, aptly titled *The Crusader*, which had a circulation of 40,000 readers. Williams also published *Negroes with Guns* (1962), which had a profound effect on the future founders of the Black Panther Party for Self-Defense, as well as many other militant African Americans during the 1960s (and 1970s). In 1969, while in China, he negotiated a deal with the Nixon administration for a return to the United States, where he became involved with the Center for Chinese Studies at the University of Michigan. Just before he died, Williams wrote his own account of his life, *While God Lay Sleeping* (1996).

REFERENCES: *AANB. Wiki.* Tyson, Timothy, in *EA-99.*

Williams, Samm-Art (né Samuel Arthur)
1/20/1946–
Plays, screenplays, documentary scripts; stage, film, and television actor

Williams's plays include *Welcome to Black River* (1975), *The Coming* (1976), *Do Unto Others* (1976), *A Love Play* (1976), *The Last Caravan* (1977, a musical), *The Frost of Renaissance* (1978), *Brass Birds Don't Sing* (1978), *The Sixteenth Round* (1980), *Eve of the Trial* (c. 1980), *Eyes of the American* (1980), *Friends* (1983), *Bojangles* (1985), *Cork* (1986), *Woman from the Town* (1990), *In My Father's House* (1996), and *The Dance on Widows' Row* (2000), as well as his Tony Award-nominated, Drama Desk Award-nominated, and Outer Critics' Circle John Gassner Playwriting Award-winning play *Home* (1979-1981). Williams also wrote scripts and edited stories for the Emmy-winning TV series *Frank's Place* (1987-1988) and for *The Fresh Prince of Bel-Air*, *Martin*, and *The Good News* (1990s). He wrote scripts for *Cagney and Lacey* and other popular TV series in the 1980s, and he wrote teleplays for the Public Broadcasting Service and other producers (e.g., *Charlotte Forten's Mission: Experiment in Freedom*, 1985, PBS; *John Henry*, Showtime; *Badges*, CBS). He also garnered a National Endowment for the Arts playwriting fellowship (1984) and a Guggenheim Foundation grant. Early in his adulthood, when not on stage or screen, Williams was a 6'8" left-handed sparring partner for world heavyweight champion **Muhammad Ali**. He is currently at work on a new play. "My whole life and my work is based on hope. It might be a desperate situation, and seemingly hopeless, but you have got to have tried" (quoted in *CAO-07*).

REFERENCES: *CAO-07. Wiki.* Harris, Trudier, in *AAW-55-85:DPW.* Kalfatovic, Mary, in *BB.* Pattillo, Laura Grace, in *GEAAL.* Walker, Robbie Jean, in *COCAAL* and *OCAAL.* Amazon.com.

Williams, Sherley Anne
8/25/1944–7/7/1999
Literary criticism, poems, novel, essays, children's book, plays, television scripts; educator

Sherley and her three sisters labored alongside their parents in the fields of California. Tuberculosis killed her father when Sherley was eight years old, and eight years later, her mother died, leaving Sherley to the care of her older sister, Ruise. Despite financial difficulties, Sherley earned her B.A. in history (1966) and her M.A. in black studies (1972). Since earning her M.A., Williams taught African-American literature at several universities and spent time in Ghana under a 1984 Fulbright grant, eventually settling at the University of California at San Diego (UCSD).

Williams's first book of literary criticism, *Give Birth to Brightness: A Thematic Study of Neo-Black Literature* (1972), explored heroism in music, poetry, folklore, and drama. For instance, she examined the heroes depicted by several African-American male writers, contrasting the European-American traditions and African-American folk traditions evident in these works. She highlighted historical continuity, showing the connections between the **Black Arts Movement** of the 1960s and the ongoing toasts and boasts originating in the **oral tradition** of African-American males. In other works of literary criticism, Williams has focused on other ways in which aspects of African-American culture interrelate, such as the relation between the blues tradition and contemporary African-American poetry.

Williams's own poetry resonates with the rhythms of the blues, and her poems frequently appear in anthologies and periodicals. Her poems were first collected in her Pulitzer Prize-nominated, National Book Award-nominated *The Peacock Poems* (1975), with poems about her own childhood and the childhood of her son, John Malcolm. Her second collection, *Some One Sweet Angel Child* (1982), traces African-American women's history from the nineteenth century through the twentieth century. She particularly highlights the life experiences of jazzy blues singer Bessie Smith and her own life experiences as a mother and an African-American woman. It, too, was nominated for a National Book Award, and a television performance of the poems won Williams an Emmy.

Williams's novel, *Dessa Rose* (1986), was inspired by historical events. The main event was an 1829 slave uprising in Kentucky, led by a pregnant African-American woman, Dessa Rose. Historically, this event was paralleled by a white North Carolinian woman (Miss Rufel in Williams's narrative) who turned her isolated farm into a sanctuary for runaway slaves. Williams brought together these two women's stories, refuting the stereotypes of antebellum Southern white women and African-American slave women, highlighting instead the strength and determination of each woman.

Through *Dessa Rose*, Williams also provided insight into the **slave narrative** form: Readers can hear Dessa's story from her own viewpoint (as omniscient narrator), through the ears of a white male amanuensis (much as traditional slave narratives were recorded), and through Miss Rufel, who is sympathetic but who cannot truly see the world as Dessa does. Thus, readers gain insight into not only how Dessa views her experiences, but also how others interpret her experiences. *Dessa Rose* was both popularly acclaimed (in its third printing within months after publication) and critically acclaimed (being called "artistically brilliant, emotionally affecting and totally unforgettable" by a *The New York Times* reviewer), a *The New York Times* Notable Book.

What genre did Williams, then a grandmother, try next? A **Coretta Scott King** Honor and Caldecott Honor children's picture book *Working Cotton* (1992, illustrated by Carole Byard) gives her child's-eye-view of picking cotton with her family, starting before dawn and finally stopping long after sunset. Her second picture book, *Girls Together* (1999, illustrated by Synthia Saint James), was published the spring before her death.

Her other writings include two TV scripts, *Ours to Make* (1973) and *The Sherley Williams Special* (1977); and two plays, *Traveling Sunshine Good Time Show and Celebration* (1973) and *Letters from a New England Negro* (1991 and 1992). She was working on a sequel to *Dessa Rose* when she died. A musical adaptation of it (by Lynn Ahrens and Stephen Flaherty) was performed at the Lincoln Center in 2005.

In addition to her specific book honors, she was a guest of honor at UCSD's "Black Women Writers and the High Art of Afro-American Letters" celebration (1998), she was honored by the San Diego mayor with "Sherley Anne Williams Day" (5/15/1998), and she won a Stephen Henderson Award for Outstanding Achievement in Literature and Poetry (1998). Her son and her three grandchildren also continue to honor her memory.

Although Williams's first book focused primarily on African-American males, her subsequent work has primarily illuminated the experiences and perspectives of African-American women. Williams observed, "I wanted specifically to write about lower-income black women.... We were missing these stories of black women's struggles and their real triumphs" (*BWWW*, p. 207). When asked about her responsibilities as a writer, she answered, "basically, to be as good as I can be and to say as much of the truth as I can see at any given time" (quoted in *LFCC-07*).

REFERENCES: *AANB. AAW:PV. BAWPP. BWWW. CAO-05. LFCC-07. MAAL. NAAAL. W. Wiki.* Beaulieu, Elizabeth Ann. "Williams, Sherley Anne (1944-1999)." In Elizabeth Ann Beaulieu (Ed.) (2006), *Writing African American Women: K-Z* (pp. 909ff). Westport, CT: Greenwood Publishing Group. Davis, Amanda, in *GEAAL*. Escamilla, Brian, in *BB*. Howard, Lillie P., in *AAP-55-85*. Mickle, Mildred R., in *COCAAL* and *OCAAL*. Schulz, Elizabeth, in *OCWW.* "Obituary." *The Horn Book Magazine.* 75.5 (Sept. 1999) p. 654. From *Literature Resource Center.* //voices.cla.umn.edu/vg/Bios/entries/williams_sherley_anne.html. //www.newsreel.org/guides/furious.htm.

FURTHER READING: *EAAWW.*

Williams, Jr., Spencer
7/14/1893–12/13/1969
Screenplays; screen actor, director

Williams started out in movies in the mid-1920s, writing the screen adaptations for the stories of Octavsus Roy Cohen for an affiliate of Paramount Pictures. Later on, Williams got into acting and wrote the screenplays for films that he directed and in which he starred, such as *Marching On* (about blacks in the military), *The Blood of Jesus* (1941, an allegory about a man who kills his wife), and *Juke Joint* (1947, a comedy). Nowadays, however, Williams is chiefly known as an actor who played the "Andy Brown" character on the much-derided popular

TV show, *Amos 'N' Andy* (1951-1954; syndicated reruns continued until 1966), which exaggerated African-American stereotypes in a comedy context.

REFERENCES: *EA-99. F. SMKC. Wiki.* Erickson, Hal, *All Movie Guide,* in *Dir.*

Williams, III, Stanley Tookie (aka inmate CDC# C29300)
12/29/1953–12/13/2005
Nonfiction, autobiography/memoir, juvenile nonfiction; criminal, gang leader

Just before abandoning his son and his son's mother, Stanley Tookie Williams II gave his son his name. By 1971, a teenage Stanley Tookie Williams III had been involved in street crime for quite a while when he and Raymond Washington formed an alliance of gangs in South Central Los Angeles. Stanley joined his own West Side gang with Washington's East Side gang to create a new alliance later known as the Crips. A decade after forming the Crips, Williams was convicted and sentenced to death (1981) for four 1979 murders, for which Williams always proclaimed his innocence.

By Williams's own admission, however, he was an unredeemed gangster until 1993, even while imprisoned. Before 1993, he was believed to have been involved in attacks on both guards and fellow inmates, for which he served more than six years in solitary confinement. Even after his release from solitary in 1993, Williams refused to assist police investigations seeking information about his gang's criminal activities. Williams did, however, undertake an extensive course of self-education and begin changing his own behavior. He outspokenly opposed gangs, and he renounced both his own former gang activities and the current activities of his former gang.

Williams created the "Tookie Speaks Out Against Gang Violence" series for children, comprising eight 1996 books cowritten with journalist Barbara Cottman Becnel. For children ages 4-8 years, they wrote *Gangs and Self-Esteem, Gangs and Violence, Gangs and Your Friends,* and *Gangs and Your Neighborhood.* For children ages 9-12 years, they wrote *Gangs and the Abuse of Power, Gangs and Drugs, Gangs and Wanting to Belong,* and *Gangs and Weapons.* In 1997, he even apologized for having founded the Crips, through a posting on his website, "Tookie's Corner." In 1998, Williams and Becnel cowrote *Life in Prison* (1998) for teenagers, offering explicit descriptions and photos of prison life. The book was named one of the American Library Association's "Quick Picks for Reluctant Readers." Williams's other books are *Redemption: From Original Gangster to Nobel Prize Nominee—The Extraordinary Life Story of Stanley Tookie Williams* (2004) and *Blue Rage, Black Redemption: A Memoir* (2005). Amazon.com also lists a posthumous volume, *Redemption: The Last Testament of Stanley "Tookie" Williams* (2006).

In 2000, Mario Fehr, a member of the Swiss Parliament, nominated Williams for the 2001 Nobel Peace Prize, the first such nomination of a death-row inmate; though controversial, other nominations followed. In 2004, *Redemption: The Stan Tookie Williams Story,* a biographical television movie, starred Jamie Foxx in the title role. In October of 2005, Williams lost his final appeal, having exhausted all of his appeal options. Worldwide pleas for clemency were denied by California's governor, former actor Arnold Schwarzenegger.

Williams spoke no last words to the prison warden at the time of his death, but hours before the execution, he had said to WBAI Pacifica radio, "I just stand strong and continue to tell you, your audience, and the world that I am innocent and, yes, I have been a wretched person, but I have redeemed myself" (quoted in //www.democracynow.org/2005/12/13/stanley_tookie_williams_i_want_the). At the time of his death, he was working on his essay collection, tentatively titled, "Thoughts of Thunder: A Manifesto for the Mind."

Williams was the father of two sons. His younger son, Stanley "Little Tookie" Williams, Jr., followed his father into the Crips, into criminal activity, and into prison for being convicted of murder. His older son, Travon Williams, is a married father who owns a home and works for a social-service agency.

REFERENCES: *W2B. Wiki.* Crosthwait, Ginny, in *AANB.* "Profile: Stanley 'Tookie' Williams Renounces Gang Violence and Changes His Life While on Death Row. *Day To Day.* (Apr. 21, 2005, 4:00-5:00 p.m.). *Literature Resource Center.* Saunders, Shellie M., and Jennifer M. York, in *BB.* //nobelprize.org/nobel_prizes/peace/laureates/. //www.democracynow.org/2005/12/13/stanley_tookie_williams_i_want_the. Amazon.com.

Williams-Garcia, Rita (né Rita Williams)
4/13/1957–
Juvenile literature, novels, short stories

At age 14, Rita Williams became a published author, with her own story published in *Highlights for Children* magazine. During Williams's college years at Hofstra University on Long Island, New York, she majored in economics and enjoyed studying dance. In her senior year, she plunged into a creative-writing class, and she started teaching remedial reading to high-school girls. She drew on all of these experiences to write the manuscript for her first book, originally titled "Blue Tights, Big Butt," in which an African-American teen with dancing talent faces both a challenging home life and discouragement from a ballet teacher who considers her full-figured body ill-suited for ballet.

Rita Williams married Peter Garcia, with whom she had two daughters, Michelle and Stephanie, and she continued to send her manuscript to a series of rejecting publishers. At last, she found Lodestar Books, which published *Blue Tights* (1988/1996). Williams-Garcia followed *Blue Tights* with *Fast Talk on a Slow Track* (1991/1998), cited as a Notable Book for Children and Young Adults by the American Library Association (ALA) (1991). Williams-Garcia's *Like Sisters on the Homefront* (1995/1998) earned a *Booklist* Editors' Choice selection (1995), another Best Books for Young Adults citation from the ALA (1996), and a **Coretta Scott King** Honor Book selection from the ALA (1996); it was also named a "Best Book of the Year" by *School Library Journal, The Bulletin of the Center for Children's Books,* and *Publishers Weekly.* The following year, she was awarded the biennial PEN/Norma Klein Award for a New Children's Fiction Writer (1997). Williams-Garcia went on to write more young-adult novels, including *Every Time a Rainbow Dies* (2001) and *No Laughter Here* (2003/2007), both of which were chosen as ALA Best Books for Young Adults, and *Jumped* (2009). She has also written a picture book for young readers, *Catching the Wild Waiyuuzee* (2000, illustrated by Mike Reed).

Amazon.com lists two other books as future releases, *One Crazy Summer* (scheduled for release Jan. 26, 2010) and *Bottle Cap Boys On Royal Street* (scheduled for release Dec. 31, 2025), and Williams-Garcia has also contributed short fiction to numerous anthologies. She is also a member of the Authors Guild and of the Society of Children's Book Writers and Illustrators, and she has been on the faculty of the Vermont College of Fine Arts in the Writing for Children & Young Adults Program.

REFERENCES: *CA/I. CAO-06.* George, Marshall A., in *WYA-2000.* Hinton-Johnson, KaaVonia, in *GEAAL.* Rochman, Hazel. "The *Booklist* Interview: Rita Williams-Garcia." *Booklist. 92.12* (Feb. 15, 1996), p. 1002. Literature Resources from Gale. //en.wikipedia.org/wiki/Highlights_Magazine. //en.wikipedia.org/wiki/Norma_Klein. //www.infoplease.com/ipa/A0154164.html. //www.myshelf.com/haveyouheard/03/garcia.htm. //www.pen.org/page.php?prmID=985. //www.ritawg.com/about-2/. //www.ritawg.com/my-books/. Amazon.com.

Wilson, August (né Frederick August Kittel)
4/27/1945–10/2/2005
Plays, poems

Young Frederick August Kittel grew up in a mixed-race neighborhood in Pittsburgh, Pennsylvania, the setting of many of his plays. Frederick's father (Frederick, Sr.), a baker, was a German immigrant, and his mother (Daisy Wilson Kittel), a cleaning woman, was an African-American native of North Carolina who had literally walked to Pittsburgh in search of better opportunities. Frederick, Sr., was rarely around, so Daisy struggled

to support herself and her six children (Frederick was the fourth) in their two-room apartment behind a grocery store, with the income she could get from her cleaning jobs and from welfare subsidies. Eventually, his parents divorced, and Frederick Sr. disappeared altogether from August's life. Despite these difficult economic circumstances, Frederick learned to read at age 4 and had started reading African-American writers such as **Arna Bontemps, Ralph Ellison, Langston Hughes,** and **Richard Wright** at age 12.

When Frederick was a teenager, his mother remarried. His stepfather, David Bedford, moved the family to a mostly white suburb, where the Bedford family confronted intense racism, including having bricks thrown through the window of their home. At the local school, his classmates refused to sit by him and left him notes saying, "Nigger go home." His teachers weren't helpful, either. When Frederick was 15 years old, a history teacher falsely accused him of plagiarizing a paper on Napoleon, suggesting that such a well-written paper could not have been written by an African-American student. That was the end of Frederick's school career, but it wasn't the end of his education.

In the Carnegie-funded public libraries of Pittsburgh, Frederick read voraciously, undertaking his own rigorous program of study. By his own account, "Basically the years from fifteen to twenty I spent in the library educating myself." Frederick also worked at various odd jobs to help support himself and his family. Over time, however, he felt sure that he would become a writer. Daisy didn't want to see her son pursue such an unstable profession, where the risk of remaining in poverty was great. Instead, she wanted him to become an attorney and forced him to leave the Bedford home if he was unwilling to return to school to make something of himself. Unable to support himself alone on his odd jobs, Frederick quickly enlisted in the U.S. Army in 1963. A year later, however, he was sure that he had to find some other way to support himself and managed to get an early discharge.

Turned loose on the streets of Pittsburgh, Frederick was unsure of how he was going to make his way in the world. On those streets, however, he managed to find a rich source of literary material: He listened to a bunch of retired railroad Pullman porters hanging out in a cigar store called "Pat's Place." These old guys would stand around and tell each other stories, anecdotes, sketches, and advice-laden parables. The cigar-store guys opened Frederick's ears to the sound of everyday black folks, and soon he started hearing their voices in barber shops, in cafés, and on street corners. About this time, he also heard, for the first time, Bessie Smith's "Nobody in Town Can Bake a Sweet Jellyroll Like Mine" and realized the value of his own cultural heritage and of the tremendous contributions African Americans had made to American culture.

By piecing together an assortment of menial jobs (short-order cook, stock boy, mail-room clerk, gardener, dishwasher, porter, etc.), Frederick managed to get by. All the while, he continued to aspire to be a writer, with poetry as his first efforts. He scribbled many of his early poems on paper bags while sitting in restaurants. On April 1, 1965, while living in a Pittsburgh rooming house, Frederick bought his first typewriter. That year, he also started getting involved in theater, helping to form the Second Avenue Poets Theatre Workshop. Soon, he started writing short fiction, as well. As Wilson later recalled, the Second Avenue poets also produced their "own stapled-together magazines with names like *Connection* and *Signal.*"

As the 1960s progressed, Frederick continually perfected his writing skills and embedded himself ever more deeply in the community of African-American writers and theater artists. He helped his friend, playwright and teacher Rob Penny, found the Black Horizons Theatre Company in his old mixed-race neighborhood in Pittsburgh. The company, of which Frederick was the director, produced various plays by and about African Americans.

As he immersed himself ever more deeply into the **Black Arts Movement**, he sought further ways in which to embrace and celebrate his African-American heritage. In 1965, he dropped his father's first name of Frederick and chose instead to be called August. In the late 1960s, he rejected his surname of Kittel, from his German-born father, and adopted his mother's maiden name, Wilson, as his own surname, honoring her and his African-American heritage. In 1969, Wilson married Brenda Burton (a Black Muslim), and the couple had a daughter, Sakina Ansari (b. 1970). The marriage didn't last long, however, and when it dissolved in 1972, Wilson turned ever more attentively to his writing.

In the late 1960s, Frederick also started publishing his poetry. The first poem of his that was published was "For **Malcolm X** and Others" (**Negro Digest**, September 1969). Subsequent poems included "Bessie" (*Black Lines*, summer of 1971, for Bessie Smith), "Morning Song," "Muhammad Ali," and "Theme One: The Variations." Although his poems appeared in such popular journals as **Black World** and in at least one anthology, he found himself turning more toward writing plays. After completing his play *Rite of Passage*, his unpublished play *Recycle* was produced in 1973, by a Pittsburgh community theater. In 1976, he wrote *The Homecoming*, about Blind Lemon Jefferson, a legendary blues singer and guitarist who froze to death in Chicago in 1930. (The play wasn't produced until 1989, however.) In 1977, Wilson wrote *Black Bart and the Sacred Hills*, about a legendary Wild West outlaw (produced in 1981 in St. Paul, Minnesota).

In 1978, Wilson moved to St. Paul, where he took a job writing plays for Claude Purdy and writing scripts for the Science Museum of Minnesota. His scripts included *An Evening with Margaret Mead, How Coyote Got His Special Power,* and *Eskimo Song Duel.* He also founded the Black Horizons Theatre Company and wrote his two-act play *Jitney,* set in 1971 in a Pittsburgh taxicab station, during that time. Wilson has claimed that he wrote *Jitney* in just 10 days, "while sitting in a fish-and-chips restaurant." In 1980, he was awarded a Jerome fellowship and named associate playwright in Minneapolis's Playwrights' Center. He also wrote his play *Fullerton Street,* set in 1949, about blacks who have migrated to the urban North from the rural South. Both *Fullerton Street* and *Jitney* were rejected by the Eugene O'Neill Theatre Center's National Playwrights Conference, and *Fullerton Street* has never been produced, but *Jitney* was produced in regional theaters in Minneapolis (1980) and Pittsburgh (1980). Wilson also wrote a few other unpublished, unproduced plays.

In 1981, Wilson married a second time, wedding Judy Oliver, a social worker of European-American ancestry. Judy encouraged August to quit his museum job, to dedicate more of his time to writing his own plays. With this encouragement, Wilson wrote **Ma Rainey**'s *Black Bottom* (1984), his first commercial success. Sadly, Wilson's mother Daisy had died the previous year, never having seen his writing career pay off financially. *Ma Rainey* is set in 1927 Chicago in a backstage room for a celebrated blues singer who verbally abuses the musicians who accompany her. The musicians talk about their experiences in the United States of the 1920s, including the exploitation of black musicians by white managers, promoters, and record producers. Their rage eventually explodes in a tragically misdirected violent outburst. Despite the gravity of the situation and the pain the speakers clearly feel, the dialogue shows great humor, and Wilson's writing shows great compassion and sensitivity for his characters.

Ma Rainey was accepted for production at the O'Neill Theatre workshop, and this production launched both Wilson's playwriting career and his collaborative relationship with Lloyd Richards, the O'Neill's director. Richards is also the dean of the highly respected Yale Drama School and director of Yale's Repertory Theatre, where Wilson's subsequent plays have been produced before going on to Broadway. *Ma Rainey* went on to be produced on Broadway in 1984 and earned a New York Drama Critics' Circle (NYDCC) Award for best new play, was nominated for several Tony Awards (nickname for the Antoinette Perry Award), and enjoyed commercial success (running for 275 performances). The play was also published as *Ma Rainey's Black Bottom: A Play in Two Acts* (paperback reissue 1988).

With *Ma Rainey*, Wilson clearly had achieved success, and his subsequent plays ensured that his success continued. Wilson announced that he planned a complete cycle of plays, with each play set in a different decade of the twentieth century, telling a distinctive aspect of the African-American experience. In 2005, he completed all the plays in his cycle—for 1900-1910: *Gem of the Ocean* (2003, Chicago; 2004, Broadway; 2008, published); for the 1910s: *Joe Turner's Come and Gone* (1986, Yale; 1988/2008, published; 1990, Broadway); the 1920s: *Ma Rainey's Black Bottom* (1984, Yale, Broadway; 1985/2008, published); the 1930s: *The Piano Lesson* (1987, Yale; 1990, Broadway, Pulitzer Prize for best drama; 1990/2007, published; 1995, television); the 1940s: *Seven Guitars* (1995; 1996/2008, published); the 1950s: *Fences* (1985, Yale; 1987, Broadway; 1986/2008, published; 1987, Pulitzer Prize and Tony for best drama); the 1960s: *Two Trains Running* (1991, Yale; 1992, Broadway; 1993/2008, published); the 1970s: *Jitney* (1982, regional; 2000, Off-Broadway; 2001/2008, published); the 1980s: *King Hedley II* (1999, Pittsburgh; 2001, Broadway; 2005/2008, published); and the 1990s: *Radio Golf* (2005, Yale; 2008, published).

After *Ma Rainey*, Wilson wrote *Fences*, about a father-son conflict set in 1957. The fences include a literal fence, which the father, Troy Maxson, is building around his yard, as well as metaphorical fences, which Troy is unwittingly building between himself and his loved ones, and which his wife, Rose, is trying to build around her family, between them and the surrounding world. Troy, a garbage collector and former Negro League baseball player, had been barred from playing Major League baseball. Based on his personal history, Troy tries to prevent his son from accepting a football scholarship, believing that he is helping his son to avoid the disappointment and heartbreak he experienced. Unlike most of Wilson's plays, *Fences* centers entirely around one main character; his others involve an ensemble of characters (or a pair of characters, as in *The Piano Lesson*).

Fences was produced at the O'Neill in 1983, at Yale Repertory Theatre in 1985, and on Broadway in 1987. The Broadway production earned Wilson the 1987 Pulitzer Prize for drama, the John Gassner Outer Critics' Circle Award for Best American Playwright, and the Drama Desk Award, as well as another NYDCC best-play award and another Tony Award for best play, in addition to Tony Awards for best director, best actor, and best featured actress. Following *Fences*, the *Chicago Tribune* also named Wilson its Artist of the Year. In addition to achieving great critical success, the play grossed a record-breaking $11 million in one year, more than any other nonmusical play at that time. A paperback reissue of the play was published in 1995. In 2002, Wilson said that Paramount was working on a film version of the play, and he described the process of adapting his play to a screenplay as "exciting" (interview with John Tibbetts).

Joe Turner's Come and Gone (written in 1984), Wilson's next play, debuted on Broadway while *Fences* was still enjoying its successful run. Like *Fences*, *Joe Turner* was first produced at the O'Neill Theatre workshop (1984), then at the Yale Rep (1986), and finally on Broadway (1988). *Joe Turner* is set in 1911 in a Pittsburgh boarding house, inhabited by former sharecroppers and other impoverished Southerners who migrated North in hopes of a better life. Wilson's story suggests that the characters must struggle to preserve their African-American roots and cultural identity after having left their Southern homeland. (Wilson's unpublished play *Fullerton Street* also highlights South-to-North migration, but during the later period of the 1940s.) In *Joe Turner*, the protagonist is a former slave and ex-convict whose wife had fled North while he was still enslaved, and he goes North hoping to find her again. The play earned Wilson another NYDCC Award (1988) and another Drama Desk Award, and its production was nominated for multiple Tonys. Wilson was also added to the New York Public Library's list of Literary Lions in 1988. A paperback reissue of *Joe Turner's Come and Gone: A Play in Two Acts* was published in 1992.

In 1986, while *Joe Turner* was working its way to Broadway, Wilson was writing *The Piano Lesson*, set in 1936, in a family living room, where the heirloom piano is the center of sibling conflict. To the brother, Boy Willie, the piano represents hope and possibilities for the future, if he can convince his sister to sell it so that he can buy some land on which his ancestors had been enslaved. To the sister, Berniece, the piano represents family, heritage, roots, and their link to the past. The siblings' grandfather had seen his "owners" sell his wife and son in exchange for the piano, and in his grief at losing them, he had carved their likenesses into the piano. Fantasy and mysticism figure into the resolution of the conflict.

Three years after its initial 1987 production at Yale Rep, the 1990 Broadway production of *The Piano Lesson* earned Wilson a second Pulitzer Prize for drama (1990), as well as an additional Tony Award for best play, another NYDCC best-play award, another Drama Desk Award, and the American Theatre Critics Outstanding Play Award. On February 5, 1995, the play was aired on CBS television for the Hallmark Hall of Fame, having been adapted to television by Wilson. A paperback reprint was published in 1990.

The year that *The Piano Lesson* debuted on Broadway, Wilson was writing his next play, *Two Trains Running*, set in 1969, in a Pittsburgh eatery inhabited by regular customers. The characters, a group of friends, discuss their experiences within the chaotic context of the Vietnam War (and opposition to it) and racial turbulence. Following its production at Yale Rep, *Two Trains*' 1992 Broadway production won another American Theatre Critics' Association Award and another NYDCC Award, and it was nominated for another Tony. A paperback of the play was published in 1993.

In 1995, Wilson wrote *Seven Guitars,* set in Pittsburgh in 1948, purportedly following the death of Floyd "Schoolboy" Barton, a local blues guitarist. Schoolboy's friends, fellow musicians, gather round to celebrate his life and to affirm their own hopes for their future. Its 1995 Broadway production won rave reviews and yet another NYDCC Award for best new play. In 1997, a paperback reprint was published.

Wilson often carries some of his characters from one play to the next. For instance, *Seven Guitars* introduced an odd character, King Hedley, who became the main character in *King Hedley II,* a released ex-convict who must reconcile his past with his present and forge a non-criminal future for himself. The star of *Gem of the Ocean,* Aunt Ester, was an offstage character in *Two Trains Running, King Hedley,* and *Radio Golf.* In *Gem of the Ocean,* Aunt Ester magically transports newly freed Citizen Barlow on a vessel made from slaves' bills of sale, to an island of bones in the middle of the Atlantic Ocean. The bones are from slaves who lost their lives during the Middle Passage and were buried at sea. "This is a journey that [Barlow] personally has to take in order to understand the source of his personal dislocation," Wilson noted (in a 2002 interview with John Tibbetts).

His final play, *Radio Golf,* departs from the first nine plays of his cycle: "One of the things with *Radio Golf* is that I realized I had to in some way deal with the black middle class, which for the most part is not in the other nine plays. My idea was that the black middle class seems to be divorcing themselves from that community, making their fortune on their own without recognizing or acknowledging their connection to the larger community," Wilson told Suzan-Lori Parks in *American Theatre* (quoted in *BB*).

His other plays include *The Coldest Day of the Year* (1989) and *The Mill Hand's Lunch Bucket* (1983), as well as his one-man play *How I Learned What I Learned* (2002-2003), telling his own life story. Wilson even starred in a production of *How I Learned.* In addition, a keynote address he gave to the Theatre Communications Group National Conference, *The Ground on Which I Stand,* was later published in *American Theatre* (1996) and then as a separate publication of the Theatre Communications Group (2000). When working on a play, Wilson's custom was to write longhand while sitting in a restaurant, starting about noon, return home, then type what he had written each night, perhaps into the wee hours of the morning. He said he avoided watching television, movies, and even plays by other authors, for the most part.

In a 2001 interview with Elisabeth J. Heard, he reflected, "I write to create a work of art that exists on its own terms and is true to itself. I don't have any particular audience in mind." When asked how he starts writing a play, he answered, "Well, I generally start with a line of dialogue. Someone says something and they're talking to someone else. I don't all the time know who's talking or who they are talking to, but you take the line of dialogue and it starts from there. The next thing you know you've got four pages of dialogue, and after a while you say, 'Well, let me name this guy; let's give him a name. Who's talking?' And in the process of him talking you find out things about him. So the more the characters talk the more you know about them. It generally starts there. And then I say, 'Okay, so where are they?' and then I'll come up with a setting or something. Once you get the set and one or two characters, then it begins to take on a life of its own. Other characters walk in, and I'm not sure how it happens from there, but it's a process. I don't, for instance, start at the beginning of the play and say, 'What's going to happen,' and go from beginning to end. Very often I don't know what the ending is or what the events of the play are going to be, but I trust that these characters will tell me or that the story will develop naturally out of the dialogue of the characters." Starting with his play *Seven Guitars,* Wilson developed a strategy for rewriting the play *during* rehearsals. He later recalled, "I had the actors there, so you could press and then you could see a response, or you could do something and see an immediate response. If you're at home doing the rewrite, you can't get that response—you're sort of working in a vacuum, so to speak."

In a 2002 interview with John Tibbetts, Wilson, said, "Regardless of the medium, rewriting and more rewriting is still necessary. No one gets anything right the first time, and since I don't write with a hammer and chisel, it's relatively easy for me to change. It's just words on paper. Words are free. You don't go to the store and order a pound of words, or five hundred words, and pay your three dollars. They're free." Wilson's words may be free to the writer, but to the listener, they're priceless.

In addition to his two Pulitzer Prizes (1987, 1990), his Tony Award (1987) and Tony nominations (1985, 1988, 1990, 1992, 2001, 2005), his seven NYDCC Awards (1985, 1987, 1988, 1990, 1992, 1996, 2000), his Drama Desk Awards (1987, 1990), his American Theatre Critics' Association Award (1987, 1990, 1992), his John Gassner Outer Critics' Circle Award for Best American Playwright (1987), Wilson was awarded a National Humanities Medal from U.S. President Clinton (1999), a British Olivier Award (2002), a Black Filmmakers Hall of Fame award (1991), the Clarence Muse Award (1992), a Harold Washington Literary Award (2001), the U.S. Comedy Arts Festival Freedom of Speech Award (2004), and a Make Shift Award at the U.S. Confederation of Play Writers (2005). In addition, his name was added to the New York Public Library's list of Literary Lions (1988), and he was honored with numerous fellowships: Jerome, Bush, McKnight, Rockefeller, and Guggenheim Foundation fellowships in playwriting. Wilson was also elected to the American Academy of Arts and Sciences (1991), and he was 1 of 10 writers to win the generous Whiting Writer's Awards (1986) in recognition of his "exceptionally promising, emerging talent." Wilson also received an honorary degree from Yale University (1988), the home of the repertory theater where most of his plays have been produced. On October 17, 2005, Broadway's Virginia Theater was renamed the August Wilson Theater, in his honor, the first Broadway theater named for an African American. On May 30, 2007, Pennsylvania declared Wilson's childhood home at 1727 Bedford Avenue in Pittsburgh to be a historic landmark. Seattle also named a street in Wilson's honor.

During the late 1980s, Wilson had moved to Seattle, and in 1990, he divorced Judy Oliver. In 1994, he married his third wife, Constanza Romero, who designed the costumes for *Seven Guitars*, among other works, and to whom he sometimes turned for advice when writing his plays. He and Constanza had his second daughter, Azula Carmen (b. 1997), whom he hoped would some day enjoy piano lessons on the piano he kept from the Yale production of *The Piano Lesson* (Tibbetts, 2002).

REFERENCES: *AA:PoP. AANB. AAW:PV. AT. B. BAWPP. BCE. CAO-06. CE. CLCS-08. EA-99. EB-BH-CD. EBLG. G-99. MWEL. NAAAL. OC20LE. W. W2B. WDAA. Wiki.* Adler, Thomas P., in *WB-99.* Carter, Linda M., in *BH2C.* Elkins, Marilyn, in *COCAAL* and *OCAAL.* Fisler, Ben, in *GEAAL.* Heard, Elisabeth J. "August Wilson on Playwriting: An Interview." *African American Review.* 35.1 (Spring 2001) p. 93. From *Literature Resource Center.* Henderson, Ashyia, Ed Decker, Christine Miner Minderovic, and Sara Pendergast, in *BB.* Little, Jonathan, in *T-CAD-2nd.* "The Piano Lesson (1990)," in *1TESK.* Saunders, James Robert. "Essential Ambiguities in the Plays of August Wilson." *Hollins Critic.* 32.5 (Dec. 1995) p. 1. From *Literature Resource Center.* Tibbetts, John C. "August Wilson Interview." *Literature Film Quarterly* 30.4 (2002), pp. 238-242. Rpt. in Jeffrey W. Hunter (Ed.) (2006), Contemporary Literary Criticism (Vol. 222). Detroit: Gale. From *Literature Resource Center.* //www.amazon.com, 8/1999, 5/2009.

Wilson, Harriet E. (née Harriet E. Adams) (aka Hattie E. Wilson)
3/15/1825?–6/28/1900?

Novel; domestic servant, possibly a beautician or a seamstress

Historians and other scholars have been able to find out very little about Harriet before 1850, when she was in her early or mid 20s. *Wikipedia,* //www.harrietwilsonproject.org/about_harriet.htm, and //www.quiltethnic.com/african-american/african-american-authors.html give the preceding birth and death dates, but other sources give other birth and death years, without specific months or days of birth or death. What is known about her is based on her autobiographical novel *Our Nig,* some of the facts of which have been confirmed or refuted by public records. According to the 1850 federal census of the state of New Hampshire, Harriet Adams was born in Milford, New Hampshire, 22 years earlier, the daughter of Charles Adams (a native of New Ipswich, New Hampshire). According to the 1860 federal census of Boston, where she was living at that time, however, she was born in Fredericksburg, Virginia, in 1807 or 1808. Other data about her life make the 1820s New Hampshire birth information seem more probable. Her birth year is given as 1827 by *BWA:AHE; OCAAL; BF:2000; EBLG* and as 1828 by *EA-99, G-99, NAAAL,* and *EB-BH-CD;* her year of death is given as 1863 in *EB-BH-CD* and 1870 in *EA-99* and *G-99.*

When Harriet published *Our Nig,* she included in it letters from three acquaintances who corroborated her account. According to one of these acquaintances, Margaret Thorn, when Harriet was just six years old, she had been hired out to the Hayward family, who made her work hard, "both in the house and in the field." Apparently, it was the female head of household who was the most abusive to Harriet. Thorn observed that the tortuous difficulty of the work ruined Harriet's health, so that by the time she was 18 years old, her poor health prevented her from doing hard labor, and she left the Hayward household. Another of the letters, written by "Allida," noted that Harriet then worked sewing straw in Massachusetts, where she lived in the home of a Mrs. Walker, probably in or near Worcester. Apparently, she was even impaired in performing this work, and Mrs. Walker kept her in a room adjoining her own, so that she could minister to Harriet, as needed. (Another source suggests, however, that Harriet was Mrs. Walker's domestic servant.)

The next documentation about Harriet shows that she was living in the Samuel Boyles household, a white family, still in Milford. The 1850 federal census listed four adults who were not family members living with them, so historians have concluded that the Boyles were running a boarding house, possibly one for which the county subsidized them for providing shelter to aged or disabled adults. The year of the census, the Fugitive Slave Act had been passed, so all African Americans living in the North were endangered, particularly if they lived or worked alone.

While living with the Boyles, Harriet met Thomas Wilson, a beguiling abolitionist lecturer who passed himself off as a Virginia-born fugitive slave reporting the horrors of his slave experiences, but who was actually a freeman. Harriet married Thomas October 6, 1851. (According to one source, however, her marriage license was issued in 1852.) Soon after, the couple left Massachusetts and moved to New Hampshire. Around the time of their marriage, Harriet had become pregnant. Before she gave birth, Thomas abandoned her and went to sea, so she had to move to the "County House," a facility for paupers, in Goffstown, New York. The facility comprised a big farm house, a barn, and several other small buildings, most of which housed paupers, all of whom suffered from malnutrition and many of whom were highly vulnerable to infectious disease. There, in late May or early June of 1852, Harriet gave birth to a son, George Mason Wilson, apparently the only child of the Wilsons.

After George's birth, Thomas returned from the sea and retrieved his wife and child. He moved them to yet another town and supported them fairly well for a while. After a bit, however, he left again, never to return, and Harriet had to place George in the care of kindly white foster parents in New Hampshire while she tried to improve her health and to make enough money to retrieve him. According to one source, Harriet was able to make money by using a sympathetic stranger's recipe for removing (or covering) gray hair in her clients; other sources suggest that she worked as a dressmaker (or even as a milliner, making women's hats); perhaps she did both, either simultaneously or consecutively. In any case, according to the Boston City Directory, by 1855, Harriet had moved to Boston, and she continued living there through 1863. Eventually, Harriet's health worsened again, confining her to bed, so she couldn't do any work outside her home. In this situation, she turned to writing, hoping to make enough to support herself and to retrieve George by writing a novel.

Wilson based her novel, *Our Nig; or, Sketches from the Life of a Free Black, in a Two-Story White House, North. Showing That Slavery's Shadows Fall Even There* (1859), on her own experiences, but she definitely freely fictionalized her account. For the most part, the plot of Wilson's *Our Nig* closely parallels the fluid, well-structured plotting found in the sentimental novels of her white female contemporaries, rather than the structure of the **slave narratives** of her era. Nonetheless, she freely borrowed the dramatic flourishes employed in slave narratives, and she frequently used many of the literary techniques employed in these narratives. Among other things, Wilson borrowed the technique of cataloging various abuses and the themes of self-empowerment through education and literacy, spiritual awakening, independent-mindedness, and even defiance in the face of oppression.

Hence, Wilson created her own unique literary contribution, drawing on the techniques of her white female contemporaries when it suited her tale, and borrowing the techniques of slave narrators when it fit her purpose.

In addition, Wilson was distinctive in speaking of the virulent racism of the North and the near-servitude of many Northern African Americans, due to extreme economic deprivation, rather than the horrors of Southern slavery or the lifestyles of Northern whites. She further broke new ground by realistically examining the life experiences of an ordinary African-American woman. Even without these distinctions, Wilson would play a significant role in the history of African-American literature, as she is widely acclaimed as the first African American to publish a novel in the United States (**William Wells Brown**'s *Clotel* and Frank J. Webb's *The Garies and Their Friends* were both published in England), the first African-American woman to publish a book of any kind in English, the fifth African American to publish a book of fiction in English, and one of the first two African-American women to publish a novel written in any language (*see also* **Frances Ellen Watkins Harper**).

Wilson's protagonist, Alfrado ("Frado"), is born out of wedlock and intentionally abandoned by her white mother, then unintentionally abandoned (through death) by her black father. From that point on, Wilson powerfully shows that "slavery's shadows fall" in the North. Like Wilson herself, Frado is physically beaten, emotionally derogated, starved, overworked, and mistreated by the mother ("Mrs. Bellmont") and one of the daughters ("Mary") of a white family to whom she is an indentured servant from early childhood. The men of the family appear relatively benign, but they do little to protect her from the abuse she receives at the hands of the females. Similarly, Frado, too, marries and becomes pregnant and is soon deserted by her husband. At the end of the novel, Frado and her infant are homeless and desperately impoverished. Her novel's ending sharply deviates from the typical ending of sentimental novels, in which the heroine is happily wedded at the conclusion of the book. Wilson closes her book with a direct appeal to her readers to help her gain enough money to retrieve her son from foster care. (Her preface made a similar appeal to her "colored brethren" to purchase her book to provide her a means of supporting herself and her son.)

Wilson finished writing her novel in 1859, and on August 18, she registered its copyright in the clerk's office of the district court, in the district of Massachusetts. On September 5, she paid to have the book published by an obscure Boston printer, the George C. Rand & Avery Company, known as a "job printer," meaning that they didn't have a regular major customer (such as a newspaper), but instead took on miscellaneous odd jobs, at a set rate per job.

Tragically, Wilson's son died before she could earn enough to retrieve him. Less than six months after her book was published, early in 1860, the *Farmer's Cabinet* of Amherst, New Hampshire, published the obituary of

George Mason Wilson, seven years old, the only son of "H. E. Wilson." The boy's death certificate listed his "color" as "Black" and identified his cause of death as "fever," a common cause of death at that time. No public records document Wilson's presence after 1863, so many scholars presume that she died about that time, but her exact location and date of death are not now known for certain.

For generations, Wilson's work had passed into obscurity. In 1984, however, **Henry Louis Gates, Jr.**, and David Curtis uncovered evidence of her work. Up until that time, any literary scholars who had come across *Our Nig* had believed that the author was white, perhaps even a male. That year, Gates affirmed that Wilson was a black woman (based largely on the evidence of George's death certificate), thereby revealing her to be the first African American to publish a novel in the United States.

Although there is wide acceptance of Gates's contention, not everyone agrees with him. Gates himself notes astonishment that such a ground-breaking work would have been published without one single notice or review of the book in any publications of the day: No report of this historical work can be found in any of the contemporary abolitionist newspapers or magazines, African-American-governed periodicals, Boston daily newspapers, or even the Amherst *Farmer's Cabinet,* which recorded George's death. If any periodical of that time did notice Wilson's remarkable achievement, no scholar has been able to find any such notices or reviews to date, despite extensive searches.

Gates's skeptics find this total lack of any notice or review all too remarkable, given that Wilson's Boston was a hotbed of zealous abolitionist reform, and the news that an African-American woman had published such an outstanding work would have greatly benefited their cause. They find it similarly implausible to think that the growing number of African-American-owned and -operated presses, eager to celebrate any noteworthy African Americans, would have ignored Wilson's work if they believed that she were of African-American descent. Similarly, historians, librarians, and bibliographers also overlooked Wilson's contribution for more than a century. Apparently, the first bibliographer to take notice of Wilson was Howard Mott, who quietly asserted that Wilson's book was the first published novel written by an African-American woman, in his 1980 catalogue of materials for antiquarians. Mott had reached this conclusion based on the three letters of recommendation appended to the novel.

Gates counters this criticism by noting that Wilson's contemporaries may have been reluctant to make much of a novel that attacks the racism of the North, particularly villainizing Northern white women. Perhaps they feared alienating Northern whites who favored abolition, wishing to focus on the horrors of Southern slavery rather than divert their readers' attention to the abuses of Northern economic oppression. Perhaps they wished not to stir up trouble because of Wilson's candid mention of a sexual relationship between a black man and a white woman (Frado's father and mother). Another argument might be made that the male-dominated presses of the day were reluctant to acknowledge the literary achievement of any woman, particularly one who had so little good to say about men of any color. Whatever the reason, Wilson's novel didn't sell well enough to lift her out of poverty or to earn her much—if any—popular or critical attention in her day.

REFERENCES: AANB. B. BCE. BF:2000. EB-BH-CD. EBLG. MWEL. NAAAL. W. Wiki. WN. Blockson, Charles L. 1998. "Damn Rare": The Memoirs of an African-American Bibliophil., Tracy, CA: Quantum Leap Publisher. Fay, Robert, in EA-99. Foreman, P. Gabrielle, in COCAAL and OCAAL. **Gates, Henry Louis, Jr.**, in AAWBHR and in BWA:AHE. Johnson, Claudia Durst, in G-99. "Our Nig (1859)," 1TESK. White, Barbara A., AWPW:1820-1870. Woodard, Helena, in OCWW. //etext.lib.virginia.edu/toc/modeng/public/WilOurn.html, electronic text of Our Nig. //www.csustan.edu/english/reuben/pal/chap3/wilson.html. //www.harrietwilsonproject.org/about_harriet.htm.

FURTHER READING: Dict. EAAWW. Saulsbury, Rebecca R., in GEAAL. Smith, Andrew, ARNE-4.

Wilson, William Julius
12/20/1935–
Nonfiction—sociology; educator

A highly influential sociologist, Wilson has written numerous books highlighting the importance of socioeconomic status. Unfortunately, his critics have often wrongly misinterpreted him as suggesting that racism has ceased to affect African Americans. Rather, Wilson illustrates how race both affects and is affected by economics, so that economic circumstances greatly compound the effects of racism. For instance, Wilson noted one way in which racism has affected economics: The racism-inspired disproportionate incarceration of black males has led to increased numbers of ex-convicts, who have increased difficulty in finding well-paid jobs. On the other hand, economic circumstances such as dramatic increases in poorly paid service-sector jobs generally held by females affects black families disproportionately. Perhaps more important, however, is Wilson's view that by dividing economically impoverished people along racial lines, they are discouraged from seeing their commonalities and uniting to overcome their economic oppression. Further, Wilson has noted, "We, as a nation, and those of us who are black, in particular, have a responsibility to help those left behind" (quoted by Golus, in BB).

The books he has authored include *Power, Racism and Privilege: Race Relations in Theoretical and Sociohistorical Perspective* (1973); *The Declining Significance of Race: Blacks and Changing America Institutions* (1978); *The Truly Disadvantaged: The Inner City, the Underclass, and Public Policy* (1987); *The Bridge over the Racial Divide: Rising Inequality and Coalition Politics* (1999); *When Work Disappears: The World of the New Urban Poor* (1996); *Good Kids from Bad Neighborhoods: Successful Development in Social Context* (2006, with Delbert S. Elliott, Scott Menard, Bruce Rankin, Amanda Elliott, and David Huizinga); *There Goes the Neighborhood: Racial, Ethnic, and Class Tensions in Four Chicago Neighborhoods and Their Meaning for America* (2006, with Richard P. Taub); and *More Than Just Race: Being Black and Poor in the Inner City* (2009). He has also edited *The Ghetto Underclass: Social Science Perspectives* (1989), *Universities and the Military, V502* (1989, Annals of the American Academy of Political and Social Science), *Sociology and the Public Agenda* (1993), *America Becoming: Racial Trends and Their Consequences* (2001; Vol. 1 with Neil Smelser and Faith Mitchell; Vol. 2, with Faith Mitchell, Neil Smelser, National Research Council, and Research Conference on Racial Trends in the United States), *Youth in Cities: A Cross-National Perspective* (2002, with Marta Tienda), and *Poverty, Inequality, and the Future of Social Policy: Western States in the New World Order* (2005, edited with Katherine McFate and Roger Lawson).

Wilson's scholarship has been recognized by his colleagues (1989, president of the American Sociological Association), by fellow scientists (1991, elected to the revered National Academy of Sciences), by other educators (elected to the American Academy of Arts and Sciences, the National Academy of Education, the American Philosophical Society, the British academy, the Institute of Medicine; received at least 41 honorary doctorates, including from Princeton, Columbia, Johns Hopkins, and University of Amsterdam in the Netherlands), and by the wider community (named one of America's 25 Most Influential People by *Time* magazine, 1996). He also received a MacArthur Foundation Fellowship, nicknamed the "genius award" (1987-1992),a National Medal of Science (1998), the Talcott Parsons Prize in the Social Sciences by the American Academy of Arts and Sciences (2003), and numerous other important prizes and awards. He has taught at the University of Chicago (1972-1996) and at Harvard University (since 1996), 1 of only 19 "University Professors" at Harvard. Wilson and his second wife, Beverly Huebner (married in 1971), have four children: Colleen, Lisa, Carter, and Paula.

REFERENCES: *AANB. BCE. CAO-07. EB-BH-CD. Wiki.* Golus, Carrie, in *BB.* Taub, Richard, in *EA-99.* Amazon.com.

Winfrey, Oprah (Gail)
1/29/1954–
Nonfiction self-help, autobiography/memoir; talk-show host, movie producer, book-club host, magazine founder and publisher

For the 2006 PBS program *African American Lives*, hosted by **Henry Louis Gates**, Winfrey was among eight participants (including Gates) offered a genetic profile of their ancestry. In the episode, "Beyond the Middle Passage" (aired 2/8/2006), Winfrey's DNA test revealed that her genetic makeup was 89% sub-Saharan African, 8% Native American, and 3% East Asian, with her mother's ancestors coming from the Kpelles who now reside in Liberia. On hearing with certitude that most of her ancestors had been brought to this country in chains, Winfrey was deeply moved.

Young Oprah, too, had an inauspicious beginning. To start with, her mother, Vernita Lee, had intended to name her "Orpah," after a biblical character in the book of Ruth, but somehow, the name ended up being spelled "Oprah" when it was registered by the clerk at the courthouse in Kosciusko, Mississippi, and the misspelling stuck. Oprah's mother wasn't married to her father, 20-year-old Vernon Winfrey, who had been on leave from the service when Oprah was conceived. After his furlough, Vernon returned to duty, unaware that he had fathered a child until he received a card from Vernita, announcing Oprah's arrival and asking him to send money for clothing.

While Oprah was still an infant, Vernita realized that she'd have to leave Kosciusko if she was to have any chance of earning a decent living, given that she had no specific skills and very little education. Vernita left Oprah in the South with Vernon's mother, and she went to Milwaukee, to earn enough to send for Oprah. At her grandmother's farm, Oprah learned to read by the time she was three years old and was in the third grade at school by the time she was six (having asked her kindergarten teacher to place her in the first grade and having skipped second grade, as well). Oprah also started performing at an early age, making her first speaking appearance at an Easter program at her grandmother's beloved church when she was just three years old.

Oprah's grandmother was desperately poor, however, and when Vernita sent for her daughter to join her in Milwaukee, Oprah went. Vernita was working long hours as a domestic servant, for $50/week, and she and Oprah shared a room in another woman's house. Oprah hated having so little of her mother's time and so little in the way of material comforts or diversions—and she made her feelings known very clearly. Pretty soon, Vernita threw up her hands and sent Oprah to live with Vernon in Nashville, Tennessee.

Meanwhile, Vernon had married and owned his own business as a barber; he and his wife welcomed Oprah's arrival during the summer of 1962. Like his mother, Vernon was active in his church, and he encouraged Oprah to get involved in the church's numerous activities and presentations. Oprah thrived in school and in the church, participating in pageants, choral performances, and whatever other opportunities she had to shine in the limelight. The following summer, however, Vernita pleaded with Vernon and his wife to have Oprah return to her for a visit, noting how much she had missed Oprah. Just as they had feared, Oprah stayed on with Vernita after the end of summer. Vernita was planning to marry a man who had his own son and daughter, and she felt sure she could provide Oprah with a more pleasant home life than she had offered her before.

For Oprah, this decision proved emotionally disastrous. For one thing, she felt physically unattractive, and her mother reinforced her negative feelings toward herself. Even more detrimental to her emotional well-being, starting when she was just nine years old, her male cousin and other male family members and acquaintances repeatedly sexually abused her. Like so many other young victims of sexual abuse, she felt confused and frightened, unsure of what to do, and she felt guilty, sensing that somehow she was to blame for the bad behavior of her abusers. Initially, she had continued to do well in school, and one of her teachers at Lincoln Middle School, Gene Abrams, helped her get a scholarship to a high-status school in an affluent suburb of Milwaukee. By the time she reached her teen years, however, she was both troubled and troublesome, running away from home, destroying her family members' possessions, and faking a burglary. When Oprah was 14 years old, she became pregnant (and later gave birth to a son who died shortly afterward), and Vernita again threw up her hands. She told Oprah that she could either go to a school for wayward girls or go to live with Vernon and his wife in Nashville.

Oprah knew that Vernon would again impose strict discipline and close supervision, but she still chose him over her other option. After initial resistance, she started again excelling academically, and again, she started performing and speaking in public, participating in speech and drama clubs and serving on the student council. While she was a senior at East High School, she got a job reading the news on local African-American-owned radio station WVOL. She also earned a partial scholarship to attend Tennessee State University (TSU) after having won an oratorical contest sponsored by the Elks Club. Although she would rather have gone to college out of town, perhaps in New England, she followed her father's wishes and attended TSU in Nashville.

At TSU, Oprah majored in speech and drama. Her freshman year, she was named Miss Black Nashville and Miss Black Tennessee and was a Miss Black America contestant. Meanwhile, she had moved from WVOL to WLAC, a more mainstream radio station. After appearing in the beauty contests, WLAC's CBS television affiliate (later WTVF) offered Oprah a job as Nashville's first woman coanchor (and reporter), with a five-figure salary—*very* unusual for a college student in the early 1970s. In her new job, she was not only the first African American to anchor a newscast in Nashville, but also one of the youngest persons (at age 19) to do so.

Pretty soon, Oprah's career success made it difficult to continue to conform to Vernon's strict guidance, and she looked for a job outside of Nashville. In 1976, a few months before Oprah would have earned her bachelor's degree, WJZ-TV, an ABC affiliate station in Baltimore, Maryland, offered her a job as reporter and coanchor, and she jumped at the chance to leave. In 1988, TSU invited her to give a commencement address, at which they awarded her an honorary degree. Oprah has since established a scholarship fund at TSU, which pays the expenses for 10 students whom she chooses and gets to know each year.

At WJZ-TV, Oprah—and the station management—quickly discovered that her lack of journalistic training made her ill prepared for objective reporting. She had signed a very favorable contract, however, so the management needed to find a way to use the talents she had. They soon discovered that the very characteristics that essentially disqualified her from journalism made her beautifully suited to a talk-show format: empathy, passion and compassion, and subjectivity. From 1977 to 1984, she cohosted *Baltimore Is Talking* (or *People Are Talking*) with Richard Sher, helping to boost the popularity of that show.

In 1984, she went on to host a half-hour television talk show, *A.M. Chicago,* which aired against the highly popular national talk-show host Phil Donahue; no previous hosts had been able to touch Donahue in the ratings. Within a month, however, Oprah's ratings were equaling Phil's. In 1985, the expanded hour-long show was renamed *The Oprah Winfrey Show,* and Phil moved his show from Chicago to New York. In 1986, Oprah's show was syndicated (broadcast nationally), and over time, she topped Phil's national ratings. A decade later, she was still the tops in national syndication, when she decided to refocus her show toward positive themes and away from sensationalism. In a television market crowded with sensationalized talk shows, she was taking a big chance, but she has continued to make syndication history. Her show has earned her 6 Emmy awards for best host, as well as 19 other Emmys, a People's Choice Award for favorite talk show host (2004), and the highly esteemed Peabody

Award (both for her talk show and for her charitable work; 1996).

In 2008, her worldwide audience had reached about 30 million people each week, including 140 countries, many in Arab lands. *Time* magazine named her 1 of the 25 most influential people in the world six times between 1996 and 2008, and 1 of the top 100 people of the twentieth century in 1998. A December 2007 Gallup poll of American woman ranked her the most admired woman in the world. Researchers at the University of Maryland, College Park, estimated that she delivered more than 1 million extra votes to Obama in the 2008 Democratic primary, thanks to her early support of him.

Winfrey owns her own production company, Harpo Productions ("Oprah" spelled backwards; founded in 1986). Harpo Productions has enabled Winfrey to produce television and film projects she believes in, such as the 1988 television miniseries *The Women of Brewster Place* (based on **Gloria Naylor**'s novel; Winfrey acted in it), the 1998 television movie *The Wedding* (based on **Dorothy West**'s novel), the 1998 film *Beloved* (based on **Toni Morrison**'s novel; Winfrey starred in it), and the 2005 television movie *Their Eyes Were Watching God* (based on **Zora Neale Hurston**'s novel and **Suzan-Lori Parks**'s teleplay). She also owns the screen rights to other noteworthy novels. In addition to her roles in *Brewster Place* and in *Beloved*, Winfrey gave an Oscar-nominated performance in **Alice Walker**'s *The Color Purple* (1985).

Not only has Oprah promoted the works of individual women writers whom she has invited as guests to her show, but Oprah has also done much to promote reading through "Oprah's Book Club," launched in 1996. A few of the books she has highlighted include **Maya Angelou**'s *The Heart of a Woman* (1997), **Ernest J. Gaines**'s *A Lesson Before Dying* (1997), and **Pearl Cleage**'s *What Looks Like Crazy on an Ordinary Day* (1998), as well as multiple books by Toni Morrison (*Song of Solomon*, 1996; *Paradise*, 1998; *The Bluest Eye*, 2000; *Sula*, 2002), by **Bill Cosby** (three books), by Jane Hamilton (two), by Wally Lamb (two), and by Gabriel García Márquez (two). Through her club, she announces in advance particular books to read and then discusses these books with viewers on subsequent shows. A profile on Oprah's Book Club essentially ensures that a book will become a best-seller, often selling half a million to a million copies following a Club endorsement.

Sadly, following Oprah's selection of Jonathan Franzen's *The Corrections* in September of 2001, Franzen questioned the ability of her mostly female audience to grasp his "hard book." In spring of 2002, she said she planned to end her club, but the following year, she said announced her plans to start anew, focusing on literary classics. By January of 2004, only five more books had been chosen for the club after Franzen's, three of them literary

classics (by Nobel laureates Toni Morrison and John Steinbeck and by Alan Paton). Between January 2004 and June 2005, Oprah chose five more literary classics, then in September 2005, she chose James Frey's *A Million Little Pieces,* which rocketed to the tippy top of best-sellers, attracting much wanted attention for Frey, as well as unwanted attention when skeptics questioned the veracity of his "memoir." Oprah invited Frey to return, and under her questioning, he revealed that much of his story was false. In 2006 and 2007, Oprah returned to focusing on literary classics. In 2008, her club recommended a contemporary book, *A New Earth* by Eckhart Tolle, which prompted criticism by some Christian leaders for its New Age philosophy. Nine months later, her club recommended first-time novelist David Wroblewski's *The Story of Edgar Sawtelle,* a contemporary retelling of Hamlet.

Oprah has also been involved with several book projects of her own: *Oprah: An Autobiography* (Oprah Winfrey and Joan Barthel); *In the Kitchen with Rosie: Oprah's Favorite Recipes* (1994, Rosie Daley; introduced by Oprah); *The Uncommon Wisdom of Oprah Winfrey: A Portrait in Her Own Words* (Bill Adler and Oprah Winfrey; 1996); *Oprah Winfrey Speaks: Insights from the World's Most Influential Voice* (Janet C. Lowe and Oprah Winfrey, 1998); *Make the Connection: 10 Steps to a Better Body—And a Better Life* (1996, Bob Greene and Oprah Winfrey, hardcover, audio cassettes); *Journey to Beloved* (1998, Oprah Winfrey, with photographer Ken Regan and with Jonathan Demme), about her decade-long process of getting Toni Morrison's *Beloved* onto the silver screen; *What I Know for Sure* (2005, Winfrey); and *The Best Life Diet Revised and Updated* (2008, Bob Greene and Oprah Winfrey). The Oprah Magazine Editors of O have authored several additional titles: *Live Your Best Life: A Treasury of Wisdom, Wit, Advice, Interviews, and Inspiration from O, The Oprah Magazine* (2005); *O, The Oprah Magazine Cookbook* (2008); and *O's Big Book of Happiness: The Best of O, The Oprah Magazine: Wisdom, Wit, Advice, Interviews, and Inspiration* (2008). In 1999, Winfrey was given an honorary National Book Award, and the National Book Foundation gave her its 50th Anniversary Medal.

In 2000, Oprah started a new publishing venture, *O: The Oprah Magazine,* which has topped 2 million circulation and which grossed more than $140 million in 2001. In 2003, *O* launched a quarterly offshoot, *O at Home,* but it folded after the Winter 2008 issue. As she has said when advising others, "There are no failures, only lessons to be learned" and "Failure is another steppingstone to greatness" (from *QB*).

In October of 1995, Winfrey had already launched Oprah Online, initially at America Online; now, Internet surfers can go to //www.oprah.com/index to find "TV & Films," "O Magazine," "Radio," her charitable "Angel

Network," "Book Club," "O Store," "Spirit," "Health," "Style," "Relationships," "Home," "Food," "Money," "World," and "Hot Topics." Her website generates more than 70 million page views by more than 6 million users each month; the site receives, on average, nearly 3,000 e-mails each day (*Wiki,* May 7, 2009). In 1998, Oprah founded Oxygen Media, to produce women's programs both for the Internet and for cable television. In 2006, she launched a new Sirius and XM Satellite radio channel, "Oprah & Friends," a 24/7 channel that features a half-hour weekly show with Oprah and her dear friend Gayle King (39 weeks/year). Before the end of 2009, Winfrey is planning to debut OWN: The Oprah Winfrey Network, a health-oriented cable channel, in concert with Discovery Communications. In exchange for taking over the former Discovery Health Channel, Winfrey will turn over control of her Oprah.com website to Discovery Communications. Winfrey has also hosted innumerable television specials, including her own *Oprah: Behind the Scenes, Oprah Live,* and *Dinner with Oprah* shows. Even the youngest among us can enjoy listening to Oprah's voice as "Gussie the Goose" in the 2006 animated film *Charlotte's Web* or as "Judge Bumbledeen" in the 2007 animated film *Bee Movie.* Oprah's multimedia domain now offers readers, broadcast and cable TV viewers, radio listeners, filmgoers, and web surfers multiple easy ways to find her.

In 2008, Winfrey's assets were estimated at $2.7 billion, according to *Forbes* (cited in *Wikipedia*). She has been not only "the richest African American of the 20th century" and the "first black woman billionaire in world history," but also "the most philanthropic African American of all time" and "one of America's top 50 most generous philanthropists" (*Wiki*). Though her many endeavors have made her wealthy, she contributes at least 10% of her income ($385 million in 2008) to charities, mostly projects related to education, youths, and literature. In addition to funding scholarships, Winfrey finances numerous charitable and philanthropic endeavors, having donated millions to her alma mater, other colleges and universities (e.g., Morehouse), the United Negro College Fund, the Harold Washington Library, a program for economically disadvantaged Chicago-area young girls, her Oprah Winfrey Leadership Academy for Girls near Johannesburg in South Africa, a program for training people of color to get jobs in TV and film, and numerous other worthy projects and institutions. She has also been instrumental in lobbying for national laws aimed at protecting children from abuse. Winfrey is also famously generous with her guests and her employees, such as having taken 1,065 of her staff members and their families to Hawaii for a vacation in the summer of 2006. For her achievements and her philanthropy, Winfrey has been honored with the Woman of Achievement Award from

the National Organization for Women (1986), the NAACP's Image Award four years in a row (1989-1992), a Lifetime Achievement Award from the Academy of Television Arts and Sciences (1998), a Bob Hope Humanitarian Award (2002), a Candle for Lifetime Achievement in Humanitarian Service from Morehouse College (2004), a Global Leadership Award from the United Nations (2004), and a People for the Ethical Treatment of Animals Person of the Year award (2008).

In addition to her best friend, Gayle King, who also currently edits *O,* Winfrey has close ties to journalist and California First Lady Maria Shriver and to writer Maya Angelou. Angelou's decade birthdays have been occasions for gala celebrations hosted by Winfrey. Winfrey has also had a long-term close relationship with Stedman Graham, Jr. (since 1986). Though marriage plans have been discussed at times, they have remained single but committed to each other. She considers the girls at her South African Leadership Academy to be her cherished daughters, and she plans to move to the academy when she retires, to live exactly as they do.

REFERENCES: *AANB. B. BCE. BF:2000. CAO-03. CE. EB-BH-CD. F. G-99. PGAA. QB. RWTC. SEW. W2B. WDAW. Wiki.* Angelou, Maya, in *L:WW.* Beetz, Kirk H., in *BusB.* Brennan, Sandra, *All Movie Guide,* in *Act.* Dunn, Lois L., & Michelle Banks, in *BH2C.* Fay, Robert, in *EA-99.* Feder, Robert, in *WB-99.* Joyce, Donald Franklin, in *AA:PoP.* Simonson, J'Lyn, in *GEAAL.* Taylor, B. Kimberly, and David Oblender, in *BB.* Thompson, Kathleen, in *BWA:AHE.* Zanoza, Melanie. "Oprah's Book Club Past, Present & Future (In the Margin)." *Book* (May-June 2003), p. 13. From *Literature Resource Center.* //en.wikipedia.org/wiki/ Oprah%27s_Book_Club. //www.answers.com/topic/quote-4?author= Winfrey,%20Oprah&s2=Oprah%20Winfrey. //www.oprah.com/index. //www.pbs.org/previews/africanamericanlives/. //www.pbs.org/previews/ oprahs-roots/. //www.pdnonline.com/pdn/content_display/photo-news/editorial/e3if0819d6addd2a0fe43517898b5b2579c. Amazon.com.

The Woman's Era See **Ruffin, Josephine, et al.**

Wonder, Stevie (né Stevland [Hardaway] Judkins Morris)
5/13/1950–
Songs; performer, pianist, singer

Wonder has written many of the popular songs he has recorded, such as the title songs on his albums *You Are the Sunshine of My Life* (1972), *Isn't She Lovely* (1972), *I Just Called to Say I Love You* (1984), and *Don't You Worry 'bout a Thing* (1999). In 1983, he was inducted into the Songwriters Hall of Fame. His print publications include *Portrait of Stevie Wonder* (1971), *The Songs of Stevie Wonder* (1973, with Bill Radics), *Stevie Wonder: Fulfillingness' First Finale* (1974), *Stevie Wonder Gold* (1975), *The Stevie Wonder Anthology* (1975; revised, 2002), *Stevie Wonder Songs in the Key of Life* (1976), *Stevie Wonder: Journey through the Secret Life of Plants* (1980), *Stevie Wonder Thought Shares* (1984), *It's Easy to Play Stevie Wonder* (1985), *Stevie Wonder Greatest Hits Updated!* (1985), *Stevie Wonder Characters* (1988), *Stevie Wonder—Easy Piano Anthology* (1998), *Stevie Wonder—Written Musiquarium* (1999), *Stevie Wonder Guitar Collection* (2000), *Stevie Wonder Hits* (2000), *The Best of Stevie Wonder* (2002, with Todd Lowry), *Stevie Wonder—Greatest Hits: E-Z Play Today Volume 277* (2003), *Stevie Wonder—Innervisions: Smart PianoSoft* (2005), *Stevie Wonder—A Musical Guide to the Classic Albums* (2005, with Steve Lodder), and *Stevie Wonder: Jazz Play Along Volume 52* (2006).

His hit singles and albums sold exceed 100 million, and he has been inducted into both the Rock and Roll Hall of Fame (1989) and the Michigan Walk of Fame (2006). *Rolling Stone Magazine* listed him as number 15 on its list of "100 Greatest Rock and Roll Artists of All Time" (2004). Wonder, blind since birth, has richly colored his listeners' auditory world. For his songwriting and his musical performance, he earned the second Gershwin Prize for Popular Song, awarded by the Library of Congress, and presented by President Barack Obama at a White House ceremony (February, 2009). Wonder had previously performed at Obama's Democratic Party nomination acceptance (2008), at Lincoln Memorial festivities honoring his inauguration (January 18, 2009), and at the Neighborhood Inaugural Ball honoring Obama on Inauguration Day (January 20, 2009). He has been honored with a Grammy Lifetime Achievement Award from the National Academy of Recording Arts and Sciences of the United States (1996), a George and Ira Gershwin Lifetime Achievement Award from the University of California at Los Angeles Student Alumni Association (2002), the Sammy Cahn Lifetime Achievement Award from the Songwriter's Hall of Fame (2002), and the Lifetime Achievement Award from the National Civil Rights Museum in Memphis (2006). His other honors include 21 other Grammys (the most for a male solo artist), an Academy Award for Best Song (1984), a Polar Music Prize (1999), Kennedy Center Honors (1999), and the Billboard Century Award (2004). Though he has recorded his music for Motown Records since age 11, Wonder also founded Black Bull Music publishing company (1971) and Wondirection Records (1982), and he sponsored the Stevie Wonder Home for Blind and Retarded Children (1976). He has also championed numerous political and social causes, most notably the campaign to establish a national holiday honoring **Martin Luther King, Jr.**, but also Mothers Against Drunk Driving, resistance to South African apartheid, and awareness of AIDS. His seven children (surnamed Morris) are Aisha, Keita, Kwame, Mumtaz, Sophia, Kailand (who sometimes drums on stage with his father), and Mandla, who was born on his father's 55th birthday (5/13/2005).

REFERENCES: *AANB. B. BCE. CAO-06. D. EB-98. EB-BH-CD. QB. W2B. Wiki.* Fay, Robert, in *EA-99.* Glickman, Simon, and Tom Pendergast, in *BB.* Huey, Steve, *All Music Guide,* in *A.* //en.wikipedia.org/wiki/Gershwin_Prize_for_Popular_Song. //en.wikipedia.org/wiki/Grammy. //en.wikipedia.org/wiki/Grammy_Award_records. //en.wikipedia.org/wiki/UCLA_Spring_Sing#The_George_and_Ira_Gershwin_Award. //www.npr.org/templates/story/story.php?storyId=101024299. Amazon.com.

Woodson, Carter G. (Godwin)
12/19/1875–4/3/1950
Nonfiction—history; scholar

Dire poverty didn't stop young Carter from getting the education he sought. While working in the coal mines of West Virginia, he managed to get in some schooling, at least some of the time, and after finishing high school (c. 1895), he went on to get a bachelor's degree, then a master's degree, and finally—in that exalted Cambridge, Massachusetts, institution of higher learning—he earned his Ph.D. in history from Harvard (1912). In Cambridge, he also taught school to earn his way through to his doctorate. Throughout all his studies, one thing emerged more clearly than all the things he saw in his readings: what *wasn't* in the history books he read. Where were all the African Americans while the European Americans were fighting this or that battle, making this or that discovery, or inventing this or that new product? Where were they in the world of business and industry? What had they contributed to the world of literature, art, and music? Ironically, perhaps, Woodson never noticed the distinct absence of women in history, and he rarely mentioned their contributions in his work.

These were not idle musings for Carter G. Woodson. No, he made up his mind to do something about these lacks. He spent the next four or so decades of his life doing whatever he could to unearth the unspoken contributions of African Americans to their country of birth, to probe the hidden lives of African Americans, and to unveil the secrets of African-American culture and lift up the glories of the African past. In 1915, Woodson cofounded the Association for the Study of Negro (renamed Afro-American) Life and History (ASNLH) in Washington, D.C., with the aim of collecting "sociological and historical data on the Negro, the study of peoples of African blood, the publishing of books in the field, and the promoting of harmony between the races by acquainting the one with the other." Through the ASNLH, young scholars were encouraged to conduct research and to publish their findings. Natural outgrowths of this association were two journals: The *Journal of Negro History* (starting in 1916) was aimed at scholars, and the *Negro*

History Bulletin (starting in 1937) was intended to aid schoolteachers from the primary grades through high school. Another vehicle for scholars in this field was the ASNLH's Associated Publishers, which was established (in 1920) to put out publications (e.g., books and other materials) on African-American history, which would otherwise never reach their increasingly numerous readers.

Woodson's own works in this field were probably enough to justify the establishment of Associated Publishers. His 20 or so books include many that he authored, such as *Education of the Negro Prior to 1861* (1915), *A Century of Negro Migration* (1918), *The History of the Negro Church* (1921), *Negro Makers of History* (1928), *The Rural Negro* (1930), *The African Background Outlined* (1936), and *African Heroes and Heroines* (1944). Important collections that he edited include *Negro Orators and Orations* (1925); *Mind of the Negro as Reflected in Letters Written During the Crisis, 1800-1860* (1926); *African Myths, Together with Proverbs, A Supplementary Reader Composed of Folk Tales from Various Parts of Africa* (1928); and *The Works of* **Francis J. Grimké** (1942, 4 vols.). Two of the books he authored deserve special notice. First, for decades, his *The Negro in Our History* (1922; 10th ed., 1962) was the primary textbook on African-American history, used chiefly in colleges, but also in high schools.

Second, his *The Mis-Education of the Negro* (1933) provoked a lot of thought. The title itself gives you an idea of where he was going with his book. He saw the miseducation of African Americans as a tragic waste of potential, and he urged readers to focus on developing the most precious resource of the African-American community: the minds of black people. He pointed out the absence of African Americans in textbooks and in the curricula, starting in the primary grades and continuing through college and even into graduate schools. He repudiated the self-loathing that a flawed education can wreak.

One of the ways in which Woodson attempted to correct the educational failures he saw was by initiating Negro History Week (starting in 1926). Initially set for the second week in February, embracing the birthdays of **Frederick Douglass** and Abraham Lincoln, the celebration has since expanded to make all of February Black History Month. A lifelong bachelor, Woodson devoted his every waking moment and his every last dime to his noble purpose. In gratitude for all he gave, he is called the "Father of Black History."

REFERENCES: *E-98. EB-98. SMKC.* Ashill, Gary, in *COCAAL* and *OCAAL.* Bolden, Tonya. 1997. *Through Loona's Door: A Tammy and Owen Adventure with Carter G. Woodson.* Oakland, CA: Corporation for Cultural Literacy. Myers, Aaron, in *EA-99.*

FURTHER READING: *AANB. B. BCE. CAO-03. CE. W. Wiki.* Ashill, Gary, in *COCAAL.* Cox, Edward L., in *T-CAH.* Dagbovie, Pero Gaglo. "Black Women, Carter G. Woodson, and the Association for the Study of Negro Life and History, 1915-1950." *The Journal of African American History. 88.1* (Winter 2003) p. 21. From *Literature Resource Center.* Dailey, Maceo Crenshaw, Sr. "Carter G. Woodson: A Life in Black History." *The Journal of Negro History. 79.3* (Summer 1994) p. 304. From *Literature Resource Center.* [Gates, Henry Louis, Jr.] "Henry Louis Gates, Jr. on Carter G. Woodson." *The Journal of African American History. 88.3* (Summer 2003) p. 325. From *Literature Resource Center.* Goggin, Jacqueline, in *USHC.* Harris, Janette Hoston. "Woodson and Wesley: a Partnership in Building the Association for the Study of Afro-American Life and History." *The Journal of Negro History. 83.2* (Spring 1998) p. 109. From *Literature Resource Center.* Knight, Gladys L., in *GEAAL.* Peters, Ann M., in *BB.* Watkins, William H., in *EE.* Wesley, Charles H. "Recollections of Carter G. Woodson." *The Journal of Negro History, 83.2* (Spring 1998) p. 143. From *Literature Resource Center. See also* Carter G. Woodson Distinguished Lecturers 2003-2004, 2004-2005, 2005-2006, 2006-2007, and 2008-2009. *The Journal of African American History* (Fall or Winter, 2003, 2004, 2005, 2006, 2007, 2008). From *Literature Resource Center.*

Woodson, Jacqueline (Amanda)
2/12/1963–
Juvenile literature, novels, family memoir, anthologies, gay/lesbian literature; educator, drama therapist, assistant editor

Editor's note: Woodson's birth year is given as 1963 in six sources (e.g., Hayn, *WYA-2000*; Smith, 1999), but as 1964 in five sources (e.g., *CAO-06, GEAAL*).

Photos of Jacqueline Woodson appeared in the pages of *Ebony* magazine when she was still a toddler, advertising Alaga Syrup. Though Woodson had the first inklings of her homosexual identity while in her early teens, she did not come out as a lesbian until she was in a creative-writing class at Adelphi University in Garden City, New York. After earning her B.A., Woodson worked at a children's book packaging company.

In 1990, Woodson published a nonfiction children's picture book, **Martin Luther King, Jr. and His Birthday** (1990). She also wrote the first in her trilogy of young-adult novels, *Last Summer with Maizon* (1990/2002), followed by *Maizon at Blue Hill* (1992/2002), cited as a Best Book for Young Adults by the American Library Association (ALA) (1993), and *Between Madison and Palmetto* (1993/2002). Between the first and second novel in her trilogy, Woodson wrote *The Dear One* (1991/2004), about a 12-year-old girl whose mother takes in a pregnant 15-year-old. During this time, Woodson also received two MacDowell Colony fellowships (1990, 1994), a fellowship for the Fine Arts Work Center in Provincetown, Massachusetts (1991-1992), and associate professorships at Goddard College's M.F.A. Writing Program Vermont (1993-1995) and at New

School University's Eugene Lang College in New York City (1994).

In 1994, Woodson wrote a novel for adults, *Autobiography of a Family Photo* (1994), for which she received her second *Kenyon Review* Award for Literary Excellence in Fiction (1995). She also wrote two companion books to public television's *Ghostwriter* series: *Book Chase* (1994), a book-length mystery, and *Write Now!* (1994), an activity book. For young-adult readers, she wrote the **Coretta Scott King** Honor Book (1995) *I Hadn't Meant to Tell You This* (1994/2006), the first of two books about an interracial friendship between Lena and Marie. Both girls miss their mothers, and Lena confides in Marie that she is being molested by her own father. In the sequel, *Lena* (1998), Lena and her little sister Dion run away to escape their sexually abusive father.

Meanwhile, Woodson wrote another Coretta Scott King Honor Book (1996), *From the Notebooks of Melanin Sun* (1995), about a 14-year-old African-American boy who struggles to deal his mother's now-public interracial homosexual relationship. In Woodson's Lambda Literary Award-winning *The House You Pass on the Way* (1997/2003), the 14-year-old protagonist, Staggerlee, is coming to terms with her sexual identity, beginning to realize that she is gay, while also dealing with her biracial identity.

As the old millennium drew to a close, Woodson was employed as a writer in residence for the National Book Foundation (1995, 1996) and an associate faculty member in the M.F.A. program at Vermont College in Montpelier (1996). She also edited *A Way Out of No Way: Writing about Growing Up Black in America* (1996), a short-story collection, and *Just a Writer's Thing: A Collection of Prose and Poetry from the National Book Foundation's 1995 Summer Writing Camp* (1996, with Norma Fox Mazer). She also contributed to other anthologies (e.g., *Am I Blue? Coming Out from the Silence*, 1994) and to numerous periodicals (e.g., *American Identities: Contemporary Multi-Cultural Voices, American Voice, Common Lives Quarterly, Conditions, Essence, Horn Book, Kenyon Review, Out/Look*), and she is a member of the editorial board of *Portable Lower East Side/Queer City*.

Woodson finished out the old millennium with *If You Come Softly* (1998/2006), cited as both a Best Book for Young Readers by the ALA (2000) and a *Bulletin* Blue Ribbon Book. In it, an interracial romance blossoms between an upper-middle-class European-American girl and an African-American boy whose celebrity parents have just separated. Years later, Woodson wrote *Behind You* (2004), a sequel following the lives of the boy's loved ones in the aftermath of a tragedy; it was named one of the Top Ten Best Books for Young Adults by the Young Adult Library Services Association (2005).

For young readers, Woodson has written many more picture books, including *We Had a Picnic This Sunday Past* (1997/2007), celebrating the joys of feasting with family and friends; *Sweet, Sweet Memory* (2000), about finding comfort while grieving; *The Other Side* (2001), which won a Time of Wonder Award (2001) and numerous distinguished citations; *Our Gracie Aunt* (2002), which addresses parental neglect and foster care; *Visiting Day* (2002), in which a young girl and her grandmother happily prepare to visit her imprisoned father; and *Coming on Home Soon* (2004), nominated for a Caldecott Medal and named a *Child* magazine Best of 2004 (2005), a Charlotte Zolotow Award Honor Book (2005), an ALA Notable Book, and a *Booklist* Editor's Choice selection. Woodson's *Show Way* (2005) offers a multigenerational family memoir, as viewed through her family's quilt-making tradition, culminating with a photo of Woodson's own baby daughter, Toshi. It was awarded a Newbery Honor (2006), a *Booklist* Editor's Choice selection (2005), and a Best Children's Books citation from *Kirkus Reviews* (2005).

For young adults, Woodson has written *Miracle's Boys* (2000), winner of the Coretta Scott King Book Award (2001) and the Los Angeles Times Book Award for young-adult fiction and named one of the Best Books for Young Adults by the ALA. *Hush* (2002) was nominated for the National Book Award for young people's literature (2002) and was chosen as a *Booklist* Editor's Choice (2002), a Best Book for Young Adults by the ALA (2003), a Best Book by *School Library Journal*, and one of the Bank Street Best Children's Books of the Year. Woodson's second National Book Award finalist (2004), *Locomotion* (2003), was nominated for a *Boston Globe-Horn Book* Award in the fiction and poetry category (2003), selected as a Children's Choice by the International Reading Association (IRA) and Children's Book Council (CBC) (2004), named a Coretta Scott King Honor Book, and cited as a Best Book by *School Library Journal*. Woodson's sequel, *Peace, Locomotion* (2009), an epistolary novel, has also been critically acclaimed as "moving, thought-provoking, and brilliantly executed, this is the rare sequel that lives up to the promise of its predecessor" (*School Library Journal*, quoted in //www.amazon.com). Woodson's other two young-adult books are *Feathers* (2007/2009), a Newbery Honor Book chosen as an Oprah's Book Club Kids Reading List selection; and *After Tupac and D Foster* (2008/2010), about the close friendship among three 11-year-old girls as they move into their teens.

In addition to the many aforementioned awards and honors, Woodson won an American Film Institute award, a *Publishers Weekly* Best Book citation (1994), two Jane Addams Children's Book Awards (1995, 1996), and a Granta Fifty Best American Authors under 40 Award (1996). The Young Adult Library Services Association also honored her with the Margaret A. Edwards Award for life-time achievement in writing for young adults (2006).

REFERENCES: CAO-06. Wiki. Allister, Jan (July 2003), "Jacqueline Woodson," EBSCO Publishing, Salem Press, in //0-web.ebscohost.com.dbpcosdcsgt.co.san-diego.ca.us/novelist/detail?vid=77&hid=16&sid=02bf6a41-8618-414c-abf5-13f22fd219a5%40sessionmgr7&bdata=JnNpdGU9bm92ZWxpc3QtbGl2ZQ%3d%3. Brown, Jennifer M. "From Outsider to Insider. (PW Interview)." Publishers Weekly. 249.6 (Feb. 11, 2002), p. 156. Literature Resources from Gale. Day, Frances Ann. 2000. Lesbian and Gay Voices: an Annotated Bibliography and Guide to Literature for Children and Young Adults. Westport, CT: Greenwood Publishing Group. Drew, Bernard Alger. 2007. 100 Most Popular African American Authors: Biographical Sketches and Bibliographies. Santa Barbara, CA: Libraries Unlimited. Editors of the Gale Group. 2003. Something about the Author: Facts and Pictures about Contemporary Authors and Illustrators of Books for Young People (Volume 139). Farmington Hills, MI: Gale Research International, Limited, Gale Group. Green, Heidi Hauser, in GEAAL. Hayn, Judith A., in WYA-2000. Hine, Darlene Clark. 2005. Black Women in America (2nd ed.). New York: Oxford University Press. Johnson, Virginia (CRRL Staff), "Jacqueline Woodson: Love Is Tough, But Words Are Beautiful," in //www.kidspoint.org/columns2.asp?column_id=1634&column_type=author. Knowles, Elizabeth, and Martha Smith. 2007. Understanding Diversity through Novels and Picture Books. Santa Barbara, CA: Libraries. Malinowski, Sharon, et al. 1998. Gay & Lesbian Literature. Belmont, CA: St. James Press. Nelson, Emmanuel Sampath. 1999. Contemporary African American Novelists: a Bio-bibliographical Critical Sourcebook. Westport, CT: Greenwood Publishing Group. Robotham, Rosemarie, Pearl Cleage, Maya Angelou. 2004. Mending the World: Stories of Family by Contemporary Black Writers. New York: Basic Civitas Books. Rochman, Hazel, "Jacqueline Woodson," Booklist. 101.11 (Feb. 1, 2005), p. 968. Literature Resources from Gale. Smith, Henrietta M., American Library Association, Coretta Scott King Task Force. 1999. The Coretta Scott King Awards Book, 1970-1999. Chicago: ALA Editions. //en.wikipedia.org/wiki/Book_packaging. //en.wikipedia.org/wiki/Ghostwriter_(TV_series). //us.penguingroup.com/static/images/yr/pdf/tl-guide-jacquelinewood.pdf. //wiki.answers.com/Q/How_old_is_jacqueline_woodson. //www.amazon.com. //www.jacquelinewoodson.com/. //www.jacquelinewoodson.com/bio.shtml. //www.jacquelinewoodson.com/faq.shtml. //www.jacquelinewoodson.com/teachers.shtml. //www.library.ci.corpus-christi.tx.us/readingroomafrauthos.htm. San Diego Public Library catalog, summary of Hinton, 2008 (see Further Readings).

FURTHER READING: Hinton, KaaVonia. (2008). Jacqueline Woodson. Hockessin, DE: Mitchell Lane Publishers.

Wright, Charles S. (Stevenson)
6/4/1932–

Journalism, columns, novels, short stories; journalist, columnist, odd-jobs worker

Highly regarded as a satirist, a surrealist, and an experimentalist, Charles Stevenson Wright left public high school in his junior year, and his only further somewhat formal education came from occasional summer stays at the Lowney Handy Writers Colony in Marshall, Illinois. Even as a teenager, however, he wrote a regular column for the Kansas City Call, which also paid Wright a

dollar for his first published short story. While carrying out a variety of odd jobs, such as being a messenger in New York City, Wright earned a little income from free-lance writing. He had written two unpublished novels before he wrote his first published novel, The Messenger (1963; London, 1964). His first-person narrative by "Charles Stevenson" so closely follows his experiences that at times the line between fact and fiction seems blurry. The book not only brought Wright critical acclaim, but also some modest financial rewards.

Wright's next novel, The Wig: A Mirror Image (1966/2003; London, 1967), did not fare as well, either critically or in terms of sales. **Ishmael Reed** called it "one of the most underrated novels by a black person in [the 20th] century" (to John O'Brien, 1973, quoted in Weixlmann, COCAAL). Discouraged by his second novel's financial failure, Wright traveled extensively, both abroad and in the States. On returning to New York City in 1971, he started writing his "Wright's World" columns for New York City's Village Voice.

In Wright's third novel, Absolutely Nothing to Get Alarmed About (1973), he again blurs genre boundaries, interweaving into the novel some personal essays about his own experiences, drawn from his columns, as might be inferred from Wright's original title, "Black Studies: A Journal." Two decades after Wright published his third novel, HarperCollins published the collection Absolutely Nothing to Get Alarmed About: The Complete Novels of Charles Wright (1993) Other writings attributed to Wright include his short stories printed in anthologies, periodicals, and his short story collection Erotic Landslide (n.d.), in addition to his unpublished, unproduced play titled "Madam Is on the Veranda."

REFERENCES: BAWPP. CAO-01. Campenni, Frank, in //biography.jrank.org/pages/4848/Wright-Charles-Stevenson.html. Natambu, Kofi, in AANB. Weixlmann, Joe, in AAFW-55-84 and in COCAAL. //en.wikipedia.org/wiki/Village_Voice. //worldcat.org/identities/lccn-n85-50261. Amazon.com.

FURTHER READING: Ostrom, Hans, in GEAAL.

Wright, Courtni (né Crump)
6/24/1950–

Literary criticism, juvenile literature, romance novels

Courtni Crump earned her B.A. in English literature from Trinity College (1972), worked for a telephone company (1972-1975, 1977-1987), and taught English (1975-1977) for years when she married Grant Wright (1979), with whom she later had their son, Ashley. Soon after marrying, she earned her M.Ed. from Johns Hopkins University (1980) and returned to teaching English to middle-school and high-school students (1987-).

In her fifth decade, Courtni Wright was awarded a fellowship from the National Endowment for the Humanities and the Council for Basic Education (1990). Her first book was *The Women of Shakespeare's Plays: Analysis of the Role of the Women in Selected Plays with Plot Synopses and Selected One-Act Plays* (1993). Next, she wrote juvenile fiction: *Jumping the Broom* (1994), a children's picture book set in the days of slavery, was cited as one of the Best Books of 1994 by the Society of School Librarians International. Her next two children's picture books also highlighted historical experiences of African Americans: *Wagon Train: A Family Goes West in 1865* (1995) and *Journey to Freedom: A Story of the Underground Railroad* (1995), cited as a Teachers' Choice from the International Reading Association (IRA).

In 1997, Wright plunged into romance novels, including *Blush* (1997), *It Had to Be You* (1998), *Paradise* (1999), *A Sure Thing* (1999), *All That Matters* (1994/2000), *A Forgotten Love* (2000), *A New Beginning* (2000), *Recipe for Love* (2001), *A Charmed Love* (2002), *Uncovered Passion* (2002), *The Music of Love* (2003), *The Last Christmas Gift* (2003), *Summer Breeze* (2004), *Espresso for Two* (2004), *Windswept Love* (2005), and *Love Under Construction* (2006). She also contributed to *Season's Greetings* (1998, with Margie Walker and Roberta Gayle) and *A Very Special Love: The Key to My Heart* (2000/2006, with Janice Sims). She has also consulted with the National Geographic Society to edit several educational videos.

REFERENCES: CAO-07. Courtot, Marilyn, "Courtni C. Wright," in //www.childrenslit.com/childrenslit/mai_wright_courtni.html. Guyant, Valerie Lynn, in *GEAAL*. Amazon.com.

Wright, Jay
5/25/1935–
Poems, plays; educator

Wright's mother is of African and Native American descent, and his father is of Cherokee, African-American, and Irish-American descent, and Jay himself spent most of his childhood living in foster homes in Albuquerque, New Mexico. When Jay reached his teens, he moved to San Pedro, California, to live with his father. There, he started playing bass guitar and playing baseball in the minor leagues about the time he finished high school. Soon after, he served in the army medical corps (1954-1957), spending most of his time in Germany, from which he traveled extensively throughout Europe whenever he could. After his military service ended, he used the G.I. Bill (government allotments to pay for veterans' education) to attend the University of California at Berkeley, from which he graduated in comparative literature within three years. From Berkeley, he went to the Union Theological Seminary in New York on a Rockefeller Brothers

theological fellowship, after which he went to Rutgers University (in 1962), to continue his postgraduate study of literature. In 1964, Wright took a year out to teach English and medieval history in Guadalajara, Mexico (at the Butler Institute). After returning to Rutgers, he completed all his coursework for a doctorate in comparative literature. He has been an itinerant poet-in-residence at the historically black colleges Talledega and Tougaloo (1968-1970, intermittently), as well as Texas Southern University, Princeton University (1970-1971, on a playwriting fellowship), Dundee University (Scotland; 1971-1973, on a creative-writing fellowship), and Yale University (1975-1979).

While at Rutgers, Wright lived in Harlem and associated with writers of the **Black Arts Movement**. There, Wright was invited to contribute to **Langston Hughes's** *New Negro Poets* (1964), **Dudley Randall** and **Margaret Burroughs's** *For Malcolm: Poems on the Life and Death of Malcolm X* (1967), and LeRoi Jones (**Amiri Baraka**), and **Larry Neal's** *Black Fire* (1968). After **Henry Dumas**, a year older than Wright, died in 1968, Wright wrote the introduction to his posthumous collection *Poetry for My People* (1970; retitled *Play Ebony, Play Ivory: Poetry*, 1974). Unlike these writers, Wright has embraced both African-American cultural traditions and European-American ones in his writing, in what has been called the "poetics of a cross-cultural imagination." By 1973, he had spent years living in Mexico and in Scotland, and his poems traverse Africa, Asia, the Caribbean, South America, Western Europe, and North America. Even his North American locales range from New Hampshire (where he has lived since 1973) to California, to Mexico. Though his philosophical, cross-cultural, abstract, allusive poems may make his work more difficult for popular audiences, they have been highly praised by literary critics. For instance, esteemed literary critic Harold Bloom said, "Jay Wright is one of the five or six living American poets whose work will survive" (//www.amazon.com).

In addition to having individual poems published in periodicals (e.g., **Callaloo**, *Nation*) and anthologies (e.g., Arnold Adoff's *The Poetry of Black America*, 1972), Wright has produced a chapbook, *Death as History* (1967), and numerous poetry collections, including *The Homecoming Singer* (1971), *Soothsayers and Omens* (1976), *Dimensions of History* (1976), *Elaine's Book* (1986), *Explications/Interpretations* (1984), *Selected Poems of Jay Wright* (1987, edited by Robert B. Stepto), and *Boleros* (1991); these poems were then collected in *Transfigurations: Collected Poems* (2000), which also included some additional new poems. His more recent collections include *The Guide Signs: Book One and Book Two* (2007), which "exhibits a free-flowing, semi-improvisational energy focused and intensified by carefully constructed lines and stanzas . . . impeccable musicality and craftsmanship"; *Music's Mask and Measure* (2007), a "terse series of short free verse stanzas, split into five shorter sequences called equations"; and *Polynomials and Pollen: Parables, Proverbs, Paradigms, and Praise for Lois* (2008), described as having "poems beautifully balanced and feathered with slant rhymes" (*Booklist,* quoted in //www.amazon.com). In addition to his collections, Wright wrote his book-length poem *The Double Invention of Komo* (1980/1998), evoking the Komo initiation rites of the Bambara people of Africa, and his book-length poem *The Presentable Art of Reading Absence* (2008), following a "meditating pilgrim" through the natural and cultural transatlantic world.

Wright has also written more than 30 plays, 12 of which have been published (e.g., *Balloons: A Comedy in One Act,* 1968), and he won a Hodder fellowship in playwriting at Princeton University (1970-1971). In addition, Wright has been recognized as a musician, and his *GAS—Living With Guitar Acquisition Syndrome* (2006) offers a "hilarious, tongue-in-cheek book . . . [with] insights, tips, confessions, and stories from over 200 'afflicted' enthusiasts from 23 countries. . . . All royalties from this book will be used to buy starter guitars and basses for deserving musician wannabes" (quoted in //www.amazon.com).

Wright has been awarded numerous fellowships, including two from the Guggenheim Foundation (1974, 1975), the John D. and Catherine T. MacArthur Foundation genius fellowship (1986-1991), and the prestigious Academy of American Poets's poetry fellowship (1996), as well as grants from the Ingram Merrill Foundation and the National Endowment for the Arts. He has also been honored with the lucrative Lannan Literary Award for Poetry (2000) and the Before Columbus Foundation's American Book Award Lifetime Achievement Award (2006), as well as a literary award from the American Academy and Institute of Arts and Letters and an annual poetry award originally sponsored by husband and wife poets Oscar Williams and Gene Derwood. In 2005, Wright became the first African American to receive the biennial Bollingen Prize for Lifetime Achievement in Poetry from the Beinecke Library at Yale.

REFERENCES: *BAWPP. CAO-05. W. Wiki.* Christensen, Paul, *CP-6.* Kutzinski, Vera M., in *COCAAL* and *OCAAL.* Richard, Phillip M., in *AAP-55-85.* Shepherd, Reginald, in *GEAAL.* Welburn, Ron. "Jay Wright's Poetics: An Appreciation. *MELUS. 18.3* (Fall 1993) p. 51. From *Literature Resource Center.* //en.wikipedia.org/wiki/Lannan_Literary_Award. //en.wikipedia.org/wiki/Oscar_Williams. //www.poets.org/poet.php/prmPID/365. Amazon.com.

Wright, Richard (Nathaniel)
9/4/1908–11/28/1960
Autobiography/memoir, novels, short stories, essays, nonfiction, travelogues, poems

Richard Wright was born on a sharecropper's farm (formerly a plantation) in Roxie, Mississippi, where Richard was immersed in the hateful hostility of the local white folks. His area of Mississippi, near Natchez, has been called one of the most racist regions in the most racist state in the land. Richard's grandparents had been slaves, and his alcoholic father fared little better as a sharecropper. When Richard was three or four years old, his father moved the family to Memphis, Tennessee, where he abandoned Richard and Richard's mother and younger brother (Leon Alan) two years later, running off with another woman.

Richard's mother, Ella Wilson Wright, had been a schoolteacher, but in Memphis, with two young sons to support, she had to get work right away in a series of low-pay, unskilled jobs. In a desperate attempt to eke out enough of a living to support her children, Ella moved them from town to town and from state to state, everywhere finding it impossible to keep her children from their perennial companion, hunger. On flipping through his autobiography *Black Boy,* the word *hunger* appears frequently, and he had originally called his full autobiography *American Hunger.* Ella also suffered from health problems, including a stroke that partially paralyzed her, and at one point, Richard and his brother were briefly placed in an orphanage.

When Ella recovered, she retrieved them, taking them first to Jackson, Mississippi, and then to Elaine, Arkansas. In Elaine, they stayed with Ella's sister and her husband, a successful property owner. Richard adored his uncle, and the Wright family enjoyed an all-too-brief period of respite from desperate poverty and deprivation. All too soon, his uncle was lynched and murdered by whites who seized his property. Terrified, Ella, her sister, and the boys left town and returned to drifting from place to place, with Ella's ill health increasingly limiting her ability to provide for the boys. After a while, young Leon was sent to live with relatives in the North, and Richard was sent back down to Mississippi, to be passed around among his maternal grandparents and other relatives in Jackson and other places in the deep South. Between his mother's moves and the moves among relatives, Richard figured he had moved about 20 times.

After a year of being passed around, Richard settled into the household dominated by his tyrannical grandmother, a fanatical Seventh-Day Adventist. She and he were at odds from the start, and she was soon openly—and lastingly—hostile toward him. Prior to the move to his grandmother's home, Richard's formal schooling had

Richard Wright

been a string of segregated—separate and definitely un-equal—schools. His constant hunger, frequent illnesses, sporadic attendance, frequent moves, and other distractions from concentrating on his schoolwork made it unlikely that Richard would profit much from his formal education, although he enjoyed writing from an early age. While in ninth grade, his "The Voodoo of Hell's Half-Acre" was published in the local black-owned Jackson, Mississippi *Southern Register*.

Following his completion of the ninth grade, Richard's formal education ended. His informal education suffered for these reasons, too. Also, when he was living with his grandmother and at last had a fairly consistent place to call home, her zealously held religious beliefs opposed nonreligious books of any kind—especially novels—and she barred them from her home. Fascinated with literature, Richard surreptitiously pored over whatever cheap fiction he could put his hands on, but he had to carefully guard it from discovery by his grandmother and his aunt.

Anyone who saw Richard in 1925, with this inauspicious beginning—desperate poverty, inadequate nutrition, poor health, a highly dysfunctional family life, utter lack of a decent education, oppressive racism including racial prejudice, hostility, and segregation—would surely have concluded that the chances of his being an acclaimed writer, gifted in his command of the language and of literature, were between zero and none. Richard himself concluded that if he were to have a chance of having

a decent life of any kind, he would have to escape the racism of the deep South and the anything-but-warm bosom of his family. To be sure, Richard's childhood gave him a bleak outlook that continued throughout his life, but the surprising observation is that he felt any hope at all for his own future based on his early experiences. In 1925, he left his family and Mississippi behind and proceeded North to Memphis, Tennessee, desperately hoping that life could hold some possibility for anything but hatred, hunger, and hopelessness.

In Memphis, Richard roomed with a warm, loving family and found work as an errand boy for an optical company. There, his hunger for literature was again whetted, and he voraciously devoured whatever literature he could put his hands on, starting with national magazines such as *Atlantic Monthly*, *Harper's*, and *American Mercury*. He was particularly interested in the writing by the editor of *American Mercury* magazine, H. L. Mencken. When he heard that Mencken had written books, he was interested in reading more. He couldn't afford to buy books on his errand-boy salary, and even if he could, a black person seen buying books would immediately become suspect and would call unwanted attention to himself. Lynchings were still quite common in the South at that time, and unwanted attention was *definitely* unwanted.

The library in Memphis was for whites only, so he knew that he would have to find a white person to help him get access to the library's books. His boss at the optical company was a Northerner, and he treated Richard well enough, so Richard asked him if he could use his library card to check out some books. Although his boss was at first reluctant, he later agreed to give him his library card, saying he could use his wife's library card for checking out books of his own.

Even with the library card of a white man in hand, Richard knew he couldn't just walk in, present the card, and ask for books. He'd need to convince the librarian that he was obtaining books for the white man to read. He forged a note to the librarian, saying, "Dear Madam: Will you please let this nigger boy have some books by H. L. Mencken?" The ploy worked. The librarian never suspected that a note referring to "this nigger boy" would have been forged by the young man presenting the note. She was a little annoyed that the requestor didn't specify which book by Mencken he wanted, but she still complied with the request. Richard was careful not to glance at the book until he got home.

In his autobiography *Black Boy*, Wright described his experience of reading Mencken's book in this way: "I opened [Mencken's] *A Book of Prefaces* and began to read. I was jarred and shocked by the style, the clear, clean, sweeping sentences. Why did he write like that? And how did one write like that? I stood up, trying to realize what reality lay behind the meaning of the words. Yes, this man was fighting, fighting with words. He was using words as a weapon, using them as one would use a club. Could words be weapons? Well, yes, for here they were. Then, maybe, perhaps, I would use them as a weapon?"

After that, Richard read other books by Mencken, as well as books by Sherwood Anderson, Fyodor Dostoyevsky, Theodore Dreiser, Alexandre Dumas (a French writer of African descent), Frank Harris, O. Henry, Sinclair Lewis, and Edgar Lee Masters, among others. After two years of Richard's self-education in Memphis, he moved North to Chicago (in 1927), where he continued his self-study, reading more modern, experimental authors such as Henry James, Marcel Proust, and Gertrude Stein. Wright later reflected that in Stein's *Three Lives,* her character Melanctha was among the few African-American characters portrayed by a white author, who was believably realistic. Wright later said of this awakened passion, "I had once tried to write, had once reveled in feeling, had let my crude imagination roam, but the impulse to dream had been slowly beaten out of me by experience. Now it surged up again and I hungered for books, new ways of looking and seeing."

In Chicago, Wright was joined by masses of other African Americans fleeing the harshness and hopelessness of the Jim Crow South. Once there, he worked in a series of menial jobs, when he heard that jobs at the post office paid quite well, particularly for someone with as little formal education as Wright. Wright took the competitive civil-service exam and scored high on it. The federal government was barred from considering race in hiring decisions, so Wright was hired as a postal clerk. At the post office, Wright worked alongside blacks and whites as coequals. This was the first time in his life when he had interacted with whites on an equal footing. Many of his coworkers were left-wing intellectuals, and one of his white coworkers was Abraham Aaron, who invited him to find out about communism at a Chicago-area John Reed Club, a fellowship of writers with left-wing views.

As Wright attended meetings of the (mostly white) John Reed Club, he felt increasingly drawn to communism, as did many workers, writers, and other intellectuals during this time. As the Great Depression pervaded the landscape, many observers felt that capitalism was disproportionately impoverishing and oppressing workers, at the bottom of the economic scale, compared with capitalist owners of companies, at the top of the economic scale. Communists asserted the absolute right of all races to be given equal rights and equal opportunities and was dedicated to changing the political and economic system so that the kind of desperate poverty Wright had known as a youth would be eliminated.

By 1933, Wright had joined the Communist Party, despite his numerous disagreements with the Party regarding Marxist doctrine, especially concerning the relationship of African Americans to the American political, economic, and social system. Other than his first two published short stories ("Voodoo . . . ," published in the Jackson newspaper, and "Superstition," published in **Robert Abbott**'s *Monthly Magazine,* 1931), most of his early short stories, essays, and poems were printed in various communist-affiliated or at least leftist periodicals (newspapers and journals). Wright continued to be associated with the Communist Party and leftist causes until 1944, but when the John Reed Club disbanded (in 1935), Wright turned his attention to writing longer fiction works, rather than the short, principally nonfiction pieces he had written earlier. In 1937, Wright's focus on literature, rather than rigidly ideological polemics, led to strong disagreements with the party; in 1942, he officially resigned from the Communist Party, chiefly over artistic freedom, but also because the party failed to speak out against racial discrimination in the military during World War II, as well as other issues of civil rights for African Americans. In 1944, his break with the party became public when "I Tried to Be a Communist," an excerpt from his *American Hunger,* was published in the *Atlantic Monthly.* He later elaborated his rationale in an essay included in Richard Crossman's symposium anthology of essays by former communists, *The God That Failed* (1950).

In 1934, Wright got a job with the Illinois Federal Writers' Project (FWP) of the Works Progress Administration (WPA). This was the first job at which Wright was paid to write full-time—writing travel guides and doing historical research for the FWP. In 1936, Wright also became involved in the Chicago-area Negro Federal Theatre, working as its press agent and literary adviser, as well as being involved in various dramatic productions at the Theatre. During this time, he also joined Chicago's new South Side Writers' Group, where he met **Arna Bontemps**, a fellow writer and FWP employee, as well as a former postal employee and a Seventh Day Adventist, though Wright was definitely not a practicing Adventist after his youth. Other Chicagoans he met included **Frank Marshall Davis**, **Fenton Johnson**, and **Theodore Ward**, as well as sociologist **Horace Cayton**, with whom he later became a close friend, and **Margaret Walker**, with whom he was a close friend while he was in Chicago and remained friends for a short time afterward. Walker later wrote *Richard Wright, Daemonic Genius: A Portrait of the Man, A Critical Look at His Work* (1988), including details of their relationship.

In May of 1937, Wright moved to Harlem, where he initially continued to work for the FWP while contributing articles and poems to such leftist magazines as the *Partisan Review, Left Front, New Masses,* and *International Literature,* as well as the *Communist Daily Worker,* of which he became the Harlem editor and chief correspondent. By the time he reached New York, he had also written at least two of the four novellas in his collection *Uncle Tom's*

Children and most of his manuscript for *Lawd Today,* the first novel he wrote (which wasn't published until after his death).

One of his earliest pieces in New York, however, was "Blueprint for Negro Writing," Wright's outline of what African-American literature should be—as distinct from what it had been. In Wright's view, the black writers of the **Harlem Renaissance** and earlier eras had kowtowed to wealthy white patrons and bourgeois blacks. He urged fellow writers to turn away from European-American-centered writing and to embrace both Marxism and African-American-centered writing, targeted to working-class African-American readers. "Blueprint" was printed in the first (and only) issue of *New Challenge* magazine, which he coedited with **Dorothy West** and Marian Minus.

The first of Wright's book-length projects to appear in print was his collection *Uncle Tom's Children: Four Novellas* (1938). Each of the novellas shows how the racial hatred of the Jim Crow South affected various African-American males and how they attempted to resist or escape those effects. Although the book sold well and was critically acclaimed, Wright had hoped his readers would come away with a greater awareness of how racism harms all Americans, not just its direct victims. The stories distinctively blend African-American literary traditions with then-contemporary Marxist thinking, as well as Wright's personal take on his deplorably miserable experiences in the deep South. He also never hesitated to twist the plot, as needed, to convey his political and race-related statements. Wright's opinion of the work differed from those of his critics: He called the stories too sentimental.

The original 1938 edition comprised these four novellas: "Big Boy Leaves Home" (a *Story* magazine prize winner when it was first published in 1936), "Fire and Cloud" (second-prize winner of an O. Henry award and first-prize winner of a 1938 *Story* magazine award), "Down by the Riverside" (written while Wright was still living in Chicago), and "Long Black Song." Although "Long Black Song" is purportedly written from the point of view of a woman (a rare stance in Wright's work), the protagonist's experiences are still described in terms of their effects on men. For instance, when she is raped, it is described as an affront to her husband's pride and masculinity, rather than as a violation of her body, her dignity, and her sense of humanity. One critic pointed out that the protagonists resist racism in three different ways: through individual escape ("Big Boy"), through protecting the family ("Down by the Riverside" and "Long Black Song"), and through banding together with others to take collective action ("Fire and Cloud"). Three of the four stories end with tragic deaths (e.g., at the hands of lynch mobs, appallingly common in those times).

Wright's collection was awarded the 1938 *Story* magazine prize for the best book written by anyone involved in the WPA's FWP. It also won Wright a 1939 Guggenheim fellowship with enough money ($2,500) to stop writing for the *Daily Worker,* to quit his New York FWP job, and to focus on writing a novel full time. About this time, Wright married Rose Meadman, a Russian-Jewish dance teacher; the couple separated in 1940 and divorced soon after. The following March (1941), Wright married Ellen Poplar, the Polish-Jewish head of his cell in the Communist Party in New York. Later on, Ellen and Richard had two daughters: Julia (b. 4/14/1942) and Rachel (b. 1/17/1949).

In 1940, a second edition of the volume was expanded to include an introductory semiautobiographical essay, "The Ethics of Living Jim Crow," and a fifth story, "Bright and Morning Star," and the subtitle was changed to "Five Long Stories" (instead of "Four Novellas"). Many critics observed that these additions not only added little, but even disrupted the integrity of the original work. Wright reworked much of "The Ethics of Living Jim Crow" to form the central core of his 1945 autobiography, *Black Boy.* A 1993 reissue paperback includes all the works from the 1940 edition, as well as passages that were deleted by the publishers in the original and earlier expanded editions.

The novel Wright finished writing while living on his Guggenheim fellowship money was *Native Son,* published in 1940, the same year as his expanded version of *Uncle Tom's Children.* The novel was inspired by the actual case of Robert Nixon of Chicago. Because Wright was living in Brooklyn while writing the book, he asked his old pal Margaret Walker to send him newspaper clippings about the case from Chicago, which she did. Around the time he finished writing the book, however, he abruptly ended their friendship.

The story revolves around Bigger Thomas, an African American from the South (Mississippi) who has moved to the urban North (Chicago) in the hope of finding greater opportunities for himself. He finds work as a chauffeur for a wealthy white family, in which the mother is blind and the daughter is involved with a young communist white man. The daughter and her boyfriend attempt to befriend Bigger and to treat him as an equal, but their behavior only confuses Bigger, as he doesn't know how to respond to their overtures. On one occasion, he drives the young woman home after she has had too much to drink, so he helps her to her bed. While he is beside her bed, her mother comes to the bedroom door, calling to her daughter, to see whether her daughter is home yet. Fearing the consequences of being in a drunk white girl's room, he puts a pillow over her head to keep her quiet until her mother leaves. Unfortunately, the girl suffocates to death before her mother has gone.

Up until this time, Bigger has not intentionally done anything wrong, but again fearing what will happen to him if he is found out, he burns the girl's body in the family's furnace. He then flees and meets up with his girlfriend, to whom he tells all. As his girlfriend sleeps, he suddenly realizes that she, too, is now a threat to him, and he intentionally kills her. When his link to the deaths is discovered, the white girl's boyfriend gets a Communist Party attorney to defend him (partly to use him as a cause célèbre for the Party), but Bigger's conviction and death sentence are inevitable. Wright's story shows how the environment in which a person lives almost fatalistically determines what the person will do and what will befall the person.

Wright purposely wrote Bigger's character to be unsympathetic, so that the intensity of his story would be, as he said, "so hard and deep that [readers] would have to face it without the consolation of tears." Indeed, Bigger's character inspires anger and fear, not sympathy. (Wright had titled the first of three parts of the book "Fear.") Even so, Wright's editors had toned down his original manuscript, and it wasn't until 1992 that the restored original text that Wright intended was published. Jack Miles, a *Los Angeles Times* reviewer (December, 1997, quoted in //www.amazon.com), noted that "This new edition gives us a *Native Son* in which the key line in the key scene is restored, to the great good fortune of American letters. The scene as we now have it is central both to an ongoing conversation among African-American writers and critics and to the consciousness among all American readers of what it means to live in a multi-racial society in which power splits along racial lines." In 1940, however, Wright's toned-down text stirred a maelstrom of heated response.

Native Son also gained critical acclaim and commercial success right away, nearly a first for an African-American writer at that time. To this day, literary scholars and critics credit it as a landmark in African-American literature, not just for its success, but also for its heralding of a new era of protest novels, which were to come into vogue following World War II. Within three weeks of its publication, 200,000 copies had been sold, breaking a 20-year sales record for its mainstream publisher, Harper & Brothers. It even outsold John Steinbeck's Pulitzer Prize-winning *Grapes of Wrath,* which appeared at about the same time. It was also a Book-of-the-Month Club selection—probably the surest sign of commercial success at the time, much like being chosen for **Oprah**'s Book Club now—the first such selection of a book by an African-American author, and it was reviewed in every major periodical in the country.

Most literary reviewers enthusiastically raved about the work, whether they were American or foreign, black or white, communist or not. Critics particularly remarked on Wright's skill in forcing white American readers to see their own part in Bigger's crime, despite depicting Bigger unsympathetically. Nonetheless, many African Americans criticized Wright for depicting yet another African-American victim and for portraying him as little more than a stereotype; they criticized the unsympathetic characterization with which Wright was so pleased, and of which many of his critics were so appreciative. Naturally, conservative whites refuted Wright's theme that Bigger's environment created who he was; in their view, he was just a bad man, doing bad things—no excuses!

Wright was invited to travel all over the country, giving lectures, talks, and readings, and the book thrust Wright not only to national prominence but also to international celebrity; it was translated into at least six languages and quickly sold more than 300,000 copies worldwide. The money from the sales of *Native Son* enabled Wright to buy his mother a house in Chicago, as well as to purchase a lot of freedom from want for himself. Among other honors, it earned Wright a prestigious **Spingarn** Medal from the NAACP. Perhaps one of the greatest honors in American response to novels is to adapt them to stage and to film. Wright and a collaborator (at first, Paul Green, and then John Houseman) adapted the novel to a play (*Native Son: The Biography of a Young American: A Play in Eleven Scenes to Be Performed without Intermission*), which Orson Welles dramatized on Broadway; the play's Broadway run was followed by a national tour. A decade later, Wright participated in making the play into a film (*Sangre Negra*), produced in Argentina, with Wright playing the part of Bigger. Critics noted that he didn't miss his calling by returning to writing instead of sticking to acting.

Wright's next project was *12 Million Black Voices: A Folk History of the American Negro* (1941), a pictorial (photographic) history of Africa's descendants in America. Most of the photographs were culled from the federal government's Farm Security Administration files. Wright's underlying Marxist sentiments were evident throughout the text. In it, he analyzed how the Great Migration from the rural South to the urban North affected African Americans in both locations. In his view, lack of property ownership oppressed African Americans both North and South. The Southern blacks who were left behind were doomed to sharecropping and tenant farming, unable to reap the rich rewards of their own labor or of the crops they sowed. The Northern blacks were doomed to perpetually paying rent to live in kitchenette apartments they would never own and to working in lightless, airless factories, with their labor enriching the owners of the factories, but doing little to lift them out of poverty. The U.S. government didn't take kindly to Wright's commentary, believing it to be subversive and perhaps even seditious. In 1943, they started keeping a file on Wright's writings and activities. In 1988, a paperback edition of the book was reissued by Thunder's Mouth Press.

Although Wright continued to write shorter works (e.g., his 1944 surrealistic novella *The Man Who Lived Underground*), his next major work was his powerful autobiography *Black Boy: A Record of Childhood and Youth* (1945). In it, Wright candidly and compellingly tells readers how he experienced life as a boy in the Jim Crow South, bereft of the basic sustenance of plentiful and nourishing food, a consistent place to call home, a dependable and loving family. Avoiding sentimentality, he shows his readers exactly how his hellish upbringing affected him. He never tries to evoke sympathy, yet readers cannot help but wish to shield young Richard from the harsh brutalities of his early environment.

The book, another Book-of-the-Month Club selection, outsold even *Native Son*, having sold more than 400,000 copies within months of its publication. It was also translated into six languages and was critically acclaimed, both at the time and by literary scholars ever since. Many don't hesitate to call it Wright's finest work. Originally, Wright had written a more comprehensive autobiography, which he had titled *American Hunger.* His publishers cut out the second section, on his adulthood, and this section was never published during Wright's lifetime, although it was published as a separate volume in 1977.

More recently, the prestigious Library of America reunited the two as the originally intended single work, which also restores much of Wright's original text (again, edited out by his publisher at the time). The Library of America volume, *Richard Wright, Later Works: Black Boy (American Hunger) / The Outsider / 2 Books in 1* (1991, edited by **Arnold Rampersad**), also includes a novel Wright wrote years later. Another volume published by Library of America is *Richard Wright, Early Works: Lawd Today! / Uncle Tom's Children / Native Son* (1991, edited by Arnold Rampersad). In reviewing these volumes, Alfred Kazin, of *The New York Times Book Review* (quoted in //www.amazon.com) said, "Superb . . . The Library of America has insured that most of Wright's major texts are now available as he wanted them to be read. . . . Most important of all is the opportunity we now have to hear a great American writer speak with his own voice about matters that still resonate at the center of our lives." Andrew Delbanco, in *New Republic* (also quoted in //www.amazon.com), observed, "The publication of this new edition is not just an editorial innovation, it is a major event in American literary history." A paperback edition of the complete autobiography was published by Perennial Classics in 1998.

During this time, Wright also wrote a novella for juveniles: *Rite of Passage*, which wasn't published until 1993 (with an afterword by Rampersad). In it, 15-year-old Johnny Gibbs takes home his usual straight-A report, when he is greeted with shocking news: The people whom he believed to be his parents (since he was six months old) are actually his foster parents, and a heartless bureaucrat has decided that it's time for him to be switched to a new family. Confused, hurt, betrayed, he flees into the cold, damp night, feeling utterly alone, orphaned, lost, homeless, and hungry for the first time in his life. Soon, he hooks up with a brutal street gang, and after winning a challenge to the gang's leader (rather improbable, but it *is* fiction), he participates in a mugging and then becomes embroiled in a theft scheme with corrupt police officers who pay the gang members to steal.

Despite Wright's literary successes, he was not immune to racial prejudice. As an example, after traveling in Mexico (in 1940), fellow writer John Steinbeck was seeing him off at a train station in Mexico. Steinbeck urged Wright to ship, rather than carry in his bags, some communist literature he had. Steinbeck warned Wright that he would have trouble getting the materials through American customs at the Texas border. Indeed, the customs official in Texas started to focus on the books, when he noticed Wright's typewriter, as well. The official was so shocked to see an African American who identified himself as a writer that he neglected to pursue his interest in the books.

Far more insulting and distressing incidents occurred every hour of every day, everywhere in America, and in 1946, Wright happily accepted an invitation from the French government to be limelighted as a literary luminary. Actually, noted existentialist Jean-Paul Sartre had invited him originally, but when the U.S. government refused to give him a passport, Gertrude Stein, Claude Levi-Strauss, and Dorothy Norman helped him get an official invitation, which smoothed the passport process. The contrast between his gracious reception in France and his hostile one at home in America was stark. Having abandoned all hope of eliminating—or even diminishing—racism in the United States, in August 1947, Wright and his family settled permanently in Paris.

In Paris, Wright became associated with existentialist writers such as Jean-Paul Sartre, Albert Camus, and Simone de Beauvoir, as well as fellow expatriates such as Gertrude Stein. Although their cultures and life experiences sharply differed, Wright shared their sense of alienation. His own outlook fit well with that of existentialism, a philosophy that highlighted each individual's isolation in an inhospitable and apathetic cosmos. To many literary scholars, the move to Paris may have given Wright his first opportunity to experience life without feeling the constant oppressive burden of racism every moment of every day, but it had deleterious effects on his writing. They suggest that it blunted the edge of his passionate opposition to racism, it deprived him of hearing the lyrical nuances and cadences of African-American speech, it dimmed his memories of his tortured childhood and youth, and it removed him from the changing political, economic, and social circumstances of African Americans (e.g., the emerging civil-rights movement).

Back in the United States, Wright was targeted by Senator McCarthy's red-baiting witch hunts, searching for "dirty commies" in every nook and cranny. Even though Wright had pointedly resigned from the Communist Party in the early 1940s, he was still subject to CIA and FBI surveillance, even in France. He frequently had to report to the U.S. embassy in Paris, to undergo lengthy interrogations about his activities and his writings. He had trouble getting a passport, and he was prevented from moving to England by both the U.S. and the British governments, even though his family had moved to London, in anticipation that he would soon follow. The U.S. State Department may even have interfered with the publication and sales of his books, although that has not been confirmed, and his U.S. sales would probably have waned in any case.

Though Wright's U.S. sales declined (and therefore his income), his literary output did not. He became involved with poets and novelists of the Négritude movement, including Leopold Senghor and Aime Cesaire, with whom he founded *Présence Africaine*. This association and his travels throughout Europe and Africa during the 1950s gave Wright a more enriched global perspective on how economic and racial oppression affect persons around the world. Communism had offered him a philosophical framework for taking a global view, but his international experiences and associations put flesh on this skeleton.

During his Parisian exile, Wright wrote seven more books: three more novels, a collection of lectures, a conference report, and two other works of nonfiction. His novels include *The Outsider* (1953; reprinted in 1993, with lengthy editorial cuts restored), *Savage Holiday* (1954; reprinted 1995), and *The Long Dream* (1958). His conference report was *The Color Curtain: A Report of the Bandung Conference* (1956; reprinted in 1995), about the 1955 Conference of Asian and African nations, held in Bandung, Indonesia; and his lecture collection was *White Man, Listen!* (1957), essays gathered from a European lecture series (1950-1956) on racial issues from a global perspective. His other two nonfiction works were *Black Power: A Record of Reactions in a Land of Pathos* (1954), about his observations of colonialism and independence movements in Africa, particularly the Gold Coast, and *Pagan Spain* (1957), a highly readable travelogue and political commentary on Spain.

Among the last Americans to see Wright was **Langston Hughes**, who visited Wright at Wright's home, just before Wright entered a clinic. At the time, Wright was just 52 years old, but he was again impoverished, in ill health (with amoebic dysentery), separated from his family, constantly harassed with interrogations by federal

agents, and estranged from many fellow expatriates and French existentialists for various reasons. Sadly, Wright's life was characterized by frequent instances of close associations terminated abruptly because of conflict or perceived betrayal, perhaps one of the consequences of his turbulent childhood and youth. Two days after Hughes's visit, Wright died, with the cause of death listed as heart attack. Wright's chief biographer, Michel Fabre, has said that all of these factors combined to lead to Wright's premature death.

Others have suggested more sinister causes due to foul play, noting that he died in a hospital almost immediately following an injection; he was cremated right away, thereby making autopsy impossible; the cremation was performed without familial consent, and in fact, his family wasn't informed of his death until after the cremation. Some have even posited that he was killed by the CIA or other federal agents. Fabre disagrees, saying that their frequent harassment may have contributed to Wright's stress and his early death, but Fabre doubts that they directly assaulted him. In any case, when Wright died, he had been working on several literary projects, including a short-story collection, some radio plays, a novella, and an autobiographical essay.

Following his death, several of his works have been published. In 1961, a collection of short stories he had written previously, *Eight Men*, was published (paperback reprint, 1996). Each of the stories in the collection presents a different slant on how black men struggle to survive in the racial hatred of white-dominated America.

In 1963, the novel he had written in the mid-1930s, *Lawd Today!* was published by Walker & Co. The novel humorously treats the events in the life of an angry, unhappy African-American postal worker in Chicago on one day: February 12, 1936. Wright had originally titled the manuscript "Cesspool." The 1963 version, like so many of Wright's works, was expurgated, and in 1993, the Northeastern Library of Black Literature published an unexpurgated paperback edition, two years after the Library of America published an uncut version in its *Early Works* volume (1991, hardcover).

In 1978, Wright's biographer (Michel Fabre) and Wright's widow (Ellen Wright) collaborated to edit *A Richard Wright Reader*. Not intended to be a comprehensive tome, it omits some of his works and includes only excerpts from some of his novels and other book-length works. It also includes some of his short stories, his journalistic pieces, his memoirs, his poems, and even some of his correspondence. In addition, Fabre introduced the works, offering an overview of Wright's contribution and setting his work in historical context.

Early in his career, Wright had written poetry, and during his final illness, the majority of his writing again turned to poems. About two years before he died, Wright was introduced to an English translation of Japanese haiku. Wright was captivated by the form and proceeded to write more than 4,000 haiku poems, strictly following the traditional three-line format (with five syllables in the first line, seven in the second, and five in the last line), with some implicit or explicit reference to the season within the body of the poem. Before he died, Wright had chosen more than 800 of his haikus for publication. It took nearly 40 years for them to reach print, but in 1998, a hardcover collection was published, *Haiku: This Other World* (edited by Yoshinobu Hakutani and Robert L. Tener). Two of the poems quoted in *Library Journal* (September 15, by Judy Clarence, quoted in //www.amazon.com) illustrate the gentle tenderness and even whimsy of Wright's final writings: "As my delegate / The spring wind has its fingers / In a young girl's hair." "For seven seconds / The steam from the train whistle / Blew out the spring moon."

The breadth and variety of Wright's literary contribution cannot be doubted, and his contributions to each genre was significant. Probably most important, however, were his contributions to contemporary African-American novels and autobiographies. His novel *Native Son* and his autobiography *Black Boy* are often required reading in high schools and colleges throughout the land, and his works have been translated into 50 or more languages. Further, **James Baldwin** (whom he had befriended while living in Harlem), **Ralph Ellison** (who had been the best man at Wright's first wedding, during his Chicago days), and numerous other important writers have credited Wright with blazing the trail for fellow African-American novelists to follow. He pulled no punches in assaulting white America for its treatment of black compatriots, yet he never sentimentalized the victims of racism, and he frankly depicted the consequences of racism in terms of black rage and violence. In looking over his literary career, Wright could definitely answer "yes," to the question he had asked himself in his youth, "Could words be weapons? . . . Then, maybe, perhaps, I would use them as a weapon?" Occasionally using them as a sledgehammer and at other times as a razor, he definitely mastered the ability to use words to disarm his readers and render them defenseless against his attacks on their beliefs about racism and their misconceptions about how many young black boys (and men) have been treated in white America.

REFERENCES: *AAL. AT. BAL-1-P. BAWPP. BC. BWA. EA-99. EB-BH-CD. EBLG. LFCC-07. MWEL. NAAL. NYTBC. OC20LE. PGAA. RG20. W. W2B. WDAA. Wiki.* "Native Son, (1940)" in *1TESK.* "Native Son," in *BF:2000.* Felgar, Robert. (1980). "Author's Works," "Chapter 1: An American Son's Life." *Richard Wright: Twayne's United States Authors* (Series 386). Boston: Twayne Publishers. From *The Twayne Authors Series.* Fisher, Vivian Njeri, in *BH2C.* Gayle, Addison, in *G-99.* Gibson, Donald B., in *COCAAL* and *OCAAL.* Hakutani, Yoshinobu, in *ASSW-1910-1945-2.* McKay, Nellie Y., in *WB-99.* Miller, Leah, in //www.coe.ohio-state.edu/ beverlygordon/834/miller.html. Rampersad, Arnold, in *USHC.* Rampson, Nancy, in *AA:PoP.* //library.msstate.edu/special_interest/ Mississippi_African-American_Authors.asp. //www.amazon.com, 8/1999, 5/2009.

FURTHER READING: *B. BCE. CAO-02. CE. CLCS-08.* Bone, Robert, in *AW:ACLB-74-4.* Clark, Edward D., in *AAW-40-55.* Cohassey, John, in *BB.* Davis, Lawrence A., in *GEAAL.*

Wright, Sarah E. (Elizabeth)
12/9/1928–
Novels, short stories, poems, nonfiction, essays, biography; educator, poetry therapist

In Wetipquin, Maryland, Sarah was born to Willis Charles and Mary Amelia Moore Wright. By the time she was in third grade, she was already starting to write, and her parents and teachers encouraged her to keep it up. At Howard University, she received further encouragement from renowned poet and literary critic **Sterling Brown** and then from poet and novelist **Owen Dodson**. During her years at Howard (1945-1949), she also became active in various literary and journalistic organizations, and she was inspired by the writing of **Langston Hughes**, who became her lifelong friend.

After graduating from Howard, Wright first moved to New York City and then to Philadelphia, where she worked as a teacher and then in a publishing house. There, she also cofounded the Philadelphia Writers' Workshop, dedicated to promoting the work of African-American writers. In 1955, she and Lucy Smith coauthored their poetry collection *Give Me a Child* (1955), to which Wright contributed 7 of 17 poems about African Americans struggling to survive despite racist oppression. One such poem was her oft-anthologized "To Some Millions Who Survive Joseph Mander, Sr." Since its publication, she contributed numerous short stories and essays to such publications as *Freedomways, American Pen,* the *Amsterdam News* (New York), the **Black Scholar**, and the **African American Review**, as well as various anthologies.

In 1957, Wright returned to New York, where she was drawn to the Harlem Writers' Guild (HWG). There, she associated with authors such as **Alice Childress, John Henrik Clarke, John Oliver Killens,** and **Paule Marshall,** who were quickly becoming well known, as well as such up-and-coming authors as **Maya Angelou, Ossie Davis, Lonnie Elder III, Rosa Guy, Audre Lorde, Julian Mayfield,** and **Douglas Turner Ward**. Wright remained actively involved in the Guild until 1972, when she started turning her attention to teaching workshops showing others how to write. Around that time, Wright also joined Guy and Angelou and dramatist Aminata Moseka (Abby Lincoln) in forming the Cultural Association for Women of African Heritage, dedicated to promoting racial pride and self-esteem.

Other organizations in which she has been involved include PEN, the Authors Guild, the International Women's Writing Guild, and Pen & Brush, Inc. (president, 1992-1993), said to be the oldest U.S. professional organization for women. She also helped organize the First (1959) and the Second National Conference of Black Writers, as well as the Congress of American Writers (1971). In addition to these organizations and her workshops, she is certified as a poetry therapist and has presented readings, lectures, and television and radio talk shows at high schools, libraries, community centers, and various other locations.

Wright's main literary contribution is her novel *This Child's Gonna Live* (1969; 2002, republished for Contemporary Classics by Women), about an impoverished African-American mother, her husband (Jacob), and their children, who are desperately struggling to survive in Tangierneck, a rural Maryland fishing town. The mother, Mariah Upshur, physically and verbally abuses her children, particularly her son Rabbit, who eventually dies, perhaps in part because of willful maternal neglect. Previously, her infant daughter had died due to an infection caused by an unsanitary bandage. Mariah constantly calls on Jesus and on God to help her, but apparently to no avail. She nonetheless remains hopeful that she can get herself and her children out of "the Neck" (Tangierneck), and when she finds herself pregnant again, she continu-

ally asserts her determination that this unborn child's gonna live. When the novel was first published, *The New York Times* named it one of the most important books of the year, and the *Baltimore Sun* gave it the year's Readability Award. The Feminist Press reissued it in 1986, with an essay by HWG founder **John Oliver Killens**; in 1994, the press issued a silver anniversary edition, and the press and Pen & Brush, Inc., celebrated its 25 years of continuous sales. In the mid-1990s, Wright was reported to be working on a sequel to *This Child*, tentatively titled, *Twelve Gates to the City, Halleluh, Halleluh!*

Wright also wrote an important nonfiction work, a biography of the activist, union organizer, and cofounder of the *Messenger* magazine, **Asa Philip Randolph**. The resulting *A. Philip Randolph: Integration in the Workplace* (1990) was included in a history series on the civil-rights movement. The New York Public Library chose it as one of the Best Books for Young Adults for that year (1990).

In addition to awards for her individual works, she has been given two MacDowell Colony fellowships for creative writing, the CAPS Award for Fiction (1975), the Howard University Novelist-Poet Award (1976), and the Zora Neale Hurston Award.

REFERENCES: *BAWPP. CAO-02. EBLG. TAWH.* Campbell, Jennifer, in *GEAAL.* Ferguson, Sally Ann H., in *OCWW.* Guilford, Virginia B., in *AAFW-55-84.* Houston, Helen R., in *COCAAL* and *OCAAL.* //www.amazon.com, 9/1999, 5/2009.

FURTHER READING: *EAAWW.*

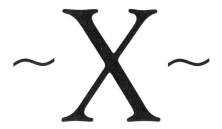

X, Malcolm (né Malcolm Little; Islamic name: El-Hajj Malik El-Shabazz)
5/19/1925–2/21/1965
Autobiography, speeches; newspaper founder, orator

Itinerant Baptist minister Earl Little, a fierce follower of Marcus Garvey, was constantly moving from church to church, moving his wife and eight children from town to town across the Midwest and the Northeast. After Ku Klux Klan members burned down one of their homes, the friction between Earl and his wife, Louise, intensified, and he beat her more frequently and severely. Earl's seventh son, Malcolm, was six years old when irate Ku Klux Klaners finally murdered Reverend Earl. Louise was ill equipped to handle the financial, emotional, and physical burden of caring for her children. After doing her best to hold things together, in 1937, she ended up in a mental institution, her family fell apart, and Malcolm and his siblings were dispersed to various foster homes.

Academically, Malcolm showed great promise and was popular in his almost-all-white classroom, where he was elected class president in the seventh grade. His optimistic outlook was squelched, however, when his teacher told him that his intelligence would in no way help him escape his certain destiny as a Negro: to become a laborer—at best, a skilled laborer. When he left school, he drifted through a series of jobs into a life as a drug dealer, burglar, and petty criminal. Following a few narrow escapes and some clever dodges, he was eventually busted for burglary.

At age 21, in 1946, convicted burglar Malcolm Little started serving 6 years of his 10-year prison sentence in the Charlestown State Prison in Massachusetts. In prison, he underwent a spiritual awakening and conversion to the Black Muslim faith, following the teachings of the Honorable Elijah Muhammad. Following his conversion, he became highly disciplined, educating himself in

the prison library and beginning a daily correspondence with the Nation of Islam's spiritual leader. To expand his vocabulary and his knowledge, he copied every page of the dictionary, and he read African-American history so prodigiously that he needed glasses by the time he left prison.

On being released from prison in 1952, he immediately went to Detroit, to work for the Black Muslims. He also rejected the surname given to his family by his ancestor's slave owner and adopted the surname "X," signifying his lost and unknown African family name. Malcolm's oratory skills were soon recognized, and in 1954, Elijah Muhammad moved him to Harlem's prominent Temple (Mosque) Seven, where he gained prominence as the primary spokesperson for the Black Muslims across the nation.

To audiences everywhere, Malcolm called for African Americans to work together, independently from European Americans, to form their own businesses, schools, and communities; to patronize businesses run by African Americans and avoid or even boycott businesses run by racists of other races; and to take pride in their own distinctive cultural heritage. He opposed the nonviolent struggle for civil rights as an ineffectual means of gaining equality and integration. Further, he held that the goals of racial equality and integration were unworthy goals in a racist nation. Though he never advocated violence as a form of aggression, he did say that African Americans should defend themselves and their communities "by any means necessary," including violent means. A powerful and charismatic orator, his speeches weren't published in book form until after his death. Since his death, many of his key speeches have been published, such as in the collections *Malcolm X Speaks: Selected Speeches and Statements* (1965) and *By Any Means Necessary: Speeches, Interviews, and a Letter* (1970), both edited by George Breitman; and *The Speeches of Malcolm X at Harvard* (1968), edited by Archie Epps.

In 1956, Sister Betty (a nursing student) joined Temple Seven. After a respectable and courtly courtship, he married Betty on January 14, 1958. Over the next seven years, they had four daughters: Attalah, Qubilah, Ilyasah, and Gamilah; Betty was also pregnant with their fifth and sixth daughters, Malaak and Malikah, when Malcolm was shot in February 1965.

Malcolm's oratory skills were matched by his leadership skills, and he directed the establishment of two academies of Islam, to provide a Black Muslim education to school-age children in Detroit and Chicago. He also founded many new mosques and recruited countless new members, lecturing around the nation on college campuses and anywhere else he could gather listeners. In 1961, he founded the official publication of the Nation of

Islam, *Muhammad Speaks.* He was soon considered second only to Elijah Muhammad in the Nation of Islam.

After a while, however, Muhammad started to envy his chief aide's fame. Often in the press and on television news, Malcolm's face and name were far more widely recognized than were Muhammad's. For his part, Malcolm was an extremely devoted follower until becoming aware of Muhammad's sexual promiscuity and excessive use of Muslim resources for his own material gain. Meanwhile, Muhammad's envy increased. Following the November 22, 1963, assassination of President John Kennedy, Malcolm remarked that this was a "case of chickens coming home to roost," meaning that the violence of powerful white men was being turned back against them. The nation—and the Nation—bristled at Malcolm's cavalier attitude. He was chastised by Muhammad and ordered to be silent for 90 days. Malcolm complied obediently, but his period of silence allowed him to reflect on his allegiance to a leader who so betrayed what he believed to be the core principles of Islam.

When Malcolm learned that Muhammad was also badmouthing him behind his back, he foresaw the next steps to come: He was suspended as a minister, then ostracized ("isolated"). Before he was expelled altogether, Malcolm split from the Nation of Islam and organized his own Muslim Mosque, Inc., in Harlem. He also decided to dedicate himself to traditional Islam, as it is practiced throughout the world. Traditional Islam rests on five pillars, or sacred obligations. Pillar 1: Profess aloud, "There is no god but God, and Muhammad is God's Prophet" in Arabic. Pillar 2: Pray five times each day: at dawn, noon, midafternoon, sunset, and night. Pillar 3: Give alms—at least 2.5% of personal wealth—to those in need. Pillar 4: Fast during the holy month Ramadan, to gain deeper empathy with those who suffer, to atone for past sins, and to express gratitude to God. Pillar 5: Each Muslim must make a pilgrimage (known as the *hajj*) to Mecca, the holy city of all followers of Islam, at some time during her or his lifetime, if the person is physically and financially able to do so. In April 1964, Malcolm made his first *hajj.*

His first *hajj* offered him a second spiritual awakening. By sharing the spiritual rituals of the *hajj* with fellow Muslims from Asia, Africa, Europe, and the Americas, he realized that whites were not by nature evil, but that racism was the evil he righteously hated. Instead of advocating racial division and separatism, he wished to promote international solidarity to overcome the evils of racism. He changed his name from Malcolm X to the Arabic name El-Hajj Malik El-Shabazz.

On his return to the United States, El-Shabazz formed the secular Organization of Afro-American Unity (OAAU), to promote African-American cultural pride through an internationalist framework of brotherhood, linking Africans, Asians, and Americans of all racial and cultural heritages. He was soon traveling throughout the Middle East, Africa, and Europe, giving speeches reflecting his new worldly attitude, urging others around the world to help African Americans in the fight against racism and oppression. He also spoke to the United Nations in New York, charging the United States with denying human rights to African Americans.

Once he embraced traditional Islam and renounced the Nation of Islam as inauthentic, the hostility between him and the Nation intensified. Threats of violence assaulted him and his family at an increasing rate. On February 21, 1965, when he was addressing an OAAU rally at the Audubon Ballroom in Harlem, he was assassinated. Three Black Muslims were later convicted of his murder. In a *60 Minutes* television interview, Nation of Islam leader Louis Farrakhan acknowledged that his vituperative denunciation of X to his followers may have led to the assassination. "I may have been complicit in words that I spoke. I acknowledge that and regret that any word that I have said caused the loss of life of a human being" (2000; quoted in *Wiki*). After his death, it became clear that Black Muslims' accusations that he hoarded huge caches of money while he worked for the Nation of Islam were false. In fact, he left his wife and six children almost destitute; he hadn't even bought life insurance to provide for them after his death. Just as he had always claimed, all of his earnings had gone to the Nation of Islam.

Months before Malcolm X broke with Elijah Muhammad, he had—with Elijah Muhammad's permission—begun working with Alex Haley to write his autobiography. Haley had interviewed Malcolm for a *Playboy* article, and he had found Malcolm reluctant to say much about himself, focusing instead on the worthiness of Elijah Muhammad, the Nation of Islam, and the black-nationalist outlook they proposed. In writing the autobiography, however, Malcolm still sought to promote the Nation of Islam, but he had no intention of producing a puff piece touting his own accomplishments.

In the autobiography, Malcolm was surprisingly frank, candidly revealing his own past crimes and misdeeds. Just as he was brutally honest in addressing America about its past and present atrocities, he was unhesitatingly open about his own unworthy actions, thoughts, and feelings. For instance, he frankly described his use of drugs, his mistreatment of women, his thefts and burglaries, and his neglect of his family. He even revealed the extent of his own limitations, such as when describing the first letter he wrote to Elijah Muhammad: "At least twenty-five times I must have written that first one-page letter to him, over and over. I was trying to make it both legible and understandable. I practically couldn't read my handwriting myself; it shames even to remember it. My spelling and my grammar were as bad, if not worse" (p. 11, *Autobiography*). Later on, he wrote that he regretted his lack

Malcolm X (right) with Martin Luther King, Jr.

of formal education more than he regretted any of the numerous mistakes he had made.

When establishing their relationship, Malcolm and Haley agreed that Haley would include everything that Malcolm had said, leaving nothing out, and that Haley would not add anything that Malcolm did not say. After Malcolm died, Haley did add a lengthy epilogue, but this was in keeping with their agreement, as Haley clearly distinguished it from the text that Malcolm had authored. Stylistically, the book retains much of the lively oratory flair of Malcolm's speaking voice. Haley's writing is transparent, so each reader can readily hear Malcolm's voice. We hear his passions, practical advice, and moral pronouncements; his changing political and religious philosophy; his impatience, frustration, and humor; his personal gibes and his feelings of hurt when duped or betrayed; and his loving appreciation of those who had shown him kindness and care.

Although the book clearly expresses Malcolm's political and religious philosophy, it does so through the narrative of his life experiences, without going into lengthy diatribes many might have suspected he would infuse into the work. When he underwent his radical transformation in 1964, Haley and he agreed not to revise the work to focus on attacking the Nation of Islam to which he had previously been so devoted. He did, however, inject a few comments into the earlier portion of the book, reflecting his later hindsight on the events that transpired.

Almost immediately after its posthumous publication, the book became a national best-seller, selling more than 6 million copies; an internationally acclaimed work, translated into eight or more languages; the object of extensive scholarly interest; required reading for various college courses; and even modern classic. In 1992, Spike Lee translated the story into a popular movie. As a literary work, it has been compared to slave narratives, with its authentic autobiographical commentary, and to *bil-*

dungsromans, in its revelation of Malcolm's personal development. Although he left his family without financial resources, he left the world much enriched by his words.

Many people regard the phrase "Black is beautiful," and the Black Power and the Black Arts movements to be the legacy of Malcolm X. Among the many namesakes honoring him are Malcolm X Community College in Chicago, Malcolm X Liberation University in Durham (North Carolina), as well as dozens of high schools and other public schools. Among the many streets named for him are New York City's Malcolm X Boulevard, formerly Lenox Avenue (renamed in the late 1980s). The Audubon Ballroom where he was assassinated now houses the Malcolm X and Dr. Betty Shabazz Memorial and Educational Center (starting in 2005).

REFERENCES: *1TESK. AA:PoP. B. BaD. BAL-1-P. BAWPP. BC. BCE. BF:2000. BWA. DA. E-98. EB-98. EBLG. G-95. MAAL. NAAAL. PGAA. W2B. Wiki.* Ferran, Christine, in *BB.* Scrimgeour, J. D., in *COCAAL* and *OCAAL.* X, Malcolm, with the assistance of Alex Haley. 1965. *The Autobiography of Malcolm X.* New York: Grove Press.

FURTHER READING: *AANB. CAO-03. CE. HD. LE. QB.* Gordon, Stephanie, in *GEAAL.* Jacoby, Tamar, *Commentary.* 95.2 (Feb. 1993) p. 27. From *Literature Resource Center.* "Malcolm X," and "Malcolm Little," in *CLCS-08.* Mervin, David, in *PD.* Stuckey, Sterling, in *USHC.*

X, Marvin (né Marvin Ellis Jackmon) (aka El Muhajir; aka Nazzam al Fitnah Muhajir; aka Marvin X Jackmon)
5/29/1944–

Poems, plays, essays, autobiography/memoir; theater founder/director, performer, educator, self-publisher

With fellow students Bobby Seale and Huey Newton, Marvin attended Merritt College (now Oakland City College), where got his A.A. degree in 1964, then he eventually earned his B.A. and his M.A. from San Francisco State College (now University) in 1975. A key participant in the Black Arts Movement, Marvin cofounded the Black Arts/West Theatre (with Ed Bullins, 1966), and cofounded the Black House political and cultural center (1967, with Bullins and Marvin's close friend Eldridge Cleaver). He has also worked as a producer, director, lecturer, editor, and spokesperson on behalf of the Nation of Islam. Marvin's produced plays include *Flowers for the Trashman* (1965, one act; musical adaptation *Take Care of Business,* 1971), *Come Next Summer* (1966), *The Black Bird* (1969, one-act parable), *The Trial* (1970), *Resurrection of the Dead* (1972), *Woman-Man's Best Friend* (1973, musical drama based on his same-titled poetry book), *In the Name of Love* (1981), *One Day in the Life* (2000), and *Sergeant Santa* (2002). One source says that his recovery-themed play *One Day in the Life* is the longest running African-American drama in Northern California.

By the late 1960s, X had become involved in the Nation of Islam, and he remains an advocate for Black Muslims today. Like others in the Nation, during the Vietnam War, X defied induction into the U.S. military, and he was arrested and convicted. Unlike Muhammad Ali and some other Black Muslims, however, while awaiting sentencing, he fled to Canada and then to Central America. There, he was arrested, then returned to the United States, where he was sentenced to a five-month federal prison term. Then-governor of California Ronald Reagan banned him from teaching at state universities in the 1960s, but he later lectured at the University of California, Berkeley (1972) and at Mills College (1973). He also founded and directed Your Black Educational Theatre (1971–1972).

In 1967, X founded his first publishing house, Al Kitab Sudan Publishing, which published volumes of his proverbs (*Black Dialectic,* 1967; *The Son of Man,* 1969), his parable *Black Bird* (1972), his collection *Woman-Man's Best Friend (Proverbs, Parables, Poems, Songs)* (1973), and his poetry. His self-published poetry volumes included *Sudan Rajuli Samia* (1967), *Fly to Allah: Poems* (1969), *Selected Poems* (1979), *Confession of a Wife Beater and Other Poems* (1981), and *Liberation Poems for North American Africans* (1982). Dudley Randall's Broadside Press published X's *Black Man Listen: Poems and Proverbs* (1969), which therefore received wider distribution and more public attention. X's writings were also published in numerous periodicals (e.g., *Black Scholar, Muhammad Speaks*), and he was the fiction editor for *Black Dialogue* (since 1965).

During the late 1980s and the 1990s, like his close friend Eldridge Cleaver, X became addicted to crack cocaine. After his recovery, he founded Recovery Theatre, which he also directs, and he has since worked to help other recovering addicts. In the late 1990s, he also became active in the movement to gain reparations for African Americans whose ancestors had endured slavery. He has since written his autobiography, *Somethin' Proper: The Life and Times of a North American African Poet* (1998); his psychological memoir, *In the Crazy House Called America* (2002); his poetry collections, *Love and War: Poems* (1995) and *Land of My Daughters: Poems 1995–2005* (2005); and his essay collections, *Wish I Could Tell You The Truth: Essays* (2005) and *Beyond Religion Toward Spirituality, Essays on Consciousness* (2007); all self-published by Black Bird Press, his second publishing house. The //www.nathanielturner.com/firstmuslim americanpoet3.htm website lists the following Black Bird Press "Works In Progress": *It Don't Matter: Essays* (2006), *You Don't Know Me and Other Poems* (2006), *In Sha Allah, A History of Black Muslims in the San Francisco Bay Area, 1954–2004* (2006), and *Seven Years in the House of Elijah, A Woman's Search for Love and Spirituality by Nisa Islam as told to Marvin X* (2006). A few of his more recent works are penned under the name Marvin Jackmon.

Marvin X's works may also be found in video and audio format, including *One Day in the Life* (videodrama and soundtrack, 2002), *The Kings and Queens of Black Consciousness* (video documentary of key leaders such as Amina and Amiri Baraka, Julia and Nathan Hare, Ishmael Reed, Kalamu Ya Salaam, Askia Touré, Cornel West, and others, 2002), and *Love and War* (poetry reading published on CD, 2001). In 2005, the Los Angeles Black Book Expo honored X with its Lifetime Achievement Award.

REFERENCES: *AANB. CAO-08. CBAPD.* Greene, Michael E., in *COCAAL* and *OCAAL.* "Muhajir, El; (né Marvin Jackmon)," *BAWPP.* Routledge, Chris, in *BB.* Thomas, Lorenzo. "El Muhajir." *AAW-55–85:DPW.* //aalbc.com/authors/marvinx.htm. //www.labbx. com/awards.htm. //www.nathanielturner.com/blackbirdfablepost blacknegro.htm. //www.nathanielturner.com/firstmuslimamerican poet3.htm. Amazon.com.

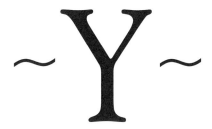

ya Salaam, Kalamu *See* Salaam, Kalamu ya

Yarbrough, Camille (aka Nana Camille Yarbrough; enthroned titles, Naa Kuokor Agyman I Queen Mother, Nana Tabuoa Tonko II)
?/1938–

Children's and young-adult books; dance, song, and theater performer, storyteller/griot, educator

Yarbrough started out as a stage and film actor (e.g., in productions of works by Lorraine Hansberry and by James Weldon Johnson; the sister of *Shaft* in the popular movie; some television soap opera parts), a dancer (e.g., touring with the Katherine Dunham Dance Company), and a singer, when she turned to writing her own songs and other poems. The celebrated Nina Simone performed some of Yarbrough's poetry and songs at New York's Philharmonic Hall (1972) and on tour. Yarbrough has developed her storytelling skills enough to consider herself a griot. She noted, "The artist should function in the tradition of the 'griot,' the African oral historian, preacher, teacher, social catalyst who uses song, rhyme, dance, and mime to illuminate and perpetuate, to revitalize and redirect the culture which he or she serves" (quoted in *BAWPP*). Her one-woman show *Tales and Tunes of an African American Griot* (toured nationally in the 1970s and 1980s) was recorded as *The Iron Pot Cooker* (1975; 2000, released on CD). British DJ Fatboy Slim sampled Yarbrough's "Take Yo' Praise" (from her *Iron Pot Cooker* album) on his track "Praise You" (1998), which has been aired in movies, television shows, and commercials.

She has developed some of her stories into books for children and juveniles, such as *Cornrows* (1979/2002, for ages 4–8), a Coretta Scott King Award winner weaving tales of African-American history and biography while interlacing a child's hair into cornrows. Similarly, *The Little Tree Growing in the Shade* (1985/1996, for ages 6–10) offers children insights into the history of enslaved African Americans, highlighting the ways in which spirituals and other music has uplifted and strengthened Americans of African descent. For slightly older readers, Yarbrough wrote *The Shimmershine Queens* (1989/2002, novel for ages 9–13), a Parents Choice Award–winner that encourages African-American girls to strive for success in school and to take pride in their gender and their cultural heritage, interspersing African proverbs and other traditions throughout the text. She also wrote *Tamika and the Wisdom Rings* (1994/2005, an easy chapter book for ages 7–11), about how an 8-year-old girl and her family recover when drug dealers murder her father; and *UC Watch Hour* (2003). All of her books reflect her finely tuned sense of rhythm and cadence in storytelling. Her website at //www.ancestorhouse.net/index.htm notes that she is working on two more children's books.

In the 1970s and 1980s, when not telling stories on stage or on the page, Yarbrough was a talk-show host, and she taught African and diaspora dance in the African Studies Department of the City College of New York. In 2002, she hosted the annual "African Voices Rhymes, Rhythms and Rituals Music and Poetry Concert" in New York City's Harlem. Also in 2002, she founded Ancestor House Productions and the Ancestor House Band. Through her company, she has produced a CD and an MP3 download of *Ancestor House* (2004), "a stage presentation of song, story, music and dance."

Yarbrough was named Griot of the Year by the Griot Society of New York (1975) and Woman of the Month by *Essence* (1979), and she was honored with a Unity Award in Media by Lincoln University (1982). She was enstooled (enthroned) as "Naa Kuokor Agyman 1 Queen Mother" by Abladei, Inc. (Ghanaian, 1994), founder of the Throne House of Harriet Tubman; a decade later, she was enthroned in Agogo-Asanti, Ghana as "Nana Tabuoa Tonko II."

When asked about what motivates her to continue, Yarbrough has answered, "Being a griot or storyteller is not a role that I choose to play. I know this is what I was born to do. What fuels me is the richness of African/African-American culture. This is what energizes me. I come from a kinship line that was **reborn** to **retell** our story over and over again. As its been said, 'if we don't tell our story, we will surely die.' We must tell it to the young, tell it to the old ... everyone grows when our family story is told!" (quoted in //www.ancestorhouse.net/index.htm).

REFERENCES: *BAWPP. CAO-02. Wiki.* Bethel, Kari, in *BB.* Harris, Violet J., in *COCAAL* and *OCAAL.* Ratcliff, Anthony J., in *GEAAL.* //aalbc.com/authors/camille.htm. //www.ancestorhouse.net/index.htm. Amazon.com. San Diego Public Library catalog.

Yerby, Frank G. (Garvin)
9/5/1916–11/29/1991
Novels, short stories, poems; educator, factory worker

In Augusta, Georgia, Frank was the second of four children of racially mixed parents, Rufus Garvin and Wilhelmina Yerby. The South's racial segregation and discrimination made a lifelong impression on young Frank, and decades after he had fled North, he still used the South as the setting—and the subject—of much of his fiction.

The South wasn't able to prevent Frank from getting a good education, however, as he was an outstanding student in the Haines Institute, the private black school he attended. In college, he started writing his own poetry, fiction, and drama while earning his bachelor's degree in English from Paine College (B.A., 1937). While he was still at Paine, Frank's sister showed some of his poems to James Weldon Johnson, who taught at Fisk. Johnson liked what he saw and urged Frank to do his postgraduate studies at Fisk University—which he did, earning an M.A. in English (1938) and continuing to write. After earning his master's degree, he moved to Chicago and started working toward a Ph.D. in English.

Nine months into Yerby's Ph.D. program, he ran into financial difficulties and left school to start working with the Federal Writers Project (FWP) of the Works Progress Administration. While working with the FWP, he met other up-and-coming Chicago-area writers, including Arna Bontemps, Margaret Walker, and Richard Wright. Within months, however, Yerby decided that he wanted to try working in academia, and in 1939, he went back South to teach at Florida A&M University and then at Louisiana's Southern University. In 1941, however, he decided he couldn't take Southern living any more, so he quit academia, and he and his first wife moved first to Dearborn, Michigan, where he worked as a technician in a defense plant for Ford Motor Company (1941–1944), and then to Jamaica, New York, where he worked for Ranger (Fairchild) Aircraft (1944–1945).

Throughout this time, Yerby was continuing to write short stories, and he wrote a protest novel about an African-American steelworker. He sent the novel to *Redbook* magazine, which sometimes published serialized versions of novels. The editor there, Muriel Fuller, rejected his novel as unsuitable for her almost-all-female audience, but she encouraged him to send her another piece. He sent her his short story "Health Card," about a racist encounter between a white congressman and a black GI's girlfriend. Fuller decided that the story didn't suit her audience, but she liked the writing and sent it on to an editor at *Harper's* magazine, a highly esteemed and popular general-interest magazine. As a result, in 1944, Yerby's writing first appeared in print: "Health Card" was pub-

lished in *Harper's*. The story won the O. Henry Memorial Award for best first published short story (1944), and Yerby's career as a writer was launched. "Health Card" was followed in short order by various other short stories, including "White Magnolias," "Homecoming," and "My Brother Went to College."

While continuing to write (and to publish) short stories, Yerby continued to try to sell the manuscript for his protest novel—without success. Eventually, he gave up on it and turned his attention to writing historical fiction, a popular genre at that time. He also switched to featuring mostly white protagonists in his works. The switch in genre and in protagonists did the trick. His next novel, *The Foxes of Harrow* (1946), a historical romance set in New Orleans in the nineteenth century, was an immediate best-seller, selling millions of copies and making him one of the first African Americans to publish a best-seller. It was also translated into at least 12 languages and was adapted to film (1947), making him the first African American to have a book purchased for screen adaptation. The book is still being read—and praised—by contemporary readers; numerous readers took the time to comment on it in 1998 and 1999 (on Amazon.com), identifying it as "very moving!" and "the best book I've ever read!!!" Some who commented also recalled having read the book 20, 30, or more years earlier, yet still recalled savoring it.

Yerby followed this success with more than 30 other novels, becoming the first African American to write a series of best-selling novels in his day, having sold more than 55 million copies of his works—published in 82 countries and in 23 languages. Probably surprising to many of his critics, Yerby's books continue to be printed and sold to this day. Some of his books were also made into successful movies: In addition to *The Foxes of Harrow*, his *The Golden Hawk* (1948) and *The Saracen Blade* (1952/1985) were made into movies. The first book after *Foxes* was *The Vixens* (1947), followed by a trilogy of novels beginning in the Civil War era, *Pride's Castle* (1949).

Yerby's next book, *The Devil's Laughter* (1953), centers around the French Revolution. It was at about this time that Yerby himself moved to Europe. After spending time in France, he eventually settled himself into self-imposed exile in Franco-tyrannized Spain, where he married his second wife and continued to live until his death nearly four decades later.

Among the books he wrote in Europe were *Fair Oaks* (1957), followed by a series that again returned to issues of race in the historical U.S. South, including *The Serpent and the Staff* (1958), *The Garfield Honor* (1961), and *Tents of Shem* (1963). He followed those with a novel set in medieval, Moor-dominated Spain, *An Odor of Sanctity* (1965). Next was *Judas, My Brother* (1968), followed by *Speak Now* (1969), about a contemporary (1968) Parisian romance between an African-American jazz musician and a European-American student from the South. Surprisingly, *Speak Now* was his first published novel with an African-American protagonist, though not the last. In *The Dahomean* (1971; later titled *The Man from Dahomey: An Historical Novel*), Yerby directly addresses issues of race and America's shameful history with slavery. Readers follow the protagonist, Hwesu, from his home in the Dahomean empire in Africa, through his capture by neighboring Africans, his sale to white slave merchants, and his subsequent life as "Wesley Parks," in America. Yerby wrote *The Voyage Unplanned* (1974) and *Tobias and the Angel* (1975) before returning to African-American characters and themes in *A Darkness at Ingraham's Crest* (1979). Other novels of his included *Floodtide* (1950), *A Woman Called Fancy* (1951), *Bride of Liberty* (1954), *Benton's Row* (1954), *The Treasure of Pleasant Valley* (1955), *Captain Rebel* (1955/1983), *Jarrett's Jade* (1959), *Gillian* (1960), *Griffin's Way* (1962), *The Old Gods Laugh* (1964), *Goat Song* (1967, set in ancient Greece, where a Spartan youth is enslaved by Athenians), *The Girl from Storeyville: A Victorian Novel* (1972), *A Rose for Ana Maria: A Novel* (1976), *Hail the Conquering Hero* (1977), *Western: A Saga of the Great Plains* (1982), *Devilseed* (1984), *McKenzie's Hundred* (1985), and *Mayo Fue el Fin del Mundo* (date unknown).

Part of Yerby's appeal is his tight, action-packed writing. He has been quoted as saying, "It is my contention that a really great novel is made with a knife and not a pen. A novelist must have the intestinal fortitude to cut out even the most brilliant passage so long as it doesn't advance the [story]" (quoted in //www.mtsu.edu/~vvesper/afam.html).

No one can fault Yerby for his ability to tell an appealing story or for working hard to put out a large volume of literary works, but he is not without his detractors. Many literary critics scorned him for using the very sensationalizing writing techniques that won him countless fans around the world. Also, fellow African-American writers continually pleaded with him to pay more attention to racial concerns in his works, and although he did so in some works, he was never able to please many writers and other prominent figures in the African-American community.

Even more irritating to fellow African Americans was his writing about European-American protagonists, which appealed to white readers but provoked black ones. Only rarely did Yerby tell stories with African-American protagonists. When he did, however, he shrewdly targeted Southern myths about American history and stereotypes of African Americans, and he savagely attacked American racism.

Even in his novels set in distant times and places (e.g., in the early days of Christianity or during the thir-teenth-century Crusades) or featuring European Americans, Yerby savored debunking myths and setting the historical record straight through his fictional narratives. On the other hand, Yerby's action-packed novels with strong male heroes did manage to perpetuate gender stereotypes, past and present. In this regard, some of his critics have labeled him misogynistic and homophobic.

Yerby's proponents point to his intricate and intriguing story lines, his colorful language, and his inclusion of characters with diverse ethnic backgrounds. Most of all, they say that Yerby offers "a good read." Yerby himself managed to elude definition, and little is known about his life after he moved to Europe. Other than occasional business or personal trips to the States, he never returned to live here. Even his death was mysterious, as he made his wife promise to keep his death a secret for five weeks—which she did. If only we had a good storyteller to give an account of why he made this request . . . .

REFERENCES: *BF:2000. EB-BH-CD. EBLG. G-99. OC20LE. WDAA.* Hill, James L., in *COCAAL* and *OCAAL.* Holliday, Deloice, in *GEAAL.* Amazon.com, 8/1999.

FURTHER READING: *AANB. B. BAWPP. CAO-07. MWEL. W. Wiki.* Bargainnier, Earl F., in *T-CR&HW.* Moore, Jack B., and Craig Bryson. *RGAL-3.* Parker, Jeffrey D., in *AAW-40–55.* //www.mtsu.edu/~vvesper/afam.html.

Young, Al (né Albert James Young)
5/31/1939–
Novels, poems, short stories, screenplays, essays; educator, musician

Young's screenplays include *Nigger* (1972), *Sparkle* (1972), and *Bustin Loose* (1981, for Richard Pryor). Young also collaborated with Ishmael Reed on a television screenplay, *Personal Problems* (1982). His "musical memoirs" include *Bodies & Soul: Musical Memoirs* (1966/1981), *Kinds of Blue: Musical Memoirs* (1984), *Things Ain't What They Used to Be: Musical Memoirs* (1987), and *Drowning in the Sea of Love: Musical Memoirs* (1995). Music also sets the rhythm for his poetry collections, *Dancing: Poems* (1969), *The Song Turning Back into Itself* (1971), *Geography of the Near Past* (1979), *The Blues Don't Change: New and Selected Poems* (1982), *Heaven: Collected Poems 1958–1988* (1989; 1992, subtitled *Collected Poems, 1956–90*), *Straight No Chaser* (1994, a chapbook), *Conjugal Visits* (1996, a chapbook), American Book Award-winning *The Sound of Dreams Remembered: Poems 1990–2000* (2001/2006), *Coastal Nights and Inland Afternoons: Poems 2001–2006: The Poetry of Al Young* (2006), and *Something About the Blues: An Unlikely Collection of Poetry* (2007; book and CD). Music also underlies his biography *Mingus/Mingus: Two Memoirs* (1989, with Janet Coleman, about jazz bassist, composer, and bandleader Charles Mingus) and his first novel *Snakes* (1970). His other novels include *Who Is Angelina?* (1975), *Sitting Pretty* (1976), *Ask Me Now* (1980), and *Seduction by Light* (1988).

Young has also edited, founded, or cofounded numerous literary journals. He and Ishmael Reed cofounded the *Yardbird Reader* (1972–1976); they also edited both *Yardbird Lives!* (1978) and *Calafia: The California Poetry* (1979). Young's other anthologies include *Believers* (1993), *African American Literature: A Brief Introduction and Anthology* (1995), and *The Literature of California, Volume 1: Native American Beginnings to 1945* (2000, with Jack Hicks, James D. Houston, and Maxine Hong Kingston) and *Volume 2* (2002).

Young has taught at several institutions in California (e.g., Stanford University, 1969–1976) and other locations (e.g., Charles University in the Czech Republic, 2001). In addition, he has served on the faculty of the Cave Canem summer workshops for African-American poets (2003–2006), and he has lectured in Europe, the Middle East, and South Asia. His poetry and prose have been translated into at least eight European languages, three Asian languages, and Urdu.

In 2005, Republican Governor Arnold Schwarzenegger named Young Poet Laureate of California. Among his many other honors are a Wallace Stegner fellowship (1966–1967), a Joseph Henry Jackson Award from the San Francisco Foundation (1969), National Arts Council awards for editing and poetry (1968–1970), National Endowment for the Arts fellowships (1968, 1969, 1975), an American Library Association Notable Book of the Year citation (1970), a California Association of Teachers of English Special Award (1973), a Guggenheim Memorial Foundation fellowship (1974), two Pushcart Prizes (1976, 1980), a *The New York Times* Outstanding Book of the Year citation (1980), two Before Columbus Foundation American Book Awards (1982, 2002), a Fulbright fellowship (1984), a Rita and Mel Cohen Award for Poetry from *Ploughshares* (1987), a PEN–Library of Congress Award for Short Fiction (1991), the PEN-USA Award for Best Non-Fiction Book of the Year (1996), the Stephen Henderson Achievement Award for Poetry from the African American Literature and Culture Society, the Glenna Luschei Distinguished Poetry Fellowship, and the Richard Wright Award for Excellence in Literature. He and his wife Arlin (or Arline; married in 1963) also share a legacy: their son Michael (b. 1971).

REFERENCES: *AANB. AAW:PV. AT. BAWPP. CAO-03. LFCC-07. NAAAL. W. Wiki.* Chirico, Miriam M., in *COCAAL* and *OCAAL.* Harris, William J., in *AAFW-55–84.* Hunt, Imelda, in *GEAAL.* Reilly, John M., in *CN-6,* and in *CP-6.* //www.cavecanempoets.org/pages/programs_faculty.php. //www.poets.org/poet.php/prmPID/466. //www.ucsc.edu/news_events/text.asp?pid=2209. Amazon.com.

Young, Kevin
11/8/1970–
Poems, essays, anthologies; educator

While earning his B.A. from Harvard University (1992), Kevin Young participated in the **Dark Room Collective** of African-American poets. After graduating, Young was awarded a Stegner fellowship in poetry at Stanford University in California (1992–1994) and two fellowships to the MacDowell Colony in New Hampshire (1993, 1995). While working on his M.F.A. in creative writing from Brown University in Rhode Island (1996), Young published his critically acclaimed first collection *Most Way Home: Poems* (1995/1998), which won the John C. Zacharis First Book Award from *Ploughshares* (1996) and was chosen for the National Poetry Series (1995). While working on his next collection, he edited an anthology of fiction, poetry, and essays, *Giant Steps: The New Generation of African American Writers* (2000).

Young's next poetry collection was *To Repel Ghosts: Five Sides in B Minor* (2001), a finalist for the James Laughlin Award from the Academy of American Poets; both it and its condensed version, *To Repel Ghosts: The Remix* (2005), honor visual artist Jean-Michel Basquiat. Between the first and second *Ghosts,* Young published *Jelly Roll: A Blues* (2003), nominated both for the National Book Award in Poetry and the *Los Angeles Times* Book Prize in Poetry (both 2003), and was awarded the Paterson Poetry Prize from the Poetry Center (2004). He also edited two more works: an anthology of poetry, *Blues Poems* (2003), and a Library of America volume, *John Berryman: Selected Poems* (2003).

Young's next poetry collection was *Black Maria: Being the Adventures of Delilah Redbone & A.K.A. Jones* (2005; also subtitled *Poems Produced and Directed by Kevin Young*), a series of narrative poems. Next, he edited the anthology *Jazz Poems* (2006). Young's subsequent poetry collections include *For the Confederate Dead* (2007) and *Dear Darkness: Poems* (2008). In addition to his collections, Young has published both his poems and his essays in numerous periodicals (e.g., **Callaloo**, *Paris Review*) and in some anthologies (e.g., *The Best American Poetry 2005*).

As an educator, Young has taught at the University of Georgia in Athens and at Indiana University, where he was the Ruth Lilly Professor of Poetry. At Emory University in Atlanta since 2005, Young has become the university's Atticus Haygood Professor of English and Creative Writing and curator of the Raymond Danowski Poetry Library. In addition to his many other honors, Young received a Guggenheim Foundation fellowship (2003) and a National Endowment for the Arts literary fellowship (2004).

REFERENCES: *CAO-06. Wiki.* Gerrity, Maggie, in *AANB.* Powers, Stephen Roger, in *GEAAL.* Rowell, Charles Henry, and Carl Phillips

(Eds.). 2002. *Making Callaloo: 25 Years of Black Literature.* New York: St. Martin's Griffin. //en.wikipedia.org/wiki/James_Laughlin_Award. //en.wikipedia.org/wiki/John_berryman. //en.wikipedia.org/ wiki/Lucie_Brock-Broido. //en.wikipedia.org/wiki/Passaic_ County_Community_College. //en.wikipedia.org/wiki/ Seamus_Heaney. //www.poets.org/poet.php/prmPID/416. //www.poets.org/viewmedia.php/prmMID/5652. Amazon.com.

Whitney Young, Jr.

Young, Jr., Whitney M. (Moore)
7/31/1921–3/11/1971
Nonfiction—politics and race, columns; civil-rights activist, organization executive

In 1958, Young coauthored *A Second Look: The Negro Citizen in Atlanta* (1958), published in connection with Atlanta's Committee for Cooperative Action, a civil-rights organization he helped found. Six years later, Young's weekly political-opinion columns ("To Be Equal," in Harlem's *Amsterdam News*) were collected into the book *To Be Equal* (1964). This book included what he called a "domestic Marshall Plan," developed while he was the executive director of the National Urban League, and designed to expand both economic and educational opportunities for African Americans—much as the European Marshall Plan had done for Europeans, following World War II. Many aspects of Young's plan were incorporated into President Lyndon Johnson's War on Poverty program—much of which ended up being siderailed by the Vietnam War. Young also wrote *Beyond Racism: Building an Open Society* (1970), which won a Christopher Book Award. Since Young's death (in 1971), his widow, Margaret Buckner Young (whom he married in 1944 and with whom he had two daughters, Marcia Elaine and Lauren Lee), has written several children's books on history, focusing especially on the civil-rights struggle.

REFERENCES: *AANB. B. CAO-02. EA-99. EB-BH-CD. EBLG. G-97. PGAA. Wiki.* McDaniel, Karen Cotton, in *BH2C.* Wankoff, Jordan, in *BB.*

~Z~

Zu-Bolton, III, Ahmos
10/21/1935–3/8/2005
Poems, plays, anthology; journals editor, bookstore owner, event organizer

Zu-Bolton's free-verse poems reflective of the **Black Arts Movement** have been collected in his *A Niggered Amen: Poems* (1975) and have been anthologized in several works. His plays include *The Widow Paris: A Folklore of Marie Laveau*, *The Funeral*, *Family Reunion*, and *The Break-In*. With **E. Ethelbert Miller**, he edited widely read *Synergy D.C. Anthology* (1975). Zu-Bolton was also deeply involved in the literary journals *Energy West Poetry Journal* (1970–1972, editor), *HooDoo* (1971–1978, founder and editor), and *Blackbox* (1974–1977, coeditor with Alan Austin and **Etheridge Knight**), a poetry journal published on audiotapes. His own writings have appeared in New Orleans's *Times-Picayune* and the *Louisiana Weekly*.

In addition to his writing, Zu-Bolton taught intermittently at Tulane, Xavier, and various other colleges and universities; he organized HooDoo Festivals in Texas and Louisiana, featuring writers and musicians performing their works (1977–1980); and he owned the Copasetic Bookstore and Gallery in New Orleans, which hosted countless literary and cultural events for about a decade (1982–1992). In addition to his literary and cultural children, he and his former wife, Kathy, parented Bojavai, Sonoma, and Amber Easter.

REFERENCES: *AT. CAO-07. Wiki.* Hall, John Greer, in *GEAAL*. Thomas, Lorenzo, in *AAP-55–85*, in *COCAAL* and *OCAAL*. Amazon.com.

Primary Documents

Africans were first kidnapped in their homeland, transported in chains across the Middle Passage, and sold to English-speaking buyers on the American continent in 1619. For the next 150-plus years, their written record was documented by their captors, their enslavers, and a few of their own, brave enough to protest against their enslavement. This section includes documents that offer insight into the life experiences of African Americans during this first century and a half of their residence on this continent, including a *sample contract for indentured servitude* (much like the contracts under which the earliest African arrivals were bound), *a letter from an indentured servant to this family,* and the *first slave narrative written in the English language.*

You will also read *laws from 1639 to 1682* (showing how slavery differentiated Africans, not only from all other residents, but also from other servants, and bound them and their children in lifelong servitude); the *1688 petition by Quakers* (members of the Religious Society of Friends), pleading for an end to slavery and the slave trade; a *1788 account by a firsthand observer of the slave trade;* and an *1752 inventory of the estate of a slaveholder.*

This section also includes the *earliest remaining writing by an African American* and a *poem by Phillis Wheatley,* one of the earliest known African-American writers.

The Forme of a Binding Servant, 1635

THIS INDENTURE made the _____ day of _____ in the _____ yeere of our Soveraigne Lord King Charles, etc. betweene _____ of the one party, and _____ on the other party, Witnesseth, that the said _____ doth hereby covenant promise, and grant, to and with the said _____ his Executors and Assignes, to serve him from the day of the date hereof, untill his first and next arrivall in Maryland; and after for and during the tearme of _____ yeeres, in such service and imployment, as the said _____ or his assignes shall there imploy him, according to the custome of the Countrey in the like kind. In consideration whereof, the said _____ doth promise and grant, to and with the said _____ to pay for his passing, and to find him with Meat, Drink, Apparell and Lodging, with other necessaries during the said terme; and at the end of the said terme, to give him one whole yeeres provision of Corne, and fifty acres of Land, according to the order of the countrey. In witnesse whereof, the said _____ _____ hath hereunto put his hand and seale, the day and yeere above written.

Sealed and delivered in

The presence of

The usuall terme of binding a servant, is for five yeers; but for any artificer, or one that shall deserve more then ordinary, the Adventurer shall doe well to shorten that time, and adde encouragements of another nature (as he shall see cause) rather then to want such usefull men.

From *A Relation of Maryland, 1635* (reprinted in Clayton Colman Hall, editor. *Narratives of Early Maryland, 1633-1684*. New York: Charles Scribner's Sons, 1910. 99-100)

An Indentured Servant's Letter Home, 1623

Richard Frethorne was one of the earliest indentured servants to come to the colony of Virginia. The first came in 1619. He wrote this letter to his parents in 1623. The letter, in fact, is a series of short letters, much like diary or journal entries. You will notice that he signed the letter three times. He was writing from Martin's Hundred, the name of a specific place in Virginia. The original letter is almost impossible to read because of different grammar, punctuation and spelling. Historians have translated it into modern English, and their version follows. This letter is quoted widely as one of the only surviving letters from an indentured servant in the early 1600s. Most surviving documents were written by the leaders of the colony. No one knows what happened to Richard Frethorne. He may have died of starvation or disease shortly after he wrote this letter, or his father may have sent him some goods to trade for money to get free of his indenture contract. Richard Frethorne is only known for this letter. Nothing else is known.

Loving and kind father and mother:

...this is to let you understand that I your child am in a most heavy case by reason of the nature of the country.... . And when we are sick there is nothing to comfort us; for since I came out of the ship I never ate anything but peas and loblollie (water gruel). As for deer and venison I never saw any since I came into this land. There is indeed some fowl, but we are not allowed to go and get it... A mouthful of bread for a penny loaf must serve for four men. ...When people cry out day and night-Oh! that they were in England without their limbs-and would not care to lose any limb to be in England again, yea though they beg from door to door. ...And there was some five or six of the late year's twenty (total Indentured Servants who came the previous year)...and yet we are but 32 (Englishmen) to fight against 3,000 (Indians) if they should come. And the nighest (nearest) help that we have is ten miles of (from) us, and when the rogues (Indians) overcame this place last they slew (killed) 80 persons. ...

And I have nothing to comfort me, nor is there nothing to be gotten here but sickness and death. ...But I have nothing at all-no, not a shirt to my back but two rags (2), nor no clothes but one poor suit, nor but one pair of shoes, but one pair of stockings, but one cap,...My cloak is stolen by one of my own fellows, and to his dying hour (he would not tell me what he did with it; but some of my fellows saw him have butter and beef out of a ship, which my cloak I doubt (not) paid for. So that I have not a penny, nor a penny worth, to help me to either spice or sugar or strong waters, without the which one cannot live here.

...But I am not half a quarter so strong as I was in England, and all is for want of victuals (food), for I do protest unto you that I have eaten more in (one) day at home that I have allowed me here for a week. You have given more than my day's allowance to a beggar at the door. ...

(Goodman Jackson, a gunsmith in Jamestown befriended Richard Frethorne) And he (Goodman Jackson)much marveled that you would send me a servant to the Company;, you must have a care how you pack it in ballels; and you ust put cooper's chips between every cheese, or else the heat of the hold will rot them. he saith I had been better knocked on the head. And indeed I so find it now, to my great grief and misery; and (I) saith that if you love me you will redeem me suddenly, for which I do entreat and beg. And if you cannot get the merchants to redeem me for some little money, for for God's sake get a gathering, or entreat some good folks to lay out some little sum of money in meal and cheese and butter and beef. Any eating meat will yield great profit. Oil and vinegar is very good, but father, there is great loss in leaking. But for God's sake send beef and cheese and butter, or the more of one sort and none of another. ...But iif you send cheese. ...I will send it (the profits) over (to his father), and beg the profit to redeem me; and if I die before it come, I have entreated Goodman Jackson to send you the worth of it, who hath promised he will. ...

Good father, do not forget me, but have mercy and pity my miserable case. I know if you did but see me, you would weep to see me; for I hath but one suit, (But though it is a strange one, it is very well guarded.) Wherefore, for God's sake, pity me. I pray you to remember my love to all my friends and kindred. I hope all my brothers and sisters are in good health, and as for my part...the answer to this letter will be life or death to me. Therefore, good father, send as soon as you can....

Richard Frethorne
Martin's Hundred

The names of them that be dead of the company (that) came over with us to serve under our Lieutenants:

John Flower	George Goulding
John Thomas	Jos. Johnson
Thos. Howes	our lieutenant, his father and brother
John Butcher	Thos. Giblin
John Sanderford	George Banum
Rich. Smith	a little Dutchman
John Olive	one woman

From *Records of the Virginia Company, 1606-26,* Volume IV. Edited by Susan Myra Kingsbury. Washington, D.C.: Government Printing Office

Thos. Peirsman   one maid
William Cerrell   one child

All these died out of my master's house, since I came; and we came in but at Christmas, and this is the 20th day of March. And the sailors say that there is twothirds of the 150 dead already. ...

Therefore if you love or respect me as your child, release me from this bondage and save my life. ...

Your loving son,
Richard Frethorne

...But what shall it be when we shall go a month or two and never see a bit of bread, as my master doth say we must do? And he said he is not able to keep us all. Then, we shall be turned up to the land and eat barks of trees or molds of the ground; therefore with weeping tears I beg of you to help me. Oh, that you did see my daily and hourly sighs, groans, and tears, and (the) thumps that I afford mine own breast, (beating myself upon the chest)...I thought no head had been able to hold so much water as hath and doth daily flow from mine eyes (crying).

But this is certain: I never felt the want of father and mother till now... .

I pray you talk with this honest man (the person bringing the letter to his parents). He will tell you more than now in my haste I can set down.

Your loving son, Richard
Frethorne Virginia, 3rd
April, 1623

Colonial Laws

Virginia, 1639

Act X. All persons except negroes are to be provided with arms and ammunition or be fined at the pleasure of the Governor and Council.

Maryland, 1664

That whatsoever free-born [English] woman shall intermarry with any slave. . . shall serve the master of such slave during the life of her husband; and that all the issue of such free-born women, so married shall be slaves as their fathers were.

Virginia, 1667

Act III. Whereas some doubts have risen whether children that are slaves by birth. . . should by virtue of their baptism be made free, it is enacted...that baptism does not alter the condition of the person as to his bondage or freedom; masters freed from this doubt may more carefully propagate Christianity by permitting children, though slaves ...to be admitted to that sacrament.

Virginia, 1682

Act I. It is enacted that all servants...being imported into this country either by sea or land, whether Negroes, Moors [Muslim North Africans], mulattoes or Indians who and whose parentage and native countries are not Christian at the time of their first purchase by some Christian. . . and all Indians, which shall be sold by our neighboring Indians, or any other trafficing with us for slaves, are hereby adjudged, deemed and taken to be slaves to all intents and purposes any law, usage, or custom to the contrary notwithstanding.

A Minute Against Slavery, Addressed to Germantown Monthly Meeting, 1688

This is to ye Monthly Meeting held at Richard Worrell's.

These are the reasons why we are against the traffick of men-body, as foloweth. Is there any that would be done or handled at this manner? viz., to be sold or made a slave for all the time of his life? How fearful and faint-hearted are many on sea, when they see a strange vessel, — being afraid it should be a Turk, and they should be taken, and sold for slaves into Turkey. Now what is this better done, as Turks doe? Yea, rather it is worse for them, which say they are Christians; for we hear that ye most part of such negers are brought hither against their will and consent,and that many of them are stolen. Now, tho they are black, we can not conceive there is more liberty to have them slaves, as it is to have other white ones. There is a saying that we shall doe to all men like as we will be done ourselves; making no difference of what generation, descent or colour they are. And those who steal or robb men, and those who buy or purchase them, are they not all alike? Here is liberty of conscience wch is right and reasonable; here ought to be liberty of ye body, except of evil-doers,wch is an other case. But to bring men hither, or to rob and sell them against their will, we stand against. In Europe there are many oppressed for conscience sake; and here there are those oppressed whare of a black colour. And we who know than men must not comitt adultery, — some do committ adultery, in separating wives from their husbands and giving them to others; and some sell the children of these poor creatures to other men. Ah! doe consider will this thing, you who doe it, if you would be done at this manner? And if it is done according to Christianity? You surpass Holland and Germany in this thing. This makes an ill report in all those countries of Europe, where they hear of, that ye Quakers doe here handel men as they handel there ye cattle. And for that reason some have no mind or inclination to come hither. And who shall maintain this your cause, or pleid for it. Truly we can not do so, except you shall inform us better hereof, viz., that Christians have liberty to practise these things. Pray, what thing in the world can be done worse towards us, than if men should rob or steal us away, and sell us for slaves to strange countries; separating husbands from their wives and children. Being now that this is not done in the manner we would be done at therefore we contradict and are against this traffic of men-body. And we who profess that is is not lawful to steal, must, likewise, avoid to purchase such things as are stolen, but rather help to stop this robbing and stealing if possible. And such men ought to be delivered out of ye hands of ye robbers,and set free as well as in Europe. Then is Pennsylvania to have a good report, instead it hath now a bad one for this sake in other countries. Especially whereas ye Europeans are desirous to know in what manner ye Quakers doe rule in their province; — and most of them doe look upon us with an envious eye. But if this is done well, what shall we say is done evil?

If once these slaves (wch they say are so wicked and stubbern men) should join themselves, — fight for their freedom, — and handel their masters and mastrisses as they did handel them before; will these masters and mastrisses take the sword at hand and warr against these poor slaves, licke, we are able to believe, some will not refuse to doe; or have these negers not as much right to fight for their freedom, as you have to keep them slaves?

Now consider will this thing, if it is good or bad? And in case you find it to be good to handle these blacks at that manner, we desire and require you hereby lovingly, that you may inform us herein, which at this time never was done, viz., that Christians have such a liberty to do so. To the end we shall be be satisfied in this point, and satisfie likewise our good friends and acquaintances in our natif country, to whose it is a terror, or fairful thing, that men should be handeld so in Pennsylvania.

This is from our meeting at Germantown, held ye 18 of the 2 month, 1688, to be delivered to the Monthly Meeting at Richard Worrell's.

Garret henderich

derick up de graeff

Francis daniell Pastorius

Abraham up Den graef.

Monthly Meeting Response: At our Monthly Meeting at Dublin, ye 30 — 2 mo., 1688, we have inspected ye matter, above mentioned, and considered of it, we find it so weighty that we think it not expedient for us to meddle with it here, but do rather commit it to ye consideration of ye Quarterly Meeting; ye tenor of it being nearly related to ye Truth. On behalf of ye Monthly Meeting,

Signed, P. Jo. Hart.

Quarterly Meeting Response: This, above mentioned, was read in our Quarterly Meeting at Philadelphia, the 4 of ye 4th mo. '88, and was from thence recommended to the

---

From *Incidentes Illustrating the Doctrines and History of the Society of Friends.* Walton, Joseph, ed. Philadelphia: Friends' Book Store, 1897.

Yearly Meeting, and the above said Derick, and the other two mentioned therein, to present the same to ^{ye} above said meeting, it being a thing of too great a weight for this meeting to determine.

Signed by order of ^{ye} meeting,
Anthony Morris.

Yearly Meeting Response: At a Yearly Meeting held at Burlington the 5th day of the 7th month, 1688. A Paper being here presented by some German Friends Concerning the Lawfulness and Unlawfulness of Buying and keeping Negroes, It was adjusted not to be so proper for this Meeting to give a Positive Judgment in the case, It having so General a Relation to many other Parts, and therefore at present they forbear It.

Alexander Falconbridge,
The African Slave Trade (1788)

Taken from An Account of the Slave Trade on the Coast of Africa *(1788), by Alexander Falconbridge. Falconbridge was a surgeon on several slave ships, and his account of the horrors of the "middle passage" made him influential among English abolitionists.*

As soon as the wretched Africans, purchased at the fairs, fall into the hands of the black traders, they experience an earnest of those dreadful sufferings which they are doomed in future to undergo. And there is not the least room to doubt, but that even before they can reach the fairs, great numbers perish from cruel usage, want of food, travelling through inhospitable deserts, etc. They are brought from the places where they are purchased to Bonny, etc. in canoes; at the bottom of which they lie, having their hands tied with a kind of willow twigs, and a strict watch is kept over them. Their usage in other respects, during the time of passage, which generally lasts several days, is equally cruel. Their allowance of food is so scanty, that it is barely sufficient to support nature. They are, besides, much exposed to the violent rains which frequently fall here, being covered only with mats that afford but a slight defense; and as there is usually water at the bottom of the canoes, from their leaking, they are scarcely every dry.

Nor do these unhappy beings, after they become the property of the Europeans (from whom as a more civilized people, more humanity might naturally be expected), find their situation in the least amended. Their treatment is no less rigorous. The men Negroes, on being brought aboard the ship, are immediately fastened together, two and two, by hand- cuffs on their wrists, and irons riveted on their legs. They are then sent down between the decks, and placed in an apartment partitioned off for that purpose. The women likewise are placed in a separate room, on the same deck, but without being ironed. And an adjoining room, on the same deck is besides appointed for the boys. Thus are they placed in different apartments.

But at the same time, they are frequently stowed so close, as to admit of no other posture than lying on their sides. Neither will the height between decks, unless directly under the grating, permit them the indulgence of an erect posture; especially where there are platforms, which is generally the case. These platforms are a kind of shelf, about eight or nine feet in breadth, extending from the side of the ship towards the centre. They are placed nearly midway between the decks, at the distance of two or three feet from each deck. Upon these the Negroes are stowed in the same manner as they are on the deck underneath. ...About eight o'clock in the morning the Negroes are generally brought upon deck. Their irons being examined, a long chain, which is locked to a ring-bolt, fixed in the deck, is run through the rings of the shackles of the men, and then locked to another ring-bolt, fixed also in the deck. By this means fifty or sixty, and sometimes more, are fastened to one chain, in order to prevent them from rising, or endeavoring to escape. If the weather proves favorable, they are permitted to remain in that situation till four or five in the afternoon, when they are disengaged from the chain, and sent down.

...Upon the Negroes refusing to take sustenance, I have seen coals of fire, glowing hot, put on a shovel, and placed so near their lips, as to scorch and burn them. And this has been accompanied with threats, of forcing them to swallow the coals, if they any longer persisted in refusing to eat. These means have generally had the desired effect. I have also been credibly informed that a certain captain in the slave trade poured melted lead on such of the Negroes as obstinately refused their food.

Exercise being deemed necessary for the preservation of their health, they are sometimes obligated to dance, when the weather will permit their coming on deck. If they go about it reluctantly, or do not move with agility, they are flogged; a person standing by them all the time with at cat-o'-nine-tails in his hand for that purpose. Their music, upon these occasions, consists of a drum, sometimes with only one head; and when that is worn out, they do not scruple to make use of the bottom of one of the tubs before described. The poor wretches are frequently compelled to sing also; but when they do so, their songs are generally, as may naturally be expected, melancholy lamentations of their exile from their native country.

...On board some ships, the common sailors are allowed to have intercourse with such of the black women whose consent they can procure. And some of them have been known to take the inconstancy of their paramours so much to heart, as to leap overboard and drown themselves. The officers are permitted to indulge their passions among them at pleasure, and sometimes are guilty of such brutal excesses as disgrace human nature. The hardships and inconveniences suffered by the Negroes during the passage are scarcely to be enumerated or conceived. They are far more violently affected by the seasickness than the Europeans. It frequently terminates in death, especially among the women. But the exclusion of the fresh air is among the most intolerable. For the purpose of admitting this needful refreshment, most of the ships in the slave trade are provided, between the decks, with five or six air-ports on each side of the ship, of about six inches in length, and four in breadth; in addition to which, some few ships, but not one in twenty, have what they denominate wind-sails. But whenever the sea is rough and the rain heavy, it becomes necessary to shut these, and every other conveyance by which the air is admitted. The fresh air being thus excluded, the Negroes' rooms very soon grow intolerably hot. The confined air, rendered noxious by the effluvia exhaled from their bodies, and by being repeatedly breathed, soon produces fevers and fluxes, which generally carries off great numbers of them.

...One morning, upon examining the place allotted for the sick Negroes, I perceived that one of them, who was so emaciated as scarcely to be able to walk, was missing, and was convinced that he must have gone overboard in the night, probably to put a more expeditious period to his sufferings. And, to conclude on this subject, I could not help being sensibly affected, on a former voyage, at observing with what apparent eagerness a black woman seized some dirt from off an African yam, and put it into her mouth, seeming to rejoice at the opportunity of possessing some of her native earth. From these instances I think it may have been clearly deduced that the unhappy Africans are not bereft of the finer feelings, but have a strong attachment to their native country, together with a just sense of the value of liberty. And the situation of the miserable beings above described, more forcibly urges the necessity of abolishing a trade which is the source of such evils, than the most eloquent harangue, or persuasive arguments could do.

Inventory of Estate of Mark Cosby
1752 November 20

An Inventory and Appraisment of the Estate of Mark Cosby decd. made by Peter Scott Thomas Hornsby and Robert Nicholson by order of York Court 1752 October 4th.

A feather Bed with Rug Blankets Bolster & Pillows 2 pr. Sheets Bedstead & Cord	£5.. 0..0
A Desk 50/. A large black walnut Table 35/. a Smaller Square Do. 12/6	4..17..6
A Looking Glass 20/. 6 Leather Chairs 30/. 1 Elbow Chair 7/6	2..17..6
1 Case with Bottles 15/. 1 Trunk 3/9 a Duroy Coat Waist Coat 3 pr. Breeches 21/6	2.. 0..3
A New Market Coat & a Cloath Coat 2 Waistcoats & 2 pr. Breeches	2.. ..
1 Serge Coat & Waist Coat 12/. a Parcel of old Books 36/	2.. 8..
8 Volumes *Turkish Spy* 20/. Josephus in folio 25/	2.. .5..
1 Bakers *Cronicle* 10/. 1 *Paradise Lost* 2/6	0..12..6
2 Volumes Hist: Egyptians &c 5/. a New hatt 24/	1.. 9..
4 Linnen Waistcoats 23/. 2 Wiggs 21/6. a Saddle & Housing 12/	2..16..6
A Horse Whip	0.. 4..
A Negro Fellow called Joe	40.. ..
A Mulatto Boy called Lewis 11 Years to Serve	11.. ..
A Negro Boy called Sam	35.. ..
A Negro Boy called Little Joe	27..10..
A Negro Winch called Hannah	45.. ..
A Negro Girl called Rachel	25.. ..
A Silver Watch £4..6/. A Set of Silver Buckles 21/6	5.. 7..6
A pr. of Gold Sleeve Buttons 13/. a pr. small Bellows 2/	0..15..
A Gun 40/. Some Pieces Shoe Leather 11/.	2..11..
2 Shirts 20/. 2 old hats 4/. Old Shoes 3/.	1.. 7..

£210.. 0..9

Peter Scott
Thomas Hornsby
Robert Nicolson

Returned into York County Court the 20th. day of November 1752 and ordered to be recorded.
Examd.
Teste
Thos. Everard Cl: Cur:

Source: The Colonial Williamsburg Foundation, 2009. Reprinted with permission.

Bars Fight
by Lucy Terry

The earliest remaining writing by an African American is this poem written in 1746. It was published in 1855 in Josiah Holland's History of Western Massachusetts.

August, 'twas the twenty-fifth,
Seventeen houndred forty-six,
The Indians did in ambush lay,
Some very valiant men to slay.
'Twas nigh unto Sam Dickinson's mill,
The Indians there five men did kill.
The names of whom I'll not leave out,
Samuel Allen like a hero fout
And though he was so brave and bold
His face no more shall we behold.
Eleazer Hawks was killed outright
Before he had time to fight
Before he did the Indians see
Was shot and killed immediately.
Oliver Amsden he was slain
Which caused his friends much grief and pain.
Simeon Amsden they found dead
Not many rods from Oliver's head.
Adonijah Gillet we do hear
Did lose his life which was so dear.
John Sadler fled across the water
And thus escaped the dreadful slaughter.
Eunice Allen see the Indians comeing
And hoped to save herself by running
And had not her petticoats stopt her
The awful creatures had not cotched her
Nor tommyhawked her on the head
And left her on the ground for dead.
Young Samuel Allen, Oh! lack-a-day
Was taken and carried to Canada.

To the Right Honourable William, Earl of Dartmouth
by Phillis Wheatley

Phillis Wheatley is one of the earliest known African-American writers.

Hail, happy day, when, smiling like the morn, Fair Freedom rose, New England to adorn: The northern clime, beneath her genial ray, Dartmouth! congratulates thy blissful sway: Elate with hope, her race no longer mourns, Each soul expands, each grateful bosom burns, While in thine hand with pleasure we behold The silken reins, and Freedom's charms unfold. Long lost to realms beneath the northern skies, She shines supreme, while hated faction dies: Soon as appeared the Goddess long desired, Sick at the view she languished and expired;

Thus from the splendors of the morning light The owl in sadness seeks the eaves of night.

No more, America, in mournful strain, Of wrongs and grievance unredressed complain; No longer shall thou dread the iron chain Which wanton Tyranny, with lawless hand, Had made, and with it meant t' enslave the land.

Should you, my lord, while you peruse my song, Wonder from whence my love of Freedom sprung, Whence flow these wishes for the common good, By feeling hearts alone best understood,- I, young in life, by seeming cruel fate Was snatched from Afric's fancied happy seat: What pangs excruciating must molest, What sorrows labour in my parent's breast! Steeled was that soul, and by no misery moved, That from a father seized his babe beloved: Such, such my case. And can I then but pray Others may never feel tyrannic sway?

For favors past, great Sir, our thanks are due, And thee we ask thy favors to renew, Since in thy power, as in thy will before, To soothe the griefs, which thou didst once deplore. May heavenly grace the sacred sanction give To all thy works, and thou forever live, Not only on the wings of fleeting Fame, Though praise immortal crowns the patriot's name, But to conduct to heaven's refulgent fane, May fiery coursers sweep the etherial plain, And bear thee upwards to that blest abode, Where, like the prophet, thou shalt find thy God.

Bars Fight: From *History of Western Massachusetts* by Josiah G. Holland. Springfield Mass.: Samuel Bowles and Company, 1855
To the Right Honourable William, Earl of Dartmouth: From *Poems on Various Subjects, Religious and Moral.* London, 1773.

A Narrative of the Most Remarkable Particulars in the Life of James Albert Ukawsaw Gronniosaw, an African Prince, as related by Himself

This autobiography is considered the first published by an African-African in Britain and the first slave narrative in the English language.

I was born in the city Bournou; my mother was the eldest daughter of the reigning King there, of which Bournou is the chief city. I was the youngest of six children, and particularly loved by my mother, and my grand-father almost doated on me.

I had, from my infancy, a curious turn of mind; was more grave and reserved in my disposition than either of my brothers and sisters. I often teazed them with questions they could not answer: for which reason they disliked me, as they supposed that I was either foolish, or insane. 'Twas certain that I was, at times, very unhappy in myself: it being strongly impressed on my mind that there was some Great Man of power which resided above the sun, moon and stars, the objects of our worship. My dear indulgent mother would bear more with me than any of my friends beside.—I often raised my hand to heaven, and asked her who lived there? was much dissatisfied when she told me the sun, moon and stars, being persuaded, in my own mind, that there must be some Superior Power.—I was frequently lost in wonder at the works of the Creation: was afraid and uneasy and restless, but could not tell for what. I wanted to be informed of things that no person could tell me; and was always dissatisfied.—These wonderful impressions begun in my childhood, and followed me continually 'till I left my parents, which affords me matter of admiration and thankfulness.

To this moment I grew more and more uneasy every day, in so much that one saturday, (which is the day on which we keep our sabbath) I laboured under anxieties and fears that cannot be expressed; and, what is more extraordinary, I could not give a reason for it.—I rose, as our custom is, about three o'clock, (as we are oblig'd to be at our place of worship an hour before the sun rise) we say nothing in our worship, but continue on our knees with our hands held up, observing a strict silence 'till the sun is at a certain height, which I suppose to be about 10 or 11 o'clock in England: when, at a certain sign made by the priest, we get up (our duty being over) and disperse to our different houses.—Our place of meeting is under a large palm tree; we divide ourselves into many congregations; as it is impossible for the same tree to cover the inhabitants of the whole City, though they are extremely large, high and majestic; the beauty and usefulness of them are not to be described; they supply the inhabitants of the country with meat, drink and clothes; the body of the palm tree is very large; at a certain season of the year they tap it, and bring vessels to receive the wine, of which they draw great quantities, the quality of which is very delicious: the leaves of this tree are of a silky nature; they are large and soft; when they are dried and pulled to pieces it has much the same appearance as the English flax, and the inhabitants of Bournou manufacture it for cloathing &c. This tree likewise produces a plant or substance which has the appearance of a cabbage, and very like it, in taste almost the same: it grows between the branches. Also the palm tree produces a nut, something like a cocoa, which contains a kernel, in which is a large quantity of milk, very pleasant to the taste: the shell is of a hard substance, and of a very beautiful appearance, and serves for basons, bowls, &c.

It is a generally received opinion, in *England*, that the natives of *Africa* go entirely unclothed; but this supposition is very unjust: they have a kind of dress so as to appear decent, though it is very slight and thin.

I hope this digression will be forgiven.—I was going to observe that after the duty of our Sabbath was over (on the day in which I was more distressed and afflicted than ever) we were all on our way home as usual, when a remarkable black cloud arose and covered the sun; then followed very heavy rain and thunder more dreadful than ever I had heard: the heav'ns roared, and the earth trembled at it: I was highly affected and cast down; in so much that I wept sadly, and could not follow my relations and friends home.—I was obliged to stop and felt as if my legs were tied, they seemed to shake under me: so I stood still, being in great fear of the Man of Power that I was persuaded in myself, lived above. One of my young companions (who entertained a particular friendship for me and I for him) came back to see for me: he asked me why I stood still in such very hard rain? I only said to him that my legs were weak, and I could not come faster: he was much affected to see me cry, and took me by the hand, and said he would lead me home, which he did. My mother was greatly alarmed at my tarrying out in such terrible weather; she asked me many questions, such as what I did so for, and if I was well? My dear mother says I, pray tell

---

Originally published by S. Southwick, Newport, R.I., 1774.

me who is the great Man of Power that makes the thunder? She said, there was no power but the sun, moon and stars; that they made all our country.—I then enquired how all our people came? She answered me, from one another; and so carried me to many generations back.—Then says I, who made the *First Man?* and who made the first Cow, and the first Lyon, and where does the fly come from, as no one can make him? My mother seemed in great trouble; she was apprehensive that my senses were impaired, or that I was foolish. My father came in, and seeing her in grief asked the cause, but when she related our conversation to him, he was exceedingly angry with me, and told me he would punish me severely if ever I was so troublesome again; so that I resolved never to say any thing more to him. But I grew very unhappy in myself; my relations and acquaintance endeavoured by all the means they could think on, to divert me, by taking me to ride upon goats, (which is much the custom of our country) and to shoot with a bow and arrow; but I experienced no satisfaction at all in any of these things; nor could I be easy by any means whatever: my parents were very unhappy to see me so dejected and melancholy.

About this time there came a merchant from the *Gold Coast* (the third city in Guinea) he traded with the inhabitants of our country in ivory &c. he took great notice of my unhappy situation, and enquired into the cause; he expressed vast concern for me, and said, if my parents would part with me for a little while, and let him take me home with him, it would be of more service to me than any thing they could do for me.—He told me that if I would go with him I should see houses with wings to them walk upon the water, and should also see the white folks; and that he had many sons of my age, which should be my companions; and he added to all this that he would bring me safe back again soon.—I was highly pleased with the account of this strange place, and was very desirous of going.—I seemed sensible of a secret impulse upon my mind which I could not resist that seemed to tell me I must go. When my dear mother saw that I was willing to leave them, she spoke to my father and grandfather and the rest of my relations, who all agreed that I should accompany the merchant to the Gold Coast. I was the more willing as my brothers and sisters despised me, and looked on me with contempt on the account of my unhappy disposition; and even my servants slighted me, and disregarded all I said to them. I had one sister who was always exceeding fond of me, and I loved her entirely; her name was Logwy, she was quite white, and fair, with fine light hair though my father and mother were black.—I was truly concerned to leave my beloved sister, and she cry'd most sadly to part with me, wringing her hands, and discovered every sign of grief that can be imagined. Indeed if I could have known when I left my friends and country that I should never return to them again my misery on that oc-

casion would have been inexpressible. All my relations were sorry to part with me; my dear mother came with me upon a camel more than three hundred miles, the first of our journey lay chiefly through woods: at night we secured ourselves from the wild beasts by making fires all around us; we and our camels kept within the circle, or we must have been torn to pieces by the Lyons, and other wild creatures, that roared terribly as soon as night came on, and continued to do so 'till morning.—There can be little said in favour of the country through which we passed; only a valley of marble that we came through which is unspeakably beautiful.—On each side of this valley are exceedingly high and almost inaccessible mountains-Some of these pieces of marble are of prodigious length and breadth but of different sizes and colour, and shaped in a variety of forms, in a wonderful manner.—It is most of it veined with gold mixed with striking and beautiful colours; so that when the sun darts upon it, it is as pleasing a sight as can be imagined.—The merchant that brought me from Bournou, was in partnership with another gentleman who accompanied us; he was very unwilling that he should take me from home, as, he said, he foresaw many difficulties that would attend my going with them.—He endeavoured to prevail on the merchant to throw me into a very deep pit that was in the valley, but he refused to listen to him, and said, he was resolved to take care of me: but the other was greatly dissatisfied; and when we came to a river, which we were obliged to pass through, he purpos'd throwing me in and drowning me; but the Merchant would not consent to it, so that I was preserv'd.

We travel'd 'till about four o'clock every day, and then began to make preparations for night, by cutting down large quantities of wood, to make fires to preserve us from the wild beasts.—I had a very unhappy and discontented journey, being in continual fear that the people I was with would murder me. I often reflected with extreme regret on the kind friends I had left, and the idea of my dear mother frequently drew tears from my eyes.—I cannot recollect how long we were in going from Bournou to the Gold Coast; but as there is no shipping nearer to Bournou than that City, it was tedious in travelling so far by land, being upwards of a thousand miles.—I was heartily rejoic'd when we arriv'd at the end of our journey: I now vainly imagin'd that all my troubles and inquietudes would terminate here; but could I have looked into futurity, I should have perceiv'd that I had much more to suffer than I had before experienc'd, and that they had as yet but barely commenc'd.

I was now more than a thousand miles from home, without a friend or any means to procure one. Soon after I came to the merchant's house I heard the drums beat remarkably loud, and the trumpets blow-the persons accustom'd to this employ, are oblig'd to go upon a very high structure appointed for that purpose, that the sound might be heard at a great distance: They are higher than the steeples are in England. I was mightily pleas'd with sounds so entirely new to me, and was very inquisitive to know the cause of this rejoicing, and ask'd many questions concerning it: I was answer'd that it was meant as a compliment to me, because I was Grandson to the King of Bournou.

This account gave me a secret pleasure; but I was not suffer'd long to enjoy this satisfaction, for in the evening of the same day, two of the merchant's sons (boys about my own age) came running to me, and told me, that the next day I was to die, for the King intended to behead me.—I reply'd that I was sure it could not be true, for that I came there to play with them, and to see houses walk upon the water with wings to them, and the white folks; but I was soon inform'd that their King imagined that I was sent by my father as a spy, and would make such discoveries at my return home that would enable them to make war with the greater advantage to ourselves; and for these reasons he had resolved I should never return to my native country.—When I heard this I suffered misery that cannot be described.—I wished a thousand times that I had never left my friends and country.—But still the Almighty was pleased to work miracles for me.

The morning I was to die, I was washed and all my gold ornaments made bright and shining, and then carried to the palace, where the King was to behead me himself (as is the custom of the place).—He was seated upon a throne at the top of an exceeding large yard, or court, which you must go through to enter the palace, it is as wide and spacious as a large field in England.—I had a lane of lifeguards to go through.—I guessed it to be about three hundred paces.

I was conducted by my friend, the merchant, about half way up; then he durst proceed no further: I went up to the King alone-I went with an undaunted courage, and it pleased God to melt the heart of the King, who sat with his scymitar in his hand ready to behead me; yet, being himself so affected, he dropped it out of his hand, and took me upon his knee and wept over me. I put my right hand round his neck, and prest him to my heart.—He sat me down and blest me; and added that he would not kill me, and that I should not go home, but be sold, for a slave, so then I was conducted back again to the merchant's house.

The next day he took me on board a French brig; but the Captain did not chuse to buy me: he said I was too small; so the merchant took me home with him again.

The partner, whom I have spoken of as my enemy, was very angry to see me return, and again purposed putting an end to my life; for he represented to the other, that I should bring them into troubles and difficulties, and that I was so little that no person would buy me.

The merchant's resolution began to waver, and I was indeed afraid that I should be put to death: but however he said he would try me once more.

A few days after a Dutch ship came into the harbour, and they carried me on board, in hopes that the Captain would purchase me.—As they went, I heard them agree, that, if they could not sell me *then*, they would throw me overboard.—I was in extreme agonies when I heard this; and as soon as ever I saw the Dutch Captain, I ran to him, and put my arms round him, and said, "father, save me." (for I knew that if he did not buy me, I should be treated very ill, or, possibly, murdered) And though he did not understand my language, yet it pleased the Almighty to influence him in my behalf, and he bought me *for two yards of check*, which is of more value *there*, than in England.

When I left my dear mother I had a large quantity of gold about me, as is the custom of our country, it was made into rings, and they were linked into one another, and formed into a kind of chain, and so put round my neck, and arms and legs, and a large piece hanging at one ear almost in the shape of a pear. I found all this troublesome, and was glad when my new Master took it from me-I was now washed, and clothed in the Dutch or English manner.—My master grew very fond of me, and I loved him exceedingly. I watched every look, was always ready when he wanted me, and endeavoured to convince him, by every action, that my only pleasure was to serve him well.—I have since thought that he must have been a serious man. His actions corresponded very well with such a character.—He used to read prayers in public to the ship's crew every Sabbath day; and when first I saw him read, I was never so surprised in my whole life as when I saw the book talk to my master; for I thought it did, as I observed him to look upon it, and move his lips.—I wished it would do so to me.—As soon as my master had done reading I follow'd him to the place where he put the book, being mightily delighted with it, and when nobody saw me, I open'd it and put my ear down close upon it, in great hope that it wou'd say something to me; but was very sorry and greatly disappointed when I found it would not speak, this thought immediately presented itself to me, that every body and every thing despis'd me because I was black.

I was exceedingly sea-sick at first; but when I became more accustom'd to the sea, it wore off.—My master's ship was bound for Barbadoes. When we came there, he thought fit to speak of me to several gentlemen of his acquaintance, and one of them exprest a particular desire to see me.—He had a great mind to buy me; but the Captain could not immediately be prevail'd on to part with me; but however, as the gentleman seem'd very solicitous, he at length let me go, and I was sold for fifty dollars (*four and sixpenny-pieces in English*). My new master's name was Vanhorn, a young Gentleman; his home was in New-England in the City of New-York; to which place he took me with him. He dress'd me in his livery, and was very good to me. My chief business was to wait at table, and tea, and clean knives, and I had a very easy place; but the servants us'd to curse and swear surprizingly; which I learnt faster than any thing, 'twas almost the first English I could speak. If any of them affronted me, I was sure to call upon God to damn them immediately; but I was broke of it all at once, occasioned by the correction of an old black servant that liv'd in the family-One day I had just clean'd the knives for dinner, when one of the maids took one to cut bread and butter with; I was very angry with her, and called upon God to damn her; when this old black man told me I must not say so. I ask'd him why? He replied there was a wicked man call'd the Devil, that liv'd in hell, and would take all that said these words, and put them in the fire and burn them.—This terrified me greatly, and I was entirely broke of swearing.—Soon after this, as I was placing the china for tea, my mistress came into the room just as the maid had been cleaning it; the girl had unfortunately sprinkled the wainscot with the mop; at which my mistress was angry; the girl very foolishly answer'd her again, which made her worse, and she call'd upon God to damn her.—I was vastly concern'd to hear this, as she was a fine young lady, and very good to me, insomuch that I could not help speaking to her, "Madam, says I, you must not say so," Why, says she? Because there is a black man call'd the Devil that lives in hell, and he will put you in the fire and burn you, and I shall be very sorry for that. Who told you this replied my lady? Old Ned, says I. Very well was all her answer; but she told my master of it, and he order'd that old Ned should be tyed up and whipp'd, and was never suffer'd to come into the kitchen with the rest of the servants afterwards.—My mistress was not angry with me, but rather diverted with my simplicity and, by way of talk, She repeated what I had said, to many of her acquaintance that visited her; among the rest, Mr. Freelandhouse, a very gracious, good Minister, heard it, and he took a great deal of notice of me, and desired my master to part with me to him. He would not hear of it at first, but, being greatly persuaded, he let me go, and Mr. Freelandhouse gave £50. for me.—He took me home with him, and made me kneel down, and put my two hands together, and pray'd for me, and every night and morning he did the same.—I could not make out what it was for, nor the meaning of it, nor what they spoke to when they talk'd-I thought it comical, but I lik'd it very

well.—After I had been a little while with my new master I grew more familiar, and ask'd him the meaning of prayer: (I could hardly speak english to be understood) he took great pains with me, and made me understand that he pray'd to God, who liv'd in Heaven; that He was my Father and best Friend.—I told him that this must be a mistake; that *my* father liv'd at Bournou, and I wanted very much to see him, and likewise my dear mother, and sister, and I wish'd he would be so good as to send me home to them; and I added, all I could think of to induce him to convey me back. I appeared in great trouble, and my good master was so much affected that the tears ran down his face. He told me that God was a Great and Good Spirit, that He created all the world, and every person and thing in it, in Ethiopia, Africa, and America, and every where. I was delighted when I heard this: There, says I, I always thought so when I liv'd at home! Now if I had wings like an Eagle I would fly to tell my dear mother that God is greater than the sun, moon, and stars; and that they were made by Him.

I was exceedingly pleas'd with this information of my master's, because it corresponded so well with my own opinion; I thought now if I could but get home, I should be wiser than all my country-folks, my grandfather, or father, or mother, or any of them-But though I was somewhat enlighten'd by this information of my master's, yet, I had no other knowledge of God but that He was a Good Spirit, and created every body, and every thing-I never was sensible in myself, nor had any one ever told me, that He would punish the wicked, and love the just. I was only glad that I had been told there was a God because I had always thought so.

My dear kind master grew very fond of me, as was his Lady; she put me to School, but I was uneasy at that, and did not like to go; but my master and mistress requested me to learn in the gentlest terms, and persuaded me to attend my school without any anger at all; that, at last, I came to like it better, and learnt to read pretty well. My schoolmaster was a good man, his name was Vanosdore, and very indulgent to me.—I was in this state when, one Sunday, I heard my master preach from these words out of the Revelations, chap. i. v. 7. *"Behold, He cometh in the clouds and every eye shall see him and they that pierc'd Him."* These words affected me excessively; I was in great agonies because I thought my master directed them to me only; and, I fancied, that he observ'd me with unusual earnestness-I was farther confirm'd in this belief as I look'd round the church, and could see no one person beside myself in such grief and distress as I was; I began to think that my master hated me, and was very desirous to go home, to my own country; for I thought that if God did come (as he said) He would be sure to be most angry with me, as I did not know what He was, nor had ever heard of him before.

I went home in great trouble, but said nothing to any body.—I was somewhat afraid of my master; I thought he disliked me.—The next text I heard him preach from was, Heb. xii. 14. *"follow peace with all men, and holiness, without which no man shall see the LORD."* he preached the law so severely, that it made me tremble.—he said, that GOD would judge the whole world; Ethiopia, Asia, and Africa, and every where.—I was now excessively perplexed, and undetermined what to do; as I had now reason to believe my situation would be equally bad to go, as to stay.—I kept these thoughts to myself, and said nothing to any person whatever.

I should have complained to my good mistress of this great trouble of mind, but she had been a little strange to me for several days before this happened, occasioned by a story told of me by one of the maids. The servants were all jealous, and envied me the regard, and favour shewn me by my master and mistress; and the Devil being always ready, and diligent in wickedness, had influenced this girl, to make a lye on me.—This happened about hay-harvest, and one day when I was unloading the waggon to put the hay into the barn, she watched an opportunity, in my absence, to take the fork out of the stick, and hide it: when I came again to my work, and could not find it, I was a good deal vexed, but I concluded it was dropt somewhere among the hay; so I went and bought another with my own money: when the girl saw that I had another, she was so malicious that she told my mistress I was very unfaithful, and not the person she took me for; and that she knew, I had, without my master's permission, order'd many things in his name, that he must pay for; and as a proof of my carelessness produc'd the fork she had taken out of the stick, and said, she had found it out of doors-My Lady, not knowing the truth of these things, was a little shy to me, till she mention'd it, and then I soon cleared myself, and convinc'd her that these accusations were false.

I continued in a most unhappy state for many days. My good mistress insisted on knowing what was the matter. When I made known my situation she gave me John Bunyan on the holy war, to read; I found his experience similar to my own, which gave me reason to suppose he must be a bad man; as I was convinc'd of my own corrupt nature, and the misery of my own heart: and as he acknowledg'd that he was likewise in the same condition, I experienc'd no relief at all in reading his work, but rather the reverse.—I took the book to my lady, and inform'd her I did not like it at all, it was concerning a wicked man as bad as myself; and I did not chuse to read it, and I desir'd her to give me another, wrote by a better

man that was holy and without sin.—She assur'd me that John Bunyan was a good man, but she could not convince me; I thought him to be too much like myself to be upright, as his experience seem'd to answer with my own.

I am very sensible that nothing but the great power and unspeakable mercies of the Lord could relieve my soul from the heavy burden it laboured under at that time.—A few days after my master gave me Baxter's *Call to the unconverted*. This was no relief to me neither; on the contrary it occasioned as much distress in me as the other had before done, *as it* invited all to come to *Christ* and I found myself so wicked and miserable that I could not come-This consideration threw me into agonies that cannot be described; insomuch that I even attempted to put an end to my life-I took one of the large case-knives, and went into the stable with an intent to destroy myself; and as I endeavoured with all my strength to force the knife into my side, it bent double. I was instantly struck with horror at the thought of my own rashness, and my conscience told me that had I succeeded in this attempt I should probably have gone to hell.

I could find no relief, nor the least shadow of comfort; the extreme distress of my mind so affected my health that I continued very ill for three Days, and Nights; and would admit of no means to be taken for my recovery, though my lady was very kind, and sent many things to me; but I rejected every means of relief and wished to die-I would not go into my own bed, but lay in the stable upon straw-I felt all the horrors of a troubled conscience, so hard to be born, and saw all the vengeance of God ready to overtake me-I was sensible that there was no way for me to be saved unless I came to *Christ,* and I could not come to Him: I thought that it was impossible He should receive such a sinner as me.

The last night that I continued in this place, in the midst of my distress these words were brought home upon my mind, *"Behold the Lamb of God."* I was something comforted at this, and began to grow easier and wished for day that I might find these words in my bible-I rose very early the following morning, and went to my school-master, Mr. Vanosdore, and communicated the situation of my mind to him; he was greatly rejoiced to find me enquiring the way to Zion, and blessed the Lord who had worked so wonderfully for me a poor heathen.—I was more familiar with this good gentleman than with my master, or any other person; and found myself more at liberty to talk to him: he encouraged me greatly, and prayed with me frequently, and I was always benefited by his discourse.

About a quarter of a mile from my Master's house stood a large remarkably fine Oak-tree, in the midst of a wood; I often used to be employed there in cutting down trees, (a work I was very fond of) I seldom failed going to this place every day; sometimes twice a day if I could be spared. It was the highest pleasure I ever experienced to set under this Oak; for there I used to pour out all my complaints to the LORD: and when I had any particular grievance I used to go there, and talk to the tree, and tell my sorrows, as if it had been to a friend.

Here I often lamented my own wicked heart, and undone state; and found more comfort and consolation than I ever was sensible of before.—Whenever I was treated with ridicule or contempt, I used to come here and find peace. I now began to relish the book my Master gave me, Baxter's *Call to the unconverted*, and took great delight in it. I was always glad to be employ'd in cutting wood, 'twas a great part of my business, and I follow'd it with delight, as I was then quite alone and my heart lifted up to GOD, and I was enabled to pray continually; and blessed for ever be his Holy Name, he faithfully answer'd my prayers. I can never be thankful enough to Almighty GOD for the many comfortable opportunities I experienced there.

It is possible the circumstance I am going to relate will not gain credit with many; but this I know, that the joy and comfort it conveyed to me, cannot be expressed and only conceived by those who have experienced the like.

I was one day in a most delightful frame of mind; my heart so overflowed with love and gratitude to the Author of all my comforts.—I was so drawn out of myself, and so fill'd and awed by the Presence of God that I saw (or thought I saw) light inexpressible dart down from heaven upon me, and shone around me for the space of a minute.—I continued on my knees, and joy unspeakable took possession of my soul.—The peace and serenity which filled my mind after this was wonderful, and cannot be told.—I would not have changed situations, or been any one but myself for the whole world. I blest God for my poverty, that I had no worldly riches or grandeur to draw my heart from Him. I wish'd at that time, if it had been possible for me, to have continued on that spot for ever. I felt an unwillingness in myself to have any thing more to do with the world, or to mix with society again. I seemed to possess a full assurance that my sins were forgiven me. I went home all my way rejoicing, and this text of scripture came full upon my mind. *"And I will make an everlasting covenant with them, that I will not turn away from them, to do them good; but I will put my fear in their hearts that they shall not depart from me."* The first opportunity that presented itself, I went to my old school-master, and made known to him the happy state of my soul who joined with me in praise to God for his mercy to me the vilest of sinners.—I was now perfectly easy, and had hardly a wish to make beyond what I possess'd, when my temporal comforts were all blasted by the death of my dear and worthy Master Mr. Freelandhouse, who was taken from this world rather

suddenly: he had but a short illness, and died of a fever. I held his hand in mine when he departed; he told me he had given me my freedom. I was at liberty to go where I would.—He added that he had always pray'd for me and hop'd I should be kept unto the end. My master left me by his will ten pounds, and my freedom.

I found that if he had lived 'twas his intention to take me with him to Holland, as he had often mention'd me to some friends of his there that were desirous to see me; but I chose to continue with my Mistress who was as good to me as if she had been my mother.

The loss of Mr. Freelandhouse distress'd me greatly, but I was render'd still more unhappy by the clouded and perplex'd situation of my mind; the great enemy of my soul being ready to torment me, would present my own misery to me in such striking light, and distress me with doubts, fears, and such a deep sense of my own unworthiness, that after all the comfort and encouragement I had received, I was often tempted to believe I should be a Cast-away at last.—The more I saw of the Beauty and Glory of God, the more I was humbled under a sense of my own vileness. I often repair'd to my old place of prayer; I seldom came away without consolation. One day this Scripture was wonderfully apply'd to my mind, *"And ye are compleat in Him which is the Head of all principalities and power."*-The Lord was pleas'd to comfort me by the application of many gracious promises at times when I was ready to sink under my troubles. *"Wherefore He is able also to save them to the uttermost that come unto God by Him seeing He ever liveth to make intercession for them. Hebrews x. ver. 14. For by one offering He hath perfected for ever them that are sanctified."*

My kind, indulgent Mistress liv'd but two years after my Master. Her death was a great affliction to me. She left five sons, all gracious young men, and Ministers of the Gospel.—I continued with them all, one after another, till they died; they liv'd but four years after their parents. When it pleased God to take them to Himself, I was left quite destitute, without a friend in the world. But I who had so often experienced the Goodness of GOD, trusted in Him to do what He pleased with me.—In this helpless condition I went in the wood to prayer as usual; and tho' the snow was a considerable height, I was not sensible of cold, or any other inconveniency.—At times indeed when I saw the world frowning round me, I was tempted to think that the LORD had forsaken me. I found great relief from the contemplation of these words in Isaiah xlix. v. 16. *"Behold I have graven thee on the palms of my hands; thy walls are continually before me."* And very many comfortable promises were sweetly applied to me. The lxxxix. Psalm and 34th verse, *"My covenant will I not break nor alter the thing that is gone out of my lips."* Hebrews, chap. xvi. v. 17, 18. Phillipians, chap. i. v. 6; and several more.

As I had now lost all my dear and valued friends every place in the world was alike to me. I had for a great while entertain'd a desire to come to England.—I imagined that all the Inhabitants of this Island were *Holy*; because all those that had visited my Master from thence were good, (Mr. Whitefield was his particular friend) and the authors of the books that had been given me were all English. But above all places in the world I wish'd to see Kidderminster, for I could not but think that on the spot where Mr. Baxter had liv'd, and preach'd, the people must be all *Righteous.*

The situation of my affairs requir'd that I should tarry a little longer in New-York, as I was something in debt, and was embarrass'd how to pay it.—About this time a young Gentleman that was a particular acquaintance of one of my young Master's, pretended to be a friend to me, and promis'd to pay my debts, which was three pounds; and he assur'd me he would never expect the money again.—But, in less than a month, he came and demanded it; and when I assur'd him I had nothing to pay, he threatened to sell me.—Though I knew he had no right to do that, yet as I had no friend in the world to go to, it alarm'd me greatly.—At length he purpos'd my going a Privateering, that I might by these means, be enabled to pay him, to which I agreed.—Our Captain's name was — I went in Character of Cook to him.—Near St. Domingo we came up to five French ships, Merchant-men.—We had a very smart engagement that continued from eight in the morning till three in the afternoon; when victory declar'd on our side.-Soon after this we were met by three English ships which join'd us, and that encourag'd us to attack a fleet of 36 Ships.-We boarded the three first and then follow'd the others; and had the same success with twelve; but the rest escap'd us.-There was a great deal of blood shed, and I was near death several times, but the LORD preserv'd me.

I met with many enemies, and much persecution, among the sailors; one of them was particularly unkind to me, and studied ways to vex and teaze me.—I can't help mentioning one circumstance that hurt me more than all the rest, which was, that he snatched a book out of my hand that I was very fond of, and used frequently to amuse myself with, and threw it into the sea.—But what is remarkable he was the first that was killed in our engagement.—I don't pretend to say that this happen'd because he was not my friend: but I thought 'twas a very awful Providence to see how the enemies of the LORD are cut off.

Our Captain was a cruel hard-hearted man. I was excessively sorry for the prisoners we took in general; but the pitiable case of one young Gentleman grieved me to the heart.—He appear'd very amiable; was strikingly handsome. Our Captain took four thousand pounds from him; but that did not satisfy him, as he imagin'd he was possess'd of more, and had somewhere conceal'd it, so that the Captain threatened him with death, at which he appear'd in the deepest distress, and took the buckles out of his shoes, and untied his hair, which was very fine, and long; and in which several very valuable rings were fasten'd. He came into the Cabbin to me, and in the most obliging terms imaginable ask'd for something to eat and drink; which when I gave him, he was so thankful and pretty in his manner that my heart bled for him; and I heartily wish'd that I could have spoken in any language in which the ship's crew would not have understood me; that I might have let him know his danger; for I heard the Captain say he was resolv'd upon his death; and he put his barbarous design into execution, for he took him on shore with one of the sailors, and there they shot him.

This circumstance affected me exceedingly, I could not put him out of my mind a long while.—When we return'd to New-York the Captain divided the prize-money among us, that we had taken. When I was call'd upon to receive my part, I waited upon Mr. —, (the Gentleman that paid my debt and was the occasion of my going abroad) to know if he chose to go with me to receive my money or if I should bring him what I owed.—He chose to go with me; and when the Captain laid my money on the table ('twas an hundred and thirty-five pounds) I desir'd Mr. — to take what I was indebted to him; and he swept it all into his handkerchief, and would never be prevail'd on to give a farthing of money, nor any thing at all beside.—And he likewise secur'd a hogshead of sugar which was my due from the same ship. The Captain was very angry with him for this piece of cruelty to me, as was every other person that heard it.—But I have reason to believe (as he was one of the Principal Merchants in the city) that he transacted business for him and on that account did not chuse to quarrel with him.

At this time a very worthy Gentleman, a Wine Merchant, his name Dunscum, took me under his protection, and would have recovered my money for me if I had chose it; but I told him to let it alone; that I wou'd rather be quiet.—I believed that it would not prosper with him, and so it happen'd, for by a series of losses and misfortunes he became poor, and was soon after drowned, as he was on a party of pleasure.—The vessel was driven out to sea, and struck against a rock by which means every soul perished.

I was very much distress'd when I heard it, and felt greatly for his family who were reduc'd to very low circumstances.—I never knew how to set a proper value on money. If I had but a little meat and drink to supply the present necessaries of life, I never wish'd for more; and when I had any I always gave it if ever I saw an object in distress. If it was not for my dear Wife and Children I should pay as little regard to money now as I did at that time.—I continu'd some time with Mr. Dunscum as his servant; he was very kind to me.—But I had a vast inclination to visit England, and wish'd continually that it would please Providence to make a clear way for me to see this Island. I entertain'd a notion that if I could get to England I should never more experience either cruelty or ingratitude, so that I was very desirous to get among Christians. I knew Mr. Whitefield very well.—I had heard him preach often at New-York. In this disposition I listed in the twenty-eighth Regiment of Foot, who were design'd for Martinico in the late war.—We went in Admiral Pocock's fleet from New-York to Barbadoes; from thence to Martinico.—When that was taken we proceeded to the Havannah, and took that place likewise.—There I got discharged.

I was then worth about thirty pounds, but I never regarded money in the least, nor would I tarry to receive my prize-money least I should lose my chance of going to England.—I went with the Spanish prisoners to Spain; and came to Old-England with the English prisoners.—I cannot describe my joy when we were within sight of Portsmouth. But I was astonished when we landed to hear the inhabitants of that place curse and swear, and otherwise profane. I expected to find nothing but goodness, gentleness and meekness in this Christian Land, I then suffer'd great perplexities of mind.

I enquir'd if any serious Christian people resided there, the woman I made this enquiry of, answer'd me in the affirmative; and added that she was one of them.—I was heartily glad to hear her say so. I thought I could give her my whole heart: she kept a Public-House. I deposited with her all the money that I had not an immediate occasion for; as I thought it would be safer with her.—It was 25 guineas but 6 of them I desired her to lay out to the best advantage, to buy me some shirts, hat and some other necessaries. I made her a present of a very handsome large looking glass that I brought with me from Martinico, in order to recompence her for the trouble I had given her. I must do this woman the justice to acknowledge that she did lay out some little for my use, but the 19 guineas and part of the 6, with my watch, she would not return, but denied that I ever gave it her.

I soon perceived that I was got among bad people, who defrauded me of my money and watch; and that all my promis'd happiness was blasted, I had no friend but GOD and I pray'd to Him earnestly. I could scarcely believe it possible that the place where so many eminent Christians

had lived and preached could abound with so much wickedness and deceit. I thought it worse than *Sodom* (considering the great advantages they have) I cryed like a child and that almost continually: at length GOD heard my prayers and rais'd me a friend indeed.

This publican had a brother who lived on Portsmouth-common, his wife was a very serious good woman.—When she heard of the treatment I had met with, she came and enquired into my real situation and was greatly troubled at the ill usage I had received, and took me home to her own house.—I began now to rejoice, and my prayer was turned into praise. She made use of all the arguments in her power to prevail on her who had wronged me, to return my watch and money, but it was to no purpose, as she had given me no receipt and I had nothing to show for it, I could not demand it.—My good friend was excessively angry with her and obliged her to give me back four guineas, which she said she gave me out of charity: Though in fact it was my own, and much more. She would have employed some rougher means to oblige her to give up my money, but I would not suffer her, let it go says I "My GOD is in heaven." Still I did not mind my loss in the least; all that grieved me was, that I had been disappointed in finding some Christian friends, with whom I hoped to enjoy a little sweet and comfortable society.

I thought the best method that I could take now, was to go to London, and find out Mr. Whitefield, who was the only living soul I knew in England, and get him to direct me to some way or other to procure a living without being troublesome to any Person.—I took leave of my Christian friend at Portsmouth, and went in the stage to London.—A creditable tradesman in the City, who went up with me in the stage, offer'd to show me the way to Mr. Whitefield's Tabernacle. Knowing that I was a perfect stranger, I thought it very kind, and accepted his offer; but he obliged me to give him half-a-crown for going with me, and likewise insisted on my giving him five shillings more for conducting me to Dr. Gifford's Meeting.

I began now to entertain a very different idea of the inhabitants of England than what I had figur'd to myself before I came amongst them.—Mr. Whitefield receiv'd me very friendly, was heartily glad to see me, and directed me to a proper place to board and lodge in Petticoat-Lane, till he could think of some way to settle me in, and paid for my lodging, and all my expences. The morning after I came to my new lodging, as I was at breakfast with the gentlewoman of the house, I heard the noise of some looms over our heads: I enquir'd what it was; she told me a person was weaving silk.—I express'd a great desire to see it, and ask'd if I might: She told me she would go up with me; she was sure I should be very welcome. She was as good as her word, and as soon as we enter'd the room, the person that was weaving look'd about, and smiled upon us, and I loved her from that moment.—She ask'd me many questions, and I in turn talk'd a great deal to her. I found she was a member of Mr. Allen's Meeting, and I begun to entertain a good opinion of her, though I was almost afraid to indulge this inclination, least she should prove like all the rest I had met with at Portsmouth, &c. and which had almost given me a dislike to all white women.—But after a short acquaintance I had the happiness to find she was very different, and quite sincere, and I was not without hope that she entertain'd some esteem for me. We often went together to hear Dr. Gifford, and as I had always a propensity to relieve every object in distress as far as I was able, I used to give to all that complain'd to me; sometimes half a guinea at a time, as I did not understand the real value of it.—This gracious, good woman took great pains to correct and advise me in that and many other respects.

After I had been in London about six weeks I was recommended to the notice of some of my late Master Mr. Freelandhouse's acquaintance, who had heard him speak frequently of me. I was much persuaded by them to go to Holland.—My Master lived there before he bought me, and used to speak of me so respectfully among his friends there, that it raised in them a curiosity to see me; particularly the Gentlemen engaged in the Ministry, who expressed a desire to hear my experience and examine me. I found that it was my good old Master's design that I should have gone if he had lived; for which reason I resolved upon going to Holland, and informed my dear friend Mr. Whitefield of my intention; he was much averse to my going at first, but after I gave him my reasons appeared very well satisfied. I likewise informed my Betty (the good woman that I have mentioned above) of my determination to go to Holland and I told her that I believed she was to be my Wife: that if it was the LORD's Will I desired it, but not else.—She made me very little answer, but has since told me, she did not think it at that time.

I embarked at Tower-wharf at four o'clock in the morning, and arriv'd at Amsterdam the next day by three o'clock in the afternoon. I had several letters of recommendation to my old master's friends, who receiv'd me very graciously. Indeed, one of the chief Ministers was particularly good to me; he kept me at his house a long while, and took great pleasure in asking questions, which I answer'd with delight, being always ready to say, "*Come unto me all ye that fear GOD, and I will tell what he hath done for my Soul.*" I cannot but admire the footsteps of Providence; astonish'd that I should be so wonderfully preserved! Though the Grandson of a King, I have wanted bread, and should have been glad of the hardest

crust I ever saw. I who, at home, was surrounded and guarded by slaves, so that no indifferent person might approach me, and clothed with gold, have been inhumanly threatened with death; and frequently wanted clothing to defend me from the inclemency of the weather; yet I never murmured, nor was I discontented.—I am willing, and even desirous to be counted as nothing, a stranger in the world, and a pilgrim here; for "*I know that my Redeemer liveth,*" and I'm thankful for every trial and trouble that I've met with, as I am not without hope that they have been all sanctified to me.

The Calvinist Ministers desired to hear my Experience from myself, which proposal I was very well pleased with: So I stood before 38 Ministers every Thursday for seven weeks together, and they were all very well satisfied, and persuaded I was what I pretended to be.—They wrote down my experience as I spoke it; and the Lord Almighty was with me at that time in a remarkable manner, and gave me words and enabled me to answer them; so great was his mercy to take me in hand a poor blind heathen.

At this time a very rich Merchant at Amsterdam offered to take me into his family in the capacity of his Butler, and I very willingly accepted it.—He was a gracious worthy Gentleman and very good to me.—He treated me more like a friend than a servant.—I tarried there a twelvemonth but was not thoroughly contented, I wanted to see my wife; (that is now) and for that reason I wished to return to *England,* I wrote to her once in my absence, but she did not answer my letter; and I must acknowledge if she had, it would have given me a less opinion of her.—My Master and Mistress persuaded me much not to leave them and likewise their two Sons who entertained a good opinion of me; and if I had found my Betty married on my arrival in England, I should have returned to them again immediately.

My Lady purposed my marrying her maid; she was an agreeable young woman, had saved a good deal of money, but I could not fancy her, though she was willing to accept of me, but I told her my inclinations were engaged in England, and I could think of no other Person.—On my return home, I found my Betty disengaged.—She had refused several offers in my absence, and told her sister that, she thought, if ever she married I was to be her husband.

Soon after I came home, I waited on Doctor Gifford who took me into his family and was exceedingly, good to me. The character of this pious worthy Gentleman is well known; my praise can be of no use or signification at all.—I hope I shall ever gratefully remember the many favours I have received from him.—Soon after I came to Doctor Gifford I expressed a desire to be admitted into their Church, and set down with them; they told me I must first be baptized; so I gave in my experience before the Church, with which they were very well satisfied, and I was baptized by Doctor Gifford with some others. I then made known my intentions of being married; but I found there were many objections against it because the person I had fixed on was poor. She was a widow, her husband had left her in debt, and with a child, so that they persuaded me against it out of real regard to me.—But I had promised and was resolved to have her; as I knew her to be a gracious woman, her poverty was no objection to me, as they had nothing else to say against her. When my friends found that they could not alter my opinion respecting her, they wrote to Mr. Allen, the Minister she attended, to persuade her to leave me; but he replied that he would not interfere at all, that we might do as we would. I was resolved that all my wife's little debt should be paid before we were married; so that I sold almost every thing I had and with all the money I could raise cleared all that she owed, and I never did any thing with a better will in all my Life, because I firmly believed that we should be very happy together, and so it prov'd, for she was given me from the LORD. And I have found her a blessed partner, and we have never repented, tho' we have gone through many great troubles and difficulties.

My wife got a very good living by weaving, and could do extremely well; but just at that time there was great disturbance among the weavers; so that I was afraid to let my wife work, least they should insist on my joining the rioters which I could not think of, and, possibly, if I had refused to do so they would have knock'd me on the head.—So that by these means my wife could get no employ, neither had I work enough to maintain my family. We had not yet been married a year before all these misfortunes overtook us.

Just at this time a gentleman, that seemed much concerned for us, advised me to go into Essex with him and promised to get me employed.—I accepted his kind proposal, and he spoke to a friend of his, a Quaker, a gentleman of large fortune, who resided a little way out of the town of *Colchester*; his name was *Handbarar*; he ordered his steward to set me to work. There were several employed in the same way with myself. I was very thankful and contented though my wages were but small.-I was allowed but eight pence a day, and found myself; but after I had been in this situation for a fortnight, my Master, being told that a Black was at work for him, had an inclination to see me. He was pleased to talk to me for some time, and at last enquired what wages I had; when I told him he declared, it was too little, and immediately ordered his Steward to let me have eighteen pence a day, which he constantly gave me after; and I then did extremely well.

I did not bring my wife with me: I came first alone and it was my design, if things answered according to our wishes, to send for her-I was now thinking to desire her to come to me when I receiv'd a letter to inform me she was just brought to bed and in want of many necessaries.—This news was a great trial to me and a fresh affliction: but my God, *faithful and abundant in mercy*, forsook me not in this trouble.—As I could not read *English*, I was obliged to apply to some one to read the letter I received, relative to my wife. I was directed by the good Providence of God to a worthy young gentleman, a Quaker, and friend of my Master.—I desired he would take the trouble to read my letter for me, which he readily comply'd with and was greatly moved and affected at the contents; insomuch that he said he would undertake to make a gathering for me, which he did and was the first to contribute to it himself. The money was sent that evening to London by a person who happen'd to be going there: nor was this All the goodness that I experienced from these kind friends, for, as soon as my wife came about and was fit to travel, they sent for her to me, and were at the whole expence of her coming; so evidently has the love and mercy of God appeared through every trouble that ever I experienced. We went on very comfortably all the summer.—We lived in a little cottage near Mr. *Handbarrar's* House; but when the winter came on I was discharged, as he had no further occasion for me. And now the prospect began to darken upon us again. We thought it most adviseable to move our habitation a little nearer to the Town, as the house we lived in was very cold, and wet, and ready to tumble down.

The boundless goodness of GOD to me has been so very great, that with the most humble gratitude I desire to prostrate myself before Him; for I have been wonderfully supported in every affliction. My GOD never left me. I perceived light still through the thickest darkness.

My dear wife and I were now both unemployed, we could get nothing to do. The winter prov'd remarkably severe, and we were reduc'd to the greatest distress imaginable.—I was always very shy of asking for any thing; I could never beg; neither did I chuse to make known our wants to any person, for fear of offending as we were entire strangers; but our last bit of bread was gone, and I was obliged to think of something to do for our support.—I did not mind for myself at all; but to see my dear wife and children in want pierc'd me to the heart.—I now blam'd myself for bringing her from London, as doubtless had we continued there we might have found friends to keep us from starving. The snow was at this season remarkably deep; so that we could see no prospect of being relieved. In this melancholy situation, not knowing what step to pursue, I resolved to make my case known to a Gentleman's Gardiner that lived near us, and entreat him to employ me: but when I came to him, my courage failed me, and I was ashamed to make known our real situation.—I endeavoured all I could to prevail on him to set me to work, but to no purpose: he assur'd me it was not in his power: but just as I was about to leave him, he asked me if I would accept of some Carrots? I took them with great thankfulness and carried them home: he gave me four, they were very large and fine.—We had nothing to make fire with, so consequently could not boil them: But was glad to have them to eat *raw*. Our youngest child was quite an infant; so that my wife was obliged to chew it, and fed her in that manner for several days.—We allowed ourselves but one every day, least they should not last 'till we could get some other supply. I was unwilling to eat at all myself; nor would I take any the last day that we continued in this situation, as I could not bear the thought that my dear wife and children would be in want of every means of support. We lived in this manner, 'till our carrots were all gone: then my Wife began to lament because of our poor babies: but I comforted her all I could; still hoping, and believing that *my* GOD would not let us die: but that it would please Him to relieve us, which *He* did by almost a Miracle.

We went to bed, as usual, before it was quite dark, (as we had neither fire nor candle) but had not been there long before some person knocked at the door & enquir'd if *James Albert* lived there? I answer'd in the affirmative, and rose immediately; as soon as I open'd the door I found it was the servant of an eminent Attorney who resided at *Colchester*.—He ask'd me how it was with me? if I was not almost starv'd? I burst out a crying, and told him I was indeed. He said his master suppos'd so, and that he wanted to speak with me, and I must return with him. This Gentleman's name was *Danniel*, he was a sincere, good Christian. He used to stand and talk with me frequently when I work'd in the road for Mr. *Handbarrar*, and would have employed me himself, if I had wanted work.—When I came to his house he told me that he had thought a good deal about me of late, and was apprehensive that I must be in want, and could not be satisfied till he sent to enquire after me. I made known my distress to him, at which he was greatly affected; and generously gave me a guinea; and promis'd to be kind to me in future. I could not help exclaiming. *O the boundless mercies of my God!* I pray'd unto Him, and He has heard me; I trusted in Him and He has preserv'd me: where shall I begin to praise Him, or how shall I love Him enough?

I went immediately and bought some bread and cheese and coal and carried it home. My dear wife was rejoiced to see me return with something to eat. She instantly got up and dressed our Babies, while I made a fire, and the first Nobility in the land never made a more comfortable meal.—We did not forget to thank the LORD for all his goodness to us.—Soon after this, as the spring came on, Mr. Peter *Daniel* employed me in helping to pull down a house, and rebuilding it. I had then very good work, and full employ: he sent for my wife, and children to *Colchester*, and provided us a house where we lived very comfortably.—I hope I shall always gratefully acknowledge his kindness to myself and family. I worked at this house for more than a year, till it was finished; and after that I was employed by several successively, and was never so happy as when I had something to do; but perceiving the winter coming on, and work rather slack, I was apprehensive that we should again be in want or become troublesome to our friends.

I had at this time an offer made me of going to *Norwich* and having constant employ.—My wife seemed pleased with this proposal, as she supposed she might get work there in the weaving-manufactory, being the business she was brought up to, and more likely to succeed there than any other place; and we thought as we had an opportunity of moving to a Town where we could both be employ'd it was most adviseable to do so; and that probably we might settle there for our lives.—When this step was resolv'd on, I went first alone to see how it would answer; which I very much repented after, for it was not in my power immediately to send my wife any supply, as I fell into the hands of a Master that was neither kind nor considerate; and she was reduced to great distress, so that she was oblig'd to sell the few goods that we had, and when I sent for her was under the disagreeable necessity of parting with our bed.

When she came to *Norwich* I hired a room ready furnished.—I experienced a great deal of difference in the carriage of my Master from what I had been accustomed to from some of my other Masters. He was very irregular in his payments to me.—My wife hired a loom and wove all the leisure time she had and we began to do very well, till we were overtaken by fresh misfortunes. Our three poor children fell ill of the small pox; this was a great trial to us; but still I was persuaded in myself we should not be forsaken.—And I did all in my power to keep my dear partner's spirits from sinking. Her whole attention now was taken up with the children as she could mind nothing else, and all I could get was but little to support a family in such a situation, beside paying for the hire of our room, which I was obliged to omit doing for several weeks: but the woman to whom we were indebted would not excuse us, tho' I promised she should have the very first money we could get after my children came about, but she would not be satisfied and had the cruelty to threaten us that if we did not pay her immediately she would turn us all into the street.

The apprehension of this plunged me in the deepest distress, considering the situation of my poor babies: if they had been in health I should have been less sensible of this misfortune. But My GOD, *still faithful to his promise*, raised me a friend. Mr. Henry Gurdney, a Quaker, a gracious gentleman heard of our distress, he sent a servant of his own to the woman we hired the room of, paid our rent, and bought all the goods with my wife's loom and gave it us all.

Some other gentlemen, hearing of his design, were pleased to assist him in these generous acts, for which we never can be thankful enough; after this my children soon came about; we began to do pretty well again; my dear wife work'd hard and constant when she could get work, but it was upon a disagreeable footing as her employ was so uncertain, sometimes she could get nothing to do and at other times when the weavers of *Norwich* had orders from London they were so excessively hurried, that the people they employ'd were often oblig'd to work on the *Sabbath-day*; but this my wife would never do, and it was matter of uneasiness to us that we could not get our living in a regular manner, though we were both diligent, industrious, and willing to work. I was far from being happy in my Master, he did not use me well. I could scarcely ever get my money from him; but I continued patient 'till it pleased GOD to alter my situation.

My worthy friend Mr. Gurdney advised me to follow the employ of chopping chaff, and bought me an instrument for that purpose. There were but few people in the town that made this their business beside myself; so that I did very well indeed and we became easy and happy.—But we did not continue long in this comfortable state: Many of the inferior people were envious and ill-natur'd and set up the same employ and work'd under price on purpose to get my business from me, and they succeeded so well that I could hardly get any thing to do, and became again unfortunate: Nor did this misfortune come alone, for just at this time we lost one of our little girls who died of a fever; this circumstance occasion'd us new troubles, for the Baptist Minister refused to bury her because we were not their members. The Parson of the parish denied us because she had never been baptized. I applied to the Quakers, but met with no success; this was one of the greatest trials I ever met with, as we did not know what to do with our poor baby.—At length I resolv'd to dig a grave in the garden behind the house, and bury her there; when the Parson of the parish sent for me to tell me he would bury the child, but did not chuse to read the burial service over her. I told him I did not mind whether he would or not, as the child could not hear it.

We met with a great deal of ill treatment after this, and found it very difficult to live.—We could scarcely get work to do, and were obliged to pawn our cloaths. We were ready to sink under our troubles.—When I purposed to my wife to go to *Kidderminster* and try if we could do there. I had always an inclination for that place, and now more than ever as I had heard *Mr. Fawcet* mentioned in the most respectful manner, as a pious worthy Gentleman; and I had seen his name in a favourite book of mine, Baxter's *Saints everlasting rest*, and as the Manufactory of *Kidderminster* seemed to promise my wife some employment, she readily came into my way of thinking.

I left her once more, and set out for *Kidderminster*, in order to judge if the situation would suit us.—As soon as I came there I waited immediately on *Mr. Fawcet*, who was pleased to receive me very kindly and recommended me to *Mr. Watson* who employed me in twisting silk and worsted together. I continued here about a fortnight, and when I thought it would answer our expectation, I returned to *Norwich* to fetch my wife; she was then near her time, and too much indisposed. So we were obliged to tarry until she was brought to bed, and as soon as she could conveniently travel we came to *Kidderminster*, but we brought nothing with us as we were obliged to sell all we had to pay our debts and the expences of my wife's illness, &c.

Such is our situation at present.—My wife, by hard labor at the loom, does every thing that can be expected from her towards the maintenance of our family; and God is pleased to incline the hearts of his People at times to yield us their charitable assistance; being myself through age and infirmity able to contribute but little to their support. As Pilgrims, and very poor Pilgrims, we are travelling through many difficulties towards our Heavenly Home, and waiting patiently for his gracious call, when the Lord shall deliver us out of the evils of this present world and bring us to the Everlasting Glories of the world to come.—To HIM be Praise for Ever and Ever, AMEN.

FINIS.

Before the Revolutionary War, more Southerners owned slaves than did Northerners, but slavery was neither abolished in the North nor illegal, and many Northerners held people in bondage. Jefferson's original draft of the Declaration of Independence revealed the irony of demanding liberty while holding others in bondage. The British Lord Dunmore exploited this hypocrisy in his proclamation offering liberty to all slaves who left their rebellious masters to join the British forces. The legislators in Vermont, however, rectified this hypocrisy by becoming the first to abolish slavery in their 1777 constitution. Starting in the mid-1770s, enslaved African Americans began petitioning the Massachusetts courts for their freedom.

Here you will read the *Lord Dunmore Proclamation* and the *1777 Vermont Constitution.*

Proclamation of Earl of Dunmore

By His Excellency the Right Honorable JOHN Earl of DUNMORE, His MAJESTY'S Lieutenant and Governor General of the Colony and Dominion of VIRGINIA, and Vice Admiral of the fame.

A PROCLAMATION.

As I have ever entertained Hopes that an Accommodation might have taken Place between GREAT- BRITAIN and this colony, without being compelled by my Duty to this moft difagreeable but now abfolutely neceffary Step, rendered fo by a Body of armed Men unlawfully affembled, bring on His MAJESTY'S [Tenders], and the formation of an Army, and that Army now on their March to attack His MAJESTY'S troops and deftroy the well difpofed Subjects of this Colony. To defeat fuch unreafonable Purpofes, and that all fuch Traitors, and their Abetters, may be brought to Juftice, and that the Peace, and good Order of this Colony may be again reftored, which the ordinary Courfe of the Civil Law is unable to effect; I have thought fit to iffue this my Proclamation, hereby declaring, that until the aforefaid good Purpofes can be obtained, I do in Virtue of the Power and Authority to ME given, by His MAJESTY, determine to execute Martial Law, and caufe the fame to be executed throughout this Colony: and to the end that Peace and good Order may the fooner be [effected], I do require every Person capable of bearing Arms, to [refort] to His MAJESTY'S STANDARD, or be looked upon as Traitors to His MAJESTY'S Crown and Government, and thereby become liable to the Penalty the Law inflicts upon fuch Offences; fuch as forfeiture of Life, confifcation of Lands, &c. &c. And I do hereby further declare all indentured Servants, Negroes, or others, (appertaining to Rebels,) free that are able and willing to bear Arms, they joining His MAJESTY'S Troops as foon as may be, for the more fpeedily reducing this Colony to a proper Senfe of their Duty, to His MAJESTY'S Leige Subjects, to retain their [Qui?rents], or any other Taxes due or that may become due, in their own Cuftody, till fuch Time as Peace may be again reftored to this at prefent moft unhappy Country, or demanded of them for their former falutary Purpofes, by Officers properly authorifed to receive the fame.

GIVEN under my Hand on board the ship WILLIAM, off NORPOLE, the 7th Day of NOVEMBER, in the SIXTEENTH Year of His MAJESTY'S Reign.

DUNMORE.

(GOD fave the KING.)

Source: http://www.nationalarchives.gov.uk

Vermont's 1777 Constitution, the First to Outlaw Slavery

CHAPTER I

A DECLARATION OF THE RIGHTS OF THE INHABITANTS OF THE STATE OF VERMONT

THAT all men are born equally free and independent, and have certain natural, inherent and unalienable rights, amongst which are the enjoying and defending life and liberty; acquiring, possessing and protecting property, and pursuing and obtaining happiness and safety. Therefore, no male person, born in this country, or brought from over sea, ought to be holden by law, to serve any person, as a servant, slave or apprentice, after he arrives to the age of twenty-one Years, nor female, in like manner, after she arrives to the age of eighteen years, unless they are bound by their own consent, after they arrive to such age, or bound by law, for the payment of debts, damages, fines, costs, or the like.

Source: http://avalon.law.yale.edu/18th_century/vt01.asp

During its early years, the U.S. Congress failed to limit slavery in the nation. Nonetheless, legislators in the Northern states gradually—sometimes very gradually—ended slavery and emancipated former slaves or at least the children of slaves. This created a refuge, if not a truly safe haven, to which Southern slaves could escape. Among slaves, who were legally compelled to remain illiterate, the *oral tradition* offered expression of their longings for freedom, as did *spirituals*.

Samples of both of these expressions are reprinted here.

Free at Last

from American Negro Songs
by J. W. Work

Free at last, free at last
I thank God I'm free at last
Free at last, free at last
I thank God I'm free at last
Way down yonder in the graveyard walk
I thank God I'm free at last
Me and my Jesus going to meet and talk
I thank God I'm free at last
On my knees when the light pass'd by
I thank God I'm free at last
Tho't my soul would rise and fly
I thank God I'm free at last
Some of these mornings, bright and fair
I thank God I'm free at last
Goin' meet King Jesus in the air
I thank God I'm free at last

Steal Away to Jesus

from The Books of American Negro Spirituals
by J. W. Johnson, J. R. Johnson

Steal away, steal away, steal away to Jesus
Steal away, steal away home
I ain't got long to stay here My Lord, He calls me
He calls me by the thunder
The trumpet sounds within-a my soul
I ain't got long to stay here Green trees are bending
Po' sinner stand a-trembling
The trumpet sounds within-a my soul
I ain't got long to stay here

Swing Low Sweet Chariot

First version

Swing low, sweet chariot
Coming for to carry me home..
I looked over Jordan and what did I see
Coming for to carry me home
A band of angels coming after me
Coming for to carry me home
If you get there before I do
Coming for to carry me home
Tell all my friends I'm coming to
Coming for to carry me home

Source: http://www.negrospirituals.com

The end of slavery in the North facilitated the growth of many communities of free African Americans there, who could offer one another mutual support. Also, having a refuge from slavery in the North made possible the Underground Railroad and led to an explosion of abolitionist activity in the North and *antislavery periodicals.* Starting in the late 1700s and continuing through 1865, African Americans, including freeborn, emancipated, self-liberated, and even enslaved, began telling their own stories and writing their own histories. Primarily, these included slave narratives, such as the well-known *1789 narrative of Olaudah Equiano,* and the numerous narratives authored by *Frederick Douglass.*

In addition, however, writers such as Quaker astronomer *Benjamin Banneker* wrote essays, analyses, and opinion pieces decrying the existence of slavery, samples of which are included here.

Absalom Jones and Richard Allen
Preamble of the Free African Society,
12 April 1787

"Philadelphia"

"(12th, 4th mo., 1787) — Whereas, Absalom Jones and Richard Allen, two men of the African race, who, for their religious life and conversation have obtained a good report among men, these persons, from a love to the people of their complexion whom they beheld with sorrow, because of their irreligious and uncivilized state, often communed together upon this painful and important subject in order to form some kind of religious society, but there being too few to be found under the like concern, and those who were, differed in their religious sentiments; with these circumstances they labored for some time, till it was proposed, after a serious communication of sentiments, that a society should be formed, without regard to religious tenets, provided, the persons lived an orderly and sober life, in order to support one another in sickness, and for the benefit of their widows and fatherless children."

ARTICLES.

"[17th, 5th mo., 1787] - We, the free Africans and their descendants, of the City of Philadelphia, in the State of Pennsylvania, or elsewhere, do unanimously agree, for the benefit of each other, to advance one shilling in silver Pennsylvania currency a month; and after one year's subscription from the date hereof, then to hand forth to the needy of this Society, if any should require, the sum of three shillings and nine pence per week of the said money: provided, this necessity is not brought on them by their own imprudence.

And it is further agreed, that no drunkard nor disorderly person be admitted as a member, and if any should prove disorderly after having been received, the said disorderly person shall be disjointed from us if there is not nit amendment, by being informed by two of the members, without having any of his subscription money returned.

And if any should neglect paying his monthly subscription for three months, and after having been informed of the same by two of the members, and no sufficient reason appearing for such neglect, if he do not pay the whole the next ensuing meeting, he shall be disjointed from us, by being informed by two of the members its an offender, without hiving any of his subscription money returned.

Also, if any person neglect meeting every month, for every omission he shall pay three pence, except in case or sickness or any other complaint that should require the assistance of the Society, then, and in such a case, he shall be exempt from the fines and subscription during the said sickness.

Also, we apprehend it to be just and reasonable, that the surviving widow of a deceased member should enjoy the benefit of this Society so long as she remains his widow, complying with the, rules thereof, excepting the subscriptions.

And we apprehend it to be necessary, that the children of our deceased members be under the care of the Society, so far as to pay for the education of their children, if they cannot attend the free school; also to put them out apprentices to suitable trades or places, if required.

Also, that no member shall convene the Society together; but, it shall be the sole business of the committee, and that only on special occasions, and to dispose of the money in hand to the best advantage, for the use of the Society, after they are granted the liberty at a monthly meeting, and to transact all other business whatsoever, except that of Clerk and Treasurer.

And we unanimously agree to choose Joseph Clarke to be our Clerk and Treasurer; and whenever another should succeed him, it is always understood, that one of the people called Quakers, belonging to one of tile three monthly meetings in Philadelphia, is to be chosen to act as Clerk and 'Treasurer of this useful Institution.

The following persons met, viz., Absalom Jones, Richard Allen, Samuel Baston, Joseph Johnson, Cato Freeman, Caesar Cranchell, and James Potter, also William White, whose early assistance and useful remarks we found truly profitable. This evening the articles were read, and after some beneficial remarks were made, they were agreed unto."

From *Annals of the First African Church in the United States of America Now Styled the African Episcopal Church of St. Thomas, Philadelphia...*, by the Rev. Wm. Douglass, Philadelphia: King & Baird Printers, 1862.

Excerpt from Olaudah Equiano's Slave Narrative, 1789

...One day, when all our people were gone out to their works as usual and only I and my dear sister were left to mind the house, two men and a woman got over our walls, and in a moment seized us both, and without giving us time to cry out or make resistance they stopped our mouths and ran off with us into the nearest wood. Here they tied our hands and continued to carry us as far as they could till night came on, when we reached a small house where the robbers halted for refreshment and spent the night. We were then unbound but were unable to take any food, and being quite overpowered by fatigue and grief, our only relief was some sleep, which allayed our misfortune for a short time. The next morning we left the house and continued travelling all the day. For a long time we had kept to the woods, but at last we came into a road which I believed I knew. I had now some hopes of being delivered, for we had advanced but a little way before I discovered some people at a distance, on which I began to cry out for their assistance: but my cries had no other effect than to make them tie me faster and stop my mouth, and then they put me into a large sack. They also stopped my sister's mouth and tied her hands and in this manner we proceeded till we were out of the sight of these people. When we went to rest the following night they offered us some victuals, but we refused it, and the only comfort we had was in being in one another's arms all that night and bathing each other with our tears. But alas! we were soon deprived of even the small comfort of weeping together. The next day proved a day of greater sorrow than I had yet experienced, for my sister and I were then separated while we lay clasped in each other's arms. It was in vain that we besought them not to part us; she was torn from me and immediately carried away, while I was left in a state of distraction not to be described. I cried and grieved continually, and for several days I did not eat anything but what they forced into my mouth

I now saw myself deprived of all chance of returning to my native country or even the least glimpse of hope of gaining the shore, which I now considered as friendly; and I even wished for my former slavery in preference to my present situation, which was filled with horrors of every kind, still heightened by my ignorance of what I was to undergo. I was not long suffered to indulge my grief; I was soon put down under the decks, and there I received such a salutation in my nostrils as I had never experienced in my life: so that with the loathsomeness of the stench and crying together, I became so sick and low that I was not able to eat, nor had I the least desire to taste anything. I

now wished for the last friend, death, to relieve me; but soon, to my grief, two of the white men offered me eatables, and on my refusing to eat, one of them held me fast by the hands and laid me across I think the windlass, and tied my feet while the other flogged me severely. I had never experienced anything of this kind before, and although, not being used to the water, I naturally feared that element the first time I saw it, yet nevertheless could I have got over the nettings I would have jumped over the side, but I could not; and besides, the crew used to watch us very closely who were not chained down to the decks, lest we should leap into the water: and I have seen some of these poor African prisoners most severely cut for attempting to do so, and hourly whipped for not eating. This indeed was often the case with myself. In a little time after, amongst the poor chained men I found some of my own nation, which in a small degree gave ease to my mind. I inquired of these what was to be done with us; they gave me to understand we were to be carried to these white people's country to work for them. I then was a little revived, and thought if it were no worse than working, my situation was not so desperate: but still I feared I should be put to death, the white people looked and acted, as I thought, in so savage a manner; for I had never seen among my people such instances of brutal cruelty, and this not only shewn towards us blacks but also to some of the whites themselves. One white man in particular I saw, when we were permitted to be on deck, flogged so unmercifully with a large rope near the foremast that he died in consequence of it; and they tossed him over the side as they would have done a brute. This made me fear these people the more, and I expected nothing less than to be treated in the same manner. . . .

The stench of the hold while we were on the coast was so intolerably loathsome that it was dangerous to remain there for any time, and some of us had been permitted to stay on the deck for the fresh air; but now that the whole ship's cargo were confined together it became absolutely pestilential. The closeness of the place and the heat of the climate, added to the number in the ship, which was so crowded that each had scarcely room to turn himself, almost suffocated us. This produced copious perspirations, so that the air soon became unfit for respiration from a variety of loathsome smells, and brought on a sickness among the slaves, of which many died, thus falling victims to the improvident avarice, as I may call it, of their purchasers. This wretched situation was again aggravated by the galling of the chains, now become insupportable and the filth of the necessary tubs, into which the chil-

From *The Interesting Narrative of the Life of Olaudah Equiano, or Gustavus Vassa, The African Written by Himself*

dren often fell and were almost suffocated. The shrieks of the women and the groans of the dying rendered the whole a scene of horror almost inconceivable. Happily perhaps for myself I was soon reduced so low here that it was thought necessary to keep me almost always on deck, and from my extreme youth I was not put in fetters. In this situation I expected every hour to share the fate of my companions, some of whom were almost daily brought upon deck at the point of death, which I began to hope would soon put an end to my miseries. Often did I think many of the inhabitants of the deep much more happy than myself. I envied them the freedom they enjoyed, and as often wished I could change my condition for theirs. Every circumstance I met with served only to render my state more painful, and heighten my apprehensions and my opinion of the cruelty of the whites. One day they had taken a number of fishes, and when they had killed and satisfied themselves with as many as they thought fit, to our astonishment who were on the deck, rather than give any of them to us to eat as we expected, they tossed the remaining fish into the sea again, although we begged and prayed for some as well as we could, but in vain; and some of my countrymen, being pressed by hunger, took an opportunity when they thought no one saw them of trying to get a little privately; but they were discovered, and the attempt procured them some very severe floggings. One day, when we had a smooth sea and moderate wind, two of my wearied countrymen who were chained together (I was near them at the time), preferring death to such a life of misery, somehow made through the nettings and jumped into the sea: immediately another quite dejected fellow, who on account of his illness was suffered to be out of irons, also followed their example; and I believe many more would very soon have done the same if they had not been prevented by the ship's crew, who were instantly alarmed. Those of us that were the most active were in a moment put down under the deck, and there was such a noise and confusion amongst the people of the ship as I never heard before, to stop her and get the boat out to go after the slaves. However two of the wretches were drowned, but they got the other and afterwards flogged him unmercifully for thus attempting to prefer death to slavery. In this manner we continued to undergo more hardships than I can now relate, hardships which are inseparable from this accursed trade.

Letter from Benjamin Banneker to Thomas Jefferson

On August 19, 1791, Benjamin Banneker wrote a lengthy letter to Thomas Jefferson, then Secretary of State, decrying the existence of slavery. Banneker was a Quaker astronomer who wrote essays, analyses, and opinion pieces on this subject.

SIR,

I AM fully sensible of the greatness of that freedom, which I take with you on the present occasion ; a liberty which seemed to me scarcely allowable, when I reflected on that distinguished and dignified station in which you stand, and the almost general prejudice and prepossession, which is so prevalent in the world against those of my complexion.

I suppose it is a truth too well attested to you, to need a proof here, that we are a race of beings, who have long labored under the abuse and censure of the world ; that we have long been looked upon with an eye of contempt ; and that we have long been considered rather as brutish than human, and scarcely capable of mental endowments.

Sir, I hope I may safely admit, in consequence of that report which hath reached me, that you are a man far less inflexible in sentiments of this nature, than many others ; that you are measurably friendly, and well disposed towards us ; and that you are willing and ready to lend your aid and assistance to our relief, from those many distresses, and numerous calamities, to which we are reduced. Now Sir, if this is founded in truth, I apprehend you will embrace every opportunity, to eradicate that train of absurd and false ideas and opinions, which so generally prevails with respect to us ; and that your sentiments are concurrent with mine, which are, that one universal Father hath given being to us all ; and that he hath not only made us all of one flesh, but that he hath also, without partiality, afforded us all the same sensations and endowed us all with the same faculties ; and that however variable we may be in society or religion, however diversified in situation or color, we are all of the same family, and stand in the same relation to him.

Sir, if these are sentiments of which you are fully persuaded, I hope you cannot but acknowledge, that it is the indispensible duty of those, who maintain for themselves the rights of human nature, and who possess the obligations of Christianity, to extend their power and influence to the relief of every part of the human race, from whatever burden or oppression they may unjustly labor under ; and this, I apprehend, a full conviction of the truth and obligation of these principles should lead all to. Sir, I have

long been convinced, that if your love for yourselves, and for those inestimable laws, which preserved to you the rights of human nature, was founded on sincerity, you could not but be solicitous, that every individual, of whatever rank or distinction, might with you equally enjoy the blessings thereof ; neither could you rest satisfied short of the most active effusion of your exertions, in order to their promotion from any state of degradation, to which the unjustifiable cruelty and barbarism of men may have reduced them.

Sir, I freely and cheerfully acknowledge, that I am of the African race, and in that color which is natural to them of the deepest dye ; and it is under a sense of the most profound gratitude to the Supreme Ruler of the Universe, that I now confess to you, that I am not under that state of tyrannical thraldom, and inhuman captivity, to which too many of my brethren are doomed, but that I have abundantly tasted of the fruition of those blessings, which proceed from that free and unequalled liberty with which you are favored ; and which, I hope, you will willingly allow you have mercifully received, from the immediate hand of that Being, from whom proceedeth every good and perfect Gift.

Sir, suffer me to recal to your mind that time, in which the arms and tyranny of the British crown were exerted, with every powerful effort, in order to reduce you to a state of servitude : look back, I entreat you, on the variety of dangers to which you were exposed ; reflect on that time, in which every human aid appeared unavailable, and in which even hope and fortitude wore the aspect of inability to the conflict, and you cannot but be led to a serious and grateful sense of your miraculous and providential preservation ; you cannot but acknowledge, that the present freedom and tranquility which you enjoy you have mercifully received, and that it is the peculiar blessing of Heaven.

This, Sir, was a time when you cleary saw into the injustice of a state of slavery, and in which you had just apprehensions of the horrors of its condition. It was now that your abhorrence thereof was so excited, that you publicly held forth this true and invaluable doctrine, which is worthy to be recorded and remembered in all succeeding ages : "We hold these truths to be self-evident, that all men are created equal ; that they are endowed by their Creator with certain unalienable rights, and that among these are, life, liberty, and the pursuit of happiness." Here was a time, in which your tender feelings for yourselves had en-

Copy of a letter from Benjamin Banneker, to the Secretary of State, with his Answer. Philadelphia: Printed and Sold by Daniel Lawrence, No. 33. North Fourth-Street, near Race. M. DCC. XCII. (1792)

gaged you thus to declare, you were then impressed with proper ideas of the great violation of liberty, and the free possession of those blessings, to which you were entitled by nature ; but, Sir, how pitiable is it to reflect, that although you were so fully convinced of the benevolence of the Father of Mankind, and of his equal and impartial distribution of these rights and privileges, which he hath conferred upon them, that you should at the same time counteract his mercies, in detaining by fraud and violence so numerous a part of my brethren, under groaning captivity and cruel oppression, that you should at the same time be found guilty of that most criminal act, which you professedly detested in others, with respect to yourselves.

I suppose that your knowledge of the situation of my brethren, is too extensive to need a recital here ; neither shall I presume to prescribe methods by which they may be relieved, otherwise than by recommending to you and all others, to wean yourselves from those narrow prejudices which you have imbibed with respect to them, and as Job proposed to his friends, "put your soul in their souls' stead ;" thus shall your hearts be enlarged with kindness and benevolence towards them ; and thus shall you need neither the direction of myself or others, in what manner to proceed herein. And now, Sir, although my sympathy and affection for my brethren hath caused my enlargement thus far, I ardently hope, that your candor and generosity will plead with you in my behalf, when I make known to you, that it was not originally my design ; but having taken up my pen in order to direct to you, as a present, a copy of an Almanac, which I have calculated for the succeeding year, I was unexpectedly and unavoidably led thereto. This calculation is the production of my arduous study, in this my advanced stage of life ; for having long had unbounded desires to become acquainted with the secrets of nature, I have had to gratify my curiosity herein, through my own assiduous application to Astronomical Study, in which I need not recount to you the many difficulties and disadvantages, which I have had to encounter.

And although I had almost declined to make my calculation for the ensuing year, in consequence of that time which I had allotted therefor, being taken up at the Federal Territory, by the request of Mr. Andrew Ellicott, yet finding myself under several engagements to Printers of this state, to whom I had communicated my design, on my return to my place of residence, I industriously applied myself thereto, which I hope I have accomplished with correctness and accuracy; a copy of which I have taken the liberty to direct to you, and which I humbly request you will favorably receive ; and although you may have the opportunity of perusing it after its publication, yet I choose to send it to you in manuscript previous thereto,

that thereby you might not only have an earlier inspection, but that you might also view it in my own hand writing.

And now, Sir, I shall conclude, and subscribe myself, with the most profound respect,
Your most obedient humble servant,

BENJAMIN
BANNEKER.

Response to Benjamin Banneker

Philadelphia, August 30, 1791. SIR, **I** THANK you, sincerely, for your letter of the 19th instant, and for the Almanac it contained. No body wishes more than I do, to see such proofs as you exhibit, that nature has given to our black brethren talents equal to those of the other colors of men ; and that the appearance of the want of them, is owing merely to the degraded condition of their existence, both in Africa and America. I can add with truth, that no body wishes more ardently to see a good system commenced, for raising the condition, both of their body and mind, to what it ought to be, as far as the imbecility of their present existence, and other circumstances, which cannot be neglected, will admit.

I have taken the liberty of sending your Almanac to Monsieur de Condozett, Secretary of the Academy of Sciences at Paris, and Member of the Philanthropic Society, because I considered it as a document, to which your whole color had a right for their justification, against the doubts which have been entertained of them. I am with great esteem, Sir, Your most obedient Humble Servant,

THOMAS
JEFFERSON.

While most African Americans continued to live in slavery, the writings of others continued to powerfully affect their lives. The European-American Congress banned the legal slave trade in 1808, passed numerous Fugitive Slave Acts (e.g., 1793, 1850), and passed the 1820 Missouri Compromise dictating where slavery could or could not continue legally. In addition, state and local legislators passed various slave codes that continually eroded any remaining liberties and rights extended to African Americans, both enslaved and free. Each time a slave revolt or insurrection erupted, further legislation would tighten the chokehold on the lives of African Americans, whether or not they had participated in, supported, or even endorsed such rebellions. This section includes abolitionist writing—a letter, a poem, and an interview with a Negro leader in Birmingham, Alabama.

In addition, you will read the *Supreme Court's Dred Scott decision*, and the mission of an antislavery journal by Frederick Douglass.

Letter to William Basset

Phila [Penn.] December, 1837.

Esteemed Friend.

Your favor of the 7th came safe to hand. It needed no apology. The fact of your being an abolitionist; the friend of my beloved sisters Sarah and Angelina Grimké, the friend of my poor and oppressed bretheren and sisters enti[t]les you to my warmest gratitude and esteem. I thank God that he has enabled you to renounce error and strengthened you to come up to the help of the Lord against the mighty. I pray that you may run the race set before you without halting, keeping your eye ste[a]dfastly fixed on the great Captain of our salvation.

The questions you ask me, make me feel my weakness, and in view of the great responsibility that rests upon me in answering them, my flesh trembles; yet will I cast my burden on Him, who is strength in weakness and resolve to do my duty; to tell the truth and leave the consequences to God. I thank you for the "Letter to a member of the Society of Friends". I can set my seal to the truth of the following paragraph, extracted from it. "It will be allowed that the Negro Pew or its equivalent may be found in some of our meeting houses where men and women bretheren and sisters by creat[i]on and heirs of the same glorious immortality are seated by themselves on a back bench for no other reason but because it has pleased God to give them a complexion darker than our own." And as you request to know particularly about Arch Street Meeting, I may say that the experience of years has made me wise in this fact, that there is a bench set apart at that meeting for our people, whether *officially* appointed or not I cannot say; but this I am free to say that my mother and myself were told to sit there, and that a friends sat at each end of the bench to prevent white persons from sitting there. And even when a child my soul was made sad with hearing five or six times during the course of one meeting this language of remonstrance addressed to those who were willing to sit by us. "This bench is for the black people." "This bench is for the people of color." And oftentimes I wept, at other times I felt indignant and queried in my own mind are these people Christians. Now it seems clear to me that had not this bench been set apart for oppressed Americans, there would have been no necessity for the oft-repeated and galling remonstrance, galling indeed, because *I believe they despise us for our color.* I have not been in Arch Street meeting for four years; but my mother goes once a week and frequently she has a *whole long bench* to herself. The assertion that our people who attend their meetings prefer sitting by themselves, is not true. A very near friend of ours, that fears God and who has been a constant attender of Friends meeting from his childhood, says "Thou mayest tell William Basset, that I know that "Friends" appointed a seat for our people at the meeting which I attend. Several years ago a friend came to me and told me that "Friends" had appointed a back bench for us. I told him with some warmth that I had just as lief sit on the floor as sit there. I do not care about it, Friends do not do the thing that is right." Judge now, I pray you, whether this man preferred sitting by himself. Two sons of the person I have just mentioned, have left attending Friends meetings within the last few months, because they could no longer endure the "scorning of those that are at ease, and the contempt of the proud." Conversing with one of them today, I asked, why did you leave Friends. "Because they do not know how to treat me, I do not like to sit on a back bench and be treated with contempt, so I go where I am better treated." Do you not like their principles and their mode of worship? "Yes, I like their principles, but not their practice. They make the *highest* profession of any sect of Christians, and are the most deficient in practice." In reply to your question "whether there appears to be a diminution of prejudice towards you among Friends," I unhesitatingly answer, no. I have heard it frequently remarked and have observed it myself, that in proportion as we become intellectual and respectable, so in proportion does their disgust and prejudice increase.

Yet while I speak this of Friends as a body, I am happy to say that there is in this city a "noble few", who have cleansed their garments from the foul stain of prejudice, and are doing all their hands find to do in promoting the moral and mental elevation of oppressed Americans.

Some of these are members of Anti-Slavery Societies and others belong to the old abolition School.

While I have been penning this letter living desires have sprung up in my soul that I might "nothing extenuate nor set down ought in malice". Doubtless you know that our beloved A. E. G[rimké] is convalescent. Did all the members of Friends society feel for us, as the sisters Grimké do, how soon, how very soon would the fetters be stricken from the captive and cruel prejudice be driven from the bosoms of the professed followers of Christ. We were lying wounded and bleeding, trampled to the very dust by the heel of our bretheren and our

Reprinted with permission. Weld-Grimké Collection, Clements Library, University of Michigan, Ann Arbor

sisters, when Sarah and Angelina Grimke passed by; they saw our low estate and their hearts melted within them; with the tenderness of ministering angels they lifted us from the dust and poured the oil of consolation, the balm of sympathy into our lacerated bosoms; they identified themselves with us, took our wrongs upon them, and made our oppression and woe theirs. Is it any marvel then that we call them blessed among women? We value them not because they belong to the great and the mighty of our land, but because they love Christ and our afflicted bretheren. Most cordially do we approve every step they have taken since they left us, believing that the unerring spirit of truth is their leader [and] friend. I hope this letter may be satisfactory to you; use it, and the account of my brother in any way you may think proper, but do not give my name unless it is absolutely necessary. Please tell our beloved A. E. G. that her friends entreat her not to exert herself until she is quite strong. May the Lord bless you, and may you anchor your little bark on the rock, Christ Jesus; that so, when the storm of persecution arises, You may suffer no loss.

Prays fervently
Sarah M. Douglass

Excerpt from The Poetical Works of George M. Horton, the Colored Bard of North Carolina To Which is Prefixed The Life Of The Author, Written by Himself

On one very calm Sabbath morning, a while before the time of preaching, I undertook to compose a divine hymn, being under some serious impression of mind:

Rise up, my soul and let us go
Up to the gospel feast;
Gird on the garment white as snow,
To join and be a guest.

Dost thou not hear the trumpet call
For thee, my soul, for thee?
Not only thee, my soul, but all,
May rise and enter free.

From *The Poetical Works of George M. Horton, the Colored Bard of North Carolina To Which is Prefixed The Life Of The Author, Written by Himself.* George Moses Horton. Hillsborough: Heartt, 1845.

Our Paper and Its Prospects

by Frederick Douglass

We are now about to assume the management of the editorial department of a newspaper, devoted to the cause of Liberty, Humanity and Progress. The position is one which, with the purest motives, we have long desired to occupy. It has long been our anxious wish to see, in this slave-holding, slave-trading, and Negro-hating land, a printing-press and paper, permanently established, under the complete control and direction of the immediate victims of slavery and oppression.

Animated by this intense desire, we have pursued our object, till on the threshold of obtaining it. Our press and printing materials are bought, and paid for. Our office secured, and is well situated, in the centre of business, in this enterprising city. Our office Agent, an industrious and amiable young man, thoroughly devoted to the interests of humanity, has already entered upon his duties. Printers well recommended have offered their services, and are ready to work as soon as we are prepared for the regular publication of our paper. Kind friends are rallying round us, with words and deeds of encouragement. Subscribers are steadily, if not rapidly coming in, and some of the best minds in the country are generously offering to lend us the powerful aid of their pens. The sincere wish of our heart, so long and so devoutly cherished seems now upon the eve of complete realization.

It is scarcely necessary for us to say that our desire to occupy our present position at the head of an Antislavery Journal, has resulted from no unworthy distrust or ungrateful want of appreciation of the zeal, integrity, or ability of the noble band of white laborers, in this department of our cause; but, from a sincere and settled conviction that such a Journal, if conducted with only moderate skill and ability, would do a most important and indispensable work, which it would be wholly impossible for our white friends to do for us.

It is neither a reflection on the fidelity, nor a disparagement of the ability of our friends and fellow-laborers, to assert what "common sense affirms and only folly denies," that the man who has *suffered the wrong* is the man to *demand redress,*—that the man STRUCK is the man to CRY OUT—and that he who has *endured the cruel pangs of Slavery* is the man to *advocate Liberty*. It is evident we must be our own representatives and advocates, not exclusively, but peculiarly—not distinct from, but in connection with our white friends. In the grand struggle for liberty and equality now waging, it is meet, right and essential that there should arise in our ranks authors and editors, as well as orators, for it is in these capacities that the most permanent good can be rendered to our cause.

Hitherto the immediate victims of slavery and prejudice, owing to various causes, have had little share in this department of effort: they have frequently undertaken, and almost as frequently failed. This latter fact has often been urged by our friends against our engaging in the present enterprise; but, so far from convincing us of the impolicy of our course, it serves to confirm us in the necessity, if not the wisdom of our undertaking. That others have failed, is a reason for OUR earnestly endeavoring to succeed. Our race must be vindicated from the embarrassing imputations resulting from former non-success. We believe that what *ought* to be done, *can* be done. We say this, in no self-confident or boastful spirit, but with a full sense of our weakness and unworthiness, relying upon the Most High for wisdom and strength to support us in our righteous undertaking. We are not wholly unaware of the duties, hardships and responsibilities of our position. We have easily imagined some, and friends have not hesitated to inform us of others. Many doubtless are yet to be revealed by that infallible teacher, experience. A view of them solemnize, but do not appal us. We have counted the cost. Our mind is made up, and we are resolved to go forward.

In aspiring to our present position, the aid of circumstances has been so strikingly apparent as to almost stamp our humble aspirations with the solemn sanctions of a Divine Providence. Nine years ago, as most of our readers are aware, we were held as a slave, shrouded in the midnight ignorance of that infernal system-sunken in the depths of senility and degradation-registered with four footed beasts and creeping things- regarded as property-compelled to toil without wages-with a heart swollen with bitter anguish-and a spirit crushed and broken. By a singular combination of circumstances we finally succeeded in escaping from the grasp of the man who claimed us as his property, and succeeded in safely reaching New Bedford, Mass. In this town we worked three years as a daily laborer on the wharves. Six years ago we became a Lecturer on Slavery. Under the apprehension of being re-taken into bondage, two years ago we embarked for England. During our stay in that country, kind friends, anxious for our safety, ransomed us from slavery, by the payment of a large sum. The same friends, as unexpectedly as generously, placed in our hands the necessary means of purchasing a printing press and printing materials. Finding ourself now in a favorable position for aiming an important blow at slavery and prejudice, we feel urged on in our enterprise by a sense of duty to God and man, firmly believing that our effort will be crowned with entire success.

From *The North Star*, 3 December 1847. Digital document courtesy of the Gilder Lehrman Center for the Study of Slavery, Resistance, and Abolition.

Excerpt from the *Dred Scott v. Sanford* Decision, 1857

They had for more than a century before been regarded as beings of an inferior order, and altogether unfit to associate with the white race either in social or political relations, and so far inferior that they had no rights which the white man was bound to respect, and that the negro might justly and lawfully be reduced to slavery for his benefit. He was bought and sold, and treated as an ordinary article of merchandise and traffic whenever a profit could be made by it. This opinion was at that time fixed and universal in the civilized portion of the white race. It was regarded as an axiom in morals as well as in politics which no one thought of disputing or supposed to be open to dispute, and men in every grade and position in society daily and habitually acted upon it in their private pursuits, as well as in matters of public concern, without doubting for a moment the correctness of this opinion.

Interview with Walter Calloway

Interviewed by W.P. Jordan
"OLE JOE HAD REAL 'LIGION"

Walter Calloway lives alone half a block off Avenue F, the thoroughfare on the southside of Birmingham on which live many of the leaders in the Negro life of the city. For his eighty-nine years he was apparently vigorous except for temporary illness. A glance at the interior of his cabin disclosed the fact that it was scrupulously neat and quite orderly in its arrangement, a characteristic of many ex-slaves. As he sat in the sunshine on his tiny front porch, his greeting was: "Come in, white folks. You ain't no doctor is you?"

To a negative reply, he explained as he continued, "Fo' de las' past twenty-five years I been keepin' right on, wukkin' for de city in de street department. 'Bout two mont's ago dis mis'ry attackted me an' don't 'pear lak nothin' dem doctors gimme do no good. De preacher he come to see me dis mornin' an' he say he know a white gemman doctor, what he gwine to sen' him to see me. I sho' wants to get well ag'in pow'ful bad, but mebby I done live long 'nuff an' my time 'bout come."

Quizzed about his age and antecedents, he began his story: "Well, Sir, Cap'n, I was born in Richmond, Virginny, in 1848. Befo' I was ole 'nuff to 'member much, my mammy wid me an' my older brudder was sold to Marse John Calloway at Snodoun in Montgomery County, ten miles south of de town of Montgomery. "Marse John hab a big plantation an' lots of slaves. Dey treated us purty good, but we hab to wuk hard. Time I was ten years ole I was makin' a reg'lar han' 'hin de plow. Oh, yassuh, Marse John good 'nough to us an' we get plenty to eat, but he had a oberseer name Green Bush what sho' whup us iffen we don't do to suit him. Yassuh, he mighty rough wid us be he didn't do de whippin' hisse'f. He had a big black boy name Mose, mean as de debil an' strong as a ox, and de oberseer let him do all de whuppin'. An', man, he could sho' lay on dat rawhide lash. He whupped a nigger gal 'bout thirteen years old so hard she nearly die, an' allus atterwa'ds she hab spells of fits or somp'n. Dat make Marse John pow'ful mad, so he run dat oberseer off de place an' Mose didn' do no mo' whuppin'. "Same time Marse John buy mammy an' us boys, he buy a black man name Joe. He a preacher an' de marster let de slaves buil' a bresh arbor in de pecan grove over in de big pastur', an' when de wedder warn't too cold all de slaves was 'lowed to meet dar on Sunday fo' preachin'.

Yassuh, ole Joe do purty good. I speck he had mo' 'ligion dan some of de hifalutin' niggers 'tendin' to preach nowadays. De white folks chu'ch, hit at Hope Hill over on de stage road, an' sometimes dey fetch 'dere preacher to de plantation to preach to de slaves. But dey druther heah Joe.

"Nawsuh, we didn't git no schoolin' 'cep'in' befo' we got big 'nough to wuk in de fiel' we go 'long to school wid de white chillun to take care of 'em. Dey show us pictures an' tell us all dey kin, but it didn't 'mount to much.

"When de war started 'mos' all I know 'bout it was all de white mens go to Montgomery an' jine de army. My brudder, he 'bout fifteen year ole, so he go 'long wid de ration wagon to Montgomery 'mos' ebry week. One day he come back from Montgomery an' he say, 'Hell done broke loose in Gawgy.' He couldn't tell us much 'bout what done happen, but de slaves dey get all 'cited 'caze dey didn' know what to 'spect. Purty soon we fin' out day some of de big mens call a meetin' at de capitol on Goat Hill in Montgomery. Dey 'lected Mista Jeff Davis president an' done busted de Nunited States wide open.

"Atter dat dar warn't much happen on de plantation 'cep'in' gangs of so'jers passin' th'ough gwine off to de war. Den 'bout ebry so often a squad of Confederate so'jers would come to de neighborhood gatherin' up rations for Gin'ral Lee's army dey say. Dat make it purty hard on bofe whites an' blacks, takin' off some of de bes' stock an' runnin' us low on grub.

"But we wuk right on 'twell one day somebody seen a runner sayin' de Yankees comin'. Ole mistis tell me to hurry ober to Mrs. Freeman's an' tell 'em Wilson's Yankee raiders was on de way an' comin' lak a harrikin. I hop on a mule an' go jes' as fas' as I can make him trabel, but befo' I git back dey done retch de plantation, smashin' things comin' an' gwine.

"Dey broke in de smoke house an' tuk all de hams an' yuther rations dey fin' what dey want an' burn up de res'. Den dey ramshack de big house lookin' fo' money an' jewelry an' raise Cain wid de wimmin folks 'caze dey didn't fin' what dey wanted. Den dey leave dere ole hosses an' mules an' take de bes' we got. Atter dey don dat, dey burn de smoke house, de barns, de cribs an' some yuther prop'ty. Den dey skedaddle some place else.

"I warn't up dar but I heern tell dey burn up piles an' piles of cotton an' lots of steamboats at Montgomery an' lef' de ole town jes' 'bout ruint'. Twarn't long atter dat dey tell us we'se free. But lawdy, Cap'n, we ain't nebber been what I calls free. 'Cose ole marster didn' own us no mo', an' all de folks soon scatter all ober, but iffen dey all lak me day still hafter wuk jes' as hard, an some times hab less dan we useter hab when we stay on Marster John's plantation. "Well, Cap'n, dat's 'bout all I know. I feel dat misery comin' on me now. Will you please, suh, gimme a lif' back in de house. I wisht dat white gemman doctor come on iffen he comin'."

During the Civil War, President Abraham Lincoln's Emancipation Proclamation emancipated slaves within all of the rebelling territories, but his executive powers could not abolish slavery except within the context of this wartime proclamation. Following the Civil War, the 13th Amendment to the U.S. Constitution abolished slavery within the United States, and the 14th and 15th Amendments defined citizenship in the United States as extending to all persons born in this country, regardless of "race, color, or previous condition of servitude."

The end of slavery in the South heralded the start of rampant terrorist activities by European-American Southerners, typified by lynchings of African-American men who questioned the status quo or who challenged the supremacy of European Americans by owning businesses, educating themselves or others, or otherwise succeeding despite Jim Crow practices in the South. Though many European Americans supported and aided in this battle, African Americans were free—literally—to lead the charge.

This section includes the *Emancipation Proclamation*, the *13th Amendment*, and Ida B. Well's documentation of how lynchings targeted Negroes.

The Emancipation Proclamation

January 1, 1863

Whereas, on the twenty-second day of September, in the year of our Lord one thousand eight hundred and sixty-two, a proclamation was issued by the President of the United States, containing, among other things, the following, to wit:

"That on the first day of January, in the year of our Lord one thousand eight hundred and sixty-three, all persons held as slaves within any State or designated part of a State, the people whereof shall then be in rebellion against the United States, shall be then, thenceforward, and forever free; and the Executive Government of the United States, including the military and naval authority thereof, will recognize and maintain the freedom of such persons, and will do no act or acts to repress such persons, or any of them, in any efforts they may make for their actual freedom.

"That the Executive will, on the first day of January afore-said, by proclamation, designate the States and parts of States, if any, in which the people thereof, respectively, shall then be in rebellion against the United States; and the fact that any State, or the people thereof, shall on that day be, in good faith, represented in the Congress of the United States by members chosen thereto at elections wherein a majority of the qualified voters of such State shall have participated, shall, in the absence of strong countervailing testimony, be deemed conclusive evidence that such State, and the people thereof, are not then in rebellion against the United States."

Now, therefore I, Abraham Lincoln, President of the United States, by virtue of the power in me vested as Commander-in-Chief, of the Army and Navy of the United States in time of actual armed rebellion against the authority and government of the United States, and as a fit and necessary war measure for suppressing said rebellion, do, on this first day of January, in the year of our Lord one thousand eight hundred and sixty-three, and in accordance with my purpose so to do publicly proclaimed for the full period of one hundred days, from the day first above mentioned, order and designate as the States and parts of States wherein the people thereof respectively, are this day in rebellion against the United States, the following, to wit:

Arkansas, Texas, Louisiana, (except the Parishes of St. Bernard, Plaquemines, Jefferson, St. John, St. Charles, St. James Ascension, Assumption, Terrebonne, Lafourche, St. Mary, St. Martin, and Orleans, including the City of New Orleans) Mississippi, Alabama, Florida, Georgia, South Carolina, North Carolina, and Virginia, (except the forty-eight counties designated as West Virginia, and also the counties of Berkley, Accomac, Northampton, Elizabeth City, York, Princess Ann, and Norfolk, including the cities of Norfolk and Portsmouth[)], and which excepted parts, are for the present, left precisely as if this proclamation were not issued.

And by virtue of the power, and for the purpose aforesaid, I do order and declare that all persons held as slaves within said designated States, and parts of States, are, and henceforward shall be free; and that the Executive government of the United States, including the military and naval authorities thereof, will recognize and maintain the freedom of said persons.

And I hereby enjoin upon the people so declared to be free to abstain from all violence, unless in necessary self-defence; and I recommend to them that, in all cases when allowed, they labor faithfully for reasonable wages.

And I further declare and make known, that such persons of suitable condition, will be received into the armed service of the United States to garrison forts, positions, stations, and other places, and to man vessels of all sorts in said service.

And upon this act, sincerely believed to be an act of justice, warranted by the Constitution, upon military necessity, I invoke the considerate judgment of mankind, and the gracious favor of Almighty God.

In witness whereof, I have hereunto set my hand and caused the seal of the United States to be affixed.

Done at the City of Washington, this first day of January, in the year of our Lord one thousand eight hundred and sixty three, and of the Independence of the United States of America the eighty-seventh.

By the President: ABRAHAM LINCOLN
WILLIAM H. SEWARD, Secretary of State.

Amendment XIII

Section 1. Neither slavery nor involuntary servitude, except as a punishment for crime whereof the party shall have been duly convicted, shall exist within the United States, or any place subject to their jurisdiction.
Section 2. Congress shall have power to enforce this article by appropriate legislation.

Source: http://avalon.law.yale.edu/19th_century/emancipa.asp

Excerpts from Crusade for Justice:
The Autobiography of Ida B. Wells

Excerpt One. On a discussion about lynching with British social and religious leaders during a speaking tour of England in 1894; pp. 154-155.

THE TROUBLESOME QUESTION IGNORED

Again the question was asked where were all the legal and civil authorities of the country, to say nothing of the Christian churches, that they permitted such things to be? I could only say that despite the axiom that there is a remedy for every wrong, everybody in authority from the President of the United States down, had declared their inability to do anything; and that the Christian bodies and moral associations do not touch the question. It is the easiest way to get along in the South (and those portions in the North where lynchings take place) to ignore the question altogether; our American Christians are too busy saving the souls of white Christians from burning in hell-fire to save the lives of black ones from present burning in fires kindled by white Christians. The feelings of the people who commit these acts must not be hurt by protesting against this sort of thing, and so the bodies of the victims of mob hate must be sacrificed, and the country disgraced because of that fear to speak out.

NEGRO COMMUNICANTS REFUSED SEATS

It seems incredible to them that the Christian churches of the South refuse to admit Negro communicants into their houses of worship save in the galleries or in the back seats. When I told of a young mulatto named James Cotton who was dragged out of one of the leading churches in Memphis, Tennessee, by a policeman and shut up in the station house all day Sunday, for taking a seat in the church, one lady remarked that it was easy to believe anything after that.

I was asked if Northern churches knew of this discrimination and continued fellowship with the churches which practiced it. Truth compelled me to reply in the affirmative, and to give instances which showed that in every case the Northern churches, which do not practice these things themselves, tacitly agreed to them by the southern churches; and that so far as I knew principle has always yielded to prejudice in the hope of gaining the good will of the South.

I had especially in mind the National Baptist Convention, which met in Philadelphia in June 1892. An effort was made to have a resolution passed by that convention condemning lynching, as the Methodist Episcopal Conference had done at Omaha in May. The committee on resolutions decided that it could not be done as they had too many southern delegates present and did not wish to offend them.

Excerpt Two. On the response to rioting in Springfield, Illinois in 1908; at this time Wells was living in Chicago and teaching Sunday school in her Presbyterian church; pp. 299-300

During this time the riot broke out in Springfield, Illinois, and raged there for three days. Several daily papers called me up to know if we were going to hold an indignation meeting or what action, if any, was to be undertaken by us. The only church in which we had been wont to have such meetings would not, I was sure, give permission for me to hold one there and I felt sure that no one else would undertake it. . . .

I had such a feeling of impotency through the whole matter. Our race had not yet perfected an organization which was prepared to take old of this situation, which seemed to be becoming as bad in Illinois as it had hitherto been in Georgia. As I wended my way tyo Sunday school that bright Sabbath day, brooding over what was still going on at our state capital, I passed numbers of people out parading in their Sunday finery. None of them seemed to be worried by the fact of this three days' riot going on less than two hundred miles away. I do not remember what the lesson was about that Sunday, but when I came to myself I found I had given vent to a passionate denunciation of the apathy of our people over this terrible thing. I told those young men that we should be stirring ourselves to see what could be done. When one of them asked, "What can we do about it?" I replied that they could at least get together and ask themselves that question. The fact that nobody seemed worried was as terrible a thing as the riot itself. One of the young men said our leaders ought to take some action about it, and I said, "That does not absolve you from responsibility." He replied, "We have no place to meet," and I quickly answered, "If there are any of you who desire to come together to consider this thing, I here and now invite you to my home this afternoon." Three out of those thirty responded to my invitation! We discussed the situation from every angle and decided that we ought to try to get an organization among the young men which would undertake to consider such matters. Every one of the three was doubtful as to whether we could get such an organization going, but I urged them to try and see if each could report next Sunday with at least one other person. That was the beginning of what was afterward to be known as the Negro Fellowship League.

The Honorable Frederick Douglass's
Letter to Ida Wells

DEAR MISS WELLS:

Let me give you thanks for your faithful paper on the lynch abomination now generally practiced against colored people in the South. There has been no word equal to it in convincing power. I have spoken, but my word is feeble in comparison. You give us what you know and testify from actual knowledge. You have dealt with the facts with cool, painstaking fidelity, and left those naked and uncontradicted facts to speak for themselves.

Brave woman! you have done your people and mine a service which can neither be weighed nor measured. If the American conscience were only half alive, if the American church and clergy were only half Christianized, if American moral sensibility were not hardened by persistent infliction of outrage and crime against colored people, a scream of horror, shame, and indignation would rise to Heaven wherever your pamphlet shall be read.

But alas! even crime has power to reproduce itself and create conditions favorable to its own existence. It sometimes seems we are deserted by earth and Heaven-yet we must still think, speak and work, and trust in the power of a merciful God for final deliverance.

Very truly and gratefully yours,

FREDERICK DOUGLASS
Cedar Hill, Anacostia, D.C.

THE CASE STATED

The student of American sociology will find the year 1894 marked by a pronounced awakening of the public conscience to a system of anarchy and outlawry which had grown during a series of ten years to be so common, that scenes of unusual brutality failed to have any visible effect upon the humane sentiments of the people of our land.

Beginning with the emancipation of the Negro, the inevitable result of unbribled power exercised for two and a half centuries, by the white man over the Negro, began to show itself in acts of conscienceless outlawry. During the slave regime, the Southern white man owned the Negro body and soul. It was to his interest to dwarf the soul and preserve the body. Vested with unlimited power over his slave, to subject him to any and all kinds of physical pun-

ishment, the white man was still restrained from such punishment as tended to injure the slave by abating his physical powers and thereby reducing his financial worth. While slaves were scourged mercilessly, and in countless cases inhumanly treated in other respects, still the white owner rarely permitted his anger to go so far as to take a life, which would entail upon him a loss of several hundred dollars. The slave was rarely killed, he was too valuable; it was easier and quite as effective, for discipline or revenge, to sell him "Down South."

But Emancipation came and the vested interests of the white man in the Negro's body were lost. The white man had no right to scourge the emancipated Negro, still less has he a right to kill him. But the Southern white people had been educated so long in that school of practice, in which might makes right, that they disdained to draw strict lines of action in dealing with the Negro. In slave times the Negro was kept subservient and submissive by the frequency and severity of the scourging, but, with freedom, a new system of intimidation came into vogue; the Negro was not only whipped and scourged; he was killed.

Not all nor nearly all of the murders done by white men, during the past thirty years in the South, have come to light, but the statistics as gathered and preserved by white men, and which have not been questioned, show that during these years more than ten thousand Negroes have been killed in cold blood, without the formality of judicial trial and legal execution. And yet, as evidence of the absolute impunity with which the white man dares to kill a Negro, the same record shows that during all these years, and for all these murders only three white men have been tried, convicted, and executed. As no white man has been lynched for the murder of colored people, these three executions are the only instances of the death penalty being visited upon white men for murdering Negroes.

Naturally enough the commission of these crimes began to tell upon the public conscience, and the Southern white man, as a tribute to the nineteenth-century civilization, was in a manner compelled to give excuses for his barbarism. His excuses have adapted themselves to the emergency, and are aptly outlined by that greatest of all Negroes, Frederick Douglass, in an article of recent date, in which he shows that there have been three distinct eras of Southern barbarism, to account for which three distinct excuses have been made.

From *The Red Record* by Ida B. Wells-Barnett, 1895.

The first excuse given to the civilized world for the murder of unoffending Negroes was the necessity of the white man to repress and stamp out alleged "race riots." For years immediately succeeding the war there was an appalling slaughter of colored people, and the wires usually conveyed to northern people and the world the intelligence, first, that an insurrection was being planned by Negroes, which, a few hours later, would prove to have been vigorously resisted by white men, and controlled with a resulting loss of several killed and wounded. It was always a remarkable feature in these insurrections and riots that only Negroes were killed during the rioting, and that all the white men escaped unharmed.

From 1865 to 1872, hundreds of colored men and women were mercilessly murdered and the almost invariable reason assigned was that they met their death by being alleged participants in an insurrection or riot. But this story at last wore itself out. No insurrection ever materialized; no Negro rioter was ever apprehended and proven guilty, and no dynamite ever recorded the black man's protest against oppression and wrong. It was too much to ask thoughtful people to believe this transparent story, and the southern white people at last made up their minds that some other excuse must be had.

Then came the second excuse, which had its birth during the turbulent times of reconstruction. By an amendment to the Constitution the Negro was given the right of franchise, and, theoretically at least, his ballot became his invaluable emblem of citizenship. In a government "of the people, for the people, and by the people," the Negro's vote became an important factor in all matters of state and national politics. But this did not last long. The southern white man would not consider that the Negro had any right, which a white man was bound to respect, and the idea of a republican form of government in the southern states grew into general contempt. It was maintained that "This is a white man's government," and regardless of numbers the white man should rule. "No Negro domination" became the new legend on the sanguinary banner of the sunny South, and under it rode the Ku Klux Klan, the Regulators, and the lawless mobs, which for any cause chose to murder one man or a dozen as suited their purpose best. It was a long, gory campaign; the blood chills and the heart almost loses faith in Christianity when one thinks of Yazoo, Hamburg, Edgefield, Copiah, and the countless massacres of defenseless Negroes, whose only crime was the attempt to exercise their right to vote.

But it was a bootless strife for colored people. The government which had made the Negro a citizen found itself unable to protect him. It gave him the right to vote, but denied him the protection which should have maintained

that right. Scourged from his home; hunted through the swamps; hung by midnight raiders, and openly murdered in the light of day, the Negro clung to his right of franchise with a heroism which would have wrung admiration from the hearts of savages. He believed that in that small white ballot there was a subtle something which stood for manhood as well as citizenship, and thousands of brave black men went to their graves, exemplifying the one by dying for the other.

The white man's victory soon became complete by fraud, violence, intimidation and murder. The franchise vouchsafed to the Negro grew to be a "barren ideality," and regardless of numbers, the colored people found themselves voiceless in the councils of those whose duty it was to rule. With no longer the fear of "Negro Domination" before their eyes, the white man's second excuse became valueless. With the Southern governments all subverted and the Negro actually eliminated from all participation in state and national elections, there could be no longer an excuse for killing Negroes to prevent "Negro Domination."

Brutality still continued; Negroes were whipped, scourged, exiled, shot and hung whenever and wherever it pleased the white man so to treat them, and as the civilized world with increasing persistency held the white people of the South to account for its outlawry, the murderers invented the third excuse-that Negroes had to be killed to avenge their assaults upon women. There could be framed no possible excuse more harmful to the Negro and more unanswerable if true in its sufficiency for the white man.

Humanity abhors the assailant of womanhood, and this charge upon the Negro at once placed him beyond the pale of human sympathy. With such unanimity, earnestness and apparent candor was this charge made and reiterated that the world has accepted the story that the Negro is a monster which the Southern white man has painted him. And today, the Christian world feels, that while lynching is a crime, and lawlessness and anarchy the certain precursors of a nation's fall, it can not by word or deed, extend sympathy or help to a race of outlaws, who might mistake their plea for justice and deem it an excuse for their continued wrongs.

The Negro has suffered much and is willing to suffer more. He recognizes that the wrongs of two centuries can not be righted in a day, and he tries to bear his burden with patience for today and be hopeful for tomorrow. But there comes a time when the veriest worm will turn, and the Negro feels today that after all the work he has done, all the sacrifices he has made, and all the suffering he has endured, if he did not, now, defend his name and manhood from this vile accusation, he would be unworthy even of the contempt of mankind. It is to this charge he now feels he must make answer.

If the Southern people in defense of their lawlessness, would tell the truth and admit that colored men and women are lynched for almost any offense, from murder to a misdemeanor, there would not now be the necessity for this defense. But when they intentionally, maliciously and constantly belie the record and bolster up these falsehoods by the words of legislators, preachers, governors and bishops, then the Negro must give to the world his side of the awful story.

A word as to the charge itself. In considering the third reason assigned by the Southern white people for the butchery of blacks, the question must be asked, what the white man means when he charges the black man with rape. Does he mean the crime which the statutes of the civilized states describe as such? Not by any means. With the Southern white man, any mesalliance existing between a white woman and a colored man is a sufficient foundation for the charge of rape. The Southern white man says that it is impossible for a voluntary alliance to exist between a white woman and a colored man, and therefore, the fact of an alliance is a proof of force. In numerous instances where colored men have have been lynched on the charge of rape, it was positively known at the time of lynching, and indisputably proven after the victim's death, that the relationship sustained between the man and woman was voluntary and clandestine, and that in no court of law could even the charge of assault have been successfully maintained.

It was for the assertion of this fact, in the defense of her own race, that the writer hereof became an exile; her property destroyed and her return to her home forbidden under penalty of death, for writing the following editorial which was printed in her paper, the Free Speech, in Memphis, Tenn., May 21, 1892:

> Eight Negroes lynched since last issue of the Free Speech one at Little Rock, Ark., last Saturday morning where the citizens broke(?) into the penitentiary and got their

man; three near Anniston, Ala., one near New Orleans; and three at Clarksville, Ga., the last three for killing a white man, and five on the same old racket-the new alarm about raping white women. The same programme of hanging, then shooting bullets into the lifeless bodies was carried out to the letter. Nobody in this section of the country believes the old threadbare lie that Negro men rape white women. If Southern white men are not careful, they will overreach themselves and public sentiment will have a reaction; a conclusion will then be reached which will be very damaging to the moral reputation of their women.

But threats cannot suppress the truth, and while the Negro suffers the soul deformity, resultant from two and a half centuries of slavery, he is no more guilty of this vilest of all vile charges than the white man who would blacken his name.

During all the years of slavery, no such charge was ever made, not even during the dark days of the rebellion, when the white man, following the fortunes of war went to do battle for the maintenance of slavery. While the master was away fighting to forge the fetters upon the slave, he left his wife and children with no protectors save the Negroes themselves. And yet during those years of trust and peril, no Negro proved recreant to his trust and no white man returned to a home that had been dispoiled.

Likewise during the period of alleged "insurrection," and alarming "race riots," it never occurred to the white man, that his wife and children were in danger of assault. Nor in the Reconstruction era, when the hue and cry was against "Negro Domination," was there ever a thought that the domination would ever contaminate a fireside or strike to death the virtue of womanhood. It must appear strange indeed, to every thoughtful and candid man that more than a quarter of a century elapsed before the Negro began to show signs of such infamous degeneration.

The early 1900s were also a time of intellectual flowering. The Harlem Renaissance, an African-American cultural movement centered in Harlem, New York City, showcased many writers, who started their careers during this time. Many of them continued to contribute to African-American literature over the next several decades.

This section includes a *poem by James Weldon Johnson,* and an excerpt from *Zora Neale Hurston's play, Cold Keener, A Revue.*

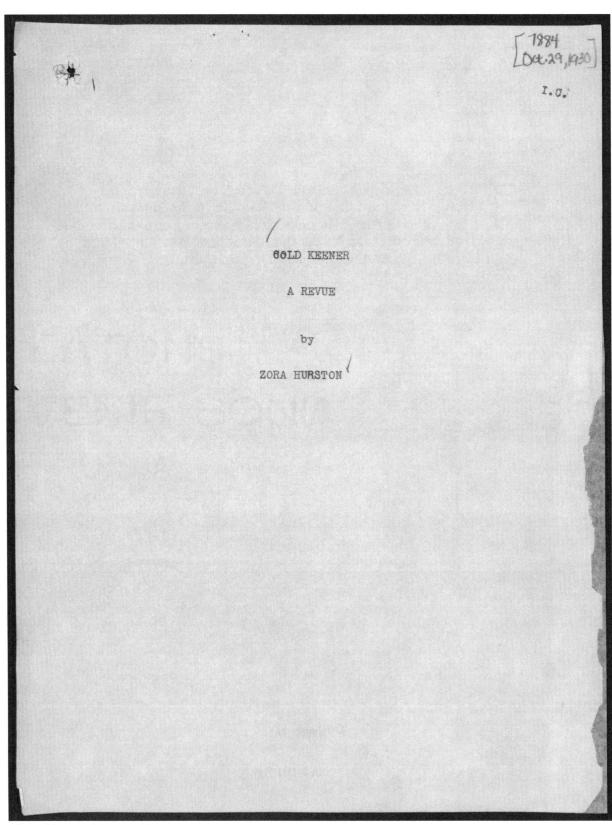

COLD KEENER

A REVUE

by

ZORA HURSTON

Excerpt from Zora Neale Hurston's
Cold Keener, A Revue

Scene: FILLING STATION

Time: Present.

Place: A point on the Alabama-Georgia state line.

Setting: A filling station upstage center. It stretches nearly across the stage. The road passes before and through it. There is a line down the center of the stage from the center of the filling station to the footlights that says on the left side, "Alabama state Line", and on the right, "Georgia State Line". The name of the station is "The State Line Filling Station". There are two gas pumps equal distance from the center of the station, so that the door of the house appears between them.

Action: When the curtain goes up a fat Negro is rared back in a chair beside the door of the station asleep and snoring. There is an inner tube lying beside him that has fallen out of his hand as he slept. It is a bright afternoon. There is the sound of a car approaching from the Alabama side and a Model T Ford rattles to the pump on the upstage side of the pumps and stops at the one nearest to the left entrance. He stops his car with a jerk. The proprietor is still asleep. The Ford driver blows his horn rigorously and wakes him. He picks up the tube beside him and arises with it in his hand, stretching and yawning.

Proprietor (Sleepily): How many?

Ford Driver: Two.

Proprietor: Two what?

Ford Driver: Two pints.

(The Proprietor gets a quart cup and measures the gas and wrings the hose to be sure to get it all, then he pours it in the tank.)

Ford Driver: You better look at my water and air, too.

(He has a very expensive and ornate cap on the radiator, but otherwise the car is most dilapidated. As the Proprietor pours the water into the radiator, the driver gets out of the car and stands off from it looking it over.)

Ford Driver: Say, Jimpson, they tells me you got a new mechanic round here that's just too tight.

Proprietor: That's right. He kin do more wid 'em than the man that made 'em.

Ford Driver: Well, looka here. My car kinda needs overhauling and maybe a little point. Look her over and tell me just what you could make her look like a brand new car for.

(Proprietor lifts the hood and looks. Walks around and studies the car from all angles. Then stops at the front and examines the radiator cap.)
Proprietor: Well, I tell you. You see it's like this. This car needs a whole heap of things done to it. But being as you'se a friend of mine-tell you what I'll do. I'll just jack that radiator cap up and run a brand new Ford under it for four hundred and ninety-five dollars.

Ford Driver (Indignantly): Whut de hen-fire you think I'm gointuh let you rob me outa my car. That's a good car.

(A car enters from the Alabama side with a good-looking girl in it alone. She stops on the downstage side of the pumps, but somewhat ahead of the Ford. The Proprietor rushes over to the left side of her car.)

Proprietor (Pleasantly): Yes, ma'am!

Girl: I had a flat down the road and I changed it, but it's not fixed. Do you vulcanize?

Proprietor: We do everything but the buzzard lope-and that's gone outa style.

(He takes the tire off the back and goes inside, and comes right out again with it.)

Proprietor: Do you want it on the wheel or on the spare?

(Girl alights and goes round to back of car.)

Girl: On the spare, I guess.

(The Proprietor tries to put it on. The Ford Driver tries to help. They get in each other's way.)

Proprietor: (peeved) Man, let go this thing.

Ford Driver: (peeved) Don't you see I'm helpin' you?

Proprietor: (Angry) Leggo! I can't utilize my self for you!

(Ford Driver lets go so suddenly that the tire falls to the ground. The girl grabs it before either of them end lifts it on the rack and gives it a good kick and the tire goes into place perfectly. She gets into the car, hands the Proprietor a dollar and drives off.)

From *The Zora Neale Hurston Plays at the Library of Congress. Cold Keener* (1930) Library of Congress, Manuscript Division

Proprietor: (admiringly) That's a tight little piece of pig-meat! Damned if I don't believe I'll go to Georgia!

Ford Driver: She ain't no pig-meat. That's a married 'oman.

Proprietor: You know her?

Ford Driver: Nope, never seen her before.

Proprietor: Well, how can you tell she's married?

Ford Driver: Didn't you see that kick? A woman that can kick like that done had some man to practise on.

(Enter from Georgia side a man driving a Chevrolet-old and battered. He stops on the downstage side of the right hand pump.)

Proprietor: (advancing to the car) what's yours?

Chevrolet Driver: Make it a gallon-goin' way over in Alabama.

(He alights and strolls towards the center of the stage where the Ford Driver is already standing.)

Chevrolet Driver: 'Lo stranger, how's Alabama?

Ford Driver: Just fine-couldn't be no better. How's you Georgy folks starvin'?

Chevrolet Driver: Starvin'? Who ever heard tell of anybody starvin' in Georgy-people so fat in Georgy till I speck Gabriel gointuh have to knock us in de heed on judgment day so we kin go long wid de rest.

Ford Driver: He might have to knock some of then Georgy crackers in de head, but you niggers will be all reedy and waitin' for de trumpet.

Chevrolet Driver: How come?

Ford Driver: (snickering) Cause dem crackers y'all got over there sho is hard on zigaboos.

Chevrolet Driver: (peeved) Lemme tell you something, coon. We got nice white folks in Georgy! But them Ala-

bama red-necks is too mean to give God a honest prayer without snatchin' back amen!

Ford Driver: Who mean? I know you ain't talkin' 'bout them white folks in my state. Alabama is de best state in de world. If you can't git along there, you can't get along nowhere. But in Georgy they hates niggers so bad till one day they lynched a black mule for kickin a white one.

Chevrolet Driver: Well, in Alabama a black horse run away with a white woman, and they lynched the horse, and burnt the buggy and hung the harness.

Ford Driver: Well, in Georgy they don't low y'all to call a white female mule Maud.
Chevrolet: What they call her then?

Ford Driver: Miss Maud-and you know it durn well, too.
Chevrolet Driver: Well, they tell me y'all can't go into a store and ask for a can of Prince Albert tobacco-not wid dat white man on it-you got to ask for Cap'n Albert.

Ford Driver: Well, they tell me they don't 'low y'all niggers to laugh on de streets in Georgy. They got laughin' barrels on certain corners for niggers, and when you gets tickled you got to hold it till you can make it to one of them barrels and stick yo' head in. Then you can cut loose. Laughin' any old place just ain't allowed.

Chevrolet Driver: Well, over in Alabama, if they tell a funny joke in the theatre, y'all ain't allowed to laugh till the white folks git through. Then a white man way down front turns round and look way up in the peanut gallery and say, "All right, niggers, y'all kin laugh now." Then y'all just "kah, kah"!

Ford Driver: That's all right. They don't 'low y'all to ride no faster than ten miles an hour. If you ride any faster-you liable to get in front of some white folks.

Chevrolet Driver: Well, they don't 'low y'all to ride nothin' but Fords so you can't pass nobody.

Ford Driver: Now, what's de matter wid a Ford?

Lift Every Voice and Sing

by James Weldon Johnson
Sometimes called the "Negro National Anthem"

Lift ev'ry voice and sing,
Till earth and heaven ring,
Ring with the harmonies of Liberty;
Let our rejoicing rise
High as the list'ning skies,
Let it resound loud as the rolling sea.
Sing a song full of the faith that the dark past has taught us,
Sing a song full of the hope that the present has brought us;
Facing the rising sun of our new day begun,
Let us march on till victory is won.
Stony the road we trod,
Bitter the chast'ning rod,
Felt in the days when hope unborn had died;
Yet with a steady beat,
Have not our weary feet
Come to the place for which our fathers sighed?
We have come over a way that with tears has been watered.
We have come, treading our path through the blood of the slaughtered,
Out from the gloomy past, Till now we stand at last Where the white gleam of our bright star is cast.
God of our weary years,
God of our silent tears,
Thou who hast brought us thus far on the way;
Thou who hast by Thy might,
Led us into the light,
Keep us forever in the path, we pray.
Lest our feet stray from the places, our God, where we met Thee,

Lest our hearts, drunk with the wine of the world, we forget Thee;
Shadowed beneath Thy hand,
May we forever stand,
True to our God,
True to our native land.

Once America moved beyond the Great Depression and World War II, the fight for equality and civil rights began in earnest. Some of the first battles were fought in the courts. Following some early victories in the courts, the Jim Crow South fought back even more virulently to keep African Americans from enjoying dignity, full rights of citizenship, and even basic safety. Many of the leaders in the struggle for civil rights were inspired by their faith to make the sacrifices needed to succeed.

This section includes such documents as *"We Shall Overcome,"* writings of *Martin Luther King, Jr.* and *Malcolm X, Testimony of Fannie Lou Hamer,* and *Stokely Carmichael's Black Power speech.*

We Shall Overcome

We shall overcome, we shall overcome
We shall overcome some day
Oh, deep in my heart, I do believe
We shall overcome some day
The Lord will see us through, the Lord will see us through
The lord will see us through some day
Oh, deep in my heart, I do believe
We shall overcome some day.

We'll walk hand in hand, we'll walk hand in hand
We'll walk hand in hand some day
Oh, deep in my heart, I do believe
We shall overcome some day.

We are not afraid, we are not afraid
We are not afraid today
Oh, deep in my heart, I do believe
We shall overcome some day
The truth shall make us free, the truth shall make us free
The truth shall make us free some day
Oh, deep in my heart, I do believe
We shall overcome some day.

We shall live in peace, we shall live in peace
We shall live in peace some day
Oh, deep in my heart, I do believe
We shall overcome some day.

Excerpt from Letter from a Birmingham Jail

by Martin Luther King, Jr.

16 April 1963

My Dear Fellow Clergymen:

While confined here in the Birmingham city jail, I came across your recent statement calling my present activities "unwise and untimely." Seldom do I pause to answer criticism of my work and ideas. If I sought to answer all the criticisms that cross my desk, my secretaries would have little time for anything other than such correspondence in the course of the day, and I would have no time for constructive work. But since I feel that you are men of genuine good will and that your criticisms are sincerely set forth, I want to try to answer your statement in what I hope will be patient and reasonable terms.

I think I should indicate why I am here in Birmingham, since you have been influenced by the view which argues against "outsiders coming in." I have the honor of serving as president of the Southern Christian Leadership Conference, an organization operating in every southern state, with headquarters in Atlanta, Georgia. We have some eighty five affiliated organizations across the South, and one of them is the Alabama Christian Movement for Human Rights. Frequently we share staff, educational and financial resources with our affiliates. Several months ago the affiliate here in Birmingham asked us to be on call to engage in a nonviolent direct action program if such were deemed necessary. We readily consented, and when the hour came we lived up to our promise. So I, along with several members of my staff, am here because I was invited here. I am here because I have organizational ties here.

But more basically, I am in Birmingham because injustice is here. Just as the prophets of the eighth century B.C. left their villages and carried their "thus saith the Lord" far beyond the boundaries of their home towns, and just as the Apostle Paul left his village of Tarsus and carried the gospel of Jesus Christ to the far corners of the Greco Roman world, so am I compelled to carry the gospel of freedom beyond my own home town. Like

Paul, I must constantly respond to the Macedonian call for aid.

Moreover, I am cognizant of the interrelatedness of all communities and states. I cannot sit idly by in Atlanta and not be concerned about what happens in Birmingham. Injustice anywhere is a threat to justice everywhere. We are caught in an inescapable network of mutuality, tied in a single garment of destiny. Whatever affects one directly, affects all indirectly. Never again can we afford to live with the narrow, provincial "outside agitator" idea. Anyone who lives inside the United States can never be considered an outsider anywhere within its bounds.

You deplore the demonstrations taking place in Birmingham. But your statement, I am sorry to say, fails to express a similar concern for the conditions that brought about the demonstrations. I am sure that none of you would want to rest content with the superficial kind of social analysis that deals merely with effects and does not grapple with underlying causes. It is unfortunate that demonstrations are taking place in Birmingham, but it is even more unfortunate that the city's white power structure left the Negro community with no alternative.

In any nonviolent campaign there are four basic steps: collection of the facts to determine whether injustices exist; negotiation; self purification; and direct action. We have gone through all these steps in Birmingham. There can be no gainsaying the fact that racial injustice engulfs this community. Birmingham is probably the most thoroughly segregated city in the United States. Its ugly record of brutality is widely known. Negroes have experienced grossly unjust treatment in the courts. There have been more unsolved bombings of Negro homes and churches in Birmingham than in any other city in the nation. These are the hard, brutal facts of the case. On the basis of these conditions, Negro leaders sought to negotiate with the city fathers. But the latter consistently refused to engage in good faith negotiation.

I've Been to the Mountaintop
by Martin Luther King, Jr.

Delivered 3 April 1968, Mason Temple (Church of God in Christ Headquarters), Memphis, Tennessee

Thank you very kindly, my friends. As I listened to Ralph Abernathy and his eloquent and generous introduction and then thought about myself, I wondered who he was talking about. It's always good to have your closest friend and associate to say something good about you. And Ralph Abernathy is the best friend that I have in the world. I'm delighted to see each of you here tonight in spite of a storm warning. You reveal that you are determined to go on anyhow.

Something is happening in Memphis; something is happening in our world. And you know, if I were standing at the beginning of time, with the possibility of taking a kind of general and panoramic view of the whole of human history up to now, and the Almighty said to me, "Martin Luther King, which age would you like to live in?" I would take my mental flight by Egypt and I would watch God's children in their magnificent trek from the dark dungeons of Egypt through, or rather across the Red Sea, through the wilderness on toward the promised land. And in spite of its magnificence, I wouldn't stop there. I would move on by Greece and take my mind to Mount Olympus. And I would see Plato, Aristotle, Socrates, Euripides and Aristophanes assembled around the Parthenon. And I would watch them around the Parthenon as they discussed the great and eternal issues of reality. But I wouldn't stop there.

I would go on, even to the great heyday of the Roman Empire. And I would see developments around there, through various emperors and leaders. But I wouldn't stop there. I would even come up to the day of the Renaissance, and get a quick picture of all that the Renaissance did for the cultural and aesthetic life of man. But I wouldn't stop there. I would even go by the way that the man for whom I am named had his habitat. And I would watch Martin Luther as he tacked his ninety-five theses on the door at the church of Wittenberg. But I wouldn't stop there. I would come on up even to 1863, and watch a vacillating President by the name of Abraham Lincoln finally come to the conclusion that he had to sign the Emancipation Proclamation. But I wouldn't stop there.

I would even come up to the early thirties, and see a man grappling with the problems of the bankruptcy of his nation. And come with an eloquent cry that we have nothing to fear but "fear itself." But I wouldn't stop there.

Strangely enough, I would turn to the Almighty, and say, "If you allow me to live just a few years in the second half of the 20th century, I will be happy." Now that's a strange statement to make, because the world is all messed up. The nation is sick. Trouble is in the land; confusion all around. That's a strange statement. But I know, somehow, that only when it is dark enough can you see the stars. And I see God working in this period of the twentieth century in a way that men, in some strange way, are responding. Something is happening in our world. The masses of people are rising up. And wherever they are assembled today, whether they are in Johannesburg, South Africa; Nairobi, Kenya; Accra, Ghana; New York City; Atlanta, Georgia; Jackson, Mississippi; or Memphis, Tennessee - the cry is always the same: "We want to be free." And another reason that I'm happy to live in this period is that we have been forced to a point where we are going to have to grapple with the problems that men have been trying to grapple with through history, but the demands didn't force them to do it. Survival demands that we grapple with them. Men, for years now, have been talking about war and peace. But now, no longer can they just talk about it. It is no longer a choice between violence and nonviolence in this world; it's nonviolence or nonexistence. That is where we are today.

And also in the human rights revolution, if something isn't done, and done in a hurry, to bring the colored peoples of the world out of their long years of poverty, their long years of hurt and neglect, the whole world is doomed. Now, I'm just happy that God has allowed me to live in this period to see what is unfolding. And I'm happy that He's allowed me to be in Memphis.

I can remember - I can remember when Negroes were just going around as Ralph has said, so often, scratching where they didn't itch, and laughing when they were not tickled. But that day is all over. We mean business now, and we are determined to gain our rightful place in God's world.

And that's all this whole thing is about. We aren't engaged in any negative protest and in any negative arguments with anybody. We are saying that we are determined to be men. We are determined to be people. We are saying - We are saying that we are God's children. And that we are God's children, we don't have to live like we are forced to live.

Now, what does all of this mean in this great period of history? It means that we've got to stay together. We've got to stay together and maintain unity. You know, whenever Pharaoh wanted to prolong the period of slavery in Egypt, he had a favorite, favorite formula for doing it. What was that? He kept the slaves fighting among themselves. But whenever the slaves get together, something happens in Pharaoh's court, and he cannot hold the slaves in slavery. When the slaves get together, that's the beginning of getting out of slavery. Now let us maintain unity.

Secondly, let us keep the issues where they are. The issue is injustice. The issue is the refusal of Memphis to be fair and honest in its dealings with its public servants, who happen to be sanitation workers. Now, we've got to keep attention on that. That's always the problem with a little violence. You know what happened the other day, and the press dealt only with the window-breaking. I read the articles. They very seldom got around to mentioning the fact that one thousand, three hundred sanitation workers are on strike, and that Memphis is not being fair to them, and that Mayor Loeb is in dire need of a doctor. They didn't get around to that.

Now we're going to march again, and we've got to march again, in order to put the issue where it is supposed to be - and force everybody to see that there are thirteen hundred of God's children here suffering, sometimes going hungry, going through dark and dreary nights wondering how this thing is going to come out. That's the issue. And we've got to say to the nation: We know how it's coming out. For when people get caught up with that which is right and they are willing to sacrifice for it, there is no stopping point short of victory.

We aren't going to let any mace stop us. We are masters in our nonviolent movement in disarming police forces; they don't know what to do. I've seen them so often. I remember in Birmingham, Alabama, when we were in that majestic struggle there, we would move out of the 16th Street Baptist Church day after day; by the hundreds we would move out. And Bull Connor would tell them to send the dogs forth, and they did come; but we just went before the dogs singing, "Ain't gonna let nobody turn me around."

Bull Connor next would say, "Turn the fire hoses on." And as I said to you the other night, Bull Connor didn't know history. He knew a kind of physics that somehow didn't relate to the transphysics that we knew about. And that was the fact that there was a certain kind of fire that no water could put out. And we went before the fire hoses; we had known water. If we were Baptist or some other denominations, we had been immersed. If we were Methodist, and some others, we had been sprinkled, but we knew water. That couldn't stop us.

And we just went on before the dogs and we would look at them; and we'd go on before the water hoses and we would look at it, and we'd just go on singing "Over my head I see freedom in the air." And then we would be thrown in the paddy wagons, and sometimes we were stacked in there like sardines in a can. And they would throw us in, and old Bull would say, "Take 'em off," and they did; and we would just go in the paddy wagon singing, "We Shall Overcome." And every now and then we'd get in jail, and we'd see the jailers looking through the windows being moved by our prayers, and being moved by our words and our songs. And there was a power there which Bull Connor couldn't adjust to; and so we ended up transforming Bull into a steer, and we won our struggle in Birmingham. Now we've got to go on in Memphis just like that. I call upon you to be with us when we go out Monday.

Now about injunctions: We have an injunction and we're going into court tomorrow morning to fight this illegal, unconstitutional injunction. All we say to America is, "Be true to what you said on paper." If I lived in China or even Russia, or any totalitarian country, maybe I could understand some of these illegal injunctions. Maybe I could understand the denial of certain basic First Amendment privileges, because they hadn't committed themselves to that over there. But somewhere I read of the freedom of assembly. Somewhere I read of the freedom of speech. Somewhere I read of the freedom of press. Somewhere I read that the greatness of America is the right to protest for right. And so just as I say, we aren't going to let dogs or water hoses turn us around, we aren't going to let any injunction turn us around. We are going on.

We need all of you. And you know what's beautiful to me is to see all of these ministers of the Gospel. It's a marvelous picture. Who is it that is supposed to articulate the longings and aspirations of the people more than the preacher? Somehow the preacher must have a kind of fire shut up in his bones. And whenever injustice is around he tell it. Somehow the preacher must be an Amos, and saith, "When God speaks who can but prophesy?" Again with Amos, "Let justice roll down like waters and righteousness like a mighty stream." Somehow the preacher must say with Jesus, "The Spirit of the Lord is upon me, because he hath anointed me," and he's anointed me to deal with the problems of the poor.

And I want to commend the preachers, under the leadership of these noble men: James Lawson, one who has been in this struggle for many years; he's been to jail for struggling; he's been kicked out of Vanderbilt University for this struggle, but he's still going on, fighting for the rights of his people. Reverend Ralph Jackson, Billy Kiles; I could just go right on down the list, but time will not permit.

But I want to thank all of them. And I want you to thank them, because so often, preachers aren't concerned about anything but themselves. And I'm always happy to see a relevant ministry.

It's all right to talk about "long white robes over yonder," in all of its symbolism. But ultimately people want some suits and dresses and shoes to wear down here! It's all right to talk about "streets flowing with milk and honey," but God has commanded us to be concerned about the slums down here, and his children who can't eat three square meals a day. It's all right to talk about the new Jerusalem, but one day, God's preacher must talk about the new New York, the new Atlanta, the new Philadelphia, the new Los Angeles, the new Memphis, Tennessee. This is what we have to do.

Now the other thing we'll have to do is this: Always anchor our external direct action with the power of economic withdrawal. Now, we are poor people. Individually, we are poor when you compare us with white society in America. We are poor. Never stop and forget that collectively—that means all of us together—collectively we are richer than all the nations in the world, with the exception of nine. Did you ever think about that? After you leave the United States, Soviet Russia, Great Britain, West Germany, France, and I could name the others, the American Negro collectively is richer than most nations of the world. We have an annual income of more than thirty billion dollars a year, which is more than all of the exports of the United States, and more than the national budget of Canada. Did you know that? That's power right there, if we know how to pool it.

We don't have to argue with anybody. We don't have to curse and go around acting bad with our words. We don't need any bricks and bottles. We don't need any Molotov cocktails. We just need to go around to these stores, and to these massive industries in our country, and say, "God sent us by here, to say to you that you're not treating his children right. And we've come by here to ask you to make the first item on your agenda fair treatment, where God's children are concerned. Now, if you are not prepared to do that, we do have an agenda that we must follow. And our agenda calls for withdrawing economic support from you."

And so, as a result of this, we are asking you tonight, to go out and tell your neighbors not to buy Coca-Cola in Memphis. Go by and tell them not to buy Sealtest milk. Tell them not to buy —what is the other bread?—Wonder Bread. And what is the other bread company, Jesse? Tell them not to buy Hart's bread. As Jesse Jackson has said, up to now, only the garbage men have been feeling pain; now we must kind of redistribute the pain. We are choosing these companies because they haven't been fair in their hiring policies; and we are choosing them because they can begin the process of saying they are going to support the needs and the rights of these men who are on strike. And then they can move on town— downtown and tell Mayor Loeb to do what is right.

But not only that, we've got to strengthen black institutions. I call upon you to take your money out of the banks downtown and deposit your money in Tri-State Bank. We want a "bank-in" movement in Memphis. Go by the savings and loan association. I'm not asking you something that we don't do ourselves at SCLC. Judge Hooks and others will tell you that we have an account here in the savings and loan association from the Southern Christian Leadership Conference. We are telling you to follow what we are doing. Put your money there. You have six or seven black insurance companies here in the city of Memphis. Take out your insurance there. We want to have an "insurance-in."

Now these are some practical things that we can do. We begin the process of building a greater economic base. And at the same time, we are putting pressure where it really hurts. I ask you to follow through here.

Now, let me say as I move to my conclusion that we've got to give ourselves to this struggle until the end. Nothing would be more tragic than to stop at this point in Memphis. We've got to see it through. And when we have our march, you need to be there. If it means leaving work, if it means leaving school—be there. Be concerned about your brother. You may not be on strike. But either we go up together, or we go down together.

Let us develop a kind of dangerous unselfishness. One day a man came to Jesus, and he wanted to raise some questions about some vital matters of life. At points he wanted to trick Jesus, and show him that he knew a little more than Jesus knew and throw him off base....

Now that question could have easily ended up in a philosophical and theological debate. But Jesus immediately pulled that question from mid-air, and placed it on a dangerous curve between Jerusalem and Jericho. And he talked about a certain man, who fell among thieves. You remember that a Levite and a priest passed by on the other side. They didn't stop to help him. And finally a man of another race came by. He got down from his beast, decided not to be compassionate by proxy. But he got down with him, administered first aid, and helped the man in need. Jesus ended up saying, this was the good man, this was the great man, because he had the capacity to project the "I" into the "thou," and to be concerned about his brother.

Now you know, we use our imagination a great deal to try to determine why the priest and the Levite didn't stop. At times we say they were busy going to a church meeting, an ecclesiastical gathering, and they had to get on down to Jerusalem so they wouldn't be late for their meeting. At other times we would speculate that there was a religious law that "One who was engaged in religious ceremonials was not to touch a human body twenty-four hours before the ceremony." And every now and then we begin to wonder whether maybe they were not going down to Jerusalem - or down to Jericho, rather to organize a "Jericho Road Improvement Association." That's a possibility. Maybe they felt that it was better to deal with the problem from the causal root, rather than to get bogged down with an individual effect.

But I'm going to tell you what my imagination tells me. It's possible that those men were afraid. You see, the Jericho road is a dangerous road. I remember when Mrs. King and I were first in Jerusalem. We rented a car and drove from Jerusalem down to Jericho. And as soon as we got on that road, I said to my wife, "I can see why Jesus used this as the setting for his parable." It's a winding, meandering road. It's really conducive for ambushing. You start out in Jerusalem, which is about 1200 miles - or rather 1200 feet above sea level. And by the time you get down to Jericho, fifteen or twenty minutes later, you're about 2200 feet below sea level. That's a dangerous road. In the days of Jesus it came to be known as the "Bloody Pass." And you know, it's possible that the priest and the Levite looked over that man on the ground and wondered if the robbers were still around. Or it's possible that they felt that the man on the ground was merely faking. And he was acting like he had been robbed and hurt, in order to seize them over there, lure them there for quick and easy seizure. And so the first question that the priest asked—the first question that the Levite asked was, "If I stop to help this man, what will happen to me?" But then the Good Samaritan came by. And he reversed the question: "If I do not stop to help this man, what will happen to him?"

That's the question before you tonight. Not, "If I stop to help the sanitation workers, what will happen to my job. Not, "If I stop to help the sanitation workers what will happen to all of the hours that I usually spend in my office every day and every week as a pastor?" The question is not, "If I stop to help this man in need, what will happen to me?" The question is, "If I do not stop to help the sanitation workers, what will happen to them?" That's the question.

Let us rise up tonight with a greater readiness. Let us stand with a greater determination. And let us move on in these powerful days, these days of challenge to make America what it ought to be. We have an opportunity to make America a better nation. And I want to thank God, once more, for allowing me to be here with you.

You know, several years ago, I was in New York City autographing the first book that I had written. And while sitting there autographing books, a demented black woman came up. The only question I heard from her was, "Are you Martin Luther King?" And I was looking down writing, and I said, "Yes." And the next minute I felt something beating on my chest. Before I knew it I had been stabbed by this demented woman. I was rushed to Harlem Hospital. It was a dark Saturday afternoon. And that blade had gone through, and the X-rays revealed that the tip of the blade was on the edge of my aorta, the main artery. And once that's punctured, your drowned in your own blood—that's the end of you.

It came out in the *New York Times* the next morning, that if I had merely sneezed, I would have died. Well, about four days later, they allowed me, after the operation, after my chest had been opened, and the blade had been taken out, to move around in the wheel chair in the hospital. They allowed me to read some of the mail that came in, and from all over the states and the world, kind letters came in. I read a few, but one of them I will never forget. I had received one from the President and the Vice-President. I've forgotten what those telegrams said. I'd received a visit and a letter from the Governor of New York, but I've forgotten what that letter said. But there was another letter that came from a little girl, a young girl who was a student at the White Plains High School. And I looked at that letter, and I'll never forget it. It said simply,

Dear Dr. King,

I am a ninth-grade student at the White Plains High School.

And she said,

While it should not matter, I would like to mention that I'm a white girl. I read in the paper of your misfortune, and of your suffering. And I read that if you had sneezed, you would have died. And I'm simply writing you to say that I'm so happy that you didn't sneeze.

And I want to say tonight— I want to say tonight that I too am happy that I didn't sneeze. Because if I had sneezed, I wouldn't have been around here in 1960, when students all over the South started sitting-in at lunch counters. And I knew that as they were sitting in, they were really standing up for the best in the American dream, and taking the whole nation back to those great wells of democracy which were dug deep by the Founding Fathers in the Declaration of Independence and the Constitution.

If I had sneezed, I wouldn't have been around here in 1961, when we decided to take a ride for freedom and ended segregation in inter-state travel.

If I had sneezed, I wouldn't have been around here in 1962, when Negroes in Albany, Georgia, decided to straighten their backs up. And whenever men and women straighten their backs up, they are going somewhere, because a man can't ride your back unless it is bent.

If I had sneezed—If I had sneezed I wouldn't have been here in 1963, when the black people of Birmingham, Alabama, aroused the conscience of this nation, and brought into being the Civil Rights Bill.

If I had sneezed, I wouldn't have had a chance later that year, in August, to try to tell America about a dream that I had had.

If I had sneezed, I wouldn't have been down in Selma, Alabama, to see the great Movement there.

If I had sneezed, I wouldn't have been in Memphis to see a community rally around those brothers and sisters who are suffering.

I'm so happy that I didn't sneeze.

And they were telling me—. Now, it doesn't matter, now. It really doesn't matter what happens now. I left Atlanta this morning, and as we got started on the plane, there were six of us. The pilot said over the public address system, "We are sorry for the delay, but we have Dr. Martin Luther King on the plane. And to be sure that all of the bags were checked, and to be sure that nothing would be wrong with on the plane, we had to check out everything carefully. And we've had the plane protected and guarded all night."

And then I got into Memphis. And some began to say the threats, or talk about the threats that were out. What would happen to me from some of our sick white brothers?

Well, I don't know what will happen now. We've got some difficult days ahead. But it really doesn't matter with me now, because I've been to the mountaintop.

And I don't mind.

Like anybody, I would like to live a long life. Longevity has its place. But I'm not concerned about that now. I just want to do God's will. And He's allowed me to go up to the mountain. And I've looked over. And I've seen the Promised Land. I may not get there with you. But I want you to know tonight, that we, as a people, will get to the promised land!

And so I'm happy, tonight. I'm not worried about anything. I'm not fearing any man! Mine eyes have seen the glory of the coming of the Lord!!

Testimony of Fannie Lou Hamer

Mr. Chairman, and the Credentials Committee, my name is Mrs. Fanny Lou Hamer, and I live at 626 East Lafayette Street, Ruleville, Mississippi, Sunflower County, the home of Senator James O. Eastland, and Senator Stennis.

It was the 31st of August in 1962 that 18 of us traveled 26 miles to the country courthouse in Indianola to try to register to try to become first-class citizens.

We was met in Indianola by Mississippi men, Highway Patrolmens and they only allowed two of us in to take the literacy test at the time. After we had taken this test and started back to Ruleville, we was held up by the City Police and the State Highway Patrolmen and carried back to Indianola where the bus driver was charged that day with driving a bus the wrong color.

After we paid the fine among us, we continued on to Ruleville, and Reverend Jeff Sunny carried me four miles in the rural area where I had worked as a timekeeper and sharecropper for 18 years. I was met there by my children, who told me that the plantation owner was angry because I had gone down to try to register.

After they told me, my husband came, and said that the plantation owner was raising cain because I had tired to register, and before he quit talking the plantation owner came, and said, "Fanny Lou, do you know-did Pap tell you what I said?"

And I said, "yes, sir."

He said, "I mean that," he said, "If you don't go down and withdraw your registration, you will have to leave," said, "Then if you go down and withdraw," he said, "You will-you might have to go because we are not ready for that in Mississippi."

And I addressed him and told him and said, "I didn't try to register for you. I tried to register for myself."

I had to leave that same night

On the 10th of September 1962, 16 bullets was fired into the home of Mr. and Mrs. Robert Tucker for me. That same night two girls were shot in Ruleville, Mississippi. Also Mr. Joe McDonald's house was shot in.

And in June the 9th, 1963, I had attended a voter registration workshop, was returning back to Mississippi. Ten of us was traveling by the Continental Trailway bus. When we got to Winona, Mississippi, which is in Montgomery County, four of the people got off to use the washroom, and two of the people-to use the restaurant-two of the people wanted to use the washroom.

The four people that had gone in to use the restaurant was ordered out. During this time I was on the bus. But when I looked through the window and saw they had rushed out I got off of the bus to see what had happened, and one of the ladies said, "It was a State Highway Patrolman and a Chief of Police ordered us out."

I got back on the bus and one of the persons had used the washroom got back on the bus, too.

As soon as I was seated on the bus, I saw when they began to get the four people in a highway patrolman's car, I stepped off of the bus to see what was happening and somebody screamed from the car that the four workers was in and said, "Get that one there," and when I went to get in the car, when the man told me I was under arrest, he kicked me.

I was carried to the county jail, and put in the booking room. They left some of the people in the booking room and began to place us in cells. I was placed in a cell with a young woman called Miss Ivesta Simpson. After I was placed in the cell I began to hear the sound of kicks and horrible screams, and I could hear somebody say, "Can you say, yes, sir, nigger? Can you say yes, sir?"

And they would say other horrible names.

She would say, "Yes, I can say yes, sir."

"So say it."

She says, "I don't know you well enough."

They beat her, I don't know how long, and after a while she began to pray, and asked God to have mercy on those people.

And it wasn't too long before three white men came to my cell. One of these men was a State Highway Patrolman and he asked me where I was from, and I told him Ruleville, he said, "We are going to check this."

And they left my cell and it wasn't too long before they came back. He said, "You are from Ruleville all right," and he used a curse work, and he said, "We are going to make you wish you was dead."

I was carried out of that cell into another cell where they had two Negro prisoners. The State Highway Patrolmen ordered the first Negro to take the blackjack.

The first Negro prisoner ordered me, by orders from the State Highway Patrolman for me, to lay down on a bunk bed on my face, and I laid on my face.

The first Negro began to beat, and I was beat by the first Negro until he was exhausted, and I was holding my hands behind me at that time on my left side because I suffered from polio when I was six years old.

After the first Negro had beat until he was exhausted the State Highway Patrolman ordered the second Negro to take the blackjack.

The second Negro began to beat and I began to work my feet, and the State Highway Patrolman ordered the first Negro who had beat me to sit upon my feet to keep me from working my feet. I began to scream and one white man got up and began to beat me my head and told me to hush.

One white man-since my dress had worked up high, walked over and pulled my dress down and he pulled my dress back, back up

I was in jail when Medgar Evers was murdered

All of this is on account of us wanting to register, to become first-class citizens, and if the freedom Democratic Party is not seated now, I question America, is this America, the land of the free and the home of the brave where we have to sleep with our telephones off of the hooks because our lives be threatened daily because we want to live as decent human beings, in America?

Thank you.

The Ballot or the Bullet

by Malcolm X

April 3, 1964
Cleveland, Ohio

Mr. Moderator, Brother Lomax, brothers and sisters, friends and enemies: I just can't believe everyone in here is a friend, and I don't want to leave anybody out. The question tonight, as I understand it, is "The Negro Revolt, and Where Do We Go From Here?" or What Next?" In my little humble way of understanding it, it points toward either the ballot or the bullet.

Before we try and explain what is meant by the ballot or the bullet, I would like to clarify something concerning myself. I'm still a Muslim; my religion is still Islam. That's my personal belief. Just as Adam Clayton Powell is a Christian minister who heads the Abyssinian Baptist Church in New York, but at the same time takes part in the political struggles to try and bring about rights to the black people in this country; and Dr. Martin Luther King is a Christian minister down in Atlanta, Georgia, who heads another organization fighting for the civil rights of black people in this country; and Reverend Galamison, I guess you've heard of him, is another Christian minister in New York who has been deeply involved in the school boycotts to eliminate segregated education; well, I myself am a minister, not a Christian minister, but a Muslim minister; and I believe in action on all fronts by whatever means necessary.

Although I'm still a Muslim, I'm not here tonight to discuss my religion. I'm not here to try and change your religion. I'm not here to argue or discuss anything that we differ about, because it's time for us to submerge our differences and realize that it is best for us to first see that we have the same problem, a common problem, a problem that will make you catch hell whether you're a Baptist, or a Methodist, or a Muslim, or a nationalist. Whether you're educated or illiterate, whether you live on the boulevard or in the alley, you're going to catch hell just like I am. We're all in the same boat and we all are going to catch the same hell from the same man. He just happens to be a white man. All of us have suffered here, in this country, political oppression at the hands of the white man, economic exploitation at the hands of the white man, and social degradation at the hands of the white man.

Now in speaking like this, it doesn't mean that we're anti-white, but it does mean we're anti-exploitation, we're anti-degradation, we're anti-oppression. And if the white man doesn't want us to be anti-him, let him stop oppressing and exploiting and degrading us. Whether we are Christians or Muslims or nationalists or agnostics or atheists, we must first learn to forget our differences. If we have differences, let us differ in the closet; when we come out in front, let us not have anything to argue about until we get finished arguing with the man. If the late President Kennedy could get together with Khrushchev and exchange some wheat, we certainly have more in common with each other than Kennedy and Khrushchev had with each other.

If we don't do something real soon, I think you'll have to agree that we're going to be forced either to use the ballot or the bullet. It's one or the other in 1964. It isn't that time is running out—time has run out!

1964 threatens to be the most explosive year America has ever witnessed. The most explosive year. Why? It's also a political year. It's the year when all of the white politicians will be back in the so-called Negro community jiving you and me for some votes. The year when all of the white political crooks will be right back in your and my community with their false promises, building up our hopes for a letdown, with their trickery and their treachery, with their false promises which they don't intend to keep. As they nourish these dissatisfactions, it can only lead to one thing, an explosion; and now we have the type of black man on the scene in America today—I'm sorry, Brother Lomax—who just doesn't intend to turn the other cheek any longer.

Don't let anybody tell you anything about the odds are against you. If they draft you, they send you to Korea and make you face 800 million Chinese. If you can be brave over there, you can be brave right here. These odds aren't as great as those odds. And if you fight here, you will at least know what you're fighting for.

I'm not a politician, not even a student of politics; in fact, I'm not a student of much of anything. I'm not a Democrat. I'm not a Republican, and I don't even consider myself an American. If you and I were Americans, there'd be no problem. Those Honkies that just got off the boat, they're already Americans; Polacks are already Americans; the Italian refugees are already Americans. Everything that came out of Europe, every blue-eyed thing, is already an American. And as long as you and I have been over here, we aren't Americans yet.

Well, I am one who doesn't believe in deluding myself. I'm not going to sit at your table and watch you eat, with nothing on my plate, and call myself a diner. Sitting at the table doesn't make you a diner, unless you eat some of what's on that plate. Being here in America doesn't make you an American. Being born here in America doesn't make you an American. Why, if birth made you American, you wouldn't need any legislation; you wouldn't need any amendments to the Constitution; you wouldn't be faced with civil-rights filibustering in Washington, D.C., right now. They don't have to pass civil-rights legislation to make a Polack an American.

No, I'm not an American. I'm one of the 22 million black people who are the victims of Americanism. One of the 22 million black people who are the victims of democracy, nothing but disguised hypocrisy. So, I'm not standing here speaking to you as an American, or a patriot, or a flag-saluter, or a flag-waver—no, not I. I'm speaking as a victim of this American system. And I see America through the eyes of the victim. I don't see any American dream; I see an American nightmare.

These 22 million victims are waking up. Their eyes are coming open. They're beginning to see what they used to only look at. They're becoming politically mature. They are realizing that there are new political trends from coast to coast. As they see these new political trends, it's possible for them to see that every time there's an election the races are so close that they have to have a recount. They had to recount in Massachusetts to see who was going to be governor, it was so close. It was the same way in Rhode Island, in Minnesota, and in many other parts of the country. And the same with Kennedy and Nixon when they ran for president. It was so close they had to count all over again. Well, what does this mean? It means that when white people are evenly divided, and black people have a bloc of votes of their own, it is left up to them to determine who's going to sit in the White House and who's going to be in the dog house.

lt. was the black man's vote that put the present administration in Washington, D.C. Your vote, your dumb vote, your ignorant vote, your wasted vote put in an administration in Washington, D.C., that has seen fit to pass every kind of legislation imaginable, saving you until last, then filibustering on top of that. And your and my leaders have the audacity to run around clapping their hands and talk about how much progress we're making. And what a good president we have. If he wasn't good in Texas, he sure can't be good in Washington, D.C. Because Texas is a lynch state. It is in the same breath as Mississippi, no different; only they lynch you in Texas with a Texas accent and lynch you in Mississippi with a Mississippi accent. And these Negro leaders have the audacity to go and have some coffee in the White House with a Texan, a Southern cracker—that's all he is—and then come out

and tell you and me that he's going to be better for us because, since he's from the South, he knows how to deal with the Southerners. What kind of logic is that? Let Eastland be president, he's from the South too. He should be better able to deal with them than Johnson.

In this present administration they have in the House of Representatives 257 Democrats to only 177 Republicans. They control two-thirds of the House vote. Why can't they pass something that will help you and me? In the Senate, there are 67 senators who are of the Democratic Party. Only 33 of them are Republicans. Why, the Democrats have got the government sewed up, and you're the one who sewed it up for them. And what have they given you for it? Four years in office, and just now getting around to some civil-rights legislation. Just now, after everything else is gone, out of the way, they're going to sit down now and play with you all summer long—the same old giant con game that they call filibuster. All those are in cahoots together. Don't you ever think they're not in cahoots together, for the man that is heading the civil-rights filibuster is a man from Georgia named Richard Russell. When Johnson became president, the first man he asked for when he got back to Washington, D.C., was "Dicky"—that's how tight they are. That's his boy, that's his pal, that's his buddy. But they're playing that old con game. One of them makes believe he's for you, and he's got it fixed where the other one is so tight against you, he never has to keep his promise.

So it's time in 1964 to wake up. And when you see them coming up with that kind of conspiracy, let them know your eyes are open. And let them know you—something else that's wide open too. It's got to be the ballot or the bullet. The ballot or the bullet. If you're afraid to use an expression like that, you should get on out of the country; you should get back in the cotton patch; you should get back in the alley. They get all the Negro vote, and after they get it, the Negro gets nothing in return. All they did when they got to Washington was give a few big Negroes big jobs. Those big Negroes didn't need big jobs, they already had jobs. That's camouflage, that's trickery, that's treachery, window-dressing. I'm not trying to knock out the Democrats for the Republicans. We'll get to them in a minute. But it is true; you put the Democrats first and the Democrats put you last.

Look at it the way it is. What alibis do they use, since they control Congress and the Senate? What alibi do they use when you and I ask, "Well, when are you going to keep your promise?" They blame the Dixiecrats. What is a Dixiecrat? A Democrat. A Dixiecrat is nothing but a Democrat in disguise. The titular head of the Democrats is also the head of the Dixiecrats, because the Dixiecrats are a part of the Democratic Party. The Democrats have never kicked the Dixiecrats out of the party. The Dixiecrats bolted themselves once, but the Democrats didn't put them out. Imagine, these lowdown Southern segregationists put the Northern Democrats down. But the Northern Democrats have never put the Dixiecrats down. No, look at that thing the way it is. They have got a con game going on, a political con game, and you and I are in the middle. It's time for you and me to wake up and start looking at it like it is, and trying to understand it like it is; and then we can deal with it like it is.

The Dixiecrats in Washington, D.C., control the key committees that run the government. The only reason the Dixiecrats control these committees is because they have seniority. The only reason they have seniority is because they come from states where Negroes can't vote. This is not even a government that's based on democracy. It. is not a government that is made up of representatives of the people. Half of the people in the South can't even vote. Eastland is not even supposed to be in Washington. Half of the senators and congressmen who occupy these key positions in Washington, D.C., are there illegally, are there unconstitutionally.

I was in Washington, D.C., a week ago Thursday, when they were debating whether or not they should let the bill come onto the floor. And in the back of the room where the Senate meets, there's a huge map of the United States, and on that map it shows the location of Negroes throughout the country. And it shows that the Southern section of the country, the states that are most heavily concentrated with Negroes, are the ones that have senators and congressmen standing up filibustering and doing all other kinds of trickery to keep the Negro from being able to vote. This is pitiful. But it's not pitiful for us any longer; it's actually pitiful for the white man, because soon now, as the Negro awakens a little more and sees the vise that he's in, sees the bag that he's in, sees the real game that he's in, then the Negro's going to develop a new tactic.

These senators and congressmen actually violate the constitutional amendments that guarantee the people of that particular state or county the right to vote. And the Constitution itself has within it the machinery to expel any representative from a state where the voting rights of the people are violated. You don't even need new legislation. Any person in Congress right now, who is there from a state or a district where the voting rights of the people are violated, that particular person should be expelled from Congress. And when you expel him, you've removed one of the obstacles in the path of any real meaningful legislation in this country. In fact, when you expel them, you don't need new legislation, because they will be replaced by black representatives from counties and dis-

tricts where the black man is in the majority, not in the minority.

If the black man in these Southern states had his full voting rights, the key Dixiecrats in Washington, D. C., which means the key Democrats in Washington, D.C., would lose their seats. The Democratic Party itself would lose its power. It would cease to be powerful as a party. When you see the amount of power that would be lost by the Democratic Party if it were to lose the Dixiecrat wing, or branch, or element, you can see where it's against the interests of the Democrats to give voting rights to Negroes in states where the Democrats have been in complete power and authority ever since the Civil War. You just can't belong to that Party without analyzing it.

I say again, I'm not anti-Democrat, I'm not anti-Republican, I'm not anti-anything. I'm just questioning their sincerity, and some of the strategy that they've been using on our people by promising them promises that they don't intend to keep. When you keep the Democrats in power, you're keeping the Dixiecrats in power. I doubt that my good Brother Lomax will deny that. A vote for a Democrat is a vote for a Dixiecrat. That's why, in 1964, it's time now for you and me to become more politically mature and realize what the ballot is for; what we're supposed to get when we cast a ballot; and that if we don't cast a ballot, it's going to end up in a situation where we're going to have to cast a bullet. It's either a ballot or a bullet.

In the North, they do it a different way. They have a system that's known as gerrymandering, whatever that means. It means when Negroes become too heavily concentrated in a certain area, and begin to gain too much political power, the white man comes along and changes the district lines. You may say, "Why do you keep saying white man?" Because it's the white man who does it. I haven't ever seen any Negro changing any lines. They don't let him get near the line. It's the white man who does this. And usually, it's the white man who grins at you the most, and pats you on the back, and is supposed to be your friend. He may be friendly, but he's not your friend.

So, what I'm trying to impress upon you, in essence, is this: You and I in America are faced not with a segregationist conspiracy, we're faced with a government conspiracy. Everyone who's filibustering is a senator—that's the government. Everyone who's finagling in Washington, D.C., is a congressman—that's the government. You don't have anybody putting blocks in your path but people who are a part of the government. The same government that you go abroad to fight for and die for is the government that is in a conspiracy to deprive you of your voting rights, deprive you of your economic opportunities, deprive you of decent housing, deprive you of decent education. You don't need to go to the employer alone, it is the government itself, the government of America, that is responsible for the oppression and exploitation and degradation of black people in this country. And you should drop it in their lap. This government has failed the Negro. This so-called democracy has failed the Negro. And all these white liberals have definitely failed the Negro.

So, where do we go from here? First, we need some friends. We need some new allies. The entire civil-rights struggle needs a new interpretation, a broader interpretation. We need to look at this civil-rights thing from another angle—from the inside as well as from the outside. To those of us whose philosophy is black nationalism, the only way you can get involved in the civil-rights struggle is give it a new interpretation. That old interpretation excluded us. It kept us out. So, we're giving a new interpretation to the civil-rights struggle, an interpretation that will enable us to come into it, take part in it. And these handkerchief-heads who have been dillydallying and pussy footing and compromising—we don't intend to let them pussyfoot and dillydally and compromise any longer.

How can you thank a man for giving you what's already yours? How then can you thank him for giving you only part of what's already yours? You haven't even made progress, if what's being given to you, you should have had already. That's not progress. And I love my Brother Lomax, the way he pointed out we're right back where we were in 1954. We're not even as far up as we were in 1954. We're behind where we were in 1954. There's more segregation now than there was in 1954. There's more racial animosity, more racial hatred, more racial violence today in 1964, than there was in 1954. Where is the progress?

And now you're facing a situation where the young Negro's coming up. They don't want to hear that "turn the-other-cheek" stuff, no. In Jacksonville, those were teenagers, they were throwing Molotov cocktails. Negroes have never done that before. But it shows you there's a new deal coming in. There's new thinking coming in. There's new strategy coming in. It'll be Molotov cocktails this month, hand grenades next month, and something else next month. It'll be ballots, or it'll be bullets. It'll be liberty, or it will be death. The only difference about this kind of death—it'll be reciprocal. You know what is meant by "reciprocal"? That's one of Brother Lomax's words. I stole it from him. I don't usually deal with those big words because I don't usually deal with big people. I deal with small people. I find you can get a whole lot of small people and whip hell out of a whole lot of big people. They haven't got anything to lose, and they've got everything to gain. And they'll let you know in a minute: "It takes two to tango; when I go, you go."

The black nationalists, those whose philosophy is black nationalism, in bringing about this new interpretation of the entire meaning of civil rights, look upon it as meaning, as Brother Lomax has pointed out, equality of opportunity. Well, we're justified in seeking civil rights, if it means equality of opportunity, because all we're doing there is trying to collect for our investment. Our mothers and fathers invested sweat and blood. Three hundred and ten years we worked in this country without a dime in return—I mean without a dime in return. You let the white man walk around here talking about how rich this country is, but you never stop to think how it got rich so quick. It got rich because you made it rich.

You take the people who are in this audience right now. They're poor. We're all poor as individuals. Our weekly salary individually amounts to hardly anything. But if you take the salary of everyone in here collectively, it'll fill up a whole lot of baskets. It's a lot of wealth. If you can collect the wages of just these people right here for a year, you'll be rich—richer than rich. When you look at it like that, think how rich Uncle Sam had to become, not with this handful, but millions of black people. Your and my mother and father, who didn't work an eight-hour shift, but worked from "can't see" in the morning until "can't see" at night, and worked for nothing, making the white man rich, making Uncle Sam rich. This is our investment. This is our contribution, our blood.

Not only did we give of our free labor, we gave of our blood. Every time he had a call to arms, we were the first ones in uniform. We died on every battlefield the white man had. We have made a greater sacrifice than anybody who's standing up in America today. We have made a greater contribution and have collected less. Civil rights, for those of us whose philosophy is black nationalism, means: "Give it to us now. Don't wait for next year. Give it to us yesterday, and that's not fast enough."

I might stop right here to point out one thing. Whenever you're going after something that belongs to you, anyone who's depriving you of the right to have it is a criminal. Understand that. Whenever you are going after something that is yours, you are within your legal rights to lay claim to it. And anyone who puts forth any effort to deprive you of that which is yours, is breaking the law, is a criminal. And this was pointed out by the Supreme Court decision. It outlawed segregation.

Which means segregation is against the law. Which means a segregationist is breaking the law. A segregationist is a criminal. You can't label him as anything other than that. And when you demonstrate against segregation, the law is on your side. The Supreme Court is on your side.

Now, who is it that opposes you in carrying out the law? The police department itself. With police dogs and clubs. Whenever you demonstrate against segregation, whether it is segregated education, segregated housing, or anything else, the law is on your side, and anyone who stands in the way is not the law any longer. They are breaking the law; they are not representatives of the law. Any time you demonstrate against segregation and a man has the audacity to put a police dog on you, kill that dog, kill him, I'm telling you, kill that dog. I say it, if they put me in jail tomorrow, kill that dog. Then you'll put a stop to it. Now, if these white people in here don't want to see that kind of action, get down and tell the mayor to tell the police department to pull the dogs in. That's all you have to do. If you don't do it, someone else will.

If you don't take this kind of stand, your little children will grow up and look at you and think "shame." If you don't take an uncompromising stand, I don't mean go out and get violent; but at the same time you should never be nonviolent unless you run into some nonviolence. I'm nonviolent with those who are nonviolent with me. But when you drop that violence on me, then you've made me go insane, and I'm not responsible for what I do. And that's the way every Negro should get. Any time you know you're within the law, within your legal rights, within your moral rights, in accord with justice, then die for what you believe in. But don't die alone. Let your dying be reciprocal. This is what is meant by equality. What's good for the goose is good for the gander.

When we begin to get in this area, we need new friends, we need new allies. We need to expand the civil-rights struggle to a higher level—to the level of human rights. Whenever you are in a civil-rights struggle, whether you know it or not, you are confining yourself to the jurisdiction of Uncle Sam. No one from the outside world can speak out in your behalf as long as your struggle is a civil-rights struggle. Civil rights comes within the domestic affairs of this country. All of our African brothers and our Asian brothers and our Latin-American brothers cannot open their mouths and interfere in the domestic affairs of the United States. And as long as it's civil rights, this comes under the jurisdiction of Uncle Sam.

But the United Nations has what's known as the charter of human rights; it has a committee that deals in human rights. You may wonder why all of the atrocities that have been committed in Africa and in Hungary and in Asia, and in Latin America are brought before the UN, and the Negro problem is never brought before the UN. This is part of the conspiracy. This old, tricky blue eyed liberal who is supposed to be your and my friend, supposed to be in our corner, supposed to be subsidizing our struggle, and supposed to be acting in the capacity of an adviser, never

tells you anything about human rights. They keep you wrapped up in civil rights. And you spend so much time barking up the civil-rights tree, you don't even know there's a human-rights tree on the same floor.

When you expand the civil-rights struggle to the level of human rights, you can then take the case of the black man in this country before the nations in the UN. You can take it before the General Assembly. You can take Uncle Sam before a world court. But the only level you can do it on is the level of human rights. Civil rights keeps you under his restrictions, under his jurisdiction. Civil rights keeps you in his pocket. Civil rights means you're asking Uncle Sam to treat you right. Human rights are something you were born with. Human rights are your God-given rights. Human rights are the rights that are recognized by all nations of this earth. And any time any one violates your human rights, you can take them to the world court.

Uncle Sam's hands are dripping with blood, dripping with the blood of the black man in this country. He's the earth's number-one hypocrite. He has the audacity—yes, he has—imagine him posing as the leader of the free world. The free world! And you over here singing "We Shall Overcome." Expand the civil-rights struggle to the level of human rights. Take it into the United Nations, where our African brothers can throw their weight on our side, where our Asian brothers can throw their weight on our side, where our Latin-American brothers can throw their weight on our side, and where 800 million Chinamen are sitting there waiting to throw their weight on our side.

Let the world know how bloody his hands are. Let the world know the hypocrisy that's practiced over here. Let it be the ballot or the bullet. Let him know that it must be the ballot or the bullet.

When you take your case to Washington, D.C., you're taking it to the criminal who's responsible; it's like running from the wolf to the fox. They're all in cahoots together. They all work political chicanery and make you look like a chump before the eyes of the world. Here you are walking around in America, getting ready to be drafted and sent abroad, like a tin soldier, and when you get over there, people ask you what are you fighting for, and you have to stick your tongue in your cheek. No, take Uncle Sam to court, take him before the world.

By ballot I only mean freedom. Don't you know—I disagree with Lomax on this issue—that the ballot is more important than the dollar? Can I prove it? Yes. Look in the UN. There are poor nations in the UN; yet those poor nations can get together with their voting power and keep the rich nations from making a move. They have one nation—one vote, everyone has an equal vote. And when those brothers from Asia, and Africa and the darker parts of this earth get together, their voting power is sufficient to hold Sam in check. Or Russia in check. Or some other section of the earth in check. So, the ballot is most important.

Right now, in this country, if you and I, 22 million African-Americans—that's what we are—Africans who are in America. You're nothing but Africans. Nothing but Africans. In fact, you'd get farther calling yourself African instead of Negro. Africans don't catch hell. You're the only one catching hell. They don't have to pass civil-rights bills for Africans. An African can go anywhere he wants right now. All you've got to do is tie your head up. That's right, go anywhere you want. Just stop being a Negro. Change your name to Hoogagagooba. That'll show you how silly the white man is. You're dealing with a silly man. A friend of mine who's very dark put a turban on his head and went into a restaurant in Atlanta before they called themselves desegregated. He went into a white restaurant, he sat down, they served him, and he said, "What would happen if a Negro came in here? And there he's sitting, black as night, but because he had his head wrapped up the waitress looked back at him and says, "Why, there wouldn't no nigger dare come in here."

So, you're dealing with a man whose bias and prejudice are making him lose his mind, his intelligence, every day. He's frightened. He looks around and sees what's taking place on this earth, and he sees that the pendulum of time is swinging in your direction. The dark people are waking up. They're losing their fear of the white man. No place where he's fighting right now is he winning. Everywhere he's fighting, he's fighting someone your and my complexion. And they're beating him. He can't win any more. He's won his last battle. He failed to win the Korean War. He couldn't win it. He had to sign a truce. That's a loss.

Any time Uncle Sam, with all his machinery for warfare, is held to a draw by some rice eaters, he's lost the battle. He had to sign a truce. America's not supposed to sign a truce. She's supposed to be bad. But she's not bad any more. She's bad as long as she can use her hydrogen bomb, but she can't use hers for fear Russia might use hers. Russia can't use hers, for fear that Sam might use his. So, both of them are weapon-less. They can't use the weapon because each's weapon nullifies the other's. So the only place where action can take place is on the ground. And the white man can't win another war fighting on the ground. Those days are over The black man knows it, the brown man knows it, the red man knows it, and the yellow man knows it. So they engage him in guerrilla warfare. That's not his style. You've got to have heart to be a guerrilla warrior, and he hasn't got any heart. I'm telling you now.

I just want to give you a little briefing on guerrilla warfare because, before you know it, before you know it. It takes heart to be a guerrilla warrior because you're on your own. In conventional warfare you have tanks and a whole lot of other people with you to back you up—planes over your head and all that kind of stuff. But a guerrilla is on his own. All you have is a rifle, some sneakers and a bowl of rice, and that's all you need—and a lot of heart. The Japanese on some of those islands in the Pacific, when the American soldiers landed, one Japanese sometimes could hold the whole army off. He'd just wait until the sun went down, and when the sun went down they were all equal. He would take his little blade and slip from bush to bush, and from American to American. The white soldiers couldn't cope with that. Whenever you see a white soldier that fought in the Pacific, he has the shakes, he has a nervous condition, because they scared him to death.

The same thing happened to the French up in French Indochina. People who just a few years previously were rice farmers got together and ran the heavily-mechanized French army out of Indochina. You don't need it—modern warfare today won't work. This is the day of the guerrilla. They did the same thing in Algeria. Algerians, who were nothing but Bedouins, took a rine and sneaked off to the hills, and de Gaulle and all of his highfalutin' war machinery couldn't defeat those guerrillas. Nowhere on this earth does the white man win in a guerrilla warfare. It's not his speed. Just as guerrilla warfare is prevailing in Asia and in parts of Africa and in parts of Latin America, you've got to be mighty naive, or you've got to play the black man cheap, if you don't think some day he's going to wake up and find that it's got to be the ballot or the bullet.

l would like to say, in closing, a few things concerning the Muslim Mosque, Inc., which we established recently in New York City. It's true we're Muslims and our religion is Islam, but we don't mix our religion with our politics and our economics and our social and civil activities—not any more We keep our religion in our mosque. After our religious services are over, then as Muslims we become involved in political action, economic action and social and civic action. We become involved with anybody, any where, any time and in any manner that's designed to eliminate the evils, the political, economic and social evils that are afflicting the people of our community.

The political philosophy of black nationalism means that the black man should control the politics and the politicians in his own community; no more. The black man in the black community has to be re-educated into the science of politics so he will know what politics is supposed to bring him in return. Don't be throwing out any ballots. A ballot is like a bullet. You don't throw your ballots until you see a target, and if that target is not within your reach, keep your ballot in your pocket.

The political philosophy of black nationalism is being taught in the Christian church. It's being taught in the NAACP. It's being taught in CORE meetings. It's being taught in SNCC Student Nonviolent Coordinating Committee meetings. It's being taught in Muslim meetings. It's being taught where nothing but atheists and agnostics come together. It's being taught everywhere. Black people are fed up with the dillydallying, pussyfooting, compromising approach that we've been using toward getting our freedom. We want freedom now, but we're not going to get it saying "We Shall Overcome." We've got to fight until we overcome.

The economic philosophy of black nationalism is pure and simple. It only means that we should control the economy of our community. Why should white people be running all the stores in our community? Why should white people be running the banks of our community? Why should the economy of our community be in the hands of the white man? Why? If a black man can't move his store into a white community, you tell me why a white man should move his store into a black community. The philosophy of black nationalism involves a re-education program in the black community in regards to economics. Our people have to be made to see that any time you take your dollar out of your community and spend it in a community where you don't live, the community where you live will get poorer and poorer, and the community where you spend your money will get richer and richer.

Then you wonder why where you live is always a ghetto or a slum area. And where you and I are concerned, not only do we lose it when we spend it out of the community, but the white man has got all our stores in the community tied up; so that though we spend it in the community, at sundown the man who runs the store takes it over across town somewhere. He's got us in a vise. So the economic philosophy of black nationalism means in every church, in every civic organization, in every fraternal order, it's time now for our people to be come conscious of the importance of controlling the economy of our community. If we own the stores, if we operate the businesses, if we try and establish some industry in our own community, then we're developing to the position where we are creating employment for our own kind. Once you gain control of the economy of your own community, then you don't have to picket and boycott and beg some cracker downtown for a job in his business.

The social philosophy of black nationalism only means that we have to get together and remove the evils, the vices, alcoholism, drug addiction, and other evils that are destroying the moral fiber of our community. We our selves have to lift the level of our community, the standard of our community to a higher level, make our own society beautiful so that we will be satisfied in our own social circles and won't be running around here trying to knock our way into a social circle where we're not wanted. So I say, in spreading a gospel such as black nationalism, it is not designed to make the black man re-evaluate the white man—you know him already—but to make the black man re-evaluate himself. Don't change the white man's mind—you can't change his mind, and that whole thing about appealing to the moral conscience of America—America's conscience is bankrupt. She lost all conscience a long time ago. Uncle Sam has no conscience.

They don't know what morals are. They don't try and eliminate an evil because it's evil, or because it's illegal, or because it's immoral; they eliminate it only when it threatens their existence. So you're wasting your time appealing to the moral conscience of a bankrupt man like Uncle Sam. If he had a conscience, he'd straighten this thing out with no more pressure being put upon him. So it is not necessary to change the white man's mind. We have to change our own mind. You can't change his mind about us. We've got to change our own minds about each other. We have to see each other with new eyes. We have to see each other as brothers and sisters. We have to come together with warmth so we can develop unity and harmony that's necessary to get this problem solved ourselves. How can we do this? How can we avoid jealousy? How can we avoid the suspicion and the divisions that exist in the community? I'll tell you how.

I have watched how Billy Graham comes into a city, spreading what he calls the gospel of Christ, which is only white nationalism. That's what he is. Billy Graham is a white nationalist; I'm a black nationalist. But since it's the natural tendency for leaders to be jealous and look upon a powerful figure like Graham with suspicion and envy, how is it possible for him to come into a city and get all the cooperation of the church leaders? Don't think because they're church leaders that they don't have weaknesses that make them envious and jealous—no, everybody's got it. It's not an accident that when they want to choose a cardinal, as Pope I over there in Rome, they get in a closet so you can't hear them cussing and fighting and carrying on.

Billy Graham comes in preaching the gospel of Christ. He evangelizes the gospel. He stirs everybody up, but he never tries to start a church. If he came in trying to start a church, all the churches would be against him. So, he just comes in talking about Christ and tells everybody who gets Christ to go to any church where Christ is; and in this way the church cooperates with him. So we're going to take a page from his book.

Our gospel is black nationalism. We're not trying to threaten the existence of any organization, but we're spreading the gospel of black nationalism. Anywhere there's a church that is also preaching and practicing the gospel of black nationalism, join that church. If the NAACP is preaching and practicing the gospel of black nationalism, join the NAACP. If CORE is spreading and practicing the gospel of black nationalism, join CORE. Join any organization that has a gospel that's for the uplift of the black man. And when you get into it and see them pussyfooting or compromising, pull out of it because that's not black nationalism. We'll find another one.

And in this manner, the organizations will increase in number and in quantity and in quality, and by August, it is then our intention to have a black nationalist convention which will consist of delegates from all over the country who are interested in the political, economic and social philosophy of black nationalism. After these delegates convene, we will hold a seminar; we will hold discussions; we will listen to everyone. We want to hear new ideas and new solutions and new answers. And at that time, if we see fit then to form a black nationalist party, we'll form a black nationalist party. If it's necessary to form a black nationalist army, we'll form a black nationalist army. It'll be the ballot or the bullet. It'll be liberty or it'll be death.

It's time for you and me to stop sitting in this country, letting some cracker senators, Northern crackers and Southern crackers, sit there in Washington, D.C., and come to a conclusion in their mind that you and I are supposed to have civil rights. There's no white man going to tell me anything about my rights. Brothers and sisters, always remember, if it doesn't take senators and congressmen and presidential proclamations to give freedom to the white man, it is not necessary for legislation or proclamation or Supreme Court decisions to give freedom to the black man. You let that white man know, if this is a country of freedom, let it be a country of freedom; and if it's not a country of freedom, change it.

We will work with anybody, anywhere, at any time, who is genuinely interested in tackling the problem head-on, nonviolently as long as the enemy is nonviolent, but violent when the enemy gets violent. We'll work with you on the voter-registration drive, we'll work with you on rent strikes, we'll work with you on school boycotts; I don't believe in any kind of integration; I'm not even worried about it, because I know you're not going to get it anyway; you're not going to get it because you're afraid to die; you've got to be ready to die if you try and force yourself on the white man, because he'll get just as violent as those crackers in Mississippi, right here in Cleveland. But we will still work with you on the school boycotts because we're against a segregated school system. A segregated school system produces children who, when they graduate, graduate with crippled minds. But this does not mean that a school is segregated because it's all black. A segregated school means a school that is controlled by people who have no real interest in it whatsoever.

Let me explain what I mean. A segregated district or community is a community in which people live, but outsiders control the politics and the economy of that community. They never refer to the white section as a segregated community. It's the all-Negro section that's a segregated community. Why? The white man controls his own school, his own bank, his own economy, his own politics, his own everything, his own community; but he also controls yours. When you're under someone else's control, you're segregated. They'll always give you the lowest or the worst that there is to offer, but it doesn't mean you're segregated just because you have your own. You've got to control your own. Just like the white man has control of his, you need to control yours.

You know the best way to get rid of segregation? The white man is more afraid of separation than he is of integration. Segregation means that he puts you away from him, but not far enough for you to be out of his jurisdiction; separation means you're gone. And the white man will integrate faster than he'll let you separate. So we will work with you against the segregated school system because it's criminal, because it is absolutely destructive, in every way imaginable, to the minds of the children who have to be exposed to that type of crippling education.

Last but not least, I must say this concerning the great controversy over rifles and shotguns. The only thing that I've ever said is that in areas where the government has proven itself either unwilling or unable to defend the lives and the property of Negroes, it's time for Negroes to defend themselves. Article number two of the constitutional amendments provides you and me the right to own a rifle or a shotgun. It is constitutionally legal to own a shotgun or a rifle. This doesn't mean you're going to get a rifle and form battalions and go out looking for white folks, although you'd be within your rights—I mean, you'd be justified; but that would be illegal and we don't do anything illegal. If the white man doesn't want the black man buying rifles and shotguns, then let the government do its job.

That's all. And don't let the white man come to you and ask you what you think about what Malcolm says—why, you old Uncle Tom. He would never ask you if he thought you were going to say, "Amen!" No, he is making a Tom out of you." So, this doesn't mean forming rifle clubs and going out looking for people, but it is time, in 1964, if you are a man, to let that man know. If he's not going to do his job in running the government and providing you and me with the protection that our taxes are supposed to be for, since he spends all those billions for his defense budget, he certainly can't begrudge you and me spending $12 or $15 for a single-shot, or double-action. I hope you understand. Don't go out shooting people, but any time—brothers and sisters, and especially the men in this audience; some of you wearing Congressional Medals of Honor, with shoulders this wide, chests this big, muscles that big—any time you and I sit around and read where they bomb a church and murder in cold blood, not some grownups, but four little girls while they were praying to the same God the white man taught them to pray to, and you and I see the government go down and can't find who did it.

Why, this man—he can find Eichmann hiding down in Argentina somewhere. Let two or three American soldiers, who are minding somebody else's business way over in South Vietnam, get killed, and he'll send battleships, sticking his nose in their business. He wanted to send troops down to Cuba and make them have what he calls free elections—this old cracker who doesn't have free elections in his own country.

No, if you never see me another time in your life, if I die in the morning, I'll die saying one thing: the ballot or the bullet, the ballot or the bullet.

If a Negro in 1964 has to sit around and wait for some cracker senator to filibuster when it comes to the rights of black people, why, you and I should hang our heads in shame. You talk about a march on Washington in 1963, you haven't seen anything. There's some more going down in '64.

And this time they're not going like they went last year. They're not going singing "We Shall Overcome." They're not going with white friends. They're not going with placards already painted for them. They're not going with round-trip tickets. They're going with one way tickets. And if they don't want that non-nonviolent army going down there, tell them to bring the filibuster to a halt.

The black nationalists aren't going to wait. Lyndon B. Johnson is the head of the Democratic Party. If he's for civil rights, let him go into the Senate next week and declare himself. Let him go in there right now and declare himself. Let him go in there and denounce the Southern branch of his party. Let him go in there right now and take a moral stand—right now, not later. Tell him, don't wait until election time. If he waits too long, brothers and sisters, he will be responsible for letting a condition develop in this country which will create a climate that will bring seeds up out of the ground with vegetation on the end of them looking like something these people never dreamed of. In 1964, it's the ballot or the bullet.

Thank you.

Excerpt from Black Power Speech

by Stokely Carmichael

Thank you very much. It's a privilege and an honor to be in the white intellectual ghetto of the West. We wanted to do a couple of things before we started. The first is that, based on the fact that SNCC, through the articulation of its program by its chairman, has been able to win elections in Georgia, Alabama, Maryland, and by our appearance here will win an election in California, in 1968 I'm going to run for President of the United States. I just can't make it, 'cause I wasn't born in the United States. That's the only thing holding me back.

We wanted to say that this is a student conference, as it should be, held on a campus, and that we're not ever to be caught up in the intellectual masturbation of the question of Black Power. That's a function of people who are advertisers that call themselves reporters. Oh, for my members and friends of the press, my self-appointed white critics, I was reading Mr. Bernard Shaw two days ago, and I came across a very important quote which I think is most apropos for you. He says, "All criticism is a[n] autobiography." Dig yourself. Okay.

The philosophers Camus and Sartre raise the question whether or not a man can condemn himself. The black existentialist philosopher who is pragmatic, Frantz Fanon, answered the question. He said that man could not. Camus and Sartre was not. We in SNCC tend to agree with Camus and Sartre, that a man cannot condemn himself.[1] Were he to condemn himself, he would then have to inflict punishment upon himself. An example would be the Nazis. Any prisoner who—any of the Nazi prisoners who admitted, after he was caught and incarcerated, that he committed crimes, that he killed all the many people that he killed, he committed suicide. The only ones who were able to stay alive were the ones who never admitted that they committed a crimes [sic] against people—that is, the ones who rationalized that Jews were not human beings and deserved to be killed, or that they were only following orders.

On a more immediate scene, the officials and the population—the white population—in Neshoba County, Mississippi—that's where Philadelphia is—could not—could not condemn [Sheriff] Rainey, his deputies, and the other fourteen men that killed three human beings. They could not because they elected Mr. Rainey to do precisely what he did; and that for them to condemn him will be for them to condemn themselves.

In a much larger view, SNCC says that white America cannot condemn herself. And since we are liberal, we have done it: You stand condemned. Now, a number of things that arises from that answer of how do you condemn yourselves. Seems to me that the institutions that function in this country are clearly racist, and that they're built upon racism. And the question, then, is how can black people inside of this country move? And then how can white people who say they're not a part of those institutions begin to move? And how then do we begin to clear away the obstacles that we have in this society, that make us live like human beings? How can we begin to build institutions that will allow people to relate with each other as human beings? This country has never done that, especially around the country of white or black.

Now, several people have been upset because we've said that integration was irrelevant when initiated by blacks, and that in fact it was a subterfuge, an insidious subterfuge, for the maintenance of white supremacy. Now we maintain that in the past six years or so, this country has been feeding us a "thalidomide drug of integration," and that some negroes have been walking down a dream street talking about sitting next to white people; and that that does not begin to solve the problem; that when we went to Mississippi we did not go to sit next to Ross Barnett[2]; we did not go to sit next to Jim Clark[3]; we went to get them out of our way; and that people ought to understand that; that we were never fighting for the right to integrate, we were fighting against white supremacy.

Now, then, in order to understand white supremacy we must dismiss the fallacious notion that white people can give anybody their freedom. No man can give anybody his freedom. A man is born free. You may enslave a man after he is born free, and that is in fact what this country does. It enslaves black people after they're born, so that the only acts that white people can do is to stop denying black people their freedom; that is, they must stop denying freedom. They never give it to anyone.

Now we want to take that to its logical extension, so that we could understand, then, what its relevancy would be in terms of new civil rights bills. I maintain that every civil rights bill in this country was passed for white people, not for black people. For example, I am black. I know that. I also know that while I am black I am a human being, and therefore I have the right to go into any public place. White people didn't know that. Every time I tried to go into a place they stopped me. So some boys had to write a bill to tell that white man, "He's a human being; don't

Source: http://www.americanrhetoric.com/speeches/stokelycarmichaelblackpower.html

stop him." That bill was for that white man, not for me. I knew it all the time. I knew it all the time.

I knew that I could vote and that that wasn't a privilege; it was my right. Every time I tried I was shot, killed or jailed, beaten or economically deprived. So somebody had to write a bill for white people to tell them, "When a black man comes to vote, don't bother him." That bill, again, was for white people, not for black people; so that when you talk about open occupancy, I know I can live any-place I want to live. It is white people across this country who are incapable of allowing me to live where I want to live. You need a civil rights bill, not me. I know I can live where I want to live.

So that the failures to pass a civil rights bill isn't because of Black Power, isn't because of the Student Nonviolent Coordinating Committee; it's not because of the rebellions that are occurring in the major cities. It is incapability of whites to deal with their own problems inside their own communities. That is the problem of the failure of the civil rights bill.

And so in a larger sense we must then ask, How is it that black people move? And what do we do? But the question in a greater sense is, How can white people who are the majority—and who are responsible for making democracy work—make it work? They have miserably failed to this point. They have never made democracy work, be it inside the United States, Vietnam, South Africa, Philippines, South America, Puerto Rico. Wherever American has been, she has not been able to make democracy work; so that in a larger sense, we not only condemn the country for what it's done internally, but we must condemn it for what it does externally. We see this country trying to rule the world, and someone must stand up and start articulating that this country is not God, and cannot rule the world.

The Black Panther Platform, October 1966

1. *We want freedom. We want power to determine the destiny of our Black Community.*

We believe that black people will not be free until we are able to determine our destiny.

2. *We want full employment for our people.*

We believe that the federal government is responsible and obligated to give every man employment or a guaranteed income. We believe that if the white American businessmen will not give full employment, then the means of production should be taken from the businessmen and placed in the community so that the people of the community can organize and employ all of its people and give a high standard of living.

3. *We want an end to the robbery by the white man of our Black Community.*

We believe that this racist government has robbed us and now we are demanding the overdue debt of forty acres and two mules. Forty acres and two mules was promised 100 years ago as restitution for slave labor and mass murder of black people. We will accept the payment as currency which will be distributed to our many communities. The Germans are now aiding the Jews in Israel for the genocide of the Jewish people. The Germans murdered six million Jews. The American racist has taken part in the slaughter of over twenty million black people; therefore, we feel that this is a modest demand that we make.

4. *We want decent housing, fit for shelter of human beings.*

We believe that if the white landlords will not give decent housing to our black community, then the housing and the land should be made into cooperatives so that our community, with government aid, can build and make decent housing for its people.

5. *We want education for our people that exposes the true nature of this decadent American society. We want education that teaches us our true history and our role in the present-day society.*

We believe in an educational system that will give to our people a knowledge of self. If a man does not have knowledge of himself and his position in society and the world, then he has little chance to relate to anything else.

6. *We want all black men to be exempt from military service.*

We believe that Black people should not be forced to fight in the military service to defend a racist government that does not protect us. We will not fight and kill other people of color in the world who, like black people, are being victimized by the white racist government of America. We will protect ourselves from the force and violence of the racist police and the racist military, by whatever means necessary.

7. *We want an immediate end to* **police brutality** *and* **murder** *of black people.*

We believe we can end police brutality in our black community by organizing black self-defense groups that are dedicated to defending our black community from racist police oppression and brutality. The Second Amendment to the Constitution of the United States gives a right to bear arms. We therefore believe that all black people should arm themselves for self defense.

8. *We want freedom for all black men held in federal, state, county and city prisons and jails.*

We believe that all black people should be released from the many jails and prisons because they have not received a fair and impartial trial.

9. *We want all black people when brought to trial to be tried in court by a jury of their peer group or people from their black communities, as defined by the Constitution of the United States.*

We believe that the courts should follow the United States Constitution so that black people will receive fair trials. The 14th Amendment of the U.S. Constitution gives a man a right to be tried by his peer group. A peer is a person from a similar economic, social, religious, geographical, environmental, historical and racial background. To do this the court will be forced to select a jury from the black community from which the black defendant came. We have been, and are being tried by all-white juries that have no understanding of the "average reasoning man" of the black community.

10. *We want land, bread, housing, education, clothing, justice and peace. And as our major political objective, a United Nations-supervised plebiscite to be held throughout the black colony in which only black colonial subjects will be*

Source: *The Black Panther.* 23 Nov. 1967:3. Reprinted from http://www.stanford.edu/group/blackpanthers/history.shtml

allowed to participate for the purpose of determining the will of black people as to their national destiny.

When in the course of human events, it becomes necessary for one people to dissolve the political bands which have connected them with another, and to assume, among the powers of the earth, the separate and equal station to which the laws of nature and nature's God entitle them, a decent respect to the opinions of mankind requires that they should declare the causes which impel them to the separation.

We hold these truths to be self evident, that all men are created equal; that they are endowed by their Creator with certain unalienable rights; that among these are life, liberty, and the pursuit of happiness. *That, to secure these rights, governments are instituted among men, deriving their just powers from the consent of the governed; that, whenever any form of government becomes destructive of these ends, it is the right of the people to alter or to abolish it, and to institute a new government, laying its foundation on such principles, and organizing its powers in such form, as to them shall seem most likely to effect their safety and happiness.* Prudence, indeed, will dictate that governments long established should not be changed for light and transient causes; and accordingly, all experience hath shown, that mankind are more disposed to suffer, while evils are sufferable, than to right themselves by abolishing the forms to which they are accustomed. *But, when a long train of abuses and usurpations, pursuing invariably the same object, evinces a design to reduce them under absolute despotism, it is their right, it is their duty, to throw off such government, and to provide new guards for their future security.*

During the 1960s and 1970s, many laws were changed, which overturned legal segregation, legal racial discrimination, and legal oppression of African Americans. During the 1980s and the 1990s, as opportunities for middle- and upper-income African Americans increased and opened, the gap between rich and poor African Americans also widened. As some African Americans were winning prestigious awards and honors, others were being sent to prison, made homeless, and falling through the increasingly large holes in the social safety net so tenuously woven during the 1960s.

This section includes *presidential inaugural poems by Maya Angelou and Elizabeth Alexander,* and *writings of Toni Morrison.*

Inauguration Poem

by Maya Angelou

Written for Bill Clinton's Presidential Inauguration.

Mr. President and Mrs. Clinton,
Mr. Vice-President and Mrs. Gore,
And Americans Everywhere...
A Rock, A River, A Tree
Hosts to species long since departed,
Marked the mastodon.
The dinosaur, who left dry tokens
Of their sojourn here
On our planet floor,
Any broad alarm of their hastening doom
Is lost in the gloom of dust and ages.
But today, the Rock cries out to us, clearly, forcefully,
Come, you may stand upon my
Back and face your distant destiny,
But seek no haven in my shadow.
I will give you no hiding place down here.
You, created only a little lower than
The angels, have crouched too long in
The bruising darkness,
Have lain too long
Face down in ignorance.
Your mouths spilling words
Armed for slaughter.
The Rock cries out to us today, you may stand on me,
But do not hide your face.
Across the wall of the world,
A River sings a beautiful song,
It says come rest here by my side.
Each of you a bordered country,
Delicate and strangely made proud,
Yet thrusting perpetually under siege.
Your armed struggles for profit
Have left collars of waste upon
My shore, currents of debris upon my breast.
Yet, today I call you to my riverside,
If you will study war no more.
Come, Clad in peace and I will sing the songs
The Creator gave to me when I and the
Tree and the rock were one.
Before cynicism was a bloody sear across your
Brow and when you yet knew you still
Knew nothing.
The River sang and sings on.
There is a true yearning to respond to
The singing River and the wise Rock.
So say the Asian, the Hispanic, the Jew
The African, the Native American, the Sioux,
The Catholic, the Muslim, the French, the Greek

The Irish, the Rabbi, the Priest, the Sheikh,
The Gay, the Straight, the Preacher,
The privileged, the homeless, the Teacher.
They all hear
The speaking of the Tree.
They hear the the first and last of every Tree
Speak to humankind today.
Come to me, here beside the River.
Plant yourself beside the River.
Each of you, descendant of some passed
On traveller, has been paid for.
You, who gave me my first name, you
Pawnee, Apache, Seneca, you
Cherokee Nation, who rested with me, then
Forced on bloody feet, left me to the employment of
Other seekers—desperate for gain,
Starving for gold.
You, the Turk, the Swede, the German, the Eskimo,
    the Scot...
You the Ashanti, the Yoruba, the Kru, bought
Sold, stolen, arriving on a nightmare
Praying for a dream.
Here, root yourselves beside me.
I am that Tree planted by the River,
Which will not be moved.
I, the Rock, I the River, I the Tree
I am yours—your Passages have been paid.
Lift up your faces, you have a piercing need
For this bright morning dawning for you.
History, despite its wrenching pain,
Cannot be unlived, but if faced
With courage, need not be lived again.
Lift up your eyes upon
This day breaking for you.
Give birth again
To the dream.
Women, children, men,
Take it into the palms of your hands.
Mold it into the shape of your most
Private need. Sculpt it into
The image of your most public self.
Lift up your hearts
Each new hour holds new chances
For new beginnings.
Do not be wedded forever
To fear, yoked eternally
To brutishness.
The horizon leans forward,
Offering you space to place new steps of change.
Here, on the pulse of this fine day

You may have the courage
To look up and out and upon me, the
Rock, the River, the Tree, your country.
No less to Midas than the mendicant.
No less to you now than the mastodon then.
Here on the pulse of this new day
You may have the grace to look up and out
And into your sister's eyes, and into
Your brother's face, your country
And say simply
Very simply
With hope
Good morning.

Praise Song for the Day

by Elizabeth Alexander

Written for Barack Obama's Presidential Inauguration

Each day we go about our business,
walking past each other, catching each other's
eyes or not, about to speak or speaking.

All about us is noise. All about us is
noise and bramble, thorn and din, each
one of our ancestors on our tongues.

Someone is stitching up a hem, darning
a hole in a uniform, patching a tire,
repairing the things in need of repair.

Someone is trying to make music somewhere,
with a pair of wooden spoons on an oil drum,
with cello, boom box, harmonica, voice.

A woman and her son wait for the bus.
A farmer considers the changing sky.
A teacher says, Take out your pencils. Begin.

We encounter each other in words, words
spiny or smooth, whispered or declaimed,
words to consider, reconsider.

We cross dirt roads and highways that mark
the will of some one and then others, who said
I need to see what's on the other side.

I know there's something better down the road.
We need to find a place where we are safe.
We walk into that which we cannot yet see.

Say it plain: that many have died for this day.
Sing the names of the dead who brought us here,
who laid the train tracks, raised the bridges,

picked the cotton and the lettuce, built
brick by brick the glittering edifices
they would then keep clean and work inside of.

Praise song for struggle, praise song for the day.
Praise song for every hand-lettered sign,
the figuring-it-out at kitchen tables.

Some live by love thy neighbor as thyself,
others by first do no harm or take no more
than you need. What if the mightiest word is love?

Love beyond marital, filial, national,
love that casts a widening pool of light,
love with no need to pre-empt grievance.

In today's sharp sparkle, this winter air,
any thing can be made, any sentence begun.
On the brink, on the brim, on the cusp,

praise song for walking forward in that light.

Nobel Lecture, December 7, 1993

by Toni Morrison on winning The Nobel Prize in Literature

"Once upon a time there was an old woman. Blind but wise." Or was it an old man? A guru, perhaps. Or a griot soothing restless children. I have heard this story, or one exactly like it, in the lore of several cultures.

"Once upon a time there was an old woman. Blind. Wise."

In the version I know the woman is the daughter of slaves, black, American, and lives alone in a small house outside of town. Her reputation for wisdom is without peer and without question. Among her people she is both the law and its transgression. The honor she is paid and the awe in which she is held reach beyond her neighborhood to places far away; to the city where the intelligence of rural prophets is the source of much amusement.

One day the woman is visited by some young people who seem to be bent on disproving her clairvoyance and showing her up for the fraud they believe she is. Their plan is simple: they enter her house and ask the one question the answer to which rides solely on her difference from them, a difference they regard as a profound disability: her blindness. They stand before her, and one of them says, "Old woman, I hold in my hand a bird. Tell me whether it is living or dead."

She does not answer, and the question is repeated. "Is the bird I am holding living or dead?"

Still she doesn't answer. She is blind and cannot see her visitors, let alone what is in their hands. She does not know their color, gender or homeland. She only knows their motive.

The old woman's silence is so long, the young people have trouble holding their laughter.

Finally she speaks and her voice is soft but stern. "I don't know", she says. "I don't know whether the bird you are holding is dead or alive, but what I do know is that it is in your hands. It is in your hands."

Her answer can be taken to mean: if it is dead, you have either found it that way or you have killed it. If it is alive, you can still kill it. Whether it is to stay alive, it is your decision. Whatever the case, it is your responsibility.

For parading their power and her helplessness, the young visitors are reprimanded, told they are responsible not only for the act of mockery but also for the small bundle of life sacrificed to achieve its aims. The blind woman shifts attention away from assertions of power to the instrument through which that power is exercised.

Speculation on what (other than its own frail body) that bird-in-the-hand might signify has always been attractive to me, but especially so now thinking, as I have been, about the work I do that has brought me to this company. So I choose to read the bird as language and the woman as a practiced writer. She is worried about how the language she dreams in, given to her at birth, is handled, put into service, even withheld from her for certain nefarious purposes. Being a writer she thinks of language partly as a system, partly as a living thing over which one has control, but mostly as agency—as an act with consequences. So the question the children put to her: "Is it living or dead?" is not unreal because she thinks of language as susceptible to death, erasure; certainly imperiled and salvageable only by an effort of the will. She believes that if the bird in the hands of her visitors is dead the custodians are responsible for the corpse. For her a dead language is not only one no longer spoken or written, it is unyielding language content to admire its own paralysis. Like statist language, censored and censoring. Ruthless in its policing duties, it has no desire or purpose other than maintaining the free range of its own narcotic narcissism, its own exclusivity and dominance. However moribund, it is not without effect for it actively thwarts the intellect, stalls conscience, suppresses human potential. Unreceptive to interrogation, it cannot form or tolerate new ideas, shape other thoughts, tell another story, fill baffling silences. Official language smitheryed to sanction ignorance and preserve privilege is a suit of armor polished to shocking glitter, a husk from which the knight departed long ago. Yet there it is: dumb, predatory, sentimental. Exciting reverence in schoolchildren, providing shelter for despots, summoning false memories of stability, harmony among the public.

She is convinced that when language dies, out of carelessness, disuse, indifference and absence of esteem, or killed by fiat, not only she herself, but all users and makers are accountable for its demise. In her country children have bitten their tongues off and use bullets instead to iterate the voice of speechlessness, of disabled and disabling language, of language adults have abandoned altogether as a device for grappling with meaning, providing guidance, or expressing love. But she knows tongue-suicide is not only the choice of children. It is common among the infantile heads of state and power merchants whose evacuated language leaves them with no access to what is left of their human instincts for they speak only to those who obey, or in order to force obedience.

The systematic looting of language can be recognized by the tendency of its users to forgo its nuanced, complex, mid-wifery properties for menace and subjugation. Oppressive language does more than represent violence; it is violence; does more than represent the limits of knowledge; it limits knowledge. Whether it is obscuring state language or the faux-language of mindless media;

whether it is the proud but calcified language of the academy or the commodity driven language of science; whether it is the malign language of law-without-ethics, or language designed for the estrangement of minorities, hiding its racist plunder in its literary cheek—it must be rejected, altered and exposed. It is the language that drinks blood, laps vulnerabilities, tucks its fascist boots under crinolines of respectability and patriotism as it moves relentlessly toward the bottom line and the bottomed-out mind. Sexist language, racist language, theistic language—all are typical of the policing languages of mastery, and cannot, do not permit new knowledge or encourage the mutual exchange of ideas.

The old woman is keenly aware that no intellectual mercenary, nor insatiable dictator, no paid-for politician or demagogue; no counterfeit journalist would be persuaded by her thoughts. There is and will be rousing language to keep citizens armed and arming; slaughtered and slaughtering in the malls, courthouses, post offices, playgrounds, bedrooms and boulevards; stirring, memorializing language to mask the pity and waste of needless death. There will be more diplomatic language to countenance rape, torture, assassination. There is and will be more seductive, mutant language designed to throttle women, to pack their throats like paté-producing geese with their own unsayable, transgressive words; there will be more of the language of surveillance disguised as research; of politics and history calculated to render the suffering of millions mute; language glamorized to thrill the dissatisfied and bereft into assaulting their neighbors; arrogant pseudo-empirical language crafted to lock creative people into cages of inferiority and hopelessness.

Underneath the eloquence, the glamor, the scholarly associations, however stirring or seductive, the heart of such language is languishing, or perhaps not beating at all—if the bird is already dead.

She has thought about what could have been the intellectual history of any discipline if it had not insisted upon, or been forced into, the waste of time and life that rationalizations for and representations of dominance required—lethal discourses of exclusion blocking access to cognition for both the excluder and the excluded.

The conventional wisdom of the Tower of Babel story is that the collapse was a misfortune. That it was the distraction, or the weight of many languages that precipitated the tower's failed architecture. That one monolithic language would have expedited the building and heaven would have been reached. Whose heaven, she wonders? And what kind? Perhaps the achievement of Paradise was premature, a little hasty if no one could take the time to understand other languages, other views, other narratives period. Had they, the heaven they imagined might have been found at their feet. Complicated, demanding, yes, but a view of heaven as life; not heaven as post-life.

She would not want to leave her young visitors with the impression that language should be forced to stay alive merely to be. The vitality of language lies in its ability to limn the actual, imagined and possible lives of its speakers, readers, writers. Although its poise is sometimes in displacing experience it is not a substitute for it. It arcs toward the place where meaning may lie. When a President of the United States thought about the graveyard his country had become, and said, "The world will little note nor long remember what we say here. But it will never forget what they did here," his simple words are exhilarating in their life-sustaining properties because they refused to encapsulate the reality of 600, 000 dead men in a cataclysmic race war. Refusing to monumentalize, disdaining the "final word", the precise "summing up", acknowledging their "poor power to add or detract", his words signal deference to the uncapturability of the life it mourns. It is the deference that moves her, that recognition that language can never live up to life once and for all. Nor should it. Language can never "pin down" slavery, genocide, war. Nor should it yearn for the arrogance to be able to do so. Its force, its felicity is in its reach toward the ineffable.

Be it grand or slender, burrowing, blasting, or refusing to sanctify; whether it laughs out loud or is a cry without an alphabet, the choice word, the chosen silence, unmolested language surges toward knowledge, not its destruction. But who does not know of literature banned because it is interrogative; discredited because it is critical; erased because alternate? And how many are outraged by the thought of a self-ravaged tongue?

Word-work is sublime, she thinks, because it is generative; it makes meaning that secures our difference, our human difference—the way in which we are like no other life.

We die. That may be the meaning of life. But we do language. That may be the measure of our lives.

"Once upon a time, ..." visitors ask an old woman a question. Who are they, these children? What did they make of that encounter? What did they hear in those final words: "The bird is in your hands"? A sentence that gestures towards possibility or one that drops a latch? Perhaps what the children heard was "It's not my problem. I am old, female, black, blind. What wisdom I have now is in knowing I cannot help you. The future of language is yours."

They stand there. Suppose nothing was in their hands? Suppose the visit was only a ruse, a trick to get to be spoken to, taken seriously as they have not been before? A chance to interrupt, to violate the adult world, its miasma of discourse about them, for them, but never to them? Urgent questions are at stake, including the one they have asked: "Is the bird we hold living or dead?" Perhaps the question meant: "Could someone tell us what is life? What is death?" No trick at all; no silliness. A straightforward question worthy of the attention of a wise one. An old one. And if the old and wise who have lived life and faced death cannot describe either, who can?

But she does not; she keeps her secret; her good opinion of herself; her gnomic pronouncements; her art without commitment. She keeps her distance, enforces it and retreats into the singularity of isolation, in sophisticated, privileged space.

Nothing, no word follows her declaration of transfer. That silence is deep, deeper than the meaning available in the words she has spoken. It shivers, this silence, and the children, annoyed, fill it with language invented on the spot.

"Is there no speech," they ask her, "no words you can give us that helps us break through your dossier of failures? Through the education you have just given us that is no education at all because we are paying close attention to what you have done as well as to what you have said? To the barrier you have erected between generosity and wisdom?

"We have no bird in our hands, living or dead. We have only you and our important question. Is the nothing in our hands something you could not bear to contemplate, to even guess? Don't you remember being young when language was magic without meaning? When what you could say, could not mean? When the invisible was what imagination strove to see? When questions and demands for answers burned so brightly you trembled with fury at not knowing?

"Do we have to begin consciousness with a battle heroines and heroes like you have already fought and lost leaving us with nothing in our hands except what you have imagined is there? Your answer is artful, but its artfulness embarrasses us and ought to embarrass you. Your answer is indecent in its self-congratulation. A made-for-television script that makes no sense if there is nothing in our hands.

"Why didn't you reach out, touch us with your soft fingers, delay the sound bite, the lesson, until you knew who we were? Did you so despise our trick, our modus operandi you could not see that we were baffled about how to get your attention? We are young. Unripe. We have heard all our short lives that we have to be responsible. What could that possibly mean in the catastrophe this world has become; where, as a poet said, "nothing needs to be exposed since it is already barefaced." Our inheritance is an affront. You want us to have your old, blank eyes and see only cruelty and mediocrity. Do you think we are stupid enough to perjure ourselves again and again with the fiction of nationhood? How dare you talk to us of duty when we stand waist deep in the toxin of your past?

"You trivialize us and trivialize the bird that is not in our hands. Is there no context for our lives? No song, no literature, no poem full of vitamins, no history connected to experience that you can pass along to help us start strong?

You are an adult. The old one, the wise one. Stop thinking about saving your face. Think of our lives and tell us your particularized world. Make up a story. Narrative is radical, creating us at the very moment it is being created. We will not blame you if your reach exceeds your grasp; if love so ignites your words they go down in flames and nothing is left but their scald. Or if, with the reticence of a surgeon's hands, your words suture only the places where blood might flow. We know you can never do it properly—once and for all. Passion is never enough; neither is skill. But try. For our sake and yours forget your name in the street; tell us what the world has been to you in the dark places and in the light. Don't tell us what to believe, what to fear. Show us belief's wide skirt and the stitch that unravels fear's caul. You, old woman, blessed with blindness, can speak the language that tells us what only language can: how to see without pictures. Language alone protects us from the scariness of things with no names. Language alone is meditation.

"Tell us what it is to be a woman so that we may know what it is to be a man. What moves at the margin. What it is to have no home in this place. To be set adrift from the one you knew. What it is to live at the edge of towns that cannot bear your company.

"Tell us about ships turned away from shorelines at Easter, placenta in a field. Tell us about a wagonload of slaves, how they sang so softly their breath was indistinguishable from the falling snow. How they knew from the hunch of the nearest shoulder that the next stop would be their last. How, with hands prayered in their sex, they thought of heat, then sun. Lifting their faces as though is was there for the taking. Turning as though there for the taking. They stop at an inn. The driver and his mate go in with the lamp leaving them humming in the dark. The horse's void steams into the snow beneath its hooves and its hiss and melt are the envy of the freezing slaves.

"The inn door opens: a girl and a boy step away from its light. They climb into the wagon bed. The boy will have a gun in three years, but now he carries a lamp and a jug of warm cider. They pass it from mouth to mouth. The girl offers bread, pieces of meat and something more: a glance into the eyes of the one she serves. One helping for each man, two for each woman. And a look. They look back. The next stop will be their last. But not this one. This one is warmed."

It's quiet again when the children finish speaking, until the woman breaks into the silence.

"Finally", she says, "I trust you now. I trust you with the bird that is not in your hands because you have truly caught it. Look. How lovely it is, this thing we have done—together."

Appendices

Appendix A: Chronology of Writers

1700-1749

Hammon, Briton (1700s)
Fortune, Amos (1710?-1801)
Hammon, Jupiter (1711-c. 1806)
Smith, Venture (c. 1729-1805)
Terry, Lucy (c. 1730-1821)
Banneker, Benjamin (1731-1806)
Equiano, Olaudah (c. 1745-1797)

1750-1799

Haynes, Lemuel (1753-1833)
Wheatley, Phillis (c. 1753-1784)
Marrant, John (1755-1791)
Allen, Richard (1760-1831)
Forten, James (1766-1842)
Williams, Jr., Peter (1780-1840)
Lee, Jarena (1783-c. 1850)
Forten, Charlotte Vandine (1784-1884)
Walker, David (1785-1830)
Prince, Mary (c. 1788-after 1833)
Grimké, Sarah (1792-1873)
Cornish, Samuel E. (1795-1858)
Jackson, Rebecca Cox (1795-1871)
Horton, George Moses (1797?-1883?)
Truth, Sojourner (c. 1797 or
    1799-1883)
Prince, Nancy Gardner (1799-1856 or
    after)
Russwurm, John Brown (1799-1851)

1800-1849

Bayley, Solomon (c. 1800s)
Dave, the Potter (c. 1800-after 1862,
    perhaps the mid-1870s)
Plato, Ann (fl. 1800s)
Turner, Nat (1800-1831)
Child, Lydia Maria (1802-1880)
Stewart, Maria W. (1803-1879)
Whipper, William (1804-1876)
Grimké (Weld), Angelina (1805-1879)
Douglass, Sarah Mapps (1806-1882)
Pennington, James W. C. (1807-1870)
Northup, Solomon (1808-1863 or after)
Johnson, William (1809-1851)
Purvis, Robert (1810-1898)
Ruggles, David (1810-1849)
Payne, Daniel A. (1811-1893)
Stowe, Harriet Beecher (1811-1896)
Delany, Martin R. (1812-1885)
Green, J. D. (1813-?)
Jacobs, Harriet Ann (c. 1813-1897)
Brown, William Wells (1814?-1884)

Forten, Sarah (1814-1883)
Bibb, Henry (1815-1854)
Garnet, Henry Highland (1815-1882)
Nell, William C. (1816-1874)
Roper, Moses (1816-1891)
Séjour, Victor (1817-1874)
Ward, Samuel (1817-1864)
Willson, Joseph (1817-1895)
Douglass, Frederick (1818-1895)
Reason, Charles L. (1818-1893)
Crummell, Alexander (1819-1898)
Tubman, Harriet (c. 1820-1913)
Still, William (1821-1902)
Whitfield, James Monroe (1822-1871)
Cary, Mary Ann Shadd (1823-1893)
Keckley, Elizabeth (c. 1824-1907)
Vashon, George B. (1824?-1878)
Harper, Frances Ellen Watkins
    (1825-1911)
Bell, James Madison (1826-1902)
Craft, William (c. 1826-1900)
Remond, Sarah Parker (1826-1894)
Webb, Frank J. (1828-1894)
Wilson, Harriet E. (1828 or 1827 -
    1863? or 1870?)
Holly, James Theodore (1829-1911)
Langston, John Mercer (1829-1897)
Fisher, Abby (c. 1832-?)
Ruffin, George Lewis (1834-1886)
Turner, Henry McNeal (1834-1915)
Tanner, Benjamin Tucker (1835-1923)
Bruce, Henry Clay (1836-1902)
Grimké, Charlotte L. Forten
    (1837?-1914)
Smith, Amanda Berry (1837-1915)
Bruce, Blanche K. (Kelso) (1841-1898)
Ruffin, Josephine St. Pierre
    (1842-1924)
Trotter, James Monroe (1842-1892)
Steward, Theophilus Gould
    (1843-1924)
Brown, Hallie Quinn (1845-1949)
Whipper, Frances A. Rollin
    (1845-1901)
Jackson, Mattie J. (c. 1846-?)
Lynch, John R. (Roy) (1847-1939)
Harris, Joel Chandler (1848-1908)
Latimer, Lewis Howard (1848-1928)
Taylor, Susie Baker King (1848-1912)
Grimké, Archibald Henry (1849-1930)
Ray, Henrietta Cordelia (c. 1849-1916)
Simmons, William J. (1849-1890)

Williams, George Washington
    (1849-1891)

1850-1899

Grimké, Francis J. (1850-1937)
Whitman, Albery Allson (1851-1901)
Scarborough, William Sanders
    (1852-1926)
Murray, Daniel Alexander Payne
    (1852-1925)
Bruce, Josephine Beall Willson
    (1853-1923)
Parsons, Lucy Gonzalez (1853-1942)
Love, Nat (aka "Deadwood Dick")
    (1854-1921)
Mossell, Gertrude Bustill (1855-1948)
Fortune, T. Thomas (1856-1928)
Washington, Booker T. (1856-1915)
Chesnutt, Charles Waddell
    (1858-1932)
Johnson, Amelia E. (1858-1922)
Cooper, Anna Julia (1859-1964)
Hopkins, Pauline (1859-1930)
Cotter, Sr., Joseph Seamon (1861-1949)
Matthews, Victoria Earle (1861-1907)
Ridley, Florida Ruffin (1861-1943)
Paynter, John H. (1862-1947)
Wells-Barnett, Ida B. (1862-1931)
Miller, Kelly (1863-1939)
Terrell, Mary Eliza Church (1863-1954)
Park, Robert E. (1864-1944)
Powell, Sr., Adam Clayton (1865-1953)
Henson, Matthew Alexander
    (1866-1955)
Campbell, James Edwin (1867-1896)
Abbott, Robert S. (1868-1940)
Du Bois, W. E. B. (1868-1963)
Corrothers, James D. (1869-1917)
Coston, Julia Ringwood (fl. 1891-1895)
Kelley, Emma Dunham (1863-1938)
Tillman, Katherine Davis Chapman
    (1870-?)
Johnson, James Weldon (1871-1938)
Williams, Edward Christopher
    (1871-1929)
Beasley, Delilah (1872-1934)
Dunbar, Paul Laurence (1872-1906)
Griggs, Sutton E. (1872-1933)
Trotter, Geraldine Pindell (1872-1918)
Trotter, William Monroe (1872-1934)
Handy, W. C. (1873-1958)
Bass, Charlotta Spears (1874-1969)

Hare, Maud Cuney (1874-1936)
McGirt, James E. (1874-1930)
Schomburg, Arthur A. (1874-1938)
Dunbar Nelson, Alice Ruth
    (1875-1935)
Morgan, Garrett A. (1875-1963)
Spingarn, Joel Elias (1875-1939)
Woodson, Carter G. (1875-1950)
Houston, Drusilla Dunjee (1876-1941)
Johnson, Georgia Douglas (1877-1966)
Barber, Jesse Max (1878-1949)
Braithwaite, William Stanley Beaumont
    (1878-1962)
Johnson, Kathryn Magnolia (c.
    1878-1955)
Spingarn, Arthur B. (1878-1971)
Bruce, Sr., Roscoe Conkling
    (1879-1950)
Burroughs, Nannie Helen (1879-1961)
Smith, Effie Waller (1879-1960)
Vann, Robert Lee (1879-1940)
Bass, Charlotta Spears (1880-1969)
Grimké, Angelina Weld (1880-1958)
Rogers, Joel Augustus (1880?-1966)
Rush, Gertrude E. Durden (1880-1962)
Van Vechten, Carl (1880-1964)
Pickens, William (1881-1954)
Brawley, Benjamin (1882-1939)
Dandridge, Raymond G. (Garfield)
    (1882-1930)
Fauset, Jessie Redmon (1882-1961)
Spencer, "Anne" (1882-1975)
Brown, "Charlotte Eugenia"
    (1883-1961)
Haynes, Elizabeth Ross (1883-1953)
Just, Ernest Everett (1883-1941)
Micheaux, Oscar (1884-1951)
Heyward, DuBose (1885-1940)
Newsome, Effie Lee (1885-1979)
Walker, A'Lelia (1885-1931)
Locke, Alain (1886-1954)
Rainey, "Ma" (1886-1939)
Garvey, Jr., Marcus (1887-1940)
Matheus, John F. (1887-1983)
Briggs, Cyril Valentine (1888-1966)
Johnson, Fenton (1888-1958)
Barnett, Claude Albert (1889-1967)
Delaney, Sara Marie Johnson
    (1889-1958)
Delany, Sarah "Sadie" (1889-1999)
Murphy, Carl (1889-1967)
Owen, Chandler (1889-1967?)
Randolph, A. Philip (1889-1979)
Richardson, Willis (1889-1977)
Sissle, Noble (1889-1975)
McKay, Claude (1890 or 1889-1948)
Merrick, Lyda Moore (1890-1987)
Turner, Lorenzo Dow (1890-1969)
Delany, Annie Elizabeth "Bessie"
    (1891-1995)
Hurston, Zora Neale (1891-1960)

Larsen, Nella (1891-1964)
Patterson, William (1891-1980)
Wesley, Charles Harris (1891-1987)
Crosswaith, Frank Rudolph
    (1892-1965)
Johnson, Charles (Spurgeon)
    (1893-1956)
White, Walter F. (1893-1955)
Williams, Jr., Spencer (1893-1969)
Frazier, E. (Edward) Franklin
    (1894-1962)
Hansberry, William Leo (1894-1965)
Mays, Benjamin Elijah (1894-1984)
Spence, Eulalie (1894-1981)
Toomer, Jean (1894-1967)
Cotter, Jr., Joseph Seamon (1895-1919)
Houston, Charles (1895-1950)
Hunter, Alberta (1895-1984)
Latimer, Catherine A. (c. 1895-1948)
Razaf, Andy (1895-1973)
Schuyler, George Samuel (1895-1977)
Du Bois, Shirley Graham (1896?-1977)
Garvey, Amy Jacques (1896-1973)
Robeson, Eslanda Cardozo Goode
    (1896-1965)
Waters, Ethel (1896-1977)
Anderson, Marian (1897-1993)
Fisher, Rudolph (1897-1934)
Logan, Rayford (1897-1982)
Rollins, Charlemae Hill (1897-1979)
Smith, Lillian Eugenia (1897-1966)
Clark, Septima Poinsette (1898-1987)
Love, Rose Leary (1898-1969)
Robeson, Paul (1898-1976)
Tolson, Melvin B. (1898?-1966)
Walrond, Eric (1898-1966)
Williams, Chancellor (1898-1992)
Bonner, Marita (1899-1971)
Dorsey, Thomas (1899-1993)
Miller, May (1899-1995)

1900-1949
Cabrera, Lydia (1900-1991)
Christian, Marcus Bruce (1900-1976)
Jackson, Joseph Harrison (1900-1990)
Thurman, Howard (1900-1981)
Anderson, Regina M. (1901-1993)
Brown, Sterling Allen (1901-1989)
Colón, Jesús (1901-1974)
Delany, Clarissa (1901-1927)
Wilkins, Roy (Ottaway) (1901-1981)
Bennett, Gwendolyn B. (1902-1981)
Bontemps, Arna Wendell (1902-1973)
Graham, Lorenz (1902-1989)
Hughes, Langston (1902-1967)
Thurman, Wallace (1902-1934)
Ward, Theodore (1902-1983)
Cayton, Jr., Horace Roscoe (1903-1970)
Cullen, Countee (1903-1946)
Bunche, Ralph (1904-1971)
Cobb, William Montague (1904-1990)

Davis, Arthur P. (1904-1996)
Ford, Nick Aaron (1904-1982)
Quarles, Benjamin (1904-1996)
Davis, Frank Marshall (1905-1987)
Porter, James Amos (1905-1970)
Porter Wesley, Dorothy Burnett
    (1905-1995)
Thompson, Era Bell (1905-1986)
Johnson, Helene (1906-1995)
Nugent, Richard Bruce (1906-1987)
Poston, Ted (1906-1974)
Redding, Jay Saunders (1906-1988)
Spivey, Victoria Regina (1906-1976)
Tarry, Ellen (1906-2008)
Weaver, Robert C. (1907-1997)
West, Dorothy (1907-1998)
Jackson, Jesse (1908-1983)
Marshall, Thurgood (1908-1993)
Murphy, Beatrice M. (1908-1992)
Petry, Ann (1908-1997)
Powell, Jr., Adam Clayton (1908-1972)
Wright, Richard (1908-1960)
Fax, Elton C. (Clay) (1909-1993)
Himes, Chester (1909-1984)
Motley, Willard (1909-1965)
Dunham, Katherine (1909-2006)
Colter, Cyrus (1910-2002)
Murray, Pauli (1910-1985)
Rustin, Bayard (1910-1987)
Turpin, Waters (1910-1968)
Attaway, William (1911-1986)
Baker, Augusta (1911-1998)
Drake, St. Clair (1911-1990)
Hercules, Frank (1911-1996)
Jackson, Mahalia (1911-1972)
Payne, Ethel L. (1911-1991)
Damas, Léon-Gontran (1912-1978)
Harrington, Oliver Wendell
    (1912-1995)
Parks, Gordon (1912-2006)
Brown, Lloyd (1913-2003)
Garland, Hazel B. (1913-1988)
Hayden, Robert (1913-1980)
Sterling, Dorothy (1913-2008)
Clark, Kenneth B. (1914-2005)
de Burgos, Julia (1914-1953)
Dodson, Owen (1914-1983)
Ellison, Ralph (1914-1994)
Hutson, Jean Blackwell (1914-1998)
Randall, Dudley (1914-2000)
Clarke, John Henrik (1915-1998)
Danner, Margaret (1915-1984)
Franklin, John Hope (1915-2009)
Holiday, Billie (1915-1959)
McGhee, "Brownie" (1915-1996)
Walker, Margaret (1915-1998)
Childress, Alice (1916-1994)
Cruse, Harold Wright (1916-2005)
Killens, John Oliver (1916-1987)
Murray, Albert L. (1916-)
Pharr, Robert Deane (1916-1992)

Yerby, Frank G. (1916-1991)
Allen, Samuel W. (1917-)
Brooks, Gwendolyn (1917-2000)
Burroughs, Margaret Taylor (1917-)
Clark, Mamie Phipps (1917-1983)
Davis, Ossie (1917-2005)
Ormes, Jackie (1917-1985)
Patterson, Lillie (1917-1999)
Ferguson, Lloyd Noel (1918-)
Iceberg Slim (1918-1992)
Johnson, John H. (1918-2005)
Holman, M. (Moses) Carl (1919-1988)
Jeffers, Lance (1919-1985)
Mitchell, Loften (1919-2001)
Millican, Arthenia J. Bates (1920-)
Southern, Eileen Stanza Jackson (1920-2002)
Emanuel, Sr., James A. (1921-)
Haley, Alex (1921-1992)
Young, Whitney M. (1921-1971)
Carroll, Vinnette (1922-2002)
Deal, Borden (1922-1985)
Lomax, Louis E. (1922-1970)
Peterson, Louis (1922-1998)
Walter, Mildred Pitts (1922-)
Bryan, Ashley F. (1923-)
Evans, Mari (1923-)
Fuller, Hoyt (1923-1981)
Lane, Pinkie (1923-)
Madgett, Naomi Long (1923-)
Meriwether, Louise (1923-)
Vroman, Mary Elizabeth (c. 1923?-1967)
Baldwin, James (1924-1987)
Chisholm, Shirley (1924-2005)
Cobb, Jewell Plummer (1924-)
Dee, Ruby (1924-)
Granville, Evelyn Boyd (1924-)
Josey, E. J. (1924-)
Lewis, Samella Sanders (1924-)
Stone, Chuck (1924-)
Gordone, Charles (1925-1995)
Guy, Rosa Cuthbert (1925 or 1928-)
Kaufman, Bob (1925-1986)
King, "B. B." (1925-)
Rowan, Carl T. (1925-2000)
Scott, Jr., Nathan A. (1925-2006)
Williams, John A. (1925-)
Williams, Robert Franklin (1925-1996)
X, Malcolm (1925-1965)
Atkins, Russell (1926-)
Greaves, "Bill" (1926-)
Richards, Beah (1926-2000)
Brown, Frank London (1927-1962)
King, Coretta Scott (1927-2006)
Shockley, Ann (1927-)
Smith, William Gardner (1927-1974)
Angelou, Maya (1928-)
Bennett, Jr., Lerone (1928-)
Collier, Eugenia (Williams) (1928-)
Diddley, Bo (1928-2008)

Domino, "Fats" (1928-)
Fabio, Sarah (1928-1979)
Higginbotham, Jr., A. Leon (1928-1998)
Joans, Ted (1928-2003)
Mayfield, Julian (1928-1984)
Thomas, Piri (1928-)
Van Dyke, Henry (1928-)
Wright, Sarah E. (1928-)
Greenfield, Eloise (1929-)
King, Jr., Martin Luther (1929-1968)
Marshall, Paule (1929-)
Patterson, Raymond R. (1929-2001)
Walker, Wyatt Tee (1929-)
Aubert, Alvin (1930-)
Bennett, Hal (1930-)
Brathwaite, Edward Kamau (1930-)
Crayton, Pearl (1930-)
Greenlee, Sam (1930-)
Hansberry, Lorraine (1930-1965)
McKay, Nellie Yvonne (1930-2006)
Ringgold, Faith (1930-)
Sanders, Dori (1930?/1934?/1935?-)
Simmons, Herbert Alfred (1930-)
Smith, Jessie Carney (1930-)
Walcott, Derek (1930-)
Ward, Douglas Turner (1930-)
Driskell, David (1931-)
Elder, III, Lonne (1931-1996)
Hunter, Kristin Eggleston (1931-)
Kennedy, Adrienne (1931-)
Knight, Etheridge (1931-1991)
Morrison, Toni (1931-)
Schuyler, Philippa Duke (1931-1967)
Shine, Ted (1931-)
Turner, Darwin T. (1931-1991)
Demby, William (1932-1998)
Dent, Tom (1932-)
Gayle, Jr., Addison (1932-1991)
Gregory, "Dick" (1932-)
Hernton, Calvin C. (1932-2001)
Perkins, Eugene (1932-)
Polite, Carlene Hatcher (1932-)
Van Peebles, Melvin (1932-)
Wilkins, Roger Wood (1932-)
Wright, Charles S. (1932-)
Barrax, Gerald W. (1933-)
Evers-Williams, Myrlie (1933-)
Feelings, Tom (1933-2003)
Gaines, Ernest J. (1933-)
Mebane, Mary E. (1933-1992)
Rivers, Conrad Kent (1933-1968)
Andrews, Raymond (1934-1991)
Baraka, Amiri (a.k.a. LeRoi Jones) (1934-)
Dumas, Henry L. (1934-1968)
Hare, Nathan (1934-)
Lorde, Audre (1934-1992)
Poussaint, Alvin Francis (1934-)
Sanchez, Sonia (1934-)
Amini, Johari (1935-)

Bullins, Ed (1935-)
Cleaver, Eldridge (1935-1998)
Cornish, Sam (Samuel) (James) (1935-)
McElroy, Colleen (1935-)
Raspberry, William (1935-)
van Sertima, Ivan (Gladstone) (1935-2009)
Welsing, Frances Cress (1935-)
Wilson, William Julius (1935-)
Wright, Jay (1935-)
Zu-Bolton, III, Ahmos (1935-)
Clifton, Lucille (1936-)
Cole, Johnnetta (née) Betsch (1936-)
Cortez, Jayne (1936-)
Hamilton, Virginia (1936-2002)
Heard, Nathan C. (1936-2004)
Jordan, Barbara (1936-1996)
Jordan, June (1936-2002)
Lewis, David Levering (1936-)
Major, Clarence (1936-)
Rahman, Aishah (1936-)
Brown, Claude (1937-2002)
Cosby, Bill (1937-)
Forrest, Leon (1937-1997)
Franklin, J. E. (1937-)
Goines, Donald (1937-1974)
Kelley, William Melvin (1937-)
King, Jr., Woodie (1937-)
Mathis, Sharon Bell (1937-)
Maynard, Robert (1937-1993)
Myers, Walter Dean (1937-)
Neal, Larry (1937-1981)
Redmond, Eugene (1937-)
Berry, Mary Frances (1938-)
Cone, James H. (Hal or Hall) (1938-)
Crews, Donald (1938-)
Fields, Julia (1938-)
Harper, Michael S. (1938-)
Milner, Ronald (1938-2004)
Reed, Ishmael (1938-)
Thomas, Joyce Carol (1938-)
Touré, Askia M. (1938-)
Yarbrough, Camille (1938-)
Bambara, Toni Cade (1939-1995)
Brown, Linda Beatrice (1939-)
Chase-Riboud, Barbara (1939-)
Edelman, Marian Wright (1939-)
Fuller, Charles H. (1939-)
Lester, Julius (1939-)
Robinson, Max (1939-1988)
Young, Al (1939-)
Moody, Anne (1940-)
Patterson, Orlando (1940-)
Plumpp, Sterling (1940-)
Pryor, Richard (1940-2005)
Smitherman, Geneva (1940-)
Carmichael, Stokely (1941-1998)
Derricotte, Toi (1941-)
Haskins, James S. (1941-2005)
Jackson, George Lester (1941-1971)
Jackson, Sr., Jesse (1941-)

Karenga, Maulana Ron (1941-)
Neely, Barbara (1941-)
Pickett, Wilson (1941-2006)
Rampersad, Arnold (1941-)
Redding, Otis (1941-1967)
Robinson, Randall (1941-)
Wideman, John Edgar (1941-)
Asante, Molefi Kete (1942-)
Collins, Kathleen (1942-1988)
Delany, Samuel R. (1942-)
Hansen, Joyce (1942-)
Hoagland, III, Everett H. (1942-)
Hunter-Gault, Charlayne (1942-)
Madhubuti, Haki (né Don Lee) (1942-)
Mayfield, Curtis (1942-1999)
Painter, Nell Irvin (1942-)
Reagon, Bernice Johnson (1942-)
Ross-Barnett, Marguerite (1942-1992)
Weatherly, Tom (1942-)
Ashe, Arthur (1943-1993)
Baker, Houston A. (1943-)
Bourne, St. Claire (1943-2007)
Brown, Cecil (1943-)
Brown, Elaine (1943-)
Christian, Barbara (Theresa)
   (1943-2000)
Cobb, Charles E. (1943-)
French, William P. (1943-1997)
Giovanni, Nikki (1943-)
Jackson, Elaine (1943-)
Ladner, Joyce A. (1943-)
McPherson, James Alan (1943-)
Oliver, Diane (1943-1966)
Pietri, Pedro Juan (1943-2004)
Southerland, Ellease (1943-)
Taylor, Mildred D. (1943-)
Troupe, Quincy (1943-)
Beckham, Barry (1944-)
Bogle, Donald (1944-)
Davis, Angela (1944-)
Foster, Frances Smith (1944-)
Hull, Akasha (Gloria) (1944-)
Lawrence-Lightfoot, Sara (1944-)
McKissack, Pat (1944-)
Parker, Pat (1944-1989)
Senna, Carl (1944-)
Spillers, Hortense J (c. 1944-)
Thomas, Lorenzo (1944-2005)
Torrence, Jackie (1944-2004)
Walker, Alice (1944-)
Williams, Sherley Anne (1944-1999)
X, Marvin (1944-)
Crouch, Stanley (1945-)
Higginbotham, Evelyn Brooks (1945-)
Rodgers, Carolyn M. (1945-)
Sundiata, Sekou (c. 1945-2007)
Wesley, Richard (1945-)
Wilson, August (1945-2005)
Cliff, Michelle (1946-)
Coleman, Wanda (1946-)
Gerima, Haile (1946-)

Hudson, Wade (1946-)
Jackson, Mae (1946-)
Lee, Barbara (1946-)
Maynard, Nancy Hicks (1946-2008)
Smith, Barbara (1946-)
Steele, Claude M. (1946-)
Steele, Shelby (1946-)
Tate, Claudia (1946-2002)
Taylor, Susan L. (1946-)
Waniek, Marilyn Nelson (1946-)
Wilkinson, Brenda (1946-)
Williams, Samm-Art (1946-)
Ai (Florence Ai Ogawa) (1947-)
Butler, Octavia E. (1947-2006)
Giddings, Paula (1947-)
Herron, Carolivia (1947-)
Hine, Darlene Clark (1947-)
Komunyakaa, Yusef (1947-)
Mackey, Nathaniel (1947-)
Page, Clarence (1947-)
Salaam, Kalamu ya (1947-)
Shakur, Assata Olugbala (1947-)
Wesley, Valerie Wilson (1947-)
Cleage, Pearl (1948-)
De Veaux, Alexis (aka Deveaux)
   (1948-)
Davis, Thulani (1948-)
Gomez, Jewelle (1948-)
Harris, Trudier (aka Trudier
   Harris-Lopez) (1948-)
Hudson, Cheryl (Willis) (1948-)
Johnson, Charles (Richard) (1948-)
Shange, Ntozake (1948-)
Tate, Eleanora (1948-)
White, Paulette Childress (1948-)
Ansa, Tina McElroy (1949-)
Goldberg, Whoopi (1949-)
Jones, Gayl (1949-)
Kincaid, Jamaica (1949-)
Scott-Heron, Gil (1949-)
Monroe, Mary (1949/1951-)
Cooper, J. California (mid-1900s?-)

1950-Present
Boyd, Melba (1950-)
Bradley, David (1950-)
Braxton, Joanne M. (1950-)
Campbell, Bebe Moore (1950-2006)
Gates, Jr., Henry Louis (1950-)
Giscombe, C. S. (1950-)
Golden, Marita (1950-)
Guinier, Lani (1950-)
Jones, Edward P. (1950-)
Miller, E. Ethelbert (1950-)
Naylor, Gloria (1950-)
Sapphire (1950-)
Smith, Anna Deveare (1950-)
Steptoe, John (1950-1989)
Wonder, Stevie (1950-)
Wright, Courtni (1950-)
Cose, Ellis (Jonathan) (1951-)

Jackson, Angela (1951-)
Jenkins, Beverly (1951-)
McMillan, Terry (1951-)
Moutoussamy-Ashe, Jeanne (1951-)
Weaver, Afaa M. (1951-)
Williams, Patricia J. (1951-)
Barnes, Steven Emory (1952-)
Dash, Julie (1952-)
Dove, Rita (1952-)
Draper, Sharon M. (1952-)
Early, Gerald (1952-)
Gibson, P. J. (1952-)
hooks, bell (1952?-)
Mosley, Walter (1952-)
Nelson, Jill (1952-)
Curtis, Christopher Paul (1953-)
Jones-Meadows, Karen (1953-)
Lee, Andrea (1953-)
Malveaux, Julianne (1953-)
McDonald, Janet A. (1953-2007)
Moore, Opal (1953-)
Mullen, Harryette (1953-)
West, Cornel (1953-)
Williams, III, Stanley Tookie
   (1953-2005)
Abu-Jamal, Mumia (1954-)
Eady, Cornelius (1954-)
Moss, Thylias (1954-)
Rhodes, Jewell Parker (1954-)
Winfrey, Oprah (1954-)
Grooms, Anthony (1955-)
Harris, E. Lynn (1955-2009)
Hill, Donna (1955-)
Everett, II, Percival (Leonard), (1956-)
Hill, Anita Faye (1956-)
Cassells, Cyrus (1957-)
Hemphill, Essex (1957-1995)
Jakes, T. D. (1957-)
Lee, Spike (1957-)
Osbey, Brenda Marie (1957-)
Riggs, Marlon Troy (1957-1994)
Williams-Garcia, Rita (1957-)
Brandon, Barbara (1958-)
Dyson, Michael Eric (1958-)
Ice-T (1958-)
Maynard, Dori J. (1958-)
Tyson, Neil deGrasse (1958-)
Banks, Leslie Esdaile (1959-)
Bolden, Tonya (1959-)
Edmonds, Kenneth (1959-)
Phillips, Carl (1959-)
Randall, Alice (1959-)
Mowry, Jess (1960-)
Walton, Anthony (1960-)
Fishburne, III, Laurence (1961-)
Johnson, Angela (1961-)
Obama, II, Barack (Hussein) (1961-)
Alexander, Elizabeth (1962-)
Joe, Yolanda (1962?-)
Baisden, Michael (1963-)
Channer, Colin (1963-)

Gladwell, Malcolm (1963-)
Kenan, Randall (1963-)
Parks, Suzan-Lori (1963-)
Shepherd, Reginald (1963-2008)
Woodson, Jacqueline (1963-)
Chapman, Tracy (1964-)
Keene, Jr., John R. (1965-)
McFadden, Bernice L. (1965-)
Ridley, John (1965-)
Rock, Chris (1965-)
Due, Tananarive (1966-)
Powell, Kevin (1966-)
Trethewey, Natasha (1966-)
Rux, Carl Hancock (1968/1974?-)
Danticat, Edwidge (1969-)
Tyree, Omar (1969-)
Walker, Rebecca (1969-)
Jones, Tayari (1970-)
Latifah, Queen (1970-)
Senna, Danzy (1970-)
Young, Kevin (1970-)
Shakur, Tupac (1971-1996)
LaValle, Victor (1972-)
Packer, ZZ (1973-)
Vernon, Olympia (1973-)
Jones, Sarah (1974-)
McGruder, Aaron (1974-)
Kweli, Talib (1975-)
Hunter, Latoya (1978-)

Appendix B: Chronology of Firsts

Year	First	Details	Page(s)
	Autobiographical Firsts		
1760	Probably the first published narrative written by an African-American slave:	*A Narrative of the Uncommon Sufferings, and Surprising Deliverance of Briton Hammon, A Negro Man-Servant to General Winslow* (U.S.; 14-page memoir allegedly authored by Briton Hammon, but Hammon's authorship has been questioned)	250-251
1789/1791	First African American to write and publish his own candid account of his life, without help or direction from white ghostwriters, amanuenses, or editors:	Olaudah Equiano, *The Interesting Narrative of the Life of Olaudah Equiano, or Gustavus Vassa, the African* (1789, England; 1791, United States); *see* 1831	189-191
1825	One of the first to write his own spiritual slave narrative (without the aid of an amanuensis):	Solomon Bayley, *A Narrative of Some Remarkable Incidents in the Life of Solomon Bayley, Formerly a Slave in the State of Delaware, North America; Written by Himself, and Published for His Benefit* (2nd London ed.)	58
1831	First published slave narrative written by an African-American woman:	*The History of Mary Prince, a West Indian Slave, Related by Herself* (published in London); *cf.* 1861	468-469
1833	One of the first African-American autobiographies (other than a slave narrative):	*The Life, Experience and Gospel Labors of the Right Reverend Richard Allen* (published posthumously)	9-10
1845	Most successful, best-selling slave narrative:	*Narrative of the Life of Frederick Douglass, an American Slave, Written by Himself*	161-163
1861	First U.S.-published slave narrative by an African-American woman:	*Incidents in the Life of a Slave Girl: Written by Herself* (Harriet Jacobs); also the first such narrative to describe the sexual exploitation and other physical abuse of African-American women slaves; *cf.* 1831	302-304
	Book-Publishing Firsts		
1773	First African-American writer to publish a book of any kind:	Phillis Wheatley (*Poems on Various Subjects, Religious and Moral by Phillis Wheatley, Negro Servant to Mr. John Wheatley, of Boston, in New England*, published in London)	614-615
1845	First anthology written by Americans of African descent:	*Les Cenelles*, French poems, written by freeborn New Orleans Creoles	18
1852	Probably the first published travel book by an African American:	*Three Years in Europe* (by William Wells Brown)	88
1859	Probably the first African-American woman to publish a book in English:	Harriet Wilson (*Our Nig*; second: Frances Ellen Watkins Harper, *Iola Leroy*, 1892)	635-637
1980	First press to publish the writings of such notable poets as Houston A. Baker, Lance Jeffers, Gayl Jones, Pinkie Lane, and Paulette Childress White:	Lotus Press (owned and operated by Naomi Long Madgett)	366-368, 372

Year	First	Details	Page(s)
1981	First U.S. publisher dedicated to publishing the writings of women of color:	Kitchen Table: Women of Color Press (cofounded by Barbara Smith, Myrna Bain, Cherríe Moraga, and Mariana Romo-Carmona)	344-345, 529
by the 1990s	One of the largest African-American publishers in the United States and abroad:	Third World Press (founded by Don Lee [Haki Madhubuti], Carolyn Rogers, and Johari Amini)	554; *see also* 373-375

Drama Firsts

Year	First	Details	Page(s)
1856	Perhaps the first play written by an African American:	*Experience; or, How to Give a Northern Man a Backbone* (by William Wells Brown; written in 1856, never published, now lost)	88
1858	First published play written by an African American:	*The Escape; or, A Leap for Freedom* (by William Wells Brown; actually the second play he wrote)	88
1916/1920	First successful full-length drama written by an African-American woman and performed by African-American actors, for a European-American audience:	*Rachel* (first produced in 1916 and published in 1920, written by Angelina Weld Grimké)	208
1921	One of the first musicals to be written, directed, produced, and performed by African Americans:	*Shuffle Along* (lyrics by Noble Sissle, music by Eubie Blake); also the first all-black musical that didn't cater to white audience tastes	524
1923	First African American to have a nonmusical play produced on Broadway (in New York):	Willis Richardson (*The Chip Woman's Fortune*)	486-487
1899-1995	Probably the most widely published and produced woman playwright of the Harlem Renaissance:	May Miller	405-406
1927	First collection of African-American dramatic works:	*Plays of Negro Life: A Source-book of Native American Drama* (edited by Alain Locke and T. Montgomery Gregory)	24, 362
c. 1910	One of the first African-American movie companies:	Lincoln Film Motion Picture Company	403
1931	First all-black-cast talkie (nonsilent movie with audible sound):	*The Exile* (by Oscar Micheaux)	403
1932	First major opera written and produced by a woman, featuring an all-black cast:	*Tom-Tom: An Epic of Music and the Negro* (written by Shirley Graham [Du Bois])	168
1935	Set records as the longest-running play on Broadway, written by an African American:	*Mulatto* (Langston Hughes); kept this record until 1955; *see* 1955	289
1953	First African-American woman to join the Screen Writers Guild:	Mary Elizabeth Vroman (on writing the screenplay *Bright Road*)	587
1955	First African-American woman to have a play produced on Broadway:	Lorraine Hansberry (*A Raisin in the Sun*); set records as the longest-running play on Broadway, written by an African American; *see also* Ntozake Shange (1970s), *for colored girls . . .* ; Anna Deveare Smith (1993), *Twilight*	252-254
1968	First African American to produce, direct, and script a major Hollywood movie:	Gordon Parks, Sr. (*The Learning Tree*); *see* 1989	454-455
1976	First American feature film that was filmed entirely in Africa, using only black professionals:	*Countdown at Kusini* (coproduced by Ossie Davis and Ruby Dee)	149

Year	First	Details	Page(s)
1989	One of the top 25 most significant U.S. films, as identified by the National Film Registry of the Library of Congress:	*The Learning Tree* (by Gordon Parks, Sr.); *see* 1968	454-455
1991	First full-length general-release film with a screenplay by an African-American woman:	*Daughters of the Dust* (by Julie Dash)	145

Fiction Firsts

Year	First	Details	Page(s)
1853	Probably the first published novel by an African American:	*Clotel; or, the President's Daughter: A Narrative of Slave Life in the United States* (by William Wells Brown, published in England)	88
1859	Generally considered the first published short story by an African American:	"The Two Offers" (by Frances Ellen Watkins [Harper])	262
1859	Probably the first African-American woman to publish a novel in English:	Harriet Wilson (*Our Nig*; second: Frances Ellen Watkins Harper, *Iola Leroy*, 1892)	635-637
		Editor's Note: Harriet Wilson (*Our Nig*) may also be the fifth African American to publish a book of fiction in English.	
1859	Probably the first U.S.-published novel by an African American:	*Our Nig* (Harriet E. Wilson)	635-637
1859	Considered the first black-nationalist novel:	*Blake, or the Huts of America* (written by Martin R. Delany)	154
1887	First short story by an African-American writer to be published in the prestigious *Atlantic Monthly*:	"The Goophered Grapevine" (written by Charles Waddell Chesnutt)	104-106
1900	First African-American novel published by a major (white-owned) American publishing company:	*The House Behind the Cedars* (by Charles Waddell Chesnutt)	104-106
c. 1900	Often considered the first major African-American novelist:	Charles Waddell Chesnutt; also one of the first American writers published by mainstream publishers to realistically portray African-American experiences	104-106
1912	First novel to describe the tension within the African-American community between light-skinned and dark-skinned blacks:	*The Autobiography of an Ex-Coloured Man* (by James Weldon Johnson)	315-316
1926	Probably the first published short story written by an African American, which explicitly depicts a homosexual encounter:	"Smoke, Lilies and Jade" (by Richard Bruce Nugent)	440-441
1928	First best-selling, commercially successful novel written by an African American:	*Home to Harlem* (by Claude McKay)	389-391
1932	First African-American detective novel:	*The Conjure-Man Dies: A Mystery Tale of Dark Harlem* (by Rudolph Fisher)	200-201
1940	One of the first novels by an African-American writer to gain both critical acclaim and commercial success immediately after publication:	*Native Son* (by Richard Wright)	650-651
1940s	First African American to write a series of best-selling novels:	Frank Yerby	664-665
1945	One of the first young-adult books to address racial prejudice as a central theme:	*Call Me Charley* (Jesse Jackson)	300

Year	First	Details	Page(s)
1946	First African-American woman to write a book selling more than a million copies:	Ann Petry, *The Street* (novel)	460-461
1927-1935	First African American to collect (1927-1931) and publish (1935) African-American folklore:	Zora Neale Hurston	293
1972-1974 to present	At one time, the best-selling African-American author:	Donald Goines	233-234

Journal and Magazine Firsts

Year	First	Details	Page(s)
1826-1834	First U.S. periodical published for children:	*Juvenile Miscellany* (founded and edited by Lydia Maria Child)	109
1838	Perhaps the first African-American weekly magazine in the United States:	*Mirror of Liberty* (founded and published by David Ruggles)	500-501
c. 1830	First African American to edit a national magazine:	William Whipper (*National Reformer*, journal he cofounded and edited for the American Moral Reform Society)	327, 616-617
1859	Probably the earliest African-American literary journal:	*Anglo-African Magazine* (coedited by Frederick Douglass, Frances Ellen Watkins [Harper], and others)	262, 327
1884-1909	First African-American scholarly journal:	*A.M.E. Church Review* (a quarterly founded [1884] and edited [1884-1888] by Benjamin Tucker Tanner)	549
1891	First fashion magazine for African-American women:	*Ringwood's Afro-American Journal of Fashion* (published by Julia Ringwood Coston)	135
1893	First women's home magazine for African-American women:	*Ringwood's Home Magazine* (published by Julia Ringwood Coston)	135
Early 1920s	First African-American to serve on the editorial board of the *Harvard Law Review*:	Charles Houston	284-285; *see also* 443
1936	First journal published by a white Southerner, which regularly printed literary and scholarly writings by blacks:	*The North Georgia Review* (founded by Lillian Eugenia Smith)	531
1950	One of the first few African-American reporters to be employed by a major white-owned and -operated urban daily newspaper:	Carl Rowan (for the *Minneapolis Tribune*)	497-499
c. 1957	First African-American member of the Gridiron Club (founded in 1885):	Carl Rowan	497-499
1964	First African-American director of the United States Information Agency (USIA):	Carl Rowan	497-499
1964	First African American to be named *Time* magazine's "Man of the Year":	Martin Luther King, Jr.	343

Journalism Firsts

Year	First	Details	Page(s)
1827-1829	First African-American weekly newspaper:	*Freedom's Journal* (founding editors Samuel E. Cornish and John Brown Russwurm)	213-214; *see also* 36, 130, 501-502

Year	First	Details	Page(s)
1853	First African-American woman to own and operate a periodical of any kind:	Mary Ann Shadd (Cary) (with Samuel Ringgold Ward, founded, published, edited, and contributed to the weekly newspaper *Provincial Freeman*)	100-101
1892	Oldest continuously published family-owned African-American newspaper still being published:	*Baltimore Afro-American* (published by John Henry Murphy, then by Carl Murphy)	50; *see also* 436-437
before 1910	Oldest African-American newspaper in the West:	*Eagle* (later the *California Eagle*)	57-58
1937	First comic strip to feature an African-American female:	"Torchy Brown in Dixie to Harlem" (*Pittsburgh Courier*, by Jackie Ormes)	448
early 1940s	First African-American woman cartoonist to be nationally syndicated:	Jackie Ormes ("Patty Jo 'n' Ginger," first appearing in the *Chicago Defender*); *cf.* 1990	448
1955	First African-American journalist to start a column critiquing television:	Hazel B. Garland, *Pittsburgh Courier*	221-222
1955-1988	One of the longest-running newspaper columns about television ever published:	"Video Vignettes" (by Hazel B. Garland, *Pittsburgh Courier*)	221-222
1972	First woman to head a nationally circulated African-American newspaper chain:	Hazel B. Garland (editor-in-chief, *Pittsburgh Courier*)	221-222
1990	First African-American woman to have her cartoons syndicated nationally in mainstream, white-owned newspapers:	Barbara Brandon (for United Press Syndicate); *cf.* 1937; early 1940s	77; *cf.* 448
1990	First African-American woman journalist to win placement on a U.S. postage stamp:	Ida B. Wells-Barnett	606-608

Nonfiction Firsts

Year	First	Details	Page(s)
1833	Probably the first published nonautobiographical book denouncing slavery, segregation, and other mistreatment of African Americans:	*An Appeal in Favor of That Class of Americans Called Africans* (by Lydia Maria Child and David Lee Child)	109
1834ff	Probably the African American to self-publish his own pamphlets:	David Ruggles	500-501
1837-1838	Two of the first American writings calling for women's rights:	Angelina Grimké's *Letters to Catherine Beecher in Reply to an Essay on Slavery and Abolitionism Addressed to A. E. Grimké* (1837) and Sarah Grimké's *Letters on the Equality of the Sexes, and the Condition of Woman* (1838); *cf.* 1892	206
1852	Probably the first published pamphlet written by an African-American woman, which based a persuasive message on a factual database:	*Notes on Canada West* (written and published by Mary Ann Shadd [Cary])	100-101
1867	First military history of African Americans:	*The Negro in the American Rebellion: His Heroism and Fidelity* (by William Wells Brown)	88
1849-1891	Considered the first major African-American historian:	George Washington Williams	626
1881	First published cookbook authored by an African-American woman:	*What Mrs. Fisher Knows about Old Southern Cooking* (by Abby Fisher)	200
1883	Generally considered the first fully encompassing history of African Americans up to 1880:	*History of the Negro Race in America from 1619 to 1880* (by George Washington Williams)	626

Year	First	Details	Page(s)
1892	Cited as the first book-length work of African-American feminism:	*A Voice from the South by a Black Woman of the South* (written by Anna Julia Cooper); *cf.* 1837-1838	128
1899	Cited as the first published sociological study of African Americans:	*The Philadelphia Negro* (by W. E. B. Du Bois)	169
1935	One of the earliest efforts to accurately record the oral tradition of African-American communities:	*Mules and Men* (by Zora Neale Hurston)	203; *see also* 228, 294, 447

Poetry and Song Firsts

Year	First	Details	Page(s)
1746/1855	First African American to have written a poem that survives to this day:	Lucy Terry (Prince) ("Bars Fight," written in 1746, but published in 1855)	553-553; *see also* 251
1761	First literary work written by an African American and published in the United States:	"An Evening Thought. Salvation by Christ with Penitential Cries: Composed by Jupiter Hammon, a Negro belonging to Mr. Lloyd of Queen's Village, on Long Island, the 25th of December, 1760" (88-line poem, published as a broadside)	251; *see also* 553-554
1761	First African American to have his own writing published:	Jupiter Hammon	251
1773	First African-American writer to publish a poetry book:	Phillis Wheatley (*Poems on Various Subjects, Religious and Moral by Phillis Wheatley, Negro Servant to Mr. John Wheatley, of Boston, in New England*, published in London)	614-615
1773	First African-American woman to have her works published:	Phillis Wheatley (*Poems on Various Subjects, Religious and Moral by Phillis Wheatley, Negro Servant to Mr. John Wheatley, of Boston, in New England*, published in London)	614-615
By 1801	First distinctive song form to emerge in the United States:	Spirituals	537-539; *see also* 9-10
1801	First black hymnal:	*Collection of Spiritual Songs and Hymns, Selected from Various Authors* (included lyrics only; compiled by Richard Allen)	9-10
1829	First book of any kind authored by an African American, which was published in the South, and the third book of poetry by an African American published in the United States:	*The Hope of Liberty, Containing a Number of Poetical Pieces* (George Moses Horton)	283-284
1797?-1883?	Preeminent nineteenth-century African-American male poet	George Moses Horton	283-284
1825-1911	Preeminent nineteenth-century African-American female poet	Frances Ellen Watkins Harper	261-264
1845	First anthology of poetry written by Americans of African descent:	*Les Cenelles*, in New Orleans	18; *see also* 28, 517
1872-1906	Generally recognized as the first major African-American poet:	Paul Laurence Dunbar	172-174
1912	Reportedly the first blues song to be published as sheet music:	"Memphis Blues" (W. C. Handy; written in 1909 (p. 336, *The Music of Black Americans*); in 1908, Handy and lyricist Harry Pace founded the Pace and Handy Music Company, which published songs; *cf.* 1931 (p. 336, *The Music of Black Americans*))	251-252

Year	First	Details	Page(s)
1889/ 1890-1948	Considered the first major poet of the Harlem Renaissance	Claude McKay	389-391
1903-1946	First African-American poet to receive wide acclaim in the United States	Countee Cullen	138-139
1928	First twentieth-century African-American woman to gain national attention for her poetry:	Georgia Douglas Johnson (*An Autumn Love Cycle*)	312-314
1931	First gospel music publishing company:	The Dorsey House of Music (p. 453, *The Music of Black Americans*), founded by Thomas Dorsey; *cf.* 1912	161
1941	Probably the first anthology of African-American poetry for youths:	*Golden Slippers, an Anthology of Negro Poetry for Young Readers* (compiled by Arna Bontemps)	34, 74; *see also* 419
1976	First African-American poet named consultant in poetry to the Library of Congress (position later renamed poet laureate):	Robert Hayden	270-271
1985	First African-American woman to serve as poetry advisor to the Library of Congress (position later renamed poet laureate):	Gwendolyn Brooks	79-81
1988	First poet laureate of Rhode Island:	Michael S. Harper	264-265
1993-1995	First African American, first woman, and youngest person to be named poet laureate of the United States:	Rita Dove	164-166

Prize-Winning Firsts

Year	First	Details	Page(s)
1912	First black writer to receive a medal from the Jamaican Institute of Arts and Sciences:	Claude McKay	389
1915	First winner of the National Association for the Advancement of Colored People (NAACP) Spingarn Medal:	Everett Just (for his scientific research and publications)	327-328
1925	First winner of *Crisis* magazine's drama contest (established by W. E. B. Du Bois):	Willis Richardson (*Broken Banjo, a Folk Tragedy*)	486-487
1930	First African-American woman to win a Guggenheim fellowship:	Nella Larsen	351
1942	First African-American woman to win a prestigious mainstream national literary competition:	Margaret Walker (Yale University Younger Poet's Award, for *For My People*)	594
1949	First African American to win the Pulitzer Prize for poetry:	Gwendolyn Brooks (*Annie Allen*)	79-81
1950	First African American to win the Nobel Peace Prize:	Ralph Bunche; *see* 1964	93
1953	First African American to win the National Book Award for fiction:	Ralph Ellison (*Invisible Man*, published in 1952); *see* 1990	186
1956	First woman of any race to receive an Obie for writing a play:	Alice Childress (for her 1954-1955 *Trouble in Mind*)	110
1959	First African American, youngest person, and fifth woman to win the New York Drama Critics Circle Award for the Best Play:	Lorraine Hansberry (*Raisin in the Sun*)	253

Year	First	Details	Page(s)
1964	Second African American (and youngest person) to win the Nobel Peace Prize:	Martin Luther King, Jr.; *see* 1950	343
1967	First African-American writer to receive the John Newbery Award:	Virginia Hamilton (for *Zeely*)	249-250
1969	First African American and the first person from an African-American-owned and -operated periodical to win a Pulitzer Prize for photojournalism:	Moneta Sleet, Jr., for *Ebony*	181, 317
1970	First African American to win the Pulitzer Prize for drama:	Charles Gordone (*No Place To Be Somebody*, produced in 1969)	236-237
1971	First book to win both the National Book Award and the John Newbery Award:	*M. C. Higgins, the Great* (by Virginia Hamilton)	249-250
1978	First novel to win the James Baldwin Prize for literature:	*Appalachee Road* (by Raymond Andrews)	14
1983	First African-American woman to win a Pulitzer Prize for a novel:	Alice Walker (American Book Award-winning *The Color Purple*, 1982)	591
1990	Second African American to win the National Book Award for fiction:	Charles (Richard) Johnson, for *Middle Passage; see* 1953	309-310
1991	First African-American author to receive two PEN/Faulkner awards:	John Edgar Wideman (*Brothers and Keepers*, 1984; *Philadelphia Fire*, 1990)	619-622
1993	First African-American woman to receive the Nobel Prize for literature:	Toni Morrison, also the eighth woman to receive the prize	409-412
2000	First book to win both a Coretta Scott King Award and a Newbery Medal:	*Bud, Not Buddy* (by Christopher Paul Curtis)	139-141
2000	First book to win a Michael L. Printz Award, awarded by the American Library Association:	*Monster* (1999, by Walter Dean Myers)	424

Professional Firsts

Year	First	Details	Page(s)
1832	First American-born woman documented to have given a public lecture to a "promiscuous audience" (both men and women) on political topics:	Maria W. Stewart (in the 1830s, the Grimké sisters Sarah and Angelina also lectured to "promiscuous audiences," the first European-American women to do so)	542-543; *see also* 206
1834	Cited as the first person to open a bookshop for works by or about African Americans:	David Ruggles (in New York City)	500-501
1892	First African-American hired as a professionally trained librarian	Edward Christopher Williams	625-626
1920	First African-American professional librarian hired by the New York Public Library:	Catherine A. Latimer	352
1928	One of the first African Americans to be hired as an editor by a major (white-owned and -operated) book-publishing house:	Wallace Thurman (Macaulay's Publishing Company)	558

1619–1779...

...African Americans land at Jamestown, to the American Revolution

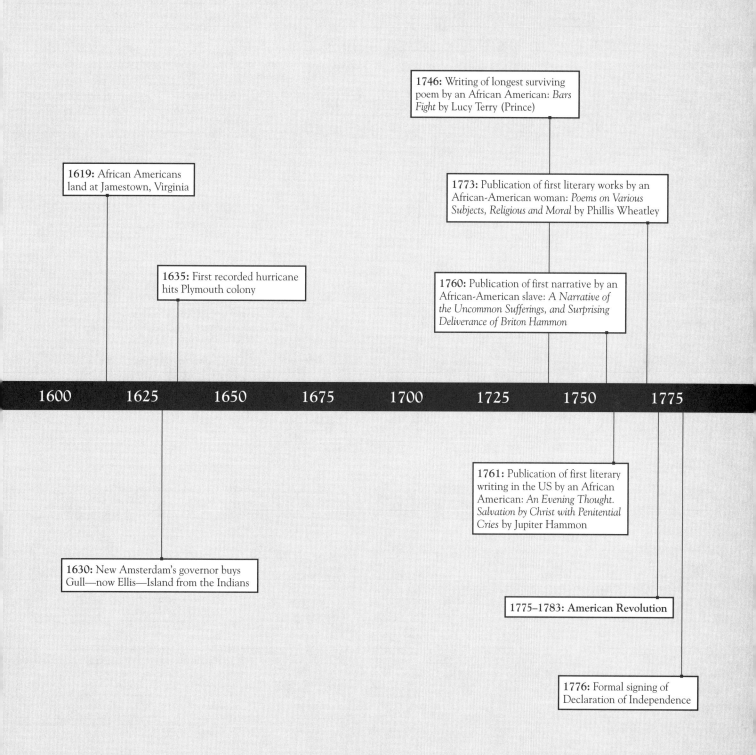

1746: Writing of longest surviving poem by an African American: *Bars Fight* by Lucy Terry (Prince)

1619: African Americans land at Jamestown, Virginia

1773: Publication of first literary works by an African-American woman: *Poems on Various Subjects, Religious and Moral* by Phillis Wheatley

1635: First recorded hurricane hits Plymouth colony

1760: Publication of first narrative by an African-American slave: *A Narrative of the Uncommon Sufferings, and Surprising Deliverance of Briton Hammon*

1600   1625   1650   1675   1700   1725   1750   1775

1761: Publication of first literary writing in the US by an African American: *An Evening Thought. Salvation by Christ with Penitential Cries* by Jupiter Hammon

1630: New Amsterdam's governor buys Gull—now Ellis—Island from the Indians

1775–1783: American Revolution

1776: Formal signing of Declaration of Independence

1780–1869...

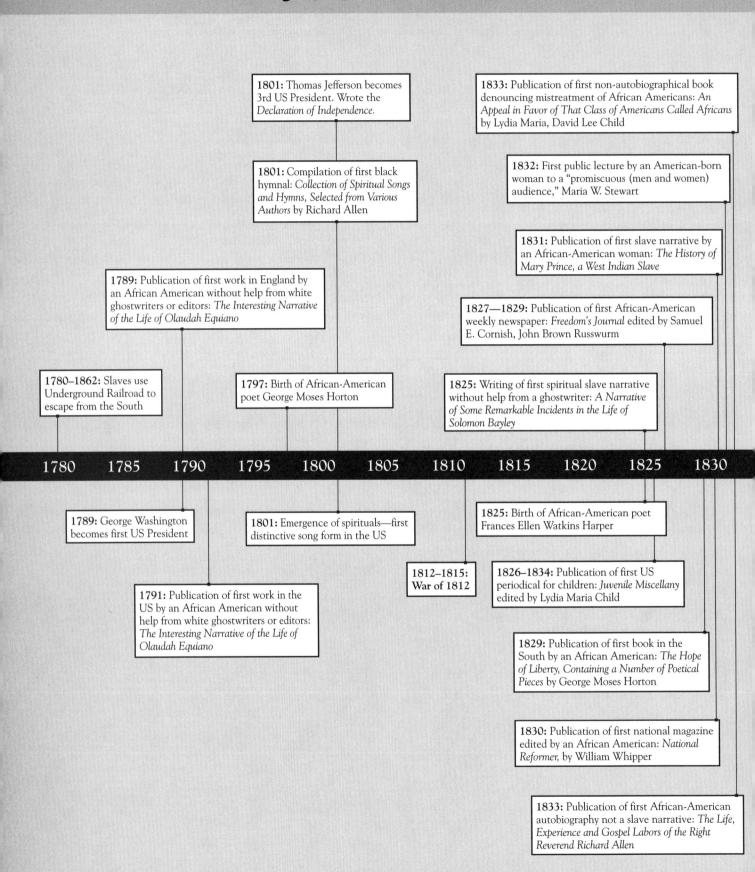

1801: Thomas Jefferson becomes 3rd US President. Wrote the *Declaration of Independence.*

1833: Publication of first non-autobiographical book denouncing mistreatment of African Americans: *An Appeal in Favor of That Class of Americans Called Africans* by Lydia Maria, David Lee Child

1801: Compilation of first black hymnal: *Collection of Spiritual Songs and Hymns, Selected from Various Authors* by Richard Allen

1832: First public lecture by an American-born woman to a "promiscuous (men and women) audience," Maria W. Stewart

1831: Publication of first slave narrative by an African-American woman: *The History of Mary Prince, a West Indian Slave*

1789: Publication of first work in England by an African American without help from white ghostwriters or editors: *The Interesting Narrative of the Life of Olaudah Equiano*

1827—1829: Publication of first African-American weekly newspaper: *Freedom's Journal* edited by Samuel E. Cornish, John Brown Russwurm

1780–1862: Slaves use Underground Railroad to escape from the South

1797: Birth of African-American poet George Moses Horton

1825: Writing of first spiritual slave narrative without help from a ghostwriter: *A Narrative of Some Remarkable Incidents in the Life of Solomon Bayley*

| 1780 | 1785 | 1790 | 1795 | 1800 | 1805 | 1810 | 1815 | 1820 | 1825 | 1830 |

1789: George Washington becomes first US President

1801: Emergence of spirituals—first distinctive song form in the US

1825: Birth of African-American poet Frances Ellen Watkins Harper

1812–1815: War of 1812

1826–1834: Publication of first US periodical for children: *Juvenile Miscellany* edited by Lydia Maria Child

1791: Publication of first work in the US by an African American without help from white ghostwriters or editors: *The Interesting Narrative of the Life of Olaudah Equiano*

1829: Publication of first book in the South by an African American: *The Hope of Liberty, Containing a Number of Poetical Pieces* by George Moses Horton

1830: Publication of first national magazine edited by an African American: *National Reformer,* by William Whipper

1833: Publication of first African-American autobiography not a slave narrative: *The Life, Experience and Gospel Labors of the Right Reverend Richard Allen*

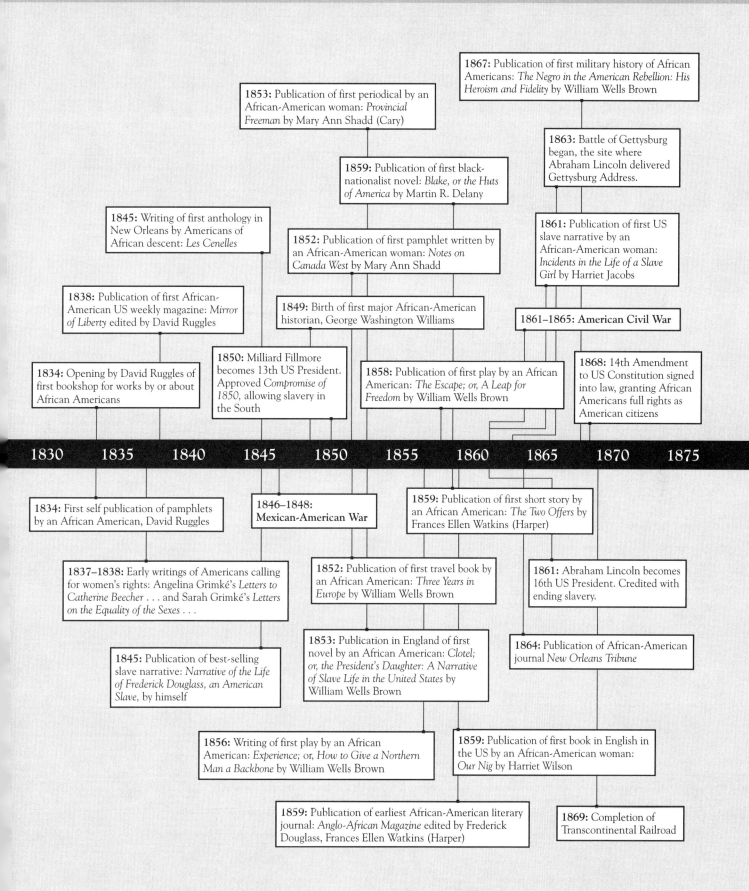

1867: Publication of first military history of African Americans: *The Negro in the American Rebellion: His Heroism and Fidelity* by William Wells Brown

1853: Publication of first periodical by an African-American woman: *Provincial Freeman* by Mary Ann Shadd (Cary)

1863: Battle of Gettysburg began, the site where Abraham Lincoln delivered Gettysburg Address.

1859: Publication of first black-nationalist novel: *Blake, or the Huts of America* by Martin R. Delany

1845: Writing of first anthology in New Orleans by Americans of African descent: *Les Cenelles*

1852: Publication of first pamphlet written by an African-American woman: *Notes on Canada West* by Mary Ann Shadd

1861: Publication of first US slave narrative by an African-American woman: *Incidents in the Life of a Slave Girl* by Harriet Jacobs

1838: Publication of first African-American US weekly magazine: *Mirror of Liberty* edited by David Ruggles

1849: Birth of first major African-American historian, George Washington Williams

1861–1865: American Civil War

1834: Opening by David Ruggles of first bookshop for works by or about African Americans

1850: Milliard Fillmore becomes 13th US President. Approved *Compromise of 1850*, allowing slavery in the South

1858: Publication of first play by an African American: *The Escape; or, A Leap for Freedom* by William Wells Brown

1868: 14th Amendment to US Constitution signed into law, granting African Americans full rights as American citizens

1830	1835	1840	1845	1850	1855	1860	1865	1870	1875

1834: First self publication of pamphlets by an African American, David Ruggles

1846–1848: Mexican-American War

1859: Publication of first short story by an African American: *The Two Offers* by Frances Ellen Watkins (Harper)

1837–1838: Early writings of Americans calling for women's rights: Angelina Grimké's *Letters to Catherine Beecher . . .* and Sarah Grimké's *Letters on the Equality of the Sexes . . .*

1852: Publication of first travel book by an African American: *Three Years in Europe* by William Wells Brown

1861: Abraham Lincoln becomes 16th US President. Credited with ending slavery.

1845: Publication of best-selling slave narrative: *Narrative of the Life of Frederick Douglass, an American Slave*, by himself

1853: Publication in England of first novel by an African American: *Clotel; or, the President's Daughter: A Narrative of Slave Life in the United States* by William Wells Brown

1864: Publication of African-American journal *New Orleans Tribune*

1856: Writing of first play by an African American: *Experience; or, How to Give a Northern Man a Backbone* by William Wells Brown

1859: Publication of first book in English in the US by an African-American woman: *Our Nig* by Harriet Wilson

1859: Publication of earliest African-American literary journal: *Anglo-African Magazine* edited by Frederick Douglass, Frances Ellen Watkins (Harper)

1869: Completion of Transcontinental Railroad

1870–1934...

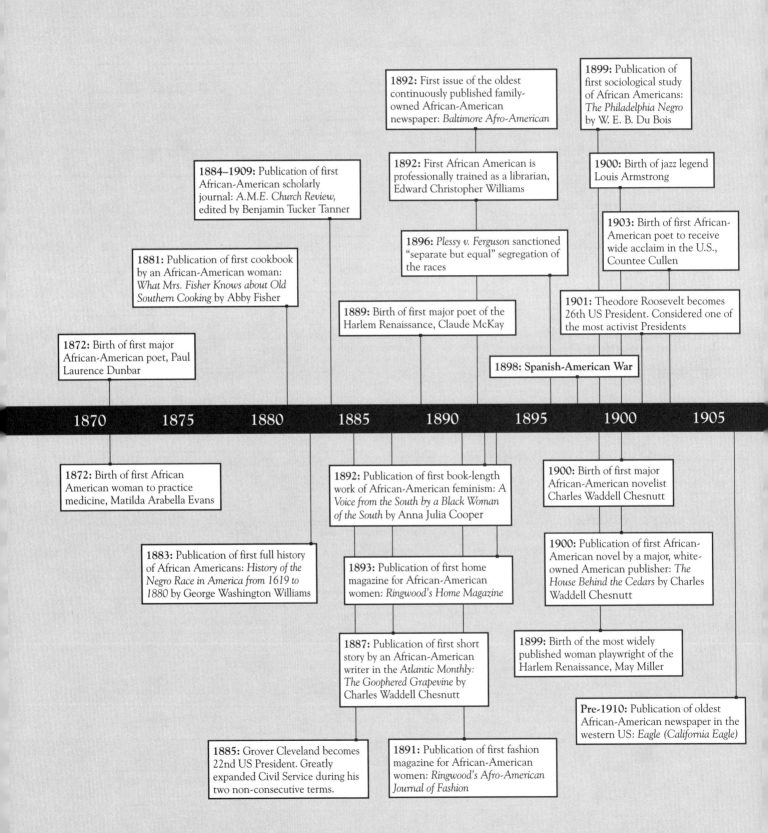

1892: First issue of the oldest continuously published family-owned African-American newspaper: *Baltimore Afro-American*

1899: Publication of first sociological study of African Americans: *The Philadelphia Negro* by W. E. B. Du Bois

1884–1909: Publication of first African-American scholarly journal: *A.M.E. Church Review*, edited by Benjamin Tucker Tanner

1892: First African American is professionally trained as a librarian, Edward Christopher Williams

1900: Birth of jazz legend Louis Armstrong

1881: Publication of first cookbook by an African-American woman: *What Mrs. Fisher Knows about Old Southern Cooking* by Abby Fisher

1896: *Plessy v. Ferguson* sanctioned "separate but equal" segregation of the races

1903: Birth of first African-American poet to receive wide acclaim in the U.S., Countee Cullen

1872: Birth of first major African-American poet, Paul Laurence Dunbar

1889: Birth of first major poet of the Harlem Renaissance, Claude McKay

1901: Theodore Roosevelt becomes 26th US President. Considered one of the most activist Presidents

1898: Spanish-American War

| 1870 | 1875 | 1880 | 1885 | 1890 | 1895 | 1900 | 1905 |

1872: Birth of first African American woman to practice medicine, Matilda Arabella Evans

1892: Publication of first book-length work of African-American feminism: *A Voice from the South by a Black Woman of the South* by Anna Julia Cooper

1900: Birth of first major African-American novelist Charles Waddell Chesnutt

1883: Publication of first full history of African Americans: *History of the Negro Race in America from 1619 to 1880* by George Washington Williams

1893: Publication of first home magazine for African-American women: *Ringwood's Home Magazine*

1900: Publication of first African-American novel by a major, white-owned American publisher: *The House Behind the Cedars* by Charles Waddell Chesnutt

1887: Publication of first short story by an African-American writer in the *Atlantic Monthly*: *The Goophered Grapevine* by Charles Waddell Chesnutt

1899: Birth of the most widely published woman playwright of the Harlem Renaissance, May Miller

Pre-1910: Publication of oldest African-American newspaper in the western US: *Eagle (California Eagle)*

1885: Grover Cleveland becomes 22nd US President. Greatly expanded Civil Service during his two non-consecutive terms.

1891: Publication of first fashion magazine for African-American women: *Ringwood's Afro-American Journal of Fashion*

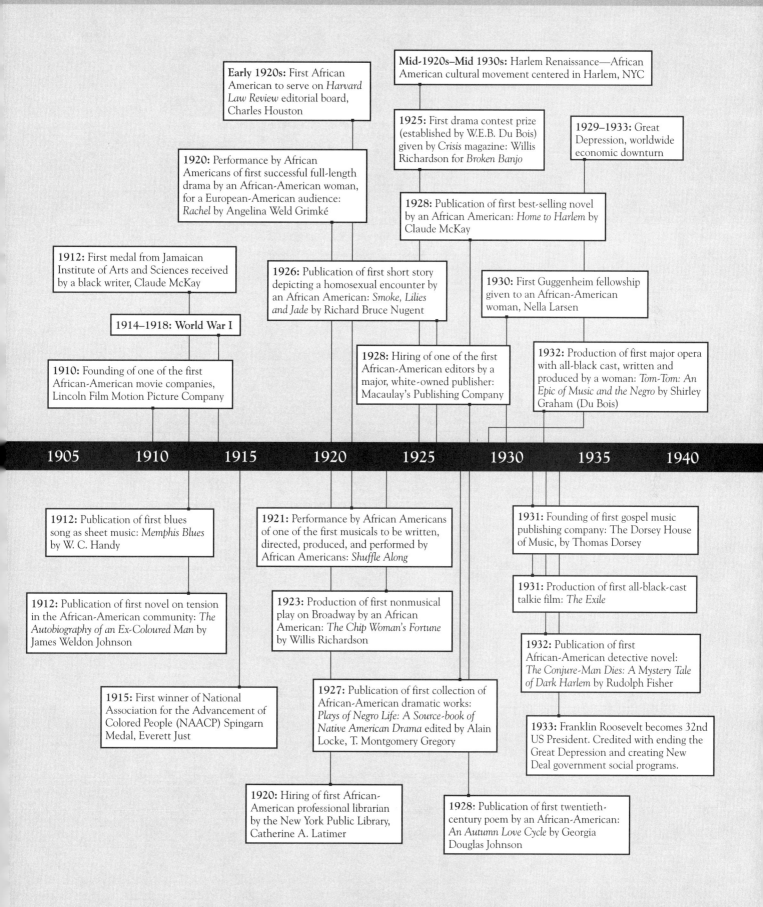

Early 1920s: First African American to serve on *Harvard Law Review* editorial board, Charles Houston

Mid-1920s–Mid 1930s: Harlem Renaissance—African American cultural movement centered in Harlem, NYC

1925: First drama contest prize (established by W.E.B. Du Bois) given by *Crisis* magazine: Willis Richardson for *Broken Banjo*

1929–1933: Great Depression, worldwide economic downturn

1920: Performance by African Americans of first successful full-length drama by an African-American woman, for a European-American audience: *Rachel* by Angelina Weld Grimké

1928: Publication of first best-selling novel by an African American: *Home to Harlem* by Claude McKay

1912: First medal from Jamaican Institute of Arts and Sciences received by a black writer, Claude McKay

1926: Publication of first short story depicting a homosexual encounter by an African American: *Smoke, Lilies and Jade* by Richard Bruce Nugent

1930: First Guggenheim fellowship given to an African-American woman, Nella Larsen

1914–1918: World War I

1910: Founding of one of the first African-American movie companies, Lincoln Film Motion Picture Company

1928: Hiring of one of the first African-American editors by a major, white-owned publisher: Macaulay's Publishing Company

1932: Production of first major opera with all-black cast, written and produced by a woman: *Tom-Tom: An Epic of Music and the Negro* by Shirley Graham (Du Bois)

| 1905 | 1910 | 1915 | 1920 | 1925 | 1930 | 1935 | 1940 |

1912: Publication of first blues song as sheet music: *Memphis Blues* by W. C. Handy

1921: Performance by African Americans of one of the first musicals to be written, directed, produced, and performed by African Americans: *Shuffle Along*

1931: Founding of first gospel music publishing company: The Dorsey House of Music, by Thomas Dorsey

1912: Publication of first novel on tension in the African-American community: *The Autobiography of an Ex-Coloured Man* by James Weldon Johnson

1923: Production of first nonmusical play on Broadway by an African American: *The Chip Woman's Fortune* by Willis Richardson

1931: Production of first all-black-cast talkie film: *The Exile*

1915: First winner of National Association for the Advancement of Colored People (NAACP) Spingarn Medal, Everett Just

1927: Publication of first collection of African-American dramatic works: *Plays of Negro Life: A Source-book of Native American Drama* edited by Alain Locke, T. Montgomery Gregory

1932: Publication of first African-American detective novel: *The Conjure-Man Dies: A Mystery Tale of Dark Harlem* by Rudolph Fisher

1933: Franklin Roosevelt becomes 32nd US President. Credited with ending the Great Depression and creating New Deal government social programs.

1920: Hiring of first African-American professional librarian by the New York Public Library, Catherine A. Latimer

1928: Publication of first twentieth-century poem by an African-American: *An Autumn Love Cycle* by Georgia Douglas Johnson

1935–1959...

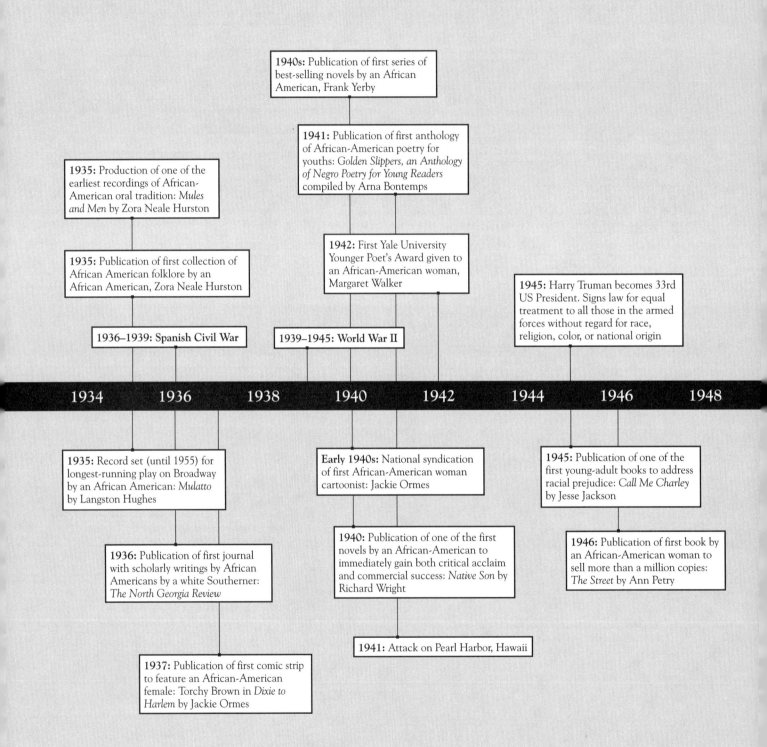

1940s: Publication of first series of best-selling novels by an African American, Frank Yerby

1941: Publication of first anthology of African-American poetry for youths: *Golden Slippers, an Anthology of Negro Poetry for Young Readers* compiled by Arna Bontemps

1935: Production of one of the earliest recordings of African-American oral tradition: *Mules and Men* by Zora Neale Hurston

1942: First Yale University Younger Poet's Award given to an African-American woman, Margaret Walker

1935: Publication of first collection of African American folklore by an African American, Zora Neale Hurston

1945: Harry Truman becomes 33rd US President. Signs law for equal treatment to all those in the armed forces without regard for race, religion, color, or national origin

1936–1939: Spanish Civil War

1939–1945: World War II

| 1934 | 1936 | 1938 | 1940 | 1942 | 1944 | 1946 | 1948 |

1935: Record set (until 1955) for longest-running play on Broadway by an African American: *Mulatto* by Langston Hughes

Early 1940s: National syndication of first African-American woman cartoonist: Jackie Ormes

1945: Publication of one of the first young-adult books to address racial prejudice: *Call Me Charley* by Jesse Jackson

1936: Publication of first journal with scholarly writings by African Americans by a white Southerner: *The North Georgia Review*

1940: Publication of one of the first novels by an African-American to immediately gain both critical acclaim and commercial success: *Native Son* by Richard Wright

1946: Publication of first book by an African-American woman to sell more than a million copies: *The Street* by Ann Petry

1937: Publication of first comic strip to feature an African-American female: Torchy Brown in *Dixie to Harlem* by Jackie Ormes

1941: Attack on Pearl Harbor, Hawaii

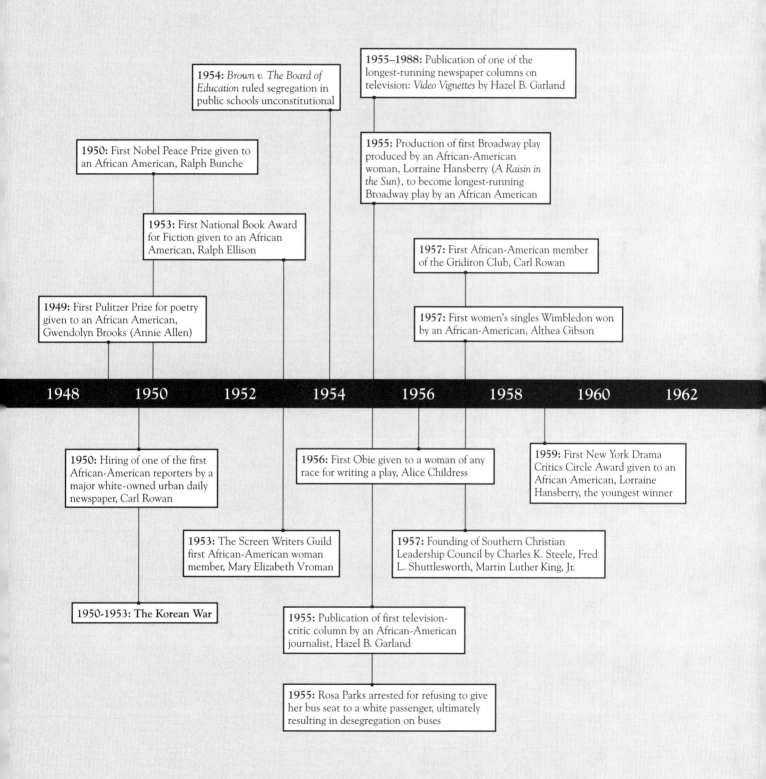

1955–1988: Publication of one of the longest-running newspaper columns on television: *Video Vignettes* by Hazel B. Garland

1954: *Brown v. The Board of Education* ruled segregation in public schools unconstitutional

1950: First Nobel Peace Prize given to an African American, Ralph Bunche

1955: Production of first Broadway play produced by an African-American woman, Lorraine Hansberry (*A Raisin in the Sun*), to become longest-running Broadway play by an African American

1953: First National Book Award for Fiction given to an African American, Ralph Ellison

1957: First African-American member of the Gridiron Club, Carl Rowan

1949: First Pulitzer Prize for poetry given to an African American, Gwendolyn Brooks (Annie Allen)

1957: First women's singles Wimbledon won by an African-American, Althea Gibson

1948	1950	1952	1954	1956	1958	1960	1962

1950: Hiring of one of the first African-American reporters by a major white-owned urban daily newspaper, Carl Rowan

1956: First Obie given to a woman of any race for writing a play, Alice Childress

1959: First New York Drama Critics Circle Award given to an African American, Lorraine Hansberry, the youngest winner

1953: The Screen Writers Guild first African-American woman member, Mary Elizabeth Vroman

1957: Founding of Southern Christian Leadership Council by Charles K. Steele, Fred L. Shuttlesworth, Martin Luther King, Jr.

1950-1953: The Korean War

1955: Publication of first television-critic column by an African-American journalist, Hazel B. Garland

1955: Rosa Parks arrested for refusing to give her bus seat to a white passenger, ultimately resulting in desegregation on buses

1960–1979...

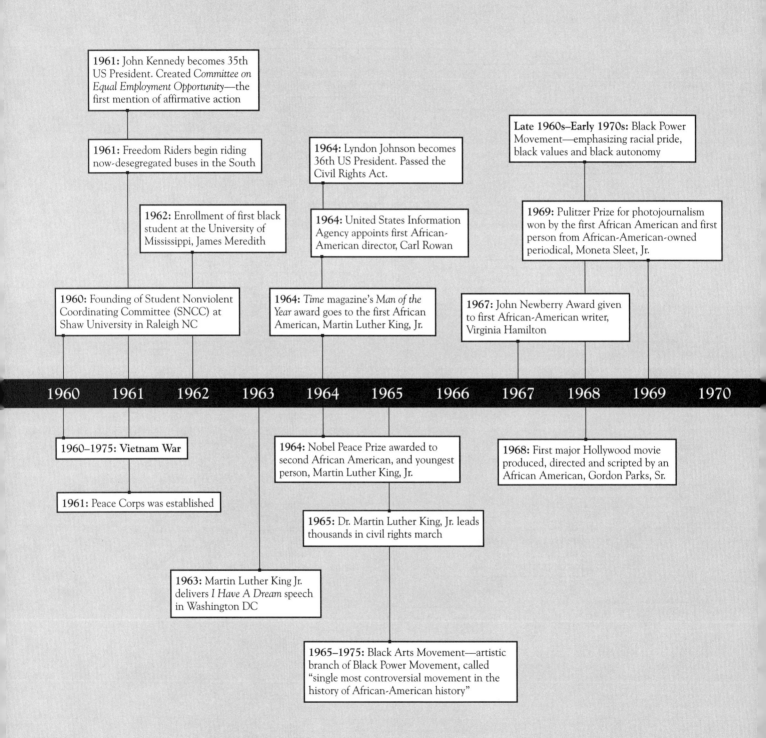

1961: John Kennedy becomes 35th US President. Created *Committee on Equal Employment Opportunity*—the first mention of affirmative action

1961: Freedom Riders begin riding now-desegregated buses in the South

1962: Enrollment of first black student at the University of Mississippi, James Meredith

1960: Founding of Student Nonviolent Coordinating Committee (SNCC) at Shaw University in Raleigh NC

1964: Lyndon Johnson becomes 36th US President. Passed the Civil Rights Act.

1964: United States Information Agency appoints first African-American director, Carl Rowan

1964: *Time* magazine's *Man of the Year* award goes to the first African American, Martin Luther King, Jr.

Late 1960s–Early 1970s: Black Power Movement—emphasizing racial pride, black values and black autonomy

1969: Pulitzer Prize for photojournalism won by the first African American and first person from African-American-owned periodical, Moneta Sleet, Jr.

1967: John Newberry Award given to first African-American writer, Virginia Hamilton

| 1960 | 1961 | 1962 | 1963 | 1964 | 1965 | 1966 | 1967 | 1968 | 1969 | 1970 |

1960–1975: Vietnam War

1961: Peace Corps was established

1964: Nobel Peace Prize awarded to second African American, and youngest person, Martin Luther King, Jr.

1968: First major Hollywood movie produced, directed and scripted by an African American, Gordon Parks, Sr.

1965: Dr. Martin Luther King, Jr. leads thousands in civil rights march

1963: Martin Luther King Jr. delivers *I Have A Dream* speech in Washington DC

1965–1975: Black Arts Movement—artistic branch of Black Power Movement, called "single most controversial movement in the history of African-American history"

...Civil Rights & Black Power Movements

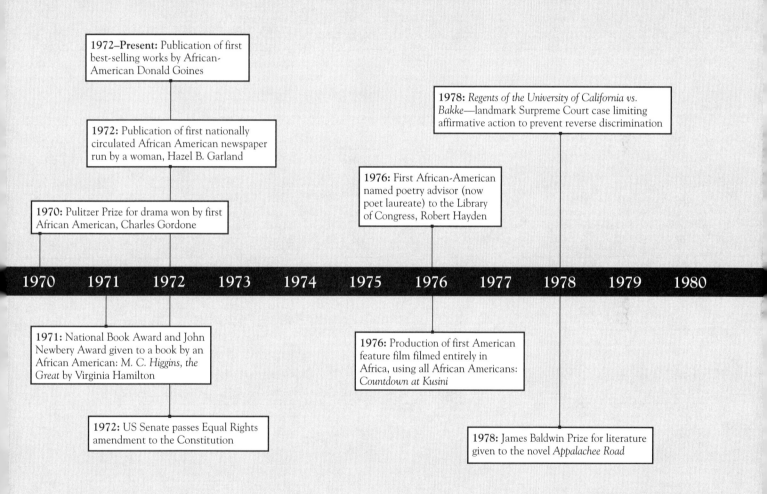

1972–Present: Publication of first best-selling works by African-American Donald Goines

1972: Publication of first nationally circulated African American newspaper run by a woman, Hazel B. Garland

1970: Pulitzer Prize for drama won by first African American, Charles Gordone

1978: *Regents of the University of California vs. Bakke*—landmark Surpreme Court case limiting affirmative action to prevent reverse discrimination

1976: First African-American named poetry advisor (now poet laureate) to the Library of Congress, Robert Hayden

| 1970 | 1971 | 1972 | 1973 | 1974 | 1975 | 1976 | 1977 | 1978 | 1979 | 1980 |

1971: National Book Award and John Newbery Award given to a book by an African American: *M. C. Higgins, the Great* by Virginia Hamilton

1976: Production of first American feature film filmed entirely in Africa, using all African Americans: *Countdown at Kusini*

1972: US Senate passes Equal Rights amendment to the Constitution

1978: James Baldwin Prize for literature given to the novel *Appalachee Road*

1980–Present...

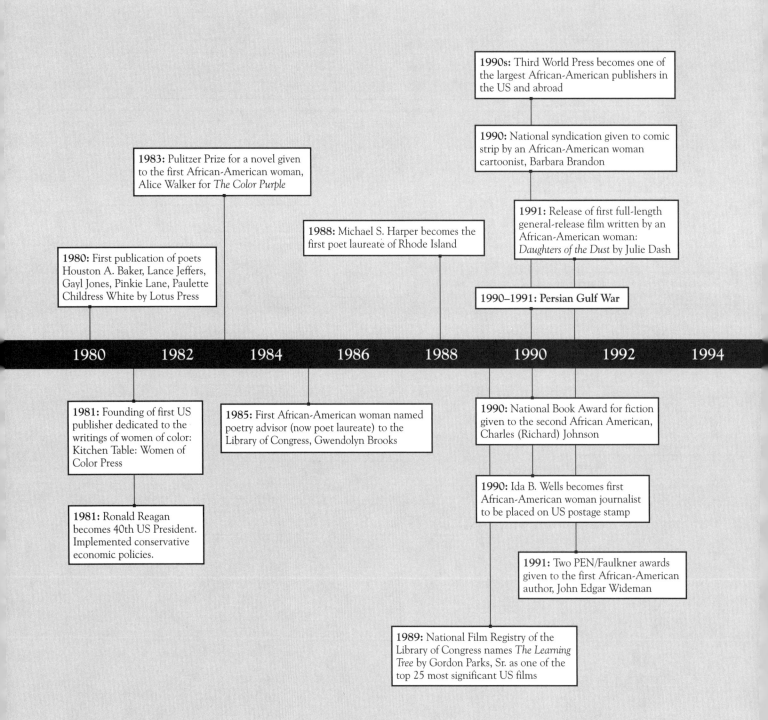

1990s: Third World Press becomes one of the largest African-American publishers in the US and abroad

1990: National syndication given to comic strip by an African-American woman cartoonist, Barbara Brandon

1983: Pulitzer Prize for a novel given to the first African-American woman, Alice Walker for *The Color Purple*

1991: Release of first full-length general-release film written by an African-American woman: *Daughters of the Dust* by Julie Dash

1988: Michael S. Harper becomes the first poet laureate of Rhode Island

1980: First publication of poets Houston A. Baker, Lance Jeffers, Gayl Jones, Pinkie Lane, Paulette Childress White by Lotus Press

1990–1991: Persian Gulf War

1980   1982   1984   1986   1988   1990   1992   1994

1981: Founding of first US publisher dedicated to the writings of women of color: Kitchen Table: Women of Color Press

1985: First African-American woman named poetry advisor (now poet laureate) to the Library of Congress, Gwendolyn Brooks

1990: National Book Award for fiction given to the second African American, Charles (Richard) Johnson

1981: Ronald Reagan becomes 40th US President. Implemented conservative economic policies.

1990: Ida B. Wells becomes first African-American woman journalist to be placed on US postage stamp

1991: Two PEN/Faulkner awards given to the first African-American author, John Edgar Wideman

1989: National Film Registry of the Library of Congress names *The Learning Tree* by Gordon Parks, Sr. as one of the top 25 most significant US films

...Reagan Era through Obama Era

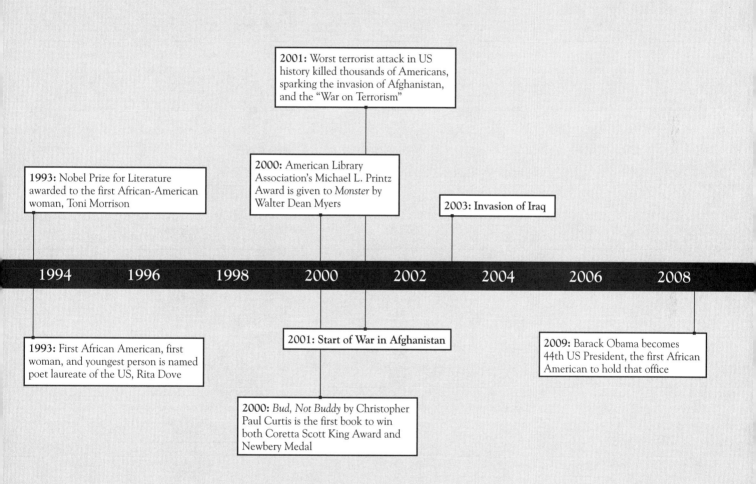

2001: Worst terrorist attack in US history killed thousands of Americans, sparking the invasion of Afghanistan, and the "War on Terrorism"

1993: Nobel Prize for Literature awarded to the first African-American woman, Toni Morrison

2000: American Library Association's Michael L. Printz Award is given to *Monster* by Walter Dean Myers

2003: Invasion of Iraq

1994   1996   1998   2000   2002   2004   2006   2008

1993: First African American, first woman, and youngest person is named poet laureate of the US, Rita Dove

2001: Start of War in Afghanistan

2009: Barack Obama becomes 44th US President, the first African American to hold that office

2000: *Bud, Not Buddy* by Christopher Paul Curtis is the first book to win both Coretta Scott King Award and Newbery Medal

Appendix D: Writers by Genre

Includes non-writer entries, such as publications and organizations.

Anthologies and Bibliographies

Anthologies of African-American literature

Anthologies of African-American literature, from literary journals

Anthologies of African-American literature, regional of African-American literature

Anthologies of African-American literature, special topics and audiences

Anthologies of African-American literature, specific genres, drama and plays

Anthologies of African-American literature, specific genres, fiction

Anthologies of African-American literature, specific genres, nonfiction

Anthologies of African-American literature, specific genres, poetry, verse, and song

Anthologies of African-American literature, written by and for gay or heterosexual men

Anthologies of African-American literature, written by and for heterosexual or lesbian women

Anthologies of African-American literature, written by and for juveniles

Anthologies of African-American literature, writers from 1619 through 1865

Anthologies of African-American literature, writers from 1920 to the early 1940s

Black Fire: An Anthology of African American Writing

Negro: An Anthology

Allen, Samuel W.

Baisden, Michael

Baker, Augusta

Bambara, Toni Cade

Baraka, Amiri

Bontemps, Arna Wendell

Braithwaite, William Stanley Beaumont

Brown, William Wells

Clarke, John Henrik

Collier, Eugenia (Williams)

Colón, Jesús

Cornish, Sam

Damas, Léon-Gontran

Danticat, Edwidge

Davis, Arthur P.

Delaney, Sara ("Sadie") Marie

Dunbar Nelson, Alice

Early, Gerald

Emanuel, James A.

Evans, Mari

Ford, Nick Aaron

Foster, Frances Smith

French, William P.

Giddings, Paula

Giovanni, Nikki

Golden, Marita

Gomez, Jewelle

Guy, Rosa Cuthbert

Handy, W. C.

Hare, Maud Cuney

Hare, Nathan

Harper, Michael S.

Harris, Trudier

Hemphill, Essex

Hernton, Calvin S.

hooks, bell

Hughes, Langston

Hutson, Jean Blackwell

Johnson, Charles (Spurgeon)

Johnson, James Weldon

Jordan, June

Josey, E. J.

Kincaid, Jamaica

King, Jr., Woodie

Knight, Etheridge

Ladner, Joyce A.

Lane, Pinkie

Latimer, Catherine A.

Lewis, David Levering

Locke, Alain

Mackey, Nathaniel

Madgett, Naomi Long

Major, Clarence

Mayfield, Julian

McElroy, Colleen

McKay, Nellie Yvonne

McMillan, Terry

Milner, Ronald

Mitchell, Loften

Morrison, Toni

Mosley, Walter

Murphy, Beatrice M.

Murray, Daniel Alexander Payne

Neal, Larry

Nelson, Jill

Packer, ZZ

Patterson, William

Perkins, Eugene

Porter Wesley, Dorothy Burnett

Powell, Kevin

Rahman, Aishah

Randall, Dudley

Reagon, Bernice Johnson

Redmond, Eugene

Reed, Ishmael

Richardson, Willis

Rollins, Charlemae Hill

Schomburg, Arthur A.

Scott, Nathan A.

Senna, Carl

Shepherd, Reginald

Shine, Ted

Shockley, Ann

Smith, Barbara

Smith, Jessie Carney

Southern, Eileen Stanza Johnson

Sterling, Dorothy

Tate, Eleanora

Thomas, Joyce Carol

Thomas, Lorenzo

Troupe, Quincy

Turner, Darwin T.

Turner, Lorenzo Dow

Turpin, Waters

Van Vechten, Carl

Walker, Alice

Walker, Rebecca

Walton, Anthony

Weaver, Afaa M.

Wilkins, Roger Wood

Williams, John A.

Woodson, Carter G.

Woodson, Jacqueline

Young, Al

Young, Kevin

Zu-Bolton, III, Ahmos

Biographies and Sketches

(individuals or groups)

Bennett, Jr., Lerone

Bolden, Tonya

Bontemps, Arna Wendell

Boyd, Melba

Braithwaite, William Stanley Beaumont

Brawley, Benjamin
Brown, Hallie Quinn
Chesnutt, Charles Waddell
De Veaux, Alexis
Du Bois, Shirley Graham
Du Bois, W. E. B.
Dyson, Michael Eric
Emanuel, James A.
Fauset, Jessie Redmon
Fax, Elton C.
Foster, Frances Smith
Franklin, John Hope
French, William P.
Garvey, Amy Jacques
Gates, Jr., Henry Louis
Gayle, Jr., Addison
Giddings, Paula
Graham, Lorenz
Greenfield, Eloise
Griggs, Sutton E.
Grimké, Archibald Henry
Haley, Alex
Hare, Maud Cuney
Harris, Trudier
Haskins, James S.
Haynes, Elizabeth Ross
Higginbotham, Evelyn (Titania) (née)
    Brooks
Hine, Darlene Clark
Hopkins, Pauline
Jackson, Jesse
Kenan, Randall
Killens, John Oliver
Lewis, David Levering
Locke, Alain
Logan, Rayford
Mathis, Sharon Bell
McKay, Nellie Yvonne
McKissack, Pat
Meriwether, Louise
Millican, Arthenia J. Bates
Murray, Albert L.
Myers, Walter Dean
Painter, Nell Irvin
Patterson, Lillie
Petry, Ann
Plato, Ann
Porter, James Amos
Quarles, Benjamin
Rampersad, Arnold
Redding, Jay Saunders
Robeson, Eslanda
Robinson, Randall
Rogers, Joel Augustus
Rollins, Charlemae Hill
Rowan, Carl T.
Senna, Carl
Shockley, Ann
Simmons, William J.
Smith, Jessie Carney
Southern, Eileen Stanza Johnson

Sterling, Dorothy
Stowe, Harriet Beecher
Tarry, Ellen
Tate, Claudia
Touré, Askia M.
Troupe, Quincy
Walker, Alice
Walker, Margaret
Walton, Anthony
Waniek, Marilyn Nelson
Wesley, Charles Harris
Whipper, Frances A. Rollin
Wilkins, Roger Wood
Wilkinson, Brenda
Williams, John A.
Wright, Sarah E.
Young, Al

Champions of Literature
(booksellers, literary salon hosts, founders of
foundations/organizations, literary executors,
bibliotherapists)
Barnett, Claude Albert
Cornish, Sam
Delaney, Sara ("Sadie") Marie
Gerima, Haile
Johnson, Kathryn Magnolia
Kweli, Talib
Maynard, Nancy Hicks
Maynard, Robert
Redmond, Eugene
Reed, Ishmael
Ruggles, David
Stone, Chuck
Van Vechten, Carl
Walker, A'Lelia
Zu-Bolton, III, Ahmos

Comic Strips/Books, Cartoons, Graphic Novels
Brandon, Barbara
Fax, Elton C.
Feelings, Tom
Graham, Lorenz
Johnson, Charles (Richard)
McGruder, Aaron
Ormes, Jackie
Van Peebles, Melvin

Criticism
(literary, music, theater, movies, media)
Alexander, Elizabeth
Allen, Samuel W.
Amini, Johari
Aubert, Alvin
Baker, Jr., Houston A.
Barrax, Gerald W.
Bennett, Gwendolyn B.
Bogle, Donald
Bolden, Tonya
Bradley, Jr., David

Braithwaite, William Stanley Beaumont
Brathwaite, Edward Kamau
Brawley, Benjamin
Braxton, Joanne M.
Brown, Sterling Allen
Cassells, Cyrus
Christian, Barbara
Coleman, Wanda
Collier, Eugenia (Williams)
Crosswaith, Frank Rudolph
Crouch, Stanley
Davis, Arthur P.
Davis, Frank Marshall
Delany, Samuel R.
Dunbar Nelson, Alice
Dyson, Michael Eric
Early, Gerald
Ellison, Ralph
Emanuel, James A.
Evans, Mari
Fauset, Jessie Redmon
Ford, Nick Aaron
Foster, Frances Smith
Fuller, Hoyt
Gates, Jr., Henry Louis
Gayle, Jr., Addison
Giddings, Paula
Giovanni, Nikki
Harris, Trudier
Haskins, James S.
Hull, Akasha (née Gloria Theresa
    Thompson)
Johnson, Charles (Richard)
Johnson, James Weldon
Jones, Gayl
Kenan, Randall
King, Jr., Woodie
Lewis, David Levering
Locke, Alain
Mackey, Nathaniel
Matheus, John F.
Mayfield, Julian
McKay, Nellie Yvonne
Mebane, Mary E.
Meriwether, Louise
Miller, E. Ethelbert
Milner, Ronald
Moore, Opal
Morrison, Toni
Mullen, Harryette
Murphy, Beatrice M.
Murray, Albert L.
Neal, Larry
Plumpp, Sterling
Rampersad, Arnold
Redding, Jay Saunders
Redmond, Eugene
Rodgers, Carolyn
Ruffin, George Lewis
Salaam, Kalamu ya
Scott, Nathan A.

Senna, Carl
Shockley, Ann
Smitherman, Geneva
Southern, Eileen Stanza Johnson
Spillers, Hortense J.
Spingarn, Joel Elias
Tate, Claudia
Thomas, Lorenzo
Thompson, Era Bell
Thurman, Wallace
Turner, Darwin T.
Turpin, Waters
Van Vechten, Carl
Walcott, Derek
Walker, Margaret
Williams, Patricia J.
Williams, Sherley Anne
Wright, Courtni

Editors
(journal, newspaper, book-acquisitions, founding)
Amini, Johari
Ansa, Tina McElroy
Asante, Molefi Kete
Baker, Jr., Houston A.
Bennett, Jr., Lerone
Bolden, Tonya
Brown, Lloyd
Bruce, Sr., Roscoe Conkling
Channer, Colin
Clarke, John Henrik
Cleage, Pearl
Cornish, Sam
Crosswaith, Frank Rudolph
Davis, Frank Marshall
De Veaux, Alexis
Du Bois, W. E. B.
Ellison, Ralph (Waldo)
Fauset, Jessie Redmon
Fuller, Hoyt
Gomez, Jewelle
Grimké, Archibald Henry
Hansberry, Lorraine
Harper, Frances Ellen Watkins
Herron, Carolivia
Holman, M. (Moses) Carl
Houston, Charles
Johnson, Charles (Spurgeon)
Kaufman, "Bob"
Keene, Jr., John R.
Kenan, Randall
Knight, Etheridge
Mackey, Nathaniel
Major, Clarence
Mayfield, Julian
Maynard, Robert
McElroy, Colleen
McKay, Claude
Miller, E. Ethelbert
Morrison, Toni

Murphy, Beatrice M.
Newsome, Effie Lee
Obama, II, Barack
Oliver, Diane
Patterson, William
Perkins, Eugene
Quarles, Benjamin
Redmond, Eugene
Reed, Ishmael
Scott, Nathan A.
Senna, Carl
Shockley, Ann
Simmons, Herbert Alfred
Simmons, William J.
Steele, Claude M.
Tate, Claudia
Thomas, Joyce Carol
Thomas, Lorenzo
Thompson, Era Bell
Touré, Askia M.
Troupe, Quincy
Turpin, Waters
Van Dyke, Henry
Van Peebles, Melvin
Walrond, Eric
Weaver, Afaa M.
Wells-Barnett, Ida B.
Wesley, Valerie Wilson
Whipper, William
Wilkins, Roy
Williams, Edward Christopher
Woodson, Jacqueline
Wright, Richard
X, Marvin
Young, Al
Zu-Bolton, III, Ahmos

Fiction
(novels of various genres)
Andrews, Raymond
Ansa, Tina McElroy
Attaway, William
Baisden, Michael
Baldwin, James
Bambara, Toni Cade
Banks, Leslie Esdaile
Baraka, Amiri
Barnes, Steven Emory
Beckham, Barry
Bennett, Hal
Bontemps, Arna Wendell
Bradley, Jr., David
Brooks, Gwendolyn
Brown, Cecil
Brown, Claude
Brown, Frank London
Brown, Linda Beatrice
Brown, Lloyd
Brown, William Wells
Bullins, Ed
Butler, Octavia E.

Campbell, Bebe Moore
Channer, Colin
Chase-Riboud, Barbara
Chesnutt, Charles Waddell
Child, Lydia Maria
Childress, Alice
Cleage, Pearl
Cliff, Michelle
Clifton, Lucille
Coleman, Wanda
Collins, Kathleen
Colter, Cyrus
Cooper, J. California
Cose, Ellis
Cullen, Countee
Danticat, Edwidge
Davis, Ossie
Davis, Thulani
De Veaux, Alexis
Deal, Borden
Delany, Martin R.
Delany, Samuel R.
Demby, William
Dodson, Owen
Dove, Rita
Du Bois, Shirley Graham
Du Bois, W. E. B.
Due, Tananarive
Dunbar Nelson, Alice
Ellison, Ralph
Everett, II, Percival
Fauset, Jessie Redmon
Fisher, Rudolph ("Bud")
Forrest, Leon
Gaines, Ernest J.
Goines, Donald
Golden, Marita
Gomez, Jewelle
Graham, Lorenz
Greenlee, Sam
Griggs, Sutton E.
Grooms, Anthony
Guy, Rosa Cuthbert
Hamilton, Virginia
Hansen, Joyce
Harper, Frances Ellen Watkins
Harris, E. Lynn
Harris, Joel Chandler
Heard, Nathan C.
Hercules, Frank
Hernton, Calvin C.
Herron, Carolivia
Heyward, DuBose
Hill, Donna
Himes, Chester
Hopkins, Pauline
Hughes, Langston
Hunter, Kristin Eggleston
Hurston, Zora Neale
Iceberg Slim
Jakes, T. D.

Jeffers, Lance
Jenkins, Beverly
Joe, Yolanda (aka Garland, Ardella)
Johnson, Amelia E.
Johnson, Angela
Johnson, Charles (Richard)
Johnson, James Weldon
Jones, Edward P.
Jones, Gayl
Jones, Tayari
Jordan, June
Keene, Jr., John R.
Kelley, William Melvin
Kenan, Randall
Killens, John Oliver
Kincaid, Jamaica
Larsen, Nella
LaValle, Victor
Lee, Andrea
Lester, Julius
Mackey, Nathaniel
Major, Clarence
Marshall, Paule
Matthews, Victoria Earle
Mayfield, Julian
McElroy, Colleen
McFadden, Bernice L.
McKay, Claude
McMillan, Terry
Meriwether, Louise
Micheaux, Oscar
Millican, Arthenia J. Bates
Milner, Ronald
Mitchell, Loften
Monroe, Mary
Morrison, Toni
Mosley, Walter
Motley, Willard
Murray, Albert L.
Myers, Walter Dean
Naylor, Gloria
Neely, Barbara
Nelson, Jill
Parks, Sr., Gordon
Patterson, Orlando
Paynter, John H.
Petry, Ann
Pharr, Robert Deane
Pickens, William
Polite, Carlene Hatcher
Randall, Alice
Redding, Jay Saunders
Reed, Ishmael
Rhodes, Jewell Parker
Ridley, John
Robinson, Randall
Rodgers, Carolyn
Rogers, Joel Augustus
Rux, Carl Hancock
Sapphire
Schuyler, George Samuel

Scott-Heron, Gil
Séjour, Victor
Senna, Danzy
Shange, Ntozake
Shockley, Ann
Simmons, Herbert Alfred
Smith, Lillian Eugenia
Smith, William Gardner
Southerland, Ellease
Steward, Theophilus Gould
Stone, Chuck
Stowe, Harriet Beecher
Taylor, Mildred Delois
Thomas, Joyce Carol
Thurman, Wallace
Tillman, Katherine Davis Chapman
Tolson, Melvin
Toomer, Jean
Turpin, Waters
Tyree, Omar
van Sertima, Ivan
Van Dyke, Henry
Van Peebles, Melvin
Van Vechten, Carl
Vernon, Olympia
Vroman, Mary Elizabeth
Walker, Alice
Walker, Margaret
Walrond, Eric
Walter, Mildred Pitts
Webb, Frank J.
Wesley, Valerie Wilson
West, Dorothy
White, Walter F.
Wideman, John Edgar
Wilkinson, Brenda
Williams, Chancellor
Williams, Edward Christopher
Williams, John A.
Williams, Sherley Anne
Wilson, Harriet E.
Woodson, Jacqueline
Wright, Charles S.
Wright, Courtni
Wright, Richard
Wright, Sarah E.
Yerby, Frank G.
Young, Al

Fiction
(short stories and sketches)
Amini, Johari
Aubert, Alvin
Baker, Augusta
Baldwin, James
Bambara, Toni Cade
Banneker, Benjamin
Bennett, Gwendolyn B.
Bennett, Hal
Bonner, Marita
Bontemps, Arna Wendell

Brown, Cecil
Brown, Charlotte Eugenia
Brown, Frank London
Burroughs, Margaret Taylor
Cabrera, Lydia
Campbell, Bebe Moore
Channer, Colin
Clarke, John Henrik
Cleage, Pearl
Cliff, Michelle
Clifton, Lucille
Coleman, Wanda
Collier, Eugenia (Williams)
Colón, Jesús
Colter, Cyrus
Cooper, J. California
Corrothers, James D.
Cotter, Sr., Joseph Seamon
Crayton, Pearl
Danticat, Edwidge
De Veaux, Alexis
Deal, Borden
Dee, Ruby
Delany, Samuel R.
Dove, Rita
Draper, Sharon M.
Dumas, Henry L.
Dunbar, Paul Laurence
Dunbar Nelson, Alice
Ellison, Ralph
Evans, Mari
Everett, II, Percival
Fields, Julia
Fisher, Rudolph ("Bud")
Ford, Nick Aaron
Forrest, Leon
Fuller, Jr., Charles H.
Gaines, Ernest J.
Gayle, Jr., Addison
Gibson, P. J.
Gomez, Jewelle
Graham, Lorenz
Greenfield, Eloise
Grimké, Angelina Weld
Harper, Frances Ellen Watkins
Harris, Joel Chandler
Herron, Carolivia
Himes, Chester
Hopkins, Pauline
Hughes, Langston
Hunter, Kristin Eggleston
Hurston, Zora Neale
Hutson, Jean Blackwell
Iceberg Slim
Jackson, Angela
Joans, Ted
Johnson, Amelia E.
Johnson, Charles (Richard)
Johnson, Fenton
Johnson, Georgia Douglas
Jones, Edward P.

Jones, Gayl
Jordan, June
Keene, Jr., John R.
Kelley, William Melvin
Kincaid, Jamaica
King, Jr., Woodie
Larsen, Nella
Lester, Julius
Major, Clarence
Marshall, Paule
Matheus, John F.
McElroy, Colleen
McFadden, Bernice L.
McGirt, James E.
McKissack, Pat
McPherson, James Alan
Meriwether, Louise
Millican, Arthenia J. Bates
Milner, Ronald
Monroe, Mary
Moody, Anne
Moore, Opal
Mosley, Walter
Mullen, Harryette
Neely, Barbara
Nugent, Richard Bruce
Oliver, Diane
Packer, ZZ
Petry, Ann
Pharr, Robert Deane
Poston, Ted
Rahman, Aishah
Ridley, Florida Ruffin
Rivers, Conrad Kent
Robeson, Paul
Rodgers, Carolyn
Salaam, Kalamu ya
Shockley, Ann
Smith, Effie Waller
Southerland, Ellease
Stowe, Harriet Beecher
Tate, Eleanora
Terry, Lucy
Thomas, Piri
Thurman, Wallace
Torrence, Jackie
Touré, Askia M.
Turpin, Waters
Van Dyke, Henry
Vroman, Mary Elizabeth
Walker, Alice
Walrond, Eric
West, Dorothy
White, Paulette Childress
Wideman, John Edgar
Wilkinson, Brenda
Williams, Edward Christopher
Wright, Charles S.
Wright, Richard
Wright, Sarah E.
Yerby, Frank G.

Young, Al

Journalists
(reporter, staffer, freelancer, correspondent)
Campbell, James Edwin
Christian, Marcus Bruce
Deal, Borden
Demby, William
Due, Tananarive
Dyson, Michael Eric
Forrest, Leon
Gladwell, Malcolm
Holly, James Theodore
Jackson, Jesse
Maynard, Dori J.
Maynard, Nancy Hicks
Maynard, Robert
McDonald, Janet A.
Nelson, Jill
Page, Clarence
Poston, Ted
Powell, Kevin
Redmond, Eugene
Ridley, Florida Ruffin
Robeson, Eslanda
Robinson, Max
Rogers, Joel Augustus
Ruffin, Josephine St. Pierre
Schuyler, George Samuel
Schuyler, Philippa Duke
Senna, Carl
Sterling, Dorothy
Stone, Chuck
Thomas, Lorenzo
Tyree, Omar
Van Peebles, Melvin
Van Vechten, Carl
Wilkins, Roger Wood
Wilkins, Roy

Folktales and Juvenile Literature
(fiction and nonfiction)
Folktales
Oral tradition
Trickster tales
Baker, Augusta
Baldwin, James
Bolden, Tonya
Bontemps, Arna Wendell
Bryan, Ashley F.
Burroughs, Margaret Taylor
Campbell, Bebe Moore
Child, Lydia Maria
Childress, Alice
Christian, Marcus Bruce
Clifton, Lucille
Cosby, Bill
Crews, Donald
Curtis, Christopher Paul
Danticat, Edwidge
De Veaux, Alexis

Dee, Ruby
Draper, Sharon M.
Evans, Mari
Everett, II, Percival
Fauset, Jessie Redmon
Fax, Elton C.
Feelings, Tom
Fields, Julia
Giovanni, Nikki
Goldberg, Whoopi
Graham, Lorenz
Greenfield, Eloise
Guy, Rosa Cuthbert
Hamilton, Virginia
Hansen, Joyce
Harris, Joel Chandler
Haskins, James S.
Herron, Carolivia
hooks, bell
Hudson, Cheryl (Willis)
Hudson, Wade
Hughes, Langston
Hunter, Kristin Eggleston
Jackson, Jesse
Joe, Yolanda (aka Garland, Ardella)
Johnson, Angela
Jordan, June
Kenan, Randall
Killens, John Oliver
Lester, Julius
Love, Rose Leary
Mathis, Sharon Bell
Matthews, Victoria Earle
McDonald, Janet A.
McKissack, Pat
Mebane, Mary E.
Meriwether, Louise
Miller, May
Morrison, Toni
Moss, Thylias
Mossell, Gertrude Bustill
Mowry, Jess
Myers, Walter Dean
Newsome, Effie Lee
Patterson, Lillie
Petry, Ann
Richards, Beah
Richardson, Willis
Ringgold, Faith
Rollins, Charlemae Hill
Sanders, Dori
Senna, Carl
Shange, Ntozake
Steptoe, John
Sterling, Dorothy
Stone, Chuck
Tarry, Ellen
Tate, Eleanora
Taylor, Mildred Delois
Thomas, Joyce Carol
Thomas, Piri

Torrence, Jackie
Tyree, Omar
Vroman, Mary Elizabeth
Walker, Alice
Walter, Mildred Pitts
Waniek, Marilyn Nelson
Wesley, Valerie Wilson
Wilkinson, Brenda
Williams, Sherley Anne
Williams, III, Stanley Tookie
Williams-Garcia, Rita
Woodson, Jacqueline
Wright, Courtni
Wright, Richard
Yarbrough, Camille

Library Champions
*(librarians, library assistants, library
founders, archivists, collection founders,
donors)*
Anderson, Regina M.
Baker, Augusta
Bontemps, Arna Wendell
Christian, Marcus Bruce
Cornish, Sam
Delaney, Sara ("Sadie") Marie
Dunham, Katherine
Fortune, Amos
Hurston, Zora Neale
Hutson, Jean Blackwell
Jenkins, Beverly
Josey, E. J.
Keene, Jr., John R.
Larsen, Nella
Latimer, Catherine A.
Lorde, Audre
Marshall, Paule
Mathis, Sharon Bell
Matthews, Victoria Earle
McMillan, Terry
Merrick, Lyda Moore
Murphy, Beatrice M.
Murray, Daniel Alexander Payne
Osbey, Brenda Marie
Patterson, Lillie
Porter Wesley, Dorothy Burnett
Randall, Dudley
Rollins, Charlemae Hill
Schomburg, Arthur A.
Shockley, Ann
Smith, Jessie Carney
Spencer, "Anne"
Spingarn, Arthur B.
Thomas, Lorenzo
Torrence, Jackie
Van Vechten, Carl
Whipper, William
Williams, Edward Christopher

Nonfiction
(essays, articles, books, reports)

Abu-Jamal, Mumia
Alexander, Elizabeth
Amini, Johari
Andrews, Raymond
Ansa, Tina McElroy
Ashe, Arthur
Baker, Jr., Houston A.
Baldwin, James
Bambara, Toni Cade
Banks, Leslie Esdaile
Banneker, Benjamin
Baraka, Amiri
Barber, Jesse Max
Barnett, Claude Albert
Bass, Charlotta Spears
Beasley, Delilah
Beckham. Barry
Bennett, Gwendolyn B.
Bennett, Jr., Lerone
Berry, Mary Frances
Bibb, Henry
BlackBoard African-American
   Bestsellers
Bogle, Donald
Bolden, Tonya
Bonner, Marita
Bontemps, Arna Wendell
Boyd, Melba
Bradley, Jr., David
Brandon, Barbara
Brawley, Benjamin
Brown, Charlotte Eugenia
Brown, Claude
Brown, Frank London
Brown, Hallie Quinn
Brown, Lloyd
Brown, William Wells
Bruce, Josephine Beall Willson
Burroughs, Nannie Helen
Cabrera, Lydia
Campbell, Bebe Moore
Carmichael, Stokely
Cary, Mary Ann Shadd
Chase-Riboud, Barbara
Chesnutt, Charles Waddell
Childress, Alice
Christian, Marcus Bruce
Clarke, John Henrik
Cleage, Pearl
Cleaver, Eldridge
Cliff, Michelle
Clifton, Lucille
Cobb, Jr., Charles E.
Cobb, William Montague
Cole, Johnnetta Betsch
Colón, Jesús
Cone, James H.
Cooper, Anna Julia
Cornish, Sam
Cose, Ellis
Coston, Julia

Cotter, Jr., Joseph Seamon
Crosswaith, Frank Rudolph
Crouch, Stanley
Cruse, Harold Wright
Cullen, Countee
Davis, Angela Yvonne
Davis, Thulani
De Veaux, Alexis
Deal, Borden
Delany, Clarissa
Delany, Martin R.
Delany, Samuel R.
Dent, Tom
Douglass, Frederick
Douglass, Sarah Mapps
Dove, Rita
Draper, Sharon M.
Du Bois, W. E. B.
Dunbar, Paul Laurence
Dunbar Nelson, Alice
Dunham, Katherine
Early, Gerald
Ellison, Ralph
Emanuel, James A.
Evans, Mari
Ferguson, Lloyd Noel
Fisher, Abby
Forrest, Leon
Forten (Grimké), Charlotte L.
Forten (Purvis), Sarah (Louisa)
Fortune, T. Thomas
Franklin, John Hope
Frazier, Edward Franklin
Fuller, Jr., Charles H.
Fuller, Hoyt
Gaines, Ernest J.
Garland, Hazel B.
Garvey, Amy Jacques
Garvey, Marcus
Gates, Jr., Henry Louis
Gayle, Jr., Addison
Giddings, Paula
Giovanni, Nikki
Gladwell, Malcolm
Gomez, Jewelle
Greenlee, Sam
Griggs, Sutton E.
Grimké (Weld), Angelina (Emily)
Grimké, Angelina Weld
Grimké, Archibald Henry
Grimké, Sarah Moore
Guinier, Lani
Haley, Alex
Hammon, Jupiter
Hansberry, Lorraine
Hare, Maud Cuney
Hare, Nathan
Harper, Frances Ellen Watkins
Harrington, Oliver Wendell
Haskins, James S.
Haynes, Elizabeth Ross

Haynes, Lemuel
Heard, Nathan C.
Hemphill, Essex
Hercules, Frank
Hernton, Calvin C.
Higginbotham, Jr., A. (Aloysius) Leon
Hine, Darlene Clark
Holly, James Theodore
hooks, bell
Hopkins, Pauline
Houston, Charles
Hudson, Wade
Hunter, Kristin Eggleston
Hunter-Gault, Charlayne
Hurston, Zora Neale
Iceberg Slim
Jackson, Sr., Jesse Louis
Jackson, Rebecca Cox
Jakes, T. D.
Johnson, Amelia E.
Johnson, Charles (Richard)
Johnson, Charles (Spurgeon)
Johnson, Fenton
Jordan, June
Karenga, Maulana Ron
Kelley, William Melvin
Kenan, Randall
Killens, John Oliver
Kincaid, Jamaica
King, Jr., Martin Luther
King, Jr., Woodie
Latimer, Catherine A.
Latimer, Lewis Howard
Lawrence-Lightfoot, Sara
Lee, Spike
Lester, Julius
Lewis, David Levering
Lewis, Samella Sanders
Locke, Alain
Logan, Rayford
Lomax, Louis E.
Lorde, Audre
Lynch, John R.
Mackey, Nathaniel
Madgett, Naomi Long
Major, Clarence
Malveaux, Julianne
Marshall, Paule
Matthews, Victoria Earle
Mayfield, Julian
Mays, Benjamin Elijah
McDonald, Janet A.
McElroy, Colleen
McKay, Claude
McKissack, Pat
McPherson, James Alan
Meriwether, Louise
Merrick, Lyda Moore
Miller, E. Ethelbert
Miller, Kelly
Millican, Arthenia J. Bates

Mitchell, Loften
Moody, Anne
Moore, Opal
Mosley, Walter
Mossell, Gertrude Bustill
Motley, Willard
Moutoussamy-Ashe, Jeanne
Murphy, Beatrice M.
Murray, Albert L.
Murray, Daniel Alexander Payne
Murray, Pauli
Myers, Walter Dean
Naylor, Gloria
Neal, Larry
Nell, William C.
Nelson, Jill
Ormes, Jackie
Page, Clarence
Painter, Nell Irvin
Park, Robert E.
Parks, Sr., Gordon
Parsons, Lucy Gonzalez
Patterson, Orlando
Payne, Daniel A.
Payne, Ethel L.
Pennington, James W. C.
Perkins, Eugene
Petry, Ann
Pickens, William
Plato, Ann
Polite, Carlene Hatcher
Porter, James Amos
Poston, Ted
Poussaint, Alvin Francis
Powell, Jr., Adam Clayton
Powell, Kevin
Purvis, Sr., Robert
Quarles, Benjamin
Randall, Alice
Randolph, A. Philip
Reagon, Bernice Johnson
Reason, Charles L.
Redding, Jay Saunders
Reed, Ishmael
Ridley, Florida Ruffin
Rogers, Joel Augustus
Rowan, Carl T.
Rustin, Bayard
Rux, Carl Hancock
Salaam, Kalamu ya
Sanders, Dori
Schomburg, Arthur A.
Schuyler, George Samuel
Schuyler, Philippa Duke
Scott, Nathan A.
Senna, Carl
Senna, Danzy
Shange, Ntozake
Shepherd, Reginald
Shockley, Ann
Smith, Barbara

Smith, Jessie Carney
Smith, Lillian Eugenia
Smitherman, Geneva
Southerland, Ellease
Southern, Eileen Stanza Johnson
Spillers, Hortense J.
Steele, Claude M.
Steele, Shelby
Sterling, Dorothy
Steward, Theophilus Gould
Stewart, Maria W.
Still, William
Stone, Chuck
Stowe, Harriet Beecher
Tanner, Benjamin Tucker
Terrell, Mary Eliza Church
Thomas, Lorenzo
Thompson, Era Bell
Thurman, Wallace
Tillman, Katherine Davis Chapman
Toomer, Jean
Touré, Askia M.
Trotter, Geraldine Pindell
Trotter, James Monroe
Trotter, William Monroe
Turner, Henry McNeal
Turpin, Waters
Tyree, Omar
Tyson, Neil deGrasse
van Sertima, Ivan
Van Peebles, Melvin
Van Vechten, Carl
Vashon, George B.
Vroman, Mary Elizabeth
Walcott, Derek
Walker, Alice
Walker, Margaret
Walker, Rebecca
Walker, Wyatt Tee
Walrond, Eric
Walter, Mildred Pitts
Walton, Anthony
Ward, Douglas Turner
Ward, Samuel
Washington, Booker T.
Weaver, Robert C.
Wells-Barnett, Ida B.
Wesley, Charles Harris
Wesley, Valerie Wilson
West, Cornel
West, Dorothy
Whipper, William
White, Walter F.
Whitfield, James Monroe
Wideman, John Edgar
Wilkins, Roger Wood
Williams, Chancellor
Williams, Edward Christopher
Williams, George Washington
Williams, John A.
Williams, Patricia J.

Williams, Robert Franklin
Williams, Sherley Anne
Williams, III, Stanley Tookie
Willson, Joseph
Wilson, William Julius
Winfrey, Oprah
Woodson, Carter G.
Wright, Richard
Wright, Sarah E.
X, Marvin
Young, Al
Young, Kevin
Young, Jr., Whitney M.

Opinion
(columns, editorials, commentaries, blogs)
Abbott, Robert S.
Abu-Jamal, Mumia
Baldwin, James
Banneker, Benjamin
Baraka, Amiri
Barnes, Steven Emory
Bass, Charlotta Spears
Beasley, Delilah
Bennett, Gwendolyn B.
Bibb, Henry
Bolden, Tonya
Briggs, Cyril Valentine
Bunche, Ralph
Burroughs, Nannie Helen
Carmichael, Stokely
Cary, Mary Ann Shadd
Cayton, Jr., Horace Roscoe
Child, Lydia Maria
Childress, Alice
Cleage, Pearl
Cleaver, Eldridge
Coleman, Wanda
Colón, Jesús
Cornish, Samuel E.
Cose, Ellis
Crosswaith, Frank Rudolph
Crouch, Stanley
Crummell, Alexander
Davis, Angela Yvonne
Davis, Arthur P.
Davis, Frank Marshall
Delany, Martin R.
Douglass, Frederick
Douglass, Sarah Mapps
Du Bois, W. E. B.
Dunbar Nelson, Alice
Edelman, Marian Wright
Forten, Sr., James
Fortune, T. Thomas
Fuller, Hoyt
Garland, Hazel B.
Garnet, Henry Highland
Garvey, Amy Jacques
Garvey, Marcus
Gregory, "Dick"

Guinier, Lani
Hammon, Jupiter
Hare, Maud Cuney
Harper, Frances Ellen Watkins
Harris, Trudier
Hernton, Calvin C.
Hill, Donna
Hoagland, III, Everett H.
Hopkins, Pauline
Houston, Charles
Houston, Drusilla Dunjee
Hughes, Langston
Hunter, Kristin Eggleston
Ice-T
Jackson, Sr., Jesse Louis
Jackson, Joseph Harrison
Johnson, Georgia Douglas
Johnson, James Weldon
Jones, Edward P.
Jordan, Barbara
Jordan, June
Karenga, Maulana Ron
Kenan, Randall
Kincaid, Jamaica
King, Coretta Scott
King, Jr., Martin Luther
Lester, Julius
Lomax, Louis E.
Major, Clarence
Malveaux, Julianne
Marshall, Thurgood
Mathis, Sharon Bell
McKay, Claude
Miller, Kelly
Mosley, Walter
Motley, Willard
Murphy, Beatrice M.
Murphy, Carl
Nelson, Jill
Obama, II, Barack
Owen, Chandler
Page, Clarence
Park, Robert E.
Parsons, Lucy Gonzalez
Patterson, Raymond R.
Patterson, William
Payne, Ethel L.
Perkins, Eugene
Petry, Ann
Poston, Ted
Powell, Jr., Adam Clayton
Randolph, A. Philip
Raspberry, William
Reed, Ishmael
Ridley, John
Robeson, Eslanda
Robeson, Paul
Robinson, Randall
Rogers, Joel Augustus
Rowan, Carl T.
Ruffin, George Lewis

Ruffin, Josephine St. Pierre
Ruggles, David
Russwurm, John Brown
Rustin, Bayard
Scarborough, William Saunders
Schuyler, George Samuel
Schuyler, Philippa Duke
Senna, Carl
Smith, Barbara
Smith, Lillian Eugenia
Steele, Shelby
Stewart, Maria W.
Stone, Chuck
Tanner, Benjamin Tucker
Tarry, Ellen
Taylor, Susan L.
Thurman, Wallace
Tolson, Melvin
Trotter, Geraldine Pindell
Trotter, William Monroe
Van Vechten, Carl
Walker, David
Ward, Samuel
Washington, Booker T.
Wells-Barnett, Ida B.
Welsing, Frances Cress
West, Cornel
West, Dorothy
Whipper, William
White, Walter F.
Wilkins, Roger Wood
Wilkins, Roy
Williams, George Washington
Williams, Patricia J.
Williams, Robert Franklin
Woodson, Carter G.
Wright, Charles S.
Wright, Richard
X, Malcolm
Young, Jr., Whitney M.

Organizations
(organizations, clubs, collectives)
Affrilachian Poets
American Negro Academy
Black Opals
Cave Canem
Combahee River Collective (CRC)
Free Southern Theater (FST)
Harlem Writers Guild
National Association of Black
    Journalists
OBAC, Organization of Black
    American Culture
Quill Club
Umbra Workshop (Society of Umbra)

Other Writings
(translations, legal briefs, legislation, petitions, letters, ghostwriting)
Allen, Samuel W.

Banneker, Benjamin
Cassells, Cyrus
Chisholm, Shirley
Dunbar Nelson, Alice
Houston, Charles
King, Coretta Scott
Lee, Barbara
Matthews, Victoria Earle
Page, Clarence
Park, Robert E.
Purvis, Sr., Robert
Scarborough, William Sanders
Thomas, Lorenzo
Waniek, Marilyn Nelson
Whipper, William

Periodicals

African American Review (also *Negro American Literature Forum, Black American Literature Forum*)
Alexander's Magazine
Amsterdam News
Antislavery periodicals, 1819-1829
Antislavery periodicals, 1830-1839
Antislavery periodicals, 1840-1849
Antislavery periodicals, 1850-1865
Baltimore Afro-American
Black Opals
Black Scholar
Brownies' Book
Callaloo
Chicago Defender and *Chicago Daily Defender*
Colored American Magazine
Crisis
Ebony
Fire!!
Freedom's Journal
Freedomways: A Quarterly Review of the Negro Freedom Movement
Harlem Renaissance, literary and scholarly journals of the "New Negro" era
Journals and magazines, literary
Messenger, The
Negro Digest
Negro World
New York Age
Newspapers
Nkombo
NOMMO
North Star, Frederick Douglass' Paper, and *Douglass Monthly*
Obsidian: Black Literature in Review, Obsidian II: Black Literature in Review, and *Obsidian III: Literature in the African Diaspora, Obsidian: Literature in the African Diaspora*
Opportunity: A Journal of Negro Life
Phylon
Pittsburgh Courier and *New Pittsburgh Courier*

Sage: A Scholarly Journal on Black Women
Saturday Evening Quill (see Quill Club)
Survey Graphic
Umbra
Voice of the Negro, The
Woman's Era, The

Personal Narrative
(autobiography, memoir, diary, journal, personal letters; see also Slave Narrative)
Allen, Richard
Anderson, Marian
Andrews, Raymond
Angelou, Maya
Ashe, Arthur
Banneker, Benjamin
Bass, Charlotta Spears
Braithwaite, William Stanley Beaumont
Brooks, Gwendolyn
Brown, Cecil
Brown, Claude
Brown, Elaine
Brown, William Wells
Bruce, Henry Clay
Bruce, Sr., Roscoe Conkling
Bryan, Ashley F.
Bunche, Ralph
Campbell, Bebe Moore
Chisholm, Shirley
Clark, Septima Poinsette
Cleaver, Eldridge
Cliff, Michelle
Clifton, Lucille
Cobb, Jr., Charles E.
Cone, James H.
Cornish, Sam
Corrothers, James D.
Cosby, Bill
Damas, Léon-Gontran
Danticat, Edwidge
Davis, Angela Yvonne
Davis, Frank Marshall
Davis, Ossie
Davis, Thulani
Dee, Ruby
Delany, "Bessie"
Delany, Samuel R.
Delany, Sarah "Sadie"
Dent, Tom
Derricotte, Toi
Douglass, Frederick
Du Bois, W. E. B.
Due, Tananarive
Dunbar Nelson, Alice
Dunham, Katherine
Early, Gerald
Edelman, Marian Wright
Evers-Williams, Myrlie
Fax, Elton C.
Ford, Nick Aaron

Forten (Grimké), Charlotte L.
Franklin, J. E.
Gates, Jr., Henry Louis
Gayle, Jr., Addison
Goldberg, Whoopi
Golden, Marita
Green, J. D.
Greenfield, Eloise
Gregory, "Dick"
Haley, Alex
Hammon, Briton
Handy, W. C.
Harris, E. Lynn
Harris, Joel Chandler
Harris, Trudier
Haskins, James S.
Henson, Matthew Alexander
Hill, Anita Faye
Himes, Chester
Holiday, Billie
Holly, James Theodore
hooks, bell
Hughes, Langston
Hunter, Latoya
Hunter-Gault, Charlayne
Hurston, Zora Neale
Iceberg Slim
Jackson, George Lester
Jackson, Sr., Jesse Louis
Jackson, Mahalia
Jackson, Mattie J.
Jackson, Rebecca Cox
Johnson, James Weldon
Johnson, John H.
Johnson, Kathryn Magnolia
Johnson, William
Jordan, Barbara
Keckley, Elizabeth Hobbs
Kenan, Randall
Kincaid, Jamaica
King, "B. B."
King, Coretta Scott
Ladner, Joyce A.
Langston, John Mercer
Latifah, Queen
Lee, Andrea
Lee, Barbara
Lee, Jarena
Lee, Spike
Lester, Julius
Lorde, Audre
Love, Nat
Love, Rose Leary
Lynch, John R.
Madgett, Naomi Long
Major, Clarence
Marrant, John
Mays, Benjamin Elijah
McDonald, Janet A.
McElroy, Colleen
McPherson, James Alan

Mebane, Mary E.
Miller, E. Ethelbert
Moody, Anne
Moss, Thylias
Motley, Willard
Murray, Pauli
Naylor, Gloria
Nelson, Jill
Northup, Solomon
Obama, II, Barack
Parks, Sr., Gordon
Patterson, William
Payne, Daniel A.
Paynter, John H.
Pickens, William
Poston, Ted
Powell, Kevin
Prince, Nancy Gardner
Pryor, Richard
Rahman, Aishah
Randall, Dudley
Reagon, Bernice Johnson
Rhodes, Jewell Parker
Ringgold, Faith
Robeson, Eslanda
Robeson, Paul
Robinson, Randall
Rock, Chris
Rowan, Carl T.
Sanders, Dori
Schuyler, George Samuel
Schuyler, Philippa Duke
Senna, Danzy
Shakur, Assata Olugbala
Shepherd, Reginald
Smith, Amanda Berry
Southerland, Ellease
Sterling, Dorothy
Tarry, Ellen
Taylor, Susan L.
Taylor, Susie Baker King
Terrell, Mary Eliza Church
Thomas, Piri
Thompson, Era Bell
Thurman, Howard
Turner, Nat
Tyson, Neil deGrasse
Van Peebles, Melvin
Van Vechten, Carl
Walker, Alice
Walker, Margaret
Walker, Rebecca
Walton, Anthony
Washington, Booker T.
Waters, Ethel
Wells-Barnett, Ida B.
Whipper, Frances A. Rollin
White, Walter F.
Wideman, John Edgar
Wilkins, Roger Wood
Wilkins, Roy

Williams, John A.
Williams, Patricia J.
Williams, Robert Franklin
Williams, III, Stanley Tookie
Winfrey, Oprah
Woodson, Jacqueline
Wright, Richard
X, Malcolm
X, Marvin
Young, Al

Play, Screenplay and Script
*(television/film, fiction/nonfiction,
documentary)*
Anderson, Regina M.
Angelou, Maya
Atkins, Russell
Attaway, William
Aubert, Alvin
Baisden, Michael
Baldwin, James
Bambara, Toni Cade
Baraka, Amiri
Barnes, Steven Emory
Bonner, Marita
Bourne, St. Claire
Brathwaite, Edward Kamau
Brown, Cecil
Brown, William Wells
Bullins, Ed
Burroughs, Nannie Helen
Campbell, Bebe Moore
Carroll, Vinnette
Childress, Alice
Cleage, Pearl
Clifton, Lucille
Coleman, Wanda
Collier, Eugenia (Williams)
Collins, Kathleen
Cooper, J. California
Cotter, Jr., Joseph Seamon
Cotter, Sr., Joseph Seamon
Cullen, Countee
Danticat, Edwidge
Dash, Julie
Davis, Ossie
De Veaux, Alexis
Dee, Ruby
Demby, William
Dent, Tom
Dodson, Owen
Dove, Rita
Du Bois, Shirley Graham
Elder, III, Lonne
Evans, Mari
Fields, Julia
Fishburne, III, Laurence
Franklin, J. E.
Fuller, Jr., Charles H.
Gerima, Haile
Gibson, P. J.

Gordone, Charles
Greaves, "Bill"
Greenlee, Sam
Grimké, Angelina Weld
Guy, Rosa Cuthbert
Hansberry, Lorraine
Hare, Maud Cuney
Hernton, Calvin S.
Heyward, DuBose
Holman, M. (Moses) Carl
Hopkins, Pauline
Hudson, Wade
Hughes, Langston
Hunter, Kristin Eggleston
Jackson, Angela
Jackson, Elaine
Johnson, Charles (Richard)
Johnson, Fenton
Johnson, Georgia Douglas
Jones, Gayl
Jones, Sarah
Jones-Meadows, Karen
Jordan, June
Kennedy, Adrienne
Killens, John Oliver
King, Jr., Woodie
Lee, Spike
Lewis, Samella Sanders
Matheus, John F.
Mayfield, Julian
McElroy, Colleen
McKissack, Pat
Mebane, Mary E.
Micheaux, Oscar
Miller, May
Milner, Ronald
Mitchell, Loften
Moss, Thylias
Naylor, Gloria
Neal, Larry
Nelson, Jill
Nugent, Richard Bruce
Parks, Sr., Gordon
Parks, Suzan-Lori
Perkins, Eugene
Peterson, Louis Stamford
Pietri, Pedro Juan
Powell, Kevin
Pryor, Richard
Rahman, Aishah
Randall, Alice
Redmond, Eugene
Reed, Ishmael
Rhodes, Jewell Parker
Richards, Beah
Richardson, Willis
Ridley, John
Riggs, Marlon Troy
Rivers, Conrad Kent
Rock, Chris
Rush, Gertrude E.

Rux, Carl Hancock
Salaam, Kalamu ya
Séjour, Victor
Shange, Ntozake
Shine, Ted
Simmons, Herbert Alfred
Smith, Anna Deveare
Spence, Eulalie
Thomas, Joyce Carol
Thomas, Piri
Thurman, Wallace
Tillman, Katherine Davis Chapman
Tolson, Melvin
Toomer, Jean
Touré, Askia M.
Turpin, Waters
Tyree, Omar
Van Peebles, Melvin
Vroman, Mary Elizabeth
Walcott, Derek
Ward, Douglas Turner
Ward, Theodore
Weaver, Afaa M.
Wesley, Richard (Errol) Wesley
Wideman, John Edgar
Wilkins, Roger Wood
Williams, Edward Christopher
Williams, John A.
Williams, Samm-Art
Williams, Sherley Anne
Williams, Jr., Spencer
Wilson, August
Wright, Jay
X, Marvin
Young, Al
Zu-Bolton, III, Ahmos

Poetry
Ai (Florence Ai Ogawa)
Alexander, Elizabeth
Allen, Samuel W.
Amini, Johari
Angelou, Maya
Atkins, Russell
Aubert, Alvin
Baker, Jr., Houston A.
Baldwin, James
Banneker, Benjamin
Baraka, Amiri
Barrax, Gerald W.
Bell, James Madison
Bennett, Gwendolyn B.
Bontemps, Arna Wendell
Boyd, Melba
Braithwaite, William Stanley Beaumont
Brathwaite, Edward Kamau
Brawley, Benjamin
Braxton, Joanne M.
Brooks, Gwendolyn
Brown, Linda Beatrice
Brown, Sterling Allen

Bullins, Ed
Burroughs, Margaret Taylor
Campbell, James Edwin
Cassells, Cyrus
Chase-Riboud, Barbara
Christian, Marcus Bruce
Cleage, Pearl
Cliff, Michelle
Clifton, Lucille
Cobb, Jr., Charles E.
Coleman, Wanda
Cornish, Sam
Corrothers, James D.
Cortez, Jayne
Cotter, Jr., Joseph Seamon
Cotter, Sr., Joseph Seamon
Crayton, Pearl
Cullen, Countee
Damas, Léon-Gontran
Dandridge, Raymond G.
Danner, Margaret
Dave, the Potter (aka David Drake)
Davis, Frank Marshall
Davis, Thulani
de Burgos, Julia
De Veaux, Alexis
Dee, Ruby
Delany, Clarissa
Dent, Tom
Derricotte, Toi
Dodson, Owen
Dove, Rita
Draper, Sharon M.
Dumas, Henry L.
Dunbar, Paul Laurence
Dunbar Nelson, Alice
Eady, Cornelius
Emanuel, James A.
Evans, Mari
Fabio, Sarah
Fields, Julia
Ford, Nick Aaron
Forten (Grimké), Charlotte L.
Forten (Purvis), Sarah (Louisa)
Fortune, T. Thomas
Fuller, Jr., Charles H.
Garvey, Marcus
Gayle, Jr., Addison
Gibson, P. J.
Giovanni, Nikki
Golden, Marita
Gomez, Jewelle
Greenfield, Eloise
Greenlee, Sam
Grimké, Angelina Weld
Grooms, Anthony
Hammon, Jupiter
Hansberry, Lorraine
Harper, Frances Ellen Watkins
Harper, Michael S.
Hayden, Robert

Hemphill, Essex
Hernton, Calvin C.
Heyward, DuBose
Hoagland, III, Everett H.
Holman, M. (Moses) Carl
hooks, bell
Horton, George Moses
Hughes, Langston
Hull, Akasha (née Gloria Theresa Thompson)
Ice-T
Iceberg Slim
Jackson, Angela
Jackson, Mae
Jeffers, Lance
Joans, Ted
Johnson, Amelia E.
Johnson, Angela
Johnson, Fenton
Johnson, Georgia Douglas
Johnson, Helene
Johnson, James Weldon
Jones, Gayl
Jones, Sarah
Jordan, June
Kaufman, "Bob"
Keene, Jr., John R.
Knight, Etheridge
Komunyakaa, Yusef
Kweli, Talib
Lane, Pinkie
Lester, Julius
Lorde, Audre
Love, Rose Leary
Mackey, Nathaniel
Madgett, Naomi Long
Madhubuti, Haki
Major, Clarence
Mathis, Sharon Bell
McElroy, Colleen
McGirt, James E.
McKay, Claude
Miller, E. Ethelbert
Miller, Kelly
Miller, May
Millican, Arthenia J. Bates
Moore, Opal
Moss, Thylias
Mossell, Gertrude Bustill
Mullen, Harryette
Murphy, Beatrice M.
Murray, Albert L.
Murray, Pauli
Myers, Walter Dean
Neal, Larry
Newsome, Effie Lee
Nugent, Richard Bruce
Osbey, Brenda Marie
Parker, Pat
Patterson, Raymond R.
Payne, Daniel A.

Perkins, Eugene
Petry, Ann
Phillips, Carl
Pietri, Pedro Juan
Plato, Ann
Plumpp, Sterling
Powell, Kevin
Randall, Dudley
Ray, Henrietta Cordelia
Reason, Charles L.
Redmond, Eugene
Reed, Ishmael
Richards, Beah
Rivers, Conrad Kent
Rodgers, Carolyn
Rux, Carl Hancock
Salaam, Kalamu ya
Sanchez, Sonia
Sapphire
Scott-Heron, Gil
Séjour, Victor
Shange, Ntozake
Shepherd, Reginald
Simmons, Herbert Alfred
Smith, Effie Waller
Southerland, Ellease
Spencer, "Anne"
Stewart, Maria W.
Stowe, Harriet Beecher
Sundiata, Sekou
Tanner, Benjamin Tucker
Tate, Eleanora
Terry, Lucy
Thomas, Joyce Carol
Thomas, Lorenzo
Thurman, Wallace
Tillman, Katherine Davis Chapman
Tolson, Melvin
Toomer, Jean
Touré, Askia M.
Trethewey, Natasha
Troupe, Quincy
Turner, Darwin T.
van Sertima, Ivan
Vashon, George B.
Walcott, Derek
Walker, Alice
Walker, Margaret
Walton, Anthony
Waniek, Marilyn Nelson
Weatherly, Tom
Weaver, Afaa M.
Wheatley, Phillis
White, Paulette Childress
Whitfield, James Monroe
Whitman, Albery Allson
Wilkinson, Brenda
Williams, Edward Christopher
Williams, John A.
Williams, Sherley Anne
Wilson, August

Wright, Jay
Wright, Richard
Wright, Sarah E.
X, Marvin
Yerby, Frank G.
Young, Al
Young, Kevin
Zu-Bolton, III, Ahmos

Publishers
(books, periodicals, self-publisher, founder)
Abbott, Robert S.
Amini, Johari
Ansa, Tina McElroy
Baisden, Michael
Barber, Jesse Max
Bass, Charlotte Spears
Beasley, Delilah
Beckham, Barry
Bibb, Henry
Braithwaite, William Stanley Beaumont
Brathwaite, Edward Kamau
Briggs, Cyril Valentine
Broadside Press
Bullins, Ed
Cary, Mary Ann Shadd
Child, Lydia Maria
Christian, Marcus Bruce
Cornish, Sam
Cornish, Samuel E.
Cortez, Jayne
Coston, Julia Ringwood
Delany, Martin R.
Dent, Tom
Douglass, Frederick
Du Bois, Shirley Graham
Dunbar, Paul Laurence
Dunbar Nelson, Alice
Fortune, T. Thomas
Garland, Hazel B.
Garnet, Henry Highland
Garvey, Amy Jacques
Garvey, Marcus
Giddings, Paula
Griggs, Sutton E.
Handy, W. C.
Hare, Nathan
Harris, E. Lynn
Harris, Joel Chandler
Hemphill, Essex
Hernton, Calvin C.
Hopkins, Pauline
Houston, Drusilla Dunjee
Howard University Press
Hudson, Cheryl (Willis)
Hudson, Wade
Johnson, Fenton
Johnson, Georgia Douglas
Johnson, James Weldon
Johnson, John H.
Johnson Publishing Company

Just Us Books
Kitchen Table: Women of Color Press
Lewis, Samella Sanders
Lotus Press
Madgett, Naomi Long
Madhubuti, Haki
Major, Clarence
Maynard, Nancy Hicks
Maynard, Robert
McGirt, James E.
Merrick, Lyda Moore
Micheaux, Oscar
Motley, Willard
Murphy, Carl
Neal, Larry
Nell, William C.
Nugent, Richard Bruce
Owen, Chandler
Park, Robert E.
Parker, Pat
Parsons, Lucy Gonzalez
Powell, Jr., Adam Clayton
Publishers
Randall, Dudley
Randolph, A. Philip
Redbone Press
Redmond, Eugene
Reed, Ishmael
Robeson, Paul
Rodgers, Carolyn
Rogers, Joel Augustus
Ruffin, Josephine St. Pierre
Ruggles, David
Russwurm, John Brown
Senna, Carl
Smith, Amanda Berry
Smith, Barbara
Smith, Lillian Eugenia
Southerland, Ellease
Southern, Eileen Stanza Johnson
Spingarn, Joel Elias
Tanner, Benjamin Tucker
Third World Press
Thurman, Wallace
Trotter, Geraldine Pindell
Trotter, William Monroe
Turner, Henry McNeal
Tyree, Omar
van Sertima, Ivan
Vann, Robert Lee
Walcott, Derek
Walker, Alice
Walker, David
Walrond, Eric
Weaver, Afaa M.
Wells-Barnett, Ida B.
West, Dorothy
Wilkins, Roger Wood
Williams, George Washington
Williams, Jr., Peter
Williams, Robert Franklin

Winfrey, Oprah
Woodson, Carter G.
X, Malcolm
X, Marvin

Satire, Parody, and other Humor
Cosby, Bill
Goldberg, Whoopi
Gregory, "Dick"
Harrington, Oliver Wendell
Reed, Ishmael
Rock, Chris
Schuyler, George Samuel

Scholarly Works
Asante, Molefi Kete
Baker, Augusta
Beasley, Delilah
Berry, Mary Frances
Bogle, Donald
Bontemps, Arna Wendell
Brawley, Benjamin
Brown, William Wells
Cabrera, Lydia
Cayton, Jr., Horace Roscoe
Christian, Barbara
Clark, Kenneth B.
Clark, Mamie
Clarke, John Henrik
Cobb, Jewell Plummer
Cobb, William Montague
Cole, Johnnetta Betsch
Davis, Arthur P.
Delaney, Sara ("Sadie") Marie
Delany, Martin R.
Dent, Tom
Drake, St. Clair
Driskell, David
Du Bois, W. E. B.
Dunham, Katherine
Early, Gerald
Franklin, John Hope
Frazier, Edward Franklin
French, William P.
Gates, Jr., Henry Louis
Giddings, Paula
Granville, Evelyn Boyd
Grimké, Archibald Henry
Guinier, Lani
Hansberry, William Leo
Hare, Maud Cuney
Hare, Nathan
Harris, Trudier
Haynes, Elizabeth Ross
Haynes, Lemuel
Hernton, Calvin C.
Herron, Carolivia
Higginbotham, Evelyn (Titania) (née
    Brooks)
Hill, Anita Faye
Hine, Darlene Clark

hooks, bell
Houston, Drusilla Dunjee
Hull, Akasha (née Gloria Theresa
    Thompson)
Hurston, Zora Neale
Hutson, Jean Blackwell
Johnson, Charles (Spurgeon)
Josey, E. J.
Just, Ernest Everett
Karenga, Maulana Ron
Ladner, Joyce A.
Latimer, Catherine A.
Latimer, Lewis Howard
Lawrence-Lightfoot, Sara
Lewis, David Levering
Lewis, Samella Sanders
Locke, Alain
Logan, Rayford
Malveaux, Julianne
McKay, Nellie Yvonne
Millican, Arthenia J. Bates
Mitchell, Loften
Murray, Pauli
Nell, William C.
Painter, Nell Irvin
Park, Robert E.
Patterson, Orlando
Payne, Daniel A.
Porter, James Amos
Porter Wesley, Dorothy Burnett
Poussaint, Alvin Francis
Quarles, Benjamin
Rampersad, Arnold
Redding, Jay Saunders
Rollins, Charlemae Hill
Ross-Barnett, Marguerite
Scarborough, William Sanders
Shine, Ted
Shockley, Ann
Smith, Barbara
Smith, Jessie Carney
Smitherman, Geneva
Southern, Eileen Stanza Johnson
Steele, Claude M.
Steward, Theophilus Gould
Tanner, Benjamin Tucker
Thurman, Howard
Turner, Lorenzo Dow
van Sertima, Ivan
Weaver, Robert C.
Wesley, Charles Harris
West, Cornel
Wilkins, Roger Wood
Williams, George Washington
Williams, Patricia J.
Williams, Sherley Anne
Wilson, William Julius
Woodson, Carter G.

Slave Narrative
(see also *Personal Narrative*)

Bayley, Solomon
Bibb, Henry
Brown, William Wells
Craft, William
Douglass, Frederick
Equiano, Olaudah
Green, J. D.
Hammon, Briton
Jackson, Mattie J.
Jacobs, Harriet Ann
Johnson, William
Keckley, Elizabeth Hobbs
Love, Nat
Northup, Solomon
Pennington, James W. C.
Prince, Mary
Roper, Moses
Slave narratives
Smith, Venture
Truth, Sojourner
Ward, Samuel
Washington, Booker T.

Songs, Lyrics, Libretti
Allen, Richard
Attaway, William
Brown, Elaine
Chapman, Tracy
Dandridge, Raymond G.
Davis, Thulani
Diddley, "Bo"
Domino, Antoine ("Fats")
Dorsey, Thomas
Du Bois, Shirley Graham
Dunbar, Paul Laurence
Edmonds, Kenneth ("Babyface")
Forrest, Leon
Handy, W. C.
Holiday, Billie
Hunter, Alberta
Ice-T
Johnson, James Weldon
Jordan, June
King, "B.B."
Latifah, Queen
Mayfield, Curtis
McGhee, "Brownie"
McGirt, James E.
Morrison, Toni
Pickett, Wilson
Rahman, Aishah
Rainey, Gertrude ("Ma")
Randall, Alice
Razaf, Andy
Reagon, Bernice Johnson
Redding, Otis
Reed, Ishmael
Rhodes, Jewell Parker
Rush, Gertrude E.
Scott-Heron, Gil
Shakur, Tupac

Sissle, Noble
Spivey, Victoria Regina
Tolson, Melvin
Tubman, Harriet
Turner, Henry McNeal
Turpin, Waters
Van Peebles, Melvin
Williams, John A.
Williams, Jr., Peter
Wonder, Stevie

Spoken Word
(oratory, storytelling, other performances,
media host)
Allen, Richard
Baker, Augusta
Brown, Hallie Quinn
Bruce, Blanche K.
Bruce, Sr., Roscoe Conkling
Bunche, Ralph
Campbell, James Edwin
Carmichael, Stokely
Cary, Mary Ann Shadd
Cooper, Anna Julia
Cosby, Bill
Crummell, Alexander
Davis, Angela Yvonne
Davis, Thulani
Edelman, Marian Wright
Ellison, Ralph (Waldo)
Equiano, Olaudah
Evans, Mari
Fortune, T. Thomas
Garnet, Henry Highland
Garvey, Marcus
Goldberg, Whoopi
Gregory, "Dick"
Griggs, Sutton E.
Grimké (Weld), Angelina (Emily)
Grimké, Francis J.
Grimké, Sarah Moore
Hammon, Jupiter
Harper, Frances Ellen Watkins
Harris, E. Lynn
Haynes, Lemuel
Heard, Nathan C.
Hemphill, Essex
Holly, James Theodore
Jackson, Sr., Jesse Louis
Jakes, T. D.
Johnson, Georgia Douglas
Jones, Sarah
Jordan, Barbara
Kennedy, Adrienne
King, Jr., Martin Luther
Kweli, Talib
Langston, John Mercer
Lee, Barbara
Lee, Jarena
Lynch, John R.
Matthews, Victoria Earle

Mays, Benjamin Elijah
Murray, Albert L.
Nell, William C.
Northup, Solomon
Obama, II, Barack
Owen, Chandler
Parker, Pat
Parsons, Lucy Gonzalez
Payne, Daniel A.
Pennington, James W. C.
Powell, Jr., Adam Clayton
Powell, Sr., Adam Clayton
Powell, Kevin
Pryor, Richard
Purvis, Sr., Robert
Redmond, Eugene
Reed, Ishmael
Remond, Sarah Parker
Ridley, John
Rock, Chris
Rodgers, Carolyn
Ruggles, David
Rustin, Bayard
Rux, Carl Hancock
Sapphire
Scott-Heron, Gil
Smith, Anna Deveare
Stewart, Maria W.
Stone, Chuck
Sundiata, Sekou
Terrell, Mary Eliza Church
Thomas, Piri
Torrence, Jackie
Troupe, Quincy
Truth, Sojourner
Tubman, Harriet
Turner, Henry McNeal
Tyree, Omar
Tyson, Neil deGrasse
Washington, Booker T.
Whipper, William
Wilkins, Roy
Williams, George Washington
Williams, Patricia J.
Williams, Jr., Peter
Winfrey, Oprah
Wright, Richard
X, Malcolm
Yarbrough, Camille

Themes
African-American Vernacular English
Anthologies of African-American
    literature
Anthologies of African-American
    literature, from literary journals
Anthologies of African-American
    literature, regional of
    African-American literature

Anthologies of African-American
    literature, special topics and
    audiences
Anthologies of African-American
    literature, specific genres, drama and
    plays
Anthologies of African-American
    literature, specific genres, fiction
Anthologies of African-American
    literature, specific genres, nonfiction
Anthologies of African-American
    literature, specific genres, poetry,
    verse, and song
Anthologies of African-American
    literature, writers from 1619 through
    1865
Anthologies of African-American
    literature, writers from 1920 to the
    early 1940s
Anthologies of African-American
    literature, written by and for gay or
    heterosexual men
Anthologies of African-American
    literature, written by and for
    heterosexual or lesbian women
Anthologies of African-American
    literature, written by and for
    juveniles
Antislavery periodicals, 1819-1829
Antislavery periodicals, 1830-1839
Antislavery periodicals, 1840-1849
Antislavery periodicals, 1850-1865
Black Aesthetic
Black Arts Movement
Black Power
Folktales
Harlem Renaissance
Harlem Renaissance, literary and
    scholarly journals of the "New
    Negro" era
Oral tradition
Organizations, clubs, and collectives
Proverbs
Publishers
Slave narratives
Spirituals
Trickster tales

Appendix E: Writers By Occupation

Abolitionist
Child, Lydia Maria
Cornish, Samuel E.
Equiano, Olaudah
Garnet, Henry Highland
Langston, John Mercer
Northup, Solomon
Pennington, James W. C.
Remond, Sarah
Ruggles, David
Still, William
Truth, Sojourner
Tubman, Harriet
Walker, David
Ward, Samuel
Webb, Frank J.

Activist
Bass, Charlotta Amanda
Bell, James Madison
Brown, Elaine
Brown, Frank London
Carmichael, Stokely
Chisholm, Shirley
Clark, Septima
Cobb, Jr., Charles E.
Cone, James H.
Cornish, Samuel E.
Crosswaith, Frank Rudolph
Davis, Angela
Dee, Ruby
Franklin, J. E.
Gregory, "Dick"
Harper, Frances Ellen Watkins
Hemphill, Essex
Holman, M. Carl
Jackson, Mae
Jackson, Sr., Jesse
Jordan, June
Karenga, Maulana Ron
Kweli, Talib
Lee, Barbara
Matthews, Victoria
Moody, Anne
Murray, "Pauli"
Neely, Barbara
Patterson, William
Pennington, James W. C.
Polite, Carlene
Randall, Alice
Randolph, A. Philip
Reason, Charles L.
Riggs, Marlon Troy

Ruffin Ridley, Florida
Ruffin, George Lewis
Ruffin, Josephine St. Pierre
Stewart, Maria W.
Trotter, Geraldine
Walker, Alice
Walker, Rebecca
Wilkins, Roy
Young, Jr., Whitney M.

Actor
Amini, Johari
Angelou, Maya
Carroll, Vinnette
Cassells, Cyrus
Childress, Alice
Cosby, Jr., Bill
Davis, Ossie
Dee, Ruby
Fishburne, III, Laurence
Goldberg, Whoopi
Gordone, Charles
Greaves, "Bill"
Ice-T
Jackson, Elaine
Jones, Sarah
King, Jr., Woodie
Latifah, Queen
Peterson, Louis
Pryor, Richard
Redmond, Eugene
Richards, Beah
Rock, Chris
Spence, Eulalie
Taylor, Susan L.
Van Peebles, Melvin
Ward, Douglas Turner
Williams, Jr., Spencer
Williams, Samm-Art

Administrator
Cobb, Jewell
Ladner, Joyce A.
Langston, John Mercer
Malveaux, Julianne
Mays, Benjamin Elijah
Ross-Barnett, Marguerite
Scarborough, William Sanders
Simmons, William J.
Vashon, George B.
Wesley, Charles Harris

Advertising Copywriter
Demby, William
Hunter, Kristin

Airman
Stone, Chuck

Amateur Engineer
Banneker, Benjamin

Archivist
Murphy, Beatrice M.
Shockley, Ann

Art Curator
Driskell, David Clyde

Artist
Bennett, Gwendolyn B.
Bryan, Ashley F.
Burroughs, Margaret
Chase-Riboud, Barbara
Coleman, Wanda
Cooper, J. California
Cortez, Jayne
Davis, Angela
Davis, Thulani
De Veaux, Alexis
Fabio, Sarah
Feelings, Tom
Hemphill, Essex
Jones, Sarah
Lewis, Samella Sanders
McElroy, Colleen
McGruder, Aaron
Nugent, Richard
Ormes, "Jackie"
Parks, Sr., Gordon
Porter, James Amos
Ringgold, Faith
Rux, Carl Hancock
Sapphire
Steptoe, John

Artistic Director
Channer, Colin
Cleage, Pearl

Assistant Editor
Woodson, Jacqueline

Astronomer
Banneker, Benjamin

Attorney
Allen, Samuel W.
Chesnutt, Charles Waddell
Colter, Cyrus
Edelman, Marian Wright
Houston, Charles
Johnson, James Weldon
Jordan, Barbara
Langston, John Mercer
Lynch, John R.
Marshall, Thurgood
McDonald, Janet A.
Murray, "Pauli"
Patterson, William
Ruffin, George Lewis
Rush, Gertrude E.
Vann, Robert Lee
Vashon, George B.
Williams, George Washington
Williams, Patricia J.

Auto Plant Worker
Curtis, Christopher Paul

Bibliophile
Schomburg, Arthur A.
Spingarn, Arthur B.

Bookseller
Cornish, Sam
Johnson, Kathryn Magnolia
Ruggles, David

Bookstore Owner
Kweli, Talib
Zu-Bolton, III, Ahmos

Business Executive
Gomez, Jewelle
Lee, Spike
Lynch, John R.
Malveaux, Julianne
Obama, II, Barack
Taylor, Susan L.
Young, Jr., Whitney M.

Business Owner
Christian, Marcus Bruce
Herron, Carolivia
King, B. B.
Latifah, Queen
Lee, Spike
Rainey, Gertrude "Ma"
Trotter, Monroe

Cartoonist
Fax, Elton C.

Cellular Zoologist
Just, Ernest Everett

Chemist
Ferguson, Lloyd Noel

Chiropractor
Amini, Johari

Choreographer
Dunham, Katherine

Civil Libertarian
Josey, E. J.

Civil Servant
Berry, Mary Frances
Bruce, Henry Clay
Colter, Cyrus
Drake, St. Clair
Hill, Anita Faye
Johnson, Georgia Douglas
Langston, John Mercer
Logan, Rayford W.
Lynch, John R.
Murray, "Pauli"
Paynter, John H.
Trotter, James Monroe

Civil-Rights Activist
Bell, James Madison
Brown, Frank London
Cobb, Jr., Charles E.
Cornish, Samuel E.
Gregory, "Dick"
Riggs, Marlon Troy
Walker, Alice
Young, Jr., Whitney M.

Cleric
Dyson, Michael Eric
Garnet, Henry Highland
Holly, James Theodore
Jakes, T. D.
Murray, "Pauli"
Pennington, James W. C.
Powell, Jr., Adam Clayton
Powell, Sr., Adam Clayton
Steward, Theophilus Gould
Tanner, Benjamin Tucker
Thurman, Howard
Turner, Henry McNeal
Wesley, Charles Harris
Williams, George Washington

Clinical Psychologist
Hare, Nathan

Clubwoman
Bruce, Josephine Beall

Co-owner, Newspaper
Wells-Barnett, Ida B.

Cofounder, Library
Whipper, William

Cofounder, Newspaper
Cary, Mary Ann

Collaborator
Bennett, Jr., Lerone
Dent, Tom

College Administrator
Cobb, Jewell

College President
Cole, Johnnetta

Colonizationist
Holly, James Theodore

Columnist
Beasley, Delilah
Bolden, Tonya
Harper, Frances Ellen Watkins
Hunter, Kristin
Jones, Edward P.
Murphy, Beatrice M.
Newsome, Effie
Petry, Ann
Ruffin, Josephine St. Pierre
Shockley, Ann
Stone, Chuck
White, Walter F.
Wright, Charles S.

Commentator, Radio
Campbell, Bebe

Construction Worker
Bruce, Henry Clay

Consultant
Childress, Alice
Clark, Kenneth B.
Poussaint, Alvin Francis
Smitherman, Geneva

Convict
Garvey, Jr., Marcus
Goines, Donald
Iceberg Slim
Williams, III, Stanley Tookie

Cosmetologist
Taylor, Susan L.

Cultural Activist
Dent, Tom
Karenga, Maulana Ron
Randall, Alice

Curator
Burroughs, Margaret
Driskell, David Clyde
Lewis, Samella Sanders
Porter Wesley, Dorothy Louise
Schomburg, Arthur A.

Dancer
Dunham, Katherine
Greaves, "Bill"

Dentist
Delany, Annie Elizabeth
Willson, Joseph

Diplomat
Bunche, Ralph
Johnson, James Weldon

Director
Angelou, Maya
Bullins, Ed
Carroll, Vinnette
Channer, Colin
Childress, Alice
Cleage, Pearl
Collins, Kathleen
Dash, Julie
Davis, Ossie
Elder, III, Lonne
Fishburne, III, Laurence
Fuller, Jr., Charles H.
Gibson, P. J.
Gordone, Charles
Greaves, "Bill"
King, Jr., Woodie
Lee, Spike
Milner, Ronald
Parker, Pat
Richardson, Willis
Shange, Ntozake
Smith, Anna Deveare
Van Peebles, Melvin
Williams, Jr., Spencer
X, Marvin

Director, Film
Greaves, "Bill"

Director, Health-Care Center
Parker, Pat

Director, Theater
Bullins, Ed
Gibson, P. J.
Milner, Ronald
Richardson, Willis
X, Marvin

Domestic Servant
Stewart, Maria W.
Taylor, Susie
Truth, Sojourner
Wheatley, Phillis
Wilson, Harriet E.

Drama Therapist
Woodson, Jacqueline

Dramaturge
Jones-Meadows, Karen

Economist
Delany, Sarah "Sadie"

Malveaux, Julianne

Editor
Abbott, Robert S.
Amini, Johari
Ansa, Tina McElroy
Asante, Molefi Kete
Baker, Jr., Houston A.
Bass, Charlotta Amanda
Bennett, Gwendolyn B.
Bennett, Jr., Lerone
Bibb, Henry
Bolden, Tonya
Braithwaite, William Stanley Beaumont
Brown, Lloyd
Bruce, Sr., Roscoe Conkling
Bullins, Ed
Channer, Colin
Clarke, John Henrik
Cleage, Pearl
Cliff, Michelle
Cobb, William Montague
Coleman, Wanda
Cornish, Sam
De Veaux, Alexis
Early, Gerald
Fauset, Jessie Redmon
Fortune, T. Thomas
Garland, Hazel B.
Garvey, Amy Euphemia
Garvey, Jr., Marcus
Giddings, Paula
Gomez, Jewelle
Greaves, "Bill"
Heard, Nathan C.
Hemphill, Essex
Holman, M. Carl
Hopkins, Pauline
Houston, Charles
Johnson, John H.
Kaufman, "Bob"
Keene, Jr., John R.
Kelley, William Melvin
Kenan, Randall
Mackey, Nathaniel
Maynard, Robert
McGirt, James E.
McKay, Nellie Yvonne
Morrison, Toni
Murphy, Beatrice M.
Myers, Walter Dean
Neal, "Larry"
Obama, II, Barack
Plumpp, Sterling
Randall, Dudley
Reed, Ishmael
Ruffin, Josephine St. Pierre
Russwurm, John
Scott, Jr., Nathan A.
Senna, Carl
Shine, Ted

Simmons, William J.
Smith, Lillian Eugenia
Southern, Eileen Stanza
Stone, Chuck
Tanner, Benjamin Tucker
Taylor, Mildred
Taylor, Susan L.
Thurman, Wallace
Turner, Henry McNeal
Van Dyke, Henry
Vann, Robert Lee
Walrond, Eric
Weaver, Afaa M.
Wesley, Valerie Wilson
West, Dorothy
Whipper, William
Wilkins, Roy
Williams, Edward Christopher
Woodson, Jacqueline
Young, Kevin
Zu-Bolton, III, Ahmos

Editor, Journal
Kaufman, "Bob"
Mackey, Nathaniel
Obama, II, Barack
Thurman, Wallace
Wilkins, Roy
Williams, Edward Christopher

Editor, Literary
Fauset, Jessie Redmon
West, Dorothy

Editor, Magazine
Coleman, Wanda
McGirt, James E.
Simmons, William J.

Editor, Newspaper
Abbott, Robert S.
Bass, Charlotta Amanda
Bibb, Henry
Garvey, Jr., Marcus
Stone, Chuck
Turner, Henry McNeal
Vann, Robert Lee

Editor, Periodical
Channer, Colin

Educator
Ai
Alexander, Elizabeth
Allen, Samuel W.
Amini, Johari
Angelou, Maya
Ansa, Tina McElroy
Asante, Molefi Kete
Atkins, Russell
Baker, Jr., Houston A.
Barrax, Gerald W.
Beckham, Barry

Bennett, Gwendolyn B.
Berry, Mary Frances
Bonner, Marita
Bontemps, Arna Wendell
Boyd, Melba
Bradley, Jr., David
Braithwaite, William Stanley Beaumont
Brathwaite, Edward Kamau
Brawley, Benjamin
Braxton, Joanne
Brooks, Gwendolyn
Brown, Cecil
Brown, Linda Beatrice
Brown, Sterling Allen
Bruce, Josephine Beall
Bruce, Sr., Roscoe Conkling
Bryan, Ashley F.
Bullins, Ed
Campbell, James Edwin
Cary, Mary Ann
Cassells, Cyrus
Chesnutt, Charles Waddell
Chisholm, Shirley
Christian, Barbara
Christian, Marcus Bruce
Clark, Kenneth B.
Clark, Mamie
Clark, Septima
Clarke, John Henrik
Cleage, Pearl
Cliff, Michelle
Clifton, Lucille
Cobb, Jewell
Cole, Johnnetta
Coleman, Wanda
Collier, Eugenia
Collins, Kathleen
Cone, James H.
Cooper, Anna Julia
Cornish, Sam
Cotter, Sr., Joseph Seamon
Crayton, Pearl
Cullen, Countee
Danticat, Edwidge
Davis, Angela
Davis, Arthur P.
Davis, Thulani
Delany, Jr., Samuel R.
Delany, Sarah "Sadie"
Demby, William
Derricotte, Toi
Dove, Rita
Drake, St. Clair
Draper, Sharon M.
Driskell, David Clyde
Dunbar Nelson, Alice Ruth
Dunham, Katherine
Dyson, Michael Eric
Eady, Cornelius
Early, Gerald
Ellison, Ralph

Emanuel, Sr., James A.
Evans, Mari
Everett, II, Percival
Fabio, Sarah
Fauset, Jessie Redmon
Ferguson, Lloyd Noel
Fields, Julia
Ford, Nick Aaron
Forrest, Leon
Foster, Frances Smith
Franklin, J. E.
Franklin, John Hope
Frazier, E. Franklin
Fuller, Hoyt
Fuller, Jr., Charles H.
Gaines, Ernest J.
Gates, Jr., Henry Louis "Skip,"
Gayle, Jr., Addison
Gibson, P. J.
Giddings, Paula
Golden, Marita
Gomez, Jewelle
Gordone, Charles
Graham, Lorenz
Granville, Evelyn
Greenlee, Sam
Griggs, Sutton E.
Grooms, Anthony
Guinier, Lani
Hansberry, William Leo
Hansen, Joyce
Hare, Nathan
Harper, Michael S.
Harris, Trudier
Haskins, James S.
Heard, Nathan C.
Hernton, Calvin C.
Herron, Carolivia
Higginbotham, Evelyn
Hill, Anita Faye
Hoagland, III, Everett H.
Holman, M. Carl
Houston, Charles
Houston, Drusilla
Hull, Akasha
Hunter, Kristin
Hurston, Zora Neale
Jackson, Angela
Jackson, Elaine
Jackson, Jesse
Jackson, Mae
Johnson, Angela
Johnson, Charles
Johnson, Fenton
Johnson, Georgia Douglas
Johnson, James Weldon
Johnson, Kathryn Magnolia
Jones, Edward P.
Jones, Gayl
Jones, Tayari
Jordan, Barbara

Jordan, June
Josey, E. J.
Just, Ernest Everett
Keene, Jr., John R.
Kelley, William Melvin
Kenan, Randall
Kennedy, Adrienne
King, Jr., Woodie
Knight, Etheridge
Komunyakaa, Yusef
Lavalle, Victor
Ladner, Joyce A.
Lane, Pinkie
Langston, John Mercer
Lester, Julius
Lewis, David Levering
Lewis, Samella Sanders
Locke, Alain
Logan, Rayford W.
Lorde, Audre
Love, Rose Leary
Mackey, Nathaniel
Major, Clarence
Malveaux, Julianne
Marshall, Paule
Mathis, Sharon
Maynard, Dori J.
Maynard, Nancy Hicks
Maynard, Robert
Mays, Benjamin Elijah
McElroy, Colleen
McKay, Nellie Yvonne
McPherson, James Alan
Mebane, Mary E.
Miller, E. Ethelbert
Miller, Kelly
Miller, May
Millican, Arthenia J. Bates
Milner, Ronald
Mitchell, Loften
Moore, Opal
Morrison, Toni
Mosley, Walter
Moss, Thylias
Mullen, Harryette
Murray, Albert L.
Osbey, Brenda Marie
Packer, Zz
Painter, Nell
Parks, Suzan-Lori
Patterson, Lillie
Patterson, Raymond R.
Payne, Daniel A.
Pennington, James W. C.
Peterson, Louis
Phillips, Carl
Pietri, Pedro Juan
Plumpp, Sterling
Polite, Carlene
Poussaint, Alvin Francis
Powell, Kevin

Quarles, Benjamin
Randall, Dudley
Ray, Henrietta Cordelia
Reagon, Bernice
Reason, Charles L.
Redding, "Jay" Saunders
Redmond, Eugene
Rhodes, Jewell Parker
Riggs, Marlon Troy
Ringgold, Faith
Rodgers, Carolyn
Ross-Barnett, Marguerite
Ruffin Ridley, Florida
Salaam, Kalamu Ya
Sanchez, Sonia
Scarborough, William Sanders
Senna, Carl
Shange, Ntozake
Shepherd, Reginald
Shockley, Ann
Simmons, William J.
Smith, Anna Deveare
Smith, Barbara
Smith, Jessie
Smitherman, Geneva
Southerland, Ellease
Southern, Eileen Stanza
Spence, Eulalie
Spillers, Hortense J.
Steele, Claude M.
Steele, Shelby
Stone, Chuck
Tarry, Ellen
Tate, Claudia
Tate, Eleanora E.
Taylor, Mildred
Taylor, Susie
Thomas, Joyce Carol
Thomas, Piri
Thurman, Howard
Tolson, Melvin
Touré, Askia Muhammad Abu Bakr El
Trethewey, Natasha
Turner, Darwin T.
Turner, Lorenzo Dow
Turpin, Waters
Tyson, Neil Degrasse
Vashon, George B.
Walcott, Derek
Walker, Alice
Walker, Margaret
Waniek, Marilyn
Weaver, Afaa M.
Wesley, Charles Harris
Wesley, Richard
West, Cornel
Wideman, John Edgar
Wilkins, Roger Wood
Williams, Chancellor
Williams, Edward Christopher
Williams, John A.

Williams, Patricia J.
Williams, Sherley Anne
Wilson, William Julius
Woodson, Jacqueline
Wright, Jay
Wright, Sarah E.
X, Marvin
Yarbrough, Camille
Yerby, Frank G.
Young, Al
Young, Kevin
De Burgos, Julia
hooks, bell

Emigrationist
Holly, James Theodore

Enslaved Domestic Servant
Truth, Sojourner
Wheatley, Phillis

Enslaved Laborer
Northup, Solomon
Terry, Lucy
Tubman, Harriet
Turner, Nat
Ward, Samuel

Enslaved Plantation Worker
Lynch, John R.

Enslaved Potter
Dave, The Potter

Entrepreneur
Garvey, Jr., Marcus
Malveaux, Julianne

Factory Worker
Weaver, Afaa M.
Yerby, Frank G.

Feminist
Walker, Rebecca
hooks, bell

Filmmaker
Collins, Kathleen
Dash, Julie
Gerima, Haile
Parks, Sr., Gordon
Riggs, Marlon Troy
Van Peebles, Melvin

Founder, Business
Barnett, Claude Albert

Founder, Journal
Brathwaite, Edward Kamau
Dent, Tom

Founder, Magazine
Garvey, Jr., Marcus

Founder, Museum
Burroughs, Margaret

Founder, Newspaper
Fortune, T. Thomas
Garvey, Jr., Marcus
Trotter, Monroe
Williams, Jr., Peter
X, Malcolm

Founder, Organization
Robinson, Randall

Founder, Theater
Carroll, Vinnette
Elder, III, Lonne
Milner, Ronald
Neal, "Larry"
X, Marvin

Founding Editor, Magazine
Cleage, Pearl

Gang Leader
Williams, III, Stanley Tookie

Gay-Rights Activist
Hemphill, Essex
Riggs, Marlon Troy

Graphic Artist
Bennett, Gwendolyn B.
Feelings, Tom
McGruder, Aaron

Griot
Yarbrough, Camille

Hairdresser
Equiano, Olaudah
Wilson, Harriet E.

Health Advocate
Gregory, "Dick"

Home Economist
Delany, Sarah "Sadie"

Homemaker
Terry, Lucy
Wilkinson, Brenda

Host
Abu-Jamal, Mumia
Anderson, Regina M.
Baisden, Michael
Coleman, Wanda
Cosby, Jr., Bill
Tyson, Neil Degrasse
Walker, A'lelia
Winfrey, Oprah

Host, Book Club
Winfrey, Oprah

Host, Literary Salon
Walker, A'lelia

Host, Media
Baisden, Michael

Host, Talk Show
Abu-Jamal, Mumia
Winfrey, Oprah

Host, Television
Cosby, Jr., Bill
Tyson, Neil Degrasse

Illustrator
Bryan, Ashley F.
De Veaux, Alexis
Fax, Elton C.

Inventor
Banneker, Benjamin
Latimer, Lewis Howard

Itinerant Preacher
Lee, Jarena
Truth, Sojourner

Journalist
Angelou, Maya
Ansa, Tina McElroy
Bennett, Jr., Lerone
Brown, Elaine
Bruce, Blanche K.
Bruce, Sr., Roscoe Conkling
Bullins, Ed
Campbell, James Edwin
Christian, Marcus Bruce
Cliff, Michelle
Cornish, Samuel E.
Corrothers, James D.
Cose, Ellis
Cotter, Jr., Joseph Seamon
Crosswaith, Frank Rudolph
Davis, Frank Marshall
Deal, Borden
Demby, William
Douglass, Frederick
Due, Tananarive
Dunbar Nelson, Alice Ruth
Dyson, Michael Eric
Forrest, Leon
Fortune, T. Thomas
Fuller, Hoyt
Garland, Hazel B.
Garvey, Amy Euphemia
Giddings, Paula
Gladwell, Malcolm
Hansberry, Lorraine Vivian
Harper, Frances Ellen Watkins
Hernton, Calvin C.
Holly, James Theodore
Hopkins, Pauline
Houston, Drusilla

Hunter, Kristin
Hunter-Gault, Charlayne
Hurston, Zora Neale
Jackson, Jesse
Johnson, Fenton
Johnson, James Weldon
Jordan, June
Kincaid, Jamaica
Lee, Andrea
Lester, Julius
Lomax, Louis E.
Marshall, Paule
Matthews, Victoria
Nell, William C.
Nelson, Jill
Nugent, Richard
Oliver, Diane
Ormes, "Jackie"
Owen, Chandler
Page, Clarence
Park, Robert E.
Payne, Ethel L.
Poston, Ted
Powell, Kevin
Redmond, Eugene
Riggs, Marlon Troy
Robinson, Max
Rogers, Joel Augustus
Rowan, Carl T.
Ruffin Ridley, Florida
Ruffin, Josephine St. Pierre
Ruggles, David
Russwurm, John
Schuyler, Philippa Duke
Senna, Carl
Senna, Danzy
Shockley, Ann
Simmons, Herbert Alfred
Sterling, Dorothy
Stone, Chuck
Tarry, Ellen
Tate, Eleanora E.
Terrell, Mary Eliza
Tolson, Melvin
Tyree, Omar
Van Dyke, Henry
Van Vechten, Carl
Vann, Robert Lee
Walrond, Eric
Ward, Douglas Turner
Wells-Barnett, Ida B.
Whipper, William
Wilkins, Roger Wood
Wilkins, Roy
Wright, Charles S.

Journalist, Broadcast
Hunter-Gault, Charlayne
Robinson, Max

Judge
Ruffin, George Lewis

Jurist
Higginbotham, Jr., A. Leon

Justice Activist
Lee, Barbara

Justice of the Peace
Lynch, John R.

Language Consultant
Smitherman, Geneva

Language-Policy Expert
Smitherman, Geneva

Leader, Labor
Crosswaith, Frank Rudolph
Patterson, William
Randolph, A. Philip

Leader, Organization
Evers-Williams, Myrlie
Johnson, James Weldon
Logan, Rayford W.
Maynard, Dori J.
Neely, Barbara
Robinson, Randall
Ruffin, Josephine St. Pierre
Wilkins, Roy

Leader, Rebel
Turner, Nat

Leader, Workshop
Jackson, Angela

Lecturer
Brown, Claude
Brown, Elaine
Brown, William Wells
Childress, Alice
De Veaux, Alexis
Equiano, Olaudah
Harris, E. Lynn
Northup, Solomon
Rodgers, Carolyn
Terrell, Mary Eliza
Touré, Askia Muhammad Abu Bakr El
Wells-Barnett, Ida B.
Williams, George Washington

Legal Clerk
Chesnutt, Charles Waddell

Librarian
Anderson, Regina M.
Christian, Marcus Bruce
Hurston, Zora Neale
Hutson, Jean
Jenkins, Beverly
Josey, E. J.
Keene, Jr., John R.
Larsen, Nella
Lorde, Audre

Mathis, Sharon
Matthews, Victoria
Murray, Daniel Alexander Payne
Osbey, Brenda Marie
Patterson, Lillie
Porter Wesley, Dorothy Louise
Rollins, Charlemae
Shockley, Ann
Smith, Jessie
Spencer, "Anne"
Williams, Edward Christopher

Librarian, Media
Patterson, Lillie

Literary Executor
Redmond, Eugene

Manager, Theater
Rainey, Gertrude "Ma"

Manual Laborer
Northup, Solomon

Mathematician
Banneker, Benjamin

Mentor
Dent, Tom

Military Careerman
Murray, Albert L.

Military Chaplain
Steward, Theophilus Gould

Military Nurse
Truth, Sojourner

Military Recruiter
Truth, Sojourner

Military Scout
Tubman, Harriet

Minister
Allen, Richard
Cone, James H.
Cornish, Samuel E.
Corrothers, James D.
Griggs, Sutton E.

Missionary
Crummell, Alexander
Graham, Lorenz
Holly, James Theodore
Marrant, John

Musician
Brown, Frank London
Demby, William
Diddley, Bo
Edmonds, Kenneth "Babyface"
Joans, Ted
Lester, Julius

Pickett, Wilson
Reed, Ishmael
Scott-Heron, Gil
Young, Al

Musician, Composer
Johnson, Georgia Douglas
Parks, Sr., Gordon
Van Peebles, Melvin

Musician, Concert Pianist
Southern, Eileen Stanza

Musician, Guitarist
King, B. B.

Musician, Jazz
Brown, Frank London

Musician, Pianist
Southern, Eileen Stanza
Wonder, Stevie

Musician, Singer
Anderson, Marian
Angelou, Maya
Brown, Elaine
Chapman, Tracy
Edmonds, Kenneth "Babyface"
Holiday, Billie
Hunter, Alberta
King, B. B.
Wonder, Stevie

Naturalist
Banneker, Benjamin

Newspaper Worker
Bourne, St. Clair

Newswriter, Radio
Joe, Yolanda

Newswriter, Television
Joe, Yolanda

Nurse
Hunter, Alberta
Larsen, Nella
Taylor, Susie
Truth, Sojourner
Tubman, Harriet

Odd-Jobs Worker
Wright, Charles S.

Ombudsman
Maynard, Robert

Orator
Bell, James Madison
Dent, Tom
Douglass, Frederick
Harper, Frances Ellen Watkins
Matthews, Victoria

Nell, William C.
Truth, Sojourner
X, Malcolm

Organization Activist
Randall, Alice
Ruffin Ridley, Florida

Organization Executive
Young, Jr., Whitney M.

Organizer
Brown, Frank London
Chisholm, Shirley
Guy, Rosa
Matthews, Victoria
Moody, Anne
Zu-Bolton, III, Ahmos

Organizer, Union
Brown, Frank London

Painter
Driskell, David Clyde
Joans, Ted

Peace Activist
Lee, Barbara
Walker, Alice

Performer
Angelou, Maya
Chapman, Tracy
Coleman, Wanda
Cooper, J. California
Cortez, Jayne
Davis, Thulani
De Veaux, Alexis
Diddley, Bo
Gregory, "Dick"
Heard, Nathan C.
Hemphill, Essex
Ice-T
Joans, Ted
Jones, Sarah
King, B. B.
Kweli, Talib
Latifah, Queen
Pietri, Pedro Juan
Polite, Carlene
Powell, Kevin
Pryor, Richard
Rainey, Gertrude "Ma"
Redding, Otis
Redmond, Eugene
Rock, Chris
Rux, Carl Hancock
Salaam, Kalamu Ya
Sapphire
Scott-Heron, Gil
Shange, Ntozake
Smith, Anna Deveare
Sundiata, Sekou

Waters, Ethel
Wonder, Stevie
X, Marvin
Yarbrough, Camille

Photographer
Lynch, John R.
Parks, Sr., Gordon
Van Vechten, Carl

Physician
Brown, William Wells
Fisher, Rudolph

Plasterer
Bell, James Madison

Poetry Slam Artist
Jones, Sarah

Poetry Therapist
Wright, Sarah E.

Political Activist
Bass, Charlotta Amanda
Bell, James Madison
Jordan, June
Karenga, Maulana Ron
Patterson, William
Randolph, A. Philip

Politician
Bass, Charlotta Amanda
Bruce, Blanche K.
Chisholm, Shirley
Jackson, Sr., Jesse
Jordan, Barbara
Langston, John Mercer
Lee, Barbara
Lynch, John R.
Obama, II, Barack
Powell, Jr., Adam Clayton
Ruffin, George Lewis

Porter, Pullman
Rogers, Joel Augustus

Preacher
Crummell, Alexander
Jackson, Sr., Jesse
Lee, Jarena
Truth, Sojourner

Press Agent
Weatherly, Tom

Printer
Braithwaite, William Stanley Beaumont
Willson, Joseph

Prison Counselor
Thomas, Piri

Producer
Angelou, Maya
Danticat, Edwidge
Edmonds, Kenneth "Babyface"
Fishburne, III, Laurence
Greaves, "Bill"
Joe, Yolanda
King, Jr., Woodie
Lee, Spike
Neely, Barbara
Weatherly, Tom
Winfrey, Oprah

Producer, Film
Danticat, Edwidge
Edmonds, Kenneth "Babyface"
Greaves, "Bill"

Producer, Movie
Winfrey, Oprah

Producer, Radio
Joe, Yolanda
Neely, Barbara

Producer, Record
Edmonds, Kenneth "Babyface"

Producer, Television
Joe, Yolanda

Producer, Theater
Weatherly, Tom

Psychiatrist
Poussaint, Alvin Francis

Psychologist
Clark, Kenneth B.
Clark, Mamie
Hare, Nathan
Steele, Claude M.

Public Speaker
Dunbar Nelson, Alice Ruth
Whipper, William

Publisher
Abbott, Robert S.
Amini, Johari
Ansa, Tina McElroy
Baisden, Michael
Bass, Charlotta Amanda
Beckham, Barry
Bibb, Henry
Braithwaite, William Stanley Beaumont
Brathwaite, Edward Kamau
Cary, Mary Ann
Christian, Marcus Bruce
Cornish, Sam
Cornish, Samuel E.
Cortez, Jayne
Dunbar Nelson, Alice Ruth
Fortune, T. Thomas

Griggs, Sutton E.
Harris, E. Lynn
Hopkins, Pauline
Hudson, Cheryl
Hudson, Wade
Johnson, Fenton
Johnson, James Weldon
Johnson, John H.
Maynard, Nancy Hicks
Maynard, Robert
McGirt, James E.
Murphy, Carl
Randall, Dudley
Redmond, Eugene
Reed, Ishmael
Rogers, Joel Augustus
Ruffin, Josephine St. Pierre
Ruggles, David
Senna, Danzy
Smith, Barbara
Smith, Lillian Eugenia
Southerland, Ellease
Southern, Eileen Stanza
Spingarn, Joel Elias
Tanner, Benjamin Tucker
Thurman, Wallace
Trotter, Geraldine
Trotter, Monroe
Turner, Henry McNeal
Tyree, Omar
Walcott, Derek
Walker, David
Walrond, Eric
West, Dorothy
X, Marvin

Publisher, Book
Beckham, Barry
Brathwaite, Edward Kamau
Cornish, Sam
Cortez, Jayne
Hudson, Cheryl
Hudson, Wade
Johnson, John H.
Turner, Henry McNeal

Publisher, Journal
Ruffin, Josephine St. Pierre
Southern, Eileen Stanza

Publisher, Magazine
Johnson, John H.
McGirt, James E.

Publisher, Newspaper
Abbott, Robert S.
Cornish, Samuel E.
Dunbar Nelson, Alice Ruth
Fortune, T. Thomas
Maynard, Nancy Hicks
Maynard, Robert
Murphy, Carl

Trotter, Monroe

Publisher, Recording
Cortez, Jayne

Publisher, Self
Cornish, Sam
Harris, E. Lynn
Johnson, Fenton
Rogers, Joel Augustus
Tyree, Omar
Walcott, Derek
X, Marvin

Reader
Jackson, Jesse

Reporter
Haley, Alex
Maynard, Dori J.
Maynard, Nancy Hicks
Maynard, Robert
Petry, Ann

Researcher
Clark, Kenneth B.
Clark, Mamie
Drake, St. Clair

Sailor
Equiano, Olaudah

Salesperson
Harris, E. Lynn
Iceberg Slim
Johnson, Kathryn Magnolia

Scholar
Jordan, Barbara
Malveaux, Julianne
Scarborough, William Sanders
Turner, Lorenzo Dow
Wilkins, Roger Wood
Williams, Chancellor
Woodson, Carter G.
hooks, bell

Scientist
Cobb, Jewell

Screenwriter
Thurman, Wallace

Scriptwriter, Television
Coleman, Wanda

Sculptor
Chase-Riboud, Barbara

Seamstress
Wilson, Harriet E.

Slave
Bruce, Blanche K.
Bruce, Henry Clay

Social Activist
Harper, Frances Ellen Watkins
Kweli, Talib
Murray, "Pauli"
Pennington, James W. C.

Social Psychologist
Steele, Claude M.

Social Reformer
Harper, Frances Ellen Watkins

Social Worker
Drake, St. Clair
Graham, Lorenz
Griggs, Sutton E.
Hernton, Calvin C.
Jackson, Mae
Perkins, Eugene
Rodgers, Carolyn
Tarry, Ellen
Tubman, Harriet
Turpin, Waters
Walker, Alice

Soldier
Lynch, John R.
Trotter, James Monroe
Williams, George Washington

Speaker
Dunbar Nelson, Alice Ruth
Tyree, Omar
Whipper, William

Speech Clinician
McElroy, Colleen

Spoken-Word Artist
Davis, Angela

Spy
Tubman, Harriet

Storyteller
Tate, Eleanora E.
Yarbrough, Camille

Tennis Player
Ashe, Jr., Arthur Robert

Theologian
Steward, Theophilus Gould
Tanner, Benjamin Tucker
Thurman, Howard
Williams, George Washington

Typesetter
Dave, The Potter

U.S. Congresswoman
Lee, Barbara

U.S. President
Obama, II, Barack

U.S. Senator
Bruce, Blanche K.

U.S. Supreme Court Justice
Marshall, Thurgood

U.S. Vice-Presidential Candidate
Bass, Charlotta Amanda

Underground Railroad Conductor
Still, William
Tubman, Harriet

Underground Railroad Station Master
Still, William
Whipper, William

Visual Artist
Chase-Riboud, Barbara
McElroy, Colleen
Nugent, Richard
Ormes, "Jackie"
Parks, Sr., Gordon
Porter, James Amos
Ringgold, Faith
Steptoe, John

Appendix F: References

Full citations for abbreviated references that appear at the end of each biography.

A Dictionary of Political Biography. 1998, 2003. New York: Oxford University Press.

African-American Biographies. 1995. Paramus, NJ: Globe Fearon Educational Publisher.

American Heritage® Dictionary of the English Language, The (4th ed.). 2000, 2007. Boston: Houghton Mifflin Company.

American Radical and Reform Writers: Second Series. 2009. In *Dictionary of Literary Biography* (Vol. 345). Detroit: Gale Research.

Anderson, George Parker (Ed.). 2005. *American Mystery and Detective Writers.* In *Dictionary of Literary Biography* (Vol. 306). Detroit: Gale.

Andrews, William L., Frances Smith Foster, and Trudier Harris (Eds.). 1997. *The Oxford Companion to African American Literature.* New York: Oxford University Press.

Appiah, Kwame Anthony, and Henry Louis Gates, Jr. (Eds.). 1999. *Encarta Africana CD-ROM Encyclopedia.* Seattle, WA: Microsoft.

Aptheker, Herbert (Ed.). 1951, 1973. *A Documentary of the Negro People in the United States* (3 vols.). Secaucus, NJ: Citadel Press.

Ashby, Ruth, and Deborah Gore Ohrn. 1995. *Herstory: Women Who Changed the World.* New York: Viking.

Ashley, Perry J. (Ed.). 1983. *American Newspaper Journalists, 1873-1900. Dictionary of Literary Biography* (Vol. 23). Detroit: Gale Research.

_____. 1984. *American Newspaper Journalists, 1926-1950.* In *Dictionary of Literary Biography* (Vol. 29). Detroit: Gale Research. (1984). Literature Resources from Gale.

_____. 1985. *American Newspaper Journalists, 1690-1872.* In *Dictionary of Literary Biography* (Vol. 43). Detroit: Gale Research.

Baechler, Lea, and A. Walton Litz. (Eds.). (1991. *African American Writers* (Vol. 1: Suppl. 3). New York: Charles Scribner's Sons. From *Scribner Writers Series.*

_____. 1991. *American Writers: A Collection of Literary Biographies.* New York: Charles Scribner's Sons. From *Scribner Writers Series.*

_____. 1991. *American Writers: A Collection of Literary Biographies.* (Vol. 1: Suppl. 3). New York: Charles Scribner's Sons. From *Scribner Writers Series.*

_____. 1991. *American Writers: A Collection of Literary Biographies.* (Vol. 2: Suppl. 3). New York: Charles Scribner's Sons. From *Scribner Writers Series.*

Bailey, Brooke. 1994. *The Remarkable Lives of 100 Women Healers and Scientists.* Holbrook, MA: Bob Adams.

_____. *The Remarkable Lives of 100 Women Writers and Journalists.* Holbrook, MA: Bob Adams.

Baker, William, and Kenneth Womack. (Eds.). 1999. *Twentieth-Century British Book Collectors and Bibliographers: 1st Series.* In *Dictionary of Literary Biography* (Vol. 201). Detroit: Gale Research.

Barksdale, Richard, and Keneth Kinnamon (Eds.). 1972. *Black Writers of America: A Comprehensive Anthology.* New York: Macmillan.

Beeching, Cyril Leslie. 1997. *A Dictionary of Dates* (2nd ed.). New York: Oxford University Press.

Bennett, Lerone, Jr. 1993. *The Shaping of Black America: The Struggles and Triumphs of African-Americans, 1619 to the 1990s* (2nd ed.). Chicago: Johnson Publishing Co.

_____. 1968. *Pioneers in Protest.* Chicago: Johnson Publishing Co.

Benét, William Rose. 1945/1987) *Benét's Reader's Encyclopedia* (3rd ed.). New York: Harper & Row.

Berger, Laura Standley. (Ed.). 1994. *Twentieth-Century Young Adult Writers. Twentieth-Century Writers Series.* Detroit: St. James Press.

_____. 1995. *Twentieth-Century Children's Writers, 4th ed. Twentieth-Century Writers Series.* Detroit: St. James Press.

Berney, K. A. 1993. *Contemporary Dramatists* (5th ed.). London: St. James Press.

Bernikow, Louise, and the National Women's History Project. 1997. *The American Women's Almanac: An Inspiring and Irreverent Women's History.* New York: Berkley Books.

Bigsby, C. W.E. (Ed.). 1981. *The Black American Writer: Poetry and Drama.* 1969. Everett/ Edwards, Inc.. Rpt. in Sharon R. Gunton (Ed.), in *Contemporary Literary Criticism* (Vol. 17, pp. 157-170). Detroit: Gale Research.

Bingham, Jane M. (Ed.). 1987. *Writers for Children.* New York: Charles Scribner's Sons. From *Scribner Writers Series.*

Blassingame, John W. (Ed.). 1977. *Slave Testimony: Two Centuries of Letters, Speeches, Interviews and Autobiographies.* Baton Rouge: Louisiana State University Press.

Bleiler, Everett Franklin. (Ed.). 1982. *Science Fiction Writers: Critical Studies of the Major Authors from the Early Nineteenth Century to the Present Day.* New York: Charles Scribner's Sons. From *Scribner Writers Series.*

Bolden, Tonya (Ed.). 1998. *And Not Afraid to Dare: The Stories of Ten African American Women.* New York: Scholastic Press.

_____. 1994. *Rites of Passage: Stories about Growing Up by Black Writers from around the World.* New York: Hyperion Books for Children.

_____. 1996. *The Book of African-American Women: 150 Crusaders, Creators, and Uplifters.* Holbrook, MA: Adams Media Corporation.

_____. 1999. *Strong Men Keep Coming: The Book of African-American Men.* New York: Wiley.

_____. 1998. *33 Things Every Girl Should Know: Stories, Songs, Poems, and Smart Talk by 33 Extraordinary Women.* New York: Crown.

Boyd, Herb. 1995. *Down the Glory Road: Contributions of African Americans in United States History and Culture.* New York: Avon.

Bradbury, Malcolm (Ed.). 1996. *The Atlas of Literature.* New York: De Agostini Editions.

Brawley, Benjamin. 1937. *Negro Builders and Heroes.* Chapel Hill: University of North Carolina Press.

Britannica Concise Encyclopedia. 2006. Encyclopædia Britannica.

Brown, Susan Windisch. (Ed.). 1996. *Contemporary Novelists* (6th ed.). New York: St. James Press.

Burt, Daniel S. (Ed.). 2004. *Works. The Chronology of American Literature.* Boston: Houghton Mifflin Company.

Cade [Bambara], Toni. 1970. *The Black Woman: An Anthology.* New York: Mentor, New American Library.

Champion, Laurie. (Ed.). 2007. *American Women Writers, 1900-1945: A Bio-Bibliographical Critical Sourcebook.* Westport, CT: Greenwood. 2000. Rpt. in Michelle Lee (Ed.), *Poetry Criticism* (Vol. 77, pp. 312-317). Detroit: Gale.

Chapman, Abraham (Ed.). 1968. *Black Voices: An Anthology of Afro-American Literature.* New York: Mentor, New American Library.

Charters, Ann, (Ed.). 1983. *The Beats: Literary Bohemians in Postwar America. Dictionary of Literary Biography* (Vol. 16). Detroit: Gale Research.

Chase, Henry (Ed.). 1994. *In Their Footsteps: The American Visions Guide to African-American Heritage Sites.* New York: Henry Holt.

Christian, Barbara. 1985. *Black Feminist Criticism: Perspectives on Black Women Writers* (Athene Series). New York: Pergamon Press.

Christian, Charles M. 1995. *Black Saga: The African American Experience.* Boston: Houghton Mifflin.

Clark, Randall. (Ed.). 1986. *American Screenwriters: 2nd Series. Dictionary of Literary Biography* (Vol. 44). Detroit: Gale Research.

Clarke, John Henrik (Ed.). 1966/1993. *Black American Short Stories: 100 Years of the Best.* New York: Hill and Wang; Farrar, Straus and Giroux.

Clifton, Lucille. 1991. *Quilting: Poems, 1987-1990.* Brockport, NY: BOA Editions, Ltd.

_____. 1996. *The Terrible Stories.* Brockport, NY: BOA Editions, Ltd.

Columbia Electronic Encyclopedia, The (6th ed.). 2003. Columbia University Press. //www.cc.columbia.edu/cu/cup/

Concise Grove Dictionary of Art, The. 2002. Oxford University Press.

Concise Grove Dictionary of Music, The. 1994. New York: Oxford University Press.

Concise Oxford Companion to African American Literature, The. 2001, 2002. New York: Oxford University Press.

Concise Oxford Dictionary of Music, The (5th ed.). 2007. Oxford University Press.

Concise Oxford Dictionary of Politics, The. 1996, 2003. New York: Oxford University Press.

Conte, Joseph Mark (Ed.). 1996. *American Poets Since World War II: 5th Series.* In *Dictionary of Literary Biography* (Vol. 169). Detroit: Gale Research.

_____. 1996. *American Poets Since World War II: 4th Series. Dictionary of Literary Biography* (Vol. 165). Detroit: Gale Research.

Contemporary Authors Online. Detroit: Gale. 1998. 2000. 2001. 2002. 2003. 2004. 2005. 2006. 2007. 2008. 2009. From *Literature Resource Center.*

Contemporary Black Biography. 2006. Detroit: Gale Group.

Contemporary Literary Criticism (Vols. 246, 253, 261). Detroit: Gale.

Contemporary Literary Criticism Select. Detroit: Gale.

Conyers, James L. 2005. *Afrocentric Traditions* (Chapter 7, "Selected Bibliography"). Edison, NJ: Transaction Publishers. Available at //books.google.com/books.

Cowart, David, and Thomas L. Wymer. (Eds.). 1981. *Twentieth-Century American Science-Fiction Writers. Dictionary of Literary Biography* (Vol. 8). Detroit: Gale Research.

Cracroft, Richard H. (Ed.). 1999. *Twentieth-Century American Western Writers: 2nd Series.* In *Dictionary of Literary Biography* (Vol. 212). Detroit: Gale Group.

Craughwell, Thomas. 1998. *I Can't Decide What to Read . . . Great Books for Every Book Lover: 2002 Great Reading Suggestions for the Discriminating Bibliophile.* New York: Black Dog and Leventhal Publishers, Workman.

Crystal, David (Ed.). 1990. *Cambridge Biographical Dictionary.* Cambridge, England: Cambridge University Press.

_____. 1994. *The Cambridge Biographical Encyclopedia.* Cambridge, England: Cambridge University Press.

Cullen-DuPont (with Annelise Orleck, historical consultant). 1998. *The Encyclopedia of Women's History in America.* New York: Da Capo Press.

Currie, Stephen. 1996. *Birthday a Day: Grades 3 and Up.* Glenview, IL: GoodYearBooks.

Dalin, Anne Safran (Ed.). 1997. *Creme de la Femme: A Collection of the Best Contemporary Women Writers, Lyricists, Playwrights and Cartoonists.* New York: Random House.

Davidson, Cathy N., and Linda Wagner-Martin (Eds.). 1995. *The Oxford Companion to Women's Writing in the United States.* New York: Oxford University Press.

Davis, Thadious M., and Trudier Harris-Lopez. (Eds.). 1984. *Afro-American Fiction Writers After 1955.* In *Dictionary of Literary Biography* (Vol. 33). Detroit: Gale Research. From *Literature Resource Center.*

_____. 1985. *Afro-American Poets Since 1955.* In *Dictionary of Literary Biography* (Vol. 41). Detroit: Gale Research.

_____. 1985. *Afro-American Writers After 1955: Dramatists and Prose Writers.* In *Dictionary of Literary Biography* (Vol. 38). Detroit: Gale Research.

Diefendorf, Elizabeth. 1996) *New York Public Library's Books of the Century.* New York: Oxford University Press.

Draper, James P. (Ed.). 1992. *Black Literature Criticism* (Vols. 1, 2, 3). Detroit: Gale Research.

Dunaway, David King, and Sara L. Spurgeon. 1995. *Writing the Southwest.* New York: Plume, Penguin.

Edgarian, Carol, and Tom Jenks. 1997. *The Writer's Life: Intimate Thoughts on Work, Love, Inspiration, and Fame from the Diaries of the World's Great Writers.* New York: Vintage Books, Random House.

Eisler, Garrett. (Ed.). 2008. *Twentieth-Century American Dramatists: 5th Series.* In *Dictionary of Literary Biography* (Vol. 341). Detroit: Gale.

Elliott, Emory (Ed.). 1984. *American Colonial Writers, 1735-1781.* In *Dictionary of Literary Biography* (Vol. 31). Detroit: Gale Research.

_____. 1985. *American Writers of the Early Republic.* In *Dictionary of Literary Biography* (Vol. 37). Detroit: Gale Research.

Emanuel, James A., and Theodore L. Gross (Eds.). 1968. *Dark Symphony: Negro Literature in America.* New York: Free Press.

Encarta. 1994. 1995. 1997. 1998. 1999. *Encarta Encyclopedia: The Ultimate Learning Resource* (deluxe ed.). Seattle, WA: Microsoft.

Encyclopædia Britannica Profiles: Black History CD. 1997. Springfield, MA: Merriam-Webster.

Encyclopædia Britannica CD: Knowledge for the Information Age. 1998. 1999. (multimedia ed.). Springfield, MA: Merriam-Webster.

Encyclopedia of Education. 2002. Detroit: Gale Group.

Encyclopedia of the Modern Middle East and North Africa. 2004. Detroit: Gale Group.

Ervin, Hazel Arnett. 2004. "Appendix 1. Outlines of Literary History: African American, African, and Anglophone Caribbean." *The Handbook of African American Literature.* Gainesville: University Press of Florida.

Estell, Kenneth. 1994. *African America: Portrait of a People.* New York: Visible Ink.

Estes, Glenn E. (Ed.). 1985. *American Writers for Children Before 1900. Dictionary of Literary Biography* (Vol. 42). Detroit: Gale Research.

_____. 1986. *American Writers for Children Since 1960: Fiction.* In *Dictionary of Literary Biography* (Vol. 52). Detroit: Gale Research.

Evans, Mari (Ed.). 1984. *Black Women Writers (1950-1980).* New York: Anchor, Doubleday.

Fadiman, Anne. 1998. *Ex Libris: Confessions of a Common Reader.* New York: Farrar, Straus and Giroux.

Female Poets of America, The. 1986. Rpt. in James E. Person, Jr. (Ed.), in *Literature Criticism from 1400 to 1800* (Vol. 3). Detroit: Gale Research.

Foner, Eric, and John A. Garraty. (Eds.). 1991. *US History Companion: The Reader's Companion to American History.* Boston: Houghton Mifflin Company.

Foner, Philip S. (Ed.). 1972. *The Voice of Black America: Major Speeches by Negroes in the United States, 1797-1971.* New York: Simon and Schuster.

Franklin, John Hope, and Alfred A. Moss, Jr. 1988. *From Slavery to Freedom: A History of Negro Americans* (6th ed.). New York: Knopf.

Furia, Philip. (Ed.). 2002. *American Song Lyricists, 1920-1960.* In *Dictionary of Literary Biography* (Vol. 265). Detroit: Gale.

Furman, Laura, and Elinore Standard (Eds.). 1997. *Bookworms: Great Writers and Readers Celebrate Reading.* New York: Carroll & Graph Publishers.

Gale Online Encyclopedia. Detroit: Gale. From *Literature Resource Center.*

Gates, Henry Louis, Jr., and Nellie Y. McKay (Eds.). 1997. *The Norton Anthology of African American Literature*. New York: Norton.

Gates, Henry Louis, Jr., and Evelyn Brooks Higginbotham (Eds.). 2008. *African American National Biography (8 vols.)*. New York: Oxford University Press.

Gates, Henry Louis, Jr. (Ed.). 1987. *The Classic Slave Narratives*. New York: Penguin Books, Mentor.

Gay & Lesbian Literature (Vol. 1, 2). 1994, 1998. Detroit: Gale.

Giles, James R., and Wanda H. Giles. (Eds.). 1994. *American Novelists Since World War II: 3rd Series*. In *Dictionary of Literary Biography* (Vol. 143). Detroit: Gale Research.

_____. 1995. *American Novelists Since World War II: 4th Series*. In *Dictionary of Literary Biography* (Vol. 152). Detroit: Gale Research.

_____. 1996. *American Novelists Since World War II: 5th Series*. In *Dictionary of Literary Biography* (Vol. 173). Detroit: Gale Research.

_____. 2000. *American Novelists Since World War II: 6th Series*. In *Dictionary of Literary Biography* (Vol. 227). Detroit: Gale Group.

_____. 2003. *American Novelists Since World War II: 7th Series*. In *Dictionary of Literary Biography* (Vol. 278). Detroit: Gale.

Goldberg, Bonni. 1996. *Room to Write: Daily Invitations to a Writer's Life*. New York: Jeremy P. Tarcher / Putnam, Penguin.

Golden, Kristen, and Barbara Findlen. 1998. *Remarkable Women of the Twentieth Century: 100 Portraits of Achievement*. New York: Friedman/Fairfax Publishers.

Goring, Rosemary (Ed.). 1994. *Larousse Dictionary of Writers*. New York: Larousse.

Greiner, Donald J. (Ed.). 1980. *American Poets Since World War II*. In *Dictionary of Literary Biography* (Vol. 5). Detroit: Gale Research.

Grolier Multimedia Encyclopedia. 1994. 1995. 1997. 1999. Danbury, CT: Grolier Interactive.

Gwynn, R. S. (Ed.). 1992. *American Poets Since World War II: 3rd Series*. In *Dictionary of Literary Biography* (Vol. 120). Detroit: Gale Research.

Haber, Louis. 1970. *Black Pioneers of Science and Invention*. New York: Harcourt Brace.

Halpern, Daniel (Ed.). 1988. *Our Private Lives: Journals, Notebooks, and Diaries*. Hopewell, NJ: The Ecco Press.

Hansom, Paul. (Ed.). 2001. *Twentieth-Century American Cultural Theorists*. In *Dictionary of Literary Biography* (Vol. 246). Detroit: Gale Group. From *Literature Resource Center*.

Harper, Michael S., and Anthony Walton (Eds.). 2000. *The Vintage Book of African American Poetry: 200 Years of Vision, Struggle, Power, Beauty, and Triumph from 50 Outstanding Poets*. New York: Vintage Books, a Division of Random House.

Harris, Sharon M., Heidi L. M. Jacobs, and Jennifer Putzi. (Eds.). 2000. *American Women Prose Writers, 1870-1920*. In *Dictionary of Literary Biography* (Vol. 221). Detroit: Gale Group.

Harris-Lopez, Trudier (Ed.). 1988. *Afro-American Writers, 1940-1955*. in *Dictionary of Literary Biography* (Vol. 76). Detroit: Gale Research.

Harris-Lopez, Trudier, and Thadious M. Davis. (Eds.). 1986. *Afro-American Writers Before the Harlem Renaissance*. In *Dictionary of Literary Biography* (Vol. 50-51). Detroit: Gale Research.

_____. (1987). *Afro-American Writers From the Harlem Renaissance to 1940*. In *Dictionary of Literary Biography* (Vol. 51). Detroit: Gale Research.

Hass, Robert (Ed.). 1998. *Poet's Choice: Poems for Everyday Life*. Hopewell, NJ: Ecco Press.

Hedgepeth, Chester M., Jr. (Ed.). 1971. *Twentieth-Century African American Writers and Artists*. Washington, DC: American Library Association.

Heinemann, Sue. 1996. *Timelines of American Women's History*. New York: A Roundtable Press Book / Perigree Book, Berkley Publishing Group.

Helicon Publishing. 1996. *On This Date*. New York: Random House (Reference & Information Publishing).

Helterman, Jeffrey, and Richard Layman. (Eds.). 1978. *American Novelists Since World War II: First Series*. *Dictionary of Literary Biography* (Vol. 2). Detroit: Gale Research. From *Literature Resource Center*.

Hendrickson, Robert. 1990. *American Literary Anecdotes*. New York: Penguin.

Hine, Darlene Clark, Elsa Barkley Brown, and Rosalyn Terborg-Penn. (Eds.). 1993. *Black Women in America: An Historical Encyclopedia* (Vols. 1, 2). Bloomington: University of Indiana Press.

Hipple, Ted. (Ed.). 1997. *Writers for Young Adults* (Vol. 1). New York: Charles Scribner's Sons. Literature Resources from Gale.

_____. 1997. *Writers for Young Adults* (Vol. 2). New York: Charles Scribner's Sons. Literature Resources from Gale.

_____. 1997. *Writers for Young Adults* (Vol. 3). New York: Charles Scribner's Sons. Literature Resources from Gale.

_____. 2000. *Writers for Young Adults*. Ed. Ted Hipple. New York: Charles Scribner's Sons. From *Scribner Writers Series*.

Hirsch, E.D. Jr., Joseph F. Kett, and James Trefil. (Eds.). 2002. *Fine Arts Dictionary. The New Dictionary of Cultural Literacy* (3rd ed.). Boston: Houghton Mifflin Company.

_____. 2002. *History Dictionary. The New Dictionary of Cultural Literacy* (3rd ed.). Boston: Houghton Mifflin Company.

_____. 2002. *Science Dictionary. The New Dictionary of Cultural Literacy* (3rd ed.). Boston: Houghton Mifflin Company.

Holman, C. Hugh, and William Harmon. 1936/1992. *A Handbook to Literature* (6th ed.). New York: Macmillan.

Hudock, Amy E., and Katharine Rodier. (Eds.). 2001. *American Women Prose Writers: 1820-1870. Dictionary of Literary Biography* (Vol. 239). Detroit: Gale Group.

Hudson, Wade, and Cheryl Willis Hudson. 1997. *In Praise of Our Fathers and Our Mothers: A Black Family Treasury by Outstanding Authors and Artists.* East Orange, NJ: Just Us Books.

Hull, Gloria T., Patricia Bell Scott, and Barbara Smith (Eds.). 1982. *All the Women Are White, All the Blacks Are Men, But Some of Us Are Brave: Black Women's Studies.* Old Westbury, NY: Feminist Press.

Hunter, Jeffrey W. (Ed.) 2007. *Contemporary Literary Criticism* (Vol. 241). Detroit: Gale.

Hymowitz, Carol, and Michaele Weissman. 1978. *A History of Women in America.* New York: Bantam.

Jay, Gregory S. (Ed.). 1988. *Modern American Critics Since 1955.* In *Dictionary of Literary Biography* (Vol. 67). Detroit: Gale Research.

Jay, Gregory S. (Ed.). 1988. *Modern American Critics, 1920-1955.* In *Dictionary of Literary Biography* (Vol. 63). Detroit: Gale Research.

Johnson, Charles [Spurgeon], Patricia Smith, and WGBH Series Research Team. 1998. *Africans in America: America's Journey through Slavery.* New York: Harcourt Brace.

Johnson, James Weldon (Ed.). 1922/1959. *The Book of American Negro Poetry.* New York: Harcourt Brace Jovanovich.

Jonathan N. Barron and Bruce Meyer. (Eds.). 2003. *New Formalist Poets.* In *Dictionary of Literary Biography* (Vol. 282). Detroit: Gale.

Kamp, Jim. (Ed.). 1994. *Reference Guide to American Literature* (3rd ed.). Detroit: St. James Press. From *Literature Resource Center.*

Kanigel, Robert. 1998. *Vintage Reading, from Plato to Bradbury: A Personal Tour of Some of the World's Best Books.* Baltimore: Bancroft Press.

Kaplan, Sidney, and Emma Nogrady Kaplan. 1989. *The Black Presence in the Era of the American Revolution, 1770-1880* (rev. ed.; original 1975). Amherst: University of Massachusetts Press.

Katz, William Loren. 1974. *Eyewitness: The Negro in American History.* Belmont, CA: Pitman Learning.

Keenan, Sheila. 1996. *Scholastic Encyclopedia of Women in the United States.* New York: Scholastic Reference.

Kellner, Bruce (Ed.). 1987. *The Harlem Renaissance: A Historical Dictionary for the Era.* New York: Methuen.

Kester-Shelton, Pamela. (Ed.). 1996. *Feminist Writers.* Detroit: St. James Press.

Kibler, James E. (Ed.) 1980. *American Novelists Since World War II: 2nd Series.* In *Dictionary of Literary Biography* (Vol. 6). Detroit: Gale Research. From *Literature Resource Center.*

Kimbel, Bobby Ellen, and William E. Grant. (Eds.). 1988. *American Short-Story Writers Before 1880.* In *Dictionary of Literary Biography* (Vol. 74). Detroit: Gale Research.

_____. 1989. *American Short-Story Writers, 1880-1910.* In *Dictionary of Literary Biography* (Vol. 78). Detroit: Gale Research.

Kimbel, Bobby Ellen. (Ed.). 1991. *American Short-Story Writers, 1910-1945: Second Series.* In *Dictionary of Literary Biography* (Vol. 102). Detroit: Gale Research.

Koolish, Lynda. 2001. *African American Writers: Portraits and Visions.* Jackson: University Press of Mississippi.

Kothari, Geeta (Ed.). 1994. *Did My Mama Like to Dance? and Other Stories about Mothers and Daughters.* New York: Avon.

Kovacs, Deborah, and James Preller. 1991. *Meet the Authors and Illustrators: Vol. 1. 60 Creators of Favorite Children's Books Talk about Their Works.* New York: Scholastic.

_____. 1994. *Meet the Authors and Illustrators: Vol. 2. 60 Creators of Favorite Children's Books Talk about Their Works.* New York: Scholastic.

Kranz, Rachel, and Philip J. Koslow. 1999. *The Biographical Dictionary of African Americans.* New York: Checkmark Books, Facts on File.

Kremer, John. 1996. *Celebrate Today! More Than 4,000 Holidays, Celebrations, Origins, and Anniversaries.* Rocklin, CA: Prima Publishing.

Leslau, Charlotte, and Wolf Leslau. 1985. *African Proverbs.* White Plains, NY: Peter Pauper Press.

Lindfors, Bernth, and Reinhard Sander. (Eds.). 1992. *Twentieth-Century Caribbean and Black African Writers: 1st Series. Dictionary of Literary Biography* (Vol. 117). Detroit: Gale Research.

_____. 1993. *Twentieth-Century Caribbean and Black African Writers: Second Series.* In *Dictionary of Literary Biography* (Vol. 125). Detroit: Gale Research.

_____. 1996. *Twentieth-Century Caribbean and Black African Writers: 3rd Series.* In *Dictionary of Literary Biography* (Vol. 157). Detroit: Gale Research.

Literary Almanac: The Best of the Printed Word, 1900 to the Present, The. 1997. Kansas City, MO: A High Tide Press Book, Andrews McMeel Publishing.

LitFinder Contemporary Collection. 2007. Detroit: Gale Group.

Litz, A. Walton (Ed.). 1981. *African American Writers*. New York: Charles Scribner's Sons. From *Scribner Writers Series*.

_____. 1981. *American Writers: A Collection of Literary Biographies*. New York: Charles Scribner's Sons. From *Scribner Writers Series*.

_____. 1981. *American Writers: A Collection of Literary Biographies* (Vol. 2). New York: Charles Scribner's Sons. From *Scribner Writers Series*.

Litz, A. Walton, and Molly Weigel. (Eds.).(1996). *African American Writers*. New York: Charles Scribner's Sons. From *Scribner Writers Series*.

_____. 1996. *American Writers: A Collection of Literary Biographies*. New York: Charles Scribner's Sons. From *Scribner Writers Series*.

Livingston, Michael E. 1997. *The African-American Book of Lists*. New York: Perigee Books, Berkley Publishing Group, Putnam.

Ljungquist, Kent P. (Ed.). 2001. *Antebellum Writers in the South: 2nd Series. Dictionary of Literary Biography* (Vol. 248). Detroit: Gale Group.

Logan, Rayford W., and Michael R. Winston (Eds.). 1982. *Dictionary of American Negro Biography*. New York: W. W. Norton.

Long, Richard A., and Eugenia W. Collier (Eds.). 1985. *Afro-American Writing: An Anthology of Prose and Poetry* (2nd, enlarged ed.). University Park: Pennsylvania State University Press.

Luis, William, and Ann Gonzalez. (Eds.). 1994. *Modern Latin-American Fiction Writers: 2nd Series*. In *Dictionary of Literary Biography* (Vol. 145). Detroit: Gale Research.

MacNicholas, John. (Ed.). 1981. *Twentieth-Century American Dramatists. Dictionary of Literary Biography* (Vol. 7). Detroit: Gale Research.

Madison, D. Soyini (Ed.). 1994. *The Woman That I Am: The Literature and Culture of Contemporary Women of Color*. New York: St. Martin's Griffin.

Magill, Frank (Ed.). 1992. *Masterpieces of African-American Literature*. New York: HarperCollins.

Martine, James J. (Ed.). 1981. *American Novelists, 1910-1945*. In *Dictionary of Literary Biography* (Vol. 9). Detroit: Gale Research.

McCrum, Robert, William Cran, and Robert MacNeil. 1986. *The Story of English*. New York: Viking.

McElmeel, Sharron L. 1999. *100 Most Popular Children's Authors: Biographical Sketches and Bibliographies*. Englewood, CO: Libraries Unlimited.

_____. 2000. *100 Most Popular Picture Book Authors and Illustrators : Biographical Sketches and Bibliographies*. Englewood, CO: Libraries Unlimited.

_____. 2004. *Children's Authors and Illustrators Too Good to Miss : Biographical Sketches and Bibliographies*. Westport, CT: Libraries Unlimited.

McGrath, Charles, and the staff of the *New York Times Book Review* (Eds.). 1998. *Books of the Century: A Hundred Years of Authors, Ideas, and Literature*. New York: Random House, Time Books.

McKissack, Patricia. 1997. *Can You Imagine?* Katonah, NY: Richard C. Owen Publishers.

McMillan, Terry (Ed.). 1990. *Breaking Ice: An Anthology of Contemporary African-American Fiction*. New York: Penguin.

Meanor, Patrick, and Gwen Crane. (Ed.). 2000. *American Short-Story Writers Since World War II: 2nd Series*. In *Dictionary of Literary Biography* (Vol. 218). Detroit: Gale Group.

Meanor, Patrick, and Joseph McNicholas (Eds.). 2001. *American Short-Story Writers Since World War II: 4th Series*. In *Dictionary of Literary Biography* (Vol. 244). Detroit: Gale Group.

Meanor, Patrick. (Ed.). 1993. *American Short-Story Writers Since World War II*. In *Dictionary of Literary Biography* (Vol. 130). Detroit: Gale Research.

Merriam-Webster's Collegiate Dictionary 1993. (10th ed.). Springfield, MA: Merriam-Webster.

Merriam-Webster Encyclopedia of Literature. 1995. Springfield, MA: Merriam-Webster. Also available through Literature Resources from Gale.

Metcalf, Fred (Ed.). 1986. *The Penguin Dictionary of Modern Humorous Quotations*. London: Penguin Books.

Metzger, Linda. 1989. *Black Writers: A Selection of Sketches from Contemporary Authors*. Detroit, Michigan: Gale Research, Book Tower.

MicroSoft Reference Library, CD version: Almanac. Chronology. Dictionary. Encyclopedia. Internet. Quotations. 1998.

Miller, John. 1998. *Legends: Women Who Have Changed the World, through the Eyes of Great Women Writers*. Novato, CA: New World Library.

Miller, Ruth (Ed.). 1971. *Black American Literature, 1760-Present*. Beverly Hills, CA: Glencoe Press (Macmillan).

Mote, Dave. (Ed.). 1997. *Contemporary Popular Writers*. Detroit: St. James Press.

Mott, Wesley T. (Ed.). 2001. *The American Renaissance in New England: Fourth Series*. In *Dictionary of Literary Biography* (Vol. 243). Detroit: Gale Group.

Moyers, Bill D. 1990. *A World of Ideas: Conversations with Thoughtful Men and Women about American Life Today and the Ideas Shaping Our Future*. New York: Doubleday.

_____. 1995. *Language of Life: A Festival of Poets*. New York: Doubleday.

Mullen, Bill (Ed.). 1995. *Revolutionary Tales: African American Women's Short Stories, from the First Story to the Present.* New York: Dell.

Myerson, Joel. (Ed.). 1978. *The American Renaissance in New England. Dictionary of Literary Biography* (Vol. 1). Detroit: Gale Research.

_____. 1979. *Antebellum Writers in New York and the South.* In *Dictionary of Literary Biography* (Vol. 3). Detroit: Gale Research.

Negro in Literature and Art in the United States, The. 1930. New York: Duffield & Company. Rpt. in David M. Galens (Ed.), 2004, in *Poetry Criticism* (Vol. 52, pp. 89-96). Detroit: Gale.

Nelson, Emmanuel S. (Ed.). 2000. *African American Authors, 1745-1945.* Westport, CT: Greenwood Press. Rpt. in *Poetry Criticism (Vol. 88).* Detroit: Gale. From *Literature Resource Center.*

New Oxford Companion to Literature in French, The. 1995, 2005. New York: Oxford University Press.

New York Public Library African-American Desk Reference. 1999. New York: Wiley.

Ostrom, Hans, and J. David Macey, Jr. (Eds.). 2005. *The Greenwood Encyclopedia of African American Literature.* Westport, CT: Greenwood Press.

Oxford Companion to American Military History, The. 2000. New York: Oxford University Press.

Oxford Companion to American Theatre, The. 2004. New York: Oxford University Press.

Oxford Companion to Fairy Tales, The. 2000, 2002, 2005. New York: Oxford University Press.

Oxford Companion to the Photograph, The. 2005. New York: Oxford University Press.

Oxford Companion to the Supreme Court of the United States, The. 1992, 2005. New York: Oxford University Press.

Oxford Dictionary of Dance, The. 2000, 2004. New York: Oxford University Press.

Oxford Essential Dictionary of the U.S. Military, The. 2001, 2002. New York: Oxford University Press.

Page, Yolanda Williams. 2007. *Encyclopedia of African American Women Writers.* Greenwood Publishing Group.

Parini, Jay (Ed.). 2004. *African American Writers.* Detroit: Charles Scribner's Sons. From *Scribner Writers Series.*

_____. 2001. *American Writers: A Collection of Literary Biographies.* New York: Charles Scribner's Sons. From *Scribner Writers Series.*

_____. 2002. *American Writers: A Collection of Literary Biographies.* New York: Charles Scribner's Sons. From *Scribner Writers Series.*

_____. 2003. *American Writers: A Collection of Literary Biographies.* New York: Charles Scribner's Sons. From *Scribner Writers Series.*

_____. 2004. *American Writers: A Collection of Literary Biographies.* Detroit: Charles Scribner's Sons. From *Scribner Writers Series.*

_____. 2007. *British Writers.* Detroit: Charles Scribner's Sons. From *Scribner Writers Series.*

_____. 2008. *American Writers: A Collection of Literary Biographies.* Detroit: Charles Scribner's Sons. From *Scribner Writers Series.*

_____. 2009. *American Writers: A Collection of Literary Biographies.* New York: Charles Scribner's Sons. From *Scribner Writers Series.*

Parini, Jay, and Suzanne Disheroon Green (Eds.). 2004. *Twenty-first-Century American Novelists. Dictionary of Literary Biography (Vol. 292).* Detroit: Gale. *Literature Resources from Gale.*

Parker, Peter (Ed.). 1995/1996. *A Reader's Guide to Twentieth-Century Writers.* New York: Oxford University Press.

Parker, Tony. 1996. *Studs Terkel: A Life in Words.* New York: Henry Holt.

Patrick, John J., Richard M. Pious, and Donald M. Ritchie. 1993, 1994, 1998, 2001, 2002. *US Government Guide: The Oxford Guide to the United States Government.*

Payne, Tom. 1997. *Encyclopedia of Great Writers: The World's Leading Authors and Their Works.* New York: Barnes & Noble Books.

Pearlman, Mickey, and Katherine Usher Henderson. 1990, 1992. *A Voice of One's Own: Conversations with America's Writing Women.* Boston: Houghton Mifflin.

Pederson, Jay P. (Ed.). 1996. *St. James Guide to Crime & Mystery Writers (4th ed.): St. James Guide to Writers Series.* Detroit: St. James Press. From *Literature Resource Center.*

_____. 1996. *St. James Guide to Science Fiction Writers* (4th ed.). New York: St. James Press. From *Literature Resource Center.*

Pizer, Donald, and Earl N. Harbert. (Eds.). 1982. *American Realists and Naturalists.* In *Dictionary of Literary Biography* (Vol. 12). Detroit: Gale Research.

Plimpton, George. 1989. *The Writer's Chapbook: A Compendium of Fact, Opinion, Wit, and Advice from the 20th Century's Preeminent Writers [Edited from* The Paris Review Interviews*].* New York: Penguin Books.

Porter, Dorothy. 1971/1995. *Early Negro Writing, 1760-1837.* Baltimore: Black Classic Press.

Price-Groff, Claire. 1997. *Extraordinary Women Journalists.* Chicago: Children's Press.

Quarles, Benjamin. 1988. *Black Mosaic: Essays in Afro-American History and Historiography.* Amherst: University of Massachusetts Press.

_____. 1969. *Black Abolitionists.* New York: Oxford University Press.

Quartermain, Peter. (Ed.). 1986. *American Poets, 1880-1945: 1st Series.* In *Dictionary of Literary Biography* (Vol. 45). Detroit: Gale Research.

_____. 1986. *American Poets, 1880-1945: 2nd Series. Dictionary of Literary Biography* (Vol. 48). Detroit: Gale Research.

_____. 1987. *American Poets, 1880-1945: Third Series.* In *Dictionary of Literary Biography* (Vol. 54). Detroit: Gale Research.

Rand, Donna, Toni Trent Parker, and Sheila Foster. 1998. *Black Books Galore! Guide to Great African American Children's Books.* New York: John Wiley & Sons.

Random House Webster's Dictionary of Scientists. 1996/1997. New York: Random House.

Riggs, Thomas. (Ed.). 1995. *Contemporary Poets* (6th ed.). New York: St. James Press.

Riley, Sam G. (Ed.). 1989. *American Magazine Journalists, 1850-1900.* In *Dictionary of Literary Biography* (Vol. 79). Detroit: Gale Research.

_____. 1990. *American Magazine Journalists, 1900-1960: First Series.* In *Dictionary of Literary Biography* (Vol. 91). Detroit: Gale Research.

_____. 1994. *American Magazine Journalists, 1900-1960: Second Series.* In *Dictionary of Literary Biography* (Vol. 137). Detroit: Gale Research.

Rood, Karen Lane. (Ed.). 1980. *American Writers in Paris, 1920-1939. Dictionary of Literary Biography* (Vol. 4). Detroit: Gale Research.

Roses, Lorraine Elena. 1990. *Harlem Renaissance and Beyond: Literary Biographies of 100 Black Women Writers 1900-1945.* Boston, MA: G.K. Hall.

Ross, Donald, and James Schramer. (Eds.). 1998. *American Travel Writers, 1850-1915.* In *Dictionary of Literary Biography* (Vol. 189). Detroit: Gale Research.

Rush, Theressa Gunnels, Carol Fairbanks Myers, and Esther Spring Arata. (Eds.). 1975. *Black American Writers Past and Present: A Biographical and Bibliographical Dictionary* (Vol. 2). Metuchen, NJ: Scarecrow Press.

Safire, William, and Leonard Safir (Eds.). 1989. *Words of Wisdom: More Good Advice.* New York: Fireside, Simon & Schuster.

Salgado, Maria Antonia (Ed.). 2004. *Modern Spanish American Poets: Second Series. Dictionary of Literary Biography* (Vol. 290). Detroit: Gale.

Salzman, Jack, David Lionel Smith, and Cornel West Eds.. (1996). *Encyclopedia of African-American Culture and History.* New York: Macmillan.

Schramer, James, and Donald Ross. (Eds.). 1997. *American Travel Writers, 1776-1864.* In *Dictionary of Literary Biography* (Vol. 183). Detroit: Gale Research.

Serafin, Steven (Ed.). 1991. *American Literary Biographers: Second Series. Dictionary of Literary Biography* (Vol. 111). Detroit: Gale Research. From *Literature Resource Center.*

Sherrin, Ned (Ed.). 1995. *The Oxford Dictionary of Humorous Quotations.* New York: Oxford University Press.

Shockley, Ann Allen. 1988/1989. *Afro-American Women Writers, 1746-1933: An Anthology and Critical Guide.* Boston: G. K. Hall (1988); New York: Meridian/NAL (1989).

Showalter, Elaine, Lea Baechler, and A. Walton Litz. (Eds.). 1991. *Modern American Women Writers.* New York: Charles Scribner's Sons. Literature Resources from Gale.

Silvey, Anita (Ed.). 1995. *Children's Books and Their Creators.* Boston: Houghton Mifflin.

Smallwood, David, Stan West, and Allison Keyes. 1998. *Profiles of Great African Americans.* Lincolnwood, IL: Publications, International.

Smith, Jessie Carney (Ed.). 1996. *Powerful Black Women.* New York: Visible Ink.

_____. 1998. *Black Heroes of the 20th Century.* New York: Visible Ink.

_____. 1992. *Notable Black American Women.* Detroit: Gale Research.

Smith, Jessie Carney (Ed.), with Casper L. Jordan and Robert L. Johns. 1994. *Black Firsts: 2,000 Years of Extraordinary Achievement.* New York: Visible Ink.

Smith, Valerie (Consulting Ed.), Lea Baechler and A. Walton Litz (General Eds.). 1991. *African American Writers.* New York: Charles Scribner's Sons.

Smith, Valerie, Lea Baechler, and A. Walton Litz. (Eds.). 1991. *African American Writers.* New York: Charles Scribner's Sons. From *Scribner Writers Series.*

Smitherman, Geneva. 1977. *Talkin and Testifyin: The Language of Black America.* Boston: Houghton Mifflin.

Steinberg, Sybil. 1995. *Writing for Your Life #2: 50 Outstanding Authors Talk about the Art of Writing and the Job of Publishing.* Wainscott, NY: Pushcart Press, W. W. Norton.

Stephens, Autumn. 1992. *Wild Women: Crusaders, Curmudgeons and Completely Corsetless Ladies in the Otherwise Virtuous Victorian Era.* Berkeley, CA: Conari Press.

Stewart, Jeffrey C. 1996. *1001 Things Everyone Should Know about African American History.* New York: Doubleday.

Stewart, Julia. 1997. *African Proverbs and Wisdom: A Collection for Every Day of the Year from More Than 40 African Nations.* Secaucus, NJ: Citadel Press, Carol Publishing Group.

Stille, Darlene R. 1995. *Extraordinary Women Scientists.* Chicago: Children's Press.

Strickland, Michael R. 1996. *African-American Poets.* Springfield, NJ: Enslow Publishers.

Stringer, Jenny (Ed.). 1996. *Oxford Companion to Twentieth Century Literature in English.* New York: Oxford University Press.

Strouf, Judie L. H. 1998. *Literature Lover's Book of Lists: Serious Trivia for the Bibliophile.* Paramus, NJ: Prentice Hall Press.

Tate, Claudia. (Ed.). 1983/1984. *Black Women Writers at Work.* New York: Continuum.

Twayne Authors Series, The. (290, 383). 1978. 1980. Boston: Twayne Publishers.

Tyrkus, Michael J. and Michael Bronski. (Eds.). 1997. *Gay & Lesbian Biography.* Detroit: St. James Press.

Unger, Leonard. (Ed.). 1974. *American Writers: A Collection of Literary Biographies.* (Vol. 4). New York: Charles Scribner's Sons. From *Scribner Writers Series.*

_____. 1979. *American Writers: A Collection of Literary Biographies.* New York: Charles Scribner's Sons. From *Scribner Writers Series.*

_____. 1979. *American Writers: A Collection of Literary Biographies: Vol. 2, Suppl. 1. Vachel Lindsay to Elinor Wylie.* New York: Charles Scribner's Sons. From *Scribner Writers Series.*

Valade, Roger M., III. 1996. *The Essential Black Literature Guide.* Detroit: Visible Ink Press.

Vasudevan, Aruna. (Eds.). 1994. *Twentieth-Century Romance & Historical Writers, 3rd ed. Twentieth-Century Writers Series.* New York: St. James Press.

Ward, Jerry W., Jr. (Ed.). 1997) *Trouble the Waters: 250 Years of African-American Poetry.* New York: Penguin (Mentor Books).

Webster's Concise Encyclopedia (in CD-ROM form). 1994.

Webster's Dictionary of American Authors. 1996. New York: Smithmark Reference, US Media Holdings.

Webster's Dictionary of American Women. 1996. New York: Smithmark Reference, US Media Holdings.

Webster's New Biographical Dictionary. 1988. Springfield, MA: Merriam-Webster.

Weekly Reader. 1995. *Dear Author: Students Write about the Books that Changed Their Lives.* Berkeley, CA: Conari Press.

West's Encyclopedia of American Law. 1998. Detroit: Gale Group.

Wettenstein, Beverley. 1994/1998. *A Woman's Book of Days.* New York: Barnes & Noble.

Wheatley, Christopher J. (Ed.). 2000. *Twentieth-Century American Dramatists: Second Series. Dictionary of Literary Biography* (Vol. 228). Detroit: Gale Group.

_____. 2002. *Twentieth-Century American Dramatists: 3rd Series.* In *Dictionary of Literary Biography* (Vol. 249). Detroit: Gale Group.

_____. 2003. *Twentieth-Century American Dramatists: Fourth Series. Dictionary of Literary Biography* (Vol. 266). Detroit: Gale.

Wilson, Clyde Norman. (Ed.). 1983. *Twentieth-Century American Historians. Dictionary of Literary Biography* (Vol. 17). Detroit: Gale Research.

Woman Artists Book of Days, The. 1988. New York: Hugh Lauter Levin Associates, Inc., Macmillan.

World Book Multimedia Encyclopedia. 1998. 1999. (CD-ROM)

Worley, Demetrice A., and Jesse Perry, Jr. (with foreword by Nikki Giovanni). 1993. *African American Literature: An Anthology of Nonfiction, Fiction, Poetry, and Drama.* Lincolnwood, IL: National Textbook Company, NTC Publishing Group.

Writers for Young Adults. Charles Scribner's Sons. 1993. Rpt. in *Children's Literature Review.* Detroit: Gale.

Appendix G: Key to References

Full citations for abbreviated references that appear at the end of each entry.
All electronic references were retrieved between June 1, 2008 and August 9, 2009.

Abbreviation	Bibliographical Citation
1MPCA:BSB	McElmeel, Sharron L. 1999. *100 Most Popular Children's Authors: Biographical Sketches and Bibliographies.* Englewood, CO: Libraries Unlimited.
1MPPBAI	McElmeel, Sharron L. 2000. *100 Most Popular Picture Book Authors and Illustrators : Biographical Sketches and Bibliographies.* Englewood, CO: Libraries Unlimited.
1TESK	Stewart, Jeffrey C. 1996. *1001 Things Everyone Should Know about African American History.* New York: Doubleday.
2CAAWA	Hedgepeth, Chester M., Jr. (Ed.). 1971. *Twentieth-Century African American Writers and Artists.* Washington, DC: American Library Association.
21-CAN	Parini, Jay, and Suzanne Disheroon Green (Eds.). 2004. *Twenty-first-Century American Novelists. Dictionary of Literary Biography* (Vol. 292). Detroit: Gale. *Literature Resources from Gale.*
33T	**Bolden, Tonya** (Ed.). 1998. *33 Things Every Girl Should Know: Stories, Songs, Poems, and Smart Talk by 33 Extraordinary Women.* New York: Crown.
A	Artist. Copyright (c) 2009 All Media Guide, LLC. Content provided by All Music Guide (r) , a trademark of All Media Guide, LLC. Available at Answers.com.
AA	American Author. (c) 1999-2009 by Answers Corporation. Available at Answers.com.
AA:AJS	**Johnson, Charles [Spurgeon]**, Patricia Smith, and WGBH Series Research Team. 1998. *Africans in America: America's Journey through Slavery.* New York: Harcourt Brace.
AA:PoP	Estell, Kenneth. 1994. *African America: Portrait of a People.* New York: Visible Ink.
AAA-1745-1945	Nelson, Emmanuel S. (Ed.). 2000. *African American Authors, 1745-1945.* Westport, CT: Greenwood Press. Rpt. in *Poetry Criticism* (Vol. 88). Detroit: Gale. From *Literature Resource Center.*
AAB	Editors at Globe Fearon. 1995. *African-American Biographies.* Paramus, NJ: Globe Fearon Educational Publisher.
AABL	Livingston, Michael E. 1997. *The African-American Book of Lists.* New York: Perigee Books, Berkley Publishing Group, Putnam.
AAFW-55-84	Davis, Thadious M., and **Trudier Harris-Lopez**. (Eds.). 1984. *Afro-American Fiction Writers After 1955.* In *Dictionary of Literary Biography* (Vol. 33). Detroit: Gale Research. From *Literature Resource Center.*
AAL	Worley, Demetrice A., and Jesse Perry, Jr. (with foreword by **Nikki Giovanni**). 1993. *African American Literature: An Anthology of Nonfiction, Fiction, Poetry, and Drama.* Lincolnwood, IL: National Textbook Company, NTC Publishing Group.
AANB	Gates, Henry Louis, Jr., and Evelyn Brooks Higginbotham (Eds.). 2008. *African American National Biography (8 vols.).* New York: Oxford University Press.
AAP	Strickland, Michael R. 1996. *African-American Poets.* Springfield, NJ: Enslow Publishers.
AAP-55-85	Davis, Thadious M., and Trudier Harris-Lopez. (Eds.). 1985. *Afro-American Poets Since 1955.* In *Dictionary of Literary Biography* (Vol. 41). Detroit: Gale Research.
AAP-WWII-1996-5th	Conte, Joseph Mark (Ed.). *American Poets Since World War II: Fifth Series.* In *Dictionary of Literary Biography* (Vol. 169). Detroit: Gale Research. 1995.
AAW	Smith, Valerie (Consulting Ed.); Lea Baechler and A. Walton Litz (General Eds.). 1991. *African American Writers.* New York: Charles Scribner's Sons.
AAW-40-55	Harris-Lopez, Trudier (Ed.). 1988. *Afro-American Writers, 1940-1955.* in *Dictionary of Literary Biography* (Vol. 76). Detroit: Gale Research.
AAW-55-85: DPW	Davis, Thadious M., and Trudier Harris-Lopez. (Eds.). 1985. *Afro-American Writers After 1955: Dramatists and Prose Writers.* In *Dictionary of Literary Biography* (Vol. 38). Detroit: Gale Research.
AAW-1981	Litz, A. Walton (Ed.). 1981. *African American Writers.* New York: Charles Scribner's Sons. From *Scribner Writers Series.*

AAW-1991	Smith, Valerie, Lea Baechler, and A. Walton Litz. (Eds.). 1991. *African American Writers.* New York: Charles Scribner's Sons. From *Scribner Writers Series.*
AAW-1991-Vol1/Sup3.	Baechler, Lea, and A. Walton Litz. (Eds.). (1991. *African American Writers* (Vol. 1: Suppl. 3). New York: Charles Scribner's Sons. From *Scribner Writers Series.*
AAW-1996	Litz, A. Walton, and Molly Weigel. (Eds.).(1996). *African American Writers.* New York: Charles Scribner's Sons. From *Scribner Writers Series.*
AAW-2004	Parini, Jay (Ed.). 2004. *African American Writers.* Detroit: Charles Scribner's Sons. From *Scribner Writers Series.*
AAW:AAPP	Long, Richard A., and Eugenia W. Collier (Eds.). 1985. *Afro-American Writing: An Anthology of Prose and Poetry* (2nd, enlarged ed.). University Park: Pennsylvania State University Press.
AAW:PV	Koolish, Lynda. 2001. *African American Writers: Portraits and Visions.* Jackson: University Press of Mississippi.
AAWBHR	Harris-Lopez, Trudier, and Thadious M. Davis. (Eds.). 1986. *Afro-American Writers Before the Harlem Renaissance.* In *Dictionary of Literary Biography* (Vol. 50-51). Detroit: Gale Research.
AAWHR-40	Harris-Lopez, Trudier, and Thadious M. Davis. Eds.. (1987). *Afro-American Writers From the Harlem Renaissance to 1940.* In *Dictionary of Literary Biography* (Vol. 51). Detroit: Gale Research.
AAWW	**Shockley, Ann Allen.** 1988/1989. *Afro-American Women Writers, 1746-1933: An Anthology and Critical Guide.* Boston: G. K. Hall (1988); New York: Meridian/NAL (1989).
Act	Actor. 2009. All Media Guide, LLC. Available at Answers.com.
ACW	Elliott, Emory (Ed.). 1984. *American Colonial Writers, 1735-1781.* In *Dictionary of Literary Biography* (Vol. 31). Detroit: Gale Research.
ADD	Beeching, Cyril Leslie. 1997. *A Dictionary of Dates* (2nd ed.). New York: Oxford University Press.
AE	Art Encyclopedia. 2002. In *The Concise Grove Dictionary of Art.* by Oxford University Press. Available at Answers.com.
AHL	Holman, C. Hugh, and William Harmon. 1936/1992. *A Handbook to Literature* (6th ed.). New York: Macmillan.
AL	Bradbury, Malcolm (Ed.). 1996. *The Atlas of Literature.* New York: De Agostini Editions.
ALA	Hendrickson, Robert. 1990. *American Literary Anecdotes.* New York: Penguin.
ALB-2	Serafin, Steven (Ed.). 1991. *American Literary Biographers: Second Series. Dictionary of Literary Biography* (Vol. 111). Detroit: Gale Research. From *Literature Resource Center.*
Amazon.com	This database resource is available from any Internet-friendly computer. To find this resource, go to //Amazon.com, and type in the author's name, from first name to surname.
AMDW	Anderson, George Parker (Ed.). 2005. *American Mystery and Detective Writers.* In *Dictionary of Literary Biography* (Vol. 306). Detroit: Gale.
AMJ-00-60-1	Riley, Sam G. (Ed.). 1990. *American Magazine Journalists, 1900-1960: First Series.* In *Dictionary of Literary Biography* (Vol. 91). Detroit: Gale Research.
AMJ-00-60-2	Riley, Sam G. (Ed.). 1994. *American Magazine Journalists, 1900-1960: Second Series.* In *Dictionary of Literary Biography* (Vol. 137). Detroit: Gale Research.
AMJ-1850-1900-1	Riley, Sam G. (Ed.). 1989. *American Magazine Journalists, 1850-1900.* In *Dictionary of Literary Biography* (Vol. 79). Detroit: Gale Research.
AN	AnswerNote. 1999-2009. Answers Corporation. Available at Answers.com.
AN-1910-45	Martine, James J. (Ed.). 1981. *American Novelists, 1910-1945.* In *Dictionary of Literary Biography* (Vol. 9). Detroit: Gale Research.
ANAD	Bolden, Tonya (Ed.). 1998. *And Not Afraid to Dare: The Stories of Ten African American Women.* New York: Scholastic Press.
ANJ-1690-1872-1.	Ashley, Perry J. (Ed.). 1985. *American Newspaper Journalists, 1690-1872.* In *Dictionary of Literary Biography* (Vol. 43). Detroit: Gale Research.
ANJ-1873-1900	Ashley, Perry J. (Ed.). 1983. *American Newspaper Journalists, 1873-1900. Dictionary of Literary Biography* (Vol. 23). Detroit: Gale Research.
ANJ-26-50-1	Ashley, Perry J. (Ed.). 1984. *American Newspaper Journalists, 1926-1950.* In *Dictionary of Literary Biography* (Vol. 29). Detroit: Gale Research. (1984). Literature Resources from Gale.
ANSWWII-1st	Helterman, Jeffrey, and Richard Layman. (Eds.). 1978. *American Novelists Since World War II: First Series. Dictionary of Literary Biography* (Vol. 2). Detroit: Gale Research. From *Literature Resource Center.*
ANSWWII-2nd	Kibler, James E. (Ed.) 1980. *American Novelists Since World War II: 2nd Series.* In *Dictionary of Literary Biography* (Vol. 6). Detroit: Gale Research. From *Literature Resource Center.*

ANSWWII-3rd	Giles, James R., and Wanda H. Giles. (Eds.). 1994. *American Novelists Since World War II: 3rd Series.* In *Dictionary of Literary Biography* (Vol. 143). Detroit: Gale Research.	*ARN*	Pizer, Donald, and Earl N. Harbert. (Eds.). 1982. *American Realists and Naturalists.* In *Dictionary of Literary Biography* (Vol. 12). Detroit: Gale Research.
ANSWWII-4th	Giles, James R., and Wanda H. Giles. (Eds.). 1995. *American Novelists Since World War II: 4th Series.* In *Dictionary of Literary Biography* (Vol. 152). Detroit: Gale Research.	*ARNE-1*	Myerson, Joel. (Ed.). 1978. *The American Renaissance in New England. Dictionary of Literary Biography* (Vol. 1). Detroit: Gale Research.
ANSWWII-5th	Giles, James R., and Wanda H. Giles. (Eds.). 1996. *American Novelists Since World War II: 5th Series.* In *Dictionary of Literary Biography* (Vol. 173). Detroit: Gale Research.	*ARNE-4*	Mott, Wesley T. (Ed.). 2001. *The American Renaissance in New England: Fourth Series.* In *Dictionary of Literary Biography* (Vol. 243). Detroit: Gale Group.
ANSWWII-6th	Giles, James R., and Wanda H. Giles. (Eds.). 2000. *American Novelists Since World War II: 6th Series.* In *Dictionary of Literary Biography* (Vol. 227). Detroit: Gale Group.	*ARRW-2*	American Radical and Reform Writers: Second Series. 2009. In *Dictionary of Literary Biography* (Vol. 345). Detroit: Gale Research.
ANSWWII-7th	Giles, James R., and Wanda H. Giles. (Eds.). 2003. *American Novelists Since World War II: 7th Series.* In *Dictionary of Literary Biography* (Vol. 278). Detroit: Gale.	*AS-2*	Clark, Randall. (Ed.). 1986. *American Screenwriters: 2nd Series. Dictionary of Literary Biography* (Vol. 44). Detroit: Gale Research.
AP	Leslau, Charlotte, and Wolf Leslau. 1985. *African Proverbs.* White Plains, NY: Peter Pauper Press.	*ASL-00-60*	Furia, Philip. (Ed.). 2002. *American Song Lyricists, 1920-1960.* In *Dictionary of Literary Biography* (Vol. 265). Detroit: Gale.
AP1880-1945-1	Quartermain, Peter. (Ed.). 1986. *American Poets, 1880-1945: 1st Series.* In *Dictionary of Literary Biography* (Vol. 45). Detroit: Gale Research.	*ASSW-to1880*	Kimbel, Bobby Ellen, and William E. Grant. (Eds.). 1988. *American Short-Story Writers Before 1880.* In *Dictionary of Literary Biography* (Vol. 74). Detroit: Gale Research.
AP1880-1945-2	Quartermain, Peter. (Ed.). 1986. *American Poets, 1880-1945: 2nd Series. Dictionary of Literary Biography* (Vol. 48). Detroit: Gale Research.	*ASSW-1880-1910*	Kimbel, Bobby Ellen, and William E. Grant. (Eds.). 1989. *American Short-Story Writers, 1880-1910.* In *Dictionary of Literary Biography* (Vol. 78). Detroit: Gale Research.
AP1880-1945-3	Quartermain, Peter. (Ed.). 1987. *American Poets, 1880-1945: Third Series.* In *Dictionary of Literary Biography* (Vol. 54). Detroit: Gale Research.	*ASSW-1910-1945-2*	Kimbel, Bobby Ellen. (Ed.). 1991. *American Short-Story Writers, 1910-1945: Second Series.* In *Dictionary of Literary Biography* (Vol. 102). Detroit: Gale Research.
APSWWII-1	Greiner, Donald J. (Ed.). 1980. *American Poets Since World War II.* In *Dictionary of Literary Biography* (Vol. 5). Detroit: Gale Research.	*ASSWSWWII-1*	Meanor, Patrick. (Ed.). 1993. *American Short-Story Writers Since World War II.* In *Dictionary of Literary Biography* (Vol. 130). Detroit: Gale Research.
APSWWII-3	Gwynn, R. S. (Ed.). 1992. *American Poets Since World War II: 3rd Series.* In *Dictionary of Literary Biography* (Vol. 120). Detroit: Gale Research.	*ASSWSWWII-2nd*	Meanor, Patrick, and Gwen Crane. (Ed.). 2000. *American Short-Story Writers Since World War II: 2nd Series.* In *Dictionary of Literary Biography* (Vol. 218). Detroit: Gale Group.
APSWWII-4	Conte, Joseph Mark. (Ed.). 1996. *American Poets Since World War II: 4th Series. Dictionary of Literary Biography* (Vol. 165). Detroit: Gale Research.	*ASSWSWWII-4th*	Meanor, Patrick, and Joseph McNicholas (Eds.). 2001. *American Short-Story Writers Since World War II: 4th Series.* In *Dictionary of Literary Biography* (Vol. 244). Detroit: Gale Group.
APSWWII-5	Conte, Joseph Mark. (Ed.).1996. *American Poets Since World War II: 5th Series. Dictionary of Literary Biography* (Vol. 169). Detroit: Gale Research.	*AT*	Conyers, James L. 2005. *Afrocentric Traditions* (Chapter 7, "Selected Bibliography"). Edison, NJ: Transaction Publishers. Available at //books.google.com/books.
AP&W	Stewart, Julia. 1997. *African Proverbs and Wisdom: A Collection for Every Day of the Year from More Than 40 African Nations.* Secaucus, NJ: Citadel Press, Carol Publishing Group.	*ATG*	"American Theater Guide." 2004. *The Oxford Companion to American Theatre.* New York; Oxford University Press. Available at Answers.com.

ATW   Schramer, James, and Donald Ross. (Eds.).
               1997. *American Travel Writers, 1776-1864*.
               In *Dictionary of Literary Biography* (Vol.
               183). Detroit: Gale Research.

ATW-1850-1915 Ross, Donald, and James Schramer. (Eds.).
               1998. *American Travel Writers, 1850-1915*.
               In *Dictionary of Literary Biography* (Vol.
               189). Detroit: Gale Research.

AW:ACLB-01   Parini, Jay. (Ed.). 2001. *American Writers: A
               Collection of Literary Biographies*. New York:
               Charles Scribner's Sons. From *Scribner
               Writers Series*.

AW:ACLB-02   Parini, Jay. (Ed.). 2002. *American Writers: A
               Collection of Literary Biographies*. New York:
               Charles Scribner's Sons. From *Scribner
               Writers Series*.

AW:ACLB-02-   Baechler, Lea, and A. Walton Litz. (Eds.).
S3.   1991. *American Writers: A Collection of
               Literary Biographies*. (Vol. 2: Suppl. 3). New
               York: Charles Scribner's Sons. From *Scribner
               Writers Series*.

AW:ACLB-03   Parini, Jay. (Ed.). 2003. *American Writers: A
               Collection of Literary Biographies*. New York:
               Charles Scribner's Sons. From *Scribner
               Writers Series*.

AW:ACLB-04   Parini, Jay. (Ed.). 2004. *American Writers: A
               Collection of Literary Biographies*. Detroit:
               Charles Scribner's Sons. From *Scribner
               Writers Series*.

AW:ACLB-08   Parini, Jay. (Ed.). 2008. *American Writers: A
               Collection of Literary Biographies*. Detroit:
               Charles Scribner's Sons. From *Scribner
               Writers Series*.

AW:ACLB-09   Parini, Jay. (Ed.). 2009. *American Writers: A
               Collection of Literary Biographies*. New York:
               Charles Scribner's Sons. From *Scribner
               Writers Series*.

AW:ACLB-74-4   Unger, Leonard. (Ed.). 1974. *American
               Writers: A Collection of Literary
               Biographies*.(Vol. 4). New York: Charles
               Scribner's Sons. From *Scribner Writers Series*.

AW:ACLB-79   Unger, Leonard. (Ed.). 1979. *American
               Writers: A Collection of Literary Biographies*.
               New York: Charles Scribner's Sons. From
               Scribner Writers Series.

AW:ACLB-79-   Unger, Leonard. (Ed.). 1979. *American
V2-S1   Writers: A Collection of Literary Biographies:
               Vol. 2, Suppl. 1. Vachel Lindsay to Elinor
               Wylie*. New York: Charles Scribner's Sons.
               From *Scribner Writers Series*.

AW:ACLB-81   Litz, A. Walton. (Ed.). 1981. *American
               Writers: A Collection of Literary Biographies*.
               New York: Charles Scribner's Sons. From
               Scribner Writers Series.

AW:ACLB-81-2   Litz, A. Walton. (Ed.). 1981. *American
               Writers: A Collection of Literary Biographies*
               (Vol. 2). New York: Charles Scribner's Sons.
               From *Scribner Writers Series*.

AW:ACLB-91   Baechler, Lea, and A. Walton Litz. (Eds.).
               1991. *American Writers: A Collection of
               Literary Biographies*. New York: Charles
               Scribner's Sons. From *Scribner Writers Series*.

AW:ACLB-91-   Baechler, Lea, and A. Walton Litz. (Eds.).
Sup3   1991. *American Writers: A Collection of
               Literary Biographies*. (Vol. 1: Suppl. 3). New
               York: Charles Scribner's Sons. From *Scribner
               Writers Series*.

AW:ACLB-96   Litz, A. Walton, and Molly Weigel. 1996.
               *American Writers: A Collection of Literary
               Biographies*. New York: Charles Scribner's
               Sons. From *Scribner Writers Series*.

AWA   Bernikow, Louise, and the National
               Women's History Project. 1997. *The
               American Women's Almanac: An Inspiring and
               Irreverent Women's History*. New York:
               Berkley Books.

AWAW   **Hull, Gloria T.**, Patricia Bell Scott, and
               Barbara Smith (Eds.). 1982. *All the Women
               Are White, All the Blacks Are Men, But Some
               of Us Are Brave: Black Women's Studies*. Old
               Westbury, NY: Feminist Press.

AWBD   Wettenstein, Beverley. 1994/1998. *A
               Woman's Book of Days*. New York: Barnes &
               Noble Books.

AWER   Emory Elliott. (Ed.). 1985. *American Writers
               of the Early Republic*. In *Dictionary of Literary
               Biography* (Vol. 37). Detroit: Gale Research.

AWC to 1900   Estes, Glenn E. (Ed.). 1985. *American
               Writers for Children Before 1900. Dictionary
               of Literary Biography* (Vol. 42). Detroit: Gale
               Research.

AWC-1960-86   Estes, Glenn E. (Ed.). 1986. *American
               Writers for Children Since 1960: Fiction*. In
               Dictionary of Literary Biography (Vol. 52).
               Detroit: Gale Research.

AWNYS   Myerson, Joel. (Ed.). 1979. *Antebellum
               Writers in New York and the South*. In
               Dictionary of Literary Biography (Vol. 3).
               Detroit: Gale Research.

AWP-1920-1939 Rood, Karen Lane. (Ed.). 1980. *American
               Writers in Paris, 1920-1939. Dictionary of
               Literary Biography* (Vol. 4). Detroit: Gale
               Research.

AWPW:1820-   Hudock, Amy E., and Katharine Rodier.
1870   (Eds.). 2001. *American Women Prose Writers:
               1820-1870. Dictionary of Literary Biography*
               (Vol. 239). Detroit: Gale Group.

AWPW:1870-   Harris, Sharon M., Heidi L. M. Jacobs, and
1920   Jennifer Putzi. (Eds.). 2000. *American
               Women Prose Writers, 1870-1920*. In
               Dictionary of Literary Biography (Vol. 221).
               Detroit: Gale Group.

AWS-2   Ljungquist, Kent P. (Ed.). 2001. *Antebellum
               Writers in the South: 2nd Series. Dictionary of
               Literary Biography* (Vol. 248). Detroit: Gale
               Group.

AWW-1900-45   Champion, Laurie. (Ed.). 2007. *American Women Writers, 1900-1945: A Bio-Bibliographical Critical Sourcebook*. Westport, CT: Greenwood. 2000. Rpt. in Michelle Lee (Ed.), *Poetry Criticism* (Vol. 77, pp. 312-317). Detroit: Gale.

B   Biography. 2006. Available at Answers.com.

BA   **Quarles, Benjamin**. 1969. *Black Abolitionists*. New York: Oxford University Press.

BAAW   Bolden, Tonya. 1996. *The Book of African-American Women: 150 Crusaders, Creators, and Uplifters*. Holbrook, MA: Adams Media Corporation.

BaD   Currie, Stephen. 1996. *Birthday a Day: Grades 3 and Up*. Glenview, IL: GoodYearBooks.

BAL-1-P   Miller, Ruth (Ed.). 1971. *Black American Literature, 1760-Present*. Beverly Hills, CA: Glencoe Press (Macmillan).

BANP   **Johnson, James Weldon** (Ed.). 1922/1959. *The Book of American Negro Poetry*. New York: Harcourt Brace Jovanovich.

BASS   **Clarke, John Henrik** (Ed.). 1966/1993. *Black American Short Stories: 100 Years of the Best*. New York: Hill and Wang; Farrar, Straus and Giroux.

BAW:P&D   Bigsby, C. W.E. (Ed.). 1981. *The Black American Writer: Poetry and Drama*.1969. Everett/ Edwards, Inc.. Rpt. in Sharon R. Gunton (Ed.), in *Contemporary Literary Criticism* (Vol. 17, pp. 157-170). Detroit: Gale Research.

BAWPP   Rush, Theressa Gunnels, Carol Fairbanks Myers, and Esther Spring Arata. (Eds.). 1975. *Black American Writers Past and Present: A Biographical and Bibliographical Dictionary* (Vol. 2). Metuchen, NJ: Scarecrow Press.

BB   Black Biography: Contemporary Black Biography. 2006. Detroit: Gale Group. Available at Answers.com.

BBG   Rand, Donna, Toni Trent Parker, and Sheila Foster. 1998. *Black Books Galore! Guide to Great African American Children's Books*. New York: John Wiley & Sons.

BC   Diefendorf, Elizabeth. 1996) *New York Public Library's Books of the Century*. New York: Oxford University Press.

BCE   Britannica Concise Encyclopedia. 2006. *Britannica Concise Encyclopedia*. Encyclopædia Britannica. Available at Answers.com.

BDAA   Kranz, Rachel, and Philip J. Koslow. 1999. *The Biographical Dictionary of African Americans*. New York: Checkmark Books, Facts on File.

BF:2000   **Smith, Jessie Carney** (Ed.), with Casper L. Jordan and Robert L. Johns. 1994. *Black Firsts: 2,000 Years of Extraordinary Achievement*. New York: Visible Ink.

BFC   **Christian, Barbara**. 1985. *Black Feminist Criticism: Perspectives on Black Women Writers* (Athene Series). New York: Pergamon Press.

BH2C   Smith, Jessie Carney (Ed.). 1998. *Black Heroes of the 20th Century*. New York: Visible Ink.

BI   **McMillan, Terry** (Ed.). 1990. *Breaking Ice: An Anthology of Contemporary African-American Fiction*. New York: Penguin.

BLC-1   Draper, James P. (Ed.). 1992. *Black Literature Criticism* (Vol. 1). Detroit: Gale Research.

BLC-2   Draper, James P. (Ed.). 1992. *Black Literature Criticism* (Vol. 2). Detroit: Gale Research.

BLC-3   Draper, James P. (Ed.). 1992. *Black Literature Criticism* (Vol. 3). Detroit: Gale Research.

BM: EAAHH   Quarles, Benjamin. 1988. *Black Mosaic: Essays in Afro-American History and Historiography*. Amherst: University of Massachusetts Press.

BPEAR   Kaplan, Sidney, and Emma Nogrady Kaplan. 1989. *The Black Presence in the Era of the American Revolution, 1770-1880* (rev. ed.; original 1975). Amherst: University of Massachusetts Press.

BPSI   Haber, Louis. 1970. *Black Pioneers of Science and Invention*. New York: Harcourt Brace.

BRE   Benét, William Rose. 1945/1987) *Benét's Reader's Encyclopedia* (3rd ed.). New York: Harper & Row.

BrWr   Parini, Jay (Ed.). 2007. *British Writers*. Detroit: Charles Scribner's Sons. From *Scribner Writers Series*.

BS:AAE   Christian, Charles M. 1995. *Black Saga: The African American Experience*. Boston: Houghton Mifflin.

BusB   Business Biographies. 2006) Available at Answers.com.

BV   Chapman, Abraham (Ed.). 1968. *Black Voices: An Anthology of Afro-American Literature*. New York: Mentor, New American Library.

BW   Furman, Laura, and Elinore Standard (Eds.). 1997. *Bookworms: Great Writers and Readers Celebrate Reading*. New York: Carroll & Graph Publishers.

BW:AA   **Cade [Bambara], Toni**. 1970. *The Black Woman: An Anthology*. New York: Mentor, New American Library.

BW:SSCA   Metzger, Linda. 1989. *Black Writers: A Selection of Sketches from Contemporary Authors*. Detroit, Michigan: Gale Research, Book Tower.

BWA	Barksdale, Richard, and Keneth Kinnamon (Eds.). 1972. *Black Writers of America: A Comprehensive Anthology*. New York: Macmillan.	CdlF	Dalin, Anne Safran (Ed.). 1997. *Creme de la Femme: A Collection of the Best Contemporary Women Writers, Lyricists, Playwrights and Cartoonists*. New York: Random House.
BWA:AHE	**Hine, Darlene Clark**, Elsa Barkley Brown, and Rosalyn Terborg-Penn. (Eds.). 1993. *Black Women in America: An Historical Encyclopedia* (Vols. 1, 2). Bloomington: University of Indiana Press.	CE	Columbia Encyclopedia: The Columbia Electronic Encyclopedia (6th ed.). 2003. Columbia University Press. //www.cc.columbia.edu/cu/cup/ Available at Answers.com.
BWW	**Evans, Mari** (Ed.). 1984. *Black Women Writers (1950-1980)*. New York: Anchor, Doubleday.	CLC-241	Hunter, Jeffrey W. (Ed.) 2007. *Contemporary Literary Criticism* (Vol. 241). Detroit: Gale.
BWWW	**Tate, Claudia**. (Ed.). 1983/1984. *Black Women Writers at Work*. New York: Continuum.	CLC-246	Contemporary Literary Criticism (Vol. 246). Detroit: Gale.
CA/I	Children's Author/Illustrator. 2006. Available at Answers.com.	CLC-253	Contemporary Literary Criticism (Vol. 253). Detroit: Gale.
CAITGM	McElmeel, Sharron L. 2004. *Children's Authors and Illustrators Too Good to Miss : Biographical Sketches and Bibliographies*. Westport, CT: Libraries Unlimited.	CLC-261	Contemporary Literary Criticism (Vol. 261). Detroit: Gale.
CAO-00	Contemporary Authors Online. Detroit: Gale. 2000. Literature Resources from Gale.	CLCS	Contemporary Literary Criticism Select. Detroit: Gale.
CAO-01	Contemporary Authors Online. Detroit: Gale. 2001. Literature Resources from Gale.	CN-6	Brown, Susan Windisch. (Ed.). 1996. *Contemporary Novelists* (6th ed.). New York: St. James Press.
CAO-02	Contemporary Authors Online. Detroit: Gale. 2002. Literature Resources from Gale.	COCAAL	African American Literature: The Concise Oxford Companion to African American Literature. 2001, 2002. New York: Oxford University Press. Available at Answers.com.
CAO-03	Contemporary Authors Online. Detroit: Gale. 2003. From *Literature Resource Center*.	CP-6	Riggs, Thomas. (Ed.). 1995. *Contemporary Poets* (6th ed.). New York: St. James Press.
CAO-04	Contemporary Authors Online. Detroit: Gale. 2004. Literature Resources from Gale.	CPW	Mote, Dave. (Ed.). 1997. *Contemporary Popular Writers*. Detroit: St. James Press.
CAO-05	Contemporary Authors Online. Detroit: Gale. 2005. Literature Resources from Gale.	CSN	**Gates, Henry Louis, Jr.** (Ed.). 1987. *The Classic Slave Narratives*. New York: Penguin Books, Mentor.
CAO-06	Contemporary Authors Online. Detroit: Gale. 2006. Literature Resources from Gale.	CT	Kremer, John. 1996. *Celebrate Today! More Than 4,000 Holidays, Celebrations, Origins, and Anniversaries*. Rocklin, CA: Prima Publishing.
CAO-07	Contemporary Authors Online. Detroit: Gale. 2007. Literature Resources from Gale.	CYI	**McKissack, Patricia**. 1997. *Can You Imagine?* Katonah, NY: Richard C. Owen Publishers.
CAO-08	Contemporary Authors Online. Detroit: Gale. 2008. Literature Resources from Gale.	D	Discography. Links to shopping at Answers.com.
CAO-09	Contemporary Authors Online. Detroit: Gale. 2009. Literature Resources from Gale.	DA	Weekly Reader. 1995. *Dear Author: Students Write about the Books that Changed Their Lives*. Berkeley, CA: Conari Press.
CAO-1998	Contemporary Authors Online. Detroit: Gale. 1998. From *Literature Resource Center*.	DANB	**Logan, Rayford W.**, and Michael R. Winston (Eds.). 1982. *Dictionary of American Negro Biography*. New York: W. W. Norton.
CBC	Silvey, Anita (Ed.). 1995. *Children's Books and Their Creators*. Boston: Houghton Mifflin.	DD	Dictionary of Dance: The Oxford Dictionary of Dance. 2000, 2004. New York: Oxford University Press. Available at Answers.com.
CBD	Crystal, David (Ed.). 1990. *Cambridge Biographical Dictionary*. Cambridge, England: Cambridge University Press.	DGR	Boyd, Herb. 1995. *Down the Glory Road: Contributions of African Americans in United States History and Culture*. New York: Avon.
CBE	Crystal, David (Ed.). 1994. *The Cambridge Biographical Encyclopedia*. Cambridge, England: Cambridge University Press.		
CD-5	Berney, K. A. 1993. *Contemporary Dramatists* (5th ed.). London: St. James Press.		

Dict	Dictionary: The American Heritage(r) Dictionary of the English Language (4th ed.). 2000, 2007. Boston: Houghton Mifflin Company.
Dir	Director. 2009. All Media Guide, LLC. Available at Answers.com.
DMM	Kothari, Geeta (Ed.). 1994. *Did My Mama Like to Dance? and Other Stories about Mothers and Daughters.* New York: Avon.
DNPUS	Aptheker, Herbert (Ed.). 1951, 1973. *A Documentary of the Negro People in the United States* (3 vols.). Secaucus, NJ: Citadel Press.
DW:NLA	Emanuel, James A., and Theodore L. Gross (Eds.). 1968. *Dark Symphony: Negro Literature in America.* New York: Free Press.
E-94	Encarta. 1994. *Encarta 94 Encyclopedia: The Ultimate Learning Resource* (deluxe ed.). Seattle, WA: Microsoft.
E-95	Encarta. 1995. *Encarta 95 Encyclopedia: The Ultimate Learning Resource* (deluxe ed.). Seattle, WA: Microsoft.
E-97	Encarta. 1997. *Encarta 97 Encyclopedia: The Ultimate Learning Resource* (deluxe ed.). Seattle, WA: Microsoft.
E-98	Encarta. 1998. *Encarta 98 Encyclopedia: The Ultimate Learning Resource* (deluxe ed.). Seattle, WA: Microsoft.
E-99	Encarta. 1999. *Encarta 99 Encyclopedia: The Ultimate Learning Resource* (deluxe ed.). Seattle, WA: Microsoft.
E:NAH	Katz, William Loren. 1974. *Eyewitness: The Negro in American History.* Belmont, CA: Pitman Learning.
EA-99	Appiah, Kwame Anthony, and **Henry Louis Gates, Jr.** (Eds.). 1999. *Encarta Africana CD-ROM Encyclopedia.* Seattle, WA: Microsoft.
EAACH	Salzman, Jack, David Lionel Smith, and **Cornel West** Eds.. (1996). *Encyclopedia of African-American Culture and History.* New York: Macmillan.
EAAWW	Page, Yolanda Williams. 2007. *Encyclopedia of African American Women Writers.* Greenwood Publishing Group.
EB-98	Encyclopædia Britannica 1998. *Encyclopædia Britannica CD 98: Knowledge for the Information Age* (multimedia ed.). Springfield, MA: Merriam-Webster.
EB-99	Encyclopædia Britannica 1999. *Encyclopædia Britannica CD 98: Knowledge for the Information Age* (multimedia ed.). Springfield, MA: Merriam-Webster.
EB-BH-CD	Encyclopædia Britannica 1997. *Encyclopædia Britannica Profiles: Black History CD.* Springfield, MA: Merriam-Webster.
EBLG	Valade, Roger M., III. 1996. *The Essential Black Literature Guide.* Detroit: Visible Ink Press.
EE	Education Encyclopedia. Encyclopedia of Education. 2002. Detroit: Gale Group.
EGW	Payne, Tom. 1997. *Encyclopedia of Great Writers: The World's Leading Authors and Their Works.* New York: Barnes & Noble Books.
EL:CCR	Fadiman, Anne. 1998. *Ex Libris: Confessions of a Common Reader.* New York: Farrar, Straus and Giroux.
ENW	**Porter, Dorothy.** 1971/1995. *Early Negro Writing, 1760-1837.* Baltimore: Black Classic Press.
EWHA	Cullen-DuPont (with Annelise Orleck, historical consultant). 1998. *The Encyclopedia of Women's History in America.* New York: Da Capo Press.
EWJ	Price-Groff, Claire. 1997. *Extraordinary Women Journalists.* Chicago: Children's Press.
EWS	Stille, Darlene R. 1995. *Extraordinary Women Scientists.* Chicago: Children's Press.
F	Filmography. Links to shopping at Answers.com
FAD	Hirsch, E.D. Jr., Joseph F. Kett, and James Trefil. (Eds.). 2002. *Fine Arts Dictionary. The New Dictionary of Cultural Literacy* (3rd ed.). Boston: Houghton Mifflin Company. Available at Answers.com.
FLC	French Literature Companion: The New Oxford Companion to Literature in French. 1995, 2005. New York: Oxford University Press. Available at Answers.com.
FPA	The Female Poets of America. 1986. Rpt. in James E. Person, Jr. (Ed.), in *Literature Criticism from 1400 to 1800* (Vol. 3). Detroit: Gale Research.
FSF	**Franklin, John Hope,** and Alfred A. Moss, Jr. 1988. *From Slavery to Freedom: A History of Negro Americans* (6th ed.). New York: Knopf.
FTC	Fairy Tale Companion: The Oxford Companion to Fairy Tales. 2000, 2002, 2005. New York: Oxford University Press. Available at Answers.com.
FW	Kester-Shelton, Pamela. (Ed.). 1996. *Feminist Writers.* Detroit: St. James Press.
G-94	1994 Grolier Multimedia Encyclopedia. Danbury, CT: Grolier Interactive.
G-95	1995 Grolier Multimedia Encyclopedia. Danbury, CT: Grolier Interactive.
G-97	1997 Grolier Multimedia Encyclopedia. Danbury, CT: Grolier Interactive.

G-99	1999 Grolier Multimedia Encyclopedia (Deluxe ed., 2 CDs). Danbury, CT: Grolier Interactive.
G&LL-98-2	Gay & Lesbian Literature (Vol. 2). Detroit: Gale. 1998. From *Literature Resource Center*.
GEAAL	Ostrom, Hans, and J. David Macey, Jr. (Eds.). 2005. *The Greenwood Encyclopedia of African American Literature*. Westport, CT: Greenwood Press.
GLB	Tyrkus, Michael J. and Michael Bronski. (Eds.). 1997. *Gay & Lesbian Biography*. Detroit: St. James Press.
GLL	Gay & Lesbian Literature (Vol. 1). 1994. Detroit: Gale.
GOE	Gale Online Encyclopedia. Detroit: Gale. From *Literature Resource Center*.
H	Ashby, Ruth, and Deborah Gore Ohrn. 1995. *Herstory: Women Who Changed the World*. New York: Viking.
HAAL	Ervin, Hazel Arnett. 2004. "Appendix 1. Outlines of Literary History: African American, African, and Anglophone Caribbean." *The Handbook of African American Literature*. Gainesville: University Press of Florida.
HD	Hirsch, E.D., Jr., Joseph F. Kett, and James Trefil. (Eds.). 2002. *History Dictionary. The New Dictionary of Cultural Literacy* (3rd ed.). Boston: Houghton Mifflin Company. Available at Answers.com.
HR:AHD	Kellner, Bruce (Ed.). 1987. *The Harlem Renaissance: A Historical Dictionary for the Era*. New York: Methuen.
HR&B	Roses, Lorraine Elena. 1990. *Harlem Renaissance and Beyond: Literary Biographies of 100 Black Women Writers 1900-1945*. Boston, MA: G.K. Hall.
HWA	Hymowitz, Carol, and Michaele Weissman. 1978. *A History of Women in America*. New York: Bantam.
ICDWR	Craughwell, Thomas. 1998. *I Can't Decide What to Read . . . Great Books for Every Book Lover: 2002 Great Reading Suggestions for the Discriminating Bibliophile*. New York: Black Dog and Leventhal Publishers, Workman.
IPOF	**Hudson, Wade**, and **Cheryl Willis Hudson**. 1997. *In Praise of Our Fathers and Our Mothers: A Black Family Treasury by Outstanding Authors and Artists*. East Orange, NJ: **Just Us Books**.
ITF	Chase, Henry (Ed.). 1994. *In Their Footsteps: The American Visions Guide to African-American Heritage Sites*. New York: Henry Holt.
L:WW	Miller, John. 1998. *Legends: Women Who Have Changed the World, through the Eyes of Great Women Writers*. Novato, CA: New World Library.
LA	The Literary Almanac: The Best of the Printed Word, 1900 to the Present. 1997. Kansas City, MO: A High Tide Press Book, Andrews McMeel Publishing.
LDW	Goring, Rosemary (Ed.). 1994. *Larousse Dictionary of Writers*. New York: Larousse.
LE	Legal Encyclopedia: West's Encyclopedia of American Law. 1998. Detroit: Gale Group. Available at Answers.com.
LF-07	LitFinder. 2007. Detroit: Gale.
LFCC-07	LitFinder Contemporary Collection. 2007. Detroit: Gale Group.
LLBL	Strouf, Judie L. H. 1998. *Literature Lover's Book of Lists: Serious Trivia for the Bibliophile*. Paramus, NJ: Prentice Hall Press.
LoL	Moyers, Bill. 1995. *Language of Life: A Festival of Poets*. New York: Doubleday.
MAAL	Magill, Frank (Ed.). 1992. *Masterpieces of African-American Literature*. New York: HarperCollins.
MAC-20-55	Jay, Gregory S. (Ed.). 1988. *Modern American Critics, 1920-1955*. In *Dictionary of Literary Biography* (Vol. 63). Detroit: Gale Research.
MAC-55-88	Jay, Gregory S. (Ed.). 1988. *Modern American Critics Since 1955*. In *Dictionary of Literary Biography* (Vol. 67). Detroit: Gale Research.
MAI-1	Kovacs, Deborah, and James Preller. 1991. *Meet the Authors and Illustrators: Vol. 1. 60 Creators of Favorite Children's Books Talk about Their Works*. New York: Scholastic.
MAI-2	Kovacs, Deborah, and James Preller. 1994. *Meet the Authors and Illustrators: Vol. 2. 60 Creators of Favorite Children's Books Talk about Their Works*. New York: Scholastic.
MAWW	Showalter, Elaine, Lea Baechler, and A. Walton Litz. (Eds.). 1991. *Modern American Women Writers*. New York: Charles Scribner's Sons. Literature Resources from Gale.
MD	Music Dictionary. The Concise Oxford Dictionary of Music (5th ed.). 2007. Oxford University Press.
ME	Music Encyclopedia: The Concise Grove Dictionary of Music. 1994. New York: Oxford University Press. Available at Answers.com.
MLAFW-2	Luis, William, and Ann Gonzalez. (Eds.). 1994. *Modern Latin-American Fiction Writers: 2nd Series*. In *Dictionary of Literary Biography* (Vol. 145). Detroit: Gale Research.
MNAE	Mideast & N. Africa Encyclopedia. Encyclopedia of the Modern Middle East and North Africa. 2004. Detroit: Gale Group. Available at Answers.com.
MSA	MicroSoft Reference Library, CD version: Almanac. 1998.

MSAP-2	Salgado, Maria Antonia (Ed.). 2004. *Modern Spanish American Poets: Second Series. Dictionary of Literary Biography* (Vol. 290). Detroit: Gale.
MSC	MicroSoft Reference Library, CD version: Chronology. 1998.
MSD	MicroSoft Reference Library, CD version: Dictionary. 1998.
MSD-AHD-3	MicroSoft Reference Library, CD version: Dictionary. 1998. *American Heritage Dictionary* (3rd ed.).
MSE	MicroSoft Reference Library, CD version: Encyclopedia. 1998.
MSI	MicroSoft Reference Library, CD version: Internet. 1998.
MSQ	MicroSoft Reference Library, CD version: Quotations. 1998.
MW-10	Merriam-Webster. 1993. *Merriam-Webster's Collegiate Dictionary* (10th ed.). Springfield, MA: Merriam-Webster.
MWEL	Merriam-Webster. 1995. *Merriam-Webster Encyclopedia of Literature.* Springfield, MA: Merriam-Webster. Also available through Literature Resources from Gale.
MWBD	Merriam-Webster. 1988. *Webster's New Biographical Dictionary.* Springfield, MA: Merriam-Webster.
NAAAL	Gates, Henry Louis, Jr., and **Nellie Y. McKay** (Eds.). 1997. *The Norton Anthology of African American Literature.* New York: Norton.
NBAW	**Smith, Jessie Carney** (Ed.). 1992. *Notable Black American Women.* Detroit: Gale Research.
NBH	**Brawley, Benjamin.** 1937. *Negro Builders and Heroes.* Chapel Hill: University of North Carolina Press.
NFP	Jonathan N. Barron and Bruce Meyer. (Eds.). 2003. *New Formalist Poets.* In *Dictionary of Literary Biography* (Vol. 282). Detroit: Gale.
NPR-ME	National Public Radio, *Morning Edition.*
NYPL-AADR	New York Public Library (Eds.). 1999. *New York Public Library African-American Desk Reference.* New York: Wiley.
NYTBC	McGrath, Charles, and the staff of the *New York Times Book Review* (Eds.). 1998. *Books of the Century: A Hundred Years of Authors, Ideas, and Literature.* New York: Random House, Time Books.
OC20LE	Stringer, Jenny (Ed.). 1996. *Oxford Companion to Twentieth Century Literature in English.* New York: Oxford University Press.
OCAAL	Andrews, William L., **Frances Smith Foster,** and Trudier Harris (Eds.). 1997. *The Oxford Companion to African American Literature.* New York: Oxford University Press.
OCWW	Davidson, Cathy N., and Linda Wagner-Martin (Eds.). 1995. *The Oxford Companion to Women's Writing in the United States.* New York: Oxford University Press.
ODHQ	Sherrin, Ned (Ed.). 1995. *The Oxford Dictionary of Humorous Quotations.* New York: Oxford University Press.
OPL	Halpern, Daniel (Ed.). 1988. *Our Private Lives: Journals, Notebooks, and Diaries.* Hopewell, NJ: The Ecco Press.
OTD	Helicon Publishing. 1996. *On This Date.* New York: Random House (Reference & Information Publishing).
P	Posters. 1998-2003. AllPosters.com, Inc. Available at Answers.com.
PB	Political Biography: A Dictionary of Political Biography. 1998, 2003. New York: Oxford University Press.
PBW	Smith, Jessie Carney (Ed.). 1996. *Powerful Black Women.* New York: Visible Ink.
PC:PEL	Hass, Robert (Ed.). 1998. *Poet's Choice: Poems for Everyday Life.* Hopewell, NJ: Ecco Press.
PD	Political Dictionary: The Concise Oxford Dictionary of Politics. 1996, 2003. New York: Oxford University Press.
PDMHQ	Metcalf, Fred (Ed.). 1986. *The Penguin Dictionary of Modern Humorous Quotations.* London: Penguin Books.
PE	Photography Encyclopedia: The Oxford Companion to the Photograph. 2005. New York: Oxford University Press.
PGAA	Smallwood, David, Stan West, and Allison Keyes. 1998. *Profiles of Great African Americans.* Lincolnwood, IL: Publications, International.
PiP	**Bennett, Lerone, Jr.** 1968. *Pioneers in Protest.* Chicago: **Johnson Publishing Co.**
Q:P	Clifton, Lucille. 1991. *Quilting: Poems, 1987-1990.* Brockport, NY: BOA Editions.
QB	Quotes By. 2008. QuotationsBook.com. Available at Answers.com.
RG20	Parker, Peter (Ed.). 1995/1996. *A Reader's Guide to Twentieth-Century Writers.* New York: Oxford University Press.
RGAL-3	Kamp, Jim. (Ed.). 1994. *Reference Guide to American Literature* (3rd ed.). Detroit: St. James Press. From *Literature Resource Center.*
RHWDS	Random House Webster's Dictionary of Scientists. 1996/1997. New York: Random House.

RLWHS   Bailey, Brooke. 1994. *The Remarkable Lives of 100 Women Healers and Scientists.* Holbrook, MA: Bob Adams.

RLWWJ   Bailey, Brooke. 1994. *The Remarkable Lives of 100 Women Writers and Journalists.* Holbrook, MA: Bob Adams.

RP   Bolden, Tonya. 1994. *Rites of Passage: Stories about Growing Up by Black Writers from around the World.* New York: Hyperion Books for Children.

RT   Mullen, Bill (Ed.). 1995. *Revolutionary Tales: African American Women's Short Stories, from the First Story to the Present.* New York: Dell.

RtW   Goldberg, Bonni. 1996. *Room to Write: Daily Invitations to a Writer's Life.* New York: Jeremy P. Tarcher / Putnam, Penguin.

RWTC   Golden, Kristen, and Barbara Findlen. 1998. *Remarkable Women of the Twentieth Century: 100 Portraits of Achievement.* New York: Friedman/Fairfax Publishers.

S   Spotlight. 1999-2009. Available at Answers.com.

SBA   Bennett, Lerone, Jr. 1993. *The Shaping of Black America: The Struggles and Triumphs of African-Americans, 1619 to the 1990s* (2nd ed.). Chicago: Johnson Publishing Co.

SD   Hirsch, E.D., Jr., Joseph F. Kett, and James Trefil. (Eds.). 2002. *Science Dictionary. The New Dictionary of Cultural Literacy* (3rd ed.). Boston: Houghton Mifflin Company. Available at Answers.com.

SDPL catalog The online catalog of the San Diego Public Library is available from any Internet-friendly computer. To find this resource, go to at //www.sandiego.gov/public-library/, and type in the author's surname and then first name, and choose the search category "Author."

SEW   Keenan, Sheila. 1996. *Scholastic Encyclopedia of Women in the United States.* New York: Scholastic Reference.

SFW:CSMA Bleiler, Everett Franklin. (Ed.). 1982. *Science Fiction Writers: Critical Studies of the Major Authors from the Early Nineteenth Century to the Present Day.* New York: Charles Scribner's Sons. From *Scribner Writers Series.*

SJGCMW   Pederson, Jay P. (Ed.). 1996. *St. James Guide to Crime & Mystery Writers* (4th ed.): *St. James Guide to Writers Series.* Detroit: St. James Press. From *Literature Resource Center.*

SJGSFW   Pederson, Jay P. (Ed.). 1996. *St. James Guide to Science Fiction Writers* (4th ed.). New York: St. James Press. From *Literature Resource Center.*

SMKC   Bolden, Tonya. 1999. *Strong Men Keep Coming: The Book of African-American Men.* New York: Wiley.

SofE   McCrum, Robert, William Cran, and Robert MacNeil. 1986. *The Story of English.* New York: Viking.

ST:2C   Blassingame, John W. (Ed.). 1977. *Slave Testimony: Two Centuries of Letters, Speeches, Interviews and Autobiographies.* Baton Rouge: Louisiana State University Press.

ST:LW   Parker, Tony. 1996. *Studs Terkel: A Life in Words.* New York: Henry Holt.

T-CACT   Hansom, Paul. (Ed.). 2001. *Twentieth-Century American Cultural Theorists.* In *Dictionary of Literary Biography* (Vol. 246). Detroit: Gale Group. From *Literature Resource Center.*

T-CAD-1st MacNicholas, John. (Ed.). 1981. *Twentieth-Century American Dramatists. Dictionary of Literary Biography* (Vol. 7). Detroit: Gale Research.

T-CAD-2nd Wheatley, Christopher J. (Ed.). 2000. *Twentieth-Century American Dramatists: Second Series. Dictionary of Literary Biography* (Vol. 228). Detroit: Gale Group.

T-CAD-3rd Wheatley, Christopher J. (Ed.). 2002. *Twentieth-Century American Dramatists: 3rd Series.* In *Dictionary of Literary Biography* (Vol. 249). Detroit: Gale Group.

T-CAD-4th Wheatley, Christopher J. (Ed.). 2003. *Twentieth-Century American Dramatists: Fourth Series. Dictionary of Literary Biography* (Vol. 266). Detroit: Gale.

T-CAD-5th Eisler, Garrett. (Ed.). 2008. *Twentieth-Century American Dramatists: 5th Series.* In *Dictionary of Literary Biography* (Vol. 341). Detroit: Gale.

T-CAH   Wilson, Clyde Norman. (Ed.). 1983. *Twentieth-Century American Historians. Dictionary of Literary Biography* (Vol. 17). Detroit: Gale Research.

T-CASFW Cowart, David, and Thomas L. Wymer. (Eds.). 1981. *Twentieth-Century American Science-Fiction Writers. Dictionary of Literary Biography* (Vol. 8). Detroit: Gale Research.

T-CAWW-2 Cracroft, Richard H. (Ed.). 1999. *Twentieth-Century American Western Writers: 2nd Series.* In *Dictionary of Literary Biography* (Vol. 212). Detroit: Gale Group.

T-CBBCB-1 Baker, William, and Kenneth Womack. (Eds.). 1999. *Twentieth-Century British Book Collectors and Bibliographers: 1st Series.* In *Dictionary of Literary Biography* (Vol. 201). Detroit: Gale Research.

T-CCBAW-1 Lindfors, Bernth, and Reinhard Sander. (Eds.). 1992. *Twentieth-Century Caribbean and Black African Writers: 1st Series. Dictionary of Literary Biography* (Vol. 117). Detroit: Gale Research.

T-CCBAW-2	Lindfors, Bernth, and Reinhard Sander. (Eds.). 1993. *Twentieth-Century Caribbean and Black African Writers: Second Series*. In *Dictionary of Literary Biography* (Vol. 125). Detroit: Gale Research.	USGG	Patrick, John J., Richard M. Pious, and Donald M. Ritchie. 1993, 1994, 1998, 2001, 2002. *US Government Guide: The Oxford Guide to the United States Government*. Available at Answers.com.
T-CCBAW-3	Lindfors, Bernth, and Reinhard Sander. (Eds.). 1996. *Twentieth-Century Caribbean and Black African Writers: 3rd Series*. In *Dictionary of Literary Biography* (Vol. 157). Detroit: Gale Research.	USHC	Foner, Eric, and John A. Garraty. (Eds.). 1991. *US History Companion: The Reader's Companion to American History*. Boston: Houghton Mifflin Company. Available at Answers.com.
T-CCW-4	Berger, Laura Standley. (Ed.). 1995. *Twentieth-Century Children's Writers, 4th ed. Twentieth-Century Writers Series*. Detroit: St. James Press.	USHE	US History Encyclopedia. 2006. Available at Answers.com.
T-CR&HW	Vasudevan, Aruna. (Ed.). 1994. *Twentieth-Century Romance & Historical Writers, 3rd ed. Twentieth-Century Writers Series*. New York: St. James Press.	USMD	US Military Dictionary. The Oxford Essential Dictionary of the U.S. Military. 2001, 2002. New York: Oxford University Press.
T-CYAW	Berger, Laura Standley. (Ed.). 1994. *Twentieth-Century Young Adult Writers. Twentieth-Century Writers Series*. Detroit: St. James Press.	USMHC	US Military History Companion. The Oxford Companion to American Military History. 2000. New York: Oxford University Press. Available at Answers.com.
T&T	**Smitherman, Geneva**. 1977. *Talkin and Testifyin: The Language of Black America*. Boston: Houghton Mifflin.	USSC	US Supreme Court. The Oxford Companion to the Supreme Court of the United States. 1992, 2005. New York: Oxford University Press. Available at Answers.com.
TAWH	Heinemann, Sue. 1996. *Timelines of American Women's History*. New York: A Roundtable Press Book / Perigree Book, Berkley Publishing Group.	VBA	Foner, Philip S. (Ed.). 1972. *The Voice of Black America: Major Speeches by Negroes in the United States, 1797-1971*. New York: Simon and Schuster.
TB:LBPA	Charters, Ann, (Ed.). 1983. *The Beats: Literary Bohemians in Postwar America. Dictionary of Literary Biography* (Vol. 16). Detroit: Gale Research.	VBAAP	**Harper, Michael S.**, and **Anthony Walton** (Eds.). 2000. *The Vintage Book of African American Poetry: 200 Years of Vision, Struggle, Power, Beauty, and Triumph from 50 Outstanding Poets*. New York: Vintage Books, a Division of Random House.
TNLAUS	The Negro in Literature and Art in the United States. 1930. New York: Duffield & Company. Rpt. in David M. Galens (Ed.), 2004, in *Poetry Criticism* (Vol. 52, pp. 89-96). Detroit: Gale.	VOO	Pearlman, Mickey, and Katherine Usher Henderson. 1990, 1992. *A Voice of One's Own: Conversations with America's Writing Women*. Boston: Houghton Mifflin.
TTS	Clifton, Lucille. 1996. *The Terrible Stories*. Brockport, NY: BOA Editions, Ltd.	VR	Kanigel, Robert. 1998. *Vintage Reading, from Plato to Bradbury: A Personal Tour of Some of the World's Best Books*. Baltimore: Bancroft Press.
TtW	Ward, Jerry W., Jr. (Ed.). 1997) *Trouble the Waters: 250 Years of African-American Poetry*. New York: Penguin (Mentor Books).	W	Burt, Daniel S. (Ed.). 2004. *Works. The Chronology of American Literature*. Boston: Houghton Mifflin Company. Available at Answers.com.
TUSAS-290	Twayne's United States Authors Series 290. 1978. Boston: Twayne Publishers. From *The Twayne Authors Series*.	W2B	Who2 Biography. 1998-2008. Who2, LLC. Available at Answers.com.
TUSAS-383	Twayne's United States Authors Series 383. 1980. Boston: Twayne Publishers. From *The Twayne Authors Series*.	WABD	The Woman Artists Book of Days. 1988. New York: Hugh Lauter Levin Associates, Inc., Macmillan.
TWL	Edgarian, Carol, and Tom Jenks. 1997. *The Writer's Life: Intimate Thoughts on Work, Love, Inspiration, and Fame from the Diaries of the World's Great Writers*. New York: Vintage Books, Random House.	WB-98	World Book 1998 Multimedia Encyclopedia. (CD-ROM)
TWT	Madison, D. Soyini (Ed.). 1994. *The Woman That I Am: The Literature and Culture of Contemporary Women of Color*. New York: St. Martin's Griffin.	WB-99	World Book 1999 Multimedia Encyclopedia. (CD-ROM)

WC   Plimpton, George. 1989. *The Writer's Chapbook: A Compendium of Fact, Opinion, Wit, and Advice from the 20th Century's Preeminent Writers [Edited from* The Paris Review *Interviews]*. New York: Penguin Books.

WCE-CD   Webster's Concise Encyclopedia (in CD-ROM form). 1994.

WDAA   Webster's Dictionary of American Authors, Created in Cooperation with the Editors of Merriam-Webster Inc. 1996. New York: Smithmark Reference, US Media Holdings.

WDAW   Webster's Dictionary of American Women, Created in Cooperation with the Editors of Merriam-Webster Inc. 1996. New York: Smithmark Reference, US Media Holdings.

WfC   Bingham, Jane M. (Ed.). 1987. *Writers for Children.* New York: Charles Scribner's Sons. From *Scribner Writers Series.*

WI   Moyers, Bill D. 1990. *A World of Ideas: Conversations with Thoughtful Men and Women about American Life Today and the Ideas Shaping Our Future.* New York: Doubleday.

Wiki   This database resource is available from any Internet-friendly computer. To find this resource, go to //en.wikipedia.org/wiki/Main_Page, and type in the author's name, from first name to surname. When compared with *Encyclopædia Britannica*, its accuracy was deemed comparable for most entries. In addition, when reached through Answers.com, these articles are licensed under the GNU Free Documentation License and use material from a Wikipedia article.

WN   WordNet. WordNet 1.7.1 2001. Princeton University.

Wr   Writer. 2009. All Media Guide, LLC. Available at Answers.com.

WS   Dunaway, David King, and Sara L. Spurgeon. 1995. *Writing the Southwest.* New York: Plume, Penguin.

WT   Word Tutor. 2004-2009. eSpindle Learning, a 501(c) nonprofit organization. Available at Answers.com.

WW:CCC   Stephens, Autumn. 1992. *Wild Women: Crusaders, Curmudgeons and Completely Corsetless Ladies in the Otherwise Virtuous Victorian Era.* Berkeley, CA: Conari Press.

WWMGA   Safire, William, and Leonard Safir (Eds.). 1989. *Words of Wisdom: More Good Advice.* New York: Fireside, Simon & Schuster.

WYA-1993   Writers for Young Adults. Charles Scribner's Sons. 1993. Rpt. in *Children's Literature Review.* Detroit: Gale.

WYA-1997-1 Hipple, Ted. (Ed.). 1997. *Writers for Young Adults* (Vol. 1). New York: Charles Scribner's Sons. Literature Resources from Gale.

WYA-1997-2 Hipple, Ted. (Ed.). 1997. *Writers for Young Adults* (Vol. 2). New York: Charles Scribner's Sons. Literature Resources from Gale.

WYA-1997-3 Hipple, Ted. (Ed.). 1997. *Writers for Young Adults* (Vol. 3). New York: Charles Scribner's Sons. Literature Resources from Gale.

WYA-2000   Hipple, Ted. (Ed.). 2000. *Writers for Young Adults.* Ed. Ted Hipple. New York: Charles Scribner's Sons. From *Scribner Writers Series.*

WYL2   Steinberg, Sybil. 1995. *Writing for Your Life #2: 50 Outstanding Authors Talk about the Art of Writing and the Job of Publishing.* Wainscott, NY: Pushcart Press, W. W. Norton.

Illustration Credits

Page numbers precede credit line.

L

351 The Granger Collection, New York
357 The Granger Collection, New York
361 The Granger Collection, New York
364 The Granger Collection, New York
368 The Granger Collection, New York
369 The Granger Collection, New York

M

378 AP/Wide World Photos
380 Library of Congress, Prints & Photographs Division,
     LC-DIG-ppmsc-01271
383 Library of Congress, Prints & Photographs Division, Carl
     Van Vechten Collection, LC-USZ62-114419
408 AP/Wide World Photos
410 ullstein bild/The Granger Collection, New York

P

460 The Granger Collection, New York
462 Library of Congress, Prints & Photographs Division,
     FSA/OWI Collection, LC-USE6-D-005480

R

478 Library of Congress, Prints & Photographs Division,
     FSA/OWI Collection, LC-USW3-011696-C
491 Library of Congress, Prints & Photographs Division,
     FSA/OWI Collection, LC-USF34-013481-C
502 Library of Congress, Prints & Photographs Division,
     LC-USZ62-133369

S

511 Library of Congress, Prints & Photographs Division,
     WPA Poster Collection, LC-USZC2-1124
514 Library of Congress, Prints & Photographs Division, Carl
     Van Vechten Collection, LC-USZ62-95999
515 Library of Congress, Prints & Photographs Division, Carl
     Van Vechten Collection, LC-USZ62-132150
524 Library of Congress, Prints & Photographs Division, Carl
     Van Vechten Collection, LC-USZ62-131764
531 Library of Congress, Prints & Photographs Division,
     LC-USZ62-109699

T

537 Library of Congress, Prints & Photographs Division,
     LC-DIG-ggbain-06079
544 "The Underground Railroad from Slavery to Freedom,"
     by Wilbur Henry Siebert, The Macmillan Company, NY
     1898, pg 74
545 Library of Congress, Prints & Photographs Division,
     LC-USZC4-10250

T

571 Library of Congress, Prints & Photographs Division,
     LC-USZ62-119343
572 Library of Congress, Prints & Photographs Division,
     LC-USZ62-7816

V

581 Library of Congress, Prints & Photographs Division, Carl
     Van Vechten Collection, LC-USZ62-117655
584 Rue des Archives/The Granger Collection, New York

W

601 Library of Congress, Prints & Photographs Division,
     WPA Poster Collection, LC-USZC2-5590
602 Library of Congress, Prints & Photographs Division,
     LC-USZ62-49568
605 Library of Congress, Prints & Photographs Division,
     FSA/OWI Collection, LC-USW3-001658-C
606 The Granger Collection, New York
613 AP/Wide World Photos/Alison Shaw
614 Library of Congress, Prints & Photographs Division,
     LC-USZC4-5316
648 Library of Congress, Prints & Photographs Division,
     FSA/OWI Collection, LC-USW3-030298-D

X

659 Library of Congress, Prints & Photographs Division,
     LC-USZ6-1847

Y

667 Library of Congress, Prints & Photographs Division,
     LC-USZ62-121755

Index

Cole, Johnnetta (née) Betsch, **122-123**, 377
Cole, Nat King, 269
Coleman, Emmett, 484
Coleman, Gerald, 3
Coleman, Ornette, 131
Coleman, Wanda (née Evans), **123**
Coleridge, Samuel Taylor, 173
college newspapers
    Fisk Herald, 135, 157, 523
    Howard Review, The, 259, 285
    Howard University Record, 259, 625
Collier, Bryan, 555
Collier, Eugenia (Williams), **123-124**, 20
Collins, Kathleen (née Conwell), **124**
Collins fellowship from the United States Artists Foundation, 323
Colón, Jesús, **124**
Colon, Ricardo Nazario, 3
"Colonial Laws", 675
colonization. *See* American Colonization Society; emigration.
Color Purple, The (1982, by Alice Walker), 112, 234, 591, 592, 593, 596, 640
Colored American, The (newspaper, 1836-1842), 37, 130, 458, 501, 616
Colored American Magazine, The (1900-1909), **124-125**, 8, 33, 37, 64, 130, 258, 282, 283, 327, 422, 616
Colored Cooperative Publishing Company (Boston), 282
Colter, Cyrus, **125-126**
Coltrane, John, 62, 131, 215, 264
column(s). *See* Appendix D: Writers by Genre, 788.
Combahee River Collective (CRC), **126-127**, 344, 345, 448, 529
comedy, 45, 69, 73, 94, 132, 160, 168, 194, 197, 228, 234-236, 242, 243, 307, 315, 322, 389, 463, 471, 472, 475, 487, 494, 576, 589, 627, 629, 630, 634, 647. *See also* Appendix D: Writers by Genre, 793.
Comer, James, 467
comic(s), 24, 86, 95, 155, 156, 193, 234, 242, 292, 487, 491, 494, 538. *See also* comic book(s); comic strip(s).
comic book(s), 237, 398
    writer(s) of, 56. *See also* Appendix D: Writers by Genre, 782.
comic strip(s), 77, 107, 198, 265, 388, 389, 436, 448. *See also* Appendix D: Writers by Genre, 782.
coming-of-age literature, 17, 237, 378, 386, 445, 575, 660
commentary/commentaries, 2, 3, 23, 40, 77, 97, 98, 112, 133, 134, 136, 147, 177, 192, 199, 213, 214, 227, 238, 242, 263, 282, 311, 331, 335, 347, 348, 356, 363, 371, 375, 377, 412, 419, 434, 437, 452, 457, 478, 483, 479, 484, 487, 492, 497, 514, 575, 583, 608, 612, 622, 626, 651, 653, 659, 660. *See also* commentator; Appendix D: Writers by Genre, 788.
commentator, 42, 97, 159, 349, 363, 458, 507, 544, 622. *See also* commentary/commentaries.
Committee for the Negro in the Arts, 245
Commodore, Chester, 108
Commoner, The (Washington), 626
Commonplace (organization), 245
Commonwealth Club, 220
communism, 58, 85, 148, 170, 186, 289, 491, 492, 653
    anticommunism. *See* House Un-American Activities Committee; McCarthyism.
communist, 54, 55, 60, 79, 85, 86, 146, 148, 169, 185, 197, 214, 289, 363, 390, 452, 457, 491, 649-653
    newspapers and other periodicals
        Communist Daily Worker (newspaper), 649
        Daily Record (newspaper), 457
        Freedom: A Revolutionary and Anarchist-Communist Monthly (1892), 456
        Harlem Liberator (1929, communist-aligned), 79
        Masses and Mainstream, 85
        New Masses, 85, 186, 649
Communist Party, 79, 86, 146, 148, 185, 214, 363, 649-651, 653
Concise Oxford Companion to African American Literature, The (2001), 268
Cone, James H. (Hal or Hall), **127-128**

Congress of Racial Equality (CORE), 21, 99, 152, 213, 214, 372, 399, 400, 404, 409, 422, 487, 507, 570, 599, 621, 650, 658. *See also* civil rights activism/advocacy/movement.
Conkling, Roscoe, 90
Conover, Marion G., 473
Conrad, Joseph, 185
Conroy, Jack, 73, 74
Consultant in Poetry to the Library of Congress, 270
Conwell, Kathleen. *See* Collins, Kathleen (née Conwell)
cookbook(s), 69, 182, 200, 305, 319, 640
Coombs, Orde, 25, 29
Cooper, Anna Julia (née Haywood), **128**, 22, 388
Cooper, Floyd, 35, 240, 555
Cooper, J. (Joan) California, **128-129**, 6
Copasetic Bookstore and Gallery, 669
CORE. *See* Congress of Racial Equality.
Coretta Scott King Book Awards and Honors, 309. *See also* King, Coretta Scott.
    Award, 91, 121, 139, 149, 159, 167, 197, 198, 239, 246, 250, 250, 255, 269, 308, 340, 358, 381, 412, 425, 489, 497, 541, 597, 597, 644, 645, 663
    Author Award, 140, 140, 167, 393, 393, 424, 426, 456, 551
    Illustrator Award, 91, 232, 393, 541
    Honor, 70, 91, 110, 139, 159, 167, 198, 255, 269, 308, 309, 329, 381, 393, 424, 425, 554, 555, 599, 629, 631, 644
    Author Honor, 393, 456, 533
    Illustrator Honor, 476, 555
    John Steptoe Genesis Award, 167
    John Steptoe New Talent Award, 386
Cornell, Adrienne. *See* Kennedy, Adrienne.
Cornish, Sam (Samuel James), **129**, 35
Cornish, Samuel E., **130**, 36, 37, 213, 430, 501
Corrothers, James D. (David), **130**, 55, 586
Cortez, Jayne, **130-131**, 63
Cosby, Bill (William Henry, Jr.), **132-133**, 123, 153, 202, 269, 467, 640,
Cosby, Camille, 133, 153, 467, 530
Cose, Ellis (Jonathan), **133-134**
Coston, Julia (née) Ringwood, **135**
Coston, William Harry, 135
Cotter, Joseph Seamon, Jr., **135**, 28
Cotter, Joseph Seamon, Sr., **135**, 5, 28
Cotton, Elizabeth, 129
Couch, William, 24
Council on Interracial Books, 240, 291, 381, 426, 459, 551
Courlander, Harold, 23, 248
Cowdery, Mae V., 64
Cox, Clinton, 624
Craft, Ellen, 314, 542
Craft, William, **135**, 314, 542
Crafts, Hannah, 228
Crandall, Prudence, 222. *See also* Miss Crandall's School for Young Ladies, 8, 599
Crayton, Pearl, **135**
Creative Artists Public Service Program, 93
Creole ancestry (typically in Louisiana, especially New Orleans), 18, 28, 71, 175, 213, 219, 437, 597, 618
Creole culture, 97, 175
Creole dialect, 6, 71, 72, 245
Creole heritage, free Creole of color, 517
creole language (linguistic term), 4
Creole society, 77
Creole song(s), 255
Crew, Louie, 368
Crews, Donald, **136**
Cricket (magazine), 433, 598
Crisis, The, **136**, 18, 21, 28, 31, 33, 59, 64, 70, 71, 73, 88, 113, 135, 170, 175, 195, 208, 255, 258, 261, 288, 311, 312, 317, 327, 352, 402, 405, 406, 407, 419, 430, 434, 436, 441, 460, 486, 496, 514, 534, 535, 590, 594, 622
criticism (literary, cultural, music, theater, movies, media, book reviews, etc.). *See* Appendix D: Writers by Genre, 782-783.

256-259, 262, 263, 271, 275-276, 280-283, 300, 309, 311, 313, 344,
350, 356, 357, 359, 374, 379, 381-383, 392, 395, 398, 405, 406,
411-412, 415, 417-419, 422, 423, 426, 430, 433, 444, 452, 453,
459, 468, 476, 485, 495, 496, 499, 507, 512, 514, 515, 523, 529,
531, 534, 536, 540-543, 550, 552, 560-563, 585, 587, 594, 596,
602, 606-608, 611, 612, 615, 617-618, 620-621, 625, 627, 631, 632,
637, 649, 650, 664, 665, 667
race relations, 93, 96, 103, 166, 204, 212, 231, 274, 289, 310, 311,
314, 360-362, 385, 390, 413, 473, 481, 568, 597, 619, 622, 626,
638 . *See also* civil-rights movement.
racial identity, 48, 105, 175, 256, 270, 351, 431, 518, 528, 562, 563.
See also Black Aesthetic; Black Arts movement; black nationalism;
Black Power.
racism/racist, 17, 41, 48, 49, 53, 61, 70, 84, 87, 106, 107, 110, 119,
125, 126, 129, 130, 138-140, 144, 152, 164, 193, 208, 211, 219,
224, 231, 245, 254, 256-258, 262, 264, 273, 274, 281-283, 288,
289, 300, 307, 310, 313, 338, 340, 345, 346, 356, 362, 364, 365,
389-391, 409, 410, 413, 420, 423, 427, 429, 448, 460, 467, 477,
480, 484, 492, 507, 517, 519, 523, 529, 539, 552, 553, 560, 569,
573, 575, 579, 594, 597, 605-608, 610, 611, 613, 617, 626, 631,
636-638, 648, 650, 652, 654, 658, 665, 667. *See also Birth of a
Nation*; bombing of Birmingham church; Brownsville (Texas)
incident; Jim Crow; Ku Klux Klan; lynchings; Scottsboro Boys;
Till, Emmett.
Radical Abolitionist (1855-1858), 40
Rael, Patrick, 27
Rahman, Aishah (née Virginia Hughes), **475**
Rainey, Gertrude (née) Pridgett "Ma", **475**, 161, 215, 632
Raisin in the Sun (1959, play by Lorraine Hansberry), 253
Ralph Waldo Emerson Award from Phi Beta Kappa, 359
Ram's Horn, The (1847-1848?), 39
Rampersad, Arnold, **475-476**, 24, 29, 42, 72, 134, 170, 187, 257, 290,
652
Randall, Alice (née Mari-Alice Randall) (aka Alice Randall Ewing),
476
Randall, Dudley (Felker), **476-478**, 11, 63, 75, 79, 94, 144, 148, 345,
365, 367, 368, 494, 646, 660
Randolph, A. (Asa) Philip, **478**, 22, 31, 225, 258, 258, 401, 403, 449,
456, 502, 514, 585, 623, 655
Randolph, Ruth Elizabeth, 31
Rangel, Charles, 434
Rankine, Claudia, 101
Ransom, Birdelle Wycoff, 22
Ransome, James, 255, 308, 308
rap (lyrics), 20, 23, 46, 49, 83, 131, 177, 192, 203, 269, 287, 297, 347,
348, 352, 424, 425, 463, 480, 495, 519, 581
Raphael, Lennox, 579
Raschka, Chris, 282
Raspberry, William (James), **478-479**
Rawls, Isetta Crawford, 368
Ray, Charles Bennett, 37
Ray, Charles E., 479
Ray, Francis, 278
Ray, Henrietta Cordelia, **479**, 28, 32, 480
Razaf, Andy, **479**, 295
Reader's Digest, 151, 180, 247, 248, 273, 274, 316, 318, 408, 434, 618
Reading Black, Reading Feminist (1990), 112
Reagon, Bernice (née) Johnson, **479-480**
Reagon, Toshi, 480
Reason, Charles L., **480-481**, 222
*Reason Why the Colored American Is Not in the World's Columbian
Exposition, The* (1893, by Ida B. Wells), 607
*Red Record: Tabulated Statistics and Alleged Causes of Lynching in the
United States, 1892 -, 1893 -, 1894, A* (1895, by Ida B.
Wells-Barnett)
Redbone Press, **481**, 32, 34, 472
Redding, (James) "Jay" Saunders, **481-482**, 20, 147, 516
Redding, Otis, **482**
Redmond, Eugene, **482-483**, 63, 172, 367
Reed, Cannon & Johnson Communications, 483
Reed, Ishmael, **483-485**, 6, 29, 62, 63, 66, 119, 158, 261, 387, 394,
567, 579, 645, 661, 665
Reed, Mike, 631

Reese, Sarah Carolyn, 368
References, Appendix F, 805-813
Key to References, Appendix G, 815-826
religion(s). *See* African Methodist Episcopal (AME) Church; Baha'i
faith; Judaism; Methodist(s); Nation of Islam; Quaker(s); Religious
Society of Friends; Seventh Day Adventist(s).
Religious Society of Friends, 35, 166, 206. *See also* Quaker(s).
Remond, Charles Lenox, 485
Remond, Sarah (née Parker), **485**
"Response to Benjamin Banneker", 704
Revels, Hiram, 102
revolt(s). *See* slave rebellion(s) and uprising(s).
Rey, Margo Okazawa, 127
Reynolds, Burt, 150
Reynolds, Evelyn Crawford, 64
Rhodes, Jewell Parker, **485-486**, 117, 323
Rhodes scholarships, 360, 620
Rice, Linda Johnson, 60, 316
Rich, Adrienne, 118, 233, 365, 366
Richard Wright Award for Excellence in Literature, 666
Richards, Beah (aka Beulah Richardson), **486**, 215
Richards, I. A., 390
Richards, Lloyd, 632
Richardson, Willis, **486-487**, 24, 70, 406
Ricks, Willie, 65
Ridley, Florida Ruffin, **499-500**, 473. *See* also Ruffin, Josephine, et al.
Ridley, Ulysses A., 500
Ridley, John, **487**
Riggs, Marlon Troy, **488**
Rights of All (newspaper), 37, 130, 502
Riley, James Whitcomb, 173
Ringgold, Faith (née Faith Willi Jones), **488-490**, 555
Ringwood's Afro-American Journal of Fashion, 135
Ringwood's Home Magazine, 135
Ripley, C. Peter, 27
Ritchie, Sharon Page, 127
Ritz Paris Hemingway Award, 338
Rive, Richard, 199
Rivers, Conrad Kent, **490**
Robb, Stephen, 27
Robbins, Hollis, 228
Roberson, Ed, 101
Robert F. Kennedy
Book Award, 423
Lifetime Achievement Award, 183
Robeson, Eslanda ("Essie") Cardozo (née Goode), **490-491**
Robeson, Paul (Bustill), **491-492**, 22, 75, 85, 148, 168, 169, 200, 214,
215, 239, 240, 249, 252, 253, 289, 337, 373, 403, 403, 417, 457,
459, 465, 490, 536, 619, 626
Robinson, D. W., 319
Robinson, Edwin Arlington, 86
Robinson, Jackie, 12
Robinson, Louie, Jr., 42
Robinson, Max (né Maxie), **492-493**, 430
Robinson, Randall, **492-493**
Robinson, William Henry, 21, 438
Robotham, Rosemarie, 18, 23, 645
Rock and Roll Hall of Fame, 160, 161, 463, 475, 642
Rock, Chris (né Christopher Julius Rock III), **493-494**, 202
Rockabilly Hall of Fame, 160
Rockefeller Foundation (grants, fellowships, scholarships), 93, 101,
111, 131, 134, 145, 160, 165, 168, 176, 179, 198, 211, 216, 220,
254, 268, 274, 284, 290, 299, 326, 337, 377, 387, 399, 455, 461,
475, 481, 482, 522, 589, 609, 635, 646
Rodgers, Carolyn (Marie), **494-495**, 6, 11, 217, 299, 373, 438, 443,
477
Rodriguez, Junius, 457
Roethke, Theodore, 56
Rogers, J. (Joel) A. (Augustus), **495-496**, 215, 362, 403, 464, 547
Rollin (Whipper), Frances A., 154. *See also* Whipper, Frances A.
Rollin.
Rollins, Charlemae (née Hill), **496-497**, 911

Rollins, Sonny, 64
Rona Jaffe Writers Foundation Grant, 451
Roosevelt, Eleanor, 324, 531. *See also* Eleanor Roosevelt Humanities
    Award.
Roosevelt, Franklin D., as U.S. president, 449.
    Roosevelt's "Black Cabinet", 362
Roosevelt, Theodore "Teddy," as U.S. president, 9, 209, 216, 602
Roots (1976, by Alex Haley), 171, 248, 595
Roots (literary journal of Texas Southern University), 556
Roper, Moses, **497**, 22, 468, 528
Rosa Parks Woman of Courage Award, 232. *See also* Parks, Rosa.
Rosenthal Foundation, 333, 334, 485, 586, 593
Rosenwald Fund/Foundation
    fellowship, 48, 73, 74, 113, 175-176, 186, 280, 595, 624, 625
    grant, 72, 160
Roses, Lorraine Elena, 31, 549
Ross, Diana, 269
Ross-Barnett, Marguerite, **497**
Rowan, Carl T. (Thomas), **497-499**, 182, 430
Rowell, Charles Henry, 22, 26, 32, 437
Royster, Jacqueline Jones, 505
Ruffin, George Lewis, **499-500**
Ruffin, Josephine St. Pierre, **499-500**, 22, 28, 32, 448, 473
Ruggles, David, **500-501**, 38, 571
Rukeyser, Muriel, 591
Rush, Gertrude E. (née Durden), **501**
Russ, Robert A., 31
Russell, Sandi, 33
Russwurm Award from the National Newspaper Publishers, 386
Russwurm, John (né Brown), **501-502**, 36, 130, 213, 430
Rustin, Bayard, **502**, 269
Rux, Carl Hancock (né Carl Stephen Hancock), **503**

S

Sage: A Scholarly Journal on Black Women, **505**, 327
Saint, Assoto, 32
Salaam, Kalamu ya (né Vallery Ferdinand III), **505-506**, 63, 66, 158,
    213, 437, 438, 507, 661
Sales, Ruby, 505
Salinger, J. D., 186
Sanchez, Sonia (Benita) (née Wilsonia Driver), **506-509**, 6, 25, 63,
    66, 79, 92, 101, 263, 290, 345, 346, 477, 506
Sandburg, Carl, 86, 148, 288, 313
Sanders, Dori, **509**
Sapin, Louis, 600
Sapphire (née Ramona Lofton), **509-510**
Saroyan, William, 197
Sartre, Jean-Paul, 48, 309, 569, 652
Satiafa (Vivian V. Gordon), 368
satire, parody, and other humor. *See* Appendix D: Writers by Genre,
    793.
Saturday Evening Quill, **473-474**. *See also* Quill Club.
Saturday Evening Quill Club, 500. *See also* Quill Club.
Saunders, Doris, 108
Sayer, Mandy Jane, 347
Scarborough, William Sanders, **510**, 5, 11, 422, 586
Schalk, Gertrude, 473
scholarly writings. *See* Appendix D: Writers by Genre, 793.
Schomburg, Arthur A. (né Arturo Alfonso Schomburg; occasional
    pseudonym: Guarionex), **510-514**, 11, 90, 113, 115, 215, 285, 295,
    422, 433, 547
Schomburg Center for Research in Black Culture (of the New York
    Public Library), 18, 28, 32, 46, 116, 165, 215, 260, 295, 352, 487,
    513
Schomburg Collection, 295, 352, 479, 513
*Schomburg Library of African American Women Writers of the
    Nineteenth Century*, 28, 32. *See also* Schomburg Library of
    Nineteenth-Century Black Women Writers.
Schomburg Library of Nineteenth-Century Black Women Writers (1980s
    and beyond), 33, 210, 227, 268, 274, 333, 530, 560. *See also*
    Schomburg Library of African American Women Writers of the
    Nineteenth Century
Schomburg Library Scholars-in-Residencies, 475

Schuster, Max Lincoln, 320
Schuyler, George Samuel, **514-515**, 402, 403, 433, 434, 515, 558
Schuyler, Philippa Duke, **515**, 514
Schwarz, A. B. Christa, 31, 32
science, 3, 55, 56, 66, 72, 73, 95, 96, 122, 129, 136, 154-156, 158,
    166, 171, 199, 233, 236, 238, 243, 259, 274, 285, 286, 293, 327,
    328, 354, 359, 361, 363, 364, 383, 412, 414, 420, 423, 429, 431,
    435, 453, 457, 477, 495, 497, 505, 506, 514, 522, 523, 530, 535,
    544, 556, 561, 575-577, 583, 586, 632, 638
science fiction, 3, 55, 56, 95, 96, 154-156, 171, 236, 309, 414, 420
sci-fi. *See* science fiction.
Scisney-Givens, Daudra, 3
SCLC. *See* Southern Christian Leadership Conference.
Scorpions (1988, by Walter Dean Myers), 425
Scott, Coretta, 521. *See also* King, Coretta Scott.
Scott, Dred, 39
Scott, Emmett Jay, 586
Scott, Nathan A. (Alexander), Jr., **515-516**
Scott, Patricia Bell, 33, 34, 127, 290, 505, 529
Scott-Heron, Gil, **516-517**
Scottsboro Boys, 269, 466
Screen Actor's Guild Lifetime Achievement Award, 150
Screen Writers Guild, 587
screenplay(s), 14, 15, 17, 52, 55, 56, 82, 102, 110, 119, 121, 124, 145,
    149, 150, 151, 155, 156, 157, 184, 192, 200, 211, 216, 229, 236,
    237, 241, 261, 266, 277, 288, 291, 309, 323, 338, 355, 386, 387,
    395, 403, 407, 418, 430, 432, 435, 454, 455, 460, 463, 468, 471,
    476, 487, 488, 493, 494, 521, 559, 564, 570, 575, 576, 581, 582,
    587, 609, 621, 628, 629, 633, 665. *See also* Appendix D: Writers by
    Genre, 790-791.
script(s), 148, 152, 168, 179, 216, 291, 355, 376, 393, 412, 415, 424,
    448, 454, 485, 546, 570, 581, 582, 587. *See also* Appendix D:
    Writers by Genre, 790-791.
Sea Island(s), 4, 16, 98, 207, 274, 275, 401, 417, 583
Sea Island Writers Retreats, 16
Seale, Bobby, 92, 117, 118, 660
Sebastian, Ellen, 234
Second Book of American Negro Spirituals, The (1926), 316. *See also*
    spirituals.
See, Carolyn, 193
Seeger, Pete, 357, 387. *See also* folk songs.
Séjour, Victor (né Juan Victor Séjour Marcon-Ferrand), **517-518**
self-publishing and self-publishers, 58, 272, 285, 311, 347, 494, 505,
    506, 589. *See also* Appendix D: Writers by Genre, 792-793.
    Down South Press, 17
    Eneke Publications, 533
    P. E. Hopkins & Co., 472
    Wild Trees Press, 591
Senghor, Léopold Sédar, 143, 653
Sengstacke Enterprises, 108, 109
Sengstacke, John, 1
Sengstacke, John H. (Herman Henry) III, 2, 108-109, 221, 222, 430,
    436, 464. *See also* Chicago Defender.
Sengstacke Newspapers (now Real Times, LLC), 464
Sengstacke, Robert Abbott, 109. *See also* Chicago Defender.
Senna, Carl, **518-519**
Senna, Danzy (Maria), **518-519**, 194
Serling, Rod, 44
sermon(s), 9, 10, 23, 87, 137, 138, 206, 223, 272, 280, 304, 316, 341,
    342, 352, 355, 385, 422, 446, 458, 459, 467, 501, 534, 538, 570,
    571, 573, 594, 597, 628. *See also* Appendix D: Writers by Genre,
    794.
Seventh Day Adventist(s), 72, 649
Shadd, Mary Ann, 40, 154. *See also* Cary, Mary Ann Shadd.
Shakespeare, William, 160, 199, 432, 519, 594
Shakur, Afeni, 519
Shakur, Assata Olugbala (née JoAnne Deborah Byron), **519**
Shakur, Tupac (2Pac), **519**, 231, 234, 468, 519
shamans, 445
Shange, Ntozake (née Paulette Williams), **519-521**, 6, 63, 101, 150,
    236, 261, 344, 447, 463
Shapiro, Bruce, 300
Shapiro, Karl, 144

Shari Dorantes Hatch worked as an editor for Academic Press and McGraw-Hill, and as a copyeditor and developmental editor for Harper-Collins, John Wiley & Sons, and others. She did developmental and ghost writing for private individuals. She was co-editor for the first edition of *African American Writers: A Dictionary*. Shari is a free-lance writer specializing in history, biography and social sciences, and lives in California with her husband Bernie.